from Sue
Christmas 1991
Started 1-92

Job

# THE ONE YEAR BIBLE

## NEW REVISED STANDARD VERSION

Fruit not fruits

Sam 7:18
20b

I Chron 28:20b

Acts 17:

ngel = Spirits sent to minister to believers in Christ.
r angel can/might even appear disguised as a human being

Nov 6 = U.S.

Col 13 } Aug 20 this Bible
Ps. 37

II Chron 15:2 "..... if you seek Him He
will be found :4 ..... turned to the
Lord ..... sought Him ..... found "
:12 entered into a covenant to seek the Lord Him
..... w/ all soul & heart :15 sought Him w/
their (all my) desire & He was found
And the Lord gave rest.

1 John 5:3

### Arranged in 365 Daily Readings

## New Revised Standard Version

Published by
WORLD BIBLE PUBLISHERS, INC.
Iowa Falls, Iowa

Also distributed by
TYNDALE HOUSE PUBLISHERS, INC.
Wheaton, Illinois

Library of Congress Cataloging-in-Publication Data

Bible. English. New Revised Standard.   1991.
     The one year Bible : New Revised Standard Version.
          p.    cm.
     "Arranged in 365 daily readings."
     Includes index.
     ISBN 0-8423-4742-9 (cloth)—ISBN 0-8423-4744-5 (kivar)
     1.  Devotional calendars.     I.  Title.
BS191.5.A1    1991.I59
220.5'20434—dc20                                        91-25325

THE ONE YEAR is a registered trademark of Tyndale House
Publishers, Inc.

THE ONE YEAR BIBLE NEW REVISED STANDARD VERSION

*The One Year Bible* © 1985, 1986, 1987, 1989, 1991 by Tyndale House
Publishers, Inc., Wheaton, Illinois 60189. All rights reserved.

The Bible text used in this edition of THE ONE YEAR BIBLE is the New
Revised Standard Version Bible.



Printed in the United States of America.

97   96   95   94   93   92   91
7    6    5    4    3    2    1

# INDEX
## TO THE BOOKS OF THE BIBLE

*Book . . . begins on:*

| | |
|---|---|
| GENESIS ...............January 1 | NAHUM ..............December 17 |
| EXODUS...............January 25 | HABAKKUK ..........December 18 |
| LEVITICUS ...........February 16 | ZEPHANIAH ..........December 19 |
| NUMBERS .............. March 3 | HAGGAI .............December 20 |
| DEUTERONOMY ........ March 23 | ZECHARIAH ..........December 21 |
| JOSHUA ..................April 10 | MALACHI ............December 30 |
| JUDGES ..................April 23 | MATTHEW ............. January 1 |
| RUTH .................... May 5 | MARK .................February 15 |
| 1 SAMUEL ............... May 7 | LUKE ................. March 13 |
| 2 SAMUEL ............... May 22 | JOHN ...................April 30 |
| 1 KINGS ................June 6 | ACTS.................... June 3 |
| 2 KINGS ................June 21 | ROMANS ...............July 12 |
| 1 CHRONICLES ..............July 5 | 1 CORINTHIANS ..........August 4 |
| 2 CHRONICLES ..............July 20 | 2 CORINTHIANS .........August 26 |
| EZRA ....................August 5 | GALATIANS ..........September 14 |
| NEHEMIAH ..............August 11 | EPHESIANS ..........September 22 |
| ESTHER ................August 18 | PHILIPPIANS .........September 29 |
| JOB ....................August 21 | COLOSSIANS ............ October 4 |
| PSALMS ........January 1 And July 3 | 1 THESSALONIANS ....... October 9 |
| PROVERBS .............. January 1 | 2 THESSALONIANS ...... October 13 |
| ECCLESIASTES ........September 2 | 1 TIMOTHY .............October 16 |
| SONG OF SOLOMON ...September 6 | 2 TIMOTHY .............October 22 |
| ISAIAH ...............September 8 | TITUS .................October 26 |
| JEREMIAH ...............October 3 | PHILEMON .............October 29 |
| LAMENTATIONS ........October 29 | HEBREWS ..............October 30 |
| EZEKIEL .............November 1 | JAMES ..............November 17 |
| DANIEL ..............November 25 | 1 PETER ..............November 22 |
| HOSEA ................December 5 | 2 PETER ..............November 27 |
| JOEL ..................December 9 | 1 JOHN ..............November 30 |
| AMOS .................December 10 | 2 JOHN ...............December 6 |
| OBADIAH ..........December 13 | 3 JOHN ...............December 7 |
| JONAH ...............December 14 | JUDE..................December 8 |
| MICAH ................December 15 | REVELATION ..........December 9 |

# ALPHABETICAL INDEX
## TO THE BOOKS OF THE BIBLE

*Book . . . begins on:*

# PUBLISHER'S NOTE

*The One Year Bible* has been prepared especially for regular Bible readers who wish to read through the entire Bible in one year.

Each day you will read a passage from the Old Testament and one from the New, along with a Psalm and one or two Proverbs. This gives variety and freshness to your daily reading.

Instead of following a Bible reading chart and experiencing the delay of turning from place to place, you will find the text here in sequence, ready for your quiet reading and meditation.

In this edition of *The One Year Bible* you will find bracketed noun insertions at the beginning of readings where the primary speakers and actors are only represented by pronouns. These bracketed nouns are not part of The New Revised Standard Version text, but they will ensure clarity as you begin each day's new reading.

May this year and every year be enriched as you enjoy daily portions from God's Word!

# WAYS TO USE THE ONE YEAR BIBLE

*The One Year Bible* is divided into daily readings. For each day there is a portion of the Old Testament, the New Testament, Psalms, and Proverbs. These four separate daily readings are grouped on consecutive pages, giving freshness and diversity to each day's reading. This also makes it easy to use *The One Year Bible* in a variety of ways.

*The One Year Bible* has led thousands of readers through the Bible in one year. Its arrangement, however, is equally useful for guiding a reader through the Bible in two, or even three, years. If you feel too rushed or want to spend more time on each day's selections, here are a few other suggested reading plans:

### The Revised One-Year Plan

Schedule some time both in the morning and evening. Then read the New Testament selection with the Psalms in the morning and the Old Testament selection with the Proverbs in the evening.

### The Two-Year Plan

During the first year just read the Old Testament selection with the Proverbs. Then during the second year, read the New Testament with the Psalms.

### The Three-Year Plan

Read the Old Testament selection the first year, the New Testament the second year, and the Psalms and Proverbs selections during the third.

### Words of Praise and Wisdom in One Year

Read the Psalms and Proverbs selected for each day. This will take you through the Psalms twice and Proverbs once during the year, giving you words of praise and wisdom to live by each day.

And you need not limit yourself to these suggested plans, either. The arrangement of *The One Year Bible* makes it easy to devise any number of Bible reading plans to meet your particular needs.

# PREFACE

This preface is addressed to you by the Committee of translators, who wish to explain, as briefly as possible, the origin and character of our work. The publication of our revision is yet another step in the long, continual process of making the Bible available in the form of the English language that is most widely current in our day. To summarize in a single sentence: the New Revised Standard Version of the Bible is an authorized revision of the Revised Standard Version, published in 1952, which was a revision of the American Standard Version, published in 1901, which, in turn, embodied earlier revisions of the King James Version, published in 1611.

In the course of time, the King James Version came to be regarded as "the Authorized Version." With good reason it has been termed "the noblest monument of English prose," and it has entered, as no other book has, into the making of the personal character and the public institutions of the English-speaking peoples. We owe to it an incalculable debt.

Yet the King James Version has serious defects. By the middle of the nineteenth century, the development of biblical studies and the discovery of many biblical manuscripts more ancient than those on which the King James Version was based made it apparent that these defects were so many as to call for revision. The task was begun, by authority of the Church of England, in 1870. The (British) Revised Version of the Bible was published in 1881-1885; and the American Standard Version, its variant embodying the preferences of the American scholars associated with the work, was published as was mentioned above, in 1901. In 1928 the copyright of the latter was acquired by the International Council of Religious Education and thus passed into the ownership of the churches of the United States and Canada that were associated in this Council through their boards of education and publication.

The Council appointed a committee of scholars to have charge of the text of the American Standard Version and to undertake inquiry concerning the need for further revision. After studying the questions whether or not revision should be undertake,, and if so, what its nature and extent should be, in 1937 the Council authorized a revision. The scholars who served as members of the Committee worked in two sections, one dealing with the Old Testament and one with the New Testament. In 1946 the Revised Standard Version of the New Testament was published. The publication of the Revised Standard Version of the Bible, containing the Old and New Testaments, took place on September 30, 1952. A translation of the Apocryphal/Deuterocanonical Books of the Old Testament followed in 1957. In 1977 this collection was issued in an expanded edition, containing three additional texts received by Eastern Orthodox communions (3 and 4 Maccabees and Psalm 151). Thereafter the Revised Standard Version gained the distinction of being officially authorized for use by all major Christian churches: Protestant, Anglican, Roman Catholic, and Eastern Orthodox.

The Revised Standard Version Bible Committee is a continuing body, comprising about thirty members, both men and women, Ecumenical in representation, it includes scholars affiliated with various Protestant denominations, as well as several Roman Catholic members, and Eastern Orthodox member, and a Jewish member who serves in the Old Testament section. For a period of time the Committee included several members from Canada and from England.

Because no translation of the Bible is perfect or is acceptable to all groups of readers, and because discoveries of older manuscripts and further investigation of linguistic features of the text continue to become available, renderings of the Bile have proliferated. During the years following the publication of the Revised Standard Version, twenty-six other English translations and revisions of the Bible were produced by committees and by individual scholars—not to mention twenty-five other translations and revisions of the New Testament alone. One of the latter was the second edition of the RSV New Testament, issued in 1971, twenty five years after its initial publication.

Following the publication of the RSV Old Testament in 1952, significant advances were made in the discovery and interpretation of documents in Semitic languages related to Hebrew. In addition to the information that had become available in the late 1940s from the Dead Sea texts of Isaiah and Habakkuk, subsequent acquisitions from the same area brought to light many other early copies of all the books of the Hebrew Scriptures (except Esther), though most of these copies are fragmentary. During the same period early Greek manuscript copies of books of the New Testament also became available.

In order to take these discoveries into account, along with recent studies of documents in Semitic languages related to Hebrew, in 1974 the Policies Committee of the Revised Standard Version, which is a standing committee of the National Council of the Churches of Christ in the U.S.A., authorized the preparation of a revision of the entire RSV Bible.

For the Old Testament the Committee has made use of the Biblia Hebraica Stuttgartensia (1977; ed. sec. emendata, 1983). This is an edition of the Hebrew and Aramaic text as current early in the Christian era and fixed by Jewish scholars (the "Masoretes") of the sixth to the ninth centuries. The vowel signs, which were added by the Masoretes, are accepted in the main, but where a more probable and convincing reading can be obtained by assuming different vowels, this has been done. No notes are given in such cases, because the vowel points are less ancient and reliable than the consonants. When an alternative reading given by the Masoretes is translated in a footnote, this is identified by the words, "Another reading is."

Departures from the consonantal text of the best manuscripts have been made only where it seems clear that errors in copying had been made before the text was standardized. Most of the corrections adopted are based on the ancient versions (translations into Greek, Aramaic, Syriac, and Latin), which were made prior to the time of the work of the Masoretes and which therefore may reflect earlier forms of the Hebrew text. In such instances a footnote specifies the version or versions from which the correction has been derived and also gives a translation of the Masoretic Text. Where it was deemed appropriate to do so, information is supplied in footnotes from subsidiary Jewish traditions concerning other textual readings (the *Tiqqune Sopherim,* "emendations of the scribes"). These are identified in the footnotes as "Ancient Heb tradition."

Occasionally it is evident that the text has suffered in transmission and that none of the versions provides a satisfactory restoration. Here were can only follow the best judgment of competent scholars as to the most probable reconstruction of the original text. Such reconstructions are indicated in footnotes by the abbreviation Cn ("Correction"), and a translation of the Masoretic Text is added.

For the New Testament the Committee has based its work on the most recent edition of *The Greek New Testament,* prepared by an interconfessional and international committee and published by the United Bible Societies (1966; 3rd ed. corrected, 1983; information concerning changes to be introduced into the critical apparatus of the forth coming 4th edition was available to the Committee). As in that edition, double brackets are used to enclose a few passages that are generally regarded to be later additions to the text, but which we have retained because of their evident antiquity and their importance in the textual tradition. Only in very rare instances have we replaced the text or the punctuation of the Bible Societies; edition by an alternative that seemed to us to be superior. Here and there in the footnotes the phrase, "Other ancient authorities read," identifies alternative readings preserved by Greek manuscripts and early versions. In both Testaments, alternative renderings of the text are indicated by the word "Or."

As for the style of English adopted for the present revision, among the mandates given to the Committee in 1980 by the Division of Education and Ministry of the National Council of Churches of Christ (which now holds the copyright of the RSV Bible) was the directive to continue in the tradition of the King James Bible, but to introduce such changes as are warranted on the basis of accuracy, clarity, euphony, and current English usage. Within the constraints set by the original texts and by the mandates of the Division, the Committee has followed the maxim, "As literal as possible, as free as necessary." As a consequence, the New Revised Standard Version remains essentially a literal translation. paraphrastic renderings have been adopted only sparingly, and then chiefly to compensate for a deficiency in the English language—the lack of a common gender third person singular pronoun.

During the almost half a century since the publication of the RSV, many in the churches have become sensitive to the danger on linguistic sexism arising from the inherent bias of the English language towards the masculine gender, a bias that in the case of the Bible has often restricted or obscured the meaning of the original text. The mandates from the Division specified that, in references to men and women, masculine-oriented language should be eliminated as far as this can be done without altering passages that reflect the historical situation of ancient patriarchal culture. As can be appreciated, more than once the Committee found that the several mandates stood in tension and even in conflict. The various concerns had to be balanced case by case in order to provide a faithful and acceptable rendering without using contrived English. Only very occasionally has the pronoun "he" or "him" been retained in passages where the reference may have been to a woman as well as to a man; for example, in several legal texts in Leviticus and Deuteronomy. In such instances of formal, legal language, the options of either putting the passage in the plural or of introducing additional nouns to avoid masculine pronouns in English seemed to the Committee to obscure the historic structure and literacy character of the original. In the vast majority of cases, however, inclusiveness has bee attained by simple rephrasing of by introducing plural forms when this does not distort the meaning of the passage. Of course, in narrative and in parable no attempt was made to generalize the sex of individual persons.

Another aspect of style will be detected by readers who compare the more stately English rendering of the Old Testament with the less formal rendering adopted for the New Testament. For example, the traditional distinction between shall and will in English has been retained in the Old Testament as appropriate in rendering a document that embodies what may be termed the classic form of Hebrew, while in the New Testament the abandonment of such distinctions in the usage of the future tense in English reflects the more colloquial nature of the koine Greek used by most New Testament authors except when they are quoting the Old Testament.

Careful readers will notice that here and there in the Old Testament the word LORD (or in certain cases GOD is printed in capital letters. This represents the traditional manner in English versions of rendering the Divine Name, the "Tetragrammaton" (see the notes on Exodus 3.14, 15), following the precedent of the ancient Greek and Latin translators and the long established practice in the reading of the Hebrew Scriptures in the synagogue. While it is almost if not quite certain that the Name was originally pronounced "Yahweh," this pronunciation was not indicated when the Masoretes added vowel sounds to the consonantal Hebrew text. To the four consonants YHWH of the Name, which had come to be regarded as too sacred to be pronounced, they attached vowel signs indicating that in its place should be read the Hebrew word *Adonai* meaning "Lord" (or *Elohim* meaning "God"). Ancient Greek translators employed the word *Kyrios* ("Lord"). The form "Jehovah" is of late medieval origin; it is a combination of the consonants for the Diving Name and the vowels attached to it by the Masoretes but belonging to an entirely different word. Although the American Standard Version (1901) had used "Jehovah" to render the Tetragrammaton (the sound of Y being represented by J and the sound of W by V, and in Latin), for two reasons the Committees that produced the RSV and the NRSV returned to the more familiar usage of the King James Version. (1) The word "Jehovah" does not accurately represent any form of the Name ever used in Hebrew. (2) The use of any proper name for the one and only God, as though there were other gods from whom the true God had to be distinguished, began to be discontinued in Judaism before the Christian era and is inappropriate for the universal faith of the Christian Church.

It will be seen that in the Psalms and in other prayers addressed to God the archaic second person singular pronouns (*thee, thou, thine*) and verb forms (*art hast, hadst*) are no longer used. Although some readers may regret this change, it should be pointed out that in the original languages neither the Old Testament nor the New makes any linguistic distinction between addressing a human being and addressing the Deity. Furthermore, in the tradition of the King James Version one will not expect to find the use of capital letters for pronouns that refer to the Deity—such capitalization is an unnecessary innovation that has only recently been introduced into a few English translations of the Bible. Finally, we have left to the discretion of the licensed publishers such matters as section headings, cross-references, and clues to the pronunciation of proper names.

This new version seeks to preserve all that is best in the English Bible as it has been known and used through the years. It is intended for use in public reading and congregational worship, as well as in private study, instruction, and meditation. We have resisted the temptation to introduce terms and phrases that merely reflect current moods, and have tried to put the message of the Scriptures in simple, enduring words and expressions that are worthy to stand in the great tradition of the King James Bible and its predecessors.

In traditional Judaism and Christianity, the Bible has been more than a historical document to be preserved or a classic of literature to be cherished and admired; it is recognized as the unique record of God's dealings with people over the ages. The Old Testament sets forth the call of a special people to enter into covenant relation with the God of justice and steadfast love and to bring God's law to the nations. The New Testament records the life and work of Jesus Christ, the one in whom "the Word became flesh," as well as describes the rise and spread of the early Christian noble literary heritage of the past or who wish to use it to enhance political purposes and advance otherwise desirable goals, but to all persons and communities who read it so that they may discern and understand what God is saying to them. That message must not be disguised in phrases that are no longer clear, or hidden under words that have changed or lost their meaning; it must be presented in language that is direct and plain and meaningful to people today. It is the hope and prayer of the translators that this version of the Bible may continue to hold a large place in congregational life and to speak to all readers, young and old alike, helping them to understand and believe and respond to its message

For the Committee,
BRUCE M. METZGER

# JANUARY 1

## GENESIS 1.1—2.25

**I**N the beginning when God cre-ated[a] the heavens and the earth, [2]the earth was a formless void and darkness covered the face of the deep, while a wind from God[b] swept over the face of the waters. [3]Then God said, "Let there be light"; and there was light. [4]And God saw that the light was good; and God separated the light from the darkness. [5]God called the light Day, and the darkness he called Night. And there was evening and there was morning, the first day.

6 And God said, "Let there be a dome in the midst of the waters, and let it separate the waters from the wa-ters." [7]So God made the dome and sep-arated the waters that were under the dome from the waters that were above the dome. And it was so. [8]God called the dome Sky. And there was evening and there was morning, the second day.

9 And God said, "Let the waters under the sky be gathered together into one place, and let the dry land ap-pear." And it was so. [10]God called the dry land Earth, and the waters that were gathered together he called Seas. And God saw that it was good. [11]Then God said, "Let the earth put forth veg-etation: plants yielding seed, and fruit trees of every kind on earth that bear fruit with the seed in it." And it was so. [12]The earth brought forth vegetation: plants yielding seed of every kind, and trees of every kind bearing fruit with the seed in it. And God saw that it was good. [13]And there was evening and there was morning, the third day.

14 And God said, "Let there be lights in the dome of the sky to separate the day from the night; and let them be for signs and for seasons and for days and years, [15]and let them be lights in the dome of the sky to give light upon the earth." And it was so. [16]God made the two great lights—the greater light to rule the day and the lesser light to rule the night—and the stars. [17]God set them in the dome of the sky to give

a Or *when God began to create* or *In the beginning God created*   b Or *while the spirit of God* or *while a mighty wind* light upon the earth, [18]to rule over the day and over the night, and to separate the light from the darkness. And God saw that it was good. [19]And there was evening and there was morning, the fourth day.

20  And God said, "Let the waters bring forth swarms of living creatures, and let birds fly above the earth across the dome of the sky." [21]So God created the great sea monsters and every living creature that moves, of every kind, with which the waters swarm, and every winged bird of every kind. And God saw that it was good. [22]God blessed them, saying, "Be fruitful and multiply and fill the waters in the seas, and let birds multiply on the earth." [23]And there was evening and there was morning, the fifth day.

24  And God said, "Let the earth bring forth living creatures of every kind: cattle and creeping things and wild animals of the earth of every kind." And it was so. [25]God made the wild animals of the earth of every kind, and the cattle of every kind, and everything that creeps upon the ground of every kind. And God saw that it was good.

26  Then God said, "Let us make humankind[a] in our image, according to our likeness; and let them have dominion over the fish of the sea, and over the birds of the air, and over the cattle, and over all the wild animals of the earth,[b] and over every creeping thing that creeps upon the earth."

[27]  So God created humankind[a] in
            his image,
      in the image of God he
            created them;[c]
      male and female he created
            them.

[28]God blessed them, and God said to them, "Be fruitful and multiply, and fill the earth and subdue it; and have dominion over the fish of the sea and over the birds of the air and over every living

thing that moves upon the earth." [29]God said, "See, I have given you every plant yielding seed that is upon the face of all the earth, and every tree with seed in its fruit; you shall have them for food. [30]And to every beast of the earth, and to every bird of the air, and to everything that creeps on the earth, everything that has the breath of life, I have given every green plant for food." And it was so. [31]God saw everything that he had made, and indeed, it was very good. And there was evening and there was morning, the sixth day.

2.1  THUS the heavens and the earth were finished, and all their multitude. [2]And on the seventh day God finished the work that he had done, and he rested on the seventh day from all the work that he had done. [3]So God blessed the seventh day and hallowed it, because on it God rested from all the work that he had done in creation.

4  These are the generations of the heavens and the earth when they were created.

In the day that the LORD God made the earth and the heavens, [5]when no plant of the field was yet in the earth and no herb of the field had yet sprung up—for the LORD God had not caused it to rain upon the earth, and there was no one to till the ground; [6]but a stream would rise from the earth, and water the whole face of the ground— [7]then the LORD God formed man from the dust of the ground,[d] and breathed into his nostrils the breath of life; and the man became a living being. [8]And the LORD God planted a garden in Eden, in the east; and there he put the man whom he had formed. [9]Out of the ground the LORD God made to grow every tree that is pleasant to the sight and good for food, the tree of life also in the midst of the garden, and the tree of the knowledge of good and evil.

---

[a]Heb *adam*  [b]Syr: Heb *and over all the earth*  [c]Heb *him*  [d]Or *formed a man* (Heb *adam*) *of dust from the ground* (Heb *adamah*)

10  A river flows out of Eden to water the garden, and from there it divides and becomes four branches. [11]The name of the first is Pishon; it is the one that flows around the whole land of Havilah, where there is gold; [12]and the gold of that land is good; bdellium and onyx stone are there. [13]The name of the second river is Gihon; it is the one that flows around the whole land of Cush. [14]The name of the third river is Tigris, which flows east of Assyria. And the fourth river is the Euphrates.

15  The LORD God took the man and put him in the garden of Eden to till it and keep it. [16]And the LORD God commanded the man, "You may freely eat of every tree of the garden; [17]but of the tree of the knowledge of good and evil you shall not eat, for in the day that you eat of it you shall die."

18  Then the LORD God said, "It is not good that the man should be alone; I will make him a helper as his partner." [19]So out of the ground the LORD God formed every animal of the field and every bird of the air, and brought them to the man to see what he would call them; and whatever the man called every living creature, that was its name. [20]The man gave names to all cattle, and to the birds of the air, and to every animal of the field; but for the man[a] there was not found a helper as his partner. [21]So the LORD God caused a deep sleep to fall upon the man, and he slept; then he took one of his ribs and closed up its place with flesh. [22]And the rib that the LORD God had taken from the man he made into a woman and brought her to the man. [23]Then the man said,

"This at last is bone of my
 bones
and flesh of my flesh;
this one shall be called
 Woman,[b]

for out of Man[c] this one was
 taken."
[24]Therefore a man leaves his father and his mother and clings to his wife, and they become one flesh. [25]And the man and his wife were both naked, and were not ashamed.

## MATTHEW 1.1—2.12

An account of the genealogy[d] of Jesus the Messiah, [e] the son of David, the son of Abraham.
2  Abraham was the father of Isaac, and Isaac the father of Jacob, and Jacob the father of Judah and his brothers, [3]and Judah the father of Perez and Zerah by Tamar, and Perez the father of Hezron, and Hezron the father of Aram, [4]and Aram the father of Aminadab, and Aminadab the father of Nahshon, and Nahshon the father of Salmon, [5]and Salmon the father of Boaz by Rahab, and Boaz the father of Obed by Ruth, and Obed the father of Jesse, [6]and Jesse the father of King David.

And David was the father of Solomon by the wife of Uriah, [7]and Solomon the father of Rehoboam, and Rehoboam the father of Abijah, and Abijah the father of Asaph,[f] [8]and Asaph[f] the father of Jehoshaphat, and Jehoshaphat the father of Joram, and Joram the father of Uzziah, [9]and Uzziah the father of Jotham, and Jotham the father of Ahaz, and Ahaz the father of Hezekiah, [10]and Hezekiah the father of Manasseh, and Manasseh the father of Amos,[g] and Amos[g] the father of Josiah, [11]and Josiah the father of Jechoniah and his brothers, at the time of the deportation to Babylon.

12  And after the deportation to Babylon: Jechoniah was the father of Salathiel, and Salathiel the father of Zerubbabel, [13]and Zerubbabel the father of Abiud, and Abiud the father of Eliakim, and Eliakim the father of Azor,

aOr *for Adam*  bHeb *ishshah*  cHeb *ish*  dOr *birth*  eOr *Jesus Christ*  fOther ancient authorities read *Asa*  gOther ancient authorities read *Amon*

[14]and Azor the father of Zadok, and Zadok the father of Achim, and Achim the father of Eliud, [15]and Eliud the father of Eleazar, and Eleazar the father of Matthan, and Matthan the father of Jacob, [16]and Jacob the father of Joseph the husband of Mary, of whom Jesus was born, who is called the Messiah. [a]

17 So all the generations from Abraham to David are fourteen generations; and from David to the deportation to Babylon, fourteen generations; and from the deportation to Babylon to the Messiah, [a] fourteen generations.

18 Now the birth of Jesus the Messiah[b] took place in this way. When his mother Mary had been engaged to Joseph, but before they lived together, she was found to be with child from the Holy Spirit. [19]Her husband Joseph, being a righteous man and unwilling to expose her to public disgrace, planned to dismiss her quietly. [20]But just when he had resolved to do this, an angel of the Lord appeared to him in a dream and said, "Joseph, son of David, do not be afraid to take Mary as your wife, for the child conceived in her is from the Holy Spirit. [21]She will bear a son, and you are to name him Jesus, for he will save his people from their sins." [22]All this took place to fulfill what had been spoken by the Lord through the prophet:
23　"Look, the virgin shall conceive
　　　　and bear a son,
　　and they shall name him
　　　　Emmanuel,"
which means, "God is with us." [24]When Joseph awoke from sleep, he did as the angel of the Lord commanded him; he took her as his wife, [25]but had no marital relations with her until she had borne a son;[c] and he named him Jesus.

2.1 In the time of King Herod, after Jesus was born in Bethlehem of Judea, wise men[d] from the East came to Jerusalem, [2]asking, "Where is the child who has been born king of the Jews? For we observed his star at its rising, [e] and have come to pay him homage." [3]When King Herod heard this, he was frightened, and all Jerusalem with him; [4]and calling together all the chief priests and scribes of the people, he inquired of them where the Messiah[a] was to be born. [5]They told him, "In Bethlehem of Judea; for so it has been written by the prophet:
6　'And you, Bethlehem, in the
　　　　land of Judah,
　　are by no means least among
　　　　the rulers of Judah;
　for from you shall come a ruler
　　who is to shepherd[f] my
　　　　people Israel.' "
7 Then Herod secretly called for the wise men[d] and learned from them the exact time when the star had appeared. [8]Then he sent them to Bethlehem, saying, "Go and search diligently for the child; and when you have found him, bring me word so that I may also go and pay him homage." [9]When they had heard the king, they set out; and there, ahead of them, went the star that they had seen at its rising, [e] until it stopped over the place where the child was. [10]When they saw that the star had stopped, [g] they were overwhelmed with joy. [11]On entering the house, they saw the child with Mary his mother; and they knelt down and paid him homage. Then, opening their treasure chests, they offered him gifts of gold, frankincense, and myrrh. [12]And having been warned in a dream not to return to Herod, they left for their own country by another road.

---

a Or *the Christ*　b Or *Jesus Christ*　c Other ancient authorities read *her firstborn son*　d Or *astrologers;* Gk *magi*　e Or *in the East*　f Or *rule*　g Gk *saw the star*

## PSALM 1.1–6

**H**APPY are those
who do not follow the
advice of the wicked,
or take the path that sinners
tread,
or sit in the seat of scoffers;
2 but their delight is in the law of
the LORD,
and on his law they meditate
day and night.
3 They are like trees
planted by streams of water,
which yield their fruit in its
season,
and their leaves do not
wither.
In all that they do, they
prosper.

4 The wicked are not so,
but are like chaff that the
wind drives away.
5 Therefore the wicked will not
stand in the judgment,
nor sinners in the
congregation of the
righteous;
6 for the LORD watches over the
way of the righteous,
but the way of the wicked will
perish.

## PROVERBS 1.1–6

**T**HE proverbs of Solomon son of
David, king of Israel:

2 For learning about wisdom and
instruction,
for understanding words of
insight,
3 for gaining instruction in wise
dealing,
righteousness, justice, and
equity;
4 to teach shrewdness to the
simple,
knowledge and prudence to
the young—
5 Let the wise also hear and gain
in learning,
and the discerning acquire
skill,
6 to understand a proverb and a
figure,
the words of the wise and
their riddles.

# JANUARY 2

## GENESIS 3.1—4.26

**N**OW the serpent was more crafty than any other wild animal that the LORD God had made. He said to the woman, "Did God say, 'You shall not eat from any tree in the garden'?" 2The woman said to the serpent, "We may eat of the fruit of the trees in the garden; 3but God said, 'You shall not eat of the fruit of the tree that is in the middle of the garden, nor shall you touch it, or you shall die.' " 4But the serpent said to the woman, "You will not die; 5for God knows that when you eat of it your eyes will be opened, and you will be like God, a knowing good and evil." 6So when the woman saw that the tree was good for food, and

aOr *gods*

that it was a delight to the eyes, and that the tree was to be desired to make one wise, she took of its fruit and ate; and she also gave some to her husband, who was with her, and he ate. 7Then the eyes of both were opened, and they knew that they were naked; and they sewed fig leaves together and made loincloths for themselves.

8 They heard the sound of the LORD God walking in the garden at the time of the evening breeze, and the man and his wife hid themselves from the presence of the LORD God among the trees of the garden. 9But the LORD God called to the man, and said to him, "Where are you?" 10He said, "I heard the sound of you in the garden, and I was afraid, because I was naked; and I hid myself." 11He said, "Who told you that you were naked? Have you eaten from the tree of which I commanded you not to eat?" 12The man said, "The woman whom you gave to be with me, she gave me fruit from the tree, and I ate." 13Then the LORD God said to the woman, "What is this that you have done?" The woman said, "The serpent tricked me, and I ate." 14The LORD God said to the serpent,

"Because you have done this,
    cursed are you among all
        animals
    and among all wild creatures;
upon your belly you shall go,
    and dust you shall eat
    all the days of your life.
15 I will put enmity between you
        and the woman,
    and between your offspring
        and hers;
he will strike your head,
    and you will strike his heel."
16To the woman he said,
"I will greatly increase your
        pangs in childbearing;
    in pain you shall bring forth
        children,

yet your desire shall be for your
        husband,
    and he shall rule over you."
17And to the mana he said,
"Because you have listened to
        the voice of your wife,
    and have eaten of the tree
about which I commanded you,
    'You shall not eat of it,'
cursed is the ground because of
        you;
    in toil you shall eat of it all
        the days of your life;
18    thorns and thistles it shall bring
        forth for you;
    and you shall eat the plants of
        the field.
19    By the sweat of your face
        you shall eat bread
    until you return to the ground,
        for out of it you were taken;
    you are dust,
        and to dust you shall return."

20 The man named his wife Eve,b because she was the mother of all living. 21And the LORD God made garments of skins for the manc and for his wife, and clothed them.

22 Then the LORD God said, "See, the man has become like one of us, knowing good and evil; and now, he might reach out his hand and take also from the tree of life, and eat, and live forever"— 23therefore the LORD God sent him forth from the garden of Eden, to till the ground from which he was taken. 24He drove out the man; and at the east of the garden of Eden he placed the cherubim, and a sword flaming and turning to guard the way to the tree of life.

4.1 Now the man knew his wife Eve, and she conceived and bore Cain, saying, "I have producedd a man with the help of the LORD." 2Next she bore his brother Abel. Now Abel was a keeper of sheep, and Cain a tiller of the ground. 3In the

aOr to Adam  bIn Heb Eve resembles the word for living  cOr for Adam  dThe verb in Heb resembles the word for Cain

course of time Cain brought to the Lord an offering of the fruit of the ground, [4]and Abel for his part brought of the firstlings of his flock, their fat portions. And the Lord had regard for Abel and his offering, [5]but for Cain and his offering he had no regard. So Cain was very angry, and his countenance fell. [6]The Lord said to Cain, "Why are you angry, and why has your countenance fallen? [7]If you do well, will you not be accepted? And if you do not do well, sin is lurking at the door; its desire is for you, but you must master it."

8 Cain said to his brother Abel, "Let us go out to the field."[a] And when they were in the field, Cain rose up against his brother Abel, and killed him. [9]Then the Lord said to Cain, "Where is your brother Abel?" He said, "I do not know; am I my brother's keeper?" [10]And the Lord said, "What have you done? Listen; your brother's blood is crying out to me from the ground! [11]And now you are cursed from the ground, which has opened its mouth to receive your brother's blood from your hand. [12]When you till the ground, it will no longer yield to you its strength; you will be a fugitive and a wanderer on the earth." [13]Cain said to the Lord, "My punishment is greater than I can bear! [14]Today you have driven me away from the soil, and I shall be hidden from your face; I shall be a fugitive and a wanderer on the earth, and anyone who meets me may kill me." [15]Then the Lord said to him, "Not so![b] Whoever kills Cain will suffer a sevenfold vengeance." And the Lord put a mark on Cain, so that no one who came upon him would kill him. [16]Then Cain went away from the presence of the Lord, and settled in the land of Nod,[c] east of Eden.

17 Cain knew his wife, and she conceived and bore Enoch; and he built a city, and named it Enoch after his son Enoch. [18]To Enoch was born Irad; and Irad was the father of Mehujael, and Mehujael the father of Methushael, and Methushael the father of Lamech. [19]Lamech took two wives; the name of the one was Adah, and the name of the other Zillah. [20]Adah bore Jabal; he was the ancestor of those who live in tents and have livestock. [21]His brother's name was Jubal; he was the ancestor of all those who play the lyre and pipe. [22]Zillah bore Tubal-cain, who made all kinds of bronze and iron tools. The sister of Tubal-cain was Naamah.

23 Lamech said to his wives:
"Adah and Zillah, hear my voice;
    you wives of Lamech, listen
        to what I say:
I have killed a man for wounding
        me,
    a young man for striking me.
24 If Cain is avenged sevenfold,
    truly Lamech
        seventy-sevenfold."

25 Adam knew his wife again, and she bore a son and named him Seth, for she said, "God has appointed[d] for me another child instead of Abel, because Cain killed him." [26]To Seth also a son was born, and he named him Enosh. At that time people began to invoke the name of the Lord.

# MATTHEW 2.13—3.6

Now after they [the wise men] had left, an angel of the Lord appeared to Joseph in a dream and said, "Get up, take the child and his mother, and flee to Egypt, and remain there until I tell you; for Herod is about to search for the child, to destroy him." [14]Then Joseph[e] got up, took the child and his mother by night, and went to Egypt, [15]and remained there until the death of Herod. This was to fulfill what had been spoken by the Lord through the prophet, "Out of Egypt I have called my son."

a Sam Gk Syr Compare Vg: MT lacks *Let us go out to the field*   b Gk Syr Vg: Heb *Therefore*   c That is *Wandering*   d The verb in Heb resembles the word for *Seth*   e Gk *he*

16 When Herod saw that he had been tricked by the wise men, [a] he was infuriated, and he sent and killed all the children in and around Bethlehem who were two years old or under, according to the time that he had learned from the wise men. [a] 17 Then was fulfilled what had been spoken through the prophet Jeremiah:

18   "A voice was heard in Ramah,
     wailing and loud lamentation,
  Rachel weeping for her children;
     she refused to be consoled,
       because they are no
        more."

19 When Herod died, an angel of the Lord suddenly appeared in a dream to Joseph in Egypt and said, 20 "Get up, take the child and his mother, and go to the land of Israel, for those who were seeking the child's life are dead." 21 Then Joseph [b] got up, took the child and his mother, and went to the land of Israel. 22 But when he heard that Archelaus was ruling over Judea in place of his father Herod, he was afraid to go there. And after being warned in a dream, he went away to the district of Galilee. 23 There he made his home in a town called Nazareth, so that what had been spoken through the prophets might be fulfilled, "He will be called a Nazorean."

3.1 In those days John the Baptist appeared in the wilderness of Judea, proclaiming, 2 "Repent, for the kingdom of heaven has come near." [c] 3 This is the one of whom the prophet Isaiah spoke when he said,

  "The voice of one crying out in
     the wilderness:
  'Prepare the way of the Lord,
     make his paths straight.' "

4 Now John wore clothing of camel's hair with a leather belt around his waist, and his food was locusts and wild honey. 5 Then the people of Jerusalem and all Judea were going out to him, and all the region along the Jordan, 6 and they were baptized by him in the river Jordan, confessing their sins.

## PSALM 2.1–12

WHY do the nations conspire,
    and the peoples plot in
     vain?
2   The kings of the earth set
     themselves,
  and the rulers take counsel
     together,
  against the LORD and his
     anointed, saying,
3   "Let us burst their bonds
     asunder,
  and cast their cords from us."

4   He who sits in the heavens
     laughs;
  the LORD has them in
     derision.
5   Then he will speak to them in
     his wrath,
  and terrify them in his fury,
     saying,
6   "I have set my king on Zion, my
     holy hill."

7   I will tell of the decree of the
     LORD:
  He said to me, "You are my
     son;
  today I have begotten you.
8   Ask of me, and I will make the
     nations your heritage,
  and the ends of the earth
     your possession.
9   You shall break them with a rod
     of iron,
  and dash them in pieces like a
     potter's vessel."

10   Now therefore, O kings, be
     wise;

a Or *astrologers*; Gk *magi*   b Gk *he*   c Or *is at hand*

be warned, O rulers of the
earth.
11 Serve the LORD with fear,
with trembling [12]kiss his
feet, [a]
or he will be angry, and you will
perish in the way;
for his wrath is quickly
kindled.

Happy are all who take refuge
in him.

## PROVERBS 1.7–9

THE fear of the LORD is the
beginning of
knowledge;
fools despise wisdom and
instruction.

8 Hear, my child, your father's
instruction,
and do not reject your
mother's teaching;
9 for they are a fair garland for
your head,
and pendants for your neck.

# JANUARY 3

## GENESIS 5.1—7.24

THIS is the list of the descendants of Adam. When God created humankind,[b] he made them[c] in the likeness of God. [2]Male and female he created them, and he blessed them and named them "Humankind"[b] when they were created.

3 When Adam had lived one hundred thirty years, he became the father of a son in his likeness, according to his image, and named him Seth. [4]The days of Adam after he became the father of Seth were eight hundred years; and he had other sons and daughters. [5]Thus all the days that Adam lived were nine hundred thirty years; and he died.

6 When Seth had lived one hundred five years, he became the father of Enosh. [7]Seth lived after the birth of Enosh eight hundred seven years, and had other sons and daughters. [8]Thus all the days of Seth were nine hundred twelve years; and he died.

9 When Enosh had lived ninety years, he became the father of Kenan. [10]Enosh lived after the birth of Kenan eight hundred fifteen years, and had other sons and daughters. [11]Thus all the days of Enosh were nine hundred five years; and he died.

12 When Kenan had lived seventy years, he became the father of Mahalalel. [13]Kenan lived after the birth of Mahalalel eight hundred and forty years, and had other sons and daughters. [14]Thus all the days of Kenan were nine hundred and ten years; and he died.

15 When Mahalalel had lived sixty-five years, he became the father of Jared. [16]Mahalalel lived after the birth of Jared eight hundred thirty years, and had other sons and daughters. [17]Thus all the days of Mahalalel were eight hundred ninety-five years; and he died.

[a]Cn: Meaning of Heb of verses 11b and 12a is uncertain   [b]Heb *adam*   [c]Heb *him*

18  When Jared had lived one hundred sixty-two years he became the father of Enoch. [19]Jared lived after the birth of Enoch eight hundred years, and had other sons and daughters. [20]Thus all the days of Jared were nine hundred sixty-two years; and he died.

21  When Enoch had lived sixty-five years, he became the father of Methuselah. [22]Enoch walked with God after the birth of Methuselah three hundred years, and had other sons and daughters. [23]Thus all the days of Enoch were three hundred sixty-five years. [24]Enoch walked with God; then he was no more, because God took him.

25  When Methuselah had lived one hundred eighty-seven years, he became the father of Lamech. [26]Methuselah lived after the birth of Lamech seven hundred eighty-two years, and had other sons and daughters. [27]Thus all the days of Methuselah were nine hundred sixty-nine years; and he died.

28  When Lamech had lived one hundred eighty-two years, he became the father of a son; [29]he named him Noah, saying, "Out of the ground that the Lord has cursed this one shall bring us relief from our work and from the toil of our hands." [30]Lamech lived after the birth of Noah five hundred ninety-five years, and had other sons and daughters. [31]Thus all the days of Lamech were seven hundred seventy-seven years; and he died.

32  After Noah was five hundred years old, Noah became the father of Shem, Ham, and Japheth.

6.1  WHEN people began to multiply on the face of the ground, and daughters were born to them, [2]the sons of God saw that they were fair; and they took wives for themselves of all that they chose. [3]Then the Lord said, "My spirit shall not abide[a] in mortals forever, for they are flesh; their days shall be one hundred twenty years." [4]The Nephilim were on the earth in those days—and also afterward—when the sons of God went in to the daughters of humans, who bore children to them. These were the heroes that were of old, warriors of renown.

5  The Lord saw that the wickedness of humankind was great in the earth, and that every inclination of the thoughts of their hearts was only evil continually. [6]And the Lord was sorry that he had made humankind on the earth, and it grieved him to his heart. [7]So the Lord said, "I will blot out from the earth the human beings I have created—people together with animals and creeping things and birds of the air, for I am sorry that I have made them." [8]But Noah found favor in the sight of the Lord.

9  These are the descendants of Noah. Noah was a righteous man, blameless in his generation; Noah walked with God. [10]And Noah had three sons, Shem, Ham, and Japheth.

11  Now the earth was corrupt in God's sight, and the earth was filled with violence. [12]And God saw that the earth was corrupt; for all flesh had corrupted its ways upon the earth. [13]And God said to Noah, "I have determined to make an end of all flesh, for the earth is filled with violence because of them; now I am going to destroy them along with the earth. [14]Make yourself an ark of cypress[a] wood; make rooms in the ark, and cover it inside and out with pitch. [15]This is how you are to make it: the length of the ark three hundred cubits, its width fifty cubits, and its height thirty cubits. [16]Make a roof[b] for the ark, and finish it to a cubit above; and put the door of the ark in its side; make it with lower, second, and third decks. [17]For my part, I am going to bring a flood of waters on the earth, to destroy from under heaven all flesh in which is

[a]Meaning of Heb uncertain   [b]Or *window*

the breath of life; everything that is on the earth shall die. [18]But I will establish my covenant with you; and you shall come into the ark, you, your sons, your wife, and your sons' wives with you. [19]And of every living thing, of all flesh, you shall bring two of every kind into the ark, to keep them alive with you; they shall be male and female. [20]Of the birds according to their kinds, and of the animals according to their kinds, of every creeping thing of the ground according to its kind, two of every kind shall come in to you, to keep them alive. [21]Also take with you every kind of food that is eaten, and store it up; and it shall serve as food for you and for them." [22]Noah did this; he did all that God commanded him.

[7.1] THEN the LORD said to Noah, "Go into the ark, you and all your household, for I have seen that you alone are righteous before me in this generation. [2]Take with you seven pairs of all clean animals, the male and its mate; and a pair of the animals that are not clean, the male and its mate; [3]and seven pairs of the birds of the air also, male and female, to keep their kind alive on the face of all the earth. [4]For in seven days I will send rain on the earth for forty days and forty nights; and every living thing that I have made I will blot out from the face of the ground." [5]And Noah did all that the LORD had commanded him.

[6] Noah was six hundred years old when the flood of waters came on the earth. [7]And Noah with his sons and his wife and his sons' wives went into the ark to escape the waters of the flood. [8]Of clean animals, and of animals that are not clean, and of birds, and of everything that creeps on the ground, [9]two and two, male and female, went into the ark with Noah, as God had commanded Noah. [10]And after seven days the waters of the flood came on the earth.

[11] In the six hundredth year of Noah's life, in the second month, on the seventeenth day of the month, on that day all the fountains of the great deep burst forth, and the windows of the heavens were opened. [12]The rain fell on the earth forty days and forty nights. [13]On the very same day Noah with his sons, Shem and Ham and Japheth, and Noah's wife and the three wives of his sons entered the ark, [14]they and every wild animal of every kind, and all domestic animals of every kind, and every creeping thing that creeps on the earth, and every bird of every kind—every bird, every winged creature. [15]They went into the ark with Noah, two and two of all flesh in which there was the breath of life. [16]And those that entered, male and female of all flesh, went in as God had commanded him; and the LORD shut him in.

[17] The flood continued forty days on the earth; and the waters increased, and bore up the ark, and it rose high above the earth. [18]The waters swelled and increased greatly on the earth; and the ark floated on the face of the waters. [19]The waters swelled so mightily on the earth that all the high mountains under the whole heaven were covered; [20]the waters swelled above the mountains, covering them fifteen cubits deep. [21]And all flesh died that moved on the earth, birds, domestic animals, wild animals, all swarming creatures that swarm on the earth, and all human beings; [22]everything on dry land in whose nostrils was the breath of life died. [23]He blotted out every living thing that was on the face of the ground, human beings and animals and creeping things and birds of the air; they were blotted out from the earth. Only Noah was left, and those that were with him in the ark. [24]And the waters swelled on the earth for one hundred fifty days.

## MATTHEW 3.7—4.11

**B**UT when he [John the Baptist] saw many Pharisees and Sadducees coming for baptism, he said to them, "You brood of vipers! Who warned you to flee from the wrath to come? 8Bear fruit worthy of repentance. 9Do not presume to say to yourselves, 'We have Abraham as our ancestor'; for I tell you, God is able from these stones to raise up children to Abraham. 10Even now the ax is lying at the root of the trees; every tree therefore that does not bear good fruit is cut down and thrown into the fire.

11 "I baptize you witha water for repentance, but one who is more powerful than I is coming after me; I am not worthy to carry his sandals. He will baptize you witha the Holy Spirit and fire. 12His winnowing fork is in his hand, and he will clear his threshing floor and will gather his wheat into the granary; but the chaff he will burn with unquenchable fire."

13 Then Jesus came from Galilee to John at the Jordan, to be baptized by him. 14John would have prevented him, saying, "I need to be baptized by you, and do you come to me?" 15But Jesus answered him, "Let it be so now; for it is proper for us in this way to fulfill all righteousness." Then he consented. 16And when Jesus had been baptized, just as he came up from the water, suddenly the heavens were opened to him and he saw the Spirit of God descending like a dove and alighting on him. 17And a voice from heaven said, "This is my Son, the Beloved,b with whom I am well pleased."

4.1 THEN Jesus was led up by the Spirit into the wilderness to be tempted by the devil. 2He fasted forty days and forty nights, and afterwards he was famished. 3The tempter came and said to him, "If you are the Son of God, command these stones to become loaves of bread." 4But he answered, "It is written,

'One does not live by bread
　　alone,
but by every word that comes
　　from the mouth of
　　God.' "

5 Then the devil took him to the holy city and placed him on the pinnacle of the temple, 6saying to him, "If you are the Son of God, throw yourself down; for it is written,

'He will command his angels
　　concerning you,'
and 'On their hands they will
　　bear you up,
so that you will not dash your
　　foot against a stone.' "

7Jesus said to him, "Again it is written, 'Do not put the Lord your God to the test.' "

8 Again, the devil took him to a very high mountain and showed him all the kingdoms of the world and their splendor; 9and he said to him, "All these I will give you, if you will fall down and worship me." 10Jesus said to him, "Away with you, Satan! for it is written,

'Worship the Lord your God,
　　and serve only him.' "

11Then the devil left him, and suddenly angels came and waited on him.

## PSALM 3.1–8

*A Psalm of David, when he fled from his son Absalom.*

**O** LORD, how many are my foes!
Many are rising against me;
　2　many are saying to me,
"There is no help for youc in
　　God." 　　　　*Selah*

3　But you, O LORD, are a shield
　　around me,
my glory, and the one who
　　lifts up my head.

aOr *in*　bOr *my beloved Son*　cSyr: Heb *him*

4  I cry aloud to the Lord,
    and he answers me from his
        holy hill.                    *Selah*

5  I lie down and sleep;
    I wake again, for the Lord
        sustains me.
6  I am not afraid of ten thousands
        of people
    who have set themselves
        against me all around.

7  Rise up, O Lord!
    Deliver me, O my God!
  For you strike all my enemies
        on the cheek;
    you break the teeth of the
        wicked.

8  Deliverance belongs to the
        Lord;
    may your blessing be on your
        people!                  *Selah*


## PROVERBS 1.10–19

My child, if sinners entice
    you,
  do not consent.
11  If they say, "Come with us, let
        us lie in wait for blood;

let us wantonly ambush the
    innocent;
12  like Sheol let us swallow them
        alive
    and whole, like those who go
        down to the Pit.
13  We shall find all kinds of costly
        things;
    we shall fill our houses with
        booty.
14  Throw in your lot among us;
    we will all have one purse"—
15  my child, do not walk in their
        way,
    keep your foot from their
        paths;
16  for their feet run to evil,
    and they hurry to shed blood.
17  For in vain is the net baited
    while the bird is looking on;
18  yet they lie in wait—to kill
        themselves!
    and set an ambush—for their
        own lives!
19  Such is the end[a] of all who are
        greedy for gain;
    it takes away the life of its
        possessors.


# JANUARY 4

## GENESIS 8.1—10.32

But God remembered Noah and all the wild animals and all the domestic animals that were with him in the ark. And God made a wind blow over the earth, and the waters subsided; 2the fountains of the deep and the windows of the heavens were closed, the rain from the heavens was restrained, 3and the waters gradually receded from the earth. At the end of one hundred fifty days the waters had abated; 4and in the seventh month, on the seventeenth day of the month, the ark came to rest on the mountains of Ararat. 5The waters continued to

a Gk: Heb *ways*

abate until the tenth month; in the tenth month, on the first day of the month, the tops of the mountains appeared.

6 At the end of forty days Noah opened the window of the ark that he had made [7]and sent out the raven; and it went to and fro until the waters were dried up from the earth. [8]Then he sent out the dove from him, to see if the waters had subsided from the face of the ground; [9]but the dove found no place to set its foot, and it returned to him to the ark, for the waters were still on the face of the whole earth. So he put out his hand and took it and brought it into the ark with him. [10]He waited another seven days, and again he sent out the dove from the ark; [11]and the dove came back to him in the evening, and there in its beak was a freshly plucked olive leaf; so Noah knew that the waters had subsided from the earth. [12]Then he waited another seven days, and sent out the dove; and it did not return to him any more.

13 In the six hundred first year, in the first month, the first day of the month, the waters were dried up from the earth; and Noah removed the covering of the ark, and looked, and saw that the face of the ground was drying. [14]In the second month, on the twenty-seventh day of the month, the earth was dry. [15]Then God said to Noah, [16]"Go out of the ark, you and your wife, and your sons and your sons' wives with you. [17]Bring out with you every living thing that is with you of all flesh—birds and animals and every creeping thing that creeps on the earth—so that they may abound on the earth, and be fruitful and multiply on the earth." [18]So Noah went out with his sons and his wife and his sons' wives. [19]And every animal, every creeping thing, and every bird, everything that moves on the earth, went out of the ark by families.

20 Then Noah built an altar to the LORD, and took of every clean animal and of every clean bird, and offered burnt offerings on the altar. [21]And when the LORD smelled the pleasing odor, the LORD said in his heart, "I will never again curse the ground because of humankind, for the inclination of the human heart is evil from youth; nor will I ever again destroy every living creature as I have done.

22 As long as the earth endures,
seedtime and harvest, cold
and heat,
summer and winter, day and
night,
shall not cease."

**9.**1 GOD blessed Noah and his sons, and said to them, "Be fruitful and multiply, and fill the earth. [2]The fear and dread of you shall rest on every animal of the earth, and on every bird of the air, on everything that creeps on the ground, and on all the fish of the sea; into your hand they are delivered. [3]Every moving thing that lives shall be food for you; and just as I gave you the green plants, I give you everything. [4]Only, you shall not eat flesh with its life, that is, its blood. [5]For your own lifeblood I will surely require a reckoning: from every animal I will require it and from human beings, each one for the blood of another, I will require a reckoning for human life.

6 Whoever sheds the blood of a
human,
by a human shall that person's
blood be shed;
for in his own image
God made humankind.

[7]And you, be fruitful and multiply, abound on the earth and multiply in it."

8 Then God said to Noah and to his sons with him, [9]"As for me, I am establishing my covenant with you and your descendants after you, [10]and with every living creature that is with you, the birds, the domestic animals, and every animal of the earth with you, as many

as came out of the ark. a 11I establish my covenant with you, that never again shall all flesh be cut off by the waters of a flood, and never again shall there be a flood to destroy the earth." 12God said, "This is the sign of the covenant that I make between me and you and every living creature that is with you, for all future generations: 13I have set my bow in the clouds, and it shall be a sign of the covenant between me and the earth. 14When I bring clouds over the earth and the bow is seen in the clouds, 15I will remember my covenant that is between me and you and every living creature of all flesh; and the waters shall never again become a flood to destroy all flesh. 16When the bow is in the clouds, I will see it and remember the everlasting covenant between God and every living creature of all flesh that is on the earth." 17God said to Noah, "This is the sign of the covenant that I have established between me and all flesh that is on the earth."

18  The sons of Noah who went out of the ark were Shem, Ham, and Japheth. Ham was the father of Canaan. 19These three were the sons of Noah; and from these the whole earth was peopled.

20  Noah, a man of the soil, was the first to plant a vineyard. 21He drank some of the wine and became drunk, and he lay uncovered in his tent. 22And Ham, the father of Canaan, saw the nakedness of his father, and told his two brothers outside. 23Then Shem and Japheth took a garment, laid it on both their shoulders, and walked backward and covered the nakedness of their father; their faces were turned away, and they did not see their father's nakedness. 24When Noah awoke from his wine and knew what his youngest son had done to him, 25he said,

"Cursed be Canaan;

lowest of slaves shall he be to
his brothers."
26He also said,

"Blessed by the Lord my God
be Shem;
and let Canaan be his slave.
27  May God make space forb
Japheth,
and let him live in the tents of
Shem;
and let Canaan be his slave."

28  After the flood Noah lived three hundred fifty years. 29All the days of Noah were nine hundred fifty years; and he died.

10.1  These are the descendants of Noah's sons, Shem, Ham, and Japheth; children were born to them after the flood.

2  The descendants of Japheth: Gomer, Magog, Madai, Javan, Tubal, Meshech, and Tiras. 3The descendants of Gomer: Ashkenaz, Riphath, and Togarmah. 4The descendants of Javan: Elishah, Tarshish, Kittim, and Rodanim. c 5From these the coastland peoples spread. These are the descendants of Japhethd in their lands, with their own language, by their families, in their nations.

6  The descendants of Ham: Cush, Egypt, Put, and Canaan. 7The descendants of Cush: Seba, Havilah, Sabtah, Raamah, and Sabteca. The descendants of Raamah: Sheba and Dedan. 8Cush became the father of Nimrod; he was the first on earth to become a mighty warrior. 9He was a mighty hunter before the Lord; therefore it is said, "Like Nimrod a mighty hunter before the Lord." 10The beginning of his kingdom was Babel, Erech, and Accad, all of them in the land of Shinar. 11From that land he went into Assyria, and built Nineveh, Rehoboth-ir, Calah, and 12Resen between Nineveh and Calah; that is the great city. 13Egypt became

aGk: Heb adds *every animal of the earth*  bHeb *yapht,* a play on *Japheth*  cHeb Mss Sam Gk See 1 Chr 1.7: MT *Dodanim*  dCompare verses 20, 31. Heb lacks *These are the descendants of Japheth*

the father of Ludim, Anamim, Lehabim, Naphtuhim, [14]Pathrusim, Casluhim, and Caphtorim, from which the Philistines come. [a]

15 Canaan became the father of Sidon his firstborn, and Heth, [16]and the Jebusites, the Amorites, the Girgashites, [17]the Hivites, the Arkites, the Sinites, [18]the Arvadites, the Zemarites, and the Hamathites. Afterward the families of the Canaanites spread abroad. [19]And the territory of the Canaanites extended from Sidon, in the direction of Gerar, as far as Gaza, and in the direction of Sodom, Gomorrah, Admah, and Zeboiim, as far as Lasha. [20]These are the descendants of Ham, by their families, their languages, their lands, and their nations.

21 To Shem also, the father of all the children of Eber, the elder brother of Japheth, children were born. [22]The descendants of Shem: Elam, Asshur, Arpachshad, Lud, and Aram. [23]The descendants of Aram: Uz, Hul, Gether, and Mash. [24]Arpachshad became the father of Shelah; and Shelah became the father of Eber. [25]To Eber were born two sons: the name of the one was Peleg, [b] for in his days the earth was divided, and his brother's name was Joktan. [26]Joktan became the father of Almodad, Sheleph, Hazarmaveth, Jerah, [27]Hadoram, Uzal, Diklah, [28]Obal, Abimael, Sheba, [29]Ophir, Havilah, and Jobab; all these were the descendants of Joktan. [30]The territory in which they lived extended from Mesha in the direction of Sephar, the hill country of the east. [31]These are the descendants of Shem, by their families, their languages, their lands, and their nations.

32 These are the families of Noah's sons, according to their genealogies, in their nations; and from these the nations spread abroad on the earth after the flood.

## MATTHEW 4.12–25

Now when Jesus[c] heard that John had been arrested, he withdrew to Galilee. [13]He left Nazareth and made his home in Capernaum by the sea, in the territory of Zebulun and Naphtali, [14]so that what had been spoken through the prophet Isaiah might be fulfilled:
15 "Land of Zebulun, land of
        Naphtali,
    on the road by the sea,
        across the Jordan, Galilee
        of the Gentiles—
16  the people who sat in darkness
        have seen a great light,
    and for those who sat in the
        region and shadow of
        death
    light has dawned."
[17]From that time Jesus began to proclaim, "Repent, for the kingdom of heaven has come near."[d]

18 As he walked by the Sea of Galilee, he saw two brothers, Simon, who is called Peter, and Andrew his brother, casting a net into the sea—for they were fishermen. [19]And he said to them, "Follow me, and I will make you fish for people." [20]Immediately they left their nets and followed him. [21]As he went from there, he saw two other brothers, James son of Zebedee and his brother John, in the boat with their father Zebedee, mending their nets, and he called them. [22]Immediately they left the boat and their father, and followed him.

23 Jesus[e] went throughout Galilee, teaching in their synagogues and proclaiming the good news[f] of the kingdom and curing every disease and every sickness among the people. [24]So his fame spread throughout all Syria, and they brought to him all the sick,

---

a Cn: Heb *Casluhim, from which the Philistines come, and Caphtorim*  b That is *Division*  c Gk *he*
d Or *is at hand*  e Gk *He*  f Gk *gospel*

those who were afflicted with various diseases and pains, demoniacs, epileptics, and paralytics, and he cured them. 25And great crowds followed him from Galilee, the Decapolis, Jerusalem, Judea, and from beyond the Jordan.

## PSALM 4.1–8

*To the leader: with stringed instruments. A Psalm of David.*

Answer me when I call, O God
        of my right!
    You gave me room when I
        was in distress.
    Be gracious to me, and hear
        my prayer.
2  How long, you people, shall my
        honor suffer shame?
    How long will you love vain
        words, and seek after
        lies?                    *Selah*
3  But know that the Lord has set
        apart the faithful for
        himself;
    the Lord hears when I call to
        him.

4  When you are disturbed, a do
        not sin;
    ponder it on your beds, and
        be silent.               *Selah*
5  Offer right sacrifices,
    and put your trust in the
        Lord.

6  There are many who say,
        "O that we might see
        some good!
    Let the light of your face
        shine on us, O Lord!"
7  You have put gladness in my
        heart
    more than when their grain
        and wine abound.

8  I will both lie down and sleep in
        peace;
    for you alone, O Lord, make
        me lie down in safety.

## PROVERBS 1.20–23

Wisdom cries out in the
        street;
    in the squares she raises
        her voice.
21  At the busiest corner she cries
        out;
    at the entrance of the city
        gates she speaks:
22  "How long, O simple ones, will
        you love being simple?
    How long will scoffers delight in
        their scoffing
    and fools hate knowledge?
23  Give heed to my reproof;
    I will pour out my thoughts to
        you;
    I will make my words known
        to you.

a Or *are angry*

# JANUARY 5

## GENESIS 11.1—13.4

**N**ow the whole earth had one language and the same words. [2]And as they migrated from the east,[a] they came upon a plain in the land of Shinar and settled there. [3]And they said to one another, "Come, let us make bricks, and burn them thoroughly." And they had brick for stone, and bitumen for mortar. [4]Then they said, "Come, let us build ourselves a city, and a tower with its top in the heavens, and let us make a name for ourselves; otherwise we shall be scattered abroad upon the face of the whole earth." [5]The LORD came down to see the city and the tower, which mortals had built. [6]And the LORD said, "Look, they are one people, and they have all one language; and this is only the beginning of what they will do; nothing that they propose to do will now be impossible for them. [7]Come, let us go down, and confuse their language there, so that they will not understand one another's speech." [8]So the LORD scattered them abroad from there over the face of all the earth, and they left off building the city. [9]Therefore it was called Babel, because there the LORD confused[b] the language of all the earth; and from there the LORD scattered them abroad over the face of all the earth.

10 These are the descendants of Shem. When Shem was one hundred years old, he became the father of Arpachshad two years after the flood; [11]and Shem lived after the birth of Arpachshad five hundred years, and had other sons and daughters.

12 When Arpachshad had lived thirty-five years, he became the father of Shelah; [13]and Arpachshad lived after the birth of Shelah four hundred three years, and had other sons and daughters.

14 When Shelah had lived thirty years, he became the father of Eber; [15]and Shelah lived after the birth of Eber four hundred three years, and had other sons and daughters.

16 When Eber had lived thirty-four years, he became the father of Peleg; [17]and Eber lived after the birth of Peleg four hundred thirty years, and had other sons and daughters.

18 When Peleg had lived thirty years, he became the father of Reu; [19]and Peleg lived after the birth of Reu two hundred nine years, and had other sons and daughters.

20 When Reu had lived thirty-two years, he became the father of Serug; [21]and Reu lived after the birth of Serug two hundred seven years, and had other sons and daughters.

22 When Serug had lived thirty years, he became the father of Nahor; [23]and Serug lived after the birth of Nahor two hundred years, and had other sons and daughters.

24 When Nahor had lived twenty-nine years, he became the father of Terah; [25]and Nahor lived after the birth of Terah one hundred nineteen years, and had other sons and daughters.

26 When Terah had lived seventy years, he became the father of Abram, Nahor, and Haran.

27 Now these are the descendants of Terah. Terah was the father of Abram, Nahor, and Haran; and Haran was the father of Lot. [28]Haran died before his father Terah in the land of his birth, in Ur of the Chaldeans. [29]Abram

---

a Or *migrated eastward*   b Heb *balal,* meaning *to confuse* and Nahor took wives; the name of Abram's wife was Sarai, and the name of Nahor's wife was Milcah. She was the daughter of Haran the father of Milcah and Iscah. ³⁰Now Sarai was barren; she had no child.

31 Terah took his son Abram and his grandson Lot son of Haran, and his daughter-in-law Sarai, his son Abram's wife, and they went out together from Ur of the Chaldeans to go into the land of Canaan; but when they came to Haran, they settled there. ³²The days of Terah were two hundred five years; and Terah died in Haran.

**12.**1 Now the LORD said to Abram, "Go from your country and your kindred and your father's house to the land that I will show you. ²I will make of you a great nation, and I will bless you, and make your name great, so that you will be a blessing. ³I will bless those who bless you, and the one who curses you I will curse; and in you all the families of the earth shall be blessed."ᵃ

4 So Abram went, as the LORD had told him; and Lot went with him. Abram was seventy-five years old when he departed from Haran. ⁵Abram took his wife Sarai and his brother's son Lot, and all the possessions that they had gathered, and the persons whom they had acquired in Haran; and they set forth to go to the land of Canaan. When they had come to the land of Canaan, ⁶Abram passed through the land to the place at Shechem, to the oakᵇ of Moreh. At that time the Canaanites were in the land. ⁷Then the LORD appeared to Abram, and said, "To your offspringᶜ I will give this land." So he built there an altar to the LORD, who had appeared to him. ⁸From there he moved on to the hill country on the east of Bethel, and pitched his tent, with Bethel on the west and Ai on the east; and there he built an altar to the LORD

and invoked the name of the LORD. ⁹And Abram journeyed on by stages toward the Negeb.

10 Now there was a famine in the land. So Abram went down to Egypt to reside there as an alien, for the famine was severe in the land. ¹¹When he was about to enter Egypt, he said to his wife Sarai, "I know well that you are a woman beautiful in appearance; ¹²and when the Egyptians see you, they will say, 'This is his wife'; then they will kill me, but they will let you live. ¹³Say you are my sister, so that it may go well with me because of you, and that my life may be spared on your account." ¹⁴When Abram entered Egypt the Egyptians saw that the woman was very beautiful. ¹⁵When the officials of Pharaoh saw her, they praised her to Pharaoh. And the woman was taken into Pharaoh's house. ¹⁶And for her sake he dealt well with Abram; and he had sheep, oxen, male donkeys, male and female slaves, female donkeys, and camels.

17 But the LORD afflicted Pharaoh and his house with great plagues because of Sarai, Abram's wife. ¹⁸So Pharaoh called Abram, and said, "What is this you have done to me? Why did you not tell me that she was your wife? ¹⁹Why did you say, 'She is my sister,' so that I took her for my wife? Now then, here is your wife, take her, and be gone." ²⁰And Pharaoh gave his men orders concerning him; and they set him on the way, with his wife and all that he had.

**13.**1 So Abram went up from Egypt, he and his wife, and all that he had, and Lot with him, into the Negeb.

2 Now Abram was very rich in livestock, in silver, and in gold. ³He journeyed on by stages from the Negeb as far as Bethel, to the place where his tent had been at the beginning, be-

ᵃOr *by you all the families of the earth shall bless themselves*  ᵇOr *terebinth*  ᶜHeb *seed*

tween Bethel and Ai, [4]to the place where he had made an altar at the first; and there Abram called on the name of the LORD.

## MATTHEW 5.1–26

WHEN Jesus[a] saw the crowds, he went up the mountain; and after he sat down, his disciples came to him. [2]Then he began to speak, and taught them, saying:

3 "Blessed are the poor in spirit, for theirs is the kingdom of heaven.

4 "Blessed are those who mourn, for they will be comforted.

5 "Blessed are the meek, for they will inherit the earth.

6 "Blessed are those who hunger and thirst for righteousness, for they will be filled.

7 "Blessed are the merciful, for they will receive mercy.

8 "Blessed are the pure in heart, for they will see God.

9 "Blessed are the peacemakers, for they will be called children of God.

10 "Blessed are those who are persecuted for righteousness' sake, for theirs is the kingdom of heaven.

11 "Blessed are you when people revile you and persecute you and utter all kinds of evil against you falsely[b] on my account. [12]Rejoice and be glad, for your reward is great in heaven, for in the same way they persecuted the prophets who were before you.

13 "You are the salt of the earth; but if salt has lost its taste, how can its saltiness be restored? It is no longer good for anything, but is thrown out and trampled under foot.

14 "You are the light of the world. A city built on a hill cannot be hid. [15]No one after lighting a lamp puts it under the bushel basket, but on the lampstand, and it gives light to all in the house. [16]In the same way, let your light shine before others, so that they may see your good works and give glory to your Father in heaven.

17 "Do not think that I have come to abolish the law or the prophets; I have come not to abolish but to fulfill. [18]For truly I tell you, until heaven and earth pass away, not one letter,[c] not one stroke of a letter, will pass from the law until all is accomplished. [19]Therefore, whoever breaks[d] one of the least of these commandments, and teaches others to do the same, will be called least in the kingdom of heaven; but whoever does them and teaches them will be called great in the kingdom of heaven. [20]For I tell you, unless your righteousness exceeds that of the scribes and Pharisees, you will never enter the kingdom of heaven.

21 "You have heard that it was said to those of ancient times, 'You shall not murder'; and 'whoever murders shall be liable to judgment.' [22]But I say to you that if you are angry with a brother or sister,[e] you will be liable to judgment; and if you insult[f] a brother or sister,[g] you will be liable to the council; and if you say, 'You fool,' you will be liable to the hell[h] of fire. [23]So when you are offering your gift at the altar, if you remember that your brother or sister[i] has something against you, [24]leave your gift there before the altar and go; first be reconciled to your brother or sister,[i] and then come and offer your gift. [25]Come to terms quickly with your accuser while you are on the way to court[j] with him, or your accuser may hand you over to the judge, and the judge to the guard, and you will be thrown into prison. [26]Truly I tell you, you will never get out until you have paid the last penny.

aGk *he*  bOther ancient authorities lack *falsely*  cGk *one iota*  dOr *annuls*  eGk *a brother*; other ancient authorities add *without cause*  fGk *say Raca to* (an obscure term of abuse)  gGk *a brother* hGk *Gehenna*  iGk *your brother*  jGk lacks *to court*

## PSALM 5.1–12

*To the leader: for the flutes. A Psalm of David.*

Give ear to my words, O Lord;
   give heed to my sighing.
2  Listen to the sound of
     my cry,
  my King and my God,
   for to you I pray.
3  O Lord, in the morning you
     hear my voice;
  in the morning I plead my
      case to you, and watch.

4  For you are not a God who
     delights in wickedness;
  evil will not sojourn with you.
5  The boastful will not stand
     before your eyes;
  you hate all evildoers.
6  You destroy those who speak
     lies;
  the Lord abhors the
     bloodthirsty and
     deceitful.

7  But I, through the abundance of
     your steadfast love,
  will enter your house,
  I will bow down toward your
     holy temple
  in awe of you.
8  Lead me, O Lord, in your
     righteousness
  because of my enemies;
  make your way straight
     before me.

9  For there is no truth in their
     mouths;
  their hearts are destruction;
  their throats are open graves;
  they flatter with their
     tongues.
10  Make them bear their guilt,
     O God;

let them fall by their own
     counsels;
because of their many
     transgressions cast them
     out,
for they have rebelled against
     you.

11  But let all who take refuge in
     you rejoice;
  let them ever sing for joy.
  Spread your protection over
     them,
  so that those who love your
     name may exult in you.
12  For you bless the righteous,
     O Lord;
  you cover them with favor as
     with a shield.

## PROVERBS 1.24–28

Because I have called and you
     refused,
have stretched out my hand
     and no one heeded,
25  and because you have ignored
     all my counsel
  and would have none of my
     reproof,
26  I also will laugh at your
     calamity;
  I will mock when panic strikes
     you,
27  when panic strikes you like a
     storm,
  and your calamity comes like
     a whirlwind,
  when distress and anguish
     come upon you.
28  Then they will call upon me, but
     I will not answer;
  they will seek me diligently,
     but will not find me.

# JANUARY 6

## GENESIS 13.5—15.21

Now Lot, who went with Abram, also had flocks and herds and tents, 6so that the land could not support both of them living together; for their possessions were so great that they could not live together, 7and there was strife between the herders of Abram's livestock and the herders of Lot's livestock. At that time the Canaanites and the Perizzites lived in the land.

8 Then Abram said to Lot, "Let there be no strife between you and me, and between your herders and my herders; for we are kindred. 9Is not the whole land before you? Separate yourself from me. If you take the left hand, then I will go to the right; or if you take the right hand, then I will go to the left." 10Lot looked about him, and saw that the plain of the Jordan was well watered everywhere like the garden of the LORD, like the land of Egypt, in the direction of Zoar; this was before the LORD had destroyed Sodom and Gomorrah. 11So Lot chose for himself all the plain of the Jordan, and Lot journeyed eastward; thus they separated from each other. 12Abram settled in the land of Canaan, while Lot settled among the cities of the Plain and moved his tent as far as Sodom. 13Now the people of Sodom were wicked, great sinners against the LORD.

14 The LORD said to Abram, after Lot had separated from him, "Raise your eyes now, and look from the place where you are, northward and southward and eastward and westward; 15for all the land that you see I will give to you and to your offspringa forever. 16I will make your offspring like the dust of the earth; so that if one can count the dust of the earth, your offspring also can be counted. 17Rise up, walk through the length and the breadth of the land, for I will give it to you." 18So Abram moved his tent, and came and settled by the oaksb of Mamre, which are at Hebron; and there he built an altar to the LORD.

14.1 IN the days of King Amraphel of Shinar, King Arioch of Ellasar, King Chedorlaomer of Elam, and King Tidal of Goiim, 2these kings made war with King Bera of Sodom, King Birsha of Gomorrah, King Shinab of Admah, King Shemeber of Zeboiim, and the king of Bela (that is, Zoar). 3All these joined forces in the Valley of Siddim (that is, the Dead Sea). c 4Twelve years they had served Chedorlaomer, but in the thirteenth year they rebelled. 5In the fourteenth year Chedorlaomer and the kings who were with him came and subdued the Rephaim in Ashteroth-karnaim, the Zuzim in Ham, the Emim in Shaveh-kiriathaim, 6and the Horites in the hill country of Seir as far as El-paran on the edge of the wilderness; 7then they turned back and came to En-mishpat (that is, Kadesh), and subdued all the country of the Amalekites, and also the Amorites who lived in Hazazon-tamar. 8Then the king of Sodom, the king of Gomorrah, the king of Admah, the king of Zeboiim, and the king of Bela (that is, Zoar) went out, and they joined battle in the Valley of Siddim 9with King Chedorlaomer of Elam, King Tidal of Goiim, King Amraphel of Shinar, and King Arioch of Ellasar, four kings against five. 10Now the Valley of Siddim was full of bitumen

---

aHeb *seed*   bOr *terebinths*   cHeb *Salt Sea*

pits; and as the kings of Sodom and Gomorrah fled, some fell into them, and the rest fled to the hill country. ¹¹So the enemy took all the goods of Sodom and Gomorrah, and all their provisions, and went their way; ¹²they also took Lot, the son of Abram's brother, who lived in Sodom, and his goods, and departed.

13 Then one who had escaped came and told Abram the Hebrew, who was living by the oaksᵃ of Mamre the Amorite, brother of Eshcol and of Aner; these were allies of Abram. ¹⁴When Abram heard that his nephew had been taken captive, he led forth his trained men, born in his house, three hundred eighteen of them, and went in pursuit as far as Dan. ¹⁵He divided his forces against them by night, he and his servants, and routed them and pursued them to Hobah, north of Damascus. ¹⁶Then he brought back all the goods, and also brought back his nephew Lot with his goods, and the women and the people.

17 After his return from the defeat of Chedorlaomer and the kings who were with him, the king of Sodom went out to meet him at the Valley of Shaveh (that is, the King's Valley). ¹⁸And King Melchizedek of Salem brought out bread and wine; he was priest of God Most High.ᵇ ¹⁹He blessed him and said,

"Blessed be Abram by God
Most High,ᵇ
maker of heaven and earth;
20 and blessed be God Most
High,ᵇ
who has delivered your
enemies into your hand!"

And Abram gave him one tenth of everything. ²¹Then the king of Sodom said to Abram, "Give me the persons, but take the goods for yourself." ²²But Abram said to the king of Sodom, "I have sworn to the LORD, God Most High,ᵇ maker of heaven and earth, ²³that I would not take a thread or a sandal-thong or anything that is yours, so that you might not say, 'I have made Abram rich.' ²⁴I will take nothing but what the young men have eaten, and the share of the men who went with me—Aner, Eshcol, and Mamre. Let them take their share."

15.1 AFTER these things the word of the LORD came to Abram in a vision, "Do not be afraid, Abram, I am your shield; your reward shall be very great." ²But Abram said, "O Lord GOD, what will you give me, for I continue childless, and the heir of my house is Eliezer of Damascus?"ᶜ ³And Abram said, "You have given me no offspring, and so a slave born in my house is to be my heir." ⁴But the word of the LORD came to him, "This man shall not be your heir; no one but your very own issue shall be your heir." ⁵He brought him outside and said, "Look toward heaven and count the stars, if you are able to count them." Then he said to him, "So shall your descendants be." ⁶And he believed the LORD; and the LORDᵈ reckoned it to him as righteousness.

7 Then he said to him, "I am the LORD who brought you from Ur of the Chaldeans, to give you this land to possess." ⁸But he said, "O Lord GOD, how am I to know that I shall possess it?" ⁹He said to him, "Bring me a heifer three years old, a female goat three years old, a ram three years old, a turtledove, and a young pigeon." ¹⁰He brought him all these and cut them in two, laying each half over against the other; but he did not cut the birds in two. ¹¹And when birds of prey came down on the carcasses, Abram drove them away.

12 As the sun was going down, a deep sleep fell upon Abram, and a deep and terrifying darkness descended upon him. ¹³Then the LORDᵈ said to

ᵃOr *terebinths*  ᵇHeb *El Elyon*  ᶜMeaning of Heb uncertain  ᵈHeb *he*

Abram, "Know this for certain, that your offspring shall be aliens in a land that is not theirs, and shall be slaves there, and they shall be oppressed for four hundred years; ¹⁴but I will bring judgment on the nation that they serve, and afterward they shall come out with great possessions. ¹⁵As for yourself, you shall go to your ancestors in peace; you shall be buried in a good old age. ¹⁶And they shall come back here in the fourth generation; for the iniquity of the Amorites is not yet complete."

17 When the sun had gone down and it was dark, a smoking fire pot and a flaming torch passed between these pieces. ¹⁸On that day the LORD made a covenant with Abram, saying, "To your descendants I give this land, from the river of Egypt to the great river, the river Euphrates, ¹⁹the land of the Kenites, the Kenizzites, the Kadmonites, ²⁰the Hittites, the Perizzites, the Rephaim, ²¹the Amorites, the Canaanites, the Girgashites, and the Jebusites."

## MATTHEW 5.27–48

"**Y**OU have heard that it was said, 'You shall not commit adultery.' ²⁸But I say to you that everyone who looks at a woman with lust has already committed adultery with her in his heart. ²⁹If your right eye causes you to sin, tear it out and throw it away; it is better for you to lose one of your members than for your whole body to be thrown into hell. ª ³⁰And if your right hand causes you to sin, cut it off and throw it away; it is better for you to lose one of your members than for your whole body to go into hell. ª

31 "It was also said, 'Whoever divorces his wife, let him give her a certificate of divorce.' ³²But I say to you that anyone who divorces his wife, except on the ground of unchastity, causes her to commit adultery; and whoever marries a divorced woman commits adultery.

33 "Again, you have heard that it was said to those of ancient times, 'You shall not swear falsely, but carry out the vows you have made to the Lord.' ³⁴But I say to you, Do not swear at all, either by heaven, for it is the throne of God, ³⁵or by the earth, for it is his footstool, or by Jerusalem, for it is the city of the great King. ³⁶And do not swear by your head, for you cannot make one hair white or black. ³⁷Let your word be 'Yes, Yes' or 'No, No'; anything more than this comes from the evil one. ᵇ

38 "You have heard that it was said, 'An eye for an eye and a tooth for a tooth.' ³⁹But I say to you, Do not resist an evildoer. But if anyone strikes you on the right cheek, turn the other also; ⁴⁰and if anyone wants to sue you and take your coat, give your cloak as well; ⁴¹and if anyone forces you to go one mile, go also the second mile. ⁴²Give to everyone who begs from you, and do not refuse anyone who wants to borrow from you.

43 "You have heard that it was said, 'You shall love your neighbor and hate your enemy.' ⁴⁴But I say to you, Love your enemies and pray for those who persecute you, ⁴⁵so that you may be children of your Father in heaven; for he makes his sun rise on the evil and on the good, and sends rain on the righteous and on the unrighteous. ⁴⁶For if you love those who love you, what reward do you have? Do not even the tax collectors do the same? ⁴⁷And if you greet only your brothers and sisters, ᶜ what more are you doing than others? Do not even the Gentiles do the same? ⁴⁸Be perfect, therefore, as your heavenly Father is perfect.

ªGk *Gehenna*  ᵇOr *evil*  ᶜGk *your brothers*

## PSALM 6.1–10

*To the leader: with stringed instruments;*
*according to The Sheminith. A Psalm of David.*

O LORD, do not rebuke me in
  your anger,
or discipline me in your
  wrath.
2 Be gracious to me, O LORD, for
  I am languishing;
  O LORD, heal me, for my
  bones are shaking with
  terror.
3 My soul also is struck with
  terror,
  while you, O LORD—how
  long?

4 Turn, O LORD, save my life;
  deliver me for the sake of
  your steadfast love.
5 For in death there is no
  remembrance of you;
  in Sheol who can give you
  praise?

6 I am weary with my moaning;
  every night I flood my bed
  with tears;
  I drench my couch with my
  weeping.
7 My eyes waste away because of
  grief;
  they grow weak because of all
  my foes.

8 Depart from me, all you
  workers of evil,
  for the LORD has heard the
  sound of my weeping.
9 The LORD has heard my
  supplication;
  the LORD accepts my prayer.
10 All my enemies shall be
  ashamed and struck with
  terror;
  they shall turn back, and in a
  moment be put to
  shame.

## PROVERBS 1.29–33

BECAUSE they hated knowledge
  and did not choose the fear
  of the LORD,
30 would have none of my counsel,
  and despised all my reproof,
31 therefore they shall eat the fruit
  of their way
  and be sated with their own
  devices.
32 For waywardness kills the
  simple,
  and the complacency of fools
  destroys them;
33 but those who listen to me will
  be secure
  and will live at ease, without
  dread of disaster."

## GENESIS 16.1—18.19

**N**ow Sarai, Abram's wife, bore him no children. She had an Egyptian slave-girl whose name was Hagar, ²and Sarai said to Abram, "You see that the Lord has prevented me from bearing children; go in to my slave-girl; it may be that I shall obtain children by her." And Abram listened to the voice of Sarai. ³So, after Abram had lived ten years in the land of Canaan, Sarai, Abram's wife, took Hagar the Egyptian, her slave-girl, and gave her to her husband Abram as a wife. ⁴He went in to Hagar, and she conceived; and when she saw that she had conceived, she looked with contempt on her mistress. ⁵Then Sarai said to Abram, "May the wrong done to me be on you! I gave my slave-girl to your embrace, and when she saw that she had conceived, she looked on me with contempt. May the Lord judge between you and me!" ⁶But Abram said to Sarai, "Your slave-girl is in your power; do to her as you please." Then Sarai dealt harshly with her, and she ran away from her.

7  The angel of the Lord found her by a spring of water in the wilderness, the spring on the way to Shur. ⁸And he said, "Hagar, slave-girl of Sarai, where have you come from and where are you going?" She said, "I am running away from my mistress Sarai." ⁹The angel of the Lord said to her, "Return to your mistress, and submit to her." ¹⁰The angel of the Lord also said to her, "I will so greatly multiply your offspring that they cannot be counted for multitude." ¹¹And the angel of the Lord said to her,

"Now you have conceived and
    shall bear a son;
you shall call him Ishmael, ᵃ
for the Lord has given heed
    to your affliction.
12  He shall be a wild ass of a man,
with his hand against everyone,
    and everyone's hand against
    him;
and he shall live at odds with all
    his kin."

¹³So she named the Lord who spoke to her, "You are El-roi"; ᵇ for she said, "Have I really seen God and remained alive after seeing him?"ᶜ ¹⁴Therefore the well was called Beer-lahai-roi; ᵈ it lies between Kadesh and Bered.

15  Hagar bore Abram a son; and Abram named his son, whom Hagar bore, Ishmael. ¹⁶Abram was eighty-six years old when Hagar bore himᵉ Ishmael.

17.1 When Abram was ninety-nine years old, the Lord appeared to Abram, and said to him, "I am God Almighty;ᶠ walk before me, and be blameless. ²And I will make my covenant between me and you, and will make you exceedingly numerous." ³Then Abram fell on his face; and God said to him, ⁴"As for me, this is my covenant with you: You shall be the ancestor of a multitude of nations. ⁵No longer shall your name be Abram,ᵍ but your name shall be Abraham;ʰ for I have made you the ancestor of a multitude of nations. ⁶I will make you exceedingly fruitful; and I will make nations of you, and kings shall come from you. ⁷I will establish my covenant between me and you, and

---

ᵃThat is *God hears*  ᵇPerhaps *God of seeing* or *God who sees*  ᶜMeaning of Heb uncertain  ᵈThat is *the Well of the Living One who sees me*  ᵉHeb *Abram*  ᶠTraditional rendering of Heb *El Shaddai*
ᵍThat is *exalted ancestor*  ʰHere taken to mean *ancestor of a multitude*

your offspring after you throughout their generations, for an everlasting covenant, to be God to you and to your offspring[a] after you. [8]And I will give to you, and to your offspring after you, the land where you are now an alien, all the land of Canaan, for a perpetual holding; and I will be their God."

9 God said to Abraham, "As for you, you shall keep my covenant, you and your offspring after you throughout their generations. [10]This is my covenant, which you shall keep, between me and you and your offspring after you: Every male among you shall be circumcised. [11]You shall circumcise the flesh of your foreskins, and it shall be a sign of the covenant between me and you. [12]Throughout your generations every male among you shall be circumcised when he is eight days old, including the slave born in your house and the one bought with your money from any foreigner who is not of your offspring. [13]Both the slave born in your house and the one bought with your money must be circumcised. So shall my covenant be in your flesh an everlasting covenant. [14]Any uncircumcised male who is not circumcised in the flesh of his foreskin shall be cut off from his people; he has broken my covenant."

15 God said to Abraham, "As for Sarai your wife, you shall not call her Sarai, but Sarah shall be her name. [16]I will bless her, and moreover I will give you a son by her. I will bless her, and she shall give rise to nations; kings of peoples shall come from her." [17]Then Abraham fell on his face and laughed, and said to himself, "Can a child be born to a man who is a hundred years old? Can Sarah, who is ninety years old, bear a child?" [18]And Abraham said to God, "O that Ishmael might live in your sight!" [19]God said, "No, but your wife Sarah shall bear you a son, and you shall name him Isaac.[b]

I will establish my covenant with him as an everlasting covenant for his offspring after him. [20]As for Ishmael, I have heard you; I will bless him and make him fruitful and exceedingly numerous; he shall be the father of twelve princes, and I will make him a great nation. [21]But my covenant I will establish with Isaac, whom Sarah shall bear to you at this season next year." [22]And when he had finished talking with him, God went up from Abraham.

23 Then Abraham took his son Ishmael and all the slaves born in his house or bought with his money, every male among the men of Abraham's house, and he circumcised the flesh of their foreskins that very day, as God had said to him. [24]Abraham was ninety-nine years old when he was circumcised in the flesh of his foreskin. [25]And his son Ishmael was thirteen years old when he was circumcised in the flesh of his foreskin. [26]That very day Abraham and his son Ishmael were circumcised; [27]and all the men of his house, slaves born in the house and those bought with money from a foreigner, were circumcised with him.

18.1 THE LORD appeared to Abraham[c] by the oaks[d] of Mamre, as he sat at the entrance of his tent in the heat of the day. [2]He looked up and saw three men standing near him. When he saw them, he ran from the tent entrance to meet them, and bowed down to the ground. [3]He said, "My lord, if I find favor with you, do not pass by your servant. [4]Let a little water be brought, and wash your feet, and rest yourselves under the tree. [5]Let me bring a little bread, that you may refresh yourselves, and after that you may pass on—since you have come to your servant." So they said, "Do as you have said." [6]And Abraham hastened into the tent to Sarah, and said, "Make ready quickly three mea-

aHeb seed   bThat is he laughs   cHeb him   dOr terebinths

sures<sup>a</sup> of choice flour, knead it, and make cakes." <sup>7</sup>Abraham ran to the herd, and took a calf, tender and good, and gave it to the servant, who hastened to prepare it. <sup>8</sup>Then he took curds and milk and the calf that he had prepared, and set it before them; and he stood by them under the tree while they ate.

9 They said to him, "Where is your wife Sarah?" And he said, "There, in the tent." <sup>10</sup>Then one said, "I will surely return to you in due season, and your wife Sarah shall have a son." And Sarah was listening at the tent entrance behind him. <sup>11</sup>Now Abraham and Sarah were old, advanced in age; it had ceased to be with Sarah after the manner of women. <sup>12</sup>So Sarah laughed to herself, saying, "After I have grown old, and my husband is old, shall I have pleasure?" <sup>13</sup>The LORD said to Abraham, "Why did Sarah laugh, and say, 'Shall I indeed bear a child, now that I am old?' <sup>14</sup>Is anything too wonderful for the LORD? At the set time I will return to you, in due season, and Sarah shall have a son." <sup>15</sup>But Sarah denied, saying, "I did not laugh"; for she was afraid. He said, "Oh yes, you did laugh."

16 Then the men set out from there, and they looked toward Sodom; and Abraham went with them to set them on their way. <sup>17</sup>The LORD said, "Shall I hide from Abraham what I am about to do, <sup>18</sup>seeing that Abraham shall become a great and mighty nation, and all the nations of the earth shall be blessed in him?<sup>b</sup> <sup>19</sup>No, for I have chosen<sup>c</sup> him, that he may charge his children and his household after him to keep the way of the LORD by doing righteousness and justice; so that the LORD may bring about for Abraham what he has promised him."

## MATTHEW 6.1–24

"**B**EWARE of practicing your piety before others in order to be seen by them; for then you have no reward from your Father in heaven.

2 "So whenever you give alms, do not sound a trumpet before you, as the hypocrites do in the synagogues and in the streets, so that they may be praised by others. Truly I tell you, they have received their reward. <sup>3</sup>But when you give alms, do not let your left hand know what your right hand is doing, <sup>4</sup>so that your alms may be done in secret; and your Father who sees in secret will reward you. <sup>d</sup>

5 "And whenever you pray, do not be like the hypocrites; for they love to stand and pray in the synagogues and at the street corners, so that they may be seen by others. Truly I tell you, they have received their reward. <sup>6</sup>But whenever you pray, go into your room and shut the door and pray to your Father who is in secret; and your Father who sees in secret will reward you. <sup>d</sup>

7 "When you are praying, do not heap up empty phrases as the Gentiles do; for they think that they will be heard because of their many words. <sup>8</sup>Do not be like them, for your Father knows what you need before you ask him.

9 "Pray then in this way:
Our Father in heaven,
    hallowed be your name.
10    Your kingdom come.
    Your will be done,
        on earth as it is in heaven.
11    Give us this day our daily
            bread. <sup>e</sup>
12    And forgive us our debts,
        as we also have forgiven
        our debtors.

13 And do not bring us to the
   time of trial, **ᵃ**
  but rescue us from the
   evil one. **ᵇ**

¹⁴For if you forgive others their trespasses, your heavenly Father will also forgive you; ¹⁵but if you do not forgive others, neither will your Father forgive your trespasses.

16 "And whenever you fast, do not look dismal, like the hypocrites, for they disfigure their faces so as to show others that they are fasting. Truly I tell you, they have received their reward. ¹⁷But when you fast, put oil on your head and wash your face, ¹⁸so that your fasting may be seen not by others but by your Father who is in secret; and your Father who sees in secret will reward you. **ᶜ**

19 "Do not store up for yourselves treasures on earth, where moth and rust**ᵈ** consume and where thieves break in and steal; ²⁰but store up for yourselves treasures in heaven, where neither moth nor rust**ᵈ** consumes and where thieves do not break in and steal. ²¹For where your treasure is, there your heart will be also.

22 "The eye is the lamp of the body. So, if your eye is healthy, your whole body will be full of light; ²³but if your eye is unhealthy, your whole body will be full of darkness. If then the light in you is darkness, how great is the darkness!

24 "No one can serve two masters; for a slave will either hate the one and love the other, or be devoted to the one and despise the other. You cannot serve God and wealth. **ᵉ**

## PSALM 7.1–17

*A Shiggaion of David, which he sang to the Lord concerning Cush, a Benjaminite.*

O LORD my God, in you I take
  refuge;
 save me from all my
  pursuers, and deliver
  me,
2 or like a lion they will tear me
   apart;
  they will drag me away, with
   no one to rescue.

3 O Lord my God, if I have done
   this,
  if there is wrong in my hands,
4 if I have repaid my ally with
   harm
  or plundered my foe without
   cause,
5 then let the enemy pursue and
   overtake me,
  trample my life to the ground,
  and lay my soul in the dust.
        *Selah*

6 Rise up, O Lord, in your anger;
  lift yourself up against the
   fury of my enemies;
  awake, O my God; **ᶠ** you
   have appointed a
   judgment.
7 Let the assembly of the peoples
   be gathered around you,
  and over it take your seat**ᵍ**
   on high.
8 The Lord judges the peoples;
  judge me, O Lord, according
   to my righteousness
  and according to the integrity
   that is in me.

9 O let the evil of the wicked
   come to an end,
  but establish the righteous,

---

**ᵃ**Or *us into temptation* **ᵇ**Or *from evil.* Other ancient authorities add, in some form, *For the kingdom and the power and the glory are yours forever. Amen.* **ᶜ**Other ancient authorities add *openly* **ᵈ**Gk *eating* **ᵉ**Gk *mammon* **ᶠ**Or *awake for me* **ᵍ**Cn: Heb *return*

you who test the minds and
 hearts,
  O righteous God.
10 God is my shield,
 who saves the upright in
  heart.
11 God is a righteous judge,
 and a God who has
  indignation every day.

12 If one does not repent, God[a]
 will whet his sword;
  he has bent and strung his
   bow;
13 he has prepared his deadly
 weapons,
  making his arrows fiery
   shafts.
14 See how they conceive evil,
 and are pregnant with
  mischief,
 and bring forth lies.
15 They make a pit, digging it out,
 and fall into the hole that they
  have made.
16 Their mischief returns upon
 their own heads,
  and on their own heads their
   violence descends.

17 I will give to the LORD the
 thanks due to his
  righteousness,
 and sing praise to the name of
  the LORD, the Most High.

## PROVERBS 2.1–5

My child, if you accept my words
 and treasure up my
  commandments within
   you,
2 making your ear attentive to
 wisdom
  and inclining your heart to
   understanding;
3 if you indeed cry out for insight,
 and raise your voice for
  understanding;
4 if you seek it like silver,
 and search for it as for hidden
  treasures—
5 then you will understand the
 fear of the LORD
  and find the knowledge of
   God.

# JANUARY 8

## GENESIS 18.20—19.38

Then the LORD said, "How great is the outcry against Sodom and Gomorrah and how very grave their sin! 21I must go down and see whether they have done altogether according to the outcry that has come to me; and if not, I will know."

22 So the men turned from there, and went toward Sodom, while Abraham remained standing before the LORD.[b] 23Then Abraham came near and said, "Will you indeed sweep away the righteous with the wicked? 24Suppose there are fifty righteous within the city; will you then sweep away the place and not forgive it for the fifty righteous who are in it? 25Far be it from you to do such a thing, to slay the righteous with the wicked, so that the righteous

a Heb *he*   b Another ancient tradition reads *while the* LORD *remained standing before Abraham*

fare as the wicked! Far be that from you! Shall not the Judge of all the earth do what is just?" 26And the LORD said, "If I find at Sodom fifty righteous in the city, I will forgive the whole place for their sake." 27Abraham answered, "Let me take it upon myself to speak to the Lord, I who am but dust and ashes. 28Suppose five of the fifty righteous are lacking? Will you destroy the whole city for lack of five?" And he said, "I will not destroy it if I find forty-five there." 29Again he spoke to him, "Suppose forty are found there." He answered, "For the sake of forty I will not do it." 30Then he said, "Oh do not let the Lord be angry if I speak. Suppose thirty are found there." He answered, "I will not do it, if I find thirty there." 31He said, "Let me take it upon myself to speak to the Lord. Suppose twenty are found there." He answered, "For the sake of twenty I will not destroy it." 32Then he said, "Oh do not let the Lord be angry if I speak just once more. Suppose ten are found there." He answered, "For the sake of ten I will not destroy it." 33And the LORD went his way, when he had finished speaking to Abraham; and Abraham returned to his place.

**19.**1 THE two angels came to Sodom in the evening, and Lot was sitting in the gateway of Sodom. When Lot saw them, he rose to meet them, and bowed down with his face to the ground. 2He said, "Please, my lords, turn aside to your servant's house and spend the night, and wash your feet; then you can rise early and go on your way." They said, "No; we will spend the night in the square." 3But he urged them strongly; so they turned aside to him and entered his house; and he made them a feast, and baked unleavened bread, and they ate. 4But before they lay down, the men of the city, the men of Sodom, both young and old, all the people to the last man, surrounded the house; 5and they called to Lot, "Where are the men who came to you tonight? Bring them out to us, so that we may know them." 6Lot went out of the door to the men, shut the door after him, 7and said, "I beg you, my brothers, do not act so wickedly. 8Look, I have two daughters who have not known a man; let me bring them out to you, and do to them as you please; only do nothing to these men, for they have come under the shelter of my roof." 9But they replied, "Stand back!" And they said, "This fellow came here as an alien, and he would play the judge! Now we will deal worse with you than with them." Then they pressed hard against the man Lot, and came near the door to break it down. 10But the men inside reached out their hands and brought Lot into the house with them, and shut the door. 11And they struck with blindness the men who were at the door of the house, both small and great, so that they were unable to find the door.

12 Then the men said to Lot, "Have you anyone else here? Sons-in-law, sons, daughters, or anyone you have in the city—bring them out of the place. 13For we are about to destroy this place, because the outcry against its people has become great before the LORD, and the LORD has sent us to destroy it." 14So Lot went out and said to his sons-in-law, who were to marry his daughters, "Up, get out of this place; for the LORD is about to destroy the city." But he seemed to his sons-in-law to be jesting.

15 When morning dawned, the angels urged Lot, saying, "Get up, take your wife and your two daughters who are here, or else you will be consumed in the punishment of the city." 16But he lingered; so the men seized him and his wife and his two daughters by the hand, the LORD being merciful to him, and they brought him out and left him outside the city. 17When they had brought

them outside, they[a] said, "Flee for your life; do not look back or stop anywhere in the Plain; flee to the hills, or else you will be consumed." [18]And Lot said to them, "Oh, no, my lords; [19]your servant has found favor with you, and you have shown me great kindness in saving my life; but I cannot flee to the hills, for fear the disaster will overtake me and I die. [20]Look, that city is near enough to flee to, and it is a little one. Let me escape there—is it not a little one?—and my life will be saved!" [21]He said to him, "Very well, I grant you this favor too, and will not overthrow the city of which you have spoken. [22]Hurry, escape there, for I can do nothing until you arrive there." Therefore the city was called Zoar.[b] [23]The sun had risen on the earth when Lot came to Zoar.

24  Then the LORD rained on Sodom and Gomorrah sulfur and fire from the LORD out of heaven; [25]and he overthrew those cities, and all the Plain, and all the inhabitants of the cities, and what grew on the ground. [26]But Lot's wife, behind him, looked back, and she became a pillar of salt.

27  Abraham went early in the morning to the place where he had stood before the LORD; [28]and he looked down toward Sodom and Gomorrah and toward all the land of the Plain and saw the smoke of the land going up like the smoke of a furnace.

29  So it was that, when God destroyed the cities of the Plain, God remembered Abraham, and sent Lot out of the midst of the overthrow, when he overthrew the cities in which Lot had settled.

30  Now Lot went up out of Zoar and settled in the hills with his two daughters, for he was afraid to stay in Zoar; so he lived in a cave with his two daughters. [31]And the firstborn said to the younger, "Our father is old, and there is not a man on earth to come in to us after the manner of all the world. [32]Come, let us make our father drink wine, and we will lie with him, so that we may preserve offspring through our father." [33]So they made their father drink wine that night; and the firstborn went in, and lay with her father; he did not know when she lay down or when she rose. [34]On the next day, the firstborn said to the younger, "Look, I lay last night with my father; let us make him drink wine tonight also; then you go in and lie with him, so that we may preserve offspring through our father." [35]So they made their father drink wine that night also; and the younger rose, and lay with him; and he did not know when she lay down or when she rose. [36]Thus both the daughters of Lot became pregnant by their father. [37]The firstborn bore a son, and named him Moab; he is the ancestor of the Moabites to this day. [38]The younger also bore a son and named him Ben-ammi; he is the ancestor of the Ammonites to this day.

# MATTHEW 6.25—7.14

"THEREFORE I tell you, do not worry about your life, what you will eat or what you will drink,[c] or about your body, what you will wear. Is not life more than food, and the body more than clothing? [26]Look at the birds of the air; they neither sow nor reap nor gather into barns, and yet your heavenly Father feeds them. Are you not of more value than they? [27]And can any of you by worrying add a single hour to your span of life?[d] [28]And why do you worry about clothing? Consider the lilies of the field, how they grow; they neither toil nor spin, [29]yet I tell you, even Solomon in all his glory was not clothed like one of these. [30]But if God so clothes the grass of the field, which is alive today and tomorrow is thrown into the oven, will he not much more clothe you—you of little faith? [31]Therefore do not worry, saying, 'What will we eat?' or 'What will we drink?' or 'What will we wear?' [32]For it is the Gentiles who strive for all these things; and indeed your heavenly Father knows that you need all these things. [33]But strive first for the kingdom of God[a] and his[b] righteousness, and all these things will be given to you as well.

34 "So do not worry about tomorrow, for tomorrow will bring worries of its own. Today's trouble is enough for today.

[7.1] "Do not judge, so that you may not be judged. [2]For with the judgment you make you will be judged, and the measure you give will be the measure you get. [3]Why do you see the speck in your neighbor's[c] eye, but do not notice the log in your own eye? [4]Or how can you say to your neighbor, [d] 'Let me take the speck out of your eye,' while the log is in your own eye? [5]You hypocrite, first take the log out of your own eye, and then you will see clearly to take the speck out of your neighbor's[c] eye.

6 "Do not give what is holy to dogs; and do not throw your pearls before swine, or they will trample them under foot and turn and maul you.

7 "Ask, and it will be given you; search, and you will find; knock, and the door will be opened for you. [8]For everyone who asks receives, and everyone who searches finds, and for everyone who knocks, the door will be opened. [9]Is there anyone among you who, if your child asks for bread, will give a stone? [10]Or if the child asks for a fish, will give a snake? [11]If you then, who are evil, know how to give good gifts to your children, how much more

will your Father in heaven give good things to those who ask him!

12 "In everything do to others as you would have them do to you; for this is the law and the prophets.

13 "Enter through the narrow gate; for the gate is wide and the road is easy[e] that leads to destruction, and there are many who take it. [14]For the gate is narrow and the road is hard that leads to life, and there are few who find it.

## PSALM 8.1–9

*To the leader: according to The Gittith. A Psalm of David.*

O LORD, our Sovereign,
  how majestic is your name
    in all the earth!

You have set your glory above
    the heavens.
2     Out of the mouths of babes
      and infants
you have founded a bulwark
      because of your foes,
  to silence the enemy and the
      avenger.

3   When I look at your heavens,
      the work of your fingers,
  the moon and the stars that
      you have established;
4   what are human beings that you
      are mindful of them,
  mortals[f] that you care for
      them?

5   Yet you have made them a little
      lower than God,[g]
  and crowned them with glory
      and honor.
6   You have given them dominion
      over the works of your
      hands;

[a]Other ancient authorities lack *of God*  [b]Or *its*  [c]Gk *brother's*  [d]Gk *brother*  [e]Other ancient authorities read *for the road is wide and easy*  [f]Heb *ben adam*, lit. *son of man*  [g]Or *than the divine beings* or *angels*: Heb *elohim*

you have put all things under
their feet,
7 all sheep and oxen,
and also the beasts of the
field,
8 the birds of the air, and the fish
of the sea,
whatever passes along the
paths of the seas.

9 O Lord, our Sovereign,
how majestic is your name in
all the earth!

## PROVERBS 2.6–15

For the Lord gives wisdom;
from his mouth come
knowledge and
understanding;
7 he stores up sound wisdom for
the upright;
he is a shield to those who
walk blamelessly,
8 guarding the paths of justice

and preserving the way of his
faithful ones.
9 Then you will understand
righteousness and justice
and equity, every good path;
10 for wisdom will come into your
heart,
and knowledge will be
pleasant to your soul;
11 prudence will watch over you;
and understanding will
guard you.
12 It will save you from the way of
evil,
from those who speak
perversely,
13 who forsake the paths of
uprightness
to walk in the ways of
darkness,
14 who rejoice in doing evil
and delight in the
perverseness of evil;
15 those whose paths are crooked,
and who are devious in their
ways.

# JANUARY 9

## GENESIS 20.1—22.24

From there Abraham journeyed toward the region of the Negeb, and settled between Kadesh and Shur. While residing in Gerar as an alien, 2Abraham said of his wife Sarah, "She is my sister." And King Abimelech of Gerar sent and took Sarah. 3But God came to Abimelech in a dream by night, and said to him, "You are about to die because of the woman whom you have taken; for she is a married woman." 4Now Abimelech had not approached her; so he said, "Lord, will

you destroy an innocent people? 5Did he not himself say to me, 'She is my sister'? And she herself said, 'He is my brother.' I did this in the integrity of my heart and the innocence of my hands." 6Then God said to him in the dream, "Yes, I know that you did this in the integrity of your heart; furthermore it was I who kept you from sinning against me. Therefore I did not let you touch her. 7Now then, return the man's wife; for he is a prophet, and he will pray for you and you shall live. But if you do not restore her, know that you shall surely die, you and all that are yours."

8 So Abimelech rose early in the morning, and called all his servants and told them all these things; and the men were very much afraid. 9Then Abimelech called Abraham, and said to him, "What have you done to us? How have I sinned against you, that you have brought such great guilt on me and my kingdom? You have done things to me that ought not to be done." 10And Abimelech said to Abraham, "What were you thinking of, that you did this thing?" 11Abraham said, "I did it because I thought, There is no fear of God at all in this place, and they will kill me because of my wife. 12Besides, she is indeed my sister, the daughter of my father but not the daughter of my mother; and she became my wife. 13And when God caused me to wander from my father's house, I said to her, 'This is the kindness you must do me: at every place to which we come, say of me, He is my brother.'" 14Then Abimelech took sheep and oxen, and male and female slaves, and gave them to Abraham, and restored his wife Sarah to him. 15Abimelech said, "My land is before you; settle where it pleases you." 16To Sarah he said, "Look, I have given your brother a thousand pieces of silver; it is your exoneration before all who are with you; you are completely vindicated." 17Then Abraham prayed to God; and God healed Abimelech, and also healed his wife and female slaves so that they bore children. 18For the LORD had closed fast all the wombs of the house of Abimelech because of Sarah, Abraham's wife.

21.1 THE LORD dealt with Sarah as he had said, and the LORD did for Sarah as he had promised. 2Sarah conceived and bore Abraham a son in his old age, at the time of which God had spoken to him. 3Abraham gave the name Isaac to his son whom Sarah bore him. 4And Abraham circumcised his son Isaac when he was eight days old, as God had commanded him. 5Abraham was a hundred years old when his son Isaac was born to him. 6Now Sarah said, "God has brought laughter for me; everyone who hears will laugh with me." 7And she said, "Who would ever have said to Abraham that Sarah would nurse children? Yet I have borne him a son in his old age."

8 The child grew, and was weaned; and Abraham made a great feast on the day that Isaac was weaned. 9But Sarah saw the son of Hagar the Egyptian, whom she had borne to Abraham, playing with her son Isaac. a 10So she said to Abraham, "Cast out this slave woman with her son; for the son of this slave woman shall not inherit along with my son Isaac." 11The matter was very distressing to Abraham on account of his son. 12But God said to Abraham, "Do not be distressed because of the boy and because of your slave woman; whatever Sarah says to you, do as she tells you, for it is through Isaac that offspring shall be named for you. 13As for the son of the slave woman, I will make a nation of him also, because he is your offspring." 14So Abraham rose early in the morning, and took bread and a skin of water, and gave it to Hagar, putting it on her shoulder, along with the child, and sent her away. And she departed, and wandered about in the wilderness of Beer-sheba.

15 When the water in the skin was gone, she cast the child under one of the bushes. 16Then she went and sat down opposite him a good way off, about the distance of a bowshot; for she said, "Do not let me look on the death of the child." And as she sat opposite him, she lifted up her voice and wept.

aGk Vg: Heb lacks *with her son Isaac*

[17]And God heard the voice of the boy; and the angel of God called to Hagar from heaven, and said to her, "What troubles you, Hagar? Do not be afraid; for God has heard the voice of the boy where he is. [18]Come, lift up the boy and hold him fast with your hand, for I will make a great nation of him." [19]Then God opened her eyes and she saw a well of water. She went, and filled the skin with water, and gave the boy a drink.

20  God was with the boy, and he grew up; he lived in the wilderness, and became an expert with the bow. [21]He lived in the wilderness of Paran; and his mother got a wife for him from the land of Egypt.

22  At that time Abimelech, with Phicol the commander of his army, said to Abraham, "God is with you in all that you do; [23]now therefore swear to me here by God that you will not deal falsely with me or with my offspring or with my posterity, but as I have dealt loyally with you, you will deal with me and with the land where you have resided as an alien." [24]And Abraham said, "I swear it."

25  When Abraham complained to Abimelech about a well of water that Abimelech's servants had seized, [26]Abimelech said, "I do not know who has done this; you did not tell me, and I have not heard of it until today." [27]So Abraham took sheep and oxen and gave them to Abimelech, and the two men made a covenant. [28]Abraham set apart seven ewe lambs of the flock. [29]And Abimelech said to Abraham, "What is the meaning of these seven ewe lambs that you have set apart?" [30]He said, "These seven ewe lambs you shall accept from my hand, in order that you may be a witness for me that I dug this well." [31]Therefore that place was called Beer-sheba;[a] because there both of them swore an oath. [32]When they had made a covenant at Beer-sheba, Abimelech, with Phicol the commander of his army, left and returned to the land of the Philistines. [33]Abraham[b] planted a tamarisk tree in Beer-sheba, and called there on the name of the LORD, the Everlasting God.[c] [34]And Abraham resided as an alien many days in the land of the Philistines.

22.1 AFTER these things God tested Abraham. He said to him, "Abraham!" And he said, "Here I am." [2]He said, "Take your son, your only son Isaac, whom you love, and go to the land of Moriah, and offer him there as a burnt offering on one of the mountains that I shall show you." [3]So Abraham rose early in the morning, saddled his donkey, and took two of his young men with him, and his son Isaac; he cut the wood for the burnt offering, and set out and went to the place in the distance that God had shown him. [4]On the third day Abraham looked up and saw the place far away. [5]Then Abraham said to his young men, "Stay here with the donkey; the boy and I will go over there; we will worship, and then we will come back to you." [6]Abraham took the wood of the burnt offering and laid it on his son Isaac, and he himself carried the fire and the knife. So the two of them walked on together. [7]Isaac said to his father Abraham, "Father!" And he said, "Here I am, my son." He said, "The fire and the wood are here, but where is the lamb for a burnt offering?" [8]Abraham said, "God himself will provide the lamb for a burnt offering, my son." So the two of them walked on together.

9  When they came to the place that God had shown him, Abraham built an altar there and laid the wood in order. He bound his son Isaac, and laid him on the altar, on top of the wood. [10]Then

---

a That is *Well of seven* or *Well of the oath*   b Heb *He*   c Or *the* LORD, *El Olam*

Abraham reached out his hand and took the knife to kill[a] his son. 11But the angel of the Lord called to him from heaven, and said, "Abraham, Abraham!" And he said, "Here I am." 12He said, "Do not lay your hand on the boy or do anything to him; for now I know that you fear God, since you have not withheld your son, your only son, from me." 13And Abraham looked up and saw a ram, caught in a thicket by its horns. Abraham went and took the ram and offered it up as a burnt offering instead of his son. 14So Abraham called that place "The Lord will provide"; [b] as it is said to this day, "On the mount of the Lord it shall be provided."[c]

15 The angel of the Lord called to Abraham a second time from heaven, 16and said, "By myself I have sworn, says the Lord: Because you have done this, and have not withheld your son, your only son, 17I will indeed bless you, and I will make your offspring as numerous as the stars of heaven and as the sand that is on the seashore. And your offspring shall possess the gate of their enemies, 18and by your offspring shall all the nations of the earth gain blessing for themselves, because you have obeyed my voice." 19So Abraham returned to his young men, and they arose and went together to Beersheba; and Abraham lived at Beersheba.

20 Now after these things it was told Abraham, "Milcah also has borne children, to your brother Nahor: 21Uz the firstborn, Buz his brother, Kemuel the father of Aram, 22Chesed, Hazo, Pildash, Jidlaph, and Bethuel." 23Bethuel became the father of Rebekah. These eight Milcah bore to Nahor, Abraham's brother. 24Moreover, his concubine, whose name was Reumah, bore Tebah, Gaham, Tahash, and Maacah.

## MATTHEW 7.15–29

"**B**EWARE of false prophets, who come to you in sheep's clothing but inwardly are ravenous wolves. 16You will know them by their fruits. Are grapes gathered from thorns, or figs from thistles? 17In the same way, every good tree bears good fruit, but the bad tree bears bad fruit. 18A good tree cannot bear bad fruit, nor can a bad tree bear good fruit. 19Every tree that does not bear good fruit is cut down and thrown into the fire. 20Thus you will know them by their fruits.

21 "Not everyone who says to me, 'Lord, Lord,' will enter the kingdom of heaven, but only the one who does the will of my Father in heaven. 22On that day many will say to me, 'Lord, Lord, did we not prophesy in your name, and cast out demons in your name, and do many deeds of power in your name?' 23Then I will declare to them, 'I never knew you; go away from me, you evildoers.'

24 "Everyone then who hears these words of mine and acts on them will be like a wise man who built his house on rock. 25The rain fell, the floods came, and the winds blew and beat on that house, but it did not fall, because it had been founded on rock. 26And everyone who hears these words of mine and does not act on them will be like a foolish man who built his house on sand. 27The rain fell, and the floods came, and the winds blew and beat against that house, and it fell—and great was its fall!"

28 Now when Jesus had finished saying these things, the crowds were astounded at his teaching, 29for he taught them as one having authority, and not as their scribes.

---

a Or *to slaughter*   b Or *will see*; Heb traditionally transliterated *Jehovah Jireh*   c Or *he shall be seen*

## PSALM 9.1–12

*To the leader: according to Muth-labben. A Psalm of David.*

I WILL give thanks to the LORD with
    my whole heart;
    I will tell of all your wonderful
        deeds.
2  I will be glad and exult in you;
    I will sing praise to your
        name, O Most High.

3  When my enemies turned back,
    they stumbled and perished
        before you.
4  For you have maintained my
        just cause;
    you have sat on the throne
        giving righteous
        judgment.

5  You have rebuked the nations,
    you have destroyed the
        wicked;
    you have blotted out their
        name forever and ever.
6  The enemies have vanished in
        everlasting ruins;
    their cities you have rooted
        out;
    the very memory of them has
        perished.

7  But the LORD sits enthroned
        forever,
    he has established his throne
        for judgment.
8  He judges the world with
        righteousness;
    he judges the peoples with
        equity.

9  The LORD is a stronghold for the
        oppressed,
    a stronghold in times of
        trouble.

10  And those who know your name
        put their trust in you,
    for you, O LORD, have not
        forsaken those who seek
        you.

11  Sing praises to the LORD, who
        dwells in Zion.
    Declare his deeds among the
        peoples.
12  For he who avenges blood is
        mindful of them;
    he does not forget the cry of
        the afflicted.

## PROVERBS 2.16–22

YOU will be saved from the
    loose[a] woman,
    from the adulteress with her
        smooth words,
17  who forsakes the partner of her
        youth
    and forgets her sacred
        covenant;
18  for her way[b] leads down to
        death,
    and her paths to the shades;
19  those who go to her never
        come back,
    nor do they regain the paths
        of life.

20  Therefore walk in the way of
        the good,
    and keep to the paths of the
        just.
21  For the upright will abide in the
        land,
    and the innocent will remain
        in it;
22  but the wicked will be cut off
        from the land,
    and the treacherous will be
        rooted out of it.

aHeb *strange*  bCn: Heb *house*

# JANUARY 10

## GENESIS 23.1—24.51

Sᴀʀᴀʜ lived one hundred twenty-seven years; this was the length of Sarah's life. ²And Sarah died at Kiriath-arba (that is, Hebron) in the land of Canaan; and Abraham went in to mourn for Sarah and to weep for her. ³Abraham rose up from beside his dead, and said to the Hittites, ⁴"I am a stranger and an alien residing among you; give me property among you for a burying place, so that I may bury my dead out of my sight." ⁵The Hittites answered Abraham, ⁶"Hear us, my lord; you are a mighty prince among us. Bury your dead in the choicest of our burial places; none of us will withhold from you any burial ground for burying your dead." ⁷Abraham rose and bowed to the Hittites, the people of the land. ⁸He said to them, "If you are willing that I should bury my dead out of my sight, hear me, and entreat for me Ephron son of Zohar, ⁹so that he may give me the cave of Machpelah, which he owns; it is at the end of his field. For the full price let him give it to me in your presence as a possession for a burying place." ¹⁰Now Ephron was sitting among the Hittites; and Ephron the Hittite answered Abraham in the hearing of the Hittites, of all who went in at the gate of his city, ¹¹"No, my lord, hear me; I give you the field, and I give you the cave that is in it; in the presence of my people I give it to you; bury your dead." ¹²Then Abraham bowed down before the people of the land. ¹³He said to Ephron in the hearing of the people of the land, "If you only will listen to me! I will give the price of the field; accept it from me, so that I may bury my dead there." ¹⁴Ephron answered Abraham, ¹⁵"My lord, listen to me; a piece of land worth four hundred shekels of silver—what is that between you and me? Bury your dead." ¹⁶Abraham agreed with Ephron; and Abraham weighed out for Ephron the silver that he had named in the hearing of the Hittites, four hundred shekels of silver, according to the weights current among the merchants.

17 So the field of Ephron in Machpelah, which was to the east of Mamre, the field with the cave that was in it and all the trees that were in the field, throughout its whole area, passed ¹⁸to Abraham as a possession in the presence of the Hittites, in the presence of all who went in at the gate of his city. ¹⁹After this, Abraham buried Sarah his wife in the cave of the field of Machpelah facing Mamre (that is, Hebron) in the land of Canaan. ²⁰The field and the cave that is in it passed from the Hittites into Abraham's possession as a burying place.

24.1 Now Abraham was old, well advanced in years; and the Lᴏʀᴅ had blessed Abraham in all things. ²Abraham said to his servant, the oldest of his house, who had charge of all that he had, "Put your hand under my thigh ³and I will make you swear by the Lᴏʀᴅ, the God of heaven and earth, that you will not get a wife for my son from the daughters of the Canaanites, among whom I live, ⁴but will go to my country and to my kindred and get a wife for my son Isaac." ⁵The servant said to him, "Perhaps the woman may not be willing to follow me to this land; must I then take your son back to the land from which you came?" ⁶Abraham said to him, "See to it that you do not take my son back there. ⁷The Lᴏʀᴅ, the God of heaven, who took me from my father's house and from the land of my birth, and who spoke to me and swore to me, 'To your offspring I will give this land,' he will send his angel before you, and you shall take a wife for my son from there. [8]But if the woman is not willing to follow you, then you will be free from this oath of mine; only you must not take my son back there." [9]So the servant put his hand under the thigh of Abraham his master and swore to him concerning this matter.

10  Then the servant took ten of his master's camels and departed, taking all kinds of choice gifts from his master; and he set out and went to Aram-naharaim, to the city of Nahor. [11]He made the camels kneel down outside the city by the well of water; it was toward evening, the time when women go out to draw water. [12]And he said, "O Lord, God of my master Abraham, please grant me success today and show steadfast love to my master Abraham. [13]I am standing here by the spring of water, and the daughters of the townspeople are coming out to draw water. [14]Let the girl to whom I shall say, 'Please offer your jar that I may drink,' and who shall say, 'Drink, and I will water your camels'—let her be the one whom you have appointed for your servant Isaac. By this I shall know that you have shown steadfast love to my master."

15  Before he had finished speaking, there was Rebekah, who was born to Bethuel son of Milcah, the wife of Nahor, Abraham's brother, coming out with her water jar on her shoulder. [16]The girl was very fair to look upon, a virgin, whom no man had known. She went down to the spring, filled her jar, and came up. [17]Then the servant ran to meet her and said, "Please let me sip a little water from your jar." [18]"Drink, my lord," she said, and quickly lowered her jar upon her hand and gave him a drink. [19]When she had finished giving him a drink, she said, "I will draw for your camels also, until they have fin-ished drinking." [20]So she quickly emp-tied her jar into the trough and ran again to the well to draw, and she drew for all his camels. [21]The man gazed at her in silence to learn whether or not the Lord had made his journey successful.

22  When the camels had finished drinking, the man took a gold nose-ring weighing a half shekel, and two brace-lets for her arms weighing ten gold shekels, [23]and said, "Tell me whose daughter you are. Is there room in your father's house for us to spend the night?" [24]She said to him, "I am the daughter of Bethuel son of Milcah, whom she bore to Nahor." [25]She added, "We have plenty of straw and fodder and a place to spend the night." [26]The man bowed his head and wor-shiped the Lord [27]and said, "Blessed be the Lord, the God of my master Abra-ham, who has not forsaken his stead-fast love and his faithfulness toward my master. As for me, the Lord has led me on the way to the house of my master's kin."

28  Then the girl ran and told her mother's household about these things. [29]Rebekah had a brother whose name was Laban; and Laban ran out to the man, to the spring. [30]As soon as he had seen the nose-ring, and the bracelets on his sister's arms, and when he heard the words of his sister Rebekah, "Thus the man spoke to me," he went to the man; and there he was, standing by the camels at the spring. [31]He said, "Come in, O blessed of the Lord. Why do you stand outside when I have prepared the house and a place for the camels?" [32]So the man came into the house; and La-ban unloaded the camels, and gave him straw and fodder for the camels, and water to wash his feet and the feet of the men who were with him. [33]Then food was set before him to eat; but he said, "I will not eat until I have told my errand." He said, "Speak on."

34  So he said, "I am Abraham's servant. [35]The Lord has greatly

blessed my master, and he has become wealthy; he has given him flocks and herds, silver and gold, male and female slaves, camels and donkeys. 36And Sarah my master's wife bore a son to my master when she was old; and he has given him all that he has. 37My master made me swear, saying, 'You shall not take a wife for my son from the daughters of the Canaanites, in whose land I live; 38but you shall go to my father's house, to my kindred, and get a wife for my son.' 39I said to my master, 'Perhaps the woman will not follow me.' 40But he said to me, 'The LORD, before whom I walk, will send his angel with you and make your way successful. You shall get a wife for my son from my kindred, from my father's house. 41Then you will be free from my oath, when you come to my kindred; even if they will not give her to you, you will be free from my oath.'

42 "I came today to the spring, and said, 'O LORD, the God of my master Abraham, if now you will only make successful the way I am going! 43I am standing here by the spring of water; let the young woman who comes out to draw, to whom I shall say, "Please give me a little water from your jar to drink," 44and who will say to me, "Drink, and I will draw for your camels also"—let her be the woman whom the LORD has appointed for my master's son.'

45 "Before I had finished speaking in my heart, there was Rebekah coming out with her water jar on her shoulder; and she went down to the spring, and drew. I said to her, 'Please let me drink.' 46She quickly let down her jar from her shoulder, and said, 'Drink, and I will also water your camels.' So I drank, and she also watered the camels. 47Then I asked her, 'Whose daughter are you?' She said, 'The daughter of Bethuel, Nahor's son, whom Milcah bore to him.' So I put the ring on her nose, and the bracelets on her arms. 48Then I bowed my head and worshiped the LORD, and blessed the LORD, the God of my master Abraham, who had led me by the right way to obtain the daughter of my master's kinsman for his son. 49Now then, if you will deal loyally and truly with my master, tell me; and if not, tell me, so that I may turn either to the right hand or to the left."

50 Then Laban and Bethuel answered, "The thing comes from the LORD; we cannot speak to you anything bad or good. 51Look, Rebekah is before you, take her and go, and let her be the wife of your master's son, as the LORD has spoken."

# MATTHEW 8.1–17

WHEN Jesusa had come down from the mountain, great crowds followed him; 2and there was a leperb who came to him and knelt before him, saying, "Lord, if you choose, you can make me clean." 3He stretched out his hand and touched him, saying, "I do choose. Be made clean!" Immediately his leprosyb was cleansed. 4Then Jesus said to him, "See that you say nothing to anyone; but go, show yourself to the priest, and offer the gift that Moses commanded, as a testimony to them."

5 When he entered Capernaum, a centurion came to him, appealing to him 6and saying, "Lord, my servant is lying at home paralyzed, in terrible distress." 7And he said to him, "I will come and cure him." 8The centurion answered, "Lord, I am not worthy to have you come under my roof; but only speak the word, and my servant will be healed. 9For I also am a man under authority, with soldiers under me; and I say to one, 'Go,' and he goes, and to another, 'Come,' and he comes, and to

aGk *he*  bThe terms *leper* and *leprosy* can refer to several diseases

my slave, 'Do this,' and the slave does it." [10]When Jesus heard him, he was amazed and said to those who followed him, "Truly I tell you, in no one[a] in Israel have I found such faith. [11]I tell you, many will come from east and west and will eat with Abraham and Isaac and Jacob in the kingdom of heaven, [12]while the heirs of the kingdom will be thrown into the outer darkness, where there will be weeping and gnashing of teeth." [13]And to the centurion Jesus said, "Go; let it be done for you according to your faith." And the servant was healed in that hour.

14 When Jesus entered Peter's house, he saw his mother-in-law lying in bed with a fever; [15]he touched her hand, and the fever left her, and she got up and began to serve him. [16]That evening they brought to him many who were possessed with demons; and he cast out the spirits with a word, and cured all who were sick. [17]This was to fulfill what had been spoken through the prophet Isaiah, "He took our infirmities and bore our diseases."

## PSALM 9.13–20

BE gracious to me, O LORD.
    See what I suffer from those
        who hate me;
    you are the one who lifts me
        up from the gates of
        death,
14  so that I may recount all your
        praises,
    and, in the gates of daughter
        Zion,
    rejoice in your deliverance.

15  The nations have sunk in the pit
        that they made;
    in the net that they hid has
        their own foot been
        caught.

16  The LORD has made himself
        known, he has executed
        judgment;
    the wicked are snared in the
        work of their own hands.
            *Higgaion. Selah*

17  The wicked shall depart to
        Sheol,
    all the nations that forget
        God.

18  For the needy shall not always
        be forgotten,
    nor the hope of the poor
        perish forever.

19  Rise up, O LORD! Do not let
        mortals prevail;
    let the nations be judged
        before you.
20  Put them in fear, O LORD;
    let the nations know that they
        are only human.      *Selah*

## PROVERBS 3.1–6

MY child, do not forget my
        teaching,
    but let your heart keep
        my commandments;
2   for length of days and years of
        life
    and abundant welfare they will
        give you.

3   Do not let loyalty and
        faithfulness forsake you;
    bind them around your neck,
    write them on the tablet of
        your heart.
4   So you will find favor and good
        repute
    in the sight of God and of
        people.

a Other ancient authorities read *Truly I tell you, not even*

5 Trust in the L<sub>ORD</sub> with all your
heart,
and do not rely on your own
insight.

6 In all your ways acknowledge
him,
and he will make straight your
paths.

# JANUARY 11

## GENESIS 24.52—26.16

W<sub>HEN</sub> Abraham's servant heard their words, he bowed himself to the ground before the L<sub>ORD</sub>. <sup>53</sup>And the servant brought out jewelry of silver and of gold, and garments, and gave them to Rebekah; he also gave to her brother and to her mother costly ornaments. <sup>54</sup>Then he and the men who were with him ate and drank, and they spent the night there. When they rose in the morning, he said, "Send me back to my master." <sup>55</sup>Her brother and her mother said, "Let the girl remain with us a while, at least ten days; after that she may go." <sup>56</sup>But he said to them, "Do not delay me, since the L<sub>ORD</sub> has made my journey successful; let me go that I may go to my master." <sup>57</sup>They said, "We will call the girl, and ask her." <sup>58</sup>And they called Rebekah, and said to her, "Will you go with this man?" She said, "I will." <sup>59</sup>So they sent away their sister Rebekah and her nurse along with Abraham's servant and his men. <sup>60</sup>And they blessed Rebekah and said to her,

"May you, our sister, become
thousands of myriads;
may your offspring gain
possession
of the gates of their foes."

<sup>61</sup>Then Rebekah and her maids rose up, mounted the camels, and followed the man; thus the servant took Rebekah, and went his way.

62 Now Isaac had come from<sup>a</sup> Beer-lahai-roi, and was settled in the Negeb. <sup>63</sup>Isaac went out in the evening to walk<sup>b</sup> in the field; and looking up, he saw camels coming. <sup>64</sup>And Rebekah looked up, and when she saw Isaac, she slipped quickly from the camel, <sup>65</sup>and said to the servant, "Who is the man over there, walking in the field to meet us?" The servant said, "It is my master." So she took her veil and covered herself. <sup>66</sup>And the servant told Isaac all the things that he had done. <sup>67</sup>Then Isaac brought her into his mother Sarah's tent. He took Rebekah, and she became his wife; and he loved her. So Isaac was comforted after his mother's death.

<sup>25.1</sup> A<sub>BRAHAM</sub> took another wife, whose name was Keturah. <sup>2</sup>She bore him Zimran, Jokshan, Medan, Midian, Ishbak, and Shuah. <sup>3</sup>Jokshan was the father of Sheba and Dedan. The sons of Dedan were Asshurim, Letushim, and Leummim. <sup>4</sup>The sons of Midian were Ephah, Epher, Hanoch, Abida, and Eldaah. All these were the children of Keturah. <sup>5</sup>Abraham gave all he had to Isaac. <sup>6</sup>But to the sons of his concubines Abraham gave gifts, while he was still living, and he sent them away from his son Isaac, eastward to the east country.

7 This is the length of Abraham's life, one hundred seventy-five years. <sup>8</sup>Abraham breathed his last and died in a good old age, an old man and full of

---

<sup>a</sup>Syr Tg: Heb *from coming to*   <sup>b</sup>Meaning of Heb word is uncertain

years, and was gathered to his people. [9]His sons Isaac and Ishmael buried him in the cave of Machpelah, in the field of Ephron son of Zohar the Hittite, east of Mamre, [10]the field that Abraham purchased from the Hittites. There Abraham was buried, with his wife Sarah. [11]After the death of Abraham God blessed his son Isaac. And Isaac settled at Beer-lahai-roi.

12 These are the descendants of Ishmael, Abraham's son, whom Hagar the Egyptian, Sarah's slave-girl, bore to Abraham. [13]These are the names of the sons of Ishmael, named in the order of their birth: Nebaioth, the firstborn of Ishmael; and Kedar, Adbeel, Mibsam, [14]Mishma, Dumah, Massa, [15]Hadad, Tema, Jetur, Naphish, and Kedemah. [16]These are the sons of Ishmael and these are their names, by their villages and by their encampments, twelve princes according to their tribes. [17](This is the length of the life of Ishmael, one hundred thirty-seven years; he breathed his last and died, and was gathered to his people.) [18]They settled from Havilah to Shur, which is opposite Egypt in the direction of Assyria; he settled down[a] alongside of[b] all his people.

19 These are the descendants of Isaac, Abraham's son: Abraham was the father of Isaac, [20]and Isaac was forty years old when he married Rebekah, daughter of Bethuel the Aramean of Paddan-aram, sister of Laban the Aramean. [21]Isaac prayed to the Lord for his wife, because she was barren; and the Lord granted his prayer, and his wife Rebekah conceived. [22]The children struggled together within her; and she said, "If it is to be this way, why do I live?"[c] So she went to inquire of the Lord. [23]And the Lord said to her,

"Two nations are in your womb,
        and two peoples born of you
        shall be divided;
the one shall be stronger than
        the other,
the elder shall serve the
        younger."

[24]When her time to give birth was at hand, there were twins in her womb. [25]The first came out red, all his body like a hairy mantle; so they named him Esau. [26]Afterward his brother came out, with his hand gripping Esau's heel; so he was named Jacob.[d] Isaac was sixty years old when she bore them.

27 When the boys grew up, Esau was a skillful hunter, a man of the field, while Jacob was a quiet man, living in tents. [28]Isaac loved Esau, because he was fond of game; but Rebekah loved Jacob.

29 Once when Jacob was cooking a stew, Esau came in from the field, and he was famished. [30]Esau said to Jacob, "Let me eat some of that red stuff, for I am famished!" (Therefore he was called Edom.[e]) [31]Jacob said, "First sell me your birthright." [32]Esau said, "I am about to die; of what use is a birthright to me?" [33]Jacob said, "Swear to me first."[f] So he swore to him, and sold his birthright to Jacob. [34]Then Jacob gave Esau bread and lentil stew, and he ate and drank, and rose and went his way. Thus Esau despised his birthright.

26.1 Now there was a famine in the land, besides the former famine that had occurred in the days of Abraham. And Isaac went to Gerar, to King Abimelech of the Philistines. [2]The Lord appeared to Isaac[g] and said, "Do not go down to Egypt; settle in the land that I shall show you. [3]Reside in this land as an alien, and I will be with you, and will bless you; for to you and to your descendants I will give all these lands, and I will fulfill the oath that I swore to your father Abraham. [4]I will make your offspring as numerous as the stars of

---

[a]Heb *he fell*   [b]Or *down in opposition to*   [c]Syr: Meaning of Heb uncertain   [d]That is *He takes by the heel* or *He supplants*   [e]That is *Red*   [f]Heb *today*   [g]Heb *him*

heaven, and will give to your offspring all these lands; and all the nations of the earth shall gain blessing for themselves through your offspring, ⁵because Abraham obeyed my voice and kept my charge, my commandments, my statutes, and my laws."

6  So Isaac settled in Gerar. ⁷When the men of the place asked him about his wife, he said, "She is my sister"; for he was afraid to say, "My wife," thinking, "or else the men of the place might kill me for the sake of Rebekah, because she is attractive in appearance." ⁸When Isaac had been there a long time, King Abimelech of the Philistines looked out of a window and saw him fondling his wife Rebekah. ⁹So Abimelech called for Isaac, and said, "So she is your wife! Why then did you say, 'She is my sister'?" Isaac said to him, "Because I thought I might die because of her." ¹⁰Abimelech said, "What is this you have done to us? One of the people might easily have lain with your wife, and you would have brought guilt upon us." ¹¹So Abimelech warned all the people, saying, "Whoever touches this man or his wife shall be put to death."

12  Isaac sowed seed in that land, and in the same year reaped a hundredfold. The Lord blessed him, ¹³and the man became rich; he prospered more and more until he became very wealthy. ¹⁴He had possessions of flocks and herds, and a great household, so that the Philistines envied him. ¹⁵(Now the Philistines had stopped up and filled with earth all the wells that his father's servants had dug in the days of his father Abraham.) ¹⁶And Abimelech said to Isaac, "Go away from us; you have become too powerful for us."

# MATTHEW 8.18–34

Now when Jesus saw great crowds around him, he gave orders to go over to the other side. ¹⁹A scribe then approached and said, "Teacher, I will follow you wherever you go." ²⁰And Jesus said to him, "Foxes have holes, and birds of the air have nests; but the Son of Man has nowhere to lay his head." ²¹Another of his disciples said to him, "Lord, first let me go and bury my father." ²²But Jesus said to him, "Follow me, and let the dead bury their own dead."

23  And when he got into the boat, his disciples followed him. ²⁴A windstorm arose on the sea, so great that the boat was being swamped by the waves; but he was asleep. ²⁵And they went and woke him up, saying, "Lord, save us! We are perishing!" ²⁶And he said to them, "Why are you afraid, you of little faith?" Then he got up and rebuked the winds and the sea; and there was a dead calm. ²⁷They were amazed, saying, "What sort of man is this, that even the winds and the sea obey him?"

28  When he came to the other side, to the country of the Gadarenes, ᵃ two demoniacs coming out of the tombs met him. They were so fierce that no one could pass that way. ²⁹Suddenly they shouted, "What have you to do with us, Son of God? Have you come here to torment us before the time?" ³⁰Now a large herd of swine was feeding at some distance from them. ³¹The demons begged him, "If you cast us out, send us into the herd of swine." ³²And he said to them, "Go!" So they came out and entered the swine; and suddenly, the whole herd rushed down the steep bank into the sea and perished in the water. ³³The swineherds ran off, and on going into the town, they told the whole story about what had happened to the demoniacs. ³⁴Then the

---

ᵃ Other ancient authorities read *Gergesenes*; others, *Gerasenes*

whole town came out to meet Jesus; and when they saw him, they begged him to leave their neighborhood.

## PSALM 10.1–15

WHY, O LORD, do you stand far off?
Why do you hide yourself
in times of trouble?
2 In arrogance the wicked
persecute the poor—
let them be caught in the
schemes they have
devised.

3 For the wicked boast of the
desires of their heart,
those greedy for gain curse
and renounce the LORD.
4 In the pride of their
countenance the wicked
say, "God will not seek it
out";
all their thoughts are, "There
is no God."

5 Their ways prosper at all times;
your judgments are on high,
out of their sight;
as for their foes, they scoff at
them.
6 They think in their heart, "We
shall not be moved;
throughout all generations we
shall not meet
adversity."

7 Their mouths are filled with
cursing and deceit and
oppression;
under their tongues are
mischief and iniquity.
8 They sit in ambush in the
villages;
in hiding places they murder
the innocent.

Their eyes stealthily watch for
the helpless;

9 they lurk in secret like a lion
in its covert;
they lurk that they may seize
the poor;
they seize the poor and drag
them off in their net.

10 They stoop, they crouch,
and the helpless fall by their
might.
11 They think in their heart, "God
has forgotten,
he has hidden his face, he will
never see it."

12 Rise up, O LORD; O God, lift up
your hand;
do not forget the oppressed.
13 Why do the wicked renounce
God,
and say in their hearts, "You
will not call us to
account"?

14 But you do see! Indeed you
note trouble and grief,
that you may take it into your
hands;
the helpless commit themselves
to you;
you have been the helper of
the orphan.

15 Break the arm of the wicked
and evildoers;
seek out their wickedness
until you find none.

## PROVERBS 3.7–8

DO not be wise in your own
eyes;
fear the LORD, and turn
away from evil.
8 It will be a healing for your flesh
and a refreshment for your
body.

# JANUARY 12

## GENESIS 26.17—27.46

So Isaac departed from there and camped in the valley of Gerar and settled there. ¹⁸Isaac dug again the wells of water that had been dug in the days of his father Abraham; for the Philistines had stopped them up after the death of Abraham; and he gave them the names that his father had given them. ¹⁹But when Isaac's servants dug in the valley and found there a well of spring water, ²⁰the herders of Gerar quarreled with Isaac's herders, saying, "The water is ours." So he called the well Esek,ᵃ because they contended with him. ²¹Then they dug another well, and they quarreled over that one also; so he called it Sitnah.ᵇ ²²He moved from there and dug another well, and they did not quarrel over it; so he called it Rehoboth,ᶜ saying, "Now the Lord has made room for us, and we shall be fruitful in the land."

23 From there he went up to Beersheba. ²⁴And that very night the Lord appeared to him and said, "I am the God of your father Abraham; do not be afraid, for I am with you and will bless you and make your offspring numerous for my servant Abraham's sake." ²⁵So he built an altar there, called on the name of the Lord, and pitched his tent there. And there Isaac's servants dug a well.

26 Then Abimelech went to him from Gerar, with Ahuzzath his adviser and Phicol the commander of his army. ²⁷Isaac said to them, "Why have you come to me, seeing that you hate me and have sent me away from you?" ²⁸They said, "We see plainly that the Lord has been with you; so we say, let there be an oath between you and us, and let us make a covenant with you ²⁹so that you will do us no harm, just as we have not touched you and have done to you nothing but good and have sent you away in peace. You are now the blessed of the Lord." ³⁰So he made them a feast, and they ate and drank. ³¹In the morning they rose early and exchanged oaths; and Isaac set them on their way, and they departed from him in peace. ³²That same day Isaac's servants came and told him about the well that they had dug, and said to him, "We have found water!" ³³He called it Shibah;ᵈ therefore the name of the city is Beer-shebaᵉ to this day.

34 When Esau was forty years old, he married Judith daughter of Beeri the Hittite, and Basemath daughter of Elon the Hittite; ³⁵and they made life bitter for Isaac and Rebekah.

**27.1** When Isaac was old and his eyes were dim so that he could not see, he called his elder son Esau and said to him, "My son"; and he answered, "Here I am." ²He said, "See, I am old; I do not know the day of my death. ³Now then, take your weapons, your quiver and your bow, and go out to the field, and hunt game for me. ⁴Then prepare for me savory food, such as I like, and bring it to me to eat, so that I may bless you before I die."

5 Now Rebekah was listening when Isaac spoke to his son Esau. So when Esau went to the field to hunt for game and bring it, ⁶Rebekah said to her son Jacob, "I heard your father say to your brother Esau, ⁷'Bring me game, and prepare for me savory food to eat, that I may bless you before the Lord before I die.' ⁸Now therefore, my son, obey

ᵃ That is *Contention*  ᵇ That is *Enmity*  ᶜ That is *Broad places* or *Room*  ᵈ A word resembling the word for *oath*  ᵉ That is *Well of the oath* or *Well of seven*

my word as I command you. ⁹Go to the flock, and get me two choice kids, so that I may prepare from them savory food for your father, such as he likes; ¹⁰and you shall take it to your father to eat, so that he may bless you before he dies." ¹¹But Jacob said to his mother Rebekah, "Look, my brother Esau is a hairy man, and I am a man of smooth skin. ¹²Perhaps my father will feel me, and I shall seem to be mocking him, and bring a curse on myself and not a blessing." ¹³His mother said to him, "Let your curse be on me, my son; only obey my word, and go, get them for me." ¹⁴So he went and got them and brought them to his mother; and his mother prepared savory food, such as his father loved. ¹⁵Then Rebekah took the best garments of her elder son Esau, which were with her in the house, and put them on her younger son Jacob; ¹⁶and she put the skins of the kids on his hands and on the smooth part of his neck. ¹⁷Then she handed the savory food, and the bread that she had prepared, to her son Jacob.

18 So he went in to his father, and said, "My father"; and he said, "Here I am; who are you, my son?" ¹⁹Jacob said to his father, "I am Esau your first-born. I have done as you told me; now sit up and eat of my game, so that you may bless me." ²⁰But Isaac said to his son, "How is it that you have found it so quickly, my son?" He answered, "Because the LORD your God granted me success." ²¹Then Isaac said to Jacob, "Come near, that I may feel you, my son, to know whether you are really my son Esau or not." ²²So Jacob went up to his father Isaac, who felt him and said, "The voice is Jacob's voice, but the hands are the hands of Esau." ²³He did not recognize him, because his hands were hairy like his brother Esau's hands; so he blessed him. ²⁴He said, "Are you really my son Esau?" He

answered, "I am." ²⁵Then he said, "Bring it to me, that I may eat of my son's game and bless you." So he brought it to him, and he ate; and he brought him wine, and he drank. ²⁶Then his father Isaac said to him, "Come near and kiss me, my son." ²⁷So he came near and kissed him; and he smelled the smell of his garments, and blessed him, and said,

> "Ah, the smell of my son
>     is like the smell of a field that
>         the LORD has blessed.
>
> 28  May God give you of the dew of
>         heaven,
>     and of the fatness of the
>         earth,
>     and plenty of grain and wine.
> 29  Let peoples serve you,
>     and nations bow down to you.
> Be lord over your brothers,
>     and may your mother's sons
>         bow down to you.
> Cursed be everyone who curses
>         you,
>     and blessed be everyone who
>         blesses you!"

30 As soon as Isaac had finished blessing Jacob, when Jacob had scarcely gone out from the presence of his father Isaac, his brother Esau came in from his hunting. ³¹He also prepared savory food, and brought it to his father. And he said to his father, "Let my father sit up and eat of his son's game, so that you may bless me." ³²His father Isaac said to him, "Who are you?" He answered, "I am your firstborn son, Esau." ³³Then Isaac trembled violently, and said, "Who was it then that hunted game and brought it to me, and I ate it all[a] before you came, and I have blessed him?—yes, and blessed he shall be!" ³⁴When Esau heard his father's words, he cried out with an exceedingly great and bitter cry, and said to his father, "Bless me, me also, father!" ³⁵But he said, "Your brother

---

[a] Cn: Heb *of all*

came deceitfully, and he has taken away your blessing." ³⁶Esau said, "Is he not rightly named Jacob?ᵃ For he has supplanted me these two times. He took away my birthright; and look, now he has taken away my blessing." Then he said, "Have you not reserved a blessing for me?" ³⁷Isaac answered Esau, "I have already made him your lord, and I have given him all his brothers as servants, and with grain and wine I have sustained him. What then can I do for you, my son?" ³⁸Esau said to his father, "Have you only one blessing, father? Bless me, me also, father!" And Esau lifted up his voice and wept.

39 Then his father Isaac answered him:

> "See, away fromᵇ the fatness
>     of the earth shall your
>     home be,
> and away fromᶜ the dew of
>     heaven on high.
> ⁴⁰ By your sword you shall live,
>     and you shall serve your
>     brother;
> but when you break loose, ᵈ
>     you shall break his yoke from
>     your neck."

41 Now Esau hated Jacob because of the blessing with which his father had blessed him, and Esau said to himself, "The days of mourning for my father are approaching; then I will kill my brother Jacob." ⁴²But the words of her elder son Esau were told to Rebekah; so she sent and called her younger son Jacob and said to him, "Your brother Esau is consoling himself by planning to kill you. ⁴³Now therefore, my son, obey my voice; flee at once to my brother Laban in Haran, ⁴⁴and stay with him a while, until your brother's fury turns away— ⁴⁵until your brother's anger against you turns away, and he forgets what you have done to him; then I will send, and bring you back from there. Why should I lose both of you in one day?"

46 Then Rebekah said to Isaac, "I am weary of my life because of the Hittite women. If Jacob marries one of the Hittite women such as these, one of the women of the land, what good will my life be to me?"

## MATTHEW 9.1–17

AND after getting into a boat he [Jesus] crossed the sea and came to his own town. 2 And just then some people were carrying a paralyzed man lying on a bed. When Jesus saw their faith, he said to the paralytic, "Take heart, son; your sins are forgiven." ³Then some of the scribes said to themselves, "This man is blaspheming." ⁴But Jesus, perceiving their thoughts, said, "Why do you think evil in your hearts? ⁵For which is easier, to say, 'Your sins are forgiven,' or to say, 'Stand up and walk'? ⁶But so that you may know that the Son of Man has authority on earth to forgive sins"—he then said to the paralytic—"Stand up, take your bed and go to your home." ⁷And he stood up and went to his home. ⁸When the crowds saw it, they were filled with awe, and they glorified God, who had given such authority to human beings.

9 As Jesus was walking along, he saw a man called Matthew sitting at the tax booth; and he said to him, "Follow me." And he got up and followed him.

10 And as he sat at dinnerᵉ in the house, many tax collectors and sinners came and were sittingᶠ with him and his disciples. ¹¹When the Pharisees saw this, they said to his disciples, "Why does your teacher eat with tax collectors and sinners?" ¹²But when he heard this, he said, "Those who are well have no need of a physician, but

---

ᵃThat is *He supplants* or *He takes by the heel*  ᵇOr *See, of*  ᶜOr *and of*  ᵈMeaning of Heb uncertain
ᵉGk *reclined*  ᶠGk *were reclining*

those who are sick. ¹³Go and learn what this means, 'I desire mercy, not sacrifice.' For I have come to call not the righteous but sinners."

14  Then the disciples of John came to him, saying, "Why do we and the Pharisees fast often,ᵃ but your disciples do not fast?" ¹⁵And Jesus said to them, "The wedding guests cannot mourn as long as the bridegroom is with them, can they? The days will come when the bridegroom is taken away from them, and then they will fast. ¹⁶No one sews a piece of unshrunk cloth on an old cloak, for the patch pulls away from the cloak, and a worse tear is made. ¹⁷Neither is new wine put into old wineskins; otherwise, the skins burst, and the wine is spilled, and the skins are destroyed; but new wine is put into fresh wineskins, and so both are preserved."

## PSALM 10.16–18

The Lord is king forever and
          ever;
     the nations shall perish from
          his land.

17  O Lord, you will hear the desire
          of the meek;
     you will strengthen their
          heart, you will incline
          your ear
18  to do justice for the orphan and
          the oppressed,
     so that those from earth may
          strike terror no more.ᵇ

## PROVERBS 3.9–10

Honor the Lord with your
          substance
     and with the first fruits of
          all your produce;
10  then your barns will be filled
          with plenty,
     and your vats will be bursting
          with wine.

# JANUARY 13

## GENESIS 28.1—29.35

Then Isaac called Jacob and blessed him, and charged him, "You shall not marry one of the Canaanite women. ²Go at once to Paddan-aram to the house of Bethuel, your mother's father; and take as wife from there one of the daughters of Laban, your mother's brother. ³May God Almightyᶜ bless you and make you fruitful and numerous, that you may become a company of peoples. ⁴May he give to you the blessing of Abraham, to you and to your offspring with you, so that you may take possession of the land where you now live as an alien— land that God gave to Abraham." ⁵Thus Isaac sent Jacob away; and he went to Paddan-aram, to Laban son of Bethuel the Aramean, the brother of Rebekah,

aOther ancient authorities lack *often*   bMeaning of Heb uncertain   cTraditional rendering of Heb *El Shaddai*

Jacob's and Esau's mother.

6 Now Esau saw that Isaac had blessed Jacob and sent him away to Paddan-aram to take a wife from there, and that as he blessed him he charged him, "You shall not marry one of the Canaanite women," [7]and that Jacob had obeyed his father and his mother and gone to Paddan-aram. [8]So when Esau saw that the Canaanite women did not please his father Isaac, [9]Esau went to Ishmael and took Mahalath daughter of Abraham's son Ishmael, and sister of Nebaioth, to be his wife in addition to the wives he had.

10 Jacob left Beer-sheba and went toward Haran. [11]He came to a certain place and stayed there for the night, because the sun had set. Taking one of the stones of the place, he put it under his head and lay down in that place. [12]And he dreamed that there was a ladder[a] set up on the earth, the top of it reaching to heaven; and the angels of God were ascending and descending on it. [13]And the LORD stood beside him[b] and said, "I am the LORD, the God of Abraham your father and the God of Isaac; the land on which you lie I will give to you and to your offspring; [14]and your offspring shall be like the dust of the earth, and you shall spread abroad to the west and to the east and to the north and to the south; and all the families of the earth shall be blessed[c] in you and in your offspring. [15]Know that I am with you and will keep you wherever you go, and will bring you back to this land; for I will not leave you until I have done what I have promised you." [16]Then Jacob woke from his sleep and said, "Surely the LORD is in this place—and I did not know it!" [17]And he was afraid, and said, "How awesome is this place! This is none other than the house of God, and this is the gate of heaven."

18 So Jacob rose early in the morning, and he took the stone that he had put under his head and set it up for a pillar and poured oil on the top of it. [19]He called that place Bethel;[d] but the name of the city was Luz at the first. [20]Then Jacob made a vow, saying, "If God will be with me, and will keep me in this way that I go, and will give me bread to eat and clothing to wear, [21]so that I come again to my father's house in peace, then the LORD shall be my God, [22]and this stone, which I have set up for a pillar, shall be God's house; and of all that you give me I will surely give one tenth to you."

29.1 THEN Jacob went on his journey, and came to the land of the people of the east. [2]As he looked, he saw a well in the field and three flocks of sheep lying there beside it; for out of that well the flocks were watered. The stone on the well's mouth was large, [3]and when all the flocks were gathered there, the shepherds would roll the stone from the mouth of the well, and water the sheep, and put the stone back in its place on the mouth of the well.

4 Jacob said to them, "My brothers, where do you come from?" They said, "We are from Haran." [5]He said to them, "Do you know Laban son of Nahor?" They said, "We do." [6]He said to them, "Is it well with him?" "Yes," they replied, "and here is his daughter Rachel, coming with the sheep." [7]He said, "Look, it is still broad daylight; it is not time for the animals to be gathered together. Water the sheep, and go, pasture them." [8]But they said, "We cannot until all the flocks are gathered together, and the stone is rolled from the mouth of the well; then we water the sheep."

9 While he was still speaking with them, Rachel came with her father's sheep; for she kept them. [10]Now when

[a]Or *stairway* or *ramp*   [b]Or *stood above it*   [c]Or *shall bless themselves*   [d]That is *House of God*

Jacob saw Rachel, the daughter of his mother's brother Laban, and the sheep of his mother's brother Laban, Jacob went up and rolled the stone from the well's mouth, and watered the flock of his mother's brother Laban. ¹¹Then Jacob kissed Rachel, and wept aloud. ¹²And Jacob told Rachel that he was her father's kinsman, and that he was Rebekah's son; and she ran and told her father.

13 When Laban heard the news about his sister's son Jacob, he ran to meet him; he embraced him and kissed him, and brought him to his house. Jacobᵃ told Laban all these things, ¹⁴and Laban said to him, "Surely you are my bone and my flesh!" And he stayed with him a month.

15 Then Laban said to Jacob, "Because you are my kinsman, should you therefore serve me for nothing? Tell me, what shall your wages be?" ¹⁶Now Laban had two daughters; the name of the elder was Leah, and the name of the younger was Rachel. ¹⁷Leah's eyes were lovely, ᵇ and Rachel was graceful and beautiful. ¹⁸Jacob loved Rachel; so he said, "I will serve you seven years for your younger daughter Rachel." ¹⁹Laban said, "It is better that I give her to you than that I should give her to any other man; stay with me." ²⁰So Jacob served seven years for Rachel, and they seemed to him but a few days because of the love he had for her.

21 Then Jacob said to Laban, "Give me my wife that I may go in to her, for my time is completed." ²²So Laban gathered together all the people of the place, and made a feast. ²³But in the evening he took his daughter Leah and brought her to Jacob; and he went in to her. ²⁴(Laban gave his maid Zilpah to his daughter Leah to be her maid.) ²⁵When morning came, it was Leah! And Jacob said to Laban, "What is this you have done to me? Did I not serve with you for Rachel? Why then have you deceived me?" ²⁶Laban said, "This is not done in our country—giving the younger before the firstborn. ²⁷Complete the week of this one, and we will give you the other also in return for serving me another seven years." ²⁸Jacob did so, and completed her week; then Laban gave him his daughter Rachel as a wife. ²⁹(Laban gave his maid Bilhah to his daughter Rachel to be her maid.) ³⁰So Jacob went in to Rachel also, and he loved Rachel more than Leah. He served Labanᶜ for another seven years.

31 When the LORD saw that Leah was unloved, he opened her womb; but Rachel was barren. ³²Leah conceived and bore a son, and she named him Reuben;ᵈ for she said, "Because the LORD has looked on my affliction; surely now my husband will love me." ³³She conceived again and bore a son, and said, "Because the LORD has heardᵉ that I am hated, he has given me this son also"; and she named him Simeon. ³⁴Again she conceived and bore a son, and said, "Now this time my husband will be joinedᶠ to me, because I have borne him three sons"; therefore he was named Levi. ³⁵She conceived again and bore a son, and said, "This time I will praiseᵍ the LORD"; therefore she named him Judah; then she ceased bearing.

## MATTHEW 9.18–38

WHILE he [Jesus] was saying these things to them, suddenly a leader of the synagogueʰ came in and knelt before him, saying, "My daughter has just died; but come and lay your hand on her, and she will live." ¹⁹And Jesus got up and followed him, with his disciples. ²⁰Then suddenly a woman who had been suffering from hemorrhages for twelve

ᵃHeb *He*  ᵇMeaning of Heb uncertain  ᶜHeb *him*  ᵈThat is *See, a son*  ᵉHeb *shama*  ᶠHeb *lawah*
ᵍHeb *hodah*  ʰGk lacks *of the synagogue*

years came up behind him and touched the fringe of his cloak, ²¹for she said to herself, "If I only touch his cloak, I will be made well." ²²Jesus turned, and seeing her he said, "Take heart, daughter; your faith has made you well." And instantly the woman was made well. ²³When Jesus came to the leader's house and saw the flute players and the crowd making a commotion, ²⁴he said, "Go away; for the girl is not dead but sleeping." And they laughed at him. ²⁵But when the crowd had been put outside, he went in and took her by the hand, and the girl got up. ²⁶And the report of this spread throughout that district.

27 As Jesus went on from there, two blind men followed him, crying loudly, "Have mercy on us, Son of David!" ²⁸When he entered the house, the blind men came to him; and Jesus said to them, "Do you believe that I am able to do this?" They said to him, "Yes, Lord." ²⁹Then he touched their eyes and said, "According to your faith let it be done to you." ³⁰And their eyes were opened. Then Jesus sternly ordered them, "See that no one knows of this." ³¹But they went away and spread the news about him throughout that district.

32 After they had gone away, a demoniac who was mute was brought to him. ³³And when the demon had been cast out, the one who had been mute spoke; and the crowds were amazed and said, "Never has anything like this been seen in Israel." ³⁴But the Pharisees said, "By the ruler of the demons he casts out the demons."[a]

35 Then Jesus went about all the cities and villages, teaching in their synagogues, and proclaiming the good news of the kingdom, and curing every disease and every sickness. ³⁶When he saw the crowds, he had compassion for them, because they were harassed and helpless, like sheep without a shepherd. ³⁷Then he said to his disciples, "The harvest is plentiful, but the laborers are few; ³⁸therefore ask the Lord of the harvest to send out laborers into his harvest."

## PSALM 11.1–7

*To the leader. Of David.*

I<sub></sub>N the LORD I take refuge; how
    can you say to me,
  "Flee like a bird to the
    mountains;[b]
2  for look, the wicked bend the
    bow,
  they have fitted their arrow
    to the string,
  to shoot in the dark at the
    upright in heart.
3  If the foundations are
    destroyed,
  what can the righteous do?"

4  The LORD is in his holy temple;
  the LORD's throne is in
    heaven.
  His eyes behold, his gaze
    examines humankind.
5  The LORD tests the righteous
    and the wicked,
  and his soul hates the lover of
    violence.
6  On the wicked he will rain coals
    of fire and sulfur;
  a scorching wind shall be the
    portion of their cup.
7  For the LORD is righteous;
  he loves righteous deeds;
    the upright shall behold his
     face.

---

a Other ancient authorities lack this verse    b Gk Syr Jerome Tg: Heb *flee to your mountain, O bird*

## PROVERBS 3.11–12

My child, do not despise the
    Lord's discipline
or be weary of his
    reproof,

12  for the Lord reproves the one
    he loves,
    as a father the son in whom
      he delights.

# JANUARY 14

## GENESIS 30.1—31.16

When Rachel saw that she bore Jacob no children, she envied her sister; and she said to Jacob, "Give me children, or I shall die!" ²Jacob became very angry with Rachel and said, "Am I in the place of God, who has withheld from you the fruit of the womb?" ³Then she said, "Here is my maid Bilhah; go in to her, that she may bear upon my knees and that I too may have children through her." ⁴So she gave him her maid Bilhah as a wife; and Jacob went in to her. ⁵And Bilhah conceived and bore Jacob a son. ⁶Then Rachel said, "God has judged me, and has also heard my voice and given me a son"; therefore she named him Dan.[a] ⁷Rachel's maid Bilhah conceived again and bore Jacob a second son. ⁸Then Rachel said, "With mighty wrestlings I have wrestled[b] with my sister, and have prevailed"; so she named him Naphtali.

9 When Leah saw that she had ceased bearing children, she took her maid Zilpah and gave her to Jacob as a wife. ¹⁰Then Leah's maid Zilpah bore Jacob a son. ¹¹And Leah said, "Good fortune!" so she named him Gad.[c] ¹²Leah's maid Zilpah bore Jacob a second son. ¹³And Leah said, "Happy am I! For the women will call me happy"; so she named him Asher.[d]

14 In the days of wheat harvest Reuben went and found mandrakes in the field, and brought them to his mother Leah. Then Rachel said to Leah, "Please give me some of your son's mandrakes." ¹⁵But she said to her, "Is it a small matter that you have taken away my husband? Would you take away my son's mandrakes also?" Rachel said, "Then he may lie with you tonight for your son's mandrakes." ¹⁶When Jacob came from the field in the evening, Leah went out to meet him, and said, "You must come in to me; for I have hired you with my son's mandrakes." So he lay with her that night. ¹⁷And God heeded Leah, and she conceived and bore Jacob a fifth son. ¹⁸Leah said, "God has given me my hire[e] because I gave my maid to my husband"; so she named him Issachar. ¹⁹And Leah conceived again, and she bore Jacob a sixth son. ²⁰Then Leah said, "God has endowed me with a good dowry; now my husband will honor[f] me, because I have borne him six sons"; so she named him Zebulun. ²¹Afterwards she bore a daughter, and named her Dinah.

22 Then God remembered Rachel, and God heeded her and opened her womb. ²³She conceived and bore a son, and said, "God has taken away my reproach"; ²⁴and she named him Joseph,[g] saying, "May the Lord add to me another son!"

a That is *He judged*   b Heb *niphtal*   c That is *Fortune*   d That is *Happy*   e Heb *sakar*   f Heb *zabal*
g That is *He adds*

25 When Rachel had borne Joseph, Jacob said to Laban, "Send me away, that I may go to my own home and country. 26Give me my wives and my children for whom I have served you, and let me go; for you know very well the service I have given you." 27But Laban said to him, "If you will allow me to say so, I have learned by divination that the LORD has blessed me because of you; 28name your wages, and I will give it." 29Jacob said to him, "You yourself know how I have served you, and how your cattle have fared with me. 30For you had little before I came, and it has increased abundantly; and the LORD has blessed you wherever I turned. But now when shall I provide for my own household also?" 31He said, "What shall I give you?" Jacob said, "You shall not give me anything; if you will do this for me, I will again feed your flock and keep it: 32let me pass through all your flock today, removing from it every speckled and spotted sheep and every black lamb, and the spotted and speckled among the goats; and such shall be my wages. 33So my honesty will answer for me later, when you come to look into my wages with you. Every one that is not speckled and spotted among the goats and black among the lambs, if found with me, shall be counted stolen." 34Laban said, "Good! Let it be as you have said." 35But that day Laban removed the male goats that were striped and spotted, and all the female goats that were speckled and spotted, every one that had white on it, and every lamb that was black, and put them in charge of his sons; 36and he set a distance of three days' journey between himself and Jacob, while Jacob was pasturing the rest of Laban's flock.

37 Then Jacob took fresh rods of poplar and almond and plane, and peeled white streaks in them, exposing the white of the rods. 38He set the rods that he had peeled in front of the flocks in the troughs, that is, the watering places, where the flocks came to drink. And since they bred when they came to drink, 39the flocks bred in front of the rods, and so the flocks produced young that were striped, speckled, and spotted. 40Jacob separated the lambs, and set the faces of the flocks toward the striped and the completely black animals in the flock of Laban; and he put his own droves apart, and did not put them with Laban's flock. 41Whenever the stronger of the flock were breeding, Jacob laid the rods in the troughs before the eyes of the flock, that they might breed among the rods, 42but for the feebler of the flock he did not lay them there; so the feebler were Laban's, and the stronger Jacob's. 43Thus the man grew exceedingly rich, and had large flocks, and male and female slaves, and camels and donkeys.

31.1 Now Jacob heard that the sons of Laban were saying, "Jacob has taken all that was our father's; he has gained all this wealth from what belonged to our father." 2And Jacob saw that Laban did not regard him as favorably as he did before. 3Then the LORD said to Jacob, "Return to the land of your ancestors and to your kindred, and I will be with you." 4So Jacob sent and called Rachel and Leah into the field where his flock was, 5and said to them, "I see that your father does not regard me as favorably as he did before. But the God of my father has been with me. 6You know that I have served your father with all my strength; 7yet your father has cheated me and changed my wages ten times, but God did not permit him to harm me. 8If he said, 'The speckled shall be your wages,' then all the flock bore speckled; and if he said, 'The striped shall be your wages,' then all the flock bore striped. 9Thus God has taken away the livestock of your father, and given them to me.

10 During the mating of the flock I once had a dream in which I looked up and saw that the male goats that leaped upon the flock were striped, speckled, and mottled. [11]Then the angel of God said to me in the dream, 'Jacob,' and I said, 'Here I am!' [12]And he said, 'Look up and see that all the goats that leap on the flock are striped, speckled, and mottled; for I have seen all that Laban is doing to you. [13]I am the God of Bethel,[a] where you anointed a pillar and made a vow to me. Now leave this land at once and return to the land of your birth.' " [14]Then Rachel and Leah answered him, "Is there any portion or inheritance left to us in our father's house? [15]Are we not regarded by him as foreigners? For he has sold us, and he has been using up the money given for us. [16]All the property that God has taken away from our father belongs to us and to our children; now then, do whatever God has said to you."

## MATTHEW 10.1–23

THEN Jesus[b] summoned his twelve disciples and gave them authority over unclean spirits, to cast them out, and to cure every disease and every sickness. [2]These are the names of the twelve apostles: first, Simon, also known as Peter, and his brother Andrew; James son of Zebedee, and his brother John; [3]Philip and Bartholomew; Thomas and Matthew the tax collector; James son of Alphaeus, and Thaddaeus;[c] [4]Simon the Cananaean, and Judas Iscariot, the one who betrayed him.

5 These twelve Jesus sent out with the following instructions: "Go nowhere among the Gentiles, and enter no town of the Samaritans, [6]but go rather to the lost sheep of the house of Israel. [7]As you go, proclaim the good news, 'The kingdom of heaven has come near.'[d] [8]Cure the sick, raise the dead, cleanse the lepers,[e] cast out demons. You received without payment; give without payment. [9]Take no gold, or silver, or copper in your belts, [10]no bag for your journey, or two tunics, or sandals, or a staff; for laborers deserve their food. [11]Whatever town or village you enter, find out who in it is worthy, and stay there until you leave. [12]As you enter the house, greet it. [13]If the house is worthy, let your peace come upon it; but if it is not worthy, let your peace return to you. [14]If anyone will not welcome you or listen to your words, shake off the dust from your feet as you leave that house or town. [15]Truly I tell you, it will be more tolerable for the land of Sodom and Gomorrah on the day of judgment than for that town.

16 "See, I am sending you out like sheep into the midst of wolves; so be wise as serpents and innocent as doves. [17]Beware of them, for they will hand you over to councils and flog you in their synagogues; [18]and you will be dragged before governors and kings because of me, as a testimony to them and the Gentiles. [19]When they hand you over, do not worry about how you are to speak or what you are to say; for what you are to say will be given to you at that time; [20]for it is not you who speak, but the Spirit of your Father speaking through you. [21]Brother will betray brother to death, and a father his child, and children will rise against parents and have them put to death; [22]and you will be hated by all because of my name. But the one who endures to the end will be saved. [23]When they persecute you in one town, flee to the next; for truly I tell you, you will not have gone through all the towns of Israel before the Son of Man comes.

[a]Cn: Meaning of Heb uncertain  [b]Gk *he*  [c]Other ancient authorities read *Lebbaeus*, or *Lebbaeus called Thaddaeus*  [d]Or *is at hand*  [e]The terms *leper* and *leprosy* can refer to several diseases

## PSALM 12.1–8

*To the leader: according to The Sheminith. A Psalm of David.*

Help, O Lord, for there is no
 longer anyone who is
 godly;
 the faithful have disappeared
 from humankind.
2 They utter lies to each other;
 with flattering lips and a
 double heart they speak.

3 May the Lord cut off all
 flattering lips,
 the tongue that makes great
 boasts,
4 those who say, "With our
 tongues we will prevail;
 our lips are our own—who is
 our master?"

5 "Because the poor are
 despoiled, because the
 needy groan,
 I will now rise up," says the
 Lord;
 "I will place them in the
 safety for which they
 long."

6 The promises of the Lord are
 promises that are pure,
 silver refined in a furnace on
 the ground,
 purified seven times.

7 You, O Lord, will protect us;
 you will guard us from this
 generation forever.
8 On every side the wicked
 prowl,
 as vileness is exalted among
 humankind.

## PROVERBS 3.13–15

Happy are those who find
 wisdom,
 and those who get
 understanding,
14 for her income is better than
 silver,
 and her revenue better than
 gold.
15 She is more precious than
 jewels,
 and nothing you desire can
 compare with her.

# JANUARY 15

## GENESIS 31.17—32.12

So Jacob arose, and set his children and his wives on camels; 18and he drove away all his livestock, all the property that he had gained, the livestock in his possession that he had acquired in Paddan-aram, to go to his father Isaac in the land of Canaan.

19 Now Laban had gone to shear his sheep, and Rachel stole her father's household gods. 20And Jacob deceived Laban the Aramean, in that he did not tell him that he intended to flee. 21So he fled with all that he had; starting out he crossed the Euphrates, a and set his face toward the hill country of Gilead.

22 On the third day Laban was told that Jacob had fled. 23So he took his

a Heb *the river*

kinsfolk with him and pursued him for seven days until he caught up with him in the hill country of Gilead. ²⁴But God came to Laban the Aramean in a dream by night, and said to him, "Take heed that you say not a word to Jacob, either good or bad."

25 Laban overtook Jacob. Now Jacob had pitched his tent in the hill country, and Laban with his kinsfolk camped in the hill country of Gilead. ²⁶Laban said to Jacob, "What have you done? You have deceived me, and carried away my daughters like captives of the sword. ²⁷Why did you flee secretly and deceive me and not tell me? I would have sent you away with mirth and songs, with tambourine and lyre. ²⁸And why did you not permit me to kiss my sons and my daughters farewell? What you have done is foolish. ²⁹It is in my power to do you harm; but the God of your father spoke to me last night, saying, 'Take heed that you speak to Jacob neither good nor bad.' ³⁰Even though you had to go because you longed greatly for your father's house, why did you steal my gods?" ³¹Jacob answered Laban, "Because I was afraid, for I thought that you would take your daughters from me by force. ³²But anyone with whom you find your gods shall not live. In the presence of our kinsfolk, point out what I have that is yours, and take it." Now Jacob did not know that Rachel had stolen the gods. ᵃ

33 So Laban went into Jacob's tent, and into Leah's tent, and into the tent of the two maids, but he did not find them. And he went out of Leah's tent, and entered Rachel's. ³⁴Now Rachel had taken the household gods and put them in the camel's saddle, and sat on them. Laban felt all about in the tent, but did not find them. ³⁵And she said to her father, "Let not my lord be angry that I cannot rise before you, for the way of women is upon me." So he searched, but did not find the household gods.

36 Then Jacob became angry, and upbraided Laban. Jacob said to Laban, "What is my offense? What is my sin, that you have hotly pursued me? ³⁷Although you have felt about through all my goods, what have you found of all your household goods? Set it here before my kinsfolk and your kinsfolk, so that they may decide between us two. ³⁸These twenty years I have been with you; your ewes and your female goats have not miscarried, and I have not eaten the rams of your flocks. ³⁹That which was torn by wild beasts I did not bring to you; I bore the loss of it myself; of my hand you required it, whether stolen by day or stolen by night. ⁴⁰It was like this with me: by day the heat consumed me, and the cold by night, and my sleep fled from my eyes. ⁴¹These twenty years I have been in your house; I served you fourteen years for your two daughters, and six years for your flock, and you have changed my wages ten times. ⁴²If the God of my father, the God of Abraham and the Fearᵇ of Isaac, had not been on my side, surely now you would have sent me away empty-handed. God saw my affliction and the labor of my hands, and rebuked you last night."

43 Then Laban answered and said to Jacob, "The daughters are my daughters, the children are my children, the flocks are my flocks, and all that you see is mine. But what can I do today about these daughters of mine, or about their children whom they have borne? ⁴⁴Come now, let us make a covenant, you and I; and let it be a witness between you and me." ⁴⁵So Jacob took a stone, and set it up as a pillar. ⁴⁶And Jacob said to his kinsfolk, "Gather stones," and they took stones, and made a heap; and they ate there by the heap. ⁴⁷Laban called it Jegar-

ᵃHeb *them*   ᵇMeaning of Heb uncertain

sahadutha:[a] but Jacob called it Galeed.[b] 48Laban said, "This heap is a witness between you and me today." Therefore he called it Galeed, 49and the pillar[c] Mizpah,[d] for he said, "The LORD watch between you and me, when we are absent one from the other. 50If you ill-treat my daughters, or if you take wives in addition to my daughters, though no one else is with us, remember that God is witness between you and me."

51 Then Laban said to Jacob, "See this heap and see the pillar, which I have set between you and me. 52This heap is a witness, and the pillar is a witness, that I will not pass beyond this heap to you, and you will not pass beyond this heap and this pillar to me, for harm. 53May the God of Abraham and the God of Nahor"—the God of their father—"judge between us." So Jacob swore by the Fear[e] of his father Isaac, 54and Jacob offered a sacrifice on the height and called his kinsfolk to eat bread; and they ate bread and tarried all night in the hill country.

55[f] Early in the morning Laban rose up, and kissed his grandchildren and his daughters and blessed them; then he departed and returned home.

32.1 JACOB went on his way and the angels of God met him; 2and when Jacob saw them he said, "This is God's camp!" So he called that place Mahanaim.[g]

3 Jacob sent messengers before him to his brother Esau in the land of Seir, the country of Edom, 4instructing them, "Thus you shall say to my lord Esau: Thus says your servant Jacob, 'I have lived with Laban as an alien, and stayed until now; 5and I have oxen, donkeys, flocks, male and female slaves; and I have sent to tell my lord,

in order that I may find favor in your sight.'"

6 The messengers returned to Jacob, saying, "We came to your brother Esau, and he is coming to meet you, and four hundred men are with him." 7Then Jacob was greatly afraid and distressed; and he divided the people that were with him, and the flocks and herds and camels, into two companies, 8thinking, "If Esau comes to the one company and destroys it, then the company that is left will escape."

9 And Jacob said, "O God of my father Abraham and God of my father Isaac, O LORD who said to me, 'Return to your country and to your kindred, and I will do you good,' 10I am not worthy of the least of all the steadfast love and all the faithfulness that you have shown to your servant, for with only my staff I crossed this Jordan; and now I have become two companies. 11Deliver me, please, from the hand of my brother, from the hand of Esau, for I am afraid of him; he may come and kill us all, the mothers with the children. 12Yet you have said, 'I will surely do you good, and make your offspring as the sand of the sea, which cannot be counted because of their number.'"

## MATTHEW 10.24—11.6

"A DISCIPLE is not above the teacher, nor a slave above the master; 25it is enough for the disciple to be like the teacher, and the slave like the master. If they have called the master of the house Beelzebul, how much more will they malign those of his household!

26 "So have no fear of them; for nothing is covered up that will not be uncovered, and nothing secret that will not become known. 27What I say to you in the dark, tell in the light; and what

aIn Aramaic *The heap of witness*  bIn Hebrew *The heap of witness*  cCompare Sam: MT lacks *the pillar*  dThat is *Watchpost*  eMeaning of Heb uncertain  fCh 32.1 in Heb  gHere taken to mean *Two camps*

you hear whispered, proclaim from the housetops. 28Do not fear those who kill the body but cannot kill the soul; rather fear him who can destroy both soul and body in hell. a 29Are not two sparrows sold for a penny? Yet not one of them will fall to the ground apart from your Father. 30And even the hairs of your head are all counted. 31So do not be afraid; you are of more value than many sparrows.

32 "Everyone therefore who acknowledges me before others, I also will acknowledge before my Father in heaven; 33but whoever denies me before others, I also will deny before my Father in heaven.

34 "Do not think that I have come to bring peace to the earth; I have not come to bring peace, but a sword.

35 For I have come to set a man
          against his father,
     and a daughter against her
          mother,
     and a daughter-in-law against
          her mother-in-law;
36 and one's foes will be members
          of one's own household.
37Whoever loves father or mother more than me is not worthy of me; and whoever loves son or daughter more than me is not worthy of me; 38and whoever does not take up the cross and follow me is not worthy of me. 39Those who find their life will lose it, and those who lose their life for my sake will find it.

40 "Whoever welcomes you welcomes me, and whoever welcomes me welcomes the one who sent me. 41Whoever welcomes a prophet in the name of a prophet will receive a prophet's reward; and whoever welcomes a righteous person in the name of a righteous person will receive the reward of the righteous; 42and whoever gives even a cup of cold water to one of these little ones in the name of a

disciple—truly I tell you, none of these will lose their reward."

11.1 Now when Jesus had finished instructing his twelve disciples, he went on from there to teach and proclaim his message in their cities.

2 When John heard in prison what the Messiahb was doing, he sent word by hisc disciples 3and said to him, "Are you the one who is to come, or are we to wait for another?" 4Jesus answered them, "Go and tell John what you hear and see: 5the blind receive their sight, the lame walk, the lepersd are cleansed, the deaf hear, the dead are raised, and the poor have good news brought to them. 6And blessed is anyone who takes no offense at me."

# PSALM 13.1–6

*To the leader. A Psalm of David.*

**H**ow long, O Lord? Will you
          forget me forever?
     How long will you hide
          your face from me?
2  How long must I bear paine in
          my soul,
     and have sorrow in my heart
          all day long?
     How long shall my enemy be
          exalted over me?

3  Consider and answer me,
          O Lord my God!
     Give light to my eyes, or I
          will sleep the sleep of
          death,
4  and my enemy will say, "I have
          prevailed";
     my foes will rejoice because I
          am shaken.

5  But I trusted in your steadfast
          love;
     my heart shall rejoice in your
          salvation.

aGk *Gehenna*  bOr *the Christ*  cOther ancient authorities read *two of his*  dThe terms *leper* and *leprosy* can refer to several diseases  eSyr: Heb *hold counsels*

6  I will sing to the LORD,
     because he has dealt
       bountifully with me.

## PROVERBS 3.16–18

Long life is in her [wisdom's]
     right hand;
   in her left hand are riches
     and honor.

17  Her ways are ways of
       pleasantness,
     and all her paths are peace.
18  She is a tree of life to those
       who lay hold of her;
     those who hold her fast are
       called happy.

# JANUARY 16

## GENESIS 32.13—34.31

So he [Jacob] spent that night there, and from what he had with him he took a present for his brother Esau, 14two hundred female goats and twenty male goats, two hundred ewes and twenty rams, 15thirty milch camels and their colts, forty cows and ten bulls, twenty female donkeys and ten male donkeys. 16These he delivered into the hand of his servants, every drove by itself, and said to his servants, "Pass on ahead of me, and put a space between drove and drove." 17He instructed the foremost, "When Esau my brother meets you, and asks you, 'To whom do you belong? Where are you going? And whose are these ahead of you?' 18then you shall say, 'They belong to your servant Jacob; they are a present sent to my lord Esau; and moreover he is behind us.'" 19He likewise instructed the second and the third and all who followed the droves, "You shall say the same thing to Esau when you meet him, 20and you shall say, 'Moreover your servant Jacob is behind us.'" For he thought, "I may appease him with the present that goes ahead of me, and afterwards I shall see his face; perhaps he will accept me." 21So the present passed on ahead of him; and he himself spent that night in the camp.

22  The same night he got up and took his two wives, his two maids, and his eleven children, and crossed the ford of the Jabbok. 23He took them and sent them across the stream, and likewise everything that he had. 24Jacob was left alone; and a man wrestled with him until daybreak. 25When the man saw that he did not prevail against Jacob, he struck him on the hip socket; and Jacob's hip was put out of joint as he wrestled with him. 26Then he said, "Let me go, for the day is breaking." But Jacob said, "I will not let you go, unless you bless me." 27So he said to him, "What is your name?" And he said, "Jacob." 28Then the man[a] said, "You shall no longer be called Jacob, but Israel,[b] for you have striven with God and with humans,[c] and have prevailed." 29Then Jacob asked him, "Please tell me your name." But he said, "Why is it that you ask my name?" And there he blessed him. 30So Jacob

[a]Heb *he*   [b]That is *The one who strives with God* or *God strives*   [c]Or *with divine and human beings*

called the place Peniel, [a] saying, "For I have seen God face to face, and yet my life is preserved." [31]The sun rose upon him as he passed Penuel, limping because of his hip. [32]Therefore to this day the Israelites do not eat the thigh muscle that is on the hip socket, because he struck Jacob on the hip socket at the thigh muscle.

[33.1] Now Jacob looked up and saw Esau coming, and four hundred men with him. So he divided the children among Leah and Rachel and the two maids. [2]He put the maids with their children in front, then Leah with her children, and Rachel and Joseph last of all. [3]He himself went on ahead of them, bowing himself to the ground seven times, until he came near his brother.

[4] But Esau ran to meet him, and embraced him, and fell on his neck and kissed him, and they wept. [5]When Esau looked up and saw the women and children, he said, "Who are these with you?" Jacob said, "The children whom God has graciously given your servant." [6]Then the maids drew near, they and their children, and bowed down; [7]Leah likewise and her children drew near and bowed down; and finally Joseph and Rachel drew near, and they bowed down. [8]Esau said, "What do you mean by all this company that I met?" Jacob answered, "To find favor with my lord." [9]But Esau said, "I have enough, my brother; keep what you have for yourself." [10]Jacob said, "No, please; if I find favor with you, then accept my present from my hand; for truly to see your face is like seeing the face of God—since you have received me with such favor. [11]Please accept my gift that is brought to you, because God has dealt graciously with me, and because I have everything I want." So he urged him, and he took it.

[12] Then Esau said, "Let us journey on our way, and I will go alongside you." [13]But Jacob said to him, "My lord knows that the children are frail and that the flocks and herds, which are nursing, are a care to me; and if they are overdriven for one day, all the flocks will die. [14]Let my lord pass on ahead of his servant, and I will lead on slowly, according to the pace of the cattle that are before me and according to the pace of the children, until I come to my lord in Seir."

[15] So Esau said, "Let me leave with you some of the people who are with me." But he said, "Why should my lord be so kind to me?" [16]So Esau returned that day on his way to Seir. [17]But Jacob journeyed to Succoth, [b] and built himself a house, and made booths for his cattle; therefore the place is called Succoth.

[18] Jacob came safely to the city of Shechem, which is in the land of Canaan, on his way from Paddan-aram; and he camped before the city. [19]And from the sons of Hamor, Shechem's father, he bought for one hundred pieces of money[c] the plot of land on which he had pitched his tent. [20]There he erected an altar and called it El-Elohe-Israel. [d]

[34.1] Now Dinah the daughter of Leah, whom she had borne to Jacob, went out to visit the women of the region. [2]When Shechem son of Hamor the Hivite, prince of the region, saw her, he seized her and lay with her by force. [3]And his soul was drawn to Dinah daughter of Jacob; he loved the girl, and spoke tenderly to her. [4]So Shechem spoke to his father Hamor, saying, "Get me this girl to be my wife."

[5] Now Jacob heard that Shechem[e] had defiled his daughter Dinah; but his sons were with his cattle in the field, so Jacob held his peace until they came. [6]And Hamor the father of Shechem

a That is *The face of God*   b That is *Booths*   c Heb *one hundred qesitah*   d That is *God, the God of Israel*   e Heb *he*

went out to Jacob to speak with him, [7]just as the sons of Jacob came in from the field. When they heard of it, the men were indignant and very angry, because he had committed an outrage in Israel by lying with Jacob's daughter, for such a thing ought not to be done.

8 But Hamor spoke with them, saying, "The heart of my son Shechem longs for your daughter; please give her to him in marriage. [9]Make marriages with us; give your daughters to us, and take our daughters for yourselves. [10]You shall live with us; and the land shall be open to you; live and trade in it, and get property in it." [11]Shechem also said to her father and to her brothers, "Let me find favor with you, and whatever you say to me I will give. [12]Put the marriage present and gift as high as you like, and I will give whatever you ask me; only give me the girl to be my wife."

13 The sons of Jacob answered Shechem and his father Hamor deceitfully, because he had defiled their sister Dinah. [14]They said to them, "We cannot do this thing, to give our sister to one who is uncircumcised, for that would be a disgrace to us. [15]Only on this condition will we consent to you: that you will become as we are and every male among you be circumcised. [16]Then we will give our daughters to you, and we will take your daughters for ourselves, and we will live among you and become one people. [17]But if you will not listen to us and be circumcised, then we will take our daughter and be gone."

18 Their words pleased Hamor and Hamor's son Shechem. [19]And the young man did not delay to do the thing, because he was delighted with Jacob's daughter. Now he was the most honored of all his family. [20]So Hamor and his son Shechem came to the gate of their city and spoke to the men of their city, saying, [21]"These people are friendly with us; let them live in the land and trade in it, for the land is large enough for them; let us take their daughters in marriage, and let us give them our daughters. [22]Only on this condition will they agree to live among us, to become one people: that every male among us be circumcised as they are circumcised. [23]Will not their livestock, their property, and all their animals be ours? Only let us agree with them, and they will live among us." [24]And all who went out of the city gate heeded Hamor and his son Shechem; and every male was circumcised, all who went out of the gate of his city.

25 On the third day, when they were still in pain, two of the sons of Jacob, Simeon and Levi, Dinah's brothers, took their swords and came against the city unawares, and killed all the males. [26]They killed Hamor and his son Shechem with the sword, and took Dinah out of Shechem's house, and went away. [27]And the other sons of Jacob came upon the slain, and plundered the city, because their sister had been defiled. [28]They took their flocks and their herds, their donkeys, and whatever was in the city and in the field. [29]All their wealth, all their little ones and their wives, all that was in the houses, they captured and made their prey. [30]Then Jacob said to Simeon and Levi, "You have brought trouble on me by making me odious to the inhabitants of the land, the Canaanites and the Perizzites; my numbers are few, and if they gather themselves against me and attack me, I shall be destroyed, both I and my household." [31]But they said, "Should our sister be treated like a whore?"

## MATTHEW 11.7–30

As they went away, Jesus began to speak to the crowds about John: "What did you go out into the wilderness to look at? A reed shaken by the wind? [8]What then did you go out to see? Someone[a] dressed in soft robes? Look, those who wear soft robes are in royal palaces. 9What then did you go out to see? A prophet?[b] Yes, I tell you, and more than a prophet. 10This is the one about whom it is written,

> 'See, I am sending my
>       messenger ahead of you,
>    who will prepare your way
>       before you.'

11Truly I tell you, among those born of women no one has arisen greater than John the Baptist; yet the least in the kingdom of heaven is greater than he. 12From the days of John the Baptist until now the kingdom of heaven has suffered violence, [c] and the violent take it by force. 13For all the prophets and the law prophesied until John came; 14and if you are willing to accept it, he is Elijah who is to come. 15Let anyone with ears[d] listen!

16 "But to what will I compare this generation? It is like children sitting in the marketplaces and calling to one another,

> 17 'We played the flute for you,
>        and you did not dance;
>     we wailed, and you did not
>        mourn.'

18For John came neither eating nor drinking, and they say, 'He has a demon'; 19the Son of Man came eating and drinking, and they say, 'Look, a glutton and a drunkard, a friend of tax collectors and sinners!' Yet wisdom is vindicated by her deeds."[e]

20 Then he began to reproach the cities in which most of his deeds of power had been done, because they did not repent. 21"Woe to you, Chorazin! Woe to you, Bethsaida! For if the deeds of power done in you had been done in Tyre and Sidon, they would have repented long ago in sackcloth and ashes. 22But I tell you, on the day of judgment it will be more tolerable for Tyre and Sidon than for you. 23And you, Capernaum,

> will you be exalted to heaven?
>    No, you will be brought down
>       to Hades.

For if the deeds of power done in you had been done in Sodom, it would have remained until this day. 24But I tell you that on the day of judgment it will be more tolerable for the land of Sodom than for you."

25 At that time Jesus said, "I thank[f] you, Father, Lord of heaven and earth, because you have hidden these things from the wise and the intelligent and have revealed them to infants; 26yes, Father, for such was your gracious will. [g] 27All things have been handed over to me by my Father; and no one knows the Son except the Father, and no one knows the Father except the Son and anyone to whom the Son chooses to reveal him.

28 "Come to me, all you that are weary and are carrying heavy burdens, and I will give you rest. 29Take my yoke upon you, and learn from me; for I am gentle and humble in heart, and you will find rest for your souls. 30For my yoke is easy, and my burden is light."

## PSALM 14.1–7

*To the leader. Of David.*

Fools say in their hearts,
>       "There is no God."
>    They are corrupt, they do
>       abominable deeds;
>    there is no one who does
>       good.
> 2 The Lord looks down from
>       heaven on humankind
>    to see if there are any who
>       are wise,
>    who seek after God.

a Or *Why then did you go out? To see someone*   b Other ancient authorities read *Why then did you go out? To see a prophet?*   c Or *has been coming violently*   d Other ancient authorities add *to hear*   e Other ancient authorities read *children*   f Or *praise*   g Or *for so it was well-pleasing in your sight*

3 They have all gone astray, they
    are all alike perverse;
  there is no one who does
    good,
  no, not one.

4 Have they no knowledge, all the
    evildoers
  who eat up my people as they
    eat bread,
  and do not call upon the
    LORD?

5 There they shall be in great
    terror,
  for God is with the company
    of the righteous.
6 You would confound the plans of
    the poor,

  but the LORD is their refuge.

7 O that deliverance for Israel
    would come from Zion!
  When the LORD restores the
    fortunes of his people,
  Jacob will rejoice; Israel will
    be glad.

## PROVERBS 3.19–20

THE LORD by wisdom founded
    the earth;
  by understanding he
    established the heavens;
20 by his knowledge the deeps
    broke open,
  and the clouds drop down the
    dew.

# JANUARY 17

## GENESIS 35.1—36.43

GOD said to Jacob, "Arise, go up to Bethel, and settle there. Make an altar there to the God who appeared to you when you fled from your brother Esau." 2So Jacob said to his household and to all who were with him, "Put away the foreign gods that are among you, and purify yourselves, and change your clothes; 3then come, let us go up to Bethel, that I may make an altar there to the God who answered me in the day of my distress and has been with me wherever I have gone." 4So they gave to Jacob all the foreign gods that they had, and the rings that were in their ears; and Jacob hid them under the oak that was near Shechem.

5 As they journeyed, a terror from God fell upon the cities all around them, so that no one pursued them. 6Jacob came to Luz (that is, Bethel), which is in the land of Canaan, he and all the people who were with him, 7and there he built an altar and called the place El-bethel, a because it was there that God had revealed himself to him when he fled from his brother. 8And Deborah, Rebekah's nurse, died, and she was buried under an oak below Bethel. So it was called Allon-bacuth. b

9 God appeared to Jacob again when he came from Paddan-aram, and he blessed him. 10God said to him, "Your name is Jacob; no longer shall you be called Jacob, but Israel shall be your name." So he was called Israel.

a That is *God of Bethel*  b That is *Oak of weeping*

11God said to him, "I am God Almighty:a be fruitful and multiply; a nation and a company of nations shall come from you, and kings shall spring from you. 12The land that I gave to Abraham and Isaac I will give to you, and I will give the land to your offspring after you." 13Then God went up from him at the place where he had spoken with him. 14Jacob set up a pillar in the place where he had spoken with him, a pillar of stone; and he poured out a drink offering on it, and poured oil on it. 15So Jacob called the place where God had spoken with him Bethel.

16 Then they journeyed from Bethel; and when they were still some distance from Ephrath, Rachel was in childbirth, and she had hard labor. 17When she was in her hard labor, the midwife said to her, "Do not be afraid; for now you will have another son." 18As her soul was departing (for she died), she named him Ben-oni;b but his father called him Benjamin.c 19So Rachel died, and she was buried on the way to Ephrath (that is, Bethlehem), 20and Jacob set up a pillar at her grave; it is the pillar of Rachel's tomb, which is there to this day. 21Israel journeyed on, and pitched his tent beyond the tower of Eder.

22 While Israel lived in that land, Reuben went and lay with Bilhah his father's concubine; and Israel heard of it.

Now the sons of Jacob were twelve. 23The sons of Leah: Reuben (Jacob's firstborn), Simeon, Levi, Judah, Issachar, and Zebulun. 24The sons of Rachel: Joseph and Benjamin. 25The sons of Bilhah, Rachel's maid: Dan and Naphtali. 26The sons of Zilpah, Leah's maid: Gad and Asher. These were the sons of Jacob who were born to him in Paddan-aram.

27 Jacob came to his father Isaac at Mamre, or Kiriath-arba (that is, Hebron), where Abraham and Isaac had resided as aliens. 28Now the days of Isaac were one hundred eighty years. 29And Isaac breathed his last; he died and was gathered to his people, old and full of days; and his sons Esau and Jacob buried him.

36.1 These are the descendants of Esau (that is, Edom). 2Esau took his wives from the Canaanites: Adah daughter of Elon the Hittite, Oholibamah daughter of Anah sond of Zibeon the Hivite, 3and Basemath, Ishmael's daughter, sister of Nebaioth. 4Adah bore Eliphaz to Esau; Basemath bore Reuel; 5and Oholibamah bore Jeush, Jalam, and Korah. These are the sons of Esau who were born to him in the land of Canaan.

6 Then Esau took his wives, his sons, his daughters, and all the members of his household, his cattle, all his livestock, and all the property he had acquired in the land of Canaan; and he moved to a land some distance from his brother Jacob. 7For their possessions were too great for them to live together; the land where they were staying could not support them because of their livestock. 8So Esau settled in the hill country of Seir; Esau is Edom.

9 These are the descendants of Esau, ancestor of the Edomites, in the hill country of Seir. 10These are the names of Esau's sons: Eliphaz son of Adah the wife of Esau; Reuel, the son of Esau's wife Basemath. 11The sons of Eliphaz were Teman, Omar, Zepho, Gatam, and Kenaz. 12(Timna was a concubine of Eliphaz, Esau's son; she bore Amalek to Eliphaz.) These were the sons of Adah, Esau's wife. 13These were the sons of Reuel: Nahath, Zerah, Shammah, and Mizzah. These were the sons of Esau's wife, Basemath. 14These were the sons of Esau's wife Oholibamah, daughter of Anah sone of Zibeon: she bore to Esau Jeush, Jalam, and Korah.

aTraditional rendering of Heb *El Shaddai*   bThat is *Son of my sorrow*   cThat is *Son of the right hand* or *Son of the South*   dSam Gk Syr: Heb *daughter*   eGk Syr: Heb *daughter*

15 These are the clans[a] of the sons of Esau. The sons of Eliphaz the firstborn of Esau: the clans[a] Teman, Omar, Zepho, Kenaz, [16]Korah, Gatam, and Amalek; these are the clans[a] of Eliphaz in the land of Edom; they are the sons of Adah. [17]These are the sons of Esau's son Reuel: the clans[a] Nahath, Zerah, Shammah, and Mizzah; these are the clans[a] of Reuel in the land of Edom; they are the sons of Esau's wife Basemath. [18]These are the sons of Esau's wife Oholibamah: the clans[a] Jeush, Jalam, and Korah; these are the clans[a] born of Esau's wife Oholibamah, the daughter of Anah. [19]These are the sons of Esau (that is, Edom), and these are their clans. [a]

20 These are the sons of Seir the Horite, the inhabitants of the land: Lotan, Shobal, Zibeon, Anah, [21]Dishon, Ezer, and Dishan; these are the clans[a] of the Horites, the sons of Seir in the land of Edom. [22]The sons of Lotan were Hori and Heman; and Lotan's sister was Timna. [23]These are the sons of Shobal: Alvan, Manahath, Ebal, Shepho, and Onam. [24]These are the sons of Zibeon: Aiah and Anah; he is the Anah who found the springs[b] in the wilderness, as he pastured the donkeys of his father Zibeon. [25]These are the children of Anah: Dishon and Oholibamah daughter of Anah. [26]These are the sons of Dishon: Hemdan, Eshban, Ithran, and Cheran. [27]These are the sons of Ezer: Bilhan, Zaavan, and Akan. [28]These are the sons of Dishan: Uz and Aran. [29]These are the clans[a] of the Horites: the clans[a] Lotan, Shobal, Zibeon, Anah, [30]Dishon, Ezer, and Dishan; these are the clans[a] of the Horites, clan by clan[c] in the land of Seir.

31 These are the kings who reigned in the land of Edom, before any king reigned over the Israelites. [32]Bela son of Beor reigned in Edom, the name of his city being Dinhabah. [33]Bela died, and Jobab son of Zerah of Bozrah succeeded him as king. [34]Jobab died, and Husham of the land of the Temanites succeeded him as king. [35]Husham died, and Hadad son of Bedad, who defeated Midian in the country of Moab, succeeded him as king, the name of his city being Avith. [36]Hadad died, and Samlah of Masrekah succeeded him as king. [37]Samlah died, and Shaul of Rehoboth on the Euphrates succeeded him as king. [38]Shaul died, and Baal-hanan son of Achbor succeeded him as king. [39]Baal-hanan son of Achbor died, and Hadar succeeded him as king, the name of his city being Pau; his wife's name was Mehetabel, the daughter of Matred, daughter of Me-zahab.

40 These are the names of the clans[a] of Esau, according to their families and their localities by their names: the clans[a] Timna, Alvah, Jetheth, [41]Oholibamah, Elah, Pinon, [42]Kenaz, Teman, Mibzar, [43]Magdiel, and Iram; these are the clans[a] of Edom (that is, Esau, the father of Edom), according to their settlements in the land that they held.

## MATTHEW 12. 1–21

At that time Jesus went through the grainfields on the sabbath; his disciples were hungry, and they began to pluck heads of grain and to eat. [2]When the Pharisees saw it, they said to him, "Look, your disciples are doing what is not lawful to do on the sabbath." [3]He said to them, "Have you not read what David did when he and his companions were hungry? [4]He entered the house of God and ate the bread of the Presence, which it was not lawful for him or his companions to eat, but only for the priests. [5]Or have you not read in the law that on the sabbath the priests in the temple break the sab-

aOr *chiefs*   bMeaning of Heb uncertain   cOr *chief by chief* bath and yet are guiltless? [6]I tell you, something greater than the temple is here. [7]But if you had known what this means, 'I desire mercy and not sacrifice,' you would not have condemned the guiltless. [8]For the Son of Man is lord of the sabbath."

9 He left that place and entered their synagogue; [10]a man was there with a withered hand, and they asked him, "Is it lawful to cure on the sabbath?" so that they might accuse him. [11]He said to them, "Suppose one of you has only one sheep and it falls into a pit on the sabbath; will you not lay hold of it and lift it out? [12]How much more valuable is a human being than a sheep! So it is lawful to do good on the sabbath." [13]Then he said to the man, "Stretch out your hand." He stretched it out, and it was restored, as sound as the other. [14]But the Pharisees went out and conspired against him, how to destroy him.

15 When Jesus became aware of this, he departed. Many crowds[a] followed him, and he cured all of them, [16]and he ordered them not to make him known. [17]This was to fulfill what had been spoken through the prophet Isaiah:

[18]    "Here is my servant, whom I
            have chosen,
        my beloved, with whom my
            soul is well pleased.
    I will put my Spirit upon him,
        and he will proclaim justice
            to the Gentiles.
[19]    He will not wrangle or cry
            aloud,
        nor will anyone hear his voice
            in the streets.
[20]    He will not break a bruised reed
            or quench a smoldering wick
        until he brings justice to victory.
[21]        And in his name the Gentiles
                will hope."

## PSALM 15.1–5

*A Psalm of David.*

O LORD, who may abide in your
            tent?
    Who may dwell on your
            holy hill?
[2]  Those who walk blamelessly,
        and do what is right,
        and speak the truth from their
            heart;
[3]  who do not slander with their
            tongue,
        and do no evil to their
            friends,
        nor take up a reproach
            against their neighbors;
[4]  in whose eyes the wicked are
            despised,
        but who honor those who fear
            the LORD;
    who stand by their oath even to
            their hurt;
[5]  who do not lend money at
            interest,
        and do not take a bribe
            against the innocent.

    Those who do these things shall
        never be moved.

## PROVERBS 3.21–26

My child, do not let these
            escape from your
            sight:
    keep sound wisdom and
            prudence,
[22]  and they will be life for your
            soul
        and adornment for your neck.
[23]  Then you will walk on your way
            securely
        and your foot will not
            stumble.
[24]  If you sit down,[b] you will not
            be afraid;

[a]Other ancient authorities lack *crowds*  [b]Gk: Heb *lie down*

> when you lie down, your
>   sleep will be sweet.
> <sup>25</sup> Do not be afraid of sudden
>     panic,
>   or of the storm that strikes
>     the wicked;

> <sup>26</sup>  for the LORD will be your
>     confidence
>   and will keep your foot from
>     being caught.

# JANUARY 18

## GENESIS 37.1—38.30

JACOB settled in the land where his father had lived as an alien, the land of Canaan. <sup>2</sup>This is the story of the family of Jacob.

Joseph, being seventeen years old, was shepherding the flock with his brothers; he was a helper to the sons of Bilhah and Zilpah, his father's wives; and Joseph brought a bad report of them to their father. <sup>3</sup>Now Israel loved Joseph more than any other of his children, because he was the son of his old age; and he had made him a long robe with sleeves. <sup>a</sup> <sup>4</sup>But when his brothers saw that their father loved him more than all his brothers, they hated him, and could not speak peaceably to him.

5 Once Joseph had a dream, and when he told it to his brothers, they hated him even more. <sup>6</sup>He said to them, "Listen to this dream that I dreamed. <sup>7</sup>There we were, binding sheaves in the field. Suddenly my sheaf rose and stood upright; then your sheaves gathered around it, and bowed down to my sheaf." <sup>8</sup>His brothers said to him, "Are you indeed to reign over us? Are you indeed to have dominion over us?" So they hated him even more because of his dreams and his words.

9 He had another dream, and told it to his brothers, saying, "Look, I have had another dream: the sun, the moon, and eleven stars were bowing down to me." <sup>10</sup>But when he told it to his father and to his brothers, his father rebuked him, and said to him, "What kind of dream is this that you have had? Shall we indeed come, I and your mother and your brothers, and bow to the ground before you?" <sup>11</sup>So his brothers were jealous of him, but his father kept the matter in mind.

12 Now his brothers went to pasture their father's flock near Shechem. <sup>13</sup>And Israel said to Joseph, "Are not your brothers pasturing the flock at Shechem? Come, I will send you to them." He answered, "Here I am." <sup>14</sup>So he said to him, "Go now, see if it is well with your brothers and with the flock; and bring word back to me." So he sent him from the valley of Hebron.

He came to Shechem, <sup>15</sup>and a man found him wandering in the fields; the man asked him, "What are you seeking?" <sup>16</sup>"I am seeking my brothers," he said; "tell me, please, where they are pasturing the flock." <sup>17</sup>The man said, "They have gone away, for I heard them say, 'Let us go to Dothan.'" So Joseph went after his brothers, and found them at Dothan. <sup>18</sup>They saw him from a distance, and before he came near to them, they conspired to kill

---

<sup>a</sup> Traditional rendering (compare Gk): *a coat of many colors*; Meaning of Heb uncertain

him. ¹⁹They said to one another, "Here comes this dreamer. ²⁰Come now, let us kill him and throw him into one of the pits; then we shall say that a wild animal has devoured him, and we shall see what will become of his dreams." ²¹But when Reuben heard it, he delivered him out of their hands, saying, "Let us not take his life." ²²Reuben said to them, "Shed no blood; throw him into this pit here in the wilderness, but lay no hand on him"—that he might rescue him out of their hand and restore him to his father. ²³So when Joseph came to his brothers, they stripped him of his robe, the long robe with sleevesᵃ that he wore; ²⁴and they took him and threw him into a pit. The pit was empty; there was no water in it.

25 Then they sat down to eat; and looking up they saw a caravan of Ishmaelites coming from Gilead, with their camels carrying gum, balm, and resin, on their way to carry it down to Egypt. ²⁶Then Judah said to his brothers, "What profit is it if we kill our brother and conceal his blood? ²⁷Come, let us sell him to the Ishmaelites, and not lay our hands on him, for he is our brother, our own flesh." And his brothers agreed. ²⁸When some Midianite traders passed by, they drew Joseph up, lifting him out of the pit, and sold him to the Ishmaelites for twenty pieces of silver. And they took Joseph to Egypt.

29 When Reuben returned to the pit and saw that Joseph was not in the pit, he tore his clothes. ³⁰He returned to his brothers, and said, "The boy is gone; and I, where can I turn?" ³¹Then they took Joseph's robe, slaughtered a goat, and dipped the robe in the blood. ³²They had the long robe with sleevesᵃ taken to their father, and they said, "This we have found; see now whether it is your son's robe or not." ³³He recognized it, and said, "It is my son's robe! A wild animal has de-

voured him; Joseph is without doubt torn to pieces." ³⁴Then Jacob tore his garments, and put sackcloth on his loins, and mourned for his son many days. ³⁵All his sons and all his daughters sought to comfort him; but he refused to be comforted, and said, "No, I shall go down to Sheol to my son, mourning." Thus his father bewailed him. ³⁶Meanwhile the Midianites had sold him in Egypt to Potiphar, one of Pharaoh's officials, the captain of the guard.

**38.**¹Iᴛ happened at that time that Judah went down from his brothers and settled near a certain Adullamite whose name was Hirah. ²There Judah saw the daughter of a certain Canaanite whose name was Shua; he married her and went in to her. ³She conceived and bore a son; and he named him Er. ⁴Again she conceived and bore a son whom she named Onan. ⁵Yet again she bore a son, and she named him Shelah. Sheᵇ was in Chezib when she bore him. ⁶Judah took a wife for Er his firstborn; her name was Tamar. ⁷But Er, Judah's firstborn, was wicked in the sight of the Lᴏʀᴅ, and the Lᴏʀᴅ put him to death. ⁸Then Judah said to Onan, "Go in to your brother's wife and perform the duty of a brother-in-law to her; raise up offspring for your brother." ⁹But since Onan knew that the offspring would not be his, he spilled his semen on the ground whenever he went in to his brother's wife, so that he would not give offspring to his brother. ¹⁰What he did was displeasing in the sight of the Lᴏʀᴅ, and he put him to death also. ¹¹Then Judah said to his daughter-in-law Tamar, "Remain a widow in your father's house until my son Shelah grows up"—for he feared that he too would die, like his brothers. So Tamar went to live in her father's house.

ᵃSee note on 37.3   ᵇGk: Heb *He*

12   In course of time the wife of Judah, Shua's daughter, died; when Judah's time of mourning was over, [a] he went up to Timnah to his sheepshearers, he and his friend Hirah the Adullamite. [13]When Tamar was told, "Your father-in-law is going up to Timnah to shear his sheep," [14]she put off her widow's garments, put on a veil, wrapped herself up, and sat down at the entrance to Enaim, which is on the road to Timnah. She saw that Shelah was grown up, yet she had not been given to him in marriage. [15]When Judah saw her, he thought her to be a prostitute, for she had covered her face. [16]He went over to her at the road side, and said, "Come, let me come in to you," for he did not know that she was his daughter-in-law. She said, "What will you give me, that you may come in to me?" [17]He answered, "I will send you a kid from the flock." And she said, "Only if you give me a pledge, until you send it." [18]He said, "What pledge shall I give you?" She replied, "Your signet and your cord, and the staff that is in your hand." So he gave them to her, and went in to her, and she conceived by him. [19]Then she got up and went away, and taking off her veil she put on the garments of her widowhood.

20   When Judah sent the kid by his friend the Adullamite, to recover the pledge from the woman, he could not find her. [21]He asked the townspeople, "Where is the temple prostitute who was at Enaim by the wayside?" But they said, "No prostitute has been here." [22]So he returned to Judah, and said, "I have not found her; moreover the townspeople said, 'No prostitute has been here.'" [23]Judah replied, "Let her keep the things as her own, otherwise we will be laughed at; you see, I sent this kid, and you could not find her."

24   About three months later Judah was told, "Your daughter-in-law Tamar has played the whore; moreover she is pregnant as a result of whoredom." And Judah said, "Bring her out, and let her be burned." [25]As she was being brought out, she sent word to her father-in-law, "It was the owner of these who made me pregnant." And she said, "Take note, please, whose these are, the signet and the cord and the staff." [26]Then Judah acknowledged them and said, "She is more in the right than I, since I did not give her to my son Shelah." And he did not lie with her again.

27   When the time of her delivery came, there were twins in her womb. [28]While she was in labor, one put out a hand; and the midwife took and bound on his hand a crimson thread, saying, "This one came out first." [29]But just then he drew back his hand, and out came his brother; and she said, "What a breach you have made for yourself!" Therefore he was named Perez. [b] [30]Afterward his brother came out with the crimson thread on his hand; and he was named Zerah. [c]

## MATTHEW 12.22–45

THEN they brought to him a demoniac who was blind and mute; and he [Jesus] cured him, so that the one who had been mute could speak and see. [23]All the crowds were amazed and said, "Can this be the Son of David?" [24]But when the Pharisees heard it, they said, "It is only by Beelzebul, the ruler of the demons, that this fellow casts out the demons." [25]He knew what they were thinking and said to them, "Every kingdom divided against itself is laid waste, and no city or house divided against itself will stand. [26]If Satan casts out Satan, he is divided against himself; how then will his kingdom stand? [27]If I cast out de-

a Heb *when Judah was comforted*   b That is *A breach*   c That is *Brightness*; perhaps alluding to the
crimson thread

mons by Beelzebul, by whom do your own exorcists[a] cast them out? Therefore they will be your judges. 28But if it is by the Spirit of God that I cast out demons, then the kingdom of God has come to you. 29Or how can one enter a strong man's house and plunder his property, without first tying up the strong man? Then indeed the house can be plundered. 30Whoever is not with me is against me, and whoever does not gather with me scatters. 31Therefore I tell you, people will be forgiven for every sin and blasphemy, but blasphemy against the Spirit will not be forgiven. 32Whoever speaks a word against the Son of Man will be forgiven, but whoever speaks against the Holy Spirit will not be forgiven, either in this age or in the age to come.

33 "Either make the tree good, and its fruit good; or make the tree bad, and its fruit bad; for the tree is known by its fruit. 34You brood of vipers! How can you speak good things, when you are evil? For out of the abundance of the heart the mouth speaks. 35The good person brings good things out of a good treasure, and the evil person brings evil things out of an evil treasure. 36I tell you, on the day of judgment you will have to give an account for every careless word you utter; 37for by your words you will be justified, and by your words you will be condemned."

38 Then some of the scribes and Pharisees said to him, "Teacher, we wish to see a sign from you." 39But he answered them, "An evil and adulterous generation asks for a sign, but no sign will be given to it except the sign of the prophet Jonah. 40For just as Jonah was three days and three nights in the belly of the sea monster, so for three days and three nights the Son of Man will be in the heart of the earth. 41The people of Nineveh will rise up at the judgment with this generation and condemn it, because they repented at the proclamation of Jonah, and see, something greater than Jonah is here! 42The queen of the South will rise up at the judgment with this generation and condemn it, because she came from the ends of the earth to listen to the wisdom of Solomon, and see, something greater than Solomon is here!

43 "When the unclean spirit has gone out of a person, it wanders through waterless regions looking for a resting place, but it finds none. 44Then it says, 'I will return to my house from which I came.' When it comes, it finds it empty, swept, and put in order. 45Then it goes and brings along seven other spirits more evil than itself, and they enter and live there; and the last state of that person is worse than the first. So will it be also with this evil generation."

## PSALM 16.1–11

*A Miktam of David.*

PROTECT me, O God, for in you
    I take refuge.
2  I say to the LORD, "You
    are my Lord;
I have no good apart from
    you."[b]

3  As for the holy ones in the land,
    they are the noble,
in whom is all my delight.

4  Those who choose another god
    multiply their sorrows;[c]
their drink offerings of blood I
    will not pour out
or take their names upon my
    lips.

5  The LORD is my chosen portion
    and my cup;
you hold my lot.
6  The boundary lines have fallen

---

for me in pleasant places;
  I have a goodly heritage.

7  I bless the Lord who gives me
      counsel;
    in the night also my heart
      instructs me.
8  I keep the Lord always before
      me;
    because he is at my right
      hand, I shall not be
      moved.

9  Therefore my heart is glad, and
      my soul rejoices;
    my body also rests secure.
10 For you do not give me up to
      Sheol,
    or let your faithful one see
      the Pit.

11 You show me the path of life.
    In your presence there is
      fullness of joy;
    in your right hand are
      pleasures forevermore.

## PROVERBS 3.27–32

**D**o not withhold good from
      those to whom it is
      due, **a**
    when it is in your power to
      do it.
28 Do not say to your neighbor,
      "Go, and come again,
    tomorrow I will give
      it"—when you have it
      with you.
29 Do not plan harm against your
      neighbor
    who lives trustingly beside
      you.
30 Do not quarrel with anyone
      without cause,
    when no harm has been done
      to you.
31 Do not envy the violent
    and do not choose any of
      their ways;
32 for the perverse are an
      abomination to the Lord,
    but the upright are in his
      confidence.

# JANUARY 19

## GENESIS 39.1—41.16

**N**ow Joseph was taken down to Egypt, and Potiphar, an officer of Pharaoh, the captain of the guard, an Egyptian, bought him from the Ishmaelites who had brought him down there. [2]The Lord was with Joseph, and he became a successful man; he was in the house of his Egyptian master. [3]His master saw that the Lord was with him, and that the Lord caused all that he did to prosper in his hands. [4]So Joseph found favor in his sight and attended him; he made him overseer of his house and put him in charge of all that he had. [5]From the time that he made him overseer in his house and over all that he had, the Lord blessed the Egyptian's house for Joseph's sake; the blessing of the Lord was on all that

**a** Heb *from its owners*

he had, in house and field. ⁶So he left all that he had in Joseph's charge; and, with him there, he had no concern for anything but the food that he ate.

Now Joseph was handsome and good-looking. ⁷And after a time his master's wife cast her eyes on Joseph and said, "Lie with me." ⁸But he refused and said to his master's wife, "Look, with me here, my master has no concern about anything in the house, and he has put everything that he has in my hand. ⁹He is not greater in this house than I am, nor has he kept back anything from me except yourself, because you are his wife. How then could I do this great wickedness, and sin against God?" ¹⁰And although she spoke to Joseph day after day, he would not consent to lie beside her or to be with her. ¹¹One day, however, when he went into the house to do his work, and while no one else was in the house, ¹²she caught hold of his garment, saying, "Lie with me!" But he left his garment in her hand, and fled and ran outside. ¹³When she saw that he had left his garment in her hand and had fled outside, ¹⁴she called out to the members of her household and said to them, "See, my husbandᵃ has brought among us a Hebrew to insult us! He came in to me to lie with me, and I cried out with a loud voice; ¹⁵and when he heard me raise my voice and cry out, he left his garment beside me, and fled outside." ¹⁶Then she kept his garment by her until his master came home, ¹⁷and she told him the same story, saying, "The Hebrew servant, whom you have brought among us, came in to me to insult me; ¹⁸but as soon as I raised my voice and cried out, he left his garment beside me, and fled outside."

19 When his master heard the words that his wife spoke to him, saying, "This is the way your servant treated me," he became enraged. ²⁰And Joseph's master took him and put him into the prison, the place where the king's prisoners were confined; he remained there in prison. ²¹But the Lord was with Joseph and showed him steadfast love; he gave him favor in the sight of the chief jailer. ²²The chief jailer committed to Joseph's care all the prisoners who were in the prison, and whatever was done there, he was the one who did it. ²³The chief jailer paid no heed to anything that was in Joseph's care, because the Lord was with him; and whatever he did, the Lord made it prosper.

40.1 Some time after this, the cupbearer of the king of Egypt and his baker offended their lord the king of Egypt. ²Pharaoh was angry with his two officers, the chief cupbearer and the chief baker, ³and he put them in custody in the house of the captain of the guard, in the prison where Joseph was confined. ⁴The captain of the guard charged Joseph with them, and he waited on them; and they continued for some time in custody. ⁵One night they both dreamed—the cupbearer and the baker of the king of Egypt, who were confined in the prison—each his own dream, and each dream with its own meaning. ⁶When Joseph came to them in the morning, he saw that they were troubled. ⁷So he asked Pharaoh's officers, who were with him in custody in his master's house, "Why are your faces downcast today?" ⁸They said to him, "We have had dreams, and there is no one to interpret them." And Joseph said to them, "Do not interpretations belong to God? Please tell them to me."

9 So the chief cupbearer told his dream to Joseph, and said to him, "In my dream there was a vine before me, ¹⁰and on the vine there were three branches. As soon as it budded, its

ᵃHeb *he*

blossoms came out and the clusters ripened into grapes. [11]Pharaoh's cup was in my hand; and I took the grapes and pressed them into Pharaoh's cup, and placed the cup in Pharaoh's hand." [12]Then Joseph said to him, "This is its interpretation: the three branches are three days; [13]within three days Pharaoh will lift up your head and restore you to your office; and you shall place Pharaoh's cup in his hand, just as you used to do when you were his cupbearer. [14]But remember me when it is well with you; please do me the kindness to make mention of me to Pharaoh, and so get me out of this place. [15]For in fact I was stolen out of the land of the Hebrews; and here also I have done nothing that they should have put me into the dungeon."

16 When the chief baker saw that the interpretation was favorable, he said to Joseph, "I also had a dream: there were three cake baskets on my head, [17]and in the uppermost basket there were all sorts of baked food for Pharaoh, but the birds were eating it out of the basket on my head." [18]And Joseph answered, "This is its interpretation: the three baskets are three days; [19]within three days Pharaoh will lift up your head—from you!—and hang you on a pole; and the birds will eat the flesh from you."

20 On the third day, which was Pharaoh's birthday, he made a feast for all his servants, and lifted up the head of the chief cupbearer and the head of the chief baker among his servants. [21]He restored the chief cupbearer to his cupbearing, and he placed the cup in Pharaoh's hand; [22]but the chief baker he hanged, just as Joseph had interpreted to them. [23]Yet the chief cupbearer did not remember Joseph, but forgot him.

**41.1** AFTER two whole years, Pharaoh dreamed that he was standing by the Nile, [2]and there came up out of the Nile seven sleek and fat cows, and they grazed in the reed grass. [3]Then seven other cows, ugly and thin, came up out of the Nile after them, and stood by the other cows on the bank of the Nile. [4]The ugly and thin cows ate up the seven sleek and fat cows. And Pharaoh awoke. [5]Then he fell asleep and dreamed a second time; seven ears of grain, plump and good, were growing on one stalk. [6]Then seven ears, thin and blighted by the east wind, sprouted after them. [7]The thin ears swallowed up the seven plump and full ears. Pharaoh awoke, and it was a dream. [8]In the morning his spirit was troubled; so he sent and called for all the magicians of Egypt and all its wise men. Pharaoh told them his dreams, but there was no one who could interpret them to Pharaoh.

9 Then the chief cupbearer said to Pharaoh, "I remember my faults today. [10]Once Pharaoh was angry with his servants, and put me and the chief baker in custody in the house of the captain of the guard. [11]We dreamed on the same night, he and I, each having a dream with its own meaning. [12]A young Hebrew was there with us, a servant of the captain of the guard. When we told him, he interpreted our dreams to us, giving an interpretation to each according to his dream. [13]As he interpreted to us, so it turned out; I was restored to my office, and the baker was hanged."

14 Then Pharaoh sent for Joseph, and he was hurriedly brought out of the dungeon. When he had shaved himself and changed his clothes, he came in before Pharaoh. [15]And Pharaoh said to Joseph, "I have had a dream, and there is no one who can interpret it. I have heard it said of you that when you hear a dream you can interpret it." [16]Joseph answered Pharaoh, "It is not I; God will give Pharaoh a favorable answer."

## MATTHEW 12.46—13.23

WHILE he [Jesus] was still speaking to the crowds, his mother and his brothers were standing outside, wanting to speak to him. [47]Someone told him, "Look, your mother and your brothers are standing outside, wanting to speak to you."[a] [48]But to the one who had told him this, Jesus[b] replied, "Who is my mother, and who are my brothers?" [49]And pointing to his disciples, he said, "Here are my mother and my brothers! [50]For whoever does the will of my Father in heaven is my brother and sister and mother."

**13.**[1] THAT same day Jesus went out of the house and sat beside the sea. [2]Such great crowds gathered around him that he got into a boat and sat there, while the whole crowd stood on the beach. [3]And he told them many things in parables, saying: "Listen! A sower went out to sow. [4]And as he sowed, some seeds fell on the path, and the birds came and ate them up. [5]Other seeds fell on rocky ground, where they did not have much soil, and they sprang up quickly, since they had no depth of soil. [6]But when the sun rose, they were scorched; and since they had no root, they withered away. [7]Other seeds fell among thorns, and the thorns grew up and choked them. [8]Other seeds fell on good soil and brought forth grain, some a hundredfold, some sixty, some thirty. [9]Let anyone with ears[c] listen!"

10 Then the disciples came and asked him, "Why do you speak to them in parables?" [11]He answered, "To you it has been given to know the secrets[d] of the kingdom of heaven, but to them it has not been given. [12]For to those who have, more will be given, and they will have an abundance; but from those who have nothing, even what they have will be taken away. [13]The reason I speak to them in parables is that 'seeing they do not perceive, and hearing they do not listen, nor do they understand.' [14]With them indeed is fulfilled the prophecy of Isaiah that says:

'You will indeed listen, but
    never understand,
and you will indeed look, but
    never perceive.
15  For this people's heart has
    grown dull,
and their ears are hard of
    hearing,
   and they have shut their
    eyes;
   so that they might not look
    with their eyes,
and listen with their ears,
and understand with their heart
    and turn—
and I would heal them.'

[16]But blessed are your eyes, for they see, and your ears, for they hear. [17]Truly I tell you, many prophets and righteous people longed to see what you see, but did not see it, and to hear what you hear, but did not hear it.

18 "Hear then the parable of the sower. [19]When anyone hears the word of the kingdom and does not understand it, the evil one comes and snatches away what is sown in the heart; this is what was sown on the path. [20]As for what was sown on rocky ground, this is the one who hears the word and immediately receives it with joy; [21]yet such a person has no root, but endures only for a while, and when trouble or persecution arises on account of the word, that person immediately falls away.[e] [22]As for what was sown among thorns, this is the one who hears the word, but the cares of the world and the lure of wealth choke the word, and it yields nothing. [23]But as for what was sown on good soil, this is the one who hears the word and under-

stands it, who indeed bears fruit and yields, in one case a hundredfold, in another sixty, and in another thirty."

## PSALM 17.1–15

*A Prayer of David.*

HEAR a just cause, O LORD;
    attend to my cry;
    give ear to my prayer from
      lips free of deceit.
2 From you let my vindication
      come;
    let your eyes see the right.

3 If you try my heart, if you visit
      me by night,
    if you test me, you will find
      no wickedness in me;
    my mouth does not
      transgress.
4 As for what others do, by the
      word of your lips
    I have avoided the ways of
      the violent.
5 My steps have held fast to your
      paths;
    my feet have not slipped.

6 I call upon you, for you will
      answer me, O God;
    incline your ear to me, hear
      my words.
7 Wondrously show your steadfast
      love,
    O savior of those who seek
      refuge
    from their adversaries at your
      right hand.

8 Guard me as the apple of the
      eye;
    hide me in the shadow of
      your wings,
9 from the wicked who despoil
      me,
    my deadly enemies who
      surround me.

10 They close their hearts to pity;
    with their mouths they speak
      arrogantly.
11 They track me down;[a] now
      they surround me;
    they set their eyes to cast me
      to the ground.
12 They are like a lion eager to
      tear,
    like a young lion lurking in
      ambush.

13 Rise up, O LORD, confront them,
      overthrow them!
    By your sword deliver my life
      from the wicked,
14 from mortals—by your hand,
      O LORD—
    from mortals whose portion in
      life is in this world.
    May their bellies be filled with
      what you have stored up
      for them;
    may their children have more
      than enough;
    may they leave something
      over to their little ones.

15 As for me, I shall behold your
      face in righteousness;
    when I awake I shall be
      satisfied, beholding your
      likeness.

## PROVERBS 3.33–35

THE LORD's curse is on the
    house of the wicked,
    but he blesses the abode of
      the righteous.
34 Toward the scorners he is
      scornful,
    but to the humble he shows
      favor.
35 The wise will inherit honor,
    but stubborn fools, disgrace.

a One Ms Compare Syr: MT *Our steps*

# JANUARY 20

## GENESIS 41.17—42.17

THEN Pharaoh said to Joseph, "In my dream I was standing on the banks of the Nile; [18]and seven cows, fat and sleek, came up out of the Nile and fed in the reed grass. [19]Then seven other cows came up after them, poor, very ugly, and thin. Never had I seen such ugly ones in all the land of Egypt. [20]The thin and ugly cows ate up the first seven fat cows, [21]but when they had eaten them no one would have known that they had done so, for they were still as ugly as before. Then I awoke. [22]I fell asleep a second time[a] and I saw in my dream seven ears of grain, full and good, growing on one stalk, [23]and seven ears, withered, thin, and blighted by the east wind, sprouting after them; [24]and the thin ears swallowed up the seven good ears. But when I told it to the magicians, there was no one who could explain it to me."

25 Then Joseph said to Pharaoh, "Pharaoh's dreams are one and the same; God has revealed to Pharaoh what he is about to do. [26]The seven good cows are seven years, and the seven good ears are seven years; the dreams are one. [27]The seven lean and ugly cows that came up after them are seven years, as are the seven empty ears blighted by the east wind. They are seven years of famine. [28]It is as I told Pharaoh; God has shown to Pharaoh what he is about to do. [29]There will come seven years of great plenty throughout all the land of Egypt. [30]After them there will arise seven years of famine, and all the plenty will be forgotten in the land of Egypt; the famine will consume the land. [31]The plenty will no longer be known in the land because of the famine that will follow, for it will be very grievous. [32]And the doubling of Pharaoh's dream means that the thing is fixed by God, and God will shortly bring it about. [33]Now therefore let Pharaoh select a man who is discerning and wise, and set him over the land of Egypt. [34]Let Pharaoh proceed to appoint overseers over the land, and take one-fifth of the produce of the land of Egypt during the seven plenteous years. [35]Let them gather all the food of these good years that are coming, and lay up grain under the authority of Pharaoh for food in the cities, and let them keep it. [36]That food shall be a reserve for the land against the seven years of famine that are to befall the land of Egypt, so that the land may not perish through the famine."

37 The proposal pleased Pharaoh and all his servants. [38]Pharaoh said to his servants, "Can we find anyone else like this—one in whom is the spirit of God?" [39]So Pharaoh said to Joseph, "Since God has shown you all this, there is no one so discerning and wise as you. [40]You shall be over my house, and all my people shall order themselves as you command; only with regard to the throne will I be greater than you." [41]And Pharaoh said to Joseph, "See, I have set you over all the land of Egypt." [42]Removing his signet ring from his hand, Pharaoh put it on Joseph's hand; he arrayed him in garments of fine linen, and put a gold chain around his neck. [43]He had him ride in the chariot of his second-in-command; and they cried out in front of him, "Bow the knee!"[b] Thus he set him over all the land of Egypt. [44]Moreover Pharaoh said to Joseph, "I am Pharaoh, and

without your consent no one shall lift up hand or foot in all the land of Egypt." ⁴⁵Pharaoh gave Joseph the name Zaphenath-paneah; and he gave him Asenath daughter of Potiphera, priest of On, as his wife. Thus Joseph gained authority over the land of Egypt.

46 Joseph was thirty years old when he entered the service of Pharaoh king of Egypt. And Joseph went out from the presence of Pharaoh, and went through all the land of Egypt. ⁴⁷During the seven plenteous years the earth produced abundantly. ⁴⁸He gathered up all the food of the seven years when there was plenty[a] in the land of Egypt, and stored up food in the cities; he stored up in every city the food from the fields around it. ⁴⁹So Joseph stored up grain in such abundance—like the sand of the sea—that he stopped measuring it; it was beyond measure.

50 Before the years of famine came, Joseph had two sons, whom Asenath daughter of Potiphera, priest of On, bore to him. ⁵¹Joseph named the firstborn Manasseh,[b] "For," he said, "God has made me forget all my hardship and all my father's house." ⁵²The second he named Ephraim,[c] "For God has made me fruitful in the land of my misfortunes."

53 The seven years of plenty that prevailed in the land of Egypt came to an end; ⁵⁴and the seven years of famine began to come, just as Joseph had said. There was famine in every country, but throughout the land of Egypt there was bread. ⁵⁵When all the land of Egypt was famished, the people cried to Pharaoh for bread. Pharaoh said to all the Egyptians, "Go to Joseph; what he says to you, do." ⁵⁶And since the famine had spread over all the land, Joseph opened all the storehouses,[d] and sold to the Egyptians, for the famine was severe in the land of Egypt. ⁵⁷Moreover, all the world came to Joseph in Egypt to buy grain, because the famine became severe throughout the world.

**42.**1 WHEN Jacob learned that there was grain in Egypt, he said to his sons, "Why do you keep looking at one another? ²I have heard," he said, "that there is grain in Egypt; go down and buy grain for us there, that we may live and not die." ³So ten of Joseph's brothers went down to buy grain in Egypt. ⁴But Jacob did not send Joseph's brother Benjamin with his brothers, for he feared that harm might come to him. ⁵Thus the sons of Israel were among the other people who came to buy grain, for the famine had reached the land of Canaan.

6 Now Joseph was governor over the land; it was he who sold to all the people of the land. And Joseph's brothers came and bowed themselves before him with their faces to the ground. ⁷When Joseph saw his brothers, he recognized them, but he treated them like strangers and spoke harshly to them. "Where do you come from?" he said. They said, "From the land of Canaan, to buy food." ⁸Although Joseph had recognized his brothers, they did not recognize him. ⁹Joseph also remembered the dreams that he had dreamed about them. He said to them, "You are spies; you have come to see the nakedness of the land!" ¹⁰They said to him, "No, my lord; your servants have come to buy food. ¹¹We are all sons of one man; we are honest men; your servants have never been spies." ¹²But he said to them, "No, you have come to see the nakedness of the land!" ¹³They said, "We, your servants, are twelve brothers, the sons of a certain man in the land of Canaan; the youngest, however, is now with our father, and one is no more." ¹⁴But Joseph said to them, "It is just as I have said to you; you are spies! ¹⁵Here is how you shall be

---

[a] Sam Gk: MT *the seven years that were*   [b] That is *Making to forget*   [c] From a Hebrew word meaning *to be fruitful*   [d] Gk Vg Compare Syr: Heb *opened all that was in* (or, *among*) *them*

tested: as Pharaoh lives, you shall not leave this place unless your youngest brother comes here! [16]Let one of you go and bring your brother, while the rest of you remain in prison, in order that your words may be tested, whether there is truth in you; or else, as Pharaoh lives, surely you are spies." [17]And he put them all together in prison for three days.

## MATTHEW 13.24–46

**H**E [Jesus] put before them another parable: "The kingdom of heaven may be compared to someone who sowed good seed in his field; [25]but while everybody was asleep, an enemy came and sowed weeds among the wheat, and then went away. [26]So when the plants came up and bore grain, then the weeds appeared as well. [27]And the slaves of the householder came and said to him, 'Master, did you not sow good seed in your field? Where, then, did these weeds come from?' [28]He answered, 'An enemy has done this.' The slaves said to him, 'Then do you want us to go and gather them?' [29]But he replied, 'No; for in gathering the weeds you would uproot the wheat along with them. [30]Let both of them grow together until the harvest; and at harvest time I will tell the reapers, Collect the weeds first and bind them in bundles to be burned, but gather the wheat into my barn.'"

31  He put before them another parable: "The kingdom of heaven is like a mustard seed that someone took and sowed in his field; [32]it is the smallest of all the seeds, but when it has grown it is the greatest of shrubs and becomes a tree, so that the birds of the air come and make nests in its branches."

33  He told them another parable: "The kingdom of heaven is like yeast that a woman took and mixed in with[a] three measures of flour until all of it was leavened."

34  Jesus told the crowds all these things in parables; without a parable he told them nothing. [35]This was to fulfill what had been spoken through the prophet:[b]

"I will open my mouth to speak
    in parables;
  I will proclaim what has been
      hidden from the
      foundation of the
      world."[c]

36  Then he left the crowds and went into the house. And his disciples approached him, saying, "Explain to us the parable of the weeds of the field." [37]He answered, "The one who sows the good seed is the Son of Man; [38]the field is the world, and the good seed are the children of the kingdom; the weeds are the children of the evil one, [39]and the enemy who sowed them is the devil; the harvest is the end of the age, and the reapers are angels. [40]Just as the weeds are collected and burned up with fire, so will it be at the end of the age. [41]The Son of Man will send his angels, and they will collect out of his kingdom all causes of sin and all evildoers, [42]and they will throw them into the furnace of fire, where there will be weeping and gnashing of teeth. [43]Then the righteous will shine like the sun in the kingdom of their Father. Let anyone with ears[d] listen!

44  "The kingdom of heaven is like treasure hidden in a field, which someone found and hid; then in his joy he goes and sells all that he has and buys that field.

45  "Again, the kingdom of heaven is like a merchant in search of fine pearls; [46]on finding one pearl of great value, he went and sold all that he had and bought it.

[a]Gk *hid in*   [b]Other ancient authorities read *the prophet Isaiah*   [c]Other ancient authorities lack *of the world*   [d]Other ancient authorities add *to hear*

## PSALM 18.1–15

*To the leader. A Psalm of David the servant of the L*ORD*, who addressed the words of this song to the L*ORD *on the day when the L*ORD *delivered him from the hand of all his enemies, and from the hand of Saul. He said:*

I LOVE you, O LORD, my strength.
2    The LORD is my rock, my
      fortress, and my
      deliverer,
  my God, my rock in whom I
      take refuge,
  my shield, and the horn of my
      salvation, my stronghold.
3  I call upon the LORD, who is
      worthy to be praised,
  so I shall be saved from my
      enemies.

4  The cords of death
      encompassed me;
  the torrents of perdition
      assailed me;
5  the cords of Sheol entangled
      me;
  the snares of death
      confronted me.

6  In my distress I called upon the
      LORD;
  to my God I cried for help.
  From his temple he heard my
      voice,
  and my cry to him reached
      his ears.

7  Then the earth reeled and
      rocked;
  the foundations also of the
      mountains trembled
  and quaked, because he was
      angry.
8  Smoke went up from his
      nostrils,
  and devouring fire from his
      mouth;
  glowing coals flamed forth
      from him.

9  He bowed the heavens, and
      came down;
  thick darkness was under his
      feet.
10  He rode on a cherub, and flew;
  he came swiftly upon the
      wings of the wind.
11  He made darkness his covering
      around him,
  his canopy thick clouds dark
      with water.
12  Out of the brightness before
      him
  there broke through his
      clouds
  hailstones and coals of fire.
13  The LORD also thundered in the
      heavens,
  and the Most High uttered his
      voice. [a]
14  And he sent out his arrows, and
      scattered them;
  he flashed forth lightnings,
      and routed them.
15  Then the channels of the sea
      were seen,
  and the foundations of the
      world were laid bare
 at your rebuke, O LORD,
  at the blast of the breath of
      your nostrils.

## PROVERBS 4.1–6

L ISTEN, children, to a father's
      instruction,
 and be attentive, that you
      may gain[b] insight;
2  for I give you good precepts:
  do not forsake my teaching.
3  When I was a son with my
      father,
  tender, and my mother's
      favorite,
4  he taught me, and said to me,
  "Let your heart hold fast my
      words;
  keep my commandments,
      and live.

a Gk See 2 Sam 22.14: Heb adds *hailstones and coals of fire*  b Heb *know*

5  Get wisdom; get insight: do not
      forget, nor turn away
   from the words of my mouth.

6  Do not forsake her, and she will
      keep you;
   love her, and she will guard
      you.

# JANUARY 21

## GENESIS 42.18—43.34

ON the third day Joseph said to them, "Do this and you will live, for I fear God: <sup>19</sup>if you are honest men, let one of your brothers stay here where you are imprisoned. The rest of you shall go and carry grain for the famine of your households, <sup>20</sup>and bring your youngest brother to me. Thus your words will be verified, and you shall not die." And they agreed to do so. <sup>21</sup>They said to one another, "Alas, we are paying the penalty for what we did to our brother; we saw his anguish when he pleaded with us, but we would not listen. That is why this anguish has come upon us." <sup>22</sup>Then Reuben answered them, "Did I not tell you not to wrong the boy? But you would not listen. So now there comes a reckoning for his blood." <sup>23</sup>They did not know that Joseph understood them, since he spoke with them through an interpreter. <sup>24</sup>He turned away from them and wept; then he returned and spoke to them. And he picked out Simeon and had him bound before their eyes. <sup>25</sup>Joseph then gave orders to fill their bags with grain, to return every man's money to his sack, and to give them provisions for their journey. This was done for them.

26  They loaded their donkeys with their grain, and departed. <sup>27</sup>When one of them opened his sack to give his donkey fodder at the lodging place, he saw his money at the top of the sack. <sup>28</sup>He said to his brothers, "My money has been put back; here it is in my sack!" At this they lost heart and turned trembling to one another, saying, "What is this that God has done to us?"

29  When they came to their father Jacob in the land of Canaan, they told him all that had happened to them, saying, <sup>30</sup>"The man, the lord of the land, spoke harshly to us, and charged us with spying on the land. <sup>31</sup>But we said to him, 'We are honest men, we are not spies. <sup>32</sup>We are twelve brothers, sons of our father; one is no more, and the youngest is now with our father in the land of Canaan.' <sup>33</sup>Then the man, the lord of the land, said to us, 'By this I shall know that you are honest men: leave one of your brothers with me, take grain for the famine of your households, and go your way. <sup>34</sup>Bring your youngest brother to me, and I shall know that you are not spies but honest men. Then I will release your brother to you, and you may trade in the land.'"

35  As they were emptying their sacks, there in each one's sack was his bag of money. When they and their father saw their bundles of money, they were dismayed. <sup>36</sup>And their father Jacob said to them, "I am the one you have bereaved of children: Joseph is no more, and Simeon is no more, and now you would take Benjamin. All this has happened to me!" <sup>37</sup>Then Reuben said

to his father, "You may kill my two sons if I do not bring him back to you. Put him in my hands, and I will bring him back to you." 38But he said, "My son shall not go down with you, for his brother is dead, and he alone is left. If harm should come to him on the journey that you are to make, you would bring down my gray hairs with sorrow to Sheol."

43.1 Now the famine was severe in the land. 2And when they had eaten up the grain that they had brought from Egypt, their father said to them, "Go again, buy us a little more food." 3But Judah said to him, "The man solemnly warned us, saying, 'You shall not see my face unless your brother is with you.' 4If you will send our brother with us, we will go down and buy you food; 5but if you will not send him, we will not go down, for the man said to us, 'You shall not see my face, unless your brother is with you.'" 6Israel said, "Why did you treat me so badly as to tell the man that you had another brother?" 7They replied, "The man questioned us carefully about ourselves and our kindred, saying, 'Is your father still alive? Have you another brother?' What we told him was in answer to these questions. Could we in any way know that he would say, 'Bring your brother down'?" 8Then Judah said to his father Israel, "Send the boy with me, and let us be on our way, so that we may live and not die—you and we and also our little ones. 9I myself will be surety for him; you can hold me accountable for him. If I do not bring him back to you and set him before you, then let me bear the blame forever. 10If we had not delayed, we would now have returned twice."

11 Then their father Israel said to them, "If it must be so, then do this: take some of the choice fruits of the land in your bags, and carry them down as a present to the man—a little balm and a little honey, gum, resin, pistachio nuts, and almonds. 12Take double the money with you. Carry back with you the money that was returned in the top of your sacks; perhaps it was an oversight. 13Take your brother also, and be on your way again to the man; 14may God Almightya grant you mercy before the man, so that he may send back your other brother and Benjamin. As for me, if I am bereaved of my children, I am bereaved." 15So the men took the present, and they took double the money with them, as well as Benjamin. Then they went on their way down to Egypt, and stood before Joseph.

16 When Joseph saw Benjamin with them, he said to the steward of his house, "Bring the men into the house, and slaughter an animal and make ready, for the men are to dine with me at noon." 17The man did as Joseph said, and brought the men to Joseph's house. 18Now the men were afraid because they were brought to Joseph's house, and they said, "It is because of the money, replaced in our sacks the first time, that we have been brought in, so that he may have an opportunity to fall upon us, to make slaves of us and take our donkeys." 19So they went up to the steward of Joseph's house and spoke with him at the entrance to the house. 20They said, "Oh, my lord, we came down the first time to buy food; 21and when we came to the lodging place we opened our sacks, and there was each one's money in the top of his sack, our money in full weight. So we have brought it back with us. 22Moreover we have brought down with us additional money to buy food. We do not know who put our money in our sacks." 23He replied, "Rest assured, do not be afraid; your God and the God of your father must have put treasure in your

---

a Traditional rendering of Heb *El Shaddai*

sacks for you; I received your money." Then he brought Simeon out to them. ²⁴When the steward[a] had brought the men into Joseph's house, and given them water, and they had washed their feet, and when he had given their donkeys fodder, ²⁵they made the present ready for Joseph's coming at noon, for they had heard that they would dine there.

26 When Joseph came home, they brought him the present that they had carried into the house, and bowed to the ground before him. ²⁷He inquired about their welfare, and said, "Is your father well, the old man of whom you spoke? Is he still alive?" ²⁸They said, "Your servant our father is well; he is still alive." And they bowed their heads and did obeisance. ²⁹Then he looked up and saw his brother Benjamin, his mother's son, and said, "Is this your youngest brother, of whom you spoke to me? God be gracious to you, my son!" ³⁰With that, Joseph hurried out, because he was overcome with affection for his brother, and he was about to weep. So he went into a private room and wept there. ³¹Then he washed his face and came out; and controlling himself he said, "Serve the meal." ³²They served him by himself, and them by themselves, and the Egyptians who ate with him by themselves, because the Egyptians could not eat with the Hebrews, for that is an abomination to the Egyptians. ³³When they were seated before him, the firstborn according to his birthright and the youngest according to his youth, the men looked at one another in amazement. ³⁴Portions were taken to them from Joseph's table, but Benjamin's portion was five times as much as any of theirs. So they drank and were merry with him.

# MATTHEW 13.47—14.12

"**A**GAIN, the kingdom of heaven is like a net that was thrown into the sea and caught fish of every kind; ⁴⁸when it was full, they drew it ashore, sat down, and put the good into baskets but threw out the bad. ⁴⁹So it will be at the end of the age. The angels will come out and separate the evil from the righteous ⁵⁰and throw them into the furnace of fire, where there will be weeping and gnashing of teeth.

51 "Have you understood all this?" They answered, "Yes." ⁵²And he said to them, "Therefore every scribe who has been trained for the kingdom of heaven is like the master of a household who brings out of his treasure what is new and what is old." ⁵³When Jesus had finished these parables, he left that place.

54 He came to his hometown and began to teach the people[b] in their synagogue, so that they were astounded and said, "Where did this man get this wisdom and these deeds of power? ⁵⁵Is not this the carpenter's son? Is not his mother called Mary? And are not his brothers James and Joseph and Simon and Judas? ⁵⁶And are not all his sisters with us? Where then did this man get all this?" ⁵⁷And they took offense at him. But Jesus said to them, "Prophets are not without honor except in their own country and in their own house." ⁵⁸And he did not do many deeds of power there, because of their unbelief.

14.1 AT that time Herod the ruler[c] heard reports about Jesus; ²and he said to his servants, "This is John the Baptist; he has been raised from the dead, and for this reason these powers are at work in him." ³For Herod had arrested John, bound him, and put him in prison on account of Herodias, his brother

a Heb *the man*   b Gk *them*   c Gk *tetrarch*

Philip's wife, a 4because John had been telling him, "It is not lawful for you to have her." 5Though Herodb wanted to put him to death, he feared the crowd, because they regarded him as a prophet. 6But when Herod's birthday came, the daughter of Herodias danced before the company, and she pleased Herod 7so much that he promised on oath to grant her whatever she might ask. 8Prompted by her mother, she said, "Give me the head of John the Baptist here on a platter." 9The king was grieved, yet out of regard for his oaths and for the guests, he commanded it to be given; 10he sent and had John beheaded in the prison. 11The head was brought on a platter and given to the girl, who brought it to her mother. 12His disciples came and took the body and buried it; then they went and told Jesus.

## PSALM 18.16–36

**H**E reached down from on
    high, he took me;
he drew me out of mighty
    waters.
17 He delivered me from my
    strong enemy,
    and from those who hated
      me;
    for they were too mighty for
      me.
18 They confronted me in the day
    of my calamity;
    but the LORD was my support.
19 He brought me out into a broad
    place;
    he delivered me, because he
      delighted in me.

20 The LORD rewarded me
    according to my
      righteousness;
    according to the cleanness of
      my hands he
      recompensed me.

21 For I have kept the ways of the
    LORD,
    and have not wickedly
      departed from my God.
22 For all his ordinances were
    before me,
    and his statutes I did not put
      away from me.
23 I was blameless before him,
    and I kept myself from guilt.
24 Therefore the LORD has
    recompensed me
      according to my
      righteousness,
    according to the cleanness of
      my hands in his sight.

25 With the loyal you show
    yourself loyal;
    with the blameless you show
      yourself blameless;
26 with the pure you show yourself
    pure;
    and with the crooked you
      show yourself perverse.
27 For you deliver a humble
    people,
    but the haughty eyes you
      bring down.
28 It is you who light my lamp;
    the LORD, my God, lights up
      my darkness.
29 By you I can crush a troop,
    and by my God I can leap
      over a wall.
30 This God—his way is perfect;
    the promise of the LORD
      proves true;
    he is a shield for all who take
      refuge in him.

31 For who is God except the
    LORD?
    And who is a rock besides
      our God?—
32 the God who girded me with
    strength,
    and made my way safe.

aOther ancient authorities read *his brother's wife*   bGk *he*

33  He made my feet like the feet
        of a deer,
      and set me secure on the
        heights.
34  He trains my hands for war,
      so that my arms can bend a
        bow of bronze.
35  You have given me the shield of
        your salvation,
      and your right hand has
        supported me;
      your help[a] has made me
        great.
36  You gave me a wide place for
        my steps under me,
      and my feet did not slip.

PROVERBS 4.7–10

THE beginning of wisdom is this:
        Get wisdom,
      and whatever else you get,
        get insight.
8   Prize her highly, and she will
        exalt you;
      she will honor you if you
        embrace her.
9   She will place on your head a
        fair garland;
      she will bestow on you a
        beautiful crown."

10  Hear, my child, and accept my
        words,
      that the years of your life
        may be many.

# JANUARY 22

GENESIS 44.1—45.28

THEN he [Joseph] commanded the steward of his house, "Fill the men's sacks with food, as much as they can carry, and put each man's money in the top of his sack. [2]Put my cup, the silver cup, in the top of the sack of the youngest, with his money for the grain." And he did as Joseph told him. [3]As soon as the morning was light, the men were sent away with their donkeys. [4]When they had gone only a short distance from the city, Joseph said to his steward, "Go, follow after the men; and when you overtake them, say to them, 'Why have you returned evil for good? Why have you stolen my silver cup?[b] [5]Is it not from this that my lord drinks? Does he not indeed use it for divination? You have done wrong in doing this.' "

6  When he overtook them, he repeated these words to them. [7]They said to him, "Why does my lord speak such words as these? Far be it from your servants that they should do such a thing! [8]Look, the money that we found at the top of our sacks, we brought back to you from the land of Canaan; why then would we steal silver or gold from your lord's house? [9]Should it be found with any one of your servants, let him die; moreover the rest of us will become my lord's slaves." [10]He said, "Even so; in accordance with your words, let it be: he with whom it is found shall become my slave, but the rest of you shall go free." [11]Then each

a Or *gentleness*   b Gk Compare Vg: Heb lacks *Why have you stolen my silver cup?*

one quickly lowered his sack to the ground, and each opened his sack. [12]He searched, beginning with the eldest and ending with the youngest; and the cup was found in Benjamin's sack. [13]At this they tore their clothes. Then each one loaded his donkey, and they returned to the city.

14 Judah and his brothers came to Joseph's house while he was still there; and they fell to the ground before him. [15]Joseph said to them, "What deed is this that you have done? Do you not know that one such as I can practice divination?" [16]And Judah said, "What can we say to my lord? What can we speak? How can we clear ourselves? God has found out the guilt of your servants; here we are then, my lord's slaves, both we and also the one in whose possession the cup has been found." [17]But he said, "Far be it from me that I should do so! Only the one in whose possession the cup was found shall be my slave; but as for you, go up in peace to your father."

18 Then Judah stepped up to him and said, "O my lord, let your servant please speak a word in my lord's ears, and do not be angry with your servant; for you are like Pharaoh himself. [19]My lord asked his servants, saying, 'Have you a father or a brother?' [20]And we said to my lord, 'We have a father, an old man, and a young brother, the child of his old age. His brother is dead; he alone is left of his mother's children, and his father loves him.' [21]Then you said to your servants, 'Bring him down to me, so that I may set my eyes on him.' [22]We said to my lord, 'The boy cannot leave his father, for if he should leave his father, his father would die.' [23]Then you said to your servants, 'Unless your youngest brother comes down with you, you shall see my face no more.' [24]When we went back to your servant my father we told him the words of my lord. [25]And when our father said, 'Go again, buy us a little food,' [26]we said, 'We cannot go down. Only if our youngest brother goes with us, will we go down; for we cannot see the man's face unless our youngest brother is with us.' [27]Then your servant my father said to us, 'You know that my wife bore me two sons; [28]one left me, and I said, Surely he has been torn to pieces; and I have never seen him since. [29]If you take this one also from me, and harm comes to him, you will bring down my gray hairs in sorrow to Sheol.' [30]Now therefore, when I come to your servant my father and the boy is not with us, then, as his life is bound up in the boy's life, [31]when he sees that the boy is not with us, he will die; and your servants will bring down the gray hairs of your servant our father with sorrow to Sheol. [32]For your servant became surety for the boy to my father, saying, 'If I do not bring him back to you, then I will bear the blame in the sight of my father all my life.' [33]Now therefore, please let your servant remain as a slave to my lord in place of the boy; and let the boy go back with his brothers. [34]For how can I go back to my father if the boy is not with me? I fear to see the suffering that would come upon my father."

45.1 THEN Joseph could no longer control himself before all those who stood by him, and he cried out, "Send everyone away from me." So no one stayed with him when Joseph made himself known to his brothers. [2]And he wept so loudly that the Egyptians heard it, and the household of Pharaoh heard it. [3]Joseph said to his brothers, "I am Joseph. Is my father still alive?" But his brothers could not answer him, so dismayed were they at his presence.

4 Then Joseph said to his brothers, "Come closer to me." And they came closer. He said, "I am your brother, Joseph, whom you sold into Egypt. [5]And now do not be distressed, or angry with yourselves, because you sold me here;

for God sent me before you to preserve life. ⁶For the famine has been in the land these two years; and there are five more years in which there will be neither plowing nor harvest. ⁷God sent me before you to preserve for you a remnant on earth, and to keep alive for you many survivors. ⁸So it was not you who sent me here, but God; he has made me a father to Pharaoh, and lord of all his house and ruler over all the land of Egypt. ⁹Hurry and go up to my father and say to him, 'Thus says your son Joseph, God has made me lord of all Egypt; come down to me, do not delay. ¹⁰You shall settle in the land of Goshen, and you shall be near me, you and your children and your children's children, as well as your flocks, your herds, and all that you have. ¹¹I will provide for you there—since there are five more years of famine to come—so that you and your household, and all that you have, will not come to poverty.' ¹²And now your eyes and the eyes of my brother Benjamin see that it is my own mouth that speaks to you. ¹³You must tell my father how greatly I am honored in Egypt, and all that you have seen. Hurry and bring my father down here." ¹⁴Then he fell upon his brother Benjamin's neck and wept, while Benjamin wept upon his neck. ¹⁵And he kissed all his brothers and wept upon them; and after that his brothers talked with him.

16 When the report was heard in Pharaoh's house, "Joseph's brothers have come," Pharaoh and his servants were pleased. ¹⁷Pharaoh said to Joseph, "Say to your brothers, 'Do this: load your animals and go back to the land of Canaan. ¹⁸Take your father and your households and come to me, so that I may give you the best of the land of Egypt, and you may enjoy the fat of the land.' ¹⁹You are further charged to say, 'Do this: take wagons from the land of Egypt for your little ones and for your wives, and bring your father, and come. ²⁰Give no thought to your possessions, for the best of all the land of Egypt is yours.' "

21 The sons of Israel did so. Joseph gave them wagons according to the instruction of Pharaoh, and he gave them provisions for the journey. ²²To each one of them he gave a set of garments; but to Benjamin he gave three hundred pieces of silver and five sets of garments. ²³To his father he sent the following: ten donkeys loaded with the good things of Egypt, and ten female donkeys loaded with grain, bread, and provision for his father on the journey. ²⁴Then he sent his brothers on their way, and as they were leaving he said to them, "Do not quarrel[a] along the way."

25 So they went up out of Egypt and came to their father Jacob in the land of Canaan. ²⁶And they told him, "Joseph is still alive! He is even ruler over all the land of Egypt." He was stunned; he could not believe them. ²⁷But when they told him all the words of Joseph that he had said to them, and when he saw the wagons that Joseph had sent to carry him, the spirit of their father Jacob revived. ²⁸Israel said, "Enough! My son Joseph is still alive. I must go and see him before I die."

## MATTHEW 14.13–36

**N**ow when Jesus heard this, he withdrew from there in a boat to a deserted place by himself. But when the crowds heard it, they followed him on foot from the towns. ¹⁴When he went ashore, he saw a great crowd; and he had compassion for them and cured their sick. ¹⁵When it was evening, the disciples came to him and said, "This is a deserted place, and the hour is now late; send the crowds away so that they may go into the villages and

a Or *be agitated*

buy food for themselves." ¹⁶Jesus said to them, "They need not go away; you give them something to eat." ¹⁷They replied, "We have nothing here but five loaves and two fish." ¹⁸And he said, "Bring them here to me." ¹⁹Then he ordered the crowds to sit down on the grass. Taking the five loaves and the two fish, he looked up to heaven, and blessed and broke the loaves, and gave them to the disciples, and the disciples gave them to the crowds. ²⁰And all ate and were filled; and they took up what was left over of the broken pieces, twelve baskets full. ²¹And those who ate were about five thousand men, besides women and children.

22  Immediately he made the disciples get into the boat and go on ahead to the other side, while he dismissed the crowds. ²³And after he had dismissed the crowds, he went up the mountain by himself to pray. When evening came, he was there alone, ²⁴but by this time the boat, battered by the waves, was far from the land,ᵃ for the wind was against them. ²⁵And early in the morning he came walking toward them on the sea. ²⁶But when the disciples saw him walking on the sea, they were terrified, saying, "It is a ghost!" And they cried out in fear. ²⁷But immediately Jesus spoke to them and said, "Take heart, it is I; do not be afraid."

28  Peter answered him, "Lord, if it is you, command me to come to you on the water." ²⁹He said, "Come." So Peter got out of the boat, started walking on the water, and came toward Jesus. ³⁰But when he noticed the strong wind,ᵇ he became frightened, and beginning to sink, he cried out, "Lord, save me!" ³¹Jesus immediately reached out his hand and caught him, saying to him, "You of little faith, why did you doubt?" ³²When they got into the boat, the wind ceased. ³³And those in the boat worshiped him, saying, "Truly

you are the Son of God."

34  When they had crossed over, they came to land at Gennesaret. ³⁵After the people of that place recognized him, they sent word throughout the region and brought all who were sick to him, ³⁶and begged him that they might touch even the fringe of his cloak; and all who touched it were healed.

## PSALM 18.37–50

I PURSUED my enemies and
        overtook them;
    and did not turn back until
        they were consumed.
38  I struck them down, so that
        they were not able to
        rise;
    they fell under my feet.
39  For you girded me with
        strength for the battle;
    you made my assailants sink
        under me.
40  You made my enemies turn
        their backs to me,
    and those who hated me I
        destroyed.
41  They cried for help, but there
        was no one to save
        them;
    they cried to the LORD, but he
        did not answer them.
42  I beat them fine, like dust
        before the wind;
    I cast them out like the mire
        of the streets.

43  You delivered me from strife
        with the peoples;ᶜ
    you made me head of the
        nations;
    people whom I had not known
        served me.
44  As soon as they heard of me
        they obeyed me;
    foreigners came cringing to
        me.

ᵃOther ancient authorities read *was out on the sea*  ᵇOther ancient authorities read *the wind*
ᶜGk Tg: Heb *people*

45  Foreigners lost heart,
        and came trembling out of
            their strongholds.

46  The LORD lives! Blessed be my
        rock,
        and exalted be the God of my
            salvation,
47  the God who gave me
            vengeance
        and subdued peoples under
            me;
48  who delivered me from my
            enemies;
        indeed, you exalted me above
            my adversaries;
        you delivered me from the
            violent.

49  For this I will extol you,
        O LORD, among the
            nations,

and sing praises to your
    name.
50  Great triumphs he gives to his
        king,
        and shows steadfast love to
            his anointed,
        to David and his descendants
            forever.

## PROVERBS 4.11–13

I HAVE taught you the way of
        wisdom;
        I have led you in the paths of
            uprightness.
12  When you walk, your step will
            not be hampered;
        and if you run, you will not
            stumble.
13  Keep hold of instruction; do not
            let go;
        guard her, for she is your life.

# JANUARY 23

## GENESIS 46.1—47.31

W HEN Israel set out on his journey with all that he had and
came to Beer-sheba, he of-
fered sacrifices to the God of his father
Isaac. [2]God spoke to Israel in visions of
the night, and said, "Jacob, Jacob." And
he said, "Here I am." [3]Then he said, "I
am God, [a] the God of your father; do
not be afraid to go down to Egypt, for
I will make of you a great nation there.
[4]I myself will go down with you to
Egypt, and I will also bring you up
again; and Joseph's own hand shall
close your eyes."

5  Then Jacob set out from Beer-
sheba; and the sons of Israel carried
their father Jacob, their little ones, and
their wives, in the wagons that Pharaoh
had sent to carry him. [6]They also took
their livestock and the goods that they
had acquired in the land of Canaan, and
they came into Egypt, Jacob and all his
offspring with him, [7]his sons, and his
sons' sons with him, his daughters, and
his sons' daughters; all his offspring he
brought with him into Egypt.

8  Now these are the names of the
Israelites, Jacob and his offspring, who
came to Egypt. Reuben, Jacob's firstborn, [9]and the children of Reuben: Hanoch, Pallu, Hezron, and Carmi. [10]The
children of Simeon: Jemuel, Jamin,
Ohad, Jachin, Zohar, and Shaul, [b] the

son of a Canaanite woman. [11]The children of Levi: Gershon, Kohath, and Merari. [12]The children of Judah: Er, Onan, Shelah, Perez, and Zerah (but Er and Onan died in the land of Canaan); and the children of Perez were Hezron and Hamul. [13]The children of Issachar: Tola, Puvah, Jashub, [a] and Shimron. [14]The children of Zebulun: Sered, Elon, and Jahleel [15](these are the sons of Leah, whom she bore to Jacob in Paddan-aram, together with his daughter Dinah; in all his sons and his daughters numbered thirty-three). [16]The children of Gad: Ziphion, Haggi, Shuni, Ezbon, Eri, Arodi, and Areli. [17]The children of Asher: Imnah, Ishvah, Ishvi, Beriah, and their sister Serah. The children of Beriah: Heber and Malchiel [18](these are the children of Zilpah, whom Laban gave to his daughter Leah; and these she bore to Jacob—sixteen persons). [19]The children of Jacob's wife Rachel: Joseph and Benjamin. [20]To Joseph in the land of Egypt were born Manasseh and Ephraim, whom Asenath daughter of Potiphera, priest of On, bore to him. [21]The children of Benjamin: Bela, Becher, Ashbel, Gera, Naaman, Ehi, Rosh, Muppim, Huppim, and Ard [22](these are the children of Rachel, who were born to Jacob—fourteen persons in all). [23]The children of Dan: Hashum. [b] [24]The children of Naphtali: Jahzeel, Guni, Jezer, and Shillem [25](these are the children of Bilhah, whom Laban gave to his daughter Rachel, and these she bore to Jacob—seven persons in all). [26]All the persons belonging to Jacob who came into Egypt, who were his own offspring, not including the wives of his sons, were sixty-six persons in all. [27]The children of Joseph, who were born to him in Egypt, were two; all the persons of the house of Jacob who came into Egypt were seventy.

28 Israel[c] sent Judah ahead to Joseph to lead the way before him into Goshen. When they came to the land of Goshen, [29]Joseph made ready his chariot and went up to meet his father Israel in Goshen. He presented himself to him, fell on his neck, and wept on his neck a good while. [30]Israel said to Joseph, "I can die now, having seen for myself that you are still alive." [31]Joseph said to his brothers and to his father's household, "I will go up and tell Pharaoh, and will say to him, 'My brothers and my father's household, who were in the land of Canaan, have come to me. [32]The men are shepherds, for they have been keepers of livestock; and they have brought their flocks, and their herds, and all that they have.' [33]When Pharaoh calls you, and says, 'What is your occupation?' [34]you shall say, 'Your servants have been keepers of livestock from our youth even until now, both we and our ancestors'—in order that you may settle in the land of Goshen, because all shepherds are abhorrent to the Egyptians.'"

**47.**1 So Joseph went and told Pharaoh, "My father and my brothers, with their flocks and herds and all that they possess, have come from the land of Canaan; they are now in the land of Goshen." [2]From among his brothers he took five men and presented them to Pharaoh. [3]Pharaoh said to his brothers, "What is your occupation?" And they said to Pharaoh, "Your servants are shepherds, as our ancestors were." [4]They said to Pharaoh, "We have come to reside as aliens in the land; for there is no pasture for your servants' flocks because the famine is severe in the land of Canaan. Now, we ask you, let your servants settle in the land of Goshen." [5]Then Pharaoh said to Joseph, "Your father and your brothers have come to you. [6]The land of Egypt is before you;

aCompare Sam Gk Num 26.24 1 Chr 7.1: MT *Iob*   bGk: Heb *Hushim*   cHeb *He*

settle your father and your brothers in the best part of the land; let them live in the land of Goshen; and if you know that there are capable men among them, put them in charge of my livestock."

7 Then Joseph brought in his father Jacob, and presented him before Pharaoh, and Jacob blessed Pharaoh. <sup>8</sup>Pharaoh said to Jacob, "How many are the years of your life?" <sup>9</sup>Jacob said to Pharaoh, "The years of my earthly sojourn are one hundred thirty; few and hard have been the years of my life. They do not compare with the years of the life of my ancestors during their long sojourn." <sup>10</sup>Then Jacob blessed Pharaoh, and went out from the presence of Pharaoh. <sup>11</sup>Joseph settled his father and his brothers, and granted them a holding in the land of Egypt, in the best part of the land, in the land of Rameses, as Pharaoh had instructed. <sup>12</sup>And Joseph provided his father, his brothers, and all his father's household with food, according to the number of their dependents.

13 Now there was no food in all the land, for the famine was very severe. The land of Egypt and the land of Canaan languished because of the famine. <sup>14</sup>Joseph collected all the money to be found in the land of Egypt and in the land of Canaan, in exchange for the grain that they bought; and Joseph brought the money into Pharaoh's house. <sup>15</sup>When the money from the land of Egypt and from the land of Canaan was spent, all the Egyptians came to Joseph, and said, "Give us food! Why should we die before your eyes? For our money is gone." <sup>16</sup>And Joseph answered, "Give me your livestock, and I will give you food in exchange for your livestock, if your money is gone." <sup>17</sup>So they brought their livestock to Joseph; and Joseph gave them food in exchange for the horses, the flocks, the herds,

and the donkeys. That year he supplied them with food in exchange for all their livestock. <sup>18</sup>When that year was ended, they came to him the following year, and said to him, "We can not hide from my lord that our money is all spent; and the herds of cattle are my lord's. There is nothing left in the sight of my lord but our bodies and our lands. <sup>19</sup>Shall we die before your eyes, both we and our land? Buy us and our land in exchange for food. We with our land will become slaves to Pharaoh; just give us seed, so that we may live and not die, and that the land may not become desolate."

20 So Joseph bought all the land of Egypt for Pharaoh. All the Egyptians sold their fields, because the famine was severe upon them; and the land became Pharaoh's. <sup>21</sup>As for the people, he made slaves of them<sup>a</sup> from one end of Egypt to the other. <sup>22</sup>Only the land of the priests he did not buy; for the priests had a fixed allowance from Pharaoh, and lived on the allowance that Pharaoh gave them; therefore they did not sell their land. <sup>23</sup>Then Joseph said to the people, "Now that I have this day bought you and your land for Pharaoh, here is seed for you; sow the land. <sup>24</sup>And at the harvests you shall give one-fifth to Pharaoh, and four-fifths shall be your own, as seed for the field and as food for yourselves and your households, and as food for your little ones." <sup>25</sup>They said, "You have saved our lives; may it please my lord, we will be slaves to Pharaoh." <sup>26</sup>So Joseph made it a statute concerning the land of Egypt, and it stands to this day, that Pharaoh should have the fifth. The land of the priests alone did not become Pharaoh's.

27 Thus Israel settled in the land of Egypt, in the region of Goshen; and they gained possessions in it, and were fruitful and multiplied exceedingly. <sup>28</sup>Jacob lived in the land of Egypt seventeen

---

a Sam Gk Compare Vg: MT *He removed them to the cities*

years; so the days of Jacob, the years of his life, were one hundred forty-seven years.

29 When the time of Israel's death drew near, he called his son Joseph and said to him, "If I have found favor with you, put your hand under my thigh and promise to deal loyally and truly with me. Do not bury me in Egypt. [30]When I lie down with my ancestors, carry me out of Egypt and bury me in their burial place." He answered, "I will do as you have said." [31]And he said, "Swear to me"; and he swore to him. Then Israel bowed himself on the head of his bed.

## MATTHEW 15.1–28

THEN Pharisees and scribes came to Jesus from Jerusalem and said, [2]"Why do your disciples break the tradition of the elders? For they do not wash their hands before they eat." [3]He answered them, "And why do you break the commandment of God for the sake of your tradition? [4]For God said,[a] 'Honor your father and your mother,' and, 'Whoever speaks evil of father or mother must surely die.' [5]But you say that whoever tells father or mother, 'Whatever support you might have had from me is given to God,'[b] then that person need not honor the father.[c] [6]So, for the sake of your tradition, you make void the word[d] of God. [7]You hypocrites! Isaiah prophesied rightly about you when he said:

8 'This people honors me with
  their lips,
 but their hearts are far from
  me;
9 in vain do they worship me,
  teaching human precepts as
   doctrines.'"

10 Then he called the crowd to him and said to them, "Listen and under-

stand: [11]it is not what goes into the mouth that defiles a person, but it is what comes out of the mouth that defiles." [12]Then the disciples approached and said to him, "Do you know that the Pharisees took offense when they heard what you said?" [13]He answered, "Every plant that my heavenly Father has not planted will be uprooted. [14]Let them alone; they are blind guides of the blind.[e] And if one blind person guides another, both will fall into a pit." [15]But Peter said to him, "Explain this parable to us." [16]Then he said, "Are you also still without understanding? [17]Do you not see that whatever goes into the mouth enters the stomach, and goes out into the sewer? [18]But what comes out of the mouth proceeds from the heart, and this is what defiles. [19]For out of the heart come evil intentions, murder, adultery, fornication, theft, false witness, slander. [20]These are what defile a person, but to eat with unwashed hands does not defile."

21 Jesus left that place and went away to the district of Tyre and Sidon. [22]Just then a Canaanite woman from that region came out and started shouting, "Have mercy on me, Lord, Son of David; my daughter is tormented by a demon." [23]But he did not answer her at all. And his disciples came and urged him, saying, "Send her away, for she keeps shouting after us." [24]He answered, "I was sent only to the lost sheep of the house of Israel." [25]But she came and knelt before him, saying, "Lord, help me." [26]He answered, "It is not fair to take the children's food and throw it to the dogs." [27]She said, "Yes, Lord, yet even the dogs eat the crumbs that fall from their masters' table." [28]Then Jesus answered her, "Woman, great is your faith! Let it be done for you as you wish." And her daughter was healed instantly.

[a]Other ancient authorities read *commanded, saying* [b]Or *is an offering* [c]Other ancient authorities add *or the mother* [d]Other ancient authorities read *law*; others, *commandment* [e]Other ancient authorities lack *of the blind*

## PSALM 19.1–14

*To the leader. A Psalm of David.*

THE heavens are telling the
glory of God;
and the firmament[a]
proclaims his handiwork.
2 Day to day pours forth speech,
and night to night declares
knowledge.
3 There is no speech, nor are
there words;
their voice is not heard;
4 yet their voice[b] goes out
through all the earth,
and their words to the end of
the world.

In the heavens[c] he has set a
tent for the sun,
5 which comes out like a
bridegroom from his
wedding canopy,
and like a strong man runs its
course with joy.
6 Its rising is from the end of the
heavens,
and its circuit to the end of
them;
and nothing is hid from its
heat.

7 The law of the LORD is perfect,
reviving the soul;
the decrees of the LORD are
sure,
making wise the simple;
8 the precepts of the LORD are
right,
rejoicing the heart;
the commandment of the LORD
is clear,
enlightening the eyes;
9 the fear of the LORD is pure,
enduring forever;
the ordinances of the LORD are
true
and righteous altogether.

10 More to be desired are they
than gold,
even much fine gold;
sweeter also than honey,
and drippings of the
honeycomb.

11 Moreover by them is your
servant warned;
in keeping them there is great
reward.
12 But who can detect their
errors?
Clear me from hidden faults.
13 Keep back your servant also
from the insolent;[d]
do not let them have
dominion over me.
Then I shall be blameless,
and innocent of great
transgression.

14 Let the words of my mouth and
the meditation of my
heart
be acceptable to you,
O LORD, my rock and my
redeemer.

## PROVERBS 4.14–19

DO not enter the path of the
wicked,
and do not walk in the way
of evildoers.
15 Avoid it; do not go on it;
turn away from it and pass
on.
16 For they cannot sleep unless
they have done wrong;
they are robbed of sleep
unless they have made
someone stumble.
17 For they eat the bread of
wickedness
and drink the wine of
violence.

a Or *dome*　b Gk Jerome Compare Syr: Heb *line*　c Heb *In them*　d Or *from proud thoughts*

18  But the path of the righteous is
      like the light of dawn,
    which shines brighter and
      brighter until full day.

19  The way of the wicked is like
      deep darkness;
    they do not know what they
      stumble over.

# JANUARY 24

## GENESIS 48.1—49.33

AFTER this Joseph was told, "Your father is ill." So he took with him his two sons, Manasseh and Ephraim. 2When Jacob was told, "Your son Joseph has come to you," he[a] summoned his strength and sat up in bed. 3And Jacob said to Joseph, "God Almighty[b] appeared to me at Luz in the land of Canaan, and he blessed me, 4and said to me, 'I am going to make you fruitful and increase your numbers; I will make of you a company of peoples, and will give this land to your offspring after you for a perpetual holding.' 5Therefore your two sons, who were born to you in the land of Egypt before I came to you in Egypt, are now mine; Ephraim and Manasseh shall be mine, just as Reuben and Simeon are. 6As for the offspring born to you after them, they shall be yours. They shall be recorded under the names of their brothers with regard to their inheritance. 7For when I came from Paddan, Rachel, alas, died in the land of Canaan on the way, while there was still some distance to go to Ephrath; and I buried her there on the way to Ephrath" (that is, Bethlehem).

8  When Israel saw Joseph's sons, he said, "Who are these?" 9Joseph said to his father, "They are my sons, whom God has given me here." And he said, "Bring them to me, please, that I may bless them." 10Now the eyes of Israel were dim with age, and he could not see well. So Joseph brought them near him; and he kissed them and embraced them. 11Israel said to Joseph, "I did not expect to see your face; and here God has let me see your children also." 12Then Joseph removed them from his father's knees,[c] and he bowed himself with his face to the earth. 13Joseph took them both, Ephraim in his right hand toward Israel's left, and Manasseh in his left hand toward Israel's right, and brought them near him. 14But Israel stretched out his right hand and laid it on the head of Ephraim, who was the younger, and his left hand on the head of Manasseh, crossing his hands, for Manasseh was the firstborn. 15He blessed Joseph, and said,

"The God before whom my
    ancestors Abraham and
    Isaac walked,
the God who has been my
    shepherd all my life to
    this day,
16  the angel who has redeemed me
    from all harm, bless the
    boys;
and in them let my name be
    perpetuated, and the
    name of my ancestors
    Abraham and Isaac;

a Heb *Israel*   b Traditional rendering of Heb *El Shaddai*   c Heb *from his knees*

and let them grow into a
    multitude on the earth."
17  When Joseph saw that his father
laid his right hand on the head of
Ephraim, it displeased him; so he took
his father's hand, to remove it from
Ephraim's head to Manasseh's head.
18Joseph said to his father, "Not so, my
father! Since this one is the firstborn,
put your right hand on his head." 19But
his father refused, and said, "I know,
my son, I know; he also shall become
a people, and he also shall be great.
Nevertheless his younger brother shall
be greater than he, and his offspring
shall become a multitude of nations."
20So he blessed them that day, saying,
    "By youa Israel will invoke
        blessings, saying,
   'God make youa like Ephraim
        and like Manasseh.'"
So he put Ephraim ahead of Manasseh.
21Then Israel said to Joseph, "I am
about to die, but God will be with you
and will bring you again to the land of
your ancestors. 22I now give to you
one portionb more than to your brothers, the portionb that I took from the
hand of the Amorites with my sword
and with my bow."

49.1 THEN Jacob called his sons, and
said: "Gather around, that I may tell
you what will happen to you in days to
come.
2  Assemble and hear, O sons of
    Jacob;
    listen to Israel your father.

3  Reuben, you are my firstborn,
    my might and the first fruits
        of my vigor,
    excelling in rank and excelling
        in power.
4  Unstable as water, you shall no
    longer excel

    because you went up onto
        your father's bed;
    then you defiled it—youc
        went up onto my couch!

5  Simeon and Levi are brothers;
    weapons of violence are their
        swords.
6  May I never come into their
        council;
    may I not be joined to their
        company—
  for in their anger they killed
        men,
  and at their whim they
        hamstrung oxen.
7  Cursed be their anger, for it is
        fierce,
    and their wrath, for it is
        cruel!
  I will divide them in Jacob,
    and scatter them in Israel.

8  Judah, your brothers shall praise
        you;
    your hand shall be on the
        neck of your enemies;
    your father's sons shall bow
        down before you.
9  Judah is a lion's whelp;
    from the prey, my son, you
        have gone up.
  He crouches down, he stretches
        out like a lion,
    like a lioness—who dares
        rouse him up?
10  The scepter shall not depart
        from Judah,
    nor the ruler's staff from
        between his feet,
  until tribute comes to him;d
    and the obedience of the
        peoples is his.
11  Binding his foal to the vine
    and his donkey's colt to the
        choice vine,
  he washes his garments in wine

and his robe in the blood of
    grapes;
12  his eyes are darker than wine,
    and his teeth whiter than
      milk.

13  Zebulun shall settle at the shore
    of the sea;
    he shall be a haven for ships,
    and his border shall be at
      Sidon.

14  Issachar is a strong donkey,
    lying down between the
      sheepfolds;
15  he saw that a resting place was
    good,
    and that the land was
      pleasant;
  so he bowed his shoulder to the
    burden,
    and became a slave at forced
      labor.

16  Dan shall judge his people
    as one of the tribes of Israel.
17  Dan shall be a snake by the
    roadside,
    a viper along the path,
  that bites the horse's heels
  so that its rider falls
    backward.

18  I wait for your salvation,
    O LORD.

19  Gad shall be raided by raiders,
    but he shall raid at their
      heels.

20  Asher's[a] food shall be rich,
    and he shall provide royal
      delicacies.

21  Naphtali is a doe let loose
    that bears lovely fawns. [b]

22  Joseph is a fruitful bough,
    a fruitful bough by a spring;
    his branches run over the
      wall. [c]
23  The archers fiercely attacked
    him;
    they shot at him and pressed
      him hard.
24  Yet his bow remained taut,
    and his arms[d] were made
      agile
  by the hands of the Mighty One
    of Jacob,
    by the name of the Shepherd,
      the Rock of Israel,
25  by the God of your father, who
    will help you,
    by the Almighty[e] who will
      bless you
    with blessings of heaven
      above,
  blessings of the deep that lies
      beneath,
    blessings of the breasts and
      of the womb.
26  The blessings of your father
    are stronger than the
      blessings of the eternal
      mountains,
    the bounties[f] of the
      everlasting hills;
  may they be on the head of
      Joseph,
    on the brow of him who was
      set apart from his
      brothers.

27  Benjamin is a ravenous wolf,
    in the morning devouring the
      prey,
    and at evening dividing the
      spoil."

28  All these are the twelve tribes of
Israel, and this is what their father said
to them when he blessed them, bless-

---

a Gk Vg Syr: Heb *From Asher*  b Or *that gives beautiful words*  c Meaning of Heb uncertain  d Heb *the arms of his hands*  e Traditional rendering of Heb *Shaddai*  f Cn Compare Gk: Heb *of my progenitors to the boundaries*

ing each one of them with a suitable blessing.

29 Then he charged them, saying to them, "I am about to be gathered to my people. Bury me with my ancestors—in the cave in the field of Ephron the Hittite, 30in the cave in the field at Machpelah, near Mamre, in the land of Canaan, in the field that Abraham bought from Ephron the Hittite as a burial site. 31There Abraham and his wife Sarah were buried; there Isaac and his wife Rebekah were buried; and there I buried Leah— 32the field and the cave that is in it were purchased from the Hittites." 33When Jacob ended his charge to his sons, he drew up his feet into the bed, breathed his last, and was gathered to his people.

## MATTHEW 15.29—16.12

AFTER Jesus had left that place, he passed along the Sea of Galilee, and he went up the mountain, where he sat down. 30Great crowds came to him, bringing with them the lame, the maimed, the blind, the mute, and many others. They put them at his feet, and he cured them, 31so that the crowd was amazed when they saw the mute speaking, the maimed whole, the lame walking, and the blind seeing. And they praised the God of Israel.

32 Then Jesus called his disciples to him and said, "I have compassion for the crowd, because they have been with me now for three days and have nothing to eat; and I do not want to send them away hungry, for they might faint on the way." 33The disciples said to him, "Where are we to get enough bread in the desert to feed so great a crowd?" 34Jesus asked them, "How many loaves have you?" They said, "Seven, and a few small fish." 35Then ordering the crowd to sit down on the

ground, 36he took the seven loaves and the fish; and after giving thanks he broke them and gave them to the disciples, and the disciples gave them to the crowds. 37And all of them ate and were filled; and they took up the broken pieces left over, seven baskets full. 38Those who had eaten were four thousand men, besides women and children. 39After sending away the crowds, he got into the boat and went to the region of Magadan. a

16.1 THE Pharisees and Sadducees came, and to test Jesusb they asked him to show them a sign from heaven. 2He answered them, "When it is evening, you say, 'It will be fair weather, for the sky is red.' 3And in the morning, 'It will be stormy today, for the sky is red and threatening.' You know how to interpret the appearance of the sky, but you cannot interpret the signs of the times. c4An evil and adulterous generation asks for a sign, but no sign will be given to it except the sign of Jonah." Then he left them and went away.

5 When the disciples reached the other side, they had forgotten to bring any bread. 6Jesus said to them, "Watch out, and beware of the yeast of the Pharisees and Sadducees." 7They said to one another, "It is because we have brought no bread." 8And becoming aware of it, Jesus said, "You of little faith, why are you talking about having no bread? 9Do you still not perceive? Do you not remember the five loaves for the five thousand, and how many baskets you gathered? 10Or the seven loaves for the four thousand, and how many baskets you gathered? 11How could you fail to perceive that I was not speaking about bread? Beware of the yeast of the Pharisees and Sadducees!" 12Then they understood that he had not told them to beware of the yeast of

aOther ancient authorities read *Magdala* or *Magdalan*  bGk *him*  cOther ancient authorities lack
*2When it is . . . of the times*

bread, but of the teaching of the Pharisees and Sadducees.

## PSALM 20.1–9

*To the leader. A Psalm of David.*

THE LORD answer you in the day
of trouble!
The name of the God of
Jacob protect you!
2  May he send you help from the
sanctuary,
and give you support from
Zion.
3  May he remember all your
offerings,
and regard with favor your
burnt sacrifices.          *Selah*

4  May he grant you your heart's
desire,
and fulfill all your plans.
5  May we shout for joy over your
victory,
and in the name of our God
set up our banners.
May the LORD fulfill all your
petitions.

6  Now I know that the LORD will
help his anointed;
he will answer him from his
holy heaven
with mighty victories by his
right hand.
7  Some take pride in chariots, and
some in horses,
but our pride is in the name
of the LORD our God.

8  They will collapse and fall,
but we shall rise and stand
upright.

9  Give victory to the king,
O LORD;
answer us when we call. [a]

## PROVERBS 4.20–27

MY child, be attentive to my
words;
incline your ear to my
sayings.
21  Do not let them escape from
your sight;
keep them within your heart.
22  For they are life to those who
find them,
and healing to all their flesh.
23  Keep your heart with all
vigilance,
for from it flow the springs
of life.
24  Put away from you crooked
speech,
and put devious talk far
from you.
25  Let your eyes look directly
forward,
and your gaze be straight
before you.
26  Keep straight the path of your
feet,
and all your ways will be
sure.
27  Do not swerve to the right or
to the left;
turn your foot away from evil.

aGk: Heb *give victory, O LORD; let the King answer us when we call*

# JANUARY 25

## GENESIS 50.1—EXODUS 2.10

**T**HEN Joseph threw himself on his father's face and wept over him and kissed him. 2Joseph commanded the physicians in his service to embalm his father. So the physicians embalmed Israel; 3they spent forty days in doing this, for that is the time required for embalming. And the Egyptians wept for him seventy days.

4 When the days of weeping for him were past, Joseph addressed the household of Pharaoh, "If now I have found favor with you, please speak to Pharaoh as follows: 5My father made me swear an oath; he said, 'I am about to die. In the tomb that I hewed out for myself in the land of Canaan, there you shall bury me.' Now therefore let me go up, so that I may bury my father; then I will return." 6Pharaoh answered, "Go up, and bury your father, as he made you swear to do."

7 So Joseph went up to bury his father. With him went up all the servants of Pharaoh, the elders of his household, and all the elders of the land of Egypt, 8as well as all the household of Joseph, his brothers, and his father's household. Only their children, their flocks, and their herds were left in the land of Goshen. 9Both chariots and charioteers went up with him. It was a very great company. 10When they came to the threshing floor of Atad, which is beyond the Jordan, they held there a very great and sorrowful lamentation; and he observed a time of mourning for his father seven days. 11When the Canaanite inhabitants of the land saw the mourning on the threshing floor of Atad, they said, "This is a grievous mourning on the part of the Egyptians."

Therefore the place was named Abel-mizraim;a it is beyond the Jordan. 12Thus his sons did for him as he had instructed them. 13They carried him to the land of Canaan and buried him in the cave of the field at Machpelah, the field near Mamre, which Abraham bought as a burial site from Ephron the Hittite. 14After he had buried his father, Joseph returned to Egypt with his brothers and all who had gone up with him to bury his father.

15 Realizing that their father was dead, Joseph's brothers said, "What if Joseph still bears a grudge against us and pays us back in full for all the wrong that we did to him?" 16So they approachedb Joseph, saying, "Your father gave this instruction before he died, 17'Say to Joseph: I beg you, forgive the crime of your brothers and the wrong they did in harming you.' Now therefore please forgive the crime of the servants of the God of your father." Joseph wept when they spoke to him. 18Then his brothers also wept,c fell down before him, and said, "We are here as your slaves." 19But Joseph said to them, "Do not be afraid! Am I in the place of God? 20Even though you intended to do harm to me, God intended it for good, in order to preserve a numerous people, as he is doing today. 21So have no fear; I myself will provide for you and your little ones." In this way he reassured them, speaking kindly to them.

22 So Joseph remained in Egypt, he and his father's household; and Joseph lived one hundred ten years. 23Joseph saw Ephraim's children of the third generation; the children of Machir

son of Manasseh were also born on Joseph's knees.

24 Then Joseph said to his brothers, "I am about to die; but God will surely come to you, and bring you up out of this land to the land that he swore to Abraham, to Isaac, and to Jacob." [25]So Joseph made the Israelites swear, saying, "When God comes to you, you shall carry up my bones from here." [26]And Joseph died, being one hundred ten years old; he was embalmed and placed in a coffin in Egypt.

[1.1] THESE are the names of the sons of Israel who came to Egypt with Jacob, each with his household: [2]Reuben, Simeon, Levi, and Judah, [3]Issachar, Zebulun, and Benjamin, [4]Dan and Naphtali, Gad and Asher. [5]The total number of people born to Jacob was seventy. Joseph was already in Egypt. [6]Then Joseph died, and all his brothers, and that whole generation. [7]But the Israelites were fruitful and prolific; they multiplied and grew exceedingly strong, so that the land was filled with them.

8 Now a new king arose over Egypt, who did not know Joseph. [9]He said to his people, "Look, the Israelite people are more numerous and more powerful than we. [10]Come, let us deal shrewdly with them, or they will increase and, in the event of war, join our enemies and fight against us and escape from the land." [11]Therefore they set taskmasters over them to oppress them with forced labor. They built supply cities, Pithom and Rameses, for Pharaoh. [12]But the more they were oppressed, the more they multiplied and spread, so that the Egyptians came to dread the Israelites. [13]The Egyptians became ruthless in imposing tasks on the Israelites, [14]and made their lives bitter with hard service in mortar and brick and in every kind of field labor.

They were ruthless in all the tasks that they imposed on them.

15 The king of Egypt said to the Hebrew midwives, one of whom was named Shiphrah and the other Puah, [16]"When you act as midwives to the Hebrew women, and see them on the birthstool, if it is a boy, kill him; but if it is a girl, she shall live." [17]But the midwives feared God; they did not do as the king of Egypt commanded them, but they let the boys live. [18]So the king of Egypt summoned the midwives and said to them, "Why have you done this, and allowed the boys to live?" [19]The midwives said to Pharaoh, "Because the Hebrew women are not like the Egyptian women; for they are vigorous and give birth before the midwife comes to them." [20]So God dealt well with the midwives; and the people multiplied and became very strong. [21]And because the midwives feared God, he gave them families. [22]Then Pharaoh commanded all his people, "Every boy that is born to the Hebrews[a] you shall throw into the Nile, but you shall let every girl live."

[2.1] Now a man from the house of Levi went and married a Levite woman. [2]The woman conceived and bore a son; and when she saw that he was a fine baby, she hid him three months. [3]When she could hide him no longer she got a papyrus basket for him, and plastered it with bitumen and pitch; she put the child in it and placed it among the reeds on the bank of the river. [4]His sister stood at a distance, to see what would happen to him.

5 The daughter of Pharaoh came down to bathe at the river, while her attendants walked beside the river. She saw the basket among the reeds and sent her maid to bring it. [6]When she opened it, she saw the child. He was crying, and she took pity on him,

[a]Sam Gk Tg: Heb lacks *to the Hebrews*

"This must be one of the Hebrews' children," she said. [7]Then his sister said to Pharaoh's daughter, "Shall I go and get you a nurse from the Hebrew women to nurse the child for you?" [8]Pharaoh's daughter said to her, "Yes." So the girl went and called the child's mother. [9]Pharaoh's daughter said to her, "Take this child and nurse it for me, and I will give you your wages." So the woman took the child and nursed it. [10]When the child grew up, she brought him to Pharaoh's daughter, and she took him as her son. She named him Moses,[a] "because," she said, "I drew him out[b] of the water."

## MATTHEW 16.13—17.9

Now when Jesus came into the district of Caesarea Philippi, he asked his disciples, "Who do people say that the Son of Man is?" [14]And they said, "Some say John the Baptist, but others Elijah, and still others Jeremiah or one of the prophets." [15]He said to them, "But who do you say that I am?" [16]Simon Peter answered, "You are the Messiah,[c] the Son of the living God." [17]And Jesus answered him, "Blessed are you, Simon son of Jonah! For flesh and blood has not revealed this to you, but my Father in heaven. [18]And I tell you, you are Peter,[d] and on this rock[e] I will build my church, and the gates of Hades will not prevail against it. [19]I will give you the keys of the kingdom of heaven, and whatever you bind on earth will be bound in heaven, and whatever you loose on earth will be loosed in heaven." [20]Then he sternly ordered the disciples not to tell anyone that he was[f] the Messiah.[c]

21 From that time on, Jesus began to show his disciples that he must go to Jerusalem and undergo great suffering at the hands of the elders and chief priests and scribes, and be killed, and on the third day be raised. [22]And Peter took him aside and began to rebuke him, saying, "God forbid it, Lord! This must never happen to you." [23]But he turned and said to Peter, "Get behind me, Satan! You are a stumbling block to me; for you are setting your mind not on divine things but on human things."

24 Then Jesus told his disciples, "If any want to become my followers, let them deny themselves and take up their cross and follow me. [25]For those who want to save their life will lose it, and those who lose their life for my sake will find it. [26]For what will it profit them if they gain the whole world but forfeit their life? Or what will they give in return for their life?

27 "For the Son of Man is to come with his angels in the glory of his Father, and then he will repay everyone for what has been done. [28]Truly I tell you, there are some standing here who will not taste death before they see the Son of Man coming in his kingdom."

[17.1] Six days later, Jesus took with him Peter and James and his brother John and led them up a high mountain, by themselves. [2]And he was transfigured before them, and his face shone like the sun, and his clothes became dazzling white. [3]Suddenly there appeared to them Moses and Elijah, talking with him. [4]Then Peter said to Jesus, "Lord, it is good for us to be here; if you wish, I[g] will make three dwellings[h] here, one for you, one for Moses, and one for Elijah." [5]While he was still speaking, suddenly a bright cloud overshadowed them, and from the cloud a voice said, "This is my Son, the Beloved;[i] with him I am well pleased; listen to him!" [6]When the disciples heard this, they fell to the ground and were overcome by fear. [7]But Jesus came and touched them, saying, "Get up and do not be

a Heb *Mosheh*  b Heb *mashah*  c Or *the Christ*  d Gk *Petros*  e Gk *petra*  f Other ancient authorities add *Jesus*  g Other ancient authorities read *we*  h Or *tents*  i Or *my beloved Son*

afraid." [8]And when they looked up, they saw no one except Jesus himself alone.

9 As they were coming down the mountain, Jesus ordered them, "Tell no one about the vision until after the Son of Man has been raised from the dead."

## PSALM 21.1–13
*To the leader. A Psalm of David.*

IN your strength the king
    rejoices, O LORD,
    and in your help how greatly
      he exults!
2 You have given him his heart's
      desire,
    and have not withheld the
      request of his lips.  *Selah*
3 For you meet him with rich
      blessings;
    you set a crown of fine gold
      on his head.
4 He asked you for life; you gave
      it to him—
    length of days forever and
      ever.
5 His glory is great through your
      help;
    splendor and majesty you
      bestow on him.
6 You bestow on him blessings
      forever;
    you make him glad with the
      joy of your presence.
7 For the king trusts in the LORD,
    and through the steadfast love
      of the Most High he shall
      not be moved.

8 Your hand will find out all your
      enemies;
    your right hand will find out
      those who hate you.

9 You will make them like a fiery
      furnace
    when you appear.
    The LORD will swallow them up
      in his wrath,
    and fire will consume them.
10 You will destroy their offspring
      from the earth,
    and their children from among
      humankind.
11 If they plan evil against you,
    if they devise mischief, they
      will not succeed.
12 For you will put them to flight;
    you will aim at their faces
      with your bows.

13 Be exalted, O LORD, in your
      strength!
    We will sing and praise your
      power.

## PROVERBS 5.1–6

MY child, be attentive to my
      wisdom;
    incline your ear to my
      understanding,
2 so that you may hold on to
      prudence,
    and your lips may guard
      knowledge.
3 For the lips of a loose[a] woman
      drip honey,
    and her speech is smoother
      than oil;
4 but in the end she is bitter as
      wormwood,
    sharp as a two-edged sword.
5 Her feet go down to death;
    her steps follow the path to
      Sheol.
6 She does not keep straight to
      the path of life;
    her ways wander, and she
      does not know it.

[a] Heb *strange*

EXODUS 2.11—3.22

Ne day, after Moses had grown up, he went out to his people and saw their forced labor. He saw an Egyptian beating a Hebrew, one of his kinsfolk. ¹²He looked this way and that, and seeing no one he killed the Egyptian and hid him in the sand. ¹³When he went out the next day, he saw two Hebrews fighting; and he said to the one who was in the wrong, "Why do you strike your fellow Hebrew?" ¹⁴He answered, "Who made you a ruler and judge over us? Do you mean to kill me as you killed the Egyptian?" Then Moses was afraid and thought, "Surely the thing is known." ¹⁵When Pharaoh heard of it, he sought to kill Moses.

But Moses fled from Pharaoh. He settled in the land of Midian, and sat down by a well. ¹⁶The priest of Midian had seven daughters. They came to draw water, and filled the troughs to water their father's flock. ¹⁷But some shepherds came and drove them away. Moses got up and came to their defense and watered their flock. ¹⁸When they returned to their father Reuel, he said, "How is it that you have come back so soon today?" ¹⁹They said, "An Egyptian helped us against the shepherds; he even drew water for us and watered the flock." ²⁰He said to his daughters, "Where is he? Why did you leave the man? Invite him to break bread." ²¹Moses agreed to stay with the man, and he gave Moses his daughter Zipporah in marriage. ²²She bore a son, and he named him Gershom; for he said, "I have been an alien^a residing in a foreign land."

23 After a long time the king of Egypt died. The Israelites groaned under their slavery, and cried out. Out of the slavery their cry for help rose up to God. ²⁴God heard their groaning, and God remembered his covenant with Abraham, Isaac, and Jacob. ²⁵God looked upon the Israelites, and God took notice of them.

3.1 Moses was keeping the flock of his father-in-law Jethro, the priest of Midian; he led his flock beyond the wilderness, and came to Horeb, the mountain of God. ²There the angel of the Lord appeared to him in a flame of fire out of a bush; he looked, and the bush was blazing, yet it was not consumed. ³Then Moses said, "I must turn aside and look at this great sight, and see why the bush is not burned up." ⁴When the Lord saw that he had turned aside to see, God called to him out of the bush, "Moses, Moses!" And he said, "Here I am." ⁵Then he said, "Come no closer! Remove the sandals from your feet, for the place on which you are standing is holy ground." ⁶He said further, "I am the God of your father, the God of Abraham, the God of Isaac, and the God of Jacob." And Moses hid his face, for he was afraid to look at God.

7 Then the Lord said, "I have observed the misery of my people who are in Egypt; I have heard their cry on account of their taskmasters. Indeed, I know their sufferings, ⁸and I have come down to deliver them from the Egyptians, and to bring them up out of that land to a good and broad land, a land flowing with milk and honey, to the country of the Canaanites, the Hittites, the Amorites, the Perizzites, the Hivites, and the Jebusites. ⁹The cry of the Israelites has now come to me; I

a Heb *ger*

have also seen how the Egyptians oppress them. [10]So come, I will send you to Pharaoh to bring my people, the Israelites, out of Egypt." [11]But Moses said to God, "Who am I that I should go to Pharaoh, and bring the Israelites out of Egypt?" [12]He said, "I will be with you; and this shall be the sign for you that it is I who sent you: when you have brought the people out of Egypt, you shall worship God on this mountain."

13 But Moses said to God, "If I come to the Israelites and say to them, 'The God of your ancestors has sent me to you,' and they ask me, 'What is his name?' what shall I say to them?" [14]God said to Moses, "I AM WHO I AM."[a] He said further, "Thus you shall say to the Israelites, 'I AM has sent me to you.'" [15]God also said to Moses, "Thus you shall say to the Israelites, 'The LORD,[b] the God of your ancestors, the God of Abraham, the God of Isaac, and the God of Jacob, has sent me to you':

This is my name forever,
and this my title for all
generations.

[16]Go and assemble the elders of Israel, and say to them, 'The LORD, the God of your ancestors, the God of Abraham, of Isaac, and of Jacob, has appeared to me, saying: I have given heed to you and to what has been done to you in Egypt. [17]I declare that I will bring you up out of the misery of Egypt, to the land of the Canaanites, the Hittites, the Amorites, the Perizzites, the Hivites, and the Jebusites, a land flowing with milk and honey.' [18]They will listen to your voice; and you and the elders of Israel shall go to the king of Egypt and say to him, 'The LORD, the God of the Hebrews, has met with us; let us now go a three days' journey into the wilderness, so that we may sacrifice to the LORD our God.' [19]I know, however, that the king of Egypt will not let you go unless compelled by a mighty hand.[c] [20]So I will stretch out my hand and strike Egypt with all my wonders that I will perform in it; after that he will let you go. [21]I will bring this people into such favor with the Egyptians that, when you go, you will not go empty-handed; [22]each woman shall ask her neighbor and any woman living in the neighbor's house for jewelry of silver and of gold, and clothing, and you shall put them on your sons and on your daughters; and so you shall plunder the Egyptians."

## MATTHEW 17.10–27

AND the disciples asked him, "Why, then, do the scribes say that Elijah must come first?" [11]He [Jesus] replied, "Elijah is indeed coming and will restore all things; [12]but I tell you that Elijah has already come, and they did not recognize him, but they did to him whatever they pleased. So also the Son of Man is about to suffer at their hands." [13]Then the disciples understood that he was speaking to them about John the Baptist.

14 When they came to the crowd, a man came to him, knelt before him, [15]and said, "Lord, have mercy on my son, for he is an epileptic and he suffers terribly; he often falls into the fire and often into the water. [16]And I brought him to your disciples, but they could not cure him." [17]Jesus answered, "You faithless and perverse generation, how much longer must I be with you? How much longer must I put up with you? Bring him here to me." [18]And Jesus rebuked the demon,[d] and it[e] came out of him, and the boy was cured instantly. [19]Then the disciples came to Jesus privately and said, "Why could we not cast it out?" [20]He said to them, "Because of

---

[a]Or *I AM WHAT I AM* or *I WILL BE WHAT I WILL BE*   [b]The word "LORD" when spelled with capital letters stands for the divine name, *YHWH,* which is here connected with the verb *hayah,* "to be"   [c]Gk Vg: Heb *no, not by a mighty hand*   [d]Gk *it* or *him*   [e]Gk *the demon*

your little faith. For truly I tell you, if you have faith the size of a[a] mustard seed, you will say to this mountain, 'Move from here to there,' and it will move; and nothing will be impossible for you."[b]

22 As they were gathering[c] in Galilee, Jesus said to them, "The Son of Man is going to be betrayed into human hands, [23]and they will kill him, and on the third day he will be raised." And they were greatly distressed.

24 When they reached Capernaum, the collectors of the temple tax[d] came to Peter and said, "Does your teacher not pay the temple tax?"[d] [25]He said, "Yes, he does." And when he came home, Jesus spoke of it first, asking, "What do you think, Simon? From whom do kings of the earth take toll or tribute? From their children or from others?" [26]When Peter[e] said, "From others," Jesus said to him, "Then the children are free. [27]However, so that we do not give offense to them, go to the sea and cast a hook; take the first fish that comes up; and when you open its mouth, you will find a coin;[f] take that and give it to them for you and me."

## PSALM 22.1–18

*To the leader: according to The Deer of the Dawn. A Psalm of David.*

My God, my God, why have
  you forsaken me?
 Why are you so far from
  helping me, from the
  words of my groaning?
2 O my God, I cry by day, but
  you do not answer;
 and by night, but find no rest.

3 Yet you are holy,
  enthroned on the praises of
  Israel.

4 In you our ancestors trusted;
  they trusted, and you
   delivered them.
5 To you they cried, and were
   saved;
  in you they trusted, and were
   not put to shame.

6 But I am a worm, and not
   human;
  scorned by others, and
   despised by the people.
7 All who see me mock at me;
  they make mouths at me,
   they shake their heads;
8 "Commit your cause to the
   Lord; let him deliver—
  let him rescue the one in
   whom he delights!"

9 Yet it was you who took me
   from the womb;
  you kept me safe on my
   mother's breast.
10 On you I was cast from my
   birth,
  and since my mother bore me
   you have been my God.
11 Do not be far from me,
  for trouble is near
  and there is no one to help.

12 Many bulls encircle me,
  strong bulls of Bashan
   surround me;
13 they open wide their mouths at
   me,
  like a ravening and roaring
   lion.

14 I am poured out like water,
  and all my bones are out of
   joint;
  my heart is like wax;
   it is melted within my breast;
15 my mouth[g] is dried up like a
   potsherd,

---

aGk *faith as a grain of*  bOther ancient authorities add verse 21, *But this kind does not come out except by prayer and fasting*  cOther ancient authorities read *living*  dGk *didrachma*  eGk *he*  fGk *stater*; the stater was worth two didrachmas  gCn: Heb *strength*

and my tongue sticks to my
    jaws;
you lay me in the dust of
    death.

16  For dogs are all around me;
    a company of evildoers
       encircles me.
  My hands and feet have
    shriveled; a
17  I can count all my bones.
  They stare and gloat over me;
18  they divide my clothes among
    themselves,
    and for my clothing they cast
      lots.

## PROVERBS 5.7–14

**A**ND now, my child, b listen to
    me,
and do not depart from the
    words of my mouth.
8  Keep your way far from her,

and do not go near the door
    of her house;
9  or you will give your honor to
    others,
    and your years to the
      merciless,
10  and strangers will take their fill
    of your wealth,
    and your labors will go to the
      house of an alien;
11  and at the end of your life you
    will groan,
    when your flesh and body are
      consumed,
12  and you say, "Oh, how I hated
    discipline,
    and my heart despised
      reproof!
13  I did not listen to the voice of
    my teachers
    or incline my ear to my
      instructors.
14  Now I am at the point of utter
    ruin
    in the public assembly."

# JANUARY 27

## EXODUS 4.1—5.21

**T**HEN Moses answered, "But suppose they do not believe me or listen to me, but say, 'The LORD did not appear to you.'" 2 The LORD said to him, "What is that in your hand?" He said, "A staff." 3 And he said, "Throw it on the ground." So he threw the staff on the ground, and it became a snake; and Moses drew back from it. 4 Then the LORD said to Moses, "Reach out your hand, and seize it by the tail"—so he reached out his hand and grasped it, and it became a staff in his hand— 5 "so that they may believe that the LORD, the God of their ancestors, the God of Abraham, the God of Isaac, and the God of Jacob, has appeared to you."

6  Again, the LORD said to him, "Put your hand inside your cloak." He put his hand into his cloak; and when he took it out, his hand was leprous, c as white as snow. 7 Then God said, "Put your hand back into your cloak"—so he put his hand back into his cloak, and when he took it out, it was restored like

a Meaning of Heb uncertain   b Gk Vg: Heb *children*   c A term for several skin diseases; precise
meaning uncertain

the rest of his body— [8]"If they will not believe you or heed the first sign, they may believe the second sign. [9]If they will not believe even these two signs or heed you, you shall take some water from the Nile and pour it on the dry ground; and the water that you shall take from the Nile will become blood on the dry ground."

10 But Moses said to the LORD, "O my Lord, I have never been eloquent, neither in the past nor even now that you have spoken to your servant; but I am slow of speech and slow of tongue." [11]Then the LORD said to him, "Who gives speech to mortals? Who makes them mute or deaf, seeing or blind? Is it not I, the LORD? [12]Now go, and I will be with your mouth and teach you what you are to speak." [13]But he said, "O my Lord, please send someone else." [14]Then the anger of the LORD was kindled against Moses and he said, "What of your brother Aaron, the Levite? I know that he can speak fluently; even now he is coming out to meet you, and when he sees you his heart will be glad. [15]You shall speak to him and put the words in his mouth; and I will be with your mouth and with his mouth, and will teach you what you shall do. [16]He indeed shall speak for you to the people; he shall serve as a mouth for you, and you shall serve as God for him. [17]Take in your hand this staff, with which you shall perform the signs."

18 Moses went back to his father-in-law Jethro and said to him, "Please let me go back to my kindred in Egypt and see whether they are still living." And Jethro said to Moses, "Go in peace." [19]The LORD said to Moses in Midian, "Go back to Egypt; for all those who were seeking your life are dead." [20]So Moses took his wife and his sons, put them on a donkey and went back to the land of Egypt; and Moses carried the staff of God in his hand.

21 And the LORD said to Moses, "When you go back to Egypt, see that you perform before Pharaoh all the wonders that I have put in your power; but I will harden his heart, so that he will not let the people go. [22]Then you shall say to Pharaoh, 'Thus says the LORD: Israel is my firstborn son. [23]I said to you, "Let my son go that he may worship me." But you refused to let him go; now I will kill your firstborn son.' "

24 On the way, at a place where they spent the night, the LORD met him and tried to kill him. [25]But Zipporah took a flint and cut off her son's foreskin, and touched Moses'[a] feet with it, and said, "Truly you are a bridegroom of blood to me!" [26]So he let him alone. It was then she said, "A bridegroom of blood by circumcision."

27 The LORD said to Aaron, "Go into the wilderness to meet Moses." So he went; and he met him at the mountain of God and kissed him. [28]Moses told Aaron all the words of the LORD with which he had sent him, and all the signs with which he had charged him. [29]Then Moses and Aaron went and assembled all the elders of the Israelites. [30]Aaron spoke all the words that the LORD had spoken to Moses, and performed the signs in the sight of the people. [31]The people believed; and when they heard that the LORD had given heed to the Israelites and that he had seen their misery, they bowed down and worshiped.

5.1 AFTERWARD Moses and Aaron went to Pharaoh and said, "Thus says the LORD, the God of Israel, 'Let my people go, so that they may celebrate a festival to me in the wilderness.' " [2]But Pharaoh said, "Who is the LORD, that I should heed him and let Israel go? I do not know the LORD, and I will not let Israel go." [3]Then they said, "The God

a Heb *his*

of the Hebrews has revealed himself to us; let us go a three days' journey into the wilderness to sacrifice to the LORD our God, or he will fall upon us with pestilence or sword." [4]But the king of Egypt said to them, "Moses and Aaron, why are you taking the people away from their work? Get to your labors!" [5]Pharaoh continued, "Now they are more numerous than the people of the land [a] and yet you want them to stop working!" [6]That same day Pharaoh commanded the taskmasters of the people, as well as their supervisors, [7]"You shall no longer give the people straw to make bricks, as before; let them go and gather straw for themselves. [8]But you shall require of them the same quantity of bricks as they have made previously; do not diminish it, for they are lazy; that is why they cry, 'Let us go and offer sacrifice to our God.' [9]Let heavier work be laid on them; then they will labor at it and pay no attention to deceptive words."

10 So the taskmasters and the supervisors of the people went out and said to the people, "Thus says Pharaoh, 'I will not give you straw. [11]Go and get straw yourselves, wherever you can find it; but your work will not be lessened in the least.' " [12]So the people scattered throughout the land of Egypt, to gather stubble for straw. [13]The taskmasters were urgent, saying, "Complete your work, the same daily assignment as when you were given straw." [14]And the supervisors of the Israelites, whom Pharaoh's taskmasters had set over them, were beaten, and were asked, "Why did you not finish the required quantity of bricks yesterday and today, as you did before?"

15 Then the Israelite supervisors came to Pharaoh and cried, "Why do you treat your servants like this? [16]No straw is given to your servants, yet they say to us, 'Make bricks!' Look how your servants are beaten! You are unjust to your own people."[b] [17]He said, "You are lazy, lazy; that is why you say, 'Let us go and sacrifice to the LORD.' [18]Go now, and work; for no straw shall be given you, but you shall still deliver the same number of bricks." [19]The Israelite supervisors saw that they were in trouble when they were told, "You shall not lessen your daily number of bricks." [20]As they left Pharaoh, they came upon Moses and Aaron who were waiting to meet them. [21]They said to them, "The LORD look upon you and judge! You have brought us into bad odor with Pharaoh and his officials, and have put a sword in their hand to kill us."

## MATTHEW 18.1–22

AT that time the disciples came to Jesus and asked, "Who is the greatest in the kingdom of heaven?" [2]He called a child, whom he put among them, [3]and said, "Truly I tell you, unless you change and become like children, you will never enter the kingdom of heaven. [4]Whoever becomes humble like this child is the greatest in the kingdom of heaven. [5]Whoever welcomes one such child in my name welcomes me.

6 "If any of you put a stumbling block before one of these little ones who believe in me, it would be better for you if a great millstone were fastened around your neck and you were drowned in the depth of the sea. [7]Woe to the world because of stumbling blocks! Occasions for stumbling are bound to come, but woe to the one by whom the stumbling block comes!

8 "If your hand or your foot causes you to stumble, cut it off and throw it away; it is better for you to enter life maimed or lame than to have two hands or two feet and to be thrown into the

---

a Sam: Heb *The people of the land are now many*   b Gk Compare Syr Vg: Heb *beaten, and the sin of your people*

eternal fire. [9]And if your eye causes you to stumble, tear it out and throw it away; it is better for you to enter life with one eye than to have two eyes and to be thrown into the hell[a] of fire.

10 "Take care that you do not despise one of these little ones; for, I tell you, in heaven their angels continually see the face of my Father in heaven.[b] [12]What do you think? If a shepherd has a hundred sheep, and one of them has gone astray, does he not leave the ninety-nine on the mountains and go in search of the one that went astray? [13]And if he finds it, truly I tell you, he rejoices over it more than over the ninety-nine that never went astray. [14]So it is not the will of your[c] Father in heaven that one of these little ones should be lost.

15 "If another member of the church[d] sins against you,[e] go and point out the fault when the two of you are alone. If the member listens to you, you have regained that one.[f] [16]But if you are not listened to, take one or two others along with you, so that every word may be confirmed by the evidence of two or three witnesses. [17]If the member refuses to listen to them, tell it to the church; and if the offender refuses to listen even to the church, let such a one be to you as a Gentile and a tax collector. [18]Truly I tell you, whatever you bind on earth will be bound in heaven, and whatever you loose on earth will be loosed in heaven. [19]Again, truly I tell you, if two of you agree on earth about anything you ask, it will be done for you by my Father in heaven. [20]For where two or three are gathered in my name, I am there among them."

21 Then Peter came and said to him, "Lord, if another member of the church[g] sins against me, how often should I forgive? As many as seven times?" [22]Jesus said to him, "Not seven times, but, I tell you, seventy-seven[h] times.

## PSALM 22. 19–31

**B**UT you, O LORD, do not be far away!
O my help, come quickly to my aid!
20   Deliver my soul from the sword,
my life[i] from the power of the dog!
21   Save me from the mouth of the lion!

From the horns of the wild oxen
you have rescued[j] me.
22   I will tell of your name to my brothers and sisters;[k]
in the midst of the congregation I will praise you:
23   You who fear the LORD, praise him!
All you offspring of Jacob, glorify him;
stand in awe of him, all you offspring of Israel!
24   For he did not despise or abhor the affliction of the afflicted;
he did not hide his face from me,[l]
but heard when I[m] cried to him.

25   From you comes my praise in the great congregation;
my vows I will pay before those who fear him.
26   The poor[n] shall eat and be satisfied;
those who seek him shall praise the LORD.

aGk *Gehenna*   bOther ancient authorities add verse 11, *For the Son of Man came to save the lost*
cOther ancient authorities read *my*   dGk *If your brother*   eOther ancient authorities lack *against you*
fGk *the brother*   gGk *if my brother*   hOr *seventy times seven*   iHeb *my only one*   jHeb *answered*
kOr *kindred*   lHeb *him*   mHeb *he*   nOr *afflicted*

May your hearts live forever!

27 All the ends of the earth shall
        remember
    and turn to the LORD;
    and all the families of the
        nations
        shall worship before him. a
28 For dominion belongs to the
        LORD,
    and he rules over the nations.

29 To him, b indeed, shall all who
        sleep in c the earth bow
        down;
    before him shall bow all who
        go down to the dust,
    and I shall live for him. d
30 Posterity will serve him;
    future generations will be told
        about the Lord,
31 and e proclaim his deliverance to
        a people yet unborn,
    saying that he has done it.

16 Should your springs be
        scattered abroad,
    streams of water in the
        streets?
17 Let them be for yourself alone,
    and not for sharing with
        strangers.
18 Let your fountain be blessed,
    and rejoice in the wife of your
        youth,
19    a lovely deer, a graceful doe.
    May her breasts satisfy you at
        all times;
    may you be intoxicated
        always by her love.
20 Why should you be intoxicated,
        my son, by another
        woman
    and embrace the bosom of an
        adulteress?
21 For human ways are under the
        eyes of the LORD,
    and he examines all their
        paths.

## PROVERBS 5.15–21

Drink water from your own cistern,
flowing water from your own well.

# JANUARY 28

## EXODUS 5.22—7.24

Then Moses turned again to the Lord and said, "O Lord, why have you mistreated this people? Why did you ever send me? 23Since I first came to Pharaoh to speak in your name, he has mistreated this people, and you have done nothing at all to deliver your people."

6.1 Then the Lord said to Moses, "Now you shall see what I will do to Pharaoh:

aGk Syr Jerome: Heb *you*   bCn: Heb *They have eaten and*   cCn: Heb *all the fat ones*   dCompare Gk
Syr Vg: Heb *and he who cannot keep himself alive*   eCompare Gk: Heb *it will be told about the Lord
to the generation, 31they will come and*

Indeed, by a mighty hand he will let them go; by a mighty hand he will drive them out of his land."

2 God also spoke to Moses and said to him: "I am the LORD. ³I appeared to Abraham, Isaac, and Jacob as God Almighty,ᵃ but by my name 'The LORD'ᵇ I did not make myself known to them. ⁴I also established my covenant with them, to give them the land of Canaan, the land in which they resided as aliens. ⁵I have also heard the groaning of the Israelites whom the Egyptians are holding as slaves, and I have remembered my covenant. ⁶Say therefore to the Israelites, 'I am the LORD, and I will free you from the burdens of the Egyptians and deliver you from slavery to them. I will redeem you with an outstretched arm and with mighty acts of judgment. ⁷I will take you as my people, and I will be your God. You shall know that I am the LORD your God, who has freed you from the burdens of the Egyptians. ⁸I will bring you into the land that I swore to give to Abraham, Isaac, and Jacob; I will give it to you for a possession. I am the LORD.'" ⁹Moses told this to the Israelites; but they would not listen to Moses, because of their broken spirit and their cruel slavery.

10 Then the LORD spoke to Moses, ¹¹"Go and tell Pharaoh king of Egypt to let the Israelites go out of his land." ¹²But Moses spoke to the LORD, "The Israelites have not listened to me; how then shall Pharaoh listen to me, poor speaker that I am?"ᶜ ¹³Thus the LORD spoke to Moses and Aaron, and gave them orders regarding the Israelites and Pharaoh king of Egypt, charging them to free the Israelites from the land of Egypt.

14 The following are the heads of their ancestral houses: the sons of Reuben, the firstborn of Israel: Hanoch, Pallu, Hezron, and Carmi; these are the families of Reuben. ¹⁵The sons of Simeon: Jemuel, Jamin, Ohad, Jachin, Zohar, and Shaul,ᵈ the son of a Canaanite woman; these are the families of Simeon. ¹⁶The following are the names of the sons of Levi according to their genealogies: Gershon,ᵉ Kohath, and Merari, and the length of Levi's life was one hundred thirty-seven years. ¹⁷The sons of Gershon:ᵉ Libni and Shimei, by their families. ¹⁸The sons of Kohath: Amram, Izhar, Hebron, and Uzziel, and the length of Kohath's life was one hundred thirty-three years. ¹⁹The sons of Merari: Mahli and Mushi. These are the families of the Levites according to their genealogies. ²⁰Amram married Jochebed his father's sister and she bore him Aaron and Moses, and the length of Amram's life was one hundred thirty-seven years. ²¹The sons of Izhar: Korah, Nepheg, and Zichri. ²²The sons of Uzziel: Mishael, Elzaphan, and Sithri. ²³Aaron married Elisheba, daughter of Amminadab and sister of Nahshon, and she bore him Nadab, Abihu, Eleazar, and Ithamar. ²⁴The sons of Korah: Assir, Elkanah, and Abiasaph; these are the families of the Korahites. ²⁵Aaron's son Eleazar married one of the daughters of Putiel, and she bore him Phinehas. These are the heads of the ancestral houses of the Levites by their families.

26 It was this same Aaron and Moses to whom the LORD said, "Bring the Israelites out of the land of Egypt, company by company." ²⁷It was they who spoke to Pharaoh king of Egypt to bring the Israelites out of Egypt, the same Moses and Aaron.

28 On the day when the LORD spoke to Moses in the land of Egypt, ²⁹he said to him, "I am the LORD; tell Pharaoh king of Egypt all that I am speaking to you." ³⁰But Moses said in

the Lord's presence, "Since I am a poor speaker, [a] why would Pharaoh listen to me?"

**7.1** The Lord said to Moses, "See, I have made you like God to Pharaoh, and your brother Aaron shall be your prophet. [2]You shall speak all that I command you, and your brother Aaron shall tell Pharaoh to let the Israelites go out of his land. [3]But I will harden Pharaoh's heart, and I will multiply my signs and wonders in the land of Egypt. [4]When Pharaoh does not listen to you, I will lay my hand upon Egypt and bring my people the Israelites, company by company, out of the land of Egypt by great acts of judgment. [5]The Egyptians shall know that I am the Lord, when I stretch out my hand against Egypt and bring the Israelites out from among them." [6]Moses and Aaron did so; they did just as the Lord commanded them. [7]Moses was eighty years old and Aaron eighty-three when they spoke to Pharaoh.

8 The Lord said to Moses and Aaron, [9]"When Pharaoh says to you, 'Perform a wonder,' then you shall say to Aaron, 'Take your staff and throw it down before Pharaoh, and it will become a snake.'" [10]So Moses and Aaron went to Pharaoh and did as the Lord had commanded; Aaron threw down his staff before Pharaoh and his officials, and it became a snake. [11]Then Pharaoh summoned the wise men and the sorcerers; and they also, the magicians of Egypt, did the same by their secret arts. [12]Each one threw down his staff, and they became snakes; but Aaron's staff swallowed up theirs. [13]Still Pharaoh's heart was hardened, and he would not listen to them, as the Lord had said.

14 Then the Lord said to Moses, "Pharaoh's heart is hardened; he refuses to let the people go. [15]Go to Pharaoh in the morning, as he is going out to the water; stand by at the river bank to meet him, and take in your hand the staff that was turned into a snake. [16]Say to him, 'The Lord, the God of the Hebrews, sent me to you to say, "Let my people go, so that they may worship me in the wilderness." But until now you have not listened.' [17]Thus says the Lord, "By this you shall know that I am the Lord." See, with the staff that is in my hand I will strike the water that is in the Nile, and it shall be turned to blood. [18]The fish in the river shall die, the river itself shall stink, and the Egyptians shall be unable to drink water from the Nile.'" [19]The Lord said to Moses, "Say to Aaron, 'Take your staff and stretch out your hand over the waters of Egypt—over its rivers, its canals, and its ponds, and all its pools of water—so that they may become blood; and there shall be blood throughout the whole land of Egypt, even in vessels of wood and in vessels of stone.'"

20 Moses and Aaron did just as the Lord commanded. In the sight of Pharaoh and of his officials he lifted up the staff and struck the water in the river, and all the water in the river was turned into blood, [21]and the fish in the river died. The river stank so that the Egyptians could not drink its water, and there was blood throughout the whole land of Egypt. [22]But the magicians of Egypt did the same by their secret arts; so Pharaoh's heart remained hardened, and he would not listen to them; as the Lord had said. [23]Pharaoh turned and went into his house, and he did not take even this to heart. [24]And all the Egyptians had to dig along the Nile for water to drink, for they could not drink the water of the river.

**a** Heb *am uncircumcised of lips*; see 6.12

## MATTHEW 18.23—19.12

"For this reason the kingdom of heaven may be compared to a king who wished to settle accounts with his slaves. 24When he began the reckoning, one who owed him ten thousand talents[a] was brought to him; 25and, as he could not pay, his lord ordered him to be sold, together with his wife and children and all his possessions, and payment to be made. 26So the slave fell on his knees before him, saying, 'Have patience with me, and I will pay you everything.' 27And out of pity for him, the lord of that slave released him and forgave him the debt. 28But that same slave, as he went out, came upon one of his fellow slaves who owed him a hundred denarii;[b] and seizing him by the throat, he said, 'Pay what you owe.' 29Then his fellow slave fell down and pleaded with him, 'Have patience with me, and I will pay you.' 30But he refused; then he went and threw him into prison until he would pay the debt. 31When his fellow slaves saw what had happened, they were greatly distressed, and they went and reported to their lord all that had taken place. 32Then his lord summoned him and said to him, 'You wicked slave! I forgave you all that debt because you pleaded with me. 33Should you not have had mercy on your fellow slave, as I had mercy on you?' 34And in anger his lord handed him over to be tortured until he would pay his entire debt. 35So my heavenly Father will also do to every one of you, if you do not forgive your brother or sister[c] from your heart."

19.1 When Jesus had finished saying these things, he left Galilee and went to the region of Judea beyond the Jordan. 2Large crowds followed him, and he cured them there.

3 Some Pharisees came to him, and to test him they asked, "Is it lawful for a man to divorce his wife for any cause?" 4He answered, "Have you not read that the one who made them at the beginning 'made them male and female,' 5and said, 'For this reason a man shall leave his father and mother and be joined to his wife, and the two shall become one flesh'? 6So they are no longer two, but one flesh. Therefore what God has joined together, let no one separate." 7They said to him, "Why then did Moses command us to give a certificate of dismissal and to divorce her?" 8He said to them, "It was because you were so hard-hearted that Moses allowed you to divorce your wives, but from the beginning it was not so. 9And I say to you, whoever divorces his wife, except for unchastity, and marries another commits adultery."[d]

10 His disciples said to him, "If such is the case of a man with his wife, it is better not to marry." 11But he said to them, "Not everyone can accept this teaching, but only those to whom it is given. 12For there are eunuchs who have been so from birth, and there are eunuchs who have been made eunuchs by others, and there are eunuchs who have made themselves eunuchs for the sake of the kingdom of heaven. Let anyone accept this who can."

## PSALM 23.1–6

*A Psalm of David.*

The Lord is my shepherd, I
    shall not want.
2    He makes me lie down
    in green pastures;
he leads me beside still
    waters;[e]
3    he restores my soul.[f]

aA talent was worth more than fifteen years' wages of a laborer   bThe denarius was the usual day's wage for a laborer   cGk *brother*   dOther ancient authorities read *except on the ground of unchastity, causes her to commit adultery*; others add at the end of the verse *and he who marries a divorced woman commits adultery*   eHeb *waters of rest*   fOr *life*

He leads me in right paths[a]
   for his name's sake.

4 Even though I walk through the
   darkest valley,[b]
I fear no evil;
   for you are with me;
     your rod and your staff—
     they comfort me.

5 You prepare a table before me
   in the presence of my
     enemies;
you anoint my head with oil;
   my cup overflows.

6 Surely[c] goodness and mercy[d]
   shall follow me
   all the days of my life,
and I shall dwell in the house of
   the LORD
   my whole life long.[e]

## PROVERBS 5.22–23

THE iniquities of the wicked
   ensnare them,
   and they are caught in the
     toils of their sin.
23 They die for lack of discipline,
   and because of their great
     folly they are lost.

# JANUARY 29

## EXODUS 7.25—9.35

SEVEN days passed after the LORD had struck the Nile.

**8f.1** THEN the LORD said to Moses, "Go to Pharaoh and say to him, 'Thus says the LORD: Let my people go, so that they may worship me. [2]If you refuse to let them go, I will plague your whole country with frogs. [3]The river shall swarm with frogs; they shall come up into your palace, into your bedchamber and your bed, and into the houses of your officials and of your people,[g] and into your ovens and your kneading bowls. [4]The frogs shall come up on you and on your people and on all your officials.' " [5h]And the LORD said to Moses, "Say to Aaron, 'Stretch out your hand with your staff over the rivers, the canals, and the pools, and make frogs come up on the land of Egypt.' " [6]So Aaron stretched out his hand over the waters of Egypt; and the frogs came up and covered the land of Egypt. [7]But the magicians did the same by their secret arts, and brought frogs up on the land of Egypt.

8 Then Pharaoh called Moses and Aaron, and said, "Pray to the LORD to take away the frogs from me and my people, and I will let the people go to sacrifice to the LORD." [9]Moses said to Pharaoh, "Kindly tell me when I am to pray for you and for your officials and for your people, that the frogs may be removed from you and your houses and be left only in the Nile." [10]And he said, "Tomorrow." Moses said, "As you say! So that you may know that there is no one like the LORD our God, [11]the frogs shall leave you and your houses and your officials and your people; they shall be left only in the Nile." [12]Then

a Or *paths of righteousness*   b Or *the valley of the shadow of death*   c Or *Only*   d Or *kindness*   e Heb *for length of days*   f Ch 7.26 in Heb   g Gk: Heb *upon your people*   h Ch 8.1 in Heb

Moses and Aaron went out from Pharaoh; and Moses cried out to the Lord concerning the frogs that he had brought upon Pharaoh. [a] 13And the Lord did as Moses requested: the frogs died in the houses, the courtyards, and the fields. 14And they gathered them together in heaps, and the land stank. 15But when Pharaoh saw that there was a respite, he hardened his heart, and would not listen to them, just as the Lord had said.

16 Then the Lord said to Moses, "Say to Aaron, 'Stretch out your staff and strike the dust of the earth, so that it may become gnats throughout the whole land of Egypt.'" 17And they did so; Aaron stretched out his hand with his staff and struck the dust of the earth, and gnats came on humans and animals alike; all the dust of the earth turned into gnats throughout the whole land of Egypt. 18The magicians tried to produce gnats by their secret arts, but they could not. There were gnats on both humans and animals. 19And the magicians said to Pharaoh, "This is the finger of God!" But Pharaoh's heart was hardened, and he would not listen to them, just as the Lord had said.

20 Then the Lord said to Moses, "Rise early in the morning and present yourself before Pharaoh, as he goes out to the water, and say to him, 'Thus says the Lord: Let my people go, so that they may worship me. 21For if you will not let my people go, I will send swarms of flies on you, your officials, and your people, and into your houses; and the houses of the Egyptians shall be filled with swarms of flies; so also the land where they live. 22But on that day I will set apart the land of Goshen, where my people live, so that no swarms of flies shall be there, that you may know that I the Lord am in this land. 23Thus I will make a distinction[b] between my people and your people.

This sign shall appear tomorrow.'" 24The Lord did so, and great swarms of flies came into the house of Pharaoh and into his officials' houses; in all of Egypt the land was ruined because of the flies.

25 Then Pharaoh summoned Moses and Aaron, and said, "Go, sacrifice to your God within the land." 26But Moses said, "It would not be right to do so; for the sacrifices that we offer to the Lord our God are offensive to the Egyptians. If we offer in the sight of the Egyptians sacrifices that are offensive to them, will they not stone us? 27We must go a three days' journey into the wilderness and sacrifice to the Lord our God as he commands us." 28So Pharaoh said, "I will let you go to sacrifice to the Lord your God in the wilderness, provided you do not go very far away. Pray for me." 29Then Moses said, "As soon as I leave you, I will pray to the Lord that the swarms of flies may depart tomorrow from Pharaoh, from his officials, and from his people; only do not let Pharaoh again deal falsely by not letting the people go to sacrifice to the Lord."

30 So Moses went out from Pharaoh and prayed to the Lord. 31And the Lord did as Moses asked: he removed the swarms of flies from Pharaoh, from his officials, and from his people; not one remained. 32But Pharaoh hardened his heart this time also, and would not let the people go.

9.1 Then the Lord said to Moses, "Go to Pharaoh, and say to him, 'Thus says the Lord, the God of the Hebrews: Let my people go, so that they may worship me. 2For if you refuse to let them go and still hold them, 3the hand of the Lord will strike with a deadly pestilence your livestock in the field: the horses, the donkeys, the camels, the herds, and the flocks. 4But the Lord will make

a Or *frogs, as he had agreed with Pharaoh*   b Gk Vg: Heb *will set redemption*

a distinction between the livestock of Israel and the livestock of Egypt, so that nothing shall die of all that belongs to the Israelites.'" 5The LORD set a time, saying, "Tomorrow the LORD will do this thing in the land." 6And on the next day the LORD did so; all the livestock of the Egyptians died, but of the livestock of the Israelites not one died. 7Pharaoh inquired and found that not one of the livestock of the Israelites was dead. But the heart of Pharaoh was hardened, and he would not let the people go.

8 Then the LORD said to Moses and Aaron, "Take handfuls of soot from the kiln, and let Moses throw it in the air in the sight of Pharaoh. 9It shall become fine dust all over the land of Egypt, and shall cause festering boils on humans and animals throughout the whole land of Egypt." 10So they took soot from the kiln, and stood before Pharaoh, and Moses threw it in the air, and it caused festering boils on humans and animals. 11The magicians could not stand before Moses because of the boils, for the boils afflicted the magicians as well as all the Egyptians. 12But the LORD hardened the heart of Pharaoh, and he would not listen to them, just as the LORD had spoken to Moses.

13 Then the LORD said to Moses, "Rise up early in the morning and present yourself before Pharaoh, and say to him, 'Thus says the LORD, the God of the Hebrews: Let my people go, so that they may worship me. 14For this time I will send all my plagues upon you yourself, and upon your officials, and upon your people, so that you may know that there is no one like me in all the earth. 15For by now I could have stretched out my hand and struck you and your people with pestilence, and you would have been cut off from the earth. 16But this is why I have let you live: to show you my power, and to make my name resound through all the earth. 17You are still exalting yourself

against my people, and will not let them go. 18Tomorrow at this time I will cause the heaviest hail to fall that has ever fallen in Egypt from the day it was founded until now. 19Send, therefore, and have your livestock and everything that you have in the open field brought to a secure place; every human or animal that is in the open field and is not brought under shelter will die when the hail comes down upon them.'" 20Those officials of Pharaoh who feared the word of the LORD hurried their slaves and livestock off to a secure place. 21Those who did not regard the word of the LORD left their slaves and livestock in the open field.

22 The LORD said to Moses, "Stretch out your hand toward heaven so that hail may fall on the whole land of Egypt, on humans and animals and all the plants of the field in the land of Egypt." 23Then Moses stretched out his staff toward heaven, and the LORD sent thunder and hail, and fire came down on the earth. And the LORD rained hail on the land of Egypt; 24there was hail with fire flashing continually in the midst of it, such heavy hail as had never fallen in all the land of Egypt since it became a nation. 25The hail struck down everything that was in the open field throughout all the land of Egypt, both human and animal; the hail also struck down all the plants of the field, and shattered every tree in the field. 26Only in the land of Goshen, where the Israelites were, there was no hail.

27 Then Pharaoh summoned Moses and Aaron, and said to them, "This time I have sinned; the LORD is in the right, and I and my people are in the wrong. 28Pray to the LORD! Enough of God's thunder and hail! I will let you go; you need stay no longer." 29Moses said to him, "As soon as I have gone out of the city, I will stretch out my hands to the LORD; the thunder will cease, and there will be no more hail, so that you may know that the earth is the LORD's.

30But as for you and your officials, I know that you do not yet fear the Lord God." 31(Now the flax and the barley were ruined, for the barley was in the ear and the flax was in bud. 32But the wheat and the spelt were not ruined, for they are late in coming up.) 33So Moses left Pharaoh, went out of the city, and stretched out his hands to the Lord; then the thunder and the hail ceased, and the rain no longer poured down on the earth. 34But when Pharaoh saw that the rain and the hail and the thunder had ceased, he sinned once more and hardened his heart, he and his officials. 35So the heart of Pharaoh was hardened, and he would not let the Israelites go, just as the Lord had spoken through Moses.

## MATTHEW 19.13–30

THEN little children were being brought to him in order that he might lay his hands on them and pray. The disciples spoke sternly to those who brought them; 14but Jesus said, "Let the little children come to me, and do not stop them; for it is to such as these that the kingdom of heaven belongs." 15And he laid his hands on them and went on his way.

16 Then someone came to him and said, "Teacher, what good deed must I do to have eternal life?" 17And he said to him, "Why do you ask me about what is good? There is only one who is good. If you wish to enter into life, keep the commandments." 18He said to him, "Which ones?" And Jesus said, "You shall not murder; You shall not commit adultery; You shall not steal; You shall not bear false witness; 19Honor your father and mother; also, You shall love your neighbor as yourself." 20The young man said to him, "I have kept all these;a what do I still lack?" 21Jesus said to him, "If you wish to be perfect, go, sell your possessions, and give the moneyb to the poor, and you will have treasure in heaven; then come, follow me." 22When the young man heard this word, he went away grieving, for he had many possessions.

23 Then Jesus said to his disciples, "Truly I tell you, it will be hard for a rich person to enter the kingdom of heaven. 24Again I tell you, it is easier for a camel to go through the eye of a needle than for someone who is rich to enter the kingdom of God." 25When the disciples heard this, they were greatly astounded and said, "Then who can be saved?" 26But Jesus looked at them and said, "For mortals it is impossible, but for God all things are possible."

27 Then Peter said in reply, "Look, we have left everything and followed you. What then will we have?" 28Jesus said to them, "Truly I tell you, at the renewal of all things, when the Son of Man is seated on the throne of his glory, you who have followed me will also sit on twelve thrones, judging the twelve tribes of Israel. 29And everyone who has left houses or brothers or sisters or father or mother or children or fields, for my name's sake, will receive a hundredfold, c and will inherit eternal life. 30But many who are first will be last, and the last will be first.

## PSALM 24.1–10

*Of David. A Psalm.*

THE earth is the Lord's and all
    that is in it,
  the world, and those who
    live in it;
2  for he has founded it on the
    seas,
  and established it on the
    rivers.

3  Who shall ascend the hill of the
    Lord?

aOther ancient authorities add *from my youth*  bGk lacks *the money*  cOther ancient authorities read *manifold*

And who shall stand in his
   holy place?
4 Those who have clean hands
   and pure hearts,
  who do not lift up their souls
   to what is false,
  and do not swear deceitfully.
5 They will receive blessing from
   the LORD,
  and vindication from the God
   of their salvation.
6 Such is the company of those
   who seek him,
  who seek the face of the God
   of Jacob. a      *Selah*

7 Lift up your heads, O gates!
  and be lifted up, O ancient
   doors!
  that the King of glory may
   come in.
8 Who is the King of glory?
  The LORD, strong and mighty,
  the LORD, mighty in battle.
9 Lift up your heads, O gates!
  and be lifted up, O ancient
   doors!

  that the King of glory may
   come in.
10 Who is this King of glory?
  The LORD of hosts,
  he is the King of glory.  *Selah*

## PROVERBS 6.1–5

My child, if you have given your pledge to your neighbor,
  if you have bound yourself to
   another, b
2 you are snared by the utterance
   of your lips, c
  caught by the words of your
   mouth.
3 So do this, my child, and save
   yourself,
  for you have come into your
   neighbor's power:
  go, hurry, d and plead with
   your neighbor.
4 Give your eyes no sleep
  and your eyelids no slumber;
5 save yourself like a gazelle from
   the hunter, e
  like a bird from the hand of
   the fowler.

# JANUARY 30

## EXODUS 10.1—12.13

THEN the LORD said to Moses, "Go to Pharaoh; for I have hardened his heart and the heart of his officials, in order that I may show these signs of mine among them, 2and that you may tell your children and grandchildren how I have made fools of the Egyptians and what signs I have done among them—so that you may know that I am the LORD."

3 So Moses and Aaron went to Pharaoh, and said to him, "Thus says the LORD, the God of the Hebrews, 'How long will you refuse to humble yourself before me? Let my people go, so that they may worship me. 4For if you refuse to let my people go, tomorrow I will bring locusts into your coun-

a Gk Syr: Heb *your face, O Jacob*  b Or *a stranger*  c Cn Compare Gk Syr: Heb *the words of your mouth*  d Or *humble yourself*  e Cn: Heb *from the hand*

try. [5]They shall cover the surface of the land, so that no one will be able to see the land. They shall devour the last remnant left you after the hail, and they shall devour every tree of yours that grows in the field. [6]They shall fill your houses, and the houses of all your officials and of all the Egyptians— something that neither your parents nor your grandparents have seen, from the day they came on earth to this day.'" Then he turned and went out from Pharaoh.

7 Pharaoh's officials said to him, "How long shall this fellow be a snare to us? Let the people go, so that they may worship the LORD their God; do you not yet understand that Egypt is ruined?" [8]So Moses and Aaron were brought back to Pharaoh, and he said to them, "Go, worship the LORD your God! But which ones are to go?" [9]Moses said, "We will go with our young and our old; we will go with our sons and daughters and with our flocks and herds, because we have the LORD's festival to celebrate." [10]He said to them, "The LORD indeed will be with you, if ever I let your little ones go with you! Plainly, you have some evil purpose in mind. [11]No, never! Your men may go and worship the LORD, for that is what you are asking." And they were driven out from Pharaoh's presence.

12 Then the LORD said to Moses, "Stretch out your hand over the land of Egypt, so that the locusts may come upon it and eat every plant in the land, all that the hail has left." [13]So Moses stretched out his staff over the land of Egypt, and the LORD brought an east wind upon the land all that day and all that night; when morning came, the east wind had brought the locusts. [14]The locusts came upon all the land of Egypt and settled on the whole country of Egypt, such a dense swarm of locusts as had never been before, nor

ever shall be again. [15]They covered the surface of the whole land, so that the land was black; and they ate all the plants in the land and all the fruit of the trees that the hail had left; nothing green was left, no tree, no plant in the field, in all the land of Egypt. [16]Pharaoh hurriedly summoned Moses and Aaron and said, "I have sinned against the LORD your God, and against you. [17]Do forgive my sin just this once, and pray to the LORD your God that at the least he remove this deadly thing from me." [18]So he went out from Pharaoh and prayed to the LORD. [19]The LORD changed the wind into a very strong west wind, which lifted the locusts and drove them into the Red Sea;[a] not a single locust was left in all the country of Egypt. [20]But the LORD hardened Pharaoh's heart, and he would not let the Israelites go.

21 Then the LORD said to Moses, "Stretch out your hand toward heaven so that there may be darkness over the land of Egypt, a darkness that can be felt." [22]So Moses stretched out his hand toward heaven, and there was dense darkness in all the land of Egypt for three days. [23]People could not see one another, and for three days they could not move from where they were; but all the Israelites had light where they lived. [24]Then Pharaoh summoned Moses, and said, "Go, worship the LORD. Only your flocks and your herds shall remain behind. Even your children may go with you." [25]But Moses said, "You must also let us have sacrifices and burnt offerings to sacrifice to the LORD our God. [26]Our livestock also must go with us; not a hoof shall be left behind, for we must choose some of them for the worship of the LORD our God, and we will not know what to use to worship the LORD until we arrive there." [27]But the LORD hardened Pharaoh's heart, and he was unwilling to let

[a] Or *Sea of Reeds*

them go. <sup>28</sup>Then Pharaoh said to him, "Get away from me! Take care that you do not see my face again, for on the day you see my face you shall die." <sup>29</sup>Moses said, "Just as you say! I will never see your face again."

11.1 THE LORD said to Moses, "I will bring one more plague upon Pharaoh and upon Egypt; afterwards he will let you go from here; indeed, when he lets you go, he will drive you away. <sup>2</sup>Tell the people that every man is to ask his neighbor and every woman is to ask her neighbor for objects of silver and gold." <sup>3</sup>The LORD gave the people favor in the sight of the Egyptians. Moreover, Moses himself was a man of great importance in the land of Egypt, in the sight of Pharaoh's officials and in the sight of the people.

4 Moses said, "Thus says the LORD: About midnight I will go out through Egypt. <sup>5</sup>Every firstborn in the land of Egypt shall die, from the first-born of Pharaoh who sits on his throne to the firstborn of the female slave who is behind the handmill, and all the firstborn of the livestock. <sup>6</sup>Then there will be a loud cry throughout the whole land of Egypt, such as has never been or will ever be again. <sup>7</sup>But not a dog shall growl at any of the Israelites—not at people, not at animals—so that you may know that the LORD makes a distinction between Egypt and Israel. <sup>8</sup>Then all these officials of yours shall come down to me, and bow low to me, saying, 'Leave us, you and all the people who follow you.' After that I will leave." And in hot anger he left Pharaoh.

9 The LORD said to Moses, "Pharaoh will not listen to you, in order that my wonders may be multiplied in the land of Egypt." <sup>10</sup>Moses and Aaron performed all these wonders before Pharaoh; but the LORD hardened Pharaoh's heart, and he did not let the people of Israel go out of his land.

12.1 THE LORD said to Moses and Aaron in the land of Egypt: <sup>2</sup>This month shall mark for you the beginning of months; it shall be the first month of the year for you. <sup>3</sup>Tell the whole congregation of Israel that on the tenth of this month they are to take a lamb for each family, a lamb for each household. <sup>4</sup>If a household is too small for a whole lamb, it shall join its closest neighbor in obtaining one; the lamb shall be divided in proportion to the number of people who eat of it. <sup>5</sup>Your lamb shall be without blemish, a year-old male; you may take it from the sheep or from the goats. <sup>6</sup>You shall keep it until the fourteenth day of this month; then the whole assembled congregation of Israel shall slaughter it at twilight. <sup>7</sup>They shall take some of the blood and put it on the two doorposts and the lintel of the houses in which they eat it. <sup>8</sup>They shall eat the lamb that same night; they shall eat it roasted over the fire with unleavened bread and bitter herbs. <sup>9</sup>Do not eat any of it raw or boiled in water, but roasted over the fire, with its head, legs, and inner organs. <sup>10</sup>You shall let none of it remain until the morning; anything that remains until the morning you shall burn. <sup>11</sup>This is how you shall eat it: your loins girded, your sandals on your feet, and your staff in your hand; and you shall eat it hurriedly. It is the passover of the LORD. <sup>12</sup>For I will pass through the land of Egypt that night, and I will strike down every firstborn in the land of Egypt, both human beings and animals; on all the gods of Egypt I will execute judgments: I am the LORD. <sup>13</sup>The blood shall be a sign for you on the houses where you live: when I see the blood, I will pass over you, and no plague shall destroy you when I strike the land of Egypt.

## MATTHEW 20.1–28

"**F**OR the kingdom of heaven is like a landowner who went out early in the morning to hire laborers for his vineyard. ²After agreeing with the laborers for the usual daily wage,ᵃ he sent them into his vineyard. ³When he went out about nine o'clock, he saw others standing idle in the marketplace; ⁴and he said to them, 'You also go into the vineyard, and I will pay you whatever is right.' So they went. ⁵When he went out again about noon and about three o'clock, he did the same. ⁶And about five o'clock he went out and found others standing around; and he said to them, 'Why are you standing here idle all day?' ⁷They said to him, 'Because no one has hired us.' He said to them, 'You also go into the vineyard.' ⁸When evening came, the owner of the vineyard said to his manager, 'Call the laborers and give them their pay, beginning with the last and then going to the first.' ⁹When those hired about five o'clock came, each of them received the usual daily wage.ᵃ ¹⁰Now when the first came, they thought they would receive more; but each of them also received the usual daily wage.ᵃ ¹¹And when they received it, they grumbled against the landowner, ¹²saying, 'These last worked only one hour, and you have made them equal to us who have borne the burden of the day and the scorching heat.' ¹³But he replied to one of them, 'Friend, I am doing you no wrong; did you not agree with me for the usual daily wage?ᵃ ¹⁴Take what belongs to you and go; I choose to give to this last the same as I give to you. ¹⁵Am I not allowed to do what I choose with what belongs to me? Or are you envious because I am generous?'ᵇ ¹⁶So the last will be first, and the first will be last."ᶜ

17 While Jesus was going up to Jerusalem, he took the twelve disciples aside by themselves, and said to them on the way, ¹⁸"See, we are going up to Jerusalem, and the Son of Man will be handed over to the chief priests and scribes, and they will condemn him to death; ¹⁹then they will hand him over to the Gentiles to be mocked and flogged and crucified; and on the third day he will be raised."

20 Then the mother of the sons of Zebedee came to him with her sons, and kneeling before him, she asked a favor of him. ²¹And he said to her, "What do you want?" She said to him, "Declare that these two sons of mine will sit, one at your right hand and one at your left, in your kingdom." ²²But Jesus answered, "You do not know what you are asking. Are you able to drink the cup that I am about to drink?"ᵈ They said to him, "We are able." ²³He said to them, "You will indeed drink my cup, but to sit at my right hand and at my left, this is not mine to grant, but it is for those for whom it has been prepared by my Father."

24 When the ten heard it, they were angry with the two brothers. ²⁵But Jesus called them to him and said, "You know that the rulers of the Gentiles lord it over them, and their great ones are tyrants over them. ²⁶It will not be so among you; but whoever wishes to be great among you must be your servant, ²⁷and whoever wishes to be first among you must be your slave; ²⁸just as the Son of Man came not to be served but to serve, and to give his life a ransom for many."

---

ᵃGk *a denarius*  ᵇGk *is your eye evil because I am good?*  ᶜOther ancient authorities add *for many are called but few are chosen*  ᵈOther ancient authorities add *or to be baptized with the baptism that I am baptized with?*

## PSALM 25.1–15

*Of David.*

**T**o you, O LORD, I lift up my
    soul.
2  O my God, in you I trust;
    do not let me be put to
      shame;
    do not let my enemies exult
      over me.
3  Do not let those who wait for
      you be put to shame;
    let them be ashamed who are
      wantonly treacherous.

4  Make me to know your ways,
      O LORD;
    teach me your paths.
5  Lead me in your truth, and
      teach me,
    for you are the God of my
      salvation;
    for you I wait all day long.

6  Be mindful of your mercy,
      O LORD, and of your
      steadfast love,
    for they have been from of
      old.
7  Do not remember the sins of
      my youth or my
      transgressions;
    according to your steadfast
      love remember me,
    for your goodness' sake,
      O LORD!

8  Good and upright is the LORD;
    therefore he instructs sinners
      in the way.
9  He leads the humble in what is
      right,
    and teaches the humble his
      way.
10  All the paths of the LORD are
      steadfast love and
      faithfulness,

    for those who keep his
      covenant and his
      decrees.
11  For your name's sake, O LORD,
      pardon my guilt, for it is
      great.
12  Who are they that fear the
      LORD?
    He will teach them the way
      that they should choose.
13  They will abide in prosperity,
    and their children shall
      possess the land.
14  The friendship of the LORD is for
      those who fear him,
    and he makes his covenant
      known to them.
15  My eyes are ever toward the
      LORD,
    for he will pluck my feet out
      of the net.

## PROVERBS 6.6–11

**G**o to the ant, you lazybones;
    consider its ways, and be
      wise.
7  Without having any chief
    or officer or ruler,
8  it prepares its food in summer,
    and gathers its sustenance in
      harvest.
9  How long will you lie there,
      O lazybones?
    When will you rise from your
      sleep?
10  A little sleep, a little slumber,
    a little folding of the hands
      to rest,
11  and poverty will come upon you
      like a robber,
    and want, like an armed
      warrior.

# JANUARY 31

EXODUS 12.14—13.16

THIS day shall be a day of remembrance for you. You shall celebrate it as a festival to the LORD; throughout your generations you shall observe it as a perpetual ordinance. [15]Seven days you shall eat unleavened bread; on the first day you shall remove leaven from your houses, for whoever eats leavened bread from the first day until the seventh day shall be cut off from Israel. [16]On the first day you shall hold a solemn assembly, and on the seventh day a solemn assembly; no work shall be done on those days; only what everyone must eat, that alone may be prepared by you. [17]You shall observe the festival of unleavened bread, for on this very day I brought your companies out of the land of Egypt: you shall observe this day throughout your generations as a perpetual ordinance. [18]In the first month, from the evening of the fourteenth day until the evening of the twenty-first day, you shall eat unleavened bread. [19]For seven days no leaven shall be found in your houses; for whoever eats what is leavened shall be cut off from the congregation of Israel, whether an alien or a native of the land. [20]You shall eat nothing leavened; in all your settlements you shall eat unleavened bread.

21 Then Moses called all the elders of Israel and said to them, "Go, select lambs for your families, and slaughter the passover lamb. [22]Take a bunch of hyssop, dip it in the blood that is in the basin, and touch the lintel and the two doorposts with the blood in the basin. None of you shall go outside the door of your house until morning. [23]For the LORD will pass through to strike down the Egyptians; when he sees the blood on the lintel and on the two doorposts, the LORD will pass over that door and will not allow the destroyer to enter your houses to strike you down. [24]You shall observe this rite as a perpetual ordinance for you and your children. [25]When you come to the land that the LORD will give you, as he has promised, you shall keep this observance. [26]And when your children ask you, 'What do you mean by this observance?' [27]you shall say, 'It is the passover sacrifice to the LORD, for he passed over the houses of the Israelites in Egypt, when he struck down the Egyptians but spared our houses.'" And the people bowed down and worshiped.

28 The Israelites went and did just as the LORD had commanded Moses and Aaron.

29 At midnight the LORD struck down all the firstborn in the land of Egypt, from the firstborn of Pharaoh who sat on his throne to the firstborn of the prisoner who was in the dungeon, and all the firstborn of the livestock. [30]Pharaoh arose in the night, he and all his officials and all the Egyptians; and there was a loud cry in Egypt, for there was not a house without someone dead. [31]Then he summoned Moses and Aaron in the night, and said, "Rise up, go away from my people, both you and the Israelites! Go, worship the LORD, as you said. [32]Take your flocks and your herds, as you said, and be gone. And bring a blessing on me too!"

33 The Egyptians urged the people to hasten their departure from the land, for they said, "We shall all be dead." [34]So the people took their dough before it was leavened, with their kneading bowls wrapped up in their cloaks on their shoulders. [35]The Israelites had done as Moses told them; they had asked the Egyptians for jewelry of sil-

ver and gold, and for clothing, ³⁶and the LORD had given the people favor in the sight of the Egyptians, so that they let them have what they asked. And so they plundered the Egyptians.

37 The Israelites journeyed from Rameses to Succoth, about six hundred thousand men on foot, besides children. ³⁸A mixed crowd also went up with them, and livestock in great numbers, both flocks and herds. ³⁹They baked unleavened cakes of the dough that they had brought out of Egypt; it was not leavened, because they were driven out of Egypt and could not wait, nor had they prepared any provisions for themselves.

40 The time that the Israelites had lived in Egypt was four hundred thirty years. ⁴¹At the end of four hundred thirty years, on that very day, all the companies of the LORD went out from the land of Egypt. ⁴²That was for the LORD a night of vigil, to bring them out of the land of Egypt. That same night is a vigil to be kept for the LORD by all the Israelites throughout their generations.

43 The LORD said to Moses and Aaron: This is the ordinance for the passover: no foreigner shall eat of it, ⁴⁴but any slave who has been purchased may eat of it after he has been circumcised; ⁴⁵no bound or hired servant may eat of it. ⁴⁶It shall be eaten in one house; you shall not take any of the animal outside the house, and you shall not break any of its bones. ⁴⁷The whole congregation of Israel shall celebrate it. ⁴⁸If an alien who resides with you wants to celebrate the passover to the LORD, all his males shall be circumcised; then he may draw near to celebrate it; he shall be regarded as a native of the land. But no uncircumcised person shall eat of it; ⁴⁹there shall be one law for the native and for the alien who resides among you.

50 All the Israelites did just as the LORD had commanded Moses and Aaron. ⁵¹That very day the LORD brought the Israelites out of the land of Egypt, company by company.

13.1 THE LORD said to Moses: ²Consecrate to me all the firstborn; whatever is the first to open the womb among the Israelites, of human beings and animals, is mine.

3 Moses said to the people, "Remember this day on which you came out of Egypt, out of the house of slavery, because the LORD brought you out from there by strength of hand; no leavened bread shall be eaten. ⁴Today, in the month of Abib, you are going out. ⁵When the LORD brings you into the land of the Canaanites, the Hittites, the Amorites, the Hivites, and the Jebusites, which he swore to your ancestors to give you, a land flowing with milk and honey, you shall keep this observance in this month. ⁶Seven days you shall eat unleavened bread, and on the seventh day there shall be a festival to the LORD. ⁷Unleavened bread shall be eaten for seven days; no leavened bread shall be seen in your possession, and no leaven shall be seen among you in all your territory. ⁸You shall tell your child on that day, 'It is because of what the LORD did for me when I came out of Egypt.' ⁹It shall serve for you as a sign on your hand and as a reminder on your forehead, so that the teaching of the LORD may be on your lips; for with a strong hand the LORD brought you out of Egypt. ¹⁰You shall keep this ordinance at its proper time from year to year.

11 "When the LORD has brought you into the land of the Canaanites, as he swore to you and your ancestors, and has given it to you, ¹²you shall set apart to the LORD all that first opens the womb. All the firstborn of your livestock that are males shall be the LORD's. ¹³But every firstborn donkey you shall redeem with a sheep; if you do not redeem it, you must break its neck.

Every firstborn male among your children you shall redeem. [14]When in the future your child asks you, 'What does this mean?' you shall answer, 'By strength of hand the LORD brought us out of Egypt, from the house of slavery. [15]When Pharaoh stubbornly refused to let us go, the LORD killed all the firstborn in the land of Egypt, from human firstborn to the firstborn of animals. Therefore I sacrifice to the LORD every male that first opens the womb, but every firstborn of my sons I redeem.' [16]It shall serve as a sign on your hand and as an emblem[a] on your forehead that by strength of hand the LORD brought us out of Egypt."

## MATTHEW 20.29—21.22

As they [Jesus and his disciples] were leaving Jericho, a large crowd followed him. [30]There were two blind men sitting by the roadside. When they heard that Jesus was passing by, they shouted, "Lord,[b] have mercy on us, Son of David!" [31]The crowd sternly ordered them to be quiet; but they shouted even more loudly, "Have mercy on us, Lord, Son of David!" [32]Jesus stood still and called them, saying, "What do you want me to do for you?" [33]They said to him, "Lord, let our eyes be opened." [34]Moved with compassion, Jesus touched their eyes. Immediately they regained their sight and followed him.

[21.1] WHEN they had come near Jerusalem and had reached Bethphage, at the Mount of Olives, Jesus sent two disciples, [2]saying to them, "Go into the village ahead of you, and immediately you will find a donkey tied, and a colt with her; untie them and bring them to me. [3]If anyone says anything to you, just say this, 'The Lord needs them.' And he will send them immediately.[c]" [4]This took place to fulfill what had been spoken through the prophet, saying,

[5] "Tell the daughter of Zion,
Look, your king is coming to
  you,
  humble, and mounted on
    a donkey,
    and on a colt, the foal of
    a donkey."

[6]The disciples went and did as Jesus had directed them; [7]they brought the donkey and the colt, and put their cloaks on them, and he sat on them. [8]A very large crowd[d] spread their cloaks on the road, and others cut branches from the trees and spread them on the road. [9]The crowds that went ahead of him and that followed were shouting,

"Hosanna to the Son of David!
  Blessed is the one who
    comes in the name of the
    Lord!
  Hosanna in the highest heaven!"

[10]When he entered Jerusalem, the whole city was in turmoil, asking, "Who is this?" [11]The crowds were saying, "This is the prophet Jesus from Nazareth in Galilee."

12 Then Jesus entered the temple[e] and drove out all who were selling and buying in the temple, and he overturned the tables of the money changers and the seats of those who sold doves. [13]He said to them, "It is written,

'My house shall be called a
    house of prayer';
  but you are making it a den
    of robbers."

14 The blind and the lame came to him in the temple, and he cured them. [15]But when the chief priests and the scribes saw the amazing things that he did, and heard[f] the children crying out in the temple, "Hosanna to the Son of

aOr *as a frontlet*; Meaning of Heb uncertain  bOther ancient authorities lack *Lord*  cOr '*The Lord needs them and will send them back immediately.*'  dOr *Most of the crowd*  eOther ancient authorities add *of God*  fGk lacks *heard*

David," they became angry [16]and said to him, "Do you hear what these are saying?" Jesus said to them, "Yes; have you never read,

> 'Out of the mouths of infants
> and nursing babies
> you have prepared praise for
> yourself'?"

[17]He left them, went out of the city to Bethany, and spent the night there.

18 In the morning, when he returned to the city, he was hungry. [19]And seeing a fig tree by the side of the road, he went to it and found nothing at all on it but leaves. Then he said to it, "May no fruit ever come from you again!" And the fig tree withered at once. [20]When the disciples saw it, they were amazed, saying, "How did the fig tree wither at once?" [21]Jesus answered them, "Truly I tell you, if you have faith and do not doubt, not only will you do what has been done to the fig tree, but even if you say to this mountain, 'Be lifted up and thrown into the sea,' it will be done. [22]Whatever you ask for in prayer with faith, you will receive."

## PSALM 25.16–22

Turn to me and be gracious to me,
> for I am lonely and afflicted.
[17] Relieve the troubles of my
> heart,

and bring me[a] out of my
> distress.
[18] Consider my affliction and my
> trouble,
> and forgive all my sins.

[19] Consider how many are my
> foes,
> and with what violent hatred
> they hate me.
[20] O guard my life, and deliver me;
> do not let me be put to
> shame, for I take refuge
> in you.
[21] May integrity and uprightness
> preserve me,
> for I wait for you.

[22] Redeem Israel, O God,
> out of all its troubles.

## PROVERBS 6.12–15

A scoundrel and a villain goes around with crooked speech,
[13] winking the eyes, shuffling the
> feet,
> pointing the fingers,
[14] with perverted mind devising
> evil,
> continually sowing discord;
[15] on such a one calamity will
> descend suddenly;
> in a moment, damage beyond
> repair.

a Or *The troubles of my heart are enlarged; bring me*

# FEBRUARY 1

EXODUS 13.17—15.18

WHEN Pharaoh let the people go, God did not lead them by way of the land of the Philistines, although that was nearer; for God thought, "If the people face war, they may change their minds and return to Egypt." 18So God led the people by the roundabout way of the wilderness toward the Red Sea.a The Israelites went up out of the land of Egypt prepared for battle. 19And Moses took with him the bones of Joseph who had required a solemn oath of the Israelites, saying, "God will surely take notice of you, and then you must carry my bones with you from here." 20They set out from Succoth, and camped at Etham, on the edge of the wilderness. 21The LORD went in front of them in a pillar of cloud by day, to lead them along the way, and in a pillar of fire by night, to give them light, so that they might travel by day and by night. 22Neither the pillar of cloud by day nor the pillar of fire by night left its place in front of the people.

14.1 THEN the LORD said to Moses: 2Tell the Israelites to turn back and camp in front of Pi-hahiroth, between Migdol and the sea, in front of Baal-zephon; you shall camp opposite it, by the sea. 3Pharaoh will say of the Israelites, 'They are wandering aimlessly in the land; the wilderness has closed in on them.' 4I will harden Pharaoh's heart, and he will pursue them, so that I will gain glory for myself over Pharaoh and all his army; and the Egyptians shall know that I am the LORD. And they did so.

5 When the king of Egypt was told that the people had fled, the minds of Pharaoh and his officials were changed toward the people, and they said, "What have we done, letting Israel leave our service?" 6So he had his chariot made ready, and took his army with him; 7he took six hundred picked chariots and all the other chariots of Egypt with officers over all of them. 8The LORD hardened the heart of Pharaoh king of Egypt and he pursued the Israelites, who were going out boldly. 9The Egyptians pursued them, all Pharaoh's horses and chariots, his chariot drivers and his army; they overtook them camped by the sea, by Pi-hahiroth, in front of Baal-zephon.

10 As Pharaoh drew near, the Israelites looked back, and there were the Egyptians advancing on them. In great fear the Israelites cried out to the LORD. 11They said to Moses, "Was it because there were no graves in Egypt that you have taken us away to die in the wilderness? What have you done to us, bringing us out of Egypt? 12Is this not the very thing we told you in Egypt, 'Let us alone and let us serve the Egyptians'? For it would have been better for us to serve the Egyptians than to die in the wilderness." 13But Moses said to the people, "Do not be afraid, stand firm, and see the deliverance that the LORD will accomplish for you today; for the Egyptians whom you see today you shall never see again. 14The LORD will fight for you, and you have only to keep still."

15 Then the LORD said to Moses, "Why do you cry out to me? Tell the Israelites to go forward. 16But you lift up your staff, and stretch out your hand over the sea and divide it, that the Isra-

a Or Sea of Reeds

elites may go into the sea on dry ground. ¹⁷Then I will harden the hearts of the Egyptians so that they will go in after them; and so I will gain glory for myself over Pharaoh and all his army, his chariots, and his chariot drivers. ¹⁸And the Egyptians shall know that I am the LORD, when I have gained glory for myself over Pharaoh, his chariots, and his chariot drivers."

19   The angel of God who was going before the Israelite army moved and went behind them; and the pillar of cloud moved from in front of them and took its place behind them. ²⁰It came between the army of Egypt and the army of Israel. And so the cloud was there with the darkness, and it lit up the night; one did not come near the other all night.

21   Then Moses stretched out his hand over the sea. The LORD drove the sea back by a strong east wind all night, and turned the sea into dry land; and the waters were divided. ²²The Israelites went into the sea on dry ground, the waters forming a wall for them on their right and on their left. ²³The Egyptians pursued, and went into the sea after them, all of Pharaoh's horses, chariots, and chariot drivers. ²⁴At the morning watch the LORD in the pillar of fire and cloud looked down upon the Egyptian army, and threw the Egyptian army into panic. ²⁵He cloggedᵃ their chariot wheels so that they turned with difficulty. The Egyptians said, "Let us flee from the Israelites, for the LORD is fighting for them against Egypt."

26   Then the LORD said to Moses, "Stretch out your hand over the sea, so that the water may come back upon the Egyptians, upon their chariots and chariot drivers." ²⁷So Moses stretched out his hand over the sea, and at dawn the sea returned to its normal depth. As the Egyptians fled before it, the LORD tossed the Egyptians into the sea.

²⁸The waters returned and covered the chariots and the chariot drivers, the entire army of Pharaoh that had followed them into the sea; not one of them remained. ²⁹But the Israelites walked on dry ground through the sea, the waters forming a wall for them on their right and on their left.

30   Thus the LORD saved Israel that day from the Egyptians; and Israel saw the Egyptians dead on the seashore. ³¹Israel saw the great work that the LORD did against the Egyptians. So the people feared the LORD and believed in the LORD and in his servant Moses.

15.1 THEN Moses and the Israelites sang this song to the LORD:

"I will sing to the LORD, for he
    has triumphed gloriously;
horse and rider he has thrown
    into the sea.
2  The LORD is my strength and
    my might, ᵇ
  and he has become my
    salvation;
this is my God, and I will praise
    him,
  my father's God, and I will
    exalt him.
3  The LORD is a warrior;
    the LORD is his name.

4  "Pharaoh's chariots and his
    army he cast into the
    sea;
  his picked officers were sunk
    in the Red Sea. ᶜ
5  The floods covered them;
  they went down into the
    depths like a stone.
6  Your right hand, O LORD,
    glorious in power—
  your right hand, O LORD,
    shattered the enemy.
7  In the greatness of your majesty
    you overthrew your
    adversaries;

ᵃSam Gk Syr: MT *removed*  ᵇOr *song*  ᶜOr *Sea of Reeds*

you sent out your fury, it
    consumed them like
    stubble.
8  At the blast of your nostrils the
    waters piled up,
    the floods stood up in a heap;
    the deeps congealed in the
    heart of the sea.
9  The enemy said, 'I will pursue,
    I will overtake,
    I will divide the spoil, my
    desire shall have its fill of
    them.
    I will draw my sword, my
    hand shall destroy them.'
10  You blew with your wind, the
    sea covered them;
    they sank like lead in the
    mighty waters.

11  "Who is like you, O Lord,
    among the gods?
    Who is like you, majestic in
    holiness,
    awesome in splendor, doing
    wonders?
12  You stretched out your right
    hand,
    the earth swallowed them.

13  "In your steadfast love you led
    the people whom you
    redeemed;
    you guided them by your
    strength to your holy
    abode.
14  The peoples heard, they
    trembled;
    pangs seized the inhabitants
    of Philistia.
15  Then the chiefs of Edom were
    dismayed;
    trembling seized the leaders
    of Moab;
    all the inhabitants of Canaan
    melted away.
16  Terror and dread fell upon
    them;

    by the might of your arm,
    they became still as a
    stone
  until your people, O Lord,
    passed by,
  until the people whom you
    acquired passed by.
17  You brought them in and planted
    them on the mountain of
    your own possession,
    the place, O Lord, that you
    made your abode,
    the sanctuary, O Lord, that
    your hands have
    established.
18  The Lord will reign forever and
    ever."

## MATTHEW 21.23–46

WHEN he entered the temple, the chief priests and the elders of the people came to him as he was teaching, and said, "By what authority are you doing these things, and who gave you this authority?" 24Jesus said to them, "I will also ask you one question; if you tell me the answer, then I will also tell you by what authority I do these things. 25Did the baptism of John come from heaven, or was it of human origin?" And they argued with one another, "If we say, 'From heaven,' he will say to us, 'Why then did you not believe him?' 26But if we say, 'Of human origin,' we are afraid of the crowd; for all regard John as a prophet." 27So they answered Jesus, "We do not know." And he said to them, "Neither will I tell you by what authority I am doing these things.

28  "What do you think? A man had two sons; he went to the first and said, 'Son, go and work in the vineyard today.' 29He answered, 'I will not'; but later he changed his mind and went. 30The father[a] went to the second and said the same; and he answered, 'I go, sir'; but he did not go. 31Which of the

aGk *He*

two did the will of his father?" They said, "The first." Jesus said to them, "Truly I tell you, the tax collectors and the prostitutes are going into the kingdom of God ahead of you. 32For John came to you in the way of righteousness and you did not believe him, but the tax collectors and the prostitutes believed him; and even after you saw it, you did not change your minds and believe him.

33 "Listen to another parable. There was a landowner who planted a vineyard, put a fence around it, dug a wine press in it, and built a watchtower. Then he leased it to tenants and went to another country. 34When the harvest time had come, he sent his slaves to the tenants to collect his produce. 35But the tenants seized his slaves and beat one, killed another, and stoned another. 36Again he sent other slaves, more than the first; and they treated them in the same way. 37Finally he sent his son to them, saying, 'They will respect my son.' 38But when the tenants saw the son, they said to themselves, 'This is the heir; come, let us kill him and get his inheritance.' 39So they seized him, threw him out of the vineyard, and killed him. 40Now when the owner of the vineyard comes, what will he do to those tenants?" 41They said to him, "He will put those wretches to a miserable death, and lease the vineyard to other tenants who will give him the produce at the harvest time."

42 Jesus said to them, "Have you never read in the scriptures:

'The stone that the builders
    rejected
  has become the
    cornerstone;[a]
this was the Lord's doing,
  and it is amazing in our eyes'?

43Therefore I tell you, the kingdom of God will be taken away from you and given to a people that produces the fruits of the kingdom.[b] 44The one who falls on this stone will be broken to pieces; and it will crush anyone on whom it falls."[c]

45 When the chief priests and the Pharisees heard his parables, they realized that he was speaking about them. 46They wanted to arrest him, but they feared the crowds, because they regarded him as a prophet.

## PSALM 26. 1–12

*Of David.*

VINDICATE me, O Lord,
  for I have walked in my
    integrity,
  and I have trusted in the
    Lord without wavering.
2  Prove me, O Lord, and try me;
    test my heart and mind.
3  For your steadfast love is
    before my eyes,
  and I walk in faithfulness to
    you.[d]

4  I do not sit with the worthless,
    nor do I consort with
      hypocrites;
5  I hate the company of evildoers,
    and will not sit with the
      wicked.

6  I wash my hands in innocence,
    and go around your altar,
      O Lord,
7  singing aloud a song of
    thanksgiving,
  and telling all your wondrous
    deeds.

8  O Lord, I love the house in
    which you dwell,
  and the place where your
    glory abides.
9  Do not sweep me away with
    sinners,

---

aOr *keystone*  bGk *the fruits of it*  cOther ancient authorities lack verse 44  dOr *in your faithfulness*

nor my life with the
    bloodthirsty,
10 those in whose hands are evil
    devices,
    and whose right hands are full
        of bribes.

11 But as for me, I walk in my
    integrity;
    redeem me, and be gracious
        to me.
12 My foot stands on level ground;
    in the great congregation I
        will bless the LORD.

## PROVERBS 6.16–19

THERE are six things that the
    LORD hates,
    seven that are an
        abomination to him:
17 haughty eyes, a lying tongue,
    and hands that shed innocent
        blood,
18 a heart that devises wicked
    plans,
    feet that hurry to run to evil,
19 a lying witness who testifies
    falsely,
    and one who sows discord in
        a family.

# FEBRUARY 2

## EXODUS 15.19—17.7

WHEN the horses of Pharaoh with his chariots and his chariot drivers went into the sea, the LORD brought back the waters of the sea upon them; but the Israelites walked through the sea on dry ground.

20 Then the prophet Miriam, Aaron's sister, took a tambourine in her hand; and all the women went out after her with tambourines and with dancing. 21 And Miriam sang to them:

    "Sing to the LORD, for he has
        triumphed gloriously;
    horse and rider he has thrown
        into the sea."

22 Then Moses ordered Israel to set out from the Red Sea, a and they went into the wilderness of Shur. They went three days in the wilderness and found no water. 23 When they came to Marah, they could not drink the water of Marah because it was bitter. That is why it was called Marah. b 24 And the people complained against Moses, saying, "What shall we drink?" 25 He cried out to the LORD; and the LORD showed him a piece of wood; c he threw it into the water, and the water became sweet.

There the LORD d made for them a statute and an ordinance and there he put them to the test. 26 He said, "If you will listen carefully to the voice of the LORD your God, and do what is right in his sight, and give heed to his commandments and keep all his statutes, I will not bring upon you any of the diseases that I brought upon the Egyptians; for I am the LORD who heals you."

27 Then they came to Elim, where there were twelve springs of water and seventy palm trees; and they camped there by the water.

a Or *Sea of Reeds*  b That is *Bitterness*  c Or *a tree*  d Heb *he*

16.1 THE whole congregation of the Israelites set out from Elim; and Israel came to the wilderness of Sin, which is between Elim and Sinai, on the fifteenth day of the second month after they had departed from the land of Egypt. 2The whole congregation of the Israelites complained against Moses and Aaron in the wilderness. 3The Israelites said to them, "If only we had died by the hand of the LORD in the land of Egypt, when we sat by the fleshpots and ate our fill of bread; for you have brought us out into this wilderness to kill this whole assembly with hunger."

4 Then the LORD said to Moses, "I am going to rain bread from heaven for you, and each day the people shall go out and gather enough for that day. In that way I will test them, whether they will follow my instruction or not. 5On the sixth day, when they prepare what they bring in, it will be twice as much as they gather on other days." 6So Moses and Aaron said to all the Israelites, "In the evening you shall know that it was the LORD who brought you out of the land of Egypt, 7and in the morning you shall see the glory of the LORD, because he has heard your complaining against the LORD. For what are we, that you complain against us?" 8And Moses said, "When the LORD gives you meat to eat in the evening and your fill of bread in the morning, because the LORD has heard the complaining that you utter against him—what are we? Your complaining is not against us but against the LORD."

9 Then Moses said to Aaron, "Say to the whole congregation of the Israelites, 'Draw near to the LORD, for he has heard your complaining.'" 10And as Aaron spoke to the whole congregation of the Israelites, they looked toward the wilderness, and the glory of the LORD appeared in the cloud. 11The LORD spoke to Moses and said, 12"I have heard the complaining of the Israelites; say to them, 'At twilight you shall eat meat, and in the morning you shall have your fill of bread; then you shall know that I am the LORD your God.'"

13 In the evening quails came up and covered the camp; and in the morning there was a layer of dew around the camp. 14When the layer of dew lifted, there on the surface of the wilderness was a fine flaky substance, as fine as frost on the ground. 15When the Israelites saw it, they said to one another, "What is it?"a For they did not know what it was. Moses said to them, "It is the bread that the LORD has given you to eat. 16This is what the LORD has commanded: 'Gather as much of it as each of you needs, an omer to a person according to the number of persons, all providing for those in their own tents.'" 17The Israelites did so, some gathering more, some less. 18But when they measured it with an omer, those who gathered much had nothing over, and those who gathered little had no shortage; they gathered as much as each of them needed. 19And Moses said to them, "Let no one leave any of it over until morning." 20But they did not listen to Moses; some left part of it until morning, and it bred worms and became foul. And Moses was angry with them. 21Morning by morning they gathered it, as much as each needed; but when the sun grew hot, it melted.

22 On the sixth day they gathered twice as much food, two omers apiece. When all the leaders of the congregation came and told Moses, 23he said to them, "This is what the LORD has commanded: 'Tomorrow is a day of solemn rest, a holy sabbath to the LORD; bake what you want to bake and boil what you want to boil, and all that is left over put aside to be kept until morning.'" 24So they put it aside until morning, as Moses commanded them; and it did not

aOr "It is manna" (Heb man hu, see verse 31)

become foul, and there were no worms in it. 25Moses said, "Eat it today, for today is a sabbath to the Lord; today you will not find it in the field. 26Six days you shall gather it; but on the seventh day, which is a sabbath, there will be none."

27  On the seventh day some of the people went out to gather, and they found none. 28The Lord said to Moses, "How long will you refuse to keep my commandments   and   instructions? 29See! The Lord has given you the sabbath, therefore on the sixth day he gives you food for two days; each of you stay where you are; do not leave your place on the seventh day." 30So the people rested on the seventh day.

31  The house of Israel called it manna; it was like coriander seed, white, and the taste of it was like wafers made with honey. 32Moses said, "This is what the Lord has commanded: 'Let an omer of it be kept throughout your generations, in order that they may see the food with which I fed you in the wilderness, when I brought you out of the land of Egypt.' " 33And Moses said to Aaron, "Take a jar, and put an omer of manna in it, and place it before the Lord, to be kept throughout your generations." 34As the Lord commanded Moses, so Aaron placed it before the covenant, a for safekeeping. 35The Israelites ate manna forty years, until they came to a habitable land; they ate manna, until they came to the border of the land of Canaan. 36An omer is a tenth of an ephah.

17.1 From the wilderness of Sin the whole congregation of the Israelites journeyed by stages, as the Lord commanded. They camped at Rephidim, but there was no water for the people to drink. 2The people quarreled with Moses, and said, "Give us water to drink." Moses said to them, "Why do you quarrel with me? Why do you test the Lord?" 3But the people thirsted there for water; and the people complained against Moses and said, "Why did you bring us out of Egypt, to kill us and our children and livestock with thirst?" 4So Moses cried out to the Lord, "What shall I do with this people? They are almost ready to stone me." 5The Lord said to Moses, "Go on ahead of the people, and take some of the elders of Israel with you; take in your hand the staff with which you struck the Nile, and go. 6I will be standing there in front of you on the rock at Horeb. Strike the rock, and water will come out of it, so that the people may drink." Moses did so, in the sight of the elders of Israel. 7He called the place Massahb and Meribah, c because the Israelites quarreled and tested the Lord, saying, "Is the Lord among us or not?"

## MATTHEW 22.1–33

ONCE more Jesus spoke to them in parables, saying: 2"The kingdom of heaven may be compared to a king who gave a wedding banquet for his son. 3He sent his slaves to call those who had been invited to the wedding banquet, but they would not come. 4Again he sent other slaves, saying, 'Tell those who have been invited: Look, I have prepared my dinner, my oxen and my fat calves have been slaughtered, and everything is ready; come to the wedding banquet.' 5But they made light of it and went away, one to his farm, another to his business, 6while the rest seized his slaves, mistreated them, and killed them. 7The king was enraged. He sent his troops, destroyed those murderers, and burned their city. 8Then he said to his slaves, 'The wedding is ready, but those invited were not worthy. 9Go therefore into the main

aOr *treaty* or *testimony*; Heb *eduth*   bThat is *Test*   cThat is *Quarrel*

streets, and invite everyone you find to the wedding banquet.' [10]Those slaves went out into the streets and gathered all whom they found, both good and bad; so the wedding hall was filled with guests.

11 "But when the king came in to see the guests, he noticed a man there who was not wearing a wedding robe, [12]and he said to him, 'Friend, how did you get in here without a wedding robe?' And he was speechless. [13]Then the king said to the attendants, 'Bind him hand and foot, and throw him into the outer darkness, where there will be weeping and gnashing of teeth.' [14]For many are called, but few are chosen."

15 Then the Pharisees went and plotted to entrap him in what he said. [16]So they sent their disciples to him, along with the Herodians, saying, "Teacher, we know that you are sincere, and teach the way of God in accordance with truth, and show deference to no one; for you do not regard people with partiality. [17]Tell us, then, what you think. Is it lawful to pay taxes to the emperor, or not?" [18]But Jesus, aware of their malice, said, "Why are you putting me to the test, you hypocrites? [19]Show me the coin used for the tax." And they brought him a denarius. [20]Then he said to them, "Whose head is this, and whose title?" [21]They answered, "The emperor's." Then he said to them, "Give therefore to the emperor the things that are the emperor's, and to God the things that are God's." [22]When they heard this, they were amazed; and they left him and went away.

23 The same day some Sadducees came to him, saying there is no resurrection;[a] and they asked him a question, saying, [24]"Teacher, Moses said, 'If a man dies childless, his brother shall marry the widow, and raise up children for his brother.' [25]Now there were seven brothers among us; the first married, and died childless, leaving the widow to his brother. [26]The second did the same, so also the third, down to the seventh. [27]Last of all, the woman herself died. [28]In the resurrection, then, whose wife of the seven will she be? For all of them had married her."

29 Jesus answered them, "You are wrong, because you know neither the scriptures nor the power of God. [30]For in the resurrection they neither marry nor are given in marriage, but are like angels[b] in heaven. [31]And as for the resurrection of the dead, have you not read what was said to you by God, [32]'I am the God of Abraham, the God of Isaac, and the God of Jacob'? He is God not of the dead, but of the living." [33]And when the crowd heard it, they were astounded at his teaching.

## PSALM 27.1–6

*Of David.*

THE LORD is my light and my
    salvation;
  whom shall I fear?
The LORD is the stronghold[c] of
    my life;
  of whom shall I be afraid?
2  When evildoers assail me
    to devour my flesh—
my adversaries and foes—
  they shall stumble and fall.

3  Though an army encamp against
    me,
    my heart shall not fear;
though war rise up against me,
  yet I will be confident.

4  One thing I asked of the LORD,
    that will I seek after:
to live in the house of the LORD
  all the days of my life,
to behold the beauty of the
    LORD,

and to inquire in his temple.

5  For he will hide me in his
       shelter
     in the day of trouble;
   he will conceal me under the
       cover of his tent;
     he will set me high on a rock.

6  Now my head is lifted up
       above my enemies all around
       me,
   and I will offer in his tent
       sacrifices with shouts of joy;
   I will sing and make melody to
       the LORD.

## PROVERBS 6.20–26

**M**Y child, keep your father's
       commandment,
   and do not forsake your
       mother's teaching.
21  Bind them upon your heart
       always;

      tie them around your neck.
22  When you walk, they a will
       lead you;
     when you lie down, they a
       will watch over you;
     and when you awake, they a
       will talk with you.
23  For the commandment is a lamp
       and the teaching a light,
     and the reproofs of discipline
       are the way of life,
24  to preserve you from the wife
       of another, b
     from the smooth tongue of
       the adulteress.
25  Do not desire her beauty in
       your heart,
     and do not let her capture
       you with her eyelashes;
26  for a prostitute's fee is only a
       loaf of bread, c
     but the wife of another stalks
       a man's very life.

# FEBRUARY 3

## EXODUS 17.8—19.15

**T**HEN Amalek came and fought with Israel at Rephidim. 9Moses said to Joshua, "Choose some men for us and go out, fight with Amalek. Tomorrow I will stand on the top of the hill with the staff of God in my hand." 10So Joshua did as Moses told him, and fought with Amalek, while Moses, Aaron, and Hur went up to the top of the hill. 11Whenever Moses held up his hand, Israel prevailed; and whenever he lowered his hand, Amalek prevailed. 12But Moses' hands grew weary; so they took a stone and put it under him, and he sat on it. Aaron and Hur held up his hands, one on one side, and the other on the other side; so his hands were steady until the sun set. 13And Joshua defeated Amalek and his people with the sword.

14  Then the LORD said to Moses, "Write this as a reminder in a book and recite it in the hearing of Joshua: I will utterly blot out the remembrance of Amalek from under heaven." 15And Moses built an altar and called it, The LORD is my banner. 16He said, "A hand

aHeb it   bGk: MT *the evil woman*   cCn Compare Gk Syr Vg Tg: Heb *for because of a harlot to a piece of bread* upon the banner of the LORD.ᵃ The LORD will have war with Amalek from generation to generation."

18.1 JETHRO, the priest of Midian, Moses' father-in-law, heard of all that God had done for Moses and for his people Israel, how the LORD had brought Israel out of Egypt. 2After Moses had sent away his wife Zipporah, his father-in-law Jethro took her back, 3along with her two sons. The name of the one was Gershom (for he said, "I have been an alienᵇ in a foreign land"), 4and the name of the other, Eliezerᶜ (for he said, "The God of my father was my help, and delivered me from the sword of Pharaoh"). 5Jethro, Moses' father-in-law, came into the wilderness where Moses was encamped at the mountain of God, bringing Moses' sons and wife to him. 6He sent word to Moses, "I, your father-in-law Jethro, am coming to you, with your wife and her two sons." 7Moses went out to meet his father-in-law; he bowed down and kissed him; each asked after the other's welfare, and they went into the tent. 8Then Moses told his father-in-law all that the LORD had done to Pharaoh and to the Egyptians for Israel's sake, all the hardship that had beset them on the way, and how the LORD had delivered them. 9Jethro rejoiced for all the good that the LORD had done to Israel, in delivering them from the Egyptians.

10 Jethro said, "Blessed be the LORD, who has delivered you from the Egyptians and from Pharaoh. 11Now I know that the LORD is greater than all gods, because he delivered the people from the Egyptians,ᵈ when they dealt arrogantly with them." 12And Jethro, Moses' father-in-law, brought a burnt offering and sacrifices to God; and Aaron came with all the elders of Israel to eat bread with Moses' father-in-law in the presence of God.

13 The next day Moses sat as judge for the people, while the people stood around him from morning until evening. 14When Moses' father-in-law saw all that he was doing for the people, he said, "What is this that you are doing for the people? Why do you sit alone, while all the people stand around you from morning until evening?" 15Moses said to his father-in-law, "Because the people come to me to inquire of God. 16When they have a dispute, they come to me and I decide between one person and another, and I make known to them the statutes and instructions of God." 17Moses' father-in-law said to him, "What you are doing is not good. 18You will surely wear yourself out, both you and these people with you. For the task is too heavy for you; you cannot do it alone. 19Now listen to me. I will give you counsel, and God be with you! You should represent the people before God, and you should bring their cases before God; 20teach them the statutes and instructions and make known to them the way they are to go and the things they are to do. 21You should also look for able men among all the people, men who fear God, are trustworthy, and hate dishonest gain; set such men over them as officers over thousands, hundreds, fifties and tens. 22Let them sit as judges for the people at all times; let them bring every important case to you, but decide every minor case themselves. So it will be easier for you, and they will bear the burden with you. 23If you do this, and God so commands you, then you will be able to endure, and all these people will go to their home in peace."

24 So Moses listened to his father-in-law and did all that he had said. 25Moses chose able men from all Israel and appointed them as heads over the people, as officers over thousands, hundreds, fifties, and tens. 26And they

ᵃCn: Meaning of Heb uncertain  ᵇHeb *ger*  ᶜHeb *Eli*, my God; *ezer*, help  ᵈThe clause *because . . . Egyptians* has been transposed from verse 10

judged the people at all times; hard cases they brought to Moses, but any minor case they decided themselves. ²⁷Then Moses let his father-in-law depart, and he went off to his own country.

¹⁹·¹ On the third new moon after the Israelites had gone out of the land of Egypt, on that very day, they came into the wilderness of Sinai. ²They had journeyed from Rephidim, entered the wilderness of Sinai, and camped in the wilderness; Israel camped there in front of the mountain. ³Then Moses went up to God; the Lord called to him from the mountain, saying, "Thus you shall say to the house of Jacob, and tell the Israelites: ⁴You have seen what I did to the Egyptians, and how I bore you on eagles' wings and brought you to myself. ⁵Now therefore, if you obey my voice and keep my covenant, you shall be my treasured possession out of all the peoples. Indeed, the whole earth is mine, ⁶but you shall be for me a priestly kingdom and a holy nation. These are the words that you shall speak to the Israelites."

7 So Moses came, summoned the elders of the people, and set before them all these words that the Lord had commanded him. ⁸The people all answered as one: "Everything that the Lord has spoken we will do." Moses reported the words of the people to the Lord. ⁹Then the Lord said to Moses, "I am going to come to you in a dense cloud, in order that the people may hear when I speak with you and so trust you ever after."

When Moses had told the words of the people to the Lord, ¹⁰the Lord said to Moses: "Go to the people and consecrate them today and tomorrow. Have them wash their clothes ¹¹and prepare for the third day, because on the third day the Lord will come down upon Mount Sinai in the sight of all the people. ¹²You shall set limits for the people all around, saying, 'Be careful not to go up the mountain or to touch the edge of it. Any who touch the mountain shall be put to death. ¹³No hand shall touch them, but they shall be stoned or shot with arrows;ᵃ whether animal or human being, they shall not live.' When the trumpet sounds a long blast, they may go up on the mountain." ¹⁴So Moses went down from the mountain to the people. He consecrated the people, and they washed their clothes. ¹⁵And he said to the people, "Prepare for the third day; do not go near a woman."

## MATTHEW 22.34—23.12

WHEN the Pharisees heard that he [Jesus] had silenced the Sadducees, they gathered together, ³⁵and one of them, a lawyer, asked him a question to test him. ³⁶"Teacher, which commandment in the law is the greatest?" ³⁷He said to him, " 'You shall love the Lord your God with all your heart, and with all your soul, and with all your mind.' ³⁸This is the greatest and first commandment. ³⁹And a second is like it: 'You shall love your neighbor as yourself.' ⁴⁰On these two commandments hang all the law and the prophets."

41 Now while the Pharisees were gathered together, Jesus asked them this question: ⁴²"What do you think of the Messiah?ᵇ Whose son is he?" They said to him, "The son of David." ⁴³He said to them, "How is it then that David by the Spiritᶜ calls him Lord, saying,

⁴⁴ 'The Lord said to my Lord,
    "Sit at my right hand,
        until I put your enemies
            under your feet" '?
⁴⁵If David thus calls him Lord, how can he be his son?" ⁴⁶No one was able to give him an answer, nor from that day

ᵃHeb lacks *with arrows*  ᵇOr *Christ*  ᶜGk *in spirit*

did anyone dare to ask him any more questions.

**23.1** THEN Jesus said to the crowds and to his disciples, 2"The scribes and the Pharisees sit on Moses' seat; 3therefore, do whatever they teach you and follow it; but do not do as they do, for they do not practice what they teach. 4They tie up heavy burdens, hard to bear, a and lay them on the shoulders of others; but they themselves are unwilling to lift a finger to move them. 5They do all their deeds to be seen by others; for they make their phylacteries broad and their fringes long. 6They love to have the place of honor at banquets and the best seats in the synagogues, 7and to be greeted with respect in the marketplaces, and to have people call them rabbi. 8But you are not to be called rabbi, for you have one teacher, and you are all students. b 9And call no one your father on earth, for you have one Father—the one in heaven. 10Nor are you to be called instructors, for you have one instructor, the Messiah. c 11The greatest among you will be your servant. 12All who exalt themselves will be humbled, and all who humble themselves will be exalted.

## PSALM 27.7–14

**H**EAR, O LORD, when I cry aloud,
    be gracious to me and answer me!
8  "Come," my heart says, "seek his face!"
    Your face, LORD, do I seek.
9    Do not hide your face from me.

Do not turn your servant away in anger,
    you who have been my help.

Do not cast me off, do not forsake me,
    O God of my salvation!
10  If my father and mother forsake me,
    the LORD will take me up.

11  Teach me your way, O LORD,
    and lead me on a level path because of my enemies.
12  Do not give me up to the will of my adversaries,
    for false witnesses have risen against me,
    and they are breathing out violence.

13  I believe that I shall see the goodness of the LORD
    in the land of the living.
14  Wait for the LORD;
    be strong, and let your heart take courage;
    wait for the LORD!

## PROVERBS 6.27–35

**C**AN fire be carried in the bosom
    without burning one's clothes?
28  Or can one walk on hot coals
    without scorching the feet?
29  So is he who sleeps with his neighbor's wife;
    no one who touches her will go unpunished.
30  Thieves are not despised who steal only
    to satisfy their appetite when they are hungry.
31  Yet if they are caught, they will pay sevenfold;
    they will forfeit all the goods of their house.
32  But he who commits adultery has no sense;
    he who does it destroys himself.

aOther ancient authorities lack *hard to bear*  bGk *brothers*  cOr *the Christ*

33 He will get wounds and
    dishonor,
  and his disgrace will not be
    wiped away.
34 For jealousy arouses a
    husband's fury,

and he shows no restraint
  when he takes revenge.
35 He will accept no compensation,
  and refuses a bribe no matter
    how great.

# FEBRUARY 4

## EXODUS 19.16—21.21

On the morning of the third day there was thunder and lightning, as well as a thick cloud on the mountain, and a blast of a trumpet so loud that all the people who were in the camp trembled. 17Moses brought the people out of the camp to meet God. They took their stand at the foot of the mountain. 18Now Mount Sinai was wrapped in smoke, because the Lord had descended upon it in fire; the smoke went up like the smoke of a kiln, while the whole mountain shook violently. 19As the blast of the trumpet grew louder and louder, Moses would speak and God would answer him in thunder. 20When the Lord descended upon Mount Sinai, to the top of the mountain, the Lord summoned Moses to the top of the mountain, and Moses went up. 21Then the Lord said to Moses, "Go down and warn the people not to break through to the Lord to look; otherwise many of them will perish. 22Even the priests who approach the Lord must consecrate themselves or the Lord will break out against them." 23Moses said to the Lord, "The people are not permitted to come up to Mount Sinai; for you yourself warned us, saying, 'Set limits around the mountain and keep it holy.' " 24The Lord said to him, "Go down, and come up bringing Aaron with you; but do not let either the priests or the people break through to come up to the Lord; otherwise he will break out against them." 25So Moses went down to the people and told them.

20.1 Then God spoke all these words:

2 I am the Lord your God, who brought you out of the land of Egypt, out of the house of slavery; 3you shall have no other gods beforea me.

4 You shall not make for yourself an idol, whether in the form of anything that is in heaven above, or that is on the earth beneath, or that is in the water under the earth. 5You shall not bow down to them or worship them; for I the Lord your God am a jealous God, punishing children for the iniquity of parents, to the third and the fourth generation of those who reject me, 6but showing steadfast love to the thousandth generationb of those who love me and keep my commandments.

7 You shall not make wrongful use of the name of the Lord your God, for the Lord will not acquit anyone who misuses his name.

8 Remember the sabbath day, and keep it holy. 9Six days you shall labor and do all your work. 10But the seventh day is a sabbath to the Lord your God;

a Or *besides*  b Or *to thousands*

you shall not do any work—you, your son or your daughter, your male or female slave, your livestock, or the alien resident in your towns. ¹¹For in six days the LORD made heaven and earth, the sea, and all that is in them, but rested the seventh day; therefore the LORD blessed the sabbath day and consecrated it.

12 Honor your father and your mother, so that your days may be long in the land that the LORD your God is giving you.

13 You shall not murder. [a]

14 You shall not commit adultery.

15 You shall not steal.

16 You shall not bear false witness against your neighbor.

17 You shall not covet your neighbor's house; you shall not covet your neighbor's wife, or male or female slave, or ox, or donkey, or anything that belongs to your neighbor.

18 When all the people witnessed the thunder and lightning, the sound of the trumpet, and the mountain smoking, they were afraid[b] and trembled and stood at a distance, ¹⁹and said to Moses, "You speak to us, and we will listen; but do not let God speak to us, or we will die." ²⁰Moses said to the people, "Do not be afraid; for God has come only to test you and to put the fear of him upon you so that you do not sin." ²¹Then the people stood at a distance, while Moses drew near to the thick darkness where God was.

22 The LORD said to Moses: Thus you shall say to the Israelites: "You have seen for yourselves that I spoke with you from heaven. ²³You shall not make gods of silver alongside me, nor shall you make for yourselves gods of gold. ²⁴You need make for me only an altar of earth and sacrifice on it your burnt offerings and your offerings of well-being, your sheep and your oxen; in every place where I cause my name

to be remembered I will come to you and bless you. ²⁵But if you make for me an altar of stone, do not build it of hewn stones; for if you use a chisel upon it you profane it. ²⁶You shall not go up by steps to my altar, so that your nakedness may not be exposed on it."

21.1 THESE are the ordinances that you shall set before them:

2 When you buy a male Hebrew slave, he shall serve six years, but in the seventh he shall go out a free person, without debt. ³If he comes in single, he shall go out single; if he comes in married, then his wife shall go out with him. ⁴If his master gives him a wife and she bears him sons or daughters, the wife and her children shall be her master's and he shall go out alone. ⁵But if the slave declares, "I love my master, my wife, and my children; I will not go out a free person," ⁶then his master shall bring him before God. [c] He shall be brought to the door or the doorpost; and his master shall pierce his ear with an awl; and he shall serve him for life.

7 When a man sells his daughter as a slave, she shall not go out as the male slaves do. ⁸If she does not please her master, who designated her for himself, then he shall let her be redeemed; he shall have no right to sell her to a foreign people, since he has dealt unfairly with her. ⁹If he designates her for his son, he shall deal with her as with a daughter. ¹⁰If he takes another wife to himself, he shall not diminish the food, clothing, or marital rights of the first wife. [d] ¹¹And if he does not do these three things for her, she shall go out without debt, without payment of money.

12 Whoever strikes a person mortally shall be put to death. ¹³If it was not premeditated, but came about by an act of God, then I will appoint for you a place to which the killer may flee. ¹⁴But

if someone willfully attacks and kills another by treachery, you shall take the killer from my altar for execution.

15 Whoever strikes father or mother shall be put to death.

16 Whoever kidnaps a person, whether that person has been sold or is still held in possession, shall be put to death.

17 Whoever curses father or mother shall be put to death.

18 When individuals quarrel and one strikes the other with a stone or fist so that the injured party, though not dead, is confined to bed, [19]but recovers and walks around outside with the help of a staff, then the assailant shall be free of liability, except to pay for the loss of time, and to arrange for full recovery.

20 When a slaveowner strikes a male or female slave with a rod and the slave dies immediately, the owner shall be punished. [21]But if the slave survives a day or two, there is no punishment; for the slave is the owner's property.

## MATTHEW 23.13–39

"**B**UT woe to you, scribes and Pharisees, hypocrites! For you lock people out of the kingdom of heaven. For you do not go in yourselves, and when others are going in, you stop them. [a] [15]Woe to you, scribes and Pharisees, hypocrites! For you cross sea and land to make a single convert, and you make the new convert twice as much a child of hell[b] as yourselves.

16 "Woe to you, blind guides, who say, 'Whoever swears by the sanctuary is bound by nothing, but whoever swears by the gold of the sanctuary is bound by the oath.' [17]You blind fools! For which is greater, the gold or the sanctuary that has made the gold sa-

cred? [18]And you say, 'Whoever swears by the altar is bound by nothing, but whoever swears by the gift that is on the altar is bound by the oath.' [19]How blind you are! For which is greater, the gift or the altar that makes the gift sacred? [20]So whoever swears by the altar, swears by it and by everything on it; [21]and whoever swears by the sanctuary, swears by it and by the one who dwells in it; [22]and whoever swears by heaven, swears by the throne of God and by the one who is seated upon it.

23 "Woe to you, scribes and Pharisees, hypocrites! For you tithe mint, dill, and cummin, and have neglected the weightier matters of the law: justice and mercy and faith. It is these you ought to have practiced without neglecting the others. [24]You blind guides! You strain out a gnat but swallow a camel!

25 "Woe to you, scribes and Pharisees, hypocrites! For you clean the outside of the cup and of the plate, but inside they are full of greed and self-indulgence. [26]You blind Pharisee! First clean the inside of the cup, [c] so that the outside also may become clean.

27 "Woe to you, scribes and Pharisees, hypocrites! For you are like whitewashed tombs, which on the outside look beautiful, but inside they are full of the bones of the dead and of all kinds of filth. [28]So you also on the outside look righteous to others, but inside you are full of hypocrisy and lawlessness.

29 "Woe to you, scribes and Pharisees, hypocrites! For you build the tombs of the prophets and decorate the graves of the righteous, [30]and you say, 'If we had lived in the days of our ancestors, we would not have taken part with them in shedding the blood of the prophets.' [31]Thus you testify against

a Other authorities add here (or after verse 12) verse 14, *Woe to you, scribes and Pharisees, hypocrites! For you devour widows' houses and for the sake of appearance you make long prayers; therefore you will receive the greater condemnation*   b Gk *Gehenna*   c Other ancient authorities add *and of the plate*

yourselves that you are descendants of those who murdered the prophets. [32]Fill up, then, the measure of your ancestors. [33]You snakes, you brood of vipers! How can you escape being sentenced to hell?[a] [34]Therefore I send you prophets, sages, and scribes, some of whom you will kill and crucify, and some you will flog in your synagogues and pursue from town to town, [35]so that upon you may come all the righteous blood shed on earth, from the blood of righteous Abel to the blood of Zechariah son of Barachiah, whom you murdered between the sanctuary and the altar. [36]Truly I tell you, all this will come upon this generation.

37 "Jerusalem, Jerusalem, the city that kills the prophets and stones those who are sent to it! How often have I desired to gather your children together as a hen gathers her brood under her wings, and you were not willing! [38]See, your house is left to you, desolate.[b] [39]For I tell you, you will not see me again until you say, 'Blessed is the one who comes in the name of the Lord.'"

## PSALM 28.1–9

*Of David.*

To you, O LORD, I call;
   my rock, do not refuse to
      hear me,
  for if you are silent to me,
    I shall be like those who go
      down to the Pit.
2  Hear the voice of my
     supplication,
   as I cry to you for help,
  as I lift up my hands
    toward your most holy
      sanctuary.[c]

3  Do not drag me away with the
     wicked,
   with those who are workers
    of evil,

who speak peace with their
    neighbors,
  while mischief is in their
    hearts.
4  Repay them according to their
    work,
  and according to the evil of
    their deeds;
  repay them according to the
    work of their hands;
  render them their due
    reward.
5  Because they do not regard the
    works of the LORD,
  or the work of his hands,
  he will break them down and
    build them up no more.

6  Blessed be the LORD,
   for he has heard the sound of
    my pleadings.
7  The LORD is my strength and
    my shield;
   in him my heart trusts;
  so I am helped, and my heart
    exults,
   and with my song I give
    thanks to him.

8  The LORD is the strength of his
    people;
   he is the saving refuge of his
    anointed.
9  O save your people, and bless
    your heritage;
   be their shepherd, and carry
    them forever.

## PROVERBS 7.1–5

My child, keep my words
  and store up my
   commandments with you;
2  keep my commandments and
    live,
  keep my teachings as the
    apple of your eye;
3  bind them on your fingers,

---

a Gk *Gehenna*  b Other ancient authorities lack *desolate*  c Heb *your innermost sanctuary*

> write them on the tablet of
>   your heart.
> 4 Say to wisdom, "You are my
>     sister,"
>   and call insight your intimate
>     friend,

> 5  that they may keep you from
>     the loose[a] woman,
>   from the adulteress with her
>     smooth words.

# FEBRUARY 5

## EXODUS 21.22—23.13

WHEN people who are fighting injure a pregnant woman so that there is a miscarriage, and yet no further harm follows, the one responsible shall be fined what the woman's husband demands, paying as much as the judges determine. 23 If any harm follows, then you shall give life for life, 24 eye for eye, tooth for tooth, hand for hand, foot for foot, 25 burn for burn, wound for wound, stripe for stripe.

26 When a slaveowner strikes the eye of a male or female slave, destroying it, the owner shall let the slave go, a free person, to compensate for the eye. 27 If the owner knocks out a tooth of a male or female slave, the slave shall be let go, a free person, to compensate for the tooth.

28 When an ox gores a man or a woman to death, the ox shall be stoned, and its flesh shall not be eaten; but the owner of the ox shall not be liable. 29 If the ox has been accustomed to gore in the past, and its owner has been warned but has not restrained it, and it kills a man or a woman, the ox shall be stoned, and its owner also shall be put to death. 30 If a ransom is imposed on the owner, then the owner shall pay whatever is imposed for the redemption of the victim's life. 31 If it gores a boy or a girl, the owner shall be dealt with according to this same rule. 32 If the ox gores a male or female slave, the owner shall pay to the slaveowner thirty shekels of silver, and the ox shall be stoned.

33 If someone leaves a pit open, or digs a pit and does not cover it, and an ox or a donkey falls into it, 34 the owner of the pit shall make restitution, giving money to its owner, but keeping the dead animal.

35 If someone's ox hurts the ox of another, so that it dies, then they shall sell the live ox and divide the price of it; and the dead animal they shall also divide. 36 But if it was known that the ox was accustomed to gore in the past, and its owner has not restrained it, the owner shall restore ox for ox, but keep the dead animal.

22 [b].1 WHEN someone steals an ox or a sheep, and slaughters it or sells it, the thief shall pay five oxen for an ox, and four sheep for a sheep. [c] The thief shall make restitution, but if unable to do so, shall be sold for the theft. 4 When the animal, whether ox or donkey or sheep, is found alive in the thief's possession, the thief shall pay double.

2 [d] If a thief is found breaking in, and

---

[a] Heb *strange*  [b] Ch 21.37 in Heb  [c] Verses 2, 3, and 4 rearranged thus: 3b, 4, 2, 3a  [d] Ch 22.1 in Heb

is beaten to death, no bloodguilt is incurred; ³but if it happens after sunrise, bloodguilt is incurred.

5  When someone causes a field or vineyard to be grazed over, or lets livestock loose to graze in someone else's field, restitution shall be made from the best in the owner's field or vineyard.

6  When fire breaks out and catches in thorns so that the stacked grain or the standing grain or the field is consumed, the one who started the fire shall make full restitution.

7  When someone delivers to a neighbor money or goods for safekeeping, and they are stolen from the neighbor's house, then the thief, if caught, shall pay double. ⁸If the thief is not caught, the owner of the house shall be brought before God, ª to determine whether or not the owner had laid hands on the neighbor's goods.

9  In any case of disputed ownership involving ox, donkey, sheep, clothing, or any other loss, of which one party says, "This is mine," the case of both parties shall come before God; ª the one whom God condemns ᵇ shall pay double to the other.

10  When someone delivers to another a donkey, ox, sheep, or any other animal for safekeeping, and it dies or is injured or is carried off, without anyone seeing it, ¹¹an oath before the Lᴏʀᴅ shall decide between the two of them that the one has not laid hands on the property of the other; the owner shall accept the oath, and no restitution shall be made. ¹²But if it was stolen, restitution shall be made to its owner. ¹³If it was mangled by beasts, let it be brought as evidence; restitution shall not be made for the mangled remains.

14  When someone borrows an animal from another and it is injured or dies, the owner not being present, full restitution shall be made. ¹⁵If the owner was present, there shall be no restitution; if it was hired, only the hiring fee is due.

16  When a man seduces a virgin who is not engaged to be married, and lies with her, he shall give the bride-price for her and make her his wife. ¹⁷But if her father refuses to give her to him, he shall pay an amount equal to the bride-price for virgins.

18  You shall not permit a female sorcerer to live.

19  Whoever lies with an animal shall be put to death.

20  Whoever sacrifices to any god, other than the Lᴏʀᴅ alone, shall be devoted to destruction.

21  You shall not wrong or oppress a resident alien, for you were aliens in the land of Egypt. ²²You shall not abuse any widow or orphan. ²³If you do abuse them, when they cry out to me, I will surely heed their cry; ²⁴my wrath will burn, and I will kill you with the sword, and your wives shall become widows and your children orphans.

25  If you lend money to my people, to the poor among you, you shall not deal with them as a creditor; you shall not exact interest from them. ²⁶If you take your neighbor's cloak in pawn, you shall restore it before the sun goes down; ²⁷for it may be your neighbor's only clothing to use as cover; in what else shall that person sleep? And if your neighbor cries out to me, I will listen, for I am compassionate.

28  You shall not revile God, or curse a leader of your people.

29  You shall not delay to make offerings from the fullness of your harvest and from the outflow of your presses. ᶜ

The firstborn of your sons you shall give to me. ³⁰You shall do the same with your oxen and with your sheep: seven days it shall remain with its mother; on the eighth day you shall give it to me.

---

ªOr *before the judges*   ᵇOr *the judges condemn*   ᶜMeaning of Heb uncertain

31 You shall be people consecrated to me; therefore you shall not eat any meat that is mangled by beasts in the field; you shall throw it to the dogs.

**23.**1 You shall not spread a false report. You shall not join hands with the wicked to act as a malicious witness. 2You shall not follow a majority in wrongdoing; when you bear witness in a lawsuit, you shall not side with the majority so as to pervert justice; 3nor shall you be partial to the poor in a lawsuit.

4 When you come upon your enemy's ox or donkey going astray, you shall bring it back.

5 When you see the donkey of one who hates you lying under its burden and you would hold back from setting it free, you must help to set it free. a

6 You shall not pervert the justice due to your poor in their lawsuits. 7Keep far from a false charge, and do not kill the innocent and those in the right, for I will not acquit the guilty. 8You shall take no bribe, for a bribe blinds the officials, and subverts the cause of those who are in the right.

9 You shall not oppress a resident alien; you know the heart of an alien, for you were aliens in the land of Egypt.

10 For six years you shall sow your land and gather in its yield; 11but the seventh year you shall let it rest and lie fallow, so that the poor of your people may eat; and what they leave the wild animals may eat. You shall do the same with your vineyard, and with your olive orchard.

12 Six days you shall do your work, but on the seventh day you shall rest, so that your ox and your donkey may have relief, and your homeborn slave and the resident alien may be refreshed. 13Be attentive to all that I have said to you. Do not invoke the names of other gods; do not let them be heard on your lips.

## MATTHEW 24.1–28

As Jesus came out of the temple and was going away, his disciples came to point out to him the buildings of the temple. 2Then he asked them, "You see all these, do you not? Truly I tell you, not one stone will be left here upon another; all will be thrown down."

3 When he was sitting on the Mount of Olives, the disciples came to him privately, saying, "Tell us, when will this be, and what will be the sign of your coming and of the end of the age?" 4Jesus answered them, "Beware that no one leads you astray. 5For many will come in my name, saying, 'I am the Messiah!'b and they will lead many astray. 6And you will hear of wars and rumors of wars; see that you are not alarmed; for this must take place, but the end is not yet. 7For nation will rise against nation, and kingdom against kingdom, and there will be faminesc and earthquakes in various places: 8all this is but the beginning of the birth pangs.

9 "Then they will hand you over to be tortured and will put you to death, and you will be hated by all nations because of my name. 10Then many will fall away, d and they will betray one another and hate one another. 11And many false prophets will arise and lead many astray. 12And because of the increase of lawlessness, the love of many will grow cold. 13But the one who endures to the end will be saved. 14And this good newse of the kingdom will be proclaimed throughout the world, as a testimony to all the nations; and then the end will come.

15 "So when you see the desolating sacrilege standing in the holy place, as was spoken of by the prophet Daniel (let the reader understand), 16then

a Meaning of Heb uncertain   b Or *the Christ*   c Other ancient authorities add *and pestilences*
d Or *stumble*   e Or *gospel*

those in Judea must flee to the mountains; [17]the one on the housetop must not go down to take what is in the house; [18]the one in the field must not turn back to get a coat. [19]Woe to those who are pregnant and to those who are nursing infants in those days! [20]Pray that your flight may not be in winter or on a sabbath. [21]For at that time there will be great suffering, such as has not been from the beginning of the world until now, no, and never will be. [22]And if those days had not been cut short, no one would be saved; but for the sake of the elect those days will be cut short. [23]Then if anyone says to you, 'Look! Here is the Messiah!'[a] or 'There he is!'—do not believe it. [24]For false messiahs[b] and false prophets will appear and produce great signs and omens, to lead astray, if possible, even the elect. [25]Take note, I have told you beforehand. [26]So, if they say to you, 'Look! He is in the wilderness,' do not go out. If they say, 'Look! He is in the inner rooms,' do not believe it. [27]For as the lightning comes from the east and flashes as far as the west, so will be the coming of the Son of Man. [28]Wherever the corpse is, there the vultures will gather.

## PSALM 29.1–11

*A Psalm of David.*

Ascribe to the LORD,
  O heavenly beings,[c]
ascribe to the LORD glory
    and strength.
2  Ascribe to the LORD the glory of
      his name;
    worship the LORD in holy
      splendor.

3  The voice of the LORD is over
      the waters;
    the God of glory thunders,
    the LORD, over mighty
      waters.

4  The voice of the LORD is
      powerful;
    the voice of the LORD is full of
      majesty.

5  The voice of the LORD breaks
      the cedars;
    the LORD breaks the cedars of
      Lebanon.
6  He makes Lebanon skip like a
      calf,
    and Sirion like a young wild
      ox.

7  The voice of the LORD flashes
      forth flames of fire.
8  The voice of the LORD shakes
      the wilderness;
    the LORD shakes the
      wilderness of Kadesh.

9  The voice of the LORD causes
      the oaks to whirl,[d]
    and strips the forest bare;
    and in his temple all say,
      "Glory!"

10  The LORD sits enthroned over
      the flood;
    the LORD sits enthroned as
      king forever.
11  May the LORD give strength to
      his people!
    May the LORD bless his
      people with peace!

## PROVERBS 7.6–23

For at the window of my house
  I looked out through my
      lattice,
7  and I saw among the simple
      ones,
    I observed among the youths,
    a young man without sense,
8  passing along the street near
      her corner,
    taking the road to her house
9  in the twilight, in the evening,

a Or *the Christ*  b Or *christs*  c Heb *sons of gods*  d Or *causes the deer to calve*

at the time of night and
    darkness.

10 Then a woman comes toward
    him,
    decked out like a prostitute,
        wily of heart. [a]
11 She is loud and wayward;
    her feet do not stay at home;
12 now in the street, now in the
    squares,
    and at every corner she lies
        in wait.
13 She seizes him and kisses him,
    and with impudent face she
        says to him:
14 "I had to offer sacrifices,
    and today I have paid my
        vows;
15 so now I have come out to
    meet you,
    to seek you eagerly, and I
        have found you!
16 I have decked my couch with
    coverings,
    colored spreads of Egyptian
        linen;
17 I have perfumed my bed with
    myrrh,

    aloes, and cinnamon.
18 Come, let us take our fill of love
    until morning;
    let us delight ourselves with
        love.
19 For my husband is not at home;
    he has gone on a long
        journey.
20 He took a bag of money with
    him;
    he will not come home until
        full moon."

21 With much seductive speech she
    persuades him;
    with her smooth talk she
        compels him.
22 Right away he follows her,
    and goes like an ox to the
        slaughter,
    or bounds like a stag toward
        the trap [b]
23 until an arrow pierces its
    entrails.
    He is like a bird rushing into a
    snare,
    not knowing that it will cost
        him his life.

# FEBRUARY 6

## EXODUS 23.14—25.40

**T**HREE times in the year you shall hold a festival for me. [15]You shall observe the festival of unleavened bread; as I commanded you, you shall eat unleavened bread for seven days at the appointed time in the month of Abib, for in it you came out of Egypt.

No one shall appear before me empty-handed.

16 You shall observe the festival of harvest, of the first fruits of your labor, of what you sow in the field. You shall observe the festival of ingathering at the end of the year, when you gather in from the field the fruit of your labor. [17]Three times in the year all your males shall appear before the Lord GOD.

18 You shall not offer the blood of

[a] Meaning of Heb uncertain  [b] Cn Compare Gk: Meaning of Heb uncertain

my sacrifice with anything leavened, or let the fat of my festival remain until the morning.

19 The choicest of the first fruits of your ground you shall bring into the house of the LORD your God.

You shall not boil a kid in its mother's milk.

20 I am going to send an angel in front of you, to guard you on the way and to bring you to the place that I have prepared. [21]Be attentive to him and listen to his voice; do not rebel against him, for he will not pardon your transgression; for my name is in him.

22 But if you listen attentively to his voice and do all that I say, then I will be an enemy to your enemies and a foe to your foes.

23 When my angel goes in front of you, and brings you to the Amorites, the Hittites, the Perizzites, the Canaanites, the Hivites, and the Jebusites, and I blot them out, [24]you shall not bow down to their gods, or worship them, or follow their practices, but you shall utterly demolish them and break their pillars in pieces. [25]You shall worship the LORD your God, and I[a] will bless your bread and your water; and I will take sickness away from among you. [26]No one shall miscarry or be barren in your land; I will fulfill the number of your days. [27]I will send my terror in front of you, and will throw into confusion all the people against whom you shall come, and I will make all your enemies turn their backs to you. [28]And I will send the pestilence[b] in front of you, which shall drive out the Hivites, the Canaanites, and the Hittites from before you. [29]I will not drive them out from before you in one year, or the land would become desolate and the wild animals would multiply against you. [30]Little by little I will drive them out from before you, until you have increased and possess the land. [31]I will set your borders from the Red Sea[c] to the sea of the Philistines, and from the wilderness to the Euphrates; for I will hand over to you the inhabitants of the land, and you shall drive them out before you. [32]You shall make no covenant with them and their gods. [33]They shall not live in your land, or they will make you sin against me; for if you worship their gods, it will surely be a snare to you.

**24.**1 THEN he said to Moses, "Come up to the LORD, you and Aaron, Nadab, and Abihu, and seventy of the elders of Israel, and worship at a distance. [2]Moses alone shall come near the LORD; but the others shall not come near, and the people shall not come up with him."

3 Moses came and told the people all the words of the LORD and all the ordinances; and all the people answered with one voice, and said, "All the words that the LORD has spoken we will do." [4]And Moses wrote down all the words of the LORD. He rose early in the morning, and built an altar at the foot of the mountain, and set up twelve pillars, corresponding to the twelve tribes of Israel. [5]He sent young men of the people of Israel, who offered burnt offerings and sacrificed oxen as offerings of well-being to the LORD. [6]Moses took half of the blood and put it in basins, and half of the blood he dashed against the altar. [7]Then he took the book of the covenant, and read it in the hearing of the people; and they said, "All that the LORD has spoken we will do, and we will be obedient." [8]Moses took the blood and dashed it on the people, and said, "See the blood of the covenant that the LORD has made with you in accordance with all these words."

9 Then Moses and Aaron, Nadab, and Abihu, and seventy of the elders of Israel went up, [10]and they saw the God of Israel. Under his feet there was

---

a Gk Vg: Heb *he*   b Or *hornets*: Meaning of Heb uncertain   c Or *Sea of Reeds* something like a pavement of sapphire stone, like the very heaven for clearness. [11]God[a] did not lay his hand on the chief men of the people of Israel; also they beheld God, and they ate and drank.

12 The LORD said to Moses, "Come up to me on the mountain, and wait there; and I will give you the tablets of stone, with the law and the commandment, which I have written for their instruction." [13]So Moses set out with his assistant Joshua, and Moses went up into the mountain of God. [14]To the elders he had said, "Wait here for us, until we come to you again; for Aaron and Hur are with you; whoever has a dispute may go to them."

15 Then Moses went up on the mountain, and the cloud covered the mountain. [16]The glory of the LORD settled on Mount Sinai, and the cloud covered it for six days; on the seventh day he called to Moses out of the cloud. [17]Now the appearance of the glory of the LORD was like a devouring fire on the top of the mountain in the sight of the people of Israel. [18]Moses entered the cloud, and went up on the mountain. Moses was on the mountain for forty days and forty nights.

**25.**[1] THE LORD said to Moses: [2]Tell the Israelites to take for me an offering; from all whose hearts prompt them to give you shall receive the offering for me. [3]This is the offering that you shall receive from them: gold, silver, and bronze, [4]blue, purple, and crimson yarns and fine linen, goats' hair, [5]tanned rams' skins, fine leather,[b] acacia wood, [6]oil for the lamps, spices for the anointing oil and for the fragrant incense, [7]onyx stones and gems to be set in the ephod and for the breastpiece. [8]And have them make me a sanctuary, so that I may dwell among them. [9]In accordance with all that I show you con-

cerning the pattern of the tabernacle and of all its furniture, so you shall make it.

10 They shall make an ark of acacia wood; it shall be two and a half cubits long, a cubit and a half wide, and a cubit and a half high. [11]You shall overlay it with pure gold, inside and outside you shall overlay it, and you shall make a molding of gold upon it all around. [12]You shall cast four rings of gold for it and put them on its four feet, two rings on the one side of it, and two rings on the other side. [13]You shall make poles of acacia wood, and overlay them with gold. [14]And you shall put the poles into the rings on the sides of the ark, by which to carry the ark. [15]The poles shall remain in the rings of the ark; they shall not be taken from it. [16]You shall put into the ark the covenant[c] that I shall give you.

17 Then you shall make a mercy seat[d] of pure gold; two cubits and a half shall be its length, and a cubit and a half its width. [18]You shall make two cherubim of gold; you shall make them of hammered work, at the two ends of the mercy seat.[e] [19]Make one cherub at the one end, and one cherub at the other; of one piece with the mercy seat[e] you shall make the cherubim at its two ends. [20]The cherubim shall spread out their wings above, overshadowing the mercy seat[e] with their wings. They shall face one to another; the faces of the cherubim shall be turned toward the mercy seat.[e] [21]You shall put the mercy seat[e] on the top of the ark; and in the ark you shall put the covenant[c] that I shall give you. [22]There I will meet with you, and from above the mercy seat,[e] from between the two cherubim that are on the ark of the covenant,[c] I will deliver to you all my commands for the Israelites.

23 You shall make a table of acacia wood, two cubits long, one cubit wide,

aHeb *He*  bMeaning of Heb uncertain  cOr *treaty,* or *testimony;* Heb *eduth*  dOr *a cover*  eOr *the cover*

and a cubit and a half high. $^{24}$You shall overlay it with pure gold, and make a molding of gold around it. $^{25}$You shall make around it a rim a handbreadth wide, and a molding of gold around the rim. $^{26}$You shall make for it four rings of gold, and fasten the rings to the four corners at its four legs. $^{27}$The rings that hold the poles used for carrying the table shall be close to the rim. $^{28}$You shall make the poles of acacia wood, and overlay them with gold, and the table shall be carried with these. $^{29}$You shall make its plates and dishes for incense, and its flagons and bowls with which to pour drink offerings; you shall make them of pure gold. $^{30}$And you shall set the bread of the Presence on the table before me always.

31 You shall make a lampstand of pure gold. The base and the shaft of the lampstand shall be made of hammered work; its cups, its calyxes, and its petals shall be of one piece with it; $^{32}$and there shall be six branches going out of its sides, three branches of the lampstand out of one side of it and three branches of the lampstand out of the other side of it; $^{33}$three cups shaped like almond blossoms, each with calyx and petals, on one branch, and three cups shaped like almond blossoms, each with calyx and petals, on the other branch—so for the six branches going out of the lampstand. $^{34}$On the lampstand itself there shall be four cups shaped like almond blossoms, each with its calyxes and petals. $^{35}$There shall be a calyx of one piece with it under the first pair of branches, a calyx of one piece with it under the next pair of branches, and a calyx of one piece with it under the last pair of branches—so for the six branches that go out of the lampstand. $^{36}$Their calyxes and their branches shall be of one piece with it, the whole of it one hammered piece of pure gold. $^{37}$You shall make the seven

lamps for it; and the lamps shall be set up so as to give light on the space in front of it. $^{38}$Its snuffers and trays shall be of pure gold. $^{39}$It, and all these utensils, shall be made from a talent of pure gold. $^{40}$And see that you make them according to the pattern for them, which is being shown you on the mountain.

## MATTHEW 24.29–51

"IMMEDIATELY after the suffering of those days
the sun will be darkened,
 and the moon will not give
  its light;
the stars will fall from heaven,
 and the powers of heaven will
  be shaken.

$^{30}$Then the sign of the Son of Man will appear in heaven, and then all the tribes of the earth will mourn, and they will see 'the Son of Man coming on the clouds of heaven' with power and great glory. $^{31}$And he will send out his angels with a loud trumpet call, and they will gather his elect from the four winds, from one end of heaven to the other.

32 "From the fig tree learn its lesson: as soon as its branch becomes tender and puts forth its leaves, you know that summer is near. $^{33}$So also, when you see all these things, you know that he[a] is near, at the very gates. $^{34}$Truly I tell you, this generation will not pass away until all these things have taken place. $^{35}$Heaven and earth will pass away, but my words will not pass away.

36 "But about that day and hour no one knows, neither the angels of heaven, nor the Son,[b] but only the Father. $^{37}$For as the days of Noah were, so will be the coming of the Son of Man. $^{38}$For as in those days before the flood they were eating and drinking, marrying and giving in marriage, until the day Noah entered the ark, $^{39}$and they knew nothing until the flood came and swept

a Or *it*  b Other ancient authorities lack *nor the Son*

them all away, so too will be the coming of the Son of Man. [40]Then two will be in the field; one will be taken and one will be left. [41]Two women will be grinding meal together; one will be taken and one will be left. [42]Keep awake therefore, for you do not know on what day[a] your Lord is coming. [43]But understand this: if the owner of the house had known in what part of the night the thief was coming, he would have stayed awake and would not have let his house be broken into. [44]Therefore you also must be ready, for the Son of Man is coming at an unexpected hour.

45 "Who then is the faithful and wise slave, whom his master has put in charge of his household, to give the other slaves[b] their allowance of food at the proper time? [46]Blessed is that slave whom his master will find at work when he arrives. [47]Truly I tell you, he will put that one in charge of all his possessions. [48]But if that wicked slave says to himself, 'My master is delayed,' [49]and he begins to beat his fellow slaves, and eats and drinks with drunkards, [50]the master of that slave will come on a day when he does not expect him and at an hour that he does not know. [51]He will cut him in pieces[c] and put him with the hypocrites, where there will be weeping and gnashing of teeth.

## PSALM 30.1–12

*A Psalm. A Song at the dedication of the temple. Of David.*

I WILL extol you, O LORD, for you
    have drawn me up,
  and did not let my foes
    rejoice over me.
2  O LORD my God, I cried to you
    for help,
  and you have healed me.
3  O LORD, you brought up my soul
    from Sheol,

restored me to life from
  among those gone down
  to the Pit. [d]

4  Sing praises to the LORD, O you
    his faithful ones,
  and give thanks to his holy
    name.
5  For his anger is but for a
    moment;
  his favor is for a lifetime.
Weeping may linger for the
    night,
  but joy comes with the
    morning.

6  As for me, I said in my
    prosperity,
  "I shall never be moved."
7  By your favor, O LORD,
  you had established me as a
    strong mountain;
you hid your face;
  I was dismayed.

8  To you, O LORD, I cried,
  and to the LORD I made
    supplication:
9  "What profit is there in my
    death,
  if I go down to the Pit?
Will the dust praise you?
  Will it tell of your
    faithfulness?
10  Hear, O LORD, and be gracious
    to me!
  O LORD, be my helper!"

11  You have turned my mourning
    into dancing;
  you have taken off my
    sackcloth
  and clothed me with joy,
12  so that my soul[e] may praise
    you and not be silent.
  O LORD my God, I will give
    thanks to you forever.

---

a Other ancient authorities read *at what hour*  b Gk *to give them*  c Or *cut him off*  d Or *that I should not go down to the Pit*  e Heb *that glory*

## PROVERBS 7.24–27

**A**ND now, my children, listen
to me,
and be attentive to the
words of my mouth.
25 Do not let your hearts turn
aside to her ways;
do not stray into her paths.

26 for many are those she has
laid low,
and numerous are her
victims.
27 Her house is the way to Sheol,
going down to the chambers
of death.

# FEBRUARY 7

## EXODUS 26.1—27.21

**M**OREOVER you shall make the tabernacle with ten curtains of fine twisted linen, and blue, purple, and crimson yarns; you shall make them with cherubim skillfully worked into them. 2The length of each curtain shall be twenty-eight cubits, and the width of each curtain four cubits; all the curtains shall be of the same size. 3Five curtains shall be joined to one another; and the other five curtains shall be joined to one another. 4You shall make loops of blue on the edge of the outermost curtain in the first set; and likewise you shall make loops on the edge of the outermost curtain in the second set. 5You shall make fifty loops on the one curtain, and you shall make fifty loops on the edge of the curtain that is in the second set; the loops shall be opposite one another. 6You shall make fifty clasps of gold, and join the curtains to one another with the clasps, so that the tabernacle may be one whole.

7 You shall also make curtains of goats' hair for a tent over the tabernacle; you shall make eleven curtains. 8The length of each curtain shall be thirty cubits, and the width of each curtain four cubits; the eleven curtains shall be of the same size. 9You shall join five curtains by themselves, and six curtains by themselves, and the sixth curtain you shall double over at the front of the tent. 10You shall make fifty loops on the edge of the curtain that is outermost in one set, and fifty loops on the edge of the curtain that is outermost in the second set.

11 You shall make fifty clasps of bronze, and put the clasps into the loops, and join the tent together, so that it may be one whole. 12The part that remains of the curtains of the tent, the half curtain that remains, shall hang over the back of the tabernacle. 13The cubit on the one side, and the cubit on the other side, of what remains in the length of the curtains of the tent, shall hang over the sides of the tabernacle, on this side and that side, to cover it. 14You shall make for the tent a covering of tanned rams' skins and an outer covering of fine leather. a

15 You shall make upright frames of acacia wood for the tabernacle. 16Ten cubits shall be the length of a frame, and a cubit and a half the width of each frame. 17There shall be two pegs in each frame to fit the frames to-

a Meaning of Heb uncertain

gether; you shall make these for all the frames of the tabernacle. [18]You shall make the frames for the tabernacle: twenty frames for the south side; [19]and you shall make forty bases of silver under the twenty frames, two bases under the first frame for its two pegs, and two bases under the next frame for its two pegs; [20]and for the second side of the tabernacle, on the north side twenty frames, [21]and their forty bases of silver, two bases under the first frame, and two bases under the next frame; [22]and for the rear of the tabernacle westward you shall make six frames. [23]You shall make two frames for corners of the tabernacle in the rear; [24]they shall be separate beneath, but joined at the top, at the first ring; it shall be the same with both of them; they shall form the two corners. [25]And so there shall be eight frames, with their bases of silver, sixteen bases; two bases under the first frame, and two bases under the next frame.

26 You shall make bars of acacia wood, five for the frames of the one side of the tabernacle, [27]and five bars for the frames of the other side of the tabernacle, and five bars for the frames of the side of the tabernacle at the rear westward. [28]The middle bar, halfway up the frames, shall pass through from end to end. [29]You shall overlay the frames with gold, and shall make their rings of gold to hold the bars; and you shall overlay the bars with gold. [30]Then you shall erect the tabernacle according to the plan for it that you were shown on the mountain.

31 You shall make a curtain of blue, purple, and crimson yarns, and of fine twisted linen; it shall be made with cherubim skillfully worked into it. [32]You shall hang it on four pillars of acacia overlaid with gold, which have hooks of gold and rest on four bases of silver. [33]You shall hang the curtain under the clasps, and bring the ark of the covenant [a] in there, within the curtain; and the curtain shall separate for you the holy place from the most holy. [34]You shall put the mercy seat [b] on the ark of the covenant [a] in the most holy place. [35]You shall set the table outside the curtain, and the lampstand on the south side of the tabernacle opposite the table; and you shall put the table on the north side.

36 You shall make a screen for the entrance of the tent, of blue, purple, and crimson yarns, and of fine twisted linen, embroidered with needlework. [37]You shall make for the screen five pillars of acacia, and overlay them with gold; their hooks shall be of gold, and you shall cast five bases of bronze for them.

**27**.1 You shall make the altar of acacia wood, five cubits long and five cubits wide; the altar shall be square, and it shall be three cubits high. [2]You shall make horns for it on its four corners; its horns shall be of one piece with it, and you shall overlay it with bronze. [3]You shall make pots for it to receive its ashes, and shovels and basins and forks and firepans; you shall make all its utensils of bronze. [4]You shall also make for it a grating, a network of bronze; and on the net you shall make four bronze rings at its four corners. [5]You shall set it under the ledge of the altar so that the net shall extend halfway down the altar. [6]You shall make poles for the altar, poles of acacia wood, and overlay them with bronze; [7]the poles shall be put through the rings, so that the poles shall be on the two sides of the altar when it is carried. [8]You shall make it hollow, with boards. They shall be made just as you were shown on the mountain.

9 You shall make the court of the tabernacle. On the south side the court

---

a Or *treaty*, or *testimony*; Heb *eduth*   b Or *the cover* shall have hangings of fine twisted linen one hundred cubits long for that side; ¹⁰its twenty pillars and their twenty bases shall be of bronze, but the hooks of the pillars and their bands shall be of silver. ¹¹Likewise for its length on the north side there shall be hangings one hundred cubits long, their pillars twenty and their bases twenty, of bronze, but the hooks of the pillars and their bands shall be of silver. ¹²For the width of the court on the west side there shall be fifty cubits of hangings, with ten pillars and ten bases. ¹³The width of the court on the front to the east shall be fifty cubits. ¹⁴There shall be fifteen cubits of hangings on the one side, with three pillars and three bases. ¹⁵There shall be fifteen cubits of hangings on the other side, with three pillars and three bases. ¹⁶For the gate of the court there shall be a screen twenty cubits long, of blue, purple, and crimson yarns, and of fine twisted linen, embroidered with needlework; it shall have four pillars and with them four bases. ¹⁷All the pillars around the court shall be banded with silver; their hooks shall be of silver, and their bases of bronze. ¹⁸The length of the court shall be one hundred cubits, the width fifty, and the height five cubits, with hangings of fine twisted linen and bases of bronze. ¹⁹All the utensils of the tabernacle for every use, and all its pegs and all the pegs of the court, shall be of bronze.

20 You shall further command the Israelites to bring you pure oil of beaten olives for the light, so that a lamp may be set up to burn regularly. ²¹In the tent of meeting, outside the curtain that is before the covenant, ᵃ Aaron and his sons shall tend it from evening to morning before the Lord. It shall be a perpetual ordinance to be observed throughout their generations by the Israelites.

## MATTHEW 25. 1–30

"THEN the kingdom of heaven will be like this. Ten bridesmaids ᵇ took their lamps and went to meet the bridegroom. ᶜ ²Five of them were foolish, and five were wise. ³When the foolish took their lamps, they took no oil with them; ⁴but the wise took flasks of oil with their lamps. ⁵As the bridegroom was delayed, all of them became drowsy and slept. ⁶But at midnight there was a shout, 'Look! Here is the bridegroom! Come out to meet him.' ⁷Then all those bridesmaids ᵇ got up and trimmed their lamps. ⁸The foolish said to the wise, 'Give us some of your oil, for our lamps are going out.' ⁹But the wise replied, 'No! there will not be enough for you and for us; you had better go to the dealers and buy some for yourselves.' ¹⁰And while they went to buy it, the bridegroom came, and those who were ready went with him into the wedding banquet; and the door was shut. ¹¹Later the other bridesmaids ᵇ came also, saying, 'Lord, lord, open to us.' ¹²But he replied, 'Truly I tell you, I do not know you.' ¹³Keep awake therefore, for you know neither the day nor the hour. ᵈ

14 "For it is as if a man, going on a journey, summoned his slaves and entrusted his property to them; ¹⁵to one he gave five talents, ᵉ to another two, to another one, to each according to his ability. Then he went away. ¹⁶The one who had received the five talents went off at once and traded with them, and made five more talents. ¹⁷In the same way, the one who had the two talents made two more talents. ¹⁸But the one who had received the one talent went off and dug a hole in the ground and hid his master's money. ¹⁹After a long time the master of those slaves came and

---

ᵃOr *treaty*, or *testimony*; Heb *eduth*   ᵇGk *virgins*   ᶜOther ancient authorities add *and the bride*
ᵈOther ancient authorities add *in which the Son of Man is coming*   ᵉA talent was worth more than fifteen years' wages of a laborer

settled accounts with them. <sup>20</sup>Then the one who had received the five talents came forward, bringing five more talents, saying, 'Master, you handed over to me five talents; see, I have made five more talents.' <sup>21</sup>His master said to him, 'Well done, good and trustworthy slave; you have been trustworthy in a few things, I will put you in charge of many things; enter into the joy of your master.' <sup>22</sup>And the one with the two talents also came forward, saying, 'Master, you handed over to me two talents; see, I have made two more talents.' <sup>23</sup>His master said to him, 'Well done, good and trustworthy slave; you have been trustworthy in a few things, I will put you in charge of many things; enter into the joy of your master.' <sup>24</sup>Then the one who had received the one talent also came forward, saying, 'Master, I knew that you were a harsh man, reaping where you did not sow, and gathering where you did not scatter seed; <sup>25</sup>so I was afraid, and I went and hid your talent in the ground. Here you have what is yours.' <sup>26</sup>But his master replied, 'You wicked and lazy slave! You knew, did you, that I reap where I did not sow, and gather where I did not scatter? <sup>27</sup>Then you ought to have invested my money with the bankers, and on my return I would have received what was my own with interest. <sup>28</sup>So take the talent from him, and give it to the one with the ten talents. <sup>29</sup>For to all those who have, more will be given, and they will have an abundance; but from those who have nothing, even what they have will be taken away. <sup>30</sup>As for this worthless slave, throw him into the outer darkness, where there will be weeping and gnashing of teeth.'

## PSALM 31.1–8

*To the leader. A Psalm of David.*

IN you, O LORD, I seek refuge;
    do not let me ever be put to
        shame;
  in your righteousness deliver
      me.
2  Incline your ear to me;
    rescue me speedily.
Be a rock of refuge for me,
  a strong fortress to save me.

3  You are indeed my rock and my
      fortress;
  for your name's sake lead me
    and guide me,
4  take me out of the net that is
      hidden for me,
  for you are my refuge.
5  Into your hand I commit my
      spirit;
  you have redeemed me,
    O LORD, faithful God.

6  You hate[a] those who pay
      regard to worthless idols,
  but I trust in the LORD.
7  I will exult and rejoice in your
      steadfast love,
  because you have seen my
    affliction;
  you have taken heed of my
    adversities,
8  and have not delivered me into
      the hand of the enemy;
  you have set my feet in a
    broad place.

## PROVERBS 8.1–11

DOES not wisdom call,
  and does not understanding
    raise her voice?
2  On the heights, beside the way,
  at the crossroads she takes
    her stand;

---

[a] One Heb Ms Gk Syr Jerome: MT *I hate*

<sup>3</sup> beside the gates in front of the
   town,
     at the entrance of the portals
      she cries out:
<sup>4</sup> "To you, O people, I call,
     and my cry is to all that live.
<sup>5</sup> O simple ones, learn prudence;
     acquire intelligence, you who
      lack it.
<sup>6</sup> Hear, for I will speak noble
   things,
     and from my lips will come
      what is right;
<sup>7</sup> for my mouth will utter truth;
     wickedness is an abomination
      to my lips.

<sup>8</sup> All the words of my mouth are
   righteous;
     there is nothing twisted or
      crooked in them.
<sup>9</sup> They are all straight to one who
   understands
     and right to those who find
      knowledge.
<sup>10</sup> Take my instruction instead of
   silver,
     and knowledge rather than
      choice gold;
<sup>11</sup> for wisdom is better than
   jewels,
     and all that you may desire
      cannot compare with her.

# FEBRUARY 8

## EXODUS 28.1–43

**T**HEN bring near to you your brother Aaron, and his sons with him, from among the Israelites, to serve me as priests—Aaron and Aaron's sons, Nadab and Abihu, Eleazar and Ithamar. <sup>2</sup>You shall make sacred vestments for the glorious adornment of your brother Aaron. <sup>3</sup>And you shall speak to all who have ability, whom I have endowed with skill, that they make Aaron's vestments to consecrate him for my priesthood. <sup>4</sup>These are the vestments that they shall make: a breastpiece, an ephod, a robe, a checkered tunic, a turban, and a sash. When they make these sacred vestments for your brother Aaron and his sons to serve me as priests, <sup>5</sup>they shall use gold, blue, purple, and crimson yarns, and fine linen.

6 They shall make the ephod of gold, of blue, purple, and crimson yarns, and of fine twisted linen, skillfully worked. <sup>7</sup>It shall have two shoulder-pieces attached to its two edges, so that it may be joined together. <sup>8</sup>The decorated band on it shall be of the same workmanship and materials, of gold, of blue, purple, and crimson yarns, and of fine twisted linen. <sup>9</sup>You shall take two onyx stones, and engrave on them the names of the sons of Israel, <sup>10</sup>six of their names on the one stone, and the names of the remaining six on the other stone, in the order of their birth. <sup>11</sup>As a gem-cutter engraves signets, so you shall engrave the two stones with the names of the sons of Israel; you shall mount them in settings of gold filigree. <sup>12</sup>You shall set the two stones on the shoulder-pieces of the ephod, as stones of remembrance for the sons of Israel; and Aaron shall bear their names before the LORD on his two shoulders for remembrance. <sup>13</sup>You shall make settings of gold filigree, <sup>14</sup>and two chains of pure gold, twisted like cords; and you shall attach the corded chains to the settings.

15 You shall make a breastpiece of judgment, in skilled work; you shall make it in the style of the ephod; of gold, of blue and purple and crimson yarns, and of fine twisted linen you shall make it. [16]It shall be square and doubled, a span in length and a span in width. [17]You shall set in it four rows of stones. A row of carnelian,[a] chrysolite, and emerald shall be the first row; [18]and the second row a turquoise, a sapphire[b] and a moonstone; [19]and the third row a jacinth, an agate, and an amethyst; [20]and the fourth row a beryl, an onyx, and a jasper; they shall be set in gold filigree. [21]There shall be twelve stones with names corresponding to the names of the sons of Israel; they shall be like signets, each engraved with its name, for the twelve tribes. [22]You shall make for the breastpiece chains of pure gold, twisted like cords; [23]and you shall make for the breastpiece two rings of gold, and put the two rings on the two edges of the breastpiece. [24]You shall put the two cords of gold in the two rings at the edges of the breastpiece; [25]the two ends of the two cords you shall attach to the two settings, and so attach it in front to the shoulder-pieces of the ephod. [26]You shall make two rings of gold, and put them at the two ends of the breastpiece, on its inside edge next to the ephod. [27]You shall make two rings of gold, and attach them in front to the lower part of the two shoulder-pieces of the ephod, at its joining above the decorated band of the ephod. [28]The breastpiece shall be bound by its rings to the rings of the ephod with a blue cord, so that it may lie on the decorated band of the ephod, and so that the breastpiece shall not come loose from the ephod. [29]So Aaron shall bear the names of the sons of Israel in the breastpiece of judgment on his heart when he goes into the holy place, for a continual remembrance before the Lord. [30]In the breastpiece of judgment you shall put the Urim and the Thummim, and they shall be on Aaron's heart when he goes in before the Lord; thus Aaron shall bear the judgment of the Israelites on his heart before the Lord continually.

31 You shall make the robe of the ephod all of blue. [32]It shall have an opening for the head in the middle of it, with a woven binding around the opening, like the opening in a coat of mail,[c] so that it may not be torn. [33]On its lower hem you shall make pomegranates of blue, purple, and crimson yarns, all around the lower hem, with bells of gold between them all around—[34]a golden bell and a pomegranate alternating all around the lower hem of the robe. [35]Aaron shall wear it when he ministers, and its sound shall be heard when he goes into the holy place before the Lord, and when he comes out, so that he may not die.

36 You shall make a rosette of pure gold, and engrave on it, like the engraving of a signet, "Holy to the Lord." [37]You shall fasten it on the turban with a blue cord; it shall be on the front of the turban. [38]It shall be on Aaron's forehead, and Aaron shall take on himself any guilt incurred in the holy offering that the Israelites consecrate as their sacred donations; it shall always be on his forehead, in order that they may find favor before the Lord.

39 You shall make the checkered tunic of fine linen, and you shall make a turban of fine linen, and you shall make a sash embroidered with needlework.

40 For Aaron's sons you shall make tunics and sashes and headdresses; you shall make them for their glorious adornment. [41]You shall put them on your brother Aaron, and on his sons with him, and shall anoint them and or-

[a]The identity of several of these stones is uncertain  [b]Or *lapis lazuli*  [c]Meaning of Heb uncertain

dain them and consecrate them, so that they may serve me as priests. ⁴²You shall make for them linen undergarments to cover their naked flesh; they shall reach from the hips to the thighs; ⁴³Aaron and his sons shall wear them when they go into the tent of meeting, or when they come near the altar to minister in the holy place; or they will bring guilt on themselves and die. This shall be a perpetual ordinance for him and for his descendants after him.

## MATTHEW 25.31—26.13

"**W**HEN the Son of Man comes in his glory, and all the angels with him, then he will sit on the throne of his glory. ³²All the nations will be gathered before him, and he will separate people one from another as a shepherd separates the sheep from the goats, ³³and he will put the sheep at his right hand and the goats at the left. ³⁴Then the king will say to those at his right hand, 'Come, you that are blessed by my Father, inherit the kingdom prepared for you from the foundation of the world; ³⁵for I was hungry and you gave me food, I was thirsty and you gave me something to drink, I was a stranger and you welcomed me, ³⁶I was naked and you gave me clothing, I was sick and you took care of me, I was in prison and you visited me.' ³⁷Then the righteous will answer him, 'Lord, when was it that we saw you hungry and gave you food, or thirsty and gave you something to drink? ³⁸And when was it that we saw you a stranger and welcomed you, or naked and gave you clothing? ³⁹And when was it that we saw you sick or in prison and visited you?' ⁴⁰And the king will answer them, 'Truly I tell you, just as you did it to one of the least of these who are members of my family, [a] you did it to me.' ⁴¹Then he will say to those at his left hand, 'You that are accursed, depart from me into the eternal fire prepared for the devil and his angels; ⁴²for I was hungry and you gave me no food, I was thirsty and you gave me nothing to drink, ⁴³I was a stranger and you did not welcome me, naked and you did not give me clothing, sick and in prison and you did not visit me.' ⁴⁴Then they also will answer, 'Lord, when was it that we saw you hungry or thirsty or a stranger or naked or sick or in prison, and did not take care of you?' ⁴⁵Then he will answer them, 'Truly I tell you, just as you did not do it to one of the least of these, you did not do it to me.' ⁴⁶And these will go away into eternal punishment, but the righteous into eternal life."

²⁶·¹ WHEN Jesus had finished saying all these things, he said to his disciples, ²"You know that after two days the Passover is coming, and the Son of Man will be handed over to be crucified."

3  Then the chief priests and the elders of the people gathered in the palace of the high priest, who was called Caiaphas, ⁴and they conspired to arrest Jesus by stealth and kill him. ⁵But they said, "Not during the festival, or there may be a riot among the people."

6  Now while Jesus was at Bethany in the house of Simon the leper, [b] ⁷a woman came to him with an alabaster jar of very costly ointment, and she poured it on his head as he sat at the table. ⁸But when the disciples saw it, they were angry and said, "Why this waste? ⁹For this ointment could have been sold for a large sum, and the money given to the poor." ¹⁰But Jesus, aware of this, said to them, "Why do you trouble the woman? She has performed a good service for me. ¹¹For you always have the poor with you, but you will not always have me. ¹²By pouring this ointment on my body she has prepared me for burial. ¹³Truly I tell

aGk *these my brothers*  bThe terms *leper* and *leprosy* can refer to several diseases

you, wherever this good news<sup>a</sup> is proclaimed in the whole world, what she has done will be told in remembrance of her."

## PSALM 31.9–18

**B**E gracious to me, O Lord, for
    I am in distress;
  my eye wastes away from
    grief,
  my soul and body also.
10  For my life is spent with
    sorrow,
  and my years with sighing;
  my strength fails because of my
    misery,<sup>b</sup>
  and my bones waste away.

11  I am the scorn of all my
    adversaries,
  a horror<sup>c</sup> to my neighbors,
  an object of dread to my
    acquaintances;
  those who see me in the
    street flee from me.
12  I have passed out of mind like
    one who is dead;
  I have become like a broken
    vessel.
13  For I hear the whispering of
    many—
    terror all around!—
  as they scheme together against
    me,
  as they plot to take my life.

14  But I trust in you, O Lord;
  I say, "You are my God."
15  My times are in your hand;
  deliver me from the hand of
    my enemies and
    persecutors.
16  Let your face shine upon your
    servant;
  save me in your steadfast
    love.
17  Do not let me be put to shame,
    O Lord,
  for I call on you;
  let the wicked be put to shame;
  let them go dumbfounded to
    Sheol.
18  Let the lying lips be stilled
  that speak insolently against
    the righteous
  with pride and contempt.

## PROVERBS 8.12–13

**I**, wisdom, live with prudence,<sup>d</sup>
  and I attain knowledge and
    discretion.
13  The fear of the Lord is hatred
    of evil.
  Pride and arrogance and the
    way of evil
  and perverted speech I hate.

## EXODUS 29.1—30.10

Now this is what you shall do to them to consecrate them, so that they may serve me as priests. Take one young bull and two rams without blemish, [2]and unleavened bread, unleavened cakes mixed with oil, and unleavened wafers spread with oil. You shall make them of choice wheat flour. [3]You shall put them in one basket and bring them in the basket, and bring the bull and the two rams. [4]You shall bring Aaron and his sons to the entrance of the tent of meeting, and wash them with water. [5]Then you shall take the vestments, and put on Aaron the tunic and the robe of the ephod, and the ephod, and the breastpiece, and gird him with the decorated band of the ephod; [6]and you shall set the turban on his head, and put the holy diadem on the turban. [7]You shall take the anointing oil, and pour it on his head and anoint him. [8]Then you shall bring his sons, and put tunics on them, [9]and you shall gird them with sashes[a] and tie headdresses on them; and the priesthood shall be theirs by a perpetual ordinance. You shall then ordain Aaron and his sons.

10 You shall bring the bull in front of the tent of meeting. Aaron and his sons shall lay their hands on the head of the bull, [11]and you shall slaughter the bull before the LORD, at the entrance of the tent of meeting, [12]and shall take some of the blood of the bull and put it on the horns of the altar with your finger, and all the rest of the blood you shall pour out at the base of the altar. [13]You shall take all the fat that covers the entrails, and the appendage of the liver, and the two kidneys with the fat that is on them, and turn them into smoke on the altar. [14]But the flesh of the bull, and its skin, and its dung, you shall burn with fire outside the camp; it is a sin offering.

15 Then you shall take one of the rams, and Aaron and his sons shall lay their hands on the head of the ram, [16]and you shall slaughter the ram, and shall take its blood and dash it against all sides of the altar. [17]Then you shall cut the ram into its parts, and wash its entrails and its legs, and put them with its parts and its head, [18]and turn the whole ram into smoke on the altar; it is a burnt offering to the LORD; it is a pleasing odor, an offering by fire to the LORD.

19 You shall take the other ram; and Aaron and his sons shall lay their hands on the head of the ram, [20]and you shall slaughter the ram, and take some of its blood and put it on the lobe of Aaron's right ear and on the lobes of the right ears of his sons, and on the thumbs of their right hands, and on the big toes of their right feet, and dash the rest of the blood against all sides of the altar. [21]Then you shall take some of the blood that is on the altar, and some of the anointing oil, and sprinkle it on Aaron and his vestments and on his sons and his sons' vestments with him; then he and his vestments shall be holy, as well as his sons and his sons' vestments.

22 You shall also take the fat of the ram, the fat tail, the fat that covers the entrails, the appendage of the liver, the two kidneys with the fat that is on them, and the right thigh (for it is a ram of ordination), [23]and one loaf of bread, one cake of bread made with oil, and

aGk: Heb *sashes, Aaron and his sons*

one wafer, out of the basket of unleavened bread that is before the LORD; [24]and you shall place all these on the palms of Aaron and on the palms of his sons, and raise them as an elevation offering before the LORD. [25]Then you shall take them from their hands, and turn them into smoke on the altar on top of the burnt offering of pleasing odor before the LORD; it is an offering by fire to the LORD.

26 You shall take the breast of the ram of Aaron's ordination and raise it as an elevation offering before the LORD; and it shall be your portion. [27]You shall consecrate the breast that was raised as an elevation offering and the thigh that was raised as an elevation offering from the ram of ordination, from that which belonged to Aaron and his sons. [28]These things shall be a perpetual ordinance for Aaron and his sons from the Israelites, for this is an offering; and it shall be an offering by the Israelites from their sacrifice of offerings of well-being, their offering to the LORD.

29 The sacred vestments of Aaron shall be passed on to his sons after him; they shall be anointed in them and ordained in them. [30]The son who is priest in his place shall wear them seven days, when he comes into the tent of meeting to minister in the holy place.

31 You shall take the ram of ordination, and boil its flesh in a holy place; [32]and Aaron and his sons shall eat the flesh of the ram and the bread that is in the basket, at the entrance of the tent of meeting. [33]They themselves shall eat the food by which atonement is made, to ordain and consecrate them, but no one else shall eat of them, because they are holy. [34]If any of the flesh for the ordination, or of the bread, remains until the morning, then you shall burn the remainder with fire; it shall not be eaten, because it is holy.

35 Thus you shall do to Aaron and to his sons, just as I have commanded you; through seven days you shall or-dain them. [36]Also every day you shall offer a bull as a sin offering for atonement. Also you shall offer a sin offering for the altar, when you make atonement for it, and shall anoint it, to consecrate it. [37]Seven days you shall make atonement for the altar, and consecrate it, and the altar shall be most holy; whatever touches the altar shall become holy.

38 Now this is what you shall offer on the altar: two lambs a year old regularly each day. [39]One lamb you shall offer in the morning, and the other lamb you shall offer in the evening; [40]and with the first lamb one-tenth of a measure of choice flour mixed with one-fourth of a hin of beaten oil, and one-fourth of a hin of wine for a drink offering. [41]And the other lamb you shall offer in the evening, and shall offer with it a grain offering and its drink offering, as in the morning, for a pleasing odor, an offering by fire to the LORD. [42]It shall be a regular burnt offering throughout your generations at the entrance of the tent of meeting before the LORD, where I will meet with you, to speak to you there. [43]I will meet with the Israelites there, and it shall be sanctified by my glory; [44]I will consecrate the tent of meeting and the altar; Aaron also and his sons I will consecrate, to serve me as priests. [45]I will dwell among the Israelites, and I will be their God. [46]And they shall know that I am the LORD their God, who brought them out of the land of Egypt that I might dwell among them; I am the LORD their God.

30.1 You shall make an altar on which to offer incense; you shall make it of acacia wood. [2]It shall be one cubit long, and one cubit wide; it shall be square, and shall be two cubits high; its horns shall be of one piece with it. [3]You shall overlay it with pure gold, its top, and its sides all around and its horns; and you shall make for it a molding of gold all around. [4]And you shall make two golden rings for it; under its molding on two opposite sides of it you shall make them, and they shall hold the poles with which to carry it. [5]You shall make the poles of acacia wood, and overlay them with gold. [6]You shall place it in front of the curtain that is above the ark of the covenant, [a] in front of the mercy seat[b] that is over the covenant, [a] where I will meet with you. [7]Aaron shall offer fragrant incense on it; every morning when he dresses the lamps he shall offer it, [8]and when Aaron sets up the lamps in the evening, he shall offer it, a regular incense offering before the LORD throughout your generations. [9]You shall not offer unholy incense on it, or a burnt offering, or a grain offering; and you shall not pour a drink offering on it. [10]Once a year Aaron shall perform the rite of atonement on its horns. Throughout your generations he shall perform the atonement for it once a year with the blood of the atoning sin offering. It is most holy to the LORD.

## MATTHEW 26.14–46

THEN one of the twelve, who was called Judas Iscariot, went to the chief priests [15]and said, "What will you give me if I betray him to you?" They paid him thirty pieces of silver. [16]And from that moment he began to look for an opportunity to betray him.

17  On the first day of Unleavened Bread the disciples came to Jesus, saying, "Where do you want us to make the preparations for you to eat the Passover?" [18]He said, "Go into the city to a certain man, and say to him, 'The Teacher says, My time is near; I will keep the Passover at your house with my disciples.' " [19]So the disciples did as Jesus had directed them, and they prepared the Passover meal.

20  When it was evening, he took his place with the twelve; [c] [21]and while they were eating, he said, "Truly I tell you, one of you will betray me." [22]And they became greatly distressed and began to say to him one after another, "Surely not I, Lord?" [23]He answered, "The one who has dipped his hand into the bowl with me will betray me. [24]The Son of Man goes as it is written of him, but woe to that one by whom the Son of Man is betrayed! It would have been better for that one not to have been born." [25]Judas, who betrayed him, said, "Surely not I, Rabbi?" He replied, "You have said so."

26  While they were eating, Jesus took a loaf of bread, and after blessing it he broke it, gave it to the disciples, and said, "Take, eat; this is my body." [27]Then he took a cup, and after giving thanks he gave it to them, saying, "Drink from it, all of you; [28]for this is my blood of the[d] covenant, which is poured out for many for the forgiveness of sins. [29]I tell you, I will never again drink of this fruit of the vine until that day when I drink it new with you in my Father's kingdom."

30  When they had sung the hymn, they went out to the Mount of Olives.

31  Then Jesus said to them, "You will all become deserters because of me this night; for it is written,

'I will strike the shepherd,
    and the sheep of the flock will
        be scattered.'

[32]But after I am raised up, I will go ahead of you to Galilee." [33]Peter said to him, "Though all become deserters because of you, I will never desert you." [34]Jesus said to him, "Truly I tell you, this very night, before the cock crows, you will deny me three times." [35]Peter said to him, "Even though I must die with you, I will not deny you." And so said all the disciples.

36  Then Jesus went with them to a

place called Gethsemane; and he said to his disciples, "Sit here while I go over there and pray." [37]He took with him Peter and the two sons of Zebedee, and began to be grieved and agitated. [38]Then he said to them, "I am deeply grieved, even to death; remain here, and stay awake with me." [39]And going a little farther, he threw himself on the ground and prayed, "My Father, if it is possible, let this cup pass from me; yet not what I want but what you want." [40]Then he came to the disciples and found them sleeping; and he said to Peter, "So, could you not stay awake with me one hour? [41]Stay awake and pray that you may not come into the time of trial;[a] the spirit indeed is willing, but the flesh is weak." [42]Again he went away for the second time and prayed, "My Father, if this cannot pass unless I drink it, your will be done." [43]Again he came and found them sleeping, for their eyes were heavy. [44]So leaving them again, he went away and prayed for the third time, saying the same words. [45]Then he came to the disciples and said to them, "Are you still sleeping and taking your rest? See, the hour is at hand, and the Son of Man is betrayed into the hands of sinners. [46]Get up, let us be going. See, my betrayer is at hand."

## PSALM 31.19–24

O HOW abundant is your
    goodness
  that you have laid up for
    those who fear you,
and accomplished for those who
    take refuge in you,
  in the sight of everyone!
[20] In the shelter of your presence
    you hide them
    from human plots;
  you hold them safe under your
    shelter
    from contentious tongues.

[21] Blessed be the LORD,
  for he has wondrously shown
    his steadfast love to me
  when I was beset as a city
    under siege.
[22] I had said in my alarm,
  "I am driven far[b] from your
    sight."
But you heard my supplications
  when I cried out to you for
    help.

[23] Love the LORD, all you his
    saints.
  The LORD preserves the
    faithful,
  but abundantly repays the one
    who acts haughtily.
[24] Be strong, and let your heart
    take courage,
  all you who wait for the LORD.

## PROVERBS 8.14–26

I [wisdom] HAVE good advice and
    sound wisdom;
  I have insight, I have
    strength.
[15] By me kings reign,
  and rulers decree what is
    just;
[16] by me rulers rule,
  and nobles, all who govern
    rightly.
[17] I love those who love me,
  and those who seek me
    diligently find me.
[18] Riches and honor are with me,
  enduring wealth and
    prosperity.
[19] My fruit is better than gold,
    even fine gold,
  and my yield than choice
    silver.
[20] I walk in the way of
    righteousness,
  along the paths of justice,

---

aOr *into temptation*  bAnother reading is *cut off*

21  endowing with wealth those who
       love me,
    and filling their treasuries.
22  The Lord created me at the
       beginning[a] of his
       work, [b]
    the first of his acts of long
       ago.
23  Ages ago I was set up,
    at the first, before the
       beginning of the earth.

24  When there were no depths I
       was brought forth,
    when there were no springs
       abounding with water.
25  Before the mountains had been
       shaped,
    before the hills, I was brought
       forth—
26  when he had not yet made earth
       and fields, [c]
    or the world's first bits of
       soil.

# FEBRUARY 10

## EXODUS 30.11—31.18

THE Lord spoke to Moses: [12]When you take a census of the Israelites to register them, at registration all of them shall give a ransom for their lives to the Lord, so that no plague may come upon them for being registered. [13]This is what each one who is registered shall give: half a shekel according to the shekel of the sanctuary (the shekel is twenty gerahs), half a shekel as an offering to the Lord. [14]Each one who is registered, from twenty years old and upward, shall give the Lord's offering. [15]The rich shall not give more, and the poor shall not give less, than the half shekel, when you bring this offering to the Lord to make atonement for your lives. [16]You shall take the atonement money from the Israelites and shall designate it for the service of the tent of meeting; before the Lord it will be a reminder to the Israelites of the ransom given for your lives.

17 The Lord spoke to Moses: [18]You shall make a bronze basin with a bronze stand for washing. You shall put it between the tent of meeting and the altar, and you shall put water in it; [19]with the water[d] Aaron and his sons shall wash their hands and their feet. [20]When they go into the tent of meeting, or when they come near the altar to minister, to make an offering by fire to the Lord, they shall wash with water, so that they may not die. [21]They shall wash their hands and their feet, so that they may not die: it shall be a perpetual ordinance for them, for him and for his descendants throughout their generations.

22 The Lord spoke to Moses: [23]Take the finest spices: of liquid myrrh five hundred shekels, and of sweet-smelling cinnamon half as much, that is, two hundred fifty, and two hundred fifty of aromatic cane, [24]and five hundred of cassia—measured by the sanctuary shekel—and a hin of olive oil; [25]and you shall make of these a sacred anointing oil blended as by the perfumer; it shall be a holy anointing oil. [26]With it you shall anoint the tent of meeting and the

a Or *me as the beginning*  b Heb *way*  c Meaning of Heb uncertain  d Heb *it*

ark of the covenant, [a] 27and the table and all its utensils, and the lampstand and its utensils, and the altar of incense, 28and the altar of burnt offering with all its utensils, and the basin with its stand; 29you shall consecrate them, so that they may be most holy; whatever touches them will become holy. 30You shall anoint Aaron and his sons, and consecrate them, in order that they may serve me as priests. 31You shall say to the Israelites, "This shall be my holy anointing oil throughout your generations. 32It shall not be used in any ordinary anointing of the body, and you shall make no other like it in composition; it is holy, and it shall be holy to you. 33Whoever compounds any like it or whoever puts any of it on an unqualified person shall be cut off from the people."

34 The Lord said to Moses: Take sweet spices, stacte, and onycha, and galbanum, sweet spices with pure frankincense (an equal part of each), 35and make an incense blended as by the perfumer, seasoned with salt, pure and holy; 36and you shall beat some of it into powder, and put part of it before the covenant[a] in the tent of meeting where I shall meet with you; it shall be for you most holy. 37When you make incense according to this composition, you shall not make it for yourselves; it shall be regarded by you as holy to the Lord. 38Whoever makes any like it to use as perfume shall be cut off from the people.

31.1 The Lord spoke to Moses: 2See, I have called by name Bezalel son of Uri son of Hur, of the tribe of Judah: 3and I have filled him with divine spirit,[b] with ability, intelligence, and knowledge in every kind of craft, 4to devise artistic designs, to work in gold, silver, and bronze, 5in cutting stones for setting, and in carving wood, in every kind of craft. 6Moreover, I have appointed with him Oholiab son of Ahisamach, of the tribe of Dan; and I have given skill to all the skillful, so that they may make all that I have commanded you: 7the tent of meeting, and the ark of the covenant,[a] and the mercy seat[c] that is on it, and all the furnishings of the tent, 8the table and its utensils, and the pure lampstand with all its utensils, and the altar of incense, 9and the altar of burnt offering with all its utensils, and the basin with its stand, 10and the finely worked vestments, the holy vestments for the priest Aaron and the vestments of his sons, for their service as priests, 11and the anointing oil and the fragrant incense for the holy place. They shall do just as I have commanded you.

12 The Lord said to Moses: 13You yourself are to speak to the Israelites: "You shall keep my sabbaths, for this is a sign between me and you throughout your generations, given in order that you may know that I, the Lord, sanctify you. 14You shall keep the sabbath, because it is holy for you; everyone who profanes it shall be put to death; whoever does any work on it shall be cut off from among the people. 15Six days shall work be done, but the seventh day is a sabbath of solemn rest, holy to the Lord; whoever does any work on the sabbath day shall be put to death. 16Therefore the Israelites shall keep the sabbath, observing the sabbath throughout their generations, as a perpetual covenant. 17It is a sign forever between me and the people of Israel that in six days the Lord made heaven and earth, and on the seventh day he rested, and was refreshed."

18 When God[d] finished speaking with Moses on Mount Sinai, he gave him the two tablets of the covenant,[a] tablets of stone, written with the finger of God.

## MATTHEW 26.47–68

WHILE he [Jesus] was still speaking, Judas, one of the twelve, arrived; with him was a large crowd with swords and clubs, from the chief priests and the elders of the people. [48]Now the betrayer had given them a sign, saying, "The one I will kiss is the man; arrest him." [49]At once he came up to Jesus and said, "Greetings, Rabbi!" and kissed him. [50]Jesus said to him, "Friend, do what you are here to do." Then they came and laid hands on Jesus and arrested him. [51]Suddenly, one of those with Jesus put his hand on his sword, drew it, and struck the slave of the high priest, cutting off his ear. [52]Then Jesus said to him, "Put your sword back into its place; for all who take the sword will perish by the sword. [53]Do you think that I cannot appeal to my Father, and he will at once send me more than twelve legions of angels? [54]But how then would the scriptures be fulfilled, which say it must happen in this way?" [55]At that hour Jesus said to the crowds, "Have you come out with swords and clubs to arrest me as though I were a bandit? Day after day I sat in the temple teaching, and you did not arrest me. [56]But all this has taken place, so that the scriptures of the prophets may be fulfilled." Then all the disciples deserted him and fled.

57 Those who had arrested Jesus took him to Caiaphas the high priest, in whose house the scribes and the elders had gathered. [58]But Peter was following him at a distance, as far as the courtyard of the high priest; and going inside, he sat with the guards in order to see how this would end. [59]Now the chief priests and the whole council were looking for false testimony against Jesus so that they might put him to death, [60]but they found none, though many false witnesses came forward. At last two came forward [61]and said, "This fellow said, 'I am able to destroy the temple of God and to build it in three days.' " [62]The high priest stood up and said, "Have you no answer? What is it that they testify against you?" [63]But Jesus was silent. Then the high priest said to him, "I put you under oath before the living God, tell us if you are the Messiah,[a] the Son of God." [64]Jesus said to him, "You have said so. But I tell you,

> From now on you will see the
> Son of Man
> seated at the right hand of
> Power
> and coming on the clouds
> of heaven."

[65]Then the high priest tore his clothes and said, "He has blasphemed! Why do we still need witnesses? You have now heard his blasphemy. [66]What is your verdict?" They answered, "He deserves death." [67]Then they spat in his face and struck him; and some slapped him, [68]saying, "Prophesy to us, you Messiah![a] Who is it that struck you?"

## PSALM 32.1–11

*Of David. A Maskil.*

HAPPY are those whose transgression is forgiven,
> whose sin is covered.
2 Happy are those to whom the
> LORD imputes no iniquity,
> and in whose spirit there is
> no deceit.

3 While I kept silence, my body
> wasted away
> through my groaning all day
> long.
4 For day and night your hand
> was heavy upon me;
> my strength was dried up[b]
> as by the heat of
> summer.                    *Selah*

[a]Or *Christ*   [b]Meaning of Heb uncertain

5 Then I acknowledged my sin to
      you,
    and I did not hide my iniquity;
  I said, "I will confess my
      transgressions to the
      LORD,"
    and you forgave the guilt of
      my sin.                    *Selah*

6 Therefore let all who are faithful
      offer prayer to you;
    at a time of distress, **a** the rush
      of mighty waters
    shall not reach them.
7 You are a hiding place for me;
    you preserve me from
      trouble;
    you surround me with glad
      cries of deliverance.
                               *Selah*

8 I will instruct you and teach you
      the way you should go;
    I will counsel you with my
      eye upon you.
9 Do not be like a horse or a
      mule, without
      understanding,
    whose temper must be
      curbed with bit and
      bridle,
    else it will not stay near you.

10 Many are the torments of the
      wicked,
    but steadfast love surrounds
      those who trust in the
      LORD.
11 Be glad in the LORD and rejoice,
      O righteous,
    and shout for joy, all you
      upright in heart.

## PROVERBS 8.27–31

WHEN he established the
      heavens, I was there,
    when he drew a circle on
      the face of the deep,
28    when he made firm the skies
      above,
    when he established the
      fountains of the deep,
29    when he assigned to the sea its
      limit,
    so that the waters might not
      transgress his command,
    when he marked out the
      foundations of the earth,
30    then I was beside him, like a
      master worker; **b**
    and I was daily his **c** delight,
      rejoicing before him always,
31    rejoicing in his inhabited world
      and delighting in the
      human race.

**a** Cn: Heb *at a time of finding only*   **b** Another reading is *little child*   **c** Gk: Heb lacks *his*

# FEBRUARY 11

EXODUS 32.1—33.23

WHEN the people saw that Moses delayed to come down from the mountain, the people gathered around Aaron, and said to him, "Come, make gods for us, who shall go before us; as for this Moses, the man who brought us up out of the land of Egypt, we do not know what has become of him." 2Aaron said to them, "Take off the gold rings that are on the ears of your wives, your sons, and your daughters, and bring them to me." 3So all the people took off the gold rings from their ears, and brought them to Aaron. 4He took the gold from them, formed it in a mold, a and cast an image of a calf; and they said, "These are your gods, O Israel, who brought you up out of the land of Egypt!" 5When Aaron saw this, he built an altar before it; and Aaron made proclamation and said, "Tomorrow shall be a festival to the LORD." 6They rose early the next day, and offered burnt offerings and brought sacrifices of well-being; and the people sat down to eat and drink, and rose up to revel.

7 The LORD said to Moses, "Go down at once! Your people, whom you brought up out of the land of Egypt, have acted perversely; 8they have been quick to turn aside from the way that I commanded them; they have cast for themselves an image of a calf, and have worshiped it and sacrificed to it, and said, 'These are your gods, O Israel, who brought you up out of the land of Egypt!' " 9The LORD said to Moses, "I have seen this people, how stiffnecked they are. 10Now let me alone, so that my wrath may burn hot against them and I may consume them; and of you I will make a great nation."

11 But Moses implored the LORD his God, and said, "O LORD, why does your wrath burn hot against your people, whom you brought out of the land of Egypt with great power and with a mighty hand? 12Why should the Egyptians say, 'It was with evil intent that he brought them out to kill them in the mountains, and to consume them from the face of the earth'? Turn from your fierce wrath; change your mind and do not bring disaster on your people. 13Remember Abraham, Isaac, and Israel, your servants, how you swore to them by your own self, saying to them, 'I will multiply your descendants like the stars of heaven, and all this land that I have promised I will give to your descendants, and they shall inherit it forever.' " 14And the LORD changed his mind about the disaster that he planned to bring on his people.

15 Then Moses turned and went down from the mountain, carrying the two tablets of the covenant b in his hands, tablets that were written on both sides, written on the front and on the back. 16The tablets were the work of God, and the writing was the writing of God, engraved upon the tablets. 17When Joshua heard the noise of the people as they shouted, he said to Moses, "There is a noise of war in the camp." 18But he said,

> "It is not the sound made by
>     victors,
> or the sound made by losers;
> it is the sound of revelers that I
>     hear."

19As soon as he came near the camp and saw the calf and the dancing, Mo-

---

a Or *fashioned it with a graving tool*; Meaning of Heb uncertain    b Or *treaty*, or *testimony*; Heb *eduth*

ses' anger burned hot, and he threw the tablets from his hands and broke them at the foot of the mountain. 20He took the calf that they had made, burned it with fire, ground it to powder, scattered it on the water, and made the Israelites drink it.

21 Moses said to Aaron, "What did this people do to you that you have brought so great a sin upon them?" 22And Aaron said, "Do not let the anger of my lord burn hot; you know the people, that they are bent on evil. 23They said to me, 'Make us gods, who shall go before us; as for this Moses, the man who brought us up out of the land of Egypt, we do not know what has become of him.' 24So I said to them, 'Whoever has gold, take it off'; so they gave it to me, and I threw it into the fire, and out came this calf!"

25 When Moses saw that the people were running wild (for Aaron had let them run wild, to the derision of their enemies), 26then Moses stood in the gate of the camp, and said, "Who is on the LORD's side? Come to me!" And all the sons of Levi gathered around him. 27He said to them, "Thus says the LORD, the God of Israel, 'Put your sword on your side, each of you! Go back and forth from gate to gate throughout the camp, and each of you kill your brother, your friend, and your neighbor.' " 28The sons of Levi did as Moses commanded, and about three thousand of the people fell on that day. 29Moses said, "Today you have ordained yourselves[a] for the service of the LORD, each one at the cost of a son or a brother, and so have brought a blessing on yourselves this day."

30 On the next day Moses said to the people, "You have sinned a great sin. But now I will go up to the LORD; perhaps I can make atonement for your sin." 31So Moses returned to the LORD and said, "Alas, this people has sinned a great sin; they have made for themselves gods of gold. 32But now, if you will only forgive their sin—but if not, blot me out of the book that you have written." 33But the LORD said to Moses, "Whoever has sinned against me I will blot out of my book. 34But now go, lead the people to the place about which I have spoken to you; see, my angel shall go in front of you. Nevertheless, when the day comes for punishment, I will punish them for their sin."

35 Then the LORD sent a plague on the people, because they made the calf—the one that Aaron made.

33.1 THE LORD said to Moses, "Go, leave this place, you and the people whom you have brought up out of the land of Egypt, and go to the land of which I swore to Abraham, Isaac, and Jacob, saying, 'To your descendants I will give it.' 2I will send an angel before you, and I will drive out the Canaanites, the Amorites, the Hittites, the Perizzites, the Hivites, and the Jebusites. 3Go up to a land flowing with milk and honey; but I will not go up among you, or I would consume you on the way, for you are a stiff-necked people."

4 When the people heard these harsh words, they mourned, and no one put on ornaments. 5For the LORD had said to Moses, "Say to the Israelites, 'You are a stiff-necked people; if for a single moment I should go up among you, I would consume you. So now take off your ornaments, and I will decide what to do to you.' " 6Therefore the Israelites stripped themselves of their ornaments, from Mount Horeb onward.

7 Now Moses used to take the tent and pitch it outside the camp, far off from the camp; he called it the tent of meeting. And everyone who sought the LORD would go out to the tent of meeting, which was outside the camp.

aGk Vg Compare Tg: Heb *Today ordain yourselves*

[8]Whenever Moses went out to the tent, all the people would rise and stand, each of them, at the entrance of their tents and watch Moses until he had gone into the tent. [9]When Moses entered the tent, the pillar of cloud would descend and stand at the entrance of the tent, and the LORD would speak with Moses. [10]When all the people saw the pillar of cloud standing at the entrance of the tent, all the people would rise and bow down, all of them, at the entrance of their tent. [11]Thus the LORD used to speak to Moses face to face, as one speaks to a friend. Then he would return to the camp; but his young assistant, Joshua son of Nun, would not leave the tent.

12 Moses said to the LORD, "See, you have said to me, 'Bring up this people'; but you have not let me know whom you will send with me. Yet you have said, 'I know you by name, and you have also found favor in my sight.' [13]Now if I have found favor in your sight, show me your ways, so that I may know you and find favor in your sight. Consider too that this nation is your people." [14]He said, "My presence will go with you, and I will give you rest." [15]And he said to him, "If your presence will not go, do not carry us up from here. [16]For how shall it be known that I have found favor in your sight, I and your people, unless you go with us? In this way, we shall be distinct, I and your people, from every people on the face of the earth."

17 The LORD said to Moses, "I will do the very thing that you have asked; for you have found favor in my sight, and I know you by name." [18]Moses said, "Show me your glory, I pray." [19]And he said, "I will make all my goodness pass before you, and will proclaim before you the name, 'The LORD'; [a] and I will be gracious to whom I will be gracious, and will show mercy on whom I will show mercy. [20]But," he said, "you cannot see my face; for no one shall see me and live." [21]And the LORD continued, "See, there is a place by me where you shall stand on the rock; [22]and while my glory passes by I will put you in a cleft of the rock, and I will cover you with my hand until I have passed by; [23]then I will take away my hand, and you shall see my back; but my face shall not be seen."

## MATTHEW 26.69—27.14

Now Peter was sitting outside in the courtyard. A servant-girl came to him and said, "You also were with Jesus the Galilean." [70]But he denied it before all of them, saying, "I do not know what you are talking about." [71]When he went out to the porch, another servant-girl saw him, and she said to the bystanders, "This man was with Jesus of Nazareth."[b] [72]Again he denied it with an oath, "I do not know the man." [73]After a little while the bystanders came up and said to Peter, "Certainly you are also one of them, for your accent betrays you." [74]Then he began to curse, and he swore an oath, "I do not know the man!" At that moment the cock crowed. [75]Then Peter remembered what Jesus had said: "Before the cock crows, you will deny me three times." And he went out and wept bitterly.

27.1 WHEN morning came, all the chief priests and the elders of the people conferred together against Jesus in order to bring about his death. [2]They bound him, led him away, and handed him over to Pilate the governor.

3 When Judas, his betrayer, saw that Jesus[c] was condemned, he repented and brought back the thirty pieces of silver to the chief priests and the elders. [4]He said, "I have sinned by

---

a Heb *YHWH*; see note at 3.15   b Gk *the Nazorean*   c Gk *he*

betraying innocent[a] blood." But they said, "What is that to us? See to it yourself." 5Throwing down the pieces of silver in the temple, he departed; and he went and hanged himself. 6But the chief priests, taking the pieces of silver, said, "It is not lawful to put them into the treasury, since they are blood money." 7After conferring together, they used them to buy the potter's field as a place to bury foreigners. 8For this reason that field has been called the Field of Blood to this day. 9Then was fulfilled what had been spoken through the prophet Jeremiah,[b] "And they took[c] the thirty pieces of silver, the price of the one on whom a price had been set,[d] on whom some of the people of Israel had set a price, 10and they gave[e] them for the potter's field, as the Lord commanded me."

11 Now Jesus stood before the governor; and the governor asked him, "Are you the King of the Jews?" Jesus said, "You say so." 12But when he was accused by the chief priests and elders, he did not answer. 13Then Pilate said to him, "Do you not hear how many accusations they make against you?" 14But he gave him no answer, not even to a single charge, so that the governor was greatly amazed.

## PSALM 33.1–11

REJOICE in the LORD, O you righteous.
Praise befits the upright.
2　Praise the LORD with the lyre;
　　make melody to him with the
　　　harp of ten strings.
3　Sing to him a new song;
　　play skillfully on the strings,
　　　with loud shouts.

4　For the word of the LORD is
　　upright,
　　and all his work is done in
　　　faithfulness.
5　He loves righteousness and
　　justice;
　　the earth is full of the
　　　steadfast love of the
　　　LORD.

6　By the word of the LORD the
　　　heavens were made,
　　and all their host by the
　　　breath of his mouth.
7　He gathered the waters of the
　　　sea as in a bottle;
　　he put the deeps in
　　　storehouses.

8　Let all the earth fear the LORD;
　　let all the inhabitants of the
　　　world stand in awe of
　　　him.
9　For he spoke, and it came to
　　　be;
　　he commanded, and it stood
　　　firm.

10　The LORD brings the counsel of
　　　the nations to nothing;
　　he frustrates the plans of the
　　　peoples.
11　The counsel of the LORD stands
　　　forever,
　　the thoughts of his heart to all
　　　generations.

## PROVERBS 8.32–36

AND now, my children, listen to me:
happy are those who keep my ways.
33　Hear instruction and be wise,
　　and do not neglect it.
34　Happy is the one who listens to
　　me,
　　watching daily at my gates,
　　waiting beside my doors.

aOther ancient authorities read *righteous*　bOther ancient authorities read *Zechariah* or *Isaiah*
cOr *I took*　dOr *the price of the precious One*　eOther ancient authorities read *I gave*

35 For whoever finds me finds life
and obtains favor from the
LORD;

36 but those who miss me injure
themselves;
all who hate me love death."

# FEBRUARY 12

## EXODUS 34.1—35.9

THE LORD said to Moses, "Cut two tablets of stone like the former ones, and I will write on the tablets the words that were on the former tablets, which you broke. 2Be ready in the morning, and come up in the morning to Mount Sinai and present yourself there to me, on the top of the mountain. 3No one shall come up with you, and do not let anyone be seen throughout all the mountain; and do not let flocks or herds graze in front of that mountain." 4So Moses cut two tablets of stone like the former ones; and he rose early in the morning and went up on Mount Sinai, as the LORD had commanded him, and took in his hand the two tablets of stone. 5The LORD descended in the cloud and stood with him there, and proclaimed the name, "The LORD."a 6The LORD passed before him, and proclaimed,

"The LORD, the LORD,
a God merciful and gracious,
slow to anger,
and abounding in steadfast love
and faithfulness,
7 keeping steadfast love for the
thousandth generation, b
forgiving iniquity and
transgression and sin,
yet by no means clearing the
guilty,
but visiting the iniquity of the
parents

upon the children
and the children's children,
to the third and the fourth
generation."
8And Moses quickly bowed his head toward the earth, and worshiped. 9He said, "If now I have found favor in your sight, O Lord, I pray, let the Lord go with us. Although this is a stiff-necked people, pardon our iniquity and our sin, and take us for your inheritance."

10 He said: I hereby make a covenant. Before all your people I will perform marvels, such as have not been performed in all the earth or in any nation; and all the people among whom you live shall see the work of the LORD; for it is an awesome thing that I will do with you.

11 Observe what I command you today. See, I will drive out before you the Amorites, the Canaanites, the Hittites, the Perizzites, the Hivites, and the Jebusites. 12Take care not to make a covenant with the inhabitants of the land to which you are going, or it will become a snare among you. 13You shall tear down their altars, break their pillars, and cut down their sacred polesc 14(for you shall worship no other god, because the LORD, whose name is Jealous, is a jealous God). 15You shall not make a covenant with the inhabitants of the land, for when they prostitute themselves to their gods and sacrifice to their gods, someone among them

aHeb YHWH; see note at 3.15   bOr for thousands   cHeb Asherim

will invite you, and you will eat of the sacrifice. <sup>16</sup>And you will take wives from among their daughters for your sons, and their daughters who prostitute themselves to their gods will make your sons also prostitute themselves to their gods.

17 You shall not make cast idols.

18 You shall keep the festival of unleavened bread. Seven days you shall eat unleavened bread, as I commanded you, at the time appointed in the month of Abib; for in the month of Abib you came out from Egypt.

19 All that first opens the womb is mine, all your male[a] livestock, the firstborn of cow and sheep. <sup>20</sup>The firstborn of a donkey you shall redeem with a lamb, or if you will not redeem it you shall break its neck. All the firstborn of your sons you shall redeem.

No one shall appear before me empty-handed.

21 Six days you shall work, but on the seventh day you shall rest; even in plowing time and in harvest time you shall rest. <sup>22</sup>You shall observe the festival of weeks, the first fruits of wheat harvest, and the festival of ingathering at the turn of the year. <sup>23</sup>Three times in the year all your males shall appear before the Lord God, the God of Israel. <sup>24</sup>For I will cast out nations before you, and enlarge your borders; no one shall covet your land when you go up to appear before the Lord your God three times in the year.

25 You shall not offer the blood of my sacrifice with leaven, and the sacrifice of the festival of the passover shall not be left until the morning.

26 The best of the first fruits of your ground you shall bring to the house of the Lord your God.

You shall not boil a kid in its mother's milk.

27 The Lord said to Moses: Write these words; in accordance with these words I have made a covenant with you and with Israel. <sup>28</sup>He was there with the Lord forty days and forty nights; he neither ate bread nor drank water. And he wrote on the tablets the words of the covenant, the ten commandments. [b]

29 Moses came down from Mount Sinai. As he came down from the mountain with the two tablets of the covenant[c] in his hand, Moses did not know that the skin of his face shone because he had been talking with God. <sup>30</sup>When Aaron and all the Israelites saw Moses, the skin of his face was shining, and they were afraid to come near him. <sup>31</sup>But Moses called to them; and Aaron and all the leaders of the congregation returned to him, and Moses spoke with them. <sup>32</sup>Afterward all the Israelites came near, and he gave them in commandment all that the Lord had spoken with him on Mount Sinai. <sup>33</sup>When Moses had finished speaking with them, he put a veil on his face; <sup>34</sup>but whenever Moses went in before the Lord to speak with him, he would take the veil off, until he came out; and when he came out, and told the Israelites what he had been commanded, <sup>35</sup>the Israelites would see the face of Moses, that the skin of his face was shining; and Moses would put the veil on his face again, until he went in to speak with him.

35.1 Moses assembled all the congregation of the Israelites and said to them: These are the things that the Lord has commanded you to do:

2 Six days shall work be done, but on the seventh day you shall have a holy sabbath of solemn rest to the Lord; whoever does any work on it shall be put to death. <sup>3</sup>You shall kindle no fire in all your dwellings on the sabbath day.

4 Moses said to all the congregation of the Israelites: This is the thing

aGk Theodotion Vg Tg: Meaning of Heb uncertain  bHeb *words*  cOr *treaty*, or *testimony*; Heb *eduth*

that the LORD has commanded: [5]Take from among you an offering to the LORD; let whoever is of a generous heart bring the LORD's offering: gold, silver, and bronze; [6]blue, purple, and crimson yarns, and fine linen; goats' hair, [7]tanned rams' skins, and fine leather;[a] acacia wood, [8]oil for the light, spices for the anointing oil and for the fragrant incense, [9]and onyx stones and gems to be set in the ephod and the breastpiece.

## MATTHEW 27.15–31

Now at the festival the governor was accustomed to release a prisoner for the crowd, anyone whom they wanted. [16]At that time they had a notorious prisoner, called Jesus[b] Barabbas. [17]So after they had gathered, Pilate said to them, "Whom do you want me to release for you, Jesus[b] Barabbas or Jesus who is called the Messiah?"[c] [18]For he realized that it was out of jealousy that they had handed him over. [19]While he was sitting on the judgment seat, his wife sent word to him, "Have nothing to do with that innocent man, for today I have suffered a great deal because of a dream about him." [20]Now the chief priests and the elders persuaded the crowds to ask for Barabbas and to have Jesus killed. [21]The governor again said to them, "Which of the two do you want me to release for you?" And they said, "Barabbas." [22]Pilate said to them, "Then what should I do with Jesus who is called the Messiah?"[c] All of them said, "Let him be crucified!" [23]Then he asked, "Why, what evil has he done?" But they shouted all the more, "Let him be crucified!"

24 So when Pilate saw that he could do nothing, but rather that a riot was beginning, he took some water and washed his hands before the crowd, saying, "I am innocent of this man's blood;[d] see to it yourselves." [25]Then the people as a whole answered, "His blood be on us and on our children!" [26]So he released Barabbas for them; and after flogging Jesus, he handed him over to be crucified.

27 Then the soldiers of the governor took Jesus into the governor's headquarters,[e] and they gathered the whole cohort around him. [28]They stripped him and put a scarlet robe on him, [29]and after twisting some thorns into a crown, they put it on his head. They put a reed in his right hand and knelt before him and mocked him, saying, "Hail, King of the Jews!" [30]They spat on him, and took the reed and struck him on the head. [31]After mocking him, they stripped him of the robe and put his own clothes on him. Then they led him away to crucify him.

## PSALM 33.12–22

Happy is the nation whose God
      is the LORD,
   the people whom he has
      chosen as his heritage.

13   The LORD looks down from
         heaven;
      he sees all humankind.
14   From where he sits enthroned
         he watches
      all the inhabitants of the
         earth—
15   he who fashions the hearts of
         them all,
      and observes all their deeds.
16   A king is not saved by his great
         army;
      a warrior is not delivered by
         his great strength.
17   The war horse is a vain hope
         for victory,
      and by its great might it
         cannot save.

aMeaning of Heb uncertain   bOther ancient authorities lack *Jesus*   cOr *the Christ*   dOther ancient authorities read *this righteous blood*, or *this righteous man's blood*   eGk *the praetorium*

18 Truly the eye of the Lord is on
    those who fear him,
  on those who hope in his
    steadfast love,
19 to deliver their soul from death,
  and to keep them alive in
    famine.

20 Our soul waits for the Lord;
  he is our help and shield.
21 Our heart is glad in him,
  because we trust in his holy
    name.
22 Let your steadfast love,
    O Lord, be upon us,
  even as we hope in you.

## PROVERBS 9.1–6

WISDOM has built her house,
she has hewn her seven
  pillars.
2 She has slaughtered her
  animals, she has mixed
  her wine,
she has also set her table.
3 She has sent out her
  servant-girls, she calls
  from the highest places in
    the town,
4 "You that are simple, turn in
    here!"
To those without sense she
    says,
5 "Come, eat of my bread
  and drink of the wine I have
    mixed.
6 Lay aside immaturity, [a] and
    live,
  and walk in the way of
    insight."

# FEBRUARY 13

## EXODUS 35.10—36.38

ALL who are skillful among you shall come and make all that the Lord has commanded: the tabernacle, [11]its tent and its covering, its clasps and its frames, its bars, its pillars, and its bases; [12]the ark with its poles, the mercy seat, [b] and the curtain for the screen; [13]the table with its poles and all its utensils, and the bread of the Presence; [14]the lampstand also for the light, with its utensils and its lamps, and the oil for the light; [15]and the altar of incense, with its poles, and the anointing oil and the fragrant incense, and the screen for the entrance, the entrance of the tabernacle; [16]the altar of burnt offering, with its grating of bronze, its poles, and all its utensils, the basin with its stand; [17]the hangings of the court, its pillars and its bases, and the screen for the gate of the court; [18]the pegs of the tabernacle and the pegs of the court, and their cords; [19]the finely worked vestments for ministering in the holy place, the holy vestments for the priest Aaron, and the vestments of his sons, for their service as priests.

a Or *simpleness*   b Or *the cover*

20 Then all the congregation of the Israelites withdrew from the presence of Moses. [21]And they came, everyone whose heart was stirred, and everyone whose spirit was willing, and brought the Lord's offering to be used for the tent of meeting, and for all its service, and for the sacred vestments. [22]So they came, both men and women; all who were of a willing heart brought brooches and earrings and signet rings and pendants, all sorts of gold objects, everyone bringing an offering of gold to the Lord. [23]And everyone who possessed blue or purple or crimson yarn or fine linen or goats' hair or tanned rams' skins or fine leather,[a] brought them. [24]Everyone who could make an offering of silver or bronze brought it as the Lord's offering; and everyone who possessed acacia wood of any use in the work, brought it. [25]All the skillful women spun with their hands, and brought what they had spun in blue and purple and crimson yarns and fine linen; [26]all the women whose hearts moved them to use their skill spun the goats' hair. [27]And the leaders brought onyx stones and gems to be set in the ephod and the breastpiece, [28]and spices and oil for the light, and for the anointing oil, and for the fragrant incense. [29]All the Israelite men and women whose hearts made them willing to bring anything for the work that the Lord had commanded by Moses to be done, brought it as a freewill offering to the Lord.

30 Then Moses said to the Israelites: See, the Lord has called by name Bezalel son of Uri son of Hur, of the tribe of Judah; [31]he has filled him with divine spirit,[b] with skill, intelligence, and knowledge in every kind of craft, [32]to devise artistic designs, to work in gold, silver, and bronze, [33]in cutting stones for setting, and in carving wood, in every kind of craft. [34]And he has inspired him to teach, both him and Oho-liab son of Ahisamach, of the tribe of Dan. [35]He has filled them with skill to do every kind of work done by an artisan or by a designer or by an embroiderer in blue, purple, and crimson yarns, and in fine linen, or by a weaver—by any sort of artisan or skilled designer.

36.1 Bezalel and Oholiab and every skillful one to whom the Lord has given skill and understanding to know how to do any work in the construction of the sanctuary shall work in accordance with all that the Lord has commanded.

2 Moses then called Bezalel and Oholiab and every skillful one to whom the Lord had given skill, everyone whose heart was stirred to come to do the work; [3]and they received from Moses all the freewill offerings that the Israelites had brought for doing the work on the sanctuary. They still kept bringing him freewill offerings every morning, [4]so that all the artisans who were doing every sort of task on the sanctuary came, each from the task being performed, [5]and said to Moses, "The people are bringing much more than enough for doing the work that the Lord has commanded us to do." [6]So Moses gave command, and word was proclaimed throughout the camp: "No man or woman is to make anything else as an offering for the sanctuary." So the people were restrained from bringing; [7]for what they had already brought was more than enough to do all the work.

8 All those with skill among the workers made the tabernacle with ten curtains; they were made of fine twisted linen, and blue, purple, and crimson yarns, with cherubim skillfully worked into them. [9]The length of each curtain was twenty-eight cubits, and the width of each curtain four cubits; all the curtains were of the same size.

10 He joined five curtains to one

another, and the other five curtains he joined to one another. [11]He made loops of blue on the edge of the outermost curtain of the first set; likewise he made them on the edge of the outermost curtain of the second set; [12]he made fifty loops on the one curtain, and he made fifty loops on the edge of the curtain that was in the second set; the loops were opposite one another. [13]And he made fifty clasps of gold, and joined the curtains one to the other with clasps; so the tabernacle was one whole.

14 He also made curtains of goats' hair for a tent over the tabernacle; he made eleven curtains. [15]The length of each curtain was thirty cubits, and the width of each curtain four cubits; the eleven curtains were of the same size. [16]He joined five curtains by themselves, and six curtains by themselves. [17]He made fifty loops on the edge of the outermost curtain of the one set, and fifty loops on the edge of the other connecting curtain. [18]He made fifty clasps of bronze to join the tent together so that it might be one whole. [19]And he made for the tent a covering of tanned rams' skins and an outer covering of fine leather. [a]

20 Then he made the upright frames for the tabernacle of acacia wood. [21]Ten cubits was the length of a frame, and a cubit and a half the width of each frame. [22]Each frame had two pegs for fitting together; he did this for all the frames of the tabernacle. [23]The frames for the tabernacle he made in this way: twenty frames for the south side; [24]and he made forty bases of silver under the twenty frames, two bases under the first frame for its two pegs, and two bases under the next frame for its two pegs. [25]For the second side of the tabernacle, on the north side, he made twenty frames [26]and their forty bases of silver, two bases under the first frame and two bases under the next frame. [27]For the rear of the tabernacle westward he made six frames. [28]He made two frames for corners of the tabernacle in the rear. [29]They were separate beneath, but joined at the top, at the first ring; he made two of them in this way, for the two corners. [30]There were eight frames with their bases of silver: sixteen bases, under every frame two bases.

31 He made bars of acacia wood, five for the frames of the one side of the tabernacle, [32]and five bars for the frames of the other side of the tabernacle, and five bars for the frames of the tabernacle at the rear westward. [33]He made the middle bar to pass through from end to end halfway up the frames. [34]And he overlaid the frames with gold, and made rings of gold for them to hold the bars, and overlaid the bars with gold.

35 He made the curtain of blue, purple, and crimson yarns, and fine twisted linen, with cherubim skillfully worked into it. [36]For it he made four pillars of acacia, and overlaid them with gold; their hooks were of gold, and he cast for them four bases of silver. [37]He also made a screen for the entrance to the tent, of blue, purple, and crimson yarns, and fine twisted linen, embroidered with needlework; [38]and its five pillars with their hooks. He overlaid their capitals and their bases with gold, but their five bases were of bronze.

# MATTHEW 27.32–66

As they [Jesus and the soldiers] went out, they came upon a man from Cyrene named Simon; they compelled this man to carry his cross. [33]And when they came to a place called Golgotha (which means Place of a Skull), [34]they offered him

[a]Meaning of Heb uncertain

wine to drink, mixed with gall; but when he tasted it, he would not drink it. 35And when they had crucified him, they divided his clothes among themselves by casting lots;a 36then they sat down there and kept watch over him. 37Over his head they put the charge against him, which read, "This is Jesus, the King of the Jews."

38 Then two bandits were crucified with him, one on his right and one on his left. 39Those who passed by deridedb him, shaking their heads 40and saying, "You who would destroy the temple and build it in three days, save yourself! If you are the Son of God, come down from the cross." 41In the same way the chief priests also, along with the scribes and elders, were mocking him, saying, 42"He saved others; he cannot save himself.c He is the King of Israel; let him come down from the cross now, and we will believe in him. 43He trusts in God; let God deliver him now, if he wants to; for he said, 'I am God's Son.'" 44The bandits who were crucified with him also taunted him in the same way.

45 From noon on, darkness came over the whole landd until three in the afternoon. 46And about three o'clock Jesus cried with a loud voice, "Eli, Eli, lema sabachthani?" that is, "My God, my God, why have you forsaken me?" 47When some of the bystanders heard it, they said, "This man is calling for Elijah." 48At once one of them ran and got a sponge, filled it with sour wine, put it on a stick, and gave it to him to drink. 49But the others said, "Wait, let us see whether Elijah will come to save him."e 50Then Jesus cried again with a loud voice and breathed his last.f 51At that moment the curtain of the temple was torn in two, from top to bottom.

The earth shook, and the rocks were split. 52The tombs also were opened, and many bodies of the saints who had fallen asleep were raised. 53After his resurrection they came out of the tombs and entered the holy city and appeared to many. 54Now when the centurion and those with him, who were keeping watch over Jesus, saw the earthquake and what took place, they were terrified and said, "Truly this man was God's Son!"g

55 Many women were also there, looking on from a distance; they had followed Jesus from Galilee and had provided for him. 56Among them were Mary Magdalene, and Mary the mother of James and Joseph, and the mother of the sons of Zebedee.

57 When it was evening, there came a rich man from Arimathea, named Joseph, who was also a disciple of Jesus. 58He went to Pilate and asked for the body of Jesus; then Pilate ordered it to be given to him. 59So Joseph took the body and wrapped it in a clean linen cloth 60and laid it in his own new tomb, which he had hewn in the rock. He then rolled a great stone to the door of the tomb and went away. 61Mary Magdalene and the other Mary were there, sitting opposite the tomb.

62 The next day, that is, after the day of Preparation, the chief priests and the Pharisees gathered before Pilate 63and said, "Sir, we remember what that impostor said while he was still alive, 'After three days I will rise again.' 64Therefore command the tomb to be made secure until the third day; otherwise his disciples may go and steal him away, and tell the people, 'He has been raised from the dead,' and the last deception would be worse than the first." 65Pilate said to them, "You have

aOther ancient authorities add *in order that what had been spoken through the prophet might be fulfilled, "They divided my clothes among themselves, and for my clothing they cast lots."* bOr *blasphemed* cOr *is he unable to save himself?* dOr *earth* eOther ancient authorities add *And another took a spear and pierced his side, and out came water and blood* fOr *gave up his spirit* gOr *a son of God*

a guard[a] of soldiers; go, make it as secure as you can."[b] <sup>66</sup>So they went with the guard and made the tomb secure by sealing the stone.

## PSALM 34.1–10

*Of David, when he feigned madness before Abimelech, so that he drove him out, and he went away.*

I WILL bless the LORD at all times;
　　his praise shall continually be
　　　in my mouth.
2　My soul makes its boast in the
　　　LORD;
　　let the humble hear and be
　　　glad.
3　O magnify the LORD with me,
　　and let us exalt his name
　　　together.

4　I sought the LORD, and he
　　　answered me,
　　and delivered me from all my
　　　fears.
5　Look to him, and be radiant;
　　so your[c] faces shall never be
　　　ashamed.
6　This poor soul cried, and was
　　　heard by the LORD,

　　and was saved from every
　　　trouble.
7　The angel of the LORD encamps
　　　around those who fear him,
　　　　and delivers them.
8　O taste and see that the LORD is
　　　good;
　　happy are those who take
　　　refuge in him.
9　O fear the LORD, you his holy
　　　ones,
　　for those who fear him have
　　　no want.
10　The young lions suffer want and
　　　hunger,
　　but those who seek the LORD
　　　lack no good thing.

## PROVERBS 9.7–8

WHOEVER corrects a scoffer
　　　wins abuse;
　whoever rebukes the
　　wicked gets hurt.
8　A scoffer who is rebuked will
　　　only hate you;
　　the wise, when rebuked, will
　　　love you.

# FEBRUARY 14

## EXODUS 37.1—38.31

BEZALEL made the ark of acacia wood; it was two and a half cubits long, a cubit and a half wide, and a cubit and a half high. <sup>2</sup>He overlaid it with pure gold inside and outside, and made a molding of gold around it. <sup>3</sup>He cast for it four rings of gold for its four feet, two rings on its one side and two rings on its other side. <sup>4</sup>He made poles of acacia wood, and overlaid them with gold, <sup>5</sup>and put the poles into the rings on the sides of the ark, to carry the ark. <sup>6</sup>He made a mercy seat[d] of pure gold; two cubits and a half was its length, and a cubit and a half its width. <sup>7</sup>He made two cherubim of hammered gold; at the two ends of the mercy seat[e] he made them, <sup>8</sup>one cherub at the one end, and one

aOr *Take a guard*　bGk *you know how*　cGk Syr Jerome: Heb *their*　dOr *a cover*　eOr *the cover*

cherub at the other end; of one piece with the mercy seat[a] he made the cherubim at its two ends. [9]The cherubim spread out their wings above, overshadowing the mercy seat[a] with their wings. They faced one another; the faces of the cherubim were turned toward the mercy seat. [a]

10 He also made the table of acacia wood, two cubits long, one cubit wide, and a cubit and a half high. [11]He overlaid it with pure gold, and made a molding of gold around it. [12]He made around it a rim a handbreadth wide, and made a molding of gold around the rim. [13]He cast for it four rings of gold, and fastened the rings to the four corners at its four legs. [14]The rings that held the poles used for carrying the table were close to the rim. [15]He made the poles of acacia wood to carry the table, and overlaid them with gold. [16]And he made the vessels of pure gold that were to be on the table, its plates and dishes for incense, and its bowls and flagons with which to pour drink offerings.

17 He also made the lampstand of pure gold. The base and the shaft of the lampstand were made of hammered work; its cups, its calyxes, and its petals were of one piece with it. [18]There were six branches going out of its sides, three branches of the lampstand out of one side of it and three branches of the lampstand out of the other side of it; [19]three cups shaped like almond blossoms, each with calyx and petals, on one branch, and three cups shaped like almond blossoms, each with calyx and petals, on the other branch—so for the six branches going out of the lampstand. [20]On the lampstand itself there were four cups shaped like almond blossoms, each with its calyxes and petals. [21]There was a calyx of one piece with it under the first pair of branches, a calyx of one piece with it under the next pair of branches, and a calyx of one

piece with it under the last pair of branches. [22]Their calyxes and their branches were of one piece with it, the whole of it one hammered piece of pure gold. [23]He made its seven lamps and its snuffers and its trays of pure gold. [24]He made it and all its utensils of a talent of pure gold.

25 He made the altar of incense of acacia wood, one cubit long, and one cubit wide; it was square, and was two cubits high; its horns were of one piece with it. [26]He overlaid it with pure gold, its top, and its sides all around, and its horns; and he made for it a molding of gold all around, [27]and made two golden rings for it under its molding, on two opposite sides of it, to hold the poles with which to carry it. [28]And he made the poles of acacia wood, and overlaid them with gold.

29 He made the holy anointing oil also, and the pure fragrant incense, blended as by the perfumer.

**38.1** HE made the altar of burnt offering also of acacia wood; it was five cubits long, and five cubits wide; it was square, and three cubits high. [2]He made horns for it on its four corners; its horns were of one piece with it, and he overlaid it with bronze. [3]He made all the utensils of the altar, the pots, the shovels, the basins, the forks, and the firepans: all its utensils he made of bronze. [4]He made for the altar a grating, a network of bronze, under its ledge, extending halfway down. [5]He cast four rings on the four corners of the bronze grating to hold the poles; [6]he made the poles of acacia wood, and overlaid them with bronze. [7]And he put the poles through the rings on the sides of the altar, to carry it with them; he made it hollow, with boards.

8 He made the basin of bronze with its stand of bronze, from the mirrors of

the women who served at the entrance to the tent of meeting.

9 He made the court; for the south side the hangings of the court were of fine twisted linen, one hundred cubits long; [10]its twenty pillars and their twenty bases were of bronze, but the hooks of the pillars and their bands were of silver. [11]For the north side there were hangings one hundred cubits long; its twenty pillars and their twenty bases were of bronze, but the hooks of the pillars and their bands were of silver. [12]For the west side there were hangings fifty cubits long, with ten pillars and ten bases; the hooks of the pillars and their bands were of silver. [13]And for the front to the east, fifty cubits. [14]The hangings for one side of the gate were fifteen cubits, with three pillars and three bases. [15]And so for the other side; on each side of the gate of the court were hangings of fifteen cubits, with three pillars and three bases. [16]All the hangings around the court were of fine twisted linen. [17]The bases for the pillars were of bronze, but the hooks of the pillars and their bands were of silver; the overlaying of their capitals was also of silver, and all the pillars of the court were banded with silver. [18]The screen for the entrance to the court was embroidered with needlework in blue, purple, and crimson yarns and fine twisted linen. It was twenty cubits long and, along the width of it, five cubits high, corresponding to the hangings of the court. [19]There were four pillars; their four bases were of bronze, their hooks of silver, and the overlaying of their capitals and their bands of silver. [20]All the pegs for the tabernacle and for the court all around were of bronze.

21 These are the records of the tabernacle, the tabernacle of the covenant,[a] which were drawn up at the commandment of Moses, the work of the Levites being under the direction of Ithamar son of the priest Aaron. [22]Bezalel son of Uri son of Hur, of the tribe of Judah, made all that the LORD commanded Moses; [23]and with him was Oholiab son of Ahisamach, of the tribe of Dan, engraver, designer, and embroiderer in blue, purple, and crimson yarns, and in fine linen.

24 All the gold that was used for the work, in all the construction of the sanctuary, the gold from the offering, was twenty-nine talents and seven hundred thirty shekels, measured by the sanctuary shekel. [25]The silver from those of the congregation who were counted was one hundred talents and one thousand seven hundred seventy-five shekels, measured by the sanctuary shekel; [26]a beka a head (that is, half a shekel, measured by the sanctuary shekel), for everyone who was counted in the census, from twenty years old and upward, for six hundred three thousand, five hundred fifty men. [27]The hundred talents of silver were for casting the bases of the sanctuary, and the bases of the curtain; one hundred bases for the hundred talents, a talent for a base. [28]Of the thousand seven hundred seventy-five shekels he made hooks for the pillars, and overlaid their capitals and made bands for them. [29]The bronze that was contributed was seventy talents, and two thousand four hundred shekels; [30]with it he made the bases for the entrance of the tent of meeting, the bronze altar and the bronze grating for it and all the utensils of the altar, [31]the bases all around the court, and the bases of the gate of the court, all the pegs of the tabernacle, and all the pegs around the court.

a Or *treaty*, or *testimony*; Heb *eduth*

## MATTHEW 28.1–20

AFTER the sabbath, as the first day of the week was dawning, Mary Magdalene and the other Mary went to see the tomb. ²And suddenly there was a great earthquake; for an angel of the Lord, descending from heaven, came and rolled back the stone and sat on it. ³His appearance was like lightning, and his clothing white as snow. ⁴For fear of him the guards shook and became like dead men. ⁵But the angel said to the women, "Do not be afraid; I know that you are looking for Jesus who was crucified. ⁶He is not here; for he has been raised, as he said. Come, see the place where he[a] lay. ⁷Then go quickly and tell his disciples, 'He has been raised from the dead,[b] and indeed he is going ahead of you to Galilee; there you will see him.' This is my message for you." ⁸So they left the tomb quickly with fear and great joy, and ran to tell his disciples. ⁹Suddenly Jesus met them and said, "Greetings!" And they came to him, took hold of his feet, and worshiped him. ¹⁰Then Jesus said to them, "Do not be afraid; go and tell my brothers to go to Galilee; there they will see me."

11 While they were going, some of the guard went into the city and told the chief priests everything that had happened. ¹²After the priests[c] had assembled with the elders, they devised a plan to give a large sum of money to the soldiers, ¹³telling them, "You must say, 'His disciples came by night and stole him away while we were asleep.' ¹⁴If this comes to the governor's ears, we will satisfy him and keep you out of trouble." ¹⁵So they took the money and did as they were directed. And this story is still told among the Jews to this day.

16 Now the eleven disciples went to Galilee, to the mountain to which Jesus had directed them. ¹⁷When they saw him, they worshiped him; but some doubted. ¹⁸And Jesus came and said to them, "All authority in heaven and on earth has been given to me. ¹⁹Go therefore and make disciples of all nations, baptizing them in the name of the Father and of the Son and of the Holy Spirit, ²⁰and teaching them to obey everything that I have commanded you. And remember, I am with you always, to the end of the age."[d]

## PSALM 34.11–22

COME, O children, listen to me;
   I will teach you the fear of
     the Lord.
12 Which of you desires life,
   and covets many days to
     enjoy good?
13 Keep your tongue from evil,
   and your lips from speaking
     deceit.
14 Depart from evil, and do good;
   seek peace, and pursue it.

15 The eyes of the Lord are on the
     righteous,
   and his ears are open to their
     cry.
16 The face of the Lord is against
     evildoers,
   to cut off the remembrance of
     them from the earth.
17 When the righteous cry for
     help, the Lord hears,
   and rescues them from all
     their troubles.
18 The Lord is near to the
     brokenhearted,
   and saves the crushed in
     spirit.

19 Many are the afflictions of the
     righteous,
   but the Lord rescues them
     from them all.

a Other ancient authorities read *the Lord*  b Other ancient authorities lack *from the dead*  c Gk *they*
d Other ancient authorities add *Amen*

20 He keeps all their bones;
>     not one of them will be
>       broken.
21 Evil brings death to the wicked,
>     and those who hate the
>       righteous will be
>       condemned.
22 The Lord redeems the life of
>     his servants;
>   none of those who take
>     refuge in him will be
>     condemned.

## PROVERBS 9.9–10

Give instruction[a] to the wise,
>     and they will become
>       wiser still;
>   teach the righteous and they
>     will gain in learning.
10 The fear of the Lord is the
>     beginning of wisdom,
>   and the knowledge of the
>     Holy One is insight.

# FEBRUARY 15

## EXODUS 39.1—40.38

Of the blue, purple, and crimson yarns they made finely worked vestments, for ministering in the holy place; they made the sacred vestments for Aaron; as the Lord had commanded Moses.

2 He made the ephod of gold, of blue, purple, and crimson yarns, and of fine twisted linen. 3Gold leaf was hammered out and cut into threads to work into the blue, purple, and crimson yarns and into the fine twisted linen, in skilled design. 4They made for the ephod shoulder-pieces, joined to it at its two edges. 5The decorated band on it was of the same materials and workmanship, of gold, of blue, purple, and crimson yarns, and of fine twisted linen; as the Lord had commanded Moses.

6 The onyx stones were prepared, enclosed in settings of gold filigree and engraved like the engravings of a signet, according to the names of the sons of Israel. 7He set them on the shoulder-pieces of the ephod, to be stones of re-membrance for the sons of Israel; as the Lord had commanded Moses.

8 He made the breastpiece, in skilled work, like the work of the ephod, of gold, of blue, purple, and crimson yarns, and of fine twisted linen. 9It was square; the breastpiece was made double, a span in length and a span in width when doubled. 10They set in it four rows of stones. A row of carnelian,[b] chrysolite, and emerald was the first row; 11and the second row, a turquoise, a sapphire,[c] and a moonstone; 12and the third row, a jacinth, an agate, and an amethyst; 13and the fourth row, a beryl, an onyx, and a jasper; they were enclosed in settings of gold filigree. 14There were twelve stones with names corresponding to the names of the sons of Israel; they were like signets, each engraved with its name, for the twelve tribes. 15They made on the breastpiece chains of pure gold, twisted like cords; 16and they made two settings of gold filigree and two gold rings, and put the two rings on

---

a Heb lacks *instruction*   b The identification of several of these stones is uncertain   c Or *lapis lazuli*

the two edges of the breastpiece; [17]and they put the two cords of gold in the two rings at the edges of the breast-piece. [18]Two ends of the two cords they had attached to the two settings of filigree; in this way they attached it in front to the shoulder-pieces of the ephod. [19]Then they made two rings of gold, and put them at the two ends of the breastpiece, on its inside edge next to the ephod. [20]They made two rings of gold, and attached them in front to the lower part of the two shoulder-pieces of the ephod, at its joining above the decorated band of the ephod. [21]They bound the breastpiece by its rings to the rings of the ephod with a blue cord, so that it should lie on the decorated band of the ephod, and that the breast-piece should not come loose from the ephod; as the Lord had commanded Moses.

22 He also made the robe of the ephod woven all of blue yarn; [23]and the opening of the robe in the middle of it was like the opening in a coat of mail, [a] with a binding around the opening, so that it might not be torn. [24]On the lower hem of the robe they made pomegran-ates of blue, purple, and crimson yarns, and of fine twisted linen. [25]They also made bells of pure gold, and put the bells between the pomegranates on the lower hem of the robe all around, be-tween the pomegranates; [26]a bell and a pomegranate, a bell and a pomegranate all around on the lower hem of the robe for ministering; as the Lord had com-manded Moses.

27 They also made the tunics, wo-ven of fine linen, for Aaron and his sons, [28]and the turban of fine linen, and the headdresses of fine linen, and the linen undergarments of fine twisted linen, [29]and the sash of fine twisted linen, and of blue, purple, and crimson yarns, embroidered with needlework; as the Lord had commanded Moses.

30 They made the rosette of the holy diadem of pure gold, and wrote on it an inscription, like the engraving of a signet, "Holy to the Lord." [31]They tied to it a blue cord, to fasten it on the tur-ban above; as the Lord had commanded Moses.

32 In this way all the work of the tabernacle of the tent of meeting was finished; the Israelites had done every-thing just as the Lord had commanded Moses. [33]Then they brought the taber-nacle to Moses, the tent and all its utensils, its hooks, its frames, its bars, its pillars, and its bases; [34]the covering of tanned rams' skins and the covering of fine leather, [a] and the curtain for the screen; [35]the ark of the covenant[b] with its poles and the mercy seat; [c] [36]the table with all its utensils, and the bread of the Presence; [37]the pure lampstand with its lamps set on it and all its uten-sils, and the oil for the light; [38]the golden altar, the anointing oil and the fragrant incense, and the screen for the entrance of the tent; [39]the bronze altar, and its grating of bronze, its poles, and all its utensils; the basin with its stand; [40]the hangings of the court, its pillars, and its bases, and the screen for the gate of the court, its cords, and its pegs; and all the utensils for the service of the tabernacle, for the tent of meet-ing; [41]the finely worked vestments for ministering in the holy place, the sacred vestments for the priest Aaron, and the vestments of his sons to serve as priests. [42]The Israelites had done all of the work just as the Lord had com-manded Moses. [43]When Moses saw that they had done all the work just as the Lord had commanded, he blessed them.

40.1 The Lord spoke to Moses: [2]On the first day of the first month you shall set up the tabernacle of the tent of meet-ing. [3]You shall put in it the ark of the

---

[a]Meaning of Heb uncertain   [b]Or *treaty*, or *testimony*; Heb *eduth*   [c]Or *the cover*

covenant,ᵃ and you shall screen the ark with the curtain. ⁴You shall bring in the table, and arrange its setting; and you shall bring in the lampstand, and set up its lamps. ⁵You shall put the golden altar for incense before the ark of the covenant,ᵃ and set up the screen for the entrance of the tabernacle. ⁶You shall set the altar of burnt offering before the entrance of the tabernacle of the tent of meeting, ⁷and place the basin between the tent of meeting and the altar, and put water in it. ⁸You shall set up the court all around, and hang up the screen for the gate of the court. ⁹Then you shall take the anointing oil, and anoint the tabernacle and all that is in it, and consecrate it and all its furniture, so that it shall become holy. ¹⁰You shall also anoint the altar of burnt offering and all its utensils, and consecrate the altar, so that the altar shall be most holy. ¹¹You shall also anoint the basin with its stand, and consecrate it. ¹²Then you shall bring Aaron and his sons to the entrance of the tent of meeting, and shall wash them with water, ¹³and put on Aaron the sacred vestments, and you shall anoint him and consecrate him, so that he may serve me as priest. ¹⁴You shall bring his sons also and put tunics on them, ¹⁵and anoint them, as you anointed their father, that they may serve me as priests: and their anointing shall admit them to a perpetual priesthood throughout all generations to come.

16 Moses did everything just as the Lᴏʀᴅ had commanded him. ¹⁷In the first month in the second year, on the first day of the month, the tabernacle was set up. ¹⁸Moses set up the tabernacle; he laid its bases, and set up its frames, and put in its poles, and raised up its pillars; ¹⁹and he spread the tent over the tabernacle, and put the covering of the tent over it; as the Lᴏʀᴅ had com-

manded Moses. ²⁰He took the covenantᵃ and put it into the ark, and put the poles on the ark, and set the mercy seatᵇ above the ark; ²¹and he brought the ark into the tabernacle, and set up the curtain for screening, and screened the ark of the covenant;ᵃ as the Lᴏʀᴅ had commanded Moses. ²²He put the table in the tent of meeting, on the north side of the tabernacle, outside the curtain, ²³and set the bread in order on it before the Lᴏʀᴅ; as the Lᴏʀᴅ had commanded Moses. ²⁴He put the lampstand in the tent of meeting, opposite the table on the south side of the tabernacle, ²⁵and set up the lamps before the Lᴏʀᴅ; as the Lᴏʀᴅ had commanded Moses. ²⁶He put the golden altar in the tent of meeting before the curtain, ²⁷and offered fragrant incense on it; as the Lᴏʀᴅ had commanded Moses. ²⁸He also put in place the screen for the entrance of the tabernacle. ²⁹He set the altar of burnt offering at the entrance of the tabernacle of the tent of meeting, and offered on it the burnt offering and the grain offering as the Lᴏʀᴅ had commanded Moses. ³⁰He set the basin between the tent of meeting and the altar, and put water in it for washing, ³¹with which Moses and Aaron and his sons washed their hands and their feet. ³²When they went into the tent of meeting, and when they approached the altar, they washed; as the Lᴏʀᴅ had commanded Moses. ³³He set up the court around the tabernacle and the altar, and put up the screen at the gate of the court. So Moses finished the work.

34 Then the cloud covered the tent of meeting, and the glory of the Lᴏʀᴅ filled the tabernacle. ³⁵Moses was not able to enter the tent of meeting because the cloud settled upon it, and the glory of the Lᴏʀᴅ filled the tabernacle. ³⁶Whenever the cloud was taken up from the tabernacle, the Israelites

ᵃOr *treaty*, or *testimony*; Heb *eduth*  ᵇOr *the cover*

would set out on each stage of their journey; [37]but if the cloud was not taken up, then they did not set out until the day that it was taken up. [38]For the cloud of the LORD was on the tabernacle by day, and fire was in the cloud[a] by night, before the eyes of all the house of Israel at each stage of their journey.

## MARK 1.1–28

THE beginning of the good news[b] of Jesus Christ, the Son of God. [c]

2  As it is written in the prophet Isaiah, [d]

"See, I am sending my
        messenger ahead of
        you, [e]
who will prepare your way;
3    the voice of one crying out in
        the wilderness:
'Prepare the way of the Lord,
    make his paths straight,'"

[4]John the baptizer appeared[f] in the wilderness, proclaiming a baptism of repentance for the forgiveness of sins. [5]And people from the whole Judean countryside and all the people of Jerusalem were going out to him, and were baptized by him in the river Jordan, confessing their sins. [6]Now John was clothed with camel's hair, with a leather belt around his waist, and he ate locusts and wild honey. [7]He proclaimed, "The one who is more powerful than I is coming after me; I am not worthy to stoop down and untie the thong of his sandals. [8]I have baptized you with[g] water; but he will baptize you with[g] the Holy Spirit."

9  In those days Jesus came from Nazareth of Galilee and was baptized by John in the Jordan. [10]And just as he was coming up out of the water, he saw the heavens torn apart and the Spirit descending like a dove on him. [11]And a voice came from heaven, "You are my Son, the Beloved;[h] with you I am well pleased."

12  And the Spirit immediately drove him out into the wilderness. [13]He was in the wilderness forty days, tempted by Satan; and he was with the wild beasts; and the angels waited on him.

14  Now after John was arrested, Jesus came to Galilee, proclaiming the good news[b] of God,[i] [15]and saying, "The time is fulfilled, and the kingdom of God has come near;[j] repent, and believe in the good news."[b]

16  As Jesus passed along the Sea of Galilee, he saw Simon and his brother Andrew casting a net into the sea—for they were fishermen. [17]And Jesus said to them, "Follow me and I will make you fish for people." [18]And immediately they left their nets and followed him. [19]As he went a little farther, he saw James son of Zebedee and his brother John, who were in their boat mending the nets. [20]Immediately he called them; and they left their father Zebedee in the boat with the hired men, and followed him.

21  They went to Capernaum; and when the sabbath came, he entered the synagogue and taught. [22]They were astounded at his teaching, for he taught them as one having authority, and not as the scribes. [23]Just then there was in their synagogue a man with an unclean spirit, [24]and he cried out, "What have you to do with us, Jesus of Nazareth? Have you come to destroy us? I know who you are, the Holy One of God." [25]But Jesus rebuked him, saying, "Be silent, and come out of him!" [26]And the unclean spirit, convulsing him and crying with a loud voice, came out of him. [27]They were all amazed, and they kept on asking one another, "What is this? A

aHeb *it*  bOr *gospel*  cOther ancient authorities lack *the Son of God*  dOther ancient authorities read *in the prophets*  eGk *before your face*  fOther ancient authorities read *John was baptizing*  gOr *in*  hOr *my beloved Son*  iOther ancient authorities read *of the kingdom*  jOr *is at hand*

new teaching—with authority! He[a] commands even the unclean spirits, and they obey him." 28 At once his fame began to spread throughout the surrounding region of Galilee.

## PSALM 35.1–16

*Of David.*

CONTEND, O LORD, with those
    who contend with me;
  fight against those who fight
    against me!
2 Take hold of shield and buckler,
    and rise up to help me!
3 Draw the spear and javelin
    against my pursuers;
say to my soul,
    "I am your salvation."

4 Let them be put to shame and
    dishonor
  who seek after my life.
Let them be turned back and
    confounded
  who devise evil against me.
5 Let them be like chaff before
    the wind,
  with the angel of the LORD
    driving them on.
6 Let their way be dark and
    slippery,
  with the angel of the LORD
    pursuing them.

7 For without cause they hid their
    net[b] for me;
  without cause they dug a pit[c]
    for my life.
8 Let ruin come on them
    unawares.
And let the net that they hid
    ensnare them;
  let them fall in it—to their
    ruin.

9 Then my soul shall rejoice in the
    LORD,
  exulting in his deliverance.
10 All my bones shall say,
  "O LORD, who is like you?
You deliver the weak
  from those too strong for
    them,
  the weak and needy from
    those who despoil them."

11 Malicious witnesses rise up;
  they ask me about things I do
    not know.
12 They repay me evil for good;
  my soul is forlorn.
13 But as for me, when they were
    sick,
  I wore sackcloth;
  I afflicted myself with fasting.
I prayed with head bowed[d] on
    my bosom,
14   as though I grieved for a
    friend or a brother;
I went about as one who
    laments for a mother,
  bowed down and in mourning.

15 But at my stumbling they
    gathered in glee,
  they gathered together
    against me;
ruffians whom I did not know
    tore at me without ceasing;
16 they impiously mocked more
    and more, [e]
  gnashing at me with their
    teeth.

## PROVERBS 9.11–12

FOR by me [wisdom] your days
    will be multiplied,
  and years will be added to
    your life.

a Or *A new teaching! With authority he*  b Heb *a pit, their net*  c The word *pit* is transposed from the preceding line  d Or *My prayer turned back*  e Cn Compare Gk: Heb *like the profanest of mockers of a cake*

12   If you are wise, you are wise
            for yourself;

if you scoff, you alone will
            bear it.

# FEBRUARY 16

## LEVITICUS 1.1—3.17

THE LORD summoned Moses and spoke to him from the tent of meeting, saying: 2Speak to the people of Israel and say to them: When any of you bring an offering of livestock to the LORD, you shall bring your offering from the herd or from the flock.

3  If the offering is a burnt offering from the herd, you shall offer a male without blemish; you shall bring it to the entrance of the tent of meeting, for acceptance in your behalf before the LORD. 4You shall lay your hand on the head of the burnt offering, and it shall be acceptable in your behalf as atonement for you. 5The bull shall be slaughtered before the LORD; and Aaron's sons the priests shall offer the blood, dashing the blood against all sides of the altar that is at the entrance of the tent of meeting. 6The burnt offering shall be flayed and cut up into its parts. 7The sons of the priest Aaron shall put fire on the altar and arrange wood on the fire. 8Aaron's sons the priests shall arrange the parts, with the head and the suet, on the wood that is on the fire on the altar; 9but its entrails and its legs shall be washed with water. Then the priest shall turn the whole into smoke on the altar as a burnt offering, an offering by fire of pleasing odor to the LORD.

10  If your gift for a burnt offering is from the flock, from the sheep or goats, your offering shall be a male without blemish. 11It shall be slaughtered on the north side of the altar before the LORD, and Aaron's sons the priests shall dash its blood against all sides of the altar. 12It shall be cut up into its parts, with its head and its suet, and the priest shall arrange them on the wood that is on the fire on the altar; 13but the entrails and the legs shall be washed with water. Then the priest shall offer the whole and turn it into smoke on the altar; it is a burnt offering, an offering by fire of pleasing odor to the LORD.

14  If your offering to the LORD is a burnt offering of birds, you shall choose your offering from turtledoves or pigeons. 15The priest shall bring it to the altar and wring off its head, and turn it into smoke on the altar; and its blood shall be drained out against the side of the altar. 16He shall remove its crop with its contentsa and throw it at the east side of the altar, in the place for ashes. 17He shall tear it open by its wings without severing it. Then the priest shall turn it into smoke on the altar, on the wood that is on the fire; it is a burnt offering, an offering by fire of pleasing odor to the LORD.

2.1 WHEN anyone presents a grain offering to the LORD, the offering shall be of choice flour; the worshiper shall pour oil on it, and put frankincense on it, 2and bring it to Aaron's sons the priests. After taking from it a handful of the choice flour and oil, with all its

aMeaning of Heb uncertain

frankincense, the priest shall turn this token portion into smoke on the altar, an offering by fire of pleasing odor to the LORD. 3And what is left of the grain offering shall be for Aaron and his sons, a most holy part of the offerings by fire to the LORD.

4 When you present a grain offering baked in the oven, it shall be of choice flour: unleavened cakes mixed with oil, or unleavened wafers spread with oil. 5If your offering is grain prepared on a griddle, it shall be of choice flour mixed with oil, unleavened; 6break it in pieces, and pour oil on it; it is a grain offering. 7If your offering is grain prepared in a pan, it shall be made of choice flour in oil. 8You shall bring to the LORD the grain offering that is prepared in any of these ways; and when it is presented to the priest, he shall take it to the altar. 9The priest shall remove from the grain offering its token portion and turn this into smoke on the altar, an offering by fire of pleasing odor to the LORD. 10And what is left of the grain offering shall be for Aaron and his sons; it is a most holy part of the offerings by fire to the LORD.

11 No grain offering that you bring to the LORD shall be made with leaven, for you must not turn any leaven or honey into smoke as an offering by fire to the LORD. 12You may bring them to the LORD as an offering of choice products, but they shall not be offered on the altar for a pleasing odor. 13You shall not omit from your grain offerings the salt of the covenant with your God; with all your offerings you shall offer salt.

14 If you bring a grain offering of first fruits to the LORD, you shall bring as the grain offering of your first fruits coarse new grain from fresh ears, parched with fire. 15You shall add oil to it and lay frankincense on it; it is a grain offering. 16And the priest shall turn a token portion of it into smoke—some of the coarse grain and oil with all its

frankincense; it is an offering by fire to the LORD.

3.1 IF the offering is a sacrifice of well-being, if you offer an animal of the herd, whether male or female, you shall offer one without blemish before the LORD. 2You shall lay your hand on the head of the offering and slaughter it at the entrance of the tent of meeting; and Aaron's sons the priests shall dash the blood against all sides of the altar. 3You shall offer from the sacrifice of well-being, as an offering by fire to the LORD, the fat that covers the entrails and all the fat that is around the entrails; 4the two kidneys with the fat that is on them at the loins, and the appendage of the liver, which he shall remove with the kidneys. 5Then Aaron's sons shall turn these into smoke on the altar, with the burnt offering that is on the wood on the fire, as an offering by fire of pleasing odor to the LORD.

6 If your offering for a sacrifice of well-being to the LORD is from the flock, male or female, you shall offer one without blemish. 7If you present a sheep as your offering, you shall bring it before the LORD 8and lay your hand on the head of the offering. It shall be slaughtered before the tent of meeting, and Aaron's sons shall dash its blood against all sides of the altar. 9You shall present its fat from the sacrifice of well-being, as an offering by fire to the LORD: the whole broad tail, which shall be removed close to the backbone, the fat that covers the entrails, and all the fat that is around the entrails; 10the two kidneys with the fat that is on them at the loins, and the appendage of the liver, which you shall remove with the kidneys. 11Then the priest shall turn these into smoke on the altar as a food offering by fire to the LORD.

12 If your offering is a goat, you shall bring it before the LORD 13and lay your hand on its head; it shall be slaughtered before the tent of meeting; and

the sons of Aaron shall dash its blood against all sides of the altar. [14]You shall present as your offering from it, as an offering by fire to the LORD, the fat that covers the entrails, and all the fat that is around the entrails; [15]the two kidneys with the fat that is on them at the loins, and the appendage of the liver, which you shall remove with the kidneys. [16]Then the priest shall turn these into smoke on the altar as a food offering by fire for a pleasing odor.

All fat is the LORD's. [17]It shall be a perpetual statute throughout your generations, in all your settlements: you must not eat any fat or any blood.

## MARK 1.29—2.12

As soon as they[a] [Jesus and his disciples] left the synagogue, they entered the house of Simon and Andrew, with James and John. [30]Now Simon's mother-in-law was in bed with a fever, and they told him about her at once. [31]He came and took her by the hand and lifted her up. Then the fever left her, and she began to serve them.

32 That evening, at sundown, they brought to him all who were sick or possessed with demons. [33]And the whole city was gathered around the door. [34]And he cured many who were sick with various diseases, and cast out many demons; and he would not permit the demons to speak, because they knew him.

35 In the morning, while it was still very dark, he got up and went out to a deserted place, and there he prayed. [36]And Simon and his companions hunted for him. [37]When they found him, they said to him, "Everyone is searching for you." [38]He answered, "Let us go on to the neighboring towns, so that I may proclaim the message there also; for that is what I came out to do." [39]And he went throughout Galilee, proclaiming the message in their synagogues and casting out demons.

40 A leper[b] came to him begging him, and kneeling[c] he said to him, "If you choose, you can make me clean." [41]Moved with pity, [d] Jesus[e] stretched out his hand and touched him, and said to him, "I do choose. Be made clean!" [42]Immediately the leprosy[b] left him, and he was made clean. [43]After sternly warning him he sent him away at once, [44]saying to him, "See that you say nothing to anyone; but go, show yourself to the priest, and offer for your cleansing what Moses commanded, as a testimony to them." [45]But he went out and began to proclaim it freely, and to spread the word, so that Jesus[e] could no longer go into a town openly, but stayed out in the country; and people came to him from every quarter.

[2.1] WHEN he returned to Capernaum after some days, it was reported that he was at home. [2]So many gathered around that there was no longer room for them, not even in front of the door; and he was speaking the word to them. [3]Then some people[f] came, bringing to him a paralyzed man, carried by four of them. [4]And when they could not bring him to Jesus because of the crowd, they removed the roof above him; and after having dug through it, they let down the mat on which the paralytic lay. [5]When Jesus saw their faith, he said to the paralytic, "Son, your sins are forgiven." [6]Now some of the scribes were sitting there, questioning in their hearts, [7]"Why does this fellow speak in this way? It is blasphemy! Who can forgive sins but God alone?" [8]At once Jesus perceived in his spirit that they were discussing these questions among themselves; and he said to them, "Why do you raise such questions in your hearts? [9]Which is easier,

aOther ancient authorities read *he*  bThe terms *leper* and *leprosy* can refer to several diseases
cOther ancient authorities lack *kneeling*  dOther ancient authorities read *anger*  eGk *he*  fGk *they*

to say to the paralytic, 'Your sins are forgiven,' or to say, 'Stand up and take your mat and walk'? [10]But so that you may know that the Son of Man has authority on earth to forgive sins"—he said to the paralytic— [11]"I say to you, stand up, take your mat and go to your home." [12]And he stood up, and immediately took the mat and went out before all of them; so that they were all amazed and glorified God, saying, "We have never seen anything like this!"

## PSALM 35.17–28

How long, O LORD, will you
    look on?
Rescue me from their
    ravages,
    my life from the lions!
18  Then I will thank you in the
    great congregation;
    in the mighty throng I will
    praise you.

19  Do not let my treacherous
    enemies rejoice over me,
    or those who hate me without
    cause wink the eye.
20  For they do not speak peace,
    but they conceive deceitful
    words
    against those who are quiet in
    the land.
21  They open wide their mouths
    against me;
    they say, "Aha, Aha,
    our eyes have seen it."

22  You have seen, O LORD; do not
    be silent!
    O Lord, do not be far from
    me!
23  Wake up! Bestir yourself for my
    defense,
    for my cause, my God and
    my Lord!
24  Vindicate me, O LORD, my God,
    according to your
    righteousness,
    and do not let them rejoice
    over me.
25  Do not let them say to
    themselves,
    "Aha, we have our heart's
    desire."
    Do not let them say, "We have
    swallowed you[a] up."

26  Let all those who rejoice at my
    calamity
    be put to shame and
    confusion;
    let those who exalt themselves
    against me
    be clothed with shame and
    dishonor.

27  Let those who desire my
    vindication
    shout for joy and be glad,
    and say evermore,
    "Great is the LORD,
    who delights in the welfare of
    his servant."
28  Then my tongue shall tell of
    your righteousness
    and of your praise all day
    long.

## PROVERBS 9.13–18

THE foolish woman is loud;
    she is ignorant and knows
    nothing.
14  She sits at the door of her
    house,
    on a seat at the high places of
    the town,
15  calling to those who pass by,
    who are going straight on
    their way,
16  "You who are simple, turn in
    here!"
    And to those without sense
    she says,
17  "Stolen water is sweet,

a Heb *him*

and bread eaten in secret is
pleasant."
18 But they do not know that the
dead[a] are there,

that her guests are in the
depths of Sheol.

# FEBRUARY 17

## LEVITICUS 4.1—5.19

THE LORD spoke to Moses, saying, [2]Speak to the people of Israel, saying: When anyone sins unintentionally in any of the LORD's commandments about things not to be done, and does any one of them:

3 If it is the anointed priest who sins, thus bringing guilt on the people, he shall offer for the sin that he has committed a bull of the herd without blemish as a sin offering to the LORD. [4]He shall bring the bull to the entrance of the tent of meeting before the LORD and lay his hand on the head of the bull; the bull shall be slaughtered before the LORD. [5]The anointed priest shall take some of the blood of the bull and bring it into the tent of meeting. [6]The priest shall dip his finger in the blood and sprinkle some of the blood seven times before the LORD in front of the curtain of the sanctuary. [7]The priest shall put some of the blood on the horns of the altar of fragrant incense that is in the tent of meeting before the LORD; and the rest of the blood of the bull he shall pour out at the base of the altar of burnt offering, which is at the entrance of the tent of meeting. [8]He shall remove all the fat from the bull of sin offering: the fat that covers the entrails and all the fat that is around the entrails; [9]the two kidneys with the fat that is on them at the loins; and the appendage of the liver, which he shall remove with the kidneys, [10]just as these are removed from the ox of the sacrifice of well-being. The priest shall turn them into smoke upon the altar of burnt offering. [11]But the skin of the bull and all its flesh, as well as its head, its legs, its entrails, and its dung— [12]all the rest of the bull—he shall carry out to a clean place outside the camp, to the ash heap, and shall burn it on a wood fire; at the ash heap it shall be burned.

13 If the whole congregation of Israel errs unintentionally and the matter escapes the notice of the assembly, and they do any one of the things that by the LORD's commandments ought not to be done and incur guilt; [14]when the sin that they have committed becomes known, the assembly shall offer a bull of the herd for a sin offering and bring it before the tent of meeting. [15]The elders of the congregation shall lay their hands on the head of the bull before the LORD, and the bull shall be slaughtered before the LORD. [16]The anointed priest shall bring some of the blood of the bull into the tent of meeting, [17]and the priest shall dip his finger in the blood and sprinkle it seven times before the LORD, in front of the curtain. [18]He shall put some of the blood on the horns of the altar that is before the LORD in the tent of meeting; and the rest of the blood he shall pour out at the base of

[a] Heb *shades*

the altar of burnt offering that is at the entrance of the tent of meeting. <sup>19</sup>He shall remove all its fat and turn it into smoke on the altar. <sup>20</sup>He shall do with the bull just as is done with the bull of sin offering; he shall do the same with this. The priest shall make atonement for them, and they shall be forgiven. <sup>21</sup>He shall carry the bull outside the camp, and burn it as he burned the first bull; it is the sin offering for the assembly.

22   When a ruler sins, doing unintentionally any one of all the things that by commandments of the Lord his God ought not to be done and incurs guilt, <sup>23</sup>once the sin that he has committed is made known to him, he shall bring as his offering a male goat without blemish. <sup>24</sup>He shall lay his hand on the head of the goat; it shall be slaughtered at the spot where the burnt offering is slaughtered before the Lord; it is a sin offering. <sup>25</sup>The priest shall take some of the blood of the sin offering with his finger and put it on the horns of the altar of burnt offering, and pour out the rest of its blood at the base of the altar of burnt offering. <sup>26</sup>All its fat he shall turn into smoke on the altar, like the fat of the sacrifice of well-being. Thus the priest shall make atonement on his behalf for his sin, and he shall be forgiven.

27   If anyone of the ordinary people among you sins unintentionally in doing any one of the things that by the Lord's commandments ought not to be done and incurs guilt, <sup>28</sup>when the sin that you have committed is made known to you, you shall bring a female goat without blemish as your offering, for the sin that you have committed. <sup>29</sup>You shall lay your hand on the head of the sin offering; and the sin offering shall be slaughtered at the place of the burnt offering. <sup>30</sup>The priest shall take some of its blood with his finger and put it on the horns of the altar of burnt offering, and he shall pour out the rest of its blood at the base of the altar. <sup>31</sup>He shall remove all its fat, as the fat is removed from the offering of well-being, and the priest shall turn it into smoke on the altar for a pleasing odor to the Lord. Thus the priest shall make atonement on your behalf, and you shall be forgiven.

32   If the offering you bring as a sin offering is a sheep, you shall bring a female without blemish. <sup>33</sup>You shall lay your hand on the head of the sin offering; and it shall be slaughtered as a sin offering at the spot where the burnt offering is slaughtered. <sup>34</sup>The priest shall take some of the blood of the sin offering with his finger and put it on the horns of the altar of burnt offering, and pour out the rest of its blood at the base of the altar. <sup>35</sup>You shall remove all its fat, as the fat of the sheep is removed from the sacrifice of well-being, and the priest shall turn it into smoke on the altar, with the offerings by fire to the Lord. Thus the priest shall make atonement on your behalf for the sin that you have committed, and you shall be forgiven.

<sup>5.1</sup> When any of you sin in that you have heard a public adjuration to testify and—though able to testify as one who has seen or learned of the matter—does not speak up, you are subject to punishment. <sup>2</sup>Or when any of you touch any unclean thing—whether the carcass of an unclean beast or the carcass of unclean livestock or the carcass of an unclean swarming thing—and are unaware of it, you have become unclean, and are guilty. <sup>3</sup>Or when you touch human uncleanness—any uncleanness by which one can become unclean—and are unaware of it, when you come to know it, you shall be guilty. <sup>4</sup>Or when any of you utter aloud a rash oath for a bad or a good purpose, whatever people utter in an oath, and are unaware of it, when you come to know it, you shall in any of these be guilty. <sup>5</sup>When you realize your guilt in any of these, you shall confess the sin that you have com-

mitted. [6]And you shall bring to the LORD, as your penalty for the sin that you have committed, a female from the flock, a sheep or a goat, as a sin offering; and the priest shall make atonement on your behalf for your sin.

7 But if you cannot afford a sheep, you shall bring to the LORD, as your penalty for the sin that you have committed, two turtledoves or two pigeons, one for a sin offering and the other for a burnt offering. [8]You shall bring them to the priest, who shall offer first the one for the sin offering, wringing its head at the nape without severing it. [9]He shall sprinkle some of the blood of the sin offering on the side of the altar, while the rest of the blood shall be drained out at the base of the altar; it is a sin offering. [10]And the second he shall offer for a burnt offering according to the regulation. Thus the priest shall make atonement on your behalf for the sin that you have committed, and you shall be forgiven.

11 But if you cannot afford two turtledoves or two pigeons, you shall bring as your offering for the sin that you have committed one-tenth of an ephah of choice flour for a sin offering; you shall not put oil on it or lay frankincense on it, for it is a sin offering. [12]You shall bring it to the priest, and the priest shall scoop up a handful of it as its memorial portion, and turn this into smoke on the altar, with the offerings by fire to the LORD; it is a sin offering. [13]Thus the priest shall make atonement on your behalf for whichever of these sins you have committed, and you shall be forgiven. Like the grain offering, the rest shall be for the priest.

14 The LORD spoke to Moses, saying: [15]When any of you commit a trespass and sins unintentionally in any of the holy things of the LORD, you shall bring, as your guilt offering to the LORD, a ram without blemish from the flock,

convertible into silver by the sanctuary shekel; it is a guilt offering. [16]And you shall make restitution for the holy thing in which you were remiss, and shall add one-fifth to it and give it to the priest. The priest shall make atonement on your behalf with the ram of the guilt offering, and you shall be forgiven.

17 If any of you sin without knowing it, doing any of the things that by the LORD's commandments ought not to be done, you have incurred guilt, and are subject to punishment. [18]You shall bring to the priest a ram without blemish from the flock, or the equivalent, as a guilt offering; and the priest shall make atonement on your behalf for the error that you committed unintentionally, and you shall be forgiven. [19]It is a guilt offering; you have incurred guilt before the LORD.

## MARK 2.13—3.6

J ESUS[a] went out again beside the sea; the whole crowd gathered around him, and he taught them. [14]As he was walking along, he saw Levi son of Alphaeus sitting at the tax booth, and he said to him, "Follow me." And he got up and followed him.

15 And as he sat at dinner[b] in Levi's[c] house, many tax collectors and sinners were also sitting[d] with Jesus and his disciples—for there were many who followed him. [16]When the scribes of[e] the Pharisees saw that he was eating with sinners and tax collectors, they said to his disciples, "Why does he eat[f] with tax collectors and sinners?" [17]When Jesus heard this, he said to them, "Those who are well have no need of a physician, but those who are sick; I have come to call not the righteous but sinners."

18 Now John's disciples and the Pharisees were fasting; and people[g] came and said to him, "Why do John's

a gk *he*  b Gk *reclined*  c Gk *his*  d Gk *reclining*  e Other ancient authorities read *and*  f Other ancient authorities add *and drink*  g Gk *they*

disciples and the disciples of the Pharisees fast, but your disciples do not fast?" 19Jesus said to them, "The wedding guests cannot fast while the bridegroom is with them, can they? As long as they have the bridegroom with them, they cannot fast. 20The days will come when the bridegroom is taken away from them, and then they will fast on that day.

21 "No one sews a piece of unshrunk cloth on an old cloak; otherwise, the patch pulls away from it, the new from the old, and a worse tear is made. 22And no one puts new wine into old wineskins; otherwise, the wine will burst the skins, and the wine is lost, and so are the skins; but one puts new wine into fresh wineskins."a

23 One sabbath he was going through the grainfields; and as they made their way his disciples began to pluck heads of grain. 24The Pharisees said to him, "Look, why are they doing what is not lawful on the sabbath?" 25And he said to them, "Have you never read what David did when he and his companions were hungry and in need of food? 26He entered the house of God, when Abiathar was high priest, and ate the bread of the Presence, which it is not lawful for any but the priests to eat, and he gave some to his companions." 27Then he said to them, "The sabbath was made for humankind, and not humankind for the sabbath; 28so the Son of Man is lord even of the sabbath."

3.1 AGAIN he entered the synagogue, and a man was there who had a withered hand. 2They watched him to see whether he would cure him on the sabbath, so that they might accuse him. 3And he said to the man who had the withered hand, "Come forward." 4Then he said to them, "Is it lawful to do good or to do harm on the sabbath, to save life or to kill?" But they were silent. 5He looked around at them with anger; he was grieved at their hardness of heart and said to the man, "Stretch out your hand." He stretched it out, and his hand was restored. 6The Pharisees went out and immediately conspired with the Herodians against him, how to destroy him.

## PSALM 36.1–12

*To the leader. Of David, the servant of the LORD.*

TRANSGRESSION speaks to the
   wicked
   deep in their hearts;
there is no fear of God
   before their eyes.
2  For they flatter themselves in
    their own eyes
  that their iniquity cannot be
    found out and hated.
3  The words of their mouths are
    mischief and deceit;
  they have ceased to act
    wisely and do good.
4  They plot mischief while on
    their beds;
  they are set on a way that is
    not good;
  they do not reject evil.

5  Your steadfast love, O LORD,
    extends to the heavens,
  your faithfulness to the
    clouds.
6  Your righteousness is like the
    mighty mountains,
  your judgments are like the
    great deep;
  you save humans and animals
    alike, O LORD.

7  How precious is your steadfast
    love, O God!
  All people may take refuge in
    the shadow of your
    wings.

aOther ancient authorities lack *but one puts new wine into fresh wineskins*

8  They feast on the abundance of
      your house,
   and you give them drink from
      the river of your
      delights.
9  For with you is the fountain of
      life;
   in your light we see light.

10  O continue your steadfast love
      to those who know you,
   and your salvation to the
      upright of heart!
11  Do not let the foot of the
      arrogant tread on me,
   or the hand of the wicked
      drive me away.

12  There the evildoers lie
      prostrate;
   they are thrust down, unable
      to rise.

## PROVERBS 10.1–2

THE proverbs of Solomon.

   A wise child makes a glad
      father,
   but a foolish child is a
      mother's grief.
2  Treasures gained by wickedness
      do not profit,
   but righteousness delivers
      from death.

# FEBRUARY 18

## LEVITICUS 6a.1—7.27

THE LORD spoke to Moses, saying: 2When any of you sin and commit a trespass against the LORD by deceiving a neighbor in a matter of a deposit or a pledge, or by robbery, or if you have defrauded a neighbor, 3or have found something lost and lied about it—if you swear falsely regarding any of the various things that one may do and sin thereby— 4when you have sinned and realize your guilt, and would restore what you took by robbery or by fraud or the deposit that was committed to you, or the lost thing that you found, 5or anything else about which you have sworn falsely, you shall repay the principal amount and shall add one-fifth to it. You shall pay it to its owner when you realize your guilt. 6And you shall bring to the priest, as your guilt offering to the LORD, a ram without blemish from the flock, or its equivalent, for a guilt offering. 7The priest shall make atonement on your behalf before the LORD, and you shall be forgiven for any of the things that one may do and incur guilt thereby.

8b The LORD spoke to Moses, saying: 9Command Aaron and his sons, saying: This is the ritual of the burnt offering. The burnt offering itself shall remain on the hearth upon the altar all night until the morning, while the fire on the altar shall be kept burning. 10The priest shall put on his linen vestments after putting on his linen undergarments next to his body; and he shall take up the ashes to which the fire has reduced the burnt offering on the altar, and place them beside the altar. 11Then

aCh 5.20 in Heb   bCh 6.1 in Heb

he shall take off his vestments and put on other garments, and carry the ashes out to a clean place outside the camp. 12The fire on the altar shall be kept burning; it shall not go out. Every morning the priest shall add wood to it, lay out the burnt offering on it, and turn into smoke the fat pieces of the offerings of well-being. 13A perpetual fire shall be kept burning on the altar; it shall not go out.

14  This is the ritual of the grain offering: The sons of Aaron shall offer it before the LORD, in front of the altar. 15They shall take from it a handful of the choice flour and oil of the grain offering, with all the frankincense that is on the offering, and they shall turn its memorial portion into smoke on the altar as a pleasing odor to the LORD. 16Aaron and his sons shall eat what is left of it; it shall be eaten as unleavened cakes in a holy place; in the court of the tent of meeting they shall eat it. 17It shall not be baked with leaven. I have given it as their portion of my offerings by fire; it is most holy, like the sin offering and the guilt offering. 18Every male among the descendants of Aaron shall eat of it, as their perpetual due throughout your generations, from the LORD's offerings by fire; anything that touches them shall become holy.

19  The LORD spoke to Moses, saying: 20This is the offering that Aaron and his sons shall offer to the LORD on the day when he is anointed: one-tenth of an ephah of choice flour as a regular offering, half of it in the morning and half in the evening. 21It shall be made with oil on a griddle; you shall bring it well soaked, as a grain offering of baked[a] pieces, and you shall present it as a pleasing odor to the LORD. 22And so the priest, anointed from among Aaron's descendants as a successor, shall prepare it; it is the LORD's—a perpetual due—to be turned entirely into smoke. 23Every grain offering of a priest shall be wholly burned; it shall not be eaten.

24  The LORD spoke to Moses, saying: 25Speak to Aaron and his sons, saying: This is the ritual of the sin offering. The sin offering shall be slaughtered before the LORD at the spot where the burnt offering is slaughtered; it is most holy. 26The priest who offers it as a sin offering shall eat of it; it shall be eaten in a holy place, in the court of the tent of meeting. 27Whatever touches its flesh shall become holy; and when any of its blood is spattered on a garment, you shall wash the bespattered part in a holy place. 28An earthen vessel in which it was boiled shall be broken; but if it is boiled in a bronze vessel, that shall be scoured and rinsed in water. 29Every male among the priests shall eat of it; it is most holy. 30But no sin offering shall be eaten from which any blood is brought into the tent of meeting for atonement in the holy place; it shall be burned with fire.

7.1 THIS is the ritual of the guilt offering. It is most holy; 2at the spot where the burnt offering is slaughtered, they shall slaughter the guilt offering, and its blood shall be dashed against all sides of the altar. 3All its fat shall be offered: the broad tail, the fat that covers the entrails, 4the two kidneys with the fat that is on them at the loins, and the appendage of the liver, which shall be removed with the kidneys. 5The priest shall turn them into smoke on the altar as an offering by fire to the LORD; it is a guilt offering. 6Every male among the priests shall eat of it; it shall be eaten in a holy place; it is most holy.

7  The guilt offering is like the sin offering, there is the same ritual for them; the priest who makes atonement with it shall have it. 8So, too, the priest who offers anyone's burnt offering shall

a Meaning of Heb uncertain

keep the skin of the burnt offering that he has offered. ⁹And every grain offering baked in the oven, and all that is prepared in a pan or on a griddle, shall belong to the priest who offers it. ¹⁰But every other grain offering, mixed with oil or dry, shall belong to all the sons of Aaron equally.

11 This is the ritual of the sacrifice of the offering of well-being that one may offer to the Lord. ¹²If you offer it for thanksgiving, you shall offer with the thank offering unleavened cakes mixed with oil, unleavened wafers spread with oil, and cakes of choice flour well soaked in oil. ¹³With your thanksgiving sacrifice of well-being you shall bring your offering with cakes of leavened bread. ¹⁴From this you shall offer one cake from each offering, as a gift to the Lord; it shall belong to the priest who dashes the blood of the offering of well-being. ¹⁵And the flesh of your thanksgiving sacrifice of well-being shall be eaten on the day it is offered; you shall not leave any of it until morning. ¹⁶But if the sacrifice you offer is a votive offering or a freewill offering, it shall be eaten on the day that you offer your sacrifice, and what is left of it shall be eaten the next day; ¹⁷but what is left of the flesh of the sacrifice shall be burned up on the third day. ¹⁸If any of the flesh of your sacrifice of well-being is eaten on the third day, it shall not be acceptable, nor shall it be credited to the one who offers it; it shall be an abomination, and the one who eats of it shall incur guilt.

19 Flesh that touches any unclean thing shall not be eaten; it shall be burned up. As for other flesh, all who are clean may eat such flesh. ²⁰But those who eat flesh from the Lord's sacrifice of well-being while in a state of uncleanness shall be cut off from their kin. ²¹When any one of you touches any unclean thing—human uncleanness or

an unclean animal or any unclean creature—and then eats flesh from the Lord's sacrifice of well-being, you shall be cut off from your kin.

22 The Lord spoke to Moses, saying: ²³Speak to the people of Israel, saying: You shall eat no fat of ox or sheep or goat. ²⁴The fat of an animal that died or was torn by wild animals may be put to any use, but you must not eat it. ²⁵If any one of you eats the fat from an animal of which an offering by fire may be made to the Lord, you who eat it shall be cut off from your kin. ²⁶You must not eat any blood whatever, either of bird or of animal, in any of your settlements. ²⁷Any one of you who eats any blood shall be cut off from your kin.

## MARK 3. 7–30

JESUS departed with his disciples to the sea, and a great multitude from Galilee followed him; ⁸hearing all that he was doing, they came to him in great numbers from Judea, Jerusalem, Idumea, beyond the Jordan, and the region around Tyre and Sidon. ⁹He told his disciples to have a boat ready for him because of the crowd, so that they would not crush him; ¹⁰for he had cured many, so that all who had diseases pressed upon him to touch him. ¹¹Whenever the unclean spirits saw him, they fell down before him and shouted, "You are the Son of God!" ¹²But he sternly ordered them not to make him known.

13 He went up the mountain and called to him those whom he wanted, and they came to him. ¹⁴And he appointed twelve, whom he also named apostles, ᵃ to be with him, and to be sent out to proclaim the message, ¹⁵and to have authority to cast out demons. ¹⁶So he appointed the twelve: ᵇ Simon (to whom he gave the name Peter); ¹⁷James son of Zebedee and John the

---

ᵃOther ancient authorities lack *whom he also named apostles*   ᵇOther ancient authorities lack *So he appointed the twelve*

brother of James (to whom he gave the name Boanerges, that is, Sons of Thunder); [18]and Andrew, and Philip, and Bartholomew, and Matthew, and Thomas, and James son of Alphaeus, and Thaddaeus, and Simon the Cananaean, [19]and Judas Iscariot, who betrayed him.

Then he went home; [20]and the crowd came together again, so that they could not even eat. [21]When his family heard it, they went out to restrain him, for people were saying, "He has gone out of his mind." [22]And the scribes who came down from Jerusalem said, "He has Beelzebul, and by the ruler of the demons he casts out demons." [23]And he called them to him, and spoke to them in parables, "How can Satan cast out Satan? [24]If a kingdom is divided against itself, that kingdom cannot stand. [25]And if a house is divided against itself, that house will not be able to stand. [26]And if Satan has risen up against himself and is divided, he cannot stand, but his end has come. [27]But no one can enter a strong man's house and plunder his property without first tying up the strong man; then indeed the house can be plundered.

28 "Truly I tell you, people will be forgiven for their sins and whatever blasphemies they utter; [29]but whoever blasphemes against the Holy Spirit can never have forgiveness, but is guilty of an eternal sin"— [30]for they had said, "He has an unclean spirit."

## PSALM 37.1–11

*Of David.*

**D**o not fret because of the
    wicked;
  do not be envious of
    wrongdoers,
2  for they will soon fade like the
    grass,
    and wither like the green
      herb.

3  Trust in the LORD, and do good;
    so you will live in the land,
      and enjoy security.
4  Take delight in the LORD,
    and he will give you the
      desires of your heart.

5  Commit your way to the LORD;
    trust in him, and he will act.
6  He will make your vindication
    shine like the light,
    and the justice of your cause
      like the noonday.

7  Be still before the LORD, and
    wait patiently for him;
  do not fret over those who
    prosper in their way,
  over those who carry out evil
    devices.

8  Refrain from anger, and forsake
    wrath.
  Do not fret—it leads only to
    evil.
9  For the wicked shall be cut off,
    but those who wait for the
      LORD shall inherit the
      land.

10  Yet a little while, and the
    wicked will be no more;
  though you look diligently for
    their place, they will not
    be there.
11  But the meek shall inherit the
    land,
  and delight themselves in
    abundant prosperity.

## PROVERBS 10.3–4

**T**HE LORD does not let the
    righteous go hungry,
  but he thwarts the craving of
    the wicked.
4  A slack hand causes poverty,
    but the hand of the diligent
    makes rich.

# FEBRUARY 19



## LEVITICUS 7.28—9.6

THE LORD spoke to Moses, saying: <sup>29</sup>Speak to the people of Israel, saying: Any one of you who would offer to the LORD your sacrifice of well-being must yourself bring to the LORD your offering from your sacrifice of well-being. <sup>30</sup>Your own hands shall bring the LORD's offering by fire; you shall bring the fat with the breast, so that the breast may be raised as an elevation offering before the LORD. <sup>31</sup>The priest shall turn the fat into smoke on the altar, but the breast shall belong to Aaron and his sons. <sup>32</sup>And the right thigh from your sacrifices of well-being you shall give to the priest as an offering; <sup>33</sup>the one among the sons of Aaron who offers the blood and fat of the offering of well-being shall have the right thigh for a portion. <sup>34</sup>For I have taken the breast of the elevation offering, and the thigh that is offered, from the people of Israel, from their sacrifices of well-being, and have given them to Aaron the priest and to his sons, as a perpetual due from the people of Israel. <sup>35</sup>This is the portion allotted to Aaron and to his sons from the offerings made by fire to the LORD, once they have been brought forward to serve the LORD as priests; <sup>36</sup>these the LORD commanded to be given them, when he anointed them, as a perpetual due from the people of Israel throughout their generations.

37 This is the ritual of the burnt offering, the grain offering, the sin offering, the guilt offering, the offering of ordination, and the sacrifice of well-being, <sup>38</sup>which the LORD commanded Moses on Mount Sinai, when he commanded the people of Israel to bring their offerings to the LORD, in the wilderness of Sinai.

<sup>8.1</sup>THE LORD spoke to Moses, saying: <sup>2</sup>Take Aaron and his sons with him, the vestments, the anointing oil, the bull of sin offering, the two rams, and the basket of unleavened bread; <sup>3</sup>and assemble the whole congregation at the entrance of the tent of meeting. <sup>4</sup>And Moses did as the LORD commanded him. When the congregation was assembled at the entrance of the tent of meeting, <sup>5</sup>Moses said to the congregation, "This is what the LORD has commanded to be done."

6 Then Moses brought Aaron and his sons forward, and washed them with water. <sup>7</sup>He put the tunic on him, fastened the sash around him, clothed him with the robe, and put the ephod on him. He then put the decorated band of the ephod around him, tying the ephod to him with it. <sup>8</sup>He placed the breastpiece on him, and in the breastpiece he put the Urim and the Thummim. <sup>9</sup>And he set the turban on his head, and on the turban, in front, he set the golden ornament, the holy crown, as the LORD commanded Moses.

10 Then Moses took the anointing oil and anointed the tabernacle and all that was in it, and consecrated them. <sup>11</sup>He sprinkled some of it on the altar seven times, and anointed the altar and all its utensils, and the basin and its base, to consecrate them. <sup>12</sup>He poured some of the anointing oil on Aaron's head and anointed him, to consecrate him. <sup>13</sup>And Moses brought forward Aaron's sons, and clothed them with tunics, and fastened sashes around them, and tied headdresses on them, as the LORD commanded Moses.

14 He led forward the bull of sin offering; and Aaron and his sons laid their hands upon the head of the bull of sin

offering, [15]and it was slaughtered. Moses took the blood and with his finger put some on each of the horns of the altar, purifying the altar; then he poured out the blood at the base of the altar. Thus he consecrated it, to make atonement for it. [16]Moses took all the fat that was around the entrails, and the appendage of the liver, and the two kidneys with their fat, and turned them into smoke on the altar. [17]But the bull itself, its skin and flesh and its dung, he burned with fire outside the camp, as the LORD commanded Moses.

18 Then he brought forward the ram of burnt offering. Aaron and his sons laid their hands on the head of the ram, [19]and it was slaughtered. Moses dashed the blood against all sides of the altar. [20]The ram was cut into its parts, and Moses turned into smoke the head and the parts and the suet. [21]And after the entrails and the legs were washed with water, Moses turned into smoke the whole ram on the altar; it was a burnt offering for a pleasing odor, an offering by fire to the LORD, as the LORD commanded Moses.

22 Then he brought forward the second ram, the ram of ordination. Aaron and his sons laid their hands on the head of the ram, [23]and it was slaughtered. Moses took some of its blood and put it on the lobe of Aaron's right ear and on the thumb of his right hand and on the big toe of his right foot. [24]After Aaron's sons were brought forward, Moses put some of the blood on the lobes of their right ears and on the thumbs of their right hands and on the big toes of their right feet; and Moses dashed the rest of the blood against all sides of the altar. [25]He took the fat— the broad tail, all the fat that was around the entrails, the appendage of the liver, and the two kidneys with their fat—and the right thigh. [26]From the basket of unleavened bread that was before the LORD, he took one cake of unleavened bread, one cake of bread with oil, and one wafer, and placed them on the fat and on the right thigh. [27]He placed all these on the palms of Aaron and on the palms of his sons, and raised them as an elevation offering before the LORD. [28]Then Moses took them from their hands and turned them into smoke on the altar with the burnt offering. This was an ordination offering for a pleasing odor, an offering by fire to the LORD. [29]Moses took the breast and raised it as an elevation offering before the LORD; it was Moses' portion of the ram of ordination, as the LORD commanded Moses.

30 Then Moses took some of the anointing oil and some of the blood that was on the altar and sprinkled them on Aaron and his vestments, and also on his sons and their vestments. Thus he consecrated Aaron and his vestments, and also his sons and their vestments.

31 And Moses said to Aaron and his sons, "Boil the flesh at the entrance of the tent of meeting, and eat it there with the bread that is in the basket of ordination offerings, as I was commanded, 'Aaron and his sons shall eat it'; [32]and what remains of the flesh and the bread you shall burn with fire. [33]You shall not go outside the entrance of the tent of meeting for seven days, until the day when your period of ordination is completed. For it will take seven days to ordain you; [34]as has been done today, the LORD has commanded to be done to make atonement for you. [35]You shall remain at the entrance of the tent of meeting day and night for seven days, keeping the LORD's charge so that you do not die; for so I am commanded." [36]Aaron and his sons did all the things that the LORD commanded through Moses.

9.1 ON the eighth day Moses summoned Aaron and his sons and the elders of Israel. [2]He said to Aaron, "Take a bull calf for a sin offering and a ram for a burnt offering, without blemish, and offer them before the LORD. <sup>3</sup>And say to the people of Israel, 'Take a male goat for a sin offering; a calf and a lamb, yearlings without blemish, for a burnt offering; <sup>4</sup>and an ox and a ram for an offering of well-being to sacrifice before the LORD; and a grain offering mixed with oil. For today the LORD will appear to you.' " <sup>5</sup>They brought what Moses commanded to the front of the tent of meeting; and the whole congregation drew near and stood before the LORD. <sup>6</sup>And Moses said, "This is the thing that the LORD commanded you to do, so that the glory of the LORD may appear to you."

## MARK 3.31—4.25

THEN his [Jesus'] mother and his brothers came; and standing outside, they sent to him and called him. <sup>32</sup>A crowd was sitting around him; and they said to him, "Your mother and your brothers and sisters[a] are outside, asking for you." <sup>33</sup>And he replied, "Who are my mother and my brothers?" <sup>34</sup>And looking at those who sat around him, he said, "Here are my mother and my brothers! <sup>35</sup>Whoever does the will of God is my brother and sister and mother."

<sup>4.1</sup>AGAIN he began to teach beside the sea. Such a very large crowd gathered around him that he got into a boat on the sea and sat there, while the whole crowd was beside the sea on the land. <sup>2</sup>He began to teach them many things in parables, and in his teaching he said to them: <sup>3</sup>"Listen! A sower went out to sow. <sup>4</sup>And as he sowed, some seed fell on the path, and the birds came and ate it up. <sup>5</sup>Other seed fell on rocky ground, where it did not have much soil, and it sprang up quickly, since it had no depth of soil. <sup>6</sup>And when the sun rose, it was scorched; and since it had no root, it withered away. <sup>7</sup>Other seed fell among thorns, and the thorns grew up and choked it, and it yielded no grain. <sup>8</sup>Other seed fell into good soil and brought forth grain, growing up and increasing and yielding thirty and sixty and a hundredfold." <sup>9</sup>And he said, "Let anyone with ears to hear listen!"

10 When he was alone, those who were around him along with the twelve asked him about the parables. <sup>11</sup>And he said to them, "To you has been given the secret[b] of the kingdom of God, but for those outside, everything comes in parables; <sup>12</sup>in order that

'they may indeed look, but not perceive,
  and may indeed listen, but not understand;
so that they may not turn again and be forgiven.' "

13 And he said to them, "Do you not understand this parable? Then how will you understand all the parables? <sup>14</sup>The sower sows the word. <sup>15</sup>These are the ones on the path where the word is sown: when they hear, Satan immediately comes and takes away the word that is sown in them. <sup>16</sup>And these are the ones sown on rocky ground: when they hear the word, they immediately receive it with joy. <sup>17</sup>But they have no root, and endure only for a while; then, when trouble or persecution arises on account of the word, immediately they fall away.[c] <sup>18</sup>And others are those sown among the thorns: these are the ones who hear the word, <sup>19</sup>but the cares of the world, and the lure of wealth, and the desire for other things come in and choke the word, and it yields nothing. <sup>20</sup>And these are the ones sown on the good soil: they hear the word and accept it and bear fruit, thirty and sixty and a hundredfold."

21 He said to them, "Is a lamp brought in to be put under the bushel basket, or under the bed, and not on

a Other ancient authorities lack *and sisters*  b Or *mystery*  c Or *stumble* the lampstand? <sup>22</sup>For there is nothing hidden, except to be disclosed; nor is anything secret, except to come to light. <sup>23</sup>Let anyone with ears to hear listen!" <sup>24</sup>And he said to them, "Pay attention to what you hear; the measure you give will be the measure you get, and still more will be given you. <sup>25</sup>For to those who have, more will be given; and from those who have nothing, even what they have will be taken away."

## PSALM 37.12–29

THE wicked plot against the
   righteous,
  and gnash their teeth at
   them;
13  but the LORD laughs at the
   wicked,
    for he sees that their day is
    coming.

14  The wicked draw the sword and
   bend their bows
    to bring down the poor and
    needy,
    to kill those who walk
    uprightly;
15  their sword shall enter their
   own heart,
    and their bows shall be
    broken.

16  Better is a little that the
   righteous person has
    than the abundance of many
    wicked.
17  For the arms of the wicked shall
   be broken,
    but the LORD upholds the
    righteous.

18  The LORD knows the days of the
   blameless,
    and their heritage will abide
    forever;
19  they are not put to shame in
   evil times,

in the days of famine they
  have abundance.

20  But the wicked perish,
   and the enemies of the LORD
    are like the glory of the
    pastures;
   they vanish—like smoke they
    vanish away.

21  The wicked borrow, and do not
   pay back,
   but the righteous are
    generous and keep
    giving;
22  for those blessed by the LORD
   shall inherit the land,
   but those cursed by him shall
    be cut off.

23  Our steps<sup>a</sup> are made firm by
   the LORD,
   when he delights in our<sup>b</sup>
    way;
24  though we stumble,<sup>c</sup> we<sup>d</sup> shall
   not fall headlong,
   for the LORD holds us<sup>e</sup> by the
    hand.

25  I have been young, and now am
   old,
   yet I have not seen the
    righteous forsaken
   or their children begging
    bread.
26  They are ever giving liberally
   and lending,
   and their children become a
    blessing.

27  Depart from evil, and do good;
   so you shall abide forever.
28  For the LORD loves justice;
   he will not forsake his faithful
    ones.

The righteous shall be kept safe
  forever,

<sup>a</sup>Heb *a man's steps*  <sup>b</sup>Heb *his*  <sup>c</sup>Heb *he stumbles*  <sup>d</sup>Heb *he*  <sup>e</sup>Heb *him*

but the children of the wicked
shall be cut off.
29 The righteous shall inherit the
land,
and live in it forever.

## PROVERBS 10.5

A CHILD who gathers in summer
is prudent,
but a child who sleeps in
harvest brings shame.

# FEBRUARY 20

## LEVITICUS 9.7—10.20

THEN Moses said to Aaron, "Draw near to the altar and sacrifice your sin offering and your burnt offering, and make atonement for yourself and for the people; and sacrifice the offering of the people, and make atonement for them; as the LORD has commanded."

8 Aaron drew near to the altar, and slaughtered the calf of the sin offering, which was for himself. 9The sons of Aaron presented the blood to him, and he dipped his finger in the blood and put it on the horns of the altar; and the rest of the blood he poured out at the base of the altar. 10But the fat, the kidneys, and the appendage of the liver from the sin offering he turned into smoke on the altar, as the LORD commanded Moses; 11and the flesh and the skin he burned with fire outside the camp.

12 Then he slaughtered the burnt offering. Aaron's sons brought him the blood, and he dashed it against all sides of the altar. 13And they brought him the burnt offering piece by piece, and the head, which he turned into smoke on the altar. 14He washed the entrails and the legs and, with the burnt offering, turned them into smoke on the altar.

15 Next he presented the people's offering. He took the goat of the sin offering that was for the people, and slaughtered it, and presented it as a sin offering like the first one. 16He presented the burnt offering, and sacrificed it according to regulation. 17He presented the grain offering, and, taking a handful of it, he turned it into smoke on the altar, in addition to the burnt offering of the morning.

18 He slaughtered the ox and the ram as a sacrifice of well-being for the people. Aaron's sons brought him the blood, which he dashed against all sides of the altar, 19and the fat of the ox and of the ram—the broad tail, the fat that covers the entrails, the two kidneys and the fat on them, a and the appendage of the liver. 20They first laid the fat on the breasts, and the fat was turned into smoke on the altar; 21and the breasts and the right thigh Aaron raised as an elevation offering before the LORD, as Moses had commanded.

22 Aaron lifted his hands toward the people and blessed them; and he came down after sacrificing the sin offering, the burnt offering, and the offering of well-being. 23Moses and Aaron entered the tent of meeting, and then came out and blessed the people; and the glory of the LORD appeared to all the

a Gk: Heb *the broad tail, and that which covers, and the kidneys* people. ²⁴Fire came out from the Lᴏʀᴅ and consumed the burnt offering and the fat on the altar; and when all the people saw it, they shouted and fell on their faces.

¹⁰·¹ Nᴏᴡ Aaron's sons, Nadab and Abihu, each took his censer, put fire in it, and laid incense on it; and they offered unholy fire before the Lᴏʀᴅ, such as he had not commanded them. ²And fire came out from the presence of the Lᴏʀᴅ and consumed them, and they died before the Lᴏʀᴅ. ³Then Moses said to Aaron, "This is what the Lᴏʀᴅ meant when he said,

'Through those who are near me
I will show myself holy,
and before all the people
I will be glorified.' "
And Aaron was silent.

4 Moses summoned Mishael and Elzaphan, sons of Uzziel the uncle of Aaron, and said to them, "Come forward, and carry your kinsmen away from the front of the sanctuary to a place outside the camp." ⁵They came forward and carried them by their tunics out of the camp, as Moses had ordered. ⁶And Moses said to Aaron and to his sons Eleazar and Ithamar, "Do not dishevel your hair, and do not tear your vestments, or you will die and wrath will strike all the congregation; but your kindred, the whole house of Israel, may mourn the burning that the Lᴏʀᴅ has sent. ⁷You shall not go outside the entrance of the tent of meeting, or you will die; for the anointing oil of the Lᴏʀᴅ is on you." And they did as Moses had ordered.

8 And the Lᴏʀᴅ spoke to Aaron: ⁹Drink no wine or strong drink, neither you nor your sons, when you enter the tent of meeting, that you may not die; it is a statute forever throughout your generations. ¹⁰You are to distinguish between the holy and the common, and between the unclean and the clean; ¹¹and you are to teach the people of Israel all the statutes that the Lᴏʀᴅ has spoken to them through Moses.

12 Moses spoke to Aaron and to his remaining sons, Eleazar and Ithamar: Take the grain offering that is left from the Lᴏʀᴅ's offerings by fire, and eat it unleavened beside the altar, for it is most holy; ¹³you shall eat it in a holy place, because it is your due and your sons' due, from the offerings by fire to the Lᴏʀᴅ; for so I am commanded. ¹⁴But the breast that is elevated and the thigh that is raised, you and your sons and daughters as well may eat in any clean place; for they have been assigned to you and your children from the sacrifices of the offerings of well-being of the people of Israel. ¹⁵The thigh that is raised and the breast that is elevated they shall bring, together with the offerings by fire of the fat, to raise for an elevation offering before the Lᴏʀᴅ; they are to be your due and that of your children forever, as the Lᴏʀᴅ has commanded.

16 Then Moses made inquiry about the goat of the sin offering, and—it had already been burned! He was angry with Eleazar and Ithamar, Aaron's remaining sons, and said, ¹⁷"Why did you not eat the sin offering in the sacred area? For it is most holy, and Godᵃ has given it to you that you may remove the guilt of the congregation, to make atonement on their behalf before the Lᴏʀᴅ. ¹⁸Its blood was not brought into the inner part of the sanctuary. You should certainly have eaten it in the sanctuary, as I commanded." ¹⁹And Aaron spoke to Moses, "See, today they offered their sin offering and their burnt offering before the Lᴏʀᴅ; and yet such things as these have befallen me! If I had eaten the sin offering today, would it have been agreeable to the

ᵃHeb he

LORD?" [20]And when Moses heard that, he agreed.

## MARK 4.26—5.20

HE [Jesus] also said, "The kingdom of God is as if someone would scatter seed on the ground, [27]and would sleep and rise night and day, and the seed would sprout and grow, he does not know how. [28]The earth produces of itself, first the stalk, then the head, then the full grain in the head. [29]But when the grain is ripe, at once he goes in with his sickle, because the harvest has come."

30  He also said, "With what can we compare the kingdom of God, or what parable will we use for it? [31]It is like a mustard seed, which, when sown upon the ground, is the smallest of all the seeds on earth; [32]yet when it is sown it grows up and becomes the greatest of all shrubs, and puts forth large branches, so that the birds of the air can make nests in its shade."

33  With many such parables he spoke the word to them, as they were able to hear it; [34]he did not speak to them except in parables, but he explained everything in private to his disciples.

35  On that day, when evening had come, he said to them, "Let us go across to the other side." [36]And leaving the crowd behind, they took him with them in the boat, just as he was. Other boats were with him. [37]A great windstorm arose, and the waves beat into the boat, so that the boat was already being swamped. [38]But he was in the stern, asleep on the cushion; and they woke him up and said to him, "Teacher, do you not care that we are perishing?" [39]He woke up and rebuked the wind, and said to the sea, "Peace! Be still!" Then the wind ceased, and there was a dead calm. [40]He said to them, "Why are you afraid? Have you still no faith?" [41]And they were filled with great awe and said to one another, "Who then is this, that even the wind and the sea obey him?"

[5.1] THEY came to the other side of the sea, to the country of the Gerasenes. [a] [2]And when he had stepped out of the boat, immediately a man out of the tombs with an unclean spirit met him. [3]He lived among the tombs; and no one could restrain him any more, even with a chain; [4]for he had often been restrained with shackles and chains, but the chains he wrenched apart, and the shackles he broke in pieces; and no one had the strength to subdue him. [5]Night and day among the tombs and on the mountains he was always howling and bruising himself with stones. [6]When he saw Jesus from a distance, he ran and bowed down before him; [7]and he shouted at the top of his voice, "What have you to do with me, Jesus, Son of the Most High God? I adjure you by God, do not torment me." [8]For he had said to him, "Come out of the man, you unclean spirit!" [9]Then Jesus[b] asked him, "What is your name?" He replied, "My name is Legion; for we are many." [10]He begged him earnestly not to send them out of the country. [11]Now there on the hillside a great herd of swine was feeding; [12]and the unclean spirits[c] begged him, "Send us into the swine; let us enter them." [13]So he gave them permission. And the unclean spirits came out and entered the swine; and the herd, numbering about two thousand, rushed down the steep bank into the sea, and were drowned in the sea.

14  The swineherds ran off and told it in the city and in the country. Then people came to see what it was that had happened. [15]They came to Jesus and saw the demoniac sitting there, clothed and in his right mind, the very man who

a Other ancient authorities read *Gergesenes*; others, *Gadarenes*   b Gk *he*   c Gk *they* had had the legion; and they were afraid. [16]Those who had seen what had happened to the demoniac and to the swine reported it. [17]Then they began to beg Jesus[a] to leave their neighborhood. [18]As he was getting into the boat, the man who had been possessed by demons begged him that he might be with him. [19]But Jesus[b] refused, and said to him, "Go home to your friends, and tell them how much the Lord has done for you, and what mercy he has shown you." [20]And he went away and began to proclaim in the Decapolis how much Jesus had done for him; and everyone was amazed.

## PSALM 37.30–40

THE mouths of the righteous
        utter wisdom,
    and their tongues speak
        justice.
31  The law of their God is in their
        hearts;
    their steps do not slip.

32  The wicked watch for the
        righteous,
    and seek to kill them.
33  The LORD will not abandon them
        to their power,
    or let them be condemned
        when they are brought to
        trial.

34  Wait for the LORD, and keep to
        his way,
    and he will exalt you to
        inherit the land;
    you will look on the
        destruction of the
        wicked.

35  I have seen the wicked
        oppressing,
    and towering like a cedar of
        Lebanon. [c]
36  Again I[d] passed by, and they
        were no more;
    though I sought them, they
        could not be found.

37  Mark the blameless, and behold
        the upright,
    for there is posterity for the
        peaceable.
38  But transgressors shall be
        altogether destroyed;
    the posterity of the wicked
        shall be cut off.

39  The salvation of the righteous is
        from the LORD;
    he is their refuge in the time
        of trouble.
40  The LORD helps them and
        rescues them;
    he rescues them from the
        wicked, and saves them,
    because they take refuge in
        him.

## PROVERBS 10.6–7

BLESSINGS are on the head of
        the righteous,
    but the mouth of the wicked
        conceals violence.
7   The memory of the righteous is
        a blessing,
    but the name of the wicked
        will rot.

aGk *him*  bGk *he*  cGk: Meaning of Heb uncertain  dGk Syr Jerome: Heb *he*

## LEVITICUS 11.1—12.8

THE LORD spoke to Moses and Aaron, saying to them: ²Speak to the people of Israel, saying:

From among all the land animals, these are the creatures that you may eat. ³Any animal that has divided hoofs and is cleft-footed and chews the cud—such you may eat. ⁴But among those that chew the cud or have divided hoofs, you shall not eat the following: the camel, for even though it chews the cud, it does not have divided hoofs; it is unclean for you. ⁵The rock badger, for even though it chews the cud, it does not have divided hoofs; it is unclean for you. ⁶The hare, for even though it chews the cud, it does not have divided hoofs; it is unclean for you. ⁷The pig, for even though it has divided hoofs and is cleft-footed, it does not chew the cud; it is unclean for you. ⁸Of their flesh you shall not eat, and their carcasses you shall not touch; they are unclean for you.

9 These you may eat, of all that are in the waters. Everything in the waters that has fins and scales, whether in the seas or in the streams—such you may eat. ¹⁰But anything in the seas or the streams that does not have fins and scales, of the swarming creatures in the waters and among all the other living creatures that are in the waters—they are detestable to you ¹¹and detestable they shall remain. Of their flesh you shall not eat, and their carcasses you shall regard as detestable. ¹²Everything in the waters that does not have fins and scales is detestable to you.

13 These you shall regard as detestable among the birds. They shall not be eaten; they are an abomination: the eagle, the vulture, the osprey, ¹⁴the buzzard, the kite of any kind; ¹⁵every raven of any kind; ¹⁶the ostrich, the nighthawk, the sea gull, the hawk of any kind; ¹⁷the little owl, the cormorant, the great owl, ¹⁸the water hen, the desert owl, ᵃ the carrion vulture, ¹⁹the stork, the heron of any kind, the hoopoe, and the bat. ᵇ

20 All winged insects that walk upon all fours are detestable to you. ²¹But among the winged insects that walk on all fours you may eat those that have jointed legs above their feet, with which to leap on the ground. ²²Of them you may eat: the locust according to its kind, the bald locust according to its kind, the cricket according to its kind, and the grasshopper according to its kind. ²³But all other winged insects that have four feet are detestable to you.

24 By these you shall become unclean; whoever touches the carcass of any of them shall be unclean until the evening, ²⁵and whoever carries any part of the carcass of any of them shall wash his clothes and be unclean until the evening. ²⁶Every animal that has divided hoofs but is not cleft-footed or does not chew the cud is unclean for you; everyone who touches one of them shall be unclean. ²⁷All that walk on their paws, among the animals that walk on all fours, are unclean for you; whoever touches the carcass of any of them shall be unclean until the evening, ²⁸and the one who carries the carcass shall wash his clothes and be unclean until the evening; they are unclean for you.

29 These are unclean for you among the creatures that swarm upon

---

ᵃ Or *pelican*  ᵇ Identification of several of the birds in verses 13-19 is uncertain

the earth: the weasel, the mouse, the great lizard according to its kind, ³⁰the gecko, the land crocodile, the lizard, the sand lizard, and the chameleon. ³¹These are unclean for you among all that swarm; whoever touches one of them when they are dead shall be unclean until the evening. ³²And anything upon which any of them falls when they are dead shall be unclean, whether an article of wood or cloth or skin or sacking, any article that is used for any purpose; it shall be dipped into water, and it shall be unclean until the evening, and then it shall be clean. ³³And if any of them falls into any earthen vessel, all that is in it shall be unclean, and you shall break the vessel. ³⁴Any food that could be eaten shall be unclean if water from any such vessel comes upon it; and any liquid that could be drunk shall be unclean if it was in any such vessel. ³⁵Everything on which any part of the carcass falls shall be unclean; whether an oven or stove, it shall be broken in pieces; they are unclean, and shall remain unclean for you. ³⁶But a spring or a cistern holding water shall be clean, while whatever touches the carcass in it shall be unclean. ³⁷If any part of their carcass falls upon any seed set aside for sowing, it is clean; ³⁸but if water is put on the seed and any part of their carcass falls on it, it is unclean for you.

39  If an animal of which you may eat dies, anyone who touches its carcass shall be unclean until the evening. ⁴⁰Those who eat of its carcass shall wash their clothes and be unclean until the evening; and those who carry the carcass shall wash their clothes and be unclean until the evening.

41  All creatures that swarm upon the earth are detestable; they shall not be eaten. ⁴²Whatever moves on its belly, and whatever moves on all fours, or whatever has many feet, all the creatures that swarm upon the earth, you shall not eat; for they are detestable. ⁴³You shall not make yourselves detestable with any creature that swarms; you shall not defile yourselves with them, and so become unclean. ⁴⁴For I am the Lᴏʀᴅ your God; sanctify yourselves therefore, and be holy, for I am holy. You shall not defile yourselves with any swarming creature that moves on the earth. ⁴⁵For I am the Lᴏʀᴅ who brought you up from the land of Egypt, to be your God; you shall be holy, for I am holy.

46  This is the law pertaining to land animal and bird and every living creature that moves through the waters and every creature that swarms upon the earth, ⁴⁷to make a distinction between the unclean and the clean, and between the living creature that may be eaten and the living creature that may not be eaten.

12.1 Tʜᴇ Lᴏʀᴅ spoke to Moses, saying: ²Speak to the people of Israel, saying:

If a woman conceives and bears a male child, she shall be ceremonially unclean seven days; as at the time of her menstruation, she shall be unclean. ³On the eighth day the flesh of his foreskin shall be circumcised. ⁴Her time of blood purification shall be thirty-three days; she shall not touch any holy thing, or come into the sanctuary, until the days of her purification are completed. ⁵If she bears a female child, she shall be unclean two weeks, as in her menstruation; her time of blood purification shall be sixty-six days.

6  When the days of her purification are completed, whether for a son or for a daughter, she shall bring to the priest at the entrance of the tent of meeting a lamb in its first year for a burnt offering, and a pigeon or a turtledove for a sin offering. ⁷He shall offer it before the Lᴏʀᴅ, and make atonement on her behalf; then she shall be clean from her flow of blood. This is the law for her who bears a child, male or female. ⁸If she cannot afford a sheep, she shall take two turtledoves or two pigeons,

one for a burnt offering and the other for a sin offering; and the priest shall make atonement on her behalf, and she shall be clean.

## MARK 5.21–43

WHEN Jesus had crossed again in the boat[a] to the other side, a great crowd gathered around him; and he was by the sea. 22Then one of the leaders of the synagogue named Jairus came and, when he saw him, fell at his feet 23and begged him repeatedly, "My little daughter is at the point of death. Come and lay your hands on her, so that she may be made well, and live." 24So he went with him.

And a large crowd followed him and pressed in on him. 25Now there was a woman who had been suffering from hemorrhages for twelve years. 26She had endured much under many physicians, and had spent all that she had; and she was no better, but rather grew worse. 27She had heard about Jesus, and came up behind him in the crowd and touched his cloak, 28for she said, "If I but touch his clothes, I will be made well." 29Immediately her hemorrhage stopped; and she felt in her body that she was healed of her disease. 30Immediately aware that power had gone forth from him, Jesus turned about in the crowd and said, "Who touched my clothes?" 31And his disciples said to him, "You see the crowd pressing in on you; how can you say, 'Who touched me?'" 32He looked all around to see who had done it. 33But the woman, knowing what had happened to her, came in fear and trembling, fell down before him, and told him the whole truth. 34He said to her, "Daughter, your faith has made you well; go in peace, and be healed of your disease."

35 While he was still speaking, some people came from the leader's house to say, "Your daughter is dead. Why trouble the teacher any further?" 36But overhearing[b] what they said, Jesus said to the leader of the synagogue, "Do not fear, only believe." 37He allowed no one to follow him except Peter, James, and John, the brother of James. 38When they came to the house of the leader of the synagogue, he saw a commotion, people weeping and wailing loudly. 39When he had entered, he said to them, "Why do you make a commotion and weep? The child is not dead but sleeping." 40And they laughed at him. Then he put them all outside, and took the child's father and mother and those who were with him, and went in where the child was. 41He took her by the hand and said to her, "Talitha cum," which means, "Little girl, get up!" 42And immediately the girl got up and began to walk about (she was twelve years of age). At this they were overcome with amazement. 43He strictly ordered them that no one should know this, and told them to give her something to eat.

## PSALM 38.1–22

*A Psalm of David, for the memorial offering.*

O LORD, do not rebuke me in
      your anger,
   or discipline me in your
      wrath.
2  For your arrows have sunk into
      me,
   and your hand has come down
      on me.

3  There is no soundness in my
      flesh
   because of your indignation;
   there is no health in my bones
      because of my sin.
4  For my iniquities have gone
      over my head;
   they weigh like a burden too
      heavy for me.

aOther ancient authorities lack *in the boat*   bOr *ignoring*; other ancient authorities read *hearing*

5  My wounds grow foul and fester
       because of my foolishness;
6  I am utterly bowed down and
       prostrate;
   all day long I go around
       mourning.
7  For my loins are filled with
       burning,
   and there is no soundness in
       my flesh.
8  I am utterly spent and crushed;
   I groan because of the tumult
       of my heart.

9  O Lord, all my longing is known
       to you;
   my sighing is not hidden from
       you.
10 My heart throbs, my strength
       fails me;
   as for the light of my
       eyes—it also has gone
       from me.
11 My friends and companions
       stand aloof from my
       affliction,
   and my neighbors stand far
       off.

12 Those who seek my life lay
       their snares;
   those who seek to hurt me
       speak of ruin,
   and meditate treachery all day
       long.

13 But I am like the deaf, I do not
       hear;
   like the mute, who cannot
       speak.
14 Truly, I am like one who does
       not hear,

and in whose mouth is no
       retort.
15 But it is for you, O Lord, that I
       wait;
   it is you, O Lord my God,
       who will answer.
16 For I pray, "Only do not let
       them rejoice over me,
   those who boast against me
       when my foot slips."

17 For I am ready to fall,
   and my pain is ever with me.
18 I confess my iniquity;
   I am sorry for my sin.
19 Those who are my foes without
       cause[a] are mighty,
   and many are those who hate
       me wrongfully.
20 Those who render me evil for
       good
   are my adversaries because I
       follow after good.

21 Do not forsake me, O Lord;
   O my God, do not be far
       from me;
22 make haste to help me,
   O Lord, my salvation.

## PROVERBS 10.8–9

THE wise of heart will heed
       commandments,
   but a babbling fool will come
       to ruin.
9  Whoever walks in integrity
       walks securely,
   but whoever follows perverse
       ways will be found out.

# FEBRUARY 22

## LEVITICUS 13.1–59

THE LORD spoke to Moses and Aaron, saying: 2 When a person has on the skin of his body a swelling or an eruption or a spot, and it turns into a leprous[a] disease on the skin of his body, he shall be brought to Aaron the priest or to one of his sons the priests. [3]The priest shall examine the disease on the skin of his body, and if the hair in the diseased area has turned white and the disease appears to be deeper than the skin of his body, it is a leprous[a] disease; after the priest has examined him he shall pronounce him ceremonially unclean. [4]But if the spot is white in the skin of his body, and appears no deeper than the skin, and the hair in it has not turned white, the priest shall confine the diseased person for seven days. [5]The priest shall examine him on the seventh day, and if he sees that the disease is checked and the disease has not spread in the skin, then the priest shall confine him seven days more. [6]The priest shall examine him again on the seventh day, and if the disease has abated and the disease has not spread in the skin, the priest shall pronounce him clean; it is only an eruption; and he shall wash his clothes, and be clean. [7]But if the eruption spreads in the skin after he has shown himself to the priest for his cleansing, he shall appear again before the priest. [8]The priest shall make an examination, and if the eruption has spread in the skin, the priest shall pronounce him unclean; it is a leprous[a] disease.

9 When a person contracts a leprous[a] disease, he shall be brought to the priest. [10]The priest shall make an examination, and if there is a white swelling in the skin that has turned the hair white, and there is quick raw flesh in the swelling, [11]it is a chronic leprous[a] disease in the skin of his body. The priest shall pronounce him unclean; he shall not confine him, for he is unclean. [12]But if the disease breaks out in the skin, so that it covers all the skin of the diseased person from head to foot, so far as the priest can see, [13]then the priest shall make an examination, and if the disease has covered all his body, he shall pronounce him clean of the disease; since it has all turned white, he is clean. [14]But if raw flesh ever appears on him, he shall be unclean; [15]the priest shall examine the raw flesh and pronounce him unclean. Raw flesh is unclean, for it is a leprous[a] disease. [16]But if the raw flesh again turns white, he shall come to the priest; [17]the priest shall examine him, and if the disease has turned white, the priest shall pronounce the diseased person clean. He is clean.

18 When there is on the skin of one's body a boil that has healed, [19]and in the place of the boil there appears a white swelling or a reddish-white spot, it shall be shown to the priest. [20]The priest shall make an examination, and if it appears deeper than the skin and its hair has turned white, the priest shall pronounce him unclean; this is a leprous[a] disease, broken out in the boil. [21]But if the priest examines it and the hair on it is not white, nor is it deeper than the skin but has abated, the priest shall confine him seven days. [22]If it spreads in the skin, the priest shall pronounce him unclean; it is diseased. [23]But if the spot remains in one place

---

[a]A term for several skin diseases; precise meaning uncertain

and does not spread, it is the scar of the boil; the priest shall pronounce him clean.

24  Or, when the body has a burn on the skin and the raw flesh of the burn becomes a spot, reddish-white or white, [25]the priest shall examine it. If the hair in the spot has turned white and it appears deeper than the skin, it is a leprous[a] disease; it has broken out in the burn, and the priest shall pronounce him unclean. This is a leprous[a] disease. [26]But if the priest examines it and the hair in the spot is not white, and it is no deeper than the skin but has abated, the priest shall confine him seven days. [27]The priest shall examine him the seventh day; if it is spreading in the skin, the priest shall pronounce him unclean. This is a leprous[a] disease. [28]But if the spot remains in one place and does not spread in the skin but has abated, it is a swelling from the burn, and the priest shall pronounce him clean; for it is the scar of the burn.

29  When a man or woman has a disease on the head or in the beard, [30]the priest shall examine the disease. If it appears deeper than the skin and the hair in it is yellow and thin, the priest shall pronounce him unclean; it is an itch, a leprous[a] disease of the head or the beard. [31]If the priest examines the itching disease, and it appears no deeper than the skin and there is no black hair in it, the priest shall confine the person with the itching disease for seven days. [32]On the seventh day the priest shall examine the itch; if the itch has not spread, and there is no yellow hair in it, and the itch appears to be no deeper than the skin, [33]he shall shave, but the itch he shall not shave. The priest shall confine the person with the itch for seven days more. [34]On the seventh day the priest shall examine the itch; if the itch has not spread in the skin and it appears to be no deeper than

the skin, the priest shall pronounce him clean. He shall wash his clothes and be clean. [35]But if the itch spreads in the skin after he was pronounced clean, [36]the priest shall examine him. If the itch has spread in the skin, the priest need not seek for the yellow hair; he is unclean. [37]But if in his eyes the itch is checked, and black hair has grown in it, the itch is healed, he is clean; and the priest shall pronounce him clean.

38  When a man or a woman has spots on the skin of the body, white spots, [39]the priest shall make an examination, and if the spots on the skin of the body are of a dull white, it is a rash that has broken out on the skin; he is clean.

40  If anyone loses the hair from his head, he is bald but he is clean. [41]If he loses the hair from his forehead and temples, he has baldness of the forehead but he is clean. [42]But if there is on the bald head or the bald forehead a reddish-white diseased spot, it is a leprous[a] disease breaking out on his bald head or his bald forehead. [43]The priest shall examine him; if the diseased swelling is reddish-white on his bald head or on his bald forehead, which resembles a leprous[a] disease in the skin of the body, [44]he is leprous, [a] he is unclean. The priest shall pronounce him unclean; the disease is on his head.

45  The person who has the leprous[a] disease shall wear torn clothes and let the hair of his head be disheveled; and he shall cover his upper lip and cry out, "Unclean, unclean." [46]He shall remain unclean as long as he has the disease; he is unclean. He shall live alone; his dwelling shall be outside the camp.

47  Concerning clothing: when a leprous[a] disease appears in it, in woolen or linen cloth, [48]in warp or woof of linen or wool, or in a skin or in anything made of skin, [49]if the disease

<hr>

aA term for several skin diseases; precise meaning uncertain

shows greenish or reddish in the garment, whether in warp or woof or in skin or in anything made of skin, it is a leprous[a] disease and shall be shown to the priest. [50]The priest shall examine the disease, and put the diseased article aside for seven days. [51]He shall examine the disease on the seventh day. If the disease has spread in the cloth, in warp or woof, or in the skin, whatever be the use of the skin, this is a spreading leprous[a] disease; it is unclean. [52]He shall burn the clothing, whether diseased in warp or woof, woolen or linen, or anything of skin, for it is a spreading leprous[a] disease; it shall be burned in fire.

53  If the priest makes an examination, and the disease has not spread in the clothing, in warp or woof or in anything of skin, [54]the priest shall command them to wash the article in which the disease appears, and he shall put it aside seven days more. [55]The priest shall examine the diseased article after it has been washed. If the diseased spot has not changed color, though the disease has not spread, it is unclean; you shall burn it in fire, whether the leprous[a] spot is on the inside or on the outside.

56  If the priest makes an examination, and the disease has abated after it is washed, he shall tear the spot out of the cloth, in warp or woof, or out of skin. [57]If it appears again in the garment, in warp or woof, or in anything of skin, it is spreading; you shall burn with fire that in which the disease appears. [58]But the cloth, warp or woof, or anything of skin from which the disease disappears when you have washed it, shall then be washed a second time, and it shall be clean.

59  This is the ritual for a leprous[a] disease in a cloth of wool or linen, either in warp or woof, or in anything of

skin, to decide whether it is clean or unclean.

## MARK 6. 1–29

**H**E [Jesus] left that place and came to his hometown, and his disciples followed him. [2]On the sabbath he began to teach in the synagogue, and many who heard him were astounded. They said, "Where did this man get all this? What is this wisdom that has been given to him? What deeds of power are being done by his hands! [3]Is not this the carpenter, the son of Mary[b] and brother of James and Joses and Judas and Simon, and are not his sisters here with us?" And they took offense[c] at him. [4]Then Jesus said to them, "Prophets are not without honor, except in their hometown, and among their own kin, and in their own house." [5]And he could do no deed of power there, except that he laid his hands on a few sick people and cured them. [6]And he was amazed at their unbelief.

Then he went about among the villages teaching. [7]He called the twelve and began to send them out two by two, and gave them authority over the unclean spirits. [8]He ordered them to take nothing for their journey except a staff; no bread, no bag, no money in their belts; [9]but to wear sandals and not to put on two tunics. [10]He said to them, "Wherever you enter a house, stay there until you leave the place. [11]If any place will not welcome you and they refuse to hear you, as you leave, shake off the dust that is on your feet as a testimony against them." [12]So they went out and proclaimed that all should repent. [13]They cast out many demons, and anointed with oil many who were sick and cured them.

---

[a]A term for several skin diseases; precise meaning uncertain   [b]Other ancient authorities read *son of the carpenter and of Mary*   [c]Or *stumbled*

14 King Herod heard of it, for Jesus'[a] name had become known. Some were[b] saying, "John the baptizer has been raised from the dead; and for this reason these powers are at work in him." [15]But others said, "It is Elijah." And others said, "It is a prophet, like one of the prophets of old." [16]But when Herod heard of it, he said, "John, whom I beheaded, has been raised."

17 For Herod himself had sent men who arrested John, bound him, and put him in prison on account of Herodias, his brother Philip's wife, because Herod[c] had married her. [18]For John had been telling Herod, "It is not lawful for you to have your brother's wife." [19]And Herodias had a grudge against him, and wanted to kill him. But she could not, [20]for Herod feared John, knowing that he was a righteous and holy man, and he protected him. When he heard him, he was greatly perplexed;[d] and yet he liked to listen to him. [21]But an opportunity came when Herod on his birthday gave a banquet for his courtiers and officers and for the leaders of Galilee. [22]When his daughter Herodias[e] came in and danced, she pleased Herod and his guests; and the king said to the girl, "Ask me for whatever you wish, and I will give it." [23]And he solemnly swore to her, "Whatever you ask me, I will give you, even half of my kingdom." [24]She went out and said to her mother, "What should I ask for?" She replied, "The head of John the baptizer." [25]Immediately she rushed back to the king and requested, "I want you to give me at once the head of John the Baptist on a platter." [26]The king was deeply grieved; yet out of regard for his oaths and for the guests, he did not want to refuse her. [27]Immediately the king sent a soldier of the guard with orders to bring John's[a] head. He went and beheaded him in the prison, [28]brought his head on a platter, and gave it to the girl. Then the girl gave it to her mother. [29]When his disciples heard about it, they came and took his body, and laid it in a tomb.

## PSALM 39.1–13

*To the leader: to Jeduthun. A Psalm of David.*

I SAID, "I will guard my ways
    that I may not sin with my
        tongue;
  I will keep a muzzle on my
      mouth
    as long as the wicked are in
      my presence."
2  I was silent and still;
    I held my peace to no avail;
  my distress grew worse,
3     my heart became hot within
      me.
  While I mused, the fire burned;
    then I spoke with my tongue:

4  "LORD, let me know my end,
    and what is the measure of
      my days;
    let me know how fleeting my
      life is.
5  You have made my days a few
      handbreadths,
    and my lifetime is as nothing
      in your sight.
  Surely everyone stands as a
      mere breath.    *Selah*
6     Surely everyone goes about
      like a shadow.
  Surely for nothing they are in
      turmoil;
    they heap up, and do not
      know who will gather.

7  "And now, O Lord, what do I
      wait for?
  My hope is in you.
8  Deliver me from all my
      transgressions.

a Gk *his*   b Other ancient authorities read *He was many things*   c Gk *he*   d Other ancient authorities read *he did*   e Other ancient authorities read *the daughter of Herodias herself*

Do not make me the scorn of
    the fool.
9  I am silent; I do not open my
    mouth,
    for it is you who have done
      it.
10  Remove your stroke from me;
    I am worn down by the
      blows[a] of your hand.

11  "You chastise mortals
    in punishment for sin,
    consuming like a moth what is
      dear to them;
    surely everyone is a mere
      breath.         *Selah*

12  "Hear my prayer, O Lord,
and give ear to my cry;
    do not hold your peace at my
      tears.
    For I am your passing guest,
      an alien, like all my forebears.
13  Turn your gaze away from me,
    that I may smile again,
    before I depart and am no
      more."

## PROVERBS 10.10

WHOEVER winks the eye
    causes trouble,
but the one who rebukes
    boldly makes peace. [b]

# FEBRUARY 23

## LEVITICUS 14.1–57

THE Lord spoke to Moses, saying: [2]This shall be the ritual for the leprous[c] person at the time of his cleansing:

He shall be brought to the priest; [3]the priest shall go out of the camp, and the priest shall make an examination. If the disease is healed in the leprous[c] person, [4]the priest shall command that two living clean birds and cedarwood and crimson yarn and hyssop be brought for the one who is to be cleansed. [5]The priest shall command that one of the birds be slaughtered over fresh water in an earthen vessel. [6]He shall take the living bird with the cedarwood and the crimson yarn and the hyssop, and dip them and the living bird in the blood of the bird that was slaughtered over the fresh water. [7]He shall sprinkle it seven times upon the one who is to be cleansed of the leprous[c] disease; then he shall pronounce him clean, and he shall let the living bird go into the open field. [8]The one who is to be cleansed shall wash his clothes, and shave off all his hair, and bathe himself in water, and he shall be clean. After that he shall come into the camp, but shall live outside his tent seven days. [9]On the seventh day he shall shave all his hair: of head, beard, eyebrows; he shall shave all his hair. Then he shall wash his clothes, and bathe his body in water, and he shall be clean.

10  On the eighth day he shall take two male lambs without blemish, and one ewe lamb in its first year without blemish, and a grain offering of three-tenths of an ephah of choice flour mixed with oil, and one log[d] of oil. [11]The priest who cleanses shall set the person to be cleansed, along with these things,

a Heb *hostility*   b Gk: Heb *but a babbling fool will come to ruin*   c A term for several skin diseases; precise meaning uncertain   d A liquid measure

before the LORD, at the entrance of the tent of meeting. ¹²The priest shall take one of the lambs, and offer it as a guilt offering, along with the log[a] of oil, and raise them as an elevation offering before the LORD. ¹³He shall slaughter the lamb in the place where the sin offering and the burnt offering are slaughtered in the holy place; for the guilt offering, like the sin offering, belongs to the priest: it is most holy. ¹⁴The priest shall take some of the blood of the guilt offering and put it on the lobe of the right ear of the one to be cleansed, and on the thumb of the right hand, and on the big toe of the right foot. ¹⁵The priest shall take some of the log[a] of oil and pour it into the palm of his own left hand, ¹⁶and dip his right finger in the oil that is in his left hand and sprinkle some oil with his finger seven times before the LORD. ¹⁷Some of the oil that remains in his hand the priest shall put on the lobe of the right ear of the one to be cleansed, and on the thumb of the right hand, and on the big toe of the right foot, on top of the blood of the guilt offering. ¹⁸The rest of the oil that is in the priest's hand he shall put on the head of the one to be cleansed. Then the priest shall make atonement on his behalf before the LORD: ¹⁹the priest shall offer the sin offering, to make atonement for the one to be cleansed from his uncleanness. Afterward he shall slaughter the burnt offering; ²⁰and the priest shall offer the burnt offering and the grain offering on the altar. Thus the priest shall make atonement on his behalf and he shall be clean.

21  But if he is poor and cannot afford so much, he shall take one male lamb for a guilt offering to be elevated, to make atonement on his behalf, and one-tenth of an ephah of choice flour mixed with oil for a grain offering and a log[a] of oil; ²²also two turtledoves or two pigeons, such as he can afford, one for a sin offering and the other for a burnt offering. ²³On the eighth day he shall bring them for his cleansing to the priest, to the entrance of the tent of meeting, before the LORD; ²⁴and the priest shall take the lamb of the guilt offering and the log[a] of oil, and the priest shall raise them as an elevation offering before the LORD. ²⁵The priest shall slaughter the lamb of the guilt offering and shall take some of the blood of the guilt offering, and put it on the lobe of the right ear of the one to be cleansed, and on the thumb of the right hand, and on the big toe of the right foot. ²⁶The priest shall pour some of the oil into the palm of his own left hand, ²⁷and shall sprinkle with his right finger some of the oil that is in his left hand seven times before the LORD. ²⁸The priest shall put some of the oil that is in his hand on the lobe of the right ear of the one to be cleansed, and on the thumb of the right hand, and the big toe of the right foot, where the blood of the guilt offering was placed. ²⁹The rest of the oil that is in the priest's hand he shall put on the head of the one to be cleansed, to make atonement on his behalf before the LORD. ³⁰And he shall offer, of the turtledoves or pigeons such as he can afford, ³¹one[b] for a sin offering and the other for a burnt offering, along with a grain offering; and the priest shall make atonement before the LORD on behalf of the one being cleansed. ³²This is the ritual for the one who has a leprous[c] disease, who cannot afford the offerings for his cleansing.

33  The LORD spoke to Moses and Aaron, saying:

34  When you come into the land of Canaan, which I give you for a possession, and I put a leprous[c] disease in a house in the land of your possession, ³⁵the owner of the house shall come and tell the priest, saying, "There

[a] A liquid measure  [b] Gk Syr: Heb *afford, 31such as he can afford, one*  [c] A term for several skin diseases; precise meaning uncertain

seems to me to be some sort of disease in my house." [36]The priest shall command that they empty the house before the priest goes to examine the disease, or all that is in the house will become unclean; and afterward the priest shall go in to inspect the house. [37]He shall examine the disease; if the disease is in the walls of the house with greenish or reddish spots, and if it appears to be deeper than the surface, [38]the priest shall go outside to the door of the house and shut up the house seven days. [39]The priest shall come again on the seventh day and make an inspection; if the disease has spread in the walls of the house, [40]the priest shall command that the stones in which the disease appears be taken out and thrown into an unclean place outside the city. [41]He shall have the inside of the house scraped thoroughly, and the plaster that is scraped off shall be dumped in an unclean place outside the city. [42]They shall take other stones and put them in the place of those stones, and take other plaster and plaster the house.

43  If the disease breaks out again in the house, after he has taken out the stones and scraped the house and plastered it, [44]the priest shall go and make inspection; if the disease has spread in the house, it is a spreading leprous[a] disease in the house; it is unclean. [45]He shall have the house torn down, its stones and timber and all the plaster of the house, and taken outside the city to an unclean place. [46]All who enter the house while it is shut up shall be unclean until the evening; [47]and all who sleep in the house shall wash their clothes; and all who eat in the house shall wash their clothes.

48  If the priest comes and makes an inspection, and the disease has not spread in the house after the house was plastered, the priest shall pronounce the house clean; the disease is healed.

[49]For the cleansing of the house he shall take two birds, with cedarwood and crimson yarn and hyssop, [50]and shall slaughter one of the birds over fresh water in an earthen vessel, [51]and shall take the cedarwood and the hyssop and the crimson yarn, along with the living bird, and dip them in the blood of the slaughtered bird and the fresh water, and sprinkle the house seven times. [52]Thus he shall cleanse the house with the blood of the bird, and with the fresh water, and with the living bird, and with the cedarwood and hyssop and crimson yarn; [53]and he shall let the living bird go out of the city into the open field; so he shall make atonement for the house, and it shall be clean.

54  This is the ritual for any leprous[a] disease: for an itch, [55]for leprous[a] diseases in clothing and houses, [56]and for a swelling or an eruption or a spot, [57]to determine when it is unclean and when it is clean. This is the ritual for leprous[a] diseases.

## MARK 6.30–56

THE apostles gathered around Jesus, and told him all that they had done and taught. [31]He said to them, "Come away to a deserted place all by yourselves and rest a while." For many were coming and going, and they had no leisure even to eat. [32]And they went away in the boat to a deserted place by themselves. [33]Now many saw them going and recognized them, and they hurried there on foot from all the towns and arrived ahead of them. [34]As he went ashore, he saw a great crowd; and he had compassion for them, because they were like sheep without a shepherd; and he began to teach them many things. [35]When it grew late, his disciples came to him and said, "This is a deserted place, and the hour is now very late; [36]send them away so that they may go into the sur-

---

[a]A term for several skin diseases; precise meaning uncertain

rounding country and villages and buy something for themselves to eat." [37]But he answered them, "You give them something to eat." They said to him, "Are we to go and buy two hundred denarii[a] worth of bread, and give it to them to eat?" [38]And he said to them, "How many loaves have you? Go and see." When they had found out, they said, "Five, and two fish." [39]Then he ordered them to get all the people to sit down in groups on the green grass. [40]So they sat down in groups of hundreds and of fifties. [41]Taking the five loaves and the two fish, he looked up to heaven, and blessed and broke the loaves, and gave them to his disciples to set before the people; and he divided the two fish among them all. [42]And all ate and were filled; [43]and they took up twelve baskets full of broken pieces and of the fish. [44]Those who had eaten the loaves numbered five thousand men.

45 Immediately he made his disciples get into the boat and go on ahead to the other side, to Bethsaida, while he dismissed the crowd. [46]After saying farewell to them, he went up on the mountain to pray.

47 When evening came, the boat was out on the sea, and he was alone on the land. [48]When he saw that they were straining at the oars against an adverse wind, he came towards them early in the morning, walking on the sea. He intended to pass them by. [49]But when they saw him walking on the sea, they thought it was a ghost and cried out; [50]for they all saw him and were terrified. But immediately he spoke to them and said, "Take heart, it is I; do not be afraid." [51]Then he got into the boat with them and the wind ceased. And they were utterly astounded, [52]for they did not understand about the loaves, but their hearts were hardened.

53 When they had crossed over, they came to land at Gennesaret and moored the boat. [54]When they got out of the boat, people at once recognized him, [55]and rushed about that whole region and began to bring the sick on mats to wherever they heard he was. [56]And wherever he went, into villages or cities or farms, they laid the sick in the marketplaces, and begged him that they might touch even the fringe of his cloak; and all who touched it were healed.

## PSALM 40.1–10

*To the leader. Of David. A Psalm.*

I WAITED patiently for the LORD;
    he inclined to me and heard
        my cry.
2  He drew me up from the
        desolate pit, [b]
    out of the miry bog,
  and set my feet upon a rock,
    making my steps secure.
3  He put a new song in my
        mouth,
    a song of praise to our God.
Many will see and fear,
    and put their trust in the
        LORD.

4  Happy are those who make
      the LORD their trust,
  who do not turn to the proud,
    to those who go astray after
        false gods.
5  You have multiplied, O LORD my
        God,
    your wondrous deeds and
        your thoughts toward us;
    none can compare with you.
Were I to proclaim and tell of
        them,
    they would be more than can
        be counted.
6  Sacrifice and offering you do not
        desire,

---

[a]The denarius was the usual day's wage for a laborer   [b]Cn: Heb *pit of tumult*

but you have given me an
    open ear. ᵃ
Burnt offering and sin offering
    you have not required.
7 Then I said, "Here I am;
    in the scroll of the book it is
      written of me. ᵇ
8 I delight to do your will, O my
      God;
    your law is within my heart."

9 I have told the glad news of
      deliverance
    in the great congregation;
see, I have not restrained my
      lips,
    as you know, O Lord.

10 I have not hidden your saving
      help within my heart,
I have spoken of your
    faithfulness and your
    salvation;
I have not concealed your
    steadfast love and your
    faithfulness
from the great congregation.

## PROVERBS 10.11–12

THE mouth of the righteous is a
    fountain of life,
    but the mouth of the wicked
      conceals violence.
12 Hatred stirs up strife,
    but love covers all offenses.

# FEBRUARY 24

## LEVITICUS 15.1—16.28

THE Lord spoke to Moses and Aaron, saying: ²Speak to the people of Israel and say to them: When any man has a discharge from his member, ᶜ his discharge makes him ceremonially unclean. ³The uncleanness of his discharge is this: whether his memberᶜ flows with his discharge, or his memberᶜ is stopped from discharging, it is uncleanness for him. ⁴Every bed on which the one with the discharge lies shall be unclean; and everything on which he sits shall be unclean. ⁵Anyone who touches his bed shall wash his clothes, and bathe in water, and be unclean until the evening. ⁶All who sit on anything on which the one with the discharge has sat shall wash their clothes, and bathe in water, and be unclean until the evening. ⁷All who touch the body of the one with the discharge shall wash their clothes, and bathe in water, and be unclean until the evening. ⁸If the one with the discharge spits on persons who are clean, then they shall wash their clothes, and bathe in water, and be unclean until the evening. ⁹Any saddle on which the one with the discharge rides shall be unclean. ¹⁰All who touch anything that was under him shall be unclean until the evening, and all who carry such a thing shall wash their clothes, and bathe in water, and be unclean until the evening. ¹¹All those whom the one with the discharge touches without his having rinsed his hands in water shall wash their clothes, and bathe in water, and be unclean until the evening. ¹²Any earthen vessel that the one with the discharge touches shall be broken; and every vessel of wood shall be rinsed in water.

13 When the one with a discharge is cleansed of his discharge, he shall count seven days for his cleansing; he shall wash his clothes and bathe his body in fresh water, and he shall be clean. [14]On the eighth day he shall take two turtledoves or two pigeons and come before the Lord to the entrance of the tent of meeting and give them to the priest. [15]The priest shall offer them, one for a sin offering and the other for a burnt offering; and the priest shall make atonement on his behalf before the Lord for his discharge.

16 If a man has an emission of semen, he shall bathe his whole body in water, and be unclean until the evening. [17]Everything made of cloth or of skin on which the semen falls shall be washed with water, and be unclean until the evening. [18]If a man lies with a woman and has an emission of semen, both of them shall bathe in water, and be unclean until the evening.

19 When a woman has a discharge of blood that is her regular discharge from her body, she shall be in her impurity for seven days, and whoever touches her shall be unclean until the evening. [20]Everything upon which she lies during her impurity shall be unclean; everything also upon which she sits shall be unclean. [21]Whoever touches her bed shall wash his clothes, and bathe in water, and be unclean until the evening. [22]Whoever touches anything upon which she sits shall wash his clothes, and bathe in water, and be unclean until the evening; [23]whether it is the bed or anything upon which she sits, when he touches it he shall be unclean until the evening. [24]If any man lies with her, and her impurity falls on him, he shall be unclean seven days; and every bed on which he lies shall be unclean.

25 If a woman has a discharge of blood for many days, not at the time of her impurity, or if she has a discharge beyond the time of her impurity, all the days of the discharge she shall continue in uncleanness; as in the days of her impurity, she shall be unclean. [26]Every bed on which she lies during all the days of her discharge shall be treated as the bed of her impurity; and everything on which she sits shall be unclean, as in the uncleanness of her impurity. [27]Whoever touches these things shall be unclean, and shall wash his clothes, and bathe in water, and be unclean until the evening. [28]If she is cleansed of her discharge, she shall count seven days, and after that she shall be clean. [29]On the eighth day she shall take two turtledoves or two pigeons and bring them to the priest to the entrance of the tent of meeting. [30]The priest shall offer one for a sin offering and the other for a burnt offering; and the priest shall make atonement on her behalf before the Lord for her unclean discharge.

31 Thus you shall keep the people of Israel separate from their uncleanness, so that they do not die in their uncleanness by defiling my tabernacle that is in their midst.

32 This is the ritual for those who have a discharge: for him who has an emission of semen, becoming unclean thereby, [33]for her who is in the infirmity of her period, for anyone, male or female, who has a discharge, and for the man who lies with a woman who is unclean.

16.1 The Lord spoke to Moses after the death of the two sons of Aaron, when they drew near before the Lord and died. [2]The Lord said to Moses:

Tell your brother Aaron not to come just at any time into the sanctuary inside the curtain before the mercy seat[a] that is upon the ark, or he will

a Or *the cover*

die; for I appear in the cloud upon the mercy seat. [a] [3]Thus shall Aaron come into the holy place: with a young bull for a sin offering and a ram for a burnt offering. [4]He shall put on the holy linen tunic, and shall have the linen undergarments next to his body, fasten the linen sash, and wear the linen turban; these are the holy vestments. He shall bathe his body in water, and then put them on. [5]He shall take from the congregation of the people of Israel two male goats for a sin offering, and one ram for a burnt offering.

6 Aaron shall offer the bull as a sin offering for himself, and shall make atonement for himself and for his house. [7]He shall take the two goats and set them before the LORD at the entrance of the tent of meeting; [8]and Aaron shall cast lots on the two goats, one lot for the LORD and the other lot for Azazel. [b] [9]Aaron shall present the goat on which the lot fell for the LORD, and offer it as a sin offering; [10]but the goat on which the lot fell for Azazel[b] shall be presented alive before the LORD to make atonement over it, that it may be sent away into the wilderness to Azazel. [b]

11 Aaron shall present the bull as a sin offering for himself, and shall make atonement for himself and for his house; he shall slaughter the bull as a sin offering for himself. [12]He shall take a censer full of coals of fire from the altar before the LORD, and two handfuls of crushed sweet incense, and he shall bring it inside the curtain [13]and put the incense on the fire before the LORD, that the cloud of the incense may cover the mercy seat[a] that is upon the covenant, [c] or he will die. [14]He shall take some of the blood of the bull, and sprinkle it with his finger on the front of the mercy seat, [a] and before the mercy seat[a] he shall sprinkle the blood with his finger seven times.

15 He shall slaughter the goat of the sin offering that is for the people and bring its blood inside the curtain, and do with its blood as he did with the blood of the bull, sprinkling it upon the mercy seat[a] and before the mercy seat. [a] [16]Thus he shall make atonement for the sanctuary, because of the uncleannesses of the people of Israel, and because of their transgressions, all their sins; and so he shall do for the tent of meeting, which remains with them in the midst of their uncleannesses. [17]No one shall be in the tent of meeting from the time he enters to make atonement in the sanctuary until he comes out and has made atonement for himself and for his house and for all the assembly of Israel. [18]Then he shall go out to the altar that is before the LORD and make atonement on its behalf, and shall take some of the blood of the bull and of the blood of the goat, and put it on each of the horns of the altar. [19]He shall sprinkle some of the blood on it with his finger seven times, and cleanse it and hallow it from the uncleannesses of the people of Israel.

20 When he has finished atoning for the holy place and the tent of meeting and the altar, he shall present the live goat. [21]Then Aaron shall lay both his hands on the head of the live goat, and confess over it all the iniquities of the people of Israel, and all their transgressions, all their sins, putting them on the head of the goat, and sending it away into the wilderness by means of someone designated for the task. [d] [22]The goat shall bear on itself all their iniquities to a barren region; and the goat shall be set free in the wilderness.

23 Then Aaron shall enter the tent of meeting, and shall take off the linen vestments that he put on when he went into the holy place, and shall leave them there. [24]He shall bathe his body in water in a holy place, and put on his vest-

aOr *the cover*  bTraditionally rendered *a scapegoat*  cOr *treaty,* or *testament;* Heb *eduth*  dMeaning of Heb uncertain

ments; then he shall come out and offer his burnt offering and the burnt offering of the people, making atonement for himself and for the people. 25 The fat of the sin offering he shall turn into smoke on the altar. 26 The one who sets the goat free for Azazela shall wash his clothes and bathe his body in water, and afterward may come into the camp. 27 The bull of the sin offering and the goat of the sin offering, whose blood was brought in to make atonement in the holy place, shall be taken outside the camp; their skin and their flesh and their dung shall be consumed in fire. 28 The one who burns them shall wash his clothes and bathe his body in water, and afterward may come into the camp.

## MARK 7.1–23

Now when the Pharisees and some of the scribes who had come from Jerusalem gathered around him [Jesus], 2 they noticed that some of his disciples were eating with defiled hands, that is, without washing them. 3 (For the Pharisees, and all the Jews, do not eat unless they thoroughly wash their hands, b thus observing the tradition of the elders; 4 and they do not eat anything from the market unless they wash it; c and there are also many other traditions that they observe, the washing of cups, pots, and bronze kettles. d) 5 So the Pharisees and the scribes asked him, "Why do your disciples not live e according to the tradition of the elders, but eat with defiled hands?" 6 He said to them, "Isaiah prophesied rightly about you hypocrites, as it is written,

'This people honors me with
their lips,
but their hearts are far from
me;

7  in vain do they worship me,
teaching human precepts as
doctrines.'

8 You abandon the commandment of God and hold to human tradition."

9  Then he said to them, "You have a fine way of rejecting the commandment of God in order to keep your tradition! 10 For Moses said, 'Honor your father and your mother'; and, 'Whoever speaks evil of father or mother must surely die.' 11 But you say that if anyone tells father or mother, 'Whatever support you might have had from me is Corban' (that is, an offering to Godf)— 12 then you no longer permit doing anything for a father or mother, 13 thus making void the word of God through your tradition that you have handed on. And you do many things like this."

14  Then he called the crowd again and said to them, "Listen to me, all of you, and understand: 15 there is nothing outside a person that by going in can defile, but the things that come out are what defile."g

17  When he had left the crowd and entered the house, his disciples asked him about the parable. 18 He said to them, "Then do you also fail to understand? Do you not see that whatever goes into a person from outside cannot defile, 19 since it enters, not the heart but the stomach, and goes out into the sewer?" (Thus he declared all foods clean.) 20 And he said, "It is what comes out of a person that defiles. 21 For it is from within, from the human heart, that evil intentions come: fornication, theft, murder, 22 adultery, avarice, wickedness, deceit, licentiousness, envy, slander, pride, folly. 23 All these evil things come from within, and they defile a person."

a Traditionally rendered *a scapegoat*  b Meaning of Gk uncertain  c Other ancient authorities read *and when they come from the marketplace, they do not eat unless they purify themselves*  d Other ancient authorities add *and beds*  e Gk *walk*  f Gk lacks *to God*  g Other ancient authorities add verse 16, *"Let anyone with ears to hear listen"*

## PSALM 40.11–17

Do not, O Lord, withhold
your mercy from me;
let your steadfast love and
your faithfulness
keep me safe forever.
12 For evils have encompassed me
without number;
my iniquities have overtaken
me,
until I cannot see;
they are more than the hairs of
my head,
and my heart fails me.

13 Be pleased, O Lord, to deliver
me;
O Lord, make haste to help
me.
14 Let all those be put to shame
and confusion
who seek to snatch away my
life;
let those be turned back and
brought to dishonor
who desire my hurt.

15 Let those be appalled because
of their shame
who say to me, "Aha, Aha!"

16 But may all who seek you
rejoice and be glad in you;
may those who love your
salvation
say continually, "Great is the
Lord!"
17 As for me, I am poor and
needy,
but the Lord takes thought
for me.
You are my help and my
deliverer;
do not delay, O my God.

## PROVERBS 10.13–14

On the lips of one who has
understanding wisdom
is found,
but a rod is for the back of
one who lacks sense.
14 The wise lay up knowledge,
but the babbling of a fool
brings ruin near.

# FEBRUARY 25

## LEVITICUS 16.29—18.30

This shall be a statute to you forever: In the seventh month, on the tenth day of the month, you shall deny yourselves, a and shall do no work, neither the citizen nor the alien who resides among you. 30For on this day atonement shall be made for you, to cleanse you; from all your sins you shall be clean before the Lord. 31It is a sabbath of complete rest to you, and you shall deny yourselves; a it is a statute forever. 32The priest who is anointed and consecrated as priest in his father's place shall make atonement, wearing the linen vestments, the holy vestments. 33He shall make atonement for the sanctuary, and he shall make atonement for the tent of meeting and for the altar, and he shall make atonement for the priests and for all the people of the assembly. 34This shall be

a Or *shall fast*

an everlasting statute for you, to make atonement for the people of Israel once in the year for all their sins. And Moses did as the LORD had commanded him.

17.1 THE LORD spoke to Moses:

2 Speak to Aaron and his sons and to all the people of Israel and say to them: This is what the LORD has commanded. ³If anyone of the house of Israel slaughters an ox or a lamb or a goat in the camp, or slaughters it outside the camp, ⁴and does not bring it to the entrance of the tent of meeting, to present it as an offering to the LORD before the tabernacle of the LORD, he shall be held guilty of bloodshed; he has shed blood, and he shall be cut off from the people. ⁵This is in order that the people of Israel may bring their sacrifices that they offer in the open field, that they may bring them to the LORD, to the priest at the entrance of the tent of meeting, and offer them as sacrifices of well-being to the LORD. ⁶The priest shall dash the blood against the altar of the LORD at the entrance of the tent of meeting, and turn the fat into smoke as a pleasing odor to the LORD, ⁷so that they may no longer offer their sacrifices for goat-demons, to whom they prostitute themselves. This shall be a statute forever to them throughout their generations.

8 And say to them further: Anyone of the house of Israel or of the aliens who reside among them who offers a burnt offering or sacrifice, ⁹and does not bring it to the entrance of the tent of meeting, to sacrifice it to the LORD, shall be cut off from the people.

10 If anyone of the house of Israel or of the aliens who reside among them eats any blood, I will set my face against that person who eats blood, and will cut that person off from the people. ¹¹For the life of the flesh is in the blood; and I have given it to you for making atonement for your lives on the altar; for, as life, it is the blood that makes atonement. ¹²Therefore I have said to the people of Israel: No person among you shall eat blood, nor shall any alien who resides among you eat blood. ¹³And anyone of the people of Israel, or of the aliens who reside among them, who hunts down an animal or bird that may be eaten shall pour out its blood and cover it with earth.

14 For the life of every creature— its blood is its life; therefore I have said to the people of Israel: You shall not eat the blood of any creature, for the life of every creature is its blood; whoever eats it shall be cut off. ¹⁵All persons, citizens or aliens, who eat what dies of itself or what has been torn by wild animals, shall wash their clothes, and bathe themselves in water, and be unclean until the evening; then they shall be clean. ¹⁶But if they do not wash themselves or bathe their body, they shall bear their guilt.

18.1 THE LORD spoke to Moses, saying:

2 Speak to the people of Israel and say to them: I am the LORD your God. ³You shall not do as they do in the land of Egypt, where you lived, and you shall not do as they do in the land of Canaan, to which I am bringing you. You shall not follow their statutes. ⁴My ordinances you shall observe and my statutes you shall keep, following them: I am the LORD your God. ⁵You shall keep my statutes and my ordinances; by doing so one shall live: I am the LORD.

6 None of you shall approach anyone near of kin to uncover nakedness: I am the LORD. ⁷You shall not uncover the nakedness of your father, which is the nakedness of your mother; she is your mother, you shall not uncover her nakedness. ⁸You shall not uncover the nakedness of your father's wife; it is the nakedness of your father. ⁹You shall not uncover the nakedness of your sister, your father's daughter or your mother's daughter, whether born at

home or born abroad. ¹⁰You shall not uncover the nakedness of your son's daughter or of your daughter's daughter, for their nakedness is your own nakedness. ¹¹You shall not uncover the nakedness of your father's wife's daughter, begotten by your father, since she is your sister. ¹²You shall not uncover the nakedness of your father's sister; she is your father's flesh. ¹³You shall not uncover the nakedness of your mother's sister, for she is your mother's flesh. ¹⁴You shall not uncover the nakedness of your father's brother, that is, you shall not approach his wife; she is your aunt. ¹⁵You shall not uncover the nakedness of your daughter-in-law: she is your son's wife; you shall not uncover her nakedness. ¹⁶You shall not uncover the nakedness of your brother's wife; it is your brother's nakedness. ¹⁷You shall not uncover the nakedness of a woman and her daughter, and you shall not take[a] her son's daughter or her daughter's daughter to uncover her nakedness; they are your[b] flesh; it is depravity. ¹⁸And you shall not take[a] a woman as a rival to her sister, uncovering her nakedness while her sister is still alive.

19 You shall not approach a woman to uncover her nakedness while she is in her menstrual uncleanness. ²⁰You shall not have sexual relations with your kinsman's wife, and defile yourself with her. ²¹You shall not give any of your offspring to sacrifice them[c] to Molech, and so profane the name of your God: I am the LORD. ²²You shall not lie with a male as with a woman; it is an abomination. ²³You shall not have sexual relations with any animal and defile yourself with it, nor shall any woman give herself to an animal to have sexual relations with it: it is perversion.

24 Do not defile yourselves in any of these ways, for by all these practices the nations I am casting out before you have defiled themselves. ²⁵Thus the land became defiled; and I punished it for its iniquity, and the land vomited out its inhabitants. ²⁶But you shall keep my statutes and my ordinances and commit none of these abominations, either the citizen or the alien who resides among you ²⁷(for the inhabitants of the land, who were before you, committed all of these abominations, and the land became defiled); ²⁸otherwise the land will vomit you out for defiling it, as it vomited out the nation that was before you. ²⁹For whoever commits any of these abominations shall be cut off from their people. ³⁰So keep my charge not to commit any of these abominations that were done before you, and not to defile yourselves by them: I am the LORD your God.

## MARK 7.24—8.10

FROM there he [Jesus] set out and went away to the region of Tyre.[d] He entered a house and did not want anyone to know he was there. Yet he could not escape notice, ²⁵but a woman whose little daughter had an unclean spirit immediately heard about him, and she came and bowed down at his feet. ²⁶Now the woman was a Gentile, of Syrophoenician origin. She begged him to cast the demon out of her daughter. ²⁷He said to her, "Let the children be fed first, for it is not fair to take the children's food and throw it to the dogs." ²⁸But she answered him, "Sir,[e] even the dogs under the table eat the children's crumbs." ²⁹Then he said to her, "For saying that, you may go—the demon has left your daughter." ³⁰So she went home, found the child lying on the bed, and the demon gone.

31 Then he returned from the region of Tyre, and went by way of Sidon towards the Sea of Galilee, in the re-

[a] Or *marry*  [b] Gk: Heb lacks *your*  [c] Heb *to pass them over*  [d] Other ancient authorities add *and Sidon*
[e] Or *Lord*; other ancient authorities prefix *Yes*

gion of the Decapolis. ³²They brought to him a deaf man who had an impediment in his speech; and they begged him to lay his hand on him. ³³He took him aside in private, away from the crowd, and put his fingers into his ears, and he spat and touched his tongue. ³⁴Then looking up to heaven, he sighed and said to him, "Ephphatha," that is, "Be opened." ³⁵And immediately his ears were opened, his tongue was released, and he spoke plainly. ³⁶Then Jesusª ordered them to tell no one; but the more he ordered them, the more zealously they proclaimed it. ³⁷They were astounded beyond measure, saying, "He has done everything well; he even makes the deaf to hear and the mute to speak."

8.1 IN those days when there was again a great crowd without anything to eat, he called his disciples and said to them, ²"I have compassion for the crowd, because they have been with me now for three days and have nothing to eat. ³If I send them away hungry to their homes, they will faint on the way—and some of them have come from a great distance." ⁴His disciples replied, "How can one feed these people with bread here in the desert?" ⁵He asked them, "How many loaves do you have?" They said, "Seven." ⁶Then he ordered the crowd to sit down on the ground; and he took the seven loaves, and after giving thanks he broke them and gave them to his disciples to distribute; and they distributed them to the crowd. ⁷They had also a few small fish; and after blessing them, he ordered that these too should be distributed. ⁸They ate and were filled; and they took up the broken pieces left over, seven baskets full. ⁹Now there were about four thousand people. And he sent them away. ¹⁰And immediately he got into the boat with his disciples and went to the district of Dalmanutha. ᵇ

## PSALM 41.1–13

*To the leader. A Psalm of David.*

HAPPY are those who consider the poor; ᶜ
the LORD delivers them in the day of trouble.
2  The LORD protects them and keeps them alive;
they are called happy in the land.
You do not give them up to the will of their enemies.
3  The LORD sustains them on their sickbed;
in their illness you heal all their infirmities. ᵈ

4  As for me, I said, "O LORD, be gracious to me;
heal me, for I have sinned against you."
5  My enemies wonder in malice when I will die, and my name perish.
6  And when they come to see me, they utter empty words,
while their hearts gather mischief;
when they go out, they tell it abroad.
7  All who hate me whisper together about me;
they imagine the worst for me.

8  They think that a deadly thing has fastened on me,
that I will not rise again from where I lie.
9  Even my bosom friend in whom I trusted,

ªGk *he*  ᵇOther ancient authorities read *Mageda* or *Magdala*  ᶜOr *weak*  ᵈHeb *you change all his bed*

who ate of my bread, has
    lifted the heel against
    me.
10 But you, O LORD, be gracious
    to me,
    and raise me up, that I may
    repay them.

11 By this I know that you are
    pleased with me;
    because my enemy has not
    triumphed over me.
12 But you have upheld me
    because of my integrity,
    and set me in your presence
    forever.

13 Blessed be the LORD, the God
    of Israel,
    from everlasting to
    everlasting.
    Amen and Amen.

## PROVERBS 10.15–16

THE wealth of the rich is their
    fortress;
    the poverty of the poor is
    their ruin.
16 The wage of the righteous leads
    to life,
    the gain of the wicked to sin.

# FEBRUARY 26

## LEVITICUS 19.1—20.21

THE LORD spoke to Moses, saying:
2 Speak to all the congregation of the people of Israel and say to them: You shall be holy, for I the LORD your God am holy. 3You shall each revere your mother and father, and you shall keep my sabbaths: I am the LORD your God. 4Do not turn to idols or make cast images for yourselves: I am the LORD your God.

5 When you offer a sacrifice of well-being to the LORD, offer it in such a way that it is acceptable on your behalf. 6It shall be eaten on the same day you offer it, or on the next day; and anything left over until the third day shall be consumed in fire. 7If it is eaten at all on the third day, it is an abomination; it will not be acceptable. 8All who eat it shall be subject to punishment, because they have profaned what is holy to the LORD;

and any such person shall be cut off from the people.

9 When you reap the harvest of your land, you shall not reap to the very edges of your field, or gather the gleanings of your harvest. 10You shall not strip your vineyard bare, or gather the fallen grapes of your vineyard; you shall leave them for the poor and the alien: I am the LORD your God.

11 You shall not steal; you shall not deal falsely; and you shall not lie to one another. 12And you shall not swear falsely by my name, profaning the name of your God: I am the LORD.

13 You shall not defraud your neighbor; you shall not steal; and you shall not keep for yourself the wages of a laborer until morning. 14You shall not revile the deaf or put a stumbling block before the blind; you shall fear your God: I am the LORD.

15 You shall not render an unjust

judgment; you shall not be partial to the poor or defer to the great: with justice you shall judge your neighbor. 16You shall not go around as a slandererᵃ among your people, and you shall not profit by the bloodᵇ of your neighbor: I am the LORD.

17 You shall not hate in your heart anyone of your kin; you shall reprove your neighbor, or you will incur guilt yourself. 18You shall not take vengeance or bear a grudge against any of your people, but you shall love your neighbor as yourself: I am the LORD.

19 You shall keep my statutes. You shall not let your animals breed with a different kind; you shall not sow your field with two kinds of seed; nor shall you put on a garment made of two different materials.

20 If a man has sexual relations with a woman who is a slave, designated for another man but not ransomed or given her freedom, an inquiry shall be held. They shall not be put to death, since she has not been freed; 21but he shall bring a guilt offering for himself to the LORD, at the entrance of the tent of meeting, a ram as guilt offering. 22And the priest shall make atonement for him with the ram of guilt offering before the LORD for his sin that he committed; and the sin he committed shall be forgiven him.

23 When you come into the land and plant all kinds of trees for food, then you shall regard their fruit as forbidden;ᶜ three years it shall be forbiddenᵈ to you, it must not be eaten. 24In the fourth year all their fruit shall be set apart for rejoicing in the LORD. 25But in the fifth year you may eat of their fruit, that their yield may be increased for you: I am the LORD your God.

26 You shall not eat anything with its blood. You shall not practice augury or witchcraft. 27You shall not round off the hair on your temples or mar the edges of your beard. 28You shall not make any gashes in your flesh for the dead or tattoo any marks upon you: I am the LORD.

29 Do not profane your daughter by making her a prostitute, that the land not become prostituted and full of depravity. 30You shall keep my sabbaths and reverence my sanctuary: I am the LORD.

31 Do not turn to mediums or wizards; do not seek them out, to be defiled by them: I am the LORD your God.

32 You shall rise before the aged, and defer to the old; and you shall fear your God: I am the LORD.

33 When an alien resides with you in your land, you shall not oppress the alien. 34The alien who resides with you shall be to you as the citizen among you; you shall love the alien as yourself, for you were aliens in the land of Egypt: I am the LORD your God.

35 You shall not cheat in measuring length, weight, or quantity. 36You shall have honest balances, honest weights, an honest ephah, and an honest hin: I am the LORD your God, who brought you out of the land of Egypt. 37You shall keep all my statutes and all my ordinances, and observe them: I am the LORD.

20.1 THE LORD spoke to Moses, saying: 2Say further to the people of Israel:

Any of the people of Israel, or of the aliens who reside in Israel, who give any of their offspring to Molech shall be put to death; the people of the land shall stone them to death. 3I myself will set my face against them, and will cut them off from the people, because they have given of their offspring to Molech, defiling my sanctuary and profaning my holy name. 4And if the people of the land should ever close their eyes to them, when they give of their offspring to Molech, and do not put them to death, 5I

ᵃMeaning of Heb uncertain   ᵇHeb *stand against the blood*   ᶜHeb *as their uncircumcision*
ᵈHeb *uncircumcision*

myself will set my face against them and against their family, and will cut them off from among their people, them and all who follow them in prostituting themselves to Molech.

6  If any turn to mediums and wizards, prostituting themselves to them, I will set my face against them, and will cut them off from the people. [7]Consecrate yourselves therefore, and be holy; for I am the LORD your God. [8]Keep my statutes, and observe them; I am the LORD; I sanctify you. [9]All who curse father or mother shall be put to death; having cursed father or mother, their blood is upon them.

10  If a man commits adultery with the wife of[a] his neighbor, both the adulterer and the adulteress shall be put to death. [11]The man who lies with his father's wife has uncovered his father's nakedness; both of them shall be put to death; their blood is upon them. [12]If a man lies with his daughter-in-law, both of them shall be put to death; they have committed perversion, their blood is upon them. [13]If a man lies with a male as with a woman, both of them have committed an abomination; they shall be put to death; their blood is upon them. [14]If a man takes a wife and her mother also, it is depravity; they shall be burned to death, both he and they, that there may be no depravity among you. [15]If a man has sexual relations with an animal, he shall be put to death; and you shall kill the animal. [16]If a woman approaches any animal and has sexual relations with it, you shall kill the woman and the animal; they shall be put to death, their blood is upon them.

17  If a man takes his sister, a daughter of his father or a daughter of his mother, and sees her nakedness, and she sees his nakedness, it is a disgrace, and they shall be cut off in the sight of their people; he has uncovered his sister's nakedness, he shall be subject to punishment. [18]If a man lies with a woman having her sickness and uncovers her nakedness, he has laid bare her flow and she has laid bare her flow of blood; both of them shall be cut off from their people. [19]You shall not uncover the nakedness of your mother's sister or of your father's sister, for that is to lay bare one's own flesh; they shall be subject to punishment. [20]If a man lies with his uncle's wife, he has uncovered his uncle's nakedness; they shall be subject to punishment; they shall die childless. [21]If a man takes his brother's wife, it is impurity; he has uncovered his brother's nakedness; they shall be childless.

## MARK 8.11—9.1

**T**HE Pharisees came and began to argue with him [Jesus], asking him for a sign from heaven, to test him. [12]And he sighed deeply in his spirit and said, "Why does this generation ask for a sign? Truly I tell you, no sign will be given to this generation." [13]And he left them, and getting into the boat again, he went across to the other side.

14  Now the disciples[b] had forgotten to bring any bread; and they had only one loaf with them in the boat. [15]And he cautioned them, saying, "Watch out—beware of the yeast of the Pharisees and the yeast of Herod."[c] [16]They said to one another, "It is because we have no bread." [17]And becoming aware of it, Jesus said to them, "Why are you talking about having no bread? Do you still not perceive or understand? Are your hearts hardened? [18]Do you have eyes, and fail to see? Do you have ears, and fail to hear? And do you not remember? [19]When I broke the five loaves for the five thousand, how many baskets full of broken pieces did you collect?" They

[a]Heb repeats *if a man commits adultery with the wife of*   [b]Gk *they*   [c]Other ancient authorities read *the Herodians*

said to him, "Twelve." [20]"And the seven for the four thousand, how many baskets full of broken pieces did you collect?" And they said to him, "Seven." [21]Then he said to them, "Do you not yet understand?"

22 They came to Bethsaida. Some people[a] brought a blind man to him and begged him to touch him. [23]He took the blind man by the hand and led him out of the village; and when he had put saliva on his eyes and laid his hands on him, he asked him, "Can you see anything?" [24]And the man[b] looked up and said, "I can see people, but they look like trees, walking." [25]Then Jesus[b] laid his hands on his eyes again; and he looked intently and his sight was restored, and he saw everything clearly. [26]Then he sent him away to his home, saying, "Do not even go into the village."[c]

27 Jesus went on with his disciples to the villages of Caesarea Philippi; and on the way he asked his disciples, "Who do people say that I am?" [28]And they answered him, "John the Baptist; and others, Elijah; and still others, one of the prophets." [29]He asked them, "But who do you say that I am?" Peter answered him, "You are the Messiah."[d] [30]And he sternly ordered them not to tell anyone about him.

31 Then he began to teach them that the Son of Man must undergo great suffering, and be rejected by the elders, the chief priests, and the scribes, and be killed, and after three days rise again. [32]He said all this quite openly. And Peter took him aside and began to rebuke him. [33]But turning and looking at his disciples, he rebuked Peter and said, "Get behind me, Satan! For you are setting your mind not on divine things but on human things."

34 He called the crowd with his disciples, and said to them, "If any want to become my followers, let them deny themselves and take up their cross and follow me. [35]For those who want to save their life will lose it, and those who lose their life for my sake, and for the sake of the gospel,[e] will save it. [36]For what will it profit them to gain the whole world and forfeit their life? [37]Indeed, what can they give in return for their life? [38]Those who are ashamed of me and of my words[f] in this adulterous and sinful generation, of them the Son of Man will also be ashamed when he comes in the glory of his Father with the holy angels." [9.1]And he said to them, "Truly I tell you, there are some standing here who will not taste death until they see that the kingdom of God has come with[g] power."

## PSALM 42.1–11

*To the leader. A Maskil of the Korahites.*

A s a deer longs for flowing
        streams,
    so my soul longs for you,
        O God.
2   My soul thirsts for God,
        for the living God.
    When shall I come and behold
        the face of God?
3   My tears have been my food
        day and night,
    while people say to me
            continually,
        "Where is your God?"

4   These things I remember,
        as I pour out my soul:
    how I went with the throng,[h]
        and led them in procession to
            the house of God,
    with glad shouts and songs of
            thanksgiving,

aGk *They*   bGk *he*   cOther ancient authorities add *or tell anyone in the village*   dOr *the Christ*
eOther ancient authorities read *lose their life for the sake of the gospel*   fOther ancient authorities
read *and of mine*   gOr *in*   hMeaning of Heb uncertain

a multitude keeping festival.
5 Why are you cast down, O my
     soul,
   and why are you disquieted
        within me?
   Hope in God; for I shall again
        praise him,
   my help 6and my God.

   My soul is cast down within me;
      therefore I remember you
   from the land of Jordan and of
        Hermon,
      from Mount Mizar.
7 Deep calls to deep
     at the thunder of your
        cataracts;
   all your waves and your billows
      have gone over me.
8 By day the LORD commands his
        steadfast love,
   and at night his song is with
        me,
   a prayer to the God of my
        life.

9 I say to God, my rock,

"Why have you forgotten me?
   Why must I walk about
        mournfully
      because the enemy oppresses
        me?"
10 As with a deadly wound in my
        body,
   my adversaries taunt me,
   while they say to me
        continually,
   "Where is your God?"

11 Why are you cast down, O my
     soul,
   and why are you disquieted
        within me?
   Hope in God; for I shall again
        praise him,
   my help and my God.

## PROVERBS 10.17

WHOEVER heeds instruction is on the path to life, but one who rejects a rebuke goes astray.

# FEBRUARY 27

## LEVITICUS 20.22—22.16

YOU shall keep all my statutes and all my ordinances, and observe them, so that the land to which I bring you to settle in may not vomit you out. 23You shall not follow the practices of the nation that I am driving out before you. Because they did all these things, I abhorred them. 24But I have said to you: You shall inherit their land, and I will give it to you to possess, a land flowing with milk and honey. I am the LORD your God; I have separated you from the peoples. 25You shall

therefore make a distinction between the clean animal and the unclean, and between the unclean bird and the clean; you shall not bring abomination on yourselves by animal or by bird or by anything with which the ground teems, which I have set apart for you to hold unclean. 26You shall be holy to me; for I the LORD am holy, and I have separated you from the other peoples to be mine.

27 A man or a woman who is a medium or a wizard shall be put to death;

they shall be stoned to death, their blood is upon them.

21.1 THE LORD said to Moses: Speak to the priests, the sons of Aaron, and say to them:

No one shall defile himself for a dead person among his relatives, 2except for his nearest kin: his mother, his father, his son, his daughter, his brother; 3likewise, for a virgin sister, close to him because she has had no husband, he may defile himself for her. 4But he shall not defile himself as a husband among his people and so profane himself. 5They shall not make bald spots upon their heads, or shave off the edges of their beards, or make any gashes in their flesh. 6They shall be holy to their God, and not profane the name of their God; for they offer the LORD's offerings by fire, the food of their God; therefore they shall be holy. 7They shall not marry a prostitute or a woman who has been defiled; neither shall they marry a woman divorced from her husband. For they are holy to their God, 8and you shall treat them as holy, since they offer the food of your God; they shall be holy to you, for I the LORD, I who sanctify you, am holy. 9When the daughter of a priest profanes herself through prostitution, she profanes her father; she shall be burned to death.

10  The priest who is exalted above his fellows, on whose head the anointing oil has been poured and who has been consecrated to wear the vestments, shall not dishevel his hair, nor tear his vestments. 11He shall not go where there is a dead body; he shall not defile himself even for his father or mother. 12He shall not go outside the sanctuary and thus profane the sanctuary of his God; for the consecration of the anointing oil of his God is upon him: I am the LORD. 13He shall marry only a woman who is a virgin. 14A widow, or a divorced woman, or a woman who has been defiled, a prostitute, these he shall not marry. He shall marry a virgin of his own kin, 15that he may not profane his offspring among his kin; for I am the LORD; I sanctify him.

16  The LORD spoke to Moses, saying: 17Speak to Aaron and say: No one of your offspring throughout their generations who has a blemish may approach to offer the food of his God. 18For no one who has a blemish shall draw near, one who is blind or lame, or one who has a mutilated face or a limb too long, 19or one who has a broken foot or a broken hand, 20or a hunchback, or a dwarf, or a man with a blemish in his eyes or an itching disease or scabs or crushed testicles. 21No descendant of Aaron the priest who has a blemish shall come near to offer the LORD's offerings by fire; since he has a blemish, he shall not come near to offer the food of his God. 22He may eat the food of his God, of the most holy as well as of the holy. 23But he shall not come near the curtain or approach the altar, because he has a blemish, that he may not profane my sanctuaries; for I am the LORD; I sanctify them. 24Thus Moses spoke to Aaron and to his sons and to all the people of Israel.

22.1 THE LORD spoke to Moses, saying: 2Direct Aaron and his sons to deal carefully with the sacred donations of the people of Israel, which they dedicate to me, so that they may not profane my holy name; I am the LORD. 3Say to them: If anyone among all your offspring throughout your generations comes near the sacred donations, which the people of Israel dedicate to the LORD, while he is in a state of uncleanness, that person shall be cut off from my presence: I am the LORD. 4No one of Aaron's offspring who has a leprousa disease or suffers a discharge

aA term for several skin diseases; precise meaning uncertain

may eat of the sacred donations until he is clean. Whoever touches anything made unclean by a corpse or a man who has had an emission of semen, 5and whoever touches any swarming thing by which he may be made unclean or any human being by whom he may be made unclean—whatever his uncleanness may be— 6the person who touches any such shall be unclean until evening and shall not eat of the sacred donations unless he has washed his body in water. 7When the sun sets he shall be clean; and afterward he may eat of the sacred donations, for they are his food. 8That which died or was torn by wild animals he shall not eat, becoming unclean by it: I am the LORD. 9They shall keep my charge, so that they may not incur guilt and die in the sanctuarya for having profaned it: I am the LORD; I sanctify them.

10　No lay person shall eat of the sacred donations. No bound or hired servant of the priest shall eat of the sacred donations; 11but if a priest acquires anyone by purchase, the person may eat of them; and those that are born in his house may eat of his food. 12If a priest's daughter marries a layman, she shall not eat of the offering of the sacred donations; 13but if a priest's daughter is widowed or divorced, without offspring, and returns to her father's house, as in her youth, she may eat of her father's food. No lay person shall eat of it. 14If a man eats of the sacred donation unintentionally, he shall add one-fifth of its value to it, and give the sacred donation to the priest. 15No one shall profane the sacred donations of the people of Israel, which they offer to the LORD, 16causing them to bear guilt requiring a guilt offering, by eating their sacred donations: for I am the LORD; I sanctify them.

## MARK 9.2–29

SIX days later, Jesus took with him Peter and James and John, and led them up a high mountain apart, by themselves. And he was transfigured before them, 3and his clothes became dazzling white, such as no oneb on earth could bleach them. 4And there appeared to them Elijah with Moses, who were talking with Jesus. 5Then Peter said to Jesus, "Rabbi, it is good for us to be here; let us make three dwellings,c one for you, one for Moses, and one for Elijah." 6He did not know what to say, for they were terrified. 7Then a cloud overshadowed them, and from the cloud there came a voice, "This is my Son, the Beloved;d listen to him!" 8Suddenly when they looked around, they saw no one with them any more, but only Jesus.

9　As they were coming down the mountain, he ordered them to tell no one about what they had seen, until after the Son of Man had risen from the dead. 10So they kept the matter to themselves, questioning what this rising from the dead could mean. 11Then they asked him, "Why do the scribes say that Elijah must come first?" 12He said to them, "Elijah is indeed coming first to restore all things. How then is it written about the Son of Man, that he is to go through many sufferings and be treated with contempt? 13But I tell you that Elijah has come, and they did to him whatever they pleased, as it is written about him."

14　When they came to the disciples, they saw a great crowd around them, and some scribes arguing with them. 15When the whole crowd saw him, they were immediately overcome with awe, and they ran forward to greet him. 16He asked them, "What are you arguing about with them?" 17Someone from the crowd answered him,

aVg: Heb *incur guilt for it and die in it*　bGk *no fuller*　cOr *tents*　dOr *my beloved Son*

"Teacher, I brought you my son; he has a spirit that makes him unable to speak; [18] and whenever it seizes him, it dashes him down; and he foams and grinds his teeth and becomes rigid; and I asked your disciples to cast it out, but they could not do so." [19] He answered them, "You faithless generation, how much longer must I be among you? How much longer must I put up with you? Bring him to me." [20] And they brought the boy[a] to him. When the spirit saw him, immediately it convulsed the boy,[a] and he fell on the ground and rolled about, foaming at the mouth. [21] Jesus[b] asked the father, "How long has this been happening to him?" And he said, "From childhood. [22] It has often cast him into the fire and into the water, to destroy him; but if you are able to do anything, have pity on us and help us." [23] Jesus said to him, "If you are able!—All things can be done for the one who believes." [24] Immediately the father of the child cried out,[c] "I believe; help my unbelief!" [25] When Jesus saw that a crowd came running together, he rebuked the unclean spirit, saying to it, "You spirit that keeps this boy from speaking and hearing, I command you, come out of him, and never enter him again!" [26] After crying out and convulsing him terribly, it came out, and the boy was like a corpse, so that most of them said, "He is dead." [27] But Jesus took him by the hand and lifted him up, and he was able to stand. [28] When he had entered the house, his disciples asked him privately, "Why could we not cast it out?" [29] He said to them, "This kind can come out only through prayer."[d]

## PSALM 43.1–5

VINDICATE me, O God, and
    defend my cause
against an ungodly people;
from those who are deceitful
    and unjust
    deliver me!
2  For you are the God in whom I
        take refuge;
    why have you cast me off?
    Why must I walk about
        mournfully
    because of the oppression of
        the enemy?

3  O send out your light and your
        truth;
    let them lead me;
    let them bring me to your holy
        hill
    and to your dwelling.
4  Then I will go to the altar of
        God,
    to God my exceeding joy;
    and I will praise you with the
        harp,
    O God, my God.

5  Why are you cast down, O my
        soul,
    and why are you disquieted
        within me?
    Hope in God; for I shall again
        praise him,
    my help and my God.

## PROVERBS 10.18

LYING lips conceal hatred,
    and whoever utters slander
        is a fool.

a Gk *him*   b Gk *He*   c Other ancient authorities add *with tears*   d Other ancient authorities add *and fasting*

## LEVITICUS 22.17—23.44

THE LORD spoke to Moses, saying: ¹⁸Speak to Aaron and his sons and all the people of Israel and say to them: When anyone of the house of Israel or of the aliens residing in Israel presents an offering, whether in payment of a vow or as a freewill offering that is offered to the LORD as a burnt offering, ¹⁹to be acceptable in your behalf it shall be a male without blemish, of the cattle or the sheep or the goats. ²⁰You shall not offer anything that has a blemish, for it will not be acceptable in your behalf.

21  When anyone offers a sacrifice of well-being to the LORD, in fulfillment of a vow or as a freewill offering, from the herd or from the flock, to be acceptable it must be perfect; there shall be no blemish in it. ²²Anything blind, or injured, or maimed, or having a discharge or an itch or scabs—these you shall not offer to the LORD or put any of them on the altar as offerings by fire to the LORD. ²³An ox or a lamb that has a limb too long or too short you may present for a freewill offering; but it will not be accepted for a vow. ²⁴Any animal that has its testicles bruised or crushed or torn or cut, you shall not offer to the LORD; such you shall not do within your land, ²⁵nor shall you accept any such animals from a foreigner to offer as food to your God; since they are mutilated, with a blemish in them, they shall not be accepted in your behalf.

26  The LORD spoke to Moses, saying: ²⁷When an ox or a sheep or a goat is born, it shall remain seven days with its mother, and from the eighth day on it shall be acceptable as the LORD's offering by fire. ²⁸But you shall not slaughter, from the herd or the flock, an animal with its young on the same day. ²⁹When you sacrifice a thanksgiving offering to the LORD, you shall sacrifice it so that it may be acceptable in your behalf. ³⁰It shall be eaten on the same day; you shall not leave any of it until morning: I am the LORD.

31  Thus you shall keep my commandments and observe them: I am the LORD. ³²You shall not profane my holy name, that I may be sanctified among the people of Israel: I am the LORD; I sanctify you, ³³I who brought you out of the land of Egypt to be your God: I am the LORD.

**23.**¹ THE LORD spoke to Moses, saying: ²Speak to the people of Israel and say to them: These are the appointed festivals of the LORD that you shall proclaim as holy convocations, my appointed festivals.

3  Six days shall work be done; but the seventh day is a sabbath of complete rest, a holy convocation; you shall do no work: it is a sabbath to the LORD throughout your settlements.

4  These are the appointed festivals of the LORD, the holy convocations, which you shall celebrate at the time appointed for them. ⁵In the first month, on the fourteenth day of the month, at twilight, ᵃ there shall be a passover offering to the LORD, ⁶and on the fifteenth day of the same month is the festival of unleavened bread to the LORD; seven days you shall eat unleavened bread. ⁷On the first day you shall have a holy convocation; you shall not work at your occupations. ⁸For seven days you shall present the LORD's offerings by fire; on the seventh day there shall be a holy

---

ᵃ Heb *between the two evenings*

convocation: you shall not work at your occupations.

9 The Lord spoke to Moses: <sup>10</sup>Speak to the people of Israel and say to them: When you enter the land that I am giving you and you reap its harvest, you shall bring the sheaf of the first fruits of your harvest to the priest. <sup>11</sup>He shall raise the sheaf before the Lord, that you may find acceptance; on the day after the sabbath the priest shall raise it. <sup>12</sup>On the day when you raise the sheaf, you shall offer a lamb a year old, without blemish, as a burnt offering to the Lord. <sup>13</sup>And the grain offering with it shall be two-tenths of an ephah of choice flour mixed with oil, an offering by fire of pleasing odor to the Lord; and the drink offering with it shall be of wine, one-fourth of a hin. <sup>14</sup>You shall eat no bread or parched grain or fresh ears until that very day, until you have brought the offering of your God: it is a statute forever throughout your generations in all your settlements.

15 And from the day after the sabbath, from the day on which you bring the sheaf of the elevation offering, you shall count off seven weeks; they shall be complete. <sup>16</sup>You shall count until the day after the seventh sabbath, fifty days; then you shall present an offering of new grain to the Lord. <sup>17</sup>You shall bring from your settlements two loaves of bread as an elevation offering, each made of two-tenths of an ephah; they shall be of choice flour, baked with leaven, as first fruits to the Lord. <sup>18</sup>You shall present with the bread seven lambs a year old without blemish, one young bull, and two rams; they shall be a burnt offering to the Lord, along with their grain offering and their drink offerings, an offering by fire of pleasing odor to the Lord. <sup>19</sup>You shall also offer one male goat for a sin offering, and two male lambs a year old as a sacrifice of well-being. <sup>20</sup>The priest shall raise them with the bread of the first fruits as an elevation offering before the Lord, together with the two lambs; they shall be holy to the Lord for the priest. <sup>21</sup>On that same day you shall make proclamation; you shall hold a holy convocation; you shall not work at your occupations. This is a statute forever in all your settlements throughout your generations.

22 When you reap the harvest of your land, you shall not reap to the very edges of your field, or gather the gleanings of your harvest; you shall leave them for the poor and for the alien: I am the Lord your God.

23 The Lord spoke to Moses, saying: <sup>24</sup>Speak to the people of Israel, saying: In the seventh month, on the first day of the month, you shall observe a day of complete rest, a holy convocation commemorated with trumpet blasts. <sup>25</sup>You shall not work at your occupations; and you shall present the Lord's offering by fire.

26 The Lord spoke to Moses, saying: <sup>27</sup>Now, the tenth day of this seventh month is the day of atonement; it shall be a holy convocation for you: you shall deny yourselves<sup>a</sup> and present the Lord's offering by fire; <sup>28</sup>and you shall do no work during that entire day; for it is a day of atonement, to make atonement on your behalf before the Lord your God. <sup>29</sup>For anyone who does not practice self-denial<sup>b</sup> during that entire day shall be cut off from the people. <sup>30</sup>And anyone who does any work during that entire day, such a one I will destroy from the midst of the people. <sup>31</sup>You shall do no work: it is a statute forever throughout your generations in all your settlements. <sup>32</sup>It shall be to you a sabbath of complete rest, and you shall deny yourselves;<sup>a</sup> on the ninth day of the month at evening, from evening to evening you shall keep your sabbath.

33 The Lord spoke to Moses, say-

<sup>a</sup>Or *shall fast*   <sup>b</sup>Or *does not fast*

ing: ³⁴Speak to the people of Israel, saying: On the fifteenth day of this seventh month, and lasting seven days, there shall be the festival of booths[a] to the LORD. ³⁵The first day shall be a holy convocation; you shall not work at your occupations. ³⁶Seven days you shall present the LORD's offerings by fire; on the eighth day you shall observe a holy convocation and present the LORD's offerings by fire; it is a solemn assembly; you shall not work at your occupations.

37 These are the appointed festivals of the LORD, which you shall celebrate as times of holy convocation, for presenting to the LORD offerings by fire—burnt offerings and grain offerings, sacrifices and drink offerings, each on its proper day— ³⁸apart from the sabbaths of the LORD, and apart from your gifts, and apart from all your votive offerings, and apart from all your freewill offerings, which you give to the LORD.

39 Now, the fifteenth day of the seventh month, when you have gathered in the produce of the land, you shall keep the festival of the LORD, lasting seven days; a complete rest on the first day, and a complete rest on the eighth day. ⁴⁰On the first day you shall take the fruit of majestic[b] trees, branches of palm trees, boughs of leafy trees, and willows of the brook; and you shall rejoice before the LORD your God for seven days. ⁴¹You shall keep it as a festival to the LORD seven days in the year; you shall keep it in the seventh month as a statute forever throughout your generations. ⁴²You shall live in booths for seven days; all that are citizens in Israel shall live in booths, ⁴³so that your generations may know that I made the people of Israel live in booths when I brought them out of the land of Egypt: I am the LORD your God.

44 Thus Moses declared to the people of Israel the appointed festivals of the LORD.

## MARK 9.30—10.12

THEY [Jesus and his disciples] went on from there and passed through Galilee. He did not want anyone to know it; ³¹for he was teaching his disciples, saying to them, "The Son of Man is to be betrayed into human hands, and they will kill him, and three days after being killed, he will rise again." ³²But they did not understand what he was saying and were afraid to ask him.

33 Then they came to Capernaum; and when he was in the house he asked them, "What were you arguing about on the way?" ³⁴But they were silent, for on the way they had argued with one another who was the greatest. ³⁵He sat down, called the twelve, and said to them, "Whoever wants to be first must be last of all and servant of all." ³⁶Then he took a little child and put it among them; and taking it in his arms, he said to them, ³⁷"Whoever welcomes one such child in my name welcomes me, and whoever welcomes me welcomes not me but the one who sent me."

38 John said to him, "Teacher, we saw someone[c] casting out demons in your name, and we tried to stop him, because he was not following us." ³⁹But Jesus said, "Do not stop him; for no one who does a deed of power in my name will be able soon afterward to speak evil of me. ⁴⁰Whoever is not against us is for us. ⁴¹For truly I tell you, whoever gives you a cup of water to drink because you bear the name of Christ will by no means lose the reward.

42 "If any of you put a stumbling block before one of these little ones who believe in me,[d] it would be better for you if a great millstone were hung

---

[a] Or *tabernacles*: Heb *succoth*  [b] Meaning of Heb uncertain  [c] Other ancient authorities add *who does not follow us*  [d] Other ancient authorities lack *in me*

around your neck and you were thrown into the sea. [43]If your hand causes you to stumble, cut it off; it is better for you to enter life maimed than to have two hands and to go to hell,[a] to the unquenchable fire.[b] [45]And if your foot causes you to stumble, cut it off; it is better for you to enter life lame than to have two feet and to be thrown into hell.[a,b] [47]And if your eye causes you to stumble, tear it out; it is better for you to enter the kingdom of God with one eye than to have two eyes and to be thrown into hell,[a] [48]where their worm never dies, and the fire is never quenched.

49 "For everyone will be salted with fire.[c] [50]Salt is good; but if salt has lost its saltiness, how can you season it?[d] Have salt in yourselves, and be at peace with one another."

10.1 He left that place and went to the region of Judea and[e] beyond the Jordan. And crowds again gathered around him; and, as was his custom, he again taught them. 2 Some Pharisees came, and to test him they asked, "Is it lawful for a man to divorce his wife?" [3]He answered them, "What did Moses command you?" [4]They said, "Moses allowed a man to write a certificate of dismissal and to divorce her." [5]But Jesus said to them, "Because of your hardness of heart he wrote this commandment for you. [6]But from the beginning of creation, 'God made them male and female.' [7]'For this reason a man shall leave his father and mother and be joined to his wife,[f] [8]and the two shall become one flesh.' So they are no longer two, but one flesh. [9]Therefore what God has joined together, let no one separate."

10 Then in the house the disciples asked him again about this matter. [11]He said to them, "Whoever divorces his wife and marries another commits adultery against her; [12]and if she divorces her husband and marries another, she commits adultery."

## PSALM 44.1–8

*To the leader. Of the Korahites. A Maskil.*

We have heard with our ears, O God,
   our ancestors have told
      us,
what deeds you performed in
      their days,
   in the days of old:
2  you with your own hand drove
      out the nations,
   but them you planted;
   you afflicted the peoples,
      but them you set free;
3  for not by their own sword did
      they win the land,
   nor did their own arm give
      them victory;
   but your right hand, and your
      arm,
   and the light of your
      countenance,
   for you delighted in them.

4  You are my King and my God;
   you command[g] victories for
      Jacob.
5  Through you we push down our
      foes;
   through your name we tread
      down our assailants.
6  For not in my bow do I trust,
   nor can my sword save me.
7  But you have saved us from our
      foes,
   and have put to confusion
      those who hate us.

aGk *Gehenna*   bVerses 44 and 46 (which are identical with verse 48) are lacking in the best ancient authorities   cOther ancient authorities either add or substitute *and every sacrifice will be salted with salt*   dOr *how can you restore its saltiness?*   eOther ancient authorities lack *and*   fOther ancient authorities lack *and be joined to his wife*   gGk Syr: Heb *You are my King, O God; command*

8  In God we have boasted
   continually,
   and we will give thanks to
   your name forever.  *Selah*

## PROVERBS 10.19

**W**HEN words are many,
transgression is not
lacking,
but the prudent are restrained
in speech.

# MARCH 1

## LEVITICUS 24.1—25.46

**T**HE LORD spoke to Moses, saying: [2]Command the people of Israel to bring you pure oil of beaten olives for the lamp, that a light may be kept burning regularly. [3]Aaron shall set it up in the tent of meeting, outside the curtain of the covenant, [a] to burn from evening to morning before the LORD regularly; it shall be a statute forever throughout your generations. [4]He shall set up the lamps on the lampstand of pure gold[b] before the LORD regularly.

5  You shall take choice flour, and bake twelve loaves of it; two-tenths of an ephah shall be in each loaf. [6]You shall place them in two rows, six in a row, on the table of pure gold. [c] [7]You shall put pure frankincense with each row, to be a token offering for the bread, as an offering by fire to the LORD. [8]Every sabbath day Aaron shall set them in order before the LORD regularly as a commitment of the people of Israel, as a covenant forever. [9]They shall be for Aaron and his descendants, who shall eat them in a holy place, for they are most holy portions for him from the offerings by fire to the LORD, a perpetual due.

10  A man whose mother was an Israelite and whose father was an Egyptian came out among the people of Israel; and the Israelite woman's son and a certain Israelite began fighting in the camp. [11]The Israelite woman's son blasphemed the Name in a curse. And they brought him to Moses—now his mother's name was Shelomith, daughter of Dibri, of the tribe of Dan— [12]and they put him in custody, until the decision of the LORD should be made clear to them.

13  The LORD said to Moses, saying: [14]Take the blasphemer outside the camp; and let all who were within hearing lay their hands on his head, and let the whole congregation stone him. [15]And speak to the people of Israel, saying: Anyone who curses God shall bear the sin. [16]One who blasphemes the name of the LORD shall be put to death; the whole congregation shall stone the blasphemer. Aliens as well as citizens, when they blaspheme the Name, shall be put to death. [17]Anyone who kills a human being shall be put to death. [18]Anyone who kills an animal shall make restitution for it, life for life. [19]Anyone who maims another shall suffer the same injury in return: [20]fracture for fracture, eye for eye, tooth for

---

**a** Or *treaty*, or *testament*; Heb *eduth*   **b** Heb *pure lampstand*   **c** Heb *pure table*

tooth; the injury inflicted is the injury to be suffered. ²¹One who kills an animal shall make restitution for it; but one who kills a human being shall be put to death. ²²You shall have one law for the alien and for the citizen: for I am the Lord your God. ²³Moses spoke thus to the people of Israel; and they took the blasphemer outside the camp, and stoned him to death. The people of Israel did as the Lord had commanded Moses.

**25.**1 The Lord spoke to Moses on Mount Sinai, saying: ²Speak to the people of Israel and say to them: When you enter the land that I am giving you, the land shall observe a sabbath for the Lord. ³Six years you shall sow your field, and six years you shall prune your vineyard, and gather in their yield; ⁴but in the seventh year there shall be a sabbath of complete rest for the land, a sabbath for the Lord: you shall not sow your field or prune your vineyard. ⁵You shall not reap the aftergrowth of your harvest or gather the grapes of your unpruned vine: it shall be a year of complete rest for the land. ⁶You may eat what the land yields during its sabbath—you, your male and female slaves, your hired and your bound laborers who live with you; ⁷for your livestock also, and for the wild animals in your land all its yield shall be for food.

8 You shall count off seven weeks[a] of years, seven times seven years, so that the period of seven weeks of years gives forty-nine years. ⁹Then you shall have the trumpet sounded loud; on the tenth day of the seventh month—on the day of atonement—you shall have the trumpet sounded throughout all your land. ¹⁰And you shall hallow the fiftieth year and you shall proclaim liberty throughout the land to all its inhabitants. It shall be a jubilee for you: you shall return, every one of you, to your property and every one of you to your family. ¹¹That fiftieth year shall be a jubilee for you: you shall not sow, or reap the aftergrowth, or harvest the unpruned vines. ¹²For it is a jubilee; it shall be holy to you: you shall eat only what the field itself produces.

13 In this year of jubilee you shall return, every one of you, to your property. ¹⁴When you make a sale to your neighbor or buy from your neighbor, you shall not cheat one another. ¹⁵When you buy from your neighbor, you shall pay only for the number of years since the jubilee; the seller shall charge you only for the remaining crop years. ¹⁶If the years are more, you shall increase the price, and if the years are fewer, you shall diminish the price; for it is a certain number of harvests that are being sold to you. ¹⁷You shall not cheat one another, but you shall fear your God; for I am the Lord your God.

18 You shall observe my statutes and faithfully keep my ordinances, so that you may live on the land securely. ¹⁹The land will yield its fruit, and you will eat your fill and live on it securely. ²⁰Should you ask, What shall we eat in the seventh year, if we may not sow or gather in our crop? ²¹I will order my blessing for you in the sixth year, so that it will yield a crop for three years. ²²When you sow in the eighth year, you will be eating from the old crop; until the ninth year, when its produce comes in, you shall eat the old. ²³The land shall not be sold in perpetuity, for the land is mine; with me you are but aliens and tenants. ²⁴Throughout the land that you hold, you shall provide for the redemption of the land.

25 If anyone of your kin falls into difficulty and sells a piece of property, then the next of kin shall come and redeem what the relative has sold. ²⁶If the person has no one to redeem it, but

a Or *sabbaths*

then prospers and finds sufficient means to do so, [27]the years since its sale shall be computed and the difference shall be refunded to the person to whom it was sold, and the property shall be returned. [28]But if there is not sufficient means to recover it, what was sold shall remain with the purchaser until the year of jubilee; in the jubilee it shall be released, and the property shall be returned.

29  If anyone sells a dwelling house in a walled city, it may be redeemed until a year has elapsed since its sale; the right of redemption shall be one year. [30]If it is not redeemed before a full year has elapsed, a house that is in a walled city shall pass in perpetuity to the purchaser, throughout the generations; it shall not be released in the jubilee. [31]But houses in villages that have no walls around them shall be classed as open country; they may be redeemed, and they shall be released in the jubilee. [32]As for the cities of the Levites, the Levites shall forever have the right of redemption of the houses in the cities belonging to them. [33]Such property as may be redeemed from the Levites—houses sold in a city belonging to them—shall be released in the jubilee; because the houses in the cities of the Levites are their possession among the people of Israel. [34]But the open land around their cities may not be sold; for that is their possession for all time.

35  If any of your kin fall into difficulty and become dependent on you, [a] you shall support them; they shall live with you as though resident aliens. [36]Do not take interest in advance or otherwise make a profit from them, but fear your God; let them live with you. [37]You shall not lend them your money at interest taken in advance, or provide them food at a profit. [38]I am the Lord your God, who brought you out of the land of Egypt, to give you the land of Canaan, to be your God.

39  If any who are dependent on you become so impoverished that they sell themselves to you, you shall not make them serve as slaves. [40]They shall remain with you as hired or bound laborers. They shall serve with you until the year of the jubilee. [41]Then they and their children with them shall be free from your authority; they shall go back to their own family and return to their ancestral property. [42]For they are my servants, whom I brought out of the land of Egypt; they shall not be sold as slaves are sold. [43]You shall not rule over them with harshness, but shall fear your God. [44]As for the male and female slaves whom you may have, it is from the nations around you that you may acquire male and female slaves. [45]You may also acquire them from among the aliens residing with you, and from their families that are with you, who have been born in your land; and they may be your property. [46]You may keep them as a possession for your children after you, for them to inherit as property. These you may treat as slaves, but as for your fellow Israelites, no one shall rule over the other with harshness.

## MARK 10.13–31

PEOPLE were bringing little children to him in order that he might touch them; and the disciples spoke sternly to them. [14]But when Jesus saw this, he was indignant and said to them, "Let the little children come to me; do not stop them; for it is to such as these that the kingdom of God belongs. [15]Truly I tell you, whoever does not receive the kingdom of God as a little child will never enter it." [16]And he took them up in his arms, laid his hands on them, and blessed them.

a Meaning of Heb uncertain

17  As he was setting out on a journey, a man ran up and knelt before him, and asked him, "Good Teacher, what must I do to inherit eternal life?" 18Jesus said to him, "Why do you call me good? No one is good but God alone. 19You know the commandments: 'You shall not murder; You shall not commit adultery; You shall not steal; You shall not bear false witness; You shall not defraud; Honor your father and mother.'" 20He said to him, "Teacher, I have kept all these since my youth." 21Jesus, looking at him, loved him and said, "You lack one thing; go, sell what you own, and give the money[a] to the poor, and you will have treasure in heaven; then come, follow me." 22When he heard this, he was shocked and went away grieving, for he had many possessions.

23  Then Jesus looked around and said to his disciples, "How hard it will be for those who have wealth to enter the kingdom of God!" 24And the disciples were perplexed at these words. But Jesus said to them again, "Children, how hard it is[b] to enter the kingdom of God! 25It is easier for a camel to go through the eye of a needle than for someone who is rich to enter the kingdom of God." 26They were greatly astounded and said to one another,[c] "Then who can be saved?" 27Jesus looked at them and said, "For mortals it is impossible, but not for God; for God all things are possible."

28  Peter began to say to him, "Look, we have left everything and followed you." 29Jesus said, "Truly I tell you, there is no one who has left house or brothers or sisters or mother or father or children or fields, for my sake and for the sake of the good news,[d] 30who will not receive a hundredfold now in this age—houses, brothers and sisters, mothers and children, and fields with persecutions—and in the age to come eternal life. 31But many who are first will be last, and the last will be first."

## PSALM 44.9–26

YET you have rejected us and
      abased us,
   and have not gone out with
      our armies.
10   You made us turn back from
         the foe,
      and our enemies have gotten
         spoil.
11   You have made us like sheep for
         slaughter,
      and have scattered us among
         the nations.
12   You have sold your people for a
         trifle,
      demanding no high price for
         them.

13   You have made us the taunt of
         our neighbors,
      the derision and scorn of
         those around us.
14   You have made us a byword
         among the nations,
      a laughingstock[e] among the
         peoples.
15   All day long my disgrace is
         before me,
      and shame has covered my
         face
16   at the words of the taunters and
         revilers,
      at the sight of the enemy and
         the avenger.

17   All this has come upon us,
      yet we have not forgotten
         you,
      or been false to your
         covenant.
18   Our heart has not turned back,
      nor have our steps departed
         from your way,

---

a Gk lacks *the money*   b Other ancient authorities add *for those who trust in riches*   c Other ancient authorities read *to him*   d Or *gospel*   e Heb *a shaking of the head*

19 yet you have broken us in the
      haunt of jackals,
   and covered us with deep
      darkness.

20 If we had forgotten the name of
      our God,
   or spread out our hands to a
      strange god,
21 would not God discover this?
   For he knows the secrets of
      the heart.
22 Because of you we are being
      killed all day long,
   and accounted as sheep for
      the slaughter.

23 Rouse yourself! Why do you
      sleep, O Lord?
   Awake, do not cast us off
      forever!
24 Why do you hide your face?
   Why do you forget our
      affliction and oppression?
25 For we sink down to the dust;
   our bodies cling to the
      ground.
26 Rise up, come to our help.
   Redeem us for the sake of
      your steadfast love.

## PROVERBS 10.20–21

THE tongue of the righteous is
      choice silver;
   the mind of the wicked is of
      little worth.
21 The lips of the righteous feed
      many,
   but fools die for lack of sense.

# MARCH 2

## LEVITICUS 25.47—27.13

IF resident aliens among you prosper, and if any of your kin fall into difficulty with one of them and sell themselves to an alien, or to a branch of the alien's family, 48after they have sold themselves they shall have the right of redemption; one of their brothers may redeem them, 49or their uncle or their uncle's son may redeem them, or anyone of their family who is of their own flesh may redeem them; or if they prosper they may redeem themselves. 50They shall compute with the purchaser the total from the year when they sold themselves to the alien until the jubilee year; the price of the sale shall be applied to the number of years: the time they were with the owner shall be rated as the time of a hired laborer. 51If many years remain, they shall pay for their redemption in proportion to the purchase price; 52and if few years remain until the jubilee year, they shall compute thus: according to the years involved they shall make payment for their redemption. 53As a laborer hired by the year they shall be under the alien's authority, who shall not, however, rule with harshness over them in your sight. 54And if they have not been redeemed in any of these ways, they and their children with them shall go free in the jubilee year. 55For to me the people of Israel are servants; they are my servants whom I brought out from the land of Egypt: I am the LORD your God.

26.1 You shall make for yourselves no idols and erect no carved images or pillars, and you shall not place figured stones in your land, to worship at them; for I am the LORD your God. 2You shall keep my sabbaths and reverence my sanctuary: I am the LORD.

3 If you follow my statutes and keep my commandments and observe them faithfully, 4I will give you your rains in their season, and the land shall yield its produce, and the trees of the field shall yield their fruit. 5Your threshing shall overtake the vintage, and the vintage shall overtake the sowing; you shall eat your bread to the full, and live securely in your land. 6And I will grant peace in the land, and you shall lie down, and no one shall make you afraid; I will remove dangerous animals from the land, and no sword shall go through your land. 7You shall give chase to your enemies, and they shall fall before you by the sword. 8Five of you shall give chase to a hundred, and a hundred of you shall give chase to ten thousand; your enemies shall fall before you by the sword. 9I will look with favor upon you and make you fruitful and multiply you; and I will maintain my covenant with you. 10You shall eat old grain long stored, and you shall have to clear out the old to make way for the new. 11I will place my dwelling in your midst, and I shall not abhor you. 12And I will walk among you, and will be your God, and you shall be my people. 13I am the LORD your God who brought you out of the land of Egypt, to be their slaves no more; I have broken the bars of your yoke and made you walk erect.

14 But if you will not obey me, and do not observe all these commandments, 15if you spurn my statutes, and abhor my ordinances, so that you will not observe all my commandments, and you break my covenant, 16I in turn will do this to you: I will bring terror on you; consumption and fever that waste the eyes and cause life to pine away.

You shall sow your seed in vain, for your enemies shall eat it. 17I will set my face against you, and you shall be struck down by your enemies; your foes shall rule over you, and you shall flee though no one pursues you. 18And if in spite of this you will not obey me, I will continue to punish you sevenfold for your sins. 19I will break your proud glory, and I will make your sky like iron and your earth like copper. 20Your strength shall be spent to no purpose: your land shall not yield its produce, and the trees of the land shall not yield their fruit.

21 If you continue hostile to me, and will not obey me, I will continue to plague you sevenfold for your sins. 22I will let loose wild animals against you, and they shall bereave you of your children and destroy your livestock; they shall make you few in number, and your roads shall be deserted.

23 If in spite of these punishments you have not turned back to me, but continue hostile to me, 24then I too will continue hostile to you: I myself will strike you sevenfold for your sins. 25I will bring the sword against you, executing vengeance for the covenant; and if you withdraw within your cities, I will send pestilence among you, and you shall be delivered into enemy hands. 26When I break your staff of bread, ten women shall bake your bread in a single oven, and they shall dole out your bread by weight; and though you eat, you shall not be satisfied.

27 But if, despite this, you disobey me, and continue hostile to me, 28I will continue hostile to you in fury; I in turn will punish you myself sevenfold for your sins. 29You shall eat the flesh of your sons, and you shall eat the flesh of your daughters. 30I will destroy your high places and cut down your incense altars; I will heap your carcasses on the carcasses of your idols. I will abhor you. 31I will lay your cities waste, will make your sanctuaries desolate, and I

will not smell your pleasing odors. ³²I will devastate the land, so that your enemies who come to settle in it shall be appalled at it. ³³And you I will scatter among the nations, and I will unsheathe the sword against you; your land shall be a desolation, and your cities a waste.

34 Then the land shall enjoyᵃ its sabbath years as long as it lies desolate, while you are in the land of your enemies; then the land shall rest, and enjoyᵃ its sabbath years. ³⁵As long as it lies desolate, it shall have the rest it did not have on your sabbaths when you were living on it. ³⁶And as for those of you who survive, I will send faintness into their hearts in the lands of their enemies; the sound of a driven leaf shall put them to flight, and they shall flee as one flees from the sword, and they shall fall though no one pursues. ³⁷They shall stumble over one another, as if to escape a sword, though no one pursues; and you shall have no power to stand against your enemies. ³⁸You shall perish among the nations, and the land of your enemies shall devour you. ³⁹And those of you who survive shall languish in the land of your enemies because of their iniquities; also they shall languish because of the iniquities of their ancestors.

40 But if they confess their iniquity and the iniquity of their ancestors, in that they committed treachery against me and, moreover, that they continued hostile to me— ⁴¹so that I, in turn, continued hostile to them and brought them into the land of their enemies; if then their uncircumcised heart is humbled and they make amends for their iniquity, ⁴²then will I remember my covenant with Jacob; I will remember also my covenant with Isaac and also my covenant with Abraham, and I will remember the land. ⁴³For the land shall be deserted by them, and enjoyᵃ its sabbath years by lying desolate without

them, while they shall make amends for their iniquity, because they dared to spurn my ordinances, and they abhorred my statutes. ⁴⁴Yet for all that, when they are in the land of their enemies, I will not spurn them, or abhor them so as to destroy them utterly and break my covenant with them; for I am the LORD their God; ⁴⁵but I will remember in their favor the covenant with their ancestors whom I brought out of the land of Egypt in the sight of the nations, to be their God: I am the LORD.

46 These are the statutes and ordinances and laws that the LORD established between himself and the people of Israel on Mount Sinai through Moses.

27.1 THE LORD spoke to Moses, saying: ²Speak to the people of Israel and say to them: When a person makes an explicit vow to the LORD concerning the equivalent for a human being, ³the equivalent for a male shall be: from twenty to sixty years of age the equivalent shall be fifty shekels of silver by the sanctuary shekel. ⁴If the person is a female, the equivalent is thirty shekels. ⁵If the age is from five to twenty years of age, the equivalent is twenty shekels for a male and ten shekels for a female. ⁶If the age is from one month to five years, the equivalent for a male is five shekels of silver, and for a female the equivalent is three shekels of silver. ⁷And if the person is sixty years old or over, then the equivalent for a male is fifteen shekels, and for a female ten shekels. ⁸If any cannot afford the equivalent, they shall be brought before the priest and the priest shall assess them; the priest shall assess them according to what each one making a vow can afford.

9 If it concerns an animal that may be brought as an offering to the LORD,

<hr>

ᵃOr *make up for*

any such that may be given to the Lord shall be holy. [10]Another shall not be exchanged or substituted for it, either good for bad or bad for good; and if one animal is substituted for another, both that one and its substitute shall be holy. [11]If it concerns any unclean animal that may not be brought as an offering to the Lord, the animal shall be presented before the priest. [12]The priest shall assess it: whether good or bad, according to the assessment of the priest, so it shall be. [13]But if it is to be redeemed, one-fifth must be added to the assessment.

## MARK 10.32–52

THEY [the disciples] were on the road, going up to Jerusalem, and Jesus was walking ahead of them; they were amazed, and those who followed were afraid. He took the twelve aside again and began to tell them what was to happen to him, [33]saying, "See, we are going up to Jerusalem, and the Son of Man will be handed over to the chief priests and the scribes, and they will condemn him to death; then they will hand him over to the Gentiles; [34]they will mock him, and spit upon him, and flog him, and kill him; and after three days he will rise again."

35 James and John, the sons of Zebedee, came forward to him and said to him, "Teacher, we want you to do for us whatever we ask of you." [36]And he said to them, "What is it you want me to do for you?" [37]And they said to him, "Grant us to sit, one at your right hand and one at your left, in your glory." [38]But Jesus said to them, "You do not know what you are asking. Are you able to drink the cup that I drink, or be baptized with the baptism that I am baptized with?" [39]They replied, "We are able." Then Jesus said to them, "The cup that I drink you will drink; and

with the baptism with which I am baptized, you will be baptized; [40]but to sit at my right hand or at my left is not mine to grant, but it is for those for whom it has been prepared."

41 When the ten heard this, they began to be angry with James and John. [42]So Jesus called them and said to them, "You know that among the Gentiles those whom they recognize as their rulers lord it over them, and their great ones are tyrants over them. [43]But it is not so among you; but whoever wishes to become great among you must be your servant, [44]and whoever wishes to be first among you must be slave of all. [45]For the Son of Man came not to be served but to serve, and to give his life a ransom for many."

46 They came to Jericho. As he and his disciples and a large crowd were leaving Jericho, Bartimaeus son of Timaeus, a blind beggar, was sitting by the roadside. [47]When he heard that it was Jesus of Nazareth, he began to shout out and say, "Jesus, Son of David, have mercy on me!" [48]Many sternly ordered him to be quiet, but he cried out even more loudly, "Son of David, have mercy on me!" [49]Jesus stood still and said, "Call him here." And they called the blind man, saying to him, "Take heart; get up, he is calling you." [50]So throwing off his cloak, he sprang up and came to Jesus. [51]Then Jesus said to him, "What do you want me to do for you?" The blind man said to him, "My teacher,[a] let me see again." [52]Jesus said to him, "Go; your faith has made you well." Immediately he regained his sight and followed him on the way.

[a]Aramaic *Rabbouni*

## PSALM 45.1–17

*To the leader: according to Lilies. Of the
Korahites. A Maskil. A love song.*

**M**Y heart overflows with a
    goodly theme;
    I address my verses to
      the king;
    my tongue is like the pen of a
      ready scribe.
2 You are the most handsome of
      men;
    grace is poured upon your
      lips;
    therefore God has blessed
      you forever.
3 Gird your sword on your thigh,
      O mighty one,
    in your glory and majesty.

4 In your majesty ride on
      victoriously
    for the cause of truth and to
      defend[a] the right;
    let your right hand teach you
      dread deeds.
5 Your arrows are sharp
    in the heart of the king's
      enemies;
    the peoples fall under you.

6 Your throne, O God,[b] endures
      forever and ever.
    Your royal scepter is a
      scepter of equity;
7   you love righteousness and
      hate wickedness.
    Therefore God, your God, has
      anointed you
    with the oil of gladness
      beyond your companions;
8   your robes are all fragrant
      with myrrh and aloes and
      cassia.
    From ivory palaces stringed
      instruments make you
      glad;

9   daughters of kings are among
      your ladies of honor;
    at your right hand stands the
      queen in gold of Ophir.

10 Hear, O daughter, consider and
      incline your ear;
    forget your people and your
      father's house,
11   and the king will desire your
      beauty.
    Since he is your lord, bow to
      him;
12   the people[c] of Tyre will seek
      your favor with gifts,
    the richest of the people
      13with all kinds of wealth.

The princess is decked in her
      chamber with gold-woven
      robes;[d]
14   in many-colored robes she is
      led to the king;
    behind her the virgins, her
      companions, follow.
15 With joy and gladness they are
      led along
    as they enter the palace of
      the king.

16 In the place of ancestors you,
      O king,[e] shall have
      sons;
    you will make them princes in
      all the earth.
17 I will cause your name to be
      celebrated in all
      generations;
    therefore the peoples will
      praise you forever and
      ever.

---

a Cn: Heb *and the meekness of*  b Or *Your throne is a throne of God, it*  c Heb *daughter*  d Or *people.*
*13All glorious is the princess within, gold embroidery is her clothing*  e Heb lacks *O king*

PROVERBS 10.22

THE blessing of the LORD makes
      rich,
    and he adds no sorrow with
      it. [a]

# MARCH 3

## LEVITICUS 27.14—
## NUMBERS 1.54

IF a person consecrates a house to the LORD, the priest shall assess it: whether good or bad, as the priest assesses it, so it shall stand. 15And if the one who consecrates the house wishes to redeem it, one-fifth shall be added to its assessed value, and it shall revert to the original owner.

16  If a person consecrates to the LORD any inherited landholding, its assessment shall be in accordance with its seed requirements: fifty shekels of silver to a homer of barley seed. 17If the person consecrates the field as of the year of jubilee, that assessment shall stand; 18but if the field is consecrated after the jubilee, the priest shall compute the price for it according to the years that remain until the year of jubilee, and the assessment shall be reduced. 19And if the one who consecrates the field wishes to redeem it, then one-fifth shall be added to its assessed value, and it shall revert to the original owner; 20but if the field is not redeemed, or if it has been sold to someone else, it shall no longer be redeemable. 21But when the field is released in the jubilee, it shall be holy to the LORD as a devoted field; it becomes the priest's holding. 22If someone consecrates to the LORD a field that has been purchased, which is not a part of the inherited landholding, 23the priest shall compute for it the proportionate assessment up to the year of jubilee, and the assessment shall be paid as of that day, a sacred donation to the LORD. 24In the year of jubilee the field shall return to the one from whom it was bought, whose holding the land is. 25All assessments shall be by the sanctuary shekel: twenty gerahs shall make a shekel.

26  A firstling of animals, however, which as a firstling belongs to the LORD, cannot be consecrated by anyone; whether ox or sheep, it is the LORD's. 27If it is an unclean animal, it shall be ransomed at its assessment, with one-fifth added; if it is not redeemed, it shall be sold at its assessment.

28  Nothing that a person owns that has been devoted to destruction for the LORD, be it human or animal, or inherited landholding, may be sold or redeemed; every devoted thing is most holy to the LORD. 29No human beings who have been devoted to destruction can be ransomed; they shall be put to death.

30  All tithes from the land, whether the seed from the ground or the fruit from the tree, are the LORD's; they are holy to the LORD. 31If persons wish to redeem any of their tithes, they must

a Or *and toil adds nothing to it*

add one-fifth to them. ³²All tithes of herd and flock, every tenth one that passes under the shepherd's staff, shall be holy to the LORD. ³³Let no one inquire whether it is good or bad, or make substitution for it; if one makes substitution for it, then both it and the substitute shall be holy and cannot be redeemed.

34 These are the commandments that the LORD gave to Moses for the people of Israel on Mount Sinai.

1.1 THE LORD spoke to Moses in the wilderness of Sinai, in the tent of meeting, on the first day of the second month, in the second year after they had come out of the land of Egypt, saying: ²Take a census of the whole congregation of Israelites, in their clans, by ancestral houses, according to the number of names, every male individually; ³from twenty years old and upward, everyone in Israel able to go to war. You and Aaron shall enroll them, company by company. ⁴A man from each tribe shall be with you, each man the head of his ancestral house. ⁵These are the names of the men who shall assist you:

From Reuben, Elizur son of
    Shedeur.
6  From Simeon, Shelumiel son of
    Zurishaddai.
7  From Judah, Nahshon son of
    Amminadab.
8  From Issachar, Nethanel son of
    Zuar.
9  From Zebulun, Eliab son of
    Helon.
10  From the sons of Joseph:
  from Ephraim, Elishama son of
    Ammihud;
  from Manasseh, Gamaliel son of
    Pedahzur.
11  From Benjamin, Abidan son of
    Gideoni.
12  From Dan, Ahiezer son of
    Ammishaddai.
13  From Asher, Pagiel son of
    Ochran.
14  From Gad, Eliasaph son of
    Deuel.
15  From Naphtali, Ahira son of
    Enan.

¹⁶These were the ones chosen from the congregation, the leaders of their ancestral tribes, the heads of the divisions of Israel.

17 Moses and Aaron took these men who had been designated by name, ¹⁸and on the first day of the second month they assembled the whole congregation together. They registered themselves in their clans, by their ancestral houses, according to the number of names from twenty years old and upward, individually, ¹⁹as the LORD commanded Moses. So he enrolled them in the wilderness of Sinai.

20 The descendants of Reuben, Israel's firstborn, their lineage, in their clans, by their ancestral houses, according to the number of names, individually, every male from twenty years old and upward, everyone able to go to war: ²¹those enrolled of the tribe of Reuben were forty-six thousand five hundred.

22 The descendants of Simeon, their lineage, in their clans, by their ancestral houses, those of them that were numbered, according to the number of names, individually, every male from twenty years old and upward, everyone able to go to war: ²³those enrolled of the tribe of Simeon were fifty-nine thousand three hundred.

24 The descendants of Gad, their lineage, in their clans, by their ancestral houses, according to the number of the names, from twenty years old and upward, everyone able to go to war: ²⁵those enrolled of the tribe of Gad were forty-five thousand six hundred fifty.

26 The descendants of Judah, their lineage, in their clans, by their ancestral houses, according to the number of names, from twenty years old and upward, everyone able to go to war:

27those enrolled of the tribe of Judah were seventy-four thousand six hundred.

28 The descendants of Issachar, their lineage, in their clans, by their ancestral houses, according to the number of names, from twenty years old and upward, everyone able to go to war: 29those enrolled of the tribe of Issachar were fifty-four thousand four hundred.

30 The descendants of Zebulun, their lineage, in their clans, by their ancestral houses, according to the number of names, from twenty years old and upward, everyone able to go to war: 31those enrolled of the tribe of Zebulun were fifty-seven thousand four hundred.

32 The descendants of Joseph, namely, the descendants of Ephraim, their lineage, in their clans, by their ancestral houses, according to the number of names, from twenty years old and upward, everyone able to go to war: 33those enrolled of the tribe of Ephraim were forty thousand five hundred.

34 The descendants of Manasseh, their lineage, in their clans, by their ancestral houses, according to the number of names, from twenty years old and upward, everyone able to go to war: 35those enrolled of the tribe of Manasseh were thirty-two thousand two hundred.

36 The descendants of Benjamin, their lineage, in their clans, by their ancestral houses, according to the number of names, from twenty years old and upward, everyone able to go to war: 37those enrolled of the tribe of Benjamin were thirty-five thousand four hundred.

38 The descendants of Dan, their lineage, in their clans, by their ancestral houses, according to the number of names, from twenty years old and upward, everyone able to go to war: 39those enrolled of the tribe of Dan were sixty-two thousand seven hundred.

40 The descendants of Asher, their lineage, in their clans, by their ancestral houses, according to the number of names, from twenty years old and upward, everyone able to go to war: 41those enrolled of the tribe of Asher were forty-one thousand five hundred.

42 The descendants of Naphtali, their lineage, in their clans, by their ancestral houses, according to the number of names, from twenty years old and upward, everyone able to go to war: 43those enrolled of the tribe of Naphtali were fifty-three thousand four hundred.

44 These are those who were enrolled, whom Moses and Aaron enrolled with the help of the leaders of Israel, twelve men, each representing his ancestral house. 45So the whole number of the Israelites, by their ancestral houses, from twenty years old and upward, everyone able to go to war in Israel— 46their whole number was six hundred three thousand five hundred fifty. 47The Levites, however, were not numbered by their ancestral tribe along with them.

48 The Lord had said to Moses: 49Only the tribe of Levi you shall not enroll, and you shall not take a census of them with the other Israelites. 50Rather you shall appoint the Levites over the tabernacle of the covenant, a and over all its equipment, and over all that belongs to it; they are to carry the tabernacle and all its equipment, and they shall tend it, and shall camp around the tabernacle. 51When the tabernacle is to set out, the Levites shall take it down; and when the tabernacle is to be pitched, the Levites shall set it up. And any outsider who comes near shall be put to death. 52The other Israelites

a Or *treaty*, or *testimony*; Heb *eduth*

shall camp in their respective regimental camps, by companies; ⁵³but the Levites shall camp around the tabernacle of the covenant, ᵃ that there may be no wrath on the congregation of the Israelites; and the Levites shall perform the guard duty of the tabernacle of the covenant. ᵃ ⁵⁴The Israelites did so; they did just as the Lᴏʀᴅ commanded Moses.

# MARK 11.1–26

WHEN they [Jesus and his disciples] were approaching Jerusalem, at Bethphage and Bethany, near the Mount of Olives, he sent two of his disciples ²and said to them, "Go into the village ahead of you, and immediately as you enter it, you will find tied there a colt that has never been ridden; untie it and bring it. ³If anyone says to you, 'Why are you doing this?' just say this, 'The Lord needs it and will send it back here immediately.'" ⁴They went away and found a colt tied near a door, outside in the street. As they were untying it, ⁵some of the bystanders said to them, "What are you doing, untying the colt?" ⁶They told them what Jesus had said; and they allowed them to take it. ⁷Then they brought the colt to Jesus and threw their cloaks on it; and he sat on it. ⁸Many people spread their cloaks on the road, and others spread leafy branches that they had cut in the fields. ⁹Then those who went ahead and those who followed were shouting,

"Hosanna!
    Blessed is the one who
        comes in the name of the
        Lord!
10    Blessed is the coming
        kingdom of our ancestor
        David!
    Hosanna in the highest heaven!"

11  Then he entered Jerusalem and went into the temple; and when he had looked around at everything, as it was already late, he went out to Bethany with the twelve.

12  On the following day, when they came from Bethany, he was hungry. ¹³Seeing in the distance a fig tree in leaf, he went to see whether perhaps he would find anything on it. When he came to it, he found nothing but leaves, for it was not the season for figs. ¹⁴He said to it, "May no one ever eat fruit from you again." And his disciples heard it.

15  Then they came to Jerusalem. And he entered the temple and began to drive out those who were selling and those who were buying in the temple, and he overturned the tables of the money changers and the seats of those who sold doves; ¹⁶and he would not allow anyone to carry anything through the temple. ¹⁷He was teaching and saying, "Is it not written,

'My house shall be called a
    house of prayer for all
    the nations'?
But you have made it a den
    of robbers.'"

¹⁸And when the chief priests and the scribes heard it, they kept looking for a way to kill him; for they were afraid of him, because the whole crowd was spellbound by his teaching. ¹⁹And when evening came, Jesus and his disciplesᵇ went out of the city.

20  In the morning as they passed by, they saw the fig tree withered away to its roots. ²¹Then Peter remembered and said to him, "Rabbi, look! The fig tree that you cursed has withered." ²²Jesus answered them, "Haveᶜ faith in God. ²³Truly I tell you, if you say to this mountain, 'Be taken up and thrown into the sea,' and if you do not doubt in your heart, but believe that what you say will come to pass, it will be done for you. ²⁴So I tell you, whatever you ask

ᵃOr *treaty,* or *testimony*; Heb *eduth*  ᵇGk *they*: other ancient authorities read *he*  ᶜOther ancient authorities read *"If you have*

for in prayer, believe that you have received[a] it, and it will be yours.

25 "Whenever you stand praying, forgive, if you have anything against anyone; so that your Father in heaven may also forgive you your trespasses."[b]

## PSALM 46.1–11

*To the leader. Of the Korahites. According to Alamoth. A Song.*

**G**OD is our refuge and strength,
    a very present[c] help in trouble.
2 Therefore we will not fear,
    though the earth should change,
    though the mountains shake in the heart of the sea;
3 though its waters roar and foam,
    though the mountains tremble with its tumult.    *Selah*

4 There is a river whose streams make glad the city of God,
    the holy habitation of the Most High.
5 God is in the midst of the city;[d] it shall not be moved;
    God will help it when the morning dawns.
6 The nations are in an uproar, the kingdoms totter;
    he utters his voice, the earth melts.
7 The LORD of hosts is with us;
    the God of Jacob is our refuge.[e]    *Selah*

8 Come, behold the works of the LORD;
    see what desolations he has brought on the earth.
9 He makes wars cease to the end of the earth;
    he breaks the bow, and shatters the spear;
    he burns the shields with fire.
10 "Be still, and know that I am God!
    I am exalted among the nations,
    I am exalted in the earth."
11 The LORD of hosts is with us;
    the God of Jacob is our refuge.[e]    *Selah*

## PROVERBS 10.23

**D**OING wrong is like sport to a fool,
    but wise conduct is pleasure to a person of understanding.

[a] Other ancient authorities read *are receiving*  [b] Other ancient authorities add verse 26, *"But if you do not forgive, neither will your Father in heaven forgive your trespasses."*  [c] Or *well proved*  [d] Heb *of it*  [e] Or *fortress*

## NUMBERS 2.1—3.51

THE LORD spoke to Moses and Aaron, saying: [2]The Israelites shall camp each in their respective regiments, under ensigns by their ancestral houses; they shall camp facing the tent of meeting on every side. [3]Those to camp on the east side toward the sunrise shall be of the regimental encampment of Judah by companies. The leader of the people of Judah shall be Nahshon son of Amminadab, [4]with a company as enrolled of seventy-four thousand six hundred. [5]Those to camp next to him shall be the tribe of Issachar. The leader of the Issacharites shall be Nethanel son of Zuar, [6]with a company as enrolled of fifty-four thousand four hundred. [7]Then the tribe of Zebulun: The leader of the Zebulunites shall be Eliab son of Helon, [8]with a company as enrolled of fifty-seven thousand four hundred. [9]The total enrollment of the camp of Judah, by companies, is one hundred eighty-six thousand four hundred. They shall set out first on the march.

10 On the south side shall be the regimental encampment of Reuben by companies. The leader of the Reubenites shall be Elizur son of Shedeur, [11]with a company as enrolled of forty-six thousand five hundred. [12]And those to camp next to him shall be the tribe of Simeon. The leader of the Simeonites shall be Shelumiel son of Zurishaddai, [13]with a company as enrolled of fifty-nine thousand three hundred. [14]Then the tribe of Gad: The leader of the Gadites shall be Eliasaph son of Reuel, [15]with a company as enrolled of forty-five thousand six hundred fifty. [16]The total enrollment of the camp of Reuben, by companies, is one hundred fifty-one thousand four hundred fifty. They shall set out second.

17 The tent of meeting, with the camp of the Levites, shall set out in the center of the camps; they shall set out just as they camp, each in position, by their regiments.

18 On the west side shall be the regimental encampment of Ephraim by companies. The leader of the people of Ephraim shall be Elishama son of Ammihud, [19]with a company as enrolled of forty thousand five hundred. [20]Next to him shall be the tribe of Manasseh. The leader of the people of Manasseh shall be Gamaliel son of Pedahzur, [21]with a company as enrolled of thirty-two thousand two hundred. [22]Then the tribe of Benjamin: The leader of the Benjaminites shall be Abidan son of Gideoni, [23]with a company as enrolled of thirty-five thousand four hundred. [24]The total enrollment of the camp of Ephraim, by companies, is one hundred eight thousand one hundred. They shall set out third on the march.

25 On the north side shall be the regimental encampment of Dan by companies. The leader of the Danites shall be Ahiezer son of Ammishaddai, [26]with a company as enrolled of sixty-two thousand seven hundred. [27]Those to camp next to him shall be the tribe of Asher. The leader of the Asherites shall be Pagiel son of Ochran, [28]with a company as enrolled of forty-one thousand five hundred. [29]Then the tribe of Naphtali: The leader of the Naphtalites shall be Ahira son of Enan, [30]with a company as enrolled of fifty-three thousand four hundred. [31]The total enrollment of the camp of Dan is one hundred fifty-seven thousand six hundred. They

shall set out last, by companies. [a]

32  This was the enrollment of the Israelites by their ancestral houses; the total enrollment in the camps by their companies was six hundred three thousand five hundred fifty. [33]Just as the Lord had commanded Moses, the Levites were not enrolled among the other Israelites.

34  The Israelites did just as the Lord had commanded Moses: They camped by regiments, and they set out the same way, everyone by clans, according to ancestral houses.

3.1  THIS is the lineage of Aaron and Moses at the time when the Lord spoke with Moses on Mount Sinai. [2]These are the names of the sons of Aaron: Nadab the firstborn, and Abihu, Eleazar, and Ithamar; [3]these are the names of the sons of Aaron, the anointed priests, whom he ordained to minister as priests. [4]Nadab and Abihu died before the Lord when they offered illicit fire before the Lord in the wilderness of Sinai, and they had no children. Eleazar and Ithamar served as priests in the lifetime of their father Aaron.

5  Then the Lord spoke to Moses, saying: [6]Bring the tribe of Levi near, and set them before Aaron the priest, so that they may assist him. [7]They shall perform duties for him and for the whole congregation in front of the tent of meeting, doing service at the tabernacle; [8]they shall be in charge of all the furnishings of the tent of meeting, and attend to the duties for the Israelites as they do service at the tabernacle. [9]You shall give the Levites to Aaron and his descendants; they are unreservedly given to him from among the Israelites. [10]But you shall make a register of Aaron and his descendants; it is they who shall attend to the priesthood, and

any outsider who comes near shall be put to death.

11  Then the Lord spoke to Moses, saying: [12]I hereby accept the Levites from among the Israelites as substitutes for all the firstborn that open the womb among the Israelites. The Levites shall be mine, [13]for all the firstborn are mine; when I killed all the firstborn in the land of Egypt, I consecrated for my own all the firstborn in Israel, both human and animal; they shall be mine. I am the Lord.

14  Then the Lord spoke to Moses in the wilderness of Sinai, saying: [15]Enroll the Levites by ancestral houses and by clans. You shall enroll every male from a month old and upward. [16]So Moses enrolled them according to the word of the Lord, as he was commanded. [17]The following were the sons of Levi, by their names: Gershon, Kohath, and Merari. [18]These are the names of the sons of Gershon by their clans: Libni and Shimei. [19]The sons of Kohath by their clans: Amram, Izhar, Hebron, and Uzziel. [20]The sons of Merari by their clans: Mahli and Mushi. These are the clans of the Levites, by their ancestral houses.

21  To Gershon belonged the clan of the Libnites and the clan of the Shimeites; these were the clans of the Gershonites. [22]Their enrollment, counting all the males from a month old and upward, was seven thousand five hundred. [23]The clans of the Gershonites were to camp behind the tabernacle on the west, [24]with Eliasaph son of Lael as head of the ancestral house of the Gershonites. [25]The responsibility of the sons of Gershon in the tent of meeting was to be the tabernacle, the tent with its covering, the screen for the entrance of the tent of meeting, [26]the hangings of the court, the screen for the entrance of the court that is around the tabernacle and the altar, and its

a Compare verses 9, 16, 24: Heb *by their regiments*

cords—all the service pertaining to these.

27  To Kohath belonged the clan of the Amramites, the clan of the Izharites, the clan of the Hebronites, and the clan of the Uzzielites; these are the clans of the Kohathites. <sup>28</sup>Counting all the males, from a month old and upward, there were eight thousand six hundred, attending to the duties of the sanctuary. <sup>29</sup>The clans of the Kohathites were to camp on the south side of the tabernacle, <sup>30</sup>with Elizaphan son of Uzziel as head of the ancestral house of the clans of the Kohathites. <sup>31</sup>Their responsibility was to be the ark, the table, the lampstand, the altars, the vessels of the sanctuary with which the priests minister, and the screen—all the service pertaining to these. <sup>32</sup>Eleazar son of Aaron the priest was to be chief over the leaders of the Levites, and to have oversight of those who had charge of the sanctuary.

33  To Merari belonged the clan of the Mahlites and the clan of the Mushites: these are the clans of Merari. <sup>34</sup>Their enrollment, counting all the males from a month old and upward, was six thousand two hundred. <sup>35</sup>The head of the ancestral house of the clans of Merari was Zuriel son of Abihail; they were to camp on the north side of the tabernacle. <sup>36</sup>The responsibility assigned to the sons of Merari was to be the frames of the tabernacle, the bars, the pillars, the bases, and all their accessories—all the service pertaining to these; <sup>37</sup>also the pillars of the court all around, with their bases and pegs and cords.

38  Those who were to camp in front of the tabernacle on the east—in front of the tent of meeting toward the east—were Moses and Aaron and Aaron's sons, having charge of the rites within the sanctuary, whatever had to be done for the Israelites; and any outsider who came near was to be put to death. <sup>39</sup>The total enrollment of the Levites whom Moses and Aaron enrolled at the commandment of the LORD, by their clans, all the males from a month old and upward, was twenty-two thousand.

40  Then the LORD said to Moses: Enroll all the firstborn males of the Israelites, from a month old and upward, and count their names. <sup>41</sup>But you shall accept the Levites for me—I am the LORD—as substitutes for all the firstborn among the Israelites, and the livestock of the Levites as substitutes for all the firstborn among the livestock of the Israelites. <sup>42</sup>So Moses enrolled all the firstborn among the Israelites, as the LORD commanded him. <sup>43</sup>The total enrollment, all the firstborn males from a month old and upward, counting the number of names, was twenty-two thousand two hundred seventy-three.

44  Then the LORD spoke to Moses, saying: <sup>45</sup>Accept the Levites as substitutes for all the firstborn among the Israelites, and the livestock of the Levites as substitutes for their livestock; and the Levites shall be mine. I am the LORD. <sup>46</sup>As the price of redemption of the two hundred seventy-three of the firstborn of the Israelites, over and above the number of the Levites, <sup>47</sup>you shall accept five shekels apiece, reckoning by the shekel of the sanctuary, a shekel of twenty gerahs. <sup>48</sup>Give to Aaron and his sons the money by which the excess number of them is redeemed. <sup>49</sup>So Moses took the redemption money from those who were over and above those redeemed by the Levites; <sup>50</sup>from the firstborn of the Israelites he took the money, one thousand three hundred sixty-five shekels, reckoned by the shekel of the sanctuary; <sup>51</sup>and Moses gave the redemption money to Aaron and his sons, according to the word of the LORD, as the LORD had commanded Moses.

## MARK 11.27—12.17

**A**GAIN they [Jesus and his disciples] came to Jerusalem. As he was walking in the temple, the chief priests, the scribes, and the elders came to him [28]and said, "By what authority are you doing these things? Who gave you this authority to do them?" [29]Jesus said to them, "I will ask you one question; answer me, and I will tell you by what authority I do these things. [30]Did the baptism of John come from heaven, or was it of human origin? Answer me." [31]They argued with one another, "If we say, 'From heaven,' he will say, 'Why then did you not believe him?' [32]But shall we say, 'Of human origin'?"—they were afraid of the crowd, for all regarded John as truly a prophet. [33]So they answered Jesus, "We do not know." And Jesus said to them, "Neither will I tell you by what authority I am doing these things."

**12.1** THEN he began to speak to them in parables. "A man planted a vineyard, put a fence around it, dug a pit for the wine press, and built a watchtower; then he leased it to tenants and went to another country. [2]When the season came, he sent a slave to the tenants to collect from them his share of the produce of the vineyard. [3]But they seized him, and beat him, and sent him away empty-handed. [4]And again he sent another slave to them; this one they beat over the head and insulted. [5]Then he sent another, and that one they killed. And so it was with many others; some they beat, and others they killed. [6]He had still one other, a beloved son. Finally he sent him to them, saying, 'They will respect my son.' [7]But those tenants said to one another, 'This is the heir; come, let us kill him, and the inheritance will be ours.' [8]So they seized him, killed him, and threw him out of the vineyard. [9]What then will the owner of the vineyard do? He will come and destroy the tenants and give the vineyard to others. [10]Have you not read this scripture:

'The stone that the builders rejected
has become the cornerstone; [a]
[11]   this was the Lord's doing,
and it is amazing in our eyes'?"

12   When they realized that he had told this parable against them, they wanted to arrest him, but they feared the crowd. So they left him and went away.

13   Then they sent to him some Pharisees and some Herodians to trap him in what he said. [14]And they came and said to him, "Teacher, we know that you are sincere, and show deference to no one; for you do not regard people with partiality, but teach the way of God in accordance with truth. Is it lawful to pay taxes to the emperor, or not? [15]Should we pay them, or should we not?" But knowing their hypocrisy, he said to them, "Why are you putting me to the test? Bring me a denarius and let me see it." [16]And they brought one. Then he said to them, "Whose head is this, and whose title?" They answered, "The emperor's." [17]Jesus said to them, "Give to the emperor the things that are the emperor's, and to God the things that are God's." And they were utterly amazed at him.

## PSALM 47.1–9

*To the leader. Of the Korahites. A Psalm.*

**C**LAP your hands, all you peoples;
shout to God with loud songs of joy.
[2]   For the LORD, the Most High, is awesome,
a great king over all the earth.

a Or *keystone*

3 He subdued peoples under us,
    and nations under our feet.
4 He chose our heritage for us,
    the pride of Jacob whom he
        loves.        *Selah*

5 God has gone up with a shout,
    the Lord with the sound of a
        trumpet.
6 Sing praises to God, sing
        praises;
    sing praises to our King, sing
        praises.
7 For God is the king of all the
        earth;
    sing praises with a psalm. a

8 God is king over the nations;
    God sits on his holy throne.

9 The princes of the peoples
        gather
    as the people of the God of
        Abraham.
For the shields of the earth
    belong to God;
    he is highly exalted.

## PROVERBS 10.24–25

WHAT the wicked dread will come upon them, but the desire of the righteous will be granted. 25 When the tempest passes, the wicked are no more, but the righteous are established forever.

# MARCH 5

## NUMBERS 4.1—5.31

THE Lord spoke to Moses and Aaron, saying: 2Take a census of the Kohathites separate from the other Levites, by their clans and their ancestral houses, 3from thirty years old up to fifty years old, all who qualify to do work relating to the tent of meeting. 4The service of the Kohathites relating to the tent of meeting concerns the most holy things.

5 When the camp is to set out, Aaron and his sons shall go in and take down the screening curtain, and cover the ark of the covenant b with it; 6then they shall put on it a covering of fine leather, c and spread over that a cloth all of blue, and shall put its poles in place. 7Over the table of the bread of the Presence they shall spread a blue cloth, and put on it the plates, the dishes for incense, the bowls, and the flagons for the drink offering; the regular bread also shall be on it; 8then they shall spread over them a crimson cloth, and cover it with a covering of fine leather, c and shall put its poles in place. 9They shall take a blue cloth, and cover the lampstand for the light, with its lamps, its snuffers, its trays, and all the vessels for oil with which it is supplied; 10and they shall put it with all its utensils in a covering of fine leather, c and put it on the carrying frame. 11Over the golden altar they shall spread a blue cloth, and cover it with a covering of fine leather, c and shall put its poles in place; 12and they shall take all the utensils of the service that are used in the sanctuary, and put them in a blue cloth,

aHeb *Maskil*   bOr *treaty,* or *testimony*; Heb *eduth*   cMeaning of Heb uncertain and cover them with a covering of fine leather, a and put them on the carrying frame. [13]They shall take away the ashes from the altar, and spread a purple cloth over it; [14]and they shall put on it all the utensils of the altar, which are used for the service there, the firepans, the forks, the shovels, and the basins, all the utensils of the altar; and they shall spread on it a covering of fine leather, a and shall put its poles in place. [15]When Aaron and his sons have finished covering the sanctuary and all the furnishings of the sanctuary, as the camp sets out, after that the Kohathites shall come to carry these, but they must not touch the holy things, or they will die. These are the things of the tent of meeting that the Kohathites are to carry.

16   Eleazar son of Aaron the priest shall have charge of the oil for the light, the fragrant incense, the regular grain offering, and the anointing oil, the oversight of all the tabernacle and all that is in it, in the sanctuary and in its utensils.

17   Then the LORD spoke to Moses and Aaron, saying: [18]You must not let the tribe of the clans of the Kohathites be destroyed from among the Levites. [19]This is how you must deal with them in order that they may live and not die when they come near to the most holy things: Aaron and his sons shall go in and assign each to a particular task or burden. [20]But the Kohathites b must not go in to look on the holy things even for a moment; otherwise they will die.

21   Then the LORD spoke to Moses, saying: [22]Take a census of the Gershonites also, by their ancestral houses and by their clans; [23]from thirty years old up to fifty years old you shall enroll them, all who qualify to do work in the tent of meeting. [24]This is the service of the clans of the Gershonites, in serving and bearing burdens: [25]They shall carry the curtains of the tabernacle, and the tent of meeting with its covering, and the outer covering of fine leather a that is on top of it, and the screen for the entrance of the tent of meeting, [26]and the hangings of the court, and the screen for the entrance of the gate of the court that is around the tabernacle and the altar, and their cords, and all the equipment for their service; and they shall do all that needs to be done with regard to them. [27]All the service of the Gershonites shall be at the command of Aaron and his sons, in all that they are to carry, and in all that they have to do; and you shall assign to their charge all that they are to carry. [28]This is the service of the clans of the Gershonites relating to the tent of meeting, and their responsibilities are to be under the oversight of Ithamar son of Aaron the priest.

29   As for the Merarites, you shall enroll them by their clans and their ancestral houses; [30]from thirty years old up to fifty years old you shall enroll them, everyone who qualifies to do the work of the tent of meeting. [31]This is what they are charged to carry, as the whole of their service in the tent of meeting: the frames of the tabernacle, with its bars, pillars, and bases, [32]and the pillars of the court all around with their bases, pegs, and cords, with all their equipment and all their related service; and you shall assign by name the objects that they are required to carry. [33]This is the service of the clans of the Merarites, the whole of their service relating to the tent of meeting, under the hand of Ithamar son of Aaron the priest.

34   So Moses and Aaron and the leaders of the congregation enrolled the Kohathites, by their clans and their ancestral houses, [35]from thirty years old up to fifty years old, everyone who qualified for work relating to the tent of meeting; [36]and their enrollment by

a Meaning of Heb uncertain   b Heb *they*

clans was two thousand seven hundred fifty. <sup>37</sup>This was the enrollment of the clans of the Kohathites, all who served at the tent of meeting, whom Moses and Aaron enrolled according to the commandment of the LORD by Moses.

38 The enrollment of the Gershonites, by their clans and their ancestral houses, <sup>39</sup>from thirty years old up to fifty years old, everyone who qualified for work relating to the tent of meeting— <sup>40</sup>their enrollment by their clans and their ancestral houses was two thousand six hundred thirty. <sup>41</sup>This was the enrollment of the clans of the Gershonites, all who served at the tent of meeting, whom Moses and Aaron enrolled according to the commandment of the LORD.

42 The enrollment of the clans of the Merarites, by their clans and their ancestral houses, <sup>43</sup>from thirty years old up to fifty years old, everyone who qualified for work relating to the tent of meeting— <sup>44</sup>their enrollment by their clans was three thousand two hundred. <sup>45</sup>This is the enrollment of the clans of the Merarites, whom Moses and Aaron enrolled according to the commandment of the LORD by Moses.

46 All those who were enrolled of the Levites, whom Moses and Aaron and the leaders of Israel enrolled, by their clans and their ancestral houses, <sup>47</sup>from thirty years old up to fifty years old, everyone who qualified to do the work of service and the work of bearing burdens relating to the tent of meeting, <sup>48</sup>their enrollment was eight thousand five hundred eighty. <sup>49</sup>According to the commandment of the LORD through Moses they were appointed to their several tasks of serving or carrying; thus they were enrolled by him, as the LORD commanded Moses.

<sup>5.1</sup> THE LORD spoke to Moses, saying: <sup>2</sup>Command the Israelites to put out of the camp everyone who is leprous, [a] or has a discharge, and everyone who is unclean through contact with a corpse; <sup>3</sup>you shall put out both male and female, putting them outside the camp; they must not defile their camp, where I dwell among them. <sup>4</sup>The Israelites did so, putting them outside the camp; as the LORD had spoken to Moses, so the Israelites did.

5 The LORD spoke to Moses, saying: <sup>6</sup>Speak to the Israelites: When a man or a woman wrongs another, breaking faith with the LORD, that person incurs guilt <sup>7</sup>and shall confess the sin that has been committed. The person shall make full restitution for the wrong, adding one fifth to it, and giving it to the one who was wronged. <sup>8</sup>If the injured party has no next of kin to whom restitution may be made for the wrong, the restitution for wrong shall go to the LORD for the priest, in addition to the ram of atonement with which atonement is made for the guilty party. <sup>9</sup>Among all the sacred donations of the Israelites, every gift that they bring to the priest shall be his. <sup>10</sup>The sacred donations of all are their own; whatever anyone gives to the priest shall be his.

11 The LORD spoke to Moses, saying: <sup>12</sup>Speak to the Israelites and say to them: If any man's wife goes astray and is unfaithful to him, <sup>13</sup>if a man has had intercourse with her but it is hidden from her husband, so that she is undetected though she has defiled herself, and there is no witness against her since she was not caught in the act; <sup>14</sup>if a spirit of jealousy comes on him, and he is jealous of his wife who has defiled herself; or if a spirit of jealousy comes on him, and he is jealous of his wife, though she has not defiled herself; <sup>15</sup>then the man shall bring his wife to the priest. And he shall bring the offering required for her, one-tenth of an ephah of barley flour. He shall pour no

---

[a] A term for several skin diseases; precise meaning uncertain

oil on it and put no frankincense on it, for it is a grain offering of jealousy, a grain offering of remembrance, bringing iniquity to remembrance.

16 Then the priest shall bring her near, and set her before the LORD; [17]the priest shall take holy water in an earthen vessel, and take some of the dust that is on the floor of the tabernacle and put it into the water. [18]The priest shall set the woman before the LORD, dishevel the woman's hair, and place in her hands the grain offering of remembrance, which is the grain offering of jealousy. In his own hand the priest shall have the water of bitterness that brings the curse. [19]Then the priest shall make her take an oath, saying, "If no man has lain with you, if you have not turned aside to uncleanness while under your husband's authority, be immune to this water of bitterness that brings the curse. [20]But if you have gone astray while under your husband's authority, if you have defiled yourself and some man other than your husband has had intercourse with you," [21]—let the priest make the woman take the oath of the curse and say to the woman—"the LORD make you an execration and an oath among your people, when the LORD makes your uterus drop, your womb discharge; [22]now may this water that brings the curse enter your bowels and make your womb discharge, your uterus drop!" And the woman shall say, "Amen. Amen."

23 Then the priest shall put these curses in writing, and wash them off into the water of bitterness. [24]He shall make the woman drink the water of bitterness that brings the curse, and the water that brings the curse shall enter her and cause bitter pain. [25]The priest shall take the grain offering of jealousy out of the woman's hand, and shall elevate the grain offering before the LORD and bring it to the altar; [26]and the priest shall take a handful of the grain offering, as its memorial portion, and turn it into smoke on the altar, and afterward shall make the woman drink the water. [27]When he has made her drink the water, then, if she has defiled herself and has been unfaithful to her husband, the water that brings the curse shall enter into her and cause bitter pain, and her womb shall discharge, her uterus drop, and the woman shall become an execration among her people. [28]But if the woman has not defiled herself and is clean, then she shall be immune and be able to conceive children.

29 This is the law in cases of jealousy, when a wife, while under her husband's authority, goes astray and defiles herself, [30]or when a spirit of jealousy comes on a man and he is jealous of his wife; then he shall set the woman before the LORD, and the priest shall apply this entire law to her. [31]The man shall be free from iniquity, but the woman shall bear her iniquity.

## MARK 12.18–37

SOME Sadducees, who say there is no resurrection, came to him [Jesus] and asked him a question, saying, [19]"Teacher, Moses wrote for us that 'if a man's brother dies, leaving a wife but no child, the man[a] shall marry the widow and raise up children for his brother.' [20]There were seven brothers; the first married and, when he died, left no children; [21]and the second married her and died, leaving no children; and the third likewise; [22]none of the seven left children. Last of all the woman herself died. [23]In the resurrection[b] whose wife will she be? For the seven had married her."

24 Jesus said to them, "Is not this the reason you are wrong, that you know neither the scriptures nor the power of God? [25]For when they rise from the dead, they neither marry nor

[a]Gk *his brother*   [b]Other ancient authorities add *when they rise*

are given in marriage, but are like angels in heaven. <sup>26</sup>And as for the dead being raised, have you not read in the book of Moses, in the story about the bush, how God said to him, 'I am the God of Abraham, the God of Isaac, and the God of Jacob'? <sup>27</sup>He is God not of the dead, but of the living; you are quite wrong."

28 One of the scribes came near and heard them disputing with one another, and seeing that he answered them well, he asked him, "Which commandment is the first of all?" <sup>29</sup>Jesus answered, "The first is, 'Hear, O Israel: the Lord our God, the Lord is one; <sup>30</sup>you shall love the Lord your God with all your heart, and with all your soul, and with all your mind, and with all your strength.' <sup>31</sup>The second is this, 'You shall love your neighbor as yourself.' There is no other commandment greater than these." <sup>32</sup>Then the scribe said to him, "You are right, Teacher; you have truly said that 'he is one, and besides him there is no other'; <sup>33</sup>and 'to love him with all the heart, and with all the understanding, and with all the strength,' and 'to love one's neighbor as oneself,'—this is much more important than all whole burnt offerings and sacrifices." <sup>34</sup>When Jesus saw that he answered wisely, he said to him, "You are not far from the kingdom of God." After that no one dared to ask him any question.

35 While Jesus was teaching in the temple, he said, "How can the scribes say that the Messiah[a] is the son of David? <sup>36</sup>David himself, by the Holy Spirit, declared,

'The Lord said to my Lord,
"Sit at my right hand,
until I put your enemies
under your feet." '

<sup>37</sup>David himself calls him Lord; so how can he be his son?" And the large crowd was listening to him with delight.



## PSALM 48.1–14

*A Song. A Psalm of the Korahites.*

GREAT is the Lord and greatly
        to be praised
    in the city of our God.
His holy mountain, <sup>2</sup>beautiful in
        elevation,
    is the joy of all the earth,
Mount Zion, in the far north,
    the city of the great King.
3   Within its citadels God
        has shown himself a sure
            defense.

4   Then the kings assembled,
        they came on together.
5   As soon as they saw it, they
            were astounded;
        they were in panic, they took
            to flight;
6   trembling took hold of them
            there,
        pains as of a woman in labor,
7   as when an east wind shatters
        the ships of Tarshish.
8   As we have heard, so have we
            seen
        in the city of the Lord of
            hosts,
    in the city of our God,
        which God establishes
            forever.            *Selah*

9   We ponder your steadfast love,
            O God,
        in the midst of your temple.
10  Your name, O God, like your
            praise,
        reaches to the ends of the
            earth.
    Your right hand is filled with
            victory.
11      Let Mount Zion be glad,
        let the towns[b] of Judah rejoice
        because of your judgments.

12  Walk about Zion, go all around
        it,
      count its towers,
13  consider well its ramparts;
      go through its citadels,
    that you may tell the next
        generation
14    that this is God,

our God forever and ever.
He will be our guide forever.

## PROVERBS 10.26

Like vinegar to the teeth, and
        smoke to the eyes,
so are the lazy to their
    employers.

# MARCH 6

## NUMBERS 6.1—7.89

The Lord spoke to Moses, saying: [2]Speak to the Israelites and say to them: When either men or women make a special vow, the vow of a nazirite,[a] to separate themselves to the Lord, [3]they shall separate themselves from wine and strong drink; they shall drink no wine vinegar or other vinegar, and shall not drink any grape juice or eat grapes, fresh or dried. [4]All their days as nazirites[b] they shall eat nothing that is produced by the grapevine, not even the seeds or the skins.

5  All the days of their nazirite vow no razor shall come upon the head; until the time is completed for which they separate themselves to the Lord, they shall be holy; they shall let the locks of the head grow long.

6  All the days that they separate themselves to the Lord they shall not go near a corpse. [7]Even if their father or mother, brother or sister, should die, they may not defile themselves; because their consecration to God is upon the head. [8]All their days as nazirites[b] they are holy to the Lord.

9  If someone dies very suddenly nearby, defiling the consecrated head, then they shall shave the head on the day of their cleansing; on the seventh day they shall shave it. [10]On the eighth day they shall bring two turtledoves or two young pigeons to the priest at the entrance of the tent of meeting, [11]and the priest shall offer one as a sin offering and the other as a burnt offering, and make atonement for them, because they incurred guilt by reason of the corpse. They shall sanctify the head that same day, [12]and separate themselves to the Lord for their days as nazirites,[b] and bring a male lamb a year old as a guilt offering. The former time shall be void, because the consecrated head was defiled.

13  This is the law for the nazirites[b] when the time of their consecration has been completed: they shall be brought to the entrance of the tent of meeting, [14]and they shall offer their gift to the Lord, one male lamb a year old without blemish as a burnt offering, one ewe lamb a year old without blemish as a sin offering, one ram without blemish as an offering of well-being, [15]and a basket of unleavened bread, cakes of choice flour mixed with oil and unleavened wafers spread with oil, with their grain offering

aThat is *one separated* or *one consecrated*   bThat is *those separated* or *those consecrated*

and their drink offerings. <sup>16</sup>The priest shall present them before the Lord and offer their sin offering and burnt offering, <sup>17</sup>and shall offer the ram as a sacrifice of well-being to the Lord, with the basket of unleavened bread; the priest also shall make the accompanying grain offering and drink offering. <sup>18</sup>Then the nazirites[a] shall shave the consecrated head at the entrance of the tent of meeting, and shall take the hair from the consecrated head and put it on the fire under the sacrifice of well-being. <sup>19</sup>The priest shall take the shoulder of the ram, when it is boiled, and one unleavened cake out of the basket, and one unleavened wafer, and shall put them in the palms of the nazirites, [a] after they have shaved the consecrated head. <sup>20</sup>Then the priest shall elevate them as an elevation offering before the Lord; they are a holy portion for the priest, together with the breast that is elevated and the thigh that is offered. After that the nazirites[a] may drink wine.

21  This is the law for the nazirites[a] who take a vow. Their offering to the Lord must be in accordance with the nazirite[b] vow, apart from what else they can afford. In accordance with whatever vow they take, so they shall do, following the law for their consecration.

22  The Lord spoke to Moses, saying: <sup>23</sup>Speak to Aaron and his sons, saying, Thus you shall bless the Israelites: You shall say to them,

24  The Lord bless you and keep
        you;
25  the Lord make his face to shine
        upon you, and be
        gracious to you;
26  the Lord lift up his countenance
        upon you, and give you
        peace.
27  So they shall put my name on the Israelites, and I will bless them.

<sup>7.1</sup> On the day when Moses had finished setting up the tabernacle, and had anointed and consecrated it with all its furnishings, and had anointed and consecrated the altar with all its utensils, <sup>2</sup>the leaders of Israel, heads of their ancestral houses, the leaders of the tribes, who were over those who were enrolled, made offerings. <sup>3</sup>They brought their offerings before the Lord, six covered wagons and twelve oxen, a wagon for every two of the leaders, and for each one an ox; they presented them before the tabernacle. <sup>4</sup>Then the Lord said to Moses: <sup>5</sup>Accept these from them, that they may be used in doing the service of the tent of meeting, and give them to the Levites, to each according to his service. <sup>6</sup>So Moses took the wagons and the oxen, and gave them to the Levites. <sup>7</sup>Two wagons and four oxen he gave to the Gershonites, according to their service; <sup>8</sup>and four wagons and eight oxen he gave to the Merarites, according to their service, under the direction of Ithamar son of Aaron the priest. <sup>9</sup>But to the Kohathites he gave none, because they were charged with the care of the holy things that had to be carried on the shoulders.

10  The leaders also presented offerings for the dedication of the altar at the time when it was anointed; the leaders presented their offering before the altar. <sup>11</sup>The Lord said to Moses: They shall present their offerings, one leader each day, for the dedication of the altar.

12  The one who presented his offering the first day was Nahshon son of Amminadab, of the tribe of Judah; <sup>13</sup>his offering was one silver plate weighing one hundred thirty shekels, one silver basin weighing seventy shekels, according to the shekel of the sanctuary, both of them full of choice flour mixed with oil for a grain offering; <sup>14</sup>one

---

a That is *those separated* or *those consecrated*  b That is *one separated* or *one consecrated*

golden dish weighing ten shekels, full of incense; [15]one young bull, one ram, one male lamb a year old, for a burnt offering; [16]one male goat for a sin offering; [17]and for the sacrifice of well-being, two oxen, five rams, five male goats, and five male lambs a year old. This was the offering of Nahshon son of Amminadab.

18  On the second day Nethanel son of Zuar, the leader of Issachar, presented an offering; [19]he presented for his offering one silver plate weighing one hundred thirty shekels, one silver basin weighing seventy shekels, according to the shekel of the sanctuary, both of them full of choice flour mixed with oil for a grain offering; [20]one golden dish weighing ten shekels, full of incense; [21]one young bull, one ram, one male lamb a year old, as a burnt offering; [22]one male goat as a sin offering; [23]and for the sacrifice of well-being, two oxen, five rams, five male goats, and five male lambs a year old. This was the offering of Nethanel son of Zuar.

24  On the third day Eliab son of Helon, the leader of the Zebulunites: [25]his offering was one silver plate weighing one hundred thirty shekels, one silver basin weighing seventy shekels, according to the shekel of the sanctuary, both of them full of choice flour mixed with oil for a grain offering; [26]one golden dish weighing ten shekels, full of incense; [27]one young bull, one ram, one male lamb a year old, for a burnt offering; [28]one male goat for a sin offering; [29]and for the sacrifice of well-being, two oxen, five rams, five male goats, and five male lambs a year old. This was the offering of Eliab son of Helon.

30  On the fourth day Elizur son of Shedeur, the leader of the Reubenites: [31]his offering was one silver plate weighing one hundred thirty shekels, one silver basin weighing seventy shekels, according to the shekel of the sanctuary, both of them full of choice flour mixed with oil for a grain offering; [32]one golden dish weighing ten shekels, full of incense; [33]one young bull, one ram, one male lamb a year old, for a burnt offering; [34]one male goat for a sin offering; [35]and for the sacrifice of well-being, two oxen, five rams, five male goats, and five male lambs a year old. This was the offering of Elizur son of Shedeur.

36  On the fifth day Shelumiel son of Zurishaddai, the leader of the Simeonites: [37]his offering was one silver plate weighing one hundred thirty shekels, one silver basin weighing seventy shekels, according to the shekel of the sanctuary, both of them full of choice flour mixed with oil for a grain offering; [38]one golden dish weighing ten shekels, full of incense; [39]one young bull, one ram, one male lamb a year old, for a burnt offering; [40]one male goat for a sin offering; [41]and for the sacrifice of well-being, two oxen, five rams, five male goats, and five male lambs a year old. This was the offering of Shelumiel son of Zurishaddai.

42  On the sixth day Eliasaph son of Deuel, the leader of the Gadites: [43]his offering was one silver plate weighing one hundred thirty shekels, one silver basin weighing seventy shekels, according to the shekel of the sanctuary, both of them full of choice flour mixed with oil for a grain offering; [44]one golden dish weighing ten shekels, full of incense; [45]one young bull, one ram, one male lamb a year old, for a burnt offering; [46]one male goat for a sin offering; [47]and for the sacrifice of well-being, two oxen, five rams, five male goats, and five male lambs a year old. This was the offering of Eliasaph son of Deuel.

48  On the seventh day Elishama son of Ammihud, the leader of the Ephraimites: [49]his offering was one silver plate weighing one hundred thirty shekels, one silver basin weighing seventy shekels, according to the shekel of

the sanctuary, both of them full of choice flour mixed with oil for a grain offering; [50]one golden dish weighing ten shekels, full of incense; [51]one young bull, one ram, one male lamb a year old, for a burnt offering; [52]one male goat for a sin offering; [53]and for the sacrifice of well-being, two oxen, five rams, five male goats, and five male lambs a year old. This was the offering of Elishama son of Ammihud.

54  On the eighth day Gamaliel son of Pedahzur, the leader of the Manassites: [55]his offering was one silver plate weighing one hundred thirty shekels, one silver basin weighing seventy shekels, according to the shekel of the sanctuary, both of them full of choice flour mixed with oil for a grain offering; [56]one golden dish weighing ten shekels, full of incense; [57]one young bull, one ram, one male lamb a year old, for a burnt offering; [58]one male goat for a sin offering; [59]and for the sacrifice of well-being, two oxen, five rams, five male goats, and five male lambs a year old. This was the offering of Gamaliel son of Pedahzur.

60  On the ninth day Abidan son of Gideoni, the leader of the Benjaminites: [61]his offering was one silver plate weighing one hundred thirty shekels, one silver basin weighing seventy shekels, according to the shekel of the sanctuary, both of them full of choice flour mixed with oil for a grain offering; [62]one golden dish weighing ten shekels, full of incense; [63]one young bull, one ram, one male lamb a year old, for a burnt offering; [64]one male goat for a sin offering; [65]and for the sacrifice of well-being, two oxen, five rams, five male goats, and five male lambs a year old. This was the offering of Abidan son of Gideoni.

66  On the tenth day Ahiezer son of Ammishaddai, the leader of the Danites: [67]his offering was one silver plate weighing one hundred thirty shekels, one silver basin weighing seventy shekels, according to the shekel of the sanctuary, both of them full of choice flour mixed with oil for a grain offering; [68]one golden dish weighing ten shekels, full of incense; [69]one young bull, one ram, one male lamb a year old, for a burnt offering; [70]one male goat for a sin offering; [71]and for the sacrifice of well-being, two oxen, five rams, five male goats, and five male lambs a year old. This was the offering of Ahiezer son of Ammishaddai.

72  On the eleventh day Pagiel son of Ochran, the leader of the Asherites: [73]his offering was one silver plate weighing one hundred thirty shekels, one silver basin weighing seventy shekels, according to the shekel of the sanctuary, both of them full of choice flour mixed with oil for a grain offering; [74]one golden dish weighing ten shekels, full of incense; [75]one young bull, one ram, one male lamb a year old, for a burnt offering; [76]one male goat for a sin offering; [77]and for the sacrifice of well-being, two oxen, five rams, five male goats, and five male lambs a year old. This was the offering of Pagiel son of Ochran.

78  On the twelfth day Ahira son of Enan, the leader of the Naphtalites: [79]his offering was one silver plate weighing one hundred thirty shekels, one silver basin weighing seventy shekels, according to the shekel of the sanctuary, both of them full of choice flour mixed with oil for a grain offering; [80]one golden dish weighing ten shekels, full of incense; [81]one young bull, one ram, one male lamb a year old, for a burnt offering; [82]one male goat for a sin offering; [83]and for the sacrifice of well-being, two oxen, five rams, five male goats, and five male lambs a year old. This was the offering of Ahira son of Enan.

84  This was the dedication offering for the altar, at the time when it was anointed, from the leaders of Israel: twelve silver plates, twelve silver ba-

sins, twelve golden dishes, [85]each silver plate weighing one hundred thirty shekels and each basin seventy, all the silver of the vessels two thousand four hundred shekels according to the shekel of the sanctuary, [86]the twelve golden dishes, full of incense, weighing ten shekels apiece according to the shekel of the sanctuary, all the gold of the dishes being one hundred twenty shekels; [87]all the livestock for the burnt offering twelve bulls, twelve rams, twelve male lambs a year old, with their grain offering; and twelve male goats for a sin offering; [88]and all the livestock for the sacrifice of well-being twenty-four bulls, the rams sixty, the male goats sixty, the male lambs a year old sixty. This was the dedication offering for the altar, after it was anointed.

89   When Moses went into the tent of meeting to speak with the LORD, [a] he would hear the voice speaking to him from above the mercy seat[b] that was on the ark of the covenant[c] from between the two cherubim; thus it spoke to him.

# MARK 12.38—13.13

As he [Jesus] taught, he said, "Beware of the scribes, who like to walk around in long robes, and to be greeted with respect in the marketplaces, [39]and to have the best seats in the synagogues and places of honor at banquets! [40]They devour widows' houses and for the sake of appearance say long prayers. They will receive the greater condemnation."

41   He sat down opposite the treasury, and watched the crowd putting money into the treasury. Many rich people put in large sums. [42]A poor widow came and put in two small copper coins, which are worth a penny. [43]Then he called his disciples and said to them, "Truly I tell you, this poor widow has put in more than all those who are contributing to the treasury. [44]For all of them have contributed out of their abundance; but she out of her poverty has put in everything she had, all she had to live on."

[13.1] As he came out of the temple, one of his disciples said to him, "Look, Teacher, what large stones and what large buildings!" [2]Then Jesus asked him, "Do you see these great buildings? Not one stone will be left here upon another; all will be thrown down."

3   When he was sitting on the Mount of Olives opposite the temple, Peter, James, John, and Andrew asked him privately, [4]"Tell us, when will this be, and what will be the sign that all these things are about to be accomplished?" [5]Then Jesus began to say to them, "Beware that no one leads you astray. [6]Many will come in my name and say, 'I am he!'[d] and they will lead many astray. [7]When you hear of wars and rumors of wars, do not be alarmed; this must take place, but the end is still to come. [8]For nation will rise against nation, and kingdom against kingdom; there will be earthquakes in various places; there will be famines. This is but the beginning of the birth pangs.

9   "As for yourselves, beware; for they will hand you over to councils; and you will be beaten in synagogues; and you will stand before governors and kings because of me, as a testimony to them. [10]And the good news[e] must first be proclaimed to all nations. [11]When they bring you to trial and hand you over, do not worry beforehand about what you are to say; but say whatever is given you at that time, for it is not you who speak, but the Holy Spirit. [12]Brother will betray brother to death, and a father his child, and children will rise against parents and have them put to death; [13]and you will be hated by all

aHeb *him*   bOr *the cover*   cOr *treaty*, or *testimony*; Heb *eduth*   dGk *I am*   eGk *gospel*

because of my name. But the one who endures to the end will be saved.

## PSALM 49. 1–20

*To the leader. Of the Korahites. A Psalm.*

HEAR this, all you peoples;
 give ear, all inhabitants of
  the world,
2 both low and high,
  rich and poor together.
3 My mouth shall speak wisdom;
  the meditation of my heart
   shall be understanding.
4 I will incline my ear to a
   proverb;
  I will solve my riddle to the
   music of the harp.

5 Why should I fear in times of
   trouble,
  when the iniquity of my
   persecutors surrounds
   me,
6 those who trust in their wealth
  and boast of the abundance of
   their riches?
7 Truly, no ransom avails for
   one's life, [a]
  there is no price one can give
   to God for it.
8 For the ransom of life is costly,
  and can never suffice
9 that one should live on forever
  and never see the grave. [b]

10 When we look at the wise, they
   die;
  fool and dolt perish together
  and leave their wealth to
   others.
11 Their graves [c] are their homes
   forever,
  their dwelling places to all
   generations,
  though they named lands their
   own.

12 Mortals cannot abide in their
   pomp;
  they are like the animals that
   perish.

13 Such is the fate of the
   foolhardy,
  the end of those [d] who are
   pleased with their lot.
    *Selah*
14 Like sheep they are appointed
   for Sheol;
  Death shall be their shepherd;
 straight to the grave they
   descend, [e]
  and their form shall waste
   away;
  Sheol shall be their home. [f]
15 But God will ransom my soul
   from the power of Sheol,
  for he will receive me. *Selah*

16 Do not be afraid when some
   become rich,
  when the wealth of their
   houses increases.
17 For when they die they will
   carry nothing away;
  their wealth will not go down
   after them.
18 Though in their lifetime they
   count themselves happy
  —for you are praised when
   you do well for
   yourself—
19 they [g] will go to the company of
   their ancestors,
  who will never again see the
   light.
20 Mortals cannot abide in their
   pomp;
  they are like the animals that
   perish.

[a] Another reading is *no one can ransom a brother*   [b] Heb *the pit*   [c] Gk Syr Compare Tg: Heb *their inward* (thought)   [d] Tg: Heb *after them*   [e] Cn: Heb *the upright shall have dominion over them in the morning*   [f] Meaning of Heb uncertain   [g] Cn: Heb *you*

## PROVERBS 10.27–28

**T**HE fear of the LORD prolongs
 life,
 but the years of the wicked
 will be short.

28 The hope of the righteous ends
 in gladness,
 but the expectation of the
 wicked comes to nothing.

# MARCH 7

## NUMBERS 8.1—9.23

**T**HE LORD spoke to Moses, saying: [2]Speak to Aaron and say to him: When you set up the lamps, the seven lamps shall give light in front of the lampstand. [3]Aaron did so; he set up its lamps to give light in front of the lampstand, as the LORD had commanded Moses. [4]Now this was how the lampstand was made, out of hammered work of gold. From its base to its flowers, it was hammered work; according to the pattern that the LORD had shown Moses, so he made the lampstand.

5 The LORD spoke to Moses, saying: [6]Take the Levites from among the Israelites and cleanse them. [7]Thus you shall do to them, to cleanse them: sprinkle the water of purification on them, have them shave their whole body with a razor and wash their clothes, and so cleanse themselves. [8]Then let them take a young bull and its grain offering of choice flour mixed with oil, and you shall take another young bull for a sin offering. [9]You shall bring the Levites before the tent of meeting, and assemble the whole congregation of the Israelites. [10]When you bring the Levites before the LORD, the Israelites shall lay their hands on the Levites, [11]and Aaron shall present the Levites before the LORD as an elevation offering from the Israelites, that they may do the service of the LORD. [12]The Levites shall lay their hands on the heads of the bulls, and he shall offer the one for a sin offering and the other for a burnt offering to the LORD, to make atonement for the Levites. [13]Then you shall have the Levites stand before Aaron and his sons, and you shall present them as an elevation offering to the LORD.

14 Thus you shall separate the Levites from among the other Israelites, and the Levites shall be mine. [15]Thereafter the Levites may go in to do service at the tent of meeting, once you have cleansed them and presented them as an elevation offering. [16]For they are unreservedly given to me from among the Israelites; I have taken them for myself, in place of all that open the womb, the firstborn of all the Israelites. [17]For all the firstborn among the Israelites are mine, both human and animal. On the day that I struck down all the firstborn in the land of Egypt I consecrated them for myself, [18]but I have taken the Levites in place of all the firstborn among the Israelites. [19]Moreover, I have given the Levites as a gift to Aaron and his sons from among the Israelites, to do the service for the Israelites at the tent of meeting, and to make atonement for the Israelites, in order that there may be no plague among the Israelites for coming too close to the sanctuary.

20 Moses and Aaron and the whole congregation of the Israelites did with the Levites accordingly; the Israelites did with the Levites just as the LORD had commanded Moses concerning them. 21The Levites purified themselves from sin and washed their clothes; then Aaron presented them as an elevation offering before the LORD, and Aaron made atonement for them to cleanse them. 22Thereafter the Levites went in to do their service in the tent of meeting in attendance on Aaron and his sons. As the LORD had commanded Moses concerning the Levites, so they did with them.

23 The LORD spoke to Moses, saying: 24This applies to the Levites: from twenty-five years old and upward they shall begin to do duty in the service of the tent of meeting; 25and from the age of fifty years they shall retire from the duty of the service and serve no more. 26They may assist their brothers in the tent of meeting in carrying out their duties, but they shall perform no service. Thus you shall do with the Levites in assigning their duties.

9.1 THE LORD spoke to Moses in the wilderness of Sinai, in the first month of the second year after they had come out of the land of Egypt, saying: 2Let the Israelites keep the passover at its appointed time. 3On the fourteenth day of this month, at twilight,a you shall keep it at its appointed time; according to all its statutes and all its regulations you shall keep it. 4So Moses told the Israelites that they should keep the passover. 5They kept the passover in the first month, on the fourteenth day of the month, at twilight,a in the wilderness of Sinai. Just as the LORD had commanded Moses, so the Israelites did. 6Now there were certain people who were unclean through touching a corpse, so that they could not keep the passover on that day. They came before Moses and Aaron on that day, 7and said to him, "Although we are unclean through touching a corpse, why must we be kept from presenting the LORD's offering at its appointed time among the Israelites?" 8Moses spoke to them, "Wait, so that I may hear what the LORD will command concerning you."

9 The LORD spoke to Moses, saying: 10Speak to the Israelites, saying: Anyone of you or your descendants who is unclean through touching a corpse, or is away on a journey, shall still keep the passover to the LORD. 11In the second month on the fourteenth day, at twilight,a they shall keep it; they shall eat it with unleavened bread and bitter herbs. 12They shall leave none of it until morning, nor break a bone of it; according to all the statute for the passover they shall keep it. 13But anyone who is clean and is not on a journey, and yet refrains from keeping the passover, shall be cut off from the people for not presenting the LORD's offering at its appointed time; such a one shall bear the consequences for the sin. 14Any alien residing among you who wishes to keep the passover to the LORD shall do so according to the statute of the passover and according to its regulation; you shall have one statute for both the resident alien and the native.

15 On the day the tabernacle was set up, the cloud covered the tabernacle, the tent of the covenant;b and from evening until morning it was over the tabernacle, having the appearance of fire. 16It was always so: the cloud covered it by dayc and the appearance of fire by night. 17Whenever the cloud lifted from over the tent, then the Israelites would set out; and in the place where the cloud settled down, there the Israelites would camp. 18At the command of the LORD the Israelites

aHeb *between the two evenings*   bOr *treaty*, or *testimony*; Heb *eduth*   cGk Syr Vg: Heb lacks *by day*

would set out, and at the command of the Lord they would camp. As long as the cloud rested over the tabernacle, they would remain in camp. [19]Even when the cloud continued over the tabernacle many days, the Israelites would keep the charge of the Lord, and would not set out. [20]Sometimes the cloud would remain a few days over the tabernacle, and according to the command of the Lord they would remain in camp; then according to the command of the Lord they would set out. [21]Sometimes the cloud would remain from evening until morning; and when the cloud lifted in the morning, they would set out, or if it continued for a day and a night, when the cloud lifted they would set out. [22]Whether it was two days, or a month, or a longer time, that the cloud continued over the tabernacle, resting upon it, the Israelites would remain in camp and would not set out; but when it lifted they would set out. [23]At the command of the Lord they would camp, and at the command of the Lord they would set out. They kept the charge of the Lord, at the command of the Lord by Moses.

## MARK 13.14–37

"**B**UT when you see the desolating sacrilege set up where it ought not to be (let the reader understand), then those in Judea must flee to the mountains; [15]the one on the housetop must not go down or enter the house to take anything away; [16]the one in the field must not turn back to get a coat. [17]Woe to those who are pregnant and to those who are nursing infants in those days! [18]Pray that it may not be in winter. [19]For in those days there will be suffering, such as has not been from the beginning of the creation that God created until now, no, and never will be. [20]And if the Lord had not cut short those days, no one would be saved; but for the sake of the elect, whom he chose, he has cut short those days. [21]And if anyone says to you at that time, 'Look! Here is the Messiah!'[a] or 'Look! There he is!'—do not believe it. [22]False messiahs[b] and false prophets will appear and produce signs and omens, to lead astray, if possible, the elect. [23]But be alert; I have already told you everything.

24 "But in those days, after that suffering,

the sun will be darkened,
    and the moon will not give
        its light,
25   and the stars will be falling
        from heaven,
    and the powers in the
        heavens will be shaken.

[26]Then they will see 'the Son of Man coming in clouds' with great power and glory. [27]Then he will send out the angels, and gather his elect from the four winds, from the ends of the earth to the ends of heaven.

28 "From the fig tree learn its lesson: as soon as its branch becomes tender and puts forth its leaves, you know that summer is near. [29]So also, when you see these things taking place, you know that he[c] is near, at the very gates. [30]Truly I tell you, this generation will not pass away until all these things have taken place. [31]Heaven and earth will pass away, but my words will not pass away.

32 "But about that day or hour no one knows, neither the angels in heaven, nor the Son, but only the Father. [33]Beware, keep alert;[d] for you do not know when the time will come. [34]It is like a man going on a journey, when he leaves home and puts his slaves in charge, each with his work, and commands the doorkeeper to be on the watch. [35]Therefore, keep awake—for you do not know when the master

---

aOr *the Christ*  bOr *christs*  cOr *it*  dOther ancient authorities add *and pray*

of the house will come, in the evening, or at midnight, or at cockcrow, or at dawn, 36or else he may find you asleep when he comes suddenly. 37And what I say to you I say to all: Keep awake."

## PSALM 50.1–23

*A Psalm of Asaph.*

THE mighty one, God the LORD,
 speaks and summons the
  earth
 from the rising of the sun to
  its setting.
2 Out of Zion, the perfection of
  beauty,
 God shines forth.

3 Our God comes and does not
  keep silence,
 before him is a devouring fire,
 and a mighty tempest all
  around him.
4 He calls to the heavens above
 and to the earth, that he may
  judge his people:
5 "Gather to me my faithful ones,
 who made a covenant with
  me by sacrifice!"
6 The heavens declare his
  righteousness,
 for God himself is judge.
            *Selah*

7 "Hear, O my people, and I will
  speak,
 O Israel, I will testify against
  you.
 I am God, your God.
8 Not for your sacrifices do I
  rebuke you;
 your burnt offerings are
  continually before me.
9 I will not accept a bull from
  your house,
 or goats from your folds.
10 For every wild animal of the
  forest is mine,
 the cattle on a thousand hills.

11 I know all the birds of the air, a
 and all that moves in the field
  is mine.

12 "If I were hungry, I would not
  tell you,
 for the world and all that is in
  it is mine.
13 Do I eat the flesh of bulls,
 or drink the blood of goats?
14 Offer to God a sacrifice of
  thanksgiving, b
 and pay your vows to the
  Most High.
15 Call on me in the day of trouble;
 I will deliver you, and you
  shall glorify me."

16 But to the wicked God says:
 "What right have you to
  recite my statutes,
 or take my covenant on your
  lips?
17 For you hate discipline,
 and you cast my words
  behind you.
18 You make friends with a thief
  when you see one,
 and you keep company with
  adulterers.

19 "You give your mouth free rein
  for evil,
 and your tongue frames
  deceit.
20 You sit and speak against your
  kin;
 you slander your own
  mother's child.
21 These things you have done and
  I have been silent;
 you thought that I was one
  just like yourself.
 But now I rebuke you, and lay
  the charge before you.

22 "Mark this, then, you who
  forget God,

aGk Syr Tg: Heb *mountains*  bOr *make thanksgiving your sacrifice to God*

or I will tear you apart, and
    there will be no one to
    deliver.
23  Those who bring thanksgiving
    as their sacrifice honor
    me;
to those who go the right
    way[a]
I will show the salvation of
    God."

## PROVERBS 10.29–30

THE way of the LORD is a
    stronghold for the
    upright,
but destruction for evildoers.
30  The righteous will never be
    removed,
but the wicked will not remain
    in the land.

# MARCH 8

## NUMBERS 10.1—11.23

THE LORD spoke to Moses, saying: [2]Make two silver trumpets; you shall make them of hammered work; and you shall use them for summoning the congregation, and for breaking camp. [3]When both are blown, the whole congregation shall assemble before you at the entrance of the tent of meeting. [4]But if only one is blown, then the leaders, the heads of the tribes of Israel, shall assemble before you. [5]When you blow an alarm, the camps on the east side shall set out; [6]when you blow a second alarm, the camps on the south side shall set out. An alarm is to be blown whenever they are to set out. [7]But when the assembly is to be gathered, you shall blow, but you shall not sound an alarm. [8]The sons of Aaron, the priests, shall blow the trumpets; this shall be a perpetual institution for you throughout your generations. [9]When you go to war in your land against the adversary who oppresses you, you shall sound an alarm with the trumpets, so that you may be remembered before the LORD your God and be saved from your enemies. [10]Also on your days of rejoicing, at your appointed festivals, and at the beginnings of your months, you shall blow the trumpets over your burnt offerings and over your sacrifices of well-being; they shall serve as a reminder on your behalf before the LORD your God: I am the LORD your God.

11  In the second year, in the second month, on the twentieth day of the month, the cloud lifted from over the tabernacle of the covenant.[b] [12]Then the Israelites set out by stages from the wilderness of Sinai, and the cloud settled down in the wilderness of Paran. [13]They set out for the first time at the command of the LORD by Moses. [14]The standard of the camp of Judah set out first, company by company, and over the whole company was Nahshon son of Amminadab. [15]Over the company of the tribe of Issachar was Nethanel son of Zuar; [16]and over the company of the tribe of Zebulun was Eliab son of Helon.

17  Then the tabernacle was taken down, and the Gershonites and the Me-

[a]Heb *who set a way*   [b]Or *treaty,* or *testimony*; Heb *eduth*

rarites, who carried the tabernacle, set out. [18]Next the standard of the camp of Reuben set out, company by company; and over the whole company was Elizur son of Shedeur. [19]Over the company of the tribe of Simeon was Shelumiel son of Zurishaddai, [20]and over the company of the tribe of Gad was Eliasaph son of Deuel.

21 Then the Kohathites, who carried the holy things, set out; and the tabernacle was set up before their arrival. [22]Next the standard of the Ephraimite camp set out, company by company, and over the whole company was Elishama son of Ammihud. [23]Over the company of the tribe of Manasseh was Gamaliel son of Pedahzur, [24]and over the company of the tribe of Benjamin was Abidan son of Gideoni.

25 Then the standard of the camp of Dan, acting as the rear guard of all the camps, set out, company by company, and over the whole company was Ahiezer son of Ammishaddai. [26]Over the company of the tribe of Asher was Pagiel son of Ochran, [27]and over the company of the tribe of Naphtali was Ahira son of Enan. [28]This was the order of march of the Israelites, company by company, when they set out.

29 Moses said to Hobab son of Reuel the Midianite, Moses' father-in-law, "We are setting out for the place of which the LORD said, 'I will give it to you'; come with us, and we will treat you well; for the LORD has promised good to Israel." [30]But he said to him, "I will not go, but I will go back to my own land and to my kindred." [31]He said, "Do not leave us, for you know where we should camp in the wilderness, and you will serve as eyes for us. [32]Moreover, if you go with us, whatever good the LORD does for us, the same we will do for you."

33 So they set out from the mount of the LORD three days' journey with the ark of the covenant of the LORD going before them three days' journey, to seek out a resting place for them, [34]the cloud of the LORD being over them by day when they set out from the camp.

35 Whenever the ark set out, Moses would say,

"Arise, O LORD, let your
enemies be scattered,
and your foes flee before
you."
[36]And whenever it came to rest, he would say,

"Return, O LORD of the ten
thousand thousands of
Israel."[a]

**11.**[1] Now when the people complained in the hearing of the LORD about their misfortunes, the LORD heard it and his anger was kindled. Then the fire of the LORD burned against them, and consumed some outlying parts of the camp. [2]But the people cried out to Moses; and Moses prayed to the LORD, and the fire abated. [3]So that place was called Taberah,[b] because the fire of the LORD burned against them.

4 The rabble among them had a strong craving; and the Israelites also wept again, and said, "If only we had meat to eat! [5]We remember the fish we used to eat in Egypt for nothing, the cucumbers, the melons, the leeks, the onions, and the garlic; [6]but now our strength is dried up, and there is nothing at all but this manna to look at."

7 Now the manna was like coriander seed, and its color was like the color of gum resin. [8]The people went around and gathered it, ground it in mills or beat it in mortars, then boiled it in pots and made cakes of it; and the taste of it was like the taste of cakes baked with oil. [9]When the dew fell on the camp in the night, the manna would fall with it.

[a]Meaning of Heb uncertain   [b]That is *Burning*

10 Moses heard the people weeping throughout their families, all at the entrances of their tents. Then the Lord became very angry, and Moses was displeased. ¹¹So Moses said to the Lord, "Why have you treated your servant so badly? Why have I not found favor in your sight, that you lay the burden of all this people on me? ¹²Did I conceive all this people? Did I give birth to them, that you should say to me, 'Carry them in your bosom, as a nurse carries a sucking child,' to the land that you promised on oath to their ancestors? ¹³Where am I to get meat to give to all this people? For they come weeping to me and say, 'Give us meat to eat!' ¹⁴I am not able to carry all this people alone, for they are too heavy for me. ¹⁵If this is the way you are going to treat me, put me to death at once—if I have found favor in your sight—and do not let me see my misery."

16 So the Lord said to Moses, "Gather for me seventy of the elders of Israel, whom you know to be the elders of the people and officers over them; bring them to the tent of meeting, and have them take their place there with you. ¹⁷I will come down and talk with you there; and I will take some of the spirit that is on you and put it on them; and they shall bear the burden of the people along with you so that you will not bear it all by yourself. ¹⁸And say to the people: Consecrate yourselves for tomorrow, and you shall eat meat; for you have wailed in the hearing of the Lord, saying, 'If only we had meat to eat! Surely it was better for us in Egypt.' Therefore the Lord will give you meat, and you shall eat. ¹⁹You shall eat not only one day, or two days, or five days, or ten days, or twenty days, ²⁰but for a whole month—until it comes out of your nostrils and becomes loathsome to you—because you have rejected the Lord who is among you, and

have wailed before him, saying, 'Why did we ever leave Egypt?' " ²¹But Moses said, "The people I am with number six hundred thousand on foot; and you say, 'I will give them meat, that they may eat for a whole month'! ²²Are there enough flocks and herds to slaughter for them? Are there enough fish in the sea to catch for them?" ²³The Lord said to Moses, "Is the Lord's power limited?ᵃ Now you shall see whether my word will come true for you or not."

# MARK 14.1–21

IT was two days before the Passover and the festival of Unleavened Bread. The chief priests and the scribes were looking for a way to arrest Jesusᵇ by stealth and kill him; ²for they said, "Not during the festival, or there may be a riot among the people."

3 While he was at Bethany in the house of Simon the leper, ᶜ as he sat at the table, a woman came with an alabaster jar of very costly ointment of nard, and she broke open the jar and poured the ointment on his head. ⁴But some were there who said to one another in anger, "Why was the ointment wasted in this way? ⁵For this ointment could have been sold for more than three hundred denarii, ᵈ and the money given to the poor." And they scolded her. ⁶But Jesus said, "Let her alone; why do you trouble her? She has performed a good service for me. ⁷For you always have the poor with you, and you can show kindness to them whenever you wish; but you will not always have me. ⁸She has done what she could; she has anointed my body beforehand for its burial. ⁹Truly I tell you, wherever the good newsᵉ is proclaimed in the whole world, what she has done will be told in remembrance of her."

---

ᵃHeb Lord's hand too short?  ᵇGk him  ᶜThe terms leper and leprosy can refer to several diseases
ᵈThe denarius was the usual day's wage for a laborer  ᵉOr gospel

10 Then Judas Iscariot, who was one of the twelve, went to the chief priests in order to betray him to them. ¹¹When they heard it, they were greatly pleased, and promised to give him money. So he began to look for an opportunity to betray him.

12 On the first day of Unleavened Bread, when the Passover lamb is sacrificed, his disciples said to him, "Where do you want us to go and make the preparations for you to eat the Passover?" ¹³So he sent two of his disciples, saying to them, "Go into the city, and a man carrying a jar of water will meet you; follow him, ¹⁴and wherever he enters, say to the owner of the house, 'The Teacher asks, Where is my guest room where I may eat the Passover with my disciples?' ¹⁵He will show you a large room upstairs, furnished and ready. Make preparations for us there." ¹⁶So the disciples set out and went to the city, and found everything as he had told them; and they prepared the Passover meal.

17 When it was evening, he came with the twelve. ¹⁸And when they had taken their places and were eating, Jesus said, "Truly I tell you, one of you will betray me, one who is eating with me." ¹⁹They began to be distressed and to say to him one after another, "Surely, not I?" ²⁰He said to them, "It is one of the twelve, one who is dipping bread[a] into the bowl[b] with me. ²¹For the Son of Man goes as it is written of him, but woe to that one by whom the Son of Man is betrayed! It would have been better for that one not to have been born."

## PSALM 51.1–19

*To the leader. A Psalm of David, when the prophet Nathan came to him, after he had gone in to Bathsheba.*

**H**AVE mercy on me, O God,
  according to your steadfast love;
according to your abundant mercy
  blot out my transgressions.
2 Wash me thoroughly from my iniquity,
  and cleanse me from my sin.

3 For I know my transgressions,
  and my sin is ever before me.
4 Against you, you alone, have I sinned,
  and done what is evil in your sight,
so that you are justified in your sentence
  and blameless when you pass judgment.
5 Indeed, I was born guilty,
  a sinner when my mother conceived me.

6 You desire truth in the inward being;[c]
  therefore teach me wisdom in my secret heart.
7 Purge me with hyssop, and I shall be clean;
  wash me, and I shall be whiter than snow.
8 Let me hear joy and gladness;
  let the bones that you have crushed rejoice.
9 Hide your face from my sins,
  and blot out all my iniquities.

10 Create in me a clean heart, O God,
  and put a new and right[d] spirit within me.

[a]Gk lacks *bread*   [b]Other ancient authorities read *same bowl*   [c]Meaning of Heb uncertain
[d]Or *steadfast*

11  Do not cast me away from your
        presence,
      and do not take your holy
        spirit from me.
12  Restore to me the joy of your
        salvation,
      and sustain in me a willing[a]
        spirit.

13  Then I will teach transgressors
        your ways,
      and sinners will return to you.
14  Deliver me from bloodshed,
        O God,
      O God of my salvation,
      and my tongue will sing aloud
        of your deliverance.

15  O Lord, open my lips,
      and my mouth will declare
        your praise.
16  For you have no delight in
        sacrifice;
      if I were to give a burnt
        offering, you would not
        be pleased.

17  The sacrifice acceptable to
        God[b] is a broken spirit;
      a broken and contrite heart,
        O God, you will not
        despise.

18  Do good to Zion in your good
        pleasure;
      rebuild the walls of Jerusalem,
19  then you will delight in right
        sacrifices,
      in burnt offerings and whole
        burnt offerings;
      then bulls will be offered on
        your altar.

## PROVERBS 10.31–32

THE mouth of the righteous
      brings forth wisdom,
  but the perverse tongue will
      be cut off.
32  The lips of the righteous know
        what is acceptable,
      but the mouth of the wicked
        what is perverse.

# MARCH 9

## NUMBERS 11.24—13.33

So Moses went out and told the
people the words of the LORD;
and he gathered seventy elders
of the people, and placed them all
around the tent. 25 Then the LORD came
down in the cloud and spoke to him, and
took some of the spirit that was on him
and put it on the seventy elders; and
when the spirit rested upon them, they
prophesied. But they did not do so
again.

26  Two men remained in the camp,
one named Eldad, and the other named
Medad, and the spirit rested on them;
they were among those registered, but
they had not gone out to the tent, and
so they prophesied in the camp. 27 And
a young man ran and told Moses, "Eldad and Medad are prophesying in the
camp." 28 And Joshua son of Nun, the
assistant of Moses, one of his chosen
men,[c] said, "My lord Moses, stop
them!" 29 But Moses said to him, "Are

a Or generous   b Or My sacrifice, O God,   c Or of Moses from his youth you jealous for my sake? Would that all the LORD's people were prophets, and that the LORD would put his spirit on them!" 30And Moses and the elders of Israel returned to the camp.

31 Then a wind went out from the LORD, and it brought quails from the sea and let them fall beside the camp, about a day's journey on this side and a day's journey on the other side, all around the camp, about two cubits deep on the ground. 32So the people worked all that day and night and all the next day, gathering the quails; the least anyone gathered was ten homers; and they spread them out for themselves all around the camp. 33But while the meat was still between their teeth, before it was consumed, the anger of the LORD was kindled against the people, and the LORD struck the people with a very great plague. 34So that place was called Kibroth-hattaavah, a because there they buried the people who had the craving. 35From Kibroth-hattaavah the people journeyed to Hazeroth.

12.1 WHILE they were at Hazeroth, Miriam and Aaron spoke against Moses because of the Cushite woman whom he had married (for he had indeed married a Cushite woman); 2and they said, "Has the LORD spoken only through Moses? Has he not spoken through us also?" And the LORD heard it. 3Now the man Moses was very humble, b more so than anyone else on the face of the earth. 4Suddenly the LORD said to Moses, Aaron, and Miriam, "Come out, you three, to the tent of meeting." So the three of them came out. 5Then the LORD came down in a pillar of cloud, and stood at the entrance of the tent, and called Aaron and Miriam; and they both came forward. 6And he said, "Hear my words:

When there are prophets among
        you,
        I the LORD make myself
            known to them in
            visions;
        I speak to them in dreams.
7   Not so with my servant Moses;
        he is entrusted with all my
            house.
8   With him I speak face to
            face—clearly, not in
            riddles;
        and he beholds the form of
            the LORD.
Why then were you not afraid to speak against my servant Moses?" 9And the anger of the LORD was kindled against them, and he departed.

10 When the cloud went away from over the tent, Miriam had become leprous, c as white as snow. And Aaron turned towards Miriam and saw that she was leprous. 11Then Aaron said to Moses, "Oh, my lord, do not punish usd for a sin that we have so foolishly committed. 12Do not let her be like one stillborn, whose flesh is half consumed when it comes out of its mother's womb." 13And Moses cried to the LORD, "O God, please heal her." 14But the LORD said to Moses, "If her father had but spit in her face, would she not bear her shame for seven days? Let her be shut out of the camp for seven days, and after that she may be brought in again." 15So Miriam was shut out of the camp for seven days; and the people did not set out on the march until Miriam had been brought in again. 16After that the people set out from Hazeroth, and camped in the wilderness of Paran.

13.1 THE LORD said to Moses, 2"Send men to spy out the land of Canaan, which I am giving to the Israelites; from each of their ancestral tribes you shall send a man, every one a leader among them." 3So Moses sent them from the wilderness of Paran, according to the command of the LORD, all of them lead-

aThat is *Graves of craving*   bOr *devout*   cA term for several skin diseases; precise meaning uncertain   dHeb *do not lay sin upon us*

ing men among the Israelites. <sup>4</sup>These were their names: From the tribe of Reuben, Shammua son of Zaccur; <sup>5</sup>from the tribe of Simeon, Shaphat son of Hori; <sup>6</sup>from the tribe of Judah, Caleb son of Jephunneh; <sup>7</sup>from the tribe of Issachar, Igal son of Joseph; <sup>8</sup>from the tribe of Ephraim, Hoshea son of Nun; <sup>9</sup>from the tribe of Benjamin, Palti son of Raphu; <sup>10</sup>from the tribe of Zebulun, Gaddiel son of Sodi; <sup>11</sup>from the tribe of Joseph (that is, from the tribe of Manasseh), Gaddi son of Susi; <sup>12</sup>from the tribe of Dan, Ammiel son of Gemalli; <sup>13</sup>from the tribe of Asher, Sethur son of Michael; <sup>14</sup>from the tribe of Naphtali, Nahbi son of Vophsi; <sup>15</sup>from the tribe of Gad, Geuel son of Machi. <sup>16</sup>These were the names of the men whom Moses sent to spy out the land. And Moses changed the name of Hoshea son of Nun to Joshua.

17  Moses sent them to spy out the land of Canaan, and said to them, "Go up there into the Negeb, and go up into the hill country, <sup>18</sup>and see what the land is like, and whether the people who live in it are strong or weak, whether they are few or many, <sup>19</sup>and whether the land they live in is good or bad, and whether the towns that they live in are unwalled or fortified, <sup>20</sup>and whether the land is rich or poor, and whether there are trees in it or not. Be bold, and bring some of the fruit of the land." Now it was the season of the first ripe grapes.

21  So they went up and spied out the land from the wilderness of Zin to Rehob, near Lebo-hamath. <sup>22</sup>They went up into the Negeb, and came to Hebron; and Ahiman, Sheshai, and Talmai, the Anakites, were there. (Hebron was built seven years before Zoan in Egypt.) <sup>23</sup>And they came to the Wadi Eshcol, and cut down from there a branch with a single cluster of grapes, and they carried it on a pole between two of them. They also brought some pomegranates and figs. <sup>24</sup>That place was called the Wadi Eshcol,<sup>a</sup> because of the cluster that the Israelites cut down from there.

25  At the end of forty days they returned from spying out the land. <sup>26</sup>And they came to Moses and Aaron and to all the congregation of the Israelites in the wilderness of Paran, at Kadesh; they brought back word to them and to all the congregation, and showed them the fruit of the land. <sup>27</sup>And they told him, "We came to the land to which you sent us; it flows with milk and honey, and this is its fruit. <sup>28</sup>Yet the people who live in the land are strong, and the towns are fortified and very large; and besides, we saw the descendants of Anak there. <sup>29</sup>The Amalekites live in the land of the Negeb; the Hittites, the Jebusites, and the Amorites live in the hill country; and the Canaanites live by the sea, and along the Jordan."

30  But Caleb quieted the people before Moses, and said, "Let us go up at once and occupy it, for we are well able to overcome it." <sup>31</sup>Then the men who had gone up with him said, "We are not able to go up against this people, for they are stronger than we." <sup>32</sup>So they brought to the Israelites an unfavorable report of the land that they had spied out, saying, "The land that we have gone through as spies is a land that devours its inhabitants; and all the people that we saw in it are of great size. <sup>33</sup>There we saw the Nephilim (the Anakites come from the Nephilim); and to ourselves we seemed like grasshoppers, and so we seemed to them."

# MARK 14.22–52

**W**HILE they [Jesus and his disciples] were eating, he took a loaf of bread, and after blessing it he broke it, gave it to them, and said, "Take; this is my body." <sup>23</sup>Then

<sup>a</sup>That is *Cluster*

he took a cup, and after giving thanks he gave it to them, and all of them drank from it. ²⁴He said to them, "This is my blood of theᵃ covenant, which is poured out for many. ²⁵Truly I tell you, I will never again drink of the fruit of the vine until that day when I drink it new in the kingdom of God."

26  When they had sung the hymn, they went out to the Mount of Olives. ²⁷And Jesus said to them, "You will all become deserters; for it is written,

'I will strike the shepherd,
    and the sheep will be
        scattered.'

²⁸But after I am raised up, I will go before you to Galilee." ²⁹Peter said to him, "Even though all become deserters, I will not." ³⁰Jesus said to him, "Truly I tell you, this day, this very night, before the cock crows twice, you will deny me three times." ³¹But he said vehemently, "Even though I must die with you, I will not deny you." And all of them said the same.

32  They went to a place called Gethsemane; and he said to his disciples, "Sit here while I pray." ³³He took with him Peter and James and John, and began to be distressed and agitated. ³⁴And he said to them, "I am deeply grieved, even to death; remain here, and keep awake." ³⁵And going a little farther, he threw himself on the ground and prayed that, if it were possible, the hour might pass from him. ³⁶He said, "Abba,ᵇ Father, for you all things are possible; remove this cup from me; yet, not what I want, but what you want." ³⁷He came and found them sleeping; and he said to Peter, "Simon, are you asleep? Could you not keep awake one hour? ³⁸Keep awake and pray that you may not come into the time of trial;ᶜ the spirit indeed is willing, but the flesh is weak." ³⁹And again he went away and prayed, saying the same words. ⁴⁰And once more he came

and found them sleeping, for their eyes were very heavy; and they did not know what to say to him. ⁴¹He came a third time and said to them, "Are you still sleeping and taking your rest? Enough! The hour has come; the Son of Man is betrayed into the hands of sinners. ⁴²Get up, let us be going. See, my betrayer is at hand."

43  Immediately, while he was still speaking, Judas, one of the twelve, arrived; and with him there was a crowd with swords and clubs, from the chief priests, the scribes, and the elders. ⁴⁴Now the betrayer had given them a sign, saying, "The one I will kiss is the man; arrest him and lead him away under guard." ⁴⁵So when he came, he went up to him at once and said, "Rabbi!" and kissed him. ⁴⁶Then they laid hands on him and arrested him. ⁴⁷But one of those who stood near drew his sword and struck the slave of the high priest, cutting off his ear. ⁴⁸Then Jesus said to them, "Have you come out with swords and clubs to arrest me as though I were a bandit? ⁴⁹Day after day I was with you in the temple teaching, and you did not arrest me. But let the scriptures be fulfilled." ⁵⁰All of them deserted him and fled.

51  A certain young man was following him, wearing nothing but a linen cloth. They caught hold of him, ⁵²but he left the linen cloth and ran off naked.

## PSALM 52.1–9

*To the leader. A Maskil of David, when Doeg the Edomite came to Saul and said to him, "David has come to the house of Ahimelech."*

Why do you boast, O mighty one,
    of mischief done against
        the godly?ᵈ
All day long ²you are plotting
        destruction.

---

ᵃOther ancient authorities add *new*   ᵇAramaic for *Father*   ᶜOr *into temptation*   ᵈCn Compare Syr: Heb *the kindness of God*

Your tongue is like a sharp
    razor,
  you worker of treachery.
3 You love evil more than good,
  and lying more than speaking
    the truth.    *Selah*
4 You love all words that devour,
  O deceitful tongue.

5 But God will break you down
    forever;
  he will snatch and tear you
    from your tent;
  he will uproot you from the
    land of the living.   *Selah*
6 The righteous will see, and fear,
  and will laugh at the
    evildoer, **a** saying,
7 "See the one who would not
    take
  refuge in God,
  but trusted in abundant riches,
  and sought refuge in
    wealth!"**b**

8 But I am like a green olive tree
  in the house of God.

I trust in the steadfast love of
    God
  forever and ever.
9 I will thank you forever,
  because of what you have
    done.
In the presence of the faithful
  I will proclaim**c** your name,
    for it is good.

## PROVERBS 11.1–3

A false balance is an
    abomination to the
    LORD,
  but an accurate weight is his
    delight.
2 When pride comes, then comes
    disgrace;
  but wisdom is with the humble.
3 The integrity of the upright
    guides them,
  but the crookedness of the
    treacherous destroys
    them.

# MARCH 10

## NUMBERS 14.1—15.16

THEN all the congregation raised a loud cry, and the people wept that night. 2And all the Israelites complained against Moses and Aaron; the whole congregation said to them, "Would that we had died in the land of Egypt! Or would that we had died in this wilderness! 3Why is the LORD bringing us into this land to fall by the sword? Our wives and our little ones will become booty; would it not be better for us to go back to Egypt?" 4So they said to one another, "Let us choose a captain, and go back to Egypt."

5 Then Moses and Aaron fell on their faces before all the assembly of the congregation of the Israelites. 6And Joshua son of Nun and Caleb son of Jephunneh, who were among those who had spied out the land, tore their clothes 7and said to all the congregation of the Israelites, "The land that we went through as spies is an exceedingly good land. 8If the LORD is pleased with

aHeb *him*   bSyr Tg: Heb *in his destruction*   cCn: Heb *wait for* us, he will bring us into this land and give it to us, a land that flows with milk and honey. ⁹Only, do not rebel against the Lord; and do not fear the people of the land, for they are no more than bread for us; their protection is removed from them, and the Lord is with us; do not fear them." ¹⁰But the whole congregation threatened to stone them.

Then the glory of the Lord appeared at the tent of meeting to all the Israelites. ¹¹And the Lord said to Moses, "How long will this people despise me? And how long will they refuse to believe in me, in spite of all the signs that I have done among them? ¹²I will strike them with pestilence and disinherit them, and I will make of you a nation greater and mightier than they."

13 But Moses said to the Lord, "Then the Egyptians will hear of it, for in your might you brought up this people from among them, ¹⁴and they will tell the inhabitants of this land. They have heard that you, O Lord, are in the midst of this people; for you, O Lord, are seen face to face, and your cloud stands over them and you go in front of them, in a pillar of cloud by day and in a pillar of fire by night. ¹⁵Now if you kill this people all at one time, then the nations who have heard about you will say, ¹⁶'It is because the Lord was not able to bring this people into the land he swore to give them that he has slaughtered them in the wilderness.' ¹⁷And now, therefore, let the power of the Lord be great in the way that you promised when you spoke, saying,

18 'The Lord is slow to anger,
   and abounding in steadfast love,
   forgiving iniquity and
      transgression,
   but by no means clearing the
      guilty,
   visiting the iniquity of the
      parents

upon the children
   to the third and the fourth
      generation.'
¹⁹Forgive the iniquity of this people according to the greatness of your steadfast love, just as you have pardoned this people, from Egypt even until now."

20 Then the Lord said, "I do forgive, just as you have asked; ²¹nevertheless—as I live, and as all the earth shall be filled with the glory of the Lord— ²²none of the people who have seen my glory and the signs that I did in Egypt and in the wilderness, and yet have tested me these ten times and have not obeyed my voice, ²³shall see the land that I swore to give to their ancestors; none of those who despised me shall see it. ²⁴But my servant Caleb, because he has a different spirit and has followed me wholeheartedly, I will bring into the land into which he went, and his descendants shall possess it. ²⁵Now, since the Amalekites and the Canaanites live in the valleys, turn tomorrow and set out for the wilderness by the way to the Red Sea."ᵃ

26 And the Lord spoke to Moses and to Aaron, saying: ²⁷How long shall this wicked congregation complain against me? I have heard the complaints of the Israelites, which they complain against me. ²⁸Say to them, "As I live," says the Lord, "I will do to you the very things I heard you say: ²⁹your dead bodies shall fall in this very wilderness; and of all your number, included in the census, from twenty years old and upward, who have complained against me, ³⁰not one of you shall come into the land in which I swore to settle you, except Caleb son of Jephunneh and Joshua son of Nun. ³¹But your little ones, who you said would become booty, I will bring in, and they shall know the land that you have despised. ³²But as for you, your dead

ᵃ Or *Sea of Reeds*

bodies shall fall in this wilderness. ³³And your children shall be shepherds in the wilderness for forty years, and shall suffer for your faithlessness, until the last of your dead bodies lies in the wilderness. ³⁴According to the number of the days in which you spied out the land, forty days, for every day a year, you shall bear your iniquity, forty years, and you shall know my displeasure." ³⁵I the LORD have spoken; surely I will do thus to all this wicked congregation gathered together against me: in this wilderness they shall come to a full end, and there they shall die.

36 And the men whom Moses sent to spy out the land, who returned and made all the congregation complain against him by bringing a bad report about the land— ³⁷the men who brought an unfavorable report about the land died by a plague before the LORD. ³⁸But Joshua son of Nun and Caleb son of Jephunneh alone remained alive, of those men who went to spy out the land.

39 When Moses told these words to all the Israelites, the people mourned greatly. ⁴⁰They rose early in the morning and went up to the heights of the hill country, saying, "Here we are. We will go up to the place that the LORD has promised, for we have sinned." ⁴¹But Moses said, "Why do you continue to transgress the command of the LORD? That will not succeed. ⁴²Do not go up, for the LORD is not with you; do not let yourselves be struck down before your enemies. ⁴³For the Amalekites and the Canaanites will confront you there, and you shall fall by the sword; because you have turned back from following the LORD, the LORD will not be with you." ⁴⁴But they presumed to go up to the heights of the hill country, even though the ark of the covenant of the LORD, and Moses, had not left the camp. ⁴⁵Then the Amalekites and the Canaanites who lived in that hill country came down and defeated them, pursuing them as far as Hormah.

15.1 THE LORD spoke to Moses, saying: ²Speak to the Israelites and say to them: When you come into the land you are to inhabit, which I am giving you, ³and you make an offering by fire to the LORD from the herd or from the flock— whether a burnt offering or a sacrifice, to fulfill a vow or as a freewill offering or at your appointed festivals—to make a pleasing odor for the LORD, ⁴then whoever presents such an offering to the LORD shall present also a grain offering, one-tenth of an ephah of choice flour, mixed with one-fourth of a hin of oil. ⁵Moreover, you shall offer one-fourth of a hin of wine as a drink offering with the burnt offering or the sacrifice, for each lamb. ⁶For a ram, you shall offer a grain offering, two-tenths of an ephah of choice flour mixed with one-third of a hin of oil; ⁷and as a drink offering you shall offer one-third of a hin of wine, a pleasing odor to the LORD. ⁸When you offer a bull as a burnt offering or a sacrifice, to fulfill a vow or as an offering of well-being to the LORD, ⁹then you shall present with the bull a grain offering, three-tenths of an ephah of choice flour, mixed with half a hin of oil, ¹⁰and you shall present as a drink offering half a hin of wine, as an offering by fire, a pleasing odor to the LORD.

11 Thus it shall be done for each ox or ram, or for each of the male lambs or the kids. ¹²According to the number that you offer, so you shall do with each and every one. ¹³Every native Israelite shall do these things in this way, in presenting an offering by fire, a pleasing odor to the LORD. ¹⁴An alien who lives with you, or who takes up permanent residence among you, and wishes to offer an offering by fire, a pleasing odor to the LORD, shall do as you do. ¹⁵As for the assembly, there shall be for both you and the resident alien a single statute, a perpetual statute throughout

your generations; you and the alien shall be alike before the Lord. [16]You and the alien who resides with you shall have the same law and the same ordinance.

## MARK 14.53–72

THEY took Jesus to the high priest; and all the chief priests, the elders, and the scribes were assembled. [54]Peter had followed him at a distance, right into the courtyard of the high priest; and he was sitting with the guards, warming himself at the fire. [55]Now the chief priests and the whole council were looking for testimony against Jesus to put him to death; but they found none. [56]For many gave false testimony against him, and their testimony did not agree. [57]Some stood up and gave false testimony against him, saying, [58]"We heard him say, 'I will destroy this temple that is made with hands, and in three days I will build another, not made with hands.' " [59]But even on this point their testimony did not agree. [60]Then the high priest stood up before them and asked Jesus, "Have you no answer? What is it that they testify against you?" [61]But he was silent and did not answer. Again the high priest asked him, "Are you the Messiah,[a] the Son of the Blessed One?" [62]Jesus said, "I am; and

'you will see the Son of Man
    seated at the right hand of
        the Power,'
and 'coming with the clouds
    of heaven.' "

[63]Then the high priest tore his clothes and said, "Why do we still need witnesses? [64]You have heard his blasphemy! What is your decision?" All of them condemned him as deserving death. [65]Some began to spit on him, to blindfold him, and to strike him, saying to him, "Prophesy!" The guards also took him over and beat him.

66 While Peter was below in the courtyard, one of the servant-girls of the high priest came by. [67]When she saw Peter warming himself, she stared at him and said, "You also were with Jesus, the man from Nazareth." [68]But he denied it, saying, "I do not know or understand what you are talking about." And he went out into the forecourt.[b] Then the cock crowed.[c] [69]And the servant-girl, on seeing him, began again to say to the bystanders, "This man is one of them." [70]But again he denied it. Then after a little while the bystanders again said to Peter, "Certainly you are one of them; for you are a Galilean." [71]But he began to curse, and he swore an oath, "I do not know this man you are talking about." [72]At that moment the cock crowed for the second time. Then Peter remembered that Jesus had said to him, "Before the cock crows twice, you will deny me three times." And he broke down and wept.

## PSALM 53.1–6

*To the leader: according to Mahalath. A Maskil of David.*

FOOLS say in their hearts,
        "There is no God."
    They are corrupt, they
        commit abominable acts;
    there is no one who does
        good.
2   God looks down from heaven on
        humankind
    to see if there are any who
        are wise,
    who seek after God.

3   They have all fallen away, they
        are all alike perverse;
    there is no one who does
        good,
    no, not one.

<hr>

[a]Or *the Christ*   [b]Or *gateway*   [c]Other ancient authorities lack *Then the cock crowed*

4 Have they no knowledge, those
    evildoers,
  who eat up my people as they
    eat bread,
  and do not call upon God?

5 There they shall be in great
    terror,
  in terror such as has not
    been.
  For God will scatter the bones
    of the ungodly; a
  they will be put to shame, b
    for God has rejected
    them.

6 O that deliverance for Israel
    would come from Zion!
  When God restores the
    fortunes of his people,
  Jacob will rejoice; Israel will
    be glad.

## PROVERBS 11.4

RICHES do not profit in the day
    of wrath,
but righteousness delivers
    from death.

# MARCH 11

## NUMBERS 15.17—16.40

THE LORD spoke to Moses, saying: 18Speak to the Israelites and say to them: After you come into the land to which I am bringing you, 19whenever you eat of the bread of the land, you shall present a donation to the LORD. 20From your first batch of dough you shall present a loaf as a donation; you shall present it just as you present a donation from the threshing floor. 21Throughout your generations you shall give to the LORD a donation from the first of your batch of dough.

22 But if you unintentionally fail to observe all these commandments that the LORD has spoken to Moses— 23everything that the LORD has commanded you by Moses, from the day the LORD gave commandment and thereafter, throughout your generations— 24then if it was done unintentionally without the knowledge of the congregation, the whole congregation shall offer one young bull for a burnt offering, a pleasing odor to the LORD, together with its grain offering and its drink offering, according to the ordinance, and one male goat for a sin offering. 25The priest shall make atonement for all the congregation of the Israelites, and they shall be forgiven; it was unintentional, and they have brought their offering, an offering by fire to the LORD, and their sin offering before the LORD, for their error. 26All the congregation of the Israelites shall be forgiven, as well as the aliens residing among them, because the whole people was involved in the error.

27 An individual who sins unintentionally shall present a female goat a year old for a sin offering. 28And the priest shall make atonement before the LORD for the one who commits an error, when it is unintentional, to make atonement for the person, who then shall be forgiven. 29For both the native among the Israelites and the alien residing

aCn Compare Gk Syr: Heb *him who encamps against you*  bGk: Heb *you will put to shame*

among them—you shall have the same law for anyone who acts in error. ³⁰But whoever acts high-handedly, whether a native or an alien, affronts the LORD, and shall be cut off from among the people. ³¹Because of having despised the word of the LORD and broken his commandment, such a person shall be utterly cut off and bear the guilt.

32 When the Israelites were in the wilderness, they found a man gathering sticks on the sabbath day. ³³Those who found him gathering sticks brought him to Moses, Aaron, and to the whole congregation. ³⁴They put him in custody, because it was not clear what should be done to him. ³⁵Then the LORD said to Moses, "The man shall be put to death; all the congregation shall stone him outside the camp." ³⁶The whole congregation brought him outside the camp and stoned him to death, just as the LORD had commanded Moses.

37 The LORD said to Moses: ³⁸Speak to the Israelites, and tell them to make fringes on the corners of their garments throughout their generations and to put a blue cord on the fringe at each corner. ³⁹You have the fringe so that, when you see it, you will remember all the commandments of the LORD and do them, and not follow the lust of your own heart and your own eyes. ⁴⁰So you shall remember and do all my commandments, and you shall be holy to your God. ⁴¹I am the LORD your God, who brought you out of the land of Egypt, to be your God: I am the LORD your God.

**16.**1 Now Korah son of Izhar son of Kohath son of Levi, along with Dathan and Abiram sons of Eliab, and On son of Peleth—descendants of Reuben—took ²two hundred fifty Israelite men, leaders of the congregation, chosen from the assembly, well-known men, ᵃ and they confronted Moses. ³They assembled against Moses and against Aaron, and said to them, "You have gone too far! All the congregation are holy, everyone of them, and the LORD is among them. So why then do you exalt yourselves above the assembly of the LORD?" ⁴When Moses heard it, he fell on his face. ⁵Then he said to Korah and all his company, "In the morning the LORD will make known who is his, and who is holy, and who will be allowed to approach him; the one whom he will choose he will allow to approach him. ⁶Do this: take censers, Korah and all yourᵇ company, ⁷and tomorrow put fire in them, and lay incense on them before the LORD; and the man whom the LORD chooses shall be the holy one. You Levites have gone too far!" ⁸Then Moses said to Korah, "Hear now, you Levites! ⁹Is it too little for you that the God of Israel has separated you from the congregation of Israel, to allow you to approach him in order to perform the duties of the LORD's tabernacle, and to stand before the congregation and serve them? ¹⁰He has allowed you to approach him, and all your brother Levites with you; yet you seek the priesthood as well! ¹¹Therefore you and all your company have gathered together against the LORD. What is Aaron that you rail against him?"

12 Moses sent for Dathan and Abiram sons of Eliab; but they said, "We will not come! ¹³Is it too little that you have brought us up out of a land flowing with milk and honey to kill us in the wilderness, that you must also lord it over us? ¹⁴It is clear you have not brought us into a land flowing with milk and honey, or given us an inheritance of fields and vineyards. Would you put out the eyes of these men? We will not come!"

15 Moses was very angry and said to the LORD, "Pay no attention to their offering. I have not taken one donkey from them, and I have not harmed any

---

ᵃCn: Heb *and they confronted Moses, and two hundred fifty men . . . well-known men*   ᵇHeb *his*

one of them." ¹⁶And Moses said to Korah, "As for you and all your company, be present tomorrow before the LORD, you and they and Aaron; ¹⁷and let each one of you take his censer, and put incense on it, and each one of you present his censer before the LORD, two hundred fifty censers; you also, and Aaron, each his censer." ¹⁸So each man took his censer, and they put fire in the censers and laid incense on them, and they stood at the entrance of the tent of meeting with Moses and Aaron. ¹⁹Then Korah assembled the whole congregation against them at the entrance of the tent of meeting. And the glory of the LORD appeared to the whole congregation.

20  Then the LORD spoke to Moses and to Aaron, saying: ²¹Separate yourselves from this congregation, so that I may consume them in a moment. ²²They fell on their faces, and said, "O God, the God of the spirits of all flesh, shall one person sin and you become angry with the whole congregation?"

23  And the LORD spoke to Moses, saying: ²⁴Say to the congregation: Get away from the dwellings of Korah, Dathan, and Abiram. ²⁵So Moses got up and went to Dathan and Abiram; the elders of Israel followed him. ²⁶He said to the congregation, "Turn away from the tents of these wicked men, and touch nothing of theirs, or you will be swept away for all their sins." ²⁷So they got away from the dwellings of Korah, Dathan, and Abiram; and Dathan and Abiram came out and stood at the entrance of their tents, together with their wives, their children, and their little ones. ²⁸And Moses said, "This is how you shall know that the LORD has sent me to do all these works; it has not been of my own accord: ²⁹If these people die a natural death, or if a natural fate comes on them, then the LORD has not sent me. ³⁰But if the LORD creates something new, and the ground opens its mouth and swallows them up, with all that belongs to them, and they go down alive into Sheol, then you shall know that these men have despised the LORD."

31  As soon as he finished speaking all these words, the ground under them was split apart. ³²The earth opened its mouth and swallowed them up, along with their households—everyone who belonged to Korah and all their goods. ³³So they with all that belonged to them went down alive into Sheol; the earth closed over them, and they perished from the midst of the assembly. ³⁴All Israel around them fled at their outcry, for they said, "The earth will swallow us too!" ³⁵And fire came out from the LORD and consumed the two hundred fifty men offering the incense.

36ᵃ Then the LORD spoke to Moses, saying: ³⁷Tell Eleazar son of Aaron the priest to take the censers out of the blaze; then scatter the fire far and wide. ³⁸For the censers of these sinners have become holy at the cost of their lives. Make them into hammered plates as a covering for the altar, for they presented them before the LORD and they became holy. Thus they shall be a sign to the Israelites. ³⁹So Eleazar the priest took the bronze censers that had been presented by those who were burned; and they were hammered out as a covering for the altar— ⁴⁰a reminder to the Israelites that no outsider, who is not of the descendants of Aaron, shall approach to offer incense before the LORD, so as not to become like Korah and his company—just as the LORD had said to him through Moses.

ᵃCh 17.1 in Heb

## MARK 15.1–47

**A**s soon as it was morning, the chief priests held a consultation with the elders and scribes and the whole council. They bound Jesus, led him away, and handed him over to Pilate. 2Pilate asked him, "Are you the King of the Jews?" He answered him, "You say so." 3Then the chief priests accused him of many things. 4Pilate asked him again, "Have you no answer? See how many charges they bring against you." 5But Jesus made no further reply, so that Pilate was amazed.

6 Now at the festival he used to release a prisoner for them, anyone for whom they asked. 7Now a man called Barabbas was in prison with the rebels who had committed murder during the insurrection. 8So the crowd came and began to ask Pilate to do for them according to his custom. 9Then he answered them, "Do you want me to release for you the King of the Jews?" 10For he realized that it was out of jealousy that the chief priests had handed him over. 11But the chief priests stirred up the crowd to have him release Barabbas for them instead. 12Pilate spoke to them again, "Then what do you wish me to do[a] with the man you call[b] the King of the Jews?" 13They shouted back, "Crucify him!" 14Pilate asked them, "Why, what evil has he done?" But they shouted all the more, "Crucify him!" 15So Pilate, wishing to satisfy the crowd, released Barabbas for them; and after flogging Jesus, he handed him over to be crucified.

16 Then the soldiers led him into the courtyard of the palace (that is, the governor's headquarters[c]); and they called together the whole cohort. 17And they clothed him in a purple cloak; and after twisting some thorns into a crown, they put it on him. 18And they began saluting him, "Hail, King of the Jews!" 19They struck his head with a reed, spat upon him, and knelt down in homage to him. 20After mocking him, they stripped him of the purple cloak and put his own clothes on him. Then they led him out to crucify him.

21 They compelled a passer-by, who was coming in from the country, to carry his cross; it was Simon of Cyrene, the father of Alexander and Rufus. 22Then they brought Jesus[d] to the place called Golgotha (which means the place of a skull). 23And they offered him wine mixed with myrrh; but he did not take it. 24And they crucified him, and divided his clothes among them, casting lots to decide what each should take.

25 It was nine o'clock in the morning when they crucified him. 26The inscription of the charge against him read, "The King of the Jews." 27And with him they crucified two bandits, one on his right and one on his left. [e] 29Those who passed by derided[f] him, shaking their heads and saying, "Aha! You who would destroy the temple and build it in three days, 30save yourself, and come down from the cross!" 31In the same way the chief priests, along with the scribes, were also mocking him among themselves and saying, "He saved others; he cannot save himself. 32Let the Messiah, [g] the King of Israel, come down from the cross now, so that we may see and believe." Those who were crucified with him also taunted him.

33 When it was noon, darkness came over the whole land[h] until three in the afternoon. 34At three o'clock Jesus cried out with a loud voice, "Eloi, Eloi, lema sabachthani?" which means, "My God, my God, why have you forsaken me?"[i] 35When some of the by-

aOther ancient authorities read *what should I do*   bOther ancient authorities lack *the man you call*
cGk *the praetorium*   dGk *him*   eOther ancient authorities add verse 28, *And the scripture was fulfilled that says, "And he was counted among the lawless."*   fOr *blasphemed*   gOr *the Christ*
hOr *earth*   iOther ancient authorities read *made me a reproach*

standers heard it, they said, "Listen, he is calling for Elijah." [36]And someone ran, filled a sponge with sour wine, put it on a stick, and gave it to him to drink, saying, "Wait, let us see whether Elijah will come to take him down." [37]Then Jesus gave a loud cry and breathed his last. [38]And the curtain of the temple was torn in two, from top to bottom. [39]Now when the centurion, who stood facing him, saw that in this way he[a] breathed his last, he said, "Truly this man was God's Son!"[b]

40 There were also women looking on from a distance; among them were Mary Magdalene, and Mary the mother of James the younger and of Joses, and Salome. [41]These used to follow him and provided for him when he was in Galilee; and there were many other women who had come up with him to Jerusalem.

42 When evening had come, and since it was the day of Preparation, that is, the day before the sabbath, [43]Joseph of Arimathea, a respected member of the council, who was also himself waiting expectantly for the kingdom of God, went boldly to Pilate and asked for the body of Jesus. [44]Then Pilate wondered if he were already dead; and summoning the centurion, he asked him whether he had been dead for some time. [45]When he learned from the centurion that he was dead, he granted the body to Joseph. [46]Then Joseph[c] bought a linen cloth, and taking down the body,[d] wrapped it in the linen cloth, and laid it in a tomb that had been hewn out of the rock. He then rolled a stone against the door of the tomb. [47]Mary Magdalene and Mary the mother of Joses saw where the body[d] was laid.

## PSALM 54.1–7

*To the leader: with stringed instruments. A Maskil of David, when the Ziphites went and told Saul, "David is in hiding among us."*

Save me, O God, by your name,
and vindicate me by your
might.
2 Hear my prayer, O God;
give ear to the words of my
mouth.

3 For the insolent have risen
against me,
the ruthless seek my life;
they do not set God before
them. *Selah*

4 But surely, God is my helper;
the Lord is the upholder of[e]
my life.
5 He will repay my enemies for
their evil.
In your faithfulness, put an
end to them.

6 With a freewill offering I will
sacrifice to you;
I will give thanks to your
name, O LORD, for it is
good.
7 For he has delivered me from
every trouble,
and my eye has looked in
triumph on my enemies.

## PROVERBS 11.5–6

The righteousness of the
blameless keeps their
ways straight,
but the wicked fall by their
own wickedness.
6 The righteousness of the
upright saves them,
but the treacherous are taken
captive by their schemes.

---

[a]Other ancient authorities add *cried out and*   [b]Or *a son of God*   [c]Gk *he*   [d]Gk *it*   [e]Gk Syr Jerome: Heb *is of those who uphold* or *is with those who uphold*

# MARCH 12

NUMBERS 16.41—18.32

O N the next day, however, the whole congregation of the Israelites rebelled against Moses and against Aaron, saying, "You have killed the people of the LORD." [42]And when the congregation had assembled against them, Moses and Aaron turned toward the tent of meeting; the cloud had covered it and the glory of the LORD appeared. [43]Then Moses and Aaron came to the front of the tent of meeting, [44]and the LORD spoke to Moses, saying, [45]"Get away from this congregation, so that I may consume them in a moment." And they fell on their faces. [46]Moses said to Aaron, "Take your censer, put fire on it from the altar and lay incense on it, and carry it quickly to the congregation and make atonement for them. For wrath has gone out from the LORD; the plague has begun." [47]So Aaron took it as Moses had ordered, and ran into the middle of the assembly, where the plague had already begun among the people. He put on the incense, and made atonement for the people. [48]He stood between the dead and the living; and the plague was stopped. [49]Those who died by the plague were fourteen thousand seven hundred, besides those who died in the affair of Korah. [50]When the plague was stopped, Aaron returned to Moses at the entrance of the tent of meeting.

there shall be one staff for the head of each ancestral house. [4]Place them in the tent of meeting before the covenant,[b] where I meet with you. [5]And the staff of the man whom I choose shall sprout; thus I will put a stop to the complaints of the Israelites that they continually make against you. [6]Moses spoke to the Israelites; and all their leaders gave him staffs, one for each leader, according to their ancestral houses, twelve staffs; and the staff of Aaron was among theirs. [7]So Moses placed the staffs before the LORD in the tent of the covenant.[b]

8 When Moses went into the tent of the covenant[b] on the next day, the staff of Aaron for the house of Levi had sprouted. It put forth buds, produced blossoms, and bore ripe almonds. [9]Then Moses brought out all the staffs from before the LORD to all the Israelites; and they looked, and each man took his staff. [10]And the LORD said to Moses, "Put back the staff of Aaron before the covenant,[b] to be kept as a warning to rebels, so that you may make an end of their complaints against me, or else they will die." [11]Moses did so; just as the LORD commanded him, so he did.

12 The Israelites said to Moses, "We are perishing; we are lost, all of us are lost! [13]Everyone who approaches the tabernacle of the LORD will die. Are we all to perish?"

[17a.1] THE LORD spoke to Moses, saying: [2]Speak to the Israelites, and get twelve staffs from them, one for each ancestral house, from all the leaders of their ancestral houses. Write each man's name on his staff, [3]and write Aaron's name on the staff of Levi. For

[18.1] THE LORD said to Aaron: You and your sons and your ancestral house with you shall bear responsibility for offenses connected with the sanctuary, while you and your sons alone shall bear responsibility for offenses con-

[a]Ch 17.16 in Heb  [b]Or *treaty*, or *testimony*; Heb *eduth*

nected with the priesthood. ²So bring with you also your brothers of the tribe of Levi, your ancestral tribe, in order that they may be joined to you, and serve you while you and your sons with you are in front of the tent of the covenant.ᵃ ³They shall perform duties for you and for the whole tent. But they must not approach either the utensils of the sanctuary or the altar, otherwise both they and you will die. ⁴They are attached to you in order to perform the duties of the tent of meeting, for all the service of the tent; no outsider shall approach you. ⁵You yourselves shall perform the duties of the sanctuary and the duties of the altar, so that wrath may never again come upon the Israelites. ⁶It is I who now take your brother Levites from among the Israelites; they are now yours as a gift, dedicated to the Lord, to perform the service of the tent of meeting. ⁷But you and your sons with you shall diligently perform your priestly duties in all that concerns the altar and the area behind the curtain. I give your priesthood as a gift;ᵇ any outsider who approaches shall be put to death.

8  The Lord spoke to Aaron: I have given you charge of the offerings made to me, all the holy gifts of the Israelites; I have given them to you and your sons as a priestly portion due you in perpetuity. ⁹This shall be yours from the most holy things, reserved from the fire: every offering of theirs that they render to me as a most holy thing, whether grain offering, sin offering, or guilt offering, shall belong to you and your sons. ¹⁰As a most holy thing you shall eat it; every male may eat it; it shall be holy to you. ¹¹This also is yours: I have given to you, together with your sons and daughters, as a perpetual due, whatever is set aside from the gifts of all the elevation offerings of the Israelites; everyone who is clean in your house may eat them. ¹²All the best of the oil and all the best of the wine and of the grain, the choice produce that they give to the Lord, I have given to you. ¹³The first fruits of all that is in their land, which they bring to the Lord, shall be yours; everyone who is clean in your house may eat of it. ¹⁴Every devoted thing in Israel shall be yours. ¹⁵The first issue of the womb of all creatures, human and animal, which is offered to the Lord, shall be yours; but the firstborn of human beings you shall redeem, and the firstborn of unclean animals you shall redeem. ¹⁶Their redemption price, reckoned from one month of age, you shall fix at five shekels of silver, according to the shekel of the sanctuary (that is, twenty gerahs). ¹⁷But the firstborn of a cow, or the firstborn of a sheep, or the firstborn of a goat, you shall not redeem; they are holy. You shall dash their blood on the altar, and shall turn their fat into smoke as an offering by fire for a pleasing odor to the Lord; ¹⁸but their flesh shall be yours, just as the breast that is elevated and as the right thigh are yours. ¹⁹All the holy offerings that the Israelites present to the Lord I have given to you, together with your sons and daughters, as a perpetual due; it is a covenant of salt forever before the Lord for you and your descendants as well. ²⁰Then the Lord said to Aaron: You shall have no allotment in their land, nor shall you have any share among them; I am your share and your possession among the Israelites.

21  To the Levites I have given every tithe in Israel for a possession in return for the service that they perform, the service in the tent of meeting. ²²From now on the Israelites shall no longer approach the tent of meeting, or else they will incur guilt and die. ²³But the Levites shall perform the service of the tent of meeting, and they

shall bear responsibility for their own offenses; it shall be a perpetual statute throughout your generations. But among the Israelites they shall have no allotment, 24because I have given to the Levites as their portion the tithe of the Israelites, which they set apart as an offering to the LORD. Therefore I have said of them that they shall have no allotment among the Israelites.

25   Then the LORD spoke to Moses, saying: 26You shall speak to the Levites, saying: When you receive from the Israelites the tithe that I have given you from them for your portion, you shall set apart an offering from it to the LORD, a tithe of the tithe. 27It shall be reckoned to you as your gift, the same as the grain of the threshing floor and the fullness of the wine press. 28Thus you also shall set apart an offering to the LORD from all the tithes that you receive from the Israelites; and from them you shall give the LORD's offering to the priest Aaron. 29Out of all the gifts to you, you shall set apart every offering due to the LORD; the best of all of them is the part to be consecrated. 30Say also to them: When you have set apart the best of it, then the rest shall be reckoned to the Levites as produce of the threshing floor, and as produce of the wine press. 31You may eat it in any place, you and your households; for it is your payment for your service in the tent of meeting. 32You shall incur no guilt by reason of it, when you have offered the best of it. But you shall not profane the holy gifts of the Israelites, on pain of death.

# MARK 16.1–20

WHEN the sabbath was over, Mary Magdalene, and Mary the mother of James, and Salome bought spices, so that they might go and anoint him. 2And very early on the first day of the week, when the sun had risen, they went to the tomb. 3They had been saying to one another, "Who will roll away the stone for us from the entrance to the tomb?" 4When they looked up, they saw that the stone, which was very large, had already been rolled back. 5As they entered the tomb, they saw a young man, dressed in a white robe, sitting on the right side; and they were alarmed. 6But he said to them, "Do not be alarmed; you are looking for Jesus of Nazareth, who was crucified. He has been raised; he is not here. Look, there is the place they laid him. 7But go, tell his disciples and Peter that he is going ahead of you to Galilee; there you will see him, just as he told you." 8So they went out and fled from the tomb, for terror and amazement had seized them; and they said nothing to anyone, for they were afraid. a

### THE SHORTER ENDING OF MARK

[And all that had been commanded them they told briefly to those around Peter. And afterward Jesus himself sent out through them, from east to west, the sacred and imperishable proclamation of eternal salvation. b]

### THE LONGER ENDING OF MARK

9 [Now after he rose early on the first day of the week, he appeared first to Mary Magdalene, from whom he had cast out seven demons. 10She went out

---

aSome of the most ancient authorities bring the book to a close at the end of verse 8. One authority concludes the book with the shorter ending; others include the shorter ending and then continue with verses 9-20. In most authorities verses 9-20 follow immediately after verse 8, though in some of these authorities the passage is marked as being doubtful.   bOther ancient authorities add *Amen*

and told those who had been with him, while they were mourning and weeping. [11] But when they heard that he was alive and had been seen by her, they would not believe it.

12 After this he appeared in another form to two of them, as they were walking into the country. [13] And they went back and told the rest, but they did not believe them.

14 Later he appeared to the eleven themselves as they were sitting at the table; and he upbraided them for their lack of faith and stubbornness, because they had not believed those who saw him after he had risen. [a] [15] And he said to them, "Go into all the world and proclaim the good news [b] to the whole creation. [16] The one who believes and is baptized will be saved; but the one who does not believe will be condemned. [17] And these signs will accompany those who believe: by using my name they will cast out demons; they will speak in new tongues; [18] they will pick up snakes in their hands, [c] and if they drink any deadly thing, it will not hurt them; they will lay their hands on the sick, and they will recover."

19 So then the Lord Jesus, after he had spoken to them, was taken up into heaven and sat down at the right hand of God. [20] And they went out and proclaimed the good news everywhere, while the Lord worked with them and confirmed the message by the signs that accompanied it. [d]⟧

## PSALM 55.1–23

*To the leader: with stringed instruments. A Maskil of David.*

G IVE ear to my prayer, O God;
do not hide yourself from
my supplication.
2 Attend to me, and answer me;
I am troubled in my
complaint.
I am distraught [3] by the noise of
the enemy,
because of the clamor of the
wicked.
For they bring [e] trouble upon
me,
and in anger they cherish
enmity against me.

4 My heart is in anguish within
me,
the terrors of death have
fallen upon me.
5 Fear and trembling come upon
me,
and horror overwhelms me.
6 And I say, "O that I had wings
like a dove!
I would fly away and be at
rest;
7 truly, I would flee far away;
I would lodge in the
wilderness;          *Selah*
8 I would hurry to find a shelter
for myself
from the raging wind and
tempest."

9 Confuse, O Lord, confound their
speech;
for I see violence and strife in
the city.

---

[a] Other ancient authorities add, in whole or in part, *And they excused themselves, saying, "This age of lawlessness and unbelief is under Satan, who does not allow the truth and power of God to prevail over the unclean things of the spirits. Therefore reveal your righteousness now"—thus they spoke to Christ. And Christ replied to them, "The term of years of Satan's power has been fulfilled, but other terrible things draw near. And for those who have sinned I was handed over to death, that they may return to the truth and sin no more, that they may inherit the spiritual and imperishable glory of righteousness that is in heaven."* [b] Or *gospel* [c] Other ancient authorities lack *in their hands* [d] Other ancient authorities add *Amen* [e] Cn Compare Gk: Heb *they cause to totter*

10 Day and night they go around it
        on its walls,
    and iniquity and trouble are
        within it;
11     ruin is in its midst;
    oppression and fraud
        do not depart from its
        marketplace.

12 It is not enemies who taunt
        me—
        I could bear that;
    it is not adversaries who deal
            insolently with me—
        I could hide from them.
13 But it is you, my equal,
        my companion, my familiar
        friend,
14 with whom I kept pleasant
            company;
        we walked in the house of
        God with the throng.
15 Let death come upon them;
        let them go down alive to
            Sheol;
        for evil is in their homes and
            in their hearts.

16 But I call upon God,
        and the LORD will save me.
17 Evening and morning and at
            noon
        I utter my complaint and
            moan,
        and he will hear my voice.
18 He will redeem me unharmed
        from the battle that I wage,
        for many are arrayed against
            me.

19 God, who is enthroned from of
            old,                    *Selah*
        will hear, and will humble
            them—
    because they do not change,
        and do not fear God.

20 My companion laid hands on a
            friend
        and violated a covenant with
            me[a]
21 with speech smoother than
            butter,
        but with a heart set on war;
    with words that were softer
            than oil,
        but in fact were drawn
            swords.

22 Cast your burden[b] on the LORD,
        and he will sustain you;
    he will never permit
        the righteous to be moved.

23 But you, O God, will cast them
            down
        into the lowest pit;
    the bloodthirsty and treacherous
        shall not live out half their
            days.
    But I will trust in you.

## PROVERBS 11.7

WHEN the wicked die, their
        hope perishes,
    and the expectation of the
        godless comes to
        nothing.

aHeb lacks *with me*   bOr *Cast what he has given you*

# MARCH 13

NUMBERS 19.1—20.29

THE LORD spoke to Moses and Aaron, saying: ²This is a statute of the law that the LORD has commanded: Tell the Israelites to bring you a red heifer without defect, in which there is no blemish and on which no yoke has been laid. ³You shall give it to the priest Eleazar, and it shall be taken outside the camp and slaughtered in his presence. ⁴The priest Eleazar shall take some of its blood with his finger and sprinkle it seven times towards the front of the tent of meeting. ⁵Then the heifer shall be burned in his sight; its skin, its flesh, and its blood, with its dung, shall be burned. ⁶The priest shall take cedarwood, hyssop, and crimson material, and throw them into the fire in which the heifer is burning. ⁷Then the priest shall wash his clothes and bathe his body in water, and afterwards he may come into the camp; but the priest shall remain unclean until evening. ⁸The one who burns the heifer[a] shall wash his clothes in water and bathe his body in water; he shall remain unclean until evening. ⁹Then someone who is clean shall gather up the ashes of the heifer, and deposit them outside the camp in a clean place; and they shall be kept for the congregation of the Israelites for the water for cleansing. It is a purification offering. ¹⁰The one who gathers the ashes of the heifer shall wash his clothes and be unclean until evening.

This shall be a perpetual statute for the Israelites and for the alien residing among them. ¹¹Those who touch the dead body of any human being shall be unclean seven days. ¹²They shall purify themselves with the water on the third day and on the seventh day, and so be clean; but if they do not purify themselves on the third day and on the seventh day, they will not become clean. ¹³All who touch a corpse, the body of a human being who has died, and do not purify themselves, defile the tabernacle of the LORD; such persons shall be cut off from Israel. Since water for cleansing was not dashed on them, they remain unclean; their uncleanness is still on them.

14 This is the law when someone dies in a tent: everyone who comes into the tent, and everyone who is in the tent, shall be unclean seven days. ¹⁵And every open vessel with no cover fastened on it is unclean. ¹⁶Whoever in the open field touches one who has been killed by a sword, or who has died naturally,[b] or a human bone, or a grave, shall be unclean seven days. ¹⁷For the unclean they shall take some ashes of the burnt purification offering, and running water shall be added in a vessel; ¹⁸then a clean person shall take hyssop, dip it in the water, and sprinkle it on the tent, on all the furnishings, on the persons who were there, and on whoever touched the bone, the slain, the corpse, or the grave. ¹⁹The clean person shall sprinkle the unclean ones on the third day and on the seventh day, thus purifying them on the seventh day. Then they shall wash their clothes and bathe themselves in water, and at evening they shall be clean. ²⁰Any who are unclean but do not purify themselves, those persons shall be cut off from the assembly, for they have defiled the sanctuary of the LORD. Since the water for cleansing has not been dashed on them, they are unclean.

a Heb it   b Heb lacks *naturally*

21 It shall be a perpetual statute for them. The one who sprinkles the water for cleansing shall wash his clothes, and whoever touches the water for cleansing shall be unclean until evening. 22Whatever the unclean person touches shall be unclean, and anyone who touches it shall be unclean until evening.

20.1 THE Israelites, the whole congregation, came into the wilderness of Zin in the first month, and the people stayed in Kadesh. Miriam died there, and was buried there.

2 Now there was no water for the congregation; so they gathered together against Moses and against Aaron. 3The people quarreled with Moses and said, "Would that we had died when our kindred died before the LORD! 4Why have you brought the assembly of the LORD into this wilderness for us and our livestock to die here? 5Why have you brought us up out of Egypt, to bring us to this wretched place? It is no place for grain, or figs, or vines, or pomegranates; and there is no water to drink." 6Then Moses and Aaron went away from the assembly to the entrance of the tent of meeting; they fell on their faces, and the glory of the LORD appeared to them. 7The LORD spoke to Moses, saying: 8Take the staff, and assemble the congregation, you and your brother Aaron, and command the rock before their eyes to yield its water. Thus you shall bring water out of the rock for them; thus you shall provide drink for the congregation and their livestock.

9 So Moses took the staff from before the LORD, as he had commanded him. 10Moses and Aaron gathered the assembly together before the rock, and he said to them, "Listen, you rebels, shall we bring water for you out of this rock?" 11Then Moses lifted up his hand and struck the rock twice with his staff; water came out abundantly, and the congregation and their livestock drank. 12But the LORD said to Moses and Aaron, "Because you did not trust in me, to show my holiness before the eyes of the Israelites, therefore you shall not bring this assembly into the land that I have given them." 13These are the waters of Meribah, a where the people of Israel quarreled with the LORD, and by which he showed his holiness.

14 Moses sent messengers from Kadesh to the king of Edom, "Thus says your brother Israel: You know all the adversity that has befallen us: 15how our ancestors went down to Egypt, and we lived in Egypt a long time; and the Egyptians oppressed us and our ancestors; 16and when we cried to the LORD, he heard our voice, and sent an angel and brought us out of Egypt; and here we are in Kadesh, a town on the edge of your territory. 17Now let us pass through your land. We will not pass through field or vineyard, or drink water from any well; we will go along the King's Highway, not turning aside to the right hand or to the left until we have passed through your territory."

18 But Edom said to him, "You shall not pass through, or we will come out with the sword against you." 19The Israelites said to him, "We will stay on the highway; and if we drink of your water, we and our livestock, then we will pay for it. It is only a small matter; just let us pass through on foot." 20But he said, "You shall not pass through." And Edom came out against them with a large force, heavily armed. 21Thus Edom refused to give Israel passage through their territory; so Israel turned away from them.

22 They set out from Kadesh, and the Israelites, the whole congregation,

a That is *Quarrel*

came to Mount Hor. [23]Then the LORD said to Moses and Aaron at Mount Hor, on the border of the land of Edom, [24]"Let Aaron be gathered to his people. For he shall not enter the land that I have given to the Israelites, because you rebelled against my command at the waters of Meribah. [25]Take Aaron and his son Eleazar, and bring them up Mount Hor; [26]strip Aaron of his vestments, and put them on his son Eleazar. But Aaron shall be gathered to his people, [a] and shall die there." [27]Moses did as the LORD had commanded; they went up Mount Hor in the sight of the whole congregation. [28]Moses stripped Aaron of his vestments, and put them on his son Eleazar; and Aaron died there on the top of the mountain. Moses and Eleazar came down from the mountain. [29]When all the congregation saw that Aaron had died, all the house of Israel mourned for Aaron thirty days.

## LUKE 1.1–25

SINCE many have undertaken to set down an orderly account of the events that have been fulfilled among us, [2]just as they were handed on to us by those who from the beginning were eyewitnesses and servants of the word, [3]I too decided, after investigating everything carefully from the very first, [b] to write an orderly account for you, most excellent Theophilus, [4]so that you may know the truth concerning the things about which you have been instructed.

5 In the days of King Herod of Judea, there was a priest named Zechariah, who belonged to the priestly order of Abijah. His wife was a descendant of Aaron, and her name was Elizabeth. [6]Both of them were righteous before God, living blamelessly according to all the commandments and regulations of the Lord. [7]But they had no children, because Elizabeth was barren, and both were getting on in years.

8 Once when he was serving as priest before God and his section was on duty, [9]he was chosen by lot, according to the custom of the priesthood, to enter the sanctuary of the Lord and offer incense. [10]Now at the time of the incense offering, the whole assembly of the people was praying outside. [11]Then there appeared to him an angel of the Lord, standing at the right side of the altar of incense. [12]When Zechariah saw him, he was terrified; and fear overwhelmed him. [13]But the angel said to him, "Do not be afraid, Zechariah, for your prayer has been heard. Your wife Elizabeth will bear you a son, and you will name him John. [14]You will have joy and gladness, and many will rejoice at his birth, [15]for he will be great in the sight of the Lord. He must never drink wine or strong drink; even before his birth he will be filled with the Holy Spirit. [16]He will turn many of the people of Israel to the Lord their God. [17]With the spirit and power of Elijah he will go before him, to turn the hearts of parents to their children, and the disobedient to the wisdom of the righteous, to make ready a people prepared for the Lord." [18]Zechariah said to the angel, "How will I know that this is so? For I am an old man, and my wife is getting on in years." [19]The angel replied, "I am Gabriel. I stand in the presence of God, and I have been sent to speak to you and to bring you this good news. [20]But now, because you did not believe my words, which will be fulfilled in their time, you will become mute, unable to speak, until the day these things occur."

21 Meanwhile the people were waiting for Zechariah, and wondered at his delay in the sanctuary. [22]When he

---

[a]Heb lacks *to his people*   [b]Or *for a long time*

did come out, he could not speak to them, and they realized that he had seen a vision in the sanctuary. He kept motioning to them and remained unable to speak. ²³When his time of service was ended, he went to his home.

24  After those days his wife Elizabeth conceived, and for five months she remained in seclusion. She said, ²⁵"This is what the Lord has done for me when he looked favorably on me and took away the disgrace I have endured among my people."

## PSALM 56.1–13

*To the leader: according to The Dove on Far-off Terebinths. Of David. A Miktam, when the Philistines seized him in Gath.*

**B**E gracious to me, O God, for people trample on me; all day long foes oppress me;
2  my enemies trample on me all day long,
for many fight against me.
O Most High, ³when I am afraid,
I put my trust in you.
4  In God, whose word I praise,
in God I trust; I am not afraid;
what can flesh do to me?

5  All day long they seek to injure my cause;
all their thoughts are against me for evil.
6  They stir up strife, they lurk, they watch my steps.

As they hoped to have my life,
7      so repayᵃ them for their crime;
in wrath cast down the peoples, O God!

8  You have kept count of my tossings;
put my tears in your bottle.
Are they not in your record?
9  Then my enemies will retreat in the day when I call.
This I know, thatᵇ God is for me.
10  In God, whose word I praise,
in the LORD, whose word I praise,
11  in God I trust; I am not afraid.
What can a mere mortal do to me?

12  My vows to you I must perform, O God;
I will render thank offerings to you.
13  For you have delivered my soul from death,
and my feet from falling,
so that I may walk before God in the light of life.

## PROVERBS 11.8

**T**HE righteous are delivered from trouble,
and the wicked get into it instead.

aCn: Heb *rescue*   bOr *because*

# MARCH 14



WHEN the Canaanite, the king of Arad, who lived in the Negeb, heard that Israel was coming by the way of Atharim, he fought against Israel and took some of them captive. [2]Then Israel made a vow to the LORD and said, "If you will indeed give this people into our hands, then we will utterly destroy their towns." [3]The LORD listened to the voice of Israel, and handed over the Canaanites; and they utterly destroyed them and their towns; so the place was called Hormah. [a]

4 From Mount Hor they set out by the way to the Red Sea, [b] to go around the land of Edom; but the people became impatient on the way. [5]The people spoke against God and against Moses, "Why have you brought us up out of Egypt to die in the wilderness? For there is no food and no water, and we detest this miserable food." [6]Then the LORD sent poisonous[c] serpents among the people, and they bit the people, so that many Israelites died. [7]The people came to Moses and said, "We have sinned by speaking against the LORD and against you; pray to the LORD to take away the serpents from us." So Moses prayed for the people. [8]And the LORD said to Moses, "Make a poisonous[d] serpent, and set it on a pole; and everyone who is bitten shall look at it and live." [9]So Moses made a serpent of bronze, and put it upon a pole; and whenever a serpent bit someone, that person would look at the serpent of bronze and live.

10 The Israelites set out, and camped in Oboth. [11]They set out from Oboth, and camped at Iye-abarim, in the wilderness bordering Moab toward the sunrise. [12]From there they set out, and camped in the Wadi Zered. [13]From there they set out, and camped on the other side of the Arnon, in[e] the wilderness that extends from the boundary of the Amorites; for the Arnon is the boundary of Moab, between Moab and the Amorites. [14]Wherefore it is said in the Book of the Wars of the LORD,

"Waheb in Suphah and the
wadis.
The Arnon [15]and the slopes of
the wadis
that extend to the seat of Ar,
and lie along the border of
Moab."[f]

16 From there they continued to Beer;[g] that is the well of which the LORD said to Moses, "Gather the people together, and I will give them water." [17]Then Israel sang this song:

"Spring up, O well!—Sing to
it!—
[18] the well that the leaders sank,
that the nobles of the people
dug,
with the scepter, with the
staff."

From the wilderness to Mattanah, [19]from Mattanah to Nahaliel, from Nahaliel to Bamoth, [20]and from Bamoth to the valley lying in the region of Moab by the top of Pisgah that overlooks the wasteland. [h]

21 Then Israel sent messengers to King Sihon of the Amorites, saying, [22]"Let me pass through your land; we will not turn aside into field or vineyard; we will not drink the water of any well; we will go by the King's Highway until we have passed through your territory." [23]But Sihon would not allow Is-

rael to pass through his territory. Sihon gathered all his people together, and went out against Israel to the wilderness; he came to Jahaz, and fought against Israel. ²⁴Israel put him to the sword, and took possession of his land from the Arnon to the Jabbok, as far as to the Ammonites; for the boundary of the Ammonites was strong. ²⁵Israel took all these towns, and Israel settled in all the towns of the Amorites, in Heshbon, and in all its villages. ²⁶For Heshbon was the city of King Sihon of the Amorites, who had fought against the former king of Moab and captured all his land as far as the Arnon. ²⁷Therefore the ballad singers say,

> "Come to Heshbon, let it be
> built;
> let the city of Sihon be
> established.
> 28 For fire came out from
> Heshbon,
> flame from the city of Sihon.
> It devoured Ar of Moab,
> and swallowed upᵃ the
> heights of the Arnon.
> 29 Woe to you, O Moab!
> You are undone, O people of
> Chemosh!
> He has made his sons fugitives,
> and his daughters captives,
> to an Amorite king, Sihon.
> 30 So their posterity perished
> from Heshbonᵇ to Dibon,
> and we laid waste until fire
> spread to Medeba."ᶜ

31 Thus Israel settled in the land of the Amorites. ³²Moses sent to spy out Jazer; and they captured its villages, and dispossessed the Amorites who were there.

33 Then they turned and went up the road to Bashan; and King Og of Bashan came out against them, he and all his people, to battle at Edrei. ³⁴But the LORD said to Moses, "Do not be afraid of him; for I have given him into your hand, with all his people, and all his land. You shall do to him as you did to King Sihon of the Amorites, who ruled in Heshbon." ³⁵So they killed him, his sons, and all his people, until there was no survivor left; and they took possession of his land.

22.1 THE Israelites set out, and camped in the plains of Moab across the Jordan from Jericho. ²Now Balak son of Zippor saw all that Israel had done to the Amorites. ³Moab was in great dread of the people, because they were so numerous; Moab was overcome with fear of the people of Israel. ⁴And Moab said to the elders of Midian, "This horde will now lick up all that is around us, as an ox licks up the grass of the field." Now Balak son of Zippor was king of Moab at that time. ⁵He sent messengers to Balaam son of Beor at Pethor, which is on the Euphrates, in the land of Amaw, ᵈ to summon him, saying, "A people has come out of Egypt; they have spread over the face of the earth, and they have settled next to me. ⁶Come now, curse this people for me, since they are stronger than I; perhaps I shall be able to defeat them and drive them from the land; for I know that whomever you bless is blessed, and whomever you curse is cursed."

7 So the elders of Moab and the elders of Midian departed with the fees for divination in their hand; and they came to Balaam, and gave him Balak's message. ⁸He said to them, "Stay here tonight, and I will bring back word to you, just as the LORD speaks to me"; so the officials of Moab stayed with Balaam. ⁹God came to Balaam and said, "Who are these men with you?" ¹⁰Balaam said to God, "King Balak son of Zippor of Moab, has sent me this message: ¹¹'A people has come out of Egypt and has spread over the face of the earth; now come, curse them for

---

ᵃGk: Heb *and the lords of*  ᵇGk: Heb *we have shot at them; Heshbon has perished*  ᶜCompare Sam Gk: Meaning of MT uncertain  ᵈOr *land of his kinsfolk*

me; perhaps I shall be able to fight against them and drive them out.'" [12]God said to Balaam, "You shall not go with them; you shall not curse the people, for they are blessed." [13]So Balaam rose in the morning, and said to the officials of Balak, "Go to your own land, for the LORD has refused to let me go with you." [14]So the officials of Moab rose and went to Balak, and said, "Balaam refuses to come with us."

15 Once again Balak sent officials, more numerous and more distinguished than these. [16]They came to Balaam and said to him, "Thus says Balak son of Zippor: 'Do not let anything hinder you from coming to me; [17]for I will surely do you great honor, and whatever you say to me I will do; come, curse this people for me.'" [18]But Balaam replied to the servants of Balak, "Although Balak were to give me his house full of silver and gold, I could not go beyond the command of the LORD my God, to do less or more. [19]You remain here, as the others did, so that I may learn what more the LORD may say to me." [20]That night God came to Balaam and said to him, "If the men have come to summon you, get up and go with them; but do only what I tell you to do."

## LUKE 1.26–56

In the sixth month the angel Gabriel was sent by God to a town in Galilee called Nazareth, [27]to a virgin engaged to a man whose name was Joseph, of the house of David. The virgin's name was Mary. [28]And he came to her and said, "Greetings, favored one! The Lord is with you."[a] [29]But she was much perplexed by his words and pondered what sort of greeting this might be. [30]The angel said to her, "Do not be afraid, Mary, for you have found favor with God. [31]And now, you will conceive in your womb and bear a son, and you will name him Jesus. [32]He will be great, and will be called the Son of the Most High, and the Lord God will give to him the throne of his ancestor David. [33]He will reign over the house of Jacob forever, and of his kingdom there will be no end." [34]Mary said to the angel, "How can this be, since I am a virgin?"[b] [35]The angel said to her, "The Holy Spirit will come upon you, and the power of the Most High will overshadow you; therefore the child to be born[c] will be holy; he will be called Son of God. [36]And now, your relative Elizabeth in her old age has also conceived a son; and this is the sixth month for her who was said to be barren. [37]For nothing will be impossible with God." [38]Then Mary said, "Here am I, the servant of the Lord; let it be with me according to your word." Then the angel departed from her.

39 In those days Mary set out and went with haste to a Judean town in the hill country, [40]where she entered the house of Zechariah and greeted Elizabeth. [41]When Elizabeth heard Mary's greeting, the child leaped in her womb. And Elizabeth was filled with the Holy Spirit [42]and exclaimed with a loud cry, "Blessed are you among women, and blessed is the fruit of your womb. [43]And why has this happened to me, that the mother of my Lord comes to me? [44]For as soon as I heard the sound of your greeting, the child in my womb leaped for joy. [45]And blessed is she who believed that there would be[d] a fulfillment of what was spoken to her by the Lord."

46 And Mary[e] said,
  "My soul magnifies the Lord,
[47]    and my spirit rejoices in God
        my Savior,

---

[a]Other ancient authorities add *Blessed are you among women*  [b]Gk *I do not know a man*  [c]Other ancient authorities add *of you*  [d]Or *believed, for there will be*  [e]Other ancient authorities read *Elizabeth*

48  for he has looked with favor on
        the lowliness of his
        servant.
      Surely, from now on all
        generations will call
        me blessed;
49  for the Mighty One has done
        great things for me,
      and holy is his name.
50  His mercy is for those who fear
        him
      from generation to
        generation.
51  He has shown strength with
        his arm;
      he has scattered the proud in
        the thoughts of their
        hearts.
52  He has brought down the
        powerful from their
        thrones,
      and lifted up the lowly;
53  he has filled the hungry with
        good things,
      and sent the rich away
        empty.
54  He has helped his servant
        Israel,
      in remembrance of his mercy,
55  according to the promise he
        made to our ancestors,
      to Abraham and to his
        descendants forever."

56  And Mary remained with her
about three months and then returned
to her home.


## PSALM 57.1–11

*To the leader: Do Not Destroy. Of David. A*
*Miktam, when he fled from Saul, in the cave.*

B E merciful to me, O God, be
        merciful to me,
    for in you my soul takes
        refuge;
  in the shadow of your wings I
        will take refuge,
      until the destroying storms
        pass by.

2  I cry to God Most High,
      to God who fulfills his
        purpose for me.
3  He will send from heaven and
        save me,
      he will put to shame those
        who trample on me.
                              *Selah*
  God will send forth his steadfast
        love and his faithfulness.

4  I lie down among lions
      that greedily devour[a] human
        prey;
    their teeth are spears and
        arrows,
      their tongues sharp swords.

5  Be exalted, O God, above the
        heavens.
      Let your glory be over all the
        earth.

6  They set a net for my steps;
      my soul was bowed down.
    They dug a pit in my path,
      but they have fallen into it
        themselves.          *Selah*
7  My heart is steadfast, O God,
      my heart is steadfast.
    I will sing and make melody.
8      Awake, my soul!
  Awake, O harp and lyre!
    I will awake the dawn.
9  I will give thanks to you,
        O Lord, among the
        peoples;
      I will sing praises to you
        among the nations.
10  For your steadfast love is as
        high as the heavens;
      your faithfulness extends to
        the clouds.

11  Be exalted, O God, above the
        heavens.
      Let your glory be over all the
        earth.

a Cn: Heb *are aflame for*

## PROVERBS 11.9–11

**W**ITH their mouths the godless
would destroy their
neighbors,
but by knowledge the
righteous are delivered.
10 When it goes well with the
righteous, the city
rejoices;
and when the wicked perish,
there is jubilation.
11 By the blessing of the upright a
city is exalted,
but it is overthrown by the
mouth of the wicked.

# MARCH 15

## NUMBERS 22.21—23.30

**S**o Balaam got up in the morning, saddled his donkey, and went with the officials of Moab.

22 God's anger was kindled because he was going, and the angel of the Lord took his stand in the road as his adversary. Now he was riding on the donkey, and his two servants were with him. 23 The donkey saw the angel of the Lord standing in the road, with a drawn sword in his hand; so the donkey turned off the road, and went into the field; and Balaam struck the donkey, to turn it back onto the road. 24 Then the angel of the Lord stood in a narrow path between the vineyards, with a wall on either side. 25 When the donkey saw the angel of the Lord, it scraped against the wall, and scraped Balaam's foot against the wall; so he struck it again. 26 Then the angel of the Lord went ahead, and stood in a narrow place, where there was no way to turn either to the right or to the left. 27 When the donkey saw the angel of the Lord, it lay down under Balaam; and Balaam's anger was kindled, and he struck the donkey with his staff. 28 Then the Lord opened the mouth of the donkey, and it said to Balaam, "What have I done to you, that you have struck me these three times?" 29 Balaam said to the donkey, "Because you have made a fool of me! I wish I had a sword in my hand! I would kill you right now!" 30 But the donkey said to Balaam, "Am I not your donkey, which you have ridden all your life to this day? Have I been in the habit of treating you this way?" And he said, "No."

31 Then the Lord opened the eyes of Balaam, and he saw the angel of the Lord standing in the road, with his drawn sword in his hand; and he bowed down, falling on his face. 32 The angel of the Lord said to him, "Why have you struck your donkey these three times? I have come out as an adversary, because your way is perverse[a] before me. 33 The donkey saw me, and turned away from me these three times. If it had not turned away from me, surely just now I would have killed you and let it live." 34 Then Balaam said to the angel of the Lord, "I have sinned, for I did not know that you were standing in the road to oppose me. Now therefore, if it is displeasing to you, I will return home." 35 The angel of the Lord said to

a Meaning of Heb uncertain

Balaam, "Go with the men; but speak only what I tell you to speak." So Balaam went on with the officials of Balak.

36 When Balak heard that Balaam had come, he went out to meet him at Ir-moab, on the boundary formed by the Arnon, at the farthest point of the boundary. <sup>37</sup>Balak said to Balaam, "Did I not send to summon you? Why did you not come to me? Am I not able to honor you?" <sup>38</sup>Balaam said to Balak, "I have come to you now, but do I have power to say just anything? The word God puts in my mouth, that is what I must say." <sup>39</sup>Then Balaam went with Balak, and they came to Kiriath-huzoth. <sup>40</sup>Balak sacrificed oxen and sheep, and sent them to Balaam and to the officials who were with him.

41 On the next day Balak took Balaam and brought him up to Bamoth-baal; and from there he could see part of the people of Israel. <sup>a</sup> <sup>23.1</sup> Then Balaam said to Balak, "Build me seven altars here, and prepare seven bulls and seven rams for me." <sup>2</sup>Balak did as Balaam had said; and Balak and Balaam offered a bull and a ram on each altar. <sup>3</sup>Then Balaam said to Balak, "Stay here beside your burnt offerings while I go aside. Perhaps the Lord will come to meet me. Whatever he shows me I will tell you." And he went to a bare height.

4 Then God met Balaam; and Balaam said to him, "I have arranged the seven altars, and have offered a bull and a ram on each altar." <sup>5</sup>The Lord put a word in Balaam's mouth, and said, "Return to Balak, and this is what you must say." <sup>6</sup>So he returned to Balak, <sup>b</sup> who was standing beside his burnt offerings with all the officials of Moab. <sup>7</sup>Then Balaam<sup>c</sup> uttered his oracle, saying:

"Balak has brought me from
Aram,
the king of Moab from the
eastern mountains:

'Come, curse Jacob for me;
Come, denounce Israel!'
8 How can I curse whom God has
not cursed?
How can I denounce those
whom the Lord has not
denounced?
9 For from the top of the crags I
see him,
from the hills I behold him;
Here is a people living alone,
and not reckoning itself
among the nations!
10 Who can count the dust of
Jacob,
or number the dust-cloud<sup>d</sup> of
Israel?
Let me die the death of the
upright,
and let my end be like his!"

11 Then Balak said to Balaam, "What have you done to me? I brought you to curse my enemies, but now you have done nothing but bless them." <sup>12</sup>He answered, "Must I not take care to say what the Lord puts into my mouth?"

13 So Balak said to him, "Come with me to another place from which you may see them; you shall see only part of them, and shall not see them all; then curse them for me from there." <sup>14</sup>So he took him to the field of Zophim, to the top of Pisgah. He built seven altars, and offered a bull and a ram on each altar. <sup>15</sup>Balaam said to Balak, "Stand here beside your burnt offerings, while I meet the Lord over there. <sup>16</sup>The Lord met Balaam, put a word into his mouth, and said, "Return to Balak, and this is what you shall say." <sup>17</sup>When he came to him, he was standing beside his burnt offerings with the officials of Moab. Balak said to him, "What has the Lord said?" <sup>18</sup>Then Balaam uttered his oracle, saying:

"Rise, Balak, and hear;
listen to me, O son of Zippor:

<sup>a</sup>Heb lacks *of Israel*   <sup>b</sup>Heb *him*   <sup>c</sup>Heb *he*   <sup>d</sup>Or *fourth part*

<sup>19</sup> God is not a human being, that
    he should lie,
  or a mortal, that he should
    change his mind.
  Has he promised, and will he
    not do it?
  Has he spoken, and will he
    not fulfill it?
<sup>20</sup> See, I received a command to
    bless;
  he has blessed, and I cannot
    revoke it.
<sup>21</sup> He has not beheld misfortune in
    Jacob;
  nor has he seen trouble in
    Israel.
  The LORD their God is with
    them,
  acclaimed as a king among
    them.
<sup>22</sup> God, who brings them out of
    Egypt,
  is like the horns of a wild ox
    for them.
<sup>23</sup> Surely there is no enchantment
    against Jacob,
  no divination against Israel;
  now it shall be said of Jacob and
    Israel,
  'See what God has done!'
<sup>24</sup> Look, a people rising up like a
    lioness,
  and rousing itself like a lion!
  It does not lie down until it has
    eaten the prey
  and drunk the blood of the
    slain."

25 Then Balak said to Balaam, "Do not curse them at all, and do not bless them at all." <sup>26</sup>But Balaam answered Balak, "Did I not tell you, 'Whatever the LORD says, that is what I must do'?"

27 So Balak said to Balaam, "Come now, I will take you to another place; perhaps it will please God that you may curse them for me from there." <sup>28</sup>So Balak took Balaam to the top of Peor, which overlooks the wasteland. ª <sup>29</sup>Balaam said to Balak, "Build me seven altars here, and prepare seven bulls and seven rams for me." <sup>30</sup>So Balak did as Balaam had said, and offered a bull and a ram on each altar.

## LUKE 1.57–80

Now the time came for Elizabeth to give birth, and she bore a son. <sup>58</sup>Her neighbors and relatives heard that the Lord had shown his great mercy to her, and they rejoiced with her.

59 On the eighth day they came to circumcise the child, and they were going to name him Zechariah after his father. <sup>60</sup>But his mother said, "No; he is to be called John." <sup>61</sup>They said to her, "None of your relatives has this name." <sup>62</sup>Then they began motioning to his father to find out what name he wanted to give him. <sup>63</sup>He asked for a writing tablet and wrote, "His name is John." And all of them were amazed. <sup>64</sup>Immediately his mouth was opened and his tongue freed, and he began to speak, praising God. <sup>65</sup>Fear came over all their neighbors, and all these things were talked about throughout the entire hill country of Judea. <sup>66</sup>All who heard them pondered them and said, "What then will this child become?" For, indeed, the hand of the Lord was with him.

67 Then his father Zechariah was filled with the Holy Spirit and spoke this prophecy:
<sup>68</sup> "Blessed be the Lord God of
    Israel,
  for he has looked favorably on
    his people and redeemed
    them.
<sup>69</sup> He has raised up a mighty
    savior[b] for us
  in the house of his servant
    David,
<sup>70</sup> as he spoke through the mouth
    of his holy prophets from
    of old,

ª Or *overlooks Jeshimon*  b Gk *a horn of salvation*

71 that we would be saved from
our enemies and from
the hand of all who hate
us.
72 Thus he has shown the mercy
promised to our
ancestors,
and has remembered his
holy covenant,
73 the oath that he swore to our
ancestor Abraham,
to grant us 74that we, being
rescued from the hands
of our enemies,
might serve him without fear,
75in holiness and
righteousness
before him all our days.
76 And you, child, will be called the
prophet of the Most
High;
for you will go before the
Lord to prepare his
ways,
77 to give knowledge of salvation
to his people
by the forgiveness of their
sins.
78 By the tender mercy of our
God,
the dawn from on high will
break upon[a] us,
79 to give light to those who sit in
darkness and in the
shadow of death,
to guide our feet into the way
of peace."

80 The child grew and became strong in spirit, and he was in the wilderness until the day he appeared publicly to Israel.

## PSALM 58. 1–11

*To the leader: Do Not Destroy. Of David. A Miktam.*

D o you indeed decree what is
right, you gods?[b]
Do you judge people fairly?
2 No, in your hearts you devise
wrongs;
your hands deal out violence
on earth.

3 The wicked go astray from the
womb;
they err from their birth,
speaking lies.
4 They have venom like the
venom of a serpent,
like the deaf adder that stops
its ear,
5 so that it does not hear the
voice of charmers
or of the cunning enchanter.

6 O God, break the teeth in their
mouths;
tear out the fangs of the
young lions, O Lord!
7 Let them vanish like water that
runs away;
like grass let them be trodden
down[c] and wither.
8 Let them be like the snail that
dissolves into slime;
like the untimely birth that
never sees the sun.
9 Sooner than your pots can feel
the heat of thorns,
whether green or ablaze, may
he sweep them away!

10 The righteous will rejoice when
they see vengeance
done;
they will bathe their feet in
the blood of the wicked.

[a]Other ancient authorities read *has broken upon*  [b]Or *mighty lords*  [c]Cn: Meaning of Heb uncertain

11 People will say, "Surely there is
a reward for the
righteous;
surely there is a God who
judges on earth."

## PROVERBS 11.12–13

Whoever belittles another
lacks sense,
but an intelligent person
remains silent.
13 A gossip goes about telling
secrets,
but one who is trustworthy in
spirit keeps a confidence.

# MARCH 16

## NUMBERS 24.1—25.18

Now Balaam saw that it pleased the Lord to bless Israel, so he did not go, as at other times, to look for omens, but set his face toward the wilderness. [2]Balaam looked up and saw Israel camping tribe by tribe. Then the spirit of God came upon him, [3]and he uttered his oracle, saying:

"The oracle of Balaam son of
Beor,
the oracle of the man whose
eye is clear, [a]
4 the oracle of one who hears the
words of God,
who sees the vision of the
Almighty, [b]
who falls down, but with eyes
uncovered:
5 how fair are your tents,
O Jacob,
your encampments, O Israel!
6 Like palm groves that stretch
far away,
like gardens beside a river,
like aloes that the Lord has
planted,

like cedar trees beside the
waters.
7 Water shall flow from his
buckets,
and his seed shall have
abundant water,
his king shall be higher than
Agag,
and his kingdom shall be
exalted.
8 God who brings him out of
Egypt,
is like the horns of a wild ox
for him;
he shall devour the nations that
are his foes
and break their bones.
He shall strike with his
arrows. [c]
9 He crouched, he lay down like a
lion,
and like a lioness; who will
rouse him up?
Blessed is everyone who
blesses you,
and cursed is everyone who
curses you."

a Or *closed* or *open*  b Traditional rendering of Heb *Shaddai*  c Meaning of Heb uncertain

10  Then Balak's anger was kindled against Balaam, and he struck his hands together. Balak said to Balaam, "I summoned you to curse my enemies, but instead you have blessed them these three times. [11]Now be off with you! Go home! I said, 'I will reward you richly,' but the LORD has denied you any reward." [12]And Balaam said to Balak, "Did I not tell your messengers whom you sent to me, [13]'If Balak should give me his house full of silver and gold, I would not be able to go beyond the word of the LORD, to do either good or bad of my own will; what the LORD says, that is what I will say'? [14]So now, I am going to my people; let me advise you what this people will do to your people in days to come."

15  So he uttered his oracle, saying:
"The oracle of Balaam son of
      Beor,
    the oracle of the man whose
      eye is clear,[a]
[16]  the oracle of one who hears the
      words of God,
    and knows the knowledge of
      the Most High,[b]
  who sees the vision of the
      Almighty,[c]
    who falls down, but with his
      eyes uncovered:
[17]  I see him, but not now;
    I behold him, but not near—
  a star shall come out of Jacob,
    and a scepter shall rise out of
      Israel;
  it shall crush the borderlands[d]
      of Moab,
    and the territory[e] of all the
      Shethites.
[18]  Edom will become a possession,
    Seir a possession of its
      enemies,[f]
  while Israel does valiantly.
[19]  One out of Jacob shall rule,
    and destroy the survivors of
      Ir."

20  Then he looked on Amalek, and uttered his oracle, saying:
"First among the nations was
      Amalek,
    but its end is to perish forever."
21  Then he looked on the Kenite, and uttered his oracle, saying:
"Enduring is your dwelling
      place,
    and your nest is set in the
      rock;
[22]  yet Kain is destined for burning.
    How long shall Asshur take
      you away captive?"
23  Again he uttered his oracle, saying:
"Alas, who shall live when God
      does this?
[24]    But ships shall come from
      Kittim
  and shall afflict Asshur and
      Eber;
    and he also shall perish
      forever."

25  Then Balaam got up and went back to his place, and Balak also went his way.

25.1 WHILE Israel was staying at Shittim, the people began to have sexual relations with the women of Moab. [2]These invited the people to the sacrifices of their gods, and the people ate and bowed down to their gods. [3]Thus Israel yoked itself to the Baal of Peor, and the LORD's anger was kindled against Israel. [4]The LORD said to Moses, "Take all the chiefs of the people, and impale them in the sun before the LORD, in order that the fierce anger of the LORD may turn away from Israel." [5]And Moses said to the judges of Israel, "Each of you shall kill any of your people who have yoked themselves to the Baal of Peor."

6  Just then one of the Israelites came and brought a Midianite woman into his family, in the sight of Moses

[a]Or *closed* or *open*  [b]Or *of Elyon*  [c]Traditional rendering of Heb *Shaddai*  [d]Or *forehead*  [e]Some Mss read *skull*  [f]Heb *Seir, its enemies, a possession*

and in the sight of the whole congregation of the Israelites, while they were weeping at the entrance of the tent of meeting. 7When Phinehas son of Eleazar, son of Aaron the priest, saw it, he got up and left the congregation. Taking a spear in his hand, 8he went after the Israelite man into the tent, and pierced the two of them, the Israelite and the woman, through the belly. So the plague was stopped among the people of Israel. 9Nevertheless those that died by the plague were twenty-four thousand.

10 The LORD spoke to Moses, saying: 11"Phinehas son of Eleazar, son of Aaron the priest, has turned back my wrath from the Israelites by manifesting such zeal among them on my behalf that in my jealousy I did not consume the Israelites. 12Therefore say, 'I hereby grant him my covenant of peace. 13It shall be for him and for his descendants after him a covenant of perpetual priesthood, because he was zealous for his God, and made atonement for the Israelites.' "

14 The name of the slain Israelite man, who was killed with the Midianite woman, was Zimri son of Salu, head of an ancestral house belonging to the Simeonites. 15The name of the Midianite woman who was killed was Cozbi daughter of Zur, who was the head of a clan, an ancestral house in Midian.

16 The LORD said to Moses, 17"Harass the Midianites, and defeat them; 18for they have harassed you by the trickery with which they deceived you in the affair of Peor, and in the affair of Cozbi, the daughter of a leader of Midian, their sister; she was killed on the day of the plague that resulted from Peor."

## LUKE 2.1–35

IN those days a decree went out from Emperor Augustus that all the world should be registered. 2This was the first registration and was taken while Quirinius was governor of Syria. 3All went to their own towns to be registered. 4Joseph also went from the town of Nazareth in Galilee to Judea, to the city of David called Bethlehem, because he was descended from the house and family of David. 5He went to be registered with Mary, to whom he was engaged and who was expecting a child. 6While they were there, the time came for her to deliver her child. 7And she gave birth to her firstborn son and wrapped him in bands of cloth, and laid him in a manger, because there was no place for them in the inn.

8 In that region there were shepherds living in the fields, keeping watch over their flock by night. 9Then an angel of the Lord stood before them, and the glory of the Lord shone around them, and they were terrified. 10But the angel said to them, "Do not be afraid; for see—I am bringing you good news of great joy for all the people: 11to you is born this day in the city of David a Savior, who is the Messiah,a the Lord. 12This will be a sign for you: you will find a child wrapped in bands of cloth and lying in a manger." 13And suddenly there was with the angel a multitude of the heavenly host,b praising God and saying,

14 "Glory to God in the highest
        heaven,
    and on earth peace among
        those whom he
        favors!"c

15 When the angels had left them and gone into heaven, the shepherds said to one another, "Let us go now to Bethlehem and see this thing that has taken place, which the Lord has made

---

a Or *the Christ*　b Gk *army*　c Other ancient authorities read *peace, goodwill among people*

known to us." ¹⁶So they went with haste and found Mary and Joseph, and the child lying in the manger. ¹⁷When they saw this, they made known what had been told them about this child; ¹⁸and all who heard it were amazed at what the shepherds told them. ¹⁹But Mary treasured all these words and pondered them in her heart. ²⁰The shepherds returned, glorifying and praising God for all they had heard and seen, as it had been told them.

21 After eight days had passed, it was time to circumcise the child; and he was called Jesus, the name given by the angel before he was conceived in the womb.

22 When the time came for their purification according to the law of Moses, they brought him up to Jerusalem to present him to the Lord ²³(as it is written in the law of the Lord, "Every firstborn male shall be designated as holy to the Lord"), ²⁴and they offered a sacrifice according to what is stated in the law of the Lord, "a pair of turtledoves or two young pigeons."

25 Now there was a man in Jerusalem whose name was Simeon;ᵃ this man was righteous and devout, looking forward to the consolation of Israel, and the Holy Spirit rested on him. ²⁶It had been revealed to him by the Holy Spirit that he would not see death before he had seen the Lord's Messiah.ᵇ ²⁷Guided by the Spirit, Simeonᶜ came into the temple; and when the parents brought in the child Jesus, to do for him what was customary under the law, ²⁸Simeonᵈ took him in his arms and praised God, saying,

29 "Master, now you are
        dismissing your servantᵉ
        in peace,
    according to your word;
30 for my eyes have seen your
        salvation,
31    which you have prepared in
        the presence of all
        peoples,
32    a light for revelation to the
        Gentiles
    and for glory to your people
        Israel."

33 And the child's father and mother were amazed at what was being said about him. ³⁴Then Simeonᵃ blessed them and said to his mother Mary, "This child is destined for the falling and the rising of many in Israel, and to be a sign that will be opposed ³⁵so that the inner thoughts of many will be revealed—and a sword will pierce your own soul too."

## PSALM 59.1–17

*To the leader: Do Not Destroy. Of David. A Miktam, when Saul ordered his house to be watched in order to kill him.*

**D**ELIVER me from my enemies,
        O my God;
    protect me from those who
        rise up against me.
2    Deliver me from those who
        work evil;
    from the bloodthirsty save
        me.

3    Even now they lie in wait for
        my life;
    the mighty stir up strife
        against me.
    For no transgression or sin of
        mine, O LORD,
4        for no fault of mine, they run
        and make ready.

    Rouse yourself, come to my
        help and see!
5    You, LORD God of hosts, are
        God of Israel.
    Awake to punish all the nations;
        spare none of those who
        treacherously plot evil.
                        *Selah*

ᵃGk *Symeon*  ᵇOr *the Lord's Christ*  ᶜGk *In the Spirit, he*  ᵈGk *he*  ᵉGk *slave*

6 Each evening they come back,
  howling like dogs
  and prowling about the city.
7 There they are, bellowing with
    their mouths,
  with sharp words<sup>a</sup> on their
    lips—
  for "Who," they think, <sup>b</sup> "will
    hear us?"

8 But you laugh at them, O LORD;
  you hold all the nations in
    derision.
9 O my strength, I will watch for
    you;
  for you, O God, are my
    fortress.
10 My God in his steadfast love
    will meet me;
  my God will let me look in
    triumph on my enemies.

11 Do not kill them, or my people
    may forget;
  make them totter by your
    power, and bring them
    down,
  O Lord, our shield.
12 For the sin of their mouths, the
    words of their lips,
  let them be trapped in their
    pride.
  For the cursing and lies that
    they utter,
13  consume them in wrath;

consume them until they are
  no more.
Then it will be known to the
  ends of the earth
that God rules over Jacob.
                    *Selah*

14 Each evening they come back,
  howling like dogs
  and prowling about the city.
15 They roam about for food,
  and growl if they do not get
    their fill.

16 But I will sing of your might;
  I will sing aloud of your
    steadfast love in the
    morning.
  For you have been a fortress
    for me
  and a refuge in the day of my
    distress.
17 O my strength, I will sing
    praises to you,
  for you, O God, are my
    fortress,
  the God who shows me
    steadfast love.

## PROVERBS 11.14

**W**HERE there is no guidance, a
    nation<sup>c</sup> falls,
  but in an abundance of
    counselors there is
    safety.

---

<sup>a</sup>Heb *with swords*   <sup>b</sup>Heb lacks *they think*   <sup>c</sup>Or *an army*

## NUMBERS 26.1–51

AFTER the plague the LORD said to Moses and to Eleazar son of Aaron the priest, 2"Take a census of the whole congregation of the Israelites, from twenty years old and upward, by their ancestral houses, everyone in Israel able to go to war." 3Moses and Eleazar the priest spoke with them in the plains of Moab by the Jordan opposite Jericho, saying, 4"Take a census of the people, a from twenty years old and upward," as the LORD commanded Moses.

The Israelites, who came out of the land of Egypt, were:

5 Reuben, the firstborn of Israel. The descendants of Reuben: of Hanoch, the clan of the Hanochites; of Pallu, the clan of the Palluites; 6of Hezron, the clan of the Hezronites; of Carmi, the clan of the Carmites. 7These are the clans of the Reubenites; the number of those enrolled was forty-three thousand seven hundred thirty. 8And the descendants of Pallu: Eliab. 9The descendants of Eliab: Nemuel, Dathan, and Abiram. These are the same Dathan and Abiram, chosen from the congregation, who rebelled against Moses and Aaron in the company of Korah, when they rebelled against the LORD, 10and the earth opened its mouth and swallowed them up along with Korah, when that company died, when the fire devoured two hundred fifty men; and they became a warning. 11Notwithstanding, the sons of Korah did not die.

12 The descendants of Simeon by their clans: of Nemuel, the clan of the Nemuelites; of Jamin, the clan of the Jaminites; of Jachin, the clan of the Jachinites; 13of Zerah, the clan of the Zerahites; of Shaul, the clan of the Shaulites. b 14These are the clans of the Simeonites, twenty-two thousand two hundred.

15 The children of Gad by their clans: of Zephon, the clan of the Zephonites; of Haggi, the clan of the Haggites; of Shuni, the clan of the Shunites; 16of Ozni, the clan of the Oznites; of Eri, the clan of the Erites; 17of Arod, the clan of the Arodites; of Areli, the clan of the Arelites. 18These are the clans of the Gadites: the number of those enrolled was forty thousand five hundred.

19 The sons of Judah: Er and Onan; Er and Onan died in the land of Canaan. 20The descendants of Judah by their clans were: of Shelah, the clan of the Shelanites; of Perez, the clan of the Perezites; of Zerah, the clan of the Zerahites. 21The descendants of Perez were: of Hezron, the clan of the Hezronites; of Hamul, the clan of the Hamulites. 22These are the clans of Judah: the number of those enrolled was seventy-six thousand five hundred.

23 The descendants of Issachar by their clans: of Tola, the clan of the Tolaites; of Puvah, the clan of the Punites; 24of Jashub, the clan of the Jashubites; of Shimron, the clan of the Shimronites. 25These are the clans of Issachar: sixty-four thousand three hundred enrolled.

26 The descendants of Zebulun by their clans: of Sered, the clan of the Seredites; of Elon, the clan of the Elonites; of Jahleel, the clan of the Jahleelites. 27These are the clans of the Zebulunites; the number of those enrolled was sixty thousand five hundred.

28 The sons of Joseph by their

clans: Manasseh and Ephraim. ²⁹The descendants of Manasseh: of Machir, the clan of the Machirites; and Machir was the father of Gilead; of Gilead, the clan of the Gileadites. ³⁰These are the descendants of Gilead: of Iezer, the clan of the Iezerites; of Helek, the clan of the Helekites; ³¹and of Asriel, the clan of the Asrielites; and of Shechem, the clan of the Shechemites; ³²and of Shemida, the clan of the Shemidaites; and of Hepher, the clan of the Hepherites. ³³Now Zelophehad son of Hepher had no sons, but daughters: and the names of the daughters of Zelophehad were Mahlah, Noah, Hoglah, Milcah, and Tirzah. ³⁴These are the clans of Manasseh; the number of those enrolled was fifty-two thousand seven hundred.

35 These are the descendants of Ephraim according to their clans: of Shuthelah, the clan of the Shuthelahites; of Becher, the clan of the Becherites; of Tahan, the clan of the Tahanites. ³⁶And these are the descendants of Shuthelah: of Eran, the clan of the Eranites. ³⁷These are the clans of the Ephraimites: the number of those enrolled was thirty-two thousand five hundred. These are the descendants of Joseph by their clans.

38 The descendants of Benjamin by their clans: of Bela, the clan of the Belaites; of Ashbel, the clan of the Ashbelites; of Ahiram, the clan of the Ahiramites; ³⁹of Shephupham, the clan of the Shuphamites; of Hupham, the clan of the Huphamites. ⁴⁰And the sons of Bela were Ard and Naaman: of Ard, the clan of the Ardites; of Naaman, the clan of the Naamites. ⁴¹These are the descendants of Benjamin by their clans; the number of those enrolled was forty-five thousand six hundred.

42 These are the descendants of Dan by their clans: of Shuham, the clan of the Shuhamites. These are the clans of Dan by their clans. ⁴³All the clans of the Shuhamites: sixty-four thousand four hundred enrolled.

44 The descendants of Asher by their families: of Imnah, the clan of the Imnites; of Ishvi, the clan of the Ishvites; of Beriah, the clan of the Beriites. ⁴⁵Of the descendants of Beriah: of Heber, the clan of the Heberites; of Malchiel, the clan of the Malchielites. ⁴⁶And the name of the daughter of Asher was Serah. ⁴⁷These are the clans of the Asherites: the number of those enrolled was fifty-three thousand four hundred.

48 The descendants of Naphtali by their clans: of Jahzeel, the clan of the Jahzeelites; of Guni, the clan of the Gunites; ⁴⁹of Jezer, the clan of the Jezerites; of Shillem, the clan of the Shillemites. ⁵⁰These are the Naphtalitesᵃ by their clans: the number of those enrolled was forty-five thousand four hundred.

51 This was the number of the Israelites enrolled: six hundred and one thousand seven hundred thirty.

# LUKE 2.36–52

THERE was also a prophet, Annaᵇ the daughter of Phanuel, of the tribe of Asher. She was of a great age, having lived with her husband seven years after her marriage, ³⁷then as a widow to the age of eighty-four. She never left the temple but worshiped there with fasting and prayer night and day. ³⁸At that moment she came, and began to praise God and to speak about the childᶜ to all who were looking for the redemption of Jerusalem.

39 When they had finished everything required by the law of the Lord, they returned to Galilee, to their own town of Nazareth. ⁴⁰The child grew and became strong, filled with wisdom; and the favor of God was upon him.

41 Now every year his parents went to Jerusalem for the festival of the Passover. ⁴²And when he was twelve years old, they went up as usual for the festival. ⁴³When the festival was ended and they started to return, the boy Jesus stayed behind in Jerusalem, but his parents did not know it. ⁴⁴Assuming that he was in the group of travelers, they went a day's journey. Then they started to look for him among their relatives and friends. ⁴⁵When they did not find him, they returned to Jerusalem to search for him. ⁴⁶After three days they found him in the temple, sitting among the teachers, listening to them and asking them questions. ⁴⁷And all who heard him were amazed at his understanding and his answers. ⁴⁸When his parents[a] saw him they were astonished; and his mother said to him, "Child, why have you treated us like this? Look, your father and I have been searching for you in great anxiety." ⁴⁹He said to them, "Why were you searching for me? Did you not know that I must be in my Father's house?"[b] ⁵⁰But they did not understand what he said to them. ⁵¹Then he went down with them and came to Nazareth, and was obedient to them. His mother treasured all these things in her heart.

52 And Jesus increased in wisdom and in years,[c] and in divine and human favor.

## PSALM 60.1–12

*To the leader: according to the Lily of the Covenant. A Miktam of David; for instruction; when he struggled with Aram-naharaim and with Aram-zobah, and when Joab on his return killed twelve thousand Edomites in the Valley of Salt.*

O GOD, you have rejected us,
    broken our defenses;
you have been angry; now
    restore us!
2  You have caused the land to
    quake; you have torn it
    open;
  repair the cracks in it, for it
    is tottering.
3  You have made your people
    suffer hard things;
  you have given us wine to
    drink that made us reel.

4  You have set up a banner for
    those who fear you,
  to rally to it out of bowshot.[d]
               *Selah*
5  Give victory with your right
    hand, and answer us,[e]
  so that those whom you love
    may be rescued.

6  God has promised in his
    sanctuary:[f]
  "With exultation I will divide
    up Shechem,
  and portion out the Vale of
    Succoth.
7  Gilead is mine, and Manasseh is
    mine;
  Ephraim is my helmet;
  Judah is my scepter.
8  Moab is my washbasin;
  on Edom I hurl my shoe;
  over Philistia I shout in
    triumph."

9  Who will bring me to the
    fortified city?
  Who will lead me to Edom?
10  Have you not rejected us,
    O God?
  You do not go out, O God,
    with our armies.
11  O grant us help against the foe,
    for human help is worthless.
12  With God we shall do valiantly;
    it is he who will tread down
    our foes.

[a] Gk *they*   [b] Or *be about my Father's interests?*   [c] Or *in stature*   [d] Gk Syr Jerome: Heb *because of the truth*   [e] Another reading is *me*   [f] Or *by his holiness*

## PROVERBS 11.15

To guarantee loans for a
 stranger brings
 trouble,
but there is safety in refusing
 to do so.

# MARCH 18

## NUMBERS 26.52—28.15

THE LORD spoke to Moses, saying: ⁵³To these the land shall be apportioned for inheritance according to the number of names. ⁵⁴To a large tribe you shall give a large inheritance, and to a small tribe you shall give a small inheritance; every tribe shall be given its inheritance according to its enrollment. ⁵⁵But the land shall be apportioned by lot; according to the names of their ancestral tribes they shall inherit. ⁵⁶Their inheritance shall be apportioned according to lot between the larger and the smaller.

57 This is the enrollment of the Levites by their clans: of Gershon, the clan of the Gershonites; of Kohath, the clan of the Kohathites; of Merari, the clan of the Merarites. ⁵⁸These are the clans of Levi: the clan of the Libnites, the clan of the Hebronites, the clan of the Mahlites, the clan of the Mushites, the clan of the Korahites. Now Kohath was the father of Amram. ⁵⁹The name of Amram's wife was Jochebed daughter of Levi, who was born to Levi in Egypt; and she bore to Amram: Aaron, Moses, and their sister Miriam. ⁶⁰To Aaron were born Nadab, Abihu, Eleazar, and Ithamar. ⁶¹But Nadab and Abihu died when they offered illicit fire before the LORD. ⁶²The number of those enrolled was twenty-three thousand, every male one month old and up; for they were not enrolled among the Israelites because there was no allotment given to them among the Israelites.

63 These were those enrolled by Moses and Eleazar the priest, who enrolled the Israelites in the plains of Moab by the Jordan opposite Jericho. ⁶⁴Among these there was not one of those enrolled by Moses and Aaron the priest, who had enrolled the Israelites in the wilderness of Sinai. ⁶⁵For the LORD had said of them, "They shall die in the wilderness." Not one of them was left, except Caleb son of Jephunneh and Joshua son of Nun.

27.1 THEN the daughters of Zelophehad came forward. Zelophehad was son of Hepher son of Gilead son of Machir son of Manasseh son of Joseph, a member of the Manassite clans. The names of his daughters were: Mahlah, Noah, Hoglah, Milcah, and Tirzah. ²They stood before Moses, Eleazar the priest, the leaders, and all the congregation, at the entrance of the tent of meeting, and they said, ³"Our father died in the wilderness; he was not among the company of those who gathered themselves together against the

LORD in the company of Korah, but died for his own sin; and he had no sons. ⁴Why should the name of our father be taken away from his clan because he had no son? Give to us a possession among our father's brothers."

5 Moses brought their case before the LORD. ⁶And the LORD spoke to Moses, saying: ⁷The daughters of Zelophehad are right in what they are saying; you shall indeed let them possess an inheritance among their father's brothers and pass the inheritance of their father on to them. ⁸You shall also say to the Israelites, "If a man dies, and has no son, then you shall pass his inheritance on to his daughter. ⁹If he has no daughter, then you shall give his inheritance to his brothers. ¹⁰If he has no brothers, then you shall give his inheritance to his father's brothers. ¹¹And if his father has no brothers, then you shall give his inheritance to the nearest kinsman of his clan, and he shall possess it. It shall be for the Israelites a statute and ordinance, as the LORD commanded Moses."

12 The LORD said to Moses, "Go up this mountain of the Abarim range, and see the land that I have given to the Israelites. ¹³When you have seen it, you also shall be gathered to your people, as your brother Aaron was, ¹⁴because you rebelled against my word in the wilderness of Zin when the congregation quarreled with me. ᵃ You did not show my holiness before their eyes at the waters." (These are the waters of Meribath-kadesh in the wilderness of Zin.) ¹⁵Moses spoke to the LORD, saying, ¹⁶"Let the LORD, the God of the spirits of all flesh, appoint someone over the congregation ¹⁷who shall go out before them and come in before them, who shall lead them out and bring them in, so that the congregation of the LORD may not be like sheep without a shepherd." ¹⁸So the LORD said to Moses, "Take Joshua son of Nun, a man in whom is the spirit, and lay your hand upon him; ¹⁹have him stand before Eleazar the priest and all the congregation, and commission him in their sight. ²⁰You shall give him some of your authority, so that all the congregation of the Israelites may obey. ²¹But he shall stand before Eleazar the priest, who shall inquire for him by the decision of the Urim before the LORD; at his word they shall go out, and at his word they shall come in, both he and all the Israelites with him, the whole congregation." ²²So Moses did as the LORD commanded him. He took Joshua and had him stand before Eleazar the priest and the whole congregation; ²³he laid his hands on him and commissioned him— as the LORD had directed through Moses.

**28**.1 THE LORD spoke to Moses, saying: ²Command the Israelites, and say to them: My offering, the food for my offerings by fire, my pleasing odor, you shall take care to offer to me at its appointed time. ³And you shall say to them, This is the offering by fire that you shall offer to the LORD: two male lambs a year old without blemish, daily, as a regular offering. ⁴One lamb you shall offer in the morning, and the other lamb you shall offer at twilightᵇ ⁵also one-tenth of an ephah of choice flour for a grain offering, mixed with one-fourth of a hin of beaten oil. ⁶It is a regular burnt offering, ordained at Mount Sinai for a pleasing odor, an offering by fire to the LORD. ⁷Its drink offering shall be one-fourth of a hin for each lamb; in the sanctuary you shall pour out a drink offering of strong drink to the LORD. ⁸The other lamb you shall offer at twilightᵇ with a grain offering and a drink offering like the one in the morning; you shall

ᵃHeb lacks *with me*   ᵇHeb *between the two evenings*

offer it as an offering by fire, a pleasing odor to the LORD.

9 On the sabbath day: two male lambs a year old without blemish, and two-tenths of an ephah of choice flour for a grain offering, mixed with oil, and its drink offering— ¹⁰this is the burnt offering for every sabbath, in addition to the regular burnt offering and its drink offering.

11 At the beginnings of your months you shall offer a burnt offering to the LORD: two young bulls, one ram, seven male lambs a year old without blemish; ¹²also three-tenths of an ephah of choice flour for a grain offering, mixed with oil, for each bull; and two-tenths of choice flour for a grain offering, mixed with oil, for the one ram; ¹³and one-tenth of choice flour mixed with oil as a grain offering for every lamb—a burnt offering of pleasing odor, an offering by fire to the LORD. ¹⁴Their drink offerings shall be half a hin of wine for a bull, one-third of a hin for a ram, and one-fourth of a hin for a lamb. This is the burnt offering of every month throughout the months of the year. ¹⁵And there shall be one male goat for a sin offering to the LORD; it shall be offered in addition to the regular burnt offering and its drink offering.

## LUKE 3.1–22

IN the fifteenth year of the reign of Emperor Tiberius, when Pontius Pilate was governor of Judea, and Herod was rulerᵃ of Galilee, and his brother Philip rulerᵃ of the region of Ituraea and Trachonitis, and Lysanias rulerᵃ of Abilene, ²during the high priesthood of Annas and Caiaphas, the word of God came to John son of Zechariah in the wilderness. ³He went into all the region around the Jordan, proclaiming a baptism of repentance for the for-

giveness of sins, ⁴as it is written in the book of the words of the prophet Isaiah,

"The voice of one crying out in
  the wilderness:
 'Prepare the way of the Lord,
  make his paths straight.
5  Every valley shall be filled,
  and every mountain and hill
   shall be made low,
 and the crooked shall be made
   straight,
  and the rough ways made
   smooth;
6  and all flesh shall see the
   salvation of God.' "

7 John said to the crowds that came out to be baptized by him, "You brood of vipers! Who warned you to flee from the wrath to come? ⁸Bear fruits worthy of repentance. Do not begin to say to yourselves, 'We have Abraham as our ancestor'; for I tell you, God is able from these stones to raise up children to Abraham. ⁹Even now the ax is lying at the root of the trees; every tree therefore that does not bear good fruit is cut down and thrown into the fire."

10 And the crowds asked him, "What then should we do?" ¹¹In reply he said to them, "Whoever has two coats must share with anyone who has none; and whoever has food must do likewise." ¹²Even tax collectors came to be baptized, and they asked him, "Teacher, what should we do?" ¹³He said to them, "Collect no more than the amount prescribed for you." ¹⁴Soldiers also asked him, "And we, what should we do?" He said to them, "Do not extort money from anyone by threats or false accusation, and be satisfied with your wages."

15 As the people were filled with expectation, and all were questioning in their hearts concerning John, whether he might be the Messiah, ᵇ ¹⁶John answered all of them by saying, "I baptize

aGk *tetrarch*  bOr *the Christ*

you with water; but one who is more powerful than I is coming; I am not worthy to untie the thong of his sandals. He will baptize you with[a] the Holy Spirit and fire. [17]His winnowing fork is in his hand, to clear his threshing floor and to gather the wheat into his granary; but the chaff he will burn with unquenchable fire."

18 So, with many other exhortations, he proclaimed the good news to the people. [19]But Herod the ruler,[b] who had been rebuked by him because of Herodias, his brother's wife, and because of all the evil things that Herod had done, [20]added to them all by shutting up John in prison.

21 Now when all the people were baptized, and when Jesus also had been baptized and was praying, the heaven was opened, [22]and the Holy Spirit descended upon him in bodily form like a dove. And a voice came from heaven, "You are my Son, the Beloved;[c] with you I am well pleased."[d]

## PSALM 61.1–8

*To the leader: with stringed instruments. Of David.*

HEAR my cry, O God;
    listen to my prayer.
2  From the end of the
      earth I call to you,
  when my heart is faint.

  Lead me to the rock
    that is higher than I;
3  for you are my refuge,
    a strong tower against the
      enemy.

4  Let me abide in your tent
    forever,
  find refuge under the shelter
    of your wings.    *Selah*
5  For you, O God, have heard my
    vows;
  you have given me the
    heritage of those who
    fear your name.

6  Prolong the life of the king;
    may his years endure to all
    generations!
7  May he be enthroned forever
    before God;
  appoint steadfast love and
    faithfulness to watch
    over him!

8  So I will always sing praises to
    your name,
  as I pay my vows day after
    day.

## PROVERBS 11.16–17

A GRACIOUS woman gets honor,
  but she who hates virtue is
    covered with shame.[e]
The timid become destitute,[f]
  but the aggressive gain
    riches.
17  Those who are kind reward
    themselves,
  but the cruel do themselves
    harm.

---

[a]Or *in*  [b]Gk *tetrarch*  [c]Or *my beloved Son*  [d]Other ancient authorities read *You are my Son, today I have begotten you*  [e]Compare Gk Syr: Heb lacks *but she . . . shame*  [f]Gk: Heb lacks *The timid . . . destitute*

# MARCH 19

NUMBERS 28.16—29.40

O<sup>N</sup> the fourteenth day of the first month there shall be a passover offering to the LORD. <sup>17</sup>And on the fifteenth day of this month is a festival; seven days shall unleavened bread be eaten. <sup>18</sup>On the first day there shall be a holy convocation. You shall not work at your occupations. <sup>19</sup>You shall offer an offering by fire, a burnt offering to the LORD: two young bulls, one ram, and seven male lambs a year old; see that they are without blemish. <sup>20</sup>Their grain offering shall be of choice flour mixed with oil: three-tenths of an ephah shall you offer for a bull, and two-tenths for a ram; <sup>21</sup>one-tenth shall you offer for each of the seven lambs; <sup>22</sup>also one male goat for a sin offering, to make atonement for you. <sup>23</sup>You shall offer these in addition to the burnt offering of the morning, which belongs to the regular burnt offering. <sup>24</sup>In the same way you shall offer daily, for seven days, the food of an offering by fire, a pleasing odor to the LORD; it shall be offered in addition to the regular burnt offering and its drink offering. <sup>25</sup>And on the seventh day you shall have a holy convocation; you shall not work at your occupations.

26 On the day of the first fruits, when you offer a grain offering of new grain to the LORD at your festival of weeks, you shall have a holy convocation; you shall not work at your occupations. <sup>27</sup>You shall offer a burnt offering, a pleasing odor to the LORD: two young bulls, one ram, seven male lambs a year old. <sup>28</sup>Their grain offering shall be of choice flour mixed with oil, three-tenths of an ephah for each bull, two-tenths for one ram, <sup>29</sup>one-tenth for each of the seven lambs; <sup>30</sup>with one male goat, to make atonement for you. <sup>31</sup>In addition to the regular burnt offering with its grain offering, you shall offer them and their drink offering. They shall be without blemish.

**29.1** O<sup>N</sup> the first day of the seventh month you shall have a holy convocation; you shall not work at your occupations. It is a day for you to blow the trumpets, <sup>2</sup>and you shall offer a burnt offering, a pleasing odor to the LORD: one young bull, one ram, seven male lambs a year old without blemish. <sup>3</sup>Their grain offering shall be of choice flour mixed with oil, three-tenths of one ephah for the bull, two-tenths for the ram, <sup>4</sup>and one-tenth for each of the seven lambs; <sup>5</sup>with one male goat for a sin offering, to make atonement for you. <sup>6</sup>These are in addition to the burnt offering of the new moon and its grain offering, and the regular burnt offering and its grain offering, and their drink offerings, according to the ordinance for them, a pleasing odor, an offering by fire to the LORD.

7 On the tenth day of this seventh month you shall have a holy convocation, and deny yourselves;<sup>a</sup> you shall do no work. <sup>8</sup>You shall offer a burnt offering to the LORD, a pleasing odor: one young bull, one ram, seven male lambs a year old. They shall be without blemish. <sup>9</sup>Their grain offering shall be of choice flour mixed with oil, three-tenths of an ephah for the bull, two-tenths for the one ram, <sup>10</sup>one-tenth for each of the seven lambs; <sup>11</sup>with one male goat for a sin offering, in addition to the sin offering of atonement, and

the regular burnt offering and its grain offering, and their drink offerings.

12 On the fifteenth day of the seventh month you shall have a holy convocation; you shall not work at your occupations. You shall celebrate a festival to the LORD seven days. 13You shall offer a burnt offering, an offering by fire, a pleasing odor to the LORD: thirteen young bulls, two rams, fourteen male lambs a year old. They shall be without blemish. 14Their grain offering shall be of choice flour mixed with oil, three-tenths of an ephah for each of the thirteen bulls, two-tenths for each of the two rams, 15and one-tenth for each of the fourteen lambs; 16also one male goat for a sin offering, in addition to the regular burnt offering, its grain offering and its drink offering.

17 On the second day: twelve young bulls, two rams, fourteen male lambs a year old without blemish, 18with the grain offering and the drink offerings for the bulls, for the rams, and for the lambs, as prescribed in accordance with their number; 19also one male goat for a sin offering, in addition to the regular burnt offering and its grain offering, and their drink offerings.

20 On the third day: eleven bulls, two rams, fourteen male lambs a year old without blemish, 21with the grain offering and the drink offerings for the bulls, for the rams, and for the lambs, as prescribed in accordance with their number; 22also one male goat for a sin offering, in addition to the regular burnt offering and its grain offering and its drink offering.

23 On the fourth day: ten bulls, two rams, fourteen male lambs a year old without blemish, 24with the grain offering and the drink offerings for the bulls, for the rams, and for the lambs, as prescribed in accordance with their number; 25also one male goat for a sin offering, in addition to the regular burnt offering, its grain offering and its drink offering.

26 On the fifth day: nine bulls, two rams, fourteen male lambs a year old without blemish, 27with the grain offering and the drink offerings for the bulls, for the rams, and for the lambs, as prescribed in accordance with their number; 28also one male goat for a sin offering, in addition to the regular burnt offering and its grain offering and its drink offering.

29 On the sixth day: eight bulls, two rams, fourteen male lambs a year old without blemish, 30with the grain offering and the drink offerings for the bulls, for the rams, and for the lambs, as prescribed in accordance with their number; 31also one male goat for a sin offering, in addition to the regular burnt offering, its grain offering, and its drink offerings.

32 On the seventh day: seven bulls, two rams, fourteen male lambs a year old without blemish, 33with the grain offering and the drink offerings for the bulls, for the rams, and for the lambs, as prescribed in accordance with their number; 34also one male goat for a sin offering, besides the regular burnt offering, its grain offering, and its drink offering.

35 On the eighth day you shall have a solemn assembly; you shall not work at your occupations. 36You shall offer a burnt offering, an offering by fire, a pleasing odor to the LORD: one bull, one ram, seven male lambs a year old without blemish, 37and the grain offering and the drink offerings for the bull, for the ram, and for the lambs, as prescribed in accordance with their number; 38also one male goat for a sin offering, in addition to the regular burnt offering and its grain offering and its drink offering.

39 These you shall offer to the LORD at your appointed festivals, in addition to your votive offerings and your freewill offerings, as your burnt offerings, your grain offerings, your drink

offerings, and your offerings of well-being.

40ᵃ So Moses told the Israelites everything just as the Lord had commanded Moses.

## LUKE 3.23–38

Jᴇsus was about thirty years old when he began his work. He was the son (as was thought) of Joseph son of Heli, 24son of Matthat, son of Levi, son of Melchi, son of Jannai, son of Joseph, 25son of Mattathias, son of Amos, son of Nahum, son of Esli, son of Naggai, 26son of Maath, son of Mattathias, son of Semein, son of Josech, son of Joda, 27son of Joanan, son of Rhesa, son of Zerubbabel, son of Shealtiel,ᵇ son of Neri, 28son of Melchi, son of Addi, son of Cosam, son of Elmadam, son of Er, 29son of Joshua, son of Eliezer, son of Jorim, son of Matthat, son of Levi, 30son of Simeon, son of Judah, son of Joseph, son of Jonam, son of Eliakim, 31son of Melea, son of Menna, son of Mattatha, son of Nathan, son of David, 32son of Jesse, son of Obed, son of Boaz, son of Sala,ᶜ son of Nahshon, 33son of Amminadab, son of Admin, son of Arni,ᵈ son of Hezron, son of Perez, son of Judah, 34son of Jacob, son of Isaac, son of Abraham, son of Terah, son of Nahor, 35son of Serug, son of Reu, son of Peleg, son of Eber, son of Shelah, 36son of Cainan, son of Arphaxad, son of Shem, son of Noah, son of Lamech, 37son of Methuselah, son of Enoch, son of Jared, son of Mahalaleel, son of Cainan, 38son of Enos, son of Seth, son of Adam, son of God.

## PSALM 62.1–12

*To the leader: according to Jeduthun. A Psalm of David.*

Fᴏʀ God alone my soul waits in
      silence;
   from him comes my
      salvation.
2  He alone is my rock and my
      salvation,
   my fortress; I shall never be
      shaken.

3  How long will you assail a
      person,
   will you batter your victim, all
      of you,
   as you would a leaning wall, a
      tottering fence?
4  Their only plan is to bring down
      a person of prominence.
   They take pleasure in
      falsehood;
   they bless with their mouths,
   but inwardly they curse.
                        *Selah*

5  For God alone my soul waits in
      silence,
   for my hope is from him.
6  He alone is my rock and my
      salvation,
   my fortress; I shall not be
      shaken.
7  On God rests my deliverance
      and my honor;
   my mighty rock, my refuge is
      in God.

8  Trust in him at all times,
      O people;
   pour out your heart before
      him;
   God is a refuge for us.   *Selah*

9  Those of low estate are but a
      breath,

ᵃCh 30.1 in Heb   ᵇGk *Salathiel*   ᶜOther ancient authorities read *Salmon*   ᵈOther ancient authorities read *Amminadab, son of Aram*; others vary widely

those of high estate are a
  delusion;
  in the balances they go up;
    they are together lighter than
      a breath.
10  Put no confidence in extortion,
      and set no vain hopes on
        robbery;
    if riches increase, do not set
      your heart on them.

11  Once God has spoken;
      twice have I heard this:
    that power belongs to God,

12      and steadfast love belongs to
          you, O Lord.
    For you repay to all
      according to their work.

## PROVERBS 11.18–19

THE wicked earn no real gain,
    but those who sow
      righteousness get a true
        reward.
19  Whoever is steadfast in
      righteousness will live,
    but whoever pursues evil will
      die.

# MARCH 20

## NUMBERS 30.1—31.54

THEN Moses said to the heads of the tribes of the Israelites: This is what the Lord has commanded. ²When a man makes a vow to the Lord, or swears an oath to bind himself by a pledge, he shall not break his word; he shall do according to all that proceeds out of his mouth.

3 When a woman makes a vow to the Lord, or binds herself by a pledge, while within her father's house, in her youth, ⁴and her father hears of her vow or her pledge by which she has bound herself, and says nothing to her; then all her vows shall stand, and any pledge by which she has bound herself shall stand. ⁵But if her father expresses disapproval to her at the time that he hears of it, no vow of hers, and no pledge by which she has bound herself, shall stand; and the Lord will forgive her, because her father had expressed to her his disapproval.

6 If she marries, while obligated by her vows or any thoughtless utterance of her lips by which she has bound herself, ⁷and her husband hears of it and says nothing to her at the time that he hears, then her vows shall stand, and her pledges by which she has bound herself shall stand. ⁸But if, at the time that her husband hears of it, he expresses disapproval to her, then he shall nullify the vow by which she was obligated, or the thoughtless utterance of her lips, by which she bound herself; and the Lord will forgive her. ⁹(But every vow of a widow or of a divorced woman, by which she has bound herself, shall be binding upon her.) ¹⁰And if she made a vow in her husband's house, or bound herself by a pledge with an oath, ¹¹and her husband heard it and said nothing to her, and did not express disapproval to her, then all her vows shall stand, and any pledge by which she bound herself shall stand. ¹²But if her husband nullifies them at the time that he hears them, then what-

ever proceeds out of her lips concerning her vows, or concerning her pledge of herself, shall not stand. Her husband has nullified them, and the LORD will forgive her. [13]Any vow or any binding oath to deny herself,[a] her husband may allow to stand, or her husband may nullify. [14]But if her husband says nothing to her from day to day,[b] then he validates all her vows, or all her pledges, by which she is obligated; he has validated them, because he said nothing to her at the time that he heard of them. [15]But if he nullifies them some time after he has heard of them, then he shall bear her guilt.

16  These are the statutes that the LORD commanded Moses concerning a husband and his wife, and a father and his daughter while she is still young and in her father's house.

**31.**[1] THE LORD spoke to Moses, saying, [2]"Avenge the Israelites on the Midianites; afterward you shall be gathered to your people." [3]So Moses said to the people, "Arm some of your number for the war, so that they may go against Midian, to execute the LORD's vengeance on Midian. [4]You shall send a thousand from each of the tribes of Israel to the war." [5]So out of the thousands of Israel, a thousand from each tribe were conscripted, twelve thousand armed for battle. [6]Moses sent them to the war, a thousand from each tribe, along with Phinehas son of Eleazar the priest,[c] with the vessels of the sanctuary and the trumpets for sounding the alarm in his hand. [7]They did battle against Midian, as the LORD had commanded Moses, and killed every male. [8]They killed the kings of Midian: Evi, Rekem, Zur, Hur, and Reba, the five kings of Midian, in addition to others who were slain by them; and they also killed Balaam son of Beor with the

sword. [9]The Israelites took the women of Midian and their little ones captive; and they took all their cattle, their flocks, and all their goods as booty. [10]All their towns where they had settled, and all their encampments, they burned, [11]but they took all the spoil and all the booty, both people and animals. [12]Then they brought the captives and the booty and the spoil to Moses, to Eleazar the priest, and to the congregation of the Israelites, at the camp on the plains of Moab by the Jordan at Jericho.

13  Moses, Eleazar the priest, and all the leaders of the congregation went to meet them outside the camp. [14]Moses became angry with the officers of the army, the commanders of thousands and the commanders of hundreds, who had come from service in the war. [15]Moses said to them, "Have you allowed all the women to live? [16]These women here, on Balaam's advice, made the Israelites act treacherously against the LORD in the affair of Peor, so that the plague came among the congregation of the LORD. [17]Now therefore, kill every male among the little ones, and kill every woman who has known a man by sleeping with him. [18]But all the young girls who have not known a man by sleeping with him, keep alive for yourselves. [19]Camp outside the camp seven days; whoever of you has killed any person or touched a corpse, purify yourselves and your captives on the third and on the seventh day. [20]You shall purify every garment, every article of skin, everything made of goats' hair, and every article of wood."

21  Eleazar the priest said to the troops who had gone to battle: "This is the statute of the law that the LORD has commanded Moses: [22]gold, silver, bronze, iron, tin, and lead— [23]everything that can withstand fire, shall be passed through fire, and it shall be

---

**a** Or *to fast*   **b** Or *from that day to the next*   **c** Gk: Heb adds *to the war*

clean. Nevertheless it shall also be purified with the water for purification; and whatever cannot withstand fire, shall be passed through the water. [24]You must wash your clothes on the seventh day, and you shall be clean; afterward you may come into the camp."

25  The Lord spoke to Moses, saying, [26]"You and Eleazar the priest and the heads of the ancestral houses of the congregation make an inventory of the booty captured, both human and animal. [27]Divide the booty into two parts, between the warriors who went out to battle and all the congregation. [28]From the share of the warriors who went out to battle, set aside as tribute for the Lord, one item out of every five hundred, whether persons, oxen, donkeys, sheep, or goats. [29]Take it from their half and give it to Eleazar the priest as an offering to the Lord. [30]But from the Israelites' half you shall take one out of every fifty, whether persons, oxen, donkeys, sheep, or goats—all the animals—and give them to the Levites who have charge of the tabernacle of the Lord."

31  Then Moses and Eleazar the priest did as the Lord had commanded Moses:

32  The booty remaining from the spoil that the troops had taken totaled six hundred seventy-five thousand sheep, [33]seventy-two thousand oxen, [34]sixty-one thousand donkeys, [35]and thirty-two thousand persons in all, women who had not known a man by sleeping with him.

36  The half-share, the portion of those who had gone out to war, was in number three hundred thirty-seven thousand five hundred sheep and goats, [37]and the Lord's tribute of sheep and goats was six hundred seventy-five. [38]The oxen were thirty-six thousand, of which the Lord's tribute was seventy-two. [39]The donkeys were thirty thousand five hundred, of which the Lord's tribute was sixty-one. [40]The persons were sixteen thousand, of which the Lord's tribute was thirty-two persons. [41]Moses gave the tribute, the offering for the Lord, to Eleazar the priest, as the Lord had commanded Moses.

42  As for the Israelites' half, which Moses separated from that of the troops, [43]the congregation's half was three hundred thirty-seven thousand five hundred sheep and goats, [44]thirty-six thousand oxen, [45]thirty thousand five hundred donkeys, [46]and sixteen thousand persons. [47]From the Israelites' half Moses took one of every fifty, both of persons and of animals, and gave them to the Levites who had charge of the tabernacle of the Lord; as the Lord had commanded Moses.

48  Then the officers who were over the thousands of the army, the commanders of thousands and the commanders of hundreds, approached Moses, [49]and said to Moses, "Your servants have counted the warriors who are under our command, and not one of us is missing. [50]And we have brought the Lord's offering, what each of us found, articles of gold, armlets and bracelets, signet rings, earrings, and pendants, to make atonement for ourselves before the Lord." [51]Moses and Eleazar the priest received the gold from them, all in the form of crafted articles. [52]And all the gold of the offering that they offered to the Lord, from the commanders of thousands and the commanders of hundreds, was sixteen thousand seven hundred fifty shekels. [53](The troops had all taken plunder for themselves.) [54]So Moses and Eleazar the priest received the gold from the commanders of thousands and of hundreds, and brought it into the tent of meeting as a memorial for the Israelites before the Lord.

## LUKE 4.1–30

JESUS, full of the Holy Spirit, returned from the Jordan and was led by the Spirit in the wilderness, ²where for forty days he was tempted by the devil. He ate nothing at all during those days, and when they were over, he was famished. ³The devil said to him, "If you are the Son of God, command this stone to become a loaf of bread." ⁴Jesus answered him, "It is written, 'One does not live by bread alone.'"

5 Then the devilᵃ led him up and showed him in an instant all the kingdoms of the world. ⁶And the devilᵃ said to him, "To you I will give their glory and all this authority; for it has been given over to me, and I give it to anyone I please. ⁷If you, then, will worship me, it will all be yours." ⁸Jesus answered him, "It is written,

'Worship the Lord your God,
    and serve only him.'"

9 Then the devilᵃ took him to Jerusalem, and placed him on the pinnacle of the temple, saying to him, "If you are the Son of God, throw yourself down from here, ¹⁰for it is written,

'He will command his angels
        concerning you,
    to protect you,'

¹¹and

'On their hands they will bear
        you up,
    so that you will not dash your
        foot against a stone.'"

¹²Jesus answered him, "It is said, 'Do not put the Lord your God to the test.'" ¹³When the devil had finished every test, he departed from him until an opportune time.

14 Then Jesus, filled with the power of the Spirit, returned to Galilee, and a report about him spread through all the surrounding country. ¹⁵He began to teach in their synagogues and was praised by everyone.

16 When he came to Nazareth, where he had been brought up, he went to the synagogue on the sabbath day, as was his custom. He stood up to read, ¹⁷and the scroll of the prophet Isaiah was given to him. He unrolled the scroll and found the place where it was written:

¹⁸    "The Spirit of the Lord is upon
            me,
        because he has anointed me
            to bring good news to the
                poor.
    He has sent me to proclaim
            release to the captives
        and recovery of sight to the
            blind,
            to let the oppressed go
                free,
¹⁹    to proclaim the year of the
            Lord's favor."

²⁰And he rolled up the scroll, gave it back to the attendant, and sat down. The eyes of all in the synagogue were fixed on him. ²¹Then he began to say to them, "Today this scripture has been fulfilled in your hearing." ²²All spoke well of him and were amazed at the gracious words that came from his mouth. They said, "Is not this Joseph's son?" ²³He said to them, "Doubtless you will quote to me this proverb, 'Doctor, cure yourself!' And you will say, 'Do here also in your hometown the things that we have heard you did at Capernaum.'" ²⁴And he said, "Truly I tell you, no prophet is accepted in the prophet's hometown. ²⁵But the truth is, there were many widows in Israel in the time of Elijah, when the heaven was shut up three years and six months, and there was a severe famine over all the land; ²⁶yet Elijah was sent to none of them except to a widow at Zarephath in Sidon. ²⁷There were also many lep-

a Gk *he*

ers[a] in Israel in the time of the prophet Elisha, and none of them was cleansed except Naaman the Syrian." 28When they heard this, all in the synagogue were filled with rage. 29They got up, drove him out of the town, and led him to the brow of the hill on which their town was built, so that they might hurl him off the cliff. 30But he passed through the midst of them and went on his way.

## PSALM 63.1–11

*A Psalm of David, when he was in the Wilderness of Judah.*

O GOD, you are my God, I seek you,
  my soul thirsts for you;
my flesh faints for you,
    as in a dry and weary land
      where there is no water.
2  So I have looked upon you in
      the sanctuary,
    beholding your power and
      glory.
3  Because your steadfast love is
      better than life,
    my lips will praise you.
4  So I will bless you as long as I
      live;
    I will lift up my hands and call
      on your name.

5  My soul is satisfied as with a
      rich feast,[b]
and my mouth praises you
    with joyful lips
6  when I think of you on my bed,
    and meditate on you in the
      watches of the night;
7  for you have been my help,
    and in the shadow of your
      wings I sing for joy.
8  My soul clings to you;
    your right hand upholds me.

9  But those who seek to destroy
      my life
    shall go down into the depths
      of the earth;
10  they shall be given over to the
      power of the sword,
    they shall be prey for jackals.
11  But the king shall rejoice in
      God;
    all who swear by him shall
      exult,
    for the mouths of liars will be
      stopped.

## PROVERBS 11.20–21

CROOKED minds are an
      abomination to the
      LORD,
    but those of blameless ways
      are his delight.
21  Be assured, the wicked will not
      go unpunished,
    but those who are righteous
      will escape.

---

aThe terms *leper* and *leprosy* can refer to several diseases   bHeb *with fat and fatness*

# MARCH 21



Now the Reubenites and the Gadites owned a very great number of cattle. When they saw that the land of Jazer and the land of Gilead was a good place for cattle, ²the Gadites and the Reubenites came and spoke to Moses, to Eleazar the priest, and to the leaders of the congregation, saying, ³"Ataroth, Dibon, Jazer, Nimrah, Heshbon, Elealeh, Sebam, Nebo, and Beon— ⁴the land that the LORD subdued before the congregation of Israel—is a land for cattle; and your servants have cattle." ⁵They continued, "If we have found favor in your sight, let this land be given to your servants for a possession; do not make us cross the Jordan."

6 But Moses said to the Gadites and to the Reubenites, "Shall your brothers go to war while you sit here? ⁷Why will you discourage the hearts of the Israelites from going over into the land that the LORD has given them? ⁸Your fathers did this, when I sent them from Kadesh-barnea to see the land. ⁹When they went up to the Wadi Eshcol and saw the land, they discouraged the hearts of the Israelites from going into the land that the LORD had given them. ¹⁰The LORD's anger was kindled on that day and he swore, saying, ¹¹'Surely none of the people who came up out of Egypt, from twenty years old and upward, shall see the land that I swore to give to Abraham, to Isaac, and to Jacob, because they have not unreservedly followed me— ¹²none except Caleb son of Jephunneh the Kenizzite and Joshua son of Nun, for they have unreservedly followed the LORD.' ¹³And the LORD's anger was kindled against Israel, and he made them wander in the wilderness for forty years, until all the generation that had done evil in the sight of the LORD had disappeared. ¹⁴And now you, a brood of sinners, have risen in place of your fathers, to increase the LORD's fierce anger against Israel! ¹⁵If you turn away from following him, he will again abandon them in the wilderness; and you will destroy all this people."

16 Then they came up to him and said, "We will build sheepfolds here for our flocks, and towns for our little ones, ¹⁷but we will take up arms as a vanguardᵃ before the Israelites, until we have brought them to their place. Meanwhile our little ones will stay in the fortified towns because of the inhabitants of the land. ¹⁸We will not return to our homes until all the Israelites have obtained their inheritance. ¹⁹We will not inherit with them on the other side of the Jordan and beyond, because our inheritance has come to us on this side of the Jordan to the east."

20 So Moses said to them, "If you do this—if you take up arms to go before the LORD for the war, ²¹and all those of you who bear arms cross the Jordan before the LORD, until he has driven out his enemies from before him ²²and the land is subdued before the LORD—then after that you may return and be free of obligation to the LORD and to Israel, and this land shall be your possession before the LORD. ²³But if you do not do this, you have sinned against the LORD; and be sure your sin will find you out. ²⁴Build towns for your little ones, and folds for your flocks; but do what you have promised."

25 Then the Gadites and the Reu-

---

ᵃCn: Heb *hurrying*

benites said to Moses, "Your servants will do as my lord commands. <sup>26</sup>Our little ones, our wives, our flocks, and all our livestock shall remain there in the towns of Gilead; <sup>27</sup>but your servants will cross over, everyone armed for war, to do battle for the LORD, just as my lord orders."

28 So Moses gave command concerning them to Eleazar the priest, to Joshua son of Nun, and to the heads of the ancestral houses of the Israelite tribes. <sup>29</sup>And Moses said to them, "If the Gadites and the Reubenites, everyone armed for battle before the LORD, will cross over the Jordan with you and the land shall be subdued before you, then you shall give them the land of Gilead for a possession; <sup>30</sup>but if they will not cross over with you armed, they shall have possessions among you in the land of Canaan." <sup>31</sup>The Gadites and the Reubenites answered, "As the LORD has spoken to your servants, so we will do. <sup>32</sup>We will cross over armed before the LORD into the land of Canaan, but the possession of our inheritance shall remain with us on this side of[a] the Jordan."

33 Moses gave to them—to the Gadites and to the Reubenites and to the half-tribe of Manasseh son of Joseph—the kingdom of King Sihon of the Amorites and the kingdom of King Og of Bashan, the land and its towns, with the territories of the surrounding towns. <sup>34</sup>And the Gadites rebuilt Dibon, Ataroth, Aroer, <sup>35</sup>Atrothshophan, Jazer, Jogbehah; <sup>36</sup>Bethnimrah, and Beth-haran, fortified cities, and folds for sheep. <sup>37</sup>And the Reubenites rebuilt Heshbon, Elealeh, Kiriathaim, <sup>38</sup>Nebo, and Baalmeon (some names being changed), and Sibmah; and they gave names to the towns that they rebuilt. <sup>39</sup>The descendants of Machir son of Manasseh went to Gilead, captured it, and dispossessed the Amorites who were there; <sup>40</sup>so Moses gave Gilead to Machir son of Manasseh, and he settled there. <sup>41</sup>Jair son of Manasseh went and captured their villages, and renamed them Havvoth-jair.[b] <sup>42</sup>And Nobah went and captured Kenath and its villages, and renamed it Nobah after himself.

<sup>33.1</sup> THESE are the stages by which the Israelites went out of the land of Egypt in military formation under the leadership of Moses and Aaron. <sup>2</sup>Moses wrote down their starting points, stage by stage, by command of the LORD; and these are their stages according to their starting places. <sup>3</sup>They set out from Rameses in the first month, on the fifteenth day of the first month; on the day after the passover the Israelites went out boldly in the sight of all the Egyptians, <sup>4</sup>while the Egyptians were burying all their firstborn, whom the LORD had struck down among them. The LORD executed judgments even against their gods.

5 So the Israelites set out from Rameses, and camped at Succoth. <sup>6</sup>They set out from Succoth, and camped at Etham, which is on the edge of the wilderness. <sup>7</sup>They set out from Etham, and turned back to Pi-hahiroth, which faces Baal-zephon; and they camped before Migdol. <sup>8</sup>They set out from Pi-hahiroth, passed through the sea into the wilderness, went a three days' journey in the wilderness of Etham, and camped at Marah. <sup>9</sup>They set out from Marah and came to Elim; at Elim there were twelve springs of water and seventy palm trees, and they camped there. <sup>10</sup>They set out from Elim and camped by the Red Sea.[c] <sup>11</sup>They set out from the Red Sea[c] and camped in the wilderness of Sin. <sup>12</sup>They set out from the wilderness of Sin and camped at Dophkah. <sup>13</sup>They set

aHeb *beyond*   bThat is *the villages of Jair*   cOr *Sea of Reeds*

out from Dophkah and camped at Alush. ¹⁴They set out from Alush and camped at Rephidim, where there was no water for the people to drink. ¹⁵They set out from Rephidim and camped in the wilderness of Sinai. ¹⁶They set out from the wilderness of Sinai and camped at Kibroth-hattaavah. ¹⁷They set out from Kibroth-hattaavah and camped at Hazeroth. ¹⁸They set out from Hazeroth and camped at Rithmah. ¹⁹They set out from Rithmah and camped at Rimmon-perez. ²⁰They set out from Rimmon-perez and camped at Libnah. ²¹They set out from Libnah and camped at Rissah. ²²They set out from Rissah and camped at Kehelathah. ²³They set out from Kehelathah and camped at Mount Shepher. ²⁴They set out from Mount Shepher and camped at Haradah. ²⁵They set out from Haradah and camped at Makheloth. ²⁶They set out from Makheloth and camped at Tahath. ²⁷They set out from Tahath and camped at Terah. ²⁸They set out from Terah and camped at Mithkah. ²⁹They set out from Mithkah and camped at Hashmonah. ³⁰They set out from Hashmonah and camped at Moseroth. ³¹They set out from Moseroth and camped at Bene-jaakan. ³²They set out from Bene-jaakan and camped at Hor-haggidgad. ³³They set out from Hor-haggidgad and camped at Jotbathah. ³⁴They set out from Jotbathah and camped at Abronah. ³⁵They set out from Abronah and camped at Ezion-geber. ³⁶They set out from Ezion-geber and camped in the wilderness of Zin (that is, Kadesh). ³⁷They set out from Kadesh and camped at Mount Hor, on the edge of the land of Edom.

38 Aaron the priest went up Mount Hor at the command of the LORD and died there in the fortieth year after the Israelites had come out of the land of Egypt, on the first day of the fifth month. ³⁹Aaron was one hundred twenty-three years old when he died on Mount Hor.

## LUKE 4.31—5.11

**H**E [Jesus] went down to Capernaum, a city in Galilee, and was teaching them on the sabbath. ³²They were astounded at his teaching, because he spoke with authority. ³³In the synagogue there was a man who had the spirit of an unclean demon, and he cried out with a loud voice, ³⁴"Let us alone! What have you to do with us, Jesus of Nazareth? Have you come to destroy us? I know who you are, the Holy One of God." ³⁵But Jesus rebuked him, saying, "Be silent, and come out of him!" When the demon had thrown him down before them, he came out of him without having done him any harm. ³⁶They were all amazed and kept saying to one another, "What kind of utterance is this? For with authority and power he commands the unclean spirits, and out they come!" ³⁷And a report about him began to reach every place in the region.

38 After leaving the synagogue he entered Simon's house. Now Simon's mother-in-law was suffering from a high fever, and they asked him about her. ³⁹Then he stood over her and rebuked the fever, and it left her. Immediately she got up and began to serve them.

40 As the sun was setting, all those who had any who were sick with various kinds of diseases brought them to him; and he laid his hands on each of them and cured them. ⁴¹Demons also came out of many, shouting, "You are the Son of God!" But he rebuked them and would not allow them to speak, because they knew that he was the Messiah. [a]

42 At daybreak he departed and went into a deserted place. And the

[a] Or *the Christ*

crowds were looking for him; and when they reached him, they wanted to prevent him from leaving them. ⁴³But he said to them, "I must proclaim the good news of the kingdom of God to the other cities also; for I was sent for this purpose." ⁴⁴So he continued proclaiming the message in the synagogues of Judea. ᵃ

5.1 ONCE while Jesusᵇ was standing beside the lake of Gennesaret, and the crowd was pressing in on him to hear the word of God, ²he saw two boats there at the shore of the lake; the fishermen had gone out of them and were washing their nets. ³He got into one of the boats, the one belonging to Simon, and asked him to put out a little way from the shore. Then he sat down and taught the crowds from the boat. ⁴When he had finished speaking, he said to Simon, "Put out into the deep water and let down your nets for a catch." ⁵Simon answered, "Master, we have worked all night long but have caught nothing. Yet if you say so, I will let down the nets." ⁶When they had done this, they caught so many fish that their nets were beginning to break. ⁷So they signaled their partners in the other boat to come and help them. And they came and filled both boats, so that they began to sink. ⁸But when Simon Peter saw it, he fell down at Jesus' knees, saying, "Go away from me, Lord, for I am a sinful man!" ⁹For he and all who were with him were amazed at the catch of fish that they had taken; ¹⁰and so also were James and John, sons of Zebedee, who were partners with Simon. Then Jesus said to Simon, "Do not be afraid; from now on you will be catching people." ¹¹When they had brought their boats to shore, they left everything and followed him.

## PSALM 64. 1–10

*To the leader. A Psalm of David.*

H EAR my voice, O God, in my
    complaint;
preserve my life from the
    dread enemy.
2 Hide me from the secret plots
    of the wicked,
  from the scheming of
    evildoers,
3 who whet their tongues like
    swords,
  who aim bitter words like
    arrows,
4 shooting from ambush at the
    blameless;
  they shoot suddenly and
    without fear.
5 They hold fast to their evil
    purpose;
  they talk of laying snares
    secretly,
thinking, "Who can see us?ᶜ
6   Who can search out our
    crimes?ᵈ
We have thought out a
    cunningly conceived
    plot."
For the human heart and
    mind are deep.

7 But God will shoot his arrow at
    them;
  they will be wounded
    suddenly.
8 Because of their tongue he will
    bring them to ruin;ᵉ
all who see them will shake
    with horror.
9 Then everyone will fear;
  they will tell what God has
    brought about,
  and ponder what he has done.

10 Let the righteous rejoice in the
    LORD

ᵃOther ancient authorities read *Galilee*  ᵇGk *he*  ᶜSyr: Heb *them*  ᵈCn: Heb *They search out crimes*
ᵉCn: Heb *They will bring him to ruin, their tongue being against them*

and take refuge in him.
Let all the upright in heart
glory.

## PROVERBS 11.22

Like a gold ring in a pig's snout
is a beautiful woman without
good sense.

# MARCH 22

## NUMBERS 33.40—35.34

The Canaanite, the king of Arad, who lived in the Negeb in the land of Canaan, heard of the coming of the Israelites.

41 They set out from Mount Hor and camped at Zalmonah. [42] They set out from Zalmonah and camped at Punon. [43] They set out from Punon and camped at Oboth. [44] They set out from Oboth and camped at Iye-abarim, in the territory of Moab. [45] They set out from Iyim and camped at Dibon-gad. [46] They set out from Dibon-gad and camped at Almon-diblathaim. [47] They set out from Almon-diblathaim and camped in the mountains of Abarim, before Nebo. [48] They set out from the mountains of Abarim and camped in the plains of Moab by the Jordan at Jericho; [49] they camped by the Jordan from Beth-jeshimoth as far as Abel-shittim in the plains of Moab.

50 In the plains of Moab by the Jordan at Jericho, the LORD spoke to Moses, saying: [51] Speak to the Israelites, and say to them: When you cross over the Jordan into the land of Canaan, [52] you shall drive out all the inhabitants of the land from before you, destroy all their figured stones, destroy all their cast images, and demolish all their high places. [53] You shall take possession of the land and settle in it, for I have given you the land to possess. [54] You shall apportion the land by lot according to your clans; to a large one you shall give a large inheritance, and to a small one you shall give a small inheritance; the inheritance shall belong to the person on whom the lot falls; according to your ancestral tribes you shall inherit. [55] But if you do not drive out the inhabitants of the land from before you, then those whom you let remain shall be as barbs in your eyes and thorns in your sides; they shall trouble you in the land where you are settling. [56] And I will do to you as I thought to do to them.

34.1 THE LORD spoke to Moses, saying: [2] Command the Israelites, and say to them: When you enter the land of Canaan (this is the land that shall fall to you for an inheritance, the land of Canaan, defined by its boundaries), [3] your south sector shall extend from the wilderness of Zin along the side of Edom. Your southern boundary shall begin from the end of the Dead Sea[a] on the east; [4] your boundary shall turn south of the ascent of Akrabbim, and cross to Zin, and its outer limit shall be south of Kadesh-barnea; then it shall go on to Hazar-addar, and cross to Azmon; [5] the boundary shall turn from Azmon to the

aHeb *Salt Sea*

Wadi of Egypt, and its termination shall be at the Sea.

6 For the western boundary, you shall have the Great Sea and its[a] coast; this shall be your western boundary.

7 This shall be your northern boundary: from the Great Sea you shall mark out your line to Mount Hor; [8]from Mount Hor you shall mark it out to Lebo-hamath, and the outer limit of the boundary shall be at Zedad; [9]then the boundary shall extend to Ziphron, and its end shall be at Hazar-enan; this shall be your northern boundary.

10 You shall mark out your eastern boundary from Hazar-enan to Shepham; [11]and the boundary shall continue down from Shepham to Riblah on the east side of Ain; and the boundary shall go down, and reach the eastern slope of the sea of Chinnereth; [12]and the boundary shall go down to the Jordan, and its end shall be at the Dead Sea.[b] This shall be your land with its boundaries all around.

13 Moses commanded the Israelites, saying: This is the land that you shall inherit by lot, which the Lord has commanded to give to the nine tribes and to the half-tribe; [14]for the tribe of the Reubenites by their ancestral houses and the tribe of the Gadites by their ancestral houses have taken their inheritance, and also the half-tribe of Manasseh; [15]the two tribes and the half-tribe have taken their inheritance beyond the Jordan at Jericho eastward, toward the sunrise.

16 The Lord spoke to Moses, saying: [17]These are the names of the men who shall apportion the land to you for inheritance: the priest Eleazar and Joshua son of Nun. [18]You shall take one leader of every tribe to apportion the land for inheritance. [19]These are the names of the men: Of the tribe of Judah, Caleb son of Jephunneh. [20]Of the tribe of the Simeonites, Shemuel son of Ammihud. [21]Of the tribe of Benjamin, Elidad son of Chislon. [22]Of the tribe of the Danites a leader, Bukki son of Jogli. [23]Of the Josephites: of the tribe of the Manassites a leader, Hanniel son of Ephod, [24]and of the tribe of the Ephraimites a leader, Kemuel son of Shiphtan. [25]Of the tribe of the Zebulunites a leader, Eli-zaphan son of Parnach. [26]Of the tribe of the Issacharites a leader, Paltiel son of Azzan. [27]And of the tribe of the Asherites a leader, Ahihud son of Shelomi. [28]Of the tribe of the Naphtalites a leader, Pedahel son of Ammihud. [29]These were the ones whom the Lord commanded to apportion the inheritance for the Israelites in the land of Canaan.

35.1 In the plains of Moab by the Jordan at Jericho, the Lord spoke to Moses, saying: [2]Command the Israelites to give, from the inheritance that they possess, towns for the Levites to live in; you shall also give to the Levites pasture lands surrounding the towns. [3]The towns shall be theirs to live in, and their pasture lands shall be for their cattle, for their livestock, and for all their animals. [4]The pasture lands of the towns, which you shall give to the Levites, shall reach from the wall of the town outward a thousand cubits all around. [5]You shall measure, outside the town, for the east side two thousand cubits, for the south side two thousand cubits, for the west side two thousand cubits, and for the north side two thousand cubits, with the town in the middle; this shall belong to them as pasture land for their towns.

6 The towns that you give to the Levites shall include the six cities of refuge, where you shall permit a slayer to flee, and in addition to them you shall give forty-two towns. [7]The towns that

a Syr: Heb lacks *its*   b Heb *Salt Sea*

you give to the Levites shall total forty-eight, with their pasture lands. ⁸And as for the towns that you shall give from the possession of the Israelites, from the larger tribes you shall take many, and from the smaller tribes you shall take few; each, in proportion to the inheritance that it obtains, shall give of its towns to the Levites.

9 The LORD spoke to Moses, saying: ¹⁰Speak to the Israelites, and say to them: When you cross the Jordan into the land of Canaan, ¹¹then you shall select cities to be cities of refuge for you, so that a slayer who kills a person without intent may flee there. ¹²The cities shall be for you a refuge from the avenger, so that the slayer may not die until there is a trial before the congregation.

13 The cities that you designate shall be six cities of refuge for you: ¹⁴you shall designate three cities beyond the Jordan, and three cities in the land of Canaan, to be cities of refuge. ¹⁵These six cities shall serve as refuge for the Israelites, for the resident or transient alien among them, so that anyone who kills a person without intent may flee there.

16 But anyone who strikes another with an iron object, and death ensues, is a murderer; the murderer shall be put to death. ¹⁷Or anyone who strikes another with a stone in hand that could cause death, and death ensues, is a murderer; the murderer shall be put to death. ¹⁸Or anyone who strikes another with a weapon of wood in hand that could cause death, and death ensues, is a murderer; the murderer shall be put to death. ¹⁹The avenger of blood is the one who shall put the murderer to death; when they meet, the avenger of blood shall execute the sentence. ²⁰Likewise, if someone pushes another from hatred, or hurls something at another, lying in wait, and death ensues,

²¹or in enmity strikes another with the hand, and death ensues, then the one who struck the blow shall be put to death; that person is a murderer; the avenger of blood shall put the murderer to death, when they meet.

22 But if someone pushes another suddenly without enmity, or hurls any object without lying in wait, ²³or, while handling any stone that could cause death, unintentionallyᵃ drops it on another and death ensues, though they were not enemies, and no harm was intended, ²⁴then the congregation shall judge between the slayer and the avenger of blood, in accordance with these ordinances; ²⁵and the congregation shall rescue the slayer from the avenger of blood. Then the congregation shall send the slayer back to the original city of refuge. The slayer shall live in it until the death of the high priest who was anointed with the holy oil. ²⁶But if the slayer shall at any time go outside the bounds of the original city of refuge, ²⁷and is found by the avenger of blood outside the bounds of the city of refuge, and is killed by the avenger, no bloodguilt shall be incurred. ²⁸For the slayer must remain in the city of refuge until the death of the high priest; but after the death of the high priest the slayer may return home.

29 These things shall be a statute and ordinance for you throughout your generations wherever you live.

30 If anyone kills another, the murderer shall be put to death on the evidence of witnesses; but no one shall be put to death on the testimony of a single witness. ³¹Moreover you shall accept no ransom for the life of a murderer who is subject to the death penalty; a murderer must be put to death. ³²Nor shall you accept ransom for one who has fled to a city of refuge, enabling the fugitive to return to live in the land before the death of the high priest. ³³You

ᵃHeb *without seeing*

shall not pollute the land in which you live; for blood pollutes the land, and no expiation can be made for the land, for the blood that is shed in it, except by the blood of the one who shed it. [34]You shall not defile the land in which you live, in which I also dwell; for I the LORD dwell among the Israelites.

## LUKE 5.12–28

ONCE, when he [Jesus] was in one of the cities, there was a man covered with leprosy.[a] When he saw Jesus, he bowed with his face to the ground and begged him, "Lord, if you choose, you can make me clean." [13]Then Jesus[b] stretched out his hand, touched him, and said, "I do choose. Be made clean." Immediately the leprosy[a] left him. [14]And he ordered him to tell no one. "Go," he said, "and show yourself to the priest, and, as Moses commanded, make an offering for your cleansing, for a testimony to them." [15]But now more than ever the word about Jesus[c] spread abroad; many crowds would gather to hear him and to be cured of their diseases. [16]But he would withdraw to deserted places and pray.

17  One day, while he was teaching, Pharisees and teachers of the law were sitting near by (they had come from every village of Galilee and Judea and from Jerusalem); and the power of the Lord was with him to heal.[d] [18]Just then some men came, carrying a paralyzed man on a bed. They were trying to bring him in and lay him before Jesus;[c] [19]but finding no way to bring him in because of the crowd, they went up on the roof and let him down with his bed through the tiles into the middle of the crowd[e] in front of Jesus. [20]When he saw their faith, he said, "Friend,[f] your sins are forgiven you." [21]Then the scribes and the Pharisees began to question, "Who is this who is speaking blasphemies? Who can forgive sins but God alone?" [22]When Jesus perceived their questionings, he answered them, "Why do you raise such questions in your hearts? [23]Which is easier, to say, 'Your sins are forgiven you,' or to say, 'Stand up and walk'? [24]But so that you may know that the Son of Man has authority on earth to forgive sins"—he said to the one who was paralyzed—"I say to you, stand up and take your bed and go to your home." [25]Immediately he stood up before them, took what he had been lying on, and went to his home, glorifying God. [26]Amazement seized all of them, and they glorified God and were filled with awe, saying, "We have seen strange things today."

27  After this he went out and saw a tax collector named Levi, sitting at the tax booth; and he said to him, "Follow me." [28]And he got up, left everything, and followed him.

## PSALM 65.1–13

*To the leader. A Psalm of David. A Song.*

PRAISE is due to you,
    O God, in Zion;
        and to you shall vows be
            performed,
2       O you who answer prayer!
    To you all flesh shall come.
3   When deeds of iniquity
            overwhelm us,
        you forgive our
            transgressions.
4   Happy are those whom you
            choose and bring near
        to live in your courts.
    We shall be satisfied with the
            goodness of your house,
        your holy temple.

5   By awesome deeds you answer
            us with deliverance,

aThe terms *leper* and *leprosy* can refer to several diseases  bGk *he*  cGk *him*  dOther ancient authorities read *was present to heal them*  eGk *into the midst*  fGk *Man*

O God of our salvation;
    you are the hope of all the ends
        of the earth
    and of the farthest seas.
6   By your[a] strength you
        established the
        mountains;
    you are girded with might.
7   You silence the roaring of the
        seas,
    the roaring of their waves,
    the tumult of the peoples.
8   Those who live at earth's
        farthest bounds are awed
        by your signs;
    you make the gateways of the
        morning and the evening
        shout for joy.

9   You visit the earth and water it,
        you greatly enrich it;
    the river of God is full of water;
    you provide the people with
        grain,
    for so you have prepared it.

10  You water its furrows
        abundantly,
    settling its ridges,
    softening it with showers,
        and blessing its growth.
11  You crown the year with your
        bounty;
    your wagon tracks overflow
        with richness.
12  The pastures of the wilderness
        overflow,
    the hills gird themselves with
        joy,
13  the meadows clothe themselves
        with flocks,
    the valleys deck themselves
        with grain,
    they shout and sing together
        for joy.

## PROVERBS 11.23

THE desire of the righteous
    ends only in good;
the expectation of the wicked
    in wrath.

# MARCH 23

## NUMBERS 36.1— DEUTERONOMY 1.45

THE heads of the ancestral houses of the clans of the descendants of Gilead son of Machir son of Manasseh, of the Josephite clans, came forward and spoke in the presence of Moses and the leaders, the heads of the ancestral houses of the Israelites; 2they said, "The LORD commanded my lord to give the land for inheritance by lot to the Israelites; and my lord was commanded by the LORD to give the inheritance of our brother Zelophehad to his daughters. 3But if they are married into another Israelite tribe, then their inheritance will be taken from the inheritance of our ancestors and added to the inheritance of the tribe into which they marry; so it will be taken away from the allotted portion of our inheritance. 4And when the jubilee of the Israelites comes, then their inheritance will be added to the inheritance of the tribe into which they have married; and their inheritance will be taken from the

[a] Gk Jerome: Heb *his*

inheritance of our ancestral tribe."

5 Then Moses commanded the Israelites according to the word of the LORD, saying, "The descendants of the tribe of Joseph are right in what they are saying. ⁶This is what the LORD commands concerning the daughters of Zelophehad, 'Let them marry whom they think best; only it must be into a clan of their father's tribe that they are married, ⁷so that no inheritance of the Israelites shall be transferred from one tribe to another; for all Israelites shall retain the inheritance of their ancestral tribes. ⁸Every daughter who possesses an inheritance in any tribe of the Israelites shall marry one from the clan of her father's tribe, so that all Israelites may continue to possess their ancestral inheritance. ⁹No inheritance shall be transferred from one tribe to another; for each of the tribes of the Israelites shall retain its own inheritance.' "

10 The daughters of Zelophehad did as the LORD had commanded Moses. ¹¹Mahlah, Tirzah, Hoglah, Milcah, and Noah, the daughters of Zelophehad, married sons of their father's brothers. ¹²They were married into the clans of the descendants of Manasseh son of Joseph, and their inheritance remained in the tribe of their father's clan.

13 These are the commandments and the ordinances that the LORD commanded through Moses to the Israelites in the plains of Moab by the Jordan at Jericho.

1.1 THESE are the words that Moses spoke to all Israel beyond the Jordan—in the wilderness, on the plain opposite Suph, between Paran and Tophel, Laban, Hazeroth, and Di-zahab. ²(By the way of Mount Seir it takes eleven days to reach Kadesh-barnea from Horeb.)

³In the fortieth year, on the first day of the eleventh month, Moses spoke to the Israelites just as the LORD had commanded him to speak to them. ⁴This was after he had defeated King Sihon of the Amorites, who reigned in Heshbon, and King Og of Bashan, who reigned in Ashtaroth andᵃ in Edrei. ⁵Beyond the Jordan in the land of Moab, Moses undertook to expound this law as follows:

6 The LORD our God spoke to us at Horeb, saying, "You have stayed long enough at this mountain. ⁷Resume your journey, and go into the hill country of the Amorites as well as into the neighboring regions—the Arabah, the hill country, the Shephelah, the Negeb, and the seacoast—the land of the Canaanites and the Lebanon, as far as the great river, the river Euphrates. ⁸See, I have set the land before you; go in and take possession of the land that Iᵇ swore to your ancestors, to Abraham, to Isaac, and to Jacob, to give to them and to their descendants after them."

9 At that time I said to you, "I am unable by myself to bear you. ¹⁰The LORD your God has multiplied you, so that today you are as numerous as the stars of heaven. ¹¹May the LORD, the God of your ancestors, increase you a thousand times more and bless you, as he has promised you! ¹²But how can I bear the heavy burden of your disputes all by myself? ¹³Choose for each of your tribes individuals who are wise, discerning, and reputable to be your leaders." ¹⁴You answered me, "The plan you have proposed is a good one." ¹⁵So I took the leaders of your tribes, wise and reputable individuals, and installed them as leaders over you, commanders of thousands, commanders of hundreds, commanders of fifties, commanders of tens, and officials, throughout your tribes. ¹⁶I charged your judges at that time: "Give the members of your community a fair

ᵃGk Syr Vg Compare Josh 12.4: Heb lacks *and*   ᵇSam Gk: MT *the LORD*

hearing, and judge rightly between one person and another, whether citizen or resident alien. [17]You must not be partial in judging: hear out the small and the great alike; you shall not be intimidated by anyone, for the judgment is God's. Any case that is too hard for you, bring to me, and I will hear it." [18]So I charged you at that time with all the things that you should do.

19 Then, just as the LORD our God had ordered us, we set out from Horeb and went through all that great and terrible wilderness that you saw, on the way to the hill country of the Amorites, until we reached Kadesh-barnea. [20]I said to you, "You have reached the hill country of the Amorites, which the LORD our God is giving us. [21]See, the LORD your God has given the land to you; go up, take possession, as the LORD, the God of your ancestors, has promised you; do not fear or be dismayed."

22 All of you came to me and said, "Let us send men ahead of us to explore the land for us and bring back a report to us regarding the route by which we should go up and the cities we will come to." [23]The plan seemed good to me, and I selected twelve of you, one from each tribe. [24]They set out and went up into the hill country, and when they reached the Valley of Eshcol they spied it out [25]and gathered some of the land's produce, which they brought down to us. They brought back a report to us, and said, "It is a good land that the LORD our God is giving us."

26 But you were unwilling to go up. You rebelled against the command of the LORD your God; [27]you grumbled in your tents and said, "It is because the LORD hates us that he has brought us out of the land of Egypt, to hand us over to the Amorites to destroy us. [28]Where are we headed? Our kindred have made our hearts melt by reporting, 'The peo-

ple are stronger and taller than we; the cities are large and fortified up to heaven! We actually saw there the offspring of the Anakim!' " [29]I said to you, "Have no dread or fear of them. [30]The LORD your God, who goes before you, is the one who will fight for you, just as he did for you in Egypt before your very eyes, [31]and in the wilderness, where you saw how the LORD your God carried you, just as one carries a child, all the way that you traveled until you reached this place. [32]But in spite of this, you have no trust in the LORD your God, [33]who goes before you on the way to seek out a place for you to camp, in fire by night, and in the cloud by day, to show you the route you should take."

34 When the LORD heard your words, he was wrathful and swore: [35]"Not one of these—not one of this evil generation—shall see the good land that I swore to give to your ancestors, [36]except Caleb son of Jephunneh. He shall see it, and to him and to his descendants I will give the land on which he set foot, because of his complete fidelity to the LORD." [37]Even with me the LORD was angry on your account, saying, "You also shall not enter there. [38]Joshua son of Nun, your assistant, shall enter there; encourage him, for he is the one who will secure Israel's possession of it. [39]And as for your little ones, who you thought would become booty, your children, who today do not yet know right from wrong, they shall enter there; to them I will give it, and they shall take possession of it. [40]But as for you, journey back into the wilderness, in the direction of the Red Sea."[a]

41 You answered me, "We have sinned against the LORD! We are ready to go up and fight, just as the LORD our God commanded us." So all of you strapped on your battle gear, and

thought it easy to go up into the hill country. ⁴²The L‍ORD said to me, "Say to them, 'Do not go up and do not fight, for I am not in the midst of you; otherwise you will be defeated by your enemies.'" ⁴³Although I told you, you would not listen. You rebelled against the command of the L‍ORD and presumptuously went up into the hill country. ⁴⁴The Amorites who lived in that hill country then came out against you and chased you as bees do. They beat you down in Seir as far as Hormah. ⁴⁵When you returned and wept before the L‍ORD, the L‍ORD would neither heed your voice nor pay you any attention.

## LUKE 5.29—6.11

THEN Levi gave a great banquet for him [Jesus] in his house; and there was a large crowd of tax collectors and others sitting at the table[a] with them. ³⁰The Pharisees and their scribes were complaining to his disciples, saying, "Why do you eat and drink with tax collectors and sinners?" ³¹Jesus answered, "Those who are well have no need of a physician, but those who are sick; ³²I have come to call not the righteous but sinners to repentance."

33 Then they said to him, "John's disciples, like the disciples of the Pharisees, frequently fast and pray, but your disciples eat and drink. ³⁴Jesus said to them, "You cannot make wedding guests fast while the bridegroom is with them, can you? ³⁵The days will come when the bridegroom will be taken away from them, and then they will fast in those days." ³⁶He also told them a parable: "No one tears a piece from a new garment and sews it on an old garment; otherwise the new will be torn, and the piece from the new will not match the old. ³⁷And no one puts new wine into old wineskins; otherwise

the new wine will burst the skins and will be spilled, and the skins will be destroyed. ³⁸But new wine must be put into fresh wineskins. ³⁹And no one after drinking old wine desires new wine, but says, 'The old is good.'"[b]

6.1 ONE sabbath[c] while Jesus[d] was going through the grainfields, his disciples plucked some heads of grain, rubbed them in their hands, and ate them. ²But some of the Pharisees said, "Why are you doing what is not lawful[e] on the sabbath?" ³Jesus answered, "Have you not read what David did when he and his companions were hungry? ⁴He entered the house of God and took and ate the bread of the Presence, which it is not lawful for any but the priests to eat, and gave some to his companions?" ⁵Then he said to them, "The Son of Man is lord of the sabbath."

6 On another sabbath he entered the synagogue and taught, and there was a man there whose right hand was withered. ⁷The scribes and the Pharisees watched him to see whether he would cure on the sabbath, so that they might find an accusation against him. ⁸Even though he knew what they were thinking, he said to the man who had the withered hand, "Come and stand here." He got up and stood there. ⁹Then Jesus said to them, "I ask you, is it lawful to do good or to do harm on the sabbath, to save life or to destroy it?" ¹⁰After looking around at all of them, he said to him, "Stretch out your hand." He did so, and his hand was restored. ¹¹But they were filled with fury and discussed with one another what they might do to Jesus.

---

[a]Gk *reclining*   [b]Other ancient authorities read *better*; others lack verse 39   [c]Other ancient authorities read *On the second first sabbath*   [d]Gk *he*   [e]Other ancient authorities add *to do*

## PSALM 66.1–20

*To the leader. A Song. A Psalm.*

**M**AKE a joyful noise to God,
    all the earth;
2    sing the glory of his
      name;
    give to him glorious praise.
3  Say to God, "How awesome are
      your deeds!
    Because of your great power,
      your enemies cringe
      before you.
4  All the earth worships you;
    they sing praises to you,
    sing praises to your name."
              *Selah*

5  Come and see what God has
      done:
    he is awesome in his deeds
      among mortals.
6  He turned the sea into dry land;
    they passed through the river
      on foot.
    There we rejoiced in him,
7    who rules by his might
      forever,
    whose eyes keep watch on the
      nations—
    let the rebellious not exalt
      themselves.      *Selah*

8  Bless our God, O peoples,
    let the sound of his praise be
      heard,
9  who has kept us among the
      living,
    and has not let our feet slip.
10  For you, O God, have tested
      us;
    you have tried us as silver is
      tried.
11  You brought us into the net;
    you laid burdens on our
      backs;
12  you let people ride over our
      heads;

    we went through fire and
      through water;
    yet you have brought us out to
      a spacious place. **a**

13  I will come into your house with
      burnt offerings;
    I will pay you my vows,
14  those that my lips uttered
    and my mouth promised when
      I was in trouble.
15  I will offer to you burnt
      offerings of fatlings,
    with the smoke of the
      sacrifice of rams;
    I will make an offering of bulls
      and goats.      *Selah*

16  Come and hear, all you who fear
      God,
    and I will tell what he has
      done for me.
17  I cried aloud to him,
    and he was extolled with my
      tongue.
18  If I had cherished iniquity in my
      heart,
    the Lord would not have
      listened.
19  But truly God has listened;
    he has given heed to the
      words of my prayer.

20  Blessed be God,
    because he has not rejected
      my prayer
    or removed his steadfast love
      from me.

## PROVERBS 11.24–26

**S**OME give freely, yet grow all
    the richer;
  others withhold what is due,
    and only suffer want.
25  A generous person will be
      enriched,
    and one who gives water will
      get water.

**a** Cn Compare Gk Syr Jerome Tg: Heb *to a saturation*

<sup>26</sup> The people curse those who
hold back grain,

but a blessing is on the head
of those who sell it.

# MARCH 24

## DEUTERONOMY 1.46—3.29

A FTER you [the Israelites] had stayed at Kadesh as many days as you did, <sup>2.1</sup> we [Moses and the Israelites] journeyed back into the wilderness, in the direction of the Red Sea, [a] as the LORD had told me and skirted Mount Seir for many days. <sup>2</sup>Then the LORD said to me: <sup>3</sup>"You have been skirting this hill country long enough. Head north, <sup>4</sup>and charge the people as follows: You are about to pass through the territory of your kindred, the descendants of Esau, who live in Seir. They will be afraid of you, so, be very careful <sup>5</sup>not to engage in battle with them, for I will not give you even so much as a foot's length of their land, since I have given Mount Seir to Esau as a possession. <sup>6</sup>You shall purchase food from them for money, so that you may eat; and you shall also buy water from them for money, so that you may drink. <sup>7</sup>Surely the LORD your God has blessed you in all your undertakings; he knows your going through this great wilderness. These forty years the LORD your God has been with you; you have lacked nothing." <sup>8</sup>So we passed by our kin, the descendants of Esau who live in Seir, leaving behind the route of the Arabah, and leaving behind Elath and Ezion-geber.

When we had headed out along the route of the wilderness of Moab, <sup>9</sup>the LORD said to me: "Do not harass Moab or engage them in battle, for I will not give you any of its land as a possession, since I have given Ar as a possession to the descendants of Lot." <sup>10</sup>(The Emim—a large and numerous people, as tall as the Anakim—had formerly inhabited it. <sup>11</sup>Like the Anakim, they are usually reckoned as Rephaim, though the Moabites call them Emim. <sup>12</sup>Moreover, the Horim had formerly inhabited Seir, but the descendants of Esau dispossessed them, destroying them and settling in their place, as Israel has done in the land that the LORD gave them as a possession.) <sup>13</sup>"Now then, proceed to cross over the Wadi Zered."

So we crossed over the Wadi Zered. <sup>14</sup>And the length of time we had traveled from Kadesh-barnea until we crossed the Wadi Zered was thirty-eight years, until the entire generation of warriors had perished from the camp, as the LORD had sworn concerning them. <sup>15</sup>Indeed, the LORD's own hand was against them, to root them out from the camp, until all had perished.

16 Just as soon as all the warriors had died off from among the people, <sup>17</sup>the LORD spoke to me, saying, <sup>18</sup>"Today you are going to cross the boundary of Moab at Ar. <sup>19</sup>When you approach the frontier of the Ammonites, do not harass them or engage them in battle, for I will not give the land of the Ammonites to you as a possession, because I have given it to the descendants of Lot." <sup>20</sup>(It also is usu-

a Or *Sea of Reeds*

ally reckoned as a land of Rephaim. Rephaim formerly inhabited it, though the Ammonites call them Zamzummim, [21]a strong and numerous people, as tall as the Anakim. But the LORD destroyed them from before the Ammonites so that they could dispossess them and settle in their place. [22]He did the same for the descendants of Esau, who live in Seir, by destroying the Horim before them so that they could dispossess them and settle in their place even to this day. [23]As for the Avvim, who had lived in settlements in the vicinity of Gaza, the Caphtorim, who came from Caphtor, destroyed them and settled in their place.) [24]"Proceed on your journey and cross the Wadi Arnon. See, I have handed over to you King Sihon the Amorite of Heshbon, and his land. Begin to take possession by engaging him in battle. [25]This day I will begin to put the dread and fear of you upon the peoples everywhere under heaven; when they hear report of you, they will tremble and be in anguish because of you."

26 So I sent messengers from the wilderness of Kedemoth to King Sihon of Heshbon with the following terms of peace: [27]"If you let me pass through your land, I will travel only along the road; I will turn aside neither to the right nor to the left. [28]You shall sell me food for money, so that I may eat, and supply me water for money, so that I may drink. Only allow me to pass through on foot— [29]just as the descendants of Esau who live in Seir have done for me and likewise the Moabites who live in Ar—until I cross the Jordan into the land that the LORD our God is giving us." [30]But King Sihon of Heshbon was not willing to let us pass through, for the LORD your God had hardened his spirit and made his heart defiant in order to hand him over to you, as he has now done.

31 The LORD said to me, "See, I have begun to give Sihon and his land over to you. Begin now to take possession of his land." [32]So when Sihon came out against us, he and all his people for battle at Jahaz, [33]the LORD our God gave him over to us; and we struck him down, along with his offspring and all his people. [34]At that time we captured all his towns, and in each town we utterly destroyed men, women, and children. We left not a single survivor. [35]Only the livestock we kept as spoil for ourselves, as well as the plunder of the towns that we had captured. [36]From Aroer on the edge of the Wadi Arnon (including the town that is in the wadi itself) as far as Gilead, there was no citadel too high for us. The LORD our God gave everything to us. [37]You did not encroach, however, on the land of the Ammonites, avoiding the whole upper region of the Wadi Jabbok as well as the towns of the hill country, just as[a] the LORD our God had charged.

3.1 WHEN we headed up the road to Bashan, King Og of Bashan came out against us, he and all his people, for battle at Edrei. [2]The LORD said to me, "Do not fear him, for I have handed him over to you, along with his people and his land. Do to him as you did to King Sihon of the Amorites, who reigned in Heshbon." [3]So the LORD our God also handed over to us King Og of Bashan and all his people. We struck him down until not a single survivor was left. [4]At that time we captured all his towns; there was no citadel that we did not take from them—sixty towns, the whole region of Argob, the kingdom of Og in Bashan. [5]All these were fortress towns with high walls, double gates, and bars, besides a great many villages. [6]And we utterly destroyed them, as we had done to King Sihon of Heshbon, in each city utterly destroying men, women, and children. [7]But all the live-

aGk Tg: Heb *and all*

stock and the plunder of the towns we kept as spoil for ourselves.

8 So at that time we took from the two kings of the Amorites the land beyond the Jordan, from the Wadi Arnon to Mount Hermon [9](the Sidonians call Hermon Sirion, while the Amorites call it Senir), [10]all the towns of the tableland, the whole of Gilead, and all of Bashan, as far as Salecah and Edrei, towns of Og's kingdom in Bashan. [11](Now only King Og of Bashan was left of the remnant of the Rephaim. In fact his bed, an iron bed, can still be seen in Rabbah of the Ammonites. By the common cubit it is nine cubits long and four cubits wide.) [12]As for the land that we took possession of at that time, I gave to the Reubenites and Gadites the territory north of Aroer, [a] that is on the edge of the Wadi Arnon, as well as half the hill country of Gilead with its towns, [13]and I gave to the half-tribe of Manasseh the rest of Gilead and all of Bashan, Og's kingdom. (The whole region of Argob: all that portion of Bashan used to be called a land of Rephaim; [14]Jair the Manassite acquired the whole region of Argob as far as the border of the Geshurites and the Maacathites, and he named them—that is, Bashan—after himself, Havvoth-jair, [b] as it is to this day.) [15]To Machir I gave Gilead. [16]And to the Reubenites and the Gadites I gave the territory from Gilead as far as the Wadi Arnon, with the middle of the wadi as a boundary, and up to the Jabbok, the wadi being boundary of the Ammonites; [17]the Arabah also, with the Jordan and its banks, from Chinnereth down to the sea of the Arabah, the Dead Sea, [c] with the lower slopes of Pisgah on the east.

18 At that time, I charged you as follows: "Although the LORD your God has given you this land to occupy, all your troops shall cross over armed as the vanguard of your Israelite kin.

[19]Only your wives, your children, and your livestock—I know that you have much livestock—shall stay behind in the towns that I have given to you. [20]When the LORD gives rest to your kindred, as to you, and they too have occupied the land that the LORD your God is giving them beyond the Jordan, then each of you may return to the property that I have given to you." [21]And I charged Joshua as well at that time, saying: "Your own eyes have seen everything that the LORD your God has done to these two kings; so the LORD will do to all the kingdoms into which you are about to cross. [22]Do not fear them, for it is the LORD your God who fights for you."

23 At that time, too, I entreated the LORD, saying: [24]"O Lord GOD, you have only begun to show your servant your greatness and your might; what god in heaven or on earth can perform deeds and mighty acts like yours! [25]Let me cross over to see the good land beyond the Jordan, that good hill country and the Lebanon." [26]But the LORD was angry with me on your account and would not heed me. The LORD said to me, "Enough from you! Never speak to me of this matter again! [27]Go up to the top of Pisgah and look around you to the west, to the north, to the south, and to the east. Look well, for you shall not cross over this Jordan. [28]But charge Joshua, and encourage and strengthen him, because it is he who shall cross over at the head of this people and who shall secure their possession of the land that you will see." [29]So we remained in the valley opposite Beth-peor.

## LUKE 6.12–38

Now during those days he [Jesus] went out to the mountain to pray; and he spent the night in prayer to God. [13]And when day came, he called his disciples and chose

---

[a]Heb *territory from Aroer*   [b]That is *Settlement of Jair*   [c]Heb *Salt Sea*

twelve of them, whom he also named apostles: [14]Simon, whom he named Peter, and his brother Andrew, and James, and John, and Philip, and Bartholomew, [15]and Matthew, and Thomas, and James son of Alphaeus, and Simon, who was called the Zealot, [16]and Judas son of James, and Judas Iscariot, who became a traitor.

17  He came down with them and stood on a level place, with a great crowd of his disciples and a great multitude of people from all Judea, Jerusalem, and the coast of Tyre and Sidon. [18]They had come to hear him and to be healed of their diseases; and those who were troubled with unclean spirits were cured. [19]And all in the crowd were trying to touch him, for power came out from him and healed all of them.

20  Then he looked up at his disciples and said:

"Blessed are you who are poor,
　for yours is the kingdom of
　　God.
[21] "Blessed are you who are
　　hungry now,
　for you will be filled.
"Blessed are you who weep
　　now,
　for you will laugh.

22  "Blessed are you when people hate you, and when they exclude you, revile you, and defame you[a] on account of the Son of Man. [23]Rejoice in that day and leap for joy, for surely your reward is great in heaven; for that is what their ancestors did to the prophets.

[24] "But woe to you who are rich,
　for you have received your
　　consolation.
[25] "Woe to you who are full now,
　for you will be hungry.
"Woe to you who are laughing
　　now,
　for you will mourn and weep.

26  "Woe to you when all speak well of you, for that is what their ancestors did to the false prophets.

27  "But I say to you that listen, Love your enemies, do good to those who hate you, [28]bless those who curse you, pray for those who abuse you. [29]If anyone strikes you on the cheek, offer the other also; and from anyone who takes away your coat do not withhold even your shirt. [30]Give to everyone who begs from you; and if anyone takes away your goods, do not ask for them again. [31]Do to others as you would have them do to you.

32  "If you love those who love you, what credit is that to you? For even sinners love those who love them. [33]If you do good to those who do good to you, what credit is that to you? For even sinners do the same. [34]If you lend to those from whom you hope to receive, what credit is that to you? Even sinners lend to sinners, to receive as much again. [35]But love your enemies, do good, and lend, expecting nothing in return.[b] Your reward will be great, and you will be children of the Most High; for he is kind to the ungrateful and the wicked. [36]Be merciful, just as your Father is merciful.

37  "Do not judge, and you will not be judged; do not condemn, and you will not be condemned. Forgive, and you will be forgiven; [38]give, and it will be given to you. A good measure, pressed down, shaken together, running over, will be put into your lap; for the measure you give will be the measure you get back."

## PSALM 67.1–7

*To the leader: with stringed instruments. A Psalm. A Song.*

**M**AY God be gracious to us
　　and bless us
and make his face to shine
　　upon us,　　　　　*Selah*

2  that your way may be known
         upon earth,
      your saving power among all
         nations.
3  Let the peoples praise you,
      O God;
   let all the peoples praise you.

4  Let the nations be glad and sing
         for joy,
      for you judge the peoples
         with equity
      and guide the nations upon
         earth.          *Selah*
5  Let the peoples praise you,
      O God;

   let all the peoples praise you.

6  The earth has yielded its
      increase;
   God, our God, has blessed
      us.
7  May God continue to bless us;
   let all the ends of the earth
      revere him.

## PROVERBS 11.27

Whoever diligently seeks good
      seeks favor,
   but evil comes to the one
      who searches for it.

# MARCH 25

## DEUTERONOMY 4.1–49

So now, Israel, give heed to the statutes and ordinances that I am teaching you to observe, so that you may live to enter and occupy the land that the Lord, the God of your ancestors, is giving you. ²You must neither add anything to what I command you nor take away anything from it, but keep the commandments of the Lord your God with which I am charging you. ³You have seen for yourselves what the Lord did with regard to the Baal of Peor—how the Lord your God destroyed from among you everyone who followed the Baal of Peor, ⁴while those of you who held fast to the Lord your God are all alive today.

5  See, just as the Lord my God has charged me, I now teach you statutes and ordinances for you to observe in the land that you are about to enter and occupy. ⁶You must observe them diligently, for this will show your wisdom and discernment to the peoples, who, when they hear all these statutes, will say, "Surely this great nation is a wise and discerning people!" ⁷For what other great nation has a god so near to it as the Lord our God is whenever we call to him? ⁸And what other great nation has statutes and ordinances as just as this entire law that I am setting before you today?

9  But take care and watch yourselves closely, so as neither to forget the things that your eyes have seen nor to let them slip from your mind all the days of your life; make them known to your children and your children's children— ¹⁰how you once stood before the Lord your God at Horeb, when the Lord said to me, "Assemble the people for me, and I will let them hear my words, so that they may learn to fear me as long as they live on the earth, and may teach their children so"; ¹¹you approached and stood at the foot

of the mountain while the mountain was blazing up to the very heavens, shrouded in dark clouds. ¹²Then the LORD spoke to you out of the fire. You heard the sound of words but saw no form; there was only a voice. ¹³He declared to you his covenant, which he charged you to observe, that is, the ten commandments;ᵃ and he wrote them on two stone tablets. ¹⁴And the LORD charged me at that time to teach you statutes and ordinances for you to observe in the land that you are about to cross into and occupy.

15 Since you saw no form when the LORD spoke to you at Horeb out of the fire, take care and watch yourselves closely, ¹⁶so that you do not act corruptly by making an idol for yourselves, in the form of any figure—the likeness of male or female, ¹⁷the likeness of any animal that is on the earth, the likeness of any winged bird that flies in the air, ¹⁸the likeness of anything that creeps on the ground, the likeness of any fish that is in the water under the earth. ¹⁹And when you look up to the heavens and see the sun, the moon, and the stars, all the host of heaven, do not be led astray and bow down to them and serve them, things that the LORD your God has allotted to all the peoples everywhere under heaven. ²⁰But the LORD has taken you and brought you out of the iron-smelter, out of Egypt, to become a people of his very own possession, as you are now.

21 The LORD was angry with me because of you, and he vowed that I should not cross the Jordan and that I should not enter the good land that the LORD your God is giving for your possession. ²²For I am going to die in this land without crossing over the Jordan, but you are going to cross over to take possession of that good land. ²³So be careful not to forget the covenant that the LORD your God made with you, and

not to make for yourselves an idol in the form of anything that the LORD your God has forbidden you. ²⁴For the LORD your God is a devouring fire, a jealous God.

25 When you have had children and children's children, and become complacent in the land, if you act corruptly by making an idol in the form of anything, thus doing what is evil in the sight of the LORD your God, and provoking him to anger, ²⁶I call heaven and earth to witness against you today that you will soon utterly perish from the land that you are crossing the Jordan to occupy; you will not live long on it, but will be utterly destroyed. ²⁷The LORD will scatter you among the peoples; only a few of you will be left among the nations where the LORD will lead you. ²⁸There you will serve other gods made by human hands, objects of wood and stone that neither see, nor hear, nor eat, nor smell. ²⁹From there you will seek the LORD your God, and you will find him if you search after him with all your heart and soul. ³⁰In your distress, when all these things have happened to you in time to come, you will return to the LORD your God and heed him. ³¹Because the LORD your God is a merciful God, he will neither abandon you nor destroy you; he will not forget the covenant with your ancestors that he swore to them.

32 For ask now about former ages, long before your own, ever since the day that God created human beings on the earth; ask from one end of heaven to the other: has anything so great as this ever happened or has its like ever been heard of? ³³Has any people ever heard the voice of a god speaking out of a fire, as you have heard, and lived? ³⁴Or has any god ever attempted to go and take a nation for himself from the midst of another nation, by trials, by signs and wonders, by war, by a mighty

ᵃ Heb *the ten words*

hand and an outstretched arm, and by terrifying displays of power, as the LORD your God did for you in Egypt before your very eyes? [35]To you it was shown so that you would acknowledge that the LORD is God; there is no other besides him. [36]From heaven he made you hear his voice to discipline you. On earth he showed you his great fire, while you heard his words coming out of the fire. [37]And because he loved your ancestors, he chose their descendants after them. He brought you out of Egypt with his own presence, by his great power, [38]driving out before you nations greater and mightier than yourselves, to bring you in, giving you their land for a possession, as it is still today. [39]So acknowledge today and take to heart that the LORD is God in heaven above and on the earth beneath; there is no other. [40]Keep his statutes and his commandments, which I am commanding you today for your own well-being and that of your descendants after you, so that you may long remain in the land that the LORD your God is giving you for all time.

41 Then Moses set apart on the east side of the Jordan three cities [42]to which a homicide could flee, someone who unintentionally kills another person, the two not having been at enmity before; the homicide could flee to one of these cities and live: [43]Bezer in the wilderness on the tableland belonging to the Reubenites, Ramoth in Gilead belonging to the Gadites, and Golan in Bashan belonging to the Manassites.

44 This is the law that Moses set before the Israelites. [45]These are the decrees and the statutes and ordinances that Moses spoke to the Israelites when they had come out of Egypt, [46]beyond the Jordan in the valley opposite Beth-peor, in the land of King Sihon of the Amorites, who reigned at Heshbon, whom Moses and the Israelites defeated when they came out of Egypt. [47]They occupied his land and the land of King Og of Bashan, the two kings of the Amorites on the eastern side of the Jordan: [48]from Aroer, which is on the edge of the Wadi Arnon, as far as Mount Sirion[a] (that is, Hermon), [49]together with all the Arabah on the east side of the Jordan as far as the Sea of the Arabah, under the slopes of Pisgah.

## LUKE 6.39—7.10

HE [Jesus] also told them a parable: "Can a blind person guide a blind person? Will not both fall into a pit? [40]A disciple is not above the teacher, but everyone who is fully qualified will be like the teacher. [41]Why do you see the speck in your neighbor's[b] eye, but do not notice the log in your own eye? [42]Or how can you say to your neighbor, [c] 'Friend, [c] let me take out the speck in your eye,' when you yourself do not see the log in your own eye? You hypocrite, first take the log out of your own eye, and then you will see clearly to take the speck out of your neighbor's[b] eye.

43 "No good tree bears bad fruit, nor again does a bad tree bear good fruit; [44]for each tree is known by its own fruit. Figs are not gathered from thorns, nor are grapes picked from a bramble bush. [45]The good person out of the good treasure of the heart produces good, and the evil person out of evil treasure produces evil; for it is out of the abundance of the heart that the mouth speaks.

46 "Why do you call me 'Lord, Lord,' and do not do what I tell you? [47]I will show you what someone is like who comes to me, hears my words, and acts on them. [48]That one is like a man building a house, who dug deeply and laid

aSyr: Heb *Sion*  bGk *brother's*  cGk *brother*

the foundation on rock; when a flood arose, the river burst against that house but could not shake it, because it had been well built. [a] 49But the one who hears and does not act is like a man who built a house on the ground without a foundation. When the river burst against it, immediately it fell, and great was the ruin of that house."

7.1 AFTER Jesus[b] had finished all his sayings in the hearing of the people, he entered Capernaum. 2A centurion there had a slave whom he valued highly, and who was ill and close to death. 3When he heard about Jesus, he sent some Jewish elders to him, asking him to come and heal his slave. 4When they came to Jesus, they appealed to him earnestly, saying, "He is worthy of having you do this for him, 5for he loves our people, and it is he who built our synagogue for us." 6And Jesus went with them, but when he was not far from the house, the centurion sent friends to say to him, "Lord, do not trouble yourself, for I am not worthy to have you come under my roof; 7therefore I did not presume to come to you. But only speak the word, and let my servant be healed. 8For I also am a man set under authority, with soldiers under me; and I say to one, 'Go,' and he goes, and to another, 'Come,' and he comes, and to my slave, 'Do this,' and the slave does it." 9When Jesus heard this he was amazed at him, and turning to the crowd that followed him, he said, "I tell you, not even in Israel have I found such faith." 10When those who had been sent returned to the house, they found the slave in good health.

## PSALM 68.1–18

*To the leader. Of David. A Psalm. A Song.*

LET God rise up, let his
enemies be scattered;
let those who hate him flee
before him.
2 As smoke is driven away, so
drive them away;
as wax melts before the fire,
let the wicked perish before
God.
3 But let the righteous be joyful;
let them exult before God;
let them be jubilant with joy.

4 Sing to God, sing praises to his
name;
lift up a song to him who
rides upon the
clouds[c]—
his name is the LORD—
be exultant before him.

5 Father of orphans and protector
of widows
is God in his holy habitation.
6 God gives the desolate a home
to live in;
he leads out the prisoners to
prosperity,
but the rebellious live in a
parched land.

7 O God, when you went out
before your people,
when you marched through
the wilderness, *Selah*
8 the earth quaked, the heavens
poured down rain
at the presence of God, the
God of Sinai,
at the presence of God, the
God of Israel.
9 Rain in abundance, O God, you
showered abroad;

[a]Other ancient authorities read *founded upon the rock*  [b]Gk *he*  [c]Or *cast up a highway for him who rides through the deserts*

you restored your heritage
when it languished;
10   your flock found a dwelling in it;
in your goodness, O God, you
provided for the needy.

11   The Lord gives the command;
great is the company of
those[a] who bore the
tidings:
12       "The kings of the armies,
they flee, they flee!"
The women at home divide the
spoil,
13       though they stay among the
sheepfolds—
the wings of a dove covered
with silver,
its pinions with green gold.
14   When the Almighty[b] scattered
kings there,
snow fell on Zalmon.

15   O mighty mountain, mountain of
Bashan;
O many-peaked mountain,
mountain of Bashan!

16   Why do you look with envy,
O many-peaked
mountain,
at the mount that God desired
for his abode,
where the Lord will reside
forever?

17   With mighty chariotry, twice ten
thousand,
thousands upon thousands,
the Lord came from Sinai into
the holy place. [c]
18   You ascended the high mount,
leading captives in your train
and receiving gifts from
people,
even from those who rebel
against the Lord God's
abiding there.

## PROVERBS 11.28

THOSE who trust in their riches
will wither, [d]
but the righteous will flourish
like green leaves.

# MARCH 26

## DEUTERONOMY 5.1—6.25

MOSES convened all Israel, and said to them:
Hear, O Israel, the statutes and ordinances that I am addressing to you today; you shall learn them and observe them diligently. [2]The Lord our God made a covenant with us at Horeb. [3]Not with our ancestors did the Lord make this covenant, but with us, who are all of us here alive today. [4]The Lord spoke with you face to face at the mountain, out of the fire. [5](At that time I was standing between the Lord and you to declare to you the words[e] of the Lord; for you were afraid because of the fire and did not go up the mountain.) And he said:

6 I am the Lord your God, who brought you out of the land of Egypt, out of the house of slavery; [7]you shall have no other gods before[f] me.

[a]Or *company of the women*   [b]Traditional rendering of Heb *Shaddai*   [c]Cn: Heb *The Lord among them Sinai in the holy* (place)   [d]Cn: Heb *fall*   [e]Q Mss Sam Gk Syr Vg Tg: MT *word*   [f]Or *besides*

8/ You shall not make for yourself an idol, whether in the form of anything that is in heaven above, or that is on the earth beneath, or that is in the water under the earth. 9You shall not bow down to them or worship them; for I the LORD your God am a jealous God, punishing children for the iniquity of parents, to the third and fourth generation of those who reject me, 10but showing steadfast love to the thousandth generation[a] of those who love me and keep my commandments.

11 You shall not make wrongful use of the name of the LORD your God, for the LORD will not acquit anyone who misuses his name.

12/ Observe the sabbath day and keep it holy, as the LORD your God commanded you. 13Six days you shall labor and do all your work. 14But the seventh day is a sabbath to the LORD your God; you shall not do any work—you, or your son or your daughter, or your male or female slave, or your ox or your donkey, or any of your livestock, or the resident alien in your towns, so that your male and female slave may rest as well as you. 15Remember that you were a slave in the land of Egypt, and the LORD your God brought you out from there with a mighty hand and an outstretched arm; therefore the LORD your God commanded you to keep the sabbath day.

16/ Honor your father and your mother, as the LORD your God commanded you, so that your days may be long and that it may go well with you in the land that the LORD your God is giving you.

17 You shall not murder.[b]

18 Neither shall you commit adultery.

19 Neither shall you steal.

20 Neither shall you bear false witness against your neighbor.

21 Neither shall you covet your neighbor's wife.

Neither shall you desire your neighbor's house, or field, or male or female slave, or ox, or donkey, or anything that belongs to your neighbor.

22 These words the LORD spoke with a loud voice to your whole assembly at the mountain, out of the fire, the cloud, and the thick darkness, and he added no more. He wrote them on two stone tablets, and gave them to me. 23When you heard the voice out of the darkness, while the mountain was burning with fire, you approached me, all the heads of your tribes and your elders; 24and you said, "Look, the LORD our God has shown us his glory and greatness, and we have heard his voice out of the fire. Today we have seen that God may speak to someone and the person may still live. 25So now why should we die? For this great fire will consume us; if we hear the voice of the LORD our God any longer, we shall die. 26For who is there of all flesh that has heard the voice of the living God speaking out of fire, as we have, and remained alive? 27Go near, you yourself, and hear all that the LORD our God will say. Then tell us everything that the LORD our God tells you, and we will listen and do it."

28 The LORD heard your words when you spoke to me, and the LORD said to me: "I have heard the words of this people, which they have spoken to you; they are right in all that they have spoken. 29If only they had such a mind as this, to fear me and to keep all my commandments always, so that it might go well with them and with their children forever! 30Go say to them, 'Return to your tents.' 31But you, stand here by me, and I will tell you all the commandments, the statutes and the ordinances, that you shall teach them,

so that they may do them in the land that I am giving them to possess." <sup>32</sup>You must therefore be careful to do as the Lord your God has commanded you; you shall not turn to the right or to the left. <sup>33</sup>You must follow exactly the path that the Lord your God has commanded you, so that you may live, and that it may go well with you, and that you may live long in the land that you are to possess.

**6.**1 Now this is the commandment—the statutes and the ordinances—that the Lord your God charged me to teach you to observe in the land that you are about to cross into and occupy, <sup>2</sup>so that you and your children and your children's children may fear the Lord your God all the days of your life, and keep all his decrees and his commandments that I am commanding you, so that your days may be long. <sup>3</sup>Hear therefore, O Israel, and observe them diligently, so that it may go well with you, and so that you may multiply greatly in a land flowing with milk and honey, as the Lord, the God of your ancestors, has promised you.

4 Hear, O Israel: The Lord is our God, the Lord alone.<sup>a</sup> <sup>5</sup>You shall love the Lord your God with all your heart, and with all your soul, and with all your might. <sup>6</sup>Keep these words that I am commanding you today in your heart. <sup>7</sup>Recite them to your children and talk about them when you are at home and when you are away, when you lie down and when you rise. <sup>8</sup>Bind them as a sign on your hand, fix them as an emblem<sup>b</sup> on your forehead, <sup>9</sup>and write them on the doorposts of your house and on your gates.

10 When the Lord your God has brought you into the land that he swore to your ancestors, to Abraham, to Isaac, and to Jacob, to give you—a land with fine, large cities that you did not build, <sup>11</sup>houses filled with all sorts of goods that you did not fill, hewn cisterns that you did not hew, vineyards and olive groves that you did not plant—and when you have eaten your fill, <sup>12</sup>take care that you do not forget the Lord, who brought you out of the land of Egypt, out of the house of slavery. <sup>13</sup>The Lord your God you shall fear; him you shall serve, and by his name alone you shall swear. <sup>14</sup>Do not follow other gods, any of the gods of the peoples who are all around you, <sup>15</sup>because the Lord your God, who is present with you, is a jealous God. The anger of the Lord your God would be kindled against you and he would destroy you from the face of the earth.

16 Do not put the Lord your God to the test, as you tested him at Massah. <sup>17</sup>You must diligently keep the commandments of the Lord your God, and his decrees, and his statutes that he has commanded you. <sup>18</sup>Do what is right and good in the sight of the Lord, so that it may go well with you, and so that you may go in and occupy the good land that the Lord swore to your ancestors to give you, <sup>19</sup>thrusting out all your enemies from before you, as the Lord has promised.

20 When your children ask you in time to come, "What is the meaning of the decrees and the statutes and the ordinances that the Lord our God has commanded you?" <sup>21</sup>then you shall say to your children, "We were Pharaoh's slaves in Egypt, but the Lord brought us out of Egypt with a mighty hand. <sup>22</sup>The Lord displayed before our eyes great and awesome signs and wonders against Egypt, against Pharaoh and all his household. <sup>23</sup>He brought us out from there in order to bring us in, to give us the land that he promised on oath to our ancestors. <sup>24</sup>Then the Lord commanded us to observe all these statutes, to fear the Lord our God, for

a Or *The Lord our God is one Lord,* or *The Lord our God, the Lord is one,* or *The Lord is our God, the Lord is one*   b Or *as a frontlet*

our lasting good, so as to keep us alive, as is now the case. ²⁵If we diligently observe this entire commandment before the Lord our God, as he has commanded us, we will be in the right."

## LUKE 7.11–35

Soon afterwards[a] he [Jesus] went to a town called Nain, and his disciples and a large crowd went with him. ¹²As he approached the gate of the town, a man who had died was being carried out. He was his mother's only son, and she was a widow; and with her was a large crowd from the town. ¹³When the Lord saw her, he had compassion for her and said to her, "Do not weep." ¹⁴Then he came forward and touched the bier, and the bearers stood still. And he said, "Young man, I say to you, rise!" ¹⁵The dead man sat up and began to speak, and Jesus[b] gave him to his mother. ¹⁶Fear seized all of them; and they glorified God, saying, "A great prophet has risen among us!" and "God has looked favorably on his people!" ¹⁷This word about him spread throughout Judea and all the surrounding country.

18 The disciples of John reported all these things to him. So John summoned two of his disciples ¹⁹and sent them to the Lord to ask, "Are you the one who is to come, or are we to wait for another?" ²⁰When the men had come to him, they said, "John the Baptist has sent us to you to ask, 'Are you the one who is to come, or are we to wait for another?'" ²¹Jesus[c] had just then cured many people of diseases, plagues, and evil spirits, and had given sight to many who were blind. ²²And he answered them, "Go and tell John what you have seen and heard: the blind receive their sight, the lame walk, the lepers[d] are cleansed, the deaf hear, the dead are raised, the poor have good news brought to them. ²³And blessed is anyone who takes no offense at me."

24 When John's messengers had gone, Jesus[b] began to speak to the crowds about John:[e] "What did you go out into the wilderness to look at? A reed shaken by the wind? ²⁵What then did you go out to see? Someone[f] dressed in soft robes? Look, those who put on fine clothing and live in luxury are in royal palaces. ²⁶What then did you go out to see? A prophet? Yes, I tell you, and more than a prophet. ²⁷This is the one about whom it is written,

'See, I am sending my
    messenger ahead of you,
who will prepare your way
    before you.'

²⁸I tell you, among those born of women no one is greater than John; yet the least in the kingdom of God is greater than he." ²⁹(And all the people who heard this, including the tax collectors, acknowledged the justice of God,[g] because they had been baptized with John's baptism. ³⁰But by refusing to be baptized by him, the Pharisees and the lawyers rejected God's purpose for themselves.)

31 "To what then will I compare the people of this generation, and what are they like? ³²They are like children sitting in the marketplace and calling to one another,

'We played the flute for you,
    and you did not dance;
we wailed, and you did not
    weep.'

³³For John the Baptist has come eating no bread and drinking no wine, and you say, 'He has a demon'; ³⁴the Son of Man has come eating and drinking, and you say, 'Look, a glutton and a drunkard, a friend of tax collectors and sinners!' ³⁵Nevertheless, wisdom is vindicated by all her children."

a Other ancient authorities read *Next day*  b Gk *he*  c Gk *He*  d The terms *leper* and *leprosy* can refer to several diseases  e Gk *him*  f Or *Why then did you go out? To see someone*  g Or *praised God*

## PSALM 68.19–35

**B**LESSED be the Lord,
  who daily bears us up;
  God is our salvation.   *Selah*
20 Our God is a God of salvation,
    and to GOD, the Lord, belongs
      escape from death.

21 But God will shatter the heads
    of his enemies,
    the hairy crown of those who
      walk in their guilty ways.
22 The Lord said,
    "I will bring them back from
      Bashan,
  I will bring them back from the
    depths of the sea,
23 so that you may bathe[a] your
    feet in blood,
  so that the tongues of your
    dogs may have their
    share from the foe."

24 Your solemn processions are
    seen,[b] O God,
  the processions of my God,
    my King, into the
    sanctuary—
25 the singers in front, the
    musicians last,
  between them girls playing
    tambourines:
26 "Bless God in the great
    congregation,
  the LORD, O you who are of
    Israel's fountain!"
27 There is Benjamin, the least of
    them, in the lead,
  the princes of Judah in a
    body,
  the princes of Zebulun, the
    princes of Naphtali.

28 Summon your might, O God;
  show your strength, O God,
    as you have done for us
    before.

29 Because of your temple at
    Jerusalem
  kings bear gifts to you.
30 Rebuke the wild animals that
    live among the reeds,
  the herd of bulls with the
    calves of the peoples.
  Trample[c] under foot those who
    lust after tribute;
  scatter the peoples who
    delight in war. [d]
31 Let bronze be brought from
    Egypt;
  let Ethiopia[e] hasten to
    stretch out its hands to
    God.

32 Sing to God, O kingdoms of the
    earth;
  sing praises to the Lord,
        *Selah*
33 O rider in the heavens, the
    ancient heavens;
  listen, he sends out his voice,
    his mighty voice.
34 Ascribe power to God,
  whose majesty is over Israel;
  and whose power is in the
    skies.
35 Awesome is God in his[f]
    sanctuary,
  the God of Israel;
  he gives power and strength
    to his people.

Blessed be God!

## PROVERBS 11.29–31

**T**HOSE who trouble their
    households will inherit
    wind,
  and the fool will be servant to
    the wise.
30 The fruit of the righteous is a
    tree of life,
  but violence[g] takes lives
    away.

[a]Gk Syr Tg: Heb *shatter*   [b]Or *have been seen*   [c]Cn: Heb *Trampling*   [d]Meaning of Heb of verse 30 is uncertain   [e]Or *Nubia*; Heb *Cush*   [f]Gk: Heb *from your*   [g]Cn Compare Gk Syr: Heb *a wise man*

<sup>31</sup>  If the righteous are repaid on
earth,

how much more the wicked
and the sinner!

# MARCH 27

## DEUTERONOMY 7.1—8.20

**W**HEN the LORD your God brings you into the land that you are about to enter and occupy, and he clears away many nations before you—the Hittites, the Girgashites, the Amorites, the Canaanites, the Perizzites, the Hivites, and the Jebusites, seven nations mightier and more numerous than you— <sup>2</sup>and when the LORD your God gives them over to you and you defeat them, then you must utterly destroy them. Make no covenant with them and show them no mercy. <sup>3</sup>Do not intermarry with them, giving your daughters to their sons or taking their daughters for your sons, <sup>4</sup>for that would turn away your children from following me, to serve other gods. Then the anger of the LORD would be kindled against you, and he would destroy you quickly. <sup>5</sup>But this is how you must deal with them: break down their altars, smash their pillars, hew down their sacred poles,<sup>a</sup> and burn their idols with fire. <sup>6</sup>For you are a people holy to the LORD your God; the LORD your God has chosen you out of all the peoples on earth to be his people, his treasured possession.

7  It was not because you were more numerous than any other people that the LORD set his heart on you and chose you—for you were the fewest of all peoples. <sup>8</sup>It was because the LORD loved you and kept the oath that he swore to your ancestors, that the LORD has brought you out with a mighty hand, and redeemed you from the house of slavery, from the hand of Pharaoh king of Egypt. <sup>9</sup>Know therefore that the LORD your God is God, the faithful God who maintains covenant loyalty with those who love him and keep his commandments, to a thousand generations, <sup>10</sup>and who repays in their own person those who reject him. He does not delay but repays in their own person those who reject him. <sup>11</sup>Therefore, observe diligently the commandment—the statutes, and the ordinances—that I am commanding you today.

12  If you heed these ordinances, by diligently observing them, the LORD your God will maintain with you the covenant loyalty that he swore to your ancestors; <sup>13</sup>he will love you, bless you, and multiply you; he will bless the fruit of your womb and the fruit of your ground, your grain and your wine and your oil, the increase of your cattle and the issue of your flock, in the land that he swore to your ancestors to give you. <sup>14</sup>You shall be the most blessed of peoples, with neither sterility nor barrenness among you or your livestock. <sup>15</sup>The LORD will turn away from you every illness; all the dread diseases of Egypt that you experienced, he will not inflict on you, but he will lay them on all who hate you. <sup>16</sup>You shall devour all the peoples that the LORD your God is giving over to you, showing them no pity;

a Heb *Asherim*

you shall not serve their gods, for that would be a snare to you.

17 If you say to yourself, "These nations are more numerous than I; how can I dispossess them?" [18]do not be afraid of them. Just remember what the Lord your God did to Pharaoh and to all Egypt, [19]the great trials that your eyes saw, the signs and wonders, the mighty hand and the outstretched arm by which the Lord your God brought you out. The Lord your God will do the same to all the peoples of whom you are afraid. [20]Moreover, the Lord your God will send the pestilence[a] against them, until even the survivors and the fugitives are destroyed. [21]Have no dread of them, for the Lord your God, who is present with you, is a great and awesome God. [22]The Lord your God will clear away these nations before you little by little; you will not be able to make a quick end of them, otherwise the wild animals would become too numerous for you. [23]But the Lord your God will give them over to you, and throw them into great panic, until they are destroyed. [24]He will hand their kings over to you and you shall blot out their name from under heaven; no one will be able to stand against you, until you have destroyed them. [25]The images of their gods you shall burn with fire. Do not covet the silver or the gold that is on them and take it for yourself, because you could be ensnared by it; for it is abhorrent to the Lord your God. [26]Do not bring an abhorrent thing into your house, or you will be set apart for destruction like it. You must utterly detest and abhor it, for it is set apart for destruction.

**8.**1 This entire commandment that I command you today you must diligently observe, so that you may live and increase, and go in and occupy the land that the Lord promised on oath to your ancestors. [2]Remember the long way that the Lord your God has led you these forty years in the wilderness, in order to humble you, testing you to know what was in your heart, whether or not you would keep his commandments. [3]He humbled you by letting you hunger, then by feeding you with manna, with which neither you nor your ancestors were acquainted, in order to make you understand that one does not live by bread alone, but by every word that comes from the mouth of the Lord.[b] [4]The clothes on your back did not wear out and your feet did not swell these forty years. [5]Know then in your heart that as a parent disciplines a child so the Lord your God disciplines you. [6]Therefore keep the commandments of the Lord your God, by walking in his ways and by fearing him. [7]For the Lord your God is bringing you into a good land, a land with flowing streams, with springs and underground waters welling up in valleys and hills, [8]a land of wheat and barley, of vines and fig trees and pomegranates, a land of olive trees and honey, [9]a land where you may eat bread without scarcity, where you will lack nothing, a land whose stones are iron and from whose hills you may mine copper. [10]You shall eat your fill and bless the Lord your God for the good land that he has given you.

11 Take care that you do not forget the Lord your God, by failing to keep his commandments, his ordinances, and his statutes, which I am commanding you today. [12]When you have eaten your fill and have built fine houses and live in them, [13]and when your herds and flocks have multiplied, and your silver and gold is multiplied, and all that you have is multiplied, [14]then do not exalt yourself, forgetting the Lord your God, who brought you out of the land of Egypt, out of the house of slavery, [15]who led you through the great and

a Or *hornets*: Meaning of Heb uncertain   b Or *by anything that the Lord decrees* terrible wilderness, an arid wasteland with poisonous[a] snakes and scorpions. He made water flow for you from flint rock, [16]and fed you in the wilderness with manna that your ancestors did not know, to humble you and to test you, and in the end to do you good. [17]Do not say to yourself, "My power and the might of my own hand have gotten me this wealth." [18]But remember the LORD your God, for it is he who gives you power to get wealth, so that he may confirm his covenant that he swore to your ancestors, as he is doing today. [19]If you do forget the LORD your God and follow other gods to serve and worship them, I solemnly warn you today that you shall surely perish. [20]Like the nations that the LORD is destroying before you, so shall you perish, because you would not obey the voice of the LORD your God.

## LUKE 7.36—8.3

ONE of the Pharisees asked Jesus[b] to eat with him, and he went into the Pharisee's house and took his place at the table. [37]And a woman in the city, who was a sinner, having learned that he was eating in the Pharisee's house, brought an alabaster jar of ointment. [38]She stood behind him at his feet, weeping, and began to bathe his feet with her tears and to dry them with her hair. Then she continued kissing his feet and anointing them with the ointment. [39]Now when the Pharisee who had invited him saw it, he said to himself, "If this man were a prophet, he would have known who and what kind of woman this is who is touching him— that she is a sinner." [40]Jesus spoke up and said to him, "Simon, I have something to say to you." "Teacher," he replied, "Speak." [41]"A certain creditor had two debtors; one owed five hundred denarii,[c] and the other fifty.

[42]When they could not pay, he canceled the debts for both of them. Now which of them will love him more?" [43]Simon answered, "I suppose the one for whom he canceled the greater debt." And Jesus[d] said to him, "You have judged rightly." [44]Then turning toward the woman, he said to Simon, "Do you see this woman? I entered your house; you gave me no water for my feet, but she has bathed my feet with her tears and dried them with her hair. [45]You gave me no kiss, but from the time I came in she has not stopped kissing my feet. [46]You did not anoint my head with oil, but she has anointed my feet with ointment. [47]Therefore, I tell you, her sins, which were many, have been forgiven; hence she has shown great love. But the one to whom little is forgiven, loves little." [48]Then he said to her, "Your sins are forgiven." [49]But those who were at the table with him began to say among themselves, "Who is this who even forgives sins?" [50]And he said to the woman, "Your faith has saved you; go in peace."

[8.1] SOON afterwards he went on through cities and villages, proclaiming and bringing the good news of the kingdom of God. The twelve were with him, [2]as well as some women who had been cured of evil spirits and infirmities: Mary, called Magdalene, from whom seven demons had gone out, [3]and Joanna, the wife of Herod's steward Chuza, and Susanna, and many others, who provided for them[e] out of their resources.

## PSALM 69.1–18

*To the leader: according to Lilies. Of David.*

SAVE me, O God,
for the waters have come up
    to my neck.
2   I sink in deep mire,

where there is no foothold;
I have come into deep waters,
   and the flood sweeps over
     me.
3 I am weary with my crying;
   my throat is parched.
My eyes grow dim
   with waiting for my God.

4 More in number than the hairs
    of my head
   are those who hate me
    without cause;
many are those who would
    destroy me,
   my enemies who accuse me
    falsely.
What I did not steal
   must I now restore?
5 O God, you know my folly;
   the wrongs I have done are
    not hidden from you.

6 Do not let those who hope in
    you be put to shame
    because of me,
   O Lord GOD of hosts;
do not let those who seek you
    be dishonored because of
    me,
   O God of Israel.
7 It is for your sake that I have
    borne reproach,
   that shame has covered my
    face.
8 I have become a stranger to my
    kindred,
   an alien to my mother's
    children.

9 It is zeal for your house that
    has consumed me;
   the insults of those who insult
    you have fallen on me.
10 When I humbled my soul with
    fasting, a
   they insulted me for doing so.

11 When I made sackcloth my
    clothing,
   I became a byword to them.
12 I am the subject of gossip for
    those who sit in the
    gate,
   and the drunkards make
    songs about me.

13 But as for me, my prayer is to
    you, O LORD.
   At an acceptable time,
    O God,
   in the abundance of your
    steadfast love, answer
    me.
With your faithful help 14rescue
    me
   from sinking in the mire;
let me be delivered from my
    enemies
   and from the deep waters.
15 Do not let the flood sweep over
    me,
   or the deep swallow me up,
   or the Pit close its mouth
    over me.

16 Answer me, O LORD, for your
    steadfast love is good;
   according to your abundant
    mercy, turn to me.
17 Do not hide your face from your
    servant,
   for I am in distress—make
    haste to answer me.
18 Draw near to me, redeem me,
   set me free because of my
    enemies.

# PROVERBS 12.1

WHOEVER loves discipline loves
    knowledge,
   but those who hate to be
    rebuked are stupid.

a Gk Syr: Heb *I wept, with fasting my soul,* or *I made my soul mourn with fasting*

## DEUTERONOMY 9.1—10.22

HEAR, O Israel! You are about to cross the Jordan today, to go in and dispossess nations larger and mightier than you, great cities, fortified to the heavens, ²a strong and tall people, the offspring of the Anakim, whom you know. You have heard it said of them, "Who can stand up to the Anakim?" ³Know then today that the LORD your God is the one who crosses over before you as a devouring fire; he will defeat them and subdue them before you, so that you may dispossess and destroy them quickly, as the LORD has promised you.

4 When the LORD your God thrusts them out before you, do not say to yourself, "It is because of my righteousness that the LORD has brought me in to occupy this land"; it is rather because of the wickedness of these nations that the LORD is dispossessing them before you. ⁵It is not because of your righteousness or the uprightness of your heart that you are going in to occupy their land; but because of the wickedness of these nations the LORD your God is dispossessing them before you, in order to fulfill the promise that the LORD made on oath to your ancestors, to Abraham, to Isaac, and to Jacob.

6 Know, then, that the LORD your God is not giving you this good land to occupy because of your righteousness; for you are a stubborn people. ⁷Remember and do not forget how you provoked the LORD your God to wrath in the wilderness; you have been rebellious against the LORD from the day you came out of the land of Egypt until you came to this place.

8 Even at Horeb you provoked the LORD to wrath, and the LORD was so angry with you that he was ready to destroy you. ⁹When I went up the mountain to receive the stone tablets, the tablets of the covenant that the LORD made with you, I remained on the mountain forty days and forty nights; I neither ate bread nor drank water. ¹⁰And the LORD gave me the two stone tablets written with the finger of God; on them were all the words that the LORD had spoken to you at the mountain out of the fire on the day of the assembly. ¹¹At the end of forty days and forty nights the LORD gave me the two stone tablets, the tablets of the covenant. ¹²Then the LORD said to me, "Get up, go down quickly from here, for your people whom you have brought from Egypt have acted corruptly. They have been quick to turn from the way that I commanded them; they have cast an image for themselves." ¹³Furthermore the LORD said to me, "I have seen that this people is indeed a stubborn people. ¹⁴Let me alone that I may destroy them and blot out their name from under heaven; and I will make of you a nation mightier and more numerous than they."

15 So I turned and went down from the mountain, while the mountain was ablaze; the two tablets of the covenant were in my two hands. ¹⁶Then I saw that you had indeed sinned against the LORD your God, by casting for yourselves an image of a calf; you had been quick to turn from the way that the LORD had commanded you. ¹⁷So I took hold of the two tablets and flung them from my two hands, smashing them before your eyes. ¹⁸Then I lay prostrate before the LORD as before, forty days and forty nights; I neither ate bread nor drank water, because of all the sin you had committed, provoking the LORD by

doing what was evil in his sight. [19]For I was afraid that the anger that the LORD bore against you was so fierce that he would destroy you. But the LORD listened to me that time also. [20]The LORD was so angry with Aaron that he was ready to destroy him, but I interceded also on behalf of Aaron at that same time. [21]Then I took the sinful thing you had made, the calf, and burned it with fire and crushed it, grinding it thoroughly, until it was reduced to dust; and I threw the dust of it into the stream that runs down the mountain.

22  At Taberah also, and at Massah, and at Kibroth-hattaavah, you provoked the LORD to wrath. [23]And when the LORD sent you from Kadesh-barnea, saying, "Go up and occupy the land that I have given you," you rebelled against the command of the LORD your God, neither trusting him nor obeying him. [24]You have been rebellious against the LORD as long as he has[a] known you.

25  Throughout the forty days and forty nights that I lay prostrate before the LORD when the LORD intended to destroy you, [26]I prayed to the LORD and said, "Lord GOD, do not destroy the people who are your very own possession, whom you redeemed in your greatness, whom you brought out of Egypt with a mighty hand. [27]Remember your servants, Abraham, Isaac, and Jacob; pay no attention to the stubbornness of this people, their wickedness and their sin, [28]otherwise the land from which you have brought us might say, 'Because the LORD was not able to bring them into the land that he promised them, and because he hated them, he has brought them out to let them die in the wilderness.' [29]For they are the people of your very own possession, whom you brought out by your great power and by your outstretched arm."

10.[1] AT that time the LORD said to me, "Carve out two tablets of stone like the former ones, and come up to me on the mountain, and make an ark of wood. [2]I will write on the tablets the words that were on the former tablets, which you smashed, and you shall put them in the ark." [3]So I made an ark of acacia wood, cut two tablets of stone like the former ones, and went up the mountain with the two tablets in my hand. [4]Then he wrote on the tablets the same words as before, the ten commandments[b] that the LORD had spoken to you on the mountain out of the fire on the day of the assembly; and the LORD gave them to me. [5]So I turned and came down from the mountain, and put the tablets in the ark that I had made; and there they are, as the LORD commanded me.

6  (The Israelites journeyed from Beeroth-bene-jaakan[c] to Moserah. There Aaron died, and there he was buried; his son Eleazar succeeded him as priest. [7]From there they journeyed to Gudgodah, and from Gudgodah to Jotbathah, a land with flowing streams. [8]At that time the LORD set apart the tribe of Levi to carry the ark of the covenant of the LORD, to stand before the LORD to minister to him, and to bless in his name, to this day. [9]Therefore Levi has no allotment or inheritance with his kindred; the LORD is his inheritance, as the LORD your God promised him.)

10  I stayed on the mountain forty days and forty nights, as I had done the first time. And once again the LORD listened to me. The LORD was unwilling to destroy you. [11]The LORD said to me, "Get up, go on your journey at the head of the people, that they may go in and occupy the land that I swore to their ancestors to give them."

12  So now, O Israel, what does the LORD your God require of you? Only to fear the LORD your God, to walk in all

a Sam Gk: MT *I have*   b Heb *the ten words*   c Or *the wells of the Bene-jaakan*

his ways, to love him, to serve the Lord your God with all your heart and with all your soul, [13]and to keep the commandments of the Lord your God[a] and his decrees that I am commanding you today, for your own well-being. [14]Although heaven and the heaven of heavens belong to the Lord your God, the earth with all that is in it, [15]yet the Lord set his heart in love on your ancestors alone and chose you, their descendants after them, out of all the peoples, as it is today. [16]Circumcise, then, the foreskin of your heart, and do not be stubborn any longer. [17]For the Lord your God is God of gods and Lord of lords, the great God, mighty and awesome, who is not partial and takes no bribe, [18]who executes justice for the orphan and the widow, and who loves the strangers, providing them food and clothing. [19]You shall also love the stranger, for you were strangers in the land of Egypt. [20]You shall fear the Lord your God; him alone you shall worship; to him you shall hold fast, and by his name you shall swear. [21]He is your praise; he is your God, who has done for you these great and awesome things that your own eyes have seen. [22]Your ancestors went down to Egypt seventy persons; and now the Lord your God has made you as numerous as the stars in heaven.

## LUKE 8.4–21

WHEN a great crowd gathered and people from town after town came to him, he [Jesus] said in a parable: [5]"A sower went out to sow his seed; and as he sowed, some fell on the path and was trampled on, and the birds of the air ate it up. [6]Some fell on the rock; and as it grew up, it withered for lack of moisture. [7]Some fell among thorns, and the thorns grew with it and choked it. [8]Some fell into good soil, and when it grew, it pro-

duced a hundredfold." As he said this, he called out, "Let anyone with ears to hear listen!"

9 Then his disciples asked him what this parable meant. [10]He said, "To you it has been given to know the secrets[b] of the kingdom of God; but to others I speak[c] in parables, so that

'looking they may not perceive,
    and listening they may not
        understand.'

11 "Now the parable is this: The seed is the word of God. [12]The ones on the path are those who have heard; then the devil comes and takes away the word from their hearts, so that they may not believe and be saved. [13]The ones on the rock are those who, when they hear the word, receive it with joy. But these have no root; they believe only for a while and in a time of testing fall away. [14]As for what fell among the thorns, these are the ones who hear; but as they go on their way, they are choked by the cares and riches and pleasures of life, and their fruit does not mature. [15]But as for that in the good soil, these are the ones who, when they hear the word, hold it fast in an honest and good heart, and bear fruit with patient endurance.

16 "No one after lighting a lamp hides it under a jar, or puts it under a bed, but puts it on a lampstand, so that those who enter may see the light. [17]For nothing is hidden that will not be disclosed, nor is anything secret that will not become known and come to light. [18]Then pay attention to how you listen; for to those who have, more will be given; and from those who do not have, even what they seem to have will be taken away."

19 Then his mother and his brothers came to him, but they could not reach him because of the crowd. [20]And he was told, "Your mother and your brothers are standing outside, wanting

a Q Ms Gk Syr: MT lacks *your God*   b Or *mysteries*   c Gk lacks *I speak* to see you." [21] But he said to them, "My mother and my brothers are those who hear the word of God and do it."

## PSALM 69.19–36

Y OU know the insults I receive,
and my shame and dishonor;
my foes are all known to
you.
[20] Insults have broken my heart,
so that I am in despair.
I looked for pity, but there was
none;
and for comforters, but I
found none.
[21] They gave me poison for food,
and for my thirst they gave
me vinegar to drink.

[22] Let their table be a trap for
them,
a snare for their allies.
[23] Let their eyes be darkened so
that they cannot see,
and make their loins tremble
continually.
[24] Pour out your indignation upon
them,
and let your burning anger
overtake them.
[25] May their camp be a desolation;
let no one live in their tents.
[26] For they persecute those whom
you have struck down,
and those whom you have
wounded, they attack still
more. [a]
[27] Add guilt to their guilt;
may they have no acquittal
from you.
[28] Let them be blotted out of the
book of the living;
let them not be enrolled
among the righteous.

[29] But I am lowly and in pain;
let your salvation, O God,
protect me.

[30] I will praise the name of God
with a song;
I will magnify him with
thanksgiving.
[31] This will please the LORD more
than an ox
or a bull with horns and
hoofs.
[32] Let the oppressed see it and be
glad;
you who seek God, let your
hearts revive.
[33] For the LORD hears the needy,
and does not despise his own
that are in bonds.

[34] Let heaven and earth praise
him,
the seas and everything that
moves in them.
[35] For God will save Zion
and rebuild the cities of
Judah;
and his servants shall live [b]
there and possess it;
[36] the children of his servants
shall inherit it,
and those who love his name
shall live in it.

## PROVERBS 12.2–3

T HE good obtain favor from the
LORD,
but those who devise evil he
condemns.
[3] No one finds security by
wickedness,
but the root of the righteous
will never be moved.

a Gk Syr: Heb *recount the pain of*    b Syr: Heb *and they shall live*

# MARCH 29



You shall love the LORD your God, therefore, and keep his charge, his decrees, his ordinances, and his commandments always. ²Remember today that it was not your children (who have not known or seen the discipline of the LORD your God), but it is you who must acknowledge his greatness, his mighty hand and his outstretched arm, ³his signs and his deeds that he did in Egypt to Pharaoh, the king of Egypt, and to all his land; ⁴what he did to the Egyptian army, to their horses and chariots, how he made the water of the Red Sea*a* flow over them as they pursued you, so that the LORD has destroyed them to this day; ⁵what he did to you in the wilderness, until you came to this place; ⁶and what he did to Dathan and Abiram, sons of Eliab son of Reuben, how in the midst of all Israel the earth opened its mouth and swallowed them up, along with their households, their tents, and every living being in their company; ⁷for it is your own eyes that have seen every great deed that the LORD did.

8 Keep, then, this entire commandment that I am commanding you today, so that you may have strength to go in and occupy the land that you are crossing over to occupy, ⁹and so that you may live long in the land that the LORD swore to your ancestors to give them and to their descendants, a land flowing with milk and honey. ¹⁰For the land that you are about to enter to occupy is not like the land of Egypt, from which you have come, where you sow your seed and irrigate by foot like a vegetable garden. ¹¹But the land that you are crossing over to occupy is a land of hills and valleys, watered by rain from the sky, ¹²a land that the LORD your God looks after. The eyes of the LORD your God are always on it, from the beginning of the year to the end of the year.

13 If you will only heed his every commandment*b* that I am commanding you today—loving the LORD your God, and serving him with all your heart and with all your soul— ¹⁴then he*c* will give the rain for your land in its season, the early rain and the later rain, and you will gather in your grain, your wine, and your oil; ¹⁵and he*c* will give grass in your fields for your livestock, and you will eat your fill. ¹⁶Take care, or you will be seduced into turning away, serving other gods and worshiping them, ¹⁷for then the anger of the LORD will be kindled against you and he will shut up the heavens, so that there will be no rain and the land will yield no fruit; then you will perish quickly off the good land that the LORD is giving you.

18 You shall put these words of mine in your heart and soul, and you shall bind them as a sign on your hand, and fix them as an emblem*d* on your forehead. ¹⁹Teach them to your children, talking about them when you are at home and when you are away, when you lie down and when you rise. ²⁰Write them on the doorposts of your house and on your gates, ²¹so that your days and the days of your children may be multiplied in the land that the LORD swore to your ancestors to give them, as long as the heavens are above the earth.

22 If you will diligently observe this entire commandment that I am com-

---

a Or *Sea of Reeds*    b Compare Gk: Heb *my commandments*    c Sam Gk Vg: MT *I*    d Or *as a frontlet*

manding you, loving the LORD your God, walking in all his ways, and holding fast to him, 23then the LORD will drive out all these nations before you, and you will dispossess nations larger and mightier than yourselves. 24Every place on which you set foot shall be yours; your territory shall extend from the wilderness to the Lebanon and from the River, the river Euphrates, to the Western Sea. 25No one will be able to stand against you; the LORD your God will put the fear and dread of you on all the land on which you set foot, as he promised you.

26 See, I am setting before you today a blessing and a curse: 27the blessing, if you obey the commandments of the LORD your God that I am commanding you today; 28and the curse, if you do not obey the commandments of the LORD your God, but turn from the way that I am commanding you today, to follow other gods that you have not known.

29 When the LORD your God has brought you into the land that you are entering to occupy, you shall set the blessing on Mount Gerizim and the curse on Mount Ebal. 30As you know, they are beyond the Jordan, some distance to the west, in the land of the Canaanites who live in the Arabah, opposite Gilgal, beside the oaka of Moreh.

31 When you cross the Jordan to go in to occupy the land that the LORD your God is giving you, and when you occupy it and live in it, 32you must diligently observe all the statutes and ordinances that I am setting before you today.

12.1 THESE are the statutes and ordinances that you must diligently observe in the land that the LORD, the God of your ancestors, has given you to occupy all the days that you live on the earth.

2 You must demolish completely all the places where the nations whom you are about to dispossess served their gods, on the mountain heights, on the hills, and under every leafy tree. 3Break down their altars, smash their pillars, burn their sacred polesb with fire, and hew down the idols of their gods, and thus blot out their name from their places. 4You shall not worship the LORD your God in such ways. 5But you shall seek the place that the LORD your God will choose out of all your tribes as his habitation to put his name there. You shall go there, 6bringing there your burnt offerings and your sacrifices, your tithes and your donations, your votive gifts, your freewill offerings, and the firstlings of your herds and flocks. 7And you shall eat there in the presence of the LORD your God, you and your households together, rejoicing in all the undertakings in which the LORD your God has blessed you.

8 You shall not act as we are acting here today, all of us according to our own desires, 9for you have not yet come into the rest and the possession that the LORD your God is giving you. 10When you cross over the Jordan and live in the land that the LORD your God is allotting to you, and when he gives you rest from your enemies all around so that you live in safety, 11then you shall bring everything that I command you to the place that the LORD your God will choose as a dwelling for his name: your burnt offerings and your sacrifices, your tithes and your donations, and all your choice votive gifts that you vow to the LORD. 12And you shall rejoice before the LORD your God, you together with your sons and your daughters, your male and female slaves, and the Levites who reside in

aGk Syr: Compare Gen 12.6; Heb oaks or terebinths  bHeb Asherim your towns (since they have no allotment or inheritance with you).

13 Take care that you do not offer your burnt offerings at any place you happen to see. ¹⁴But only at the place that the LORD will choose in one of your tribes—there you shall offer your burnt offerings and there you shall do everything I command you.

15 Yet whenever you desire you may slaughter and eat meat within any of your towns, according to the blessing that the LORD your God has given you; the unclean and the clean may eat of it, as they would of gazelle or deer. ¹⁶The blood, however, you must not eat; you shall pour it out on the ground like water. ¹⁷Nor may you eat within your towns the tithe of your grain, your wine, and your oil, the firstlings of your herds and your flocks, any of your votive gifts that you vow, your freewill offerings, or your donations; ¹⁸these you shall eat in the presence of the LORD your God at the place that the LORD your God will choose, you together with your son and your daughter, your male and female slaves, and the Levites resident in your towns, rejoicing in the presence of the LORD your God in all your undertakings. ¹⁹Take care that you do not neglect the Levite as long as you live in your land.

20 When the LORD your God enlarges your territory, as he has promised you, and you say, "I am going to eat some meat," because you wish to eat meat, you may eat meat whenever you have the desire. ²¹If the place where the LORD your God will choose to put his name is too far from you, and you slaughter as I have commanded you any of your herd or flock that the LORD has given you, then you may eat within your towns whenever you desire. ²²Indeed, just as gazelle or deer is eaten, so you may eat it; the unclean and the clean alike may eat it. ²³Only be sure that you do not eat the blood; for the blood is the life, and you shall not eat the life with the meat. ²⁴Do not eat it; you shall pour it out on the ground like water. ²⁵Do not eat it, so that all may go well with you and your children after you, because you do what is right in the sight of the LORD. ²⁶But the sacred donations that are due from you, and your votive gifts, you shall bring to the place that the LORD will choose. ²⁷You shall present your burnt offerings, both the meat and the blood, on the altar of the LORD your God; the blood of your other sacrifices shall be poured out beside[a] the altar of the LORD your God, but the meat you may eat.

28 Be careful to obey all these words that I command you today,[b] so that it may go well with you and with your children after you forever, because you will be doing what is good and right in the sight of the LORD your God.

29 When the LORD your God has cut off before you the nations whom you are about to enter to dispossess them, when you have dispossessed them and live in their land, ³⁰take care that you are not snared into imitating them, after they have been destroyed before you: do not inquire concerning their gods, saying, "How did these nations worship their gods? I also want to do the same." ³¹You must not do the same for the LORD your God, because every abhorrent thing that the LORD hates they have done for their gods. They would even burn their sons and their daughters in the fire to their gods. ³²[c]You must diligently observe everything that I command you; do not add to it or take anything from it.

a Or *on*   b Gk Sam Syr: MT lacks *today*   c Ch 13.1 in Heb

## LUKE 8.22–39

O NE day he [Jesus] got into a boat with his disciples, and he said to them, "Let us go across to the other side of the lake." So they put out, [23]and while they were sailing he fell asleep. A windstorm swept down on the lake, and the boat was filling with water, and they were in danger. [24]They went to him and woke him up, shouting, "Master, Master, we are perishing!" And he woke up and rebuked the wind and the raging waves; they ceased, and there was a calm. [25]He said to them, "Where is your faith?" They were afraid and amazed, and said to one another, "Who then is this, that he commands even the winds and the water, and they obey him?"

26  Then they arrived at the country of the Gerasenes, [a] which is opposite Galilee. [27]As he stepped out on land, a man of the city who had demons met him. For a long time he had worn[b] no clothes, and he did not live in a house but in the tombs. [28]When he saw Jesus, he fell down before him and shouted at the top of his voice, "What have you to do with me, Jesus, Son of the Most High God? I beg you, do not torment me"— [29]for Jesus[c] had commanded the unclean spirit to come out of the man. (For many times it had seized him; he was kept under guard and bound with chains and shackles, but he would break the bonds and be driven by the demon into the wilds.) [30]Jesus then asked him, "What is your name?" He said, "Legion"; for many demons had entered him. [31]They begged him not to order them to go back into the abyss.

32  Now there on the hillside a large herd of swine was feeding; and the demons[d] begged Jesus[e] to let them enter these. So he gave them permission. [33]Then the demons came out of the man and entered the swine, and the herd rushed down the steep bank into the lake and was drowned.

34  When the swineherds saw what had happened, they ran off and told it in the city and in the country. [35]Then people came out to see what had happened, and when they came to Jesus, they found the man from whom the demons had gone sitting at the feet of Jesus, clothed and in his right mind. And they were afraid. [36]Those who had seen it told them how the one who had been possessed by demons had been healed. [37]Then all the people of the surrounding country of the Gerasenes[a] asked Jesus[e] to leave them; for they were seized with great fear. So he got into the boat and returned. [38]The man from whom the demons had gone begged that he might be with him; but Jesus[c] sent him away, saying, [39]"Return to your home, and declare how much God has done for you." So he went away, proclaiming throughout the city how much Jesus had done for him.

## PSALM 70.1–5

*To the leader. Of David, for the memorial offering.*

B E pleased, O God, to deliver
         me.
    O LORD, make haste to help
         me!
[2]  Let those be put to shame and
         confusion
     who seek my life.
   Let those be turned back and
         brought to dishonor
     who desire to hurt me.
[3]  Let those who say, "Aha, Aha!"
     turn back because of their
         shame.

[4]  Let all who seek you
     rejoice and be glad in you.
   Let those who love your
         salvation

---

[a]Other ancient authorities read *Gadarenes*; others, *Gergesenes*  [b]Other ancient authorities read *a man of the city who had had demons for a long time met him. He wore*  [c]Gk *he*  [d]Gk *they*  [e]Gk *him*

say evermore, "God is
great!"
5 But I am poor and needy;
hasten to me, O God!
You are my help and my
deliverer;
O Lord, do not delay!

## PROVERBS 12.4

A GOOD wife is the crown of her husband, but she who brings shame is like rottenness in his bones.

# MARCH 30

## DEUTERONOMY 13a.1—15.23

IF prophets or those who divine by dreams appear among you and promise you omens or portents, 2and the omens or the portents declared by them take place, and they say, "Let us follow other gods" (whom you have not known) "and let us serve them," 3you must not heed the words of those prophets or those who divine by dreams; for the Lord your God is testing you, to know whether you indeed love the Lord your God with all your heart and soul. 4The Lord your God you shall follow, him alone you shall fear, his commandments you shall keep, his voice you shall obey, him you shall serve, and to him you shall hold fast. 5But those prophets or those who divine by dreams shall be put to death for having spoken treason against the Lord your God—who brought you out of the land of Egypt and redeemed you from the house of slavery—to turn you from the way in which the Lord your God commanded you to walk. So you shall purge the evil from your midst.

6 If anyone secretly entices you—even if it is your brother, your father's son orb your mother's son, or your own son or daughter, or the wife you embrace, or your most intimate friend—saying, "Let us go worship other gods," whom neither you nor your ancestors have known, 7any of the gods of the peoples that are around you, whether near you or far away from you, from one end of the earth to the other, 8you must not yield to or heed any such persons. Show them no pity or compassion and do not shield them. 9But you shall surely kill them; your own hand shall be first against them to execute them, and afterwards the hand of all the people. 10Stone them to death for trying to turn you away from the Lord your God, who brought you out of the land of Egypt, out of the house of slavery. 11Then all Israel shall hear and be afraid, and never again do any such wickedness.

12 If you hear it said about one of the towns that the Lord your God is giving you to live in, 13that scoundrels from among you have gone out and led the inhabitants of the town astray, saying, "Let us go and worship other gods," whom you have not known, 14then you shall inquire and make a thorough investigation. If the charge is established that such an abhorrent

a Ch 13.2 in Heb   b Sam Gk Compare Tg: MT lacks *your father's son or* thing has been done among you, ¹⁵you shall put the inhabitants of that town to the sword, utterly destroying it and everything in it—even putting its livestock to the sword. ¹⁶All of its spoil you shall gather into its public square; then burn the town and all its spoil with fire, as a whole burnt offering to the LORD your God. It shall remain a perpetual ruin, never to be rebuilt. ¹⁷Do not let anything devoted to destruction stick to your hand, so that the LORD may turn from his fierce anger and show you compassion, and in his compassion multiply you, as he swore to your ancestors, ¹⁸if you obey the voice of the LORD your God by keeping all his commandments that I am commanding you today, doing what is right in the sight of the LORD your God.

14.1 YOU are children of the LORD your God. You must not lacerate yourselves or shave your forelocks for the dead. ²For you are a people holy to the LORD your God; it is you the LORD has chosen out of all the peoples on earth to be his people, his treasured possession.

3 You shall not eat any abhorrent thing. ⁴These are the animals you may eat: the ox, the sheep, the goat, ⁵the deer, the gazelle, the roebuck, the wild goat, the ibex, the antelope, and the mountain-sheep. ⁶Any animal that divides the hoof and has the hoof cleft in two, and chews the cud, among the animals, you may eat. ⁷Yet of those that chew the cud or have the hoof cleft you shall not eat these: the camel, the hare, and the rock badger, because they chew the cud but do not divide the hoof; they are unclean for you. ⁸And the pig, because it divides the hoof but does not chew the cud, is unclean for you. You shall not eat their meat, and you shall not touch their carcasses.

9 Of all that live in water you may eat these: whatever has fins and scales you may eat. ¹⁰And whatever does not have fins and scales you shall not eat; it is unclean for you.

11 You may eat any clean birds. ¹²But these are the ones that you shall not eat: the eagle, the vulture, the osprey, ¹³the buzzard, the kite, of any kind; ¹⁴every raven of any kind; ¹⁵the ostrich, the nighthawk, the sea gull, the hawk, of any kind; ¹⁶the little owl and the great owl, the water hen ¹⁷and the desert owl, ᵃ the carrion vulture and the cormorant, ¹⁸the stork, the heron, of any kind; the hoopoe and the bat. ᵇ ¹⁹And all winged insects are unclean for you; they shall not be eaten. ²⁰You may eat any clean winged creature.

21 You shall not eat anything that dies of itself; you may give it to aliens residing in your towns for them to eat, or you may sell it to a foreigner. For you are a people holy to the LORD your God.

You shall not boil a kid in its mother's milk.

22 Set apart a tithe of all the yield of your seed that is brought in yearly from the field. ²³In the presence of the LORD your God, in the place that he will choose as a dwelling for his name, you shall eat the tithe of your grain, your wine, and your oil, as well as the firstlings of your herd and flock, so that you may learn to fear the LORD your God always. ²⁴But if, when the LORD your God has blessed you, the distance is so great that you are unable to transport it, because the place where the LORD your God will choose to set his name is too far away from you, ²⁵then you may turn it into money. With the money secure in hand, go to the place that the LORD your God will choose; ²⁶spend the money for whatever you wish—oxen, sheep, wine, strong drink, or whatever you desire. And you shall eat there in the presence of the LORD your God, you and your household rejoicing together.

ᵃOr *pelican*  ᵇIdentification of several of the birds in verses 12-18 is uncertain

27As for the Levites resident in your towns, do not neglect them, because they have no allotment or inheritance with you. 28 Every third year you shall bring out the full tithe of your produce for that year, and store it within your towns; 29the Levites, because they have no allotment or inheritance with you, as well as the resident aliens, the orphans, and the widows in your towns, may come and eat their fill so that the Lord your God may bless you in all the work that you undertake.

15.1 Every seventh year you shall grant a remission of debts. 2And this is the manner of the remission: every creditor shall remit the claim that is held against a neighbor, not exacting it of a neighbor who is a member of the community, because the Lord's remission has been proclaimed. 3Of a foreigner you may exact it, but you must remit your claim on whatever any member of your community owes you. 4There will, however, be no one in need among you, because the Lord is sure to bless you in the land that the Lord your God is giving you as a possession to occupy, 5if only you will obey the Lord your God by diligently observing this entire commandment that I command you today. 6When the Lord your God has blessed you, as he promised you, you will lend to many nations, but you will not borrow; you will rule over many nations, but they will not rule over you.

7 If there is among you anyone in need, a member of your community in any of your towns within the land that the Lord your God is giving you, do not be hard-hearted or tight-fisted toward your needy neighbor. 8You should rather open your hand, willingly lending enough to meet the need, whatever it may be. 9Be careful that you do not entertain a mean thought, thinking, "The seventh year, the year of remission, is near," and therefore view your needy neighbor with hostility and give nothing; your neighbor might cry to the Lord against you, and you would incur guilt. 10Give liberally and be ungrudging when you do so, for on this account the Lord your God will bless you in all your work and in all that you undertake. 11Since there will never cease to be some in need on the earth, I therefore command you, "Open your hand to the poor and needy neighbor in your land."

12 If a member of your community, whether a Hebrew man or a Hebrew woman, is sold[a] to you and works for you six years, in the seventh year you shall set that person free. 13And when you send a male slave[b] out from you a free person, you shall not send him out empty-handed. 14Provide liberally out of your flock, your threshing floor, and your wine press, thus giving to him some of the bounty with which the Lord your God has blessed you. 15Remember that you were a slave in the land of Egypt, and the Lord your God redeemed you; for this reason I lay this command upon you today. 16But if he says to you, "I will not go out from you," because he loves you and your household, since he is well off with you, 17then you shall take an awl and thrust it through his earlobe into the door, and he shall be your slave[c] forever.

You shall do the same with regard to your female slave. [d]

18 Do not consider it a hardship when you send them out from you free persons, because for six years they have given you services worth the wages of hired laborers; and the Lord your God will bless you in all that you do.

19 Every firstling male born of your herd and flock you shall consecrate to the Lord your God; you shall not do work with your firstling ox nor shear

aOr *sells himself or herself*  bHeb *him*  cOr *bondman*  dOr *bondwoman* the firstling of your flock. [20]You shall eat it, you together with your household, in the presence of the LORD your God year by year at the place that the LORD will choose. [21]But if it has any defect—any serious defect, such as lameness or blindness—you shall not sacrifice it to the LORD your God; [22]within your towns you may eat it, the unclean and the clean alike, as you would a gazelle or deer. [23]Its blood, however, you must not eat; you shall pour it out on the ground like water.

## LUKE 8.40—9.6

Now when Jesus returned, the crowd welcomed him, for they were all waiting for him. [41]Just then there came a man named Jairus, a leader of the synagogue. He fell at Jesus' feet and begged him to come to his house, [42]for he had an only daughter, about twelve years old, who was dying.

As he went, the crowds pressed in on him. [43]Now there was a woman who had been suffering from hemorrhages for twelve years; and though she had spent all she had on physicians,[a] no one could cure her. [44]She came up behind him and touched the fringe of his clothes, and immediately her hemorrhage stopped. [45]Then Jesus asked, "Who touched me?" When all denied it, Peter[b] said, "Master, the crowds surround you and press in on you." [46]But Jesus said, "Someone touched me; for I noticed that power had gone out from me." [47]When the woman saw that she could not remain hidden, she came trembling; and falling down before him, she declared in the presence of all the people why she had touched him, and how she had been immediately healed. [48]He said to her, "Daughter, your faith has made you well; go in peace."

49 While he was still speaking, someone came from the leader's house to say, "Your daughter is dead; do not trouble the teacher any longer." [50]When Jesus heard this, he replied, "Do not fear. Only believe, and she will be saved." [51]When he came to the house, he did not allow anyone to enter with him, except Peter, John, and James, and the child's father and mother. [52]They were all weeping and wailing for her; but he said, "Do not weep; for she is not dead but sleeping." [53]And they laughed at him, knowing that she was dead. [54]But he took her by the hand and called out, "Child, get up!" [55]Her spirit returned, and she got up at once. Then he directed them to give her something to eat. [56]Her parents were astounded; but he ordered them to tell no one what had happened.

[9.1] THEN Jesus[c] called the twelve together and gave them power and authority over all demons and to cure diseases, [2]and he sent them out to proclaim the kingdom of God and to heal. [3]He said to them, "Take nothing for your journey, no staff, nor bag, nor bread, nor money—not even an extra tunic. [4]Whatever house you enter, stay there, and leave from there. [5]Wherever they do not welcome you, as you are leaving that town shake the dust off your feet as a testimony against them." [6]They departed and went through the villages, bringing the good news and curing diseases everywhere.

## PSALM 71.1–24

In you, O LORD, I take refuge;
   let me never be put to
      shame.
2  In your righteousness deliver
      me and rescue me;
   incline your ear to me and
      save me.
3  Be to me a rock of refuge,

aOther ancient authorities lack *and had spent all she had on physicians*  bOther ancient authorities add *and those who were with him*  cGk *he*

a strong fortress, **a** to save
    me,
  for you are my rock and my
    fortress.

4 Rescue me, O my God, from
    the hand of the wicked,
  from the grasp of the unjust
    and cruel.
5 For you, O Lord, are my hope,
  my trust, O LORD, from my
    youth.
6 Upon you I have leaned from
    my birth;
  it was you who took me from
    my mother's womb.
  My praise is continually of you.

7 I have been like a portent to
    many,
  but you are my strong refuge.
8 My mouth is filled with your
    praise,
  and with your glory all day
    long.
9 Do not cast me off in the time
    of old age;
  do not forsake me when my
    strength is spent.
10 For my enemies speak
    concerning me,
  and those who watch for my
    life consult together.
11 They say, "Pursue and seize
    that person
  whom God has forsaken,
  for there is no one to
    deliver."

12 O God, do not be far from me;
  O my God, make haste to
    help me!
13 Let my accusers be put to
    shame and consumed;
  let those who seek to hurt
    me
  be covered with scorn and
    disgrace.

14 But I will hope continually,
  and will praise you yet more
    and more.
15 My mouth will tell of your
    righteous acts,
  of your deeds of salvation all
    day long,
  though their number is past
    my knowledge.
16 I will come praising the mighty
    deeds of the Lord GOD,
  I will praise your
    righteousness, yours
    alone.

17 O God, from my youth you have
    taught me,
  and I still proclaim your
    wondrous deeds.
18 So even to old age and gray
    hairs,
  O God, do not forsake me,
  until I proclaim your might
  to all the generations to
    come. **b**
  Your power 19and your
    righteousness, O God,
  reach the high heavens.

  You who have done great
    things,
  O God, who is like you?
20 You who have made me see
    many troubles and
    calamities
  will revive me again;
  from the depths of the earth
  you will bring me up again.
21 You will increase my honor,
  and comfort me once again.

22 I will also praise you with the
    harp
  for your faithfulness, O my
    God;
  I will sing praises to you with
    the lyre,
  O Holy One of Israel.

aGk Compare 31.3: Heb *to come continually you have commanded*   bGk Compare Syr: Heb *to a generation, to all that come*

23 My lips will shout for joy
    when I sing praises to you;
    my soul also, which you have
        rescued.
24 All day long my tongue will talk
    of your righteous help,
  for those who tried to do me
        harm
    have been put to shame, and
        disgraced.

## PROVERBS 12.5–7

THE thoughts of the righteous
    are just;
  the advice of the wicked is
    treacherous.
6 The words of the wicked are a
    deadly ambush,
  but the speech of the upright
    delivers them.
7 The wicked are overthrown and
    are no more,
  but the house of the righteous
    will stand.

# MARCH 31

## DEUTERONOMY 16.1—17.20

OBSERVE the month[a] of Abib by keeping the passover for the LORD your God, for in the month of Abib the LORD your God brought you out of Egypt by night. 2You shall offer the passover sacrifice for the LORD your God, from the flock and the herd, at the place that the LORD will choose as a dwelling for his name. 3You must not eat with it anything leavened. For seven days you shall eat unleavened bread with it—the bread of affliction—because you came out of the land of Egypt in great haste, so that all the days of your life you may remember the day of your departure from the land of Egypt. 4No leaven shall be seen with you in all your territory for seven days; and none of the meat of what you slaughter on the evening of the first day shall remain until morning. 5You are not permitted to offer the passover sacrifice within any of your towns that the LORD your God is giving you. 6But at the place that the LORD your God will choose as a dwelling for his name, only there shall you offer the passover sacrifice, in the evening at sunset, the time of day when you departed from Egypt. 7You shall cook it and eat it at the place that the LORD your God will choose; the next morning you may go back to your tents. 8For six days you shall continue to eat unleavened bread, and on the seventh day there shall be a solemn assembly for the LORD your God, when you shall do no work.

9 You shall count seven weeks; begin to count the seven weeks from the time the sickle is first put to the standing grain. 10Then you shall keep the festival of weeks for the LORD your God, contributing a freewill offering in proportion to the blessing that you have received from the LORD your God. 11Rejoice before the LORD your God—

a Or *new moon*

you and your sons and your daughters, your male and female slaves, the Levites resident in your towns, as well as the strangers, the orphans, and the widows who are among you—at the place that the LORD your God will choose as a dwelling for his name. [12]Remember that you were a slave in Egypt, and diligently observe these statutes.

13 You shall keep the festival of booths[a] for seven days, when you have gathered in the produce from your threshing floor and your wine press. [14]Rejoice during your festival, you and your sons and your daughters, your male and female slaves, as well as the Levites, the strangers, the orphans, and the widows resident in your towns. [15]Seven days you shall keep the festival for the LORD your God at the place that the LORD will choose; for the LORD your God will bless you in all your produce and in all your undertakings, and you shall surely celebrate.

16 Three times a year all your males shall appear before the LORD your God at the place that he will choose: at the festival of unleavened bread, at the festival of weeks, and at the festival of booths. [a] They shall not appear before the LORD empty-handed; [17]all shall give as they are able, according to the blessing of the LORD your God that he has given you.

18 You shall appoint judges and officials throughout your tribes, in all your towns that the LORD your God is giving you, and they shall render just decisions for the people. [19]You must not distort justice; you must not show partiality; and you must not accept bribes, for a bribe blinds the eyes of the wise and subverts the cause of those who are in the right. [20]Justice, and only justice, you shall pursue, so that you may live and occupy the land that the LORD your God is giving you.

21 You shall not plant any tree as a sacred pole[b] beside the altar that you make for the LORD your God; [22]nor shall you set up a stone pillar—things that the LORD your God hates.

[17.1] You must not sacrifice to the LORD your God an ox or a sheep that has a defect, anything seriously wrong; for that is abhorrent to the LORD your God.

2 If there is found among you, in one of your towns that the LORD your God is giving you, a man or woman who does what is evil in the sight of the LORD your God, and transgresses his covenant [3]by going to serve other gods and worshiping them—whether the sun or the moon or any of the host of heaven, which I have forbidden— [4]and if it is reported to you or you hear of it, and you make a thorough inquiry, and the charge is proved true that such an abhorrent thing has occurred in Israel, [5]then you shall bring out to your gates that man or that woman who has committed this crime and you shall stone the man or woman to death. [6]On the evidence of two or three witnesses the death sentence shall be executed; a person must not be put to death on the evidence of only one witness. [7]The hands of the witnesses shall be the first raised against the person to execute the death penalty, and afterward the hands of all the people. So you shall purge the evil from your midst.

8 If a judicial decision is too difficult for you to make between one kind of bloodshed and another, one kind of legal right and another, or one kind of assault and another—any such matters of dispute in your towns—then you shall immediately go up to the place that the LORD your God will choose, [9]where you shall consult with the levitical priests and the judge who is in office in those days; they shall announce to you the decision in the case. [10]Carry out ex-

---

a Or *tabernacles*; Heb *succoth*   b Heb *Asherah*

actly the decision that they announce to you from the place that the LORD will choose, diligently observing everything they instruct you. [11]You must carry out fully the law that they interpret for you or the ruling that they announce to you; do not turn aside from the decision that they announce to you, either to the right or to the left. [12]As for anyone who presumes to disobey the priest appointed to minister there to the LORD your God, or the judge, that person shall die. So you shall purge the evil from Israel. [13]All the people will hear and be afraid, and will not act presumptuously again.

14 When you have come into the land that the LORD your God is giving you, and have taken possession of it and settled in it, and you say, "I will set a king over me, like all the nations that are around me," [15]you may indeed set over you a king whom the LORD your God will choose. One of your own community you may set as king over you; you are not permitted to put a foreigner over you, who is not of your own community. [16]Even so, he must not acquire many horses for himself, or return the people to Egypt in order to acquire more horses, since the LORD has said to you, "You must never return that way again." [17]And he must not acquire many wives for himself, or else his heart will turn away; also silver and gold he must not acquire in great quantity for himself. [18]When he has taken the throne of his kingdom, he shall have a copy of this law written for him in the presence of the levitical priests. [19]It shall remain with him and he shall read in it all the days of his life, so that he may learn to fear the LORD his God, diligently observing all the words of this law and these statutes, [20]neither exalting himself above other members of the community nor turning aside from the commandment, either to the right or to

the left, so that he and his descendants may reign long over his kingdom in Israel.

## LUKE 9. 7–27

Now Herod the ruler[a] heard about all that had taken place, and he was perplexed, because it was said by some that John had been raised from the dead, [8]by some that Elijah had appeared, and by others that one of the ancient prophets had arisen. [9]Herod said, "John I beheaded; but who is this about whom I hear such things?" And he tried to see him.

10 On their return the apostles told Jesus[b] all they had done. He took them with him and withdrew privately to a city called Bethsaida. [11]When the crowds found out about it, they followed him; and he welcomed them, and spoke to them about the kingdom of God, and healed those who needed to be cured.

12 The day was drawing to a close, and the twelve came to him and said, "Send the crowd away, so that they may go into the surrounding villages and countryside, to lodge and get provisions; for we are here in a deserted place." [13]But he said to them, "You give them something to eat." They said, "We have no more than five loaves and two fish—unless we are to go and buy food for all these people." [14]For there were about five thousand men. And he said to his disciples, "Make them sit down in groups of about fifty each." [15]They did so and made them all sit down. [16]And taking the five loaves and the two fish, he looked up to heaven, and blessed and broke them, and gave them to the disciples to set before the crowd. [17]And all ate and were filled. What was left over was gathered up, twelve baskets of broken pieces.

18 Once when Jesus[c] was praying

aGk *tetrarch*   bGk *him*   cGk *he*

alone, with only the disciples near him, he asked them, "Who do the crowds say that I am?" [19]They answered, "John the Baptist; but others, Elijah; and still others, that one of the ancient prophets has arisen." [20]He said to them, "But who do you say that I am?" Peter answered, "The Messiah[a] of God."

21 He sternly ordered and commanded them not to tell anyone, [22]saying, "The Son of Man must undergo great suffering, and be rejected by the elders, chief priests, and scribes, and be killed, and on the third day be raised."

23 Then he said to them all, "If any want to become my followers, let them deny themselves and take up their cross daily and follow me. [24]For those who want to save their life will lose it, and those who lose their life for my sake will save it. [25]What does it profit them if they gain the whole world, but lose or forfeit themselves? [26]Those who are ashamed of me and of my words, of them the Son of Man will be ashamed when he comes in his glory and the glory of the Father and of the holy angels. [27]But truly I tell you, there are some standing here who will not taste death before they see the kingdom of God."

# PSALM 72. 1–20

*Of Solomon.*

**G**IVE the king your justice,
O God,
and your righteousness to a
king's son.
2 May he judge your people with
righteousness,
and your poor with justice.
3 May the mountains yield
prosperity for the people,
and the hills, in
righteousness.

4 May he defend the cause of the
poor of the people,
give deliverance to the needy,
and crush the oppressor.

5 May he live[b] while the sun
endures,
and as long as the moon,
throughout all
generations.
6 May he be like rain that falls on
the mown grass,
like showers that water the
earth.
7 In his days may righteousness
flourish
and peace abound, until the
moon is no more.

8 May he have dominion from sea
to sea,
and from the River to the
ends of the earth.
9 May his foes[c] bow down before
him,
and his enemies lick the dust.
10 May the kings of Tarshish and
of the isles
render him tribute,
may the kings of Sheba and
Seba
bring gifts.
11 May all kings fall down before
him,
all nations give him service.

12 For he delivers the needy when
they call,
the poor and those who have
no helper.
13 He has pity on the weak and
the needy,
and saves the lives of the
needy.
14 From oppression and violence
he redeems their life;
and precious is their blood in
his sight.

aOr *The Christ*  bGk: Heb *may they fear you*  cCn: Heb *those who live in the wilderness*

15  Long may he live!
        May gold of Sheba be given
            to him.
        May prayer be made for him
            continually,
        and blessings invoked for him
            all day long.
16  May there be abundance of
            grain in the land;
        may it wave on the tops of
            the mountains;
        may its fruit be like Lebanon;
        and may people blossom in the
            cities
        like the grass of the field.
17  May his name endure forever,
        his fame continue as long as
            the sun.
    May all nations be blessed in
            him; a
        may they pronounce him
            happy.

18  Blessed be the Lord, the God
            of Israel,
        who alone does wondrous
            things.
19  Blessed be his glorious name
            forever;
        may his glory fill the whole
            earth.
        Amen and Amen.

20  The prayers of David son of
            Jesse are ended.

## PROVERBS 12.8–9

ONE is commended for good
        sense,
    but a perverse mind is
        despised.
9  Better to be despised and have
        a servant,
        than to be self-important and
            lack food.

# APRIL 1

## DEUTERONOMY 18.1—20.20

THE levitical priests, the whole tribe of Levi, shall have no allotment or inheritance within Israel. They may eat the sacrifices that are the Lord's portion b 2but they shall have no inheritance among the other members of the community; the Lord is their inheritance, as he promised them.

3  This shall be the priests' due from the people, from those offering a sacrifice, whether an ox or a sheep: they shall give to the priest the shoulder, the two jowls, and the stomach. 4The first fruits of your grain, your wine, and your oil, as well as the first of the fleece of your sheep, you shall give him. 5For the Lord your God has chosen Levi c out of all your tribes, to stand and minister in the name of the Lord, him and his sons for all time.

6  If a Levite leaves any of your towns, from wherever he has been residing in Israel, and comes to the place that the Lord will choose (and he may come whenever he wishes), 7then he may minister in the name of the Lord his God, like all his fellow-Levites who stand to minister there before the Lord. 8They shall have equal portions to eat, even though they have income from the sale of family possessions. b

a Or *bless themselves by him*   b Meaning of Heb uncertain   c Heb *him*

9   When you come into the land that the Lord your God is giving you, you must not learn to imitate the abhorrent practices of those nations. [10]No one shall be found among you who makes a son or daughter pass through fire, or who practices divination, or is a soothsayer, or an augur, or a sorcerer, [11]or one who casts spells, or who consults ghosts or spirits, or who seeks oracles from the dead. [12]For whoever does these things is abhorrent to the Lord; it is because of such abhorrent practices that the Lord your God is driving them out before you. [13]You must remain completely loyal to the Lord your God. [14]Although these nations that you are about to dispossess do give heed to soothsayers and diviners, as for you, the Lord your God does not permit you to do so.

15   The Lord your God will raise up for you a prophet[a] like me from among your own people; you shall heed such a prophet.[b] [16]This is what you requested of the Lord your God at Horeb on the day of the assembly when you said: "If I hear the voice of the Lord my God any more, or ever again see this great fire, I will die." [17]Then the Lord replied to me: "They are right in what they have said. [18]I will raise up for them a prophet[a] like you from among their own people; I will put my words in the mouth of the prophet,[c] who shall speak to them everything that I command. [19]Anyone who does not heed the words that the prophet[d] shall speak in my name, I myself will hold accountable. [20]But any prophet who speaks in the name of other gods, or who presumes to speak in my name a word that I have not commanded the prophet to speak—that prophet shall die." [21]You may say to yourself, "How can we recognize a word that the Lord has not spoken?" [22]If a prophet speaks in the name of the Lord but the thing does not take place or prove true, it is a word that the Lord has not spoken. The prophet has spoken it presumptuously; do not be frightened by it.

[19.1]When the Lord your God has cut off the nations whose land the Lord your God is giving you, and you have dispossessed them and settled in their towns and in their houses, [2]you shall set apart three cities in the land that the Lord your God is giving you to possess. [3]You shall calculate the distances[e] and divide into three regions the land that the Lord your God gives you as a possession, so that any homicide can flee to one of them.

4   Now this is the case of a homicide who might flee there and live, that is, someone who has killed another person unintentionally when the two had not been at enmity before: [5]Suppose someone goes into the forest with another to cut wood, and when one of them swings the ax to cut down a tree, the head slips from the handle and strikes the other person who then dies; the killer may flee to one of these cities and live. [6]But if the distance is too great, the avenger of blood in hot anger might pursue and overtake and put the killer to death, although a death sentence was not deserved, since the two had not been at enmity before. [7]Therefore I command you: You shall set apart three cities.

8   If the Lord your God enlarges your territory, as he swore to your ancestors—and he will give you all the land that he promised your ancestors to give you, [9]provided you diligently observe this entire commandment that I command you today, by loving the Lord your God and walking always in his ways—then you shall add three more cities to these three, [10]so that the blood of an innocent person may not be shed in the land that the Lord your God is

---

a Or *prophets*   b Or *such prophets*   c Or *mouths of the prophets*   d Heb *he*   e Or *prepare roads to them*

giving you as an inheritance, thereby bringing bloodguilt upon you.

11 But if someone at enmity with another lies in wait and attacks and takes the life of that person, and flees into one of these cities, 12then the elders of the killer's city shall send to have the culprit taken from there and handed over to the avenger of blood to be put to death. 13Show no pity; you shall purge the guilt of innocent blood from Israel, so that it may go well with you.

14 You must not move your neighbor's boundary marker, set up by former generations, on the property that will be allotted to you in the land that the Lord your God is giving you to possess.

15 A single witness shall not suffice to convict a person of any crime or wrongdoing in connection with any offense that may be committed. Only on the evidence of two or three witnesses shall a charge be sustained. 16If a malicious witness comes forward to accuse someone of wrongdoing, 17then both parties to the dispute shall appear before the Lord, before the priests and the judges who are in office in those days, 18and the judges shall make a thorough inquiry. If the witness is a false witness, having testified falsely against another, 19then you shall do to the false witness just as the false witness had meant to do to the other. So you shall purge the evil from your midst. 20The rest shall hear and be afraid, and a crime such as this shall never again be committed among you. 21Show no pity: life for life, eye for eye, tooth for tooth, hand for hand, foot for foot.

**20.1** When you go out to war against your enemies, and see horses and chariots, an army larger than your own, you shall not be afraid of them; for the Lord your God is with you, who brought you up from the land of Egypt. 2Before you engage in battle, the priest shall come forward and speak to the troops, 3and shall say to them: "Hear, O Israel! Today you are drawing near to do battle against your enemies. Do not lose heart, or be afraid, or panic, or be in dread of them; 4for it is the Lord your God who goes with you, to fight for you against your enemies, to give you victory." 5Then the officials shall address the troops, saying, "Has anyone built a new house but not dedicated it? He should go back to his house, or he might die in the battle and another dedicate it. 6Has anyone planted a vineyard but not yet enjoyed its fruit? He should go back to his house, or he might die in the battle and another be first to enjoy its fruit. 7Has anyone become engaged to a woman but not yet married her? He should go back to his house, or he might die in the battle and another marry her." 8The officials shall continue to address the troops, saying, "Is anyone afraid or disheartened? He should go back to his house, or he might cause the heart of his comrades to melt like his own." 9When the officials have finished addressing the troops, then the commanders shall take charge of them.

10 When you draw near to a town to fight against it, offer it terms of peace. 11If it accepts your terms of peace and surrenders to you, then all the people in it shall serve you at forced labor. 12If it does not submit to you peacefully, but makes war against you, then you shall besiege it; 13and when the Lord your God gives it into your hand, you shall put all its males to the sword. 14You may, however, take as your booty the women, the children, livestock, and everything else in the town, all its spoil. You may enjoy the spoil of your enemies, which the Lord your God has given you. 15Thus you shall treat all the towns that are very far from you, which are not towns of the nations here. 16But as for the towns of

these peoples that the Lord your God is giving you as an inheritance, you must not let anything that breathes remain alive. [17]You shall annihilate them—the Hittites and the Amorites, the Canaanites and the Perizzites, the Hivites and the Jebusites—just as the Lord your God has commanded, [18]so that they may not teach you to do all the abhorrent things that they do for their gods, and you thus sin against the Lord your God.

19  If you besiege a town for a long time, making war against it in order to take it, you must not destroy its trees by wielding an ax against them. Although you may take food from them, you must not cut them down. Are trees in the field human beings that they should come under siege from you? [20]You may destroy only the trees that you know do not produce food; you may cut them down for use in building siegeworks against the town that makes war with you, until it falls.

## LUKE 9.28–50

Now about eight days after these sayings Jesus[a] took with him Peter and John and James, and went up on the mountain to pray. [29]And while he was praying, the appearance of his face changed, and his clothes became dazzling white. [30]Suddenly they saw two men, Moses and Elijah, talking to him. [31]They appeared in glory and were speaking of his departure, which he was about to accomplish at Jerusalem. [32]Now Peter and his companions were weighed down with sleep; but since they had stayed awake,[b] they saw his glory and the two men who stood with him. [33]Just as they were leaving him, Peter said to Jesus, "Master, it is good for us to be here; let us make three dwellings,[c] one for you, one for Moses, and one for Elijah"—

not knowing what he said. [34]While he was saying this, a cloud came and overshadowed them; and they were terrified as they entered the cloud. [35]Then from the cloud came a voice that said, "This is my Son, my Chosen;[d] listen to him!" [36]When the voice had spoken, Jesus was found alone. And they kept silent and in those days told no one any of the things they had seen.

37  On the next day, when they had come down from the mountain, a great crowd met him. [38]Just then a man from the crowd shouted, "Teacher, I beg you to look at my son; he is my only child. [39]Suddenly a spirit seizes him, and all at once he[e] shrieks. It convulses him until he foams at the mouth; it mauls him and will scarcely leave him. [40]I begged your disciples to cast it out, but they could not." [41]Jesus answered, "You faithless and perverse generation, how much longer must I be with you and bear with you? Bring your son here." [42]While he was coming, the demon dashed him to the ground in convulsions. But Jesus rebuked the unclean spirit, healed the boy, and gave him back to his father. [43]And all were astounded at the greatness of God.

While everyone was amazed at all that he was doing, he said to his disciples, [44]"Let these words sink into your ears: The Son of Man is going to be betrayed into human hands." [45]But they did not understand this saying; its meaning was concealed from them, so that they could not perceive it. And they were afraid to ask him about this saying.

46  An argument arose among them as to which one of them was the greatest. [47]But Jesus, aware of their inner thoughts, took a little child and put it by his side, [48]and said to them, "Whoever welcomes this child in my name welcomes me, and whoever welcomes me welcomes the one who sent me; for the

[a]Gk *he*  [b]Or *but when they were fully awake*  [c]Or *tents*  [d]Other ancient authorities read *my Beloved*  [e]Or *it*

least among all of you is the greatest."

49 John answered, "Master, we saw someone casting out demons in your name, and we tried to stop him, because he does not follow with us." ⁵⁰But Jesus said to him, "Do not stop him; for whoever is not against you is for you."

## PSALM 73.1–28

*A Psalm of Asaph.*

T RULY God is good to the upright, ᵃ
to those who are pure in
heart.
2  But as for me, my feet had
almost stumbled;
my steps had nearly slipped.
3  For I was envious of the
arrogant;
I saw the prosperity of the
wicked.

4  For they have no pain;
their bodies are sound and
sleek.
5  They are not in trouble as
others are;
they are not plagued like
other people.
6  Therefore pride is their
necklace;
violence covers them like a
garment.
7  Their eyes swell out with
fatness;
their hearts overflow with
follies.
8  They scoff and speak with
malice;
loftily they threaten
oppression.
9  They set their mouths against
heaven,
and their tongues range over
the earth.

10  Therefore the people turn and
praise them, ᵇ
and find no fault in them. ᶜ
11  And they say, "How can God
know?
Is there knowledge in the
Most High?"
12  Such are the wicked;
always at ease, they increase
in riches.
13  All in vain I have kept my heart
clean
and washed my hands in
innocence.
14  For all day long I have been
plagued,
and am punished every
morning.

15  If I had said, "I will talk on in
this way,"
I would have been untrue to
the circle of your
children.
16  But when I thought how to
understand this,
it seemed to me a wearisome
task,
17  until I went into the sanctuary
of God;
then I perceived their end.
18  Truly you set them in slippery
places;
you make them fall to ruin.
19  How they are destroyed in a
moment,
swept away utterly by
terrors!
20  They areᵈ like a dream when
one awakes;
on awaking you despise their
phantoms.

21  When my soul was embittered,
when I was pricked in heart,
22  I was stupid and ignorant;

ᵃOr *good to Israel*   ᵇCn: Heb *his people return here*   ᶜCn: Heb *abundant waters are drained by them*
ᵈCn: Heb *Lord*

I was like a brute beast
toward you.
23 Nevertheless I am continually
with you;
you hold my right hand.
24 You guide me with your
counsel,
and afterward you will receive
me with honor. a
25 Whom have I in heaven but
you?
And there is nothing on earth
that I desire other than
you.
26 My flesh and my heart may fail,
but God is the strengthb of
my heart and my portion
forever.

27 Indeed, those who are far from
you will perish;
you put an end to those who
are false to you.
28 But for me it is good to be near
God;
I have made the Lord God
my refuge,
to tell of all your works.

## PROVERBS 12.10

THE righteous know the needs
of their animals,
but the mercy of the wicked
is cruel.

# APRIL 2

## DEUTERONOMY 21.1—22.30

IF, in the land that the Lord your God is giving you to possess, a body is found lying in open country, and it is not known who struck the person down, 2then your elders and your judges shall come out to measure the distances to the towns that are near the body. 3The elders of the town nearest the body shall take a heifer that has never been worked, one that has not pulled in the yoke; 4the elders of that town shall bring the heifer down to a wadi with running water, which is neither plowed nor sown, and shall break the heifer's neck there in the wadi. 5Then the priests, the sons of Levi, shall come forward, for the Lord your God has chosen them to minister to him and to pronounce blessings in the name of the Lord, and by their decision all cases of dispute and assault shall be settled. 6All the elders of that town nearest the body shall wash their hands over the heifer whose neck was broken in the wadi, 7and they shall declare: "Our hands did not shed this blood, nor were we witnesses to it. 8Absolve, O Lord, your people Israel, whom you redeemed; do not let the guilt of innocent blood remain in the midst of your people Israel." Then they will be absolved of bloodguilt. 9So you shall purge the guilt of innocent blood from your midst, because you must do what is right in the sight of the Lord.

10 When you go out to war against your enemies, and the Lord your God hands them over to you and you take them captive, 11suppose you see among the captives a beautiful woman

a Or *to glory*  b Heb *rock*

whom you desire and want to marry, ¹²and so you bring her home to your house: she shall shave her head, pare her nails, ¹³discard her captive's garb, and shall remain in your house a full month, mourning for her father and mother; after that you may go in to her and be her husband, and she shall be your wife. ¹⁴But if you are not satisfied with her, you shall let her go free and not sell her for money. You must not treat her as a slave, since you have dishonored her.

15 If a man has two wives, one of them loved and the other disliked, and if both the loved and the disliked have borne him sons, the firstborn being the son of the one who is disliked, ¹⁶then on the day when he wills his possessions to his sons, he is not permitted to treat the son of the loved as the firstborn in preference to the son of the disliked, who is the firstborn. ¹⁷He must acknowledge as firstborn the son of the one who is disliked, giving him a double portionᵃ of all that he has; since he is the first issue of his virility, the right of the firstborn is his.

18 If someone has a stubborn and rebellious son who will not obey his father and mother, who does not heed them when they discipline him, ¹⁹then his father and his mother shall take hold of him and bring him out to the elders of his town at the gate of that place. ²⁰They shall say to the elders of his town, "This son of ours is stubborn and rebellious. He will not obey us. He is a glutton and a drunkard." ²¹Then all the men of the town shall stone him to death. So you shall purge the evil from your midst; and all Israel will hear, and be afraid.

22 When someone is convicted of a crime punishable by death and is executed, and you hang him on a tree, ²³his corpse must not remain all night upon the tree; you shall bury him that same day, for anyone hung on a tree is under God's curse. You must not defile the land that the Lord your God is giving you for possession.

22.¹ You shall not watch your neighbor's ox or sheep straying away and ignore them; you shall take them back to their owner. ²If the owner does not reside near you or you do not know who the owner is, you shall bring it to your own house, and it shall remain with you until the owner claims it; then you shall return it. ³You shall do the same with a neighbor's donkey; you shall do the same with a neighbor's garment; and you shall do the same with anything else that your neighbor loses and you find. You may not withhold your help.

4 You shall not see your neighbor's donkey or ox fallen on the road and ignore it; you shall help to lift it up.

5 A woman shall not wear a man's apparel, nor shall a man put on a woman's garment; for whoever does such things is abhorrent to the Lord your God.

6 If you come on a bird's nest, in any tree or on the ground, with fledglings or eggs, with the mother sitting on the fledglings or on the eggs, you shall not take the mother with the young. ⁷Let the mother go, taking only the young for yourself, in order that it may go well with you and you may live long.

8 When you build a new house, you shall make a parapet for your roof; otherwise you might have bloodguilt on your house, if anyone should fall from it.

9 You shall not sow your vineyard with a second kind of seed, or the whole yield will have to be forfeited, both the crop that you have sown and the yield of the vineyard itself.

10 You shall not plow with an ox and a donkey yoked together.

ᵃHeb *two-thirds*

11 You shall not wear clothes made of wool and linen woven together.

12 You shall make tassels on the four corners of the cloak with which you cover yourself.

13 Suppose a man marries a woman, but after going in to her, he dislikes her ¹⁴and makes up charges against her, slandering her by saying, "I married this woman; but when I lay with her, I did not find evidence of her virginity." ¹⁵The father of the young woman and her mother shall then submit the evidence of the young woman's virginity to the elders of the city at the gate. ¹⁶The father of the young woman shall say to the elders: "I gave my daughter in marriage to this man but he dislikes her; ¹⁷now he has made up charges against her, saying, 'I did not find evidence of your daughter's virginity.' But here is the evidence of my daughter's virginity." Then they shall spread out the cloth before the elders of the town. ¹⁸The elders of that town shall take the man and punish him; ¹⁹they shall fine him one hundred shekels of silver (which they shall give to the young woman's father) because he has slandered a virgin of Israel. She shall remain his wife; he shall not be permitted to divorce her as long as he lives.

20 If, however, this charge is true, that evidence of the young woman's virginity was not found, ²¹then they shall bring the young woman out to the entrance of her father's house and the men of her town shall stone her to death, because she committed a disgraceful act in Israel by prostituting herself in her father's house. So you shall purge the evil from your midst.

22 If a man is caught lying with the wife of another man, both of them shall die, the man who lay with the woman as well as the woman. So you shall purge the evil from Israel.

23 If there is a young woman, a virgin already engaged to be married, and a man meets her in the town and lies with her, ²⁴you shall bring both of them to the gate of that town and stone them to death, the young woman because she did not cry for help in the town and the man because he violated his neighbor's wife. So you shall purge the evil from your midst.

25 But if the man meets the engaged woman in the open country, and the man seizes her and lies with her, then only the man who lay with her shall die. ²⁶You shall do nothing to the young woman; the young woman has not committed an offense punishable by death, because this case is like that of someone who attacks and murders a neighbor. ²⁷Since he found her in the open country, the engaged woman may have cried for help, but there was no one to rescue her.

28 If a man meets a virgin who is not engaged, and seizes her and lies with her, and they are caught in the act, ²⁹the man who lay with her shall give fifty shekels of silver to the young woman's father, and she shall become his wife. Because he violated her he shall not be permitted to divorce her as long as he lives.

30ᵃ A man shall not marry his father's wife, thereby violating his father's rights. ᵇ

## LUKE 9.51—10.12

WHEN the days drew near for him to be taken up, he [Jesus] set his face to go to Jerusalem. ⁵²And he sent messengers ahead of him. On their way they entered a village of the Samaritans to make ready for him; ⁵³but they did not receive him, because his face was set toward Jerusalem. ⁵⁴When his disciples James and John saw it, they said, "Lord, do you want us to command fire

ᵃCh 23.1 in Heb  ᵇHeb *uncovering his father's skirt*

to come down from heaven and consume them?"a 55But he turned and rebuked them. 56Thenb they went on to another village.

57 As they were going along the road, someone said to him, "I will follow you wherever you go." 58And Jesus said to him, "Foxes have holes, and birds of the air have nests; but the Son of Man has nowhere to lay his head." 59To another he said, "Follow me." But he said, "Lord, first let me go and bury my father." 60But Jesusc said to him, "Let the dead bury their own dead; but as for you, go and proclaim the kingdom of God." 61Another said, "I will follow you, Lord; but let me first say farewell to those at my home." 62Jesus said to him, "No one who puts a hand to the plow and looks back is fit for the kingdom of God."

10.1 AFTER this the Lord appointed seventyd others and sent them on ahead of him in pairs to every town and place where he himself intended to go. 2He said to them, "The harvest is plentiful, but the laborers are few; therefore ask the Lord of the harvest to send out laborers into his harvest. 3Go on your way. See, I am sending you out like lambs into the midst of wolves. 4Carry no purse, no bag, no sandals; and greet no one on the road. 5Whatever house you enter, first say, 'Peace to this house!' 6And if anyone is there who shares in peace, your peace will rest on that person; but if not, it will return to you. 7Remain in the same house, eating and drinking whatever they provide, for the laborer deserves to be paid. Do not move about from house to house. 8Whenever you enter a town and its people welcome you, eat what is set before you; 9cure the sick who are there, and say to them, 'The kingdom of God has come near to you.'e 10But whenever you enter a town and they do not welcome you, go out into its streets and say, 11'Even the dust of your town that clings to our feet, we wipe off in protest against you. Yet know this: the kingdom of God has come near.'f 12I tell you, on that day it will be more tolerable for Sodom than for that town.

## PSALM 74.1–23

*A Maskil of Asaph.*

O GOD, why do you cast us off
    forever?
Why does your anger
    smoke against the sheep
    of your pasture?
2 Remember your congregation,
    which you acquired long
    ago,
  which you redeemed to be
    the tribe of your
    heritage.
  Remember Mount Zion,
    where you came to
    dwell.
3 Direct your steps to the
    perpetual ruins;
  the enemy has destroyed
    everything in the
    sanctuary.

4 Your foes have roared within
    your holy place;
  they set up their emblems
    there.
5 At the upper entrance they
    hacked
  the wooden trellis with
    axes.g
6 And then, with hatchets and
    hammers,
  they smashed all its carved
    work.
7 They set your sanctuary on fire;

---

aOther ancient authorities add *as Elijah did*   bOther ancient authorities read *rebuked them, and said, "You do not know what spirit you are of, 56for the Son of Man has not come to destroy the lives of human beings but to save them." Then*   cGk *he*   dOther ancient authorities read *seventy-two*   eOr *is at hand for you*   fOr *is at hand*   gCn Compare Gk Syr: Meaning of Heb uncertain

they desecrated the dwelling
  place of your name,
  bringing it to the ground.
8 They said to themselves, "We
    will utterly subdue
    them";
  they burned all the meeting
    places of God in the land.

9 We do not see our emblems;
    there is no longer any
    prophet,
  and there is no one among us
    who knows how long.
10 How long, O God, is the foe to
    scoff?
  Is the enemy to revile your
    name forever?
11 Why do you hold back your
    hand;
  why do you keep your hand
    in[a] your bosom?

12 Yet God my King is from of old,
    working salvation in the
    earth.
13 You divided the sea by your
    might;
  you broke the heads of the
    dragons in the waters.
14 You crushed the heads of
    Leviathan;
  you gave him as food[b] for
    the creatures of the
    wilderness.
15 You cut openings for springs
    and torrents;
  you dried up ever-flowing
    streams.
16 Yours is the day, yours also the
    night;

  you established the
    luminaries[c] and the sun.
17 You have fixed all the bounds of
    the earth;
  you made summer and
    winter.

18 Remember this, O LORD, how
    the enemy scoffs,
  and an impious people reviles
    your name.
19 Do not deliver the soul of your
    dove to the wild animals;
  do not forget the life of your
    poor forever.

20 Have regard for your[d]
    covenant,
  for the dark places of the land
    are full of the haunts of
    violence.
21 Do not let the downtrodden be
    put to shame;
  let the poor and needy praise
    your name.
22 Rise up, O God, plead your
    cause;
  remember how the impious
    scoff at you all day long.
23 Do not forget the clamor of
    your foes,
  the uproar of your
    adversaries that goes up
    continually.

## PROVERBS 12.11

THOSE who till their land will
    have plenty of food,
  but those who follow
    worthless pursuits have
    no sense.

---

aCn: Heb *do you consume your right hand from*   bHeb *food for the people*   cOr *moon*; Heb *light*
dGk Syr: Heb *the*

# APRIL 3

DEUTERONOMY 23.1—25.19

No one whose testicles are crushed or whose penis is cut off shall be admitted to the assembly of the LORD.

2  Those born of an illicit union shall not be admitted to the assembly of the LORD. Even to the tenth generation, none of their descendants shall be admitted to the assembly of the LORD.

3  No Ammonite or Moabite shall be admitted to the assembly of the LORD. Even to the tenth generation, none of their descendants shall be admitted to the assembly of the LORD, [4]because they did not meet you with food and water on your journey out of Egypt, and because they hired against you Balaam son of Beor, from Pethor of Mesopotamia, to curse you. [5](Yet the LORD your God refused to heed Balaam; the LORD your God turned the curse into a blessing for you, because the LORD your God loved you.) [6]You shall never promote their welfare or their prosperity as long as you live.

7  You shall not abhor any of the Edomites, for they are your kin. You shall not abhor any of the Egyptians, because you were an alien residing in their land. [8]The children of the third generation that are born to them may be admitted to the assembly of the LORD.

9  When you are encamped against your enemies you shall guard against any impropriety.

10  If one of you becomes unclean because of a nocturnal emission, then he shall go outside the camp; he must not come within the camp. [11]When evening comes, he shall wash himself with water, and when the sun has set, he may come back into the camp.

12  You shall have a designated area outside the camp to which you shall go. [13]With your utensils you shall have a trowel; when you relieve yourself outside, you shall dig a hole with it and then cover up your excrement. [14]Because the LORD your God travels along with your camp, to save you and to hand over your enemies to you, therefore your camp must be holy, so that he may not see anything indecent among you and turn away from you.

15  Slaves who have escaped to you from their owners shall not be given back to them. [16]They shall reside with you, in your midst, in any place they choose in any one of your towns, wherever they please; you shall not oppress them.

17  None of the daughters of Israel shall be a temple prostitute; none of the sons of Israel shall be a temple prostitute. [18]You shall not bring the fee of a prostitute or the wages of a male prostitute[a] into the house of the LORD your God in payment for any vow, for both of these are abhorrent to the LORD your God.

19  You shall not charge interest on loans to another Israelite, interest on money, interest on provisions, interest on anything that is lent. [20]On loans to a foreigner you may charge interest, but on loans to another Israelite you may not charge interest, so that the LORD your God may bless you in all your undertakings in the land that you are about to enter and possess.

21  If you make a vow to the LORD your God, do not postpone fulfilling it; for the LORD your God will surely re-

---

[a] Heb *a dog*

quire it of you, and you would incur guilt. [22]But if you refrain from vowing, you will not incur guilt. [23]Whatever your lips utter you must diligently perform, just as you have freely vowed to the LORD your God with your own mouth.

24 If you go into your neighbor's vineyard, you may eat your fill of grapes, as many as you wish, but you shall not put any in a container.

25 If you go into your neighbor's standing grain, you may pluck the ears with your hand, but you shall not put a sickle to your neighbor's standing grain.

24.1 SUPPOSE a man enters into marriage with a woman, but she does not please him because he finds something objectionable about her, and so he writes her a certificate of divorce, puts it in her hand, and sends her out of his house; she then leaves his house [2]and goes off to become another man's wife. [3]Then suppose the second man dislikes her, writes her a bill of divorce, puts it in her hand, and sends her out of his house (or the second man who married her dies); [4]her first husband, who sent her away, is not permitted to take her again to be his wife after she has been defiled; for that would be abhorrent to the LORD, and you shall not bring guilt on the land that the LORD your God is giving you as a possession.

5 When a man is newly married, he shall not go out with the army or be charged with any related duty. He shall be free at home one year, to be happy with the wife whom he has married.

6 No one shall take a mill or an upper millstone in pledge, for that would be taking a life in pledge.

7 If someone is caught kidnaping another Israelite, enslaving or selling the Israelite, then that kidnaper shall die. So you shall purge the evil from your midst.

8 Guard against an outbreak of a leprous[a] skin disease by being very careful; you shall carefully observe whatever the levitical priests instruct you, just as I have commanded them. [9]Remember what the LORD your God did to Miriam on your journey out of Egypt.

10 When you make your neighbor a loan of any kind, you shall not go into the house to take the pledge. [11]You shall wait outside, while the person to whom you are making the loan brings the pledge out to you. [12]If the person is poor, you shall not sleep in the garment given you as[b] the pledge. [13]You shall give the pledge back by sunset, so that your neighbor may sleep in the cloak and bless you; and it will be to your credit before the LORD your God.

14 You shall not withhold the wages of poor and needy laborers, whether other Israelites or aliens who reside in your land in one of your towns. [15]You shall pay them their wages daily before sunset, because they are poor and their livelihood depends on them; otherwise they might cry to the LORD against you, and you would incur guilt.

16 Parents shall not be put to death for their children, nor shall children be put to death for their parents; only for their own crimes may persons be put to death.

17 You shall not deprive a resident alien or an orphan of justice; you shall not take a widow's garment in pledge. [18]Remember that you were a slave in Egypt and the LORD your God redeemed you from there; therefore I command you to do this.

19 When you reap your harvest in your field and forget a sheaf in the field, you shall not go back to get it; it shall be left for the alien, the orphan, and the

---

[a]A term for several skin diseases; precise meaning uncertain   [b]Heb lacks *the garment given you as*

widow, so that the Lord your God may bless you in all your undertakings. 20When you beat your olive trees, do not strip what is left; it shall be for the alien, the orphan, and the widow.

21 When you gather the grapes of your vineyard, do not glean what is left; it shall be for the alien, the orphan, and the widow. 22Remember that you were a slave in the land of Egypt; therefore I am commanding you to do this.

25.1 Suppose two persons have a dispute and enter into litigation, and the judges decide between them, declaring one to be in the right and the other to be in the wrong. 2If the one in the wrong deserves to be flogged, the judge shall make that person lie down and be beaten in his presence with the number of lashes proportionate to the offense. 3Forty lashes may be given but not more; if more lashes than these are given, your neighbor will be degraded in your sight.

4 You shall not muzzle an ox while it is treading out the grain.

5 When brothers reside together, and one of them dies and has no son, the wife of the deceased shall not be married outside the family to a stranger. Her husband's brother shall go in to her, taking her in marriage, and performing the duty of a husband's brother to her, 6and the firstborn whom she bears shall succeed to the name of the deceased brother, so that his name may not be blotted out of Israel. 7But if the man has no desire to marry his brother's widow, then his brother's widow shall go up to the elders at the gate and say, "My husband's brother refuses to perpetuate his brother's name in Israel; he will not perform the duty of a husband's brother to me." 8Then the elders of his town shall summon him and speak to him. If he persists, saying, "I have no desire to marry her," 9then his brother's wife shall go up to him in the presence of the elders, pull his sandal off his foot, spit in his face, and declare, "This is what is done to the man who does not build up his brother's house." 10Throughout Israel his family shall be known as "the house of him whose sandal was pulled off."

11 If men get into a fight with one another, and the wife of one intervenes to rescue her husband from the grip of his opponent by reaching out and seizing his genitals, 12you shall cut off her hand; show no pity.

13 You shall not have in your bag two kinds of weights, large and small. 14You shall not have in your house two kinds of measures, large and small. 15You shall have only a full and honest weight; you shall have only a full and honest measure, so that your days may be long in the land that the Lord your God is giving you. 16For all who do such things, all who act dishonestly, are abhorrent to the Lord your God.

17 Remember what Amalek did to you on your journey out of Egypt, 18how he attacked you on the way, when you were faint and weary, and struck down all who lagged behind you; he did not fear God. 19Therefore when the Lord your God has given you rest from all your enemies on every hand, in the land that the Lord your God is giving you as an inheritance to possess, you shall blot out the remembrance of Amalek from under heaven; do not forget.

## LUKE 10.13–37

"Woe to you, Chorazin! Woe to you, Bethsaida! For if the deeds of power done in you had been done in Tyre and Sidon, they would have repented long ago, sitting in sackcloth and ashes. 14But at the judgment it will be more tolerable for Tyre and Sidon than for you. 15And you, Capernaum,

will you be exalted to heaven?

No, you will be brought down
to Hades.

16 "Whoever listens to you listens to me, and whoever rejects you rejects me, and whoever rejects me rejects the one who sent me."

17 The seventy[a] returned with joy, saying, "Lord, in your name even the demons submit to us!" [18]He said to them, "I watched Satan fall from heaven like a flash of lightning. [19]See, I have given you authority to tread on snakes and scorpions, and over all the power of the enemy; and nothing will hurt you. [20]Nevertheless, do not rejoice at this, that the spirits submit to you, but rejoice that your names are written in heaven."

21 At that same hour Jesus[b] rejoiced in the Holy Spirit[c] and said, "I thank[d] you, Father, Lord of heaven and earth, because you have hidden these things from the wise and the intelligent and have revealed them to infants; yes, Father, for such was your gracious will. [e] [22]All things have been handed over to me by my Father; and no one knows who the Son is except the Father, or who the Father is except the Son and anyone to whom the Son chooses to reveal him."

23 Then turning to the disciples, Jesus[b] said to them privately, "Blessed are the eyes that see what you see! [24]For I tell you that many prophets and kings desired to see what you see, but did not see it, and to hear what you hear, but did not hear it."

25 Just then a lawyer stood up to test Jesus. [f] "Teacher," he said, "what must I do to inherit eternal life?" [26]He said to him, "What is written in the law? What do you read there?" [27]He answered, "You shall love the Lord your God with all your heart, and with all your soul, and with all your strength, and with all your mind; and your neigh-bor as yourself." [28]And he said to him, "You have given the right answer; do this, and you will live."

29 But wanting to justify himself, he asked Jesus, "And who is my neighbor?" [30]Jesus replied, "A man was going down from Jerusalem to Jericho, and fell into the hands of robbers, who stripped him, beat him, and went away, leaving him half dead. [31]Now by chance a priest was going down that road; and when he saw him, he passed by on the other side. [32]So likewise a Levite, when he came to the place and saw him, passed by on the other side. [33]But a Samaritan while traveling came near him; and when he saw him, he was moved with pity. [34]He went to him and bandaged his wounds, having poured oil and wine on them. Then he put him on his own animal, brought him to an inn, and took care of him. [35]The next day he took out two denarii, [g] gave them to the innkeeper, and said, 'Take care of him; and when I come back, I will repay you whatever more you spend.' [36]Which of these three, do you think, was a neighbor to the man who fell into the hands of the robbers?" [37]He said, "The one who showed him mercy." Jesus said to him, "Go and do likewise."

## PSALM 75.1–10

*To the leader: Do Not Destroy. A Psalm of Asaph. A Song.*

WE give thanks to you,
O God;
we give thanks; your
name is near.
People tell of your wondrous
deeds.
2 At the set time that I appoint
I will judge with equity.
3 When the earth totters, with all
its inhabitants,

aOther ancient authorities read *seventy-two*  bGk *he*  cOther authorities read *in the spirit*
dOr *praise*  eOr *for so it was well-pleasing in your sight*  fGk *him*  gThe denarius was the usual day's wage for a laborer

it is I who keep its pillars
    steady.     *Selah*
4 I say to the boastful, "Do not
    boast,"
  and to the wicked, "Do not
    lift up your horn;
5 do not lift up your horn on high,
    or speak with insolent neck."

6 For not from the east or from
    the west
  and not from the wilderness
    comes lifting up;
7 but it is God who executes
    judgment,
  putting down one and lifting
    up another.
8 For in the hand of the Lord
    there is a cup
  with foaming wine, well
    mixed;
  he will pour a draught from it,
  and all the wicked of the
    earth

  shall drain it down to the
    dregs.
9 But I will rejoice[a] forever;
  I will sing praises to the God
    of Jacob.

10 All the horns of the wicked I
    will cut off,
  but the horns of the righteous
    shall be exalted.

## PROVERBS 12.12–14

THE wicked covet the proceeds
    of wickedness,[b]
  but the root of the righteous
    bears fruit.
13 The evil are ensnared by the
    transgression of their
    lips,
  but the righteous escape from
    trouble.
14 From the fruit of the mouth one
    is filled with good things,
  and manual labor has its
    reward.

# APRIL 4

## DEUTERONOMY 26.1—27.26

WHEN you have come into the land that the Lord your God is giving you as an inheritance to possess, and you possess it, and settle in it, 2you shall take some of the first of all the fruit of the ground, which you harvest from the land that the Lord your God is giving you, and you shall put it in a basket and go to the place that the Lord your God will choose as a dwelling for his name. 3You shall go to the priest who is in office at that time, and say to him, "Today I declare to the Lord your God that I have come into the land that the Lord swore to our ancestors to give us." 4When the priest takes the basket from your hand and sets it down before the altar of the Lord your God, 5you shall make this response before the Lord your God: "A wandering Aramean was my ancestor; he went down into Egypt and lived there as an alien, few in number, and there he became a great nation, mighty

[a] Gk: Heb *declare*   [b] Or *covet the catch of the wicked*

and populous. [6]When the Egyptians treated us harshly and afflicted us, by imposing hard labor on us, [7]we cried to the LORD, the God of our ancestors; the LORD heard our voice and saw our affliction, our toil, and our oppression. [8]The LORD brought us out of Egypt with a mighty hand and an outstretched arm, with a terrifying display of power, and with signs and wonders; [9]and he brought us into this place and gave us this land, a land flowing with milk and honey. [10]So now I bring the first of the fruit of the ground that you, O LORD, have given me." You shall set it down before the LORD your God and bow down before the LORD your God. [11]Then you, together with the Levites and the aliens who reside among you, shall celebrate with all the bounty that the LORD your God has given to you and to your house.

12 When you have finished paying all the tithe of your produce in the third year (which is the year of the tithe), giving it to the Levites, the aliens, the orphans, and the widows, so that they may eat their fill within your towns, [13]then you shall say before the LORD your God: "I have removed the sacred portion from the house, and I have given it to the Levites, the resident aliens, the orphans, and the widows, in accordance with your entire commandment that you commanded me; I have neither transgressed nor forgotten any of your commandments: [14]I have not eaten of it while in mourning; I have not removed any of it while I was unclean; and I have not offered any of it to the dead. I have obeyed the LORD my God, doing just as you commanded me. [15]Look down from your holy habitation, from heaven, and bless your people Israel and the ground that you have given us, as you swore to our ancestors—a land flowing with milk and honey."

16 This very day the LORD your God is commanding you to observe these statutes and ordinances; so observe them diligently with all your heart and with all your soul. [17]Today you have obtained the LORD's agreement: to be your God; and for you to walk in his ways, to keep his statutes, his commandments, and his ordinances, and to obey him. [18]Today the LORD has obtained your agreement: to be his treasured people, as he promised you, and to keep his commandments; [19]for him to set you high above all nations that he has made, in praise and in fame and in honor; and for you to be a people holy to the LORD your God, as he promised.

**27.**[1] THEN Moses and the elders of Israel charged all the people as follows: Keep the entire commandment that I am commanding you today. [2]On the day that you cross over the Jordan into the land that the LORD your God is giving you, you shall set up large stones and cover them with plaster. [3]You shall write on them all the words of this law when you have crossed over, to enter the land that the LORD your God is giving you, a land flowing with milk and honey, as the LORD, the God of your ancestors, promised you. [4]So when you have crossed over the Jordan, you shall set up these stones, about which I am commanding you today, on Mount Ebal, and you shall cover them with plaster. [5]And you shall build an altar there to the LORD your God, an altar of stones on which you have not used an iron tool. [6]You must build the altar of the LORD your God of unhewn[a] stones. Then offer up burnt offerings on it to the LORD your God, [7]make sacrifices of well-being, and eat them there, rejoicing before the LORD your God. [8]You shall write on the stones all the words of this law very clearly.

9 Then Moses and the levitical

---

priests spoke to all Israel, saying: Keep silence and hear, O Israel! This very day you have become the people of the LORD your God. [10]Therefore obey the LORD your God, observing his commandments and his statutes that I am commanding you today.

11 The same day Moses charged the people as follows: [12]When you have crossed over the Jordan, these shall stand on Mount Gerizim for the blessing of the people: Simeon, Levi, Judah, Issachar, Joseph, and Benjamin. [13]And these shall stand on Mount Ebal for the curse: Reuben, Gad, Asher, Zebulun, Dan, and Naphtali. [14]Then the Levites shall declare in a loud voice to all the Israelites:

15 "Cursed be anyone who makes an idol or casts an image, anything abhorrent to the LORD, the work of an artisan, and sets it up in secret." All the people shall respond, saying, "Amen!"

16 "Cursed be anyone who dishonors father or mother." All the people shall say, "Amen!"

17 "Cursed be anyone who moves a neighbor's boundary marker." All the people shall say, "Amen!"

18 "Cursed be anyone who misleads a blind person on the road." All the people shall say, "Amen!"

19 "Cursed be anyone who deprives the alien, the orphan, and the widow of justice." All the people shall say, "Amen!"

20 "Cursed be anyone who lies with his father's wife, because he has violated his father's rights."[a] All the people shall say, "Amen!"

21 "Cursed be anyone who lies with any animal." All the people shall say, "Amen!"

22 "Cursed be anyone who lies with his sister, whether the daughter of his father or the daughter of his mother." All the people shall say, "Amen!"

23 "Cursed be anyone who lies with his mother-in-law." All the people shall say, "Amen!"

24 "Cursed be anyone who strikes down a neighbor in secret." All the people shall say, "Amen!"

25 "Cursed be anyone who takes a bribe to shed innocent blood." All the people shall say, "Amen!"

26 "Cursed be anyone who does not uphold the words of this law by observing them." All the people shall say, "Amen!"

## LUKE 10.38—11.13

Now as they went on their way, he [Jesus] entered a certain village, where a woman named Martha welcomed him into her home. [39]She had a sister named Mary, who sat at the Lord's feet and listened to what he was saying. [40]But Martha was distracted by her many tasks; so she came to him and asked, "Lord, do you not care that my sister has left me to do all the work by myself? Tell her then to help me." [41]But the Lord answered her, "Martha, Martha, you are worried and distracted by many things; [42]there is need of only one thing.[b] Mary has chosen the better part, which will not be taken away from her."

[11.1] HE was praying in a certain place, and after he had finished, one of his disciples said to him, "Lord, teach us to pray, as John taught his disciples." [2]He said to them, "When you pray, say:

Father,[c] hallowed be your
   name.
Your kingdom come.[d]
3   Give us each day our daily
   bread.[e]

---

[a]Heb *uncovered his father's skirt*   [b]Other ancient authorities read *few things are necessary, or only one*   [c]Other ancient authorities read *Our Father in heaven*   [d]A few ancient authorities read *Your Holy Spirit come upon us and cleanse us.* Other ancient authorities add *Your will be done, on earth as in heaven*   [e]Or *our bread for tomorrow*

4 And forgive us our sins,
 for we ourselves forgive
  everyone indebted to us.
 And do not bring us to the
  time of trial."a

5 And he said to them, "Suppose one of you has a friend, and you go to him at midnight and say to him, 'Friend, lend me three loaves of bread; 6for a friend of mine has arrived, and I have nothing to set before him.' 7And he answers from within, 'Do not bother me; the door has already been locked, and my children are with me in bed; I cannot get up and give you anything.' 8I tell you, even though he will not get up and give him anything because he is his friend, at least because of his persistence he will get up and give him whatever he needs.

9 "So I say to you, Ask, and it will be given you; search, and you will find; knock, and the door will be opened for you. 10For everyone who asks receives, and everyone who searches finds, and for everyone who knocks, the door will be opened. 11Is there anyone among you who, if your child asks forb a fish, will give a snake instead of a fish? 12Or if the child asks for an egg, will give a scorpion? 13If you then, who are evil, know how to give good gifts to your children, how much more will the heavenly Father give the Holy Spiritc to those who ask him!"

## PSALM 76.1–12

*To the leader: with stringed instruments. A
Psalm of Asaph. A Song.*

IN Judah God is known,
 his name is great in Israel.
2 His abode has been
  established in Salem,
 his dwelling place in Zion.

3 There he broke the flashing
  arrows,
 the shield, the sword, and the
  weapons of war.    *Selah*

4 Glorious are you, more majestic
 than the everlasting
  mountains. d
5 The stouthearted were stripped
  of their spoil;
 they sank into sleep;
none of the troops
 was able to lift a hand.
6 At your rebuke, O God of
  Jacob,
 both rider and horse lay
  stunned.

7 But you indeed are awesome!
 Who can stand before you
  when once your anger is
   roused?
8 From the heavens you uttered
  judgment;
 the earth feared and was still
9 when God rose up to establish
  judgment,
 to save all the oppressed of
  the earth.    *Selah*

10 Human wrath serves only to
  praise you,
 when you bind the last bit of
  youre wrath around you.
11 Make vows to the LORD your
  God, and perform them;
 let all who are around him
  bring gifts
 to the one who is awesome,
12 who cuts off the spirit of
  princes,
 who inspires fear in the kings
  of the earth.

---

aOr *us into temptation.* Other ancient authorities add *but rescue us from the evil one* (or *from evil*)
bOther ancient authorities add *bread, will give a stone; or if your child asks for*   cOther ancient
authorities read *the Father give the Holy Spirit from heaven*   dGk: Heb *the mountains of prey*
eHeb lacks *your*

## PROVERBS 12.15–17

**F**OOLS think their own way is right,
but the wise listen to advice.
16 Fools show their anger at once,
but the prudent ignore an insult.
17 Whoever speaks the truth gives honest evidence,
but a false witness speaks deceitfully.

# APRIL 5

## DEUTERONOMY 28.1–68

**I**F you will only obey the LORD your God, by diligently observing all his commandments that I am commanding you today, the LORD your God will set you high above all the nations of the earth; 2all these blessings shall come upon you and overtake you, if you obey the LORD your God:

3 Blessed shall you be in the city, and blessed shall you be in the field.

4 Blessed shall be the fruit of your womb, the fruit of your ground, and the fruit of your livestock, both the increase of your cattle and the issue of your flock.

5 Blessed shall be your basket and your kneading bowl.

6 Blessed shall you be when you come in, and blessed shall you be when you go out.

7 The LORD will cause your enemies who rise against you to be defeated before you; they shall come out against you one way, and flee before you seven ways. 8The LORD will command the blessing upon you in your barns, and in all that you undertake; he will bless you in the land that the LORD your God is giving you. 9The LORD will establish you as his holy people, as he has sworn to you, if you keep the commandments of the LORD your God and walk in his ways. 10All the peoples of the earth shall see that you are called by the name of the LORD, and they shall be afraid of you. 11The LORD will make you abound in prosperity, in the fruit of your womb, in the fruit of your livestock, and in the fruit of your ground in the land that the LORD swore to your ancestors to give you. 12The LORD will open for you his rich storehouse, the heavens, to give the rain of your land in its season and to bless all your undertakings. You will lend to many nations, but you will not borrow. 13The LORD will make you the head, and not the tail; you shall be only at the top, and not at the bottom—if you obey the commandments of the LORD your God, which I am commanding you today, by diligently observing them, 14and if you do not turn aside from any of the words that I am commanding you today, either to the right or to the left, following other gods to serve them.

15 But if you will not obey the LORD your God by diligently observing all his commandments and decrees, which I am commanding you today, then all these curses shall come upon you and overtake you:

16 Cursed shall you be in the city, and cursed shall you be in the field.

17 Cursed shall be your basket and your kneading bowl.

18 Cursed shall be the fruit of your

womb, the fruit of your ground, the increase of your cattle and the issue of your flock.

19 Cursed shall you be when you come in, and cursed shall you be when you go out.

20 The Lord will send upon you disaster, panic, and frustration in everything you attempt to do, until you are destroyed and perish quickly, on account of the evil of your deeds, because you have forsaken me. <sup>21</sup>The Lord will make the pestilence cling to you until it has consumed you off the land that you are entering to possess. <sup>22</sup>The Lord will afflict you with consumption, fever, inflammation, with fiery heat and drought, and with blight and mildew; they shall pursue you until you perish. <sup>23</sup>The sky over your head shall be bronze, and the earth under you iron. <sup>24</sup>The Lord will change the rain of your land into powder, and only dust shall come down upon you from the sky until you are destroyed.

25 The Lord will cause you to be defeated before your enemies; you shall go out against them one way and flee before them seven ways. You shall become an object of horror to all the kingdoms of the earth. <sup>26</sup>Your corpses shall be food for every bird of the air and animal of the earth, and there shall be no one to frighten them away. <sup>27</sup>The Lord will afflict you with the boils of Egypt, with ulcers, scurvy, and itch, of which you cannot be healed. <sup>28</sup>The Lord will afflict you with madness, blindness, and confusion of mind; <sup>29</sup>you shall grope about at noon as blind people grope in darkness, but you shall be unable to find your way; and you shall be continually abused and robbed, without anyone to help. <sup>30</sup>You shall become engaged to a woman, but another man shall lie with her. You shall build a house, but not live in it. You shall plant a vineyard, but not enjoy its fruit. <sup>31</sup>Your ox shall be butchered before your eyes, but you shall not eat of it.

Your donkey shall be stolen in front of you, and shall not be restored to you. Your sheep shall be given to your enemies, without anyone to help you. <sup>32</sup>Your sons and daughters shall be given to another people, while you look on; you will strain your eyes looking for them all day but be powerless to do anything. <sup>33</sup>A people whom you do not know shall eat up the fruit of your ground and of all your labors; you shall be continually abused and crushed, <sup>34</sup>and driven mad by the sight that your eyes shall see. <sup>35</sup>The Lord will strike you on the knees and on the legs with grievous boils of which you cannot be healed, from the sole of your foot to the crown of your head. <sup>36</sup>The Lord will bring you, and the king whom you set over you, to a nation that neither you nor your ancestors have known, where you shall serve other gods, of wood and stone. <sup>37</sup>You shall become an object of horror, a proverb, and a byword among all the peoples where the Lord will lead you.

38 You shall carry much seed into the field but shall gather little in, for the locust shall consume it. <sup>39</sup>You shall plant vineyards and dress them, but you shall neither drink the wine nor gather the grapes, for the worm shall eat them. <sup>40</sup>You shall have olive trees throughout all your territory, but you shall not anoint yourself with the oil, for your olives shall drop off. <sup>41</sup>You shall have sons and daughters, but they shall not remain yours, for they shall go into captivity. <sup>42</sup>All your trees and the fruit of your ground the cicada shall take over. <sup>43</sup>Aliens residing among you shall ascend above you higher and higher, while you shall descend lower and lower. <sup>44</sup>They shall lend to you but you shall not lend to them; they shall be the head and you shall be the tail.

45 All these curses shall come upon you, pursuing and overtaking you until you are destroyed, because you did not obey the Lord your God, by observing

the commandments and the decrees that he commanded you. ⁴⁶They shall be among you and your descendants as a sign and a portent forever.

47 Because you did not serve the LORD your God joyfully and with gladness of heart for the abundance of everything, ⁴⁸therefore you shall serve your enemies whom the LORD will send against you, in hunger and thirst, in nakedness and lack of everything. He will put an iron yoke on your neck until he has destroyed you. ⁴⁹The LORD will bring a nation from far away, from the end of the earth, to swoop down on you like an eagle, a nation whose language you do not understand, ⁵⁰a grim-faced nation showing no respect to the old or favor to the young. ⁵¹It shall consume the fruit of your livestock and the fruit of your ground until you are destroyed, leaving you neither grain, wine, and oil, nor the increase of your cattle and the issue of your flock, until it has made you perish. ⁵²It shall besiege you in all your towns until your high and fortified walls, in which you trusted, come down throughout your land; it shall besiege you in all your towns throughout the land that the LORD your God has given you. ⁵³In the desperate straits to which the enemy siege reduces you, you will eat the fruit of your womb, the flesh of your own sons and daughters whom the LORD your God has given you. ⁵⁴Even the most refined and gentle of men among you will begrudge food to his own brother, to the wife whom he embraces, and to the last of his remaining children, ⁵⁵giving to none of them any of the flesh of his children whom he is eating, because nothing else remains to him, in the desperate straits to which the enemy siege will reduce you in all your towns. ⁵⁶She who is the most refined and gentle among you, so gentle and refined that she does not venture to set the sole of her foot on the ground, will begrudge food to the husband whom she embraces, to her own son, and to her own daughter, ⁵⁷begrudging even the afterbirth that comes out from between her thighs, and the children that she bears, because she is eating them in secret for lack of anything else, in the desperate straits to which the enemy siege will reduce you in your towns.

58 If you do not diligently observe all the words of this law that are written in this book, fearing this glorious and awesome name, the LORD your God, ⁵⁹then the LORD will overwhelm both you and your offspring with severe and lasting afflictions and grievous and lasting maladies. ⁶⁰He will bring back upon you all the diseases of Egypt, of which you were in dread, and they shall cling to you. ⁶¹Every other malady and affliction, even though not recorded in the book of this law, the LORD will inflict on you until you are destroyed. ⁶²Although once you were as numerous as the stars in heaven, you shall be left few in number, because you did not obey the LORD your God. ⁶³And just as the LORD took delight in making you prosperous and numerous, so the LORD will take delight in bringing you to ruin and destruction; you shall be plucked off the land that you are entering to possess. ⁶⁴The LORD will scatter you among all peoples, from one end of the earth to the other; and there you shall serve other gods, of wood and stone, which neither you nor your ancestors have known. ⁶⁵Among those nations you shall find no ease, no resting place for the sole of your foot. There the LORD will give you a trembling heart, failing eyes, and a languishing spirit. ⁶⁶Your life shall hang in doubt before you; night and day you shall be in dread, with no assurance of your life. ⁶⁷In the morning you shall say, "If only it were evening!" and at evening you shall say, "If only it were morning!"—because of the dread that your heart shall feel and the sights that your eyes shall see. ⁶⁸The LORD will bring you back in ships to Egypt, by a

route that I promised you would never see again; and there you shall offer yourselves for sale to your enemies as male and female slaves, but there will be no buyer.

## LUKE 11.14–36

Now he [Jesus] was casting out a demon that was mute; when the demon had gone out, the one who had been mute spoke, and the crowds were amazed. 15But some of them said, "He casts out demons by Beelzebul, the ruler of the demons." 16Others, to test him, kept demanding from him a sign from heaven. 17But he knew what they were thinking and said to them, "Every kingdom divided against itself becomes a desert, and house falls on house. 18If Satan also is divided against himself, how will his kingdom stand? —for you say that I cast out the demons by Beelzebul. 19Now if I cast out the demons by Beelzebul, by whom do your exorcists[a] cast them out? Therefore they will be your judges. 20But if it is by the finger of God that I cast out the demons, then the kingdom of God has come to you. 21When a strong man, fully armed, guards his castle, his property is safe. 22But when one stronger than he attacks him and overpowers him, he takes away his armor in which he trusted and divides his plunder. 23Whoever is not with me is against me, and whoever does not gather with me scatters.

24 "When the unclean spirit has gone out of a person, it wanders through waterless regions looking for a resting place, but not finding any, it says, 'I will return to my house from which I came.' 25When it comes, it finds it swept and put in order. 26Then it goes and brings seven other spirits more evil than itself, and they enter and live there; and the last state of that person is worse than the first."

27 While he was saying this, a woman in the crowd raised her voice and said to him, "Blessed is the womb that bore you and the breasts that nursed you!" 28But he said, "Blessed rather are those who hear the word of God and obey it!"

29 When the crowds were increasing, he began to say, "This generation is an evil generation; it asks for a sign, but no sign will be given to it except the sign of Jonah. 30For just as Jonah became a sign to the people of Nineveh, so the Son of Man will be to this generation. 31The queen of the South will rise at the judgment with the people of this generation and condemn them, because she came from the ends of the earth to listen to the wisdom of Solomon, and see, something greater than Solomon is here! 32The people of Nineveh will rise up at the judgment with this generation and condemn it, because they repented at the proclamation of Jonah, and see, something greater than Jonah is here!

33 "No one after lighting a lamp puts it in a cellar,[b] but on the lampstand so that those who enter may see the light. 34Your eye is the lamp of your body. If your eye is healthy, your whole body is full of light; but if it is not healthy, your body is full of darkness. 35Therefore consider whether the light in you is not darkness. 36If then your whole body is full of light, with no part of it in darkness, it will be as full of light as when a lamp gives you light with its rays."

aGk *sons*   bOther ancient authorities add *or under the bushel basket*

## PSALM 77.1–20

*To the leader: according to Jeduthun. Of Asaph.*
*A Psalm.*

I CRY aloud to God,
 aloud to God, that he may
  hear me.
2 In the day of my trouble I seek
  the Lord;
 in the night my hand is
  stretched out without
  wearying;
 my soul refuses to be
  comforted.
3 I think of God, and I moan;
 I meditate, and my spirit
  faints.              *Selah*

4 You keep my eyelids from
  closing;
 I am so troubled that I cannot
  speak.
5 I consider the days of old,
 and remember the years of
  long ago.
6 I commune[a] with my heart in
  the night;
 I meditate and search my
  spirit: [b]
7 "Will the Lord spurn forever,
 and never again be favorable?
8 Has his steadfast love ceased
  forever?
 Are his promises at an end
  for all time?
9 Has God forgotten to be
  gracious?
 Has he in anger shut up his
  compassion?"          *Selah*
10 And I say, "It is my grief
 that the right hand of the
  Most High has changed."

11 I will call to mind the deeds of
  the LORD;
 I will remember your
  wonders of old.

12 I will meditate on all your work,
 and muse on your mighty
  deeds.
13 Your way, O God, is holy.
 What god is so great as our
  God?
14 You are the God who works
  wonders;
 you have displayed your
  might among the
  peoples.
15 With your strong arm you
  redeemed your people,
 the descendants of Jacob and
  Joseph.            *Selah*

16 When the waters saw you,
  O God,
 when the waters saw you,
  they were afraid;
 the very deep trembled.
17 The clouds poured out water;
 the skies thundered;
 your arrows flashed on every
  side.
18 The crash of your thunder was
  in the whirlwind;
 your lightnings lit up the
  world;
 the earth trembled and shook.
19 Your way was through the sea,
 your path, through the mighty
  waters;
 yet your footprints were
  unseen.
20 You led your people like a flock
 by the hand of Moses and
  Aaron.

## PROVERBS 12.18

R ASH words are like sword
  thrusts,
 but the tongue of the wise
  brings healing.

aGk Syr: Heb *My music*   bSyr Jerome: Heb *my spirit searches*

# APRIL 6

## DEUTERONOMY 29[a].1—30.20

THESE are the words of the covenant that the LORD commanded Moses to make with the Israelites in the land of Moab, in addition to the covenant that he had made with them at Horeb.

2[b] Moses summoned all Israel and said to them: You have seen all that the LORD did before your eyes in the land of Egypt, to Pharaoh and to all his servants and to all his land, [3]the great trials that your eyes saw, the signs, and those great wonders. [4]But to this day the LORD has not given you a mind to understand, or eyes to see, or ears to hear. [5]I have led you forty years in the wilderness. The clothes on your back have not worn out, and the sandals on your feet have not worn out; [6]you have not eaten bread, and you have not drunk wine or strong drink—so that you may know that I am the LORD your God. [7]When you came to this place, King Sihon of Heshbon and King Og of Bashan came out against us for battle, but we defeated them. [8]We took their land and gave it as an inheritance to the Reubenites, the Gadites, and the half-tribe of Manasseh. [9]Therefore diligently observe the words of this covenant, in order that you may succeed[c] in everything that you do.

10 You stand assembled today, all of you, before the LORD your God—the leaders of your tribes,[d] your elders, and your officials, all the men of Israel, [11]your children, your women, and the aliens who are in your camp, both those who cut your wood and those who draw your water— [12]to enter into the covenant of the LORD your God, sworn by an oath, which the LORD your God is making with you today; [13]in order that he may establish you today as his people, and that he may be your God, as he promised you and as he swore to your ancestors, to Abraham, to Isaac, and to Jacob. [14]I am making this covenant, sworn by an oath, not only with you who stand here with us today before the LORD our God, [15]but also with those who are not here with us today. [16]You know how we lived in the land of Egypt, and how we came through the midst of the nations through which you passed. [17]You have seen their detestable things, the filthy idols of wood and stone, of silver and gold, that were among them. [18]It may be that there is among you a man or woman, or a family or tribe, whose heart is already turning away from the LORD our God to serve the gods of those nations. It may be that there is among you a root sprouting poisonous and bitter growth. [19]All who hear the words of this oath and bless themselves, thinking in their hearts, "We are safe even though we go our own stubborn ways" (thus bringing disaster on moist and dry alike)[e]— [20]the LORD will be unwilling to pardon them, for the LORD's anger and passion will smoke against them. All the curses written in this book will descend on them, and the LORD will blot out their names from under heaven. [21]The LORD will single them out from all the tribes of Israel for calamity, in accordance with all the curses of the covenant written in this book of the law. [22]The next generation, your children who rise up after you, as well as the foreigner who comes from a distant country, will see

the devastation of that land and the afflictions with which the Lord has afflicted it— 23all its soil burned out by sulfur and salt, nothing planted, nothing sprouting, unable to support any vegetation, like the destruction of Sodom and Gomorrah, Admah and Zeboiim, which the Lord destroyed in his fierce anger— 24they and indeed all the nations will wonder, "Why has the Lord done thus to this land? What caused this great display of anger?" 25They will conclude, "It is because they abandoned the covenant of the Lord, the God of their ancestors, which he made with them when he brought them out of the land of Egypt. 26They turned and served other gods, worshiping them, gods whom they had not known and whom he had not allotted to them; 27so the anger of the Lord was kindled against that land, bringing on it every curse written in this book. 28The Lord uprooted them from their land in anger, fury, and great wrath, and cast them into another land, as is now the case." 29The secret things belong to the Lord our God, but the revealed things belong to us and to our children forever, to observe all the words of this law.

30.1 When all these things have happened to you, the blessings and the curses that I have set before you, if you call them to mind among all the nations where the Lord your God has driven you, 2and return to the Lord your God, and you and your children obey him with all your heart and with all your soul, just as I am commanding you today, 3then the Lord your God will restore your fortunes and have compassion on you, gathering you again from all the peoples among whom the Lord your God has scattered you. 4Even if you are exiled to the ends of the world, a from there the Lord your God will gather you, and from there he will bring you back. 5The Lord your God will bring you into the land that your ancestors possessed, and you will possess it; he will make you more prosperous and numerous than your ancestors.

6 Moreover, the Lord your God will circumcise your heart and the heart of your descendants, so that you will love the Lord your God with all your heart and with all your soul, in order that you may live. 7The Lord your God will put all these curses on your enemies and on the adversaries who took advantage of you. 8Then you shall again obey the Lord, observing all his commandments that I am commanding you today, 9and the Lord your God will make you abundantly prosperous in all your undertakings, in the fruit of your body, in the fruit of your livestock, and in the fruit of your soil. For the Lord will again take delight in prospering you, just as he delighted in prospering your ancestors, 10when you obey the Lord your God by observing his commandments and decrees that are written in this book of the law, because you turn to the Lord your God with all your heart and with all your soul.

11 Surely, this commandment that I am commanding you today is not too hard for you, nor is it too far away. 12It is not in heaven, that you should say, "Who will go up to heaven for us, and get it for us so that we may hear it and observe it?" 13Neither is it beyond the sea, that you should say, "Who will cross to the other side of the sea for us, and get it for us so that we may hear it and observe it?" 14No, the word is very near to you; it is in your mouth and in your heart for you to observe.

15 See, I have set before you today life and prosperity, death and adversity. 16If you obey the commandments of the Lord your Godb that I am commanding you today, by loving the Lord

aHeb *of heaven*   bGk: Heb lacks *If you obey the commandments of the Lord your God* your God, walking in his ways, and observing his commandments, decrees, and ordinances, then you shall live and become numerous, and the LORD your God will bless you in the land that you are entering to possess. [17]But if your heart turns away and you do not hear, but are led astray to bow down to other gods and serve them, [18]I declare to you today that you shall perish; you shall not live long in the land that you are crossing the Jordan to enter and possess. [19]I call heaven and earth to witness against you today that I have set before you life and death, blessings and curses. Choose life so that you and your descendants may live, [20]loving the LORD your God, obeying him, and holding fast to him; for that means life to you and length of days, so that you may live in the land that the LORD swore to give to your ancestors, to Abraham, to Isaac, and to Jacob.

## LUKE 11.37—12.7

WHILE he [Jesus] was speaking, a Pharisee invited him to dine with him; so he went in and took his place at the table. [38]The Pharisee was amazed to see that he did not first wash before dinner. [39]Then the Lord said to him, "Now you Pharisees clean the outside of the cup and of the dish, but inside you are full of greed and wickedness. [40]You fools! Did not the one who made the outside make the inside also? [41]So give for alms those things that are within; and see, everything will be clean for you.

42 "But woe to you Pharisees! For you tithe mint and rue and herbs of all kinds, and neglect justice and the love of God; it is these you ought to have practiced, without neglecting the others. [43]Woe to you Pharisees! For you love to have the seat of honor in the synagogues and to be greeted with respect in the marketplaces. [44]Woe to you! For you are like unmarked graves, and people walk over them without realizing it."

45 One of the lawyers answered him, "Teacher, when you say these things, you insult us too." [46]And he said, "Woe also to you lawyers! For you load people with burdens hard to bear, and you yourselves do not lift a finger to ease them. [47]Woe to you! For you build the tombs of the prophets whom your ancestors killed. [48]So you are witnesses and approve of the deeds of your ancestors; for they killed them, and you build their tombs. [49]Therefore also the Wisdom of God said, 'I will send them prophets and apostles, some of whom they will kill and persecute,' [50]so that this generation may be charged with the blood of all the prophets shed since the foundation of the world, [51]from the blood of Abel to the blood of Zechariah, who perished between the altar and the sanctuary. Yes, I tell you, it will be charged against this generation. [52]Woe to you lawyers! For you have taken away the key of knowledge; you did not enter yourselves, and you hindered those who were entering."

53 When he went outside, the scribes and the Pharisees began to be very hostile toward him and to cross-examine him about many things, [54]lying in wait for him, to catch him in something he might say.

12.1 MEANWHILE, when the crowd gathered by the thousands, so that they trampled on one another, he began to speak first to his disciples, "Beware of the yeast of the Pharisees, that is, their hypocrisy. [2]Nothing is covered up that will not be uncovered, and nothing secret that will not become known. [3]Therefore whatever you have said in the dark will be heard in the light, and what you have whispered behind closed doors will be proclaimed from the housetops.

4 "I tell you, my friends, do not fear

those who kill the body, and after that can do nothing more. ⁵But I will warn you whom to fear: fear him who, after he has killed, has authority[a] to cast into hell.[b] Yes, I tell you, fear him! ⁶Are not five sparrows sold for two pennies? Yet not one of them is forgotten in God's sight. ⁷But even the hairs of your head are all counted. Do not be afraid; you are of more value than many sparrows.

## PSALM 78.1–31

*A Maskil of Asaph.*

G IVE ear, O my people, to my
    teaching;
  incline your ears to the
    words of my mouth.
2 I will open my mouth in a
    parable;
  I will utter dark sayings from
    of old,
3 things that we have heard and
    known,
  that our ancestors have told
    us.
4 We will not hide them from
    their children;
  we will tell to the coming
    generation
the glorious deeds of the Lord,
    and his might,
  and the wonders that he has
    done.

5 He established a decree in
    Jacob,
  and appointed a law in Israel,
which he commanded our
    ancestors
  to teach to their children;
6 that the next generation might
    know them,
  the children yet unborn,
and rise up and tell them to
    their children,
7   so that they should set their
    hope in God,

and not forget the works of
    God,
  but keep his commandments;
8 and that they should not be like
    their ancestors,
  a stubborn and rebellious
    generation,
a generation whose heart was
    not steadfast,
  whose spirit was not faithful
    to God.

9 The Ephraimites, armed with[c]
    the bow,
  turned back on the day of
    battle.
10 They did not keep God's
    covenant,
  but refused to walk according
    to his law.
11 They forgot what he had done,
  and the miracles that he had
    shown them.
12 In the sight of their ancestors
    he worked marvels
  in the land of Egypt, in the
    fields of Zoan.
13 He divided the sea and let them
    pass through it,
  and made the waters stand
    like a heap.
14 In the daytime he led them with
    a cloud,
  and all night long with a fiery
    light.
15 He split rocks open in the
    wilderness,
  and gave them drink
    abundantly as from the
    deep.
16 He made streams come out of
    the rock,
  and caused waters to flow
    down like rivers.

17 Yet they sinned still more
    against him,

a Or *power*  b Gk *Gehenna*  c Heb *armed with shooting*

rebelling against the Most
High in the desert.
18 They tested God in their heart
by demanding the food they
craved.
19 They spoke against God,
saying,
"Can God spread a table in
the wilderness?
20 Even though he struck the rock
so that water gushed out
and torrents overflowed,
can he also give bread,
or provide meat for his
people?"

21 Therefore, when the Lord
heard, he was full of
rage;
a fire was kindled against
Jacob,
his anger mounted against
Israel,
22 because they had no faith in
God,
and did not trust his saving
power.
23 Yet he commanded the skies
above,
and opened the doors of
heaven;
24 he rained down on them manna
to eat,
and gave them the grain of
heaven.
25 Mortals ate of the bread of
angels;

he sent them food in
abundance.
26 He caused the east wind to
blow in the heavens,
and by his power he led out
the south wind;
27 he rained flesh upon them like
dust,
winged birds like the sand of
the seas;
28 he let them fall within their
camp,
all around their dwellings.
29 And they ate and were well
filled,
for he gave them what they
craved.
30 But before they had satisfied
their craving,
while the food was still in
their mouths,
31 the anger of God rose against
them
and he killed the strongest of
them,
and laid low the flower of
Israel.

## PROVERBS 12.19–20

TRUTHFUL lips endure forever,
but a lying tongue lasts only
a moment.
20 Deceit is in the mind of those
who plan evil,
but those who counsel peace
have joy.

# APRIL 7

## DEUTERONOMY 31.1—32.27

WHEN Moses had finished speaking all[a] these words to all Israel, [2]he said to them: "I am now one hundred twenty years old. I am no longer able to get about, and the LORD has told me, 'You shall not cross over this Jordan.' [3]The LORD your God himself will cross over before you. He will destroy these nations before you, and you shall dispossess them. Joshua also will cross over before you, as the LORD promised. [4]The LORD will do to them as he did to Sihon and Og, the kings of the Amorites, and to their land, when he destroyed them. [5]The LORD will give them over to you and you shall deal with them in full accord with the command that I have given to you. [6]Be strong and bold; have no fear or dread of them, because it is the LORD your God who goes with you; he will not fail you or forsake you."

7 Then Moses summoned Joshua and said to him in the sight of all Israel: "Be strong and bold, for you are the one who will go with this people into the land that the LORD has sworn to their ancestors to give them; and you will put them in possession of it. [8]It is the LORD who goes before you. He will be with you; he will not fail you or forsake you. Do not fear or be dismayed."

9 Then Moses wrote down this law, and gave it to the priests, the sons of Levi, who carried the ark of the covenant of the LORD, and to all the elders of Israel. [10]Moses commanded them: "Every seventh year, in the scheduled year of remission, during the festival of booths, [b] [11]when all Israel comes to appear before the LORD your God at the place that he will choose, you shall read this law before all Israel in their hearing. [12]Assemble the people—men, women, and children, as well as the aliens residing in your towns—so that they may hear and learn to fear the LORD your God and to observe diligently all the words of this law, [13]and so that their children, who have not known it, may hear and learn to fear the LORD your God, as long as you live in the land that you are crossing over the Jordan to possess."

14 The LORD said to Moses, "Your time to die is near; call Joshua and present yourselves in the tent of meeting, so that I may commission him." So Moses and Joshua went and presented themselves in the tent of meeting, [15]and the LORD appeared at the tent in a pillar of cloud; the pillar of cloud stood at the entrance to the tent.

16 The LORD said to Moses, "Soon you will lie down with your ancestors. Then this people will begin to prostitute themselves to the foreign gods in their midst, the gods of the land into which they are going; they will forsake me, breaking my covenant that I have made with them. [17]My anger will be kindled against them in that day. I will forsake them and hide my face from them; they will become easy prey, and many terrible troubles will come upon them. In that day they will say, 'Have not these troubles come upon us because our God is not in our midst?' [18]On that day I will surely hide my face on account of all the evil they have done by turning to other gods. [19]Now therefore write this song, and teach it to the Israelites; put it in their mouths, in order that this song may be a witness for me against

aQ Ms Gk: MT *Moses went and spoke*   bOr *tabernacles*; Heb *succoth* the Israelites. [20]For when I have brought them into the land flowing with milk and honey, which I promised on oath to their ancestors, and they have eaten their fill and grown fat, they will turn to other gods and serve them, despising me and breaking my covenant. [21]And when many terrible troubles come upon them, this song will confront them as a witness, because it will not be lost from the mouths of their descendants. For I know what they are inclined to do even now, before I have brought them into the land that I promised them on oath." [22]That very day Moses wrote this song and taught it to the Israelites.

23 Then the LORD commissioned Joshua son of Nun and said, "Be strong and bold, for you shall bring the Israelites into the land that I promised them; I will be with you."

24 When Moses had finished writing down in a book the words of this law to the very end, [25]Moses commanded the Levites who carried the ark of the covenant of the LORD, saying, [26]"Take this book of the law and put it beside the ark of the covenant of the LORD your God; let it remain there as a witness against you. [27]For I know well how rebellious and stubborn you are. If you already have been so rebellious toward the LORD while I am still alive among you, how much more after my death! [28]Assemble to me all the elders of your tribes and your officials, so that I may recite these words in their hearing and call heaven and earth to witness against them. [29]For I know that after my death you will surely act corruptly, turning aside from the way that I have commanded you. In time to come trouble will befall you, because you will do what is evil in the sight of the LORD, provoking him to anger through the work of your hands."

30 Then Moses recited the words of this song, to the very end, in the hearing of the whole assembly of Israel:

32.1   GIVE ear, O heavens, and I
     will speak;
  let the earth hear the words
     of my mouth.
2  May my teaching drop like the
     rain,
  my speech condense like the
     dew;
  like gentle rain on grass,
     like showers on new growth.
3  For I will proclaim the name of
     the LORD;
  ascribe greatness to our God!

4  The Rock, his work is perfect,
     and all his ways are just.
  A faithful God, without deceit,
     just and upright is he;
5  yet his degenerate children have
     dealt falsely with him, [a]
  a perverse and crooked
     generation.
6  Do you thus repay the LORD,
     O foolish and senseless
     people?
  Is not he your father, who
     created you,
  who made you and
     established you?
7  Remember the days of old,
     consider the years long past;
  ask your father, and he will
     inform you;
  your elders, and they will tell
     you.
8  When the Most High[b]
     apportioned the nations,
  when he divided humankind,
  he fixed the boundaries of the
     peoples
  according to the number of
     the gods;[c]
9  the LORD's own portion was his
     people,
  Jacob his allotted share.

[a]Meaning of Heb uncertain   [b]Traditional rendering of Heb *Elyon*   [c]Q Ms Compare Gk Tg: MT *the Israelites*

10  He sustained<sup>a</sup> him in a desert
        land,
      in a howling wilderness
        waste;
    he shielded him, cared for him,
      guarded him as the apple of
        his eye.
11  As an eagle stirs up its nest,
      and hovers over its young;
    as it spreads its wings, takes
        them up,
      and bears them aloft on its
        pinions,
12  the LORD alone guided him;
      no foreign god was with him.
13  He set him atop the heights of
        the land,
      and fed him with<sup>b</sup> produce of
        the field;
    he nursed him with honey from
        the crags,
      with oil from flinty rock;
14  curds from the herd, and milk
        from the flock,
      with fat of lambs and rams;
    Bashan bulls and goats,
      together with the choicest
        wheat—
    you drank fine wine from the
        blood of grapes.
15  Jacob ate his fill;<sup>c</sup>
      Jeshurun grew fat, and
        kicked.
    You grew fat, bloated, and
        gorged!
    He abandoned God who made
        him,
      and scoffed at the Rock of his
        salvation.
16  They made him jealous with
        strange gods,
      with abhorrent things they
        provoked him.
17  They sacrificed to demons, not
        God,
      to deities they had never
        known,

to new ones recently arrived,
    whom your ancestors had not
        feared.
18  You were unmindful of the Rock
        that bore you;<sup>d</sup>
      you forgot the God who gave
        you birth.

19  The LORD saw it, and was
        jealous<sup>e</sup>
      he spurned<sup>f</sup> his sons and
        daughters.
20  He said: I will hide my face
        from them,
      I will see what their end will
        be;
    for they are a perverse
        generation,
      children in whom there is no
        faithfulness.
21  They made me jealous with
        what is no god,
      provoked me with their idols.
    So I will make them jealous with
        what is no people,
      provoke them with a foolish
        nation.
22  For a fire is kindled by my
        anger,
      and burns to the depths of
        Sheol;
    it devours the earth and its
        increase,
      and sets on fire the
        foundations of the
        mountains.
23  I will heap disasters upon them,
      spend my arrows against
        them:
24  wasting hunger,
      burning consumption,
      bitter pestilence.
    The teeth of beasts I will send
        against them,
      with venom of things crawling
        in the dust.

aSam Gk Compare Tg: MT *found*  bSam Gk Syr Tg: MT *he ate*  cQ Mss Sam Gk: MT lacks *Jacob ate his fill*  dOr *that begot you*  eQ Mss Gk: MT lacks *was jealous*  fCn: Heb *he spurned because of provocation*

25 In the street the sword shall
    bereave,
    and in the chambers terror,
    for young man and woman alike,
    nursing child and old gray
    head.
26 I thought to scatter them[a]
    and blot out the memory of
    them from humankind;
27 but I feared provocation by the
    enemy,
    for their adversaries might
    misunderstand
    and say, "Our hand is
    triumphant;
    it was not the LORD who did
    all this."

## LUKE 12.8–34

"AND I tell you, everyone who acknowledges me before others, the Son of Man also will acknowledge before the angels of God; [9]but whoever denies me before others will be denied before the angels of God. [10]And everyone who speaks a word against the Son of Man will be forgiven; but whoever blasphemes against the Holy Spirit will not be forgiven. [11]When they bring you before the synagogues, the rulers, and the authorities, do not worry about how[b] you are to defend yourselves or what you are to say; [12]for the Holy Spirit will teach you at that very hour what you ought to say."

13 Someone in the crowd said to him, "Teacher, tell my brother to divide the family inheritance with me." [14]But he said to him, "Friend, who set me to be a judge or arbitrator over you?" [15]And he said to them, "Take care! Be on your guard against all kinds of greed; for one's life does not consist in the abundance of possessions." [16]Then he told them a parable: "The land of a rich man produced abundantly.

[17]And he thought to himself, 'What should I do, for I have no place to store my crops?' [18]Then he said, 'I will do this: I will pull down my barns and build larger ones, and there I will store all my grain and my goods. [19]And I will say to my soul, 'Soul, you have ample goods laid up for many years; relax, eat, drink, be merry.' [20]But God said to him, 'You fool! This very night your life is being demanded of you. And the things you have prepared, whose will they be?' [21]So it is with those who store up treasures for themselves but are not rich toward God."

22 He said to his disciples, "Therefore I tell you, do not worry about your life, what you will eat, or about your body, what you will wear. [23]For life is more than food, and the body more than clothing. [24]Consider the ravens: they neither sow nor reap, they have neither storehouse nor barn, and yet God feeds them. Of how much more value are you than the birds! [25]And can any of you by worrying add a single hour to your span of life?[c] [26]If then you are not able to do so small a thing as that, why do you worry about the rest? [27]Consider the lilies, how they grow: they neither toil nor spin;[d] yet I tell you, even Solomon in all his glory was not clothed like one of these. [28]But if God so clothes the grass of the field, which is alive today and tomorrow is thrown into the oven, how much more will he clothe you—you of little faith! [29]And do not keep striving for what you are to eat and what you are to drink, and do not keep worrying. [30]For it is the nations of the world that strive after all these things, and your Father knows that you need them. [31]Instead, strive for his[e] kingdom, and these things will be given to you as well.

32 "Do not be afraid, little flock, for it is your Father's good pleasure to give

you the kingdom. ³³Sell your possessions, and give alms. Make purses for
yourselves that do not wear out, an un-
failing treasure in heaven, where no
thief comes near and no moth destroys.
³⁴For where your treasure is, there
your heart will be also.

## PSALM 78.32–55

IN spite of all this they still
        sinned;
    they did not believe in his
        wonders.
33  So he made their days vanish
        like a breath,
    and their years in terror.
34  When he killed them, they
        sought for him;
    they repented and sought
        God earnestly.
35  They remembered that God was
        their rock,
    the Most High God their
        redeemer.
36  But they flattered him with their
        mouths;
    they lied to him with their
        tongues.
37  Their heart was not steadfast
        toward him;
    they were not true to his
        covenant.
38  Yet he, being compassionate,
        forgave their iniquity,
    and did not destroy them;
    often he restrained his anger,
        and did not stir up all his
        wrath.
39  He remembered that they were
        but flesh,
    a wind that passes and does
        not come again.
40  How often they rebelled against
        him in the wilderness
    and grieved him in the desert!
41  They tested God again and
        again,
    and provoked the Holy One of
        Israel.
42  They did not keep in mind his
        power,
    or the day when he redeemed
        them from the foe;
43  when he displayed his signs in
        Egypt,
    and his miracles in the fields
        of Zoan.
44  He turned their rivers to blood,
    so that they could not drink of
        their streams.
45  He sent among them swarms of
        flies, which devoured
        them,
    and frogs, which destroyed
        them.
46  He gave their crops to the
        caterpillar,
    and the fruit of their labor to
        the locust.
47  He destroyed their vines with
        hail,
    and their sycamores with
        frost.
48  He gave over their cattle to the
        hail,
    and their flocks to
        thunderbolts.
49  He let loose on them his fierce
        anger,
    wrath, indignation, and
        distress,
    a company of destroying
        angels.
50  He made a path for his anger;
    he did not spare them from
        death,
    but gave their lives over to
        the plague.
51  He struck all the firstborn in
        Egypt,
    the first issue of their
        strength in the tents of
        Ham.
52  Then he led out his people like
        sheep,
    and guided them in the
        wilderness like a flock.
53  He led them in safety, so that
        they were not afraid;

but the sea overwhelmed
   their enemies.
54 And he brought them to his holy
   hill,
   to the mountain that his right
   hand had won.
55 He drove out nations before
   them;
   he apportioned them for a
   possession
   and settled the tribes of Israel
   in their tents.

## PROVERBS 12.21–23

No harm happens to the
   righteous,
   but the wicked are filled
   with trouble.
22 Lying lips are an abomination to
   the LORD,
   but those who act faithfully
   are his delight.
23 One who is clever conceals
   knowledge,
   but the mind of a fool[a]
   broadcasts folly.

# APRIL 8

## DEUTERONOMY 32.28–52

THEY [the Israelites] are a
   nation void of sense;
   there is no understanding in
   them.
29 If they were wise, they would
   understand this;
   they would discern what the
   end would be.
30 How could one have routed a
   thousand,
   and two put a myriad to
   flight,
   unless their Rock had sold
   them,
   the LORD had given them up?
31 Indeed their rock is not like our
   Rock;
   our enemies are fools.[b]
32 Their vine comes from the
   vinestock of Sodom,
   from the vineyards of
   Gomorrah;
   their grapes are grapes of
   poison,
   their clusters are bitter;
33 their wine is the poison of
   serpents,
   the cruel venom of asps.

34 Is not this laid up in store with
   me,
   sealed up in my treasuries?
35 Vengeance is mine, and
   recompense,
   for the time when their foot
   shall slip;
   because the day of their
   calamity is at hand,
   their doom comes swiftly.

36 Indeed the LORD will vindicate
   his people,
   have compassion on his
   servants,
   when he sees that their power
   is gone,

a Heb *the heart of fools*  b Gk: Meaning of Heb uncertain

neither bond nor free
   remaining.
37 Then he will say: Where are
   their gods,
   the rock in which they took
     refuge,
38 who ate the fat of their
     sacrifices,
   and drank the wine of their
     libations?
   Let them rise up and help you,
     let them be your protection!

39 See now that I, even I, am he;
     there is no god besides me.
   I kill and I make alive;
     I wound and I heal;
     and no one can deliver from
      my hand.
40 For I lift up my hand to heaven,
     and swear: As I live forever,
41 when I whet my flashing sword,
     and my hand takes hold on
      judgment;
   I will take vengeance on my
      adversaries,
   and will repay those who hate
     me.
42 I will make my arrows drunk
     with blood,
   and my sword shall devour
     flesh—
   with the blood of the slain and
     the captives,
   from the long-haired enemy.

43 Praise, O heavens, [a] his people,
     worship him, all you gods! [b]
   For he will avenge the blood of
     his children, [c]
   and take vengeance on his
     adversaries;
   he will repay those who hate
     him, [b]
   and cleanse the land for his
     people. [d]

44 Moses came and recited all the words of this song in the hearing of the people, he and Joshua [e] son of Nun. 45When Moses had finished reciting all these words to all Israel, 46he said to them: "Take to heart all the words that I am giving in witness against you today; give them as a command to your children, so that they may diligently observe all the words of this law. 47This is no trifling matter for you, but rather your very life; through it you may live long in the land that you are crossing over the Jordan to possess."

48 On that very day the LORD addressed Moses as follows: 49"Ascend this mountain of the Abarim, Mount Nebo, which is in the land of Moab, across from Jericho, and view the land of Canaan, which I am giving to the Israelites for a possession; 50you shall die there on the mountain that you ascend and shall be gathered to your kin, as your brother Aaron died on Mount Hor and was gathered to his kin; 51because both of you broke faith with me among the Israelites at the waters of Meribath-kadesh in the wilderness of Zin, by failing to maintain my holiness among the Israelites. 52Although you may view the land from a distance, you shall not enter it—the land that I am giving to the Israelites."

## LUKE 12.35–59

"**B**E dressed for action and have your lamps lit; 36be like those who are waiting for their master to return from the wedding banquet, so that they may open the door for him as soon as he comes and knocks. 37Blessed are those slaves whom the master finds alert when he comes; truly I tell you, he will fasten his belt and have them sit down to eat, and he will come and serve them. 38If he comes during the middle of the night, or near dawn, and finds them so, blessed are those slaves.

a Q Ms Gk: MT *nations*  b Q Ms Gk: MT lacks this line  c Q Ms Gk: MT *his servants*  d Q Ms Sam Gk Vg: MT *his land his people*  e Sam Gk Syr Vg: MT *Hoshea*

39 "But know this: if the owner of the house had known at what hour the thief was coming, he[a] would not have let his house be broken into. 40 You also must be ready, for the Son of Man is coming at an unexpected hour."

41 Peter said, "Lord, are you telling this parable for us or for everyone?" 42 And the Lord said, "Who then is the faithful and prudent manager whom his master will put in charge of his slaves, to give them their allowance of food at the proper time? 43 Blessed is that slave whom his master will find at work when he arrives. 44 Truly I tell you, he will put that one in charge of all his possessions. 45 But if that slave says to himself, 'My master is delayed in coming,' and if he begins to beat the other slaves, men and women, and to eat and drink and get drunk, 46 the master of that slave will come on a day when he does not expect him and at an hour that he does not know, and will cut him in pieces,[b] and put him with the unfaithful. 47 That slave who knew what his master wanted, but did not prepare himself or do what was wanted, will receive a severe beating. 48 But the one who did not know and did what deserved a beating will receive a light beating. From everyone to whom much has been given, much will be required; and from the one to whom much has been entrusted, even more will be demanded.

49 "I came to bring fire to the earth, and how I wish it were already kindled! 50 I have a baptism with which to be baptized, and what stress I am under until it is completed! 51 Do you think that I have come to bring peace to the earth? No, I tell you, but rather division! 52 From now on five in one household will be divided, three against two and two against three; 53 they will be divided:

father against son
and son against father,
mother against daughter
and daughter against mother,
mother-in-law against her
daughter-in-law
and daughter-in-law against
mother-in-law."

54 He also said to the crowds, "When you see a cloud rising in the west, you immediately say, 'It is going to rain'; and so it happens. 55 And when you see the south wind blowing, you say, 'There will be scorching heat'; and it happens. 56 You hypocrites! You know how to interpret the appearance of earth and sky, but why do you not know how to interpret the present time?

57 "And why do you not judge for yourselves what is right? 58 Thus, when you go with your accuser before a magistrate, on the way make an effort to settle the case,[c] or you may be dragged before the judge, and the judge hand you over to the officer, and the officer throw you in prison. 59 I tell you, you will never get out until you have paid the very last penny."

## PSALM 78.56–64

Y ET they tested the Most High God,
    and rebelled against him.
    They did not observe his
        decrees,
57  but turned away and were
        faithless like their
        ancestors;
    they twisted like a
        treacherous bow.
58  For they provoked him to anger
        with their high places;
    they moved him to jealousy
        with their idols.
59  When God heard, he was full of
        wrath,
    and he utterly rejected Israel.

---

[a] Other ancient authorities add *would have watched and*   [b] Or *cut him off*   [c] Gk *settle with him*

60 He abandoned his dwelling at
      Shiloh,
    the tent where he dwelt
      among mortals,
61 and delivered his power to
      captivity,
    his glory to the hand of the
      foe.
62 He gave his people to the
      sword,
    and vented his wrath on his
      heritage.
63 Fire devoured their young men,

and their girls had no
      marriage song.
64 Their priests fell by the sword,
    and their widows made no
      lamentation.

## PROVERBS 12.24

THE hand of the diligent will
    rule,
while the lazy will be put to
    forced labor.

# APRIL 9

## DEUTERONOMY 33.1–29

THIS is the blessing with which
Moses, the man of God, blessed
the Israelites before his death.
²He said:
    The LORD came from Sinai,
      and dawned from Seir upon
        us; ᵃ
    he shone forth from Mount
      Paran.
    With him were myriads of holy
      ones; ᵇ
    at his right, a host of his
      own. ᶜ
3 Indeed, O favorite amongᵈ
      peoples,
    all his holy ones were in your
      charge;
    they marched at your heels,
      accepted direction from you.
4 Moses charged us with the law,
    as a possession for the
      assembly of Jacob.
5 There arose a king in Jeshurun,

when the leaders of the
      people assembled—
    the united tribes of Israel.

6 May Reuben live, and not die
      out,
    even though his numbers are
      few.

⁷And this he said of Judah:
    O LORD, give heed to Judah,
      and bring him to his people;
    strengthen his hands for him, ᵉ
      and be a help against his
        adversaries.

⁸And of Levi he said:
    Give to Leviᶠ your Thummim,
      and your Urim to your loyal
        one,
    whom you tested at Massah,
      with whom you contended at
        the waters of Meribah;

ᵃGk Syr Vg Compare Tg: Heb *upon them*   ᵇCn Compare Gk Sam Syr Vg: MT *He came from Ribeboth-kodesh,*   ᶜCn Compare Gk: meaning of Heb uncertain   ᵈOr *O lover of the*   ᵉCn: Heb *with his hands he contended*   ᶠQ Ms Gk: MT lacks *Give to Levi*

9 who said of his father and
    mother,
    "I regard them not";
  he ignored his kin,
    and did not acknowledge his
    children.
  For they observed your word,
    and kept your covenant.
10 They teach Jacob your
    ordinances,
    and Israel your law;
  they place incense before you,
    and whole burnt offerings on
    your altar.
11 Bless, O LORD, his substance,
    and accept the work of his
    hands;
  crush the loins of his
    adversaries,
    of those that hate him, so
    that they do not rise
    again.

12 Of Benjamin he said:
  The beloved of the LORD rests
    in safety—
  the High God[a] surrounds him
    all day long—
    the beloved[b] rests between
    his shoulders.

13 And of Joseph he said:
  Blessed by the LORD be his
    land,
    with the choice gifts of
    heaven above,
  and of the deep that lies
    beneath;
14 with the choice fruits of the sun,
    and the rich yield of the
    months;
15 with the finest produce of the
    ancient mountains,
    and the abundance of the
    everlasting hills;
16 with the choice gifts of the earth
    and its fullness,

  and the favor of the one who
    dwells on Sinai.[c]
  Let these come on the head of
    Joseph,
    on the brow of the prince
    among his brothers.
17 A firstborn[d] bull—majesty is
    his!
  His horns are the horns of a
    wild ox;
  with them he gores the peoples,
    driving them to[e] the ends of
    the earth;
  such are the myriads of
    Ephraim,
    such the thousands of
    Manasseh.

18 And of Zebulun he said:
  Rejoice, Zebulun, in your going
    out;
    and Issachar, in your tents.
19 They call peoples to the
    mountain;
    there they offer the right
    sacrifices;
  for they suck the affluence of
    the seas
    and the hidden treasures of
    the sand.

20 And of Gad he said:
  Blessed be the enlargement of
    Gad!
  Gad lives like a lion;
    he tears at arm and scalp.
21 He chose the best for himself,
    for there a commander's
    allotment was reserved;
  he came at the head of the
    people,
    he executed the justice of the
    LORD,
    and his ordinances for Israel.

22 And of Dan he said:
  Dan is a lion's whelp
    that leaps forth from Bashan.

a Heb *above him*  b Heb *he*  c Cn: Heb *in the bush*  d Q Ms Gk Syr Vg: MT *His firstborn*  e Cn: Heb *the peoples, together*

23 And of Naphtali he said:
  O Naphtali, sated with favor,
    full of the blessing of the
      LORD,
    possess the west and the
      south.

24 And of Asher he said:
  Most blessed of sons be Asher;
    may he be the favorite of his
      brothers,
    and may he dip his foot in oil.
25   Your bars are iron and bronze;
    and as your days, so is your
      strength.

26   There is none like God,
        O Jeshurun,
    who rides through the
        heavens to your help,
    majestic through the skies.
27   He subdues the ancient gods, a
    shatters b the forces of old; c
  he drove out the enemy before
      you,
    and said, "Destroy!"
28   So Israel lives in safety,
    untroubled is Jacob's abode d
  in a land of grain and wine,
    where the heavens drop down
      dew.
29   Happy are you, O Israel! Who is
      like you,
    a people saved by the LORD,
  the shield of your help,
    and the sword of your
      triumph!
  Your enemies shall come
      fawning to you,
    and you shall tread on their
      backs.

## LUKE 13.1–21

**A**T that very time there were
some present who told him
[Jesus] about the Galileans
whose blood Pilate had mingled with
their sacrifices. 2He asked them, "Do
you think that because these Galileans
suffered in this way they were worse
sinners than all other Galileans? 3No, I
tell you; but unless you repent, you will
all perish as they did. 4Or those eighteen who were killed when the tower of
Siloam fell on them—do you think that
they were worse offenders than all the
others living in Jerusalem? 5No, I tell
you; but unless you repent, you will all
perish just as they did."

6  Then he told this parable: "A man
had a fig tree planted in his vineyard;
and he came looking for fruit on it and
found none. 7So he said to the gardener, 'See here! For three years I
have come looking for fruit on this fig
tree, and still I find none. Cut it down!
Why should it be wasting the soil?' 8He
replied, 'Sir, let it alone for one more
year, until I dig around it and put manure on it. 9If it bears fruit next year,
well and good; but if not, you can cut it
down.' "

10  Now he was teaching in one of
the synagogues on the sabbath. 11And
just then there appeared a woman with
a spirit that had crippled her for eighteen years. She was bent over and was
quite unable to stand up straight.
12When Jesus saw her, he called her
over and said, "Woman, you are set
free from your ailment." 13When he laid
his hands on her, immediately she
stood up straight and began praising
God. 14But the leader of the synagogue, indignant because Jesus had
cured on the sabbath, kept saying to
the crowd, "There are six days on
which work ought to be done; come on
those days and be cured, and not on the
sabbath day." 15But the Lord answered
him and said, "You hypocrites! Does
not each of you on the sabbath untie his
ox or his donkey from the manger, and
lead it away to give it water? 16And
ought not this woman, a daughter of

a Or *The eternal God is a dwelling place*   b Cn: Heb *from underneath*   c Or *the everlasting arms*
d Or *fountain*

Abraham whom Satan bound for eighteen long years, be set free from this bondage on the sabbath day?" ¹⁷When he said this, all his opponents were put to shame; and the entire crowd was rejoicing at all the wonderful things that he was doing.

18  He said therefore, "What is the kingdom of God like? And to what should I compare it? ¹⁹It is like a mustard seed that someone took and sowed in the garden; it grew and became a tree, and the birds of the air made nests in its branches."

20  And again he said, "To what should I compare the kingdom of God? ²¹It is like yeast that a woman took and mixed in with ᵃ three measures of flour until all of it was leavened."

## PSALM 78.65–72

Then the Lord awoke as from
　　　sleep,
　like a warrior shouting
　　　because of wine.
⁶⁶ He put his adversaries to rout;
　　he put them to everlasting
　　　disgrace.

⁶⁷ He rejected the tent of Joseph,
　　he did not choose the tribe of
　　　Ephraim;
⁶⁸ but he chose the tribe of Judah,
　　Mount Zion, which he loves.
⁶⁹ He built his sanctuary like the
　　　high heavens,
　　like the earth, which he has
　　　founded forever.
⁷⁰ He chose his servant David,
　　and took him from the
　　　sheepfolds;
⁷¹ from tending the nursing ewes
　　　he brought him
　to be the shepherd of his
　　　people Jacob,
　of Israel, his inheritance.
⁷² With upright heart he tended
　　　them,
　　and guided them with skillful
　　　hand.

## PROVERBS 12.25

Anxiety weighs down the
　　　human heart,
but a good word cheers it
　up.

# APRIL 10

## DEUTERONOMY 34.1— JOSHUA 2.24

Then Moses went up from the plains of Moab to Mount Nebo, to the top of Pisgah, which is opposite Jericho, and the Lord showed him the whole land: Gilead as far as Dan, ²all Naphtali, the land of Ephraim and Manasseh, all the land of Judah as far as the Western Sea, ³the Negeb, and the Plain—that is, the valley of Jericho, the city of palm trees—as far as Zoar. ⁴The Lord said to him, "This is the land of which I swore to Abraham, to Isaac, and to Jacob, saying, 'I will give it to your descendants'; I have let you see it with your eyes, but you shall not cross over there." ⁵Then Moses, the servant of the Lord, died there in the land of Moab, at the Lord's command. ⁶He was buried in a valley in the land of Moab, opposite Beth-peor, but

ᵃGk *hid in*

no one knows his burial place to this day. ⁷Moses was one hundred twenty years old when he died; his sight was unimpaired and his vigor had not abated. ⁸The Israelites wept for Moses in the plains of Moab thirty days; then the period of mourning for Moses was ended.

9 Joshua son of Nun was full of the spirit of wisdom, because Moses had laid his hands on him; and the Israelites obeyed him, doing as the Lord had commanded Moses.

10 Never since has there arisen a prophet in Israel like Moses, whom the Lord knew face to face. ¹¹He was unequaled for all the signs and wonders that the Lord sent him to perform in the land of Egypt, against Pharaoh and all his servants and his entire land, ¹²and for all the mighty deeds and all the terrifying displays of power that Moses performed in the sight of all Israel.

1.1 After the death of Moses the servant of the Lord, the Lord spoke to Joshua son of Nun, Moses' assistant, saying, ²"My servant Moses is dead. Now proceed to cross the Jordan, you and all this people, into the land that I am giving to them, to the Israelites. ³Every place that the sole of your foot will tread upon I have given to you, as I promised to Moses. ⁴From the wilderness and the Lebanon as far as the great river, the river Euphrates, all the land of the Hittites, to the Great Sea in the west shall be your territory. ⁵No one shall be able to stand against you all the days of your life. As I was with Moses, so I will be with you; I will not fail you or forsake you. ⁶Be strong and courageous; for you shall put this people in possession of the land that I swore to their ancestors to give them. ⁷Only be strong and very courageous, being careful to act in accordance with all the law that my servant Moses commanded you; do not turn from it to the right hand or to the left, so that you

may be successful wherever you go. ⁸This book of the law shall not depart out of your mouth; you shall meditate on it day and night, so that you may be careful to act in accordance with all that is written in it. For then you shall make your way prosperous, and then you shall be successful. ⁹I hereby command you: Be strong and courageous; do not be frightened or dismayed, for the Lord your God is with you wherever you go."

10 Then Joshua commanded the officers of the people, ¹¹"Pass through the camp, and command the people: 'Prepare your provisions; for in three days you are to cross over the Jordan, to go in to take possession of the land that the Lord your God gives you to possess.'"

12 To the Reubenites, the Gadites, and the half-tribe of Manasseh Joshua said, ¹³"Remember the word that Moses the servant of the Lord commanded you, saying, 'The Lord your God is providing you a place of rest, and will give you this land.' ¹⁴Your wives, your little ones, and your livestock shall remain in the land that Moses gave you beyond the Jordan. But all the warriors among you shall cross over armed before your kindred and shall help them, ¹⁵until the Lord gives rest to your kindred as well as to you, and they too take possession of the land that the Lord your God is giving them. Then you shall return to your own land and take possession of it, the land that Moses the servant of the Lord gave you beyond the Jordan to the east."

16 They answered Joshua: "All that you have commanded us we will do, and wherever you send us we will go. ¹⁷Just as we obeyed Moses in all things, so we will obey you. Only may the Lord your God be with you, as he was with Moses! ¹⁸Whoever rebels against your orders and disobeys your words, whatever you command, shall

be put to death. Only be strong and courageous."

2.1 THEN Joshua son of Nun sent two men secretly from Shittim as spies, saying, "Go, view the land, especially Jericho." So they went, and entered the house of a prostitute whose name was Rahab, and spent the night there. 2The king of Jericho was told, "Some Israelites have come here tonight to search out the land." 3Then the king of Jericho sent orders to Rahab, "Bring out the men who have come to you, who entered your house, for they have come only to search out the whole land." 4But the woman took the two men and hid them. Then she said, "True, the men came to me, but I did not know where they came from. 5And when it was time to close the gate at dark, the men went out. Where the men went I do not know. Pursue them quickly, for you can overtake them." 6She had, however, brought them up to the roof and hidden them with the stalks of flax that she had laid out on the roof. 7So the men pursued them on the way to the Jordan as far as the fords. As soon as the pursuers had gone out, the gate was shut.

8  Before they went to sleep, she came up to them on the roof 9and said to the men: "I know that the LORD has given you the land, and that dread of you has fallen on us, and that all the inhabitants of the land melt in fear before you. 10For we have heard how the LORD dried up the water of the Red Sea[a] before you when you came out of Egypt, and what you did to the two kings of the Amorites that were beyond the Jordan, to Sihon and Og, whom you utterly destroyed. 11As soon as we heard it, our hearts melted, and there was no courage left in any of us because of you. The LORD your God is indeed God in heaven above and on earth be-

low. 12Now then, since I have dealt kindly with you, swear to me by the LORD that you in turn will deal kindly with my family. Give me a sign of good faith 13that you will spare my father and mother, my brothers and sisters, and all who belong to them, and deliver our lives from death." 14The men said to her, "Our life for yours! If you do not tell this business of ours, then we will deal kindly and faithfully with you when the LORD gives us the land."

15  Then she let them down by a rope through the window, for her house was on the outer side of the city wall and she resided within the wall itself. 16She said to them, "Go toward the hill country, so that the pursuers may not come upon you. Hide yourselves there three days, until the pursuers have returned; then afterward you may go your way." 17The men said to her, "We will be released from this oath that you have made us swear to you 18if we invade the land and you do not tie this crimson cord in the window through which you let us down, and you do not gather into your house your father and mother, your brothers, and all your family. 19If any of you go out of the doors of your house into the street, they shall be responsible for their own death, and we shall be innocent; but if a hand is laid upon any who are with you in the house, we shall bear the responsibility for their death. 20But if you tell this business of ours, then we shall be released from this oath that you made us swear to you." 21She said, "According to your words, so be it." She sent them away and they departed. Then she tied the crimson cord in the window.

22  They departed and went into the hill country and stayed there three days, until the pursuers returned. The pursuers had searched all along the way and found nothing. 23Then the two men

a Or *Sea of Reeds*

came down again from the hill country. They crossed over, came to Joshua son of Nun, and told him all that had happened to them. [24]They said to Joshua, "Truly the LORD has given all the land into our hands; moreover all the inhabitants of the land melt in fear before us."

## LUKE 13.22—14.6

JESUS[a] went through one town and village after another, teaching as he made his way to Jerusalem. [23]Someone asked him, "Lord, will only a few be saved?" He said to them, [24]"Strive to enter through the narrow door; for many, I tell you, will try to enter and will not be able. [25]When once the owner of the house has got up and shut the door, and you begin to stand outside and to knock at the door, saying, 'Lord, open to us,' then in reply he will say to you, 'I do not know where you come from.' [26]Then you will begin to say, 'We ate and drank with you, and you taught in our streets.' [27]But he will say, 'I do not know where you come from; go away from me, all you evildoers!' [28]There will be weeping and gnashing of teeth when you see Abraham and Isaac and Jacob and all the prophets in the kingdom of God, and you yourselves thrown out. [29]Then people will come from east and west, from north and south, and will eat in the kingdom of God. [30]Indeed, some are last who will be first, and some are first who will be last."

31 At that very hour some Pharisees came and said to him, "Get away from here, for Herod wants to kill you." [32]He said to them, "Go and tell that fox for me,[b] 'Listen, I am casting out demons and performing cures today and tomorrow, and on the third day I finish my work. [33]Yet today, tomorrow, and the next day I must be on my way, because it is impossible for a prophet to be killed outside of Jerusalem.' [34]Jerusalem, Jerusalem, the city that kills the prophets and stones those who are sent to it! How often have I desired to gather your children together as a hen gathers her brood under her wings, and you were not willing! [35]See, your house is left to you. And I tell you, you will not see me until the time comes when[c] you say, 'Blessed is the one who comes in the name of the Lord.' "

[14.1] ON one occasion when Jesus[d] was going to the house of a leader of the Pharisees to eat a meal on the sabbath, they were watching him closely. [2]Just then, in front of him, there was a man who had dropsy. [3]And Jesus asked the lawyers and Pharisees, "Is it lawful to cure people on the sabbath, or not?" [4]But they were silent. So Jesus[d] took him and healed him, and sent him away. [5]Then he said to them, "If one of you has a child[e] or an ox that has fallen into a well, will you not immediately pull it out on a sabbath day?" [6]And they could not reply to this.

## PSALM 79.1–13

*A Psalm of Asaph.*

O GOD, the nations have come
  into your inheritance;
 they have defiled your holy
  temple;
 they have laid Jerusalem in
  ruins.
2 They have given the bodies of
  your servants
  to the birds of the air for
   food,
  the flesh of your faithful to
   the wild animals of the
   earth.
3 They have poured out their
   blood like water
  all around Jerusalem,

a Gk *he* bGk lacks *for me* cOther ancient authorities lack *the time comes when* dGk *he* eOther ancient authorities read *a donkey*

and there was no one to bury
  them.
4 We have become a taunt to our
    neighbors,
  mocked and derided by those
    around us.

5 How long, O Lord? Will you be
    angry forever?
  Will your jealous wrath burn
    like fire?
6 Pour out your anger on the
    nations
  that do not know you,
and on the kingdoms
  that do not call on your name.
7 For they have devoured Jacob
    and laid waste his habitation.

8 Do not remember against us the
    iniquities of our
    ancestors;
  let your compassion come
    speedily to meet us,
  for we are brought very low.
9 Help us, O God of our salvation,
  for the glory of your name;
  deliver us, and forgive our sins,
    for your name's sake.
10 Why should the nations say,

"Where is their God?"
Let the avenging of the
    outpoured blood of your
    servants
  be known among the nations
    before our eyes.

11 Let the groans of the prisoners
    come before you;
  according to your great power
    preserve those doomed
    to die.
12 Return sevenfold into the bosom
    of our neighbors
  the taunts with which they
    taunted you, O Lord!
13 Then we your people, the flock
    of your pasture,
  will give thanks to you
    forever;
  from generation to generation
    we will recount your
    praise.

## PROVERBS 12.26

THE righteous gives good advice
to friends, [a]
but the way of the wicked
leads astray.

# APRIL 11

## JOSHUA 3.1—4.24

EARLY in the morning Joshua rose
and set out from Shittim with all
the Israelites, and they came to
the Jordan. They camped there before
crossing over. 2At the end of three
days the officers went through the
camp 3and commanded the people,

"When you see the ark of the covenant
of the Lord your God being carried by
the levitical priests, then you shall set
out from your place. Follow it, 4so that
you may know the way you should go,
for you have not passed this way before. Yet there shall be a space between you and it, a distance of about

a Syr: Meaning of Heb uncertain

two thousand cubits; do not come any nearer to it." [5]Then Joshua said to the people, "Sanctify yourselves; for tomorrow the LORD will do wonders among you." [6]To the priests Joshua said, "Take up the ark of the covenant, and pass on in front of the people." So they took up the ark of the covenant and went in front of the people.

7 The LORD said to Joshua, "This day I will begin to exalt you in the sight of all Israel, so that they may know that I will be with you as I was with Moses. [8]You are the one who shall command the priests who bear the ark of the covenant, 'When you come to the edge of the waters of the Jordan, you shall stand still in the Jordan.'" [9]Joshua then said to the Israelites, "Draw near and hear the words of the LORD your God." [10]Joshua said, "By this you shall know that among you is the living God who without fail will drive out from before you the Canaanites, Hittites, Hivites, Perizzites, Girgashites, Amorites, and Jebusites: [11]the ark of the covenant of the Lord of all the earth is going to pass before you into the Jordan. [12]So now select twelve men from the tribes of Israel, one from each tribe. [13]When the soles of the feet of the priests who bear the ark of the LORD, the Lord of all the earth, rest in the waters of the Jordan, the waters of the Jordan flowing from above shall be cut off; they shall stand in a single heap."

14 When the people set out from their tents to cross over the Jordan, the priests bearing the ark of the covenant were in front of the people. [15]Now the Jordan overflows all its banks throughout the time of harvest. So when those who bore the ark had come to the Jordan, and the feet of the priests bearing the ark were dipped in the edge of the water, [16]the waters flowing from above stood still, rising up in a single heap far off at Adam, the city that is beside Zar-

ethan, while those flowing toward the sea of the Arabah, the Dead Sea, [a] were wholly cut off. Then the people crossed over opposite Jericho. [17]While all Israel were crossing over on dry ground, the priests who bore the ark of the covenant of the LORD stood on dry ground in the middle of the Jordan, until the entire nation finished crossing over the Jordan.

4.1 WHEN the entire nation had finished crossing over the Jordan, the LORD said to Joshua: [2]"Select twelve men from the people, one from each tribe, [3]and command them, 'Take twelve stones from here out of the middle of the Jordan, from the place where the priests' feet stood, carry them over with you, and lay them down in the place where you camp tonight.'" [4]Then Joshua summoned the twelve men from the Israelites, whom he had appointed, one from each tribe. [5]Joshua said to them, "Pass on before the ark of the LORD your God into the middle of the Jordan, and each of you take up a stone on his shoulder, one for each of the tribes of the Israelites, [6]so that this may be a sign among you. When your children ask in time to come, 'What do those stones mean to you?' [7]then you shall tell them that the waters of the Jordan were cut off in front of the ark of the covenant of the LORD. When it crossed over the Jordan, the waters of the Jordan were cut off. So these stones shall be to the Israelites a memorial forever."

8 The Israelites did as Joshua commanded. They took up twelve stones out of the middle of the Jordan, according to the number of the tribes of the Israelites, as the LORD told Joshua, carried them over with them to the place where they camped, and laid them down there. [9](Joshua set up twelve stones in the middle of the Jordan, in

the place where the feet of the priests bearing the ark of the covenant had stood; and they are there to this day.)

10  The priests who bore the ark remained standing in the middle of the Jordan, until everything was finished that the LORD commanded Joshua to tell the people, according to all that Moses had commanded Joshua. The people crossed over in haste. [11]As soon as all the people had finished crossing over, the ark of the LORD, and the priests, crossed over in front of the people. [12]The Reubenites, the Gadites, and the half-tribe of Manasseh crossed over armed before the Israelites, as Moses had ordered them. [13]About forty thousand armed for war crossed over before the LORD to the plains of Jericho for battle.

14  On that day the LORD exalted Joshua in the sight of all Israel; and they stood in awe of him, as they had stood in awe of Moses, all the days of his life.

15  The LORD said to Joshua, [16]"Command the priests who bear the ark of the covenant,[a] to come up out of the Jordan." [17]Joshua therefore commanded the priests, "Come up out of the Jordan." [18]When the priests bearing the ark of the covenant of the LORD came up from the middle of the Jordan, and the soles of the priests' feet touched dry ground, the waters of the Jordan returned to their place and overflowed all its banks, as before.

19  The people came up out of the Jordan on the tenth day of the first month, and they camped in Gilgal on the east border of Jericho. [20]Those twelve stones, which they had taken out of the Jordan, Joshua set up in Gilgal, [21]saying to the Israelites, "When your children ask their parents in time to come, 'What do these stones mean?' [22]then you shall let your children know, 'Israel crossed over the Jordan here on dry ground.' [23]For the LORD your God dried up the waters of the Jordan for you until you crossed over, as the LORD your God did to the Red Sea,[b] which he dried up for us until we crossed over, [24]so that all the peoples of the earth may know that the hand of the LORD is mighty, and so that you may fear the LORD your God forever."

# LUKE 14.7–35

WHEN he [Jesus] noticed how the guests chose the places of honor, he told them a parable. [8]"When you are invited by someone to a wedding banquet, do not sit down at the place of honor, in case someone more distinguished than you has been invited by your host; [9]and the host who invited both of you may come and say to you, 'Give this person your place,' and then in disgrace you would start to take the lowest place. [10]But when you are invited, go and sit down at the lowest place, so that when your host comes, he may say to you, 'Friend, move up higher'; then you will be honored in the presence of all who sit at the table with you. [11]For all who exalt themselves will be humbled, and those who humble themselves will be exalted."

12  He said also to the one who had invited him, "When you give a luncheon or a dinner, do not invite your friends or your brothers or your relatives or rich neighbors, in case they may invite you in return, and you would be repaid. [13]But when you give a banquet, invite the poor, the crippled, the lame, and the blind. [14]And you will be blessed, because they cannot repay you, for you will be repaid at the resurrection of the righteous."

15  One of the dinner guests, on hearing this, said to him, "Blessed is anyone who will eat bread in the kingdom of God!" [16]Then Jesus[c] said to

---

[a]Or *treaty*, or *testimony*; Heb *eduth*   [b]Or *Sea of Reeds*   [c]Gk *he*

him, "Someone gave a great dinner and invited many. [17]At the time for the dinner he sent his slave to say to those who had been invited, 'Come; for everything is ready now.' [18]But they all alike began to make excuses. The first said to him, 'I have bought a piece of land, and I must go out and see it; please accept my regrets.' [19]Another said, 'I have bought five yoke of oxen, and I am going to try them out; please accept my regrets.' [20]Another said, 'I have just been married, and therefore I cannot come.' [21]So the slave returned and reported this to his master. Then the owner of the house became angry and said to his slave, 'Go out at once into the streets and lanes of the town and bring in the poor, the crippled, the blind, and the lame.' [22]And the slave said, 'Sir, what you ordered has been done, and there is still room.' [23]Then the master said to the slave, 'Go out into the roads and lanes, and compel people to come in, so that my house may be filled. [24]For I tell you, [a] none of those who were invited will taste my dinner.' "

25 Now large crowds were traveling with him; and he turned and said to them, [26]"Whoever comes to me and does not hate father and mother, wife and children, brothers and sisters, yes, and even life itself, cannot be my disciple. [27]Whoever does not carry the cross and follow me cannot be my disciple. [28]For which of you, intending to build a tower, does not first sit down and estimate the cost, to see whether he has enough to complete it? [29]Otherwise, when he has laid a foundation and is not able to finish, all who see it will begin to ridicule him, [30]saying, 'This fellow began to build and was not able to finish.' [31]Or what king, going out to wage war against another king, will not sit down first and consider whether he is able with ten thousand to oppose the one who comes against him with twenty thousand? [32]If he cannot, then, while the other is still far away, he sends a delegation and asks for the terms of peace. [33]So therefore, none of you can become my disciple if you do not give up all your possessions.

34 "Salt is good; but if salt has lost its taste, how can its saltiness be restored? [b] [35]It is fit neither for the soil nor for the manure pile; they throw it away. Let anyone with ears to hear listen!"

## PSALM 80. 1–19

*To the leader: on Lilies, a Covenant. Of Asaph. A Psalm.*

G IVE ear, O Shepherd of Israel,
    you who lead Joseph like a
       flock!
  You who are enthroned upon
       the cherubim, shine forth
2     before Ephraim and Benjamin
       and Manasseh.
  Stir up your might,
     and come to save us!

3  Restore us, O God;
     let your face shine, that we
       may be saved.

4  O LORD God of hosts,
     how long will you be angry
       with your people's
       prayers?
5  You have fed them with the
       bread of tears,
    and given them tears to drink
       in full measure.
6  You make us the scorn [c] of our
       neighbors;
    our enemies laugh among
       themselves.

7  Restore us, O God of hosts;
     let your face shine, that we
       may be saved.

a The Greek word for *you* here is plural  b Or *how can it be used for seasoning?*  c Syr: Heb *strife*

8  You brought a vine out of
    Egypt;
  you drove out the nations and
    planted it.
9  You cleared the ground for it;
  it took deep root and filled
    the land.
10  The mountains were covered
    with its shade,
  the mighty cedars with its
    branches;
11  it sent out its branches to the
    sea,
  and its shoots to the River.
12  Why then have you broken
    down its walls,
  so that all who pass along the
    way pluck its fruit?
13  The boar from the forest
    ravages it,
  and all that move in the field
    feed on it.

14  Turn again, O God of hosts;
  look down from heaven, and
    see;
  have regard for this vine,
15    the stock that your right hand
    planted. a

16  They have burned it with fire,
    they have cut it down; b
  may they perish at the rebuke
    of your countenance.
17  But let your hand be upon the
    one at your right hand,
  the one whom you made
    strong for yourself.
18  Then we will never turn back
    from you;
  give us life, and we will call
    on your name.

19  Restore us, O LORD God of
    hosts;
  let your face shine, that we
    may be saved.

## PROVERBS 12.27–28

THE lazy do not roast c their
    game,
  but the diligent obtain
    precious wealth. c
28  In the path of righteousness
    there is life,
  in walking its path there is no
    death.

# APRIL 12

## JOSHUA 5.1—7.15

WHEN all the kings of the Amorites beyond the Jordan to the west, and all the kings of the Canaanites by the sea, heard that the LORD had dried up the waters of the Jordan for the Israelites until they had crossed over, their hearts melted, and there was no longer any spirit in them, because of the Israelites.

2 At that time the LORD said to Joshua, "Make flint knives and circumcise the Israelites a second time." 3So Joshua made flint knives, and circumcised the Israelites at Gibeath-haaraloth. d 4This is the reason why Joshua circumcised them: all the males

aHeb adds from verse 17 *and upon the one whom you made strong for yourself*  bCn: Heb *it is cut down*  cMeaning of Heb uncertain  dThat is *the Hill of the Foreskins*

of the people who came out of Egypt, all the warriors, had died during the journey through the wilderness after they had come out of Egypt. 5Although all the people who came out had been circumcised, yet all the people born on the journey through the wilderness after they had come out of Egypt had not been circumcised. 6For the Israelites traveled forty years in the wilderness, until all the nation, the warriors who came out of Egypt, perished, not having listened to the voice of the LORD. To them the LORD swore that he would not let them see the land that he had sworn to their ancestors to give us, a land flowing with milk and honey. 7So it was their children, whom he raised up in their place, that Joshua circumcised; for they were uncircumcised, because they had not been circumcised on the way.

8 When the circumcising of all the nation was done, they remained in their places in the camp until they were healed. 9The LORD said to Joshua, "Today I have rolled away from you the disgrace of Egypt." And so that place is called Gilgala to this day.

10 While the Israelites were camped in Gilgal they kept the passover in the evening on the fourteenth day of the month in the plains of Jericho. 11On the day after the passover, on that very day, they ate the produce of the land, unleavened cakes and parched grain. 12The manna ceased on the day they ate the produce of the land, and the Israelites no longer had manna; they ate the crops of the land of Canaan that year.

13 Once when Joshua was by Jericho, he looked up and saw a man standing before him with a drawn sword in his hand. Joshua went to him and said to him, "Are you one of us, or one of our adversaries?" 14He replied, "Neither; but as commander of the army of the LORD I have now come." And Joshua fell on his face to the earth and worshiped, and he said to him, "What do you command your servant, my lord?" 15The commander of the army of the LORD said to Joshua, "Remove the sandals from your feet, for the place where you stand is holy." And Joshua did so.

6.1 NOW Jericho was shut up inside and out because of the Israelites; no one came out and no one went in. 2The LORD said to Joshua, "See, I have handed Jericho over to you, along with its king and soldiers. 3You shall march around the city, all the warriors circling the city once. Thus you shall do for six days, 4with seven priests bearing seven trumpets of rams' horns before the ark. On the seventh day you shall march around the city seven times, the priests blowing the trumpets. 5When they make a long blast with the ram's horn, as soon as you hear the sound of the trumpet, then all the people shall shout with a great shout; and the wall of the city will fall down flat, and all the people shall charge straight ahead." 6So Joshua son of Nun summoned the priests and said to them, "Take up the ark of the covenant, and have seven priests carry seven trumpets of rams' horns in front of the ark of the LORD." 7To the people he said, "Go forward and march around the city; have the armed men pass on before the ark of the LORD."

8 As Joshua had commanded the people, the seven priests carrying the seven trumpets of rams' horns before the LORD went forward, blowing the trumpets, with the ark of the covenant of the LORD following them. 9And the armed men went before the priests who blew the trumpets; the rear guard came after the ark, while the trumpets blew continually. 10To the people

aRelated to Heb *galal* to roll

Joshua gave this command: "You shall not shout or let your voice be heard, nor shall you utter a word, until the day I tell you to shout. Then you shall shout." ¹¹So the ark of the LORD went around the city, circling it once; and they came into the camp, and spent the night in the camp.

12 Then Joshua rose early in the morning, and the priests took up the ark of the LORD. ¹³The seven priests carrying the seven trumpets of rams' horns before the ark of the LORD passed on, blowing the trumpets continually. The armed men went before them, and the rear guard came after the ark of the LORD, while the trumpets blew continually. ¹⁴On the second day they marched around the city once and then returned to the camp. They did this for six days.

15 On the seventh day they rose early, at dawn, and marched around the city in the same manner seven times. It was only on that day that they marched around the city seven times. ¹⁶And at the seventh time, when the priests had blown the trumpets, Joshua said to the people, "Shout! For the LORD has given you the city. ¹⁷The city and all that is in it shall be devoted to the LORD for destruction. Only Rahab the prostitute and all who are with her in her house shall live because she hid the messengers we sent. ¹⁸As for you, keep away from the things devoted to destruction, so as not to covetᵃ and take any of the devoted things and make the camp of Israel an object for destruction, bringing trouble upon it. ¹⁹But all silver and gold, and vessels of bronze and iron, are sacred to the LORD; they shall go into the treasury of the LORD." ²⁰So the people shouted, and the trumpets were blown. As soon as the people heard the sound of the trumpets, they raised a great shout, and the wall fell down flat; so the people charged straight ahead into the city and captured it. ²¹Then they devoted to destruction by the edge of the sword all in the city, both men and women, young and old, oxen, sheep, and donkeys.

22 Joshua said to the two men who had spied out the land, "Go into the prostitute's house, and bring the woman out of it and all who belong to her, as you swore to her." ²³So the young men who had been spies went in and brought Rahab out, along with her father, her mother, her brothers, and all who belonged to her—they brought all her kindred out—and set them outside the camp of Israel. ²⁴They burned down the city, and everything in it; only the silver and gold, and the vessels of bronze and iron, they put into the treasury of the house of the LORD. ²⁵But Rahab the prostitute, with her family and all who belonged to her, Joshua spared. Her familyᵇ has lived in Israel ever since. For she hid the messengers whom Joshua sent to spy out Jericho.

26 Joshua then pronounced this oath, saying,

"Cursed before the LORD be
    anyone who tries
  to build this city—this
      Jericho!
At the cost of his firstborn he
    shall lay its foundation,
  and at the cost of his
    youngest he shall set up
      its gates!"

27 So the LORD was with Joshua; and his fame was in all the land.

**7.1** BUT the Israelites broke faith in regard to the devoted things: Achan son of Carmi son of Zabdi son of Zerah, of the tribe of Judah, took some of the devoted things; and the anger of the LORD burned against the Israelites.

2 Joshua sent men from Jericho to Ai, which is near Beth-aven, east of Bethel, and said to them, "Go up and spy out the land." And the men went up

---

ᵃGk: Heb *devote to destruction* Compare 7.21   ᵇHeb *She*

and spied out Ai. [3]Then they returned to Joshua and said to him, "Not all the people need go up; about two or three thousand men should go up and attack Ai. Since they are so few, do not make the whole people toil up there." [4]So about three thousand of the people went up there; and they fled before the men of Ai. [5]The men of Ai killed about thirty-six of them, chasing them from outside the gate as far as Shebarim and killing them on the slope. The hearts of the people melted and turned to water.

6  Then Joshua tore his clothes, and fell to the ground on his face before the ark of the LORD until the evening, he and the elders of Israel; and they put dust on their heads. [7]Joshua said, "Ah, Lord GOD! Why have you brought this people across the Jordan at all, to hand us over to the Amorites so as to destroy us? Would that we had been content to settle beyond the Jordan! [8]O Lord, what can I say, now that Israel has turned their backs to their enemies! [9]The Canaanites and all the inhabitants of the land will hear of it, and surround us, and cut off our name from the earth. Then what will you do for your great name?"

10  The LORD said to Joshua, "Stand up! Why have you fallen upon your face? [11]Israel has sinned; they have transgressed my covenant that I imposed on them. They have taken some of the devoted things; they have stolen, they have acted deceitfully, and they have put them among their own belongings. [12]Therefore the Israelites are unable to stand before their enemies; they turn their backs to their enemies, because they have become a thing devoted for destruction themselves. I will be with you no more, unless you destroy the devoted things from among you. [13]Proceed to sanctify the people, and say, 'Sanctify yourselves for tomorrow; for thus says the LORD, the God of Israel, "There are devoted things among you, O Israel; you will be unable to stand before your enemies until you take away the devoted things from among you." [14]In the morning therefore you shall come forward tribe by tribe. The tribe that the LORD takes shall come near by clans, the clan that the LORD takes shall come near by households, and the household that the LORD takes shall come near one by one. [15]And the one who is taken as having the devoted things shall be burned with fire, together with all that he has, for having transgressed the covenant of the LORD, and for having done an outrageous thing in Israel.' "

## LUKE 15. 1–32

Now all the tax collectors and sinners were coming near to listen to him [Jesus]. [2]And the Pharisees and the scribes were grumbling and saying, "This fellow welcomes sinners and eats with them."

3  So he told them this parable: [4]"Which one of you, having a hundred sheep and losing one of them, does not leave the ninety-nine in the wilderness and go after the one that is lost until he finds it? [5]When he has found it, he lays it on his shoulders and rejoices. [6]And when he comes home, he calls together his friends and neighbors, saying to them, 'Rejoice with me, for I have found my sheep that was lost.' [7]Just so, I tell you, there will be more joy in heaven over one sinner who repents than over ninety-nine righteous persons who need no repentance.

8  "Or what woman having ten silver coins, [a] if she loses one of them, does not light a lamp, sweep the house, and search carefully until she finds it? [9]When she has found it, she calls together her friends and neighbors, saying, 'Rejoice with me, for I have found

aGk *drachmas*, each worth about a day's wage for a laborer

the coin that I had lost.' ¹⁰Just so, I tell you, there is joy in the presence of the angels of God over one sinner who repents."

11   Then Jesus[a] said, "There was a man who had two sons. ¹²The younger of them said to his father, 'Father, give me the share of the property that will belong to me.' So he divided his property between them. ¹³A few days later the younger son gathered all he had and traveled to a distant country, and there he squandered his property in dissolute living. ¹⁴When he had spent everything, a severe famine took place throughout that country, and he began to be in need. ¹⁵So he went and hired himself out to one of the citizens of that country, who sent him to his fields to feed the pigs. ¹⁶He would gladly have filled himself with[b] the pods that the pigs were eating; and no one gave him anything. ¹⁷But when he came to himself he said, 'How many of my father's hired hands have bread enough and to spare, but here I am dying of hunger! ¹⁸I will get up and go to my father, and I will say to him, "Father, I have sinned against heaven and before you; ¹⁹I am no longer worthy to be called your son; treat me like one of your hired hands."' ²⁰So he set off and went to his father. But while he was still far off, his father saw him and was filled with compassion; he ran and put his arms around him and kissed him. ²¹Then the son said to him, 'Father, I have sinned against heaven and before you; I am no longer worthy to be called your son.'[c] ²²But the father said to his slaves, 'Quickly, bring out a robe—the best one—and put it on him; put a ring on his finger and sandals on his feet. ²³And get the fatted calf and kill it, and let us eat and celebrate; ²⁴for this son of mine was dead and is alive again; he was lost and is found!' And they began to celebrate.

25   "Now his elder son was in the field; and when he came and approached the house, he heard music and dancing. ²⁶He called one of the slaves and asked what was going on. ²⁷He replied, 'Your brother has come, and your father has killed the fatted calf, because he has got him back safe and sound.' ²⁸Then he became angry and refused to go in. His father came out and began to plead with him. ²⁹But he answered his father, 'Listen! For all these years I have been working like a slave for you, and I have never disobeyed your command; yet you have never given me even a young goat so that I might celebrate with my friends. ³⁰But when this son of yours came back, who has devoured your property with prostitutes, you killed the fatted calf for him!' ³¹Then the father[a] said to him, 'Son, you are always with me, and all that is mine is yours. ³²But we had to celebrate and rejoice, because this brother of yours was dead and has come to life; he was lost and has been found.'"

## PSALM 81.1–16

*To the leader: according to The Gittith.*
*Of Asaph.*

SING aloud to God our strength;
       shout for joy to the God of
              Jacob.
2   Raise a song, sound the
              tambourine,
       the sweet lyre with the harp.
3   Blow the trumpet at the new
              moon,
       at the full moon, on our
              festal day.
4   For it is a statute for Israel,
       an ordinance of the God of
              Jacob.
5   He made it a decree in Joseph,
       when he went out over[d] the
              land of Egypt.

[a]Gk *he*   [b]Other ancient authorities read *filled his stomach with*   [c]Other ancient authorities add *treat me as one of your hired servants*   [d]Or *against*

I hear a voice I had not known:
6   "I relieved your[a] shoulder of
      the burden;
    your[a] hands were freed from
      the basket.
7   In distress you called, and I
      rescued you;
    I answered you in the secret
      place of thunder;
    I tested you at the waters of
      Meribah.      *Selah*
8   Hear, O my people, while I
      admonish you;
    O Israel, if you would but
      listen to me!
9   There shall be no strange god
      among you;
    you shall not bow down to a
      foreign god.
10  I am the LORD your God,
    who brought you up out of
      the land of Egypt.
    Open your mouth wide and I
      will fill it.

11   "But my people did not listen to
    my voice;

    Israel would not submit to
      me.
12  So I gave them over to their
      stubborn hearts,
    to follow their own counsels.
13  O that my people would listen
      to me,
    that Israel would walk in my
      ways!
14  Then I would quickly subdue
      their enemies,
    and turn my hand against
      their foes.
15  Those who hate the LORD would
      cringe before him,
    and their doom would last
      forever.
16  I would feed you[b] with the
      finest of the wheat,
    and with honey from the rock
      I would satisfy you."

## PROVERBS 13.1

A WISE child loves discipline,[c]
but a scoffer does not listen
to rebuke.

# APRIL 13

## JOSHUA 7.16—9.2

So Joshua rose early in the morning, and brought Israel near tribe by tribe, and the tribe of Judah was taken. [17]He brought near the clans of Judah, and the clan of the Zerahites was taken; and he brought near the clan of the Zerahites, family by family,[d] and Zabdi was taken. [18]And he brought near his household one by one, and Achan son of Carmi son of Zabdi son of Zerah, of the tribe of Judah, was taken. [19]Then Joshua said to Achan, "My son, give glory to the LORD God of Israel and make confession to him. Tell me now what you have done; do not hide it from me." [20]And Achan answered Joshua, "It is true; I am the one who sinned against the LORD God of Israel. This is what I did: [21]when I saw among the spoil a beautiful mantle from Shinar, and two hundred shekels of silver, and

aHeb *his*   bCn Compare verse 16b: Heb *he would feed him*   cCn: Heb *A wise child the discipline of his father*   dMss Syr: MT *man by man*

a bar of gold weighing fifty shekels, then I coveted them and took them. They now lie hidden in the ground inside my tent, with the silver underneath."

22  So Joshua sent messengers, and they ran to the tent; and there it was, hidden in his tent with the silver underneath. [23]They took them out of the tent and brought them to Joshua and all the Israelites; and they spread them out before the Lord. [24]Then Joshua and all Israel with him took Achan son of Zerah, with the silver, the mantle, and the bar of gold, with his sons and daughters, with his oxen, donkeys, and sheep, and his tent and all that he had; and they brought them up to the Valley of Achor. [25]Joshua said, "Why did you bring trouble on us? The Lord is bringing trouble on you today." And all Israel stoned him to death; they burned them with fire, cast stones on them, [26]and raised over him a great heap of stones that remains to this day. Then the Lord turned from his burning anger. Therefore that place to this day is called the Valley of Achor. [a]

8.1 Then the Lord said to Joshua, "Do not fear or be dismayed; take all the fighting men with you, and go up now to Ai. See, I have handed over to you the king of Ai with his people, his city, and his land. [2]You shall do to Ai and its king as you did to Jericho and its king; only its spoil and its livestock you may take as booty for yourselves. Set an ambush against the city, behind it."

3  So Joshua and all the fighting men set out to go up against Ai. Joshua chose thirty thousand warriors and sent them out by night [4]with the command, "You shall lie in ambush against the city, behind it; do not go very far from the city, but all of you stay alert. [5]I and all the people who are with me will approach the city. When they come out against us, as before, we shall flee from them. [6]They will come out after us until we have drawn them away from the city; for they will say, 'They are fleeing from us, as before.' While we flee from them, [7]you shall rise up from the ambush and seize the city; for the Lord your God will give it into your hand. [8]And when you have taken the city, you shall set the city on fire, doing as the Lord has ordered; see, I have commanded you." [9]So Joshua sent them out; and they went to the place of ambush, and lay between Bethel and Ai, to the west of Ai; but Joshua spent that night in the camp. [b]

10  In the morning Joshua rose early and mustered the people, and went up, with the elders of Israel, before the people to Ai. [11]All the fighting men who were with him went up, and drew near before the city, and camped on the north side of Ai, with a ravine between them and Ai. [12]Taking about five thousand men, he set them in ambush between Bethel and Ai, to the west of the city. [13]So they stationed the forces, the main encampment that was north of the city and its rear guard west of the city. But Joshua spent that night in the valley. [14]When the king of Ai saw this, he and all his people, the inhabitants of the city, hurried out early in the morning to the meeting place facing the Arabah to meet Israel in battle; but he did not know that there was an ambush against him behind the city. [15]And Joshua and all Israel made a pretense of being beaten before them, and fled in the direction of the wilderness. [16]So all the people who were in the city were called together to pursue them, and as they pursued Joshua they were drawn away from the city. [17]There was not a man left in Ai or Bethel who did not go out after Israel; they left the city open, and pursued Israel.

18  Then the Lord said to Joshua,

<hr>

a That is *Trouble*  b Heb *among the people*

"Stretch out the sword that is in your hand toward Ai; for I will give it into your hand." And Joshua stretched out the sword that was in his hand toward the city. [19]As soon as he stretched out his hand, the troops in ambush rose quickly out of their place and rushed forward. They entered the city, took it, and at once set the city on fire. [20]So when the men of Ai looked back, the smoke of the city was rising to the sky. They had no power to flee this way or that, for the people who fled to the wilderness turned back against the pursuers. [21]When Joshua and all Israel saw that the ambush had taken the city and that the smoke of the city was rising, then they turned back and struck down the men of Ai. [22]And the others came out from the city against them; so they were surrounded by Israelites, some on one side, and some on the other; and Israel struck them down until no one was left who survived or escaped. [23]But the king of Ai was taken alive and brought to Joshua.

24 When Israel had finished slaughtering all the inhabitants of Ai in the open wilderness where they pursued them, and when all of them to the very last had fallen by the edge of the sword, all Israel returned to Ai, and attacked it with the edge of the sword. [25]The total of those who fell that day, both men and women, was twelve thousand—all the people of Ai. [26]For Joshua did not draw back his hand, with which he stretched out the sword, until he had utterly destroyed all the inhabitants of Ai. [27]Only the livestock and the spoil of that city Israel took as their booty, according to the word of the LORD that he had issued to Joshua. [28]So Joshua burned Ai, and made it forever a heap of ruins, as it is to this day. [29]And he hanged the king of Ai on a tree until evening; and at sunset Joshua commanded, and they took his body down from the tree, threw it down at the entrance of the gate of the city, and raised over it a great heap of stones, which stands there to this day.

30 Then Joshua built on Mount Ebal an altar to the LORD, the God of Israel, [31]just as Moses the servant of the LORD had commanded the Israelites, as it is written in the book of the law of Moses, "an altar of unhewn[a] stones, on which no iron tool has been used"; and they offered on it burnt offerings to the LORD, and sacrificed offerings of well-being. [32]And there, in the presence of the Israelites, Joshua[b] wrote on the stones a copy of the law of Moses, which he had written. [33]All Israel, alien as well as citizen, with their elders and officers and their judges, stood on opposite sides of the ark in front of the levitical priests who carried the ark of the covenant of the LORD, half of them in front of Mount Gerizim and half of them in front of Mount Ebal, as Moses the servant of the LORD had commanded at the first, that they should bless the people of Israel. [34]And afterward he read all the words of the law, blessings and curses, according to all that is written in the book of the law. [35]There was not a word of all that Moses commanded that Joshua did not read before all the assembly of Israel, and the women, and the little ones, and the aliens who resided among them.

**9.**[1] Now when all the kings who were beyond the Jordan in the hill country and in the lowland all along the coast of the Great Sea toward Lebanon—the Hittites, the Amorites, the Canaanites, the Perizzites, the Hivites, and the Jebusites—heard of this, [2]they gathered together with one accord to fight Joshua and Israel.

aHeb *whole*   bHeb *he*

## LUKE 16.1–18

**T**HEN Jesus[a] said to the disciples, "There was a rich man who had a manager, and charges were brought to him that this man was squandering his property. [2]So he summoned him and said to him, 'What is this that I hear about you? Give me an accounting of your management, because you cannot be my manager any longer.' [3]Then the manager said to himself, 'What will I do, now that my master is taking the position away from me? I am not strong enough to dig, and I am ashamed to beg. [4]I have decided what to do so that, when I am dismissed as manager, people may welcome me into their homes.' [5]So, summoning his master's debtors one by one, he asked the first, 'How much do you owe my master?' [6]He answered, 'A hundred jugs of olive oil.' He said to him, 'Take your bill, sit down quickly, and make it fifty.' [7]Then he asked another, 'And how much do you owe?' He replied, 'A hundred containers of wheat.' He said to him, 'Take your bill and make it eighty.' [8]And his master commended the dishonest manager because he had acted shrewdly; for the children of this age are more shrewd in dealing with their own generation than are the children of light. [9]And I tell you, make friends for yourselves by means of dishonest wealth[b] so that when it is gone, they may welcome you into the eternal homes. [c]

10 "Whoever is faithful in a very little is faithful also in much; and whoever is dishonest in a very little is dishonest also in much. [11]If then you have not been faithful with the dishonest wealth,[b] who will entrust to you the true riches? [12]And if you have not been faithful with what belongs to another, who will give you what is your own? [13]No slave can serve two masters; for a slave will either hate the one and love the other, or be devoted to the one and despise the other. You cannot serve God and wealth."[b]

14 The Pharisees, who were lovers of money, heard all this, and they ridiculed him. [15]So he said to them, "You are those who justify yourselves in the sight of others; but God knows your hearts; for what is prized by human beings is an abomination in the sight of God.

16 "The law and the prophets were in effect until John came; since then the good news of the kingdom of God is proclaimed, and everyone tries to enter it by force. [d] [17]But it is easier for heaven and earth to pass away, than for one stroke of a letter in the law to be dropped.

18 "Anyone who divorces his wife and marries another commits adultery, and whoever marries a woman divorced from her husband commits adultery.

## PSALM 82.1–8

*A Psalm of Asaph.*

**G**OD has taken his place in the
　　divine council;
in the midst of the gods he
　　holds judgment:
2　"How long will you judge
　　　unjustly
　　and show partiality to the
　　　wicked?　　　　　*Selah*
3　Give justice to the weak and the
　　　orphan;
　　maintain the right of the lowly
　　　and the destitute.
4　Rescue the weak and the
　　　needy;
　　deliver them from the hand of
　　　the wicked."

5　They have neither knowledge
　　　nor understanding,
　　they walk around in darkness;

---

aGk *he*　bGk *mammon*　cGk *tents*　dOr *everyone is strongly urged to enter it*

all the foundations of the
earth are shaken.

6 I say, "You are gods,
children of the Most High, all
of you;
7 nevertheless, you shall die like
mortals,
and fall like any prince."[a]

8 Rise up, O God, judge the
earth;
for all the nations belong to
you!

## PROVERBS 13.2–3

FROM the fruit of their words
good persons eat good
things,
but the desire of the
treacherous is for
wrongdoing.
3 Those who guard their mouths
preserve their lives;
those who open wide their
lips come to ruin.

# APRIL 14

## JOSHUA 9.3—10.43

BUT when the inhabitants of Gibeon heard what Joshua had done to Jericho and to Ai, [4]they on their part acted with cunning: they went and prepared provisions,[b] and took worn-out sacks for their donkeys, and wineskins, worn-out and torn and mended, [5]with worn-out, patched sandals on their feet, and worn-out clothes; and all their provisions were dry and moldy. [6]They went to Joshua in the camp at Gilgal, and said to him and to the Israelites, "We have come from a far country; so now make a treaty with us." [7]But the Israelites said to the Hivites, "Perhaps you live among us; then how can we make a treaty with you?" [8]They said to Joshua, "We are your servants." And Joshua said to them, "Who are you? And where do you come from?" [9]They said to him, "Your servants have come from a very far country, because of the name of the LORD your God; for we have heard a report of him, of all that he did in Egypt, [10]and of all that he did to the two kings of the Amorites who were beyond the Jordan, King Sihon of Heshbon, and King Og of Bashan who lived in Ashtaroth. [11]So our elders and all the inhabitants of our country said to us, 'Take provisions in your hand for the journey; go to meet them, and say to them, "We are your servants; come now, make a treaty with us." ' [12]Here is our bread; it was still warm when we took it from our houses as our food for the journey, on the day we set out to come to you, but now, see, it is dry and moldy; [13]these wineskins were new when we filled them, and see, they are burst; and these garments and sandals of ours are worn out from the very long journey." [14]So the leaders[c] partook of their provisions, and did not ask direction from the LORD. [15]And Joshua made peace with them, guaranteeing their

[a]Or *fall as one man, O princes*   [b]Cn: Meaning of Heb uncertain   [c]Gk: Heb *men*

lives by a treaty; and the leaders of the congregation swore an oath to them.

16 But when three days had passed after they had made a treaty with them, they heard that they were their neighbors and were living among them. [17]So the Israelites set out and reached their cities on the third day. Now their cities were Gibeon, Chephirah, Beeroth, and Kiriath-jearim. [18]But the Israelites did not attack them, because the leaders of the congregation had sworn to them by the LORD, the God of Israel. Then all the congregation murmured against the leaders. [19]But all the leaders said to all the congregation, "We have sworn to them by the LORD, the God of Israel, and now we must not touch them. [20]This is what we will do to them: We will let them live, so that wrath may not come upon us, because of the oath that we swore to them." [21]The leaders said to them, "Let them live." So they became hewers of wood and drawers of water for all the congregation, as the leaders had decided concerning them.

22 Joshua summoned them, and said to them, "Why did you deceive us, saying, 'We are very far from you,' while in fact you are living among us? [23]Now therefore you are cursed, and some of you shall always be slaves, hewers of wood and drawers of water for the house of my God." [24]They answered Joshua, "Because it was told to your servants for a certainty that the LORD your God had commanded his servant Moses to give you all the land, and to destroy all the inhabitants of the land before you; so we were in great fear for our lives because of you, and did this thing. [25]And now we are in your hand: do as it seems good and right in your sight to do to us." [26]This is what he did for them: he saved them from the Israelites; and they did not kill them. [27]But on that day Joshua made them hewers of wood and drawers of water for the congregation and for the altar of the LORD, to continue to this day, in the place that he should choose.

10.1 WHEN King Adoni-zedek of Jerusalem heard how Joshua had taken Ai, and had utterly destroyed it, doing to Ai and its king as he had done to Jericho and its king, and how the inhabitants of Gibeon had made peace with Israel and were among them, [2]he[a] became greatly frightened, because Gibeon was a large city, like one of the royal cities, and was larger than Ai, and all its men were warriors. [3]So King Adoni-zedek of Jerusalem sent a message to King Hoham of Hebron, to King Piram of Jarmuth, to King Japhia of Lachish, and to King Debir of Eglon, saying, [4]"Come up and help me, and let us attack Gibeon; for it has made peace with Joshua and with the Israelites." [5]Then the five kings of the Amorites—the king of Jerusalem, the king of Hebron, the king of Jarmuth, the king of Lachish, and the king of Eglon—gathered their forces, and went up with all their armies and camped against Gibeon, and made war against it.

6 And the Gibeonites sent to Joshua at the camp in Gilgal, saying, "Do not abandon your servants; come up to us quickly, and save us, and help us; for all the kings of the Amorites who live in the hill country are gathered against us." [7]So Joshua went up from Gilgal, he and all the fighting force with him, all the mighty warriors. [8]The LORD said to Joshua, "Do not fear them, for I have handed them over to you; not one of them shall stand before you." [9]So Joshua came upon them suddenly, having marched up all night from Gilgal. [10]And the LORD threw them into a panic before Israel, who inflicted a great slaughter on them at Gibeon, chased them by the way of the ascent of Beth-

a Heb *they*

horon, and struck them down as far as Azekah and Makkedah. [11]As they fled before Israel, while they were going down the slope of Beth-horon, the LORD threw down huge stones from heaven on them as far as Azekah, and they died; there were more who died because of the hailstones than the Israelites killed with the sword.

12  On the day when the LORD gave the Amorites over to the Israelites, Joshua spoke to the LORD; and he said in the sight of Israel,

>"Sun, stand still at Gibeon,
>    and Moon, in the valley of
>        Aijalon."
[13]  And the sun stood still, and the
>        moon stopped,
>    until the nation took
>        vengeance on their
>        enemies.

Is this not written in the Book of Jashar? The sun stopped in midheaven, and did not hurry to set for about a whole day. [14]There has been no day like it before or since, when the LORD heeded a human voice; for the LORD fought for Israel.

15  Then Joshua returned, and all Israel with him, to the camp at Gilgal.

16  Meanwhile, these five kings fled and hid themselves in the cave at Makkedah. [17]And it was told Joshua, "The five kings have been found, hidden in the cave at Makkedah." [18]Joshua said, "Roll large stones against the mouth of the cave, and set men by it to guard them; [19]but do not stay there yourselves; pursue your enemies, and attack them from the rear. Do not let them enter their towns, for the LORD your God has given them into your hand." [20]When Joshua and the Israelites had finished inflicting a very great slaughter on them, until they were wiped out, and when the survivors had entered into the fortified towns, [21]all the people returned safe to Joshua in the camp at Makkedah; no one dared to speak[a] against any of the Israelites.

22  Then Joshua said, "Open the mouth of the cave, and bring those five kings out to me from the cave." [23]They did so, and brought the five kings out to him from the cave, the king of Jerusalem, the king of Hebron, the king of Jarmuth, the king of Lachish, and the king of Eglon. [24]When they brought the kings out to Joshua, Joshua summoned all the Israelites, and said to the chiefs of the warriors who had gone with him, "Come near, put your feet on the necks of these kings." Then they came near and put their feet on their necks. [25]And Joshua said to them, "Do not be afraid or dismayed; be strong and courageous; for thus the LORD will do to all the enemies against whom you fight." [26]Afterward Joshua struck them down and put them to death, and he hung them on five trees. And they hung on the trees until evening. [27]At sunset Joshua commanded, and they took them down from the trees and threw them into the cave where they had hidden themselves; they set large stones against the mouth of the cave, which remain to this very day.

28  Joshua took Makkedah on that day, and struck it and its king with the edge of the sword; he utterly destroyed every person in it; he left no one remaining. And he did to the king of Makkedah as he had done to the king of Jericho.

29  Then Joshua passed on from Makkedah, and all Israel with him, to Libnah, and fought against Libnah. [30]The LORD gave it also and its king into the hand of Israel; and he struck it with the edge of the sword, and every person in it; he left no one remaining in it; and he did to its king as he had done to the king of Jericho.

31  Next Joshua passed on from Libnah, and all Israel with him, to La-

---

a Heb *moved his tongue*

chish, and laid siege to it, and assaulted it. <sup>32</sup>The Lord gave Lachish into the hand of Israel, and he took it on the second day, and struck it with the edge of the sword, and every person in it, as he had done to Libnah.

33 Then King Horam of Gezer came up to help Lachish; and Joshua struck him and his people, leaving him no survivors.

34 From Lachish Joshua passed on with all Israel to Eglon; and they laid siege to it, and assaulted it; <sup>35</sup>and they took it that day, and struck it with the edge of the sword; and every person in it he utterly destroyed that day, as he had done to Lachish.

36 Then Joshua went up with all Israel from Eglon to Hebron; they assaulted it, <sup>37</sup>and took it, and struck it with the edge of the sword, and its king and its towns, and every person in it; he left no one remaining, just as he had done to Eglon, and utterly destroyed it with every person in it.

38 Then Joshua, with all Israel, turned back to Debir and assaulted it, <sup>39</sup>and he took it with its king and all its towns; they struck them with the edge of the sword, and utterly destroyed every person in it; he left no one remaining; just as he had done to Hebron, and, as he had done to Libnah and its king, so he did to Debir and its king.

40 So Joshua defeated the whole land, the hill country and the Negeb and the lowland and the slopes, and all their kings; he left no one remaining, but utterly destroyed all that breathed, as the Lord God of Israel commanded. <sup>41</sup>And Joshua defeated them from Kadesh-barnea to Gaza, and all the country of Goshen, as far as Gibeon. <sup>42</sup>Joshua took all these kings and their land at one time, because the Lord God of Israel fought for Israel. <sup>43</sup>Then Joshua returned, and all Israel with him, to the camp at Gilgal.

## LUKE 16.19—17.10

"THERE was a rich man who was dressed in purple and fine linen and who feasted sumptuously every day. <sup>20</sup>And at his gate lay a poor man named Lazarus, covered with sores, <sup>21</sup>who longed to satisfy his hunger with what fell from the rich man's table; even the dogs would come and lick his sores. <sup>22</sup>The poor man died and was carried away by the angels to be with Abraham. [a] The rich man also died and was buried. <sup>23</sup>In Hades, where he was being tormented, he looked up and saw Abraham far away with Lazarus by his side. [b] <sup>24</sup>He called out, 'Father Abraham, have mercy on me, and send Lazarus to dip the tip of his finger in water and cool my tongue; for I am in agony in these flames.' <sup>25</sup>But Abraham said, 'Child, remember that during your lifetime you received your good things, and Lazarus in like manner evil things; but now he is comforted here, and you are in agony. <sup>26</sup>Besides all this, between you and us a great chasm has been fixed, so that those who might want to pass from here to you cannot do so, and no one can cross from there to us.' <sup>27</sup>He said, 'Then, father, I beg you to send him to my father's house— <sup>28</sup>for I have five brothers—that he may warn them, so that they will not also come into this place of torment.' <sup>29</sup>Abraham replied, 'They have Moses and the prophets; they should listen to them.' <sup>30</sup>He said, 'No, father Abraham; but if someone goes to them from the dead, they will repent.' <sup>31</sup>He said to him, 'If they do not listen to Moses and the prophets, neither will they be convinced even if someone rises from the dead.' "

<sup>17.1</sup> Jesus[c] said to his disciples, "Occasions for stumbling are bound to come, but woe to anyone by whom they

come! ²It would be better for you if a millstone were hung around your neck and you were thrown into the sea than for you to cause one of these little ones to stumble. ³Be on your guard! If another disciple[a] sins, you must rebuke the offender, and if there is repentance, you must forgive. ⁴And if the same person sins against you seven times a day, and turns back to you seven times and says, 'I repent,' you must forgive."

5 The apostles said to the Lord, "Increase our faith!" ⁶The Lord replied, "If you had faith the size of a[b] mustard seed, you could say to this mulberry tree, 'Be uprooted and planted in the sea,' and it would obey you.

7 "Who among you would say to your slave who has just come in from plowing or tending sheep in the field, 'Come here at once and take your place at the table'? ⁸Would you not rather say to him, 'Prepare supper for me, put on your apron and serve me while I eat and drink; later you may eat and drink'? ⁹Do you thank the slave for doing what was commanded? ¹⁰So you also, when you have done all that you were ordered to do, say, 'We are worthless slaves; we have done only what we ought to have done!' "

## PSALM 83.1–18

*A Song. A Psalm of Asaph.*

O GOD, do not keep silence;
do not hold your peace or
be still, O God!
2 Even now your enemies are in
tumult;
those who hate you have
raised their heads.
3 They lay crafty plans against
your people;
they consult together against
those you protect.

4 They say, "Come, let us wipe
them out as a nation;
let the name of Israel be
remembered no more."
5 They conspire with one accord;
against you they make a
covenant—
6 the tents of Edom and the
Ishmaelites,
Moab and the Hagrites,
7 Gebal and Ammon and Amalek,
Philistia with the inhabitants
of Tyre;
8 Assyria also has joined them;
they are the strong arm of
the children of Lot. *Selah*

9 Do to them as you did to
Midian,
as to Sisera and Jabin at the
Wadi Kishon,
10 who were destroyed at En-dor,
who became dung for the
ground.
11 Make their nobles like Oreb and
Zeeb,
all their princes like Zebah
and Zalmunna,
12 who said, "Let us take the
pastures of God
for our own possession."

13 O my God, make them like
whirling dust,[c]
like chaff before the wind.
14 As fire consumes the forest,
as the flame sets the
mountains ablaze,
15 so pursue them with your
tempest
and terrify them with your
hurricane.
16 Fill their faces with shame,
so that they may seek your
name, O LORD.
17 Let them be put to shame and
dismayed forever;
let them perish in disgrace.

aGk *your brother*  bGk *faith as a grain of*  cOr *a tumbleweed*

[18] Let them know that you alone,
    whose name is the Lord,
    are the Most High over all
      the earth.

## PROVERBS 13.4

THE appetite of the lazy craves,
    and gets nothing,
while the appetite of the
    diligent is richly supplied.

# APRIL 15

## JOSHUA 11.1—12.24

WHEN King Jabin of Hazor heard of this, he sent to King Jobab of Madon, to the king of Shimron, to the king of Achshaph, [2] and to the kings who were in the northern hill country, and in the Arabah south of Chinneroth, and in the lowland, and in Naphoth-dor on the west, [3] to the Canaanites in the east and the west, the Amorites, the Hittites, the Perizzites, and the Jebusites in the hill country, and the Hivites under Hermon in the land of Mizpah. [4] They came out, with all their troops, a great army, in number like the sand on the seashore, with very many horses and chariots. [5] All these kings joined their forces, and came and camped together at the waters of Merom, to fight with Israel.

6 And the Lord said to Joshua, "Do not be afraid of them, for tomorrow at this time I will hand over all of them, slain, to Israel; you shall hamstring their horses, and burn their chariots with fire." [7] So Joshua came suddenly upon them with all his fighting force, by the waters of Merom, and fell upon them. [8] And the Lord handed them over to Israel, who attacked them and chased them as far as Great Sidon and Misrephoth-maim, and eastward as far as the valley of Mizpeh. They struck them down, until they had left no one remaining. [9] And Joshua did to them as the Lord commanded him; he hamstrung their horses, and burned their chariots with fire.

10 Joshua turned back at that time, and took Hazor, and struck its king down with the sword. Before that time Hazor was the head of all those kingdoms. [11] And they put to the sword all who were in it, utterly destroying them; there was no one left who breathed, and he burned Hazor with fire. [12] And all the towns of those kings, and all their kings, Joshua took, and struck them with the edge of the sword, utterly destroying them, as Moses the servant of the Lord had commanded. [13] But Israel burned none of the towns that stood on mounds except Hazor, which Joshua did burn. [14] All the spoil of these towns, and the livestock, the Israelites took for their booty; but all the people they struck down with the edge of the sword, until they had destroyed them, and they did not leave any who breathed. [15] As the Lord had commanded his servant Moses, so Moses commanded Joshua, and so Joshua did; he left nothing undone of all that the Lord had commanded Moses.

16 So Joshua took all that land: the

hill country and all the Negeb and all the land of Goshen and the lowland and the Arabah and the hill country of Israel and its lowland, <sup>17</sup>from Mount Halak, which rises toward Seir, as far as Baal-gad in the valley of Lebanon below Mount Hermon. He took all their kings, struck them down, and put them to death. <sup>18</sup>Joshua made war a long time with all those kings. <sup>19</sup>There was not a town that made peace with the Israelites, except the Hivites, the inhabitants of Gibeon; all were taken in battle. <sup>20</sup>For it was the LORD's doing to harden their hearts so that they would come against Israel in battle, in order that they might be utterly destroyed, and might receive no mercy, but be exterminated, just as the LORD had commanded Moses.

21 At that time Joshua came and wiped out the Anakim from the hill country, from Hebron, from Debir, from Anab, and from all the hill country of Judah, and from all the hill country of Israel; Joshua utterly destroyed them with their towns. <sup>22</sup>None of the Anakim was left in the land of the Israelites; some remained only in Gaza, in Gath, and in Ashdod. <sup>23</sup>So Joshua took the whole land, according to all that the LORD had spoken to Moses; and Joshua gave it for an inheritance to Israel according to their tribal allotments. And the land had rest from war.

**12.**1 Now these are the kings of the land, whom the Israelites defeated, whose land they occupied beyond the Jordan toward the east, from the Wadi Arnon to Mount Hermon, with all the Arabah eastward: <sup>2</sup>King Sihon of the Amorites who lived at Heshbon, and ruled from Aroer, which is on the edge of the Wadi Arnon, and from the middle of the valley as far as the river Jabbok, the boundary of the Ammonites, that is, half of Gilead, <sup>3</sup>and the Arabah to the Sea of Chinneroth eastward, and in the direction of Beth-jeshimoth, to the sea of the Arabah, the Dead Sea,<sup>a</sup> southward to the foot of the slopes of Pisgah; <sup>4</sup>and King Og<sup>b</sup> of Bashan, one of the last of the Rephaim, who lived at Ashtaroth and at Edrei <sup>5</sup>and ruled over Mount Hermon and Salecah and all Bashan to the boundary of the Geshurites and the Maacathites, and over half of Gilead to the boundary of King Sihon of Heshbon. <sup>6</sup>Moses, the servant of the LORD, and the Israelites defeated them; and Moses the servant of the LORD gave their land for a possession to the Reubenites and the Gadites and the half-tribe of Manasseh.

7 The following are the kings of the land whom Joshua and the Israelites defeated on the west side of the Jordan, from Baal-gad in the valley of Lebanon to Mount Halak, that rises toward Seir (and Joshua gave their land to the tribes of Israel as a possession according to their allotments, <sup>8</sup>in the hill country, in the lowland, in the Arabah, in the slopes, in the wilderness, and in the Negeb, the land of the Hittites, Amorites, Canaanites, Perizzites, Hivites, and Jebusites):

| | | |
|---|---|---|
| 9 | the king of Jericho | one |
| | the king of Ai, which is next to Bethel | one |
| 10 | the king of Jerusalem | one |
| | the king of Hebron | one |
| 11 | the king of Jarmuth | one |
| | the king of Lachish | one |
| 12 | the king of Eglon | one |
| | the king of Gezer | one |
| 13 | the king of Debir | one |
| | the king of Geder | one |
| 14 | the king of Hormah | one |
| | the king of Arad | one |
| 15 | the king of Libnah | one |
| | the king of Adullam | one |
| 16 | the king of Makkedah | one |
| | the king of Bethel | one |
| 17 | the king of Tappuah | one |

aHeb *Salt Sea*   bGk: Heb *the boundary of King Og*

| | | |
|---|---|---|
| | the king of Hepher | one |
| 18 | the king of Aphek | one |
| | the king of Lasharon | one |
| 19 | the king of Madon | one |
| | the king of Hazor | one |
| 20 | the king of Shimron-meron | one |
| | the king of Achshaph | one |
| 21 | the king of Taanach | one |
| | the king of Megiddo | one |
| 22 | the king of Kedesh | one |
| | the king of Jokneam in Carmel | one |
| 23 | the king of Dor in Naphath-dor | one |
| | the king of Goiim in Galilee, [a] | one |
| 24 | the king of Tirzah | one |

thirty-one kings in all.

## LUKE 17.11–37

O[N] the way to Jerusalem Jesus[b] was going through the region between Samaria and Galilee. [12]As he entered a village, ten lepers[c] approached him. Keeping their distance, [13]they called out, saying, "Jesus, Master, have mercy on us!" [14]When he saw them, he said to them, "Go and show yourselves to the priests." And as they went, they were made clean. [15]Then one of them, when he saw that he was healed, turned back, praising God with a loud voice. [16]He prostrated himself at Jesus'[d] feet and thanked him. And he was a Samaritan. [17]Then Jesus asked, "Were not ten made clean? But the other nine, where are they? [18]Was none of them found to return and give praise to God except this foreigner?" [19]Then he said to him, "Get up and go on your way; your faith has made you well."

20 Once Jesus[b] was asked by the Pharisees when the kingdom of God was coming, and he answered, "The kingdom of God is not coming with things that can be observed; [21]nor will they say, 'Look, here it is!' or 'There it is!' For, in fact, the kingdom of God is among[e] you."

22 Then he said to the disciples, "The days are coming when you will long to see one of the days of the Son of Man, and you will not see it. [23]They will say to you, 'Look there!' or 'Look here!' Do not go, do not set off in pursuit. [24]For as the lightning flashes and lights up the sky from one side to the other, so will the Son of Man be in his day.[f] [25]But first he must endure much suffering and be rejected by this generation. [26]Just as it was in the days of Noah, so too it will be in the days of the Son of Man. [27]They were eating and drinking, and marrying and being given in marriage, until the day Noah entered the ark, and the flood came and destroyed all of them. [28]Likewise, just as it was in the days of Lot: they were eating and drinking, buying and selling, planting and building, [29]but on the day that Lot left Sodom, it rained fire and sulfur from heaven and destroyed all of them [30]—it will be like that on the day that the Son of Man is revealed. [31]On that day, anyone on the housetop who has belongings in the house must not come down to take them away; and likewise anyone in the field must not turn back. [32]Remember Lot's wife. [33]Those who try to make their life secure will lose it, but those who lose their life will keep it. [34]I tell you, on that night there will be two in one bed; one will be taken and the other left. [35]There will be two women grinding meal together; one will be taken and the other left."[g] [37]Then they asked him, "Where, Lord?" He said to them, "Where the corpse is, there the vultures will gather."

---

a Gk: Heb *Gilgal*   b Gk *he*   c The terms *leper* and *leprosy* can refer to several diseases   d Gk *his*
e Or *within*   f Other ancient authorities lack *in his day*   g Other ancient authorities add verse 36,
*"Two will be in the field; one will be taken and the other left."*

## PSALM 84.1–12

*To the leader: according to The Gittith. Of the
Korahites. A Psalm.*

How lovely is your dwelling
      place,
  O Lord of hosts!
2 My soul longs, indeed it faints
    for the courts of the Lord;
  my heart and my flesh sing for
      joy
    to the living God.

3 Even the sparrow finds a home,
    and the swallow a nest for
      herself,
  where she may lay her
      young,
  at your altars, O Lord of hosts,
    my King and my God.
4 Happy are those who live in
    your house,
  ever singing your praise.
                *Selah*

5 Happy are those whose strength
    is in you,
  in whose heart are the
    highways to Zion. [a]
6 As they go through the valley of
    Baca
  they make it a place of
    springs;
  the early rain also covers it
    with pools.
7 They go from strength to
    strength;
  the God of gods will be seen
    in Zion.

8 O Lord God of hosts, hear my
    prayer;
  give ear, O God of Jacob!
                *Selah*
9 Behold our shield, O God;
  look on the face of your
    anointed.

10 For a day in your courts is
    better
  than a thousand elsewhere.
I would rather be a doorkeeper
    in the house of my God
  than live in the tents of
    wickedness.
11 For the Lord God is a sun and
    shield;
  he bestows favor and honor.
No good thing does the Lord
    withhold
  from those who walk
    uprightly.
12 O Lord of hosts,
  happy is everyone who trusts
    in you.

## PROVERBS 13.5–6

The righteous hate falsehood,
  but the wicked act
    shamefully and
    disgracefully.
6 Righteousness guards one
    whose way is upright,
  but sin overthrows the
    wicked.

a Heb lacks *to Zion*

# APRIL 16

JOSHUA 13.1—14.15

Now Joshua was old and advanced in years; and the LORD said to him, "You are old and advanced in years, and very much of the land still remains to be possessed. ²This is the land that still remains: all the regions of the Philistines, and all those of the Geshurites ³(from the Shihor, which is east of Egypt, northward to the boundary of Ekron, it is reckoned as Canaanite; there are five rulers of the Philistines, those of Gaza, Ashdod, Ashkelon, Gath, and Ekron), and those of the Avvim, ⁴in the south, all the land of the Canaanites, and Mearah that belongs to the Sidonians, to Aphek, to the boundary of the Amorites, ⁵and the land of the Gebalites, and all Lebanon, toward the east, from Baal-gad below Mount Hermon to Lebo-hamath, ⁶all the inhabitants of the hill country from Lebanon to Misrephoth-maim, even all the Sidonians. I will myself drive them out from before the Israelites; only allot the land to Israel for an inheritance, as I have commanded you. ⁷Now therefore divide this land for an inheritance to the nine tribes and the half-tribe of Manasseh."

8 With the other half-tribe of Manasseh[a] the Reubenites and the Gadites received their inheritance, which Moses gave them, beyond the Jordan eastward, as Moses the servant of the LORD gave them: ⁹from Aroer, which is on the edge of the Wadi Arnon, and the town that is in the middle of the valley, and all the tableland from[b] Medeba as far as Dibon; ¹⁰and all the cities of King Sihon of the Amorites, who reigned in Heshbon, as far as the boundary of the Ammonites; ¹¹and Gilead, and the region of the Geshurites and Maacathites, and all Mount Hermon, and all Bashan to Salecah; ¹²all the kingdom of Og in Bashan, who reigned in Ashtaroth and in Edrei (he alone was left of the survivors of the Rephaim); these Moses had defeated and driven out. ¹³Yet the Israelites did not drive out the Geshurites or the Maacathites; but Geshur and Maacath live within Israel to this day.

14 To the tribe of Levi alone Moses gave no inheritance; the offerings by fire to the LORD God of Israel are their inheritance, as he said to them.

15 Moses gave an inheritance to the tribe of the Reubenites according to their clans. ¹⁶Their territory was from Aroer, which is on the edge of the Wadi Arnon, and the town that is in the middle of the valley, and all the tableland by Medeba; ¹⁷with Heshbon, and all its towns that are in the tableland; Dibon, and Bamoth-baal, and Beth-baal-meon, ¹⁸and Jahaz, and Kedemoth, and Mephaath, ¹⁹and Kiriathaim, and Sibmah, and Zereth-shahar on the hill of the valley, ²⁰and Beth-peor, and the slopes of Pisgah, and Beth-jeshimoth, ²¹that is, all the towns of the tableland, and all the kingdom of King Sihon of the Amorites, who reigned in Heshbon, whom Moses defeated with the leaders of Midian, Evi and Rekem and Zur and Hur and Reba, as princes of Sihon, who lived in the land. ²²Along with the rest of those they put to death, the Israelites also put to the sword Balaam son of Beor, who practiced divination. ²³And the border of the Reubenites was the Jordan and its banks. This was the inheritance of the Reubenites, according to

---

a Cn: Heb *With it*   b Compare Gk: Heb lacks *from*

their families with their towns and villages.

24 Moses gave an inheritance also to the tribe of the Gadites, according to their families. 25Their territory was Jazer, and all the towns of Gilead, and half the land of the Ammonites, to Aroer, which is east of Rabbah, 26and from Heshbon to Ramath-mizpeh and Betonim, and from Mahanaim to the territory of Debir,ᵃ 27and in the valley Beth-haram, Beth-nimrah, Succoth, and Zaphon, the rest of the kingdom of King Sihon of Heshbon, the Jordan and its banks, as far as the lower end of the Sea of Chinnereth, eastward beyond the Jordan. 28This is the inheritance of the Gadites according to their clans, with their towns and villages.

29 Moses gave an inheritance to the half-tribe of Manasseh; it was allotted to the half-tribe of the Manassites according to their families. 30Their territory extended from Mahanaim, through all Bashan, the whole kingdom of King Og of Bashan, and all the settlements of Jair, which are in Bashan, sixty towns, 31and half of Gilead, and Ashtaroth, and Edrei, the towns of the kingdom of Og in Bashan; these were allotted to the people of Machir son of Manasseh according to their clans—for half the Machirites.

32 These are the inheritances that Moses distributed in the plains of Moab, beyond the Jordan east of Jericho. 33But to the tribe of Levi Moses gave no inheritance; the Lord God of Israel is their inheritance, as he said to them.

14.1 These are the inheritances that the Israelites received in the land of Canaan, which the priest Eleazar, and Joshua son of Nun, and the heads of the families of the tribes of the Israelites distributed to them. 2Their inheritance was by lot, as the Lord had commanded Moses for the nine and one-half tribes. 3For Moses had given an inheritance to the two and one-half tribes beyond the Jordan; but to the Levites he gave no inheritance among them. 4For the people of Joseph were two tribes, Manasseh and Ephraim; and no portion was given to the Levites in the land, but only towns to live in, with their pasture lands for their flocks and herds. 5The Israelites did as the Lord commanded Moses; they allotted the land.

6 Then the people of Judah came to Joshua at Gilgal; and Caleb son of Jephunneh the Kenizzite said to him, "You know what the Lord said to Moses the man of God in Kadesh-barnea concerning you and me. 7I was forty years old when Moses the servant of the Lord sent me from Kadesh-barnea to spy out the land; and I brought him an honest report. 8But my companions who went up with me made the heart of the people melt; yet I wholeheartedly followed the Lord my God. 9And Moses swore on that day, saying, 'Surely the land on which your foot has trodden shall be an inheritance for you and your children forever, because you have wholeheartedly followed the Lord my God.' 10And now, as you see, the Lord has kept me alive, as he said, these forty-five years since the time that the Lord spoke this word to Moses, while Israel was journeying through the wilderness; and here I am today, eighty-five years old. 11I am still as strong today as I was on the day that Moses sent me; my strength now is as my strength was then, for war, and for going and coming. 12So now give me this hill country of which the Lord spoke on that day; for you heard on that day how the Anakim were there, with great fortified cities; it may be that the Lord will be with me, and I shall drive them out, as the Lord said."

ᵃGk Syr Vg: Heb *Lidebir*

13 Then Joshua blessed him, and gave Hebron to Caleb son of Jephunneh for an inheritance. [14]So Hebron became the inheritance of Caleb son of Jephunneh the Kenizzite to this day, because he wholeheartedly followed the LORD, the God of Israel. [15]Now the name of Hebron formerly was Kiriath-arba;[a] this Arba was[b] the greatest man among the Anakim. And the land had rest from war.

## LUKE 18.1–17

THEN Jesus[c] told them [the disciples] a parable about their need to pray always and not to lose heart. [2]He said, "In a certain city there was a judge who neither feared God nor had respect for people. [3]In that city there was a widow who kept coming to him and saying, 'Grant me justice against my opponent.' [4]For a while he refused; but later he said to himself, 'Though I have no fear of God and no respect for anyone, [5]yet because this widow keeps bothering me, I will grant her justice, so that she may not wear me out by continually coming.' "[d] [6]And the Lord said, "Listen to what the unjust judge says. [7]And will not God grant justice to his chosen ones who cry to him day and night? Will he delay long in helping them? [8]I tell you, he will quickly grant justice to them. And yet, when the Son of Man comes, will he find faith on earth?"

9 He also told this parable to some who trusted in themselves that they were righteous and regarded others with contempt: [10]"Two men went up to the temple to pray, one a Pharisee and the other a tax collector. [11]The Pharisee, standing by himself, was praying thus, 'God, I thank you that I am not like other people: thieves, rogues, adulterers, or even like this tax collector. [12]I fast twice a week; I give a tenth of all my income.' [13]But the tax collector, standing far off, would not even look up to heaven, but was beating his breast and saying, 'God, be merciful to me, a sinner!' [14]I tell you, this man went down to his home justified rather than the other; for all who exalt themselves will be humbled, but all who humble themselves will be exalted."

15 People were bringing even infants to him that he might touch them; and when the disciples saw it, they sternly ordered them not to do it. [16]But Jesus called for them and said, "Let the little children come to me, and do not stop them; for it is to such as these that the kingdom of God belongs. [17]Truly I tell you, whoever does not receive the kingdom of God as a little child will never enter it."

## PSALM 85.1–13

*To the leader. Of the Korahites. A Psalm.*

LORD, you were favorable to
    your land;
  you restored the fortunes of
    Jacob.
2  You forgave the iniquity of your
    people;
  you pardoned all their sin.
                *Selah*
3  You withdrew all your wrath;
  you turned from your hot
    anger.

4  Restore us again, O God of our
    salvation,
  and put away your indignation
    toward us.
5  Will you be angry with us
    forever?
  Will you prolong your anger
    to all generations?
6  Will you not revive us again,
  so that your people may
    rejoice in you?

a That is *the city of Arba*   b Heb lacks *this Arba was and slap me in the face*   c Gk *he*   d Or *so that she may not finally come*

7 Show us your steadfast love,
    O Lord,
  and grant us your salvation.

8 Let me hear what God the Lord
    will speak,
  for he will speak peace to his
    people,
  to his faithful, to those who
    turn to him in their
    hearts. a
9 Surely his salvation is at hand
    for those who fear him,
  that his glory may dwell in
    our land.

10 Steadfast love and faithfulness
    will meet;
  righteousness and peace will
    kiss each other.

11 Faithfulness will spring up from
    the ground,
  and righteousness will look
    down from the sky.
12 The Lord will give what is
    good,
  and our land will yield its
    increase.
13 Righteousness will go before
    him,
  and will make a path for his
    steps.

## PROVERBS 13.7–8

Some pretend to be rich, yet
    have nothing;
  others pretend to be poor,
    yet have great wealth.
8 Wealth is a ransom for a
    person's life,
  but the poor get no threats.

# APRIL 17

## JOSHUA 15.1–63

The lot for the tribe of the people of Judah according to their families reached southward to the boundary of Edom, to the wilderness of Zin at the farthest south. 2And their south boundary ran from the end of the Dead Sea, b from the bay that faces southward; 3it goes out southward of the ascent of Akrabbim, passes along to Zin, and goes up south of Kadesh-barnea, along by Hezron, up to Addar, makes a turn to Karka, 4passes along to Azmon, goes out by the Wadi of Egypt, and comes to its end at the sea. This shall be your south boundary. 5And the east boundary is the Dead Sea, b to the mouth of the Jordan. And the boundary on the north side runs from the bay of the sea at the mouth of the Jordan; 6and the boundary goes up to Beth-hoglah, and passes along north of Beth-arabah; and the boundary goes up to the Stone of Bohan, Reuben's son; 7and the boundary goes up to Debir from the Valley of Achor, and so northward, turning toward Gilgal, which is opposite the ascent of Adummim, which is on the south side of the valley; and the boundary passes along to the waters of En-shemesh, and ends at En-rogel; 8then the boundary goes up by the valley of the son of Hinnom at the southern slope of the Jebusites (that is,

aGk: Heb *but let them not turn back to folly*   bHeb *Salt Sea*

Jerusalem); and the boundary goes up to the top of the mountain that lies over against the valley of Hinnom, on the west, at the northern end of the valley of Rephaim; [9]then the boundary extends from the top of the mountain to the spring of the Waters of Nephtoah, and from there to the towns of Mount Ephron; then the boundary bends around to Baalah (that is, Kiriath-jearim); [10]and the boundary circles west of Baalah to Mount Seir, passes along to the northern slope of Mount Jearim (that is, Chesalon), and goes down to Beth-shemesh, and passes along by Timnah; [11]the boundary goes out to the slope of the hill north of Ekron, then the boundary bends around to Shikkeron, and passes along to Mount Baalah, and goes out to Jabneel; then the boundary comes to an end at the sea. [12]And the west boundary was the Mediterranean with its coast. This is the boundary surrounding the people of Judah according to their families.

13 According to the commandment of the LORD to Joshua, he gave to Caleb son of Jephunneh a portion among the people of Judah, Kiriath-arba, [a] that is, Hebron (Arba was the father of Anak). [14]And Caleb drove out from there the three sons of Anak: Sheshai, Ahiman, and Talmai, the descendants of Anak. [15]From there he went up against the inhabitants of Debir; now the name of Debir formerly was Kiriath-sepher. [16]And Caleb said, "Whoever attacks Kiriath-sepher and takes it, to him I will give my daughter Achsah as wife." [17]Othniel son of Kenaz, the brother of Caleb, took it; and he gave him his daughter Achsah as wife. [18]When she came to him, she urged him to ask her father for a field. As she dismounted from her donkey, Caleb said to her, "What do you wish?" [19]She said to him, "Give me a present; since you have set me in the land of the Negeb, give me

springs of water as well." So Caleb gave her the upper springs and the lower springs.

20 This is the inheritance of the tribe of the people of Judah according to their families. [21]The towns belonging to the tribe of the people of Judah in the extreme South, toward the boundary of Edom, were Kabzeel, Eder, Jagur, [22]Kinah, Dimonah, Adadah, [23]Kedesh, Hazor, Ithnan, [24]Ziph, Telem, Bealoth, [25]Hazor-hadattah, Kerioth-hezron (that is, Hazor), [26]Amam, Shema, Moladah, [27]Hazar-gaddah, Heshmon, Beth-pelet, [28]Hazar-shual, Beer-sheba Biziothiah, [29]Baalah, Iim, Ezem, [30]Eltolad, Chesil, Hormah, [31]Ziklag, Madmannah, Sansannah, [32]Lebaoth, Shilhim, Ain, and Rimmon: in all, twenty-nine towns, with their villages.

33 And in the Lowland, Eshtaol, Zorah, Ashnah, [34]Zanoah, En-gannim, Tappuah, Enam, [35]Jarmuth, Adullam, Socoh, Azekah, [36]Shaaraim, Adithaim, Gederah, Gederothaim: fourteen towns with their villages.

37 Zenan, Hadashah, Migdal-gad, [38]Dilan, Mizpeh, Jokthe-el, [39]Lachish, Bozkath, Eglon, [40]Cabbon, Lahmam, Chitlish, [41]Gederoth, Beth-dagon, Naamah, and Makkedah: sixteen towns with their villages.

42 Libnah, Ether, Ashan, [43]Iphtah, Ashnah, Nezib, [44]Keilah, Achzib, and Mareshah: nine towns with their villages.

45 Ekron, with its dependencies and its villages; [46]from Ekron to the sea, all that were near Ashdod, with their villages.

47 Ashdod, its towns and its villages; Gaza, its towns and its villages; to the Wadi of Egypt, and the Great Sea with its coast.

48 And in the hill country, Shamir, Jattir, Socoh, [49]Dannah, Kiriath-sannah (that is, Debir), [50]Anab, Eshtemoh,

---

[a] That is *the city of Arba*

Anim, ⁵¹Goshen, Holon, and Giloh: eleven towns with their villages.

52 Arab, Dumah, Eshan, ⁵³Janim, Beth-tappuah, Aphekah, ⁵⁴Humtah, Kiriath-arba (that is, Hebron), and Zior: nine towns with their villages.

55 Maon, Carmel, Ziph, Juttah, ⁵⁶Jezreel, Jokdeam, Zanoah, ⁵⁷Kain, Gibeah, and Timnah: ten towns with their villages.

58 Halhul, Beth-zur, Gedor, ⁵⁹Maarath, Beth-anoth, and Eltekon: six towns with their villages.

60 Kiriath-baal (that is, Kiriath-jearim), and Rabbah: two towns with their villages.

61 In the wilderness, Beth-arabah, Middin, Secacah, ⁶²Nibshan, the City of Salt, and En-gedi: six towns with their villages.

63 But the people of Judah could not drive out the Jebusites, the inhabitants of Jerusalem; so the Jebusites live with the people of Judah in Jerusalem to this day.

## LUKE 18.18–43

A CERTAIN ruler asked him, "Good Teacher, what must I do to inherit eternal life?" ¹⁹Jesus said to him, "Why do you call me good? No one is good but God alone. ²⁰You know the commandments: 'You shall not commit adultery; You shall not murder; You shall not steal; You shall not bear false witness; Honor your father and mother.'" ²¹He replied, "I have kept all these since my youth." ²²When Jesus heard this, he said to him, "There is still one thing lacking. Sell all that you own and distribute the money[a] to the poor, and you will have treasure in heaven; then come, follow me." ²³But when he heard this, he became sad; for he was very rich. ²⁴Jesus looked at him and said, "How hard it is for those who have wealth to enter the kingdom of God!

²⁵Indeed, it is easier for a camel to go through the eye of a needle than for someone who is rich to enter the kingdom of God."

26 Those who heard it said, "Then who can be saved?" ²⁷He replied, "What is impossible for mortals is possible for God."

28 Then Peter said, "Look, we have left our homes and followed you." ²⁹And he said to them, "Truly I tell you, there is no one who has left house or wife or brothers or parents or children, for the sake of the kingdom of God, ³⁰who will not get back very much more in this age, and in the age to come eternal life."

31 Then he took the twelve aside and said to them, "See, we are going up to Jerusalem, and everything that is written about the Son of Man by the prophets will be accomplished. ³²For he will be handed over to the Gentiles; and he will be mocked and insulted and spat upon. ³³After they have flogged him, they will kill him, and on the third day he will rise again." ³⁴But they understood nothing about all these things; in fact, what he said was hidden from them, and they did not grasp what was said.

35 As he approached Jericho, a blind man was sitting by the roadside begging. ³⁶When he heard a crowd going by, he asked what was happening. ³⁷They told him, "Jesus of Nazareth[b] is passing by." ³⁸Then he shouted, "Jesus, Son of David, have mercy on me!" ³⁹Those who were in front sternly ordered him to be quiet; but he shouted even more loudly, "Son of David, have mercy on me!" ⁴⁰Jesus stood still and ordered the man to be brought to him; and when he came near, he asked him, ⁴¹"What do you want me to do for you?" He said, "Lord, let me see again." ⁴²Jesus said to him, "Receive your

a Gk lacks *the money*   b Gk *the Nazorean*

sight; your faith has saved you." <sup>43</sup>Immediately he regained his sight and followed him, glorifying God; and all the people, when they saw it, praised God.

## PSALM 86.1–17

*A Prayer of David.*

INCLINE your ear, O LORD, and
    answer me,
  for I am poor and needy.
2  Preserve my life, for I am
    devoted to you;
    save your servant who trusts
      in you.
  You are my God; <sup>3</sup>be gracious
    to me, O Lord,
    for to you do I cry all day
      long.
4  Gladden the soul of your
    servant,
    for to you, O Lord, I lift up
      my soul.
5  For you, O Lord, are good and
    forgiving,
    abounding in steadfast love to
      all who call on you.
6  Give ear, O LORD, to my
    prayer;
    listen to my cry of
      supplication.
7  In the day of my trouble I call
    on you,
    for you will answer me.

8  There is none like you among
    the gods, O Lord,
    nor are there any works like
      yours.
9  All the nations you have made
    shall come
    and bow down before you,
      O Lord,
    and shall glorify your name.
10  For you are great and do
    wondrous things;
    you alone are God.
11  Teach me your way, O LORD,
    that I may walk in your truth;
    give me an undivided heart to
      revere your name.
12  I give thanks to you, O Lord
    my God, with my whole
      heart,
    and I will glorify your name
      forever.
13  For great is your steadfast love
    toward me;
    you have delivered my soul
      from the depths of Sheol.

14  O God, the insolent rise up
    against me;
    a band of ruffians seeks my
      life,
    and they do not set you
      before them.
15  But you, O Lord, are a God
    merciful and gracious,
    slow to anger and abounding
      in steadfast love and
      faithfulness.
16  Turn to me and be gracious to
    me;
    give your strength to your
      servant;
    save the child of your serving
      girl.
17  Show me a sign of your favor,
    so that those who hate me
      may see it and be put to
      shame,
    because you, LORD, have
      helped me and comforted
      me.

## PROVERBS 13.9–10

THE light of the righteous
    rejoices,
  but the lamp of the wicked
    goes out.
10  By insolence the heedless make
    strife,
    but wisdom is with those who
      take advice.

# APRIL 18

JOSHUA 16.1—18.28

THE allotment of the Josephites went from the Jordan by Jericho, east of the waters of Jericho, into the wilderness, going up from Jericho into the hill country to Bethel; ²then going from Bethel to Luz, it passes along to Ataroth, the territory of the Archites; ³then it goes down westward to the territory of the Japhletites, as far as the territory of Lower Beth-horon, then to Gezer, and it ends at the sea.

4 The Josephites—Manasseh and Ephraim—received their inheritance.

5 The territory of the Ephraimites by their families was as follows: the boundary of their inheritance on the east was Ataroth-addar as far as Upper Beth-horon, ⁶and the boundary goes from there to the sea; on the north is Michmethath; then on the east the boundary makes a turn toward Taanath-shiloh, and passes along beyond it on the east to Janoah, ⁷then it goes down from Janoah to Ataroth and to Naarah, and touches Jericho, ending at the Jordan. ⁸From Tappuah the boundary goes westward to the Wadi Kanah, and ends at the sea. Such is the inheritance of the tribe of the Ephraimites by their families, ⁹together with the towns that were set apart for the Ephraimites within the inheritance of the Manassites, all those towns with their villages. ¹⁰They did not, however, drive out the Canaanites who lived in Gezer: so the Canaanites have lived within Ephraim to this day but have been made to do forced labor.

**17.1** THEN allotment was made to the tribe of Manasseh, for he was the firstborn of Joseph. To Machir the firstborn of Manasseh, the father of Gilead, were allotted Gilead and Bashan, because he was a warrior. ²And allotments were made to the rest of the tribe of Manasseh, by their families, Abiezer, Helek, Asriel, Shechem, Hepher, and Shemida; these were the male descendants of Manasseh son of Joseph, by their families.

3 Now Zelophehad son of Hepher son of Gilead son of Machir son of Manasseh had no sons, but only daughters; and these are the names of his daughters: Mahlah, Noah, Hoglah, Milcah, and Tirzah. ⁴They came before the priest Eleazar and Joshua son of Nun and the leaders, and said, "The LORD commanded Moses to give us an inheritance along with our male kin." So according to the commandment of the LORD he gave them an inheritance among the kinsmen of their father. ⁵Thus there fell to Manasseh ten portions, besides the land of Gilead and Bashan, which is on the other side of the Jordan, ⁶because the daughters of Manasseh received an inheritance along with his sons. The land of Gilead was allotted to the rest of the Manassites.

7 The territory of Manasseh reached from Asher to Michmethath, which is east of Shechem; then the boundary goes along southward to the inhabitants of En-tappuah. ⁸The land of Tappuah belonged to Manasseh, but the town of Tappuah on the boundary of Manasseh belonged to the Ephraimites. ⁹Then the boundary went down to the Wadi Kanah. The towns here, to the south of the wadi, among the towns of Manasseh, belong to Ephraim. Then the boundary of Manasseh goes along the north side of the wadi and ends at the sea. ¹⁰The land to the south is Ephraim's and that to the north is Ma-

nasseh's, with the sea forming its boundary; on the north Asher is reached, and on the east Issachar. [11]Within Issachar and Asher, Manasseh had Beth-shean and its villages, Ibleam and its villages, the inhabitants of Dor and its villages, the inhabitants of En-dor and its villages, the inhabitants of Taanach and its villages, and the inhabitants of Megiddo and its villages (the third is Naphath). [a] [12]Yet the Manassites could not take possession of those towns; but the Canaanites continued to live in that land. [13]But when the Israelites grew strong, they put the Canaanites to forced labor, but did not utterly drive them out.

14 The tribe of Joseph spoke to Joshua, saying, "Why have you given me but one lot and one portion as an inheritance, since we are a numerous people, whom all along the LORD has blessed?" [15]And Joshua said to them, "If you are a numerous people, go up to the forest, and clear ground there for yourselves in the land of the Perizzites and the Rephaim, since the hill country of Ephraim is too narrow for you." [16]The tribe of Joseph said, "The hill country is not enough for us; yet all the Canaanites who live in the plain have chariots of iron, both those in Beth-shean and its villages and those in the Valley of Jezreel." [17]Then Joshua said to the house of Joseph, to Ephraim and Manasseh, "You are indeed a numerous people, and have great power; you shall not have one lot only, [18]but the hill country shall be yours, for though it is a forest, you shall clear it and possess it to its farthest borders; for you shall drive out the Canaanites, though they have chariots of iron, and though they are strong."

**18.**[1]THEN the whole congregation of the Israelites assembled at Shiloh, and set up the tent of meeting there. The land lay subdued before them.

2 There remained among the Israelites seven tribes whose inheritance had not yet been apportioned. [3]So Joshua said to the Israelites, "How long will you be slack about going in and taking possession of the land that the LORD, the God of your ancestors, has given you? [4]Provide three men from each tribe, and I will send them out that they may begin to go throughout the land, writing a description of it with a view to their inheritances. Then come back to me. [5]They shall divide it into seven portions, Judah continuing in its territory on the south, and the house of Joseph in their territory on the north. [6]You shall describe the land in seven divisions and bring the description here to me; and I will cast lots for you here before the LORD our God. [7]The Levites have no portion among you, for the priesthood of the LORD is their heritage; and Gad and Reuben and the half-tribe of Manasseh have received their inheritance beyond the Jordan eastward, which Moses the servant of the LORD gave them."

8 So the men started on their way; and Joshua charged those who went to write the description of the land, saying, "Go throughout the land and write a description of it, and come back to me; and I will cast lots for you here before the LORD in Shiloh." [9]So the men went and traversed the land and set down in a book a description of it by towns in seven divisions; then they came back to Joshua in the camp at Shiloh, [10]and Joshua cast lots for them in Shiloh before the LORD; and there Joshua apportioned the land to the Israelites, to each a portion.

11 The lot of the tribe of Benjamin according to its families came up, and the territory allotted to it fell between the tribe of Judah and the tribe of Jo-

[a]Meaning of Heb uncertain

seph. ¹²On the north side their boundary began at the Jordan; then the boundary goes up to the slope of Jericho on the north, then up through the hill country westward; and it ends at the wilderness of Beth-aven. ¹³From there the boundary passes along southward in the direction of Luz, to the slope of Luz (that is, Bethel), then the boundary goes down to Ataroth-addar, on the mountain that lies south of Lower Beth-horon. ¹⁴Then the boundary goes in another direction, turning on the western side southward from the mountain that lies to the south, opposite Beth-horon, and it ends at Kiriath-baal (that is, Kiriath-jearim), a town belonging to the tribe of Judah. This forms the western side. ¹⁵The southern side begins at the outskirts of Kiriath-jearim; and the boundary goes from there to Ephron, ª to the spring of the Waters of Nephtoah; ¹⁶then the boundary goes down to the border of the mountain that overlooks the valley of the son of Hinnom, which is at the north end of the valley of Rephaim; and it then goes down the valley of Hinnom, south of the slope of the Jebusites, and downward to En-rogel; ¹⁷then it bends in a northerly direction going on to En-shemesh, and from there goes to Geliloth, which is opposite the ascent of Adummim; then it goes down to the Stone of Bohan, Reuben's son; ¹⁸and passing on to the north of the slope of Beth-arabahᵇ it goes down to the Arabah; ¹⁹then the boundary passes on to the north of the slope of Beth-hoglah; and the boundary ends at the northern bay of the Dead Sea, ᶜ at the south end of the Jordan: this is the southern border. ²⁰The Jordan forms its boundary on the eastern side. This is the inheritance of the tribe of Benjamin, according to its families, boundary by boundary all around.

21 Now the towns of the tribe of Benjamin according to their families were Jericho, Beth-hoglah, Emekkeziz, ²²Beth-arabah, Zemaraim, Bethel, ²³Avvim, Parah, Ophrah, ²⁴Chephar-ammoni, Ophni, and Geba—twelve towns with their villages: ²⁵Gibeon, Ramah, Beeroth, ²⁶Mizpeh, Chephirah, Mozah, ²⁷Rekem, Irpeel, Taralah, ²⁸Zela, Haeleph, Jebusᵈ (that is Jerusalem), Gibeahᵉ and Kiriath-jearimᶠ—fourteen towns with their villages. This is the inheritance of the tribe of Benjamin according to its families.

## LUKE 19. 1–27

**H**E [Jesus] entered Jericho and was passing through it. ²A man was there named Zacchaeus; he was a chief tax collector and was rich. ³He was trying to see who Jesus was, but on account of the crowd he could not, because he was short in stature. ⁴So he ran ahead and climbed a sycamore tree to see him, because he was going to pass that way. ⁵When Jesus came to the place, he looked up and said to him, "Zacchaeus, hurry and come down; for I must stay at your house today." ⁶So he hurried down and was happy to welcome him. ⁷All who saw it began to grumble and said, "He has gone to be the guest of one who is a sinner." ⁸Zacchaeus stood there and said to the Lord, "Look, half of my possessions, Lord, I will give to the poor; and if I have defrauded anyone of anything, I will pay back four times as much." ⁹Then Jesus said to him, "Today salvation has come to this house, because he too is a son of Abraham. ¹⁰For the Son of Man came to seek out and to save the lost."

11 As they were listening to this, he went on to tell a parable, because he was near Jerusalem, and because they supposed that the kingdom of God was

ªCn See 15.9. Heb *westward*   ᵇGk: Heb *to the slope over against the Arabah*   ᶜHeb *Salt Sea*
ᵈGk Syr Vg: Heb *the Jebusite*   ᵉHeb *Gibeath*   ᶠGk: Heb *Kiriath*

to appear immediately. ¹²So he said, "A nobleman went to a distant country to get royal power for himself and then return. ¹³He summoned ten of his slaves, and gave them ten pounds,ᵃ and said to them, 'Do business with these until I come back.' ¹⁴But the citizens of his country hated him and sent a delegation after him, saying, 'We do not want this man to rule over us.' ¹⁵When he returned, having received royal power, he ordered these slaves, to whom he had given the money, to be summoned so that he might find out what they had gained by trading. ¹⁶The first came forward and said, 'Lord, your pound has made ten more pounds.' ¹⁷He said to him, 'Well done, good slave! Because you have been trustworthy in a very small thing, take charge of ten cities.' ¹⁸Then the second came, saying, 'Lord, your pound has made five pounds.' ¹⁹He said to him, 'And you, rule over five cities.' ²⁰Then the other came, saying, 'Lord, here is your pound. I wrapped it up in a piece of cloth, ²¹for I was afraid of you, because you are a harsh man; you take what you did not deposit, and reap what you did not sow.' ²²He said to him, 'I will judge you by your own words, you wicked slave! You knew, did you, that I was a harsh man, taking what I did not deposit and reaping what I did not sow? ²³Why then did you not put my money into the bank? Then when I returned, I could have collected it with interest.' ²⁴He said to the bystanders, 'Take the pound from him and give it to the one who has ten pounds.' ²⁵(And they said to him, 'Lord, he has ten pounds!') ²⁶'I tell you, to all those who have, more will be given; but from those who have nothing, even what they have will be taken away. ²⁷But as for these enemies of mine who did not want me to be king over them—bring them here and slaughter them in my presence.' "

## PSALM 87.1–7

*Of the Korahites. A Psalm. A Song.*

O N the holy mount stands the
    city he founded;
²    the Lord loves the
    gates of Zion
more than all the dwellings of
    Jacob.
³ Glorious things are spoken of
    you,
   O city of God.     *Selah*

⁴ Among those who know me I
    mention Rahab and
    Babylon;
   Philistia too, and Tyre, with
    Ethiopiaᵇ—
   "This one was born there,"
    they say.

⁵ And of Zion it shall be said,
   "This one and that one were
    born in it";
   for the Most High himself will
    establish it.
⁶ The Lord records, as he
    registers the peoples,
   "This one was born there."
       *Selah*

⁷ Singers and dancers alike say,
   "All my springs are in you."

## PROVERBS 13.11

W EALTH hastily gottenᶜ will
    dwindle,
  but those who gather little
    by little will increase it.

ᵃThe mina, rendered here by *pound,* was about three months' wages for a laborer   ᵇOr *Nubia*; Heb *Cush*   ᶜGk Vg: Heb *from vanity*

# APRIL 19



THE second lot came out for Simeon, for the tribe of Simeon, according to its families; its inheritance lay within the inheritance of the tribe of Judah. [2]It had for its inheritance Beer-sheba, Sheba, Moladah, [3]Hazar-shual, Balah, Ezem, [4]Eltolad, Bethul, Hormah, [5]Ziklag, Beth-marcaboth, Hazar-susah, [6]Beth-lebaoth, and Sharuhen—thirteen towns with their villages; [7]Ain, Rimmon, Ether, and Ashan—four towns with their villages; [8]together with all the villages all around these towns as far as Baalath-beer, Ramah of the Negeb. This was the inheritance of the tribe of Simeon according to its families. [9]The inheritance of the tribe of Simeon formed part of the territory of Judah; because the portion of the tribe of Judah was too large for them, the tribe of Simeon obtained an inheritance within their inheritance.

10 The third lot came up for the tribe of Zebulun, according to its families. The boundary of its inheritance reached as far as Sarid; [11]then its boundary goes up westward, and on to Maralah, and touches Dabbesheth, then the wadi that is east of Jokneam; [12]from Sarid it goes in the other direction eastward toward the sunrise to the boundary of Chisloth-tabor; from there it goes to Daberath, then up to Japhia; [13]from there it passes along on the east toward the sunrise to Gath-hepher, to Eth-kazin, and going on to Rimmon it bends toward Neah; [14]then on the north the boundary makes a turn to Hannathon, and it ends at the valley of Iphtah-el; [15]and Kattath, Nahalal, Shimron, Idalah, and Bethlehem— twelve towns with their villages. [16]This is the inheritance of the tribe of Zebulun, according to its families—these towns with their villages.

17 The fourth lot came out for Issachar, for the tribe of Issachar, according to its families. [18]Its territory included Jezreel, Chesulloth, Shunem, [19]Hapharaim, Shion, Anaharath, [20]Rabbith, Kishion, Ebez, [21]Remeth, En-gannim, En-haddah, Beth-pazzez; [22]the boundary also touches Tabor, Shahazumah, and Beth-shemesh, and its boundary ends at the Jordan— sixteen towns with their villages. [23]This is the inheritance of the tribe of Issachar, according to its families—the towns with their villages.

24 The fifth lot came out for the tribe of Asher according to its families. [25]Its boundary included Helkath, Hali, Beten, Achshaph, [26]Allammelech, Amad, and Mishal; on the west it touches Carmel and Shihor-libnath, [27]then it turns eastward, goes to Beth-dagon, and touches Zebulun and the valley of Iphtah-el northward to Beth-emek and Neiel; then it continues in the north to Cabul, [28]Ebron, Rehob, Hammon, Kanah, as far as Great Sidon; [29]then the boundary turns to Ramah, reaching to the fortified city of Tyre; then the boundary turns to Hosah, and it ends at the sea; Mahalab,[a] Achzib, [30]Ummah, Aphek, and Rehob— twenty-two towns with their villages. [31]This is the inheritance of the tribe of Asher according to its families—these towns with their villages.

32 The sixth lot came out for the tribe of Naphtali, for the tribe of Naphtali, according to its families. [33]And its boundary ran from Heleph, from the

---

aCn Compare Gk: Heb *Mehebel*

oak in Zaanannim, and Adami-nekeb, and Jabneel, as far as Lakkum; and it ended at the Jordan; ³⁴then the boundary turns westward to Aznoth-tabor, and goes from there to Hukkok, touching Zebulun at the south, and Asher on the west, and Judah on the east at the Jordan. ³⁵The fortified towns are Ziddim, Zer, Hammath, Rakkath, Chinnereth, ³⁶Adamah, Ramah, Hazor, ³⁷Kedesh, Edrei, En-hazor, ³⁸Iron, Migdal-el, Horem, Beth-anath, and Beth-shemesh—nineteen towns with their villages. ³⁹This is the inheritance of the tribe of Naphtali according to its families—the towns with their villages.

40 The seventh lot came out for the tribe of Dan, according to its families. ⁴¹The territory of its inheritance included Zorah, Eshtaol, Ir-shemesh, ⁴²Shaalabbin, Aijalon, Ithlah, ⁴³Elon, Timnah, Ekron, ⁴⁴Eltekeh, Gibbethon, Baalath, ⁴⁵Jehud, Bene-berak, Gathrimmon, ⁴⁶Me-jarkon, and Rakkon at the border opposite Joppa. ⁴⁷When the territory of the Danites was lost to them, the Danites went up and fought against Leshem, and after capturing it and putting it to the sword, they took possession of it and settled in it, calling Leshem, Dan, after their ancestor Dan. ⁴⁸This is the inheritance of the tribe of Dan, according to their families—these towns with their villages.

49 When they had finished distributing the several territories of the land as inheritances, the Israelites gave an inheritance among them to Joshua son of Nun. ⁵⁰By command of the Lord they gave him the town that he asked for, Timnath-serah in the hill country of Ephraim; he rebuilt the town, and settled in it.

51 These are the inheritances that the priest Eleazar and Joshua son of Nun and the heads of the families of the tribes of the Israelites distributed by lot at Shiloh before the Lord, at the entrance of the tent of meeting. So they finished dividing the land.

²⁰·¹ Then the Lord spoke to Joshua, saying, ²"Say to the Israelites, 'Appoint the cities of refuge, of which I spoke to you through Moses, ³so that anyone who kills a person without intent or by mistake may flee there; they shall be for you a refuge from the avenger of blood. ⁴The slayer shall flee to one of these cities and shall stand at the entrance of the gate of the city, and explain the case to the elders of that city; then the fugitive shall be taken into the city, and given a place, and shall remain with them. ⁵And if the avenger of blood is in pursuit, they shall not give up the slayer, because the neighbor was killed by mistake, there having been no enmity between them before. ⁶The slayer shall remain in that city until there is a trial before the congregation, until the death of the one who is high priest at the time: then the slayer may return home, to the town in which the deed was done.' "

7 So they set apart Kedesh in Galilee in the hill country of Naphtali, and Shechem in the hill country of Ephraim, and Kiriath-arba (that is, Hebron) in the hill country of Judah. ⁸And beyond the Jordan east of Jericho, they appointed Bezer in the wilderness on the tableland, from the tribe of Reuben, and Ramoth in Gilead, from the tribe of Gad, and Golan in Bashan, from the tribe of Manasseh. ⁹These were the cities designated for all the Israelites, and for the aliens residing among them, that anyone who killed a person without intent could flee there, so as not to die by the hand of the avenger of blood, until there was a trial before the congregation.

# LUKE 19.28–48

**A**FTER he [Jesus] had said this, he went on ahead, going up to Jerusalem.

29 When he had come near Bethphage and Bethany, at the place called the Mount of Olives, he sent two of the disciples, <sup>30</sup>saying, "Go into the village ahead of you, and as you enter it you will find tied there a colt that has never been ridden. Untie it and bring it here. <sup>31</sup>If anyone asks you, 'Why are you untying it?' just say this, 'The Lord needs it.' " <sup>32</sup>So those who were sent departed and found it as he had told them. <sup>33</sup>As they were untying the colt, its owners asked them, "Why are you untying the colt?" <sup>34</sup>They said, "The Lord needs it." <sup>35</sup>Then they brought it to Jesus; and after throwing their cloaks on the colt, they set Jesus on it. <sup>36</sup>As he rode along, people kept spreading their cloaks on the road. <sup>37</sup>As he was now approaching the path down from the Mount of Olives, the whole multitude of the disciples began to praise God joyfully with a loud voice for all the deeds of power that they had seen, <sup>38</sup>saying,

> "Blessed is the king
> > who comes in the name of
> > the Lord!
> Peace in heaven,
> > and glory in the highest
> > heaven!"

<sup>39</sup>Some of the Pharisees in the crowd said to him, "Teacher, order your disciples to stop." <sup>40</sup>He answered, "I tell you, if these were silent, the stones would shout out."

41 As he came near and saw the city, he wept over it, <sup>42</sup>saying, "If you, even you, had only recognized on this day the things that make for peace! But now they are hidden from your eyes. <sup>43</sup>Indeed, the days will come upon you, when your enemies will set up ramparts around you and surround you, and hem you in on every side. <sup>44</sup>They will crush you to the ground, you and your children within you, and they will not leave within you one stone upon another; because you did not recognize the time of your visitation from God."<sup>a</sup>

45 Then he entered the temple and began to drive out those who were selling things there; <sup>46</sup>and he said, "It is written,

> 'My house shall be a house
> > of prayer';
> but you have made it a den
> > of robbers.' "

47 Every day he was teaching in the temple. The chief priests, the scribes, and the leaders of the people kept looking for a way to kill him; <sup>48</sup>but they did not find anything they could do, for all the people were spellbound by what they heard.

# PSALM 88.1–18

*A Song. A Psalm of the Korahites. To the leader: according to Mahalath Leannoth. A Maskil of Heman the Ezrahite.*

**O** LORD, God of my salvation,
> > when, at night, I cry out in
> > your presence,
> 2 let my prayer come before you;
> > incline your ear to my cry.

> 3 For my soul is full of troubles,
> > and my life draws near to
> > Sheol.
> 4 I am counted among those who
> > go down to the Pit;
> > I am like those who have no
> > help,
> 5 like those forsaken among the
> > dead,
> > like the slain that lie in the
> > grave,
> > like those whom you remember
> > no more,
> > for they are cut off from your
> > hand.

a Gk lacks *from God*

6 You have put me in the depths
        of the Pit,
    in the regions dark and deep.
7 Your wrath lies heavy upon me,
    and you overwhelm me with
        all your waves.        *Selah*

8 You have caused my
        companions to shun me;
    you have made me a thing of
        horror to them.
    I am shut in so that I cannot
        escape;
9     my eye grows dim through
        sorrow.
    Every day I call on you,
        O Lord;
    I spread out my hands to you.
10 Do you work wonders for the
        dead?
    Do the shades rise up to
        praise you?        *Selah*
11 Is your steadfast love declared
        in the grave,
    or your faithfulness in
        Abaddon?
12 Are your wonders known in the
        darkness,
    or your saving help in the
        land of forgetfulness?

13 But I, O Lord, cry out to you;
    in the morning my prayer
        comes before you.

14 O Lord, why do you cast me
        off?
    Why do you hide your face
        from me?
15 Wretched and close to death
        from my youth up,
    I suffer your terrors; I am
        desperate. ᵃ
16 Your wrath has swept over me;
    your dread assaults destroy
        me.
17 They surround me like a flood
        all day long;
    from all sides they close in on
        me.
18 You have caused friend and
        neighbor to shun me;
    my companions are in
        darkness.

# PROVERBS 13.12–14

Hope deferred makes the
        heart sick,
    but a desire fulfilled is a
        tree of life.
13 Those who despise the word
        bring destruction on
        themselves,
    but those who respect the
        commandment will be
        rewarded.
14 The teaching of the wise is a
        fountain of life,
    so that one may avoid the
        snares of death.

# APRIL 20

JOSHUA 21.1—22.20

THEN the heads of the families of the Levites came to the priest Eleazar and to Joshua son of Nun and to the heads of the families of the tribes of the Israelites; ²they said to them at Shiloh in the land of Canaan, "The LORD commanded through Moses that we be given towns to live in, along with their pasture lands for our livestock." ³So by command of the LORD the Israelites gave to the Levites the following towns and pasture lands out of their inheritance.

4 The lot came out for the families of the Kohathites. So those Levites who were descendants of Aaron the priest received by lot thirteen towns from the tribes of Judah, Simeon, and Benjamin.

5 The rest of the Kohathites received by lot ten towns from the families of the tribe of Ephraim, from the tribe of Dan, and the half-tribe of Manasseh.

6 The Gershonites received by lot thirteen towns from the families of the tribe of Issachar, from the tribe of Asher, from the tribe of Naphtali, and from the half-tribe of Manasseh in Bashan.

7 The Merarites according to their families received twelve towns from the tribe of Reuben, the tribe of Gad, and the tribe of Zebulun.

8 These towns and their pasture lands the Israelites gave by lot to the Levites, as the LORD had commanded through Moses.

9 Out of the tribe of Judah and the tribe of Simeon they gave the following towns mentioned by name, ¹⁰which went to the descendants of Aaron, one of the families of the Kohathites who belonged to the Levites, since the lot fell to them first. ¹¹They gave them Kiriath-arba (Arba being the father of Anak), that is Hebron, in the hill country of Judah, along with the pasture lands around it. ¹²But the fields of the town and its villages had been given to Caleb son of Jephunneh as his holding.

13 To the descendants of Aaron the priest they gave Hebron, the city of refuge for the slayer, with its pasture lands, Libnah with its pasture lands, ¹⁴Jattir with its pasture lands, Eshtemoa with its pasture lands, ¹⁵Holon with its pasture lands, Debir with its pasture lands, ¹⁶Ain with its pasture lands, Juttah with its pasture lands, and Beth-shemesh with its pasture lands— nine towns out of these two tribes. ¹⁷Out of the tribe of Benjamin: Gibeon with its pasture lands, Geba with its pasture lands, ¹⁸Anathoth with its pasture lands, and Almon with its pasture lands—four towns. ¹⁹The towns of the descendants of Aaron—the priests— were thirteen in all, with their pasture lands.

20 As to the rest of the Kohathites belonging to the Kohathite families of the Levites, the towns allotted to them were out of the tribe of Ephraim. ²¹To them were given Shechem, the city of refuge for the slayer, with its pasture lands in the hill country of Ephraim, Gezer with its pasture lands, ²²Kibzaim with its pasture lands, and Beth-horon with its pasture lands—four towns. ²³Out of the tribe of Dan: Elteke with its pasture lands, Gibbethon with its pasture lands, ²⁴Aijalon with its pasture lands, Gath-rimmon with its pasture lands—four towns. ²⁵Out of the half-tribe of Manasseh: Taanach with its pasture lands, and Gath-rimmon with its pasture lands—two towns. ²⁶The towns of the families of the rest of the

Kohathites were ten in all, with their pasture lands.

27 To the Gershonites, one of the families of the Levites, were given out of the half-tribe of Manasseh, Golan in Bashan with its pasture lands, the city of refuge for the slayer, and Beeshterah with its pasture lands—two towns. [28]Out of the tribe of Issachar: Kishion with its pasture lands, Daberath with its pasture lands, [29]Jarmuth with its pasture lands, En-gannim with its pasture lands—four towns; [30]Out of the tribe of Asher: Mishal with its pasture lands, Abdon with its pasture lands, [31]Helkath with its pasture lands, and Rehob with its pasture lands—four towns. [32]Out of the tribe of Naphtali: Kedesh in Galilee with its pasture lands, the city of refuge for the slayer, Hammoth-dor with its pasture lands, and Kartan with its pasture lands— three towns. [33]The towns of the several families of the Gershonites were in all thirteen, with their pasture lands.

34 To the rest of the Levites—the Merarite families—were given out of the tribe of Zebulun: Jokneam with its pasture lands, Kartah with its pasture lands, [35]Dimnah with its pasture lands, Nahalal with its pasture lands—four towns. [36]Out of the tribe of Reuben: Bezer with its pasture lands, Jahzah with its pasture lands, [37]Kedemoth with its pasture lands, and Mephaath with its pasture lands—four towns. [38]Out of the tribe of Gad: Ramoth in Gilead with its pasture lands, the city of refuge for the slayer, Mahanaim with its pasture lands, [39]Heshbon with its pasture lands, Jazer with its pasture lands—four towns in all. [40]As for the towns of the several Merarite families, that is, the remainder of the families of the Levites, those allotted to them were twelve in all.

41 The towns of the Levites within the holdings of the Israelites were in all forty-eight towns with their pasture lands. [42]Each of these towns had its pasture lands around it; so it was with all these towns.

43 Thus the LORD gave to Israel all the land that he swore to their ancestors that he would give them; and having taken possession of it, they settled there. [44]And the LORD gave them rest on every side just as he had sworn to their ancestors; not one of all their enemies had withstood them, for the LORD had given all their enemies into their hands. [45]Not one of all the good promises that the LORD had made to the house of Israel had failed; all came to pass.

22.1 THEN Joshua summoned the Reubenites, the Gadites, and the half-tribe of Manasseh, [2]and said to them, "You have observed all that Moses the servant of the LORD commanded you, and have obeyed me in all that I have commanded you; [3]you have not forsaken your kindred these many days, down to this day, but have been careful to keep the charge of the LORD your God. [4]And now the LORD your God has given rest to your kindred, as he promised them; therefore turn and go to your tents in the land where your possession lies, which Moses the servant of the LORD gave you on the other side of the Jordan. [5]Take good care to observe the commandment and instruction that Moses the servant of the LORD commanded you, to love the LORD your God, to walk in all his ways, to keep his commandments, and to hold fast to him, and to serve him with all your heart and with all your soul." [6]So Joshua blessed them and sent them away, and they went to their tents.

7 Now to the one half of the tribe of Manasseh Moses had given a possession in Bashan; but to the other half Joshua had given a possession beside their fellow Israelites in the land west of the Jordan. And when Joshua sent them away to their tents and blessed them, [8]he said to them, "Go back to

your tents with much wealth, and with very much livestock, with silver, gold, bronze, and iron, and with a great quantity of clothing; divide the spoil of your enemies with your kindred." [9]So the Reubenites and the Gadites and the half-tribe of Manasseh returned home, parting from the Israelites at Shiloh, which is in the land of Canaan, to go to the land of Gilead, their own land of which they had taken possession by command of the Lord through Moses.

10 When they came to the region[a] near the Jordan that lies in the land of Canaan, the Reubenites and the Gadites and the half-tribe of Manasseh built there an altar by the Jordan, an altar of great size. [11]The Israelites heard that the Reubenites and the Gadites and the half-tribe of Manasseh had built an altar at the frontier of the land of Canaan, in the region[b] near the Jordan, on the side that belongs to the Israelites. [12]And when the people of Israel heard of it, the whole assembly of the Israelites gathered at Shiloh, to make war against them.

13 Then the Israelites sent the priest Phinehas son of Eleazar to the Reubenites and the Gadites and the half-tribe of Manasseh, in the land of Gilead, [14]and with him ten chiefs, one from each of the tribal families of Israel, every one of them the head of a family among the clans of Israel. [15]They came to the Reubenites, the Gadites, and the half-tribe of Manasseh, in the land of Gilead, and they said to them, [16]"Thus says the whole congregation of the Lord, 'What is this treachery that you have committed against the God of Israel in turning away today from following the Lord, by building yourselves an altar today in rebellion against the Lord? [17]Have we not had enough of the sin at Peor from which even yet we have not cleansed ourselves, and for which a plague came upon the congregation of the Lord, [18]that you must turn away today from following the Lord! If you rebel against the Lord today, he will be angry with the whole congregation of Israel tomorrow. [19]But now, if your land is unclean, cross over into the Lord's land where the Lord's tabernacle now stands, and take for yourselves a possession among us; only do not rebel against the Lord, or rebel against us[c] by building yourselves an altar other than the altar of the Lord our God. [20]Did not Achan son of Zerah break faith in the matter of the devoted things, and wrath fell upon all the congregation of Israel? And he did not perish alone for his iniquity!' "

## LUKE 20.1–26

ONE day, as he [Jesus] was teaching the people in the temple and telling the good news, the chief priests and the scribes came with the elders [2]and said to him, "Tell us, by what authority are you doing these things? Who is it who gave you this authority?" [3]He answered them, "I will also ask you a question, and you tell me: [4]Did the baptism of John come from heaven, or was it of human origin?" [5]They discussed it with one another, saying, "If we say, 'From heaven,' he will say, 'Why did you not believe him?' [6]But if we say, 'Of human origin,' all the people will stone us; for they are convinced that John was a prophet." [7]So they answered that they did not know where it came from. [8]Then Jesus said to them, "Neither will I tell you by what authority I am doing these things."

9 He began to tell the people this parable: "A man planted a vineyard, and leased it to tenants, and went to another country for a long time. [10]When the season came, he sent a slave to the tenants in order that they

might give him his share of the produce of the vineyard; but the tenants beat him and sent him away empty-handed. <sup>11</sup>Next he sent another slave; that one also they beat and insulted and sent away empty-handed. <sup>12</sup>And he sent still a third; this one also they wounded and threw out. <sup>13</sup>Then the owner of the vineyard said, 'What shall I do? I will send my beloved son; perhaps they will respect him.' <sup>14</sup>But when the tenants saw him, they discussed it among themselves and said, 'This is the heir; let us kill him so that the inheritance may be ours.' <sup>15</sup>So they threw him out of the vineyard and killed him. What then will the owner of the vineyard do to them? <sup>16</sup>He will come and destroy those tenants and give the vineyard to others." When they heard this, they said, "Heaven forbid!" <sup>17</sup>But he looked at them and said, "What then does this text mean:

'The stone that the builders rejected
has become the cornerstone'?<sup>a</sup>

<sup>18</sup>Everyone who falls on that stone will be broken to pieces; and it will crush anyone on whom it falls." <sup>19</sup>When the scribes and chief priests realized that he had told this parable against them, they wanted to lay hands on him at that very hour, but they feared the people.

20 So they watched him and sent spies who pretended to be honest, in order to trap him by what he said, so as to hand him over to the jurisdiction and authority of the governor. <sup>21</sup>So they asked him, "Teacher, we know that you are right in what you say and teach, and you show deference to no one, but teach the way of God in accordance with truth. <sup>22</sup>Is it lawful for us to pay taxes to the emperor, or not?" <sup>23</sup>But he perceived their craftiness and said to them, <sup>24</sup>"Show me a denarius. Whose head and whose title does it bear?"

They said, "The emperor's." <sup>25</sup>He said to them, "Then give to the emperor the things that are the emperor's, and to God the things that are God's." <sup>26</sup>And they were not able in the presence of the people to trap him by what he said; and being amazed by his answer, they became silent.

## PSALM 89. 1–13

*A Maskil of Ethan the Ezrahite.*

I WILL sing of your steadfast love,
  O LORD, <sup>b</sup> forever;
  with my mouth I will proclaim
    your faithfulness to all
    generations.
2  I declare that your steadfast
    love is established
    forever;
  your faithfulness is as firm as
    the heavens.

3  You said, "I have made a
    covenant with my chosen
    one,
  I have sworn to my servant
    David:
4  'I will establish your
    descendants forever,
  and build your throne for all
    generations.'"          *Selah*

5  Let the heavens praise your
    wonders, O LORD,
  your faithfulness in the
    assembly of the holy
    ones.
6  For who in the skies can be
    compared to the LORD?
  Who among the heavenly
    beings is like the LORD,
7  a God feared in the council of
    the holy ones,
  great and awesome<sup>c</sup> above
    all that are around him?
8  O LORD God of hosts,
  who is as mighty as you,
    O LORD?

<sup>a</sup>Or *keystone*   <sup>b</sup>Gk: Heb *the steadfast love of the* LORD   <sup>c</sup>Gk Syr: Heb *greatly awesome*

Your faithfulness surrounds
you.

9 You rule the raging of the sea;
when its waves rise, you still
them.

10 You crushed Rahab like a
carcass;
you scattered your enemies
with your mighty arm.

11 The heavens are yours, the
earth also is yours;
the world and all that is in
it—you have founded
them.

12 The north and the south[a]—you
created them;
Tabor and Hermon joyously
praise your name.

13 You have a mighty arm;
strong is your hand, high your
right hand.

## PROVERBS 13.15–16

GOOD sense wins favor,
but the way of the faithless
is their ruin.[b]

16 The clever do all things
intelligently,
but the fool displays folly.

# APRIL 21

## JOSHUA 22.21—23.16

THEN the Reubenites, the Gadites, and the half-tribe of Manasseh said in answer to the heads of the families of Israel, 22"The LORD, God of gods! The LORD, God of gods! He knows; and let Israel itself know! If it was in rebellion or in breach of faith toward the LORD, do not spare us today 23for building an altar to turn away from following the LORD; or if we did so to offer burnt offerings or grain offerings or offerings of well-being on it, may the LORD himself take vengeance. 24No! We did it from fear that in time to come your children might say to our children, 'What have you to do with the LORD, the God of Israel? 25For the LORD has made the Jordan a boundary between us and you, you Reubenites and Gadites; you have no portion in the LORD.' So your children might make our children cease to worship the LORD. 26Therefore we said, 'Let us now build an altar, not for burnt offering, nor for sacrifice, 27but to be a witness between us and you, and between the generations after us, that we do perform the service of the LORD in his presence with our burnt offerings and sacrifices and offerings of well-being; so that your children may never say to our children in time to come, "You have no portion in the LORD."' 28And we thought, If this should be said to us or to our descendants in time to come, we could say, 'Look at this copy of the altar of the LORD, which our ancestors made, not for burnt offerings, nor for sacrifice, but to be a witness between us and you.' 29Far be it from us that we should rebel against the LORD, and turn away this day from following the LORD by building an altar for burnt offering, grain offering, or sacrifice, other than the altar of the LORD our God that stands before his tabernacle!"

a Or *Zaphon and Yamin*   b Cn Compare Gk Syr Vg Tg: Heb *is enduring*

30 When the priest Phinehas and the chiefs of the congregation, the heads of the families of Israel who were with him, heard the words that the Reubenites and the Gadites and the Manassites spoke, they were satisfied. [31]The priest Phinehas son of Eleazar said to the Reubenites and the Gadites and the Manassites, "Today we know that the Lord is among us, because you have not committed this treachery against the Lord; now you have saved the Israelites from the hand of the Lord."

32 Then the priest Phinehas son of Eleazar and the chiefs returned from the Reubenites and the Gadites in the land of Gilead to the land of Canaan, to the Israelites, and brought back word to them. [33]The report pleased the Israelites; and the Israelites blessed God and spoke no more of making war against them, to destroy the land where the Reubenites and the Gadites were settled. [34]The Reubenites and the Gadites called the altar Witness;[a] "For," said they, "it is a witness between us that the Lord is God."

[23.1] A long time afterward, when the Lord had given rest to Israel from all their enemies all around, and Joshua was old and well advanced in years, [2]Joshua summoned all Israel, their elders and heads, their judges and officers, and said to them, "I am now old and well advanced in years; [3]and you have seen all that the Lord your God has done to all these nations for your sake, for it is the Lord your God who has fought for you. [4]I have allotted to you as an inheritance for your tribes those nations that remain, along with all the nations that I have already cut off, from the Jordan to the Great Sea in the west. [5]The Lord your God will push them back before you, and drive them out of your sight; and you shall possess their land, as the Lord your God promised you. [6]Therefore be very steadfast to observe and do all that is written in the book of the law of Moses, turning aside from it neither to the right nor to the left, [7]so that you may not be mixed with these nations left here among you, or make mention of the names of their gods, or swear by them, or serve them, or bow yourselves down to them, [8]but hold fast to the Lord your God, as you have done to this day. [9]For the Lord has driven out before you great and strong nations; and as for you, no one has been able to withstand you to this day. [10]One of you puts to flight a thousand, since it is the Lord your God who fights for you, as he promised you. [11]Be very careful, therefore, to love the Lord your God. [12]For if you turn back, and join the survivors of these nations left here among you, and intermarry with them, so that you marry their women and they yours, [13]know assuredly that the Lord your God will not continue to drive out these nations before you; but they shall be a snare and a trap for you, a scourge on your sides, and thorns in your eyes, until you perish from this good land that the Lord your God has given you.

14 "And now I am about to go the way of all the earth, and you know in your hearts and souls, all of you, that not one thing has failed of all the good things that the Lord your God promised concerning you; all have come to pass for you, not one of them has failed. [15]But just as all the good things that the Lord your God promised concerning you have been fulfilled for you, so the Lord will bring upon you all the bad things, until he has destroyed you from this good land that the Lord your God has given you. [16]If you transgress the covenant of the Lord your God, which he enjoined on you, and go and serve other gods and bow down to them, then

a Cn Compare Syr: Heb lacks *Witness*

the anger of the LORD will be kindled against you, and you shall perish quickly from the good land that he has given to you."

## LUKE 20.27–47

SOME Sadducees, those who say there is no resurrection, came to him [Jesus] [28]and asked him a question, "Teacher, Moses wrote for us that if a man's brother dies, leaving a wife but no children, the man[a] shall marry the widow and raise up children for his brother. [29]Now there were seven brothers; the first married, and died childless; [30]then the second [31]and the third married her, and so in the same way all seven died childless. [32]Finally the woman also died. [33]In the resurrection, therefore, whose wife will the woman be? For the seven had married her."

34 Jesus said to them, "Those who belong to this age marry and are given in marriage; [35]but those who are considered worthy of a place in that age and in the resurrection from the dead neither marry nor are given in marriage. [36]Indeed they cannot die anymore, because they are like angels and are children of God, being children of the resurrection. [37]And the fact that the dead are raised Moses himself showed, in the story about the bush, where he speaks of the Lord as the God of Abraham, the God of Isaac, and the God of Jacob. [38]Now he is God not of the dead, but of the living; for to him all of them are alive." [39]Then some of the scribes answered, "Teacher, you have spoken well." [40]For they no longer dared to ask him another question.

41 Then he said to them, "How can they say that the Messiah[b] is David's son? [42]For David himself says in the book of Psalms,

'The Lord said to my Lord,

"Sit at my right hand,
[43]    until I make your enemies
        your footstool." '
[44]David thus calls him Lord; so how can he be his son?"

45 In the hearing of all the people he said to the[c] disciples, [46]"Beware of the scribes, who like to walk around in long robes, and love to be greeted with respect in the marketplaces, and to have the best seats in the synagogues and places of honor at banquets. [47]They devour widows' houses and for the sake of appearance say long prayers. They will receive the greater condemnation."

## PSALM 89.14–37

RIGHTEOUSNESS and justice are
        the foundation of your
        throne;
    steadfast love and faithfulness
        go before you.
[15]  Happy are the people who know
        the festal shout,
    who walk, O LORD, in the
        light of your
        countenance;
[16]  they exult in your name all day
        long,
    and extol[d] your
        righteousness.
[17]  For you are the glory of their
        strength;
    by your favor our horn is
        exalted.
[18]  For our shield belongs to the
        LORD,
    our king to the Holy One of
        Israel.

[19]  Then you spoke in a vision to
        your faithful one, and
        said:
    "I have set the crown[e] on
        one who is mighty,

---

aGk *his brother*   bOr *the Christ*   cOther ancient authorities read *his*   dCn: Heb *are exalted in*
eCn: Heb *help*

    I have exalted one chosen
      from the people.
20 I have found my servant David;
    with my holy oil I have
      anointed him;
21 my hand shall always remain
    with him;
    my arm also shall strengthen
      him.
22 The enemy shall not outwit him,
    the wicked shall not humble
      him.
23 I will crush his foes before him
    and strike down those who
      hate him.
24 My faithfulness and steadfast
    love shall be with him;
    and in my name his horn shall
      be exalted.
25 I will set his hand on the sea
    and his right hand on the
      rivers.
26 He shall cry to me, 'You are my
    Father,
    my God, and the Rock of my
      salvation!'
27 I will make him the firstborn,
    the highest of the kings of the
      earth.
28 Forever I will keep my steadfast
    love for him,
    and my covenant with him will
      stand firm.
29 I will establish his line forever,
    and his throne as long as the
      heavens endure.
30 If his children forsake my law
    and do not walk according to
      my ordinances,

31 if they violate my statutes
    and do not keep my
      commandments,
32 then I will punish their
    transgression with the
      rod
    and their iniquity with
      scourges;
33 but I will not remove from him
    my steadfast love,
    or be false to my faithfulness.
34 I will not violate my covenant,
    or alter the word that went
      forth from my lips.
35 Once and for all I have sworn
    by my holiness;
    I will not lie to David.
36 His line shall continue forever,
    and his throne endure before
      me like the sun.
37 It shall be established forever
    like the moon,
    an enduring witness in the
      skies."     *Selah*

# PROVERBS 13.17–19

**A** BAD messenger brings
    trouble,
    but a faithful envoy, healing.
18 Poverty and disgrace are for the
    one who ignores
      instruction,
    but one who heeds reproof is
      honored.
19 A desire realized is sweet to
    the soul,
    but to turn away from evil is
      an abomination to fools.

# APRIL 22

## JOSHUA 24.1–33

THEN Joshua gathered all the tribes of Israel to Shechem, and summoned the elders, the heads, the judges, and the officers of Israel; and they presented themselves before God. ²And Joshua said to all the people, "Thus says the LORD, the God of Israel: Long ago your ancestors—Terah and his sons Abraham and Nahor—lived beyond the Euphrates and served other gods. ³Then I took your father Abraham from beyond the River and led him through all the land of Canaan and made his offspring many. I gave him Isaac; ⁴and to Isaac I gave Jacob and Esau. I gave Esau the hill country of Seir to possess, but Jacob and his children went down to Egypt. ⁵Then I sent Moses and Aaron, and I plagued Egypt with what I did in its midst; and afterwards I brought you out. ⁶When I brought your ancestors out of Egypt, you came to the sea; and the Egyptians pursued your ancestors with chariots and horsemen to the Red Sea.ᵃ ⁷When they cried out to the LORD, he put darkness between you and the Egyptians, and made the sea come upon them and cover them; and your eyes saw what I did to Egypt. Afterwards you lived in the wilderness a long time. ⁸Then I brought you to the land of the Amorites, who lived on the other side of the Jordan; they fought with you, and I handed them over to you, and you took possession of their land, and I destroyed them before you. ⁹Then King Balak son of Zippor of Moab, set out to fight against Israel. He sent and invited Balaam son of Beor to curse you, ¹⁰but I would not listen to Balaam; therefore he blessed you; so I rescued you out of his hand. ¹¹When you went over the Jordan and came to Jericho, the citizens of Jericho fought against you, and also the Amorites, the Perizzites, the Canaanites, the Hittites, the Girgashites, the Hivites, and the Jebusites; and I handed them over to you. ¹²I sent the hornetᵇ ahead of you, which drove out before you the two kings of the Amorites; it was not by your sword or by your bow. ¹³I gave you a land on which you had not labored, and towns that you had not built, and you live in them; you eat the fruit of vineyards and oliveyards that you did not plant.

14 "Now therefore revere the LORD, and serve him in sincerity and in faithfulness; put away the gods that your ancestors served beyond the River and in Egypt, and serve the LORD. ¹⁵Now if you are unwilling to serve the LORD, choose this day whom you will serve, whether the gods your ancestors served in the region beyond the River or the gods of the Amorites in whose land you are living; but as for me and my household, we will serve the LORD."

16 Then the people answered, "Far be it from us that we should forsake the LORD to serve other gods; ¹⁷for it is the LORD our God who brought us and our ancestors up from the land of Egypt, out of the house of slavery, and who did those great signs in our sight. He protected us along all the way that we went, and among all the peoples through whom we passed; ¹⁸and the LORD drove out before us all the peoples, the Amorites who lived in the land. Therefore we also will serve the LORD, for he is our God."

ᵃOr *Sea of Reeds*    ᵇMeaning of Heb uncertain

19 But Joshua said to the people, "You cannot serve the LORD, for he is a holy God. He is a jealous God; he will not forgive your transgressions or your sins. 20If you forsake the LORD and serve foreign gods, then he will turn and do you harm, and consume you, after having done you good." 21And the people said to Joshua, "No, we will serve the LORD!" 22Then Joshua said to the people, "You are witnesses against yourselves that you have chosen the LORD, to serve him." And they said, "We are witnesses." 23He said, "Then put away the foreign gods that are among you, and incline your hearts to the LORD, the God of Israel." 24The people said to Joshua, "The LORD our God we will serve, and him we will obey." 25So Joshua made a covenant with the people that day, and made statutes and ordinances for them at Shechem. 26Joshua wrote these words in the book of the law of God; and he took a large stone, and set it up there under the oak in the sanctuary of the LORD. 27Joshua said to all the people, "See, this stone shall be a witness against us; for it has heard all the words of the LORD that he spoke to us; therefore it shall be a witness against you, if you deal falsely with your God." 28So Joshua sent the people away to their inheritances.

29 After these things Joshua son of Nun, the servant of the LORD, died, being one hundred ten years old. 30They buried him in his own inheritance at Timnath-serah, which is in the hill country of Ephraim, north of Mount Gaash.

31 Israel served the LORD all the days of Joshua, and all the days of the elders who outlived Joshua and had known all the work that the LORD did for Israel.

32 The bones of Joseph, which the Israelites had brought up from Egypt, were buried at Shechem, in the portion of ground that Jacob had bought from the children of Hamor, the father of Shechem, for one hundred pieces of money;a it became an inheritance of the descendants of Joseph.

33 Eleazar son of Aaron died; and they buried him at Gibeah, the town of his son Phinehas, which had been given him in the hill country of Ephraim.

## LUKE 21.1–28

HE [Jesus] looked up and saw rich people putting their gifts into the treasury; 2he also saw a poor widow put in two small copper coins. 3He said, "Truly I tell you, this poor widow has put in more than all of them; 4for all of them have contributed out of their abundance, but she out of her poverty has put in all she had to live on."

5 When some were speaking about the temple, how it was adorned with beautiful stones and gifts dedicated to God, he said, 6"As for these things that you see, the days will come when not one stone will be left upon another; all will be thrown down."

7 They asked him, "Teacher, when will this be, and what will be the sign that this is about to take place?" 8And he said, "Beware that you are not led astray; for many will come in my name and say, 'I am he!'b and, 'The time is near!'c Do not go after them.

9 "When you hear of wars and insurrections, do not be terrified; for these things must take place first, but the end will not follow immediately." 10Then he said to them, "Nation will rise against nation, and kingdom against kingdom; 11there will be great earthquakes, and in various places famines and plagues; and there will be dreadful portents and great signs from heaven.

12 "But before all this occurs, they

aHeb *one hundred qesitah* bGk *I am* cOr *at hand*

will arrest you and persecute you; they will hand you over to synagogues and prisons, and you will be brought before kings and governors because of my name. ¹³This will give you an opportunity to testify. ¹⁴So make up your minds not to prepare your defense in advance; ¹⁵for I will give you words[a] and a wisdom that none of your opponents will be able to withstand or contradict. ¹⁶You will be betrayed even by parents and brothers, by relatives and friends; and they will put some of you to death. ¹⁷You will be hated by all because of my name. ¹⁸But not a hair of your head will perish. ¹⁹By your endurance you will gain your souls.

20 "When you see Jerusalem surrounded by armies, then know that its desolation has come near.[b] ²¹Then those in Judea must flee to the mountains, and those inside the city must leave it, and those out in the country must not enter it; ²²for these are days of vengeance, as a fulfillment of all that is written. ²³Woe to those who are pregnant and to those who are nursing infants in those days! For there will be great distress on the earth and wrath against this people; ²⁴they will fall by the edge of the sword and be taken away as captives among all nations; and Jerusalem will be trampled on by the Gentiles, until the times of the Gentiles are fulfilled.

25 "There will be signs in the sun, the moon, and the stars, and on the earth distress among nations confused by the roaring of the sea and the waves. ²⁶People will faint from fear and foreboding of what is coming upon the world, for the powers of the heavens will be shaken. ²⁷Then they will see 'the Son of Man coming in a cloud' with power and great glory. ²⁸Now when these things begin to take place, stand up and raise your heads, because your redemption is drawing near."

## PSALM 89.38–52

**B**UT now you have spurned and rejected him;
   you are full of wrath against your anointed.

39 You have renounced the covenant with your servant;
   you have defiled his crown in the dust.

40 You have broken through all his walls;
   you have laid his strongholds in ruins.

41 All who pass by plunder him;
   he has become the scorn of his neighbors.

42 You have exalted the right hand of his foes;
   you have made all his enemies rejoice.

43 Moreover, you have turned back the edge of his sword,
   and you have not supported him in battle.

44 You have removed the scepter from his hand,[c]
   and hurled his throne to the ground.

45 You have cut short the days of his youth;
   you have covered him with shame.    *Selah*

46 How long, O LORD? Will you hide yourself forever?
   How long will your wrath burn like fire?

47 Remember how short my time is—[d]
   for what vanity you have created all mortals!

48 Who can live and never see death?
   Who can escape the power of Sheol?    *Selah*

---

aGk *a mouth*  bOr *is at hand*  cCn: Heb *removed his cleanness*  dMeaning of Heb uncertain

49  Lord, where is your steadfast
       love of old,
     which by your faithfulness you
       swore to David?
50  Remember, O Lord, how your
       servant is taunted;
     how I bear in my bosom the
       insults of the peoples, a
51  with which your enemies taunt,
       O Lord,
     with which they taunted the
       footsteps of your
       anointed.

52  Blessed be the Lord forever.
       Amen and Amen.

## PROVERBS 13.20–23

WHOEVER walks with the wise
       becomes wise,
     but the companion of fools
       suffers harm.
21  Misfortune pursues sinners,
     but prosperity rewards the
       righteous.
22  The good leave an inheritance
       to their children's
       children,
     but the sinner's wealth is laid
       up for the righteous.
23  The field of the poor may yield
       much food,
     but it is swept away through
       injustice.

# APRIL 23

## JUDGES 1.1—2.9

AFTER the death of Joshua, the Israelites inquired of the Lord, "Who shall go up first for us against the Canaanites, to fight against them?" 2The Lord said, "Judah shall go up. I hereby give the land into his hand." 3Judah said to his brother Simeon, "Come up with me into the territory allotted to me, that we may fight against the Canaanites; then I too will go with you into the territory allotted to you." So Simeon went with him. 4Then Judah went up and the Lord gave the Canaanites and the Perizzites into their hand; and they defeated ten thousand of them at Bezek. 5They came upon Adoni-bezek at Bezek, and fought against him, and defeated the Canaanites and the Perizzites. 6Adoni-bezek fled; but they pursued him, and caught him, and cut off his thumbs and big toes. 7Adoni-bezek said, "Seventy kings with their thumbs and big toes cut off used to pick up scraps under my table; as I have done, so God has paid me back." They brought him to Jerusalem, and he died there.

8 Then the people of Judah fought against Jerusalem and took it. They put it to the sword and set the city on fire. 9Afterward the people of Judah went down to fight against the Canaanites who lived in the hill country, in the Negeb, and in the lowland. 10Judah went against the Canaanites who lived in Hebron (the name of Hebron was formerly Kiriath-arba); and they defeated Sheshai and Ahiman and Talmai.

11 From there they went against

a Cn: Heb *bosom all of many peoples*

the inhabitants of Debir (the name of Debir was formerly Kiriath-sepher). ¹²Then Caleb said, "Whoever attacks Kiriath-sepher and takes it, I will give him my daughter Achsah as wife." ¹³And Othniel son of Kenaz, Caleb's younger brother, took it; and he gave him his daughter Achsah as wife. ¹⁴When she came to him, she urged him to ask her father for a field. As she dismounted from her donkey, Caleb said to her, "What do you wish?" ¹⁵She said to him, "Give me a present; since you have set me in the land of the Negeb, give me also Gulloth-mayim."ᵃ So Caleb gave her Upper Gulloth and Lower Gulloth.

16 The descendants of Hobabᵇ the Kenite, Moses' father-in-law, went up with the people of Judah from the city of palms into the wilderness of Judah, which lies in the Negeb near Arad. Then they went and settled with the Amalekites.ᶜ ¹⁷Judah went with his brother Simeon, and they defeated the Canaanites who inhabited Zephath, and devoted it to destruction. So the city was called Hormah. ¹⁸Judah took Gaza with its territory, Ashkelon with its territory, and Ekron with its territory. ¹⁹The Lord was with Judah, and he took possession of the hill country, but could not drive out the inhabitants of the plain, because they had chariots of iron. ²⁰Hebron was given to Caleb, as Moses had said; and he drove out from it the three sons of Anak. ²¹But the Benjaminites did not drive out the Jebusites who lived in Jerusalem; so the Jebusites have lived in Jerusalem among the Benjaminites to this day.

22 The house of Joseph also went up against Bethel; and the Lord was with them. ²³The house of Joseph sent out spies to Bethel (the name of the city was formerly Luz). ²⁴When the spies saw a man coming out of the city, they said to him, "Show us the way into the city, and we will deal kindly with you." ²⁵So he showed them the way into the city; and they put the city to the sword, but they let the man and all his family go. ²⁶So the man went to the land of the Hittites and built a city, and named it Luz; that is its name to this day.

27 Manasseh did not drive out the inhabitants of Beth-shean and its villages, or Taanach and its villages, or the inhabitants of Dor and its villages, or the inhabitants of Ibleam and its villages, or the inhabitants of Megiddo and its villages; but the Canaanites continued to live in that land. ²⁸When Israel grew strong, they put the Canaanites to forced labor, but did not in fact drive them out.

29 And Ephraim did not drive out the Canaanites who lived in Gezer; but the Canaanites lived among them in Gezer.

30 Zebulun did not drive out the inhabitants of Kitron, or the inhabitants of Nahalol; but the Canaanites lived among them, and became subject to forced labor.

31 Asher did not drive out the inhabitants of Acco, or the inhabitants of Sidon, or of Ahlab, or of Achzib, or of Helbah, or of Aphik, or of Rehob; ³²but the Asherites lived among the Canaanites, the inhabitants of the land; for they did not drive them out.

33 Naphtali did not drive out the inhabitants of Beth-shemesh, or the inhabitants of Beth-anath, but lived among the Canaanites, the inhabitants of the land; nevertheless the inhabitants of Beth-shemesh and of Beth-anath became subject to forced labor for them.

34 The Amorites pressed the Danites back into the hill country; they did not allow them to come down to the plain. ³⁵The Amorites continued to live in Har-heres, in Aijalon, and in Shaal-bim, but the hand of the house of Jo-

---

ᵃ That is *Basins of Water*   ᵇ Gk: Heb lacks *Hobab*   ᶜ See 1 Sam 15.6: Heb *people*

seph rested heavily on them, and they became subject to forced labor. ³⁶The border of the Amorites ran from the ascent of Akrabbim, from Sela and upward.

2.1 Now the angel of the LORD went up from Gilgal to Bochim, and said, "I brought you up from Egypt, and brought you into the land that I had promised to your ancestors. I said, 'I will never break my covenant with you. ²For your part, do not make a covenant with the inhabitants of this land; tear down their altars.' But you have not obeyed my command. See what you have done! ³So now I say, I will not drive them out before you; but they shall become adversaries[a] to you, and their gods shall be a snare to you." ⁴When the angel of the LORD spoke these words to all the Israelites, the people lifted up their voices and wept. ⁵So they named that place Bochim,[b] and there they sacrificed to the LORD.

6 When Joshua dismissed the people, the Israelites all went to their own inheritances to take possession of the land. ⁷The people worshiped the LORD all the days of Joshua, and all the days of the elders who outlived Joshua, who had seen all the great work that the LORD had done for Israel. ⁸Joshua son of Nun, the servant of the LORD, died at the age of one hundred ten years. ⁹So they buried him within the bounds of his inheritance in Timnath-heres, in the hill country of Ephraim, north of Mount Gaash.

## LUKE 21.29—22.13

Then he [Jesus] told them a parable: "Look at the fig tree and all the trees; ³⁰as soon as they sprout leaves you can see for yourselves and know that summer is already near. ³¹So also, when you see these things taking place, you know that the kingdom of God is near. ³²Truly I tell you, this generation will not pass away until all things have taken place. ³³Heaven and earth will pass away, but my words will not pass away.

34 "Be on guard so that your hearts are not weighed down with dissipation and drunkenness and the worries of this life, and that day catch you unexpectedly, ³⁵like a trap. For it will come upon all who live on the face of the whole earth.[c] ³⁶Be alert at all times, praying that you may have the strength to escape all these things that will take place, and to stand before the Son of Man."

37 Every day he was teaching in the temple, and at night he would go out and spend the night on the Mount of Olives, as it was called. ³⁸And all the people would get up early in the morning to listen to him in the temple.

22.1 Now the festival of Unleavened Bread, which is called the Passover, was near. ²The chief priests and the scribes were looking for a way to put Jesus[c] to death, for they were afraid of the people.

3 Then Satan entered into Judas called Iscariot, who was one of the twelve; ⁴he went away and conferred with the chief priests and officers of the temple police about how he might betray him to them. ⁵They were greatly pleased and agreed to give him money. ⁶So he consented and began to look for an opportunity to betray him to them when no crowd was present.

7 Then came the day of Unleavened Bread, on which the Passover lamb had to be sacrificed. ⁸So Jesus[d] sent Peter and John, saying, "Go and prepare the Passover meal for us that we may eat it." ⁹They asked him, "Where do you want us to make preparations for it?" ¹⁰"Listen," he said to

a OL Vg Compare Gk: Heb *sides*  b That is *Weepers*  c Gk *him*  d Gk *he* them, "when you have entered the city, a man carrying a jar of water will meet you; follow him into the house he enters ¹¹and say to the owner of the house, 'The teacher asks you, "Where is the guest room, where I may eat the Passover with my disciples?" ' ¹²He will show you a large room upstairs, already furnished. Make preparations for us there." ¹³So they went and found everything as he had told them; and they prepared the Passover meal.

## PSALM 90.1—91.16

*A Prayer of Moses, the man of God.*

Lord, you have been our
  dwelling place[a]
 in all generations.
2 Before the mountains were
   brought forth,
  or ever you had formed the
   earth and the world,
  from everlasting to
   everlasting you are God.

3 You turn us[b] back to dust,
  and say, "Turn back, you
   mortals."
4 For a thousand years in your
   sight
  are like yesterday when it is
   past,
  or like a watch in the night.

5 You sweep them away; they are
   like a dream,
  like grass that is renewed in
   the morning;
6 in the morning it flourishes and
   is renewed;
  in the evening it fades and
   withers.

7 For we are consumed by your
   anger;
  by your wrath we are
   overwhelmed.

8 You have set our iniquities
   before you,
  our secret sins in the light of
   your countenance.

9 For all our days pass away
   under your wrath;
  our years come to an end[c]
   like a sigh.
10 The days of our life are seventy
   years,
  or perhaps eighty, if we are
   strong;
  even then their span[d] is only
   toil and trouble;
  they are soon gone, and we
   fly away.

11 Who considers the power of
   your anger?
  Your wrath is as great as the
   fear that is due you.
12 So teach us to count our days
  that we may gain a wise
   heart.

13 Turn, O Lord! How long?
  Have compassion on your
   servants!
14 Satisfy us in the morning with
   your steadfast love,
  so that we may rejoice and be
   glad all our days.
15 Make us glad as many days as
   you have afflicted us,
  and as many years as we
   have seen evil.
16 Let your work be manifest to
   your servants,
  and your glorious power to
   their children.
17 Let the favor of the Lord our
   God be upon us,
  and prosper for us the work
   of our hands—
  O prosper the work of our
   hands!

aAnother reading is *our refuge* bHeb *humankind* cSyr: Heb *we bring our years to an end*
dCn Compare Gk Syr Jerome Tg: Heb *pride*

**91.1** You who live in the shelter of
    the Most High,
  who abide in the shadow of
    the Almighty, **a**
2  will say to the Lord, "My
    refuge and my fortress;
  my God, in whom I trust."
3  For he will deliver you from the
    snare of the fowler
  and from the deadly
    pestilence;
4  he will cover you with his
    pinions,
  and under his wings you will
    find refuge;
  his faithfulness is a shield and
    buckler.
5  You will not fear the terror of
    the night,
  or the arrow that flies by day,
6  or the pestilence that stalks in
    darkness,
  or the destruction that wastes
    at noonday.

7  A thousand may fall at your
    side,
  ten thousand at your right
    hand,
  but it will not come near you.
8  You will only look with your
    eyes
  and see the punishment of the
    wicked.

9  Because you have made the
    Lord your refuge, **b**
  the Most High your dwelling
    place,
10  no evil shall befall you,

  no scourge come near your
    tent.

11  For he will command his angels
    concerning you
  to guard you in all your ways.
12  On their hands they will bear
    you up,
  so that you will not dash your
    foot against a stone.
13  You will tread on the lion and
    the adder,
  the young lion and the
    serpent you will trample
    under foot.

14  Those who love me, I will
    deliver;
  I will protect those who know
    my name.
15  When they call to me, I will
    answer them;
  I will be with them in trouble,
  I will rescue them and honor
    them.
16  With long life I will satisfy them,
  and show them my salvation.

# PROVERBS 13.24–25

Those who spare the rod hate
    their children,
but those who love them are
    diligent to discipline
    them.
25  The righteous have enough to
    satisfy their appetite,
  but the belly of the wicked is
    empty.

---

**a** Traditional rendering of Heb *Shaddai*  **b** Cn: Heb *Because you, Lord, are my refuge; you have made*

# APRIL 24

JUDGES 2.10—3.31

**M**OREOVER, that whole generation was gathered to their ancestors, and another generation grew up after them, who did not know the LORD or the work that he had done for Israel.

11 Then the Israelites did what was evil in the sight of the LORD and worshiped the Baals; <sup>12</sup>and they abandoned the LORD, the God of their ancestors, who had brought them out of the land of Egypt; they followed other gods, from among the gods of the peoples who were all around them, and bowed down to them; and they provoked the LORD to anger. <sup>13</sup>They abandoned the LORD, and worshiped Baal and the Astartes. <sup>14</sup>So the anger of the LORD was kindled against Israel, and he gave them over to plunderers who plundered them, and he sold them into the power of their enemies all around, so that they could no longer withstand their enemies. <sup>15</sup>Whenever they marched out, the hand of the LORD was against them to bring misfortune, as the LORD had warned them and sworn to them; and they were in great distress.

16 Then the LORD raised up judges, who delivered them out of the power of those who plundered them. <sup>17</sup>Yet they did not listen even to their judges; for they lusted after other gods and bowed down to them. They soon turned aside from the way in which their ancestors had walked, who had obeyed the commandments of the LORD; they did not follow their example. <sup>18</sup>Whenever the LORD raised up judges for them, the LORD was with the judge, and he delivered them from the hand of their enemies all the days of the judge; for the LORD would be moved to pity by their groaning because of those who persecuted and oppressed them. <sup>19</sup>But whenever the judge died, they would relapse and behave worse than their ancestors, following other gods, worshiping them and bowing down to them. They would not drop any of their practices or their stubborn ways. <sup>20</sup>So the anger of the LORD was kindled against Israel; and he said, "Because this people have transgressed my covenant that I commanded their ancestors, and have not obeyed my voice, <sup>21</sup>I will no longer drive out before them any of the nations that Joshua left when he died." <sup>22</sup>In order to test Israel, whether or not they would take care to walk in the way of the LORD as their ancestors did, <sup>23</sup>the LORD had left those nations, not driving them out at once, and had not handed them over to Joshua.

<sup>3.1</sup> Now these are the nations that the LORD left to test all those in Israel who had no experience of any war in Canaan <sup>2</sup>(it was only that successive generations of Israelites might know war, to teach those who had no experience of it before): <sup>3</sup>the five lords of the Philistines, and all the Canaanites, and the Sidonians, and the Hivites who lived on Mount Lebanon, from Mount Baal-hermon as far as Lebo-hamath. <sup>4</sup>They were for the testing of Israel, to know whether Israel would obey the commandments of the LORD, which he commanded their ancestors by Moses. <sup>5</sup>So the Israelites lived among the Canaanites, the Hittites, the Amorites, the Perizzites, the Hivites, and the Jebusites; <sup>6</sup>and they took their daughters as wives for themselves, and their own daughters they gave to their sons; and they worshiped their gods.

7 The Israelites did what was evil in

the sight of the Lord, forgetting the Lord their God, and worshiping the Baals and the Asherahs. 8Therefore the anger of the Lord was kindled against Israel, and he sold them into the hand of King Cushan-rishathaim of Aram-naharaim; and the Israelites served Cushan-rishathaim eight years. 9But when the Israelites cried out to the Lord, the Lord raised up a deliverer for the Israelites, who delivered them, Othniel son of Kenaz, Caleb's younger brother. 10The spirit of the Lord came upon him, and he judged Israel; he went out to war, and the Lord gave King Cushan-rishathaim of Aram into his hand; and his hand prevailed over Cushan-rishathaim. 11So the land had rest forty years. Then Othniel son of Kenaz died.

12 The Israelites again did what was evil in the sight of the Lord; and the Lord strengthened King Eglon of Moab against Israel, because they had done what was evil in the sight of the Lord. 13In alliance with the Ammonites and the Amalekites, he went and defeated Israel; and they took possession of the city of palms. 14So the Israelites served King Eglon of Moab eighteen years.

15 But when the Israelites cried out to the Lord, the Lord raised up for them a deliverer, Ehud son of Gera, the Benjaminite, a left-handed man. The Israelites sent tribute by him to King Eglon of Moab. 16Ehud made for himself a sword with two edges, a cubit in length; and he fastened it on his right thigh under his clothes. 17Then he presented the tribute to King Eglon of Moab. Now Eglon was a very fat man. 18When Ehud had finished presenting the tribute, he sent the people who carried the tribute on their way. 19But he himself turned back at the sculptured stones near Gilgal, and said, "I have a secret message for you, O king." So the king said, a "Silence!" and all his attendants went out from his presence. 20Ehud came to him, while he was sitting alone in his cool roof chamber, and said, "I have a message from God for you." So he rose from his seat. 21Then Ehud reached with his left hand, took the sword from his right thigh, and thrust it into Eglon'sb belly; 22the hilt also went in after the blade, and the fat closed over the blade, for he did not draw the sword out of his belly; and the dirt came out. c 23Then Ehud went out into the vestibule, d and closed the doors of the roof chamber on him, and locked them.

24 After he had gone, the servants came. When they saw that the doors of the roof chamber were locked, they thought, "He must be relieving himselfe in the cool chamber." 25So they waited until they were embarrassed. When he still did not open the doors of the roof chamber, they took the key and opened them. There was their lord lying dead on the floor.

26 Ehud escaped while they delayed, and passed beyond the sculptured stones, and escaped to Seirah. 27When he arrived, he sounded the trumpet in the hill country of Ephraim; and the Israelites went down with him from the hill country, having him at their head. 28He said to them, "Follow after me; for the Lord has given your enemies the Moabites into your hand." So they went down after him, and seized the fords of the Jordan against the Moabites, and allowed no one to cross over. 29At that time they killed about ten thousand of the Moabites, all strong, able-bodied men; no one escaped. 30So Moab was subdued that day under the hand of Israel. And the land had rest eighty years.

31 After him came Shamgar son of

a Heb *he said*   b Heb *his*   c With Tg Vg: Meaning of Heb uncertain   d Meaning of Heb uncertain
e Heb *covering his feet*

Anath, who killed six hundred of the Philistines with an oxgoad. He too delivered Israel.

## LUKE 22.14–34

**W**HEN the hour came, he [Jesus] took his place at the table, and the apostles with him. [15]He said to them, "I have eagerly desired to eat this Passover with you before I suffer; [16]for I tell you, I will not eat it[a] until it is fulfilled in the kingdom of God." [17]Then he took a cup, and after giving thanks he said, "Take this and divide it among yourselves; [18]for I tell you that from now on I will not drink of the fruit of the vine until the kingdom of God comes." [19]Then he took a loaf of bread, and when he had given thanks, he broke it and gave it to them, saying, "This is my body, which is given for you. Do this in remembrance of me." [20]And he did the same with the cup after supper, saying, "This cup that is poured out for you is the new covenant in my blood.[b] [21]But see, the one who betrays me is with me, and his hand is on the table. [22]For the Son of Man is going as it has been determined, but woe to that one by whom he is betrayed!" [23]Then they began to ask one another, which one of them it could be who would do this.

24 A dispute also arose among them as to which one of them was to be regarded as the greatest. [25]But he said to them, "The kings of the Gentiles lord it over them; and those in authority over them are called benefactors. [26]But not so with you; rather the greatest among you must become like the youngest, and the leader like one who serves. [27]For who is greater, the one who is at the table or the one who serves? Is it not the one at the table? But I am among you as one who serves.

28 "You are those who have stood by me in my trials; [29]and I confer on you, just as my Father has conferred on me, a kingdom, [30]so that you may eat and drink at my table in my kingdom, and you will sit on thrones judging the twelve tribes of Israel.

31 "Simon, Simon, listen! Satan has demanded[c] to sift all of you like wheat, [32]but I have prayed for you that your own faith may not fail; and you, when once you have turned back, strengthen your brothers." [33]And he said to him, "Lord, I am ready to go with you to prison and to death!" [34]Jesus[d] said, "I tell you, Peter, the cock will not crow this day, until you have denied three times that you know me."

## PSALM 92.1—93.5

*A Psalm. A Song for the Sabbath Day.*

**I**T is good to give thanks to the LORD,
　　to sing praises to your name,
　　　　O Most High;
2　to declare your steadfast love in
　　　　the morning,
　　and your faithfulness by night,
3　to the music of the lute and the
　　　　harp,
　　to the melody of the lyre.
4　For you, O LORD, have made
　　　　me glad by your work;
　　at the works of your hands I
　　　　sing for joy.

5　How great are your works,
　　　　O LORD!
　　Your thoughts are very deep!
6　The dullard cannot know,
　　　　the stupid cannot understand
　　　　　　this:
7　though the wicked sprout like
　　　　grass
　　and all evildoers flourish,
　　they are doomed to destruction
　　　　forever,

8  but you, O Lord, are on high
       forever.
9  For your enemies, O Lord,
     for your enemies shall perish;
     all evildoers shall be
       scattered.

10  But you have exalted my horn
        like that of the wild ox;
      you have poured over me[a]
        fresh oil.
11  My eyes have seen the downfall
        of my enemies;
      my ears have heard the doom
        of my evil assailants.

12  The righteous flourish like the
        palm tree,
      and grow like a cedar in
        Lebanon.
13  They are planted in the house of
        the Lord;
      they flourish in the courts of
        our God.
14  In old age they still produce
        fruit;
      they are always green and full
        of sap,
15  showing that the Lord is
        upright;
      he is my rock, and there is
        no unrighteousness in
        him.

93.1  The Lord is king, he is robed in
          majesty;
        the Lord is robed, he is
          girded with strength.
      He has established the world; it
          shall never be moved;
2       your throne is established
          from of old;
        you are from everlasting.

3  The floods have lifted up,
        O Lord,
      the floods have lifted up their
        voice;
      the floods lift up their roaring.
4  More majestic than the thunders
        of mighty waters,
      more majestic than the
        waves[b] of the sea,
      majestic on high is the Lord!

5  Your decrees are very sure;
      holiness befits your house,
      O Lord, forevermore.

## PROVERBS 14.1–2

The wise woman[c] builds her
        house,
      but the foolish tears it down
        with her own hands.
2  Those who walk uprightly fear
        the Lord,
      but one who is devious in
        conduct despises him.

[a] Syr: Meaning of Heb uncertain   [b] Cn: Heb *majestic are the waves*   [c] Heb *Wisdom of women*

# APRIL 25



THE Israelites again did what was evil in the sight of the LORD, after Ehud died. [2]So the LORD sold them into the hand of King Jabin of Canaan, who reigned in Hazor; the commander of his army was Sisera, who lived in Harosheth-ha-goiim. [3]Then the Israelites cried out to the LORD for help; for he had nine hundred chariots of iron, and had oppressed the Israelites cruelly twenty years.

4 At that time Deborah, a prophetess, wife of Lappidoth, was judging Israel. [5]She used to sit under the palm of Deborah between Ramah and Bethel in the hill country of Ephraim; and the Israelites came up to her for judgment. [6]She sent and summoned Barak son of Abinoam from Kedesh in Naphtali, and said to him, "The LORD, the God of Israel, commands you, 'Go, take position at Mount Tabor, bringing ten thousand from the tribe of Naphtali and the tribe of Zebulun. [7]I will draw out Sisera, the general of Jabin's army, to meet you by the Wadi Kishon with his chariots and his troops; and I will give him into your hand.' " [8]Barak said to her, "If you will go with me, I will go; but if you will not go with me, I will not go." [9]And she said, "I will surely go with you; nevertheless, the road on which you are going will not lead to your glory, for the LORD will sell Sisera into the hand of a woman." Then Deborah got up and went with Barak to Kedesh. [10]Barak summoned Zebulun and Naphtali to Kedesh; and ten thousand warriors went up behind him; and Deborah went up with him.

11 Now Heber the Kenite had separated from the other Kenites,[a] that is, the descendants of Hobab the father-in-law of Moses, and had encamped as far away as Elon-bezaanannim, which is near Kedesh.

12 When Sisera was told that Barak son of Abinoam had gone up to Mount Tabor, [13]Sisera called out all his chariots, nine hundred chariots of iron, and all the troops who were with him, from Harosheth-ha-goiim to the Wadi Kishon. [14]Then Deborah said to Barak, "Up! For this is the day on which the LORD has given Sisera into your hand. The LORD is indeed going out before you." So Barak went down from Mount Tabor with ten thousand warriors following him. [15]And the LORD threw Sisera and all his chariots and all his army into a panic[b] before Barak; Sisera got down from his chariot and fled away on foot, [16]while Barak pursued the chariots and the army to Harosheth-ha-goiim. All the army of Sisera fell by the sword; no one was left.

17 Now Sisera had fled away on foot to the tent of Jael wife of Heber the Kenite; for there was peace between King Jabin of Hazor and the clan of Heber the Kenite. [18]Jael came out to meet Sisera, and said to him, "Turn aside, my lord, turn aside to me; have no fear." So he turned aside to her into the tent, and she covered him with a rug. [19]Then he said to her, "Please give me a little water to drink; for I am thirsty." So she opened a skin of milk and gave him a drink and covered him. [20]He said to her, "Stand at the entrance of the tent, and if anybody comes and asks you, 'Is anyone here?' say, 'No.' " [21]But Jael wife of Heber took a tent peg, and took a hammer in her hand, and went softly to him and drove the

---

a Heb *from the Kain*   b Heb adds *to the sword*; compare verse 16

peg into his temple, until it went down into the ground—he was lying fast asleep from weariness—and he died. <sup>22</sup>Then, as Barak came in pursuit of Sisera, Jael went out to meet him, and said to him, "Come, and I will show you the man whom you are seeking." So he went into her tent; and there was Sisera lying dead, with the tent peg in his temple.

23 So on that day God subdued King Jabin of Canaan before the Israelites. <sup>24</sup>Then the hand of the Israelites bore harder and harder on King Jabin of Canaan, until they destroyed King Jabin of Canaan.

<sup>5.1</sup> THEN Deborah and Barak son of Abinoam sang on that day, saying:
2   "When locks are long in Israel,
        when the people offer
            themselves willingly—
        bless <sup>a</sup> the LORD!

3   "Hear, O kings; give ear,
        O princes;
    to the LORD I will sing,
    I will make melody to the
        LORD, the God of Israel.

4   "LORD, when you went out from
        Seir,
    when you marched from the
        region of Edom,
    the earth trembled,
    and the heavens poured,
    the clouds indeed poured
        water.
5   The mountains quaked before
        the LORD, the One of
        Sinai,
    before the LORD, the God of
        Israel.

6   "In the days of Shamgar son of
        Anath,
    in the days of Jael, caravans
        ceased

and travelers kept to the
    byways.
7   The peasantry prospered in
        Israel,
    they grew fat on plunder,
because you arose, Deborah,
    arose as a mother in Israel.
8   When new gods were chosen,
        then war was in the gates.
    Was shield or spear to be seen
        among forty thousand in
        Israel?
9   My heart goes out to the
            commanders of Israel
    who offered themselves
            willingly among the
            people.
    Bless the LORD.

10  "Tell of it, you who ride on
            white donkeys,
    you who sit on rich carpets<sup>b</sup>
    and you who walk by the
        way.
11  To the sound of musicians<sup>b</sup> at
            the watering places,
    there they repeat the
            triumphs of the LORD,
    the triumphs of his peasantry
        in Israel.

    "Then down to the gates
            marched the people of
            the LORD.

12  "Awake, awake, Deborah!
        Awake, awake, utter a song!
    Arise, Barak, lead away your
            captives,
        O son of Abinoam.
13  Then down marched the
            remnant of the noble;
    the people of the LORD
            marched down for him<sup>c</sup>
            against the mighty.
14  From Ephraim they set out<sup>d</sup>
            into the valley,<sup>e</sup>

<sup>a</sup>Or *You who offer yourselves willingly among the people, bless*   <sup>b</sup>Meaning of Heb uncertain
<sup>c</sup>Gk: Heb *me*   <sup>d</sup>Cn: Heb *From Ephraim their root*   <sup>e</sup>Gk: Heb *in Amalek*

following you, Benjamin, with
    your kin;
from Machir marched down the
    commanders,
    and from Zebulun those who
        bear the marshal's staff;
15 the chiefs of Issachar came with
    Deborah,
    and Issachar faithful to Barak;
    into the valley they rushed
        out at his heels.
Among the clans of Reuben
    there were great searchings
        of heart.
16 Why did you tarry among the
    sheepfolds,
    to hear the piping for the
        flocks?
Among the clans of Reuben
    there were great searchings
        of heart.
17 Gilead stayed beyond the
    Jordan;
    and Dan, why did he abide
        with the ships?
Asher sat still at the coast of
    the sea,
    settling down by his landings.
18 Zebulun is a people that scorned
    death;
    Naphtali too, on the heights
        of the field.

19 "The kings came, they fought;
    then fought the kings of
        Canaan,
at Taanach, by the waters of
    Megiddo;
    they got no spoils of silver.
20 The stars fought from heaven,
    from their courses they
        fought against Sisera.
21 The torrent Kishon swept them
    away,
    the onrushing torrent, the
        torrent Kishon.
    March on, my soul, with
        might!

22 "Then loud beat the horses'
    hoofs
    with the galloping, galloping of
        his steeds.

23 "Curse Meroz, says the angel of
    the LORD,
    curse bitterly its inhabitants,
because they did not come to
    the help of the LORD,
    to the help of the LORD
        against the mighty.

24 "Most blessed of women be
    Jael,
    the wife of Heber the Kenite,
    of tent-dwelling women most
        blessed.
25 He asked water and she gave
    him milk,
    she brought him curds in a
        lordly bowl.
26 She put her hand to the tent
    peg
    and her right hand to the
        workmen's mallet;
she struck Sisera a blow,
    she crushed his head,
    she shattered and pierced his
        temple.
27 He sank, he fell,
    he lay still at her feet;
at her feet he sank, he fell;
    where he sank, there he fell
        dead.

28 "Out of the window she peered,
    the mother of Sisera gazed[a]
        through the lattice:
'Why is his chariot so long in
    coming?
    Why tarry the hoofbeats of
        his chariots?'
29 Her wisest ladies make answer,
    indeed, she answers the
        question herself:

a Gk Compare Tg: Heb *exclaimed*

30 'Are they not finding and
    dividing the spoil?—
  A girl or two for every man;
spoil of dyed stuffs for Sisera,
    spoil of dyed stuffs
      embroidered,
  two pieces of dyed work
      embroidered for my neck
      as spoil?'

31 "So perish all your enemies,
    O Lord!
  But may your friends be like
      the sun as it rises in its
      might."

And the land had rest forty years.

## LUKE 22.35–53

H E [Jesus] said to them, "When I sent you out without a purse, bag, or sandals, did you lack anything?" They said, "No, not a thing." 36He said to them, "But now, the one who has a purse must take it, and likewise a bag. And the one who has no sword must sell his cloak and buy one. 37For I tell you, this scripture must be fulfilled in me, 'And he was counted among the lawless'; and indeed what is written about me is being fulfilled." 38They said, "Lord, look, here are two swords." He replied, "It is enough."

39 He came out and went, as was his custom, to the Mount of Olives; and the disciples followed him. 40When he reached the place, he said to them, "Pray that you may not come into the time of trial."a 41Then he withdrew from them about a stone's throw, knelt down, and prayed, 42"Father, if you are willing, remove this cup from me; yet, not my will but yours be done." ⟦43Then an angel from heaven appeared to him and gave him strength. 44In his anguish he prayed more earnestly, and his sweat became like great drops of blood falling down on the ground.⟧b 45When he got up from prayer, he came to the disciples and found them sleeping because of grief, 46and he said to them, "Why are you sleeping? Get up and pray that you may not come into the time of trial."a

47 While he was still speaking, suddenly a crowd came, and the one called Judas, one of the twelve, was leading them. He approached Jesus to kiss him; 48but Jesus said to him, "Judas, is it with a kiss that you are betraying the Son of Man?" 49When those who were around him saw what was coming, they asked, "Lord, should we strike with the sword?" 50Then one of them struck the slave of the high priest and cut off his right ear. 51But Jesus said, "No more of this!" And he touched his ear and healed him. 52Then Jesus said to the chief priests, the officers of the temple police, and the elders who had come for him, "Have you come out with swords and clubs as if I were a bandit? 53When I was with you day after day in the temple, you did not lay hands on me. But this is your hour, and the power of darkness!"

## PSALM 94.1–23

O LORD, you God of vengeance,
  you God of vengeance,
    shine forth!
2 Rise up, O judge of the earth;
  give to the proud what they
    deserve!
3 O Lord, how long shall the
    wicked,
  how long shall the wicked
    exult?

4 They pour out their arrogant
    words;
  all the evildoers boast.
5 They crush your people,
    O Lord,
  and afflict your heritage.

a Or *into temptation*  b Other ancient authorities lack verses 43 and 44

6 They kill the widow and the
    stranger,
  they murder the orphan,
7 and they say, "The LORD does
    not see;
  the God of Jacob does not
    perceive."

8 Understand, O dullest of the
    people;
  fools, when will you be wise?
9 He who planted the ear, does
    he not hear?
  He who formed the eye, does
    he not see?
10 He who disciplines the nations,
  he who teaches knowledge to
    humankind,
  does he not chastise?
11 The LORD knows our thoughts, [a]
    that they are but an empty
    breath.

12 Happy are those whom you
    discipline, O LORD,
  and whom you teach out of
    your law,
13 giving them respite from days of
    trouble,
  until a pit is dug for the
    wicked.
14 For the LORD will not forsake
    his people;
  he will not abandon his
    heritage;
15 for justice will return to the
    righteous,
  and all the upright in heart
    will follow it.

16 Who rises up for me against the
    wicked?
Who stands up for me against
    evildoers?
17 If the LORD had not been my
    help,
  my soul would soon have
    lived in the land of
    silence.
18 When I thought, "My foot is
    slipping,"
  your steadfast love, O LORD,
    held me up.
19 When the cares of my heart are
    many,
  your consolations cheer my
    soul.
20 Can wicked rulers be allied
    with you,
  those who contrive mischief
    by statute?
21 They band together against the
    life of the righteous,
  and condemn the innocent to
    death.
22 But the LORD has become my
    stronghold,
  and my God the rock of my
    refuge.
23 He will repay them for their
    iniquity
  and wipe them out for their
    wickedness;
  the LORD our God will wipe
    them out.

# PROVERBS 14.3–4

THE talk of fools is a rod for
    their backs, [b]
  but the lips of the wise
    preserve them.
4 Where there are no oxen, there
    is no grain;
  abundant crops come by the
    strength of the ox.

[a] Heb *the thoughts of humankind*   [b] Cn: Heb *a rod of pride*

# APRIL 26

## JUDGES 6.1–40

THE Israelites did what was evil in the sight of the LORD, and the LORD gave them into the hand of Midian seven years. ²The hand of Midian prevailed over Israel; and because of Midian the Israelites provided for themselves hiding places in the mountains, caves and strongholds. ³For whenever the Israelites put in seed, the Midianites and the Amalekites and the people of the east would come up against them. ⁴They would encamp against them and destroy the produce of the land, as far as the neighborhood of Gaza, and leave no sustenance in Israel, and no sheep or ox or donkey. ⁵For they and their livestock would come up, and they would even bring their tents, as thick as locusts; neither they nor their camels could be counted; so they wasted the land as they came in. ⁶Thus Israel was greatly impoverished because of Midian; and the Israelites cried out to the LORD for help.

7 When the Israelites cried to the LORD on account of the Midianites, ⁸the LORD sent a prophet to the Israelites; and he said to them, "Thus says the LORD, the God of Israel: I led you up from Egypt, and brought you out of the house of slavery; ⁹and I delivered you from the hand of the Egyptians, and from the hand of all who oppressed you, and drove them out before you, and gave you their land; ¹⁰and I said to you, 'I am the LORD your God; you shall not pay reverence to the gods of the Amorites, in whose land you live.' But you have not given heed to my voice."

11 Now the angel of the LORD came and sat under the oak at Ophrah, which belonged to Joash the Abiezrite, as his son Gideon was beating out wheat in the wine press, to hide it from the Midianites. ¹²The angel of the LORD appeared to him and said to him, "The LORD is with you, you mighty warrior." ¹³Gideon answered him, "But sir, if the LORD is with us, why then has all this happened to us? And where are all his wonderful deeds that our ancestors recounted to us, saying, 'Did not the LORD bring us up from Egypt?' But now the LORD has cast us off, and given us into the hand of Midian." ¹⁴Then the LORD turned to him and said, "Go in this might of yours and deliver Israel from the hand of Midian; I hereby commission you." ¹⁵He responded, "But sir, how can I deliver Israel? My clan is the weakest in Manasseh, and I am the least in my family." ¹⁶The LORD said to him, "But I will be with you, and you shall strike down the Midianites, every one of them." ¹⁷Then he said to him, "If now I have found favor with you, then show me a sign that it is you who speak with me. ¹⁸Do not depart from here until I come to you, and bring out my present, and set it before you." And he said, "I will stay until you return."

19 So Gideon went into his house and prepared a kid, and unleavened cakes from an ephah of flour; the meat he put in a basket, and the broth he put in a pot, and brought them to him under the oak and presented them. ²⁰The angel of God said to him, "Take the meat and the unleavened cakes, and put them on this rock, and pour out the broth." And he did so. ²¹Then the angel of the LORD reached out the tip of the staff that was in his hand, and touched the meat and the unleavened cakes; and fire sprang up from the rock and consumed the meat and the unleavened cakes; and the angel of the LORD vanished from his sight. ²²Then Gideon perceived that it was the angel of the

Lord; and Gideon said, "Help me, Lord God! For I have seen the angel of the Lord face to face." ²³But the Lord said to him, "Peace be to you; do not fear, you shall not die." ²⁴Then Gideon built an altar there to the Lord, and called it, The Lord is peace. To this day it still stands at Ophrah, which belongs to the Abiezrites.

25  That night the Lord said to him, "Take your father's bull, the second bull seven years old, and pull down the altar of Baal that belongs to your father, and cut down the sacred pole<sup>a</sup> that is beside it; ²⁶and build an altar to the Lord your God on the top of the stronghold here, in proper order; then take the second bull, and offer it as a burnt offering with the wood of the sacred pole<sup>a</sup> that you shall cut down." ²⁷So Gideon took ten of his servants, and did as the Lord had told him; but because he was too afraid of his family and the townspeople to do it by day, he did it by night.

28  When the townspeople rose early in the morning, the altar of Baal was broken down, and the sacred pole<sup>a</sup> beside it was cut down, and the second bull was offered on the altar that had been built. ²⁹So they said to one another, "Who has done this?" After searching and inquiring, they were told, "Gideon son of Joash did it." ³⁰Then the townspeople said to Joash, "Bring out your son, so that he may die, for he has pulled down the altar of Baal and cut down the sacred pole<sup>a</sup> beside it." ³¹But Joash said to all who were arrayed against him, "Will you contend for Baal? Or will you defend his cause? Whoever contends for him shall be put to death by morning. If he is a god, let him contend for himself, because his altar has been pulled down." ³²Therefore on that day Gideon<sup>b</sup> was called Jerubbaal, that is to say, "Let Baal contend against him," because he pulled down his altar.

33  Then all the Midianites and the Amalekites and the people of the east came together, and crossing the Jordan they encamped in the Valley of Jezreel. ³⁴But the spirit of the Lord took possession of Gideon; and he sounded the trumpet, and the Abiezrites were called out to follow him. ³⁵He sent messengers throughout all Manasseh, and they too were called out to follow him. He also sent messengers to Asher, Zebulun, and Naphtali, and they went up to meet them.

36  Then Gideon said to God, "In order to see whether you will deliver Israel by my hand, as you have said, ³⁷I am going to lay a fleece of wool on the threshing floor; if there is dew on the fleece alone, and it is dry on all the ground, then I shall know that you will deliver Israel by my hand, as you have said." ³⁸And it was so. When he rose early next morning and squeezed the fleece, he wrung enough dew from the fleece to fill a bowl with water. ³⁹Then Gideon said to God, "Do not let your anger burn against me, let me speak one more time; let me, please, make trial with the fleece just once more; let it be dry only on the fleece, and on all the ground let there be dew." ⁴⁰And God did so that night. It was dry on the fleece only, and on all the ground there was dew.

## LUKE 22.54—23.12

THEN they seized him [Jesus] and led him away, bringing him into the high priest's house. But Peter was following at a distance. ⁵⁵When they had kindled a fire in the middle of the courtyard and sat down together, Peter sat among them. ⁵⁶Then a servant-girl, seeing him in the firelight, stared at him and said, "This man also was with him." ⁵⁷But he denied it, saying, "Woman, I do not know him." [58]A little later someone else, on seeing him, said, "You also are one of them." But Peter said, "Man, I am not!" [59]Then about an hour later still another kept insisting, "Surely this man also was with him; for he is a Galilean." [60]But Peter said, "Man, I do not know what you are talking about!" At that moment, while he was still speaking, the cock crowed. [61]The Lord turned and looked at Peter. Then Peter remembered the word of the Lord, how he had said to him, "Before the cock crows today, you will deny me three times." [62]And he went out and wept bitterly.

63 Now the men who were holding Jesus began to mock him and beat him; [64]they also blindfolded him and kept asking him, "Prophesy! Who is it that struck you?" [65]They kept heaping many other insults on him.

66 When day came, the assembly of the elders of the people, both chief priests and scribes, gathered together, and they brought him to their council. [67]They said, "If you are the Messiah, [a] tell us." He replied, "If I tell you, you will not believe; [68]and if I question you, you will not answer. [69]But from now on the Son of Man will be seated at the right hand of the power of God." [70]All of them asked, "Are you, then, the Son of God?" He said to them, "You say that I am." [71]Then they said, "What further testimony do we need? We have heard it ourselves from his own lips!"

[23.1] THEN the assembly rose as a body and brought Jesus[b] before Pilate. [2]They began to accuse him, saying, "We found this man perverting our nation, forbidding us to pay taxes to the emperor, and saying that he himself is the Messiah, a king."[c] [3]Then Pilate asked him, "Are you the king of the Jews?" He answered, "You say so." [4]Then Pilate said to the chief priests and the crowds, "I find no basis for an accusation against this man." [5]But they were insistent and said, "He stirs up the people by teaching throughout all Judea, from Galilee where he began even to this place."

6 When Pilate heard this, he asked whether the man was a Galilean. [7]And when he learned that he was under Herod's jurisdiction, he sent him off to Herod, who was himself in Jerusalem at that time. [8]When Herod saw Jesus, he was very glad, for he had been wanting to see him for a long time, because he had heard about him and was hoping to see him perform some sign. [9]He questioned him at some length, but Jesus[d] gave him no answer. [10]The chief priests and the scribes stood by, vehemently accusing him. [11]Even Herod with his soldiers treated him with contempt and mocked him; then he put an elegant robe on him, and sent him back to Pilate. [12]That same day Herod and Pilate became friends with each other; before this they had been enemies.

## PSALM 95.1—96.13

O COME, let us sing to the LORD;
   let us make a joyful noise to
      the rock of our salvation!
2 Let us come into his presence
   with thanksgiving;
  let us make a joyful noise to
      him with songs of praise!
3 For the LORD is a great God,
  and a great King above all
     gods.
4 In his hand are the depths of
   the earth;
  the heights of the mountains
     are his also.
5 The sea is his, for he made it,
  and the dry land, which his
     hands have formed.

[a]Or the Christ  [b]Gk him  [c]Or is an anointed king  [d]Gk he

6 O come, let us worship and bow
down,
let us kneel before the LORD,
our Maker!
7 For he is our God,
and we are the people of his
pasture,
and the sheep of his hand.

O that today you would listen to
his voice!
8 Do not harden your hearts, as
at Meribah,
as on the day at Massah in
the wilderness,
9 when your ancestors tested me,
and put me to the proof,
though they had seen my
work.
10 For forty years I loathed that
generation
and said, "They are a people
whose hearts go astray,
and they do not regard my
ways."
11 Therefore in my anger I swore,
"They shall not enter my
rest."

96.1 O sing to the LORD a new song;
sing to the LORD, all the
earth.
2 Sing to the LORD, bless his
name;
tell of his salvation from day
to day.
3 Declare his glory among the
nations,
his marvelous works among
all the peoples.
4 For great is the LORD, and
greatly to be praised;
he is to be revered above
all gods.
5 For all the gods of the peoples
are idols,
but the LORD made the
heavens.
6 Honor and majesty are before
him;

strength and beauty are in his
sanctuary.
7 Ascribe to the LORD, O families
of the peoples,
ascribe to the LORD glory and
strength.
8 Ascribe to the LORD the glory
due his name;
bring an offering, and come
into his courts.
9 Worship the LORD in holy
splendor;
tremble before him, all the
earth.

10 Say among the nations, "The
LORD is king!
The world is firmly
established; it shall never
be moved.
He will judge the peoples with
equity."
11 Let the heavens be glad, and let
the earth rejoice;
let the sea roar, and all that
fills it;
12 let the field exult, and
everything in it.
Then shall all the trees of the
forest sing for joy
13 before the LORD; for he is
coming,
for he is coming to judge the
earth.
He will judge the world with
righteousness,
and the peoples with his
truth.

## PROVERBS 14.5–6

A FAITHFUL witness does not lie,
but a false witness breathes
out lies.
6 A scoffer seeks wisdom in vain,
but knowledge is easy for one
who understands.

# APRIL 27

**JUDGES 7.1—8.17**

**T**HEN Jerubbaal (that is, Gideon) and all the troops that were with him rose early and encamped beside the spring of Harod; and the camp of Midian was north of them, below[a] the hill of Moreh, in the valley.

2 The LORD said to Gideon, "The troops with you are too many for me to give the Midianites into their hand. Israel would only take the credit away from me, saying, 'My own hand has delivered me.' [3]Now therefore proclaim this in the hearing of the troops, 'Whoever is fearful and trembling, let him return home.' " Thus Gideon sifted them out;[b] twenty-two thousand returned, and ten thousand remained.

4 Then the LORD said to Gideon, "The troops are still too many; take them down to the water and I will sift them out for you there. When I say, 'This one shall go with you,' he shall go with you; and when I say, 'This one shall not go with you,' he shall not go." [5]So he brought the troops down to the water; and the LORD said to Gideon, "All those who lap the water with their tongues, as a dog laps, you shall put to one side; all those who kneel down to drink, putting their hands to their mouths,[c] you shall put to the other side." [6]The number of those that lapped was three hundred; but all the rest of the troops knelt down to drink water. [7]Then the LORD said to Gideon, "With the three hundred that lapped I will deliver you, and give the Midianites into your hand. Let all the others go to their homes." [8]So he took the jars of the troops from their hands,[d] and their trumpets; and he sent all the rest of Is-

rael back to their own tents, but retained the three hundred. The camp of Midian was below him in the valley.

9 That same night the LORD said to him, "Get up, attack the camp; for I have given it into your hand. [10]But if you fear to attack, go down to the camp with your servant Purah; [11]and you shall hear what they say, and afterward your hands shall be strengthened to attack the camp." Then he went down with his servant Purah to the outposts of the armed men that were in the camp. [12]The Midianites and the Amalekites and all the people of the east lay along the valley as thick as locusts; and their camels were without number, countless as the sand on the seashore. [13]When Gideon arrived, there was a man telling a dream to his comrade; and he said, "I had a dream, and in it a cake of barley bread tumbled into the camp of Midian, and came to the tent, and struck it so that it fell; it turned upside down, and the tent collapsed." [14]And his comrade answered, "This is no other than the sword of Gideon son of Joash, a man of Israel; into his hand God has given Midian and all the army."

15 When Gideon heard the telling of the dream and its interpretation, he worshiped; and he returned to the camp of Israel, and said, "Get up; for the LORD has given the army of Midian into your hand." [16]After he divided the three hundred men into three companies, and put trumpets into the hands of all of them, and empty jars, with torches inside the jars, [17]he said to them, "Look at me, and do the same; when I come to the outskirts of the camp, do as I do. [18]When I blow the

---

aHeb *from*   bCn: Heb *home, and depart from Mount Gilead' "*   cHeb places the words *putting their hands to their mouths* after the word *lapped* in verse 6   dCn: Heb *So the people took provisions in their hands*

trumpet, I and all who are with me, then you also blow the trumpets around the whole camp, and shout, 'For the LORD and for Gideon!' "

19  So Gideon and the hundred who were with him came to the outskirts of the camp at the beginning of the middle watch, when they had just set the watch; and they blew the trumpets and smashed the jars that were in their hands. [20]So the three companies blew the trumpets and broke the jars, holding in their left hands the torches, and in their right hands the trumpets to blow; and they cried, "A sword for the LORD and for Gideon!" [21]Every man stood in his place all around the camp, and all the men in camp ran; they cried out and fled. [22]When they blew the three hundred trumpets, the LORD set every man's sword against his fellow and against all the army; and the army fled as far as Beth-shittah toward Zererah, [a] as far as the border of Abel-meholah, by Tabbath. [23]And the men of Israel were called out from Naphtali and from Asher and from all Manasseh, and they pursued after the Midianites.

24  Then Gideon sent messengers throughout all the hill country of Ephraim, saying, "Come down against the Midianites and seize the waters against them, as far as Beth-barah, and also the Jordan." So all the men of Ephraim were called out, and they seized the waters as far as Beth-barah, and also the Jordan. [25]They captured the two captains of Midian, Oreb and Zeeb; they killed Oreb at the rock of Oreb, and Zeeb they killed at the wine press of Zeeb, as they pursued the Midianites. They brought the heads of Oreb and Zeeb to Gideon beyond the Jordan.

**8.**[1] THEN the Ephraimites said to him, "What have you done to us, not to call us when you went to fight against the Midianites?" And they upbraided him violently. [2]So he said to them, "What have I done now in comparison with you? Is not the gleaning of the grapes of Ephraim better than the vintage of Abiezer? [3]God has given into your hands the captains of Midian, Oreb and Zeeb; what have I been able to do in comparison with you?" When he said this, their anger against him subsided.

4  Then Gideon came to the Jordan and crossed over, he and the three hundred who were with him, exhausted and famished. [b] [5]So he said to the people of Succoth, "Please give some loaves of bread to my followers, for they are exhausted, and I am pursuing Zebah and Zalmunna, the kings of Midian." [6]But the officials of Succoth said, "Do you already have in your possession the hands of Zebah and Zalmunna, that we should give bread to your army?" [7]Gideon replied, "Well then, when the LORD has given Zebah and Zalmunna into my hand, I will trample your flesh on the thorns of the wilderness and on briers." [8]From there he went up to Penuel, and made the same request of them; and the people of Penuel answered him as the people of Succoth had answered. [9]So he said to the people of Penuel, "When I come back victorious, I will break down this tower."

10  Now Zebah and Zalmunna were in Karkor with their army, about fifteen thousand men, all who were left of all the army of the people of the east; for one hundred twenty thousand men bearing arms had fallen. [11]So Gideon went up by the caravan route east of Nobah and Jogbehah, and attacked the army; for the army was off its guard. [12]Zebah and Zalmunna fled; and he pursued them and took the two kings of Midian, Zebah and Zalmunna, and threw all the army into a panic.

13  When Gideon son of Joash returned from the battle by the ascent of

---

a Another reading is *Zeredah*   b Gk: Heb *pursuing*

Heres, [14]he caught a young man, one of the people of Succoth, and questioned him; and he listed for him the officials and elders of Succoth, seventy-seven people. [15]Then he came to the people of Succoth, and said, "Here are Zebah and Zalmunna, about whom you taunted me, saying, 'Do you already have in your possession the hands of Zebah and Zalmunna, that we should give bread to your troops who are exhausted?' " [16]So he took the elders of the city and he took thorns of the wilderness and briers and with them he trampled[a] the people of Succoth. [17]He also broke down the tower of Penuel, and killed the men of the city.

## LUKE 23.13–43

**P**ILATE then called together the chief priests, the leaders, and the people, [14]and said to them, "You brought me this man as one who was perverting the people; and here I have examined him in your presence and have not found this man guilty of any of your charges against him. [15]Neither has Herod, for he sent him back to us. Indeed, he has done nothing to deserve death. [16]I will therefore have him flogged and release him."[b]

18 Then they all shouted out together, "Away with this fellow! Release Barabbas for us!" [19](This was a man who had been put in prison for an insurrection that had taken place in the city, and for murder.) [20]Pilate, wanting to release Jesus, addressed them again; [21]but they kept shouting, "Crucify, crucify him!" [22]A third time he said to them, "Why, what evil has he done? I have found in him no ground for the sentence of death; I will therefore have him flogged and then release him." [23]But they kept urgently demanding with loud shouts that he should be crucified; and their voices prevailed. [24]So Pilate gave his verdict that their demand should be granted. [25]He released the man they asked for, the one who had been put in prison for insurrection and murder, and he handed Jesus over as they wished.

26 As they led him away, they seized a man, Simon of Cyrene, who was coming from the country, and they laid the cross on him, and made him carry it behind Jesus. [27]A great number of the people followed him, and among them were women who were beating their breasts and wailing for him. [28]But Jesus turned to them and said, "Daughters of Jerusalem, do not weep for me, but weep for yourselves and for your children. [29]For the days are surely coming when they will say, 'Blessed are the barren, and the wombs that never bore, and the breasts that never nursed.' [30]Then they will begin to say to the mountains, 'Fall on us'; and to the hills, 'Cover us.' [31]For if they do this when the wood is green, what will happen when it is dry?"

32 Two others also, who were criminals, were led away to be put to death with him. [33]When they came to the place that is called The Skull, they crucified Jesus[c] there with the criminals, one on his right and one on his left. [[34]Then Jesus said, "Father, forgive them; for they do not know what they are doing."][d] And they cast lots to divide his clothing. [35]And the people stood by, watching; but the leaders scoffed at him, saying, "He saved others; let him save himself if he is the Messiah[e] of God, his chosen one!" [36]The soldiers also mocked him, coming up and offering him sour wine, [37]and saying, "If you are the King of the Jews, save yourself!" [38]There was also

---

[a]With verse 7, Compare Gk: Heb *he taught*   [b]Here, or after verse 19, other ancient authorities add verse 17, *Now he was obliged to release someone for them at the festival*   [c]Gk *him*   [d]Other ancient authorities lack the sentence *Then Jesus . . . what they are doing*   [e]Or *the Christ*

an inscription over him,[a] "This is the King of the Jews."

39 One of the criminals who were hanged there kept deriding[b] him and saying, "Are you not the Messiah?[c] Save yourself and us!" 40But the other rebuked him, saying, "Do you not fear God, since you are under the same sentence of condemnation? 41And we indeed have been condemned justly, for we are getting what we deserve for our deeds, but this man has done nothing wrong." 42Then he said, "Jesus, remember me when you come into[d] your kingdom." 43He replied, "Truly I tell you, today you will be with me in Paradise."

## PSALM 97.1—98.9

THE LORD is king! Let the earth rejoice;
    let the many coastlands be
        glad!
2 Clouds and thick darkness are
        all around him;
    righteousness and justice are
        the foundation of his
        throne.
3 Fire goes before him,
    and consumes his adversaries
        on every side.
4 His lightnings light up the world;
    the earth sees and trembles.
5 The mountains melt like wax
        before the LORD,
    before the Lord of all the
        earth.

6 The heavens proclaim his
        righteousness;
    and all the peoples behold his
        glory.
7 All worshipers of images are put
        to shame,
    those who make their boast in
        worthless idols;

all gods bow down before
    him.
8 Zion hears and is glad,
    and the towns[e] of Judah
        rejoice,
    because of your judgments,
        O God.
9 For you, O LORD, are most high
        over all the earth;
    you are exalted far above
        all gods.

10 The LORD loves those who
        hate[f] evil;
    he guards the lives of his
        faithful;
    he rescues them from the
        hand of the wicked.
11 Light dawns[g] for the righteous,
    and joy for the upright in
        heart.
12 Rejoice in the LORD, O you
        righteous,
    and give thanks to his holy
        name!

*A Psalm.*

98.1 O sing to the LORD a new song,
    for he has done marvelous
        things.
    His right hand and his holy arm
        have gotten him victory.
2 The LORD has made known his
        victory;
    he has revealed his
        vindication in the sight of
        the nations.
3 He has remembered his
        steadfast love and
        faithfulness
    to the house of Israel.
    All the ends of the earth have
        seen
    the victory of our God.

4 Make a joyful noise to the LORD,
    all the earth;

[a]Other ancient authorities add *written in Greek and Latin and Hebrew* (that is, *Aramaic*)
[b]Or *blaspheming*  [c]Or *the Christ*  [d]Other ancient authorities read *in*  [e]Heb *daughters*  [f]Cn: Heb *You who love the LORD hate*  [g]Gk Syr Jerome: Heb *is sown*

> break forth into joyous song
> and sing praises.
> 5 Sing praises to the LORD with
> the lyre,
> with the lyre and the sound of
> melody.
> 6 With trumpets and the sound of
> the horn
> make a joyful noise before the
> King, the LORD.
>
> 7 Let the sea roar, and all that
> fills it;
> the world and those who live
> in it.
> 8 Let the floods clap their hands;

> let the hills sing together for
> joy
> 9 at the presence of the LORD, for
> he is coming
> to judge the earth.
> He will judge the world with
> righteousness,
> and the peoples with equity.

## PROVERBS 14. 7–8

LEAVE the presence of a fool,
for there you do not find
words of knowledge.
8 It is the wisdom of the clever to
understand where they
go,
but the folly of fools misleads.

# APRIL 28

## JUDGES 8. 18—9. 21

THEN he [Gideon] said to Zebah and Zalmunna, "What about the men whom you killed at Tabor?" They answered, "As you are, so were they, every one of them; they resembled the sons of a king." 19And he replied, "They were my brothers, the sons of my mother; as the LORD lives, if you had saved them alive, I would not kill you." 20So he said to Jether his first-born, "Go kill them!" But the boy did not draw his sword, for he was afraid, because he was still a boy. 21Then Zebah and Zalmunna said, "You come and kill us; for as the man is, so is his strength." So Gideon proceeded to kill Zebah and Zalmunna; and he took the crescents that were on the necks of their camels.

22 Then the Israelites said to Gideon, "Rule over us, you and your son and your grandson also; for you have delivered us out of the hand of Midian." 23Gideon said to them, "I will not rule over you, and my son will not rule over you; the LORD will rule over you." 24Then Gideon said to them, "Let me make a request of you; each of you give me an earring he has taken as booty." (For the enemya had golden earrings, because they were Ishmaelites.) 25"We will willingly give them," they answered. So they spread a garment, and each threw into it an earring he had taken as booty. 26The weight of the golden earrings that he requested was one thousand seven hundred shekels of gold (apart from the crescents and the pendants and the purple garments worn by the kings of Midian, and the collars that were on the necks of their

aHeb *they*

camels). ²⁷Gideon made an ephod of it and put it in his town, in Ophrah; and all Israel prostituted themselves to it there, and it became a snare to Gideon and to his family. ²⁸So Midian was subdued before the Israelites, and they lifted up their heads no more. So the land had rest forty years in the days of Gideon.

29 Jerubbaal son of Joash went to live in his own house. ³⁰Now Gideon had seventy sons, his own offspring, for he had many wives. ³¹His concubine who was in Shechem also bore him a son, and he named him Abimelech. ³²Then Gideon son of Joash died at a good old age, and was buried in the tomb of his father Joash at Ophrah of the Abiezrites.

33 As soon as Gideon died, the Israelites relapsed and prostituted themselves with the Baals, making Baal-berith their god. ³⁴The Israelites did not remember the Lord their God, who had rescued them from the hand of all their enemies on every side; ³⁵and they did not exhibit loyalty to the house of Jerubbaal (that is, Gideon) in return for all the good that he had done to Israel.

9.1 Now Abimelech son of Jerubbaal went to Shechem to his mother's kinsfolk and said to them and to the whole clan of his mother's family, ²"Say in the hearing of all the lords of Shechem, 'Which is better for you, that all seventy of the sons of Jerubbaal rule over you, or that one rule over you?' Remember also that I am your bone and your flesh." ³So his mother's kinsfolk spoke all these words on his behalf in the hearing of all the lords of Shechem; and their hearts inclined to follow Abimelech, for they said, "He is our brother." ⁴They gave him seventy pieces of silver out of the temple of Baal-berith with which Abimelech hired

worthless and reckless fellows, who followed him. ⁵He went to his father's house at Ophrah, and killed his brothers the sons of Jerubbaal, seventy men, on one stone; but Jotham, the youngest son of Jerubbaal, survived, for he hid himself. ⁶Then all the lords of Shechem and all Beth-millo came together, and they went and made Abimelech king, by the oak of the pillar[a] at Shechem.

7 When it was told to Jotham, he went and stood on the top of Mount Gerizim, and cried aloud and said to them, "Listen to me, you lords of Shechem, so that God may listen to you.

8   The trees once went out
     to anoint a king over
       themselves.
  So they said to the olive tree,
    'Reign over us.'
9   The olive tree answered them,
    'Shall I stop producing my
      rich oil
     by which gods and mortals
     are honored,
     and go to sway over the
     trees?'
10   Then the trees said to the fig
     tree,
    'You come and reign over us.'
11   But the fig tree answered them,
    'Shall I stop producing my
      sweetness
     and my delicious fruit,
     and go to sway over the
     trees?'
12   Then the trees said to the vine,
    'You come and reign over us.'
13   But the vine said to them,
    'Shall I stop producing my
      wine
     that cheers gods and
     mortals,
     and go to sway over the
     trees?'
14   So all the trees said to the
     bramble,
    'You come and reign over us.'

---

a Cn: Meaning of Heb uncertain

15 And the bramble said to the
        trees,
      'If in good faith you are
        anointing me king over
        you,
        then come and take refuge
        in my shade;
      but if not, let fire come out of
        the bramble
        and devour the cedars of
        Lebanon.'

16 "Now therefore, if you acted in good faith and honor when you made Abimelech king, and if you have dealt well with Jerubbaal and his house, and have done to him as his actions deserved— [17]for my father fought for you, and risked his life, and rescued you from the hand of Midian; [18]but you have risen up against my father's house this day, and have killed his sons, seventy men on one stone, and have made Abimelech, the son of his slave woman, king over the lords of Shechem, because he is your kinsman— [19]if, I say, you have acted in good faith and honor with Jerubbaal and with his house this day, then rejoice in Abimelech, and let him also rejoice in you; [20]but if not, let fire come out from Abimelech, and devour the lords of Shechem, and Beth-millo; and let fire come out from the lords of Shechem, and from Beth-millo, and devour Abimelech." [21]Then Jotham ran away and fled, going to Beer, where he remained for fear of his brother Abimelech.

## LUKE 23.44—24.12

IT was now about noon, and darkness came over the whole land[a] until three in the afternoon, [45]while the sun's light failed;[b] and the curtain of the temple was torn in two. [46]Then Jesus, crying with a loud voice, said, "Father, into your hands I commend my spirit." Having said this, he breathed his last. [47]When the centurion saw what had taken place, he praised God and said, "Certainly this man was innocent."[c] [48]And when all the crowds who had gathered there for this spectacle saw what had taken place, they returned home, beating their breasts. [49]But all his acquaintances, including the women who had followed him from Galilee, stood at a distance, watching these things.

50 Now there was a good and righteous man named Joseph, who, though a member of the council, [51]had not agreed to their plan and action. He came from the Jewish town of Arimathea, and he was waiting expectantly for the kingdom of God. [52]This man went to Pilate and asked for the body of Jesus. [53]Then he took it down, wrapped it in a linen cloth, and laid it in a rock-hewn tomb where no one had ever been laid. [54]It was the day of Preparation, and the sabbath was beginning.[d] [55]The women who had come with him from Galilee followed, and they saw the tomb and how his body was laid. [56]Then they returned, and prepared spices and ointments.

On the sabbath they rested according to the commandment.

24.1 BUT on the first day of the week, at early dawn, they came to the tomb, taking the spices that they had prepared. [2]They found the stone rolled away from the tomb, [3]but when they went in, they did not find the body.[e] [4]While they were perplexed about this, suddenly two men in dazzling clothes stood beside them. [5]The women[f] were terrified and bowed their faces to the ground, but the men[g] said to them, "Why do you look for the living among the dead? He is not here, but has risen.[h] [6]Remember how he told you, while he was still in Galilee, [7]that the Son of Man must be handed over to sinners, and be crucified, and on the third day rise again." [8]Then they remembered his words, [9]and returning from the tomb, they told all this to the eleven and to all the rest. [10]Now it was Mary Magdalene, Joanna, Mary the mother of James, and the other women with them who told this to the apostles. [11]But these words seemed to them an idle tale, and they did not believe them. [12]But Peter got up and ran to the tomb; stooping and looking in, he saw the linen cloths by themselves; then he went home, amazed at what had happened. [a]

## PSALM 99.1–9

THE LORD is king; let the
        peoples tremble!
He sits enthroned upon the
        cherubim; let the earth
        quake!
2   The LORD is great in Zion;
        he is exalted over all the
        peoples.
3   Let them praise your great and
        awesome name.
    Holy is he!
4   Mighty King, [b] lover of justice,
        you have established equity;
    you have executed justice
        and righteousness in Jacob.
5   Extol the LORD our God;

worship at his footstool.
    Holy is he!

6   Moses and Aaron were among
        his priests,
    Samuel also was among those
        who called on his name.
    They cried to the LORD, and
        he answered them.
7   He spoke to them in the pillar
        of cloud;
    they kept his decrees,
        and the statutes that he gave
        them.

8   O LORD our God, you answered
        them;
    you were a forgiving God to
        them,
    but an avenger of their
        wrongdoings.
9   Extol the LORD our God,
        and worship at his holy
        mountain;
    for the LORD our God is holy.

## PROVERBS 14.9–10

FOOLS mock at the guilt
        offering, [c]
but the upright enjoy God's
        favor.
10  The heart knows its own
        bitterness,
    and no stranger shares its
        joy.

# APRIL 29

JUDGES 9.22—10.18

**A**BIMELECH ruled over Israel three years. <sup>23</sup>But God sent an evil spirit between Abimelech and the lords of Shechem; and the lords of Shechem dealt treacherously with Abimelech. <sup>24</sup>This happened so that the violence done to the seventy sons of Jerubbaal might be avenged[a] and their blood be laid on their brother Abimelech, who killed them, and on the lords of Shechem, who strengthened his hands to kill his brothers. <sup>25</sup>So, out of hostility to him, the lords of Shechem set ambushes on the mountain tops. They robbed all who passed by them along that way; and it was reported to Abimelech.

26  When Gaal son of Ebed moved into Shechem with his kinsfolk, the lords of Shechem put confidence in him. <sup>27</sup>They went out into the field and gathered the grapes from their vineyards, trod them, and celebrated. Then they went into the temple of their god, ate and drank, and ridiculed Abimelech. <sup>28</sup>Gaal son of Ebed said, "Who is Abimelech, and who are we of Shechem, that we should serve him? Did not the son of Jerubbaal and Zebul his officer serve the men of Hamor father of Shechem? Why then should we serve him? <sup>29</sup>If only this people were under my command! Then I would remove Abimelech; I would say[b] to him, 'Increase your army, and come out.'"

30  When Zebul the ruler of the city heard the words of Gaal son of Ebed, his anger was kindled. <sup>31</sup>He sent messengers to Abimelech at Arumah,[c] saying, "Look, Gaal son of Ebed and his kinsfolk have come to Shechem, and they are stirring up[d] the city against you. <sup>32</sup>Now therefore, go by night, you and the troops that are with you, and lie in wait in the fields. <sup>33</sup>Then early in the morning, as soon as the sun rises, get up and rush on the city; and when he and the troops that are with him come out against you, you may deal with them as best you can."

34  So Abimelech and all the troops with him got up by night and lay in wait against Shechem in four companies. <sup>35</sup>When Gaal son of Ebed went out and stood in the entrance of the gate of the city, Abimelech and the troops with him rose from the ambush. <sup>36</sup>And when Gaal saw them, he said to Zebul, "Look, people are coming down from the mountain tops!" And Zebul said to him, "The shadows on the mountains look like people to you." <sup>37</sup>Gaal spoke again and said, "Look, people are coming down from Tabbur-erez, and one company is coming from the direction of Elon-meonenim."[e] <sup>38</sup>Then Zebul said to him, "Where is your boast[f] now, you who said, 'Who is Abimelech, that we should serve him?' Are not these the troops you made light of? Go out now and fight with them." <sup>39</sup>So Gaal went out at the head of the lords of Shechem, and fought with Abimelech. <sup>40</sup>Abimelech chased him, and he fled before him. Many fell wounded, up to the entrance of the gate. <sup>41</sup>So Abimelech resided at Arumah; and Zebul drove out Gaal and his kinsfolk, so that they could not live on at Shechem.

42  On the following day the people went out into the fields. When Abimelech was told, <sup>43</sup>he took his troops and divided them into three companies, and lay in wait in the fields. When he looked and saw the people coming out of the

aHeb *might come*  bGk: Heb *and he said*  cCn See 9.41. Heb *Tormah*  dCn: Heb *are besieging*
eThat is *Diviners' Oak*  fHeb *mouth*

city, he rose against them and killed them. [44]Abimelech and the company that was[a] with him rushed forward and stood at the entrance of the gate of the city, while the two companies rushed on all who were in the fields and killed them. [45]Abimelech fought against the city all that day; he took the city, and killed the people that were in it; and he razed the city and sowed it with salt.

46 When all the lords of the Tower of Shechem heard of it, they entered the stronghold of the temple of El-berith. [47]Abimelech was told that all the lords of the Tower of Shechem were gathered together. [48]So Abimelech went up to Mount Zalmon, he and all the troops that were with him. Abime-lech took an ax in his hand, cut down a bundle of brushwood, and took it up and laid it on his shoulder. Then he said to the troops with him, "What you have seen me do, do quickly, as I have done." [49]So every one of the troops cut down a bundle and following Abimelech put it against the stronghold, and they set the stronghold on fire over them, so that all the people of the Tower of She-chem also died, about a thousand men and women.

50 Then Abimelech went to The-bez, and encamped against Thebez, and took it. [51]But there was a strong tower within the city, and all the men and women and all the lords of the city fled to it and shut themselves in; and they went to the roof of the tower. [52]Abimelech came to the tower, and fought against it, and came near to the entrance of the tower to burn it with fire. [53]But a certain woman threw an upper millstone on Abimelech's head, and crushed his skull. [54]Immediately he called to the young man who carried his armor and said to him, "Draw your sword and kill me, so people will not say about me, 'A woman killed him.'" So the young man thrust him through,

and he died. [55]When the Israelites saw that Abimelech was dead, they all went home. [56]Thus God repaid Abimelech for the crime he committed against his father in killing his seventy brothers; [57]and God also made all the wickedness of the people of Shechem fall back on their heads, and on them came the curse of Jotham son of Jerubbaal.

[10.1] AFTER Abimelech, Tola son of Puah son of Dodo, a man of Issachar, who lived at Shamir in the hill country of Ephraim, rose to deliver Israel. [2]He judged Israel twenty-three years. Then he died, and was buried at Sha-mir.

3 After him came Jair the Gileadite, who judged Israel twenty-two years. [4]He had thirty sons who rode on thirty donkeys; and they had thirty towns, which are in the land of Gilead, and are called Havvoth-jair to this day. [5]Jair died, and was buried in Kamon.

6 The Israelites again did what was evil in the sight of the LORD, worshiping the Baals and the Astartes, the gods of Aram, the gods of Sidon, the gods of Moab, the gods of the Ammonites, and the gods of the Philistines. Thus they abandoned the LORD, and did not wor-ship him. [7]So the anger of the LORD was kindled against Israel, and he sold them into the hand of the Philistines and into the hand of the Ammonites, [8]and they crushed and oppressed the Israelites that year. For eighteen years they op-pressed all the Israelites that were be-yond the Jordan in the land of the Amorites, which is in Gilead. [9]The Am-monites also crossed the Jordan to fight against Judah and against Benjamin and against the house of Ephraim; so that Israel was greatly distressed.

10 So the Israelites cried to the LORD, saying, "We have sinned against you, because we have abandoned our God and have worshiped the Baals."

---

[a]Vg and some Gk Mss: Heb *companies that were*

[11]And the LORD said to the Israelites, "Did I not deliver you[a] from the Egyptians and from the Amorites, from the Ammonites and from the Philistines? [12]The Sidonians also, and the Amalekites, and the Maonites, oppressed you; and you cried to me, and I delivered you out of their hand. [13]Yet you have abandoned me and worshiped other gods; therefore I will deliver you no more. [14]Go and cry to the gods whom you have chosen; let them deliver you in the time of your distress." [15]And the Israelites said to the LORD, "We have sinned; do to us whatever seems good to you; but deliver us this day!" [16]So they put away the foreign gods from among them and worshiped the LORD; and he could no longer bear to see Israel suffer.

17 Then the Ammonites were called to arms, and they encamped in Gilead; and the Israelites came together, and they encamped at Mizpah. [18]The commanders of the people of Gilead said to one another, "Who will begin the fight against the Ammonites? He shall be head over all the inhabitants of Gilead."

## LUKE 24.13–53

Now on that same day two of them were going to a village called Emmaus, about seven miles[b] from Jerusalem, [14]and talking with each other about all these things that had happened. [15]While they were talking and discussing, Jesus himself came near and went with them, [16]but their eyes were kept from recognizing him. [17]And he said to them, "What are you discussing with each other while you walk along?" They stood still, looking sad.[c] [18]Then one of them, whose name was Cleopas, answered him, "Are you the only stranger in Jerusalem who does not know the things that have taken place there in these days?" [19]He asked them, "What things?" They replied, "The things about Jesus of Nazareth,[d] who was a prophet mighty in deed and word before God and all the people, [20]and how our chief priests and leaders handed him over to be condemned to death and crucified him. [21]But we had hoped that he was the one to redeem Israel.[e] Yes, and besides all this, it is now the third day since these things took place. [22]Moreover, some women of our group astounded us. They were at the tomb early this morning, [23]and when they did not find his body there, they came back and told us that they had indeed seen a vision of angels who said that he was alive. [24]Some of those who were with us went to the tomb and found it just as the women had said; but they did not see him." [25]Then he said to them, "Oh, how foolish you are, and how slow of heart to believe all that the prophets have declared! [26]Was it not necessary that the Messiah[f] should suffer these things and then enter into his glory?" [27]Then beginning with Moses and all the prophets, he interpreted to them the things about himself in all the scriptures.

28 As they came near the village to which they were going, he walked ahead as if he were going on. [29]But they urged him strongly, saying, "Stay with us, because it is almost evening and the day is now nearly over." So he went in to stay with them. [30]When he was at the table with them, he took bread, blessed and broke it, and gave it to them. [31]Then their eyes were opened, and they recognized him; and he vanished from their sight. [32]They said to each other, "Were not our hearts burning within us[g] while he was talking to us on the road, while he was opening

---

[a]Heb lacks *Did I not deliver you*   [b]Gk *sixty stadia;* other ancient authorities read *a hundred sixty stadia*   [c]Other ancient authorities read *walk along, looking sad?"*   [d]Other ancient authorities read *Jesus the Nazorean*   [e]Or *to set Israel free*   [f]Or *the Christ*   [g]Other ancient authorities lack *within us*

the scriptures to us?" [33] That same hour they got up and returned to Jerusalem; and they found the eleven and their companions gathered together. [34] They were saying, "The Lord has risen indeed, and he has appeared to Simon!" [35] Then they told what had happened on the road, and how he had been made known to them in the breaking of the bread.

36 While they were talking about this, Jesus himself stood among them and said to them, "Peace be with you." [a] [37] They were startled and terrified, and thought that they were seeing a ghost. [38] He said to them, "Why are you frightened, and why do doubts arise in your hearts? [39] Look at my hands and my feet; see that it is I myself. Touch me and see; for a ghost does not have flesh and bones as you see that I have." [40] And when he had said this, he showed them his hands and his feet. [b] [41] While in their joy they were disbelieving and still wondering, he said to them, "Have you anything here to eat?" [42] They gave him a piece of broiled fish, [43] and he took it and ate in their presence.

44 Then he said to them, "These are my words that I spoke to you while I was still with you—that everything written about me in the law of Moses, the prophets, and the psalms must be fulfilled." [45] Then he opened their minds to understand the scriptures, [46] and he said to them, "Thus it is written, that the Messiah [c] is to suffer and to rise from the dead on the third day, [47] and that repentance and forgiveness of sins is to be proclaimed in his name to all nations, [d] beginning from Jerusalem. [48] You are witnesses of these things. [49] And see, I am sending upon you what my Father promised; so stay here in the city until you have been clothed with power from on high."

50 Then he led them out as far as Bethany, and, lifting up his hands, he blessed them. [51] While he was blessing them, he withdrew from them and was carried up into heaven. [e] [52] And they worshiped him, and [f] returned to Jerusalem with great joy; [53] and they were continually in the temple blessing God. [g]

## PSALM 100.1–5

*A Psalm of thanksgiving.*

**M**AKE a joyful noise to the LORD, all the earth.
 2    Worship the LORD
    with gladness;
come into his presence with
    singing.

3  Know that the LORD is God.
    It is he that made us, and we
        are his; [h]
    we are his people, and the
        sheep of his pasture.

4  Enter his gates with
        thanksgiving,
    and his courts with praise.
    Give thanks to him, bless his
        name.

5  For the LORD is good;
    his steadfast love endures
        forever,
    and his faithfulness to all
        generations.

## PROVERBS 14.11–12

**T**HE house of the wicked is
        destroyed,
    but the tent of the upright
        flourishes.



---

a Other ancient authorities lack *and said to them, "Peace be with you."*  b Other ancient authorities lack verse 40  c Or *the Christ*  d Or *nations. Beginning from Jerusalem you are witnesses*  e Other ancient authorities lack *and was carried up into heaven*  f Other ancient authorities lack *worshiped him, and*  g Other ancient authorities add *Amen*  h Another reading is *and not we ourselves*

12  There is a way that seems right
      to a person,

      but its end is the way to
      death. [a]

# APRIL 30

## JUDGES 11.1—12.15

Now Jephthah the Gileadite, the son of a prostitute, was a mighty warrior. Gilead was the father of Jephthah. [2]Gilead's wife also bore him sons; and when his wife's sons grew up, they drove Jephthah away, saying to him, "You shall not inherit anything in our father's house; for you are the son of another woman." [3]Then Jephthah fled from his brothers and lived in the land of Tob. Outlaws collected around Jephthah and went raiding with him.

4 After a time the Ammonites made war against Israel. [5]And when the Ammonites made war against Israel, the elders of Gilead went to bring Jephthah from the land of Tob. [6]They said to Jephthah, "Come and be our commander, so that we may fight with the Ammonites." [7]But Jephthah said to the elders of Gilead, "Are you not the very ones who rejected me and drove me out of my father's house? So why do you come to me now when you are in trouble?" [8]The elders of Gilead said to Jephthah, "Nevertheless, we have now turned back to you, so that you may go with us and fight with the Ammonites, and become head over us, over all the inhabitants of Gilead." [9]Jephthah said to the elders of Gilead, "If you bring me home again to fight with the Ammonites, and the LORD gives them over to me, I will be your head." [10]And the elders of Gilead said to Jephthah, "The LORD will be witness between us; we will surely do as you say." [11]So Jephthah went with the elders of Gilead, and the people made him head and commander over them; and Jephthah spoke all his words before the LORD at Mizpah.

12 Then Jephthah sent messengers to the king of the Ammonites and said, "What is there between you and me, that you have come to me to fight against my land?" [13]The king of the Ammonites answered the messengers of Jephthah, "Because Israel, on coming from Egypt, took away my land from the Arnon to the Jabbok and to the Jordan; now therefore restore it peaceably." [14]Once again Jephthah sent messengers to the king of the Ammonites [15]and said to him: "Thus says Jephthah: Israel did not take away the land of Moab or the land of the Ammonites, [16]but when they came up from Egypt, Israel went through the wilderness to the Red Sea[b] and came to Kadesh. [17]Israel then sent messengers to the king of Edom, saying, 'Let us pass through your land'; but the king of Edom would not listen. They also sent to the king of Moab, but he would not consent. So Israel remained at Kadesh. [18]Then they journeyed through the wilderness, went around the land of Edom and the land of Moab, arrived on the east side of the land of Moab, and camped on the other side of the Arnon. They did not enter the territory of

a Heb *ways of death*  b Or *Sea of Reeds*

Moab, for the Arnon was the boundary of Moab. 19Israel then sent messengers to King Sihon of the Amorites, king of Heshbon; and Israel said to him, 'Let us pass through your land to our country.' 20But Sihon did not trust Israel to pass through his territory; so Sihon gathered all his people together, and encamped at Jahaz, and fought with Israel. 21Then the LORD, the God of Israel, gave Sihon and all his people into the hand of Israel, and they defeated them; so Israel occupied all the land of the Amorites, who inhabited that country. 22They occupied all the territory of the Amorites from the Arnon to the Jabbok and from the wilderness to the Jordan. 23So now the LORD, the God of Israel, has conquered the Amorites for the benefit of his people Israel. Do you intend to take their place? 24Should you not possess what your god Chemosh gives you to possess? And should we not be the ones to possess everything that the LORD our God has conquered for our benefit? 25Now are you any better than King Balak son of Zippor of Moab? Did he ever enter into conflict with Israel, or did he ever go to war with them? 26While Israel lived in Heshbon and its villages, and in Aroer and its villages, and in all the towns that are along the Arnon, three hundred years, why did you not recover them within that time? 27It is not I who have sinned against you, but you are the one who does me wrong by making war on me. Let the LORD, who is judge, decide today for the Israelites or for the Ammonites." 28But the king of the Ammonites did not heed the message that Jephthah sent him.

29 Then the spirit of the LORD came upon Jephthah, and he passed through Gilead and Manasseh. He passed on to Mizpah of Gilead, and from Mizpah of Gilead he passed on to the Ammonites. 30And Jephthah made a vow to the LORD, and said, "If you will give the Ammonites into my hand, 31then whoever comes out of the doors of my house to meet me, when I return victorious from the Ammonites, shall be the LORD's, to be offered up by me as a burnt offering." 32So Jephthah crossed over to the Ammonites to fight against them; and the LORD gave them into his hand. 33He inflicted a massive defeat on them from Aroer to the neighborhood of Minnith, twenty towns, and as far as Abel-keramim. So the Ammonites were subdued before the people of Israel.

34 Then Jephthah came to his home at Mizpah; and there was his daughter coming out to meet him with timbrels and with dancing. She was his only child; he had no son or daughter except her. 35When he saw her, he tore his clothes, and said, "Alas, my daughter! You have brought me very low; you have become the cause of great trouble to me. For I have opened my mouth to the LORD, and I cannot take back my vow." 36She said to him, "My father, if you have opened your mouth to the LORD, do to me according to what has gone out of your mouth, now that the LORD has given you vengeance against your enemies, the Ammonites." 37And she said to her father, "Let this thing be done for me: Grant me two months, so that I may go and wandera on the mountains, and bewail my virginity, my companions and I." 38"Go," he said and sent her away for two months. So she departed, she and her companions, and bewailed her virginity on the mountains. 39At the end of two months, she returned to her father, who did with her according to the vow he had made. She had never slept with a man. So there arose an Israelite custom that 40for four days every year the daughters of Israel would go out to lament the daughter of Jephthah the Gileadite.

aCn: Heb go down

12.1 The men of Ephraim were called to arms, and they crossed to Zaphon and said to Jephthah, "Why did you cross over to fight against the Ammonites, and did not call us to go with you? We will burn your house down over you!" 2Jephthah said to them, "My people and I were engaged in conflict with the Ammonites who oppressed us<sup>a</sup> severely. But when I called you, you did not deliver me from their hand. 3When I saw that you would not deliver me, I took my life in my hand, and crossed over against the Ammonites, and the Lord gave them into my hand. Why then have you come up to me this day, to fight against me?" 4Then Jephthah gathered all the men of Gilead and fought with Ephraim; and the men of Gilead defeated Ephraim, because they said, "You are fugitives from Ephraim, you Gileadites—in the heart of Ephraim and Manasseh."<sup>b</sup> 5Then the Gileadites took the fords of the Jordan against the Ephraimites. Whenever one of the fugitives of Ephraim said, "Let me go over," the men of Gilead would say to him, "Are you an Ephraimite?" When he said, "No," 6they said to him, "Then say Shibboleth," and he said, "Sibboleth," for he could not pronounce it right. Then they seized him and killed him at the fords of the Jordan. Forty-two thousand of the Ephraimites fell at that time.

7 Jephthah judged Israel six years. Then Jephthah the Gileadite died, and was buried in his town in Gilead.<sup>c</sup>

8 After him Ibzan of Bethlehem judged Israel. 9He had thirty sons. He gave his thirty daughters in marriage outside his clan and brought in thirty young women from outside for his sons. He judged Israel seven years. 10Then Ibzan died, and was buried at Bethlehem.

11 After him Elon the Zebulunite judged Israel; and he judged Israel ten years. 12Then Elon the Zebulunite died, and was buried at Aijalon in the land of Zebulun.

13 After him Abdon son of Hillel the Pirathonite judged Israel. 14He had forty sons and thirty grandsons, who rode on seventy donkeys; he judged Israel eight years. 15Then Abdon son of Hillel the Pirathonite died, and was buried at Pirathon in the land of Ephraim, in the hill country of the Amalekites.

# JOHN 1.1–28

In the beginning was the Word, and the Word was with God, and the Word was God. 2He was in the beginning with God. 3All things came into being through him, and without him not one thing came into being. What has come into being 4in him was life,<sup>d</sup> and the life was the light of all people. 5The light shines in the darkness, and the darkness did not overcome it.

6 There was a man sent from God, whose name was John. 7He came as a witness to testify to the light, so that all might believe through him. 8He himself was not the light, but he came to testify to the light. 9The true light, which enlightens everyone, was coming into the world.<sup>e</sup>

10 He was in the world, and the world came into being through him; yet the world did not know him. 11He came to what was his own,<sup>f</sup> and his own people did not accept him. 12But to all who received him, who believed in his name, he gave power to become children of God, 13who were born, not of blood or of the will of the flesh or of the will of man, but of God.

14 And the Word became flesh and lived among us, and we have seen his

glory, the glory as of a father's only son,[a] full of grace and truth. [15](John testified to him and cried out, "This was he of whom I said, 'He who comes after me ranks ahead of me because he was before me.' ") [16]From his fullness we have all received, grace upon grace. [17]The law indeed was given through Moses; grace and truth came through Jesus Christ. [18]No one has ever seen God. It is God the only Son,[b] who is close to the Father's heart,[c] who has made him known.

19 This is the testimony given by John when the Jews sent priests and Levites from Jerusalem to ask him, "Who are you?" [20]He confessed and did not deny it, but confessed, "I am not the Messiah."[d] [21]And they asked him, "What then? Are you Elijah?" He said, "I am not." "Are you the prophet?" He answered, "No." [22]Then they said to him, "Who are you? Let us have an answer for those who sent us. What do you say about yourself?" [23]He said,

"I am the voice of one crying
        out in the wilderness,
'Make straight the way of
        the Lord,' "

as the prophet Isaiah said.

24 Now they had been sent from the Pharisees. [25]They asked him, "Why then are you baptizing if you are neither the Messiah,[d] nor Elijah, nor the prophet?" [26]John answered them, "I baptize with water. Among you stands one whom you do not know, [27]the one who is coming after me; I am not worthy to untie the thong of his sandal." [28]This took place in Bethany across the Jordan where John was baptizing.

## PSALM 101.1–8

*Of David. A Psalm.*

I WILL sing of loyalty and of justice;
    to you, O LORD, I will sing.
[2] I will study the way that is
        blameless.
    When shall I attain it?

I will walk with integrity of
        heart
    within my house;
[3] I will not set before my eyes
    anything that is base.

I hate the work of those who
        fall away;
    it shall not cling to me.
[4] Perverseness of heart shall be
        far from me;
    I will know nothing of evil.

[5] One who secretly slanders a
        neighbor
    I will destroy.
A haughty look and an arrogant
        heart
    I will not tolerate.

[6] I will look with favor on the
        faithful in the land,
    so that they may live with
        me;
    whoever walks in the way that
        is blameless
    shall minister to me.

[7] No one who practices deceit
        shall remain in my house;
no one who utters lies
        shall continue in my presence.

[8] Morning by morning I will
        destroy
    all the wicked in the land,
cutting off all evildoers
        from the city of the LORD.

---

[a]Or *the Father's only Son*  [b]Other ancient authorities read *It is an only Son, God,* or *It is the only Son*  [c]Gk *bosom*  [d]Or *the Christ*

## PROVERBS 14.13–14

**E**VEN in laughter the heart is
sad,
and the end of joy is grief.

[14] The perverse get what their
ways deserve,
and the good, what their
deeds deserve. [a]

# MAY 1

## JUDGES 13.1—14.20

**T**HE Israelites again did what was evil in the sight of the LORD, and the LORD gave them into the hand of the Philistines forty years.

2 There was a certain man of Zorah, of the tribe of the Danites, whose name was Manoah. His wife was barren, having borne no children. [3]And the angel of the LORD appeared to the woman and said to her, "Although you are barren, having borne no children, you shall conceive and bear a son. [4]Now be careful not to drink wine or strong drink, or to eat anything unclean, [5]for you shall conceive and bear a son. No razor is to come on his head, for the boy shall be a nazirite[b] to God from birth. It is he who shall begin to deliver Israel from the hand of the Philistines." [6]Then the woman came and told her husband, "A man of God came to me, and his appearance was like that of an angel[c] of God, most awe-inspiring; I did not ask him where he came from, and he did not tell me his name; [7]but he said to me, 'You shall conceive and bear a son. So then drink no wine or strong drink, and eat nothing unclean, for the boy shall be a nazirite[b] to God from birth to the day of his death.' "

8 Then Manoah entreated the LORD, and said, "O, LORD, I pray, let the man of God whom you sent come to us again and teach us what we are to do concerning the boy who will be born." [9]God listened to Manoah, and the angel of God came again to the woman as she sat in the field; but her husband Manoah was not with her. [10]So the woman ran quickly and told her husband, "The man who came to me the other day has appeared to me." [11]Manoah got up and followed his wife, and came to the man and said to him, "Are you the man who spoke to this woman?" And he said, "I am." [12]Then Manoah said, "Now when your words come true, what is to be the boy's rule of life; what is he to do?" [13]The angel of the LORD said to Manoah, "Let the woman give heed to all that I said to her. [14]She may not eat of anything that comes from the vine. She is not to drink wine or strong drink, or eat any unclean thing. She is to observe everything that I commanded her."

15 Manoah said to the angel of the LORD, "Allow us to detain you, and prepare a kid for you." [16]The angel of the LORD said to Manoah, "If you detain me, I will not eat your food; but if you want to prepare a burnt offering, then offer it to the LORD." (For Manoah did

---

aCn: Heb *from upon him*   bThat is *one separated* or *one consecrated*   cOr *the angel*

not know that he was the angel of the Lord.) [17]Then Manoah said to the angel of the Lord, "What is your name, so that we may honor you when your words come true?" [18]But the angel of the Lord said to him, "Why do you ask my name? It is too wonderful."

19  So Manoah took the kid with the grain offering, and offered it on the rock to the Lord, to him who works[a] wonders.[b] [20]When the flame went up toward heaven from the altar, the angel of the Lord ascended in the flame of the altar while Manoah and his wife looked on; and they fell on their faces to the ground. [21]The angel of the Lord did not appear again to Manoah and his wife. Then Manoah realized that it was the angel of the Lord. [22]And Manoah said to his wife, "We shall surely die, for we have seen God." [23]But his wife said to him, "If the Lord had meant to kill us, he would not have accepted a burnt offering and a grain offering at our hands, or shown us all these things, or now announced to us such things as these."

24  The woman bore a son, and named him Samson. The boy grew, and the Lord blessed him. [25]The spirit of the Lord began to stir him in Mahaneh-dan, between Zorah and Eshtaol.

14.1 Once Samson went down to Timnah, and at Timnah he saw a Philistine woman. [2]Then he came up, and told his father and mother, "I saw a Philistine woman at Timnah; now get her for me as my wife." [3]But his father and mother said to him, "Is there not a woman among your kin, or among all our[c] people, that you must go to take a wife from the uncircumcised Philistines?" But Samson said to his father, "Get her for me, because she pleases me." [4]His father and mother did not know that this was from the Lord; for he was seeking a pretext to act against the Philistines. At that time the Philistines had dominion over Israel.

5  Then Samson went down with his father and mother to Timnah. When he came to the vineyards of Timnah, suddenly a young lion roared at him. [6]The spirit of the Lord rushed on him, and he tore the lion apart barehanded as one might tear apart a kid. But he did not tell his father or his mother what he had done. [7]Then he went down and talked with the woman, and she pleased Samson. [8]After a while he returned to marry her, and he turned aside to see the carcass of the lion, and there was a swarm of bees in the body of the lion, and honey. [9]He scraped it out into his hands, and went on, eating as he went. When he came to his father and mother, he gave some to them, and they ate it. But he did not tell them that he had taken the honey from the carcass of the lion.

10  His father went down to the woman, and Samson made a feast there as the young men were accustomed to do. [11]When the people saw him, they brought thirty companions to be with him. [12]Samson said to them, "Let me now put a riddle to you. If you can explain it to me within the seven days of the feast, and find it out, then I will give you thirty linen garments and thirty festal garments. [13]But if you cannot explain it to me, then you shall give me thirty linen garments and thirty festal garments." So they said to him, "Ask your riddle; let us hear it." [14]He said to them,

"Out of the eater came
    something to eat.
Out of the strong came
    something sweet."
But for three days they could not explain the riddle.

15  On the fourth[d] day they said to Samson's wife, "Coax your husband to explain the riddle to us, or we will burn

aGk Vg: Heb *and working*   bHeb *wonders, while Manoah and his wife looked on*   cCn: Heb *my*
dGk Syr: Heb *seventh*

you and your father's house with fire. Have you invited us here to impoverish us?" [16]So Samson's wife wept before him, saying, "You hate me; you do not really love me. You have asked a riddle of my people, but you have not explained it to me." He said to her, "Look, I have not told my father or my mother. Why should I tell you?" [17]She wept before him the seven days that their feast lasted; and because she nagged him, on the seventh day he told her. Then she explained the riddle to her people. [18]The men of the town said to him on the seventh day before the sun went down,

"What is sweeter than honey?
What is stronger than a lion?"

And he said to them,

"If you had not plowed with my
    heifer,
you would not have found out
    my riddle."

[19]Then the spirit of the LORD rushed on him, and he went down to Ashkelon. He killed thirty men of the town, took their spoil, and gave the festal garments to those who had explained the riddle. In hot anger he went back to his father's house. [20]And Samson's wife was given to his companion, who had been his best man.

# JOHN 1.29–51

THE next day he [John the Baptist] saw Jesus coming toward him and declared, "Here is the Lamb of God who takes away the sin of the world! [30]This is he of whom I said, 'After me comes a man who ranks ahead of me because he was before me.' [31]I myself did not know him; but I came baptizing with water for this reason, that he might be revealed to Israel." [32]And John testified, "I saw the Spirit descending from heaven like a dove, and it remained on him. [33]I myself did not know him, but the one who sent me to baptize with water said to me, 'He on whom you see the Spirit descend and remain is the one who baptizes with the Holy Spirit.' [34]And I myself have seen and have testified that this is the Son of God."[a]

35 The next day John again was standing with two of his disciples, [36]and as he watched Jesus walk by, he exclaimed, "Look, here is the Lamb of God!" [37]The two disciples heard him say this, and they followed Jesus. [38]When Jesus turned and saw them following, he said to them, "What are you looking for?" They said to him, "Rabbi" (which translated means Teacher), "where are you staying?" [39]He said to them, "Come and see." They came and saw where he was staying, and they remained with him that day. It was about four o'clock in the afternoon. [40]One of the two who heard John speak and followed him was Andrew, Simon Peter's brother. [41]He first found his brother Simon and said to him, "We have found the Messiah" (which is translated Anointed[b]). [42]He brought Simon[c] to Jesus, who looked at him and said, "You are Simon son of John. You are to be called Cephas" (which is translated Peter[d]).

43 The next day Jesus decided to go to Galilee. He found Philip and said to him, "Follow me." [44]Now Philip was from Bethsaida, the city of Andrew and Peter. [45]Philip found Nathanael and said to him, "We have found him about whom Moses in the law and also the prophets wrote, Jesus son of Joseph from Nazareth." [46]Nathanael said to him, "Can anything good come out of Nazareth?" Philip said to him, "Come and see." [47]When Jesus saw Nathanael coming toward him, he said of him, "Here is truly an Israelite in whom there is no deceit!" [48]Nathanael asked him, "Where did you get to know me?"

[a]Other ancient authorities read *is God's chosen one*  [b]Or *Christ*  [c]Gk *him*  [d]From the word for *rock* in Aramaic (*kepha*) and Greek (*petra*), respectively

Jesus answered, "I saw you under the fig tree before Philip called you." [49]Nathanael replied, "Rabbi, you are the Son of God! You are the King of Israel!" [50]Jesus answered, "Do you believe because I told you that I saw you under the fig tree? You will see greater things than these." [51]And he said to him, "Very truly, I tell you, [a] you will see heaven opened and the angels of God ascending and descending upon the Son of Man."

## PSALM 102.1–28

*A prayer of one afflicted, when faint and pleading before the LORD.*

HEAR my prayer, O LORD;
  let my cry come to you.
2  Do not hide your face
      from me
  in the day of my distress.
Incline your ear to me;
  answer me speedily in the
      day when I call.

3  For my days pass away like
      smoke,
  and my bones burn like a
      furnace.
4  My heart is stricken and
      withered like grass;
  I am too wasted to eat my
      bread.
5  Because of my loud groaning
  my bones cling to my skin.
6  I am like an owl of the
      wilderness,
  like a little owl of the waste
      places.
7  I lie awake;
  I am like a lonely bird on the
      housetop.
8  All day long my enemies taunt
      me;
  those who deride me use my
      name for a curse.
9  For I eat ashes like bread,

  and mingle tears with my
      drink,
10  because of your indignation and
      anger;
  for you have lifted me up and
      thrown me aside.
11  My days are like an evening
      shadow;
  I wither away like grass.

12  But you, O LORD, are enthroned
      forever;
  your name endures to all
      generations.
13  You will rise up and have
      compassion on Zion,
  for it is time to favor it;
  the appointed time has come.
14  For your servants hold its
      stones dear,
  and have pity on its dust.
15  The nations will fear the name
      of the LORD,
  and all the kings of the earth
      your glory.
16  For the LORD will build up Zion;
  he will appear in his glory.
17  He will regard the prayer of the
      destitute,
  and will not despise their
      prayer.

18  Let this be recorded for a
      generation to come,
  so that a people yet unborn
      may praise the LORD:
19  that he looked down from his
      holy height,
  from heaven the LORD looked
      at the earth,
20  to hear the groans of the
      prisoners,
  to set free those who were
      doomed to die;
21  so that the name of the LORD
      may be declared in Zion,
  and his praise in Jerusalem,
22  when peoples gather together,

---

aBoth instances of the Greek word for *you* in this verse are plural

and kingdoms, to worship the
     LORD.

23  He has broken my strength in
         midcourse;
     he has shortened my days.
24  "O my God," I say, "do not
         take me away
     at the mid-point of my life,
     you whose years endure
         throughout all generations."

25  Long ago you laid the foundation
         of the earth,
     and the heavens are the work
         of your hands.
26  They will perish, but you
         endure;
     they will all wear out like a
         garment.

You change them like clothing,
     and they pass away;
27  but you are the same, and
         your years have no end.
28  The children of your servants
         shall live secure;
     their offspring shall be
         established in your
         presence.

## PROVERBS 14.15–16

THE simple believe everything,
     but the clever consider
         their steps.
16  The wise are cautious and turn
         away from evil,
     but the fool throws off
         restraint and is careless.

# MAY 2

## JUDGES 15.1—16.31

AFTER a while, at the time of the wheat harvest, Samson went to visit his wife, bringing along a kid. He said, "I want to go into my wife's room." But her father would not allow him to go in. ²Her father said, "I was sure that you had rejected her; so I gave her to your companion. Is not her younger sister prettier than she? Why not take her instead?" ³Samson said to them, "This time, when I do mischief to the Philistines, I will be without blame." ⁴So Samson went and caught three hundred foxes, and took some torches; and he turned the foxesª tail to tail, and put a torch between each pair of tails. ⁵When he had set fire to the torches, he let the foxes go into the standing grain of the Philistines, and burned up the shocks and the standing grain, as well as the vineyards andᵇ olive groves. ⁶Then the Philistines asked, "Who has done this?" And they said, "Samson, the son-in-law of the Timnite, because he has taken Samson's wife and given her to his companion." So the Philistines came up, and burned her and her father. ⁷Samson said to them, "If this is what you do, I swear I will not stop until I have taken revenge on you." ⁸He struck them down hip and thigh with great slaughter; and he went down and stayed in the cleft of the rock of Etam.

9  Then the Philistines came up and encamped in Judah, and made a raid on Lehi. ¹⁰The men of Judah said, "Why

aHeb *them*   bGk Tg Vg: Heb lacks *and*

have you come up against us?" They said, "We have come up to bind Samson, to do to him as he did to us." ¹¹Then three thousand men of Judah went down to the cleft of the rock of Etam, and they said to Samson, "Do you not know that the Philistines are rulers over us? What then have you done to us?" He replied, "As they did to me, so I have done to them." ¹²They said to him, "We have come down to bind you, so that we may give you into the hands of the Philistines." Samson answered them, "Swear to me that you yourselves will not attack me." ¹³They said to him, "No, we will only bind you and give you into their hands; we will not kill you." So they bound him with two new ropes, and brought him up from the rock.

14 When he came to Lehi, the Philistines came shouting to meet him; and the spirit of the LORD rushed on him, and the ropes that were on his arms became like flax that has caught fire, and his bonds melted off his hands. ¹⁵Then he found a fresh jawbone of a donkey, reached down and took it, and with it he killed a thousand men. ¹⁶And Samson said,

"With the jawbone of a donkey,
  heaps upon heaps,
with the jawbone of a donkey
  I have slain a thousand men."

¹⁷When he had finished speaking, he threw away the jawbone; and that place was called Ramath-lehi. ª

18 By then he was very thirsty, and he called on the LORD, saying, "You have granted this great victory by the hand of your servant. Am I now to die of thirst, and fall into the hands of the uncircumcised?" ¹⁹So God split open the hollow place that is at Lehi, and water came from it. When he drank, his spirit returned, and he revived. Therefore it was named En-hakkore, ᵇ which is at Lehi to this day. ²⁰And he judged Israel in the days of the Philistines twenty years.

16.1 ONCE Samson went to Gaza, where he saw a prostitute and went in to her. ²The Gazites were told, ᶜ "Samson has come here." So they circled around and lay in wait for him all night at the city gate. They kept quiet all night, thinking, "Let us wait until the light of the morning; then we will kill him." ³But Samson lay only until midnight. Then at midnight he rose up, took hold of the doors of the city gate and the two posts, pulled them up, bar and all, put them on his shoulders, and carried them to the top of the hill that is in front of Hebron.

4 After this he fell in love with a woman in the valley of Sorek, whose name was Delilah. ⁵The lords of the Philistines came to her and said to her, "Coax him, and find out what makes his strength so great, and how we may overpower him, so that we may bind him in order to subdue him; and we will each give you eleven hundred pieces of silver." ⁶So Delilah said to Samson, "Please tell me what makes your strength so great, and how you could be bound, so that one could subdue you." ⁷Samson said to her, "If they bind me with seven fresh bowstrings that are not dried out, then I shall become weak, and be like anyone else." ⁸Then the lords of the Philistines brought her seven fresh bowstrings that had not dried out, and she bound him with them. ⁹While men were lying in wait in an inner chamber, she said to him, "The Philistines are upon you, Samson!" But he snapped the bowstrings, as a strand of fiber snaps when it touches the fire. So the secret of his strength was not known.

10 Then Delilah said to Samson, "You have mocked me and told me lies; please tell me how you could be

ª That is *The Hill of the Jawbone*   ᵇ That is *The Spring of the One who Called*   ᶜ Gk: Heb lacks *were told*

bound." [11]He said to her, "If they bind me with new ropes that have not been used, then I shall become weak, and be like anyone else." [12]So Delilah took new ropes and bound him with them, and said to him, "The Philistines are upon you, Samson!" (The men lying in wait were in an inner chamber.) But he snapped the ropes off his arms like a thread.

13 Then Delilah said to Samson, "Until now you have mocked me and told me lies; tell me how you could be bound." He said to her, "If you weave the seven locks of my head with the web and make it tight with the pin, then I shall become weak, and be like anyone else." [14]So while he slept, Delilah took the seven locks of his head and wove them into the web,[a] and made them tight with the pin. Then she said to him, "The Philistines are upon you, Samson!" But he awoke from his sleep, and pulled away the pin, the loom, and the web.

15 Then she said to him, "How can you say, 'I love you,' when your heart is not with me? You have mocked me three times now and have not told me what makes your strength so great." [16]Finally, after she had nagged him with her words day after day, and pestered him, he was tired to death. [17]So he told her his whole secret, and said to her, "A razor has never come upon my head; for I have been a nazirite[b] to God from my mother's womb. If my head were shaved, then my strength would leave me; I would become weak, and be like anyone else."

18 When Delilah realized that he had told her his whole secret, she sent and called the lords of the Philistines, saying, "This time come up, for he has told his whole secret to me." Then the lords of the Philistines came up to her, and brought the money in their hands.

[19]She let him fall asleep on her lap; and she called a man, and had him shave off the seven locks of his head. He began to weaken,[c] and his strength left him. [20]Then she said, "The Philistines are upon you, Samson!" When he awoke from his sleep, he thought, "I will go out as at other times, and shake myself free." But he did not know that the Lord had left him. [21]So the Philistines seized him and gouged out his eyes. They brought him down to Gaza and bound him with bronze shackles; and he ground at the mill in the prison. [22]But the hair of his head began to grow again after it had been shaved.

23 Now the lords of the Philistines gathered to offer a great sacrifice to their god Dagon, and to rejoice; for they said, "Our god has given Samson our enemy into our hand." [24]When the people saw him, they praised their god; for they said, "Our god has given our enemy into our hand, the ravager of our country, who has killed many of us." [25]And when their hearts were merry, they said, "Call Samson, and let him entertain us." So they called Samson out of the prison, and he performed for them. They made him stand between the pillars; [26]and Samson said to the attendant who held him by the hand, "Let me feel the pillars on which the house rests, so that I may lean against them." [27]Now the house was full of men and women; all the lords of the Philistines were there, and on the roof there were about three thousand men and women, who looked on while Samson performed.

28 Then Samson called to the Lord and said, "Lord God, remember me and strengthen me only this once, O God, so that with this one act of revenge I may pay back the Philistines for my two eyes."[d] [29]And Samson grasped the two middle pillars on which

---

[a]Compare Gk: in verses 13-14, Heb lacks *and make it tight . . . into the web*  [b]That is *one separated* or *one consecrated*  [c]Gk: Heb *She began to torment him*  [d]Or *so that I may be avenged upon the Philistines for one of my two eyes*

the house rested, and he leaned his weight against them, his right hand on the one and his left hand on the other. ³⁰Then Samson said, "Let me die with the Philistines." He strained with all his might; and the house fell on the lords and all the people who were in it. So those he killed at his death were more than those he had killed during his life. ³¹Then his brothers and all his family came down and took him and brought him up and buried him between Zorah and Eshtaol in the tomb of his father Manoah. He had judged Israel twenty years.

## JOHN 2.1–25

On the third day there was a wedding in Cana of Galilee, and the mother of Jesus was there. ²Jesus and his disciples had also been invited to the wedding. ³When the wine gave out, the mother of Jesus said to him, "They have no wine." ⁴And Jesus said to her, "Woman, what concern is that to you and to me? My hour has not yet come." ⁵His mother said to the servants, "Do whatever he tells you." ⁶Now standing there were six stone water jars for the Jewish rites of purification, each holding twenty or thirty gallons. ⁷Jesus said to them, "Fill the jars with water." And they filled them up to the brim. ⁸He said to them, "Now draw some out, and take it to the chief steward." So they took it. ⁹When the steward tasted the water that had become wine, and did not know where it came from (though the servants who had drawn the water knew), the steward called the bridegroom ¹⁰and said to him, "Everyone serves the good wine first, and then the inferior wine after the guests have become drunk. But you have kept the good wine until now." ¹¹Jesus did this, the first of his signs, in Cana of Galilee, and revealed his glory; and his disciples believed in him.

12 After this he went down to Capernaum with his mother, his brothers, and his disciples; and they remained there a few days.

13 The Passover of the Jews was near, and Jesus went up to Jerusalem. ¹⁴In the temple he found people selling cattle, sheep, and doves, and the money changers seated at their tables. ¹⁵Making a whip of cords, he drove all of them out of the temple, both the sheep and the cattle. He also poured out the coins of the money changers and overturned their tables. ¹⁶He told those who were selling the doves, "Take these things out of here! Stop making my Father's house a marketplace!" ¹⁷His disciples remembered that it was written, "Zeal for your house will consume me." ¹⁸The Jews then said to him, "What sign can you show us for doing this?" ¹⁹Jesus answered them, "Destroy this temple, and in three days I will raise it up." ²⁰The Jews then said, "This temple has been under construction for forty-six years, and will you raise it up in three days?" ²¹But he was speaking of the temple of his body. ²²After he was raised from the dead, his disciples remembered that he had said this; and they believed the scripture and the word that Jesus had spoken.

23 When he was in Jerusalem during the Passover festival, many believed in his name because they saw the signs that he was doing. ²⁴But Jesus on his part would not entrust himself to them, because he knew all people ²⁵and needed no one to testify about anyone; for he himself knew what was in everyone.

## PSALM 103.1–22
*Of David.*

Bless the Lord, O my soul,
and all that is within me,
bless his holy name.
² Bless the Lord, O my soul,

and do not forget all his
    benefits—
3 who forgives all your iniquity,
    who heals all your diseases,
4 who redeems your life from the
    Pit,
    who crowns you with
        steadfast love and mercy,
5 who satisfies you with good as
    long as you live[a]
    so that your youth is renewed
    like the eagle's.

6 The LORD works vindication
    and justice for all who are
        oppressed.
7 He made known his ways to
    Moses,
    his acts to the people of
        Israel.
8 The LORD is merciful and
    gracious,
    slow to anger and abounding
    in steadfast love.
9 He will not always accuse,
    nor will he keep his anger
    forever.
10 He does not deal with us
    according to our sins,
    nor repay us according to our
    iniquities.
11 For as the heavens are high
    above the earth,
    so great is his steadfast love
    toward those who fear
    him;
12 as far as the east is from the
    west,
    so far he removes our
    transgressions from us.
13 As a father has compassion for
    his children,
    so the LORD has compassion
    for those who fear him.
14 For he knows how we were
    made;
    he remembers that we are
    dust.

15 As for mortals, their days are
    like grass;
    they flourish like a flower of
    the field;
16 for the wind passes over it, and
    it is gone,
    and its place knows it no
    more.
17 But the steadfast love of the
    LORD is from everlasting
    to everlasting
    on those who fear him,
    and his righteousness to
    children's children,
18 to those who keep his covenant
    and remember to do his
    commandments.

19 The LORD has established his
    throne in the heavens,
    and his kingdom rules over
    all.
20 Bless the LORD, O you his
    angels,
    you mighty ones who do his
    bidding,
    obedient to his spoken word.
21 Bless the LORD, all his hosts,
    his ministers that do his will.
22 Bless the LORD, all his works,
    in all places of his dominion.
    Bless the LORD, O my soul.

# PROVERBS 14.17–19

One who is quick-tempered
    acts foolishly,
    and the schemer is hated.
18 The simple are adorned with[b]
    folly,
    but the clever are crowned
    with knowledge.
19 The evil bow down before the
    good,
    the wicked at the gates of the
    righteous.

[a] Meaning of Heb uncertain    [b] Or *inherit*

# MAY 3

## JUDGES 17.1—18.31

**T**HERE was a man in the hill country of Ephraim whose name was Micah. ²He said to his mother, "The eleven hundred pieces of silver that were taken from you, about which you uttered a curse, and even spoke it in my hearing,—that silver is in my possession; I took it; but now I will return it to you."ᵃ And his mother said, "May my son be blessed by the LORD!" ³Then he returned the eleven hundred pieces of silver to his mother; and his mother said, "I consecrate the silver to the LORD from my hand for my son, to make an idol of cast metal." ⁴So when he returned the money to his mother, his mother took two hundred pieces of silver, and gave it to the silversmith, who made it into an idol of cast metal; and it was in the house of Micah. ⁵This man Micah had a shrine, and he made an ephod and teraphim, and installed one of his sons, who became his priest. ⁶In those days there was no king in Israel; all the people did what was right in their own eyes.

7 Now there was a young man of Bethlehem in Judah, of the clan of Judah. He was a Levite residing there. ⁸This man left the town of Bethlehem in Judah, to live wherever he could find a place. He came to the house of Micah in the hill country of Ephraim to carry on his work.ᵇ ⁹Micah said to him, "From where do you come?" He replied, "I am a Levite of Bethlehem in Judah, and I am going to live wherever I can find a place." ¹⁰Then Micah said to him, "Stay with me, and be to me a father and a priest, and I will give you ten pieces of silver a year, a set of clothes, and your living."ᶜ ¹¹The Levite agreed to stay with the man; and the young man became to him like one of his sons. ¹²So Micah installed the Levite, and the young man became his priest, and was in the house of Micah. ¹³Then Micah said, "Now I know that the LORD will prosper me, because the Levite has become my priest."

**18.**¹ IN those days there was no king in Israel. And in those days the tribe of the Danites was seeking for itself a territory to live in; for until then no territory among the tribes of Israel had been allotted to them. ²So the Danites sent five valiant men from the whole number of their clan, from Zorah and from Eshtaol, to spy out the land and to explore it; and they said to them, "Go, explore the land." When they came to the hill country of Ephraim, to the house of Micah, they stayed there. ³While they were at Micah's house, they recognized the voice of the young Levite; so they went over and asked him, "Who brought you here? What are you doing in this place? What is your business here?" ⁴He said to them, "Micah did such and such for me, and he hired me, and I have become his priest." ⁵Then they said to him, "Inquire of God that we may know whether the mission we are undertaking will succeed." ⁶The priest replied, "Go in peace. The mission you are on is under the eye of the LORD."

7 The five men went on, and when they came to Laish, they observed the people who were there living securely, after the manner of the Sidonians, quiet and unsuspecting, lackingᵈ nothing on

---

ᵃThe words *but now I will return it to you* are transposed from the end of verse 3 in Heb
ᵇOr *Ephraim, continuing his journey*   ᶜHeb *living, and the Levite went*   ᵈCn Compare 18.10: Meaning of Heb uncertain

earth, and possessing wealth.[a] Furthermore, they were far from the Sidonians and had no dealings with Aram.[b] [8]When they came to their kinsfolk at Zorah and Eshtaol, they said to them, "What do you report?" [9]They said, "Come, let us go up against them; for we have seen the land, and it is very good. Will you do nothing? Do not be slow to go, but enter in and possess the land. [10]When you go, you will come to an unsuspecting people. The land is broad—God has indeed given it into your hands—a place where there is no lack of anything on earth."

11 Six hundred men of the Danite clan, armed with weapons of war, set out from Zorah and Eshtaol, [12]and went up and encamped at Kiriath-jearim in Judah. On this account that place is called Mahaneh-dan[c] to this day; it is west of Kiriath-jearim. [13]From there they passed on to the hill country of Ephraim, and came to the house of Micah.

14 Then the five men who had gone to spy out the land (that is, Laish) said to their comrades, "Do you know that in these buildings there are an ephod, teraphim, and an idol of cast metal? Now therefore consider what you will do." [15]So they turned in that direction and came to the house of the young Levite, at the home of Micah, and greeted him. [16]While the six hundred men of the Danites, armed with their weapons of war, stood by the entrance of the gate, [17]the five men who had gone to spy out the land proceeded to enter and take the idol of cast metal, the ephod, and the teraphim.[d] The priest was standing by the entrance of the gate with the six hundred men armed with weapons of war. [18]When the men went into Micah's house and took the idol of cast metal, the ephod, and the teraphim, the priest said to them, "What are you doing?" [19]They said to him, "Keep quiet! Put your hand over your mouth, and come with us, and be to us a father and a priest. Is it better for you to be priest to the house of one person, or to be priest to a tribe and clan in Israel?" [20]Then the priest accepted the offer. He took the ephod, the teraphim, and the idol, and went along with the people.

21 So they resumed their journey, putting the little ones, the livestock, and the goods in front of them. [22]When they were some distance from the home of Micah, the men who were in the houses near Micah's house were called out, and they overtook the Danites. [23]They shouted to the Danites, who turned around and said to Micah, "What is the matter that you come with such a company?" [24]He replied, "You take my gods that I made, and the priest, and go away, and what have I left? How then can you ask me, 'What is the matter?' " [25]And the Danites said to him, "You had better not let your voice be heard among us or else hot-tempered fellows will attack you, and you will lose your life and the lives of your household." [26]Then the Danites went their way. When Micah saw that they were too strong for him, he turned and went back to his home.

27 The Danites, having taken what Micah had made, and the priest who belonged to him, came to Laish, to a people quiet and unsuspecting, put them to the sword, and burned down the city. [28]There was no deliverer, because it was far from Sidon and they had no dealings with Aram.[e] It was in the valley that belongs to Beth-rehob. They rebuilt the city, and lived in it. [29]They named the city Dan, after their ancestor Dan, who was born to Israel; but the name of the city was formerly Laish. [30]Then the Danites set up the idol for themselves. Jonathan son of

[a]Meaning of Heb uncertain   [b]Symmachus: Heb *with anyone*   [c]That is *Camp of Dan*   [d]Compare 17.4, 5; 18.14: Heb *teraphim and the cast metal*   [e]Cn Compare verse 7: Heb *with anyone*

Gershom, son of Moses, [a] and his sons were priests to the tribe of the Danites until the time the land went into captivity. [31]So they maintained as their own Micah's idol that he had made, as long as the house of God was at Shiloh.

## JOHN 3.1–21

Now there was a Pharisee named Nicodemus, a leader of the Jews. [2]He came to Jesus[b] by night and said to him, "Rabbi, we know that you are a teacher who has come from God; for no one can do these signs that you do apart from the presence of God." [3]Jesus answered him, "Very truly, I tell you, no one can see the kingdom of God without being born from above."[c] [4]Nicodemus said to him, "How can anyone be born after having grown old? Can one enter a second time into the mother's womb and be born?" [5]Jesus answered, "Very truly, I tell you, no one can enter the kingdom of God without being born of water and Spirit. [6]What is born of the flesh is flesh, and what is born of the Spirit is spirit. [d] [7]Do not be astonished that I said to you, 'You[e] must be born from above.'[f] [8]The wind[d] blows where it chooses, and you hear the sound of it, but you do not know where it comes from or where it goes. So it is with everyone who is born of the Spirit." [9]Nicodemus said to him, "How can these things be?" [10]Jesus answered him, "Are you a teacher of Israel, and yet you do not understand these things?

11 "Very truly, I tell you, we speak of what we know and testify to what we have seen; yet you[g] do not receive our testimony. [12]If I have told you about earthly things and you do not believe, how can you believe if I tell you about heavenly things? [13]No one has ascended into heaven except the one who descended from heaven, the Son of Man. [h] [14]And just as Moses lifted up the serpent in the wilderness, so must the Son of Man be lifted up, [15]that whoever believes in him may have eternal life. [i]

16 "For God so loved the world that he gave his only Son, so that everyone who believes in him may not perish but may have eternal life.

17 "Indeed, God did not send the Son into the world to condemn the world, but in order that the world might be saved through him. [18]Those who believe in him are not condemned; but those who do not believe are condemned already, because they have not believed in the name of the only Son of God. [19]And this is the judgment, that the light has come into the world, and people loved darkness rather than light because their deeds were evil. [20]For all who do evil hate the light and do not come to the light, so that their deeds may not be exposed. [21]But those who do what is true come to the light, so that it may be clearly seen that their deeds have been done in God."[i]

## PSALM 104.1–23

Bless the Lord, O my soul.
   O Lord my God, you are
      very great.
You are clothed with honor and
      majesty,
2    wrapped in light as with a
      garment.
You stretch out the heavens like
      a tent,
3    you set the beams of your[j]
      chambers on the waters,
you make the clouds your[j]
      chariot,

[a]Another reading is *son of Manasseh*  [b]Gk *him*  [c]Or *born anew*  [d]The same Greek word means both *wind* and *spirit*  [e]The Greek word for *you* here is plural  [f]Or *anew*  [g]The Greek word for *you* here and in verse 12 is plural  [h]Other ancient authorities add *who is in heaven*  [i]Some interpreters hold that the quotation concludes with verse 15  [j]Heb *his*

you ride on the wings of the
    wind,
4 you make the winds your[a]
    messengers,
  fire and flame your[a]
    ministers.

5 You set the earth on its
    foundations,
  so that it shall never be
    shaken.
6 You cover it with the deep as
    with a garment;
  the waters stood above the
    mountains.
7 At your rebuke they flee;
  at the sound of your thunder
    they take to flight.
8 They rose up to the mountains,
    ran down to the valleys
  to the place that you
    appointed for them.
9 You set a boundary that they
    may not pass,
  so that they might not again
    cover the earth.

10 You make springs gush forth in
    the valleys;
  they flow between the hills,
11 giving drink to every wild
    animal;
  the wild asses quench their
    thirst.
12 By the streams[b] the birds of
    the air have their
    habitation;
  they sing among the
    branches.
13 From your lofty abode you
    water the mountains;
  the earth is satisfied with the
    fruit of your work.

14 You cause the grass to grow for
    the cattle,
  and plants for people to
    use,[c]

to bring forth food from the
    earth,
15   and wine to gladden the
    human heart,
oil to make the face shine,
  and bread to strengthen the
    human heart.
16 The trees of the LORD are
    watered abundantly,
  the cedars of Lebanon that he
    planted.
17 In them the birds build their
    nests;
  the stork has its home in the
    fir trees.
18 The high mountains are for the
    wild goats;
  the rocks are a refuge for the
    coneys.
19 You have made the moon to
    mark the seasons;
  the sun knows its time for
    setting.
20 You make darkness, and it is
    night,
  when all the animals of the
    forest come creeping
    out.
21 The young lions roar for their
    prey,
  seeking their food from God.
22 When the sun rises, they
    withdraw
  and lie down in their dens.
23 People go out to their work
  and to their labor until the
    evening.


## PROVERBS 14.20–21

THE poor are disliked even by
    their neighbors,
  but the rich have many
    friends.
21 Those who despise their
    neighbors are sinners,
  but happy are those who are
    kind to the poor.

[a] Heb *his*  [b] Heb *By them*  [c] Or *to cultivate*

## JUDGES 19.1—20.48

IN those days, when there was no king in Israel, a certain Levite, residing in the remote parts of the hill country of Ephraim, took to himself a concubine from Bethlehem in Judah. [2]But his concubine became angry with[a] him, and she went away from him to her father's house at Bethlehem in Judah, and was there some four months. [3]Then her husband set out after her, to speak tenderly to her and bring her back. He had with him his servant and a couple of donkeys. When he reached[b] her father's house, the girl's father saw him and came with joy to meet him. [4]His father-in-law, the girl's father, made him stay, and he remained with him three days; so they ate and drank, and he[c] stayed there. [5]On the fourth day they got up early in the morning, and he prepared to go; but the girl's father said to his son-in-law, "Fortify yourself with a bit of food, and after that you may go." [6]So the two men sat and ate and drank together; and the girl's father said to the man, "Why not spend the night and enjoy yourself?" [7]When the man got up to go, his father-in-law kept urging him until he spent the night there again. [8]On the fifth day he got up early in the morning to leave; and the girl's father said, "Fortify yourself." So they lingered[d] until the day declined, and the two of them ate and drank. [e] [9]When the man with his concubine and his servant got up to leave, his father-in-law, the girl's father, said to him, "Look, the day has worn on until it is almost evening. Spend the night. See, the day has drawn to a close. Spend the night here and enjoy yourself. Tomorrow you can get up early in the morning for your journey, and go home."

10 But the man would not spend the night; he got up and departed, and arrived opposite Jebus (that is, Jerusalem). He had with him a couple of saddled donkeys, and his concubine was with him. [11]When they were near Jebus, the day was far spent, and the servant said to his master, "Come now, let us turn aside to this city of the Jebusites, and spend the night in it." [12]But his master said to him, "We will not turn aside into a city of foreigners, who do not belong to the people of Israel; but we will continue on to Gibeah." [13]Then he said to his servant, "Come, let us try to reach one of these places, and spend the night at Gibeah or at Ramah." [14]So they passed on and went their way; and the sun went down on them near Gibeah, which belongs to Benjamin. [15]They turned aside there, to go in and spend the night at Gibeah. He went in and sat down in the open square of the city, but no one took them in to spend the night.

16 Then at evening there was an old man coming from his work in the field. The man was from the hill country of Ephraim, and he was residing in Gibeah. (The people of the place were Benjaminites.) [17]When the old man looked up and saw the wayfarer in the open square of the city, he said, "Where are you going and where do you come from?" [18]He answered him, "We are passing from Bethlehem in Judah to the remote parts of the hill country of Ephraim, from which I come. I went to Bethlehem in Judah; and I am

---

aGk OL: Heb *prostituted herself against*   bGk: Heb *she brought him*   cCompare verse 7 and Gk: Heb *they*   dCn: Heb *Linger*   eGk: Heb lacks *and drank*

going to my home. a Nobody has offered to take me in. ¹⁹We your servants have straw and fodder for our donkeys, with bread and wine for me and the woman and the young man along with us. We need nothing more." ²⁰The old man said, "Peace be to you. I will care for all your wants; only do not spend the night in the square." ²¹So he brought him into his house, and fed the donkeys; they washed their feet, and ate and drank.

22 While they were enjoying themselves, the men of the city, a perverse lot, surrounded the house, and started pounding on the door. They said to the old man, the master of the house, "Bring out the man who came into your house, so that we may have intercourse with him." ²³And the man, the master of the house, went out to them and said to them, "No, my brothers, do not act so wickedly. Since this man is my guest, do not do this vile thing. ²⁴Here are my virgin daughter and his concubine; let me bring them out now. Ravish them and do whatever you want to them; but against this man do not do such a vile thing." ²⁵But the men would not listen to him. So the man seized his concubine, and put her out to them. They wantonly raped her, and abused her all through the night until the morning. And as the dawn began to break, they let her go. ²⁶As morning appeared, the woman came and fell down at the door of the man's house where her master was, until it was light.

27 In the morning her master got up, opened the doors of the house, and when he went out to go on his way, there was his concubine lying at the door of the house, with her hands on the threshold. ²⁸"Get up," he said to her, "we are going." But there was no answer. Then he put her on the donkey; and the man set out for his home. ²⁹When he had entered his house, he took a knife, and grasping his concubine he cut her into twelve pieces, limb by limb, and sent her throughout all the territory of Israel. ³⁰Then he commanded the men whom he sent, saying, "Thus shall you say to all the Israelites, 'Has such a thing ever happened b since the day that the Israelites came up from the land of Egypt until this day? Consider it, take counsel, and speak out.' "

20.1 THEN all the Israelites came out, from Dan to Beer-sheba, including the land of Gilead, and the congregation assembled in one body before the LORD at Mizpah. ²The chiefs of all the people, of all the tribes of Israel, presented themselves in the assembly of the people of God, four hundred thousand foot-soldiers bearing arms. ³(Now the Benjaminites heard that the people of Israel had gone up to Mizpah.) And the Israelites said, "Tell us, how did this criminal act come about?" ⁴The Levite, the husband of the woman who was murdered, answered, "I came to Gibeah that belongs to Benjamin, I and my concubine, to spend the night. ⁵The lords of Gibeah rose up against me, and surrounded the house at night. They intended to kill me, and they raped my concubine until she died. ⁶Then I took my concubine and cut her into pieces, and sent her throughout the whole extent of Israel's territory; for they have committed a vile outrage in Israel. ⁷So now, you Israelites, all of you, give your advice and counsel here."

8 All the people got up as one, saying, "We will not any of us go to our tents, nor will any of us return to our houses. ⁹But now this is what we will do to Gibeah: we will go up c against it by lot. ¹⁰We will take ten men of a hundred throughout all the tribes of Israel, and a hundred of a thousand, and a thousand of ten thousand, to bring pro-

visions for the troops, who are going to repay[a] Gibeah of Benjamin for all the disgrace that they have done in Israel." [11]So all the men of Israel gathered against the city, united as one.

12 The tribes of Israel sent men through all the tribe of Benjamin, saying, "What crime is this that has been committed among you? [13]Now then, hand over those scoundrels in Gibeah, so that we may put them to death, and purge the evil from Israel." But the Benjaminites would not listen to their kinsfolk, the Israelites. [14]The Benjaminites came together out of the towns to Gibeah, to go out to battle against the Israelites. [15]On that day the Benjaminites mustered twenty-six thousand armed men from their towns, besides the inhabitants of Gibeah. [16]Of all this force, there were seven hundred picked men who were left-handed; every one could sling a stone at a hair, and not miss. [17]And the Israelites, apart from Benjamin, mustered four hundred thousand armed men, all of them warriors.

18 The Israelites proceeded to go up to Bethel, where they inquired of God, "Which of us shall go up first to battle against the Benjaminites?" And the LORD answered, "Judah shall go up first."

19 Then the Israelites got up in the morning, and encamped against Gibeah. [20]The Israelites went out to battle against Benjamin; and the Israelites drew up the battle line against them at Gibeah. [21]The Benjaminites came out of Gibeah, and struck down on that day twenty-two thousand of the Israelites. [23b]The Israelites went up and wept before the LORD until the evening; and they inquired of the LORD, "Shall we again draw near to battle against our kinsfolk the Benjaminites?" And the LORD said, "Go up against them." [22]The Israelites took courage, and again formed the battle line in the same place where they had formed it on the first day.

24 So the Israelites advanced against the Benjaminites the second day. [25]Benjamin moved out against them from Gibeah the second day, and struck down eighteen thousand of the Israelites, all of them armed men. [26]Then all the Israelites, the whole army, went back to Bethel and wept, sitting there before the LORD; they fasted that day until evening. Then they offered burnt offerings and sacrifices of well-being before the LORD. [27]And the Israelites inquired of the LORD (for the ark of the covenant of God was there in those days, [28]and Phinehas son of Eleazar, son of Aaron, ministered before it in those days), saying, "Shall we go out once more to battle against our kinsfolk the Benjaminites, or shall we desist?" The LORD answered, "Go up, for tomorrow I will give them into your hand."

29 So Israel stationed men in ambush around Gibeah. [30]Then the Israelites went up against the Benjaminites on the third day, and set themselves in array against Gibeah, as before. [31]When the Benjaminites went out against the army, they were drawn away from the city. As before they began to inflict casualties on the troops, along the main roads, one of which goes up to Bethel and the other to Gibeah, as well as in the open country, killing about thirty men of Israel. [32]The Benjaminites thought, "They are being routed before us, as previously." But the Israelites said, "Let us retreat and draw them away from the city toward the roads." [33]The main body of the Israelites drew back its battle line to Baal-tamar, while those Israelites who were in ambush rushed out of their place west[c] of Geba. [34]There came against Gibeah ten thousand picked

men out of all Israel, and the battle was fierce. But the Benjaminites did not realize that disaster was close upon them.

35 The Lord defeated Benjamin before Israel; and the Israelites destroyed twenty-five thousand one hundred men of Benjamin that day, all of them armed.

36 Then the Benjaminites saw that they were defeated. [a]

The Israelites gave ground to Benjamin, because they trusted to the troops in ambush that they had stationed against Gibeah. [37]The troops in ambush rushed quickly upon Gibeah. Then they put the whole city to the sword. [38]Now the agreement between the main body of Israel and the men in ambush was that when they sent up a cloud of smoke out of the city [39]the main body of Israel should turn in battle. But Benjamin had begun to inflict casualties on the Israelites, killing about thirty of them; so they thought, "Surely they are defeated before us, as in the first battle." [40]But when the cloud, a column of smoke, began to rise out of the city, the Benjaminites looked behind them—and there was the whole city going up in smoke toward the sky! [41]Then the main body of Israel turned, and the Benjaminites were dismayed, for they saw that disaster was close upon them. [42]Therefore they turned away from the Israelites in the direction of the wilderness; but the battle overtook them, and those who came out of the city[b] were slaughtering them in between. [c] [43]Cutting down[d] the Benjaminites, they pursued them from Nohah[e] and trod them down as far as a place east of Gibeah. [44]Eighteen thousand Benjaminites fell, all of them courageous fighters. [45]When they turned and fled toward the wilderness to the rock of Rimmon, five thousand of them

were cut down on the main roads, and they were pursued as far as Gidom, and two thousand of them were slain. [46]So all who fell that day of Benjamin were twenty-five thousand arms-bearing men, all of them courageous fighters. [47]But six hundred turned and fled toward the wilderness to the rock of Rimmon, and remained at the rock of Rimmon for four months. [48]Meanwhile, the Israelites turned back against the Benjaminites, and put them to the sword—the city, the people, the animals, and all that remained. Also the remaining towns they set on fire.

## JOHN 3.22—4.3

AFTER this Jesus and his disciples went into the Judean countryside, and he spent some time there with them and baptized. [23]John also was baptizing at Aenon near Salim because water was abundant there; and people kept coming and were being baptized [24]—John, of course, had not yet been thrown into prison.

25 Now a discussion about purification arose between John's disciples and a Jew. [f] [26]They came to John and said to him, "Rabbi, the one who was with you across the Jordan, to whom you testified, here he is baptizing, and all are going to him." [27]John answered, "No one can receive anything except what has been given from heaven. [28]You yourselves are my witnesses that I said, 'I am not the Messiah, [g] but I have been sent ahead of him.' [29]He who has the bride is the bridegroom. The friend of the bridegroom, who stands and hears him, rejoices greatly at the bridegroom's voice. For this reason my joy has been fulfilled. [30]He must increase, but I must decrease." [h]

31 The one who comes from above

---

a This sentence is continued by verse 45.   b Compare Vg and some Gk Mss: Heb *cities*   c Compare Syr: Meaning of Heb uncertain   d Gk: Heb *Surrounding*   e Gk: Heb *pursued them at their resting place*   f Other ancient authorities read *the Jews*   g Or *the Christ*   h Some interpreters hold that the quotation continues through verse 36

is above all; the one who is of the earth belongs to the earth and speaks about earthly things. The one who comes from heaven is above all. [32]He testifies to what he has seen and heard, yet no one accepts his testimony. [33]Whoever has accepted his testimony has certi- fied[a] this, that God is true. [34]He whom God has sent speaks the words of God, for he gives the Spirit without measure. [35]The Father loves the Son and has placed all things in his hands. [36]Who- ever believes in the Son has eternal life; whoever disobeys the Son will not see life, but must endure God's wrath.

[4.1] Now when Jesus[b] learned that the Pharisees had heard, "Jesus is making and baptizing more disciples than John" [2]—although it was not Jesus himself but his disciples who baptized— [3]he left Judea and started back to Galilee.

## PSALM 104.22–35

O LORD, how manifold are your
    works!
In wisdom you have made
    them all;
    the earth is full of your
      creatures.
[25] Yonder is the sea, great and
      wide,
    creeping things innumerable
      are there,
    living things both small and
      great.
[26] There go the ships,
    and Leviathan that you
      formed to sport in it.

[27] These all look to you
    to give them their food in due
      season;
[28] when you give to them, they
      gather it up;

    when you open your hand,
      they are filled with good
      things.
[29] When you hide your face, they
      are dismayed;
    when you take away their
      breath, they die
    and return to their dust.
[30] When you send forth your
      spirit,[c] they are created;
    and you renew the face of the
      ground.

[31] May the glory of the LORD
      endure forever;
    may the LORD rejoice in his
      works—
[32] who looks on the earth and it
      trembles,
    who touches the mountains
      and they smoke.
[33] I will sing to the LORD as long as
      I live;
    I will sing praise to my God
      while I have being.
[34] May my meditation be pleasing
      to him,
    for I rejoice in the LORD.
[35] Let sinners be consumed from
      the earth,
    and let the wicked be no
      more.
Bless the LORD, O my soul.
Praise the LORD!

## PROVERBS 14.22–24

D o they not err that plan evil?
    Those who plan good find
      loyalty and faithfulness.
[23] In all toil there is profit,
    but mere talk leads only
      to poverty.
[24] The crown of the wise is their
      wisdom,[d]
    but folly is the garland[e] of
      fools.

a Gk *set a seal to*   b Other ancient authorities read *the Lord*   c Or *your breath*   d Cn Compare Gk: Heb *riches*   e Cn: Heb *is the folly*

## JUDGES 21.1—RUTH 1.22

Now the Israelites had sworn at Mizpah, "No one of us shall give his daughter in marriage to Benjamin." ²And the people came to Bethel, and sat there until evening before God, and they lifted up their voices and wept bitterly. ³They said, "O LORD, the God of Israel, why has it come to pass that today there should be one tribe lacking in Israel?" ⁴On the next day, the people got up early, and built an altar there, and offered burnt offerings and sacrifices of well-being. ⁵Then the Israelites said, "Which of all the tribes of Israel did not come up in the assembly to the LORD?" For a solemn oath had been taken concerning whoever did not come up to the LORD to Mizpah, saying, "That one shall be put to death." ⁶But the Israelites had compassion for Benjamin their kin, and said, "One tribe is cut off from Israel this day. ⁷What shall we do for wives for those who are left, since we have sworn by the LORD that we will not give them any of our daughters as wives?"

8 Then they said, "Is there anyone from the tribes of Israel who did not come up to the LORD to Mizpah?" It turned out that no one from Jabesh-gilead had come to the camp, to the assembly. ⁹For when the roll was called among the people, not one of the inhabitants of Jabesh-gilead was there. ¹⁰So the congregation sent twelve thousand soldiers there and commanded them, "Go, put the inhabitants of Jabesh-gilead to the sword, including the women and the little ones. ¹¹This is what you shall do; every male and every woman that has lain with a male you shall devote to destruction." ¹²And they found among the inhabitants of Jabesh-gilead four hundred young virgins who had never slept with a man and brought them to the camp at Shiloh, which is in the land of Canaan.

13 Then the whole congregation sent word to the Benjaminites who were at the rock of Rimmon, and proclaimed peace to them. ¹⁴Benjamin returned at that time; and they gave them the women whom they had saved alive of the women of Jabesh-gilead; but they did not suffice for them.

15 The people had compassion on Benjamin because the LORD had made a breach in the tribes of Israel. ¹⁶So the elders of the congregation said, "What shall we do for wives for those who are left, since there are no women left in Benjamin?" ¹⁷And they said, "There must be heirs for the survivors of Benjamin, in order that a tribe may not be blotted out from Israel. ¹⁸Yet we cannot give any of our daughters to them as wives." For the Israelites had sworn, "Cursed be anyone who gives a wife to Benjamin." ¹⁹So they said, "Look, the yearly festival of the LORD is taking place at Shiloh, which is north of Bethel, on the east of the highway that goes up from Bethel to Shechem, and south of Lebonah." ²⁰And they instructed the Benjaminites, saying, "Go and lie in wait in the vineyards, ²¹and watch; when the young women of Shiloh come out to dance in the dances, then come out of the vineyards and each of you carry off a wife for himself from the young women of Shiloh, and go to the land of Benjamin. ²²Then if their fathers or their brothers come to complain to us, we will say to them, 'Be generous and allow us to have them; because we did not capture in battle a wife for each man. But neither did you incur guilt by giving your daughters to them.' " ²³The Benjaminites did so;

they took wives for each of them from the dancers whom they abducted. Then they went and returned to their territory, and rebuilt the towns, and lived in them. 24So the Israelites departed from there at that time by tribes and families, and they went out from there to their own territories.

25  In those days there was no king in Israel; all the people did what was right in their own eyes.

1.1 IN the days when the judges ruled, there was a famine in the land, and a certain man of Bethlehem in Judah went to live in the country of Moab, he and his wife and two sons. 2The name of the man was Elimelech and the name of his wife Naomi, and the names of his two sons were Mahlon and Chilion; they were Ephrathites from Bethlehem in Judah. They went into the country of Moab and remained there. 3But Elimelech, the husband of Naomi, died, and she was left with her two sons. 4These took Moabite wives; the name of the one was Orpah and the name of the other Ruth. When they had lived there about ten years, 5both Mahlon and Chilion also died, so that the woman was left without her two sons and her husband.

6  Then she started to return with her daughters-in-law from the country of Moab, for she had heard in the country of Moab that the LORD had considered his people and given them food. 7So she set out from the place where she had been living, she and her two daughters-in-law, and they went on their way to go back to the land of Judah. 8But Naomi said to her two daughters-in-law, "Go back each of you to your mother's house. May the LORD deal kindly with you, as you have dealt with the dead and with me. 9The LORD grant that you may find security, each of you in the house of your husband."

Then she kissed them, and they wept aloud. 10They said to her, "No, we will return with you to your people." 11But Naomi said, "Turn back, my daughters, why will you go with me? Do I still have sons in my womb that they may become your husbands? 12Turn back, my daughters, go your way, for I am too old to have a husband. Even if I thought there was hope for me, even if I should have a husband tonight and bear sons, 13would you then wait until they were grown? Would you then refrain from marrying? No, my daughters, it has been far more bitter for me than for you, because the hand of the LORD has turned against me." 14Then they wept aloud again. Orpah kissed her mother-in-law, but Ruth clung to her.

15  So she said, "See, your sister-in-law has gone back to her people and to her gods; return after your sister-in-law." 16But Ruth said,

"Do not press me to leave you
    or to turn back from following
        you!
Where you go, I will go;
    Where you lodge, I will lodge;
your people shall be my people,
    and your God my God.
17  Where you die, I will die—
    there will I be buried.
May the LORD do thus and so to
        me,
    and more as well,
if even death parts me from
        you!"

18When Naomi saw that she was determined to go with her, she said no more to her.

19  So the two of them went on until they came to Bethlehem. When they came to Bethlehem, the whole town was stirred because of them; and the women said, "Is this Naomi?" 20She said to them,

"Call me no longer Naomi, a
    call me Mara, b

a That is Pleasant   b That is Bitter

for the Almighty[a] has dealt
   bitterly with me.
21  I went away full,
   but the Lord has brought me
    back empty;
  why call me Naomi
   when the Lord has dealt
    harshly with[b] me,
   and the Almighty[a] has
    brought calamity upon
    me?"

22 So Naomi returned together with Ruth the Moabite, her daughter-in-law, who came back with her from the country of Moab. They came to Bethlehem at the beginning of the barley harvest.

## JOHN 4.4–42

**B**UT he [Jesus] had to go through Samaria. [5]So he came to a Samaritan city called Sychar, near the plot of ground that Jacob had given to his son Joseph. [6]Jacob's well was there, and Jesus, tired out by his journey, was sitting by the well. It was about noon.

7 A Samaritan woman came to draw water, and Jesus said to her, "Give me a drink." [8](His disciples had gone to the city to buy food.) [9]The Samaritan woman said to him, "How is it that you, a Jew, ask a drink of me, a woman of Samaria?" (Jews do not share things in common with Samaritans.)[c] [10]Jesus answered her, "If you knew the gift of God, and who it is that is saying to you, 'Give me a drink,' you would have asked him, and he would have given you living water." [11]The woman said to him, "Sir, you have no bucket, and the well is deep. Where do you get that living water? [12]Are you greater than our ancestor Jacob, who gave us the well, and with his sons and his flocks drank from it?" [13]Jesus said to her, "Everyone who drinks of this wa-

ter will be thirsty again, [14]but those who drink of the water that I will give them will never be thirsty. The water that I will give will become in them a spring of water gushing up to eternal life." [15]The woman said to him, "Sir, give me this water, so that I may never be thirsty or have to keep coming here to draw water."

16 Jesus said to her, "Go, call your husband, and come back." [17]The woman answered him, "I have no husband." Jesus said to her, "You are right in saying, 'I have no husband'; [18]for you have had five husbands, and the one you have now is not your husband. What you have said is true!" [19]The woman said to him, "Sir, I see that you are a prophet. [20]Our ancestors worshiped on this mountain, but you[d] say that the place where people must worship is in Jerusalem." [21]Jesus said to her, "Woman, believe me, the hour is coming when you will worship the Father neither on this mountain nor in Jerusalem. [22]You worship what you do not know; we worship what we know, for salvation is from the Jews. [23]But the hour is coming, and is now here, when the true worshipers will worship the Father in spirit and truth, for the Father seeks such as these to worship him. [24]God is spirit, and those who worship him must worship in spirit and truth." [25]The woman said to him, "I know that Messiah is coming" (who is called Christ). "When he comes, he will proclaim all things to us." [26]Jesus said to her, "I am he,[e] the one who is speaking to you."

27 Just then his disciples came. They were astonished that he was speaking with a woman, but no one said, "What do you want?" or, "Why are you speaking with her?" [28]Then the woman left her water jar and went back to the city. She said to the people, [29]"Come and see a man who told me

everything I have ever done! He cannot be the Messiah, a can he?" 30They left the city and were on their way to him.

31 Meanwhile the disciples were urging him, "Rabbi, eat something." 32But he said to them, "I have food to eat that you do not know about." 33So the disciples said to one another, "Surely no one has brought him something to eat?" 34Jesus said to them, "My food is to do the will of him who sent me and to complete his work. 35Do you not say, 'Four months more, then comes the harvest'? But I tell you, look around you, and see how the fields are ripe for harvesting. 36The reaper is already receivingb wages and is gathering fruit for eternal life, so that sower and reaper may rejoice together. 37For here the saying holds true, 'One sows and another reaps.' 38I sent you to reap that for which you did not labor. Others have labored, and you have entered into their labor."

39 Many Samaritans from that city believed in him because of the woman's testimony, "He told me everything I have ever done." 40So when the Samaritans came to him, they asked him to stay with them; and he stayed there two days. 41And many more believed because of his word. 42They said to the woman, "It is no longer because of what you said that we believe, for we have heard for ourselves, and we know that this is truly the Savior of the world."

## PSALM 105. 1–15

O GIVE thanks to the LORD, call
  on his name,
make known his deeds
  among the peoples.
2 Sing to him, sing praises to him;
  tell of all his wonderful works.
3 Glory in his holy name;

let the hearts of those who
  seek the LORD rejoice.
4 Seek the LORD and his strength;
  seek his presence continually.
5 Remember the wonderful works
  he has done,
his miracles, and the
  judgments he uttered,
6 O offspring of his servant
  Abraham, c
children of Jacob, his chosen
  ones.

7 He is the LORD our God;
  his judgments are in all the
  earth.
8 He is mindful of his covenant
  forever,
of the word that he
  commanded, for a
  thousand generations,
9 the covenant that he made with
  Abraham,
his sworn promise to Isaac,
10 which he confirmed to Jacob as
  a statute,
to Israel as an everlasting
  covenant,
11 saying, "To you I will give the
  land of Canaan
as your portion for an
  inheritance."

12 When they were few in number,
  of little account, and
  strangers in it,
13 wandering from nation to nation,
  from one kingdom to another
  people,
14 he allowed no one to oppress
  them;
he rebuked kings on their
  account,
15 saying, "Do not touch my
  anointed ones;
do my prophets no harm."

aOr *the Christ*  bOr *35. . . the fields are already ripe for harvesting. 36The reaper is receiving*
cAnother reading is *Israel* (compare 1 Chr 16.13)

## PROVERBS 14.25

A TRUTHFUL witness saves lives, but one who utters lies is a betrayer.

# MAY 6

## RUTH 2.1—4.22

Now Naomi had a kinsman on her husband's side, a prominent rich man, of the family of Elimelech, whose name was Boaz. [2]And Ruth the Moabite said to Naomi, "Let me go to the field and glean among the ears of grain, behind someone in whose sight I may find favor." She said to her, "Go, my daughter." [3]So she went. She came and gleaned in the field behind the reapers. As it happened, she came to the part of the field belonging to Boaz, who was of the family of Elimelech. [4]Just then Boaz came from Bethlehem. He said to the reapers, "The LORD be with you." They answered, "The LORD bless you." [5]Then Boaz said to his servant who was in charge of the reapers, "To whom does this young woman belong?" [6]The servant who was in charge of the reapers answered, "She is the Moabite who came back with Naomi from the country of Moab. [7]She said, 'Please, let me glean and gather among the sheaves behind the reapers.' So she came, and she has been on her feet from early this morning until now, without resting even for a moment."[a]

8 Then Boaz said to Ruth, "Now listen, my daughter, do not go to glean in another field or leave this one, but keep close to my young women. [9]Keep your eyes on the field that is being reaped, and follow behind them. I have ordered the young men not to bother you. If you get thirsty, go to the vessels and drink from what the young men have drawn." [10]Then she fell prostrate, with her face to the ground, and said to him, "Why have I found favor in your sight, that you should take notice of me, when I am a foreigner?" [11]But Boaz answered her, "All that you have done for your mother-in-law since the death of your husband has been fully told me, and how you left your father and mother and your native land and came to a people that you did not know before. [12]May the LORD reward you for your deeds, and may you have a full reward from the LORD, the God of Israel, under whose wings you have come for refuge!" [13]Then she said, "May I continue to find favor in your sight, my lord, for you have comforted me and spoken kindly to your servant, even though I am not one of your servants."

14 At mealtime Boaz said to her, "Come here, and eat some of this bread, and dip your morsel in the sour wine." So she sat beside the reapers, and he heaped up for her some parched grain. She ate until she was satisfied, and she had some left over. [15]When she got up to glean, Boaz instructed his young men, "Let her glean even among the standing sheaves, and do not re-

[a]Compare Gk Vg: Meaning of Heb uncertain

proach her. ¹⁶You must also pull out some handfuls for her from the bundles, and leave them for her to glean, and do not rebuke her."

17  So she gleaned in the field until evening. Then she beat out what she had gleaned, and it was about an ephah of barley. ¹⁸She picked it up and came into the town, and her mother-in-law saw how much she had gleaned. Then she took out and gave her what was left over after she herself had been satisfied. ¹⁹Her mother-in-law said to her, "Where did you glean today? And where have you worked? Blessed be the man who took notice of you." So she told her mother-in-law with whom she had worked, and said, "The name of the man with whom I worked today is Boaz." ²⁰Then Naomi said to her daughter-in-law, "Blessed be he by the LORD, whose kindness has not forsaken the living or the dead!" Naomi also said to her, "The man is a relative of ours, one of our nearest kin."ᵃ ²¹Then Ruth the Moabite said, "He even said to me, 'Stay close by my servants, until they have finished all my harvest.' " ²²Naomi said to Ruth, her daughter-in-law, "It is better, my daughter, that you go out with his young women, otherwise you might be bothered in another field." ²³So she stayed close to the young women of Boaz, gleaning until the end of the barley and wheat harvests; and she lived with her mother-in-law.

3.1 NAOMI her mother-in-law said to her, "My daughter, I need to seek some security for you, so that it may be well with you. ²Now here is our kinsman Boaz, with whose young women you have been working. See, he is winnowing barley tonight at the threshing floor. ³Now wash and anoint yourself, and put on your best clothes and go down to the threshing floor; but do not make yourself known to the man until he has fin-

ished eating and drinking. ⁴When he lies down, observe the place where he lies; then, go and uncover his feet and lie down; and he will tell you what to do." ⁵She said to her, "All that you tell me I will do."

6  So she went down to the threshing floor and did just as her mother-in-law had instructed her. ⁷When Boaz had eaten and drunk, and he was in a contented mood, he went to lie down at the end of the heap of grain. Then she came stealthily and uncovered his feet, and lay down. ⁸At midnight the man was startled, and turned over, and there, lying at his feet, was a woman! ⁹He said, "Who are you?" And she answered, "I am Ruth, your servant; spread your cloak over your servant, for you are next-of-kin."ᵃ ¹⁰He said, "May you be blessed by the LORD, my daughter; this last instance of your loyalty is better than the first; you have not gone after young men, whether poor or rich. ¹¹And now, my daughter, do not be afraid, I will do for you all that you ask, for all the assembly of my people know that you are a worthy woman. ¹²But now, though it is true that I am a near kinsman, there is another kinsman more closely related than I. ¹³Remain this night, and in the morning, if he will act as next-of-kinᵃ for you, good; let him do it. If he is not willing to act as next-of-kinᵃ for you, then, as the LORD lives, I will act as next-of-kinᵃ for you. Lie down until the morning."

14  So she lay at his feet until morning, but got up before one person could recognize another; for he said, "It must not be known that the woman came to the threshing floor." ¹⁵Then he said, "Bring the cloak you are wearing and hold it out." So she held it, and he measured out six measures of barley, and put it on her back; then he went into the city. ¹⁶She came to her mother-in-law, who said, "How did things go with

ᵃOr *one with the right to redeem*

you,[a] my daughter?" Then she told her all that the man had done for her, [17]saying, "He gave me these six measures of barley, for he said, 'Do not go back to your mother-in-law empty-handed.'" [18]She replied, "Wait, my daughter, until you learn how the matter turns out, for the man will not rest, but will settle the matter today."

[4].[1] No sooner had Boaz gone up to the gate and sat down there than the next-of-kin,[b] of whom Boaz had spoken, came passing by. So Boaz said, "Come over, friend; sit down here." And he went over and sat down. [2]Then Boaz took ten men of the elders of the city, and said, "Sit down here"; so they sat down. [3]He then said to the next-of-kin,[b] "Naomi, who has come back from the country of Moab, is selling the parcel of land that belonged to our kinsman Elimelech. [4]So I thought I would tell you of it, and say: Buy it in the presence of those sitting here, and in the presence of the elders of my people. If you will redeem it, redeem it; but if you will not, tell me, so that I may know; for there is no one prior to you to redeem it, and I come after you." So he said, "I will redeem it." [5]Then Boaz said, "The day you acquire the field from the hand of Naomi, you are also acquiring Ruth[c] the Moabite, the widow of the dead man, to maintain the dead man's name on his inheritance." [6]At this, the next-of-kin[b] said, "I cannot redeem it for myself without damaging my own inheritance. Take my right of redemption yourself, for I cannot redeem it."

7 Now this was the custom in former times in Israel concerning redeeming and exchanging: to confirm a transaction, the one took off a sandal and gave it to the other; this was the manner of attesting in Israel. [8]So when the next-of-kin[b] said to Boaz, "Acquire it for yourself," he took off his sandal. [9]Then Boaz said to the elders and all the people, "Today you are witnesses that I have acquired from the hand of Naomi all that belonged to Elimelech and all that belonged to Chilion and Mahlon. [10]I have also acquired Ruth the Moabite, the wife of Mahlon, to be my wife, to maintain the dead man's name on his inheritance, in order that the name of the dead may not be cut off from his kindred and from the gate of his native place; today you are witnesses." [11]Then all the people who were at the gate, along with the elders, said, "We are witnesses. May the Lord make the woman who is coming into your house like Rachel and Leah, who together built up the house of Israel. May you produce children in Ephrathah and bestow a name in Bethlehem; [12]and, through the children that the Lord will give you by this young woman, may your house be like the house of Perez, whom Tamar bore to Judah."

13 So Boaz took Ruth and she became his wife. When they came together, the Lord made her conceive, and she bore a son. [14]Then the women said to Naomi, "Blessed be the Lord, who has not left you this day without next-of-kin;[b] and may his name be renowned in Israel! [15]He shall be to you a restorer of life and a nourisher of your old age; for your daughter-in-law who loves you, who is more to you than seven sons, has borne him." [16]Then Naomi took the child and laid him in her bosom, and became his nurse. [17]The women of the neighborhood gave him a name, saying, "A son has been born to Naomi." They named him Obed; he became the father of Jesse, the father of David.

18 Now these are the descendants

---

[a]Or *"Who are you,*   [b]Or *one with the right to redeem*   [c]OL Vg: Heb *from the hand of Naomi and* *from Ruth*

of Perez: Perez became the father of Hezron, [19]Hezron of Ram, Ram of Amminadab, [20]Amminadab of Nahshon, Nahshon of Salmon, [21]Salmon of Boaz, Boaz of Obed, [22]Obed of Jesse, and Jesse of David.

## JOHN 4.43–54

WHEN the two days were over, he [Jesus] went from that place to Galilee [44](for Jesus himself had testified that a prophet has no honor in the prophet's own country). [45]When he came to Galilee, the Galileans welcomed him, since they had seen all that he had done in Jerusalem at the festival; for they too had gone to the festival.

46 Then he came again to Cana in Galilee where he had changed the water into wine. Now there was a royal official whose son lay ill in Capernaum. [47]When he heard that Jesus had come from Judea to Galilee, he went and begged him to come down and heal his son, for he was at the point of death. [48]Then Jesus said to him, "Unless you[a] see signs and wonders you will not believe." [49]The official said to him, "Sir, come down before my little boy dies." [50]Jesus said to him, "Go; your son will live." The man believed the word that Jesus spoke to him and started on his way. [51]As he was going down, his slaves met him and told him that his child was alive. [52]So he asked them the hour when he began to recover, and they said to him, "Yesterday at one in the afternoon the fever left him." [53]The father realized that this was the hour when Jesus had said to him, "Your son will live." So he himself believed, along with his whole household. [54]Now this was the second sign that Jesus did after coming from Judea to Galilee.

## PSALM 105.16–36

WHEN he summoned famine against the land,
and broke every staff of bread,
[17] he had sent a man ahead of them,
Joseph, who was sold as a slave.
[18] His feet were hurt with fetters,
his neck was put in a collar of iron;
[19] until what he had said came to pass,
the word of the LORD kept testing him.
[20] The king sent and released him;
the ruler of the peoples set him free.
[21] He made him lord of his house,
and ruler of all his possessions,
[22] to instruct[b] his officials at his pleasure,
and to teach his elders wisdom.

[23] Then Israel came to Egypt;
Jacob lived as an alien in the land of Ham.
[24] And the LORD made his people very fruitful,
and made them stronger than their foes,
[25] whose hearts he then turned to hate his people,
to deal craftily with his servants.

[26] He sent his servant Moses,
and Aaron whom he had chosen.
[27] They performed his signs among them,
and miracles in the land of Ham.
[28] He sent darkness, and made the land dark;

---

[a]Both instances of the Greek word for *you* in this verse are plural   [b]Gk Syr Jerome: Heb *to bind*

they rebelled[a] against his
words.
29 He turned their waters into
blood,
and caused their fish to die.
30 Their land swarmed with frogs,
even in the chambers of their
kings.
31 He spoke, and there came
swarms of flies,
and gnats throughout their
country.
32 He gave them hail for rain,
and lightning that flashed
through their land.
33 He struck their vines and fig
trees,
and shattered the trees of
their country.
34 He spoke, and the locusts
came,
and young locusts without
number;
35 they devoured all the vegetation
in their land,
and ate up the fruit of their
ground.
36 He struck down all the firstborn
in their land,
the first issue of all their
strength.

## PROVERBS 14.26–27

IN the fear of the LORD one has
strong confidence,
and one's children will have a
refuge.
27 The fear of the LORD is a
fountain of life,
so that one may avoid the
snares of death.

# MAY 7

## 1 SAMUEL 1.1—2.21

THERE was a certain man of Rama-
thaim, a Zuphite[b] from the hill
country of Ephraim, whose
name was Elkanah son of Jeroham son
of Elihu son of Tohu son of Zuph, an
Ephraimite. [2]He had two wives; the
name of the one was Hannah, and the
name of the other Peninnah. Peninnah
had children, but Hannah had no children.

3 Now this man used to go up year
by year from his town to worship and
to sacrifice to the LORD of hosts at Shiloh, where the two sons of Eli, Hophni
and Phinehas, were priests of the
LORD. [4]On the day when Elkanah sacrificed, he would give portions to his wife
Peninnah and to all her sons and daughters; [5]but to Hannah he gave a double
portion,[c] because he loved her,
though the LORD had closed her womb.
[6]Her rival used to provoke her severely, to irritate her, because the
LORD had closed her womb. [7]So it went
on year by year; as often as she went
up to the house of the LORD, she used
to provoke her. Therefore Hannah
wept and would not eat. [8]Her husband
Elkanah said to her, "Hannah, why do
you weep? Why do you not eat? Why is

a Cn Compare Gk Syr: Heb *they did not rebel*  b Compare Gk and 1 Chr 6.35-36: Heb
*Ramathaim-zophim*  c Syr: Meaning of Heb uncertain

your heart sad? Am I not more to you than ten sons?"

9   After they had eaten and drunk at Shiloh, Hannah rose and presented herself before the LORD. [a] Now Eli the priest was sitting on the seat beside the doorpost of the temple of the LORD. [10]She was deeply distressed and prayed to the LORD, and wept bitterly. [11]She made this vow: "O LORD of hosts, if only you will look on the misery of your servant, and remember me, and not forget your servant, but will give to your servant a male child, then I will set him before you as a nazirite[b] until the day of his death. He shall drink neither wine nor intoxicants, [c] and no razor shall touch his head."

12   As she continued praying before the LORD, Eli observed her mouth. [13]Hannah was praying silently; only her lips moved, but her voice was not heard; therefore Eli thought she was drunk. [14]So Eli said to her, "How long will you make a drunken spectacle of yourself? Put away your wine." [15]But Hannah answered, "No, my lord, I am a woman deeply troubled; I have drunk neither wine nor strong drink, but I have been pouring out my soul before the LORD. [16]Do not regard your servant as a worthless woman, for I have been speaking out of my great anxiety and vexation all this time." [17]Then Eli answered, "Go in peace; the God of Israel grant the petition you have made to him." [18]And she said, "Let your servant find favor in your sight." Then the woman went to her quarters, [d] ate and drank with her husband, [e] and her countenance was sad no longer. [f]

19   They rose early in the morning and worshiped before the LORD; then they went back to their house at Ra-mah. Elkanah knew his wife Hannah, and the LORD remembered her. [20]In due time Hannah conceived and bore a son. She named him Samuel, for she said, "I have asked him of the LORD."

21   The man Elkanah and all his household went up to offer to the LORD the yearly sacrifice, and to pay his vow. [22]But Hannah did not go up, for she said to her husband, "As soon as the child is weaned, I will bring him, that he may appear in the presence of the LORD, and remain there forever; I will offer him as a nazirite[b] for all time."[g] [23]Her husband Elkanah said to her, "Do what seems best to you, wait until you have weaned him; only—may the LORD establish his word."[h] So the woman remained and nursed her son, until she weaned him. [24]When she had weaned him, she took him up with her, along with a three-year-old bull, [i] an ephah of flour, and a skin of wine. She brought him to the house of the LORD at Shiloh; and the child was young. [25]Then they slaughtered the bull, and they brought the child to Eli. [26]And she said, "Oh, my lord! As you live, my lord, I am the woman who was standing here in your presence, praying to the LORD. [27]For this child I prayed; and the LORD has granted me the petition that I made to him. [28]Therefore I have lent him to the LORD; as long as he lives, he is given to the LORD."

She left him there for[j] the LORD.

2.1 HANNAH prayed and said,
   "My heart exults in the LORD;
      my strength is exalted in my
         God. [k]
   My mouth derides my enemies,
      because I rejoice in my[l]
         victory.

aGk: Heb lacks *and presented herself before the LORD*   bThat is *one separated* or *one consecrated*
cCn Compare Gk Q Ms 1.22: MT *then I will give him to the LORD all the days of his life*   dGk: Heb *went her way*   eGk: Heb lacks *and drank with her husband*   fGk: Meaning of Heb uncertain
gCn Compare Q Ms: MT lacks *I will offer him as a nazirite for all time*   hMT: Q Ms Gk Compare Syr *that which goes out of your mouth*   iQ Ms Gk Syr: MT *three bulls*   jGk (Compare Q Ms) and Gk at 2.11: MT *And he* (that is, Elkanah) *worshiped there before*   kGk: Heb *the LORD*   lQ Ms: MT *your*

2 "There is no Holy One like the
  Lord,
    no one besides you;
    there is no Rock like our
      God.
3 Talk no more so very proudly,
    let not arrogance come from
      your mouth;
  for the Lord is a God of
      knowledge,
    and by him actions are
      weighed.
4 The bows of the mighty are
      broken,
    but the feeble gird on
      strength.
5 Those who were full have hired
      themselves out for
      bread,
    but those who were hungry
      are fat with spoil.
  The barren has borne seven,
    but she who has many
      children is forlorn.
6 The Lord kills and brings to life;
    he brings down to Sheol and
      raises up.
7 The Lord makes poor and
      makes rich;
    he brings low, he also exalts.
8 He raises up the poor from the
      dust;
    he lifts the needy from the
      ash heap,
  to make them sit with princes
    and inherit a seat of honor. a
  For the pillars of the earth are
      the Lord's,
    and on them he has set the
      world.

9 "He will guard the feet of his
      faithful ones,
    but the wicked shall be cut off
      in darkness;
  for not by might does one
      prevail.

10 The Lord! His adversaries shall
      be shattered;
    the Most High b will thunder
      in heaven.
  The Lord will judge the ends of
      the earth;
    he will give strength to his
      king,
    and exalt the power of his
      anointed."

11 Then Elkanah went home to Ramah, while the boy remained to minister to the Lord, in the presence of the priest Eli.

12 Now the sons of Eli were scoundrels; they had no regard for the Lord 13or for the duties of the priests to the people. When anyone offered sacrifice, the priest's servant would come, while the meat was boiling, with a three-pronged fork in his hand, 14and he would thrust it into the pan, or kettle, or caldron, or pot; all that the fork brought up the priest would take for himself. c This is what they did at Shiloh to all the Israelites who came there. 15Moreover, before the fat was burned, the priest's servant would come and say to the one who was sacrificing, "Give meat for the priest to roast; for he will not accept boiled meat from you, but only raw." 16And if the man said to him, "Let them burn the fat first, and then take whatever you wish," he would say, "No, you must give it now; if not, I will take it by force." 17Thus the sin of the young men was very great in the sight of the Lord; for they treated the offerings of the Lord with contempt.

18 Samuel was ministering before the Lord, a boy wearing a linen ephod. 19His mother used to make for him a little robe and take it to him each year, when she went up with her husband to offer the yearly sacrifice. 20Then Eli would bless Elkanah and his wife, and say, "May the Lord repayd you with

aGk (Compare Q Ms) adds *He grants the vow of the one who vows, and blesses the years of the just*
bCn Heb *against him he*   cGk Syr Vg: Heb *with it*   dQ Ms Gk: MT *give*

children by this woman for the gift that she made to[a] the LORD"; and then they would return to their home.

21 And[b] the LORD took note of Hannah; she conceived and bore three sons and two daughters. And the boy Samuel grew up in the presence of the LORD.

## JOHN 5.1–24

AFTER this there was a festival of the Jews, and Jesus went up to Jerusalem.

2 Now in Jerusalem by the Sheep Gate there is a pool, called in Hebrew[c] Beth-zatha,[d] which has five porticoes. [3]In these lay many invalids—blind, lame, and paralyzed.[e] [5]One man was there who had been ill for thirty-eight years. [6]When Jesus saw him lying there and knew that he had been there a long time, he said to him, "Do you want to be made well?" [7]The sick man answered him, "Sir, I have no one to put me into the pool when the water is stirred up; and while I am making my way, someone else steps down ahead of me." [8]Jesus said to him, "Stand up, take your mat and walk." [9]At once the man was made well, and he took up his mat and began to walk.

Now that day was a sabbath. [10]So the Jews said to the man who had been cured, "It is the sabbath; it is not lawful for you to carry your mat." [11]But he answered them, "The man who made me well said to me, 'Take up your mat and walk.'" [12]They asked him, "Who is the man who said to you, 'Take it up and walk'?" [13]Now the man who had been healed did not know who it was, for Jesus had disappeared in[f] the crowd that was there. [14]Later Jesus found him in the temple and said to him,

"See, you have been made well! Do not sin any more, so that nothing worse happens to you." [15]The man went away and told the Jews that it was Jesus who had made him well. [16]Therefore the Jews started persecuting Jesus, because he was doing such things on the sabbath. [17]But Jesus answered them, "My Father is still working, and I also am working." [18]For this reason the Jews were seeking all the more to kill him, because he was not only breaking the sabbath, but was also calling God his own Father, thereby making himself equal to God.

19 Jesus said to them, "Very truly, I tell you, the Son can do nothing on his own, but only what he sees the Father doing; for whatever the Father[g] does, the Son does likewise. [20]The Father loves the Son and shows him all that he himself is doing; and he will show him greater works than these, so that you will be astonished. [21]Indeed, just as the Father raises the dead and gives them life, so also the Son gives life to whomever he wishes. [22]The Father judges no one but has given all judgment to the Son, [23]so that all may honor the Son just as they honor the Father. Anyone who does not honor the Son does not honor the Father who sent him. [24]Very truly, I tell you, anyone who hears my word and believes him who sent me has eternal life, and does not come under judgment, but has passed from death to life.

## PSALM 105.37–45

THEN he brought Israel[h] out
        with silver and gold,
    and there was no one among
        their tribes who
        stumbled.

aQ Ms Gk: MT *for the petition that she asked of*   bQ Ms Gk: MT *When*   cThat is, *Aramaic*   dOther ancient authorities read *Bethesda*, others *Bethsaida*   eOther ancient authorities add, wholly or in part, *waiting for the stirring of the water; 4for an angel of the Lord went down at certain seasons into the pool, and stirred up the water; whoever stepped in first after the stirring of the water was made well from whatever disease that person had.*   fOr *had left because of*   gGk *that one*   hHeb *them*

38 Egypt was glad when they
        departed,
    for dread of them had fallen
        upon it.
39 He spread a cloud for a
        covering,
    and fire to give light by night.
40 They asked, and he brought
        quails,
    and gave them food from
        heaven in abundance.
41 He opened the rock, and water
        gushed out;
    it flowed through the desert
        like a river.
42 For he remembered his holy
        promise,
    and Abraham, his servant.

43 So he brought his people out
        with joy,
    his chosen ones with singing.
44 He gave them the lands of the
        nations,
    and they took possession of
        the wealth of the
        peoples,
45 that they might keep his
        statutes
    and observe his laws.
Praise the LORD!

## PROVERBS 14.28–29

THE glory of a king is a
        multitude of people;
    without people a prince is
        ruined.
29 Whoever is slow to anger has
        great understanding,
    but one who has a hasty
        temper exalts folly.

# MAY 8

## 1 SAMUEL 2.22—4.22

Now Eli was very old. He heard all that his sons were doing to all Israel, and how they lay with the women who served at the entrance to the tent of meeting. 23He said to them, "Why do you do such things? For I hear of your evil dealings from all these people. 24No, my sons; it is not a good report that I hear the people of the LORD spreading abroad. 25If one person sins against another, someone can intercede for the sinner with the LORD;a but if someone sins against the LORD, who can make intercession?" But they would not listen to the voice of their father; for it was the will of the LORD to kill them.

26 Now the boy Samuel continued to grow both in stature and in favor with the LORD and with the people.

27 A man of God came to Eli and said to him, "Thus the LORD has said, 'I revealedb myself to the family of your ancestor in Egypt when they were slavesc to the house of Pharaoh. 28I chose him out of all the tribes of Israel to be my priest, to go up to my altar, to offer incense, to wear an ephod before me; and I gave to the family of your ancestor all my offerings by fire from the people of Israel. 29Why then look with greedy eyed at my sacrifices and

aGk Compare Q Ms: MT *another, God will mediate for him*   bGk Tg Syr: Heb *Did I reveal*   cQ Ms
Gk: MT lacks *slaves*   dQ Ms Gk: MT *then kick*

my offerings that I commanded, and honor your sons more than me by fattening yourselves on the choicest parts of every offering of my people Israel?' [30]Therefore the LORD the God of Israel declares: 'I promised that your family and the family of your ancestor should go in and out before me forever'; but now the LORD declares: 'Far be it from me; for those who honor me I will honor, and those who despise me shall be treated with contempt. [31]See, a time is coming when I will cut off your strength and the strength of your ancestor's family, so that no one in your family will live to old age. [32]Then in distress you will look with greedy eye[a] on all the prosperity that shall be bestowed upon Israel; and no one in your family shall ever live to old age. [33]The only one of you whom I shall not cut off from my altar shall be spared to weep out his[b] eyes and grieve his[c] heart; all the members of your household shall die by the sword.[d] [34]The fate of your two sons, Hophni and Phinehas, shall be the sign to you—both of them shall die on the same day. [35]I will raise up for myself a faithful priest, who shall do according to what is in my heart and in my mind. I will build him a sure house, and he shall go in and out before my anointed one forever. [36]Everyone who is left in your family shall come to implore him for a piece of silver or a loaf of bread, and shall say, Please put me in one of the priest's places, that I may eat a morsel of bread.'"

**3.**[1] Now the boy Samuel was ministering to the LORD under Eli. The word of the LORD was rare in those days; visions were not widespread.

[2] At that time Eli, whose eyesight had begun to grow dim so that he could not see, was lying down in his room; [3]the lamp of God had not yet gone out, and Samuel was lying down in the temple of the LORD, where the ark of God was. [4]Then the LORD called, "Samuel! Samuel!"[e] and he said, "Here I am!" [5]and ran to Eli, and said, "Here I am, for you called me." But he said, "I did not call; lie down again." So he went and lay down. [6]The LORD called again, "Samuel!" Samuel got up and went to Eli, and said, "Here I am, for you called me." But he said, "I did not call, my son; lie down again." [7]Now Samuel did not yet know the LORD, and the word of the LORD had not yet been revealed to him. [8]The LORD called Samuel again, a third time. And he got up and went to Eli, and said, "Here I am, for you called me." Then Eli perceived that the LORD was calling the boy. [9]Therefore Eli said to Samuel, "Go, lie down; and if he calls you, you shall say, 'Speak, LORD, for your servant is listening.'" So Samuel went and lay down in his place.

[10] Now the LORD came and stood there, calling as before, "Samuel! Samuel!" And Samuel said, "Speak, for your servant is listening." [11]Then the LORD said to Samuel, "See, I am about to do something in Israel that will make both ears of anyone who hears of it tingle. [12]On that day I will fulfill against Eli all that I have spoken concerning his house, from beginning to end. [13]For I have told him that I am about to punish his house forever, for the iniquity that he knew, because his sons were blaspheming God,[f] and he did not restrain them. [14]Therefore I swear to the house of Eli that the iniquity of Eli's house shall not be expiated by sacrifice or offering forever."

[15] Samuel lay there until morning; then he opened the doors of the house of the LORD. Samuel was afraid to tell the vision to Eli. [16]But Eli called Samuel and said, "Samuel, my son." He said, "Here I am." [17]Eli said, "What was it that he told you? Do not hide it from me. May God do so to you and more

also, if you hide anything from me of all that he told you." [18] So Samuel told him everything and hid nothing from him. Then he said, "It is the LORD; let him do what seems good to him."

19 As Samuel grew up, the LORD was with him and let none of his words fall to the ground. [20] And all Israel from Dan to Beer-sheba knew that Samuel was a trustworthy prophet of the LORD. [21] The LORD continued to appear at Shiloh, for the LORD revealed himself to Samuel at Shiloh by the word of the LORD. [4.1] And the word of Samuel came to all Israel.

In those days the Philistines mustered for war against Israel,[a] and Israel went out to battle against them;[b] they encamped at Ebenezer, and the Philistines encamped at Aphek. [2] The Philistines drew up in line against Israel, and when the battle was joined,[c] Israel was defeated by the Philistines, who killed about four thousand men on the field of battle. [3] When the troops came to the camp, the elders of Israel said, "Why has the LORD put us to rout today before the Philistines? Let us bring the ark of the covenant of the LORD here from Shiloh, so that he may come among us and save us from the power of our enemies." [4] So the people sent to Shiloh, and brought from there the ark of the covenant of the LORD of hosts, who is enthroned on the cherubim. The two sons of Eli, Hophni and Phinehas, were there with the ark of the covenant of God.

5 When the ark of the covenant of the LORD came into the camp, all Israel gave a mighty shout, so that the earth resounded. [6] When the Philistines heard the noise of the shouting, they said, "What does this great shouting in the camp of the Hebrews mean?" When they learned that the ark of the LORD had come to the camp, [7] the Philistines were afraid; for they said, "Gods have[d] come into the camp." They also said, "Woe to us! For nothing like this has happened before. [8] Woe to us! Who can deliver us from the power of these mighty gods? These are the gods who struck the Egyptians with every sort of plague in the wilderness. [9] Take courage, and be men, O Philistines, in order not to become slaves to the Hebrews as they have been to you; be men and fight."

10 So the Philistines fought; Israel was defeated, and they fled, everyone to his home. There was a very great slaughter, for there fell of Israel thirty thousand foot soldiers. [11] The ark of God was captured; and the two sons of Eli, Hophni and Phinehas, died.

12 A man of Benjamin ran from the battle line, and came to Shiloh the same day, with his clothes torn and with earth upon his head. [13] When he arrived, Eli was sitting upon his seat by the road watching, for his heart trembled for the ark of God. When the man came into the city and told the news, all the city cried out. [14] When Eli heard the sound of the outcry, he said, "What is this uproar?" Then the man came quickly and told Eli. [15] Now Eli was ninety-eight years old and his eyes were set, so that he could not see. [16] The man said to Eli, "I have just come from the battle; I fled from the battle today." He said, "How did it go, my son?" [17] The messenger replied, "Israel has fled before the Philistines, and there has also been a great slaughter among the troops; your two sons also, Hophni and Phinehas, are dead, and the ark of God has been captured." [18] When he mentioned the ark of God, Eli[e] fell over backward from his seat by the side of the gate; and his neck was broken and he died, for he was an old man, and heavy. He had judged Israel forty years.

19 Now his daughter-in-law, the

[a] Gk: Heb lacks *In those days the Philistines mustered for war against Israel*   [b] Gk: Heb *against the Philistines*   [c] Meaning of Heb uncertain   [d] Or *A god has*   [e] Heb *he*

wife of Phinehas, was pregnant, about to give birth. When she heard the news that the ark of God was captured, and that her father-in-law and her husband were dead, she bowed and gave birth; for her labor pains overwhelmed her. [20]As she was about to die, the women attending her said to her, "Do not be afraid, for you have borne a son." But she did not answer or give heed. [21]She named the child Ichabod, meaning, "The glory has departed from Israel," because the ark of God had been captured and because of her father-in-law and her husband. [22]She said, "The glory has departed from Israel, for the ark of God has been captured."

## JOHN 5.25–47

"VERY truly, I tell you, the hour is coming, and is now here, when the dead will hear the voice of the Son of God, and those who hear will live. [26]For just as the Father has life in himself, so he has granted the Son also to have life in himself; [27]and he has given him authority to execute judgment, because he is the Son of Man. [28]Do not be astonished at this; for the hour is coming when all who are in their graves will hear his voice [29]and will come out—those who have done good, to the resurrection of life, and those who have done evil, to the resurrection of condemnation.

30 "I can do nothing on my own. As I hear, I judge; and my judgment is just, because I seek to do not my own will but the will of him who sent me.

31 "If I testify about myself, my testimony is not true. [32]There is another who testifies on my behalf, and I know that his testimony to me is true. [33]You sent messengers to John, and he testified to the truth. [34]Not that I accept such human testimony, but I say these things so that you may be saved. [35]He was a burning and shining lamp, and you were willing to rejoice for a while in his light. [36]But I have a testimony greater than John's. The works that the Father has given me to complete, the very works that I am doing, testify on my behalf that the Father has sent me. [37]And the Father who sent me has himself testified on my behalf. You have never heard his voice or seen his form, [38]and you do not have his word abiding in you, because you do not believe him whom he has sent.

39 "You search the scriptures because you think that in them you have eternal life; and it is they that testify on my behalf. [40]Yet you refuse to come to me to have life. [41]I do not accept glory from human beings. [42]But I know that you do not have the love of God in[a] you. [43]I have come in my Father's name, and you do not accept me; if another comes in his own name, you will accept him. [44]How can you believe when you accept glory from one another and do not seek the glory that comes from the one who alone is God? [45]Do not think that I will accuse you before the Father; your accuser is Moses, on whom you have set your hope. [46]If you believed Moses, you would believe me, for he wrote about me. [47]But if you do not believe what he wrote, how will you believe what I say?"

## PSALM 106.1–12

PRAISE the Lord!
  O give thanks to the Lord,
    for he is good;
  for his steadfast love endures
    forever.
2  Who can utter the mighty
    doings of the Lord,
  or declare all his praise?
3  Happy are those who observe
    justice,
  who do righteousness at all
    times.

a Or *among*

4 Remember me, O Lord, when
    you show favor to your
    people;
  help me when you deliver
    them;
5 that I may see the prosperity of
    your chosen ones,
  that I may rejoice in the
    gladness of your nation,
  that I may glory in your
    heritage.

6 Both we and our ancestors have
    sinned;
  we have committed iniquity,
    have done wickedly.
7 Our ancestors, when they were
    in Egypt,
  did not consider your
    wonderful works;
  they did not remember the
    abundance of your
    steadfast love,
  but rebelled against the Most
    High[a] at the Red Sea. [b]
8 Yet he saved them for his
    name's sake,

  so that he might make known
    his mighty power.
9 He rebuked the Red Sea, [b] and
    it became dry;
  he led them through the deep
    as through a desert.
10 So he saved them from the hand
    of the foe,
  and delivered them from the
    hand of the enemy.
11 The waters covered their
    adversaries;
  not one of them was left.
12 Then they believed his words;
  they sang his praise.

## PROVERBS 14.30–31

A TRANQUIL mind gives life to
    the flesh,
  but passion makes the
    bones rot.
31 Those who oppress the poor
    insult their Maker,
  but those who are kind to the
    needy honor him.

# MAY 9

## 1 SAMUEL 5.1—7.17

WHEN the Philistines captured the ark of God, they brought it from Ebenezer to Ashdod; 2then the Philistines took the ark of God and brought it into the house of Dagon and placed it beside Dagon. 3When the people of Ashdod rose early the next day, there was Dagon, fallen on his face to the ground before the ark of the Lord. So they took Dagon and put him back in his place. 4But when they rose early on the next morning, Dagon had fallen on his face to the ground before the ark of the Lord, and the head of Dagon and both his hands were lying cut off upon the threshold; only the trunk of[c] Dagon was left to him. 5This is why the priests of Dagon and all who enter the house of Dagon do not step on the threshold of Dagon in Ashdod to this day.

6 The hand of the Lord was heavy upon the people of Ashdod, and he ter-

aCn Compare 78.17, 56: Heb *rebelled at the sea*   bOr *Sea of Reeds*   cHeb lacks *the trunk of* rified and struck them with tumors, both in Ashdod and in its territory. [7]And when the inhabitants of Ashdod saw how things were, they said, "The ark of the God of Israel must not remain with us; for his hand is heavy on us and on our god Dagon." [8]So they sent and gathered together all the lords of the Philistines, and said, "What shall we do with the ark of the God of Israel?" The inhabitants of Gath replied, "Let the ark of God be moved on to us."[a] So they moved the ark of the God of Israel to Gath. [b] [9]But after they had brought it to Gath, [c] the hand of the LORD was against the city, causing a very great panic; he struck the inhabitants of the city, both young and old, so that tumors broke out on them. [10]So they sent the ark of the God of Israel[d] to Ekron. But when the ark of God came to Ekron, the people of Ekron cried out, "Why[e] have they brought around to us[f] the ark of the God of Israel to kill us[f] and our[g] people?" [11]They sent therefore and gathered together all the lords of the Philistines, and said, "Send away the ark of the God of Israel, and let it return to its own place, that it may not kill us and our people." For there was a deathly panic[h] throughout the whole city. The hand of God was very heavy there; [12]those who did not die were stricken with tumors, and the cry of the city went up to heaven.

**6.1** THE ark of the LORD was in the country of the Philistines seven months. [2]Then the Philistines called for the priests and the diviners and said, "What shall we do with the ark of the LORD? Tell us what we should send with it to its place." [3]They said, "If you send away the ark of the God of Israel, do not send it empty, but by all means re-turn him a guilt offering. Then you will be healed and will be ransomed; [i] will not his hand then turn from you?" [4]And they said, "What is the guilt offering that we shall return to him?" They answered, "Five gold tumors and five gold mice, according to the number of the lords of the Philistines; for the same plague was upon all of you and upon your lords. [5]So you must make images of your tumors and images of your mice that ravage the land, and give glory to the God of Israel; perhaps he will lighten his hand on you and your gods and your land. [6]Why should you harden your hearts as the Egyptians and Pharaoh hardened their hearts? After he had made fools of them, did they not let the people go, and they de-parted? [7]Now then, get ready a new cart and two milch cows that have never borne a yoke, and yoke the cows to the cart, but take their calves home, away from them. [8]Take the ark of the LORD and place it on the cart, and put in a box at its side the figures of gold, which you are returning to him as a guilt offering. Then send it off, and let it go its way. [9]And watch; if it goes up on the way to its own land, to Beth-shemesh, then it is he who has done us this great harm; but if not, then we shall know that it is not his hand that struck us; it happened to us by chance."

10  The men did so; they took two milch cows and yoked them to the cart, and shut up their calves at home. [11]They put the ark of the LORD on the cart, and the box with the gold mice and the images of their tumors. [12]The cows went straight in the direction of Beth-shemesh along one highway, lowing as they went; they turned neither to the right nor to the left, and the lords of the Philistines went after them as far as the border of Beth-shemesh.

[a]Gk Compare Q Ms: MT *They answered, "Let the ark of the God of Israel be brought around to Gath."* [b]Gk: Heb lacks *to Gath* [c]Q Ms: MT lacks *to Gath* [d]Q Ms Gk: MT lacks *of Israel* [e]Q Ms Gk: MT lacks *Why* [f]Heb *me* [g]Heb *my* [h]Q Ms reads *a panic from the LORD* [i]Q Ms Gk: MT *and it will be known to you*

13 Now the people of Beth-shemesh were reaping their wheat harvest in the valley. When they looked up and saw the ark, they went with rejoicing to meet it. [a] [14]The cart came into the field of Joshua of Beth-shemesh, and stopped there. A large stone was there; so they split up the wood of the cart and offered the cows as a burnt offering to the Lord. [15]The Levites took down the ark of the Lord and the box that was beside it, in which were the gold objects, and set them upon the large stone. Then the people of Beth-shemesh offered burnt offerings and presented sacrifices on that day to the Lord. [16]When the five lords of the Philistines saw it, they returned that day to Ekron.

17 These are the gold tumors, which the Philistines returned as a guilt offering to the Lord: one for Ashdod, one for Gaza, one for Ashkelon, one for Gath, one for Ekron; [18]also the gold mice, according to the number of all the cities of the Philistines belonging to the five lords, both fortified cities and unwalled villages. The great stone, beside which they set down the ark of the Lord, is a witness to this day in the field of Joshua of Beth-shemesh.

19 The descendants of Jeconiah did not rejoice with the people of Beth-shemesh when they greeted[b] the ark of the Lord; and he killed seventy men of them. [c] The people mourned because the Lord had made a great slaughter among the people. [20]Then the people of Beth-shemesh said, "Who is able to stand before the Lord, this holy God? To whom shall he go so that we may be rid of him?" [21]So they sent messengers to the inhabitants of Kiriath-jearim, saying, "The Philistines have returned the ark of the Lord. Come down and take it up to you." [7.1]And the people of Kiriath-jearim came and took up the ark of the Lord, and brought it to the house of Abinadab on the hill. They consecrated his son, Eleazar, to have charge of the ark of the Lord.

2 From the day that the ark was lodged at Kiriath-jearim, a long time passed, some twenty years, and all the house of Israel lamented[d] after the Lord.

3 Then Samuel said to all the house of Israel, "If you are returning to the Lord with all your heart, then put away the foreign gods and the Astartes from among you. Direct your heart to the Lord, and serve him only, and he will deliver you out of the hand of the Philistines." [4]So Israel put away the Baals and the Astartes, and they served the Lord only.

5 Then Samuel said, "Gather all Israel at Mizpah, and I will pray to the Lord for you." [6]So they gathered at Mizpah, and drew water and poured it out before the Lord. They fasted that day, and said, "We have sinned against the Lord." And Samuel judged the people of Israel at Mizpah.

7 When the Philistines heard that the people of Israel had gathered at Mizpah, the lords of the Philistines went up against Israel. And when the people of Israel heard of it they were afraid of the Philistines. [8]The people of Israel said to Samuel, "Do not cease to cry out to the Lord our God for us, and pray that he may save us from the hand of the Philistines." [9]So Samuel took a sucking lamb and offered it as a whole burnt offering to the Lord; Samuel cried out to the Lord for Israel, and the Lord answered him. [10]As Samuel was offering up the burnt offering, the Philistines drew near to attack Israel; but the Lord thundered with a mighty voice that day against the Philistines and threw them into confusion; and they were routed before Israel. [11]And the men of Israel went out of Mizpah and

aGk: Heb *rejoiced to see it*   bGk: Heb *And he killed some of the people of Beth-shemesh, because they looked into*   cHeb *killed seventy men, fifty thousand men*   dMeaning of Heb uncertain

pursued the Philistines, and struck them down as far as beyond Beth-car. 12 Then Samuel took a stone and set it up between Mizpah and Jeshanah,[a] and named it Ebenezer;[b] for he said, "Thus far the Lord has helped us." [13]So the Philistines were subdued and did not again enter the territory of Israel; the hand of the Lord was against the Philistines all the days of Samuel. [14]The towns that the Philistines had taken from Israel were restored to Israel, from Ekron to Gath; and Israel recovered their territory from the hand of the Philistines. There was peace also between Israel and the Amorites.

15 Samuel judged Israel all the days of his life. [16]He went on a circuit year by year to Bethel, Gilgal, and Mizpah; and he judged Israel in all these places. [17]Then he would come back to Ramah, for his home was there; he administered justice there to Israel, and built there an altar to the Lord.

## JOHN 6.1–21

AFTER this Jesus went to the other side of the Sea of Galilee, also called the Sea of Tiberias.[c] [2]A large crowd kept following him, because they saw the signs that he was doing for the sick. [3]Jesus went up the mountain and sat down there with his disciples. [4]Now the Passover, the festival of the Jews, was near. [5]When he looked up and saw a large crowd coming toward him, Jesus said to Philip, "Where are we to buy bread for these people to eat?" [6]He said this to test him, for he himself knew what he was going to do. [7]Philip answered him, "Six months' wages[d] would not buy enough bread for each of them to get a little." [8]One of his disciples, Andrew, Simon Peter's brother, said to him, [9]"There is a boy here who has five barley loaves and two fish. But what are they among so many people?" [10]Jesus said, "Make the people sit down." Now there was a great deal of grass in the place; so they[e] sat down, about five thousand in all. [11]Then Jesus took the loaves, and when he had given thanks, he distributed them to those who were seated; so also the fish, as much as they wanted. [12]When they were satisfied, he told his disciples, "Gather up the fragments left over, so that nothing may be lost." [13]So they gathered them up, and from the fragments of the five barley loaves, left by those who had eaten, they filled twelve baskets. [14]When the people saw the sign that he had done, they began to say, "This is indeed the prophet who is to come into the world."

15 When Jesus realized that they were about to come and take him by force to make him king, he withdrew again to the mountain by himself.

16 When evening came, his disciples went down to the sea, [17]got into a boat, and started across the sea to Capernaum. It was now dark, and Jesus had not yet come to them. [18]The sea became rough because a strong wind was blowing. [19]When they had rowed about three or four miles,[f] they saw Jesus walking on the sea and coming near the boat, and they were terrified. [20]But he said to them, "It is I;[g] do not be afraid." [21]Then they wanted to take him into the boat, and immediately the boat reached the land toward which they were going.

## PSALM 106.13–31

BUT they soon forgot his works;
they did not wait for his counsel.

aGk Syr: Heb *Shen*   bThat is *Stone of Help*   cGk *of Galilee of Tiberius*   dGk *Two hundred denarii*; the denarius was the usual day's wage for a laborer   eGk *the men*   fGk *about twenty-five or thirty stadia*   gGk *I am*

14 But they had a wanton craving
       in the wilderness,
    and put God to the test in the
       desert;
15  he gave them what they asked,
    but sent a wasting disease
       among them.

16  They were jealous of Moses in
       the camp,
    and of Aaron, the holy one of
       the LORD.
17  The earth opened and
       swallowed up Dathan,
    and covered the faction of
       Abiram.
18  Fire also broke out in their
       company;
    the flame burned up the
       wicked.

19  They made a calf at Horeb
    and worshiped a cast image.
20  They exchanged the glory of
       God[a]
    for the image of an ox that
       eats grass.
21  They forgot God, their Savior,
    who had done great things in
       Egypt,
22  wondrous works in the land of
       Ham,
    and awesome deeds by the
       Red Sea.[b]
23  Therefore he said he would
       destroy them—
    had not Moses, his chosen
       one,
    stood in the breach before him,
    to turn away his wrath from
       destroying them.

24  Then they despised the pleasant
       land,

    having no faith in his promise.
25  They grumbled in their tents,
    and did not obey the voice of
       the LORD.
26  Therefore he raised his hand
    and swore to them
    that he would make them fall
       in the wilderness,
27  and would disperse[c] their
       descendants among the
       nations,
    scattering them over the
       lands.

28  Then they attached themselves
       to the Baal of Peor,
    and ate sacrifices offered to
       the dead;
29  they provoked the LORD to
       anger with their deeds,
    and a plague broke out among
       them.
30  Then Phinehas stood up and
       interceded,
    and the plague was stopped.
31  And that has been reckoned to
       him as righteousness
    from generation to generation
       forever.

# PROVERBS 14.32–33

THE wicked are overthrown by
       their evildoing,
    but the righteous find a
       refuge in their
       integrity.[d]
33  Wisdom is at home in the mind
       of one who has
       understanding,
    but it is not[e] known in the
       heart of fools.

# MAY 10

1 SAMUEL 8.1—9.27

WHEN Samuel became old, he made his sons judges over Israel. ²The name of his first-born son was Joel, and the name of his second, Abijah; they were judges in Beer-sheba. ³Yet his sons did not follow in his ways, but turned aside after gain; they took bribes and perverted justice.

4 Then all the elders of Israel gathered together and came to Samuel at Ramah, ⁵and said to him, "You are old and your sons do not follow in your ways; appoint for us, then, a king to govern us, like other nations." ⁶But the thing displeased Samuel when they said, "Give us a king to govern us." Samuel prayed to the LORD, ⁷and the LORD said to Samuel, "Listen to the voice of the people in all that they say to you; for they have not rejected you, but they have rejected me from being king over them. ⁸Just as they have done to me,ᵃ from the day I brought them up out of Egypt to this day, forsaking me and serving other gods, so also they are doing to you. ⁹Now then, listen to their voice; only—you shall solemnly warn them, and show them the ways of the king who shall reign over them."

10 So Samuel reported all the words of the LORD to the people who were asking him for a king. ¹¹He said, "These will be the ways of the king who will reign over you: he will take your sons and appoint them to his chariots and to be his horsemen, and to run before his chariots; ¹²and he will appoint for himself commanders of thousands and commanders of fifties, and some to plow his ground and to reap his harvest, and to make his implements of war and the equipment of his chariots. ¹³He will take your daughters to be perfumers and cooks and bakers. ¹⁴He will take the best of your fields and vineyards and olive orchards and give them to his courtiers. ¹⁵He will take one-tenth of your grain and of your vineyards and give it to his officers and his courtiers. ¹⁶He will take your male and female slaves, and the best of your cattleᵇ and donkeys, and put them to his work. ¹⁷He will take one-tenth of your flocks, and you shall be his slaves. ¹⁸And in that day you will cry out because of your king, whom you have chosen for yourselves; but the LORD will not answer you in that day."

19 But the people refused to listen to the voice of Samuel; they said, "No! but we are determined to have a king over us, ²⁰so that we also may be like other nations, and that our king may govern us and go out before us and fight our battles." ²¹When Samuel had heard all the words of the people, he repeated them in the ears of the LORD. ²²The LORD said to Samuel, "Listen to their voice and set a king over them." Samuel then said to the people of Israel, "Each of you return home."

⁹·¹ THERE was a man of Benjamin whose name was Kish son of Abiel son of Zeror son of Becorath son of Aphiah, a Benjaminite, a man of wealth. ²He had a son whose name was Saul, a handsome young man. There was not a man among the people of Israel more handsome than he; he stood head and shoulders above everyone else.

3 Now the donkeys of Kish, Saul's father, had strayed. So Kish said to his

ᵃGk: Heb lacks *to me*  ᵇGk: Heb *young men*

son Saul, "Take one of the boys with you; go and look for the donkeys." ⁴He passed through the hill country of Ephraim and passed through the land of Shalishah, but they did not find them. And they passed through the land of Shaalim, but they were not there. Then he passed through the land of Benjamin, but they did not find them.

5 When they came to the land of Zuph, Saul said to the boy who was with him, "Let us turn back, or my father will stop worrying about the donkeys and worry about us." ⁶But he said to him, "There is a man of God in this town; he is a man held in honor. Whatever he says always comes true. Let us go there now; perhaps he will tell us about the journey on which we have set out." ⁷Then Saul replied to the boy, "But if we go, what can we bring the man? For the bread in our sacks is gone, and there is no present to bring to the man of God. What have we?" ⁸The boy answered Saul again, "Here, I have with me a quarter shekel of silver; I will give it to the man of God, to tell us our way." ⁹(Formerly in Israel, anyone who went to inquire of God would say, "Come, let us go to the seer"; for the one who is now called a prophet was formerly called a seer.) ¹⁰Saul said to the boy, "Good; come, let us go." So they went to the town where the man of God was.

11 As they went up the hill to the town, they met some girls coming out to draw water, and said to them, "Is the seer here?" ¹²They answered, "Yes, there he is just ahead of you. Hurry; he has come just now to the town, because the people have a sacrifice today at the shrine. ¹³As soon as you enter the town, you will find him, before he goes up to the shrine to eat. For the people will not eat until he comes, since he must bless the sacrifice; afterward those eat who are invited. Now go up,

for you will meet him immediately." ¹⁴So they went up to the town. As they were entering the town, they saw Samuel coming out toward them on his way up to the shrine.

15 Now the day before Saul came, the Lord had revealed to Samuel: ¹⁶"Tomorrow about this time I will send to you a man from the land of Benjamin, and you shall anoint him to be ruler over my people Israel. He shall save my people from the hand of the Philistines; for I have seen the suffering of[a] my people, because their outcry has come to me." ¹⁷When Samuel saw Saul, the Lord told him, "Here is the man of whom I spoke to you. He it is who shall rule over my people." ¹⁸Then Saul approached Samuel inside the gate, and said, "Tell me, please, where is the house of the seer?" ¹⁹Samuel answered Saul, "I am the seer; go up before me to the shrine, for today you shall eat with me, and in the morning I will let you go and will tell you all that is on your mind. ²⁰As for your donkeys that were lost three days ago, give no further thought to them, for they have been found. And on whom is all Israel's desire fixed, if not on you and on all your ancestral house?" ²¹Saul answered, "I am only a Benjaminite, from the least of the tribes of Israel, and my family is the humblest of all the families of the tribe of Benjamin. Why then have you spoken to me in this way?"

22 Then Samuel took Saul and his servant-boy and brought them into the hall, and gave them a place at the head of those who had been invited, of whom there were about thirty. ²³And Samuel said to the cook, "Bring the portion I gave you, the one I asked you to put aside." ²⁴The cook took up the thigh and what went with it[b] and set them before Saul. Samuel said, "See, what was kept is set before you. Eat; for it is set[c] before you at the appointed

[a]Gk: Heb lacks *the suffering of*   [b]Meaning of Heb uncertain   [c]Q Ms Gk: MT *it was kept*

time, so that you might eat with the guests."[a]

So Saul ate with Samuel that day. [25]When they came down from the shrine into the town, a bed was spread for Saul[b] on the roof, and he lay down to sleep.[c] [26]Then at the break of dawn[d] Samuel called to Saul upon the roof, "Get up, so that I may send you on your way." Saul got up, and both he and Samuel went out into the street.

27 As they were going down to the outskirts of the town, Samuel said to Saul, "Tell the boy to go on before us, and when he has passed on, stop here yourself for a while, that I may make known to you the word of God."

## JOHN 6.22–40

THE next day the crowd that had stayed on the other side of the sea saw that there had been only one boat there. They also saw that Jesus had not got into the boat with his disciples, but that his disciples had gone away alone. [23]Then some boats from Tiberias came near the place where they had eaten the bread after the Lord had given thanks.[e] [24]So when the crowd saw that neither Jesus nor his disciples were there, they themselves got into the boats and went to Capernaum looking for Jesus.

25 When they found him on the other side of the sea, they said to him, "Rabbi, when did you come here?" [26]Jesus answered them, "Very truly, I tell you, you are looking for me, not because you saw signs, but because you ate your fill of the loaves. [27]Do not work for the food that perishes, but for the food that endures for eternal life, which the Son of Man will give you. For it is on him that God the Father has set his seal." [28]Then they said to him, "What must we do to perform the works of God?" [29]Jesus answered them, "This is the work of God, that you believe in him whom he has sent." [30]So they said to him, "What sign are you going to give us then, so that we may see it and believe you? What work are you performing? [31]Our ancestors ate the manna in the wilderness; as it is written, 'He gave them bread from heaven to eat.'" [32]Then Jesus said to them, "Very truly, I tell you, it was not Moses who gave you the bread from heaven, but it is my Father who gives you the true bread from heaven. [33]For the bread of God is that which[f] comes down from heaven and gives life to the world." [34]They said to him, "Sir, give us this bread always."

35 Jesus said to them, "I am the bread of life. Whoever comes to me will never be hungry, and whoever believes in me will never be thirsty. [36]But I said to you that you have seen me and yet do not believe. [37]Everything that the Father gives me will come to me, and anyone who comes to me I will never drive away; [38]for I have come down from heaven, not to do my own will, but the will of him who sent me. [39]And this is the will of him who sent me, that I should lose nothing of all that he has given me, but raise it up on the last day. [40]This is indeed the will of my Father, that all who see the Son and believe in him may have eternal life; and I will raise them up on the last day."

## PSALM 106.32–48

THEY angered the LORD[g] at the
    waters of Meribah,
and it went ill with Moses on
    their account;
[33]  for they made his spirit bitter,
    and he spoke words that
      were rash.

[a]Cn: Heb *it was kept for you, saying, I have invited the people*  [b]Gk: Heb *and he spoke with Saul*
[c]Gk: Heb lacks *and he lay down to sleep*  [d]Gk: Heb *and they arose early and at break of dawn*
[e]Other ancient authorities lack *after the Lord had given thanks*  [f]Or *he who*  [g]Heb *him*

34 They did not destroy the
    peoples,
    as the Lord commanded
    them,
35 but they mingled with the
    nations
    and learned to do as they did.
36 They served their idols,
    which became a snare to
    them.
37 They sacrificed their sons
    and their daughters to the
    demons;
38 they poured out innocent blood,
    the blood of their sons and
    daughters,
whom they sacrificed to the
    idols of Canaan;
    and the land was polluted with
    blood.
39 Thus they became unclean by
    their acts,
    and prostituted themselves in
    their doings.

40 Then the anger of the Lord was
    kindled against his
    people,
    and he abhorred his heritage;
41 he gave them into the hand of
    the nations,
    so that those who hated them
    ruled over them.
42 Their enemies oppressed them,
    and they were brought into
    subjection under their
    power.
43 Many times he delivered them,

but they were rebellious in
    their purposes,
    and were brought low through
    their iniquity.
44 Nevertheless he regarded their
    distress
    when he heard their cry.
45 For their sake he remembered
    his covenant,
    and showed compassion
    according to the
    abundance of his
    steadfast love.
46 He caused them to be pitied
    by all who held them captive.

47 Save us, O Lord our God,
    and gather us from among the
    nations,
that we may give thanks to your
    holy name
    and glory in your praise.

48 Blessed be the Lord, the God
    of Israel,
    from everlasting to
    everlasting.
And let all the people say,
    "Amen."
Praise the Lord!

# PROVERBS 14.34–35

RIGHTEOUSNESS exalts a nation,
    but sin is a reproach to any
    people.
35 A servant who deals wisely has
    the king's favor,
    but his wrath falls on one who
    acts shamefully.

# MAY 11

## 1 SAMUEL 10.1—11.15

SAMUEL took a vial of oil and poured it on his [Saul's] head, and kissed him; he said, "The LORD has anointed you ruler over his people Israel. You shall reign over the people of the LORD and you will save them from the hand of their enemies all around. Now this shall be the sign to you that the LORD has anointed you ruler[a] over his heritage: [2]When you depart from me today you will meet two men by Rachel's tomb in the territory of Benjamin at Zelzah; they will say to you, 'The donkeys that you went to seek are found, and now your father has stopped worrying about them and is worrying about you, saying: What shall I do about my son?' [3]Then you shall go on from there further and come to the oak of Tabor; three men going up to God at Bethel will meet you there, one carrying three kids, another carrying three loaves of bread, and another carrying a skin of wine. [4]They will greet you and give you two loaves of bread, which you shall accept from them. [5]After that you shall come to Gibeath-elohim,[b] at the place where the Philistine garrison is; there, as you come to the town, you will meet a band of prophets coming down from the shrine with harp, tambourine, flute, and lyre playing in front of them; they will be in a prophetic frenzy. [6]Then the spirit of the LORD will possess you, and you will be in a prophetic frenzy along with them and be turned into a different person. [7]Now when these signs meet you, do whatever you see fit to do, for God is with you. [8]And you shall go down to Gilgal ahead of me; then I will come down to you to present burnt offerings and offer sacrifices of well-being. Seven days you shall wait, until I come to you and show you what you shall do."

9  As he turned away to leave Samuel, God gave him another heart; and all these signs were fulfilled that day. [10]When they were going from there[c] to Gibeah,[d] a band of prophets met him; and the spirit of God possessed him, and he fell into a prophetic frenzy along with them. [11]When all who knew him before saw how he prophesied with the prophets, the people said to one another, "What has come over the son of Kish? Is Saul also among the prophets?" [12]A man of the place answered, "And who is their father?" Therefore it became a proverb, "Is Saul also among the prophets?" [13]When his prophetic frenzy had ended, he went home. [e]

14  Saul's uncle said to him and to the boy, "Where did you go?" And he replied, "To seek the donkeys; and when we saw they were not to be found, we went to Samuel." [15]Saul's uncle said, "Tell me what Samuel said to you." [16]Saul said to his uncle, "He told us that the donkeys had been found." But about the matter of the kingship, of which Samuel had spoken, he did not tell him anything.

17  Samuel summoned the people to the LORD at Mizpah [18]and said to them,[f] "Thus says the LORD, the God of Israel, 'I brought up Israel out of Egypt, and I rescued you from the hand of the Egyptians and from the hand of all the kingdoms that were oppressing you.' [19]But today you have rejected your God, who saves you from all your calamities and your distresses; and you

a Gk: Heb lacks *over his people Israel. You shall . . . anointed you ruler*   b Or *the Hill of God*
c Gk: Heb *they came there*   d Or *the hill*   e Cn: Heb *he came to the shrine*   f Heb *to the people of Israel*

have said, 'No! but set a king over us.' Now therefore present yourselves before the LORD by your tribes and by your clans."

20 Then Samuel brought all the tribes of Israel near, and the tribe of Benjamin was taken by lot. [21] He brought the tribe of Benjamin near by its families, and the family of the Matrites was taken by lot. Finally he brought the family of the Matrites near man by man, [a] and Saul the son of Kish was taken by lot. But when they sought him, he could not be found. [22] So they inquired again of the LORD, "Did the man come here?" [b] and the LORD said, "See, he has hidden himself among the baggage." [23] Then they ran and brought him from there. When he took his stand among the people, he was head and shoulders taller than any of them. [24] Samuel said to all the people, "Do you see the one whom the LORD has chosen? There is no one like him among all the people." And all the people shouted, "Long live the king!"

25 Samuel told the people the rights and duties of the kingship; and he wrote them in a book and laid it up before the LORD. Then Samuel sent all the people back to their homes. [26] Saul also went to his home at Gibeah, and with him went warriors whose hearts God had touched. [27] But some worthless fellows said, "How can this man save us?" They despised him and brought him no present. But he held his peace.

Now Nahash, king of the Ammonites, had been grievously oppressing the Gadites and the Reubenites. He would gouge out the right eye of each of them and would not grant Israel a deliverer. No one was left of the Israelites across the Jordan whose right eye Nahash, king of the Ammonites, had not gouged out. But there were seven thousand men who had escaped from the Ammonites and had entered Jabesh-gilead. [c]

[11.1] ABOUT a month later, [d] Nahash the Ammonite went up and besieged Jabesh-gilead; and all the men of Jabesh said to Nahash, "Make a treaty with us, and we will serve you." [2] But Nahash the Ammonite said to them, "On this condition I will make a treaty with you, namely that I gouge out everyone's right eye, and thus put disgrace upon all Israel." [3] The elders of Jabesh said to him, "Give us seven days' respite that we may send messengers through all the territory of Israel. Then, if there is no one to save us, we will give ourselves up to you." [4] When the messengers came to Gibeah of Saul, they reported the matter in the hearing of the people; and all the people wept aloud.

5 Now Saul was coming from the field behind the oxen; and Saul said, "What is the matter with the people, that they are weeping?" So they told him the message from the inhabitants of Jabesh. [6] And the spirit of God came upon Saul in power when he heard these words, and his anger was greatly kindled. [7] He took a yoke of oxen, and cut them in pieces and sent them throughout all the territory of Israel by messengers, saying, "Whoever does not come out after Saul and Samuel, so shall it be done to his oxen!" Then the dread of the LORD fell upon the people, and they came out as one. [8] When he mustered them at Bezek, those from Israel were three hundred thousand, and those from Judah seventy [e] thousand. [9] They said to the messengers who had come, "Thus shall you say to the inhabitants of Jabesh-gilead: 'Tomorrow, by the time the sun is hot, you shall have deliverance.'" When the messengers came and told the inhabi-

---

a Gk: Heb lacks *Finally . . . man by man*   b Gk: Heb *Is there yet a man to come here?*   c Q Ms
Compare Josephus, *Antiquities* VI. v. 1 (68-71): MT lacks *Now Nahash . . . entered Jabesh-gilead.*
d Q Ms Gk: MT lacks *About a month later*   e Q Ms Gk: MT *thirty*

tants of Jabesh, they rejoiced. ¹⁰So the inhabitants of Jabesh said, "Tomorrow we will give ourselves up to you, and you may do to us whatever seems good to you." ¹¹The next day Saul put the people in three companies. At the morning watch they came into the camp and cut down the Ammonites until the heat of the day; and those who survived were scattered, so that no two of them were left together.

12 The people said to Samuel, "Who is it that said, 'Shall Saul reign over us?' Give them to us so that we may put them to death." ¹³But Saul said, "No one shall be put to death this day, for today the LORD has brought deliverance to Israel."

14 Samuel said to the people, "Come, let us go to Gilgal and there renew the kingship." ¹⁵So all the people went to Gilgal, and there they made Saul king before the LORD in Gilgal. There they sacrificed offerings of well-being before the LORD, and there Saul and all the Israelites rejoiced greatly.

## JOHN 6.41–71

THEN the Jews began to complain about him because he said, "I am the bread that came down from heaven." ⁴²They were saying, "Is not this Jesus, the son of Joseph, whose father and mother we know? How can he now say, 'I have come down from heaven'?" ⁴³Jesus answered them, "Do not complain among yourselves. ⁴⁴No one can come to me unless drawn by the Father who sent me; and I will raise that person up on the last day. ⁴⁵It is written in the prophets, 'And they shall all be taught by God.' Everyone who has heard and learned from the Father comes to me. ⁴⁶Not that anyone has seen the Father except the one who is from God; he has seen the Father. ⁴⁷Very truly, I tell you, whoever believes has eternal life. ⁴⁸I am the bread of life. ⁴⁹Your ancestors ate the manna in the wilderness, and they died. ⁵⁰This is the bread that comes down from heaven, so that one may eat of it and not die. ⁵¹I am the living bread that came down from heaven. Whoever eats of this bread will live forever; and the bread that I will give for the life of the world is my flesh."

52 The Jews then disputed among themselves, saying, "How can this man give us his flesh to eat?" ⁵³So Jesus said to them, "Very truly, I tell you, unless you eat the flesh of the Son of Man and drink his blood, you have no life in you. ⁵⁴Those who eat my flesh and drink my blood have eternal life, and I will raise them up on the last day; ⁵⁵for my flesh is true food and my blood is true drink. ⁵⁶Those who eat my flesh and drink my blood abide in me, and I in them. ⁵⁷Just as the living Father sent me, and I live because of the Father, so whoever eats me will live because of me. ⁵⁸This is the bread that came down from heaven, not like that which your ancestors ate, and they died. But the one who eats this bread will live forever." ⁵⁹He said these things while he was teaching in the synagogue at Capernaum.

60 When many of his disciples heard it, they said, "This teaching is difficult; who can accept it?" ⁶¹But Jesus, being aware that his disciples were complaining about it, said to them, "Does this offend you? ⁶²Then what if you were to see the Son of Man ascending to where he was before? ⁶³It is the spirit that gives life; the flesh is useless. The words that I have spoken to you are spirit and life. ⁶⁴But among you there are some who do not believe." For Jesus knew from the first who were the ones that did not believe, and who was the one that would betray him. ⁶⁵And he said, "For this reason I have told you that no one can come to me unless it is granted by the Father."

66 Because of this many of his disciples turned back and no longer went

about with him. ⁶⁷So Jesus asked the twelve, "Do you also wish to go away?" ⁶⁸Simon Peter answered him, "Lord, to whom can we go? You have the words of eternal life. ⁶⁹We have come to believe and know that you are the Holy One of God."ᵃ ⁷⁰Jesus answered them, "Did I not choose you, the twelve? Yet one of you is a devil." ⁷¹He was speaking of Judas son of Simon Iscariot,ᵇ for he, though one of the twelve, was going to betray him.

## PSALM 107.1–43

O GIVE thanks to the LORD, for
  he is good;
  for his steadfast love
    endures forever.
2 Let the redeemed of the LORD
    say so,
  those he redeemed from
    trouble
3 and gathered in from the lands,
  from the east and from the
    west,
  from the north and from the
    south. ᶜ

4 Some wandered in desert
    wastes,
  finding no way to an inhabited
    town;
5 hungry and thirsty,
  their soul fainted within them.
6 Then they cried to the LORD in
    their trouble,
  and he delivered them from
    their distress;
7 he led them by a straight way,
  until they reached an
    inhabited town.
8 Let them thank the LORD for his
    steadfast love,
  for his wonderful works to
    humankind.

9 For he satisfies the thirsty,
  and the hungry he fills with
    good things.

10 Some sat in darkness and in
    gloom,
  prisoners in misery and in
    irons,
11 for they had rebelled against the
    words of God,
  and spurned the counsel of
    the Most High.
12 Their hearts were bowed down
    with hard labor;
  they fell down, with no one
    to help.
13 Then they cried to the LORD in
    their trouble,
  and he saved them from their
    distress;
14 he brought them out of
    darkness and gloom,
  and broke their bonds
    asunder.
15 Let them thank the LORD for his
    steadfast love,
  for his wonderful works to
    humankind.
16 For he shatters the doors of
    bronze,
  and cuts in two the bars of
    iron.

17 Some were sickᵈ through their
    sinful ways,
  and because of their iniquities
    endured affliction;
18 they loathed any kind of food,
  and they drew near to the
    gates of death.
19 Then they cried to the LORD in
    their trouble,
  and he saved them from their
    distress;
20 he sent out his word and healed
    them,

ᵃOther ancient authorities read *the Christ, the Son of the living God*  ᵇOther ancient authorities read *Judas Iscariot son of Simon;* others, *Judas son of Simon from Karyot* (Kerioth)  ᶜCn: Heb *sea*  ᵈCn: Heb *fools*

and delivered them from
    destruction.
21 Let them thank the LORD for his
    steadfast love,
    for his wonderful works to
       humankind.
22 And let them offer thanksgiving
    sacrifices,
    and tell of his deeds with
       songs of joy.

23 Some went down to the sea
    in ships,
    doing business on the mighty
       waters;
24 they saw the deeds of the LORD,
    his wondrous works in the
       deep.
25 For he commanded and raised
    the stormy wind,
    which lifted up the waves of
       the sea.
26 They mounted up to heaven,
    they went down to the
       depths;
    their courage melted away in
       their calamity;
27 they reeled and staggered like
    drunkards,
    and were at their wits' end.
28 Then they cried to the LORD in
    their trouble,
    and he brought them out from
       their distress;
29 he made the storm be still,
    and the waves of the sea
       were hushed.
30 Then they were glad because
    they had quiet,
    and he brought them to their
       desired haven.
31 Let them thank the LORD for his
    steadfast love,
    for his wonderful works to
       humankind.
32 Let them extol him in the
    congregation of the
       people,
    and praise him in the
       assembly of the elders.

33 He turns rivers into a desert,
    springs of water into thirsty
       ground,
34 a fruitful land into a salty waste,
    because of the wickedness of
       its inhabitants.
35 He turns a desert into pools of
    water,
    a parched land into springs of
       water.
36 And there he lets the hungry
    live,
    and they establish a town to
       live in;
37 they sow fields, and plant
    vineyards,
    and get a fruitful yield.
38 By his blessing they multiply
    greatly,
    and he does not let their
       cattle decrease.

39 When they are diminished and
    brought low
    through oppression, trouble,
       and sorrow,
40 he pours contempt on princes
    and makes them wander in
       trackless wastes;
41 but he raises up the needy out
    of distress,
    and makes their families like
       flocks.
42 The upright see it and are glad;
    and all wickedness stops its
       mouth.
43 Let those who are wise give
    heed to these things,
    and consider the steadfast
       love of the LORD.

## PROVERBS 15.1–3

A SOFT answer turns away
    wrath,
but a harsh word stirs up
    anger.

2 The tongue of the wise
    dispenses knowledge, [a]
  but the mouths of fools pour
    out folly.

3 The eyes of the Lord are in
    every place,
  keeping watch on the evil and
    the good.

# MAY 12

## 1 SAMUEL 12.1—13.22

Samuel said to all Israel, "I have listened to you in all that you have said to me, and have set a king over you. 2See, it is the king who leads you now; I am old and gray, but my sons are with you. I have led you from my youth until this day. 3Here I am; testify against me before the Lord and before his anointed. Whose ox have I taken? Or whose donkey have I taken? Or whom have I defrauded? Whom have I oppressed? Or from whose hand have I taken a bribe to blind my eyes with it? Testify against me[b] and I will restore it to you." 4They said, "You have not defrauded us or oppressed us or taken anything from the hand of anyone." 5He said to them, "The Lord is witness against you, and his anointed is witness this day, that you have not found anything in my hand." And they said, "He is witness."

6 Samuel said to the people, "The Lord is witness, who[c] appointed Moses and Aaron and brought your ancestors up out of the land of Egypt. 7Now therefore take your stand, so that I may enter into judgment with you before the Lord, and I will declare to you[d] all the saving deeds of the Lord that he performed for you and for your ancestors. 8When Jacob went into Egypt and the Egyptians oppressed them, [e] then your ancestors cried to the Lord and the Lord sent Moses and Aaron, who brought forth your ancestors out of Egypt, and settled them in this place. 9But they forgot the Lord their God; and he sold them into the hand of Sisera, commander of the army of King Jabin of[f] Hazor, and into the hand of the Philistines, and into the hand of the king of Moab; and they fought against them. 10Then they cried to the Lord, and said, 'We have sinned, because we have forsaken the Lord, and have served the Baals and the Astartes; but now rescue us out of the hand of our enemies, and we will serve you.' 11And the Lord sent Jerubbaal and Barak, [g] and Jephthah, and Samson, [h] and rescued you out of the hand of your enemies on every side; and you lived in safety. 12But when you saw that King Nahash of the Ammonites came against you, you said to me, 'No, but a king shall reign over us,' though the Lord your God was your king. 13See, here is the king whom you have chosen, for whom you have asked; see, the Lord has set a king over you. 14If you will fear the Lord and serve him and heed his voice and not rebel against the commandment of the Lord, and if both you and the king who reigns over you will follow the Lord your God, it will be well; 15but if you will not heed the voice

a Cn: Heb *makes knowledge good*  b Gk: Heb lacks *Testify against me*  c Gk: Heb lacks *is witness, who*
d Gk: Heb lacks *and I will declare to you*  e Gk: Heb lacks *and the Egyptians oppressed them*
f Gk: Heb lacks *Jabin king of*  g Gk Syr: Heb *Bedan*  h Gk: Heb *Samuel*

of the Lord, but rebel against the commandment of the Lord, then the hand of the Lord will be against you and your king. a 16Now therefore take your stand and see this great thing that the Lord will do before your eyes. 17Is it not the wheat harvest today? I will call upon the Lord, that he may send thunder and rain; and you shall know and see that the wickedness that you have done in the sight of the Lord is great in demanding a king for yourselves." 18So Samuel called upon the Lord, and the Lord sent thunder and rain that day; and all the people greatly feared the Lord and Samuel.

19 All the people said to Samuel, "Pray to the Lord your God for your servants, so that we may not die; for we have added to all our sins the evil of demanding a king for ourselves." 20And Samuel said to the people, "Do not be afraid; you have done all this evil, yet do not turn aside from following the Lord, but serve the Lord with all your heart; 21and do not turn aside after useless things that cannot profit or save, for they are useless. 22For the Lord will not cast away his people, for his great name's sake, because it has pleased the Lord to make you a people for himself. 23Moreover as for me, far be it from me that I should sin against the Lord by ceasing to pray for you; and I will instruct you in the good and the right way. 24Only fear the Lord, and serve him faithfully with all your heart; for consider what great things he has done for you. 25But if you still do wickedly, you shall be swept away, both you and your king."

13.1 Saul was . . . b years old when he began to reign; and he reigned . . . and twoc years over Israel.

2 Saul chose three thousand out of Israel; two thousand were with Saul in Michmash and the hill country of Bethel, and a thousand were with Jonathan in Gibeah of Benjamin; the rest of the people he sent home to their tents. 3Jonathan defeated the garrison of the Philistines that was at Geba; and the Philistines heard of it. And Saul blew the trumpet throughout all the land, saying, "Let the Hebrews hear!" 4When all Israel heard that Saul had defeated the garrison of the Philistines, and also that Israel had become odious to the Philistines, the people were called out to join Saul at Gilgal.

5 The Philistines mustered to fight with Israel, thirty thousand chariots, and six thousand horsemen, and troops like the sand on the seashore in multitude; they came up and encamped at Michmash, to the east of Beth-aven. 6When the Israelites saw that they were in distress (for the troops were hard pressed), the people hid themselves in caves and in holes and in rocks and in tombs and in cisterns. 7Some Hebrews crossed the Jordan to the land of Gad and Gilead. Saul was still at Gilgal, and all the people followed him trembling.

8 He waited seven days, the time appointed by Samuel; but Samuel did not come to Gilgal, and the people began to slip away from Saul. d 9So Saul said, "Bring the burnt offering here to me, and the offerings of well-being." And he offered the burnt offering. 10As soon as he had finished offering the burnt offering, Samuel arrived; and Saul went out to meet him and salute him. 11Samuel said, "What have you done?" Saul replied, "When I saw that the people were slipping away from me, and that you did not come within the days appointed, and that the Philistines were mustering at Michmash, 12I said, 'Now the Philistines will come down upon me at Gilgal, and I have not entreated the favor of the Lord'; so I forced myself, and offered the burnt of-

aGk: Heb *and your ancestors*  bThe number is lacking in the Heb text (the verse is lacking in the Septuagint).  c*Two* is not the entire number; something has dropped out.  dHeb *him*

fering." [13]Samuel said to Saul, "You have done foolishly; you have not kept the commandment of the LORD your God, which he commanded you. The LORD would have established your kingdom over Israel forever, [14]but now your kingdom will not continue; the LORD has sought out a man after his own heart; and the LORD has appointed him to be ruler over his people, because you have not kept what the LORD commanded you." [15]And Samuel left and went on his way from Gilgal. [a] The rest of the people followed Saul to join the army; they went up from Gilgal toward Gibeah of Benjamin. [b]

Saul counted the people who were present with him, about six hundred men. [16]Saul, his son Jonathan, and the people who were present with them stayed in Geba of Benjamin; but the Philistines encamped at Michmash. [17]And raiders came out of the camp of the Philistines in three companies; one company turned toward Ophrah, to the land of Shual, [18]another company turned toward Beth-horon, and another company turned toward the mountain[c] that looks down upon the valley of Zeboim toward the wilderness.

19 Now there was no smith to be found throughout all the land of Israel; for the Philistines said, "The Hebrews must not make swords or spears for themselves"; [20]so all the Israelites went down to the Philistines to sharpen their plowshare, mattocks, axes, or sickles; [d] [21]The charge was two-thirds of a shekel[e] for the plowshares and for the mattocks, and one-third of a shekel for sharpening the axes and for setting the goads. [f] [22]So on the day of the battle neither sword nor spear was to be found in the possession of any of the people with Saul and Jonathan; but Saul and his son Jonathan had them.

## JOHN 7.1–29

AFTER this Jesus went about in Galilee. He did not wish[g] to go about in Judea because the Jews were looking for an opportunity to kill him. [2]Now the Jewish festival of Booths[h] was near. [3]So his brothers said to him, "Leave here and go to Judea so that your disciples also may see the works you are doing; [4]for no one who wants[i] to be widely known acts in secret. If you do these things, show yourself to the world." [5](For not even his brothers believed in him.) [6]Jesus said to them, "My time has not yet come, but your time is always here. [7]The world cannot hate you, but it hates me because I testify against it that its works are evil. [8]Go to the festival yourselves. I am not[j] going to this festival, for my time has not yet fully come." [9]After saying this, he remained in Galilee.

10 But after his brothers had gone to the festival, then he also went, not publicly but as it were[k] in secret. [11]The Jews were looking for him at the festival and saying, "Where is he?" [12]And there was considerable complaining about him among the crowds. While some were saying, "He is a good man," others were saying, "No, he is deceiving the crowd." [13]Yet no one would speak openly about him for fear of the Jews.

14 About the middle of the festival Jesus went up into the temple and began to teach. [15]The Jews were astonished at it, saying, "How does this man have such learning,[l] when he has

aGk: Heb *went up from Gilgal to Gibeah of Benjamin*   bGk: Heb lacks *The rest . . . of Benjamin*   cCn Compare Gk: Heb *toward the border*   dGk: Heb *plowshare*   eHeb *was a pim*   fCn: Meaning of Heb uncertain   gOther ancient authorities read *was not at liberty*   hOr *Tabernacles*   iOther ancient authorities read *wants it*   jOther ancient authorities add *yet*   kOther ancient authorities lack *as it were*   lOr *this man know his letters*

never been taught?" [16]Then Jesus answered them, "My teaching is not mine but his who sent me. [17]Anyone who resolves to do the will of God will know whether the teaching is from God or whether I am speaking on my own. [18]Those who speak on their own seek their own glory; but the one who seeks the glory of him who sent him is true, and there is nothing false in him.

19 "Did not Moses give you the law? Yet none of you keeps the law. Why are you looking for an opportunity to kill me?" [20]The crowd answered, "You have a demon! Who is trying to kill you?" [21]Jesus answered them, "I performed one work, and all of you are astonished. [22]Moses gave you circumcision (it is, of course, not from Moses, but from the patriarchs), and you circumcise a man on the sabbath. [23]If a man receives circumcision on the sabbath in order that the law of Moses may not be broken, are you angry with me because I healed a man's whole body on the sabbath? [24]Do not judge by appearances, but judge with right judgment."

25 Now some of the people of Jerusalem were saying, "Is not this the man whom they are trying to kill? [26]And here he is, speaking openly, but they say nothing to him! Can it be that the authorities really know that this is the Messiah?[a] [27]Yet we know where this man is from; but when the Messiah[a] comes, no one will know where he is from." [28]Then Jesus cried out as he was teaching in the temple, "You know me, and you know where I am from. I have not come on my own. But the one who sent me is true, and you do not know him. [29]I know him, because I am from him, and he sent me."

## PSALM 108.1–13

*A Song. A Psalm of David.*

My heart is steadfast, O God,
   my heart is
      steadfast;[b]
  I will sing and make melody.
  Awake, my soul![c]
2  Awake, O harp and lyre!
  I will awake the dawn.
3  I will give thanks to you,
    O Lord, among the
     peoples,
  and I will sing praises to you
    among the nations.
4  For your steadfast love is higher
    than the heavens,
  and your faithfulness reaches
    to the clouds.

5  Be exalted, O God, above the
    heavens,
  and let your glory be over all
    the earth.
6  Give victory with your right
    hand, and answer me,
  so that those whom you love
    may be rescued.

7  God has promised in his
    sanctuary:[d]
  "With exultation I will divide
    up Shechem,
  and portion out the Vale of
    Succoth.
8  Gilead is mine; Manasseh is
    mine;
  Ephraim is my helmet;
  Judah is my scepter.
9  Moab is my washbasin;
  on Edom I hurl my shoe;
  over Philistia I shout in
    triumph."

10  Who will bring me to the
    fortified city?
  Who will lead me to Edom?

---

aOr *the Christ*  bHeb Mss Gk Syr: MT lacks *my heart is steadfast*  cCompare 57.8: Heb *also my soul*  dOr *by his holiness*

11   Have you not rejected us,
         O God?
     You do not go out, O God,
         with our armies.
12   O grant us help against the foe,
         for human help is worthless.
13   With God we shall do valiantly;
         it is he who will tread down
             our foes.

## PROVERBS 15.4

A GENTLE tongue is a tree of
life,
but perverseness in it
breaks the spirit.

# MAY 13

## 1 SAMUEL 13.23—14.52

Now a garrison of the Philistines had gone out to the pass of Michmash. 14.1 One day Jonathan son of Saul said to the young man who carried his armor, "Come, let us go over to the Philistine garrison on the other side." But he did not tell his father. 2 Saul was staying in the outskirts of Gibeah under the pomegranate tree that is at Migron; the troops that were with him were about six hundred men, 3 along with Ahijah son of Ahitub, Ichabod's brother, son of Phinehas son of Eli, the priest of the Lord in Shiloh, carrying an ephod. Now the people did not know that Jonathan had gone. 4 In the pass,[a] by which Jonathan tried to go over to the Philistine garrison, there was a rocky crag on one side and a rocky crag on the other; the name of the one was Bozez, and the name of the other Seneh. 5 One crag rose on the north in front of Michmash, and the other on the south in front of Geba.

6 Jonathan said to the young man who carried his armor, "Come, let us go over to the garrison of these uncircumcised; it may be that the Lord will act for us; for nothing can hinder the Lord from saving by many or by few." 7 His armor-bearer said to him, "Do all that your mind inclines to.[b] I am with you; as your mind is, so is mine."[c] 8 Then Jonathan said, "Now we will cross over to those men and will show ourselves to them. 9 If they say to us, 'Wait until we come to you,' then we will stand still in our place, and we will not go up to them. 10 But if they say, 'Come up to us,' then we will go up; for the Lord has given them into our hand. That will be the sign for us." 11 So both of them showed themselves to the garrison of the Philistines; and the Philistines said, "Look, Hebrews are coming out of the holes where they have hidden themselves." 12 The men of the garrison hailed Jonathan and his armor-bearer, saying, "Come up to us, and we will show you something." Jonathan said to his armor-bearer, "Come up after me; for the Lord has given them into the hand of Israel." 13 Then Jonathan climbed up on his hands and feet, with his armor-bearer following after him. The Philistines[d] fell before Jonathan, and his armor-bearer, coming after him, killed them. 14 In that first

a Heb *Between the passes*   b Gk: Heb *Do all that is in your mind. Turn*   c Gk: Heb lacks *so is mine*
d Heb *They*

slaughter Jonathan and his armor-bearer killed about twenty men within an area about half a furrow long in an acre[a] of land. [15]There was a panic in the camp, in the field, and among all the people; the garrison and even the raiders trembled; the earth quaked; and it became a very great panic.

16 Saul's lookouts in Gibeah of Benjamin were watching as the multitude was surging back and forth.[b] [17]Then Saul said to the troops that were with him, "Call the roll and see who has gone from us." When they had called the roll, Jonathan and his armor-bearer were not there. [18]Saul said to Ahijah, "Bring the ark[c] of God here." For at that time the ark[c] of God went with the Israelites. [19]While Saul was talking to the priest, the tumult in the camp of the Philistines increased more and more; and Saul said to the priest, "Withdraw your hand." [20]Then Saul and all the people who were with him rallied and went into the battle; and every sword was against the other, so that there was very great confusion. [21]Now the Hebrews who previously had been with the Philistines and had gone up with them into the camp turned and joined the Israelites who were with Saul and Jonathan. [22]Likewise, when all the Israelites who had gone into hiding in the hill country of Ephraim heard that the Philistines were fleeing, they too followed closely after them in the battle. [23]So the LORD gave Israel the victory that day.

The battle passed beyond Beth-aven, and the troops with Saul numbered altogether about ten thousand men. The battle spread out over the hill country of Ephraim.

24 Now Saul committed a very rash act on that day.[d] He had laid an oath on the troops, saying, "Cursed be anyone who eats food before it is evening and I have been avenged on my enemies." So none of the troops tasted food. [25]All the troops[e] came upon a honeycomb; and there was honey on the ground. [26]When the troops came upon the honeycomb, the honey was dripping out; but they did not put their hands to their mouths, for they feared the oath. [27]But Jonathan had not heard his father charge the troops with the oath; so he extended the staff that was in his hand, and dipped the tip of it in the honeycomb, and put his hand to his mouth; and his eyes brightened. [28]Then one of the soldiers said, "Your father strictly charged the troops with an oath, saying, 'Cursed be anyone who eats food this day.' And so the troops are faint." [29]Then Jonathan said, "My father has troubled the land; see how my eyes have brightened because I tasted a little of this honey. [30]How much better if today the troops had eaten freely of the spoil taken from their enemies; for now the slaughter among the Philistines has not been great."

31 After they had struck down the Philistines that day from Michmash to Aijalon, the troops were very faint; [32]so the troops flew upon the spoil, and took sheep and oxen and calves, and slaughtered them on the ground; and the troops ate them with the blood. [33]Then it was reported to Saul, "Look, the troops are sinning against the LORD by eating with the blood." And he said, "You have dealt treacherously; roll a large stone before me here."[f] [34]Saul said, "Disperse yourselves among the troops, and say to them, 'Let all bring their oxen or their sheep, and slaughter them here, and eat; and do not sin against the LORD by eating with the blood.'" So all of the troops brought their oxen with them that night, and slaughtered them there. [35]And Saul built an altar to the LORD; it was the first altar that he built to the LORD.

36 Then Saul said, "Let us go down

aHeb *yoke*  bGk: Heb *they went and there*  cGk *the ephod*  dGk: Heb *The Israelites were distressed that day*  eHeb *land*  fGk: Heb *me this day*

after the Philistines by night and despoil them until the morning light; let us not leave one of them." They said, "Do whatever seems good to you." But the priest said, "Let us draw near to God here." [37]So Saul inquired of God, "Shall I go down after the Philistines? Will you give them into the hand of Israel?" But he did not answer him that day. [38]Saul said, "Come here, all you leaders of the people; and let us find out how this sin has arisen today. [39]For as the LORD lives who saves Israel, even if it is in my son Jonathan, he shall surely die!" But there was no one among all the people who answered him. [40]He said to all Israel, "You shall be on one side, and I and my son Jonathan will be on the other side." The people said to Saul, "Do what seems good to you." [41]Then Saul said, "O LORD God of Israel, why have you not answered your servant today? If this guilt is in me or in my son Jonathan, O LORD God of Israel, give Urim; but if this guilt is in your people Israel, [a] give Thummim." And Jonathan and Saul were indicated by the lot, but the people were cleared. [42]Then Saul said, "Cast the lot between me and my son Jonathan." And Jonathan was taken.

43 Then Saul said to Jonathan, "Tell me what you have done." Jonathan told him, "I tasted a little honey with the tip of the staff that was in my hand; here I am, I will die." [44]Saul said, "God do so to me and more also; you shall surely die, Jonathan!" [45]Then the people said to Saul, "Shall Jonathan die, who has accomplished this great victory in Israel? Far from it! As the LORD lives, not one hair of his head shall fall to the ground; for he has worked with God today." So the people ransomed Jonathan, and he did not die. [46]Then Saul withdrew from pursuing the Philistines; and the Philistines went to their own place.

47 When Saul had taken the kingship over Israel, he fought against all his enemies on every side—against Moab, against the Ammonites, against Edom, against the kings of Zobah, and against the Philistines; wherever he turned he routed them. [48]He did valiantly, and struck down the Amalekites, and rescued Israel out of the hands of those who plundered them.

49 Now the sons of Saul were Jonathan, Ishvi, and Malchishua; and the names of his two daughters were these: the name of the firstborn was Merab, and the name of the younger, Michal. [50]The name of Saul's wife was Ahinoam daughter of Ahimaaz. And the name of the commander of his army was Abner son of Ner, Saul's uncle; [51]Kish was the father of Saul, and Ner the father of Abner was the son of Abiel.

52 There was hard fighting against the Philistines all the days of Saul; and when Saul saw any strong or valiant warrior, he took him into his service.

## JOHN 7.30–52

THEN they tried to arrest him [Jesus], but no one laid hands on him, because his hour had not yet come. [31]Yet many in the crowd believed in him and were saying, "When the Messiah[b] comes, will he do more signs than this man has done?"[c]

32 The Pharisees heard the crowd muttering such things about him, and the chief priests and Pharisees sent temple police to arrest him. [33]Jesus then said, "I will be with you a little while longer, and then I am going to him who sent me. [34]You will search for me, but you will not find me; and where I am, you cannot come." [35]The Jews said to one another, "Where does this man intend to go that we will not find him? Does he intend to go to the Dispersion

aVg Compare Gk: Heb *41Saul said to the LORD, the God of Israel*   bOr *the Christ*   cOther ancient authorities read *is doing*

among the Greeks and teach the Greeks? [36]What does he mean by saying, 'You will search for me and you will not find me' and 'Where I am, you cannot come'?"

37 On the last day of the festival, the great day, while Jesus was standing there, he cried out, "Let anyone who is thirsty come to me, [38]and let the one who believes in me drink. As[a] the scripture has said, 'Out of the believer's heart[b] shall flow rivers of living water.'" [39]Now he said this about the Spirit, which believers in him were to receive; for as yet there was no Spirit,[c] because Jesus was not yet glorified.

40 When they heard these words, some in the crowd said, "This is really the prophet." [41]Others said, "This is the Messiah."[d] But some asked, "Surely the Messiah[d] does not come from Galilee, does he? [42]Has not the scripture said that the Messiah[d] is descended from David and comes from Bethlehem, the village where David lived?" [43]So there was a division in the crowd because of him. [44]Some of them wanted to arrest him, but no one laid hands on him.

45 Then the temple police went back to the chief priests and Pharisees, who asked them, "Why did you not arrest him?" [46]The police answered, "Never has anyone spoken like this!" [47]Then the Pharisees replied, "Surely you have not been deceived too, have you? [48]Has any one of the authorities or of the Pharisees believed in him? [49]But this crowd, which does not know the law—they are accursed." [50]Nicodemus, who had gone to Jesus[e] before, and who was one of them, asked, [51]"Our law does not judge people without first giving them a hearing to find out what they are doing, does it?"

[52]They replied, "Surely you are not also from Galilee, are you? Search and you will see that no prophet is to arise from Galilee."

## PSALM 109. 1–31

*To the leader. Of David. A Psalm.*

Do not be silent, O God of my
    praise.
2  For wicked and deceitful
    mouths are opened
    against me,
  speaking against me with
    lying tongues.
3  They beset me with words of
    hate,
  and attack me without cause.
4  In return for my love they
    accuse me,
  even while I make prayer for
    them.[f]
5  So they reward me evil for
    good,
  and hatred for my love.

6  They say,[g] "Appoint a wicked
    man against him;
  let an accuser stand on his
    right.
7  When he is tried, let him be
    found guilty;
  let his prayer be counted as
    sin.
8  May his days be few;
  may another seize his
    position.
9  May his children be orphans,
  and his wife a widow.
10  May his children wander about
    and beg;
  may they be driven out of[h]
    the ruins they inhabit.
11  May the creditor seize all that
    he has;

[a]Or *come to me and drink.* *[38]The one who believes in me, as*  [b]Gk *out of his belly*  [c]Other ancient authorities read *for as yet the Spirit* (others, *Holy Spirit*) *had not been given*  [d]Or *the Christ*  [e]Gk *him*  [f]Syr: Heb *I prayer*  [g]Heb lacks *They say*  [h]Gk: Heb *and seek*

may strangers plunder the
    fruits of his toil.
12 May there be no one to do him
    a kindness,
    nor anyone to pity his
    orphaned children.
13 May his posterity be cut off;
    may his name be blotted out
    in the second generation.
14 May the iniquity of his father[a]
    be remembered before
    the LORD,
    and do not let the sin of his
    mother be blotted out.
15 Let them be before the LORD
    continually,
    and may his[b] memory be cut
    off from the earth.
16 For he did not remember to
    show kindness,
    but pursued the poor and
    needy
    and the brokenhearted to
    their death.
17 He loved to curse; let curses
    come on him.
    He did not like blessing; may
    it be far from him.
18 He clothed himself with cursing
    as his coat,
    may it soak into his body like
    water,
    like oil into his bones.
19 May it be like a garment that he
    wraps around himself,
    like a belt that he wears
    every day."

20 May that be the reward of my
    accusers from the LORD,
    of those who speak evil
    against my life.
21 But you, O LORD my Lord,
    act on my behalf for your
    name's sake;
    because your steadfast love is
    good, deliver me.

22 For I am poor and needy,
    and my heart is pierced
    within me.
23 I am gone like a shadow at
    evening;
    I am shaken off like a locust.
24 My knees are weak through
    fasting;
    my body has become gaunt.
25 I am an object of scorn to my
    accusers;
    when they see me, they
    shake their heads.

26 Help me, O LORD my God!
    Save me according to your
    steadfast love.
27 Let them know that this is your
    hand;
    you, O LORD, have done it.
28 Let them curse, but you will
    bless.
    Let my assailants be put to
    shame;[c] may your
    servant be glad.
29 May my accusers be clothed
    with dishonor;
    may they be wrapped in their
    own shame as in a
    mantle.
30 With my mouth I will give great
    thanks to the LORD;
    I will praise him in the midst
    of the throng.
31 For he stands at the right hand
    of the needy,
    to save them from those who
    would condemn them to
    death.

## PROVERBS 15.5–7

A FOOL despises a parent's
    instruction,
but the one who heeds
    admonition is prudent.

a Cn: Heb *fathers*  b Gk: Heb *their*  c Gk: Heb *They have risen up and have been put to shame*

<sup>6</sup>  In the house of the righteous
there is much treasure,
but trouble befalls the income
of the wicked.

<sup>7</sup>  The lips of the wise spread
knowledge;
not so the minds of fools.

# MAY 14

## 1 SAMUEL 15.1—16.23

SAMUEL said to Saul, "The LORD sent me to anoint you king over his people Israel; now therefore listen to the words of the LORD. <sup>2</sup>Thus says the LORD of hosts, 'I will punish the Amalekites for what they did in opposing the Israelites when they came up out of Egypt. <sup>3</sup>Now go and attack Amalek, and utterly destroy all that they have; do not spare them, but kill both man and woman, child and infant, ox and sheep, camel and donkey.'"

4  So Saul summoned the people, and numbered them in Telaim, two hundred thousand foot soldiers, and ten thousand soldiers of Judah. <sup>5</sup>Saul came to the city of the Amalekites and lay in wait in the valley. <sup>6</sup>Saul said to the Kenites, "Go! Leave! Withdraw from among the Amalekites, or I will destroy you with them; for you showed kindness to all the people of Israel when they came up out of Egypt." So the Kenites withdrew from the Amalekites. <sup>7</sup>Saul defeated the Amalekites, from Havilah as far as Shur, which is east of Egypt. <sup>8</sup>He took King Agag of the Amalekites alive, but utterly destroyed all the people with the edge of the sword. <sup>9</sup>Saul and the people spared Agag, and the best of the sheep and of the cattle and of the fatlings, and the lambs, and all that was valuable, and would not utterly destroy them; all that was despised and worthless they utterly destroyed.

10  The word of the LORD came to Samuel: <sup>11</sup>"I regret that I made Saul king, for he has turned back from following me, and has not carried out my commands." Samuel was angry; and he cried out to the LORD all night. <sup>12</sup>Samuel rose early in the morning to meet Saul, and Samuel was told, "Saul went to Carmel, where he set up a monument for himself, and on returning he passed on down to Gilgal." <sup>13</sup>When Samuel came to Saul, Saul said to him, "May you be blessed by the LORD; I have carried out the command of the LORD." <sup>14</sup>But Samuel said, "What then is this bleating of sheep in my ears, and the lowing of cattle that I hear?" <sup>15</sup>Saul said, "They have brought them from the Amalekites; for the people spared the best of the sheep and the cattle, to sacrifice to the LORD your God; but the rest we have utterly destroyed." <sup>16</sup>Then Samuel said to Saul, "Stop! I will tell you what the LORD said to me last night." He replied, "Speak."

17  Samuel said, "Though you are little in your own eyes, are you not the head of the tribes of Israel? The LORD anointed you king over Israel. <sup>18</sup>And the LORD sent you on a mission, and said, 'Go, utterly destroy the sinners, the Amalekites, and fight against them until they are consumed.' <sup>19</sup>Why then did you not obey the voice of the LORD? Why did you swoop down on the spoil, and do what was evil in the sight of the LORD?" <sup>20</sup>Saul said to Samuel, "I have obeyed the voice of the LORD, I have gone on the mission on which the LORD sent me, I have brought Agag the king

of Amalek, and I have utterly destroyed the Amalekites. [21]But from the spoil the people took sheep and cattle, the best of the things devoted to destruction, to sacrifice to the Lord your God in Gilgal." [22]And Samuel said,

> "Has the Lord as great delight
> in burnt offerings and
> sacrifices,
> as in obeying the voice of the
> Lord?
> Surely, to obey is better than
> sacrifice,
> and to heed than the fat of
> rams.
> [23] For rebellion is no less a sin
> than divination,
> and stubbornness is like
> iniquity and idolatry.
> Because you have rejected the
> word of the Lord,
> he has also rejected you from
> being king."

[24] Saul said to Samuel, "I have sinned; for I have transgressed the commandment of the Lord and your words, because I feared the people and obeyed their voice. [25]Now therefore, I pray, pardon my sin, and return with me, so that I may worship the Lord." [26]Samuel said to Saul, "I will not return with you; for you have rejected the word of the Lord, and the Lord has rejected you from being king over Israel." [27]As Samuel turned to go away, Saul caught hold of the hem of his robe, and it tore. [28]And Samuel said to him, "The Lord has torn the kingdom of Israel from you this very day, and has given it to a neighbor of yours, who is better than you. [29]Moreover the Glory of Israel will not recant[a] or change his mind; for he is not a mortal, that he should change his mind." [30]Then Saul[b] said, "I have sinned; yet honor me now before the elders of my people and before Israel, and return with me, so that I may worship the Lord your God."

[31]So Samuel turned back after Saul; and Saul worshiped the Lord.

32  Then Samuel said, "Bring Agag king of the Amalekites here to me." And Agag came to him haltingly.[c] Agag said, "Surely this is the bitterness of death."[d] [33]But Samuel said,

> "As your sword has made
> women childless,
> so your mother shall be
> childless among women."

And Samuel hewed Agag in pieces before the Lord in Gilgal.

34  Then Samuel went to Ramah; and Saul went up to his house in Gibeah of Saul. [35]Samuel did not see Saul again until the day of his death, but Samuel grieved over Saul. And the Lord was sorry that he had made Saul king over Israel.

**16.**[1] The Lord said to Samuel, "How long will you grieve over Saul? I have rejected him from being king over Israel. Fill your horn with oil and set out; I will send you to Jesse the Bethlehemite, for I have provided for myself a king among his sons." [2]Samuel said, "How can I go? If Saul hears of it, he will kill me." And the Lord said, "Take a heifer with you, and say, 'I have come to sacrifice to the Lord.' [3]Invite Jesse to the sacrifice, and I will show you what you shall do; and you shall anoint for me the one whom I name to you." [4]Samuel did what the Lord commanded, and came to Bethlehem. The elders of the city came to meet him trembling, and said, "Do you come peaceably?" [5]He said, "Peaceably; I have come to sacrifice to the Lord; sanctify yourselves and come with me to the sacrifice." And he sanctified Jesse and his sons and invited them to the sacrifice.

6  When they came, he looked on Eliab and thought, "Surely the Lord's anointed is now before the Lord."[e] [7]But the Lord said to Samuel, "Do not

aQ Ms Gk: MT *deceive*   bHeb *he*   cCn Compare Gk: Meaning of Heb uncertain   dQ Ms Gk: MT
*Surely the bitterness of death is past*   eHeb *him*

look on his appearance or on the height of his stature, because I have rejected him; for the LORD does not see as mortals see; they look on the outward appearance, but the LORD looks on the heart." [8]Then Jesse called Abinadab, and made him pass before Samuel. He said, "Neither has the LORD chosen this one." [9]Then Jesse made Shammah pass by. And he said, "Neither has the LORD chosen this one." [10]Jesse made seven of his sons pass before Samuel, and Samuel said to Jesse, "The LORD has not chosen any of these." [11]Samuel said to Jesse, "Are all your sons here?" And he said, "There remains yet the youngest, but he is keeping the sheep." And Samuel said to Jesse, "Send and bring him; for we will not sit down until he comes here." [12]He sent and brought him in. Now he was ruddy, and had beautiful eyes, and was handsome. The LORD said, "Rise and anoint him; for this is the one." [13]Then Samuel took the horn of oil, and anointed him in the presence of his brothers; and the spirit of the LORD came mightily upon David from that day forward. Samuel then set out and went to Ramah.

14 Now the spirit of the LORD departed from Saul, and an evil spirit from the LORD tormented him. [15]And Saul's servants said to him, "See now, an evil spirit from God is tormenting you. [16]Let our lord now command the servants who attend you to look for someone who is skillful in playing the lyre; and when the evil spirit from God is upon you, he will play it, and you will feel better." [17]So Saul said to his servants, "Provide for me someone who can play well, and bring him to me." [18]One of the young men answered, "I have seen a son of Jesse the Bethlehemite who is skillful in playing, a man of valor, a warrior, prudent in speech, and a man of good presence; and the LORD is with him." [19]So Saul sent messengers to Jesse, and said, "Send me your son David who is with the sheep." [20]Jesse took a donkey loaded with bread, a skin of wine, and a kid, and sent them by his son David to Saul. [21]And David came to Saul, and entered his service. Saul loved him greatly, and he became his armor-bearer. [22]Saul sent to Jesse, saying, "Let David remain in my service, for he has found favor in my sight." [23]And whenever the evil spirit from God came upon Saul, David took the lyre and played it with his hand, and Saul would be relieved and feel better, and the evil spirit would depart from him.

## JOHN 7.53—8.20

⟦T⟧HEN each of them went home, [8.1]while Jesus went to the Mount of Olives. [2]Early in the morning he came again to the temple. All the people came to him and he sat down and began to teach them. [3]The scribes and the Pharisees brought a woman who had been caught in adultery; and making her stand before all of them, [4]they said to him, "Teacher, this woman was caught in the very act of committing adultery. [5]Now in the law Moses commanded us to stone such women. Now what do you say?" [6]They said this to test him, so that they might have some charge to bring against him. Jesus bent down and wrote with his finger on the ground. [7]When they kept on questioning him, he straightened up and said to them, "Let anyone among you who is without sin be the first to throw a stone at her." [8]And once again he bent down and wrote on the ground. [a] [9]When they heard it, they went away, one by one, beginning with the elders; and Jesus was left alone with the woman standing before him. [10]Jesus straightened up and said to her, "Woman, where are they? Has no one

a Other ancient authorities add *the sins of each of them*

condemned you?" [11]She said, "No one, sir."[a] And Jesus said, "Neither do I condemn you. Go your way, and from now on do not sin again."]][b]

12   Again Jesus spoke to them, saying, "I am the light of the world. Whoever follows me will never walk in darkness but will have the light of life." [13]Then the Pharisees said to him, "You are testifying on your own behalf; your testimony is not valid." [14]Jesus answered, "Even if I testify on my own behalf, my testimony is valid because I know where I have come from and where I am going, but you do not know where I come from or where I am going. [15]You judge by human standards;[c] I judge no one. [16]Yet even if I do judge, my judgment is valid; for it is not I alone who judge, but I and the Father[d] who sent me. [17]In your law it is written that the testimony of two witnesses is valid. [18]I testify on my own behalf, and the Father who sent me testifies on my behalf." [19]Then they said to him, "Where is your Father?" Jesus answered, "You know neither me nor my Father. If you knew me, you would know my Father also." [20]He spoke these words while he was teaching in the treasury of the temple, but no one arrested him, because his hour had not yet come.

## PSALM 110.1–7

*Of David. A Psalm.*

THE LORD says to my lord,
  "Sit at my right hand
    until I make your enemies
      your footstool."
2   The LORD sends out from Zion
    your mighty scepter.
    Rule in the midst of your
      foes.

3   Your people will offer
    themselves willingly
  on the day you lead your
    forces
  on the holy mountains.[e]
From the womb of the morning,
  like dew, your youth[f] will
    come to you.
4   The LORD has sworn and will
    not change his mind,
  "You are a priest forever
    according to the order of
    Melchizedek."[g]

5   The Lord is at your right hand;
  he will shatter kings on the
    day of his wrath.
6   He will execute judgment among
    the nations,
  filling them with corpses;
he will shatter heads
  over the wide earth.
7   He will drink from the stream
    by the path;
  therefore he will lift up his
    head.

## PROVERBS 15.8–10

THE sacrifice of the wicked is an
    abomination to the
    LORD,
  but the prayer of the upright
    is his delight.
9   The way of the wicked is an
    abomination to the LORD,
  but he loves the one who
    pursues righteousness.
10   There is severe discipline for
    one who forsakes the
    way,
  but one who hates a rebuke
    will die.

a Or *Lord*   b The most ancient authorities lack 7.53—8.11; other authorities add the passage here or after 7.36 or after 21.25 or after Luke 21.38, with variations of text; some mark the passage as doubtful.   c Gk *according to the flesh*   d Other ancient authorities read *he*   e Another reading is *in holy splendor*   f Cn: Heb *the dew of your youth*   g Or *forever, a rightful king by my edict*

# MAY 15



Now the Philistines gathered their armies for battle; they were gathered at Socoh, which belongs to Judah, and encamped between Socoh and Azekah, in Ephes-dammim. ²Saul and the Israelites gathered and encamped in the valley of Elah, and formed ranks against the Philistines. ³The Philistines stood on the mountain on the one side, and Israel stood on the mountain on the other side, with a valley between them. ⁴And there came out from the camp of the Philistines a champion named Goliath, of Gath, whose height was six[a] cubits and a span. ⁵He had a helmet of bronze on his head, and he was armed with a coat of mail; the weight of the coat was five thousand shekels of bronze. ⁶He had greaves of bronze on his legs and a javelin of bronze slung between his shoulders. ⁷The shaft of his spear was like a weaver's beam, and his spear's head weighed six hundred shekels of iron; and his shield-bearer went before him. ⁸He stood and shouted to the ranks of Israel, "Why have you come out to draw up for battle? Am I not a Philistine, and are you not servants of Saul? Choose a man for yourselves, and let him come down to me. ⁹If he is able to fight with me and kill me, then we will be your servants; but if I prevail against him and kill him, then you shall be our servants and serve us." ¹⁰And the Philistine said, "Today I defy the ranks of Israel! Give me a man, that we may fight together." ¹¹When Saul and all Israel heard these words of the Philistine, they were dismayed and greatly afraid.

12 Now David was the son of an Ephrathite of Bethlehem in Judah, named Jesse, who had eight sons. In the days of Saul the man was already old and advanced in years.[b] ¹³The three eldest sons of Jesse had followed Saul to the battle; the names of his three sons who went to the battle were Eliab the firstborn, and next to him Abinadab, and the third Shammah. ¹⁴David was the youngest; the three eldest followed Saul, ¹⁵but David went back and forth from Saul to feed his father's sheep at Bethlehem. ¹⁶For forty days the Philistine came forward and took his stand, morning and evening.

17 Jesse said to his son David, "Take for your brothers an ephah of this parched grain and these ten loaves, and carry them quickly to the camp to your brothers; ¹⁸also take these ten cheeses to the commander of their thousand. See how your brothers fare, and bring some token from them."

19 Now Saul, and they, and all the men of Israel, were in the valley of Elah, fighting with the Philistines. ²⁰David rose early in the morning, left the sheep with a keeper, took the provisions, and went as Jesse had commanded him. He came to the encampment as the army was going forth to the battle line, shouting the war cry. ²¹Israel and the Philistines drew up for battle, army against army. ²²David left the things in charge of the keeper of the baggage, ran to the ranks, and went and greeted his brothers. ²³As he talked with them, the champion, the Philistine of Gath, Goliath by name, came up out of the ranks of the Philistines, and spoke the same words as before. And David heard him.

24 All the Israelites, when they

saw the man, fled from him and were very much afraid. 25The Israelites said, "Have you seen this man who has come up? Surely he has come up to defy Israel. The king will greatly enrich the man who kills him, and will give him his daughter and make his family free in Israel." 26David said to the men who stood by him, "What shall be done for the man who kills this Philistine, and takes away the reproach from Israel? For who is this uncircumcised Philistine that he should defy the armies of the living God?" 27The people answered him in the same way, "So shall it be done for the man who kills him."

28 His eldest brother Eliab heard him talking to the men; and Eliab's anger was kindled against David. He said, "Why have you come down? With whom have you left those few sheep in the wilderness? I know your presumption and the evil of your heart; for you have come down just to see the battle." 29David said, "What have I done now? It was only a question." 30He turned away from him toward another and spoke in the same way; and the people answered him again as before.

31 When the words that David spoke were heard, they repeated them before Saul; and he sent for him. 32David said to Saul, "Let no one's heart fail because of him; your servant will go and fight with this Philistine." 33Saul said to David, "You are not able to go against this Philistine to fight with him; for you are just a boy, and he has been a warrior from his youth." 34But David said to Saul, "Your servant used to keep sheep for his father; and whenever a lion or a bear came, and took a lamb from the flock, 35I went after it and struck it down, rescuing the lamb from its mouth; and if it turned against me, I would catch it by the jaw, strike it down, and kill it. 36Your servant has killed both lions and bears; and this uncircumcised Philistine shall be like one of them, since he has defied the armies

of the living God." 37David said, "The LORD, who saved me from the paw of the lion and from the paw of the bear, will save me from the hand of this Philistine." So Saul said to David, "Go, and may the LORD be with you!"

38 Saul clothed David with his armor; he put a bronze helmet on his head and clothed him with a coat of mail. 39David strapped Saul's sword over the armor, and he tried in vain to walk, for he was not used to them. Then David said to Saul, "I cannot walk with these; for I am not used to them." So David removed them. 40Then he took his staff in his hand, and chose five smooth stones from the wadi, and put them in his shepherd's bag, in the pouch; his sling was in his hand, and he drew near to the Philistine.

41 The Philistine came on and drew near to David, with his shield-bearer in front of him. 42When the Philistine looked and saw David, he disdained him, for he was only a youth, ruddy and handsome in appearance. 43The Philistine said to David, "Am I a dog, that you come to me with sticks?" And the Philistine cursed David by his gods. 44The Philistine said to David, "Come to me, and I will give your flesh to the birds of the air and to the wild animals of the field." 45But David said to the Philistine, "You come to me with sword and spear and javelin; but I come to you in the name of the LORD of hosts, the God of the armies of Israel, whom you have defied. 46This very day the LORD will deliver you into my hand, and I will strike you down and cut off your head; and I will give the dead bodies of the Philistine army this very day to the birds of the air and to the wild animals of the earth, so that all the earth may know that there is a God in Israel, 47and that all this assembly may know that the LORD does not save by sword and spear; for the battle is the LORD's and he will give you into our hand."

48 When the Philistine drew nearer

to meet David, David ran quickly toward the battle line to meet the Philistine. [49]David put his hand in his bag, took out a stone, slung it, and struck the Philistine on his forehead; the stone sank into his forehead, and he fell face down on the ground.

50 So David prevailed over the Philistine with a sling and a stone, striking down the Philistine and killing him; there was no sword in David's hand. [51]Then David ran and stood over the Philistine; he grasped his sword, drew it out of its sheath, and killed him; then he cut off his head with it.

When the Philistines saw that their champion was dead, they fled. [52]The troops of Israel and Judah rose up with a shout and pursued the Philistines as far as Gath[a] and the gates of Ekron, so that the wounded Philistines fell on the way from Shaaraim as far as Gath and Ekron. [53]The Israelites came back from chasing the Philistines, and they plundered their camp. [54]David took the head of the Philistine and brought it to Jerusalem; but he put his armor in his tent.

55 When Saul saw David go out against the Philistine, he said to Abner, the commander of the army, "Abner, whose son is this young man?" Abner said, "As your soul lives, O king, I do not know." [56]The king said, "Inquire whose son the stripling is." [57]On David's return from killing the Philistine, Abner took him and brought him before Saul, with the head of the Philistine in his hand. [58]Saul said to him, "Whose son are you, young man?" And David answered, "I am the son of your servant Jesse the Bethlehemite."

**18.1** When David[b] had finished speaking to Saul, the soul of Jonathan was bound to the soul of David, and Jonathan loved him as his own soul. [2]Saul took him that day and would not let him return to his father's house. [3]Then Jonathan made a covenant with David, because he loved him as his own soul. [4]Jonathan stripped himself of the robe that he was wearing, and gave it to David, and his armor, and even his sword and his bow and his belt.

## JOHN 8.21–30

Again he [Jesus] said to them, "I am going away, and you will search for me, but you will die in your sin. Where I am going, you cannot come." [22]Then the Jews said, "Is he going to kill himself? Is that what he means by saying, 'Where I am going, you cannot come'?" [23]He said to them, "You are from below, I am from above; you are of this world, I am not of this world. [24]I told you that you would die in your sins, for you will die in your sins unless you believe that I am he."[c] [25]They said to him, "Who are you?" Jesus said to them, "Why do I speak to you at all?[d] [26]I have much to say about you and much to condemn; but the one who sent me is true, and I declare to the world what I have heard from him." [27]They did not understand that he was speaking to them about the Father. [28]So Jesus said, "When you have lifted up the Son of Man, then you will realize that I am he,[c] and that I do nothing on my own, but I speak these things as the Father instructed me. [29]And the one who sent me is with me; he has not left me alone, for I always do what is pleasing to him." [30]As he was saying these things, many believed in him.

## PSALM 111.1–10

Praise the Lord!
I will give thanks to the
    Lord with my whole
    heart,
in the company of the upright,
    in the congregation.

aGk Syr: Heb *Gai*   bHeb *he*   cGk *I am*   dOr *What I have told you from the beginning*

2 Great are the works of the
    Lord,
      studied by all who delight
        in them.
3 Full of honor and majesty is
      his work,
      and his righteousness endures
        forever.
4 He has gained renown by his
      wonderful deeds;
    the Lord is gracious and
      merciful.
5 He provides food for those who
      fear him;
    he is ever mindful of his
      covenant.
6 He has shown his people the
      power of his works,
    in giving them the heritage of
      the nations.
7 The works of his hands are
      faithful and just;
    all his precepts are
      trustworthy.

8 They are established forever
      and ever,
    to be performed with
      faithfulness and
      uprightness.
9 He sent redemption to his
      people;
    he has commanded his
      covenant forever.
    Holy and awesome is his
      name.
10 The fear of the Lord is the
      beginning of wisdom;
    all those who practice it[a]
      have a good
      understanding.
    His praise endures forever.

## PROVERBS 15.11

SHEOL and Abaddon lie open
      before the Lord,
how much more human
      hearts!

# MAY 16

## 1 SAMUEL 18.5—19.24

DAVID went out and was successful wherever Saul sent him; as a result, Saul set him over the army. And all the people, even the servants of Saul, approved.

6 As they were coming home, when David returned from killing the Philistine, the women came out of all the towns of Israel, singing and dancing, to meet King Saul, with tambourines, with songs of joy, and with musical instruments.[b] [7]And the women sang to one another as they made merry,

    "Saul has killed his thousands,
      and David his ten thousands."

[8]Saul was very angry, for this saying displeased him. He said, "They have ascribed to David ten thousands, and to me they have ascribed thousands; what more can he have but the kingdom?" [9]So Saul eyed David from that day on.

10 The next day an evil spirit from God rushed upon Saul, and he raved within his house, while David was play-

[a]Gk Syr: Heb *them*   [b]Or *triangles,* or *three-stringed instruments*

ing the lyre, as he did day by day. Saul had his spear in his hand; [11]and Saul threw the spear, for he thought, "I will pin David to the wall." But David eluded him twice.

12 Saul was afraid of David, because the LORD was with him but had departed from Saul. [13]So Saul removed him from his presence, and made him a commander of a thousand; and David marched out and came in, leading the army. [14]David had success in all his undertakings; for the LORD was with him. [15]When Saul saw that he had great success, he stood in awe of him. [16]But all Israel and Judah loved David; for it was he who marched out and came in leading them.

17 Then Saul said to David, "Here is my elder daughter Merab; I will give her to you as a wife; only be valiant for me and fight the LORD's battles." For Saul thought, "I will not raise a hand against him; let the Philistines deal with him." [18]David said to Saul, "Who am I and who are my kinsfolk, my father's family in Israel, that I should be son-in-law to the king?" [19]But at the time when Saul's daughter Merab should have been given to David, she was given to Adriel the Meholathite as a wife.

20 Now Saul's daughter Michal loved David. Saul was told, and the thing pleased him. [21]Saul thought, "Let me give her to him that she may be a snare for him and that the hand of the Philistines may be against him." Therefore Saul said to David a second time,[a] "You shall now be my son-in-law." [22]Saul commanded his servants, "Speak to David in private and say, 'See, the king is delighted with you, and all his servants love you; now then, become the king's son-in-law.'" [23]So Saul's servants reported these words to David in private. And David said, "Does it seem to you a little thing to become the king's son-in-law, seeing that I am a poor man and of no repute?" [24]The servants of Saul told him, "This is what David said." [25]Then Saul said, "Thus shall you say to David, 'The king desires no marriage present except a hundred foreskins of the Philistines, that he may be avenged on the king's enemies.'" Now Saul planned to make David fall by the hand of the Philistines. [26]When his servants told David these words, David was well pleased to be the king's son-in-law. Before the time had expired, [27]David rose and went, along with his men, and killed one hundred[b] of the Philistines; and David brought their foreskins, which were given in full number to the king, that he might become the king's son-in-law. Saul gave him his daughter Michal as a wife. [28]But when Saul realized that the LORD was with David, and that Saul's daughter Michal loved him, [29]Saul was still more afraid of David. So Saul was David's enemy from that time forward.

30 Then the commanders of the Philistines came out to battle; and as often as they came out, David had more success than all the servants of Saul, so that his fame became very great.

**19.**1 SAUL spoke with his son Jonathan and with all his servants about killing David. But Saul's son Jonathan took great delight in David. [2]Jonathan told David, "My father Saul is trying to kill you; therefore be on guard tomorrow morning; stay in a secret place and hide yourself. [3]I will go out and stand beside my father in the field where you are, and I will speak to my father about you; if I learn anything I will tell you." [4]Jonathan spoke well of David to his father Saul, saying to him, "The king should not sin against his servant David, because he has not sinned against you, and because his deeds have been of good service to you; [5]for he took his life

aHeb *by two*   bGk Compare 2 Sam 3.14: Heb *two hundred*

in his hand when he attacked the Philistine, and the LORD brought about a great victory for all Israel. You saw it, and rejoiced; why then will you sin against an innocent person by killing David without cause?" [6]Saul heeded the voice of Jonathan; Saul swore, "As the LORD lives, he shall not be put to death." [7]So Jonathan called David and related all these things to him. Jonathan then brought David to Saul, and he was in his presence as before.

8 Again there was war, and David went out to fight the Philistines. He launched a heavy attack on them, so that they fled before him. [9]Then an evil spirit from the LORD came upon Saul, as he sat in his house with his spear in his hand, while David was playing music. [10]Saul sought to pin David to the wall with the spear; but he eluded Saul, so that he struck the spear into the wall. David fled and escaped that night.

11 Saul sent messengers to David's house to keep watch over him, planning to kill him in the morning. David's wife Michal told him, "If you do not save your life tonight, tomorrow you will be killed." [12]So Michal let David down through the window; he fled away and escaped. [13]Michal took an idol[a] and laid it on the bed; she put a net[b] of goats' hair on its head, and covered it with the clothes. [14]When Saul sent messengers to take David, she said, "He is sick." [15]Then Saul sent the messengers to see David for themselves. He said, "Bring him up to me in the bed, that I may kill him." [16]When the messengers came in, the idol[c] was in the bed, with the covering[b] of goats' hair on its head. [17]Saul said to Michal, "Why have you deceived me like this, and let my enemy go, so that he has escaped?" Michal answered Saul, "He said to me, 'Let me go; why should I kill you?'"

18 Now David fled and escaped; he came to Samuel at Ramah, and told him all that Saul had done to him. He and Samuel went and settled at Naioth. [19]Saul was told, "David is at Naioth in Ramah." [20]Then Saul sent messengers to take David. When they saw the company of the prophets in a frenzy, with Samuel standing in charge of[b] them, the spirit of God came upon the messengers of Saul, and they also fell into a prophetic frenzy. [21]When Saul was told, he sent other messengers, and they also fell into a frenzy. Saul sent messengers again the third time, and they also fell into a frenzy. [22]Then he himself went to Ramah. He came to the great well that is in Secu;[d] he asked, "Where are Samuel and David?" And someone said, "They are at Naioth in Ramah." [23]He went there, toward Naioth in Ramah; and the spirit of God came upon him. As he was going, he fell into a prophetic frenzy, until he came to Naioth in Ramah. [24]He too stripped off his clothes, and he too fell into a frenzy before Samuel. He lay naked all that day and all that night. Therefore it is said, "Is Saul also among the prophets?"

## JOHN 8.31–59

THEN Jesus said to the Jews who had believed in him, "If you continue in my word, you are truly my disciples; [32]and you will know the truth, and the truth will make you free." [33]They answered him, "We are descendants of Abraham and have never been slaves to anyone. What do you mean by saying, 'You will be made free'?"

34 Jesus answered them, "Very truly, I tell you, everyone who commits sin is a slave to sin. [35]The slave does not have a permanent place in the household; the son has a place there forever. [36]So if the Son makes you

aHeb *took the teraphim*   bMeaning of Heb uncertain   cHeb *the teraphim*   dGk reads *to the well of the threshing floor on the bare height*

free, you will be free indeed. [37]I know that you are descendants of Abraham; yet you look for an opportunity to kill me, because there is no place in you for my word. [38]I declare what I have seen in the Father's presence; as for you, you should do what you have heard from the Father."[a]

39 They answered him, "Abraham is our father." Jesus said to them, "If you were Abraham's children, you would be doing[b] what Abraham did, [40]but now you are trying to kill me, a man who has told you the truth that I heard from God. This is not what Abraham did. [41]You are indeed doing what your father does." They said to him, "We are not illegitimate children; we have one father, God himself." [42]Jesus said to them, "If God were your Father, you would love me, for I came from God and now I am here. I did not come on my own, but he sent me. [43]Why do you not understand what I say? It is because you cannot accept my word. [44]You are from your father the devil, and you choose to do your father's desires. He was a murderer from the beginning and does not stand in the truth, because there is no truth in him. When he lies, he speaks according to his own nature, for he is a liar and the father of lies. [45]But because I tell the truth, you do not believe me. [46]Which of you convicts me of sin? If I tell the truth, why do you not believe me? [47]Whoever is from God hears the words of God. The reason you do not hear them is that you are not from God."

48 The Jews answered him, "Are we not right in saying that you are a Samaritan and have a demon?" [49]Jesus answered, "I do not have a demon; but I honor my Father, and you dishonor me. [50]Yet I do not seek my own glory; there is one who seeks it and he is the judge. [51]Very truly, I tell you, whoever keeps my word will never see death." [52]The Jews said to him, "Now we know that you have a demon. Abraham died, and so did the prophets; yet you say, 'Whoever keeps my word will never taste death.' [53]Are you greater than our father Abraham, who died? The prophets also died. Who do you claim to be?" [54]Jesus answered, "If I glorify myself, my glory is nothing. It is my Father who glorifies me, he of whom you say, 'He is our God,' [55]though you do not know him. But I know him; if I would say that I do not know him, I would be a liar like you. But I do know him and I keep his word. [56]Your ancestor Abraham rejoiced that he would see my day; he saw it and was glad." [57]Then the Jews said to him, "You are not yet fifty years old, and have you seen Abraham?"[c] [58]Jesus said to them, "Very truly, I tell you, before Abraham was, I am." [59]So they picked up stones to throw at him, but Jesus hid himself and went out of the temple.

# PSALM 112.1–10

Praise the Lord!
   Happy are those who fear
      the Lord,
   who greatly delight in his
      commandments.
2  Their descendants will be
      mighty in the land;
   the generation of the upright
      will be blessed.
3  Wealth and riches are in their
      houses,
   and their righteousness
      endures forever.
4  They rise in the darkness as a
      light for the upright;
   they are gracious, merciful,
      and righteous.

a Other ancient authorities read *you do what you have heard from your father*  b Other ancient authorities read *If you are Abraham's children, then do*  c Other ancient authorities read *has Abraham seen you?*

5 It is well with those who deal
     generously and lend,
  who conduct their affairs with
     justice.
6 For the righteous will never
     be moved;
  they will be remembered
     forever.
7 They are not afraid of evil
     tidings;
  their hearts are firm, secure
     in the LORD.
8 Their hearts are steady, they
     will not be afraid;
  in the end they will look in
     triumph on their foes.
9 They have distributed freely,
     they have given to the
     poor;
  their righteousness endures
     forever;
  their horn is exalted in honor.

10 The wicked see it and are
     angry;
  they gnash their teeth and
     melt away;
  the desire of the wicked
     comes to nothing.

## PROVERBS 15.12–14

SCOFFERS do not like to be
     rebuked;
  they will not go to the wise.
13 A glad heart makes a cheerful
     countenance,
  but by sorrow of heart the
     spirit is broken.
14 The mind of one who has
     understanding seeks
     knowledge,
  but the mouths of fools feed
     on folly.

# MAY 17

## 1 SAMUEL 20.1—21.15

DAVID fled from Naioth in Ramah. He came before Jonathan and said, "What have I done? What is my guilt? And what is my sin against your father that he is trying to take my life?" 2He said to him, "Far from it! You shall not die. My father does nothing either great or small without disclosing it to me; and why should my father hide this from me? Never!" 3But David also swore, "Your father knows well that you like me; and he thinks, 'Do not let Jonathan know this, or he will be grieved.' But truly, as the LORD lives and as you yourself live, there is but a step between me and death." 4Then Jonathan said to David, "Whatever you say, I will do for you." 5David said to Jonathan, "Tomorrow is the new moon, and I should not fail to sit with the king at the meal; but let me go, so that I may hide in the field until the third evening. 6If your father misses me at all, then say, 'David earnestly asked leave of me to run to Bethlehem his city; for there is a yearly sacrifice there for all the family.' 7If he says, 'Good!' it will be well with your servant; but if he is angry, then know that evil has been determined by him. 8Therefore deal kindly with your servant, for you have brought your servant into a sacred covenant[a] with you. But if there is

a Heb *a covenant of the LORD*

guilt in me, kill me yourself; why should you bring me to your father?" [9]Jonathan said, "Far be it from you! If I knew that it was decided by my father that evil should come upon you, would I not tell you?" [10]Then David said to Jonathan, "Who will tell me if your father answers you harshly?" [11]Jonathan replied to David, "Come, let us go out into the field." So they both went out into the field.

12 Jonathan said to David, "By the Lord, the God of Israel! When I have sounded out my father, about this time tomorrow, or on the third day, if he is well disposed toward David, shall I not then send and disclose it to you? [13]But if my father intends to do you harm, the Lord do so to Jonathan, and more also, if I do not disclose it to you, and send you away, so that you may go in safety. May the Lord be with you, as he has been with my father. [14]If I am still alive, show me the faithful love of the Lord; but if I die, [a] [15]never cut off your faithful love from my house, even if the Lord were to cut off every one of the enemies of David from the face of the earth." [16]Thus Jonathan made a covenant with the house of David, saying, "May the Lord seek out the enemies of David." [17]Jonathan made David swear again by his love for him; for he loved him as he loved his own life.

18 Jonathan said to him, "Tomorrow is the new moon; you will be missed, because your place will be empty. [19]On the day after tomorrow, you shall go a long way down; go to the place where you hid yourself earlier, and remain beside the stone there. [a] [20]I will shoot three arrows to the side of it, as though I shot at a mark. [21]Then I will send the boy, saying, 'Go, find the arrows.' If I say to the boy, 'Look, the arrows are on this side of you, collect them,' then you are to come, for, as the Lord lives, it is safe for you and there is no danger. [22]But if I say to the young

man, 'Look, the arrows are beyond you,' then go; for the Lord has sent you away. [23]As for the matter about which you and I have spoken, the Lord is witness[b] between you and me forever."

24 So David hid himself in the field. When the new moon came, the king sat at the feast to eat. [25]The king sat upon his seat, as at other times, upon the seat by the wall. Jonathan stood, while Abner sat by Saul's side; but David's place was empty.

26 Saul did not say anything that day; for he thought, "Something has befallen him; he is not clean, surely he is not clean." [27]But on the second day, the day after the new moon, David's place was empty. And Saul said to his son Jonathan, "Why has the son of Jesse not come to the feast, either yesterday or today?" [28]Jonathan answered Saul, "David earnestly asked leave of me to go to Bethlehem; [29]he said, 'Let me go; for our family is holding a sacrifice in the city, and my brother has commanded me to be there. So now, if I have found favor in your sight, let me get away, and see my brothers.' For this reason he has not come to the king's table."

30 Then Saul's anger was kindled against Jonathan. He said to him, "You son of a perverse, rebellious woman! Do I not know that you have chosen the son of Jesse to your own shame, and to the shame of your mother's nakedness? [31]For as long as the son of Jesse lives upon the earth, neither you nor your kingdom shall be established. Now send and bring him to me, for he shall surely die." [32]Then Jonathan answered his father Saul, "Why should he be put to death? What has he done?" [33]But Saul threw his spear at him to strike him; so Jonathan knew that it was the decision of his father to put David to death. [34]Jonathan rose from the table in fierce anger and ate no food on

---

aMeaning of Heb uncertain   bGk: Heb lacks *witness*

the second day of the month, for he was grieved for David, and because his father had disgraced him.

35 In the morning Jonathan went out into the field to the appointment with David, and with him was a little boy. 36He said to the boy, "Run and find the arrows that I shoot." As the boy ran, he shot an arrow beyond him. 37When the boy came to the place where Jonathan's arrow had fallen, Jonathan called after the boy and said, "Is the arrow not beyond you?" 38Jonathan called after the boy, "Hurry, be quick, do not linger." So Jonathan's boy gathered up the arrows and came to his master. 39But the boy knew nothing; only Jonathan and David knew the arrangement. 40Jonathan gave his weapons to the boy and said to him, "Go and carry them to the city." 41As soon as the boy had gone, David rose from beside the stone heapa and prostrated himself with his face to the ground. He bowed three times, and they kissed each other, and wept with each other; David wept the more. b 42Then Jonathan said to David, "Go in peace, since both of us have sworn in the name of the LORD, saying, 'The LORD shall be between me and you, and between my descendants and your descendants, forever.' " He got up and left; and Jonathan went into the city. c

21d.1 DAVID came to Nob to the priest Ahimelech. Ahimelech came trembling to meet David, and said to him, "Why are you alone, and no one with you?" 2David said to the priest Ahimelech, "The king has charged me with a matter, and said to me, 'No one must know anything of the matter about which I send you, and with which I have charged you.' I have made an appointmente with the young men for such and such a place. 3Now then, what have you at hand? Give me five loaves of bread, or whatever is here." 4The priest answered David, "I have no ordinary bread at hand, only holy bread—provided that the young men have kept themselves from women." 5David answered the priest, "Indeed women have been kept from us as always when I go on an expedition; the vessels of the young men are holy even when it is a common journey; how much more today will their vessels be holy?" 6So the priest gave him the holy bread; for there was no bread there except the bread of the Presence, which is removed from before the LORD, to be replaced by hot bread on the day it is taken away.

7 Now a certain man of the servants of Saul was there that day, detained before the LORD; his name was Doeg the Edomite, the chief of Saul's shepherds.

8 David said to Ahimelech, "Is there no spear or sword here with you? I did not bring my sword or my weapons with me, because the king's business required haste." 9The priest said, "The sword of Goliath the Philistine, whom you killed in the valley of Elah, is here wrapped in a cloth behind the ephod; if you will take that, take it, for there is none here except that one." David said, "There is none like it; give it to me."

10 David rose and fled that day from Saul; he went to King Achish of Gath. 11The servants of Achish said to him, "Is this not David the king of the land? Did they not sing to one another of him in dances,

'Saul has killed his thousands,
    and David his ten
        thousands'?"

12David took these words to heart and was very much afraid of King Achish of Gath. 13So he changed his behavior before them; he pretended to be mad when in their presence. f He scratched

aGk: Heb *from beside the south*   bVg: Meaning of Heb uncertain   cThis sentence is 21.1 in Heb
dCh 21.2 in Heb   eQ Ms Vg Compare Gk: Meaning of MT uncertain   fHeb *in their hands*

marks on the doors of the gate, and let his spittle run down his beard. [14]Achish said to his servants, "Look, you see the man is mad; why then have you brought him to me? [15]Do I lack madmen, that you have brought this fellow to play the madman in my presence? Shall this fellow come into my house?"

## JOHN 9.1–41

As he [Jesus] walked along, he saw a man blind from birth. [2]His disciples asked him, "Rabbi, who sinned, this man or his parents, that he was born blind?" [3]Jesus answered, "Neither this man nor his parents sinned; he was born blind so that God's works might be revealed in him. [4]We[a] must work the works of him who sent me[b] while it is day; night is coming when no one can work. [5]As long as I am in the world, I am the light of the world." [6]When he had said this, he spat on the ground and made mud with the saliva and spread the mud on the man's eyes, [7]saying to him, "Go, wash in the pool of Siloam" (which means Sent). Then he went and washed and came back able to see. [8]The neighbors and those who had seen him before as a beggar began to ask, "Is this not the man who used to sit and beg?" [9]Some were saying, "It is he." Others were saying, "No, but it is someone like him." He kept saying, "I am the man." [10]But they kept asking him, "Then how were your eyes opened?" [11]He answered, "The man called Jesus made mud, spread it on my eyes, and said to me, 'Go to Siloam and wash.' Then I went and washed and received my sight." [12]They said to him, "Where is he?" He said, "I do not know."

13  They brought to the Pharisees the man who had formerly been blind. [14]Now it was a sabbath day when Jesus made the mud and opened his eyes.

[15]Then the Pharisees also began to ask him how he had received his sight. He said to them, "He put mud on my eyes. Then I washed, and now I see." [16]Some of the Pharisees said, "This man is not from God, for he does not observe the sabbath." But others said, "How can a man who is a sinner perform such signs?" And they were divided. [17]So they said again to the blind man, "What do you say about him? It was your eyes he opened." He said, "He is a prophet."

18  The Jews did not believe that he had been blind and had received his sight until they called the parents of the man who had received his sight [19]and asked them, "Is this your son, who you say was born blind? How then does he now see?" [20]His parents answered, "We know that this is our son, and that he was born blind; [21]but we do not know how it is that now he sees, nor do we know who opened his eyes. Ask him; he is of age. He will speak for himself." [22]His parents said this because they were afraid of the Jews; for the Jews had already agreed that anyone who confessed Jesus[c] to be the Messiah[d] would be put out of the synagogue. [23]Therefore his parents said, "He is of age; ask him."

24  So for the second time they called the man who had been blind, and they said to him, "Give glory to God! We know that this man is a sinner." [25]He answered, "I do not know whether he is a sinner. One thing I do know, that though I was blind, now I see." [26]They said to him, "What did he do to you? How did he open your eyes?" [27]He answered them, "I have told you already, and you would not listen. Why do you want to hear it again? Do you also want to become his disciples?" [28]Then they reviled him, saying, "You are his disciple, but we are disciples of Moses. [29]We know that God has

a Other ancient authorities read *I*  b Other ancient authorities read *us*  c Gk *him*  d Or *the Christ*

spoken to Moses, but as for this man, we do not know where he comes from." [30]The man answered, "Here is an astonishing thing! You do not know where he comes from, and yet he opened my eyes. [31]We know that God does not listen to sinners, but he does listen to one who worships him and obeys his will. [32]Never since the world began has it been heard that anyone opened the eyes of a person born blind. [33]If this man were not from God, he could do nothing." [34]They answered him, "You were born entirely in sins, and are you trying to teach us?" And they drove him out.

35 Jesus heard that they had driven him out, and when he found him, he said, "Do you believe in the Son of Man?"[a] [36]He answered, "And who is he, sir?[b] Tell me, so that I may believe in him." [37]Jesus said to him, "You have seen him, and the one speaking with you is he." [38]He said, "Lord,[b] I believe." And he worshiped him. [39]Jesus said, "I came into this world for judgment so that those who do not see may see, and those who do see may become blind." [40]Some of the Pharisees near him heard this and said to him, "Surely we are not blind, are we?" [41]Jesus said to them, "If you were blind, you would not have sin. But now that you say, 'We see,' your sin remains.

# PSALM 113.1 — 114.8

P RAISE the LORD!
Praise, O servants of the
LORD;
praise the name of the LORD.

2 Blessed be the name of the
LORD
from this time on and
forevermore.
3 From the rising of the sun to its
setting

the name of the LORD is to be
praised.
4 The LORD is high above all
nations,
and his glory above the
heavens.

5 Who is like the LORD our God,
who is seated on high,
6 who looks far down
on the heavens and the earth?
7 He raises the poor from the
dust,
and lifts the needy from the
ash heap,
8 to make them sit with princes,
with the princes of his people.
9 He gives the barren woman a
home,
making her the joyous mother
of children.
Praise the LORD!
114.1 WHEN Israel went out from
Egypt,
the house of Jacob from a
people of strange
language,
2 Judah became God's[c]
sanctuary,
Israel his dominion.

3 The sea looked and fled;
Jordan turned back.
4 The mountains skipped like
rams,
the hills like lambs.

5 Why is it, O sea, that you flee?
O Jordan, that you turn back?
6 O mountains, that you skip like
rams?
O hills, like lambs?

7 Tremble, O earth, at the
presence of the LORD,
at the presence of the God of
Jacob,

aOther ancient authorities read *the Son of God*   bSir and *Lord* translate the same Greek word
cHeb *his*

8  who turns the rock into a pool
       of water,
   the flint into a spring of
       water.

## PROVERBS 15.15–17

**A**LL the days of the poor are
   hard,
   but a cheerful heart has a
   continual feast.

16  Better is a little with the fear of
       the LORD
    than great treasure and
       trouble with it.
17  Better is a dinner of vegetables
       where love is
    than a fatted ox and hatred
       with it.

# MAY 18

## 1 SAMUEL 22.1—23.29

**D**AVID left there and escaped to the cave of Adullam; when his brothers and all his father's house heard of it, they went down there to him. ²Everyone who was in distress, and everyone who was in debt, and everyone who was discontented gathered to him; and he became captain over them. Those who were with him numbered about four hundred.

3  David went from there to Mizpeh of Moab. He said to the king of Moab, "Please let my father and mother come*a* to you, until I know what God will do for me." ⁴He left them with the king of Moab, and they stayed with him all the time that David was in the stronghold. ⁵Then the prophet Gad said to David, "Do not remain in the stronghold; leave, and go into the land of Judah." So David left, and went into the forest of Hereth.

6  Saul heard that David and those who were with him had been located. Saul was sitting at Gibeah, under the tamarisk tree on the height, with his spear in his hand, and all his servants were standing around him. ⁷Saul said to his servants who stood around him, "Hear now, you Benjaminites; will the son of Jesse give every one of you fields and vineyards, will he make you all commanders of thousands and commanders of hundreds? ⁸Is that why all of you have conspired against me? No one discloses to me when my son makes a league with the son of Jesse, none of you is sorry for me or discloses to me that my son has stirred up my servant against me, to lie in wait, as he is doing today." ⁹Doeg the Edomite, who was in charge of Saul's servants, answered, "I saw the son of Jesse coming to Nob, to Ahimelech son of Ahitub; ¹⁰he inquired of the LORD for him, gave him provisions, and gave him the sword of Goliath the Philistine."

11  The king sent for the priest Ahimelech son of Ahitub and for all his father's house, the priests who were at Nob; and all of them came to the king. ¹²Saul said, "Listen now, son of Ahitub." He answered, "Here I am, my lord." ¹³Saul said to him, "Why have

---

*a*Syr Vg: Heb *come out*

you conspired against me, you and the son of Jesse, by giving him bread and a sword, and by inquiring of God for him, so that he has risen against me, to lie in wait, as he is doing today?"

14 Then Ahimelech answered the king, "Who among all your servants is so faithful as David? He is the king's son-in-law, and is quick[a] to do your bidding, and is honored in your house. [15]Is today the first time that I have inquired of God for him? By no means! Do not let the king impute anything to his servant or to any member of my father's house; for your servant has known nothing of all this, much or little." [16]The king said, "You shall surely die, Ahimelech, you and all your father's house." [17]The king said to the guard who stood around him, "Turn and kill the priests of the LORD, because their hand also is with David; they knew that he fled, and did not disclose it to me." But the servants of the king would not raise their hand to attack the priests of the LORD. [18]Then the king said to Doeg, "You, Doeg, turn and attack the priests." Doeg the Edomite turned and attacked the priests; on that day he killed eighty-five who wore the linen ephod. [19]Nob, the city of the priests, he put to the sword; men and women, children and infants, oxen, donkeys, and sheep, he put to the sword.

20 But one of the sons of Ahimelech son of Ahitub, named Abiathar, escaped and fled after David. [21]Abiathar told David that Saul had killed the priests of the LORD. [22]David said to Abiathar, "I knew on that day, when Doeg the Edomite was there, that he would surely tell Saul. I am responsible[b] for the lives of all your father's house. [23]Stay with me, and do not be afraid; for the one who seeks my life seeks your life; you will be safe with me."

23.1 Now they told David, "The Philistines are fighting against Keilah, and are robbing the threshing floors." [2]David inquired of the LORD, "Shall I go and attack these Philistines?" The LORD said to David, "Go and attack the Philistines and save Keilah." [3]But David's men said to him, "Look, we are afraid here in Judah; how much more then if we go to Keilah against the armies of the Philistines?" [4]Then David inquired of the LORD again. The LORD answered him, "Yes, go down to Keilah; for I will give the Philistines into your hand." [5]So David and his men went to Keilah, fought with the Philistines, brought away their livestock, and dealt them a heavy defeat. Thus David rescued the inhabitants of Keilah.

6 When Abiathar son of Ahimelech fled to David at Keilah, he came down with an ephod in his hand. [7]Now it was told Saul that David had come to Keilah. And Saul said, "God has given[c] him into my hand; for he has shut himself in by entering a town that has gates and bars." [8]Saul summoned all the people to war, to go down to Keilah, to besiege David and his men. [9]When David learned that Saul was plotting evil against him, he said to the priest Abiathar, "Bring the ephod here." [10]David said, "O LORD, the God of Israel, your servant has heard that Saul seeks to come to Keilah, to destroy the city on my account. [11]And now, will[d] Saul come down as your servant has heard? O LORD, the God of Israel, I beseech you, tell your servant." The LORD said, "He will come down." [12]Then David said, "Will the men of Keilah surrender me and my men into the hand of Saul?" The LORD said, "They will surrender you." [13]Then David and his men, who were about six hundred, set out and left Keilah; they wandered wherever they could go. When Saul was told that Da-

---

a Heb *and turns aside*   b Gk Vg: Meaning of Heb uncertain   c Gk Tg: Heb *made a stranger of*
d Q Ms Compare Gk: MT *Will the men of Keilah surrender me into his hand? Will*

vid had escaped from Keilah, he gave up the expedition. [14]David remained in the strongholds in the wilderness, in the hill country of the Wilderness of Ziph. Saul sought him every day, but the LORD [a] did not give him into his hand.

15 David was in the Wilderness of Ziph at Horesh when he learned that[b] Saul had come out to seek his life. [16]Saul's son Jonathan set out and came to David at Horesh; there he strengthened his hand through the LORD. [c] [17]He said to him, "Do not be afraid; for the hand of my father Saul shall not find you; you shall be king over Israel, and I shall be second to you; my father Saul also knows that this is so." [18]Then the two of them made a covenant before the LORD; David remained at Horesh, and Jonathan went home.

19 Then some Ziphites went up to Saul at Gibeah and said, "David is hiding among us in the strongholds of Horesh, on the hill of Hachilah, which is south of Jeshimon. [20]Now, O king, whenever you wish to come down, do so; and our part will be to surrender him into the king's hand." [21]Saul said, "May you be blessed by the LORD for showing me compassion! [22]Go and make sure once more; find out exactly where he is, and who has seen him there; for I am told that he is very cunning. [23]Look around and learn all the hiding places where he lurks, and come back to me with sure information. Then I will go with you; and if he is in the land, I will search him out among all the thousands of Judah." [24]So they set out and went to Ziph ahead of Saul.

David and his men were in the wilderness of Maon, in the Arabah to the south of Jeshimon. [25]Saul and his men went to search for him. When David was told, he went down to the rock and stayed in the wilderness of Maon. When Saul heard that, he pursued Da-vid into the wilderness of Maon. [26]Saul went on one side of the mountain, and David and his men on the other side of the mountain. David was hurrying to get away from Saul, while Saul and his men were closing in on David and his men to capture them. [27]Then a messenger came to Saul, saying, "Hurry and come; for the Philistines have made a raid on the land." [28]So Saul stopped pursuing David, and went against the Philistines; therefore that place was called the Rock of Escape. [d] [29e]David then went up from there, and lived in the strongholds of En-gedi.

## JOHN 10. 1–21

"VERY truly, I tell you, anyone who does not enter the sheepfold by the gate but climbs in by another way is a thief and a bandit. [2]The one who enters by the gate is the shepherd of the sheep. [3]The gatekeeper opens the gate for him, and the sheep hear his voice. He calls his own sheep by name and leads them out. [4]When he has brought out all his own, he goes ahead of them, and the sheep follow him because they know his voice. [5]They will not follow a stranger, but they will run from him because they do not know the voice of strangers." [6]Jesus used this figure of speech with them, but they did not understand what he was saying to them.

7 So again Jesus said to them, "Very truly, I tell you, I am the gate for the sheep. [8]All who came before me are thieves and bandits; but the sheep did not listen to them. [9]I am the gate. Whoever enters by me will be saved, and will come in and go out and find pasture. [10]The thief comes only to steal and kill and destroy. I came that they may have life, and have it abundantly.

11 "I am the good shepherd. The good shepherd lays down his life for the

aQ Ms Gk: MT *God*  bOr *saw that*  cCompare Q Ms Gk: MT *God*  dOr *Rock of Division*; Meaning of Heb uncertain  eCh 24.1 in Heb

sheep. ¹²The hired hand, who is not the shepherd and does not own the sheep, sees the wolf coming and leaves the sheep and runs away—and the wolf snatches them and scatters them. ¹³The hired hand runs away because a hired hand does not care for the sheep. ¹⁴I am the good shepherd. I know my own and my own know me, ¹⁵just as the Father knows me and I know the Father. And I lay down my life for the sheep. ¹⁶I have other sheep that do not belong to this fold. I must bring them also, and they will listen to my voice. So there will be one flock, one shepherd. ¹⁷For this reason the Father loves me, because I lay down my life in order to take it up again. ¹⁸No one takes[a] it from me, but I lay it down of my own accord. I have power to lay it down, and I have power to take it up again. I have received this command from my Father."

19 Again the Jews were divided because of these words. ²⁰Many of them were saying, "He has a demon and is out of his mind. Why listen to him?" ²¹Others were saying, "These are not the words of one who has a demon. Can a demon open the eyes of the blind?"

## PSALM 115.1–18

**N**ot to us, O LORD, not to us,
　　but to your name give
　　glory,
　for the sake of your steadfast
　　love and your
　　faithfulness.
2　Why should the nations say,
　　"Where is their God?"

3　Our God is in the heavens;
　　he does whatever he pleases.
4　Their idols are silver and gold,
　　the work of human hands.
5　They have mouths, but do not
　　speak;
　　eyes, but do not see.

6　They have ears, but do not
　　hear;
　　noses, but do not smell.
7　They have hands, but do not
　　feel;
　　feet, but do not walk;
　　they make no sound in their
　　throats.
8　Those who make them are like
　　them;
　　so are all who trust in them.

9　O Israel, trust in the LORD!
　　He is their help and their
　　shield.
10　O house of Aaron, trust in the
　　LORD!
　　He is their help and their
　　shield.
11　You who fear the LORD, trust in
　　the LORD!
　　He is their help and their
　　shield.

12　The LORD has been mindful of
　　us; he will bless us;
　　he will bless the house of
　　Israel;
　　he will bless the house of
　　Aaron;
13　he will bless those who fear the
　　LORD,
　　both small and great.

14　May the LORD give you
　　increase,
　　both you and your children.
15　May you be blessed by the
　　LORD,
　　who made heaven and earth.

16　The heavens are the LORD's
　　heavens,
　　but the earth he has given to
　　human beings.
17　The dead do not praise the
　　LORD,

a Other ancient authorities read *has taken*

nor do any that go down into
    silence.
18 But we will bless the LORD
    from this time on and
      forevermore.
Praise the LORD!

## PROVERBS 15.18–19

THOSE who are hot-tempered
    stir up strife,
but those who are slow to
    anger calm contention.
19 The way of the lazy is
    overgrown with thorns,
but the path of the upright is
    a level highway.

# MAY 19

## 1 SAMUEL 24.1—25.44

WHEN Saul returned from following the Philistines, he was told, "David is in the wilderness of En-gedi." 2Then Saul took three thousand chosen men out of all Israel, and went to look for David and his men in the direction of the Rocks of the Wild Goats. 3He came to the sheepfolds beside the road, where there was a cave; and Saul went in to relieve himself.[a] Now David and his men were sitting in the innermost parts of the cave. 4The men of David said to him, "Here is the day of which the LORD said to you, 'I will give your enemy into your hand, and you shall do to him as it seems good to you.' " Then David went and stealthily cut off a corner of Saul's cloak. 5Afterward David was stricken to the heart because he had cut off a corner of Saul's cloak. 6He said to his men, "The LORD forbid that I should do this thing to my lord, the LORD's anointed, to raise my hand against him; for he is the LORD's anointed." 7So David scolded his men severely and did not permit them to attack Saul. Then

Saul got up and left the cave, and went on his way.

8 Afterwards David also rose up and went out of the cave and called after Saul, "My lord the king!" When Saul looked behind him, David bowed with his face to the ground, and did obeisance. 9David said to Saul, "Why do you listen to the words of those who say, 'David seeks to do you harm'? 10This very day your eyes have seen how the LORD gave you into my hand in the cave; and some urged me to kill you, but I spared[b] you. I said, 'I will not raise my hand against my lord; for he is the LORD's anointed.' 11See, my father, see the corner of your cloak in my hand; for by the fact that I cut off the corner of your cloak, and did not kill you, you may know for certain that there is no wrong or treason in my hands. I have not sinned against you, though you are hunting me to take my life. 12May the LORD judge between me and you! May the LORD avenge me on you; but my hand shall not be against you. 13As the ancient proverb says,

aHeb *to cover his feet*  bGk Syr Tg Vg: Heb *it (my eye)* spared

'Out of the wicked comes forth wickedness'; but my hand shall not be against you. [14]Against whom has the king of Israel come out? Whom do you pursue? A dead dog? A single flea? [15]May the LORD therefore be judge, and give sentence between me and you. May he see to it, and plead my cause, and vindicate me against you."

16 When David had finished speaking these words to Saul, Saul said, "Is this your voice, my son David?" Saul lifted up his voice and wept. [17]He said to David, "You are more righteous than I; for you have repaid me good, whereas I have repaid you evil. [18]Today you have explained how you have dealt well with me, in that you did not kill me when the LORD put me into your hands. [19]For who has ever found an enemy, and sent the enemy safely away? So may the LORD reward you with good for what you have done to me this day. [20]Now I know that you shall surely be king, and that the kingdom of Israel shall be established in your hand. [21]Swear to me therefore by the LORD that you will not cut off my descendants after me, and that you will not wipe out my name from my father's house." [22]So David swore this to Saul. Then Saul went home; but David and his men went up to the stronghold.

[25.1] Now Samuel died; and all Israel assembled and mourned for him. They buried him at his home in Ramah.

Then David got up and went down to the wilderness of Paran.

2 There was a man in Maon, whose property was in Carmel. The man was very rich; he had three thousand sheep and a thousand goats. He was shearing his sheep in Carmel. [3]Now the name of the man was Nabal, and the name of his wife Abigail. The woman was clever and beautiful, but the man was surly and mean; he was a Calebite. [4]David heard in the wilderness that Nabal was shearing his sheep. [5]So David sent ten young men; and David said to the young men, "Go up to Carmel, and go to Nabal, and greet him in my name. [6]Thus you shall salute him: 'Peace be to you, and peace be to your house, and peace be to all that you have. [7]I hear that you have shearers; now your shepherds have been with us, and we did them no harm, and they missed nothing, all the time they were in Carmel. [8]Ask your young men, and they will tell you. Therefore let my young men find favor in your sight; for we have come on a feast day. Please give whatever you have at hand to your servants and to your son David.' "

9 When David's young men came, they said all this to Nabal in the name of David; and then they waited. [10]But Nabal answered David's servants, "Who is David? Who is the son of Jesse? There are many servants today who are breaking away from their masters. [11]Shall I take my bread and my water and the meat that I have butchered for my shearers, and give it to men who come from I do not know where?" [12]So David's young men turned away, and came back and told him all this. [13]David said to his men, "Every man strap on his sword!" And every one of them strapped on his sword; David also strapped on his sword; and about four hundred men went up after David, while two hundred remained with the baggage.

14 But one of the young men told Abigail, Nabal's wife, "David sent messengers out of the wilderness to salute our master; and he shouted insults at them. [15]Yet the men were very good to us, and we suffered no harm, and we never missed anything when we were in the fields, as long as we were with them; [16]they were a wall to us both by night and by day, all the while we were with them keeping the sheep. [17]Now therefore know this and consider what you should do; for evil has been decided against our master and against all his

house; he is so ill-natured that no one can speak to him."

18 Then Abigail hurried and took two hundred loaves, two skins of wine, five sheep ready dressed, five measures of parched grain, one hundred clusters of raisins, and two hundred cakes of figs. She loaded them on donkeys [19]and said to her young men, "Go on ahead of me; I am coming after you." But she did not tell her husband Nabal. [20]As she rode on the donkey and came down under cover of the mountain, David and his men came down toward her; and she met them. [21]Now David had said, "Surely it was in vain that I protected all that this fellow has in the wilderness, so that nothing was missed of all that belonged to him; but he has returned me evil for good. [22]God do so to David[a] and more also, if by morning I leave so much as one male of all who belong to him."

23 When Abigail saw David, she hurried and alighted from the donkey, fell before David on her face, bowing to the ground. [24]She fell at his feet and said, "Upon me alone, my lord, be the guilt; please let your servant speak in your ears, and hear the words of your servant. [25]My lord, do not take seriously this ill-natured fellow, Nabal; for as his name is, so is he; Nabal[b] is his name, and folly is with him; but I, your servant, did not see the young men of my lord, whom you sent.

26 Now then, my lord, as the LORD lives, and as you yourself live, since the LORD has restrained you from bloodguilt and from taking vengeance with your own hand, now let your enemies and those who seek to do evil to my lord be like Nabal. [27]And now let this present that your servant has brought to my lord be given to the young men who follow my lord. [28]Please forgive the trespass of your servant; for the LORD will certainly make my lord a sure house, because my lord is fighting the battles of the LORD; and evil shall not be found in you so long as you live. [29]If anyone should rise up to pursue you and to seek your life, the life of my lord shall be bound in the bundle of the living under the care of the LORD your God; but the lives of your enemies he shall sling out as from the hollow of a sling. [30]When the LORD has done to my lord according to all the good that he has spoken concerning you, and has appointed you prince over Israel, [31]my lord shall have no cause of grief, or pangs of conscience, for having shed blood without cause or for having saved himself. And when the LORD has dealt well with my lord, then remember your servant."

32 David said to Abigail, "Blessed be the LORD, the God of Israel, who sent you to meet me today! [33]Blessed be your good sense, and blessed be you, who have kept me today from bloodguilt and from avenging myself by my own hand! [34]For as surely as the LORD the God of Israel lives, who has restrained me from hurting you, unless you had hurried and come to meet me, truly by morning there would not have been left to Nabal so much as one male." [35]Then David received from her hand what she had brought him; he said to her, "Go up to your house in peace; see, I have heeded your voice, and I have granted your petition."

36 Abigail came to Nabal; he was holding a feast in his house, like the feast of a king. Nabal's heart was merry within him, for he was very drunk; so she told him nothing at all until the morning light. [37]In the morning, when the wine had gone out of Nabal, his wife told him these things, and his heart died within him; he became like a stone. [38]About ten days later the LORD struck Nabal, and he died.

39 When David heard that Nabal

a Gk Compare Syr: Heb *the enemies of David*   b That is *Fool*

was dead, he said, "Blessed be the LORD who has judged the case of Nabal's insult to me, and has kept back his servant from evil; the LORD has returned the evildoing of Nabal upon his own head." Then David sent and wooed Abigail, to make her his wife. 40When David's servants came to Abigail at Carmel, they said to her, "David has sent us to you to take you to him as his wife." 41She rose and bowed down, with her face to the ground, and said, "Your servant is a slave to wash the feet of the servants of my lord." 42Abigail got up hurriedly and rode away on a donkey; her five maids attended her. She went after the messengers of David and became his wife.

43 David also married Ahinoam of Jezreel; both of them became his wives. 44Saul had given his daughter Michal, David's wife, to Palti son of Laish, who was from Gallim.

## JOHN 10.22–42

**A**T that time the festival of the Dedication took place in Jerusalem. It was winter, 23and Jesus was walking in the temple, in the portico of Solomon. 24So the Jews gathered around him and said to him, "How long will you keep us in suspense? If you are the Messiah, a tell us plainly." 25Jesus answered, "I have told you, and you do not believe. The works that I do in my Father's name testify to me; 26but you do not believe, because you do not belong to my sheep. 27My sheep hear my voice. I know them, and they follow me. 28I give them eternal life, and they will never perish. No one will snatch them out of my hand. 29What my Father has given me is greater than all else, and no one can snatch it out of the Father's hand. b 30The Father and I are one."

31 The Jews took up stones again to stone him. 32Jesus replied, "I have shown you many good works from the Father. For which of these are you going to stone me?" 33The Jews answered, "It is not for a good work that we are going to stone you, but for blasphemy, because you, though only a human being, are making yourself God." 34Jesus answered, "Is it not written in your law, c 'I said, you are gods'? 35If those to whom the word of God came were called 'gods'—and the scripture cannot be annulled— 36can you say that the one whom the Father has sanctified and sent into the world is blaspheming because I said, 'I am God's Son'? 37If I am not doing the works of my Father, then do not believe me. 38But if I do them, even though you do not believe me, believe the works, so that you may know and understandd that the Father is in me and I am in the Father." 39Then they tried to arrest him again, but he escaped from their hands.

40 He went away again across the Jordan to the place where John had been baptizing earlier, and he remained there. 41Many came to him, and they were saying, "John performed no sign, but everything that John said about this man was true." 42And many believed in him there.

## PSALM 116.1–19

**I** LOVE the LORD, because he has
    heard
  my voice and my
    supplications.
2  Because he inclined his ear to
    me,
    therefore I will call on him as
    long as I live.
3  The snares of death
    encompassed me;

aOr *the Christ*  bOther ancient authorities read *My Father who has given them to me is greater than all, and no one can snatch them out of the Father's hand*  cOther ancient authorities read *in the law*
dOther ancient authorities lack *and understand*; others read *and believe*

the pangs of Sheol laid hold
   on me;
I suffered distress and
   anguish.
4 Then I called on the name of
   the LORD:
   "O LORD, I pray, save my
      life!"

5 Gracious is the LORD, and
   righteous;
   our God is merciful.
6 The LORD protects the simple;
   when I was brought low, he
      saved me.
7 Return, O my soul, to your
   rest,
   for the LORD has dealt
      bountifully with you.

8 For you have delivered my soul
   from death,
   my eyes from tears,
   my feet from stumbling.
9 I walk before the LORD
   in the land of the living.
10 I kept my faith, even when I
   said,
   "I am greatly afflicted";
11 I said in my consternation,
   "Everyone is a liar."

12 What shall I return to the LORD
   for all his bounty to me?
13 I will lift up the cup of salvation
   and call on the name of the
      LORD,
14 I will pay my vows to the LORD
   in the presence of all his
      people.
15 Precious in the sight of the
   LORD
   is the death of his faithful
      ones.
16 O LORD, I am your servant;
   I am your servant, the child
      of your serving girl.
   You have loosed my bonds.
17 I will offer to you a thanksgiving
   sacrifice
   and call on the name of the
      LORD.
18 I will pay my vows to the LORD
   in the presence of all his
      people,
19 in the courts of the house of
   the LORD,
   in your midst, O Jerusalem.
Praise the LORD!

## PROVERBS 15.20–21

A WISE child makes a glad
   father,
but the foolish despise their
   mothers.
21 Folly is a joy to one who has no
   sense,
   but a person of understanding
      walks straight ahead.

## 1 SAMUEL 26.1—28.25

Then the Ziphites came to Saul at Gibeah, saying, "David is in hiding on the hill of Hachilah, which is opposite Jeshimon."[a] 2So Saul rose and went down to the Wilderness of Ziph, with three thousand chosen men of Israel, to seek David in the Wilderness of Ziph. 3Saul encamped on the hill of Hachilah, which is opposite Jeshimon[a] beside the road. But David remained in the wilderness. When he learned that Saul came after him into the wilderness, 4David sent out spies, and learned that Saul had indeed arrived. 5Then David set out and came to the place where Saul had encamped; and David saw the place where Saul lay, with Abner son of Ner, the commander of his army. Saul was lying within the encampment, while the army was encamped around him.

6 Then David said to Ahimelech the Hittite, and to Joab's brother Abishai son of Zeruiah, "Who will go down with me into the camp to Saul?" Abishai said, "I will go down with you." 7So David and Abishai went to the army by night; there Saul lay sleeping within the encampment, with his spear stuck in the ground at his head; and Abner and the army lay around him. 8Abishai said to David, "God has given your enemy into your hand today; now therefore let me pin him to the ground with one stroke of the spear; I will not strike him twice." 9But David said to Abishai, "Do not destroy him; for who can raise his hand against the Lord's anointed, and be guiltless?" 10David said, "As the Lord lives, the Lord will strike him down; or his day will come to die; or he will go down into battle and perish.

11The Lord forbid that I should raise my hand against the Lord's anointed; but now take the spear that is at his head, and the water jar, and let us go." 12So David took the spear that was at Saul's head and the water jar, and they went away. No one saw it, or knew it, nor did anyone awake; for they were all asleep, because a deep sleep from the Lord had fallen upon them.

13 Then David went over to the other side, and stood on top of a hill far away, with a great distance between them. 14David called to the army and to Abner son of Ner, saying, "Abner! Will you not answer?" Then Abner replied, "Who are you that calls to the king?" 15David said to Abner, "Are you not a man? Who is like you in Israel? Why then have you not kept watch over your lord the king? For one of the people came in to destroy your lord the king. 16This thing that you have done is not good. As the Lord lives, you deserve to die, because you have not kept watch over your lord, the Lord's anointed. See now, where is the king's spear, or the water jar that was at his head?"

17 Saul recognized David's voice, and said, "Is this your voice, my son David?" David said, "It is my voice, my lord, O king." 18And he added, "Why does my lord pursue his servant? For what have I done? What guilt is on my hands? 19Now therefore let my lord the king hear the words of his servant. If it is the Lord who has stirred you up against me, may he accept an offering; but if it is mortals, may they be cursed before the Lord, for they have driven me out today from my share in the heritage of the Lord, saying, 'Go, serve other gods.' 20Now therefore, do not

let my blood fall to the ground, away from the presence of the LORD; for the king of Israel has come out to seek a single flea, like one who hunts a partridge in the mountains."

21 Then Saul said, "I have done wrong; come back, my son David, for I will never harm you again, because my life was precious in your sight today; I have been a fool, and have made a great mistake." 22David replied, "Here is the spear, O king! Let one of the young men come over and get it. 23The LORD rewards everyone for his righteousness and his faithfulness; for the LORD gave you into my hand today, but I would not raise my hand against the LORD's anointed. 24As your life was precious today in my sight, so may my life be precious in the sight of the LORD, and may he rescue me from all tribulation." 25Then Saul said to David, "Blessed be you, my son David! You will do many things and will succeed in them." So David went his way, and Saul returned to his place.

27.1 DAVID said in his heart, "I shall now perish one day by the hand of Saul; there is nothing better for me than to escape to the land of the Philistines; then Saul will despair of seeking me any longer within the borders of Israel, and I shall escape out of his hand." 2So David set out and went over, he and the six hundred men who were with him, to King Achish son of Maoch of Gath. 3David stayed with Achish at Gath, he and his troops, every man with his household, and David with his two wives, Ahinoam of Jezreel, and Abigail of Carmel, Nabal's widow. 4When Saul was told that David had fled to Gath, he no longer sought for him.

5 Then David said to Achish, "If I have found favor in your sight, let a place be given me in one of the country towns, so that I may live there; for why should your servant live in the royal city with you?" 6So that day Achish gave him Ziklag; therefore Ziklag has belonged to the kings of Judah to this day. 7The length of time that David lived in the country of the Philistines was one year and four months.

8 Now David and his men went up and made raids on the Geshurites, the Girzites, and the Amalekites; for these were the landed settlements from Telam[a] on the way to Shur and on to the land of Egypt. 9David struck the land, leaving neither man nor woman alive, but took away the sheep, the oxen, the donkeys, the camels, and the clothing, and came back to Achish. 10When Achish asked, "Against whom[b] have you made a raid today?" David would say, "Against the Negeb of Judah," or "Against the Negeb of the Jerahmeelites," or, "Against the Negeb of the Kenites." 11David left neither man nor woman alive to be brought back to Gath, thinking, "They might tell about us, and say, 'David has done so and so.'" Such was his practice all the time he lived in the country of the Philistines. 12Achish trusted David, thinking, "He has made himself utterly abhorrent to his people Israel; therefore he shall always be my servant."

28.1 IN those days the Philistines gathered their forces for war, to fight against Israel. Achish said to David, "You know, of course, that you and your men are to go out with me in the army." 2David said to Achish, "Very well, then you shall know what your servant can do." Achish said to David, "Very well, I will make you my bodyguard for life."

3 Now Samuel had died, and all Israel had mourned for him and buried him in Ramah, his own city. Saul had expelled the mediums and the wizards from the land. 4The Philistines assem-

a Compare Gk 15.4: Heb *from of old*    b Q Ms Gk Vg: MT lacks *whom* bled, and came and encamped at Shunem. Saul gathered all Israel, and they encamped at Gilboa. 5When Saul saw the army of the Philistines, he was afraid, and his heart trembled greatly. 6When Saul inquired of the LORD, the LORD did not answer him, not by dreams, or by Urim, or by prophets. 7Then Saul said to his servants, "Seek out for me a woman who is a medium, so that I may go to her and inquire of her." His servants said to him, "There is a medium at Endor."

8  So Saul disguised himself and put on other clothes and went there, he and two men with him. They came to the woman by night. And he said, "Consult a spirit for me, and bring up for me the one whom I name to you." 9The woman said to him, "Surely you know what Saul has done, how he has cut off the mediums and the wizards from the land. Why then are you laying a snare for my life to bring about my death?" 10But Saul swore to her by the LORD, "As the LORD lives, no punishment shall come upon you for this thing." 11Then the woman said, "Whom shall I bring up for you?" He answered, "Bring up Samuel for me." 12When the woman saw Samuel, she cried out with a loud voice; and the woman said to Saul, "Why have you deceived me? You are Saul!" 13The king said to her, "Have no fear; what do you see?" The woman said to Saul, "I see a divine beinga coming up out of the ground." 14He said to her, "What is his appearance?" She said, "An old man is coming up; he is wrapped in a robe." So Saul knew that it was Samuel, and he bowed with his face to the ground, and did obeisance.

15  Then Samuel said to Saul, "Why have you disturbed me by bringing me up?" Saul answered, "I am in great distress, for the Philistines are warring against me, and God has turned away from me and answers me no more, ei-ther by prophets or by dreams; so I have summoned you to tell me what I should do." 16Samuel said, "Why then do you ask me, since the LORD has turned from you and become your enemy? 17The LORD has done to you just as he spoke by me; for the LORD has torn the kingdom out of your hand, and given it to your neighbor, David. 18Because you did not obey the voice of the LORD, and did not carry out his fierce wrath against Amalek, therefore the LORD has done this thing to you today. 19Moreover the LORD will give Israel along with you into the hands of the Philistines; and tomorrow you and your sons shall be with me; the LORD will also give the army of Israel into the hands of the Philistines."

20  Immediately Saul fell full length on the ground, filled with fear because of the words of Samuel; and there was no strength in him, for he had eaten nothing all day and all night. 21The woman came to Saul, and when she saw that he was terrified, she said to him, "Your servant has listened to you; I have taken my life in my hand, and have listened to what you have said to me. 22Now therefore, you also listen to your servant; let me set a morsel of bread before you. Eat, that you may have strength when you go on your way." 23He refused, and said, "I will not eat." But his servants, together with the woman, urged him; and he listened to their words. So he got up from the ground and sat on the bed. 24Now the woman had a fatted calf in the house. She quickly slaughtered it, and she took flour, kneaded it, and baked unleavened cakes. 25She put them before Saul and his servants, and they ate. Then they rose and went away that night.

a Or *a god*; or *gods*

## JOHN 11.1–53

**N**ow a certain man was ill, Lazarus of Bethany, the village of Mary and her sister Martha. [2]Mary was the one who anointed the Lord with perfume and wiped his feet with her hair; her brother Lazarus was ill. [3]So the sisters sent a message to Jesus,[a] "Lord, he whom you love is ill." [4]But when Jesus heard it, he said, "This illness does not lead to death; rather it is for God's glory, so that the Son of God may be glorified through it." [5]Accordingly, though Jesus loved Martha and her sister and Lazarus, [6]after having heard that Lazarus[b] was ill, he stayed two days longer in the place where he was.

7 Then after this he said to the disciples, "Let us go to Judea again." [8]The disciples said to him, "Rabbi, the Jews were just now trying to stone you, and are you going there again?" [9]Jesus answered, "Are there not twelve hours of daylight? Those who walk during the day do not stumble, because they see the light of this world. [10]But those who walk at night stumble, because the light is not in them." [11]After saying this, he told them, "Our friend Lazarus has fallen asleep, but I am going there to awaken him." [12]The disciples said to him, "Lord, if he has fallen asleep, he will be all right." [13]Jesus, however, had been speaking about his death, but they thought that he was referring merely to sleep. [14]Then Jesus told them plainly, "Lazarus is dead. [15]For your sake I am glad I was not there, so that you may believe. But let us go to him." [16]Thomas, who was called the Twin,[c] said to his fellow disciples, "Let us also go, that we may die with him."

17 When Jesus arrived, he found that Lazarus[b] had already been in the tomb four days. [18]Now Bethany was near Jerusalem, some two miles[d] away, [19]and many of the Jews had come to Martha and Mary to console them about their brother. [20]When Martha heard that Jesus was coming, she went and met him, while Mary stayed at home. [21]Martha said to Jesus, "Lord, if you had been here, my brother would not have died. [22]But even now I know that God will give you whatever you ask of him." [23]Jesus said to her, "Your brother will rise again." [24]Martha said to him, "I know that he will rise again in the resurrection on the last day." [25]Jesus said to her, "I am the resurrection and the life.[e] Those who believe in me, even though they die, will live, [26]and everyone who lives and believes in me will never die. Do you believe this?" [27]She said to him, "Yes, Lord, I believe that you are the Messiah,[f] the Son of God, the one coming into the world."

28 When she had said this, she went back and called her sister Mary, and told her privately, "The Teacher is here and is calling for you." [29]And when she heard it, she got up quickly and went to him. [30]Now Jesus had not yet come to the village, but was still at the place where Martha had met him. [31]The Jews who were with her in the house, consoling her, saw Mary get up quickly and go out. They followed her because they thought that she was going to the tomb to weep there. [32]When Mary came where Jesus was and saw him, she knelt at his feet and said to him, "Lord, if you had been here, my brother would not have died." [33]When Jesus saw her weeping, and the Jews who came with her also weeping, he was greatly disturbed in spirit and deeply moved. [34]He said, "Where have you laid him?" They said to him, "Lord, come and see." [35]Jesus began to weep. [36]So the Jews said, "See how he loved him!" [37]But some of them said, "Could

aGk *him*  bGk *he*  cGk *Didymus*  dGk *fifteen stadia*  eOther ancient authorities lack *and the life*
fOr *the Christ*

not he who opened the eyes of the blind man have kept this man from dying?"

38 Then Jesus, again greatly disturbed, came to the tomb. It was a cave, and a stone was lying against it. ³⁹Jesus said, "Take away the stone." Martha, the sister of the dead man, said to him, "Lord, already there is a stench because he has been dead four days." ⁴⁰Jesus said to her, "Did I not tell you that if you believed, you would see the glory of God?" ⁴¹So they took away the stone. And Jesus looked upward and said, "Father, I thank you for having heard me. ⁴²I knew that you always hear me, but I have said this for the sake of the crowd standing here, so that they may believe that you sent me." ⁴³When he had said this, he cried with a loud voice, "Lazarus, come out!" ⁴⁴The dead man came out, his hands and feet bound with strips of cloth, and his face wrapped in a cloth. Jesus said to them, "Unbind him, and let him go."

45 Many of the Jews therefore, who had come with Mary and had seen what Jesus did, believed in him. ⁴⁶But some of them went to the Pharisees and told them what he had done. ⁴⁷So the chief priests and the Pharisees called a meeting of the council, and said, "What are we to do? This man is performing many signs. ⁴⁸If we let him go on like this, everyone will believe in him, and the Romans will come and destroy both our holy place[a] and our nation." ⁴⁹But one of them, Caiaphas, who was high priest that year, said to them, "You know nothing at all! ⁵⁰You do not understand that it is better for you to have one man die for the people than to have the whole nation destroyed." ⁵¹He did not say this on his own, but being high priest that year he prophesied that Jesus was about to die for the nation, ⁵²and not for the nation only, but to gather into one the dispersed children of God. ⁵³So from that day on they planned to put him to death.

## PSALM 117.1–2

Praise the Lord, all you
    nations!
  Extol him, all you peoples!
2 For great is his steadfast love
    toward us,
  and the faithfulness of the
    Lord endures forever.
Praise the Lord!

## PROVERBS 15.22–23

Without counsel, plans go
    wrong,
  but with many advisers
    they succeed.
23 To make an apt answer is a joy
    to anyone,
  and a word in season, how
    good it is!

a Or *our temple*; Greek *our place*

# MAY 21

## 1 SAMUEL 29.1—31.13

Now the Philistines gathered all their forces at Aphek, while the Israelites were encamped by the fountain that is in Jezreel. [2]As the lords of the Philistines were passing on by hundreds and by thousands, and David and his men were passing on in the rear with Achish, [3]the commanders of the Philistines said, "What are these Hebrews doing here?" Achish said to the commanders of the Philistines, "Is this not David, the servant of King Saul of Israel, who has been with me now for days and years? Since he deserted to me I have found no fault in him to this day." [4]But the commanders of the Philistines were angry with him; and the commanders of the Philistines said to him, "Send the man back, so that he may return to the place that you have assigned to him; he shall not go down with us to battle, or else he may become an adversary to us in the battle. For how could this fellow reconcile himself to his lord? Would it not be with the heads of the men here? [5]Is this not David, of whom they sing to one another in dances,

> 'Saul has killed his thousands,
>> and David his ten
>>> thousands'?"

[6] Then Achish called David and said to him, "As the LORD lives, you have been honest, and to me it seems right that you should march out and in with me in the campaign; for I have found nothing wrong in you from the day of your coming to me until today. Nevertheless the lords do not approve of you. [7]So go back now; and go peaceably; do nothing to displease the lords of the Philistines." [8]David said to Achish, "But what have I done? What have you found in your servant from the day I entered your service until now, that I should not go and fight against the enemies of my lord the king?" [9]Achish replied to David, "I know that you are as blameless in my sight as an angel of God; nevertheless, the commanders of the Philistines have said, 'He shall not go up with us to the battle.' [10]Now then rise early in the morning, you and the servants of your lord who came with you, and go to the place that I appointed for you. As for the evil report, do not take it to heart, for you have done well before me. [a] Start early in the morning, and leave as soon as you have light." [11]So David set out with his men early in the morning, to return to the land of the Philistines. But the Philistines went up to Jezreel.

[30.1] Now when David and his men came to Ziklag on the third day, the Amalekites had made a raid on the Negeb and on Ziklag. They had attacked Ziklag, burned it down, [2]and taken captive the women and all[b] who were in it, both small and great; they killed none of them, but carried them off, and went their way. [3]When David and his men came to the city, they found it burned down, and their wives and sons and daughters taken captive. [4]Then David and the people who were with him raised their voices and wept, until they had no more strength to weep. [5]David's two wives also had been taken captive, Ahinoam of Jezreel, and Abigail the widow of Nabal of Carmel. [6]David was in great danger; for the people spoke of stoning him, because all the people were bitter in spirit for their

---

a Gk: Heb lacks *and go to the place . . . done well before me*  b Gk: Heb lacks *and all*

sons and daughters. But David strengthened himself in the Lord his God.

7 David said to the priest Abiathar son of Ahimelech, "Bring me the ephod." So Abiathar brought the ephod to David. [8]David inquired of the Lord, "Shall I pursue this band? Shall I overtake them?" He answered him, "Pursue; for you shall surely overtake and shall surely rescue." [9]So David set out, he and the six hundred men who were with him. They came to the Wadi Besor, where those stayed who were left behind. [10]But David went on with the pursuit, he and four hundred men; two hundred stayed behind, too exhausted to cross the Wadi Besor.

11 In the open country they found an Egyptian, and brought him to David. They gave him bread and he ate, they gave him water to drink; [12]they also gave him a piece of fig cake and two clusters of raisins. When he had eaten, his spirit revived; for he had not eaten bread or drunk water for three days and three nights. [13]Then David said to him, "To whom do you belong? Where are you from?" He said, "I am a young man of Egypt, servant to an Amalekite. My master left me behind because I fell sick three days ago. [14]We had made a raid on the Negeb of the Cherethites and on that which belongs to Judah and on the Negeb of Caleb; and we burned Ziklag down." [15]David said to him, "Will you take me down to this raiding party?" He said, "Swear to me by God that you will not kill me, or hand me over to my master, and I will take you down to them."

16 When he had taken him down, they were spread out all over the ground, eating and drinking and dancing, because of the great amount of spoil they had taken from the land of the Philistines and from the land of Judah. [17]David attacked them from twilight until the evening of the next day. Not one of them escaped, except four hundred young men, who mounted camels and fled. [18]David recovered all that the Amalekites had taken; and David rescued his two wives. [19]Nothing was missing, whether small or great, sons or daughters, spoil or anything that had been taken; David brought back everything. [20]David also captured all the flocks and herds, which were driven ahead of the other cattle; people said, "This is David's spoil."

21 Then David came to the two hundred men who had been too exhausted to follow David, and who had been left at the Wadi Besor. They went out to meet David and to meet the people who were with him. When David drew near to the people he saluted them. [22]Then all the corrupt and worthless fellows among the men who had gone with David said, "Because they did not go with us, we will not give them any of the spoil that we have recovered, except that each man may take his wife and children, and leave." [23]But David said, "You shall not do so, my brothers, with what the Lord has given us; he has preserved us and handed over to us the raiding party that attacked us. [24]Who would listen to you in this matter? For the share of the one who goes down into the battle shall be the same as the share of the one who stays by the baggage; they shall share alike." [25]From that day forward he made it a statute and an ordinance for Israel; it continues to the present day.

26 When David came to Ziklag, he sent part of the spoil to his friends, the elders of Judah, saying, "Here is a present for you from the spoil of the enemies of the Lord"; [27]it was for those in Bethel, in Ramoth of the Negeb, in Jattir, [28]in Aroer, in Siphmoth, in Eshtemoa, [29]in Racal, in the towns of the Jerahmeelites, in the towns of the Kenites, [30]in Hormah, in Bor-ashan, in Athach, [31]in Hebron, all the places where David and his men had roamed.

31.1 Now the Philistines fought against Israel; and the men of Israel fled before the Philistines, and many fell[a] on Mount Gilboa. 2The Philistines overtook Saul and his sons; and the Philistines killed Jonathan and Abinadab and Malchishua, the sons of Saul. 3The battle pressed hard upon Saul; the archers found him, and he was badly wounded by them. 4Then Saul said to his armorbearer, "Draw your sword and thrust me through with it, so that these uncircumcised may not come and thrust me through, and make sport of me." But his armor-bearer was unwilling; for he was terrified. So Saul took his own sword and fell upon it. 5When his armor-bearer saw that Saul was dead, he also fell upon his sword and died with him. 6So Saul and his three sons and his armor-bearer and all his men died together on the same day. 7When the men of Israel who were on the other side of the valley and those beyond the Jordan saw that the men of Israel had fled and that Saul and his sons were dead, they forsook their towns and fled; and the Philistines came and occupied them.

8 The next day, when the Philistines came to strip the dead, they found Saul and his three sons fallen on Mount Gilboa. 9They cut off his head, stripped off his armor, and sent messengers throughout the land of the Philistines to carry the good news to the houses of their idols and to the people. 10They put his armor in the temple of Astarte;[b] and they fastened his body to the wall of Beth-shan. 11But when the inhabitants of Jabesh-gilead heard what the Philistines had done to Saul, 12all the valiant men set out, traveled all night long, and took the body of Saul and the bodies of his sons from the wall of Beth-shan. They came to Jabesh and burned them there. 13Then they took their bones and buried them under the tamarisk tree in Jabesh, and fasted seven days.

## JOHN 11.54—12.19

Jesus therefore no longer walked about openly among the Jews, but went from there to a town called Ephraim in the region near the wilderness; and he remained there with the disciples. 55 Now the Passover of the Jews was near, and many went up from the country to Jerusalem before the Passover to purify themselves. 56They were looking for Jesus and were asking one another as they stood in the temple, "What do you think? Surely he will not come to the festival, will he?" 57Now the chief priests and the Pharisees had given orders that anyone who knew where Jesus[c] was should let them know, so that they might arrest him.

12.1 Six days before the Passover Jesus came to Bethany, the home of Lazarus, whom he had raised from the dead. 2There they gave a dinner for him. Martha served, and Lazarus was one of those at the table with him. 3Mary took a pound of costly perfume made of pure nard, anointed Jesus' feet, and wiped them[d] with her hair. The house was filled with the fragrance of the perfume. 4But Judas Iscariot, one of his disciples (the one who was about to betray him), said, 5"Why was this perfume not sold for three hundred denarii[e] and the money given to the poor?" 6(He said this not because he cared about the poor, but because he was a thief; he kept the common purse and used to steal what was put into it.) 7Jesus said, "Leave her alone. She bought it[f] so that she might keep it for the day of my burial. 8You always have the poor with you, but you do not always have me."

aHeb *and they fell slain*  bHeb plural  cGk *he*  dGk *his feet*  eThree hundred denarii would be nearly a year's wages for a laborer  fGk lacks *She bought it*

9 When the great crowd of the Jews learned that he was there, they came not only because of Jesus but also to see Lazarus, whom he had raised from the dead. 10So the chief priests planned to put Lazarus to death as well, 11since it was on account of him that many of the Jews were deserting and were believing in Jesus.

12 The next day the great crowd that had come to the festival heard that Jesus was coming to Jerusalem. 13So they took branches of palm trees and went out to meet him, shouting,

> "Hosanna!
> Blessed is the one who comes
> in the name
> of the Lord—
> the King of Israel!"

14Jesus found a young donkey and sat on it; as it is written:

15 "Do not be afraid, daughter of
> Zion.
> Look, your king is coming,
> sitting on a donkey's colt!"

16His disciples did not understand these things at first; but when Jesus was glorified, then they remembered that these things had been written of him and had been done to him. 17So the crowd that had been with him when he called Lazarus out of the tomb and raised him from the dead continued to testify. a 18It was also because they heard that he had performed this sign that the crowd went to meet him. 19The Pharisees then said to one another, "You see, you can do nothing. Look, the world has gone after him!"

## PSALM 118. 1–18

O GIVE thanks to the Lord, for
> he is good;
> his steadfast love endures
> forever!

2 Let Israel say,

> "His steadfast love endures
> forever."
3 Let the house of Aaron say,
> "His steadfast love endures
> forever."
4 Let those who fear the Lord
> say,
> "His steadfast love endures
> forever."

5 Out of my distress I called on
> the Lord;
> the Lord answered me and
> set me in a broad place.
6 With the Lord on my side I do
> not fear.
> What can mortals do to me?
7 The Lord is on my side to help
> me;
> I shall look in triumph on
> those who hate me.
8 It is better to take refuge in the
> Lord
> than to put confidence in
> mortals.
9 It is better to take refuge in the
> Lord
> than to put confidence in
> princes.

10 All nations surrounded me;
> in the name of the Lord I cut
> them off!
11 They surrounded me,
> surrounded me on every
> side;
> in the name of the Lord I cut
> them off!
12 They surrounded me like bees;
> they blazedb like a fire of
> thorns;
> in the name of the Lord I cut
> them off!
13 I was pushed hard, c so that I
> was falling,
> but the Lord helped me.
14 The Lord is my strength and
> my might;

aOther ancient authorities read *with him began to testify that he had called. . .from the dead*
bGk: Heb *were extinguished*   cGk Syr Jerome: Heb *You pushed me hard*

he has become my salvation.

15 There are glad songs of victory
     in the tents of the
     righteous:
   "The right hand of the Lord
       does valiantly;
16   the right hand of the Lord is
       exalted;
     the right hand of the Lord
       does valiantly."
17 I shall not die, but I shall live,
     and recount the deeds of the
       Lord.
18 The Lord has punished me
     severely,

but he did not give me over
   to death.

## PROVERBS 15.24–26

FOR the wise the path of life
     leads upward,
   in order to avoid Sheol
     below.
25 The Lord tears down the house
     of the proud,
     but maintains the widow's
       boundaries.
26 Evil plans are an abomination to
     the Lord,
     but gracious words are pure.

# MAY 22

## 2 SAMUEL 1.1—2.11

AFTER the death of Saul, when David had returned from defeating the Amalekites, David remained two days in Ziklag. ²On the third day, a man came from Saul's camp, with his clothes torn and dirt on his head. When he came to David, he fell to the ground and did obeisance. ³David said to him, "Where have you come from?" He said to him, "I have escaped from the camp of Israel." ⁴David said to him, "How did things go? Tell me!" He answered, "The army fled from the battle, but also many of the army fell and died; and Saul and his son Jonathan also died." ⁵Then David asked the young man who was reporting to him, "How do you know that Saul and his son Jonathan died?" ⁶The young man reporting to him said, "I happened to be on Mount Gilboa; and there was Saul leaning on his spear, while the chariots and the horsemen drew close to him. ⁷When he looked behind him, he saw me, and called to me. I answered, 'Here sir.' ⁸And he said to me, 'Who are you?' I answered him, 'I am an Amalekite.' ⁹He said to me, 'Come, stand over me and kill me; for convulsions have seized me, and yet my life still lingers.' ¹⁰So I stood over him, and killed him, for I knew that he could not live after he had fallen. I took the crown that was on his head and the armlet that was on his arm, and I have brought them here to my lord."

11 Then David took hold of his clothes and tore them; and all the men who were with him did the same. ¹²They mourned and wept, and fasted until evening for Saul and for his son Jonathan, and for the army of the Lord and for the house of Israel, because they had fallen by the sword. ¹³David said to the young man who had reported to him, "Where do you come from?" He answered, "I am the son of

a resident alien, an Amalekite." ¹⁴David said to him, "Were you not afraid to lift your hand to destroy the Lord's anointed?" ¹⁵Then David called one of the young men and said, "Come here and strike him down." So he struck him down and he died. ¹⁶David said to him, "Your blood be on your head; for your own mouth has testified against you, saying, 'I have killed the Lord's anointed.'"

17 David intoned this lamentation over Saul and his son Jonathan. ¹⁸(He ordered that The Song of the Bow[a] be taught to the people of Judah; it is written in the Book of Jashar.) He said:

¹⁹ Your glory, O Israel, lies slain
        upon your high places!
    How the mighty have fallen!
²⁰ Tell it not in Gath,
        proclaim it not in the streets
            of Ashkelon;
    or the daughters of the
            Philistines will rejoice,
        the daughters of the
            uncircumcised will exult.

²¹ You mountains of Gilboa,
        let there be no dew or rain
            upon you,
        nor bounteous fields![b]
    For there the shield of the
            mighty was defiled,
        the shield of Saul, anointed
            with oil no more.

²² From the blood of the slain,
        from the fat of the mighty,
    the bow of Jonathan did not turn
            back,
        nor the sword of Saul return
            empty.

²³ Saul and Jonathan, beloved and
            lovely!
        In life and in death they were
            not divided;
    they were swifter than eagles,
        they were stronger than
            lions.

²⁴ O daughters of Israel, weep
            over Saul,
        who clothed you with
            crimson, in luxury,
        who put ornaments of gold on
            your apparel.

²⁵ How the mighty have fallen
        in the midst of the battle!

    Jonathan lies slain upon your
            high places.
²⁶     I am distressed for you, my
            brother Jonathan;
    greatly beloved were you to
            me;
        your love to me was
            wonderful,
        passing the love of women.

²⁷ How the mighty have fallen,
        and the weapons of war
            perished!

2.1 After this David inquired of the Lord, "Shall I go up into any of the cities of Judah?" The Lord said to him, "Go up." David said, "To which shall I go up?" He said, "To Hebron." ²So David went up there, along with his two wives, Ahinoam of Jezreel, and Abigail the widow of Nabal of Carmel. ³David brought up the men who were with him, every one with his household; and they settled in the towns of Hebron. ⁴Then the people of Judah came, and there they anointed David king over the house of Judah.

When they told David, "It was the people of Jabesh-gilead who buried Saul," ⁵David sent messengers to the people of Jabesh-gilead, and said to them, "May you be blessed by the Lord, because you showed this loyalty to Saul your lord, and buried him! ⁶Now

---

a Heb *that The Bow*   b Meaning of Heb uncertain

may the L ORD show steadfast love and faithfulness to you! And I too will reward you because you have done this thing. 7Therefore let your hands be strong, and be valiant; for Saul your lord is dead, and the house of Judah has anointed me king over them."

8 But Abner son of Ner, commander of Saul's army, had taken Ishbaala son of Saul, and brought him over to Mahanaim. 9He made him king over Gilead, the Ashurites, Jezreel, Ephraim, Benjamin, and over all Israel. 10Ishbaal, a Saul's son, was forty years old when he began to reign over Israel, and he reigned two years. But the house of Judah followed David. 11The time that David was king in Hebron over the house of Judah was seven years and six months.

## JOHN 12.20–50

Now among those who went up to worship at the festival were some Greeks. 21They came to Philip, who was from Bethsaida in Galilee, and said to him, "Sir, we wish to see Jesus." 22Philip went and told Andrew; then Andrew and Philip went and told Jesus. 23Jesus answered them, "The hour has come for the Son of Man to be glorified. 24Very truly, I tell you, unless a grain of wheat falls into the earth and dies, it remains just a single grain; but if it dies, it bears much fruit. 25Those who love their life lose it, and those who hate their life in this world will keep it for eternal life. 26Whoever serves me must follow me, and where I am, there will my servant be also. Whoever serves me, the Father will honor.

27 "Now my soul is troubled. And what should I say—'Father, save me from this hour'? No, it is for this reason that I have come to this hour. 28Father, glorify your name." Then a voice came from heaven, "I have glorified it, and I will glorify it again." 29The crowd standing there heard it and said that it was thunder. Others said, "An angel has spoken to him." 30Jesus answered, "This voice has come for your sake, not for mine. 31Now is the judgment of this world; now the ruler of this world will be driven out. 32And I, when I am lifted up from the earth, will draw all peopleb to myself." 33He said this to indicate the kind of death he was to die. 34The crowd answered him, "We have heard from the law that the Messiahc remains forever. How can you say that the Son of Man must be lifted up? Who is this Son of Man?" 35Jesus said to them, "The light is with you for a little longer. Walk while you have the light, so that the darkness may not overtake you. If you walk in the darkness, you do not know where you are going. 36While you have the light, believe in the light, so that you may become children of light."

After Jesus had said this, he departed and hid from them. 37Although he had performed so many signs in their presence, they did not believe in him. 38This was to fulfill the word spoken by the prophet Isaiah:
"Lord, who has believed our
    message,
  and to whom has the arm of
      the Lord been revealed?"
39And so they could not believe, because Isaiah also said,
40  "He has blinded their eyes
    and hardened their heart,
  so that they might not look with
      their eyes,
    and understand with their
      heart and turn—
    and I would heal them."
41Isaiah said this becaused he saw his glory and spoke about him. 42Nevertheless many, even of the authorities, believed in him. But because of the

aGk Compare 1 Chr 8.33; 9.39: Heb *Ish-bosheth,* "man of shame"    bOther ancient authorities read *all things*    cOr *the Christ*    dOther ancient witnesses read *when*

Pharisees they did not confess it, for fear that they would be put out of the synagogue; ⁴³for they loved human glory more than the glory that comes from God.

44 Then Jesus cried aloud: "Whoever believes in me believes not in me but in him who sent me. ⁴⁵And whoever sees me sees him who sent me. ⁴⁶I have come as light into the world, so that everyone who believes in me should not remain in the darkness. ⁴⁷I do not judge anyone who hears my words and does not keep them, for I came not to judge the world, but to save the world. ⁴⁸The one who rejects me and does not receive my word has a judge; on the last day the word that I have spoken will serve as judge, ⁴⁹for I have not spoken on my own, but the Father who sent me has himself given me a commandment about what to say and what to speak. ⁵⁰And I know that his commandment is eternal life. What I speak, therefore, I speak just as the Father has told me."

## PSALM 118. 19–29

OPEN to me the gates of
   righteousness,
that I may enter through them
and give thanks to the LORD.

20  This is the gate of the LORD;
   the righteous shall enter
     through it.

21  I thank you that you have
     answered me
   and have become my
     salvation.
22  The stone that the builders
     rejected

has become the chief
   cornerstone.
23  This is the LORD's doing;
   it is marvelous in our eyes.
24  This is the day that the LORD
     has made;
   let us rejoice and be glad in
     it. ᵃ
25  Save us, we beseech you,
     O LORD!
   O LORD, we beseech you,
     give us success!

26  Blessed is the one who comes
     in the name of the
     LORD. ᵇ
   We bless you from the house
     of the LORD.
27  The LORD is God,
   and he has given us light.
   Bind the festal procession with
     branches,
   up to the horns of the altar. ᶜ

28  You are my God, and I will give
     thanks to you;
   you are my God, I will extol
     you.

29  O give thanks to the LORD, for
     he is good,
   for his steadfast love endures
     forever.

## PROVERBS 15. 27–28

THOSE who are greedy for
   unjust gain make
   trouble for their
   households,
but those who hate bribes
   will live.
28  The mind of the righteous
     ponders how to answer,
   but the mouth of the wicked
     pours out evil.

ᵃOr *in him*   ᵇOr *Blessed in the name of the* LORD *is the one who comes*   ᶜMeaning of Heb uncertain

# MAY 23

---

## 2 SAMUEL 2.12—3.39

ABNER son of Ner, and the servants of Ishbaal[a] son of Saul, went out from Mahanaim to Gibeon. [13]Joab son of Zeruiah, and the servants of David, went out and met them at the pool of Gibeon. One group sat on one side of the pool, while the other sat on the other side of the pool. [14]Abner said to Joab, "Let the young men come forward and have a contest before us." Joab said, "Let them come forward." [15]So they came forward and were counted as they passed by, twelve for Benjamin and Ishbaal[a] son of Saul, and twelve of the servants of David. [16]Each grasped his opponent by the head, and thrust his sword in his opponent's side; so they fell down together. Therefore that place was called Helkath-hazzurim,[b] which is at Gibeon. [17]The battle was very fierce that day; and Abner and the men of Israel were beaten by the servants of David.

18  The three sons of Zeruiah were there, Joab, Abishai, and Asahel. Now Asahel was as swift of foot as a wild gazelle. [19]Asahel pursued Abner, turning neither to the right nor to the left as he followed him. [20]Then Abner looked back and said, "Is it you, Asahel?" He answered, "Yes, it is." [21]Abner said to him, "Turn to your right or to your left, and seize one of the young men, and take his spoil." But Asahel would not turn away from following him. [22]Abner said again to Asahel, "Turn away from following me; why should I strike you to the ground? How then could I show my face to your brother Joab?" [23]But he refused to turn away. So Abner struck him in the stomach with the butt of his spear, so that the spear came out at his back. He fell there, and died where he lay. And all those who came to the place where Asahel had fallen and died, stood still.

24  But Joab and Abishai pursued Abner. As the sun was going down they came to the hill of Ammah, which lies before Giah on the way to the wilderness of Gibeon. [25]The Benjaminites rallied around Abner and formed a single band; they took their stand on the top of a hill. [26]Then Abner called to Joab, "Is the sword to keep devouring forever? Do you not know that the end will be bitter? How long will it be before you order your people to turn from the pursuit of their kinsmen?" [27]Joab said, "As God lives, if you had not spoken, the people would have continued to pursue their kinsmen, not stopping until morning." [28]Joab sounded the trumpet and all the people stopped; they no longer pursued Israel or engaged in battle any further.

29  Abner and his men traveled all that night through the Arabah; they crossed the Jordan, and, marching the whole forenoon,[c] they came to Mahanaim. [30]Joab returned from the pursuit of Abner; and when he had gathered all the people together, there were missing of David's servants nineteen men besides Asahel. [31]But the servants of David had killed of Benjamin three hundred sixty of Abner's men. [32]They took up Asahel and buried him in the tomb of his father, which was at Bethlehem. Joab and his men marched all night, and the day broke upon them at Hebron.

3.1  THERE was a long war between the house of Saul and the house of David; David grew stronger and stronger,

---

aGk Compare 1 Chr 8.33; 9.39: Heb *Ish-bosheth,* "man of shame"    bThat is *Field of Sword-edges*
cMeaning of Heb uncertain

while the house of Saul became weaker and weaker.

2 Sons were born to David at Hebron: his firstborn was Amnon, of Ahinoam of Jezreel; <sup>3</sup>his second, Chileab, of Abigail the widow of Nabal of Carmel; the third, Absalom son of Maacah, daughter of King Talmai of Geshur; <sup>4</sup>the fourth, Adonijah son of Haggith; the fifth, Shephatiah son of Abital; <sup>5</sup>and the sixth, Ithream, of David's wife Eglah. These were born to David in Hebron.

6 While there was war between the house of Saul and the house of David, Abner was making himself strong in the house of Saul. <sup>7</sup>Now Saul had a concubine whose name was Rizpah daughter of Aiah. And Ishbaal<sup>a</sup> said to Abner, "Why have you gone in to my father's concubine?" <sup>8</sup>The words of Ishbaal<sup>b</sup> made Abner very angry; he said, "Am I a dog's head for Judah? Today I keep showing loyalty to the house of your father Saul, to his brothers, and to his friends, and have not given you into the hand of David; and yet you charge me now with a crime concerning this woman. <sup>9</sup>So may God do to Abner and so may he add to it! For just what the LORD has sworn to David, that will I accomplish for him, <sup>10</sup>to transfer the kingdom from the house of Saul, and set up the throne of David over Israel and over Judah, from Dan to Beer-sheba." <sup>11</sup>And Ishbaal<sup>a</sup> could not answer Abner another word, because he feared him.

12 Abner sent messengers to David at Hebron, <sup>c</sup> saying, "To whom does the land belong? Make your covenant with me, and I will give you my support to bring all Israel over to you." <sup>13</sup>He said, "Good; I will make a covenant with you. But one thing I require of you: you shall never appear in my presence unless you bring Saul's daughter Michal when you come to see me." <sup>14</sup>Then David sent messengers to Saul's son Ishbaal, <sup>d</sup> saying, "Give me my wife Michal, to whom I became engaged at the price of one hundred foreskins of the Philistines." <sup>15</sup>Ishbaal<sup>d</sup> sent and took her from her husband Paltiel the son of Laish. <sup>16</sup>But her husband went with her, weeping as he walked behind her all the way to Bahurim. Then Abner said to him, "Go back home!" So he went back.

17 Abner sent word to the elders of Israel, saying, "For some time past you have been seeking David as king over you. <sup>18</sup>Now then bring it about; for the LORD has promised David: Through my servant David I will save my people Israel from the hand of the Philistines, and from all their enemies." <sup>19</sup>Abner also spoke directly to the Benjaminites; then Abner went to tell David at Hebron all that Israel and the whole house of Benjamin were ready to do.

20 When Abner came with twenty men to David at Hebron, David made a feast for Abner and the men who were with him. <sup>21</sup>Abner said to David, "Let me go and rally all Israel to my lord the king, in order that they may make a covenant with you, and that you may reign over all that your heart desires." So David dismissed Abner, and he went away in peace.

22 Just then the servants of David arrived with Joab from a raid, bringing much spoil with them. But Abner was not with David at Hebron, for David<sup>e</sup> had dismissed him, and he had gone away in peace. <sup>23</sup>When Joab and all the army that was with him came, it was told Joab, "Abner son of Ner came to the king, and he has dismissed him, and he has gone away in peace." <sup>24</sup>Then Joab went to the king and said, "What have you done? Abner came to you; why did you dismiss him, so that he got away? <sup>25</sup>You know that Abner son of Ner came to deceive you, and to learn

a Heb *And he*  b Gk Compare 1 Chr 8.33; 9.39: Heb *Ish-bosheth*, "man of shame"  c Gk: Heb *where he was*  d Heb *Ish-bosheth*  e Heb *he*

your comings and goings and to learn all that you are doing."

26 When Joab came out from David's presence, he sent messengers after Abner, and they brought him back from the cistern of Sirah; but David did not know about it. [27]When Abner returned to Hebron, Joab took him aside in the gateway to speak with him privately, and there he stabbed him in the stomach. So he died for shedding[a] the blood of Asahel, Joab's[b] brother. [28]Afterward, when David heard of it, he said, "I and my kingdom are forever guiltless before the LORD for the blood of Abner son of Ner. [29]May the guilt[c] fall on the head of Joab, and on all his father's house; and may the house of Joab never be without one who has a discharge, or who is leprous,[d] or who holds a spindle, or who falls by the sword, or who lacks food!" [30]So Joab and his brother Abishai murdered Abner because he had killed their brother Asahel in the battle at Gibeon.

31 Then David said to Joab and to all the people who were with him, "Tear your clothes, and put on sackcloth, and mourn over Abner." And King David followed the bier. [32]They buried Abner at Hebron. The king lifted up his voice and wept at the grave of Abner, and all the people wept. [33]The king lamented for Abner, saying,

> "Should Abner die as a fool
>     dies?
> [34] Your hands were not bound,
>     your feet were not fettered;
> as one falls before the wicked
>     you have fallen."

And all the people wept over him again. [35]Then all the people came to persuade David to eat something while it was still day; but David swore, saying, "So may God do to me, and more, if I taste bread or anything else before the sun goes down!" [36]All the people took notice of it, and it pleased them; just as every-thing the king did pleased all the people. [37]So all the people and all Israel understood that day that the king had no part in the killing of Abner son of Ner. [38]And the king said to his servants, "Do you not know that a prince and a great man has fallen this day in Israel? [39]Today I am powerless, even though anointed king; these men, the sons of Zeruiah, are too violent for me. The LORD pay back the one who does wickedly in accordance with his wickedness!"

## JOHN 13. 1–30

Now before the festival of the Passover, Jesus knew that his hour had come to depart from this world and go to the Father. Having loved his own who were in the world, he loved them to the end. [2]The devil had already put it into the heart of Judas son of Simon Iscariot to betray him. And during supper [3]Jesus, knowing that the Father had given all things into his hands, and that he had come from God and was going to God, [4]got up from the table,[e] took off his outer robe, and tied a towel around himself. [5]Then he poured water into a basin and began to wash the disciples' feet and to wipe them with the towel that was tied around him. [6]He came to Simon Peter, who said to him, "Lord, are you going to wash my feet?" [7]Jesus answered, "You do not know now what I am doing, but later you will understand." [8]Peter said to him, "You will never wash my feet." Jesus answered, "Unless I wash you, you have no share with me." [9]Simon Peter said to him, "Lord, not my feet only but also my hands and my head!" [10]Jesus said to him, "One who has bathed does not need to wash, except for the feet,[f] but is entirely clean.

[a]Heb lacks *shedding*  [b]Heb *his*  [c]Heb *May it*  [d]A term for several skin diseases; precise meaning uncertain  [e]Gk *from supper*  [f]Other ancient authorities lack *except for the feet*

And you[a] are clean, though not all of you." [11]For he knew who was to betray him; for this reason he said, "Not all of you are clean."

12  After he had washed their feet, had put on his robe, and had returned to the table, he said to them, "Do you know what I have done to you? [13]You call me Teacher and Lord—and you are right, for that is what I am. [14]So if I, your Lord and Teacher, have washed your feet, you also ought to wash one another's feet. [15]For I have set you an example, that you also should do as I have done to you. [16]Very truly, I tell you, servants[b] are not greater than their master, nor are messengers greater than the one who sent them. [17]If you know these things, you are blessed if you do them. [18]I am not speaking of all of you; I know whom I have chosen. But it is to fulfill the scripture, 'The one who ate my bread[c] has lifted his heel against me.' [19]I tell you this now, before it occurs, so that when it does occur, you may believe that I am he.[d] [20]Very truly, I tell you, whoever receives one whom I send receives me; and whoever receives me receives him who sent me."

21  After saying this Jesus was troubled in spirit, and declared, "Very truly, I tell you, one of you will betray me." [22]The disciples looked at one another, uncertain of whom he was speaking. [23]One of his disciples—the one whom Jesus loved—was reclining next to him; [24]Simon Peter therefore motioned to him to ask Jesus of whom he was speaking. [25]So while reclining next to Jesus, he asked him, "Lord, who is it?" [26]Jesus answered, "It is the one to whom I give this piece of bread when I have dipped it in the dish."[e] So when he had dipped the piece of bread, he gave it to Judas son of Simon Iscariot.[f] [27]After he received the piece of bread,[g] Satan entered into him. Jesus said to him, "Do quickly what you are going to do." [28]Now no one at the table knew why he said this to him. [29]Some thought that, because Judas had the common purse, Jesus was telling him, "Buy what we need for the festival"; or, that he should give something to the poor. [30]So, after receiving the piece of bread, he immediately went out. And it was night.

## PSALM 119.1–16

Happy are those whose way is blameless,
who walk in the law of the LORD.
2  Happy are those who keep his decrees,
who seek him with their whole heart,
3  who also do no wrong,
but walk in his ways.
4  You have commanded your precepts
to be kept diligently.
5  O that my ways may be steadfast
in keeping your statutes!
6  Then I shall not be put to shame,
having my eyes fixed on all your commandments.
7  I will praise you with an upright heart,
when I learn your righteous ordinances.
8  I will observe your statutes;
do not utterly forsake me.

9  How can young people keep their way pure?
By guarding it according to your word.
10  With my whole heart I seek you;

---

[a]The Greek word for *you* here is plural  [b]Gk *slaves*  [c]Other ancient authorities read *ate bread with me*  [d]Gk *I am*  [e]Gk *dipped it*  [f]Other ancient authorities read *Judas Iscariot son of Simon*; others, *Judas son of Simon from Karyot* (Kerioth)  [g]Gk *After the piece of bread*

> do not let me stray from your
>   commandments.
> 11 I treasure your word in my
>   heart,
>   so that I may not sin against
>   you.
> 12 Blessed are you, O Lord;
>   teach me your statutes.
> 13 With my lips I declare
>   all the ordinances of your
>   mouth.
> 14 I delight in the way of your
>   decrees
>   as much as in all riches.
> 15 I will meditate on your
>   precepts,

> and fix my eyes on your
>   ways.
> 16 I will delight in your statutes;
>   I will not forget your word.

## PROVERBS 15.29–30

> THE Lord is far from the
>   wicked,
>   but he hears the prayer of
>   the righteous.
> 30 The light of the eyes rejoices
>   the heart,
>   and good news refreshes
>   the body.

# MAY 24

## 2 SAMUEL 4.1—6.23

WHEN Saul's son Ishbaal[a] heard that Abner had died at Hebron, his courage failed, and all Israel was dismayed. [2] Saul's son had two captains of raiding bands; the name of the one was Baanah, and the name of the other Rechab. They were sons of Rimmon a Benjaminite from Beeroth— for Beeroth is considered to belong to Benjamin. [3] (Now the people of Beeroth had fled to Gittaim and are there as resident aliens to this day).

4 Saul's son Jonathan had a son who was crippled in his feet. He was five years old when the news about Saul and Jonathan came from Jezreel. His nurse picked him up and fled; and, in her haste to flee, it happened that he fell and became lame. His name was Mephibosheth. [b]

5 Now the sons of Rimmon the Be- erothite, Rechab and Baanah, set out, and about the heat of the day they came to the house of Ishbaal, [c] while he was taking his noonday rest. [6] They came inside the house as though to take wheat, and they struck him in the stomach; then Rechab and his brother Baanah escaped. [d] [7] Now they had come into the house while he was lying on his couch in his bedchamber; they attacked him, killed him, and beheaded him. Then they took his head and traveled by way of the Arabah all night long. [8] They brought the head of Ishbaal[c] to David at Hebron and said to the king, "Here is the head of Ishbaal, [c] son of Saul, your enemy, who sought your life; the Lord has avenged my lord the king this day on Saul and on his offspring."

9 David answered Rechab and his brother Baanah, the sons of Rimmon the Beerothite, "As the Lord lives,

who has redeemed my life out of every adversity, [10]when the one who told me, 'See, Saul is dead,' thought he was bringing good news, I seized him and killed him at Ziklag—this was the reward I gave him for his news. [11]How much more then, when wicked men have killed a righteous man on his bed in his own house! And now shall I not require his blood at your hand, and destroy you from the earth?" [12]So David commanded the young men, and they killed them; they cut off their hands and feet, and hung their bodies beside the pool at Hebron. But the head of Ish-baal[a] they took and buried in the tomb of Abner at Hebron.

**5.**[1] THEN all the tribes of Israel came to David at Hebron, and said, "Look, we are your bone and flesh. [2]For some time, while Saul was king over us, it was you who led out Israel and brought it in. The LORD said to you: It is you who shall be shepherd of my people Israel, you who shall be ruler over Israel." [3]So all the elders of Israel came to the king at Hebron; and King David made a covenant with them at Hebron before the LORD, and they anointed David king over Israel. [4]David was thirty years old when he began to reign, and he reigned forty years. [5]At Hebron he reigned over Judah seven years and six months; and at Jerusalem he reigned over all Israel and Judah thirty-three years.

[6] The king and his men marched to Jerusalem against the Jebusites, the inhabitants of the land, who said to David, "You will not come in here, even the blind and the lame will turn you back"—thinking, "David cannot come in here." [7]Nevertheless David took the stronghold of Zion, which is now the city of David. [8]David had said on that day, "Whoever would strike down the Jebusites, let him get up the water shaft to attack the lame and the blind,

those whom David hates."[b] Therefore it is said, "The blind and the lame shall not come into the house." [9]David occupied the stronghold, and named it the city of David. David built the city all around from the Millo inward. [10]And David became greater and greater, for the LORD, the God of hosts, was with him.

[11] King Hiram of Tyre sent messengers to David, along with cedar trees, and carpenters and masons who built David a house. [12]David then perceived that the LORD had established him king over Israel, and that he had exalted his kingdom for the sake of his people Israel.

[13] In Jerusalem, after he came from Hebron, David took more concubines and wives; and more sons and daughters were born to David. [14]These are the names of those who were born to him in Jerusalem: Shammua, Shobab, Nathan, Solomon, [15]Ibhar, Elishua, Nepheg, Japhia, [16]Elishama, Eliada, and Eliphelet.

[17] When the Philistines heard that David had been anointed king over Israel, all the Philistines went up in search of David; but David heard about it and went down to the stronghold. [18]Now the Philistines had come and spread out in the valley of Rephaim. [19]David inquired of the LORD, "Shall I go up against the Philistines? Will you give them into my hand?" The LORD said to David, "Go up; for I will certainly give the Philistines into your hand." [20]So David came to Baal-perazim, and David defeated them there. He said, "The LORD has burst forth against[c] my enemies before me, like a bursting flood." Therefore that place is called Baal-perazim.[d] [21]The Philistines abandoned their idols there, and David and his men carried them away.

[22] Once again the Philistines came up, and were spread out in the valley of

aHeb *Ish-bosheth*  bAnother reading is *those who hate David*  cHeb *paraz*  dThat is *Lord of Bursting Forth*

Rephaim. [23]When David inquired of the Lord, he said, "You shall not go up; go around to their rear, and come upon them opposite the balsam trees. [24]When you hear the sound of marching in the tops of the balsam trees, then be on the alert; for then the Lord has gone out before you to strike down the army of the Philistines." [25]David did just as the Lord had commanded him; and he struck down the Philistines from Geba all the way to Gezer.

6.[1] David again gathered all the chosen men of Israel, thirty thousand. [2]David and all the people with him set out and went from Baale-judah, to bring up from there the ark of God, which is called by the name of the Lord of hosts who is enthroned on the cherubim. [3]They carried the ark of God on a new cart, and brought it out of the house of Abinadab, which was on the hill. Uzzah and Ahio, [a] the sons of Abinadab, were driving the new cart [4]with the ark of God; [b] and Ahio[a] went in front of the ark. [5]David and all the house of Israel were dancing before the Lord with all their might, with songs[c] and lyres and harps and tambourines and castanets and cymbals.

6  When they came to the threshing floor of Nacon, Uzzah reached out his hand to the ark of God and took hold of it, for the oxen shook it. [7]The anger of the Lord was kindled against Uzzah; and God struck him there because he reached out his hand to the ark; [d] and he died there beside the ark of God. [8]David was angry because the Lord had burst forth with an outburst upon Uzzah; so that place is called Perez-uzzah, [e] to this day. [9]David was afraid of the Lord that day; he said, "How can the ark of the Lord come into my care?" [10]So David was unwilling to take the ark of the Lord into his care in the city of David; instead David took it to the house of Obed-edom the Gittite. [11]The ark of the Lord remained in the house of Obed-edom the Gittite three months; and the Lord blessed Obed-edom and all his household.

12  It was told King David, "The Lord has blessed the household of Obed-edom and all that belongs to him, because of the ark of God." So David went and brought up the ark of God from the house of Obed-edom to the city of David with rejoicing; [13]and when those who bore the ark of the Lord had gone six paces, he sacrificed an ox and a fatling. [14]David danced before the Lord with all his might; David was girded with a linen ephod. [15]So David and all the house of Israel brought up the ark of the Lord with shouting, and with the sound of the trumpet.

16  As the ark of the Lord came into the city of David, Michal daughter of Saul looked out of the window, and saw King David leaping and dancing before the Lord; and she despised him in her heart.

17  They brought in the ark of the Lord, and set it in its place, inside the tent that David had pitched for it; and David offered burnt offerings and offerings of well-being before the Lord. [18]When David had finished offering the burnt offerings and the offerings of well-being, he blessed the people in the name of the Lord of hosts, [19]and distributed food among all the people, the whole multitude of Israel, both men and women, to each a cake of bread, a portion of meat, [f] and a cake of raisins. Then all the people went back to their homes.

20  David returned to bless his household. But Michal the daughter of Saul came out to meet David, and said, "How the king of Israel honored himself today, uncovering himself today before

aOr *and his brother*  bCompare Gk: Heb *and brought it out of the house of Abinadab, which was on the hill with the ark of God*  cQ Ms Gk 1 Chr 13.8: Heb *fir-trees*  d1 Chr 13.10 Compare Q Ms: Meaning of Heb uncertain  eThat is *Bursting Out Against Uzzah*  fVg: Meaning of Heb uncertain

the eyes of his servants' maids, as any vulgar fellow might shamelessly uncover himself!" 21David said to Michal, "It was before the LORD, who chose me in place of your father and all his household, to appoint me as prince over Israel, the people of the LORD, that I have danced before the LORD. 22I will make myself yet more contemptible than this, and I will be abased in my own eyes; but by the maids of whom you have spoken, by them I shall be held in honor." 23And Michal the daughter of Saul had no child to the day of her death.

## JOHN 13.31—14.14

WHEN he [Judas Iscariot] had gone out, Jesus said, "Now the Son of Man has been glorified, and God has been glorified in him. 32If God has been glorified in him, a God will also glorify him in himself and will glorify him at once. 33Little children, I am with you only a little longer. You will look for me; and as I said to the Jews so now I say to you, 'Where I am going, you cannot come.' 34I give you a new commandment, that you love one another. Just as I have loved you, you also should love one another. 35By this everyone will know that you are my disciples, if you have love for one another."

36 Simon Peter said to him, "Lord, where are you going?" Jesus answered, "Where I am going, you cannot follow me now; but you will follow afterward." 37Peter said to him, "Lord, why can I not follow you now? I will lay down my life for you." 38Jesus answered, "Will you lay down your life for me? Very truly, I tell you, before the cock crows, you will have denied me three times.

14.1 "Do not let your hearts be troubled. Believeb in God, believe also in me. 2In my Father's house there are many dwelling places. If it were not so, would I have told you that I go to prepare a place for you?c 3And if I go and prepare a place for you, I will come again and will take you to myself, so that where I am, there you may be also. 4And you know the way to the place where I am going."d 5Thomas said to him, "Lord, we do not know where you are going. How can we know the way?" 6Jesus said to him, "I am the way, and the truth, and the life. No one comes to the Father except through me. 7If you know me, you will knowe my Father also. From now on you do know him and have seen him."

8 Philip said to him, "Lord, show us the Father, and we will be satisfied." 9Jesus said to him, "Have I been with you all this time, Philip, and you still do not know me? Whoever has seen me has seen the Father. How can you say, 'Show us the Father'? 10Do you not believe that I am in the Father and the Father is in me? The words that I say to you I do not speak on my own; but the Father who dwells in me does his works. 11Believe me that I am in the Father and the Father is in me; but if you do not, then believe me because of the works themselves. 12Very truly, I tell you, the one who believes in me will also do the works that I do and, in fact, will do greater works than these, because I am going to the Father. 13I will do whatever you ask in my name, so that the Father may be glorified in the Son. 14If in my name you ask mef for anything, I will do it.

aOther ancient authorities lack *If God has been glorified in him*  bOr *You believe*  cOr *If it were not so, I would have told you; for I go to prepare a place for you*  dOther ancient authorities read *Where I am going you know, and the way you know*  eOther ancient authorities read *If you had known me, you would have known*  fOther ancient authorities lack *me*

## PSALM 119.17–32

**D**EAL bountifully with your
servant,
so that I may live and
observe your word.
18 Open my eyes, so that I may
behold
wondrous things out of your
law.
19 I live as an alien in the land;
do not hide your
commandments from me.
20 My soul is consumed with
longing
for your ordinances at all
times.
21 You rebuke the insolent,
accursed ones,
who wander from your
commandments;
22 take away from me their scorn
and contempt,
for I have kept your decrees.
23 Even though princes sit plotting
against me,
your servant will meditate on
your statutes.
24 Your decrees are my delight,
they are my counselors.

25 My soul clings to the dust;
revive me according to your
word.

26 When I told of my ways, you
answered me;
teach me your statutes.
27 Make me understand the way of
your precepts,
and I will meditate on your
wondrous works.
28 My soul melts away for sorrow;
strengthen me according to
your word.
29 Put false ways far from me;
and graciously teach me
your law.
30 I have chosen the way of
faithfulness;
I set your ordinances before
me.
31 I cling to your decrees, O LORD;
let me not be put to shame.
32 I run the way of your
commandments,
for you enlarge my
understanding.

## PROVERBS 15.31–32

**T**HE ear that heeds wholesome
admonition
will lodge among the wise.
32 Those who ignore instruction
despise themselves,
but those who heed
admonition gain
understanding.

# MAY 25

## 2 SAMUEL 7.1—8.18

**N**OW when the king was settled in
his house, and the LORD had
given him rest from all his enemies around him, 2the king said to the
prophet Nathan, "See now, I am living
in a house of cedar, but the ark of God
stays in a tent." 3Nathan said to the
king, "Go, do all that you have in mind;
for the LORD is with you."

4 But that same night the word of
the LORD came to Nathan: 5Go and tell

my servant David: Thus says the Lord: Are you the one to build me a house to live in? [6]I have not lived in a house since the day I brought up the people of Israel from Egypt to this day, but I have been moving about in a tent and a tabernacle. [7]Wherever I have moved about among all the people of Israel, did I ever speak a word with any of the tribal leaders[a] of Israel, whom I commanded to shepherd my people Israel, saying, "Why have you not built me a house of cedar?" [8]Now therefore thus you shall say to my servant David: Thus says the Lord of hosts: I took you from the pasture, from following the sheep to be prince over my people Israel; [9]and I have been with you wherever you went, and have cut off all your enemies from before you; and I will make for you a great name, like the name of the great ones of the earth. [10]And I will appoint a place for my people Israel and will plant them, so that they may live in their own place, and be disturbed no more; and evildoers shall afflict them no more, as formerly, [11]from the time that I appointed judges over my people Israel; and I will give you rest from all your enemies. Moreover the Lord declares to you that the Lord will make you a house. [12]When your days are fulfilled and you lie down with your ancestors, I will raise up your offspring after you, who shall come forth from your body, and I will establish his kingdom. [13]He shall build a house for my name, and I will establish the throne of his kingdom forever. [14]I will be a father to him, and he shall be a son to me. When he commits iniquity, I will punish him with a rod such as mortals use, with blows inflicted by human beings. [15]But I will not take[b] my steadfast love from him, as I took it from Saul, whom I put away from before you. [16]Your house and your kingdom shall be made sure forever before me;[c] your throne shall be established forever. [17]In accordance with all these words and with all this vision, Nathan spoke to David.

18  Then King David went in and sat before the Lord, and said, "Who am I, O Lord God, and what is my house, that you have brought me thus far? [19]And yet this was a small thing in your eyes, O Lord God; you have spoken also of your servant's house for a great while to come. May this be instruction for the people,[d] O Lord God! [20]And what more can David say to you? For you know your servant, O Lord God! [21]Because of your promise, and according to your own heart, you have wrought all this greatness, so that your servant may know it. [22]Therefore you are great, O Lord God; for there is no one like you, and there is no God besides you, according to all that we have heard with our ears. [23]Who is like your people, like Israel? Is there another[e] nation on earth whose God went to redeem it as a people, and to make a name for himself, doing great and awesome things for them,[f] by driving out[g] before his people nations and their gods?[h] [24]And you established your people Israel for yourself to be your people forever; and you, O Lord, became their God. [25]And now, O Lord God, as for the word that you have spoken concerning your servant and concerning his house, confirm it forever; do as you have promised. [26]Thus your name will be magnified forever in the saying, 'The Lord of hosts is God over Israel'; and the house of your servant David will be established before you. [27]For you, O Lord of hosts, the God of Israel, have made this revelation to your servant, saying, 'I will build you a house'; therefore your servant has

aOr *any of the tribes*  bGk Syr Vg 1 Chr 17.13: Heb *shall not depart*  cGk Heb Mss: MT *before you;* Compare 2 Sam 7.26, 29  dMeaning of Heb uncertain  eGk: Heb *one*  fHeb *you*  gGk 1 Chr 17.21: Heb *for your land*  hCn: Heb *before your people, whom you redeemed for yourself from Egypt, nations and its gods*

found courage to pray this prayer to you. ²⁸And now, O Lord God, you are God, and your words are true, and you have promised this good thing to your servant; ²⁹now therefore may it please you to bless the house of your servant, so that it may continue forever before you; for you, O Lord God, have spoken, and with your blessing shall the house of your servant be blessed forever."

**8.**1 Some time afterward, David attacked the Philistines and subdued them; David took Metheg-ammah out of the hand of the Philistines.

2 He also defeated the Moabites and, making them lie down on the ground, measured them off with a cord; he measured two lengths of cord for those who were to be put to death, and one length[a] for those who were to be spared. And the Moabites became servants to David and brought tribute.

3 David also struck down King Hadadezer son of Rehob of Zobah, as he went to restore his monument[b] at the river Euphrates. ⁴David took from him one thousand seven hundred horsemen, and twenty thousand foot soldiers. David hamstrung all the chariot horses, but left enough for a hundred chariots. ⁵When the Arameans of Damascus came to help King Hadadezer of Zobah, David killed twenty-two thousand men of the Arameans. ⁶Then David put garrisons among the Arameans of Damascus; and the Arameans became servants to David and brought tribute. The Lord gave victory to David wherever he went. ⁷David took the gold shields that were carried by the servants of Hadadezer, and brought them to Jerusalem. ⁸From Betah and from Berothai, towns of Hadadezer, King David took a great amount of bronze.

9 When King Toi of Hamath heard that David had defeated the whole army of Hadadezer, ¹⁰Toi sent his son Joram to King David, to greet him and to congratulate him because he had fought against Hadadezer and defeated him. Now Hadadezer had often been at war with Toi. Joram brought with him articles of silver, gold, and bronze; ¹¹these also King David dedicated to the Lord, together with the silver and gold that he dedicated from all the nations he subdued, ¹²from Edom, Moab, the Ammonites, the Philistines, Amalek, and from the spoil of King Hadadezer son of Rehob of Zobah.

13 David won a name for himself. When he returned, he killed eighteen thousand Edomites[c] in the Valley of Salt. ¹⁴He put garrisons in Edom; throughout all Edom he put garrisons, and all the Edomites became David's servants. And the Lord gave victory to David wherever he went.

15 So David reigned over all Israel; and David administered justice and equity to all his people. ¹⁶Joab son of Zeruiah was over the army; Jehoshaphat son of Ahilud was recorder; ¹⁷Zadok son of Ahitub and Ahimelech son of Abiathar were priests; Seraiah was secretary; ¹⁸Benaiah son of Jehoiada was over[d] the Cherethites and the Pelethites; and David's sons were priests.

# JOHN 14.15–31

"IF you love me, you will keep[e] my commandments. ¹⁶And I will ask the Father, and he will give you another Advocate,[f] to be with you forever. ¹⁷This is the Spirit of truth, whom the world cannot receive, because it neither sees him nor knows him. You know him, because he abides with you, and he will be in[g] you.

18 "I will not leave you orphaned; I

aHeb *one full length*   bCompare 1 Sam 15.12 and 2 Sam 18.18   cGk: Heb *returned from striking down eighteen thousand Arameans*   dSyr Tg Vg 20.23; 1 Chr 18.17: Heb lacks *was over*   eOther ancient authorities read *me, keep*   fOr *Helper*   gOr *among*

am coming to you. ¹⁹In a little while the world will no longer see me, but you will see me; because I live, you also will live. ²⁰On that day you will know that I am in my Father, and you in me, and I in you. ²¹They who have my commandments and keep them are those who love me; and those who love me will be loved by my Father, and I will love them and reveal myself to them." ²²Judas (not Iscariot) said to him, "Lord, how is it that you will reveal yourself to us, and not to the world?" ²³Jesus answered him, "Those who love me will keep my word, and my Father will love them, and we will come to them and make our home with them. ²⁴Whoever does not love me does not keep my words; and the word that you hear is not mine, but is from the Father who sent me.

25 "I have said these things to you while I am still with you. ²⁶But the Advocate, [a] the Holy Spirit, whom the Father will send in my name, will teach you everything, and remind you of all that I have said to you. ²⁷Peace I leave with you; my peace I give to you. I do not give to you as the world gives. Do not let your hearts be troubled, and do not let them be afraid. ²⁸You heard me say to you, 'I am going away, and I am coming to you.' If you loved me, you would rejoice that I am going to the Father, because the Father is greater than I. ²⁹And now I have told you this before it occurs, so that when it does occur, you may believe. ³⁰I will no longer talk much with you, for the ruler of this world is coming. He has no power over me; ³¹but I do as the Father has commanded me, so that the world may know that I love the Father. Rise, let us be on our way.

## PSALM 119.33–48

TEACH me, O LORD, the way of
    your statutes,
  and I will observe it to the
    end.
34 Give me understanding, that I
    may keep your law
  and observe it with my whole
    heart.
35 Lead me in the path of your
    commandments,
  for I delight in it.
36 Turn my heart to your decrees,
  and not to selfish gain.
37 Turn my eyes from looking at
    vanities;
  give me life in your ways.
38 Confirm to your servant your
    promise,
  which is for those who fear
    you.
39 Turn away the disgrace that I
    dread,
  for your ordinances are good.
40 See, I have longed for your
    precepts;
  in your righteousness give
    me life.

41 Let your steadfast love come to
    me, O LORD,
  your salvation according to
    your promise.
42 Then I shall have an answer for
    those who taunt me,
  for I trust in your word.
43 Do not take the word of truth
    utterly out of my mouth,
  for my hope is in your
    ordinances.
44 I will keep your law continually,
  forever and ever.
45 I shall walk at liberty,
  for I have sought your
    precepts.
46 I will also speak of your decrees
    before kings,

a Or *Helper*

and shall not be put to shame;
47   I find my delight in your
         commandments,
      because I love them.
48   I revere your commandments,
         which I love,
      and I will meditate on your
         statutes.

## PROVERBS 15.33

THE fear of the LORD is instruction in wisdom, and humility goes before honor.

# MAY 26

## 2 SAMUEL 9.1—11.27a

DAVID asked, "Is there still anyone left of the house of Saul to whom I may show kindness for Jonathan's sake?" ²Now there was a servant of the house of Saul whose name was Ziba, and he was summoned to David. The king said to him, "Are you Ziba?" And he said, "At your service!" ³The king said, "Is there anyone remaining of the house of Saul to whom I may show the kindness of God?" Ziba said to the king, "There remains a son of Jonathan; he is crippled in his feet." ⁴The king said to him, "Where is he?" Ziba said to the king, "He is in the house of Machir son of Ammiel, at Lo-debar." ⁵Then King David sent and brought him from the house of Machir son of Ammiel, at Lo-debar. ⁶Mephibosheth[a] son of Jonathan son of Saul came to David, and fell on his face and did obeisance. David said, "Mephibosheth!"[a] He answered, "I am your servant." ⁷David said to him, "Do not be afraid, for I will show you kindness for the sake of your father Jonathan; I will restore to you all the land of your grandfather Saul, and you yourself shall eat at my table always." ⁸He did obeisance and said, "What is your servant, that you should look upon a dead dog such as I?"

9   Then the king summoned Saul's servant Ziba, and said to him, "All that belonged to Saul and to all his house I have given to your master's grandson. ¹⁰You and your sons and your servants shall till the land for him, and shall bring in the produce, so that your master's grandson may have food to eat; but your master's grandson Mephibosheth[a] shall always eat at my table." Now Ziba had fifteen sons and twenty servants. ¹¹Then Ziba said to the king, "According to all that my lord the king commands his servant, so your servant will do." Mephibosheth[a] ate at David's[b] table, like one of the king's sons. ¹²Mephibosheth[a] had a young son whose name was Mica. And all who lived in Ziba's house became Mephibosheth's[c] servants. ¹³Mephibosheth[a] lived in Jerusalem, for he always ate at the king's table. Now he was lame in both his feet.

¹⁰·¹ SOME time afterward, the king of the Ammonites died, and his son Hanun succeeded him. ²David said, "I will deal loyally with Hanun son of Nahash, just as his father dealt loyally with me." So

---

a Or *Merib-baal*: See 4.4 note   b Gk: Heb *my*   c Or *Merib-baal's*: See 4.4 note

David sent envoys to console him concerning his father. When David's envoys came into the land of the Ammonites, <sup>3</sup>the princes of the Ammonites said to their lord Hanun, "Do you really think that David is honoring your father just because he has sent messengers with condolences to you? Has not David sent his envoys to you to search the city, to spy it out, and to overthrow it?" <sup>4</sup>So Hanun seized David's envoys, shaved off half the beard of each, cut off their garments in the middle at their hips, and sent them away. <sup>5</sup>When David was told, he sent to meet them, for the men were greatly ashamed. The king said, "Remain at Jericho until your beards have grown, and then return."

6 When the Ammonites saw that they had become odious to David, the Ammonites sent and hired the Arameans of Beth-rehob and the Arameans of Zobah, twenty thousand foot soldiers, as well as the king of Maacah, one thousand men, and the men of Tob, twelve thousand men. <sup>7</sup>When David heard of it, he sent Joab and all the army with the warriors. <sup>8</sup>The Ammonites came out and drew up in battle array at the entrance of the gate; but the Arameans of Zobah and of Rehob, and the men of Tob and Maacah, were by themselves in the open country.

9 When Joab saw that the battle was set against him both in front and in the rear, he chose some of the picked men of Israel, and arrayed them against the Arameans; <sup>10</sup>the rest of his men he put in the charge of his brother Abishai, and he arrayed them against the Ammonites. <sup>11</sup>He said, "If the Arameans are too strong for me, then you shall help me; but if the Ammonites are too strong for you, then I will come and help you. <sup>12</sup>Be strong, and let us be courageous for the sake of our people, and for the cities of our God; and may

the Lord do what seems good to him." <sup>13</sup>So Joab and the people who were with him moved forward into battle against the Arameans; and they fled before him. <sup>14</sup>When the Ammonites saw that the Arameans fled, they likewise fled before Abishai, and entered the city. Then Joab returned from fighting against the Ammonites, and came to Jerusalem.

15 But when the Arameans saw that they had been defeated by Israel, they gathered themselves together. <sup>16</sup>Hadadezer sent and brought out the Arameans who were beyond the Euphrates; and they came to Helam, with Shobach the commander of the army of Hadadezer at their head. <sup>17</sup>When it was told David, he gathered all Israel together, and crossed the Jordan, and came to Helam. The Arameans arrayed themselves against David and fought with him. <sup>18</sup>The Arameans fled before Israel; and David killed of the Arameans seven hundred chariot teams, and forty thousand horsemen,[a] and wounded Shobach the commander of their army, so that he died there. <sup>19</sup>When all the kings who were servants of Hadadezer saw that they had been defeated by Israel, they made peace with Israel, and became subject to them. So the Arameans were afraid to help the Ammonites any more.

11.1 In the spring of the year, the time when kings go out to battle, David sent Joab with his officers and all Israel with him; they ravaged the Ammonites, and besieged Rabbah. But David remained at Jerusalem.

2 It happened, late one afternoon, when David rose from his couch and was walking about on the roof of the king's house, that he saw from the roof a woman bathing; the woman was very beautiful. <sup>3</sup>David sent someone to in-

a 1 Chr 19.18 and some Gk Mss read *foot soldiers*

quire about the woman. It was reported, "This is Bathsheba daughter of Eliam, the wife of Uriah the Hittite." ⁴So David sent messengers to get her, and she came to him, and he lay with her. (Now she was purifying herself after her period.) Then she returned to her house. ⁵The woman conceived; and she sent and told David, "I am pregnant."

6 So David sent word to Joab, "Send me Uriah the Hittite." And Joab sent Uriah to David. ⁷When Uriah came to him, David asked how Joab and the people fared, and how the war was going. ⁸Then David said to Uriah, "Go down to your house, and wash your feet." Uriah went out of the king's house, and there followed him a present from the king. ⁹But Uriah slept at the entrance of the king's house with all the servants of his lord, and did not go down to his house. ¹⁰When they told David, "Uriah did not go down to his house," David said to Uriah, "You have just come from a journey. Why did you not go down to your house?" ¹¹Uriah said to David, "The ark and Israel and Judah remain in booths;ᵃ and my lord Joab and the servants of my lord are camping in the open field; shall I then go to my house, to eat and to drink, and to lie with my wife? As you live, and as your soul lives, I will not do such a thing." ¹²Then David said to Uriah, "Remain here today also, and tomorrow I will send you back." So Uriah remained in Jerusalem that day. On the next day, ¹³David invited him to eat and drink in his presence and made him drunk; and in the evening he went out to lie on his couch with the servants of his lord, but he did not go down to his house.

14 In the morning David wrote a letter to Joab, and sent it by the hand of Uriah. ¹⁵In the letter he wrote, "Set Uriah in the forefront of the hardest fighting, and then draw back from him, so that he may be struck down and die." ¹⁶As Joab was besieging the city, he assigned Uriah to the place where he knew there were valiant warriors. ¹⁷The men of the city came out and fought with Joab; and some of the servants of David among the people fell. Uriah the Hittite was killed as well. ¹⁸Then Joab sent and told David all the news about the fighting; ¹⁹and he instructed the messenger, "When you have finished telling the king all the news about the fighting, ²⁰then, if the king's anger rises, and if he says to you, 'Why did you go so near the city to fight? Did you not know that they would shoot from the wall? ²¹Who killed Abimelech son of Jerubbaal?ᵇ Did not a woman throw an upper millstone on him from the wall, so that he died at Thebez? Why did you go so near the wall?' then you shall say, 'Your servant Uriah the Hittite is dead too.' "

22 So the messenger went, and came and told David all that Joab had sent him to tell. ²³The messenger said to David, "The men gained an advantage over us, and came out against us in the field; but we drove them back to the entrance of the gate. ²⁴Then the archers shot at your servants from the wall; some of the king's servants are dead; and your servant Uriah the Hittite is dead also." ²⁵David said to the messenger, "Thus you shall say to Joab, 'Do not let this matter trouble you, for the sword devours now one and now another; press your attack on the city, and overthrow it.' And encourage him."

26 When the wife of Uriah heard that her husband was dead, she made lamentation for him. ²⁷When the mourning was over, David sent and brought her to his house, and she became his wife, and bore him a son.

---

ᵃ Or *at Succoth*   ᵇ Gk Syr Judg 7.1: Heb *Jerubbesheth*

## JOHN 15.1–27

"I AM the true vine, and my Father is the vinegrower. ²He removes every branch in me that bears no fruit. Every branch that bears fruit he prunes[a] to make it bear more fruit. ³You have already been cleansed[a] by the word that I have spoken to you. ⁴Abide in me as I abide in you. Just as the branch cannot bear fruit by itself unless it abides in the vine, neither can you unless you abide in me. ⁵I am the vine, you are the branches. Those who abide in me and I in them bear much fruit, because apart from me you can do nothing. ⁶Whoever does not abide in me is thrown away like a branch and withers; such branches are gathered, thrown into the fire, and burned. ⁷If you abide in me, and my words abide in you, ask for whatever you wish, and it will be done for you. ⁸My Father is glorified by this, that you bear much fruit and become[b] my disciples. ⁹As the Father has loved me, so I have loved you; abide in my love. ¹⁰If you keep my commandments, you will abide in my love, just as I have kept my Father's commandments and abide in his love. ¹¹I have said these things to you so that my joy may be in you, and that your joy may be complete.

12 "This is my commandment, that you love one another as I have loved you. ¹³No one has greater love than this, to lay down one's life for one's friends. ¹⁴You are my friends if you do what I command you. ¹⁵I do not call you servants[c] any longer, because the servant[d] does not know what the master is doing; but I have called you friends, because I have made known to you everything that I have heard from my Father. ¹⁶You did not choose me but I chose you. And I appointed you to go and bear fruit, fruit that will last, so that the Father will give you whatever you ask him in my name. ¹⁷I am giving you these commands so that you may love one another.

18 "If the world hates you, be aware that it hated me before it hated you. ¹⁹If you belonged to the world,[e] the world would love you as its own. Because you do not belong to the world, but I have chosen you out of the world—therefore the world hates you. ²⁰Remember the word that I said to you, 'Servants[f] are not greater than their master.' If they persecuted me, they will persecute you; if they kept my word, they will keep yours also. ²¹But they will do all these things to you on account of my name, because they do not know him who sent me. ²²If I had not come and spoken to them, they would not have sin; but now they have no excuse for their sin. ²³Whoever hates me hates my Father also. ²⁴If I had not done among them the works that no one else did, they would not have sin. But now they have seen and hated both me and my Father. ²⁵It was to fulfill the word that is written in their law, 'They hated me without a cause.'

26 "When the Advocate[g] comes, whom I will send to you from the Father, the Spirit of truth who comes from the Father, he will testify on my behalf. ²⁷You also are to testify because you have been with me from the beginning.

## PSALM 119.49–64

R EMEMBER your word to your servant,
 in which you have made
  me hope.
50  This is my comfort in my
  distress,
  that your promise gives me
   life.
51  The arrogant utterly deride me,

---

aThe same Greek root refers to pruning and cleansing  bOr be  cGk slaves  dGk slave  eGk were of the world  fGk Slaves  gOr Helper

but I do not turn away from
your law.
52 When I think of your ordinances
from of old,
I take comfort, O LORD.
53 Hot indignation seizes me
because of the wicked,
those who forsake your law.
54 Your statutes have been my
songs
wherever I make my home.
55 I remember your name in the
night, O LORD,
and keep your law.
56 This blessing has fallen to me,
for I have kept your precepts.

57 The LORD is my portion;
I promise to keep your
words.
58 I implore your favor with all my
heart;
be gracious to me according
to your promise.
59 When I think of your ways,
I turn my feet to your
decrees;
60 I hurry and do not delay

to keep your commandments.
61 Though the cords of the wicked
ensnare me,
I do not forget your law.
62 At midnight I rise to praise you,
because of your righteous
ordinances.
63 I am a companion of all who fear
you,
of those who keep your
precepts.
64 The earth, O LORD, is full of
your steadfast love;
teach me your statutes.

## PROVERBS 16.1–3

THE plans of the mind belong to
mortals,
but the answer of the tongue
is from the LORD.
2 All one's ways may be pure in
one's own eyes,
but the LORD weighs the
spirit.
3 Commit your work to the LORD,
and your plans will be
established.

# MAY 27

## 2 SAMUEL 11.27b—12.31

BUT the thing that David had done displeased the LORD, 12.1 and the LORD sent Nathan to David. He came to him, and said to him, "There were two men in a certain city, the one rich and the other poor. 2The rich man had very many flocks and herds; 3but the poor man had nothing but one little ewe lamb, which he had bought. He brought it up, and it grew up with him and with his children; it used to eat of his meager fare, and drink from his cup, and lie in his bosom, and it was like a daughter to him. 4Now there came a traveler to the rich man, and he was loath to take one of his own flock or herd to prepare for the wayfarer who had come to him, but he took the poor man's lamb, and prepared that for the guest who had come to him." 5Then David's anger was greatly kindled against the man. He said to Nathan, "As the LORD lives, the man who has done this deserves to die; ⁶he shall restore the lamb fourfold, because he did this thing, and because he had no pity."

7 Nathan said to David, "You are the man! Thus says the Lord, the God of Israel: I anointed you king over Israel, and I rescued you from the hand of Saul; ⁸I gave you your master's house, and your master's wives into your bosom, and gave you the house of Israel and of Judah; and if that had been too little, I would have added as much more. ⁹Why have you despised the word of the Lord, to do what is evil in his sight? You have struck down Uriah the Hittite with the sword, and have taken his wife to be your wife, and have killed him with the sword of the Ammonites. ¹⁰Now therefore the sword shall never depart from your house, for you have despised me, and have taken the wife of Uriah the Hittite to be your wife. ¹¹Thus says the Lord: I will raise up trouble against you from within your own house; and I will take your wives before your eyes, and give them to your neighbor, and he shall lie with your wives in the sight of this very sun. ¹²For you did it secretly; but I will do this thing before all Israel, and before the sun." ¹³David said to Nathan, "I have sinned against the Lord." Nathan said to David, "Now the Lord has put away your sin; you shall not die. ¹⁴Nevertheless, because by this deed you have utterly scorned the Lord,ᵃ the child that is born to you shall die." ¹⁵Then Nathan went to his house.

The Lord struck the child that Uriah's wife bore to David, and it became very ill. ¹⁶David therefore pleaded with God for the child; David fasted, and went in and lay all night on the ground. ¹⁷The elders of his house stood beside him, urging him to rise from the ground; but he would not, nor did he eat food with them. ¹⁸On the seventh day the child died. And the servants of David were afraid to tell him that the child was dead; for they said, "While the child was still alive, we spoke to him, and he did not listen to us; how then can we tell him the child is dead? He may do himself some harm." ¹⁹But when David saw that his servants were whispering together, he perceived that the child was dead; and David said to his servants, "Is the child dead?" They said, "He is dead."

20 Then David rose from the ground, washed, anointed himself, and changed his clothes. He went into the house of the Lord, and worshiped; he then went to his own house; and when he asked, they set food before him and he ate. ²¹Then his servants said to him, "What is this thing that you have done? You fasted and wept for the child while it was alive; but when the child died, you rose and ate food." ²²He said, "While the child was still alive, I fasted and wept; for I said, 'Who knows? The Lord may be gracious to me, and the child may live.' ²³But now he is dead; why should I fast? Can I bring him back again? I shall go to him, but he will not return to me."

24 Then David consoled his wife Bathsheba, and went to her, and lay with her; and she bore a son, and he named him Solomon. The Lord loved him, ²⁵and sent a message by the prophet Nathan; so he named him Jedidiah,ᵇ because of the Lord.

26 Now Joab fought against Rabbah of the Ammonites, and took the royal city. ²⁷Joab sent messengers to David, and said, "I have fought against Rabbah; moreover, I have taken the water city. ²⁸Now, then, gather the rest of the people together, and encamp against the city, and take it; or I myself will take the city, and it will be called by my name." ²⁹So David gathered all the people together and went to Rabbah,

ᵃAncient scribal tradition: Compare 1 Sam 25.22 note: Heb *scorned the enemies of the Lord*   ᵇThat is *Beloved of the Lord*

and fought against it and took it. [30]He took the crown of Milcom[a] from his head; the weight of it was a talent of gold, and in it was a precious stone; and it was placed on David's head. He also brought forth the spoil of the city, a very great amount. [31]He brought out the people who were in it, and set them to work with saws and iron picks and iron axes, or sent them to the brickworks. Thus he did to all the cities of the Ammonites. Then David and all the people returned to Jerusalem.

## JOHN 16.1–33

"I HAVE said these things to you to keep you from stumbling. [2]They will put you out of the synagogues. Indeed, an hour is coming when those who kill you will think that by doing so they are offering worship to God. [3]And they will do this because they have not known the Father or me. [4]But I have said these things to you so that when their hour comes you may remember that I told you about them.

"I did not say these things to you from the beginning, because I was with you. [5]But now I am going to him who sent me; yet none of you asks me, 'Where are you going?' [6]But because I have said these things to you, sorrow has filled your hearts. [7]Nevertheless I tell you the truth: it is to your advantage that I go away, for if I do not go away, the Advocate[b] will not come to you; but if I go, I will send him to you. [8]And when he comes, he will prove the world wrong about[c] sin and righteousness and judgment: [9]about sin, because they do not believe in me; [10]about righteousness, because I am going to the Father and you will see me no longer; [11]about judgment, because the ruler of this world has been condemned.

12 "I still have many things to say to you, but you cannot bear them now. [13]When the Spirit of truth comes, he will guide you into all the truth; for he will not speak on his own, but will speak whatever he hears, and he will declare to you the things that are to come. [14]He will glorify me, because he will take what is mine and declare it to you. [15]All that the Father has is mine. For this reason I said that he will take what is mine and declare it to you.

16 "A little while, and you will no longer see me, and again a little while, and you will see me." [17]Then some of his disciples said to one another, "What does he mean by saying to us, 'A little while, and you will no longer see me, and again a little while, and you will see me'; and 'Because I am going to the Father'?" [18]They said, "What does he mean by this 'a little while'? We do not know what he is talking about." [19]Jesus knew that they wanted to ask him, so he said to them, "Are you discussing among yourselves what I meant when I said, 'A little while, and you will no longer see me, and again a little while, and you will see me'? [20]Very truly, I tell you, you will weep and mourn, but the world will rejoice; you will have pain, but your pain will turn into joy. [21]When a woman is in labor, she has pain, because her hour has come. But when her child is born, she no longer remembers the anguish because of the joy of having brought a human being into the world. [22]So you have pain now; but I will see you again, and your hearts will rejoice, and no one will take your joy from you. [23]On that day you will ask nothing of me.[d] Very truly, I tell you, if you ask anything of the Father in my name, he will give it to you.[e] [24]Until now you have not asked for anything in my name. Ask and you will receive, so that your joy may be complete.

25 "I have said these things to you in figures of speech. The hour is coming when I will no longer speak to you

in figures, but will tell you plainly of the Father. 26 On that day you will ask in my name. I do not say to you that I will ask the Father on your behalf; 27 for the Father himself loves you, because you have loved me and have believed that I came from God. a 28 I came from the Father and have come into the world; again, I am leaving the world and am going to the Father."

29 His disciples said, "Yes, now you are speaking plainly, not in any figure of speech! 30 Now we know that you know all things, and do not need to have anyone question you; by this we believe that you came from God." 31 Jesus answered them, "Do you now believe? 32 The hour is coming, indeed it has come, when you will be scattered, each one to his home, and you will leave me alone. Yet I am not alone because the Father is with me. 33 I have said this to you, so that in me you may have peace. In the world you face persecution. But take courage; I have conquered the world!"

## PSALM 119.65–80

You have dealt well with your
    servant,
O Lord, according to your
    word.
66 Teach me good judgment and
    knowledge,
  for I believe in your
    commandments.
67 Before I was humbled I went
    astray,
  but now I keep your word.
68 You are good and do good;
  teach me your statutes.
69 The arrogant smear me with
    lies,
  but with my whole heart I
    keep your precepts.
70 Their hearts are fat and gross,
  but I delight in your law.

71 It is good for me that I was
    humbled,
  so that I might learn your
    statutes.
72 The law of your mouth is better
    to me
  than thousands of gold and
    silver pieces.

73 Your hands have made and
    fashioned me;
  give me understanding that I
    may learn your
    commandments.
74 Those who fear you shall see
    me and rejoice,
  because I have hoped in your
    word.
75 I know, O Lord, that your
    judgments are right,
  and that in faithfulness you
    have humbled me.
76 Let your steadfast love become
    my comfort
  according to your promise to
    your servant.
77 Let your mercy come to me,
    that I may live;
  for your law is my delight.
78 Let the arrogant be put to
    shame,
  because they have subverted
    me with guile;
  as for me, I will meditate on
    your precepts.
79 Let those who fear you turn to
    me,
  so that they may know your
    decrees.
80 May my heart be blameless in
    your statutes,
  so that I may not be put to
    shame.

a Other ancient authorities read *the Father*

## PROVERBS 16.4–5

**T**HE LORD has made everything
for its purpose,
even the wicked for the day
of trouble.

5 All those who are arrogant are
an abomination to the
LORD;
be assured, they will not go
unpunished.

# MAY 28

## 2 SAMUEL 13.1–39

**S**OME time passed. David's son Absalom had a beautiful sister whose name was Tamar; and David's son Amnon fell in love with her. [2]Amnon was so tormented that he made himself ill because of his sister Tamar, for she was a virgin and it seemed impossible to Amnon to do anything to her. [3]But Amnon had a friend whose name was Jonadab, the son of David's brother Shimeah; and Jonadab was a very crafty man. [4]He said to him, "O son of the king, why are you so haggard morning after morning? Will you not tell me?" Amnon said to him, "I love Tamar, my brother Absalom's sister." [5]Jonadab said to him, "Lie down on your bed, and pretend to be ill; and when your father comes to see you, say to him, 'Let my sister Tamar come and give me something to eat, and prepare the food in my sight, so that I may see it and eat it from her hand.'" [6]So Amnon lay down, and pretended to be ill; and when the king came to see him, Amnon said to the king, "Please let my sister Tamar come and make a couple of cakes in my sight, so that I may eat from her hand."

7 Then David sent home to Tamar, saying, "Go to your brother Amnon's house, and prepare food for him." [8]So Tamar went to her brother Amnon's house, where he was lying down. She took dough, kneaded it, made cakes in his sight, and baked the cakes. [9]Then she took the pan and set them[a] out before him, but he refused to eat. Amnon said, "Send out everyone from me." So everyone went out from him. [10]Then Amnon said to Tamar, "Bring the food into the chamber, so that I may eat from your hand." So Tamar took the cakes she had made, and brought them into the chamber to Amnon her brother. [11]But when she brought them near him to eat, he took hold of her, and said to her, "Come, lie with me, my sister." [12]She answered him, "No, my brother, do not force me; for such a thing is not done in Israel; do not do anything so vile! [13]As for me, where could I carry my shame? And as for you, you would be as one of the scoundrels in Israel. Now therefore, I beg you, speak to the king; for he will not withhold me from you." [14]But he would not listen to her; and being stronger than she, he forced her and lay with her.

15 Then Amnon was seized with a very great loathing for her; indeed, his loathing was even greater than the lust he had felt for her. Amnon said to her, "Get out!" [16]But she said to him, "No,

a Heb *and poured*

my brother; a for this wrong in sending me away is greater than the other that you did to me." But he would not listen to her. [17]He called the young man who served him and said, "Put this woman out of my presence, and bolt the door after her." [18](Now she was wearing a long robe with sleeves; for this is how the virgin daughters of the king were clothed in earlier times. b) So his servant put her out, and bolted the door after her. [19]But Tamar put ashes on her head, and tore the long robe that she was wearing; she put her hand on her head, and went away, crying aloud as she went.

20 Her brother Absalom said to her, "Has Amnon your brother been with you? Be quiet for now, my sister; he is your brother; do not take this to heart." So Tamar remained, a desolate woman, in her brother Absalom's house. [21]When King David heard of all these things, he became very angry, but he would not punish his son Amnon, because he loved him, for he was his firstborn. c [22]But Absalom spoke to Amnon neither good nor bad; for Absalom hated Amnon, because he had raped his sister Tamar.

23 After two full years Absalom had sheepshearers at Baal-hazor, which is near Ephraim, and Absalom invited all the king's sons. [24]Absalom came to the king, and said, "Your servant has sheepshearers; will the king and his servants please go with your servant?" [25]But the king said to Absalom, "No, my son, let us not all go, or else we will be burdensome to you." He pressed him, but he would not go but gave him his blessing. [26]Then Absalom said, "If not, please let my brother Amnon go with us." The king said to him, "Why should he go with you?" [27]But Absalom pressed him until he let

Amnon and all the king's sons go with him. Absalom made a feast like a king's feast. d [28]Then Absalom commanded his servants, "Watch when Amnon's heart is merry with wine, and when I say to you, 'Strike Amnon,' then kill him. Do not be afraid; have I not myself commanded you? Be courageous and valiant." [29]So the servants of Absalom did to Amnon as Absalom had commanded. Then all the king's sons rose, and each mounted his mule and fled.

30 While they were on the way, the report came to David that Absalom had killed all the king's sons, and not one of them was left. [31]The king rose, tore his garments, and lay on the ground; and all his servants who were standing by tore their garments. [32]But Jonadab, the son of David's brother Shimeah, said, "Let not my lord suppose that they have killed all the young men the king's sons; Amnon alone is dead. This has been determined by Absalom from the day Amnon e raped his sister Tamar. [33]Now therefore, do not let my lord the king take it to heart, as if all the king's sons were dead; for Amnon alone is dead."

34 But Absalom fled. When the young man who kept watch looked up, he saw many people coming from the Horonaim road f by the side of the mountain. [35]Jonadab said to the king, "See, the king's sons have come; as your servant said, so it has come about." [36]As soon as he had finished speaking, the king's sons arrived, and raised their voices and wept; and the king and all his servants also wept very bitterly.

37 But Absalom fled, and went to Talmai son of Ammihud, king of Geshur. David mourned for his son day after day. [38]Absalom, having fled to Geshur, stayed there three years. [39]And

---

aCn Compare Gk Vg: Meaning of Heb uncertain   bCn: Heb *were clothed in robes*   cQ Ms Gk: MT lacks *but he would not punish . . . firstborn*   dGk Compare Q Ms: MT lacks *Absalom made a feast like a king's feast*   eHeb *he*   fCn Compare Gk: Heb *the road behind him*

the heart of[a] the king went out, yearning for Absalom; for he was now consoled over the death of Amnon.

## JOHN 17.1–26

AFTER Jesus had spoken these words, he looked up to heaven and said, "Father, the hour has come; glorify your Son so that the Son may glorify you, [2]since you have given him authority over all people,[b] to give eternal life to all whom you have given him. [3]And this is eternal life, that they may know you, the only true God, and Jesus Christ whom you have sent. [4]I glorified you on earth by finishing the work that you gave me to do. [5]So now, Father, glorify me in your own presence with the glory that I had in your presence before the world existed.

6 "I have made your name known to those whom you gave me from the world. They were yours, and you gave them to me, and they have kept your word. [7]Now they know that everything you have given me is from you; [8]for the words that you gave to me I have given to them, and they have received them and know in truth that I came from you; and they have believed that you sent me. [9]I am asking on their behalf; I am not asking on behalf of the world, but on behalf of those whom you gave me, because they are yours. [10]All mine are yours, and yours are mine; and I have been glorified in them. [11]And now I am no longer in the world, but they are in the world, and I am coming to you. Holy Father, protect them in your name that[c] you have given me, so that they may be one, as we are one. [12]While I was with them, I protected them in your name that[c] you have given me. I guarded them, and not one of them was lost except the one destined to be lost,[d] so that the scripture

might be fulfilled. [13]But now I am coming to you, and I speak these things in the world so that they may have my joy made complete in themselves.[e] [14]I have given them your word, and the world has hated them because they do not belong to the world, just as I do not belong to the world. [15]I am not asking you to take them out of the world, but I ask you to protect them from the evil one.[f] [16]They do not belong to the world, just as I do not belong to the world. [17]Sanctify them in the truth; your word is truth. [18]As you have sent me into the world, so I have sent them into the world. [19]And for their sakes I sanctify myself, so that they also may be sanctified in truth.

20 "I ask not only on behalf of these, but also on behalf of those who will believe in me through their word, [21]that they may all be one. As you, Father, are in me and I am in you, may they also be in us,[g] so that the world may believe that you have sent me. [22]The glory that you have given me I have given them, so that they may be one, as we are one, [23]I in them and you in me, that they may become completely one, so that the world may know that you have sent me and have loved them even as you have loved me. [24]Father, I desire that those also, whom you have given me, may be with me where I am, to see my glory, which you have given me because you loved me before the foundation of the world.

25 "Righteous Father, the world does not know you, but I know you; and these know that you have sent me. [26]I made your name known to them, and I will make it known, so that the love with which you have loved me may be in them, and I in them."

[a]Q Ms Gk: MT *And David*  [b]Gk *flesh*  [c]Other ancient authorities read *protected in your name those whom*  [d]Gk *except the son of destruction*  [e]Or *among themselves*  [f]Or *from evil*  [g]Other ancient authorities read *be one in us*

## PSALM 119.81–96

**M**y soul languishes for your
   salvation;
   I hope in your word.
82 My eyes fail with watching for
     your promise;
   I ask, "When will you comfort
     me?"
83 For I have become like a
     wineskin in the smoke,
   yet I have not forgotten your
     statutes.
84 How long must your servant
     endure?
   When will you judge those
     who persecute me?
85 The arrogant have dug pitfalls
     for me;
   they flout your law.
86 All your commandments are
     enduring;
   I am persecuted without
     cause; help me!
87 They have almost made an end
     of me on earth;
   but I have not forsaken your
     precepts.
88 In your steadfast love spare my
     life,
   so that I may keep the
     decrees of your mouth.

89 The LORD exists forever;
   your word is firmly fixed in
     heaven.
90 Your faithfulness endures to all
     generations;
   you have established the
     earth, and it stands fast.
91 By your appointment they stand
     today,
   for all things are your
     servants.
92 If your law had not been my
     delight,
   I would have perished in my
     misery.
93 I will never forget your
     precepts,
   for by them you have given
     me life.
94 I am yours; save me,
   for I have sought your
     precepts.
95 The wicked lie in wait to
     destroy me,
   but I consider your decrees.
96 I have seen a limit to all
     perfection,
   but your commandment is
     exceedingly broad.

## PROVERBS 16.6–7

**B**y loyalty and faithfulness
   iniquity is atoned for,
   and by the fear of the LORD
   one avoids evil.
7 When the ways of people please
   the LORD,
   he causes even their enemies
   to be at peace with
   them.

## 2 SAMUEL 14.1—15.22

Now Joab son of Zeruiah perceived that the king's mind was on Absalom. 2Joab sent to Tekoa and brought from there a wise woman. He said to her, "Pretend to be a mourner; put on mourning garments, do not anoint yourself with oil, but behave like a woman who has been mourning many days for the dead. 3Go to the king and speak to him as follows." And Joab put the words into her mouth.

4 When the woman of Tekoa came to the king, she fell on her face to the ground and did obeisance, and said, "Help, O king!" 5The king asked her, "What is your trouble?" She answered, "Alas, I am a widow; my husband is dead. 6Your servant had two sons, and they fought with one another in the field; there was no one to part them, and one struck the other and killed him. 7Now the whole family has risen against your servant. They say, 'Give up the man who struck his brother, so that we may kill him for the life of his brother whom he murdered, even if we destroy the heir as well.' Thus they would quench my one remaining ember, and leave to my husband neither name nor remnant on the face of the earth."

8 Then the king said to the woman, "Go to your house, and I will give orders concerning you." 9The woman of Tekoa said to the king, "On me be the guilt, my lord the king, and on my father's house; let the king and his throne be guiltless." 10The king said, "If anyone says anything to you, bring him to me, and he shall never touch you again." 11Then she said, "Please, may the king keep the LORD your God in mind, so that the avenger of blood may kill no more, and my son not be destroyed." He said, "As the LORD lives, not one hair of your son shall fall to the ground."

12 Then the woman said, "Please let your servant speak a word to my lord the king." He said, "Speak." 13The woman said, "Why then have you planned such a thing against the people of God? For in giving this decision the king convicts himself, inasmuch as the king does not bring his banished one home again. 14We must all die; we are like water spilled on the ground, which cannot be gathered up. But God will not take away a life; he will devise plans so as not to keep an outcast banished forever from his presence. a 15Now I have come to say this to my lord the king because the people have made me afraid; your servant thought, 'I will speak to the king; it may be that the king will perform the request of his servant. 16For the king will hear, and deliver his servant from the hand of the man who would cut both me and my son off from the heritage of God.' 17Your servant thought, 'The word of my lord the king will set me at rest'; for my lord the king is like the angel of God, discerning good and evil. The LORD your God be with you!"

18 Then the king answered the woman, "Do not withhold from me anything I ask you." The woman said, "Let my lord the king speak." 19The king said, "Is the hand of Joab with you in all this?" The woman answered and said, "As surely as you live, my lord the king, one cannot turn right or left from anything that my lord the king has said. For it was your servant Joab who com-

a Meaning of Heb uncertain

manded me; it was he who put all these words into the mouth of your servant. ²⁰In order to change the course of affairs your servant Joab did this. But my lord has wisdom like the wisdom of the angel of God to know all things that are on the earth."

21 Then the king said to Joab, "Very well, I grant this; go, bring back the young man Absalom." ²²Joab prostrated himself with his face to the ground and did obeisance, and blessed the king; and Joab said, "Today your servant knows that I have found favor in your sight, my lord the king, in that the king has granted the request of his servant." ²³So Joab set off, went to Geshur, and brought Absalom to Jerusalem. ²⁴The king said, "Let him go to his own house; he is not to come into my presence." So Absalom went to his own house, and did not come into the king's presence.

25 Now in all Israel there was no one to be praised so much for his beauty as Absalom; from the sole of his foot to the crown of his head there was no blemish in him. ²⁶When he cut the hair of his head (for at the end of every year he used to cut it; when it was heavy on him, he cut it), he weighed the hair of his head, two hundred shekels by the king's weight. ²⁷There were born to Absalom three sons, and one daughter whose name was Tamar; she was a beautiful woman.

28 So Absalom lived two full years in Jerusalem, without coming into the king's presence. ²⁹Then Absalom sent for Joab to send him to the king; but Joab would not come to him. He sent a second time, but Joab would not come. ³⁰Then he said to his servants, "Look, Joab's field is next to mine, and he has barley there; go and set it on fire." So Absalom's servants set the field on fire. ³¹Then Joab rose and went to Absalom at his house, and said to him, "Why have your servants set my field on fire?" ³²Absalom answered Joab, "Look, I sent word to you: Come here, that I may send you to the king with the question, 'Why have I come from Geshur? It would be better for me to be there still.' Now let me go into the king's presence; if there is guilt in me, let him kill me!" ³³Then Joab went to the king and told him; and he summoned Absalom. So he came to the king and prostrated himself with his face to the ground before the king; and the king kissed Absalom.

15.1 AFTER this Absalom got himself a chariot and horses, and fifty men to run ahead of him. ²Absalom used to rise early and stand beside the road into the gate; and when anyone brought a suit before the king for judgment, Absalom would call out and say, "From what city are you?" When the person said, "Your servant is of such and such a tribe in Israel," ³Absalom would say, "See, your claims are good and right; but there is no one deputed by the king to hear you." ⁴Absalom said moreover, "If only I were judge in the land! Then all who had a suit or cause might come to me, and I would give them justice." ⁵Whenever people came near to do obeisance to him, he would put out his hand and take hold of them, and kiss them. ⁶Thus Absalom did to every Israelite who came to the king for judgment; so Absalom stole the hearts of the people of Israel.

7 At the end of four ͣ years Absalom said to the king, "Please let me go to Hebron and pay the vow that I have made to the LORD. ⁸For your servant made a vow while I lived at Geshur in Aram: If the LORD will indeed bring me back to Jerusalem, then I will worship the LORD in Hebron." ͣ ⁹The king said to him, "Go in peace." So he got up, and went to Hebron. ¹⁰But Absalom

a Gk Syr: Heb *forty*   b Gk Mss: Heb lacks *in Hebron*

sent secret messengers throughout all the tribes of Israel, saying, "As soon as you hear the sound of the trumpet, then shout: Absalom has become king at Hebron!" [11]Two hundred men from Jerusalem went with Absalom; they were invited guests, and they went in their innocence, knowing nothing of the matter. [12]While Absalom was offering the sacrifices, he sent for[a] Ahithophel the Gilonite, David's counselor, from his city Giloh. The conspiracy grew in strength, and the people with Absalom kept increasing.

13 A messenger came to David, saying, "The hearts of the Israelites have gone after Absalom." [14]Then David said to all his officials who were with him at Jerusalem, "Get up! Let us flee, or there will be no escape for us from Absalom. Hurry, or he will soon overtake us, and bring disaster down upon us, and attack the city with the edge of the sword." [15]The king's officials said to the king, "Your servants are ready to do whatever our lord the king decides." [16]So the king left, followed by all his household, except ten concubines whom he left behind to look after the house. [17]The king left, followed by all the people; and they stopped at the last house. [18]All his officials passed by him; and all the Cherethites, and all the Pelethites, and all the six hundred Gittites who had followed him from Gath, passed on before the king.

19 Then the king said to Ittai the Gittite, "Why are you also coming with us? Go back, and stay with the king; for you are a foreigner, and also an exile from your home. [20]You came only yesterday, and shall I today make you wander about with us, while I go wherever I can? Go back, and take your kinsfolk with you; and may the LORD show[b] steadfast love and faithfulness to you." [21]But Ittai answered the king, "As the LORD lives, and as my lord the king lives, wherever my lord the king may be, whether for death or for life, there also your servant will be." [22]David said to Ittai, "Go then, march on." So Ittai the Gittite marched on, with all his men and all the little ones who were with him.

## JOHN 18.1–24

AFTER Jesus had spoken these words, he went out with his disciples across the Kidron valley to a place where there was a garden, which he and his disciples entered. [2]Now Judas, who betrayed him, also knew the place, because Jesus often met there with his disciples. [3]So Judas brought a detachment of soldiers together with police from the chief priests and the Pharisees, and they came there with lanterns and torches and weapons. [4]Then Jesus, knowing all that was to happen to him, came forward and asked them, "Whom are you looking for?" [5]They answered, "Jesus of Nazareth."[c] Jesus replied, "I am he."[d] Judas, who betrayed him, was standing with them. [6]When Jesus[e] said to them, "I am he,"[d] they stepped back and fell to the ground. [7]Again he asked them, "Whom are you looking for?" And they said, "Jesus of Nazareth."[c] [8]Jesus answered, "I told you that I am he.[d] So if you are looking for me, let these men go." [9]This was to fulfill the word that he had spoken, "I did not lose a single one of those whom you gave me." [10]Then Simon Peter, who had a sword, drew it, struck the high priest's slave, and cut off his right ear. The slave's name was Malchus. [11]Jesus said to Peter, "Put your sword back into its sheath. Am I not to drink the cup that the Father has given me?"

12 So the soldiers, their officer, and the Jewish police arrested Jesus and bound him. [13]First they took him to

aOr *he sent*   bGk Compare 2.6: Heb lacks *may the* LORD *show*   cGk *the Nazorean*   dGk *I am*
eGk *he*

Annas, who was the father-in-law of Caiaphas, the high priest that year. ¹⁴Caiaphas was the one who had advised the Jews that it was better to have one person die for the people.

15 Simon Peter and another disciple followed Jesus. Since that disciple was known to the high priest, he went with Jesus into the courtyard of the high priest, ¹⁶but Peter was standing outside at the gate. So the other disciple, who was known to the high priest, went out, spoke to the woman who guarded the gate, and brought Peter in. ¹⁷The woman said to Peter, "You are not also one of this man's disciples, are you?" He said, "I am not." ¹⁸Now the slaves and the police had made a charcoal fire because it was cold, and they were standing around it and warming themselves. Peter also was standing with them and warming himself.

19 Then the high priest questioned Jesus about his disciples and about his teaching. ²⁰Jesus answered, "I have spoken openly to the world; I have always taught in synagogues and in the temple, where all the Jews come together. I have said nothing in secret. ²¹Why do you ask me? Ask those who heard what I said to them; they know what I said." ²²When he had said this, one of the police standing nearby struck Jesus on the face, saying, "Is that how you answer the high priest?" ²³Jesus answered, "If I have spoken wrongly, testify to the wrong. But if I have spoken rightly, why do you strike me?" ²⁴Then Annas sent him bound to Caiaphas the high priest.

## PSALM 119.97–112

O H, how I love your law!
It is my meditation all day
long.
98 Your commandment makes me
wiser than my enemies,
for it is always with me.

99 I have more understanding than
all my teachers,
for your decrees are my
meditation.
100 I understand more than the
aged,
for I keep your precepts.
101 I hold back my feet from every
evil way,
in order to keep your word.
102 I do not turn away from your
ordinances,
for you have taught me.
103 How sweet are your words to
my taste,
sweeter than honey to my
mouth!
104 Through your precepts I get
understanding;
therefore I hate every false
way.

105 Your word is a lamp to my feet
and a light to my path.
106 I have sworn an oath and
confirmed it,
to observe your righteous
ordinances.
107 I am severely afflicted;
give me life, O LORD,
according to your word.
108 Accept my offerings of praise,
O LORD,
and teach me your
ordinances.
109 I hold my life in my hand
continually,
but I do not forget your law.
110 The wicked have laid a snare
for me,
but I do not stray from your
precepts.
111 Your decrees are my heritage
forever;
they are the joy of my heart.
112 I incline my heart to perform
your statutes
forever, to the end.

## PROVERBS 16.8–9

**B**ETTER is a little with
righteousness
than large income with
injustice.

⁹ The human mind plans the way,
but the LORD directs the
steps.

# MAY 30

## 2 SAMUEL 15.23—16.23

**T**HE whole country wept aloud as all the people passed by; the king crossed the Wadi Kidron, and all the people moved on toward the wilderness.

24 Abiathar came up, and Zadok also, with all the Levites, carrying the ark of the covenant of God. They set down the ark of God, until the people had all passed out of the city. ²⁵Then the king said to Zadok, "Carry the ark of God back into the city. If I find favor in the eyes of the LORD, he will bring me back and let me see both it and the place where it stays. ²⁶But if he says, 'I take no pleasure in you,' here I am, let him do to me what seems good to him." ²⁷The king also said to the priest Zadok, "Look, ᵃ go back to the city in peace, you and Abiathar, ᵇ with your two sons, Ahimaaz your son, and Jonathan son of Abiathar. ²⁸See, I will wait at the fords of the wilderness until word comes from you to inform me." ²⁹So Zadok and Abiathar carried the ark of God back to Jerusalem, and they remained there.

30 But David went up the ascent of the Mount of Olives, weeping as he went, with his head covered and walking barefoot; and all the people who were with him covered their heads and went up, weeping as they went. ³¹David was told that Ahithophel was among the conspirators with Absalom. And David said, "O LORD, I pray you, turn the counsel of Ahithophel into foolishness."

32 When David came to the summit, where God was worshiped, Hushai the Archite came to meet him with his coat torn and earth on his head. ³³David said to him, "If you go on with me, you will be a burden to me. ³⁴But if you return to the city and say to Absalom, 'I will be your servant, O king; as I have been your father's servant in time past, so now I will be your servant,' then you will defeat for me the counsel of Ahithophel. ³⁵The priests Zadok and Abiathar will be with you there. So whatever you hear from the king's house, tell it to the priests Zadok and Abiathar. ³⁶Their two sons are with them there, Zadok's son Ahimaaz and Abiathar's son Jonathan; and by them you shall report to me everything you hear." ³⁷So Hushai, David's friend, came into the city, just as Absalom was entering Jerusalem.

**16.1** WHEN David had passed a little beyond the summit, Ziba the servant of Mephiboshethᶜ met him, with a couple

ᵃGk: Heb *Are you a seer* or *Do you see?*   ᵇCn: Heb lacks *and Abiathar*   ᶜOr *Merib-baal*: See 4.4 note

of donkeys saddled, carrying two hundred loaves of bread, one hundred bunches of raisins, one hundred of summer fruits, and one skin of wine. [2]The king said to Ziba, "Why have you brought these?" Ziba answered, "The donkeys are for the king's household to ride, the bread and summer fruit for the young men to eat, and the wine is for those to drink who faint in the wilderness." [3]The king said, "And where is your master's son?" Ziba said to the king, "He remains in Jerusalem; for he said, 'Today the house of Israel will give me back my grandfather's kingdom.'" [4]Then the king said to Ziba, "All that belonged to Mephibosheth[a] is now yours." Ziba said, "I do obeisance; let me find favor in your sight, my lord the king."

[5] When King David came to Bahurim, a man of the family of the house of Saul came out whose name was Shimei son of Gera; he came out cursing. [6]He threw stones at David and at all the servants of King David; now all the people and all the warriors were on his right and on his left. [7]Shimei shouted while he cursed, "Out! Out! Murderer! Scoundrel! [8]The LORD has avenged on all of you the blood of the house of Saul, in whose place you have reigned; and the LORD has given the kingdom into the hand of your son Absalom. See, disaster has overtaken you; for you are a man of blood."

[9] Then Abishai son of Zeruiah said to the king, "Why should this dead dog curse my lord the king? Let me go over and take off his head." [10]But the king said, "What have I to do with you, you sons of Zeruiah? If he is cursing because the LORD has said to him, 'Curse David,' who then shall say, 'Why have you done so?'" [11]David said to Abishai and to all his servants, "My own son seeks my life; how much more now may this Benjaminite! Let him alone, and let him curse; for the LORD has bidden him. [12]It may be that the LORD will look on my distress,[b] and the LORD will repay me with good for this cursing of me today." [13]So David and his men went on the road, while Shimei went along on the hillside opposite him and cursed as he went, throwing stones and flinging dust at him. [14]The king and all the people who were with him arrived weary at the Jordan;[c] and there he refreshed himself.

[15] Now Absalom and all the Israelites[d] came to Jerusalem; Ahithophel was with him. [16]When Hushai the Archite, David's friend, came to Absalom, Hushai said to Absalom, "Long live the king! Long live the king!" [17]Absalom said to Hushai, "Is this your loyalty to your friend? Why did you not go with your friend?" [18]Hushai said to Absalom, "No; but the one whom the LORD and this people and all the Israelites have chosen, his I will be, and with him I will remain. [19]Moreover, whom should I serve? Should it not be his son? Just as I have served your father, so I will serve you."

[20] Then Absalom said to Ahithophel, "Give us your counsel; what shall we do?" [21]Ahithophel said to Absalom, "Go in to your father's concubines, the ones he has left to look after the house; and all Israel will hear that you have made yourself odious to your father, and the hands of all who are with you will be strengthened." [22]So they pitched a tent for Absalom upon the roof; and Absalom went in to his father's concubines in the sight of all Israel. [23]Now in those days the counsel that Ahithophel gave was as if one consulted the oracle[e] of God; so all the counsel of Ahithophel was esteemed, both by David and by Absalom.

a Or *Merib-baal*: See 4.4 note   b Gk Vg: Heb *iniquity*   c Gk: Heb lacks *at the Jordan*   d Gk: Heb *all the people, the men of Israel*   e Heb *word*

## JOHN 18.25—19.22

**N**ow Simon Peter was standing and warming himself. They asked him, "You are not also one of his disciples, are you?" He denied it and said, "I am not." 26One of the slaves of the high priest, a relative of the man whose ear Peter had cut off, asked, "Did I not see you in the garden with him?" 27Again Peter denied it, and at that moment the cock crowed.

28　Then they took Jesus from Caiaphas to Pilate's headquarters. a It was early in the morning. They themselves did not enter the headquarters, a so as to avoid ritual defilement and to be able to eat the Passover. 29So Pilate went out to them and said, "What accusation do you bring against this man?" 30They answered, "If this man were not a criminal, we would not have handed him over to you." 31Pilate said to them, "Take him yourselves and judge him according to your law." The Jews replied, "We are not permitted to put anyone to death." 32(This was to fulfill what Jesus had said when he indicated the kind of death he was to die.)

33　Then Pilate entered the headquarters a again, summoned Jesus, and asked him, "Are you the King of the Jews?" 34Jesus answered, "Do you ask this on your own, or did others tell you about me?" 35Pilate replied, "I am not a Jew, am I? Your own nation and the chief priests have handed you over to me. What have you done?" 36Jesus answered, "My kingdom is not from this world. If my kingdom were from this world, my followers would be fighting to keep me from being handed over to the Jews. But as it is, my kingdom is not from here." 37Pilate asked him, "So you are a king?" Jesus answered, "You say that I am a king. For this I was born, and for this I came into the world, to testify to the truth. Everyone who belongs to the truth listens to my voice." 38Pilate asked him, "What is truth?"

After he had said this, he went out to the Jews again and told them, "I find no case against him. 39But you have a custom that I release someone for you at the Passover. Do you want me to release for you the King of the Jews?" 40They shouted in reply, "Not this man, but Barabbas!" Now Barabbas was a bandit.

19.1 THEN Pilate took Jesus and had him flogged. 2And the soldiers wove a crown of thorns and put it on his head, and they dressed him in a purple robe. 3They kept coming up to him, saying, "Hail, King of the Jews!" and striking him on the face. 4Pilate went out again and said to them, "Look, I am bringing him out to you to let you know that I find no case against him." 5So Jesus came out, wearing the crown of thorns and the purple robe. Pilate said to them, "Here is the man!" 6When the chief priests and the police saw him, they shouted, "Crucify him! Crucify him!" Pilate said to them, "Take him yourselves and crucify him; I find no case against him." 7The Jews answered him, "We have a law, and according to that law he ought to die because he has claimed to be the Son of God."

8　Now when Pilate heard this, he was more afraid than ever. 9He entered his headquarters a again and asked Jesus, "Where are you from?" But Jesus gave him no answer. 10Pilate therefore said to him, "Do you refuse to speak to me? Do you not know that I have power to release you, and power to crucify you?" 11Jesus answered him, "You would have no power over me unless it had been given you from above; therefore the one who handed me over to you is guilty of a greater sin." 12From then on Pilate tried to release him, but the Jews cried out, "If you release this

a Gk *the praetorium*

man, you are no friend of the emperor. Everyone who claims to be a king sets himself against the emperor."

13 When Pilate heard these words, he brought Jesus outside and sat[a] on the judge's bench at a place called The Stone Pavement, or in Hebrew[b] Gabbatha. [14]Now it was the day of Preparation for the Passover; and it was about noon. He said to the Jews, "Here is your King!" [15]They cried out, "Away with him! Away with him! Crucify him!" Pilate asked them, "Shall I crucify your King?" The chief priests answered, "We have no king but the emperor." [16]Then he handed him over to them to be crucified.

So they took Jesus; [17]and carrying the cross by himself, he went out to what is called The Place of the Skull, which in Hebrew[b] is called Golgotha. [18]There they crucified him, and with him two others, one on either side, with Jesus between them. [19]Pilate also had an inscription written and put on the cross. It read, "Jesus of Nazareth,[c] the King of the Jews." [20]Many of the Jews read this inscription, because the place where Jesus was crucified was near the city; and it was written in Hebrew,[b] in Latin, and in Greek. [21]Then the chief priests of the Jews said to Pilate, "Do not write, 'The King of the Jews,' but, 'This man said, I am King of the Jews.'" [22]Pilate answered, "What I have written I have written."

## PSALM 119.113–128

I HATE the double-minded,
    but I love your law.
[114]  You are my hiding place
        and my shield;
        I hope in your word.
[115]  Go away from me, you
        evildoers,

that I may keep the
    commandments of my
    God.
[116]  Uphold me according to your
        promise, that I may live,
    and let me not be put to
        shame in my hope.
[117]  Hold me up, that I may be safe
    and have regard for your
        statutes continually.
[118]  You spurn all who go astray
        from your statutes;
    for their cunning is in vain.
[119]  All the wicked of the earth you
        count as dross;
    therefore I love your decrees.
[120]  My flesh trembles for fear of
        you,
    and I am afraid of your
        judgments.

[121]  I have done what is just and
        right;
    do not leave me to my
        oppressors.
[122]  Guarantee your servant's
        well-being;
    do not let the godless oppress
        me.
[123]  My eyes fail from watching for
        your salvation,
    and for the fulfillment of your
        righteous promise.
[124]  Deal with your servant
        according to your
        steadfast love,
    and teach me your statutes.
[125]  I am your servant; give me
        understanding,
    so that I may know your
        decrees.
[126]  It is time for the LORD to act,
    for your law has been broken.
[127]  Truly I love your
        commandments
    more than gold, more than
        fine gold.

a Or *seated him*  b That is, *Aramaic*  c Gk *the Nazorean*

128   Truly I direct my steps by all
        your precepts; [a]
    I hate every false way.

## PROVERBS 16.10–11

**I**NSPIRED decisions are on the lips
    of a king;
  his mouth does not sin in
    judgment.

11   Honest balances and scales are
      the LORD's;
    all the weights in the bag are
      his work.

# MAY 31

## 2 SAMUEL 17.1–29

**M**OREOVER Ahithophel said to Absalom, "Let me choose twelve thousand men, and I will set out and pursue David tonight. [2]I will come upon him while he is weary and discouraged, and throw him into a panic; and all the people who are with him will flee. I will strike down only the king, [3]and I will bring all the people back to you as a bride comes home to her husband. You seek the life of only one man, [b] and all the people will be at peace." [4]The advice pleased Absalom and all the elders of Israel.

5   Then Absalom said, "Call Hushai the Archite also, and let us hear too what he has to say." [6]When Hushai came to Absalom, Absalom said to him, "This is what Ahithophel has said; shall we do as he advises? If not, you tell us." [7]Then Hushai said to Absalom, "This time the counsel that Ahithophel has given is not good." [8]Hushai continued, "You know that your father and his men are warriors, and that they are enraged, like a bear robbed of her cubs in the field. Besides, your father is expert in war; he will not spend the night with the troops. [9]Even now he has hidden himself in one of the pits, or in some other place. And when some of our troops[c] fall at the first attack, whoever hears it will say, 'There has been a slaughter among the troops who follow Absalom.' [10]Then even the valiant warrior, whose heart is like the heart of a lion, will utterly melt with fear; for all Israel knows that your father is a warrior, and that those who are with him are valiant warriors. [11]But my counsel is that all Israel be gathered to you, from Dan to Beer-sheba, like the sand by the sea for multitude, and that you go to battle in person. [12]So we shall come upon him in whatever place he may be found, and we shall light on him as the dew falls on the ground; and he will not survive, nor will any of those with him. [13]If he withdraws into a city, then all Israel will bring ropes to that city, and we shall drag it into the valley, until not even a pebble is to be found there." [14]Absalom and all the men of Israel said, "The counsel of Hushai the Archite is better than the counsel of Ahithophel." For the LORD had ordained to defeat the good counsel of Ahitho-

aGk Jerome: Meaning of Heb uncertain   bGk: Heb *like the return of the whole (is) the man whom you seek*   cGk Mss: Heb *some of them* phel, so that the L ord might bring ruin on Absalom.

15  Then Hushai said to the priests Zadok and Abiathar, "Thus and so did Ahithophel counsel Absalom and the elders of Israel; and thus and so I have counseled. [16]Therefore send quickly and tell David, 'Do not lodge tonight at the fords of the wilderness, but by all means cross over; otherwise the king and all the people who are with him will be swallowed up.'" [17]Jonathan and Ahimaaz were waiting at En-rogel; a servant-girl used to go and tell them, and they would go and tell King David; for they could not risk being seen entering the city. [18]But a boy saw them, and told Absalom; so both of them went away quickly, and came to the house of a man at Bahurim, who had a well in his courtyard; and they went down into it. [19]The man's wife took a covering, stretched it over the well's mouth, and spread out grain on it; and nothing was known of it. [20]When Absalom's servants came to the woman at the house, they said, "Where are Ahimaaz and Jonathan?" The woman said to them, "They have crossed over the brook[a] of water." And when they had searched and could not find them, they returned to Jerusalem.

21  After they had gone, the men came up out of the well, and went and told King David. They said to David, "Go and cross the water quickly; for thus and so has Ahithophel counseled against you." [22]So David and all the people who were with him set out and crossed the Jordan; by daybreak not one was left who had not crossed the Jordan.

23  When Ahithophel saw that his counsel was not followed, he saddled his donkey and went off home to his own city. He set his house in order, and hanged himself; he died and was buried in the tomb of his father.

24  Then David came to Mahanaim, while Absalom crossed the Jordan with all the men of Israel. [25]Now Absalom had set Amasa over the army in the place of Joab. Amasa was the son of a man named Ithra the Ishmaelite,[b] who had married Abigal daughter of Nahash, sister of Zeruiah, Joab's mother. [26]The Israelites and Absalom encamped in the land of Gilead.

27  When David came to Mahanaim, Shobi son of Nahash from Rabbah of the Ammonites, and Machir son of Ammiel from Lo-debar, and Barzillai the Gileadite from Rogelim, [28]brought beds, basins, and earthen vessels, wheat, barley, meal, parched grain, beans and lentils,[c] [29]honey and curds, sheep, and cheese from the herd, for David and the people with him to eat; for they said, "The troops are hungry and weary and thirsty in the wilderness."

## JOHN 19.23–42

WHEN the soldiers had crucified Jesus, they took his clothes and divided them into four parts, one for each soldier. They also took his tunic; now the tunic was seamless, woven in one piece from the top. [24]So they said to one another, "Let us not tear it, but cast lots for it to see who will get it." This was to fulfill what the scripture says,

"They divided my clothes
among themselves,
and for my clothing they
cast lots."

[25]And that is what the soldiers did.

Meanwhile, standing near the cross of Jesus were his mother, and his mother's sister, Mary the wife of Clopas, and Mary Magdalene. [26]When Jesus saw his mother and the disciple whom he loved standing beside her, he said to his mother, "Woman, here is your son." [27]Then he said to the disciple, "Here is your mother." And from

---

aMeaning of Heb uncertain   b1 Chr 2.17: Heb *Israelite*   cHeb *and lentils and parched grain*

that hour the disciple took her into his own home.

28 After this, when Jesus knew that all was now finished, he said (in order to fulfill the scripture), "I am thirsty." ²⁹A jar full of sour wine was standing there. So they put a sponge full of the wine on a branch of hyssop and held it to his mouth. ³⁰When Jesus had received the wine, he said, "It is finished." Then he bowed his head and gave up his spirit.

31  Since it was the day of Preparation, the Jews did not want the bodies left on the cross during the sabbath, especially because that sabbath was a day of great solemnity. So they asked Pilate to have the legs of the crucified men broken and the bodies removed. ³²Then the soldiers came and broke the legs of the first and of the other who had been crucified with him. ³³But when they came to Jesus and saw that he was already dead, they did not break his legs. ³⁴Instead, one of the soldiers pierced his side with a spear, and at once blood and water came out. ³⁵(He who saw this has testified so that you also may believe. His testimony is true, and he knowsᵃ that he tells the truth.) ³⁶These things occurred so that the scripture might be fulfilled, "None of his bones shall be broken." ³⁷And again another passage of scripture says, "They will look on the one whom they have pierced."

38  After these things, Joseph of Arimathea, who was a disciple of Jesus, though a secret one because of his fear of the Jews, asked Pilate to let him take away the body of Jesus. Pilate gave him permission; so he came and removed his body. ³⁹Nicodemus, who had at first come to Jesus by night, also came, bringing a mixture of myrrh and aloes, weighing about a hundred pounds. ⁴⁰They took the body of Jesus and wrapped it with the spices in linen cloths, according to the burial custom of the Jews. ⁴¹Now there was a garden in the place where he was crucified, and in the garden there was a new tomb in which no one had ever been laid. ⁴²And so, because it was the Jewish day of Preparation, and the tomb was nearby, they laid Jesus there.

## PSALM 119.129–152

**Y**OUR decrees are wonderful;
    therefore my soul keeps
      them.
130  The unfolding of your words
      gives light;
    it imparts understanding to
      the simple.
131  With open mouth I pant,
    because I long for your
      commandments.
132  Turn to me and be gracious to
      me,
    as is your custom toward
      those who love your
      name.
133  Keep my steps steady
      according to your
      promise,
    and never let iniquity have
      dominion over me.
134  Redeem me from human
      oppression,
    that I may keep your
      precepts.
135  Make your face shine upon
      your servant,
    and teach me your statutes.
136  My eyes shed streams of tears
    because your law is not kept.

137  You are righteous, O LORD,
    and your judgments are right.
138  You have appointed your
      decrees in righteousness
    and in all faithfulness.
139  My zeal consumes me
    because my foes forget your
      words.

ᵃ Or *there is one who knows*

140 Your promise is well tried,
     and your servant loves it.
141 I am small and despised,
     yet I do not forget your
       precepts.
142 Your righteousness is an
       everlasting
       righteousness,
     and your law is the truth.
143 Trouble and anguish have come
       upon me,
     but your commandments are
       my delight.
144 Your decrees are righteous
       forever;
     give me understanding that I
       may live.

145 With my whole heart I cry;
       answer me, O LORD.
     I will keep your statutes.
146 I cry to you; save me,
     that I may observe your
       decrees.
147 I rise before dawn and cry
       for help;
     I put my hope in your words.

148 My eyes are awake before
       each watch of the night,
     that I may meditate on your
       promise.
149 In your steadfast love hear my
       voice;
     O LORD, in your justice
       preserve my life.
150 Those who persecute me with
       evil purpose draw near;
     they are far from your law.
151 Yet you are near, O LORD,
     and all your commandments
       are true.
152 Long ago I learned from your
       decrees
     that you have established
       them forever.

## PROVERBS 16.12–13

IT is an abomination to kings to
       do evil,
     for the throne is established
       by righteousness.
13 Righteous lips are the delight of
       a king,
     and he loves those who speak
       what is right.

# JUNE 1

## 2 SAMUEL 18.1—19.10

THEN David mustered the men who were with him, and set over them commanders of thousands and commanders of hundreds. [2]And David divided the army into three groups:[a] one third under the command of Joab, one third under the command of Abishai son of Zeruiah, Joab's brother, and one third under the command of Ittai the Gittite. The king said to the men, "I myself will also go out with you." [3]But the men said, "You shall not go out. For if we flee, they will not care about us. If half of us die, they will not care about us. But you are worth ten thousand of us;[b] therefore it is better that you send us help from the city." [4]The king said to them, "Whatever seems best to you I will do." So the king stood at the side of the gate, while all the army marched out by hundreds and by thousands. ⁵The king ordered Joab and Abishai and Ittai, saying, "Deal gently for my sake with the young man Absalom." And all the people heard when the king gave orders to all the commanders concerning Absalom.

6 So the army went out into the field against Israel; and the battle was fought in the forest of Ephraim. ⁷The men of Israel were defeated there by the servants of David, and the slaughter there was great on that day, twenty thousand men. ⁸The battle spread over the face of all the country; and the forest claimed more victims that day than the sword.

9 Absalom happened to meet the servants of David. Absalom was riding on his mule, and the mule went under the thick branches of a great oak. His head caught fast in the oak, and he was left hangingᵃ between heaven and earth, while the mule that was under him went on. ¹⁰A man saw it, and told Joab, "I saw Absalom hanging in an oak." ¹¹Joab said to the man who told him, "What, you saw him! Why then did you not strike him there to the ground? I would have been glad to give you ten pieces of silver and a belt." ¹²But the man said to Joab, "Even if I felt in my hand the weight of a thousand pieces of silver, I would not raise my hand against the king's son; for in our hearing the king commanded you and Abishai and Ittai, saying: For my sake protect the young man Absalom! ¹³On the other hand, if I had dealt treacherously against his lifeᵇ (and there is nothing hidden from the king), then you yourself would have stood aloof." ¹⁴Joab said, "I will not waste time like this with you." He took three spears in his hand, and thrust them into the heart of Absalom, while he was still alive in the oak. ¹⁵And ten young men, Joab's armor-bearers, surrounded Absalom and struck him, and killed him.

16 Then Joab sounded the trumpet, and the troops came back from pursuing Israel, for Joab restrained the troops. ¹⁷They took Absalom, threw him into a great pit in the forest, and raised over him a very great heap of stones. Meanwhile all the Israelites fled to their homes. ¹⁸Now Absalom in his lifetime had taken and set up for himself a pillar that is in the King's Valley, for he said, "I have no son to keep my name in remembrance"; he called the pillar by his own name. It is called Absalom's Monument to this day.

19 Then Ahimaaz son of Zadok said, "Let me run, and carry tidings to the king that the Lᴏʀᴅ has delivered him from the power of his enemies." ²⁰Joab said to him, "You are not to carry tidings today; you may carry tidings another day, but today you shall not do so, because the king's son is dead." ²¹Then Joab said to a Cushite, "Go, tell the king what you have seen." The Cushite bowed before Joab, and ran. ²²Then Ahimaaz son of Zadok said again to Joab, "Come what may, let me also run after the Cushite." And Joab said, "Why will you run, my son, seeing that you have no rewardᶜ for the tidings?" ²³"Come what may," he said, "I will run." So he said to him, "Run." Then Ahimaaz ran by the way of the Plain, and outran the Cushite.

24 Now David was sitting between the two gates. The sentinel went up to the roof of the gate by the wall, and when he looked up, he saw a man running alone. ²⁵The sentinel shouted and told the king. The king said, "If he is alone, there are tidings in his mouth." He kept coming, and drew near. ²⁶Then the sentinel saw another man running; and the sentinel called to the gatekeeper and said, "See, another

---

ᵃGk Syr Tg: Heb *was put*   ᵇAnother reading is *at the risk of my life*   ᶜMeaning of Heb uncertain

man running alone!" The king said, "He also is bringing tidings." ²⁷The sentinel said, "I think the running of the first one is like the running of Ahimaaz son of Zadok." The king said, "He is a good man, and comes with good tidings."

28  Then Ahimaaz cried out to the king, "All is well!" He prostrated himself before the king with his face to the ground, and said, "Blessed be the LORD your God, who has delivered up the men who raised their hand against my lord the king." ²⁹The king said, "Is it well with the young man Absalom?" Ahimaaz answered, "When Joab sent your servant,ᵃ I saw a great tumult, but I do not know what it was." ³⁰The king said, "Turn aside, and stand here." So he turned aside, and stood still.

31  Then the Cushite came; and the Cushite said, "Good tidings for my lord the king! For the LORD has vindicated you this day, delivering you from the power of all who rose up against you." ³²The king said to the Cushite, "Is it well with the young man Absalom?" The Cushite answered, "May the enemies of my lord the king, and all who rise up to do you harm, be like that young man."

33ᵇ The king was deeply moved, and went up to the chamber over the gate, and wept; and as he went, he said, "O my son Absalom, my son, my son Absalom! Would I had died instead of you, O Absalom, my son, my son!"

¹⁹·¹ IT was told Joab, "The king is weeping and mourning for Absalom." ²So the victory that day was turned into mourning for all the troops; for the troops heard that day, "The king is grieving for his son." ³The troops stole into the city that day as soldiers steal in who are ashamed when they flee in battle. ⁴The king covered his face, and the king cried with a loud voice, "O my son Ab-

salom, O Absalom, my son, my son!" ⁵Then Joab came into the house to the king, and said, "Today you have covered with shame the faces of all your officers who have saved your life today, and the lives of your sons and your daughters, and the lives of your wives and your concubines, ⁶for love of those who hate you and for hatred of those who love you. You have made it clear today that commanders and officers are nothing to you; for I perceive that if Absalom were alive and all of us were dead today, then you would be pleased. ⁷So go out at once and speak kindly to your servants; for I swear by the LORD, if you do not go, not a man will stay with you this night; and this will be worse for you than any disaster that has come upon you from your youth until now." ⁸Then the king got up and took his seat in the gate. The troops were all told, "See, the king is sitting in the gate"; and all the troops came before the king.

Meanwhile, all the Israelites had fled to their homes. ⁹All the people were disputing throughout all the tribes of Israel, saying, "The king delivered us from the hand of our enemies, and saved us from the hand of the Philistines; and now he has fled out of the land because of Absalom. ¹⁰But Absalom, whom we anointed over us, is dead in battle. Now therefore why do you say nothing about bringing the king back?"

# JOHN 20.1–31

EARLY on the first day of the week, while it was still dark, Mary Magdalene came to the tomb and saw that the stone had been removed from the tomb. ²So she ran and went to Simon Peter and the other disciple, the one whom Jesus loved, and said to them, "They have taken the Lord out of the tomb, and we do not know where they have laid him." ³Then

ᵃHeb *the king's servant, your servant*  ᵇCh 19.1 in Heb

Peter and the other disciple set out and went toward the tomb. 4The two were running together, but the other disciple outran Peter and reached the tomb first. 5He bent down to look in and saw the linen wrappings lying there, but he did not go in. 6Then Simon Peter came, following him, and went into the tomb. He saw the linen wrappings lying there, 7and the cloth that had been on Jesus' head, not lying with the linen wrappings but rolled up in a place by itself. 8Then the other disciple, who reached the tomb first, also went in, and he saw and believed; 9for as yet they did not understand the scripture, that he must rise from the dead. 10Then the disciples returned to their homes.

11 But Mary stood weeping outside the tomb. As she wept, she bent over to looka into the tomb; 12and she saw two angels in white, sitting where the body of Jesus had been lying, one at the head and the other at the feet. 13They said to her, "Woman, why are you weeping?" She said to them, "They have taken away my Lord, and I do not know where they have laid him." 14When she had said this, she turned around and saw Jesus standing there, but she did not know that it was Jesus. 15Jesus said to her, "Woman, why are you weeping? Whom are you looking for?" Supposing him to be the gardener, she said to him, "Sir, if you have carried him away, tell me where you have laid him, and I will take him away." 16Jesus said to her, "Mary!" She turned and said to him in Hebrew,b "Rabbouni!" (which means Teacher). 17Jesus said to her, "Do not hold on to me, because I have not yet ascended to the Father. But go to my brothers and say to them, 'I am ascending to my Father and your Father, to my God and your God.'" 18Mary Magdalene went and announced to the disciples, "I have seen the Lord"; and she told them that he had said these things to her.

19 When it was evening on that day, the first day of the week, and the doors of the house where the disciples had met were locked for fear of the Jews, Jesus came and stood among them and said, "Peace be with you." 20After he said this, he showed them his hands and his side. Then the disciples rejoiced when they saw the Lord. 21Jesus said to them again, "Peace be with you. As the Father has sent me, so I send you." 22When he had said this, he breathed on them and said to them, "Receive the Holy Spirit. 23If you forgive the sins of any, they are forgiven them; if you retain the sins of any, they are retained."

24 But Thomas (who was called the Twinc), one of the twelve, was not with them when Jesus came. 25So the other disciples told him, "We have seen the Lord." But he said to them, "Unless I see the mark of the nails in his hands, and put my finger in the mark of the nails and my hand in his side, I will not believe."

26 A week later his disciples were again in the house, and Thomas was with them. Although the doors were shut, Jesus came and stood among them and said, "Peace be with you." 27Then he said to Thomas, "Put your finger here and see my hands. Reach out your hand and put it in my side. Do not doubt but believe." 28Thomas answered him, "My Lord and my God!" 29Jesus said to him, "Have you believed because you have seen me? Blessed are those who have not seen and yet have come to believe."

30 Now Jesus did many other signs in the presence of his disciples, which are not written in this book. 31But these are written so that you may come to believed that Jesus is the Messiah,e the Son of God, and that

aGk lacks to look  bThat is, Aramaic  cGk Didymus  dOther ancient authorities read may continue
to believe  eOr the Christ

through believing you may have life in
his name.

## PSALM 119.153–176

Look on my misery and rescue
  me,
  for I do not forget your law.
154 Plead my cause and redeem
    me;
      give me life according to your
      promise.
155 Salvation is far from the
      wicked,
      for they do not seek your
      statutes.
156 Great is your mercy, O Lord;
      give me life according to your
      justice.
157 Many are my persecutors and
      my adversaries,
      yet I do not swerve from
      your decrees.
158 I look at the faithless with
      disgust,
      because they do not keep
      your commands.
159 Consider how I love your
      precepts;
      preserve my life according to
      your steadfast love.
160 The sum of your word is truth;
      and every one of your
      righteous ordinances
      endures forever.

161 Princes persecute me without
      cause,
      but my heart stands in awe of
      your words.
162 I rejoice at your word
      like one who finds great spoil.
163 I hate and abhor falsehood,
      but I love your law.
164 Seven times a day I praise you
      for your righteous ordinances.
165 Great peace have those who
      love your law;
      nothing can make them
      stumble.

166 I hope for your salvation,
      O Lord,
      and I fulfill your
      commandments.
167 My soul keeps your decrees;
      I love them exceedingly.
168 I keep your precepts and
      decrees,
      for all my ways are before
      you.

169 Let my cry come before you,
      O Lord;
      give me understanding
      according to your word.
170 Let my supplication come
      before you;
      deliver me according to your
      promise.
171 My lips will pour forth praise,
      because you teach me your
      statutes.
172 My tongue will sing of your
      promise,
      for all your commandments
      are right.
173 Let your hand be ready to help
      me,
      for I have chosen your
      precepts.
174 I long for your salvation,
      O Lord,
      and your law is my delight.
175 Let me live that I may praise
      you,
      and let your ordinances help
      me.
176 I have gone astray like a lost
      sheep; seek out your
      servant,
      for I do not forget your
      commandments.

## PROVERBS 16.14–15

A king's wrath is a messenger
  of death,
  and whoever is wise will
    appease it.

15  In the light of a king's face
      there is life,

and his favor is like the clouds
      that bring the spring
      rain.

# JUNE 2

## 2 SAMUEL 19.11—20.13

KING David sent this message to the priests Zadok and Abiathar, "Say to the elders of Judah, 'Why should you be the last to bring the king back to his house? The talk of all Israel has come to the king.[a] [12]You are my kin, you are my bone and my flesh; why then should you be the last to bring back the king?' [13]And say to Amasa, 'Are you not my bone and my flesh? So may God do to me, and more, if you are not the commander of my army from now on, in place of Joab.' " [14]Amasa[b] swayed the hearts of all the people of Judah as one, and they sent word to the king, "Return, both you and all your servants." [15]So the king came back to the Jordan; and Judah came to Gilgal to meet the king and to bring him over the Jordan.

16  Shimei son of Gera, the Benjaminite, from Bahurim, hurried to come down with the people of Judah to meet King David; [17]with him were a thousand people from Benjamin. And Ziba, the servant of the house of Saul, with his fifteen sons and his twenty servants, rushed down to the Jordan ahead of the king, [18]while the crossing was taking place,[c] to bring over the king's household, and to do his pleasure.

Shimei son of Gera fell down before the king, as he was about to cross the Jordan, [19]and said to the king, "May my lord not hold me guilty or remember how your servant did wrong on the day my lord the king left Jerusalem; may the king not bear it in mind. [20]For your servant knows that I have sinned; therefore, see, I have come this day, the first of all the house of Joseph to come down to meet my lord the king." [21]Abishai son of Zeruiah answered, "Shall not Shimei be put to death for this, because he cursed the LORD's anointed?" [22]But David said, "What have I to do with you, you sons of Zeruiah, that you should today become an adversary to me? Shall anyone be put to death in Israel this day? For do I not know that I am this day king over Israel?" [23]The king said to Shimei, "You shall not die." And the king gave him his oath.

24  Mephibosheth[d] grandson of Saul came down to meet the king; he had not taken care of his feet, or trimmed his beard, or washed his clothes, from the day the king left until the day he came back in safety. [25]When he came from Jerusalem to meet the king, the king said to him, "Why did you not go with me, Mephibosheth?"[d] [26]He answered, "My lord, O king, my servant deceived me; for your servant said to him, 'Saddle a donkey for me,[e] so that I may ride on it and go with the king.' For your servant is lame. [27]He has slandered your servant to my lord

aGk: Heb *to the king, to his house*   bHeb *He*   cCn: Heb *the ford crossed*   dOr *Merib-baal*: See 4.4 note   eGk Syr Vg: Heb *said, I will saddle a donkey for myself*

the king. But my lord the king is like the angel of God; do therefore what seems good to you. 28For all my father's house were doomed to death before my lord the king; but you set your servant among those who eat at your table. What further right have I, then, to appeal to the king?" 29The king said to him, "Why speak any more of your affairs? I have decided: you and Ziba shall divide the land." 30Mephibosheth[a] said to the king, "Let him take it all, since my lord the king has arrived home safely."

31 Now Barzillai the Gileadite had come down from Rogelim; he went on with the king to the Jordan, to escort him over the Jordan. 32Barzillai was a very aged man, eighty years old. He had provided the king with food while he stayed at Mahanaim, for he was a very wealthy man. 33The king said to Barzillai, "Come over with me, and I will provide for you in Jerusalem at my side." 34But Barzillai said to the king, "How many years have I still to live, that I should go up with the king to Jerusalem? 35Today I am eighty years old; can I discern what is pleasant and what is not? Can your servant taste what he eats or what he drinks? Can I still listen to the voice of singing men and singing women? Why then should your servant be an added burden to my lord the king? 36Your servant will go a little way over the Jordan with the king. Why should the king recompense me with such a reward? 37Please let your servant return, so that I may die in my own town, near the graves of my father and my mother. But here is your servant Chimham; let him go over with my lord the king; and do for him whatever seems good to you." 38The king answered, "Chimham shall go over with me, and I will do for him whatever seems good to you; and all that you desire of me I will do for you." 39Then all the people

crossed over the Jordan, and the king crossed over; the king kissed Barzillai and blessed him, and he returned to his own home. 40The king went on to Gilgal, and Chimham went on with him; all the people of Judah, and also half the people of Israel, brought the king on his way.

41 Then all the people of Israel came to the king, and said to him, "Why have our kindred the people of Judah stolen you away, and brought the king and his household over the Jordan, and all David's men with him?" 42All the people of Judah answered the people of Israel, "Because the king is near of kin to us. Why then are you angry over this matter? Have we eaten at all at the king's expense? Or has he given us any gift?" 43But the people of Israel answered the people of Judah, "We have ten shares in the king, and in David also we have more than you. Why then did you despise us? Were we not the first to speak of bringing back our king?" But the words of the people of Judah were fiercer than the words of the people of Israel.

20.1 Now a scoundrel named Sheba son of Bichri, a Benjaminite, happened to be there. He sounded the trumpet and cried out,

"We have no portion in David,
no share in the son of Jesse!
Everyone to your tents,
O Israel!"

2So all the people of Israel withdrew from David and followed Sheba son of Bichri; but the people of Judah followed their king steadfastly from the Jordan to Jerusalem.

3 David came to his house at Jerusalem; and the king took the ten concubines whom he had left to look after the house, and put them in a house under guard, and provided for them, but did not go in to them. So they were shut up

---

a Or *Merib-baal*: See 4.4 note

until the day of their death, living as if in widowhood.

4 Then the king said to Amasa, "Call the men of Judah together to me within three days, and be here yourself." [5]So Amasa went to summon Judah; but he delayed beyond the set time that had been appointed him. [6]David said to Abishai, "Now Sheba son of Bichri will do us more harm than Absalom; take your lord's servants and pursue him, or he will find fortified cities for himself, and escape from us." [7]Joab's men went out after him, along with the Cherethites, the Pelethites, and all the warriors; they went out from Jerusalem to pursue Sheba son of Bichri. [8]When they were at the large stone that is in Gibeon, Amasa came to meet them. Now Joab was wearing a soldier's garment and over it was a belt with a sword in its sheath fastened at his waist; as he went forward it fell out. [9]Joab said to Amasa, "Is it well with you, my brother?" And Joab took Amasa by the beard with his right hand to kiss him. [10]But Amasa did not notice the sword in Joab's hand; Joab struck him in the belly so that his entrails poured out on the ground, and he died. He did not strike a second blow.

Then Joab and his brother Abishai pursued Sheba son of Bichri. [11]And one of Joab's men took his stand by Amasa, and said, "Whoever favors Joab, and whoever is for David, let him follow Joab." [12]Amasa lay wallowing in his blood on the highway, and the man saw that all the people were stopping. Since he saw that all who came by him were stopping, he carried Amasa from the highway into a field, and threw a garment over him. [13]Once he was removed from the highway, all the people went on after Joab to pursue Sheba son of Bichri.

## JOHN 21.1–25

AFTER these things Jesus showed himself again to the disciples by the Sea of Tiberias; and he showed himself in this way. [2]Gathered there together were Simon Peter, Thomas called the Twin,[a] Nathanael of Cana in Galilee, the sons of Zebedee, and two others of his disciples. [3]Simon Peter said to them, "I am going fishing." They said to him, "We will go with you." They went out and got into the boat, but that night they caught nothing.

4 Just after daybreak, Jesus stood on the beach; but the disciples did not know that it was Jesus. [5]Jesus said to them, "Children, you have no fish, have you?" They answered him, "No." [6]He said to them, "Cast the net to the right side of the boat, and you will find some." So they cast it, and now they were not able to haul it in because there were so many fish. [7]That disciple whom Jesus loved said to Peter, "It is the Lord!" When Simon Peter heard that it was the Lord, he put on some clothes, for he was naked, and jumped into the sea. [8]But the other disciples came in the boat, dragging the net full of fish, for they were not far from the land, only about a hundred yards[b] off.

9 When they had gone ashore, they saw a charcoal fire there, with fish on it, and bread. [10]Jesus said to them, "Bring some of the fish that you have just caught." [11]So Simon Peter went aboard and hauled the net ashore, full of large fish, a hundred fifty-three of them; and though there were so many, the net was not torn. [12]Jesus said to them, "Come and have breakfast." Now none of the disciples dared to ask him, "Who are you?" because they knew it was the Lord. [13]Jesus came and took the bread and gave it to them, and did the same with the fish. [14]This was

a Gk *Didymus*   b Gk *two hundred cubits*

now the third time that Jesus appeared to the disciples after he was raised from the dead.

15 When they had finished breakfast, Jesus said to Simon Peter, "Simon son of John, do you love me more than these?" He said to him, "Yes, Lord; you know that I love you." Jesus said to him, "Feed my lambs." [16]A second time he said to him, "Simon son of John, do you love me?" He said to him, "Yes, Lord; you know that I love you." Jesus said to him, "Tend my sheep." [17]He said to him the third time, "Simon son of John, do you love me?" Peter felt hurt because he said to him the third time, "Do you love me?" And he said to him, "Lord, you know everything; you know that I love you." Jesus said to him, "Feed my sheep. [18]Very truly, I tell you, when you were younger, you used to fasten your own belt and to go wherever you wished. But when you grow old, you will stretch out your hands, and someone else will fasten a belt around you and take you where you do not wish to go." [19](He said this to indicate the kind of death by which he would glorify God.) After this he said to him, "Follow me."

20 Peter turned and saw the disciple whom Jesus loved following them; he was the one who had reclined next to Jesus at the supper and had said, "Lord, who is it that is going to betray you?" [21]When Peter saw him, he said to Jesus, "Lord, what about him?" [22]Jesus said to him, "If it is my will that he remain until I come, what is that to you? Follow me!" [23]So the rumor spread in the community[a] that this disciple would not die. Yet Jesus did not say to him that he would not die, but, "If it is my will that he remain until I come, what is that to you?"[b]

24 This is the disciple who is testifying to these things and has written them, and we know that his testimony is true. [25]But there are also many other things that Jesus did; if every one of them were written down, I suppose that the world itself could not contain the books that would be written.

## PSALM 120.1–7

*A Song of Ascents.*

IN my distress I cry to the LORD,
that he may answer me:
2   "Deliver me, O LORD,
from lying lips,
from a deceitful tongue."

3   What shall be given to you?
And what more shall be done
to you,
you deceitful tongue?
4   A warrior's sharp arrows,
with glowing coals of the
broom tree!

5   Woe is me, that I am an alien in
Meshech,
that I must live among the
tents of Kedar.
6   Too long have I had my dwelling
among those who hate peace.
7   I am for peace;
but when I speak,
they are for war.

## PROVERBS 16.16–17

How much better to get
wisdom than gold!
To get understanding is to
be chosen rather than
silver.
17   The highway of the upright
avoids evil;
those who guard their way
preserve their lives.

---

[a] Gk *among the brothers*   [b] Other ancient authorities lack *what is that to you*

## 2 SAMUEL 20.14—22.20

Sᴴᴇʙᴀ[a] passed through all the tribes of Israel to Abel of Beth-maacah;[b] and all the Bichrites[c] assembled, and followed him inside. [15]Joab's forces[d] came and besieged him in Abel of Beth-maacah; they threw up a siege ramp against the city, and it stood against the rampart. Joab's forces were battering the wall to break it down. [16]Then a wise woman called from the city, "Listen! Listen! Tell Joab, 'Come here, I want to speak to you.'" [17]He came near her; and the woman said, "Are you Joab?" He answered, "I am." Then she said to him, "Listen to the words of your servant." He answered, "I am listening." [18]Then she said, "They used to say in the old days, 'Let them inquire at Abel'; and so they would settle a matter. [19]I am one of those who are peaceable and faithful in Israel; you seek to destroy a city that is a mother in Israel; why will you swallow up the heritage of the Lᴏʀᴅ?" [20]Joab answered, "Far be it from me, far be it, that I should swallow up or destroy! [21]That is not the case! But a man of the hill country of Ephraim, called Sheba son of Bichri, has lifted up his hand against King David; give him up alone, and I will withdraw from the city." The woman said to Joab, "His head shall be thrown over the wall to you." [22]Then the woman went to all the people with her wise plan. And they cut off the head of Sheba son of Bichri, and threw it out to Joab. So he blew the trumpet, and they dispersed from the city, and all went to their homes, while Joab returned to Jerusalem to the king.

23 Now Joab was in command of all the army of Israel;[e] Benaiah son of Jehoiada was in command of the Cherethites and the Pelethites; [24]Adoram was in charge of the forced labor; Jehoshaphat son of Ahilud was the recorder; [25]Sheva was secretary; Zadok and Abiathar were priests; [26]and Ira the Jairite was also David's priest.

[21.1] Now there was a famine in the days of David for three years, year after year; and David inquired of the Lᴏʀᴅ. The Lᴏʀᴅ said, "There is bloodguilt on Saul and on his house, because he put the Gibeonites to death." [2]So the king called the Gibeonites and spoke to them. (Now the Gibeonites were not of the people of Israel, but of the remnant of the Amorites; although the people of Israel had sworn to spare them, Saul had tried to wipe them out in his zeal for the people of Israel and Judah.) [3]David said to the Gibeonites, "What shall I do for you? How shall I make expiation, that you may bless the heritage of the Lᴏʀᴅ?" [4]The Gibeonites said to him, "It is not a matter of silver or gold between us and Saul or his house; neither is it for us to put anyone to death in Israel." He said, "What do you say that I should do for you?" [5]They said to the king, "The man who consumed us and planned to destroy us, so that we should have no place in all the territory of Israel— [6]let seven of his sons be handed over to us, and we will impale them before the Lᴏʀᴅ at Gibeon on the mountain of the Lᴏʀᴅ."[f] The king said, "I will hand them over."

7 But the king spared Mephibosheth,[g] the son of Saul's son Jonathan, because of the oath of the Lᴏʀᴅ that

aheb *he*   bCompare 20.15: Heb *and Beth-maacah*   cCompare Gk Vg: Heb *Berites*   dHeb *They*
eCn: Heb *Joab to all the army, Israel*   fCn Compare Gk and 21.9: Heb *at Gibeah of Saul, the chosen of the Lᴏʀᴅ*   gOr *Merib-baal*: See 4.4 note

was between them, between David and Jonathan son of Saul. 8The king took the two sons of Rizpah daughter of Aiah, whom she bore to Saul, Armoni and Mephibosheth;a and the five sons of Merabb daughter of Saul, whom she bore to Adriel son of Barzillai the Meholathite; 9he gave them into the hands of the Gibeonites, and they impaled them on the mountain before the LORD. The seven of them perished together. They were put to death in the first days of harvest, at the beginning of barley harvest.

10 Then Rizpah the daughter of Aiah took sackcloth, and spread it on a rock for herself, from the beginning of harvest until rain fell on them from the heavens; she did not allow the birds of the air to come on the bodiesc by day, or the wild animals by night. 11When David was told what Rizpah daughter of Aiah, the concubine of Saul, had done, 12David went and took the bones of Saul and the bones of his son Jonathan from the people of Jabesh-gilead, who had stolen them from the public square of Beth-shan, where the Philistines had hung them up, on the day the Philistines killed Saul on Gilboa. 13He brought up from there the bones of Saul and the bones of his son Jonathan; and they gathered the bones of those who had been impaled. 14They buried the bones of Saul and of his son Jonathan in the land of Benjamin in Zela, in the tomb of his father Kish; they did all that the king commanded. After that, God heeded supplications for the land.

15 The Philistines went to war again with Israel, and David went down together with his servants. They fought against the Philistines, and David grew weary. 16Ishbi-benob, one of the descendants of the giants, whose spear weighed three hundred shekels of bronze, and who was fitted out with new weapons,d said he would kill David. 17But Abishai son of Zeruiah came to his aid, and attacked the Philistine and killed him. Then David's men swore to him, "You shall not go out with us to battle any longer, so that you do not quench the lamp of Israel."

18 After this a battle took place with the Philistines, at Gob; then Sibbecai the Hushathite killed Saph, who was one of the descendants of the giants. 19Then there was another battle with the Philistines at Gob; and Elhanan son of Jaare-oregim, the Bethlehemite, killed Goliath the Gittite, the shaft of whose spear was like a weaver's beam. 20There was again war at Gath, where there was a man of great size, who had six fingers on each hand, and six toes on each foot, twenty-four in number; he too was descended from the giants. 21When he taunted Israel, Jonathan son of David's brother Shimei, killed him. 22These four were descended from the giants in Gath; they fell by the hands of David and his servants.

22.1 DAVID spoke to the LORD the words of this song on the day when the LORD delivered him from the hand of all his enemies, and from the hand of Saul. 2He said:

> The LORD is my rock, my
>     fortress, and my
>     deliverer,
> 3 my God, my rock, in whom I
>     take refuge,
> my shield and the horn of my
>     salvation,
>     my stronghold and my refuge,
>     my savior; you save me from
>     violence.
> 4 I call upon the LORD, who is
>     worthy to be praised,
>     and I am saved from my
>     enemies.
>
> 5 For the waves of death
>     encompassed me,

aOr *Merib-baal*: See 4.4 note　bTwo Heb Mss Syr Compare Gk: MT *Michal*　cHeb *them*
dHeb *was belted anew*

  the torrents of perdition
    assailed me;
6 the cords of Sheol entangled
    me,
  the snares of death
    confronted me.

7 In my distress I called upon the
    Lord;
  to my God I called.
  From his temple he heard my
    voice,
  and my cry came to his ears.

8 Then the earth reeled and
    rocked;
  the foundations of the
    heavens trembled
  and quaked, because he was
    angry.
9 Smoke went up from his
    nostrils,
  and devouring fire from his
    mouth;
  glowing coals flamed forth
    from him.
10 He bowed the heavens, and
    came down;
  thick darkness was under his
    feet.
11 He rode on a cherub, and flew;
  he was seen upon the wings
    of the wind.
12 He made darkness around him a
    canopy,
  thick clouds, a gathering of
    water.
13 Out of the brightness before
    him
  coals of fire flamed forth.
14 The Lord thundered from
    heaven;
  the Most High uttered his
    voice.
15 He sent out arrows, and
    scattered them
  —lightning, and routed them.

16 Then the channels of the sea
    were seen,
  the foundations of the world
    were laid bare
  at the rebuke of the Lord,
    at the blast of the breath of
      his nostrils.

17 He reached from on high, he
    took me,
  he drew me out of mighty
    waters.
18 He delivered me from my
    strong enemy,
  from those who hated me;
  for they were too mighty for
    me.
19 They came upon me in the day
    of my calamity,
  but the Lord was my stay.
20 He brought me out into a broad
    place;
  he delivered me, because he
    delighted in me.

## ACTS 1.1–26

In the first book, Theophilus, I wrote about all that Jesus did and taught from the beginning [2]until the day when he was taken up to heaven, after giving instructions through the Holy Spirit to the apostles whom he had chosen. [3]After his suffering he presented himself alive to them by many convincing proofs, appearing to them during forty days and speaking about the kingdom of God. [4]While staying[a] with them, he ordered them not to leave Jerusalem, but to wait there for the promise of the Father. "This," he said, "is what you have heard from me; [5]for John baptized with water, but you will be baptized with[b] the Holy Spirit not many days from now."

6 So when they had come together, they asked him, "Lord, is this the time when you will restore the kingdom to Israel?" [7]He replied, "It is not for you

a Or *eating*   b Or *by*

to know the times or periods that the Father has set by his own authority. [8]But you will receive power when the Holy Spirit has come upon you; and you will be my witnesses in Jerusalem, in all Judea and Samaria, and to the ends of the earth." [9]When he had said this, as they were watching, he was lifted up, and a cloud took him out of their sight. [10]While he was going and they were gazing up toward heaven, suddenly two men in white robes stood by them. [11]They said, "Men of Galilee, why do you stand looking up toward heaven? This Jesus, who has been taken up from you into heaven, will come in the same way as you saw him go into heaven."

12 Then they returned to Jerusalem from the mount called Olivet, which is near Jerusalem, a sabbath day's journey away. [13]When they had entered the city, they went to the room upstairs where they were staying, Peter, and John, and James, and Andrew, Philip and Thomas, Bartholomew and Matthew, James son of Alphaeus, and Simon the Zealot, and Judas son of[a] James. [14]All these were constantly devoting themselves to prayer, together with certain women, including Mary the mother of Jesus, as well as his brothers.

15 In those days Peter stood up among the believers[b] (together the crowd numbered about one hundred twenty persons) and said, [16]"Friends,[c] the scripture had to be fulfilled, which the Holy Spirit through David foretold concerning Judas, who became a guide for those who arrested Jesus— [17]for he was numbered among us and was allotted his share in this ministry." [18](Now this man acquired a field with the reward of his wickedness; and falling headlong,[d] he burst open in the middle and all his bowels gushed out. [19]This became known to all the residents of Jerusalem, so that the field was called in their language Hakeldama, that is, Field of Blood.) [20]"For it is written in the book of Psalms,

> 'Let his homestead become
>     desolate,
>   and let there be no one to
>     live in it';

and

>   'Let another take his position of
>     overseer.'

[21]So one of the men who have accompanied us during all the time that the Lord Jesus went in and out among us, [22]beginning from the baptism of John until the day when he was taken up from us—one of these must become a witness with us to his resurrection." [23]So they proposed two, Joseph called Barsabbas, who was also known as Justus, and Matthias. [24]Then they prayed and said, "Lord, you know everyone's heart. Show us which one of these two you have chosen [25]to take the place[e] in this ministry and apostleship from which Judas turned aside to go to his own place." [26]And they cast lots for them, and the lot fell on Matthias; and he was added to the eleven apostles.

## PSALM 121.1–8

*A Song of Ascents.*

I LIFT up my eyes to the hills—
    from where will my help
        come?
[2]  My help comes from the LORD,
        who made heaven and earth.

[3]  He will not let your foot be
        moved;
    he who keeps you will not
        slumber.
[4]  He who keeps Israel
        will neither slumber nor
        sleep.

[5]  The LORD is your keeper;

the Lord is your shade at
your right hand.
6 The sun shall not strike you
by day,
nor the moon by night.

7 The Lord will keep you from
all evil;
he will keep your life.
8 The Lord will keep

your going out and your
coming in
from this time on and
forevermore.

## PROVERBS 16.18

**P**RIDE goes before destruction,
and a haughty spirit before a
fall.

# JUNE 4

## 2 SAMUEL 22.21—23.23

**T**HE Lord rewarded me
according to my
righteousness;
according to the cleanness of
my hands he
recompensed me.
22 For I have kept the ways of the
Lord,
and have not wickedly
departed from my God.
23 For all his ordinances were
before me,
and from his statutes I did not
turn aside.
24 I was blameless before him,
and I kept myself from guilt.
25 Therefore the Lord has
recompensed me
according to my
righteousness,
according to my cleanness in
his sight.

26 With the loyal you show
yourself loyal;
with the blameless you show
yourself blameless;

27 with the pure you show yourself
pure,
and with the crooked you
show yourself perverse.
28 You deliver a humble people,
but your eyes are upon the
haughty to bring them
down.
29 Indeed, you are my lamp,
O Lord,
the Lord lightens my
darkness.
30 By you I can crush a troop,
and by my God I can leap
over a wall.
31 This God—his way is perfect;
the promise of the Lord
proves true;
he is a shield for all who take
refuge in him.

32 For who is God, but the Lord?
And who is a rock, except
our God?
33 The God who has girded me
with strength[a]
has opened wide my path. [b]

---

**a**Q Ms Gk Syr Vg Compare Ps 18.32: MT *God is my strong refuge*   **b**Meaning of Heb uncertain

34 He made my[a] feet like the feet
      of deer,
   and set me secure on the
      heights.
35 He trains my hands for war,
      so that my arms can bend a
      bow of bronze.
36 You have given me the shield of
      your salvation,
   and your help[b] has made me
      great.
37 You have made me stride
      freely,
   and my feet do not slip;
38 I pursued my enemies and
      destroyed them,
   and did not turn back until
      they were consumed.
39 I consumed them; I struck them
      down, so that they did
      not rise;
   they fell under my feet.
40 For you girded me with
      strength for the battle;
   you made my assailants sink
      under me.
41 You made my enemies turn
      their backs to me,
   those who hated me, and I
      destroyed them.
42 They looked, but there was no
      one to save them;
   they cried to the LORD, but he
      did not answer them.
43 I beat them fine like the dust of
      the earth,
   I crushed them and stamped
      them down like the mire
      of the streets.

44 You delivered me from strife
      with the peoples;[c]
   you kept me as the head of
      the nations;
   people whom I had not known
      served me.
45 Foreigners came cringing to me;

   as soon as they heard of me,
      they obeyed me.
46 Foreigners lost heart,
   and came trembling out of
      their strongholds.

47 The LORD lives! Blessed be my
      rock,
   and exalted be my God, the
      rock of my salvation,
48 the God who gave me
      vengeance
   and brought down peoples
      under me,
49 who brought me out from my
      enemies;
   you exalted me above my
      adversaries,
   you delivered me from the
      violent.

50 For this I will extol you,
      O LORD, among the
      nations,
   and sing praises to your
      name.
51 He is a tower of salvation for
      his king,
   and shows steadfast love to
      his anointed,
   to David and his descendants
      forever.

23.1 Now these are the last words of David:
   The oracle of David, son of
      Jesse,
   the oracle of the man whom
      God exalted,[d]
   the anointed of the God of
      Jacob,
   the favorite of the Strong One
      of Israel:

2  The spirit of the LORD speaks
      through me,
   his word is upon my tongue.
3  The God of Israel has spoken,

---

a Another reading is *his*   b Q Ms: MT *your answering*   c Gk: Heb *from strife with my people*   d Q Ms:
MT *who was raised on high*

the Rock of Israel has said to
  me:
One who rules over people
  justly,
  ruling in the fear of God,
4  is like the light of morning,
  like the sun rising on a
  cloudless morning,
  gleaming from the rain on the
  grassy land.

5  Is not my house like this with
  God?
  For he has made with me an
  everlasting covenant,
  ordered in all things and
  secure.
Will he not cause to prosper
  all my help and my desire?
6  But the godless are[a] all like
  thorns that are thrown
  away;
  for they cannot be picked up
  with the hand;
7  to touch them one uses an iron
  bar
  or the shaft of a spear.
  And they are entirely
  consumed in fire on the
  spot.[b]

8  These are the names of the warriors whom David had: Josheb-basshebeth a Tahchemonite; he was chief of the Three;[c] he wielded his spear[d] against eight hundred whom he killed at one time.

9  Next to him among the three warriors was Eleazar son of Dodo son of Ahohi. He was with David when they defied the Philistines who were gathered there for battle. The Israelites withdrew, [10]but he stood his ground. He struck down the Philistines until his arm grew weary, though his hand clung to the sword. The LORD brought about a great victory that day. Then the people came back to him—but only to strip the dead.

11  Next to him was Shammah son of Agee, the Hararite. The Philistines gathered together at Lehi, where there was a plot of ground full of lentils; and the army fled from the Philistines. [12]But he took his stand in the middle of the plot, defended it, and killed the Philistines; and the LORD brought about a great victory.

13  Towards the beginning of harvest three of the thirty[e] chiefs went down to join David at the cave of Adullam, while a band of Philistines was encamped in the valley of Rephaim. [14]David was then in the stronghold; and the garrison of the Philistines was then at Bethlehem. [15]David said longingly, "O that someone would give me water to drink from the well of Bethlehem that is by the gate!" [16]Then the three warriors broke through the camp of the Philistines, drew water from the well of Bethlehem that was by the gate, and brought it to David. But he would not drink of it; he poured it out to the LORD, [17]for he said, "The LORD forbid that I should do this. Can I drink the blood of the men who went at the risk of their lives?" Therefore he would not drink it. The three warriors did these things.

18  Now Abishai son of Zeruiah, the brother of Joab, was chief of the Thirty.[f] With his spear he fought against three hundred men and killed them, and won a name beside the Three. [19]He was the most renowned of the Thirty,[g] and became their commander; but he did not attain to the Three.

20  Benaiah son of Jehoiada was a valiant warrior[h] from Kabzeel, a doer of great deeds; he struck down two sons of Ariel[i] of Moab. He also went

aHeb *But worthlessness*   bHeb *in sitting*   cGk Vg Compare 1 Chr 11.11: Meaning of Heb uncertain
d1 Chr 11.11: Meaning of Heb uncertain   eHeb adds *head*   fTwo Heb Mss Syr: MT *Three*
gSyr Compare 1 Chr 11.25: Heb *Was he the most renowned of the Three?*   hAnother reading is *the son of Ish-hai*   iGk: Heb lacks *sons of*

down and killed a lion in a pit on a day when snow had fallen. ²¹And he killed an Egyptian, a handsome man. The Egyptian had a spear in his hand; but Benaiah went against him with a staff, snatched the spear out of the Egyptian's hand, and killed him with his own spear. ²²Such were the things Benaiah son of Jehoiada did, and won a name beside the three warriors. ²³He was renowned among the Thirty, but he did not attain to the Three. And David put him in charge of his bodyguard.

## ACTS 2.1–47

**W**HEN the day of Pentecost had come, they [the believers] were all together in one place. ²And suddenly from heaven there came a sound like the rush of a violent wind, and it filled the entire house where they were sitting. ³Divided tongues, as of fire, appeared among them, and a tongue rested on each of them. ⁴All of them were filled with the Holy Spirit and began to speak in other languages, as the Spirit gave them ability.

5 Now there were devout Jews from every nation under heaven living in Jerusalem. ⁶And at this sound the crowd gathered and was bewildered, because each one heard them speaking in the native language of each. ⁷Amazed and astonished, they asked, "Are not all these who are speaking Galileans? ⁸And how is it that we hear, each of us, in our own native language? ⁹Parthians, Medes, Elamites, and residents of Mesopotamia, Judea and Cappadocia, Pontus and Asia, ¹⁰Phrygia and Pamphylia, Egypt and the parts of Libya belonging to Cyrene, and visitors from Rome, both Jews and proselytes, ¹¹Cretans and Arabs—in our own languages we hear them speaking about God's deeds of power." ¹²All were amazed and perplexed, saying to one another, "What does this mean?" ¹³But others sneered and said, "They are filled with new wine."

14 But Peter, standing with the eleven, raised his voice and addressed them, "Men of Judea and all who live in Jerusalem, let this be known to you, and listen to what I say. ¹⁵Indeed, these are not drunk, as you suppose, for it is only nine o'clock in the morning. ¹⁶No, this is what was spoken through the prophet Joel:

17   'In the last days it will be, God
      declares,
  that I will pour out my Spirit
      upon all flesh,
  and your sons and your
      daughters shall prophesy,
  and your young men shall
      see visions,
  and your old men shall
      dream dreams.
18   Even upon my slaves, both men
      and women,
  in those days I will pour out
      my Spirit;
  and they shall prophesy.
19   And I will show portents in the
      heaven above
  and signs on the earth below,
      blood, and fire, and
      smoky mist.
20   The sun shall be turned to
      darkness
  and the moon to blood,
  before the coming of the
      Lord's great and glorious
      day.
21   Then everyone who calls on the
      name of the Lord shall
      be saved.'

22 "You that are Israelites, ᵃ listen to what I have to say: Jesus of Nazareth, ᵇ a man attested to you by God with deeds of power, wonders, and signs that God did through him among you, as you yourselves know— ²³this man, handed over to you according to

ᵃGk *Men, Israelites*  ᵇGk *the Nazorean*

the definite plan and foreknowledge of God, you crucified and killed by the hands of those outside the law. 24But God raised him up, having freed him from death,a because it was impossible for him to be held in its power. 25For David says concerning him,

'I saw the Lord always before
        me,
    for he is at my right hand so
        that I will not be shaken;
26  therefore my heart was glad,
        and my tongue rejoiced;
    moreover my flesh will live
        in hope.
27  For you will not abandon my
        soul to Hades,
    or let your Holy One
        experience corruption.
28  You have made known to me
        the ways of life;
    you will make me full of
        gladness with your
        presence.'

29 "Fellow Israelites,b I may say to you confidently of our ancestor David that he both died and was buried, and his tomb is with us to this day. 30Since he was a prophet, he knew that God had sworn with an oath to him that he would put one of his descendants on his throne. 31Foreseeing this, Davidc spoke of the resurrection of the Messiah,d saying,

'He was not abandoned to
        Hades,
    nor did his flesh experience
        corruption.'

32This Jesus God raised up, and of that all of us are witnesses. 33Being therefore exalted ate the right hand of God, and having received from the Father the promise of the Holy Spirit, he has poured out this that you both see and hear. 34For David did not ascend into the heavens, but he himself says,

'The Lord said to my Lord,
    "Sit at my right hand,
35      until I make your enemies
            your footstool." '

36Therefore let the entire house of Israel know with certainty that God has made him both Lord and Messiah,f this Jesus whom you crucified."

37 Now when they heard this, they were cut to the heart and said to Peter and to the other apostles, "Brothers,b what should we do?" 38Peter said to them, "Repent, and be baptized every one of you in the name of Jesus Christ so that your sins may be forgiven; and you will receive the gift of the Holy Spirit. 39For the promise is for you, for your children, and for all who are far away, everyone whom the Lord our God calls to him." 40And he testified with many other arguments and exhorted them, saying, "Save yourselves from this corrupt generation." 41So those who welcomed his message were baptized, and that day about three thousand persons were added. 42They devoted themselves to the apostles' teaching and fellowship, to the breaking of bread and the prayers.

43 Awe came upon everyone, because many wonders and signs were being done by the apostles. 44All who believed were together and had all things in common; 45they would sell their possessions and goods and distribute the proceedsg to all, as any had need. 46Day by day, as they spent much time together in the temple, they broke bread at homeh and ate their food with glad and generousi hearts, 47praising God and having the goodwill of all the people. And day by day the Lord added to their number those who were being saved.

aGk *the pains of death*   bGk *Men, brothers*   cGk *he*   dOr *the Christ*   eOr *by*   fOr *Christ*   gGk *them*   hOr *from house to house*   iOr *sincere*

## PSALM 122.1–9

*A Song of Ascents. Of David.*

I WAS glad when they said to me,
  "Let us go to the house of
    the LORD!"
2  Our feet are standing
    within your gates,
      O Jerusalem.

3  Jerusalem—built as a city
    that is bound firmly together.
4  To it the tribes go up,
    the tribes of the LORD,
  as was decreed for Israel,
    to give thanks to the name of
      the LORD.
5  For there the thrones for
      judgment were set up,
    the thrones of the house of
      David.

6  Pray for the peace of Jerusalem:
  "May they prosper who love
      you.
7  Peace be within your walls,
    and security within your
      towers."
8  For the sake of my relatives and
      friends
    I will say, "Peace be within
      you."
9  For the sake of the house of the
      LORD our God,
    I will seek your good.

## PROVERBS 16.19–20

I T is better to be of a lowly spirit
      among the poor
    than to divide the spoil with
      the proud.
20  Those who are attentive to a
      matter will prosper,
    and happy are those who
      trust in the LORD.

# JUNE 5

## 2 SAMUEL 23.24—24.25

A MONG the Thirty were Asahel brother of Joab; Elhanan son of Dodo of Bethlehem; 25Shammah of Harod; Elika of Harod; 26Helez the Paltite; Ira son of Ikkesh of Tekoa; 27Abiezer of Anathoth; Mebunnai the Hushathite; 28Zalmon the Ahohite; Maharai of Netophah; 29Heleb son of Baanah of Netophah; Ittai son of Ribai of Gibeah of the Benjaminites; 30Benaiah of Pirathon; Hiddai of the torrents of Gaash; 31Abi-albon the Arbathite; Azmaveth of Bahurim; 32Eliahba of Shaalbon; the sons of Jashen: Jonathan 33son ofa Shammah the Hararite; Ahiam son of Sharar the Hararite; 34Eliphelet son of Ahasbai of Maacah; Eliam son of Ahithophel the Gilonite; 35Hezrob of Carmel; Paarai the Arbite; 36Igal son of Nathan of Zobah; Bani the Gadite; 37Zelek the Ammonite; Naharai of Beeroth, the armor-bearer of Joab son of Zeruiah; 38Ira the Ithrite; Gareb the Ithrite; 39Uriah the Hittite—thirty-seven in all.

24.1 AGAIN the anger of the LORD was kindled against Israel, and he incited David against them, saying, "Go, count the people of Israel and Judah." 2So the king said to Joab and the commanders

aGk: Heb lacks *son of*   bAnother reading is *Hezrai*

of the army,[a] who were with him, "Go through all the tribes of Israel, from Dan to Beer-sheba, and take a census of the people, so that I may know how many there are." [3]But Joab said to the king, "May the LORD your God increase the number of the people a hundredfold, while the eyes of my lord the king can still see it! But why does my lord the king want to do this?" [4]But the king's word prevailed against Joab and the commanders of the army. So Joab and the commanders of the army went out from the presence of the king to take a census of the people of Israel. [5]They crossed the Jordan, and began from[b] Aroer and from the city that is in the middle of the valley, toward Gad and on to Jazer. [6]Then they came to Gilead, and to Kadesh in the land of the Hittites;[c] and they came to Dan, and from Dan[d] they went around to Sidon, [7]and came to the fortress of Tyre and to all the cities of the Hivites and Canaanites; and they went out to the Negeb of Judah at Beer-sheba. [8]So when they had gone through all the land, they came back to Jerusalem at the end of nine months and twenty days. [9]Joab reported to the king the number of those who had been recorded: in Israel there were eight hundred thousand soldiers able to draw the sword, and those of Judah were five hundred thousand.

10 But afterward, David was stricken to the heart because he had numbered the people. David said to the LORD, "I have sinned greatly in what I have done. But now, O LORD, I pray you, take away the guilt of your servant; for I have done very foolishly." [11]When David rose in the morning, the word of the LORD came to the prophet Gad, David's seer, saying, [12]"Go and say to David: Thus says the LORD: Three things I offer[e] you; choose one

of them, and I will do it to you." [13]So Gad came to David and told him; he asked him, "Shall three[f] years of famine come to you on your land? Or will you flee three months before your foes while they pursue you? Or shall there be three days' pestilence in your land? Now consider, and decide what answer I shall return to the one who sent me." [14]Then David said to Gad, "I am in great distress; let us fall into the hand of the LORD, for his mercy is great; but let me not fall into human hands."

15 So the LORD sent a pestilence on Israel from that morning until the appointed time; and seventy thousand of the people died, from Dan to Beer-sheba. [16]But when the angel stretched out his hand toward Jerusalem to destroy it, the LORD relented concerning the evil, and said to the angel who was bringing destruction among the people, "It is enough; now stay your hand." The angel of the LORD was then by the threshing floor of Araunah the Jebusite. [17]When David saw the angel who was destroying the people, he said to the LORD, "I alone have sinned, and I alone have done wickedly; but these sheep, what have they done? Let your hand, I pray, be against me and against my father's house."

18 That day Gad came to David and said to him, "Go up and erect an altar to the LORD on the threshing floor of Araunah the Jebusite." [19]Following Gad's instructions, David went up, as the LORD had commanded. [20]When Araunah looked down, he saw the king and his servants coming toward him; and Araunah went out and prostrated himself before the king with his face to the ground. [21]Araunah said, "Why has my lord the king come to his servant?" David said, "To buy the threshing floor from you in order to build an altar to the LORD, so that the plague may be

a1 Chr 21.2 Gk: Heb *to Joab the commander of the army*   bGk Mss: Heb *encamped in Aroer south of* cGk: Heb *to the land of Tahtim-hodshi*  dCn Compare Gk: Heb *they came to Dan-jaan and*   eOr *hold over*  f1 Chr 21.12 Gk: Heb *seven*

averted from the people." ²²Then Araunah said to David, "Let my lord the king take and offer up what seems good to him; here are the oxen for the burnt offering, and the threshing sledges and the yokes of the oxen for the wood. ²³All this, O king, Araunah gives to the king." And Araunah said to the king, "May the LORD your God respond favorably to you."

24 But the king said to Araunah, "No, but I will buy them from you for a price; I will not offer burnt offerings to the LORD my God that cost me nothing." So David bought the threshing floor and the oxen for fifty shekels of silver. ²⁵David built there an altar to the LORD, and offered burnt offerings and offerings of well-being. So the LORD answered his supplication for the land, and the plague was averted from Israel.

## ACTS 3.1–26

ONE day Peter and John were going up to the temple at the hour of prayer, at three o'clock in the afternoon. ²And a man lame from birth was being carried in. People would lay him daily at the gate of the temple called the Beautiful Gate so that he could ask for alms from those entering the temple. ³When he saw Peter and John about to go into the temple, he asked them for alms. ⁴Peter looked intently at him, as did John, and said, "Look at us." ⁵And he fixed his attention on them, expecting to receive something from them. ⁶But Peter said, "I have no silver or gold, but what I have I give you; in the name of Jesus Christ of Nazareth,ᵃ stand up and walk." ⁷And he took him by the right hand and raised him up; and immediately his feet and ankles were made strong. ⁸Jumping up, he stood and began to walk, and he entered the temple with them, walking and leaping and praising God. ⁹All the people saw him walking and praising God, ¹⁰and they recognized him as the one who used to sit and ask for alms at the Beautiful Gate of the temple; and they were filled with wonder and amazement at what had happened to him.

11 While he clung to Peter and John, all the people ran together to them in the portico called Solomon's Portico, utterly astonished. ¹²When Peter saw it, he addressed the people, "You Israelites,ᵇ why do you wonder at this, or why do you stare at us, as though by our own power or piety we had made him walk? ¹³The God of Abraham, the God of Isaac, and the God of Jacob, the God of our ancestors has glorified his servantᶜ Jesus, whom you handed over and rejected in the presence of Pilate, though he had decided to release him. ¹⁴But you rejected the Holy and Righteous One and asked to have a murderer given to you, ¹⁵and you killed the Author of life, whom God raised from the dead. To this we are witnesses. ¹⁶And by faith in his name, his name itself has made this man strong, whom you see and know; and the faith that is through Jesusᵈ has given him this perfect health in the presence of all of you.

17 "And now, friends,ᵉ I know that you acted in ignorance, as did also your rulers. ¹⁸In this way God fulfilled what he had foretold through all the prophets, that his Messiahᶠ would suffer. ¹⁹Repent therefore, and turn to God so that your sins may be wiped out, ²⁰so that times of refreshing may come from the presence of the Lord, and that he may send the Messiahᵍ appointed for you, that is, Jesus, ²¹who must remain in heaven until the time of universal restoration that God announced long ago through his holy prophets. ²²Moses said, 'The Lord your God will raise up for you from your

ᵃGk *the Nazorean*  ᵇGk *Men, Israelites*  ᶜOr *child* ᵈGk *him*  ᵉGk *brothers*  ᶠOr *his Christ*  ᵍOr *the Christ*

own people[a] a prophet like me. You must listen to whatever he tells you. 23And it will be that everyone who does not listen to that prophet will be utterly rooted out of the people.' 24And all the prophets, as many as have spoken, from Samuel and those after him, also predicted these days. 25You are the descendants of the prophets and of the covenant that God gave to your ancestors, saying to Abraham, 'And in your descendants all the families of the earth shall be blessed.' 26When God raised up his servant,[b] he sent him first to you, to bless you by turning each of you from your wicked ways."

## PSALM 123.1–4

*A Song of Ascents.*

To you I lift up my eyes,
O you who are enthroned in
the heavens!
2  As the eyes of servants
look to the hand of their
master,
as the eyes of a maid
to the hand of her mistress,

so our eyes look to the LORD
our God,
until he has mercy upon us.

3  Have mercy upon us, O LORD,
have mercy upon us,
for we have had more than
enough of contempt.
4  Our soul has had more than its
fill
of the scorn of those who are
at ease,
of the contempt of the proud.

## PROVERBS 16.21–23

THE wise of heart is called
perceptive,
and pleasant speech
increases
persuasiveness.
22  Wisdom is a fountain of life to
one who has it,
but folly is the punishment of
fools.
23  The mind of the wise makes
their speech judicious,
and adds persuasiveness to
their lips.

# JUNE 6

## 1 KINGS 1.1–53

KING David was old and advanced in years; and although they covered him with clothes, he could not get warm. 2So his servants said to him, "Let a young virgin be sought for my lord the king, and let her wait on the king, and be his attendant; let her lie in your bosom, so that my lord the king may be warm." 3So they searched for a beautiful girl throughout all the territory of Israel, and found Abishag the Shunammite, and brought her to the king. 4The girl was very beautiful. She became the king's attendant and served him, but the king did not know her sexually.

5 Now Adonijah son of Haggith exalted himself, saying, "I will be king"; he prepared for himself chariots and

[a]Gk *brothers*  [b]Or *child*

horsemen, and fifty men to run before him. [6]His father had never at any time displeased him by asking, "Why have you done thus and so?" He was also a very handsome man, and he was born next after Absalom. [7]He conferred with Joab son of Zeruiah and with the priest Abiathar, and they supported Adonijah. [8]But the priest Zadok, and Benaiah son of Jehoiada, and the prophet Nathan, and Shimei, and Rei, and David's own warriors did not side with Adonijah.

9 Adonijah sacrificed sheep, oxen, and fatted cattle by the stone Zoheleth, which is beside En-rogel, and he invited all his brothers, the king's sons, and all the royal officials of Judah, [10]but he did not invite the prophet Nathan or Benaiah or the warriors or his brother Solomon.

11 Then Nathan said to Bathsheba, Solomon's mother, "Have you not heard that Adonijah son of Haggith has become king and our lord David does not know it? [12]Now therefore come, let me give you advice, so that you may save your own life and the life of your son Solomon. [13]Go in at once to King David, and say to him, 'Did you not, my lord the king, swear to your servant, saying: Your son Solomon shall succeed me as king, and he shall sit on my throne? Why then is Adonijah king?' [14]Then while you are still there speaking with the king, I will come in after you and confirm your words."

15 So Bathsheba went to the king in his room. The king was very old; Abishag the Shunammite was attending the king. [16]Bathsheba bowed and did obeisance to the king, and the king said, "What do you wish?" [17]She said to him, "My lord, you swore to your servant by the LORD your God, saying: Your son Solomon shall succeed me as king, and he shall sit on my throne. [18]But now suddenly Adonijah has become king, though you, my lord the king, do not know it. [19]He has sacrificed oxen, fatted cattle, and sheep in abundance, and has invited all the children of the king, the priest Abiathar, and Joab the commander of the army; but your servant Solomon he has not invited. [20]But you, my lord the king— the eyes of all Israel are on you to tell them who shall sit on the throne of my lord the king after him. [21]Otherwise it will come to pass, when my lord the king sleeps with his ancestors, that my son Solomon and I will be counted offenders."

22 While she was still speaking with the king, the prophet Nathan came in. [23]The king was told, "Here is the prophet Nathan." When he came in before the king, he did obeisance to the king, with his face to the ground. [24]Nathan said, "My lord the king, have you said, 'Adonijah shall succeed me as king, and he shall sit on my throne'? [25]For today he has gone down and has sacrificed oxen, fatted cattle, and sheep in abundance, and has invited all the king's children, Joab the commander[a] of the army, and the priest Abiathar, who are now eating and drinking before him, and saying, 'Long live King Adonijah!' [26]But he did not invite me, your servant, and the priest Zadok, and Benaiah son of Jehoiada, and your servant Solomon. [27]Has this thing been brought about by my lord the king and you have not let your servants know who should sit on the throne of my lord the king after him?"

28 King David answered, "Summon Bathsheba to me." So she came into the king's presence, and stood before the king. [29]The king swore, saying, "As the LORD lives, who has saved my life from every adversity, [30]as I swore to you by the LORD, the God of Israel, 'Your son Solomon shall succeed me as king, and he shall sit on my throne in my place,' so will I do this

---

[a] Gk: Heb *the commanders*

day." ³¹Then Bathsheba bowed with her face to the ground, and did obeisance to the king, and said, "May my lord King David live forever!"

32 King David said, "Summon to me the priest Zadok, the prophet Nathan, and Benaiah son of Jehoiada." When they came before the king, ³³the king said to them, "Take with you the servants of your lord, and have my son Solomon ride on my own mule, and bring him down to Gihon. ³⁴There let the priest Zadok and the prophet Nathan anoint him king over Israel; then blow the trumpet, and say, 'Long live King Solomon!' ³⁵You shall go up following him. Let him enter and sit on my throne; he shall be king in my place; for I have appointed him to be ruler over Israel and over Judah." ³⁶Benaiah son of Jehoiada answered the king, "Amen! May the LORD, the God of my lord the king, so ordain. ³⁷As the LORD has been with my lord the king, so may he be with Solomon, and make his throne greater than the throne of my lord King David."

38 So the priest Zadok, the prophet Nathan, and Benaiah son of Jehoiada, and the Cherethites and the Pelethites, went down and had Solomon ride on King David's mule, and led him to Gihon. ³⁹There the priest Zadok took the horn of oil from the tent and anointed Solomon. Then they blew the trumpet, and all the people said, "Long live King Solomon!" ⁴⁰And all the people went up following him, playing on pipes and rejoicing with great joy, so that the earth quaked at their noise.

41 Adonijah and all the guests who were with him heard it as they finished feasting. When Joab heard the sound of the trumpet, he said, "Why is the city in an uproar?" ⁴²While he was still speaking, Jonathan son of the priest Abiathar arrived. Adonijah said, "Come in, for you are a worthy man and surely you bring good news." ⁴³Jonathan answered Adonijah, "No, for our lord King David has made Solomon king; ⁴⁴the king has sent with him the priest Zadok, the prophet Nathan, and Benaiah son of Jehoiada, and the Cherethites and the Pelethites; and they had him ride on the king's mule; ⁴⁵the priest Zadok and the prophet Nathan have anointed him king at Gihon; and they have gone up from there rejoicing, so that the city is in an uproar. This is the noise that you heard. ⁴⁶Solomon now sits on the royal throne. ⁴⁷Moreover the king's servants came to congratulate our lord King David, saying, 'May God make the name of Solomon more famous than yours, and make his throne greater than your throne.' The king bowed in worship on the bed ⁴⁸and went on to pray thus, 'Blessed be the LORD, the God of Israel, who today has granted one of my offspringᵃ to sit on my throne and permitted me to witness it.' "

49 Then all the guests of Adonijah got up trembling and went their own ways. ⁵⁰Adonijah, fearing Solomon, got up and went to grasp the horns of the altar. ⁵¹Solomon was informed, "Adonijah is afraid of King Solomon; see, he has laid hold of the horns of the altar, saying, 'Let King Solomon swear to me first that he will not kill his servant with the sword.' " ⁵²So Solomon responded, "If he proves to be a worthy man, not one of his hairs shall fall to the ground; but if wickedness is found in him, he shall die." ⁵³Then King Solomon sent to have him brought down from the altar. He came to do obeisance to King Solomon; and Solomon said to him, "Go home."

aGk: Heb *one*

## ACTS 4.1–37

WHILE Peter and John[a] were speaking to the people, the priests, the captain of the temple, and the Sadducees came to them, [2]much annoyed because they were teaching the people and proclaiming that in Jesus there is the resurrection of the dead. [3]So they arrested them and put them in custody until the next day, for it was already evening. [4]But many of those who heard the word believed; and they numbered about five thousand.

5 The next day their rulers, elders, and scribes assembled in Jerusalem, [6]with Annas the high priest, Caiaphas, John,[b] and Alexander, and all who were of the high-priestly family. [7]When they had made the prisoners[c] stand in their midst, they inquired, "By what power or by what name did you do this?" [8]Then Peter, filled with the Holy Spirit, said to them, "Rulers of the people and elders, [9]if we are questioned today because of a good deed done to someone who was sick and are asked how this man has been healed, [10]let it be known to all of you, and to all the people of Israel, that this man is standing before you in good health by the name of Jesus Christ of Nazareth,[d] whom you crucified, whom God raised from the dead. [11]This Jesus[e] is

'the stone that was rejected by
    you, the builders;
it has become the
    cornerstone.'[f]

[12]There is salvation in no one else, for there is no other name under heaven given among mortals by which we must be saved."

13 Now when they saw the boldness of Peter and John and realized that they were uneducated and ordinary men, they were amazed and recognized them as companions of Jesus.

[14]When they saw the man who had been cured standing beside them, they had nothing to say in opposition. [15]So they ordered them to leave the council while they discussed the matter with one another. [16]They said, "What will we do with them? For it is obvious to all who live in Jerusalem that a notable sign has been done through them; we cannot deny it. [17]But to keep it from spreading further among the people, let us warn them to speak no more to anyone in this name." [18]So they called them and ordered them not to speak or teach at all in the name of Jesus. [19]But Peter and John answered them, "Whether it is right in God's sight to listen to you rather than to God, you must judge; [20]for we cannot keep from speaking about what we have seen and heard." [21]After threatening them again, they let them go, finding no way to punish them because of the people, for all of them praised God for what had happened. [22]For the man on whom this sign of healing had been performed was more than forty years old.

23 After they were released, they went to their friends[g] and reported what the chief priests and the elders had said to them. [24]When they heard it, they raised their voices together to God and said, "Sovereign Lord, who made the heaven and the earth, the sea, and everything in them, [25]it is you who said by the Holy Spirit through our ancestor David, your servant:[h]

'Why did the Gentiles rage,
    and the peoples imagine vain
        things?
26  The kings of the earth took
        their stand,
    and the rulers have gathered
        together
    against the Lord and
        against his Messiah.'[i]

[27]For in this city, in fact, both Herod

aGk *While they*  bOther ancient authorities read *Jonathan*  cGk *them*  dGk *the Nazorean*  eGk *This*
fOr *keystone*  gGk *their own*  hOr *child*  iOr *his Christ*

and Pontius Pilate, with the Gentiles and the peoples of Israel, gathered together against your holy servant[a] Jesus, whom you anointed, [28]to do whatever your hand and your plan had predestined to take place. [29]And now, Lord, look at their threats, and grant to your servants[b] to speak your word with all boldness, [30]while you stretch out your hand to heal, and signs and wonders are performed through the name of your holy servant[a] Jesus." [31]When they had prayed, the place in which they were gathered together was shaken; and they were all filled with the Holy Spirit and spoke the word of God with boldness.

32 Now the whole group of those who believed were of one heart and soul, and no one claimed private ownership of any possessions, but everything they owned was held in common. [33]With great power the apostles gave their testimony to the resurrection of the Lord Jesus, and great grace was upon them all. [34]There was not a needy person among them, for as many as owned lands or houses sold them and brought the proceeds of what was sold. [35]They laid it at the apostles' feet, and it was distributed to each as any had need. [36]There was a Levite, a native of Cyprus, Joseph, to whom the apostles gave the name Barnabas (which means "son of encouragement"). [37]He sold a field that belonged to him, then brought the money, and laid it at the apostles' feet.

## PSALM 124.1–8

*A Song of Ascents. Of David.*

**I**F it had not been the LORD who
was on our side
—let Israel now say—
2 if it had not been the LORD who
was on our side,
when our enemies attacked
us,
3 then they would have swallowed
us up alive,
when their anger was kindled
against us;
4 then the flood would have swept
us away,
the torrent would have gone
over us;
5 then over us would have gone
the raging waters.

6 Blessed be the LORD,
who has not given us
as prey to their teeth.
7 We have escaped like a bird
from the snare of the fowlers;
the snare is broken,
and we have escaped.

8 Our help is in the name of
the LORD,
who made heaven and earth.

## PROVERBS 16.24

**P**LEASANT words are like a
honeycomb,
sweetness to the soul and
health to the body.

a Or *child*   b Gk *slaves*

# JUNE 7

## 1 KINGS 2.1—3.2

WHEN David's time to die drew near, he charged his son Solomon, saying: [2]"I am about to go the way of all the earth. Be strong, be courageous, [3]and keep the charge of the LORD your God, walking in his ways and keeping his statutes, his commandments, his ordinances, and his testimonies, as it is written in the law of Moses, so that you may prosper in all that you do and wherever you turn. [4]Then the LORD will establish his word that he spoke concerning me: 'If your heirs take heed to their way, to walk before me in faithfulness with all their heart and with all their soul, there shall not fail you a successor on the throne of Israel.'

5 "Moreover you know also what Joab son of Zeruiah did to me, how he dealt with the two commanders of the armies of Israel, Abner son of Ner, and Amasa son of Jether, whom he murdered, retaliating in time of peace for blood that had been shed in war, and putting the blood of war on the belt around his waist, and on the sandals on his feet. [6]Act therefore according to your wisdom, but do not let his gray head go down to Sheol in peace. [7]Deal loyally, however, with the sons of Barzillai the Gileadite, and let them be among those who eat at your table; for with such loyalty they met me when I fled from your brother Absalom. [8]There is also with you Shimei son of Gera, the Benjaminite from Bahurim, who cursed me with a terrible curse on the day when I went to Mahanaim; but when he came down to meet me at the Jordan, I swore to him by the LORD, 'I will not put you to death with the sword.' [9]Therefore do not hold him guiltless, for you are a wise man; you will know what you ought to do to him, and you must bring his gray head down with blood to Sheol."

10 Then David slept with his ancestors, and was buried in the city of David. [11]The time that David reigned over Israel was forty years; he reigned seven years in Hebron, and thirty-three years in Jerusalem. [12]So Solomon sat on the throne of his father David; and his kingdom was firmly established.

13 Then Adonijah son of Haggith came to Bathsheba, Solomon's mother. She asked, "Do you come peaceably?" He said, "Peaceably." [14]Then he said, "May I have a word with you?" She said, "Go on." [15]He said, "You know that the kingdom was mine, and that all Israel expected me to reign; however, the kingdom has turned about and become my brother's, for it was his from the LORD. [16]And now I have one request to make of you; do not refuse me." She said to him, "Go on." [17]He said, "Please ask King Solomon—he will not refuse you—to give me Abishag the Shunammite as my wife." [18]Bathsheba said, "Very well; I will speak to the king on your behalf."

19 So Bathsheba went to King Solomon, to speak to him on behalf of Adonijah. The king rose to meet her, and bowed down to her; then he sat on his throne, and had a throne brought for the king's mother, and she sat on his right. [20]Then she said, "I have one small request to make of you; do not refuse me." And the king said to her, "Make your request, my mother; for I will not refuse you." [21]She said, "Let Abishag the Shunammite be given to your brother Adonijah as his wife." [22]King Solomon answered his mother, "And why do you ask Abishag the Shunammite for Adonijah? Ask for him the

kingdom as well! For he is my elder brother; ask not only for him but also for the priest Abiathar and for Joab son of Zeruiah!" 23 Then King Solomon swore by the LORD, "So may God do to me, and more also, for Adonijah has devised this scheme at the risk of his life! 24 Now therefore as the LORD lives, who has established me and placed me on the throne of my father David, and who has made me a house as he promised, today Adonijah shall be put to death." 25 So King Solomon sent Benaiah son of Jehoiada; he struck him down, and he died.

26 The king said to the priest Abiathar, "Go to Anathoth, to your estate; for you deserve death. But I will not at this time put you to death, because you carried the ark of the Lord GOD before my father David, and because you shared in all the hardships my father endured." 27 So Solomon banished Abiathar from being priest to the LORD, thus fulfilling the word of the LORD that he had spoken concerning the house of Eli in Shiloh.

28 When the news came to Joab—for Joab had supported Adonijah though he had not supported Absalom—Joab fled to the tent of the LORD and grasped the horns of the altar. 29 When it was told King Solomon, "Joab has fled to the tent of the LORD and now is beside the altar," Solomon sent Benaiah son of Jehoiada, saying, "Go, strike him down." 30 So Benaiah came to the tent of the LORD and said to him, "The king commands, 'Come out.'" But he said, "No, I will die here." Then Benaiah brought the king word again, saying, "Thus said Joab, and thus he answered me." 31 The king replied to him, "Do as he has said, strike him down and bury him; and thus take away from me and from my father's house the guilt for the blood that Joab shed without cause. 32 The LORD will bring back his bloody deeds on his own head, because, without the knowledge of my father David, he attacked and killed with the sword two men more righteous and better than himself, Abner son of Ner, commander of the army of Israel, and Amasa son of Jether, commander of the army of Judah. 33 So shall their blood come back on the head of Joab and on the head of his descendants forever; but to David, and to his descendants, and to his house, and to his throne, there shall be peace from the LORD forevermore." 34 Then Benaiah son of Jehoiada went up and struck him down and killed him; and he was buried at his own house near the wilderness. 35 The king put Benaiah son of Jehoiada over the army in his place, and the king put the priest Zadok in the place of Abiathar.

36 Then the king sent and summoned Shimei, and said to him, "Build yourself a house in Jerusalem, and live there, and do not go out from there to any place whatever. 37 For on the day you go out, and cross the Wadi Kidron, know for certain that you shall die; your blood shall be on your own head." 38 And Shimei said to the king, "The sentence is fair; as my lord the king has said, so will your servant do." So Shimei lived in Jerusalem many days.

39 But it happened at the end of three years that two of Shimei's slaves ran away to King Achish son of Maacah of Gath. When it was told Shimei, "Your slaves are in Gath," 40 Shimei arose and saddled a donkey, and went to Achish in Gath, to search for his slaves; Shimei went and brought his slaves from Gath. 41 When Solomon was told that Shimei had gone from Jerusalem to Gath and returned, 42 the king sent and summoned Shimei, and said to him, "Did I not make you swear by the LORD, and solemnly adjure you, saying, 'Know for certain that on the day you go out and go to any place whatever, you shall die'? And you said to me, 'The sentence is fair; I accept.' 43 Why then have you not kept your oath to the LORD and the commandment

with which I charged you?" [44] The king also said to Shimei, "You know in your own heart all the evil that you did to my father David; so the LORD will bring back your evil on your own head. [45] But King Solomon shall be blessed, and the throne of David shall be established before the LORD forever." [46] Then the king commanded Benaiah son of Jehoiada; and he went out and struck him down, and he died.

So the kingdom was established in the hand of Solomon.

[3.1] SOLOMON made a marriage alliance with Pharaoh king of Egypt; he took Pharaoh's daughter and brought her into the city of David, until he had finished building his own house and the house of the LORD and the wall around Jerusalem. [2] The people were sacrificing at the high places, however, because no house had yet been built for the name of the LORD.

# ACTS 5.1–42

BUT a man named Ananias, with the consent of his wife Sapphira, sold a piece of property; [2] with his wife's knowledge, he kept back some of the proceeds, and brought only a part and laid it at the apostles' feet. [3] "Ananias," Peter asked, "why has Satan filled your heart to lie to the Holy Spirit and to keep back part of the proceeds of the land? [4] While it remained unsold, did it not remain your own? And after it was sold, were not the proceeds at your disposal? How is it that you have contrived this deed in your heart? You did not lie to us[a] but to God!" [5] Now when Ananias heard these words, he fell down and died. And great fear seized all who heard of it. [6] The young men came and wrapped up his body,[b] then carried him out and buried him.

[7] After an interval of about three hours his wife came in, not knowing what had happened. [8] Peter said to her, "Tell me whether you and your husband sold the land for such and such a price." And she said, "Yes, that was the price." [9] Then Peter said to her, "How is it that you have agreed together to put the Spirit of the Lord to the test? Look, the feet of those who have buried your husband are at the door, and they will carry you out." [10] Immediately she fell down at his feet and died. When the young men came in they found her dead, so they carried her out and buried her beside her husband. [11] And great fear seized the whole church and all who heard of these things.

[12] Now many signs and wonders were done among the people through the apostles. And they were all together in Solomon's Portico. [13] None of the rest dared to join them, but the people held them in high esteem. [14] Yet more than ever believers were added to the Lord, great numbers of both men and women, [15] so that they even carried out the sick into the streets, and laid them on cots and mats, in order that Peter's shadow might fall on some of them as he came by. [16] A great number of people would also gather from the towns around Jerusalem, bringing the sick and those tormented by unclean spirits, and they were all cured.

[17] Then the high priest took action; he and all who were with him (that is, the sect of the Sadducees), being filled with jealousy, [18] arrested the apostles and put them in the public prison. [19] But during the night an angel of the Lord opened the prison doors, brought them out, and said, [20] "Go, stand in the temple and tell the people the whole message about this life." [21] When they heard this, they entered the temple at daybreak and went on with their teaching.

a Gk *to men*    b Meaning of Gk uncertain

When the high priest and those with him arrived, they called together the council and the whole body of the elders of Israel, and sent to the prison to have them brought. [22]But when the temple police went there, they did not find them in the prison; so they returned and reported, [23]"We found the prison securely locked and the guards standing at the doors, but when we opened them, we found no one inside." [24]Now when the captain of the temple and the chief priests heard these words, they were perplexed about them, wondering what might be going on. [25]Then someone arrived and announced, "Look, the men whom you put in prison are standing in the temple and teaching the people!" [26]Then the captain went with the temple police and brought them, but without violence, for they were afraid of being stoned by the people.

27 When they had brought them, they had them stand before the council. The high priest questioned them, [28]saying, "We gave you strict orders not to teach in this name,[a] yet here you have filled Jerusalem with your teaching and you are determined to bring this man's blood on us." [29]But Peter and the apostles answered, "We must obey God rather than any human authority.[b] [30]The God of our ancestors raised up Jesus, whom you had killed by hanging him on a tree. [31]God exalted him at his right hand as Leader and Savior that he might give repentance to Israel and forgiveness of sins. [32]And we are witnesses to these things, and so is the Holy Spirit whom God has given to those who obey him."

33 When they heard this, they were enraged and wanted to kill them. [34]But a Pharisee in the council named Gamaliel, a teacher of the law, respected by all the people, stood up and ordered the men to be put outside for a short time. [35]Then he said to them, "Fellow Israelites,[c] consider carefully what you propose to do to these men. [36]For some time ago Theudas rose up, claiming to be somebody, and a number of men, about four hundred, joined him; but he was killed, and all who followed him were dispersed and disappeared. [37]After him Judas the Galilean rose up at the time of the census and got people to follow him; he also perished, and all who followed him were scattered. [38]So in the present case, I tell you, keep away from these men and let them alone; because if this plan or this undertaking is of human origin, it will fail; [39]but if it is of God, you will not be able to overthrow them—in that case you may even be found fighting against God!"

They were convinced by him, [40]and when they had called in the apostles, they had them flogged. Then they ordered them not to speak in the name of Jesus, and let them go. [41]As they left the council, they rejoiced that they were considered worthy to suffer dishonor for the sake of the name. [42]And every day in the temple and at home[d] they did not cease to teach and proclaim Jesus as the Messiah.[e]

## PSALM 125.1–5

*A Song of Ascents.*

THOSE who trust in the LORD are
　　　like Mount Zion,
　　which cannot be moved, but
　　　abides forever.
2 　As the mountains surround
　　　Jerusalem,
　　　so the LORD surrounds his
　　　　people,
　　from this time on and
　　　forevermore.
3 　For the scepter of wickedness
　　　shall not rest

---

a Other ancient authorities read *Did we not give you strict orders not to teach in this name?*　b Gk *than men*　c Gk *Men, Israelites*　d Or *from house to house*　e Or *the Christ*

on the land allotted to the
righteous,
so that the righteous might not
stretch out
their hands to do wrong.
4 Do good, O LORD, to those who
are good,
and to those who are upright
in their hearts.
5 But those who turn aside to
their own crooked ways

the LORD will lead away with
evildoers.
Peace be upon Israel!

## PROVERBS 16.25

SOMETIMES there is a way that
seems to be right,
but in the end it is the way
to death.

# JUNE 8

## 1 KINGS 3.3—4.34

SOLOMON loved the LORD, walking
in the statutes of his father David; only, he sacrificed and offered incense at the high places. 4The
king went to Gibeon to sacrifice there,
for that was the principal high place;
Solomon used to offer a thousand burnt
offerings on that altar. 5At Gibeon the
LORD appeared to Solomon in a dream
by night; and God said, "Ask what I
should give you." 6And Solomon said,
"You have shown great and steadfast
love to your servant my father David,
because he walked before you in faithfulness, in righteousness, and in uprightness of heart toward you; and you
have kept for him this great and steadfast love, and have given him a son to
sit on his throne today. 7And now,
O LORD my God, you have made your
servant king in place of my father David, although I am only a little child; I do
not know how to go out or come in.
8And your servant is in the midst of the
people whom you have chosen, a great
people, so numerous they cannot be
numbered or counted. 9Give your servant therefore an understanding mind

to govern your people, able to discern
between good and evil; for who can
govern this your great people?"

10 It pleased the Lord that Solomon had asked this. 11God said to him,
"Because you have asked this, and
have not asked for yourself long life or
riches, or for the life of your enemies,
but have asked for yourself understanding to discern what is right, 12I
now do according to your word. Indeed
I give you a wise and discerning mind;
no one like you has been before you and
no one like you shall arise after you. 13I
give you also what you have not asked,
both riches and honor all your life; no
other king shall compare with you. 14If
you will walk in my ways, keeping my
statutes and my commandments, as
your father David walked, then I will
lengthen your life."

15 Then Solomon awoke; it had
been a dream. He came to Jerusalem
where he stood before the ark of the
covenant of the LORD. He offered up
burnt offerings and offerings of wellbeing, and provided a feast for all his
servants.

16 Later, two women who were prostitutes came to the king and stood before him. ¹⁷The one woman said, "Please, my lord, this woman and I live in the same house; and I gave birth while she was in the house. ¹⁸Then on the third day after I gave birth, this woman also gave birth. We were together; there was no one else with us in the house, only the two of us were in the house. ¹⁹Then this woman's son died in the night, because she lay on him. ²⁰She got up in the middle of the night and took my son from beside me while your servant slept. She laid him at her breast, and laid her dead son at my breast. ²¹When I rose in the morning to nurse my son, I saw that he was dead; but when I looked at him closely in the morning, clearly it was not the son I had borne." ²²But the other woman said, "No, the living son is mine, and the dead son is yours." The first said, "No, the dead son is yours, and the living son is mine." So they argued before the king.

23 Then the king said, "The one says, 'This is my son that is alive, and your son is dead'; while the other says, 'Not so! Your son is dead, and my son is the living one.'" ²⁴So the king said, "Bring me a sword," and they brought a sword before the king. ²⁵The king said, "Divide the living boy in two; then give half to the one, and half to the other." ²⁶But the woman whose son was alive said to the king—because compassion for her son burned within her—"Please, my lord, give her the living boy; certainly do not kill him!" The other said, "It shall be neither mine nor yours; divide it." ²⁷Then the king responded: "Give the first woman the living boy; do not kill him. She is his mother." ²⁸All Israel heard of the judgment that the king had rendered; and they stood in awe of the king, because they perceived that the wisdom of God was in him, to execute justice.

⁴·¹ KING Solomon was king over all Israel, ²and these were his high officials: Azariah son of Zadok was the priest; ³Elihoreph and Ahijah sons of Shisha were secretaries; Jehoshaphat son of Ahilud was recorder; ⁴Benaiah son of Jehoiada was in command of the army; Zadok and Abiathar were priests; ⁵Azariah son of Nathan was over the officials; Zabud son of Nathan was priest and king's friend; ⁶Ahishar was in charge of the palace; and Adoniram son of Abda was in charge of the forced labor.

7 Solomon had twelve officials over all Israel, who provided food for the king and his household; each one had to make provision for one month in the year. ⁸These were their names: Benhur, in the hill country of Ephraim; ⁹Ben-deker, in Makaz, Shaalbim, Bethshemesh, and Elon-beth-hanan; ¹⁰Benhesed, in Arubboth (to him belonged Socoh and all the land of Hepher); ¹¹Ben-abinadab, in all Naphath-dor (he had Taphath, Solomon's daughter, as his wife); ¹²Baana son of Ahilud, in Taanach, Megiddo, and all Beth-shean, which is beside Zarethan below Jezreel, and from Beth-shean to Abel-meholah, as far as the other side of Jokmeam; ¹³Ben-geber, in Ramoth-gilead (he had the villages of Jair son of Manasseh, which are in Gilead, and he had the region of Argob, which is in Bashan, sixty great cities with walls and bronze bars); ¹⁴Ahinadab son of Iddo, in Mahanaim; ¹⁵Ahimaaz, in Naphtali (he had taken Basemath, Solomon's daughter, as his wife); ¹⁶Baana son of Hushai, in Asher and Bealoth; ¹⁷Jehoshaphat son of Paruah, in Issachar; ¹⁸Shimei son of Ela, in Benjamin; ¹⁹Geber son of Uri, in the land of Gilead, the country of King Sihon of the Amorites and of King Og of Bashan. And there was one official in the land of Judah.

20 Judah and Israel were as numerous as the sand by the sea; they ate and

drank and were happy. 21aSolomon was sovereign over all the kingdoms from the Euphrates to the land of the Philistines, even to the border of Egypt; they brought tribute and served Solomon all the days of his life.

22 Solomon's provision for one day was thirty cors of choice flour, and sixty cors of meal, 23ten fat oxen, and twenty pasture-fed cattle, one hundred sheep, besides deer, gazelles, roebucks, and fatted fowl. 24For he had dominion over all the region west of the Euphrates from Tiphsah to Gaza, over all the kings west of the Euphrates; and he had peace on all sides. 25During Solomon's lifetime Judah and Israel lived in safety, from Dan even to Beer-sheba, all of them under their vines and fig trees. 26Solomon also had forty thousand stalls of horses for his chariots, and twelve thousand horsemen. 27Those officials supplied provisions for King Solomon and for all who came to King Solomon's table, each one in his month; they let nothing be lacking. 28They also brought to the required place barley and straw for the horses and swift steeds, each according to his charge.

29 God gave Solomon very great wisdom, discernment, and breadth of understanding as vast as the sand on the seashore, 30so that Solomon's wisdom surpassed the wisdom of all the people of the east, and all the wisdom of Egypt. 31He was wiser than anyone else, wiser than Ethan the Ezrahite, and Heman, Calcol, and Darda, children of Mahol; his fame spread throughout all the surrounding nations. 32He composed three thousand proverbs, and his songs numbered a thousand and five. 33He would speak of trees, from the cedar that is in the Lebanon to the hyssop that grows in the wall; he would speak of animals, and birds, and reptiles, and fish. 34People came from all the nations to hear the wisdom of Solomon; they came from all the kings of the earth who had heard of his wisdom.

## ACTS 6.1–15

Now during those days, when the disciples were increasing in number, the Hellenists complained against the Hebrews because their widows were being neglected in the daily distribution of food. 2And the twelve called together the whole community of the disciples and said, "It is not right that we should neglect the word of God in order to wait on tables. b 3Therefore, friends, c select from among yourselves seven men of good standing, full of the Spirit and of wisdom, whom we may appoint to this task, 4while we, for our part, will devote ourselves to prayer and to serving the word." 5What they said pleased the whole community, and they chose Stephen, a man full of faith and the Holy Spirit, together with Philip, Prochorus, Nicanor, Timon, Parmenas, and Nicolaus, a proselyte of Antioch. 6They had these men stand before the apostles, who prayed and laid their hands on them.

7 The word of God continued to spread; the number of the disciples increased greatly in Jerusalem, and a great many of the priests became obedient to the faith.

8 Stephen, full of grace and power, did great wonders and signs among the people. 9Then some of those who belonged to the synagogue of the Freedmen (as it was called), Cyrenians, Alexandrians, and others of those from Cilicia and Asia, stood up and argued with Stephen. 10But they could not withstand the wisdom and the Spiritd with which he spoke. 11Then they secretly instigated some men to say, "We have heard him speak blasphemous

aCh 5.1 in Heb   bOr *keep accounts*   cGk *brothers*   dOr *spirit* words against Moses and God." [12]They stirred up the people as well as the elders and the scribes; then they suddenly confronted him, seized him, and brought him before the council. [13]They set up false witnesses who said, "This man never stops saying things against this holy place and the law; [14]for we have heard him say that this Jesus of Nazareth[a] will destroy this place and will change the customs that Moses handed on to us." [15]And all who sat in the council looked intently at him, and they saw that his face was like the face of an angel.

## PSALM 126.1–6

*A Song of Ascents.*

WHEN the LORD restored the fortunes of Zion,[b]
  we were like those who
    dream.
2  Then our mouth was filled with
    laughter,
    and our tongue with shouts
     of joy;

  then it was said among the
    nations,
  "The LORD has done great
    things for them."
3  The LORD has done great things
    for us,
    and we rejoiced.

4  Restore our fortunes, O LORD,
    like the watercourses in the
     Negeb.
5  May those who sow in tears
    reap with shouts of joy.
6  Those who go out weeping,
    bearing the seed for sowing,
  shall come home with shouts of
    joy,
    carrying their sheaves.

## PROVERBS 16.26–27

THE appetite of workers works
  for them;
  their hunger urges them on.
27  Scoundrels concoct evil,
    and their speech is like a
    scorching fire.

# JUNE 9

## 1 KINGS 5[c].1—6.38

NOW King Hiram of Tyre sent his servants to Solomon, when he heard that they had anointed him king in place of his father; for Hiram had always been a friend to David. [2]Solomon sent word to Hiram, saying, [3]"You know that my father David could not build a house for the name of the LORD his God because of the warfare with which his enemies surrounded him, until the LORD put them under the soles of his feet.[d] [4]But now the LORD my God has given me rest on every side; there is neither adversary nor misfortune. [5]So I intend to build a house for the name of the LORD my God, as the LORD said to my father David, 'Your son, whom I will set on your throne in your place, shall build the house for my name.' [6]Therefore command that cedars from the Lebanon be cut for me. My servants will join your servants, and I will give you whatever wages you set for your servants; for you know that there is no one among us who knows how to cut timber like the Sidonians."

7 When Hiram heard the words of Solomon, he rejoiced greatly, and said, "Blessed be the LORD today, who has given to David a wise son to be over this great people." [8]Hiram sent word to Solomon, "I have heard the message that you have sent to me; I will fulfill all your needs in the matter of cedar and cypress timber. [9]My servants shall bring it down to the sea from the Lebanon; I will make it into rafts to go by sea to the place you indicate. I will have them broken up there for you to take away. And you shall meet my needs by providing food for my household." [10]So Hiram supplied Solomon's every need for timber of cedar and cypress. [11]Solomon in turn gave Hiram twenty thousand cors of wheat as food for his household, and twenty cors of fine oil. Solomon gave this to Hiram year by year. [12]So the LORD gave Solomon wisdom, as he promised him. There was peace between Hiram and Solomon; and the two of them made a treaty.

13 King Solomon conscripted forced labor out of all Israel; the levy numbered thirty thousand men. [14]He sent them to the Lebanon, ten thousand a month in shifts; they would be a month in the Lebanon and two months at home; Adoniram was in charge of the forced labor. [15]Solomon also had seventy thousand laborers and eighty thousand stonecutters in the hill country, [16]besides Solomon's three thousand three hundred supervisors who were over the work, having charge of the people who did the work. [17]At the king's command, they quarried out great, costly stones in order to lay the foundation of the house with dressed stones. [18]So Solomon's builders and Hiram's builders and the Gebalites did the stonecutting and prepared the timber and the stone to build the house.

[6.1] IN the four hundred eightieth year after the Israelites came out of the land of Egypt, in the fourth year of Solomon's reign over Israel, in the month of Ziv, which is the second month, he began to build the house of the LORD. [2]The house that King Solomon built for the LORD was sixty cubits long, twenty cubits wide, and thirty cubits high. [3]The vestibule in front of the nave of the house was twenty cubits wide, across the width of the house. Its depth was ten cubits in front of the house. [4]For the house he made windows with recessed frames. [a] [5]He also built a structure against the wall of the house, running around the walls of the house, both the nave and the inner sanctuary; and he made side chambers all around. [6]The lowest story[b] was five cubits wide, the middle one was six cubits wide, and the third was seven cubits wide; for around the outside of the house he made offsets on the wall in order that the supporting beams should not be inserted into the walls of the house.

7 The house was built with stone finished at the quarry, so that neither hammer nor ax nor any tool of iron was heard in the temple while it was being built.

8 The entrance for the middle story was on the south side of the house: one went up by winding stairs to the middle story, and from the middle story to the third. [9]So he built the house, and finished it; he roofed the house with beams and planks of cedar. [10]He built the structure against the whole house, each story[c] five cubits high, and it was joined to the house with timbers of cedar.

11 Now the word of the LORD came

---

[a]Gk: Meaning of Heb uncertain   [b]Gk: Heb *structure*   [c]Heb lacks *each story*

to Solomon, [12]"Concerning this house that you are building, if you will walk in my statutes, obey my ordinances, and keep all my commandments by walking in them, then I will establish my promise with you, which I made to your father David. [13]I will dwell among the children of Israel and will not forsake my people Israel."

14 So Solomon built the house, and finished it. [15]He lined the walls of the house on the inside with boards of cedar; from the floor of the house to the rafters of the ceiling, he covered them on the inside with wood; and he covered the floor of the house with boards of cypress. [16]He built twenty cubits of the rear of the house with boards of cedar from the floor to the rafters, and he built this within as an inner sanctuary, as the most holy place. [17]The house, that is, the nave in front of the inner sanctuary, was forty cubits long. [18]The cedar within the house had carvings of gourds and open flowers; all was cedar, no stone was seen. [19]The inner sanctuary he prepared in the innermost part of the house to set there the ark of the covenant of the LORD. [20]The interior of the inner sanctuary was twenty cubits long, twenty cubits wide, and twenty cubits high; he overlaid it with pure gold. He also overlaid the altar with cedar. [a] [21]Solomon overlaid the inside of the house with pure gold, then he drew chains of gold across, in front of the inner sanctuary, and overlaid it with gold. [22]Next he overlaid the whole house with gold, in order that the whole house might be perfect; even the whole altar that belonged to the inner sanctuary he overlaid with gold.

23 In the inner sanctuary he made two cherubim of olivewood, each ten cubits high. [24]Five cubits was the length of one wing of the cherub, and five cubits the length of the other wing of the cherub; it was ten cubits from the tip of one wing to the tip of the other. [25]The other cherub also measured ten cubits; both cherubim had the same measure and the same form. [26]The height of one cherub was ten cubits, and so was that of the other cherub. [27]He put the cherubim in the innermost part of the house; the wings of the cherubim were spread out so that a wing of one was touching the one wall, and a wing of the other cherub was touching the other wall; their other wings toward the center of the house were touching wing to wing. [28]He also overlaid the cherubim with gold.

29 He carved the walls of the house all around about with carved engravings of cherubim, palm trees, and open flowers, in the inner and outer rooms. [30]The floor of the house he overlaid with gold, in the inner and outer rooms.

31 For the entrance to the inner sanctuary he made doors of olivewood; the lintel and the doorposts were five-sided. [a] [32]He covered the two doors of olivewood with carvings of cherubim, palm trees, and open flowers; he overlaid them with gold, and spread gold on the cherubim and on the palm trees.

33 So also he made for the entrance to the nave doorposts of olivewood, four-sided each, [34]and two doors of cypress wood; the two leaves of the one door were folding, and the two leaves of the other door were folding. [35]He carved cherubim, palm trees, and open flowers, overlaying them with gold evenly applied upon the carved work. [36]He built the inner court with three courses of dressed stone to one course of cedar beams.

37 In the fourth year the foundation of the house of the LORD was laid, in the month of Ziv. [38]In the eleventh year, in the month of Bul, which is the eighth month, the house was finished in all its parts, and according to all its specifications. He was seven years in building it.

a Meaning of Heb uncertain

## ACTS 7.1–29

**T**HEN the high priest asked him, "Are these things so?" [2]And Stephen replied:

"Brothers[a] and fathers, listen to me. The God of glory appeared to our ancestor Abraham when he was in Mesopotamia, before he lived in Haran, [3]and said to him, 'Leave your country and your relatives and go to the land that I will show you.' [4]Then he left the country of the Chaldeans and settled in Haran. After his father died, God had him move from there to this country in which you are now living. [5]He did not give him any of it as a heritage, not even a foot's length, but promised to give it to him as his possession and to his descendants after him, even though he had no child. [6]And God spoke in these terms, that his descendants would be resident aliens in a country belonging to others, who would enslave them and mistreat them during four hundred years. [7]'But I will judge the nation that they serve,' said God, 'and after that they shall come out and worship me in this place.' [8]Then he gave him the covenant of circumcision. And so Abraham[b] became the father of Isaac and circumcised him on the eighth day; and Isaac became the father of Jacob, and Jacob of the twelve patriarchs.

9 "The patriarchs, jealous of Joseph, sold him into Egypt; but God was with him, [10]and rescued him from all his afflictions, and enabled him to win favor and to show wisdom when he stood before Pharaoh, king of Egypt, who appointed him ruler over Egypt and over all his household. [11]Now there came a famine throughout Egypt and Canaan, and great suffering, and our ancestors could find no food. [12]But when Jacob heard that there was grain in Egypt, he sent our ancestors there on their first visit. [13]On the second visit Joseph made himself known to his brothers, and Joseph's family became known to Pharaoh. [14]Then Joseph sent and invited his father Jacob and all his relatives to come to him, seventy-five in all; [15]so Jacob went down to Egypt. He himself died there as well as our ancestors, [16]and their bodies[c] were brought back to Shechem and laid in the tomb that Abraham had bought for a sum of silver from the sons of Hamor in Shechem.

17 "But as the time drew near for the fulfillment of the promise that God had made to Abraham, our people in Egypt increased and multiplied [18]until another king who had not known Joseph ruled over Egypt. [19]He dealt craftily with our race and forced our ancestors to abandon their infants so that they would die. [20]At this time Moses was born, and he was beautiful before God. For three months he was brought up in his father's house; [21]and when he was abandoned, Pharaoh's daughter adopted him and brought him up as her own son. [22]So Moses was instructed in all the wisdom of the Egyptians and was powerful in his words and deeds.

23 "When he was forty years old, it came into his heart to visit his relatives, the Israelites. [d] [24]When he saw one of them being wronged, he defended the oppressed man and avenged him by striking down the Egyptian. [25]He supposed that his kinsfolk would understand that God through him was rescuing them, but they did not understand. [26]The next day he came to some of them as they were quarreling and tried to reconcile them, saying, 'Men, you are brothers; why do you wrong each other?' [27]But the man who was wronging his neighbor pushed Moses[e] aside, saying, 'Who made you a ruler and a judge over us? [28]Do you want to kill me as you killed the Egyptian yesterday?' [29]When he heard this, Moses fled and became a resident alien in the

---

aGk *Men, brothers*  bGk *he*  cGk *they*  dGk *his brothers, the sons of Israel*  eGk *him*

land of Midian. There he became the father of two sons.

## PSALM 127.1–5

*A Song of Ascents. Of Solomon.*

Unless the Lord builds the
    house,
those who build it labor in
    vain.
Unless the Lord guards the city,
    the guard keeps watch in
    vain.
2 It is in vain that you rise up
    early
    and go late to rest,
eating the bread of anxious toil;
    for he gives sleep to his
    beloved. a

3 Sons are indeed a heritage from
    the Lord,
    the fruit of the womb a
    reward.

4 Like arrows in the hand of a
    warrior
    are the sons of one's youth.
5 Happy is the man who has
    his quiver full of them.
He shall not be put to shame
    when he speaks with his
    enemies in the gate.

## PROVERBS 16.28–30

A perverse person spreads
    strife,
and a whisperer separates
    close friends.
29 The violent entice their
    neighbors,
and lead them in a way that is
    not good.
30 One who winks the eyes plans b
    perverse things;
one who compresses the lips
    brings evil to pass.

# JUNE 10

## 1 KINGS 7.1–51

Solomon was building his own house thirteen years, and he finished his entire house.

2 He built the House of the Forest of the Lebanon one hundred cubits long, fifty cubits wide, and thirty cubits high, built on four rows of cedar pillars, with cedar beams on the pillars. 3 It was roofed with cedar on the forty-five rafters, fifteen in each row, which were on the pillars. 4 There were window frames in the three rows, facing each other in the three rows. 5 All the doorways and doorposts had four-sided frames, opposite, facing each other in the three rows.

6 He made the Hall of Pillars fifty cubits long and thirty cubits wide. There was a porch in front with pillars, and a canopy in front of them.

7 He made the Hall of the Throne where he was to pronounce judgment, the Hall of Justice, covered with cedar from floor to floor.

8 His own house where he would reside, in the other court back of the hall, was of the same construction. Solomon also made a house like this hall for

a Or *for he provides for his beloved during sleep*  b Gk Syr Vg Tg: Heb *to plan*

Pharaoh's daughter, whom he had taken in marriage.

9 All these were made of costly stones, cut according to measure, sawed with saws, back and front, from the foundation to the coping, and from outside to the great court. [10]The foundation was of costly stones, huge stones, stones of eight and ten cubits. [11]There were costly stones above, cut to measure, and cedarwood. [12]The great court had three courses of dressed stone to one layer of cedar beams all around; so had the inner court of the house of the Lord, and the vestibule of the house.

13 Now King Solomon invited and received Hiram from Tyre. [14]He was the son of a widow of the tribe of Naphtali, whose father, a man of Tyre, had been an artisan in bronze; he was full of skill, intelligence, and knowledge in working bronze. He came to King Solomon, and did all his work.

15 He cast two pillars of bronze. Eighteen cubits was the height of the one, and a cord of twelve cubits would encircle it; the second pillar was the same. [a] [16]He also made two capitals of molten bronze, to set on the tops of the pillars; the height of the one capital was five cubits, and the height of the other capital was five cubits. [17]There were nets of checker work with wreaths of chain work for the capitals on the tops of the pillars; seven[b] for the one capital, and seven[b] for the other capital. [18]He made the columns with two rows around each latticework to cover the capitals that were above the pomegranates; he did the same with the other capital. [19]Now the capitals that were on the tops of the pillars in the vestibule were of lily-work, four cubits high. [20]The capitals were on the two pillars and also above the rounded projection that was beside the latticework; there were two hundred pomegranates in rows all around; and so with the other capital. [21]He set up the pillars at the vestibule of the temple; he set up the pillar on the south and called it Jachin; and he set up the pillar on the north and called it Boaz. [22]On the tops of the pillars was lily-work. Thus the work of the pillars was finished.

23 Then he made the molten sea; it was round, ten cubits from brim to brim, and five cubits high. A line of thirty cubits would encircle it completely. [24]Under its brim were panels all around it, each of ten cubits, surrounding the sea; there were two rows of panels, cast when it was cast. [25]It stood on twelve oxen, three facing north, three facing west, three facing south, and three facing east; the sea was set on them. The hindquarters of each were toward the inside. [26]Its thickness was a handbreadth; its brim was made like the brim of a cup, like the flower of a lily; it held two thousand baths. [c]

27 He also made the ten stands of bronze; each stand was four cubits long, four cubits wide, and three cubits high. [28]This was the construction of the stands: they had borders; the borders were within the frames; [29]on the borders that were set in the frames were lions, oxen, and cherubim. On the frames, both above and below the lions and oxen, there were wreaths of beveled work. [30]Each stand had four bronze wheels and axles of bronze; at the four corners were supports for a basin. The supports were cast with wreaths at the side of each. [31]Its opening was within the crown whose height was one cubit; its opening was round, as a pedestal is made; it was a cubit and a half wide. At its opening there were carvings; its borders were four-sided, not round. [32]The four wheels were underneath the borders; the axles of the

aCn: Heb *and a cord of twelve cubits encircled the second pillar*; Compare Jer 52.21   bHeb: Gk *a net*
cA Heb measure of volume

wheels were in the stands; and the height of a wheel was a cubit and a half. [33]The wheels were made like a chariot wheel; their axles, their rims, their spokes, and their hubs were all cast. [34]There were four supports at the four corners of each stand; the supports were of one piece with the stands. [35]On the top of the stand there was a round band half a cubit high; on the top of the stand, its stays and its borders were of one piece with it. [36]On the surfaces of its stays and on its borders he carved cherubim, lions, and palm trees, where each had space, with wreaths all around. [37]In this way he made the ten stands; all of them were cast alike, with the same size and the same form.

38 He made ten basins of bronze; each basin held forty baths, [a] each basin measured four cubits; there was a basin for each of the ten stands. [39]He set five of the stands on the south side of the house, and five on the north side of the house; he set the sea on the southeast corner of the house.

40 Hiram also made the pots, the shovels, and the basins. So Hiram finished all the work that he did for King Solomon on the house of the Lord: [41]the two pillars, the two bowls of the capitals that were on the tops of the pillars, the two latticeworks to cover the two bowls of the capitals that were on the tops of the pillars; [42]the four hundred pomegranates for the two latticeworks, two rows of pomegranates for each latticework, to cover the two bowls of the capitals that were on the pillars; [43]the ten stands, the ten basins on the stands; [44]the one sea, and the twelve oxen underneath the sea.

45 The pots, the shovels, and the basins, all these vessels that Hiram made for King Solomon for the house of the Lord were of burnished bronze. [46]In the plain of the Jordan the king cast them, in the clay ground between Suc-coth and Zarethan. [47]Solomon left all the vessels unweighed, because there were so many of them; the weight of the bronze was not determined.

48 So Solomon made all the vessels that were in the house of the Lord: the golden altar, the golden table for the bread of the Presence, [49]the lamp-stands of pure gold, five on the south side and five on the north, in front of the inner sanctuary; the flowers, the lamps, and the tongs, of gold; [50]the cups, snuffers, basins, dishes for incense, and firepans, of pure gold; the sockets for the doors of the innermost part of the house, the most holy place, and for the doors of the nave of the temple, of gold.

51 Thus all the work that King Solomon did on the house of the Lord was finished. Solomon brought in the things that his father David had dedicated, the silver, the gold, and the vessels, and stored them in the treasuries of the house of the Lord.

## ACTS 7.30–50

"Now when forty years had passed, an angel appeared to him in the wilderness of Mount Sinai, in the flame of a burning bush. [31]When Moses saw it, he was amazed at the sight; and as he approached to look, there came the voice of the Lord: [32]'I am the God of your ancestors, the God of Abraham, Isaac, and Jacob.' Moses began to tremble and did not dare to look. [33]Then the Lord said to him, 'Take off the sandals from your feet, for the place where you are standing is holy ground. [34]I have surely seen the mistreatment of my people who are in Egypt and have heard their groaning, and I have come down to rescue them. Come now, I will send you to Egypt.'

35 "It was this Moses whom they rejected when they said, 'Who made

you a ruler and a judge?' and whom God now sent as both ruler and liberator through the angel who appeared to him in the bush. ³⁶He led them out, having performed wonders and signs in Egypt, at the Red Sea, and in the wilderness for forty years. ³⁷This is the Moses who said to the Israelites, 'God will raise up a prophet for you from your own peopleᵃ as he raised me up.' ³⁸He is the one who was in the congregation in the wilderness with the angel who spoke to him at Mount Sinai, and with our ancestors; and he received living oracles to give to us. ³⁹Our ancestors were unwilling to obey him; instead, they pushed him aside, and in their hearts they turned back to Egypt, ⁴⁰saying to Aaron, 'Make gods for us who will lead the way for us; as for this Moses who led us out from the land of Egypt, we do not know what has happened to him.' ⁴¹At that time they made a calf, offered a sacrifice to the idol, and reveled in the works of their hands. ⁴²But God turned away from them and handed them over to worship the host of heaven, as it is written in the book of the prophets:

'Did you offer to me slain
    victims and sacrifices
forty years in the wilderness,
    O house of Israel?
43  No; you took along the tent
    of Moloch,
and the star of your god
    Rephan,
the images that you made
    to worship;
so I will remove you beyond
    Babylon.'

44 "Our ancestors had the tent of testimony in the wilderness, as Godᵇ directed when he spoke to Moses, ordering him to make it according to the pattern he had seen. ⁴⁵Our ancestors in turn brought it in with Joshua when they dispossessed the nations that God drove out before our ancestors. And it was there until the time of David, ⁴⁶who found favor with God and asked that he might find a dwelling place for the house of Jacob. ᶜ ⁴⁷But it was Solomon who built a house for him. ⁴⁸Yet the Most High does not dwell in houses made with human hands;ᵈ as the prophet says,

49  'Heaven is my throne,
    and the earth is my footstool.
What kind of house will you
    build for me, says the
    Lord,
or what is the place of my
    rest?
50  Did not my hand make all these
    things?'

## PSALM 128.1–6

*A Song of Ascents.*

**H**APPY is everyone who fears
    the LORD,
who walks in his ways.
2  You shall eat the fruit of the
    labor of your hands;
you shall be happy, and it
    shall go well with you.

3  Your wife will be like a fruitful
    vine
    within your house;
your children will be like olive
    shoots
    around your table.
4  Thus shall the man be blessed
    who fears the LORD.

5  The LORD bless you from Zion.
    May you see the prosperity
    of Jerusalem
    all the days of your life.
6  May you see your children's
    children.
    Peace be upon Israel!

ᵃGk *your brothers*  ᵇGk *he*  ᶜOther ancient authorities read *for the God of Jacob*  ᵈGk *with hands*

## PROVERBS 16.31–33

Gray hair is a crown of glory;
it is gained in a righteous
life.
32  One who is slow to anger is
better than the mighty,
and one whose temper is
controlled than one who
captures a city.
33  The lot is cast into the lap,
but the decision is the Lord's
alone.

# JUNE 11

## 1 KINGS 8.1–66

Then Solomon assembled the elders of Israel and all the heads of the tribes, the leaders of the ancestral houses of the Israelites, before King Solomon in Jerusalem, to bring up the ark of the covenant of the Lord out of the city of David, which is Zion. 2All the people of Israel assembled to King Solomon at the festival in the month Ethanim, which is the seventh month. 3And all the elders of Israel came, and the priests carried the ark. 4So they brought up the ark of the Lord, the tent of meeting, and all the holy vessels that were in the tent; the priests and the Levites brought them up. 5King Solomon and all the congregation of Israel, who had assembled before him, were with him before the ark, sacrificing so many sheep and oxen that they could not be counted or numbered. 6Then the priests brought the ark of the covenant of the Lord to its place, in the inner sanctuary of the house, in the most holy place, underneath the wings of the cherubim. 7For the cherubim spread out their wings over the place of the ark, so that the cherubim made a covering above the ark and its poles. 8The poles were so long that the ends of the poles were seen from the holy place in front of the inner sanctuary; but they could not be seen from outside; they are there to this day. 9There was nothing in the ark except the two tablets of stone that Moses had placed there at Horeb, where the Lord made a covenant with the Israelites, when they came out of the land of Egypt. 10And when the priests came out of the holy place, a cloud filled the house of the Lord, 11so that the priests could not stand to minister because of the cloud; for the glory of the Lord filled the house of the Lord.
12  Then Solomon said,
"The Lord has said that he
would dwell in thick
darkness.
13  I have built you an exalted
house,
a place for you to dwell in
forever."
14  Then the king turned around and blessed all the assembly of Israel, while all the assembly of Israel stood. 15He said, "Blessed be the Lord, the God of Israel, who with his hand has fulfilled what he promised with his mouth to my father David, saying, 16'Since the day that I brought my people Israel out of Egypt, I have not chosen a city from any of the tribes of Israel in which to build a house, that my name might be there; but I chose David

to be over my people Israel.' [17]My father David had it in mind to build a house for the name of the LORD, the God of Israel. [18]But the LORD said to my father David, 'You did well to consider building a house for my name; [19]nevertheless you shall not build the house, but your son who shall be born to you shall build the house for my name.' [20]Now the LORD has upheld the promise that he made; for I have risen in the place of my father David; I sit on the throne of Israel, as the LORD promised, and have built the house for the name of the LORD, the God of Israel. [21]There I have provided a place for the ark, in which is the covenant of the LORD that he made with our ancestors when he brought them out of the land of Egypt."

22 Then Solomon stood before the altar of the LORD in the presence of all the assembly of Israel, and spread out his hands to heaven. [23]He said, "O LORD, God of Israel, there is no God like you in heaven above or on earth beneath, keeping covenant and steadfast love for your servants who walk before you with all their heart, [24]the covenant that you kept for your servant my father David as you declared to him; you promised with your mouth and have this day fulfilled with your hand. [25]Therefore, O LORD, God of Israel, keep for your servant my father David that which you promised him, saying, 'There shall never fail you a successor before me to sit on the throne of Israel, if only your children look to their way, to walk before me as you have walked before me.' [26]Therefore, O God of Israel, let your word be confirmed, which you promised to your servant my father David.

27 "But will God indeed dwell on the earth? Even heaven and the highest heaven cannot contain you, much less this house that I have built! [28]Regard your servant's prayer and his plea, O LORD my God, heeding the cry and the prayer that your servant prays to you today; [29]that your eyes may be open night and day toward this house, the place of which you said, 'My name shall be there,' that you may heed the prayer that your servant prays toward this place. [30]Hear the plea of your servant and of your people Israel when they pray toward this place; O hear in heaven your dwelling place; heed and forgive.

31 "If someone sins against a neighbor and is given an oath to swear, and comes and swears before your altar in this house, [32]then hear in heaven, and act, and judge your servants, condemning the guilty by bringing their conduct on their own head, and vindicating the righteous by rewarding them according to their righteousness.

33 "When your people Israel, having sinned against you, are defeated before an enemy but turn again to you, confess your name, pray and plead with you in this house, [34]then hear in heaven, forgive the sin of your people Israel, and bring them again to the land that you gave to their ancestors.

35 "When heaven is shut up and there is no rain because they have sinned against you, and then they pray toward this place, confess your name, and turn from their sin, because you punish[a] them, [36]then hear in heaven, and forgive the sin of your servants, your people Israel, when you teach them the good way in which they should walk; and grant rain on your land, which you have given to your people as an inheritance.

37 "If there is famine in the land, if there is plague, blight, mildew, locust, or caterpillar; if their enemy besieges them in any[b] of their cities; whatever plague, whatever sickness there is; [38]whatever prayer, whatever plea there is from any individual or from all

a Or *when you answer*   b Gk Syr: Heb *in the land*

your people Israel, all knowing the afflictions of their own hearts so that they stretch out their hands toward this house; <sup>39</sup>then hear in heaven your dwelling place, forgive, act, and render to all whose hearts you know—according to all their ways, for only you know what is in every human heart—<sup>40</sup>so that they may fear you all the days that they live in the land that you gave to our ancestors.

41 "Likewise when a foreigner, who is not of your people Israel, comes from a distant land because of your name <sup>42</sup>—for they shall hear of your great name, your mighty hand, and your outstretched arm—when a foreigner comes and prays toward this house, <sup>43</sup>then hear in heaven your dwelling place, and do according to all that the foreigner calls to you, so that all the peoples of the earth may know your name and fear you, as do your people Israel, and so that they may know that your name has been invoked on this house that I have built.

44 "If your people go out to battle against their enemy, by whatever way you shall send them, and they pray to the Lord toward the city that you have chosen and the house that I have built for your name, <sup>45</sup>then hear in heaven their prayer and their plea, and maintain their cause.

46 "If they sin against you—for there is no one who does not sin—and you are angry with them and give them to an enemy, so that they are carried away captive to the land of the enemy, far off or near; <sup>47</sup>yet if they come to their senses in the land to which they have been taken captive, and repent, and plead with you in the land of their captors, saying, 'We have sinned, and have done wrong; we have acted wickedly'; <sup>48</sup>if they repent with all their heart and soul in the land of their enemies, who took them captive, and pray to you toward their land, which you gave to their ancestors, the city that

you have chosen, and the house that I have built for your name; <sup>49</sup>then hear in heaven your dwelling place their prayer and their plea, maintain their cause <sup>50</sup>and forgive your people who have sinned against you, and all their transgressions that they have committed against you; and grant them compassion in the sight of their captors, so that they may have compassion on them <sup>51</sup>(for they are your people and heritage, which you brought out of Egypt, from the midst of the iron-smelter). <sup>52</sup>Let your eyes be open to the plea of your servant, and to the plea of your people Israel, listening to them whenever they call to you. <sup>53</sup>For you have separated them from among all the peoples of the earth, to be your heritage, just as you promised through Moses, your servant, when you brought our ancestors out of Egypt, O Lord God."

54 Now when Solomon finished offering all this prayer and this plea to the Lord, he arose from facing the altar of the Lord, where he had knelt with hands outstretched toward heaven; <sup>55</sup>he stood and blessed all the assembly of Israel with a loud voice:

56 "Blessed be the Lord, who has given rest to his people Israel according to all that he promised; not one word has failed of all his good promise, which he spoke through his servant Moses. <sup>57</sup>The Lord our God be with us, as he was with our ancestors; may he not leave us or abandon us, <sup>58</sup>but incline our hearts to him, to walk in all his ways, and to keep his commandments, his statutes, and his ordinances, which he commanded our ancestors. <sup>59</sup>Let these words of mine, with which I pleaded before the Lord, be near to the Lord our God day and night, and may he maintain the cause of his servant and the cause of his people Israel, as each day requires; <sup>60</sup>so that all the peoples of the earth may know that the Lord is God; there is no other. <sup>61</sup>Therefore devote yourselves completely to the Lord

our God, walking in his statutes and keeping his commandments, as at this day."

62 Then the king, and all Israel with him, offered sacrifice before the Lord. 63Solomon offered as sacrifices of well-being to the Lord twenty-two thousand oxen and one hundred twenty thousand sheep. So the king and all the people of Israel dedicated the house of the Lord. 64The same day the king consecrated the middle of the court that was in front of the house of the Lord; for there he offered the burnt offerings and the grain offerings and the fat pieces of the sacrifices of well-being, because the bronze altar that was before the Lord was too small to receive the burnt offerings and the grain offerings and the fat pieces of the sacrifices of well-being.

65 So Solomon held the festival at that time, and all Israel with him—a great assembly, people from Lebo-hamath to the Wadi of Egypt—before the Lord our God, seven days. a 66On the eighth day he sent the people away; and they blessed the king, and went to their tents, joyful and in good spirits because of all the goodness that the Lord had shown to his servant David and to his people Israel.

## ACTS 7.51—8.13

"You stiff-necked people, uncircumcised in heart and ears, you are forever opposing the Holy Spirit, just as your ancestors used to do. 52Which of the prophets did your ancestors not persecute? They killed those who foretold the coming of the Righteous One, and now you have become his betrayers and murderers. 53You are the ones that received the law as ordained by angels, and yet you have not kept it."

54 When they heard these things, they became enraged and ground their teeth at Stephen. b 55But filled with the Holy Spirit, he gazed into heaven and saw the glory of God and Jesus standing at the right hand of God. 56"Look," he said, "I see the heavens opened and the Son of Man standing at the right hand of God!" 57But they covered their ears, and with a loud shout all rushed together against him. 58Then they dragged him out of the city and began to stone him; and the witnesses laid their coats at the feet of a young man named Saul. 59While they were stoning Stephen, he prayed, "Lord Jesus, receive my spirit." 60Then he knelt down and cried out in a loud voice, "Lord, do not hold this sin against them." When he had said this, he died. c 8.1And Saul approved of their killing him.

That day a severe persecution began against the church in Jerusalem, and all except the apostles were scattered throughout the countryside of Judea and Samaria. 2Devout men buried Stephen and made loud lamentation over him. 3But Saul was ravaging the church by entering house after house; dragging off both men and women, he committed them to prison.

4 Now those who were scattered went from place to place, proclaiming the word. 5Philip went down to the cityd of Samaria and proclaimed the Messiahe to them. 6The crowds with one accord listened eagerly to what was said by Philip, hearing and seeing the signs that he did, 7for unclean spirits, crying with loud shrieks, came out of many who were possessed; and many others who were paralyzed or lame were cured. 8So there was great joy in that city.

9 Now a certain man named Simon had previously practiced magic in the city and amazed the people of Samaria, saying that he was someone great. 10All of them, from the least to the greatest,

a Compare Gk: Heb *seven days and seven days, fourteen days*   b Gk *him*   c Gk *fell asleep*   d Other ancient authorities read *a city*   e Or *the Christ*

listened to him eagerly, saying, "This man is the power of God that is called Great." [11] And they listened eagerly to him because for a long time he had amazed them with his magic. [12] But when they believed Philip, who was proclaiming the good news about the kingdom of God and the name of Jesus Christ, they were baptized, both men and women. [13] Even Simon himself believed. After being baptized, he stayed constantly with Philip and was amazed when he saw the signs and great miracles that took place.

## PSALM 129.1–8

*A Song of Ascents.*

"OFTEN have they attacked me
from my youth"
—let Israel now say—
[2] "often have they attacked me
from my youth,
yet they have not prevailed
against me.
[3] The plowers plowed on my
back;
they made their furrows
long."

[4] The LORD is righteous;
he has cut the cords of the
wicked.
[5] May all who hate Zion
be put to shame and turned
backward.
[6] Let them be like the grass on
the housetops
that withers before it grows
up,
[7] with which reapers do not fill
their hands
or binders of sheaves their
arms,
[8] while those who pass by do not
say,
"The blessing of the LORD be
upon you!
We bless you in the name of
the LORD!"

## PROVERBS 17.1

BETTER is a dry morsel with quiet
than a house full of feasting
with strife.

# JUNE 12

## 1 KINGS 9.1—10.29

WHEN Solomon had finished building the house of the LORD and the king's house and all that Solomon desired to build, [2] the LORD appeared to Solomon a second time, as he had appeared to him at Gibeon. [3] The LORD said to him, "I have heard your prayer and your plea, which you made before me; I have consecrated this house that you have built, and put my name there forever; my eyes and my heart will be there for all time. [4] As for you, if you will walk before me, as David your father walked, with integrity of heart and uprightness, doing according to all that I have commanded you, and keeping my statutes and my ordinances, [5] then I will establish your royal throne over Israel forever, as I promised your father David, saying, 'There shall not fail you a successor on the throne of Israel.'

[6] "If you turn aside from following

me, you or your children, and do not keep my commandments and my statutes that I have set before you, but go and serve other gods and worship them, [7]then I will cut Israel off from the land that I have given them; and the house that I have consecrated for my name I will cast out of my sight; and Israel will become a proverb and a taunt among all peoples. [8]This house will become a heap of ruins;[a] everyone passing by it will be astonished, and will hiss; and they will say, 'Why has the LORD done such a thing to this land and to this house?' [9]Then they will say, 'Because they have forsaken the LORD their God, who brought their ancestors out of the land of Egypt, and embraced other gods, worshiping them and serving them; therefore the LORD has brought this disaster upon them.'"

10 At the end of twenty years, in which Solomon had built the two houses, the house of the LORD and the king's house, [11]King Hiram of Tyre having supplied Solomon with cedar and cypress timber and gold, as much as he desired, King Solomon gave to Hiram twenty cities in the land of Galilee. [12]But when Hiram came from Tyre to see the cities that Solomon had given him, they did not please him. [13]Therefore he said, "What kind of cities are these that you have given me, my brother?" So they are called the land of Cabul[b] to this day. [14]But Hiram had sent to the king one hundred twenty talents of gold.

15 This is the account of the forced labor that King Solomon conscripted to build the house of the LORD and his own house, the Millo and the wall of Jerusalem, Hazor, Megiddo, Gezer [16](Pharaoh king of Egypt had gone up and captured Gezer and burned it down, had killed the Canaanites who lived in the city, and had given it as dowry to his daughter, Solomon's wife; [17]so Solomon rebuilt Gezer), Lower Beth-horon, [18]Baalath, Tamar in the wilderness, within the land, [19]as well as all of Solomon's storage cities, the cities for his chariots, the cities for his cavalry, and whatever Solomon desired to build, in Jerusalem, in Lebanon, and in all the land of his dominion. [20]All the people who were left of the Amorites, the Hittites, the Perizzites, the Hivites, and the Jebusites, who were not of the people of Israel— [21]their descendants who were still left in the land, whom the Israelites were unable to destroy completely—these Solomon conscripted for slave labor, and so they are to this day. [22]But of the Israelites Solomon made no slaves; they were the soldiers, they were his officials, his commanders, his captains, and the commanders of his chariotry and cavalry.

23 These were the chief officers who were over Solomon's work: five hundred fifty, who had charge of the people who carried on the work.

24 But Pharaoh's daughter went up from the city of David to her own house that Solomon had built for her; then he built the Millo.

25 Three times a year Solomon used to offer up burnt offerings and sacrifices of well-being on the altar that he built for the LORD, offering incense[c] before the LORD. So he completed the house.

26 King Solomon built a fleet of ships at Ezion-geber, which is near Eloth on the shore of the Red Sea,[d] in the land of Edom. [27]Hiram sent his servants with the fleet, sailors who were familiar with the sea, together with the servants of Solomon. [28]They went to Ophir, and imported from there four hundred twenty talents of gold, which they delivered to King Solomon.

---

[a]Syr Old Latin: Heb *will become high*   [b]Perhaps meaning *a land good for nothing*   [c]Gk: Heb *offering incense with it that was*   [d]Or *Sea of Reeds*

**10.1** WHEN the queen of Sheba heard of the fame of Solomon, (fame due to[a] the name of the LORD), she came to test him with hard questions. 2She came to Jerusalem with a very great retinue, with camels bearing spices, and very much gold, and precious stones; and when she came to Solomon, she told him all that was on her mind. 3Solomon answered all her questions; there was nothing hidden from the king that he could not explain to her. 4When the queen of Sheba had observed all the wisdom of Solomon, the house that he had built, 5the food of his table, the seating of his officials, and the attendance of his servants, their clothing, his valets, and his burnt offerings that he offered at the house of the LORD, there was no more spirit in her.

6  So she said to the king, "The report was true that I heard in my own land of your accomplishments and of your wisdom, 7but I did not believe the reports until I came and my own eyes had seen it. Not even half had been told me; your wisdom and prosperity far surpass the report that I had heard. 8Happy are your wives![b] Happy are these your servants, who continually attend you and hear your wisdom! 9Blessed be the LORD your God, who has delighted in you and set you on the throne of Israel! Because the LORD loved Israel forever, he has made you king to execute justice and righteousness." 10Then she gave the king one hundred twenty talents of gold, a great quantity of spices, and precious stones; never again did spices come in such quantity as that which the queen of Sheba gave to King Solomon.

11  Moreover, the fleet of Hiram, which carried gold from Ophir, brought from Ophir a great quantity of almug wood and precious stones. 12From the almug wood the king made supports for the house of the LORD, and for the king's house, lyres also and harps for the singers; no such almug wood has come or been seen to this day.

13  Meanwhile King Solomon gave to the queen of Sheba every desire that she expressed, as well as what he gave her out of Solomon's royal bounty. Then she returned to her own land, with her servants.

14  The weight of gold that came to Solomon in one year was six hundred sixty-six talents of gold, 15besides that which came from the traders and from the business of the merchants, and from all the kings of Arabia and the governors of the land. 16King Solomon made two hundred large shields of beaten gold; six hundred shekels of gold went into each large shield. 17He made three hundred shields of beaten gold; three minas of gold went into each shield; and the king put them in the House of the Forest of Lebanon. 18The king also made a great ivory throne, and overlaid it with the finest gold. 19The throne had six steps. The top of the throne was rounded in the back, and on each side of the seat were arm rests and two lions standing beside the arm rests, 20while twelve lions were standing, one on each end of a step on the six steps. Nothing like it was ever made in any kingdom. 21All King Solomon's drinking vessels were of gold, and all the vessels of the House of the Forest of Lebanon were of pure gold; none were of silver—it was not considered as anything in the days of Solomon. 22For the king had a fleet of ships of Tarshish at sea with the fleet of Hiram. Once every three years the fleet of ships of Tarshish used to come bringing gold, silver, ivory, apes, and peacocks.[c]

23  Thus King Solomon excelled all the kings of the earth in riches and in

aMeaning of Heb uncertain   bGk Syr: Heb *men*   cOr *baboons*

wisdom. [24]The whole earth sought the presence of Solomon to hear his wisdom, which God had put into his mind. [25]Every one of them brought a present, objects of silver and gold, garments, weaponry, spices, horses, and mules, so much year by year.

26 Solomon gathered together chariots and horses; he had fourteen hundred chariots and twelve thousand horses, which he stationed in the chariot cities and with the king in Jerusalem. [27]The king made silver as common in Jerusalem as stones, and he made cedars as numerous as the sycamores of the Shephelah. [28]Solomon's import of horses was from Egypt and Kue, and the king's traders received them from Kue at a price. [29]A chariot could be imported from Egypt for six hundred shekels of silver, and a horse for one hundred fifty; so through the king's traders they were exported to all the kings of the Hittites and the kings of Aram.

## ACTS 8.14–40

Now when the apostles at Jerusalem heard that Samaria had accepted the word of God, they sent Peter and John to them. [15]The two went down and prayed for them that they might receive the Holy Spirit [16](for as yet the Spirit had not come[a] upon any of them; they had only been baptized in the name of the Lord Jesus). [17]Then Peter and John[b] laid their hands on them, and they received the Holy Spirit. [18]Now when Simon saw that the Spirit was given through the laying on of the apostles' hands, he offered them money, [19]saying, "Give me also this power so that anyone on whom I lay my hands may receive the Holy Spirit." [20]But Peter said to him, "May your silver perish with you, because you thought you could obtain God's gift with money! [21]You have no part or share in this, for your heart is not right before God. [22]Repent therefore of this wickedness of yours, and pray to the Lord that, if possible, the intent of your heart may be forgiven you. [23]For I see that you are in the gall of bitterness and the chains of wickedness." [24]Simon answered, "Pray for me to the Lord, that nothing of what you[c] have said may happen to me."

25 Now after Peter and John[d] had testified and spoken the word of the Lord, they returned to Jerusalem, proclaiming the good news to many villages of the Samaritans.

26 Then an angel of the Lord said to Philip, "Get up and go toward the south[e] to the road that goes down from Jerusalem to Gaza." (This is a wilderness road.) [27]So he got up and went. Now there was an Ethiopian eunuch, a court official of the Candace, queen of the Ethiopians, in charge of her entire treasury. He had come to Jerusalem to worship [28]and was returning home; seated in his chariot, he was reading the prophet Isaiah. [29]Then the Spirit said to Philip, "Go over to this chariot and join it." [30]So Philip ran up to it and heard him reading the prophet Isaiah. He asked, "Do you understand what you are reading?" [31]He replied, "How can I, unless someone guides me?" And he invited Philip to get in and sit beside him. [32]Now the passage of the scripture that he was reading was this:

> "Like a sheep he was led to the
> slaughter,
> and like a lamb silent before
> its shearer,
> so he does not open his
> mouth.
> [33] In his humiliation justice was
> denied him.
> Who can describe his
> generation?

<hr>

[a]Gk *fallen*  [b]Gk *they*  [c]The Greek word for *you* and the verb *pray* are plural  [d]Gk *after they*  [e]Or *go at noon*

For his life is taken away
from the earth."

<sup>34</sup>The eunuch asked Philip, "About whom, may I ask you, does the prophet say this, about himself or about someone else?" <sup>35</sup>Then Philip began to speak, and starting with this scripture, he proclaimed to him the good news about Jesus. <sup>36</sup>As they were going along the road, they came to some water; and the eunuch said, "Look, here is water! What is to prevent me from being baptized?"ᵃ <sup>38</sup>He commanded the chariot to stop, and both of them, Philip and the eunuch, went down into the water, and Philipᵇ baptized him. <sup>39</sup>When they came up out of the water, the Spirit of the Lord snatched Philip away; the eunuch saw him no more, and went on his way rejoicing. <sup>40</sup>But Philip found himself at Azotus, and as he was passing through the region, he proclaimed the good news to all the towns until he came to Caesarea.

## PSALM 130.1–8

*A Song of Ascents.*

Oᵁᵀ of the depths I cry to you,
O Lᴏʀᴅ.
<sup>2</sup> Lord, hear my voice!
Let your ears be attentive
to the voice of my
supplications!

<sup>3</sup> If you, O Lᴏʀᴅ, should mark
iniquities,
Lord, who could stand?
<sup>4</sup> But there is forgiveness with
you,
so that you may be revered.

<sup>5</sup> I wait for the Lᴏʀᴅ, my soul
waits,
and in his word I hope;
<sup>6</sup> my soul waits for the Lord
more than those who watch
for the morning,
more than those who watch
for the morning.

<sup>7</sup> O Israel, hope in the Lᴏʀᴅ!
For with the Lᴏʀᴅ there is
steadfast love,
and with him is great power
to redeem.
<sup>8</sup> It is he who will redeem Israel
from all its iniquities.

## PROVERBS 17.2–3

A sʟᴀᴠᴇ who deals wisely will
rule over a child who
acts shamefully,
and will share the inheritance
as one of the family.
<sup>3</sup> The crucible is for silver, and
the furnace is for gold,
but the Lᴏʀᴅ tests the heart.

---

ᵃOther ancient authorities add all or most of verse 37, *And Philip said, "If you believe with all your heart, you may." And he replied, "I believe that Jesus Christ is the Son of God."* ᵇGk *he*

# JUNE 13

## 1 KINGS 11.1—12.19

**K**ING Solomon loved many foreign women along with the daughter of Pharaoh: Moabite, Ammonite, Edomite, Sidonian, and Hittite women, [2]from the nations concerning which the LORD had said to the Israelites, "You shall not enter into marriage with them, neither shall they with you; for they will surely incline your heart to follow their gods"; Solomon clung to these in love. [3]Among his wives were seven hundred princesses and three hundred concubines; and his wives turned away his heart. [4]For when Solomon was old, his wives turned away his heart after other gods; and his heart was not true to the LORD his God, as was the heart of his father David. [5]For Solomon followed Astarte the goddess of the Sidonians, and Milcom the abomination of the Ammonites. [6]So Solomon did what was evil in the sight of the LORD, and did not completely follow the LORD, as his father David had done. [7]Then Solomon built a high place for Chemosh the abomination of Moab, and for Molech the abomination of the Ammonites, on the mountain east of Jerusalem. [8]He did the same for all his foreign wives, who offered incense and sacrificed to their gods.

9 Then the LORD was angry with Solomon, because his heart had turned away from the LORD, the God of Israel, who had appeared to him twice, [10]and had commanded him concerning this matter, that he should not follow other gods; but he did not observe what the LORD commanded. [11]Therefore the LORD said to Solomon, "Since this has been your mind and you have not kept my covenant and my statutes that I have commanded you, I will surely tear the kingdom from you and give it to your servant. [12]Yet for the sake of your father David I will not do it in your lifetime; I will tear it out of the hand of your son. [13]I will not, however, tear away the entire kingdom; I will give one tribe to your son, for the sake of my servant David and for the sake of Jerusalem, which I have chosen."

14 Then the LORD raised up an adversary against Solomon, Hadad the Edomite; he was of the royal house in Edom. [15]For when David was in Edom, and Joab the commander of the army went up to bury the dead, he killed every male in Edom [16](for Joab and all Israel remained there six months, until he had eliminated every male in Edom); [17]but Hadad fled to Egypt with some Edomites who were servants of his father. He was a young boy at that time. [18]They set out from Midian and came to Paran; they took people with them from Paran and came to Egypt, to Pharaoh king of Egypt, who gave him a house, assigned him an allowance of food, and gave him land. [19]Hadad found great favor in the sight of Pharaoh, so that he gave him his sister-in-law for a wife, the sister of Queen Tahpenes. [20]The sister of Tahpenes gave birth by him to his son Genubath, whom Tahpenes weaned in Pharaoh's house; Genubath was in Pharaoh's house among the children of Pharaoh. [21]When Hadad heard in Egypt that David slept with his ancestors and that Joab the commander of the army was dead, Hadad said to Pharaoh, "Let me depart, that I may go to my own country." [22]But Pharaoh said to him, "What do you lack with me that you now seek to go to your own country?" And he said, "No, do let me go."

23 God raised up another adver-

sary against Solomon,[a] Rezon son of Eliada, who had fled from his master, King Hadadezer of Zobah. [24]He gathered followers around him and became leader of a marauding band, after the slaughter by David; they went to Damascus, settled there, and made him king in Damascus. [25]He was an adversary of Israel all the days of Solomon, making trouble as Hadad did; he despised Israel and reigned over Aram.

26 Jeroboam son of Nebat, an Ephraimite of Zeredah, a servant of Solomon, whose mother's name was Zeruah, a widow, rebelled against the king. [27]The following was the reason he rebelled against the king. Solomon built the Millo, and closed up the gap in the wall[b] of the city of his father David. [28]The man Jeroboam was very able, and when Solomon saw that the young man was industrious he gave him charge over all the forced labor of the house of Joseph. [29]About that time, when Jeroboam was leaving Jerusalem, the prophet Ahijah the Shilonite found him on the road. Ahijah had clothed himself with a new garment. The two of them were alone in the open country [30]when Ahijah laid hold of the new garment he was wearing and tore it into twelve pieces. [31]He then said to Jeroboam: Take for yourself ten pieces; for thus says the LORD, the God of Israel, "See, I am about to tear the kingdom from the hand of Solomon, and will give you ten tribes. [32]One tribe will remain his, for the sake of my servant David and for the sake of Jerusalem, the city that I have chosen out of all the tribes of Israel. [33]This is because he has[c] forsaken me, worshiped Astarte the goddess of the Sidonians, Chemosh the god of Moab, and Milcom the god of the Ammonites, and has[c] not walked in my ways, doing what is right in my sight and keeping my statutes and my ordinances, as his father David did. [34]Nev-

ertheless I will not take the whole kingdom away from him but will make him ruler all the days of his life, for the sake of my servant David whom I chose and who did keep my commandments and my statutes; [35]but I will take the kingdom away from his son and give it to you—that is, the ten tribes. [36]Yet to his son I will give one tribe, so that my servant David may always have a lamp before me in Jerusalem, the city where I have chosen to put my name. [37]I will take you, and you shall reign over all that your soul desires; you shall be king over Israel. [38]If you will listen to all that I command you, walk in my ways, and do what is right in my sight by keeping my statutes and my commandments, as David my servant did, I will be with you, and will build you an enduring house, as I built for David, and I will give Israel to you. [39]For this reason I will punish the descendants of David, but not forever." [40]Solomon sought therefore to kill Jeroboam; but Jeroboam promptly fled to Egypt, to King Shishak of Egypt, and remained in Egypt until the death of Solomon.

41 Now the rest of the acts of Solomon, all that he did as well as his wisdom, are they not written in the Book of the Acts of Solomon? [42]The time that Solomon reigned in Jerusalem over all Israel was forty years. [43]Solomon slept with his ancestors and was buried in the city of his father David; and his son Rehoboam succeeded him.

12.1 REHOBOAM went to Shechem, for all Israel had come to Shechem to make him king. [2]When Jeroboam son of Nebat heard of it (for he was still in Egypt, where he had fled from King Solomon), then Jeroboam returned from[d] Egypt. [3]And they sent and called him; and Jeroboam and all the assembly of Israel came and said to Rehoboam, [4]"Your father made our yoke heavy. Now there-

aHeb *him*   bHeb lacks *in the wall*   cGk Syr Vg: Heb *they have*   dGk Vg Compare 2 Chr 10.2: Heb *lived in*

fore lighten the hard service of your father and his heavy yoke that he placed on us, and we will serve you." [5]He said to them, "Go away for three days, then come again to me." So the people went away.

6  Then King Rehoboam took counsel with the older men who had attended his father Solomon while he was still alive, saying, "How do you advise me to answer this people?" [7]They answered him, "If you will be a servant to this people today and serve them, and speak good words to them when you answer them, then they will be your servants forever." [8]But he disregarded the advice that the older men gave him, and consulted with the young men who had grown up with him and now attended him. [9]He said to them, "What do you advise that we answer this people who have said to me, 'Lighten the yoke that your father put on us'?" [10]The young men who had grown up with him said to him, "Thus you should say to this people who spoke to you, 'Your father made our yoke heavy, but you must lighten it for us'; thus you should say to them, 'My little finger is thicker than my father's loins. [11]Now, whereas my father laid on you a heavy yoke, I will add to your yoke. My father disciplined you with whips, but I will discipline you with scorpions.' "

12  So Jeroboam and all the people came to Rehoboam the third day, as the king had said, "Come to me again the third day." [13]The king answered the people harshly. He disregarded the advice that the older men had given him [14]and spoke to them according to the advice of the young men, "My father made your yoke heavy, but I will add to your yoke; my father disciplined you with whips, but I will discipline you with scorpions." [15]So the king did not listen to the people, because it was a turn of affairs brought about by the LORD that he might fulfill his word, which the LORD

had spoken by Ahijah the Shilonite to Jeroboam son of Nebat.

16  When all Israel saw that the king would not listen to them, the people answered the king,

> "What share do we have in
> David?
> We have no inheritance in the
> son of Jesse.
> To your tents, O Israel!
> Look now to your own house,
> O David."

So Israel went away to their tents. [17]But Rehoboam reigned over the Israelites who were living in the towns of Judah. [18]When King Rehoboam sent Adoram, who was taskmaster over the forced labor, all Israel stoned him to death. King Rehoboam then hurriedly mounted his chariot to flee to Jerusalem. [19]So Israel has been in rebellion against the house of David to this day.

## ACTS 9.1–25

MEANWHILE Saul, still breathing threats and murder against the disciples of the Lord, went to the high priest [2]and asked him for letters to the synagogues at Damascus, so that if he found any who belonged to the Way, men or women, he might bring them bound to Jerusalem. [3]Now as he was going along and approaching Damascus, suddenly a light from heaven flashed around him. [4]He fell to the ground and heard a voice saying to him, "Saul, Saul, why do you persecute me?" [5]He asked, "Who are you, Lord?" The reply came, "I am Jesus, whom you are persecuting. [6]But get up and enter the city, and you will be told what you are to do." [7]The men who were traveling with him stood speechless because they heard the voice but saw no one. [8]Saul got up from the ground, and though his eyes were open, he could see nothing; so they led him by the hand and brought him into Damascus. [9]For three days he was without sight, and neither ate nor drank.

10  Now there was a disciple in Damascus named Ananias. The Lord said to him in a vision, "Ananias." He answered, "Here I am, Lord." [11]The Lord said to him, "Get up and go to the street called Straight, and at the house of Judas look for a man of Tarsus named Saul. At this moment he is praying, [12]and he has seen in a vision[a] a man named Ananias come in and lay his hands on him so that he might regain his sight." [13]But Ananias answered, "Lord, I have heard from many about this man, how much evil he has done to your saints in Jerusalem; [14]and here he has authority from the chief priests to bind all who invoke your name." [15]But the Lord said to him, "Go, for he is an instrument whom I have chosen to bring my name before Gentiles and kings and before the people of Israel; [16]I myself will show him how much he must suffer for the sake of my name." [17]So Ananias went and entered the house. He laid his hands on Saul[b] and said, "Brother Saul, the Lord Jesus, who appeared to you on your way here, has sent me so that you may regain your sight and be filled with the Holy Spirit." [18]And immediately something like scales fell from his eyes, and his sight was restored. Then he got up and was baptized, [19]and after taking some food, he regained his strength.

For several days he was with the disciples in Damascus, [20]and immediately he began to proclaim Jesus in the synagogues, saying, "He is the Son of God." [21]All who heard him were amazed and said, "Is not this the man who made havoc in Jerusalem among those who invoked this name? And has he not come here for the purpose of bringing them bound before the chief priests?" [22]Saul became increasingly more powerful and confounded the Jews who lived in Damascus by proving that Jesus[c] was the Messiah. [d]

23  After some time had passed, the Jews plotted to kill him, [24]but their plot became known to Saul. They were watching the gates day and night so that they might kill him; [25]but his disciples took him by night and let him down through an opening in the wall, [e] lowering him in a basket.

## PSALM 131.1–3

*A Song of Ascents. Of David.*

O LORD, my heart is not lifted
    up,
my eyes are not raised too
    high;
I do not occupy myself with
    things
    too great and too marvelous
        for me.
2  But I have calmed and quieted
    my soul,
    like a weaned child with its
        mother;
    my soul is like the weaned
        child that is with me. [f]

3  O Israel, hope in the LORD
    from this time on and
        forevermore.

## PROVERBS 17.4–5

A N evildoer listens to wicked
    lips;
and a liar gives heed to a
    mischievous tongue.
5  Those who mock the poor insult
    their Maker;
    those who are glad at
    calamity will not go
    unpunished.

---

a Other ancient authorities lack *in a vision*  b Gk *him*  c Gk *that this*  d Or *the Christ*  e Gk *through the wall*  f Or *my soul within me is like a weaned child*

# JUNE 14

## 1 KINGS 12.20—13.34

WHEN all Israel heard that Jeroboam had returned, they sent and called him to the assembly and made him king over all Israel. There was no one who followed the house of David, except the tribe of Judah alone.

21 When Rehoboam came to Jerusalem, he assembled all the house of Judah and the tribe of Benjamin, one hundred eighty thousand chosen troops to fight against the house of Israel, to restore the kingdom to Rehoboam son of Solomon. ²²But the word of God came to Shemaiah the man of God: ²³Say to King Rehoboam of Judah, son of Solomon, and to all the house of Judah and Benjamin, and to the rest of the people, ²⁴"Thus says the LORD, You shall not go up or fight against your kindred the people of Israel. Let everyone go home, for this thing is from me." So they heeded the word of the LORD and went home again, according to the word of the LORD.

25 Then Jeroboam built Shechem in the hill country of Ephraim, and resided there; he went out from there and built Penuel. ²⁶Then Jeroboam said to himself, "Now the kingdom may well revert to the house of David. ²⁷If this people continues to go up to offer sacrifices in the house of the LORD at Jerusalem, the heart of this people will turn again to their master, King Rehoboam of Judah; they will kill me and return to King Rehoboam of Judah." ²⁸So the king took counsel, and made two calves of gold. He said to the people, ᵃ "You have gone up to Jerusalem long enough. Here are your gods, O Israel, who brought you up out of the land of Egypt." ²⁹He set one in Bethel, and the other he put in Dan. ³⁰And this thing became a sin, for the people went to worship before the one at Bethel and before the other as far as Dan. ᵇ ³¹He also made houses ᶜ on high places, and appointed priests from among all the people, who were not Levites. ³²Jeroboam appointed a festival on the fifteenth day of the eighth month like the festival that was in Judah, and he offered sacrifices on the altar; so he did in Bethel, sacrificing to the calves that he had made. And he placed in Bethel the priests of the high places that he had made. ³³He went up to the altar that he had made in Bethel on the fifteenth day in the eighth month, in the month that he alone had devised; he appointed a festival for the people of Israel, and he went up to the altar to offer incense.

13.1 WHILE Jeroboam was standing by the altar to offer incense, a man of God came out of Judah by the word of the LORD to Bethel ²and proclaimed against the altar by the word of the LORD, and said, "O altar, altar, thus says the LORD: 'A son shall be born to the house of David, Josiah by name; and he shall sacrifice on you the priests of the high places who offer incense on you, and human bones shall be burned on you.'" ³He gave a sign the same day, saying, "This is the sign that the LORD has spoken: 'The altar shall be torn down, and the ashes that are on it shall be poured out.'" ⁴When the king heard what the man of God cried out against the altar at Bethel, Jeroboam stretched out his hand from the altar, saying, "Seize him!" But the hand that he stretched

ᵃGk: Heb *to them*   ᵇCompare Gk: Heb *went to the one as far as Dan*   ᶜGk Vg Compare 13.32: Heb *a house*

out against him withered so that he could not draw it back to himself. ⁵The altar also was torn down, and the ashes poured out from the altar, according to the sign that the man of God had given by the word of the LORD. ⁶The king said to the man of God, "Entreat now the favor of the LORD your God, and pray for me, so that my hand may be restored to me." So the man of God entreated the LORD; and the king's hand was restored to him, and became as it was before. ⁷Then the king said to the man of God, "Come home with me and dine, and I will give you a gift." ⁸But the man of God said to the king, "If you give me half your kingdom, I will not go in with you; nor will I eat food or drink water in this place. ⁹For thus I was commanded by the word of the LORD: You shall not eat food, or drink water, or return by the way that you came." ¹⁰So he went another way, and did not return by the way that he had come to Bethel.

11 Now there lived an old prophet in Bethel. One of his sons came and told him all that the man of God had done that day in Bethel; the words also that he had spoken to the king, they told to their father. ¹²Their father said to them, "Which way did he go?" And his sons showed him the way that the man of God who came from Judah had gone. ¹³Then he said to his sons, "Saddle a donkey for me." So they saddled a donkey for him, and he mounted it. ¹⁴He went after the man of God, and found him sitting under an oak tree. He said to him, "Are you the man of God who came from Judah?" He answered, "I am." ¹⁵Then he said to him, "Come home with me and eat some food." ¹⁶But he said, "I cannot return with you, or go in with you; nor will I eat food or drink water with you in this place; ¹⁷for it was said to me by the word of the LORD: You shall not eat food

or drink water there, or return by the way that you came." ¹⁸Then the other*a* said to him, "I also am a prophet as you are, and an angel spoke to me by the word of the LORD: Bring him back with you into your house so that he may eat food and drink water." But he was deceiving him. ¹⁹Then the man of God*a* went back with him, and ate food and drank water in his house.

20 As they were sitting at the table, the word of the LORD came to the prophet who had brought him back; ²¹and he proclaimed to the man of God who came from Judah, "Thus says the LORD: Because you have disobeyed the word of the LORD, and have not kept the commandment that the LORD your God commanded you, ²²but have come back and have eaten food and drunk water in the place of which he said to you, 'Eat no food, and drink no water,' your body shall not come to your ancestral tomb." ²³After the man of God*a* had eaten food and had drunk, they saddled for him a donkey belonging to the prophet who had brought him back. ²⁴Then as he went away, a lion met him on the road and killed him. His body was thrown in the road, and the donkey stood beside it; the lion also stood beside the body. ²⁵People passed by and saw the body thrown in the road, with the lion standing by the body. And they came and told it in the town where the old prophet lived.

26 When the prophet who had brought him back from the way heard of it, he said, "It is the man of God who disobeyed the word of the LORD; therefore the LORD has given him to the lion, which has torn him and killed him according to the word that the LORD spoke to him." ²⁷Then he said to his sons, "Saddle a donkey for me." So they saddled one, ²⁸and he went and found the body thrown in the road, with the donkey and the lion standing beside

a Heb *he*

the body. The lion had not eaten the body or attacked the donkey. ²⁹The prophet took up the body of the man of God, laid it on the donkey, and brought it back to the city,ᵃ to mourn and to bury him. ³⁰He laid the body in his own grave; and they mourned over him, saying, "Alas, my brother!" ³¹After he had buried him, he said to his sons, "When I die, bury me in the grave in which the man of God is buried; lay my bones beside his bones. ³²For the saying that he proclaimed by the word of the Lᴏʀᴅ against the altar in Bethel, and against all the houses of the high places that are in the cities of Samaria, shall surely come to pass."

33 Even after this event Jeroboam did not turn from his evil way, but made priests for the high places again from among all the people; any who wanted to be priests he consecrated for the high places. ³⁴This matter became sin to the house of Jeroboam, so as to cut it off and to destroy it from the face of the earth.

## ACTS 9.26–43

WHEN he [Saul] had come to Jerusalem, he attempted to join the disciples; and they were all afraid of him, for they did not believe that he was a disciple. ²⁷But Barnabas took him, brought him to the apostles, and described for them how on the road he had seen the Lord, who had spoken to him, and how in Damascus he had spoken boldly in the name of Jesus. ²⁸So he went in and out among them in Jerusalem, speaking boldly in the name of the Lord. ²⁹He spoke and argued with the Hellenists; but they were attempting to kill him. ³⁰When the believersᵇ learned of it, they brought him down to Caesarea and sent him off to Tarsus.

31 Meanwhile the church through-out Judea, Galilee, and Samaria had peace and was built up. Living in the fear of the Lord and in the comfort of the Holy Spirit, it increased in numbers.

32 Now as Peter went here and there among all the believers,ᶜ he came down also to the saints living in Lydda. ³³There he found a man named Aeneas, who had been bedridden for eight years, for he was paralyzed. ³⁴Peter said to him, "Aeneas, Jesus Christ heals you; get up and make your bed!" And immediately he got up. ³⁵And all the residents of Lydda and Sharon saw him and turned to the Lord.

36 Now in Joppa there was a disciple whose name was Tabitha, which in Greek is Dorcas.ᵈ She was devoted to good works and acts of charity. ³⁷At that time she became ill and died. When they had washed her, they laid her in a room upstairs. ³⁸Since Lydda was near Joppa, the disciples, who heard that Peter was there, sent two men to him with the request, "Please come to us without delay." ³⁹So Peter got up and went with them; and when he arrived, they took him to the room upstairs. All the widows stood beside him, weeping and showing tunics and other clothing that Dorcas had made while she was with them. ⁴⁰Peter put all of them outside, and then he knelt down and prayed. He turned to the body and said, "Tabitha, get up." Then she opened her eyes, and seeing Peter, she sat up. ⁴¹He gave her his hand and helped her up. Then calling the saints and widows, he showed her to be alive. ⁴²This became known throughout Joppa, and many believed in the Lord. ⁴³Meanwhile he stayed in Joppa for some time with a certain Simon, a tanner.

## PSALM 132.1–18

*A Song of Ascents.*

O LORD, remember in David's
    favor
all the hardships he
    endured;
2 how he swore to the LORD
    and vowed to the Mighty One
      of Jacob,
3 "I will not enter my house
    or get into my bed;
4 I will not give sleep to my eyes
    or slumber to my eyelids,
5 until I find a place for the LORD,
    a dwelling place for the
      Mighty One of Jacob."

6 We heard of it in Ephrathah;
    we found it in the fields of
      Jaar.
7 "Let us go to his dwelling place;
    let us worship at his
      footstool."

8 Rise up, O LORD, and go to your
    resting place,
    you and the ark of your
      might.
9 Let your priests be clothed with
    righteousness,
    and let your faithful shout
      for joy.
10 For your servant David's sake
    do not turn away the face of
      your anointed one.

11 The LORD swore to David a sure
    oath
from which he will not turn
    back:
"One of the sons of your body
    I will set on your throne.
12 If your sons keep my covenant
    and my decrees that I shall
      teach them,
their sons also, forevermore,
    shall sit on your throne."

13 For the LORD has chosen Zion;
    he has desired it for his
      habitation:
14 "This is my resting place
    forever;
    here I will reside, for I have
      desired it.
15 I will abundantly bless its
    provisions;
    I will satisfy its poor with
      bread.
16 Its priests I will clothe with
    salvation,
    and its faithful will shout for
      joy.
17 There I will cause a horn to
    sprout up for David;
    I have prepared a lamp for
      my anointed one.
18 His enemies I will clothe with
    disgrace,
    but on him, his crown will
      gleam."

## PROVERBS 17.6

G RANDCHILDREN are the crown of
    the aged,
and the glory of children is
    their parents.

# JUNE 15

## 1 KINGS 14.1—15.24

**A**T that time Abijah son of Jeroboam fell sick. [2]Jeroboam said to his wife, "Go, disguise yourself, so that it will not be known that you are the wife of Jeroboam, and go to Shiloh; for the prophet Ahijah is there, who said of me that I should be king over this people. [3]Take with you ten loaves, some cakes, and a jar of honey, and go to him; he will tell you what shall happen to the child."

4 Jeroboam's wife did so; she set out and went to Shiloh, and came to the house of Ahijah. Now Ahijah could not see, for his eyes were dim because of his age. [5]But the LORD said to Ahijah, "The wife of Jeroboam is coming to inquire of you concerning her son; for he is sick. Thus and thus you shall say to her."

When she came, she pretended to be another woman. [6]But when Ahijah heard the sound of her feet, as she came in at the door, he said, "Come in, wife of Jeroboam; why do you pretend to be another? For I am charged with heavy tidings for you. [7]Go, tell Jeroboam, 'Thus says the LORD, the God of Israel: Because I exalted you from among the people, made you leader over my people Israel, [8]and tore the kingdom away from the house of David to give it to you; yet you have not been like my servant David, who kept my commandments and followed me with all his heart, doing only that which was right in my sight, [9]but you have done evil above all those who were before you and have gone and made for yourself other gods, and cast images, provoking me to anger, and have thrust me behind your back; [10]therefore, I will bring evil upon the house of Jeroboam. I will cut off from Jeroboam every male, both bond and free in Israel, and will consume the house of Jeroboam, just as one burns up dung until it is all gone. [11]Anyone belonging to Jeroboam who dies in the city, the dogs shall eat; and anyone who dies in the open country, the birds of the air shall eat; for the LORD has spoken.' [12]Therefore set out, go to your house. When your feet enter the city, the child shall die. [13]All Israel shall mourn for him and bury him; for he alone of Jeroboam's family shall come to the grave, because in him there is found something pleasing to the LORD, the God of Israel, in the house of Jeroboam. [14]Moreover the LORD will raise up for himself a king over Israel, who shall cut off the house of Jeroboam today, even right now! [a]

15 "The LORD will strike Israel, as a reed is shaken in the water; he will root up Israel out of this good land that he gave to their ancestors, and scatter them beyond the Euphrates, because they have made their sacred poles, [b] provoking the LORD to anger. [16]He will give Israel up because of the sins of Jeroboam, which he sinned and which he caused Israel to commit."

17 Then Jeroboam's wife got up and went away, and she came to Tirzah. As she came to the threshold of the house, the child died. [18]All Israel buried him and mourned for him, according to the word of the LORD, which he spoke by his servant the prophet Ahijah.

19 Now the rest of the acts of Jeroboam, how he warred and how he reigned, are written in the Book of the Annals of the Kings of Israel. [20]The

time that Jeroboam reigned was twenty-two years; then he slept with his ancestors, and his son Nadab succeeded him.

21 Now Rehoboam son of Solomon reigned in Judah. Rehoboam was forty-one years old when he began to reign, and he reigned seventeen years in Jerusalem, the city that the LORD had chosen out of all the tribes of Israel, to put his name there. His mother's name was Naamah the Ammonite. ²²Judah did what was evil in the sight of the LORD; they provoked him to jealousy with their sins that they committed, more than all that their ancestors had done. ²³For they also built for themselves high places, pillars, and sacred poles[a] on every high hill and under every green tree; ²⁴there were also male temple prostitutes in the land. They committed all the abominations of the nations that the LORD drove out before the people of Israel.

25 In the fifth year of King Rehoboam, King Shishak of Egypt came up against Jerusalem; ²⁶he took away the treasures of the house of the LORD and the treasures of the king's house; he took everything. He also took away all the shields of gold that Solomon had made; ²⁷so King Rehoboam made shields of bronze instead, and committed them to the hands of the officers of the guard, who kept the door of the king's house. ²⁸As often as the king went into the house of the LORD, the guard carried them and brought them back to the guardroom.

29 Now the rest of the acts of Rehoboam, and all that he did, are they not written in the Book of the Annals of the Kings of Judah? ³⁰There was war between Rehoboam and Jeroboam continually. ³¹Rehoboam slept with his ancestors and was buried with his ancestors in the city of David. His mother's name was Naamah the Ammonite. His son Abijam succeeded him.

15.1 Now in the eighteenth year of King Jeroboam son of Nebat, Abijam began to reign over Judah. ²He reigned for three years in Jerusalem. His mother's name was Maacah daughter of Abishalom. ³He committed all the sins that his father did before him; his heart was not true to the LORD his God, like the heart of his father David. ⁴Nevertheless for David's sake the LORD his God gave him a lamp in Jerusalem, setting up his son after him, and establishing Jerusalem; ⁵because David did what was right in the sight of the LORD, and did not turn aside from anything that he commanded him all the days of his life, except in the matter of Uriah the Hittite. ⁶The war begun between Rehoboam and Jeroboam continued all the days of his life. ⁷The rest of the acts of Abijam, and all that he did, are they not written in the Book of the Annals of the Kings of Judah? There was war between Abijam and Jeroboam. ⁸Abijam slept with his ancestors, and they buried him in the city of David. Then his son Asa succeeded him.

9 In the twentieth year of King Jeroboam of Israel, Asa began to reign over Judah; ¹⁰he reigned forty-one years in Jerusalem. His mother's name was Maacah daughter of Abishalom. ¹¹Asa did what was right in the sight of the LORD, as his father David had done. ¹²He put away the male temple prostitutes out of the land, and removed all the idols that his ancestors had made. ¹³He also removed his mother Maacah from being queen mother, because she had made an abominable image for Asherah; Asa cut down her image and burned it at the Wadi Kidron. ¹⁴But the high places were not taken away. Nevertheless the heart of Asa was true to

a Heb *Asherim*

the Lord all his days. <sup>15</sup>He brought into the house of the Lord the votive gifts of his father and his own votive gifts— silver, gold, and utensils.

16 There was war between Asa and King Baasha of Israel all their days. <sup>17</sup>King Baasha of Israel went up against Judah, and built Ramah, to prevent anyone from going out or coming in to King Asa of Judah. <sup>18</sup>Then Asa took all the silver and the gold that were left in the treasures of the house of the Lord and the treasures of the king's house, and gave them into the hands of his servants. King Asa sent them to King Ben-hadad son of Tabrimmon son of Hezion of Aram, who resided in Damascus, saying, <sup>19</sup>"Let there be an alliance between me and you, like that between my father and your father: I am sending you a present of silver and gold; go, break your alliance with King Baasha of Israel, so that he may withdraw from me." <sup>20</sup>Ben-hadad listened to King Asa, and sent the commanders of his armies against the cities of Israel. He conquered Ijon, Dan, Abel-beth-maacah, and all Chinneroth, with all the land of Naphtali. <sup>21</sup>When Baasha heard of it, he stopped building Ramah and lived in Tirzah. <sup>22</sup>Then King Asa made a proclamation to all Judah, none was exempt: they carried away the stones of Ramah and its timber, with which Baasha had been building; with them King Asa built Geba of Benjamin and Mizpah. <sup>23</sup>Now the rest of all the acts of Asa, all his power, all that he did, and the cities that he built, are they not written in the Book of the Annals of the Kings of Judah? But in his old age he was diseased in his feet. <sup>24</sup>Then Asa slept with his ancestors, and was buried with his ancestors in the city of his father David; his son Jehoshaphat succeeded him.

## ACTS 10.1–23a

In Caesarea there was a man named Cornelius, a centurion of the Italian Cohort, as it was called. <sup>2</sup>He was a devout man who feared God with all his household; he gave alms generously to the people and prayed constantly to God. <sup>3</sup>One afternoon at about three o'clock he had a vision in which he clearly saw an angel of God coming in and saying to him, "Cornelius." <sup>4</sup>He stared at him in terror and said, "What is it, Lord?" He answered, "Your prayers and your alms have ascended as a memorial before God. <sup>5</sup>Now send men to Joppa for a certain Simon who is called Peter; <sup>6</sup>he is lodging with Simon, a tanner, whose house is by the seaside." <sup>7</sup>When the angel who spoke to him had left, he called two of his slaves and a devout soldier from the ranks of those who served him, <sup>8</sup>and after telling them everything, he sent them to Joppa.

9 About noon the next day, as they were on their journey and approaching the city, Peter went up on the roof to pray. <sup>10</sup>He became hungry and wanted something to eat; and while it was being prepared, he fell into a trance. <sup>11</sup>He saw the heaven opened and something like a large sheet coming down, being lowered to the ground by its four corners. <sup>12</sup>In it were all kinds of four-footed creatures and reptiles and birds of the air. <sup>13</sup>Then he heard a voice saying, "Get up, Peter; kill and eat." <sup>14</sup>But Peter said, "By no means, Lord; for I have never eaten anything that is profane or unclean." <sup>15</sup>The voice said to him again, a second time, "What God has made clean, you must not call profane." <sup>16</sup>This happened three times, and the thing was suddenly taken up to heaven.

17 Now while Peter was greatly puzzled about what to make of the vision that he had seen, suddenly the

men sent by Cornelius appeared. They were asking for Simon's house and were standing by the gate. [18]They called out to ask whether Simon, who was called Peter, was staying there. [19]While Peter was still thinking about the vision, the Spirit said to him, "Look, three[a] men are searching for you. [20]Now get up, go down, and go with them without hesitation; for I have sent them." [21]So Peter went down to the men and said, "I am the one you are looking for; what is the reason for your coming?" [22]They answered, "Cornelius, a centurion, an upright and God-fearing man, who is well spoken of by the whole Jewish nation, was directed by a holy angel to send for you to come to his house and to hear what you have to say." [23]So Peter[b] invited them in and gave them lodging.

## PSALM 133.1–3

*A Song of Ascents.*

How very good and pleasant it is
when kindred live together
in unity!

[2] It is like the precious oil on the
head,
running down upon the beard,
on the beard of Aaron,
running down over the collar
of his robes.
[3] It is like the dew of Hermon,
which falls on the mountains
of Zion.
For there the Lord ordained his
blessing,
life forevermore.

## PROVERBS 17.7–8

Fine speech is not becoming to
a fool;
still less is false speech to a
ruler. [c]
[8] A bribe is like a magic stone in
the eyes of those who
give it;
wherever they turn they
prosper.

# JUNE 16

## 1 KINGS 15.25—17.24

Nadab son of Jeroboam began to reign over Israel in the second year of King Asa of Judah; he reigned over Israel two years. [26]He did what was evil in the sight of the Lord, walking in the way of his ancestor and in the sin that he caused Israel to commit.

27 Baasha son of Ahijah, of the house of Issachar, conspired against him; and Baasha struck him down at Gibbethon, which belonged to the Philistines; for Nadab and all Israel were laying siege to Gibbethon. [28]So Baasha killed Nadab[d] in the third year of King Asa of Judah, and succeeded him. [29]As soon as he was king, he killed all the house of Jeroboam; he left to the house of Jeroboam not one that breathed, un-

aOne ancient authority reads *two*; others lack the word   bGk *he*   cOr *a noble person*   dHeb *him* til he had destroyed it, according to the word of the Lord that he spoke by his servant Ahijah the Shilonite— ³⁰because of the sins of Jeroboam that he committed and that he caused Israel to commit, and because of the anger to which he provoked the Lord, the God of Israel.

31  Now the rest of the acts of Nadab, and all that he did, are they not written in the Book of the Annals of the Kings of Israel? ³²There was war between Asa and King Baasha of Israel all their days.

33  In the third year of King Asa of Judah, Baasha son of Ahijah began to reign over all Israel at Tirzah; he reigned twenty-four years. ³⁴He did what was evil in the sight of the Lord, walking in the way of Jeroboam and in the sin that he caused Israel to commit.

**16.**1  The word of the Lord came to Jehu son of Hanani against Baasha, saying, ²"Since I exalted you out of the dust and made you leader over my people Israel, and you have walked in the way of Jeroboam, and have caused my people Israel to sin, provoking me to anger with their sins, ³therefore, I will consume Baasha and his house, and I will make your house like the house of Jeroboam son of Nebat. ⁴Anyone belonging to Baasha who dies in the city the dogs shall eat; and anyone of his who dies in the field the birds of the air shall eat."

5  Now the rest of the acts of Baasha, what he did, and his power, are they not written in the Book of the Annals of the Kings of Israel? ⁶Baasha slept with his ancestors, and was buried at Tirzah; and his son Elah succeeded him. ⁷Moreover the word of the Lord came by the prophet Jehu son of Hanani against Baasha and his house, both because of all the evil that he did in the sight of the Lord, provoking him to anger with the work of his hands, in being like the house of Jeroboam, and also because he destroyed it.

8  In the twenty-sixth year of King Asa of Judah, Elah son of Baasha began to reign over Israel in Tirzah; he reigned two years. ⁹But his servant Zimri, commander of half his chariots, conspired against him. When he was at Tirzah, drinking himself drunk in the house of Arza, who was in charge of the palace at Tirzah, ¹⁰Zimri came in and struck him down and killed him, in the twenty-seventh year of King Asa of Judah, and succeeded him.

11  When he began to reign, as soon as he had seated himself on his throne, he killed all the house of Baasha; he did not leave him a single male of his kindred or his friends. ¹²Thus Zimri destroyed all the house of Baasha, according to the word of the Lord, which he spoke against Baasha by the prophet Jehu— ¹³because of all the sins of Baasha and the sins of his son Elah that they committed, and that they caused Israel to commit, provoking the Lord God of Israel to anger with their idols. ¹⁴Now the rest of the acts of Elah, and all that he did, are they not written in the Book of the Annals of the Kings of Israel?

15  In the twenty-seventh year of King Asa of Judah, Zimri reigned seven days in Tirzah. Now the troops were encamped against Gibbethon, which belonged to the Philistines, ¹⁶and the troops who were encamped heard it said, "Zimri has conspired, and he has killed the king"; therefore all Israel made Omri, the commander of the army, king over Israel that day in the camp. ¹⁷So Omri went up from Gibbethon, and all Israel with him, and they besieged Tirzah. ¹⁸When Zimri saw that the city was taken, he went into the citadel of the king's house; he burned down the king's house over himself with fire, and died— ¹⁹because of the sins that he committed, doing evil in the sight of the Lord, walking in the way of Jeroboam, and for the sin that he committed, causing Israel to

sin. <sup>20</sup>Now the rest of the acts of Zimri, and the conspiracy that he made, are they not written in the Book of the Annals of the Kings of Israel?

21 Then the people of Israel were divided into two parts; half of the people followed Tibni son of Ginath, to make him king, and half followed Omri. <sup>22</sup>But the people who followed Omri overcame the people who followed Tibni son of Ginath; so Tibni died, and Omri became king. <sup>23</sup>In the thirty-first year of King Asa of Judah, Omri began to reign over Israel; he reigned for twelve years, six of them in Tirzah.

24 He bought the hill of Samaria from Shemer for two talents of silver; he fortified the hill, and called the city that he built, Samaria, after the name of Shemer, the owner of the hill.

25 Omri did what was evil in the sight of the LORD; he did more evil than all who were before him. <sup>26</sup>For he walked in all the way of Jeroboam son of Nebat, and in the sins that he caused Israel to commit, provoking the LORD, the God of Israel, to anger by their idols. <sup>27</sup>Now the rest of the acts of Omri that he did, and the power that he showed, are they not written in the Book of the Annals of the Kings of Israel? <sup>28</sup>Omri slept with his ancestors, and was buried in Samaria; his son Ahab succeeded him.

29 In the thirty-eighth year of King Asa of Judah, Ahab son of Omri began to reign over Israel; Ahab son of Omri reigned over Israel in Samaria twenty-two years. <sup>30</sup>Ahab son of Omri did evil in the sight of the LORD more than all who were before him.

31 And as if it had been a light thing for him to walk in the sins of Jeroboam son of Nebat, he took as his wife Jezebel daughter of King Ethbaal of the Sidonians, and went and served Baal, and worshiped him. <sup>32</sup>He erected an altar for Baal in the house of Baal, which he built in Samaria. <sup>33</sup>Ahab also made a sacred pole.[a] Ahab did more to provoke the anger of the LORD, the God of Israel, than had all the kings of Israel who were before him. <sup>34</sup>In his days Hiel of Bethel built Jericho; he laid its foundation at the cost of Abiram his firstborn, and set up its gates at the cost of his youngest son Segub, according to the word of the LORD, which he spoke by Joshua son of Nun.

17.<sup>1</sup> Now Elijah the Tishbite, of Tishbe[b] in Gilead, said to Ahab, "As the LORD the God of Israel lives, before whom I stand, there shall be neither dew nor rain these years, except by my word." <sup>2</sup>The word of the LORD came to him, saying, <sup>3</sup>"Go from here and turn eastward, and hide yourself by the Wadi Cherith, which is east of the Jordan. <sup>4</sup>You shall drink from the wadi, and I have commanded the ravens to feed you there." <sup>5</sup>So he went and did according to the word of the LORD; he went and lived by the Wadi Cherith, which is east of the Jordan. <sup>6</sup>The ravens brought him bread and meat in the morning, and bread and meat in the evening; and he drank from the wadi. <sup>7</sup>But after a while the wadi dried up, because there was no rain in the land.

8 Then the word of the LORD came to him, saying, <sup>9</sup>"Go now to Zarephath, which belongs to Sidon, and live there; for I have commanded a widow there to feed you." <sup>10</sup>So he set out and went to Zarephath. When he came to the gate of the town, a widow was there gathering sticks; he called to her and said, "Bring me a little water in a vessel, so that I may drink." <sup>11</sup>As she was going to bring it, he called to her and said, "Bring me a morsel of bread in your hand." <sup>12</sup>But she said, "As the LORD your God lives, I have nothing baked, only a handful of meal in a jar, and a little

---

**a** Heb *Asherah*  **b** Gk: Heb *of the settlers*

oil in a jug; I am now gathering a couple of sticks, so that I may go home and prepare it for myself and my son, that we may eat it, and die." ¹³Elijah said to her, "Do not be afraid; go and do as you have said; but first make me a little cake of it and bring it to me, and afterwards make something for yourself and your son. ¹⁴For thus says the LORD the God of Israel: The jar of meal will not be emptied and the jug of oil will not fail until the day that the LORD sends rain on the earth." ¹⁵She went and did as Elijah said, so that she as well as he and her household ate for many days. ¹⁶The jar of meal was not emptied, neither did the jug of oil fail, according to the word of the LORD that he spoke by Elijah.

17 After this the son of the woman, the mistress of the house, became ill; his illness was so severe that there was no breath left in him. ¹⁸She then said to Elijah, "What have you against me, O man of God? You have come to me to bring my sin to remembrance, and to cause the death of my son!" ¹⁹But he said to her, "Give me your son." He took him from her bosom, carried him up into the upper chamber where he was lodging, and laid him on his own bed. ²⁰He cried out to the LORD, "O LORD my God, have you brought calamity even upon the widow with whom I am staying, by killing her son?" ²¹Then he stretched himself upon the child three times, and cried out to the LORD, "O LORD my God, let this child's life come into him again." ²²The LORD listened to the voice of Elijah; the life of the child came into him again, and he revived. ²³Elijah took the child, brought him down from the upper chamber into the house, and gave him to his mother; then Elijah said, "See, your son is alive." ²⁴So the woman said to Elijah, "Now I know that you are a man of God, and that the word of the LORD in your mouth is truth."

## ACTS 10.23b–48

THE next day he [Peter] got up and went with them, and some of the believers[a] from Joppa accompanied him. ²⁴The following day they came to Caesarea. Cornelius was expecting them and had called together his relatives and close friends. ²⁵On Peter's arrival Cornelius met him, and falling at his feet, worshiped him. ²⁶But Peter made him get up, saying, "Stand up; I am only a mortal." ²⁷And as he talked with him, he went in and found that many had assembled; ²⁸and he said to them, "You yourselves know that it is unlawful for a Jew to associate with or to visit a Gentile; but God has shown me that I should not call anyone profane or unclean. ²⁹So when I was sent for, I came without objection. Now may I ask why you sent for me?"

30 Cornelius replied, "Four days ago at this very hour, at three o'clock, I was praying in my house when suddenly a man in dazzling clothes stood before me. ³¹He said, 'Cornelius, your prayer has been heard and your alms have been remembered before God. ³²Send therefore to Joppa and ask for Simon, who is called Peter; he is staying in the home of Simon, a tanner, by the sea.' ³³Therefore I sent for you immediately, and you have been kind enough to come. So now all of us are here in the presence of God to listen to all that the Lord has commanded you to say."

34 Then Peter began to speak to them: "I truly understand that God shows no partiality, ³⁵but in every nation anyone who fears him and does what is right is acceptable to him. ³⁶You know the message he sent to the people of Israel, preaching peace by Jesus Christ—he is Lord of all. ³⁷That message spread throughout Judea, beginning in Galilee after the baptism that

a Gk *brothers*

John announced: [38]how God anointed Jesus of Nazareth with the Holy Spirit and with power; how he went about doing good and healing all who were oppressed by the devil, for God was with him. [39]We are witnesses to all that he did both in Judea and in Jerusalem. They put him to death by hanging him on a tree; [40]but God raised him on the third day and allowed him to appear, [41]not to all the people but to us who were chosen by God as witnesses, and who ate and drank with him after he rose from the dead. [42]He commanded us to preach to the people and to testify that He is the one ordained by God as judge of the living and the dead. [43]All the prophets testify about him that everyone who believes in him receives forgiveness of sins through his name."

44 While Peter was still speaking, the Holy Spirit fell upon all who heard the word. [45]The circumcised believers who had come with Peter were astounded that the gift of the Holy Spirit had been poured out even on the Gentiles, [46]for they heard them speaking in tongues and extolling God. Then Peter said, [47]"Can anyone withhold the water for baptizing these people who have received the Holy Spirit just as we have?" [48]So he ordered them to be baptized in the name of Jesus Christ. Then they invited him to stay for several days.

## PSALM 134.1–3

*A Song of Ascents.*

COME, bless the LORD, all you
        servants of the LORD,
    who stand by night in the
        house of the LORD!
2   Lift up your hands to the holy
        place,
    and bless the LORD.

3   May the LORD, maker of heaven
        and earth,
    bless you from Zion.

## PROVERBS 17.9–11

ONE who forgives an affront
        fosters friendship,
    but one who dwells on
        disputes will alienate a
        friend.
10  A rebuke strikes deeper into a
        discerning person
    than a hundred blows into a
        fool.
11  Evil people seek only rebellion,
    but a cruel messenger will be
        sent against them.

# JUNE 17

## 1 KINGS 18.1–46

AFTER many days the word of the LORD came to Elijah, in the third year of the drought,[a] saying, "Go, present yourself to Ahab; I will send rain on the earth." [2]So Elijah went to present himself to Ahab. The famine was severe in Samaria. [3]Ahab summoned Obadiah, who was in charge of the palace. (Now Obadiah revered the LORD greatly; [4]when Jezebel was killing off the prophets of the LORD, Obadiah took a hundred prophets, hid them fifty to a cave, and provided them

**a**Heb lacks *of the drought*

with bread and water.) ⁵Then Ahab said to Obadiah, "Go through the land to all the springs of water and to all the wadis; perhaps we may find grass to keep the horses and mules alive, and not lose some of the animals." ⁶So they divided the land between them to pass through it; Ahab went in one direction by himself, and Obadiah went in another direction by himself.

7  As Obadiah was on the way, Elijah met him; Obadiah recognized him, fell on his face, and said, "Is it you, my lord Elijah?" ⁸He answered him, "It is I. Go, tell your lord that Elijah is here." ⁹And he said, "How have I sinned, that you would hand your servant over to Ahab, to kill me? ¹⁰As the Lord your God lives, there is no nation or kingdom to which my lord has not sent to seek you; and when they would say, 'He is not here,' he would require an oath of the kingdom or nation, that they had not found you. ¹¹But now you say, 'Go, tell your lord that Elijah is here.' ¹²As soon as I have gone from you, the spirit of the Lord will carry you I know not where; so, when I come and tell Ahab and he cannot find you, he will kill me, although I your servant have revered the Lord from my youth. ¹³Has it not been told my lord what I did when Jezebel killed the prophets of the Lord, how I hid a hundred of the Lord's prophets fifty to a cave, and provided them with bread and water? ¹⁴Yet now you say, 'Go, tell your lord that Elijah is here'; he will surely kill me." ¹⁵Elijah said, "As the Lord of hosts lives, before whom I stand, I will surely show myself to him today." ¹⁶So Obadiah went to meet Ahab, and told him; and Ahab went to meet Elijah.

17  When Ahab saw Elijah, Ahab said to him, "Is it you, you troubler of Israel?" ¹⁸He answered, "I have not troubled Israel; but you have, and your father's house, because you have forsaken the commandments of the Lord and followed the Baals. ¹⁹Now therefore have all Israel assemble for me at Mount Carmel, with the four hundred fifty prophets of Baal and the four hundred prophets of Asherah, who eat at Jezebel's table."

20  So Ahab sent to all the Israelites, and assembled the prophets at Mount Carmel. ²¹Elijah then came near to all the people, and said, "How long will you go limping with two different opinions? If the Lord is God, follow him; but if Baal, then follow him." The people did not answer him a word. ²²Then Elijah said to the people, "I, even I only, am left a prophet of the Lord; but Baal's prophets number four hundred fifty. ²³Let two bulls be given to us; let them choose one bull for themselves, cut it in pieces, and lay it on the wood, but put no fire to it; I will prepare the other bull and lay it on the wood, but put no fire to it. ²⁴Then you call on the name of your god and I will call on the name of the Lord; the god who answers by fire is indeed God." All the people answered, "Well spoken!" ²⁵Then Elijah said to the prophets of Baal, "Choose for yourselves one bull and prepare it first, for you are many; then call on the name of your god, but put no fire to it." ²⁶So they took the bull that was given them, prepared it, and called on the name of Baal from morning until noon, crying, "O Baal, answer us!" But there was no voice, and no answer. They limped about the altar that they had made. ²⁷At noon Elijah mocked them, saying, "Cry aloud! Surely he is a god; either he is meditating, or he has wandered away, or he is on a journey, or perhaps he is asleep and must be awakened." ²⁸Then they cried aloud and, as was their custom, they cut themselves with swords and lances until the blood gushed out over them. ²⁹As midday passed, they raved on until the time of the offering of the oblation, but there was no voice, no answer, and no response.

30  Then Elijah said to all the peo-

ple, "Come closer to me"; and all the people came closer to him. First he repaired the altar of the LORD that had been thrown down; [31]Elijah took twelve stones, according to the number of the tribes of the sons of Jacob, to whom the word of the LORD came, saying, "Israel shall be your name"; [32]with the stones he built an altar in the name of the LORD. Then he made a trench around the altar, large enough to contain two measures of seed. [33]Next he put the wood in order, cut the bull in pieces, and laid it on the wood. He said, "Fill four jars with water and pour it on the burnt offering and on the wood." [34]Then he said, "Do it a second time"; and they did it a second time. Again he said, "Do it a third time"; and they did it a third time, [35]so that the water ran all around the altar, and filled the trench also with water.

36 At the time of the offering of the oblation, the prophet Elijah came near and said, "O LORD, God of Abraham, Isaac, and Israel, let it be known this day that you are God in Israel, that I am your servant, and that I have done all these things at your bidding. [37]Answer me, O LORD, answer me, so that this people may know that you, O LORD, are God, and that you have turned their hearts back." [38]Then the fire of the LORD fell and consumed the burnt offering, the wood, the stones, and the dust, and even licked up the water that was in the trench. [39]When all the people saw it, they fell on their faces and said, "The LORD indeed is God; the LORD indeed is God." [40]Elijah said to them, "Seize the prophets of Baal; do not let one of them escape." Then they seized them; and Elijah brought them down to the Wadi Kishon, and killed them there.

41 Elijah said to Ahab, "Go up, eat and drink; for there is a sound of rushing rain." [42]So Ahab went up to eat and to drink. Elijah went up to the top of Carmel; there he bowed himself down upon the earth and put his face between his knees. [43]He said to his servant, "Go up now, look toward the sea." He went up and looked, and said, "There is nothing." Then he said, "Go again seven times." [44]At the seventh time he said, "Look, a little cloud no bigger than a person's hand is rising out of the sea." Then he said, "Go say to Ahab, 'Harness your chariot and go down before the rain stops you.'" [45]In a little while the heavens grew black with clouds and wind; there was a heavy rain. Ahab rode off and went to Jezreel. [46]But the hand of the LORD was on Elijah; he girded up his loins and ran in front of Ahab to the entrance of Jezreel.

## ACTS 11.1–30

Now the apostles and the believers[a] who were in Judea heard that the Gentiles had also accepted the word of God. [2]So when Peter went up to Jerusalem, the circumcised believers[b] criticized him, [3]saying, "Why did you go to uncircumcised men and eat with them?" [4]Then Peter began to explain it to them, step by step, saying, [5]"I was in the city of Joppa praying, and in a trance I saw a vision. There was something like a large sheet coming down from heaven, being lowered by its four corners; and it came close to me. [6]As I looked at it closely I saw four-footed animals, beasts of prey, reptiles, and birds of the air. [7]I also heard a voice saying to me, 'Get up, Peter; kill and eat.' [8]But I replied, 'By no means, Lord; for nothing profane or unclean has ever entered my mouth.' [9]But a second time the voice answered from heaven, 'What God has made clean, you must not call profane.' [10]This happened three times; then everything was pulled up again to

a Gk *brothers*  b Gk lacks *believers*

heaven. [11]At that very moment three men, sent to me from Caesarea, arrived at the house where we were. [12]The Spirit told me to go with them and not to make a distinction between them and us.[a] These six brothers also accompanied me, and we entered the man's house. [13]He told us how he had seen the angel standing in his house and saying, 'Send to Joppa and bring Simon, who is called Peter; [14]he will give you a message by which you and your entire household will be saved.' [15]And as I began to speak, the Holy Spirit fell upon them just as it had upon us at the beginning. [16]And I remembered the word of the Lord, how he had said, 'John baptized with water, but you will be baptized with the Holy Spirit.' [17]If then God gave them the same gift that he gave us when we believed in the Lord Jesus Christ, who was I that I could hinder God?" [18]When they heard this, they were silenced. And they praised God, saying, "Then God has given even to the Gentiles the repentance that leads to life."

19 Now those who were scattered because of the persecution that took place over Stephen traveled as far as Phoenicia, Cyprus, and Antioch, and they spoke the word to no one except Jews. [20]But among them were some men of Cyprus and Cyrene who, on coming to Antioch, spoke to the Hellenists[b] also, proclaiming the Lord Jesus. [21]The hand of the Lord was with them, and a great number became believers and turned to the Lord. [22]News of this came to the ears of the church in Jerusalem, and they sent Barnabas to Antioch. [23]When he came and saw the grace of God, he rejoiced, and he exhorted them all to remain faithful to the Lord with steadfast devotion; [24]for he was a good man, full of the Holy Spirit and of faith. And a great many people

were brought to the Lord. [25]Then Barnabas went to Tarsus to look for Saul, [26]and when he had found him, he brought him to Antioch. So it was that for an entire year they met with[c] the church and taught a great many people, and it was in Antioch that the disciples were first called "Christians."

27 At that time prophets came down from Jerusalem to Antioch. [28]One of them named Agabus stood up and predicted by the Spirit that there would be a severe famine over all the world; and this took place during the reign of Claudius. [29]The disciples determined that according to their ability, each would send relief to the believers[d] living in Judea; [30]this they did, sending it to the elders by Barnabas and Saul.

## PSALM 135.1–21

Praise the Lord!
  Praise the name of the
    Lord;
  give praise, O servants of
    the Lord,
2  you that stand in the house of
    the Lord,
  in the courts of the house of
    our God.
3  Praise the Lord, for the Lord
    is good;
  sing to his name, for he is
    gracious.
4  For the Lord has chosen Jacob
    for himself,
  Israel as his own possession.

5  For I know that the Lord is
    great;
  our Lord is above all gods.
6  Whatever the Lord pleases he
    does,
  in heaven and on earth,
  in the seas and all deeps.

a Or *not to hesitate*  b Other ancient authorities read *Greeks*  c Or *were guests of*  d Gk *brothers*

7 He it is who makes the clouds
    rise at the end of the
    earth;
  he makes lightnings for the
    rain
  and brings out the wind from
    his storehouses.

8 He it was who struck down the
    firstborn of Egypt,
  both human beings and
    animals;
9 he sent signs and wonders
    into your midst, O Egypt,
  against Pharaoh and all his
    servants.
10 He struck down many nations
    and killed mighty kings—
11 Sihon, king of the Amorites,
    and Og, king of Bashan,
    and all the kingdoms of
    Canaan—
12 and gave their land as a
    heritage,
  a heritage to his people
    Israel.

13 Your name, O Lord, endures
    forever,
  your renown, O Lord,
    throughout all ages.
14 For the Lord will vindicate his
    people,
  and have compassion on his
    servants.

15 The idols of the nations are
    silver and gold,
  the work of human hands.
16 They have mouths, but they do
    not speak;
  they have eyes, but they do
    not see;
17 they have ears, but they do not
    hear,
  and there is no breath in their
    mouths.
18 Those who make them
  and all who trust them
  shall become like them.

19 O house of Israel, bless the
    Lord!
  O house of Aaron, bless the
    Lord!
20 O house of Levi, bless the
    Lord!
  You that fear the Lord, bless
    the Lord!
21 Blessed be the Lord from Zion,
  he who resides in Jerusalem.
Praise the Lord!

## PROVERBS 17.12–13

**B**ETTER to meet a she-bear
    robbed of its cubs
  than to confront a fool
    immersed in folly.
13 Evil will not depart from the
    house
  of one who returns evil for
    good.

# JUNE 18

## 1 KINGS 19.1–21

AHAB told Jezebel all that Elijah had done, and how he had killed all the prophets with the sword. ²Then Jezebel sent a messenger to Elijah, saying, "So may the gods do to me, and more also, if I do not make your life like the life of one of them by this time tomorrow." ³Then he was afraid; he got up and fled for his life, and came to Beer-sheba, which belongs to Judah; he left his servant there.

4 But he himself went a day's journey into the wilderness, and came and sat down under a solitary broom tree. He asked that he might die: "It is enough; now, O LORD, take away my life, for I am no better than my ancestors." ⁵Then he lay down under the broom tree and fell asleep. Suddenly an angel touched him and said to him, "Get up and eat." ⁶He looked, and there at his head was a cake baked on hot stones, and a jar of water. He ate and drank, and lay down again. ⁷The angel of the LORD came a second time, touched him, and said, "Get up and eat, otherwise the journey will be too much for you." ⁸He got up, and ate and drank; then he went in the strength of that food forty days and forty nights to Horeb the mount of God. ⁹At that place he came to a cave, and spent the night there.

Then the word of the LORD came to him, saying, "What are you doing here, Elijah?" ¹⁰He answered, "I have been very zealous for the LORD, the God of hosts; for the Israelites have forsaken your covenant, thrown down your altars, and killed your prophets with the sword. I alone am left, and they are seeking my life, to take it away."

11 He said, "Go out and stand on the mountain before the LORD, for the LORD is about to pass by." Now there was a great wind, so strong that it was splitting mountains and breaking rocks in pieces before the LORD, but the LORD was not in the wind; and after the wind an earthquake, but the LORD was not in the earthquake; ¹²and after the earthquake a fire, but the LORD was not in the fire; and after the fire a sound of sheer silence. ¹³When Elijah heard it, he wrapped his face in his mantle and went out and stood at the entrance of the cave. Then there came a voice to him that said, "What are you doing here, Elijah?" ¹⁴He answered, "I have been very zealous for the LORD, the God of hosts; for the Israelites have forsaken your covenant, thrown down your altars, and killed your prophets with the sword. I alone am left, and they are seeking my life, to take it away." ¹⁵Then the LORD said to him, "Go, return on your way to the wilderness of Damascus; when you arrive, you shall anoint Hazael as king over Aram. ¹⁶Also you shall anoint Jehu son of Nimshi as king over Israel; and you shall anoint Elisha son of Shaphat of Abel-meholah as prophet in your place. ¹⁷Whoever escapes from the sword of Hazael, Jehu shall kill; and whoever escapes from the sword of Jehu, Elisha shall kill. ¹⁸Yet I will leave seven thousand in Israel, all the knees that have not bowed to Baal, and every mouth that has not kissed him."

19 So he set out from there, and found Elisha son of Shaphat, who was plowing. There were twelve yoke of oxen ahead of him, and he was with the twelfth. Elijah passed by him and threw his mantle over him. ²⁰He left the oxen, ran after Elijah, and said, "Let me kiss my father and my mother, and then I

will follow you." Then Elijah[a] said to him, "Go back again; for what have I done to you?" <sup>21</sup>He returned from following him, took the yoke of oxen, and slaughtered them; using the equipment from the oxen, he boiled their flesh, and gave it to the people, and they ate. Then he set out and followed Elijah, and became his servant.

## ACTS 12.1–23

About that time King Herod laid violent hands upon some who belonged to the church. <sup>2</sup>He had James, the brother of John, killed with the sword. <sup>3</sup>After he saw that it pleased the Jews, he proceeded to arrest Peter also. (This was during the festival of Unleavened Bread.) <sup>4</sup>When he had seized him, he put him in prison and handed him over to four squads of soldiers to guard him, intending to bring him out to the people after the Passover. <sup>5</sup>While Peter was kept in prison, the church prayed fervently to God for him.

6 The very night before Herod was going to bring him out, Peter, bound with two chains, was sleeping between two soldiers, while guards in front of the door were keeping watch over the prison. <sup>7</sup>Suddenly an angel of the Lord appeared and a light shone in the cell. He tapped Peter on the side and woke him, saying, "Get up quickly." And the chains fell off his wrists. <sup>8</sup>The angel said to him, "Fasten your belt and put on your sandals." He did so. Then he said to him, "Wrap your cloak around you and follow me." <sup>9</sup>Peter[b] went out and followed him; he did not realize that what was happening with the angel's help was real; he thought he was seeing a vision. <sup>10</sup>After they had passed the first and the second guard, they came before the iron gate leading into the city. It opened for them of its own accord, and they went outside and walked along a lane, when suddenly the angel left him. <sup>11</sup>Then Peter came to himself and said, "Now I am sure that the Lord has sent his angel and rescued me from the hands of Herod and from all that the Jewish people were expecting."

12 As soon as he realized this, he went to the house of Mary, the mother of John whose other name was Mark, where many had gathered and were praying. <sup>13</sup>When he knocked at the outer gate, a maid named Rhoda came to answer. <sup>14</sup>On recognizing Peter's voice, she was so overjoyed that, instead of opening the gate, she ran in and announced that Peter was standing at the gate. <sup>15</sup>They said to her, "You are out of your mind!" But she insisted that it was so. They said, "It is his angel." <sup>16</sup>Meanwhile Peter continued knocking; and when they opened the gate, they saw him and were amazed. <sup>17</sup>He motioned to them with his hand to be silent, and described for them how the Lord had brought him out of the prison. And he added, "Tell this to James and to the believers."[c] Then he left and went to another place.

18 When morning came, there was no small commotion among the soldiers over what had become of Peter. <sup>19</sup>When Herod had searched for him and could not find him, he examined the guards and ordered them to be put to death. Then Peter[d] went down from Judea to Caesarea and stayed there.

20 Now Herod was angry with the people of Tyre and Sidon. So they came to him in a body; and after winning over Blastus, the king's chamberlain, they asked for a reconciliation, because their country depended on the king's country for food. <sup>21</sup>On an appointed day Herod put on his royal robes, took his seat on the platform, and delivered a public address to them. <sup>22</sup>The people kept shouting, "The voice of a god, and not of a mortal!" <sup>23</sup>And immediately, be-

aHeb *he*　bGk *He*　cGk *brothers*　dGk *he*

cause he had not given the glory to God, an angel of the Lord struck him down, and he was eaten by worms and died.

## PSALM 136.1–26

O GIVE thanks to the LORD, for he is good,
 for his steadfast love
  endures forever.
2 O give thanks to the God of
  gods,
  for his steadfast love endures
   forever.
3 O give thanks to the Lord of
  lords,
  for his steadfast love endures
   forever;

4 who alone does great wonders,
  for his steadfast love endures
   forever;
5 who by understanding made the
  heavens,
  for his steadfast love endures
   forever;
6 who spread out the earth on the
  waters,
  for his steadfast love endures
   forever;
7 who made the great lights,
  for his steadfast love endures
   forever;
8 the sun to rule over the day,
  for his steadfast love endures
   forever;
9 the moon and stars to rule over
  the night,
  for his steadfast love endures
   forever;

10 who struck Egypt through their
  firstborn,
  for his steadfast love endures
   forever;
11 and brought Israel out from
  among them,
  for his steadfast love endures
   forever;
12 with a strong hand and an
  outstretched arm,
  for his steadfast love endures
   forever;
13 who divided the Red Sea[a] in
  two,
  for his steadfast love endures
   forever;
14 and made Israel pass through
  the midst of it,
  for his steadfast love endures
   forever;
15 but overthrew Pharaoh and his
  army in the Red Sea, [a]
  for his steadfast love endures
   forever;
16 who led his people through the
  wilderness,
  for his steadfast love endures
   forever;
17 who struck down great kings,
  for his steadfast love endures
   forever;
18 and killed famous kings,
  for his steadfast love endures
   forever;
19 Sihon, king of the Amorites,
  for his steadfast love endures
   forever;
20 and Og, king of Bashan,
  for his steadfast love endures
   forever;
21 and gave their land as a
  heritage,
  for his steadfast love endures
   forever;
22 a heritage to his servant Israel,
  for his steadfast love endures
   forever.

23 It is he who remembered us in
  our low estate,
  for his steadfast love endures
   forever;
24 and rescued us from our foes,

a Or *Sea of Reeds*

      for his steadfast love endures
            forever;
25  who gives food to all flesh,
      for his steadfast love endures
            forever.

26  O give thanks to the God of
            heaven,
      for his steadfast love endures
            forever.

## PROVERBS 17.14–15

THE beginning of strife is like
            letting out water;
      so stop before the quarrel
            breaks out.
15  One who justifies the wicked
            and one who condemns
            the righteous
      are both alike an abomination
            to the LORD.

# JUNE 19

## 1 KINGS 20.1—21.29

KING Ben-hadad of Aram gathered all his army together; thirty-two kings were with him, along with horses and chariots. He marched against Samaria, laid siege to it, and attacked it. 2Then he sent messengers into the city to King Ahab of Israel, and said to him: "Thus says Ben-hadad: 3Your silver and gold are mine; your fairest wives and children also are mine." 4The king of Israel answered, "As you say, my lord, O king, I am yours, and all that I have." 5The messengers came again and said: "Thus says Ben-hadad: I sent to you, saying, 'Deliver to me your silver and gold, your wives and children'; 6nevertheless I will send my servants to you tomorrow about this time, and they shall search your house and the houses of your servants, and lay hands on whatever pleases them,ᵃ and take it away."

7  Then the king of Israel called all the elders of the land, and said, "Look now! See how this man is seeking trou-

ble; for he sent to me for my wives, my children, my silver, and my gold; and I did not refuse him." 8Then all the elders and all the people said to him, "Do not listen or consent." 9So he said to the messengers of Ben-hadad, "Tell my lord the king: All that you first demanded of your servant I will do; but this thing I cannot do." The messengers left and brought him word again. 10Ben-hadad sent to him and said, "The gods do so to me, and more also, if the dust of Samaria will provide a handful for each of the people who follow me." 11The king of Israel answered, "Tell him: One who puts on armor should not brag like one who takes it off." 12When Ben-hadad heard this message—now he had been drinking with the kings in the booths—he said to his men, "Take your positions!" And they took their positions against the city.

13  Then a certain prophet came up to King Ahab of Israel and said, "Thus says the LORD, Have you seen all this great multitude? Look, I will give it into your hand today; and you shall know

ᵃGk Syr Vg: Heb *you*

that I am the LORD." ¹⁴Ahab said, "By whom?" He said, "Thus says the LORD, By the young men who serve the district governors." Then he said, "Who shall begin the battle?" He answered, "You." ¹⁵Then he mustered the young men who serve the district governors, two hundred thirty-two; after them he mustered all the people of Israel, seven thousand.

16 They went out at noon, while Ben-hadad was drinking himself drunk in the booths, he and the thirty-two kings allied with him. ¹⁷The young men who serve the district governors went out first. Ben-hadad had sent out scouts, ᵃ and they reported to him, "Men have come out from Samaria." ¹⁸He said, "If they have come out for peace, take them alive; if they have come out for war, take them alive."

19 But these had already come out of the city: the young men who serve the district governors, and the army that followed them. ²⁰Each killed his man; the Arameans fled and Israel pursued them, but King Ben-hadad of Aram escaped on a horse with the cavalry. ²¹The king of Israel went out, attacked the horses and chariots, and defeated the Arameans with a great slaughter.

22 Then the prophet approached the king of Israel and said to him, "Come, strengthen yourself, and consider well what you have to do; for in the spring the king of Aram will come up against you."

23 The servants of the king of Aram said to him, "Their gods are gods of the hills, and so they were stronger than we; but let us fight against them in the plain, and surely we shall be stronger than they. ²⁴Also do this: remove the kings, each from his post, and put commanders in place of them; ²⁵and muster an army like the army that you have lost, horse for horse, and chariot for chariot; then we will fight against them in the plain, and surely we shall be stronger than they." He heeded their voice, and did so.

26 In the spring Ben-hadad mustered the Arameans and went up to Aphek to fight against Israel. ²⁷After the Israelites had been mustered and provisioned, they went out to engage them; the people of Israel encamped opposite them like two little flocks of goats, while the Arameans filled the country. ²⁸A man of God approached and said to the king of Israel, "Thus says the LORD: Because the Arameans have said, 'The LORD is a god of the hills but he is not a god of the valleys,' therefore I will give all this great multitude into your hand, and you shall know that I am the LORD." ²⁹They encamped opposite one another seven days. Then on the seventh day the battle began; the Israelites killed one hundred thousand Aramean foot soldiers in one day. ³⁰The rest fled into the city of Aphek; and the wall fell on twenty-seven thousand men that were left.

Ben-hadad also fled, and entered the city to hide. ³¹His servants said to him, "Look, we have heard that the kings of the house of Israel are merciful kings; let us put sackcloth around our waists and ropes on our heads, and go out to the king of Israel; perhaps he will spare your life." ³²So they tied sackcloth around their waists, put ropes on their heads, went to the king of Israel, and said, "Your servant Ben-hadad says, 'Please let me live.'" And he said, "Is he still alive? He is my brother." ³³Now the men were watching for an omen; they quickly took it up from him and said, "Yes, Ben-hadad is your brother." Then he said, "Go and bring him." So Ben-hadad came out to him; and he had him come up into the chariot. ³⁴Ben-hadadᵇ said to him, "I will restore the towns that my father took from your father; and you may establish bazaars for yourself in Damascus, as my father did in Samaria." The king of Israel responded, a "I will let you go on those terms." So he made a treaty with him and let him go.

35  At the command of the LORD a certain member of a company of prophets[b] said to another, "Strike me!" But the man refused to strike him. [36]Then he said to him, "Because you have not obeyed the voice of the LORD, as soon as you have left me, a lion will kill you." And when he had left him, a lion met him and killed him. [37]Then he found another man and said, "Strike me!" So the man hit him, striking and wounding him. [38]Then the prophet departed, and waited for the king along the road, disguising himself with a bandage over his eyes. [39]As the king passed by, he cried to the king and said, "Your servant went out into the thick of the battle; then a soldier turned and brought a man to me, and said, 'Guard this man; if he is missing, your life shall be given for his life, or else you shall pay a talent of silver.' [40]While your servant was busy here and there, he was gone." The king of Israel said to him, "So shall your judgment be; you yourself have decided it." [41]Then he quickly took the bandage away from his eyes. The king of Israel recognized him as one of the prophets. [42]Then he said to him, "Thus says the LORD, 'Because you have let the man go whom I had devoted to destruction, therefore your life shall be for his life, and your people for his people.' " [43]The king of Israel set out toward home, resentful and sullen, and came to Samaria.

21.1  LATER the following events took place: Naboth the Jezreelite had a vineyard in Jezreel, beside the palace of King Ahab of Samaria. [2]And Ahab said to Naboth, "Give me your vineyard, so that I may have it for a vegetable garden, because it is near my house; I will give you a better vineyard for it; or, if it seems good to you, I will give you its value in money." [3]But Naboth said to Ahab, "The LORD forbid that I should give you my ancestral inheritance." [4]Ahab went home resentful and sullen because of what Naboth the Jezreelite had said to him; for he had said, "I will not give you my ancestral inheritance." He lay down on his bed, turned away his face, and would not eat.

5  His wife Jezebel came to him and said, "Why are you so depressed that you will not eat?" [6]He said to her, "Because I spoke to Naboth the Jezreelite and said to him, 'Give me your vineyard for money; or else, if you prefer, I will give you another vineyard for it'; but he answered, 'I will not give you my vineyard.' " [7]His wife Jezebel said to him, "Do you now govern Israel? Get up, eat some food, and be cheerful; I will give you the vineyard of Naboth the Jezreelite."

8  So she wrote letters in Ahab's name and sealed them with his seal; she sent the letters to the elders and the nobles who lived with Naboth in his city. [9]She wrote in the letters, "Proclaim a fast, and seat Naboth at the head of the assembly; [10]seat two scoundrels opposite him, and have them bring a charge against him, saying, 'You have cursed God and the king.' Then take him out, and stone him to death." [11]The men of his city, the elders and the nobles who lived in his city, did as Jezebel had sent word to them. Just as it was written in the letters that she had sent to them, [12]they proclaimed a fast and seated Naboth at the head of the assembly. [13]The two scoundrels came in and sat opposite him; and the scoundrels brought a charge against Naboth, in the presence of the people, saying, "Naboth cursed

aHeb lacks *The king of Israel responded*  bHeb *of the sons of the prophets*

God and the king." So they took him outside the city, and stoned him to death. [14]Then they sent to Jezebel, saying, "Naboth has been stoned; he is dead."

15 As soon as Jezebel heard that Naboth had been stoned and was dead, Jezebel said to Ahab, "Go, take possession of the vineyard of Naboth the Jezreelite, which he refused to give you for money; for Naboth is not alive, but dead." [16]As soon as Ahab heard that Naboth was dead, Ahab set out to go down to the vineyard of Naboth the Jezreelite, to take possession of it.

17 Then the word of the LORD came to Elijah the Tishbite, saying: [18]Go down to meet King Ahab of Israel, who rules[a] in Samaria; he is now in the vineyard of Naboth, where he has gone to take possession. [19]You shall say to him, "Thus says the LORD: Have you killed, and also taken possession?" You shall say to him, "Thus says the LORD: In the place where dogs licked up the blood of Naboth, dogs will also lick up your blood."

20 Ahab said to Elijah, "Have you found me, O my enemy?" He answered, "I have found you. Because you have sold yourself to do what is evil in the sight of the LORD, [21]I will bring disaster on you; I will consume you, and will cut off from Ahab every male, bond or free, in Israel; [22]and I will make your house like the house of Jeroboam son of Nebat, and like the house of Baasha son of Ahijah, because you have provoked me to anger and have caused Israel to sin. [23]Also concerning Jezebel the LORD said, 'The dogs shall eat Jezebel within the bounds of Jezreel.' [24]Anyone belonging to Ahab who dies in the city the dogs shall eat; and anyone of his who dies in the open country the birds of the air shall eat."

25 (Indeed, there was no one like Ahab, who sold himself to do what was evil in the sight of the LORD, urged on by his wife Jezebel. [26]He acted most abominably in going after idols, as the Amorites had done, whom the LORD drove out before the Israelites.)

27 When Ahab heard those words, he tore his clothes and put sackcloth over his bare flesh; he fasted, lay in the sackcloth, and went about dejectedly. [28]Then the word of the LORD came to Elijah the Tishbite: [29]"Have you seen how Ahab has humbled himself before me? Because he has humbled himself before me, I will not bring the disaster in his days; but in his son's days I will bring the disaster on his house."

## ACTS 12.24—13.12

**B**UT the word of God continued to advance and gain adherents. [25]Then after completing their mission Barnabas and Saul returned to[b] Jerusalem and brought with them John, whose other name was Mark.

[13.1] Now in the church at Antioch there were prophets and teachers: Barnabas, Simeon who was called Niger, Lucius of Cyrene, Manaen a member of the court of Herod the ruler,[c] and Saul. [2]While they were worshiping the Lord and fasting, the Holy Spirit said, "Set apart for me Barnabas and Saul for the work to which I have called them." [3]Then after fasting and praying they laid their hands on them and sent them off.

4 So, being sent out by the Holy Spirit, they went down to Seleucia; and from there they sailed to Cyprus. [5]When they arrived at Salamis, they proclaimed the word of God in the synagogues of the Jews. And they had John also to assist them. [6]When they had gone through the whole island as far as Paphos, they met a certain magician, a Jewish false prophet, named Bar-

[a]Heb *who is*   [b]Other ancient authorities read *from*   [c]Gk *tetrarch*

Jesus. ⁷He was with the proconsul, Sergius Paulus, an intelligent man, who summoned Barnabas and Saul and wanted to hear the word of God. ⁸But the magician Elymas (for that is the translation of his name) opposed them and tried to turn the proconsul away from the faith. ⁹But Saul, also known as Paul, filled with the Holy Spirit, looked intently at him ¹⁰and said, "You son of the devil, you enemy of all righteousness, full of all deceit and villainy, will you not stop making crooked the straight paths of the Lord? ¹¹And now listen—the hand of the Lord is against you, and you will be blind for a while, unable to see the sun." Immediately mist and darkness came over him, and he went about groping for someone to lead him by the hand. ¹²When the proconsul saw what had happened, he believed, for he was astonished at the teaching about the Lord.

## PSALM 137.1–9

Bʏ the rivers of Babylon—
    there we sat down and there
        we wept
    when we remembered Zion.
2  On the willowsᵃ there
        we hung up our harps.
3  For there our captors
        asked us for songs,
    and our tormentors asked for
        mirth, saying,

"Sing us one of the songs of
    Zion!"

4  How could we sing the Lᴏʀᴅ's
        song
    in a foreign land?
5  If I forget you, O Jerusalem,
    let my right hand wither!
6  Let my tongue cling to the roof
        of my mouth,
    if I do not remember you,
    if I do not set Jerusalem
    above my highest joy.

7  Remember, O Lᴏʀᴅ, against the
        Edomites
    the day of Jerusalem's fall,
    how they said, "Tear it down!
        Tear it down!
    Down to its foundations!"
8  O daughter Babylon, you
        devastator!ᵇ
    Happy shall they be who pay
        you back
    what you have done to us!
9  Happy shall they be who take
        your little ones
    and dash them against the
        rock!

## PROVERBS 17.16

Wʜʏ should fools have a price
        in hand
    to buy wisdom, when they
        have no mind to learn?

ᵃOr *poplars*  ᵇOr *you who are devastated*

# JUNE 20



For three years Aram and Israel continued without war. [2]But in the third year King Jehoshaphat of Judah came down to the king of Israel. [3]The king of Israel said to his servants, "Do you know that Ramoth-gilead belongs to us, yet we are doing nothing to take it out of the hand of the king of Aram?" [4]He said to Jehoshaphat, "Will you go with me to battle at Ramoth-gilead?" Jehoshaphat replied to the king of Israel, "I am as you are; my people are your people, my horses are your horses."

[5] But Jehoshaphat also said to the king of Israel, "Inquire first for the word of the LORD." [6]Then the king of Israel gathered the prophets together, about four hundred of them, and said to them, "Shall I go to battle against Ramoth-gilead, or shall I refrain?" They said, "Go up; for the LORD will give it into the hand of the king." [7]But Jehoshaphat said, "Is there no other prophet of the LORD here of whom we may inquire?" [8]The king of Israel said to Jehoshaphat, "There is still one other by whom we may inquire of the LORD, Micaiah son of Imlah; but I hate him, for he never prophesies anything favorable about me, but only disaster." Jehoshaphat said, "Let the king not say such a thing." [9]Then the king of Israel summoned an officer and said, "Bring quickly Micaiah son of Imlah." [10]Now the king of Israel and King Jehoshaphat of Judah were sitting on their thrones, arrayed in their robes, at the threshing floor at the entrance of the gate of Samaria; and all the prophets were prophesying before them. [11]Zedekiah son of Chenaanah made for himself horns of iron, and he said, "Thus says the LORD: With these you shall gore the Arameans until they are destroyed." [12]All the prophets were prophesying the same and saying, "Go up to Ramoth-gilead and triumph; the LORD will give it into the hand of the king."

[13] The messenger who had gone to summon Micaiah said to him, "Look, the words of the prophets with one accord are favorable to the king; let your word be like the word of one of them, and speak favorably." [14]But Micaiah said, "As the LORD lives, whatever the LORD says to me, that I will speak."

[15] When he had come to the king, the king said to him, "Micaiah, shall we go to Ramoth-gilead to battle, or shall we refrain?" He answered him, "Go up and triumph; the LORD will give it into the hand of the king." [16]But the king said to him, "How many times must I make you swear to tell me nothing but the truth in the name of the LORD?" [17]Then Micaiah[a] said, "I saw all Israel scattered on the mountains, like sheep that have no shepherd; and the LORD said, 'These have no master; let each one go home in peace.'" [18]The king of Israel said to Jehoshaphat, "Did I not tell you that he would not prophesy anything favorable about me, but only disaster?"

[19] Then Micaiah[a] said, "Therefore hear the word of the LORD: I saw the LORD sitting on his throne, with all the host of heaven standing beside him to the right and to the left of him. [20]And the LORD said, 'Who will entice Ahab, so that he may go up and fall at Ramoth-gilead?' Then one said one thing, and another said another, [21]until a spirit came forward and stood before the

a Heb *he*

LORD, saying, 'I will entice him.' [22]'How?' the LORD asked him. He replied, 'I will go out and be a lying spirit in the mouth of all his prophets.' Then the LORD [a] said, 'You are to entice him, and you shall succeed; go out and do it.' [23]So you see, the LORD has put a lying spirit in the mouth of all these your prophets; the LORD has decreed disaster for you."

24 Then Zedekiah son of Chenaanah came up to Micaiah, slapped him on the cheek, and said, "Which way did the spirit of the LORD pass from me to speak to you?" [25]Micaiah replied, "You will find out on that day when you go in to hide in an inner chamber." [26]The king of Israel then ordered, "Take Micaiah, and return him to Amon the governor of the city and to Joash the king's son, [27]and say, 'Thus says the king: Put this fellow in prison, and feed him on reduced rations of bread and water until I come in peace.'" [28]Micaiah said, "If you return in peace, the LORD has not spoken by me." And he said, "Hear, you peoples, all of you!"

29 So the king of Israel and King Jehoshaphat of Judah went up to Ramoth-gilead. [30]The king of Israel said to Jehoshaphat, "I will disguise myself and go into battle, but you wear your robes." So the king of Israel disguised himself and went into battle. [31]Now the king of Aram had commanded the thirty-two captains of his chariots, "Fight with no one small or great, but only with the king of Israel." [32]When the captains of the chariots saw Jehoshaphat, they said, "It is surely the king of Israel." So they turned to fight against him; and Jehoshaphat cried out. [33]When the captains of the chariots saw that it was not the king of Israel, they turned back from pursuing him. [34]But a certain man drew his bow and unknowingly struck the king of Israel between the scale armor and the breastplate; so

he said to the driver of his chariot, "Turn around, and carry me out of the battle, for I am wounded." [35]The battle grew hot that day, and the king was propped up in his chariot facing the Arameans, until at evening he died; the blood from the wound had flowed into the bottom of the chariot. [36]Then about sunset a shout went through the army, "Every man to his city, and every man to his country!"

37 So the king died, and was brought to Samaria; they buried the king in Samaria. [38]They washed the chariot by the pool of Samaria; the dogs licked up his blood, and the prostitutes washed themselves in it, [b] according to the word of the LORD that he had spoken. [39]Now the rest of the acts of Ahab, and all that he did, and the ivory house that he built, and all the cities that he built, are they not written in the Book of the Annals of the Kings of Israel? [40]So Ahab slept with his ancestors; and his son Ahaziah succeeded him.

41 Jehoshaphat son of Asa began to reign over Judah in the fourth year of King Ahab of Israel. [42]Jehoshaphat was thirty-five years old when he began to reign, and he reigned twenty-five years in Jerusalem. His mother's name was Azubah daughter of Shilhi. [43]He walked in all the way of his father Asa; he did not turn aside from it, doing what was right in the sight of the LORD; yet the high places were not taken away, and the people still sacrificed and offered incense on the high places. [44]Jehoshaphat also made peace with the king of Israel.

45 Now the rest of the acts of Jehoshaphat, and his power that he showed, and how he waged war, are they not written in the Book of the Annals of the Kings of Judah? [46]The remnant of the male temple prostitutes who were still in the land in the days of his father Asa, he exterminated.

47 There was no king in Edom; a

deputy was king. [48]Jehoshaphat made ships of the Tarshish type to go to Ophir for gold; but they did not go, for the ships were wrecked at Ezion-geber. [49]Then Ahaziah son of Ahab said to Jehoshaphat, "Let my servants go with your servants in the ships," but Jehoshaphat was not willing. [50]Jehoshaphat slept with his ancestors and was buried with his ancestors in the city of his father David; his son Jehoram succeeded him.

51 Ahaziah son of Ahab began to reign over Israel in Samaria in the seventeenth year of King Jehoshaphat of Judah; he reigned two years over Israel. [52]He did what was evil in the sight of the LORD, and walked in the way of his father and mother, and in the way of Jeroboam son of Nebat, who caused Israel to sin. [53]He served Baal and worshiped him; he provoked the LORD, the God of Israel, to anger, just as his father had done.

## ACTS 13.13–41

THEN Paul and his companions set sail from Paphos and came to Perga in Pamphylia. John, however, left them and returned to Jerusalem; [14]but they went on from Perga and came to Antioch in Pisidia. And on the sabbath day they went into the synagogue and sat down. [15]After the reading of the law and the prophets, the officials of the synagogue sent them a message, saying, "Brothers, if you have any word of exhortation for the people, give it." [16]So Paul stood up and with a gesture began to speak:

"You Israelites, [a] and others who fear God, listen. [17]The God of this people Israel chose our ancestors and made the people great during their stay in the land of Egypt, and with uplifted arm he led them out of it. [18]For about forty years he put up with[b] them in the wilderness. [19]After he had destroyed seven nations in the land of Canaan, he gave them their land as an inheritance [20]for about four hundred fifty years. After that he gave them judges until the time of the prophet Samuel. [21]Then they asked for a king; and God gave them Saul son of Kish, a man of the tribe of Benjamin, who reigned for forty years. [22]When he had removed him, he made David their king. In his testimony about him he said, 'I have found David, son of Jesse, to be a man after my heart, who will carry out all my wishes.' [23]Of this man's posterity God has brought to Israel a Savior, Jesus, as he promised; [24]before his coming John had already proclaimed a baptism of repentance to all the people of Israel. [25]And as John was finishing his work, he said, 'What do you suppose that I am? I am not he. No, but one is coming after me; I am not worthy to untie the thong of the sandals[c] on his feet.'

26 "My brothers, you descendants of Abraham's family, and others who fear God, to us[d] the message of this salvation has been sent. [27]Because the residents of Jerusalem and their leaders did not recognize him or understand the words of the prophets that are read every sabbath, they fulfilled those words by condemning him. [28]Even though they found no cause for a sentence of death, they asked Pilate to have him killed. [29]When they had carried out everything that was written about him, they took him down from the tree and laid him in a tomb. [30]But God raised him from the dead; [31]and for many days he appeared to those who came up with him from Galilee to Jerusalem, and they are now his witnesses to the people. [32]And we bring you the good news that what God promised to our ancestors [33]he has fulfilled for us, their children, by raising Jesus; as also it is written in the second psalm,

[a] Gk *Men, Israelites*   [b] Other ancient authorities read *cared for*   [c] Gk *untie the sandals*   [d] Other ancient authorities read *you*

'You are my Son;
    today I have begotten you.'
[34]As to his raising him from the dead, no more to return to corruption, he has spoken in this way,
    'I will give you the holy
        promises made to David.'
[35]Therefore he has also said in another psalm,
    'You will not let your Holy One
        experience corruption.'
[36]For David, after he had served the purpose of God in his own generation, died,[a] was laid beside his ancestors, and experienced corruption; [37]but he whom God raised up experienced no corruption. [38]Let it be known to you therefore, my brothers, that through this man forgiveness of sins is proclaimed to you; [39]by this Jesus[b] everyone who believes is set free from all those sins[c] from which you could not be freed by the law of Moses. [40]Beware, therefore, that what the prophets said does not happen to you:
[41]    'Look, you scoffers!
        Be amazed and perish,
    for in your days I am doing a
        work,
    a work that you will never
        believe, even if someone
        tells you.' "

## PSALM 138. 1–8

*Of David.*

I GIVE you thanks, O LORD, with
        my whole heart;
    before the gods I sing your
        praise;
[2]    I bow down toward your holy
        temple
    and give thanks to your name
        for your steadfast love
        and your faithfulness;
for you have exalted your
    name and your word
    above everything. [d]
[3]    On the day I called, you
        answered me,
    you increased my strength of
        soul. [e]

[4]    All the kings of the earth shall
        praise you, O LORD,
    for they have heard the
        words of your mouth.
[5]    They shall sing of the ways of
        the LORD,
    for great is the glory of the
        LORD.
[6]    For though the LORD is high, he
        regards the lowly;
    but the haughty he perceives
        from far away.

[7]    Though I walk in the midst of
        trouble,
    you preserve me against the
        wrath of my enemies;
    you stretch out your hand,
        and your right hand delivers
        me.
[8]    The LORD will fulfill his purpose
        for me;
    your steadfast love, O LORD,
        endures forever.
    Do not forsake the work of
        your hands.

## PROVERBS 17. 17–18

A FRIEND loves at all times,
        and kinsfolk are born to
        share adversity.
[18]    It is senseless to give a pledge,
        to become surety for a
        neighbor.

aGk *fell asleep*   bGk *this*   cGk *all*   dCn: Heb *you have exalted your word above all your name*
eSyr Compare Gk Tg: Heb *you made me arrogant in my soul with strength*

# JUNE 21

2 KINGS 1.1—2.25

**A**FTER the death of Ahab, Moab rebelled against Israel. 2 Ahaziah had fallen through the lattice in his upper chamber in Samaria, and lay injured; so he sent messengers, telling them, "Go, inquire of Baal-zebub, the god of Ekron, whether I shall recover from this injury." ³But the angel of the LORD said to Elijah the Tishbite, "Get up, go to meet the messengers of the king of Samaria, and say to them, 'Is it because there is no God in Israel that you are going to inquire of Baal-zebub, the god of Ekron?' ⁴Now therefore thus says the LORD, 'You shall not leave the bed to which you have gone, but you shall surely die.'" So Elijah went.

5 The messengers returned to the king, who said to them, "Why have you returned?" ⁶They answered him, "There came a man to meet us, who said to us, 'Go back to the king who sent you, and say to him: Thus says the LORD: Is it because there is no God in Israel that you are sending to inquire of Baal-zebub, the god of Ekron? Therefore you shall not leave the bed to which you have gone, but shall surely die.'" ⁷He said to them, "What sort of man was he who came to meet you and told you these things?" ⁸They answered him, "A hairy man, with a leather belt around his waist." He said, "It is Elijah the Tishbite."

9 Then the king sent to him a captain of fifty with his fifty men. He went up to Elijah, who was sitting on the top of a hill, and said to him, "O man of God, the king says, 'Come down.'" ¹⁰But Elijah answered the captain of fifty, "If I am a man of God, let fire come down from heaven and consume you and your fifty." Then fire came down from heaven, and consumed him and his fifty.

11 Again the king sent to him another captain of fifty with his fifty. He went up[a] and said to him, "O man of God, this is the king's order: Come down quickly!" ¹²But Elijah answered them, "If I am a man of God, let fire come down from heaven and consume you and your fifty." Then the fire of God came down from heaven and consumed him and his fifty.

13 Again the king sent the captain of a third fifty with his fifty. So the third captain of fifty went up, and came and fell on his knees before Elijah, and entreated him, "O man of God, please let my life, and the life of these fifty servants of yours, be precious in your sight. ¹⁴Look, fire came down from heaven and consumed the two former captains of fifty men with their fifties; but now let my life be precious in your sight." ¹⁵Then the angel of the LORD said to Elijah, "Go down with him; do not be afraid of him." So he set out and went down with him to the king, ¹⁶and said to him, "Thus says the LORD: Because you have sent messengers to inquire of Baal-zebub, the god of Ekron,—is it because there is no God in Israel to inquire of his word?—therefore you shall not leave the bed to which you have gone, but you shall surely die."

17 So he died according to the word of the LORD that Elijah had spoken. His brother,[b] Jehoram succeeded him as king in the second year of King Jehoram son of Jehoshaphat of Judah, because Ahaziah had no son. ¹⁸Now the rest of

the acts of Ahaziah that he did, are they not written in the Book of the Annals of the Kings of Israel?

2.1 Now when the LORD was about to take Elijah up to heaven by a whirlwind, Elijah and Elisha were on their way from Gilgal. ²Elijah said to Elisha, "Stay here; for the LORD has sent me as far as Bethel." But Elisha said, "As the LORD lives, and as you yourself live, I will not leave you." So they went down to Bethel. ³The company of prophetsᵃ who were in Bethel came out to Elisha, and said to him, "Do you know that today the LORD will take your master away from you?" And he said, "Yes, I know; keep silent."

4 Elijah said to him, "Elisha, stay here; for the LORD has sent me to Jericho." But he said, "As the LORD lives, and as you yourself live, I will not leave you." So they came to Jericho. ⁵The company of prophetsᵃ who were at Jericho drew near to Elisha, and said to him, "Do you know that today the LORD will take your master away from you?" And he answered, "Yes, I know; be silent."

6 Then Elijah said to him, "Stay here; for the LORD has sent me to the Jordan." But he said, "As the LORD lives, and as you yourself live, I will not leave you." So the two of them went on. ⁷Fifty men of the company of prophetsᵃ also went, and stood at some distance from them, as they both were standing by the Jordan. ⁸Then Elijah took his mantle and rolled it up, and struck the water; the water was parted to the one side and to the other, until the two of them crossed on dry ground.

9 When they had crossed, Elijah said to Elisha, "Tell me what I may do for you, before I am taken from you." Elisha said, "Please let me inherit a double share of your spirit." ¹⁰He responded, "You have asked a hard thing;

yet, if you see me as I am being taken from you, it will be granted you; if not, it will not." ¹¹As they continued walking and talking, a chariot of fire and horses of fire separated the two of them, and Elijah ascended in a whirlwind into heaven. ¹²Elisha kept watching and crying out, "Father, father! The chariots of Israel and its horsemen!" But when he could no longer see him, he grasped his own clothes and tore them in two pieces.

13 He picked up the mantle of Elijah that had fallen from him, and went back and stood on the bank of the Jordan. ¹⁴He took the mantle of Elijah that had fallen from him, and struck the water, saying, "Where is the LORD, the God of Elijah?" When he had struck the water, the water was parted to the one side and to the other, and Elisha went over.

15 When the company of prophetsᵃ who were at Jericho saw him at a distance, they declared, "The spirit of Elijah rests on Elisha." They came to meet him and bowed to the ground before him. ¹⁶They said to him, "See now, we have fifty strong men among your servants; please let them go and seek your master; it may be that the spirit of the LORD has caught him up and thrown him down on some mountain or into some valley." He responded, "No, do not send them." ¹⁷But when they urged him until he was ashamed, he said, "Send them." So they sent fifty men who searched for three days but did not find him. ¹⁸When they came back to him (he had remained at Jericho), he said to them, "Did I not say to you, Do not go?"

19 Now the people of the city said to Elisha, "The location of this city is good, as my lord sees; but the water is bad, and the land is unfruitful." ²⁰He said, "Bring me a new bowl, and put salt in it." So they brought it to him.

ᵃHeb *sons of the prophets*

²¹Then he went to the spring of water and threw the salt into it, and said, "Thus says the LORD, I have made this water wholesome; from now on neither death nor miscarriage shall come from it." ²²So the water has been wholesome to this day, according to the word that Elisha spoke.

23 He went up from there to Bethel; and while he was going up on the way, some small boys came out of the city and jeered at him, saying, "Go away, baldhead! Go away, baldhead!" ²⁴When he turned around and saw them, he cursed them in the name of the LORD. Then two she-bears came out of the woods and mauled forty-two of the boys. ²⁵From there he went on to Mount Carmel, and then returned to Samaria.

## ACTS 13.42—14.7

As Paul and Barnabasᵃ were going out, the people urged them to speak about these things again the next sabbath. ⁴³When the meeting of the synagogue broke up, many Jews and devout converts to Judaism followed Paul and Barnabas, who spoke to them and urged them to continue in the grace of God.

44 The next sabbath almost the whole city gathered to hear the word of the Lord.ᵇ ⁴⁵But when the Jews saw the crowds, they were filled with jealousy; and blaspheming, they contradicted what was spoken by Paul. ⁴⁶Then both Paul and Barnabas spoke out boldly, saying, "It was necessary that the word of God should be spoken first to you. Since you reject it and judge yourselves to be unworthy of eternal life, we are now turning to the Gentiles. ⁴⁷For so the Lord has commanded us, saying,

'I have set you to be a light for
    the Gentiles,
        so that you may bring
            salvation to the ends of
                the earth.' "

48 When the Gentiles heard this, they were glad and praised the word of the Lord; and as many as had been destined for eternal life became believers. ⁴⁹Thus the word of the Lord spread throughout the region. ⁵⁰But the Jews incited the devout women of high standing and the leading men of the city, and stirred up persecution against Paul and Barnabas, and drove them out of their region. ⁵¹So they shook the dust off their feet in protest against them, and went to Iconium. ⁵²And the disciples were filled with joy and with the Holy Spirit.

14.1 THE same thing occurred in Iconium, where Paul and Barnabasᵃ went into the Jewish synagogue and spoke in such a way that a great number of both Jews and Greeks became believers. ²But the unbelieving Jews stirred up the Gentiles and poisoned their minds against the brothers. ³So they remained for a long time, speaking boldly for the Lord, who testified to the word of his grace by granting signs and wonders to be done through them. ⁴But the residents of the city were divided; some sided with the Jews, and some with the apostles. ⁵And when an attempt was made by both Gentiles and Jews, with their rulers, to mistreat them and to stone them, ⁶the apostlesᵃ learned of it and fled to Lystra and Derbe, cities of Lycaonia, and to the surrounding country; ⁷and there they continued proclaiming the good news.

ᵃGk *they*   ᵇOther ancient authorities read *God*

## PSALM 139.1–24

*To the leader. Of David. A Psalm.*

O LORD, you have searched me
and known me.
2   You know when I sit
down and when I rise up;
you discern my thoughts from
far away.
3   You search out my path and my
lying down,
and are acquainted with all
my ways.
4   Even before a word is on my
tongue,
O LORD, you know it
completely.
5   You hem me in, behind and
before,
and lay your hand upon me.
6   Such knowledge is too
wonderful for me;
it is so high that I cannot
attain it.

7   Where can I go from your
spirit?
Or where can I flee from your
presence?
8   If I ascend to heaven, you are
there;
if I make my bed in Sheol,
you are there.
9   If I take the wings of the
morning
and settle at the farthest
limits of the sea,
10   even there your hand shall
lead me,
and your right hand shall hold
me fast.
11   If I say, "Surely the darkness
shall cover me,
and the light around me
become night,"
12   even the darkness is not dark
to you;
the night is as bright as the
day,

for darkness is as light to
you.

13   For it was you who formed my
inward parts;
you knit me together in my
mother's womb.
14   I praise you, for I am fearfully
and wonderfully made.
Wonderful are your works;
that I know very well.
15   My frame was not hidden
from you,
when I was being made in
secret,
intricately woven in the
depths of the earth.
16   Your eyes beheld my unformed
substance.
In your book were written
all the days that were formed
for me,
when none of them as yet
existed.
17   How weighty to me are your
thoughts, O God!
How vast is the sum of them!
18   I try to count them—they are
more than the sand;
I come to the end[a]—I am
still with you.

19   O that you would kill the
wicked, O God,
and that the bloodthirsty
would depart from me—
20   those who speak of you
maliciously,
and lift themselves up against
you for evil![b]
21   Do I not hate those who hate
you, O LORD?
And do I not loathe those
who rise up against you?
22   I hate them with perfect hatred;
I count them my enemies.
23   Search me, O God, and know
my heart;

a Or *I awake*   b Cn: Meaning of Heb uncertain

    test me and know my
        thoughts.
24 See if there is any wicked[a] way
    in me,
    and lead me in the way
        everlasting. [b]

## PROVERBS 17.19–21

One who loves transgression
    loves strife;
one who builds a high
    threshold invites broken
    bones.

20 The crooked of mind do not
    prosper,
    and the perverse of tongue
        fall into calamity.
21 The one who begets a fool gets
    trouble;
    the parent of a fool has no
        joy.

# JUNE 22

## 2 KINGS 3.1—4.17

In the eighteenth year of King Jehoshaphat of Judah, Jehoram son of Ahab became king over Israel in Samaria; he reigned twelve years. ²He did what was evil in the sight of the Lord, though not like his father and mother, for he removed the pillar of Baal that his father had made. ³Nevertheless he clung to the sin of Jeroboam son of Nebat, which he caused Israel to commit; he did not depart from it.

4 Now King Mesha of Moab was a sheep breeder, who used to deliver to the king of Israel one hundred thousand lambs, and the wool of one hundred thousand rams. ⁵But when Ahab died, the king of Moab rebelled against the king of Israel. ⁶So King Jehoram marched out of Samaria at that time and mustered all Israel. ⁷As he went he sent word to King Jehoshaphat of Judah, "The king of Moab has rebelled against me; will you go with me to battle against Moab?" He answered, "I will; I am with you, my people are your people, my horses are your horses." ⁸Then he asked, "By which way shall we march?" Jehoram answered, "By the way of the wilderness of Edom."

9 So the king of Israel, the king of Judah, and the king of Edom set out; and when they had made a roundabout march of seven days, there was no water for the army or for the animals that were with them. ¹⁰Then the king of Israel said, "Alas! The Lord has summoned us, three kings, only to be handed over to Moab." ¹¹But Jehoshaphat said, "Is there no prophet of the Lord here, through whom we may inquire of the Lord?" Then one of the servants of the king of Israel answered, "Elisha son of Shaphat, who used to pour water on the hands of Elijah, is here." ¹²Jehoshaphat said, "The word of the Lord is with him." So the king of Israel and Jehoshaphat and the king of Edom went down to him.

13 Elisha said to the king of Israel,

aHeb *hurtful*  bOr *the ancient way*. Compare Jer 6.16

"What have I to do with you? Go to your father's prophets or to your mother's." But the king of Israel said to him, "No; it is the LORD who has summoned us, three kings, only to be handed over to Moab." [14]Elisha said, "As the LORD of hosts lives, whom I serve, were it not that I have regard for King Jehoshaphat of Judah, I would give you neither a look nor a glance. [15]But get me a musician." And then, while the musician was playing, the power of the LORD came on him. [16]And he said, "Thus says the LORD, 'I will make this wadi full of pools.' [17]For thus says the LORD, 'You shall see neither wind nor rain, but the wadi shall be filled with water, so that you shall drink, you, your cattle, and your animals.' [18]This is only a trifle in the sight of the LORD, for he will also hand Moab over to you. [19]You shall conquer every fortified city and every choice city; every good tree you shall fell, all springs of water you shall stop up, and every good piece of land you shall ruin with stones." [20]The next day, about the time of the morning offering, suddenly water began to flow from the direction of Edom, until the country was filled with water.

21 When all the Moabites heard that the kings had come up to fight against them, all who were able to put on armor, from the youngest to the oldest, were called out and were drawn up at the frontier. [22]When they rose early in the morning, and the sun shone upon the water, the Moabites saw the water opposite them as red as blood. [23]They said, "This is blood; the kings must have fought together, and killed one another. Now then, Moab, to the spoil!" [24]But when they came to the camp of Israel, the Israelites rose up and attacked the Moabites, who fled before them; as they entered Moab they continued the attack. [a] [25]The cities they overturned, and on every good piece of land everyone threw a stone, until it was covered; every spring of water they stopped up, and every good tree they felled. Only at Kir-hareseth did the stone walls remain, until the slingers surrounded and attacked it. [26]When the king of Moab saw that the battle was going against him, he took with him seven hundred swordsmen to break through, opposite the king of Edom; but they could not. [27]Then he took his firstborn son who was to succeed him, and offered him as a burnt offering on the wall. And great wrath came upon Israel, so they withdrew from him and returned to their own land.

[4.1] Now the wife of a member of the company of prophets[b] cried to Elisha, "Your servant my husband is dead; and you know that your servant feared the LORD, but a creditor has come to take my two children as slaves." [2]Elisha said to her, "What shall I do for you? Tell me, what do you have in the house?" She answered, "Your servant has nothing in the house, except a jar of oil." [3]He said, "Go outside, borrow vessels from all your neighbors, empty vessels and not just a few. [4]Then go in, and shut the door behind you and your children, and start pouring into all these vessels; when each is full, set it aside." [5]So she left him and shut the door behind her and her children; they kept bringing vessels to her, and she kept pouring. [6]When the vessels were full, she said to her son, "Bring me another vessel." But he said to her, "There are no more." Then the oil stopped flowing. [7]She came and told the man of God, and he said, "Go sell the oil and pay your debts, and you and your children can live on the rest."

8 One day Elisha was passing through Shunem, where a wealthy woman lived, who urged him to have a meal. So whenever he passed that way,

---

[a]Compare Gk Syr: Meaning of Heb uncertain   [b]Heb *the sons of the prophets*

he would stop there for a meal. ⁹She said to her husband, "Look, I am sure that this man who regularly passes our way is a holy man of God. ¹⁰Let us make a small roof chamber with walls, and put there for him a bed, a table, a chair, and a lamp, so that he can stay there whenever he comes to us."

11 One day when he came there, he went up to the chamber and lay down there. ¹²He said to his servant Gehazi, "Call the Shunammite woman." When he had called her, she stood before him. ¹³He said to him, "Say to her, Since you have taken all this trouble for us, what may be done for you? Would you have a word spoken on your behalf to the king or to the commander of the army?" She answered, "I live among my own people." ¹⁴He said, "What then may be done for her?" Gehazi answered, "Well, she has no son, and her husband is old." ¹⁵He said, "Call her." When he had called her, she stood at the door. ¹⁶He said, "At this season, in due time, you shall embrace a son." She replied, "No, my lord, O man of God; do not deceive your servant."

17 The woman conceived and bore a son at that season, in due time, as Elisha had declared to her.

## ACTS 14.8–28

IN Lystra there was a man sitting who could not use his feet and had never walked, for he had been crippled from birth. ⁹He listened to Paul as he was speaking. And Paul, looking at him intently and seeing that he had faith to be healed, ¹⁰said in a loud voice, "Stand upright on your feet." And the manᵃ sprang up and began to walk. ¹¹When the crowds saw what Paul had done, they shouted in the Lycaonian language, "The gods have come down to us in human form!" ¹²Barnabas they called Zeus, and Paul they called Hermes, because he was the chief speaker. ¹³The priest of Zeus, whose temple was just outside the city,ᵇ brought oxen and garlands to the gates; he and the crowds wanted to offer sacrifice. ¹⁴When the apostles Barnabas and Paul heard of it, they tore their clothes and rushed out into the crowd, shouting, ¹⁵"Friends,ᶜ why are you doing this? We are mortals just like you, and we bring you good news, that you should turn from these worthless things to the living God, who made the heaven and the earth and the sea and all that is in them. ¹⁶In past generations he allowed all the nations to follow their own ways; ¹⁷yet he has not left himself without a witness in doing good—giving you rains from heaven and fruitful seasons, and filling you with food and your hearts with joy." ¹⁸Even with these words, they scarcely restrained the crowds from offering sacrifice to them.

19 But Jews came there from Antioch and Iconium and won over the crowds. Then they stoned Paul and dragged him out of the city, supposing that he was dead. ²⁰But when the disciples surrounded him, he got up and went into the city. The next day he went on with Barnabas to Derbe.

21 After they had proclaimed the good news to that city and had made many disciples, they returned to Lystra, then on to Iconium and Antioch. ²²There they strengthened the souls of the disciples and encouraged them to continue in the faith, saying, "It is through many persecutions that we must enter the kingdom of God." ²³And after they had appointed elders for them in each church, with prayer and fasting they entrusted them to the Lord in whom they had come to believe.

24 Then they passed through Pisidia and came to Pamphylia. ²⁵When they had spoken the word in Perga,

ᵃGk *he*　ᵇOr *The priest of Zeus-Outside-the-City*　ᶜGk *Men*

they went down to Attalia. ²⁶From there they sailed back to Antioch, where they had been commended to the grace of God for the work[a] that they had completed. ²⁷When they arrived, they called the church together and related all that God had done with them, and how he had opened a door of faith for the Gentiles. ²⁸And they stayed there with the disciples for some time.

## PSALM 140.1–13

*To the leader. A Psalm of David.*

**D**ELIVER me, O LORD, from evildoers;
    protect me from those who are violent,
2 who plan evil things in their minds
    and stir up wars continually.
3 They make their tongue sharp as a snake's,
    and under their lips is the venom of vipers.    *Selah*

4 Guard me, O LORD, from the hands of the wicked;
    protect me from the violent who have planned my downfall.
5 The arrogant have hidden a trap for me,
    and with cords they have spread a net,[b]
    along the road they have set snares for me.    *Selah*

6 I say to the LORD, "You are my God;

give ear, O LORD, to the voice of my supplications."
7 O LORD, my Lord, my strong deliverer,
    you have covered my head in the day of battle.
8 Do not grant, O LORD, the desires of the wicked;
    do not further their evil plot.[c]    *Selah*

9 Those who surround me lift up their heads;[d]
    let the mischief of their lips overwhelm them!
10 Let burning coals fall on them!
    Let them be flung into pits, no more to rise!
11 Do not let the slanderer be established in the land;
    let evil speedily hunt down the violent!

12 I know that the LORD maintains the cause of the needy,
    and executes justice for the poor.
13 Surely the righteous shall give thanks to your name;
    the upright shall live in your presence.

## PROVERBS 17.22

**A** CHEERFUL heart is a good medicine,
    but a downcast spirit dries up the bones.

---

[a]Or *committed in the grace of God to the work*   [b]Or *they have spread cords as a net*   [c]Heb adds *they are exalted*   [d]Cn Compare Gk: Heb *those who surround me are uplifted in head*; Heb divides verses 8 and 9 differently

## 2 KINGS 4.18—5.27

**W**HEN the child was older, he went out one day to his father among the reapers. [19]He complained to his father, "Oh, my head, my head!" The father said to his servant, "Carry him to his mother." [20]He carried him and brought him to his mother; the child sat on her lap until noon, and he died. [21]She went up and laid him on the bed of the man of God, closed the door on him, and left. [22]Then she called to her husband, and said, "Send me one of the servants and one of the donkeys, so that I may quickly go to the man of God and come back again." [23]He said, "Why go to him today? It is neither new moon nor sabbath." She said, "It will be all right." [24]Then she saddled the donkey and said to her servant, "Urge the animal on; do not hold back for me unless I tell you." [25]So she set out, and came to the man of God at Mount Carmel.

When the man of God saw her coming, he said to Gehazi his servant, "Look, there is the Shunammite woman; [26]run at once to meet her, and say to her, Are you all right? Is your husband all right? Is the child all right?" She answered, "It is all right." [27]When she came to the man of God at the mountain, she caught hold of his feet. Gehazi approached to push her away. But the man of God said, "Let her alone, for she is in bitter distress; the LORD has hidden it from me and has not told me." [28]Then she said, "Did I ask my lord for a son? Did I not say, Do not mislead me?" [29]He said to Gehazi, "Gird up your loins, and take my staff in your hand, and go. If you meet anyone, give no greeting, and if anyone greets you, do not answer; and lay my staff on the face of the child." [30]Then the mother of the child said, "As the LORD lives, and as you yourself live, I will not leave without you." So he rose up and followed her. [31]Gehazi went on ahead and laid the staff on the face of the child, but there was no sound or sign of life. He came back to meet him and told him, "The child has not awakened."

32 When Elisha came into the house, he saw the child lying dead on his bed. [33]So he went in and closed the door on the two of them, and prayed to the LORD. [34]Then he got up on the bed[a] and lay upon the child, putting his mouth upon his mouth, his eyes upon his eyes, and his hands upon his hands; and while he lay bent over him, the flesh of the child became warm. [35]He got down, walked once to and fro in the room, then got up again and bent over him; the child sneezed seven times, and the child opened his eyes. [36]Elisha[b] summoned Gehazi and said, "Call the Shunammite woman." So he called her. When she came to him, he said, "Take your son." [37]She came and fell at his feet, bowing to the ground; then she took her son and left.

38 When Elisha returned to Gilgal, there was a famine in the land. As the company of prophets was[c] sitting before him, he said to his servant, "Put the large pot on, and make some stew for the company of prophets."[d] [39]One of them went out into the field to gather herbs; he found a wild vine and gathered from it a lapful of wild gourds, and came and cut them up into the pot of stew, not knowing what they were. [40]They served some for the men to eat.

---

aHeb lacks *on the bed*   bHeb *he*   cHeb *sons of the prophets were*   dHeb *sons of the prophets*

But while they were eating the stew, they cried out, "O man of God, there is death in the pot!" They could not eat it. ⁴¹He said, "Then bring some flour." He threw it into the pot, and said, "Serve the people and let them eat." And there was nothing harmful in the pot.

42 A man came from Baal-shalishah, bringing food from the first fruits to the man of God: twenty loaves of barley and fresh ears of grain in his sack. Elisha said, "Give it to the people and let them eat." ⁴³But his servant said, "How can I set this before a hundred people?" So he repeated, "Give it to the people and let them eat, for thus says the Lord, 'They shall eat and have some left.'" ⁴⁴He set it before them, they ate, and had some left, according to the word of the Lord.

5.1 Naaman, commander of the army of the king of Aram, was a great man and in high favor with his master, because by him the Lord had given victory to Aram. The man, though a mighty warrior, suffered from leprosy.ᵃ ²Now the Arameans on one of their raids had taken a young girl captive from the land of Israel, and she served Naaman's wife. ³She said to her mistress, "If only my lord were with the prophet who is in Samaria! He would cure him of his leprosy."ᵃ ⁴So Naamanᵇ went in and told his lord just what the girl from the land of Israel had said. ⁵And the king of Aram said, "Go then, and I will send along a letter to the king of Israel."

He went, taking with him ten talents of silver, six thousand shekels of gold, and ten sets of garments. ⁶He brought the letter to the king of Israel, which read, "When this letter reaches you, know that I have sent to you my servant Naaman, that you may cure him of his leprosy."ᵃ ⁷When the king of Israel read the letter, he tore his clothes and said, "Am I God, to give death or life, that this man sends word to me to cure a man of his leprosy?ᵃ Just look and see how he is trying to pick a quarrel with me."

8 But when Elisha the man of God heard that the king of Israel had torn his clothes, he sent a message to the king, "Why have you torn your clothes? Let him come to me, that he may learn that there is a prophet in Israel." ⁹So Naaman came with his horses and chariots, and halted at the entrance of Elisha's house. ¹⁰Elisha sent a messenger to him, saying, "Go, wash in the Jordan seven times, and your flesh shall be restored and you shall be clean." ¹¹But Naaman became angry and went away, saying, "I thought that for me he would surely come out, and stand and call on the name of the Lord his God, and would wave his hand over the spot, and cure the leprosy!ᵃ ¹²Are not Abanaᶜ and Pharpar, the rivers of Damascus, better than all the waters of Israel? Could I not wash in them, and be clean?" He turned and went away in a rage. ¹³But his servants approached and said to him, "Father, if the prophet had commanded you to do something difficult, would you not have done it? How much more, when all he said to you was, 'Wash, and be clean'?" ¹⁴So he went down and immersed himself seven times in the Jordan, according to the word of the man of God; his flesh was restored like the flesh of a young boy, and he was clean.

15 Then he returned to the man of God, he and all his company; he came and stood before him and said, "Now I know that there is no God in all the earth except in Israel; please accept a present from your servant." ¹⁶But he said, "As the Lord lives, whom I serve, I will accept nothing!" He urged him to accept, but he refused. ¹⁷Then Naaman said, "If not, please let two mule-loads of earth be given to your servant; for

ᵃA term for several skin diseases; precise meaning uncertain  ᵇHeb *he*  ᶜAnother reading is *Amana* your servant will no longer offer burnt offering or sacrifice to any god except the LORD. [18]But may the LORD pardon your servant on one count: when my master goes into the house of Rimmon to worship there, leaning on my arm, and I bow down in the house of Rimmon, when I do bow down in the house of Rimmon, may the LORD pardon your servant on this one count." [19]He said to him, "Go in peace."

But when Naaman had gone from him a short distance, [20]Gehazi, the servant of Elisha the man of God, thought, "My master has let that Aramean Naaman off too lightly by not accepting from him what he offered. As the LORD lives, I will run after him and get something out of him." [21]So Gehazi went after Naaman. When Naaman saw someone running after him, he jumped down from the chariot to meet him and said, "Is everything all right?" [22]He replied, "Yes, but my master has sent me to say, 'Two members of a company of prophets[a] have just come to me from the hill country of Ephraim; please give them a talent of silver and two changes of clothing.'" [23]Naaman said, "Please accept two talents." He urged him, and tied up two talents of silver in two bags, with two changes of clothing, and gave them to two of his servants, who carried them in front of Gehazi.[b] [24]When he came to the citadel, he took the bags[c] from them, and stored them inside; he dismissed the men, and they left.

25  He went in and stood before his master; and Elisha said to him, "Where have you been, Gehazi?" He answered, "Your servant has not gone anywhere at all." [26]But he said to him, "Did I not go with you in spirit when someone left his chariot to meet you? Is this a time to accept money and to accept clothing, olive orchards and vineyards, sheep and oxen, and male and female slaves?

[27]Therefore the leprosy[d] of Naaman shall cling to you, and to your descendants forever." So he left his presence leprous,[d] as white as snow.

## ACTS 15. 1–35

THEN certain individuals came down from Judea and were teaching the brothers, "Unless you are circumcised according to the custom of Moses, you cannot be saved." [2]And after Paul and Barnabas had no small dissension and debate with them, Paul and Barnabas and some of the others were appointed to go up to Jerusalem to discuss this question with the apostles and the elders. [3]So they were sent on their way by the church, and as they passed through both Phoenicia and Samaria, they reported the conversion of the Gentiles, and brought great joy to all the believers.[e] [4]When they came to Jerusalem, they were welcomed by the church and the apostles and the elders, and they reported all that God had done with them. [5]But some believers who belonged to the sect of the Pharisees stood up and said, "It is necessary for them to be circumcised and ordered to keep the law of Moses."

6  The apostles and the elders met together to consider this matter. [7]After there had been much debate, Peter stood up and said to them, "My brothers,[f] you know that in the early days God made a choice among you, that I should be the one through whom the Gentiles would hear the message of the good news and become believers. [8]And God, who knows the human heart, testified to them by giving them the Holy Spirit, just as he did to us; [9]and in cleansing their hearts by faith he has made no distinction between them and us. [10]Now therefore why are you putting God to the test by placing on the

[a]Heb sons of the prophets  [b]Heb him  [c]Heb lacks the bags  [d]A term for several skin diseases; precise meaning uncertain  [e]Gk brothers  [f]Gk Men, brothers

neck of the disciples a yoke that neither our ancestors nor we have been able to bear? [11]On the contrary, we believe that we will be saved through the grace of the Lord Jesus, just as they will."

12 The whole assembly kept silence, and listened to Barnabas and Paul as they told of all the signs and wonders that God had done through them among the Gentiles. [13]After they finished speaking, James replied, "My brothers,[a] listen to me. [14]Simeon has related how God first looked favorably on the Gentiles, to take from among them a people for his name. [15]This agrees with the words of the prophets, as it is written,

16 'After this I will return,
   and I will rebuild the dwelling of
      David, which has fallen;
     from its ruins I will rebuild it,
     and I will set it up,
17   so that all other peoples may
      seek the Lord—
   even all the Gentiles over
      whom my name has been
      called.
     Thus says the Lord, who
      has been making these
      things [18]known from long
      ago.'[b]

[19]Therefore I have reached the decision that we should not trouble those Gentiles who are turning to God, [20]but we should write to them to abstain only from things polluted by idols and from fornication and from whatever has been strangled[c] and from blood. [21]For in every city, for generations past, Moses has had those who proclaim him, for he has been read aloud every sabbath in the synagogues."

22 Then the apostles and the elders, with the consent of the whole church, decided to choose men from among their members[d] and to send them to Antioch with Paul and Barnabas. They sent Judas called Barsabbas, and Silas, leaders among the brothers, [23]with the following letter: "The brothers, both the apostles and the elders, to the believers[e] of Gentile origin in Antioch and Syria and Cilicia, greetings. [24]Since we have heard that certain persons who have gone out from us, though with no instructions from us, have said things to disturb you and have unsettled your minds,[f] [25]we have decided unanimously to choose representatives[g] and send them to you, along with our beloved Barnabas and Paul, [26]who have risked their lives for the sake of our Lord Jesus Christ. [27]We have therefore sent Judas and Silas, who themselves will tell you the same things by word of mouth. [28]For it has seemed good to the Holy Spirit and to us to impose on you no further burden than these essentials: [29]that you abstain from what has been sacrificed to idols and from blood and from what is strangled[h] and from fornication. If you keep yourselves from these, you will do well. Farewell."

30 So they were sent off and went down to Antioch. When they gathered the congregation together, they delivered the letter. [31]When its members[i] read it, they rejoiced at the exhortation. [32]Judas and Silas, who were themselves prophets, said much to encourage and strengthen the believers.[e] [33]After they had been there for some time, they were sent off in peace by the believers[e] to those who had sent them.[j] [35]But Paul and Barnabas remained in Antioch, and there, with many others, they taught and proclaimed the word of the Lord.

aGk *Men, brothers*   bOther ancient authorities read *things. 18Known to God from of old are all his works.'*   cOther ancient authorities lack *and from whatever has been strangled*   dGk *from among them*   eGk *brothers*   fOther ancient authorities add *saying, 'You must be circumcised and keep the law,'*   gGk *men*   hOther ancient authorities lack *and from what is strangled*   iGk *When they*   jOther ancient authorities add verse 34, *But it seemed good to Silas to remain there*

## PSALM 141.1–10

*A Psalm of David.*

I CALL upon you, O LORD; come
  quickly to me;
  give ear to my voice when I
  call to you.
2 Let my prayer be counted as
  incense before you,
  and the lifting up of my hands
  as an evening sacrifice.

3 Set a guard over my mouth,
  O LORD;
  keep watch over the door of
  my lips.
4 Do not turn my heart to any
  evil,
  to busy myself with wicked
  deeds
in company with those who
  work iniquity;
  do not let me eat of their
  delicacies.

5 Let the righteous strike me;
  let the faithful correct me.
Never let the oil of the wicked
  anoint my head, a
  for my prayer is continuallyb
  against their wicked
  deeds.

6 When they are given over to
  those who shall condemn
  them,
  then they shall learn that my
  words were pleasant.
7 Like a rock that one breaks
  apart and shatters on the
  land,
  so shall their bones be strewn
  at the mouth of Sheol. c

8 But my eyes are turned toward
  you, O GOD, my Lord;
  in you I seek refuge; do not
  leave me defenseless.
9 Keep me from the trap that
  they have laid for me,
  and from the snares of
  evildoers.
10 Let the wicked fall into their
  own nets,
  while I alone escape.

## PROVERBS 17.23

THE wicked accept a concealed
  bribe
  to pervert the ways of
  justice.

# JUNE 24

## 2 KINGS 6.1—7.20

Now the company of prophetsd said to Elisha, "As you see, the place where we live under your charge is too small for us. 2Let us go to the Jordan, and let us collect logs there, one for each of us, and build a place there for us to live." He answered, "Do so." 3Then one of them said, "Please come with your servants." And he answered, "I will." 4So he went with them. When they came to the Jordan, they cut down trees. 5But as one was felling a log, his ax head fell into the

aGk: Meaning of Heb uncertain  bCn: Heb *for continually and my prayer*  cMeaning of Heb of
verses 5-7 is uncertain  dHeb *sons of the prophets*

water; he cried out, "Alas, master! It was borrowed." 6Then the man of God said, "Where did it fall?" When he showed him the place, he cut off a stick, and threw it in there, and made the iron float. 7He said, "Pick it up." So he reached out his hand and took it.

8  Once when the king of Aram was at war with Israel, he took counsel with his officers. He said, "At such and such a place shall be my camp." 9But the man of God sent word to the king of Israel, "Take care not to pass this place, because the Arameans are going down there." 10The king of Israel sent word to the place of which the man of God spoke. More than once or twice he warned such a placea so that it was on the alert.

11  The mind of the king of Aram was greatly perturbed because of this; he called his officers and said to them, "Now tell me who among us sides with the king of Israel?" 12Then one of his officers said, "No one, my lord king. It is Elisha, the prophet in Israel, who tells the king of Israel the words that you speak in your bedchamber." 13He said, "Go and find where he is; I will send and seize him." He was told, "He is in Dothan." 14So he sent horses and chariots there and a great army; they came by night, and surrounded the city.

15  When an attendant of the man of God rose early in the morning and went out, an army with horses and chariots was all around the city. His servant said, "Alas, master! What shall we do?" 16He replied, "Do not be afraid, for there are more with us than there are with them." 17Then Elisha prayed: "O Lord, please open his eyes that he may see." So the Lord opened the eyes of the servant, and he saw; the mountain was full of horses and chariots of fire all around Elisha. 18When the Arameansb came down against him, Elisha prayed to the Lord, and said, "Strike this people, please, with blindness." So he struck them with blindness as Elisha had asked. 19Elisha said to them, "This is not the way, and this is not the city; follow me, and I will bring you to the man whom you seek." And he led them to Samaria.

20  As soon as they entered Samaria, Elisha said, "O Lord, open the eyes of these men so that they may see." The Lord opened their eyes, and they saw that they were inside Samaria. 21When the king of Israel saw them he said to Elisha, "Father, shall I kill them? Shall I kill them?" 22He answered, "No! Did you capture with your sword and your bow those whom you want to kill? Set food and water before them so that they may eat and drink; and let them go to their master." 23So he prepared for them a great feast; after they ate and drank, he sent them on their way, and they went to their master. And the Arameans no longer came raiding into the land of Israel.

24  Some time later King Benhadad of Aram mustered his entire army; he marched against Samaria and laid siege to it. 25As the siege continued, famine in Samaria became so great that a donkey's head was sold for eighty shekels of silver, and one-fourth of a kab of dove's dung for five shekels of silver. 26Now as the king of Israel was walking on the city wall, a woman cried out to him, "Help, my lord king!" 27He said, "No! Let the Lord help you. How can I help you? From the threshing floor or from the wine press?" 28But then the king asked her, "What is your complaint?" She answered, "This woman said to me, 'Give up your son; we will eat him today, and we will eat my son tomorrow.' 29So we cooked my son and ate him. The next day I said to her, 'Give up your son and we will eat him.' But she has hidden her son." 30When the king heard the words of the

a Heb *warned it*   b Heb *they*

woman he tore his clothes—now since he was walking on the city wall, the people could see that he had sackcloth on his body underneath— ³¹and he said, "So may God do to me, and more, if the head of Elisha son of Shaphat stays on his shoulders today." ³²So he dispatched a man from his presence.

Now Elisha was sitting in his house, and the elders were sitting with him. Before the messenger arrived, Elisha said to the elders, "Are you aware that this murderer has sent someone to take off my head? When the messenger comes, see that you shut the door and hold it closed against him. Is not the sound of his master's feet behind him?" ³³While he was still speaking with them, the king[a] came down to him and said, "This trouble is from the LORD! Why should I hope in the LORD any longer?" 7.1 But Elisha said, "Hear the word of the LORD: thus says the LORD, Tomorrow about this time a measure of choice meal shall be sold for a shekel, and two measures of barley for a shekel, at the gate of Samaria." ²Then the captain on whose hand the king leaned said to the man of God, "Even if the LORD were to make windows in the sky, could such a thing happen?" But he said, "You shall see it with your own eyes, but you shall not eat from it."

3 Now there were four leprous[b] men outside the city gate, who said to one another, "Why should we sit here until we die? ⁴If we say, 'Let us enter the city,' the famine is in the city, and we shall die there; but if we sit here, we shall also die. Therefore, let us desert to the Aramean camp; if they spare our lives, we shall live; and if they kill us, we shall but die." ⁵So they arose at twilight to go to the Aramean camp; but when they came to the edge of the Aramean camp, there was no one there at all. ⁶For the Lord had caused the Ara-

mean army to hear the sound of chariots, and of horses, the sound of a great army, so that they said to one another, "The king of Israel has hired the kings of the Hittites and the kings of Egypt to fight against us." ⁷So they fled away in the twilight and abandoned their tents, their horses, and their donkeys leaving the camp just as it was, and fled for their lives. ⁸When these leprous[b] men had come to the edge of the camp, they went into a tent, ate and drank, carried off silver, gold, and clothing, and went and hid them. Then they came back, entered another tent, carried off things from it, and went and hid them.

9 Then they said to one another, "What we are doing is wrong. This is a day of good news; if we are silent and wait until the morning light, we will be found guilty; therefore let us go and tell the king's household." ¹⁰So they came and called to the gatekeepers of the city, and told them, "We went to the Aramean camp, but there was no one to be seen or heard there, nothing but the horses tied, the donkeys tied, and the tents as they were." ¹¹Then the gatekeepers called out and proclaimed it to the king's household. ¹²The king got up in the night, and said to his servants, "I will tell you what the Arameans have prepared against us. They know that we are starving; so they have left the camp to hide themselves in the open country, thinking, 'When they come out of the city, we shall take them alive and get into the city.'" ¹³One of his servants said, "Let some men take five of the remaining horses, since those left here will suffer the fate of the whole multitude of Israel that have perished already;[c] let us send and find out." ¹⁴So they took two mounted men, and the king sent them after the Aramean army, saying, "Go and find out." ¹⁵So they went after them as far as the Jordan; the whole

[a]See 7.2: Heb *messenger*  [b]A term for several skin diseases; precise meaning uncertain  [c]Compare Gk Syr Vg: Meaning of Heb uncertain

way was littered with garments and equipment that the Arameans had thrown away in their haste. So the messengers returned, and told the king.

16 Then the people went out, and plundered the camp of the Arameans. So a measure of choice meal was sold for a shekel, and two measures of barley for a shekel, according to the word of the LORD. [17]Now the king had appointed the captain on whose hand he leaned to have charge of the gate; the people trampled him to death in the gate, just as the man of God had said when the king came down to him. [18]For when the man of God had said to the king, "Two measures of barley shall be sold for a shekel, and a measure of choice meal for a shekel, about this time tomorrow in the gate of Samaria," [19]the captain had answered the man of God, "Even if the LORD were to make windows in the sky, could such a thing happen?" And he had answered, "You shall see it with your own eyes, but you shall not eat from it." [20]It did indeed happen to him; the people trampled him to death in the gate.

## ACTS 15.36—16.15

AFTER some days Paul said to Barnabas, "Come, let us return and visit the believers[a] in every city where we proclaimed the word of the Lord and see how they are doing." [37]Barnabas wanted to take with them John called Mark. [38]But Paul decided not to take with them one who had deserted them in Pamphylia and had not accompanied them in the work. [39]The disagreement became so sharp that they parted company; Barnabas took Mark with him and sailed away to Cyprus. [40]But Paul chose Silas and set out, the believers[a] commending him to the grace of the Lord. [41]He went through Syria and Cilicia, strengthening the churches.

16.1 PAUL[b] went on also to Derbe and to Lystra, where there was a disciple named Timothy, the son of a Jewish woman who was a believer; but his father was a Greek. [2]He was well spoken of by the believers[a] in Lystra and Iconium. [3]Paul wanted Timothy to accompany him; and he took him and had him circumcised because of the Jews who were in those places, for they all knew that his father was a Greek. [4]As they went from town to town, they delivered to them for observance the decisions that had been reached by the apostles and elders who were in Jerusalem. [5]So the churches were strengthened in the faith and increased in numbers daily.

6 They went through the region of Phrygia and Galatia, having been forbidden by the Holy Spirit to speak the word in Asia. [7]When they had come opposite Mysia, they attempted to go into Bithynia, but the Spirit of Jesus did not allow them; [8]so, passing by Mysia, they went down to Troas. [9]During the night Paul had a vision: there stood a man of Macedonia pleading with him and saying, "Come over to Macedonia and help us." [10]When he had seen the vision, we immediately tried to cross over to Macedonia, being convinced that God had called us to proclaim the good news to them.

11 We set sail from Troas and took a straight course to Samothrace, the following day to Neapolis, [12]and from there to Philippi, which is a leading city of the district[c] of Macedonia and a Roman colony. We remained in this city for some days. [13]On the sabbath day we went outside the gate by the river, where we supposed there was a place of prayer; and we sat down and spoke to the women who had gathered there.

[a]Gk *brothers*  [b]Gk *He*  [c]Other authorities read *a city of the first district*

¹⁴A certain woman named Lydia, a worshiper of God, was listening to us; she was from the city of Thyatira and a dealer in purple cloth. The Lord opened her heart to listen eagerly to what was said by Paul. ¹⁵When she and her household were baptized, she urged us, saying, "If you have judged me to be faithful to the Lord, come and stay at my home." And she prevailed upon us.

## PSALM 142.1–7

*A Maskil of David. When he was in the cave. A Prayer.*

WITH my voice I cry to the LORD;
   with my voice I make
      supplication to the LORD.
2  I pour out my complaint before
     him;
   I tell my trouble before him.
3  When my spirit is faint,
   you know my way.

   In the path where I walk
     they have hidden a trap for
      me.
4  Look on my right hand and
     see—

   there is no one who takes
     notice of me;
  no refuge remains to me;
   no one cares for me.

5  I cry to you, O LORD;
   I say, "You are my refuge,
     my portion in the land of the
      living."
6  Give heed to my cry,
   for I am brought very low.

  Save me from my persecutors,
   for they are too strong for
     me.
7  Bring me out of prison,
   so that I may give thanks to
     your name.
  The righteous will surround me,
   for you will deal bountifully
     with me.

## PROVERBS 17.24–25

THE discerning person looks to
     wisdom,
   but the eyes of a fool to the
     ends of the earth.
25  Foolish children are a grief to
     their father
   and bitterness to her who
     bore them.

# JUNE 25

## 2 KINGS 8.1—9.13

NOW Elisha had said to the woman whose son he had restored to life, "Get up and go with your household, and settle wherever you can; for the LORD has called for a famine, and it will come on the land for seven years." ²So the woman got up and did according to the word of the man of God; she went with her household and settled in the land of the Philistines seven years. ³At the end of the seven years, when the woman returned from the land of the Philistines, she set out to appeal to the king for her house and her land. ⁴Now the king was talking with Gehazi the servant of the man of God, saying, "Tell me all the great things that Elisha has done." 5While he was telling the king how Elisha had restored a dead person to life, the woman whose son he had restored to life appealed to the king for her house and her land. Gehazi said, "My lord king, here is the woman, and here is her son whom Elisha restored to life." 6When the king questioned the woman, she told him. So the king appointed an official for her, saying, "Restore all that was hers, together with all the revenue of the fields from the day that she left the land until now."

7 Elisha went to Damascus while King Ben-hadad of Aram was ill. When it was told him, "The man of God has come here," 8the king said to Hazael, "Take a present with you and go to meet the man of God. Inquire of the LORD through him, whether I shall recover from this illness." 9So Hazael went to meet him, taking a present with him, all kinds of goods of Damascus, forty camel loads. When he entered and stood before him, he said, "Your son King Ben-hadad of Aram has sent me to you, saying, 'Shall I recover from this illness?'" 10Elisha said to him, "Go, say to him, 'You shall certainly recover'; but the LORD has shown me that he shall certainly die." 11He fixed his gaze and stared at him, until he was ashamed. Then the man of God wept. 12Hazael asked, "Why does my lord weep?" He answered, "Because I know the evil that you will do to the people of Israel; you will set their fortresses on fire, you will kill their young men with the sword, dash in pieces their little ones, and rip up their pregnant women." 13Hazael said, "What is your servant, who is a mere dog, that he should do this great thing?" Elisha answered, "The LORD has shown me that you are to be king over Aram."

14Then he left Elisha, and went to his master Ben-hadad,a who said to him, "What did Elisha say to you?" And he answered, "He told me that you would certainly recover." 15But the next day he took the bed-cover and dipped it in water and spread it over the king's face, until he died. And Hazael succeeded him.

16 In the fifth year of King Joram son of Ahab of Israel,b Jehoram son of King Jehoshaphat of Judah began to reign. 17He was thirty-two years old when he became king, and he reigned eight years in Jerusalem. 18He walked in the way of the kings of Israel, as the house of Ahab had done, for the daughter of Ahab was his wife. He did what was evil in the sight of the LORD. 19Yet the LORD would not destroy Judah, for the sake of his servant David, since he had promised to give a lamp to him and to his descendants forever.

20 In his days Edom revolted against the rule of Judah, and set up a king of their own. 21Then Joram crossed over to Zair with all his chariots. He set out by night and attacked the Edomites and their chariot commanders who had surrounded him;c but his army fled home. 22So Edom has been in revolt against the rule of Judah to this day. Libnah also revolted at the same time. 23Now the rest of the acts of Joram, and all that he did, are they not written in the Book of the Annals of the Kings of Judah? 24So Joram slept with his ancestors, and was buried with them in the city of David; his son Ahaziah succeeded him.

25 In the twelfth year of King Joram son of Ahab of Israel, Ahaziah son of King Jehoram of Judah began to reign. 26Ahaziah was twenty-two years old when he began to reign; he reigned one year in Jerusalem. His mother's name was Athaliah, a granddaughter of King Omri of Israel. 27He also walked

aHeb lacks *Ben-hadad*   bGk Syr: Heb adds *Jehoshaphat being king of Judah,*   cMeaning of Heb uncertain

in the way of the house of Ahab, doing what was evil in the sight of the Lord, as the house of Ahab had done, for he was son-in-law to the house of Ahab.

28  He went with Joram son of Ahab to wage war against King Hazael of Aram at Ramoth-gilead, where the Arameans wounded Joram. <sup>29</sup>King Joram returned to be healed in Jezreel of the wounds that the Arameans had inflicted on him at Ramah, when he fought against King Hazael of Aram. King Ahaziah son of Jehoram of Judah went down to see Joram son of Ahab in Jezreel, because he was wounded.

<sup>9.1</sup> Then the prophet Elisha called a member of the company of prophets[a] and said to him, "Gird up your loins; take this flask of oil in your hand, and go to Ramoth-gilead. <sup>2</sup>When you arrive, look there for Jehu son of Jehoshaphat, son of Nimshi; go in and get him to leave his companions, and take him into an inner chamber. <sup>3</sup>Then take the flask of oil, pour it on his head, and say, 'Thus says the Lord: I anoint you king over Israel.' Then open the door and flee; do not linger."

4  So the young man, the young prophet, went to Ramoth-gilead. <sup>5</sup>He arrived while the commanders of the army were in council, and he announced, "I have a message for you, commander." "For which one of us?" asked Jehu. "For you, commander." <sup>6</sup>So Jehu[b] got up and went inside; the young man poured the oil on his head, saying to him, "Thus says the Lord the God of Israel: I anoint you king over the people of the Lord, over Israel. <sup>7</sup>You shall strike down the house of your master Ahab, so that I may avenge on Jezebel the blood of my servants the prophets, and the blood of all the servants of the Lord. <sup>8</sup>For the whole house of Ahab shall perish; I will cut off from Ahab every male, bond or free, in

Israel. <sup>9</sup>I will make the house of Ahab like the house of Jeroboam son of Nebat, and like the house of Baasha son of Ahijah. <sup>10</sup>The dogs shall eat Jezebel in the territory of Jezreel, and no one shall bury her." Then he opened the door and fled.

11  When Jehu came back to his master's officers, they said to him, "Is everything all right? Why did that madman come to you?" He answered them, "You know the sort and how they babble." <sup>12</sup>They said, "Liar! Come on, tell us!" So he said, "This is just what he said to me: 'Thus says the Lord, I anoint you king over Israel.'" <sup>13</sup>Then hurriedly they all took their cloaks and spread them for him on the bare[c] steps; and they blew the trumpet, and proclaimed, "Jehu is king."

## ACTS 16.16–40

One day, as we [Luke, Paul, and companions] were going to the place of prayer, we met a slave-girl who had a spirit of divination and brought her owners a great deal of money by fortune-telling. <sup>17</sup>While she followed Paul and us, she would cry out, "These men are slaves of the Most High God, who proclaim to you[d] a way of salvation." <sup>18</sup>She kept doing this for many days. But Paul, very much annoyed, turned and said to the spirit, "I order you in the name of Jesus Christ to come out of her." And it came out that very hour.

19  But when her owners saw that their hope of making money was gone, they seized Paul and Silas and dragged them into the marketplace before the authorities. <sup>20</sup>When they had brought them before the magistrates, they said, "These men are disturbing our city; they are Jews <sup>21</sup>and are advocating customs that are not lawful for us as Romans to adopt or observe." <sup>22</sup>The

a Heb *sons of the prophets*  b Heb *he*  c Meaning of Heb uncertain  d Other ancient authorities read *to us* crowd joined in attacking them, and the magistrates had them stripped of their clothing and ordered them to be beaten with rods. [23]After they had given them a severe flogging, they threw them into prison and ordered the jailer to keep them securely. [24]Following these instructions, he put them in the innermost cell and fastened their feet in the stocks.

25 About midnight Paul and Silas were praying and singing hymns to God, and the prisoners were listening to them. [26]Suddenly there was an earthquake, so violent that the foundations of the prison were shaken; and immediately all the doors were opened and everyone's chains were unfastened. [27]When the jailer woke up and saw the prison doors wide open, he drew his sword and was about to kill himself, since he supposed that the prisoners had escaped. [28]But Paul shouted in a loud voice, "Do not harm yourself, for we are all here." [29]The jailer[a] called for lights, and rushing in, he fell down trembling before Paul and Silas. [30]Then he brought them outside and said, "Sirs, what must I do to be saved?" [31]They answered, "Believe on the Lord Jesus, and you will be saved, you and your household." [32]They spoke the word of the Lord[b] to him and to all who were in his house. [33]At the same hour of the night he took them and washed their wounds; then he and his entire family were baptized without delay. [34]He brought them up into the house and set food before them; and he and his entire household rejoiced that he had become a believer in God.

35 When morning came, the magistrates sent the police, saying, "Let those men go." [36]And the jailer reported the message to Paul, saying, "The magistrates sent word to let you go; therefore come out now and go in peace." [37]But Paul replied, "They have beaten us in public, uncondemned, men who are Roman citizens, and have thrown us into prison; and now are they going to discharge us in secret? Certainly not! Let them come and take us out themselves." [38]The police reported these words to the magistrates, and they were afraid when they heard that they were Roman citizens; [39]so they came and apologized to them. And they took them out and asked them to leave the city. [40]After leaving the prison they went to Lydia's home; and when they had seen and encouraged the brothers and sisters[c] there, they departed.

## PSALM 143. 1–12

*A Psalm of David.*

HEAR my prayer, O LORD;
  give ear to my supplications
    in your faithfulness;
  answer me in your
    righteousness.
2  Do not enter into judgment with
      your servant,
    for no one living is righteous
      before you.

3  For the enemy has pursued me,
    crushing my life to the
      ground,
    making me sit in darkness like
      those long dead.
4  Therefore my spirit faints
      within me;
    my heart within me is
      appalled.

5  I remember the days of old,
    I think about all your deeds,
    I meditate on the works of
      your hands.
6  I stretch out my hands to you;
    my soul thirsts for you like a
      parched land.          *Selah*

7  Answer me quickly, O LORD;
    my spirit fails.

[a]Gk *He*   [b]Other ancient authorities read *word of God*   [c]Gk *brothers*

Do not hide your face from me,
  or I shall be like those who
    go down to the Pit.
8 Let me hear of your steadfast
    love in the morning,
  for in you I put my trust.
Teach me the way I should go,
  for to you I lift up my soul.

9 Save me, O Lord, from my
    enemies;
  I have fled to you for
    refuge. a
10 Teach me to do your will,
  for you are my God.
Let your good spirit lead me
  on a level path.

11 For your name's sake, O Lord,
  preserve my life.
In your righteousness bring
  me out of trouble.
12 In your steadfast love cut off my
    enemies,
  and destroy all my
    adversaries,
for I am your servant.

## PROVERBS 17.26

To impose a fine on the innocent is not right, or to flog the noble for their integrity.

# JUNE 26

## 2 KINGS 9.14—10.31

Thus Jehu son of Jehoshaphat son of Nimshi conspired against Joram. Joram with all Israel had been on guard at Ramoth-gilead against King Hazael of Aram; 15but King Joram had returned to be healed in Jezreel of the wounds that the Arameans had inflicted on him, when he fought against King Hazael of Aram. So Jehu said, "If this is your wish, then let no one slip out of the city to go and tell the news in Jezreel." 16Then Jehu mounted his chariot and went to Jezreel, where Joram was lying ill. King Ahaziah of Judah had come down to visit Joram.

17 In Jezreel, the sentinel standing on the tower spied the company of Jehu arriving, and said, "I see a company." Joram said, "Take a horseman; send him to meet them, and let him say, 'Is it peace?' " 18So the horseman went to meet him; he said, "Thus says the king, 'Is it peace?' " Jehu responded, "What have you to do with peace? Fall in behind me." The sentinel reported, saying, "The messenger reached them, but he is not coming back." 19Then he sent out a second horseman, who came to them and said, "Thus says the king, 'Is it peace?' " Jehu answered, "What have you to do with peace? Fall in behind me." 20Again the sentinel reported, "He reached them, but he is not coming back. It looks like the driving of Jehu son of Nimshi; for he drives like a maniac."

21 Joram said, "Get ready." And they got his chariot ready. Then King Joram of Israel and King Ahaziah of Judah set out, each in his chariot, and went to meet Jehu; they met him at the

a One Heb Ms Gk: MT *to you I have hidden*

property of Naboth the Jezreelite. ²²When Joram saw Jehu, he said, "Is it peace, Jehu?" He answered, "What peace can there be, so long as the many whoredoms and sorceries of your mother Jezebel continue?" ²³Then Joram reined about and fled, saying to Ahaziah, "Treason, Ahaziah!" ²⁴Jehu drew his bow with all his strength, and shot Joram between the shoulders, so that the arrow pierced his heart; and he sank in his chariot. ²⁵Jehu said to his aide Bidkar, "Lift him out, and throw him on the plot of ground belonging to Naboth the Jezreelite; for remember, when you and I rode side by side behind his father Ahab how the Lord uttered this oracle against him: ²⁶'For the blood of Naboth and for the blood of his children that I saw yesterday, says the Lord, I swear I will repay you on this very plot of ground.' Now therefore lift him out and throw him on the plot of ground, in accordance with the word of the Lord."

27 When King Ahaziah of Judah saw this, he fled in the direction of Beth-haggan. Jehu pursued him, saying, "Shoot him also!" And they shot him[a] in the chariot at the ascent to Gur, which is by Ibleam. Then he fled to Megiddo, and died there. ²⁸His officers carried him in a chariot to Jerusalem, and buried him in his tomb with his ancestors in the city of David.

29 In the eleventh year of Joram son of Ahab, Ahaziah began to reign over Judah.

30 When Jehu came to Jezreel, Jezebel heard of it; she painted her eyes, and adorned her head, and looked out of the window. ³¹As Jehu entered the gate, she said, "Is it peace, Zimri, murderer of your master?" ³²He looked up to the window and said, "Who is on my side? Who?" Two or three eunuchs looked out at him. ³³He said, "Throw her down." So they threw her down;

some of her blood spattered on the wall and on the horses, which trampled on her. ³⁴Then he went in and ate and drank; he said, "See to that cursed woman and bury her; for she is a king's daughter." ³⁵But when they went to bury her, they found no more of her than the skull and the feet and the palms of her hands. ³⁶When they came back and told him, he said, "This is the word of the Lord, which he spoke by his servant Elijah the Tishbite, 'In the territory of Jezreel the dogs shall eat the flesh of Jezebel; ³⁷the corpse of Jezebel shall be like dung on the field in the territory of Jezreel, so that no one can say, This is Jezebel.'"

10.1 Now Ahab had seventy sons in Samaria. So Jehu wrote letters and sent them to Samaria, to the rulers of Jezreel,[b] to the elders, and to the guardians of the sons of[c] Ahab, saying, ²"Since your master's sons are with you and you have at your disposal chariots and horses, a fortified city, and weapons, ³select the son of your master who is the best qualified, set him on his father's throne, and fight for your master's house." ⁴But they were utterly terrified and said, "Look, two kings could not withstand him; how then can we stand?" ⁵So the steward of the palace, and the governor of the city, along with the elders and the guardians, sent word to Jehu: "We are your servants; we will do anything you say. We will not make anyone king; do whatever you think right." ⁶Then he wrote them a second letter, saying, "If you are on my side, and if you are ready to obey me, take the heads of your master's sons and come to me at Jezreel tomorrow at this time." Now the king's sons, seventy persons, were with the leaders of the city, who were charged with their upbringing. ⁷When the letter reached them, they took the

---

a Syr Vg Compare Gk: Heb lacks *and they shot him*  lacks *of the sons of*  b Or *of the city*; Vg Compare Gk  c Gk: Heb

king's sons and killed them, seventy persons; they put their heads in baskets and sent them to him at Jezreel. 8When the messenger came and told him, "They have brought the heads of the king's sons," he said, "Lay them in two heaps at the entrance of the gate until the morning." 9Then in the morning when he went out, he stood and said to all the people, "You are innocent. It was I who conspired against my master and killed him; but who struck down all these? 10Know then that there shall fall to the earth nothing of the word of the LORD, which the LORD spoke concerning the house of Ahab; for the LORD has done what he said through his servant Elijah." 11So Jehu killed all who were left of the house of Ahab in Jezreel, all his leaders, close friends, and priests, until he left him no survivor.

12 Then he set out and went to Samaria. On the way, when he was at Beth-eked of the Shepherds, 13Jehu met relatives of King Ahaziah of Judah and said, "Who are you?" They answered, "We are kin of Ahaziah; we have come down to visit the royal princes and the sons of the queen mother." 14He said, "Take them alive." They took them alive, and slaughtered them at the pit of Beth-eked, forty-two in all; he spared none of them.

15 When he left there, he met Jehonadab son of Rechab coming to meet him; he greeted him, and said to him, "Is your heart as true to mine as mine is to yours?"a Jehonadab answered, "It is." Jehu said,b "If it is, give me your hand." So he gave him his hand. Jehu took him up with him into the chariot. 16He said, "Come with me, and see my zeal for the LORD." So hec had him ride in his chariot. 17When he came to Samaria, he killed all who were left to Ahab in Samaria, until he had wiped them out, according to the word of the LORD that he spoke to Elijah.

18 Then Jehu assembled all the people and said to them, "Ahab offered Baal small service; but Jehu will offer much more. 19Now therefore summon to me all the prophets of Baal, all his worshipers, and all his priests; let none be missing, for I have a great sacrifice to offer to Baal; whoever is missing shall not live." But Jehu was acting with cunning in order to destroy the worshipers of Baal. 20Jehu decreed, "Sanctify a solemn assembly for Baal." So they proclaimed it. 21Jehu sent word throughout all Israel; all the worshipers of Baal came, so that there was no one left who did not come. They entered the temple of Baal, until the temple of Baal was filled from wall to wall. 22He said to the keeper of the wardrobe, "Bring out the vestments for all the worshipers of Baal." So he brought out the vestments for them. 23Then Jehu entered the temple of Baal with Jehonadab son of Rechab; he said to the worshipers of Baal, "Search and see that there is no worshiper of the LORD here among you, but only worshipers of Baal." 24Then they proceeded to offer sacrifices and burnt offerings.

Now Jehu had stationed eighty men outside, saying, "Whoever allows any of those to escape whom I deliver into your hands shall forfeit his life." 25As soon as he had finished presenting the burnt offering, Jehu said to the guards and to the officers, "Come in and kill them; let no one escape." So they put them to the sword. The guards and the officers threw them out, and then went into the citadel of the temple of Baal. 26They brought out the pillard that was in the temple of Baal, and burned it. 27Then they demolished the pillar of Baal, and destroyed the temple of Baal, and made it a latrine to this day.

28 Thus Jehu wiped out Baal from Israel. 29But Jehu did not turn aside from the sins of Jeroboam son of Nebat,

aGk: Heb *Is it right with your heart, as my heart is with your heart?* bGk: Heb lacks *Jehu said*
cGk Syr Tg: Heb *they* dGk Vg Syr Tg: Heb *pillars*

which he caused Israel to commit—the golden calves that were in Bethel and in Dan. [30]The Lord said to Jehu, "Because you have done well in carrying out what I consider right, and in accordance with all that was in my heart have dealt with the house of Ahab, your sons of the fourth generation shall sit on the throne of Israel." [31]But Jehu was not careful to follow the law of the Lord the God of Israel with all his heart; he did not turn from the sins of Jeroboam, which he caused Israel to commit.

## ACTS 17.1–34

AFTER Paul and Silas[a] had passed through Amphipolis and Apollonia, they came to Thessalonica, where there was a synagogue of the Jews. [2]And Paul went in, as was his custom, and on three sabbath days argued with them from the scriptures, [3]explaining and proving that it was necessary for the Messiah[b] to suffer and to rise from the dead, and saying, "This is the Messiah, [b] Jesus whom I am proclaiming to you." [4]Some of them were persuaded and joined Paul and Silas, as did a great many of the devout Greeks and not a few of the leading women. [5]But the Jews became jealous, and with the help of some ruffians in the marketplaces they formed a mob and set the city in an uproar. While they were searching for Paul and Silas to bring them out to the assembly, they attacked Jason's house. [6]When they could not find them, they dragged Jason and some believers[c] before the city authorities,[d] shouting, "These people who have been turning the world upside down have come here also, [7]and Jason has entertained them as guests. They are all acting contrary to the decrees of the emperor, saying that there is another king named Jesus." [8]The people and the city officials were disturbed when they heard this, [9]and after they had taken bail from Jason and the others, they let them go.

10 That very night the believers[c] sent Paul and Silas off to Beroea; and when they arrived, they went to the Jewish synagogue. [11]These Jews were more receptive than those in Thessalonica, for they welcomed the message very eagerly and examined the scriptures every day to see whether these things were so. [12]Many of them therefore believed, including not a few Greek women and men of high standing. [13]But when the Jews of Thessalonica learned that the word of God had been proclaimed by Paul in Beroea as well, they came there too, to stir up and incite the crowds. [14]Then the believers[c] immediately sent Paul away to the coast, but Silas and Timothy remained behind. [15]Those who conducted Paul brought him as far as Athens; and after receiving instructions to have Silas and Timothy join him as soon as possible, they left him.

16 While Paul was waiting for them in Athens, he was deeply distressed to see that the city was full of idols. [17]So he argued in the synagogue with the Jews and the devout persons, and also in the marketplace[e] every day with those who happened to be there. [18]Also some Epicurean and Stoic philosophers debated with him. Some said, "What does this babbler want to say?" Others said, "He seems to be a proclaimer of foreign divinities." (This was because he was telling the good news about Jesus and the resurrection.) [19]So they took him and brought him to the Areopagus and asked him, "May we know what this new teaching is that you are presenting? [20]It sounds rather strange to us, so we would like to know what it means." [21]Now all the Athenians and the foreigners living there would spend their time in nothing but telling or hearing something new.

---

[a] Gk *they*  [b] Or *the Christ*  [c] Gk *brothers*  [d] Gk *politarchs*  [e] Or *civic center*, Gk *agora*

22 Then Paul stood in front of the Areopagus and said, "Athenians, I see how extremely religious you are in every way. 23For as I went through the city and looked carefully at the objects of your worship, I found among them an altar with the inscription, 'To an unknown god.' What therefore you worship as unknown, this I proclaim to you. 24The God who made the world and everything in it, he who is Lord of heaven and earth, does not live in shrines made by human hands, 25nor is he served by human hands, as though he needed anything, since he himself gives to all mortals life and breath and all things. 26From one ancestor[a] he made all nations to inhabit the whole earth, and he allotted the times of their existence and the boundaries of the places where they would live, 27so that they would search for God[b] and perhaps grope for him and find him—though indeed he is not far from each one of us. 28For 'In him we live and move and have our being'; as even some of your own poets have said,

'For we too are his offspring.'
29Since we are God's offspring, we ought not to think that the deity is like gold, or silver, or stone, an image formed by the art and imagination of mortals. 30While God has overlooked the times of human ignorance, now he commands all people everywhere to repent, 31because he has fixed a day on which he will have the world judged in righteousness by a man whom he has appointed, and of this he has given assurance to all by raising him from the dead."

32 When they heard of the resurrection of the dead, some scoffed; but others said, "We will hear you again about this." 33At that point Paul left them. 34But some of them joined him and became believers, including Diony-

sius the Areopagite and a woman named Damaris, and others with them.

## PSALM 144.1–15

*Of David.*

**B**LESSED be the LORD, my rock,
    who trains my hands for
      war, and my fingers for
      battle;
2 my rock[c] and my fortress,
   my stronghold and my
      deliverer,
my shield, in whom I take
      refuge,
who subdues the peoples[d]
      under me.

3 O LORD, what are human beings
      that you regard them,
   or mortals that you think of
      them?
4 They are like a breath;
   their days are like a passing
      shadow.

5 Bow your heavens, O LORD, and
      come down;
   touch the mountains so that
      they smoke.
6 Make the lightning flash and
      scatter them;
   send out your arrows and
      rout them.
7 Stretch out your hand from on
      high;
   set me free and rescue me
      from the mighty waters,
   from the hand of aliens,
8 whose mouths speak lies,
   and whose right hands are
      false.

9 I will sing a new song to you,
      O God;
   upon a ten-stringed harp I will
      play to you,

[a]Gk *From one*; other ancient authorities read *From one blood*  [b]Other ancient authorities read *the Lord*  [c]With 18.2 and 2 Sam 22.2: Heb *my steadfast love*  [d]Heb Mss Syr Aquila Jerome: MT *my people*

10 the one who gives victory to
    kings,
      who rescues his servant
        David.
11 Rescue me from the cruel
      sword,
      and deliver me from the hand
        of aliens,
  whose mouths speak lies,
    and whose right hands are
      false.

12 May our sons in their youth
      be like plants full grown,
  our daughters like corner pillars,
    cut for the building of a
      palace.
13 May our barns be filled,
      with produce of every kind;
  may our sheep increase by
    thousands,
      by tens of thousands in our
        fields,

14 and may our cattle be heavy
      with young.
  May there be no breach in the
    walls, a no exile,
      and no cry of distress in our
        streets.

15 Happy are the people to whom
      such blessings fall;
  happy are the people whose
    God is the LORD.

## PROVERBS 17.27–28

ONE who spares words is
    knowledgeable;
  one who is cool in spirit has
    understanding.
28 Even fools who keep silent are
    considered wise;
  when they close their lips,
    they are deemed
      intelligent.

# JUNE 27

## 2 KINGS 10.32—12.21

IN those days the LORD began to trim off parts of Israel. Hazael defeated them throughout the territory of Israel: 33from the Jordan eastward, all the land of Gilead, the Gadites, the Reubenites, and the Manassites, from Aroer, which is by the Wadi Arnon, that is, Gilead and Bashan. 34Now the rest of the acts of Jehu, all that he did, and all his power, are they not written in the Book of the Annals of the Kings of Israel? 35So Jehu slept with his ancestors, and they buried him in Samaria. His son Jehoahaz succeeded him. 36The time that Jehu reigned over Israel in Samaria was twenty-eight years.

11.1 Now when Athaliah, Ahaziah's mother, saw that her son was dead, she set about to destroy all the royal family. 2But Jehosheba, King Joram's daughter, Ahaziah's sister, took Joash son of Ahaziah, and stole him away from among the king's children who were about to be killed; she put b him and his nurse in a bedroom. Thus she c hid him from Athaliah, so that he was not killed; 3he remained with her six

aHeb lacks *in the walls*   bWith 2 Chr 22.11: Heb lacks *she put*   cGk Syr Vg Compare 2 Chr 22.11: Heb *they*

years, hidden in the house of the Lord, while Athaliah reigned over the land.

4 But in the seventh year Jehoiada summoned the captains of the Carites and of the guards and had them come to him in the house of the Lord. He made a covenant with them and put them under oath in the house of the Lord; then he showed them the king's son. ⁵He commanded them, "This is what you are to do: one-third of you, those who go off duty on the sabbath and guard the king's house ⁶(another third being at the gate Sur and a third at the gate behind the guards), shall guard the palace; ⁷and your two divisions that come on duty in force on the sabbath and guard the house of the Lord ᵃ ⁸shall surround the king, each with weapons in hand; and whoever approaches the ranks is to be killed. Be with the king in his comings and goings."

9 The captains did according to all that the priest Jehoiada commanded; each brought his men who were to go off duty on the sabbath, with those who were to come on duty on the sabbath, and came to the priest Jehoiada. ¹⁰The priest delivered to the captains the spears and shields that had been King David's, which were in the house of the Lord; ¹¹the guards stood, every man with his weapons in his hand, from the south side of the house to the north side of the house, around the altar and the house, to guard the king on every side. ¹²Then he brought out the king's son, put the crown on him, and gave him the covenant;ᵇ they proclaimed him king, and anointed him; they clapped their hands and shouted, "Long live the king!"

13 When Athaliah heard the noise of the guard and of the people, she went into the house of the Lord to the people; ¹⁴when she looked, there was the king standing by the pillar, according to custom, with the captains and the trumpeters beside the king, and all the people of the land rejoicing and blowing trumpets. Athaliah tore her clothes and cried, "Treason! Treason!" ¹⁵Then the priest Jehoiada commanded the captains who were set over the army, "Bring her out between the ranks, and kill with the sword anyone who follows her." For the priest said, "Let her not be killed in the house of the Lord." ¹⁶So they laid hands on her; she went through the horses' entrance to the king's house, and there she was put to death.

17 Jehoiada made a covenant between the Lord and the king and people, that they should be the Lord's people; also between the king and the people. ¹⁸Then all the people of the land went to the house of Baal, and tore it down; his altars and his images they broke in pieces, and they killed Mattan, the priest of Baal, before the altars. The priest posted guards over the house of the Lord. ¹⁹He took the captains, the Carites, the guards, and all the people of the land; then they brought the king down from the house of the Lord, marching through the gate of the guards to the king's house. He took his seat on the throne of the kings. ²⁰So all the people of the land rejoiced; and the city was quiet after Athaliah had been killed with the sword at the king's house.

21ᶜ Jehoashᵈ was seven years old when he began to reign.

12.1 In the seventh year of Jehu, Jehoash began to reign; he reigned forty years in Jerusalem. His mother's name was Zibiah of Beer-sheba. ²Jehoash did what was right in the sight of the Lord all his days, because the priest Jehoiada instructed him. ³Nevertheless the high places were not taken away; the people

aHeb the Lord to the king   bOr treaty or testimony; Heb eduth   cCh 12.1 in Heb   dAnother spelling is Joash; see verse 19

continued to sacrifice and make offerings on the high places.

4 Jehoash said to the priests, "All the money offered as sacred donations that is brought into the house of the LORD, the money for which each person is assessed—the money from the assessment of persons—and the money from the voluntary offerings brought into the house of the LORD, 5let the priests receive from each of the donors; and let them repair the house wherever any need of repairs is discovered." 6But by the twenty-third year of King Jehoash the priests had made no repairs on the house. 7Therefore King Jehoash summoned the priest Jehoiada with the other priests and said to them, "Why are you not repairing the house? Now therefore do not accept any more money from your donors but hand it over for the repair of the house." 8So the priests agreed that they would neither accept more money from the people nor repair the house.

9 Then the priest Jehoiada took a chest, made a hole in its lid, and set it beside the altar on the right side as one entered the house of the LORD; the priests who guarded the threshold put in it all the money that was brought into the house of the LORD. 10Whenever they saw that there was a great deal of money in the chest, the king's secretary and the high priest went up, counted the money that was found in the house of the LORD, and tied it up in bags. 11They would give the money that was weighed out into the hands of the workers who had the oversight of the house of the LORD; then they paid it out to the carpenters and the builders who worked on the house of the LORD, 12to the masons and the stonecutters, as well as to buy timber and quarried stone for making repairs on the house of the LORD, as well as for any outlay for repairs of the house. 13But for the house of the LORD no basins of silver, snuffers, bowls, trumpets, or any vessels of gold, or of silver, were made from the money that was brought into the house of the LORD, 14for that was given to the workers who were repairing the house of the LORD with it. 15They did not ask an accounting from those into whose hand they delivered the money to pay out to the workers, for they dealt honestly. 16The money from the guilt offerings and the money from the sin offerings was not brought into the house of the LORD; it belonged to the priests.

17 At that time King Hazael of Aram went up, fought against Gath, and took it. But when Hazael set his face to go up against Jerusalem, 18King Jehoash of Judah took all the votive gifts that Jehoshaphat, Jehoram, and Ahaziah, his ancestors, the kings of Judah, had dedicated, as well as his own votive gifts, all the gold that was found in the treasuries of the house of the LORD and of the king's house, and sent these to King Hazael of Aram. Then Hazael withdrew from Jerusalem.

19 Now the rest of the acts of Joash, and all that he did, are they not written in the Book of the Annals of the Kings of Judah? 20His servants arose, devised a conspiracy, and killed Joash in the house of Millo, on the way that goes down to Silla. 21It was Jozacar son of Shimeath and Jehozabad son of Shomer, his servants, who struck him down, so that he died. He was buried with his ancestors in the city of David; then his son Amaziah succeeded him.

## ACTS 18.1–21

AFTER this Paul[a] left Athens and went to Corinth. 2There he found a Jew named Aquila, a native of Pontus, who had recently come from Italy with his wife Priscilla,

aGk *he*

because Claudius had ordered all Jews to leave Rome. Paul[a] went to see them, [3]and, because he was of the same trade, he stayed with them, and they worked together—by trade they were tentmakers. [4]Every sabbath he would argue in the synagogue and would try to convince Jews and Greeks.

5 When Silas and Timothy arrived from Macedonia, Paul was occupied with proclaiming the word,[b] testifying to the Jews that the Messiah[c] was Jesus. [6]When they opposed and reviled him, in protest he shook the dust from his clothes[d] and said to them, "Your blood be on your own heads! I am innocent. From now on I will go to the Gentiles." [7]Then he left the synagogue[e] and went to the house of a man named Titius[f] Justus, a worshiper of God; his house was next door to the synagogue. [8]Crispus, the official of the synagogue, became a believer in the Lord, together with all his household; and many of the Corinthians who heard Paul became believers and were baptized. [9]One night the Lord said to Paul in a vision, "Do not be afraid, but speak and do not be silent; [10]for I am with you, and no one will lay a hand on you to harm you, for there are many in this city who are my people." [11]He stayed there a year and six months, teaching the word of God among them.

12 But when Gallio was proconsul of Achaia, the Jews made a united attack on Paul and brought him before the tribunal. [13]They said, "This man is persuading people to worship God in ways that are contrary to the law." [14]Just as Paul was about to speak, Gallio said to the Jews, "If it were a matter of crime or serious villainy, I would be justified in accepting the complaint of you Jews; [15]but since it is a matter of questions about words and names and your own law, see to it yourselves; I do not wish to be a judge of these matters." [16]And he dismissed them from the tribunal. [17]Then all of them[g] seized Sosthenes, the official of the synagogue, and beat him in front of the tribunal. But Gallio paid no attention to any of these things.

18 After staying there for a considerable time, Paul said farewell to the believers[h] and sailed for Syria, accompanied by Priscilla and Aquila. At Cenchreae he had his hair cut, for he was under a vow. [19]When they reached Ephesus, he left them there, but first he himself went into the synagogue and had a discussion with the Jews. [20]When they asked him to stay longer, he declined; [21]but on taking leave of them, he said, "I[i] will return to you, if God wills." Then he set sail from Ephesus.

## PSALM 145. 1–21

*Praise. Of David.*

I WILL extol you, my God and
    King,
    and bless your name forever
      and ever.
2  Every day I will bless you,
    and praise your name forever
      and ever.
3  Great is the LORD, and greatly
      to be praised;
    his greatness is unsearchable.

4  One generation shall laud your
      works to another,
    and shall declare your mighty
      acts.
5  On the glorious splendor of your
      majesty,
    and on your wondrous works,
      I will meditate.
6  The might of your awesome
      deeds shall be
      proclaimed,

---

[a]Gk *He*  [b]Gk *with the word*  [c]Or *the Christ*  [d]Gk *reviled him, he shook out his clothes*  [e]Gk *left there*
[f]Other ancient authorities read *Titus*  [g]Other ancient authorities read *all the Greeks*  [h]Gk *brothers*
[i]Other ancient authorities read *I must at all costs keep the approaching festival in Jerusalem, but I*

and I will declare your
 greatness.
7 They shall celebrate the fame of
 your abundant goodness,
 and shall sing aloud of your
 righteousness.

8 The Lord is gracious and
 merciful,
 slow to anger and abounding
 in steadfast love.
9 The Lord is good to all,
 and his compassion is over all
 that he has made.

10 All your works shall give thanks
 to you, O Lord,
 and all your faithful shall
 bless you.
11 They shall speak of the glory of
 your kingdom,
 and tell of your power,
12 to make known to all people
 your[a] mighty deeds,
 and the glorious splendor of
 your[b] kingdom.
13 Your kingdom is an everlasting
 kingdom,
 and your dominion endures
 throughout all
 generations.

The Lord is faithful in all his
 words,
 and gracious in all his
 deeds. [c]

14 The Lord upholds all who are
 falling,
 and raises up all who are
 bowed down.
15 The eyes of all look to you,
 and you give them their food
 in due season.
16 You open your hand,
 satisfying the desire of every
 living thing.
17 The Lord is just in all his ways,
 and kind in all his doings.
18 The Lord is near to all who call
 on him,
 to all who call on him in truth.
19 He fulfills the desire of all who
 fear him;
 he also hears their cry, and
 saves them.
20 The Lord watches over all who
 love him,
 but all the wicked he will
 destroy.

21 My mouth will speak the praise
 of the Lord,
 and all flesh will bless his holy
 name forever and ever.

## PROVERBS 18.1

THE one who lives alone is
 self-indulgent,
 showing contempt for all who
 have sound judgment. [d]

aGk Jerome Syr: Heb *his*  bHeb *his*  cThese two lines supplied by Q Ms Gk Syr  dMeaning of Heb
uncertain

# JUNE 28

## 2 KINGS 13.1—14.29

IN the twenty-third year of King Joash son of Ahaziah of Judah, Jehoahaz son of Jehu began to reign over Israel in Samaria; he reigned seventeen years. ²He did what was evil in the sight of the LORD, and followed the sins of Jeroboam son of Nebat, which he caused Israel to sin; he did not depart from them. ³The anger of the LORD was kindled against Israel, so that he gave them repeatedly into the hand of King Hazael of Aram, then into the hand of Ben-hadad son of Hazael. ⁴But Jehoahaz entreated the LORD, and the LORD heeded him; for he saw the oppression of Israel, how the king of Aram oppressed them. ⁵Therefore the LORD gave Israel a savior, so that they escaped from the hand of the Arameans; and the people of Israel lived in their homes as formerly. ⁶Nevertheless they did not depart from the sins of the house of Jeroboam, which he caused Israel to sin, but walkedᵃ in them; the sacred poleᵇ also remained in Samaria. ⁷So Jehoahaz was left with an army of not more than fifty horsemen, ten chariots and ten thousand footmen; for the king of Aram had destroyed them and made them like the dust at threshing. ⁸Now the rest of the acts of Jehoahaz and all that he did, including his might, are they not written in the Book of the Annals of the Kings of Israel? ⁹So Jehoahaz slept with his ancestors, and they buried him in Samaria; then his son Joash succeeded him.

10 In the thirty-seventh year of King Joash of Judah, Jehoash son of Jehoahaz began to reign over Israel in Samaria; he reigned sixteen years. ¹¹He also did what was evil in the sight of the LORD; he did not depart from all the sins of Jeroboam son of Nebat, which he caused Israel to sin, but he walked in them. ¹²Now the rest of the acts of Joash, and all that he did, as well as the might with which he fought against King Amaziah of Judah, are they not written in the Book of the Annals of the Kings of Israel? ¹³So Joash slept with his ancestors, and Jeroboam sat upon his throne; Joash was buried in Samaria with the kings of Israel.

14 Now when Elisha had fallen sick with the illness of which he was to die, King Joash of Israel went down to him, and wept before him, crying, "My father, my father! The chariots of Israel and its horsemen!" ¹⁵Elisha said to him, "Take a bow and arrows"; so he took a bow and arrows. ¹⁶Then he said to the king of Israel, "Draw the bow"; and he drew it. Elisha laid his hands on the king's hands. ¹⁷Then he said, "Open the window eastward"; and he opened it. Elisha said, "Shoot"; and he shot. Then he said, "The LORD's arrow of victory, the arrow of victory over Aram! For you shall fight the Arameans in Aphek until you have made an end of them." ¹⁸He continued, "Take the arrows"; and he took them. He said to the king of Israel, "Strike the ground with them"; he struck three times, and stopped. ¹⁹Then the man of God was angry with him, and said, "You should have struck five or six times; then you would have struck down Aram until you had made an end of it, but now you will strike down Aram only three times."

20 So Elisha died, and they buried him. Now bands of Moabites used to invade the land in the spring of the year. ²¹As a man was being buried, a

---

ᵃGk Syr Tg Vg: Heb *he walked*  ᵇHeb *Asherah*

marauding band was seen and the man was thrown into the grave of Elisha; as soon as the man touched the bones of Elisha, he came to life and stood on his feet.

22 Now King Hazael of Aram oppressed Israel all the days of Jehoahaz. 23But the Lord was gracious to them and had compassion on them; he turned toward them, because of his covenant with Abraham, Isaac, and Jacob, and would not destroy them; nor has he banished them from his presence until now.

24 When King Hazael of Aram died, his son Ben-hadad succeeded him. 25Then Jehoash son of Jehoahaz took again from Ben-hadad son of Hazael the towns that he had taken from his father Jehoahaz in war. Three times Joash defeated him and recovered the towns of Israel.

14.1 In the second year of King Joash son of Joahaz of Israel, King Amaziah son of Joash of Judah, began to reign. 2He was twenty-five years old when he began to reign, and he reigned twenty-nine years in Jerusalem. His mother's name was Jehoaddin of Jerusalem. 3He did what was right in the sight of the Lord, yet not like his ancestor David; in all things he did as his father Joash had done. 4But the high places were not removed; the people still sacrificed and made offerings on the high places. 5As soon as the royal power was firmly in his hand he killed his servants who had murdered his father the king. 6But he did not put to death the children of the murderers; according to what is written in the book of the law of Moses, where the Lord commanded, "The parents shall not be put to death for the children, or the children be put to death for the parents; but all shall be put to death for their own sins."

7 He killed ten thousand Edomites in the Valley of Salt and took Sela by storm; he called it Jokthe-el, which is its name to this day.

8 Then Amaziah sent messengers to King Jehoash son of Jehoahaz, son of Jehu, of Israel, saying, "Come, let us look one another in the face." 9King Jehoash of Israel sent word to King Amaziah of Judah, "A thornbush on Lebanon sent to a cedar on Lebanon, saying, 'Give your daughter to my son for a wife'; but a wild animal of Lebanon passed by and trampled down the thornbush. 10You have indeed defeated Edom, and your heart has lifted you up. Be content with your glory, and stay at home; for why should you provoke trouble so that you fall, you and Judah with you?"

11 But Amaziah would not listen. So King Jehoash of Israel went up; he and King Amaziah of Judah faced one another in battle at Beth-shemesh, which belongs to Judah. 12Judah was defeated by Israel; everyone fled home. 13King Jehoash of Israel captured King Amaziah of Judah son of Jehoash, son of Ahaziah, at Beth-shemesh; he came to Jerusalem, and broke down the wall of Jerusalem from the Ephraim Gate to the Corner Gate, a distance of four hundred cubits. 14He seized all the gold and silver, and all the vessels that were found in the house of the Lord and in the treasuries of the king's house, as well as hostages; then he returned to Samaria.

15 Now the rest of the acts that Jehoash did, his might, and how he fought with King Amaziah of Judah, are they not written in the Book of the Annals of the Kings of Israel? 16Jehoash slept with his ancestors, and was buried in Samaria with the kings of Israel; then his son Jeroboam succeeded him.

17 King Amaziah son of Joash of Judah lived fifteen years after the death of King Jehoash son of Jehoahaz of Israel. 18Now the rest of the deeds of Amaziah, are they not written in the Book of the Annals of the Kings of Judah?

¹⁹They made a conspiracy against him in Jerusalem, and he fled to Lachish. But they sent after him to Lachish, and killed him there. ²⁰They brought him on horses; he was buried in Jerusalem with his ancestors in the city of David. ²¹All the people of Judah took Azariah, who was sixteen years old, and made him king to succeed his father Amaziah. ²²He rebuilt Elath and restored it to Judah, after King Amaziah[a] slept with his ancestors.

23  In the fifteenth year of King Amaziah son of Joash of Judah, King Jeroboam son of Joash of Israel began to reign in Samaria; he reigned forty-one years. ²⁴He did what was evil in the sight of the LORD; he did not depart from all the sins of Jeroboam son of Nebat, which he caused Israel to sin. ²⁵He restored the border of Israel from Lebo-hamath as far as the Sea of the Arabah, according to the word of the LORD, the God of Israel, which he spoke by his servant Jonah son of Amittai, the prophet, who was from Gath-hepher. ²⁶For the LORD saw that the distress of Israel was very bitter; there was no one left, bond or free, and no one to help Israel. ²⁷But the LORD had not said that he would blot out the name of Israel from under heaven, so he saved them by the hand of Jeroboam son of Joash.

28  Now the rest of the acts of Jeroboam, and all that he did, and his might, how he fought, and how he recovered for Israel Damascus and Hamath, which had belonged to Judah, are they not written in the Book of the Annals of the Kings of Israel? ²⁹Jeroboam slept with his ancestors, the kings of Israel; his son Zechariah succeeded him.

## ACTS 18.22—19.12

WHEN he [Paul] had landed at Caesarea, he went up to Jerusalem[b] and greeted the church, and then went down to Antioch. ²³After spending some time there he departed and went from place to place through the region of Galatia[c] and Phrygia, strengthening all the disciples.

24  Now there came to Ephesus a Jew named Apollos, a native of Alexandria. He was an eloquent man, well-versed in the scriptures. ²⁵He had been instructed in the Way of the Lord; and he spoke with burning enthusiasm and taught accurately the things concerning Jesus, though he knew only the baptism of John. ²⁶He began to speak boldly in the synagogue; but when Priscilla and Aquila heard him, they took him aside and explained the Way of God to him more accurately. ²⁷And when he wished to cross over to Achaia, the believers[d] encouraged him and wrote to the disciples to welcome him. On his arrival he greatly helped those who through grace had become believers, ²⁸for he powerfully refuted the Jews in public, showing by the scriptures that the Messiah[e] is Jesus.

19.1 WHILE Apollos was in Corinth, Paul passed through the interior regions and came to Ephesus, where he found some disciples. ²He said to them, "Did you receive the Holy Spirit when you became believers?" They replied, "No, we have not even heard that there is a Holy Spirit." ³Then he said, "Into what then were you baptized?" They answered, "Into John's baptism." ⁴Paul said, "John baptized with the baptism of repentance, telling the people to believe in the one who was to come after him, that is, in Jesus." ⁵On hearing this, they were baptized in the name of the

aHeb *the king*　bGk *went up*　cGk *the Galatian region*　dGk *brothers*　eOr *the Christ*

Lord Jesus. ⁶When Paul had laid his hands on them, the Holy Spirit came upon them, and they spoke in tongues and prophesied— ⁷altogether there were about twelve of them.

8 He entered the synagogue and for three months spoke out boldly, and argued persuasively about the kingdom of God. ⁹When some stubbornly refused to believe and spoke evil of the Way before the congregation, he left them, taking the disciples with him, and argued daily in the lecture hall of Tyrannus. a ¹⁰This continued for two years, so that all the residents of Asia, both Jews and Greeks, heard the word of the Lord.

11 God did extraordinary miracles through Paul, ¹²so that when the handkerchiefs or aprons that had touched his skin were brought to the sick, their diseases left them, and the evil spirits came out of them.

## PSALM 146.1–10

**P**RAISE the LORD!
Praise the LORD, O my soul!
² I will praise the LORD as
long as I live;
I will sing praises to my God
all my life long.

³ Do not put your trust in
princes,
in mortals, in whom there is
no help.
⁴ When their breath departs, they
return to the earth;
on that very day their plans
perish.

⁵ Happy are those whose help is
the God of Jacob,
whose hope is in the LORD
their God,
⁶ who made heaven and earth,
the sea, and all that is in
them;
who keeps faith forever;
⁷ who executes justice for the
oppressed;
who gives food to the hungry.

The LORD sets the prisoners
free;
⁸ the LORD opens the eyes of
the blind.
The LORD lifts up those who are
bowed down;
the LORD loves the righteous.
⁹ The LORD watches over the
strangers;
he upholds the orphan and the
widow,
but the way of the wicked he
brings to ruin.

¹⁰ The LORD will reign forever,
your God, O Zion, for all
generations.
Praise the LORD!

## PROVERBS 18.2–3

**A** FOOL takes no pleasure in
understanding,
but only in expressing
personal opinion.
³ When wickedness comes,
contempt comes also;
and with dishonor comes
disgrace.

---

a Other ancient authorities read *of a certain Tyrannus, from eleven o'clock in the morning to four in the afternoon*

# JUNE 29

2 KINGS 15.1—16.20

In the twenty-seventh year of King Jeroboam of Israel King Azariah son of Amaziah of Judah began to reign. ²He was sixteen years old when he began to reign, and he reigned fifty-two years in Jerusalem. His mother's name was Jecoliah of Jerusalem. ³He did what was right in the sight of the LORD, just as his father Amaziah had done. ⁴Nevertheless the high places were not taken away; the people still sacrificed and made offerings on the high places. ⁵The LORD struck the king, so that he was leprousª to the day of his death, and lived in a separate house. Jotham the king's son was in charge of the palace, governing the people of the land. ⁶Now the rest of the acts of Azariah, and all that he did, are they not written in the Book of the Annals of the Kings of Judah? ⁷Azariah slept with his ancestors; they buried him with his ancestors in the city of David; his son Jotham succeeded him.

8 In the thirty-eighth year of King Azariah of Judah, Zechariah son of Jeroboam reigned over Israel in Samaria six months. ⁹He did what was evil in the sight of the LORD, as his ancestors had done. He did not depart from the sins of Jeroboam son of Nebat, which he caused Israel to sin. ¹⁰Shallum son of Jabesh conspired against him, and struck him down in public and killed him, and reigned in place of him. ¹¹Now the rest of the deeds of Zechariah are written in the Book of the Annals of the Kings of Israel. ¹²This was the promise of the LORD that he gave to Jehu, "Your sons shall sit on the throne of Israel to the fourth generation." And so it happened.

13 Shallum son of Jabesh began to reign in the thirty-ninth year of King Uzziah of Judah; he reigned one month in Samaria. ¹⁴Then Menahem son of Gadi came up from Tirzah and came to Samaria; he struck down Shallum son of Jabesh in Samaria and killed him; he reigned in place of him. ¹⁵Now the rest of the deeds of Shallum, including the conspiracy that he made, are written in the Book of the Annals of the Kings of Israel. ¹⁶At that time Menahem sacked Tiphsah, all who were in it and its territory from Tirzah on; because they did not open it to him, he sacked it. He ripped open all the pregnant women in it.

17 In the thirty-ninth year of King Azariah of Judah, Menahem son of Gadi began to reign over Israel; he reigned ten years in Samaria. ¹⁸He did what was evil in the sight of the LORD; he did not depart all his days from any of the sins of Jeroboam son of Nebat, which he caused Israel to sin. ¹⁹King Pul of Assyria came against the land; Menahem gave Pul a thousand talents of silver, so that he might help him confirm his hold on the royal power. ²⁰Menahem exacted the money from Israel, that is, from all the wealthy, fifty shekels of silver from each one, to give to the king of Assyria. So the king of Assyria turned back, and did not stay there in the land. ²¹Now the rest of the deeds of Menahem, and all that he did, are they not written in the Book of the Annals of the Kings of Israel? ²²Menahem slept with his ancestors, and his son Pekahiah succeeded him.

23 In the fiftieth year of King Azariah of Judah, Pekahiah son of Menahem began to reign over Israel in

---

ª A term for several skin diseases; precise meaning uncertain

Samaria; he reigned two years. <sup>24</sup>He did what was evil in the sight of the LORD; he did not turn away from the sins of Jeroboam son of Nebat, which he caused Israel to sin. <sup>25</sup>Pekah son of Remaliah, his captain, conspired against him with fifty of the Gileadites, and attacked him in Samaria, in the citadel of the palace along with Argob and Arieh; he killed him, and reigned in place of him. <sup>26</sup>Now the rest of the deeds of Pekahiah, and all that he did, are written in the Book of the Annals of the Kings of Israel.

27  In the fifty-second year of King Azariah of Judah, Pekah son of Remaliah began to reign over Israel in Samaria; he reigned twenty years. <sup>28</sup>He did what was evil in the sight of the LORD; he did not depart from the sins of Jeroboam son of Nebat, which he caused Israel to sin.

29  In the days of King Pekah of Israel, King Tiglath-pileser of Assyria came and captured Ijon, Abel-beth-maacah, Janoah, Kedesh, Hazor, Gilead, and Galilee, all the land of Naphtali; and he carried the people captive to Assyria. <sup>30</sup>Then Hoshea son of Elah made a conspiracy against Pekah son of Remaliah, attacked him, and killed him; he reigned in place of him, in the twentieth year of Jotham son of Uzziah. <sup>31</sup>Now the rest of the acts of Pekah, and all that he did, are written in the Book of the Annals of the Kings of Israel.

32  In the second year of King Pekah son of Remaliah of Israel, King Jotham son of Uzziah of Judah began to reign. <sup>33</sup>He was twenty-five years old when he began to reign and reigned sixteen years in Jerusalem. His mother's name was Jerusha daughter of Zadok. <sup>34</sup>He did what was right in the sight of the LORD, just as his father Uzziah had done. <sup>35</sup>Nevertheless the high places were not removed; the people still sac-

rificed and made offerings on the high places. He built the upper gate of the house of the LORD. <sup>36</sup>Now the rest of the acts of Jotham, and all that he did, are they not written in the Book of the Annals of the Kings of Judah? <sup>37</sup>In those days the LORD began to send King Rezin of Aram and Pekah son of Remaliah against Judah. <sup>38</sup>Jotham slept with his ancestors, and was buried with his ancestors in the city of David, his ancestor; his son Ahaz succeeded him.

**16.**<sup>1</sup> IN the seventeenth year of Pekah son of Remaliah, King Ahaz son of Jotham of Judah began to reign. <sup>2</sup>Ahaz was twenty years old when he began to reign; he reigned sixteen years in Jerusalem. He did not do what was right in the sight of the LORD his God, as his ancestor David had done, <sup>3</sup>but he walked in the way of the kings of Israel. He even made his son pass through fire, according to the abominable practices of the nations whom the LORD drove out before the people of Israel. <sup>4</sup>He sacrificed and made offerings on the high places, on the hills, and under every green tree.

5  Then King Rezin of Aram and King Pekah son of Remaliah of Israel came up to wage war on Jerusalem; they besieged Ahaz but could not conquer him. <sup>6</sup>At that time the king of Edom<sup>a</sup> recovered Elath for Edom,<sup>b</sup> and drove the Judeans from Elath; and the Edomites came to Elath, where they live to this day. <sup>7</sup>Ahaz sent messengers to King Tiglath-pileser of Assyria, saying, "I am your servant and your son. Come up, and rescue me from the hand of the king of Aram and from the hand of the king of Israel, who are attacking me." <sup>8</sup>Ahaz also took the silver and gold found in the house of the LORD and in the treasures of the king's house, and sent a present to the king of Assyria. <sup>9</sup>The king of Assyria listened

**a** Cn: Heb *King Rezin of Aram*   **b** Cn: Heb *Aram*

to him; the king of Assyria marched up against Damascus, and took it, carrying its people captive to Kir; then he killed Rezin.

10 When King Ahaz went to Damascus to meet King Tiglath-pileser of Assyria, he saw the altar that was at Damascus. King Ahaz sent to the priest Uriah a model of the altar, and its pattern, exact in all its details. [11]The priest Uriah built the altar; in accordance with all that King Ahaz had sent from Damascus, just so did the priest Uriah build it, before King Ahaz arrived from Damascus. [12]When the king came from Damascus, the king viewed the altar. Then the king drew near to the altar, went up on it, [13]and offered his burnt offering and his grain offering, poured his drink offering, and dashed the blood of his offerings of well-being against the altar. [14]The bronze altar that was before the LORD he removed from the front of the house, from the place between his altar and the house of the LORD, and put it on the north side of his altar. [15]King Ahaz commanded the priest Uriah, saying, "Upon the great altar offer the morning burnt offering, and the evening grain offering, and the king's burnt offering, and his grain offering, with the burnt offering of all the people of the land, their grain offering, and their drink offering; then dash against it all the blood of the burnt offering, and all the blood of the sacrifice; but the bronze altar shall be for me to inquire by." [16]The priest Uriah did everything that King Ahaz commanded.

17 Then King Ahaz cut off the frames of the stands, and removed the laver from them; he removed the sea from the bronze oxen that were under it, and put it on a pediment of stone. [18]The covered portal for use on the sabbath that had been built inside the palace, and the outer entrance for the king he removed from[a] the house of the LORD. He did this because of the king of Assyria. [19]Now the rest of the acts of Ahaz that he did, are they not written in the Book of the Annals of the Kings of Judah? [20]Ahaz slept with his ancestors, and was buried with his ancestors in the city of David; his son Hezekiah succeeded him.

## ACTS 19.13–41

THEN some itinerant Jewish exorcists tried to use the name of the Lord Jesus over those who had evil spirits, saying, "I adjure you by the Jesus whom Paul proclaims." [14]Seven sons of a Jewish high priest named Sceva were doing this. [15]But the evil spirit said to them in reply, "Jesus I know, and Paul I know; but who are you?" [16]Then the man with the evil spirit leaped on them, mastered them all, and so overpowered them that they fled out of the house naked and wounded. [17]When this became known to all residents of Ephesus, both Jews and Greeks, everyone was awestruck; and the name of the Lord Jesus was praised. [18]Also many of those who became believers confessed and disclosed their practices. [19]A number of those who practiced magic collected their books and burned them publicly; when the value of these books[b] was calculated, it was found to come to fifty thousand silver coins. [20]So the word of the Lord grew mightily and prevailed.

21 Now after these things had been accomplished, Paul resolved in the Spirit to go through Macedonia and Achaia, and then to go on to Jerusalem. He said, "After I have gone there, I must also see Rome." [22]So he sent two of his helpers, Timothy and Erastus, to Macedonia, while he himself stayed for some time longer in Asia.

23 About that time no little disturbance broke out concerning the Way.

---

[a]Cn: Heb lacks *from*   [b]Gk *them*

[24]A man named Demetrius, a silversmith who made silver shrines of Artemis, brought no little business to the artisans. [25]These he gathered together, with the workers of the same trade, and said, "Men, you know that we get our wealth from this business. [26]You also see and hear that not only in Ephesus but in almost the whole of Asia this Paul has persuaded and drawn away a considerable number of people by saying that gods made with hands are not gods. [27]And there is danger not only that this trade of ours may come into disrepute but also that the temple of the great goddess Artemis will be scorned, and she will be deprived of her majesty that brought all Asia and the world to worship her."

28 When they heard this, they were enraged and shouted, "Great is Artemis of the Ephesians!" [29]The city was filled with the confusion; and people[a] rushed together to the theater, dragging with them Gaius and Aristarchus, Macedonians who were Paul's travel companions. [30]Paul wished to go into the crowd, but the disciples would not let him; [31]even some officials of the province of Asia,[b] who were friendly to him, sent him a message urging him not to venture into the theater. [32]Meanwhile, some were shouting one thing, some another; for the assembly was in confusion, and most of them did not know why they had come together. [33]Some of the crowd gave instructions to Alexander, whom the Jews had pushed forward. And Alexander motioned for silence and tried to make a defense before the people. [34]But when they recognized that he was a Jew, for about two hours all of them shouted in unison, "Great is Artemis of the Ephesians!" [35]But when the town clerk had quieted the crowd, he said, "Citizens of Ephesus, who is there that does not know that the city of the Ephesians is the temple keeper of the great Artemis and of the statue that fell from heaven?[c] [36]Since these things cannot be denied, you ought to be quiet and do nothing rash. [37]You have brought these men here who are neither temple robbers nor blasphemers of our[d] goddess. [38]If therefore Demetrius and the artisans with him have a complaint against anyone, the courts are open, and there are proconsuls; let them bring charges there against one another. [39]If there is anything further[e] you want to know, it must be settled in the regular assembly. [40]For we are in danger of being charged with rioting today, since there is no cause that we can give to justify this commotion." [41]When he had said this, he dismissed the assembly.

## PSALM 147.1–20

Praise the Lord!
   How good it is to sing
     praises to our God;
  for he is gracious, and a song
     of praise is fitting.
2  The Lord builds up Jerusalem;
    he gathers the outcasts of
     Israel.
3  He heals the brokenhearted,
    and binds up their wounds.
4  He determines the number of
     the stars;
    he gives to all of them their
     names.
5  Great is our Lord, and abundant
     in power;
    his understanding is beyond
     measure.
6  The Lord lifts up the
     downtrodden;
    he casts the wicked to the
     ground.

7  Sing to the Lord with
     thanksgiving;

aGk *they*  bGk *some of the Asiarchs*  cMeaning of Gk uncertain  dOther ancient authorities read *your*  eOther ancient authorities read *about other matters*

make melody to our God on
  the lyre.
8  He covers the heavens with
    clouds,
  prepares rain for the earth,
  makes grass grow on the
    hills.
9  He gives to the animals their
    food,
  and to the young ravens when
    they cry.
10  His delight is not in the strength
    of the horse,
  nor his pleasure in the speed
    of a runner; [a]
11  but the Lord takes pleasure in
    those who fear him,
  in those who hope in his
    steadfast love.

12  Praise the Lord, O Jerusalem!
  Praise your God, O Zion!
13  For he strengthens the bars of
    your gates;
  he blesses your children
    within you.
14  He grants peace [b] within your
    borders;
  he fills you with the finest of
    wheat.

15  He sends out his command to
    the earth;
  his word runs swiftly.
16  He gives snow like wool;
  he scatters frost like ashes.
17  He hurls down hail like
    crumbs—
  who can stand before his
    cold?
18  He sends out his word, and
    melts them;
  he makes his wind blow, and
    the waters flow.
19  He declares his word to Jacob,
  his statutes and ordinances to
    Israel.
20  He has not dealt thus with any
    other nation;
  they do not know his
    ordinances.
Praise the Lord!

## PROVERBS 18.4–5

THE words of the mouth are
    deep waters;
  the fountain of wisdom is a
    gushing stream.
5  It is not right to be partial to
    the guilty,
  or to subvert the innocent in
    judgment.

# JUNE 30

## 2 KINGS 17.1—18.12

IN the twelfth year of King Ahaz of Judah, Hoshea son of Elah began to reign in Samaria over Israel; he reigned nine years. [2]He did what was evil in the sight of the Lord, yet not like the kings of Israel who were before him. [3]King Shalmaneser of Assyria came up against him; Hoshea became his vassal, and paid him tribute. [4]But the king of Assyria found treachery in Hoshea; for he had sent messengers to King So of Egypt, and offered no tribute to the king of Assyria, as he had

a Heb *legs of a person*   b Or *prosperity*

done year by year; therefore the king of Assyria confined him and imprisoned him.

5 Then the king of Assyria invaded all the land and came to Samaria; for three years he besieged it. [6]In the ninth year of Hoshea the king of Assyria captured Samaria; he carried the Israelites away to Assyria. He placed them in Halah, on the Habor, the river of Gozan, and in the cities of the Medes.

7 This occurred because the people of Israel had sinned against the Lord their God, who had brought them up out of the land of Egypt from under the hand of Pharaoh king of Egypt. They had worshiped other gods [8]and walked in the customs of the nations whom the Lord drove out before the people of Israel, and in the customs that the kings of Israel had introduced. [a] [9]The people of Israel secretly did things that were not right against the Lord their God. They built for themselves high places at all their towns, from watchtower to fortified city; [10]they set up for themselves pillars and sacred poles[b] on every high hill and under every green tree; [11]there they made offerings on all the high places, as the nations did whom the Lord carried away before them. They did wicked things, provoking the Lord to anger; [12]they served idols, of which the Lord had said to them, "You shall not do this." [13]Yet the Lord warned Israel and Judah by every prophet and every seer, saying, "Turn from your evil ways and keep my commandments and my statutes, in accordance with all the law that I commanded your ancestors and that I sent to you by my servants the prophets." [14]They would not listen but were stubborn, as their ancestors had been, who did not believe in the Lord their God. [15]They despised his statutes, and his covenant that he made with their ancestors, and the warnings that he gave them. They went after

false idols and became false; they followed the nations that were around them, concerning whom the Lord had commanded them that they should not do as they did. [16]They rejected all the commandments of the Lord their God and made for themselves cast images of two calves; they made a sacred pole, [c] worshiped all the host of heaven, and served Baal. [17]They made their sons and their daughters pass through fire; they used divination and augury; and they sold themselves to do evil in the sight of the Lord, provoking him to anger. [18]Therefore the Lord was very angry with Israel and removed them out of his sight; none was left but the tribe of Judah alone.

19 Judah also did not keep the commandments of the Lord their God but walked in the customs that Israel had introduced. [20]The Lord rejected all the descendants of Israel; he punished them and gave them into the hand of plunderers, until he had banished them from his presence.

21 When he had torn Israel from the house of David, they made Jeroboam son of Nebat king. Jeroboam drove Israel from following the Lord and made them commit great sin. [22]The people of Israel continued in all the sins that Jeroboam committed; they did not depart from them [23]until the Lord removed Israel out of his sight, as he had foretold through all his servants the prophets. So Israel was exiled from their own land to Assyria until this day.

24 The king of Assyria brought people from Babylon, Cuthah, Avva, Hamath, and Sepharvaim, and placed them in the cities of Samaria in place of the people of Israel; they took possession of Samaria, and settled in its cities. [25]When they first settled there, they did not worship the Lord; therefore the Lord sent lions among them, which killed some of them. [26]So the king of

[a]Meaning of Heb uncertain   [b]Heb *Asherim*   [c]Heb *Asherah*

Assyria was told, "The nations that you have carried away and placed in the cities of Samaria do not know the law of the god of the land; therefore he has sent lions among them; they are killing them, because they do not know the law of the god of the land." ²⁷Then the king of Assyria commanded, "Send there one of the priests whom you carried away from there; let him[a] go and live there, and teach them the law of the god of the land." ²⁸So one of the priests whom they had carried away from Samaria came and lived in Bethel; he taught them how they should worship the LORD.

29 But every nation still made gods of its own and put them in the shrines of the high places that the people of Samaria had made, every nation in the cities in which they lived; ³⁰the people of Babylon made Succoth-benoth, the people of Cuth made Nergal, the people of Hamath made Ashima; ³¹the Avvites made Nibhaz and Tartak; the Sepharvites burned their children in the fire to Adrammelech and Anammelech, the gods of Sepharvaim. ³²They also worshiped the LORD and appointed from among themselves all sorts of people as priests of the high places, who sacrificed for them in the shrines of the high places. ³³So they worshiped the LORD but also served their own gods, after the manner of the nations from among whom they had been carried away. ³⁴To this day they continue to practice their former customs.

They do not worship the LORD and they do not follow the statutes or the ordinances or the law or the commandment that the LORD commanded the children of Jacob, whom he named Israel. ³⁵The LORD had made a covenant with them and commanded them, "You shall not worship other gods or bow yourselves to them or serve them or sacrifice to them, ³⁶but you shall worship the LORD, who brought you out of the land of Egypt with great power and with an outstretched arm; you shall bow yourselves to him, and to him you shall sacrifice. ³⁷The statutes and the ordinances and the law and the commandment that he wrote for you, you shall always be careful to observe. You shall not worship other gods; ³⁸you shall not forget the covenant that I have made with you. You shall not worship other gods, ³⁹but you shall worship the LORD your God; he will deliver you out of the hand of all your enemies." ⁴⁰They would not listen, however, but they continued to practice their former custom.

41 So these nations worshiped the LORD, but also served their carved images; to this day their children and their children's children continue to do as their ancestors did.

18.1 IN the third year of King Hoshea son of Elah of Israel, Hezekiah son of King Ahaz of Judah began to reign. ²He was twenty-five years old when he began to reign; he reigned twenty-nine years in Jerusalem. His mother's name was Abi daughter of Zechariah. ³He did what was right in the sight of the LORD just as his ancestor David had done. ⁴He removed the high places, broke down the pillars, and cut down the sacred pole.[b] He broke in pieces the bronze serpent that Moses had made, for until those days the people of Israel had made offerings to it; it was called Nehushtan. ⁵He trusted in the LORD the God of Israel; so that there was no one like him among all the kings of Judah after him, or among those who were before him. ⁶For he held fast to the LORD; he did not depart from following him but kept the commandments that the LORD commanded Moses. ⁷The LORD was with him; wherever he went, he prospered. He rebelled against the

---

aSyr Vg: Heb *them*  bHeb *Asherah*

king of Assyria and would not serve him. ⁸He attacked the Philistines as far as Gaza and its territory, from watchtower to fortified city.

9 In the fourth year of King Hezekiah, which was the seventh year of King Hoshea son of Elah of Israel, King Shalmaneser of Assyria came up against Samaria, besieged it, ¹⁰and at the end of three years, took it. In the sixth year of Hezekiah, which was the ninth year of King Hoshea of Israel, Samaria was taken. ¹¹The king of Assyria carried the Israelites away to Assyria, settled them in Halah, on the Habor, the river of Gozan, and in the cities of the Medes, ¹²because they did not obey the voice of the LORD their God but transgressed his covenant—all that Moses the servant of the LORD had commanded; they neither listened nor obeyed.

## ACTS 20.1–38

AFTER the uproar had ceased, Paul sent for the disciples; and after encouraging them and saying farewell, he left for Macedonia. ²When he had gone through those regions and had given the believersᵃ much encouragement, he came to Greece, ³where he stayed for three months. He was about to set sail for Syria when a plot was made against him by the Jews, and so he decided to return through Macedonia. ⁴He was accompanied by Sopater son of Pyrrhus from Beroea, by Aristarchus and Secundus from Thessalonica, by Gaius from Derbe, and by Timothy, as well as by Tychicus and Trophimus from Asia. ⁵They went ahead and were waiting for us in Troas; ⁶but we sailed from Philippi after the days of Unleavened Bread, and in five days we joined them in Troas, where we stayed for seven days.

7 On the first day of the week, when we met to break bread, Paul was holding a discussion with them; since he intended to leave the next day, he continued speaking until midnight. ⁸There were many lamps in the room upstairs where we were meeting. ⁹A young man named Eutychus, who was sitting in the window, began to sink off into a deep sleep while Paul talked still longer. Overcome by sleep, he fell to the ground three floors below and was picked up dead. ¹⁰But Paul went down, and bending over him took him in his arms, and said, "Do not be alarmed, for his life is in him." ¹¹Then Paul went upstairs, and after he had broken bread and eaten, he continued to converse with them until dawn; then he left. ¹²Meanwhile they had taken the boy away alive and were not a little comforted.

13 We went ahead to the ship and set sail for Assos, intending to take Paul on board there; for he had made this arrangement, intending to go by land himself. ¹⁴When he met us in Assos, we took him on board and went to Mitylene. ¹⁵We sailed from there, and on the following day we arrived opposite Chios. The next day we touched at Samos, andᵇ the day after that we came to Miletus. ¹⁶For Paul had decided to sail past Ephesus, so that he might not have to spend time in Asia; he was eager to be in Jerusalem, if possible, on the day of Pentecost.

17 From Miletus he sent a message to Ephesus, asking the elders of the church to meet him. ¹⁸When they came to him, he said to them:

"You yourselves know how I lived among you the entire time from the first day that I set foot in Asia, ¹⁹serving the Lord with all humility and with tears, enduring the trials that came to me through the plots of the Jews. ²⁰I did not shrink from doing anything helpful, proclaiming the message to you and

ᵃGk *given them*   ᵇOther ancient authorities add *after remaining at Trogyllium*

teaching you publicly and from house to house, 21as I testified to both Jews and Greeks about repentance toward God and faith toward our Lord Jesus. 22And now, as a captive to the Spirit, a I am on my way to Jerusalem, not knowing what will happen to me there, 23except that the Holy Spirit testifies to me in every city that imprisonment and persecutions are waiting for me. 24But I do not count my life of any value to myself, if only I may finish my course and the ministry that I received from the Lord Jesus, to testify to the good news of God's grace.

25 "And now I know that none of you, among whom I have gone about proclaiming the kingdom, will ever see my face again. 26Therefore I declare to you this day that I am not responsible for the blood of any of you, 27for I did not shrink from declaring to you the whole purpose of God. 28Keep watch over yourselves and over all the flock, of which the Holy Spirit has made you overseers, to shepherd the church of Godb that he obtained with the blood of his own Son. c 29I know that after I have gone, savage wolves will come in among you, not sparing the flock. 30Some even from your own group will come distorting the truth in order to entice the disciples to follow them. 31Therefore be alert, remembering that for three years I did not cease night or day to warn everyone with tears. 32And now I commend you to God and to the message of his grace, a message that is able to build you up and to give you the inheritance among all who are sanctified. 33I coveted no one's silver or gold or clothing. 34You know for yourselves that I worked with my own hands to support myself and my companions. 35In all this I have given you an example that by such work we must support the weak, remembering the words of the Lord Jesus, for he himself said, 'It is more blessed to give than to receive.' "

36  When he had finished speaking, he knelt down with them all and prayed. 37There was much weeping among them all; they embraced Paul and kissed him, 38grieving especially because of what he had said, that they would not see him again. Then they brought him to the ship.

## PSALM 148.1–14

Praise the Lord!
Praise the Lord from the
  heavens;
  praise him in the heights!
2  Praise him, all his angels;
  praise him, all his host!

3  Praise him, sun and moon;
  praise him, all you shining
    stars!
4  Praise him, you highest
    heavens,
  and you waters above the
    heavens!

5  Let them praise the name of
    the Lord,
  for he commanded and they
    were created.
6  He established them forever
    and ever;
  he fixed their bounds, which
    cannot be passed. d

7  Praise the Lord from the earth,
  you sea monsters and all
    deeps,
8  fire and hail, snow and frost,
  stormy wind fulfilling his
    command!

9  Mountains and all hills,
  fruit trees and all cedars!
10  Wild animals and all cattle,

aOr *And now, bound in the spirit*  bOther ancient authorities read *of the Lord*  cOr *with his own blood*; Gk *with the blood of his Own*  dOr *he set a law that cannot pass away*

> creeping things and flying
>   birds!
>
> 11  Kings of the earth and all
>       peoples,
>     princes and all rulers of the
>       earth!
> 12  Young men and women alike,
>     old and young together!
>
> 13  Let them praise the name of
>       the LORD,
>     for his name alone is exalted;
>     his glory is above earth and
>       heaven.

> 14  He has raised up a horn for his
>       people,
>     praise for all his faithful,
>     for the people of Israel who
>       are close to him.
>   Praise the LORD!

## PROVERBS 18.6–7

A FOOL'S lips bring strife,
  and a fool's mouth invites a
    flogging.
7  The mouths of fools are their
    ruin,
  and their lips a snare to
    themselves.

# JULY 1

## 2 KINGS 18.13—19.37

IN the fourteenth year of King Hezekiah, King Sennacherib of Assyria came up against all the fortified cities of Judah and captured them. ¹⁴King Hezekiah of Judah sent to the king of Assyria at Lachish, saying, "I have done wrong; withdraw from me; whatever you impose on me I will bear." The king of Assyria demanded of King Hezekiah of Judah three hundred talents of silver and thirty talents of gold. ¹⁵Hezekiah gave him all the silver that was found in the house of the LORD and in the treasuries of the king's house. ¹⁶At that time Hezekiah stripped the gold from the doors of the temple of the LORD, and from the doorposts that King Hezekiah of Judah had overlaid and gave it to the king of Assyria. ¹⁷The king of Assyria sent the Tartan, the Rabsaris, and the Rabshakeh with a great army from Lachish to King Hezekiah at Jerusalem. They went up and came to Jerusalem. When they arrived, they came and stood by the conduit of the upper pool, which is on the highway to the Fuller's Field. ¹⁸When they called for the king, there came out to them Eliakim son of Hilkiah, who was in charge of the palace, and Shebnah the secretary, and Joah son of Asaph, the recorder.

19 The Rabshakeh said to them, "Say to Hezekiah: Thus says the great king, the king of Assyria: On what do you base this confidence of yours? ²⁰Do you think that mere words are strategy and power for war? On whom do you now rely, that you have rebelled against me? ²¹See, you are relying now on Egypt, that broken reed of a staff, which will pierce the hand of anyone who leans on it. Such is Pharaoh king of Egypt to all who rely on him. ²²But if you say to me, 'We rely on the LORD our God,' is it not he whose high places and altars Hezekiah has removed, saying to Judah and to Jerusalem, 'You shall worship before this altar in Jerusalem'? ²³Come now, make a wager with my master the king of Assyria: I will give you two thousand horses, if you are able on your part to set riders on them.

²⁴How then can you repulse a single captain among the least of my master's servants, when you rely on Egypt for chariots and for horsemen? ²⁵Moreover, is it without the LORD that I have come up against this place to destroy it? The LORD said to me, Go up against this land, and destroy it.' "

26  Then Eliakim son of Hilkiah, and Shebnah, and Joah said to the Rabshakeh, "Please speak to your servants in the Aramaic language, for we understand it; do not speak to us in the language of Judah within the hearing of the people who are on the wall." ²⁷But the Rabshakeh said to them, "Has my master sent me to speak these words to your master and to you, and not to the people sitting on the wall, who are doomed with you to eat their own dung and to drink their own urine?"

28  Then the Rabshakeh stood and called out in a loud voice in the language of Judah, "Hear the word of the great king, the king of Assyria! ²⁹Thus says the king: 'Do not let Hezekiah deceive you, for he will not be able to deliver you out of my hand. ³⁰Do not let Hezekiah make you rely on the LORD by saying, The LORD will surely deliver us, and this city will not be given into the hand of the king of Assyria.' ³¹Do not listen to Hezekiah; for thus says the king of Assyria: 'Make your peace with me and come out to me; then every one of you will eat from your own vine and your own fig tree, and drink water from your own cistern, ³²until I come and take you away to a land like your own land, a land of grain and wine, a land of bread and vineyards, a land of olive oil and honey, that you may live and not die. Do not listen to Hezekiah when he misleads you by saying, The LORD will deliver us. ³³Has any of the gods of the nations ever delivered its land out of the hand of the king of Assyria? ³⁴Where are the gods of Hamath and Arpad? Where are the gods of Sepharvaim, Hena, and Ivvah? Have they delivered Samaria out of my hand? ³⁵Who among all the gods of the countries have delivered their countries out of my hand, that the LORD should deliver Jerusalem out of my hand?' "

36  But the people were silent and answered him not a word, for the king's command was, "Do not answer him." ³⁷Then Eliakim son of Hilkiah, who was in charge of the palace, and Shebna the secretary, and Joah son of Asaph, the recorder, came to Hezekiah with their clothes torn and told him the words of the Rabshakeh.


**19.1** WHEN King Hezekiah heard it, he tore his clothes, covered himself with sackcloth, and went into the house of the LORD. ²And he sent Eliakim, who was in charge of the palace, and Shebna the secretary, and the senior priests, covered with sackcloth, to the prophet Isaiah son of Amoz. ³They said to him, "Thus says Hezekiah, This day is a day of distress, of rebuke, and of disgrace; children have come to the birth, and there is no strength to bring them forth. ⁴It may be that the LORD your God heard all the words of the Rabshakeh, whom his master the king of Assyria has sent to mock the living God, and will rebuke the words that the LORD your God has heard; therefore lift up your prayer for the remnant that is left." ⁵When the servants of King Hezekiah came to Isaiah, ⁶Isaiah said to them, "Say to your master, 'Thus says the LORD: Do not be afraid because of the words that you have heard, with which the servants of the king of Assyria have reviled me. ⁷I myself will put a spirit in him, so that he shall hear a rumor and return to his own land; I will cause him to fall by the sword in his own land.' "

8  The Rabshakeh returned, and found the king of Assyria fighting against Libnah; for he had heard that the king had left Lachish. ⁹When the

king[a] heard concerning King Tirhakah of Ethiopia,[b] "See, he has set out to fight against you," he sent messengers again to Hezekiah, saying, [10]"Thus shall you speak to King Hezekiah of Judah: Do not let your God on whom you rely deceive you by promising that Jerusalem will not be given into the hand of the king of Assyria. [11]See, you have heard what the kings of Assyria have done to all lands, destroying them utterly. Shall you be delivered? [12]Have the gods of the nations delivered them, the nations that my predecessors destroyed, Gozan, Haran, Rezeph, and the people of Eden who were in Telassar? [13]Where is the king of Hamath, the king of Arpad, the king of the city of Sepharvaim, the king of Hena, or the king of Ivvah?"

14 Hezekiah received the letter from the hand of the messengers and read it; then Hezekiah went up to the house of the LORD and spread it before the LORD. [15]And Hezekiah prayed before the LORD, and said: "O LORD the God of Israel, who are enthroned above the cherubim, you are God, you alone, of all the kingdoms of the earth; you have made heaven and earth. [16]Incline your ear, O LORD, and hear; open your eyes, O LORD, and see; hear the words of Sennacherib, which he has sent to mock the living God. [17]Truly, O LORD, the kings of Assyria have laid waste the nations and their lands, [18]and have hurled their gods into the fire, though they were no gods but the work of human hands—wood and stone—and so they were destroyed. [19]So now, O LORD our God, save us, I pray you, from his hand, so that all the kingdoms of the earth may know that you, O LORD, are God alone."

20 Then Isaiah son of Amoz sent to Hezekiah, saying, "Thus says the LORD, the God of Israel: I have heard your prayer to me about King Sennacherib of Assyria. [21]This is the word that the LORD has spoken concerning him:

She despises you, she scorns
    you—
  virgin daughter Zion;
she tosses her head—behind
    your back,
  daughter Jerusalem.

22  Whom have you mocked and
    reviled?
  Against whom have you
    raised your voice
and haughtily lifted your eyes?
  Against the Holy One of
    Israel!
23  By your messengers you have
    mocked the Lord,
  and you have said, 'With my
    many chariots
I have gone up the heights of
    the mountains,
  to the far recesses of
    Lebanon;
I felled its tallest cedars,
  its choicest cypresses;
I entered its farthest retreat,
  its densest forest.
24  I dug wells
  and drank foreign waters,
I dried up with the sole of my
    foot
  all the streams of Egypt.'

25  Have you not heard
  that I determined it long ago?
I planned from days of old
  what now I bring to pass,
that you should make fortified
    cities
  crash into heaps of ruins,
26  while their inhabitants, shorn of
    strength,
  are dismayed and confounded;
they have become like plants of
    the field
  and like tender grass,
like grass on the housetops,

[a] Heb *he*  [b] Or *Nubia*; Heb *Cush*

blighted before it is grown.

27 "But I know your rising<sup>a</sup> and
> your sitting,
> your going out and coming in,
> and your raging against me.
28 Because you have raged against
> me
> and your arrogance has come
> to my ears,
> I will put my hook in your nose
> and my bit in your mouth;
> I will turn you back on the way
> by which you came.

29 "And this shall be the sign for you: This year you shall eat what grows of itself, and in the second year what springs from that; then in the third year sow, reap, plant vineyards, and eat their fruit. <sup>30</sup>The surviving remnant of the house of Judah shall again take root downward, and bear fruit upward; <sup>31</sup>for from Jerusalem a remnant shall go out, and from Mount Zion a band of survivors. The zeal of the LORD of hosts will do this.

32 "Therefore thus says the LORD concerning the king of Assyria: He shall not come into this city, shoot an arrow there, come before it with a shield, or cast up a siege ramp against it. <sup>33</sup>By the way that he came, by the same he shall return; he shall not come into this city, says the LORD. <sup>34</sup>For I will defend this city to save it, for my own sake and for the sake of my servant David."

35 That very night the angel of the LORD set out and struck down one hundred eighty-five thousand in the camp of the Assyrians; when morning dawned, they were all dead bodies. <sup>36</sup>Then King Sennacherib of Assyria left, went home, and lived at Nineveh. <sup>37</sup>As he was worshiping in the house of his god Nisroch, his sons Adrammelech and Sharezer killed him with the sword, and they escaped into the land of Ara-

rat. His son Esar-haddon succeeded him.

## ACTS 21.1–16

WHEN we [Luke, Paul, and companions] had parted from them and set sail, we came by a straight course to Cos, and the next day to Rhodes, and from there to Patara. <sup>b</sup> <sup>2</sup>When we found a ship bound for Phoenicia, we went on board and set sail. <sup>3</sup>We came in sight of Cyprus; and leaving it on our left, we sailed to Syria and landed at Tyre, because the ship was to unload its cargo there. <sup>4</sup>We looked up the disciples and stayed there for seven days. Through the Spirit they told Paul not to go on to Jerusalem. <sup>5</sup>When our days there were ended, we left and proceeded on our journey; and all of them, with wives and children, escorted us outside the city. There we knelt down on the beach and prayed <sup>6</sup>and said farewell to one another. Then we went on board the ship, and they returned home.

7 When we had finished<sup>c</sup> the voyage from Tyre, we arrived at Ptolemais; and we greeted the believers<sup>d</sup> and stayed with them for one day. <sup>8</sup>The next day we left and came to Caesarea; and we went into the house of Philip the evangelist, one of the seven, and stayed with him. <sup>9</sup>He had four unmarried daughters<sup>e</sup> who had the gift of prophecy. <sup>10</sup>While we were staying there for several days, a prophet named Agabus came down from Judea. <sup>11</sup>He came to us and took Paul's belt, bound his own feet and hands with it, and said, "Thus says the Holy Spirit, 'This is the way the Jews in Jerusalem will bind the man who owns this belt and will hand him over to the Gentiles.'" <sup>12</sup>When we heard this, we and the people there urged him not to go up to Jerusalem. <sup>13</sup>Then Paul answered,

---

<sup>a</sup>Gk Compare Isa 37.27 Q Ms: MT lacks *rising*  <sup>b</sup>Other ancient authorities add *and Myra*  <sup>c</sup>Or *continued*  <sup>d</sup>Gk *brothers*  <sup>e</sup>Gk *four daughters, virgins,*

"What are you doing, weeping and breaking my heart? For I am ready not only to be bound but even to die in Jerusalem for the name of the Lord Jesus." [14]Since he would not be persuaded, we remained silent except to say, "The Lord's will be done."

15 After these days we got ready and started to go up to Jerusalem. [16]Some of the disciples from Caesarea also came along and brought us to the house of Mnason of Cyprus, an early disciple, with whom we were to stay.

## PSALM 149.1–9

Praise the Lord!
Sing to the Lord a new song,
his praise in the assembly of the faithful.
2 Let Israel be glad in its Maker;
let the children of Zion rejoice in their King.
3 Let them praise his name with dancing,
making melody to him with tambourine and lyre.
4 For the Lord takes pleasure in his people;

he adorns the humble with victory.
5 Let the faithful exult in glory;
let them sing for joy on their couches.
6 Let the high praises of God be in their throats
and two-edged swords in their hands,
7 to execute vengeance on the nations
and punishment on the peoples,
8 to bind their kings with fetters
and their nobles with chains of iron,
9 to execute on them the judgment decreed.
This is glory for all his faithful ones.
Praise the Lord!

## PROVERBS 18.8

The words of a whisperer are like delicious morsels;
they go down into the inner parts of the body.

# JULY 2

## 2 KINGS 20.1—22.2

In those days Hezekiah became sick and was at the point of death. The prophet Isaiah son of Amoz came to him, and said to him, "Thus says the Lord: Set your house in order, for you shall die; you shall not recover." [2]Then Hezekiah turned his face to the wall and prayed to the Lord: [3]"Remember now, O Lord, I implore you, how I have walked before you in faithfulness with a whole heart, and have done what is good in your sight." Hezekiah wept bitterly. [4]Before Isaiah had gone out of the middle court, the word of the Lord came to him: [5]"Turn back, and say to Hezekiah prince of my people, Thus says the Lord, the God of your ancestor David: I have heard your prayer, I have seen your tears; indeed, I will heal you; on the third day you shall go up to the house of the Lord. [6]I will add fifteen years to your life. I will deliver you and this city out of the hand of the king of Assyria; I will defend this city for my own sake and for my servant David's sake." [7]Then Isaiah said, "Bring a lump of figs. Let them take it and apply it to the boil, so that he may recover."

8 Hezekiah said to Isaiah, "What shall be the sign that the LORD will heal me, and that I shall go up to the house of the LORD on the third day?" [9]Isaiah said, "This is the sign to you from the LORD, that the LORD will do the thing that he has promised: the shadow has now advanced ten intervals; shall it retreat ten intervals?" [10]Hezekiah answered, "It is normal for the shadow to lengthen ten intervals; rather let the shadow retreat ten intervals." [11]The prophet Isaiah cried to the LORD; and he brought the shadow back the ten intervals, by which the sun[a] had declined on the dial of Ahaz.

12 At that time King Merodach-baladan son of Baladan of Babylon sent envoys with letters and a present to Hezekiah, for he had heard that Hezekiah had been sick. [13]Hezekiah welcomed them;[b] he showed them all his treasure house, the silver, the gold, the spices, the precious oil, his armory, all that was found in his storehouses; there was nothing in his house or in all his realm that Hezekiah did not show them. [14]Then the prophet Isaiah came to King Hezekiah, and said to him, "What did these men say? From where did they come to you?" Hezekiah answered, "They have come from a far country, from Babylon." [15]He said, "What have they seen in your house?" Hezekiah answered, "They have seen all that is in my house; there is nothing in my storehouses that I did not show them."

16 Then Isaiah said to Hezekiah, "Hear the word of the LORD: [17]Days are coming when all that is in your house, and that which your ancestors have stored up until this day, shall be carried to Babylon; nothing shall be left, says the LORD. [18]Some of your own sons who are born to you shall be taken away; they shall be eunuchs in the palace of the king of Babylon." [19]Then Hezekiah said to Isaiah, "The word of the LORD that you have spoken is good." For he thought, "Why not, if there will be peace and security in my days?"

20 The rest of the deeds of Hezekiah, all his power, how he made the pool and the conduit and brought water into the city, are they not written in the Book of the Annals of the Kings of Judah? [21]Hezekiah slept with his ancestors; and his son Manasseh succeeded him.

21.1 MANASSEH was twelve years old when he began to reign; he reigned fifty-five years in Jerusalem. His mother's name was Hephzibah. [2]He did what was evil in the sight of the LORD, following the abominable practices of the nations that the LORD drove out before the people of Israel. [3]For he rebuilt the high places that his father Hezekiah had destroyed; he erected altars for Baal, made a sacred pole,[c] as King Ahab of Israel had done, worshiped all the host of heaven, and served them. [4]He built altars in the house of the LORD, of which the LORD had said, "In Jerusalem I will put my name." [5]He built altars for all the host of heaven in the two courts of the house of the LORD. [6]He made his son pass through fire; he practiced soothsaying and augury, and dealt with mediums and with wizards. He did much evil in the sight of the LORD, provoking him to anger. [7]The carved image of Asherah that he had made he set in the house of which the LORD said to David and to his

aSyr See Isa 38.8 and Tg: Heb *it*   bGk Vg Syr: Heb *When Hezekiah heard about them*
cHeb *Asherah*

son Solomon, "In this house, and in Jerusalem, which I have chosen out of all the tribes of Israel, I will put my name forever; [8]I will not cause the feet of Israel to wander any more out of the land that I gave to their ancestors, if only they will be careful to do according to all that I have commanded them, and according to all the law that my servant Moses commanded them." [9]But they did not listen; Manasseh misled them to do more evil than the nations had done that the LORD destroyed before the people of Israel.

10  The LORD said by his servants the prophets, [11]"Because King Manasseh of Judah has committed these abominations, has done things more wicked than all that the Amorites did, who were before him, and has caused Judah also to sin with his idols; [12]therefore thus says the LORD, the God of Israel, I am bringing upon Jerusalem and Judah such evil that the ears of everyone who hears of it will tingle. [13]I will stretch over Jerusalem the measuring line for Samaria, and the plummet for the house of Ahab; I will wipe Jerusalem as one wipes a dish, wiping it and turning it upside down. [14]I will cast off the remnant of my heritage, and give them into the hand of their enemies; they shall become a prey and a spoil to all their enemies, [15]because they have done what is evil in my sight and have provoked me to anger, since the day their ancestors came out of Egypt, even to this day."

16  Moreover Manasseh shed very much innocent blood, until he had filled Jerusalem from one end to another, besides the sin that he caused Judah to sin so that they did what was evil in the sight of the LORD.

17  Now the rest of the acts of Manasseh, all that he did, and the sin that he committed, are they not written in the Book of the Annals of the Kings of Judah? [18]Manasseh slept with his ancestors, and was buried in the garden of his house, in the garden of Uzza. His son Amon succeeded him.

19  Amon was twenty-two years old when he began to reign; he reigned two years in Jerusalem. His mother's name was Meshullemeth daughter of Haruz of Jotbah. [20]He did what was evil in the sight of the LORD, as his father Manasseh had done. [21]He walked in all the way in which his father walked, served the idols that his father served, and worshiped them; [22]he abandoned the LORD, the God of his ancestors, and did not walk in the way of the LORD. [23]The servants of Amon conspired against him, and killed the king in his house. [24]But the people of the land killed all those who had conspired against King Amon, and the people of the land made his son Josiah king in place of him. [25]Now the rest of the acts of Amon that he did, are they not written in the Book of the Annals of the Kings of Judah? [26]He was buried in his tomb in the garden of Uzza; then his son Josiah succeeded him.

22.1 JOSIAH was eight years old when he began to reign; he reigned thirty-one years in Jerusalem. His mother's name was Jedidah daughter of Adaiah of Bozkath. [2]He did what was right in the sight of the LORD, and walked in all the way of his father David; he did not turn aside to the right or to the left.

## ACTS 21.17–36

WHEN we [Luke, Paul, and companions] arrived in Jerusalem, the brothers welcomed us warmly. [18]The next day Paul went with us to visit James; and all the elders were present. [19]After greeting them, he related one by one the things that God had done among the Gentiles through his ministry. [20]When they heard it, they praised God. Then they said to him, "You see, brother, how many thousands of believers there are among the Jews, and they are all zealous for the law. 21They have been told about you that you teach all the Jews living among the Gentiles to forsake Moses, and that you tell them not to circumcise their children or observe the customs. 22What then is to be done? They will certainly hear that you have come. 23So do what we tell you. We have four men who are under a vow. 24Join these men, go through the rite of purification with them, and pay for the shaving of their heads. Thus all will know that there is nothing in what they have been told about you, but that you yourself observe and guard the law. 25But as for the Gentiles who have become believers, we have sent a letter with our judgment that they should abstain from what has been sacrificed to idols and from blood and from what is strangled[a] and from fornication." 26Then Paul took the men, and the next day, having purified himself, he entered the temple with them, making public the completion of the days of purification when the sacrifice would be made for each of them.

27 When the seven days were almost completed, the Jews from Asia, who had seen him in the temple, stirred up the whole crowd. They seized him, 28shouting, "Fellow Israelites, help! This is the man who is teaching everyone everywhere against our people, our law, and this place; more than that, he has actually brought Greeks into the temple and has defiled this holy place." 29For they had previously seen Trophimus the Ephesian with him in the city, and they supposed that Paul had brought him into the temple. 30Then all the city was aroused, and the people rushed together. They seized Paul and dragged him out of the temple, and immediately the doors were shut. 31While they were trying to kill him, word came to the tribune of the cohort that all Jerusalem was in an uproar. 32Immediately he took soldiers and centurions and ran down to them. When they saw the tribune and the soldiers, they stopped beating Paul. 33Then the tribune came, arrested him, and ordered him to be bound with two chains; he inquired who he was and what he had done. 34Some in the crowd shouted one thing, some another; and as he could not learn the facts because of the uproar, he ordered him to be brought into the barracks. 35When Paul[b] came to the steps, the violence of the mob was so great that he had to be carried by the soldiers. 36The crowd that followed kept shouting, "Away with him!"

## PSALM 150.1–6

PRAISE the LORD!
Praise God in his sanctuary;
    praise him in his mighty
        firmament![c]
2  Praise him for his mighty deeds;
    praise him according to his
        surpassing greatness!

3  Praise him with trumpet sound;
    praise him with lute and harp!
4  Praise him with tambourine and
        dance;
    praise him with strings and
        pipe!
5  Praise him with clanging
        cymbals;
    praise him with loud clashing
        cymbals!
6  Let everything that breathes
        praise the LORD!
    Praise the LORD!

aOther ancient authorities lack *and from what is strangled*  bGk *he*  cOr *dome*

## PROVERBS 18.9–10

**O**NE who is slack in work
is close kin to a vandal.
 [10]   The name of the LORD is
a strong tower;
the righteous run into it and
are safe.

# JULY 3

## 2 KINGS 22.3—23.30

**I**N the eighteenth year of King Josiah, the king sent Shaphan son of Azaliah, son of Meshullam, the secretary, to the house of the LORD, saying, [4]"Go up to the high priest Hilkiah, and have him count the entire sum of the money that has been brought into the house of the LORD, which the keepers of the threshold have collected from the people; [5]let it be given into the hand of the workers who have the oversight of the house of the LORD; let them give it to the workers who are at the house of the LORD, repairing the house, [6]that is, to the carpenters, to the builders, to the masons; and let them use it to buy timber and quarried stone to repair the house. [7]But no accounting shall be asked from them for the money that is delivered into their hand, for they deal honestly."

8 The high priest Hilkiah said to Shaphan the secretary, "I have found the book of the law in the house of the LORD." When Hilkiah gave the book to Shaphan, he read it. [9]Then Shaphan the secretary came to the king, and reported to the king, "Your servants have emptied out the money that was found in the house, and have delivered it into the hand of the workers who have oversight of the house of the LORD." [10]Shaphan the secretary informed the king, "The priest Hilkiah has given me a book." Shaphan then read it aloud to the king.

11 When the king heard the words of the book of the law, he tore his clothes. [12]Then the king commanded the priest Hilkiah, Ahikam son of Shaphan, Achbor son of Micaiah, Shaphan the secretary, and the king's servant Asaiah, saying, [13]"Go, inquire of the LORD for me, for the people, and for all Judah, concerning the words of this book that has been found; for great is the wrath of the LORD that is kindled against us, because our ancestors did not obey the words of this book, to do according to all that is written concerning us."

14 So the priest Hilkiah, Ahikam, Achbor, Shaphan, and Asaiah went to the prophetess Huldah the wife of Shallum son of Tikvah, son of Harhas, keeper of the wardrobe; she resided in Jerusalem in the Second Quarter, where they consulted her. [15]She declared to them, "Thus says the LORD, the God of Israel: Tell the man who sent you to me, [16]Thus says the LORD, I will indeed bring disaster on this place and on its inhabitants—all the words of the book that the king of Judah has read. [17]Because they have abandoned me and have made offerings to other gods, so that they have provoked me to anger with all the work of their hands, therefore my wrath will be kindled against this place, and it will not be quenched. [18]But as to the king of Judah, who sent you to inquire of the LORD, thus shall you say to him, Thus says the LORD, the God of Israel: Regarding the words that you have heard, [19]because your heart was penitent, and you humbled yourself before the LORD, when

you heard how I spoke against this place, and against its inhabitants, that they should become a desolation and a curse, and because you have torn your clothes and wept before me, I also have heard you, says the Lord. <sup>20</sup>Therefore, I will gather you to your ancestors, and you shall be gathered to your grave in peace; your eyes shall not see all the disaster that I will bring on this place." They took the message back to the king.

23.1 Then the king directed that all the elders of Judah and Jerusalem should be gathered to him. <sup>2</sup>The king went up to the house of the Lord, and with him went all the people of Judah, all the inhabitants of Jerusalem, the priests, the prophets, and all the people, both small and great; he read in their hearing all the words of the book of the covenant that had been found in the house of the Lord. <sup>3</sup>The king stood by the pillar and made a covenant before the Lord, to follow the Lord, keeping his commandments, his decrees, and his statutes, with all his heart and all his soul, to perform the words of this covenant that were written in this book. All the people joined in the covenant.

4 The king commanded the high priest Hilkiah, the priests of the second order, and the guardians of the threshold, to bring out of the temple of the Lord all the vessels made for Baal, for Asherah, and for all the host of heaven; he burned them outside Jerusalem in the fields of the Kidron, and carried their ashes to Bethel. <sup>5</sup>He deposed the idolatrous priests whom the kings of Judah had ordained to make offerings in the high places at the cities of Judah and around Jerusalem; those also who made offerings to Baal, to the sun, the moon, the constellations, and all the host of the heavens. <sup>6</sup>He brought out the image of<sup>a</sup> Asherah from the house of the Lord, outside Jerusalem, to the Wadi Kidron, burned it at the Wadi Kidron, beat it to dust and threw the dust of it upon the graves of the common people. <sup>7</sup>He broke down the houses of the male temple prostitutes that were in the house of the Lord, where the women did weaving for Asherah. <sup>8</sup>He brought all the priests out of the towns of Judah, and defiled the high places where the priests had made offerings, from Geba to Beer-sheba; he broke down the high places of the gates that were at the entrance of the gate of Joshua the governor of the city, which were on the left at the gate of the city. <sup>9</sup>The priests of the high places, however, did not come up to the altar of the Lord in Jerusalem, but ate unleavened bread among their kindred. <sup>10</sup>He defiled Topheth, which is in the valley of Ben-hinnom, so that no one would make a son or a daughter pass through fire as an offering to Molech. <sup>11</sup>He removed the horses that the kings of Judah had dedicated to the sun, at the entrance to the house of the Lord, by the chamber of the eunuch Nathan-melech, which was in the precincts;<sup>b</sup> then he burned the chariots of the sun with fire. <sup>12</sup>The altars on the roof of the upper chamber of Ahaz, which the kings of Judah had made, and the altars that Manasseh had made in the two courts of the house of the Lord, he pulled down from there and broke in pieces, and threw the rubble into the Wadi Kidron. <sup>13</sup>The king defiled the high places that were east of Jerusalem, to the south of the Mount of Destruction, which King Solomon of Israel had built for Astarte the abomination of the Sidonians, for Chemosh the abomination of Moab, and for Milcom the abomination of the Ammonites. <sup>14</sup>He broke the pillars in pieces, cut down sacred poles,<sup>c</sup> and covered the sites with human bones.

---

<sup>a</sup>Heb lacks *image of*   <sup>b</sup>Meaning of Heb uncertain   <sup>c</sup>Heb *Asherim*

15 Moreover, the altar at Bethel, the high place erected by Jeroboam son of Nebat, who caused Israel to sin—he pulled down that altar along with the high place. He burned the high place, crushing it to dust; he also burned the sacred pole. [a] 16As Josiah turned, he saw the tombs there on the mount; and he sent and took the bones out of the tombs, and burned them on the altar, and defiled it, according to the word of the Lord that the man of God proclaimed, [b] when Jeroboam stood by the altar at the festival; he turned and looked up at the tomb of the man of God who had predicted these things. 17Then he said, "What is that monument that I see?" The people of the city told him, "It is the tomb of the man of God who came from Judah and predicted these things that you have done against the altar at Bethel." 18He said, "Let him rest; let no one move his bones." So they let his bones alone, with the bones of the prophet who came out of Samaria. 19Moreover, Josiah removed all the shrines of the high places that were in the towns of Samaria, which kings of Israel had made, provoking the Lord to anger; he did to them just as he had done at Bethel. 20He slaughtered on the altars all the priests of the high places who were there, and burned human bones on them. Then he returned to Jerusalem.

21 The king commanded all the people, "Keep the passover to the Lord your God as prescribed in this book of the covenant." 22No such passover had been kept since the days of the judges who judged Israel, or during all the days of the kings of Israel or of the kings of Judah; 23but in the eighteenth year of King Josiah this passover was kept to the Lord in Jerusalem.

24 Moreover Josiah put away the mediums, wizards, teraphim, [c] idols, and all the abominations that were seen in the land of Judah and in Jerusalem, so that he established the words of the law that were written in the book that the priest Hilkiah had found in the house of the Lord. 25Before him there was no king like him, who turned to the Lord with all his heart, with all his soul, and with all his might, according to all the law of Moses; nor did any like him arise after him.

26 Still the Lord did not turn from the fierceness of his great wrath, by which his anger was kindled against Judah, because of all the provocations with which Manasseh had provoked him. 27The Lord said, "I will remove Judah also out of my sight, as I have removed Israel; and I will reject this city that I have chosen, Jerusalem, and the house of which I said, My name shall be there."

28 Now the rest of the acts of Josiah, and all that he did, are they not written in the Book of the Annals of the Kings of Judah? 29In his days Pharaoh Neco king of Egypt went up to the king of Assyria to the river Euphrates. King Josiah went to meet him; but when Pharaoh Neco met him at Megiddo, he killed him. 30His servants carried him dead in a chariot from Megiddo, brought him to Jerusalem, and buried him in his own tomb. The people of the land took Jehoahaz son of Josiah, anointed him, and made him king in place of his father.

## ACTS 21.37—22.16

JUST as Paul was about to be brought into the barracks, he said to the tribune, "May I say something to you?" The tribune [d] replied, "Do you know Greek? 38Then you are not the Egyptian who recently stirred up a revolt and led the four thousand assassins out into the wilderness?" 39Paul replied, "I am a Jew, from Tarsus in Cilicia, a citizen of an

aHeb *Asherah*   bGk: Heb *proclaimed, who had predicted these things*   cOr *household gods*   dGk *He*

important city; I beg you, let me speak to the people." ⁴⁰When he had given him permission, Paul stood on the steps and motioned to the people for silence; and when there was a great hush, he addressed them in the Hebrewᵃ language, saying:

**22.**¹ "BROTHERS and fathers, listen to the defense that I now make before you."

2 When they heard him addressing them in Hebrew, ᵃ they became even more quiet. Then he said:

3 "I am a Jew, born in Tarsus in Cilicia, but brought up in this city at the feet of Gamaliel, educated strictly according to our ancestral law, being zealous for God, just as all of you are today. ⁴I persecuted this Way up to the point of death by binding both men and women and putting them in prison, ⁵as the high priest and the whole council of elders can testify about me. From them I also received letters to the brothers in Damascus, and I went there in order to bind those who were there and to bring them back to Jerusalem for punishment.

6 "While I was on my way and approaching Damascus, about noon a great light from heaven suddenly shone about me. ⁷I fell to the ground and heard a voice saying to me, 'Saul, Saul, why are you persecuting me?' ⁸I answered, 'Who are you, Lord?' Then he said to me, 'I am Jesus of Nazarethᵇ whom you are persecuting.' ⁹Now those who were with me saw the light but did not hear the voice of the one who was speaking to me. ¹⁰I asked, 'What am I to do, Lord?' The Lord said to me, 'Get up and go to Damascus; there you will be told everything that has been assigned to you to do.' ¹¹Since I could not see because of the brightness of that light, those who were with me took my hand and led me to Damascus.

12 "A certain Ananias, who was a devout man according to the law and well spoken of by all the Jews living there, ¹³came to me; and standing beside me, he said, 'Brother Saul, regain your sight!' In that very hour I regained my sight and saw him. ¹⁴Then he said, 'The God of our ancestors has chosen you to know his will, to see the Righteous One and to hear his own voice; ¹⁵for you will be his witness to all the world of what you have seen and heard. ¹⁶And now why do you delay? Get up, be baptized, and have your sins washed away, calling on his name.'

## PSALM 1.1–6

Happy are those
   who do not follow the
     advice of the wicked,
  or take the path that sinners
     tread,
    or sit in the seat of scoffers;
2  but their delight is in the law of
     the LORD,
   and on his law they meditate
     day and night.
3  They are like trees
   planted by streams of water,
  which yield their fruit in its
     season,
   and their leaves do not
     wither.
  In all that they do, they
     prosper.

4  The wicked are not so,
   but are like chaff that the
     wind drives away.
5  Therefore the wicked will not
     stand in the judgment,
   nor sinners in the
     congregation of the
     righteous;
6  for the LORD watches over the
     way of the righteous,
   but the way of the wicked will
     perish.

ᵃ That is, *Aramaic*  ᵇ Gk *the Nazorean*

## PROVERBS 18.11–12

**T**HE wealth of the rich is their
strong city;
in their imagination it is like a
high wall.

<sup>12</sup> Before destruction one's heart
is haughty,
but humility goes before
honor.

# JULY 4

## 2 KINGS 23.31—25.30

**J**EHOAHAZ was twenty-three years
old when he began to reign; he
reigned three months in Jerusalem. His mother's name was Hamutal
daughter of Jeremiah of Libnah. <sup>32</sup>He
did what was evil in the sight of the
LORD, just as his ancestors had done.
<sup>33</sup>Pharaoh Neco confined him at Riblah
in the land of Hamath, so that he might
not reign in Jerusalem, and imposed
tribute on the land of one hundred talents of silver and a talent of gold.
<sup>34</sup>Pharaoh Neco made Eliakim son of
Josiah king in place of his father Josiah,
and changed his name to Jehoiakim. But
he took Jehoahaz away; he came to
Egypt, and died there. <sup>35</sup>Jehoiakim
gave the silver and the gold to Pharaoh,
but he taxed the land in order to meet
Pharaoh's demand for money. He exacted the silver and the gold from the
people of the land, from all according to
their assessment, to give it to Pharaoh
Neco.

36 Jehoiakim was twenty-five
years old when he began to reign; he
reigned eleven years in Jerusalem. His
mother's name was Zebidah daughter
of Pedaiah of Rumah. <sup>37</sup>He did what
was evil in the sight of the LORD, just as
all his ancestors had done.

<sup>24.1</sup> IN his days King Nebuchadnezzar of
Babylon came up; Jehoiakim became
his servant for three years; then he
turned and rebelled against him. <sup>2</sup>The
LORD sent against him bands of the
Chaldeans, bands of the Arameans,
bands of the Moabites, and bands of the
Ammonites; he sent them against Judah to destroy it, according to the word
of the LORD that he spoke by his servants the prophets. <sup>3</sup>Surely this came
upon Judah at the command of the
LORD, to remove them out of his sight,
for the sins of Manasseh, for all that he
had committed, <sup>4</sup>and also for the innocent blood that he had shed; for he filled
Jerusalem with innocent blood, and the
LORD was not willing to pardon. <sup>5</sup>Now
the rest of the deeds of Jehoiakim, and
all that he did, are they not written in
the Book of the Annals of the Kings of
Judah? <sup>6</sup>So Jehoiakim slept with his ancestors; then his son Jehoiachin succeeded him. <sup>7</sup>The king of Egypt did not
come again out of his land, for the king
of Babylon had taken over all that belonged to the king of Egypt from the
Wadi of Egypt to the River Euphrates.

8 Jehoiachin was eighteen years old
when he began to reign; he reigned
three months in Jerusalem. His
mother's name was Nehushta daughter
of Elnathan of Jerusalem. <sup>9</sup>He did what
was evil in the sight of the LORD, just as
his father had done.

10 At that time the servants of
King Nebuchadnezzar of Babylon came

up to Jerusalem, and the city was besieged. [11]King Nebuchadnezzar of Babylon came to the city, while his servants were besieging it; [12]King Jehoiachin of Judah gave himself up to the king of Babylon, himself, his mother, his servants, his officers, and his palace officials. The king of Babylon took him prisoner in the eighth year of his reign.

13 He carried off all the treasures of the house of the LORD, and the treasures of the king's house; he cut in pieces all the vessels of gold in the temple of the LORD, which King Solomon of Israel had made, all this as the LORD had foretold. [14]He carried away all Jerusalem, all the officials, all the warriors, ten thousand captives, all the artisans and the smiths; no one remained, except the poorest people of the land. [15]He carried away Jehoiachin to Babylon; the king's mother, the king's wives, his officials, and the elite of the land, he took into captivity from Jerusalem to Babylon. [16]The king of Babylon brought captive to Babylon all the men of valor, seven thousand, the artisans and the smiths, one thousand, all of them strong and fit for war. [17]The king of Babylon made Mattaniah, Jehoiachin's uncle, king in his place, and changed his name to Zedekiah.

18 Zedekiah was twenty-one years old when he began to reign; he reigned eleven years in Jerusalem. His mother's name was Hamutal daughter of Jeremiah of Libnah. [19]He did what was evil in the sight of the LORD, just as Jehoiakim had done. [20]Indeed, Jerusalem and Judah so angered the LORD that he expelled them from his presence.

Zedekiah rebelled against the king of Babylon. 25.1 And in the ninth year of his reign, in the tenth month, on the tenth day of the month, King Nebuchadnezzar of Babylon came with all his army against Jerusalem, and laid siege to it; they built siegeworks against it all around. [2]So the city was besieged until the eleventh year of King Zedekiah. [3]On the ninth day of the fourth month the famine became so severe in the city that there was no food for the people of the land. [4]Then a breach was made in the city wall; [a] the king with all the soldiers fled[b] by night by the way of the gate between the two walls, by the king's garden, though the Chaldeans were all around the city. They went in the direction of the Arabah. [5]But the army of the Chaldeans pursued the king, and overtook him in the plains of Jericho; all his army was scattered, deserting him. [6]Then they captured the king and brought him up to the king of Babylon at Riblah, who passed sentence on him. [7]They slaughtered the sons of Zedekiah before his eyes, then put out the eyes of Zedekiah; they bound him in fetters and took him to Babylon.

8 In the fifth month, on the seventh day of the month—which was the nineteenth year of King Nebuchadnezzar, king of Babylon—Nebuzaradan, the captain of the bodyguard, a servant of the king of Babylon, came to Jerusalem. [9]He burned the house of the LORD, the king's house, and all the houses of Jerusalem; every great house he burned down. [10]All the army of the Chaldeans who were with the captain of the guard broke down the walls around Jerusalem. [11]Nebuzaradan the captain of the guard carried into exile the rest of the people who were left in the city and the deserters who had defected to the king of Babylon—all the rest of the population. [12]But the captain of the guard left some of the poorest people of the land to be vinedressers and tillers of the soil.

13 The bronze pillars that were in the house of the LORD, as well as the stands and the bronze sea that were in the house of the LORD, the Chaldeans

aHeb lacks *wall*   bGk Compare Jer 39.4; 52.7: Heb lacks *the king* and lacks *fled*

broke in pieces, and carried the bronze to Babylon. [14]They took away the pots, the shovels, the snuffers, the dishes for incense, and all the bronze vessels used in the temple service, [15]as well as the firepans and the basins. What was made of gold the captain of the guard took away for the gold, and what was made of silver, for the silver. [16]As for the two pillars, the one sea, and the stands, which Solomon had made for the house of the LORD, the bronze of all these vessels was beyond weighing. [17]The height of the one pillar was eighteen cubits, and on it was a bronze capital; the height of the capital was three cubits; latticework and pomegranates, all of bronze, were on the capital all around. The second pillar had the same, with the latticework.

18 The captain of the guard took the chief priest Seraiah, the second priest Zephaniah, and the three guardians of the threshold; [19]from the city he took an officer who had been in command of the soldiers, and five men of the king's council who were found in the city; the secretary who was the commander of the army who mustered the people of the land; and sixty men of the people of the land who were found in the city. [20]Nebuzaradan the captain of the guard took them, and brought them to the king of Babylon at Riblah. [21]The king of Babylon struck them down and put them to death at Riblah in the land of Hamath. So Judah went into exile out of its land.

22 He appointed Gedaliah son of Ahikam son of Shaphan as governor over the people who remained in the land of Judah, whom King Nebuchadnezzar of Babylon had left. [23]Now when all the captains of the forces and their men heard that the king of Babylon had appointed Gedaliah as governor, they came with their men to Gedaliah at Mizpah, namely, Ishmael son of Netha-niah, Johanan son of Kareah, Seraiah son of Tanhumeth the Netophathite, and Jaazaniah son of the Maacathite. [24]Gedaliah swore to them and their men, saying, "Do not be afraid because of the Chaldean officials; live in the land, serve the king of Babylon, and it shall be well with you." [25]But in the seventh month, Ishmael son of Nethaniah son of Elishama, of the royal family, came with ten men; they struck down Gedaliah so that he died, along with the Judeans and Chaldeans who were with him at Mizpah. [26]Then all the people, high and low[a] and the captains of the forces set out and went to Egypt; for they were afraid of the Chaldeans.

27 In the thirty-seventh year of the exile of King Jehoiachin of Judah, in the twelfth month, on the twenty-seventh day of the month, King Evil-merodach of Babylon, in the year that he began to reign, released King Jehoiachin of Judah from prison; [28]he spoke kindly to him, and gave him a seat above the other seats of the kings who were with him in Babylon. [29]So Jehoiachin put aside his prison clothes. Every day of his life he dined regularly in the king's presence. [30]For his allowance, a regular allowance was given him by the king, a portion every day, as long as he lived.

## ACTS 22.17—23.10

"AFTER I [Paul] had returned to Jerusalem and while I was praying in the temple, I fell into a trance [18]and saw Jesus[b] saying to me, 'Hurry and get out of Jerusalem quickly, because they will not accept your testimony about me.' [19]And I said, 'Lord, they themselves know that in every synagogue I imprisoned and beat those who believed in you. [20]And while the blood of your witness Stephen was shed, I myself was standing by, approving and keeping the coats of those who

a Or *young and old*   b Gk *him*

killed him.' [21]Then he said to me, 'Go, for I will send you far away to the Gentiles.' "

22  Up to this point they listened to him, but then they shouted, "Away with such a fellow from the earth! For he should not be allowed to live." [23]And while they were shouting, throwing off their cloaks, and tossing dust into the air, [24]the tribune directed that he was to be brought into the barracks, and ordered him to be examined by flogging, to find out the reason for this outcry against him. [25]But when they had tied him up with thongs,[a] Paul said to the centurion who was standing by, "Is it legal for you to flog a Roman citizen who is uncondemned?" [26]When the centurion heard that, he went to the tribune and said to him, "What are you about to do? This man is a Roman citizen." [27]The tribune came and asked Paul,[b] "Tell me, are you a Roman citizen?" And he said, "Yes." [28]The tribune answered, "It cost me a large sum of money to get my citizenship." Paul said, "But I was born a citizen." [29]Immediately those who were about to examine him drew back from him; and the tribune also was afraid, for he realized that Paul was a Roman citizen and that he had bound him.

30  Since he wanted to find out what Paul[c] was being accused of by the Jews, the next day he released him and ordered the chief priests and the entire council to meet. He brought Paul down and had him stand before them.

[23.1] WHILE Paul was looking intently at the council he said, "Brothers,[d] up to this day I have lived my life with a clear conscience before God." [2]Then the high priest Ananias ordered those standing near him to strike him on the mouth. [3]At this Paul said to him, "God will strike you, you whitewashed wall! Are you sitting there to judge me according to the law, and yet in violation of the law you order me to be struck?" [4]Those standing nearby said, "Do you dare to insult God's high priest?" [5]And Paul said, "I did not realize, brothers, that he was high priest; for it is written, 'You shall not speak evil of a leader of your people.' "

6  When Paul noticed that some were Sadducees and others were Pharisees, he called out in the council, "Brothers, I am a Pharisee, a son of Pharisees. I am on trial concerning the hope of the resurrection[e] of the dead." [7]When he said this, a dissension began between the Pharisees and the Sadducees, and the assembly was divided. [8](The Sadducees say that there is no resurrection, or angel, or spirit; but the Pharisees acknowledge all three.) [9]Then a great clamor arose, and certain scribes of the Pharisees' group stood up and contended, "We find nothing wrong with this man. What if a spirit or an angel has spoken to him?" [10]When the dissension became violent, the tribune, fearing that they would tear Paul to pieces, ordered the soldiers to go down, take him by force, and bring him into the barracks.

## PSALM 2.1–12

WHY do the nations conspire,
  and the peoples plot in
    vain?
2  The kings of the earth set
      themselves,
    and the rulers take counsel
      together,
    against the LORD and his
      anointed, saying,
3  "Let us burst their bonds
      asunder,
    and cast their cords from us."

4  He who sits in the heavens
      laughs;

aOr *up for the lashes*  bGk *him*  cGk *he*  dGk *Men, brothers*  eGk *concerning hope and resurrection*

the Lord has them in
    derision.
5 Then he will speak to them in
    his wrath,
  and terrify them in his fury,
    saying,
6 "I have set my king on Zion, my
    holy hill."

7 I will tell of the decree of the
    Lord:
  He said to me, "You are my
    son;
  today I have begotten you.
8 Ask of me, and I will make the
    nations your heritage,
  and the ends of the earth
    your possession.
9 You shall break them with a rod
    of iron,
  and dash them in pieces like a
    potter's vessel."

10 Now therefore, O kings, be
    wise;
  be warned, O rulers of the
    earth.
11 Serve the Lord with fear,
  with trembling 12kiss his
    feet, a
  or he will be angry, and you will
    perish in the way;
  for his wrath is quickly
    kindled.

Happy are all who take refuge
  in him.

## PROVERBS 18.13

IF one gives answer before
    hearing,
  it is folly and shame.

# JULY 5

## 1 CHRONICLES 1.1—2.17

ADAM, Seth, Enosh; 2Kenan, Mahalalel, Jared; 3Enoch, Methuselah, Lamech; 4Noah, Shem, Ham, and Japheth.

5 The descendants of Japheth: Gomer, Magog, Madai, Javan, Tubal, Meshech, and Tiras. 6The descendants of Gomer: Ashkenaz, Diphath, b and Togarmah. 7The descendants of Javan: Elishah, Tarshish, Kittim, and Rodanim. c

8 The descendants of Ham: Cush, Egypt, Put, and Canaan. 9The descendants of Cush: Seba, Havilah, Sabta, Raama, and Sabteca. The descendants of Raamah: Sheba and Dedan. 10Cush became the father of Nimrod; he was the first to be a mighty one on the earth.

11 Egypt became the father of Ludim, Anamim, Lehabim, Naphtuhim, 12Pathrusim, Casluhim, and Caphtorim, from whom the Philistines come. d

13 Canaan became the father of Sidon his firstborn, and Heth, 14and the Jebusites, the Amorites, the Girgashites, 15the Hivites, the Arkites, the Sinites, 16the Arvadites, the Zema-

aCn: Meaning of Heb of verses 11b and 12a is uncertain  bGen 10.3 *Ripath*; See Gk Vg  cGen 10.4 *Dodanim*; See Syr Vg  dHeb *Casluhim, from which the Philistines come, Caphtorim*; See Am 9.7, Jer 47.4

rites, and the Hamathites.

17 The descendants of Shem: Elam, Asshur, Arpachshad, Lud, Aram, Uz, Hul, Gether, and Meshech. [a] 18Arpachshad became the father of Shelah; and Shelah became the father of Eber. 19To Eber were born two sons: the name of the one was Peleg (for in his days the earth was divided), and the name of his brother Joktan. 20Joktan became the father of Almodad, Sheleph, Hazarmaveth, Jerah, 21Hadoram, Uzal, Diklah, 22Ebal, Abimael, Sheba, 23Ophir, Havilah, and Jobab; all these were the descendants of Joktan.

24 Shem, Arpachshad, Shelah; 25Eber, Peleg, Reu; 26Serug, Nahor, Terah; 27Abram, that is, Abraham.

28 The sons of Abraham: Isaac and Ishmael. 29These are their genealogies: the firstborn of Ishmael, Nebaioth; and Kedar, Adbeel, Mibsam, 30Mishma, Dumah, Massa, Hadad, Tema, 31Jetur, Naphish, and Kedemah. These are the sons of Ishmael. 32The sons of Keturah, Abraham's concubine: she bore Zimran, Jokshan, Medan, Midian, Ishbak, and Shuah. The sons of Jokshan: Sheba and Dedan. 33The sons of Midian: Ephah, Epher, Hanoch, Abida, and Eldaah. All these were the descendants of Keturah.

34 Abraham became the father of Isaac. The sons of Isaac: Esau and Israel. 35The sons of Esau: Eliphaz, Reuel, Jeush, Jalam, and Korah. 36The sons of Eliphaz: Teman, Omar, Zephi, Gatam, Kenaz, Timna, and Amalek. 37The sons of Reuel: Nahath, Zerah, Shammah, and Mizzah.

38 The sons of Seir: Lotan, Shobal, Zibeon, Anah, Dishon, Ezer, and Dishan. 39The sons of Lotan: Hori and Homam; and Lotan's sister was Timna. 40The sons of Shobal: Alian, Manahath, Ebal, Shephi, and Onam. The sons of Zibeon: Aiah and Anah. 41The sons of

Anah: Dishon. The sons of Dishon: Hamran, Eshban, Ithran, and Cheran. 42The sons of Ezer: Bilhan, Zaavan, and Jaakan. [b] The sons of Dishan: [c] Uz and Aran.

43 These are the kings who reigned in the land of Edom before any king reigned over the Israelites: Bela son of Beor, whose city was called Dinhabah. 44When Bela died, Jobab son of Zerah of Bozrah succeeded him. 45When Jobab died, Husham of the land of the Temanites succeeded him. 46When Husham died, Hadad son of Bedad, who defeated Midian in the country of Moab, succeeded him; and the name of his city was Avith. 47When Hadad died, Samlah of Masrekah succeeded him. 48When Samlah died, Shaul[d] of Rehoboth on the Euphrates succeeded him. 49When Shaul[d] died, Baal-hanan son of Achbor succeeded him. 50When Baal-hanan died, Hadad succeeded him; the name of his city was Pai, and his wife's name Mehetabel daughter of Matred, daughter of Mezahab. 51And Hadad died.

The clans[e] of Edom were: clans[e] Timna, Aliah, [f] Jetheth, 52Oholibamah, Elah, Pinon, 53Kenaz, Teman, Mibzar, 54Magdiel, and Iram; these are the clans[e] of Edom.

2.1 THESE are the sons of Israel: Reuben, Simeon, Levi, Judah, Issachar, Zebulun, 2Dan, Joseph, Benjamin, Naphtali, Gad, and Asher. 3The sons of Judah: Er, Onan, and Shelah; these three the Canaanite woman Bath-shua bore to him. Now Er, Judah's firstborn, was wicked in the sight of the LORD, and he put him to death. 4His daughter-in-law Tamar also bore him Perez and Zerah. Judah had five sons in all.

5 The sons of Perez: Hezron and Hamul. 6The sons of Zerah: Zimri, Ethan, Heman, Calcol, and Dara, [g] five in all. 7The sons of Carmi: Achar, the

---

aMash in Gen 10.23  bOr and Akan; See Gen 36.27  cSee 1.38: Heb Dishon  dOr Saul  eOr chiefs
fOr Alvah; See Gen 36.40  gOr Darda; Compare Syr Tg some Gk Mss; See 1 Kings 4.31

troubler of Israel, who transgressed in the matter of the devoted thing; [8]and Ethan's son was Azariah.

9  The sons of Hezron, who were born to him: Jerahmeel, Ram, and Chelubai. [10]Ram became the father of Amminadab, and Amminadab became the father of Nahshon, prince of the sons of Judah. [11]Nahshon became the father of Salma, Salma of Boaz, [12]Boaz of Obed, Obed of Jesse. [13]Jesse became the father of Eliab his firstborn, Abinadab the second, Shimea the third, [14]Nethanel the fourth, Raddai the fifth, [15]Ozem the sixth, David the seventh; [16]and their sisters were Zeruiah and Abigail. The sons of Zeruiah: Abishai, Joab, and Asahel, three. [17]Abigail bore Amasa, and the father of Amasa was Jether the Ishmaelite.

## ACTS 23.11–35

**T**HAT night the Lord stood near him [Paul] and said, "Keep up your courage! For just as you have testified for me in Jerusalem, so you must bear witness also in Rome."

12  In the morning the Jews joined in a conspiracy and bound themselves by an oath neither to eat nor drink until they had killed Paul. [13]There were more than forty who joined in this conspiracy. [14]They went to the chief priests and elders and said, "We have strictly bound ourselves by an oath to taste no food until we have killed Paul. [15]Now then, you and the council must notify the tribune to bring him down to you, on the pretext that you want to make a more thorough examination of his case. And we are ready to do away with him before he arrives."

16  Now the son of Paul's sister heard about the ambush; so he went and gained entrance to the barracks and told Paul. [17]Paul called one of the centurions and said, "Take this young man to the tribune, for he has something to report to him." [18]So he took him, brought him to the tribune, and said, "The prisoner Paul called me and asked me to bring this young man to you; he has something to tell you." [19]The tribune took him by the hand, drew him aside privately, and asked, "What is it that you have to report to me?" [20]He answered, "The Jews have agreed to ask you to bring Paul down to the council tomorrow, as though they were going to inquire more thoroughly into his case. [21]But do not be persuaded by them, for more than forty of their men are lying in ambush for him. They have bound themselves by an oath neither to eat nor drink until they kill him. They are ready now and are waiting for your consent." [22]So the tribune dismissed the young man, ordering him, "Tell no one that you have informed me of this."

23  Then he summoned two of the centurions and said, "Get ready to leave by nine o'clock tonight for Caesarea with two hundred soldiers, seventy horsemen, and two hundred spearmen. [24]Also provide mounts for Paul to ride, and take him safely to Felix the governor." [25]He wrote a letter to this effect:

26  "Claudius Lysias to his Excellency the governor Felix, greetings. [27]This man was seized by the Jews and was about to be killed by them, but when I had learned that he was a Roman citizen, I came with the guard and rescued him. [28]Since I wanted to know the charge for which they accused him, I had him brought to their council. [29]I found that he was accused concerning questions of their law, but was charged with nothing deserving death or imprisonment. [30]When I was informed that there would be a plot against the man, I sent him to you at once, ordering his accusers also to state before you what they have against him. [a]"

31  So the soldiers, according to their instructions, took Paul and

[a] Other ancient authorities add *Farewell*

brought him during the night to Antipatris. [32]The next day they let the horsemen go on with him, while they returned to the barracks. [33]When they came to Caesarea and delivered the letter to the governor, they presented Paul also before him. [34]On reading the letter, he asked what province he belonged to, and when he learned that he was from Cilicia, [35]he said, "I will give you a hearing when your accusers arrive." Then he ordered that he be kept under guard in Herod's headquarters. [a]

## PSALM 3.1–8

*A Psalm of David, when he fled from his son Absalom.*

O LORD, how many are my foes!
  Many are rising against me;
[2]  many are saying to me,
  "There is no help for you[b] in
    God."          *Selah*

[3]  But you, O LORD, are a shield
    around me,
  my glory, and the one who
    lifts up my head.
[4]  I cry aloud to the LORD,
    and he answers me from his
      holy hill.          *Selah*

[5]  I lie down and sleep;
    I wake again, for the LORD
      sustains me.
[6]  I am not afraid of ten thousands
      of people
    who have set themselves
      against me all around.

[7]  Rise up, O LORD!
    Deliver me, O my God!
  For you strike all my enemies
      on the cheek;
    you break the teeth of the
      wicked.

[8]  Deliverance belongs to the
      LORD;
    may your blessing be on your
      people!          *Selah*

## PROVERBS 18.14–15

THE human spirit will endure
      sickness;
  but a broken spirit—who
      can bear?
[15]  An intelligent mind acquires
      knowledge,
    and the ear of the wise seeks
      knowledge.

# JULY 6

## 1 CHRONICLES 2.18—4.4

CALEB son of Hezron had children by his wife Azubah, and by Jerioth; these were her sons: Jesher, Shobab, and Ardon. [19]When Azubah died, Caleb married Ephrath, who bore him Hur. [20]Hur became the father of Uri, and Uri became the father of Bezalel.

21 Afterward Hezron went in to the daughter of Machir father of Gilead, whom he married when he was sixty years old; and she bore him Segub; [22]and Segub became the father of Jair,

who had twenty-three towns in the land of Gilead. 23But Geshur and Aram took from them Havvoth-jair, Kenath and its villages, sixty towns. All these were descendants of Machir, father of Gilead. 24After the death of Hezron, in Caleb-ephrathah, Abijah wife of Hezron bore him Ashhur, father of Tekoa.

25 The sons of Jerahmeel, the firstborn of Hezron: Ram his firstborn, Bunah, Oren, Ozem, and Ahijah. 26Jerahmeel also had another wife, whose name was Atarah; she was the mother of Onam. 27The sons of Ram, the firstborn of Jerahmeel: Maaz, Jamin, and Eker. 28The sons of Onam: Shammai and Jada. The sons of Shammai: Nadab and Abishur. 29The name of Abishur's wife was Abihail, and she bore him Ahban and Molid. 30The sons of Nadab: Seled and Appaim; and Seled died childless. 31The sona of Appaim: Ishi. The sona of Ishi: Sheshan. The sona of Sheshan: Ahlai. 32The sons of Jada, Shammai's brother: Jether and Jonathan; and Jether died childless. 33The sons of Jonathan: Peleth and Zaza. These were the descendants of Jerahmeel. 34Now Sheshan had no sons, only daughters; but Sheshan had an Egyptian slave, whose name was Jarha. 35So Sheshan gave his daughter in marriage to his slave Jarha; and she bore him Attai. 36Attai became the father of Nathan, and Nathan of Zabad. 37Zabad became the father of Ephlal, and Ephlal of Obed. 38Obed became the father of Jehu, and Jehu of Azariah. 39Azariah became the father of Helez, and Helez of Eleasah. 40Eleasah became the father of Sismai, and Sismai of Shallum. 41Shallum became the father of Jekamiah, and Jekamiah of Elishama.

42 The sons of Caleb brother of Jerahmeel: Meshab his firstborn, who was father of Ziph. The sons of Mareshah father of Hebron. 43The sons of Hebron: Korah, Tappuah, Rekem, and Shema. 44Shema became father of Raham, father of Jorkeam; and Rekem became the father of Shammai. 45The son of Shammai: Maon; and Maon was the father of Beth-zur. 46Ephah also, Caleb's concubine, bore Haran, Moza, and Gazez; and Haran became the father of Gazez. 47The sons of Jahdai: Regem, Jotham, Geshan, Pelet, Ephah, and Shaaph. 48Maacah, Caleb's concubine, bore Sheber and Tirhanah. 49She also bore Shaaph father of Madmannah, Sheva father of Machbenah and father of Gibea; and the daughter of Caleb was Achsah. 50These were the descendants of Caleb.

The sonsc of Hur the firstborn of Ephrathah: Shobal father of Kiriath-jearim, 51Salma father of Bethlehem, and Hareph father of Beth-gader. 52Shobal father of Kiriath-jearim had other sons: Haroeh, half of the Menuhoth. 53And the families of Kiriath-jearim: the Ithrites, the Puthites, the Shumathites, and the Mishraites; from these came the Zorathites and the Eshtaolites. 54The sons of Salma: Bethlehem, the Netophathites, Atroth-beth-joab, and half of the Manahathites, the Zorites. 55The families also of the scribes that lived at Jabez: the Tirathites, the Shimeathites, and the Sucathites. These are the Kenites who came from Hammath, father of the house of Rechab.

3.1 THESE are the sons of David who were born to him in Hebron: the firstborn Amnon, by Ahinoam the Jezreelite; the second Daniel, by Abigail the Carmelite; 2the third Absalom, son of Maacah, daughter of King Talmai of Geshur; the fourth Adonijah, son of Haggith; 3the fifth Shephatiah, by Abital; the sixth Ithream, by his wife Eglah; 4six were born to him in Hebron, where he reigned for seven years and six months. And he reigned thirty-

aHeb sons  bGk reads Mareshah  cGk Vg: Heb son

three years in Jerusalem. [5]These were born to him in Jerusalem: Shimea, Shobab, Nathan, and Solomon, four by Bath-shua, daughter of Ammiel; [6]then Ibhar, Elishama, Eliphelet, [7]Nogah, Nepheg, Japhia, [8]Elishama, Eliada, and Eliphelet, nine. [9]All these were David's sons, besides the sons of the concubines; and Tamar was their sister.

10 The descendants of Solomon: Rehoboam, Abijah his son, Asa his son, Jehoshaphat his son, [11]Joram his son, Ahaziah his son, Joash his son, [12]Amaziah his son, Azariah his son, Jotham his son, [13]Ahaz his son, Hezekiah his son, Manasseh his son, [14]Amon his son, Josiah his son. [15]The sons of Josiah: Johanan the firstborn, the second Jehoiakim, the third Zedekiah, the fourth Shallum. [16]The descendants of Jehoiakim: Jeconiah his son, Zedekiah his son; [17]and the sons of Jeconiah, the captive: Shealtiel his son, [18]Malchiram, Pedaiah, Shenazzar, Jekamiah, Hoshama, and Nedabiah; [19]The sons of Pedaiah: Zerubbabel and Shimei; and the sons of Zerubbabel: Meshullam and Hananiah, and Shelomith was their sister; [20]and Hashubah, Ohel, Berechiah, Hasadiah, and Jushab-hesed, five. [21]The sons of Hananiah: Pelatiah and Jeshaiah, his son[a] Rephaiah, his son[a] Arnan, his son[a] Obadiah, his son[a] Shecaniah. [22]The son[b] of Shecaniah: Shemaiah. And the sons of Shemaiah: Hattush, Igal, Bariah, Neariah, and Shaphat, six. [23]The sons of Neariah: Elioenai, Hizkiah, and Azrikam, three. [24]The sons of Elioenai: Hodaviah, Eliashib, Pelaiah, Akkub, Johanan, Delaiah, and Anani, seven.

[4.1] THE sons of Judah: Perez, Hezron, Carmi, Hur, and Shobal. [2]Reaiah son of Shobal became the father of Jahath, and Jahath became the father of Ahumai and Lahad. These were the families of the Zorathites. [3]These were the sons[c] of Etam: Jezreel, Ishma, and Idbash; and the name of their sister was Hazzelelponi, [4]and Penuel was the father of Gedor, and Ezer the father of Hushah. These were the sons of Hur, the firstborn of Ephrathah, the father of Bethlehem.

## ACTS 24.1–27

FIVE days later the high priest Ananias came down with some elders and an attorney, a certain Tertullus, and they reported their case against Paul to the governor. [2]When Paul[d] had been summoned, Tertullus began to accuse him, saying:

"Your Excellency,[e] because of you we have long enjoyed peace, and reforms have been made for this people because of your foresight. [3]We welcome this in every way and everywhere with utmost gratitude. [4]But, to detain you no further, I beg you to hear us briefly with your customary graciousness. [5]We have, in fact, found this man a pestilent fellow, an agitator among all the Jews throughout the world, and a ringleader of the sect of the Nazarenes.[f] [6]He even tried to profane the temple, and so we seized him.[g] [8]By examining him yourself you will be able to learn from him concerning everything of which we accuse him."

9 The Jews also joined in the charge by asserting that all this was true.

10 When the governor motioned to him to speak, Paul replied:

"I cheerfully make my defense, knowing that for many years you have been a judge over this nation. [11]As you can find out, it is not more than twelve

[a]Gk Compare Syr Vg: Heb *sons of*  [b]Heb *sons*  [c]Gk Compare Vg: Heb *the father*  [d]Gk *he*  [e]Gk lacks *Your Excellency*  [f]Gk *Nazoreans*  [g]Other ancient authorities add *and we would have judged him according to our law. [7]But the chief captain Lysias came and with great violence took him out of our hands, [8]commanding his accusers to come before you.*

days since I went up to worship in Jerusalem. ¹²They did not find me disputing with anyone in the temple or stirring up a crowd either in the synagogues or throughout the city. ¹³Neither can they prove to you the charge that they now bring against me. ¹⁴But this I admit to you, that according to the Way, which they call a sect, I worship the God of our ancestors, believing everything laid down according to the law or written in the prophets. ¹⁵I have a hope in God— a hope that they themselves also accept—that there will be a resurrection of both[a] the righteous and the unrighteous. ¹⁶Therefore I do my best always to have a clear conscience toward God and all people. ¹⁷Now after some years I came to bring alms to my nation and to offer sacrifices. ¹⁸While I was doing this, they found me in the temple, completing the rite of purification, without any crowd or disturbance. ¹⁹But there were some Jews from Asia—they ought to be here before you to make an accusation, if they have anything against me. ²⁰Or let these men here tell what crime they had found when I stood before the council, ²¹unless it was this one sentence that I called out while standing before them, 'It is about the resurrection of the dead that I am on trial before you today.' "

22  But Felix, who was rather well informed about the Way, adjourned the hearing with the comment, "When Lysias the tribune comes down, I will decide your case." ²³Then he ordered the centurion to keep him in custody, but to let him have some liberty and not to prevent any of his friends from taking care of his needs.

24  Some days later when Felix came with his wife Drusilla, who was Jewish, he sent for Paul and heard him speak concerning faith in Christ Jesus. ²⁵And as he discussed justice, self-control, and the coming judgment, Felix became frightened and said, "Go away for the present; when I have an opportunity, I will send for you." ²⁶At the same time he hoped that money would be given him by Paul, and for that reason he used to send for him very often and converse with him.

27  After two years had passed, Felix was succeeded by Porcius Festus; and since he wanted to grant the Jews a favor, Felix left Paul in prison.

## PSALM 4.1–8

*To the leader: with stringed instruments. A Psalm of David.*

ANSWER me when I call, O God
of my right!
You gave me room when I
was in distress.
Be gracious to me, and hear
my prayer.
2  How long, you people, shall my
honor suffer shame?
How long will you love vain
words, and seek after
lies?           *Selah*
3  But know that the Lord has set
apart the faithful for
himself;
the Lord hears when I call to
him.

4  When you are disturbed,[b] do
not sin;
ponder it on your beds, and
be silent.           *Selah*
5  Offer right sacrifices,
and put your trust in the
Lord.

6  There are many who say,
"O that we might see
some good!
Let the light of your face
shine on us, O Lord!"
7  You have put gladness in my
heart

---

aOther ancient authorities read *of the dead, both of*   bOr *are angry*

more than when their grain
and wine abound.

8 I will both lie down and sleep in
    peace;
for you alone, O Lord, make
    me lie down in safety.

## PROVERBS 18.16–18

A GIFT opens doors;
    it gives access to the great.
17 The one who first states
    a case seems right,
until the other comes and
    cross-examines.
18 Casting the lot puts an end to
    disputes
and decides between powerful
    contenders.

# JULY 7

## 1 CHRONICLES 4.5—5.17

A SHHUR father of Tekoa had two wives, Helah and Naarah; 6Naarah bore him Ahuzzam, Hepher, Temeni, and Haahashtari.a These were the sons of Naarah. 7The sons of Helah: Zereth, Izhar,b and Ethnan. 8Koz became the father of Anub, Zobebah, and the families of Aharhel son of Harum. 9Jabez was honored more than his brothers, and his mother named him Jabez, saying, "Because I bore him in pain." 10Jabez called on the God of Israel, saying, "Oh that you would bless me and enlarge my border, and that your hand might be with me, and that you would keep me from hurt and harm!" And God granted what he asked. 11Chelub the brother of Shuhah became the father of Mehir, who was the father of Eshton. 12Eshton became the father of Beth-rapha, Paseah, and Tehinnah the father of Irnahash. These are the men of Recah. 13The sons of Kenaz: Othniel and Sera-

iah; and the sons of Othniel: Hathath and Meonothai. c 14Meonothai became the father of Ophrah; and Seraiah became the father of Joab father of Geharashim, d so-called because they were artisans. 15The sons of Caleb son of Jephunneh: Iru, Elah, and Naam; and the sone of Elah: Kenaz. 16The sons of Jehallelel: Ziph, Ziphah, Tiria, and Asarel. 17The sons of Ezrah: Jether, Mered, Epher, and Jalon. These are the sons of Bithiah, daughter of Pharaoh, whom Mered married;f and she conceived and boreg Miriam, Shammai, and Ishbah father of Eshtemoa. 18And his Judean wife bore Jered father of Gedor, Heber father of Soco, and Jekuthiel father of Zanoah. 19The sons of the wife of Hodiah, the sister of Naham, were the fathers of Keilah the Garmite and Eshtemoa the Maacathite. 20The sons of Shimon: Amnon, Rinnah, Benhanan, and Tilon. The sons of Ishi: Zoheth and Ben-zoheth. 21The sons of Shelah son of Judah: Er father of Lecah,

a Or Ahashtari   b Another reading is Zohar   c Gk Vg: Heb lacks and Meonothai   d That is Valley of artisans   e Heb sons   f The clause: These are . . . married is transposed from verse 18   g Heb lacks and bore

Laadah father of Mareshah, and the families of the guild of linen workers at Beth-ashbea; <sup>22</sup>and Jokim, and the men of Cozeba, and Joash, and Saraph, who married into Moab but returned to Le-hem[a] (now the records[b] are ancient). <sup>23</sup>These were the potters and inhabitants of Netaim and Gederah; they lived there with the king in his service.

24 The sons of Simeon: Nemuel, Jamin, Jarib, Zerah, Shaul;[c] <sup>25</sup>Shallum was his son, Mibsam his son, Mishma his son. <sup>26</sup>The sons of Mishma: Hammuel his son, Zaccur his son, Shimei his son. <sup>27</sup>Shimei had sixteen sons and six daughters; but his brothers did not have many children, nor did all their family multiply like the Judeans. <sup>28</sup>They lived in Beer-sheba, Moladah, Hazar-shual, <sup>29</sup>Bilhah, Ezem, Tolad, <sup>30</sup>Bethuel, Hormah, Ziklag, <sup>31</sup>Beth-marcaboth, Hazar-susim, Beth-biri, and Shaaraim. These were their towns until David became king. <sup>32</sup>And their villages were Etam, Ain, Rimmon, Tochen, and Ashan, five towns, <sup>33</sup>along with all their villages that were around these towns as far as Baal. These were their settlements. And they kept a genealogical record.

34 Meshobab, Jamlech, Joshah son of Amaziah, <sup>35</sup>Joel, Jehu son of Joshibiah son of Seraiah son of Asiel, <sup>36</sup>Elioenai, Jaakobah, Jeshohaiah, Asaiah, Adiel, Jesimiel, Benaiah, <sup>37</sup>Ziza son of Shiphi son of Allon son of Jedaiah son of Shimri son of Shemaiah— <sup>38</sup>these men tioned by name were leaders in their families, and their clans increased greatly. <sup>39</sup>They journeyed to the entrance of Gedor, to the east side of the valley, to seek pasture for their flocks, <sup>40</sup>where they found rich, good pasture, and the land was very broad, quiet, and peaceful; for the former inhabitants there belonged to Ham. <sup>41</sup>These, registered by name, came in the days of King Hezekiah of Judah, and attacked their tents and the Meunim who were found there, and exterminated them to this day, and settled in their place, because there was pasture there for their flocks. <sup>42</sup>And some of them, five hundred men of the Simeonites, went to Mount Seir, having as their leaders Pelatiah, Neariah, Rephaiah, and Uzziel, sons of Ishi; <sup>43</sup>they destroyed the remnant of the Amalekites that had escaped, and they have lived there to this day.

<sup>5.1</sup> THE sons of Reuben the firstborn of Israel. (He was the firstborn, but because he defiled his father's bed his birthright was given to the sons of Joseph son of Israel, so that he is not enrolled in the genealogy according to the birthright; <sup>2</sup>though Judah became prominent among his brothers and a ruler came from him, yet the birthright belonged to Joseph.) <sup>3</sup>The sons of Reuben, the firstborn of Israel: Hanoch, Pallu, Hezron, and Carmi. <sup>4</sup>The sons of Joel: Shemaiah his son, Gog his son, Shimei his son, <sup>5</sup>Micah his son, Reaiah his son, Baal his son, <sup>6</sup>Beerah his son, whom King Tilgath-pilneser of Assyria carried away into exile; he was a chieftain of the Reubenites. <sup>7</sup>And his kindred by their families, when the genealogy of their generations was reckoned: the chief, Jeiel, and Zechariah, <sup>8</sup>and Bela son of Azaz, son of Shema, son of Joel, who lived in Aroer, as far as Nebo and Baal-meon. <sup>9</sup>He also lived to the east as far as the beginning of the desert this side of the Euphrates, because their cattle had multiplied in the land of Gilead. <sup>10</sup>And in the days of Saul they made war on the Hagrites, who fell by their hand; and they lived in their tents throughout all the region east of Gilead.

11 The sons of Gad lived beside them in the land of Bashan as far as Salecah: <sup>12</sup>Joel the chief, Shapham the sec-

<sup>a</sup>Vg Compare Gk: Heb *and Jashubi-lahem*   <sup>b</sup>Or *matters*   <sup>c</sup>Or *Saul*

ond, Janai, and Shaphat in Bashan. ¹³And their kindred according to their clans: Michael, Meshullam, Sheba, Jorai, Jacan, Zia, and Eber, seven. ¹⁴These were the sons of Abihail son of Huri, son of Jaroah, son of Gilead, son of Michael, son of Jeshishai, son of Jahdo, son of Buz; ¹⁵Ahi son of Abdiel, son of Guni, was chief in their clan; ¹⁶and they lived in Gilead, in Bashan and in its towns, and in all the pasture lands of Sharon to their limits. ¹⁷All of these were enrolled by genealogies in the days of King Jotham of Judah, and in the days of King Jeroboam of Israel.

## ACTS 25.1–27

THREE days after Festus had arrived in the province, he went up from Caesarea to Jerusalem ²where the chief priests and the leaders of the Jews gave him a report against Paul. They appealed to him ³and requested, as a favor to them against Paul, [a] to have him transferred to Jerusalem. They were, in fact, planning an ambush to kill him along the way. ⁴Festus replied that Paul was being kept at Caesarea, and that he himself intended to go there shortly. ⁵"So," he said, "let those of you who have the authority come down with me, and if there is anything wrong about the man, let them accuse him."

6 After he had stayed among them not more than eight or ten days, he went down to Caesarea; the next day he took his seat on the tribunal and ordered Paul to be brought. ⁷When he arrived, the Jews who had gone down from Jerusalem surrounded him, bringing many serious charges against him, which they could not prove. ⁸Paul said in his defense, "I have in no way committed an offense against the law of the Jews, or against the temple, or against the emperor." ⁹But Festus, wishing to do the Jews a favor, asked Paul, "Do you wish to go up to Jerusalem and be tried there before me on these charges?" ¹⁰Paul said, "I am appealing to the emperor's tribunal; this is where I should be tried. I have done no wrong to the Jews, as you very well know. ¹¹Now if I am in the wrong and have committed something for which I deserve to die, I am not trying to escape death; but if there is nothing to their charges against me, no one can turn me over to them. I appeal to the emperor." ¹²Then Festus, after he had conferred with his council, replied, "You have appealed to the emperor; to the emperor you will go."

13 After several days had passed, King Agrippa and Bernice arrived at Caesarea to welcome Festus. ¹⁴Since they were staying there several days, Festus laid Paul's case before the king, saying, "There is a man here who was left in prison by Felix. ¹⁵When I was in Jerusalem, the chief priests and the elders of the Jews informed me about him and asked for a sentence against him. ¹⁶I told them that it was not the custom of the Romans to hand over anyone before the accused had met the accusers face to face and had been given an opportunity to make a defense against the charge. ¹⁷So when they met here, I lost no time, but on the next day took my seat on the tribunal and ordered the man to be brought. ¹⁸When the accusers stood up, they did not charge him with any of the crimes[b] that I was expecting. ¹⁹Instead they had certain points of disagreement with him about their own religion and about a certain Jesus, who had died, but whom Paul asserted to be alive. ²⁰Since I was at a loss how to investigate these questions, I asked whether he wished to go to Jerusalem and be tried there on these charges. [c] ²¹But when Paul had appealed to be kept in custody for the decision of his Imperial Majesty, I or-

a Gk *him*  b Other ancient authorities read *with anything*  c Gk *on them* dered him to be held until I could send him to the emperor." ²²Agrippa said to Festus, "I would like to hear the man myself." "Tomorrow," he said, "you will hear him."

23  So on the next day Agrippa and Bernice came with great pomp, and they entered the audience hall with the military tribunes and the prominent men of the city. Then Festus gave the order and Paul was brought in. ²⁴And Festus said, "King Agrippa and all here present with us, you see this man about whom the whole Jewish community petitioned me, both in Jerusalem and here, shouting that he ought not to live any longer. ²⁵But I found that he had done nothing deserving death; and when he appealed to his Imperial Majesty, I decided to send him. ²⁶But I have nothing definite to write to our sovereign about him. Therefore I have brought him before all of you, and especially before you, King Agrippa, so that, after we have examined him, I may have something to write— ²⁷for it seems to me unreasonable to send a prisoner without indicating the charges against him."

## PSALM 5. 1–12

*To the leader: for the flutes. A Psalm of David.*

G IVE ear to my words, O LORD;
give heed to my sighing.
² Listen to the sound of
my cry,
my King and my God,
for to you I pray.
³ O LORD, in the morning you
hear my voice;
in the morning I plead my
case to you, and watch.

⁴ For you are not a God who
delights in wickedness;
evil will not sojourn with you.
⁵ The boastful will not stand
before your eyes;
you hate all evildoers.

⁶ You destroy those who speak
lies;
the LORD abhors the
bloodthirsty and
deceitful.

⁷ But I, through the abundance of
your steadfast love,
will enter your house,
I will bow down toward your
holy temple
in awe of you.
⁸ Lead me, O LORD, in your
righteousness
because of my enemies;
make your way straight
before me.

⁹ For there is no truth in their
mouths;
their hearts are destruction;
their throats are open graves;
they flatter with their
tongues.
¹⁰ Make them bear their guilt,
O God;
let them fall by their own
counsels;
because of their many
transgressions cast them
out,
for they have rebelled against
you.

¹¹ But let all who take refuge in
you rejoice;
let them ever sing for joy.
Spread your protection over
them,
so that those who love your
name may exult in you.
¹² For you bless the righteous,
O LORD;
you cover them with favor as
with a shield.

## PROVERBS 18.19

**A**N ally offended is stronger
than a city; [a]
such quarreling is like the
bars of a castle.

# JULY 8

## 1 CHRONICLES 5.18—6.81

**T**HE Reubenites, the Gadites, and the half-tribe of Manasseh had valiant warriors, who carried shield and sword, and drew the bow, expert in war, forty-four thousand seven hundred sixty, ready for service. [19]They made war on the Hagrites, Jetur, Naphish, and Nodab; [20]and when they received help against them, the Hagrites and all who were with them were given into their hands, for they cried to God in the battle, and he granted their entreaty because they trusted in him. [21]They captured their livestock: fifty thousand of their camels, two hundred fifty thousand sheep, two thousand donkeys, and one hundred thousand captives. [22]Many fell slain, because the war was of God. And they lived in their territory until the exile.

23 The members of the half-tribe of Manasseh lived in the land; they were very numerous from Bashan to Baal-hermon, Senir, and Mount Hermon. [24]These were the heads of their clans: Epher, [b] Ishi, Eliel, Azriel, Jeremiah, Hodaviah, and Jahdiel, mighty warriors, famous men, heads of their clans. [25]But they transgressed against the God of their ancestors, and prostituted themselves to the gods of the peoples of the land, whom God had destroyed before them. [26]So the God of Israel stirred up the spirit of King Pul of Assyria, the spirit of King Tilgath-pilneser of Assyria, and he carried them away, namely, the Reubenites, the Gadites, and the half-tribe of Manasseh, and brought them to Halah, Habor, Hara, and the river Gozan, to this day.

[6c.1] THE sons of Levi: Gershom, [d] Kohath, and Merari. [2]The sons of Kohath: Amram, Izhar, Hebron, and Uzziel. [3]The children of Amram: Aaron, Moses, and Miriam. The sons of Aaron: Nadab, Abihu, Eleazar, and Ithamar. [4]Eleazar became the father of Phinehas, Phinehas of Abishua, [5]Abishua of Bukki, Bukki of Uzzi, [6]Uzzi of Zerahiah, Zerahiah of Meraioth, [7]Meraioth of Amariah, Amariah of Ahitub, [8]Ahitub of Zadok, Zadok of Ahimaaz, [9]Ahimaaz of Azariah, Azariah of Johanan, [10]and Johanan of Azariah (it was he who served as priest in the house that Solomon built in Jerusalem). [11]Azariah became the father of Amariah, Amariah of Ahitub, [12]Ahitub of Zadok, Zadok of Shallum, [13]Shallum of Hilkiah, Hilkiah of Azariah, [14]Azariah of Seraiah, Seraiah of Jehozadak; [15]and Jehozadak went into exile when the LORD sent Judah and

Jerusalem into exile by the hand of Nebuchadnezzar.

16ᵃ The sons of Levi: Gershom, Kohath, and Merari. ¹⁷These are the names of the sons of Gershom: Libni and Shimei. ¹⁸The sons of Kohath: Amram, Izhar, Hebron, and Uzziel. ¹⁹The sons of Merari: Mahli and Mushi. These are the clans of the Levites according to their ancestry. ²⁰Of Gershom: Libni his son, Jahath his son, Zimmah his son, ²¹Joah his son, Iddo his son, Zerah his son, Jeatherai his son. ²²The sons of Kohath: Amminadab his son, Korah his son, Assir his son, ²³Elkanah his son, Ebiasaph his son, Assir his son, ²⁴Tahath his son, Uriel his son, Uzziah his son, and Shaul his son. ²⁵The sons of Elkanah: Amasai and Ahimoth, ²⁶Elkanah his son, Zophai his son, Nahath his son, ²⁷Eliab his son, Jeroham his son, Elkanah his son. ²⁸The sons of Samuel: Joelᵇ his firstborn, the second Abijah. ᶜ ²⁹The sons of Merari: Mahli, Libni his son, Shimei his son, Uzzah his son, ³⁰Shimea his son, Haggiah his son, and Asaiah his son.

31 These are the men whom David put in charge of the service of song in the house of the LORD, after the ark came to rest there. ³²They ministered with song before the tabernacle of the tent of meeting, until Solomon had built the house of the LORD in Jerusalem; and they performed their service in due order. ³³These are the men who served; and their sons were: Of the Kohathites: Heman, the singer, son of Joel, son of Samuel, ³⁴son of Elkanah, son of Jeroham, son of Eliel, son of Toah, ³⁵son of Zuph, son of Elkanah, son of Mahath, son of Amasai, ³⁶son of Elkanah, son of Joel, son of Azariah, son of Zephaniah, ³⁷son of Tahath, son of Assir, son of Ebiasaph, son of Korah, ³⁸son of Izhar, son of Kohath, son of Levi, son of Israel; ³⁹and his brother Asaph, who stood on his right, namely, Asaph son of Berechiah, son of Shimea, ⁴⁰son of Michael, son of Baaseiah, son of Malchijah, ⁴¹son of Ethni, son of Zerah, son of Adaiah, ⁴²son of Ethan, son of Zimmah, son of Shimei, ⁴³son of Jahath, son of Gershom, son of Levi. ⁴⁴On the left were their kindred the sons of Merari: Ethan son of Kishi, son of Abdi, son of Malluch, ⁴⁵son of Hashabiah, son of Amaziah, son of Hilkiah, ⁴⁶son of Amzi, son of Bani, son of Shemer, ⁴⁷son of Mahli, son of Mushi, son of Merari, son of Levi; ⁴⁸and their kindred the Levites were appointed for all the service of the tabernacle of the house of God.

49 But Aaron and his sons made offerings on the altar of burnt offering and on the altar of incense, doing all the work of the most holy place, to make atonement for Israel, according to all that Moses the servant of God had commanded. ⁵⁰These are the sons of Aaron: Eleazar his son, Phinehas his son, Abishua his son, ⁵¹Bukki his son, Uzzi his son, Zerahiah his son, ⁵²Meraioth his son, Amariah his son, Ahitub his son, ⁵³Zadok his son, Ahimaaz his son.

54 These are their dwelling places according to their settlements within their borders: to the sons of Aaron of the families of Kohathites—for the lot fell to them first— ⁵⁵to them they gave Hebron in the land of Judah and its surrounding pasture lands, ⁵⁶but the fields of the city and its villages they gave to Caleb son of Jephunneh. ⁵⁷To the sons of Aaron they gave the cities of refuge: Hebron, Libnah with its pasture lands, Jattir, Eshtemoa with its pasture lands, ⁵⁸Hilenᵈ with its pasture lands, Debir with its pasture lands, ⁵⁹Ashan with its pasture lands, and Beth-shemesh with its pasture lands. ⁶⁰From the tribe of Benjamin, Geba with its pasture lands, Alemeth with its pasture lands, and An-

---

ᵃCh 6.1 in Heb   ᵇGk Syr Compare verse 33 and 1 Sam 8.2: Heb lacks *Joel*   ᶜHeb reads *Vashni, and Abijah* for *the second Abijah,* taking *the second* as a proper name   ᵈOther readings *Hilez, Holon;* See Josh 21.15

athoth with its pasture lands. All their towns throughout their families were thirteen.

61 To the rest of the Kohathites were given by lot out of the family of the tribe, out of the half-tribe, the half of Manasseh, ten towns. ⁶²To the Gershomites according to their families were allotted thirteen towns out of the tribes of Issachar, Asher, Naphtali, and Manasseh in Bashan. ⁶³To the Merarites according to their families were allotted twelve towns out of the tribes of Reuben, Gad, and Zebulun. ⁶⁴So the people of Israel gave the Levites the towns with their pasture lands. ⁶⁵They also gave them by lot out of the tribes of Judah, Simeon, and Benjamin these towns that are mentioned by name.

66 And some of the families of the sons of Kohath had towns of their territory out of the tribe of Ephraim. ⁶⁷They were given the cities of refuge: Shechem with its pasture lands in the hill country of Ephraim, Gezer with its pasture lands, ⁶⁸Jokmeam with its pasture lands, Beth-horon with its pasture lands, ⁶⁹Aijalon with its pasture lands, Gath-rimmon with its pasture lands; ⁷⁰and out of the half-tribe of Manasseh, Aner with its pasture lands, and Bileam with its pasture lands, for the rest of the families of the Kohathites.

71 To the Gershomites: out of the half-tribe of Manasseh: Golan in Bashan with its pasture lands and Ashtaroth with its pasture lands; ⁷²and out of the tribe of Issachar: Kedesh with its pasture lands, Daberath* with its pasture lands, ⁷³Ramoth with its pasture lands, and Anem with its pasture lands; ⁷⁴out of the tribe of Asher: Mashal with its pasture lands, Abdon with its pasture lands, ⁷⁵Hukok with its pasture lands, and Rehob with its pasture lands; ⁷⁶and out of the tribe of Naphtali: Kedesh in Galilee with its pasture lands, Hammon with its pasture lands, and

Kiriathaim with its pasture lands. ⁷⁷To the rest of the Merarites out of the tribe of Zebulun: Rimmono with its pasture lands, Tabor with its pasture lands, ⁷⁸and across the Jordan from Jericho, on the east side of the Jordan, out of the tribe of Reuben: Bezer in the steppe with its pasture lands, Jahzah with its pasture lands, ⁷⁹Kedemoth with its pasture lands, and Mephaath with its pasture lands; ⁸⁰and out of the tribe of Gad: Ramoth in Gilead with its pasture lands, Mahanaim with its pasture lands, ⁸¹Heshbon with its pasture lands, and Jazer with its pasture lands.

## ACTS 26.1–32

AGRIPPA said to Paul, "You have permission to speak for yourself." Then Paul stretched out his hand and began to defend himself:

2 "I consider myself fortunate that it is before you, King Agrippa, I am to make my defense today against all the accusations of the Jews, ³because you are especially familiar with all the customs and controversies of the Jews; therefore I beg of you to listen to me patiently.

4 "All the Jews know my way of life from my youth, a life spent from the beginning among my own people and in Jerusalem. ⁵They have known for a long time, if they are willing to testify, that I have belonged to the strictest sect of our religion and lived as a Pharisee. ⁶And now I stand here on trial on account of my hope in the promise made by God to our ancestors, ⁷a promise that our twelve tribes hope to attain, as they earnestly worship day and night. It is for this hope, your Excellency,** that I am accused by Jews! ⁸Why is it thought incredible by any of you that God raises the dead?

9 "Indeed, I myself was convinced that I ought to do many things against the name of Jesus of Nazareth.*** ¹⁰And

ᵃOr *Dobrath*  ᵇGk *O king*  ᶜGk *the Nazorean*

that is what I did in Jerusalem; with authority received from the chief priests, I not only locked up many of the saints in prison, but I also cast my vote against them when they were being condemned to death. [11]By punishing them often in all the synagogues I tried to force them to blaspheme; and since I was so furiously enraged at them, I pursued them even to foreign cities.

12 "With this in mind, I was traveling to Damascus with the authority and commission of the chief priests, [13]when at midday along the road, your Excellency,[a] I saw a light from heaven, brighter than the sun, shining around me and my companions. [14]When we had all fallen to the ground, I heard a voice saying to me in the Hebrew[b] language, 'Saul, Saul, why are you persecuting me? It hurts you to kick against the goads.' [15]I asked, 'Who are you, Lord?' The Lord answered, 'I am Jesus whom you are persecuting. [16]But get up and stand on your feet; for I have appeared to you for this purpose, to appoint you to serve and testify to the things in which you have seen me[c] and to those in which I will appear to you. [17]I will rescue you from your people and from the Gentiles—to whom I am sending you [18]to open their eyes so that they may turn from darkness to light and from the power of Satan to God, so that they may receive forgiveness of sins and a place among those who are sanctified by faith in me.'

19 "After that, King Agrippa, I was not disobedient to the heavenly vision, [20]but declared first to those in Damascus, then in Jerusalem and throughout the countryside of Judea, and also to the Gentiles, that they should repent and turn to God and do deeds consistent with repentance. [21]For this reason the Jews seized me in the temple and tried to kill me. [22]To this day I have had help from God, and so I stand here, testifying to both small and great, saying nothing but what the prophets and Moses said would take place: [23]that the Messiah[d] must suffer, and that, by being the first to rise from the dead, he would proclaim light both to our people and to the Gentiles."

24 While he was making this defense, Festus exclaimed, "You are out of your mind, Paul! Too much learning is driving you insane!" [25]But Paul said, "I am not out of my mind, most excellent Festus, but I am speaking the sober truth. [26]Indeed the king knows about these things, and to him I speak freely; for I am certain that none of these things has escaped his notice, for this was not done in a corner. [27]King Agrippa, do you believe the prophets? I know that you believe." [28]Agrippa said to Paul, "Are you so quickly persuading me to become a Christian?"[e] [29]Paul replied, "Whether quickly or not, I pray to God that not only you but also all who are listening to me today might become such as I am—except for these chains."

30 Then the king got up, and with him the governor and Bernice and those who had been seated with them; [31]and as they were leaving, they said to one another, "This man is doing nothing to deserve death or imprisonment." [32]Agrippa said to Festus, "This man could have been set free if he had not appealed to the emperor."

## PSALM 6.1–10

*To the leader: with stringed instruments; according to The Sheminith. A Psalm of David.*

O LORD, do not rebuke me in
    your anger,
or discipline me in your
    wrath.
2  Be gracious to me, O LORD, for
    I am languishing;

---

a Gk *O king*  b That is, *Aramaic*  c Other ancient authorities read *the things that you have seen*
d Or *the Christ*  e Or *Quickly you will persuade me to play the Christian*

O Lord, heal me, for my
    bones are shaking with
    terror.
3 My soul also is struck with
    terror,
    while you, O Lord—how
    long?

4 Turn, O Lord, save my life;
    deliver me for the sake of
    your steadfast love.
5 For in death there is no
    remembrance of you;
    in Sheol who can give you
    praise?

6 I am weary with my moaning;
    every night I flood my bed
    with tears;
    I drench my couch with my
    weeping.
7 My eyes waste away because of
    grief;
    they grow weak because of all
    my foes.

8 Depart from me, all you
    workers of evil,
    for the Lord has heard the
    sound of my weeping.
9 The Lord has heard my
    supplication;
    the Lord accepts my prayer.
10 All my enemies shall be
    ashamed and struck with
    terror;
    they shall turn back, and in a
    moment be put to
    shame.

## PROVERBS 18.20–21

FROM the fruit of the mouth
    one's stomach is
    satisfied;
    the yield of the lips brings
    satisfaction.
21 Death and life are in the power
    of the tongue,
    and those who love it will eat
    its fruits.

# JULY 9

## 1 CHRONICLES 7.1—8.40

THE sons[a] of Issachar: Tola, Puah, Jashub, and Shimron, four. 2The sons of Tola: Uzzi, Rephaiah, Jeriel, Jahmai, Ibsam, and Shemuel, heads of their ancestral houses, namely of Tola, mighty warriors of their generations, their number in the days of David being twenty-two thousand six hundred. 3The son[b] of Uzzi: Izrahiah. And the sons of Izrahiah: Michael, Obadiah, Joel, and Isshiah, five, all of them chiefs; 4and along with them, by their generations, according to their ancestral houses, were units of the fighting force, thirty-six thousand, for they had many wives and sons. 5Their kindred belonging to all the families of Issachar were in all eighty-seven thousand mighty warriors, enrolled by genealogy.

6 The sons of Benjamin: Bela, Becher, and Jediael, three. 7The sons of Bela: Ezbon, Uzzi, Uzziel, Jerimoth, and Iri, five, heads of ancestral houses, mighty warriors; and their enrollment

aSyr Compare Vg: Heb *And to the sons*   bHeb *sons*

by genealogies was twenty-two thousand thirty-four. [8]The sons of Becher: Zemirah, Joash, Eliezer, Elioenai, Omri, Jeremoth, Abijah, Anathoth, and Alemeth. All these were the sons of Becher; [9]and their enrollment by genealogies, according to their generations, as heads of their ancestral houses, mighty warriors, was twenty thousand two hundred. [10]The sons of Jediael: Bilhan. And the sons of Bilhan: Jeush, Benjamin, Ehud, Chenaanah, Zethan, Tarshish, and Ahishahar. [11]All these were the sons of Jediael according to the heads of their ancestral houses, mighty warriors, seventeen thousand two hundred, ready for service in war. [12]And Shuppim and Huppim were the sons of Ir, Hushim the son[a] of Aher.

13 The descendants of Naphtali: Jahziel, Guni, Jezer, and Shallum, the descendants of Bilhah.

14 The sons of Manasseh: Asriel, whom his Aramean concubine bore; she bore Machir the father of Gilead. [15]And Machir took a wife for Huppim and for Shuppim. The name of his sister was Maacah. And the name of the second was Zelophehad; and Zelophehad had daughters. [16]Maacah the wife of Machir bore a son, and she named him Peresh; the name of his brother was Sheresh; and his sons were Ulam and Rekem. [17]The son[a] of Ulam: Bedan. These were the sons of Gilead son of Machir, son of Manasseh. [18]And his sister Hammolecheth bore Ishhod, Abiezer, and Mahlah. [19]The sons of Shemida were Ahian, Shechem, Likhi, and Aniam.

20 The sons of Ephraim: Shuthelah, and Bered his son, Tahath his son, Eleadah his son, Tahath his son, [21]Zabad his son, Shuthelah his son, and Ezer and Elead. Now the people of Gath, who were born in the land, killed them, because they came down to raid their cattle. [22]And their father Ephraim mourned many days, and his brothers came to comfort him. [23]Ephraim[b] went in to his wife, and she conceived and bore a son; and he named him Beriah, because disaster[c] had befallen his house. [24]His daughter was Sheerah, who built both Lower and Upper Beth-horon, and Uzzen-sheerah. [25]Rephah was his son, Resheph his son, Telah his son, Tahan his son, [26]Ladan his son, Ammihud his son, Elishama his son, [27]Nun[d] his son, Joshua his son. [28]Their possessions and settlements were Bethel and its towns, and eastward Naaran, and westward Gezer and its towns, Shechem and its towns, as far as Ayyah and its towns; [29]also along the borders of the Manassites, Beth-shean and its towns, Taanach and its towns, Megiddo and its towns, Dor and its towns. In these lived the sons of Joseph son of Israel.

30 The sons of Asher: Imnah, Ishvah, Ishvi, Beriah, and their sister Serah. [31]The sons of Beriah: Heber and Malchiel, who was the father of Birzaith. [32]Heber became the father of Japhlet, Shomer, Hotham, and their sister Shua. [33]The sons of Japhlet: Pasach, Bimhal, and Ashvath. These are the sons of Japhlet. [34]The sons of Shemer: Ahi, Rohgah, Hubbah, and Aram. [35]The sons of Helem[e] his brother: Zophah, Imna, Shelesh, and Amal. [36]The sons of Zophah: Suah, Harnepher, Shual, Beri, Imrah, [37]Bezer, Hod, Shamma, Shilshah, Ithran, and Beera. [38]The sons of Jether: Jephunneh, Pispa, and Ara. [39]The sons of Ulla: Arah, Hanniel, and Rizia. [40]All of these were men of Asher, heads of ancestral houses, select mighty warriors, chief of the princes. Their number enrolled by genealogies, for service in war, was twenty-six thousand men.

**8.**1 BENJAMIN became the father of Bela his firstborn, Ashbel the second,

---

aHeb *sons*  bHeb *He*  cHeb *beraah*  dHere spelled *Non*; see Ex 33.11  eOr *Hotham*; see 7.32

Aharah the third, <sup>2</sup>Nohah the fourth, and Rapha the fifth. <sup>3</sup>And Bela had sons: Addar, Gera, Abihud,ᵃ <sup>4</sup>Abishua, Naaman, Ahoah, <sup>5</sup>Gera, Shephuphan, and Huram. <sup>6</sup>These are the sons of Ehud (they were heads of ancestral houses of the inhabitants of Geba, and they were carried into exile to Manahath): <sup>7</sup>Naaman,ᵇ Ahijah, and Gera, that is, Heglam,ᶜ who became the father of Uzza and Ahihud. <sup>8</sup>And Shaharaim had sons in the country of Moab after he had sent away his wives Hushim and Baara. <sup>9</sup>He had sons by his wife Hodesh: Jobab, Zibia, Mesha, Malcam, <sup>10</sup>Jeuz, Sachia, and Mirmah. These were his sons, heads of ancestral houses. <sup>11</sup>He also had sons by Hushim: Abitub and Elpaal. <sup>12</sup>The sons of Elpaal: Eber, Misham, and Shemed, who built Ono and Lod with its towns, <sup>13</sup>and Beriah and Shema (they were heads of ancestral houses of the inhabitants of Aijalon, who put to flight the inhabitants of Gath); <sup>14</sup>and Ahio, Shashak, and Jeremoth. <sup>15</sup>Zebadiah, Arad, Eder, <sup>16</sup>Michael, Ishpah, and Joha were sons of Beriah. <sup>17</sup>Zebadiah, Meshullam, Hizki, Heber, <sup>18</sup>Ishmerai, Izliah, and Jobab were the sons of Elpaal. <sup>19</sup>Jakim, Zichri, Zabdi, <sup>20</sup>Elienai, Zillethai, Eliel, <sup>21</sup>Adaiah, Beraiah, and Shimrath were the sons of Shimei. <sup>22</sup>Ishpan, Eber, Eliel, <sup>23</sup>Abdon, Zichri, Hanan, <sup>24</sup>Hananiah, Elam, Anthothijah, <sup>25</sup>Iphdeiah, and Penuel were the sons of Shashak. <sup>26</sup>Shamsherai, Shehariah, Athaliah, <sup>27</sup>Jaareshiah, Elijah, and Zichri were the sons of Jeroham. <sup>28</sup>These were the heads of ancestral houses, according to their generations, chiefs. These lived in Jerusalem.

29 Jeielᵈ the father of Gibeon lived in Gibeon, and the name of his wife was Maacah. <sup>30</sup>His firstborn son: Abdon, then Zur, Kish, Baal,ᵉ Nadab, <sup>31</sup>Gedor, Ahio, Zecher, <sup>32</sup>and Mikloth, who became the father of Shimeah. Now these also lived opposite their kindred in Jerusalem, with their kindred. <sup>33</sup>Ner became the father of Kish, Kish of Saul,ᶠ Saulᶠ of Jonathan, Malchishua, Abinadab, and Esh-baal; <sup>34</sup>and the son of Jonathan was Merib-baal; and Meribbaal became the father of Micah. <sup>35</sup>The sons of Micah: Pithon, Melech, Tarea, and Ahaz. <sup>36</sup>Ahaz became the father of Jehoaddah; and Jehoaddah became the father of Alemeth, Azmaveth, and Zimri; Zimri became the father of Moza. <sup>37</sup>Moza became the father of Binea; Raphah was his son, Eleasah his son, Azel his son. <sup>38</sup>Azel had six sons, and these are their names: Azrikam, Bocheru, Ishmael, Sheariah, Obadiah, and Hanan; all these were the sons of Azel. <sup>39</sup>The sons of his brother Eshek: Ulam his firstborn, Jeush the second, and Eliphelet the third. <sup>40</sup>The sons of Ulam were mighty warriors, archers, having many children and grandchildren, one hundred fifty. All these were Benjaminites.

## ACTS 27.1–20

WHEN it was decided that we [Luke, Paul, and companions] were to sail for Italy, they transferred Paul and some other prisoners to a centurion of the Augustan Cohort, named Julius. <sup>2</sup>Embarking on a ship of Adramyttium that was about to set sail to the ports along the coast of Asia, we put to sea, accompanied by Aristarchus, a Macedonian from Thessalonica. <sup>3</sup>The next day we put in at Sidon; and Julius treated Paul kindly, and allowed him to go to his friends to be cared for. <sup>4</sup>Putting out to sea from there, we sailed under the lee of Cyprus, because the winds were against us. <sup>5</sup>After we had sailed across the sea that is off Cilicia and Pamphylia, we came to Myra in Lycia. <sup>6</sup>There the centurion found an Alexandrian ship

---

ᵃOr *father of Ehud*; see 8.6   ᵇHeb *and Naaman*   ᶜOr *he carried them into exile*   ᵈCompare 9.35: Heb lacks *Jeiel*   ᵉGk Ms adds *Ner*; Compare 8.33 and 9.36   ᶠOr *Shaul*

bound for Italy and put us on board. [7]We sailed slowly for a number of days and arrived with difficulty off Cnidus, and as the wind was against us, we sailed under the lee of Crete off Salmone. [8]Sailing past it with difficulty, we came to a place called Fair Havens, near the city of Lasea.

9 Since much time had been lost and sailing was now dangerous, because even the Fast had already gone by, Paul advised them, [10]saying, "Sirs, I can see that the voyage will be with danger and much heavy loss, not only of the cargo and the ship, but also of our lives." [11]But the centurion paid more attention to the pilot and to the owner of the ship than to what Paul said. [12]Since the harbor was not suitable for spending the winter, the majority was in favor of putting to sea from there, on the chance that somehow they could reach Phoenix, where they could spend the winter. It was a harbor of Crete, facing southwest and northwest.

13 When a moderate south wind began to blow, they thought they could achieve their purpose; so they weighed anchor and began to sail past Crete, close to the shore. [14]But soon a violent wind, called the northeaster, rushed down from Crete.[a] [15]Since the ship was caught and could not be turned head-on into the wind, we gave way to it and were driven. [16]By running under the lee of a small island called Cauda[b] we were scarcely able to get the ship's boat under control. [17]After hoisting it up they took measures[c] to undergird the ship; then, fearing that they would run on the Syrtis, they lowered the sea anchor and so were driven. [18]We were being pounded by the storm so violently that on the next day they began to throw the cargo overboard, [19]and on the third day with their own hands they threw the ship's tackle overboard. [20]When neither sun nor stars appeared for many days, and no small tempest raged, all hope of our being saved was at last abandoned.

## PSALM 7.1–17

*A Shiggaion of David, which he sang to the Lord concerning Cush, a Benjaminite.*

O Lord my God, in you I take
    refuge;
save me from all my
    pursuers, and deliver
    me,
2  or like a lion they will tear me
    apart;
they will drag me away, with
    no one to rescue.

3  O Lord my God, if I have done
    this,
if there is wrong in my hands,
4  if I have repaid my ally with
    harm
or plundered my foe without
    cause,
5  then let the enemy pursue and
    overtake me,
trample my life to the ground,
and lay my soul in the dust.
        *Selah*

6  Rise up, O Lord, in your anger;
lift yourself up against the
    fury of my enemies;
awake, O my God;[d] you
    have appointed a
    judgment.
7  Let the assembly of the peoples
    be gathered around you,
and over it take your seat[e]
    on high.
8  The Lord judges the peoples;
judge me, O Lord, according
    to my righteousness
and according to the integrity
    that is in me.

9  O let the evil of the wicked
    come to an end,

[a]Gk *it*  [b]Other ancient authorities read *Clauda*  [c]Gk *helps*  [d]Or *awake for me*  [e]Cn: Heb *return*

but establish the righteous,
    you who test the minds and
        hearts,
      O righteous God.
10  God is my shield,
    who saves the upright in
        heart.
11  God is a righteous judge,
    and a God who has
        indignation every day.

12  If one does not repent, God[a]
        will whet his sword;
    he has bent and strung his
        bow;
13  he has prepared his deadly
        weapons,
    making his arrows fiery
        shafts.
14  See how they conceive evil,
    and are pregnant with
        mischief,

and bring forth lies.
15  They make a pit, digging it out,
    and fall into the hole that they
        have made.
16  Their mischief returns upon
        their own heads,
    and on their own heads their
        violence descends.

17  I will give to the Lord the
        thanks due to his
        righteousness,
    and sing praise to the name of
        the Lord, the Most High.

## PROVERBS 18.22

HE who finds a wife finds a good thing, and obtains favor from the Lord.

# JULY 10

## 1 CHRONICLES 9.1—10.14

So all Israel was enrolled by gene-alogies; and these are written in the Book of the Kings of Israel. And Judah was taken into exile in Babylon because of their unfaithfulness. [2]Now the first to live again in their possessions in their towns were Israelites, priests, Levites, and temple servants.

3 And some of the people of Judah, Benjamin, Ephraim, and Manasseh lived in Jerusalem: [4]Uthai son of Ammihud, son of Omri, son of Imri, son of Bani, from the sons of Perez son of Judah. [5]And of the Shilonites: Asaiah the firstborn, and his sons. [6]Of the sons of Zerah: Jeuel and their kin, six hundred ninety. [7]Of the Benjaminites: Sallu son of Meshullam, son of Hodaviah, son of Hassenuah, [8]Ibneiah son of Jeroham, Elah son of Uzzi, son of Michri, and Meshullam son of Shephatiah, son of Reuel, son of Ibnijah; [9]and their kindred according to their generations, nine hundred fifty-six. All these were heads of families according to their ancestral houses.

10 Of the priests: Jedaiah, Jehoiarib, Jachin, [11]and Azariah son of Hilkiah, son of Meshullam, son of Zadok, son of Meraioth, son of Ahitub, the chief officer of the house of God; [12]and Adaiah son of Jeroham, son of Pashhur, son of Malchijah, and Maasai son of Adiel, son

a Heb *he*

of Jahzerah, son of Meshullam, son of Meshillemith, son of Immer; [13]besides their kindred, heads of their ancestral houses, one thousand seven hundred sixty, qualified for the work of the service of the house of God.

14 Of the Levites: Shemaiah son of Hasshub, son of Azrikam, son of Hashabiah, of the sons of Merari; [15]and Bakbakkar, Heresh, Galal, and Mattaniah son of Mica, son of Zichri, son of Asaph; [16]and Obadiah son of Shemaiah, son of Galal, son of Jeduthun, and Berechiah son of Asa, son of Elkanah, who lived in the villages of the Netophathites.

17 The gatekeepers were: Shallum, Akkub, Talmon, Ahiman; and their kindred Shallum was the chief, [18]stationed previously in the king's gate on the east side. These were the gatekeepers of the camp of the Levites. [19]Shallum son of Kore, son of Ebiasaph, son of Korah, and his kindred of his ancestral house, the Korahites, were in charge of the work of the service, guardians of the thresholds of the tent, as their ancestors had been in charge of the camp of the LORD, guardians of the entrance. [20]And Phinehas son of Eleazar was chief over them in former times; the LORD was with him. [21]Zechariah son of Meshelemiah was gatekeeper at the entrance of the tent of meeting. [22]All these, who were chosen as gatekeepers at the thresholds, were two hundred twelve. They were enrolled by genealogies in their villages. David and the seer Samuel established them in their office of trust. [23]So they and their descendants were in charge of the gates of the house of the LORD, that is, the house of the tent, as guards. [24]The gatekeepers were on the four sides, east, west, north, and south; [25]and their kindred who were in their villages were obliged to come in every seven days, in turn, to be with them;

[26]for the four chief gatekeepers, who were Levites, were in charge of the chambers and the treasures of the house of God. [27]And they would spend the night near the house of God; for on them lay the duty of watching, and they had charge of opening it every morning.

28 Some of them had charge of the utensils of service, for they were required to count them when they were brought in and taken out. [29]Others of them were appointed over the furniture, and over all the holy utensils, also over the choice flour, the wine, the oil, the incense, and the spices. [30]Others, of the sons of the priests, prepared the mixing of the spices, [31]and Mattithiah, one of the Levites, the firstborn of Shallum the Korahite, was in charge of making the flat cakes. [32]Also some of their kindred of the Kohathites had charge of the rows of bread, to prepare them for each sabbath.

33 Now these are the singers, the heads of ancestral houses of the Levites, living in the chambers of the temple free from other service, for they were on duty day and night. [34]These were heads of ancestral houses of the Levites, according to their generations; these leaders lived in Jerusalem.

35 In Gibeon lived the father of Gibeon, Jeiel, and the name of his wife was Maacah. [36]His firstborn son was Abdon, then Zur, Kish, Baal, Ner, Nadab, [37]Gedor, Ahio, Zechariah, and Mikloth; [38]and Mikloth became the father of Shimeam; and these also lived opposite their kindred in Jerusalem, with their kindred. [39]Ner became the father of Kish, Kish of Saul, Saul of Jonathan, Malchishua, Abinadab, and Eshbaal; [40]and the son of Jonathan was Merib-baal; and Merib-baal became the father of Micah. [41]The sons of Micah: Pithon, Melech, Tahrea, and Ahaz;[a] [42]and Ahaz became the father of Jarah, and Jarah of Alemeth, Azmaveth, and

[a]Compare 8.35: Heb lacks *and Ahaz*

Zimri; and Zimri became the father of Moza. ⁴³Moza became the father of Binea; and Rephaiah was his son, Eleasah his son, Azel his son. ⁴⁴Azel had six sons, and these are their names: Azrikam, Bocheru, Ishmael, Sheariah, Obadiah, and Hanan; these were the sons of Azel.

10.1 Now the Philistines fought against Israel; and the men of Israel fled before the Philistines, and fell slain on Mount Gilboa. ²The Philistines overtook Saul and his sons; and the Philistines killed Jonathan and Abinadab and Malchishua, sons of Saul. ³The battle pressed hard on Saul; and the archers found him, and he was wounded by the archers. ⁴Then Saul said to his armor-bearer, "Draw your sword, and thrust me through with it, so that these uncircumcised may not come and make sport of me." But his armor-bearer was unwilling, for he was terrified. So Saul took his own sword and fell on it. ⁵When his armor-bearer saw that Saul was dead, he also fell on his sword and died. ⁶Thus Saul died; he and his three sons and all his house died together. ⁷When all the men of Israel who were in the valley saw that the army[a] had fled and that Saul and his sons were dead, they abandoned their towns and fled; and the Philistines came and occupied them.

8 The next day when the Philistines came to strip the dead, they found Saul and his sons fallen on Mount Gilboa. ⁹They stripped him and took his head and his armor, and sent messengers throughout the land of the Philistines to carry the good news to their idols and to the people. ¹⁰They put his armor in the temple of their gods, and fastened his head in the temple of Dagon. ¹¹But when all Jabesh-gilead heard everything that the Philistines had done to Saul, ¹²all the valiant warriors got up and took away the body of Saul and the bodies of his sons, and brought them to Jabesh. Then they buried their bones under the oak in Jabesh, and fasted seven days.

13 So Saul died for his unfaithfulness; he was unfaithful to the LORD in that he did not keep the command of the LORD; moreover, he had consulted a medium, seeking guidance, ¹⁴and did not seek guidance from the LORD. Therefore the LORD[b] put him to death and turned the kingdom over to David son of Jesse.

## ACTS 27.21–44

SINCE they [the sailors] had been without food for a long time, Paul then stood up among them and said, "Men, you should have listened to me and not have set sail from Crete and thereby avoided this damage and loss. ²²I urge you now to keep up your courage, for there will be no loss of life among you, but only of the ship. ²³For last night there stood by me an angel of the God to whom I belong and whom I worship, ²⁴and he said, 'Do not be afraid, Paul; you must stand before the emperor; and indeed, God has granted safety to all those who are sailing with you.' ²⁵So keep up your courage, men, for I have faith in God that it will be exactly as I have been told. ²⁶But we will have to run aground on some island."

27 When the fourteenth night had come, as we were drifting across the sea of Adria, about midnight the sailors suspected that they were nearing land. ²⁸So they took soundings and found twenty fathoms; a little farther on they took soundings again and found fifteen fathoms. ²⁹Fearing that we might run on the rocks, they let down four anchors from the stern and prayed for day to come. ³⁰But when the sailors tried to escape from the ship and had lowered the boat into the sea, on the pretext of

aHeb *they*   bHeb *he*

putting out anchors from the bow, [31]Paul said to the centurion and the soldiers, "Unless these men stay in the ship, you cannot be saved." [32]Then the soldiers cut away the ropes of the boat and set it adrift.

33 Just before daybreak, Paul urged all of them to take some food, saying, "Today is the fourteenth day that you have been in suspense and remaining without food, having eaten nothing. [34]Therefore I urge you to take some food, for it will help you survive; for none of you will lose a hair from your heads." [35]After he had said this, he took bread; and giving thanks to God in the presence of all, he broke it and began to eat. [36]Then all of them were encouraged and took food for themselves. [37](We were in all two hundred seventy-six[a] persons in the ship.) [38]After they had satisfied their hunger, they lightened the ship by throwing the wheat into the sea.

39 In the morning they did not recognize the land, but they noticed a bay with a beach, on which they planned to run the ship ashore, if they could. [40]So they cast off the anchors and left them in the sea. At the same time they loosened the ropes that tied the steering-oars; then hoisting the foresail to the wind, they made for the beach. [41]But striking a reef,[b] they ran the ship aground; the bow stuck and remained immovable, but the stern was being broken up by the force of the waves. [42]The soldiers' plan was to kill the prisoners, so that none might swim away and escape; [43]but the centurion, wishing to save Paul, kept them from carrying out their plan. He ordered those who could swim to jump overboard first and make for the land, [44]and the rest to follow, some on planks and others on pieces of the ship. And so it was that all were brought safely to land.

## PSALM 8.1–9

*To the leader: according to The Gittith. A Psalm of David.*

O LORD, our Sovereign,
how majestic is your name
in all the earth!

You have set your glory above
the heavens.
2    Out of the mouths of babes
and infants
you have founded a bulwark
because of your foes,
to silence the enemy and the
avenger.

3  When I look at your heavens,
the work of your fingers,
the moon and the stars that
you have established;
4  what are human beings that you
are mindful of them,
mortals[c] that you care for
them?

5  Yet you have made them a little
lower than God, [d]
and crowned them with glory
and honor.
6  You have given them dominion
over the works of your
hands;
you have put all things under
their feet,
7  all sheep and oxen,
and also the beasts of the
field,
8  the birds of the air, and the fish
of the sea,
whatever passes along the
paths of the seas.

9  O LORD, our Sovereign,
how majestic is your name in
all the earth!

a Other ancient authorities read *seventy-six*; others, *about seventy-six*   b Gk *place of two seas*   c Heb *ben adam*, lit. *son of man*   d Or *than the divine beings* or *angels*: Heb *elohim*

## PROVERBS 18.23–24

**T**HE poor use entreaties,
  but the rich answer roughly.
  24 Some[a] friends play at
    friendship[b]

but a true friend sticks closer
  than one's nearest kin.

# JULY 11

## 1 CHRONICLES 11.1—12.18

**T**HEN all Israel gathered together to David at Hebron and said, "See, we are your bone and flesh. ²For some time now, even while Saul was king, it was you who commanded the army of Israel. The LORD your God said to you: It is you who shall be shepherd of my people Israel, you who shall be ruler over my people Israel." ³So all the elders of Israel came to the king at Hebron, and David made a covenant with them at Hebron before the LORD. And they anointed David king over Israel, according to the word of the LORD by Samuel.

4 David and all Israel marched to Jerusalem, that is Jebus, where the Jebusites were, the inhabitants of the land. ⁵The inhabitants of Jebus said to David, "You will not come in here." Nevertheless David took the stronghold of Zion, now the city of David. ⁶David had said, "Whoever attacks the Jebusites first shall be chief and commander." And Joab son of Zeruiah went up first, so he became chief. ⁷David resided in the stronghold; therefore it was called the city of David. ⁸He built the city all around, from the Millo in complete circuit; and Joab repaired the rest of the city. ⁹And David became greater and greater, for the LORD of hosts was with him.

10 Now these are the chiefs of David's warriors, who gave him strong support in his kingdom, together with all Israel, to make him king, according to the word of the LORD concerning Israel. ¹¹This is an account of David's mighty warriors: Jashobeam, son of Hachmoni,[c] was chief of the Three;[d] he wielded his spear against three hundred whom he killed at one time.

12 And next to him among the three warriors was Eleazar son of Dodo, the Ahohite. ¹³He was with David at Pas-dammim when the Philistines were gathered there for battle. There was a plot of ground full of barley. Now the people had fled from the Philistines, ¹⁴but he and David took their stand in the middle of the plot, defended it, and killed the Philistines; and the LORD saved them by a great victory.

15 Three of the thirty chiefs went down to the rock to David at the cave of Adullam, while the army of Philistines was encamped in the valley of Rephaim. ¹⁶David was then in the stronghold; and the garrison of the Philistines was then at Bethlehem. ¹⁷David said longingly, "O that someone would give me water to drink from the well of

---

[a]Syr Tg: Heb *A man of*   [b]Cn Compare Syr Vg Tg: Meaning of Heb uncertain   [c]Or *a Hachmonite*
[d]Compare 2 Sam 23.8: Heb *Thirty* or *captains*

Bethlehem that is by the gate!" [18]Then the Three broke through the camp of the Philistines, and drew water from the well of Bethlehem that was by the gate, and they brought it to David. But David would not drink of it; he poured it out to the LORD, [19]and said, "My God forbid that I should do this. Can I drink the blood of these men? For at the risk of their lives they brought it." Therefore he would not drink it. The three warriors did these things.

20 Now Abishai,[a] the brother of Joab, was chief of the Thirty.[b] With his spear he fought against three hundred and killed them, and won a name beside the Three. [21]He was the most renowned[c] of the Thirty,[b] and became their commander; but he did not attain to the Three.

22 Benaiah son of Jehoiada was a valiant man[d] of Kabzeel, a doer of great deeds; he struck down two sons of[e] Ariel of Moab. He also went down and killed a lion in a pit on a day when snow had fallen. [23]And he killed an Egyptian, a man of great stature, five cubits tall. The Egyptian had in his hand a spear like a weaver's beam; but Benaiah went against him with a staff, snatched the spear out of the Egyptian's hand, and killed him with his own spear. [24]Such were the things Benaiah son of Jehoiada did, and he won a name beside the three warriors. [25]He was renowned among the Thirty, but he did not attain to the Three. And David put him in charge of his bodyguard.

26 The warriors of the armies were Asahel brother of Joab, Elhanan son of Dodo of Bethlehem, [27]Shammoth of Harod,[f] Helez the Pelonite, [28]Ira son of Ikkesh of Tekoa, Abiezer of Anathoth, [29]Sibbecai the Hushathite, Ilai the Ahohite, [30]Maharai of Netophah, Heled son of Baanah of Netophah,

[31]Ithai son of Ribai of Gibeah of the Benjaminites, Benaiah of Pirathon, [32]Hurai of the wadis of Gaash, Abiel the Arbathite, [33]Azmaveth of Baharum, Eliahba of Shaalbon, [34]Hashem[g] the Gizonite, Jonathan son of Shagee the Hararite, [35]Ahiam son of Sachar the Hararite, Eliphal son of Ur, [36]Hepher the Mecherathite, Ahijah the Pelonite, [37]Hezro of Carmel, Naarai son of Ezbai, [38]Joel the brother of Nathan, Mibhar son of Hagri, [39]Zelek the Ammonite, Naharai of Beeroth, the armor-bearer of Joab son of Zeruiah, [40]Ira the Ithrite, Gareb the Ithrite, [41]Uriah the Hittite, Zabad son of Ahlai, [42]Adina son of Shiza the Reubenite, a leader of the Reubenites, and thirty with him, [43]Hanan son of Maacah, and Joshaphat the Mithnite, [44]Uzzia the Ashterathite, Shama and Jeiel sons of Hotham the Aroerite, [45]Jediael son of Shimri, and his brother Joha the Tizite, [46]Eliel the Mahavite, and Jeribai and Joshaviah sons of Elnaam, and Ithmah the Moabite, [47]Eliel, and Obed, and Jaasiel the Mezobaite.

12.1 THE following are those who came to David at Ziklag, while he could not move about freely because of Saul son of Kish; they were among the mighty warriors who helped him in war. [2]They were archers, and could shoot arrows and sling stones with either the right hand or the left; they were Benjaminites, Saul's kindred. [3]The chief was Ahiezer, then Joash, both sons of Shemaah of Gibeah; also Jeziel and Pelet sons of Azmaveth; Beracah, Jehu of Anathoth, [4]Ishmaiah of Gibeon, a warrior among the Thirty and a leader over the Thirty; Jeremiah,[h] Jahaziel, Johanan, Jozabad of Gederah, [5]Eluzai,[i] Jerimoth, Bealiah, Shemariah, Shephatiah the Haruphite; [6]Elkanah, Isshiah,

Azarel, Joezer, and Jashobeam, the Korahites; 7and Joelah and Zebadiah, sons of Jeroham of Gedor.

8 From the Gadites there went over to David at the stronghold in the wilderness mighty and experienced warriors, expert with shield and spear, whose faces were like the faces of lions, and who were swift as gazelles on the mountains: 9Ezer the chief, Obadiah second, Eliab third, 10Mishmannah fourth, Jeremiah fifth, 11Attai sixth, Eliel seventh, 12Johanan eighth, Elzabad ninth, 13Jeremiah tenth, Machbannai eleventh. 14These Gadites were officers of the army, the least equal to a hundred and the greatest to a thousand. 15These are the men who crossed the Jordan in the first month, when it was overflowing all its banks, and put to flight all those in the valleys, to the east and to the west.

16 Some Benjaminites and Judahites came to the stronghold to David. 17David went out to meet them and said to them, "If you have come to me in friendship, to help me, then my heart will be knit to you; but if you have come to betray me to my adversaries, though my hands have done no wrong, then may the God of our ancestors see and give judgment." 18Then the spirit came upon Amasai, chief of the Thirty, and he said,

> "We are yours, O David;
>     and with you, O son of Jesse!
> Peace, peace to you,
>     and peace to the one who
>         helps you!
>     For your God is the one who
>         helps you."

Then David received them, and made them officers of his troops.

## ACTS 28.1–31

AFTER we [Luke, Paul, and companions] had reached safety, we then learned that the island was called Malta. 2The natives showed us unusual kindness. Since it had begun to rain and was cold, they kindled a fire and welcomed all of us around it. 3Paul had gathered a bundle of brushwood and was putting it on the fire, when a viper, driven out by the heat, fastened itself on his hand. 4When the natives saw the creature hanging from his hand, they said to one another, "This man must be a murderer; though he has escaped from the sea, justice has not allowed him to live." 5He, however, shook off the creature into the fire and suffered no harm. 6They were expecting him to swell up or drop dead, but after they had waited a long time and saw that nothing unusual had happened to him, they changed their minds and began to say that he was a god.

7 Now in the neighborhood of that place were lands belonging to the leading man of the island, named Publius, who received us and entertained us hospitably for three days. 8It so happened that the father of Publius lay sick in bed with fever and dysentery. Paul visited him and cured him by praying and putting his hands on him. 9After this happened, the rest of the people on the island who had diseases also came and were cured. 10They bestowed many honors on us, and when we were about to sail, they put on board all the provisions we needed.

11 Three months later we set sail on a ship that had wintered at the island, an Alexandrian ship with the Twin Brothers as its figurehead. 12We put in at Syracuse and stayed there for three days; 13then we weighed anchor and came to Rhegium. After one day there a south wind sprang up, and on the second day we came to Puteoli. 14There

we found believers[a] and were invited to stay with them for seven days. And so we came to Rome. [15]The believers[a] from there, when they heard of us, came as far as the Forum of Appius and Three Taverns to meet us. On seeing them, Paul thanked God and took courage.

16 When we came into Rome, Paul was allowed to live by himself, with the soldier who was guarding him.

17 Three days later he called together the local leaders of the Jews. When they had assembled, he said to them, "Brothers, though I had done nothing against our people or the customs of our ancestors, yet I was arrested in Jerusalem and handed over to the Romans. [18]When they had examined me, the Romans[b] wanted to release me, because there was no reason for the death penalty in my case. [19]But when the Jews objected, I was compelled to appeal to the emperor—even though I had no charge to bring against my nation. [20]For this reason therefore I have asked to see you and speak with you,[c] since it is for the sake of the hope of Israel that I am bound with this chain." [21]They replied, "We have received no letters from Judea about you, and none of the brothers coming here has reported or spoken anything evil about you. [22]But we would like to hear from you what you think, for with regard to this sect we know that everywhere it is spoken against."

23 After they had set a day to meet with him, they came to him at his lodgings in great numbers. From morning until evening he explained the matter to them, testifying to the kingdom of God and trying to convince them about Jesus both from the law of Moses and from the prophets. [24]Some were convinced by what he had said, while others refused to believe. [25]So they disagreed with each other; and as they were leaving, Paul made one further statement: "The Holy Spirit was right in saying to your ancestors through the prophet Isaiah,

26 'Go to this people and say,
You will indeed listen, but never understand,
and you will indeed look, but never perceive.
27 For this people's heart has grown dull,
and their ears are hard of hearing,
and they have shut their eyes;
so that they might not look with their eyes,
and listen with their ears,
and understand with their heart and turn—
and I would heal them.'
[28]Let it be known to you then that this salvation of God has been sent to the Gentiles; they will listen."[d]

30 He lived there two whole years at his own expense[e] and welcomed all who came to him, [31]proclaiming the kingdom of God and teaching about the Lord Jesus Christ with all boldness and without hindrance.

## PSALM 9.1–12

*To the leader: according to Muth-labben. A Psalm of David.*

I WILL give thanks to the LORD with my whole heart;
I will tell of all your wonderful deeds.
2 I will be glad and exult in you;
I will sing praise to your name, O Most High.

3 When my enemies turned back,
they stumbled and perished before you.

---

a Gk *brothers*  b Gk *they*  c Or *I have asked you to see me and speak with me*  d Other ancient authorities add verse 29, *And when he had said these words, the Jews departed, arguing vigorously among themselves*  e Or *in his own hired dwelling*

4 For you have maintained my
   just cause;
 you have sat on the throne
   giving righteous
   judgment.

5 You have rebuked the nations,
   you have destroyed the
   wicked;
 you have blotted out their
   name forever and ever.
6 The enemies have vanished in
   everlasting ruins;
 their cities you have rooted
   out;
 the very memory of them has
   perished.

7 But the Lord sits enthroned
   forever,
 he has established his throne
   for judgment.
8 He judges the world with
   righteousness;
 he judges the peoples with
   equity.

9 The Lord is a stronghold for the
   oppressed,
 a stronghold in times of
   trouble.
10 And those who know your name
   put their trust in you,
 for you, O Lord, have not
   forsaken those who seek
   you.

11 Sing praises to the Lord, who
   dwells in Zion.
 Declare his deeds among the
   peoples.
12 For he who avenges blood is
   mindful of them;
 he does not forget the cry of
   the afflicted.

## PROVERBS 19.1–3

Better the poor walking in
   integrity
 than one perverse of speech
   who is a fool.
2 Desire without knowledge is
   not good,
 and one who moves too
   hurriedly misses the
   way.
3 One's own folly leads to ruin,
   yet the heart rages against
   the Lord.

# JULY 12

## 1 CHRONICLES 12.19—14.17

Some of the Manassites deserted to David when he came with the Philistines for the battle against Saul. (Yet he did not help them, for the rulers of the Philistines took counsel and sent him away, saying, "He will desert to his master Saul at the cost of our heads.") 20As he went to Ziklag these Manassites deserted to him: Adnah, Jozabad, Jediael, Michael, Jozabad, Elihu, and Zillethai, chiefs of the thousands in Manasseh. 21They helped David against the band of raiders,a for they were all warriors and commanders

aOr *as officers of his troops*

in the army. [22]Indeed from day to day people kept coming to David to help him, until there was a great army, like an army of God.

23 These are the numbers of the divisions of the armed troops who came to David in Hebron to turn the kingdom of Saul over to him, according to the word of the LORD. [24]The people of Judah bearing shield and spear numbered six thousand eight hundred armed troops. [25]Of the Simeonites, mighty warriors, seven thousand one hundred. [26]Of the Levites four thousand six hundred. [27]Jehoiada, leader of the house of Aaron, and with him three thousand seven hundred. [28]Zadok, a young warrior, and twenty-two commanders from his own ancestral house. [29]Of the Benjaminites, the kindred of Saul, three thousand, of whom the majority had continued to keep their allegiance to the house of Saul. [30]Of the Ephraimites, twenty thousand eight hundred, mighty warriors, notables in their ancestral houses. [31]Of the half-tribe of Manasseh, eighteen thousand, who were expressly named to come and make David king. [32]Of Issachar, those who had understanding of the times, to know what Israel ought to do, two hundred chiefs, and all their kindred under their command. [33]Of Zebulun, fifty thousand seasoned troops, equipped for battle with all the weapons of war, to help David[a] with singleness of purpose. [34]Of Naphtali, a thousand commanders, with whom there were thirty-seven thousand armed with shield and spear. [35]Of the Danites, twenty-eight thousand six hundred equipped for battle. [36]Of Asher, forty thousand seasoned troops ready for battle. [37]Of the Reubenites and Gadites and the half-tribe of Manasseh from beyond the Jordan, one hundred twenty thousand armed with all the weapons of war.

38 All these, warriors arrayed in battle order, came to Hebron with full intent to make David king over all Israel; likewise all the rest of Israel were of a single mind to make David king. [39]They were there with David for three days, eating and drinking, for their kindred had provided for them. [40]And also their neighbors, from as far away as Issachar and Zebulun and Naphtali, came bringing food on donkeys, camels, mules, and oxen—abundant provisions of meal, cakes of figs, clusters of raisins, wine, oil, oxen, and sheep, for there was joy in Israel.

[13.1]DAVID consulted with the commanders of the thousands and of the hundreds, with every leader. [2]David said to the whole assembly of Israel, "If it seems good to you, and if it is the will of the LORD our God, let us send abroad to our kindred who remain in all the land of Israel, including the priests and Levites in the cities that have pasture lands, that they may come together to us. [3]Then let us bring again the ark of our God to us; for we did not turn to it in the days of Saul." [4]The whole assembly agreed to do so, for the thing pleased all the people.

5 So David assembled all Israel from the Shihor of Egypt to Lebohamath, to bring the ark of God from Kiriath-jearim. [6]And David and all Israel went up to Baalah, that is, to Kiriath-jearim, which belongs to Judah, to bring up from there the ark of God, the LORD, who is enthroned on the cherubim, which is called by his[b] name. [7]They carried the ark of God on a new cart, from the house of Abinadab, and Uzzah and Ahio[c] were driving the cart. [8]David and all Israel were dancing before God with all their might, with song and lyres and harps and tambourines and cymbals and trumpets.

9 When they came to the threshing

[a]Gk: Heb lacks *David*  [b]Heb lacks *his*  [c]Or *and his brother*

floor of Chidon, Uzzah put out his hand to hold the ark, for the oxen shook it. <sup>10</sup>The anger of the Lord was kindled against Uzzah; he struck him down because he put out his hand to the ark; and he died there before God. <sup>11</sup>David was angry because the Lord had burst out against Uzzah; so that place is called Perez-uzzah[a] to this day. <sup>12</sup>David was afraid of God that day; he said, "How can I bring the ark of God into my care?" <sup>13</sup>So David did not take the ark into his care into the city of David; he took it instead to the house of Obed-edom the Gittite. <sup>14</sup>The ark of God remained with the household of Obed-edom in his house three months, and the Lord blessed the household of Obed-edom and all that he had.

<sup>14.1</sup> King Hiram of Tyre sent messengers to David, along with cedar logs, and masons and carpenters to build a house for him. <sup>2</sup>David then perceived that the Lord had established him as king over Israel, and that his kingdom was highly exalted for the sake of his people Israel.

3  David took more wives in Jerusalem, and David became the father of more sons and daughters. <sup>4</sup>These are the names of the children whom he had in Jerusalem: Shammua, Shobab, and Nathan; Solomon, <sup>5</sup>Ibhar, Elishua, and Elpelet; <sup>6</sup>Nogah, Nepheg, and Japhia; <sup>7</sup>Elishama, Beeliada, and Eliphelet.

8  When the Philistines heard that David had been anointed king over all Israel, all the Philistines went up in search of David; and David heard of it and went out against them. <sup>9</sup>Now the Philistines had come and made a raid in the valley of Rephaim. <sup>10</sup>David inquired of God, "Shall I go up against the Philistines? Will you give them into my hand?" The Lord said to him, "Go up, and I will give them into your hand." <sup>11</sup>So he went up to Baal-perazim, and David defeated them there. David said, "God has burst out[b] against my enemies by my hand, like a bursting flood." Therefore that place is called Baal-perazim.[c] <sup>12</sup>They abandoned their gods there, and at David's command they were burned.

13  Once again the Philistines made a raid in the valley. <sup>14</sup>When David again inquired of God, God said to him, "You shall not go up after them; go around and come on them opposite the balsam trees. <sup>15</sup>When you hear the sound of marching in the tops of the balsam trees, then go out to battle; for God has gone out before you to strike down the army of the Philistines." <sup>16</sup>David did as God had commanded him, and they struck down the Philistine army from Gibeon to Gezer. <sup>17</sup>The fame of David went out into all lands, and the Lord brought the fear of him on all nations.

## ROMANS 1.1–17

Paul, a servant[d] of Jesus Christ, called to be an apostle, set apart for the gospel of God, <sup>2</sup>which he promised beforehand through his prophets in the holy scriptures, <sup>3</sup>the gospel concerning his Son, who was descended from David according to the flesh <sup>4</sup>and was declared to be Son of God with power according to the spirit[e] of holiness by resurrection from the dead, Jesus Christ our Lord, <sup>5</sup>through whom we have received grace and apostleship to bring about the obedience of faith among all the Gentiles for the sake of his name, <sup>6</sup>including yourselves who are called to belong to Jesus Christ,

7  To all God's beloved in Rome, who are called to be saints:

Grace to you and peace from God our Father and the Lord Jesus Christ.

8  First, I thank my God through

a That is *Bursting Out Against Uzzah*   b Heb *paraz*   c That is *Lord of Bursting Out*   d Gk *slave*
e Or *Spirit*

Jesus Christ for all of you, because your faith is proclaimed throughout the world. [9]For God, whom I serve with my spirit by announcing the gospel[a] of his Son, is my witness that without ceasing I remember you always in my prayers, [10]asking that by God's will I may somehow at last succeed in coming to you. [11]For I am longing to see you so that I may share with you some spiritual gift to strengthen you— [12]or rather so that we may be mutually encouraged by each other's faith, both yours and mine. [13]I want you to know, brothers and sisters,[b] that I have often intended to come to you (but thus far have been prevented), in order that I may reap some harvest among you as I have among the rest of the Gentiles. [14]I am a debtor both to Greeks and to barbarians, both to the wise and to the foolish [15]—hence my eagerness to proclaim the gospel to you also who are in Rome.

16 For I am not ashamed of the gospel; it is the power of God for salvation to everyone who has faith, to the Jew first and also to the Greek. [17]For in it the righteousness of God is revealed through faith for faith; as it is written, "The one who is righteous will live by faith."[c]

## PSALM 9.13–20

Be gracious to me, O LORD.
  See what I suffer from those
    who hate me;
  you are the one who lifts me
    up from the gates of
    death,
[14]  so that I may recount all your
    praises,
  and, in the gates of daughter
    Zion,
  rejoice in your deliverance.

[15]  The nations have sunk in the pit
    that they made;
  in the net that they hid has
    their own foot been
    caught.
[16]  The LORD has made himself
    known, he has executed
    judgment;
  the wicked are snared in the
    work of their own hands.
      *Higgaion. Selah*

[17]  The wicked shall depart to
    Sheol,
  all the nations that forget
    God.

[18]  For the needy shall not always
    be forgotten,
  nor the hope of the poor
    perish forever.

[19]  Rise up, O LORD! Do not let
    mortals prevail;
  let the nations be judged
    before you.
[20]  Put them in fear, O LORD;
  let the nations know that they
    are only human.      *Selah*

## PROVERBS 19.4–5

Wealth brings many friends,
  but the poor are left
    friendless.
[5]  A false witness will not go
    unpunished,
  and a liar will not escape.

aGk *my spirit in the gospel*  bGk *brothers*  cOr *The one who is righteous through faith will live*

# JULY 13

1 CHRONICLES 15.1—16.36

D^AVID^a built houses for himself in the city of David, and he prepared a place for the ark of God and pitched a tent for it. ²Then David commanded that no one but the Levites were to carry the ark of God, for the LORD had chosen them to carry the ark of the LORD and to minister to him forever. ³David assembled all Israel in Jerusalem to bring up the ark of the LORD to its place, which he had prepared for it. ⁴Then David gathered together the descendants of Aaron and the Levites: ⁵of the sons of Kohath, Uriel the chief, with one hundred twenty of his kindred; ⁶of the sons of Merari, Asaiah the chief, with two hundred twenty of his kindred; ⁷of the sons of Gershom, Joel the chief, with one hundred thirty of his kindred; ⁸of the sons of Elizaphan, Shemaiah the chief, with two hundred of his kindred; ⁹of the sons of Hebron, Eliel the chief, with eighty of his kindred; ¹⁰of the sons of Uzziel, Amminadab the chief, with one hundred twelve of his kindred.

11 David summoned the priests Zadok and Abiathar, and the Levites Uriel, Asaiah, Joel, Shemaiah, Eliel, and Amminadab. ¹²He said to them, "You are the heads of families of the Levites; sanctify yourselves, you and your kindred, so that you may bring up the ark of the LORD, the God of Israel, to the place that I have prepared for it. ¹³Because you did not carry it the first time,ᵇ the LORD our God burst out against us, because we did not give it proper care." ¹⁴So the priests and the Levites sanctified themselves to bring up the ark of the LORD, the God of Israel. ¹⁵And the Levites carried the ark of God on their shoulders with the poles, as Moses had commanded according to the word of the LORD.

16 David also commanded the chiefs of the Levites to appoint their kindred as the singers to play on musical instruments, on harps and lyres and cymbals, to raise loud sounds of joy. ¹⁷So the Levites appointed Heman son of Joel; and of his kindred Asaph son of Berechiah; and of the sons of Merari, their kindred, Ethan son of Kushaiah; ¹⁸and with them their kindred of the second order, Zechariah, Jaaziel, Shemiramoth, Jehiel, Unni, Eliab, Benaiah, Maaseiah, Mattithiah, Eliphelehu, and Mikneiah, and the gatekeepers Obededom and Jeiel. ¹⁹The singers Heman, Asaph, and Ethan were to sound bronze cymbals; ²⁰Zechariah, Aziel, Shemiramoth, Jehiel, Unni, Eliab, Maaseiah, and Benaiah were to play harps according to Alamoth; ²¹but Mattithiah, Eliphelehu, Mikneiah, Obed-edom, Jeiel, and Azaziah were to lead with lyres according to the Sheminith. ²²Chenaniah, leader of the Levites in music, was to direct the music, for he understood it. ²³Berechiah and Elkanah were to be gatekeepers for the ark. ²⁴Shebaniah, Joshaphat, Nethanel, Amasai, Zechariah, Benaiah, and Eliezer, the priests, were to blow the trumpets before the ark of God. Obed-edom and Jehiah also were to be gatekeepers for the ark.

25 So David and the elders of Israel, and the commanders of the thousands, went to bring up the ark of the covenant of the LORD from the house of Obed-edom with rejoicing. ²⁶And because God helped the Levites who were carrying the ark of the covenant

ᵃheb *he*  ᵇMeaning of Heb uncertain

of the Lord, they sacrificed seven bulls and seven rams. <sup>27</sup>David was clothed with a robe of fine linen, as also were all the Levites who were carrying the ark, and the singers, and Chenaniah the leader of the music of the singers; and David wore a linen ephod. <sup>28</sup>So all Israel brought up the ark of the covenant of the Lord with shouting, to the sound of the horn, trumpets, and cymbals, and made loud music on harps and lyres.

29   As the ark of the covenant of the Lord came to the city of David, Michal daughter of Saul looked out of the window, and saw King David leaping and dancing; and she despised him in her heart.

**16.**1 They brought in the ark of God, and set it inside the tent that David had pitched for it; and they offered burnt offerings and offerings of well-being before God. <sup>2</sup>When David had finished offering the burnt offerings and the offerings of well-being, he blessed the people in the name of the Lord; <sup>3</sup>and he distributed to every person in Israel—man and woman alike—to each a loaf of bread, a portion of meat, [a] and a cake of raisins.

4   He appointed certain of the Levites as ministers before the ark of the Lord, to invoke, to thank, and to praise the Lord, the God of Israel. <sup>5</sup>Asaph was the chief, and second to him Zechariah, Jeiel, Shemiramoth, Jehiel, Mattithiah, Eliab, Benaiah, Obed-edom, and Jeiel, with harps and lyres; Asaph was to sound the cymbals, <sup>6</sup>and the priests Benaiah and Jahaziel were to blow trumpets regularly, before the ark of the covenant of God.

7   Then on that day David first appointed the singing of praises to the Lord by Asaph and his kindred.

8   O give thanks to the Lord, call
    on his name,
    make known his deeds among
        the peoples.
9   Sing to him, sing praises to him,
    tell of all his wonderful works.
10  Glory in his holy name;
    let the hearts of those who
        seek the Lord rejoice.
11  Seek the Lord and his strength,
    seek his presence continually.
12  Remember the wonderful works
        he has done,
    his miracles, and the
        judgments he uttered,
13  O offspring of his servant
        Israel, [b]
    children of Jacob, his chosen
        ones.

14  He is the Lord our God;
    his judgments are in all the
        earth.
15  Remember his covenant
        forever,
    the word that he commanded,
        for a thousand
        generations,
16  the covenant that he made with
        Abraham,
    his sworn promise to Isaac,
17  which he confirmed to Jacob as
        a statute,
    to Israel as an everlasting
        covenant,
18  saying, "To you I will give the
        land of Canaan
    as your portion for an
        inheritance."

19  When they were few in number,
    of little account, and
        strangers in the land, [c]
20  wandering from nation to nation,
    from one kingdom to another
        people,

a Compare Gk Syr Vg: Meaning of Heb uncertain   b Another reading is *Abraham* (compare Ps 105.6)   c Heb *in it*

21  he allowed no one to oppress
        them;
    he rebuked kings on their
        account,
22  saying, "Do not touch my
        anointed ones;
    do my prophets no harm."

23  Sing to the LORD, all the earth.
    Tell of his salvation from day
        to day.
24  Declare his glory among the
        nations,
    his marvelous works among
        all the peoples.
25  For great is the LORD, and
        greatly to be praised;
    he is to be revered above all
        gods.
26  For all the gods of the peoples
        are idols,
    but the LORD made the
        heavens.
27  Honor and majesty are before
        him;
    strength and joy are in his
        place.

28  Ascribe to the LORD, O families
        of the peoples,
    ascribe to the LORD glory and
        strength.
29  Ascribe to the LORD the glory
        due his name;
    bring an offering, and come
        before him.
    Worship the LORD in holy
        splendor;
30      tremble before him, all the
        earth.
    The world is firmly
        established; it shall never
        be moved.
31  Let the heavens be glad, and let
        the earth rejoice,
    and let them say among the
        nations, "The LORD is
        king!"
32  Let the sea roar, and all that
        fills it;

    let the field exult, and
        everything in it.
33  Then shall the trees of the
        forest sing for joy
    before the LORD, for he
        comes to judge the
        earth.
34  O give thanks to the LORD, for
        he is good;
    for his steadfast love endures
        forever.

35 Say also:
    "Save us, O God of our
        salvation,
    and gather and rescue us
        from among the nations,
    that we may give thanks to your
        holy name,
    and glory in your praise.
36  Blessed be the LORD, the God
        of Israel,
    from everlasting to
        everlasting."
Then all the people said "Amen!" and
praised the LORD.

## ROMANS 1.18–32

FOR the wrath of God is revealed
from heaven against all ungodliness and wickedness of those
who by their wickedness suppress the
truth. ¹⁹For what can be known about
God is plain to them, because God has
shown it to them. ²⁰Ever since the creation of the world his eternal power and
divine nature, invisible though they
are, have been understood and seen
through the things he has made. So
they are without excuse; ²¹for though
they knew God, they did not honor him
as God or give thanks to him, but they
became futile in their thinking, and their
senseless minds were darkened.
²²Claiming to be wise, they became
fools; ²³and they exchanged the glory of
the immortal God for images resembling a mortal human being or birds or
four-footed animals or reptiles.

24 Therefore God gave them up in the lusts of their hearts to impurity, to the degrading of their bodies among themselves, 25because they exchanged the truth about God for a lie and worshiped and served the creature rather than the Creator, who is blessed forever! Amen.

26 For this reason God gave them up to degrading passions. Their women exchanged natural intercourse for unnatural, 27and in the same way also the men, giving up natural intercourse with women, were consumed with passion for one another. Men committed shameless acts with men and received in their own persons the due penalty for their error.

28 And since they did not see fit to acknowledge God, God gave them up to a debased mind and to things that should not be done. 29They were filled with every kind of wickedness, evil, covetousness, malice. Full of envy, murder, strife, deceit, craftiness, they are gossips, 30slanderers, God-haters,a insolent, haughty, boastful, inventors of evil, rebellious toward parents, 31foolish, faithless, heartless, ruthless. 32They know God's decree, that those who practice such things deserve to die—yet they not only do them but even applaud others who practice them.

## PSALM 10.1–15

Why, O Lord, do you stand
    far off?
  Why do you hide yourself
    in times of trouble?
2  In arrogance the wicked
    persecute the poor—
    let them be caught in the
      schemes they have
      devised.

3  For the wicked boast of the
    desires of their heart,
  those greedy for gain curse
    and renounce the Lord.
4 In the pride of their
    countenance the wicked
    say, "God will not seek it
    out";
  all their thoughts are, "There
    is no God."

5  Their ways prosper at all times;
    your judgments are on high,
      out of their sight;
  as for their foes, they scoff at
    them.
6  They think in their heart, "We
    shall not be moved;
  throughout all generations we
    shall not meet
    adversity."

7  Their mouths are filled with
    cursing and deceit and
    oppression;
  under their tongues are
    mischief and iniquity.
8  They sit in ambush in the
    villages;
  in hiding places they murder
    the innocent.

  Their eyes stealthily watch for
    the helpless;
9  they lurk in secret like a lion
    in its covert;
  they lurk that they may seize
    the poor;
  they seize the poor and drag
    them off in their net.

10  They stoop, they crouch,
    and the helpless fall by their
    might.
11  They think in their heart, "God
    has forgotten,
  he has hidden his face, he will
    never see it."

aOr *God-hated*

12  Rise up, O Lord; O God, lift up
       your hand;
    do not forget the oppressed.
13  Why do the wicked renounce
       God,
    and say in their hearts, "You
       will not call us to
       account"?

14  But you do see! Indeed you
       note trouble and grief,
    that you may take it into your
       hands;
    the helpless commit themselves
       to you;
    you have been the helper of
       the orphan.

15  Break the arm of the wicked
       and evildoers;
    seek out their wickedness
       until you find none.

## PROVERBS 19.6–7

MANY seek the favor of the
    generous,
  and everyone is a friend to
     a giver of gifts.
7  If the poor are hated even by
      their kin,
   how much more are they
      shunned by their friends!
When they call after them, they
      are not there. a

# JULY 14

## 1 CHRONICLES 16.37—18.17

DAVID left Asaph and his kinsfolk there before the ark of the covenant of the Lord to minister regularly before the ark as each day required, 38and also Obed-edom and his b sixty-eight kinsfolk; while Obed-edom son of Jeduthun and Hosah were to be gatekeepers. 39And he left the priest Zadok and his kindred the priests before the tabernacle of the Lord in the high place that was at Gibeon, 40to offer burnt offerings to the Lord on the altar of burnt offering regularly, morning and evening, according to all that is written in the law of the Lord that he commanded Israel. 41With them were Heman and Jeduthun, and the rest of those chosen and expressly named to render thanks to the Lord, for his steadfast love endures forever. 42Heman and Je-duthun had with them trumpets and cymbals for the music, and instruments for sacred song. The sons of Jeduthun were appointed to the gate.

43  Then all the people departed to their homes, and David went home to bless his household.

17.1 Now when David settled in his house, David said to the prophet Nathan, "I am living in a house of cedar, but the ark of the covenant of the Lord is under a tent." 2Nathan said to David, "Do all that you have in mind, for God is with you."

3  But that same night the word of the Lord came to Nathan, saying: 4Go and tell my servant David: Thus says the Lord: You shall not build me a house to live in. 5For I have not lived

aMeaning of Heb uncertain   bGk Syr Vg: Heb their

in a house since the day I brought out Israel to this very day, but I have lived in a tent and a tabernacle. a 6Wherever I have moved about among all Israel, did I ever speak a word with any of the judges of Israel, whom I commanded to shepherd my people, saying, Why have you not built me a house of cedar? 7Now therefore thus you shall say to my servant David: Thus says the LORD of hosts: I took you from the pasture, from following the sheep, to be ruler over my people Israel; 8and I have been with you wherever you went, and have cut off all your enemies before you; and I will make for you a name, like the name of the great ones of the earth. 9I will appoint a place for my people Israel, and will plant them, so that they may live in their own place, and be disturbed no more; and evildoers shall wear them down no more, as they did formerly, 10from the time that I appointed judges over my people Israel; and I will subdue all your enemies.

Moreover I declare to you that the LORD will build you a house. 11When your days are fulfilled to go to be with your ancestors, I will raise up your offspring after you, one of your own sons, and I will establish his kingdom. 12He shall build a house for me, and I will establish his throne forever. 13I will be a father to him, and he shall be a son to me. I will not take my steadfast love from him, as I took it from him who was before you, 14but I will confirm him in my house and in my kingdom forever, and his throne shall be established forever. 15In accordance with all these words and all this vision, Nathan spoke to David.

16 Then King David went in and sat before the LORD, and said, "Who am I, O LORD God, and what is my house, that you have brought me thus far? 17And even this was a small thing in your sight, O God; you have also spoken of your servant's house for a great while to come. You regard me as someone of high rank, b O LORD God! 18And what more can David say to you for honoring your servant? You know your servant. 19For your servant's sake, O LORD, and according to your own heart, you have done all these great deeds, making known all these great things. 20There is no one like you, O LORD, and there is no God besides you, according to all that we have heard with our ears. 21Who is like your people Israel, one nation on the earth whom God went to redeem to be his people, making for yourself a name for great and terrible things, in driving out nations before your people whom you redeemed from Egypt? 22And you made your people Israel to be your people forever; and you, O LORD, became their God.

23 "And now, O LORD, as for the word that you have spoken concerning your servant and concerning his house, let it be established forever, and do as you have promised. 24Thus your name will be established and magnified forever in the saying, 'The LORD of hosts, the God of Israel, is Israel's God'; and the house of your servant David will be established in your presence. 25For you, my God, have revealed to your servant that you will build a house for him; therefore your servant has found it possible to pray before you. 26And now, O LORD, you are God, and you have promised this good thing to your servant; 27therefore may it please you to bless the house of your servant, that it may continue forever before you. For you, O LORD, have blessed and are blessed c forever."

18.1 SOME time afterward, David attacked the Philistines and subdued them; he took Gath and its villages from the Philistines.

a Gk 2 Sam 7.6: Heb *but I have been from tent to tent and from tabernacle*   b Meaning of Heb uncertain   c Or *and it is blessed*

2  He defeated Moab, and the Moabites became subject to David and brought tribute.

3  David also struck down King Hadadezer of Zobah, toward Hamath, a as he went to set up a monument at the river Euphrates. ⁴David took from him one thousand chariots, seven thousand cavalry, and twenty thousand foot soldiers. David hamstrung all the chariot horses, but left one hundred of them. ⁵When the Arameans of Damascus came to help King Hadadezer of Zobah, David killed twenty-two thousand Arameans. ⁶Then David put garrisons b in Aram of Damascus; and the Arameans became subject to David, and brought tribute. The Lᴏʀᴅ gave victory to David wherever he went. ⁷David took the gold shields that were carried by the servants of Hadadezer, and brought them to Jerusalem. ⁸From Tibhath and from Cun, cities of Hadadezer, David took a vast quantity of bronze; with it Solomon made the bronze sea and the pillars and the vessels of bronze.

9  When King Tou of Hamath heard that David had defeated the whole army of King Hadadezer of Zobah, ¹⁰he sent his son Hadoram to King David, to greet him and to congratulate him, because he had fought against Hadadezer and defeated him. Now Hadadezer had often been at war with Tou. He sent all sorts of articles of gold, of silver, and of bronze; ¹¹these also King David dedicated to the Lᴏʀᴅ, together with the silver and gold that he had carried off from all the nations, from Edom, Moab, the Ammonites, the Philistines, and Amalek.

12  Abishai son of Zeruiah killed eighteen thousand Edomites in the Valley of Salt. ¹³He put garrisons in Edom; and all the Edomites became subject to David. And the Lᴏʀᴅ gave victory to David wherever he went.

14  So David reigned over all Israel; and he administered justice and equity to all his people. ¹⁵Joab son of Zeruiah was over the army; Jehoshaphat son of Ahilud was recorder; ¹⁶Zadok son of Ahitub and Ahimelech son of Abiathar were priests; Shavsha was secretary; ¹⁷Benaiah son of Jehoiada was over the Cherethites and the Pelethites; and David's sons were the chief officials in the service of the king.

## ROMANS 2.1–24

THEREFORE you have no excuse, whoever you are, when you judge others; for in passing judgment on another you condemn yourself, because you, the judge, are doing the very same things. ²You say, c "We know that God's judgment on those who do such things is in accordance with truth." ³Do you imagine, whoever you are, that when you judge those who do such things and yet do them yourself, you will escape the judgment of God? ⁴Or do you despise the riches of his kindness and forbearance and patience? Do you not realize that God's kindness is meant to lead you to repentance? ⁵But by your hard and impenitent heart you are storing up wrath for yourself on the day of wrath, when God's righteous judgment will be revealed. ⁶For he will repay according to each one's deeds: ⁷to those who by patiently doing good seek for glory and honor and immortality, he will give eternal life; ⁸while for those who are self-seeking and who obey not the truth but wickedness, there will be wrath and fury. ⁹There will be anguish and distress for everyone who does evil, the Jew first and also the Greek, ¹⁰but glory and honor and peace for everyone who does good, the Jew first and also the Greek. ¹¹For God shows no partiality.

aMeaning of Heb uncertain   bGk Vg 2 Sam 8.6 Compare Syr: Heb lacks *garrisons*   cGk lacks *You say*

12  All who have sinned apart from the law will also perish apart from the law, and all who have sinned under the law will be judged by the law. 13For it is not the hearers of the law who are righteous in God's sight, but the doers of the law who will be justified. 14When Gentiles, who do not possess the law, do instinctively what the law requires, these, though not having the law, are a law to themselves. 15They show that what the law requires is written on their hearts, to which their own conscience also bears witness; and their conflicting thoughts will accuse or perhaps excuse them 16on the day when, according to my gospel, God, through Jesus Christ, will judge the secret thoughts of all.

17  But if you call yourself a Jew and rely on the law and boast of your relation to God 18and know his will and determine what is best because you are instructed in the law, 19and if you are sure that you are a guide to the blind, a light to those who are in darkness, 20a corrector of the foolish, a teacher of children, having in the law the embodiment of knowledge and truth, 21you, then, that teach others, will you not teach yourself? While you preach against stealing, do you steal? 22You that forbid adultery, do you commit adultery? You that abhor idols, do you rob temples? 23You that boast in the law, do you dishonor God by breaking the law? 24For, as it is written, "The name of God is blasphemed among the Gentiles because of you."

## PSALM 10.16–18

The Lord is king forever and
    ever;
  the nations shall perish from
    his land.

17  O Lord, you will hear the desire
    of the meek;
  you will strengthen their
    heart, you will incline
    your ear
18  to do justice for the orphan and
    the oppressed,
  so that those from earth may
    strike terror no more. [a]

## PROVERBS 19.8–9

To get wisdom is to love
    oneself;
  to keep understanding is
    to prosper.
9  A false witness will not go
    unpunished,
  and the liar will perish.

aMeaning of Heb uncertain

# JULY 15

## 1 CHRONICLES 19.1—21.27

SOME time afterward, King Nahash of the Ammonites died, and his son succeeded him. [2]David said, "I will deal loyally with Hanun son of Nahash, for his father dealt loyally with me." So David sent messengers to console him concerning his father. When David's servants came to Hanun in the land of the Ammonites, to console him, [3]the officials of the Ammonites said to Hanun, "Do you think, because David has sent consolers to you, that he is honoring your father? Have not his servants come to you to search and to overthrow and to spy out the land?" [4]So Hanun seized David's servants, shaved them, cut off their garments in the middle at their hips, and sent them away; [5]and they departed. When David was told about the men, he sent messengers to them, for they felt greatly humiliated. The king said, "Remain at Jericho until your beards have grown, and then return."

6 When the Ammonites saw that they had made themselves odious to David, Hanun and the Ammonites sent a thousand talents of silver to hire chariots and cavalry from Mesopotamia, from Aram-maacah and from Zobah. [7]They hired thirty-two thousand chariots and the king of Maacah with his army, who came and camped before Medeba. And the Ammonites were mustered from their cities and came to battle. [8]When David heard of it, he sent Joab and all the army of the warriors. [9]The Ammonites came out and drew up in battle array at the entrance of the city, and the kings who had come were by themselves in the open country.

10 When Joab saw that the line of battle was set against him both in front and in the rear, he chose some of the picked men of Israel and arrayed them against the Arameans; [11]the rest of his troops he put in the charge of his brother Abishai, and they were arrayed against the Ammonites. [12]He said, "If the Arameans are too strong for me, then you shall help me; but if the Ammonites are too strong for you, then I will help you. [13]Be strong, and let us be courageous for our people and for the cities of our God; and may the LORD do what seems good to him." [14]So Joab and the troops who were with him advanced toward the Arameans for battle; and they fled before him. [15]When the Ammonites saw that the Arameans fled, they likewise fled before Abishai, Joab's brother, and entered the city. Then Joab came to Jerusalem.

16 But when the Arameans saw that they had been defeated by Israel, they sent messengers and brought out the Arameans who were beyond the Euphrates, with Shophach the commander of the army of Hadadezer at their head. [17]When David was informed, he gathered all Israel together, crossed the Jordan, came to them, and drew up his forces against them. When David set the battle in array against the Arameans, they fought with him. [18]The Arameans fled before Israel; and David killed seven thousand Aramean charioteers and forty thousand foot soldiers, and also killed Shophach the commander of their army. [19]When the servants of Hadadezer saw that they had been defeated by Israel, they made peace with David, and became subject to him. So the Arameans were not willing to help the Ammonites any more.

20.1 IN the spring of the year, the time when kings go out to battle, Joab led out the army, ravaged the country of the Ammonites, and came and besieged Rabbah. But David remained at Jerusalem. Joab attacked Rabbah, and overthrew it. [2]David took the crown of Milcom[a] from his head; he found that it weighed a talent of gold, and in it was a precious stone; and it was placed on David's head. He also brought out the booty of the city, a very great amount. [3]He brought out the people who were in it, and set them to work[b] with saws and iron picks and axes. [c] Thus David did to all the cities of the Ammonites. Then David and all the people returned to Jerusalem.

4 After this, war broke out with the Philistines at Gezer; then Sibbecai the Hushathite killed Sippai, who was one of the descendants of the giants; and the Philistines were subdued. [5]Again there was war with the Philistines; and Elhanan son of Jair killed Lahmi the brother of Goliath the Gittite, the shaft of whose spear was like a weaver's beam. [6]Again there was war at Gath, where there was a man of great size, who had six fingers on each hand, and six toes on each foot, twenty-four in number; he also was descended from the giants. [7]When he taunted Israel, Jonathan son of Shimea, David's brother, killed him. [8]These were descended from the giants in Gath; they fell by the hand of David and his servants.

21.1 SATAN stood up against Israel, and incited David to count the people of Israel. [2]So David said to Joab and the commanders of the army, "Go, number Israel, from Beer-sheba to Dan, and bring me a report, so that I may know their number." [3]But Joab said, "May the LORD increase the number of his people a hundredfold! Are they not, my lord the king, all of them my lord's servants? Why then should my lord require this? Why should he bring guilt on

Israel?" [4]But the king's word prevailed against Joab. So Joab departed and went throughout all Israel, and came back to Jerusalem. [5]Joab gave the total count of the people to David. In all Israel there were one million one hundred thousand men who drew the sword, and in Judah four hundred seventy thousand who drew the sword. [6]But he did not include Levi and Benjamin in the numbering, for the king's command was abhorrent to Joab.

7 But God was displeased with this thing, and he struck Israel. [8]David said to God, "I have sinned greatly in that I have done this thing. But now, I pray you, take away the guilt of your servant; for I have done very foolishly." [9]The LORD spoke to Gad, David's seer, saying, [10]"Go and say to David, 'Thus says the LORD: Three things I offer you; choose one of them, so that I may do it to you.'" [11]So Gad came to David and said to him, "Thus says the LORD, 'Take your choice: [12]either three years of famine; or three months of devastation by your foes, while the sword of your enemies overtakes you; or three days of the sword of the LORD, pestilence on the land, and the angel of the LORD destroying throughout all the territory of Israel.' Now decide what answer I shall return to the one who sent me." [13]Then David said to Gad, "I am in great distress; let me fall into the hand of the LORD, for his mercy is very great; but let me not fall into human hands."

14 So the LORD sent a pestilence on Israel; and seventy thousand persons fell in Israel. [15]And God sent an angel to Jerusalem to destroy it; but when he was about to destroy it, the LORD took note and relented concerning the calamity; he said to the destroying angel, "Enough! Stay your hand." The angel of the LORD was then standing by the threshing floor of Ornan the Jebusite. [16]David looked up and saw the angel of

the LORD standing between earth and heaven, and in his hand a drawn sword stretched out over Jerusalem. Then David and the elders, clothed in sackcloth, fell on their faces. [17]And David said to God, "Was it not I who gave the command to count the people? It is I who have sinned and done very wickedly. But these sheep, what have they done? Let your hand, I pray, O LORD my God, be against me and against my father's house; but do not let your people be plagued!"

18  Then the angel of the LORD commanded Gad to tell David that he should go up and erect an altar to the LORD on the threshing floor of Ornan the Jebusite. [19]So David went up following Gad's instructions, which he had spoken in the name of the LORD. [20]Ornan turned and saw the angel; and while his four sons who were with him hid themselves, Ornan continued to thresh wheat. [21]As David came to Ornan, Ornan looked and saw David; he went out from the threshing floor, and did obeisance to David with his face to the ground. [22]David said to Ornan, "Give me the site of the threshing floor that I may build on it an altar to the LORD—give it to me at its full price—so that the plague may be averted from the people." [23]Then Ornan said to David, "Take it; and let my lord the king do what seems good to him; see, I present the oxen for burnt offerings, and the threshing sledges for the wood, and the wheat for a grain offering. I give it all." [24]But King David said to Ornan, "No; I will buy them for the full price. I will not take for the LORD what is yours, nor offer burnt offerings that cost me nothing." [25]So David paid Ornan six hundred shekels of gold by weight for the site. [26]David built there an altar to the LORD and presented burnt offerings and offerings of well-being. He called upon the LORD, and he answered him with fire from heaven on the altar of burnt offering. [27]Then the LORD commanded the angel, and he put his sword back into its sheath.

## ROMANS 2.25—3.8

CIRCUMCISION indeed is of value if you obey the law; but if you break the law, your circumcision has become uncircumcision. [26]So, if those who are uncircumcised keep the requirements of the law, will not their uncircumcision be regarded as circumcision? [27]Then those who are physically uncircumcised but keep the law will condemn you that have the written code and circumcision but break the law. [28]For a person is not a Jew who is one outwardly, nor is true circumcision something external and physical. [29]Rather, a person is a Jew who is one inwardly, and real circumcision is a matter of the heart—it is spiritual and not literal. Such a person receives praise not from others but from God.

[3.1] THEN what advantage has the Jew? Or what is the value of circumcision? [2]Much, in every way. For in the first place the Jews[a] were entrusted with the oracles of God. [3]What if some were unfaithful? Will their faithlessness nullify the faithfulness of God? [4]By no means! Although everyone is a liar, let God be proved true, as it is written,

"So that you may be justified in
        your words,
    and prevail in your judging."[b]

[5]But if our injustice serves to confirm the justice of God, what should we say? That God is unjust to inflict wrath on us? (I speak in a human way.) [6]By no means! For then how could God judge the world? [7]But if through my falsehood God's truthfulness abounds to his glory, why am I still being condemned as a sinner? [8]And why not say (as some

aGk *they*   bGk *when you are being judged*

people slander us by saying that we say), "Let us do evil so that good may come"? Their condemnation is deserved!

## PSALM 11.1–7

*To the leader. Of David.*

IN the LORD I take refuge; how
    can you say to me,
    "Flee like a bird to the
    mountains; [a]
2  for look, the wicked bend the
    bow,
  they have fitted their arrow
    to the string,
  to shoot in the dark at the
    upright in heart.
3  If the foundations are
    destroyed,
  what can the righteous do?"

4  The LORD is in his holy temple;
  the LORD's throne is in
    heaven.
  His eyes behold, his gaze
    examines humankind.

5  The LORD tests the righteous
    and the wicked,
  and his soul hates the lover of
    violence.
6  On the wicked he will rain coals
    of fire and sulfur;
  a scorching wind shall be the
    portion of their cup.
7  For the LORD is righteous;
  he loves righteous deeds;
  the upright shall behold his
    face.

## PROVERBS 19.10–12

IT is not fitting for a fool to live
    in luxury,
  much less for a slave to rule
    over princes.
11  Those with good sense are slow
    to anger,
  and it is their glory to
    overlook an offense.
12  A king's anger is like the
    growling of a lion,
  but his favor is like dew on
    the grass.

# JULY 16

## 1 CHRONICLES 21.28—23.32

AT that time, when David saw that the LORD had answered him at the threshing floor of Ornan the Jebusite, he made his sacrifices there. 29For the tabernacle of the LORD, which Moses had made in the wilderness, and the altar of burnt offering were at that time in the high place at Gibeon; 30but David could not go before it to inquire of God, for he was afraid of the sword of the angel of the LORD. 22.1Then David said, "Here shall be the house of the LORD God and here the altar of burnt offering for Israel."

2 David gave orders to gather together the aliens who were residing in the land of Israel, and he set stonecutters to prepare dressed stones for building the house of God. 3David also provided great stores of iron for nails for the doors of the gates and for clamps, as well as bronze in quantities

a Gk Syr Jerome Tg: Heb *flee to your mountain, O bird*

beyond weighing, [4]and cedar logs without number—for the Sidonians and Tyrians brought great quantities of cedar to David. [5]For David said, "My son Solomon is young and inexperienced, and the house that is to be built for the LORD must be exceedingly magnificent, famous and glorified throughout all lands; I will therefore make preparation for it." So David provided materials in great quantity before his death.

6 Then he called for his son Solomon and charged him to build a house for the LORD, the God of Israel. [7]David said to Solomon, "My son, I had planned to build a house to the name of the LORD my God. [8]But the word of the LORD came to me, saying, 'You have shed much blood and have waged great wars; you shall not build a house to my name, because you have shed so much blood in my sight on the earth. [9]See, a son shall be born to you; he shall be a man of peace. I will give him peace from all his enemies on every side; for his name shall be Solomon,[a] and I will give peace[b] and quiet to Israel in his days. [10]He shall build a house for my name. He shall be a son to me, and I will be a father to him, and I will establish his royal throne in Israel forever.' [11]Now, my son, the LORD be with you, so that you may succeed in building the house of the LORD your God, as he has spoken concerning you. [12]Only, may the LORD grant you discretion and understanding, so that when he gives you charge over Israel you may keep the law of the LORD your God. [13]Then you will prosper if you are careful to observe the statutes and the ordinances that the LORD commanded Moses for Israel. Be strong and of good courage. Do not be afraid or dismayed. [14]With great pains I have provided for the house of the LORD one hundred thousand talents of gold, one million talents of silver, and bronze and iron beyond weighing, for

there is so much of it; timber and stone too I have provided. To these you must add more. [15]You have an abundance of workers: stonecutters, masons, carpenters, and all kinds of artisans without number, skilled in working [16]gold, silver, bronze, and iron. Now begin the work, and the LORD be with you."

17 David also commanded all the leaders of Israel to help his son Solomon, saying, [18]"Is not the LORD your God with you? Has he not given you peace on every side? For he has delivered the inhabitants of the land into my hand; and the land is subdued before the LORD and his people. [19]Now set your mind and heart to seek the LORD your God. Go and build the sanctuary of the LORD God so that the ark of the covenant of the LORD and the holy vessels of God may be brought into a house built for the name of the LORD."

23.1 WHEN David was old and full of days, he made his son Solomon king over Israel.

2 David assembled all the leaders of Israel and the priests and the Levites. [3]The Levites, thirty years old and upward, were counted, and the total was thirty-eight thousand. [4]"Twenty-four thousand of these," David said, "shall have charge of the work in the house of the LORD, six thousand shall be officers and judges, [5]four thousand gatekeepers, and four thousand shall offer praises to the LORD with the instruments that I have made for praise." [6]And David organized them in divisions corresponding to the sons of Levi: Gershon,[c] Kohath, and Merari.

7 The sons of Gershon[d] were Ladan and Shimei. [8]The sons of Ladan: Jehiel the chief, Zetham, and Joel, three. [9]The sons of Shimei: Shelomoth, Haziel, and Haran, three. These were the heads of families of Ladan. [10]And the sons of Shimei: Jahath, Zina,

[a]Heb *Shelomoh*  [b]Heb *shalom*  [c]Or *Gershom*; See 1 Chr 6.1, note, and 23.15  [d]Vg Compare Gk Syr: Heb *to the Gershonite*

Jeush, and Beriah. These four were the sons of Shimei. ¹¹Jahath was the chief, and Zizah the second; but Jeush and Beriah did not have many sons, so they were enrolled as a single family.

12 The sons of Kohath: Amram, Izhar, Hebron, and Uzziel, four. ¹³The sons of Amram: Aaron and Moses. Aaron was set apart to consecrate the most holy things, so that he and his sons forever should make offerings before the Lord, and minister to him and pronounce blessings in his name forever; ¹⁴but as for Moses the man of God, his sons were to be reckoned among the tribe of Levi. ¹⁵The sons of Moses: Gershom and Eliezer. ¹⁶The sons of Gershom: Shebuel the chief. ¹⁷The sons of Eliezer: Rehabiah the chief; Eliezer had no other sons, but the sons of Rehabiah were very numerous. ¹⁸The sons of Izhar: Shelomith the chief. ¹⁹The sons of Hebron: Jeriah the chief, Amariah the second, Jahaziel the third, and Jekameam the fourth. ²⁰The sons of Uzziel: Micah the chief and Isshiah the second.

21 The sons of Merari: Mahli and Mushi. The sons of Mahli: Eleazar and Kish. ²²Eleazar died having no sons, but only daughters; their kindred, the sons of Kish, married them. ²³The sons of Mushi: Mahli, Eder, and Jeremoth, three.

24 These were the sons of Levi by their ancestral houses, the heads of families as they were enrolled according to the number of the names of the individuals from twenty years old and upward who were to do the work for the service of the house of the Lord. ²⁵For David said, "The Lord, the God of Israel, has given rest to his people; and he resides in Jerusalem forever. ²⁶And so the Levites no longer need to carry the tabernacle or any of the things for its service"— ²⁷for according to the last words of David these were the number of the Levites from twenty years old and upward— ²⁸"but their duty shall be to assist the descendants of Aaron for the service of the house of the Lord, having the care of the courts and the chambers, the cleansing of all that is holy, and any work for the service of the house of God; ²⁹to assist also with the rows of bread, the choice flour for the grain offering, the wafers of unleavened bread, the baked offering, the offering mixed with oil, and all measures of quantity or size. ³⁰And they shall stand every morning, thanking and praising the Lord, and likewise at evening, ³¹and whenever burnt offerings are offered to the Lord on sabbaths, new moons, and appointed festivals, according to the number required of them, regularly before the Lord. ³²Thus they shall keep charge of the tent of meeting and the sanctuary, and shall attend the descendants of Aaron, their kindred, for the service of the house of the Lord."

## ROMANS 3.9–31

WHAT then? Are we any better off?ᵃ No, not at all; for we have already charged that all, both Jews and Greeks, are under the power of sin, ¹⁰as it is written:
"There is no one who is
        righteous, not even one;
11    there is no one who has
        understanding,
    there is no one who seeks
        God.
12  All have turned aside, together
        they have become
        worthless;
    there is no one who shows
        kindness,
    there is not even one."
13  "Their throats are opened
        graves;
    they use their tongues to
        deceive."

ᵃOr *at any disadvantage?*

"The venom of vipers is under
their lips."
14   "Their mouths are full of
cursing and bitterness."
15   "Their feet are swift to shed
blood;
16   ruin and misery are in their
paths,
17   and the way of peace they have
not known."
18   "There is no fear of God
before their eyes."

19 Now we know that whatever the law says, it speaks to those who are under the law, so that every mouth may be silenced, and the whole world may be held accountable to God. 20For "no human being will be justified in his sight" by deeds prescribed by the law, for through the law comes the knowledge of sin.

21 But now, apart from law, the righteousness of God has been disclosed, and is attested by the law and the prophets, 22the righteousness of God through faith in Jesus Christ[a] for all who believe. For there is no distinction, 23since all have sinned and fall short of the glory of God; 24they are now justified by his grace as a gift, through the redemption that is in Christ Jesus, 25whom God put forward as a sacrifice of atonement[b] by his blood, effective through faith. He did this to show his righteousness, because in his divine forbearance he had passed over the sins previously committed; 26it was to prove at the present time that he himself is righteous and that he justifies the one who has faith in Jesus.[c]

27 Then what becomes of boasting? It is excluded. By what law? By that of works? No, but by the law of faith. 28For we hold that a person is justified by faith apart from works prescribed by the law. 29Or is God the God of Jews only? Is he not the God of Gentiles also? Yes, of Gentiles also, 30since God is one; and he will justify the circumcised on the ground of faith and the uncircumcised through that same faith. 31Do we then overthrow the law by this faith? By no means! On the contrary, we uphold the law.

## PSALM 12.1–8

*To the leader: according to The Sheminith. A Psalm of David.*

HELP, O LORD, for there is no
longer anyone who is
godly;
the faithful have disappeared
from humankind.
2   They utter lies to each other;
with flattering lips and a
double heart they speak.

3   May the LORD cut off all
flattering lips,
the tongue that makes great
boasts,
4   those who say, "With our
tongues we will prevail;
our lips are our own—who is
our master?"

5   "Because the poor are
despoiled, because the
needy groan,
I will now rise up," says the
LORD;
"I will place them in the
safety for which they
long."
6   The promises of the LORD are
promises that are pure,
silver refined in a furnace on
the ground,
purified seven times.

7   You, O LORD, will protect us;
you will guard us from this
generation forever.
8   On every side the wicked
prowl,

aOr *through the faith of Jesus Christ*   bOr *a place of atonement*   cOr *who has the faith of Jesus*

as vileness is exalted among
humankind.

## PROVERBS 19.13–14

A STUPID child is ruin to a
father,
and a wife's quarreling is a
continual dripping of rain.

14 House and wealth are inherited
from parents,
but a prudent wife is from
the LORD.

# JULY 17

## 1 CHRONICLES 24.1—26.11

THE divisions of the descendants of Aaron were these. The sons of Aaron: Nadab, Abihu, Eleazar, and Ithamar. 2But Nadab and Abihu died before their father, and had no sons; so Eleazar and Ithamar became the priests. 3Along with Zadok of the sons of Eleazar, and Ahimelech of the sons of Ithamar, David organized them according to the appointed duties in their service. 4Since more chief men were found among the sons of Eleazar than among the sons of Ithamar, they organized them under sixteen heads of ancestral houses of the sons of Eleazar, and eight of the sons of Ithamar. 5They organized them by lot, all alike, for there were officers of the sanctuary and officers of God among both the sons of Eleazar and the sons of Ithamar. 6The scribe Shemaiah son of Nethanel, a Levite, recorded them in the presence of the king, and the officers, and Zadok the priest, and Ahimelech son of Abiathar, and the heads of ancestral houses of the priests and of the Levites; one ancestral house being chosen for Eleazar and one chosen for Ithamar.

7 The first lot fell to Jehoiarib, the second to Jedaiah, 8the third to Harim, the fourth to Seorim, 9the fifth to Malchijah, the sixth to Mijamin, 10the seventh to Hakkoz, the eighth to Abijah, 11the ninth to Jeshua, the tenth to Shecaniah, 12the eleventh to Eliashib, the twelfth to Jakim, 13the thirteenth to Huppah, the fourteenth to Jeshebeab, 14the fifteenth to Bilgah, the sixteenth to Immer, 15the seventeenth to Hezir, the eighteenth to Happizzez, 16the nineteenth to Pethahiah, the twentieth to Jehezkel, 17the twenty-first to Jachin, the twenty-second to Gamul, 18the twenty-third to Delaiah, the twenty-fourth to Maaziah. 19These had as their appointed duty in their service to enter the house of the LORD according to the procedure established for them by their ancestor Aaron, as the LORD God of Israel had commanded him.

20 And of the rest of the sons of Levi: of the sons of Amram, Shubael; of the sons of Shubael, Jehdeiah. 21Of Rehabiah: of the sons of Rehabiah, Isshiah the chief. 22Of the Izharites, Shelomoth; of the sons of Shelomoth, Jahath. 23The sons of Hebron:a Jeriah the

aSee 23.19: Heb lacks *Hebron*

chief, [a] Amariah the second, Jahaziel the third, Jekameam the fourth. [24]The sons of Uzziel, Micah; of the sons of Micah, Shamir. [25]The brother of Micah, Isshiah; of the sons of Isshiah, Zechariah. [26]The sons of Merari: Mahli and Mushi. The sons of Jaaziah: Beno. [b] [27]The sons of Merari: of Jaaziah, Beno, [b] Shoham, Zaccur, and Ibri. [28]Of Mahli: Eleazar, who had no sons. [29]Of Kish, the sons of Kish: Jerahmeel. [30]The sons of Mushi: Mahli, Eder, and Jerimoth. These were the sons of the Levites according to their ancestral houses. [31]These also cast lots corresponding to their kindred, the descendants of Aaron, in the presence of King David, Zadok, Ahimelech, and the heads of ancestral houses of the priests and of the Levites, the chief as well as the youngest brother.

[25.1] DAVID and the officers of the army also set apart for the service the sons of Asaph, and of Heman, and of Jeduthun, who should prophesy with lyres, harps, and cymbals. The list of those who did the work and of their duties was: [2]Of the sons of Asaph: Zaccur, Joseph, Nethaniah, and Asarelah, sons of Asaph, under the direction of Asaph, who prophesied under the direction of the king. [3]Of Jeduthun, the sons of Jeduthun: Gedaliah, Zeri, Jeshaiah, Shimei, [c] Hashabiah, and Mattithiah, six, under the direction of their father Jeduthun, who prophesied with the lyre in thanksgiving and praise to the LORD. [4]Of Heman, the sons of Heman: Bukkiah, Mattaniah, Uzziel, Shebuel, and Jerimoth, Hananiah, Hanani, Eliathah, Giddalti, and Romamti-ezer, Joshbekashah, Mallothi, Hothir, Mahazioth. [5]All these were the sons of Heman the king's seer, according to the promise of God to exalt him; for God had given Heman fourteen sons and three daughters. [6]They were all under the direction of their father for the music in the house of the LORD with cymbals, harps, and lyres for the service of the house of God. Asaph, Jeduthun, and Heman were under the order of the king. [7]They and their kindred, who were trained in singing to the LORD, all of whom were skillful, numbered two hundred eighty-eight. [8]And they cast lots for their duties, small and great, teacher and pupil alike.

9  The first lot fell for Asaph to Joseph; the second to Gedaliah, to him and his brothers and his sons, twelve; [10]the third to Zaccur, his sons and his brothers, twelve; [11]the fourth to Izri, his sons and his brothers, twelve; [12]the fifth to Nethaniah, his sons and his brothers, twelve; [13]the sixth to Bukkiah, his sons and his brothers, twelve; [14]the seventh to Jesarelah, [d] his sons and his brothers, twelve; [15]the eighth to Jeshaiah, his sons and his brothers, twelve; [16]the ninth to Mattaniah, his sons and his brothers, twelve; [17]the tenth to Shimei, his sons and his brothers, twelve; [18]the eleventh to Azarel, his sons and his brothers, twelve; [19]the twelfth to Hashabiah, his sons and his brothers, twelve; [20]to the thirteenth, Shubael, his sons and his brothers, twelve; [21]to the fourteenth, Mattithiah, his sons and his brothers, twelve; [22]to the fifteenth, to Jeremoth, his sons and his brothers, twelve; [23]to the sixteenth, to Hananiah, his sons and his brothers, twelve; [24]to the seventeenth, to Joshbekashah, his sons and his brothers, twelve; [25]to the eighteenth, to Hanani, his sons and his brothers, twelve; [26]to the nineteenth, to Mallothi, his sons and his brothers, twelve; [27]to the twentieth, to Eliathah, his sons and his brothers, twelve; [28]to the twenty-first, to Hothir, his sons and his brothers, twelve; [29]to the twenty-second, to Giddalti, his sons and his brothers, twelve; [30]to the twenty-

aSee 23.19: Heb lacks *the chief*   bOr *his son*: Meaning of Heb uncertain   cOne Ms: Gk: MT lacks *Shimei*   dOr *Asarelah*; see 25.2

third, to Mahazioth, his sons and his brothers, twelve; ³¹to the twenty-fourth, to Romamti-ezer, his sons and his brothers, twelve.

**26.**1 As for the divisions of the gatekeepers: of the Korahites, Meshelemiah son of Kore, of the sons of Asaph. ²Meshelemiah had sons: Zechariah the firstborn, Jediael the second, Zebadiah the third, Jathniel the fourth, ³Elam the fifth, Jehohanan the sixth, Eliehoenai the seventh. ⁴Obed-edom had sons: Shemaiah the firstborn, Jehozabad the second, Joah the third, Sachar the fourth, Nethanel the fifth, ⁵Ammiel the sixth, Issachar the seventh, Peullethai the eighth; for God blessed him. ⁶Also to his son Shemaiah sons were born who exercised authority in their ancestral houses, for they were men of great ability. ⁷The sons of Shemaiah: Othni, Rephael, Obed, and Elzabad, whose brothers were able men, Elihu and Semachiah. ⁸All these, sons of Obed-edom with their sons and brothers, were able men qualified for the service; sixty-two of Obed-edom. ⁹Meshelemiah had sons and brothers, able men, eighteen. ¹⁰Hosah, of the sons of Merari, had sons: Shimri the chief (for though he was not the firstborn, his father made him chief), ¹¹Hilkiah the second, Tebaliah the third, Zechariah the fourth: all the sons and brothers of Hosah totaled thirteen.

## ROMANS 4.1–12

**W**HAT then are we to say was gained byᵃ Abraham, our ancestor according to the flesh? ²For if Abraham was justified by works, he has something to boast about, but not before God. ³For what does the scripture say? "Abraham believed God, and it was reckoned to him as righteousness." ⁴Now to one who works, wages are not reckoned as a gift but as something due. ⁵But to one who without works trusts him who justifies the ungodly, such faith is reckoned as righteousness. ⁶So also David speaks of the blessedness of those to whom God reckons righteousness apart from works:

7 "Blessed are those whose
    iniquities are forgiven,
  and whose sins are covered;
8 blessed is the one against whom
    the Lord will not reckon
    sin."

9 Is this blessedness, then, pronounced only on the circumcised, or also on the uncircumcised? We say, "Faith was reckoned to Abraham as righteousness." ¹⁰How then was it reckoned to him? Was it before or after he had been circumcised? It was not after, but before he was circumcised. ¹¹He received the sign of circumcision as a seal of the righteousness that he had by faith while he was still uncircumcised. The purpose was to make him the ancestor of all who believe without being circumcised and who thus have righteousness reckoned to them, ¹²and likewise the ancestor of the circumcised who are not only circumcised but who also follow the example of the faith that our ancestor Abraham had before he was circumcised.

## PSALM 13.1–6

*To the leader. A Psalm of David.*

**H**ow long, O LORD? Will you
    forget me forever?
  How long will you hide
    your face from me?
2 How long must I bear painᵇ in
    my soul,
  and have sorrow in my heart
    all day long?
  How long shall my enemy be
    exalted over me?

ᵃOther ancient authorities read *say about*   ᵇSyr: Heb *hold counsels*

3 Consider and answer me,
 O Lord my God!
Give light to my eyes, or I
 will sleep the sleep of
 death,
4 and my enemy will say, "I have
 prevailed";
 my foes will rejoice because I
 am shaken.

5 But I trusted in your steadfast
 love;
 my heart shall rejoice in your
 salvation.

6 I will sing to the Lord,
 because he has dealt
 bountifully with me.

## PROVERBS 19.15–16

Laziness brings on deep sleep;
 an idle person will suffer
 hunger.
16 Those who keep the
 commandment will live;
 those who are heedless of
 their ways will die.

# JULY 18

## 1 CHRONICLES 26.12—27.34

These divisions of the gatekeepers, corresponding to their leaders, had duties, just as their kindred did, ministering in the house of the Lord; 13and they cast lots by ancestral houses, small and great alike, for their gates. 14The lot for the east fell to Shelemiah. They cast lots also for his son Zechariah, a prudent counselor, and his lot came out for the north. 15Obed-edom's came out for the south, and to his sons was allotted the storehouse. 16For Shuppim and Hosah it came out for the west, at the gate of Shallecheth on the ascending road. Guard corresponded to guard. 17On the east there were six Levites each day, a on the north four each day, on the south four each day, as well as two and two at the storehouse; 18and for the colonnadeb on the west there were four at the road and two at the colonnade. b 19These were the divisions of the gatekeepers among the Korahites and the sons of Merari.

20 And of the Levites, Ahijah had charge of the treasuries of the house of God and the treasuries of the dedicated gifts. 21The sons of Ladan, the sons of the Gershonites belonging to Ladan, the heads of families belonging to Ladan the Gershonite: Jehieli. c

22 The sons of Jehieli, Zetham and his brother Joel, were in charge of the treasuries of the house of the Lord. 23Of the Amramites, the Izharites, the Hebronites, and the Uzzielites: 24Shebuel son of Gershom, son of Moses, was chief officer in charge of the treasuries. 25His brothers: from Eliezer were his son Rehabiah, his son Jeshaiah, his son Joram, his son Zichri, and his son Shelomoth. 26This Shelomoth and his brothers were in charge of all the treasuries of the dedicated gifts that King David, and the heads of fami-

aGk: Heb lacks *each day*   bHeb *parbar*: meaning uncertain   cThe Hebrew text of verse 21 is confused

lies, and the officers of the thousands and the hundreds, and the commanders of the army, had dedicated. [27]From booty won in battles they dedicated gifts for the maintenance of the house of the LORD. [28]Also all that Samuel the seer, and Saul son of Kish, and Abner son of Ner, and Joab son of Zeruiah had dedicated—all dedicated gifts were in the care of Shelomoth[a] and his brothers.

29  Of the Izharites, Chenaniah and his sons were appointed to outside duties for Israel, as officers and judges. [30]Of the Hebronites, Hashabiah and his brothers, one thousand seven hundred men of ability, had the oversight of Israel west of the Jordan for all the work of the LORD and for the service of the king. [31]Of the Hebronites, Jerijah was chief of the Hebronites. (In the fortieth year of David's reign search was made, of whatever genealogy or family, and men of great ability among them were found at Jazer in Gilead.) [32]King David appointed him and his brothers, two thousand seven hundred men of ability, heads of families, to have the oversight of the Reubenites, the Gadites, and the half-tribe of the Manassites for everything pertaining to God and for the affairs of the king.

**27.1** THIS is the list of the people of Israel, the heads of families, the commanders of the thousands and the hundreds, and their officers who served the king in all matters concerning the divisions that came and went, month after month throughout the year, each division numbering twenty-four thousand: [2]Jashobeam son of Zabdiel was in charge of the first division in the first month; in his division were twenty-four thousand. [3]He was a descendant of Perez, and was chief of all the commanders of the army for the first month.

[4]Dodai the Ahohite was in charge of the division of the second month; Mikloth was the chief officer of his division. In his division were twenty-four thousand. [5]The third commander, for the third month, was Benaiah son of the priest Jehoiada, as chief; in his division were twenty-four thousand. [6]This is the Benaiah who was a mighty man of the Thirty and in command of the Thirty; his son Ammizabad was in charge of his division. [b] [7]Asahel brother of Joab was fourth, for the fourth month, and his son Zebadiah after him; in his division were twenty-four thousand. [8]The fifth commander, for the fifth month, was Shamhuth, the Izrahite; in his division were twenty-four thousand. [9]Sixth, for the sixth month, was Ira son of Ikkesh the Tekoite; in his division were twenty-four thousand. [10]Seventh, for the seventh month, was Helez the Pelonite, of the Ephraimites; in his division were twenty-four thousand. [11]Eighth, for the eighth month, was Sibbecai the Hushathite, of the Zerahites; in his division were twenty-four thousand. [12]Ninth, for the ninth month, was Abiezer of Anathoth, a Benjaminite; in his division were twenty-four thousand. [13]Tenth, for the tenth month, was Maharai of Netophah, of the Zerahites; in his division were twenty-four thousand. [14]Eleventh, for the eleventh month, was Benaiah of Pirathon, of the Ephraimites; in his division were twenty-four thousand. [15]Twelfth, for the twelfth month, was Heldai the Netophathite, of Othniel; in his division were twenty-four thousand.

16  Over the tribes of Israel, for the Reubenites, Eliezer son of Zichri was chief officer; for the Simeonites, Shephatiah son of Maacah; [17]for Levi, Hashabiah son of Kemuel; for Aaron, Zadok; [18]for Judah, Elihu, one of David's brothers; for Issachar, Omri son

aGk Compare 26.28: Heb *Shelomith*   bGk Vg: Heb *Ammizabad was his division*

of Michael; ¹⁹for Zebulun, Ishmaiah son of Obadiah; for Naphtali, Jerimoth son of Azriel; ²⁰for the Ephraimites, Hoshea son of Azaziah; for the half-tribe of Manasseh, Joel son of Pedaiah; ²¹for the half-tribe of Manasseh in Gilead, Iddo son of Zechariah; for Benjamin, Jaasiel son of Abner; ²²for Dan, Azarel son of Jeroham. These were the leaders of the tribes of Israel. ²³David did not count those below twenty years of age, for the LORD had promised to make Israel as numerous as the stars of heaven. ²⁴Joab son of Zeruiah began to count them, but did not finish; yet wrath came upon Israel for this, and the number was not entered into the account of the Annals of King David.

25 Over the king's treasuries was Azmaveth son of Adiel. Over the treasuries in the country, in the cities, in the villages and in the towers, was Jonathan son of Uzziah. ²⁶Over those who did the work of the field, tilling the soil, was Ezri son of Chelub. ²⁷Over the vineyards was Shimei the Ramathite. Over the produce of the vineyards for the wine cellars was Zabdi the Shiphmite. ²⁸Over the olive and sycamore trees in the Shephelah was Baal-hanan the Gederite. Over the stores of oil was Joash. ²⁹Over the herds that pastured in Sharon was Shitrai the Sharonite. Over the herds in the valleys was Shaphat son of Adlai. ³⁰Over the camels was Obil the Ishmaelite. Over the donkeys was Jehdeiah the Meronothite. Over the flocks was Jaziz the Hagrite. ³¹All these were stewards of King David's property.

32 Jonathan, David's uncle, was a counselor, being a man of understanding and a scribe; Jehiel son of Hachmoni attended the king's sons. ³³Ahithophel was the king's counselor, and Hushai the Archite was the king's friend. ³⁴After Ahithophel came Jehoiada son of

Benaiah, and Abiathar. Joab was commander of the king's army.

## ROMANS 4.13—5.5

FOR the promise that he would inherit the world did not come to Abraham or to his descendants through the law but through the righteousness of faith. ¹⁴If it is the adherents of the law who are to be the heirs, faith is null and the promise is void. ¹⁵For the law brings wrath; but where there is no law, neither is there violation.

16 For this reason it depends on faith, in order that the promise may rest on grace and be guaranteed to all his descendants, not only to the adherents of the law but also to those who share the faith of Abraham (for he is the father of all of us, ¹⁷as it is written, "I have made you the father of many nations")—in the presence of the God in whom he believed, who gives life to the dead and calls into existence the things that do not exist. ¹⁸Hoping against hope, he believed that he would become "the father of many nations," according to what was said, "So numerous shall your descendants be." ¹⁹He did not weaken in faith when he considered his own body, which was already[a] as good as dead (for he was about a hundred years old), or when he considered the barrenness of Sarah's womb. ²⁰No distrust made him waver concerning the promise of God, but he grew strong in his faith as he gave glory to God, ²¹being fully convinced that God was able to do what he had promised. ²²Therefore his faith[b] "was reckoned to him as righteousness." ²³Now the words, "it was reckoned to him," were written not for his sake alone, ²⁴but for ours also. It will be reckoned to us who believe in him who raised Jesus our Lord from the dead, ²⁵who was handed

---

a Other ancient authorities lack *already*  b Gk *Therefore it*

over to death for our trespasses and was raised for our justification.

**5.1** THEREFORE, since we are justified by faith, we[a] have peace with God through our Lord Jesus Christ, [2]through whom we have obtained access[b] to this grace in which we stand; and we[c] boast in our hope of sharing the glory of God. [3]And not only that, but we[c] also boast in our sufferings, knowing that suffering produces endurance, [4]and endurance produces character, and character produces hope, [5]and hope does not disappoint us, because God's love has been poured into our hearts through the Holy Spirit that has been given to us.

## PSALM 14.1–7

*To the leader. Of David.*

FOOLS say in their hearts,
    "There is no God."
They are corrupt, they do
    abominable deeds;
there is no one who does
    good.
[2] The LORD looks down from
    heaven on humankind
to see if there are any who
    are wise,
who seek after God.

[3] They have all gone astray, they
    are all alike perverse;
there is no one who does
    good,
no, not one.

[4] Have they no knowledge, all the
    evildoers
who eat up my people as they
    eat bread,
and do not call upon the
    LORD?

[5] There they shall be in great
    terror,
for God is with the company
    of the righteous.
[6] You would confound the plans of
    the poor,
but the LORD is their refuge.

[7] O that deliverance for Israel
    would come from Zion!
When the LORD restores the
    fortunes of his people,
Jacob will rejoice; Israel will
    be glad.

## PROVERBS 19.17

WHOEVER is kind to the poor lends to the LORD, and will be repaid in full.

---

[a]Other ancient authorities read *let us*  [b]Other ancient authorities add *by faith*  [c]Or *let us*

## 1 CHRONICLES 28.1—29.30

DAVID assembled at Jerusalem all the officials of Israel, the officials of the tribes, the officers of the divisions that served the king, the commanders of the thousands, the commanders of the hundreds, the stewards of all the property and cattle of the king and his sons, together with the palace officials, the mighty warriors, and all the warriors. [2]Then King David rose to his feet and said: "Hear me, my brothers and my people. I had planned to build a house of rest for the ark of the covenant of the Lord, for the footstool of our God; and I made preparations for building. [3]But God said to me, 'You shall not build a house for my name, for you are a warrior and have shed blood.' [4]Yet the Lord God of Israel chose me from all my ancestral house to be king over Israel forever; for he chose Judah as leader, and in the house of Judah my father's house, and among my father's sons he took delight in making me king over all Israel. [5]And of all my sons, for the Lord has given me many, he has chosen my son Solomon to sit upon the throne of the kingdom of the Lord over Israel. [6]He said to me, 'It is your son Solomon who shall build my house and my courts, for I have chosen him to be a son to me, and I will be a father to him. [7]I will establish his kingdom forever if he continues resolute in keeping my commandments and my ordinances, as he is today.' [8]Now therefore in the sight of all Israel, the assembly of the Lord, and in the hearing of our God, observe and search out all the commandments of the Lord your God; that you may possess this good land, and leave it for an inheritance to your children after you forever.

9 "And you, my son Solomon, know the God of your father, and serve him with single mind and willing heart; for the Lord searches every mind, and understands every plan and thought. If you seek him, he will be found by you; but if you forsake him, he will abandon you forever. [10]Take heed now, for the Lord has chosen you to build a house as the sanctuary; be strong, and act."

11 Then David gave his son Solomon the plan of the vestibule of the temple, and of its houses, its treasuries, its upper rooms, and its inner chambers, and of the room for the mercy seat; [a] [12]and the plan of all that he had in mind: for the courts of the house of the Lord, all the surrounding chambers, the treasuries of the house of God, and the treasuries for dedicated gifts; [13]for the divisions of the priests and of the Levites, and all the work of the service in the house of the Lord; for all the vessels for the service in the house of the Lord, [14]the weight of gold for all golden vessels for each service, the weight of silver vessels for each service, [15]the weight of the golden lampstands and their lamps, the weight of gold for each lampstand and its lamps, the weight of silver for a lampstand and its lamps, according to the use of each in the service, [16]the weight of gold for each table for the rows of bread, the silver for the silver tables, [17]and pure gold for the forks, the basins, and the cups; for the golden bowls and the weight of each; for the silver bowls and the weight of each; [18]for the altar of incense made of refined gold, and its weight; also his plan for the

golden chariot of the cherubim that spread their wings and covered the ark of the covenant of the LORD.

19  "All this, in writing at the LORD's direction, he made clear to me—the plan of all the works."

20  David said further to his son Solomon, "Be strong and of good courage, and act. Do not be afraid or dismayed; for the LORD God, my God, is with you. He will not fail you or forsake you, until all the work for the service of the house of the LORD is finished. 21Here are the divisions of the priests and the Levites for all the service of the house of God; and with you in all the work will be every volunteer who has skill for any kind of service; also the officers and all the people will be wholly at your command."

**29.1** KING David said to the whole assembly, "My son Solomon, whom alone God has chosen, is young and inexperienced, and the work is great; for the temple[a] will not be for mortals but for the LORD God. 2So I have provided for the house of my God, so far as I was able, the gold for the things of gold, the silver for the things of silver, and the bronze for the things of bronze, the iron for the things of iron, and wood for the things of wood, besides great quantities of onyx and stones for setting, antimony, colored stones, all sorts of precious stones, and marble in abundance. 3Moreover, in addition to all that I have provided for the holy house, I have a treasure of my own of gold and silver, and because of my devotion to the house of my God I give it to the house of my God: 4three thousand talents of gold, of the gold of Ophir, and seven thousand talents of refined silver, for overlaying the walls of the house, 5and for all the work to be done by artisans, gold for the things of gold and silver for the things of silver. Who

then will offer willingly, consecrating themselves today to the LORD?"

6  Then the leaders of ancestral houses made their freewill offerings, as did also the leaders of the tribes, the commanders of the thousands and of the hundreds, and the officers over the king's work. 7They gave for the service of the house of God five thousand talents and ten thousand darics of gold, ten thousand talents of silver, eighteen thousand talents of bronze, and one hundred thousand talents of iron. 8Whoever had precious stones gave them to the treasury of the house of the LORD, into the care of Jehiel the Gershonite. 9Then the people rejoiced because these had given willingly, for with single mind they had offered freely to the LORD; King David also rejoiced greatly.

10  Then David blessed the LORD in the presence of all the assembly; David said: "Blessed are you, O LORD, the God of our ancestor Israel, forever and ever. 11Yours, O LORD, are the greatness, the power, the glory, the victory, and the majesty; for all that is in the heavens and on the earth is yours; yours is the kingdom, O LORD, and you are exalted as head above all. 12Riches and honor come from you, and you rule over all. In your hand are power and might; and it is in your hand to make great and to give strength to all. 13And now, our God, we give thanks to you and praise your glorious name.

14  "But who am I, and what is my people, that we should be able to make this freewill offering? For all things come from you, and of your own have we given you. 15For we are aliens and transients before you, as were all our ancestors; our days on the earth are like a shadow, and there is no hope. 16O LORD our God, all this abundance that we have provided for building you a house for your holy name comes from

---

aHeb *fortress*

your hand and is all your own. [17]I know, my God, that you search the heart, and take pleasure in uprightness; in the uprightness of my heart I have freely offered all these things, and now I have seen your people, who are present here, offering freely and joyously to you. [18]O Lord, the God of Abraham, Isaac, and Israel, our ancestors, keep forever such purposes and thoughts in the hearts of your people, and direct their hearts toward you. [19]Grant to my son Solomon that with single mind he may keep your commandments, your decrees, and your statutes, performing all of them, and that he may build the temple[a] for which I have made provision."

20 Then David said to the whole assembly, "Bless the Lord your God." And all the assembly blessed the Lord, the God of their ancestors, and bowed their heads and prostrated themselves before the Lord and the king. [21]On the next day they offered sacrifices and burnt offerings to the Lord, a thousand bulls, a thousand rams, and a thousand lambs, with their libations, and sacrifices in abundance for all Israel; [22]and they ate and drank before the Lord on that day with great joy.

They made David's son Solomon king a second time; they anointed him as the Lord's prince, and Zadok as priest. [23]Then Solomon sat on the throne of the Lord, succeeding his father David as king; he prospered, and all Israel obeyed him. [24]All the leaders and the mighty warriors, and also all the sons of King David, pledged their allegiance to King Solomon. [25]The Lord highly exalted Solomon in the sight of all Israel, and bestowed upon him such royal majesty as had not been on any king before him in Israel.

26 Thus David son of Jesse reigned over all Israel. [27]The period that he reigned over Israel was forty years; he reigned seven years in Hebron, and thirty-three years in Jerusalem. [28]He died in a good old age, full of days, riches, and honor; and his son Solomon succeeded him. [29]Now the acts of King David, from first to last, are written in the records of the seer Samuel, and in the records of the prophet Nathan, and in the records of the seer Gad, [30]with accounts of all his rule and his might and of the events that befell him and Israel and all the kingdoms of the earth.

## ROMANS 5.6–21

For while we were still weak, at the right time Christ died for the ungodly. [7]Indeed, rarely will anyone die for a righteous person—though perhaps for a good person someone might actually dare to die. [8]But God proves his love for us in that while we still were sinners Christ died for us. [9]Much more surely then, now that we have been justified by his blood, will we be saved through him from the wrath of God.[b] [10]For if while we were enemies, we were reconciled to God through the death of his Son, much more surely, having been reconciled, will we be saved by his life. [11]But more than that, we even boast in God through our Lord Jesus Christ, through whom we have now received reconciliation.

12 Therefore, just as sin came into the world through one man, and death came through sin, and so death spread to all because all have sinned— [13]sin was indeed in the world before the law, but sin is not reckoned when there is no law. [14]Yet death exercised dominion from Adam to Moses, even over those whose sins were not like the transgression of Adam, who is a type of the one who was to come.

15 But the free gift is not like the trespass. For if the many died through

the one man's trespass, much more surely have the grace of God and the free gift in the grace of the one man, Jesus Christ, abounded for the many. [16]And the free gift is not like the effect of the one man's sin. For the judgment following one trespass brought condemnation, but the free gift following many trespasses brings justification. [17]If, because of the one man's trespass, death exercised dominion through that one, much more surely will those who receive the abundance of grace and the free gift of righteousness exercise dominion in life through the one man, Jesus Christ.

18 Therefore just as one man's trespass led to condemnation for all, so one man's act of righteousness leads to justification and life for all. [19]For just as by the one man's disobedience the many were made sinners, so by the one man's obedience the many will be made righteous. [20]But law came in, with the result that the trespass multiplied; but where sin increased, grace abounded all the more, [21]so that, just as sin exercised dominion in death, so grace might also exercise dominion through justification[a] leading to eternal life through Jesus Christ our Lord.

## PSALM 15.1–5

*A Psalm of David.*

O LORD, who may abide in your
    tent?
Who may dwell on your
    holy hill?

2   Those who walk blamelessly,
        and do what is right,
    and speak the truth from their
        heart;
3   who do not slander with their
        tongue,
    and do no evil to their
        friends,
    nor take up a reproach
        against their neighbors;
4   in whose eyes the wicked are
        despised,
    but who honor those who fear
        the LORD;
    who stand by their oath even to
        their hurt;
5   who do not lend money at
        interest,
    and do not take a bribe
        against the innocent.

Those who do these things shall
    never be moved.

## PROVERBS 19.18–19

DISCIPLINE your children while
    there is hope;
    do not set your heart on
        their destruction.
19  A violent tempered person will
        pay the penalty;
    if you effect a rescue, you will
        only have to do it
        again. [b]

---

[a]Or *righteousness*   [b]Meaning of Heb uncertain

# JULY 20

## 2 CHRONICLES 1.1—3.17

Solomon son of David established himself in his kingdom; the Lord his God was with him and made him exceedingly great.

2 Solomon summoned all Israel, the commanders of the thousands and of the hundreds, the judges, and all the leaders of all Israel, the heads of families. ³Then Solomon, and the whole assembly with him, went to the high place that was at Gibeon; for God's tent of meeting, which Moses the servant of the Lord had made in the wilderness, was there. ⁴(But David had brought the ark of God up from Kiriath-jearim to the place that David had prepared for it; for he had pitched a tent for it in Jerusalem.) ⁵Moreover the bronze altar that Bezalel son of Uri, son of Hur, had made, was there in front of the tabernacle of the Lord. And Solomon and the assembly inquired at it. ⁶Solomon went up there to the bronze altar before the Lord, which was at the tent of meeting, and offered a thousand burnt offerings on it.

7 That night God appeared to Solomon, and said to him, "Ask what I should give you." ⁸Solomon said to God, "You have shown great and steadfast love to my father David, and have made me succeed him as king. ⁹O Lord God, let your promise to my father David now be fulfilled, for you have made me king over a people as numerous as the dust of the earth. ¹⁰Give me now wisdom and knowledge to go out and come in before this people, for who can rule this great people of yours?" ¹¹God answered Solomon, "Because this was in your heart, and you have not asked for possessions, wealth, honor, or the life of those who hate you, and have not even asked for long life, but have asked for wisdom and knowledge for yourself that you may rule my people over whom I have made you king, ¹²wisdom and knowledge are granted to you. I will also give you riches, possessions, and honor, such as none of the kings had who were before you, and none after you shall have the like." ¹³So Solomon came from^a the high place at Gibeon, from the tent of meeting, to Jerusalem. And he reigned over Israel.

14 Solomon gathered together chariots and horses; he had fourteen hundred chariots and twelve thousand horses, which he stationed in the chariot cities and with the king in Jerusalem. ¹⁵The king made silver and gold as common in Jerusalem as stone, and he made cedar as plentiful as the sycamore of the Shephelah. ¹⁶Solomon's horses were imported from Egypt and Kue; the king's traders received them from Kue at the prevailing price. ¹⁷They imported from Egypt, and then exported, a chariot for six hundred shekels of silver, and a horse for one hundred fifty; so through them these were exported to all the kings of the Hittites and the kings of Aram.

2^b.1 Solomon decided to build a temple for the name of the Lord, and a royal palace for himself. ²^cSolomon conscripted seventy thousand laborers and eighty thousand stonecutters in the hill country, with three thousand six hundred to oversee them.

3 Solomon sent word to King Huram of Tyre: "Once you dealt with my father David and sent him cedar to build himself a house to live in. ⁴I am now

about to build a house for the name of the LORD my God and dedicate it to him for offering fragrant incense before him, and for the regular offering of the rows of bread, and for burnt offerings morning and evening, on the sabbaths and the new moons and the appointed festivals of the LORD our God, as ordained forever for Israel. ⁵The house that I am about to build will be great, for our God is greater than other gods. ⁶But who is able to build him a house, since heaven, even highest heaven, cannot contain him? Who am I to build a house for him, except as a place to make offerings before him? ⁷So now send me an artisan skilled to work in gold, silver, bronze, and iron, and in purple, crimson, and blue fabrics, trained also in engraving, to join the skilled workers who are with me in Judah and Jerusalem, whom my father David provided. ⁸Send me also cedar, cypress, and algum timber from Lebanon, for I know that your servants are skilled in cutting Lebanon timber. My servants will work with your servants ⁹to prepare timber for me in abundance, for the house I am about to build will be great and wonderful. ¹⁰I will provide for your servants, those who cut the timber, twenty thousand cors of crushed wheat, twenty thousand cors of barley, twenty thousand baths[a] of wine, and twenty thousand baths of oil."

11 Then King Huram of Tyre answered in a letter that he sent to Solomon, "Because the LORD loves his people he has made you king over them." ¹²Huram also said, "Blessed be the LORD God of Israel, who made heaven and earth, who has given King David a wise son, endowed with discretion and understanding, who will build a temple for the LORD, and a royal palace for himself.

13 "I have dispatched Huram-abi, a skilled artisan, endowed with understanding, ¹⁴the son of one of the Danite women, his father a Tyrian. He is trained to work in gold, silver, bronze, iron, stone, and wood, and in purple, blue, and crimson fabrics and fine linen, and to do all sorts of engraving and execute any design that may be assigned him, with your artisans, the artisans of my lord, your father David. ¹⁵Now, as for the wheat, barley, oil, and wine, of which my lord has spoken, let him send them to his servants. ¹⁶We will cut whatever timber you need from Lebanon, and bring it to you as rafts by sea to Joppa; you will take it up to Jerusalem."

17 Then Solomon took a census of all the aliens who were residing in the land of Israel, after the census that his father David had taken; and there were found to be one hundred fifty-three thousand six hundred. ¹⁸Seventy thousand of them he assigned as laborers, eighty thousand as stonecutters in the hill country, and three thousand six hundred as overseers to make the people work.

3.1 SOLOMON began to build the house of the LORD in Jerusalem on Mount Moriah, where the LORD had appeared to his father David, at the place that David had designated, on the threshing floor of Ornan the Jebusite. ²He began to build on the second day of the second month of the fourth year of his reign. ³These are Solomon's measurements[b] for building the house of God: the length, in cubits of the old standard, was sixty cubits, and the width twenty cubits. ⁴The vestibule in front of the nave of the house was twenty cubits long, across the width of the house;[c] and its height was one hundred twenty cubits. He overlaid it on the inside with pure gold. ⁵The nave he lined with cypress, covered it with fine gold, and

a A Hebrew measure of volume   b Syr: Heb *foundations*   c Compare 1 Kings 6.3: Meaning of Heb uncertain made palms and chains on it. ⁶He adorned the house with settings of precious stones. The gold was gold from Parvaim. ⁷So he lined the house with gold—its beams, its thresholds, its walls, and its doors; and he carved cherubim on the walls.

8  He made the most holy place; its length, corresponding to the width of the house, was twenty cubits, and its width was twenty cubits; he overlaid it with six hundred talents of fine gold. ⁹The weight of the nails was fifty shekels of gold. He overlaid the upper chambers with gold.

10  In the most holy place he made two carved cherubim and overlaid[a] them with gold. ¹¹The wings of the cherubim together extended twenty cubits: one wing of the one, five cubits long, touched the wall of the house, and its other wing, five cubits long, touched the wing of the other cherub; ¹²and of this cherub, one wing, five cubits long, touched the wall of the house, and the other wing, also five cubits long, was joined to the wing of the first cherub. ¹³The wings of these cherubim extended twenty cubits; the cherubim[b] stood on their feet, facing the nave. ¹⁴And Solomon[c] made the curtain of blue and purple and crimson fabrics and fine linen, and worked cherubim into it.

15  In front of the house he made two pillars thirty-five cubits high, with a capital of five cubits on the top of each. ¹⁶He made encircling[d] chains and put them on the tops of the pillars; and he made one hundred pomegranates, and put them on the chains. ¹⁷He set up the pillars in front of the temple, one on the right, the other on the left; the one on the right he called Jachin, and the one on the left, Boaz.

## ROMANS 6.1–23

WHAT then are we to say? Should we continue in sin in order that grace may abound? ²By no means! How can we who died to sin go on living in it? ³Do you not know that all of us who have been baptized into Christ Jesus were baptized into his death? ⁴Therefore we have been buried with him by baptism into death, so that, just as Christ was raised from the dead by the glory of the Father, so we too might walk in newness of life.

5  For if we have been united with him in a death like his, we will certainly be united with him in a resurrection like his. ⁶We know that our old self was crucified with him so that the body of sin might be destroyed, and we might no longer be enslaved to sin. ⁷For whoever has died is freed from sin. ⁸But if we have died with Christ, we believe that we will also live with him. ⁹We know that Christ, being raised from the dead, will never die again; death no longer has dominion over him. ¹⁰The death he died, he died to sin, once for all; but the life he lives, he lives to God. ¹¹So you also must consider yourselves dead to sin and alive to God in Christ Jesus.

12  Therefore, do not let sin exercise dominion in your mortal bodies, to make you obey their passions. ¹³No longer present your members to sin as instruments[e] of wickedness, but present yourselves to God as those who have been brought from death to life, and present your members to God as instruments[e] of righteousness. ¹⁴For sin will have no dominion over you, since you are not under law but under grace.

15  What then? Should we sin because we are not under law but under grace? By no means! ¹⁶Do you not

---

aHeb *they overlaid*   bHeb *they*   cHeb *he*   dCn: Heb *in the inner sanctuary*   eOr *weapons*

know that if you present yourselves to anyone as obedient slaves, you are slaves of the one whom you obey, either of sin, which leads to death, or of obedience, which leads to righteousness? [17]But thanks be to God that you, having once been slaves of sin, have become obedient from the heart to the form of teaching to which you were entrusted, [18]and that you, having been set free from sin, have become slaves of righteousness. [19]I am speaking in human terms because of your natural limitations.[a] For just as you once presented your members as slaves to impurity and to greater and greater iniquity, so now present your members as slaves to righteousness for sanctification.

20 When you were slaves of sin, you were free in regard to righteousness. [21]So what advantage did you then get from the things of which you now are ashamed? The end of those things is death. [22]But now that you have been freed from sin and enslaved to God, the advantage you get is sanctification. The end is eternal life. [23]For the wages of sin is death, but the free gift of God is eternal life in Christ Jesus our Lord.

## PSALM 16.1–11

*A Miktam of David.*

PROTECT me, O God, for in you
    I take refuge.
2  I say to the LORD, "You
    are my Lord;
I have no good apart from
    you."[b]

3  As for the holy ones in the land,
    they are the noble,
in whom is all my delight.

4  Those who choose another god
    multiply their sorrows;[c]

their drink offerings of blood I
    will not pour out
or take their names upon my
    lips.

5  The LORD is my chosen portion
    and my cup;
you hold my lot.
6  The boundary lines have fallen
    for me in pleasant places;
I have a goodly heritage.

7  I bless the LORD who gives me
    counsel;
in the night also my heart
    instructs me.
8  I keep the LORD always before
    me;
because he is at my right
    hand, I shall not be
    moved.

9  Therefore my heart is glad, and
    my soul rejoices;
my body also rests secure.
10  For you do not give me up to
    Sheol,
or let your faithful one see
    the Pit.

11  You show me the path of life.
    In your presence there is
    fullness of joy;
in your right hand are
    pleasures forevermore.

## PROVERBS 19.20–21

LISTEN to advice and accept
    instruction,
that you may gain wisdom
    for the future.
21  The human mind may devise
    many plans,
but it is the purpose of the
    LORD that will be
    established.

a Gk *the weakness of your flesh*  b Jerome Tg: Meaning of Heb uncertain  c Cn: Meaning of Heb uncertain

## 2 CHRONICLES 4.1—6.11

H<sub>E</sub> [Solomon] made an altar of bronze, twenty cubits long, twenty cubits wide, and ten cubits high. 2Then he made the molten sea; it was round, ten cubits from rim to rim, and five cubits high. A line of thirty cubits would encircle it completely. 3Under it were panels all around, each of ten cubits, surrounding the sea; there were two rows of panels, cast when it was cast. 4It stood on twelve oxen, three facing north, three facing west, three facing south, and three facing east; the sea was set on them. The hindquarters of each were toward the inside. 5Its thickness was a handbreadth; its rim was made like the rim of a cup, like the flower of a lily; it held three thousand baths.ᵃ 6He also made ten basins in which to wash, and set five on the right side, and five on the left. In these they were to rinse what was used for the burnt offering. The sea was for the priests to wash in.

7 He made ten golden lampstands as prescribed, and set them in the temple, five on the south side and five on the north. 8He also made ten tables and placed them in the temple, five on the right side and five on the left. And he made one hundred basins of gold. 9He made the court of the priests, and the great court, and doors for the court; he overlaid their doors with bronze. 10He set the sea at the southeast corner of the house.

11 And Huram made the pots, the shovels, and the basins. Thus Huram finished the work that he did for King Solomon on the house of God: 12the two pillars, the bowls, and the two capitals on the top of the pillars; and the two latticeworks to cover the two bowls of the capitals that were on the top of the pillars; 13the four hundred pomegranates for the two latticeworks, two rows of pomegranates for each latticework, to cover the two bowls of the capitals that were on the pillars. 14He made the stands, the basins on the stands, 15the one sea, and the twelve oxen underneath it. 16The pots, the shovels, the forks, and all the equipment for these Huram-abi made of burnished bronze for King Solomon for the house of the L<sub>ORD</sub>. 17In the plain of the Jordan the king cast them, in the clay ground between Succoth and Zeredah. 18Solomon made all these things in great quantities, so that the weight of the bronze was not determined.

19 So Solomon made all the things that were in the house of God: the golden altar, the tables for the bread of the Presence, 20the lampstands and their lamps of pure gold to burn before the inner sanctuary, as prescribed; 21the flowers, the lamps, and the tongs, of purest gold; 22the snuffers, basins, ladles, and firepans, of pure gold. As for the entrance to the temple: the inner doors to the most holy place and the doors of the nave of the temple were of gold.

5.1 T<sub>HUS</sub> all the work that Solomon did for the house of the L<sub>ORD</sub> was finished. Solomon brought in the things that his father David had dedicated, and stored the silver, the gold, and all the vessels in the treasuries of the house of God.

2 Then Solomon assembled the elders of Israel and all the heads of the tribes, the leaders of the ancestral houses of the people of Israel, in Jeru-

---

ᵃ A Hebrew measure of volume

salem, to bring up the ark of the covenant of the Lord out of the city of David, which is Zion. ³And all the Israelites assembled before the king at the festival that is in the seventh month. ⁴And all the elders of Israel came, and the Levites carried the ark. ⁵So they brought up the ark, the tent of meeting, and all the holy vessels that were in the tent; the priests and the Levites brought them up. ⁶King Solomon and all the congregation of Israel, who had assembled before him, were before the ark, sacrificing so many sheep and oxen that they could not be numbered or counted. ⁷Then the priests brought the ark of the covenant of the Lord to its place, in the inner sanctuary of the house, in the most holy place, underneath the wings of the cherubim. ⁸For the cherubim spread out their wings over the place of the ark, so that the cherubim made a covering above the ark and its poles. ⁹The poles were so long that the ends of the poles were seen from the holy place in front of the inner sanctuary; but they could not be seen from outside; they are there to this day. ¹⁰There was nothing in the ark except the two tablets that Moses put there at Horeb, where the Lord made a covenantᵃ with the people of Israel after they came out of Egypt.

11  Now when the priests came out of the holy place (for all the priests who were present had sanctified themselves, without regard to their divisions, ¹²and all the levitical singers, Asaph, Heman, and Jeduthun, their sons and kindred, arrayed in fine linen, with cymbals, harps, and lyres, stood east of the altar with one hundred twenty priests who were trumpeters). ¹³It was the duty of the trumpeters and singers to make themselves heard in unison in praise and thanksgiving to the Lord, and when the song was raised, with trumpets and cymbals and other musical instruments, in praise to the Lord,

"For he is good,
    for his steadfast love endures
        forever,"

the house, the house of the Lord, was filled with a cloud, ¹⁴so that the priests could not stand to minister because of the cloud; for the glory of the Lord filled the house of God.

**6.1** Then Solomon said, "The Lord has said that he would reside in thick darkness. ²I have built you an exalted house, a place for you to reside in forever."

3  Then the king turned around and blessed all the assembly of Israel, while all the assembly of Israel stood. ⁴And he said, "Blessed be the Lord, the God of Israel, who with his hand has fulfilled what he promised with his mouth to my father David, saying, ⁵'Since the day that I brought my people out of the land of Egypt, I have not chosen a city from any of the tribes of Israel in which to build a house, so that my name might be there, and I chose no one as ruler over my people Israel; ⁶but I have chosen Jerusalem in order that my name may be there, and I have chosen David to be over my people Israel.' ⁷My father David had it in mind to build a house for the name of the Lord, the God of Israel. ⁸But the Lord said to my father David, 'You did well to consider building a house for my name; ⁹nevertheless you shall not build the house, but your son who shall be born to you shall build the house for my name.' ¹⁰Now the Lord has fulfilled his promise that he made; for I have succeeded my father David, and sit on the throne of Israel, as the Lord promised, and have built the house for the name of the Lord, the God of Israel. ¹¹There I have set the ark, in which is the covenant of

ᵃHeb lacks *a covenant*

the LORD that he made with the people of Israel."

## ROMANS 7.1–13

Do you not know, brothers and sisters[a]—for I am speaking to those who know the law—that the law is binding on a person only during that person's lifetime? [2]Thus a married woman is bound by the law to her husband as long as he lives; but if her husband dies, she is discharged from the law concerning the husband. [3]Accordingly, she will be called an adulteress if she lives with another man while her husband is alive. But if her husband dies, she is free from that law, and if she marries another man, she is not an adulteress.

4 In the same way, my friends,[a] you have died to the law through the body of Christ, so that you may belong to another, to him who has been raised from the dead in order that we may bear fruit for God. [5]While we were living in the flesh, our sinful passions, aroused by the law, were at work in our members to bear fruit for death. [6]But now we are discharged from the law, dead to that which held us captive, so that we are slaves not under the old written code but in the new life of the Spirit.

7 What then should we say? That the law is sin? By no means! Yet, if it had not been for the law, I would not have known sin. I would not have known what it is to covet if the law had not said, "You shall not covet." [8]But sin, seizing an opportunity in the commandment, produced in me all kinds of covetousness. Apart from the law sin lies dead. [9]I was once alive apart from the law, but when the commandment came, sin revived [10]and I died, and the very commandment that promised life proved to be death to me. [11]For sin, seizing an opportunity in the command-

ment, deceived me and through it killed me. [12]So the law is holy, and the commandment is holy and just and good.

13 Did what is good, then, bring death to me? By no means! It was sin, working death in me through what is good, in order that sin might be shown to be sin, and through the commandment might become sinful beyond measure.

## PSALM 17.1–15

*A Prayer of David.*

Hear a just cause, O LORD;
   attend to my cry;
 give ear to my prayer from
   lips free of deceit.
2  From you let my vindication
   come;
   let your eyes see the right.

3  If you try my heart, if you visit
   me by night,
   if you test me, you will find
     no wickedness in me;
   my mouth does not
     transgress.
4  As for what others do, by the
   word of your lips
   I have avoided the ways of
     the violent.
5  My steps have held fast to your
   paths;
   my feet have not slipped.

6  I call upon you, for you will
   answer me, O God;
   incline your ear to me, hear
     my words.
7  Wondrously show your steadfast
   love,
   O savior of those who seek
     refuge
   from their adversaries at your
     right hand.

8  Guard me as the apple of the
   eye;

[a]Gk *brothers*

    hide me in the shadow of
      your wings,
9  from the wicked who despoil
      me,
    my deadly enemies who
      surround me.
10  They close their hearts to pity;
    with their mouths they speak
      arrogantly.
11  They track me down;[a] now
      they surround me;
    they set their eyes to cast me
      to the ground.
12  They are like a lion eager to
      tear,
    like a young lion lurking in
      ambush.

13  Rise up, O Lord, confront them,
      overthrow them!
    By your sword deliver my life
      from the wicked,
14  from mortals—by your hand,
      O Lord—
    from mortals whose portion in
      life is in this world.

    May their bellies be filled with
      what you have stored up
      for them;
    may their children have more
      than enough;
    may they leave something
      over to their little ones.

15  As for me, I shall behold your
      face in righteousness;
    when I awake I shall be
      satisfied, beholding your
      likeness.

## PROVERBS 19.22–23

WHAT is desirable in a person
      is loyalty,
    and it is better to be poor
      than a liar.
23  The fear of the Lord is life
      indeed;
    filled with it one rests secure
    and suffers no harm.

# JULY 22

## 2 CHRONICLES 6.12—8.10

THEN Solomon[b] stood before the altar of the Lord in the presence of the whole assembly of Israel, and spread out his hands. 13Solomon had made a bronze platform five cubits long, five cubits wide, and three cubits high, and had set it in the court; and he stood on it. Then he knelt on his knees in the presence of the whole assembly of Israel, and spread out his hands toward heaven. 14He said, "O Lord, God of Israel, there is no God like you, in heaven or on earth, keeping covenant in steadfast love with your servants who walk before you with all their heart— 15you who have kept for your servant, my father David, what you promised to him. Indeed, you promised with your mouth and this day have fulfilled with your hand. 16Therefore, O Lord, God of Israel, keep for your servant, my father David, that which you promised him, saying, 'There shall never fail you a successor before me to sit on the throne of Israel, if only your

aOne Ms Compare Syr: MT *Our steps*   bHeb *he*

children keep to their way, to walk in my law as you have walked before me.' [17]Therefore, O Lord, God of Israel, let your word be confirmed, which you promised to your servant David.

18 "But will God indeed reside with mortals on earth? Even heaven and the highest heaven cannot contain you, how much less this house that I have built! [19]Regard your servant's prayer and his plea, O Lord my God, heeding the cry and the prayer that your servant prays to you. [20]May your eyes be open day and night toward this house, the place where you promised to set your name, and may you heed the prayer that your servant prays toward this place. [21]And hear the plea of your servant and of your people Israel, when they pray toward this place; may you hear from heaven your dwelling place; hear and forgive.

22 "If someone sins against another and is required to take an oath and comes and swears before your altar in this house, [23]may you hear from heaven, and act, and judge your servants, repaying the guilty by bringing their conduct on their own head, and vindicating those who are in the right by rewarding them in accordance with their righteousness.

24 "When your people Israel, having sinned against you, are defeated before an enemy but turn again to you, confess your name, pray and plead with you in this house, [25]may you hear from heaven, and forgive the sin of your people Israel, and bring them again to the land that you gave to them and to their ancestors.

26 "When heaven is shut up and there is no rain because they have sinned against you, and then they pray toward this place, confess your name, and turn from their sin, because you punish them, [27]may you hear in heaven, forgive the sin of your servants, your people Israel, when you teach them the good way in which they should walk;

and send down rain upon your land, which you have given to your people as an inheritance.

28 "If there is famine in the land, if there is plague, blight, mildew, locust, or caterpillar; if their enemies besiege them in any of the settlements of the lands; whatever suffering, whatever sickness there is; [29]whatever prayer, whatever plea from any individual or from all your people Israel, all knowing their own suffering and their own sorrows so that they stretch out their hands toward this house; [30]may you hear from heaven, your dwelling place, forgive, and render to all whose heart you know, according to all their ways, for only you know the human heart. [31]Thus may they fear you and walk in your ways all the days that they live in the land that you gave to our ancestors.

32 "Likewise when foreigners, who are not of your people Israel, come from a distant land because of your great name, and your mighty hand, and your outstretched arm, when they come and pray toward this house, [33]may you hear from heaven your dwelling place, and do whatever the foreigners ask of you, in order that all the peoples of the earth may know your name and fear you, as do your people Israel, and that they may know that your name has been invoked on this house that I have built.

34 "If your people go out to battle against their enemies, by whatever way you shall send them, and they pray to you toward this city that you have chosen and the house that I have built for your name, [35]then hear from heaven their prayer and their plea, and maintain their cause.

36 "If they sin against you—for there is no one who does not sin—and you are angry with them and give them to an enemy, so that they are carried away captive to a land far or near; [37]then if they come to their senses in the land to which they have been taken

captive, and repent, and plead with you in the land of their captivity, saying, 'We have sinned, and have done wrong; we have acted wickedly'; <sup>38</sup>if they repent with all their heart and soul in the land of their captivity, to which they were taken captive, and pray toward their land, which you gave to their ancestors, the city that you have chosen, and the house that I have built for your name, <sup>39</sup>then hear from heaven your dwelling place their prayer and their pleas, maintain their cause and forgive your people who have sinned against you. <sup>40</sup>Now, O my God, let your eyes be open and your ears attentive to prayer from this place.

<sup>41</sup>    "Now rise up, O Lᴏʀᴅ God, and
            go to your resting place,
        you and the ark of your
            might.
    Let your priests, O Lᴏʀᴅ God,
            be clothed with salvation,
        and let your faithful rejoice in
            your goodness.
<sup>42</sup>    O Lᴏʀᴅ God, do not reject your
            anointed one.
        Remember your steadfast
            love for your servant
            David."

**7.1** Wʜᴇɴ Solomon had ended his prayer, fire came down from heaven and consumed the burnt offering and the sacrifices; and the glory of the Lᴏʀᴅ filled the temple. <sup>2</sup>The priests could not enter the house of the Lᴏʀᴅ, because the glory of the Lᴏʀᴅ filled the Lᴏʀᴅ's house. <sup>3</sup>When all the people of Israel saw the fire come down and the glory of the Lᴏʀᴅ on the temple, they bowed down on the pavement with their faces to the ground, and worshiped and gave thanks to the Lᴏʀᴅ, saying,

    "For he is good,
        for his steadfast love endures
            forever."

<sup>4</sup>    Then the king and all the people offered sacrifice before the Lᴏʀᴅ. <sup>5</sup>King Solomon offered as a sacrifice twenty-two thousand oxen and one hundred twenty thousand sheep. So the king and all the people dedicated the house of God. <sup>6</sup>The priests stood at their posts; the Levites also, with the instruments for music to the Lᴏʀᴅ that King David had made for giving thanks to the Lᴏʀᴅ—for his steadfast love endures forever—whenever David offered praises by their ministry. Opposite them the priests sounded trumpets; and all Israel stood.

<sup>7</sup>    Solomon consecrated the middle of the court that was in front of the house of the Lᴏʀᴅ; for there he offered the burnt offerings and the fat of the offerings of well-being because the bronze altar Solomon had made could not hold the burnt offering and the grain offering and the fat parts.

<sup>8</sup>    At that time Solomon held the festival for seven days, and all Israel with him, a very great congregation, from Lebo-hamath to the Wadi of Egypt. <sup>9</sup>On the eighth day they held a solemn assembly; for they had observed the dedication of the altar seven days and the festival seven days. <sup>10</sup>On the twenty-third day of the seventh month he sent the people away to their homes, joyful and in good spirits because of the goodness that the Lᴏʀᴅ had shown to David and to Solomon and to his people Israel.

<sup>11</sup>    Thus Solomon finished the house of the Lᴏʀᴅ and the king's house; all that Solomon had planned to do in the house of the Lᴏʀᴅ and in his own house he successfully accomplished.

<sup>12</sup>    Then the Lᴏʀᴅ appeared to Solomon in the night and said to him: "I have heard your prayer, and have chosen this place for myself as a house of sacrifice. <sup>13</sup>When I shut up the heavens so that there is no rain, or command the locust to devour the land, or send pestilence among my people, <sup>14</sup>if my people who are called by my name humble themselves, pray, seek my face, and turn from their wicked ways, then I will

hear from heaven, and will forgive their sin and heal their land. [15]Now my eyes will be open and my ears attentive to the prayer that is made in this place. [16]For now I have chosen and consecrated this house so that my name may be there forever; my eyes and my heart will be there for all time. [17]As for you, if you walk before me, as your father David walked, doing according to all that I have commanded you and keeping my statutes and my ordinances, [18]then I will establish your royal throne, as I made covenant with your father David saying, 'You shall never lack a successor to rule over Israel.'

19 "But if you[a] turn aside and forsake my statutes and my commandments that I have set before you, and go and serve other gods and worship them, [20]then I will pluck you[b] up from the land that I have given you;[b] and this house, which I have consecrated for my name, I will cast out of my sight, and will make it a proverb and a byword among all peoples. [21]And regarding this house, now exalted, everyone passing by will be astonished, and say, 'Why has the Lord done such a thing to this land and to this house?' [22]Then they will say, 'Because they abandoned the Lord the God of their ancestors who brought them out of the land of Egypt, and they adopted other gods, and worshiped them and served them; therefore he has brought all this calamity upon them.'"

[8.1] At the end of twenty years, during which Solomon had built the house of the Lord and his own house, [2]Solomon rebuilt the cities that Huram had given to him, and settled the people of Israel in them.

3 Solomon went to Hamath-zobah, and captured it. [4]He built Tadmor in the wilderness and all the storage towns that he built in Hamath. [5]He also built Upper Beth-horon and Lower Beth-horon, fortified cities, with walls, gates, and bars, [6]and Baalath, as well as all Solomon's storage towns, and all the towns for his chariots, the towns for his cavalry, and whatever Solomon desired to build, in Jerusalem, in Lebanon, and in all the land of his dominion. [7]All the people who were left of the Hittites, the Amorites, the Perizzites, the Hivites, and the Jebusites, who were not of Israel, [8]from their descendants who were still left in the land, whom the people of Israel had not destroyed— these Solomon conscripted for forced labor, as is still the case today. [9]But of the people of Israel Solomon made no slaves for his work; they were soldiers, and his officers, the commanders of his chariotry and cavalry. [10]These were the chief officers of King Solomon, two hundred fifty of them, who exercised authority over the people.

## ROMANS 7.14—8.8

FOR we know that the law is spiritual; but I am of the flesh, sold into slavery under sin.[c] [15]I do not understand my own actions. For I do not do what I want, but I do the very thing I hate. [16]Now if I do what I do not want, I agree that the law is good. [17]But in fact it is no longer I that do it, but sin that dwells within me. [18]For I know that nothing good dwells within me, that is, in my flesh. I can will what is right, but I cannot do it. [19]For I do not do the good I want, but the evil I do not want is what I do. [20]Now if I do what I do not want, it is no longer I that do it, but sin that dwells within me.

21 So I find it to be a law that when I want to do what is good, evil lies close at hand. [22]For I delight in the law of God in my inmost self, [23]but I see in my members another law at war with the law of my mind, making me captive to

the law of sin that dwells in my members. ²⁴Wretched man that I am! Who will rescue me from this body of death? ²⁵Thanks be to God through Jesus Christ our Lord!

So then, with my mind I am a slave to the law of God, but with my flesh I am a slave to the law of sin.

**8.1** THERE is therefore now no condemnation for those who are in Christ Jesus. ²For the law of the Spirit[a] of life in Christ Jesus has set you[b] free from the law of sin and of death. ³For God has done what the law, weakened by the flesh, could not do: by sending his own Son in the likeness of sinful flesh, and to deal with sin,[c] he condemned sin in the flesh, ⁴so that the just requirement of the law might be fulfilled in us, who walk not according to the flesh but according to the Spirit.[a] ⁵For those who live according to the flesh set their minds on the things of the flesh, but those who live according to the Spirit[a] set their minds on the things of the Spirit.[a] ⁶To set the mind on the flesh is death, but to set the mind on the Spirit[a] is life and peace. ⁷For this reason the mind that is set on the flesh is hostile to God; it does not submit to God's law—indeed it cannot, ⁸and those who are in the flesh cannot please God.

## PSALM 18.1–15

*To the leader. A Psalm of David the servant of the LORD, who addressed the words of this song to the LORD on the day when the LORD delivered him from the hand of all his enemies, and from the hand of Saul. He said:*

I LOVE you, O LORD, my strength.
2   The LORD is my rock, my
    fortress, and my
    deliverer,
my God, my rock in whom I
    take refuge,
my shield, and the horn of my
    salvation, my stronghold.
3   I call upon the LORD, who is
    worthy to be praised,
so I shall be saved from my
    enemies.

4   The cords of death
    encompassed me;
the torrents of perdition
    assailed me;
5   the cords of Sheol entangled
    me;
the snares of death
    confronted me.

6   In my distress I called upon the
    LORD;
to my God I cried for help.
From his temple he heard my
    voice,
and my cry to him reached
    his ears.

7   Then the earth reeled and
    rocked;
the foundations also of the
    mountains trembled
and quaked, because he was
    angry.
8   Smoke went up from his
    nostrils,
and devouring fire from his
    mouth;
glowing coals flamed forth
    from him.
9   He bowed the heavens, and
    came down;
thick darkness was under his
    feet.
10   He rode on a cherub, and flew;
he came swiftly upon the
    wings of the wind.
11   He made darkness his covering
    around him,
his canopy thick clouds dark
    with water.

a Or *spirit*   b Here the Greek word *you* is singular number; other ancient authorities read *me* or *us*
c Or *and as a sin offering*

12 Out of the brightness before
       him
     there broke through his
       clouds
     hailstones and coals of fire.
13 The LORD also thundered in the
       heavens,
     and the Most High uttered his
       voice. [a]
14 And he sent out his arrows, and
       scattered them;
     he flashed forth lightnings,
       and routed them.
15 Then the channels of the sea
       were seen,

and the foundations of the
  world were laid bare
at your rebuke, O LORD,
  at the blast of the breath of
    your nostrils.

## PROVERBS 19.24–25

THE lazy person buries a hand
     in the dish,
   and will not even bring it
     back to the mouth.
25 Strike a scoffer, and the simple
     will learn prudence;
   reprove the intelligent, and
     they will gain knowledge.

# JULY 23

## 2 CHRONICLES 8.11—10.19

SOLOMON brought Pharaoh's daughter from the city of David to the house that he had built for her, for he said, "My wife shall not live in the house of King David of Israel, for the places to which the ark of the LORD has come are holy."

12 Then Solomon offered up burnt offerings to the LORD on the altar of the LORD that he had built in front of the vestibule, [13]as the duty of each day required, offering according to the commandment of Moses for the sabbaths, the new moons, and the three annual festivals—the festival of unleavened bread, the festival of weeks, and the festival of booths. [14]According to the ordinance of his father David, he appointed the divisions of the priests for their service, and the Levites for their offices of praise and ministry alongside the priests as the duty of each day required, and the gatekeepers in their divisions for the several gates; for so David the man of God had commanded. [15]They did not turn away from what the king had commanded the priests and Levites regarding anything at all, or regarding the treasuries.

16 Thus all the work of Solomon was accomplished from[b] the day the foundation of the house of the LORD was laid until the house of the LORD was finished completely.

17 Then Solomon went to Ezion-geber and Eloth on the shore of the sea, in the land of Edom. [18]Huram sent him, in the care of his servants, ships and servants familiar with the sea. They went to Ophir, together with the servants of Solomon, and imported from there four hundred fifty talents of gold and brought it to King Solomon.

a Gk See 2 Sam 22.14: Heb adds *hailstones and coals of fire*  b Gk Syr Vg: Heb *to*

9.1 WHEN the queen of Sheba heard of the fame of Solomon, she came to Jerusalem to test him with hard questions, having a very great retinue and camels bearing spices and very much gold and precious stones. When she came to Solomon, she discussed with him all that was on her mind. 2Solomon answered all her questions; there was nothing hidden from Solomon that he could not explain to her. 3When the queen of Sheba had observed the wisdom of Solomon, the house that he had built, 4the food of his table, the seating of his officials, and the attendance of his servants, and their clothing, his valets, and their clothing, and his burnt offeringsa that he offered at the house of the LORD, there was no more spirit left in her.

5 So she said to the king, "The report was true that I heard in my own land of your accomplishments and of your wisdom, 6but I did not believe theb reports until I came and my own eyes saw it. Not even half of the greatness of your wisdom had been told to me; you far surpass the report that I had heard. 7Happy are your people! Happy are these your servants, who continually attend you and hear your wisdom! 8Blessed be the LORD your God, who has delighted in you and set you on his throne as king for the LORD your God. Because your God loved Israel and would establish them forever, he has made you king over them, that you may execute justice and righteousness." 9Then she gave the king one hundred twenty talents of gold, a very great quantity of spices, and precious stones: there were no spices such as those that the queen of Sheba gave to King Solomon.

10 Moreover the servants of Huram and the servants of Solomon who brought gold from Ophir brought algum wood and precious stones. 11From the algum wood, the king made stepsc for the house of the LORD and for the king's house, lyres also and harps for the singers; there never was seen the like of them before in the land of Judah.

12 Meanwhile King Solomon granted the queen of Sheba every desire that she expressed, well beyond what she had brought to the king. Then she returned to her own land, with her servants.

13 The weight of gold that came to Solomon in one year was six hundred sixty-six talents of gold, 14besides that which the traders and merchants brought; and all the kings of Arabia and the governors of the land brought gold and silver to Solomon. 15King Solomon made two hundred large shields of beaten gold; six hundred shekels of beaten gold went into each large shield. 16He made three hundred shields of beaten gold; three hundred shekels of gold went into each shield; and the king put them in the House of the Forest of Lebanon. 17The king also made a great ivory throne, and overlaid it with pure gold. 18The throne had six steps and a footstool of gold, which were attached to the throne, and on each side of the seat were arm rests and two lions standing beside the arm rests, 19while twelve lions were standing, one on each end of a step on the six steps. The like of it was never made in any kingdom. 20All King Solomon's drinking vessels were of gold, and all the vessels of the House of the Forest of Lebanon were of pure gold; silver was not considered as anything in the days of Solomon. 21For the king's ships went to Tarshish with the servants of Huram; once every three years the ships of Tarshish used to come bringing gold, silver, ivory, apes, and peacocks. d

22 Thus King Solomon excelled all the kings of the earth in riches and in wisdom. 23All the kings of the earth

<hr>

aGk Syr Vg 1 Kings 10.5: Heb *ascent*   bHeb *their*   cGk Vg: Meaning of Heb uncertain   dOr *baboons*

sought the presence of Solomon to hear his wisdom, which God had put into his mind. ²⁴Every one of them brought a present, objects of silver and gold, garments, weaponry, spices, horses, and mules, so much year by year. ²⁵Solomon had four thousand stalls for horses and chariots, and twelve thousand horses, which he stationed in the chariot cities and with the king in Jerusalem. ²⁶He ruled over all the kings from the Euphrates to the land of the Philistines, and to the border of Egypt. ²⁷The king made silver as common in Jerusalem as stone, and cedar as plentiful as the sycamore of the Shephelah. ²⁸Horses were imported for Solomon from Egypt and from all lands.

29   Now the rest of the acts of Solomon, from first to last, are they not written in the history of the prophet Nathan, and in the prophecy of Ahijah the Shilonite, and in the visions of the seer Iddo concerning Jeroboam son of Nebat? ³⁰Solomon reigned in Jerusalem over all Israel forty years. ³¹Solomon slept with his ancestors and was buried in the city of his father David; and his son Rehoboam succeeded him.

10.1 REHOBOAM went to Shechem, for all Israel had come to Shechem to make him king. ²When Jeroboam son of Nebat heard of it (for he was in Egypt, where he had fled from King Solomon), then Jeroboam returned from Egypt. ³They sent and called him; and Jeroboam and all Israel came and said to Rehoboam, ⁴"Your father made our yoke heavy. Now therefore lighten the hard service of your father and his heavy yoke that he placed on us, and we will serve you." ⁵He said to them, "Come to me again in three days." So the people went away.

6   Then King Rehoboam took counsel with the older men who had attended his father Solomon while he was still alive, saying, "How do you advise me to answer this people?" ⁷They answered him, "If you will be kind to this people and please them, and speak good words to them, then they will be your servants forever." ⁸But he rejected the advice that the older men gave him, and consulted the young men who had grown up with him and now attended him. ⁹He said to them, "What do you advise that we answer this people who have said to me, 'Lighten the yoke that your father put on us'?" ¹⁰The young men who had grown up with him said to him, "Thus should you speak to the people who said to you, 'Your father made our yoke heavy, but you must lighten it for us'; tell them, 'My little finger is thicker than my father's loins. ¹¹Now, whereas my father laid on you a heavy yoke, I will add to your yoke. My father disciplined you with whips, but I will discipline you with scorpions.' "

12   So Jeroboam and all the people came to Rehoboam the third day, as the king had said, "Come to me again the third day." ¹³The king answered them harshly. King Rehoboam rejected the advice of the older men; ¹⁴he spoke to them in accordance with the advice of the young men, "My father made your yoke heavy, but I will add to it; my father disciplined you with whips, but I will discipline you with scorpions." ¹⁵So the king did not listen to the people, because it was a turn of affairs brought about by God so that the LORD might fulfill his word, which he had spoken by Ahijah the Shilonite to Jeroboam son of Nebat.

16   When all Israel saw that the king would not listen to them, the people answered the king,

> "What share do we have in
>     David?
>   We have no inheritance in the
>     son of Jesse.
> Each of you to your tents,
>     O Israel!
>   Look now to your own house,
>     O David."

So all Israel departed to their tents. [17]But Rehoboam reigned over the people of Israel who were living in the cities of Judah. [18]When King Rehoboam sent Hadoram, who was taskmaster over the forced labor, the people of Israel stoned him to death. King Rehoboam hurriedly mounted his chariot to flee to Jerusalem. [19]So Israel has been in rebellion against the house of David to this day.

## ROMANS 8.9–21

BUT you are not in the flesh; you are in the Spirit,[a] since the Spirit of God dwells in you. Anyone who does not have the Spirit of Christ does not belong to him. [10]But if Christ is in you, though the body is dead because of sin, the Spirit[a] is life because of righteousness. [11]If the Spirit of him who raised Jesus from the dead dwells in you, he who raised Christ[b] from the dead will give life to your mortal bodies also through[c] his Spirit that dwells in you.

12 So then, brothers and sisters,[d] we are debtors, not to the flesh, to live according to the flesh— [13]for if you live according to the flesh, you will die; but if by the Spirit you put to death the deeds of the body, you will live. [14]For all who are led by the Spirit of God are children of God. [15]For you did not receive a spirit of slavery to fall back into fear, but you have received a spirit of adoption. When we cry, "Abba![e] Father!" [16]it is that very Spirit bearing witness[f] with our spirit that we are children of God, [17]and if children, then heirs, heirs of God and joint heirs with Christ—if, in fact, we suffer with him so that we may also be glorified with him.

18 I consider that the sufferings of this present time are not worth comparing with the glory about to be revealed to us. [19]For the creation waits with eager longing for the revealing of the children of God; [20]for the creation was subjected to futility, not of its own will but by the will of the one who subjected it, in hope [21]that the creation itself will be set free from its bondage to decay and will obtain the freedom of the glory of the children of God.

## PSALM 18.16–36

HE reached down from on high, he took me;
he drew me out of mighty waters.
[17] He delivered me from my strong enemy,
and from those who hated me;
for they were too mighty for me.
[18] They confronted me in the day of my calamity;
but the LORD was my support.
[19] He brought me out into a broad place;
he delivered me, because he delighted in me.

[20] The LORD rewarded me according to my righteousness;
according to the cleanness of my hands he recompensed me.
[21] For I have kept the ways of the LORD,
and have not wickedly departed from my God.
[22] For all his ordinances were before me,
and his statutes I did not put away from me.
[23] I was blameless before him,
and I kept myself from guilt.

24 Therefore the Lord has
    recompensed me
    according to my
      righteousness,
    according to the cleanness of
      my hands in his sight.

25 With the loyal you show
      yourself loyal;
    with the blameless you show
      yourself blameless;
26 with the pure you show yourself
      pure;
    and with the crooked you
      show yourself perverse.
27 For you deliver a humble
      people,
    but the haughty eyes you
      bring down.
28 It is you who light my lamp;
    the Lord, my God, lights up
      my darkness.
29 By you I can crush a troop,
    and by my God I can leap
      over a wall.
30 This God—his way is perfect;
    the promise of the Lord
      proves true;
    he is a shield for all who take
      refuge in him.

31 For who is God except the
      Lord?
    And who is a rock besides
      our God?—
32 the God who girded me with
      strength,
    and made my way safe.
33 He made my feet like the feet
      of a deer,
    and set me secure on the
      heights.
34 He trains my hands for war,
    so that my arms can bend a
      bow of bronze.
35 You have given me the shield of
      your salvation,
    and your right hand has
      supported me;
    your help[a] has made me
      great.
36 You gave me a wide place for
      my steps under me,
    and my feet did not slip.

## PROVERBS 19.26

THOSE who do violence to their
      father and chase away
      their mother
are children who cause shame
      and bring reproach.

# JULY 24

## 2 CHRONICLES 11.1—13.22

WHEN Rehoboam came to Jerusalem, he assembled one hundred eighty thousand chosen troops of the house of Judah and Benjamin to fight against Israel, to restore the kingdom to Rehoboam. 2But the word of the Lord came to Shemaiah the man of God: 3Say to King Rehoboam of Judah, son of Solomon, and to all Israel in Judah and Benjamin, 4"Thus says the Lord: You shall not go up or fight against your kindred. Let everyone return home, for this thing is from

a Or *gentleness*

me." So they heeded the word of the LORD and turned back from the expedition against Jeroboam.

5 Rehoboam resided in Jerusalem, and he built cities for defense in Judah. ⁶He built up Bethlehem, Etam, Tekoa, ⁷Beth-zur, Soco, Adullam, ⁸Gath, Mareshah, Ziph, ⁹Adoraim, Lachish, Azekah, ¹⁰Zorah, Aijalon, and Hebron, fortified cities that are in Judah and in Benjamin. ¹¹He made the fortresses strong, and put commanders in them, and stores of food, oil, and wine. ¹²He also put large shields and spears in all the cities, and made them very strong. So he held Judah and Benjamin.

13 The priests and the Levites who were in all Israel presented themselves to him from all their territories. ¹⁴The Levites had left their common lands and their holdings and had come to Judah and Jerusalem, because Jeroboam and his sons had prevented them from serving as priests of the LORD, ¹⁵and had appointed his own priests for the high places, and for the goat-demons, and for the calves that he had made. ¹⁶Those who had set their hearts to seek the LORD God of Israel came after them from all the tribes of Israel to Jerusalem to sacrifice to the LORD, the God of their ancestors. ¹⁷They strengthened the kingdom of Judah, and for three years they made Rehoboam son of Solomon secure, for they walked for three years in the way of David and Solomon.

18 Rehoboam took as his wife Mahalath daughter of Jerimoth son of David, and of Abihail daughter of Eliab son of Jesse. ¹⁹She bore him sons: Jeush, Shemariah, and Zaham. ²⁰After her he took Maacah daughter of Absalom, who bore him Abijah, Attai, Ziza, and Shelomith. ²¹Rehoboam loved Maacah daughter of Absalom more than all his other wives and concubines (he took eighteen wives and sixty concubines, and became the father of twenty-eight sons and sixty daughters). ²²Rehoboam appointed Abijah son of Maacah as chief prince among his brothers, for he intended to make him king. ²³He dealt wisely, and distributed some of his sons through all the districts of Judah and Benjamin, in all the fortified cities; he gave them abundant provisions, and found many wives for them.

12.1 WHEN the rule of Rehoboam was established and he grew strong, he abandoned the law of the LORD, he and all Israel with him. ²In the fifth year of King Rehoboam, because they had been unfaithful to the LORD, King Shishak of Egypt came up against Jerusalem ³with twelve hundred chariots and sixty thousand cavalry. A countless army came with him from Egypt—Libyans, Sukkiim, and Ethiopians. ᵃ ⁴He took the fortified cities of Judah and came as far as Jerusalem. ⁵Then the prophet Shemaiah came to Rehoboam and to the officers of Judah, who had gathered at Jerusalem because of Shishak, and said to them, "Thus says the LORD: You abandoned me, so I have abandoned you to the hand of Shishak." ⁶Then the officers of Israel and the king humbled themselves and said, "The LORD is in the right." ⁷When the LORD saw that they humbled themselves, the word of the LORD came to Shemaiah, saying: "They have humbled themselves; I will not destroy them, but I will grant them some deliverance, and my wrath shall not be poured out on Jerusalem by the hand of Shishak. ⁸Nevertheless they shall be his servants, so that they may know the difference between serving me and serving the kingdoms of other lands."

9 So King Shishak of Egypt came up against Jerusalem; he took away the treasures of the house of the LORD and the treasures of the king's house; he

a Or *Nubians*; Heb *Cushites*

took everything. He also took away the shields of gold that Solomon had made; [10]but King Rehoboam made in place of them shields of bronze, and committed them to the hands of the officers of the guard, who kept the door of the king's house. [11]Whenever the king went into the house of the LORD, the guard would come along bearing them, and would then bring them back to the guard-room. [12]Because he humbled himself the wrath of the LORD turned from him, so as not to destroy them completely; moreover, conditions were good in Judah.

13 So King Rehoboam established himself in Jerusalem and reigned. Rehoboam was forty-one years old when he began to reign; he reigned seventeen years in Jerusalem, the city that the LORD had chosen out of all the tribes of Israel to put his name there. His mother's name was Naamah the Ammonite. [14]He did evil, for he did not set his heart to seek the LORD.

15 Now the acts of Rehoboam, from first to last, are they not written in the records of the prophet Shemaiah and of the seer Iddo, recorded by genealogy? There were continual wars between Rehoboam and Jeroboam. [16]Rehoboam slept with his ancestors and was buried in the city of David; and his son Abijah succeeded him.

13.1 IN the eighteenth year of King Jeroboam, Abijah began to reign over Judah. [2]He reigned for three years in Jerusalem. His mother's name was Micaiah daughter of Uriel of Gibeah.

Now there was war between Abijah and Jeroboam. [3]Abijah engaged in battle, having an army of valiant warriors, four hundred thousand picked men; and Jeroboam drew up his line of battle against him with eight hundred thousand picked mighty warriors. [4]Then Abijah stood on the slope of Mount Zemaraim that is in the hill country of Ephraim, and said, "Listen to me, Jeroboam and all Israel! [5]Do you not know that the LORD God of Israel gave the kingship over Israel forever to David and his sons by a covenant of salt? [6]Yet Jeroboam son of Nebat, a servant of Solomon son of David, rose up and rebelled against his lord; [7]and certain worthless scoundrels gathered around him and defied Rehoboam son of Solomon, when Rehoboam was young and irresolute and could not withstand them.

8 "And now you think that you can withstand the kingdom of the LORD in the hand of the sons of David, because you are a great multitude and have with you the golden calves that Jeroboam made as gods for you. [9]Have you not driven out the priests of the LORD, the descendants of Aaron, and the Levites, and made priests for yourselves like the peoples of other lands? Whoever comes to be consecrated with a young bull or seven rams becomes a priest of what are no gods. [10]But as for us, the LORD is our God, and we have not abandoned him. We have priests ministering to the LORD who are descendants of Aaron, and Levites for their service. [11]They offer to the LORD every morning and every evening burnt offerings and fragrant incense, set out the rows of bread on the table of pure gold, and care for the golden lampstand so that its lamps may burn every evening; for we keep the charge of the LORD our God, but you have abandoned him. [12]See, God is with us at our head, and his priests have their battle trumpets to sound the call to battle against you. O Israelites, do not fight against the LORD, the God of your ancestors; for you cannot succeed."

13 Jeroboam had sent an ambush around to come on them from behind; thus his troops[a] were in front of Judah,

a Heb *they*

and the ambush was behind them. ¹⁴When Judah turned, the battle was in front of them and behind them. They cried out to the LORD, and the priests blew the trumpets. ¹⁵Then the people of Judah raised the battle shout. And when the people of Judah shouted, God defeated Jeroboam and all Israel before Abijah and Judah. ¹⁶The Israelites fled before Judah, and God gave them into their hands. ¹⁷Abijah and his army defeated them with great slaughter; five hundred thousand picked men of Israel fell slain. ¹⁸Thus the Israelites were subdued at that time, and the people of Judah prevailed, because they relied on the LORD, the God of their ancestors. ¹⁹Abijah pursued Jeroboam, and took cities from him: Bethel with its villages and Jeshanah with its villages and Ephronᵃ with its villages. ²⁰Jeroboam did not recover his power in the days of Abijah; the LORD struck him down, and he died. ²¹But Abijah grew strong. He took fourteen wives, and became the father of twenty-two sons and sixteen daughters. ²²The rest of the acts of Abijah, his behavior and his deeds, are written in the story of the prophet Iddo.

## ROMANS 8.22–39

WE know that the whole creation has been groaning in labor pains until now; ²³and not only the creation, but we ourselves, who have the first fruits of the Spirit, groan inwardly while we wait for adoption, the redemption of our bodies. ²⁴For inᵇ hope we were saved. Now hope that is seen is not hope. For who hopesᶜ for what is seen? ²⁵But if we hope for what we do not see, we wait for it with patience.

26 Likewise the Spirit helps us in our weakness; for we do not know how to pray as we ought, but that very Spirit intercedesᵈ with sighs too deep for words. ²⁷And God, ᵉ who searches the heart, knows what is the mind of the Spirit, because the Spiritᶠ intercedes for the saints according to the will of God. ᵍ

28 We know that all things work together for goodʰ for those who love God, who are called according to his purpose. ²⁹For those whom he foreknew he also predestined to be conformed to the image of his Son, in order that he might be the firstborn within a large family. ⁱ ³⁰And those whom he predestined he also called; and those whom he called he also justified; and those whom he justified he also glorified.

31 What then are we to say about these things? If God is for us, who is against us? ³²He who did not withhold his own Son, but gave him up for all of us, will he not with him also give us everything else? ³³Who will bring any charge against God's elect? It is God who justifies. ³⁴Who is to condemn? It is Christ Jesus, who died, yes, who was raised, who is at the right hand of God, who indeed intercedes for us. ʲ ³⁵Who will separate us from the love of Christ? Will hardship, or distress, or persecution, or famine, or nakedness, or peril, or sword? ³⁶As it is written,

"For your sake we are being
    killed all day long;
we are accounted as sheep to
    be slaughtered."

³⁷No, in all these things we are more than conquerors through him who loved us. ³⁸For I am convinced that neither death, nor life, nor angels, nor rulers, nor things present, nor things to come, nor powers, ³⁹nor height, nor depth, nor anything else in all creation,

---

ᵃAnother reading is *Ephrain*   ᵇOr *by*   ᶜOther ancient authorities read *awaits*   ᵈOther ancient authorities add *for us*   ᵉGk *the one*   ᶠGk *he* or *it*   ᵍGk *according to God*   ʰOther ancient authorities read *God makes all things work together for good*, or *in all things God works for good*   ⁱGk *among many brothers*   ʲOr *Is it Christ Jesus . . . for us?*

will be able to separate us from the love
of God in Christ Jesus our Lord.

## PSALM 18.37–50

I PURSUED my enemies and
overtook them;
and did not turn back until
they were consumed.
38 I struck them down, so that
they were not able to
rise;
they fell under my feet.
39 For you girded me with
strength for the battle;
you made my assailants sink
under me.
40 You made my enemies turn
their backs to me,
and those who hated me I
destroyed.
41 They cried for help, but there
was no one to save
them;
they cried to the LORD, but he
did not answer them.
42 I beat them fine, like dust
before the wind;
I cast them out like the mire
of the streets.

43 You delivered me from strife
with the peoples; a
you made me head of the
nations;
people whom I had not known
served me.
44 As soon as they heard of me
they obeyed me;
foreigners came cringing to
me.
45 Foreigners lost heart,
and came trembling out of
their strongholds.

46 The LORD lives! Blessed be my
rock,
and exalted be the God of my
salvation,
47 the God who gave me
vengeance
and subdued peoples under
me;
48 who delivered me from my
enemies;
indeed, you exalted me above
my adversaries;
you delivered me from the
violent.

49 For this I will extol you,
O LORD, among the
nations,
and sing praises to your
name.
50 Great triumphs he gives to his
king,
and shows steadfast love to
his anointed,
to David and his descendants
forever.

## PROVERBS 19.27–29

C EASE straying, my child, from
the words of
knowledge,
in order that you may hear
instruction.
28 A worthless witness mocks
at justice,
and the mouth of the wicked
devours iniquity.
29 Condemnation is ready for
scoffers,
and flogging for the backs of
fools.

a Gk Tg: Heb *people*

## 2 CHRONICLES 14a.1— 16.14

So Abijah slept with his ancestors, and they buried him in the city of David. His son Asa succeeded him. In his days the land had rest for ten years. [2b]Asa did what was good and right in the sight of the LORD his God. [3]He took away the foreign altars and the high places, broke down the pillars, hewed down the sacred poles,[c] [4]and commanded Judah to seek the LORD, the God of their ancestors, and to keep the law and the commandment. [5]He also removed from all the cities of Judah the high places and the incense altars. And the kingdom had rest under him. [6]He built fortified cities in Judah while the land had rest. He had no war in those years, for the LORD gave him peace. [7]He said to Judah, "Let us build these cities, and surround them with walls and towers, gates and bars; the land is still ours because we have sought the LORD our God; we have sought him, and he has given us peace on every side." So they built and prospered. [8]Asa had an army of three hundred thousand from Judah, armed with large shields and spears, and two hundred eighty thousand troops from Benjamin who carried shields and drew bows; all these were mighty warriors.

9 Zerah the Ethiopian[d] came out against them with an army of a million men and three hundred chariots, and came as far as Mareshah. [10]Asa went out to meet him, and they drew up their lines of battle in the valley of Zephathah at Mareshah. [11]Asa cried to the LORD his God, "O LORD, there is no difference for you between helping the mighty and the weak. Help us, O LORD our God, for we rely on you, and in your name we have come against this multitude. O LORD, you are our God; let no mortal prevail against you." [12]So the LORD defeated the Ethiopians[e] before Asa and before Judah, and the Ethiopians[e] fled. [13]Asa and the army with him pursued them as far as Gerar, and the Ethiopians[e] fell until no one remained alive; for they were broken before the LORD and his army. The people of Judah[f] carried away a great quantity of booty. [14]They defeated all the cities around Gerar, for the fear of the LORD was on them. They plundered all the cities; for there was much plunder in them. [15]They also attacked the tents of those who had livestock,[g] and carried away sheep and goats in abundance, and camels. Then they returned to Jerusalem.

[15.1] THE spirit of God came upon Azariah son of Oded. [2]He went out to meet Asa and said to him, "Hear me, Asa, and all Judah and Benjamin: The LORD is with you, while you are with him. If you seek him, he will be found by you, but if you abandon him, he will abandon you. [3]For a long time Israel was without the true God, and without a teaching priest, and without law; [4]but when in their distress they turned to the LORD, the God of Israel, and sought him, he was found by them. [5]In those times it was not safe for anyone to go or come, for great disturbances afflicted all the inhabitants of the lands. [6]They were broken in pieces, nation against nation and city against city, for God troubled them with every sort of

---

aCh 13.23 in Heb   bCh 14.1 in Heb   cHeb *Asherim*   dOr *Nubian*; Heb *Cushite*   eOr *Nubians*; Heb *Cushites*   fHeb *They*   gMeaning of Heb uncertain

distress. ⁷But you, take courage! Do not let your hands be weak, for your work shall be rewarded."

8 When Asa heard these words, the prophecy of Azariah son of Oded, [a] he took courage, and put away the abominable idols from all the land of Judah and Benjamin and from the towns that he had taken in the hill country of Ephraim. He repaired the altar of the LORD that was in front of the vestibule of the house of the LORD. [b] ⁹He gathered all Judah and Benjamin, and those from Ephraim, Manasseh, and Simeon who were residing as aliens with them, for great numbers had deserted to him from Israel when they saw that the LORD his God was with him. ¹⁰They were gathered at Jerusalem in the third month of the fifteenth year of the reign of Asa. ¹¹They sacrificed to the LORD on that day, from the booty that they had brought, seven hundred oxen and seven thousand sheep. ¹²They entered into a covenant to seek the LORD, the God of their ancestors, with all their heart and with all their soul. ¹³Whoever would not seek the LORD, the God of Israel, should be put to death, whether young or old, man or woman. ¹⁴They took an oath to the LORD with a loud voice, and with shouting, and with trumpets, and with horns. ¹⁵All Judah rejoiced over the oath; for they had sworn with all their heart, and had sought him with their whole desire, and he was found by them, and the LORD gave them rest all around.

16 King Asa even removed his mother Maacah from being queen mother because she had made an abominable image for Asherah. Asa cut down her image, crushed it, and burned it at the Wadi Kidron. ¹⁷But the high places were not taken out of Israel. Nevertheless the heart of Asa was true all his days. ¹⁸He brought into the house of God the votive gifts of his fa-

ther and his own votive gifts—silver, gold, and utensils. ¹⁹And there was no more war until the thirty-fifth year of the reign of Asa.

**16.**1 IN the thirty-sixth year of the reign of Asa, King Baasha of Israel went up against Judah, and built Ramah, to prevent anyone from going out or coming into the territory of[c] King Asa of Judah. ²Then Asa took silver and gold from the treasures of the house of the LORD and the king's house, and sent them to King Ben-hadad of Aram, who resided in Damascus, saying, ³"Let there be an alliance between me and you, like that between my father and your father; I am sending to you silver and gold; go, break your alliance with King Baasha of Israel, so that he may withdraw from me." ⁴Ben-hadad listened to King Asa, and sent the commanders of his armies against the cities of Israel. They conquered Ijon, Dan, Abel-maim, and all the store-cities of Naphtali. ⁵When Baasha heard of it, he stopped building Ramah, and let his work cease. ⁶Then King Asa brought all Judah, and they carried away the stones of Ramah and its timber, with which Baasha had been building, and with them he built up Geba and Mizpah.

7 At that time the seer Hanani came to King Asa of Judah, and said to him, "Because you relied on the king of Aram, and did not rely on the LORD your God, the army of the king of Aram has escaped you. ⁸Were not the Ethiopians[d] and the Libyans a huge army with exceedingly many chariots and cavalry? Yet because you relied on the LORD, he gave them into your hand. ⁹For the eyes of the LORD range throughout the entire earth, to strengthen those whose heart is true to him. You have done foolishly in this; for from now on you will have wars." ¹⁰Then Asa was angry with the seer, and put him in the

[a]Compare Syr Vg: Heb *the prophecy, the prophet Obed*  [b]Heb *the vestibule of the LORD*  [c]Heb lacks *the territory of*  [d]Or *Nubians*; Heb *Cushites*

stocks, in prison, for he was in a rage with him because of this. And Asa inflicted cruelties on some of the people at the same time.

11 The acts of Asa, from first to last, are written in the Book of the Kings of Judah and Israel. [12]In the thirty-ninth year of his reign Asa was diseased in his feet, and his disease became severe; yet even in his disease he did not seek the LORD, but sought help from physicians. [13]Then Asa slept with his ancestors, dying in the forty-first year of his reign. [14]They buried him in the tomb that he had hewn out for himself in the city of David. They laid him on a bier that had been filled with various kinds of spices prepared by the perfumer's art; and they made a very great fire in his honor.

# ROMANS 9.1–21

I AM speaking the truth in Christ—I am not lying; my conscience confirms it by the Holy Spirit— [2]I have great sorrow and unceasing anguish in my heart. [3]For I could wish that I myself were accursed and cut off from Christ for the sake of my own people, [a] my kindred according to the flesh. [4]They are Israelites, and to them belong the adoption, the glory, the covenants, the giving of the law, the worship, and the promises; [5]to them belong the patriarchs, and from them, according to the flesh, comes the Messiah, [b] who is over all, God blessed forever. [c] Amen.

6 It is not as though the word of God had failed. For not all Israelites truly belong to Israel, [7]and not all of Abraham's children are his true descendants; but "It is through Isaac that descendants shall be named for you." [8]This means that it is not the children of the flesh who are the children of God, but the children of the promise are counted as descendants. [9]For this is what the promise said, "About this time I will return and Sarah shall have a son." [10]Nor is that all; something similar happened to Rebecca when she had conceived children by one husband, our ancestor Isaac. [11]Even before they had been born or had done anything good or bad (so that God's purpose of election might continue, [12]not by works but by his call) she was told, "The elder shall serve the younger." [13]As it is written,

"I have loved Jacob,
    but I have hated Esau."

14 What then are we to say? Is there injustice on God's part? By no means! [15]For he says to Moses,

"I will have mercy on whom I
    have mercy,
and I will have compassion on
    whom I have
    compassion."

[16]So it depends not on human will or exertion, but on God who shows mercy. [17]For the scripture says to Pharaoh, "I have raised you up for the very purpose of showing my power in you, so that my name may be proclaimed in all the earth." [18]So then he has mercy on whomever he chooses, and he hardens the heart of whomever he chooses.

19 You will say to me then, "Why then does he still find fault? For who can resist his will?" [20]But who indeed are you, a human being, to argue with God? Will what is molded say to the one who molds it, "Why have you made me like this?" [21]Has the potter no right over the clay, to make out of the same lump one object for special use and another for ordinary use?

[a] Gk *my brothers*  [b] Or *the Christ*  [c] Or *Messiah, who is God over all, blessed forever,* or *Messiah. May he who is God over all be blessed forever*

## PSALM 19.1–14

*To the leader. A Psalm of David.*

THE heavens are telling the
glory of God;
and the firmament[a]
proclaims his handiwork.
2 Day to day pours forth speech,
and night to night declares
knowledge.
3 There is no speech, nor are
there words;
their voice is not heard;
4 yet their voice[b] goes out
through all the earth,
and their words to the end of
the world.

In the heavens[c] he has set a
tent for the sun,
5 which comes out like a
bridegroom from his
wedding canopy,
and like a strong man runs its
course with joy.
6 Its rising is from the end of the
heavens,
and its circuit to the end of
them;
and nothing is hid from its
heat.

7 The law of the Lord is perfect,
reviving the soul;
the decrees of the Lord are
sure,
making wise the simple;
8 the precepts of the Lord are
right,
rejoicing the heart;
the commandment of the Lord
is clear,
enlightening the eyes;
9 the fear of the Lord is pure,
enduring forever;
the ordinances of the Lord are
true
and righteous altogether.
10 More to be desired are they
than gold,
even much fine gold;
sweeter also than honey,
and drippings of the
honeycomb.

11 Moreover by them is your
servant warned;
in keeping them there is great
reward.
12 But who can detect their
errors?
Clear me from hidden faults.
13 Keep back your servant also
from the insolent;[d]
do not let them have
dominion over me.
Then I shall be blameless,
and innocent of great
transgression.

14 Let the words of my mouth and
the meditation of my
heart
be acceptable to you,
O Lord, my rock and my
redeemer.

## PROVERBS 20.1

WINE is a mocker, strong
drink a brawler,
and whoever is led astray
by it is not wise.

---

a Or *dome*　b Gk Jerome Compare Syr: Heb *line*　c Heb *In them*　d Or *from proud thoughts*

## 2 CHRONICLES 17.1—18.34

His son Jehoshaphat succeeded him, and strengthened himself against Israel. ²He placed forces in all the fortified cities of Judah, and set garrisons in the land of Judah, and in the cities of Ephraim that his father Asa had taken. ³The Lord was with Jehoshaphat, because he walked in the earlier ways of his father; a he did not seek the Baals, ⁴but sought the God of his father and walked in his commandments, and not according to the ways of Israel. ⁵Therefore the Lord established the kingdom in his hand. All Judah brought tribute to Jehoshaphat, and he had great riches and honor. ⁶His heart was courageous in the ways of the Lord; and furthermore he removed the high places and the sacred poles b from Judah.

7 In the third year of his reign he sent his officials, Ben-hail, Obadiah, Zechariah, Nethanel, and Micaiah, to teach in the cities of Judah. ⁸With them were the Levites, Shemaiah, Nethaniah, Zebadiah, Asahel, Shemiramoth, Jehonathan, Adonijah, Tobijah, and Tob-adonijah; and with these Levites, the priests Elishama and Jehoram. ⁹They taught in Judah, having the book of the law of the Lord with them; they went around through all the cities of Judah and taught among the people.

10 The fear of the Lord fell on all the kingdoms of the lands around Judah, and they did not make war against Jehoshaphat. ¹¹Some of the Philistines brought Jehoshaphat presents, and silver for tribute; and the Arabs also brought him seven thousand seven hundred rams and seven thousand seven hundred male goats. ¹²Jehoshaphat grew steadily greater. He built fortresses and storage cities in Judah. ¹³He carried out great works in the cities of Judah. He had soldiers, mighty warriors, in Jerusalem. ¹⁴This was the muster of them by ancestral houses: Of Judah, the commanders of the thousands: Adnah the commander, with three hundred thousand mighty warriors, ¹⁵and next to him Jehohanan the commander, with two hundred eighty thousand, ¹⁶and next to him Amasiah son of Zichri, a volunteer for the service of the Lord, with two hundred thousand mighty warriors. ¹⁷Of Benjamin: Eliada, a mighty warrior, with two hundred thousand armed with bow and shield, ¹⁸and next to him Jehozabad with one hundred eighty thousand armed for war. ¹⁹These were in the service of the king, besides those whom the king had placed in the fortified cities throughout all Judah.

18.1 Now Jehoshaphat had great riches and honor; and he made a marriage alliance with Ahab. ²After some years he went down to Ahab in Samaria. Ahab slaughtered an abundance of sheep and oxen for him and for the people who were with him, and induced him to go up against Ramoth-gilead. ³King Ahab of Israel said to King Jehoshaphat of Judah, "Will you go with me to Ramoth-gilead?" He answered him, "I am with you, my people are your people. We will be with you in the war."

4 But Jehoshaphat also said to the king of Israel, "Inquire first for the word of the Lord." ⁵Then the king of Israel gathered the prophets together, four hundred of them, and said to them, "Shall we go to battle against Ramoth-

---

a Another reading is *his father David*　b Heb *Asherim*

gilead, or shall I refrain?" They said, "Go up; for God will give it into the hand of the king." 6But Jehoshaphat said, "Is there no other prophet of the LORD here of whom we may inquire?" 7The king of Israel said to Jehoshaphat, "There is still one other by whom we may inquire of the LORD, Micaiah son of Imlah; but I hate him, for he never prophesies anything favorable about me, but only disaster." Jehoshaphat said, "Let the king not say such a thing." 8Then the king of Israel summoned an officer and said, "Bring quickly Micaiah son of Imlah." 9Now the king of Israel and King Jehoshaphat of Judah were sitting on their thrones, arrayed in their robes; and they were sitting at the threshing floor at the entrance of the gate of Samaria; and all the prophets were prophesying before them. 10Zedekiah son of Chenaanah made for himself horns of iron, and he said, "Thus says the LORD: With these you shall gore the Arameans until they are destroyed." 11All the prophets were prophesying the same and saying, "Go up to Ramoth-gilead and triumph; the LORD will give it into the hand of the king."

12 The messenger who had gone to summon Micaiah said to him, "Look, the words of the prophets with one accord are favorable to the king; let your word be like the word of one of them, and speak favorably." 13But Micaiah said, "As the LORD lives, whatever my God says, that I will speak."

14 When he had come to the king, the king said to him, "Micaiah, shall we go to Ramoth-gilead to battle, or shall I refrain?" He answered, "Go up and triumph; they will be given into your hand." 15But the king said to him, "How many times must I make you swear to tell me nothing but the truth in the name of the LORD?" 16Then Micaiah[a] said, "I saw all Israel scattered on the mountains, like sheep without a shepherd; and the LORD said, 'These have no master; let each one go home in peace.'" 17The king of Israel said to Jehoshaphat, "Did I not tell you that he would not prophesy anything favorable about me, but only disaster?"

18 Then Micaiah[a] said, "Therefore hear the word of the LORD: I saw the LORD sitting on his throne, with all the host of heaven standing to the right and to the left of him. 19And the LORD said, 'Who will entice King Ahab of Israel, so that he may go up and fall at Ramoth-gilead?' Then one said one thing, and another said another, 20until a spirit came forward and stood before the LORD, saying, 'I will entice him.' The LORD asked him, 'How?' 21He replied, 'I will go out and be a lying spirit in the mouth of all his prophets.' Then the LORD[a] said, 'You are to entice him, and you shall succeed; go out and do it.' 22So you see, the LORD has put a lying spirit in the mouth of these your prophets; the LORD has decreed disaster for you."

23 Then Zedekiah son of Chenaanah came up to Micaiah, slapped him on the cheek, and said, "Which way did the spirit of the LORD pass from me to speak to you?" 24Micaiah replied, "You will find out on that day when you go in to hide in an inner chamber." 25The king of Israel then ordered, "Take Micaiah, and return him to Amon the governor of the city and to Joash the king's son; 26and say, 'Thus says the king: Put this fellow in prison, and feed him on reduced rations of bread and water until I return in peace.'" 27Micaiah said, "If you return in peace, the LORD has not spoken by me." And he said, "Hear, you peoples, all of you!"

28 So the king of Israel and King Jehoshaphat of Judah went up to Ramoth-gilead. 29The king of Israel said to Jehoshaphat, "I will disguise my-

aHeb *he*

self and go into battle, but you wear your robes." So the king of Israel disguised himself, and they went into battle. ³⁰Now the king of Aram had commanded the captains of his chariots, "Fight with no one small or great, but only with the king of Israel." ³¹When the captains of the chariots saw Jehoshaphat, they said, "It is the king of Israel." So they turned to fight against him; and Jehoshaphat cried out, and the LORD helped him. God drew them away from him, ³²for when the captains of the chariots saw that it was not the king of Israel, they turned back from pursuing him. ³³But a certain man drew his bow and unknowingly struck the king of Israel between the scale armor and the breastplate; so he said to the driver of his chariot, "Turn around, and carry me out of the battle, for I am wounded." ³⁴The battle grew hot that day, and the king of Israel propped himself up in his chariot facing the Arameans until evening; then at sunset he died.

# ROMANS 9.22—10.13

WHAT if God, desiring to show his wrath and to make known his power, has endured with much patience the objects of wrath that are made for destruction; ²³and what if he has done so in order to make known the riches of his glory for the objects of mercy, which he has prepared beforehand for glory— ²⁴including us whom he has called, not from the Jews only but also from the Gentiles? ²⁵As indeed he says in Hosea,

> "Those who were not my
> people I will call 'my
> people,'
> and her who was not beloved
> I will call 'beloved.' "

²⁶ "And in the very place where it
> was said to them, 'You
> are not my people,'
> there they shall be called
> children of the living
> God."

27 And Isaiah cries out concerning Israel, "Though the number of the children of Israel were like the sand of the sea, only a remnant of them will be saved; ²⁸for the Lord will execute his sentence on the earth quickly and decisively."ᵃ ²⁹And as Isaiah predicted,

> "If the Lord of hosts had not
> left survivorsᵇ to us,
> we would have fared like
> Sodom
> and been made like
> Gomorrah."

30 What then are we to say? Gentiles, who did not strive for righteousness, have attained it, that is, righteousness through faith; ³¹but Israel, who did strive for the righteousness that is based on the law, did not succeed in fulfilling that law. ³²Why not? Because they did not strive for it on the basis of faith, but as if it were based on works. They have stumbled over the stumbling stone, ³³as it is written,

> "See, I am laying in Zion a
> stone that will make
> people stumble, a rock
> that will make them fall,
> and whoever believes in himᶜ
> will not be put to
> shame."

¹⁰·¹ BROTHERS and sisters, ᵈ my heart's desire and prayer to God for them is that they may be saved. ²I can testify that they have a zeal for God, but it is not enlightened. ³For, being ignorant of the righteousness that comes from God, and seeking to establish their own, they have not submitted to God's

ᵃOther ancient authorities read *for he will finish his work and cut it short in righteousness, because the Lord will make the sentence shortened on the earth*   ᵇOr *descendants*; Gk *seed*   ᶜOr *trusts in it*
ᵈGk *Brothers*

righteousness. [4]For Christ is the end of the law so that there may be righteousness for everyone who believes.

5 Moses writes concerning the righteousness that comes from the law, that "the person who does these things will live by them." [6]But the righteousness that comes from faith says, "Do not say in your heart, 'Who will ascend into heaven?' " (that is, to bring Christ down) [7]"or 'Who will descend into the abyss?' " (that is, to bring Christ up from the dead). [8]But what does it say?

"The word is near you,
    on your lips and in your
        heart"

(that is, the word of faith that we proclaim); [9]because[a] if you confess with your lips that Jesus is Lord and believe in your heart that God raised him from the dead, you will be saved. [10]For one believes with the heart and so is justified, and one confesses with the mouth and so is saved. [11]The scripture says, "No one who believes in him will be put to shame." [12]For there is no distinction between Jew and Greek; the same Lord is Lord of all and is generous to all who call on him. [13]For, "Everyone who calls on the name of the Lord shall be saved."

## PSALM 20.1–9

*To the leader. A Psalm of David.*

THE LORD answer you in the day of trouble!
    The name of the God of
        Jacob protect you!
2  May he send you help from the
        sanctuary,
    and give you support from
        Zion.
3  May he remember all your
        offerings,
    and regard with favor your
        burnt sacrifices.        *Selah*

4  May he grant you your heart's
        desire,
    and fulfill all your plans.
5  May we shout for joy over your
        victory,
    and in the name of our God
        set up our banners.
May the LORD fulfill all your
        petitions.

6  Now I know that the LORD will
        help his anointed;
    he will answer him from his
        holy heaven
    with mighty victories by his
        right hand.
7  Some take pride in chariots, and
        some in horses,
    but our pride is in the name
        of the LORD our God.
8  They will collapse and fall,
    but we shall rise and stand
        upright.

9  Give victory to the king,
        O LORD;
    answer us when we call. [b]

## PROVERBS 20.2–3

THE dread anger of a king is like the growling of a lion;
    anyone who provokes him to
        anger forfeits life itself.
3  It is honorable to refrain
        from strife,
    but every fool is quick to
        quarrel.

---

[a]Or *namely, that*  [b]Gk: Heb *give victory, O* LORD; *let the King answer us when we call*

## 2 CHRONICLES 19.1—20.37

**K**ING Jehoshaphat of Judah returned in safety to his house in Jerusalem. ²Jehu son of Hanani the seer went out to meet him and said to King Jehoshaphat, "Should you help the wicked and love those who hate the LORD? Because of this, wrath has gone out against you from the LORD. ³Nevertheless, some good is found in you, for you destroyed the sacred poles[a] out of the land, and have set your heart to seek God."

4 Jehoshaphat resided at Jerusalem; then he went out again among the people, from Beer-sheba to the hill country of Ephraim, and brought them back to the LORD, the God of their ancestors. ⁵He appointed judges in the land in all the fortified cities of Judah, city by city, ⁶and said to the judges, "Consider what you are doing, for you judge not on behalf of human beings but on the LORD's behalf; he is with you in giving judgment. ⁷Now, let the fear of the LORD be upon you; take care what you do, for there is no perversion of justice with the LORD our God, or partiality, or taking of bribes."

8 Moreover in Jerusalem Jehoshaphat appointed certain Levites and priests and heads of families of Israel, to give judgment for the LORD and to decide disputed cases. They had their seat at Jerusalem. ⁹He charged them: "This is how you shall act: in the fear of the LORD, in faithfulness, and with your whole heart; ¹⁰whenever a case comes to you from your kindred who live in their cities, concerning bloodshed, law or commandment, statutes or ordinances, then you shall instruct them, so that they may not incur guilt before the LORD and wrath may not come on you and your kindred. Do so, and you will not incur guilt. ¹¹See, Amariah the chief priest is over you in all matters of the LORD; and Zebadiah son of Ishmael, the governor of the house of Judah, in all the king's matters; and the Levites will serve you as officers. Deal courageously, and may the LORD be with the good!"

20.1 AFTER this the Moabites and Ammonites, and with them some of the Meunites,[b] came against Jehoshaphat for battle. ²Messengers[c] came and told Jehoshaphat, "A great multitude is coming against you from Edom,[d] from beyond the sea; already they are at Hazazon-tamar" (that is, En-gedi). ³Jehoshaphat was afraid; he set himself to seek the LORD, and proclaimed a fast throughout all Judah. ⁴Judah assembled to seek help from the LORD; from all the towns of Judah they came to seek the LORD.

5 Jehoshaphat stood in the assembly of Judah and Jerusalem, in the house of the LORD, before the new court, ⁶and said, "O LORD, God of our ancestors, are you not God in heaven? Do you not rule over all the kingdoms of the nations? In your hand are power and might, so that no one is able to withstand you. ⁷Did you not, O our God, drive out the inhabitants of this land before your people Israel, and give it forever to the descendants of your friend Abraham? ⁸They have lived in it, and in it have built you a sanctuary for your name, saying, ⁹'If disaster comes upon us, the sword, judgment,[e] or pestilence, or famine, we will stand before this house, and before you, for your

---

aHeb *Asheroth*   bCompare 26.7: Heb *Ammonites*   cHeb *They*   dOne Ms: MT *Aram*   eOr *the sword of judgment*

name is in this house, and cry to you in our distress, and you will hear and save.' <sup>10</sup>See now, the people of Ammon, Moab, and Mount Seir, whom you would not let Israel invade when they came from the land of Egypt, and whom they avoided and did not destroy— <sup>11</sup>they reward us by coming to drive us out of your possession that you have given us to inherit. <sup>12</sup>O our God, will you not execute judgment upon them? For we are powerless against this great multitude that is coming against us. We do not know what to do, but our eyes are on you."

13 Meanwhile all Judah stood before the LORD, with their little ones, their wives, and their children. <sup>14</sup>Then the spirit of the LORD came upon Jahaziel son of Zechariah, son of Benaiah, son of Jeiel, son of Mattaniah, a Levite of the sons of Asaph, in the middle of the assembly. <sup>15</sup>He said, "Listen, all Judah and inhabitants of Jerusalem, and King Jehoshaphat: Thus says the LORD to you: 'Do not fear or be dismayed at this great multitude; for the battle is not yours but God's. <sup>16</sup>Tomorrow go down against them; they will come up by the ascent of Ziz; you will find them at the end of the valley, before the wilderness of Jeruel. <sup>17</sup>This battle is not for you to fight; take your position, stand still, and see the victory of the LORD on your behalf, O Judah and Jerusalem.' Do not fear or be dismayed; tomorrow go out against them, and the LORD will be with you."

18 Then Jehoshaphat bowed down with his face to the ground, and all Judah and the inhabitants of Jerusalem fell down before the LORD, worshiping the LORD. <sup>19</sup>And the Levites, of the Kohathites and the Korahites, stood up to praise the LORD, the God of Israel, with a very loud voice.

20 They rose early in the morning and went out into the wilderness of Te-

koa; and as they went out, Jehoshaphat stood and said, "Listen to me, O Judah and inhabitants of Jerusalem! Believe in the LORD your God and you will be established; believe his prophets." <sup>21</sup>When he had taken counsel with the people, he appointed those who were to sing to the LORD and praise him in holy splendor, as they went before the army, saying,

"Give thanks to the LORD,
for his steadfast love endures forever."

<sup>22</sup>As they began to sing and praise, the LORD set an ambush against the Ammonites, Moab, and Mount Seir, who had come against Judah, so that they were routed. <sup>23</sup>For the Ammonites and Moab attacked the inhabitants of Mount Seir, destroying them utterly; and when they had made an end of the inhabitants of Seir, they all helped to destroy one another.

24 When Judah came to the watchtower of the wilderness, they looked toward the multitude; they were corpses lying on the ground; no one had escaped. <sup>25</sup>When Jehoshaphat and his people came to take the booty from them, they found livestock[a] in great numbers, goods, clothing, and precious things, which they took for themselves until they could carry no more. They spent three days taking the booty, because of its abundance. <sup>26</sup>On the fourth day they assembled in the Valley of Beracah, for there they blessed the LORD; therefore that place has been called the Valley of Beracah[b] to this day. <sup>27</sup>Then all the people of Judah and Jerusalem, with Jehoshaphat at their head, returned to Jerusalem with joy, for the LORD had enabled them to rejoice over their enemies. <sup>28</sup>They came to Jerusalem, with harps and lyres and trumpets, to the house of the LORD. <sup>29</sup>The fear of God came on all the kingdoms of the countries when they heard

aGk: Heb *among them*   bThat is *Blessing*

that the LORD had fought against the enemies of Israel. ³⁰And the realm of Jehoshaphat was quiet, for his God gave him rest all around.

31  So Jehoshaphat reigned over Judah. He was thirty-five years old when he began to reign; he reigned twenty-five years in Jerusalem. His mother's name was Azubah daughter of Shilhi. ³²He walked in the way of his father Asa and did not turn aside from it, doing what was right in the sight of the LORD. ³³Yet the high places were not removed; the people had not yet set their hearts upon the God of their ancestors.

34  Now the rest of the acts of Jehoshaphat, from first to last, are written in the Annals of Jehu son of Hanani, which are recorded in the Book of the Kings of Israel.

35  After this King Jehoshaphat of Judah joined with King Ahaziah of Israel, who did wickedly. ³⁶He joined him in building ships to go to Tarshish; they built the ships in Ezion-geber. ³⁷Then Eliezer son of Dodavahu of Mareshah prophesied against Jehoshaphat, saying, "Because you have joined with Ahaziah, the LORD will destroy what you have made." And the ships were wrecked and were not able to go to Tarshish.

## ROMANS 10.14—11.12

**B**UT how are they to call on one in whom they have not believed? And how are they to believe in one of whom they have never heard? And how are they to hear without someone to proclaim him? ¹⁵And how are they to proclaim him unless they are sent? As it is written, "How beautiful are the feet of those who bring good news!" ¹⁶But not all have obeyed the good news;ᵃ for Isaiah says, "Lord, who has believed our message?" ¹⁷So faith comes from what is heard, and what is heard comes through the word of Christ. ᵇ

18  But I ask, have they not heard? Indeed they have; for

"Their voice has gone out to all
    the earth,
  and their words to the ends
    of the world."

¹⁹Again I ask, did Israel not understand? First Moses says,

"I will make you jealous of those
    who are not a nation;
  with a foolish nation I will
    make you angry."

²⁰Then Isaiah is so bold as to say,

"I have been found by those
    who did not seek me;
  I have shown myself to those
    who did not ask for me."

²¹But of Israel he says, "All day long I have held out my hands to a disobedient and contrary people."

11.1 I ask, then, has God rejected his people? By no means! I myself am an Israelite, a descendant of Abraham, a member of the tribe of Benjamin. ²God has not rejected his people whom he foreknew. Do you not know what the scripture says of Elijah, how he pleads with God against Israel? ³"Lord, they have killed your prophets, they have demolished your altars; I alone am left, and they are seeking my life." ⁴But what is the divine reply to him? "I have kept for myself seven thousand who have not bowed the knee to Baal." ⁵So too at the present time there is a remnant, chosen by grace. ⁶But if it is by grace, it is no longer on the basis of works, otherwise grace would no longer be grace. ᶜ

7  What then? Israel failed to obtain what it was seeking. The elect obtained it, but the rest were hardened, ⁸as it is written,

"God gave them a sluggish
    spirit,

ᵃOr *gospel*  ᵇOr *about Christ*; other ancient authorities read *of God*  ᶜOther ancient authorities add *But if it is by works, it is no longer on the basis of grace, otherwise work would no longer be work*

eyes that would not see
and ears that would not hear,
down to this very day."
⁹And David says,
"Let their table become a snare
and a trap,
a stumbling block and a
retribution for them;
10 let their eyes be darkened so
that they cannot see,
and keep their backs forever
bent."

11 So I ask, have they stumbled so as to fall? By no means! But through their stumbling[a] salvation has come to the Gentiles, so as to make Israel[b] jealous. ¹²Now if their stumbling[a] means riches for the world, and if their defeat means riches for Gentiles, how much more will their full inclusion mean!

# PSALM 21.1–13

*To the leader. A Psalm of David.*

IN your strength the king
rejoices, O LORD,
and in your help how greatly
he exults!
2 You have given him his heart's
desire,
and have not withheld the
request of his lips.  *Selah*
3 For you meet him with rich
blessings;
you set a crown of fine gold
on his head.
4 He asked you for life; you gave
it to him—
length of days forever and
ever.
5 His glory is great through your
help;
splendor and majesty you
bestow on him.
6 You bestow on him blessings
forever;

you make him glad with the
joy of your presence.
7 For the king trusts in the LORD,
and through the steadfast love
of the Most High he shall
not be moved.

8 Your hand will find out all your
enemies;
your right hand will find out
those who hate you.
9 You will make them like a fiery
furnace
when you appear.
The LORD will swallow them up
in his wrath,
and fire will consume them.
10 You will destroy their offspring
from the earth,
and their children from among
humankind.
11 If they plan evil against you,
if they devise mischief, they
will not succeed.
12 For you will put them to flight;
you will aim at their faces
with your bows.

13 Be exalted, O LORD, in your
strength!
We will sing and praise your
power.

# PROVERBS 20.4–6

THE lazy person does not plow
in season;
harvest comes, and there is
nothing to be found.
5 The purposes in the human
mind are like deep
water,
but the intelligent will draw
them out.
6 Many proclaim themselves loyal,
but who can find one worthy
of trust?

a Gk *transgression*   b Gk *them*

## 2 CHRONICLES 21.1—23.21

JEHOSHAPHAT slept with his ancestors and was buried with his ancestors in the city of David; his son Jehoram succeeded him. ²He had brothers, the sons of Jehoshaphat: Azariah, Jehiel, Zechariah, Azariah, Michael, and Shephatiah; all these were the sons of King Jehoshaphat of Judah. ª ³Their father gave them many gifts, of silver, gold, and valuable possessions, together with fortified cities in Judah; but he gave the kingdom to Jehoram, because he was the firstborn. ⁴When Jehoram had ascended the throne of his father and was established, he put all his brothers to the sword, and also some of the officials of Israel. ⁵Jehoram was thirty-two years old when he began to reign; he reigned eight years in Jerusalem. ⁶He walked in the way of the kings of Israel, as the house of Ahab had done; for the daughter of Ahab was his wife. He did what was evil in the sight of the LORD. ⁷Yet the LORD would not destroy the house of David because of the covenant that he had made with David, and since he had promised to give a lamp to him and to his descendants forever.

8 In his days Edom revolted against the rule of Judah and set up a king of their own. ⁹Then Jehoram crossed over with his commanders and all his chariots. He set out by night and attacked the Edomites, who had surrounded him and his chariot commanders. ¹⁰So Edom has been in revolt against the rule of Judah to this day. At that time Libnah also revolted against his rule, because he had forsaken the LORD, the God of his ancestors.

11 Moreover he made high places in the hill country of Judah, and led the inhabitants of Jerusalem into unfaithfulness, and made Judah go astray. ¹²A letter came to him from the prophet Elijah, saying: "Thus says the LORD, the God of your father David: Because you have not walked in the ways of your father Jehoshaphat or in the ways of King Asa of Judah, ¹³but have walked in the way of the kings of Israel, and have led Judah and the inhabitants of Jerusalem into unfaithfulness, as the house of Ahab led Israel into unfaithfulness, and because you also have killed your brothers, members of your father's house, who were better than yourself, ¹⁴see, the LORD will bring a great plague on your people, your children, your wives, and all your possessions, ¹⁵and you yourself will have a severe sickness with a disease of your bowels, until your bowels come out, day after day, because of the disease."

16 The LORD aroused against Jehoram the anger of the Philistines and of the Arabs who are near the Ethiopians. ᵇ ¹⁷They came up against Judah, invaded it, and carried away all the possessions they found that belonged to the king's house, along with his sons and his wives, so that no son was left to him except Jehoahaz, his youngest son.

18 After all this the LORD struck him in his bowels with an incurable disease. ¹⁹In course of time, at the end of two years, his bowels came out because of the disease, and he died in great agony. His people made no fire in his honor, like the fires made for his ancestors. ²⁰He was thirty-two years old when he began to reign; he reigned

ªGk Syr: Heb *Israel*   ᵇOr *Nubians*; Heb *Cushites*

eight years in Jerusalem. He departed with no one's regret. They buried him in the city of David, but not in the tombs of the kings.

22.1 THE inhabitants of Jerusalem made his youngest son Ahaziah king as his successor; for the troops who came with the Arabs to the camp had killed all the older sons. So Ahaziah son of Jehoram reigned as king of Judah. ²Ahaziah was forty-two years old when he began to reign; he reigned one year in Jerusalem. His mother's name was Athaliah, a granddaughter of Omri. ³He also walked in the ways of the house of Ahab, for his mother was his counselor in doing wickedly. ⁴He did what was evil in the sight of the LORD, as the house of Ahab had done; for after the death of his father they were his counselors, to his ruin. ⁵He even followed their advice, and went with Jehoram son of King Ahab of Israel to make war against King Hazael of Aram at Ramoth-gilead. The Arameans wounded Joram, ⁶and he returned to be healed in Jezreel of the wounds that he had received at Ramah, when he fought King Hazael of Aram. And Ahaziah son of King Jehoram of Judah went down to see Joram son of Ahab in Jezreel, because he was sick.

7  But it was ordained by God that the downfall of Ahaziah should come about through his going to visit Joram. For when he came there he went out with Jehoram to meet Jehu son of Nimshi, whom the LORD had anointed to destroy the house of Ahab. ⁸When Jehu was executing judgment on the house of Ahab, he met the officials of Judah and the sons of Ahaziah's brothers, who attended Ahaziah, and he killed them. ⁹He searched for Ahaziah, who was captured while hiding in Samaria and was brought to Jehu, and put to death. They buried him, for they said,

"He is the grandson of Jehoshaphat, who sought the LORD with all his heart." And the house of Ahaziah had no one able to rule the kingdom.

10  Now when Athaliah, Ahaziah's mother, saw that her son was dead, she set about to destroy all the royal family of the house of Judah. ¹¹But Jehoshabeath, the king's daughter, took Joash son of Ahaziah, and stole him away from among the king's children who were about to be killed; she put him and his nurse in a bedroom. Thus Jehoshabeath, daughter of King Jehoram and wife of the priest Jehoiada—because she was a sister of Ahaziah—hid him from Athaliah, so that she did not kill him; ¹²he remained with them six years, hidden in the house of God, while Athaliah reigned over the land.

23.1 BUT in the seventh year Jehoiada took courage, and entered into a compact with the commanders of the hundreds, Azariah son of Jeroham, Ishmael son of Jehohanan, Azariah son of Obed, Maaseiah son of Adaiah, and Elishaphat son of Zichri. ²They went around through Judah and gathered the Levites from all the towns of Judah, and the heads of families of Israel, and they came to Jerusalem. ³Then the whole assembly made a covenant with the king in the house of God. Jehoiadaª said to them, "Here is the king's son! Let him reign, as the LORD promised concerning the sons of David. ⁴This is what you are to do: one third of you, priests and Levites, who come on duty on the sabbath, shall be gatekeepers, ⁵one third shall be at the king's house, and one third at the Gate of the Foundation; and all the people shall be in the courts of the house of the LORD. ⁶Do not let anyone enter the house of the LORD except the priests and ministering Levites; they may enter, for they are

a Heb *He*

holy, but all the other[a] people shall observe the instructions of the LORD. [7]The Levites shall surround the king, each with his weapons in his hand; and whoever enters the house shall be killed. Stay with the king in his comings and goings."

8 The Levites and all Judah did according to all that the priest Jehoiada commanded; each brought his men, who were to come on duty on the sabbath, with those who were to go off duty on the sabbath; for the priest Jehoiada did not dismiss the divisions. [9]The priest Jehoiada delivered to the captains the spears and the large and small shields that had been King David's, which were in the house of God; [10]and he set all the people as a guard for the king, everyone with weapon in hand, from the south side of the house to the north side of the house, around the altar and the house. [11]Then he brought out the king's son, put the crown on him, and gave him the covenant;[b] they proclaimed him king, and Jehoiada and his sons anointed him; and they shouted, "Long live the king!"

12 When Athaliah heard the noise of the people running and praising the king, she went into the house of the LORD to the people; [13]and when she looked, there was the king standing by his pillar at the entrance, and the captains and the trumpeters beside the king, and all the people of the land rejoicing and blowing trumpets, and the singers with their musical instruments leading in the celebration. Athaliah tore her clothes, and cried, "Treason! Treason!" [14]Then the priest Jehoiada brought out the captains who were set over the army, saying to them, "Bring her out between the ranks; anyone who follows her is to be put to the sword." For the priest said, "Do not put her to death in the house of the LORD." [15]So they laid hands on her; she went into the entrance of the Horse Gate of the king's house, and there they put her to death.

16 Jehoiada made a covenant between himself and all the people and the king that they should be the LORD's people. [17]Then all the people went to the house of Baal, and tore it down; his altars and his images they broke in pieces, and they killed Mattan, the priest of Baal, in front of the altars. [18]Jehoiada assigned the care of the house of the LORD to the levitical priests whom David had organized to be in charge of the house of the LORD, to offer burnt offerings to the LORD, as it is written in the law of Moses, with rejoicing and with singing, according to the order of David. [19]He stationed the gatekeepers at the gates of the house of the LORD so that no one should enter who was in any way unclean. [20]And he took the captains, the nobles, the governors of the people, and all the people of the land, and they brought the king down from the house of the LORD, marching through the upper gate to the king's house. They set the king on the royal throne. [21]So all the people of the land rejoiced, and the city was quiet after Athaliah had been killed with the sword.

## ROMANS 11.13–36

Now I am speaking to you Gentiles. Inasmuch then as I am an apostle to the Gentiles, I glorify my ministry [14]in order to make my own people[c] jealous, and thus save some of them. [15]For if their rejection is the reconciliation of the world, what will their acceptance be but life from the dead! [16]If the part of the dough offered as first fruits is holy, then the whole batch is holy; and if the root is holy, then the branches also are holy.

17 But if some of the branches

---

[a]Heb lacks *other*   [b]Or *treaty*, or *testimony*; Heb *eduth*   [c]Gk *my flesh*

were broken off, and you, a wild olive shoot, were grafted in their place to share the rich root[a] of the olive tree, [18]do not boast over the branches. If you do boast, remember that it is not you that support the root, but the root that supports you. [19]You will say, "Branches were broken off so that I might be grafted in." [20]That is true. They were broken off because of their unbelief, but you stand only through faith. So do not become proud, but stand in awe. [21]For if God did not spare the natural branches, perhaps he will not spare you.[b] [22]Note then the kindness and the severity of God: severity toward those who have fallen, but God's kindness toward you, provided you continue in his kindness; otherwise you also will be cut off. [23]And even those of Israel,[c] if they do not persist in unbelief, will be grafted in, for God has the power to graft them in again. [24]For if you have been cut from what is by nature a wild olive tree and grafted, contrary to nature, into a cultivated olive tree, how much more will these natural branches be grafted back into their own olive tree.

25 So that you may not claim to be wiser than you are, brothers and sisters,[d] I want you to understand this mystery: a hardening has come upon part of Israel, until the full number of the Gentiles has come in. [26]And so all Israel will be saved; as it is written,

"Out of Zion will come the
    Deliverer;
he will banish ungodliness
    from Jacob."
27 "And this is my covenant
    with them,
when I take away their sins."
[28]As regards the gospel they are enemies of God[e] for your sake; but as regards election they are beloved, for the sake of their ancestors; [29]for the gifts and the calling of God are irrevocable.

[30]Just as you were once disobedient to God but have now received mercy because of their disobedience, [31]so they have now been disobedient in order that, by the mercy shown to you, they too may now[f] receive mercy. [32]For God has imprisoned all in disobedience so that he may be merciful to all.

33 O the depth of the riches and wisdom and knowledge of God! How unsearchable are his judgments and how inscrutable his ways!
34 "For who has known the mind
    of the Lord?
  Or who has been his
    counselor?"
35 "Or who has given a gift to him,
    to receive a gift in return?"
[36]For from him and through him and to him are all things. To him be the glory forever. Amen.

## PSALM 22.1–18

*To the leader: according to The Deer of the Dawn. A Psalm of David.*

My God, my God, why have
    you forsaken me?
Why are you so far from
    helping me, from the
    words of my groaning?
2 O my God, I cry by day, but
    you do not answer;
  and by night, but find no rest.

3 Yet you are holy,
    enthroned on the praises of
    Israel.
4 In you our ancestors trusted;
    they trusted, and you
    delivered them.
5 To you they cried, and were
    saved;
  in you they trusted, and were
    not put to shame.

6 But I am a worm, and not
    human;

---

a Other ancient authorities read *the richness*  b Other ancient authorities read *neither will he spare you*  c Gk lacks *of Israel*  d Gk *brothers*  e Gk lacks *of God*  f Other ancient authorities lack *now*

scorned by others, and
    despised by the people.
7 All who see me mock at me;
    they make mouths at me,
      they shake their heads;
8 "Commit your cause to the
      LORD; let him deliver—
    let him rescue the one in
      whom he delights!"

9 Yet it was you who took me
      from the womb;
    you kept me safe on my
      mother's breast.
10 On you I was cast from my
      birth,
    and since my mother bore me
      you have been my God.
11 Do not be far from me,
    for trouble is near
    and there is no one to help.

12 Many bulls encircle me,
    strong bulls of Bashan
      surround me;
13 they open wide their mouths at
      me,
    like a ravening and roaring
      lion.

14 I am poured out like water,
    and all my bones are out of
      joint;
    my heart is like wax;
      it is melted within my breast;
15 my mouth[a] is dried up like a
      potsherd,
    and my tongue sticks to my
      jaws;
    you lay me in the dust of
      death.

16 For dogs are all around me;
    a company of evildoers
      encircles me.
    My hands and feet have
      shriveled;[b]
17 I can count all my bones.
    They stare and gloat over me;
18 they divide my clothes among
      themselves,
    and for my clothing they cast
      lots.

## PROVERBS 20.7

THE righteous walk in
    integrity—
  happy are the children who
    follow them!

# JULY 29

## 2 CHRONICLES 24.1—25.28

JOASH was seven years old when he began to reign; he reigned forty years in Jerusalem; his mother's name was Zibiah of Beersheba. 2Joash did what was right in the sight of the LORD all the days of the priest Jehoiada. 3Jehoiada got two wives for him, and he became the father of sons and daughters.

4 Some time afterward Joash decided to restore the house of the LORD. 5He assembled the priests and the Levites and said to them, "Go out to the cities of Judah and gather money from all Israel to repair the house of your

---

[a] Cn: Heb *strength*  [b] Meaning of Heb uncertain

God, year by year; and see that you act quickly." But the Levites did not act quickly. ⁶So the king summoned Jehoiada the chief, and said to him, "Why have you not required the Levites to bring in from Judah and Jerusalem the tax levied by Moses, the servant of the LORD, on[a] the congregation of Israel for the tent of the covenant?"[b] ⁷For the children of Athaliah, that wicked woman, had broken into the house of God, and had even used all the dedicated things of the house of the LORD for the Baals.

8 So the king gave command, and they made a chest, and set it outside the gate of the house of the LORD. ⁹A proclamation was made throughout Judah and Jerusalem to bring in for the LORD the tax that Moses the servant of God laid on Israel in the wilderness. ¹⁰All the leaders and all the people rejoiced and brought their tax and dropped it into the chest until it was full. ¹¹Whenever the chest was brought to the king's officers by the Levites, when they saw that there was a large amount of money in it, the king's secretary and the officer of the chief priest would come and empty the chest and take it and return it to its place. So they did day after day, and collected money in abundance. ¹²The king and Jehoiada gave it to those who had charge of the work of the house of the LORD, and they hired masons and carpenters to restore the house of the LORD, and also workers in iron and bronze to repair the house of the LORD. ¹³So those who were engaged in the work labored, and the repairing went forward at their hands, and they restored the house of God to its proper condition and strengthened it. ¹⁴When they had finished, they brought the rest of the money to the king and Jehoiada, and with it were made utensils for the house of the LORD, utensils for the service and for the burnt offerings, and ladles, and vessels of gold and silver. They offered burnt offerings in the house of the LORD regularly all the days of Jehoiada.

15 But Jehoiada grew old and full of days, and died; he was one hundred thirty years old at his death. ¹⁶And they buried him in the city of David among the kings, because he had done good in Israel, and for God and his house.

17 Now after the death of Jehoiada the officials of Judah came and did obeisance to the king; then the king listened to them. ¹⁸They abandoned the house of the LORD, the God of their ancestors, and served the sacred poles[c] and the idols. And wrath came upon Judah and Jerusalem for this guilt of theirs. ¹⁹Yet he sent prophets among them to bring them back to the LORD; they testified against them, but they would not listen.

20 Then the spirit of God took possession of[d] Zechariah son of the priest Jehoiada; he stood above the people and said to them, "Thus says God: Why do you transgress the commandments of the LORD, so that you cannot prosper? Because you have forsaken the LORD, he has also forsaken you." ²¹But they conspired against him, and by command of the king they stoned him to death in the court of the house of the LORD. ²²King Joash did not remember the kindness that Jehoiada, Zechariah's father, had shown him, but killed his son. As he was dying, he said, "May the LORD see and avenge!"

23 At the end of the year the army of Aram came up against Joash. They came to Judah and Jerusalem, and destroyed all the officials of the people from among them, and sent all the booty they took to the king of Damascus. ²⁴Although the army of Aram had come with few men, the LORD delivered into their hand a very great army, because they had abandoned the LORD,

aCompare Vg: Heb *and*   bOr *treaty*, or *testimony*; Heb *eduth*   cHeb *Asherim*   dHeb *clothed itself with*

the God of their ancestors. Thus they executed judgment on Joash.

25 When they had withdrawn, leaving him severely wounded, his servants conspired against him because of the blood of the son[a] of the priest Jehoiada, and they killed him on his bed. So he died; and they buried him in the city of David, but they did not bury him in the tombs of the kings. [26]Those who conspired against him were Zabad son of Shimeath the Ammonite, and Jehozabad son of Shimrith the Moabite. [27]Accounts of his sons, and of the many oracles against him, and of the rebuilding[b] of the house of God are written in the Commentary on the Book of the Kings. And his son Amaziah succeeded him.

25.1 AMAZIAH was twenty-five years old when he began to reign, and he reigned twenty-nine years in Jerusalem. His mother's name was Jehoaddan of Jerusalem. [2]He did what was right in the sight of the LORD, yet not with a true heart. [3]As soon as the royal power was firmly in his hand he killed his servants who had murdered his father the king. [4]But he did not put their children to death, according to what is written in the law, in the book of Moses, where the LORD commanded, "The parents shall not be put to death for the children, or the children be put to death for the parents; but all shall be put to death for their own sins."

5 Amaziah assembled the people of Judah, and set them by ancestral houses under commanders of the thousands and of the hundreds for all Judah and Benjamin. He mustered those twenty years old and upward, and found that they were three hundred thousand picked troops fit for war, able to handle spear and shield. [6]He also hired one hundred thousand mighty warriors from Israel for one hundred talents of silver. [7]But a man of God came to him and said, "O king, do not let the army of Israel go with you, for the LORD is not with Israel—all these Ephraimites. [8]Rather, go by yourself and act; be strong in battle, or God will fling you down before the enemy; for God has power to help or to overthrow." [9]Amaziah said to the man of God, "But what shall we do about the hundred talents that I have given to the army of Israel?" The man of God answered, "The LORD is able to give you much more than this." [10]Then Amaziah discharged the army that had come to him from Ephraim, letting them go home again. But they became very angry with Judah, and returned home in fierce anger.

11 Amaziah took courage, and led out his people; he went to the Valley of Salt, and struck down ten thousand men of Seir. [12]The people of Judah captured another ten thousand alive, took them to the top of Sela, and threw them down from the top of Sela, so that all of them were dashed to pieces. [13]But the men of the army whom Amaziah sent back, not letting them go with him to battle, fell on the cities of Judah from Samaria to Beth-horon; they killed three thousand people in them, and took much booty.

14 Now after Amaziah came from the slaughter of the Edomites, he brought the gods of the people of Seir, set them up as his gods, and worshiped them, making offerings to them. [15]The LORD was angry with Amaziah and sent to him a prophet, who said to him, "Why have you resorted to a people's gods who could not deliver their own people from your hand?" [16]But as he was speaking the king[c] said to him, "Have we made you a royal counselor? Stop! Why should you be put to death?" So the prophet stopped, but said, "I know that God has determined to de-

a Gk Vg: Heb *sons*    b Heb *founding*    c Heb *he*

stroy you, because you have done this and have not listened to my advice."

17 Then King Amaziah of Judah took counsel and sent to King Joash son of Jehoahaz son of Jehu of Israel, saying, "Come, let us look one another in the face." [18]King Joash of Israel sent word to King Amaziah of Judah, "A thornbush on Lebanon sent to a cedar on Lebanon, saying, 'Give your daughter to my son for a wife'; but a wild animal of Lebanon passed by and trampled down the thornbush. [19]You say, 'See, I have defeated Edom,' and your heart has lifted you up in boastfulness. Now stay at home; why should you provoke trouble so that you fall, you and Judah with you?"

20 But Amaziah would not listen— it was God's doing, in order to hand them over, because they had sought the gods of Edom. [21]So King Joash of Israel went up; he and King Amaziah of Judah faced one another in battle at Beth-shemesh, which belongs to Judah. [22]Judah was defeated by Israel; everyone fled home. [23]King Joash of Israel captured King Amaziah of Judah, son of Joash, son of Ahaziah, at Beth-shemesh; he brought him to Jerusalem, and broke down the wall of Jerusalem from the Ephraim Gate to the Corner Gate, a distance of four hundred cubits. [24]He seized all the gold and silver, and all the vessels that were found in the house of God, and Obed-edom with them; he seized also the treasuries of the king's house, also hostages; then he returned to Samaria.

25 King Amaziah son of Joash of Judah, lived fifteen years after the death of King Joash son of Jehoahaz of Israel. [26]Now the rest of the deeds of Amaziah, from first to last, are they not written in the Book of the Kings of Judah and Israel? [27]From the time that Amaziah turned away from the LORD they made a conspiracy against him in Jerusalem, and he fled to Lachish. But they sent after him to Lachish, and killed him there. [28]They brought him back on horses; he was buried with his ancestors in the city of David.

# ROMANS 12.1–21

I APPEAL to you therefore, brothers and sisters,[a] by the mercies of God, to present your bodies as a living sacrifice, holy and acceptable to God, which is your spiritual[b] worship. [2]Do not be conformed to this world,[c] but be transformed by the renewing of your minds, so that you may discern what is the will of God—what is good and acceptable and perfect.[d]

3 For by the grace given to me I say to everyone among you not to think of yourself more highly than you ought to think, but to think with sober judgment, each according to the measure of faith that God has assigned. [4]For as in one body we have many members, and not all the members have the same function, [5]so we, who are many, are one body in Christ, and individually we are members one of another. [6]We have gifts that differ according to the grace given to us: prophecy, in proportion to faith; [7]ministry, in ministering; the teacher, in teaching; [8]the exhorter, in exhortation; the giver, in generosity; the leader, in diligence; the compassionate, in cheerfulness.

9 Let love be genuine; hate what is evil, hold fast to what is good; [10]love one another with mutual affection; outdo one another in showing honor. [11]Do not lag in zeal, be ardent in spirit, serve the Lord.[e] [12]Rejoice in hope, be patient in suffering, persevere in prayer. [13]Contribute to the needs of the saints; extend hospitality to strangers.

14 Bless those who persecute you; bless and do not curse them. [15]Rejoice

[a]Gk *brothers*  [b]Or *reasonable*  [c]Gk *age*  [d]Or *what is the good and acceptable and perfect will of God*
[e]Other ancient authorities read *serve the opportune time*

with those who rejoice, weep with those who weep. [16]Live in harmony with one another; do not be haughty, but associate with the lowly;[a] do not claim to be wiser than you are. [17]Do not repay anyone evil for evil, but take thought for what is noble in the sight of all. [18]If it is possible, so far as it depends on you, live peaceably with all. [19]Beloved, never avenge yourselves, but leave room for the wrath of God;[b] for it is written, "Vengeance is mine, I will repay, says the Lord." [20]No, "if your enemies are hungry, feed them; if they are thirsty, give them something to drink; for by doing this you will heap burning coals on their heads." [21]Do not be overcome by evil, but overcome evil with good.

## PSALM 22.19–31

But you, O Lord, do not be far
  away!
O my help, come quickly to
  my aid!
20 Deliver my soul from the
   sword,
  my life[c] from the power of
   the dog!
21 Save me from the mouth of
   the lion!

  From the horns of the wild oxen
   you have rescued[d] me.
22 I will tell of your name to my
   brothers and sisters;[e]
  in the midst of the
   congregation I will praise
   you:
23 You who fear the Lord, praise
   him!
  All you offspring of Jacob,
   glorify him;
  stand in awe of him, all you
   offspring of Israel!

24 For he did not despise or abhor
   the affliction of the afflicted;
  he did not hide his face from
   me,[f]
  but heard when I[g] cried to
   him.

25 From you comes my praise in
   the great congregation;
  my vows I will pay before
   those who fear him.
26 The poor[h] shall eat and be
   satisfied;
  those who seek him shall
   praise the Lord.
  May your hearts live forever!

27 All the ends of the earth shall
   remember
  and turn to the Lord;
  and all the families of the
   nations
  shall worship before him.[i]
28 For dominion belongs to the
   Lord,
  and he rules over the nations.

29 To him,[j] indeed, shall all who
   sleep in[k] the earth bow
   down;
  before him shall bow all who
   go down to the dust,
  and I shall live for him.[l]
30 Posterity will serve him;
  future generations will be told
   about the Lord,
31 and[m] proclaim his deliverance to
   a people yet unborn,
  saying that he has done it.

## PROVERBS 20.8–10

A king who sits on the throne
  of judgment
winnows all evil with his
  eyes.

aOr *give yourselves to humble tasks* bGk *the wrath* cHeb *my only one* dHeb *answered* eOr *kindred*
fHeb *him* gHeb *he* hOr *afflicted* iGk Syr Jerome: Heb *you* jCn: Heb *They have eaten and*
kCn: Heb *all the fat ones* lCompare Gk Syr Vg: Heb *and he who cannot keep himself alive*
mCompare Gk: Heb *it will be told about the Lord to the generation,* 31*they will come and*

9  Who can say, "I have made my
        heart clean;
     I am pure from my sin"?

10  Diverse weights and diverse
         measures
      are both alike an abomination
        to the LORD.

# JULY 30

## 2 CHRONICLES 26.1—28.27

THEN all the people of Judah took Uzziah, who was sixteen years old, and made him king to succeed his father Amaziah. ²He rebuilt Eloth and restored it to Judah, after the king slept with his ancestors. ³Uzziah was sixteen years old when he began to reign, and he reigned fifty-two years in Jerusalem. His mother's name was Jecoliah of Jerusalem. ⁴He did what was right in the sight of the LORD, just as his father Amaziah had done. ⁵He set himself to seek God in the days of Zechariah, who instructed him in the fear of God; and as long as he sought the LORD, God made him prosper.

6 He went out and made war against the Philistines, and broke down the wall of Gath and the wall of Jabneh and the wall of Ashdod; he built cities in the territory of Ashdod and elsewhere among the Philistines. ⁷God helped him against the Philistines, against the Arabs who lived in Gurbaal, and against the Meunites. ⁸The Ammonites paid tribute to Uzziah, and his fame spread even to the border of Egypt, for he became very strong. ⁹Moreover Uzziah built towers in Jerusalem at the Corner Gate, at the Valley Gate, and at the Angle, and fortified them. ¹⁰He built towers in the wilderness and hewed out many cisterns, for he had large herds, both in the Shephelah and in the plain, and he had farmers and vinedressers in the hills and in the fertile lands, for he loved the soil. ¹¹Moreover Uzziah had an army of soldiers, fit for war, in divisions according to the numbers in the muster made by the secretary Jeiel and the officer Maaseiah, under the direction of Hananiah, one of the king's commanders. ¹²The whole number of the heads of ancestral houses of mighty warriors was two thousand six hundred. ¹³Under their command was an army of three hundred seven thousand five hundred, who could make war with mighty power, to help the king against the enemy. ¹⁴Uzziah provided for all the army the shields, spears, helmets, coats of mail, bows, and stones for slinging. ¹⁵In Jerusalem he set up machines, invented by skilled workers, on the towers and the corners for shooting arrows and large stones. And his fame spread far, for he was marvelously helped until he became strong.

16 But when he had become strong he grew proud, to his destruction. For he was false to the LORD his God, and entered the temple of the LORD to make offering on the altar of incense. ¹⁷But the priest Azariah went in after him, with eighty priests of the LORD who were men of valor; ¹⁸they withstood King Uzziah, and said to him, "It is not for you, Uzziah, to make offering to the LORD, but for the priests the descendants of Aaron, who are consecrated to

make offering. Go out of the sanctuary; for you have done wrong, and it will bring you no honor from the Lord God." ¹⁹Then Uzziah was angry. Now he had a censer in his hand to make offering, and when he became angry with the priests a leprous[a] disease broke out on his forehead, in the presence of the priests in the house of the Lord, by the altar of incense. ²⁰When the chief priest Azariah, and all the priests, looked at him, he was leprous[a] in his forehead. They hurried him out, and he himself hurried to get out, because the Lord had struck him. ²¹King Uzziah was leprous[a] to the day of his death, and being leprous[a] lived in a separate house, for he was excluded from the house of the Lord. His son Jotham was in charge of the palace of the king, governing the people of the land.

22 Now the rest of the acts of Uzziah, from first to last, the prophet Isaiah son of Amoz wrote. ²³Uzziah slept with his ancestors; they buried him near his ancestors in the burial field that belonged to the kings, for they said, "He is leprous."[a] His son Jotham succeeded him.

²⁷.¹ JOTHAM was twenty-five years old when he began to reign; he reigned sixteen years in Jerusalem. His mother's name was Jerushah daughter of Zadok. ²He did what was right in the sight of the Lord just as his father Uzziah had done—only he did not invade the temple of the Lord. But the people still followed corrupt practices. ³He built the upper gate of the house of the Lord, and did extensive building on the wall of Ophel. ⁴Moreover he built cities in the hill country of Judah, and forts and towers on the wooded hills. ⁵He fought with the king of the Ammonites and prevailed against them. The Ammonites gave him that year one hundred talents of silver, ten thousand cors of

wheat and ten thousand of barley. The Ammonites paid him the same amount in the second and the third years. ⁶So Jotham became strong because he ordered his ways before the Lord his God. ⁷Now the rest of the acts of Jotham, and all his wars and his ways, are written in the Book of the Kings of Israel and Judah. ⁸He was twenty-five years old when he began to reign; he reigned sixteen years in Jerusalem. ⁹Jotham slept with his ancestors, and they buried him in the city of David; and his son Ahaz succeeded him.

²⁸.¹ AHAZ was twenty years old when he began to reign; he reigned sixteen years in Jerusalem. He did not do what was right in the sight of the Lord, as his ancestor David had done, ²but he walked in the ways of the kings of Israel. He even made cast images for the Baals; ³and he made offerings in the valley of the son of Hinnom, and made his sons pass through fire, according to the abominable practices of the nations whom the Lord drove out before the people of Israel. ⁴He sacrificed and made offerings on the high places, on the hills, and under every green tree.

5 Therefore the Lord his God gave him into the hand of the king of Aram, who defeated him and took captive a great number of his people and brought them to Damascus. He was also given into the hand of the king of Israel, who defeated him with great slaughter. ⁶Pekah son of Remaliah killed one hundred twenty thousand in Judah in one day, all of them valiant warriors, because they had abandoned the Lord, the God of their ancestors. ⁷And Zichri, a mighty warrior of Ephraim, killed the king's son Maaseiah, Azrikam the commander of the palace, and Elkanah the next in authority to the king.

8 The people of Israel took captive two hundred thousand of their kin,

aA term for several skin diseases; precise meaning uncertain

women, sons, and daughters; they also took much booty from them and brought the booty to Samaria. ⁹But a prophet of the LORD was there, whose name was Oded; he went out to meet the army that came to Samaria, and said to them, "Because the LORD, the God of your ancestors, was angry with Judah, he gave them into your hand, but you have killed them in a rage that has reached up to heaven. ¹⁰Now you intend to subjugate the people of Judah and Jerusalem, male and female, as your slaves. But what have you except sins against the LORD your God? ¹¹Now hear me, and send back the captives whom you have taken from your kindred, for the fierce wrath of the LORD is upon you." ¹²Moreover, certain chiefs of the Ephraimites, Azariah son of Johanan, Berechiah son of Meshillemoth, Jehizkiah son of Shallum, and Amasa son of Hadlai, stood up against those who were coming from the war, ¹³and said to them, "You shall not bring the captives in here, for you propose to bring on us guilt against the LORD in addition to our present sins and guilt. For our guilt is already great, and there is fierce wrath against Israel." ¹⁴So the warriors left the captives and the booty before the officials and all the assembly. ¹⁵Then those who were mentioned by name got up and took the captives, and with the booty they clothed all that were naked among them; they clothed them, gave them sandals, provided them with food and drink, and anointed them; and carrying all the feeble among them on donkeys, they brought them to their kindred at Jericho, the city of palm trees. Then they returned to Samaria.

16 At that time King Ahaz sent to the king[a] of Assyria for help. ¹⁷For the Edomites had again invaded and defeated Judah, and carried away captives. ¹⁸And the Philistines had made raids on the cities in the Shephelah and the Negeb of Judah, and had taken Beth-shemesh, Aijalon, Gederoth, Soco with its villages, Timnah with its villages, and Gimzo with its villages; and they settled there. ¹⁹For the LORD brought Judah low because of King Ahaz of Israel, for he had behaved without restraint in Judah and had been faithless to the LORD. ²⁰So King Tilgath-pilneser of Assyria came against him, and oppressed him instead of strengthening him. ²¹For Ahaz plundered the house of the LORD and the houses of the king and of the officials, and gave tribute to the king of Assyria; but it did not help him.

22 In the time of his distress he became yet more faithless to the LORD— this same King Ahaz. ²³For he sacrificed to the gods of Damascus, which had defeated him, and said, "Because the gods of the kings of Aram helped them, I will sacrifice to them so that they may help me." But they were the ruin of him, and of all Israel. ²⁴Ahaz gathered together the utensils of the house of God, and cut in pieces the utensils of the house of God. He shut up the doors of the house of the LORD and made himself altars in every corner of Jerusalem. ²⁵In every city of Judah he made high places to make offerings to other gods, provoking to anger the LORD, the God of his ancestors. ²⁶Now the rest of his acts and all his ways, from first to last, are written in the Book of the Kings of Judah and Israel. ²⁷Ahaz slept with his ancestors, and they buried him in the city, in Jerusalem; but they did not bring him into the tombs of the kings of Israel. His son Hezekiah succeeded him.

# ROMANS 13.1–14

Let every person be subject to the governing authorities; for there is no authority except

---

[a] Gk Syr Vg Compare 2 Kings 16.7: Heb *kings*

from God, and those authorities that exist have been instituted by God. 2Therefore whoever resists authority resists what God has appointed, and those who resist will incur judgment. 3For rulers are not a terror to good conduct, but to bad. Do you wish to have no fear of the authority? Then do what is good, and you will receive its approval; 4for it is God's servant for your good. But if you do what is wrong, you should be afraid, for the authoritya does not bear the sword in vain! It is the servant of God to execute wrath on the wrongdoer. 5Therefore one must be subject, not only because of wrath but also because of conscience. 6For the same reason you also pay taxes, for the authorities are God's servants, busy with this very thing. 7Pay to all what is due them—taxes to whom taxes are due, revenue to whom revenue is due, respect to whom respect is due, honor to whom honor is due.

8 Owe no one anything, except to love one another; for the one who loves another has fulfilled the law. 9The commandments, "You shall not commit adultery; You shall not murder; You shall not steal; You shall not covet"; and any other commandment, are summed up in this word, "Love your neighbor as yourself." 10Love does no wrong to a neighbor; therefore, love is the fulfilling of the law.

11 Besides this, you know what time it is, how it is now the moment for you to wake from sleep. For salvation is nearer to us now than when we became believers; 12the night is far gone, the day is near. Let us then lay aside the works of darkness and put on the armor of light; 13let us live honorably as in the day, not in reveling and drunkenness, not in debauchery and licentiousness, not in quarreling and jealousy. 14Instead, put on the Lord Jesus Christ,

and make no provision for the flesh, to gratify its desires.

## PSALM 23.1–6

*A Psalm of David.*

THE LORD is my shepherd, I
   shall not want.
2    He makes me lie down
    in green pastures;
he leads me beside still
    waters; b
3   he restores my soul. c
He leads me in right pathsd
   for his name's sake.

4  Even though I walk through the
    darkest valley, e
  I fear no evil;
for you are with me;
   your rod and your staff—
  they comfort me.

5  You prepare a table before me
   in the presence of my
   enemies;
you anoint my head with oil;
   my cup overflows.
6  Surelyf goodness and mercyg
    shall follow me
  all the days of my life,
and I shall dwell in the house of
   the LORD
  my whole life long. h

## PROVERBS 20.11

EVEN children make themselves
   known by their acts,
by whether what they do is
   pure and right.

aGk *it*  bHeb *waters of rest*  cOr *life*  dOr *paths of righteousness*  eOr *the valley of the shadow of death*  fOr *Only*  gOr *kindness*  hHeb *for length of days*

## 2 CHRONICLES 29.1–36

**H**EZEKIAH began to reign when he was twenty-five years old; he reigned twenty-nine years in Jerusalem. His mother's name was Abijah daughter of Zechariah. ²He did what was right in the sight of the LORD, just as his ancestor David had done.

3 In the first year of his reign, in the first month, he opened the doors of the house of the LORD and repaired them. ⁴He brought in the priests and the Levites and assembled them in the square on the east. ⁵He said to them, "Listen to me, Levites! Sanctify yourselves, and sanctify the house of the LORD, the God of your ancestors, and carry out the filth from the holy place. ⁶For our ancestors have been unfaithful and have done what was evil in the sight of the LORD our God; they have forsaken him, and have turned away their faces from the dwelling of the LORD, and turned their backs. ⁷They also shut the doors of the vestibule and put out the lamps, and have not offered incense or made burnt offerings in the holy place to the God of Israel. ⁸Therefore the wrath of the LORD came upon Judah and Jerusalem, and he has made them an object of horror, of astonishment, and of hissing, as you see with your own eyes. ⁹Our fathers have fallen by the sword and our sons and our daughters and our wives are in captivity for this. ¹⁰Now it is in my heart to make a covenant with the LORD, the God of Israel, so that his fierce anger may turn away from us. ¹¹My sons, do not now be negligent, for the LORD has chosen you to stand in his presence to minister to him, and to be his ministers and make offerings to him."

12 Then the Levites arose, Mahath son of Amasai, and Joel son of Azariah, of the sons of the Kohathites; and of the sons of Merari, Kish son of Abdi, and Azariah son of Jehallelel; and of the Gershonites, Joah son of Zimmah, and Eden son of Joah; ¹³and of the sons of Elizaphan, Shimri and Jeuel; and of the sons of Asaph, Zechariah and Mattaniah; ¹⁴and of the sons of Heman, Jehuel and Shimei; and of the sons of Jeduthun, Shemaiah and Uzziel. ¹⁵They gathered their brothers, sanctified themselves, and went in as the king had commanded, by the words of the LORD, to cleanse the house of the LORD. ¹⁶The priests went into the inner part of the house of the LORD to cleanse it, and they brought out all the unclean things that they found in the temple of the LORD into the court of the house of the LORD; and the Levites took them and carried them out to the Wadi Kidron. ¹⁷They began to sanctify on the first day of the first month, and on the eighth day of the month they came to the vestibule of the LORD; then for eight days they sanctified the house of the LORD, and on the sixteenth day of the first month they finished. ¹⁸Then they went inside to King Hezekiah and said, "We have cleansed all the house of the LORD, the altar of burnt offering and all its utensils, and the table for the rows of bread and all its utensils. ¹⁹All the utensils that King Ahaz repudiated during his reign when he was faithless, we have made ready and sanctified; see, they are in front of the altar of the LORD."

20 Then King Hezekiah rose early, assembled the officials of the city, and went up to the house of the LORD. ²¹They brought seven bulls, seven rams, seven lambs, and seven male goats for a sin offering for the kingdom and for the sanctuary and for Judah. He

commanded the priests the descendants of Aaron to offer them on the altar of the Lord. 22So they slaughtered the bulls, and the priests received the blood and dashed it against the altar; they slaughtered the rams and their blood was dashed against the altar; they also slaughtered the lambs and their blood was dashed against the altar. 23Then the male goats for the sin offering were brought to the king and the assembly; they laid their hands on them, 24and the priests slaughtered them and made a sin offering with their blood at the altar, to make atonement for all Israel. For the king commanded that the burnt offering and the sin offering should be made for all Israel.

25 He stationed the Levites in the house of the Lord with cymbals, harps, and lyres, according to the commandment of David and of Gad the king's seer and of the prophet Nathan, for the commandment was from the Lord through his prophets. 26The Levites stood with the instruments of David, and the priests with the trumpets. 27Then Hezekiah commanded that the burnt offering be offered on the altar. When the burnt offering began, the song to the Lord began also, and the trumpets, accompanied by the instruments of King David of Israel. 28The whole assembly worshiped, the singers sang, and the trumpeters sounded; all this continued until the burnt offering was finished. 29When the offering was finished, the king and all who were present with him bowed down and worshiped. 30King Hezekiah and the officials commanded the Levites to sing praises to the Lord with the words of David and of the seer Asaph. They sang praises with gladness, and they bowed down and worshiped.

31 Then Hezekiah said, "You have now consecrated yourselves to the Lord; come near, bring sacrifices and thank offerings to the house of the Lord." The assembly brought sacrifices and thank offerings; and all who were of a willing heart brought burnt offerings. 32The number of the burnt offerings that the assembly brought was seventy bulls, one hundred rams, and two hundred lambs; all these were for a burnt offering to the Lord. 33The consecrated offerings were six hundred bulls and three thousand sheep. 34But the priests were too few and could not skin all the burnt offerings, so, until other priests had sanctified themselves, their kindred, the Levites, helped them until the work was finished—for the Levites were more conscientious[a] than the priests in sanctifying themselves. 35Besides the great number of burnt offerings there was the fat of the offerings of well-being, and there were the drink offerings for the burnt offerings. Thus the service of the house of the Lord was restored. 36And Hezekiah and all the people rejoiced because of what God had done for the people; for the thing had come about suddenly.

## ROMANS 14. 1–23

WELCOME those who are weak in faith,[b] but not for the purpose of quarreling over opinions. 2Some believe in eating anything, while the weak eat only vegetables. 3Those who eat must not despise those who abstain, and those who abstain must not pass judgment on those who eat; for God has welcomed them. 4Who are you to pass judgment on servants of another? It is before their own lord that they stand or fall. And they will be upheld, for the Lord[c] is able to make them stand.

5 Some judge one day to be better than another, while others judge all days to be alike. Let all be fully con-

a Heb *upright in heart*   b Or *conviction*   c Other ancient authorities read *for God*

vinced in their own minds. <sup>6</sup>Those who observe the day, observe it in honor of the Lord. Also those who eat, eat in honor of the Lord, since they give thanks to God; while those who abstain, abstain in honor of the Lord and give thanks to God.

7 We do not live to ourselves, and we do not die to ourselves. <sup>8</sup>If we live, we live to the Lord, and if we die, we die to the Lord; so then, whether we live or whether we die, we are the Lord's. <sup>9</sup>For to this end Christ died and lived again, so that he might be Lord of both the dead and the living.

10 Why do you pass judgment on your brother or sister?<sup>a</sup> Or you, why do you despise your brother or sister?<sup>a</sup> For we will all stand before the judgment seat of God.<sup>b</sup> <sup>11</sup>For it is written,

> "As I live, says the Lord, every
>     knee shall bow to me,
>   and every tongue shall give
>     praise to<sup>c</sup> God."

<sup>12</sup>So then, each of us will be accountable to God.<sup>d</sup>

13 Let us therefore no longer pass judgment on one another, but resolve instead never to put a stumbling block or hindrance in the way of another.<sup>e</sup> <sup>14</sup>I know and am persuaded in the Lord Jesus that nothing is unclean in itself; but it is unclean for anyone who thinks it unclean. <sup>15</sup>If your brother or sister<sup>a</sup> is being injured by what you eat, you are no longer walking in love. Do not let what you eat cause the ruin of one for whom Christ died. <sup>16</sup>So do not let your good be spoken of as evil. <sup>17</sup>For the kingdom of God is not food and drink but righteousness and peace and joy in the Holy Spirit. <sup>18</sup>The one who thus serves Christ is acceptable to God and has human approval. <sup>19</sup>Let us then pursue what makes for peace and for mutual upbuilding. <sup>20</sup>Do not, for the sake of food, destroy the work of God. Everything is indeed clean, but it is wrong for you to make others fall by what you eat; <sup>21</sup>it is good not to eat meat or drink wine or do anything that makes your brother or sister<sup>a</sup> stumble.<sup>f</sup> <sup>22</sup>The faith that you have, have as your own conviction before God. Blessed are those who have no reason to condemn themselves because of what they approve. <sup>23</sup>But those who have doubts are condemned if they eat, because they do not act from faith;<sup>g</sup> for whatever does not proceed from faith<sup>g</sup> is sin.<sup>h</sup>

## PSALM 24.1–10

*Of David. A Psalm.*

THE earth is the LORD's and all
   that is in it,
  the world, and those who
   live in it;
<sup>2</sup> for he has founded it on the
   seas,
  and established it on the
   rivers.

<sup>3</sup> Who shall ascend the hill of the
   LORD?
  And who shall stand in his
   holy place?
<sup>4</sup> Those who have clean hands
   and pure hearts,
  who do not lift up their souls
   to what is false,
  and do not swear deceitfully.
<sup>5</sup> They will receive blessing from
   the LORD,
  and vindication from the God
   of their salvation.
<sup>6</sup> Such is the company of those
   who seek him,
  who seek the face of the God
   of Jacob.<sup>i</sup>     *Selah*

<sup>a</sup>Gk *brother*  <sup>b</sup>Other ancient authorities read *of Christ*  <sup>c</sup>Or *confess*  <sup>d</sup>Other ancient authorities lack *to God*  <sup>e</sup>Gk *of a brother*  <sup>f</sup>Other ancient authorities add *or be upset or be weakened*  <sup>g</sup>Or *conviction*  <sup>h</sup>Other authorities, some ancient, add here 16.25-27  <sup>i</sup>Gk Syr: Heb *your face, O Jacob*

7 Lift up your heads, O gates!
    and be lifted up, O ancient
       doors!
    that the King of glory may
       come in.
8 Who is the King of glory?
    The LORD, strong and mighty,
    the LORD, mighty in battle.
9 Lift up your heads, O gates!
    and be lifted up, O ancient
       doors!

    that the King of glory may
       come in.
10 Who is this King of glory?
    The LORD of hosts,
    he is the King of glory. *Selah*

## PROVERBS 20.12

THE hearing ear and the seeing
    eye—
the LORD has made them
    both.

# AUGUST 1

## 2 CHRONICLES 30.1—31.21

HEZEKIAH sent word to all Israel and Judah, and wrote letters also to Ephraim and Manasseh, that they should come to the house of the LORD at Jerusalem, to keep the passover to the LORD the God of Israel. 2For the king and his officials and all the assembly in Jerusalem had taken counsel to keep the passover in the second month 3(for they could not keep it at its proper time because the priests had not sanctified themselves in sufficient number, nor had the people assembled in Jerusalem). 4The plan seemed right to the king and all the assembly. 5So they decreed to make a proclamation throughout all Israel, from Beer-sheba to Dan, that the people should come and keep the passover to the LORD the God of Israel, at Jerusalem; for they had not kept it in great numbers as prescribed. 6So couriers went throughout all Israel and Judah with letters from the king and his officials, as the king had commanded, saying, "O people of Israel, return to the LORD, the God of Abraham, Isaac, and Israel, so that he may turn again to the remnant of you who have escaped from the hand of the kings of Assyria. 7Do not be like your ancestors and your kindred, who were faithless to the LORD God of their ancestors, so that he made them a desolation, as you see. 8Do not now be stiff-necked as your ancestors were, but yield yourselves to the LORD and come to his sanctuary, which he has sanctified forever, and serve the LORD your God, so that his fierce anger may turn away from you. 9For as you return to the LORD, your kindred and your children will find compassion with their captors, and return to this land. For the LORD your God is gracious and merciful, and will not turn away his face from you, if you return to him."

10 So the couriers went from city to city through the country of Ephraim and Manasseh, and as far as Zebulun; but they laughed them to scorn, and mocked them. 11Only a few from Asher, Manasseh, and Zebulun humbled themselves and came to Jerusalem. 12The hand of God was also on Judah to give them one heart to do what the king and the officials commanded by the word of the LORD.

13 Many people came together in Jerusalem to keep the festival of unleavened bread in the second month, a very large assembly. 14They set to work and removed the altars that were in Jerusalem, and all the altars for offering incense they took away and threw into the Wadi Kidron. 15They slaughtered the passover lamb on the fourteenth day of the second month. The priests and the Levites were ashamed, and they sanctified themselves and brought burnt offerings into the house of the Lord. 16They took their accustomed posts according to the law of Moses the man of God; the priests dashed the blood that they received[a] from the hands of the Levites. 17For there were many in the assembly who had not sanctified themselves; therefore the Levites had to slaughter the passover lamb for everyone who was not clean, to make it holy to the Lord. 18For a multitude of the people, many of them from Ephraim, Manasseh, Issachar, and Zebulun, had not cleansed themselves, yet they ate the passover otherwise than as prescribed. But Hezekiah prayed for them, saying, "The good Lord pardon all 19who set their hearts to seek God, the Lord the God of their ancestors, even though not in accordance with the sanctuary's rules of cleanness." 20The Lord heard Hezekiah, and healed the people. 21The people of Israel who were present at Jerusalem kept the festival of unleavened bread seven days with great gladness; and the Levites and the priests praised the Lord day by day, accompanied by loud instruments for the Lord. 22Hezekiah spoke encouragingly to all the Levites who showed good skill in the service of the Lord. So the people ate the food of the festival for seven days, sacrificing offerings of well-being and giving thanks to the Lord the God of their ancestors.

23 Then the whole assembly agreed together to keep the festival for another seven days; so they kept it for another seven days with gladness. 24For King Hezekiah of Judah gave the assembly a thousand bulls and seven thousand sheep for offerings, and the officials gave the assembly a thousand bulls and ten thousand sheep. The priests sanctified themselves in great numbers. 25The whole assembly of Judah, the priests and the Levites, and the whole assembly that came out of Israel, and the resident aliens who came out of the land of Israel, and the resident aliens who lived in Judah, rejoiced. 26There was great joy in Jerusalem, for since the time of Solomon son of King David of Israel there had been nothing like this in Jerusalem. 27Then the priests and the Levites stood up and blessed the people, and their voice was heard; their prayer came to his holy dwelling in heaven.

31.1 Now when all this was finished, all Israel who were present went out to the cities of Judah and broke down the pillars, hewed down the sacred poles,[b] and pulled down the high places and the altars throughout all Judah and Benjamin, and in Ephraim and Manasseh, until they had destroyed them all. Then all the people of Israel returned to their cities, all to their individual properties.

2 Hezekiah appointed the divisions of the priests and of the Levites, division by division, everyone according to his service, the priests and the Levites, for burnt offerings and offerings of well-being, to minister in the gates of the camp of the Lord and to give thanks and praise. 3The contribution of the king from his own possessions was for the burnt offerings: the burnt offerings of morning and evening, and the burnt offerings for the sabbaths, the new moons, and the appointed festivals, as

a Heb lacks *that they received*   b Heb *Asherim*

it is written in the law of the Lord. ⁴He commanded the people who lived in Jerusalem to give the portion due to the priests and the Levites, so that they might devote themselves to the law of the Lord. ⁵As soon as the word spread, the people of Israel gave in abundance the first fruits of grain, wine, oil, honey, and of all the produce of the field; and they brought in abundantly the tithe of everything. ⁶The people of Israel and Judah who lived in the cities of Judah also brought in the tithe of cattle and sheep, and the tithe of the dedicated things that had been consecrated to the Lord their God, and laid them in heaps. ⁷In the third month they began to pile up the heaps, and finished them in the seventh month. ⁸When Hezekiah and the officials came and saw the heaps, they blessed the Lord and his people Israel. ⁹Hezekiah questioned the priests and the Levites about the heaps. ¹⁰The chief priest Azariah, who was of the house of Zadok, answered him, "Since they began to bring the contributions into the house of the Lord, we have had enough to eat and have plenty to spare; for the Lord has blessed his people, so that we have this great supply left over."

11 Then Hezekiah commanded them to prepare store-chambers in the house of the Lord; and they prepared them. ¹²Faithfully they brought in the contributions, the tithes and the dedicated things. The chief officer in charge of them was Conaniah the Levite, with his brother Shimei as second; ¹³while Jehiel, Azaziah, Nahath, Asahel, Jerimoth, Jozabad, Eliel, Ismachiah, Mahath, and Benaiah were overseers assisting Conaniah and his brother Shimei, by the appointment of King Hezekiah and of Azariah the chief officer of the house of God. ¹⁴Kore son of Imnah the Levite, keeper of the east gate, was in charge of the freewill offerings to God, to apportion the contribution reserved for the Lord and the most holy offerings. ¹⁵Eden, Miniamin, Jeshua, Shemaiah, Amariah, and Shecaniah were faithfully assisting him in the cities of the priests, to distribute the portions to their kindred, old and young alike, by divisions, ¹⁶except those enrolled by genealogy, males from three years old and upwards, all who entered the house of the Lord as the duty of each day required, for their service according to their offices, by their divisions. ¹⁷The enrollment of the priests was according to their ancestral houses; that of the Levites from twenty years old and upwards was according to their offices, by their divisions. ¹⁸The priests were enrolled with all their little children, their wives, their sons, and their daughters, the whole multitude; for they were faithful in keeping themselves holy. ¹⁹And for the descendants of Aaron, the priests, who were in the fields of common land belonging to their towns, town by town, the people designated by name were to distribute portions to every male among the priests and to everyone among the Levites who was enrolled.

20 Hezekiah did this throughout all Judah; he did what was good and right and faithful before the Lord his God. ²¹And every work that he undertook in the service of the house of God, and in accordance with the law and the commandments, to seek his God, he did with all his heart; and he prospered.

## ROMANS 15.1–22

WE who are strong ought to put up with the failings of the weak, and not to please ourselves. ²Each of us must please our neighbor for the good purpose of building up the neighbor. ³For Christ did not please himself; but, as it is written, "The insults of those who insult you have fallen on me." ⁴For whatever was written in former days was written for our instruction, so that by steadfastness and by the encouragement of the scriptures we might have hope. [5]May the God of steadfastness and encouragement grant you to live in harmony with one another, in accordance with Christ Jesus, [6]so that together you may with one voice glorify the God and Father of our Lord Jesus Christ.

7 Welcome one another, therefore, just as Christ has welcomed you, for the glory of God. [8]For I tell you that Christ has become a servant of the circumcised on behalf of the truth of God in order that he might confirm the promises given to the patriarchs, [9]and in order that the Gentiles might glorify God for his mercy. As it is written,

> "Therefore I will confess[a] you
> among the Gentiles,
> and sing praises to your
> name";

[10]and again he says,

> "Rejoice, O Gentiles, with his
> people";

[11]and again,

> "Praise the Lord, all you
> Gentiles,
> and let all the peoples
> praise him";

[12]and again Isaiah says,

> "The root of Jesse shall come,
> the one who rises to rule
> the Gentiles;
> in him the Gentiles shall hope."

[13]May the God of hope fill you with all joy and peace in believing, so that you may abound in hope by the power of the Holy Spirit.

14 I myself feel confident about you, my brothers and sisters,[b] that you yourselves are full of goodness, filled with all knowledge, and able to instruct one another. [15]Nevertheless on some points I have written to you rather boldly by way of reminder, because of the grace given me by God [16]to be a minister of Christ Jesus to the Gentiles in the priestly service of the gospel of God, so that the offering of the Gentiles may be acceptable, sanctified by the Holy Spirit. [17]In Christ Jesus, then, I have reason to boast of my work for God. [18]For I will not venture to speak of anything except what Christ has accomplished[c] through me to win obedience from the Gentiles, by word and deed, [19]by the power of signs and wonders, by the power of the Spirit of God,[d] so that from Jerusalem and as far around as Illyricum I have fully proclaimed the good news[e] of Christ. [20]Thus I make it my ambition to proclaim the good news,[e] not where Christ has already been named, so that I do not build on someone else's foundation, [21]but as it is written,

> "Those who have never been
> told of him shall see,
> and those who have never
> heard of him shall
> understand."

22 This is the reason that I have so often been hindered from coming to you.

## PSALM 25.1–15

*Of David.*

> To you, O LORD, I lift up my
> soul.
> [2] O my God, in you I trust;
> do not let me be put to
> shame;
> do not let my enemies exult
> over me.
> [3] Do not let those who wait for
> you be put to shame;
> let them be ashamed who are
> wantonly treacherous.
>
> [4] Make me to know your ways,
> O LORD;
> teach me your paths.
> [5] Lead me in your truth, and
> teach me,

for you are the God of my
    salvation;
for you I wait all day long.

6 Be mindful of your mercy,
    O LORD, and of your
    steadfast love,
for they have been from of
    old.
7 Do not remember the sins of
    my youth or my
    transgressions;
according to your steadfast
    love remember me,
for your goodness' sake,
    O LORD!

8 Good and upright is the LORD;
    therefore he instructs sinners
    in the way.
9 He leads the humble in what is
    right,
    and teaches the humble his
    way.
10 All the paths of the LORD are
    steadfast love and
    faithfulness,
for those who keep his
    covenant and his
    decrees.

11 For your name's sake, O LORD,
    pardon my guilt, for it is
    great.
12 Who are they that fear the
    LORD?
    He will teach them the way
    that they should choose.

13 They will abide in prosperity,
    and their children shall
    possess the land.
14 The friendship of the LORD is for
    those who fear him,
    and he makes his covenant
    known to them.
15 My eyes are ever toward the
    LORD,
for he will pluck my feet out
    of the net.

## PROVERBS 20.13–15

Do not love sleep, or else you
    will come to poverty;
open your eyes, and you
    will have plenty of bread.
14 "Bad, bad," says the buyer,
    then goes away and boasts.
15 There is gold, and abundance of
    costly stones;
but the lips informed by
    knowledge are a
    precious jewel.

# AUGUST 2

## 2 CHRONICLES 32.1—33.13

After these things and these acts of faithfulness, King Sennacherib of Assyria came and invaded Judah and encamped against the fortified cities, thinking to win them for himself. 2When Hezekiah saw that Sennacherib had come and intended to fight against Jerusalem, 3he planned with his officers and his warriors to stop the flow of the springs that were outside the city; and they helped him. 4A great many people were gathered, and they stopped all the springs and the wadi that flowed through the land, saying, "Why should the Assyrian kings come and find water in abundance?" [5]Hezekiah[a] set to work resolutely and built up the entire wall that was broken down, and raised towers on it,[b] and outside it he built another wall; he also strengthened the Millo in the city of David, and made weapons and shields in abundance. [6]He appointed combat commanders over the people, and gathered them together to him in the square at the gate of the city and spoke encouragingly to them, saying, [7]"Be strong and of good courage. Do not be afraid or dismayed before the king of Assyria and all the horde that is with him; for there is one greater with us than with him. [8]With him is an arm of flesh; but with us is the Lord our God, to help us and to fight our battles." The people were encouraged by the words of King Hezekiah of Judah.

[9] After this, while King Sennacherib of Assyria was at Lachish with all his forces, he sent his servants to Jerusalem to King Hezekiah of Judah and to all the people of Judah that were in Jerusalem, saying, [10]"Thus says King Sennacherib of Assyria: On what are you relying, that you undergo the siege of Jerusalem? [11]Is not Hezekiah misleading you, handing you over to die by famine and by thirst, when he tells you, 'The Lord our God will save us from the hand of the king of Assyria'? [12]Was it not this same Hezekiah who took away his high places and his altars and commanded Judah and Jerusalem, saying, 'Before one altar you shall worship, and upon it you shall make your offerings'? [13]Do you not know what I and my ancestors have done to all the peoples of other lands? Were the gods of the nations of those lands at all able to save their lands out of my hand? [14]Who among all the gods of those nations that my ancestors utterly destroyed was able to save his people from my hand, that your God should be able to save

you from my hand? [15]Now therefore do not let Hezekiah deceive you or mislead you in this fashion, and do not believe him, for no god of any nation or kingdom has been able to save his people from my hand or from the hand of my ancestors. How much less will your God save you out of my hand!"

16 His servants said still more against the Lord God and against his servant Hezekiah. [17]He also wrote letters to throw contempt on the Lord the God of Israel and to speak against him, saying, "Just as the gods of the nations in other lands did not rescue their people from my hands, so the God of Hezekiah will not rescue his people from my hand." [18]They shouted it with a loud voice in the language of Judah to the people of Jerusalem who were on the wall, to frighten and terrify them, in order that they might take the city. [19]They spoke of the God of Jerusalem as if he were like the gods of the peoples of the earth, which are the work of human hands.

20 Then King Hezekiah and the prophet Isaiah son of Amoz prayed because of this and cried to heaven. [21]And the Lord sent an angel who cut off all the mighty warriors and commanders and officers in the camp of the king of Assyria. So he returned in disgrace to his own land. When he came into the house of his god, some of his own sons struck him down there with the sword. [22]So the Lord saved Hezekiah and the inhabitants of Jerusalem from the hand of King Sennacherib of Assyria and from the hand of all his enemies; he gave them rest[c] on every side. [23]Many brought gifts to the Lord in Jerusalem and precious things to King Hezekiah of Judah, so that he was exalted in the sight of all nations from that time onward.

24 In those days Hezekiah became sick and was at the point of death. He

---

ᵃVg: Heb *and raised on the towers*   ᶜGk Vg: Heb *guided them*

prayed to the Lord, and he answered him and gave him a sign. 25But Hezekiah did not respond according to the benefit done to him, for his heart was proud. Therefore wrath came upon him and upon Judah and Jerusalem. 26Then Hezekiah humbled himself for the pride of his heart, both he and the inhabitants of Jerusalem, so that the wrath of the Lord did not come upon them in the days of Hezekiah.

27 Hezekiah had very great riches and honor; and he made for himself treasuries for silver, for gold, for precious stones, for spices, for shields, and for all kinds of costly objects; 28storehouses also for the yield of grain, wine, and oil; and stalls for all kinds of cattle, and sheepfolds. a 29He likewise provided cities for himself, and flocks and herds in abundance; for God had given him very great possessions. 30This same Hezekiah closed the upper outlet of the waters of Gihon and directed them down to the west side of the city of David. Hezekiah prospered in all his works. 31So also in the matter of the envoys of the officials of Babylon, who had been sent to him to inquire about the sign that had been done in the land, God left him to himself, in order to test him and to know all that was in his heart.

32 Now the rest of the acts of Hezekiah, and his good deeds, are written in the vision of the prophet Isaiah son of Amoz in the Book of the Kings of Judah and Israel. 33Hezekiah slept with his ancestors, and they buried him on the ascent to the tombs of the descendants of David; and all Judah and the inhabitants of Jerusalem did him honor at his death. His son Manasseh succeeded him.

33.1 Manasseh was twelve years old when he began to reign; he reigned fifty-five years in Jerusalem. 2He did what was evil in the sight of the Lord, according to the abominable practices of the nations whom the Lord drove out before the people of Israel. 3For he rebuilt the high places that his father Hezekiah had pulled down, and erected altars to the Baals, made sacred poles, b worshiped all the host of heaven, and served them. 4He built altars in the house of the Lord, of which the Lord had said, "In Jerusalem shall my name be forever." 5He built altars for all the host of heaven in the two courts of the house of the Lord. 6He made his son pass through fire in the valley of the son of Hinnom, practiced soothsaying and augury and sorcery, and dealt with mediums and with wizards. He did much evil in the sight of the Lord, provoking him to anger. 7The carved image of the idol that he had made he set in the house of God, of which God said to David and to his son Solomon, "In this house, and in Jerusalem, which I have chosen out of all the tribes of Israel, I will put my name forever; 8I will never again remove the feet of Israel from the land that I appointed for your ancestors, if only they will be careful to do all that I have commanded them, all the law, the statutes, and the ordinances given through Moses." 9Manasseh misled Judah and the inhabitants of Jerusalem, so that they did more evil than the nations whom the Lord had destroyed before the people of Israel.

10 The Lord spoke to Manasseh and to his people, but they gave no heed. 11Therefore the Lord brought against them the commanders of the army of the king of Assyria, who took Manasseh captive in manacles, bound him with fetters, and brought him to Babylon. 12While he was in distress he entreated the favor of the Lord his God and humbled himself greatly before the God of his ancestors. 13He prayed to

---

a Gk Vg: Heb *flocks for folds*    b Heb *Asheroth*

him, and God received his entreaty, heard his plea, and restored him again to Jerusalem and to his kingdom. Then Manasseh knew that the Lord indeed was God.

## ROMANS 15.23—16.7

But now, with no further place for me in these regions, I desire, as I have for many years, to come to you ²⁴when I go to Spain. For I do hope to see you on my journey and to be sent on by you, once I have enjoyed your company for a little while. ²⁵At present, however, I am going to Jerusalem in a ministry to the saints; ²⁶for Macedonia and Achaia have been pleased to share their resources with the poor among the saints at Jerusalem. ²⁷They were pleased to do this, and indeed they owe it to them; for if the Gentiles have come to share in their spiritual blessings, they ought also to be of service to them in material things. ²⁸So, when I have completed this, and have delivered to them what has been collected, [a] I will set out by way of you to Spain; ²⁹and I know that when I come to you, I will come in the fullness of the blessing[b] of Christ.

30 I appeal to you, brothers and sisters, [c] by our Lord Jesus Christ and by the love of the Spirit, to join me in earnest prayer to God on my behalf, ³¹that I may be rescued from the unbelievers in Judea, and that my ministry[d] to Jerusalem may be acceptable to the saints, ³²so that by God's will I may come to you with joy and be refreshed in your company. ³³The God of peace be with all of you. [e] Amen.

16.1 I commend to you our sister Phoebe, a deacon[f] of the church at Cenchreae, ²so that you may welcome her in the Lord as is fitting for the saints, and help her in whatever she may require from you, for she has been a benefactor of many and of myself as well.

3 Greet Prisca and Aquila, who work with me in Christ Jesus, ⁴and who risked their necks for my life, to whom not only I give thanks, but also all the churches of the Gentiles. ⁵Greet also the church in their house. Greet my beloved Epaenetus, who was the first convert[g] in Asia for Christ. ⁶Greet Mary, who has worked very hard among you. ⁷Greet Andronicus and Junia,[h] my relatives[i] who were in prison with me; they are prominent among the apostles, and they were in Christ before I was.

## PSALM 25.16–22

Turn to me and be gracious to
    me,
  for I am lonely and afflicted.
17  Relieve the troubles of my
        heart,
    and bring me[j] out of my
        distress.
18  Consider my affliction and my
        trouble,
    and forgive all my sins.

19  Consider how many are my
        foes,
    and with what violent hatred
        they hate me.
20  O guard my life, and deliver me;
    do not let me be put to
        shame, for I take refuge
        in you.
21  May integrity and uprightness
        preserve me,
    for I wait for you.

---

ⁿwe sealed to them this fruit  [b]Other ancient authorities add *of the gospel*  [c]Gk *brothers*  [d]Other authorities read *my bringing of a gift*  [e]One ancient authority adds 16.25-27 here  [g]Gk *first fruits*  [h]Or *Junias*; other ancient authorities read *Julia*  [i]Or *compatriots*  ...oles of my heart are enlarged; bring me

22  Redeem Israel, O God,
    out of all its troubles.

## PROVERBS 20.16–18

**T**AKE the garment of one who
      has given surety for a
      stranger;
  seize the pledge given as
      surety for foreigners.

17  Bread gained by deceit is
      sweet,
    but afterward the mouth will
      be full of gravel.
18  Plans are established by
      taking advice;
    wage war by following wise
      guidance.

# AUGUST 3

## 2 CHRONICLES 33.14—34.33

**A**FTERWARD he [Manasseh] built an outer wall for the city of David west of Gihon, in the valley, reaching the entrance at the Fish Gate; he carried it around Ophel, and raised it to a very great height. He also put commanders of the army in all the fortified cities in Judah. 15He took away the foreign gods and the idol from the house of the LORD, and all the altars that he had built on the mountain of the house of the LORD and in Jerusalem, and he threw them out of the city. 16He also restored the altar of the LORD and offered on it sacrifices of well-being and of thanksgiving; and he commanded Judah to serve the LORD the God of Israel. 17The people, however, still sacrificed at the high places, but only to the LORD their God.

18  Now the rest of the acts of Manasseh, his prayer to his God, and the words of the seers who spoke to him in the name of the LORD God of Israel, these are in the Annals of the Kings of Israel. 19His prayer, and how God received his entreaty, all his sin and his faithlessness, the sites on which he built high places and set up the sacred poles[a] and the images, before he humbled himself, these are written in the records of the seers.[b] 20So Manasseh slept with his ancestors, and they buried him in his house. His son Amon succeeded him.

21  Amon was twenty-two years old when he began to reign; he reigned two years in Jerusalem. 22He did what was evil in the sight of the LORD, as his father Manasseh had done. Amon sacrificed to all the images that his father Manasseh had made, and served them. 23He did not humble himself before the LORD, as his father Manasseh had humbled himself, but this Amon incurred more and more guilt. 24His servants conspired against him and killed him in his house. 25But the people of the land killed all those who had conspired against King Amon; and the people of the land made his son Josiah king to succeed him.

34.1 JOSIAH was eight years old when he began to reign; he reigned thirty-one years in Jerusalem. 2He did what was right in the sight of the LORD, and walked in the ways of his ancestor Da-

a Heb *Asherim*   b One Ms Gk: MT *of Hozai*

vid; he did not turn aside to the right or to the left. ³For in the eighth year of his reign, while he was still a boy, he began to seek the God of his ancestor David, and in the twelfth year he began to purge Judah and Jerusalem of the high places, the sacred poles,ª and the carved and the cast images. ⁴In his presence they pulled down the altars of the Baals; he demolished the incense altars that stood above them. He broke down the sacred polesª and the carved and the cast images; he made dust of them and scattered it over the graves of those who had sacrificed to them. ⁵He also burned the bones of the priests on their altars, and purged Judah and Jerusalem. ⁶In the towns of Manasseh, Ephraim, and Simeon, and as far as Naphtali, in their ruinsᵇ all around, ⁷he broke down the altars, beat the sacred polesª and the images into powder, and demolished all the incense altars throughout all the land of Israel. Then he returned to Jerusalem.

8 In the eighteenth year of his reign, when he had purged the land and the house, he sent Shaphan son of Azaliah, Maaseiah the governor of the city, and Joah son of Joahaz, the recorder, to repair the house of the LORD his God. ⁹They came to the high priest Hilkiah and delivered the money that had been brought into the house of God, which the Levites, the keepers of the threshold, had collected from Manasseh and Ephraim and from all the remnant of Israel and from all Judah and Benjamin and from the inhabitants of Jerusalem. ¹⁰They delivered it to the workers who had the oversight of the house of the LORD, and the workers who were working in the house of the LORD gave it for repairing and restoring the house. ¹¹They gave it to the carpenters and the builders to buy quarried stone, and timber for binders, and beams for the buildings that the kings of Judah had let go to ruin. ¹²The people did the work faithfully. Over them were appointed the Levites Jahath and Obadiah, of the sons of Merari, along with Zechariah and Meshullam, of the sons of the Kohathites, to have oversight. Other Levites, all skillful with instruments of music, ¹³were over the burden bearers and directed all who did work in every kind of service; and some of the Levites were scribes, and officials, and gatekeepers.

14 While they were bringing out the money that had been brought into the house of the LORD, the priest Hilkiah found the book of the law of the LORD given through Moses. ¹⁵Hilkiah said to the secretary Shaphan, "I have found the book of the law in the house of the LORD"; and Hilkiah gave the book to Shaphan. ¹⁶Shaphan brought the book to the king, and further reported to the king, "All that was committed to your servants they are doing. ¹⁷They have emptied out the money that was found in the house of the LORD and have delivered it into the hand of the overseers and the workers." ¹⁸The secretary Shaphan informed the king, "The priest Hilkiah has given me a book." Shaphan then read it aloud to the king.

19 When the king heard the words of the law he tore his clothes. ²⁰Then the king commanded Hilkiah, Ahikam son of Shaphan, Abdon son of Micah, the secretary Shaphan, and the king's servant Asaiah: ²¹"Go, inquire of the LORD for me and for those who are left in Israel and in Judah, concerning the words of the book that has been found; for the wrath of the LORD that is poured out on us is great, because our ancestors did not keep the word of the LORD, to act in accordance with all that is written in this book."

22 So Hilkiah and those whom the king had sent went to the prophet Huldah, the wife of Shallum son of Tokhath

ªHeb *Asherim*  ᵇMeaning of Heb uncertain

son of Hasrah, keeper of the wardrobe (who lived in Jerusalem in the Second Quarter) and spoke to her to that effect. ²³She declared to them, "Thus says the LORD, the God of Israel: Tell the man who sent you to me, ²⁴Thus says the LORD: I will indeed bring disaster upon this place and upon its inhabitants, all the curses that are written in the book that was read before the king of Judah. ²⁵Because they have forsaken me and have made offerings to other gods, so that they have provoked me to anger with all the works of their hands, my wrath will be poured out on this place and will not be quenched. ²⁶But as to the king of Judah, who sent you to inquire of the LORD, thus shall you say to him: Thus says the LORD, the God of Israel: Regarding the words that you have heard, ²⁷because your heart was penitent and you humbled yourself before God when you heard his words against this place and its inhabitants, and you have humbled yourself before me, and have torn your clothes and wept before me, I also have heard you, says the LORD. ²⁸I will gather you to your ancestors and you shall be gathered to your grave in peace; your eyes shall not see all the disaster that I will bring on this place and its inhabitants." They took the message back to the king.

29 Then the king sent word and gathered together all the elders of Judah and Jerusalem. ³⁰The king went up to the house of the LORD, with all the people of Judah, the inhabitants of Jerusalem, the priests and the Levites, all the people both great and small; he read in their hearing all the words of the book of the covenant that had been found in the house of the LORD. ³¹The king stood in his place and made a covenant before the LORD, to follow the LORD, keeping his commandments, his decrees, and his statutes, with all his heart and all his soul, to perform the words of the covenant that were written in this book. ³²Then he made all who were present in Jerusalem and in Benjamin pledge themselves to it. And the inhabitants of Jerusalem acted according to the covenant of God, the God of their ancestors. ³³Josiah took away all the abominations from all the territory that belonged to the people of Israel, and made all who were in Israel worship the LORD their God. All his days they did not turn away from following the LORD the God of their ancestors.

## ROMANS 16.8–27

GREET Ampliatus, my beloved in the Lord. ⁹Greet Urbanus, our co-worker in Christ, and my beloved Stachys. ¹⁰Greet Apelles, who is approved in Christ. Greet those who belong to the family of Aristobulus. ¹¹Greet my relativeª Herodion. Greet those in the Lord who belong to the family of Narcissus. ¹²Greet those workers in the Lord, Tryphaena and Tryphosa. Greet the beloved Persis, who has worked hard in the Lord. ¹³Greet Rufus, chosen in the Lord; and greet his mother—a mother to me also. ¹⁴Greet Asyncritus, Phlegon, Hermes, Patrobas, Hermas, and the brothers and sistersᵇ who are with them. ¹⁵Greet Philologus, Julia, Nereus and his sister, and Olympas, and all the saints who are with them. ¹⁶Greet one another with a holy kiss. All the churches of Christ greet you.

17 I urge you, brothers and sisters,ᵇ to keep an eye on those who cause dissensions and offenses, in opposition to the teaching that you have learned; avoid them. ¹⁸For such people do not serve our Lord Christ, but their own appetites,ᶜ and by smooth talk and flattery they deceive the hearts of

ªOr *compatriot*  ᵇGk *brothers*  ᶜGk *their own belly*

the simple-minded. [19]For while your obedience is known to all, so that I rejoice over you, I want you to be wise in what is good and guileless in what is evil. [20]The God of peace will shortly crush Satan under your feet. The grace of our Lord Jesus Christ be with you. [a]

21 Timothy, my co-worker, greets you; so do Lucius and Jason and Sosipater, my relatives. [b]

22 I Tertius, the writer of this letter, greet you in the Lord. [c]

23 Gaius, who is host to me and to the whole church, greets you. Erastus, the city treasurer, and our brother Quartus, greet you. [d]

25 Now to God[e] who is able to strengthen you according to my gospel and the proclamation of Jesus Christ, according to the revelation of the mystery that was kept secret for long ages [26]but is now disclosed, and through the prophetic writings is made known to all the Gentiles, according to the command of the eternal God, to bring about the obedience of faith— [27]to the only wise God, through Jesus Christ, to whom[f] be the glory forever! Amen. [g]

## PSALM 26.1–12

*Of David.*

VINDICATE me, O LORD,
    for I have walked in my
       integrity,
    and I have trusted in the
       LORD without wavering.
2 Prove me, O LORD, and try me;
    test my heart and mind.
3 For your steadfast love is
       before my eyes,
    and I walk in faithfulness to
       you. [h]

4 I do not sit with the worthless,
    nor do I consort with
       hypocrites;
5 I hate the company of evildoers,
    and will not sit with the
       wicked.

6 I wash my hands in innocence,
    and go around your altar,
       O LORD,
7 singing aloud a song of
       thanksgiving,
    and telling all your wondrous
       deeds.

8 O LORD, I love the house in
       which you dwell,
    and the place where your
       glory abides.
9 Do not sweep me away with
       sinners,
    nor my life with the
       bloodthirsty,
10 those in whose hands are evil
       devices,
    and whose right hands are full
       of bribes.

11 But as for me, I walk in my
       integrity;
    redeem me, and be gracious
       to me.
12 My foot stands on level ground;
    in the great congregation I
       will bless the LORD.

## PROVERBS 20.19

A GOSSIP reveals secrets;
    therefore do not associate
    with a babbler.

[a]Other ancient authorities lack this sentence  [b]Or *compatriots*  [c]Or *I Tertius, writing this letter in the Lord, greet you*  [d]Other ancient authorities add verse 24, *The grace of our Lord Jesus Christ be with all of you. Amen.*  [e]Gk *the one*  [f]Other ancient authorities lack *to whom.* The verse then reads, *to the only wise God be the glory through Jesus Christ forever. Amen.*  [g]Other ancient authorities lack 16.25–27 or include it after 14.23 or 15.33; others put verse 24 after verse 27  [h]Or *in your faithfulness*

# AUGUST 4



JOSIAH kept a passover to the LORD in Jerusalem; they slaughtered the passover lamb on the fourteenth day of the first month. ²He appointed the priests to their offices and encouraged them in the service of the house of the LORD. ³He said to the Levites who taught all Israel and who were holy to the LORD, "Put the holy ark in the house that Solomon son of David, king of Israel, built; you need no longer carry it on your shoulders. Now serve the LORD your God and his people Israel. ⁴Make preparations by your ancestral houses by your divisions, following the written directions of King David of Israel and the written directions of his son Solomon. ⁵Take position in the holy place according to the groupings of the ancestral houses of your kindred the people, and let there be Levites for each division of an ancestral house.ᵃ ⁶Slaughter the passover lamb, sanctify yourselves, and on behalf of your kindred make preparations, acting according to the word of the LORD by Moses."

7 Then Josiah contributed to the people, as passover offerings for all that were present, lambs and kids from the flock to the number of thirty thousand, and three thousand bulls; these were from the king's possessions. ⁸His officials contributed willingly to the people, to the priests, and to the Levites. Hilkiah, Zechariah, and Jehiel, the chief officers of the house of God, gave to the priests for the passover offerings two thousand six hundred lambs and kids and three hundred bulls. ⁹Conaniah also, and his brothers Shemaiah and Nethanel, and Hashabiah and Jeiel and Jozabad, the chiefs of the Levites, gave to the Levites for the passover offerings five thousand lambs and kids and five hundred bulls.

10 When the service had been prepared for, the priests stood in their place, and the Levites in their divisions according to the king's command. ¹¹They slaughtered the passover lamb, and the priests dashed the blood that they receivedᵇ from them, while the Levites did the skinning. ¹²They set aside the burnt offerings so that they might distribute them according to the groupings of the ancestral houses of the people, to offer to the LORD, as it is written in the book of Moses. And they did the same with the bulls. ¹³They roasted the passover lamb with fire according to the ordinance; and they boiled the holy offerings in pots, in caldrons, and in pans, and carried them quickly to all the people. ¹⁴Afterward they made preparations for themselves and for the priests, because the priests the descendants of Aaron were occupied in offering the burnt offerings and the fat parts until night; so the Levites made preparations for themselves and for the priests, the descendants of Aaron. ¹⁵The singers, the descendants of Asaph, were in their place according to the command of David, and Asaph, and Heman, and the king's seer Jeduthun. The gatekeepers were at each gate; they did not need to interrupt their service, for their kindred the Levites made preparations for them.

16 So all the service of the LORD was prepared that day, to keep the passover and to offer burnt offerings on the altar of the LORD, according to the command of King Josiah. ¹⁷The people

---

ᵃMeaning of Heb uncertain  ᵇHeb lacks *that they received*

of Israel who were present kept the passover at that time, and the festival of unleavened bread seven days. ¹⁸No passover like it had been kept in Israel since the days of the prophet Samuel; none of the kings of Israel had kept such a passover as was kept by Josiah, by the priests and the Levites, by all Judah and Israel who were present, and by the inhabitants of Jerusalem. ¹⁹In the eighteenth year of the reign of Josiah this passover was kept.

20 After all this, when Josiah had set the temple in order, King Neco of Egypt went up to fight at Carchemish on the Euphrates, and Josiah went out against him. ²¹But Neco[a] sent envoys to him, saying, "What have I to do with you, king of Judah? I am not coming against you today, but against the house with which I am at war; and God has commanded me to hurry. Cease opposing God, who is with me, so that he will not destroy you." ²²But Josiah would not turn away from him, but disguised himself in order to fight with him. He did not listen to the words of Neco from the mouth of God, but joined battle in the plain of Megiddo. ²³The archers shot King Josiah; and the king said to his servants, "Take me away, for I am badly wounded." ²⁴So his servants took him out of the chariot and carried him in his second chariot[b] and brought him to Jerusalem. There he died, and was buried in the tombs of his ancestors. All Judah and Jerusalem mourned for Josiah. ²⁵Jeremiah also uttered a lament for Josiah, and all the singing men and singing women have spoken of Josiah in their laments to this day. They made these a custom in Israel; they are recorded in the Laments. ²⁶Now the rest of the acts of Josiah and his faithful deeds in accordance with what is written in the law of the LORD, ²⁷and his acts, first and last, are written in the Book of the Kings of Israel and Judah.

36.1 THE people of the land took Jehoahaz son of Josiah and made him king to succeed his father in Jerusalem. ²Jehoahaz was twenty-three years old when he began to reign; he reigned three months in Jerusalem. ³Then the king of Egypt deposed him in Jerusalem and laid on the land a tribute of one hundred talents of silver and one talent of gold. ⁴The king of Egypt made his brother Eliakim king over Judah and Jerusalem, and changed his name to Jehoiakim; but Neco took his brother Jehoahaz and carried him to Egypt.

5 Jehoiakim was twenty-five years old when he began to reign; he reigned eleven years in Jerusalem. He did what was evil in the sight of the LORD his God. ⁶Against him King Nebuchadnezzar of Babylon came up, and bound him with fetters to take him to Babylon. ⁷Nebuchadnezzar also carried some of the vessels of the house of the LORD to Babylon and put them in his palace in Babylon. ⁸Now the rest of the acts of Jehoiakim, and the abominations that he did, and what was found against him, are written in the Book of the Kings of Israel and Judah; and his son Jehoiachin succeeded him.

9 Jehoiachin was eight years old when he began to reign; he reigned three months and ten days in Jerusalem. He did what was evil in the sight of the LORD. ¹⁰In the spring of the year King Nebuchadnezzar sent and brought him to Babylon, along with the precious vessels of the house of the LORD, and made his brother Zedekiah king over Judah and Jerusalem.

11 Zedekiah was twenty-one years old when he began to reign; he reigned eleven years in Jerusalem. ¹²He did

aHeb *he*   bOr *the chariot of his deputy*

what was evil in the sight of the Lord his God. He did not humble himself before the prophet Jeremiah who spoke from the mouth of the Lord. [13]He also rebelled against King Nebuchadnezzar, who had made him swear by God; he stiffened his neck and hardened his heart against turning to the Lord, the God of Israel. [14]All the leading priests and the people also were exceedingly unfaithful, following all the abominations of the nations; and they polluted the house of the Lord that he had consecrated in Jerusalem.

15 The Lord, the God of their ancestors, sent persistently to them by his messengers, because he had compassion on his people and on his dwelling place; [16]but they kept mocking the messengers of God, despising his words, and scoffing at his prophets, until the wrath of the Lord against his people became so great that there was no remedy.

17 Therefore he brought up against them the king of the Chaldeans, who killed their youths with the sword in the house of their sanctuary, and had no compassion on young man or young woman, the aged or the feeble; he gave them all into his hand. [18]All the vessels of the house of God, large and small, and the treasures of the house of the Lord, and the treasures of the king and of his officials, all these he brought to Babylon. [19]They burned the house of God, broke down the wall of Jerusalem, burned all its palaces with fire, and destroyed all its precious vessels. [20]He took into exile in Babylon those who had escaped from the sword, and they became servants to him and to his sons until the establishment of the kingdom of Persia, [21]to fulfill the word of the Lord by the mouth of Jeremiah, until the land had made up for its sabbaths. All the days that it lay desolate it kept sabbath, to fulfill seventy years.

22 In the first year of King Cyrus of Persia, in fulfillment of the word of the Lord spoken by Jeremiah, the Lord stirred up the spirit of King Cyrus of Persia so that he sent a herald throughout all his kingdom and also declared in a written edict: [23]"Thus says King Cyrus of Persia: The Lord, the God of heaven, has given me all the kingdoms of the earth, and he has charged me to build him a house at Jerusalem, which is in Judah. Whoever is among you of all his people, may the Lord his God be with him! Let him go up.'"

# 1 CORINTHIANS 1.1–17

**P**AUL, called to be an apostle of Christ Jesus by the will of God, and our brother Sosthenes,

2 To the church of God that is in Corinth, to those who are sanctified in Christ Jesus, called to be saints, together with all those who in every place call on the name of our Lord Jesus Christ, both their Lord[a] and ours:

3 Grace to you and peace from God our Father and the Lord Jesus Christ.

4 I give thanks to my[b] God always for you because of the grace of God that has been given you in Christ Jesus, [5]for in every way you have been enriched in him, in speech and knowledge of every kind— [6]just as the testimony of[c] Christ has been strengthened among you— [7]so that you are not lacking in any spiritual gift as you wait for the revealing of our Lord Jesus Christ. [8]He will also strengthen you to the end, so that you may be blameless on the day of our Lord Jesus Christ. [9]God is faithful; by him you were called into the fellowship of his Son, Jesus Christ our Lord.

10 Now I appeal to you, brothers and sisters,[d] by the name of our Lord Jesus Christ, that all of you be in agree-

---

a Gk *theirs*  b Other ancient authorities lack *my*  c Or *to*  d Gk *brothers* ment and that there be no divisions among you, but that you be united in the same mind and the same purpose. [11]For it has been reported to me by Chloe's people that there are quarrels among you, my brothers and sisters. [a] [12]What I mean is that each of you says, "I belong to Paul," or "I belong to Apollos," or "I belong to Cephas," or "I belong to Christ." [13]Has Christ been divided? Was Paul crucified for you? Or were you baptized in the name of Paul? [14]I thank God[b] that I baptized none of you except Crispus and Gaius, [15]so that no one can say that you were baptized in my name. [16](I did baptize also the household of Stephanas; beyond that, I do not know whether I baptized anyone else.) [17]For Christ did not send me to baptize but to proclaim the gospel, and not with eloquent wisdom, so that the cross of Christ might not be emptied of its power.

## PSALM 27.1–6

*Of David.*

THE LORD is my light and my
  salvation;
  whom shall I fear?
The LORD is the stronghold[c] of
  my life;
  of whom shall I be afraid?
2  When evildoers assail me
    to devour my flesh—
  my adversaries and foes—
    they shall stumble and fall.

3  Though an army encamp against
    me,
  my heart shall not fear;
though war rise up against me,
  yet I will be confident.

4  One thing I asked of the LORD,
    that will I seek after:
to live in the house of the LORD
  all the days of my life,
to behold the beauty of the
    LORD,
  and to inquire in his temple.

5  For he will hide me in his
    shelter
  in the day of trouble;
he will conceal me under the
    cover of his tent;
  he will set me high on a rock.

6  Now my head is lifted up
    above my enemies all around
    me,
  and I will offer in his tent
    sacrifices with shouts of joy;
  I will sing and make melody to
    the LORD.

## PROVERBS 20.20–21

IF you curse father or mother,
  your lamp will go out in utter
    darkness.
21  An estate quickly acquired in
    the beginning
  will not be blessed in the end.

---

aGk *my brothers*   bOther ancient authorities read *I am thankful*   cOr *refuge*

# AUGUST 5

## EZRA 1.1—2.70

IN the first year of King Cyrus of Persia, in order that the word of the LORD by the mouth of Jeremiah might be accomplished, the LORD stirred up the spirit of King Cyrus of Persia so that he sent a herald throughout all his kingdom, and also in a written edict declared:

2 "Thus says King Cyrus of Persia: The LORD, the God of heaven, has given me all the kingdoms of the earth, and he has charged me to build him a house at Jerusalem in Judah. ³Any of those among you who are of his people—may their God be with them!—are now permitted to go up to Jerusalem in Judah, and rebuild the house of the LORD, the God of Israel— he is the God who is in Jerusalem; ⁴and let all survivors, in whatever place they reside, be assisted by the people of their place with silver and gold, with goods and with animals, besides freewill offerings for the house of God in Jerusalem."

5 The heads of the families of Judah and Benjamin, and the priests and the Levites—everyone whose spirit God had stirred—got ready to go up and rebuild the house of the LORD in Jerusalem. ⁶All their neighbors aided them with silver vessels, with gold, with goods, with animals, and with valuable gifts, besides all that was freely offered. ⁷King Cyrus himself brought out the vessels of the house of the LORD that Nebuchadnezzar had carried away from Jerusalem and placed in the house of his gods. ⁸King Cyrus of Persia had them released into the charge of Mithredath the treasurer, who counted them out to Sheshbazzar the prince of Judah. ⁹And this was the inventory: gold basins, thirty; silver basins, one thousand; knives, ᵃ twenty-nine; ¹⁰gold bowls, thirty; other silver bowls, four hundred ten; other vessels, one thousand; ¹¹the total of the gold and silver vessels was five thousand four hundred. All these Sheshbazzar brought up, when the exiles were brought up from Babylonia to Jerusalem.

2.1 Now these were the people of the province who came from those captive exiles whom King Nebuchadnezzar of Babylon had carried captive to Babylonia; they returned to Jerusalem and Judah, all to their own towns. ²They came with Zerubbabel, Jeshua, Nehemiah, Seraiah, Reelaiah, Mordecai, Bilshan, Mispar, Bigvai, Rehum, and Baanah.

The number of the Israelite people: ³the descendants of Parosh, two thousand one hundred seventy-two. ⁴Of Shephatiah, three hundred seventytwo. ⁵Of Arah, seven hundred seventyfive. ⁶Of Pahath-moab, namely the descendants of Jeshua and Joab, two thousand eight hundred twelve. ⁷Of Elam, one thousand two hundred fiftyfour. ⁸Of Zattu, nine hundred fortyfive. ⁹Of Zaccai, seven hundred sixty. ¹⁰Of Bani, six hundred forty-two. ¹¹Of Bebai, six hundred twenty-three. ¹²Of Azgad, one thousand two hundred twenty-two. ¹³Of Adonikam, six hundred sixty-six. ¹⁴Of Bigvai, two thousand fifty-six. ¹⁵Of Adin, four hundred fifty-four. ¹⁶Of Ater, namely of Hezekiah, ninety-eight. ¹⁷Of Bezai, three hundred twenty-three. ¹⁸Of Jorah, one hundred twelve. ¹⁹Of Hashum, two

ᵃ Vg: Meaning of Heb uncertain

hundred twenty-three. [20]Of Gibbar, ninety-five. [21]Of Bethlehem, one hundred twenty-three. [22]The people of Netophah, fifty-six. [23]Of Anathoth, one hundred twenty-eight. [24]The descendants of Azmaveth, forty-two. [25]Of Kiriatharim, Chephirah, and Beeroth, seven hundred forty-three. [26]Of Ramah and Geba, six hundred twenty-one. [27]The people of Michmas, one hundred twenty-two. [28]Of Bethel and Ai, two hundred twenty-three. [29]The descendants of Nebo, fifty-two. [30]Of Magbish, one hundred fifty-six. [31]Of the other Elam, one thousand two hundred fifty-four. [32]Of Harim, three hundred twenty. [33]Of Lod, Hadid, and Ono, seven hundred twenty-five. [34]Of Jericho, three hundred forty-five. [35]Of Senaah, three thousand six hundred thirty.

36 The priests: the descendants of Jedaiah, of the house of Jeshua, nine hundred seventy-three. [37]Of Immer, one thousand fifty-two. [38]Of Pashhur, one thousand two hundred forty-seven. [39]Of Harim, one thousand seventeen.

40 The Levites: the descendants of Jeshua and Kadmiel, of the descendants of Hodaviah, seventy-four. [41]The singers: the descendants of Asaph, one hundred twenty-eight. [42]The descendants of the gatekeepers: of Shallum, of Ater, of Talmon, of Akkub, of Hatita, and of Shobai, in all one hundred thirty-nine.

43 The temple servants: the descendants of Ziha, Hasupha, Tabbaoth, [44]Keros, Siaha, Padon, [45]Lebanah, Hagabah, Akkub, [46]Hagab, Shamlai, Hanan, [47]Giddel, Gahar, Reaiah, [48]Rezin, Nekoda, Gazzam, [49]Uzza, Paseah, Besai, [50]Asnah, Meunim, Nephisim, [51]Bakbuk, Hakupha, Harhur, [52]Bazluth, Mehida, Harsha, [53]Barkos, Sisera, Temah, [54]Neziah, and Hatipha.

55 The descendants of Solomon's servants: Sotai, Hassophereth, Peruda, [56]Jaalah, Darkon, Giddel, [57]Shephatiah, Hattil, Pochereth-hazzebaim, and Ami.

58 All the temple servants and the descendants of Solomon's servants were three hundred ninety-two.

59 The following were those who came up from Tel-melah, Tel-harsha, Cherub, Addan, and Immer, though they could not prove their families or their descent, whether they belonged to Israel: [60]the descendants of Delaiah, Tobiah, and Nekoda, six hundred fifty-two. [61]Also, of the descendants of the priests: the descendants of Habaiah, Hakkoz, and Barzillai (who had married one of the daughters of Barzillai the Gileadite, and was called by their name). [62]These looked for their entries in the genealogical records, but they were not found there, and so they were excluded from the priesthood as unclean; [63]the governor told them that they were not to partake of the most holy food, until there should be a priest to consult Urim and Thummim.

64 The whole assembly together was forty-two thousand three hundred sixty, [65]besides their male and female servants, of whom there were seven thousand three hundred thirty-seven; and they had two hundred male and female singers. [66]They had seven hundred thirty-six horses, two hundred forty-five mules, [67]four hundred thirty-five camels, and six thousand seven hundred twenty donkeys.

68 As soon as they came to the house of the Lord in Jerusalem, some of the heads of families made freewill offerings for the house of God, to erect it on its site. [69]According to their resources they gave to the building fund sixty-one thousand darics of gold, five thousand minas of silver, and one hundred priestly robes.

70 The priests, the Levites, and some of the people lived in Jerusalem

and its vicinity;[a] and the singers, the gatekeepers, and the temple servants lived in their towns, and all Israel in their towns.

## 1 CORINTHIANS 1.18—2.5

For the message about the cross is foolishness to those who are perishing, but to us who are being saved it is the power of God. [19]For it is written,

"I will destroy the wisdom of
        the wise,
    and the discernment of the
        discerning I will thwart."

[20]Where is the one who is wise? Where is the scribe? Where is the debater of this age? Has not God made foolish the wisdom of the world? [21]For since, in the wisdom of God, the world did not know God through wisdom, God decided, through the foolishness of our proclamation, to save those who believe. [22]For Jews demand signs and Greeks desire wisdom, [23]but we proclaim Christ crucified, a stumbling block to Jews and foolishness to Gentiles, [24]but to those who are the called, both Jews and Greeks, Christ the power of God and the wisdom of God. [25]For God's foolishness is wiser than human wisdom, and God's weakness is stronger than human strength.

26 Consider your own call, brothers and sisters:[b] not many of you were wise by human standards,[c] not many were powerful, not many were of noble birth. [27]But God chose what is foolish in the world to shame the wise; God chose what is weak in the world to shame the strong; [28]God chose what is low and despised in the world, things that are not, to reduce to nothing things that are, [29]so that no one[d] might boast in the presence of God. [30]He is the source of your life in Christ Jesus, who became for us wisdom from God, and righteousness and sanctification and redemption, [31]in order that, as it is written, "Let the one who boasts, boast in[e] the Lord."

[2.1]When I came to you, brothers and sisters,[b] I did not come proclaiming the mystery[f] of God to you in lofty words or wisdom. [2]For I decided to know nothing among you except Jesus Christ, and him crucified. [3]And I came to you in weakness and in fear and in much trembling. [4]My speech and my proclamation were not with plausible words of wisdom,[g] but with a demonstration of the Spirit and of power, [5]so that your faith might rest not on human wisdom but on the power of God.

## PSALM 27.7–14

Hear, O Lord, when I cry
        aloud,
    be gracious to me and
        answer me!
8   "Come," my heart says, "seek
        his face!"
    Your face, Lord, do I seek.
9   Do not hide your face from
        me.

    Do not turn your servant away
        in anger,
    you who have been my help.
    Do not cast me off, do not
        forsake me,
    O God of my salvation!
10  If my father and mother forsake
        me,
    the Lord will take me up.

11  Teach me your way, O Lord,
        and lead me on a level path
        because of my enemies.
12  Do not give me up to the will of
        my adversaries,

---

a 1 Esdras 5.46: Heb lacks *lived in Jerusalem and its vicinity*   b Gk *brothers*   c Gk *according to the flesh*   d Gk *no flesh*   e Or *of*   f Other ancient authorities read *testimony*   g Other ancient authorities read *the persuasiveness of wisdom*

for false witnesses have risen
    against me,
and they are breathing out
    violence.

13 I believe that I shall see the
    goodness of the LORD
    in the land of the living.
14 Wait for the LORD;
    be strong, and let your heart
       take courage;
    wait for the LORD!

## PROVERBS 20.22–23

Do not say, "I will repay evil";
    wait for the LORD, and he
      will help you.
23 Differing weights are an
    abomination to the LORD,
and false scales are not good.

# AUGUST 6

## EZRA 3.1—4.24

**W**HEN the seventh month came, and the Israelites were in the towns, the people gathered together in Jerusalem. ²Then Jeshua son of Jozadak, with his fellow priests, and Zerubbabel son of Shealtiel with his kin set out to build the altar of the God of Israel, to offer burnt offerings on it, as prescribed in the law of Moses the man of God. ³They set up the altar on its foundation, because they were in dread of the neighboring peoples, and they offered burnt offerings upon it to the LORD, morning and evening. ⁴And they kept the festival of booths,ᵃ as prescribed, and offered the daily burnt offerings by number according to the ordinance, as required for each day, ⁵and after that the regular burnt offerings, the offerings at the new moon and at all the sacred festivals of the LORD, and the offerings of everyone who made a freewill offering to the LORD. ⁶From the first day of the seventh month they began to offer burnt offerings to the LORD. But the foundation of the temple of the LORD was not yet laid.

⁷So they gave money to the masons and the carpenters, and food, drink, and oil to the Sidonians and the Tyrians to bring cedar trees from Lebanon to the sea, to Joppa, according to the grant that they had from King Cyrus of Persia.

8 In the second year after their arrival at the house of God at Jerusalem, in the second month, Zerubbabel son of Shealtiel and Jeshua son of Jozadak made a beginning, together with the rest of their people, the priests and the Levites and all who had come to Jerusalem from the captivity. They appointed the Levites, from twenty years old and upward, to have the oversight of the work on the house of the LORD. ⁹And Jeshua with his sons and his kin, and Kadmiel and his sons, Binnui and Hodaviahᵇ along with the sons of Henadad, the Levites, their sons and kin, together took charge of the workers in the house of God.

10 When the builders laid the foundation of the temple of the LORD, the priests in their vestments were stationed to praise the LORD with trum-

ᵃOr *tabernacles*; Heb *succoth*   ᵇCompare 2.40; Neh 7.43; 1 Esdras 5.58: Heb *sons of Judah*

pets, and the Levites, the sons of Asaph, with cymbals, according to the directions of King David of Israel; [11]and they sang responsively, praising and giving thanks to the LORD,

"For he is good,
for his steadfast love endures
forever toward Israel."

And all the people responded with a great shout when they praised the LORD, because the foundation of the house of the LORD was laid. [12]But many of the priests and Levites and heads of families, old people who had seen the first house on its foundations, wept with a loud voice when they saw this house, though many shouted aloud for joy, [13]so that the people could not distinguish the sound of the joyful shout from the sound of the people's weeping, for the people shouted so loudly that the sound was heard far away.

[4.1] WHEN the adversaries of Judah and Benjamin heard that the returned exiles were building a temple to the LORD, the God of Israel, [2]they approached Zerubbabel and the heads of families and said to them, "Let us build with you, for we worship your God as you do, and we have been sacrificing to him ever since the days of King Esar-haddon of Assyria who brought us here." [3]But Zerubbabel, Jeshua, and the rest of the heads of families in Israel said to them, "You shall have no part with us in building a house to our God; but we alone will build to the LORD, the God of Israel, as King Cyrus of Persia has commanded us."

[4] Then the people of the land discouraged the people of Judah, and made them afraid to build, [5]and they bribed officials to frustrate their plan throughout the reign of King Cyrus of Persia and until the reign of King Darius of Persia.

[6] In the reign of Ahasuerus, in his accession year, they wrote an accusation against the inhabitants of Judah and Jerusalem.

[7] And in the days of Artaxerxes, Bishlam and Mithredath and Tabeel and the rest of their associates wrote to King Artaxerxes of Persia; the letter was written in Aramaic and translated. [a] [8]Rehum the royal deputy and Shimshai the scribe wrote a letter against Jerusalem to King Artaxerxes as follows [9](then Rehum the royal deputy, Shimshai the scribe, and the rest of their associates, the judges, the envoys, the officials, the Persians, the people of Erech, the Babylonians, the people of Susa, that is, the Elamites, [10]and the rest of the nations whom the great and noble Osnappar deported and settled in the cities of Samaria and in the rest of the province Beyond the River wrote—and now [11]this is a copy of the letter that they sent):

"To King Artaxerxes: Your servants, the people of the province Beyond the River, send greeting. And now [12]may it be known to the king that the Jews who came up from you to us have gone to Jerusalem. They are rebuilding that rebellious and wicked city; they are finishing the walls and repairing the foundations. [13]Now may it be known to the king that, if this city is rebuilt and the walls finished, they will not pay tribute, custom, or toll, and the royal revenue will be reduced. [14]Now because we share the salt of the palace and it is not fitting for us to witness the king's dishonor, therefore we send and inform the king, [15]so that a search may be made in the annals of your ancestors. You will discover in the annals that this is a rebellious city, hurtful to kings and provinces, and that sedition was stirred up in it from long ago. On that account this city was laid waste. [16]We make known to the king that, if this city is rebuilt and its walls finished,

aHeb adds *in Aramaic,* indicating that 4.8-6.18 is in Aramaic. Another interpretation is *The letter was written in the Aramaic script and set forth in the Aramaic language*

you will then have no possession in the province Beyond the River."

17 The king sent an answer: "To Rehum the royal deputy and Shimshai the scribe and the rest of their associates who live in Samaria and in the rest of the province Beyond the River, greeting. And now [18]the letter that you sent to us has been read in translation before me. [19]So I made a decree, and someone searched and discovered that this city has risen against kings from long ago, and that rebellion and sedition have been made in it. [20]Jerusalem has had mighty kings who ruled over the whole province Beyond the River, to whom tribute, custom, and toll were paid. [21]Therefore issue an order that these people be made to cease, and that this city not be rebuilt, until I make a decree. [22]Moreover, take care not to be slack in this matter; why should damage grow to the hurt of the king?"

23 Then when the copy of King Artaxerxes' letter was read before Rehum and the scribe Shimshai and their associates, they hurried to the Jews in Jerusalem and by force and power made them cease. [24]At that time the work on the house of God in Jerusalem stopped and was discontinued until the second year of the reign of King Darius of Persia.

> "What no eye has seen, nor
> ear heard,
> nor the human heart
> conceived,
> what God has prepared for
> those who love him"—

[10]these things God has revealed to us through the Spirit; for the Spirit searches everything, even the depths of God. [11]For what human being knows what is truly human except the human spirit that is within? So also no one comprehends what is truly God's except the Spirit of God. [12]Now we have received not the spirit of the world, but the Spirit that is from God, so that we may understand the gifts bestowed on us by God. [13]And we speak of these things in words not taught by human wisdom but taught by the Spirit, interpreting spiritual things to those who are spiritual. [a]

14 Those who are unspiritual[b] do not receive the gifts of God's Spirit, for they are foolishness to them, and they are unable to understand them because they are spiritually discerned. [15]Those who are spiritual discern all things, and they are themselves subject to no one else's scrutiny.

16 "For who has known the mind
> of the Lord
> so as to instruct him?"

But we have the mind of Christ.

# 1 CORINTHIANS 2.6—3.4

**Y**ET among the mature we do speak wisdom, though it is not a wisdom of this age or of the rulers of this age, who are doomed to perish. [7]But we speak God's wisdom, secret and hidden, which God decreed before the ages for our glory. [8]None of the rulers of this age understood this; for if they had, they would not have crucified the Lord of glory. [9]But, as it is written,

[3.1] AND so, brothers and sisters, [c] I could not speak to you as spiritual people, but rather as people of the flesh, as infants in Christ. [2]I fed you with milk, not solid food, for you were not ready for solid food. Even now you are still not ready, [3]for you are still of the flesh. For as long as there is jealousy and quarreling among you, are you not of the flesh, and behaving according to human inclinations? [4]For when one says, "I belong to Paul," and another, "I be-

a Or *interpreting spiritual things in spiritual language,* or *comparing spiritual things with spiritual*
b Or *natural*   c Gk *brothers*

long to Apollos," are you not merely human?

## PSALM 28.1–9
*Of David.*

To you, O Lord, I call;
    my rock, do not refuse to
      hear me,
  for if you are silent to me,
    I shall be like those who go
      down to the Pit.
2 Hear the voice of my
    supplication,
  as I cry to you for help,
  as I lift up my hands
    toward your most holy
    sanctuary. [a]

3 Do not drag me away with the
    wicked,
  with those who are workers
    of evil,
  who speak peace with their
    neighbors,
  while mischief is in their
    hearts.
4 Repay them according to their
    work,
  and according to the evil of
    their deeds;
  repay them according to the
    work of their hands;
  render them their due
    reward.
5 Because they do not regard the
    works of the Lord,
or the work of his hands,
  he will break them down and
    build them up no more.

6 Blessed be the Lord,
  for he has heard the sound of
    my pleadings.
7 The Lord is my strength and
    my shield;
  in him my heart trusts;
so I am helped, and my heart
    exults,
  and with my song I give
    thanks to him.

8 The Lord is the strength of his
    people;
  he is the saving refuge of his
    anointed.
9 O save your people, and bless
    your heritage;
  be their shepherd, and carry
    them forever.

## PROVERBS 20.24–25

All our steps are ordered by
    the Lord;
  how then can we
    understand our own
    ways?
25 It is a snare for one to say
    rashly, "It is holy,"
  and begin to reflect only after
    making a vow.

a Heb *your innermost sanctuary*

# AUGUST 7

## EZRA 5.1—6.22

**N**ow the prophets, Haggai[a] and Zechariah son of Iddo, prophesied to the Jews who were in Judah and Jerusalem, in the name of the God of Israel who was over them. [2]Then Zerubbabel son of Shealtiel and Jeshua son of Jozadak set out to rebuild the house of God in Jerusalem; and with them were the prophets of God, helping them.

3 At the same time Tattenai the governor of the province Beyond the River and Shethar-bozenai and their associates came to them and spoke to them thus, "Who gave you a decree to build this house and to finish this structure?" [4]They[b] also asked them this, "What are the names of the men who are building this building?" [5]But the eye of their God was upon the elders of the Jews, and they did not stop them until a report reached Darius and then answer was returned by letter in reply to it.

6 The copy of the letter that Tattenai the governor of the province Beyond the River and Shethar-bozenai and his associates the envoys who were in the province Beyond the River sent to King Darius; [7]they sent him a report, in which was written as follows: "To Darius the king, all peace! [8]May it be known to the king that we went to the province of Judah, to the house of the great God. It is being built of hewn stone, and timber is laid in the walls; this work is being done diligently and prospers in their hands. [9]Then we spoke to those elders and asked them, 'Who gave you a decree to build this house and to finish this structure?' [10]We also asked them their names, for your information, so that we might write down the names of the men at their head. [11]This was their reply to us: 'We are the servants of the God of heaven and earth, and we are rebuilding the house that was built many years ago, which a great king of Israel built and finished. [12]But because our ancestors had angered the God of heaven, he gave them into the hand of King Nebuchadnezzar of Babylon, the Chaldean, who destroyed this house and carried away the people to Babylonia. [13]However, King Cyrus of Babylon, in the first year of his reign, made a decree that this house of God should be rebuilt. [14]Moreover, the gold and silver vessels of the house of God, which Nebuchadnezzar had taken out of the temple in Jerusalem and had brought into the temple of Babylon, these King Cyrus took out of the temple of Babylon, and they were delivered to a man named Sheshbazzar, whom he had made governor. [15]He said to him, "Take these vessels; go and put them in the temple in Jerusalem, and let the house of God be rebuilt on its site." [16]Then this Sheshbazzar came and laid the foundations of the house of God in Jerusalem; and from that time until now it has been under construction, and it is not yet finished.' [17]And now, if it seems good to the king, have a search made in the royal archives there in Babylon, to see whether a decree was issued by King Cyrus for the rebuilding of this house of God in Jerusalem. Let the king send us his pleasure in this matter."

6.1 Then King Darius made a decree, and they searched the archives where the documents were stored in Babylon.

a Aram adds *the prophet*   b Gk Syr: Aram *We*

²But it was in Ecbatana, the capital in the province of Media, that a scroll was found on which this was written: "A record. ³In the first year of his reign, King Cyrus issued a decree: Concerning the house of God at Jerusalem, let the house be rebuilt, the place where sacrifices are offered and burnt offerings are brought; ᵃ its height shall be sixty cubits and its width sixty cubits, ⁴with three courses of hewn stones and one course of timber; let the cost be paid from the royal treasury. ⁵Moreover, let the gold and silver vessels of the house of God, which Nebuchadnezzar took out of the temple in Jerusalem and brought to Babylon, be restored and brought back to the temple in Jerusalem, each to its place; you shall put them in the house of God."

6 "Now you, Tattenai, governor of the province Beyond the River, Shethar-bozenai, and you, their associates, the envoys in the province Beyond the River, keep away; ⁷let the work on this house of God alone; let the governor of the Jews and the elders of the Jews rebuild this house of God on its site. ⁸Moreover I make a decree regarding what you shall do for these elders of the Jews for the rebuilding of this house of God: the cost is to be paid to these people, in full and without delay, from the royal revenue, the tribute of the province Beyond the River. ⁹Whatever is needed—young bulls, rams, or sheep for burnt offerings to the God of heaven, wheat, salt, wine, or oil, as the priests in Jerusalem require—let that be given to them day by day without fail, ¹⁰so that they may offer pleasing sacrifices to the God of heaven, and pray for the life of the king and his children. ¹¹Furthermore I decree that if anyone alters this edict, a beam shall be pulled out of the house of the perpetrator, who then shall be impaled on it. The house shall be made a dunghill. ¹²May the God who has established his name there overthrow any king or people that shall put forth a hand to alter this, or to destroy this house of God in Jerusalem. I, Darius, make a decree; let it be done with all diligence."

13 Then, according to the word sent by King Darius, Tattenai, the governor of the province Beyond the River, Shethar-bozenai, and their associates did with all diligence what King Darius had ordered. ¹⁴So the elders of the Jews built and prospered, through the prophesying of the prophet Haggai and Zechariah son of Iddo. They finished their building by command of the God of Israel and by decree of Cyrus, Darius, and King Artaxerxes of Persia; ¹⁵and this house was finished on the third day of the month of Adar, in the sixth year of the reign of King Darius.

16 The people of Israel, the priests and the Levites, and the rest of the returned exiles, celebrated the dedication of this house of God with joy. ¹⁷They offered at the dedication of this house of God one hundred bulls, two hundred rams, four hundred lambs, and as a sin offering for all Israel, twelve male goats, according to the number of the tribes of Israel. ¹⁸Then they set the priests in their divisions and the Levites in their courses for the service of God at Jerusalem, as it is written in the book of Moses.

19 On the fourteenth day of the first month the returned exiles kept the passover. ²⁰For both the priests and the Levites had purified themselves; all of them were clean. So they killed the passover lamb for all the returned exiles, for their fellow priests, and for themselves. ²¹It was eaten by the people of Israel who had returned from exile, and also by all who had joined them and separated themselves from the pollutions of the nations of the land to worship the LORD, the God of Israel. ²²With

ᵃMeaning of Aram uncertain

joy they celebrated the festival of unleavened bread seven days; for the Lord had made them joyful, and had turned the heart of the king of Assyria to them, so that he aided them in the work on the house of God, the God of Israel.

# 1 CORINTHIANS 3.5–23

**W**HAT then is Apollos? What is Paul? Servants through whom you came to believe, as the Lord assigned to each. [6]I planted, Apollos watered, but God gave the growth. [7]So neither the one who plants nor the one who waters is anything, but only God who gives the growth. [8]The one who plants and the one who waters have a common purpose, and each will receive wages according to the labor of each. [9]For we are God's servants, working together; you are God's field, God's building.

10 According to the grace of God given to me, like a skilled master builder I laid a foundation, and someone else is building on it. Each builder must choose with care how to build on it. [11]For no one can lay any foundation other than the one that has been laid; that foundation is Jesus Christ. [12]Now if anyone builds on the foundation with gold, silver, precious stones, wood, hay, straw— [13]the work of each builder will become visible, for the Day will disclose it, because it will be revealed with fire, and the fire will test what sort of work each has done. [14]If what has been built on the foundation survives, the builder will receive a reward. [15]If the work is burned up, the builder will suffer loss; the builder will be saved, but only as through fire.

16 Do you not know that you are God's temple and that God's Spirit dwells in you?[a] [17]If anyone destroys God's temple, God will destroy that person. For God's temple is holy, and you are that temple.

18 Do not deceive yourselves. If you think that you are wise in this age, you should become fools so that you may become wise. [19]For the wisdom of this world is foolishness with God. For it is written,

> "He catches the wise in their
>    craftiness,"

[20]and again,

> "The Lord knows the thoughts
>    of the wise,
>  that they are futile."

[21]So let no one boast about human leaders. For all things are yours, [22]whether Paul or Apollos or Cephas or the world or life or death or the present or the future—all belong to you, [23]and you belong to Christ, and Christ belongs to God.

# PSALM 29.1–11

*A Psalm of David.*

**A**SCRIBE to the Lord,
    O heavenly beings,[b]
 ascribe to the Lord glory
    and strength.
2  Ascribe to the Lord the glory of
       his name;
   worship the Lord in holy
       splendor.

3  The voice of the Lord is over
       the waters;
   the God of glory thunders,
   the Lord, over mighty
       waters.
4  The voice of the Lord is
       powerful;
   the voice of the Lord is full of
       majesty.

5  The voice of the Lord breaks
       the cedars;
   the Lord breaks the cedars of
       Lebanon.

[a]In verses 16 and 17 the Greek word for *you* is plural  [b]Heb *sons of gods*

6 He makes Lebanon skip like a
    calf,
        and Sirion like a young wild
            ox.

7 The voice of the LORD flashes
        forth flames of fire.
8 The voice of the LORD shakes
        the wilderness;
    the LORD shakes the
        wilderness of Kadesh.

9 The voice of the LORD causes
        the oaks to whirl, a
    and strips the forest bare;
    and in his temple all say,
        "Glory!"

10 The LORD sits enthroned over
        the flood;
    the LORD sits enthroned as
        king forever.
11 May the LORD give strength to
        his people!
    May the LORD bless his
        people with peace!

## PROVERBS 20.26–27

A WISE king winnows the
        wicked,
    and drives the wheel over
        them.
27 The human spirit is the lamp of
        the LORD,
    searching every inmost part.

# AUGUST 8

## EZRA 7.1—8.20

AFTER this, in the reign of King Artaxerxes of Persia, Ezra son of Seraiah, son of Azariah, son of Hilkiah, 2son of Shallum, son of Zadok, son of Ahitub, 3son of Amariah, son of Azariah, son of Meraioth, 4son of Zerahiah, son of Uzzi, son of Bukki, 5son of Abishua, son of Phinehas, son of Eleazar, son of the chief priest Aaron— 6this Ezra went up from Babylonia. He was a scribe skilled in the law of Moses that the LORD the God of Israel had given; and the king granted him all that he asked, for the hand of the LORD his God was upon him.

7 Some of the people of Israel, and some of the priests and Levites, the singers and gatekeepers, and the temple servants also went up to Jerusalem, in the seventh year of King Artaxerxes. 8They came to Jerusalem in the fifth month, which was in the seventh year of the king. 9On the first day of the first month the journey up from Babylon was begun, and on the first day of the fifth month he came to Jerusalem, for the gracious hand of his God was upon him. 10For Ezra had set his heart to study the law of the LORD, and to do it, and to teach the statutes and ordinances in Israel.

11 This is a copy of the letter that King Artaxerxes gave to the priest Ezra, the scribe, a scholar of the text of the commandments of the LORD and his statutes for Israel: 12"Artaxerxes, king of kings, to the priest Ezra, the scribe of the law of the God of heaven:

aOr *causes the deer to calve*

Peace.[a] And now [13]I decree that any of the people of Israel or their priests or Levites in my kingdom who freely offers to go to Jerusalem may go with you. [14]For you are sent by the king and his seven counselors to make inquiries about Judah and Jerusalem according to the law of your God, which is in your hand, [15]and also to convey the silver and gold that the king and his counselors have freely offered to the God of Israel, whose dwelling is in Jerusalem, [16]with all the silver and gold that you shall find in the whole province of Babylonia, and with the freewill offerings of the people and the priests, given willingly for the house of their God in Jerusalem. [17]With this money, then, you shall with all diligence buy bulls, rams, and lambs, and their grain offerings and their drink offerings, and you shall offer them on the altar of the house of your God in Jerusalem. [18]Whatever seems good to you and your colleagues to do with the rest of the silver and gold, you may do, according to the will of your God. [19]The vessels that have been given you for the service of the house of your God, you shall deliver before the God of Jerusalem. [20]And whatever else is required for the house of your God, which you are responsible for providing, you may provide out of the king's treasury.

21 "I, King Artaxerxes, decree to all the treasurers in the province Beyond the River: Whatever the priest Ezra, the scribe of the law of the God of heaven, requires of you, let it be done with all diligence, [22]up to one hundred talents of silver, one hundred cors of wheat, one hundred baths[b] of wine, one hundred baths[b] of oil, and unlimited salt. [23]Whatever is commanded by the God of heaven, let it be done with zeal for the house of the God of heaven, or wrath will come upon the realm of the king and his heirs. [24]We also notify you that it shall not be lawful to impose tribute, custom, or toll on any of the priests, the Levites, the singers, the doorkeepers, the temple servants, or other servants of this house of God.

25 "And you, Ezra, according to the God-given wisdom you possess, appoint magistrates and judges who may judge all the people in the province Beyond the River who know the laws of your God; and you shall teach those who do not know them. [26]All who will not obey the law of your God and the law of the king, let judgment be strictly executed on them, whether for death or for banishment or for confiscation of their goods or for imprisonment."

27 Blessed be the LORD, the God of our ancestors, who put such a thing as this into the heart of the king to glorify the house of the LORD in Jerusalem, [28]and who extended to me steadfast love before the king and his counselors, and before all the king's mighty officers. I took courage, for the hand of the LORD my God was upon me, and I gathered leaders from Israel to go up with me.

8.1 THESE are their family heads, and this is the genealogy of those who went up with me from Babylonia, in the reign of King Artaxerxes: [2]Of the descendants of Phinehas, Gershom. Of Ithamar, Daniel. Of David, Hattush, [3]of the descendants of Shecaniah. Of Parosh, Zechariah, with whom were registered one hundred fifty males. [4]Of the descendants of Pahath-moab, Eliehoenai son of Zerahiah, and with him two hundred males. [5]Of the descendants of Zattu,[c] Shecaniah son of Jahaziel, and with him three hundred males. [6]Of the descendants of Adin, Ebed son of Jonathan, and with him fifty males. [7]Of the descendants of Elam, Jeshaiah son of Athaliah, and with him seventy males. [8]Of the descendants of Shephatiah,

aSyr Vg 1 Esdras 8.9: Aram *Perfect*   bA Heb measure of volume   cGk 1 Esdras 8.32: Heb lacks *of Zattu*

Zebadiah son of Michael, and with him eighty males. [9]Of the descendants of Joab, Obadiah son of Jehiel, and with him two hundred eighteen males. [10]Of the descendants of Bani,[a] Shelomith son of Josiphiah, and with him one hundred sixty males. [11]Of the descendants of Bebai, Zechariah son of Bebai, and with him twenty-eight males. [12]Of the descendants of Azgad, Johanan son of Hakkatan, and with him one hundred ten males. [13]Of the descendants of Adonikam, those who came later, their names being Eliphelet, Jeuel, and Shemaiah, and with them sixty males. [14]Of the descendants of Bigvai, Uthai and Zaccur, and with them seventy males.

15 I gathered them by the river that runs to Ahava, and there we camped three days. As I reviewed the people and the priests, I found there none of the descendants of Levi. [16]Then I sent for Eliezer, Ariel, Shemaiah, Elnathan, Jarib, Elnathan, Nathan, Zechariah, and Meshullam, who were leaders, and for Joiarib and Elnathan, who were wise, [17]and sent them to Iddo, the leader at the place called Casiphia, telling them what to say to Iddo and his colleagues the temple servants at Casiphia, namely, to send us ministers for the house of our God. [18]Since the gracious hand of our God was upon us, they brought us a man of discretion, of the descendants of Mahli son of Levi son of Israel, namely Sherebiah, with his sons and kin, eighteen; [19]also Hashabiah and with him Jeshaiah of the descendants of Merari, with his kin and their sons, twenty; [20]besides two hundred twenty of the temple servants, whom David and his officials had set apart to attend the Levites. These were all mentioned by name.

## 1 CORINTHIANS 4.1–21

**T**HINK of us in this way, as servants of Christ and stewards of God's mysteries. [2]Moreover, it is required of stewards that they be found trustworthy. [3]But with me it is a very small thing that I should be judged by you or by any human court. I do not even judge myself. [4]I am not aware of anything against myself, but I am not thereby acquitted. It is the Lord who judges me. [5]Therefore do not pronounce judgment before the time, before the Lord comes, who will bring to light the things now hidden in darkness and will disclose the purposes of the heart. Then each one will receive commendation from God.

6 I have applied all this to Apollos and myself for your benefit, brothers and sisters,[b] so that you may learn through us the meaning of the saying, "Nothing beyond what is written," so that none of you will be puffed up in favor of one against another. [7]For who sees anything different in you?[c] What do you have that you did not receive? And if you received it, why do you boast as if it were not a gift?

8 Already you have all you want! Already you have become rich! Quite apart from us you have become kings! Indeed, I wish that you had become kings, so that we might be kings with you! [9]For I think that God has exhibited us apostles as last of all, as though sentenced to death, because we have become a spectacle to the world, to angels and to mortals. [10]We are fools for the sake of Christ, but you are wise in Christ. We are weak, but you are strong. You are held in honor, but we in disrepute. [11]To the present hour we are hungry and thirsty, we are poorly clothed and beaten and homeless, [12]and we grow weary from the work of our own hands. When reviled, we bless;

---

aGk 1 Esdras 8.36: Heb lacks *Bani*  bGk *brothers*  cOr *Who makes you different from another?*

when persecuted, we endure; [13] when slandered, we speak kindly. We have become like the rubbish of the world, the dregs of all things, to this very day.

14 I am not writing this to make you ashamed, but to admonish you as my beloved children. [15] For though you might have ten thousand guardians in Christ, you do not have many fathers. Indeed, in Christ Jesus I became your father through the gospel. [16] I appeal to you, then, be imitators of me. [17] For this reason I sent [a] you Timothy, who is my beloved and faithful child in the Lord, to remind you of my ways in Christ Jesus, as I teach them everywhere in every church. [18] But some of you, thinking that I am not coming to you, have become arrogant. [19] But I will come to you soon, if the Lord wills, and I will find out not the talk of these arrogant people but their power. [20] For the kingdom of God depends not on talk but on power. [21] What would you prefer? Am I to come to you with a stick, or with love in a spirit of gentleness?

## PSALM 30.1–12

*A Psalm. A Song at the dedication of the temple. Of David.*

I WILL extol you, O LORD, for you
   have drawn me up,
   and did not let my foes
      rejoice over me.
2 O LORD my God, I cried to you
      for help,
   and you have healed me.
3 O LORD, you brought up my soul
      from Sheol,
   restored me to life from
      among those gone down
      to the Pit. [b]

4 Sing praises to the LORD, O you
      his faithful ones,
   and give thanks to his holy
      name.

5 For his anger is but for a
      moment;
   his favor is for a lifetime.
Weeping may linger for the
      night,
   but joy comes with the
      morning.

6 As for me, I said in my
      prosperity,
   "I shall never be moved."
7 By your favor, O LORD,
   you had established me as a
      strong mountain;
you hid your face;
   I was dismayed.

8 To you, O LORD, I cried,
   and to the LORD I made
      supplication:
9 "What profit is there in my
      death,
   if I go down to the Pit?
Will the dust praise you?
   Will it tell of your
      faithfulness?
10 Hear, O LORD, and be gracious
      to me!
   O LORD, be my helper!"

11 You have turned my mourning
      into dancing;
   you have taken off my
      sackcloth
   and clothed me with joy,
12 so that my soul [c] may praise
      you and not be silent.
   O LORD my God, I will give
      thanks to you forever.

## PROVERBS 20.28–30

L OYALTY and faithfulness
      preserve the king,
   and his throne is upheld by
      righteousness. [d]
29 The glory of youths is their
      strength,

a Or *am sending*  b Or *that I should not go down to the Pit*  c Heb *that glory*  d Gk: Heb *loyalty*

but the beauty of the aged is
their gray hair.
30 Blows that wound cleanse
away evil;

beatings make clean the
innermost parts.

# AUGUST 9

## EZRA 8.21—9.15

**T**HEN I [Ezra] proclaimed a fast there, at the river Ahava, that we might deny ourselves[a] before our God, to seek from him a safe journey for ourselves, our children, and all our possessions. 22For I was ashamed to ask the king for a band of soldiers and cavalry to protect us against the enemy on our way, since we had told the king that the hand of our God is gracious to all who seek him, but his power and his wrath are against all who forsake him. 23So we fasted and petitioned our God for this, and he listened to our entreaty.

24 Then I set apart twelve of the leading priests: Sherebiah, Hashabiah, and ten of their kin with them. 25And I weighed out to them the silver and the gold and the vessels, the offering for the house of our God that the king, his counselors, his lords, and all Israel there present had offered; 26I weighed out into their hand six hundred fifty talents of silver, and one hundred silver vessels worth . . . talents,[b] and one hundred talents of gold, 27twenty gold bowls worth a thousand darics, and two vessels of fine polished bronze as precious as gold. 28And I said to them, "You are holy to the LORD, and the vessels are holy; and the silver and the gold are a freewill offering to the LORD, the God of your ancestors. 29Guard

them and keep them until you weigh them before the chief priests and the Levites and the heads of families in Israel at Jerusalem, within the chambers of the house of the LORD." 30So the priests and the Levites took over the silver, the gold, and the vessels as they were weighed out, to bring them to Jerusalem, to the house of our God.

31 Then we left the river Ahava on the twelfth day of the first month, to go to Jerusalem; the hand of our God was upon us, and he delivered us from the hand of the enemy and from ambushes along the way. 32We came to Jerusalem and remained there three days. 33On the fourth day, within the house of our God, the silver, the gold, and the vessels were weighed into the hands of the priest Meremoth son of Uriah, and with him was Eleazar son of Phinehas, and with them were the Levites, Jozabad son of Jeshua and Noadiah son of Binnui. 34The total was counted and weighed, and the weight of everything was recorded.

35 At that time those who had come from captivity, the returned exiles, offered burnt offerings to the God of Israel, twelve bulls for all Israel, ninety-six rams, seventy-seven lambs, and as a sin offering twelve male goats; all this was a burnt offering to the LORD. 36They also delivered the king's commissions to the king's satraps and to

a Or *might fast*   b The number of talents is lacking

the governors of the province Beyond the River; and they supported the people and the house of God.

9.1 AFTER these things had been done, the officials approached me and said, "The people of Israel, the priests, and the Levites have not separated themselves from the peoples of the lands with their abominations, from the Canaanites, the Hittites, the Perizzites, the Jebusites, the Ammonites, the Moabites, the Egyptians, and the Amorites. ²For they have taken some of their daughters as wives for themselves and for their sons. Thus the holy seed has mixed itself with the peoples of the lands, and in this faithlessness the officials and leaders have led the way." ³When I heard this, I tore my garment and my mantle, and pulled hair from my head and beard, and sat appalled. ⁴Then all who trembled at the words of the God of Israel, because of the faithlessness of the returned exiles, gathered around me while I sat appalled until the evening sacrifice.

5  At the evening sacrifice I got up from my fasting, with my garments and my mantle torn, and fell on my knees, spread out my hands to the LORD my God, ⁶and said,

"O my God, I am too ashamed and embarrassed to lift my face to you, my God, for our iniquities have risen higher than our heads, and our guilt has mounted up to the heavens. ⁷From the days of our ancestors to this day we have been deep in guilt, and for our iniquities we, our kings, and our priests have been handed over to the kings of the lands, to the sword, to captivity, to plundering, and to utter shame, as is now the case. ⁸But now for a brief moment favor has been shown by the LORD our God, who has left us a remnant, and given us a stake in his holy place, in order that heª may brighten our eyes

ªHeb *our God*

and grant us a little sustenance in our slavery. ⁹For we are slaves; yet our God has not forsaken us in our slavery, but has extended to us his steadfast love before the kings of Persia, to give us new life to set up the house of our God, to repair its ruins, and to give us a wall in Judea and Jerusalem.

10  "And now, our God, what shall we say after this? For we have forsaken your commandments, ¹¹which you commanded by your servants the prophets, saying, 'The land that you are entering to possess is a land unclean with the pollutions of the peoples of the lands, with their abominations. They have filled it from end to end with their uncleanness. ¹²Therefore do not give your daughters to their sons, neither take their daughters for your sons, and never seek their peace or prosperity, so that you may be strong and eat the good of the land and leave it for an inheritance to your children forever.' ¹³After all that has come upon us for our evil deeds and for our great guilt, seeing that you, our God, have punished us less than our iniquities deserved and have given us such a remnant as this, ¹⁴shall we break your commandments again and intermarry with the peoples who practice these abominations? Would you not be angry with us until you destroy us without remnant or survivor? ¹⁵O LORD, God of Israel, you are just, but we have escaped as a remnant, as is now the case. Here we are before you in our guilt, though no one can face you because of this."

# 1 CORINTHIANS 5.1–13

IT is actually reported that there is sexual immorality among you, and of a kind that is not found even among pagans; for a man is living with his father's wife. ²And you are arrogant! Should you not rather have mourned, so that he who has done this would have been removed from among you?

3   For though absent in body, I am present in spirit; and as if present I have already pronounced judgment [4]in the name of the Lord Jesus on the man who has done such a thing. [a] When you are assembled, and my spirit is present with the power of our Lord Jesus, [5]you are to hand this man over to Satan for the destruction of the flesh, so that his spirit may be saved in the day of the Lord. [b]

6   Your boasting is not a good thing. Do you not know that a little yeast leavens the whole batch of dough? [7]Clean out the old yeast so that you may be a new batch, as you really are unleavened. For our paschal lamb, Christ, has been sacrificed. [8]Therefore, let us celebrate the festival, not with the old yeast, the yeast of malice and evil, but with the unleavened bread of sincerity and truth.

9   I wrote to you in my letter not to associate with sexually immoral persons— [10]not at all meaning the immoral of this world, or the greedy and robbers, or idolaters, since you would then need to go out of the world. [11]But now I am writing to you not to associate with anyone who bears the name of brother or sister[c] who is sexually immoral or greedy, or is an idolater, reviler, drunkard, or robber. Do not even eat with such a one. [12]For what have I to do with judging those outside? Is it not those who are inside that you are to judge? [13]God will judge those outside. "Drive out the wicked person from among you."

## PSALM 31.1–8

*To the leader. A Psalm of David.*

IN you, O LORD, I seek refuge;
>   do not let me ever be put to
>       shame;
>   in your righteousness deliver
>       me.
2   Incline your ear to me;
>       rescue me speedily.
>   Be a rock of refuge for me,
>       a strong fortress to save me.

3   You are indeed my rock and my
>           fortress;
>       for your name's sake lead me
>           and guide me,
4   take me out of the net that is
>           hidden for me,
>       for you are my refuge.
5   Into your hand I commit my
>           spirit;
>       you have redeemed me,
>           O LORD, faithful God.

6   You hate[d] those who pay
>           regard to worthless idols,
>       but I trust in the LORD.
7   I will exult and rejoice in your
>           steadfast love,
>       because you have seen my
>           affliction;
>       you have taken heed of my
>           adversities,
8   and have not delivered me into
>           the hand of the enemy;
>       you have set my feet in a
>           broad place.

a Or *on the man who has done such a thing in the name of the Lord Jesus*   b Other ancient authorities add *Jesus*   c Gk *brother*   d One Heb Ms Gk Syr Jerome: MT *I hate*

## PROVERBS 21.1–2

**T**HE king's heart is a stream of water in the hand of the LORD; he turns it wherever he will. 2 All deeds are right in the sight of the doer, but the LORD weighs the heart.

# AUGUST 10

## EZRA 10.1–44

**W**HILE Ezra prayed and made confession, weeping and throwing himself down before the house of God, a very great assembly of men, women, and children gathered to him out of Israel; the people also wept bitterly. 2Shecaniah son of Jehiel, of the descendants of Elam, addressed Ezra, saying, "We have broken faith with our God and have married foreign women from the peoples of the land, but even now there is hope for Israel in spite of this. 3So now let us make a covenant with our God to send away all these wives and their children, according to the counsel of my lord and of those who tremble at the commandment of our God; and let it be done according to the law. 4Take action, for it is your duty, and we are with you; be strong, and do it." 5Then Ezra stood up and made the leading priests, the Levites, and all Israel swear that they would do as had been said. So they swore.

6 Then Ezra withdrew from before the house of God, and went to the chamber of Jehohanan son of Eliashib, where he spent the night. a He did not eat bread or drink water, for he was mourning over the faithlessness of the exiles. 7They made a proclamation throughout Judah and Jerusalem to all the returned exiles that they should assemble at Jerusalem, 8and that if any did not come within three days, by order of the officials and the elders all their property should be forfeited, and they themselves banned from the congregation of the exiles.

9 Then all the people of Judah and Benjamin assembled at Jerusalem within the three days; it was the ninth month, on the twentieth day of the month. All the people sat in the open square before the house of God, trembling because of this matter and because of the heavy rain. 10Then Ezra the priest stood up and said to them, "You have trespassed and married foreign women, and so increased the guilt of Israel. 11Now make confession to the LORD the God of your ancestors, and do his will; separate yourselves from the peoples of the land and from the foreign wives." 12Then all the assembly answered with a loud voice, "It is so; we must do as you have said. 13But the people are many, and it is a time of heavy rain; we cannot stand in the open. Nor is this a task for one day or for two, for many of us have transgressed in this matter. 14Let our officials represent the whole assembly, and let all in our towns who have taken foreign wives come at appointed times, and with them the elders and judges of every town, until the fierce wrath of our God on this account is averted from us." 15Only Jonathan son of Asahel and Jahzeiah son of Tikvah opposed this, and Meshullam and Shabbethai the Levites supported them.

a 1 Esdras 9.2: Heb *where he went*

16 Then the returned exiles did so. Ezra the priest selected men, [a] heads of families, according to their families, each of them designated by name. On the first day of the tenth month they sat down to examine the matter. [17]By the first day of the first month they had come to the end of all the men who had married foreign women.

18 There were found of the descendants of the priests who had married foreign women, of the descendants of Jeshua son of Jozadak and his brothers: Maaseiah, Eliezer, Jarib, and Gedaliah. [19]They pledged themselves to send away their wives, and their guilt offering was a ram of the flock for their guilt. [20]Of the descendants of Immer: Hanani and Zebadiah. [21]Of the descendants of Harim: Maaseiah, Elijah, Shemaiah, Jehiel, and Uzziah. [22]Of the descendants of Pashhur: Elioenai, Maaseiah, Ishmael, Nethanel, Jozabad, and Elasah.

23 Of the Levites: Jozabad, Shimei, Kelaiah (that is, Kelita), Pethahiah, Judah, and Eliezer. [24]Of the singers: Eliashib. Of the gatekeepers: Shallum, Telem, and Uri.

25 And of Israel: of the descendants of Parosh: Ramiah, Izziah, Malchijah, Mijamin, Eleazar, Hashabiah, [b] and Benaiah. [26]Of the descendants of Elam: Mattaniah, Zechariah, Jehiel, Abdi, Jeremoth, and Elijah. [27]Of the descendants of Zattu: Elioenai, Eliashib, Mattaniah, Jeremoth, Zabad, and Aziza. [28]Of the descendants of Bebai: Jehohanan, Hananiah, Zabbai, and Athlai. [29]Of the descendants of Bani: Meshullam, Malluch, Adaiah, Jashub, Sheal, and Jeremoth. [30]Of the descendants of Pahath-moab: Adna, Chelal, Benaiah, Maaseiah, Mattaniah, Bezalel, Binnui, and Manasseh. [31]Of the descendants of Harim: Eliezer, Isshijah, Malchijah, Shemaiah, Shimeon, [32]Benjamin, Malluch, and Shemariah. [33]Of

the descendants of Hashum: Mattenai, Mattattah, Zabad, Eliphelet, Jeremai, Manasseh, and Shimei. [34]Of the descendants of Bani: Maadai, Amram, Uel, [35]Benaiah, Bedeiah, Cheluhi, [36]Vaniah, Meremoth, Eliashib, [37]Mattaniah, Mattenai, and Jaasu. [38]Of the descendants of Binnui: [c] Shimei, [39]Shelemiah, Nathan, Adaiah, [40]Machnadebai, Shashai, Sharai, [41]Azarel, Shelemiah, Shemariah, [42]Shallum, Amariah, and Joseph. [43]Of the descendants of Nebo: Jeiel, Mattithiah, Zabad, Zebina, Jaddai, Joel, and Benaiah. [44]All these had married foreign women, and they sent them away with their children. [d]

# 1 CORINTHIANS 6.1–20

WHEN any of you has a grievance against another, do you dare to take it to court before the unrighteous, instead of taking it before the saints? [2]Do you not know that the saints will judge the world? And if the world is to be judged by you, are you incompetent to try trivial cases? [3]Do you not know that we are to judge angels—to say nothing of ordinary matters? [4]If you have ordinary cases, then, do you appoint as judges those who have no standing in the church? [5]I say this to your shame. Can it be that there is no one among you wise enough to decide between one believer[e] and another, [6]but a believer[e] goes to court against a believer[e]—and before unbelievers at that?

7 In fact, to have lawsuits at all with one another is already a defeat for you. Why not rather be wronged? Why not rather be defrauded? [8]But you yourselves wrong and defraud—and believers[f] at that?

9 Do you not know that wrongdoers will not inherit the kingdom of God? Do not be deceived! Fornicators, idola-

---

[a]1 Esdra 9.16: Syr: Heb *And there were selected Ezra,*   [b]1 Esdras 9.26 Gk: Heb *Malchijah*
[c]Gk: Heb *Bani, Binnui*   [d]1 Esdras 9.36; Meaning of Heb uncertain   [e]Gk *brother*   [f]Gk *brothers*

ters, adulterers, male prostitutes, sodomites, 10thieves, the greedy, drunkards, revilers, robbers—none of these will inherit the kingdom of God. 11And this is what some of you used to be. But you were washed, you were sanctified, you were justified in the name of the Lord Jesus Christ and in the Spirit of our God.

12 "All things are lawful for me," but not all things are beneficial. "All things are lawful for me," but I will not be dominated by anything. 13"Food is meant for the stomach and the stomach for food,"a and God will destroy both one and the other. The body is meant not for fornication but for the Lord, and the Lord for the body. 14And God raised the Lord and will also raise us by his power. 15Do you not know that your bodies are members of Christ? Should I therefore take the members of Christ and make them members of a prostitute? Never! 16Do you not know that whoever is united to a prostitute becomes one body with her? For it is said, "The two shall be one flesh." 17But anyone united to the Lord becomes one spirit with him. 18Shun fornication! Every sin that a person commits is outside the body; but the fornicator sins against the body itself. 19Or do you not know that your body is a templeb of the Holy Spirit within you, which you have from God, and that you are not your own? 20For you were bought with a price; therefore glorify God in your body.

## PSALM 31.9–18

Be gracious to me, O Lord, for
  I am in distress;
  my eye wastes away from
    grief,
  my soul and body also.
10 For my life is spent with
    sorrow,
  and my years with sighing;

my strength fails because of my
    misery,c
  and my bones waste away.
11 I am the scorn of all my
    adversaries,
  a horrord to my neighbors,
an object of dread to my
    acquaintances;
  those who see me in the
    street flee from me.
12 I have passed out of mind like
    one who is dead;
  I have become like a broken
    vessel.
13 For I hear the whispering of
    many—
  terror all around!—
as they scheme together against
    me,
  as they plot to take my life.

14 But I trust in you, O Lord;
  I say, "You are my God."
15 My times are in your hand;
  deliver me from the hand of
    my enemies and
    persecutors.
16 Let your face shine upon your
    servant;
  save me in your steadfast
    love.
17 Do not let me be put to shame,
    O Lord,
  for I call on you;
let the wicked be put to shame;
  let them go dumbfounded to
    Sheol.
18 Let the lying lips be stilled
  that speak insolently against
    the righteous
  with pride and contempt.

## PROVERBS 21.3

To do righteousness and justice
  is more acceptable to the
    Lord than sacrifice.

---

aThe quotation may extend to the word *other*   bOr *sanctuary*   cGk Syr: Heb *my iniquity*
dCn: Heb *exceedingly*

## NEHEMIAH 1.1—3.14

THE words of Nehemiah son of Hacaliah. In the month of Chislev, in the twentieth year, while I was in Susa the capital, ²one of my brothers, Hanani, came with certain men from Judah; and I asked them about the Jews that survived, those who had escaped the captivity, and about Jerusalem. ³They replied, "The survivors there in the province who escaped captivity are in great trouble and shame; the wall of Jerusalem is broken down, and its gates have been destroyed by fire."

4 When I heard these words I sat down and wept, and mourned for days, fasting and praying before the God of heaven. ⁵I said, "O LORD God of heaven, the great and awesome God who keeps covenant and steadfast love with those who love him and keep his commandments; ⁶let your ear be attentive and your eyes open to hear the prayer of your servant that I now pray before you day and night for your servants, the people of Israel, confessing the sins of the people of Israel, which we have sinned against you. Both I and my family have sinned. ⁷We have offended you deeply, failing to keep the commandments, the statutes, and the ordinances that you commanded your servant Moses. ⁸Remember the word that you commanded your servant Moses, 'If you are unfaithful, I will scatter you among the peoples; ⁹but if you return to me and keep my commandments and do them, though your outcasts are under the farthest skies, I will gather them from there and bring them to the place at which I have chosen to establish my name.' ¹⁰They are your servants and your people, whom you redeemed by your great power and your strong hand. ¹¹O Lord, let your ear be attentive to the prayer of your servant, and to the prayer of your servants who delight in revering your name. Give success to your servant today, and grant him mercy in the sight of this man!"

At the time, I was cupbearer to the king.

2.1 IN the month of Nisan, in the twentieth year of King Artaxerxes, when wine was served him, I carried the wine and gave it to the king. Now, I had never been sad in his presence before. ²So the king said to me, "Why is your face sad, since you are not sick? This can only be sadness of the heart." Then I was very much afraid. ³I said to the king, "May the king live forever! Why should my face not be sad, when the city, the place of my ancestors' graves, lies waste, and its gates have been destroyed by fire?" ⁴Then the king said to me, "What do you request?" So I prayed to the God of heaven. ⁵Then I said to the king, "If it pleases the king, and if your servant has found favor with you, I ask that you send me to Judah, to the city of my ancestors' graves, so that I may rebuild it." ⁶The king said to me (the queen also was sitting beside him), "How long will you be gone, and when will you return?" So it pleased the king to send me, and I set him a date. ⁷Then I said to the king, "If it pleases the king, let letters be given me to the governors of the province Beyond the River, that they may grant me passage until I arrive in Judah; ⁸and a letter to Asaph, the keeper of the king's forest, directing him to give me timber to make beams for the gates of the temple fortress, and for the wall of the city, and for the house that I shall occupy."

And the king granted me what I asked, for the gracious hand of my God was upon me.

9 Then I came to the governors of the province Beyond the River, and gave them the king's letters. Now the king had sent officers of the army and cavalry with me. [10]When Sanballat the Horonite and Tobiah the Ammonite official heard this, it displeased them greatly that someone had come to seek the welfare of the people of Israel.

11 So I came to Jerusalem and was there for three days. [12]Then I got up during the night, I and a few men with me; I told no one what my God had put into my heart to do for Jerusalem. The only animal I took was the animal I rode. [13]I went out by night by the Valley Gate past the Dragon's Spring and to the Dung Gate, and I inspected the walls of Jerusalem that had been broken down and its gates that had been destroyed by fire. [14]Then I went on to the Fountain Gate and to the King's Pool; but there was no place for the animal I was riding to continue. [15]So I went up by way of the valley by night and inspected the wall. Then I turned back and entered by the Valley Gate, and so returned. [16]The officials did not know where I had gone or what I was doing; I had not yet told the Jews, the priests, the nobles, the officials, and the rest that were to do the work.

17 Then I said to them, "You see the trouble we are in, how Jerusalem lies in ruins with its gates burned. Come, let us rebuild the wall of Jerusalem, so that we may no longer suffer disgrace." [18]I told them that the hand of my God had been gracious upon me, and also the words that the king had spoken to me. Then they said, "Let us start building!" So they committed themselves to the common good. [19]But when Sanballat the Horonite and Tobiah the Ammonite official, and Geshem the Arab heard of it, they mocked and ridiculed us, saying, "What is this that you are doing? Are you rebelling against the king?" [20]Then I replied to them, "The God of heaven is the one who will give us success, and we his servants are going to start building; but you have no share or claim or historic right in Jerusalem."

3.1 THEN the high priest Eliashib set to work with his fellow priests and rebuilt the Sheep Gate. They consecrated it and set up its doors; they consecrated it as far as the Tower of the Hundred and as far as the Tower of Hananel. [2]And the men of Jericho built next to him. And next to them[a] Zaccur son of Imri built.

3 The sons of Hassenaah built the Fish Gate; they laid its beams and set up its doors, its bolts, and its bars. [4]Next to them Meremoth son of Uriah son of Hakkoz made repairs. Next to them Meshullam son of Berechiah son of Meshezabel made repairs. Next to them Zadok son of Baana made repairs. [5]Next to them the Tekoites made repairs; but their nobles would not put their shoulders to the work of their Lord.[b]

6 Joiada son of Paseah and Meshullam son of Besodeiah repaired the Old Gate; they laid its beams and set up its doors, its bolts, and its bars. [7]Next to them repairs were made by Melatiah the Gibeonite and Jadon the Meronothite—the men of Gibeon and of Mizpah—who were under the jurisdiction of[c] the governor of the province Beyond the River. [8]Next to them Uzziel son of Harhaiah, one of the goldsmiths, made repairs. Next to him Hananiah, one of the perfumers, made repairs; and they restored Jerusalem as far as the Broad Wall. [9]Next to them Rephaiah son of Hur, ruler of half the district of[d] Jerusalem, made repairs.

¹⁰Next to them Jedaiah son of Harumaph made repairs opposite his house; and next to him Hattush son of Hashabneiah made repairs. ¹¹Malchijah son of Harim and Hasshub son of Pahathmoab repaired another section and the Tower of the Ovens. ¹²Next to him Shallum son of Hallohesh, ruler of half the district ofᵃ Jerusalem, made repairs, he and his daughters.

13 Hanun and the inhabitants of Zanoah repaired the Valley Gate; they rebuilt it and set up its doors, its bolts, and its bars, and repaired a thousand cubits of the wall, as far as the Dung Gate.

14 Malchijah son of Rechab, ruler of the district ofᵇ Beth-haccherem, repaired the Dung Gate; he rebuilt it and set up its doors, its bolts, and its bars.

# 1 CORINTHIANS 7.1–24

Now concerning the matters about which you wrote: "It is well for a man not to touch a woman." ²But because of cases of sexual immorality, each man should have his own wife and each woman her own husband. ³The husband should give to his wife her conjugal rights, and likewise the wife to her husband. ⁴For the wife does not have authority over her own body, but the husband does; likewise the husband does not have authority over his own body, but the wife does. ⁵Do not deprive one another except perhaps by agreement for a set time, to devote yourselves to prayer, and then come together again, so that Satan may not tempt you because of your lack of self-control. ⁶This I say by way of concession, not of command. ⁷I wish that all were as I myself am. But each has a particular gift from God, one having one kind and another a different kind.

8 To the unmarried and the widows I say that it is well for them to remain unmarried as I am. ⁹But if they are not practicing self-control, they should marry. For it is better to marry than to be aflame with passion.

10 To the married I give this command—not I but the Lord—that the wife should not separate from her husband ¹¹(but if she does separate, let her remain unmarried or else be reconciled to her husband), and that the husband should not divorce his wife.

12 To the rest I say—I and not the Lord—that if any believerᶜ has a wife who is an unbeliever, and she consents to live with him, he should not divorce her. ¹³And if any woman has a husband who is an unbeliever, and he consents to live with her, she should not divorce him. ¹⁴For the unbelieving husband is made holy through his wife, and the unbelieving wife is made holy through her husband. Otherwise, your children would be unclean, but as it is, they are holy. ¹⁵But if the unbelieving partner separates, let it be so; in such a case the brother or sister is not bound. It is to peace that God has called you. ᵈ ¹⁶Wife, for all you know, you might save your husband. Husband, for all you know, you might save your wife.

17 However that may be, let each of you lead the life that the Lord has assigned, to which God called you. This is my rule in all the churches. ¹⁸Was anyone at the time of his call already circumcised? Let him not seek to remove the marks of circumcision. Was anyone at the time of his call uncircumcised? Let him not seek circumcision. ¹⁹Circumcision is nothing, and uncircumcision is nothing; but obeying the commandments of God is everything. ²⁰Let each of you remain in the condition in which you were called.

21 Were you a slave when called? Do not be concerned about it. Even if you can gain your freedom, make use of

ᵃOr *supervisor of half the portion assigned to*   ᵇOr *supervisor of the portion assigned to*   ᶜGk *brother*   ᵈOther ancient authorities read *us*

your present condition now more than ever. [a] 22 For whoever was called in the Lord as a slave is a freed person belonging to the Lord, just as whoever was free when called is a slave of Christ. 23 You were bought with a price; do not become slaves of human masters. 24 In whatever condition you were called, brothers and sisters, [b] there remain with God.

## PSALM 31.19–24

O HOW abundant is your
goodness
that you have laid up for
those who fear you,
and accomplished for those who
take refuge in you,
in the sight of everyone!
20  In the shelter of your presence
you hide them
from human plots;
you hold them safe under your
shelter
from contentious tongues.

21  Blessed be the LORD,

for he has wondrously shown
his steadfast love to me
when I was beset as a city
under siege.
22  I had said in my alarm,
"I am driven far [c] from your
sight."
But you heard my supplications
when I cried out to you for
help.

23  Love the LORD, all you his
saints.
The LORD preserves the
faithful,
but abundantly repays the one
who acts haughtily.
24  Be strong, and let your heart
take courage,
all you who wait for the LORD.

## PROVERBS 21.4

H AUGHTY eyes and a proud
heart—
the lamp of the
wicked—are sin.

# AUGUST 12

## NEHEMIAH 3.15—5.13

A ND Shallum son of Col-hozeh, ruler of the district of [d] Mizpah, repaired the Fountain Gate; he rebuilt it and covered it and set up its doors, its bolts, and its bars; and he built the wall of the Pool of Shelah of the king's garden, as far as the stairs that go down from the City of David. 16 After him Nehemiah son of Azbuk, ruler of half the district of [e] Beth-zur, repaired from a point opposite the graves of David, as far as the artificial pool and the house of the warriors. 17 After him the Levites made repairs: Rehum son of Bani; next to him Hashabiah, ruler of half the district of [e] Keilah, made repairs for his district. 18 After him their kin made repairs: Binnui, [f] son of Henadad, ruler of half the

a Or *avail yourself of the opportunity*   b Gk *brothers*   c Another reading is *cut off*   d Or *supervisor of the portion assigned to*   e Or *supervisor of half the portion assigned to*   f Gk Syr Compare verse 24, 10.9: Heb *Bavvai* district of[a] Keilah; [19]next to him Ezer son of Jeshua, ruler[b] of Mizpah, repaired another section opposite the ascent to the armory at the Angle. [20]After him Baruch son of Zabbai repaired another section from the Angle to the door of the house of the high priest Eliashib. [21]After him Meremoth son of Uriah son of Hakkoz repaired another section from the door of the house of Eliashib to the end of the house of Eliashib. [22]After him the priests, the men of the surrounding area, made repairs. [23]After them Benjamin and Hasshub made repairs opposite their house. After them Azariah son of Maaseiah son of Ananiah made repairs beside his own house. [24]After him Binnui son of Henadad repaired another section, from the house of Azariah to the Angle and to the corner. [25]Palal son of Uzai repaired opposite the Angle and the tower projecting from the upper house of the king at the court of the guard. After him Pedaiah son of Parosh [26]and the temple servants living[c] on Ophel made repairs up to a point opposite the Water Gate on the east and the projecting tower. [27]After him the Tekoites repaired another section opposite the great projecting tower as far as the wall of Ophel.

28 Above the Horse Gate the priests made repairs, each one opposite his own house. [29]After them Zadok son of Immer made repairs opposite his own house. After him Shemaiah son of Shecaniah, the keeper of the East Gate, made repairs. [30]After him Hananiah son of Shelemiah and Hanun sixth son of Zalaph repaired another section. After him Meshullam son of Berechiah made repairs opposite his living quarters. [31]After him Malchijah, one of the goldsmiths, made repairs as far as the house of the temple servants and of the merchants, opposite the Muster Gate,[d] and to the upper room of the corner. [32]And between the upper room

of the corner and the Sheep Gate the goldsmiths and the merchants made repairs.

[4e.1] Now when Sanballat heard that we were building the wall, he was angry and greatly enraged, and he mocked the Jews. [2]He said in the presence of his associates and of the army of Samaria, "What are these feeble Jews doing? Will they restore things? Will they sacrifice? Will they finish it in a day? Will they revive the stones out of the heaps of rubbish—and burned ones at that?" [3]Tobiah the Ammonite was beside him, and he said, "That stone wall they are building—any fox going up on it would break it down!" [4]Hear, O our God, for we are despised; turn their taunt back on their own heads, and give them over as plunder in a land of captivity. [5]Do not cover their guilt, and do not let their sin be blotted out from your sight; for they have hurled insults in the face of the builders.

6 So we rebuilt the wall, and all the wall was joined together to half its height; for the people had a mind to work.

[7f] But when Sanballat and Tobiah and the Arabs and the Ammonites and the Ashdodites heard that the repairing of the walls of Jerusalem was going forward and the gaps were beginning to be closed, they were very angry, [8]and all plotted together to come and fight against Jerusalem and to cause confusion in it. [9]So we prayed to our God, and set a guard as a protection against them day and night.

10 But Judah said, "The strength of the burden bearers is failing, and there is too much rubbish so that we are unable to work on the wall." [11]And our enemies said, "They will not know or see anything before we come upon them and kill them and stop the work." [12]When the Jews who lived near them

came, they said to us ten times, "From all the places where they live[a] they will come up against us."[b] ¹³So in the lowest parts of the space behind the wall, in open places, I stationed the people according to their families,[c] with their swords, their spears, and their bows. ¹⁴After I looked these things over, I stood up and said to the nobles and the officials and the rest of the people, "Do not be afraid of them. Remember the LORD, who is great and awesome, and fight for your kin, your sons, your daughters, your wives, and your homes."

15 When our enemies heard that their plot was known to us, and that God had frustrated it, we all returned to the wall, each to his work. ¹⁶From that day on, half of my servants worked on construction, and half held the spears, shields, bows, and body-armor; and the leaders posted themselves behind the whole house of Judah, ¹⁷who were building the wall. The burden bearers carried their loads in such a way that each labored on the work with one hand and with the other held a weapon. ¹⁸And each of the builders had his sword strapped at his side while he built. The man who sounded the trumpet was beside me. ¹⁹And I said to the nobles, the officials, and the rest of the people, "The work is great and widely spread out, and we are separated far from one another on the wall. ²⁰Rally to us wherever you hear the sound of the trumpet. Our God will fight for us."

21 So we labored at the work, and half of them held the spears from break of dawn until the stars came out. ²²I also said to the people at that time, "Let every man and his servant pass the night inside Jerusalem, so that they may be a guard for us by night and may labor by day." ²³So neither I nor my brothers nor my servants nor the men of the guard who followed me ever took off our clothes; each kept his weapon in his right hand. [d]

5.1 Now there was a great outcry of the people and of their wives against their Jewish kin. ²For there were those who said, "With our sons and our daughters, we are many; we must get grain, so that we may eat and stay alive." ³There were also those who said, "We are having to pledge our fields, our vineyards, and our houses in order to get grain during the famine." ⁴And there were those who said, "We are having to borrow money on our fields and vineyards to pay the king's tax. ⁵Now our flesh is the same as that of our kindred; our children are the same as their children; and yet we are forcing our sons and daughters to be slaves, and some of our daughters have been ravished; we are powerless, and our fields and vineyards now belong to others."

6 I was very angry when I heard their outcry and these complaints. ⁷After thinking it over, I brought charges against the nobles and the officials; I said to them, "You are all taking interest from your own people." And I called a great assembly to deal with them, ⁸and said to them, "As far as we were able, we have bought back our Jewish kindred who had been sold to other nations; but now you are selling your own kin, who must then be bought back by us!" They were silent, and could not find a word to say. ⁹So I said, "The thing that you are doing is not good. Should you not walk in the fear of our God, to prevent the taunts of the nations our enemies? ¹⁰Moreover I and my brothers and my servants are lending them money and grain. Let us stop this taking of interest. ¹¹Restore to them, this very day, their fields, their vineyards, their olive orchards, and their houses, and the interest on

[a] Cn: Heb *you return*   [b] Compare Gk Syr: Meaning of Heb uncertain   [c] Meaning of Heb uncertain
[d] Cn: Heb *each his weapon the water*

money, grain, wine, and oil that you have been exacting from them." [12]Then they said, "We will restore everything and demand nothing more from them. We will do as you say." And I called the priests, and made them take an oath to do as they had promised. [13]I also shook out the fold of my garment and said, "So may God shake out everyone from house and from property who does not perform this promise. Thus may they be shaken out and emptied." And all the assembly said, "Amen," and praised the LORD. And the people did as they had promised.

# 1 CORINTHIANS 7.25–40

**N**ow concerning virgins, I have no command of the Lord, but I give my opinion as one who by the Lord's mercy is trustworthy. [26]I think that, in view of the impending[a] crisis, it is well for you to remain as you are. [27]Are you bound to a wife? Do not seek to be free. Are you free from a wife? Do not seek a wife. [28]But if you marry, you do not sin, and if a virgin marries, she does not sin. Yet those who marry will experience distress in this life,[b] and I would spare you that. [29]I mean, brothers and sisters,[c] the appointed time has grown short; from now on, let even those who have wives be as though they had none, [30]and those who mourn as though they were not mourning, and those who rejoice as though they were not rejoicing, and those who buy as though they had no possessions, [31]and those who deal with the world as though they had no dealings with it. For the present form of this world is passing away.

[32] I want you to be free from anxieties. The unmarried man is anxious about the affairs of the Lord, how to please the Lord; [33]but the married man is anxious about the affairs of the world, how to please his wife, [34]and his interests are divided. And the unmarried woman and the virgin are anxious about the affairs of the Lord, so that they may be holy in body and spirit; but the married woman is anxious about the affairs of the world, how to please her husband. [35]I say this for your own benefit, not to put any restraint upon you, but to promote good order and unhindered devotion to the Lord.

[36] If anyone thinks that he is not behaving properly toward his fiancée,[d] if his passions are strong, and so it has to be, let him marry as he wishes; it is no sin. Let them marry. [37]But if someone stands firm in his resolve, being under no necessity but having his own desire under control, and has determined in his own mind to keep her as his fiancée,[d] he will do well. [38]So then, he who marries his fiancée[d] does well; and he who refrains from marriage will do better.

[39] A wife is bound as long as her husband lives. But if the husband dies,[e] she is free to marry anyone she wishes, only in the Lord. [40]But in my judgment she is more blessed if she remains as she is. And I think that I too have the Spirit of God.

# PSALM 32.1–11

*Of David. A Maskil.*

**H**APPY are those whose
    transgression is
    forgiven,
  whose sin is covered.
2  Happy are those to whom the
    LORD imputes no iniquity,
  and in whose spirit there is
    no deceit.

3  While I kept silence, my body
    wasted away
  through my groaning all day
    long.

4  For day and night your hand
      was heavy upon me;
   my strength was dried up[a]
      as by the heat of
      summer.                    *Selah*

5  Then I acknowledged my sin to
      you,
   and I did not hide my iniquity;
   I said, "I will confess my
      transgressions to the
      LORD,"
   and you forgave the guilt of
      my sin.                    *Selah*

6  Therefore let all who are faithful
      offer prayer to you;
   at a time of distress,[b] the rush
      of mighty waters
   shall not reach them.
7  You are a hiding place for me;
      you preserve me from
      trouble;
   you surround me with glad
      cries of deliverance.
                                 *Selah*

8  I will instruct you and teach you
      the way you should go;
   I will counsel you with my
      eye upon you.

9  Do not be like a horse or a
      mule, without
      understanding,
   whose temper must be
      curbed with bit and
      bridle,
   else it will not stay near you.

10  Many are the torments of the
       wicked,
    but steadfast love surrounds
       those who trust in the
       LORD.
11  Be glad in the LORD and rejoice,
       O righteous,
    and shout for joy, all you
       upright in heart.

## PROVERBS 21.5–7

THE plans of the diligent lead
      surely to abundance,
   but everyone who is hasty
      comes only to want.
6  The getting of treasures by a
      lying tongue
   is a fleeting vapor and a
      snare[c] of death.
7  The violence of the wicked will
      sweep them away,
   because they refuse to do
      what is just.

# AUGUST 13

## NEHEMIAH 5.14—7.60

MOREOVER from the time that I [Nehemiah] was appointed to be their governor in the land of Judah, from the twentieth year to the thirty-second year of King Artaxerxes, twelve years, neither I nor my brothers ate the food allowance of the governor. 15 The former governors who were before me laid heavy burdens on the people, and took food and wine from them, besides forty shekels of silver. Even their servants lorded it over the peo-

[a] Meaning of Heb uncertain   [b] Cn: Heb *at a time of finding only*   [c] Gk: Heb *seekers*

ple. But I did not do so, because of the fear of God. <sup>16</sup>Indeed, I devoted myself to the work on this wall, and acquired no land; and all my servants were gathered there for the work. <sup>17</sup>Moreover there were at my table one hundred fifty people, Jews and officials, besides those who came to us from the nations around us. <sup>18</sup>Now that which was prepared for one day was one ox and six choice sheep; also fowls were prepared for me, and every ten days skins of wine in abundance; yet with all this I did not demand the food allowance of the governor, because of the heavy burden of labor on the people. <sup>19</sup>Remember for my good, O my God, all that I have done for this people.

**6.**1 Now when it was reported to Sanballat and Tobiah and to Geshem the Arab and to the rest of our enemies that I had built the wall and that there was no gap left in it (though up to that time I had not set up the doors in the gates), <sup>2</sup>Sanballat and Geshem sent to me, saying, "Come and let us meet together in one of the villages in the plain of Ono." But they intended to do me harm. <sup>3</sup>So I sent messengers to them, saying, "I am doing a great work and I cannot come down. Why should the work stop while I leave it to come down to you?" <sup>4</sup>They sent to me four times in this way, and I answered them in the same manner. <sup>5</sup>In the same way Sanballat for the fifth time sent his servant to me with an open letter in his hand. <sup>6</sup>In it was written, "It is reported among the nations—and Geshem[a] also says it—that you and the Jews intend to rebel; that is why you are building the wall; and according to this report you wish to become their king. <sup>7</sup>You have also set up prophets to proclaim in Jerusalem concerning you, 'There is a king in Judah!' And now it will be reported to the king according to these words. So

come, therefore, and let us confer together." <sup>8</sup>Then I sent to him, saying, "No such things as you say have been done; you are inventing them out of your own mind" <sup>9</sup>—for they all wanted to frighten us, thinking, "Their hands will drop from the work, and it will not be done." But now, O God, strengthen my hands.

10 One day when I went into the house of Shemaiah son of Delaiah son of Mehetabel, who was confined to his house, he said, "Let us meet together in the house of God, within the temple, and let us close the doors of the temple, for they are coming to kill you; indeed, tonight they are coming to kill you." <sup>11</sup>But I said, "Should a man like me run away? Would a man like me go into the temple to save his life? I will not go in!" <sup>12</sup>Then I perceived and saw that God had not sent him at all, but he had pronounced the prophecy against me because Tobiah and Sanballat had hired him. <sup>13</sup>He was hired for this purpose, to intimidate me and make me sin by acting in this way, and so they could give me a bad name, in order to taunt me. <sup>14</sup>Remember Tobiah and Sanballat, O my God, according to these things that they did, and also the prophetess Noadiah and the rest of the prophets who wanted to make me afraid.

15 So the wall was finished on the twenty-fifth day of the month Elul, in fifty-two days. <sup>16</sup>And when all our enemies heard of it, all the nations around us were afraid[b] and fell greatly in their own esteem; for they perceived that this work had been accomplished with the help of our God. <sup>17</sup>Moreover in those days the nobles of Judah sent many letters to Tobiah, and Tobiah's letters came to them. <sup>18</sup>For many in Judah were bound by oath to him, because he was the son-in-law of Shecaniah son of Arah; and his son Jehohanan had married the daughter of

a Heb *Gashmu*   b Another reading is *saw*

Meshullam son of Berechiah. ¹⁹Also they spoke of his good deeds in my presence, and reported my words to him. And Tobiah sent letters to intimidate me.

**7.**¹ Now when the wall had been built and I had set up the doors, and the gatekeepers, the singers, and the Levites had been appointed, ²I gave my brother Hanani charge over Jerusalem, along with Hananiah the commander of the citadel—for he was a faithful man and feared God more than many. ³And I said to them, "The gates of Jerusalem are not to be opened until the sun is hot; while the gatekeepersᵃ are still standing guard, let them shut and bar the doors. Appoint guards from among the inhabitants of Jerusalem, some at their watch posts, and others before their own houses." ⁴The city was wide and large, but the people within it were few and no houses had been built.

5  Then my God put it into my mind to assemble the nobles and the officials and the people to be enrolled by genealogy. And I found the book of the genealogy of those who were the first to come back, and I found the following written in it:

6  These are the people of the province who came up out of the captivity of those exiles whom King Nebuchadnezzar of Babylon had carried into exile; they returned to Jerusalem and Judah, each to his town. ⁷They came with Zerubbabel, Jeshua, Nehemiah, Azariah, Raamiah, Nahamani, Mordecai, Bilshan, Mispereth, Bigvai, Nehum, Baanah.

The number of the Israelite people: ⁸the descendants of Parosh, two thousand one hundred seventy-two. ⁹Of Shephatiah, three hundred seventy-two. ¹⁰Of Arah, six hundred fifty-two. ¹¹Of Pahath-moab, namely the descendants of Jeshua and Joab, two thousand eight hundred eighteen. ¹²Of Elam, one thousand two hundred fifty-four. ¹³Of Zattu, eight hundred forty-five. ¹⁴Of Zaccai, seven hundred sixty. ¹⁵Of Binnui, six hundred forty-eight. ¹⁶Of Bebai, six hundred twenty-eight. ¹⁷Of Azgad, two thousand three hundred twenty-two. ¹⁸Of Adonikam, six hundred sixty-seven. ¹⁹Of Bigvai, two thousand sixty-seven. ²⁰Of Adin, six hundred fifty-five. ²¹Of Ater, namely of Hezekiah, ninety-eight. ²²Of Hashum, three hundred twenty-eight. ²³Of Bezai, three hundred twenty-four. ²⁴Of Hariph, one hundred twelve. ²⁵Of Gibeon, ninety-five. ²⁶The people of Bethlehem and Netophah, one hundred eighty-eight. ²⁷Of Anathoth, one hundred twenty-eight. ²⁸Of Bethazmaveth, forty-two. ²⁹Of Kiriathjearim, Chephirah, and Beeroth, seven hundred forty-three. ³⁰Of Ramah and Geba, six hundred twenty-one. ³¹Of Michmas, one hundred twenty-two. ³²Of Bethel and Ai, one hundred twenty-three. ³³Of the other Nebo, fifty-two. ³⁴The descendants of the other Elam, one thousand two hundred fifty-four. ³⁵Of Harim, three hundred twenty. ³⁶Of Jericho, three hundred forty-five. ³⁷Of Lod, Hadid, and Ono, seven hundred twenty-one. ³⁸Of Senaah, three thousand nine hundred thirty.

39  The priests: the descendants of Jedaiah, namely the house of Jeshua, nine hundred seventy-three. ⁴⁰Of Immer, one thousand fifty-two. ⁴¹Of Pashhur, one thousand two hundred forty-seven. ⁴²Of Harim, one thousand seventeen.

43  The Levites: the descendants of Jeshua, namely of Kadmiel of the descendants of Hodevah, seventy-four. ⁴⁴The singers: the descendants of Asaph, one hundred forty-eight. ⁴⁵The gatekeepers: the descendants of Shallum, of Ater, of Talmon, of Akkub, of

ᵃHeb *while they*

Hatita, of Shobai, one hundred thirty-eight.

46 The temple servants: the descendants of Ziha, of Hasupha, of Tabbaoth, ⁴⁷of Keros, of Sia, of Padon, ⁴⁸of Lebana, of Hagaba, of Shalmai, ⁴⁹of Hanan, of Giddel, of Gahar, ⁵⁰of Reaiah, of Rezin, of Nekoda, ⁵¹of Gazzam, of Uzza, of Paseah, ⁵²of Besai, of Meunim, of Nephushesim, ⁵³of Bakbuk, of Hakupha, of Harhur, ⁵⁴of Bazlith, of Mehida, of Harsha, ⁵⁵of Barkos, of Sisera, of Temah, ⁵⁶of Neziah, of Hatipha.

57 The descendants of Solomon's servants: of Sotai, of Sophereth, of Perida, ⁵⁸of Jaala, of Darkon, of Giddel, ⁵⁹of Shephatiah, of Hattil, of Pochereth-hazzebaim, of Amon.

60 All the temple servants and the descendants of Solomon's servants were three hundred ninety-two.

as food offered to an idol; and their conscience, being weak, is defiled. ⁸"Food will not bring us close to God."a We are no worse off if we do not eat, and no better off if we do. ⁹But take care that this liberty of yours does not somehow become a stumbling block to the weak. ¹⁰For if others see you, who possess knowledge, eating in the temple of an idol, might they not, since their conscience is weak, be encouraged to the point of eating food sacrificed to idols? ¹¹So by your knowledge those weak believers for whom Christ died are destroyed.b ¹²But when you thus sin against members of your family,c and wound their conscience when it is weak, you sin against Christ. ¹³Therefore, if food is a cause of their falling,d I will never eat meat, so that I may not cause one of theme to fall.

## 1 CORINTHIANS 8.1–13

Now concerning food sacrificed to idols: we know that "all of us possess knowledge." Knowledge puffs up, but love builds up. ²Anyone who claims to know something does not yet have the necessary knowledge; ³but anyone who loves God is known by him.

4 Hence, as to the eating of food offered to idols, we know that "no idol in the world really exists," and that "there is no God but one." ⁵Indeed, even though there may be so-called gods in heaven or on earth—as in fact there are many gods and many lords— ⁶yet for us there is one God, the Father, from whom are all things and for whom we exist, and one Lord, Jesus Christ, through whom are all things and through whom we exist.

7 It is not everyone, however, who has this knowledge. Since some have become so accustomed to idols until now, they still think of the food they eat

## PSALM 33.1–11

Rejoice in the Lord, O you
        righteous.
    Praise befits the upright.
2   Praise the Lord with the lyre;
        make melody to him with the
            harp of ten strings.
3   Sing to him a new song;
        play skillfully on the strings,
            with loud shouts.

4   For the word of the Lord is
            upright,
        and all his work is done in
            faithfulness.
5   He loves righteousness and
            justice;
        the earth is full of the
            steadfast love of the
            Lord.

6   By the word of the Lord the
            heavens were made,
        and all their host by the
            breath of his mouth.

aThe quotation may extend to the end of the verse  bGk *the weak brother . . . is destroyed*
cGk *against the brothers*  dGk *my brother's falling*  eGk *cause my brother*

7 He gathered the waters of the
  sea as in a bottle;
  he put the deeps in
  storehouses.

8 Let all the earth fear the LORD;
  let all the inhabitants of the
  world stand in awe of
  him.
9 For he spoke, and it came to
  be;
  he commanded, and it stood
  firm.

10 The LORD brings the counsel of
  the nations to nothing;
  he frustrates the plans of the
  peoples.

11 The counsel of the LORD stands
  forever,
  the thoughts of his heart to all
  generations.

## PROVERBS 21.8–10

THE way of the guilty is
  crooked,
  but the conduct of the pure
  is right.
9 It is better to live in a corner of
  the housetop
  than in a house shared with a
  contentious wife.
10 The souls of the wicked desire
  evil;
  their neighbors find no mercy
  in their eyes.

# AUGUST 14

## NEHEMIAH 7.61—9.21

THE following were those who came up from Tel-melah, Tel-harsha, Cherub, Addon, and Immer, but they could not prove their ancestral houses or their descent, whether they belonged to Israel: 62the descendants of Delaiah, of Tobiah, of Nekoda, six hundred forty-two. 63Also, of the priests: the descendants of Hobaiah, of Hakkoz, of Barzillai (who had married one of the daughters of Barzillai the Gileadite and was called by their name). 64These sought their registration among those enrolled in the genealogies, but it was not found there, so they were excluded from the priesthood as unclean; 65the governor told them that they were not to partake of the most holy food, until a priest with Urim and Thummim should come.

66 The whole assembly together was forty-two thousand three hundred sixty, 67besides their male and female slaves, of whom there were seven thousand three hundred thirty-seven; and they had two hundred forty-five singers, male and female. 68They had seven hundred thirty-six horses, two hundred forty-five mules, a 69four hundred thirty-five camels, and six thousand seven hundred twenty donkeys.

70 Now some of the heads of ancestral houses contributed to the work. The governor gave to the treasury one thousand darics of gold, fifty basins, and five hundred thirty priestly robes. 71And some of the heads of ancestral houses gave into the building fund

a Ezra 2.66 and the margins of some Hebrew Mss: MT lacks *They had . . . forty-five mules*

twenty thousand darics of gold and two thousand two hundred minas of silver. [72]And what the rest of the people gave was twenty thousand darics of gold, two thousand minas of silver, and sixty-seven priestly robes.

73  So the priests, the Levites, the gatekeepers, the singers, some of the people, the temple servants, and all Israel settled in their towns.

When the seventh month came— the people of Israel being settled in their towns— [8.1]all the people gathered together into the square before the Water Gate. They told the scribe Ezra to bring the book of the law of Moses, which the LORD had given to Israel. [2]Accordingly, the priest Ezra brought the law before the assembly, both men and women and all who could hear with understanding. This was on the first day of the seventh month. [3]He read from it facing the square before the Water Gate from early morning until midday, in the presence of the men and the women and those who could understand; and the ears of all the people were attentive to the book of the law. [4]The scribe Ezra stood on a wooden platform that had been made for the purpose; and beside him stood Mattithiah, Shema, Anaiah, Uriah, Hilkiah, and Maaseiah on his right hand; and Pedaiah, Mishael, Malchijah, Hashum, Hash-baddanah, Zechariah, and Meshullam on his left hand. [5]And Ezra opened the book in the sight of all the people, for he was standing above all the people; and when he opened it, all the people stood up. [6]Then Ezra blessed the LORD, the great God, and all the people answered, "Amen, Amen," lifting up their hands. Then they bowed their heads and worshiped the LORD with their faces to the ground. [7]Also Jeshua, Bani, Sherebiah, Jamin, Akkub, Shabbethai, Hodiah, Maaseiah, Kelita, Azariah, Jozabad, Hanan, Pela-

iah, the Levites, [a] helped the people to understand the law, while the people remained in their places. [8]So they read from the book, from the law of God, with interpretation. They gave the sense, so that the people understood the reading.

9  And Nehemiah, who was the governor, and Ezra the priest and scribe, and the Levites who taught the people said to all the people, "This day is holy to the LORD your God; do not mourn or weep." For all the people wept when they heard the words of the law. [10]Then he said to them, "Go your way, eat the fat and drink sweet wine and send portions of them to those for whom nothing is prepared, for this day is holy to our LORD; and do not be grieved, for the joy of the LORD is your strength." [11]So the Levites stilled all the people, saying, "Be quiet, for this day is holy; do not be grieved." [12]And all the people went their way to eat and drink and to send portions and to make great rejoicing, because they had understood the words that were declared to them.

13  On the second day the heads of ancestral houses of all the people, with the priests and the Levites, came together to the scribe Ezra in order to study the words of the law. [14]And they found it written in the law, which the LORD had commanded by Moses, that the people of Israel should live in booths[b] during the festival of the seventh month, [15]and that they should publish and proclaim in all their towns and in Jerusalem as follows, "Go out to the hills and bring branches of olive, wild olive, myrtle, palm, and other leafy trees to make booths,[b] as it is written." [16]So the people went out and brought them, and made booths[b] for themselves, each on the roofs of their houses, and in their courts and in the courts of the house of God, and in the

---

a 1 Esdras 9.48 Vg: Heb *and the Levites*   b Or *tabernacles*; Heb *succoth*

square at the Water Gate and in the square at the Gate of Ephraim. [17]And all the assembly of those who had returned from the captivity made booths[a] and lived in them; for from the days of Jeshua son of Nun to that day the people of Israel had not done so. And there was very great rejoicing. [18]And day by day, from the first day to the last day, he read from the book of the law of God. They kept the festival seven days; and on the eighth day there was a solemn assembly, according to the ordinance.

[9.1] Now on the twenty-fourth day of this month the people of Israel were assembled with fasting and in sackcloth, and with earth on their heads.[b] [2]Then those of Israelite descent separated themselves from all foreigners, and stood and confessed their sins and the iniquities of their ancestors. [3]They stood up in their place and read from the book of the law of the LORD their God for a fourth part of the day, and for another fourth they made confession and worshiped the LORD their God. [4]Then Jeshua, Bani, Kadmiel, Shebaniah, Bunni, Sherebiah, Bani, and Chenani stood on the stairs of the Levites and cried out with a loud voice to the LORD their God. [5]Then the Levites, Jeshua, Kadmiel, Bani, Hashabneiah, Sherebiah, Hodiah, Shebaniah, and Pethahiah, said, "Stand up and bless the LORD your God from everlasting to everlasting. Blessed be your glorious name, which is exalted above all blessing and praise."

6 And Ezra said:[c] "You are the LORD, you alone; you have made heaven, the heaven of heavens, with all their host, the earth and all that is on it, the seas and all that is in them. To all of them you give life, and the host of heaven worships you. [7]You are the LORD, the God who chose Abram and

brought him out of Ur of the Chaldeans and gave him the name Abraham; [8]and you found his heart faithful before you, and made with him a covenant to give to his descendants the land of the Canaanite, the Hittite, the Amorite, the Perizzite, the Jebusite, and the Girgashite; and you have fulfilled your promise, for you are righteous.

9 "And you saw the distress of our ancestors in Egypt and heard their cry at the Red Sea.[d] [10]You performed signs and wonders against Pharaoh and all his servants and all the people of his land, for you knew that they acted insolently against our ancestors. You made a name for yourself, which remains to this day. [11]And you divided the sea before them, so that they passed through the sea on dry land, but you threw their pursuers into the depths, like a stone into mighty waters. [12]Moreover, you led them by day with a pillar of cloud, and by night with a pillar of fire, to give them light on the way in which they should go. [13]You came down also upon Mount Sinai, and spoke with them from heaven, and gave them right ordinances and true laws, good statutes and commandments, [14]and you made known your holy sabbath to them and gave them commandments and statutes and a law through your servant Moses. [15]For their hunger you gave them bread from heaven, and for their thirst you brought water for them out of the rock, and you told them to go in to possess the land that you swore to give them.

16 "But they and our ancestors acted presumptuously and stiffened their necks and did not obey your commandments; [17]they refused to obey, and were not mindful of the wonders that you performed among them; but they stiffened their necks and determined to return to their slavery in Egypt. But you are a God ready to for-

---

[a]Or *tabernacles*; Heb *succoth*   [b]Heb *on them*   [c]Gk: Heb lacks *And Ezra said*   [d]Or *Sea of Reeds*

give, gracious and merciful, slow to anger and abounding in steadfast love, and you did not forsake them. [18]Even when they had cast an image of a calf for themselves and said, 'This is your God who brought you up out of Egypt,' and had committed great blasphemies, [19]you in your great mercies did not forsake them in the wilderness; the pillar of cloud that led them in the way did not leave them by day, nor the pillar of fire by night that gave them light on the way by which they should go. [20]You gave your good spirit to instruct them, and did not withhold your manna from their mouths, and gave them water for their thirst. [21]Forty years you sustained them in the wilderness so that they lacked nothing; their clothes did not wear out and their feet did not swell.

## 1 CORINTHIANS 9.1–18

**A**M I not free? Am I not an apostle? Have I not seen Jesus our Lord? Are you not my work in the Lord? [2]If I am not an apostle to others, at least I am to you; for you are the seal of my apostleship in the Lord.

3  This is my defense to those who would examine me. [4]Do we not have the right to our food and drink? [5]Do we not have the right to be accompanied by a believing wife, **a** as do the other apostles and the brothers of the Lord and Cephas? [6]Or is it only Barnabas and I who have no right to refrain from working for a living? [7]Who at any time pays the expenses for doing military service? Who plants a vineyard and does not eat any of its fruit? Or who tends a flock and does not get any of its milk?

8  Do I say this on human authority? Does not the law also say the same? [9]For it is written in the law of Moses, "You shall not muzzle an ox while it is treading out the grain." Is it for oxen that God is concerned? [10]Or does he not speak entirely for our sake? It was

**a** Gk *a sister as wife*

indeed written for our sake, for whoever plows should plow in hope and whoever threshes should thresh in hope of a share in the crop. [11]If we have sown spiritual good among you, is it too much if we reap your material benefits? [12]If others share this rightful claim on you, do not we still more?

Nevertheless, we have not made use of this right, but we endure anything rather than put an obstacle in the way of the gospel of Christ. [13]Do you not know that those who are employed in the temple service get their food from the temple, and those who serve at the altar share in what is sacrificed on the altar? [14]In the same way, the Lord commanded that those who proclaim the gospel should get their living by the gospel.

15  But I have made no use of any of these rights, nor am I writing this so that they may be applied in my case. Indeed, I would rather die than that— no one will deprive me of my ground for boasting! [16]If I proclaim the gospel, this gives me no ground for boasting, for an obligation is laid on me, and woe to me if I do not proclaim the gospel! [17]For if I do this of my own will, I have a reward; but if not of my own will, I am entrusted with a commission. [18]What then is my reward? Just this: that in my proclamation I may make the gospel free of charge, so as not to make full use of my rights in the gospel.

## PSALM 33.12–22

**H**APPY is the nation whose God
    is the LORD,
  the people whom he has
    chosen as his heritage.

13  The LORD looks down from
    heaven;
  he sees all humankind.
14  From where he sits enthroned
  he watches

all the inhabitants of the
    earth—
15 he who fashions the hearts of
    them all,
  and observes all their deeds.
16 A king is not saved by his great
    army;
  a warrior is not delivered by
    his great strength.
17 The war horse is a vain hope
    for victory,
  and by its great might it
    cannot save.

18 Truly the eye of the Lord is on
    those who fear him,
  on those who hope in his
    steadfast love,
19 to deliver their soul from death,
  and to keep them alive in
    famine.

20 Our soul waits for the Lord;
  he is our help and shield.
21 Our heart is glad in him,
  because we trust in his holy
    name.
22 Let your steadfast love,
    O Lord, be upon us,
  even as we hope in you.

## PROVERBS 21.11–12

WHEN a scoffer is punished,
    the simple become
    wiser;
  when the wise are instructed,
    they increase in
    knowledge.
12 The Righteous One observes
    the house of the wicked;
  he casts the wicked down to
    ruin.

# AUGUST 15

## NEHEMIAH 9.22—10.39

AND you gave them [the Israelites] kingdoms and peoples, and allotted to them every corner,[a] so they took possession of the land of King Sihon of Heshbon and the land of King Og of Bashan. 23 You multiplied their descendants like the stars of heaven, and brought them into the land that you had told their ancestors to enter and possess. 24 So the descendants went in and possessed the land, and you subdued before them the inhabitants of the land, the Canaanites, and gave them into their hands, with their kings and the peoples of the land, to do with them as they pleased. 25 And they captured fortress cities and a rich land, and took possession of houses filled with all sorts of goods, hewn cisterns, vineyards, olive orchards, and fruit trees in abundance; so they ate, and were filled and became fat, and delighted themselves in your great goodness.

26 "Nevertheless they were disobedient and rebelled against you and cast your law behind their backs and killed your prophets, who had warned them in order to turn them back to you, and they committed great blasphemies. 27 Therefore you gave them into the hands of their enemies, who made them suffer. Then in the time of their

a Meaning of Heb uncertain

suffering they cried out to you and you heard them from heaven, and according to your great mercies you gave them saviors who saved them from the hands of their enemies. [28]But after they had rest, they again did evil before you, and you abandoned them to the hands of their enemies, so that they had dominion over them; yet when they turned and cried to you, you heard from heaven, and many times you rescued them according to your mercies. [29]And you warned them in order to turn them back to your law. Yet they acted presumptuously and did not obey your commandments, but sinned against your ordinances, by the observance of which a person shall live. They turned a stubborn shoulder and stiffened their neck and would not obey. [30]Many years you were patient with them, and warned them by your spirit through your prophets; yet they would not listen. Therefore you handed them over to the peoples of the lands. [31]Nevertheless, in your great mercies you did not make an end of them or forsake them, for you are a gracious and merciful God.

32 "Now therefore, our God—the great and mighty and awesome God, keeping covenant and steadfast love— do not treat lightly all the hardship that has come upon us, upon our kings, our officials, our priests, our prophets, our ancestors, and all your people, since the time of the kings of Assyria until today. [33]You have been just in all that has come upon us, for you have dealt faithfully and we have acted wickedly; [34]our kings, our officials, our priests, and our ancestors have not kept your law or heeded the commandments and the warnings that you gave them. [35]Even in their own kingdom, and in the great goodness you bestowed on them, and in the large and rich land that you set before them, they did not serve you

and did not turn from their wicked works. [36]Here we are, slaves to this day—slaves in the land that you gave to our ancestors to enjoy its fruit and its good gifts. [37]Its rich yield goes to the kings whom you have set over us because of our sins; they have power also over our bodies and over our livestock at their pleasure, and we are in great distress."

38[a] Because of all this we make a firm agreement in writing, and on that sealed document are inscribed the names of our officials, our Levites, and our priests.

10[b].1 UPON the sealed document are the names of Nehemiah the governor, son of Hacaliah, and Zedekiah; [2]Seraiah, Azariah, Jeremiah, [3]Pashhur, Amariah, Malchijah, [4]Hattush, Shebaniah, Malluch, [5]Harim, Meremoth, Obadiah, [6]Daniel, Ginnethon, Baruch, [7]Meshullam, Abijah, Mijamin, [8]Maaziah, Bilgai, Shemaiah; these are the priests. [9]And the Levites: Jeshua son of Azaniah, Binnui of the sons of Henadad, Kadmiel; [10]and their associates, Shebaniah, Hodiah, Kelita, Pelaiah, Hanan, [11]Mica, Rehob, Hashabiah, [12]Zaccur, Sherebiah, Shebaniah, [13]Hodiah, Bani, Beninu. [14]The leaders of the people: Parosh, Pahath-moab, Elam, Zattu, Bani, [15]Bunni, Azgad, Bebai, [16]Adonijah, Bigvai, Adin, [17]Ater, Hezekiah, Azzur, [18]Hodiah, Hashum, Bezai, [19]Hariph, Anathoth, Nebai, [20]Magpiash, Meshullam, Hezir, [21]Meshezabel, Zadok, Jaddua, [22]Pelatiah, Hanan, Anaiah, [23]Hoshea, Hananiah, Hasshub, [24]Hallohesh, Pilha, Shobek, [25]Rehum, Hashabnah, Maaseiah, [26]Ahiah, Hanan, Anan, [27]Malluch, Harim, and Baanah.

28 The rest of the people, the priests, the Levites, the gatekeepers, the singers, the temple servants, and all who have separated themselves from the peoples of the lands to adhere

[a]Ch 10.1 in Heb   [b]Ch 10.2 in Heb

to the law of God, their wives, their sons, their daughters, all who have knowledge and understanding, <sup>29</sup>join with their kin, their nobles, and enter into a curse and an oath to walk in God's law, which was given by Moses the servant of God, and to observe and do all the commandments of the LORD our Lord and his ordinances and his statutes. <sup>30</sup>We will not give our daughters to the peoples of the land or take their daughters for our sons; <sup>31</sup>and if the peoples of the land bring in merchandise or any grain on the sabbath day to sell, we will not buy it from them on the sabbath or on a holy day; and we will forego the crops of the seventh year and the exaction of every debt.

32  We also lay on ourselves the obligation to charge ourselves yearly one-third of a shekel for the service of the house of our God: <sup>33</sup>for the rows of bread, the regular grain offering, the regular burnt offering, the sabbaths, the new moons, the appointed festivals, the sacred donations, and the sin offerings to make atonement for Israel, and for all the work of the house of our God. <sup>34</sup>We have also cast lots among the priests, the Levites, and the people, for the wood offering, to bring it into the house of our God, by ancestral houses, at appointed times, year by year, to burn on the altar of the LORD our God, as it is written in the law. <sup>35</sup>We obligate ourselves to bring the first fruits of our soil and the first fruits of all fruit of every tree, year by year, to the house of the LORD; <sup>36</sup>also to bring to the house of our God, to the priests who minister in the house of our God, the firstborn of our sons and of our livestock, as it is written in the law, and the firstlings of our herds and of our flocks; <sup>37</sup>and to bring the first of our dough, and our contributions, the fruit of every tree, the wine and the oil, to the priests, to the chambers of the house of our God; and to bring to the Levites the tithes from our soil, for it is the Levites who collect the tithes in all our rural towns. <sup>38</sup>And the priest, the descendant of Aaron, shall be with the Levites when the Levites receive the tithes; and the Levites shall bring up a tithe of the tithes to the house of our God, to the chambers of the storehouse. <sup>39</sup>For the people of Israel and the sons of Levi shall bring the contribution of grain, wine, and oil to the storerooms where the vessels of the sanctuary are, and where the priests that minister, and the gatekeepers and the singers are. We will not neglect the house of our God.

## 1 CORINTHIANS 9.19—10.13

FOR though I am free with respect to all, I have made myself a slave to all, so that I might win more of them. <sup>20</sup>To the Jews I became as a Jew, in order to win Jews. To those under the law I became as one under the law (though I myself am not under the law) so that I might win those under the law. <sup>21</sup>To those outside the law I became as one outside the law (though I am not free from God's law but am under Christ's law) so that I might win those outside the law. <sup>22</sup>To the weak I became weak, so that I might win the weak. I have become all things to all people, that I might by all means save some. <sup>23</sup>I do it all for the sake of the gospel, so that I may share in its blessings.

24  Do you not know that in a race the runners all compete, but only one receives the prize? Run in such a way that you may win it. <sup>25</sup>Athletes exercise self-control in all things; they do it to receive a perishable wreath, but we an imperishable one. <sup>26</sup>So I do not run aimlessly, nor do I box as though beating the air; <sup>27</sup>but I punish my body and enslave it, so that after proclaiming to others I myself should not be disqualified.

**10.1** I do not want you to be unaware, brothers and sisters, [a] that our ancestors were all under the cloud, and all passed through the sea, [2]and all were baptized into Moses in the cloud and in the sea, [3]and all ate the same spiritual food, [4]and all drank the same spiritual drink. For they drank from the spiritual rock that followed them, and the rock was Christ. [5]Nevertheless, God was not pleased with most of them, and they were struck down in the wilderness.

6 Now these things occurred as examples for us, so that we might not desire evil as they did. [7]Do not become idolaters as some of them did; as it is written, "The people sat down to eat and drink, and they rose up to play." [8]We must not indulge in sexual immorality as some of them did, and twenty-three thousand fell in a single day. [9]We must not put Christ[b] to the test, as some of them did, and were destroyed by serpents. [10]And do not complain as some of them did, and were destroyed by the destroyer. [11]These things happened to them to serve as an example, and they were written down to instruct us, on whom the ends of the ages have come. [12]So if you think you are standing, watch out that you do not fall. [13]No testing has overtaken you that is not common to everyone. God is faithful, and he will not let you be tested beyond your strength, but with the testing he will also provide the way out so that you may be able to endure it.

## PSALM 34.1–10

*Of David, when he feigned madness before Abimelech, so that he drove him out, and he went away.*

I WILL bless the LORD at all times;
   his praise shall continually be
      in my mouth.
2  My soul makes its boast in the
      LORD;

   let the humble hear and be
      glad.
3  O magnify the LORD with me,
   and let us exalt his name
      together.

4  I sought the LORD, and he
      answered me,
   and delivered me from all my
      fears.
5  Look to him, and be radiant;
   so your[c] faces shall never be
      ashamed.
6  This poor soul cried, and was
      heard by the LORD,
   and was saved from every
      trouble.
7  The angel of the LORD encamps
   around those who fear him,
      and delivers them.
8  O taste and see that the LORD is
      good;
   happy are those who take
      refuge in him.
9  O fear the LORD, you his holy
      ones,
   for those who fear him have
      no want.
10  The young lions suffer want and
      hunger,
   but those who seek the LORD
      lack no good thing.

## PROVERBS 21.13

IF you close your ear to the cry
      of the poor,
  you will cry out and not be
      heard.

---

a Gk *brothers*  b Other ancient authorities read *the Lord*  c Gk Syr Jerome: Heb *their*

# AUGUST 16

## NEHEMIAH 11.1—12.26

Now the leaders of the people lived in Jerusalem; and the rest of the people cast lots to bring one out of ten to live in the holy city Jerusalem, while nine-tenths remained in the other towns. ²And the people blessed all those who willingly offered to live in Jerusalem.

3 These are the leaders of the province who lived in Jerusalem; but in the towns of Judah all lived on their property in their towns: Israel, the priests, the Levites, the temple servants, and the descendants of Solomon's servants. ⁴And in Jerusalem lived some of the Judahites and of the Benjaminites. Of the Judahites: Athaiah son of Uzziah son of Zechariah son of Amariah son of Shephatiah son of Mahalalel, of the descendants of Perez; ⁵and Maaseiah son of Baruch son of Col-hozeh son of Hazaiah son of Adaiah son of Joiarib son of Zechariah son of the Shilonite. ⁶All the descendants of Perez who lived in Jerusalem were four hundred sixty-eight valiant warriors.

7 And these are the Benjaminites: Sallu son of Meshullam son of Joed son of Pedaiah son of Kolaiah son of Maaseiah son of Ithiel son of Jeshaiah. ⁸And his brothersª Gabbai, Sallai: nine hundred twenty-eight. ⁹Joel son of Zichri was their overseer; and Judah son of Hassenuah was second in charge of the city.

10 Of the priests: Jedaiah son of Joiarib, Jachin, ¹¹Seraiah son of Hilkiah son of Meshullam son of Zadok son of Meraioth son of Ahitub, officer of the house of God, ¹²and their associates who did the work of the house, eight hundred twenty-two; and Adaiah son of Jeroham son of Pelaliah son of Amzi son of Zechariah son of Pashhur son of Malchijah, ¹³and his associates, heads of ancestral houses, two hundred forty-two; and Amashsai son of Azarel son of Ahzai son of Meshillemoth son of Immer, ¹⁴and their associates, valiant warriors, one hundred twenty-eight; their overseer was Zabdiel son of Haggedolim.

15 And of the Levites: Shemaiah son of Hasshub son of Azrikam son of Hashabiah son of Bunni; ¹⁶and Shabbethai and Jozabad, of the leaders of the Levites, who were over the outside work of the house of God; ¹⁷and Mattaniah son of Mica son of Zabdi son of Asaph, who was the leader to begin the thanksgiving in prayer, and Bakbukiah, the second among his associates; and Abda son of Shammua son of Galal son of Jeduthun. ¹⁸All the Levites in the holy city were two hundred eighty-four.

19 The gatekeepers, Akkub, Talmon and their associates, who kept watch at the gates, were one hundred seventy-two. ²⁰And the rest of Israel, and of the priests and the Levites, were in all the towns of Judah, all of them in their inheritance. ²¹But the temple servants lived on Ophel; and Ziha and Gishpa were over the temple servants.

22 The overseer of the Levites in Jerusalem was Uzzi son of Bani son of Hashabiah son of Mattaniah son of Mica, of the descendants of Asaph, the singers, in charge of the work of the house of God. ²³For there was a command from the king concerning them, and a settled provision for the singers, as was required every day. ²⁴And Peth-

---

ª Gk Mss: Heb *And after him*

ahiah son of Meshezabel, of the descendants of Zerah son of Judah, was at the king's hand in all matters concerning the people.

25 And as for the villages, with their fields, some of the people of Judah lived in Kiriath-arba and its villages, and in Dibon and its villages, and in Jekabzeel and its villages, 26and in Jeshua and in Moladah and Beth-pelet, 27in Hazarshual, in Beer-sheba and its villages, 28in Ziklag, in Meconah and its villages, 29in En-rimmon, in Zorah, in Jarmuth, 30Zanoah, Adullam, and their villages, Lachish and its fields, and Azekah and its villages. So they camped from Beer-sheba to the valley of Hinnom. 31The people of Benjamin also lived from Geba onward, at Michmash, Aija, Bethel and its villages, 32Anathoth, Nob, Ananiah, 33Hazor, Ramah, Gittaim, 34Hadid, Zeboim, Neballat, 35Lod, and Ono, the valley of artisans. 36And certain divisions of the Levites in Judah were joined to Benjamin.

12.1 THESE are the priests and the Levites who came up with Zerubbabel son of Shealtiel, and Jeshua: Seraiah, Jeremiah, Ezra, 2Amariah, Malluch, Hattush, 3Shecaniah, Rehum, Meremoth, 4Iddo, Ginnethoi, Abijah, 5Mijamin, Maadiah, Bilgah, 6Shemaiah, Joiarib, Jedaiah, 7Sallu, Amok, Hilkiah, Jedaiah. These were the leaders of the priests and of their associates in the days of Jeshua.

8 And the Levites: Jeshua, Binnui, Kadmiel, Sherebiah, Judah, and Mattaniah, who with his associates was in charge of the songs of thanksgiving. 9And Bakbukiah and Unno their associates stood opposite them in the service. 10Jeshua was the father of Joiakim, Joiakim the father of Eliashib, Eliashib the father of Joiada, 11Joiada the father of Jonathan, and Jonathan the father of Jaddua.

12 In the days of Joiakim the priests, heads of ancestral houses, were: of Seraiah, Meraiah; of Jeremiah, Hananiah; 13of Ezra, Meshullam; of Amariah, Jehohanan; 14of Malluchi, Jonathan; of Shebaniah, Joseph; 15of Harim, Adna; of Meraioth, Helkai; 16of Iddo, Zechariah; of Ginnethon, Meshullam; 17of Abijah, Zichri; of Miniamin, of Moadiah, Piltai; 18of Bilgah, Shammua; of Shemaiah, Jehonathan; 19of Joiarib, Mattenai; of Jedaiah, Uzzi; 20of Sallai, Kallai; of Amok, Eber; 21of Hilkiah, Hashabiah; of Jedaiah, Nethanel.

22 As for the Levites, in the days of Eliashib, Joiada, Johanan, and Jaddua, there were recorded the heads of ancestral houses; also the priests until the reign of Darius the Persian. 23The Levites, heads of ancestral houses, were recorded in the Book of the Annals until the days of Johanan son of Eliashib. 24And the leaders of the Levites: Hashabiah, Sherebiah, and Jeshua son of Kadmiel, with their associates over against them, to praise and to give thanks, according to the commandment of David the man of God, section opposite to section. 25Mattaniah, Bakbukiah, Obadiah, Meshullam, Talmon, and Akkub were gatekeepers standing guard at the storehouses of the gates. 26These were in the days of Joiakim son of Jeshua son of Jozadak, and in the days of the governor Nehemiah and of the priest Ezra, the scribe.

# 1 CORINTHIANS
## 10.14—11.1

THEREFORE, my dear friends, a flee from the worship of idols. 15I speak as to sensible people; judge for yourselves what I say. 16The cup of blessing that we bless, is it not a sharing in the blood of Christ? The bread that we break, is it not a sharing in the body of Christ? 17Because there

aGk *my beloved*

is one bread, we who are many are one body, for we all partake of the one bread. ¹⁸Consider the people of Israel;ᵃ are not those who eat the sacrifices partners in the altar? ¹⁹What do I imply then? That food sacrificed to idols is anything, or that an idol is anything? ²⁰No, I imply that what pagans sacrifice, they sacrifice to demons and not to God. I do not want you to be partners with demons. ²¹You cannot drink the cup of the Lord and the cup of demons. You cannot partake of the table of the Lord and the table of demons. ²²Or are we provoking the Lord to jealousy? Are we stronger than he?

23 "All things are lawful," but not all things are beneficial. "All things are lawful," but not all things build up. ²⁴Do not seek your own advantage, but that of the other. ²⁵Eat whatever is sold in the meat market without raising any question on the ground of conscience, ²⁶for "the earth and its fullness are the Lord's." ²⁷If an unbeliever invites you to a meal and you are disposed to go, eat whatever is set before you without raising any question on the ground of conscience. ²⁸But if someone says to you, "This has been offered in sacrifice," then do not eat it, out of consideration for the one who informed you, and for the sake of conscience— ²⁹I mean the other's conscience, not your own. For why should my liberty be subject to the judgment of someone else's conscience? ³⁰If I partake with thankfulness, why should I be denounced because of that for which I give thanks?

31 So, whether you eat or drink, or whatever you do, do everything for the glory of God. ³²Give no offense to Jews or to Greeks or to the church of God, ³³just as I try to please everyone in everything I do, not seeking my own advantage, but that of many, so that they may be saved. ¹¹.¹Be imitators of me, as I am of Christ.

ᵃ Gk *Israel according to the flesh*

## PSALM 34.11–22

Come, O children, listen to me;
   I will teach you the fear of
      the Lord.
12 Which of you desires life,
   and covets many days to
      enjoy good?
13 Keep your tongue from evil,
   and your lips from speaking
      deceit.
14 Depart from evil, and do good;
   seek peace, and pursue it.

15 The eyes of the Lord are on the
      righteous,
   and his ears are open to their
      cry.
16 The face of the Lord is against
      evildoers,
   to cut off the remembrance of
      them from the earth.
17 When the righteous cry for
      help, the Lord hears,
   and rescues them from all
      their troubles.
18 The Lord is near to the
      brokenhearted,
   and saves the crushed in
      spirit.

19 Many are the afflictions of the
      righteous,
   but the Lord rescues them
      from them all.
20 He keeps all their bones;
   not one of them will be
      broken.
21 Evil brings death to the wicked,
   and those who hate the
      righteous will be
      condemned.
22 The Lord redeems the life of
      his servants;
   none of those who take
      refuge in him will be
      condemned.

## PROVERBS 21.14–16

**A** GIFT in secret averts anger;
and a concealed bribe in the
bosom, strong wrath.
15 When justice is done, it is a joy
to the righteous,
but dismay to evildoers.
16 Whoever wanders from the way
of understanding
will rest in the assembly of
the dead.

# AUGUST 17

## NEHEMIAH 12.27—13.31

**N**ow at the dedication of the wall of Jerusalem they sought out the Levites in all their places, to bring them to Jerusalem to celebrate the dedication with rejoicing, with thanksgivings and with singing, with cymbals, harps, and lyres. 28The companies of the singers gathered together from the circuit around Jerusalem and from the villages of the Netophathites; 29also from Beth-gilgal and from the region of Geba and Azmaveth; for the singers had built for themselves villages around Jerusalem. 30And the priests and the Levites purified themselves; and they purified the people and the gates and the wall.

31 Then I brought the leaders of Judah up onto the wall, and appointed two great companies that gave thanks and went in procession. One went to the right on the wall to the Dung Gate; 32and after them went Hoshaiah and half the officials of Judah, 33and Azariah, Ezra, Meshullam, 34Judah, Benjamin, Shemaiah, and Jeremiah, 35and some of the young priests with trumpets: Zechariah son of Jonathan son of Shemaiah son of Mattaniah son of Micaiah son of Zaccur son of Asaph; 36and his kindred, Shemaiah, Azarel, Milalai, Gilalai, Maai, Nethanel, Judah, and Hanani, with the musical instruments of David the man of God; and the scribe Ezra went in front of them. 37At the Fountain Gate, in front of them, they went straight up by the stairs of the city of David, at the ascent of the wall, above the house of David, to the Water Gate on the east.

38 The other company of those who gave thanks went to the left, a and I followed them with half of the people on the wall, above the Tower of the Ovens, to the Broad Wall, 39and above the Gate of Ephraim, and by the Old Gate, and by the Fish Gate and the Tower of Hananel and the Tower of the Hundred, to the Sheep Gate; and they came to a halt at the Gate of the Guard. 40So both companies of those who gave thanks stood in the house of God, and I and half of the officials with me; 41and the priests Eliakim, Maaseiah, Miniamin, Micaiah, Elioenai, Zechariah, and Hananiah, with trumpets; 42and Maaseiah, Shemaiah, Eleazar, Uzzi, Jehohanan, Malchijah, Elam, and Ezer. And the singers sang with Jezrahiah as their leader. 43They offered great sacrifices that day and rejoiced, for God had made them rejoice with great joy; the women and children also rejoiced. The joy of Jerusalem was heard far away.

44 On that day men were appointed

a Cn: Heb *opposite*

over the chambers for the stores, the contributions, the first fruits, and the tithes, to gather into them the portions required by the law for the priests and for the Levites from the fields belonging to the towns; for Judah rejoiced over the priests and the Levites who ministered. 45They performed the service of their God and the service of purification, as did the singers and the gatekeepers, according to the command of David and his son Solomon. 46For in the days of David and Asaph long ago there was a leader of the singers, and there were songs of praise and thanksgiving to God. 47In the days of Zerubbabel and in the days of Nehemiah all Israel gave the daily portions for the singers and the gatekeepers. They set apart that which was for the Levites; and the Levites set apart that which was for the descendants of Aaron.

13.1 On that day they read from the book of Moses in the hearing of the people; and in it was found written that no Ammonite or Moabite should ever enter the assembly of God, 2because they did not meet the Israelites with bread and water, but hired Balaam against them to curse them—yet our God turned the curse into a blessing. 3When the people heard the law, they separated from Israel all those of foreign descent.

4 Now before this, the priest Eliashib, who was appointed over the chambers of the house of our God, and who was related to Tobiah, 5prepared for Tobiah a large room where they had previously put the grain offering, the frankincense, the vessels, and the tithes of grain, wine, and oil, which were given by commandment to the Levites, singers, and gatekeepers, and the contributions for the priests. 6While this was taking place I was not in Jerusalem, for in the thirty-second year of King Artaxerxes of Babylon I went to the king. After some time I asked leave of the king 7and returned to Jerusalem. I then discovered the wrong that Eliashib had done on behalf of Tobiah, preparing a room for him in the courts of the house of God. 8And I was very angry, and I threw all the household furniture of Tobiah out of the room. 9Then I gave orders and they cleansed the chambers, and I brought back the vessels of the house of God, with the grain offering and the frankincense.

10 I also found out that the portions of the Levites had not been given to them; so that the Levites and the singers, who had conducted the service, had gone back to their fields. 11So I remonstrated with the officials and said, "Why is the house of God forsaken?" And I gathered them together and set them in their stations. 12Then all Judah brought the tithe of the grain, wine, and oil into the storehouses. 13And I appointed as treasurers over the storehouses the priest Shelemiah, the scribe Zadok, and Pedaiah of the Levites, and as their assistant Hanan son of Zaccur son of Mattaniah, for they were considered faithful; and their duty was to distribute to their associates. 14Remember me, O my God, concerning this, and do not wipe out my good deeds that I have done for the house of my God and for his service.

15 In those days I saw in Judah people treading wine presses on the sabbath, and bringing in heaps of grain and loading them on donkeys; and also wine, grapes, figs, and all kinds of burdens, which they brought into Jerusalem on the sabbath day; and I warned them at that time against selling food. 16Tyrians also, who lived in the city, brought in fish and all kinds of merchandise and sold them on the sabbath to the people of Judah, and in Jerusalem. 17Then I remonstrated with the nobles of Judah and said to them, "What is this evil thing that you are doing, profaning

the sabbath day? [18]Did not your ancestors act in this way, and did not our God bring all this disaster on us and on this city? Yet you bring more wrath on Israel by profaning the sabbath."

19 When it began to be dark at the gates of Jerusalem before the sabbath, I commanded that the doors should be shut and gave orders that they should not be opened until after the sabbath. And I set some of my servants over the gates, to prevent any burden from being brought in on the sabbath day. [20]Then the merchants and sellers of all kinds of merchandise spent the night outside Jerusalem once or twice. [21]But I warned them and said to them, "Why do you spend the night in front of the wall? If you do so again, I will lay hands on you." From that time on they did not come on the sabbath. [22]And I commanded the Levites that they should purify themselves and come and guard the gates, to keep the sabbath day holy. Remember this also in my favor, O my God, and spare me according to the greatness of your steadfast love.

23 In those days also I saw Jews who had married women of Ashdod, Ammon, and Moab; [24]and half of their children spoke the language of Ashdod, and they could not speak the language of Judah, but spoke the language of various peoples. [25]And I contended with them and cursed them and beat some of them and pulled out their hair; and I made them take an oath in the name of God, saying, "You shall not give your daughters to their sons, or take their daughters for your sons or for yourselves. [26]Did not King Solomon of Israel sin on account of such women? Among the many nations there was no king like him, and he was beloved by his God, and God made him king over all Israel; nevertheless, foreign women made even him to sin. [27]Shall we then listen to you and do all this great evil

and act treacherously against our God by marrying foreign women?"

28 And one of the sons of Jehoiada, son of the high priest Eliashib, was the son-in-law of Sanballat the Horonite; I chased him away from me. [29]Remember them, O my God, because they have defiled the priesthood, the covenant of the priests and the Levites.

30 Thus I cleansed them from everything foreign, and I established the duties of the priests and Levites, each in his work; [31]and I provided for the wood offering, at appointed times, and for the first fruits. Remember me, O my God, for good.

# 1 CORINTHIANS 11.2–16

I T commend you because you remember me in everything and maintain the traditions just as I handed them on to yo [3]But I want you to understand that Christ is the head of every man, and the husband[a] is the head of his wife, [b] and God is the head of Christ. [4]Any man who prays or prophesies with something on his head disgraces his head, [5]but any woman who prays or prophesies with her head unveiled disgraces her head—it is one and the same thing as having her head shaved. [6]For if a woman will not veil herself, then she should cut off her hair; but if it is disgraceful for a woman to have her hair cut off or to be shaved, she should wear a veil. [7]For a man ought not to have his head veiled, since he is the image and reflection[c] of God; but woman is the reflection[c] of man. [8]Indeed, man was not made from woman, but woman from man. [9]Neither was man created for the sake of woman, but woman for the sake of man. [10]For this reason a woman ought to have a symbol of[d] authority on her head, [e] because of the angels. [11]Nevertheless, in the Lord woman is not in-

aThe same Greek word means *man* or *husband*   bOr *head of the woman*   cOr *glory*   dGk lacks *a symbol of*   eOr *have freedom of choice regarding her head*

dependent of man or man independent of woman. ¹²For just as woman came from man, so man comes through woman; but all things come from God. ¹³Judge for yourselves: is it proper for a woman to pray to God with her head unveiled? ¹⁴Does not nature itself teach you that if a man wears long hair, it is degrading to him, ¹⁵but if a woman has long hair, it is her glory? For her hair is given to her for a covering. ¹⁶But if anyone is disposed to be contentious— we have no such custom, nor do the churches of God.

## PSALM 35.1–16

*Of David.*

CONTEND, O LORD, with those
who contend with me;
fight against those who fight
against me!
2  Take hold of shield and buckler,
and rise up to help me!
3  Draw the spear and javelin
against my pursuers;
say to my soul,
"I am your salvation."

4  Let them be put to shame and
dishonor
who seek after my life.
Let them be turned back and
confounded
who devise evil against me.
5  Let them be like chaff before
the wind,
with the angel of the LORD
driving them on.
6  Let their way be dark and
slippery,
with the angel of the LORD
pursuing them.

7  For without cause they hid their
netᵃ for me;
without cause they dug a pitᵇ
for my life.

8  Let ruin come on them
unawares.
And let the net that they hid
ensnare them;
let them fall in it—to their
ruin.

9  Then my soul shall rejoice in the
LORD,
exulting in his deliverance.
10  All my bones shall say,
"O LORD, who is like you?
You deliver the weak
from those too strong for
them,
the weak and needy from
those who despoil them."

11  Malicious witnesses rise up;
they ask me about things I do
not know.
12  They repay me evil for good;
my soul is forlorn.
13  But as for me, when they were
sick,
I wore sackcloth;
I afflicted myself with fasting.
I prayed with head bowedᶜ on
my bosom,
14  as though I grieved for a
friend or a brother;
I went about as one who
laments for a mother,
bowed down and in mourning.

15  But at my stumbling they
gathered in glee,
they gathered together
against me;
ruffians whom I did not know
tore at me without ceasing;
16  they impiously mocked more
and more, ᵈ
gnashing at me with their
teeth.

---

ᵃHeb *a pit, their net*   ᵇThe word *pit* is transposed from the preceding line   ᶜOr *My prayer turned back*   ᵈCn Compare Gk: Heb *like the profanest of mockers of a cake*

## PROVERBS 21.17–18

WHOEVER loves pleasure will
suffer want;
whoever loves wine and
oil will not be rich.

18 The wicked is a ransom for the
righteous,
and the faithless for the
upright.

# AUGUST 18

## ESTHER 1.1—3.15

THIS happened in the days of Ahasuerus, the same Ahasuerus who ruled over one hundred twenty-seven provinces from India to Ethiopia.[a] 2In those days when King Ahasuerus sat on his royal throne in the citadel of Susa, 3in the third year of his reign, he gave a banquet for all his officials and ministers. The army of Persia and Media and the nobles and governors of the provinces were present, 4while he displayed the great wealth of his kingdom and the splendor and pomp of his majesty for many days, one hundred eighty days in all.

5 When these days were completed, the king gave for all the people present in the citadel of Susa, both great and small, a banquet lasting for seven days, in the court of the garden of the king's palace. 6There were white cotton curtains and blue hangings tied with cords of fine linen and purple to silver rings[b] and marble pillars. There were couches of gold and silver on a mosaic pavement of porphyry, marble, mother-of-pearl, and colored stones. 7Drinks were served in golden goblets, goblets of different kinds, and the royal wine was lavished according to the bounty of the king. 8Drinking was by flagons, without restraint; for the king had given orders to all the officials of his palace to do as each one desired. 9Furthermore, Queen Vashti gave a banquet for the women in the palace of King Ahasuerus.

10 On the seventh day, when the king was merry with wine, he commanded Mehuman, Biztha, Harbona, Bigtha and Abagtha, Zethar and Carkas, the seven eunuchs who attended him, 11to bring Queen Vashti before the king, wearing the royal crown, in order to show the peoples and the officials her beauty; for she was fair to behold. 12But Queen Vashti refused to come at the king's command conveyed by the eunuchs. At this the king was enraged, and his anger burned within him.

13 Then the king consulted the sages who knew the laws[c] (for this was the king's procedure toward all who were versed in law and custom, 14and those next to him were Carshena, Shethar, Admatha, Tarshish, Meres, Marsena, and Memucan, the seven officials of Persia and Media, who had access to the king, and sat first in the kingdom): 15"According to the law, what is to be done to Queen Vashti because she has not performed the command of King Ahasuerus conveyed by the eunuchs?" 16Then Memucan said in the presence of the king and the officials, "Not only has Queen Vashti done wrong to the king, but also to all

a Or *Nubia*; Heb *Cush*   b Or *rods*   c Cn: Heb *times*

the officials and all the peoples who are in all the provinces of King Ahasuerus. [17] For this deed of the queen will be made known to all women, causing them to look with contempt on their husbands, since they will say, 'King Ahasuerus commanded Queen Vashti to be brought before him, and she did not come.' [18] This very day the noble ladies of Persia and Media who have heard of the queen's behavior will rebel against[a] the king's officials, and there will be no end of contempt and wrath! [19] If it pleases the king, let a royal order go out from him, and let it be written among the laws of the Persians and the Medes so that it may not be altered, that Vashti is never again to come before King Ahasuerus; and let the king give her royal position to another who is better than she. [20] So when the decree made by the king is proclaimed throughout all his kingdom, vast as it is, all women will give honor to their husbands, high and low alike."

21 This advice pleased the king and the officials, and the king did as Memucan proposed; [22] he sent letters to all the royal provinces, to every province in its own script and to every people in its own language, declaring that every man should be master in his own house.[b]

2.1 After these things, when the anger of King Ahasuerus had abated, he remembered Vashti and what she had done and what had been decreed against her. [2] Then the king's servants who attended him said, "Let beautiful young virgins be sought out for the king. [3] And let the king appoint commissioners in all the provinces of his kingdom to gather all the beautiful young virgins to the harem in the citadel of Susa under custody of Hegai, the king's eunuch, who is in charge of the women; let their cosmetic treatments be given

them. [4] And let the girl who pleases the king be queen instead of Vashti." This pleased the king, and he did so.

5 Now there was a Jew in the citadel of Susa whose name was Mordecai son of Jair son of Shimei son of Kish, a Benjaminite. [6] Kish[c] had been carried away from Jerusalem among the captives carried away with King Jeconiah of Judah, whom King Nebuchadnezzar of Babylon had carried away. [7] Mordecai[d] had brought up Hadassah, that is Esther, his cousin, for she had neither father nor mother; the girl was fair and beautiful, and when her father and her mother died, Mordecai adopted her as his own daughter. [8] So when the king's order and his edict were proclaimed, and when many young women were gathered in the citadel of Susa in custody of Hegai, Esther also was taken into the king's palace and put in custody of Hegai, who had charge of the women. [9] The girl pleased him and won his favor, and he quickly provided her with her cosmetic treatments and her portion of food, and with seven chosen maids from the king's palace, and advanced her and her maids to the best place in the harem. [10] Esther did not reveal her people or kindred, for Mordecai had charged her not to tell. [11] Every day Mordecai would walk around in front of the court of the harem, to learn how Esther was and how she fared.

12 The turn came for each girl to go in to King Ahasuerus, after being twelve months under the regulations for the women, since this was the regular period of their cosmetic treatment, six months with oil of myrrh and six months with perfumes and cosmetics for women. [13] When the girl went in to the king she was given whatever she asked for to take with her from the harem to the king's palace. [14] In the evening she went in; then in the morning she came back to the second harem

a Cn: Heb *will tell*   b Heb adds *and speak according to the language of his people*   c Heb *a Benjamite*   6who   d Heb *He* in custody of Shaashgaz, the king's eunuch, who was in charge of the concubines; she did not go in to the king again, unless the king delighted in her and she was summoned by name.

15 When the turn came for Esther daughter of Abihail the uncle of Mordecai, who had adopted her as his own daughter, to go in to the king, she asked for nothing except what Hegai the king's eunuch, who had charge of the women, advised. Now Esther was admired by all who saw her. 16When Esther was taken to King Ahasuerus in his royal palace in the tenth month, which is the month of Tebeth, in the seventh year of his reign, 17the king loved Esther more than all the other women; of all the virgins she won his favor and devotion, so that he set the royal crown on her head and made her queen instead of Vashti. 18Then the king gave a great banquet to all his officials and ministers—"Esther's banquet." He also granted a holidaya to the provinces, and gave gifts with royal liberality.

19 When the virgins were being gathered together, b Mordecai was sitting at the king's gate. 20Now Esther had not revealed her kindred or her people, as Mordecai had charged her; for Esther obeyed Mordecai just as when she was brought up by him. 21In those days, while Mordecai was sitting at the king's gate, Bigthan and Teresh, two of the king's eunuchs, who guarded the threshold, became angry and conspired to assassinatec King Ahasuerus. 22But the matter came to the knowledge of Mordecai, and he told it to Queen Esther, and Esther told the king in the name of Mordecai. 23When the affair was investigated and found to be so, both the men were hanged on the gallows. It was recorded in the book of the annals in the presence of the king.

3.1 AFTER these things King Ahasuerus promoted Haman son of Hammedatha the Agagite, and advanced him and set his seat above all the officials who were with him. 2And all the king's servants who were at the king's gate bowed down and did obeisance to Haman; for the king had so commanded concerning him. But Mordecai did not bow down or do obeisance. 3Then the king's servants who were at the king's gate said to Mordecai, "Why do you disobey the king's command?" 4When they spoke to him day after day and he would not listen to them, they told Haman, in order to see whether Mordecai's words would avail; for he had told them that he was a Jew. 5When Haman saw that Mordecai did not bow down or do obeisance to him, Haman was infuriated. 6But he thought it beneath him to lay hands on Mordecai alone. So, having been told who Mordecai's people were, Haman plotted to destroy all the Jews, the people of Mordecai, throughout the whole kingdom of Ahasuerus.

7 In the first month, which is the month of Nisan, in the twelfth year of King Ahasuerus, they cast Pur—which means "the lot"—before Haman for the day and for the month, and the lot fell on the thirteenth dayd of the twelfth month, which is the month of Adar. 8Then Haman said to King Ahasuerus, "There is a certain people scattered and separated among the peoples in all the provinces of your kingdom; their laws are different from those of every other people, and they do not keep the king's laws, so that it is not appropriate for the king to tolerate them. 9If it pleases the king, let a decree be issued for their destruction, and I will pay ten thousand talents of silver into the hands of those who have charge of the king's business, so that they may put it into the king's treasuries." 10So the king took his signet ring

aOr *an amnesty*   bHeb adds *a second time*   cHeb *to lay hands on*   dCn Compare Gk and verse 13 below: Heb *the twelfth month* from his hand and gave it to Haman son of Hammedatha the Agagite, the enemy of the Jews. [11]The king said to Haman, "The money is given to you, and the people as well, to do with them as it seems good to you."

12 Then the king's secretaries were summoned on the thirteenth day of the first month, and an edict, according to all that Haman commanded, was written to the king's satraps and to the governors over all the provinces and to the officials of all the peoples, to every province in its own script and every people in its own language; it was written in the name of King Ahasuerus and sealed with the king's ring. [13]Letters were sent by couriers to all the king's provinces, giving orders to destroy, to kill, and to annihilate all Jews, young and old, women and children, in one day, the thirteenth day of the twelfth month, which is the month of Adar, and to plunder their goods. [14]A copy of the document was to be issued as a decree in every province by proclamation, calling on all the peoples to be ready for that day. [15]The couriers went quickly by order of the king, and the decree was issued in the citadel of Susa. The king and Haman sat down to drink; but the city of Susa was thrown into confusion.

# 1 CORINTHIANS 11.17–34

Now in the following instructions I do not commend you, because when you come together it is not for the better but for the worse. [18]For, to begin with, when you come together as a church, I hear that there are divisions among you; and to some extent I believe it. [19]Indeed, there have to be factions among you, for only so will it become clear who among you are genuine. [20]When you come together, it is not really to eat the Lord's supper. [21]For when the time comes to eat, each of you goes ahead with your own supper, and one goes hungry and another becomes drunk. [22]What! Do you not have homes to eat and drink in? Or do you show contempt for the church of God and humiliate those who have nothing? What should I say to you? Should I commend you? In this matter I do not commend you!

23 For I received from the Lord what I also handed on to you, that the Lord Jesus on the night when he was betrayed took a loaf of bread, [24]and when he had given thanks, he broke it and said, "This is my body that is for[a] you. Do this in remembrance of me." [25]In the same way he took the cup also, after supper, saying, "This cup is the new covenant in my blood. Do this, as often as you drink it, in remembrance of me." [26]For as often as you eat this bread and drink the cup, you proclaim the Lord's death until he comes.

27 Whoever, therefore, eats the bread or drinks the cup of the Lord in an unworthy manner will be answerable for the body and blood of the Lord. [28]Examine yourselves, and only then eat of the bread and drink of the cup. [29]For all who eat and drink[b] without discerning the body,[c] eat and drink judgment against themselves. [30]For this reason many of you are weak and ill, and some have died.[d] [31]But if we judged ourselves, we would not be judged. [32]But when we are judged by the Lord, we are disciplined[e] so that we may not be condemned along with the world.

33 So then, my brothers and sisters,[f] when you come together to eat, wait for one another. [34]If you are hungry, eat at home, so that when you come together, it will not be for your

---

aOther ancient authorities read *is broken for*   bOther ancient authorities add *in an unworthy manner,*   cOther ancient authorities read *the Lord's body*   dGk *fallen asleep*   eOr *When we are judged, we are being disciplined by the Lord*   fGk *brothers*

condemnation. About the other things
I will give instructions when I come.


## PSALM 35.17–28

How long, O Lord, will you
    look on?
Rescue me from their
    ravages,
    my life from the lions!
18 Then I will thank you in the
    great congregation;
    in the mighty throng I will
    praise you.

19 Do not let my treacherous
    enemies rejoice over me,
    or those who hate me without
    cause wink the eye.
20 For they do not speak peace,
    but they conceive deceitful
    words
    against those who are quiet in
    the land.
21 They open wide their mouths
    against me;
    they say, "Aha, Aha,
    our eyes have seen it."

22 You have seen, O Lord; do not
    be silent!
    O Lord, do not be far from
    me!
23 Wake up! Bestir yourself for my
    defense,
    for my cause, my God and
    my Lord!
24 Vindicate me, O Lord, my God,
    according to your
    righteousness,

and do not let them rejoice
    over me.
25 Do not let them say to
    themselves,
    "Aha, we have our heart's
    desire."
Do not let them say, "We have
    swallowed you[a] up."

26 Let all those who rejoice at my
    calamity
    be put to shame and
    confusion;
    let those who exalt themselves
    against me
    be clothed with shame and
    dishonor.

27 Let those who desire my
    vindication
    shout for joy and be glad,
    and say evermore,
"Great is the Lord,
    who delights in the welfare of
    his servant."
28 Then my tongue shall tell of
    your righteousness
    and of your praise all day
    long.


## PROVERBS 21.19–20

It is better to live in a desert
    land
    than with a contentious and
    fretful wife.
20 Precious treasure remains[b] in
    the house of the wise,
    but the fool devours it.

aHeb *him*  bGk: Heb *and oil*

# AUGUST 19



**W**HEN Mordecai learned all that had been done, Mordecai tore his clothes and put on sackcloth and ashes, and went through the city, wailing with a loud and bitter cry; 2he went up to the entrance of the king's gate, for no one might enter the king's gate clothed with sackcloth. 3In every province, wherever the king's command and his decree came, there was great mourning among the Jews, with fasting and weeping and lamenting, and most of them lay in sackcloth and ashes.

4 When Esther's maids and her eunuchs came and told her, the queen was deeply distressed; she sent garments to clothe Mordecai, so that he might take off his sackcloth; but he would not accept them. 5Then Esther called for Hathach, one of the king's eunuchs, who had been appointed to attend her, and ordered him to go to Mordecai to learn what was happening and why. 6Hathach went out to Mordecai in the open square of the city in front of the king's gate, 7and Mordecai told him all that had happened to him, and the exact sum of money that Haman had promised to pay into the king's treasuries for the destruction of the Jews. 8Mordecai also gave him a copy of the written decree issued in Susa for their destruction, that he might show it to Esther, explain it to her, and charge her to go to the king to make supplication to him and entreat him for her people.

9 Hathach went and told Esther what Mordecai had said. 10Then Esther spoke to Hathach and gave him a message for Mordecai, saying, 11"All the king's servants and the people of the king's provinces know that if any man or woman goes to the king inside the inner court without being called, there is but one law—all alike are to be put to death. Only if the king holds out the golden scepter to someone, may that person live. I myself have not been called to come in to the king for thirty days." 12When they told Mordecai what Esther had said, 13Mordecai told them to reply to Esther, "Do not think that in the king's palace you will escape any more than all the other Jews. 14For if you keep silence at such a time as this, relief and deliverance will rise for the Jews from another quarter, but you and your father's family will perish. Who knows? Perhaps you have come to royal dignity for just such a time as this." 15Then Esther said in reply to Mordecai, 16"Go, gather all the Jews to be found in Susa, and hold a fast on my behalf, and neither eat nor drink for three days, night or day. I and my maids will also fast as you do. After that I will go to the king, though it is against the law; and if I perish, I perish." 17Mordecai then went away and did everything as Esther had ordered him.

5.1 ON the third day Esther put on her royal robes and stood in the inner court of the king's palace, opposite the king's hall. The king was sitting on his royal throne inside the palace opposite the entrance to the palace. 2As soon as the king saw Queen Esther standing in the court, she won his favor and he held out to her the golden scepter that was in his hand. Then Esther approached and touched the top of the scepter. 3The king said to her, "What is it, Queen Esther? What is your request? It shall be given you, even to the half of my kingdom." 4Then Esther said, "If it pleases the king, let the king and Haman come today to a banquet that I have prepared for the king." 5Then the king said, "Bring Haman quickly, so that we may do as Esther desires." So the king and Haman came to the banquet that Esther had prepared. 6While they were drinking wine, the king said to Esther, "What is your petition? It shall be granted you. And what is your request? Even to the half of my kingdom, it shall be fulfilled." 7Then Esther said, "This is my petition and request: 8If I have won the king's favor, and if it pleases the king to grant my petition and fulfill my request, let the king and Haman come tomorrow to the banquet that I will prepare for them, and then I will do as the king has said."

9 Haman went out that day happy and in good spirits. But when Haman saw Mordecai in the king's gate, and observed that he neither rose nor trembled before him, he was infuriated with Mordecai; 10nevertheless Haman restrained himself and went home. Then he sent and called for his friends and his wife Zeresh, 11and Haman recounted to them the splendor of his riches, the number of his sons, all the promotions with which the king had honored him, and how he had advanced him above the officials and the ministers of the king. 12Haman added, "Even Queen Esther let no one but myself come with the king to the banquet that she prepared. Tomorrow also I am invited by her, together with the king. 13Yet all this does me no good so long as I see the Jew Mordecai sitting at the king's gate." 14Then his wife Zeresh and all his friends said to him, "Let a gallows fifty cubits high be made, and in the morning tell the king to have Mordecai hanged on it; then go with the king to the banquet in good spirits." This advice pleased Haman, and he had the gallows made.

6.1 On that night the king could not sleep, and he gave orders to bring the book of records, the annals, and they were read to the king. 2It was found written how Mordecai had told about Bigthana and Teresh, two of the king's eunuchs, who guarded the threshold, and who had conspired to assassinate[a] King Ahasuerus. 3Then the king said, "What honor or distinction has been bestowed on Mordecai for this?" The king's servants who attended him said, "Nothing has been done for him." 4The king said, "Who is in the court?" Now Haman had just entered the outer court of the king's palace to speak to the king about having Mordecai hanged on the gallows that he had prepared for him. 5So the king's servants told him, "Haman is there, standing in the court." The king said, "Let him come in." 6So Haman came in, and the king said to him, "What shall be done for the man whom the king wishes to honor?" Haman said to himself, "Whom would the king wish to honor more than me?" 7So Haman said to the king, "For the man whom the king wishes to honor, 8let royal robes be brought, which the king has worn, and a horse that the king has ridden, with a royal crown on its head. 9Let the robes and the horse be handed over to one of the king's most noble officials; let him[b] robe the man whom the king wishes to honor, and let him[b] conduct the man on horseback through the open square of the city, proclaiming before him: 'Thus shall it be done for the man whom the king wishes to honor.'" 10Then the king said to Haman, "Quickly, take the robes and the horse, as you have said, and do so to the Jew Mordecai who sits at the king's gate. Leave out nothing that you have mentioned." 11So Haman took the robes and the horse and robed Mordecai and led him riding through the open

[a]Heb *to lay hands on*   [b]Heb *them*

square of the city, proclaiming, "Thus shall it be done for the man whom the king wishes to honor."

12  Then Mordecai returned to the king's gate, but Haman hurried to his house, mourning and with his head covered. [13]When Haman told his wife Zeresh and all his friends everything that had happened to him, his advisers and his wife Zeresh said to him, "If Mordecai, before whom your downfall has begun, is of the Jewish people, you will not prevail against him, but will surely fall before him."

14  While they were still talking with him, the king's eunuchs arrived and hurried Haman off to the banquet that Esther had prepared. [7.1]So the king and Haman went in to feast with Queen Esther. [2]On the second day, as they were drinking wine, the king again said to Esther, "What is your petition, Queen Esther? It shall be granted you. And what is your request? Even to the half of my kingdom, it shall be fulfilled." [3]Then Queen Esther answered, "If I have won your favor, O king, and if it pleases the king, let my life be given me—that is my petition—and the lives of my people—that is my request. [4]For we have been sold, I and my people, to be destroyed, to be killed, and to be annihilated. If we had been sold merely as slaves, men and women, I would have held my peace; but no enemy can compensate for this damage to the king."[a] [5]Then King Ahasuerus said to Queen Esther, "Who is he, and where is he, who has presumed to do this?" [6]Esther said, "A foe and enemy, this wicked Haman!" Then Haman was terrified before the king and the queen. [7]The king rose from the feast in wrath and went into the palace garden, but Haman stayed to beg his life from Queen Esther, for he saw that the king had determined to destroy him. [8]When the king returned from the palace garden to the banquet hall, Haman had thrown himself on the couch where Esther was reclining; and the king said, "Will he even assault the queen in my presence, in my own house?" As the words left the mouth of the king, they covered Haman's face. [9]Then Harbona, one of the eunuchs in attendance on the king, said, "Look, the very gallows that Haman has prepared for Mordecai, whose word saved the king, stands at Haman's house, fifty cubits high." And the king said, "Hang him on that." [10]So they hanged Haman on the gallows that he had prepared for Mordecai. Then the anger of the king abated.

# 1 CORINTHIANS 12.1–26

Now concerning spiritual gifts,[b] brothers and sisters,[c] I do not want you to be uninformed. [2]You know that when you were pagans, you were enticed and led astray to idols that could not speak. [3]Therefore I want you to understand that no one speaking by the Spirit of God ever says "Let Jesus be cursed!" and no one can say "Jesus is Lord" except by the Holy Spirit.

4  Now there are varieties of gifts, but the same Spirit; [5]and there are varieties of services, but the same Lord; [6]and there are varieties of activities, but it is the same God who activates all of them in everyone. [7]To each is given the manifestation of the Spirit for the common good. [8]To one is given through the Spirit the utterance of wisdom, and to another the utterance of knowledge according to the same Spirit, [9]to another faith by the same Spirit, to another gifts of healing by the one Spirit, [10]to another the working of miracles, to another prophecy, to another the discernment of spirits, to another various kinds of tongues, to

<hr>

a Meaning of Heb uncertain  b Or *spiritual persons*  c Gk *brothers* another the interpretation of tongues. <sup>11</sup>All these are activated by one and the same Spirit, who allots to each one individually just as the Spirit chooses.

12  For just as the body is one and has many members, and all the members of the body, though many, are one body, so it is with Christ. <sup>13</sup>For in the one Spirit we were all baptized into one body—Jews or Greeks, slaves or free—and we were all made to drink of one Spirit.

14  Indeed, the body does not consist of one member but of many. <sup>15</sup>If the foot would say, "Because I am not a hand, I do not belong to the body," that would not make it any less a part of the body. <sup>16</sup>And if the ear would say, "Because I am not an eye, I do not belong to the body," that would not make it any less a part of the body. <sup>17</sup>If the whole body were an eye, where would the hearing be? If the whole body were hearing, where would the sense of smell be? <sup>18</sup>But as it is, God arranged the members in the body, each one of them, as he chose. <sup>19</sup>If all were a single member, where would the body be? <sup>20</sup>As it is, there are many members, yet one body. <sup>21</sup>The eye cannot say to the hand, "I have no need of you," nor again the head to the feet, "I have no need of you." <sup>22</sup>On the contrary, the members of the body that seem to be weaker are indispensable, <sup>23</sup>and those members of the body that we think less honorable we clothe with greater honor, and our less respectable members are treated with greater respect; <sup>24</sup>whereas our more respectable members do not need this. But God has so arranged the body, giving the greater honor to the inferior member, <sup>25</sup>that there may be no dissension within the body, but the members may have the same care for one another. <sup>26</sup>If one member suffers, all suffer together with it; if one member is honored, all rejoice together with it.

## PSALM 36.1–12

*To the leader. Of David, the servant of the* Lord.

Transgression speaks to the wicked
  deep in their hearts;
there is no fear of God
  before their eyes.
2 For they flatter themselves in their own eyes
  that their iniquity cannot be
  found out and hated.
3 The words of their mouths are mischief and deceit;
  they have ceased to act
  wisely and do good.
4 They plot mischief while on their beds;
  they are set on a way that is not good;
  they do not reject evil.

5 Your steadfast love, O Lord,
  extends to the heavens,
  your faithfulness to the clouds.
6 Your righteousness is like the mighty mountains,
  your judgments are like the great deep;
  you save humans and animals alike, O Lord.

7 How precious is your steadfast love, O God!
  All people may take refuge in the shadow of your wings.
8 They feast on the abundance of your house,
  and you give them drink from the river of your delights.
9 For with you is the fountain of life;
  in your light we see light.

10 O continue your steadfast love to those who know you,

and your salvation to the
    upright of heart!
11  Do not let the foot of the
    arrogant tread on me,
  or the hand of the wicked
    drive me away.
12  There the evildoers lie
    prostrate;
  they are thrust down, unable
    to rise.

## PROVERBS 21.21–22

WHOEVER pursues
righteousness and
kindness
will find life[a] and honor.
22  One wise person went up
    against a city of warriors
  and brought down the
    stronghold in which they
    trusted.

# AUGUST 20

## ESTHER 8.1—10.3

ON that day King Ahasuerus gave to Queen Esther the house of Haman, the enemy of the Jews; and Mordecai came before the king, for Esther had told what he was to her. ²Then the king took off his signet ring, which he had taken from Haman, and gave it to Mordecai. So Esther set Mordecai over the house of Haman.

3 Then Esther spoke again to the king; she fell at his feet, weeping and pleading with him to avert the evil design of Haman the Agagite and the plot that he had devised against the Jews. ⁴The king held out the golden scepter to Esther, ⁵and Esther rose and stood before the king. She said, "If it pleases the king, and if I have won his favor, and if the thing seems right before the king, and I have his approval, let an order be written to revoke the letters devised by Haman son of Hammedatha the Agagite, which he wrote giving orders to destroy the Jews who are in all the provinces of the king. ⁶For how can

I bear to see the calamity that is coming on my people? Or how can I bear to see the destruction of my kindred?" ⁷Then King Ahasuerus said to Queen Esther and to the Jew Mordecai, "See, I have given Esther the house of Haman, and they have hanged him on the gallows, because he plotted to lay hands on the Jews. ⁸You may write as you please with regard to the Jews, in the name of the king, and seal it with the king's ring; for an edict written in the name of the king and sealed with the king's ring cannot be revoked."

9 The king's secretaries were summoned at that time, in the third month, which is the month of Sivan, on the twenty-third day; and an edict was written, according to all that Mordecai commanded, to the Jews and to the satraps and the governors and the officials of the provinces from India to Ethiopia,[b] one hundred twenty-seven provinces, to every province in its own script and to every people in its own language, and also to the Jews in their script and their language. ¹⁰He wrote

a Gk: Heb *life and righteousness*  b Or *Nubia*; Heb *Cush*

letters in the name of King Ahasuerus, sealed them with the king's ring, and sent them by mounted couriers riding on fast steeds bred from the royal herd. a 11By these letters the king allowed the Jews who were in every city to assemble and defend their lives, to destroy, to kill, and to annihilate any armed force of any people or province that might attack them, with their children and women, and to plunder their goods 12on a single day throughout all the provinces of King Ahasuerus, on the thirteenth day of the twelfth month, which is the month of Adar. 13A copy of the writ was to be issued as a decree in every province and published to all peoples, and the Jews were to be ready on that day to take revenge on their enemies. 14So the couriers, mounted on their swift royal steeds, hurried out, urged by the king's command. The decree was issued in the citadel of Susa.

15 Then Mordecai went out from the presence of the king, wearing royal robes of blue and white, with a great golden crown and a mantle of fine linen and purple, while the city of Susa shouted and rejoiced. 16For the Jews there was light and gladness, joy and honor. 17In every province and in every city, wherever the king's command and his edict came, there was gladness and joy among the Jews, a festival and a holiday. Furthermore, many of the peoples of the country professed to be Jews, because the fear of the Jews had fallen upon them.

9.1 Now in the twelfth month, which is the month of Adar, on the thirteenth day, when the king's command and edict were about to be executed, on the very day when the enemies of the Jews hoped to gain power over them, but which had been changed to a day when the Jews would gain power over their foes, 2the Jews gathered in their cities throughout all the provinces of King Ahasuerus to lay hands on those who had sought their ruin; and no one could withstand them, because the fear of them had fallen upon all peoples. 3All the officials of the provinces, the satraps and the governors, and the royal officials were supporting the Jews, because the fear of Mordecai had fallen upon them. 4For Mordecai was powerful in the king's house, and his fame spread throughout all the provinces as the man Mordecai grew more and more powerful. 5So the Jews struck down all their enemies with the sword, slaughtering, and destroying them, and did as they pleased to those who hated them. 6In the citadel of Susa the Jews killed and destroyed five hundred people. 7They killed Parshandatha, Dalphon, Aspatha, 8Poratha, Adalia, Aridatha, 9Parmashta, Arisai, Aridai, Vaizatha, 10the ten sons of Haman son of Hammedatha, the enemy of the Jews; but they did not touch the plunder.

11 That very day the number of those killed in the citadel of Susa was reported to the king. 12The king said to Queen Esther, "In the citadel of Susa the Jews have killed five hundred people and also the ten sons of Haman. What have they done in the rest of the king's provinces? Now what is your petition? It shall be granted you. And what further is your request? It shall be fulfilled." 13Esther said, "If it pleases the king, let the Jews who are in Susa be allowed tomorrow also to do according to this day's edict, and let the ten sons of Haman be hanged on the gallows." 14So the king commanded this to be done; a decree was issued in Susa, and the ten sons of Haman were hanged. 15The Jews who were in Susa gathered also on the fourteenth day of the month of Adar and they killed three hundred persons in Susa; but they did not touch the plunder.

a Meaning of Heb uncertain

16 Now the other Jews who were in the king's provinces also gathered to defend their lives, and gained relief from their enemies, and killed seventy-five thousand of those who hated them; but they laid no hands on the plunder. [17]This was on the thirteenth day of the month of Adar, and on the fourteenth day they rested and made that a day of feasting and gladness.

18 But the Jews who were in Susa gathered on the thirteenth day and on the fourteenth, and rested on the fifteenth day, making that a day of feasting and gladness. [19]Therefore the Jews of the villages, who live in the open towns, hold the fourteenth day of the month of Adar as a day for gladness and feasting, a holiday on which they send gifts of food to one another.

20 Mordecai recorded these things, and sent letters to all the Jews who were in all the provinces of King Ahasuerus, both near and far, [21]enjoining them that they should keep the fourteenth day of the month Adar and also the fifteenth day of the same month, year by year, [22]as the days on which the Jews gained relief from their enemies, and as the month that had been turned for them from sorrow into gladness and from mourning into a holiday; that they should make them days of feasting and gladness, days for sending gifts of food to one another and presents to the poor. [23]So the Jews adopted as a custom what they had begun to do, as Mordecai had written to them.

24 Haman son of Hammedatha the Agagite, the enemy of all the Jews, had plotted against the Jews to destroy them, and had cast Pur—that is "the lot"—to crush and destroy them; [25]but when Esther came before the king, he gave orders in writing that the wicked plot that he had devised against the Jews should come upon his own head, and that he and his sons should be hanged on the gallows. [26]Therefore these days are called Purim, from the word Pur. Thus because of all that was written in this letter, and of what they had faced in this matter, and of what had happened to them, [27]the Jews established and accepted as a custom for themselves and their descendants and all who joined them, that without fail they would continue to observe these two days every year, as it was written and at the time appointed. [28]These days should be remembered and kept throughout every generation, in every family, province, and city; and these days of Purim should never fall into disuse among the Jews, nor should the commemoration of these days cease among their descendants.

29 Queen Esther daughter of Abihail, along with the Jew Mordecai, gave full written authority, confirming this second letter about Purim. [30]Letters were sent wishing peace and security to all the Jews, to the one hundred twenty-seven provinces of the kingdom of Ahasuerus, [31]and giving orders that these days of Purim should be observed at their appointed seasons, as the Jew Mordecai and Queen Esther enjoined on the Jews, just as they had laid down for themselves and for their descendants regulations concerning their fasts and their lamentations. [32]The command of Queen Esther fixed these practices of Purim, and it was recorded in writing.

10.1 KING Ahasuerus laid tribute on the land and on the islands of the sea. [2]All the acts of his power and might, and the full account of the high honor of Mordecai, to which the king advanced him, are they not written in the annals of the kings of Media and Persia? [3]For Mordecai the Jew was next in rank to King Ahasuerus, and he was powerful among the Jews and popular with his many kindred, for he sought the good of his people and interceded for the welfare of all his descendants.

## 1 CORINTHIANS 12.27—13.13

**N**ow you are the body of Christ and individually members of it. 28And God has appointed in the church first apostles, second prophets, third teachers; then deeds of power, then gifts of healing, forms of assistance, forms of leadership, various kinds of tongues. 29Are all apostles? Are all prophets? Are all teachers? Do all work miracles? 30Do all possess gifts of healing? Do all speak in tongues? Do all interpret? 31But strive for the greater gifts. And I will show you a still more excellent way.

**13.1** If I speak in the tongues of mortals and of angels, but do not have love, I am a noisy gong or a clanging cymbal. 2And if I have prophetic powers, and understand all mysteries and all knowledge, and if I have all faith, so as to remove mountains, but do not have love, I am nothing. 3If I give away all my possessions, and if I hand over my body so that I may boast,a but do not have love, I gain nothing.

4 Love is patient; love is kind; love is not envious or boastful or arrogant 5or rude. It does not insist on its own way; it is not irritable or resentful; 6it does not rejoice in wrongdoing, but rejoices in the truth. 7It bears all things, believes all things, hopes all things, endures all things.

8 Love never ends. But as for prophecies, they will come to an end; as for tongues, they will cease; as for knowledge, it will come to an end. 9For we know only in part, and we prophesy only in part; 10but when the complete comes, the partial will come to an end. 11When I was a child, I spoke like a child, I thought like a child, I reasoned like a child; when I became an adult, I put an end to childish ways. 12For now we see in a mirror, dimly,b but then we will see face to face. Now I know only in part; then I will know fully, even as I have been fully known. 13And now faith, hope, and love abide, these three; and the greatest of these is love.

## PSALM 37.1–11

*Of David.*

**D**o not fret because of the
    wicked;
do not be envious of
    wrongdoers,
2  for they will soon fade like the
    grass,
  and wither like the green
    herb.

3  Trust in the Lord, and do good;
  so you will live in the land,
    and enjoy security.
4  Take delight in the Lord,
  and he will give you the
    desires of your heart.

5  Commit your way to the Lord;
  trust in him, and he will act.
6  He will make your vindication
    shine like the light,
  and the justice of your cause
    like the noonday.

7  Be still before the Lord, and
    wait patiently for him;
  do not fret over those who
    prosper in their way,
  over those who carry out evil
    devices.

8  Refrain from anger, and forsake
    wrath.
  Do not fret—it leads only to
    evil.
9  For the wicked shall be cut off,
  but those who wait for the
    Lord shall inherit the
    land.

aOther ancient authorities read *body to be burned* bGk *in a riddle*

10 Yet a little while, and the
    wicked will be no more;
though you look diligently for
    their place, they will not
    be there.
11 But the meek shall inherit the
    land,
    and delight themselves in
    abundant prosperity.

## PROVERBS 21.23–24

To watch over mouth and
    tongue
is to keep out of trouble.
24 The proud, haughty person,
    named "Scoffer,"
    acts with arrogant pride.

# AUGUST 21

## JOB 1.1—3.26

THERE was once a man in the land of Uz whose name was Job. That man was blameless and upright, one who feared God and turned away from evil. ²There were born to him seven sons and three daughters. ³He had seven thousand sheep, three thousand camels, five hundred yoke of oxen, five hundred donkeys, and very many servants; so that this man was the greatest of all the people of the east. ⁴His sons used to go and hold feasts in one another's houses in turn; and they would send and invite their three sisters to eat and drink with them. ⁵And when the feast days had run their course, Job would send and sanctify them, and he would rise early in the morning and offer burnt offerings according to the number of them all; for Job said, "It may be that my children have sinned, and cursed God in their hearts." This is what Job always did.

6 One day the heavenly beingsᵃ came to present themselves before the LORD, and Satanᵇ also came among them. ⁷The LORD said to Satan,ᵇ "Where have you come from?" Satanᵇ answered the LORD, "From going to and fro on the earth, and from walking up and down on it." ⁸The LORD said to Satan,ᵇ "Have you considered my servant Job? There is no one like him on the earth, a blameless and upright man who fears God and turns away from evil." ⁹Then Satanᵇ answered the LORD, "Does Job fear God for nothing? ¹⁰Have you not put a fence around him and his house and all that he has, on every side? You have blessed the work of his hands, and his possessions have increased in the land. ¹¹But stretch out your hand now, and touch all that he has, and he will curse you to your face." ¹²The LORD said to Satan,ᵇ "Very well, all that he has is in your power; only do not stretch out your hand against him!" So Satanᵇ went out from the presence of the LORD.

13 One day when his sons and daughters were eating and drinking wine in the eldest brother's house, ¹⁴a messenger came to Job and said, "The oxen were plowing and the donkeys were feeding beside them, ¹⁵and the Sabeans fell on them and carried them off, and killed the servants with the

ᵃHeb *sons of God*  ᵇOr *the Accuser*; Heb *ha-satan*

edge of the sword; I alone have escaped to tell you." 16While he was still speaking, another came and said, "The fire of God fell from heaven and burned up the sheep and the servants, and consumed them; I alone have escaped to tell you." 17While he was still speaking, another came and said, "The Chaldeans formed three columns, made a raid on the camels and carried them off, and killed the servants with the edge of the sword; I alone have escaped to tell you." 18While he was still speaking, another came and said, "Your sons and daughters were eating and drinking wine in their eldest brother's house, 19and suddenly a great wind came across the desert, struck the four corners of the house, and it fell on the young people, and they are dead; I alone have escaped to tell you."

20 Then Job arose, tore his robe, shaved his head, and fell on the ground and worshiped. 21He said, "Naked I came from my mother's womb, and naked shall I return there; the LORD gave, and the LORD has taken away; blessed be the name of the LORD."

22 In all this Job did not sin or charge God with wrongdoing.

2.1 ONE day the heavenly beings[a] came to present themselves before the LORD, and Satan[b] also came among them to present himself before the LORD. 2The LORD said to Satan, [b] "Where have you come from?" Satan[c] answered the LORD, "From going to and fro on the earth, and from walking up and down on it." 3The LORD said to Satan, [b] "Have you considered my servant Job? There is no one like him on the earth, a blameless and upright man who fears God and turns away from evil. He still persists in his integrity, although you incited me against him, to destroy him for no reason." 4Then Satan[b] answered the LORD, "Skin for skin! All that people have they will give to save their lives. [d] 5But stretch out your hand now and touch his bone and his flesh, and he will curse you to your face." 6The LORD said to Satan, [b] "Very well, he is in your power; only spare his life."

7 So Satan[b] went out from the presence of the LORD, and inflicted loathsome sores on Job from the sole of his foot to the crown of his head. 8Job[e] took a potsherd with which to scrape himself, and sat among the ashes.

9 Then his wife said to him, "Do you still persist in your integrity? Curse[f] God, and die." 10But he said to her, "You speak as any foolish woman would speak. Shall we receive the good at the hand of God, and not receive the bad?" In all this Job did not sin with his lips.

11 Now when Job's three friends heard of all these troubles that had come upon him, each of them set out from his home—Eliphaz the Temanite, Bildad the Shuhite, and Zophar the Naamathite. They met together to go and console and comfort him. 12When they saw him from a distance, they did not recognize him, and they raised their voices and wept aloud; they tore their robes and threw dust in the air upon their heads. 13They sat with him on the ground seven days and seven nights, and no one spoke a word to him, for they saw that his suffering was very great.

3.1 AFTER this Job opened his mouth and cursed the day of his birth. 2Job said:
3   "Let the day perish in which I
        was born,
    and the night that said,
    'A man-child is conceived.'
4  Let that day be darkness!
    May God above not seek it,
    or light shine on it.

aHeb *sons of God*   bOr *the Accuser,* Heb *ha-satan*   cOr *The Accuser,* Heb *ha-satan*   dOr *All that the man has he will give for his life*   eHeb *He*   fHeb *Bless*

 5 Let gloom and deep darkness
        claim it.
      Let clouds settle upon it;
      let the blackness of the day
        terrify it.
 6 That night—let thick darkness
        seize it!
      let it not rejoice among the
        days of the year;
      let it not come into the
        number of the months.
 7 Yes, let that night be barren;
      let no joyful cry be heard[a] in
        it.
 8 Let those curse it who curse
        the Sea,[b]
      those who are skilled to rouse
        up Leviathan.
 9 Let the stars of its dawn be
        dark;
      let it hope for light, but have
        none;
      may it not see the eyelids of
        the morning—
10  because it did not shut the
        doors of my mother's
        womb,
      and hide trouble from my
        eyes.

11  "Why did I not die at birth,
      come forth from the womb
        and expire?
12  Why were there knees to
        receive me,
      or breasts for me to suck?
13  Now I would be lying down and
        quiet;
      I would be asleep; then I
        would be at rest
14  with kings and counselors of the
        earth
      who rebuild ruins for
        themselves,
15  or with princes who have gold,
      who fill their houses with
        silver.

16  Or why was I not buried like a
        stillborn child,
      like an infant that never sees
        the light?
17  There the wicked cease from
        troubling,
      and there the weary are at
        rest.
18  There the prisoners are at ease
        together;
      they do not hear the voice of
        the taskmaster.
19  The small and the great are
        there,
      and the slaves are free from
        their masters.

20  "Why is light given to one in
        misery,
      and life to the bitter in soul,
21  who long for death, but it does
        not come,
      and dig for it more than for
        hidden treasures;
22  who rejoice exceedingly,
      and are glad when they find
        the grave?
23  Why is light given to one who
        cannot see the way,
      whom God has fenced in?
24  For my sighing comes like[c] my
        bread,
      and my groanings are poured
        out like water.
25  Truly the thing that I fear
        comes upon me,
      and what I dread befalls me.
26  I am not at ease, nor am I
        quiet;
      I have no rest; but trouble
        comes."

# 1 CORINTHIANS 14.1–17

PURSUE love and strive for the spiritual gifts, and especially that you may prophesy. ²For those who speak in a tongue do not speak to other people but to God; for

a Heb *come*   b Cn: Heb *day*   c Heb *before*

nobody understands them, since they are speaking mysteries in the Spirit. ³On the other hand, those who prophesy speak to other people for their upbuilding and encouragement and consolation. ⁴Those who speak in a tongue build up themselves, but those who prophesy build up the church. ⁵Now I would like all of you to speak in tongues, but even more to prophesy. One who prophesies is greater than one who speaks in tongues, unless someone interprets, so that the church may be built up.

6 Now, brothers and sisters, ᵃ if I come to you speaking in tongues, how will I benefit you unless I speak to you in some revelation or knowledge or prophecy or teaching? ⁷It is the same way with lifeless instruments that produce sound, such as the flute or the harp. If they do not give distinct notes, how will anyone know what is being played? ⁸And if the bugle gives an indistinct sound, who will get ready for battle? ⁹So with yourselves; if in a tongue you utter speech that is not intelligible, how will anyone know what is being said? For you will be speaking into the air. ¹⁰There are doubtless many different kinds of sounds in the world, and nothing is without sound. ¹¹If then I do not know the meaning of a sound, I will be a foreigner to the speaker and the speaker a foreigner to me. ¹²So with yourselves; since you are eager for spiritual gifts, strive to excel in them for building up the church.

13 Therefore, one who speaks in a tongue should pray for the power to interpret. ¹⁴For if I pray in a tongue, my spirit prays but my mind is unproductive. ¹⁵What should I do then? I will pray with the spirit, but I will pray with the mind also; I will sing praise with the spirit, but I will sing praise with the mind also. ¹⁶Otherwise, if you say a blessing with the spirit, how can any-

one in the position of an outsider say the "Amen" to your thanksgiving, since the outsider does not know what you are saying? ¹⁷For you may give thanks well enough, but the other person is not built up.

## PSALM 37.12–29

THE wicked plot against the
    righteous,
  and gnash their teeth at
    them;
13  but the LORD laughs at the
    wicked,
    for he sees that their day is
      coming.

14  The wicked draw the sword and
    bend their bows
    to bring down the poor and
      needy,
    to kill those who walk
      uprightly;
15  their sword shall enter their
    own heart,
    and their bows shall be
    broken.

16  Better is a little that the
    righteous person has
    than the abundance of many
    wicked.
17  For the arms of the wicked shall
    be broken,
    but the LORD upholds the
    righteous.

18  The LORD knows the days of the
    blameless,
    and their heritage will abide
    forever;
19  they are not put to shame in
    evil times,
    in the days of famine they
    have abundance.

20  But the wicked perish,

ᵃGk *brothers*

and the enemies of the LORD
  are like the glory of the
  pastures;
they vanish—like smoke they
  vanish away.

21  The wicked borrow, and do not
      pay back,
    but the righteous are
      generous and keep
      giving;
22  for those blessed by the LORD
      shall inherit the land,
    but those cursed by him shall
      be cut off.

23  Our steps[a] are made firm by
      the LORD,
    when he delights in our[b]
      way;
24  though we stumble,[c] we[d] shall
      not fall headlong,
    for the LORD holds us[e] by the
      hand.

25  I have been young, and now am
      old,
    yet I have not seen the
      righteous forsaken

or their children begging
  bread.
26  They are ever giving liberally
      and lending,
    and their children become a
      blessing.

27  Depart from evil, and do good;
      so you shall abide forever.
28  For the LORD loves justice;
      he will not forsake his faithful
      ones.

The righteous shall be kept safe
  forever,
but the children of the wicked
  shall be cut off.
29  The righteous shall inherit the
      land,
    and live in it forever.

## PROVERBS 21.25–26

THE craving of the lazy person
  is fatal,
for lazy hands refuse to
  labor.
26  All day long the wicked covet,[f]
    but the righteous give and do
      not hold back.

# AUGUST 22

## JOB 4.1—7.21

THEN Eliphaz the Temanite answered:
2  "If one ventures a word
    with you, will you be
    offended?
But who can keep from
    speaking?

3  See, you have instructed many;
    you have strengthened the
    weak hands.
4  Your words have supported
    those who were
    stumbling,
  and you have made firm the
    feeble knees.

[a] Heb *a man's steps*  [b] Heb *his*  [c] Heb *he stumbles*  [d] Heb *he*  [e] Heb *him*  [f] Gk: Heb *all day long one covets covetously*

5 But now it has come to you,
  and you are impatient;
  it touches you, and you are
    dismayed.
6 Is not your fear of God your
    confidence,
  and the integrity of your ways
    your hope?

7 "Think now, who that was
    innocent ever perished?
  Or where were the upright
    cut off?
8 As I have seen, those who plow
    iniquity
  and sow trouble reap the
    same.
9 By the breath of God they
    perish,
  and by the blast of his anger
    they are consumed.
10 The roar of the lion, the voice
    of the fierce lion,
  and the teeth of the young
    lions are broken.
11 The strong lion perishes for lack
    of prey,
  and the whelps of the lioness
    are scattered.

12 "Now a word came stealing to
    me,
  my ear received the whisper
    of it.
13 Amid thoughts from visions of
    the night,
  when deep sleep falls on
    mortals,
14 dread came upon me, and
    trembling,
  which made all my bones
    shake.
15 A spirit glided past my face;
  the hair of my flesh bristled.
16 It stood still,
  but I could not discern its
    appearance.
  A form was before my eyes;

  there was silence, then I
    heard a voice:
17 'Can mortals be righteous
    before[a] God?
  Can human beings be pure
    before[a] their Maker?
18 Even in his servants he puts no
    trust,
  and his angels he charges
    with error;
19 how much more those who live
    in houses of clay,
  whose foundation is in the
    dust,
  who are crushed like a moth.
20 Between morning and evening
    they are destroyed;
  they perish forever without
    any regarding it.
21 Their tent-cord is plucked up
    within them,
  and they die devoid of
    wisdom.'

5.1 "CALL now; is there anyone
    who will answer you?
  To which of the holy ones will
    you turn?
2 Surely vexation kills the fool,
  and jealousy slays the simple.
3 I have seen fools taking root,
  but suddenly I cursed their
    dwelling.
4 Their children are far from
    safety,
  they are crushed in the gate,
  and there is no one to deliver
    them.
5 The hungry eat their harvest,
  and they take it even out of
    the thorns;[b]
  and the thirsty[c] pant after
    their wealth.
6 For misery does not come from
    the earth,
  nor does trouble sprout from
    the ground;

a Or *more than*   b Meaning of Heb uncertain   c Aquila Symmachus Syr Vg: Heb *snare*

7  but human beings are born to
      trouble
   just as sparks<sup>a</sup> fly upward.

8  "As for me, I would seek God,
      and to God I would commit
         my cause.
9  He does great things and
      unsearchable,
   marvelous things without
      number.
10  He gives rain on the earth
      and sends waters on the
         fields;
11  he sets on high those who are
      lowly,
   and those who mourn are
      lifted to safety.
12  He frustrates the devices of the
      crafty,
   so that their hands achieve no
      success.
13  He takes the wise in their own
      craftiness;
   and the schemes of the wily
      are brought to a quick
         end.
14  They meet with darkness in the
      daytime,
   and grope at noonday as in
      the night.
15  But he saves the needy from
      the sword of their
         mouth,
   from the hand of the mighty.
16  So the poor have hope,
      and injustice shuts its mouth.

17  "How happy is the one whom
      God reproves;
   therefore do not despise the
      discipline of the
         Almighty.<sup>b</sup>
18  For he wounds, but he binds
      up;
   he strikes, but his hands heal.
19  He will deliver you from six
      troubles;

in seven no harm shall touch
      you.
20  In famine he will redeem you
      from death,
   and in war from the power of
      the sword.
21  You shall be hidden from the
      scourge of the tongue,
   and shall not fear destruction
      when it comes.
22  At destruction and famine you
      shall laugh,
   and shall not fear the wild
      animals of the earth.
23  For you shall be in league with
      the stones of the field,
   and the wild animals shall be
      at peace with you.
24  You shall know that your tent is
      safe,
   you shall inspect your fold and
      miss nothing.
25  You shall know that your
      descendants will be
         many,
   and your offspring like the
      grass of the earth.
26  You shall come to your grave in
      ripe old age,
   as a shock of grain comes up
      to the threshing floor in
         its season.
27  See, we have searched this out;
      it is true.
   Hear, and know it for
      yourself."

6.1  THEN Job answered:
2  "O that my vexation were
      weighed,
   and all my calamity laid in the
      balances!
3  For then it would be heavier
      than the sand of the sea;
   therefore my words have
      been rash.
4  For the arrows of the
      Almighty<sup>b</sup> are in me;

<sup>a</sup> Or *birds*; Heb *sons of Resheph*   <sup>b</sup> Traditional rendering of Heb *Shaddai*

my spirit drinks their poison;
   the terrors of God are
      arrayed against me.
5 Does the wild ass bray over its
      grass,
   or the ox low over its fodder?
6 Can that which is tasteless be
      eaten without salt,
   or is there any flavor in the
      juice of mallows? [a]
7 My appetite refuses to touch
      them;
   they are like food that is
      loathsome to me. [a]

8 "O that I might have my
      request,
   and that God would grant my
      desire;
9 that it would please God to
      crush me,
   that he would let loose his
      hand and cut me off!
10 This would be my consolation;
   I would even exult [a] in
      unrelenting pain;
   for I have not denied the
      words of the Holy One.
11 What is my strength, that I
      should wait?
   And what is my end, that I
      should be patient?
12 Is my strength the strength of
      stones,
   or is my flesh bronze?
13 In truth I have no help in me,
   and any resource is driven
      from me.

14 "Those who withhold [b] kindness
      from a friend
   forsake the fear of the
      Almighty. [c]
15 My companions are treacherous
      like a torrent-bed,
   like freshets that pass away,
16 that run dark with ice,
   turbid with melting snow.

17 In time of heat they disappear;
   when it is hot, they vanish
      from their place.
18 The caravans turn aside from
      their course;
   they go up into the waste,
      and perish.
19 The caravans of Tema look,
   the travelers of Sheba hope.
20 They are disappointed because
      they were confident;
   they come there and are
      confounded.
21 Such you have now become to
      me; [d]
   you see my calamity, and are
      afraid.
22 Have I said, 'Make me a gift'?
   Or, 'From your wealth offer a
      bribe for me'?
23 Or, 'Save me from an
      opponent's hand'?
   Or, 'Ransom me from the
      hand of oppressors'?

24 "Teach me, and I will be silent;
   make me understand how I
      have gone wrong.
25 How forceful are honest words!
   But your reproof, what does
      it reprove?
26 Do you think that you can
      reprove words,
   as if the speech of the
      desperate were wind?
27 You would even cast lots over
      the orphan,
   and bargain over your friend.

28 "But now, be pleased to look at
      me;
   for I will not lie to your face.
29 Turn, I pray, let no wrong be
      done.
   Turn now, my vindication is
      at stake.
30 Is there any wrong on my
      tongue?

a Meaning of Heb uncertain  b Syr Vg Compare Tg: Meaning of Heb uncertain  c Traditional
rendering of Heb *Shaddai*  d Cn Compare Gk Syr: Meaning of Heb uncertain

Cannot my taste discern
    calamity?

**7.1** "Do not human beings have a
    hard service on earth,
  and are not their days like the
    days of a laborer?
2 Like a slave who longs for the
    shadow,
  and like laborers who look for
    their wages,
3 so I am allotted months of
    emptiness,
  and nights of misery are
    apportioned to me.
4 When I lie down I say, 'When
    shall I rise?'
  But the night is long,
  and I am full of tossing until
    dawn.
5 My flesh is clothed with worms
    and dirt;
  my skin hardens, then breaks
    out again.
6 My days are swifter than a
    weaver's shuttle,
  and come to their end without
    hope. [a]

7 "Remember that my life is a
    breath;
  my eye will never again see
    good.
8 The eye that beholds me will
    see me no more;
  while your eyes are upon me,
    I shall be gone.
9 As the cloud fades and vanishes,
  so those who go down to
    Sheol do not come up;
10 they return no more to their
    houses,
  nor do their places know
    them any more.

11 "Therefore I will not restrain
    my mouth;
  I will speak in the anguish of
    my spirit;
  I will complain in the
    bitterness of my soul.
12 Am I the Sea, or the Dragon,
  that you set a guard over me?
13 When I say, 'My bed will
    comfort me,
  my couch will ease my
    complaint,'
14 then you scare me with dreams
  and terrify me with visions,
15 so that I would choose
    strangling
  and death rather than this
    body.
16 I loathe my life; I would not live
    forever.
  Let me alone, for my days
    are a breath.
17 What are human beings, that
    you make so much of
    them,
  that you set your mind on
    them,
18 visit them every morning,
  test them every moment?
19 Will you not look away from me
    for a while,
  let me alone until I swallow
    my spittle?
20 If I sin, what do I do to you,
    you watcher of humanity?
  Why have you made me your
    target?
  Why have I become a burden
    to you?
21 Why do you not pardon my
    transgression
  and take away my iniquity?
  For now I shall lie in the earth;
  you will seek me, but I shall
    not be."

[a] Or *as the thread runs out*

## 1 CORINTHIANS 14.18–40

I THANK God that I speak in tongues more than all of you; [19]nevertheless, in church I would rather speak five words with my mind, in order to instruct others also, than ten thousand words in a tongue.

20 Brothers and sisters,[a] do not be children in your thinking; rather, be infants in evil, but in thinking be adults. [21]In the law it is written,

"By people of strange tongues
  and by the lips of foreigners
I will speak to this people;
  yet even then they will not
    listen to me,"

says the Lord. [22]Tongues, then, are a sign not for believers but for unbelievers, while prophecy is not for unbelievers but for believers. [23]If, therefore, the whole church comes together and all speak in tongues, and outsiders or unbelievers enter, will they not say that you are out of your mind? [24]But if all prophesy, an unbeliever or outsider who enters is reproved by all and called to account by all. [25]After the secrets of the unbeliever's heart are disclosed, that person will bow down before God and worship him, declaring, "God is really among you."

26 What should be done then, my friends?[a] When you come together, each one has a hymn, a lesson, a revelation, a tongue, or an interpretation. Let all things be done for building up. [27]If anyone speaks in a tongue, let there be only two or at most three, and each in turn; and let one interpret. [28]But if there is no one to interpret, let them be silent in church and speak to themselves and to God. [29]Let two or three prophets speak, and let the others weigh what is said. [30]If a revelation is made to someone else sitting nearby, let the first person be silent. [31]For you can all prophesy one by one, so that all may learn and all be encouraged. [32]And the spirits of prophets are subject to the prophets, [33]for God is a God not of disorder but of peace.

(As in all the churches of the saints, [34]women should be silent in the churches. For they are not permitted to speak, but should be subordinate, as the law also says. [35]If there is anything they desire to know, let them ask their husbands at home. For it is shameful for a woman to speak in church.[b] [36]Or did the word of God originate with you? Or are you the only ones it has reached?)

37 Anyone who claims to be a prophet, or to have spiritual powers, must acknowledge that what I am writing to you is a command of the Lord. [38]Anyone who does not recognize this is not to be recognized. [39]So, my friends,[c] be eager to prophesy, and do not forbid speaking in tongues; [40]but all things should be done decently and in order.

## PSALM 37.30–40

T HE mouths of the righteous
      utter wisdom,
    and their tongues speak
      justice.
[31]  The law of their God is in their
      hearts;
    their steps do not slip.

[32]  The wicked watch for the
      righteous,
    and seek to kill them.
[33]  The LORD will not abandon them
      to their power,
    or let them be condemned
      when they are brought to
      trial.

[34]  Wait for the LORD, and keep to
      his way,
    and he will exalt you to
      inherit the land;

you will look on the
destruction of the
wicked.

35 I have seen the wicked
oppressing,
and towering like a cedar of
Lebanon. **a**
36 Again I**b** passed by, and they
were no more;
though I sought them, they
could not be found.

37 Mark the blameless, and behold
the upright,
for there is posterity for the
peaceable.
38 But transgressors shall be
altogether destroyed;

the posterity of the wicked
shall be cut off.

39 The salvation of the righteous is
from the LORD;
he is their refuge in the time
of trouble.
40 The LORD helps them and
rescues them;
he rescues them from the
wicked, and saves them,
because they take refuge in
him.

## PROVERBS 21.27

THE sacrifice of the wicked is an
abomination;
how much more when
brought with evil intent.

# AUGUST 23

## JOB 8.1—11.20

THEN Bildad the Shuhite answered:
2 "How long will you say
these things,
and the words of your mouth
be a great wind?
3 Does God pervert justice?
Or does the Almighty**c**
pervert the right?
4 If your children sinned against
him,
he delivered them into the
power of their
transgression.
5 If you will seek God
and make supplication to the
Almighty, **c**
6 if you are pure and upright,

surely then he will rouse
himself for you
and restore to you your
rightful place.
7 Though your beginning was
small,
your latter days will be very
great.

8 "For inquire now of bygone
generations,
and consider what their
ancestors have found;
9 for we are but of yesterday, and
we know nothing,
for our days on earth are but
a shadow.
10 Will they not teach you and tell
you

and utter words out of their
    understanding?

11 "Can papyrus grow where there
    is no marsh?
  Can reeds flourish where
    there is no water?
12 While yet in flower and not cut
    down,
  they wither before any other
    plant.
13 Such are the paths of all who
    forget God;
  the hope of the godless shall
    perish.
14 Their confidence is gossamer,
  a spider's house their trust.
15 If one leans against its house, it
    will not stand;
  if one lays hold of it, it will
    not endure.
16 The wicked thrive[a] before the
    sun,
  and their shoots spread over
    the garden.
17 Their roots twine around the
    stoneheap;
  they live among the rocks. [b]
18 If they are destroyed from their
    place,
  then it will deny them,
    saying, 'I have never
    seen you.'
19 See, these are their happy
    ways, [c]
  and out of the earth still
    others will spring.

20 "See, God will not reject a
    blameless person,
  nor take the hand of
    evildoers.
21 He will yet fill your mouth with
    laughter,
  and your lips with shouts of
    joy.
22 Those who hate you will be
    clothed with shame,

and the tent of the wicked
    will be no more."

9.1 THEN Job answered:
2 "Indeed I know that this is so;
  but how can a mortal be just
    before God?
3 If one wished to contend with
    him,
  one could not answer him
    once in a thousand.
4 He is wise in heart, and mighty
    in strength
  —who has resisted him, and
    succeeded?—
5 he who removes mountains, and
    they do not know it,
  when he overturns them in
    his anger;
6 who shakes the earth out of its
    place,
  and its pillars tremble;
7 who commands the sun, and it
    does not rise;
  who seals up the stars;
8 who alone stretched out the
    heavens
  and trampled the waves of
    the Sea; [d]
9 who made the Bear and Orion,
  the Pleiades and the
    chambers of the south;
10 who does great things beyond
    understanding,
  and marvelous things without
    number.
11 Look, he passes by me, and I
    do not see him;
  he moves on, but I do not
    perceive him.
12 He snatches away; who can
    stop him?
  Who will say to him, 'What
    are you doing?'

13 "God will not turn back his
    anger;

[a] Heb *He thrives*  [b] Gk Vg: Meaning of Heb uncertain  [c] Meaning of Heb uncertain  [d] Or *trampled the back of the sea dragon*

the helpers of Rahab bowed
    beneath him.
14 How then can I answer him,
    choosing my words with him?
15 Though I am innocent, I cannot
    answer him;
    I must appeal for mercy to
    my accuser. [a]
16 If I summoned him and he
    answered me,
    I do not believe that he would
    listen to my voice.
17 For he crushes me with a
    tempest,
    and multiplies my wounds
    without cause;
18 he will not let me get my
    breath,
    but fills me with bitterness.
19 If it is a contest of strength, he
    is the strong one!
    If it is a matter of justice,
    who can summon him? [b]
20 Though I am innocent, my own
    mouth would condemn
    me;
    though I am blameless, he
    would prove me
    perverse.
21 I am blameless; I do not know
    myself;
    I loathe my life.
22 It is all one; therefore I say,
    he destroys both the
    blameless and the
    wicked.
23 When disaster brings sudden
    death,
    he mocks at the calamity[c] of
    the innocent.
24 The earth is given into the hand
    of the wicked;
    he covers the eyes of its
    judges—
    if it is not he, who then is it?

25 "My days are swifter than a
    runner;

they flee away, they see no
    good.
26 They go by like skiffs of reed,
    like an eagle swooping on the
    prey.
27 If I say, 'I will forget my
    complaint;
    I will put off my sad
    countenance and be of
    good cheer,'
28 I become afraid of all my
    suffering,
    for I know you will not hold
    me innocent.
29 I shall be condemned;
    why then do I labor in vain?
30 If I wash myself with soap
    and cleanse my hands with
    lye,
31 yet you will plunge me into filth,
    and my own clothes will abhor
    me.
32 For he is not a mortal, as I am,
    that I might answer him,
    that we should come to trial
    together.
33 There is no umpire[d] between
    us,
    who might lay his hand on us
    both.
34 If he would take his rod away
    from me,
    and not let dread of him
    terrify me,
35 then I would speak without fear
    of him,
    for I know I am not what I
    am thought to be. [e]

10.1 "I LOATHE my life;
    I will give free utterance to
    my complaint;
    I will speak in the bitterness
    of my soul.
2 I will say to God, Do not
    condemn me;
    let me know why you contend
    against me.

[a] Or *for my right*  [b] Compare Gk: Heb *me*  [c] Meaning of Heb uncertain  [d] Another reading is *Would that there were an umpire*  [e] Cn: Heb *for I am not so in myself*

3 Does it seem good to you to
        oppress,
    to despise the work of your
        hands
    and favor the schemes of the
        wicked?
4 Do you have eyes of flesh?
    Do you see as humans see?
5 Are your days like the days of
        mortals,
    or your years like human
        years,
6 that you seek out my iniquity
    and search for my sin,
7 although you know that I am not
        guilty,
    and there is no one to deliver
        out of your hand?
8 Your hands fashioned and made
        me;
    and now you turn and destroy
        me. a
9 Remember that you fashioned
        me like clay;
    and will you turn me to dust
        again?
10 Did you not pour me out like
        milk
    and curdle me like cheese?
11 You clothed me with skin and
        flesh,
    and knit me together with
        bones and sinews.
12 You have granted me life and
        steadfast love,
    and your care has preserved
        my spirit.
13 Yet these things you hid in your
        heart;
    I know that this was your
        purpose.
14 If I sin, you watch me,
    and do not acquit me of my
        iniquity.
15 If I am wicked, woe to me!

If I am righteous, I cannot lift
        up my head,
    for I am filled with disgrace
        and look upon my affliction.
16 Bold as a lion you hunt me;
    you repeat your exploits
        against me.
17 You renew your witnesses
        against me,
    and increase your vexation
        toward me;
    you bring fresh troops against
        me. b

18 "Why did you bring me forth
        from the womb?
    Would that I had died before
        any eye had seen me,
19 and were as though I had not
        been,
    carried from the womb to the
        grave.
20 Are not the days of my life
        few? c
    Let me alone, that I may find
        a little comfort d
21 before I go, never to return,
    to the land of gloom and deep
        darkness,
22 the land of gloom e and chaos,
    where light is like darkness."

11.1 THEN Zophar the Naamathite answered:
2 "Should a multitude of words go
        unanswered,
    and should one full of talk be
        vindicated?
3 Should your babble put others
        to silence,
    and when you mock, shall no
        one shame you?
4 For you say, 'My conduct f is
        pure,
    and I am clean in God's g
        sight.'

aCn Compare Gk Syr: Heb *made me together all around, and you destroy me*   bCn Compare Gk:
Heb *toward me; changes and a troop are with me*   cCn Compare Gk Syr: Heb *Are not my days few?
Let him cease!*   dHeb *that I may brighten up a little*   eHeb *gloom as darkness, deep darkness*
fGk: Heb *teaching*   gHeb *your*

5 But oh, that God would speak,
  and open his lips to you,
6 and that he would tell you the
    secrets of wisdom!
  For wisdom is many-sided. [a]
Know then that God exacts of
    you less than your guilt
    deserves.

7 "Can you find out the deep
    things of God?
  Can you find out the limit of
    the Almighty? [b]
8 It is higher than
    heaven [c]—what can you
    do?
  Deeper than Sheol—what can
    you know?
  Its measure is longer than the
    earth,
  and broader than the sea.
10 If he passes through, and
    imprisons,
  and assembles for judgment,
    who can hinder him?
11 For he knows those who are
    worthless;
  when he sees iniquity, will he
    not consider it?
12 But a stupid person will get
    understanding,
  when a wild ass is born
    human. [a]

13 "If you direct your heart rightly,
  you will stretch out your
    hands toward him.
14 If iniquity is in your hand, put it
    far away,
  and do not let wickedness
    reside in your tents.
15 Surely then you will lift up your
    face without blemish;
  you will be secure, and will
    not fear.
16 You will forget your misery;
  you will remember it as

waters that have passed
    away.
17 And your life will be brighter
    than the noonday;
  its darkness will be like the
    morning.
18 And you will have confidence,
    because there is hope;
  you will be protected [d] and
    take your rest in safety.
19 You will lie down, and no one
    will make you afraid;
  many will entreat your favor.
20 But the eyes of the wicked will
    fail;
  all way of escape will be lost
    to them,
  and their hope is to breathe
    their last."

# 1 CORINTHIANS 15. 1–28

Now I would remind you, brothers and sisters, [e] of the good news [f] that I proclaimed to you, which you in turn received, in which also you stand, 2through which also you are being saved, if you hold firmly to the message that I proclaimed to you—unless you have come to believe in vain.

3 For I handed on to you as of first importance what I in turn had received: that Christ died for our sins in accordance with the scriptures, 4and that he was buried, and that he was raised on the third day in accordance with the scriptures, 5and that he appeared to Cephas, then to the twelve. 6Then he appeared to more than five hundred brothers and sisters [e] at one time, most of whom are still alive, though some have died. [g] 7Then he appeared to James, then to all the apostles. 8Last of all, as to one untimely born, he appeared also to me. 9For I am the least of the apostles, unfit to be called an

[a] Meaning of Heb uncertain   [b] Traditional rendering of Heb *Shaddai*   [c] Heb *The heights of heaven*
[d] Or *you will look around*   [e] Gk *brothers*   [f] Or *gospel*   [g] Gk *fallen asleep*

apostle, because I persecuted the church of God. ¹⁰But by the grace of God I am what I am, and his grace toward me has not been in vain. On the contrary, I worked harder than any of them—though it was not I, but the grace of God that is with me. ¹¹Whether then it was I or they, so we proclaim and so you have come to believe.

12 Now if Christ is proclaimed as raised from the dead, how can some of you say there is no resurrection of the dead? ¹³If there is no resurrection of the dead, then Christ has not been raised; ¹⁴and if Christ has not been raised, then our proclamation has been in vain and your faith has been in vain. ¹⁵We are even found to be misrepresenting God, because we testified of God that he raised Christ—whom he did not raise if it is true that the dead are not raised. ¹⁶For if the dead are not raised, then Christ has not been raised. ¹⁷If Christ has not been raised, your faith is futile and you are still in your sins. ¹⁸Then those also who have died[a] in Christ have perished. ¹⁹If for this life only we have hoped in Christ, we are of all people most to be pitied.

20 But in fact Christ has been raised from the dead, the first fruits of those who have died. [a] ²¹For since death came through a human being, the resurrection of the dead has also come through a human being; ²²for as all die in Adam, so all will be made alive in Christ. ²³But each in his own order: Christ the first fruits, then at his coming those who belong to Christ. ²⁴Then comes the end, [b] when he hands over the kingdom to God the Father, after he has destroyed every ruler and every authority and power. ²⁵For he must reign until he has put all his enemies under his feet. ²⁶The last enemy to be destroyed is death. ²⁷For "God[c] has put all things in subjection under his feet." But when it says, "All things are put in subjection," it is plain that this does not include the one who put all things in subjection under him. ²⁸When all things are subjected to him, then the Son himself will also be subjected to the one who put all things in subjection under him, so that God may be all in all.

## PSALM 38.1–22
*A Psalm of David, for the memorial offering.*

O LORD, do not rebuke me in
    your anger,
or discipline me in your
    wrath.
2  For your arrows have sunk into
    me,
    and your hand has come down
      on me.

3  There is no soundness in my
    flesh
    because of your indignation;
there is no health in my bones
    because of my sin.
4  For my iniquities have gone
    over my head;
    they weigh like a burden too
      heavy for me.

5  My wounds grow foul and fester
    because of my foolishness;
6  I am utterly bowed down and
    prostrate;
    all day long I go around
      mourning.
7  For my loins are filled with
    burning,
    and there is no soundness in
      my flesh.
8  I am utterly spent and crushed;
    I groan because of the tumult
      of my heart.

9  O Lord, all my longing is known
    to you;
    my sighing is not hidden from
      you.

---

a Gk *fallen asleep*  b Or *Then come the rest*  c Gk *he*

10 My heart throbs, my strength
        fails me;
    as for the light of my
        eyes—it also has gone
        from me.
11 My friends and companions
        stand aloof from my
        affliction,
    and my neighbors stand far
        off.

12 Those who seek my life lay
        their snares;
    those who seek to hurt me
        speak of ruin,
    and meditate treachery all day
        long.

13 But I am like the deaf, I do not
        hear;
    like the mute, who cannot
        speak.
14 Truly, I am like one who does
        not hear,
    and in whose mouth is no
        retort.

15 But it is for you, O Lord, that I
        wait;
    it is you, O Lord my God,
        who will answer.

16 For I pray, "Only do not let
        them rejoice over me,
    those who boast against me
        when my foot slips."
17 For I am ready to fall,
    and my pain is ever with me.
18 I confess my iniquity;
    I am sorry for my sin.
19 Those who are my foes without
        cause[a] are mighty,
    and many are those who hate
        me wrongfully.
20 Those who render me evil for
        good
    are my adversaries because I
        follow after good.

21 Do not forsake me, O Lord;
    O my God, do not be far
        from me;
22 make haste to help me,
    O Lord, my salvation.

## PROVERBS 21.28–29

A FALSE witness will perish,
but a good listener will
    testify successfully.
29 The wicked put on a bold face,
    but the upright give thought
        to[b] their ways.

# AUGUST 24

## JOB 12.1—15.35

THEN Job answered:
2 "No doubt you are the
        people,
    and wisdom will die with you.
3 But I have understanding as
        well as you;
    I am not inferior to you.
    Who does not know such
        things as these?
4 I am a laughingstock to my
        friends;
    I, who called upon God and
        he answered me,

aQ Ms: MT *my living foes*   bAnother reading is *establish*

a just and blameless man, I
    am a laughingstock.
5 Those at ease have contempt
    for misfortune, **a**
but it is ready for those
    whose feet are unstable.
6 The tents of robbers are at
    peace,
and those who provoke God
    are secure,
who bring their god in their
    hands. **b**

7 "But ask the animals, and they
    will teach you;
the birds of the air, and they
    will tell you;
8 ask the plants of the earth, **c**
    and they will teach you;
and the fish of the sea will
    declare to you.
9 Who among all these does not
    know
that the hand of the Lord has
    done this?
10 In his hand is the life of every
    living thing
and the breath of every
    human being.
11 Does not the ear test words
    as the palate tastes food?
12 Is wisdom with the aged,
and understanding in length of
    days?
13 "With God **d** are wisdom and
    strength;
he has counsel and
    understanding.
14 If he tears down, no one can
    rebuild;
if he shuts someone in, no
    one can open up.
15 If he withholds the waters, they
    dry up;
if he sends them out, they
    overwhelm the land.

16 With him are strength and
    wisdom;
the deceived and the deceiver
    are his.
17 He leads counselors away
    stripped,
and makes fools of judges.
18 He looses the sash of kings,
and binds a waistcloth on
    their loins.
19 He leads priests away stripped,
and overthrows the mighty.
20 He deprives of speech those
    who are trusted,
and takes away the
    discernment of the
    elders.
21 He pours contempt on princes,
and looses the belt of the
    strong.
22 He uncovers the deeps out of
    darkness,
and brings deep darkness to
    light.
23 He makes nations great, then
    destroys them;
he enlarges nations, then
    leads them away.
24 He strips understanding from
    the leaders **e** of the
    earth,
and makes them wander in a
    pathless waste.
25 They grope in the dark without
    light;
he makes them stagger like a
    drunkard.

13.1 "Look, my eye has seen all
    this,
my ear has heard and
    understood it.
2 What you know, I also know;
I am not inferior to you.
3 But I would speak to the
    Almighty, **f**
and I desire to argue my case
    with God.

**a** Meaning of Heb uncertain  **b** Or *whom God brought forth by his hand*; Meaning of Heb uncertain  **c** Or *speak to the earth*  **d** Heb *him*  **e** Heb adds *of the people*  **f** Traditional rendering of Heb *Shaddai*

4  As for you, you whitewash with
        lies;
     all of you are worthless
        physicians.
5  If you would only keep silent,
     that would be your wisdom!
6  Hear now my reasoning,
     and listen to the pleadings of
        my lips.
7  Will you speak falsely for God,
     and speak deceitfully for him?
8  Will you show partiality toward
        him,
     will you plead the case for
        God?
9  Will it be well with you when he
        searches you out?
     Or can you deceive him, as
        one person deceives
        another?
10  He will surely rebuke you
     if in secret you show
        partiality.
11  Will not his majesty terrify you,
     and the dread of him fall upon
        you?
12  Your maxims are proverbs of
        ashes,
     your defenses are defenses of
        clay.

13  "Let me have silence, and I will
        speak,
     and let come on me what
        may.
14  I will take my flesh in my teeth,
     and put my life in my hand. [a]
15  See, he will kill me; I have no
        hope; [b]
     but I will defend my ways to
        his face.
16  This will be my salvation,
     that the godless shall not
        come before him.
17  Listen carefully to my words,
     and let my declaration be in
        your ears.

18  I have indeed prepared my
        case;
     I know that I shall be
        vindicated.
19  Who is there that will contend
        with me?
     For then I would be silent and
        die.
20  Only grant two things to me,
     then I will not hide myself
        from your face:
21  withdraw your hand far from
        me,
     and do not let dread of you
        terrify me.
22  Then call, and I will answer;
     or let me speak, and you
        reply to me.
23  How many are my iniquities and
        my sins?
     Make me know my
        transgression and my sin.
24  Why do you hide your face,
     and count me as your enemy?
25  Will you frighten a windblown
        leaf
     and pursue dry chaff?
26  For you write bitter things
        against me,
     and make me reap [c] the
        iniquities of my youth.
27  You put my feet in the stocks,
     and watch all my paths;
     you set a bound to the soles
        of my feet.
28  One wastes away like a rotten
        thing,
     like a garment that is
        moth-eaten.

14.1  "A MORTAL, born of woman, few
        of days and full of
        trouble,
2      comes up like a flower and
        withers,
     flees like a shadow and does
        not last.

a Gk: Heb *Why should I take . . . in my hand?*  b Or *Though he kill me, yet I will trust in him*
c Heb *inherit*

3 Do you fix your eyes on such a
        one?
    Do you bring me into
        judgment with you?
4 Who can bring a clean thing out
        of an unclean?
    No one can.
5 Since their days are determined,
    and the number of their
        months is known to you,
    and you have appointed the
        bounds that they cannot
        pass,
6 look away from them, and
        desist,ᵃ
    that they may enjoy, like
        laborers, their days.

7 "For there is hope for a tree,
    if it is cut down, that it will
        sprout again,
    and that its shoots will not
        cease.
8 Though its root grows old in the
        earth,
    and its stump dies in the
        ground,
9 yet at the scent of water it will
        bud
    and put forth branches like a
        young plant.
10 But mortals die, and are laid
        low;
    humans expire, and where
        are they?
11 As waters fail from a lake,
    and a river wastes away and
        dries up,
12 so mortals lie down and do not
        rise again;
    until the heavens are no
        more, they will not
        awake
    or be roused out of their
        sleep.
13 Oh that you would hide me in
        Sheol,

that you would conceal me
        until your wrath is past,
    that you would appoint me a
        set time, and remember
        me!
14 If mortals die, will they live
        again?
    All the days of my service I
        would wait
    until my release should come.
15 You would call, and I would
        answer you;
    you would long for the work
        of your hands.
16 For then you would notᵇ
        number my steps,
    you would not keep watch
        over my sin;
17 my transgression would be
        sealed up in a bag,
    and you would cover over my
        iniquity.

18 "But the mountain falls and
        crumbles away,
    and the rock is removed from
        its place;
19 the waters wear away the
        stones;
    the torrents wash away the
        soil of the earth;
    so you destroy the hope of
        mortals.
20 You prevail forever against
        them, and they pass
        away;
    you change their countenance,
        and send them away.
21 Their children come to honor,
        and they do not know it;
    they are brought low, and it
        goes unnoticed.
22 They feel only the pain of their
        own bodies,
    and mourn only for
        themselves."

ᵃCn: Heb *that they may desist*   ᵇSyr: Heb lacks *not*

**15.1** THEN Eliphaz the Temanite answered:

2 "Should the wise answer with
  windy knowledge,
  and fill themselves with the
  east wind?
3 Should they argue in
  unprofitable talk,
  or in words with which they
  can do no good?
4 But you are doing away with the
  fear of God,
  and hindering meditation
  before God.
5 For your iniquity teaches your
  mouth,
  and you choose the tongue of
  the crafty.
6 Your own mouth condemns you,
  and not I;
  your own lips testify against
  you.

7 "Are you the firstborn of the
  human race?
  Were you brought forth
  before the hills?
8 Have you listened in the council
  of God?
  And do you limit wisdom to
  yourself?
9 What do you know that we do
  not know?
  What do you understand that
  is not clear to us?
10 The gray-haired and the aged
  are on our side,
  those older than your father.
11 Are the consolations of God too
  small for you,
  or the word that deals gently
  with you?
12 Why does your heart carry you
  away,
  and why do your eyes flash, a
13 so that you turn your spirit
  against God,

and let such words go out of
  your mouth?
14 What are mortals, that they can
  be clean?
  Or those born of woman, that
  they can be righteous?
15 God puts no trust even in his
  holy ones,
  and the heavens are not clean
  in his sight;
16 how much less one who is
  abominable and corrupt,
  one who drinks iniquity like
  water!

17 "I will show you; listen to me;
  what I have seen I will
  declare—
18 what sages have told,
  and their ancestors have not
  hidden,
19 to whom alone the land was
  given,
  and no stranger passed
  among them.
20 The wicked writhe in pain all
  their days,
  through all the years that are
  laid up for the ruthless.
21 Terrifying sounds are in their
  ears;
  in prosperity the destroyer
  will come upon them.
22 They despair of returning from
  darkness,
  and they are destined for the
  sword.
23 They wander abroad for bread,
  saying, 'Where is it?'
  They know that a day of
  darkness is ready at
  hand;
24 distress and anguish terrify
  them;
  they prevail against them, like
  a king prepared for
  battle.

a Meaning of Heb uncertain

25 Because they stretched out
     their hands against God,
   and bid defiance to the
     Almighty, a
26 running stubbornly against him
     with a thick-bossed shield;
27 because they have covered their
     faces with their fat,
   and gathered fat upon their
     loins,
28 they will live in desolate cities,
   in houses that no one should
     inhabit,
   houses destined to become
     heaps of ruins;
29 they will not be rich, and their
     wealth will not endure,
   nor will they strike root in the
     earth; b
30 they will not escape from
     darkness;
   the flame will dry up their
     shoots,
   and their blossomc will be
     swept awayd by the
     wind.
31 Let them not trust in
     emptiness, deceiving
     themselves;
   for emptiness will be their
     recompense.
32 It will be paid in full before their
     time,
   and their branch will not be
     green.
33 They will shake off their unripe
     grape, like the vine,
   and cast off their blossoms,
     like the olive tree.
34 For the company of the godless
     is barren,
   and fire consumes the tents
     of bribery.
35 They conceive mischief and
     bring forth evil
   and their heart prepares
     deceit.”

## 1 CORINTHIANS 15.29–58

OTHERWISE, what will those people do who receive baptism on behalf of the dead? If the dead are not raised at all, why are people baptized on their behalf?

30 And why are we putting ourselves in danger every hour? 31 I die every day! That is as certain, brothers and sisters, e as my boasting of you—a boast that I make in Christ Jesus our Lord. 32 If with merely human hopes I fought with wild animals at Ephesus, what would I have gained by it? If the dead are not raised,

   “Let us eat and drink,
     for tomorrow we die.”
33 Do not be deceived:
   “Bad company ruins good
     morals.”
34 Come to a sober and right mind, and sin no more; for some people have no knowledge of God. I say this to your shame.

35 But someone will ask, “How are the dead raised? With what kind of body do they come?” 36 Fool! What you sow does not come to life unless it dies. 37 And as for what you sow, you do not sow the body that is to be, but a bare seed, perhaps of wheat or of some other grain. 38 But God gives it a body as he has chosen, and to each kind of seed its own body. 39 Not all flesh is alike, but there is one flesh for human beings, another for animals, another for birds, and another for fish. 40 There are both heavenly bodies and earthly bodies, but the glory of the heavenly is one thing, and that of the earthly is another. 41 There is one glory of the sun, and another glory of the moon, and another glory of the stars; indeed, star differs from star in glory.

42 So it is with the resurrection of the dead. What is sown is perishable,

a Traditional rendering of Heb *Shaddai*   b Vg: Meaning of Heb uncertain   c Gk: Heb *mouth*
d Cn: Heb *will depart*   e Gk *brothers*

what is raised is imperishable. [43]It is sown in dishonor, it is raised in glory. It is sown in weakness, it is raised in power. [44]It is sown a physical body, it is raised a spiritual body. If there is a physical body, there is also a spiritual body. [45]Thus it is written, "The first man, Adam, became a living being"; the last Adam became a life-giving spirit. [46]But it is not the spiritual that is first, but the physical, and then the spiritual. [47]The first man was from the earth, a man of dust; the second man is[a] from heaven. [48]As was the man of dust, so are those who are of the dust; and as is the man of heaven, so are those who are of heaven. [49]Just as we have borne the image of the man of dust, we will[b] also bear the image of the man of heaven.

50  What I am saying, brothers and sisters,[c] is this: flesh and blood cannot inherit the kingdom of God, nor does the perishable inherit the imperishable. [51]Listen, I will tell you a mystery! We will not all die,[d] but we will all be changed, [52]in a moment, in the twinkling of an eye, at the last trumpet. For the trumpet will sound, and the dead will be raised imperishable, and we will be changed. [53]For this perishable body must put on imperishability, and this mortal body must put on immortality. [54]When this perishable body puts on imperishability, and this mortal body puts on immortality, then the saying that is written will be fulfilled:

"Death has been swallowed up
    in victory."
[55]  "Where, O death, is your
        victory?
    Where, O death, is your
        sting?"

[56]The sting of death is sin, and the power of sin is the law. [57]But thanks be to God, who gives us the victory through our Lord Jesus Christ.

58  Therefore, my beloved,[e] be steadfast, immovable, always excelling in the work of the Lord, because you know that in the Lord your labor is not in vain.

## PSALM 39.1–13

*To the leader: to Jeduthun. A Psalm of David.*

I SAID, "I will guard my ways
        that I may not sin with my
            tongue;
    I will keep a muzzle on my
        mouth
        as long as the wicked are in
            my presence."
[2]  I was silent and still;
        I held my peace to no avail;
    my distress grew worse,
[3]      my heart became hot within
            me.
    While I mused, the fire burned;
        then I spoke with my tongue:

[4]  "LORD, let me know my end,
        and what is the measure of
            my days;
        let me know how fleeting my
            life is.
[5]  You have made my days a few
            handbreadths,
        and my lifetime is as nothing
            in your sight.
    Surely everyone stands as a
            mere breath.        *Selah*
[6]      Surely everyone goes about
            like a shadow.
    Surely for nothing they are in
            turmoil;
        they heap up, and do not
            know who will gather.

[7]  "And now, O Lord, what do I
            wait for?
    My hope is in you.
[8]  Deliver me from all my
            transgressions.
        Do not make me the scorn of
            the fool.

aOther ancient authorities add *the Lord*   bOther ancient authorities read *let us*   cGk *brothers*
dGk *fall asleep*   eGk *beloved brothers*

9 I am silent; I do not open my
      mouth,
   for it is you who have done
      it.
10 Remove your stroke from me;
   I am worn down by the
      blows[a] of your hand.

11 "You chastise mortals
      in punishment for sin,
   consuming like a moth what is
      dear to them;
      surely everyone is a mere
      breath.                    *Selah*

12 "Hear my prayer, O LORD,
   and give ear to my cry;

   do not hold your peace at my
      tears.
   For I am your passing guest,
      an alien, like all my forebears.
13 Turn your gaze away from me,
      that I may smile again,
   before I depart and am no
      more."

## PROVERBS 21.30–31

No wisdom, no understanding,
      no counsel,
   can avail against the LORD.
31 The horse is made ready for the
      day of battle,
   but the victory belongs to
      the LORD.

# AUGUST 25

## JOB 16.1—19.29

THEN Job answered:
2    "I have heard many such
      things;
   miserable comforters are you
      all.
3 Have windy words no limit?
   Or what provokes you that
      you keep on talking?
4 I also could talk as you do,
   if you were in my place;
   I could join words together
      against you,
   and shake my head at you.
5 I could encourage you with my
      mouth,
   and the solace of my lips
      would assuage your pain.

6 "If I speak, my pain is not
      assuaged,

   and if I forbear, how much of
      it leaves me?
7 Surely now God has worn me
      out;
   he has[b] made desolate all my
      company.
8 And he has[b] shriveled me up,
   which is a witness against
      me;
   my leanness has risen up
      against me,
   and it testifies to my face.
9 He has torn me in his wrath,
      and hated me;
   he has gnashed his teeth at
      me;
   my adversary sharpens his
      eyes against me.
10 They have gaped at me with
      their mouths;

they have struck me
    insolently on the cheek;
they mass themselves
    together against me.
11 God gives me up to the
    ungodly,
    and casts me into the hands
        of the wicked.
12 I was at ease, and he broke me
    in two;
    he seized me by the neck and
        dashed me to pieces;
he set me up as his target;
13    his archers surround me.
He slashes open my kidneys,
    and shows no mercy;
    he pours out my gall on the
        ground.
14 He bursts upon me again and
    again;
    he rushes at me like a
        warrior.
15 I have sewed sackcloth upon my
    skin,
    and have laid my strength in
        the dust.
16 My face is red with weeping,
    and deep darkness is on my
        eyelids,
17 though there is no violence in
    my hands,
    and my prayer is pure.

18 "O earth, do not cover my
    blood;
    let my outcry find no resting
        place.
19 Even now, in fact, my witness
    is in heaven,
    and he that vouches for me is
        on high.
20 My friends scorn me;
    my eye pours out tears to
        God,
21 that he would maintain the right
    of a mortal with God,
    as[a] one does for a neighbor.

22 For when a few years have
    come,
    I shall go the way from which
        I shall not return.

17.1 My spirit is broken, my days
    are extinct,
    the grave is ready for me.
2 Surely there are mockers
    around me,
    and my eye dwells on their
        provocation.

3 "Lay down a pledge for me with
    yourself;
    who is there that will give
        surety for me?
4 Since you have closed their
    minds to understanding,
    therefore you will not let
        them triumph.
5 Those who denounce friends for
    reward—
    the eyes of their children will
        fail.

6 "He has made me a byword of
    the peoples,
    and I am one before whom
        people spit.
7 My eye has grown dim from
    grief,
    and all my members are like a
        shadow.
8 The upright are appalled at this,
    and the innocent stir
        themselves up against
        the godless.
9 Yet the righteous hold to their
    way,
    and they that have clean
        hands grow stronger and
        stronger.
10 But you, come back now, all of
    you,
    and I shall not find a sensible
        person among you.

[a] Syr Vg Tg: Heb *and*

11 My days are past, my plans are
    broken off,
      the desires of my heart.
12 They make night into day;
    'The light,' they say, 'is near
      to the darkness.'[a]
13 If I look for Sheol as my house,
    if I spread my couch in
      darkness,
14 if I say to the Pit, 'You are my
    father,'
    and to the worm, 'My
      mother,' or 'My sister,'
15 where then is my hope?
    Who will see my hope?
16 Will it go down to the bars of
    Sheol?
    Shall we descend together
      into the dust?"

18.1 THEN Bildad the Shuhite answered:
2 "How long will you hunt for
    words?
    Consider, and then we shall
      speak.
3 Why are we counted as cattle?
    Why are we stupid in your
      sight?
4 You who tear yourself in your
    anger—
    shall the earth be forsaken
      because of you,
    or the rock be removed out
      of its place?

5 "Surely the light of the wicked
    is put out,
    and the flame of their fire
      does not shine.
6 The light is dark in their tent,
    and the lamp above them is
      put out.
7 Their strong steps are
    shortened,
    and their own schemes throw
      them down.
8 For they are thrust into a net
    by their own feet,

    and they walk into a pitfall.
9 A trap seizes them by the heel;
    a snare lays hold of them.
10 A rope is hid for them in the
    ground,
    a trap for them in the path.
11 Terrors frighten them on every
    side,
    and chase them at their heels.
12 Their strength is consumed by
    hunger,[b]
    and calamity is ready for their
      stumbling.
13 By disease their skin is
    consumed,[c]
    the firstborn of Death
      consumes their limbs.
14 They are torn from the tent in
    which they trusted,
    and are brought to the king of
      terrors.
15 In their tents nothing remains;
    sulfur is scattered upon their
      habitations.
16 Their roots dry up beneath,
    and their branches wither
      above.
17 Their memory perishes from
    the earth,
    and they have no name in the
      street.
18 They are thrust from light into
    darkness,
    and driven out of the world.
19 They have no offspring or
    descendant among their
      people,
    and no survivor where they
      used to live.
20 They of the west are appalled at
    their fate,
    and horror seizes those of the
      east.
21 Surely such are the dwellings of
    the ungodly,
    such is the place of those who
      do not know God."

[a] Meaning of Heb uncertain  [b] Or *Disaster is hungry for them*  [c] Cn: Heb *It consumes the limbs of his skin*

**19.1** THEN Job answered:
2 "How long will you torment me,
    and break me in pieces with
        words?
3 These ten times you have cast
        reproach upon me;
    are you not ashamed to
        wrong me?
4 And even if it is true that I have
        erred,
    my error remains with me.
5 If indeed you magnify
        yourselves against me,
    and make my humiliation an
        argument against me,
6 know then that God has put me
        in the wrong,
    and closed his net around me.
7 Even when I cry out, 'Violence!'
        I am not answered;
    I call aloud, but there is no
        justice.
8 He has walled up my way so
        that I cannot pass,
    and he has set darkness upon
        my paths.
9 He has stripped my glory from
        me,
    and taken the crown from my
        head.
10 He breaks me down on every
        side, and I am gone,
    he has uprooted my hope like
        a tree.
11 He has kindled his wrath against
        me,
    and counts me as his
        adversary.
12 His troops come on together;
    they have thrown up
        siegeworks[a] against me,
    and encamp around my tent.

13 "He has put my family far from
        me,
    and my acquaintances are
        wholly estranged from
        me.
14 My relatives and my close
        friends have failed me;
15 the guests in my house have
        forgotten me;
    my serving girls count me as a
        stranger;
    I have become an alien in
        their eyes.
16 I call to my servant, but he
        gives me no answer;
    I must myself plead with him.
17 My breath is repulsive to my
        wife;
    I am loathsome to my own
        family.
18 Even young children despise
        me;
    when I rise, they talk against
        me.
19 All my intimate friends abhor
        me,
    and those whom I loved have
        turned against me.
20 My bones cling to my skin and
        to my flesh,
    and I have escaped by the
        skin of my teeth.
21 Have pity on me, have pity on
        me, O you my friends,
    for the hand of God has
        touched me!
22 Why do you, like God, pursue
        me,
    never satisfied with my flesh?

23 "O that my words were written
        down!
    O that they were inscribed in
        a book!
24 O that with an iron pen and with
        lead
    they were engraved on a rock
        forever!
25 For I know that my Redeemer[b]
        lives,
    and that at the last he[c] will
        stand upon the earth;[d]

---

**a** Cn: Heb *their way*   **b** Or *Vindicator*   **c** Or *that he the Last*   **d** Heb *dust*

26 and after my skin has been thus
    destroyed,
      then in[a] my flesh I shall see
      God,[b]
27 whom I shall see on my side,[c]
    and my eyes shall behold, and
      not another.
    My heart faints within me!
28 If you say, 'How we will
      persecute him!'
    and, 'The root of the matter
      is found in him';
29 be afraid of the sword,
    for wrath brings the
      punishment of the sword,
    so that you may know there
      is a judgment."

## 1 CORINTHIANS 16.1–24

**N**ow concerning the collection for the saints: you should follow the directions I gave to the churches of Galatia. [2]On the first day of every week, each of you is to put aside and save whatever extra you earn, so that collections need not be taken when I come. [3]And when I arrive, I will send any whom you approve with letters to take your gift to Jerusalem. [4]If it seems advisable that I should go also, they will accompany me.

5 I will visit you after passing through Macedonia—for I intend to pass through Macedonia— [6]and perhaps I will stay with you or even spend the winter, so that you may send me on my way, wherever I go. [7]I do not want to see you now just in passing, for I hope to spend some time with you, if the Lord permits. [8]But I will stay in Ephesus until Pentecost, [9]for a wide door for effective work has opened to me, and there are many adversaries.

10 If Timothy comes, see that he has nothing to fear among you, for he is doing the work of the Lord just as I am; [11]therefore let no one despise him. Send him on his way in peace, so that he may come to me; for I am expecting him with the brothers.

12 Now concerning our brother Apollos, I strongly urged him to visit you with the other brothers, but he was not at all willing[d] to come now. He will come when he has the opportunity.

13 Keep alert, stand firm in your faith, be courageous, be strong. [14]Let all that you do be done in love.

15 Now, brothers and sisters,[e] you know that members of the household of Stephanas were the first converts in Achaia, and they have devoted themselves to the service of the saints; [16]I urge you to put yourselves at the service of such people, and of everyone who works and toils with them. [17]I rejoice at the coming of Stephanas and Fortunatus and Achaicus, because they have made up for your absence; [18]for they refreshed my spirit as well as yours. So give recognition to such persons.

19 The churches of Asia send greetings. Aquila and Prisca, together with the church in their house, greet you warmly in the Lord. [20]All the brothers and sisters[e] send greetings. Greet one another with a holy kiss.

21 I, Paul, write this greeting with my own hand. [22]Let anyone be accursed who has no love for the Lord. Our Lord, come![f] [23]The grace of the Lord Jesus be with you. [24]My love be with all of you in Christ Jesus. [g]

---

[a]Or *without*  [b]Meaning of Heb of this verse uncertain  [c]Or *for myself*  [d]Or *it was not at all God's will for him*  [e]Gk *brothers*  [f]Gk *Marana tha.* These Aramaic words can also be read *Maran atha,* meaning *Our Lord has come*  [g]Other ancient authorities add *Amen*

## PSALM 40.1–10

*To the leader. Of David. A Psalm.*

**I** WAITED patiently for the LORD;
    he inclined to me and heard
       my cry.
2 He drew me up from the
       desolate pit, **a**
    out of the miry bog,
and set my feet upon a rock,
    making my steps secure.
3 He put a new song in my
       mouth,
    a song of praise to our God.
Many will see and fear,
    and put their trust in the
       LORD.

4 Happy are those who make
    the LORD their trust,
who do not turn to the proud,
    to those who go astray after
      false gods.
5 You have multiplied, O LORD my
      God,
    your wondrous deeds and
      your thoughts toward us;
    none can compare with you.
Were I to proclaim and tell of
      them,
    they would be more than can
      be counted.

6 Sacrifice and offering you do not
      desire,

    but you have given me an
      open ear. **b**
Burnt offering and sin offering
    you have not required.
7 Then I said, "Here I am;
    in the scroll of the book it is
      written of me. **c**
8 I delight to do your will, O my
      God;
    your law is within my heart."

9 I have told the glad news of
      deliverance
    in the great congregation;
see, I have not restrained my
      lips,
    as you know, O LORD.
10 I have not hidden your saving
      help within my heart,
I have spoken of your
      faithfulness and your
      salvation;
I have not concealed your
      steadfast love and your
      faithfulness
from the great congregation.

## PROVERBS 22.1

**A** GOOD name is to be chosen
      rather than great riches,
and favor is better than
      silver or gold.

---

**a** Cn: Heb *pit of tumult*  **b** Heb *ears you have dug for me*  **c** Meaning of Heb uncertain

# AUGUST 26

JOB 20.1—22.30

THEN Zophar the Naamathite answered:
2 "Pay attention! My
thoughts urge me to
answer,
because of the agitation within
me.
3 I hear censure that insults me,
and a spirit beyond my
understanding answers
me.
4 Do you not know this from of
old,
ever since mortals were
placed on earth,
5 that the exulting of the wicked
is short,
and the joy of the godless is
but for a moment?
6 Even though they mount up
high as the heavens,
and their head reaches to the
clouds,
7 they will perish forever like
their own dung;
those who have seen them
will say, 'Where are
they?'
8 They will fly away like a dream,
and not be found;
they will be chased away like
a vision of the night.
9 The eye that saw them will see
them no more,
nor will their place behold
them any longer.
10 Their children will seek the
favor of the poor,
and their hands will give back
their wealth.
11 Their bodies, once full of youth,
will lie down in the dust with
them.

12 "Though wickedness is sweet in
their mouth,
though they hide it under
their tongues,
13 though they are loath to let it
go,
and hold it in their mouths,
14 yet their food is turned in their
stomachs;
it is the venom of asps within
them.
15 They swallow down riches and
vomit them up again;
God casts them out of their
bellies.
16 They will suck the poison of
asps;
the tongue of a viper will kill
them.
17 They will not look on the rivers,
the streams flowing with
honey and curds.
18 They will give back the fruit of
their toil,
and will not swallow it down;
from the profit of their trading
they will get no enjoyment.
19 For they have crushed and
abandoned the poor,
they have seized a house that
they did not build.

20 "They knew no quiet in their
bellies;
in their greed they let nothing
escape.
21 There was nothing left after
they had eaten;
therefore their prosperity will
not endure.
22 In full sufficiency they will be in
distress;
all the force of misery will
come upon them.

23  To fill their belly to the full
        God[a] will send his fierce
            anger into them,
        and rain it upon them as their
            food. [b]
24  They will flee from an iron
        weapon;
        a bronze arrow will strike
            them through.
25  It is drawn forth and comes out
        of their body,
        and the glittering point comes
            out of their gall;
        terrors come upon them.
26  Utter darkness is laid up for
        their treasures;
        a fire fanned by no one will
            devour them;
        what is left in their tent will
            be consumed.
27  The heavens will reveal their
        iniquity,
        and the earth will rise up
            against them.
28  The possessions of their house
            will be carried away,
        dragged off in the day of
            God's[c] wrath.
29  This is the portion of the wicked
            from God,
        the heritage decreed for them
            by God."


21.1  THEN Job answered:
  2  "Listen carefully to my words,
        and let this be your
            consolation.
  3  Bear with me, and I will speak;
        then after I have spoken,
            mock on.
  4  As for me, is my complaint
            addressed to mortals?
        Why should I not be
            impatient?
  5  Look at me, and be appalled,
        and lay your hand upon your
            mouth.

  6  When I think of it I am
            dismayed,
        and shuddering seizes my
            flesh.
  7  Why do the wicked live on,
        reach old age, and grow
            mighty in power?
  8  Their children are established in
            their presence,
        and their offspring before
            their eyes.
  9  Their houses are safe from fear,
        and no rod of God is upon
            them.
10  Their bull breeds without fail;
        their cow calves and never
            miscarries.
11  They send out their little ones
            like a flock,
        and their children dance
            around.
12  They sing to the tambourine and
            the lyre,
        and rejoice to the sound of
            the pipe.
13  They spend their days in
            prosperity,
        and in peace they go down to
            Sheol.
14  They say to God, 'Leave us
            alone!
        We do not desire to know
            your ways.
15  What is the Almighty, [d] that we
            should serve him?
        And what profit do we get if
            we pray to him?'
16  Is not their prosperity indeed
            their own achievement?[e]
        The plans of the wicked are
            repugnant to me.

17  "How often is the lamp of the
            wicked put out?
        How often does calamity
            come upon them?

aHeb *he*   bCn: Meaning of Heb uncertain   cHeb *his*   dTraditional rendering of Heb *Shaddai*
eHeb *in their hand*

How often does God<sup>a</sup>
distribute pains in his
anger?
18  How often are they like straw
before the wind,
and like chaff that the storm
carries away?
19  You say, 'God stores up their
iniquity for their
children.'
Let it be paid back to them,
so that they may know
it.
20  Let their own eyes see their
destruction,
and let them drink of the
wrath of the Almighty.<sup>b</sup>
21  For what do they care for their
household after them,
when the number of their
months is cut off?
22  Will any teach God knowledge,
seeing that he judges those
that are on high?
23  One dies in full prosperity,
being wholly at ease and
secure,
24  his loins full of milk
and the marrow of his bones
moist.
25  Another dies in bitterness of
soul,
never having tasted of good.
26  They lie down alike in the dust,
and the worms cover them.

27  "Oh, I know your thoughts,
and your schemes to wrong
me.
28  For you say, 'Where is the
house of the prince?
Where is the tent in which
the wicked lived?'
29  Have you not asked those who
travel the roads,
and do you not accept their
testimony,
30  that the wicked are spared in
the day of calamity,

and are rescued in the day of
wrath?
31  Who declares their way to their
face,
and who repays them for
what they have done?
32  When they are carried to the
grave,
a watch is kept over their
tomb.
33  The clods of the valley are
sweet to them;
everyone will follow after,
and those who went before
are innumerable.
34  How then will you comfort me
with empty nothings?
There is nothing left of your
answers but falsehood."


22.1  THEN Eliphaz the Temanite answered:
2  "Can a mortal be of use to God?
Can even the wisest be of
service to him?
3  Is it any pleasure to the
Almighty<sup>b</sup> if you are
righteous,
or is it gain to him if you
make your ways
blameless?
4  Is it for your piety that he
reproves you,
and enters into judgment with
you?
5  Is not your wickedness great?
There is no end to your
iniquities.
6  For you have exacted pledges
from your family for no
reason,
and stripped the naked of
their clothing.
7  You have given no water to the
weary to drink,
and you have withheld bread
from the hungry.

<sup>a</sup>Heb *he*   <sup>b</sup>Traditional rendering of Heb *Shaddai*

8 The powerful possess the land,
   and the favored live in it.
9 You have sent widows away
     empty-handed,
   and the arms of the orphans
     you have crushed. [a]
10 Therefore snares are around
     you,
   and sudden terror
     overwhelms you,
11 or darkness so that you cannot
     see;
   a flood of water covers you.

12 "Is not God high in the
     heavens?
   See the highest stars, how
     lofty they are!
13 Therefore you say, 'What does
     God know?
   Can he judge through the
     deep darkness?
14 Thick clouds enwrap him, so
     that he does not see,
   and he walks on the dome of
     heaven.'
15 Will you keep to the old way
   that the wicked have trod?
16 They were snatched away
     before their time;
   their foundation was washed
     away by a flood.
17 They said to God, 'Leave us
     alone,'
   and 'What can the Almighty[b]
     do to us?'[c]
18 Yet he filled their houses with
     good things—
   but the plans of the wicked
     are repugnant to me.
19 The righteous see it and are
     glad;
   the innocent laugh them to
     scorn,
20 saying, 'Surely our adversaries
     are cut off,
   and what they left, the fire
     has consumed.'

21 "Agree with God, [d] and be at
     peace;
   in this way good will come to
     you.
22 Receive instruction from his
     mouth,
   and lay up his words in your
     heart.
23 If you return to the Almighty, [b]
     you will be restored,
   if you remove
     unrighteousness from
     your tents,
24 if you treat gold like dust,
   and gold of Ophir like the
     stones of the
     torrent-bed,
25 and if the Almighty[b] is your
     gold
   and your precious silver,
26 then you will delight yourself in
     the Almighty, [b]
   and lift up your face to God.
27 You will pray to him, and he will
     hear you,
   and you will pay your vows.
28 You will decide on a matter, and
     it will be established for
     you,
   and light will shine on your
     ways.
29 When others are humiliated, you
     say it is pride;
   for he saves the humble.
30 He will deliver even those who
     are guilty;
   they will escape because of
     the cleanness of your
     hands."[e]

---

[a] Gk Syr Tg Vg: Heb *were crushed*  [b] Traditional rendering of Heb *Shaddai*  [c] Gk Syr: Heb *them*
[d] Heb *him*  [e] Meaning of Heb uncertain

## 2 CORINTHIANS 1.1–11

**P**AUL, an apostle of Christ Jesus by the will of God, and Timothy our brother,

To the church of God that is in Corinth, including all the saints throughout Achaia:

2   Grace to you and peace from God our Father and the Lord Jesus Christ.

3   Blessed be the God and Father of our Lord Jesus Christ, the Father of mercies and the God of all consolation, [4]who consoles us in all our affliction, so that we may be able to console those who are in any affliction with the consolation with which we ourselves are consoled by God. [5]For just as the sufferings of Christ are abundant for us, so also our consolation is abundant through Christ. [6]If we are being afflicted, it is for your consolation and salvation; if we are being consoled, it is for your consolation, which you experience when you patiently endure the same sufferings that we are also suffering. [7]Our hope for you is unshaken; for we know that as you share in our sufferings, so also you share in our consolation.

8   We do not want you to be unaware, brothers and sisters, [a] of the affliction we experienced in Asia; for we were so utterly, unbearably crushed that we despaired of life itself. [9]Indeed, we felt that we had received the sentence of death so that we would rely not on ourselves but on God who raises the dead. [10]He who rescued us from so deadly a peril will continue to rescue us; on him we have set our hope that he will rescue us again, [11]as you also join in helping us by your prayers, so that many will give thanks on our[b] behalf for the blessing granted us through the prayers of many.

## PSALM 40.11–17

**D**o not, O LORD, withhold your mercy from me;
    let your steadfast love and
        your faithfulness
    keep me safe forever.
12  For evils have encompassed me
        without number;
    my iniquities have overtaken
        me,
        until I cannot see;
    they are more than the hairs of
        my head,
        and my heart fails me.

13  Be pleased, O LORD, to deliver
        me;
        O LORD, make haste to help
        me.
14  Let all those be put to shame
        and confusion
    who seek to snatch away my
        life;
    let those be turned back and
        brought to dishonor
    who desire my hurt.
15  Let those be appalled because
        of their shame
    who say to me, "Aha, Aha!"

16  But may all who seek you
        rejoice and be glad in you;
    may those who love your
        salvation
    say continually, "Great is the
        LORD!"
17  As for me, I am poor and
        needy,
    but the Lord takes thought
        for me.
    You are my help and my
        deliverer;
        do not delay, O my God.

---

a Gk *brothers*   b Other ancient authorities read *your*

## PROVERBS 22.2–4

THE rich and the poor have this
    in common:
the LORD is the maker of
    them all.
3  The clever see danger and hide;
    but the simple go on, and
      suffer for it.
4  The reward for humility and fear
    of the LORD
    is riches and honor and life.

# AUGUST 27

## JOB 23.1—27.23

THEN Job answered:
2  "Today also my complaint
    is bitter;ᵃ
hisᵇ hand is heavy despite
    my groaning.
3  Oh, that I knew where I might
    find him,
    that I might come even to his
      dwelling!
4  I would lay my case before him,
    and fill my mouth with
      arguments.
5  I would learn what he would
    answer me,
    and understand what he
      would say to me.
6  Would he contend with me in
    the greatness of his
      power?
    No; but he would give heed
      to me.
7  There an upright person could
    reason with him,
    and I should be acquitted
      forever by my judge.

8  "If I go forward, he is not
    there;
    or backward, I cannot
      perceive him;
9  on the left he hides, and I
    cannot behold him;
    I turnᶜ to the right, but I
      cannot see him.
10  But he knows the way that I
    take;
    when he has tested me, I
      shall come out like gold.
11  My foot has held fast to his
    steps;
    I have kept his way and have
      not turned aside.
12  I have not departed from the
    commandment of his lips;
    I have treasured inᵈ my
      bosom the words of his
      mouth.
13  But he stands alone and who
    can dissuade him?
    What he desires, that he
      does.
14  For he will complete what he
    appoints for me;
    and many such things are in
      his mind.
15  Therefore I am terrified at his
    presence;
    when I consider, I am in
      dread of him.
16  God has made my heart faint;
    the Almightyᵉ has terrified
      me;

ᵃSyr Vg Tg: Heb *rebellious*  ᵇGk Syr: Heb *my*  ᶜSyr Vg: Heb *he turns*  ᵈGk Vg: Heb *from*
ᵉTraditional rendering of Heb *Shaddai*

17  If only I could vanish in
        darkness,
      and thick darkness would
        cover my face!ᵃ

24.1  "WHY are times not kept by
        the Almighty, ᵇ
      and why do those who know
        him never see his days?
2   The wickedᶜ remove
        landmarks;
      they seize flocks and pasture
        them.
3   They drive away the donkey of
        the orphan;
      they take the widow's ox for
        a pledge.
4   They thrust the needy off the
        road;
      the poor of the earth all hide
        themselves.
5   Like wild asses in the desert
        they go out to their toil,
      scavenging in the wasteland
        food for their young.
6   They reap in a field not their
        own
      and they glean in the vineyard
        of the wicked.
7   They lie all night naked, without
        clothing,
      and have no covering in the
        cold.
8   They are wet with the rain of
        the mountains,
      and cling to the rock for want
        of shelter.

9   "There are those who snatch
        the orphan child from the
        breast,
      and take as a pledge the
        infant of the poor.
10  They go about naked, without
        clothing;
      though hungry, they carry the
        sheaves;

11  between their terracesᵈ they
        press out oil;
      they tread the wine presses,
        but suffer thirst.
12  From the city the dying groan,
        and the throat of the wounded
        cries for help;
      yet God pays no attention to
        their prayer.

13  "There are those who rebel
        against the light,
      who are not acquainted with
        its ways,
      and do not stay in its paths.
14  The murderer rises at dusk
        to kill the poor and needy,
      and in the night is like a thief.
15  The eye of the adulterer also
        waits for the twilight,
      saying, 'No eye will see me';
      and he disguises his face.
16  In the dark they dig through
        houses;
      by day they shut themselves
        up;
      they do not know the light.
17  For deep darkness is morning to
        all of them;
      for they are friends with the
        terrors of deep darkness.

18  "Swift are they on the face of
        the waters;
      their portion in the land is
        cursed;
      no treader turns toward their
        vineyards.
19  Drought and heat snatch away
        the snow waters;
      so does Sheol those who have
        sinned.
20  The womb forgets them;
      the worm finds them sweet;
      they are no longer remembered;
      so wickedness is broken like
        a tree.

ᵃOr *But I am not destroyed by the darkness; he has concealed the thick darkness from me*
ᵇTraditional rendering of Heb *Shaddai*  ᶜGk: Heb *they*  ᵈMeaning of Heb uncertain

21 "They harm[a] the childless
    woman,
      and do no good to the widow.
22 Yet God[b] prolongs the life of
    the mighty by his power;
      they rise up when they
      despair of life.
23 He gives them security, and
    they are supported;
      his eyes are upon their ways.
24 They are exalted a little while,
    and then are gone;
      they wither and fade like the
      mallow;[c]
      they are cut off like the heads
      of grain.
25 If it is not so, who will prove
    me a liar,
      and show that there is
      nothing in what I say?"

25.1 THEN Bildad the Shuhite answered:
2 "Dominion and fear are with
    God;[d]
    he makes peace in his high
    heaven.
3 Is there any number to his
    armies?
    Upon whom does his light not
    arise?
4 How then can a mortal be
    righteous before God?
    How can one born of woman
    be pure?
5 If even the moon is not bright
    and the stars are not pure in
    his sight,
6 how much less a mortal, who is
    a maggot,
    and a human being, who is a
    worm!"

26.1 THEN Job answered:
2 "How you have helped one who
    has no power!
    How you have assisted the
    arm that has no strength!
3 How you have counseled one
    who has no wisdom,
    and given much good advice!
4 With whose help have you
    uttered words,
    and whose spirit has come
    forth from you?
5 The shades below tremble,
    the waters and their
    inhabitants.
6 Sheol is naked before God,
    and Abaddon has no covering.
7 He stretches out Zaphon[e] over
    the void,
    and hangs the earth upon
    nothing.
8 He binds up the waters in his
    thick clouds,
    and the cloud is not torn open
    by them.
9 He covers the face of the full
    moon,
    and spreads over it his cloud.
10 He has described a circle on the
    face of the waters,
    at the boundary between light
    and darkness.
11 The pillars of heaven tremble,
    and are astounded at his
    rebuke.
12 By his power he stilled the Sea;
    by his understanding he
    struck down Rahab.
13 By his wind the heavens were
    made fair;
    his hand pierced the fleeing
    serpent.
14 These are indeed but the
    outskirts of his ways;
    and how small a whisper do
    we hear of him!
    But the thunder of his power
    who can understand?"

27.1 JOB again took up his discourse and
said:
2 "As God lives, who has taken
    away my right,

aGk Tg: Heb *feed on* or *associate with*  bHeb *he*  cGk: Heb *like all others*  dHeb *him*  eOr *the North*

and the Almighty, [a] who has
   made my soul bitter,
3 as long as my breath is in me
   and the spirit of God is in my
    nostrils,
4 my lips will not speak falsehood,
   and my tongue will not utter
    deceit.
5 Far be it from me to say that
   you are right;
   until I die I will not put away
    my integrity from me.
6 I hold fast my righteousness,
   and will not let it go;
   my heart does not reproach
    me for any of my days.

7 "May my enemy be like the
   wicked,
   and may my opponent be like
    the unrighteous.
8 For what is the hope of the
   godless when God cuts
    them off,
   when God takes away their
    lives?
9 Will God hear their cry
   when trouble comes upon
    them?
10 Will they take delight in the
   Almighty? [a]
   Will they call upon God at all
    times?
11 I will teach you concerning the
   hand of God;
   that which is with the
    Almighty [a] I will not
    conceal.
12 All of you have seen it
   yourselves;
   why then have you become
    altogether vain?

13 "This is the portion of the
   wicked with God,
   and the heritage that
    oppressors receive from
    the Almighty: [a]

14 If their children are multiplied, it
   is for the sword;
   and their offspring have not
    enough to eat.
15 Those who survive them the
   pestilence buries,
   and their widows make no
    lamentation.
16 Though they heap up silver like
   dust,
   and pile up clothing like
    clay—
17 they may pile it up, but the just
   will wear it,
   and the innocent will divide
    the silver.
18 They build their houses like
   nests,
   like booths made by sentinels
    of the vineyard.
19 They go to bed with wealth, but
   will do so no more;
   they open their eyes, and it is
    gone.
20 Terrors overtake them like a
   flood;
   in the night a whirlwind
    carries them off.
21 The east wind lifts them up and
   they are gone;
   it sweeps them out of their
    place.
22 It [b] hurls at them without pity;
   they flee from its [c] power in
    headlong flight.
23 It [b] claps its [c] hands at them,
   and hisses at them from its [c]
    place.

# 2 CORINTHIANS 1.12—2.11

INDEED, this is our boast, the testimony of our conscience: we have behaved in the world with frankness [d] and godly sincerity, not by earthly wisdom but by the grace of God—and all the more toward you. [13] For we write you nothing other than

a Traditional rendering of Heb *Shaddai*  b Or *He* (that is God)  c Or *his*  d Other ancient authorities
read *holiness*

what you can read and also understand; I hope you will understand until the end— [14]as you have already understood us in part—that on the day of the Lord Jesus we are your boast even as you are our boast.

15 Since I was sure of this, I wanted to come to you first, so that you might have a double favor;[a] [16]I wanted to visit you on my way to Macedonia, and to come back to you from Macedonia and have you send me on to Judea. [17]Was I vacillating when I wanted to do this? Do I make my plans according to ordinary human standards,[b] ready to say "Yes, yes" and "No, no" at the same time? [18]As surely as God is faithful, our word to you has not been "Yes and No." [19]For the Son of God, Jesus Christ, whom we proclaimed among you, Silvanus and Timothy and I, was not "Yes and No"; but in him it is always "Yes." [20]For in him every one of God's promises is a "Yes." For this reason it is through him that we say the "Amen," to the glory of God. [21]But it is God who establishes us with you in Christ and has anointed us, [22]by putting his seal on us and giving us his Spirit in our hearts as a first installment.

23 But I call on God as witness against me: it was to spare you that I did not come again to Corinth. [24]I do not mean to imply that we lord it over your faith; rather, we are workers with you for your joy, because you stand firm in the faith. [2.1]So I made up my mind not to make you another painful visit. [2]For if I cause you pain, who is there to make me glad but the one whom I have pained? [3]And I wrote as I did, so that when I came, I might not suffer pain from those who should have made me rejoice; for I am confident about all of you, that my joy would be the joy of all of you. [4]For I wrote you out of much distress and anguish of heart and with many tears, not to cause you pain, but to let you know the abundant love that I have for you.

5 But if anyone has caused pain, he has caused it not to me, but to some extent—not to exaggerate it—to all of you. [6]This punishment by the majority is enough for such a person; [7]so now instead you should forgive and console him, so that he may not be overwhelmed by excessive sorrow. [8]So I urge you to reaffirm your love for him. [9]I wrote for this reason: to test you and to know whether you are obedient in everything. [10]Anyone whom you forgive, I also forgive. What I have forgiven, if I have forgiven anything, has been for your sake in the presence of Christ. [11]And we do this so that we may not be outwitted by Satan; for we are not ignorant of his designs.

# PSALM 41.1–13

*To the leader. A Psalm of David.*

Happy are those who consider
    the poor;[c]
    the Lord delivers them in
      the day of trouble.
2  The Lord protects them and
    keeps them alive;
    they are called happy in the
      land.
    You do not give them up to
      the will of their enemies.
3  The Lord sustains them on their
    sickbed;
    in their illness you heal all
      their infirmities.[d]

4  As for me, I said, "O Lord, be
    gracious to me;
    heal me, for I have sinned
      against you."
5  My enemies wonder in malice
    when I will die, and my name
      perish.

---

[a]Other ancient authorities read *pleasure*  [b]Gk *according to the flesh*  [c]Or *weak*  [d]Heb *you change all his bed*

6 And when they come to see
me, they utter empty
words,
while their hearts gather
mischief;
when they go out, they tell it
abroad.
7 All who hate me whisper
together about me;
they imagine the worst for
me.

8 They think that a deadly thing
has fastened on me,
that I will not rise again from
where I lie.
9 Even my bosom friend in whom
I trusted,
who ate of my bread, has
lifted the heel against
me.
10 But you, O LORD, be gracious
to me,
and raise me up, that I may
repay them.

11 By this I know that you are
pleased with me;
because my enemy has not
triumphed over me.
12 But you have upheld me
because of my integrity,
and set me in your presence
forever.

13 Blessed be the LORD, the God
of Israel,
from everlasting to
everlasting.
Amen and Amen.

## PROVERBS 22.5–6

THORNS and snares are in the
way of the perverse;
the cautious will keep far
from them.
6 Train children in the right way,
and when old, they will not
stray.

# AUGUST 28

## JOB 28.1—30.31

SURELY there is a mine for
silver,
and a place for gold to be
refined.
2 Iron is taken out of the earth,
and copper is smelted from
ore.
3 Miners put[a] an end to
darkness,
and search out to the farthest
bound
the ore in gloom and deep
darkness.
4 They open shafts in a valley
away from human
habitation;
they are forgotten by
travelers,
they sway suspended, remote
from people.
5 As for the earth, out of it
comes bread;
but underneath it is turned up
as by fire.

a Heb *He puts*

6 Its stones are the place of
    sapphires, **a**
  and its dust contains gold.

7 "That path no bird of prey
    knows,
  and the falcon's eye has not
    seen it.
8 The proud wild animals have not
    trodden it;
  the lion has not passed over
    it.

9 "They put their hand to the
    flinty rock,
  and overturn mountains by
    the roots.
10 They cut out channels in the
    rocks,
  and their eyes see every
    precious thing.
11 The sources of the rivers they
    probe; **b**
  hidden things they bring to
    light.

12 "But where shall wisdom be
    found?
  And where is the place of
    understanding?
13 Mortals do not know the way to
    it, **c**
  and it is not found in the land
    of the living.
14 The deep says, 'It is not in me,'
  and the sea says, 'It is not
    with me.'
15 It cannot be gotten for gold,
  and silver cannot be weighed
    out as its price.
16 It cannot be valued in the gold
    of Ophir,
  in precious onyx or
    sapphire. **a**
17 Gold and glass cannot equal it,
  nor can it be exchanged for
    jewels of fine gold.

18 No mention shall be made of
    coral or of crystal;
  the price of wisdom is above
    pearls.
19 The chrysolite of Ethiopia **d**
    cannot compare with it,
  nor can it be valued in pure
    gold.

20 "Where then does wisdom come
    from?
  And where is the place of
    understanding?
21 It is hidden from the eyes of all
    living,
  and concealed from the birds
    of the air.
22 Abaddon and Death say,
  'We have heard a rumor of it
    with our ears.'

23 "God understands the way to it,
  and he knows its place.
24 For he looks to the ends of the
    earth,
  and sees everything under
    the heavens.
25 When he gave to the wind its
    weight,
  and apportioned out the
    waters by measure;
26 when he made a decree for the
    rain,
  and a way for the
    thunderbolt;
27 then he saw it and declared it;
  he established it, and
    searched it out.
28 And he said to humankind,
  'Truly, the fear of the Lord,
    that is wisdom;
  and to depart from evil is
    understanding.' "

29.1 JOB again took up his discourse and
said:
2 "Oh, that I were as in the
    months of old,

as in the days when God
watched over me;
3 when his lamp shone over my
head,
and by his light I walked
through darkness;
4 when I was in my prime,
when the friendship of God
was upon my tent;
5 when the Almighty[a] was still
with me,
when my children were
around me;
6 when my steps were washed
with milk,
and the rock poured out for
me streams of oil!
7 When I went out to the gate of
the city,
when I took my seat in the
square,
8 the young men saw me and
withdrew,
and the aged rose up and
stood;
9 the nobles refrained from
talking,
and laid their hands on their
mouths;
10 the voices of princes were
hushed,
and their tongues stuck to the
roof of their mouths.
11 When the ear heard, it
commended me,
and when the eye saw, it
approved;
12 because I delivered the poor
who cried,
and the orphan who had no
helper.
13 The blessing of the wretched
came upon me,
and I caused the widow's
heart to sing for joy.
14 I put on righteousness, and it
clothed me;

my justice was like a robe and
a turban.
15 I was eyes to the blind,
and feet to the lame.
16 I was a father to the needy,
and I championed the cause of
the stranger.
17 I broke the fangs of the
unrighteous,
and made them drop their
prey from their teeth.
18 Then I thought, 'I shall die in
my nest,
and I shall multiply my days
like the phoenix;[b]
19 my roots spread out to the
waters,
with the dew all night on my
branches;
20 my glory was fresh with me,
and my bow ever new in my
hand.'

21 "They listened to me, and
waited,
and kept silence for my
counsel.
22 After I spoke they did not speak
again,
and my word dropped upon
them like dew. [c]
23 They waited for me as for the
rain;
they opened their mouths as
for the spring rain.
24 I smiled on them when they had
no confidence;
and the light of my
countenance they did not
extinguish. [d]
25 I chose their way, and sat as
chief,
and I lived like a king among
his troops,
like one who comforts
mourners.

[a] Traditional rendering of Heb *Shaddai*   [b] Or *like sand*   [c] Heb lacks *like dew*   [d] Meaning of Heb
uncertain

**30.1** "But now they make sport of
me,
those who are younger than
I,
whose fathers I would have
disdained
to set with the dogs of my
flock.
2 What could I gain from the
strength of their hands?
All their vigor is gone.
3 Through want and hard hunger
they gnaw the dry and
desolate ground,
4 they pick mallow and the leaves
of bushes,
and to warm themselves the
roots of broom.
5 They are driven out from
society;
people shout after them as
after a thief.
6 In the gullies of wadis they must
live,
in holes in the ground, and in
the rocks.
7 Among the bushes they bray;
under the nettles they huddle
together.
8 A senseless, disreputable brood,
they have been whipped out
of the land.

9 "And now they mock me in
song;
I am a byword to them.
10 They abhor me, they keep aloof
from me;
they do not hesitate to spit at
the sight of me.
11 Because God has loosed my
bowstring and humbled
me,
they have cast off restraint in
my presence.
12 On my right hand the rabble
rise up;
they send me sprawling,
and build roads for my ruin.
13 They break up my path,
they promote my calamity;
no one restrains[a] them.
14 As through a wide breach they
come;
amid the crash they roll on.
15 Terrors are turned upon me;
my honor is pursued as by
the wind,
and my prosperity has passed
away like a cloud.

16 "And now my soul is poured out
within me;
days of affliction have taken
hold of me.
17 The night racks my bones,
and the pain that gnaws me
takes no rest.
18 With violence he seizes my
garment;[b]
he grasps me by[c] the collar
of my tunic.
19 He has cast me into the mire,
and I have become like dust
and ashes.
20 I cry to you and you do not
answer me;
I stand, and you merely look
at me.
21 You have turned cruel to me;
with the might of your hand
you persecute me.
22 You lift me up on the wind, you
make me ride on it,
and you toss me about in the
roar of the storm.
23 I know that you will bring me to
death,
and to the house appointed
for all living.

24 "Surely one does not turn
against the needy,[d]
when in disaster they cry for
help.[e]

25  Did I not weep for those whose
        day was hard?
      Was not my soul grieved for
        the poor?
26  But when I looked for good, evil
        came;
      and when I waited for light,
        darkness came.
27  My inward parts are in turmoil,
        and are never still;
      days of affliction come to
        meet me.
28  I go about in sunless gloom;
      I stand up in the assembly
        and cry for help.
29  I am a brother of jackals,
      and a companion of ostriches.
30  My skin turns black and falls
        from me,
      and my bones burn with heat.
31  My lyre is turned to mourning,
      and my pipe to the voice of
        those who weep.


## 2 CORINTHIANS 2.12–17

WHEN I came to Troas to proclaim the good news of Christ, a door was opened for me in the Lord; 13but my mind could not rest because I did not find my brother Titus there. So I said farewell to them and went on to Macedonia.

14  But thanks be to God, who in Christ always leads us in triumphal procession, and through us spreads in every place the fragrance that comes from knowing him. 15For we are the aroma of Christ to God among those who are being saved and among those who are perishing; 16to the one a fragrance from death to death, to the other a fragrance from life to life. Who is sufficient for these things? 17For we are not peddlers of God's word like so many; a but in Christ we speak as persons of sincerity, as persons sent from God and standing in his presence.

## PSALM 42.1–11

*To the leader. A Maskil of the Korahites.*

As a deer longs for flowing
        streams,
      so my soul longs for you,
        O God.
2  My soul thirsts for God,
      for the living God.
    When shall I come and behold
      the face of God?
3  My tears have been my food
      day and night,
    while people say to me
        continually,
      "Where is your God?"

4  These things I remember,
      as I pour out my soul:
    how I went with the throng, b
      and led them in procession to
        the house of God,
    with glad shouts and songs of
        thanksgiving,
      a multitude keeping festival.
5  Why are you cast down, O my
        soul,
      and why are you disquieted
        within me?
    Hope in God; for I shall again
        praise him,
      my help 6and my God.

    My soul is cast down within me;
      therefore I remember you
    from the land of Jordan and of
        Hermon,
      from Mount Mizar.
7  Deep calls to deep
      at the thunder of your
        cataracts;
    all your waves and your billows
      have gone over me.
8  By day the LORD commands his
        steadfast love,
      and at night his song is with
        me,
      a prayer to the God of my
        life.

aOther ancient authorities read *like the others*    bMeaning of Heb uncertain

9 I say to God, my rock,
    "Why have you forgotten me?
  Why must I walk about
      mournfully
    because the enemy oppresses
      me?"
10 As with a deadly wound in my
      body,
    my adversaries taunt me,
  while they say to me
      continually,
    "Where is your God?"
11 Why are you cast down, O my
      soul,

and why are you disquieted
    within me?
Hope in God; for I shall again
    praise him,
  my help and my God.

## PROVERBS 22.7

THE rich rules over the poor,
  and the borrower is the slave
    of the lender.

# AUGUST 29

JOB 31.1—33.33

"I HAVE made a covenant with my
      eyes;
    how then could I look upon a
      virgin?
2 What would be my portion from
      God above,
    and my heritage from the
      Almighty[a] on high?
3 Does not calamity befall the
      unrighteous,
    and disaster the workers of
      iniquity?
4 Does he not see my ways,
    and number all my steps?

5 "If I have walked with
      falsehood,
    and my foot has hurried to
      deceit—
6 let me be weighed in a just
      balance,
    and let God know my
      integrity!—

7 if my step has turned aside from
      the way,
    and my heart has followed my
      eyes,
    and if any spot has clung to
      my hands;
8 then let me sow, and another
      eat;
    and let what grows for me be
      rooted out.

9 "If my heart has been enticed
      by a woman,
    and I have lain in wait at my
      neighbor's door;
10 then let my wife grind for
      another,
    and let other men kneel over
      her.
11 For that would be a heinous
      crime;
    that would be a criminal
      offense;

a Traditional rendering of Heb *Shaddai*

12 for that would be a fire
      consuming down to
      Abaddon,
   and it would burn to the root
      all my harvest.

13 "If I have rejected the cause of
      my male or female
      slaves,
   when they brought a
      complaint against me;
14 what then shall I do when God
      rises up?
   When he makes inquiry, what
      shall I answer him?
15 Did not he who made me in the
      womb make them?
   And did not one fashion us in
      the womb?

16 "If I have withheld anything that
      the poor desired,
   or have caused the eyes of
      the widow to fail,
17 or have eaten my morsel alone,
   and the orphan has not eaten
      from it—
18 for from my youth I reared the
      orphan[a] like a father,
   and from my mother's womb
      I guided the widow[b]—
19 if I have seen anyone perish for
      lack of clothing,
   or a poor person without
      covering,
20 whose loins have not blessed
      me,
   and who was not warmed
      with the fleece of my
      sheep;
21 if I have raised my hand against
      the orphan,
   because I saw I had
      supporters at the gate;
22 then let my shoulder blade fall
      from my shoulder,
   and let my arm be broken
      from its socket.

23 For I was in terror of calamity
      from God,
   and I could not have faced his
      majesty.

24 "If I have made gold my trust,
   or called fine gold my
      confidence;
25 if I have rejoiced because my
      wealth was great,
   or because my hand had
      gotten much;
26 if I have looked at the sun[c]
      when it shone,
   or the moon moving in
      splendor,
27 and my heart has been secretly
      enticed,
   and my mouth has kissed my
      hand;
28 this also would be an iniquity to
      be punished by the
      judges,
   for I should have been false
      to God above.

29 "If I have rejoiced at the ruin of
      those who hated me,
   or exulted when evil overtook
      them—
30 I have not let my mouth sin
   by asking for their lives with
      a curse—
31 if those of my tent ever said,
   'O that we might be sated
      with his flesh!'[d]—
32 the stranger has not lodged in
      the street;
   I have opened my doors to
      the traveler—
33 if I have concealed my
      transgressions as others
      do, [e]
   by hiding my iniquity in my
      bosom,
34 because I stood in great fear of
      the multitude,

aHeb *him*   bHeb *her*   cHeb *the light*   dMeaning of Heb uncertain   eOr *as Adam did*

and the contempt of families
    terrified me,
so that I kept silence, and did
    not go out of doors—
35 Oh, that I had one to hear me!
    (Here is my signature! let the
        Almighty<sup>a</sup> answer me!)
    Oh, that I had the indictment
        written by my adversary!
36 Surely I would carry it on my
        shoulder;
    I would bind it on me like a
        crown;
37 I would give him an account of
        all my steps;
    like a prince I would approach
        him.

38 "If my land has cried out against
        me,
    and its furrows have wept
        together;
39 if I have eaten its yield without
        payment,
    and caused the death of its
        owners;
40 let thorns grow instead of
        wheat,
    and foul weeds instead of
        barley."

The words of Job are ended.

**32.**1 So these three men ceased to answer Job, because he was righteous in his own eyes. 2Then Elihu son of Barachel the Buzite, of the family of Ram, became angry. He was angry at Job because he justified himself rather than God; 3he was angry also at Job's three friends because they had found no answer, though they had declared Job to be in the wrong.<sup>b</sup> 4Now Elihu had waited to speak to Job, because they were older than he. 5But when Elihu saw that there was no answer in the mouths of these three men, he became angry.

6 Elihu son of Barachel the Buzite
answered:
    "I am young in years,
        and you are aged;
    therefore I was timid and afraid
        to declare my opinion to you.
7 I said, 'Let days speak,
    and many years teach
        wisdom.'
8 But truly it is the spirit in a
        mortal,
    the breath of the Almighty, <sup>a</sup>
        that makes for
        understanding.
9 It is not the old<sup>c</sup> that are wise,
    nor the aged that understand
        what is right.
10 Therefore I say, 'Listen to me;
    let me also declare my
        opinion.'

11 "See, I waited for your words,
    I listened for your wise
        sayings,
    while you searched out what
        to say.
12 I gave you my attention,
    but there was in fact no one
        that confuted Job,
    no one among you that
        answered his words.
13 Yet do not say, 'We have found
        wisdom;
    God may vanquish him, not a
        human.'
14 He has not directed his words
        against me,
    and I will not answer him with
        your speeches.

15 "They are dismayed, they
        answer no more;
    they have not a word to say.
16 And am I to wait, because they
        do not speak,
    because they stand there, and
        answer no more?
17 I also will give my answer;

<sup>a</sup>Traditional rendering of Heb *Shaddai*  <sup>b</sup>Another ancient tradition reads *answer, and had put God in the wrong*  <sup>c</sup>Gk Syr Vg: Heb *many*

I also will declare my opinion.
18 For I am full of words;
      the spirit within me constrains
        me.
19 My heart is indeed like wine
        that has no vent;
      like new wineskins, it is ready
        to burst.
20 I must speak, so that I may find
        relief;
      I must open my lips and
        answer.
21 I will not show partiality to any
        person
      or use flattery toward
        anyone.
22 For I do not know how to
        flatter—
      or my Maker would soon put
        an end to me!

33.1 "But now, hear my speech,
        O Job,
      and listen to all my words.
2  See, I open my mouth;
      the tongue in my mouth
        speaks.
3  My words declare the
        uprightness of my heart,
      and what my lips know they
        speak sincerely.
4  The spirit of God has made me,
      and the breath of the
        Almighty[a] gives me life.
5  Answer me, if you can;
      set your words in order
        before me; take your
        stand.
6  See, before God I am as you
        are;
      I too was formed from a piece
        of clay.
7  No fear of me need terrify you;
      my pressure will not be heavy
        on you.

8  "Surely, you have spoken in my
        hearing,
      and I have heard the sound of
        your words.
9  You say, 'I am clean, without
        transgression;
      I am pure, and there is no
        iniquity in me.
10 Look, he finds occasions against
        me,
      he counts me as his enemy;
11 he puts my feet in the stocks,
      and watches all my paths.'

12 "But in this you are not right. I
        will answer you:
      God is greater than any
        mortal.
13 Why do you contend against
        him,
      saying, 'He will answer none
        of my[b] words'?
14 For God speaks in one way,
      and in two, though people do
        not perceive it.
15 In a dream, in a vision of the
        night,
      when deep sleep falls on
        mortals,
      while they slumber on their
        beds,
16 then he opens their ears,
      and terrifies them with
        warnings,
17 that he may turn them aside
        from their deeds,
      and keep them from pride,
18 to spare their souls from the
        Pit,
      their lives from traversing the
        River.
19 They are also chastened with
        pain upon their beds,
      and with continual strife in
        their bones,
20 so that their lives loathe bread,
      and their appetites dainty
        food.
21 Their flesh is so wasted away
        that it cannot be seen;

a Traditional rendering of Heb *Shaddai*   b Compare Gk: Heb *his*

and their bones, once
  invisible, now stick out.
22 Their souls draw near the Pit,
  and their lives to those who
    bring death.
23 Then, if there should be for one
    of them an angel,
  a mediator, one of a
    thousand,
  one who declares a person
    upright,
24 and he is gracious to that
    person, and says,
  'Deliver him from going down
    into the Pit;
  I have found a ransom;
25 let his flesh become fresh with
    youth;
  let him return to the days of
    his youthful vigor.'
26 Then he prays to God, and is
    accepted by him,
  he comes into his presence
    with joy,
  and God<sup>a</sup> repays him for his
    righteousness.
27   That person sings to others
    and says,
  'I sinned, and perverted what
    was right,
  and it was not paid back to
    me.
28 He has redeemed my soul from
    going down to the Pit,
  and my life shall see the
    light.'

29   "God indeed does all these
    things,
  twice, three times, with
    mortals,
30 to bring back their souls from
    the Pit,
  so that they may see the light
    of life.<sup>b</sup>
31 Pay heed, Job, listen to me;
  be silent, and I will speak.

32   If you have anything to say,
    answer me;
  speak, for I desire to justify
    you.
33 If not, listen to me;
  be silent, and I will teach you
    wisdom."

## 2 CORINTHIANS 3.1–18

ARE we beginning to commend ourselves again? Surely we do not need, as some do, letters of recommendation to you or from you, do we? <sup>2</sup>You yourselves are our letter, written on our<sup>c</sup> hearts, to be known and read by all; <sup>3</sup>and you show that you are a letter of Christ, prepared by us, written not with ink but with the Spirit of the living God, not on tablets of stone but on tablets of human hearts.

4 Such is the confidence that we have through Christ toward God. <sup>5</sup>Not that we are competent of ourselves to claim anything as coming from us; our competence is from God, <sup>6</sup>who has made us competent to be ministers of a new covenant, not of letter but of spirit; for the letter kills, but the Spirit gives life.

7 Now if the ministry of death, chiseled in letters on stone tablets,<sup>d</sup> came in glory so that the people of Israel could not gaze at Moses' face because of the glory of his face, a glory now set aside, <sup>8</sup>how much more will the ministry of the Spirit come in glory? <sup>9</sup>For if there was glory in the ministry of condemnation, much more does the ministry of justification abound in glory! <sup>10</sup>Indeed, what once had glory has lost its glory because of the greater glory; <sup>11</sup>for if what was set aside came through glory, much more has the permanent come in glory!

12 Since, then, we have such a hope, we act with great boldness, <sup>13</sup>not

a Heb *he*   b Syr: Heb *to be lighted with the light of life*   c Other ancient authorities read *your*   d Gk *on stones* like Moses, who put a veil over his face to keep the people of Israel from gazing at the end of the glory that[a] was being set aside. [14]But their minds were hardened. Indeed, to this very day, when they hear the reading of the old covenant, that same veil is still there, since only in Christ is it set aside. [15]Indeed, to this very day whenever Moses is read, a veil lies over their minds; [16]but when one turns to the Lord, the veil is removed. [17]Now the Lord is the Spirit, and where the Spirit of the Lord is, there is freedom. [18]And all of us, with unveiled faces, seeing the glory of the Lord as though reflected in a mirror, are being transformed into the same image from one degree of glory to another; for this comes from the Lord, the Spirit.

## PSALM 43.1–5

Vindicate me, O God, and
    defend my cause
  against an ungodly people;
from those who are deceitful
    and unjust
deliver me!
2 For you are the God in whom I
    take refuge;
  why have you cast me off?
Why must I walk about
    mournfully

because of the oppression of
  the enemy?

3 O send out your light and your
    truth;
  let them lead me;
let them bring me to your holy
    hill
  and to your dwelling.
4 Then I will go to the altar of
    God,
  to God my exceeding joy;
and I will praise you with the
    harp,
  O God, my God.

5 Why are you cast down, O my
    soul,
  and why are you disquieted
    within me?
Hope in God; for I shall again
    praise him,
  my help and my God.

## PROVERBS 22.8–9

Whoever sows injustice will
    reap calamity,
  and the rod of anger will
    fail.
9 Those who are generous are
    blessed,
  for they share their bread
    with the poor.

a Gk *of what*

# AUGUST 30

JOB 34.1—36.33

T HEN Elihu continued and said:
2 "Hear my words, you
    wise men,
   and give ear to me, you who
    know;
3 for the ear tests words
   as the palate tastes food.
4 Let us choose what is right;
   let us determine among
    ourselves what is good.
5 For Job has said, 'I am innocent,
   and God has taken away my
    right;
6 in spite of being right I am
    counted a liar;
   my wound is incurable,
    though I am without
    transgression.'
7 Who is there like Job,
   who drinks up scoffing like
    water,
8 who goes in company with
    evildoers
   and walks with the wicked?
9 For he has said, 'It profits one
    nothing
   to take delight in God.'

10 "Therefore, hear me, you who
    have sense,
   far be it from God that he
    should do wickedness,
   and from the Almighty[a] that
    he should do wrong.
11 For according to their deeds he
    will repay them,
   and according to their ways
    he will make it befall
    them.
12 Of a truth, God will not do
    wickedly,
   and the Almighty[a] will not
    pervert justice.
13 Who gave him charge over the
    earth
   and who laid on him[b] the
    whole world?
14 If he should take back his
    spirit[c] to himself,
   and gather to himself his
    breath,
15 all flesh would perish together,
   and all mortals return to dust.

16 "If you have understanding,
    hear this;
   listen to what I say.
17 Shall one who hates justice
    govern?
   Will you condemn one who is
    righteous and mighty,
18 who says to a king, 'You
    scoundrel!'
   and to princes, 'You wicked
    men!';
19 who shows no partiality to
    nobles,
   nor regards the rich more
    than the poor,
   for they are all the work of
    his hands?
20 In a moment they die;
   at midnight the people are
    shaken and pass away,
   and the mighty are taken
    away by no human hand.

21 "For his eyes are upon the
    ways of mortals,
   and he sees all their steps.
22 There is no gloom or deep
    darkness
   where evildoers may hide
    themselves.

---

[a] Traditional rendering of Heb *Shaddai*  [b] Heb lacks *on him*  [c] Heb *his heart his spirit*

23 For he has not appointed a
    time[a] for anyone
  to go before God in judgment.
24 He shatters the mighty without
    investigation,
  and sets others in their place.
25 Thus, knowing their works,
  he overturns them in the
    night, and they are
    crushed.
26 He strikes them for their
    wickedness
  while others look on,
27 because they turned aside from
    following him,
  and had no regard for any of
    his ways,
28 so that they caused the cry of
    the poor to come to him,
  and he heard the cry of the
    afflicted—
29 When he is quiet, who can
    condemn?
  When he hides his face, who
    can behold him,
  whether it be a nation or an
    individual?—
30 so that the godless should not
    reign,
  or those who ensnare the
    people.

31 "For has anyone said to God,
  'I have endured punishment; I
    will not offend any more;
32 teach me what I do not see;
  if I have done iniquity, I will
    do it no more'?
33 Will he then pay back to suit
    you,
  because you reject it?
  For you must choose, and not I;
  therefore declare what you
    know. [b]
34 Those who have sense will say
    to me,
  and the wise who hear me
    will say,

35 'Job speaks without knowledge,
  his words are without insight.'
36 Would that Job were tried to the
    limit,
  because his answers are
    those of the wicked.
37 For he adds rebellion to his sin;
  he claps his hands among us,
  and multiplies his words
    against God."

35.1 ELIHU continued and said:
2 "Do you think this to be just?
  You say, 'I am in the right
    before God.'
3 If you ask, 'What advantage
    have I?
  How am I better off than if I
    had sinned?'
4 I will answer you
  and your friends with you.
5 Look at the heavens and see;
  observe the clouds, which are
    higher than you.
6 If you have sinned, what do you
    accomplish against him?
  And if your transgressions are
    multiplied, what do you
    do to him?
7 If you are righteous, what do
    you give to him;
  or what does he receive from
    your hand?
8 Your wickedness affects others
    like you,
  and your righteousness, other
    human beings.

9 "Because of the multitude of
    oppressions people cry
    out;
  they call for help because of
    the arm of the mighty.
10 But no one says, 'Where is God
    my Maker,
  who gives strength in the
    night,

---

[a]Cn: Heb *yet*  [b]Meaning of Heb of verses 29-33 uncertain

11 who teaches us more than the
    animals of the earth,
  and makes us wiser than the
    birds of the air?'
12 There they cry out, but he does
    not answer,
  because of the pride of
    evildoers.
13 Surely God does not hear an
    empty cry,
  nor does the Almighty[a]
    regard it.
14 How much less when you say
    that you do not see him,
  that the case is before him,
    and you are waiting for
    him!
15 And now, because his anger
    does not punish,
  and he does not greatly heed
    transgression, [b]
16 Job opens his mouth in empty
    talk,
  he multiplies words without
    knowledge."

**36.**1 ELIHU continued and said:
2 "Bear with me a little, and I will
    show you,
  for I have yet something to
    say on God's behalf.
3 I will bring my knowledge from
    far away,
  and ascribe righteousness to
    my Maker.
4 For truly my words are not
    false;
  one who is perfect in
    knowledge is with you.

5 "Surely God is mighty and does
    not despise any;
  he is mighty in strength of
    understanding.
6 He does not keep the wicked
    alive,
  but gives the afflicted their
    right.

7 He does not withdraw his eyes
    from the righteous,
  but with kings on the throne
  he sets them forever, and
    they are exalted.
8 And if they are bound in fetters
  and caught in the cords of
    affliction,
9 then he declares to them their
    work
  and their transgressions, that
    they are behaving
    arrogantly.
10 He opens their ears to
    instruction,
  and commands that they
    return from iniquity.
11 If they listen, and serve him,
  they complete their days in
    prosperity,
  and their years in
    pleasantness.
12 But if they do not listen, they
    shall perish by the
    sword,
  and die without knowledge.

13 "The godless in heart cherish
    anger;
  they do not cry for help when
    he binds them.
14 They die in their youth,
  and their life ends in shame. [c]
15 He delivers the afflicted by their
    affliction,
  and opens their ear by
    adversity.
16 He also allured you out of
    distress
  into a broad place where
    there was no constraint,
  and what was set on your
    table was full of fatness.

17 "But you are obsessed with the
    case of the wicked;
  judgment and justice seize
    you.

[a]Traditional rendering of Heb *Shaddai*  [b]Theodotion Symmachus Compare Vg: Meaning of Heb uncertain  [c]Heb *ends among the temple prostitutes*

18 Beware that wrath does not
        entice you into scoffing,
    and do not let the greatness
        of the ransom turn you
        aside.
19 Will your cry avail to keep you
        from distress,
    or will all the force of your
        strength?
20 Do not long for the night,
    when peoples are cut off in
        their place.
21 Beware! Do not turn to iniquity;
    because of that you have
        been tried by affliction.
22 See, God is exalted in his
        power;
    who is a teacher like him?
23 Who has prescribed for him his
        way,
    or who can say, 'You have
        done wrong'?

24 "Remember to extol his work,
    of which mortals have sung.
25 All people have looked on it;
    everyone watches it from far
        away.
26 Surely God is great, and we do
        not know him;
    the number of his years is
        unsearchable.
27 For he draws up the drops of
        water;
    he distills[a] his mist in rain,
28 which the skies pour down
    and drop upon mortals
        abundantly.
29 Can anyone understand the
        spreading of the clouds,
    the thunderings of his
        pavilion?
30 See, he scatters his lightning
        around him
    and covers the roots of the
        sea.
31 For by these he governs
        peoples;

    he gives food in abundance.
32 He covers his hands with the
        lightning,
    and commands it to strike the
        mark.
33 Its crashing[b] tells about him;
    he is jealous[b] with anger
        against iniquity.

# 2 CORINTHIANS 4.1–12

THEREFORE, since it is by God's mercy that we are engaged in this ministry, we do not lose heart. [2]We have renounced the shameful things that one hides; we refuse to practice cunning or to falsify God's word; but by the open statement of the truth we commend ourselves to the conscience of everyone in the sight of God. [3]And even if our gospel is veiled, it is veiled to those who are perishing. [4]In their case the god of this world has blinded the minds of the unbelievers, to keep them from seeing the light of the gospel of the glory of Christ, who is the image of God. [5]For we do not proclaim ourselves; we proclaim Jesus Christ as Lord and ourselves as your slaves for Jesus' sake. [6]For it is the God who said, "Let light shine out of darkness," who has shone in our hearts to give the light of the knowledge of the glory of God in the face of Jesus Christ.

7 But we have this treasure in clay jars, so that it may be made clear that this extraordinary power belongs to God and does not come from us. [8]We are afflicted in every way, but not crushed; perplexed, but not driven to despair; [9]persecuted, but not forsaken; struck down, but not destroyed; [10]always carrying in the body the death of Jesus, so that the life of Jesus may also be made visible in our bodies. [11]For while we live, we are always being given up to death for Jesus' sake, so that the life of Jesus may be made visi-

a Cn: Heb *they distill*   b Meaning of Heb uncertain

ble in our mortal flesh. [12]So death is at work in us, but life in you.

## PSALM 44.1–8

*To the leader. Of the Korahites. A Maskil.*

WE have heard with our ears, O God,
our ancestors have told us,
what deeds you performed in
their days,
in the days of old:
2 you with your own hand drove
out the nations,
but them you planted;
you afflicted the peoples,
but them you set free;
3 for not by their own sword did
they win the land,
nor did their own arm give
them victory;
but your right hand, and your
arm,
and the light of your
countenance,
for you delighted in them.

4 You are my King and my God;
you command[a] victories for
Jacob.

5 Through you we push down our
foes;
through your name we tread
down our assailants.
6 For not in my bow do I trust,
nor can my sword save me.
7 But you have saved us from our
foes,
and have put to confusion
those who hate us.
8 In God we have boasted
continually,
and we will give thanks to
your name forever. *Selah*

## PROVERBS 22.10–12

DRIVE out a scoffer, and strife
goes out;
quarreling and abuse will
cease.
11 Those who love a pure heart
and are gracious in
speech
will have the king as a friend.
12 The eyes of the LORD keep
watch over knowledge,
but he overthrows the words
of the faithless.

# AUGUST 31

## JOB 37.1—39.30

"AT this also my heart
trembles,
and leaps out of its place.
2 Listen, listen to the thunder of
his voice
and the rumbling that comes
from his mouth.

3 Under the whole heaven he lets
it loose,
and his lightning to the
corners of the earth.
4 After it his voice roars;
he thunders with his majestic
voice

aGk Syr: Heb *You are my King, O God; command*

and he does not restrain the
    lightnings[a] when his
    voice is heard.
5 God thunders wondrously with
    his voice;
    he does great things that we
      cannot comprehend.
6 For to the snow he says, 'Fall
    on the earth';
    and the shower of rain, his
      heavy shower of rain,
7 serves as a sign on everyone's
    hand,
    so that all whom he has made
      may know it. [b]
8 Then the animals go into their
    lairs
    and remain in their dens.
9 From its chamber comes the
    whirlwind,
    and cold from the scattering
      winds.
10 By the breath of God ice is
    given,
    and the broad waters are
      frozen fast.
11 He loads the thick cloud with
    moisture;
    the clouds scatter his
      lightning.
12 They turn round and round by
    his guidance,
    to accomplish all that he
      commands them
    on the face of the habitable
      world.
13 Whether for correction, or for
    his land,
    or for love, he causes it to
      happen.

14 "Hear this, O Job;
    stop and consider the
      wondrous works of God.
15 Do you know how God lays his
    command upon them,
    and causes the lightning of his
    cloud to shine?

16 Do you know the balancings of
    the clouds,
    the wondrous works of the
      one whose knowledge is
      perfect,
17 you whose garments are hot
    when the earth is still
      because of the south
      wind?
18 Can you, like him, spread out
    the skies,
    hard as a molten mirror?
19 Teach us what we shall say to
    him;
    we cannot draw up our case
      because of darkness.
20 Should he be told that I want to
    speak?
    Did anyone ever wish to be
      swallowed up?
21 Now, no one can look on the
    light
    when it is bright in the skies,
    when the wind has passed
      and cleared them.
22 Out of the north comes golden
    splendor;
    around God is awesome
      majesty.
23 The Almighty[c]—we cannot find
    him;
    he is great in power and
      justice,
    and abundant righteousness
      he will not violate.
24 Therefore mortals fear him;
    he does not regard any who
      are wise in their own
      conceit."

38.1 THEN the LORD answered Job out of
the whirlwind:
2 "Who is this that darkens
    counsel by words without
    knowledge?
3 Gird up your loins like a man,
    I will question you, and you
      shall declare to me.

a Heb *them*  b Meaning of Heb of verse 7 uncertain  c Traditional rendering of Heb *Shaddai*

4 "Where were you when I laid
      the foundation of the
      earth?
   Tell me, if you have
      understanding.
5 Who determined its
      measurements—surely
      you know!
   Or who stretched the line
      upon it?
6 On what were its bases sunk,
   or who laid its cornerstone
7 when the morning stars sang
      together
   and all the heavenly beings[a]
      shouted for joy?

8 "Or who shut in the sea with
      doors
   when it burst out from the
      womb?—
9 when I made the clouds its
      garment,
   and thick darkness its
      swaddling band,
10 and prescribed bounds for it,
   and set bars and doors,
11 and said, 'Thus far shall you
      come, and no farther,
   and here shall your proud
      waves be stopped'?

12 "Have you commanded the
      morning since your days
      began,
   and caused the dawn to know
      its place,
13 so that it might take hold of the
      skirts of the earth,
   and the wicked be shaken out
      of it?
14 It is changed like clay under the
      seal,
   and it is dyed[b] like a
      garment.
15 Light is withheld from the
      wicked,

and their uplifted arm is
      broken.
16 "Have you entered into the
      springs of the sea,
   or walked in the recesses of
      the deep?
17 Have the gates of death been
      revealed to you,
   or have you seen the gates of
      deep darkness?
18 Have you comprehended the
      expanse of the earth?
   Declare, if you know all this.

19 "Where is the way to the
      dwelling of light,
   and where is the place of
      darkness,
20 that you may take it to its
      territory
   and that you may discern the
      paths to its home?
21 Surely you know, for you were
      born then,
   and the number of your days
      is great!

22 "Have you entered the
      storehouses of the snow,
   or have you seen the
      storehouses of the hail,
23 which I have reserved for the
      time of trouble,
   for the day of battle and war?
24 What is the way to the place
      where the light is
      distributed,
   or where the east wind is
      scattered upon the earth?

25 "Who has cut a channel for the
      torrents of rain,
   and a way for the
      thunderbolt,
26 to bring rain on a land where no
      one lives,

a Heb *sons of God*   b Cn: Heb *and they stand forth*

on the desert, which is empty
of human life,
27 to satisfy the waste and
desolate land,
and to make the ground put
forth grass?

28 "Has the rain a father,
or who has begotten the
drops of dew?
29 From whose womb did the ice
come forth,
and who has given birth to
the hoarfrost of heaven?
30 The waters become hard like
stone,
and the face of the deep is
frozen.

31 "Can you bind the chains of the
Pleiades,
or loose the cords of Orion?
32 Can you lead forth the
Mazzaroth in their
season,
or can you guide the Bear
with its children?
33 Do you know the ordinances of
the heavens?
Can you establish their rule
on the earth?

34 "Can you lift up your voice to
the clouds,
so that a flood of waters may
cover you?
35 Can you send forth lightnings,
so that they may go
and say to you, 'Here we
are'?
36 Who has put wisdom in the
inward parts, a
or given understanding to the
mind? a
37 Who has the wisdom to number
the clouds?

Or who can tilt the
waterskins of the
heavens,
38 when the dust runs into a mass
and the clods cling together?

39 "Can you hunt the prey for the
lion,
or satisfy the appetite of the
young lions,
40 when they crouch in their dens,
or lie in wait in their covert?
41 Who provides for the raven its
prey,
when its young ones cry to
God,
and wander about for lack of
food?

39.1 "Do you know when the
mountain goats give
birth?
Do you observe the calving of
the deer?
2 Can you number the months
that they fulfill,
and do you know the time
when they give birth,
3 when they crouch to give birth
to their offspring,
and are delivered of their
young?
4 Their young ones become
strong, they grow up in
the open;
they go forth, and do not
return to them.

5 "Who has let the wild ass go
free?
Who has loosed the bonds of
the swift ass,
6 to which I have given the
steppe for its home,
the salt land for its dwelling
place?
7 It scorns the tumult of the city;

a Meaning of Heb uncertain

it does not hear the shouts of
the driver.
8 It ranges the mountains as its
pasture,
and it searches after every
green thing.

9 "Is the wild ox willing to serve
you?
Will it spend the night at your
crib?
10 Can you tie it in the furrow with
ropes,
or will it harrow the valleys
after you?
11 Will you depend on it because
its strength is great,
and will you hand over your
labor to it?
12 Do you have faith in it that it
will return,
and bring your grain to your
threshing floor? a

13 "The ostrich's wings flap wildly,
though its pinions lack
plumage. b
14 For it leaves its eggs to the
earth,
and lets them be warmed on
the ground,
15 forgetting that a foot may crush
them,
and that a wild animal may
trample them.
16 It deals cruelly with its young,
as if they were not its
own;
though its labor should be in
vain, yet it has no fear;
17 because God has made it forget
wisdom,
and given it no share in
understanding.
18 When it spreads its plumes
aloft, b
it laughs at the horse and its
rider.

19 "Do you give the horse its
might?
Do you clothe its neck with
mane?
20 Do you make it leap like the
locust?
Its majestic snorting is
terrible.
21 It paws c violently, exults
mightily;
it goes out to meet the
weapons.
22 It laughs at fear, and is not
dismayed;
it does not turn back from the
sword.
23 Upon it rattle the quiver,
the flashing spear, and the
javelin.
24 With fierceness and rage it
swallows the ground;
it cannot stand still at the
sound of the trumpet.
25 When the trumpet sounds, it
says 'Aha!'
From a distance it smells the
battle,
the thunder of the captains,
and the shouting.

26 "Is it by your wisdom that the
hawk soars,
and spreads its wings toward
the south?
27 Is it at your command that the
eagle mounts up
and makes its nest on high?
28 It lives on the rock and makes
its home
in the fastness of the rocky
crag.
29 From there it spies the prey;
its eyes see it from far away.
30 Its young ones suck up blood;
and where the slain are, there
it is."

a Heb *your grain and your threshing floor*   b Meaning of Heb uncertain   c Gk Syr Vg: Heb *they dig*

## 2 CORINTHIANS 4.13—5.10

**B**UT just as we have the same spirit of faith that is in accordance with scripture—"I believed, and so I spoke"—we also believe, and so we speak, [14]because we know that the one who raised the Lord Jesus will raise us also with Jesus, and will bring us with you into his presence. [15]Yes, everything is for your sake, so that grace, as it extends to more and more people, may increase thanksgiving, to the glory of God.

16 So we do not lose heart. Even though our outer nature is wasting away, our inner nature is being renewed day by day. [17]For this slight momentary affliction is preparing us for an eternal weight of glory beyond all measure, [18]because we look not at what can be seen but at what cannot be seen; for what can be seen is temporary, but what cannot be seen is eternal.

[5.1] FOR we know that if the earthly tent we live in is destroyed, we have a building from God, a house not made with hands, eternal in the heavens. [2]For in this tent we groan, longing to be clothed with our heavenly dwelling— [3]if indeed, when we have taken it off[a] we will not be found naked. [4]For while we are still in this tent, we groan under our burden, because we wish not to be unclothed but to be further clothed, so that what is mortal may be swallowed up by life. [5]He who has prepared us for this very thing is God, who has given us the Spirit as a guarantee.

6 So we are always confident; even though we know that while we are at home in the body we are away from the Lord— [7]for we walk by faith, not by sight. [8]Yes, we do have confidence, and we would rather be away from the body and at home with the Lord. [9]So whether we are at home or away, we make it our aim to please him. [10]For all of us must appear before the judgment seat of Christ, so that each may receive recompense for what has been done in the body, whether good or evil.

## PSALM 44.9–26

**Y**ET you have rejected us and abased us,
and have not gone out with
our armies.
10 You made us turn back from
the foe,
and our enemies have gotten
spoil.
11 You have made us like sheep for
slaughter,
and have scattered us among
the nations.
12 You have sold your people for a
trifle,
demanding no high price for
them.

13 You have made us the taunt of
our neighbors,
the derision and scorn of
those around us.
14 You have made us a byword
among the nations,
a laughingstock[b] among the
peoples.
15 All day long my disgrace is
before me,
and shame has covered my
face
16 at the words of the taunters and
revilers,
at the sight of the enemy and
the avenger.

17 All this has come upon us,
yet we have not forgotten
you,
or been false to your
covenant.
18 Our heart has not turned back,
nor have our steps departed
from your way,

---

[a]Other ancient authorities read *put it on*  [b]Heb *a shaking of the head*

19  yet you have broken us in the
        haunt of jackals,
    and covered us with deep
        darkness.

20  If we had forgotten the name of
        our God,
    or spread out our hands to a
        strange god,
21  would not God discover this?
        For he knows the secrets of
        the heart.
22  Because of you we are being
        killed all day long,
    and accounted as sheep for
        the slaughter.

23  Rouse yourself! Why do you
        sleep, O Lord?

    Awake, do not cast us off
        forever!
24  Why do you hide your face?
    Why do you forget our
        affliction and oppression?
25  For we sink down to the dust;
        our bodies cling to the
        ground.
26  Rise up, come to our help.
        Redeem us for the sake of
        your steadfast love.

## PROVERBS 22.13

THE lazy person says, "There is
        a lion outside!
    I shall be killed in the
        streets!"

# SEPTEMBER 1

## JOB 40.1—42.17

AND the LORD said to Job:
2  "Shall a faultfinder
    contend with the
    Almighty? a
Anyone who argues with God
    must respond."

3  Then Job answered the LORD:
4  "See, I am of small account;
        what shall I answer you?
    I lay my hand on my mouth.
5  I have spoken once, and I will
        not answer;
    twice, but will proceed no
        further."

6  Then the LORD answered Job out
of the whirlwind:
7  "Gird up your loins like a man;

    I will question you, and you
        declare to me.
8  Will you even put me in the
        wrong?
    Will you condemn me that
        you may be justified?
9  Have you an arm like God,
        and can you thunder with a
        voice like his?

10  "Deck yourself with majesty and
        dignity;
    clothe yourself with glory and
        splendor.
11  Pour out the overflowings of
        your anger,
    and look on all who are
        proud, and abase them.
12  Look on all who are proud, and
        bring them low;

a Traditional rendering of Heb *Shaddai*

tread down the wicked where
     they stand.
13  Hide them all in the dust
     together;
     bind their faces in the world
       below. ᵃ
14  Then I will also acknowledge to
       you
     that your own right hand can
       give you victory.

15   "Look at Behemoth,
     which I made just as I made
       you;
     it eats grass like an ox.
16  Its strength is in its loins,
     and its power in the muscles
       of its belly.
17  It makes its tail stiff like a
       cedar;
     the sinews of its thighs are
       knit together.
18  Its bones are tubes of bronze,
     its limbs like bars of iron.

19   "It is the first of the great acts
       of God—
     only its Maker can approach it
       with the sword.
20  For the mountains yield food for
       it
     where all the wild animals
       play.
21  Under the lotus plants it lies,
     in the covert of the reeds and
       in the marsh.
22  The lotus trees cover it for
       shade;
     the willows of the wadi
       surround it.
23  Even if the river is turbulent, it
       is not frightened;
     it is confident though Jordan
       rushes against its mouth.
24  Can one take it with hooksᵇ
     or pierce its nose with a
       snare?

41ᶜ.1  "Can you draw out
     Leviathanᵈ with a
       fishhook,
     or press down its tongue with
       a cord?
2   Can you put a rope in its nose,
     or pierce its jaw with a hook?
3   Will it make many supplications
       to you?
     Will it speak soft words to
       you?
4   Will it make a covenant with you
       to be taken as your servant
       forever?
5   Will you play with it as with a
       bird,
     or will you put it on leash for
       your girls?
6   Will traders bargain over it?
     Will they divide it up among
       the merchants?
7   Can you fill its skin with
       harpoons,
     or its head with fishing
       spears?
8   Lay hands on it;
     think of the battle; you will
       not do it again!
9ᵉ  Any hope of capturing itᶠ will
       be disappointed;
     were not even the godsᵍ
       overwhelmed at the sight
       of it?
10  No one is so fierce as to dare to
       stir it up.
     Who can stand before it?ʰ
11  Who can confront itʰ and be
       safe?ⁱ
     —under the whole heaven,
       who?ʲ

12   "I will not keep silence
       concerning its limbs,
     or its mighty strength, or its
       splendid frame.

---

ᵃHeb *the hidden place*   ᵇCn: Heb *in his eyes*   ᶜCh 40.25 in Heb   ᵈOr *the crocodile*   ᵉCh 41.1 in Heb
ᶠHeb *of it*   ᵍCn Compare Symmachus Syr: Heb *one is*   ʰHeb *me*   ⁱGk: Heb *that I shall repay*
ʲHeb *to me*

13 Who can strip off its outer
    garment?
    Who can penetrate its double
    coat of mail? [a]
14 Who can open the doors of its
    face?
    There is terror all around its
    teeth.
15 Its back [b] is made of shields in
    rows,
    shut up closely as with a seal.
16 One is so near to another
    that no air can come between
    them.
17 They are joined one to another;
    they clasp each other and
    cannot be separated.
18 Its sneezes flash forth light,
    and its eyes are like the
    eyelids of the dawn.
19 From its mouth go flaming
    torches;
    sparks of fire leap out.
20 Out of its nostrils comes smoke,
    as from a boiling pot and
    burning rushes.
21 Its breath kindles coals,
    and a flame comes out of its
    mouth.
22 In its neck abides strength,
    and terror dances before it.
23 The folds of its flesh cling
    together;
    it is firmly cast and
    immovable.
24 Its heart is as hard as stone,
    as hard as the lower
    millstone.
25 When it raises itself up the gods
    are afraid;
    at the crashing they are
    beside themselves.
26 Though the sword reaches it, it
    does not avail,
    nor does the spear, the dart,
    or the javelin.
27 It counts iron as straw,
    and bronze as rotten wood.

28 The arrow cannot make it flee;
    slingstones, for it, are turned
    to chaff.
29 Clubs are counted as chaff;
    it laughs at the rattle of
    javelins.
30 Its underparts are like sharp
    potsherds;
    it spreads itself like a
    threshing sledge on the
    mire.
31 It makes the deep boil like a
    pot;
    it makes the sea like a pot of
    ointment.
32 It leaves a shining wake behind
    it;
    one would think the deep to
    be white-haired.
33 On earth it has no equal,
    a creature without fear.
34 It surveys everything that is
    lofty;
    it is king over all that are
    proud."

42.1 THEN Job answered the LORD:
 2 "I know that you can do all
    things,
    and that no purpose of yours
    can be thwarted.
 3 'Who is this that hides counsel
    without knowledge?'
    Therefore I have uttered what I
    did not understand,
    things too wonderful for me,
    which I did not know.
 4 'Hear, and I will speak;
    I will question you, and you
    declare to me.'
 5 I had heard of you by the
    hearing of the ear,
    but now my eye sees you;
 6 therefore I despise myself,
    and repent in dust and
    ashes."

 7 After the LORD had spoken these

a Gk: Heb *bridle*   b Cn Compare Gk Vg: Heb *pride*

words to Job, the LORD said to Eliphaz the Temanite: "My wrath is kindled against you and against your two friends; for you have not spoken of me what is right, as my servant Job has. 8Now therefore take seven bulls and seven rams, and go to my servant Job, and offer up for yourselves a burnt offering; and my servant Job shall pray for you, for I will accept his prayer not to deal with you according to your folly; for you have not spoken of me what is right, as my servant Job has done." 9So Eliphaz the Temanite and Bildad the Shuhite and Zophar the Naamathite went and did what the LORD had told them; and the LORD accepted Job's prayer.

10  And the LORD restored the fortunes of Job when he had prayed for his friends; and the LORD gave Job twice as much as he had before. 11Then there came to him all his brothers and sisters and all who had known him before, and they ate bread with him in his house; they showed him sympathy and comforted him for all the evil that the LORD had brought upon him; and each of them gave him a piece of moneya and a gold ring. 12The LORD blessed the latter days of Job more than his beginning; and he had fourteen thousand sheep, six thousand camels, a thousand yoke of oxen, and a thousand donkeys. 13He also had seven sons and three daughters. 14He named the first Jemimah, the second Keziah, and the third Keren-happuch. 15In all the land there were no women so beautiful as Job's daughters; and their father gave them an inheritance along with their brothers. 16After this Job lived one hundred and forty years, and saw his children, and his children's children, four generations. 17And Job died, old and full of days.

# 2 CORINTHIANS 5.11–21

THEREFORE, knowing the fear of the Lord, we try to persuade others; but we ourselves are well known to God, and I hope that we are also well known to your consciences. 12We are not commending ourselves to you again, but giving you an opportunity to boast about us, so that you may be able to answer those who boast in outward appearance and not in the heart. 13For if we are beside ourselves, it is for God; if we are in our right mind, it is for you. 14For the love of Christ urges us on, because we are convinced that one has died for all; therefore all have died. 15And he died for all, so that those who live might live no longer for themselves, but for him who died and was raised for them.

16  From now on, therefore, we regard no one from a human point of view;b even though we once knew Christ from a human point of view,b we know him no longer in that way. 17So if anyone is in Christ, there is a new creation: everything old has passed away; see, everything has become new! 18All this is from God, who reconciled us to himself through Christ, and has given us the ministry of reconciliation; 19that is, in Christ God was reconciling the world to himself,c not counting their trespasses against them, and entrusting the message of reconciliation to us. 20So we are ambassadors for Christ, since God is making his appeal through us; we entreat you on behalf of Christ, be reconciled to God. 21For our sake he made him to be sin who knew no sin, so that in him we might become the righteousness of God.

aHeb *a qesitah*  bGk *according to the flesh*  cOr *God was in Christ reconciling the world to himself*

## PSALM 45.1–17

*To the leader: according to Lilies. Of the Korahites. A Maskil. A love song.*

**M**Y heart overflows with a
    goodly theme;
  I address my verses to
    the king;
  my tongue is like the pen of a
    ready scribe.
2 You are the most handsome of
    men;
  grace is poured upon your
    lips;
  therefore God has blessed
    you forever.
3 Gird your sword on your thigh,
    O mighty one,
  in your glory and majesty.

4 In your majesty ride on
    victoriously
  for the cause of truth and to
    defend[a] the right;
  let your right hand teach you
    dread deeds.
5 Your arrows are sharp
  in the heart of the king's
    enemies;
  the peoples fall under you.

6 Your throne, O God,[b] endures
    forever and ever.
  Your royal scepter is a
    scepter of equity;
7 you love righteousness and
    hate wickedness.
  Therefore God, your God, has
    anointed you
  with the oil of gladness
    beyond your companions;
8 your robes are all fragrant
    with myrrh and aloes and
    cassia.
  From ivory palaces stringed
    instruments make you
    glad;

9 daughters of kings are among
    your ladies of honor;
  at your right hand stands the
    queen in gold of Ophir.

10 Hear, O daughter, consider and
    incline your ear;
  forget your people and your
    father's house,
11 and the king will desire your
    beauty.
  Since he is your lord, bow to
    him;
12 the people[c] of Tyre will seek
    your favor with gifts,
  the richest of the people
    13with all kinds of wealth.

The princess is decked in her
    chamber with gold-woven
    robes;[d]
14 in many-colored robes she is
    led to the king;
  behind her the virgins, her
    companions, follow.
15 With joy and gladness they are
    led along
  as they enter the palace of
    the king.

16 In the place of ancestors you,
    O king,[e] shall have
    sons;
  you will make them princes in
    all the earth.
17 I will cause your name to be
    celebrated in all
    generations;
  therefore the peoples will
    praise you forever and
    ever.

## PROVERBS 22.14

**T**HE mouth of a loose[f] woman
    is a deep pit;
  he with whom the LORD is
    angry falls into it.

---

a Cn: Heb *and the meekness of*  b Or *Your throne is a throne of God, it*  c Heb *daughter*  d Or *people.*
13*All glorious is the princess within, gold embroidery is her clothing*  e Heb lacks *O king*  f Heb *strange*

## ECCLESIASTES 1.1—3.22

THE words of the Teacher, [a] the son of David, king in Jerusalem.
2 Vanity of vanities, says
the Teacher, [a]
vanity of vanities! All is
vanity.
3 What do people gain from all
the toil
at which they toil under the
sun?
4 A generation goes, and a
generation comes,
but the earth remains
forever.
5 The sun rises and the sun
goes down,
and hurries to the place
where it rises.
6 The wind blows to the south,
and goes around to the north;
round and round goes the wind,
and on its circuits the wind
returns.
7 All streams run to the sea,
but the sea is not full;
to the place where the streams
flow,
there they continue to flow.
8 All things [b] are wearisome;
more than one can express;
the eye is not satisfied with
seeing,
or the ear filled with hearing.
9 What has been is what will be,
and what has been done is
what will be done;
there is nothing new under
the sun.
10 Is there a thing of which it is
said,
"See, this is new"?
It has already been,
in the ages before us.
11 The people of long ago are not
remembered,
nor will there be any
remembrance
of people yet to come
by those who come after
them.

12 I, the Teacher, [a] when king over Israel in Jerusalem, 13 applied my mind to seek and to search out by wisdom all that is done under heaven; it is an unhappy business that God has given to human beings to be busy with. 14 I saw all the deeds that are done under the sun; and see, all is vanity and a chasing after wind. [c]
15 What is crooked cannot be made
straight,
and what is lacking cannot
be counted.

16 I said to myself, "I have acquired great wisdom, surpassing all who were over Jerusalem before me; and my mind has had great experience of wisdom and knowledge." 17 And I applied my mind to know wisdom and to know madness and folly. I perceived that this also is but a chasing after wind. [c]
18 For in much wisdom is much
vexation,
and those who increase
knowledge increase
sorrow.

2.1 I SAID to myself, "Come now, I will make a test of pleasure; enjoy yourself." But again, this also was vanity. 2 I said of laughter, "It is mad," and of pleasure, "What use is it?" 3 I searched with my mind how to cheer my body with wine—my mind still guiding me

---

[a] Heb *Qoheleth*, traditionally rendered *Preacher*  [b] Or *words*  [c] Or *a feeding on wind*. See Hos 12.1

with wisdom—and how to lay hold on folly, until I might see what was good for mortals to do under heaven during the few days of their life. [4]I made great works; I built houses and planted vineyards for myself; [5]I made myself gardens and parks, and planted in them all kinds of fruit trees. [6]I made myself pools from which to water the forest of growing trees. [7]I bought male and female slaves, and had slaves who were born in my house; I also had great possessions of herds and flocks, more than any who had been before me in Jerusalem. [8]I also gathered for myself silver and gold and the treasure of kings and of the provinces; I got singers, both men and women, and delights of the flesh, and many concubines. [a]

9 So I became great and surpassed all who were before me in Jerusalem; also my wisdom remained with me. [10]Whatever my eyes desired I did not keep from them; I kept my heart from no pleasure, for my heart found pleasure in all my toil, and this was my reward for all my toil. [11]Then I considered all that my hands had done and the toil I had spent in doing it, and again, all was vanity and a chasing after wind, [b] and there was nothing to be gained under the sun.

12 So I turned to consider wisdom and madness and folly; for what can the one do who comes after the king? Only what has already been done. [13]Then I saw that wisdom excels folly as light excels darkness.

[14] The wise have eyes in their
>head,
>but fools walk in darkness.

Yet I perceived that the same fate befalls all of them. [15]Then I said to myself, "What happens to the fool will happen to me also; why then have I been so very wise?" And I said to myself that this also is vanity. [16]For there is no enduring remembrance of the wise or of fools, seeing that in the days to come all will have been long forgotten. How can the wise die just like fools? [17]So I hated life, because what is done under the sun was grievous to me; for all is vanity and a chasing after wind. [b]

18 I hated all my toil in which I had toiled under the sun, seeing that I must leave it to those who come after me [19]—and who knows whether they will be wise or foolish? Yet they will be master of all for which I toiled and used my wisdom under the sun. This also is vanity. [20]So I turned and gave my heart up to despair concerning all the toil of my labors under the sun, [21]because sometimes one who has toiled with wisdom and knowledge and skill must leave all to be enjoyed by another who did not toil for it. This also is vanity and a great evil. [22]What do mortals get from all the toil and strain with which they toil under the sun? [23]For all their days are full of pain, and their work is a vexation; even at night their minds do not rest. This also is vanity.

24 There is nothing better for mortals than to eat and drink, and find enjoyment in their toil. This also, I saw, is from the hand of God; [25]for apart from him[c] who can eat or who can have enjoyment? [26]For to the one who pleases him God gives wisdom and knowledge and joy; but to the sinner he gives the work of gathering and heaping, only to give to one who pleases God. This also is vanity and a chasing after wind. [b]

[3.1] FOR everything there is a season, and a time for every matter under heaven:
[2] a time to be born, and a time
>to die;
>a time to plant, and a time to
>pluck up what is planted;
[3] a time to kill, and a time to
>heal;

a time to break down, and a
  time to build up;
4  a time to weep, and a time
  to laugh;
a time to mourn, and a time
  to dance;
5  a time to throw away stones,
  and a time to gather
  stones together;
a time to embrace, and a time
  to refrain from
  embracing;
6  a time to seek, and a time to
  lose;
a time to keep, and a time to
  throw away;
7  a time to tear, and a time to
  sew;
a time to keep silence, and a
  time to speak;
8  a time to love, and a time to
  hate;
a time for war, and a time for
  peace.

9  What gain have the workers from their toil? 10I have seen the business that God has given to everyone to be busy with. 11He has made everything suitable for its time; moreover he has put a sense of past and future into their minds, yet they cannot find out what God has done from the beginning to the end. 12I know that there is nothing better for them than to be happy and enjoy themselves as long as they live; 13moreover, it is God's gift that all should eat and drink and take pleasure in all their toil. 14I know that whatever God does endures forever; nothing can be added to it, nor anything taken from it; God has done this, so that all should stand in awe before him. 15That which is, already has been; that which is to be, already is; and God seeks out what has gone by.a

16  Moreover I saw under the sun that in the place of justice, wickedness was there, and in the place of righ-teousness, wickedness was there as well. 17I said in my heart, God will judge the righteous and the wicked, for he has appointed a time for every mat-ter, and for every work. 18I said in my heart with regard to human beings that God is testing them to show that they are but animals. 19For the fate of hu-mans and the fate of animals is the same; as one dies, so dies the other. They all have the same breath, and hu-mans have no advantage over the ani-mals; for all is vanity. 20All go to one place; all are from the dust, and all turn to dust again. 21Who knows whether the human spirit goes upward and the spirit of animals goes downward to the earth? 22So I saw that there is nothing better than that all should enjoy their work, for that is their lot; who can bring them to see what will be after them?

## 2 CORINTHIANS 6.1–13

As we work together with him,b we urge you also not to accept the grace of God in vain. 2For he says,
  "At an acceptable time I have
    listened to you,
  and on a day of salvation I
    have helped you."
See, now is the acceptable time; see, now is the day of salvation! 3We are putting no obstacle in anyone's way, so that no fault may be found with our min-istry, 4but as servants of God we have commended ourselves in every way: through great endurance, in afflictions, hardships, calamities, 5beatings, im-prisonments, riots, labors, sleepless nights, hunger; 6by purity, knowledge, patience, kindness, holiness of spirit, genuine love, 7truthful speech, and the power of God; with the weapons of righteousness for the right hand and for the left; 8in honor and dishonor, in ill repute and good repute. We are

aHeb *what is pursued*   bGk *As we work together*

treated as impostors, and yet are true; [9]as unknown, and yet are well known; as dying, and see—we are alive; as punished, and yet not killed; [10]as sorrowful, yet always rejoicing; as poor, yet making many rich; as having nothing, and yet possessing everything.

11  We have spoken frankly to you Corinthians; our heart is wide open to you. [12]There is no restriction in our affections, but only in yours. [13]In return—I speak as to children—open wide your hearts also.

## PSALM 46.1–11

*To the leader. Of the Korahites. According to Alamoth. A Song.*

G OD is our refuge and
strength,
a very present[a] help in
trouble.
2  Therefore we will not fear,
though the earth should
change,
though the mountains shake
in the heart of the sea;
3  though its waters roar and
foam,
though the mountains tremble
with its tumult.      *Selah*

4  There is a river whose streams
make glad the city of
God,
the holy habitation of the
Most High.

5  God is in the midst of the
city;[b] it shall not be
moved;
God will help it when the
morning dawns.
6  The nations are in an uproar,
the kingdoms totter;
he utters his voice, the earth
melts.
7  The LORD of hosts is with us;
the God of Jacob is our
refuge.[c]      *Selah*

8  Come, behold the works of the
LORD;
see what desolations he has
brought on the earth.
9  He makes wars cease to the
end of the earth;
he breaks the bow, and
shatters the spear;
he burns the shields with fire.
10  "Be still, and know that I am
God!
I am exalted among the
nations,
I am exalted in the earth."
11  The LORD of hosts is with us;
the God of Jacob is our
refuge.[c]      *Selah*

## PROVERBS 22.15

F OLLY is bound up in the heart
of a boy,
but the rod of discipline
drives it far away.

## ECCLESIASTES 4.1—6.12

**A**GAIN I saw all the oppressions that are practiced under the sun. Look, the tears of the oppressed—with no one to comfort them! On the side of their oppressors there was power—with no one to comfort them. [2]And I thought the dead, who have already died, more fortunate than the living, who are still alive; [3]but better than both is the one who has not yet been, and has not seen the evil deeds that are done under the sun.

4 Then I saw that all toil and all skill in work come from one person's envy of another. This also is vanity and a chasing after wind. [a]

5 Fools fold their hands
   and consume their own flesh.
6 Better is a handful with quiet
   than two handfuls with toil,
   and a chasing after wind. [a]

7 Again, I saw vanity under the sun: [8]the case of solitary individuals, without sons or brothers; yet there is no end to all their toil, and their eyes are never satisfied with riches. "For whom am I toiling," they ask, "and depriving myself of pleasure?" This also is vanity and an unhappy business.

9 Two are better than one, because they have a good reward for their toil. [10]For if they fall, one will lift up the other; but woe to one who is alone and falls and does not have another to help. [11]Again, if two lie together, they keep warm; but how can one keep warm alone? [12]And though one might prevail against another, two will withstand one. A threefold cord is not quickly broken.

13 Better is a poor but wise youth than an old but foolish king, who will no longer take advice. [14]One can indeed come out of prison to reign, even though born poor in the kingdom. [15]I saw all the living who, moving about under the sun, follow that[b] youth who replaced the king; [c] [16]there was no end to all those people whom he led. Yet those who come later will not rejoice in him. Surely this also is vanity and a chasing after wind. [a]

[5d.1] GUARD your steps when you go to the house of God; to draw near to listen is better than the sacrifice offered by fools; for they do not know how to keep from doing evil. [e] [2f]Never be rash with your mouth, nor let your heart be quick to utter a word before God, for God is in heaven, and you upon earth; therefore let your words be few.

3 For dreams come with many cares, and a fool's voice with many words.

4 When you make a vow to God, do not delay fulfilling it; for he has no pleasure in fools. Fulfill what you vow. [5]It is better that you should not vow than that you should vow and not fulfill it. [6]Do not let your mouth lead you into sin, and do not say before the messenger that it was a mistake; why should God be angry at your words, and destroy the work of your hands?

7 With many dreams come vanities and a multitude of words; [g] but fear God.

8 If you see in a province the oppression of the poor and the violation of justice and right, do not be amazed at the matter; for the high official is watched by a higher, and there are yet higher ones over them. [9]But all things

[a]Or *a feeding on wind.* See Hos 12.1   [b]Heb *the second*   [c]Heb *him*   [d]Ch 4.17 in Heb   [e]Cn: Heb *they do not know how to do evil*   [f]Ch 5.1 in Heb   [g]Meaning of Heb uncertain

considered, this is an advantage for a land: a king for a plowed field. **a**

10  The lover of money will not be satisfied with money; nor the lover of wealth, with gain. This also is vanity.

11  When goods increase, those who eat them increase; and what gain has their owner but to see them with his eyes?

12  Sweet is the sleep of laborers, whether they eat little or much; but the surfeit of the rich will not let them sleep.

13  There is a grievous ill that I have seen under the sun: riches were kept by their owners to their hurt, [14]and those riches were lost in a bad venture; though they are parents of children, they have nothing in their hands. [15]As they came from their mother's womb, so they shall go again, naked as they came; they shall take nothing for their toil, which they may carry away with their hands. [16]This also is a grievous ill: just as they came, so shall they go; and what gain do they have from toiling for the wind? [17]Besides, all their days they eat in darkness, in much vexation and sickness and resentment.

18  This is what I have seen to be good: it is fitting to eat and drink and find enjoyment in all the toil with which one toils under the sun the few days of the life God gives us; for this is our lot. [19]Likewise all to whom God gives wealth and possessions and whom he enables to enjoy them, and to accept their lot and find enjoyment in their toil—this is the gift of God. [20]For they will scarcely brood over the days of their lives, because God keeps them occupied with the joy of their hearts.

[6.1] THERE is an evil that I have seen under the sun, and it lies heavy upon humankind: [2]those to whom God gives wealth, possessions, and honor, so that they lack nothing of all that they desire,

yet God does not enable them to enjoy these things, but a stranger enjoys them. This is vanity; it is a grievous ill. [3]A man may beget a hundred children, and live many years; but however many are the days of his years, if he does not enjoy life's good things, or has no burial, I say that a stillborn child is better off than he. [4]For it comes into vanity and goes into darkness, and in darkness its name is covered; [5]moreover it has not seen the sun or known anything; yet it finds rest rather than he. [6]Even though he should live a thousand years twice over, yet enjoy no good—do not all go to one place?

7  All human toil is for the mouth, yet the appetite is not satisfied. [8]For what advantage have the wise over fools? And what do the poor have who know how to conduct themselves before the living? [9]Better is the sight of the eyes than the wandering of desire; this also is vanity and a chasing after wind. **b**

10  Whatever has come to be has already been named, and it is known what human beings are, and that they are not able to dispute with those who are stronger. [11]The more words, the more vanity, so how is one the better? [12]For who knows what is good for mortals while they live the few days of their vain life, which they pass like a shadow? For who can tell them what will be after them under the sun?

## 2 CORINTHIANS 6.14—7.7

Do not be mismatched with unbelievers. For what partnership is there between righteousness and lawlessness? Or what fellowship is there between light and darkness? [15]What agreement does Christ have with Beliar? Or what does a believer share with an unbeliever? [16]What agreement has the temple of

a Meaning of Heb uncertain   b Or *a feeding on wind.* See Hos 12.1

God with idols? For we[a] are the temple of the living God; as God said,
"I will live in them and walk
        among them,
    and I will be their God,
    and they shall be my people.
17 Therefore come out from them,
    and be separate from them,
        says the Lord,
    and touch nothing unclean;
        then I will welcome you,
18 and I will be your father,
    and you shall be my sons and
        daughters,
    says the Lord Almighty."

7.1 SINCE we have these promises, beloved, let us cleanse ourselves from every defilement of body and of spirit, making holiness perfect in the fear of God.

2 Make room in your hearts[b] for us; we have wronged no one, we have corrupted no one, we have taken advantage of no one. 3I do not say this to condemn you, for I said before that you are in our hearts, to die together and to live together. 4I often boast about you; I have great pride in you; I am filled with consolation; I am overjoyed in all our affliction.
5 For even when we came into Macedonia, our bodies had no rest, but we were afflicted in every way— disputes without and fears within. 6But God, who consoles the downcast, consoled us by the arrival of Titus, 7and not only by his coming, but also by the consolation with which he was consoled about you, as he told us of your longing, your mourning, your zeal for me, so that I rejoiced still more.

# PSALM 47.1–9

*To the leader. Of the Korahites. A Psalm.*

CLAP your hands, all you
        peoples;
    shout to God with loud
        songs of joy.
2 For the LORD, the Most High, is
        awesome,
    a great king over all the
        earth.
3 He subdued peoples under us,
    and nations under our feet.
4 He chose our heritage for us,
    the pride of Jacob whom he
        loves.            *Selah*

5 God has gone up with a shout,
    the LORD with the sound of a
        trumpet.
6 Sing praises to God, sing
        praises;
    sing praises to our King, sing
        praises.
7 For God is the king of all the
        earth;
    sing praises with a psalm. [c]

8 God is king over the nations;
    God sits on his holy throne.
9 The princes of the peoples
        gather
    as the people of the God of
        Abraham.
    For the shields of the earth
        belong to God;
    he is highly exalted.

# PROVERBS 22.16

OPPRESSING the poor in order to
        enrich oneself,
    and giving to the rich, will
        lead only to loss.

aOther ancient authorities read *you*  bGk lacks *in your hearts*  cHeb *Maskil*

ECCLESIASTES 7.1—9.18

**A** GOOD name is better than
precious ointment,
and the day of death, than
the day of birth.
2 It is better to go to the house
of mourning
than to go to the house of
feasting;
for this is the end of everyone,
and the living will lay it
to heart.
3 Sorrow is better than laughter,
for by sadness of countenance
the heart is made glad.
4 The heart of the wise is in the
house of mourning;
but the heart of fools is in the
house of mirth.
5 It is better to hear the rebuke
of the wise
than to hear the song of fools.
6 For like the crackling of thorns
under a pot,
so is the laughter of fools;
this also is vanity.
7 Surely oppression makes the
wise foolish,
and a bribe corrupts the
heart.
8 Better is the end of a thing than
its beginning;
the patient in spirit are better
than the proud in spirit.
9 Do not be quick to anger,
for anger lodges in the bosom
of fools.
10 Do not say, "Why were the
former days better than
these?"
For it is not from wisdom that
you ask this.
11 Wisdom is as good as an
inheritance,
an advantage to those who
see the sun.
12 For the protection of wisdom is
like the protection of
money,
and the advantage of
knowledge is that
wisdom gives life to the
one who possesses it.
13 Consider the work of God;
who can make straight what
he has made crooked?
14 In the day of prosperity be joyful, and in the day of adversity consider; God has made the one as well as the other, so that mortals may not find out anything that will come after them.
15 In my vain life I have seen everything; there are righteous people who perish in their righteousness, and there are wicked people who prolong their life in their evildoing. 16Do not be too righteous, and do not act too wise; why should you destroy yourself? 17Do not be too wicked, and do not be a fool; why should you die before your time? 18It is good that you should take hold of the one, without letting go of the other; for the one who fears God shall succeed with both.
19 Wisdom gives strength to the wise more than ten rulers that are in a city.
20 Surely there is no one on earth so righteous as to do good without ever sinning.
21 Do not give heed to everything that people say, or you may hear your servant cursing you; 22your heart knows that many times you have yourself cursed others.
23 All this I have tested by wisdom; I said, "I will be wise," but it was far from me. 24That which is, is far off, and deep, very deep; who can find it out?

[25]I turned my mind to know and to search out and to seek wisdom and the sum of things, and to know that wickedness is folly and that foolishness is madness. [26]I found more bitter than death the woman who is a trap, whose heart is snares and nets, whose hands are fetters; one who pleases God escapes her, but the sinner is taken by her. [27]See, this is what I found, says the Teacher, [a] adding one thing to another to find the sum, [28]which my mind has sought repeatedly, but I have not found. One man among a thousand I found, but a woman among all these I have not found. [29]See, this alone I found, that God made human beings straightforward, but they have devised many schemes.

8.1 Who is like the wise man?
　　And who knows the
　　　　interpretation of a thing?
　　Wisdom makes one's face shine,
　　　and the hardness of one's
　　　　countenance is changed.

2 Keep[b] the king's command because of your sacred oath. [3]Do not be terrified; go from his presence, do not delay when the matter is unpleasant, for he does whatever he pleases. [4]For the word of the king is powerful, and who can say to him, "What are you doing?" [5]Whoever obeys a command will meet no harm, and the wise mind will know the time and way. [6]For every matter has its time and way, although the troubles of mortals lie heavy upon them. [7]Indeed, they do not know what is to be, for who can tell them how it will be? [8]No one has power over the wind[c] to restrain the wind, [c] or power over the day of death; there is no discharge from the battle, nor does wickedness deliver those who practice it. [9]All this I observed, applying my mind to all that is done under the sun, while one person exercises authority over another to the other's hurt.

10　Then I saw the wicked buried; they used to go in and out of the holy place, and were praised in the city where they had done such things. [d] This also is vanity. [11]Because sentence against an evil deed is not executed speedily, the human heart is fully set to do evil. [12]Though sinners do evil a hundred times and prolong their lives, yet I know that it will be well with those who fear God, because they stand in fear before him, [13]but it will not be well with the wicked, neither will they prolong their days like a shadow, because they do not stand in fear before God.

14　There is a vanity that takes place on earth, that there are righteous people who are treated according to the conduct of the wicked, and there are wicked people who are treated according to the conduct of the righteous. I said that this also is vanity. [15]So I commend enjoyment, for there is nothing better for people under the sun than to eat, and drink, and enjoy themselves, for this will go with them in their toil through the days of life that God gives them under the sun.

16　When I applied my mind to know wisdom, and to see the business that is done on earth, how one's eyes see sleep neither day nor night, [17]then I saw all the work of God, that no one can find out what is happening under the sun. However much they may toil in seeking, they will not find it out; even though those who are wise claim to know, they cannot find it out.

9.1 All this I laid to heart, examining it all, how the righteous and the wise and their deeds are in the hand of God; whether it is love or hate one does not know. Everything that confronts them [2]is vanity, [e] since the same fate comes to all, to the righteous and the wicked, to the good and the evil, [a] to the clean and the unclean, to those who sacrifice and those who do not sacrifice. As are the good, so are the sinners; those who swear are like those who shun an oath. ³This is an evil in all that happens under the sun, that the same fate comes to everyone. Moreover, the hearts of all are full of evil; madness is in their hearts while they live, and after that they go to the dead. ⁴But whoever is joined with all the living has hope, for a living dog is better than a dead lion. ⁵The living know that they will die, but the dead know nothing; they have no more reward, and even the memory of them is lost. ⁶Their love and their hate and their envy have already perished; never again will they have any share in all that happens under the sun.

7  Go, eat your bread with enjoyment, and drink your wine with a merry heart; for God has long ago approved what you do. ⁸Let your garments always be white; do not let oil be lacking on your head. ⁹Enjoy life with the wife whom you love, all the days of your vain life that are given you under the sun, because that is your portion in life and in your toil at which you toil under the sun. ¹⁰Whatever your hand finds to do, do with your might; for there is no work or thought or knowledge or wisdom in Sheol, to which you are going.

11  Again I saw that under the sun the race is not to the swift, nor the battle to the strong, nor bread to the wise, nor riches to the intelligent, nor favor to the skillful; but time and chance happen to them all. ¹²For no one can anticipate the time of disaster. Like fish taken in a cruel net, and like birds caught in a snare, so mortals are snared at a time of calamity, when it suddenly falls upon them.

13  I have also seen this example of wisdom under the sun, and it seemed great to me. ¹⁴There was a little city with few people in it. A great king came against it and besieged it, building great siegeworks against it. ¹⁵Now there was found in it a poor wise man, and he by his wisdom delivered the city. Yet no one remembered that poor man. ¹⁶So I said, "Wisdom is better than might; yet the poor man's wisdom is despised, and his words are not heeded."

17  The quiet words of the wise are
     more to be heeded
   than the shouting of a ruler
     among fools.
18  Wisdom is better than weapons
     of war,
   but one bungler destroys
     much good.

# 2 CORINTHIANS 7.8–16

FOR even if I made you sorry with my letter, I do not regret it (though I did regret it, for I see that I grieved you with that letter, though only briefly). ⁹Now I rejoice, not because you were grieved, but because your grief led to repentance; for you felt a godly grief, so that you were not harmed in any way by us. ¹⁰For godly grief produces a repentance that leads to salvation and brings no regret, but worldly grief produces death. ¹¹For see what earnestness this godly grief has produced in you, what eagerness to clear yourselves, what indignation, what alarm, what longing, what zeal, what punishment! At every point you have proved yourselves guiltless in the matter. ¹²So although I wrote to you, it was not on account of the one who did the wrong, nor on account of the one who was wronged, but in order that your zeal for us might be made known to you before God. ¹³In this we find comfort.

In addition to our own consolation, we rejoiced still more at the joy of Titus, because his mind has been set at

---

ᵃGk Syr Vg: Heb lacks *and the evil*

rest by all of you. ¹⁴For if I have been somewhat boastful about you to him, I was not disgraced; but just as everything we said to you was true, so our boasting to Titus has proved true as well. ¹⁵And his heart goes out all the more to you, as he remembers the obedience of all of you, and how you welcomed him with fear and trembling. ¹⁶I rejoice, because I have complete confidence in you.

## PSALM 48.1–14

*A Song. A Psalm of the Korahites.*

**G**REAT is the LORD and greatly
    to be praised
  in the city of our God.
His holy mountain, ²beautiful in
    elevation,
  is the joy of all the earth,
Mount Zion, in the far north,
  the city of the great King.
3  Within its citadels God
    has shown himself a sure
      defense.

4  Then the kings assembled,
    they came on together.
5  As soon as they saw it, they
    were astounded;
  they were in panic, they took
    to flight;
6  trembling took hold of them
    there,
  pains as of a woman in labor,
7  as when an east wind shatters
    the ships of Tarshish.
8  As we have heard, so have we
    seen
  in the city of the LORD of
    hosts,
  in the city of our God,
  which God establishes
    forever.     *Selah*

9  We ponder your steadfast love,
    O God,
  in the midst of your temple.
10  Your name, O God, like your
    praise,
  reaches to the ends of the
    earth.
  Your right hand is filled with
    victory.
11    Let Mount Zion be glad,
  let the towns ᵃ of Judah rejoice
    because of your judgments.

12  Walk about Zion, go all around
    it,
  count its towers,
13  consider well its ramparts;
    go through its citadels,
  that you may tell the next
    generation
14    that this is God,
  our God forever and ever.
    He will be our guide forever.

## PROVERBS 22.17–19

**T**HE words of the wise:

  Incline your ear and hear my
    words, ᵇ
  and apply your mind to my
    teaching;
18  for it will be pleasant if you
    keep them within you,
  if all of them are ready on
    your lips.
19  So that your trust may be in
    the LORD,
  I have made them known to
    you today—yes, to you.

---

ᵃHeb *daughters*  ᵇCn Compare Gk: Heb *Incline your ear, and hear the words of the wise*

# SEPTEMBER 5

ECCLESIASTES 10.1—12.14

**D**EAD flies make the perfumer's
ointment give off a
foul odor;
so a little folly outweighs
wisdom and honor.
2 The heart of the wise inclines to
the right,
but the heart of a fool to the
left.
3 Even when fools walk on the
road, they lack sense,
and show to everyone that
they are fools.
4 If the anger of the ruler rises
against you, do not leave
your post,
for calmness will undo great
offenses.

5 There is an evil that I have seen under the sun, as great an error as if it proceeded from the ruler: 6folly is set in many high places, and the rich sit in a low place. 7I have seen slaves on horseback, and princes walking on foot like slaves.

8 Whoever digs a pit will fall into
it;
and whoever breaks through
a wall will be bitten by
a snake.
9 Whoever quarries stones will be
hurt by them;
and whoever splits logs will
be endangered by them.
10 If the iron is blunt, and one
does not whet the edge,
then more strength must be
exerted;
but wisdom helps one to
succeed.
11 If the snake bites before it is
charmed,
there is no advantage in a
charmer.
12 Words spoken by the wise bring
them favor,
but the lips of fools consume
them.
13 The words of their mouths
begin in foolishness,
and their talk ends in wicked
madness;
14 yet fools talk on and on.
No one knows what is to
happen,
and who can tell anyone what
the future holds?
15 The toil of fools wears them
out,
for they do not even know
the way to town.

16 Alas for you, O land, when your
king is a servant, [a]
and your princes feast in the
morning!
17 Happy are you, O land, when
your king is a nobleman,
and your princes feast at the
proper time—
for strength, and not for
drunkenness!
18 Through sloth the roof sinks in,
and through indolence the
house leaks.
19 Feasts are made for laughter;
wine gladdens life,
and money meets every
need.
20 Do not curse the king, even in
your thoughts,
or curse the rich, even in
your bedroom;

[a] Or *a child*

for a bird of the air may carry
    your voice,
  or some winged creature tell
    the matter.

11.1 SEND out your bread upon the
    waters,
  for after many days you will
    get it back.
2 Divide your means seven ways,
    or even eight,
  for you do not know what
    disaster may happen
    on earth.
3 When clouds are full,
    they empty rain on the earth;
  whether a tree falls to the south
    or to the north,
  in the place where the tree
    falls, there it will lie.
4 Whoever observes the wind will
    not sow;
  and whoever regards the
    clouds will not reap.

5 Just as you do not know how the breath comes to the bones in the mother's womb, so you do not know the work of God, who makes everything.

6 In the morning sow your seed, and at evening do not let your hands be idle; for you do not know which will prosper, this or that, or whether both alike will be good.

7 Light is sweet, and it is pleasant for the eyes to see the sun.

8 Even those who live many years should rejoice in them all; yet let them remember that the days of darkness will be many. All that comes is vanity.

9 Rejoice, young man, while you are young, and let your heart cheer you in the days of your youth. Follow the inclination of your heart and the desire of your eyes, but know that for all these things God will bring you into judgment.

10 Banish anxiety from your mind, and put away pain from your body; for youth and the dawn of life are vanity.

12.1 REMEMBER your creator in the days of your youth, before the days of trouble come, and the years draw near when you will say, "I have no pleasure in them"; 2before the sun and the light and the moon and the stars are darkened and the clouds return with[a] the rain; 3in the day when the guards of the house tremble, and the strong men are bent, and the women who grind cease working because they are few, and those who look through the windows see dimly; 4when the doors on the street are shut, and the sound of the grinding is low, and one rises up at the sound of a bird, and all the daughters of song are brought low; 5when one is afraid of heights, and terrors are in the road; the almond tree blossoms, the grasshopper drags itself along[b] and desire fails; because all must go to their eternal home, and the mourners will go about the streets; 6before the silver cord is snapped,[c] and the golden bowl is broken, and the pitcher is broken at the fountain, and the wheel broken at the cistern, 7and the dust returns to the earth as it was, and the breath[d] returns to God who gave it. 8Vanity of vanities, says the Teacher;[e] all is vanity.

9 Besides being wise, the Teacher[e] also taught the people knowledge, weighing and studying and arranging many proverbs. 10The Teacher[e] sought to find pleasing words, and he wrote words of truth plainly.

11 The sayings of the wise are like goads, and like nails firmly fixed are the collected sayings that are given by one shepherd.[f] 12Of anything beyond these, my child, beware. Of making many books there is no end, and much study is a weariness of the flesh.

a Or *after*; Heb *'ahar*  b Or *is a burden*  c Syr Vg Compare Gk: Heb *is removed*  d Or *the spirit*
e *Qoheleth,* traditionally rendered *Preacher*  f Meaning of Heb uncertain

13 The end of the matter; all has been heard. Fear God, and keep his commandments; for that is the whole duty of everyone. [14]For God will bring every deed into judgment, including[a] every secret thing, whether good or evil.

## 2 CORINTHIANS 8.1–15

WE want you to know, brothers and sisters,[b] about the grace of God that has been granted to the churches of Macedonia; [2]for during a severe ordeal of affliction, their abundant joy and their extreme poverty have overflowed in a wealth of generosity on their part. [3]For, as I can testify, they voluntarily gave according to their means, and even beyond their means, [4]begging us earnestly for the privilege[c] of sharing in this ministry to the saints— [5]and this, not merely as we expected; they gave themselves first to the Lord and, by the will of God, to us, [6]so that we might urge Titus that, as he had already made a beginning, so he should also complete this generous undertaking[d] among you. [7]Now as you excel in everything—in faith, in speech, in knowledge, in utmost eagerness, and in our love for you[e]—so we want you to excel also in this generous undertaking. [d]

8 I do not say this as a command, but I am testing the genuineness of your love against the earnestness of others. [9]For you know the generous act[f] of our Lord Jesus Christ, that though he was rich, yet for your sakes he became poor, so that by his poverty you might become rich. [10]And in this matter I am giving my advice: it is appropriate for you who began last year not only to do something but even to desire to do something— [11]now finish doing it, so that your eagerness may be matched by completing it according to your means. [12]For if the eagerness is there, the gift is acceptable according to what one has—not according to what one does not have. [13]I do not mean that there should be relief for others and pressure on you, but it is a question of a fair balance between [14]your present abundance and their need, so that their abundance may be for your need, in order that there may be a fair balance. [15]As it is written,

> "The one who had much did not
>     have too much,
> and the one who had little did
>     not have too little."

## PSALM 49.1–20

*To the leader. Of the Korahites. A Psalm.*

HEAR this, all you peoples;
    give ear, all inhabitants of
    the world,
2  both low and high,
        rich and poor together.
3  My mouth shall speak wisdom;
        the meditation of my heart
            shall be understanding.
4  I will incline my ear to a
            proverb;
        I will solve my riddle to the
            music of the harp.

5  Why should I fear in times of
            trouble,
        when the iniquity of my
            persecutors surrounds
            me,
6  those who trust in their wealth
        and boast of the abundance of
            their riches?
7  Truly, no ransom avails for
            one's life,[g]
        there is no price one can give
            to God for it.
8  For the ransom of life is costly,
        and can never suffice
9  that one should live on forever
        and never see the grave.[h]

aOr *into the judgment on*  bGk *brothers*  cGk *grace*  dGk *this grace*  eOther ancient authorities read *your love for us*  fGk *the grace*  gAnother reading is *no one can ransom a brother*  hHeb *the pit*

10 When we look at the wise, they
      die;
   fool and dolt perish together
   and leave their wealth to
      others.
11 Their graves[a] are their homes
      forever,
   their dwelling places to all
      generations,
   though they named lands their
      own.
12 Mortals cannot abide in their
      pomp;
   they are like the animals that
      perish.

13 Such is the fate of the
      foolhardy,
   the end of those[b] who are
      pleased with their lot.
                              *Selah*
14 Like sheep they are appointed
      for Sheol;
   Death shall be their shepherd;
   straight to the grave they
      descend,[c]
   and their form shall waste
      away;
   Sheol shall be their home.[d]
15 But God will ransom my soul
      from the power of Sheol,
   for he will receive me.   *Selah*

16 Do not be afraid when some
      become rich,
   when the wealth of their
      houses increases.
17 For when they die they will
      carry nothing away;
   their wealth will not go down
      after them.
18 Though in their lifetime they
      count themselves happy
   —for you are praised when
      you do well for
      yourself—
19 they[e] will go to the company of
      their ancestors,
   who will never again see the
      light.
20 Mortals cannot abide in their
      pomp;
   they are like the animals that
      perish.

# PROVERBS 22.20–21

**H**AVE I not written for you
      thirty sayings
   of admonition and
      knowledge,
21 to show you what is right and
      true,
   so that you may give a true
      answer to those who
      sent you?

aGk Syr Compare Tg: Heb *their inward* (thought)   bTg: Heb *after them*   cCn: Heb *the upright shall
have dominion over them in the morning*   dMeaning of Heb uncertain   eCn: Heb *you*

## SONG OF SOLOMON 1.1—4.16

T HE Song of Songs, which is Solomon's.

2 Let him kiss me with the kisses
    of his mouth!
For your love is better than
    wine,
3    your anointing oils are
      fragrant,
your name is perfume poured
    out;
   therefore the maidens love
      you.
4 Draw me after you, let us make
    haste.
The king has brought me into
    his chambers.
We will exult and rejoice in you;
   we will extol your love more
      than wine;
   rightly do they love you.

5 I am black and beautiful,
   O daughters of Jerusalem,
like the tents of Kedar,
   like the curtains of Solomon.
6 Do not gaze at me because I am
    dark,
   because the sun has gazed on
      me.
My mother's sons were angry
    with me;
   they made me keeper of the
      vineyards,
   but my own vineyard I have
      not kept!
7 Tell me, you whom my soul
    loves,
   where you pasture your flock,
   where you make it lie down
      at noon;

for why should I be like one
    who is veiled
beside the flocks of your
    companions?

8 If you do not know,
   O fairest among women,
follow the tracks of the flock,
   and pasture your kids
   beside the shepherds' tents.

9 I compare you, my love,
   to a mare among Pharaoh's
      chariots.
10 Your cheeks are comely with
    ornaments,
   your neck with strings of
      jewels.
11 We will make you ornaments
    of gold,
   studded with silver.

12 While the king was on his
    couch,
   my nard gave forth its
      fragrance.
13 My beloved is to me a bag of
    myrrh
   that lies between my breasts.
14 My beloved is to me a cluster
    of henna blossoms
   in the vineyards of En-gedi.

15 Ah, you are beautiful, my love;
   ah, you are beautiful;
   your eyes are doves.
16 Ah, you are beautiful, my
    beloved,
   truly lovely.
Our couch is green;
17    the beams of our house are
      cedar,
   our rafters[a] are pine.

a Meaning of Heb uncertain

2.1 I AM a rose[a] of Sharon,
   a lily of the valleys.

2  As a lily among brambles,
   so is my love among maidens.

3  As an apple tree among the
      trees of the wood,
   so is my beloved among
      young men.
   With great delight I sat in his
      shadow,
   and his fruit was sweet to
      my taste.
4  He brought me to the
      banqueting house,
   and his intention toward me
      was love.
5  Sustain me with raisins,
   refresh me with apples;
   for I am faint with love.
6  O that his left hand were under
      my head,
   and that his right hand
      embraced me!
7  I adjure you, O daughters of
      Jerusalem,
   by the gazelles or the wild
      does:
   do not stir up or awaken love
      until it is ready!

8  The voice of my beloved!
      Look, he comes,
   leaping upon the mountains,
      bounding over the hills.
9  My beloved is like a gazelle
      or a young stag.
   Look, there he stands
      behind our wall,
   gazing in at the windows,
      looking through the lattice.
10  My beloved speaks and says to
      me:
   "Arise, my love, my fair one,
      and come away;
11  for now the winter is past,
      the rain is over and gone.

12  The flowers appear on the
      earth;
   the time of singing has come,
   and the voice of the turtledove
      is heard in our land.
13  The fig tree puts forth its figs,
      and the vines are in blossom;
      they give forth fragrance.
   Arise, my love, my fair one,
      and come away.
14  O my dove, in the clefts of the
      rock,
      in the covert of the cliff,
   let me see your face,
      let me hear your voice;
   for your voice is sweet,
      and your face is lovely.
15  Catch us the foxes,
      the little foxes,
   that ruin the vineyards—
      for our vineyards are in
      blossom."

16  My beloved is mine and I am
      his;
   he pastures his flock among
      the lilies.
17  Until the day breathes
      and the shadows flee,
   turn, my beloved, be like a
      gazelle
   or a young stag on the cleft
      mountains.[b]

3.1 UPON my bed at night
   I sought him whom my soul
      loves;
   I sought him, but found him not;
   I called him, but he gave no
      answer.[c]
2  "I will rise now and go about
      the city,
      in the streets and in the
      squares;
   I will seek him whom my soul
      loves."
   I sought him, but found him
      not.

---

[a]Heb *crocus*  [b]Or *on the mountains of Bethe* : meaning of Heb uncertain  [c]Gk: Heb lacks this line

3 The sentinels found me,
    as they went about in the
      city.
  "Have you seen him whom my
      soul loves?"
4 Scarcely had I passed them,
    when I found him whom my
      soul loves.
  I held him, and would not let
      him go
    until I brought him into my
      mother's house,
    and into the chamber of her
      that conceived me.
5 I adjure you, O daughters of
      Jerusalem,
    by the gazelles or the wild
      does:
  do not stir up or awaken love
    until it is ready!

6 What is that coming up from the
      wilderness,
    like a column of smoke,
  perfumed with myrrh and
      frankincense,
    with all the fragrant powders
      of the merchant?
7 Look, it is the litter of Solomon!
  Around it are sixty mighty men
    of the mighty men of Israel,
8 all equipped with swords
    and expert in war,
  each with his sword at his thigh
    because of alarms by night.
9 King Solomon made himself a
      palanquin
    from the wood of Lebanon.
10 He made its posts of silver,
    its back of gold, its seat of
      purple;
  its interior was inlaid with
      love. a
  Daughters of Jerusalem,
11   come out.
  Look, O daughters of Zion,
    at King Solomon,

at the crown with which his
      mother crowned him
  on the day of his wedding,
  on the day of the gladness of
      his heart.

4.1 How beautiful you are, my
      love,
    how very beautiful!
  Your eyes are doves
    behind your veil.
  Your hair is like a flock of goats,
    moving down the slopes of
      Gilead.
2 Your teeth are like a flock of
      shorn ewes
    that have come up from the
      washing,
  all of which bear twins,
    and not one among them is
      bereaved.
3 Your lips are like a crimson
      thread,
    and your mouth is lovely.
  Your cheeks are like halves of a
      pomegranate
    behind your veil.
4 Your neck is like the tower of
      David,
    built in courses;
  on it hang a thousand bucklers,
    all of them shields of
      warriors.
5 Your two breasts are like two
      fawns,
    twins of a gazelle,
    that feed among the lilies.
6 Until the day breathes
    and the shadows flee,
  I will hasten to the mountain of
      myrrh
    and the hill of frankincense.
7 You are altogether beautiful,
    my love;
    there is no flaw in you.
8 Come with me from Lebanon,
    my bride;

a Meaning of Heb uncertain

come with me from Lebanon.
Depart[a] from the peak of
   Amana,
  from the peak of Senir and
   Hermon,
from the dens of lions,
  from the mountains of
   leopards.

9  You have ravished my heart, my
   sister, my bride,
  you have ravished my heart
   with a glance of your
   eyes,
  with one jewel of your
   necklace.
10  How sweet is your love, my
   sister, my bride!
  how much better is your love
   than wine,
  and the fragrance of your oils
   than any spice!
11  Your lips distill nectar, my
   bride;
  honey and milk are under
   your tongue;
  the scent of your garments is
   like the scent of
   Lebanon.
12  A garden locked is my sister,
   my bride,
  a garden locked, a fountain
   sealed.
13  Your channel[b] is an orchard of
   pomegranates
  with all choicest fruits,
  henna with nard,
14  nard and saffron, calamus and
   cinnamon,
  with all trees of frankincense,
  myrrh and aloes,
  with all chief spices—
15  a garden fountain, a well of
   living water,
  and flowing streams from
   Lebanon.

16  Awake, O north wind,
   and come, O south wind!
  Blow upon my garden
   that its fragrance may be
   wafted abroad.
  Let my beloved come to his
   garden,
   and eat its choicest fruits.

## 2 CORINTHIANS 8.16–24

**B**UT thanks be to God who put in the heart of Titus the same eagerness for you that I myself have. [17]For he not only accepted our appeal, but since he is more eager than ever, he is going to you of his own accord. [18]With him we are sending the brother who is famous among all the churches for his proclaiming the good news;[c] [19]and not only that, but he has also been appointed by the churches to travel with us while we are administering this generous undertaking[d] for the glory of the Lord himself[e] and to show our goodwill. [20]We intend that no one should blame us about this generous gift that we are administering, [21]for we intend to do what is right not only in the Lord's sight but also in the sight of others. [22]And with them we are sending our brother whom we have often tested and found eager in many matters, but who is now more eager than ever because of his great confidence in you. [23]As for Titus, he is my partner and co-worker in your service; as for our brothers, they are messengers[f] of the churches, the glory of Christ. [24]Therefore openly before the churches, show them the proof of your love and of our reason for boasting about you.

a Or *Look*  b Meaning of Heb uncertain  c Or *the gospel*  d Gk *this grace*  e Other ancient authorities lack *himself*  f Gk *apostles*

## PSALM 50.1–23

*A Psalm of Asaph.*

THE mighty one, God the LORD,
  speaks and summons the
    earth
  from the rising of the sun to
    its setting.
2 Out of Zion, the perfection of
    beauty,
  God shines forth.

3 Our God comes and does not
    keep silence,
  before him is a devouring fire,
  and a mighty tempest all
    around him.
4 He calls to the heavens above
  and to the earth, that he may
    judge his people:
5 "Gather to me my faithful ones,
  who made a covenant with
    me by sacrifice!"
6 The heavens declare his
    righteousness,
  for God himself is judge.
      *Selah*

7 "Hear, O my people, and I will
    speak,
  O Israel, I will testify against
    you.
  I am God, your God.
8 Not for your sacrifices do I
    rebuke you;
  your burnt offerings are
    continually before me.
9 I will not accept a bull from
    your house,
  or goats from your folds.
10 For every wild animal of the
    forest is mine,
  the cattle on a thousand hills.
11 I know all the birds of the air, ᵃ
  and all that moves in the field
    is mine.

12 "If I were hungry, I would not
    tell you,

for the world and all that is in
    it is mine.
13 Do I eat the flesh of bulls,
  or drink the blood of goats?
14 Offer to God a sacrifice of
    thanksgiving, ᵇ
  and pay your vows to the
    Most High.
15 Call on me in the day of trouble;
  I will deliver you, and you
    shall glorify me."

16 But to the wicked God says:
  "What right have you to
    recite my statutes,
  or take my covenant on your
    lips?
17 For you hate discipline,
  and you cast my words
    behind you.
18 You make friends with a thief
    when you see one,
  and you keep company with
    adulterers.

19 "You give your mouth free rein
    for evil,
  and your tongue frames
    deceit.
20 You sit and speak against your
    kin;
  you slander your own
    mother's child.
21 These things you have done and
    I have been silent;
  you thought that I was one
    just like yourself.
  But now I rebuke you, and lay
    the charge before you.

22 "Mark this, then, you who
    forget God,
  or I will tear you apart, and
    there will be no one to
    deliver.
23 Those who bring thanksgiving
    as their sacrifice honor
    me;

ᵃGk Syr Tg: Heb *mountains*   ᵇOr *make thanksgiving your sacrifice to God*

to those who go the right
way[a]
I will show the salvation of
God.”

## PROVERBS 22.22–23

Do not rob the poor because
they are poor,
or crush the afflicted at the
gate;
23  for the LORD pleads their cause
and despoils of life those who
despoil them.

# SEPTEMBER 7

## SONG OF SOLOMON 5.1—8.14

I come to my garden, my sister,
my brid
I gather my myrrh with my
spice,
I eat my honeycomb with my
honey,
I drink my wine with my milk.

Eat, friends, drink,
and be drunk with love.

2  I slept, but my heart was
awake.
Listen! my beloved is knocking.
“Open to me, my sister, my
love,
my dove, my perfect one;
for my head is wet with dew,
my locks with the drops of
the night.”
3  I had put off my garment;
how could I put it on again?
I had bathed my feet;
how could I soil them?
4  My beloved thrust his hand into
the opening,

and my inmost being yearned
for him.
5  I arose to open to my beloved,
and my hands dripped with
myrrh,
my fingers with liquid myrrh,
upon the handles of the bolt.
6  I opened to my beloved,
but my beloved had turned
and was gone.
My soul failed me when he
spoke.
I sought him, but did not find
him;
I called him, but he gave
no answer.
7  Making their rounds in the city
the sentinels found me;
they beat me, they wounded
me,
they took away my mantle,
those sentinels of the walls.
8  I adjure you, O daughters of
Jerusalem,
if you find my beloved,
tell him this:
I am faint with love.

[a] Heb *who set a way*

9 What is your beloved more than
        another beloved,
    O fairest among women?
  What is your beloved more than
        another beloved,
    that you thus adjure us?

10  My beloved is all radiant and
        ruddy,
    distinguished among ten
        thousand.
11  His head is the finest gold;
    his locks are wavy,
        black as a raven.
12  His eyes are like doves
        beside springs of water,
    bathed in milk,
        fitly set. a
13  His cheeks are like beds of
        spices,
    yielding fragrance.
  His lips are lilies,
    distilling liquid myrrh.
14  His arms are rounded gold,
    set with jewels.
  His body is ivory work, a
    encrusted with sapphires. b
15  His legs are alabaster columns,
    set upon bases of gold.
  His appearance is like Lebanon,
    choice as the cedars.
16  His speech is most sweet,
    and he is altogether desirable.
  This is my beloved and this is
        my friend,
    O daughters of Jerusalem.


6.1  WHERE has your beloved gone,
    O fairest among women?
  Which way has your beloved
        turned,
    that we may seek him with
        you?

2  My beloved has gone down to
        his garden,
    to the beds of spices,

  to pasture his flock in the
        gardens,
    and to gather lilies.
3  I am my beloved's and my
        beloved is mine;
    he pastures his flock among
        the lilies.

4  You are beautiful as Tirzah,
        my love,
    comely as Jerusalem,
    terrible as an army with
        banners.
5  Turn away your eyes from me,
    for they overwhelm me!
  Your hair is like a flock of goats,
    moving down the slopes of
        Gilead.
6  Your teeth are like a flock of
        ewes,
    that have come up from the
        washing;
  all of them bear twins,
    and not one among them is
        bereaved.
7  Your cheeks are like halves of a
        pomegranate
    behind your veil.
8  There are sixty queens and
        eighty concubines,
    and maidens without number.
9  My dove, my perfect one, is the
        only one,
    the darling of her mother,
    flawless to her that bore her.
  The maidens saw her and called
        her happy;
    the queens and concubines
        also, and they praised
        her.
10  "Who is this that looks forth like
        the dawn,
    fair as the moon, bright as
        the sun,
    terrible as an army with
        banners?"

11  I went down to the nut orchard,

a Meaning of Heb uncertain   b Heb *lapis lazuli*

to look at the blossoms of the
    valley,
to see whether the vines had
    budded,
    whether the pomegranates
      were in bloom.
12 Before I was aware, my fancy
      set me
    in a chariot beside my
      prince. [a]

13 [b] Return, return, O Shulammite!
    Return, return, that we may
      look upon you.

Why should you look upon the
    Shulammite,
    as upon a dance before two
      armies? [c]

7.1 How graceful are your feet in
      sandals,
    O queenly maiden!
Your rounded thighs are like
      jewels,
    the work of a master hand.
2 Your navel is a rounded bowl
    that never lacks mixed wine.
Your belly is a heap of wheat,
    encircled with lilies.
3 Your two breasts are like two
      fawns,
    twins of a gazelle.
4 Your neck is like an ivory
      tower.
Your eyes are pools in
      Heshbon,
    by the gate of Bath-rabbim.
Your nose is like a tower of
      Lebanon,
    overlooking Damascus.
5 Your head crowns you like
      Carmel,
    and your flowing locks are
      like purple;
    a king is held captive in the
      tresses. [d]

6 How fair and pleasant you are,
    O loved one, delectable
      maiden! [e]
7 You are stately [f] as a palm
      tree,
    and your breasts are like its
      clusters.
8 I say I will climb the palm tree
    and lay hold of its branches.
Oh, may your breasts be like
      clusters of the vine,
    and the scent of your breath
      like apples,
9 and your kisses [g] like the best
      wine
    that goes down [h] smoothly,
    gliding over lips and teeth. [i]

10 I am my beloved's,
    and his desire is for me.
11 Come, my beloved,
    let us go forth into the fields,
    and lodge in the villages;
12 let us go out early to the
      vineyards,
    and see whether the vines
      have budded,
    whether the grape blossoms
      have opened
    and the pomegranates are
      in bloom.
There I will give you my love.
13 The mandrakes give forth
      fragrance,
    and over our doors are all
      choice fruits,
new as well as old,
    which I have laid up for you,
      O my beloved.

8.1 O THAT you were like a
      brother to me,
    who nursed at my mother's
      breast!
If I met you outside, I would
      kiss you,

[a] Cn: Meaning of Heb uncertain   [b] Ch 7.1 in Heb   [c] Or *dance of Mahanaim*   [d] Meaning of Heb uncertain   [e] Syr: Heb *in delights*   [f] Heb *This your stature is*   [g] Heb *palate*   [h] Heb *down for my lover*   [i] Gk Syr Vg: Heb *lips of sleepers*

and no one would despise me.
2 I would lead you and bring you
into the house of my mother,
and into the chamber of the
one who bore me. ᵃ
I would give you spiced wine
to drink,
the juice of my pomegranates.
3 O that his left hand were under
my head,
and that his right hand
embraced me!
4 I adjure you, O daughters of
Jerusalem,
do not stir up or awaken love
until it is ready!

5 Who is that coming up from the
wilderness,
leaning upon her beloved?

Under the apple tree I
awakened you.
There your mother was in labor
with you;
there she who bore you was
in labor.

6 Set me as a seal upon your
heart,
as a seal upon your arm;
for love is strong as death,
passion fierce as the grave.
Its flashes are flashes of fire,
a raging flame.
7 Many waters cannot quench
love,
neither can floods drown it.
If one offered for love
all the wealth of his house,
it would be utterly scorned.

8 We have a little sister,
and she has no breasts.
What shall we do for our sister,
on the day when she is
spoken for?
9 If she is a wall,

we will build upon her a
battlement of silver;
but if she is a door,
we will enclose her with
boards of cedar.
10 I was a wall,
and my breasts were like
towers;
then I was in his eyes
as one who brings ᵇ peace.
11 Solomon had a vineyard at
Baal-hamon;
he entrusted the vineyard to
keepers;
each one was to bring for its
fruit a thousand pieces of
silver.
12 My vineyard, my very own, is
for myself;
you, O Solomon, may have
the thousand,
and the keepers of the fruit
two hundred!

13 O you who dwell in the gardens,
my companions are listening
for your voice;
let me hear it.

14 Make haste, my beloved,
and be like a gazelle
or a young stag
upon the mountains of spices!

## 2 CORINTHIANS 9.1–15

Now it is not necessary for me to write you about the ministry to the saints, ²for I know your eagerness, which is the subject of my boasting about you to the people of Macedonia, saying that Achaia has been ready since last year; and your zeal has stirred up most of them. ³But I am sending the brothers in order that our boasting about you may not prove to have been empty in this case, so that you may be ready, as I said you would

ᵃGk Syr: Heb *my mother; she* (or *you*) *will teach me*   ᵇOr *finds*

be; ⁴otherwise, if some Macedonians come with me and find that you are not ready, we would be humiliated—to say nothing of you—in this undertaking. [a] ⁵So I thought it necessary to urge the brothers to go on ahead to you, and arrange in advance for this bountiful gift that you have promised, so that it may be ready as a voluntary gift and not as an extortion.

6 The point is this: the one who sows sparingly will also reap sparingly, and the one who sows bountifully will also reap bountifully. ⁷Each of you must give as you have made up your mind, not reluctantly or under compulsion, for God loves a cheerful giver. ⁸And God is able to provide you with every blessing in abundance, so that by always having enough of everything, you may share abundantly in every good work. ⁹As it is written,

"He scatters abroad, he gives to
      the poor;
   his righteousness[b] endures
      forever."

¹⁰He who supplies seed to the sower and bread for food will supply and multiply your seed for sowing and increase the harvest of your righteousness. [b] ¹¹You will be enriched in every way for your great generosity, which will produce thanksgiving to God through us; ¹²for the rendering of this ministry not only supplies the needs of the saints but also overflows with many thanksgivings to God. ¹³Through the testing of this ministry you glorify God by your obedience to the confession of the gospel of Christ and by the generosity of your sharing with them and with all others, ¹⁴while they long for you and pray for you because of the surpassing grace of God that he has given you. ¹⁵Thanks be to God for his indescribable gift!

## PSALM 51.1–19

*To the leader. A Psalm of David, when the prophet Nathan came to him, after he had gone in to Bathsheba.*

Have mercy on me, O God,
      according to your steadfast
         love;
   according to your abundant
      mercy
   blot out my transgressions.
2   Wash me thoroughly from my
         iniquity,
      and cleanse me from my sin.

3   For I know my transgressions,
      and my sin is ever before me.
4   Against you, you alone, have I
         sinned,
      and done what is evil in your
         sight,
   so that you are justified in your
         sentence
      and blameless when you pass
         judgment.
5   Indeed, I was born guilty,
      a sinner when my mother
         conceived me.

6   You desire truth in the inward
         being; [c]
      therefore teach me wisdom in
         my secret heart.
7   Purge me with hyssop, and I
         shall be clean;
      wash me, and I shall be
         whiter than snow.
8   Let me hear joy and gladness;
      let the bones that you have
         crushed rejoice.
9   Hide your face from my sins,
      and blot out all my iniquities.

10   Create in me a clean heart,
         O God,
      and put a new and right[d]
         spirit within me.

[a]Other ancient authorities add *of boasting*   [b]Or *benevolence*   [c]Meaning of Heb uncertain
[d]Or *steadfast*

11 Do not cast me away from your
        presence,
    and do not take your holy
        spirit from me.
12 Restore to me the joy of your
        salvation,
    and sustain in me a willing[a]
        spirit.

13 Then I will teach transgressors
        your ways,
    and sinners will return to you.
14 Deliver me from bloodshed,
        O God,
    O God of my salvation,
    and my tongue will sing aloud
        of your deliverance.

15 O Lord, open my lips,
    and my mouth will declare
        your praise.
16 For you have no delight in
        sacrifice;
    if I were to give a burnt
        offering, you would not
        be pleased.

17 The sacrifice acceptable to
        God[b] is a broken spirit;
    a broken and contrite heart,
        O God, you will not
        despise.

18 Do good to Zion in your good
        pleasure;
    rebuild the walls of Jerusalem,
19 then you will delight in right
        sacrifices,
    in burnt offerings and whole
        burnt offerings;
    then bulls will be offered on
        your altar.

## PROVERBS 22.24–25

MAKE no friends with those
    given to anger,
and do not associate with
    hotheads,
25 or you may learn their ways
    and entangle yourself in a
        snare.

# SEPTEMBER 8

## ISAIAH 1.1—2.22

THE vision of Isaiah son of Amoz,
which he saw concerning Judah
and Jerusalem in the days of Uzziah, Jotham, Ahaz, and Hezekiah,
kings of Judah.
2 Hear, O heavens, and listen,
        O earth;
    for the Lord has spoken:
    I reared children and brought
        them up,
    but they have rebelled against
        me.

3 The ox knows its owner,
    and the donkey its master's
        crib;
    but Israel does not know,
    my people do not understand.

4 Ah, sinful nation,
    people laden with iniquity,
    offspring who do evil,
    children who deal corruptly,
    who have forsaken the Lord,
    who have despised the Holy
        One of Israel,

a Or *generous*   b Or *My sacrifice, O God,*

who are utterly estranged!

5  Why do you seek further
        beatings?
    Why do you continue to
        rebel?
   The whole head is sick,
        and the whole heart faint.
6  From the sole of the foot even
        to the head,
        there is no soundness in it,
   but bruises and sores
        and bleeding wounds;
   they have not been drained, or
        bound up,
        or softened with oil.

7  Your country lies desolate,
        your cities are burned with
        fire;
   in your very presence
        aliens devour your land;
        it is desolate, as overthrown
        by foreigners.
8  And daughter Zion is left
        like a booth in a vineyard,
   like a shelter in a cucumber
        field,
        like a besieged city.
9  If the Lord of hosts
        had not left us a few
        survivors,
   we would have been like
        Sodom,
        and become like Gomorrah.

10  Hear the word of the Lord,
        you rulers of Sodom!
    Listen to the teaching of our
        God,
        you people of Gomorrah!
11  What to me is the multitude of
        your sacrifices?
        says the Lord;
    I have had enough of burnt
        offerings of rams
        and the fat of fed beasts;

I do not delight in the blood
        of bulls,
        or of lambs, or of goats.
12  When you come to appear
        before me, [a]
        who asked this from your
        hand?
    Trample my courts no more;
13  bringing offerings is futile;
        incense is an abomination to
        me.
    New moon and sabbath and
        calling of convocation—
        I cannot endure solemn
        assemblies with iniquity.
14  Your new moons and your
        appointed festivals
        my soul hates;
    they have become a burden to
        me,
        I am weary of bearing them.
15  When you stretch out your
        hands,
        I will hide my eyes from you;
    even though you make many
        prayers,
        I will not listen;
        your hands are full of blood.
16  Wash yourselves; make
        yourselves clean;
        remove the evil of your
        doings
        from before my eyes;
    cease to do evil,
17      learn to do good;
    seek justice,
        rescue the oppressed,
    defend the orphan,
        plead for the widow.

18  Come now, let us argue it out,
        says the Lord:
    though your sins are like
        scarlet,
        they shall be like snow;
    though they are red like
        crimson,

they shall become like wool.
19 If you are willing and obedient,
  you shall eat the good of the
    land;
20 but if you refuse and rebel,
  you shall be devoured by the
    sword;
  for the mouth of the Lord has
    spoken.

21 How the faithful city
  has become a whore!
  She that was full of justice,
righteousness lodged in her—
  but now murderers!
22 Your silver has become dross,
  your wine is mixed with
    water.
23 Your princes are rebels
  and companions of thieves.
Everyone loves a bribe
  and runs after gifts.
They do not defend the orphan,
  and the widow's cause does
    not come before them.

24 Therefore says the Sovereign,
    the Lord of hosts, the
    Mighty One of Israel:
Ah, I will pour out my wrath on
    my enemies,
  and avenge myself on my
    foes!
25 I will turn my hand against you;
  I will smelt away your dross
    as with lye
  and remove all your alloy.
26 And I will restore your judges
    as at the first,
  and your counselors as at the
    beginning.
Afterward you shall be called
    the city of righteousness,
  the faithful city.

27 Zion shall be redeemed by
    justice,

and those in her who repent,
  by righteousness.
28 But rebels and sinners shall be
    destroyed together,
  and those who forsake the
    Lord shall be consumed.
29 For you shall be ashamed of
    the oaks
  in which you delighted;
and you shall blush for the
    gardens
  that you have chosen.
30 For you shall be like an oak
  whose leaf withers,
  and like a garden without
    water.
31 The strong shall become like
    tinder,
  and their work[a] like a spark;
they and their work shall burn
    together,
  with no one to quench them.

2.1 The word that Isaiah son of Amoz
saw concerning Judah and Jerusalem.

2 In days to come
  the mountain of the Lord's
    house
shall be established as the
    highest of the mountains,
  and shall be raised above
    the hills;
all the nations shall stream to it.
3 Many peoples shall come and
    say,
"Come, let us go up to the
    mountain of the Lord,
  to the house of the God of
    Jacob;
that he may teach us his ways
  and that we may walk in his
    paths."
For out of Zion shall go forth
    instruction,
  and the word of the Lord
    from Jerusalem.

a Or *its makers*

4 He shall judge between the
    nations,
  and shall arbitrate for many
    peoples;
  they shall beat their swords into
    plowshares,
  and their spears into pruning
    hooks;
  nation shall not lift up sword
    against nation,
  neither shall they learn war
    any more.

5 O house of Jacob,
    come, let us walk
  in the light of the Lord!
6 For you have forsaken the ways
    of[a] your people,
  O house of Jacob.
  Indeed they are full of diviners[b]
    from the east
  and of soothsayers like the
    Philistines,
  and they clasp hands with
    foreigners.
7 Their land is filled with silver
    and gold,
  and there is no end to their
    treasures;
  their land is filled with horses,
  and there is no end to their
    chariots.
8 Their land is filled with idols;
  they bow down to the work
    of their hands,
  to what their own fingers
    have made.
9 And so people are humbled,
  and everyone is brought
    low—
  do not forgive them!
10 Enter into the rock,
  and hide in the dust
  from the terror of the Lord,
  and from the glory of his
    majesty.
11 The haughty eyes of people
  shall be brought low,

  and the pride of everyone
    shall be humbled;
  and the Lord alone will be
    exalted
  in that day.
12 For the Lord of hosts has a day
  against all that is proud and
    lofty,
  against all that is lifted up
    and high;[c]
13 against all the cedars of
    Lebanon,
  lofty and lifted up;
  and against all the oaks of
    Bashan;
14 against all the high mountains,
  and against all the lofty hills;
15 against every high tower,
  and against every fortified
    wall;
16 against all the ships of Tarshish,
  and against all the beautiful
    craft.[d]
17 The haughtiness of people shall
    be humbled,
  and the pride of everyone
    shall be brought low;
  and the Lord alone will be
    exalted on that day.
18 The idols shall utterly pass
    away.
19 Enter the caves of the rocks
  and the holes of the ground,
  from the terror of the Lord,
  and from the glory of his
    majesty,
  when he rises to terrify the
    earth.
20 On that day people will throw
    away
  to the moles and to the bats
  their idols of silver and their
    idols of gold,
  which they made for
    themselves to worship,
21 to enter the caverns of the
    rocks
  and the clefts in the crags,

from the terror of the Lord,
    and from the glory of his
      majesty,
    when he rises to terrify the
      earth.
22 Turn away from mortals,
    who have only breath in their
      nostrils,
    for of what account are they?

## 2 CORINTHIANS 10.1–18

I MYSELF, Paul, appeal to you by the meekness and gentleness of Christ—I who am humble when face to face with you, but bold toward you when I am away!— 2I ask that when I am present I need not show boldness by daring to oppose those who think we are acting according to human standards. a 3Indeed, we live as human beings, b but we do not wage war according to human standards; a 4for the weapons of our warfare are not merely human, c but they have divine power to destroy strongholds. We destroy arguments 5and every proud obstacle raised up against the knowledge of God, and we take every thought captive to obey Christ. 6We are ready to punish every disobedience when your obedience is complete.

7 Look at what is before your eyes. If you are confident that you belong to Christ, remind yourself of this, that just as you belong to Christ, so also do we. 8Now, even if I boast a little too much of our authority, which the Lord gave for building you up and not for tearing you down, I will not be ashamed of it. 9I do not want to seem as though I am trying to frighten you with my letters. 10For they say, "His letters are weighty and strong, but his bodily presence is weak, and his speech contemptible." 11Let such people understand that what we say by letter when absent, we will also do when present.

12 We do not dare to classify or compare ourselves with some of those who commend themselves. But when they measure themselves by one another, and compare themselves with one another, they do not show good sense. 13We, however, will not boast beyond limits, but will keep within the field that God has assigned to us, to reach out even as far as you. 14For we were not overstepping our limits when we reached you; we were the first to come all the way to you with the good newsd of Christ. 15We do not boast beyond limits, that is, in the labors of others; but our hope is that, as your faith increases, our sphere of action among you may be greatly enlarged, 16so that we may proclaim the good newsd in lands beyond you, without boasting of work already done in someone else's sphere of action. 17"Let the one who boasts, boast in the Lord." 18For it is not those who commend themselves that are approved, but those whom the Lord commends.

## PSALM 52.1–9

*To the leader. A Maskil of David, when Doeg the Edomite came to Saul and said to him, "David has come to the house of Ahimelech."*

W HY do you boast, O mighty
      one,
    of mischief done against
      the godly?e
All day long 2you are plotting
      destruction.
Your tongue is like a sharp
      razor,
    you worker of treachery.
3 You love evil more than good,
    and lying more than speaking
      the truth.     *Selah*
4 You love all words that devour,
    O deceitful tongue.
5 But God will break you down
      forever;

aGk *according to the flesh*   bGk *in the flesh*   cGk *fleshly*   dOr *the gospel*   eCn Compare Syr: Heb *the kindness of God*

he will snatch and tear you
   from your tent;
he will uproot you from the
   land of the living.     *Selah*
6 The righteous will see, and fear,
   and will laugh at the
      evildoer, ᵃ saying,
7 "See the one who would not
      take
   refuge in God,
but trusted in abundant riches,
   and sought refuge in
      wealth!"ᵇ

8 But I am like a green olive tree
   in the house of God.
I trust in the steadfast love of
      God
   forever and ever.

9 I will thank you forever,
   because of what you have
      done.
In the presence of the faithful
   I will proclaimᶜ your name,
      for it is good.

## PROVERBS 22.26–27

Do not be one of those who
   give pledges,
who become surety for
   debts.
27 If you have nothing with which
      to pay,
   why should your bed be taken
      from under you?

# SEPTEMBER 9

## ISAIAH 3.1—5.30

For now the Sovereign, the
      Lord of hosts,
   is taking away from
      Jerusalem and from Judah
support and staff—
   all support of bread,
   and all support of water—
2 warrior and soldier,
   judge and prophet,
   diviner and elder,
3 captain of fifty
   and dignitary,
counselor and skillful magician
   and expert enchanter.
4 And I will make boys their
      princes,
   and babes shall rule over
      them.

5 The people will be oppressed,
   everyone by another
   and everyone by a neighbor;
the youth will be insolent to
      the elder,
   and the base to the
      honorable.

6 Someone will even seize a
      relative,
   a member of the clan, saying,
"You have a cloak;
   you shall be our leader,
and this heap of ruins
   shall be under your rule."
7 But the other will cry out on
      that day, saying,
"I will not be a healer;

aHeb *him*   bSyr Tg: Heb *in his destruction*   cCn: Heb *wait for*

in my house there is neither
    bread nor cloak;
you shall not make me
    leader of the people."
8   For Jerusalem has stumbled
    and Judah has fallen,
because their speech and their
    deeds are against the
    LORD,
    defying his glorious presence.

9   The look on their faces bears
    witness against them;
they proclaim their sin like
    Sodom,
    they do not hide it.
Woe to them!
    For they have brought evil on
    themselves.
10  Tell the innocent how fortunate
    they are,
    for they shall eat the fruit of
    their labors.
11  Woe to the guilty! How
    unfortunate they are,
    for what their hands have
    done shall be done to
    them.
12  My people—children are their
    oppressors,
    and women rule over them.
O my people, your leaders
    mislead you,
    and confuse the course of
    your paths.

13  The LORD rises to argue his
    case;
    he stands to judge the
    peoples.
14  The LORD enters into judgment
    with the elders and princes of
    his people:
It is you who have devoured the
    vineyard;
    the spoil of the poor is in
    your houses.

15  What do you mean by crushing
    my people,
    by grinding the face of the
    poor? says the Lord GOD
    of hosts.

16  The LORD said:
Because the daughters of Zion
    are haughty
    and walk with outstretched
    necks,
    glancing wantonly with
    their eyes,
mincing along as they go,
    tinkling with their feet;
17  the Lord will afflict with scabs
    the heads of the daughters of
    Zion,
    and the LORD will lay bare
    their secret parts.

18  In that day the Lord will take away the finery of the anklets, the headbands, and the crescents; 19the pendants, the bracelets, and the scarfs; 20the headdresses, the armlets, the sashes, the perfume boxes, and the amulets; 21the signet rings and nose rings; 22the festal robes, the mantles, the cloaks, and the handbags; 23the garments of gauze, the linen garments, the turbans, and the veils.
24  Instead of perfume there will be
    a stench;
    and instead of a sash, a rope;
and instead of well-set hair,
    baldness;
    and instead of a rich robe, a
    binding of sackcloth;
    instead of beauty, shame. a
25  Your men shall fall by the sword
    and your warriors in battle.
26  And her gates shall lament and
    mourn;
    ravaged, she shall sit upon
    the ground.

aQ Ms: MT lacks *shame*

4.1 SEVEN women shall take hold of one man in that day, saying,
> "We will eat our own bread and
> wear our own clothes;
> just let us be called by your
> name;
> take away our disgrace."

2 On that day the branch of the LORD shall be beautiful and glorious, and the fruit of the land shall be the pride and glory of the survivors of Israel. ³Whoever is left in Zion and remains in Jerusalem will be called holy, everyone who has been recorded for life in Jerusalem, ⁴once the Lord has washed away the filth of the daughters of Zion and cleansed the bloodstains of Jerusalem from its midst by a spirit of judgment and by a spirit of burning. ⁵Then the LORD will create over the whole site of Mount Zion and over its places of assembly a cloud by day and smoke and the shining of a flaming fire by night. Indeed over all the glory there will be a canopy. ⁶It will serve as a pavilion, a shade by day from the heat, and a refuge and a shelter from the storm and rain.

5.1 LET me sing for my beloved
> my love-song concerning his
> vineyard:
> My beloved had a vineyard
> on a very fertile hill.
2 He dug it and cleared it of
> stones,
> and planted it with choice
> vines;
> he built a watchtower in the
> midst of it,
> and hewed out a wine vat in
> it;
> he expected it to yield grapes,
> but it yielded wild grapes.

3 And now, inhabitants of
> Jerusalem
> and people of Judah,
> judge between me
> and my vineyard.
4 What more was there to do for
> my vineyard
> that I have not done in it?
> When I expected it to yield
> grapes,
> why did it yield wild grapes?

5 And now I will tell you
> what I will do to my vineyard.
> I will remove its hedge,
> and it shall be devoured;
> I will break down its wall,
> and it shall be trampled down.
6 I will make it a waste;
> it shall not be pruned or
> hoed,
> and it shall be overgrown with
> briers and thorns;
> I will also command the clouds
> that they rain no rain upon it.

7 For the vineyard of the LORD
> of hosts
> is the house of Israel,
> and the people of Judah
> are his pleasant planting;
> he expected justice,
> but saw bloodshed;
> righteousness,
> but heard a cry!
8 Ah, you who join house to
> house,
> who add field to field,
> until there is room for no one
> but you,
> and you are left to live alone
> in the midst of the land!
9 The LORD of hosts has sworn in
> my hearing:
> Surely many houses shall be
> desolate,
> large and beautiful houses,
> without inhabitant.
10 For ten acres of vineyard shall
> yield but one bath,

and a homer of seed shall
  yield a mere ephah. ᵃ

11 Ah, you who rise early in the
    morning
  in pursuit of strong drink,
who linger in the evening
  to be inflamed by wine,
12 whose feasts consist of lyre and
    harp,
  tambourine and flute and
    wine,
but who do not regard the
    deeds of the LORD,
  or see the work of his hands!
13 Therefore my people go into
    exile without knowledge;
their nobles are dying of
    hunger,
  and their multitude is parched
    with thirst.

14 Therefore Sheol has enlarged its
    appetite
  and opened its mouth beyond
    measure;
the nobility of Jerusalemᵇ and
    her multitude go down,
  her throng and all who exult
    in her.
15 People are bowed down,
    everyone is brought low,
  and the eyes of the haughty
    are humbled.
16 But the LORD of hosts is exalted
    by justice,
  and the Holy God shows
    himself holy by
    righteousness.
17 Then the lambs shall graze as in
    their pasture,
  fatlings and kidsᶜ shall feed
    among the ruins.

18 Ah, you who drag iniquity along
    with cords of falsehood,
  who drag sin along as with
    cart ropes,

19 who say, "Let him make haste,
  let him speed his work
    that we may see it;
let the plan of the Holy One of
    Israel hasten to
    fulfillment,
  that we may know it!"
20 Ah, you who call evil good
    and good evil,
  who put darkness for light
    and light for darkness,
  who put bitter for sweet
    and sweet for bitter!
21 Ah, you who are wise in your
    own eyes,
  and shrewd in your own
    sight!
22 Ah, you who are heroes in
    drinking wine
  and valiant at mixing drink,
23 who acquit the guilty for a
    bribe,
  and deprive the innocent of
    their rights!
24 Therefore, as the tongue of fire
    devours the stubble,
  and as dry grass sinks down
    in the flame,
so their root will become rotten,
  and their blossom go up like
    dust;
for they have rejected the
    instruction of the LORD
    of hosts,
  and have despised the word
    of the Holy One of
    Israel.

25 Therefore the anger of the LORD
    was kindled against his
    people,
  and he stretched out his hand
    against them and struck
    them;
  the mountains quaked,
and their corpses were like
    refuse
  in the streets.

ᵃThe Heb *bath*, *homer*, and *ephah* are measures of quantity  ᵇHeb *her nobility*  ᶜCn Compare Gk:
Heb *aliens*

For all this his anger has not
    turned away,
  and his hand is stretched
    out still.

26 He will raise a signal for a
    nation far away,
  and whistle for a people at
    the ends of the earth;
  Here they come, swiftly,
    speedily!
27 None of them is weary, none
    stumbles,
  none slumbers or sleeps,
  not a loincloth is loose,
  not a sandal-thong broken;
28 their arrows are sharp,
  all their bows bent,
  their horses' hoofs seem like
    flint,
  and their wheels like the
    whirlwind.
29 Their roaring is like a lion,
  like young lions they roar;
  they growl and seize their prey,
  they carry it off, and no one
    can rescue.
30 They will roar over it on that
    day,
  like the roaring of the sea.
  And if one look to the land—
  only darkness and distress;
  and the light grows dark with
    clouds.

## 2 CORINTHIANS 11.1–15

I WISH you would bear with me in a little foolishness. Do bear with me! 2I feel a divine jealousy for you, for I promised you in marriage to one husband, to present you as a chaste virgin to Christ. 3But I am afraid that as the serpent deceived Eve by its cunning, your thoughts will be led astray from a sincere and pure[a] devotion to Christ. 4For if someone comes and proclaims another Jesus than the one we proclaimed, or if you receive a different spirit from the one you received, or a different gospel from the one you accepted, you submit to it readily enough. 5I think that I am not in the least inferior to these super-apostles. 6I may be untrained in speech, but not in knowledge; certainly in every way and in all things we have made this evident to you.

7 Did I commit a sin by humbling myself so that you might be exalted, because I proclaimed God's good news[b] to you free of charge? 8I robbed other churches by accepting support from them in order to serve you. 9And when I was with you and was in need, I did not burden anyone, for my needs were supplied by the friends[c] who came from Macedonia. So I refrained and will continue to refrain from burdening you in any way. 10As the truth of Christ is in me, this boast of mine will not be silenced in the regions of Achaia. 11And why? Because I do not love you? God knows I do!

12 And what I do I will also continue to do, in order to deny an opportunity to those who want an opportunity to be recognized as our equals in what they boast about. 13For such boasters are false apostles, deceitful workers, disguising themselves as apostles of Christ. 14And no wonder! Even Satan disguises himself as an angel of light. 15So it is not strange if his ministers also disguise themselves as ministers of righteousness. Their end will match their deeds.

## PSALM 53.1–6

*To the leader: according to Mahalath. A Maskil of David.*

FOOLS say in their hearts,
    "There is no God."
  They are corrupt, they
    commit abominable acts;
  there is no one who does
    good.

a Other ancient authorities lack *and pure*    b Gk *the gospel of God*    c Gk *brothers*

2 God looks down from heaven on
      humankind
  to see if there are any who
      are wise,
  who seek after God.

3 They have all fallen away, they
      are all alike perverse;
  there is no one who does
      good,
  no, not one.

4 Have they no knowledge, those
      evildoers,
  who eat up my people as they
      eat bread,
  and do not call upon God?

5 There they shall be in great
      terror,
  in terror such as has not
      been.

For God will scatter the bones
    of the ungodly; [a]
  they will be put to shame, [b]
    for God has rejected
    them.

6 O that deliverance for Israel
    would come from Zion!
  When God restores the
    fortunes of his people,
  Jacob will rejoice; Israel will
    be glad.

## PROVERBS 22.28–29

Do not remove the ancient landmark
  that your ancestors set up.
29 Do you see those who are
    skillful in their work?
  they will serve kings;
  they will not serve common
    people.

# SEPTEMBER 10

## ISAIAH 6.1—7.25

In the year that King Uzziah died, I saw the Lord sitting on a throne, high and lofty; and the hem of his robe filled the temple. ²Seraphs were in attendance above him; each had six wings: with two they covered their faces, and with two they covered their feet, and with two they flew. ³And one called to another and said:

  "Holy, holy, holy is the Lord of
    hosts;
  the whole earth is full of his
    glory."

⁴The pivots[c] on the thresholds shook at the voices of those who called, and the house filled with smoke. ⁵And I said: "Woe is me! I am lost, for I am a man of unclean lips, and I live among a people of unclean lips; yet my eyes have seen the King, the Lord of hosts!"

6 Then one of the seraphs flew to me, holding a live coal that had been taken from the altar with a pair of tongs. ⁷The seraph[d] touched my mouth with it and said: "Now that this has touched your lips, your guilt has departed and your sin is blotted out." ⁸Then I heard the voice of the Lord saying, "Whom shall I send, and who

aCn Compare Gk Syr: Heb *him who encamps against you*   bGk: Heb *you will put to shame*
cMeaning of Heb uncertain   dHeb *He*

will go for us?" And I said, "Here am I; send me!" [9]And he said, "Go and say to this people:

'Keep listening, but do not
  comprehend;
keep looking, but do not
  understand.'
[10] Make the mind of this people
  dull,
    and stop their ears,
    and shut their eyes,
  so that they may not look with
    their eyes,
    and listen with their ears,
  and comprehend with their
    minds,
    and turn and be healed."
[11] Then I said, "How long,
    O Lord?" And he said:
  "Until cities lie waste
    without inhabitant,
  and houses without people,
    and the land is utterly
      desolate;
[12] until the Lord sends everyone
    far away,
  and vast is the emptiness in
    the midst of the land.
[13] Even if a tenth part remain in it,
    it will be burned again,
  like a terebinth or an oak
    whose stump remains
      standing
    when it is felled."[a]
The holy seed is its stump.

[7.1] In the days of Ahaz son of Jotham son of Uzziah, king of Judah, King Rezin of Aram and King Pekah son of Remaliah of Israel went up to attack Jerusalem, but could not mount an attack against it. [2]When the house of David heard that Aram had allied itself with Ephraim, the heart of Ahaz[b] and the heart of his people shook as the trees of the forest shake before the wind.

3  Then the Lord said to Isaiah, Go out to meet Ahaz, you and your son Shear-jashub,[c] at the end of the conduit of the upper pool on the highway to the Fuller's Field, [4]and say to him, Take heed, be quiet, do not fear, and do not let your heart be faint because of these two smoldering stumps of firebrands, because of the fierce anger of Rezin and Aram and the son of Remaliah. [5]Because Aram—with Ephraim and the son of Remaliah—has plotted evil against you, saying, [6]Let us go up against Judah and cut off Jerusalem[d] and conquer it for ourselves and make the son of Tabeel king in it; [7]therefore thus says the Lord God:

It shall not stand,
    and it shall not come to pass.
8  For the head of Aram is
    Damascus,
  and the head of Damascus is
    Rezin.
(Within sixty-five years Ephraim will be shattered, no longer a people.)
9  The head of Ephraim is
    Samaria,
  and the head of Samaria is the
    son of Remaliah.
If you do not stand firm in faith,
    you shall not stand at all.

10  Again the Lord spoke to Ahaz, saying, [11]Ask a sign of the Lord your God; let it be deep as Sheol or high as heaven. [12]But Ahaz said, I will not ask, and I will not put the Lord to the test. [13]Then Isaiah[e] said: "Hear then, O house of David! Is it too little for you to weary mortals, that you weary my God also? [14]Therefore the Lord himself will give you a sign. Look, the young woman[f] is with child and shall bear a son, and shall name him Immanuel.[g] [15]He shall eat curds and honey by the time he knows how to refuse the evil and choose the good. [16]For before the child knows how to refuse the evil and choose the good, the land before whose two kings you are in dread will be deserted. [17]The Lord will bring on you

and on your people and on your ancestral house such days as have not come since the day that Ephraim departed from Judah—the king of Assyria."

18 On that day the LORD will whistle for the fly that is at the sources of the streams of Egypt, and for the bee that is in the land of Assyria. ¹⁹And they will all come and settle in the steep ravines, and in the clefts of the rocks, and on all the thornbushes, and on all the pastures.

20 On that day the Lord will shave with a razor hired beyond the River— with the king of Assyria—the head and the hair of the feet, and it will take off the beard as well.

21 On that day one will keep alive a young cow and two sheep, ²²and will eat curds because of the abundance of milk that they give; for everyone that is left in the land shall eat curds and honey.

23 On that day every place where there used to be a thousand vines, worth a thousand shekels of silver, will become briers and thorns. ²⁴With bow and arrows one will go there, for all the land will be briers and thorns; ²⁵and as for all the hills that used to be hoed with a hoe, you will not go there for fear of briers and thorns; but they will become a place where cattle are let loose and where sheep tread.

## 2 CORINTHIANS 11.16–33

I REPEAT, let no one think that I am a fool; but if you do, then accept me as a fool, so that I too may boast a little. ¹⁷What I am saying in regard to this boastful confidence, I am saying not with the Lord's authority, but as a fool; ¹⁸since many boast according to human standards,ª I will also boast. ¹⁹For you gladly put up with fools, being wise

yourselves! ²⁰For you put up with it when someone makes slaves of you, or preys upon you, or takes advantage of you, or puts on airs, or gives you a slap in the face. ²¹To my shame, I must say, we were too weak for that!

But whatever anyone dares to boast of—I am speaking as a fool—I also dare to boast of that. ²²Are they Hebrews? So am I. Are they Israelites? So am I. Are they descendants of Abraham? So am I. ²³Are they ministers of Christ? I am talking like a madman—I am a better one: with far greater labors, far more imprisonments, with countless floggings, and often near death. ²⁴Five times I have received from the Jews the forty lashes minus one. ²⁵Three times I was beaten with rods. Once I received a stoning. Three times I was shipwrecked; for a night and a day I was adrift at sea; ²⁶on frequent journeys, in danger from rivers, danger from bandits, danger from my own people, danger from Gentiles, danger in the city, danger in the wilderness, danger at sea, danger from false brothers and sisters;ᵇ ²⁷in toil and hardship, through many a sleepless night, hungry and thirsty, often without food, cold and naked. ²⁸And, besides other things, I am under daily pressure because of my anxiety for all the churches. ²⁹Who is weak, and I am not weak? Who is made to stumble, and I am not indignant?

30 If I must boast, I will boast of the things that show my weakness. ³¹The God and Father of the Lord Jesus (blessed be he forever!) knows that I do not lie. ³²In Damascus, the governorᶜ under King Aretas guarded the city of Damascus in order toᵈ seize me, ³³but I was let down in a basket through a window in the wall,ᵉ and escaped from his hands.

ªGk *according to the flesh*  ᵇGk *brothers*  ᶜGk *ethnarch*  ᵈOther ancient authorities read *and wanted to*  ᵉGk *through the wall*

## PSALM 54.1–7

*To the leader: with stringed instruments. A Maskil of David, when the Ziphites went and told Saul, "David is in hiding among us."*

Save me, O God, by your name,
  and vindicate me by your
    might.
2 Hear my prayer, O God;
  give ear to the words of my
    mouth.

3 For the insolent have risen
    against me,
  the ruthless seek my life;
  they do not set God before
    them.          *Selah*

4 But surely, God is my helper;
  the Lord is the upholder of[a]
    my life.
5 He will repay my enemies for
    their evil.
  In your faithfulness, put an
    end to them.

6 With a freewill offering I will
    sacrifice to you;
  I will give thanks to your
    name, O Lord, for it is
      good.
7 For he has delivered me from
    every trouble,
  and my eye has looked in
    triumph on my enemies.

## PROVERBS 23.1–3

When you sit down to eat
    with a ruler,
  observe carefully what[b] is
    before you,
2 and put a knife to your throat
  if you have a big appetite.
3 Do not desire the ruler's[c]
    delicacies,
  for they are deceptive food.

# SEPTEMBER 11

## ISAIAH 8.1—9.21

Then the Lord said to me, Take a large tablet and write on it in common characters, "Belonging to Maher-shalal-hash-baz,"[d] 2and have it attested[e] for me by reliable witnesses, the priest Uriah and Zechariah son of Jeberechiah. 3And I went to the prophetess, and she conceived and bore a son. Then the Lord said to me, Name him Maher-shalal-hash-baz; 4for before the child knows how to call "My father" or "My mother," the wealth of Damascus and the spoil of Samaria will be carried away by the king of Assyria.

5 The Lord spoke to me again: 6Because this people has refused the waters of Shiloah that flow gently, and melt in fear before[f] Rezin and the son of Remaliah; 7therefore, the Lord is bringing up against it the mighty flood waters of the River, the king of Assyria and all his glory; it will rise above all its channels and overflow all its banks; 8it will sweep on into Judah as a flood, and, pouring over, it will reach up to the neck; and its outspread wings will fill

aGk Syr Jerome: Heb *is of those who uphold* or *is with those who uphold*   bOr *who*   cHeb *his*   dThat is *The spoil speeds, the prey hastens*   eQ Ms Gk Syr: MT *and I caused to be attested*   fCn: Meaning of Heb uncertain

the breadth of your land, O Immanuel.

9  Band together, you peoples, and
        be dismayed;
    listen, all you far countries;
    gird yourselves and be
        dismayed;
    gird yourselves and be
        dismayed!
10  Take counsel together, but it
        shall be brought to
        naught;
    speak a word, but it will not
        stand,
    for God is with us. a

11  For the LORD spoke thus to me while his hand was strong upon me, and warned me not to walk in the way of this people, saying: 12Do not call conspiracy all that this people calls conspiracy, and do not fear what it fears, or be in dread. 13But the LORD of hosts, him you shall regard as holy; let him be your fear, and let him be your dread. 14He will become a sanctuary, a stone one strikes against; for both houses of Israel he will become a rock one stumbles over—a trap and a snare for the inhabitants of Jerusalem. 15And many among them shall stumble; they shall fall and be broken; they shall be snared and taken.

16  Bind up the testimony, seal the teaching among my disciples. 17I will wait for the LORD, who is hiding his face from the house of Jacob, and I will hope in him. 18See, I and the children whom the LORD has given me are signs and portents in Israel from the LORD of hosts, who dwells on Mount Zion. 19Now if people say to you, "Consult the ghosts and the familiar spirits that chirp and mutter; should not a people consult their gods, the dead on behalf of the living, 20for teaching and for instruction?" Surely, those who speak like this will have no dawn! 21They will pass through the land, b greatly distressed and hungry; when they are hungry, they will be enraged and will cursec their king and their gods. They will turn their faces upward, 22or they will look to the earth, but will see only distress and darkness, the gloom of anguish; and they will be thrust into thick darkness. d

9e.1  BUT there will be no gloom for those who were in anguish. In the former time he brought into contempt the land of Zebulun and the land of Naphtali, but in the latter time he will make glorious the way of the sea, the land beyond the Jordan, Galilee of the nations.
2f  The people who walked in
        darkness
    have seen a great light;
    those who lived in a land of
        deep darkness—
    on them light has shined.
3  You have multiplied the nation,
    you have increased its joy;
    they rejoice before you
        as with joy at the harvest,
        as people exult when dividing
        plunder.
4  For the yoke of their burden,
    and the bar across their
        shoulders,
        the rod of their oppressor,
    you have broken as on the
        day of Midian.
5  For all the boots of the tramping
        warriors
    and all the garments rolled in
        blood
    shall be burned as fuel for
        the fire.
6  For a child has been born for
        us,
    a son given to us;
    authority rests upon his
        shoulders;
    and he is named
    Wonderful Counselor, Mighty
        God,

aHeb immanu el  bHeb it  cOr curse by  dMeaning of Heb uncertain  eCh 8.23 in Heb  fCh 9.1 in Heb

Everlasting Father, Prince of
    Peace.
7 His authority shall grow
    continually,
    and there shall be endless
      peace
for the throne of David and his
    kingdom.
He will establish and uphold it
with justice and with
    righteousness
    from this time onward and
      forevermore.
The zeal of the Lord of hosts
    will do this.

8 The Lord sent a word against
    Jacob,
    and it fell on Israel;
9 and all the people knew it—
    Ephraim and the inhabitants
      of Samaria—
    but in pride and arrogance of
      heart they said:
10 "The bricks have fallen,
    but we will build with dressed
      stones;
the sycamores have been cut
    down,
    but we will put cedars in their
      place."
11 So the Lord raised adversaries[a]
    against them,
    and stirred up their enemies,
12 the Arameans on the east and
    the Philistines on the
      west,
    and they devoured Israel with
      open mouth.
For all this his anger has not
    turned away;
    his hand is stretched out still.

13 The people did not turn to him
    who struck them,
    or seek the Lord of hosts.
14 So the Lord cut off from Israel
    head and tail,

    palm branch and reed in one
      day—
15 elders and dignitaries are the
    head,
    and prophets who teach lies
      are the tail;
16 for those who led this people
    led them astray,
    and those who were led by
      them were left in
      confusion.
17 That is why the Lord did not
    have pity on[b] their
      young people,
    or compassion on their
      orphans and widows;
for everyone was godless and
    an evildoer,
    and every mouth spoke folly.
For all this his anger has not
    turned away,
    his hand is stretched out still.

18 For wickedness burned like a
    fire,
    consuming briers and thorns;
it kindled the thickets of the
    forest,
    and they swirled upward in a
      column of smoke.
19 Through the wrath of the Lord
    of hosts
    the land was burned,
and the people became like fuel
    for the fire;
    no one spared another.
20 They gorged on the right, but
    still were hungry,
    and they devoured on the
      left, but were not
      satisfied;
they devoured the flesh of their
    own kindred;[c]
21 Manasseh devoured Ephraim,
    and Ephraim Manasseh,
    and together they were
      against Judah.

---

[a] Cn: Heb *the adversaries of Rezin*  [b] Q Ms: MT *rejoice over*  [c] Or *arm*

For all this his anger has not
turned away;
his hand is stretched out still.

## 2 CORINTHIANS 12.1–10

IT is necessary to boast; nothing is to be gained by it, but I will go on to visions and revelations of the Lord. ²I know a person in Christ who fourteen years ago was caught up to the third heaven—whether in the body or out of the body I do not know; God knows. ³And I know that such a person—whether in the body or out of the body I do not know; God knows—⁴was caught up into Paradise and heard things that are not to be told, that no mortal is permitted to repeat. ⁵On behalf of such a one I will boast, but on my own behalf I will not boast, except of my weaknesses. ⁶But if I wish to boast, I will not be a fool, for I will be speaking the truth. But I refrain from it, so that no one may think better of me than what is seen in me or heard from me, ⁷even considering the exceptional character of the revelations. Therefore, to keepᵃ me from being too elated, a thorn was given me in the flesh, a messenger of Satan to torment me, to keep me from being too elated.ᵇ ⁸Three times I appealed to the Lord about this, that it would leave me, ⁹but he said to me, "My grace is sufficient for you, for powerᶜ is made perfect in weakness." So, I will boast all the more gladly of my weaknesses, so that the power of Christ may dwell in me. ¹⁰Therefore I am content with weaknesses, insults, hardships, persecutions, and calamities for the sake of Christ; for whenever I am weak, then I am strong.

## PSALM 55.1–23

*To the leader: with stringed instruments. A Maskil of David.*

GIVE ear to my prayer, O God;
do not hide yourself from
my supplication.
2    Attend to me, and answer me;
I am troubled in my
complaint.
I am distraught ³by the noise of
the enemy,
because of the clamor of the
wicked.
For they bringᵈ trouble upon
me,
and in anger they cherish
enmity against me.

4    My heart is in anguish within
me,
the terrors of death have
fallen upon me.
5    Fear and trembling come upon
me,
and horror overwhelms me.
6    And I say, "O that I had wings
like a dove!
I would fly away and be at
rest;
7    truly, I would flee far away;
I would lodge in the
wilderness;            *Selah*
8    I would hurry to find a shelter
for myself
from the raging wind and
tempest."

9    Confuse, O Lord, confound their
speech;
for I see violence and strife in
the city.
10    Day and night they go around it
on its walls,
and iniquity and trouble are
within it;
11        ruin is in its midst;

---

ᵃOther ancient authorities read *To keep*    ᵇOther ancient authorities lack *to keep me from being too elated*    ᶜOther ancient authorities read *my power*    ᵈCn Compare Gk: Heb *they cause to totter*

oppression and fraud
   do not depart from its
     marketplace.

12 It is not enemies who taunt
   me—
   I could bear that;
it is not adversaries who deal
    insolently with me—
   I could hide from them.
13 But it is you, my equal,
   my companion, my familiar
    friend,
14 with whom I kept pleasant
    company;
   we walked in the house of
    God with the throng.
15 Let death come upon them;
   let them go down alive to
    Sheol;
   for evil is in their homes and
    in their hearts.

16 But I call upon God,
   and the LORD will save me.
17 Evening and morning and at
    noon
   I utter my complaint and
    moan,
   and he will hear my voice.
18 He will redeem me unharmed
   from the battle that I wage,
   for many are arrayed against
    me.
19 God, who is enthroned from of
    old,        *Selah*
   will hear, and will humble
    them—
because they do not change,

and do not fear God.

20 My companion laid hands on a
    friend
   and violated a covenant with
    me[a]
21 with speech smoother than
    butter,
   but with a heart set on war;
with words that were softer
    than oil,
   but in fact were drawn
    swords.

22 Cast your burden[b] on the LORD,
   and he will sustain you;
he will never permit
   the righteous to be moved.

23 But you, O God, will cast them
    down
   into the lowest pit;
the bloodthirsty and treacherous
   shall not live out half their
    days.
But I will trust in you.

## PROVERBS 23.4–5

Do not wear yourself out to
    get rich;
   be wise enough to desist.
5 When your eyes light upon it,
    it is gone;
   for suddenly it takes wings to
    itself,
   flying like an eagle toward
    heaven.

[a] Heb lacks *with me*   [b] Or *Cast what he has given you*

# SEPTEMBER 12

ISAIAH 10.1—11.16

A<sup>H</sup>, you who make iniquitous
decrees,
who write oppressive
statutes,
2  to turn aside the needy from
justice
and to rob the poor of my
people of their right,
that widows may be your spoil,
and that you may make the
orphans your prey!
3  What will you do on the day of
punishment,
in the calamity that will come
from far away?
To whom will you flee for help,
and where will you leave your
wealth,
4  so as not to crouch among the
prisoners
or fall among the slain?
For all this his anger has not
turned away;
his hand is stretched out still.

5  Ah, Assyria, the rod of my
anger—
the club in their hands is
my fury!
6  Against a godless nation I
send him,
and against the people of my
wrath I command him,
to take spoil and seize plunder,
and to tread them down like
the mire of the streets.
7  But this is not what he intends,
nor does he have this in
mind;
but it is in his heart to destroy,
and to cut off nations not a
few.

8  For he says:
"Are not my commanders all
kings?
9  Is not Calno like Carchemish?
Is not Hamath like Arpad?
Is not Samaria like
Damascus?
10  As my hand has reached to the
kingdoms of the idols
whose images were greater
than those of Jerusalem
and Samaria,
11  shall I not do to Jerusalem and
her idols
what I have done to Samaria
and her images?"

12  When the Lord has finished all
his work on Mount Zion and on Jerusalem, he<sup>a</sup> will punish the arrogant
boasting of the king of Assyria and his
haughty pride. <sup>13</sup>For he says:
"By the strength of my hand I
have done it,
and by my wisdom, for I have
understanding;
I have removed the boundaries
of peoples,
and have plundered their
treasures;
like a bull I have brought
down those who sat on
thrones.
14  My hand has found, like a nest,
the wealth of the peoples;
and as one gathers eggs that
have been forsaken,
so I have gathered all the
earth;
and there was none that moved
a wing,
or opened its mouth, or
chirped."

<sup>a</sup>Heb *I*

15 Shall the ax vaunt itself over the
    one who wields it,
      or the saw magnify itself
        against the one who
        handles it?
    As if a rod should raise the one
      who lifts it up,
      or as if a staff should lift the
        one who is not wood!
16 Therefore the Sovereign, the
    Lord of hosts,
    will send wasting sickness
      among his stout warriors,
  and under his glory a burning
    will be kindled,
    like the burning of fire.
17 The light of Israel will become
    a fire,
    and his Holy One a flame;
  and it will burn and devour
    his thorns and briers in one
    day.
18 The glory of his forest and his
    fruitful land
    the Lord will destroy, both
    soul and body,
    and it will be as when an
    invalid wastes away.
19 The remnant of the trees of his
    forest will be so few
    that a child can write them
    down.

20 On that day the remnant of Israel and the survivors of the house of Jacob will no more lean on the one who struck them, but will lean on the Lord, the Holy One of Israel, in truth. 21A remnant will return, the remnant of Jacob, to the mighty God. 22For though your people Israel were like the sand of the sea, only a remnant of them will return. Destruction is decreed, overflowing with righteousness. 23For the Lord God of hosts will make a full end, as decreed, in all the earth. a

24 Therefore thus says the Lord God of hosts: O my people, who live in Zion, do not be afraid of the Assyrians when they beat you with a rod and lift up their staff against you as the Egyptians did. 25For in a very little while my indignation will come to an end, and my anger will be directed to their destruction. 26The Lord of hosts will wield a whip against them, as when he struck Midian at the rock of Oreb; his staff will be over the sea, and he will lift it as he did in Egypt. 27On that day his burden will be removed from your shoulder, and his yoke will be destroyed from your neck.

    He has gone up from Rimmon, b
28     he has come to Aiath;
    he has passed through Migron,
      at Michmash he stores his
      baggage;
29 they have crossed over the
      pass,
    at Geba they lodge for the
      night;
  Ramah trembles,
    Gibeah of Saul has fled.
30 Cry aloud, O daughter Gallim!
    Listen, O Laishah!
    Answer her, O Anathoth!
31 Madmenah is in flight,
    the inhabitants of Gebim flee
      for safety.
32 This very day he will halt at
    Nob,
    he will shake his fist
    at the mount of daughter
    Zion,
    the hill of Jerusalem.

33 Look, the Sovereign, the Lord
    of hosts,
    will lop the boughs with
      terrifying power;
  the tallest trees will be cut
    down,
    and the lofty will be brought
    low.

a Or *land*  b Cn: Heb *and his yoke from your neck, and a yoke will be destroyed because of fatness*

34 He will hack down the thickets
        of the forest with an ax,
    and Lebanon with its majestic
        trees[a] will fall.

11.1 A SHOOT shall come out from
        the stump of Jesse,
    and a branch shall grow out of
        his roots.
2   The spirit of the LORD shall rest
        on him,
    the spirit of wisdom and
        understanding,
    the spirit of counsel and
        might,
    the spirit of knowledge and
        the fear of the LORD.
3   His delight shall be in the fear
        of the LORD.

    He shall not judge by what his
        eyes see,
    or decide by what his ears
        hear;
4   but with righteousness he shall
        judge the poor,
    and decide with equity for the
        meek of the earth;
    he shall strike the earth with
        the rod of his mouth,
    and with the breath of his lips
        he shall kill the wicked.
5   Righteousness shall be the belt
        around his waist,
    and faithfulness the belt
        around his loins.

6   The wolf shall live with the
        lamb,
    the leopard shall lie down
        with the kid,
    the calf and the lion and the
        fatling together,
    and a little child shall lead
        them.
7   The cow and the bear shall
        graze,

    their young shall lie down
        together;
    and the lion shall eat straw
        like the ox.
8   The nursing child shall play over
        the hole of the asp,
    and the weaned child shall put
        its hand on the adder's
        den.
9   They will not hurt or destroy
        on all my holy mountain;
    for the earth will be full of the
        knowledge of the LORD
        as the waters cover the sea.

10  On that day the root of Jesse
shall stand as a signal to the peoples;
the nations shall inquire of him, and his
dwelling shall be glorious.

11  On that day the Lord will extend
his hand yet a second time to recover
the remnant that is left of his people,
from Assyria, from Egypt, from Pathros, from Ethiopia,[b] from Elam, from
Shinar, from Hamath, and from the
coastlands of the sea.

12  He will raise a signal for the
        nations,
    and will assemble the outcasts
        of Israel,
    and gather the dispersed of
        Judah
    from the four corners of the
        earth.
13  The jealousy of Ephraim shall
        depart,
    the hostility of Judah shall be
        cut off;
    Ephraim shall not be jealous of
        Judah,
    and Judah shall not be hostile
        towards Ephraim.
14  But they shall swoop down on
        the backs of the
        Philistines in the west,
    together they shall plunder
        the people of the east.

aCn Compare Gk Vg: Heb *with a majestic one*   bOr *Nubia*; Heb *Cush*

They shall put forth their hand
    against Edom and Moab,
and the Ammonites shall
    obey them.
15 And the Lord will utterly
    destroy
  the tongue of the sea of
    Egypt;
and will wave his hand over
    the River
  with his scorching wind;
and will split it into seven
    channels,
  and make a way to cross on
    foot;
16 so there shall be a highway from
    Assyria
  for the remnant that is left of
    his people,
as there was for Israel
  when they came up from the
    land of Egypt.

## 2 CORINTHIANS 12.11–21

**I**HAVE been a fool! You forced me to it. Indeed you should have been the ones commending me, for I am not at all inferior to these super-apostles, even though I am nothing. [12]The signs of a true apostle were performed among you with utmost patience, signs and wonders and mighty works. [13]How have you been worse off than the other churches, except that I myself did not burden you? Forgive me this wrong!

14 Here I am, ready to come to you this third time. And I will not be a burden, because I do not want what is yours but you; for children ought not to lay up for their parents, but parents for their children. [15]I will most gladly spend and be spent for you. If I love you more, am I to be loved less? [16]Let it be assumed that I did not burden you. Nevertheless (you say) since I was crafty, I took you in by deceit. [17]Did I take advantage of you through any of those whom I sent to you? [18]I urged

Titus to go, and sent the brother with him. Titus did not take advantage of you, did he? Did we not conduct ourselves with the same spirit? Did we not take the same steps?

19 Have you been thinking all along that we have been defending ourselves before you? We are speaking in Christ before God. Everything we do, beloved, is for the sake of building you up. [20]For I fear that when I come, I may find you not as I wish, and that you may find me not as you wish; I fear that there may perhaps be quarreling, jealousy, anger, selfishness, slander, gossip, conceit, and disorder. [21]I fear that when I come again, my God may humble me before you, and that I may have to mourn over many who previously sinned and have not repented of the impurity, sexual immorality, and licentiousness that they have practiced.

## PSALM 56.1–13

*To the leader: according to The Dove on Far-off Terebinths. Of David. A Miktam, when the Philistines seized him in Gath.*

**B**E gracious to me, O God, for
    people trample on me;
  all day long foes oppress
    me;
2 my enemies trample on me all
    day long,
  for many fight against me.
O Most High, 3when I am
    afraid,
  I put my trust in you.
4 In God, whose word I praise,
  in God I trust; I am not
    afraid;
  what can flesh do to me?

5 All day long they seek to injure
    my cause;
  all their thoughts are against
    me for evil.
6 They stir up strife, they lurk,
  they watch my steps.
As they hoped to have my life,

7  so repay[a] them for their
         crime;
     in wrath cast down the
         peoples, O God!

8  You have kept count of my
         tossings;
     put my tears in your bottle.
     Are they not in your record?
9  Then my enemies will retreat
         in the day when I call.
     This I know, that[b] God is for
         me.
10  In God, whose word I praise,
     in the LORD, whose word I
         praise,
11  in God I trust; I am not afraid.
     What can a mere mortal do to
         me?

12  My vows to you I must
         perform, O God;

I will render thank offerings
     to you.
13  For you have delivered my soul
         from death,
     and my feet from falling,
     so that I may walk before God
     in the light of life.

## PROVERBS 23.6–8

Do not eat the bread of the
         stingy;
     do not desire their
         delicacies;
7  for like a hair in the throat, so
         are they.[c]
     "Eat and drink!" they say to
         you;
     but they do not mean it.
8  You will vomit up the little you
         have eaten,
     and you will waste your
         pleasant words.

# SEPTEMBER 13

## ISAIAH 12.1—14.32

You will say in that day:
     I will give thanks to you,
         O LORD,
     for though you were angry
         with me,
     your anger turned away,
     and you comforted me.

2  Surely God is my salvation;
     I will trust, and will not
         be afraid,
     for the LORD GOD[d] is my
         strength and my might;
     he has become my salvation.

3  With joy you will draw water from
the wells of salvation. 4And you will say
in that day:
     Give thanks to the LORD,
         call on his name;
     make known his deeds among
         the nations;
     proclaim that his name is
         exalted.

5  Sing praises to the LORD, for he
         has done gloriously;
     let this be known[e] in all the
         earth.

---

aCn: Heb *rescue*  bOr *because*  cMeaning of Heb uncertain  dHeb *for Yah, the* LORD  eOr *this is made known*

6  Shout aloud and sing for joy,
       O royal<sup>a</sup> Zion,
    for great in your midst is the
       Holy One of Israel.

**13.1** THE oracle concerning Babylon that Isaiah son of Amoz saw.

2  On a bare hill raise a signal,
       cry aloud to them;
    wave the hand for them to enter
       the gates of the nobles.
3  I myself have commanded my
       consecrated ones,
    have summoned my warriors,
       my proudly exulting
       ones,
    to execute my anger.

4  Listen, a tumult on the
       mountains
       as of a great multitude!
    Listen, an uproar of kingdoms,
       of nations gathering together!
    The LORD of hosts is mustering
       an army for battle.
5  They come from a distant land,
       from the end of the heavens,
    the LORD and the weapons of his
       indignation,
       to destroy the whole earth.

6  Wail, for the day of the LORD
       is near;
    it will come like destruction
       from the Almighty!<sup>b</sup>
7  Therefore all hands will be
       feeble,
    and every human heart will
       melt,
8     and they will be dismayed.
    Pangs and agony will seize
       them;
       they will be in anguish like a
       woman in labor.
    They will look aghast at one
       another;
       their faces will be aflame.

9  See, the day of the LORD
       comes,
    cruel, with wrath and fierce
       anger,
    to make the earth a desolation,
       and to destroy its sinners
       from it.
10 For the stars of the heavens
       and their constellations
    will not give their light;
    the sun will be dark at its rising,
       and the moon will not shed
       its light.
11 I will punish the world for its
       evil,
       and the wicked for their
       iniquity;
    I will put an end to the pride of
       the arrogant,
       and lay low the insolence of
       tyrants.
12 I will make mortals more rare
       than fine gold,
       and humans than the gold of
       Ophir.
13 Therefore I will make the
       heavens tremble,
       and the earth will be shaken
       out of its place,
    at the wrath of the LORD of
       hosts
       in the day of his fierce anger.
14 Like a hunted gazelle,
       or like sheep with no one to
       gather them,
    all will turn to their own people,
       and all will flee to their
       own lands.
15 Whoever is found will be thrust
       through,
       and whoever is caught will fall
       by the sword.
16 Their infants will be dashed
       to pieces
       before their eyes;
    their houses will be plundered,
       and their wives ravished.

<sup>a</sup>Or *O inhabitant of*   <sup>b</sup>Traditional rendering of Heb *Shaddai*

17 See, I am stirring up the Medes
    against them,
who have no regard for silver
    and do not delight in gold.
18 Their bows will slaughter the
    young men;
they will have no mercy on
    the fruit of the womb;
their eyes will not pity
    children.
19 And Babylon, the glory of
    kingdoms,
the splendor and pride of the
    Chaldeans,
will be like Sodom and
    Gomorrah
when God overthrew them.
20 It will never be inhabited
    or lived in for all generations;
Arabs will not pitch their
    tents there,
shepherds will not make their
    flocks lie down there.
21 But wild animals will lie
    down there,
and its houses will be full of
    howling creatures;
there ostriches will live,
and there goat-demons
    will dance.
22 Hyenas will cry in its towers,
and jackals in the pleasant
    palaces;
its time is close at hand,
and its days will not be
    prolonged.

14.1 BUT the LORD will have compassion on Jacob and will again choose Israel, and will set them in their own land; and aliens will join them and attach themselves to the house of Jacob. 2And the nations will take them and bring them to their place, and the house of Israel will possess the nations[a] as male and female slaves in the LORD's land; they will take captive those who were their captors, and rule over those who oppressed them.

3 When the LORD has given you rest from your pain and turmoil and the hard service with which you were made to serve, 4you will take up this taunt against the king of Babylon:

How the oppressor has ceased!
    How his insolence[b] has
    ceased!
5 The LORD has broken the staff
    of the wicked,
the scepter of rulers,
6 that struck down the peoples
    in wrath
with unceasing blows,
that ruled the nations in anger
    with unrelenting persecution.
7 The whole earth is at rest
    and quiet;
they break forth into singing.
8 The cypresses exult over you,
    the cedars of Lebanon,
    saying,
"Since you were laid low,
    no one comes to cut us
    down."
9 Sheol beneath is stirred up
    to meet you when you come;
it rouses the shades to greet
    you,
all who were leaders of the
    earth;
it raises from their thrones
all who were kings of the
    nations.
10 All of them will speak
    and say to you:
"You too have become as weak
    as we!
You have become like us!"
11 Your pomp is brought down
    to Sheol,
    and the sound of your harps;
maggots are the bed beneath
    you,
    and worms are your covering.

aHeb *them*  bQ Ms Compare Gk Syr Vg: Meaning of MT uncertain

12 How you are fallen from
    heaven,
  O Day Star, son of Dawn!
  How you are cut down to the
    ground,
    you who laid the nations low!
13 You said in your heart,
    "I will ascend to heaven;
  I will raise my throne
    above the stars of God;
  I will sit on the mount of
    assembly
    on the heights of Zaphon; [a]
14 I will ascend to the tops of the
    clouds,
  I will make myself like the
    Most High."
15 But you are brought down to
    Sheol,
    to the depths of the Pit.
16 Those who see you will stare
    at you,
    and ponder over you:
  "Is this the man who made the
    earth tremble,
    who shook kingdoms,
17 who made the world like a
    desert
    and overthrew its cities,
    who would not let his
    prisoners go home?"
18 All the kings of the nations lie
    in glory,
    each in his own tomb;
19 but you are cast out, away from
    your grave,
    like loathsome carrion, [b]
  clothed with the dead, those
    pierced by the sword,
    who go down to the stones of
    the Pit,
    like a corpse trampled
    underfoot.
20 You will not be joined with them
    in burial,
    because you have destroyed
    your land,
    you have killed your people.

  May the descendants of
    evildoers
    nevermore be named!
21 Prepare slaughter for his sons
    because of the guilt of their
    father. [c]
  Let them never rise to possess
    the earth
    or cover the face of the world
    with cities.

22 I will rise up against them, says the LORD of hosts, and will cut off from Babylon name and remnant, offspring and posterity, says the LORD. 23 And I will make it a possession of the hedgehog, and pools of water, and I will sweep it with the broom of destruction, says the LORD of hosts.

24 The LORD of hosts has sworn:
  As I have designed,
    so shall it be;
  and as I have planned,
    so shall it come to pass:
25 I will break the Assyrian in
    my land,
    and on my mountains trample
    him under foot;
  his yoke shall be removed
    from them,
    and his burden from their
    shoulders.
26 This is the plan that is planned
    concerning the whole earth;
  and this is the hand that is
    stretched out
    over all the nations.
27 For the LORD of hosts has
    planned,
    and who will annul it?
  His hand is stretched out,
    and who will turn it back?

28 In the year that King Ahaz died this oracle came:

---

**a** Or *assembly in the far north*    **b** Cn Compare Gk: Heb *like a loathed branch*    **c** Syr Compare Gk: Heb *fathers*

29 Do not rejoice, all you
 Philistines,
 that the rod that struck you
  is broken,
 for from the root of the snake
  will come forth an adder,
 and its fruit will be a flying
  fiery serpent.
30 The firstborn of the poor will
 graze,
 and the needy lie down in
  safety;
 but I will make your root die
  of famine,
 and your remnant I[a] will kill.
31 Wail, O gate; cry, O city;
 melt in fear, O Philistia, all
  of you!
 For smoke comes out of the
  north,
 and there is no straggler in
  its ranks.

32 What will one answer the
 messengers of the
  nation?
 "The LORD has founded Zion,
 and the needy among his
  people
 will find refuge in her."

## 2 CORINTHIANS 13.1–13

**T**HIS is the third time I am coming to you. "Any charge must be sustained by the evidence of two or three witnesses." [2]I warned those who sinned previously and all the others, and I warn them now while absent, as I did when present on my second visit, that if I come again, I will not be lenient— [3]since you desire proof that Christ is speaking in me. He is not weak in dealing with you, but is powerful in you. [4]For he was crucified in weakness, but lives by the power of God. For we are weak in him,[b] but in dealing with you we will live with him by the power of God.

5 Examine yourselves to see whether you are living in the faith. Test yourselves. Do you not realize that Jesus Christ is in you?—unless, indeed, you fail to meet the test! [6]I hope you will find out that we have not failed. [7]But we pray to God that you may not do anything wrong—not that we may appear to have met the test, but that you may do what is right, though we may seem to have failed. [8]For we cannot do anything against the truth, but only for the truth. [9]For we rejoice when we are weak and you are strong. This is what we pray for, that you may become perfect. [10]So I write these things while I am away from you, so that when I come, I may not have to be severe in using the authority that the Lord has given me for building up and not for tearing down.

11 Finally, brothers and sisters,[c] farewell.[d] Put things in order, listen to my appeal,[e] agree with one another, live in peace; and the God of love and peace will be with you. [12]Greet one another with a holy kiss. All the saints greet you.

13 The grace of the Lord Jesus Christ, the love of God, and the communion of[f] the Holy Spirit be with all of you.

## PSALM 57.1–11

*To the leader: Do Not Destroy. Of David. A Miktam, when he fled from Saul, in the cave.*

**B**E merciful to me, O God, be
 merciful to me,
 for in you my soul takes
  refuge;
 in the shadow of your wings I
  will take refuge,
 until the destroying storms
  pass by.
2 I cry to God Most High,

to God who fulfills his
    purpose for me.
3 He will send from heaven and
    save me,
he will put to shame those
    who trample on me.
               *Selah*
God will send forth his steadfast
    love and his faithfulness.

4 I lie down among lions
    that greedily devour[a] human
      prey;
their teeth are spears and
    arrows,
    their tongues sharp swords.

5 Be exalted, O God, above the
    heavens.
    Let your glory be over all the
      earth.

6 They set a net for my steps;
    my soul was bowed down.
They dug a pit in my path,
    but they have fallen into it
      themselves.     *Selah*
7 My heart is steadfast, O God,
    my heart is steadfast.
I will sing and make melody.
8     Awake, my soul!

Awake, O harp and lyre!
    I will awake the dawn.
9 I will give thanks to you,
    O Lord, among the
      peoples;
I will sing praises to you
    among the nations.
10 For your steadfast love is as
    high as the heavens;
your faithfulness extends to
    the clouds.

11 Be exalted, O God, above the
    heavens.
    Let your glory be over all the
      earth.

## PROVERBS 23.9–11

Do not speak in the hearing of
    a fool,
who will only despise the
    wisdom of your words.
10 Do not remove an ancient
    landmark
or encroach on the fields of
    orphans,
11 for their redeemer is strong;
    he will plead their cause
    against you.

# SEPTEMBER 14

## ISAIAH 15.1—18.7

An oracle concerning Moab.

Because Ar is laid waste in
    a night,
    Moab is undone;
because Kir is laid waste in
    a night,

    Moab is undone.
2 Dibon[b] has gone up to the
    temple,
    to the high places to weep;
over Nebo and over Medeba
    Moab wails.
On every head is baldness,
    every beard is shorn;

a Cn: Heb *are aflame for*    b Cn: Heb *the house and Dibon*

3  in the streets they bind on
          sackcloth;
      on the housetops and in the
          squares
      everyone wails and melts
          in tears.
4  Heshbon and Elealeh cry out,
      their voices are heard as far
          as Jahaz;
      therefore the loins of Moab
          quiver;[a]
      his soul trembles.
5  My heart cries out for Moab;
      his fugitives flee to Zoar,
      to Eglath-shelishiyah.
   For at the ascent of Luhith
      they go up weeping;
   on the road to Horonaim
      they raise a cry of
          destruction;
6  the waters of Nimrim
      are a desolation;
   the grass is withered, the new
          growth fails,
      the verdure is no more.
7  Therefore the abundance they
          have gained
      and what they have laid up
   they carry away
      over the Wadi of the Willows.
8  For a cry has gone
      around the land of Moab;
   the wailing reaches to Eglaim,
      the wailing reaches to
          Beer-elim.
9  For the waters of Dibon[b] are
          full of blood;
      yet I will bring upon Dibon[b]
          even more—
   a lion for those of Moab
      who escape,
      for the remnant of the land.

16.1  SEND lambs
      to the ruler of the land,
   from Sela, by way of the desert,
      to the mount of daughter
          Zion.

2  Like fluttering birds,
      like scattered nestlings,
   so are the daughters of Moab
      at the fords of the Arnon.
3  "Give counsel,
      grant justice;
   make your shade like night
      at the height of noon;
   hide the outcasts,
      do not betray the fugitive;
4  let the outcasts of Moab
      settle among you;
   be a refuge to them
      from the destroyer."

   When the oppressor is no more,
      and destruction has ceased,
   and marauders have vanished
          from the land,
5  then a throne shall be
          established in steadfast
          love
      in the tent of David,
      and on it shall sit in
          faithfulness
   a ruler who seeks justice
      and is swift to do what is
          right.

6  We have heard of the pride of
          Moab
      —how proud he is!—
   of his arrogance, his pride, and
          his insolence;
      his boasts are false.
7  Therefore let Moab wail,
      let everyone wail for Moab.
   Mourn, utterly stricken,
      for the raisin cakes of
          Kir-hareseth.

8  For the fields of Heshbon
          languish,
      and the vines of Sibmah,
   whose clusters once made
          drunk
      the lords of the nations,
   reached to Jazer

---

a Cn Compare Gk Syr: Heb *the armed men of Moab cry aloud*   b Q Ms Vg Compare Syr: MT *Dimon*

and strayed to the desert;
   their shoots once spread abroad
   and crossed over the sea.
9 Therefore I weep with the
     weeping of Jazer
   for the vines of Sibmah;
I drench you with my tears,
   O Heshbon and Elealeh;
for the shout over your fruit
     harvest
   and your grain harvest
     has ceased.
10 Joy and gladness are taken away
   from the fruitful field;
and in the vineyards no songs
     are sung,
   no shouts are raised;
no treader treads out wine in
     the presses;
   the vintage-shout is hushed. a
11 Therefore my heart throbs like
     a harp for Moab,
   and my very soul for
     Kir-heres.

12 When Moab presents himself, when he wearies himself upon the high place, when he comes to his sanctuary to pray, he will not prevail.

13 This was the word that the LORD spoke concerning Moab in the past. 14But now the LORD says, In three years, like the years of a hired worker, the glory of Moab will be brought into contempt, in spite of all its great multitude; and those who survive will be very few and feeble.

17.1 AN oracle concerning Damascus.

   See, Damascus will cease to be
     a city,
   and will become a heap of
     ruins.
2 Her towns will be deserted
     forever; b
   they will be places for flocks,

which will lie down, and no
     one will make them
     afraid.
3 The fortress will disappear from
     Ephraim,
   and the kingdom from
     Damascus;
and the remnant of Aram will be
   like the glory of the children
     of Israel,
       says the LORD of hosts.
4 On that day
   the glory of Jacob will be
     brought low,
   and the fat of his flesh will
     grow lean.
5 And it shall be as when reapers
     gather standing grain
   and their arms harvest the
     ears,
and as when one gleans the ears
     of grain
   in the Valley of Rephaim.
6 Gleanings will be left in it,
   as when an olive tree is
     beaten—
two or three berries
   in the top of the highest
     bough,
four or five
   on the branches of a fruit
     tree,
     says the LORD God of Israel.

7 On that day people will regard their Maker, and their eyes will look to the Holy One of Israel; 8they will not have regard for the altars, the work of their hands, and they will not look to what their own fingers have made, either the sacred polesc or the altars of incense.

9 On that day their strong cities will be like the deserted places of the Hivites and the Amorites, d which they deserted because of the children of Israel, and there will be desolation.

aGk: Heb *I have hushed*   bCn Compare Gk: Heb *the cities of Aroer are deserted*   cHeb *Asherim*
dCn Compare Gk: Heb *places of the wood and the highest bough*

10 For you have forgotten the God
        of your salvation,
    and have not remembered the
        Rock of your refuge;
    therefore, though you plant
        pleasant plants
    and set out slips of an alien
        god,
11 though you make them grow on
        the day that you plant
        them,
    and make them blossom in
        the morning that you
        sow;
    yet the harvest will flee away
        in a day of grief and incurable
        pain.

12 Ah, the thunder of many
        peoples,
    they thunder like the
        thundering of the sea!
    Ah, the roar of nations,
        they roar like the roaring of
        mighty waters!
13 The nations roar like the roaring
        of many waters,
    but he will rebuke them, and
        they will flee far away,
    chased like chaff on the
        mountains before the
        wind
    and whirling dust before the
        storm.
14 At evening time, lo, terror!
    Before morning, they are no
        more.
    This is the fate of those who
        despoil us,
    and the lot of those who
        plunder us.

18.1 Ah, land of whirring wings
        beyond the rivers of
        Ethiopia, a
2  sending ambassadors by the
        Nile

in vessels of papyrus on the
        waters!
    Go, you swift messengers,
        to a nation tall and smooth,
    to a people feared near and far,
        a nation mighty and
        conquering,
    whose land the rivers divide.

3 All you inhabitants of the world,
        you who live on the earth,
    when a signal is raised on the
        mountains, look!
    When a trumpet is blown,
        listen!
4 For thus the LORD said to me:
    I will quietly look from my
        dwelling
    like clear heat in sunshine,
    like a cloud of dew in the heat
        of harvest.
5 For before the harvest, when
        the blossom is over
    and the flower becomes a
        ripening grape,
    he will cut off the shoots with
        pruning hooks,
    and the spreading branches
        he will hew away.
6 They shall all be left
        to the birds of prey of the
        mountains
    and to the animals of the
        earth.
    And the birds of prey will
        summer on them,
    and all the animals of the
        earth will winter on
        them.

7  At that time gifts will be brought
to the LORD of hosts from^b a people tall
and smooth, from a people feared near
and far, a nation mighty and conquering, whose land the rivers divide, to
Mount Zion, the place of the name of
the LORD of hosts.

a Or *Nubia*; Heb *Cush*   b Q Ms Gk Vg: MT *of*

# GALATIANS 1.1–24

**P**AUL an apostle—sent neither by human commission nor from human authorities, but through Jesus Christ and God the Father, who raised him from the dead— 2and all the members of God's family[a] who are with me,

To the churches of Galatia:

3   Grace to you and peace from God our Father and the Lord Jesus Christ, 4who gave himself for our sins to set us free from the present evil age, according to the will of our God and Father, 5to whom be the glory forever and ever. Amen.

6   I am astonished that you are so quickly deserting the one who called you in the grace of Christ and are turning to a different gospel— 7not that there is another gospel, but there are some who are confusing you and want to pervert the gospel of Christ. 8But even if we or an angel[b] from heaven should proclaim to you a gospel contrary to what we proclaimed to you, let that one be accursed! 9As we have said before, so now I repeat, if anyone proclaims to you a gospel contrary to what you received, let that one be accursed!

10   Am I now seeking human approval, or God's approval? Or am I trying to please people? If I were still pleasing people, I would not be a servant[c] of Christ.

11   For I want you to know, brothers and sisters,[d] that the gospel that was proclaimed by me is not of human origin; 12for I did not receive it from a human source, nor was I taught it, but I received it through a revelation of Jesus Christ.

13   You have heard, no doubt, of my earlier life in Judaism. I was violently persecuting the church of God and was trying to destroy it. 14I advanced in Judaism beyond many among my people

of the same age, for I was far more zealous for the traditions of my ancestors. 15But when God, who had set me apart before I was born and called me through his grace, was pleased 16to reveal his Son to me,[e] so that I might proclaim him among the Gentiles, I did not confer with any human being, 17nor did I go up to Jerusalem to those who were already apostles before me, but I went away at once into Arabia, and afterwards I returned to Damascus.

18   Then after three years I did go up to Jerusalem to visit Cephas and stayed with him fifteen days; 19but I did not see any other apostle except James the Lord's brother. 20In what I am writing to you, before God, I do not lie! 21Then I went into the regions of Syria and Cilicia, 22and I was still unknown by sight to the churches of Judea that are in Christ; 23they only heard it said, "The one who formerly was persecuting us is now proclaiming the faith he once tried to destroy." 24And they glorified God because of me.

# PSALM 58.1–11

*To the leader: Do Not Destroy. Of David. A Miktam.*

**D**o you indeed decree what is
   right, you gods?[f]
Do you judge people fairly?
2   No, in your hearts you devise
       wrongs;
   your hands deal out violence
       on earth.

3   The wicked go astray from the
       womb;
   they err from their birth,
       speaking lies.
4   They have venom like the
       venom of a serpent,
   like the deaf adder that stops
       its ear,
5   so that it does not hear the
       voice of charmers

    or of the cunning enchanter.

6 O God, break the teeth in their
      mouths;
    tear out the fangs of the
      young lions, O Lord!
7 Let them vanish like water that
      runs away;
    like grass let them be trodden
      down[a] and wither.
8 Let them be like the snail that
      dissolves into slime;
    like the untimely birth that
      never sees the sun.
9 Sooner than your pots can feel
      the heat of thorns,
    whether green or ablaze, may
      he sweep them away!

10 The righteous will rejoice when
      they see vengeance
      done;
    they will bathe their feet in
      the blood of the wicked.
11 People will say, "Surely there is
      a reward for the
      righteous;
    surely there is a God who
      judges on earth."

•

## PROVERBS 23.12

APPLY your mind to instruction
and your ear to words of
knowledge.

# SEPTEMBER 15

## ISAIAH 19.1—21.17

AN oracle concerning Egypt.

See, the Lord is riding on a
    swift cloud
and comes to Egypt;
the idols of Egypt will tremble
      at his presence,
and the heart of the
      Egyptians will melt within
      them.
2 I will stir up Egyptians against
      Egyptians,
and they will fight, one
      against the other,
neighbor against neighbor,
city against city, kingdom
      against kingdom;
3 the spirit of the Egyptians
      within them will be
      emptied out,

and I will confound their
      plans;
they will consult the idols and
      the spirits of the dead
and the ghosts and the
      familiar spirits;
4 I will deliver the Egyptians
    into the hand of a hard
      master;
a fierce king will rule over
      them,
    says the Sovereign, the Lord
      of hosts.

5 The waters of the Nile will be
      dried up,
    and the river will be parched
      and dry;
6 its canals will become foul,

[a] Cn: Meaning of Heb uncertain

and the branches of Egypt's
    Nile will diminish and dry
    up,
    reeds and rushes will rot
    away.
7 There will be bare places by
    the Nile,
    on the brink of the Nile;
and all that is sown by the Nile
    will dry up,
    be driven away, and be no
    more.
8 Those who fish will mourn;
    all who cast hooks in the Nile
    will lament,
    and those who spread nets on
    the water will languish.
9 The workers in flax will be in
    despair,
    and the carders and those at
    the loom will grow pale.
10 Its weavers will be dismayed,
    and all who work for wages
    will be grieved.

11 The princes of Zoan are utterly
    foolish;
    the wise counselors of
    Pharaoh give stupid
    counsel.
How can you say to Pharaoh,
    "I am one of the sages,
    a descendant of ancient
    kings"?
12 Where now are your sages?
    Let them tell you and make
    known
    what the Lord of hosts has
    planned against Egypt.
13 The princes of Zoan have
    become fools,
    and the princes of Memphis
    are deluded;
those who are the cornerstones
    of its tribes
    have led Egypt astray.
14 The Lord has poured into
    them[a]

    a spirit of confusion;
    and they have made Egypt
    stagger in all its doings
    as a drunkard staggers around
    in vomit.
15 Neither head nor tail, palm
    branch or reed,
    will be able to do anything for
    Egypt.

16 On that day the Egyptians will be like women, and tremble with fear before the hand that the Lord of hosts raises against them. 17And the land of Judah will become a terror to the Egyptians; everyone to whom it is mentioned will fear because of the plan that the Lord of hosts is planning against them.

18 On that day there will be five cities in the land of Egypt that speak the language of Canaan and swear allegiance to the Lord of hosts. One of these will be called the City of the Sun.

19 On that day there will be an altar to the Lord in the center of the land of Egypt, and a pillar to the Lord at its border. 20It will be a sign and a witness to the Lord of hosts in the land of Egypt; when they cry to the Lord because of oppressors, he will send them a savior, and will defend and deliver them. 21The Lord will make himself known to the Egyptians; and the Egyptians will know the Lord on that day, and will worship with sacrifice and burnt offering, and they will make vows to the Lord and perform them. 22The Lord will strike Egypt, striking and healing; they will return to the Lord, and he will listen to their supplications and heal them.

23 On that day there will be a highway from Egypt to Assyria, and the Assyrian will come into Egypt, and the Egyptian into Assyria, and the Egyptians will worship with the Assyrians.

24 On that day Israel will be the

---

a Gk Compare Tg: Heb *it*

third with Egypt and Assyria, a blessing in the midst of the earth, 25whom the LORD of hosts has blessed, saying, "Blessed be Egypt my people, and Assyria the work of my hands, and Israel my heritage."

**20**.1 IN the year that the commander-in-chief, who was sent by King Sargon of Assyria, came to Ashdod and fought against it and took it— 2at that time the LORD had spoken to Isaiah son of Amoz, saying, "Go, and loose the sackcloth from your loins and take your sandals off your feet," and he had done so, walking naked and barefoot. 3Then the LORD said, "Just as my servant Isaiah has walked naked and barefoot for three years as a sign and a portent against Egypt and Ethiopia,a 4so shall the king of Assyria lead away the Egyptians as captives and the Ethiopiansb as exiles, both the young and the old, naked and barefoot, with buttocks uncovered, to the shame of Egypt. 5And they shall be dismayed and confounded because of Ethiopiaa their hope and of Egypt their boast. 6In that day the inhabitants of this coastland will say, 'See, this is what has happened to those in whom we hoped and to whom we fled for help and deliverance from the king of Assyria! And we, how shall we escape?' "

**21**.1 THE oracle concerning the wilderness of the sea.

As whirlwinds in the Negeb
    sweep on,
      it comes from the desert,
      from a terrible land.
2  A stern vision is told to me;
      the betrayer betrays,
      and the destroyer destroys.
    Go up, O Elam,
      lay siege, O Media;
    all the sighing she has caused

    I bring to an end.
3 Therefore my loins are filled
      with anguish;
    pangs have seized me,
    like the pangs of a woman
      in labor;
    I am bowed down so that I
      cannot hear,
    I am dismayed so that I
      cannot see.
4 My mind reels, horror has
      appalled me;
    the twilight I longed for
    has been turned for me into
      trembling.
5 They prepare the table,
    they spread the rugs,
    they eat, they drink.
    Rise up, commanders,
    oil the shield!
6 For thus the Lord said to me:
    "Go, post a lookout,
    let him announce what he
      sees.
7 When he sees riders, horsemen
      in pairs,
    riders on donkeys, riders
      on camels,
    let him listen diligently,
    very diligently."
8 Then the watcherc called out:
    "Upon a watchtower I stand,
      O Lord,
    continually by day,
    and at my post I am stationed
    throughout the night.
9 Look, there they come, riders,
    horsemen in pairs!"
    Then he responded,
    "Fallen, fallen is Babylon;
    and all the images of her gods
    lie shattered on the ground."
10 O my threshed and winnowed
      one,
    what I have heard from the
      LORD of hosts,
    the God of Israel, I announce
    to you.

aOr *Nubia*; Heb *Cush*  bOr *Nubians*; Heb *Cushites*  cQ Ms: MT *a lion*

11    The oracle concerning Dumah.

One is calling to me from Seir,
    "Sentinel, what of the night?
    Sentinel, what of the night?"
12    The sentinel says:
    "Morning comes, and also
        the night.
    If you will inquire, inquire;
    come back again."

13    The oracle concerning the
        desert plain.

In the scrub of the desert plain
        you will lodge,
    O caravans of Dedanites.
14    Bring water to the thirsty,
        meet the fugitive with bread,
    O inhabitants of the land
        of Tema.
15    For they have fled from the
        swords,
        from the drawn sword,
    from the bent bow,
        and from the stress of battle.

16  For thus the Lord said to me: Within a year, according to the years of a hired worker, all the glory of Kedar will come to an end; 17and the remaining bows of Kedar's warriors will be few; for the LORD, the God of Israel, has spoken.

## GALATIANS 2.1–16

THEN after fourteen years I went up again to Jerusalem with Barnabas, taking Titus along with me. 2I went up in response to a revelation. Then I laid before them (though only in a private meeting with the acknowledged leaders) the gospel that I proclaim among the Gentiles, in order to make sure that I was not running, or had not run, in vain. 3But even Titus, who was with me, was not compelled to be circumcised, though he was a Greek. 4But because of false believersa secretly brought in, who slipped in to spy on the freedom we have in Christ Jesus, so that they might enslave us— 5we did not submit to them even for a moment, so that the truth of the gospel might always remain with you. 6And from those who were supposed to be acknowledged leaders (what they actually were makes no difference to me; God shows no partiality)—those leaders contributed nothing to me. 7On the contrary, when they saw that I had been entrusted with the gospel for the uncircumcised, just as Peter had been entrusted with the gospel for the circumcised 8(for he who worked through Peter making him an apostle to the circumcised also worked through me in sending me to the Gentiles), 9and when James and Cephas and John, who were acknowledged pillars, recognized the grace that had been given to me, they gave to Barnabas and me the right hand of fellowship, agreeing that we should go to the Gentiles and they to the circumcised. 10They asked only one thing, that we remember the poor, which was actually what I wasb eager to do.

11  But when Cephas came to Antioch, I opposed him to his face, because he stood self-condemned; 12for until certain people came from James, he used to eat with the Gentiles. But after they came, he drew back and kept himself separate for fear of the circumcision faction. 13And the other Jews joined him in this hypocrisy, so that even Barnabas was led astray by their hypocrisy. 14But when I saw that they were not acting consistently with the truth of the gospel, I said to Cephas before them all, "If you, though a Jew, live like a Gentile and not like a Jew, how can you compel the Gentiles to live like Jews?"c

15  We ourselves are Jews by birth

aGk *false brothers*  bOr *had been*  cSome interpreters hold that the quotation extends into the following paragraph

and not Gentile sinners; [16]yet we know that a person is justified[a] not by the works of the law but through faith in Jesus Christ.[b] And we have come to believe in Christ Jesus, so that we might be justified by faith in Christ,[c] and not by doing the works of the law, because no one will be justified by the works of the law.

## PSALM 59.1–17

*To the leader: Do Not Destroy. Of David. A Miktam, when Saul ordered his house to be watched in order to kill him.*

DELIVER me from my enemies,
    O my God;
  protect me from those who
    rise up against me.
2  Deliver me from those who
    work evil;
  from the bloodthirsty save
    me.

3  Even now they lie in wait for
    my life;
  the mighty stir up strife
    against me.
  For no transgression or sin of
    mine, O LORD,
4    for no fault of mine, they run
    and make ready.

  Rouse yourself, come to my
    help and see!
5    You, LORD God of hosts, are
    God of Israel.
  Awake to punish all the nations;
    spare none of those who
    treacherously plot evil.
                *Selah*

6  Each evening they come back,
    howling like dogs
    and prowling about the city.
7  There they are, bellowing with
    their mouths,

with sharp words[d] on their
    lips—
  for "Who," they think, [e] "will
    hear us?"

8  But you laugh at them, O LORD;
    you hold all the nations in
    derision.
9  O my strength, I will watch for
    you;
  for you, O God, are my
    fortress.
10  My God in his steadfast love
    will meet me;
  my God will let me look in
    triumph on my enemies.

11  Do not kill them, or my people
    may forget;
  make them totter by your
    power, and bring them
    down,
  O Lord, our shield.
12  For the sin of their mouths, the
    words of their lips,
  let them be trapped in their
    pride.
  For the cursing and lies that
    they utter,
13    consume them in wrath;
  consume them until they are
    no more.
  Then it will be known to the
    ends of the earth
  that God rules over Jacob.
                *Selah*

14  Each evening they come back,
    howling like dogs
    and prowling about the city.
15  They roam about for food,
    and growl if they do not get
    their fill.

16  But I will sing of your might;
    I will sing aloud of your
    steadfast love in the
    morning.

---

[a] Or *reckoned as righteous;* and so elsewhere   [b] Or *the faith of Jesus Christ*   [c] Or *the faith of Christ*
[d] Heb *with swords*   [e] Heb lacks *they think*

For you have been a fortress
>  for me
and a refuge in the day of my
>  distress.
17 O my strength, I will sing
>  praises to you,
for you, O God, are my
>  fortress,
the God who shows me
>  steadfast love.

## PROVERBS 23.13–14

Do not withhold discipline from
>  your children;
if you beat them with a rod,
>  they will not die.
14 If you beat them with the rod,
>  you will save their lives from
>  Sheol.

# SEPTEMBER 16

## ISAIAH 22.1—24.23

THE oracle concerning the valley
of vision.

What do you mean that you
>  have gone up,
all of you, to the housetops,
2 you that are full of shoutings,
>  tumultuous city, exultant
>  town?
Your slain are not slain by
>  the sword,
nor are they dead in battle.
3 Your rulers have all fled
>  together;
they were captured without
>  the use of a bow. a
All of you who were found were
>  captured,
though they had fled far
>  away. b
4 Therefore I said:
Look away from me,
>  let me weep bitter tears;
do not try to comfort me
>  for the destruction of my
>  beloved people.

5 For the Lord GOD of hosts has
>  a day
of tumult and trampling and
>  confusion
in the valley of vision,
a battering down of walls
>  and a cry for help to the
>  mountains.
6 Elam bore the quiver
>  with chariots and cavalry, c
>  and Kir uncovered the shield.
7 Your choicest valleys were full
>  of chariots,
and the cavalry took their
>  stand at the gates.
8 He has taken away the covering
>  of Judah.

On that day you looked to the weapons of the House of the Forest, 9and you saw that there were many breaches in the city of David, and you collected the waters of the lower pool. 10You counted the houses of Jerusalem, and you broke down the houses to fortify the wall. 11You made a reservoir between the two walls for the water of

aOr *without their bows*  bGk Syr Vg: Heb *fled from far away*  cMeaning of Heb uncertain

the old pool. But you did not look to him who did it, or have regard for him who planned it long ago.

12  In that day the Lord God of hosts
        called to weeping and
            mourning,
        to baldness and putting on
            sackcloth;
13  but instead there was joy and
        festivity,
        killing oxen and slaughtering
            sheep,
        eating meat and drinking
            wine.
    "Let us eat and drink,
        for tomorrow we die."
14  The Lord of hosts has revealed
        himself in my ears:
    Surely this iniquity will not be
        forgiven you until you
        die,
    says the Lord God of hosts.

15 Thus says the Lord God of hosts: Come, go to this steward, to Shebna, who is master of the household, and say to him: 16What right do you have here? Who are your relatives here, that you have cut out a tomb here for yourself, cutting a tomb on the height, and carving a habitation for yourself in the rock? 17The Lord is about to hurl you away violently, my fellow. He will seize firm hold on you, 18whirl you round and round, and throw you like a ball into a wide land; there you shall die, and there your splendid chariots shall lie, O you disgrace to your master's house! 19I will thrust you from your office, and you will be pulled down from your post.

20 On that day I will call my servant Eliakim son of Hilkiah, 21and will clothe him with your robe and bind your sash on him. I will commit your authority to his hand, and he shall be a father to the inhabitants of Jerusalem and to the house of Judah. 22I will place on his shoulder the key of the house of David; he shall open, and no one shall shut; he shall shut, and no one shall open. 23I will fasten him like a peg in a secure place, and he will become a throne of honor to his ancestral house. 24And they will hang on him the whole weight of his ancestral house, the offspring and issue, every small vessel, from the cups to all the flagons. 25On that day, says the Lord of hosts, the peg that was fastened in a secure place will give way; it will be cut down and fall, and the load that was on it will perish, for the Lord has spoken.

23.1 The oracle concerning Tyre.

    Wail, O ships of Tarshish,
        for your fortress is
            destroyed. a
    When they came in from Cyprus
        they learned of it.
2   Be still, O inhabitants of
        the coast,
        O merchants of Sidon,
    your messengers crossed over
        the seab
3       and were on the mighty
            waters;
    your revenue was the grain of
        Shihor,
        the harvest of the Nile;
        you were the merchant of the
            nations.
4   Be ashamed, O Sidon, for the
        sea has spoken,
        the fortress of the sea,
            saying:
    "I have neither labored nor
        given birth,
        I have neither reared young
            men
        nor brought up young
            women."
5   When the report comes to
        Egypt,

a Cn Compare verse 14: Heb *for it is destroyed, without houses they replenished you*   b Q Ms: MT *crossing over the sea,*

they will be in anguish over
   the report about Tyre.
6 Cross over to Tarshish—
   wail, O inhabitants of the
      coast!
7 Is this your exultant city
   whose origin is from days of
      old,
whose feet carried her
   to settle far away?
8 Who has planned this
   against Tyre, the bestower
      of crowns,
whose merchants were princes,
   whose traders were the
      honored of the earth?
9 The Lord of hosts has planned
      it—
to defile the pride of all glory,
   to shame all the honored of
      the earth.
10 Cross over to your own land,
   O ships of[a] Tarshish;
   this is a harbor[b] no more.
11 He has stretched out his hand
      over the sea,
   he has shaken the kingdoms;
the Lord has given command
      concerning Canaan
to destroy its fortresses.
12 He said:
You will exult no longer,
   O oppressed virgin daughter
      Sidon;
rise, cross over to Cyprus—
   even there you will have no
      rest.

13 Look at the land of the Chaldeans! This is the people; it was not Assyria. They destined Tyre for wild animals. They erected their siege towers, they tore down her palaces, they made her a ruin. [c]
14 Wail, O ships of Tarshish,
   for your fortress is
      destroyed.
15 From that day Tyre will be forgotten for seventy years, the lifetime of one king. At the end of seventy years, it will happen to Tyre as in the song about the prostitute:
16 Take a harp,
   go about the city,
   you forgotten prostitute!
Make sweet melody,
   sing many songs,
   that you may be
      remembered.
17 At the end of seventy years, the Lord will visit Tyre, and she will return to her trade, and will prostitute herself with all the kingdoms of the world on the face of the earth. 18 Her merchandise and her wages will be dedicated to the Lord; her profits[d] will not be stored or hoarded, but her merchandise will supply abundant food and fine clothing for those who live in the presence of the Lord.

24.1 Now the Lord is about to lay
      waste the earth and
      make it desolate,
   and he will twist its surface
      and scatter its
      inhabitants.
2 And it shall be, as with the
      people, so with the
      priest;
   as with the slave, so with his
      master;
   as with the maid, so with her
      mistress;
as with the buyer, so with
      the seller;
   as with the lender, so with
      the borrower;
   as with the creditor, so with
      the debtor.
3 The earth shall be utterly laid
      waste and utterly
      despoiled;
   for the Lord has spoken
      this word.

a Cn Compare Gk: Heb *like the Nile, daughter*  b Cn: Heb *restraint*  c Meaning of Heb uncertain
d Heb *it*

4 The earth dries up and withers,
    the world languishes and
        withers;
    the heavens languish together
        with the earth.
5 The earth lies polluted
    under its inhabitants;
    for they have transgressed
        laws,
    violated the statutes,
    broken the everlasting
        covenant.
6 Therefore a curse devours
        the earth,
    and its inhabitants suffer for
        their guilt;
    therefore the inhabitants of the
        earth dwindled,
    and few people are left.
7 The wine dries up,
    the vine languishes,
    all the merry-hearted sigh.
8 The mirth of the timbrels is
        stilled,
    the noise of the jubilant
        has ceased,
    the mirth of the lyre is stilled.
9 No longer do they drink wine
        with singing;
    strong drink is bitter to those
        who drink it.
10 The city of chaos is broken
        down,
    every house is shut up so
        that no one can enter.
11 There is an outcry in the
        streets for lack of wine;
    all joy has reached its
        eventide;
    the gladness of the earth is
        banished.
12 Desolation is left in the city,
    the gates are battered into
        ruins.
13 For thus it shall be on the earth
    and among the nations,
    as when an olive tree is beaten,
    as at the gleaning when the
        grape harvest is ended.

14 They lift up their voices, they
        sing for joy;
    they shout from the west
        over the majesty of the
        LORD.
15 Therefore in the east give glory
        to the LORD;
    in the coastlands of the sea
        glorify the name of the
        LORD, the God of Israel.
16 From the ends of the earth we
        hear songs of praise,
    of glory to the Righteous
        One.
But I say, I pine away,
    I pine away. Woe is me!
For the treacherous deal
        treacherously,
    the treacherous deal very
        treacherously.

17 Terror, and the pit, and the
        snare
    are upon you, O inhabitant of
        the earth!
18 Whoever flees at the sound of
        the terror
    shall fall into the pit;
and whoever climbs out of the
        pit
    shall be caught in the snare.
For the windows of heaven are
        opened,
    and the foundations of the
        earth tremble.
19 The earth is utterly broken,
    the earth is torn asunder,
    the earth is violently shaken.
20 The earth staggers like a
        drunkard,
    it sways like a hut;
its transgression lies heavy upon
        it,
    and it falls, and will not
        rise again.

21 On that day the LORD will punish
    the host of heaven in heaven,

and on earth the kings of
    the earth.
22 They will be gathered together
    like prisoners in a pit;
  they will be shut up in a prison,
    and after many days they will
      be punished.
23 Then the moon will be abashed,
    and the sun ashamed;
  for the Lord of hosts will reign
    on Mount Zion and in
      Jerusalem,
  and before his elders he will
    manifest his glory.

## GALATIANS 2.17—3.9

**B**UT if, in our effort to be justified in Christ, we ourselves have been found to be sinners, is Christ then a servant of sin? Certainly not! [18]But if I build up again the very things that I once tore down, then I demonstrate that I am a transgressor. [19]For through the law I died to the law, so that I might live to God. I have been crucified with Christ; [20]and it is no longer I who live, but it is Christ who lives in me. And the life I now live in the flesh I live by faith in the Son of God, [a] who loved me and gave himself for me. [21]I do not nullify the grace of God; for if justification[b] comes through the law, then Christ died for nothing.

3.1 You foolish Galatians! Who has bewitched you? It was before your eyes that Jesus Christ was publicly exhibited as crucified! [2]The only thing I want to learn from you is this: Did you receive the Spirit by doing the works of the law or by believing what you heard? [3]Are you so foolish? Having started with the Spirit, are you now ending with the flesh? [4]Did you experience so much for nothing?—if it really was for nothing. [5]Well then, does God[c] supply you with the Spirit and work miracles among you by your doing the works of the law, or by your believing what you heard?

6 Just as Abraham "believed God, and it was reckoned to him as righteousness," [7]so, you see, those who believe are the descendants of Abraham. [8]And the scripture, foreseeing that God would justify the Gentiles by faith, declared the gospel beforehand to Abraham, saying, "All the Gentiles shall be blessed in you." [9]For this reason, those who believe are blessed with Abraham who believed.

## PSALM 60. 1–12

*To the leader: according to the Lily of the Covenant. A Miktam of David; for instruction; when he struggled with Aram-naharaim and with Aram-zobah, and when Joab on his return killed twelve thousand Edomites in the Valley of Salt.*

**O** GOD, you have rejected us,
    broken our defenses;
  you have been angry; now
    restore us!
2 You have caused the land to
    quake; you have torn it
    open;
  repair the cracks in it, for it
    is tottering.
3 You have made your people
    suffer hard things;
  you have given us wine to
    drink that made us reel.

4 You have set up a banner for
    those who fear you,
  to rally to it out of bowshot. [d]
         *Selah*
5 Give victory with your right
    hand, and answer us, [e]
  so that those whom you love
    may be rescued.

6 God has promised in his
    sanctuary:[f]
  "With exultation I will divide
    up Shechem,

**a** Or *by the faith of the Son of God*  **b** Or *righteousness* *truth*  **e** Another reading is *me*  **f** Or *by his holiness*  **c** Gk *he*  **d** Gk Syr Jerome: Heb *because of the*

and portion out the Vale of
 Succoth.
7 Gilead is mine, and Manasseh is
  mine;
 Ephraim is my helmet;
 Judah is my scepter.
8 Moab is my washbasin;
 on Edom I hurl my shoe;
 over Philistia I shout in
  triumph.”

9 Who will bring me to the
  fortified city?
 Who will lead me to Edom?
10 Have you not rejected us,
  O God?

You do not go out, O God,
 with our armies.
11 O grant us help against the foe,
 for human help is worthless.
12 With God we shall do valiantly;
 it is he who will tread down
  our foes.

## PROVERBS 23.15–16

My child, if your heart is
  wise,
 my heart too will be glad.
16 My soul will rejoice
 when your lips speak what
  is right.

# SEPTEMBER 17

## ISAIAH 25.1—28.13

O Lord, you are my God;
 I will exalt you, I will praise
  your name;
for you have done wonderful
  things,
 plans formed of old, faithful
  and sure.
2 For you have made the city
  a heap,
 the fortified city a ruin;
the palace of aliens is a city
  no more,
 it will never be rebuilt.
3 Therefore strong peoples will
  glorify you;
 cities of ruthless nations will
  fear you.
4 For you have been a refuge to
  the poor,
 a refuge to the needy in their
  distress,

a shelter from the rainstorm
 and a shade from the
  heat.
When the blast of the ruthless
 was like a winter
  rainstorm,
5  the noise of aliens like heat in
  a dry place,
you subdued the heat with the
  shade of clouds;
 the song of the ruthless
  was stilled.

6 On this mountain the Lord of
  hosts will make for all
  peoples
 a feast of rich food, a feast of
  well-aged wines,
of rich food filled with
  marrow, of well-aged
  wines strained clear.
7 And he will destroy on this
  mountain

the shroud that is cast over
all peoples,
the sheet that is spread over
all nations;
he will swallow up death
forever.
8 Then the Lord God will wipe
away the tears from all
faces,
and the disgrace of his people
he will take away from all
the earth,
for the Lord has spoken.
9 It will be said on that day,
Lo, this is our God; we have
waited for him, so that
he might save us.
This is the Lord for whom we
have waited;
let us be glad and rejoice in
his salvation.
10 For the hand of the Lord will
rest on this mountain.

The Moabites shall be trodden
down in their place
as straw is trodden down in a
dung-pit.
11 Though they spread out their
hands in the midst of it,
as swimmers spread out their
hands to swim,
their pride will be laid low
despite the struggle[a] of
their hands.
12 The high fortifications of his
walls will be brought
down,
laid low, cast to the ground,
even to the dust.

26.1 On that day this song will be sung
in the land of Judah:
We have a strong city;
he sets up victory
like walls and bulwarks.
2 Open the gates,

so that the righteous nation
that keeps faith
may enter in.
3 Those of steadfast mind you
keep in peace—
in peace because they trust
in you.
4 Trust in the Lord forever,
for in the Lord God [b]
you have an everlasting rock.
5 For he has brought low
the inhabitants of the height;
the lofty city he lays low.
He lays it low to the ground,
casts it to the dust.
6 The foot tramples it,
the feet of the poor,
the steps of the needy.

7 The way of the righteous is
level;
O Just One, you make
smooth the path of the
righteous.
8 In the path of your judgments,
O Lord, we wait for you;
your name and your renown
are the soul's desire.
9 My soul yearns for you in
the night,
my spirit within me earnestly
seeks you.
For when your judgments are in
the earth,
the inhabitants of the world
learn righteousness.
10 If favor is shown to the wicked,
they do not learn
righteousness;
in the land of uprightness they
deal perversely
and do not see the majesty of
the Lord.
11 O Lord, your hand is lifted up,
but they do not see it.
Let them see your zeal for your
people, and be ashamed.

a Meaning of Heb uncertain   b Heb in Yah, the Lord

Let the fire for your
    adversaries consume
    them.
12 O Lord, you will ordain peace
    for us,
    for indeed, all that we have
        done, you have done for
        us.
13 O Lord our God,
    other lords besides you have
        ruled over us,
    but we acknowledge your
        name alone.
14 The dead do not live;
    shades do not rise—
    because you have punished and
        destroyed them,
    and wiped out all memory
        of them.
15 But you have increased the
        nation, O Lord,
    you have increased the
        nation; you are glorified;
    you have enlarged all the
        borders of the land.

16 O Lord, in distress they sought
        you,
    they poured out a prayer[a]
    when your chastening was
        on them.
17 Like a woman with child,
    who writhes and cries out in
        her pangs
    when she is near her time,
    so were we because of you,
        O Lord;
18     we were with child, we
        writhed,
    but we gave birth only to
        wind.
    We have won no victories on
        earth,
    and no one is born to inhabit
        the world.
19 Your dead shall live, their
        corpses[b] shall rise.

    O dwellers in the dust, awake
        and sing for joy!
    For your dew is a radiant dew,
        and the earth will give birth
        to those long dead. [c]

20 Come, my people, enter your
        chambers,
    and shut your doors behind
        you;
    hide yourselves for a little while
        until the wrath is past.
21 For the Lord comes out from
        his place
    to punish the inhabitants of
        the earth for their
        iniquity;
    the earth will disclose the blood
        shed on it,
    and will no longer cover its
        slain.

27.1 On that day the Lord with his cruel
and great and strong sword will punish
Leviathan the fleeing serpent, Leviathan the twisting serpent, and he will
kill the dragon that is in the sea.

2 On that day:
    A pleasant vineyard, sing about
        it!
3     I, the Lord, am its keeper;
    every moment I water it.
    I guard it night and day
        so that no one can harm it;
4     I have no wrath.
    If it gives me thorns and briers,
        I will march to battle against
        it.
        I will burn it up.
5 Or else let it cling to me for
        protection,
    let it make peace with me,
    let it make peace with me.

6 In days to come[d] Jacob shall
        take root,

---

a Meaning of Heb uncertain   b Cn Compare Syr Tg: Heb *my corpse*   c Heb *to the shades*   d Heb *Those to come*

Israel shall blossom and put
forth shoots,
and fill the whole world
with fruit.

7 Has he struck them down as he
struck down those who
struck them?
Or have they been killed as
their killers were killed?
8 By expulsion, a by exile you
struggled against them;
with his fierce blast he
removed them in the day
of the east wind.
9 Therefore by this the guilt of
Jacob will be expiated,
and this will be the full fruit of
the removal of his sin:
when he makes all the stones of
the altars
like chalkstones crushed
to pieces,
no sacred poles b or incense
altars will remain
standing.
10 For the fortified city is solitary,
a habitation deserted and
forsaken, like the
wilderness;
the calves graze there,
there they lie down, and strip
its branches.
11 When its boughs are dry, they
are broken;
women come and make a fire
of them.
For this is a people without
understanding;
therefore he that made them
will not have compassion
on them,
he that formed them will
show them no favor.

12 On that day the LORD will thresh
from the channel of the Euphrates to
the Wadi of Egypt, and you will be gathered one by one, O people of Israel.
13 And on that day a great trumpet will
be blown, and those who were lost in
the land of Assyria and those who were
driven out to the land of Egypt will
come and worship the LORD on the holy
mountain at Jerusalem.

28.1 AH, the proud garland of the
drunkards of Ephraim,
and the fading flower of its
glorious beauty,
which is on the head of those
bloated with rich food, of
those overcome with
wine!
2 See, the Lord has one who is
mighty and strong;
like a storm of hail, a
destroying tempest,
like a storm of mighty,
overflowing waters;
with his hand he will hurl
them down to the earth.
3 Trampled under foot will be
the proud garland of the
drunkards of Ephraim.
4 And the fading flower of its
glorious beauty,
which is on the head of those
bloated with rich food,
will be like a first-ripe fig before
the summer;
whoever sees it, eats it up
as soon as it comes to hand.

5 In that day the LORD of hosts
will be a garland of glory,
and a diadem of beauty, to
the remnant of his
people;
6 and a spirit of justice to the one
who sits in judgment,
and strength to those who
turn back the battle at
the gate.

7 These also reel with wine

a Meaning of Heb uncertain   b Heb *Asherim*

*to affirm approve confirmation*

and stagger with strong drink;
the priest and the prophet reel
    with strong drink,
    they are confused with wine,
    they stagger with strong
        drink;
they err in vision,
    they stumble in giving
        judgment.
8 All tables are covered with
        filthy vomit;
    no place is clean.

9 "Whom will he teach
        knowledge,
    and to whom will he explain
        the message?
    Those who are weaned from
        milk,
    those taken from the breast?
10  For it is precept upon precept,
        precept upon precept,
    line upon line, line upon line,
    here a little, there a little."a

11 Truly, with stammering lip
        and with alien tongue
    he will speak to this people,
12      to whom he has said,
    "This is rest;
        give rest to the weary;
    and this is repose";
        yet they would not hear.
13 Therefore the word of the Lord
        will be to them,
    "Precept upon precept,
        precept upon precept,
    line upon line, line upon line,
    here a little, there a little;"a
    in order that they may go, and
        fall backward,
    and be broken, and snared,
        and taken.

## GALATIANS 3.10–22

For all who rely on the works of the law are under a curse; for it is written, "Cursed is everyone who does not observe and obey all the things written in the book of the law." 11Now it is evident that no one is justified before God by the law; for "The one who is righteous will live by faith."b 12But the law does not rest on faith; on the contrary, "Whoever does the works of the lawc will live by them." 13Christ redeemed us from the curse of the law by becoming a curse for us—for it is written, "Cursed is everyone who hangs on a tree"— 14in order that in Christ Jesus the blessing of Abraham might come to the Gentiles, so that we might receive the promise of the Spirit through faith.

15 Brothers and sisters,d I give an example from daily life: once a person's wille has been ratified, no one adds to it or annuls it. 16Now the promises were made to Abraham and to his offspring;f it does not say, "And to offsprings,"g as of many; but it says, "And to your offspring,"f that is, to one person, who is Christ. 17My point is this: the law, which came four hundred thirty years later, does not annul a covenant previously ratified by God, so as to nullify the promise. 18For if the inheritance comes from the law, it no longer comes from the promise; but God granted it to Abraham through the promise.

19 Why then the law? It was added because of transgressions, until the offspringf would come to whom the promise had been made; and it was ordained through angels by a mediator. 20Now a mediator involves more than one party; but God is one.

21 Is the law then opposed to the promises of God? Certainly not! For if

---

aMeaning of Heb of this verse uncertain  bOr *The one who is righteous through faith will live*
cGk *does them*  dGk *Brothers*  eOr *covenant* (as in verse 17)  fGk *seed*  gGk *seeds*

a law had been given that could make alive, then righteousness would indeed come through the law. [22]But the scripture has imprisoned all things under the power of sin, so that what was promised through faith in Jesus Christ[a] might be given to those who believe.

## PSALM 61.1–8

*To the leader: with stringed instruments. Of David.*

Hear my cry, O God;
  listen to my prayer.
[2]  From the end of the
    earth I call to you,
  when my heart is faint.

Lead me to the rock
  that is higher than I;
[3]  for you are my refuge,
    a strong tower against the
    enemy.

[4]  Let me abide in your tent
    forever,
  find refuge under the shelter
    of your wings.    *Selah*

[5]  For you, O God, have heard my
    vows;
  you have given me the
    heritage of those who
    fear your name.

[6]  Prolong the life of the king;
  may his years endure to all
    generations!
[7]  May he be enthroned forever
    before God;
  appoint steadfast love and
    faithfulness to watch
    over him!

[8]  So I will always sing praises to
    your name,
  as I pay my vows day after
    day.

## PROVERBS 23.17–18

Do not let your heart envy
    sinners,
  but always continue in the
    fear of the LORD.
[18]  Surely there is a future,
  and your hope will not be cut
    off.

# SEPTEMBER 18

## ISAIAH 28.14—30.11

Therefore hear the word of the
    LORD, you scoffers
  who rule this people in
    Jerusalem.
[15]  Because you have said, "We
    have made a covenant
    with death,
  and with Sheol we have an
    agreement;
when the overwhelming scourge
    passes through
  it will not come to us;
for we have made lies our
    refuge,
  and in falsehood we have
    taken shelter";
[16]  therefore thus says the Lord
    GOD,

[a]Or *through the faith of Jesus Christ*

See, I am laying in Zion a
    foundation stone,
a tested stone,
a precious cornerstone, a sure
    foundation:
"One who trusts will not
    panic."
17 And I will make justice the line,
    and righteousness the
        plummet;
hail will sweep away the refuge
    of lies,
and waters will overwhelm
    the shelter.
18 Then your covenant with death
    will be annulled,
and your agreement with
    Sheol will not stand;
when the overwhelming scourge
    passes through
you will be beaten down by it.
19 As often as it passes through, it
    will take you;
for morning by morning it will
    pass through,
by day and by night;
and it will be sheer terror to
    understand the message.
20 For the bed is too short to
    stretch oneself on it,
and the covering too narrow
    to wrap oneself in it.
21 For the Lord will rise up as on
    Mount Perazim,
he will rage as in the valley of
    Gibeon;
to do his deed—strange is his
    deed!
and to work his work—alien
    is his work!
22 Now therefore do not scoff,
    or your bonds will be made
        stronger;
for I have heard a decree of
    destruction
from the Lord God of hosts
    upon the whole land.

23 Listen, and hear my voice;
    Pay attention, and hear my
        speech.
24 Do those who plow for sowing
    plow continually?
Do they continually open and
    harrow their ground?
25 When they have leveled its
    surface,
do they not scatter dill, sow
    cummin,
and plant wheat in rows
    and barley in its proper place,
    and spelt as the border?
26 For they are well instructed;
    their God teaches them.

27 Dill is not threshed with a
    threshing sledge,
    nor is a cart wheel rolled over
        cummin;
but dill is beaten out with a
    stick,
and cummin with a rod.
28 Grain is crushed for bread,
    but one does not thresh it
        forever;
one drives the cart wheel and
    horses over it,
    but does not pulverize it.
29 This also comes from the Lord
    of hosts;
he is wonderful in counsel,
and excellent in wisdom.

29.1 Ah, Ariel, Ariel,
    the city where David
        encamped!
Add year to year;
    let the festivals run their
        round.
2 Yet I will distress Ariel,
    and there shall be moaning
        and lamentation,
and it shall be to me like an Ariel.[b]
    and Jerusalem[a] shall be to
        me like an Ariel.[b]

a Heb *she*  b Probable meaning, *altar hearth*; compare Ezek 43.15

3  And like David[a] I will encamp
         against you;
      I will besiege you with towers
      and raise siegeworks against
         you.
4  Then deep from the earth you
         shall speak,
      from low in the dust your
         words shall come;
   your voice shall come from the
         ground like the voice of
         a ghost,
      and your speech shall whisper
         out of the dust.

5  But the multitude of your foes[b]
         shall be like small dust,
      and the multitude of tyrants
         like flying chaff.
   And in an instant, suddenly,
6     you will be visited by the
         Lord of hosts
   with thunder and earthquake
         and great noise,
      with whirlwind and tempest,
         and the flame of a
         devouring fire.
7  And the multitude of all the
         nations that fight against
         Ariel,
      all that fight against her and
         her stronghold, and who
         distress her,
      shall be like a dream, a vision
         of the night.
8  Just as when a hungry person
         dreams of eating
      and wakes up still hungry,
   or a thirsty person dreams of
         drinking
      and wakes up faint, still
         thirsty,
   so shall the multitude of all the
         nations be
      that fight against Mount Zion.

9  Stupefy yourselves and be in a
         stupor,
      blind yourselves and be blind!
   Be drunk, but not from wine;
      stagger, but not from strong
         drink!
10  For the Lord has poured out
         upon you
      a spirit of deep sleep;
   he has closed your eyes, you
         prophets,
      and covered your heads, you
         seers.

11  The vision of all this has become for you like the words of a sealed document. If it is given to those who can read, with the command, "Read this," they say, "We cannot, for it is sealed." 12 And if it is given to those who cannot read, saying, "Read this," they say, "We cannot read."

13  The Lord said:
   Because these people draw near
         with their mouths
      and honor me with their lips,
      while their hearts are far
         from me,
   and their worship of me is a
         human commandment
         learned by rote;
14  so I will again do
      amazing things with this
         people,
      shocking and amazing.
   The wisdom of their wise shall
         perish,
      and the discernment of the
         discerning shall be
         hidden.

15  Ha! You who hide a plan too
         deep for the Lord,
      whose deeds are in the dark,
      and who say, "Who sees us?
         Who knows us?"
16  You turn things upside down!
      Shall the potter be regarded
         as the clay?

a Gk: Meaning of Heb uncertain  b Cn: Heb *strangers*

Shall the thing made say of its
    maker,
    "He did not make me";
or the thing formed say of the
    one who formed it,
    "He has no understanding"?

17 Shall not Lebanon in a very little
    while
    become a fruitful field,
    and the fruitful field be
    regarded as a forest?
18 On that day the deaf shall hear
    the words of a scroll,
    and out of their gloom and
    darkness
    the eyes of the blind shall
    see.
19 The meek shall obtain fresh joy
    in the LORD,
    and the neediest people shall
    exult in the Holy One of
    Israel.
20 For the tyrant shall be no more,
    and the scoffer shall cease to
    be;
    all those alert to do evil shall
    be cut off—
21 those who cause a person to
    lose a lawsuit,
    who set a trap for the arbiter
    in the gate,
    and without grounds deny
    justice to the one in the
    right.

22 Therefore thus says the LORD,
who redeemed Abraham, concerning
the house of Jacob:
    No longer shall Jacob be
    ashamed,
    no longer shall his face
    grow pale.
23 For when he sees his children,
    the work of my hands, in
    his midst,
    they will sanctify my name;

they will sanctify the Holy One
    of Jacob,
    and will stand in awe of the
    God of Israel.
24 And those who err in spirit will
    come to understanding,
    and those who grumble will
    accept instruction.

30.1 OH, rebellious children, says the
    LORD,
    who carry out a plan, but not
    mine;
    who make an alliance, but
    against my will,
    adding sin to sin;
2 who set out to go down to
    Egypt
    without asking for my
    counsel,
    to take refuge in the protection
    of Pharaoh,
    and to seek shelter in the
    shadow of Egypt;
3 Therefore the protection of
    Pharaoh shall become
    your shame,
    and the shelter in the shadow
    of Egypt your
    humiliation.
4 For though his officials are at
    Zoan
    and his envoys reach Hanes,
5 everyone comes to shame
    through a people that cannot
    profit them,
    that brings neither help nor
    profit,
    but shame and disgrace.

6 An oracle concerning the animals
of the Negeb.
    Through a land of trouble and
    distress,
    of lioness and roaring[a] lion,
    of viper and flying serpent,
    they carry their riches on the
    backs of donkeys,

a Cn: Heb *from them*

and their treasures on the
    humps of camels,
to a people that cannot profit
    them.
7 For Egypt's help is worthless
    and empty,
therefore I have called her,
    "Rahab who sits still."[a]

8 Go now, write it before them on
    a tablet,
and inscribe it in a book,
so that it may be for the time
    to come
    as a witness forever.
9 For they are a rebellious
    people,
    faithless children,
children who will not hear
    the instruction of the LORD;
10 who say to the seers, "Do not
    see";
and to the prophets, "Do not
    prophesy to us what is
    right;
speak to us smooth things,
    prophesy illusions,
11 leave the way, turn aside from
    the path,
let us hear no more about the
    Holy One of Israel."

## GALATIANS 3.23—4.20

Now before faith came, we were imprisoned and guarded under the law until faith would be revealed. 24Therefore the law was our disciplinarian until Christ came, so that we might be justified by faith. 25But now that faith has come, we are no longer subject to a disciplinarian, 26for in Christ Jesus you are all children of God through faith. 27As many of you as were baptized into Christ have clothed yourselves with Christ. 28There is no longer Jew or Greek, there is no longer slave or free, there is no longer male and female; for all of you are one in Christ Jesus. 29And if you belong to Christ, then you are Abraham's offspring,[b] heirs according to the promise.

4.1 MY point is this: heirs, as long as they are minors, are no better than slaves, though they are the owners of all the property; 2but they remain under guardians and trustees until the date set by the father. 3So with us; while we were minors, we were enslaved to the elemental spirits[c] of the world. 4But when the fullness of time had come, God sent his Son, born of a woman, born under the law, 5in order to redeem those who were under the law, so that we might receive adoption as children. 6And because you are children, God has sent the Spirit of his Son into our[d] hearts, crying, "Abba![e] Father!" 7So you are no longer a slave but a child, and if a child then also an heir, through God.[f]

8 Formerly, when you did not know God, you were enslaved to beings that by nature are not gods. 9Now, however, that you have come to know God, or rather to be known by God, how can you turn back again to the weak and beggarly elemental spirits?[g] How can you want to be enslaved to them again? 10You are observing special days, and months, and seasons, and years. 11I am afraid that my work for you may have been wasted.

12 Friends,[h] I beg you, become as I am, for I also have become as you are. You have done me no wrong. 13You know that it was because of a physical infirmity that I first announced the gospel to you; 14though my condition put you to the test, you did not scorn or despise me, but welcomed me as an angel of God, as Christ Jesus. 15What has become of the goodwill you felt? For I

a Meaning of Heb uncertain  b Gk *seed*  c Or *the rudiments*  d Other ancient authorities read *your*  e Aramaic for *Father*  f Other ancient authorities read *an heir of God through Christ*  g Or *beggarly rudiments*  h Gk *Brothers*

testify that, had it been possible, you would have torn out your eyes and given them to me. ¹⁶Have I now become your enemy by telling you the truth? ¹⁷They make much of you, but for no good purpose; they want to exclude you, so that you may make much of them. ¹⁸It is good to be made much of for a good purpose at all times, and not only when I am present with you. ¹⁹My little children, for whom I am again in the pain of childbirth until Christ is formed in you, ²⁰I wish I were present with you now and could change my tone, for I am perplexed about you.

## PSALM 62.1–12

*To the leader: according to Jeduthun. A Psalm of David.*

**F**OR God alone my soul waits in
    silence;
  from him comes my
    salvation.
2  He alone is my rock and my
    salvation,
  my fortress; I shall never be
    shaken.

3  How long will you assail a
    person,
  will you batter your victim, all
    of you,
  as you would a leaning wall, a
    tottering fence?
4  Their only plan is to bring down
    a person of prominence.
  They take pleasure in
    falsehood;
  they bless with their mouths,
  but inwardly they curse.
          *Selah*

5  For God alone my soul waits in
    silence,
  for my hope is from him.
6  He alone is my rock and my
    salvation,
  my fortress; I shall not be
    shaken.
7  On God rests my deliverance
    and my honor;
  my mighty rock, my refuge is
    in God.

8  Trust in him at all times,
    O people;
  pour out your heart before
    him;
  God is a refuge for us.   *Selah*

9  Those of low estate are but a
    breath,
  those of high estate are a
    delusion;
  in the balances they go up;
  they are together lighter than
    a breath.
10  Put no confidence in extortion,
  and set no vain hopes on
    robbery;
  if riches increase, do not set
    your heart on them.

11  Once God has spoken;
  twice have I heard this:
  that power belongs to God,
12   and steadfast love belongs to
    you, O Lord.
  For you repay to all
  according to their work.

## PROVERBS 23.19–21

**H**EAR, my child, and be wise,
  and direct your mind in the
    way.
20  Do not be among winebibbers,
  or among gluttonous eaters
    of meat;
21  for the drunkard and the glutton
  will come to poverty,
  and drowsiness will clothe
    them with rags.

# SEPTEMBER 19

ISAIAH 30.12—33.12

Therefore thus says the Holy
        One of Israel:
    Because you reject this
        word,
    and put your trust in
        oppression and deceit,
    and rely on them;
13  therefore this iniquity shall
        become for you
    like a break in a high wall,
        bulging out, and about to
        collapse,
    whose crash comes suddenly,
        in an instant;
14  its breaking is like that of a
        potter's vessel
    that is smashed so ruthlessly
    that among its fragments not a
        sherd is found
    for taking fire from the
        hearth,
    or dipping water out of the
        cistern.

15  For thus said the Lord God, the
        Holy One of Israel:
    In returning and rest you shall
        be saved;
    in quietness and in trust shall
        be your strength.
    But you refused 16and said,
    "No! We will flee upon
        horses"—
    therefore you shall flee!
    and, "We will ride upon swift
        steeds"—
    therefore your pursuers shall
        be swift!
17  A thousand shall flee at the
        threat of one,
    at the threat of five you
        shall flee,
    until you are left

    like a flagstaff on the top of
        a mountain,
    like a signal on a hill.

18  Therefore the Lord waits to be
        gracious to you;
    therefore he will rise up to
        show mercy to you.
    For the Lord is a God of
        justice;
    blessed are all those who wait
        for him.
19  Truly, O people in Zion, inhabitants of Jerusalem, you shall weep no
more. He will surely be gracious to you
at the sound of your cry; when he hears
it, he will answer you. 20Though the
Lord may give you the bread of adversity and the water of affliction, yet your
Teacher will not hide himself any more,
but your eyes shall see your Teacher.
21And when you turn to the right or
when you turn to the left, your ears
shall hear a word behind you, saying,
"This is the way; walk in it." 22Then
you will defile your silver-covered idols
and your gold-plated images. You will
scatter them like filthy rags; you will
say to them, "Away with you!"
23  He will give rain for the seed
with which you sow the ground, and
grain, the produce of the ground, which
will be rich and plenteous. On that day
your cattle will graze in broad pastures;
24and the oxen and donkeys that till the
ground will eat silage, which has been
winnowed with shovel and fork. 25On
every lofty mountain and every high hill
there will be brooks running with
water—on a day of the great slaughter,
when the towers fall. 26Moreover the
light of the moon will be like the light of
the sun, and the light of the sun will be
sevenfold, like the light of seven days,
on the day when the Lord binds up the

injuries of his people, and heals the wounds inflicted by his blow.

27   See, the name of the LORD
      comes from far away,
    burning with his anger, and in
      thick rising smoke; a
  his lips are full of indignation,
    and his tongue is like a
      devouring fire;
28   his breath is like an overflowing
      stream
    that reaches up to the neck—
  to sift the nations with the sieve
    of destruction,
  and to place on the jaws of
    the peoples a bridle that
    leads them astray.

29 You shall have a song as in the night when a holy festival is kept; and gladness of heart, as when one sets out to the sound of the flute to go to the mountain of the LORD, to the Rock of Israel. 30And the LORD will cause his majestic voice to be heard and the descending blow of his arm to be seen, in furious anger and a flame of devouring fire, with a cloudburst and tempest and hailstones. 31The Assyrian will be terror-stricken at the voice of the LORD, when he strikes with his rod. 32And every stroke of the staff of punishment that the LORD lays upon him will be to the sound of timbrels and lyres; battling with brandished arm he will fight with him. 33For his burning placeb has long been prepared; truly it is made ready for the king, c its pyre made deep and wide, with fire and wood in abundance; the breath of the LORD, like a stream of sulfur, kindles it.

31.1 ALAS for those who go down
    to Egypt for help
  and who rely on horses,
  who trust in chariots because
    they are many

  and in horsemen because they
    are very strong,
  but do not look to the Holy One
    of Israel
  or consult the LORD!
2  Yet he too is wise and brings
    disaster;
  he does not call back his
    words,
  but will rise against the house of
    the evildoers,
  and against the helpers of
    those who work iniquity.
3  The Egyptians are human, and
    not God;
  their horses are flesh, and
    not spirit.
  When the LORD stretches out
    his hand,
  the helper will stumble, and
    the one helped will fall,
  and they will all perish
    together.

4  For thus the LORD said to me,
  As a lion or a young lion growls
    over its prey,
  and—when a band of
    shepherds is called out
    against it—
  is not terrified by their shouting
    or daunted at their noise,
  so the LORD of hosts will
    come down
    to fight upon Mount Zion and
    upon its hill.
5  Like birds hovering overhead,
    so the LORD of hosts
  will protect Jerusalem;
  he will protect and deliver it,
    he will spare and rescue it.

6 Turn back to him whom youd have deeply betrayed, O people of Israel. 7For on that day all of you shall throw away your idols of silver and idols of gold, which your hands have sinfully made for you.

aMeaning of Heb uncertain  bOr *Topheth*  cOr *Molech*  dHeb *they*

8 "Then the Assyrian shall fall by
        a sword, not of mortals;
    and a sword, not of humans,
        shall devour him;
    he shall flee from the sword,
        and his young men shall be
            put to forced labor.
9 His rock shall pass away in
        terror,
    and his officers desert the
        standard in panic,"
    says the LORD, whose fire is in
        Zion,
    and whose furnace is in
        Jerusalem.

32.1 SEE, a king will reign in
        righteousness,
    and princes will rule with
        justice.
2 Each will be like a hiding place
        from the wind,
    a covert from the tempest,
    like streams of water in a
        dry place,
    like the shade of a great rock
        in a weary land.
3 Then the eyes of those who
        have sight will not be
        closed,
    and the ears of those who
        have hearing will listen.
4 The minds of the rash will have
        good judgment,
    and the tongues of
        stammerers will speak
        readily and distinctly.
5 A fool will no longer be called
        noble,
    nor a villain said to be
        honorable.
6 For fools speak folly,
    and their minds plot iniquity:
    to practice ungodliness,
        to utter error concerning
        the LORD,
    to leave the craving of the
        hungry unsatisfied,
    and to deprive the thirsty of
        drink.

7 The villainies of villains are evil;
    they devise wicked devices
    to ruin the poor with lying
        words,
    even when the plea of the
        needy is right.
8 But those who are noble plan
        noble things,
    and by noble things they
        stand.

9 Rise up, you women who are at
        ease, hear my voice;
    you complacent daughters,
        listen to my speech.
10 In little more than a year
    you will shudder, you
        complacent ones;
    for the vintage will fail,
        the fruit harvest will not
        come.
11 Tremble, you women who are
        at ease,
    shudder, you complacent
        ones;
    strip, and make yourselves
        bare,
    and put sackcloth on your
        loins.
12 Beat your breasts for the
        pleasant fields,
    for the fruitful vine,
13 for the soil of my people
        growing up in thorns and
        briers;
    yes, for all the joyous houses
        in the jubilant city.
14 For the palace will be forsaken,
        the populous city deserted;
    the hill and the watchtower
        will become dens forever,
    the joy of wild asses,
        a pasture for flocks;
15 until a spirit from on high is
        poured out on us,
    and the wilderness becomes a
        fruitful field,
    and the fruitful field is
        deemed a forest.

16 Then justice will dwell in the
       wilderness,
     and righteousness abide in the
       fruitful field.
17 The effect of righteousness will
       be peace,
     and the result of
       righteousness, quietness
       and trust forever.
18 My people will abide in a
       peaceful habitation,
     in secure dwellings, and in
       quiet resting places.
19 The forest will disappear
       completely, a
     and the city will be utterly
       laid low.
20 Happy will you be who sow
       beside every stream,
     who let the ox and the
       donkey range freely.

33.1 Ah, you destroyer,
     who yourself have not been
       destroyed;
   you treacherous one,
     with whom no one has dealt
       treacherously!
   When you have ceased to
       destroy,
     you will be destroyed;
   and when you have stopped
       dealing treacherously,
     you will be dealt with
       treacherously.

2 O Lord, be gracious to us; we
       wait for you.
     Be our arm every morning,
     our salvation in the time of
       trouble.
3 At the sound of tumult, peoples
       fled;
     before your majesty, nations
       scattered.
4 Spoil was gathered as the
       caterpillar gathers;

     as locusts leap, they leaped b
       upon it.
5 The Lord is exalted, he dwells
       on high;
     he filled Zion with justice and
       righteousness;
6 he will be the stability of your
       times,
     abundance of salvation,
       wisdom, and knowledge;
     the fear of the Lord is Zion's
       treasure. c

7 Listen! the valiant b cry in the
       streets;
     the envoys of peace weep
       bitterly.
8 The highways are deserted,
     travelers have quit the road.
   The treaty is broken,
     its oaths d are despised,
     its obligation e is disregarded.
9 The land mourns and
       languishes;
     Lebanon is confounded and
       withers away;
   Sharon is like a desert;
     and Bashan and Carmel shake
       off their leaves.

10 "Now I will arise," says the
       Lord,
     "now I will lift myself up;
     now I will be exalted.
11 You conceive chaff, you bring
       forth stubble;
     your breath is a fire that will
       consume you.
12 And the peoples will be as if
       burned to lime,
     like thorns cut down, that are
       burned in the fire."

a Cn: Heb *And it will hail when the forest comes down*   b Meaning of Heb uncertain   c Heb *his treasure*; meaning of Heb uncertain   d Q Ms: MT *cities*   e Or *everyone*

## GALATIANS 4.21—5.12

Tell me, you who desire to be subject to the law, will you not listen to the law? [22]For it is written that Abraham had two sons, one by a slave woman and the other by a free woman. [23]One, the child of the slave, was born according to the flesh; the other, the child of the free woman, was born through the promise. [24]Now this is an allegory: these women are two covenants. One woman, in fact, is Hagar, from Mount Sinai, bearing children for slavery. [25]Now Hagar is Mount Sinai in Arabia[a] and corresponds to the present Jerusalem, for she is in slavery with her children. [26]But the other woman corresponds to the Jerusalem above; she is free, and she is our mother. [27]For it is written,

"Rejoice, you childless one, you
  who bear no children,
  burst into song and shout,
    you who endure no birth
    pangs;
for the children of the desolate
    woman are more
    numerous
  than the children of the one
    who is married."

[28]Now you,[b] my friends,[c] are children of the promise, like Isaac. [29]But just as at that time the child who was born according to the flesh persecuted the child who was born according to the Spirit, so it is now also. [30]But what does the scripture say? "Drive out the slave and her child; for the child of the slave will not share the inheritance with the child of the free woman." [31]So then, friends,[c] we are children, not of the slave but of the free woman. [5.1]For freedom Christ has set us free. Stand firm, therefore, and do not submit again to a yoke of slavery.

2 Listen! I, Paul, am telling you that if you let yourselves be circumcised, Christ will be of no benefit to you. [3]Once again I testify to every man who lets himself be circumcised that he is obliged to obey the entire law. [4]You who want to be justified by the law have cut yourselves off from Christ; you have fallen away from grace. [5]For through the Spirit, by faith, we eagerly wait for the hope of righteousness. [6]For in Christ Jesus neither circumcision nor uncircumcision counts for anything; the only thing that counts is faith working[d] through love.

7 You were running well; who prevented you from obeying the truth? [8]Such persuasion does not come from the one who calls you. [9]A little yeast leavens the whole batch of dough. [10]I am confident about you in the Lord that you will not think otherwise. But whoever it is that is confusing you will pay the penalty. [11]But my friends,[c] why am I still being persecuted if I am still preaching circumcision? In that case the offense of the cross has been removed. [12]I wish those who unsettle you would castrate themselves!

## PSALM 63.1–11

*A Psalm of David, when he was in the Wilderness of Judah.*

O God, you are my God, I seek
      you,
  my soul thirsts for you;
my flesh faints for you,
    as in a dry and weary land
      where there is no water.
2 So I have looked upon you in
      the sanctuary,
    beholding your power and
      glory.
3 Because your steadfast love is
      better than life,
    my lips will praise you.
4 So I will bless you as long as I
      live;

aOther ancient authorities read *For Sinai is a mountain in Arabia*  bOther ancient authorities read *we*  cGk *brothers*  dOr *made effective*

I will lift up my hands and call
  on your name.

5  My soul is satisfied as with a
    rich feast, **a**
  and my mouth praises you
    with joyful lips
6  when I think of you on my bed,
    and meditate on you in the
      watches of the night;
7  for you have been my help,
    and in the shadow of your
      wings I sing for joy.
8  My soul clings to you;
    your right hand upholds me.

9  But those who seek to destroy
    my life

shall go down into the depths
  of the earth;
10  they shall be given over to the
      power of the sword,
    they shall be prey for jackals.
11  But the king shall rejoice in
      God;
    all who swear by him shall
      exult,
    for the mouths of liars will be
      stopped.

## PROVERBS 23.22

LISTEN to your father who
  begot you,
and do not despise your
  mother when she is old.

# SEPTEMBER 20

## ISAIAH 33.13—35.10

HEAR, you who are far away,
    what I have done;
  and you who are near,
    acknowledge my might.
14  The sinners in Zion are afraid;
    trembling has seized the
      godless:
  "Who among us can live with
    the devouring fire?
  Who among us can live with
    everlasting flames?"
15  Those who walk righteously and
      speak uprightly,
    who despise the gain of
      oppression,
  who wave away a bribe instead
    of accepting it,
    who stop their ears from
      hearing of bloodshed

and shut their eyes from
  looking on evil,
16  they will live on the heights;
    their refuge will be the
      fortresses of rocks;
    their food will be supplied,
      their water assured.

17  Your eyes will see the king in
      his beauty;
    they will behold a land that
      stretches far away.
18  Your mind will muse on the
      terror:
  "Where is the one who
    counted?
  Where is the one who
    weighed the tribute?
  Where is the one who
    counted the towers?"

**a** Heb *with fat and fatness*

19 No longer will you see the
        insolent people,
    the people of an obscure
        speech that you cannot
        comprehend,
    stammering in a language that
        you cannot understand.
20 Look on Zion, the city of our
        appointed festivals!
    Your eyes will see Jerusalem,
    a quiet habitation, an
        immovable tent,
    whose stakes will never be
        pulled up,
    and none of whose ropes will
        be broken.
21 But there the LORD in majesty
        will be for us
    a place of broad rivers and
        streams,
    where no galley with oars can
        go,
    nor stately ship can pass.
22 For the LORD is our judge, the
        LORD is our ruler,
    the LORD is our king; he will
        save us.

23 Your rigging hangs loose;
    it cannot hold the mast firm in
        its place,
    or keep the sail spread out.

    Then prey and spoil in
        abundance will be
        divided;
    even the lame will fall to
        plundering.
24 And no inhabitant will say, "I am
        sick";
    the people who live there will
        be forgiven their iniquity.

34.1 DRAW near, O nations, to
        hear;
    O peoples, give heed!
    Let the earth hear, and all that
        fills it;
    the world, and all that comes
        from it.

2 For the LORD is enraged against
        all the nations,
    and furious against all their
        hoards;
    he has doomed them, has
        given them over for
        slaughter.
3 Their slain shall be cast out,
    and the stench of their
        corpses shall rise;
    the mountains shall flow with
        their blood.
4 All the host of heaven shall rot
        away,
    and the skies roll up like a
        scroll.
    All their host shall wither
        like a leaf withering on a vine,
        or fruit withering on a fig
        tree.

5 When my sword has drunk its
        fill in the heavens,
    lo, it will descend upon
        Edom,
    upon the people I have
        doomed to judgment.
6 The LORD has a sword; it is
        sated with blood,
    it is gorged with fat,
        with the blood of lambs and
        goats,
    with the fat of the kidneys
        of rams.
    For the LORD has a sacrifice in
        Bozrah,
    a great slaughter in the land
        of Edom.
7 Wild oxen shall fall with them,
    and young steers with the
        mighty bulls.
    Their land shall be soaked with
        blood,
    and their soil made rich with
        fat.

8 For the LORD has a day of
        vengeance,

a year of vindication by Zion's
    cause. a
9  And the streams of Edomb
        shall be turned into pitch,
    and her soil into sulfur;
    her land shall become burning
        pitch.
10  Night and day it shall not be
        quenched;
    its smoke shall go up forever.
    From generation to generation it
        shall lie waste;
    no one shall pass through it
        forever and ever.
11  But the hawkc and the
        hedgehogc shall possess
        it;
    the owlc and the raven shall
        live in it.
    He shall stretch the line of
        confusion over it,
    and the plummet of chaos
        overd its nobles.
12  They shall name it No Kingdom
        There,
    and all its princes shall be
        nothing.
13  Thorns shall grow over its
        strongholds,
    nettles and thistles in its
        fortresses.
    It shall be the haunt of jackals,
    an abode for ostriches.
14  Wildcats shall meet with hyenas,
    goat-demons shall call to
        each other;
    there too Lilith shall repose,
    and find a place to rest.
15  There shall the owl nest
    and lay and hatch and brood
        in its shadow;
    there too the buzzards shall
        gather,
    each one with its mate.
16  Seek and read from the book of
        the LORD:
    Not one of these shall be
        missing;

none shall be without its
        mate.
    For the mouth of the LORD has
        commanded,
    and his spirit has gathered
        them.
17  He has cast the lot for them,
    his hand has portioned it out
        to them with the line;
    they shall possess it forever,
    from generation to generation
        they shall live in it.

35.1  THE wilderness and the dry land
        shall be glad,
    the desert shall rejoice and
        blossom;
    like the crocus 2it shall blossom
        abundantly,
    and rejoice with joy and
        singing.
    The glory of Lebanon shall be
        given to it,
    the majesty of Carmel and
        Sharon.
    They shall see the glory of the
        LORD,
    the majesty of our God.

3  Strengthen the weak hands,
    and make firm the feeble
        knees.
4  Say to those who are of a
        fearful heart,
    "Be strong, do not fear!
    Here is your God.
    He will come with vengeance,
    with terrible recompense.
    He will come and save you."

5  Then the eyes of the blind shall
        be opened,
    and the ears of the deaf
        unstopped;
6  then the lame shall leap like
        a deer,
    and the tongue of the
        speechless sing for joy.

a Or *of recompense by Zion's defender*   b Heb *her streams*   c Identification uncertain   d Heb lacks *over*

For waters shall break forth in
    the wilderness,
  and streams in the desert;
7  the burning sand shall become
    a pool,
  and the thirsty ground springs
    of water;
  the haunt of jackals shall
    become a swamp, [a]
  the grass shall become reeds
    and rushes.

8  A highway shall be there,
  and it shall be called the
    Holy Way;
  the unclean shall not travel on
    it, [b]
  but it shall be for God's
    people; [c]
  no traveler, not even fools,
    shall go astray.
9  No lion shall be there,
  nor shall any ravenous beast
    come up on it;
  they shall not be found there,
  but the redeemed shall walk
    there.
10  And the ransomed of the LORD
    shall return,
  and come to Zion with
    singing;
  everlasting joy shall be upon
    their heads;
  they shall obtain joy and
    gladness,
  and sorrow and sighing shall
    flee away.

# GALATIANS 5.13–26

**F**OR you were called to freedom, brothers and sisters; [d] only do not use your freedom as an opportunity for self-indulgence, [e] but through love become slaves to one another. [14]For the whole law is summed up in a single commandment, "You shall love your neighbor as yourself." [15]If,

however, you bite and devour one another, take care that you are not consumed by one another.

16  Live by the Spirit, I say, and do not gratify the desires of the flesh. [17]For what the flesh desires is opposed to the Spirit, and what the Spirit desires is opposed to the flesh; for these are opposed to each other, to prevent you from doing what you want. [18]But if you are led by the Spirit, you are not subject to the law. [19]Now the works of the flesh are obvious: fornication, impurity, licentiousness, [20]idolatry, sorcery, enmities, strife, jealousy, anger, quarrels, dissensions, factions, [21]envy, [f] drunkenness, carousing, and things like these. I am warning you, as I warned you before: those who do such things will not inherit the kingdom of God.

22  By contrast, the fruit of the Spirit is love, joy, peace, patience, kindness, generosity, faithfulness, [23]gentleness, and self-control. There is no law against such things. [24]And those who belong to Christ Jesus have crucified the flesh with its passions and desires. [25]If we live by the Spirit, let us also be guided by the Spirit. [26]Let us not become conceited, competing against one another, envying one another.

# PSALM 64.1–10

*To the leader. A Psalm of David.*

**H**EAR my voice, O God, in my
    complaint;
  preserve my life from the
    dread enemy.
2  Hide me from the secret plots
    of the wicked,
  from the scheming of
    evildoers,
3  who whet their tongues like
    swords,

---

[a]Cn: Heb *in the haunt of jackals is her resting place*   [b]Or *pass it by*   [c]Cn: Heb *for them*
[d]Gk *brothers*   [e]Gk *the flesh*   [f]Other ancient authorities add *murder*

who aim bitter words like
   arrows,
4 shooting from ambush at the
   blameless;
  they shoot suddenly and
   without fear.
5 They hold fast to their evil
   purpose;
  they talk of laying snares
   secretly,
  thinking, "Who can see us?[a]
6 Who can search out our
   crimes?[b]
  We have thought out a
   cunningly conceived
   plot."
  For the human heart and
   mind are deep.

7 But God will shoot his arrow at
   them;

  they will be wounded
   suddenly.
8 Because of their tongue he will
   bring them to ruin;[c]
  all who see them will shake
   with horror.
9 Then everyone will fear;
  they will tell what God has
   brought about,
  and ponder what he has done.

10 Let the righteous rejoice in the
   Lord
  and take refuge in him.
  Let all the upright in heart
   glory.

## PROVERBS 23.23

Buy truth, and do not sell it;
buy wisdom, instruction, and
   understanding.

# SEPTEMBER 21

## ISAIAH 36.1—37.38

In the fourteenth year of King Hezekiah, King Sennacherib of Assyria came up against all the fortified cities of Judah and captured them. 2The king of Assyria sent the Rabshakeh from Lachish to King Hezekiah at Jerusalem, with a great army. He stood by the conduit of the upper pool on the highway to the Fuller's Field. 3And there came out to him Eliakim son of Hilkiah, who was in charge of the palace, and Shebna the secretary, and Joah son of Asaph, the recorder.

4 The Rabshakeh said to them, "Say to Hezekiah: Thus says the great king, the king of Assyria: On what do you base this confidence of yours? 5Do you think that mere words are strategy and power for war? On whom do you now rely, that you have rebelled against me? 6See, you are relying on Egypt, that broken reed of a staff, which will pierce the hand of anyone who leans on it. Such is Pharaoh king of Egypt to all who rely on him. 7But if you say to me, 'We rely on the Lord our God,' is it not he whose high places and altars Hezekiah has removed, saying to Judah and to Jerusalem, 'You shall worship before this altar'? 8Come now, make a wager with my master the king

---

of Assyria: I will give you two thousand horses, if you are able on your part to set riders on them. ⁹How then can you repulse a single captain among the least of my master's servants, when you rely on Egypt for chariots and for horsemen? ¹⁰Moreover, is it without the LORD that I have come up against this land to destroy it? The LORD said to me, Go up against this land, and destroy it."

11 Then Eliakim, Shebna, and Joah said to the Rabshakeh, "Please speak to your servants in Aramaic, for we understand it; do not speak to us in the language of Judah within the hearing of the people who are on the wall." ¹²But the Rabshakeh said, "Has my master sent me to speak these words to your master and to you, and not to the people sitting on the wall, who are doomed with you to eat their own dung and drink their own urine?"

13 Then the Rabshakeh stood and called out in a loud voice in the language of Judah, "Hear the words of the great king, the king of Assyria! ¹⁴Thus says the king: 'Do not let Hezekiah deceive you, for he will not be able to deliver you. ¹⁵Do not let Hezekiah make you rely on the LORD by saying, The LORD will surely deliver us; this city will not be given into the hand of the king of Assyria.' ¹⁶Do not listen to Hezekiah; for thus says the king of Assyria: 'Make your peace with me and come out to me; then everyone of you will eat from your own vine and your own fig tree and drink water from your own cistern, ¹⁷until I come and take you away to a land like your own land, a land of grain and wine, a land of bread and vineyards. ¹⁸Do not let Hezekiah mislead you by saying, The LORD will save us. Has any of the gods of the nations saved their land out of the hand of the king of Assyria? ¹⁹Where are the gods of Hamath and Arpad? Where are the gods of Sepharvaim? Have they delivered Samaria out of my hand? ²⁰Who among all the gods of these countries have saved their countries out of my hand, that the LORD should save Jerusalem out of my hand?' "

21 But they were silent and answered him not a word, for the king's command was, "Do not answer him." ²²Then Eliakim son of Hilkiah, who was in charge of the palace, and Shebna the secretary, and Joah son of Asaph, the recorder, came to Hezekiah with their clothes torn, and told him the words of the Rabshakeh.

**37.1** WHEN King Hezekiah heard it, he tore his clothes, covered himself with sackcloth, and went into the house of the LORD. ²And he sent Eliakim, who was in charge of the palace, and Shebna the secretary, and the senior priests, covered with sackcloth, to the prophet Isaiah son of Amoz. ³They said to him, "Thus says Hezekiah, This day is a day of distress, of rebuke, and of disgrace; children have come to the birth, and there is no strength to bring them forth. ⁴It may be that the LORD your God heard the words of the Rabshakeh, whom his master the king of Assyria has sent to mock the living God, and will rebuke the words that the LORD your God has heard; therefore lift up your prayer for the remnant that is left."

5 When the servants of King Hezekiah came to Isaiah, ⁶Isaiah said to them, "Say to your master, 'Thus says the LORD: Do not be afraid because of the words that you have heard, with which the servants of the king of Assyria have reviled me. ⁷I myself will put a spirit in him, so that he shall hear a rumor, and return to his own land; I will cause him to fall by the sword in his own land.' "

8 The Rabshakeh returned, and found the king of Assyria fighting against Libnah; for he had heard that the king had left Lachish. ⁹Now the

king[a] heard concerning King Tirhakah of Ethiopia,[b] "He has set out to fight against you." When he heard it, he sent messengers to Hezekiah, saying, [10]"Thus shall you speak to King Hezekiah of Judah: Do not let your God on whom you rely deceive you by promising that Jerusalem will not be given into the hand of the king of Assyria. [11]See, you have heard what the kings of Assyria have done to all lands, destroying them utterly. Shall you be delivered? [12]Have the gods of the nations delivered them, the nations that my predecessors destroyed, Gozan, Haran, Rezeph, and the people of Eden who were in Telassar? [13]Where is the king of Hamath, the king of Arpad, the king of the city of Sepharvaim, the king of Hena, or the king of Ivvah?"

14 Hezekiah received the letter from the hand of the messengers and read it; then Hezekiah went up to the house of the LORD and spread it before the LORD. [15]And Hezekiah prayed to the LORD, saying: [16]"O LORD of hosts, God of Israel, who are enthroned above the cherubim, you are God, you alone, of all the kingdoms of the earth; you have made heaven and earth. [17]Incline your ear, O LORD, and hear; open your eyes, O LORD, and see; hear all the words of Sennacherib, which he has sent to mock the living God. [18]Truly, O LORD, the kings of Assyria have laid waste all the nations and their lands, [19]and have hurled their gods into the fire, though they were no gods, but the work of human hands—wood and stone—and so they were destroyed. [20]So now, O LORD our God, save us from his hand, so that all the kingdoms of the earth may know that you alone are the LORD."

21 Then Isaiah son of Amoz sent to Hezekiah, saying: "Thus says the LORD, the God of Israel: Because you have prayed to me concerning King Sennacherib of Assyria, [22]this is the word that the LORD has spoken concerning him:

She despises you, she scorns
	you—
	virgin daughter Zion;
she tosses her head—behind
	your back,
	daughter Jerusalem.

23	Whom have you mocked and
		reviled?
	Against whom have you
		raised your voice
	and haughtily lifted your eyes?
	Against the Holy One of
		Israel!
24	By your servants you have
		mocked the Lord,
	and you have said, 'With my
		many chariots
	I have gone up the heights of
		the mountains,
	to the far recesses of
		Lebanon;
	I felled its tallest cedars,
		its choicest cypresses;
	I came to its remotest height,
		its densest forest.
25	I dug wells
		and drank waters,
	I dried up with the sole of my
		foot
		all the streams of Egypt.'

26	Have you not heard
		that I determined it long ago?
	I planned from days of old
		what now I bring to pass,
	that you should make fortified
		cities
		crash into heaps of ruins,
27	while their inhabitants, shorn of
		strength,
	are dismayed and confounded;
	they have become like plants of
		the field
	and like tender grass,

[a]Heb *he*   [b]Or *Nubia;* Heb *Cush*

like grass on the housetops,
  blighted<sup>a</sup> before it is grown.

28 I know your rising up<sup>b</sup> and
    your sitting down,
  your going out and coming in,
  and your raging against me.
29 Because you have raged against
      me
    and your arrogance has come
      to my ears,
  I will put my hook in your nose
    and my bit in your mouth;
  I will turn you back on the way
    by which you came.

30 "And this shall be the sign for you: This year eat what grows of itself, and in the second year what springs from that; then in the third year sow, reap, plant vineyards, and eat their fruit. <sup>31</sup>The surviving remnant of the house of Judah shall again take root downward, and bear fruit upward; <sup>32</sup>for from Jerusalem a remnant shall go out, and from Mount Zion a band of survivors. The zeal of the Lord of hosts will do this.

33 "Therefore thus says the Lord concerning the king of Assyria: He shall not come into this city, shoot an arrow there, come before it with a shield, or cast up a siege ramp against it. <sup>34</sup>By the way that he came, by the same he shall return; he shall not come into this city, says the Lord. <sup>35</sup>For I will defend this city to save it, for my own sake and for the sake of my servant David."

36 Then the angel of the Lord set out and struck down one hundred eighty-five thousand in the camp of the Assyrians; when morning dawned, they were all dead bodies. <sup>37</sup>Then King Sennacherib of Assyria left, went home, and lived at Nineveh. <sup>38</sup>As he was worshiping in the house of his god Nisroch, his sons Adrammelech and

Sharezer killed him with the sword, and they escaped into the land of Ararat. His son Esar-haddon succeeded him.

## GALATIANS 6.1–18

M<sup>Y</sup> friends,<sup>c</sup> if anyone is detected in a transgression, you who have received the Spirit should restore such a one in a spirit of gentleness. Take care that you yourselves are not tempted. <sup>2</sup>Bear one another's burdens, and in this way you will fulfill<sup>d</sup> the law of Christ. <sup>3</sup>For if those who are nothing think they are something, they deceive themselves. <sup>4</sup>All must test their own work; then that work, rather than their neighbor's work, will become a cause for pride. <sup>5</sup>For all must carry their own loads.

6 Those who are taught the word must share in all good things with their teacher.

7 Do not be deceived; God is not mocked, for you reap whatever you sow. <sup>8</sup>If you sow to your own flesh, you will reap corruption from the flesh; but if you sow to the Spirit, you will reap eternal life from the Spirit. <sup>9</sup>So let us not grow weary in doing what is right, for we will reap at harvest time, if we do not give up. <sup>10</sup>So then, whenever we have an opportunity, let us work for the good of all, and especially for those of the family of faith.

11 See what large letters I make when I am writing in my own hand! <sup>12</sup>It is those who want to make a good showing in the flesh that try to compel you to be circumcised—only that they may not be persecuted for the cross of Christ. <sup>13</sup>Even the circumcised do not themselves obey the law, but they want you to be circumcised so that they may boast about your flesh. <sup>14</sup>May I never boast of anything except the cross of our Lord Jesus Christ, by

<sup>a</sup>With 2 Kings 19.26: Heb *field*  <sup>b</sup>Q Ms Gk: MT lacks *your rising up*  <sup>c</sup>Gk *Brothers*  <sup>d</sup>Other ancient authorities read *in this way fulfill*

which[a] the world has been crucified to me, and I to the world. [15]For[b] neither circumcision nor uncircumcision is anything; but a new creation is everything! [16]As for those who will follow this rule—peace be upon them, and mercy, and upon the Israel of God.

17 From now on, let no one make trouble for me; for I carry the marks of Jesus branded on my body.

18 May the grace of our Lord Jesus Christ be with your spirit, brothers and sisters.[c] Amen.

## PSALM 65.1–13

*To the leader. A Psalm of David. A Song.*

PRAISE is due to you,
O God, in Zion;
　and to you shall vows be
　　performed,
2　O you who answer prayer!
To you all flesh shall come.
3 When deeds of iniquity
　　overwhelm us,
　you forgive our
　　transgressions.
4 Happy are those whom you
　　choose and bring near
　to live in your courts.
We shall be satisfied with the
　　goodness of your house,
　your holy temple.

5 By awesome deeds you answer
　　us with deliverance,
　O God of our salvation;
　you are the hope of all the ends
　　of the earth
　and of the farthest seas.
6 By your[d] strength you
　　established the
　　mountains;
　　you are girded with might.

7 You silence the roaring of the
　　seas,
　the roaring of their waves,
　the tumult of the peoples.
8 Those who live at earth's
　　farthest bounds are awed
　　by your signs;
you make the gateways of the
　　morning and the evening
　　shout for joy.

9 You visit the earth and water it,
　you greatly enrich it;
the river of God is full of water;
　you provide the people with
　　grain,
　for so you have prepared it.
10 You water its furrows
　　abundantly,
　settling its ridges,
softening it with showers,
　and blessing its growth.
11 You crown the year with your
　　bounty;
　your wagon tracks overflow
　　with richness.
12 The pastures of the wilderness
　　overflow,
　the hills gird themselves with
　　joy,
13 the meadows clothe themselves
　　with flocks,
　the valleys deck themselves
　　with grain,
　they shout and sing together
　　for joy.

## PROVERBS 23.24

THE father of the righteous will
　　greatly rejoice;
he who begets a wise son
　　will be glad in him.

---

[a]Or *through whom*　[b]Other ancient authorities add *in Christ Jesus*　[c]Gk *brothers*　[d]Gk Jerome: Heb *his*

# SEPTEMBER 22

## ISAIAH 38.1—41.16

IN those days Hezekiah became sick and was at the point of death. The prophet Isaiah son of Amoz came to him, and said to him, "Thus says the LORD: Set your house in order, for you shall die; you shall not recover." ²Then Hezekiah turned his face to the wall, and prayed to the LORD: ³"Remember now, O LORD, I implore you, how I have walked before you in faithfulness with a whole heart, and have done what is good in your sight." And Hezekiah wept bitterly.

4 Then the word of the LORD came to Isaiah: ⁵"Go and say to Hezekiah, Thus says the LORD, the God of your ancestor David: I have heard your prayer, I have seen your tears; I will add fifteen years to your life. ⁶I will deliver you and this city out of the hand of the king of Assyria, and defend this city.

7 "This is the sign to you from the LORD, that the LORD will do this thing that he has promised: ⁸See, I will make the shadow cast by the declining sun on the dial of Ahaz turn back ten steps." So the sun turned back on the dial the ten steps by which it had declined. ᵃ

9 A writing of King Hezekiah of Judah, after he had been sick and had recovered from his sickness:

10   I said: In the noontide of my
      days
    I must depart;
  I am consigned to the gates of
      Sheol
    for the rest of my years.
11   I said, I shall not see the LORD
    in the land of the living;
  I shall look upon mortals no
      more
    among the inhabitants of
      the world.
12   My dwelling is plucked up and
      removed from me
    like a shepherd's tent;
  like a weaver I have rolled up
      my life;
    he cuts me off from the loom;
  from day to night you bring me
      to an end; ᵃ
13     I cry for helpᵇ until morning;
  like a lion he breaks all my
      bones;
    from day to night you bring
      me to an end. ᵃ

14   Like a swallow or a craneᵃ I
      clamor,
    I moan like a dove.
  My eyes are weary with looking
      upward.
    O Lord, I am oppressed; be
      my security!
15   But what can I say? For he has
      spoken to me,
    and he himself has done it.
  All my sleep has fledᶜ
    because of the bitterness of
      my soul.

16   O Lord, by these things people
      live,
    and in all these is the life of
      my spirit. ᵃ
    Oh, restore me to health and
      make me live!
17   Surely it was for my welfare
    that I had great bitterness;
  but you have held backᵈ my life
    from the pit of destruction,
  for you have cast all my sins

ᵃMeaning of Heb uncertain   ᵇCn: Meaning of Heb uncertain   ᶜCn Compare Syr: Heb *I will walk slowly all my years*   ᵈCn Compare Gk Vg: Heb *loved*

behind your back.
18 For Sheol cannot thank you,
death cannot praise you;
those who go down to the Pit
cannot hope
for your faithfulness.
19 The living, the living, they
thank you,
as I do this day;
fathers make known to children
your faithfulness.

20 The LORD will save me,
and we will sing to stringed
instruments[a]
all the days of our lives,
at the house of the LORD.

21 Now Isaiah had said, "Let them take a lump of figs, and apply it to the boil, so that he may recover." ²²Hezekiah also had said, "What is the sign that I shall go up to the house of the LORD?"

39.1 AT that time King Merodach-baladan son of Baladan of Babylon sent envoys with letters and a present to Hezekiah, for he heard that he had been sick and had recovered. ²Hezekiah welcomed them; he showed them his treasure house, the silver, the gold, the spices, the precious oil, his whole armory, all that was found in his storehouses. There was nothing in his house or in all his realm that Hezekiah did not show them. ³Then the prophet Isaiah came to King Hezekiah and said to him, "What did these men say? From where did they come to you?" Hezekiah answered, "They have come to me from a far country, from Babylon." ⁴He said, "What have they seen in your house?" Hezekiah answered, "They have seen all that is in my house; there is nothing in my storehouses that I did not show them."

5 Then Isaiah said to Hezekiah,

"Hear the word of the LORD of hosts: ⁶Days are coming when all that is in your house, and that which your ancestors have stored up until this day, shall be carried to Babylon; nothing shall be left, says the LORD. ⁷Some of your own sons who are born to you shall be taken away; they shall be eunuchs in the palace of the king of Babylon." ⁸Then Hezekiah said to Isaiah, "The word of the LORD that you have spoken is good." For he thought, "There will be peace and security in my days."

40.1 COMFORT, O comfort my
people,
says your God.
2 Speak tenderly to Jerusalem,
and cry to her
that she has served her term,
that her penalty is paid,
that she has received from the
LORD's hand
double for all her sins.

3 A voice cries out:
"In the wilderness prepare the
way of the LORD,
make straight in the desert a
highway for our God.
4 Every valley shall be lifted up,
and every mountain and hill
be made low;
the uneven ground shall become
level,
and the rough places a plain.
5 Then the glory of the LORD shall
be revealed,
and all people shall see it
together,
for the mouth of the LORD has
spoken."

6 A voice says, "Cry out!"
And I said, "What shall I
cry?"
All people are grass,

a Heb *my stringed instruments*

their constancy is like the
    flower of the field.
7 The grass withers, the flower
    fades,
    when the breath of the Lord
       blows upon it;
    surely the people are grass.
8 The grass withers, the flower
    fades;
    but the word of our God will
       stand forever.
9 Get you up to a high mountain,
    O Zion, herald of good
       tidings; a
    lift up your voice with strength,
    O Jerusalem, herald of good
       tidings, b
    lift it up, do not fear;
    say to the cities of Judah,
    "Here is your God!"
10 See, the Lord God comes with
    might,
    and his arm rules for him;
    his reward is with him,
    and his recompense before
       him.
11 He will feed his flock like a
    shepherd;
    he will gather the lambs in
       his arms,
    and carry them in his bosom,
    and gently lead the mother
       sheep.

12 Who has measured the waters
    in the hollow of his hand
    and marked off the heavens
       with a span,
    enclosed the dust of the earth in
       a measure,
    and weighed the mountains
       in scales
    and the hills in a balance?
13 Who has directed the spirit of
    the Lord,
    or as his counselor has
       instructed him?

14 Whom did he consult for his
    enlightenment,
    and who taught him the path
       of justice?
    Who taught him knowledge,
    and showed him the way of
       understanding?
15 Even the nations are like a drop
    from a bucket,
    and are accounted as dust on
       the scales;
    see, he takes up the isles like
       fine dust.
16 Lebanon would not provide fuel
    enough,
    nor are its animals enough for
       a burnt offering.
17 All the nations are as nothing
    before him;
    they are accounted by him as
       less than nothing and
       emptiness.

18 To whom then will you liken
    God,
    or what likeness compare
       with him?
19 An idol? —A workman casts it,
    and a goldsmith overlays it
       with gold,
    and casts for it silver chains.
20 As a gift one chooses mulberry
    wood c
    —wood that will not rot—
    then seeks out a skilled artisan
    to set up an image that will
       not topple.

21 Have you not known? Have you
    not heard?
    Has it not been told you from
       the beginning?
    Have you not understood
       from the foundations of
       the earth?
22 It is he who sits above the
    circle of the earth,

a Or *O herald of good tidings to Zion*   b Or *O herald of good tidings to Jerusalem*   c Meaning of Heb
uncertain

and its inhabitants are like
    grasshoppers;
who stretches out the heavens
    like a curtain,
and spreads them like a tent
    to live in;
23 who brings princes to naught,
    and makes the rulers of the
    earth as nothing.

24 Scarcely are they planted,
    scarcely sown,
    scarcely has their stem taken
    root in the earth,
when he blows upon them, and
    they wither,
    and the tempest carries them
    off like stubble.

25 To whom then will you compare
    me,
    or who is my equal? says the
    Holy One.
26 Lift up your eyes on high and
    see:
Who created these?
He who brings out their host
    and numbers them,
    calling them all by name;
because he is great in strength,
    mighty in power,
    not one is missing.

27 Why do you say, O Jacob,
    and speak, O Israel,
"My way is hidden from the
    LORD,
    and my right is disregarded
    by my God"?
28 Have you not known? Have you
    not heard?
The LORD is the everlasting
    God,
    the Creator of the ends of
    the earth.
He does not faint or grow
    weary;
    his understanding is
    unsearchable.
29 He gives power to the faint,

    and strengthens the
    powerless.
30 Even youths will faint and
    be weary,
    and the young will fall
    exhausted;
31 but those who wait for the LORD
    shall renew their
    strength,
they shall mount up with
    wings like eagles,
they shall run and not be weary,
they shall walk and not faint.

41.1 LISTEN to me in silence,
    O coastlands;
    let the peoples renew their
    strength;
let them approach, then let
    them speak;
    let us together draw near for
    judgment.

2 Who has roused a victor from
    the east,
    summoned him to his service?
He delivers up nations to him,
    and tramples kings under
    foot;
he makes them like dust with
    his sword,
    like driven stubble with his
    bow.
3 He pursues them and passes
    on safely,
    scarcely touching the path
    with his feet.
4 Who has performed and done
    this,
    calling the generations from
    the beginning?
I, the LORD, am first,
    and will be with the last.
5 The coastlands have seen and
    are afraid,
    the ends of the earth tremble;
    they have drawn near and
    come.
6 Each one helps the other,

saying to one another, "Take
        courage!"
7   The artisan encourages the
        goldsmith,
    and the one who smooths
        with the hammer
        encourages the one who
        strikes the anvil,
    saying of the soldering, "It is
        good";
    and they fasten it with nails
        so that it cannot be
        moved.
8   But you, Israel, my servant,
        Jacob, whom I have chosen,
        the offspring of Abraham,
        my friend;
9   you whom I took from the ends
        of the earth,
    and called from its farthest
        corners,
    saying to you, "You are my
        servant,
    I have chosen you and not
        cast you off";
10  do not fear, for I am with you,
        do not be afraid, for I am
        your God;
    I will strengthen you, I will help
        you,
    I will uphold you with my
        victorious right hand.

11  Yes, all who are incensed
        against you
    shall be ashamed and
        disgraced;
    those who strive against you
        shall be as nothing and
        shall perish.
12  You shall seek those who
        contend with you,
    but you shall not find them;
    those who war against you
        shall be as nothing at all.
13  For I, the LORD your God,
        hold your right hand;

it is I who say to you, "Do not
        fear,
    I will help you."

14  Do not fear, you worm Jacob,
        you insect[a] Israel!
    I will help you, says the LORD;
        your Redeemer is the Holy
        One of Israel.
15  Now, I will make of you a
        threshing sledge,
    sharp, new, and having teeth;
    you shall thresh the mountains
        and crush them,
    and you shall make the hills
        like chaff.
16  You shall winnow them and the
        wind shall carry them
        away,
    and the tempest shall scatter
        them.
    Then you shall rejoice in the
        LORD;
    in the Holy One of Israel you
        shall glory.


# EPHESIANS 1.1–23

PAUL, an apostle of Christ Jesus
by the will of God,
    To the saints who are in Ephe-
sus and are faithful[b] in Christ Jesus:
    2   Grace to you and peace from God
our Father and the Lord Jesus Christ.

    3   Blessed be the God and Father of
our Lord Jesus Christ, who has blessed
us in Christ with every spiritual blessing in the heavenly places, [4]just as he
chose us in Christ[c] before the foundation of the world to be holy and blameless before him in love. [5]He destined us
for adoption as his children through
Jesus Christ, according to the good
pleasure of his will, [6]to the praise of his
glorious grace that he freely bestowed
on us in the Beloved. [7]In him we have

aSyr: Heb *men of*   bOther ancient authorities lack *in Ephesus,* reading *saints who are also faithful*
cGk *in him*

redemption through his blood, the forgiveness of our trespasses, according to the riches of his grace ⁸that he lavished on us. With all wisdom and insight ⁹he has made known to us the mystery of his will, according to his good pleasure that he set forth in Christ, ¹⁰as a plan for the fullness of time, to gather up all things in him, things in heaven and things on earth. ¹¹In Christ we have also obtained an inheritance,[a] having been destined according to the purpose of him who accomplishes all things according to his counsel and will, ¹²so that we, who were the first to set our hope on Christ, might live for the praise of his glory. ¹³In him you also, when you had heard the word of truth, the gospel of your salvation, and had believed in him, were marked with the seal of the promised Holy Spirit; ¹⁴this[b] is the pledge of our inheritance toward redemption as God's own people, to the praise of his glory.

15  I have heard of your faith in the Lord Jesus and your love[c] toward all the saints, and for this reason ¹⁶I do not cease to give thanks for you as I remember you in my prayers. ¹⁷I pray that the God of our Lord Jesus Christ, the Father of glory, may give you a spirit of wisdom and revelation as you come to know him, ¹⁸so that, with the eyes of your heart enlightened, you may know what is the hope to which he has called you, what are the riches of his glorious inheritance among the saints, ¹⁹and what is the immeasurable greatness of his power for us who believe, according to the working of his great power. ²⁰God[d] put this power to work in Christ when he raised him from the dead and seated him at his right hand in the heavenly places, ²¹far above all rule and authority and power and dominion, and above every name that is named, not only in this age but also in the age to come. ²²And he has put all things under his feet and has made him the head over all things for the church, ²³which is his body, the fullness of him who fills all in all.

## PSALM 66.1–20

*To the leader. A Song. A Psalm.*

**M**AKE a joyful noise to God,
    all the earth;
²    sing the glory of his
    name;
  give to him glorious praise.
³ Say to God, "How awesome are
    your deeds!
  Because of your great power,
    your enemies cringe
    before you.
⁴ All the earth worships you;
    they sing praises to you,
    sing praises to your name."
                *Selah*

⁵ Come and see what God has
    done:
  he is awesome in his deeds
    among mortals.
⁶ He turned the sea into dry land;
  they passed through the river
    on foot.
  There we rejoiced in him,
⁷   who rules by his might
    forever,
  whose eyes keep watch on the
    nations—
  let the rebellious not exalt
    themselves.     *Selah*

⁸ Bless our God, O peoples,
  let the sound of his praise be
    heard,
⁹ who has kept us among the
    living,
  and has not let our feet slip.
¹⁰ For you, O God, have tested
    us;
  you have tried us as silver is
    tried.

a Or *been made a heritage*  b Other ancient authorities read *who*  c Other ancient authorities lack *and your love*  d Gk *He*

11 You brought us into the net;
    you laid burdens on our
        backs;
12 you let people ride over our
        heads;
    we went through fire and
        through water;
    yet you have brought us out to
        a spacious place. **a**

13 I will come into your house with
        burnt offerings;
    I will pay you my vows,
14 those that my lips uttered
    and my mouth promised when
        I was in trouble.
15 I will offer to you burnt
        offerings of fatlings,
    with the smoke of the
        sacrifice of rams;
    I will make an offering of bulls
        and goats.          *Selah*

16 Come and hear, all you who fear
        God,
    and I will tell what he has
        done for me.
17 I cried aloud to him,
    and he was extolled with my
        tongue.

18 If I had cherished iniquity in my
        heart,
    the Lord would not have
        listened.
19 But truly God has listened;
    he has given heed to the
        words of my prayer.

20 Blessed be God,
    because he has not rejected
        my prayer
    or removed his steadfast love
        from me.

## PROVERBS 23.25–28

Let your father and mother
        be glad;
    let her who bore you rejoice.

26 My child, give me your heart,
    and let your eyes observe **b**
        my ways.
27 For a prostitute is a deep pit;
    an adulteress **c** is a narrow
        well.
28 She lies in wait like a robber
    and increases the number of
        the faithless.

# SEPTEMBER 23

## ISAIAH 41.17—43.13

When the poor and needy
        seek water,
    and there is none,
    and their tongue is parched
        with thirst,
    I the Lord will answer them,
    I the God of Israel will not
        forsake them.
18 I will open rivers on the bare
        heights, **d**
    and fountains in the midst of
        the valleys;
    I will make the wilderness a
        pool of water,

**a**Cn Compare Gk Syr Jerome Tg: Heb *to a saturation*   **b**Another reading is *delight in*   **c**Heb *an alien woman*   **d**Or *trails*

and the dry land springs of
water.
19 I will put in the wilderness
the cedar,
the acacia, the myrtle, and
the olive;
I will set in the desert the
cypress,
the plane and the pine
together,
20 so that all may see and know,
all may consider and
understand,
that the hand of the Lord has
done this,
the Holy One of Israel has
created it.

21 Set forth your case, says the
Lord;
bring your proofs, says the
King of Jacob.
22 Let them bring them, and tell us
what is to happen.
Tell us the former things, what
they are,
so that we may consider
them,
and that we may know their
outcome;
or declare to us the things
to come.
23 Tell us what is to come
hereafter,
that we may know that you
are gods;
do good, or do harm,
that we may be afraid and
terrified.
24 You, indeed, are nothing
and your work is nothing at
all;
whoever chooses you is an
abomination.

25 I stirred up one from the north,
and he has come,

from the rising of the sun he
was summoned by
name. [a]
He shall trample [b] on rulers as
on mortar,
as the potter treads clay.
26 Who declared it from the
beginning, so that we
might know,
and beforehand, so that we
might say, "He is right"?
There was no one who declared
it, none who proclaimed,
none who heard your words.
27 I first have declared it to Zion, [c]
and I give to Jerusalem a
herald of good tidings.
28 But when I look there is no
one;
among these there is no
counselor
who, when I ask, gives an
answer.
29 No, they are all a delusion;
their works are nothing;
their images are empty wind.

42.1 Here is my servant, whom I
uphold,
my chosen, in whom my soul
delights;
I have put my spirit upon him;
he will bring forth justice to
the nations.
2 He will not cry or lift up his
voice,
or make it heard in the
street;
3 a bruised reed he will not break,
and a dimly burning wick he
will not quench;
he will faithfully bring forth
justice.
4 He will not grow faint or be
crushed
until he has established justice
in the earth;

a Cn Compare Q Ms Gk: MT *and he shall call on my name*   b Cn: Heb *come*   c Cn: Heb *First to
Zion—Behold, behold them*

and the coastlands wait for his
    teaching.

5 Thus says God, the LORD,
    who created the heavens and
        stretched them out,
    who spread out the earth and
        what comes from it,
  who gives breath to the people
        upon it
  and spirit to those who walk
        in it:
6 I am the LORD, I have called you
    in righteousness,
  I have taken you by the hand
        and kept you;
  I have given you as a covenant
    to the people, a
  a light to the nations,
7   to open the eyes that are
        blind,
  to bring out the prisoners from
    the dungeon,
  from the prison those who sit
    in darkness.
8 I am the LORD, that is my name;
    my glory I give to no other,
    nor my praise to idols.
9 See, the former things have
    come to pass,
  and new things I now declare;
  before they spring forth,
    I tell you of them.

10 Sing to the LORD a new song,
    his praise from the end of the
        earth!
  Let the sea roarb and all that
        fills it,
  the coastlands and their
        inhabitants.
11 Let the desert and its towns lift
    up their voice,
  the villages that Kedar
        inhabits;
  let the inhabitants of Sela sing
    for joy,

  let them shout from the tops
    of the mountains.
12 Let them give glory to the
    LORD,
  and declare his praise in the
    coastlands.
13 The LORD goes forth like a
    soldier,
  like a warrior he stirs up his
    fury;
  he cries out, he shouts aloud,
  he shows himself mighty
    against his foes.

14 For a long time I have held my
    peace,
  I have kept still and
    restrained myself;
  now I will cry out like a woman
    in labor,
  I will gasp and pant.
15 I will lay waste mountains and
    hills,
  and dry up all their herbage;
  I will turn the rivers into
    islands,
  and dry up the pools.
16 I will lead the blind
    by a road they do not know,
  by paths they have not known
    I will guide them.
  I will turn the darkness before
    them into light,
  the rough places into level
    ground.
  These are the things I will do,
    and I will not forsake them.
17 They shall be turned back and
    utterly put to shame—
  those who trust in carved
    images,
  who say to cast images,
    "You are our gods."

18 Listen, you that are deaf;
    and you that are blind, look
        up and see!
19 Who is blind but my servant,

---

a Meaning of Heb uncertain  b Cn Compare Ps 96.11; 98.7: Heb *Those who go down to the sea*

or deaf like my messenger
    whom I send?
Who is blind like my dedicated
    one,
or blind like the servant of
    the LORD?
20 He sees many things, but
    does[a] not observe them;
his ears are open, but he
    does not hear.
21 The LORD was pleased, for the
    sake of his
    righteousness,
to magnify his teaching and
    make it glorious.
22 But this is a people robbed and
    plundered,
    all of them are trapped in
    holes
    and hidden in prisons;
they have become a prey with
    no one to rescue,
a spoil with no one to say,
    "Restore!"
23 Who among you will give heed
    to this,
who will attend and listen for
    the time to come?
24 Who gave up Jacob to the
    spoiler,
and Israel to the robbers?
Was it not the LORD, against
    whom we have sinned,
in whose ways they would
    not walk,
and whose law they would
    not obey?
25 So he poured upon him the heat
    of his anger
    and the fury of war;
it set him on fire all around, but
    he did not understand;
it burned him, but he did not
    take it to heart.

43.1 BUT now thus says the LORD,
    he who created you, O Jacob,
    he who formed you, O Israel:

Do not fear, for I have
    redeemed you;
I have called you by name,
    you are mine.
2 When you pass through the
    waters, I will be with
    you;
and through the rivers, they
    shall not overwhelm you;
when you walk through fire you
    shall not be burned,
and the flame shall not
    consume you.
3 For I am the LORD your God,
    the Holy One of Israel, your
    Savior.
I give Egypt as your ransom,
    Ethiopia[b] and Seba in
    exchange for you.
4 Because you are precious in
    my sight,
    and honored, and I love you,
I give people in return for you,
    nations in exchange for your
    life.
5 Do not fear, for I am with you;
    I will bring your offspring
    from the east,
and from the west I will
    gather you;
6 I will say to the north, "Give
    them up,"
and to the south, "Do not
    withhold;
bring my sons from far away
    and my daughters from the
    end of the earth—
7 everyone who is called by my
    name,
whom I created for my glory,
    whom I formed and made."

8 Bring forth the people who are
    blind, yet have eyes,
who are deaf, yet have ears!
9 Let all the nations gather
    together,
and let the peoples assemble.

[a] Heb *You see many things but do*  [b] Or *Nubia*; Heb *Cush*

Who among them declared this,
    and foretold to us the former
      things?
Let them bring their witnesses
    to justify them,
    and let them hear and say, "It
      is true."
10 You are my witnesses, says the
      LORD,
    and my servant whom I have
      chosen,
so that you may know and
      believe me
and understand that I am he.
Before me no god was formed,
    nor shall there be any after
      me.
11 I, I am the LORD,
    and besides me there is no
      savior.
12 I declared and saved and
      proclaimed,
    when there was no strange
      god among you;
    and you are my witnesses,
      says the LORD.
13 I am God, and also henceforth I
      am He;
    there is no one who can
      deliver from my hand;
    I work and who can hinder it?

# EPHESIANS 2.1–22

YOU were dead through the trespasses and sins [2]in which you once lived, following the course of this world, following the ruler of the power of the air, the spirit that is now at work among those who are disobedient. [3]All of us once lived among them in the passions of our flesh, following the desires of flesh and senses, and we were by nature children of wrath, like everyone else. [4]But God, who is rich in mercy, out of the great love with which he loved us [5]even when we were dead through our trespasses, made us alive

together with Christ[a]—by grace you have been saved— [6]and raised us up with him and seated us with him in the heavenly places in Christ Jesus, [7]so that in the ages to come he might show the immeasurable riches of his grace in kindness toward us in Christ Jesus. [8]For by grace you have been saved through faith, and this is not your own doing; it is the gift of God— [9]not the result of works, so that no one may boast. [10]For we are what he has made us, created in Christ Jesus for good works, which God prepared beforehand to be our way of life.

11 So then, remember that at one time you Gentiles by birth,[b] called "the uncircumcision" by those who are called "the circumcision"—a physical circumcision made in the flesh by human hands— [12]remember that you were at that time without Christ, being aliens from the commonwealth of Israel, and strangers to the covenants of promise, having no hope and without God in the world. [13]But now in Christ Jesus you who once were far off have been brought near by the blood of Christ. [14]For he is our peace; in his flesh he has made both groups into one and has broken down the dividing wall, that is, the hostility between us. [15]He has abolished the law with its commandments and ordinances, that he might create in himself one new humanity in place of the two, thus making peace, [16]and might reconcile both groups to God in one body[c] through the cross, thus putting to death that hostility through it.[d] [17]So he came and proclaimed peace to you who were far off and peace to those who were near; [18]for through him both of us have access in one Spirit to the Father. [19]So then you are no longer strangers and aliens, but you are citizens with the saints and also members of the household of God, [20]built upon the foundation

aOther ancient authorities read *in Christ*  bGk *in the flesh*  cOr *reconcile both of us in one body for God*  dOr *in him,* or *in himself*

of the apostles and prophets, with Christ Jesus himself as the cornerstone. a 21 In him the whole structure is joined together and grows into a holy temple in the Lord; 22 in whom you also are built together spiritually b into a dwelling place for God.

## PSALM 67.1–7

*To the leader: with stringed instruments. A Psalm. A Song.*

May God be gracious to us
    and bless us
    and make his face to shine
        upon us,     *Selah*
2 that your way may be known
      upon earth,
    your saving power among all
      nations.
3 Let the peoples praise you,
    O God;
    let all the peoples praise you.

4 Let the nations be glad and sing
      for joy,
    for you judge the peoples
      with equity
    and guide the nations upon
      earth.     *Selah*
5 Let the peoples praise you,
    O God;
    let all the peoples praise you.

6 The earth has yielded its
      increase;
    God, our God, has blessed
      us.
7 May God continue to bless us;
    let all the ends of the earth
      revere him.

## PROVERBS 23.29–35

Who has woe? Who has
      sorrow?
    Who has strife? Who has
      complaining?
Who has wounds without cause?
    Who has redness of eyes?
30 Those who linger late over
      wine,
    those who keep trying
      mixed wines.
31 Do not look at wine when it is
      red,
    when it sparkles in the cup
    and goes down smoothly.
32 At the last it bites like a
      serpent,
    and stings like an adder.
33 Your eyes will see strange
      things,
    and your mind utter perverse
      things.
34 You will be like one who lies
      down in the midst of the
      sea,
    like one who lies on the top
      of a mast. c
35 "They struck me," you will
      say, d "but I was not
      hurt;
    they beat me, but I did not
      feel it.
When shall I awake?
    I will seek another drink."

a Or *keystone*   b Gk *in the Spirit*   c Meaning of Heb uncertain   d Gk Syr Vg Tg: Heb lacks *you will say*

# SEPTEMBER 24

ISAIAH 43.14—45.10

**T**HUS says the LORD,
　your Redeemer, the Holy
　　One of Israel:
For your sake I will send to
　Babylon
and break down all the bars,
and the shouting of the
　　Chaldeans will be turned
　　to lamentation. **a**

15　I am the LORD, your Holy One,
　　the Creator of Israel, your
　　King.
16　Thus says the LORD,
　　who makes a way in the sea,
　　a path in the mighty waters,
17　who brings out chariot and
　　　horse,
　　army and warrior;
they lie down, they cannot rise,
　　they are extinguished,
　　　quenched like a wick:
18　Do not remember the former
　　　things,
　　or consider the things of old.
19　I am about to do a new thing;
　　now it springs forth, do you
　　　not perceive it?
　I will make a way in the
　　　wilderness
　　and rivers in the desert.
20　The wild animals will honor me,
　　the jackals and the ostriches;
for I give water in the
　　　wilderness,
　　rivers in the desert,
to give drink to my chosen
　　　people,
21　the people whom I formed
　　　for myself
so that they might declare
　　my praise.

22　Yet you did not call upon me,
　　　O Jacob;
　　but you have been weary of
　　me, O Israel!
23　You have not brought me your
　　　sheep for burnt offerings,
　　or honored me with your
　　　sacrifices.
I have not burdened you with
　　　offerings,
　　or wearied you with
　　　frankincense.
24　You have not bought me sweet
　　　cane with money,
　　or satisfied me with the fat of
　　　your sacrifices.
But you have burdened me with
　　　your sins;
　　you have wearied me with
　　　your iniquities.

25　I, I am He
　　who blots out your
　　　transgressions for my
　　　own sake,
　　and I will not remember
　　　your sins.
26　Accuse me, let us go to trial;
　　set forth your case, so that
　　　you may be proved right.
27　Your first ancestor sinned,
　　and your interpreters
　　　transgressed against me.
28　Therefore I profaned the
　　　princes of the sanctuary,
I delivered Jacob to utter
　　　destruction,
and Israel to reviling.

44.1 BUT now hear, O Jacob
　　my servant,
　　Israel whom I have chosen

2 Thus says the Lord who made
    you,
  who formed you in the womb
    and will help you:
  Do not fear, O Jacob my
    servant,
  Jeshurun whom I have
    chosen.
3 For I will pour water on the
    thirsty land,
  and streams on the dry
    ground;
  I will pour my spirit upon your
    descendants,
  and my blessing on your
    offspring.
4 They shall spring up like a
    green tamarisk,
  like willows by flowing
    streams.
5 This one will say, "I am the
    Lord's,"
  another will be called by the
    name of Jacob,
  yet another will write on the
    hand, "The Lord's,"
  and adopt the name of Israel.

6 Thus says the Lord, the King
    of Israel,
  and his Redeemer, the Lord
    of hosts:
  I am the first and I am the last;
    besides me there is no god.
7 Who is like me? Let them
    proclaim it,
  let them declare and set it
    forth before me.
  Who has announced from of old
    the things to come?[a]
  Let them tell us[b] what is yet
    to be.
8 Do not fear, or be afraid;
  have I not told you from of
    old and declared it?
  You are my witnesses!
  Is there any god besides me?

There is no other rock; I
  know not one.

9 All who make idols are nothing, and the things they delight in do not profit; their witnesses neither see nor know. And so they will be put to shame. [10]Who would fashion a god or cast an image that can do no good? [11]Look, all its devotees shall be put to shame; the artisans too are merely human. Let them all assemble, let them stand up; they shall be terrified, they shall all be put to shame.

12 The ironsmith fashions it[c] and works it over the coals, shaping it with hammers, and forging it with his strong arm; he becomes hungry and his strength fails, he drinks no water and is faint. [13]The carpenter stretches a line, marks it out with a stylus, fashions it with planes, and marks it with a compass; he makes it in human form, with human beauty, to be set up in a shrine. [14]He cuts down cedars or chooses a holm tree or an oak and lets it grow strong among the trees of the forest. He plants a cedar and the rain nourishes it. [15]Then it can be used as fuel. Part of it he takes and warms himself; he kindles a fire and bakes bread. Then he makes a god and worships it, makes it a carved image and bows down before it. [16]Half of it he burns in the fire; over this half he roasts meat, eats it and is satisfied. He also warms himself and says, "Ah, I am warm, I can feel the fire!" [17]The rest of it he makes into a god, his idol, bows down to it and worships it; he prays to it and says, "Save me, for you are my god!"

18 They do not know, nor do they comprehend; for their eyes are shut, so that they cannot see, and their minds as well, so that they cannot understand. [19]No one considers, nor is there knowledge or discernment to say, "Half of it I burned in the fire; I also baked bread

a Cn: Heb *from my placing an eternal people and things to come*   b Tg: Heb *them*   c Cn: Heb *an ax* on its coals, I roasted meat and have eaten. Now shall I make the rest of it an abomination? Shall I fall down before a block of wood?" <sup>20</sup>He feeds on ashes; a deluded mind has led him astray, and he cannot save himself or say, "Is not this thing in my right hand a fraud?"

<sup>21</sup>   Remember these things,
          O Jacob,
      and Israel, for you are my
          servant;
      I formed you, you are my
          servant;
        O Israel, you will not be
          forgotten by me.
<sup>22</sup>  I have swept away your
          transgressions like a
          cloud,
      and your sins like mist;
      return to me, for I have
          redeemed you.

<sup>23</sup>   Sing, O heavens, for the Lord
          has done it;
        shout, O depths of the earth;
      break forth into singing,
          O mountains,
        O forest, and every tree in it!
      For the Lord has redeemed
          Jacob,
      and will be glorified in Israel.

<sup>24</sup>   Thus says the Lord, your
          Redeemer,
        who formed you in the womb:
      I am the Lord, who made all
          things,
        who alone stretched out the
          heavens,
        who by myself spread out
          the earth;
<sup>25</sup>  who frustrates the omens of
          liars,
        and makes fools of diviners;
      who turns back the wise,
        and makes their knowledge
          foolish;

<sup>26</sup>  who confirms the word of his
          servant,
      and fulfills the prediction of
          his messengers;
      who says of Jerusalem, "It shall
          be inhabited,"
      and of the cities of Judah,
          "They shall be rebuilt,
      and I will raise up their
          ruins";
<sup>27</sup>  who says to the deep, "Be
          dry—
        I will dry up your rivers";
<sup>28</sup>  who says of Cyrus, "He is my
          shepherd,
        and he shall carry out all my
          purpose";
      and who says of Jerusalem, "It
          shall be rebuilt,"
      and of the temple, "Your
          foundation shall be laid."

<sup>45.1</sup> Thus says the Lord to his
          anointed, to Cyrus,
        whose right hand I have
          grasped
      to subdue nations before him
        and strip kings of their robes,
      to open doors before him—
        and the gates shall not be
          closed:
<sup>2</sup>   I will go before you
        and level the mountains, <sup>a</sup>
      I will break in pieces the doors
          of bronze
        and cut through the bars of
          iron,
<sup>3</sup>   I will give you the treasures of
          darkness
        and riches hidden in secret
          places,
      so that you may know that it is
          I, the Lord,
        the God of Israel, who call
          you by your name.
<sup>4</sup>   For the sake of my servant
          Jacob,
        and Israel my chosen,

a Q Ms Gk: MT *the swellings*

I call you by your name,
    I surname you, though you do
      not know me.
5 I am the LORD, and there is
    no other;
    besides me there is no god.
    I arm you, though you do not
      know me,
6 so that they may know, from
      the rising of the sun
    and from the west, that there
      is no one besides me;
    I am the LORD, and there is
      no other.
7 I form light and create
      darkness,
    I make weal and create woe;
    I the LORD do all these things.

8 Shower, O heavens, from
      above,
    and let the skies rain down
      righteousness;
    let the earth open, that salvation
      may spring up, a
    and let it cause righteousness
      to sprout up also;
    I the LORD have created it.

9 Woe to you who strive with
      your Maker,
    earthen vessels with the
      potter! b
    Does the clay say to the one
      who fashions it, "What
      are you making"?
    or "Your work has no
      handles"?
10 Woe to anyone who says to a
      father, "What are you
      begetting?"
    or to a woman, "With what
      are you in labor?"

# EPHESIANS 3.1–21

THIS is the reason that I Paul am a prisoner for c Christ Jesus for the sake of you Gentiles— 2for surely you have already heard of the commission of God's grace that was given me for you, 3and how the mystery was made known to me by revelation, as I wrote above in a few words, 4a reading of which will enable you to perceive my understanding of the mystery of Christ. 5In former generations this mystery d was not made known to humankind, as it has now been revealed to his holy apostles and prophets by the Spirit: 6that is, the Gentiles have become fellow heirs, members of the same body, and sharers in the promise in Christ Jesus through the gospel.

7 Of this gospel I have become a servant according to the gift of God's grace that was given me by the working of his power. 8Although I am the very least of all the saints, this grace was given to me to bring to the Gentiles the news of the boundless riches of Christ, 9and to make everyone see e what is the plan of the mystery hidden for ages in f God who created all things; 10so that through the church the wisdom of God in its rich variety might now be made known to the rulers and authorities in the heavenly places. 11This was in accordance with the eternal purpose that he has carried out in Christ Jesus our Lord, 12in whom we have access to God in boldness and confidence through faith in him. g 13I pray therefore that you h may not lose heart over my sufferings for you; they are your glory.

14 For this reason I bow my knees before the Father, i 15from whom every family j in heaven and on earth takes its name. 16I pray that, according

aQ Ms: MT *that they may bring forth salvation*  bCn: Heb *with the potsherds*, or *with the potters*
cOr *of*  dGk *it*  eOther ancient authorities read *to bring to light*  fOr *by*  gOr *the faith of him*  hOr *I*
iOther ancient authorities add *of our Lord Jesus Christ*  jGk *fatherhood*

to the riches of his glory, he may grant that you may be strengthened in your inner being with power through his Spirit, [17]and that Christ may dwell in your hearts through faith, as you are being rooted and grounded in love. [18]I pray that you may have the power to comprehend, with all the saints, what is the breadth and length and height and depth, [19]and to know the love of Christ that surpasses knowledge, so that you may be filled with all the fullness of God.

20 Now to him who by the power at work within us is able to accomplish abundantly far more than all we can ask or imagine, [21]to him be glory in the church and in Christ Jesus to all generations, forever and ever. Amen.

## PSALM 68.1–18

*To the leader. Of David. A Psalm. A Song.*

L ET God rise up, let his
    enemies be scattered;
  let those who hate him flee
    before him.
2 As smoke is driven away, so
    drive them away;
  as wax melts before the fire,
  let the wicked perish before
    God.
3 But let the righteous be joyful;
  let them exult before God;
  let them be jubilant with joy.

4 Sing to God, sing praises to his
    name;
  lift up a song to him who
    rides upon the
    clouds[a]—
his name is the LORD—
  be exultant before him.

5 Father of orphans and protector
    of widows
  is God in his holy habitation.

6 God gives the desolate a home
    to live in;
  he leads out the prisoners to
    prosperity,
  but the rebellious live in a
    parched land.

7 O God, when you went out
    before your people,
  when you marched through
    the wilderness,     *Selah*
8 the earth quaked, the heavens
    poured down rain
  at the presence of God, the
    God of Sinai,
  at the presence of God, the
    God of Israel.
9 Rain in abundance, O God, you
    showered abroad;
  you restored your heritage
    when it languished;
10 your flock found a dwelling in it;
  in your goodness, O God, you
    provided for the needy.

11 The Lord gives the command;
  great is the company of
    those[b] who bore the
    tidings:
12 "The kings of the armies,
    they flee, they flee!"
The women at home divide the
    spoil,
13 though they stay among the
    sheepfolds—
the wings of a dove covered
    with silver,
  its pinions with green gold.
14 When the Almighty[c] scattered
    kings there,
  snow fell on Zalmon.

15 O mighty mountain, mountain of
    Bashan;
  O many-peaked mountain,
    mountain of Bashan!

[a]Or *cast up a highway for him who rides through the deserts*   [b]Or *company of the women*   [c]Traditional rendering of Heb *Shaddai*

16 Why do you look with envy,
   O many-peaked
     mountain,
  at the mount that God desired
     for his abode,
  where the LORD will reside
     forever?

17 With mighty chariotry, twice ten
     thousand,
  thousands upon thousands,
  the Lord came from Sinai into
     the holy place. a
18 You ascended the high mount,
  leading captives in your train
  and receiving gifts from
     people,
  even from those who rebel
     against the LORD God's
     abiding there.

## PROVERBS 24.1–2

Do not envy the wicked,
  nor desire to be with them;
2  for their minds devise
     violence,
  and their lips talk of mischief.

# SEPTEMBER 25

## ISAIAH 45.11—48.11

THUS says the LORD,
  the Holy One of Israel, and
     its Maker:
Will you question me b about
     my children,
  or command me concerning
     the work of my hands?
12 I made the earth,
  and created humankind upon
     it;
  it was my hands that stretched
     out the heavens,
  and I commanded all their
     host.
13 I have aroused Cyrus c in
     righteousness,
  and I will make all his paths
     straight;
  he shall build my city
     and set my exiles free,
  not for price or reward,
     says the LORD of hosts.
14 Thus says the LORD:
The wealth of Egypt and the
     merchandise of
     Ethiopia, d
  and the Sabeans, tall of
     stature,
shall come over to you and
     be yours,
  they shall follow you;
  they shall come over in chains
     and bow down to you.
They will make supplication to
     you, saying,
  "God is with you alone, and
     there is no other;
  there is no god besides him."
15 Truly, you are a God who hides
     himself,
  O God of Israel, the Savior.
16 All of them are put to shame
     and confounded,
  the makers of idols go in
     confusion together.
17 But Israel is saved by the LORD
  with everlasting salvation;

a Cn: Heb *The Lord among them Sinai in the holy* (place)  b Cn: Heb *Ask me of things to come*
c Heb *him*  d Or *Nubia*; Heb *Cush*

you shall not be put to shame or
    confounded
  to all eternity.

18 For thus says the LORD,
who created the heavens
   (he is God!),
who formed the earth and made
     it
   (he established it;
he did not create it a chaos,
   he formed it to be inhabited!):
I am the LORD, and there is
    no other.
19 I did not speak in secret,
  in a land of darkness;
I did not say to the offspring
    of Jacob,
  "Seek me in chaos."
I the LORD speak the truth,
  I declare what is right.

20 Assemble yourselves and come
    together,
  draw near, you survivors of
    the nations!
They have no knowledge—
  those who carry about their
    wooden idols,
and keep on praying to a god
  that cannot save.
21 Declare and present your case;
  let them take counsel
    together!
Who told this long ago?
  Who declared it of old?
Was it not I, the LORD?
  There is no other god besides
    me,
a righteous God and a Savior;
  there is no one besides me.

22 Turn to me and be saved,
  all the ends of the earth!
For I am God, and there is
    no other.
23 By myself I have sworn,
  from my mouth has gone
    forth in righteousness
a word that shall not return:

"To me every knee shall bow,
  every tongue shall swear."
24 Only in the LORD, it shall be said
    of me,
are righteousness and
    strength;
all who were incensed against
    him
  shall come to him and be
    ashamed.
25 In the LORD all the offspring of
    Israel
  shall triumph and glory.

46.1 BEL bows down, Nebo
    stoops,
  their idols are on beasts
    and cattle;
these things you carry are
    loaded
  as burdens on weary animals.
2 They stoop, they bow down
    together;
  they cannot save the burden,
but themselves go into
    captivity.

3 Listen to me, O house of Jacob,
  all the remnant of the house
    of Israel,
who have been borne by me
    from your birth,
  carried from the womb;
4 even to your old age I am he,
  even when you turn gray I
    will carry you.
I have made, and I will bear;
  I will carry and will save.

5 To whom will you liken me and
    make me equal,
  and compare me, as though
    we were alike?
6 Those who lavish gold from the
    purse,
  and weigh out silver in the
    scales—
they hire a goldsmith, who
    makes it into a god;

then they fall down and
    worship!
7 They lift it to their shoulders,
    they carry it,
  they set it in its place, and it
    stands there;
  it cannot move from its place.
If one cries out to it, it does
    not answer
  or save anyone from trouble.

8 Remember this and consider, a
  recall it to mind, you
    transgressors,
9   remember the former things
    of old;
for I am God, and there is no
    other;
I am God, and there is no
    one like me,
10 declaring the end from the
    beginning
  and from ancient times things
    not yet done,
saying, "My purpose shall
    stand,
  and I will fulfill my intention,"
11 calling a bird of prey from the
    east,
  the man for my purpose from
    a far country.
I have spoken, and I will bring it
    to pass;
  I have planned, and I will do
    it.

12 Listen to me, you stubborn of
    heart,
  you who are far from
    deliverance:
13 I bring near my deliverance, it
    is not far off,
  and my salvation will not
    tarry;
I will put salvation in Zion,
  for Israel my glory.

47.1 COME down and sit in the dust,
  virgin daughter Babylon!
Sit on the ground without a
    throne,
  daughter Chaldea!
For you shall no more be called
  tender and delicate.
2 Take the millstones and grind
    meal,
  remove your veil,
strip off your robe, uncover
    your legs,
  pass through the rivers.
3 Your nakedness shall be
    uncovered,
  and your shame shall be seen.
I will take vengeance,
  and I will spare no one.
4 Our Redeemer—the LORD of
    hosts is his name—
  is the Holy One of Israel.

5 Sit in silence, and go into
    darkness,
  daughter Chaldea!
For you shall no more be called
  the mistress of kingdoms.
6 I was angry with my people,
  I profaned my heritage;
I gave them into your hand,
  you showed them no mercy;
on the aged you made your
    yoke
  exceedingly heavy.
7 You said, "I shall be mistress
    forever,"
  so that you did not lay these
    things to heart
  or remember their end.

8 Now therefore hear this, you
    lover of pleasures,
  who sit securely,
who say in your heart,
  "I am, and there is no one
    besides me;

a Meaning of Heb uncertain

I shall not sit as a widow
  or know the loss of
    children"—
9  both these things shall come
      upon you
    in a moment, in one day:
  the loss of children and
    widowhood
  shall come upon you in full
    measure,
  in spite of your many sorceries
    and the great power of your
      enchantments.

10  You felt secure in your
      wickedness;
    you said, "No one sees me."
  Your wisdom and your
      knowledge
    led you astray,
  and you said in your heart,
    "I am, and there is no one
      besides me."
11  But evil shall come upon you,
    which you cannot charm
      away;
  disaster shall fall upon you,
    which you will not be able to
      ward off;
  and ruin shall come on you
      suddenly,
    of which you know nothing.

12  Stand fast in your enchantments
    and your many sorceries,
    with which you have labored
      from your youth;
  perhaps you may be able to
      succeed,
    perhaps you may inspire
      terror.
13  You are wearied with your many
      consultations;
    let those who study[a] the
      heavens
  stand up and save you,
    those who gaze at the stars,
  and at each new moon predict

what[b] shall befall you.
14  See, they are like stubble,
    the fire consumes them;
  they cannot deliver themselves
    from the power of the flame.
  No coal for warming oneself is
      this,
    no fire to sit before!
15  Such to you are those with
      whom you have labored,
    who have trafficked with you
      from your youth;
  they all wander about in their
      own paths;
    there is no one to save you.


48.1  HEAR this, O house of Jacob,
      who are called by the name of
        Israel,
    and who came forth from the
      loins[c] of Judah;
  who swear by the name of the
      LORD,
    and invoke the God of Israel,
    but not in truth or right.
2  For they call themselves after
      the holy city,
    and lean on the God of Israel;
    the LORD of hosts is his name.

3  The former things I declared
      long ago,
    they went out from my mouth
      and I made them known;
    then suddenly I did them and
      they came to pass.
4  Because I know that you are
      obstinate,
    and your neck is an iron
      sinew
    and your forehead brass,
5  I declared them to you from
      long ago,
    before they came to pass I
      announced them to you,
  so that you would not say, "My
      idol did them,

my carved image and my cast
    image commanded
    them."

6 You have heard; now see all
    this;
  and will you not declare it?
From this time forward I make
    you hear new things,
  hidden things that you have
    not known.
7 They are created now, not long
    ago;
  before today you have never
    heard of them,
so that you could not say, "I
    already knew them."
8 You have never heard, you have
    never known,
  from of old your ear has not
    been opened.
For I knew that you would deal
    very treacherously,
  and that from birth you were
    called a rebel.

9 For my name's sake I defer my
    anger,
  for the sake of my praise I
    restrain it for you,
so that I may not cut you off.
10 See, I have refined you, but not
    like[a] silver;
  I have tested you in the
    furnace of adversity.
11 For my own sake, for my own
    sake, I do it,
  for why should my name[b] be
    profaned?
My glory I will not give to
    another.

# EPHESIANS 4.1–16

I THEREFORE, the prisoner in the Lord, beg you to lead a life worthy of the calling to which you have been called, 2with all humility and gentleness, with patience, bearing with one another in love, 3making every effort to maintain the unity of the Spirit in the bond of peace. 4There is one body and one Spirit, just as you were called to the one hope of your calling, 5one Lord, one faith, one baptism, 6one God and Father of all, who is above all and through all and in all.

7 But each of us was given grace according to the measure of Christ's gift. 8Therefore it is said,

"When he ascended on high he
    made captivity itself
    a captive;
  he gave gifts to his people."

9(When it says, "He ascended," what does it mean but that he had also descended[c] into the lower parts of the earth? 10He who descended is the same one who ascended far above all the heavens, so that he might fill all things.) 11The gifts he gave were that some would be apostles, some prophets, some evangelists, some pastors and teachers, 12to equip the saints for the work of ministry, for building up the body of Christ, 13until all of us come to the unity of the faith and of the knowledge of the Son of God, to maturity, to the measure of the full stature of Christ. 14We must no longer be children, tossed to and fro and blown about by every wind of doctrine, by people's trickery, by their craftiness in deceitful scheming. 15But speaking the truth in love, we must grow up in every way into him who is the head, into Christ, 16from whom the whole body, joined and knit together by every ligament with which it is equipped, as each part is working properly, promotes the body's growth in building itself up in love.

---

aCn: Heb *with*  bGk Old Latin: Heb *for why should it*  cOther ancient authorities add *first*

## PSALM 68.19–35

**B**LESSED be the Lord,
who daily bears us up;
God is our salvation. *Selah*
20 Our God is a God of salvation,
and to GOD, the Lord, belongs
escape from death.

21 But God will shatter the heads
of his enemies,
the hairy crown of those who
walk in their guilty ways.
22 The Lord said,
"I will bring them back from
Bashan,
I will bring them back from the
depths of the sea,
23 so that you may bathe[a] your
feet in blood,
so that the tongues of your
dogs may have their
share from the foe."

24 Your solemn processions are
seen,[b] O God,
the processions of my God,
my King, into the
sanctuary—
25 the singers in front, the
musicians last,
between them girls playing
tambourines:
26 "Bless God in the great
congregation,
the LORD, O you who are of
Israel's fountain!"
27 There is Benjamin, the least of
them, in the lead,
the princes of Judah in a
body,
the princes of Zebulun, the
princes of Naphtali.

28 Summon your might, O God;
show your strength, O God,
as you have done for us
before.

29 Because of your temple at
Jerusalem
kings bear gifts to you.
30 Rebuke the wild animals that
live among the reeds,
the herd of bulls with the
calves of the peoples.
Trample[c] under foot those who
lust after tribute;
scatter the peoples who
delight in war.[d]
31 Let bronze be brought from
Egypt;
let Ethiopia[e] hasten to
stretch out its hands to
God.

32 Sing to God, O kingdoms of the
earth;
sing praises to the Lord,
*Selah*
33 O rider in the heavens, the
ancient heavens;
listen, he sends out his voice,
his mighty voice.
34 Ascribe power to God,
whose majesty is over Israel;
and whose power is in the
skies.
35 Awesome is God in his[f]
sanctuary,
the God of Israel;
he gives power and strength
to his people.

Blessed be God!

## PROVERBS 24.3–4

**B**Y wisdom a house is built,
and by understanding it is
established;
4 by knowledge the rooms are
filled
with all precious and pleasant
riches.

aGk Syr Tg: Heb *shatter*   bOr *have been seen*   cCn: Heb *Trampling*   dMeaning of Heb of verse 30
is uncertain   eOr *Nubia*; Heb *Cush*   fGk: Heb *from your*

# SEPTEMBER 26

## ISAIAH 48.12—50.11

L ISTEN to me, O Jacob,
and Israel, whom I called:
I am He; I am the first,
and I am the last.
13 My hand laid the foundation of
the earth,
and my right hand spread out
the heavens;
when I summon them,
they stand at attention.

14 Assemble, all of you, and hear!
Who among them has
declared these things?
The LORD loves him;
he shall perform his purpose
on Babylon,
and his arm shall be against
the Chaldeans.
15 I, even I, have spoken and
called him,
I have brought him, and he
will prosper in his way.
16 Draw near to me, hear this!
From the beginning I have
not spoken in secret,
from the time it came to be I
have been there.
And now the Lord GOD has sent
me and his spirit.

17 Thus says the LORD,
your Redeemer, the Holy
One of Israel:
I am the LORD your God,
who teaches you for your
own good,
who leads you in the way you
should go.
18 O that you had paid attention to
my commandments!
Then your prosperity would
have been like a river,

and your success like the
waves of the sea;
19 your offspring would have been
like the sand,
and your descendants like its
grains;
their name would never be cut
off
or destroyed from before me.

20 Go out from Babylon, flee from
Chaldea,
declare this with a shout of
joy, proclaim it,
send it forth to the end of the
earth;
say, "The LORD has redeemed
his servant Jacob!"
21 They did not thirst when he led
them through the
deserts;
he made water flow for them
from the rock;
he split open the rock and the
water gushed out.

22 "There is no peace," says the
LORD, "for the wicked."

49.1 LISTEN to me, O coastlands,
pay attention, you peoples
from far away!
The LORD called me before I
was born,
while I was in my mother's
womb he named me.
2 He made my mouth like a sharp
sword,
in the shadow of his hand he
hid me;
he made me a polished arrow,
in his quiver he hid me away.
3 And he said to me, "You are my
servant,

Israel, in whom I will be
 glorified."
4 But I said, "I have labored in
 vain,
 I have spent my strength for
  nothing and vanity;
yet surely my cause is with
 the LORD,
 and my reward with my
  God."

5 And now the LORD says,
 who formed me in the womb
  to be his servant,
to bring Jacob back to him,
 and that Israel might be
  gathered to him,
for I am honored in the sight of
 the LORD,
 and my God has become my
  strength—
6 he says,
"It is too light a thing that you
  should be my servant
 to raise up the tribes of Jacob
 and to restore the survivors
  of Israel;
I will give you as a light to the
  nations,
 that my salvation may reach
  to the end of the earth."

7 Thus says the LORD,
 the Redeemer of Israel and
  his Holy One,
to one deeply despised,
 abhorred by the nations,
 the slave of rulers,
"Kings shall see and stand up,
 princes, and they shall
  prostrate themselves,
because of the LORD, who is
 faithful,
 the Holy One of Israel, who
  has chosen you."

8 Thus says the LORD:

In a time of favor I have
 answered you,
 on a day of salvation I have
  helped you;
I have kept you and given you
 as a covenant to the people, a
to establish the land,
 to apportion the desolate
  heritages;
9 saying to the prisoners, "Come
  out,"
 to those who are in darkness,
  "Show yourselves."
They shall feed along the ways,
 on all the bare heights b shall
  be their pasture;
10 they shall not hunger or thirst,
 neither scorching wind nor
  sun shall strike them
  down,
for he who has pity on them will
 lead them,
 and by springs of water will
  guide them.
11 And I will turn all my mountains
  into a road,
 and my highways shall be
  raised up.
12 Lo, these shall come from far
  away,
 and lo, these from the north
  and from the west,
 and these from the land of
  Syene. c

13 Sing for joy, O heavens, and
  exult, O earth;
 break forth, O mountains,
  into singing!
For the LORD has comforted his
 people,
 and will have compassion on
  his suffering ones.

14 But Zion said, "The LORD has
 forsaken me,
 my Lord has forgotten me."

---

a Meaning of Heb uncertain b Or *the trails* c Q Ms: MT *Sinim*

15 Can a woman forget her nursing
       child,
    or show no compassion for
       the child of her womb?
  Even these may forget,
    yet I will not forget you.
16 See, I have inscribed you on the
       palms of my hands;
    your walls are continually
       before me.
17 Your builders outdo your
       destroyers, a
    and those who laid you waste
       go away from you.
18 Lift up your eyes all around
       and see;
    they all gather, they come to
       you.
  As I live, says the LORD,
    you shall put all of them on
       like an ornament,
    and like a bride you shall bind
       them on.

19 Surely your waste and your
       desolate places
    and your devastated land—
  surely now you will be too
       crowded for your
       inhabitants,
    and those who swallowed you
       up will be far away.
20 The children born in the time of
       your bereavement
    will yet say in your hearing:
  "The place is too crowded for
       me;
    make room for me to settle."
21 Then you will say in your heart,
    "Who has borne me these?
  I was bereaved and barren,
    exiled and put away—
    so who has reared these?
  I was left all alone—
    where then have these come
       from?"

22 Thus says the Lord GOD:

  I will soon lift up my hand to
       the nations,
    and raise my signal to the
       peoples;
  and they shall bring your sons in
       their bosom,
    and your daughters shall be
       carried on their
       shoulders.
23 Kings shall be your foster
       fathers,
    and their queens your nursing
       mothers.
  With their faces to the ground
       they shall bow down to
       you,
    and lick the dust of your feet.
  Then you will know that I am
       the LORD;
    those who wait for me shall
       not be put to shame.

24 Can the prey be taken from the
       mighty,
    or the captives of a tyrant b
       be rescued?
25 But thus says the LORD:
  Even the captives of the mighty
       shall be taken,
    and the prey of the tyrant be
       rescued;
  for I will contend with those
       who contend with you,
    and I will save your children.
26 I will make your oppressors eat
       their own flesh,
    and they shall be drunk with
       their own blood as with
       wine.
  Then all flesh shall know
    that I am the LORD your
       Savior,
    and your Redeemer, the
       Mighty One of Jacob.

50.1 THUS says the LORD:
  Where is your mother's bill of
       divorce

---

a Or *Your children come swiftly; your destroyers*   b Q Ms Syr Vg: MT *of a righteous person*

with which I put her away?
Or which of my creditors is it
to whom I have sold you?
No, because of your sins you
were sold,
and for your transgressions
your mother was put
away.
2 Why was no one there when I
came?
Why did no one answer when
I called?
Is my hand shortened, that it
cannot redeem?
Or have I no power to
deliver?
By my rebuke I dry up the sea,
I make the rivers a desert;
their fish stink for lack of water,
and die of thirst. **a**
3 I clothe the heavens with
blackness,
and make sackcloth their
covering.

4 The Lord GOD has given me
the tongue of a teacher, **b**
that I may know how to sustain
the weary with a word.
Morning by morning he
wakens—
wakens my ear
to listen as those who are
taught.
5 The Lord GOD has opened my
ear,
and I was not rebellious,
I did not turn backward.
6 I gave my back to those who
struck me,
and my cheeks to those who
pulled out the beard;
I did not hide my face
from insult and spitting.

7 The Lord GOD helps me;
therefore I have not been
disgraced;
therefore I have set my face
like flint,
and I know that I shall not be
put to shame;
8 he who vindicates me is near.
Who will contend with me?
Let us stand up together.
Who are my adversaries?
Let them confront me.
9 It is the Lord GOD who helps
me;
who will declare me guilty?
All of them will wear out like a
garment;
the moth will eat them up.

10 Who among you fears the LORD
and obeys the voice of his
servant,
who walks in darkness
and has no light,
yet trusts in the name of the
LORD
and relies upon his God?
11 But all of you are kindlers of
fire,
lighters of firebrands. **c**
Walk in the flame of your fire,
and among the brands that
you have kindled!
This is what you shall have from
my hand:
you shall lie down in torment.

# EPHESIANS 4.17—5.2

Now this I affirm and insist on in the Lord: you must no longer live as the Gentiles live, in the futility of their minds. [18]They are darkened in their understanding, alienated from the life of God because of their ignorance and hardness of heart. [19]They have lost all sensitivity and have abandoned themselves to licentiousness, greedy to practice every kind of impurity. [20]That is not the way you learned Christ! [21]For surely you have

**a**Or *die on the thirsty ground*  **b**Cn: Heb *of those who are taught*  **c**Syr: Heb *you gird yourselves with firebrands*

heard about him and were taught in him, as truth is in Jesus. <sup>22</sup>You were taught to put away your former way of life, your old self, corrupt and deluded by its lusts, <sup>23</sup>and to be renewed in the spirit of your minds, <sup>24</sup>and to clothe yourselves with the new self, created according to the likeness of God in true righteousness and holiness.

25 So then, putting away falsehood, let all of us speak the truth to our neighbors, for we are members of one another. <sup>26</sup>Be angry but do not sin; do not let the sun go down on your anger, <sup>27</sup>and do not make room for the devil. <sup>28</sup>Thieves must give up stealing; rather let them labor and work honestly with their own hands, so as to have something to share with the needy. <sup>29</sup>Let no evil talk come out of your mouths, but only what is useful for building up, [a] as there is need, so that your words may give grace to those who hear. <sup>30</sup>And do not grieve the Holy Spirit of God, with which you were marked with a seal for the day of redemption. <sup>31</sup>Put away from you all bitterness and wrath and anger and wrangling and slander, together with all malice, <sup>32</sup>and be kind to one another, tenderhearted, forgiving one another, as God in Christ has forgiven you. [b] <sup>5.1</sup>Therefore be imitators of God, as beloved children, <sup>2</sup>and live in love, as Christ loved us[c] and gave himself up for us, a fragrant offering and sacrifice to God.

## PSALM 69.1–18

*To the leader: according to Lilies. Of David.*

SAVE me, O God,
   for the waters have come up
      to my neck.
2  I sink in deep mire,
   where there is no foothold;
  I have come into deep waters,

   and the flood sweeps over
     me.
3  I am weary with my crying;
   my throat is parched.
My eyes grow dim
   with waiting for my God.

4  More in number than the hairs
     of my head
   are those who hate me
     without cause;
many are those who would
     destroy me,
   my enemies who accuse me
     falsely.
What I did not steal
   must I now restore?
5  O God, you know my folly;
   the wrongs I have done are
     not hidden from you.

6  Do not let those who hope in
     you be put to shame
     because of me,
   O Lord GOD of hosts;
do not let those who seek you
     be dishonored because of
     me,
   O God of Israel.
7  It is for your sake that I have
     borne reproach,
   that shame has covered my
     face.
8  I have become a stranger to my
     kindred,
   an alien to my mother's
     children.

9  It is zeal for your house that
     has consumed me;
   the insults of those who insult
     you have fallen on me.
10  When I humbled my soul with
     fasting, [d]
   they insulted me for doing so.
11  When I made sackcloth my
     clothing,

[a] Other ancient authorities read *building up faith*  [b] Other ancient authorities read *us*  [c] Other ancient authorities read *you*  [d] Gk Syr: Heb *I wept, with fasting my soul,* or *I made my soul mourn with fasting*

I became a byword to them.
12  I am the subject of gossip for
        those who sit in the
        gate,
    and the drunkards make
        songs about me.

13  But as for me, my prayer is to
        you, O LORD.
    At an acceptable time,
        O God,
    in the abundance of your
        steadfast love, answer
        me.
    With your faithful help 14rescue
        me
    from sinking in the mire;
    let me be delivered from my
        enemies
    and from the deep waters.
15  Do not let the flood sweep over
        me,
    or the deep swallow me up,
    or the Pit close its mouth
        over me.

16  Answer me, O LORD, for your
        steadfast love is good;
    according to your abundant
        mercy, turn to me.
17  Do not hide your face from your
        servant,
    for I am in distress—make
        haste to answer me.
18  Draw near to me, redeem me,
    set me free because of my
        enemies.

## PROVERBS 24.5–6

WISE warriors are mightier
        than strong ones,[a]
    and those who have
        knowledge than those
        who have strength;
6   for by wise guidance you can
        wage your war,
    and in abundance of
        counselors there is
        victory.

# SEPTEMBER 27

## ISAIAH 51.1—53.12

LISTEN to me, you that pursue
        righteousness,
    you that seek the LORD.
    Look to the rock from which
        you were hewn,
    and to the quarry from which
        you were dug.
2   Look to Abraham your father
        and to Sarah who bore you;
    for he was but one when I
        called him,
    but I blessed him and made
        him many.
3   For the LORD will comfort Zion;
    he will comfort all her waste
        places,
    and will make her wilderness
        like Eden,
    her desert like the garden of
        the LORD;
    joy and gladness will be found
        in her,
    thanksgiving and the voice
        of song.

aGk Compare Syr Tg: Heb *A wise man is strength*

4  Listen to me, my people,
     and give heed to me, my
       nation;
   for a teaching will go out from
       me,
     and my justice for a light to
       the peoples.
5  I will bring near my deliverance
       swiftly,
     my salvation has gone out
     and my arms will rule the
       peoples;
   the coastlands wait for me,
     and for my arm they hope.
6  Lift up your eyes to the
       heavens,
     and look at the earth beneath;
   for the heavens will vanish like
       smoke,
     the earth will wear out like a
       garment,
     and those who live on it will
       die like gnats;[a]
   but my salvation will be forever,
     and my deliverance will never
       be ended.

7  Listen to me, you who know
       righteousness,
     you people who have my
       teaching in your hearts;
   do not fear the reproach of
       others,
     and do not be dismayed when
       they revile you.
8  For the moth will eat them up
       like a garment,
     and the worm will eat them
       like wool;
   but my deliverance will be
       forever,
     and my salvation to all
       generations.

9  Awake, awake, put on strength,
     O arm of the LORD!
   Awake, as in days of old,
     the generations of long ago!
   Was it not you who cut Rahab
       in pieces,
     who pierced the dragon?
10 Was it not you who dried up
       the sea,
     the waters of the great deep;
   who made the depths of the sea
       a way
     for the redeemed to cross
       over?
11 So the ransomed of the LORD
       shall return,
     and come to Zion with
       singing;
   everlasting joy shall be upon
       their heads;
     they shall obtain joy and
       gladness,
     and sorrow and sighing shall
       flee away.

12 I, I am he who comforts you;
     why then are you afraid of a
       mere mortal who must
       die,
     a human being who fades like
       grass?
13 You have forgotten the LORD,
       your Maker,
     who stretched out the
       heavens
     and laid the foundations of
       the earth.
   You fear continually all day long
     because of the fury of the
       oppressor,
   who is bent on destruction.
     But where is the fury of the
       oppressor?
14 The oppressed shall speedily be
       released;
     they shall not die and go
       down to the Pit,
     nor shall they lack bread.
15 For I am the LORD your God,
     who stirs up the sea so that
       its waves roar—
     the LORD of hosts is his name.

a Or *in like manner*

16  I have put my words in your
        mouth,
      and hidden you in the shadow
        of my hand,
    stretching out[a] the heavens
        and laying the foundations of
          the earth,
      and saying to Zion, "You are
        my people."

17  Rouse yourself, rouse yourself!
        Stand up, O Jerusalem,
    you who have drunk at the hand
        of the LORD
      the cup of his wrath,
    who have drunk to the dregs
        the bowl of staggering.
18  There is no one to guide her
        among all the children she
          has borne;
    there is no one to take her by
        the hand
      among all the children she has
        brought up.
19  These two things have befallen
        you
      —who will grieve with
          you?—
    devastation and destruction,
        famine and sword—
      who will comfort you?[b]
20  Your children have fainted,
        they lie at the head of every
          street
      like an antelope in a net;
    they are full of the wrath of
        the LORD,
      the rebuke of your God.

21  Therefore hear this, you who
        are wounded,[c]
    who are drunk, but not
        with wine:
22  Thus says your Sovereign, the
        LORD,
      your God who pleads the
        cause of his people:

    See, I have taken from your
        hand the cup of
          staggering;
    you shall drink no more
        from the bowl of my wrath.
23  And I will put it into the hand of
        your tormentors,
      who have said to you,
      "Bow down, that we may
          walk on you";
    and you have made your back
        like the ground
      and like the street for them
        to walk on.

52.1  AWAKE, awake,
        put on your strength, O Zion!
    Put on your beautiful garments,
        O Jerusalem, the holy city;
    for the uncircumcised and the
        unclean
      shall enter you no more.
2   Shake yourself from the dust,
        rise up,
      O captive[d] Jerusalem;
    loose the bonds from your neck,
        O captive daughter Zion!

3  For thus says the LORD: You
were sold for nothing, and you shall be
redeemed without money. [4]For thus
says the Lord GOD: Long ago, my people went down into Egypt to reside
there as aliens; the Assyrian, too, has
oppressed them without cause. [5]Now
therefore what am I doing here, says
the LORD, seeing that my people are
taken away without cause? Their rulers
howl, says the LORD, and continually, all
day long, my name is despised. [6]There-
fore my people shall know my name;
therefore in that day they shall know
that it is I who speak; here am I.

7   How beautiful upon the
        mountains
      are the feet of the messenger
        who announces peace,

aSyr: Heb *planting*   bQ Ms Gk Syr Vg: MT *how may I comfort you?*   cOr *humbled*   dCn: Heb *rise up, sit*

who brings good news,
  who announces salvation,
  who says to Zion, "Your God
    reigns."
8 Listen! Your sentinels lift up
    their voices,
  together they sing for joy;
for in plain sight they see
  the return of the LORD to
    Zion.
9 Break forth together into
    singing,
  you ruins of Jerusalem;
for the LORD has comforted his
    people,
  he has redeemed Jerusalem.
10 The LORD has bared his holy
    arm
  before the eyes of all the
    nations;
and all the ends of the earth
    shall see
  the salvation of our God.

11 Depart, depart, go out from
    there!
  Touch no unclean thing;
go out from the midst of it,
    purify yourselves,
  you who carry the vessels of
    the LORD.
12 For you shall not go out in
    haste,
  and you shall not go in flight;
for the LORD will go before you,
  and the God of Israel will be
    your rear guard.

13 See, my servant shall prosper;
  he shall be exalted and lifted
    up,
  and shall be very high.
14 Just as there were many who
    were astonished at him[a]
  —so marred was his
    appearance, beyond
    human semblance,

and his form beyond that of
    mortals—
15 so he shall startle[b] many
    nations;
  kings shall shut their mouths
    because of him;
for that which had not been told
    them they shall see,
  and that which they had not
    heard they shall
    contemplate.

53.1 WHO has believed what we have
    heard?
  And to whom has the arm of
    the LORD been revealed?
2 For he grew up before him like
    a young plant,
  and like a root out of dry
    ground;
he had no form or majesty that
    we should look at him,
nothing in his appearance that
    we should desire him.
3 He was despised and rejected
    by others;
  a man of suffering[c] and
    acquainted with infirmity;
and as one from whom others
    hide their faces[d]
  he was despised, and we held
    him of no account.

4 Surely he has borne our
    infirmities
  and carried our diseases;
yet we accounted him stricken,
  struck down by God, and
    afflicted.
5 But he was wounded for our
    transgressions,
  crushed for our iniquities;
upon him was the punishment
    that made us whole,
  and by his bruises we are
    healed.
6 All we like sheep have gone
    astray;

[a] Syr Tg: Heb *you*  [b] Meaning of Heb uncertain  [c] Or *a man of sorrows*  [d] Or *as one who hides his
face from us*

we have all turned to our
    own way,
and the Lord has laid on him
    the iniquity of us all.

7  He was oppressed, and he was
    afflicted,
    yet he did not open his
      mouth;
    like a lamb that is led to the
      slaughter,
    and like a sheep that before
      its shearers is silent,
    so he did not open his mouth.
8  By a perversion of justice he
    was taken away.
    Who could have imagined his
      future?
    For he was cut off from the land
      of the living,
    stricken for the transgression
      of my people.
9  They made his grave with the
    wicked
    and his tomb[a] with the
      rich, [b]
    although he had done no
      violence,
    and there was no deceit in
      his mouth.

10  Yet it was the will of the Lord
    to crush him with pain. [c]
  When you make his life an
    offering for sin, [d]
    he shall see his offspring, and
      shall prolong his days;
  through him the will of the Lord
    shall prosper.
11    Out of his anguish he shall
      see light; [e]
  he shall find satisfaction through
    his knowledge.
    The righteous one, [f] my
      servant, shall make many
      righteous,

    and he shall bear their
      iniquities.
12  Therefore I will allot him a
      portion with the great,
    and he shall divide the spoil
      with the strong;
  because he poured out himself
      to death,
    and was numbered with the
      transgressors;
    yet he bore the sin of many,
      and made intercession for the
      transgressors.

## EPHESIANS 5.3–33

BUT fornication and impurity of any kind, or greed, must not even be mentioned among you, as is proper among saints. 4Entirely out of place is obscene, silly, and vulgar talk; but instead, let there be thanksgiving. 5Be sure of this, that no fornicator or impure person, or one who is greedy (that is, an idolater), has any inheritance in the kingdom of Christ and of God.

6 Let no one deceive you with empty words, for because of these things the wrath of God comes on those who are disobedient. 7Therefore do not be associated with them. 8For once you were darkness, but now in the Lord you are light. Live as children of light— 9for the fruit of the light is found in all that is good and right and true. 10Try to find out what is pleasing to the Lord. 11Take no part in the unfruitful works of darkness, but instead expose them. 12For it is shameful even to mention what such people do secretly; 13but everything exposed by the light becomes visible, 14for everything that becomes visible is light. Therefore it says,

    "Sleeper, awake!
      Rise from the dead,
    and Christ will shine on you."

aQ Ms: MT *and in his death*  bCn: Heb *with a rich person*  cOr *by disease*; meaning of Heb uncertain  dMeaning of Heb uncertain  eQ Mss: MT lacks *light*  fOr *and he shall find satisfaction. Through his knowledge, the righteous one*

15 Be careful then how you live, not as unwise people but as wise, [16]making the most of the time, because the days are evil. [17]So do not be foolish, but understand what the will of the Lord is. [18]Do not get drunk with wine, for that is debauchery; but be filled with the Spirit, [19]as you sing psalms and hymns and spiritual songs among yourselves, singing and making melody to the Lord in your hearts, [20]giving thanks to God the Father at all times and for everything in the name of our Lord Jesus Christ.

21 Be subject to one another out of reverence for Christ.

22 Wives, be subject to your husbands as you are to the Lord. [23]For the husband is the head of the wife just as Christ is the head of the church, the body of which he is the Savior. [24]Just as the church is subject to Christ, so also wives ought to be, in everything, to their husbands.

25 Husbands, love your wives, just as Christ loved the church and gave himself up for her, [26]in order to make her holy by cleansing her with the washing of water by the word, [27]so as to present the church to himself in splendor, without a spot or wrinkle or anything of the kind—yes, so that she may be holy and without blemish. [28]In the same way, husbands should love their wives as they do their own bodies. He who loves his wife loves himself. [29]For no one ever hates his own body, but he nourishes and tenderly cares for it, just as Christ does for the church, [30]because we are members of his body. [a] [31]"For this reason a man will leave his father and mother and be joined to his wife, and the two will become one flesh." [32]This is a great mystery, and I am applying it to Christ and the church. [33]Each of you, however, should love his wife as himself, and a wife should respect her husband.

## PSALM 69.19–36

You know the insults I receive,
   and my shame and dishonor;
   my foes are all known to
      you.
20 Insults have broken my heart,
   so that I am in despair.
I looked for pity, but there was
      none;
   and for comforters, but I
      found none.
21 They gave me poison for food,
   and for my thirst they gave
      me vinegar to drink.

22 Let their table be a trap for
      them,
   a snare for their allies.
23 Let their eyes be darkened so
      that they cannot see,
   and make their loins tremble
      continually.
24 Pour out your indignation upon
      them,
   and let your burning anger
      overtake them.
25 May their camp be a desolation;
   let no one live in their tents.
26 For they persecute those whom
      you have struck down,
   and those whom you have
      wounded, they attack still
      more. [b]
27 Add guilt to their guilt;
   may they have no acquittal
      from you.
28 Let them be blotted out of the
      book of the living;
   let them not be enrolled
      among the righteous.
29 But I am lowly and in pain;
   let your salvation, O God,
      protect me.

30 I will praise the name of God
      with a song;

---

a Other ancient authorities add *of his flesh and of his bones*   b Gk Syr: Heb *recount the pain of*

I will magnify him with
    thanksgiving.
31 This will please the LORD more
    than an ox
    or a bull with horns and
    hoofs.
32 Let the oppressed see it and be
    glad;
    you who seek God, let your
    hearts revive.
33 For the LORD hears the needy,
    and does not despise his own
    that are in bonds.

34 Let heaven and earth praise
    him,

the seas and everything that
    moves in them.
35 For God will save Zion
    and rebuild the cities of
    Judah;
    and his servants shall live[a]
    there and possess it;
36 the children of his servants
    shall inherit it,
    and those who love his name
    shall live in it.

## PROVERBS 24.7

WISDOM is too high for fools;
    in the gate they do not
    open their mouths.

# SEPTEMBER 28

## ISAIAH 54.1—57.13

SING, O barren one who did
    not bear;
burst into song and shout,
    you who have not been in
    labor!
For the children of the desolate
    woman will be more
    than the children of her that
    is married, says the
    LORD.
2 Enlarge the site of your tent,
    and let the curtains of your
    habitations be stretched
    out;
do not hold back; lengthen
    your cords
and strengthen your stakes.
3 For you will spread out to the
    right and to the left,
    and your descendants will
    possess the nations

and will settle the desolate
    towns.

4 Do not fear, for you will not be
    ashamed;
do not be discouraged, for
    you will not suffer
    disgrace;
for you will forget the shame of
    your youth,
and the disgrace of your
    widowhood you will
    remember no more.
5 For your Maker is your
    husband,
    the LORD of hosts is his name;
the Holy One of Israel is your
    Redeemer,
    the God of the whole earth he
    is called.
6 For the LORD has called you

[a] Syr: Heb *and they shall live*

like a wife forsaken and
    grieved in spirit,
like the wife of a man's youth
    when she is cast off,
    says your God.
7 For a brief moment I abandoned
    you,
    but with great compassion I
    will gather you.
8 In overflowing wrath for a
    moment
    I hid my face from you,
but with everlasting love I will
    have compassion on you,
    says the Lord, your
    Redeemer.

9 This is like the days of Noah to
    me:
    Just as I swore that the
    waters of Noah
    would never again go over
    the earth,
so I have sworn that I will not
    be angry with you
    and will not rebuke you.
10 For the mountains may depart
    and the hills be removed,
but my steadfast love shall not
    depart from you,
    and my covenant of peace
    shall not be removed,
says the Lord, who has
    compassion on you.

11 O afflicted one, storm-tossed,
    and not comforted,
    I am about to set your stones
    in antimony,
    and lay your foundations with
    sapphires. a
12 I will make your pinnacles of
    rubies,
    your gates of jewels,
    and all your wall of precious
    stones.
13 All your children shall be taught
    by the Lord,

    and great shall be the
    prosperity of your
    children.
14 In righteousness you shall be
    established;
    you shall be far from
    oppression, for you shall
    not fear;
    and from terror, for it shall
    not come near you.
15 If anyone stirs up strife,
    it is not from me;
whoever stirs up strife with you
    shall fall because of you.
16 See it is I who have created
    the smith
    who blows the fire of coals,
    and produces a weapon fit for
    its purpose;
I have also created the ravager
    to destroy.
17     No weapon that is fashioned
    against you shall prosper,
    and you shall confute every
    tongue that rises against
    you in judgment.
This is the heritage of the
    servants of the Lord
    and their vindication from me,
    says the Lord.

55.1 Ho, everyone who thirsts,
    come to the waters;
and you that have no money,
    come, buy and eat!
Come, buy wine and milk
    without money and without
    price.
2 Why do you spend your money
    for that which is not
    bread,
    and your labor for that which
    does not satisfy?
Listen carefully to me, and eat
    what is good,
    and delight yourselves in
    rich food.

a Or *lapis lazuli*

3 Incline your ear, and come to
    me;
    listen, so that you may live.
I will make with you an
        everlasting covenant,
    my steadfast, sure love for
    David.
4 See, I made him a witness to
        the peoples,
    a leader and commander for
    the peoples.
5 See, you shall call nations that
        you do not know,
    and nations that do not know
        you shall run to you,
because of the Lord your God,
        the Holy One of Israel,
    for he has glorified you.

6 Seek the Lord while he may
        be found,
    call upon him while he is
        near;
7 let the wicked forsake their
        way,
    and the unrighteous their
        thoughts;
let them return to the Lord,
        that he may have mercy
        on them,
    and to our God, for he will
        abundantly pardon.
8 For my thoughts are not your
        thoughts,
    nor are your ways my ways,
        says the Lord.
9 For as the heavens are higher
        than the earth,
    so are my ways higher than
        your ways
    and my thoughts than your
        thoughts.

10 For as the rain and the snow
        come down from heaven,
    and do not return there until
        they have watered the
        earth,
making it bring forth and sprout,

giving seed to the sower and
    bread to the eater,
11 so shall my word be that goes
        out from my mouth;
    it shall not return to me
        empty,
but it shall accomplish that
        which I purpose,
    and succeed in the thing for
        which I sent it.

12 For you shall go out in joy,
    and be led back in peace;
the mountains and the hills
        before you
    shall burst into song,
    and all the trees of the field
        shall clap their hands.
13 Instead of the thorn shall come
        up the cypress;
    instead of the brier shall come
        up the myrtle;
and it shall be to the Lord for a
        memorial,
    for an everlasting sign that
        shall not be cut off.

56.1 Thus says the Lord:
    Maintain justice, and do what
        is right,
for soon my salvation will come,
    and my deliverance be
        revealed.

2 Happy is the mortal who does
        this,
    the one who holds it fast,
who keeps the sabbath, not
        profaning it,
    and refrains from doing any
        evil.

3 Do not let the foreigner joined
        to the Lord say,
    "The Lord will surely
        separate me from his
        people";
and do not let the eunuch say,
    "I am just a dry tree."
4 For thus says the Lord:

To the eunuchs who keep my
      sabbaths,
   who choose the things that
      please me
   and hold fast my covenant,
5  I will give, in my house and
      within my walls,
   a monument and a name
   better than sons and
      daughters;
   I will give them an everlasting
      name
   that shall not be cut off.

6  And the foreigners who join
      themselves to the LORD,
   to minister to him, to love the
      name of the LORD,
   and to be his servants,
   all who keep the sabbath, and
      do not profane it,
   and hold fast my covenant—
7  these I will bring to my holy
      mountain,
   and make them joyful in my
      house of prayer;
   their burnt offerings and their
      sacrifices
   will be accepted on my altar;
   for my house shall be called a
      house of prayer
   for all peoples.
8  Thus says the Lord GOD,
   who gathers the outcasts of
      Israel,
   I will gather others to them
   besides those already
      gathered. a

9  All you wild animals,
   all you wild animals in the
      forest, come to devour!
10  Israel's b sentinels are blind,
   they are all without
      knowledge;
   they are all silent dogs
   that cannot bark;
   dreaming, lying down,

      loving to slumber.
11  The dogs have a mighty
      appetite;
   they never have enough.
   The shepherds also have no
      understanding;
   they have all turned to their
      own way,
   to their own gain, one and all.
12  "Come," they say, "let us c
      get wine;
   let us fill ourselves with
      strong drink.
   And tomorrow will be like
      today,
   great beyond measure."

57.1  THE righteous perish,
   and no one takes it to heart;
   the devout are taken away,
   while no one understands.
   For the righteous are taken
      away from calamity,
2   and they enter into peace;
   those who walk uprightly
   will rest on their couches.
3  But as for you, come here,
   you children of a sorceress,
   you offspring of an adulterer
      and a whore. d
4  Whom are you mocking?
   Against whom do you open
      your mouth wide
   and stick out your tongue?
   Are you not children of
      transgression,
   the offspring of deceit—
5  you that burn with lust among
      the oaks,
   under every green tree;
   you that slaughter your children
      in the valleys,
   under the clefts of the rocks?
6  Among the smooth stones of
      the valley is your
      portion;
   they, they, are your lot;

a Heb *besides his gathered ones*   b Heb *His*   c Q Ms Syr Vg Tg: MT *me*   d Heb *an adulterer and she plays the whore*

to them you have poured out a
drink offering,
you have brought a grain
offering.
Shall I be appeased for these
things?
7 Upon a high and lofty mountain
you have set your bed,
and there you went up to
offer sacrifice.
8 Behind the door and the
doorpost
you have set up your symbol;
for, in deserting me, [a] you have
uncovered your bed,
you have gone up to it,
you have made it wide;
and you have made a bargain for
yourself with them,
you have loved their bed,
you have gazed on their
nakedness. [b]
9 You journeyed to Molech[c] with
oil,
and multiplied your perfumes;
you sent your envoys far away,
and sent down even to Sheol.
10 You grew weary from your
many wanderings,
but you did not say, "It is
useless."
You found your desire
rekindled,
and so you did not weaken.

11 Whom did you dread and fear
so that you lied,
and did not remember me
or give me a thought?
Have I not kept silent and
closed my eyes, [d]
and so you do not fear me?
12 I will concede your
righteousness and your
works,
but they will not help you.

13 When you cry out, let your
collection of idols deliver
you!
The wind will carry them off,
a breath will take them away.
But whoever takes refuge in me
shall possess the land
and inherit my holy mountain.

# EPHESIANS 6.1–24

CHILDREN, obey your parents in the Lord, [e] for this is right. [2]"Honor your father and mother"—this is the first commandment with a promise: [3]"so that it may be well with you and you may live long on the earth."

4 And, fathers, do not provoke your children to anger, but bring them up in the discipline and instruction of the Lord.

5 Slaves, obey your earthly masters with fear and trembling, in singleness of heart, as you obey Christ; [6]not only while being watched, and in order to please them, but as slaves of Christ, doing the will of God from the heart. [7]Render service with enthusiasm, as to the Lord and not to men and women, [8]knowing that whatever good we do, we will receive the same again from the Lord, whether we are slaves or free.

9 And, masters, do the same to them. Stop threatening them, for you know that both of you have the same Master in heaven, and with him there is no partiality.

10 Finally, be strong in the Lord and in the strength of his power. [11]Put on the whole armor of God, so that you may be able to stand against the wiles of the devil. [12]For our[f] struggle is not against enemies of blood and flesh, but against the rulers, against the authorities, against the cosmic powers of this present darkness, against the spiritual forces of evil in the heavenly places.

[a]Meaning of Heb uncertain  [b]Or *their phallus*; Heb *the hand*  [c]Or *the king*  [d]Gk Vg: Heb *silent even for a long time*  [e]Other ancient authorities lack *in the Lord*  [f]Other ancient authorities read *your*

[13]Therefore take up the whole armor of God, so that you may be able to withstand on that evil day, and having done everything, to stand firm. [14]Stand therefore, and fasten the belt of truth around your waist, and put on the breastplate of righteousness. [15]As shoes for your feet put on whatever will make you ready to proclaim the gospel of peace. [16]With all of these, [a] take the shield of faith, with which you will be able to quench all the flaming arrows of the evil one. [17]Take the helmet of salvation, and the sword of the Spirit, which is the word of God.

18  Pray in the Spirit at all times in every prayer and supplication. To that end keep alert and always persevere in supplication for all the saints. [19]Pray also for me, so that when I speak, a message may be given to me to make known with boldness the mystery of the gospel, [b] [20]for which I am an ambassador in chains. Pray that I may declare it boldly, as I must speak.

21  So that you also may know how I am and what I am doing, Tychicus will tell you everything. He is a dear brother and a faithful minister in the Lord. [22]I am sending him to you for this very purpose, to let you know how we are, and to encourage your hearts.

23  Peace be to the whole community, [c] and love with faith, from God the Father and the Lord Jesus Christ. [24]Grace be with all who have an undying love for our Lord Jesus Christ. [d]

## PSALM 70.1–5

*To the leader. Of David, for the memorial offering.*

Be pleased, O God, to deliver me.
O Lord, make haste to help me!
2  Let those be put to shame and confusion
    who seek my life.
Let those be turned back and
        brought to dishonor
    who desire to hurt me.
3  Let those who say, "Aha, Aha!"
    turn back because of their
        shame.

4  Let all who seek you
    rejoice and be glad in you.
Let those who love your
        salvation
    say evermore, "God is
        great!"
5  But I am poor and needy;
    hasten to me, O God!
You are my help and my
        deliverer;
    O Lord, do not delay!

## PROVERBS 24.8–9

Whoever plans to do evil
    will be called a
    mischief-maker.
9  The devising of folly is sin,
    and the scoffer is an
        abomination to all.

---

aOr *In all circumstances*  bOther ancient authorities lack *of the gospel*  cGk *to the brothers*  dOther ancient authorities add *Amen*

## ISAIAH 57.14—59.21

I<sup>T</sup> shall be said,
"Build up, build up, prepare
the way,
remove every obstruction
from my people's way."
15 For thus says the high and
lofty one
who inhabits eternity, whose
name is Holy:
I dwell in the high and holy
place,
and also with those who are
contrite and humble in
spirit,
to revive the spirit of the
humble,
and to revive the heart of the
contrite.
16 For I will not continually accuse,
nor will I always be angry;
for then the spirits would grow
faint before me,
even the souls that I have
made.
17 Because of their wicked
covetousness I
was angry;
I struck them, I hid and was
angry;
but they kept turning back to
their own ways.
18 I have seen their ways, but I
will heal them;
I will lead them and repay
them with comfort,
creating for their mourners
the fruit of the lips. <sup>a</sup>
19 Peace, peace, to the far and the
near, says the LORD;
and I will heal them.
20 But the wicked are like the
tossing sea

that cannot keep still;
its waters toss up mire and
mud.
21 There is no peace, says my
God, for the wicked.

58.1 S<sup>HOUT</sup> out, do not hold back!
Lift up your voice like a
trumpet!
Announce to my people their
rebellion,
to the house of Jacob their
sins.
2 Yet day after day they seek me
and delight to know my ways,
as if they were a nation that
practiced righteousness
and did not forsake the
ordinance of their God;
they ask of me righteous
judgments,
they delight to draw near to
God.
3 "Why do we fast, but you do
not see?
Why humble ourselves, but
you do not notice?"
Look, you serve your own
interest on your fast day,
and oppress all your workers.
4 Look, you fast only to quarrel
and to fight
and to strike with a wicked
fist.
Such fasting as you do today
will not make your voice
heard on high.
5 Is such the fast that I choose,
a day to humble oneself?
Is it to bow down the head like
a bulrush,
and to lie in sackcloth and
ashes?

<sup>a</sup>Meaning of Heb uncertain

Will you call this a fast,
    a day acceptable to the Lord?

6 Is not this the fast that I
      choose:
    to loose the bonds of
      injustice,
    to undo the thongs of the
      yoke,
    to let the oppressed go free,
    and to break every yoke?
7 Is it not to share your bread
      with the hungry,
    and bring the homeless poor
      into your house;
    when you see the naked, to
      cover them,
    and not to hide yourself from
      your own kin?
8 Then your light shall break forth
      like the dawn,
    and your healing shall spring
      up quickly;
    your vindicator[a] shall go
      before you,
    the glory of the Lord shall be
      your rear guard.
9 Then you shall call, and the
      Lord will answer;
    you shall cry for help, and he
      will say, Here I am.

If you remove the yoke from
      among you,
    the pointing of the finger, the
      speaking of evil,
10 if you offer your food to the
      hungry
    and satisfy the needs of the
      afflicted,
    then your light shall rise in
      the darkness
    and your gloom be like the
      noonday.
11 The Lord will guide you
      continually,
    and satisfy your needs in
      parched places,

    and make your bones strong;
    and you shall be like a watered
      garden,
    like a spring of water,
    whose waters never fail.
12 Your ancient ruins shall be
      rebuilt;
    you shall raise up the
      foundations of many
      generations;
    you shall be called the repairer
      of the breach,
    the restorer of streets to live
      in.

13 If you refrain from trampling the
      sabbath,
    from pursuing your own
      interests on my holy day;
    if you call the sabbath a delight
    and the holy day of the Lord
      honorable;
    if you honor it, not going your
      own ways,
    serving your own interests,
      or pursuing your own
      affairs;[b]
14 then you shall take delight in
      the Lord,
    and I will make you ride upon
      the heights of the earth;
    I will feed you with the heritage
      of your ancestor Jacob,
    for the mouth of the Lord has
      spoken.

59.1 See, the Lord's hand is not too
      short to save,
    nor his ear too dull to hear.
2 Rather, your iniquities have
      been barriers
    between you and your God,
    and your sins have hidden his
      face from you
    so that he does not hear.
3 For your hands are defiled
      with blood,
    and your fingers with iniquity;

a Or *vindication*  b Heb *or speaking words*

your lips have spoken lies,
   your tongue mutters
     wickedness.
4 No one brings suit justly,
   no one goes to law honestly;
they rely on empty pleas, they
     speak lies,
   conceiving mischief and
     begetting iniquity.
5 They hatch adders' eggs,
   and weave the spider's web;
whoever eats their eggs dies,
   and the crushed egg hatches
     out a viper.
6 Their webs cannot serve as
     clothing;
   they cannot cover themselves
     with what they make.
Their works are works of
     iniquity,
   and deeds of violence are in
     their hands.
7 Their feet run to evil,
   and they rush to shed
     innocent blood;
their thoughts are thoughts
     of iniquity,
   desolation and destruction are
     in their highways.
8 The way of peace they do not
     know,
   and there is no justice in
     their paths.
Their roads they have made
     crooked;
   no one who walks in them
     knows peace.

9 Therefore justice is far from us,
   and righteousness does not
     reach us;
we wait for light, and lo! there
     is darkness;
   and for brightness, but we
     walk in gloom.
10 We grope like the blind along
     a wall,
groping like those who have
     no eyes;
we stumble at noon as in the
     twilight,
   among the vigorous[a] as
     though we were dead.
11 We all growl like bears;
   like doves we moan
     mournfully.
We wait for justice, but there is
     none;
   for salvation, but it is far
     from us.
12 For our transgressions before
     you are many,
   and our sins testify against
     us.
Our transgressions indeed are
     with us,
   and we know our iniquities:
13 transgressing, and denying the
     Lord,
   and turning away from
     following our God,
talking oppression and revolt,
   conceiving lying words and
     uttering them from
     the heart.
14 Justice is turned back,
   and righteousness stands at a
     distance;
for truth stumbles in the public
     square,
   and uprightness cannot enter.
15 Truth is lacking,
   and whoever turns from evil
     is despoiled.

The Lord saw it, and it
     displeased him
   that there was no justice.
16 He saw that there was no one,
   and was appalled that there
     was no one to intervene;
so his own arm brought him
     victory,
   and his righteousness upheld
     him.

a Meaning of Heb uncertain

17 He put on righteousness like a
    breastplate,
  and a helmet of salvation on
    his head;
he put on garments of
    vengeance for clothing,
  and wrapped himself in fury
    as in a mantle.
18 According to their deeds, so will
    he repay;
  wrath to his adversaries,
    requital to his enemies;
to the coastlands he will
    render requital.
19 So those in the west shall fear
    the name of the Lord,
  and those in the east, his
    glory;
for he will come like a pent-up
    stream
  that the wind of the Lord
    drives on.

20 And he will come to Zion as
    Redeemer,
  to those in Jacob who turn
    from transgression, says
    the Lord.

21 And as for me, this is my covenant with them, says the Lord: my spirit that is upon you, and my words that I have put in your mouth, shall not depart out of your mouth, or out of the mouths of your children, or out of the mouths of your children's children, says the Lord, from now on and forever.

# PHILIPPIANS 1.1–26

PAUL and Timothy, servants[a] of Christ Jesus,

To all the saints in Christ Jesus who are in Philippi, with the bishops[b] and deacons:[c]

2 Grace to you and peace from God our Father and the Lord Jesus Christ.

3 I thank my God every time I re-member you, 4 constantly praying with joy in every one of my prayers for all of you, 5 because of your sharing in the gospel from the first day until now. 6 I am confident of this, that the one who began a good work among you will bring it to completion by the day of Jesus Christ. 7 It is right for me to think this way about all of you, because you hold me in your heart,[d] for all of you share in God's grace[e] with me, both in my imprisonment and in the defense and confirmation of the gospel. 8 For God is my witness, how I long for all of you with the compassion of Christ Jesus. 9 And this is my prayer, that your love may overflow more and more with knowledge and full insight 10 to help you to determine what is best, so that in the day of Christ you may be pure and blameless, 11 having produced the harvest of righteousness that comes through Jesus Christ for the glory and praise of God.

12 I want you to know, beloved,[f] that what has happened to me has actually helped to spread the gospel, 13 so that it has become known throughout the whole imperial guard[g] and to everyone else that my imprisonment is for Christ; 14 and most of the brothers and sisters,[f] having been made confident in the Lord by my imprisonment, dare to speak the word[h] with greater boldness and without fear.

15 Some proclaim Christ from envy and rivalry, but others from goodwill. 16 These proclaim Christ out of love, knowing that I have been put here for the defense of the gospel; 17 the others proclaim Christ out of selfish ambition, not sincerely but intending to increase my suffering in my imprisonment. 18 What does it matter? Just this, that Christ is proclaimed in every way, whether out of false motives or true; and in that I rejoice.

Yes, and I will continue to rejoice,

a Gk *slaves*  b Or *overseers*  c Or *overseers and helpers*  d Or *because I hold you in my heart*  e Gk *in grace*  f Gk *brothers*  g Gk *whole praetorium*  h Other ancient authorities read *word of God*

[19]for I know that through your prayers and the help of the Spirit of Jesus Christ this will turn out for my deliverance. [20]It is my eager expectation and hope that I will not be put to shame in any way, but that by my speaking with all boldness, Christ will be exalted now as always in my body, whether by life or by death. [21]For to me, living is Christ and dying is gain. [22]If I am to live in the flesh, that means fruitful labor for me; and I do not know which I prefer. [23]I am hard pressed between the two: my desire is to depart and be with Christ, for that is far better; [24]but to remain in the flesh is more necessary for you. [25]Since I am convinced of this, I know that I will remain and continue with all of you for your progress and joy in faith, [26]so that I may share abundantly in your boasting in Christ Jesus when I come to you again.

## PSALM 71.1–24

IN you, O LORD, I take refuge;
    let me never be put to
      shame.
2  In your righteousness deliver
      me and rescue me;
   incline your ear to me and
      save me.
3  Be to me a rock of refuge,
      a strong fortress, [a] to save
      me,
      for you are my rock and my
      fortress.

4  Rescue me, O my God, from
      the hand of the wicked,
      from the grasp of the unjust
      and cruel.
5  For you, O Lord, are my hope,
      my trust, O LORD, from my
      youth.
6  Upon you I have leaned from
      my birth;
      it was you who took me from
      my mother's womb.

My praise is continually of you.
7  I have been like a portent to
      many,
      but you are my strong refuge.
8  My mouth is filled with your
      praise,
      and with your glory all day
      long.
9  Do not cast me off in the time
      of old age;
      do not forsake me when my
      strength is spent.
10  For my enemies speak
      concerning me,
      and those who watch for my
      life consult together.
11  They say, "Pursue and seize
      that person
      whom God has forsaken,
      for there is no one to
      deliver."

12  O God, do not be far from me;
      O my God, make haste to
      help me!
13  Let my accusers be put to
      shame and consumed;
      let those who seek to hurt
      me
      be covered with scorn and
      disgrace.
14  But I will hope continually,
      and will praise you yet more
      and more.
15  My mouth will tell of your
      righteous acts,
      of your deeds of salvation all
      day long,
      though their number is past
      my knowledge.
16  I will come praising the mighty
      deeds of the Lord GOD,
      I will praise your
      righteousness, yours
      alone.

a Gk Compare 31.3: Heb *to come continually you have commanded*

17 O God, from my youth you have
        taught me,
    and I still proclaim your
        wondrous deeds.
18 So even to old age and gray
        hairs,
    O God, do not forsake me,
until I proclaim your might
    to all the generations to
        come. [a]
Your power 19and your
        righteousness, O God,
    reach the high heavens.

You who have done great
        things,
    O God, who is like you?
20 You who have made me see
        many troubles and
        calamities
    will revive me again;
from the depths of the earth
    you will bring me up again.
21 You will increase my honor,
    and comfort me once again.

22 I will also praise you with the
        harp

for your faithfulness, O my
        God;
    I will sing praises to you with
        the lyre,
    O Holy One of Israel.
23 My lips will shout for joy
        when I sing praises to you;
    my soul also, which you have
        rescued.
24 All day long my tongue will talk
        of your righteous help,
for those who tried to do me
        harm
    have been put to shame, and
        disgraced.

## PROVERBS 24.10–11

IF you faint in the day of
        adversity,
    your strength being small;
11 if you hold back from rescuing
        those taken away to
        death,
    those who go staggering to
        the slaughter;

# SEPTEMBER 30

## ISAIAH 60.1—62.5

ARISE, shine; for your light
        has come,
    and the glory of the LORD
        has risen upon you.
2 For darkness shall cover the
        earth,
    and thick darkness the
        peoples;

but the LORD will arise upon you,
    and his glory will appear
        over you.
3 Nations shall come to your light,
    and kings to the brightness of
        your dawn.

4 Lift up your eyes and look
        around;

aGk Compare Syr: Heb *to a generation, to all that come*

they all gather together, they
   come to you;
your sons shall come from
   far away,
   and your daughters shall be
      carried on their nurses'
      arms.
5 Then you shall see and be
   radiant;
   your heart shall thrill and
      rejoice, **a**
because the abundance of the
   sea shall be brought to
   you,
   the wealth of the nations shall
      come to you.
6 A multitude of camels shall
   cover you,
   the young camels of Midian
      and Ephah;
   all those from Sheba shall
      come.
They shall bring gold and
   frankincense,
   and shall proclaim the praise
      of the LORD.
7 All the flocks of Kedar shall be
   gathered to you,
   the rams of Nebaioth shall
      minister to you;
they shall be acceptable on my
   altar,
   and I will glorify my glorious
      house.

8 Who are these that fly like a
   cloud,
   and like doves to their
      windows?
9 For the coastlands shall wait
   for me,
   the ships of Tarshish first,
to bring your children from far
   away,
   their silver and gold with
      them,
for the name of the LORD your
   God,

and for the Holy One of
   Israel,
   because he has glorified you.
10 Foreigners shall build up your
   walls,
   and their kings shall minister
      to you;
for in my wrath I struck you
   down,
   but in my favor I have had
      mercy on you.
11 Your gates shall always be
   open;
   day and night they shall not
      be shut,
so that nations shall bring you
   their wealth,
   with their kings led in
      procession.
12 For the nation and kingdom
   that will not serve you shall
      perish;
   those nations shall be utterly
      laid waste.
13 The glory of Lebanon shall
   come to you,
   the cypress, the plane, and
      the pine,
to beautify the place of my
   sanctuary;
   and I will glorify where my
      feet rest.
14 The descendants of those who
   oppressed you
   shall come bending low to
      you,
and all who despised you
   shall bow down at your feet;
they shall call you the City of
   the LORD,
   the Zion of the Holy One of
      Israel.
15 Whereas you have been
   forsaken and hated,
   with no one passing through,
I will make you majestic
   forever,
   a joy from age to age.

**a** Heb *be enlarged*

<sup>16</sup> You shall suck the milk of
    nations,
      you shall suck the breasts
        of kings;
    and you shall know that I, the
        LORD, am your Savior
    and your Redeemer, the
      Mighty One of Jacob.

<sup>17</sup> Instead of bronze I will bring
    gold,
      instead of iron I will bring
      silver;
    instead of wood, bronze,
      instead of stones, iron.
    I will appoint Peace as your
      overseer
    and Righteousness as your
      taskmaster.
<sup>18</sup> Violence shall no more be heard
      in your land,
    devastation or destruction
      within your borders;
    you shall call your walls
      Salvation,
    and your gates Praise.
<sup>19</sup> The sun shall no longer be
    your light by day,
    nor for brightness shall the
      moon
      give light to you by night; <sup>a</sup>
    but the LORD will be your
      everlasting light,
    and your God will be your
      glory.
<sup>20</sup> Your sun shall no more go
    down,
    or your moon withdraw itself;
    for the LORD will be your
      everlasting light,
    and your days of mourning
      shall be ended.
<sup>21</sup> Your people shall all be
    righteous;
      they shall possess the land
      forever.

They are the shoot that I
    planted, the work of my
    hands,
    so that I might be glorified.
<sup>22</sup> The least of them shall become
    a clan,
    and the smallest one a mighty
    nation;
I am the LORD;
    in its time I will accomplish
    it quickly.

<sup>61.1</sup> THE spirit of the Lord GOD is
    upon me,
    because the LORD has
    anointed me;
he has sent me to bring good
    news to the oppressed,
    to bind up the brokenhearted,
to proclaim liberty to the
    captives,
    and release to the prisoners;
<sup>2</sup> to proclaim the year of the
    LORD's favor,
    and the day of vengeance of
    our God;
    to comfort all who mourn;
<sup>3</sup> to provide for those who mourn
    in Zion—
    to give them a garland instead
    of ashes,
the oil of gladness instead of
    mourning,
    the mantle of praise instead of
    a faint spirit.
They will be called oaks of
    righteousness,
    the planting of the LORD, to
    display his glory.
<sup>4</sup> They shall build up the ancient
    ruins,
    they shall raise up the former
    devastations;
they shall repair the ruined
    cities,
    the devastations of many
    generations.

**a** Q Ms Gk Old Latin Tg: MT lacks *by night*

5 Strangers shall stand and feed
   your flocks,
      foreigners shall till your land
      and dress your vines;
6 but you shall be called priests of
   the Lord,
      you shall be named ministers
      of our God;
   you shall enjoy the wealth of
   the nations,
      and in their riches you shall
      glory.
7 Because their<sup>a</sup> shame was
   double,
      and dishonor was proclaimed
      as their lot,
   therefore they shall possess a
   double portion;
      everlasting joy shall be theirs.

8 For I the Lord love justice,
      I hate robbery and
      wrongdoing;<sup>b</sup>
   I will faithfully give them their
   recompense,
      and I will make an everlasting
      covenant with them.
9 Their descendants shall be
   known among the
   nations,
      and their offspring among the
      peoples;
   all who see them shall
   acknowledge
      that they are a people whom
      the Lord has blessed.
10 I will greatly rejoice in the
   Lord,
      my whole being shall exult in
      my God;
   for he has clothed me with the
   garments of salvation,
      he has covered me with the
      robe of righteousness,
   as a bridegroom decks himself
   with a garland,
      and as a bride adorns herself
      with her jewels.

11 For as the earth brings forth its
   shoots,
      and as a garden causes what
      is sown in it to spring
      up,
   so the Lord God will cause
      righteousness and praise
   to spring up before all the
   nations.

62.1 For Zion's sake I will not keep
   silent,
      and for Jerusalem's sake I will
      not rest,
   until her vindication shines out
      like the dawn,
      and her salvation like a
      burning torch.
2 The nations shall see your
   vindication,
      and all the kings your glory;
   and you shall be called by a
   new name
      that the mouth of the Lord
      will give.
3 You shall be a crown of beauty
      in the hand of the Lord,
      and a royal diadem in the
      hand of your God.
4 You shall no more be termed
   Forsaken,<sup>c</sup>
      and your land shall no more
      be termed Desolate;<sup>d</sup>
   but you shall be called My
   Delight Is in Her,<sup>e</sup>
      and your land Married;<sup>f</sup>
   for the Lord delights in you,
      and your land shall be
      married.
5 For as a young man marries a
   young woman,
      so shall your builder<sup>g</sup> marry
      you,
   and as the bridegroom rejoices
      over the bride,
      so shall your God rejoice
      over you.

<sup>a</sup>Heb *your*   <sup>b</sup>Or *robbery with a burnt offering*   <sup>c</sup>Heb *Azubah*   <sup>d</sup>Heb *Shemamah*   <sup>e</sup>Heb *Hephzibah*
<sup>f</sup>Heb *Beulah*   <sup>g</sup>Cn: Heb *your sons*

## PHILIPPIANS 1.27—2.18

ONLY, live your life in a manner worthy of the gospel of Christ, so that, whether I come and see you or am absent and hear about you, I will know that you are standing firm in one spirit, striving side by side with one mind for the faith of the gospel, ²⁸and are in no way intimidated by your opponents. For them this is evidence of their destruction, but of your salvation. And this is God's doing. ²⁹For he has graciously granted you the privilege not only of believing in Christ, but of suffering for him as well— ³⁰since you are having the same struggle that you saw I had and now hear that I still have.

²·¹ If then there is any encouragement in Christ, any consolation from love, any sharing in the Spirit, any compassion and sympathy, ²make my joy complete: be of the same mind, having the same love, being in full accord and of one mind. ³Do nothing from selfish ambition or conceit, but in humility regard others as better than yourselves. ⁴Let each of you look not to your own interests, but to the interests of others. ⁵Let the same mind be in you that wasᵃ in Christ Jesus,

6 who, though he was in the form
      of God,
    did not regard equality with
      God
    as something to be exploited,
7 but emptied himself,
    taking the form of a slave,
    being born in human likeness.
  And being found in human form,
8     he humbled himself
    and became obedient to the
      point of death—
    even death on a cross.

9 Therefore God also highly
      exalted him

and gave him the name
    that is above every name,
10  so that at the name of Jesus
      every knee should bend,
    in heaven and on earth and
      under the earth,
11  and every tongue should confess
      that Jesus Christ is Lord,
    to the glory of God the
      Father.

12 Therefore, my beloved, just as you have always obeyed me, not only in my presence, but much more now in my absence, work out your own salvation with fear and trembling; ¹³for it is God who is at work in you, enabling you both to will and to work for his good pleasure.

14 Do all things without murmuring and arguing, ¹⁵so that you may be blameless and innocent, children of God without blemish in the midst of a crooked and perverse generation, in which you shine like stars in the world. ¹⁶It is by your holding fast to the word of life that I can boast on the day of Christ that I did not run in vain or labor in vain. ¹⁷But even if I am being poured out as a libation over the sacrifice and the offering of your faith, I am glad and rejoice with all of you— ¹⁸and in the same way you also must be glad and rejoice with me.

## PSALM 72.1–20

*Of Solomon.*

GIVE the king your justice,
      O God,
    and your righteousness to a
      king's son.
2 May he judge your people with
      righteousness,
    and your poor with justice.
3 May the mountains yield
      prosperity for the people,
    and the hills, in
      righteousness.

ᵃ Or *that you have*

4 May he defend the cause of the
    poor of the people,
  give deliverance to the needy,
  and crush the oppressor.

5 May he live[a] while the sun
    endures,
  and as long as the moon,
    throughout all
    generations.
6 May he be like rain that falls on
    the mown grass,
  like showers that water the
    earth.
7 In his days may righteousness
    flourish
  and peace abound, until the
    moon is no more.

8 May he have dominion from sea
    to sea,
  and from the River to the
    ends of the earth.
9 May his foes[b] bow down before
    him,
  and his enemies lick the dust.
10 May the kings of Tarshish and
    of the isles
  render him tribute,
  may the kings of Sheba and
    Seba
  bring gifts.
11 May all kings fall down before
    him,
  all nations give him service.

12 For he delivers the needy when
    they call,
  the poor and those who have
    no helper.
13 He has pity on the weak and
    the needy,
  and saves the lives of the
    needy.
14 From oppression and violence
    he redeems their life;
  and precious is their blood in
    his sight.

15 Long may he live!
  May gold of Sheba be given
    to him.
  May prayer be made for him
    continually,
  and blessings invoked for him
    all day long.
16 May there be abundance of
    grain in the land;
  may it wave on the tops of
    the mountains;
  may its fruit be like Lebanon;
  and may people blossom in the
    cities
  like the grass of the field.
17 May his name endure forever,
  his fame continue as long as
    the sun.
  May all nations be blessed in
    him;[c]
  may they pronounce him
    happy.

18 Blessed be the LORD, the God
    of Israel,
  who alone does wondrous
    things.
19 Blessed be his glorious name
    forever;
  may his glory fill the whole
    earth.
    Amen and Amen.

20 The prayers of David son of
    Jesse are ended.

## PROVERBS 24.12

IF you say, "Look, we did not
    know this"—
  does not he who weighs the
    heart perceive it?
  Does not he who keeps watch
    over your soul know it?
  And will he not repay all
    according to their deeds?

a Gk: Heb *may they fear you*  b Cn: Heb *those who live in the wilderness*  c Or *bless themselves by him*

# OCTOBER 1

ISAIAH 62.6—65.25

UPON your walls, O Jerusalem,
  I have posted sentinels;
  all day and all night
  they shall never be silent.
You who remind the LORD,
  take no rest,
7  and give him no rest
  until he establishes Jerusalem
  and makes it renowned
      throughout the earth.
8  The LORD has sworn by his
      right hand
  and by his mighty arm:
I will not again give your grain
  to be food for your enemies,
and foreigners shall not drink
      the wine
  for which you have labored;
9  but those who garner it shall eat
      it
  and praise the LORD,
and those who gather it shall
      drink it
  in my holy courts.

10  Go through, go through the
      gates,
  prepare the way for the
      people;
build up, build up the highway,
  clear it of stones,
  lift up an ensign over the
      peoples.
11  The LORD has proclaimed
  to the end of the earth:
Say to daughter Zion,
  "See, your salvation comes;
his reward is with him,
  and his recompense before
      him."
12  They shall be called, "The
      Holy People,
  The Redeemed of the LORD";

and you shall be called,
  "Sought Out,
A City Not Forsaken."

63.1 "WHO is this that comes from
      Edom,
  from Bozrah in garments
      stained crimson?
Who is this so splendidly robed,
  marching in his great might?"

"It is I, announcing vindication,
  mighty to save."

2  "Why are your robes red,
  and your garments like theirs
      who tread the wine
      press?"

3  "I have trodden the wine press
      alone,
  and from the peoples no one
      was with me;
I trod them in my anger
  and trampled them in my
      wrath;
their juice spattered on my
      garments,
  and stained all my robes.
4  For the day of vengeance was in
      my heart,
  and the year for my
      redeeming work had
      come.
5  I looked, but there was no
      helper;
  I stared, but there was no
      one to sustain me;
so my own arm brought me
      victory,
  and my wrath sustained me.
6  I trampled down peoples in my
      anger,
  I crushed them in my wrath,

and I poured out their
   lifeblood on the earth.''

7  I will recount the gracious deeds
      of the LORD,
   the praiseworthy acts of the
      LORD,
   because of all that the LORD has
      done for us,
   and the great favor to the
      house of Israel
   that he has shown them
      according to his mercy,
      according to the abundance of
      his steadfast love.
8  For he said, "Surely they are
      my people,
   children who will not deal
      falsely";
   and he became their savior
9     in all their distress.
   It was no messenger[a] or angel
      but his presence that saved
      them;[b]
   in his love and in his pity he
      redeemed them;
      he lifted them up and carried
      them all the days of old.

10  But they rebelled
      and grieved his holy spirit;
   therefore he became their
      enemy;
      he himself fought against
      them.
11  Then they[c] remembered the
      days of old,
   of Moses his servant.[d]
   Where is the one who brought
      them up out of the sea
   with the shepherds of his
      flock?
   Where is the one who put
      within them
   his holy spirit,
12  who caused his glorious arm
      to march at the right hand
      of Moses,

who divided the waters before
      them
   to make for himself an
      everlasting name,
13  who led them through the
      depths?
   Like a horse in the desert,
      they did not stumble.
14  Like cattle that go down into
      the valley,
   the spirit of the LORD gave
      them rest.
   Thus you led your people,
      to make for yourself a
      glorious name.
15  Look down from heaven and
      see,
   from your holy and glorious
      habitation.
   Where are your zeal and your
      might?
   The yearning of your heart
      and your compassion?
   They are withheld from me.
16  For you are our father,
      though Abraham does not
      know us
   and Israel does not
      acknowledge us;
   you, O LORD, are our father;
      our Redeemer from of old is
      your name.
17  Why, O LORD, do you make us
      stray from your ways
      and harden our heart, so that
      we do not fear you?
   Turn back for the sake of your
      servants,
      for the sake of the tribes that
      are your heritage.
18  Your holy people took
      possession for a little
      while;
      but now our adversaries have
      trampled down your
      sanctuary.
19  We have long been like those
      whom you do not rule,

aGk: Heb *anguish*   bOr *savior. 9In all their distress he was distressed; the angel of his presence saved
them;*   cHeb *he*   dCn: Heb *his people*

like those not called by your
   name.

**64.1** O THAT you would tear open the
   heavens and come
   down,
   so that the mountains would
   quake at your
   presence—
**2a** as when fire kindles brushwood
   and the fire causes water to
   boil—
   to make your name known to
   your adversaries,
   so that the nations might
   tremble at your
   presence!
**3** When you did awesome deeds
   that we did not expect,
   you came down, the
   mountains quaked at your
   presence.
**4** From ages past no one has
   heard,
   no ear has perceived,
   no eye has seen any God
   besides you,
   who works for those who
   wait for him.
**5** You meet those who gladly do
   right,
   those who remember you in
   your ways.
   But you were angry, and we
   sinned;
   because you hid yourself we
   transgressed. **b**
**6** We have all become like one
   who is unclean,
   and all our righteous deeds
   are like a filthy cloth.
   We all fade like a leaf,
   and our iniquities, like the
   wind, take us away.
**7** There is no one who calls on
   your name,
   or attempts to take hold of
   you;

for you have hidden your face
   from us,
   and have delivered[c] us into
   the hand of our iniquity.
**8** Yet, O LORD, you are our
   Father;
   we are the clay, and you are
   our potter;
   we are all the work of your
   hand.
**9** Do not be exceedingly angry,
   O LORD,
   and do not remember iniquity
   forever.
   Now consider, we are all your
   people.
**10** Your holy cities have become a
   wilderness,
   Zion has become a
   wilderness,
   Jerusalem a desolation.
**11** Our holy and beautiful house,
   where our ancestors praised
   you,
   has been burned by fire,
   and all our pleasant places
   have become ruins.
**12** After all this, will you restrain
   yourself, O LORD?
   Will you keep silent, and
   punish us so severely?

**65.1** I WAS ready to be sought out
   by those who did not
   ask,
   to be found by those who did
   not seek me.
   I said, "Here I am, here I am,"
   to a nation that did not call on
   my name.
**2** I held out my hands all day long
   to a rebellious people,
   who walk in a way that is not
   good,
   following their own devices;
**3** a people who provoke me
   to my face continually,
sacrificing in gardens

<hr>

a Ch 64.1 in Heb   b Meaning of Heb uncertain   c Gk Syr Old Latin Tg: Heb *melted*

and offering incense on
    bricks;
4 who sit inside tombs,
    and spend the night in secret
        places;
who eat swine's flesh,
    with broth of abominable
        things in their vessels;
5 who say, "Keep to yourself,
    do not come near me, for I
        am too holy for you."
These are a smoke in my
    nostrils,
    a fire that burns all day long.
6 See, it is written before me:
    I will not keep silent, but I
        will repay;
I will indeed repay into their
    laps
7     their[a] iniquities and their[a]
        ancestors' iniquities
        together,
            says the LORD;
because they offered incense on
    the mountains
    and reviled me on the hills,
I will measure into their laps
    full payment for their actions.
8 Thus says the LORD:
As the wine is found in the
        cluster,
    and they say, "Do not
        destroy it,
    for there is a blessing in it,"
so I will do for my servants'
        sake,
    and not destroy them all.
9 I will bring forth descendants[b]
        from Jacob,
    and from Judah inheritors[c] of
        my mountains;
my chosen shall inherit it,
    and my servants shall settle
        there.
10 Sharon shall become a pasture
    for flocks,

and the Valley of Achor a
    place for herds to lie
        down,
    for my people who have
        sought me.
11 But you who forsake the LORD,
    who forget my holy mountain,
who set a table for Fortune
    and fill cups of mixed wine for
        Destiny;
12 I will destine you to the sword,
    and all of you shall bow down
        to the slaughter;
because, when I called, you did
    not answer,
    when I spoke, you did not
        listen,
but you did what was evil in
    my sight,
    and chose what I did not
        delight in.
13 Therefore thus says the Lord
    GOD:
My servants shall eat,
    but you shall be hungry;
my servants shall drink,
    but you shall be thirsty;
my servants shall rejoice,
    but you shall be put to
        shame;
14 my servants shall sing for
        gladness of heart,
    but you shall cry out for pain
        of heart,
    and shall wail for anguish
        of spirit.
15 You shall leave your name to
        my chosen to use as a
        curse,
    and the Lord GOD will put you
        to death;
    but to his servants he will
        give a different name.
16 Then whoever invokes a
        blessing in the land
    shall bless by the God of
        faithfulness,

a Gk Syr: Heb *your*  b Or *a descendant*  c Or *an inheritor*

and whoever takes an oath in
    the land
shall swear by the God of
    faithfulness;
because the former troubles are
    forgotten
and are hidden from my sight.

17 For I am about to create new
    heavens
    and a new earth;
the former things shall not be
    remembered
    or come to mind.
18 But be glad and rejoice forever
    in what I am creating;
for I am about to create
    Jerusalem as a joy,
    and its people as a delight.
19 I will rejoice in Jerusalem,
    and delight in my people;
no more shall the sound of
    weeping be heard in it,
    or the cry of distress.
20 No more shall there be in it
    an infant that lives but a
    few days,
    or an old person who does
    not live out a lifetime;
for one who dies at a hundred
    years will be considered
    a youth,
    and one who falls short of a
    hundred will be
    considered accursed.
21 They shall build houses and
    inhabit them;
    they shall plant vineyards and
    eat their fruit.
22 They shall not build and another
    inhabit;
    they shall not plant and
    another eat;
for like the days of a tree shall
    the days of my people
    be,

    and my chosen shall long
    enjoy the work of their
    hands.
23 They shall not labor in vain,
    or bear children for
    calamity; a
for they shall be offspring
    blessed by the LORD—
    and their descendants as well.
24 Before they call I will answer,
    while they are yet speaking I
    will hear.
25 The wolf and the lamb shall feed
    together,
    the lion shall eat straw like
    the ox;
    but the serpent—its food
    shall be dust!
They shall not hurt or destroy
    on all my holy mountain,
          says the LORD.

## PHILIPPIANS 2.19—3.4a

I HOPE in the Lord Jesus to send Timothy to you soon, so that I may be cheered by news of you. 20I have no one like him who will be genuinely concerned for your welfare. 21All of them are seeking their own interests, not those of Jesus Christ. 22But Timothy'sb worth you know, how like a son with a father he has served with me in the work of the gospel. 23I hope therefore to send him as soon as I see how things go with me; 24and I trust in the Lord that I will also come soon.

25 Still, I think it necessary to send to you Epaphroditus—my brother and co-worker and fellow soldier, your messengerc and minister to my need; 26for he has been longing ford all of you, and has been distressed because you heard that he was ill. 27He was indeed so ill that he nearly died. But God had mercy on him, and not only on him but on me also, so that I would not have one sorrow after another. 28I am the more eager to send him, therefore, in

a Or *sudden terror*  b Gk *his*  c Gk *apostle*  d Other ancient authorities read *longing to see* order that you may rejoice at seeing him again, and that I may be less anxious. <sup>29</sup>Welcome him then in the Lord with all joy, and honor such people, <sup>30</sup>because he came close to death for the work of Christ, **a** risking his life to make up for those services that you could not give me.

<sup>3.1</sup> FINALLY, my brothers and sisters, **b** rejoice **c** in the Lord.

To write the same things to you is not troublesome to me, and for you it is a safeguard.
2 Beware of the dogs, beware of the evil workers, beware of those who mutilate the flesh! **d** <sup>3</sup>For it is we who are the circumcision, who worship in the Spirit of God **e** and boast in Christ Jesus and have no confidence in the flesh— <sup>4</sup>even though I, too, have reason for confidence in the flesh.

## PSALM 73.1–28

*A Psalm of Asaph.*

TRULY God is good to the upright, **f**
to those who are pure in heart.
2 But as for me, my feet had almost stumbled;
my steps had nearly slipped.
3 For I was envious of the arrogant;
I saw the prosperity of the wicked.

4 For they have no pain;
their bodies are sound and sleek.
5 They are not in trouble as others are;
they are not plagued like other people.

6 Therefore pride is their necklace;
violence covers them like a garment.
7 Their eyes swell out with fatness;
their hearts overflow with follies.
8 They scoff and speak with malice;
loftily they threaten oppression.
9 They set their mouths against heaven,
and their tongues range over the earth.

10 Therefore the people turn and praise them, **g**
and find no fault in them. **h**
11 And they say, "How can God know?
Is there knowledge in the Most High?"
12 Such are the wicked;
always at ease, they increase in riches.
13 All in vain I have kept my heart clean
and washed my hands in innocence.
14 For all day long I have been plagued,
and am punished every morning.

15 If I had said, "I will talk on in this way,"
I would have been untrue to the circle of your children.
16 But when I thought how to understand this,
it seemed to me a wearisome task,
17 until I went into the sanctuary of God;

aOther ancient authorities read *of the Lord*  bGk *my brothers*  cOr *farewell*  dGk *the mutilation*  eOther ancient authorities read *worship God in spirit here*  fOr *good to Israel*  gCn: Heb *his people return*  hCn: Heb *abundant waters are drained by them*

then I perceived their end.
18 Truly you set them in slippery
        places;
    you make them fall to ruin.
19 How they are destroyed in a
        moment,
    swept away utterly by
        terrors!
20 They are[a] like a dream when
        one awakes;
    on awaking you despise their
        phantoms.

21 When my soul was embittered,
        when I was pricked in heart,
22 I was stupid and ignorant;
    I was like a brute beast
        toward you.
23 Nevertheless I am continually
        with you;
    you hold my right hand.
24 You guide me with your
        counsel,
    and afterward you will receive
        me with honor. [b]
25 Whom have I in heaven but
        you?
    And there is nothing on earth
        that I desire other than
        you.

26 My flesh and my heart may fail,
    but God is the strength[c] of
        my heart and my portion
        forever.

27 Indeed, those who are far from
        you will perish;
    you put an end to those who
        are false to you.
28 But for me it is good to be near
        God;
    I have made the Lord God
        my refuge,
    to tell of all your works.


## PROVERBS 24.13–14

My child, eat honey, for it is
        good,
    and the drippings of the
        honeycomb are sweet to
        your taste.
14 Know that wisdom is such to
        your soul;
    if you find it, you will find a
        future,
    and your hope will not be cut
        off.


# OCTOBER 2

## ISAIAH 66.1–24

Thus says the Lord:
    Heaven is my throne
        and the earth is my
        footstool;
    what is the house that you
        would build for me,
    and what is my resting place?

2 All these things my hand has
        made,
    and so all these things
        are mine, [d]
                    says the Lord.
    But this is the one to whom I
        will look,

aCn: Heb *Lord*   bOr *to glory*   cHeb *rock*   dGk Syr: Heb *these things came to be*

to the humble and contrite
in spirit,
who trembles at my word.

3    Whoever slaughters an ox is like
one who kills a human
being;
whoever sacrifices a lamb,
like one who breaks a
dog's neck;
whoever presents a grain
offering, like one who
offers swine's blood;[a]
whoever makes a memorial
offering of frankincense,
like one who blesses an
idol.
These have chosen their own
ways,
and in their abominations they
take delight;
4    I also will choose to mock[b]
them,
and bring upon them what
they fear;
because, when I called, no one
answered,
when I spoke, they did not
listen;
but they did what was evil in
my sight,
and chose what did not
please me.
5    Hear the word of the Lord,
you who tremble at his word:
Your own people who hate you
and reject you for my name's
sake
have said, "Let the Lord be
glorified,
so that we may see your
joy";
but it is they who shall be put
to shame.

6    Listen, an uproar from the city!
A voice from the temple!
The voice of the Lord,

dealing retribution to his
enemies!

7    Before she was in labor
she gave birth;
before her pain came upon her
she delivered a son.
8    Who has heard of such a thing?
Who has seen such things?
Shall a land be born in one day?
Shall a nation be delivered in
one moment?
Yet as soon as Zion was in labor
she delivered her children.
9    Shall I open the womb and not
deliver?
says the Lord;
shall I, the one who delivers,
shut the womb?
says your God.

10    Rejoice with Jerusalem, and be
glad for her,
all you who love her;
rejoice with her in joy,
all you who mourn over
her—
11    that you may nurse and be
satisfied
from her consoling breast;
that you may drink deeply with
delight
from her glorious bosom.

12    For thus says the Lord:
I will extend prosperity to her
like a river,
and the wealth of the nations
like an overflowing
stream;
and you shall nurse and be
carried on her arm,
and dandled on her knees.
13    As a mother comforts her child,
so I will comfort you;
you shall be comforted in
Jerusalem.

[a] Meaning of Heb uncertain    [b] Or *to punish*

14 You shall see, and your heart
    shall rejoice;
  your bodies[a] shall flourish
    like the grass;
  and it shall be known that the
    hand of the LORD is with
    his servants,
  and his indignation is against
    his enemies.
15 For the LORD will come in fire,
  and his chariots like the
    whirlwind,
  to pay back his anger in fury,
  and his rebuke in flames
    of fire.
16 For by fire will the LORD
    execute judgment,
  and by his sword, on all flesh;
  and those slain by the LORD
    shall be many.

17 Those who sanctify and purify themselves to go into the gardens, following the one in the center, eating the flesh of pigs, vermin, and rodents, shall come to an end together, says the LORD.

18 For I know[b] their works and their thoughts, and I am[c] coming to gather all nations and tongues; and they shall come and shall see my glory, 19and I will set a sign among them. From them I will send survivors to the nations, to Tarshish, Put,[d] and Lud—which draw the bow—to Tubal and Javan, to the coastlands far away that have not heard of my fame or seen my glory; and they shall declare my glory among the nations. 20They shall bring all your kindred from all the nations as an offering to the LORD, on horses, and in chariots, and in litters, and on mules, and on dromedaries, to my holy mountain Jerusalem, says the LORD, just as the Israelites bring a grain offering in a clean vessel to the house of the LORD. 21And I will also take some of them as

priests and as Levites, says the LORD.

22 For as the new heavens and the
    new earth,
  which I will make,
  shall remain before me, says
    the LORD;
  so shall your descendants and
    your name remain.
23 From new moon to new moon,
  and from sabbath to sabbath,
  all flesh shall come to worship
    before me,
  says the LORD.

24 And they shall go out and look at the dead bodies of the people who have rebelled against me; for their worm shall not die, their fire shall not be quenched, and they shall be an abhorrence to all flesh.

# PHILIPPIANS 3.4b—4.1

IF anyone else has reason to be confident in the flesh, I have more: 5circumcised on the eighth day, a member of the people of Israel, of the tribe of Benjamin, a Hebrew born of Hebrews; as to the law, a Pharisee; 6as to zeal, a persecutor of the church; as to righteousness under the law, blameless.

7 Yet whatever gains I had, these I have come to regard as loss because of Christ. 8More than that, I regard everything as loss because of the surpassing value of knowing Christ Jesus my Lord. For his sake I have suffered the loss of all things, and I regard them as rubbish, in order that I may gain Christ 9and be found in him, not having a righteousness of my own that comes from the law, but one that comes through faith in Christ,[e] the righteousness from God based on faith. 10I want to know Christ[f] and the power of his res-

urrection and the sharing of his sufferings by becoming like him in his death, [11]if somehow I may attain the resurrection from the dead.

12 Not that I have already obtained this or have already reached the goal;[a] but I press on to make it my own, because Christ Jesus has made me his own. [13]Beloved,[b] I do not consider that I have made it my own;[c] but this one thing I do: forgetting what lies behind and straining forward to what lies ahead, [14]I press on toward the goal for the prize of the heavenly[d] call of God in Christ Jesus. [15]Let those of us then who are mature be of the same mind; and if you think differently about anything, this too God will reveal to you. [16]Only let us hold fast to what we have attained.

17 Brothers and sisters,[b] join in imitating me, and observe those who live according to the example you have in us. [18]For many live as enemies of the cross of Christ; I have often told you of them, and now I tell you even with tears. [19]Their end is destruction; their god is the belly; and their glory is in their shame; their minds are set on earthly things. [20]But our citizenship[e] is in heaven, and it is from there that we are expecting a Savior, the Lord Jesus Christ. [21]He will transform the body of our humiliation[f] that it may be conformed to the body of his glory,[g] by the power that also enables him to make all things subject to himself. [4.1]Therefore, my brothers and sisters,[h] whom I love and long for, my joy and crown, stand firm in the Lord in this way, my beloved.

## PSALM 74. 1–23

*A Maskil of Asaph.*

O GOD, why do you cast us off
  forever?
Why does your anger
  smoke against the sheep
  of your pasture?
2 Remember your congregation,
  which you acquired long
  ago,
  which you redeemed to be
  the tribe of your
  heritage.
  Remember Mount Zion,
  where you came to
  dwell.
3 Direct your steps to the
  perpetual ruins;
  the enemy has destroyed
  everything in the
  sanctuary.

4 Your foes have roared within
  your holy place;
  they set up their emblems
  there.
5 At the upper entrance they
  hacked
  the wooden trellis with
  axes.[i]
6 And then, with hatchets and
  hammers,
  they smashed all its carved
  work.
7 They set your sanctuary on fire;
  they desecrated the dwelling
  place of your name,
  bringing it to the ground.
8 They said to themselves, "We
  will utterly subdue
  them";
  they burned all the meeting
  places of God in the land.

9 We do not see our emblems;

---

aOr *have already been made perfect*   bGk *Brothers*   cOther ancient authorities read *my own yet*
dGk *upward*   eOr *commonwealth*   fOr *our humble bodies*   gOr *his glorious body*   hGk *my brothers*
iCn Compare Gk Syr: Meaning of Heb uncertain

there is no longer any
    prophet,
and there is no one among us
    who knows how long.
10 How long, O God, is the foe to
    scoff?
Is the enemy to revile your
    name forever?
11 Why do you hold back your
    hand;
why do you keep your hand
    in[a] your bosom?

12 Yet God my King is from of old,
    working salvation in the
    earth.
13 You divided the sea by your
    might;
you broke the heads of the
    dragons in the waters.
14 You crushed the heads of
    Leviathan;
you gave him as food[b] for
    the creatures of the
    wilderness.
15 You cut openings for springs
    and torrents;
you dried up ever-flowing
    streams.
16 Yours is the day, yours also the
    night;
you established the
    luminaries[c] and the sun.
17 You have fixed all the bounds of
    the earth;
you made summer and
    winter.

18 Remember this, O LORD, how
    the enemy scoffs,
and an impious people reviles
    your name.
19 Do not deliver the soul of your
    dove to the wild animals;
do not forget the life of your
    poor forever.

20 Have regard for your[d]
    covenant,
for the dark places of the land
    are full of the haunts of
    violence.
21 Do not let the downtrodden be
    put to shame;
let the poor and needy praise
    your name.
22 Rise up, O God, plead your
    cause;
remember how the impious
    scoff at you all day long.
23 Do not forget the clamor of
    your foes,
the uproar of your
    adversaries that goes up
    continually.

## PROVERBS 24.15–16

Do not lie in wait like an
    outlaw against the
    home of the righteous;
do no violence to the place
    where the righteous live;
16 for though they fall seven times,
    they will rise again;
but the wicked are
    overthrown by calamity.

a Cn: Heb *do you consume your right hand from*  b Heb *food for the people*  c Or *moon*; Heb *light*
d Gk Syr: Heb *the*

## JEREMIAH 1.1—2.30

THE words of Jeremiah son of Hilkiah, of the priests who were in Anathoth in the land of Benjamin, ²to whom the word of the LORD came in the days of King Josiah son of Amon of Judah, in the thirteenth year of his reign. ³It came also in the days of King Jehoiakim son of Josiah of Judah, and until the end of the eleventh year of King Zedekiah son of Josiah of Judah, until the captivity of Jerusalem in the fifth month.

4 Now the word of the LORD came to me saying,
5 "Before I formed you in the
womb I knew you,
and before you were born I
consecrated you;
I appointed you a prophet to the
nations."
⁶Then I said, "Ah, Lord GOD! Truly I do not know how to speak, for I am only a boy." ⁷But the LORD said to me,
"Do not say, 'I am only a boy';
for you shall go to all to whom I
send you,
and you shall speak whatever I
command you,
8 Do not be afraid of them,
for I am with you to deliver
you,
says the LORD."
⁹Then the LORD put out his hand and touched my mouth; and the LORD said to me,
"Now I have put my words in
your mouth.
10 See, today I appoint you over
nations and over
kingdoms,
to pluck up and to pull down,
to destroy and to overthrow,
to build and to plant."

11 The word of the LORD came to me, saying, "Jeremiah, what do you see?" And I said, "I see a branch of an almond tree."ᵃ ¹²Then the LORD said to me, "You have seen well, for I am watchingᵇ over my word to perform it." ¹³The word of the LORD came to me a second time, saying, "What do you see?" And I said, "I see a boiling pot, tilted away from the north."

14 Then the LORD said to me: Out of the north disaster shall break out on all the inhabitants of the land. ¹⁵For now I am calling all the tribes of the kingdoms of the north, says the LORD; and they shall come and all of them shall set their thrones at the entrance of the gates of Jerusalem, against all its surrounding walls and against all the cities of Judah. ¹⁶And I will utter my judgments against them, for all their wickedness in forsaking me; they have made offerings to other gods, and worshiped the works of their own hands. ¹⁷But you, gird up your loins; stand up and tell them everything that I command you. Do not break down before them, or I will break you before them. ¹⁸And I for my part have made you today a fortified city, an iron pillar, and a bronze wall, against the whole land— against the kings of Judah, its princes, its priests, and the people of the land. ¹⁹They will fight against you; but they shall not prevail against you, for I am with you, says the LORD, to deliver you.

2.1 THE word of the LORD came to me, saying: ²Go and proclaim in the hearing of Jerusalem, Thus says the LORD:
I remember the devotion of
your youth,

your love as a bride,
how you followed me in the
wilderness,
in a land not sown.
3 Israel was holy to the LORD,
the first fruits of his harvest.
All who ate of it were held
guilty;
disaster came upon them,
says the LORD.

4 Hear the word of the LORD, O house of Jacob, and all the families of the house of Israel. 5Thus says the LORD:
What wrong did your ancestors
find in me
that they went far from me,
and went after worthless things,
and became worthless
themselves?
6 They did not say, "Where is
the LORD
who brought us up from the
land of Egypt,
who led us in the wilderness,
in a land of deserts and pits,
in a land of drought and deep
darkness,
in a land that no one passes
through,
where no one lives?"
7 I brought you into a plentiful
land
to eat its fruits and its good
things.
But when you entered you
defiled my land,
and made my heritage an
abomination.
8 The priests did not say, "Where
is the LORD?"
Those who handle the law did
not know me;
the rulersa transgressed against
me;
the prophets prophesied by
Baal,

and went after things that do
not profit.
9 Therefore once more I accuse
you,
says the LORD,
and I accuse your children's
children.
10 Cross to the coasts of Cyprus
and look,
send to Kedar and examine
with care;
see if there has ever been
such a thing.
11 Has a nation changed its gods,
even though they are no
gods?
But my people have changed
their glory
for something that does not
profit.
12 Be appalled, O heavens, at this,
be shocked, be utterly
desolate,
says the LORD,
13 for my people have committed
two evils:
they have forsaken me,
the fountain of living water,
and dug out cisterns for
themselves,
cracked cisterns
that can hold no water.

14 Is Israel a slave? Is he a
homeborn servant?
Why then has he become
plunder?
15 The lions have roared against
him,
they have roared loudly.
They have made his land a
waste;
his cities are in ruins, without
inhabitant.
16 Moreover, the people of
Memphis and Tahpanhes

aHeb *shepherds*

have broken the crown of
    your head.
17 Have you not brought this upon
    yourself
  by forsaking the Lord your
    God,
  while he led you in the way?
18 What then do you gain by going
    to Egypt,
  to drink the waters of the
    Nile?
  Or what do you gain by going to
    Assyria,
  to drink the waters of the
    Euphrates?
19 Your wickedness will punish
    you,
  and your apostasies will
    convict you.
  Know and see that it is evil
    and bitter
  for you to forsake the Lord
    your God;
  the fear of me is not in you,
    says the Lord God of hosts.

20 For long ago you broke your
    yoke
  and burst your bonds,
  and you said, "I will not
    serve!"
  On every high hill
    and under every green tree
  you sprawled and played
    the whore.
21 Yet I planted you as a choice
    vine,
    from the purest stock.
  How then did you turn
    degenerate
    and become a wild vine?
22 Though you wash yourself with
    lye
    and use much soap,
  the stain of your guilt is still
    before me,
      says the Lord God.
23 How can you say, "I am not
    defiled,

    I have not gone after the
    Baals"?
  Look at your way in the valley;
    know what you have done—
  a restive young camel
    interlacing her tracks,
24   a wild ass at home in the
    wilderness,
  in her heat sniffing the wind!
    Who can restrain her lust?
  None who seek her need weary
    themselves;
    in her month they will find
    her.
25 Keep your feet from going
    unshod
    and your throat from thirst.
  But you said, "It is hopeless,
    for I have loved strangers,
    and after them I will go."

26 As a thief is shamed when
    caught,
  so the house of Israel shall be
    shamed—
  they, their kings, their officials,
    their priests, and their
    prophets,
27 who say to a tree, "You are
    my father,"
    and to a stone, "You gave
    me birth."
  For they have turned their
    backs to me,
    and not their faces.
  But in the time of their trouble
    they say,
    "Come and save us!"
28 But where are your gods
    that you made for yourself?
  Let them come, if they can
    save you,
    in your time of trouble;
  for you have as many gods
    as you have towns, O Judah.

29 Why do you complain against
    me?

You have all rebelled against
    me,

             says the LORD.
30  In vain I have struck down
    your children;
  they accepted no correction.
Your own sword devoured your
    prophets
  like a ravening lion.

## PHILIPPIANS 4. 2–23

I URGE Euodia and I urge Syntyche to be of the same mind in the Lord. [3]Yes, and I ask you also, my loyal companion,[a] help these women, for they have struggled beside me in the work of the gospel, together with Clement and the rest of my co-workers, whose names are in the book of life.

4 Rejoice[b] in the Lord always; again I will say, Rejoice.[b] [5]Let your gentleness be known to everyone. The Lord is near. [6]Do not worry about anything, but in everything by prayer and supplication with thanksgiving let your requests be made known to God. [7]And the peace of God, which surpasses all understanding, will guard your hearts and your minds in Christ Jesus.

8 Finally, beloved,[c] whatever is true, whatever is honorable, whatever is just, whatever is pure, whatever is pleasing, whatever is commendable, if there is any excellence and if there is anything worthy of praise, think about[d] these things. [9]Keep on doing the things that you have learned and received and heard and seen in me, and the God of peace will be with you.

10 I rejoice[e] in the Lord greatly that now at last you have revived your concern for me; indeed, you were concerned for me, but had no opportunity to show it.[f] [11]Not that I am referring to being in need; for I have learned to be content with whatever I have. [12]I know what it is to have little, and I know what it is to have plenty. In any and all circumstances I have learned the secret of being well-fed and of going hungry, of having plenty and of being in need. [13]I can do all things through him who strengthens me. [14]In any case, it was kind of you to share my distress.

15 You Philippians indeed know that in the early days of the gospel, when I left Macedonia, no church shared with me in the matter of giving and receiving, except you alone. [16]For even when I was in Thessalonica, you sent me help for my needs more than once. [17]Not that I seek the gift, but I seek the profit that accumulates to your account. [18]I have been paid in full and have more than enough; I am fully satisfied, now that I have received from Epaphroditus the gifts you sent, a fragrant offering, a sacrifice acceptable and pleasing to God. [19]And my God will fully satisfy every need of yours according to his riches in glory in Christ Jesus. [20]To our God and Father be glory forever and ever. Amen.

21 Greet every saint in Christ Jesus. The friends[c] who are with me greet you. [22]All the saints greet you, especially those of the emperor's household.

23 The grace of the Lord Jesus Christ be with your spirit.[g]

## PSALM 75. 1–10

*To the leader: Do Not Destroy. A Psalm of Asaph. A Song.*

WE give thanks to you,
    O God;
we give thanks; your
    name is near.
People tell of your wondrous
    deeds.

a Or *loyal Syzygus*  b Or *Farewell*  c Gk *brothers*  d Gk *take account of*  e Gk *I rejoiced*  f Gk lacks *to show it*  g Other ancient authorities add *Amen*

2 At the set time that I appoint
    I will judge with equity.
3 When the earth totters, with all
        its inhabitants,
    it is I who keep its pillars
        steady.                    *Selah*
4 I say to the boastful, "Do not
        boast,"
    and to the wicked, "Do not
        lift up your horn;
5 do not lift up your horn on high,
    or speak with insolent neck."

6 For not from the east or from
        the west
    and not from the wilderness
        comes lifting up;
7 but it is God who executes
        judgment,
    putting down one and lifting
        up another.
8 For in the hand of the Lord
        there is a cup
    with foaming wine, well
        mixed;
    he will pour a draught from it,
        and all the wicked of the
        earth

shall drain it down to the
        dregs.
9 But I will rejoice[a] forever;
    I will sing praises to the God
        of Jacob.

10 All the horns of the wicked I
        will cut off,
    but the horns of the righteous
        shall be exalted.

## PROVERBS 24.17–20

Do not rejoice when your
        enemies fall,
    and do not let your heart be
        glad when they stumble,
18 or else the Lord will see it and
        be displeased,
    and turn away his anger
        from them.

19 Do not fret because of
        evildoers.
    Do not envy the wicked;
20 for the evil have no future;
    the lamp of the wicked will
        go out.

# OCTOBER 4

## JEREMIAH 2.31—4.18

And you, O generation, behold
        the word of the
        Lord![b]
Have I been a wilderness to
        Israel,
    or a land of thick darkness?
Why then do my people say,
        "We are free,
    we will come to you no
        more"?

32 Can a girl forget her ornaments,
    or a bride her attire?
Yet my people have forgotten
        me,
    days without number.

33 How well you direct your
        course
    to seek lovers!
So that even to wicked women
    you have taught your ways.

a Gk: Heb *declare*   b Meaning of Heb uncertain

34 Also on your skirts is found
   the lifeblood of the innocent
      poor,
   though you did not catch them
      breaking in.
   Yet in spite of all these
      things a
35 you say, "I am innocent;
   surely his anger has turned
      from me."
   Now I am bringing you to
      judgment
   for saying, "I have not
      sinned."
36 How lightly you gad about,
   changing your ways!
   You shall be put to shame
      by Egypt
   as you were put to shame
      by Assyria.
37 From there also you will
      come away
   with your hands on your
      head;
   for the Lord has rejected those
      in whom you trust,
   and you will not prosper
      through them.

3.1 If b a man divorces his wife
   and she goes from him
   and becomes another man's wife,
   will he return to her?
   Would not such a land be
      greatly polluted?
   You have played the whore with
      many lovers;
   and would you return to me?
                        says the Lord.
2  Look up to the bare heights, c
      and see!
   Where have you not been
      lain with?
   By the waysides you have sat
      waiting for lovers,
   like a nomad in the
      wilderness.
   You have polluted the land

   with your whoring and
      wickedness.
3  Therefore the showers have
      been withheld,
   and the spring rain has not
      come;
   yet you have the forehead of
      a whore,
   you refuse to be ashamed.
4  Have you not just now called to
      me,
   "My Father, you are the
      friend of my youth—
5  will he be angry forever,
   will he be indignant to the
      end?"
   This is how you have spoken,
   but you have done all the evil
      that you could.

6  The Lord said to me in the days
of King Josiah: Have you seen what she
did, that faithless one, Israel, how she
went up on every high hill and under
every green tree, and played the whore
there? 7And I thought, "After she has
done all this she will return to me"; but
she did not return, and her false sister
Judah saw it. 8She d saw that for all the
adulteries of that faithless one, Israel,
I had sent her away with a decree of
divorce; yet her false sister Judah did
not fear, but she too went and played
the whore. 9Because she took her
whoredom so lightly, she polluted the
land, committing adultery with stone
and tree. 10Yet for all this her false sister Judah did not return to me with her
whole heart, but only in pretense, says
the Lord.

11 Then the Lord said to me:
Faithless Israel has shown herself less
guilty than false Judah. 12Go, and proclaim these words toward the north,
and say:

   Return, faithless Israel,
                        says the Lord.
   I will not look on you in anger,

a Meaning of Heb uncertain   b Q Ms Gk Syr: MT *Saying, If*   c Or *the trails*   d Q Ms Gk Mss Syr:
MT *I*

for I am merciful,
   says the LORD;
I will not be angry forever.
13 Only acknowledge your guilt,
  that you have rebelled against
   the LORD your God,
 and scattered your favors
   among strangers under
    every green tree,
 and have not obeyed my
   voice,
    says the LORD.
14 Return, O faithless children,
   says the LORD,
 for I am your master;
 I will take you, one from a city
   and two from a family,
 and I will bring you to Zion.

15 I will give you shepherds after my own heart, who will feed you with knowledge and understanding. 16And when you have multiplied and increased in the land, in those days, says the LORD, they shall no longer say, "The ark of the covenant of the LORD." It shall not come to mind, or be remembered, or missed; nor shall another one be made. 17At that time Jerusalem shall be called the throne of the LORD, and all nations shall gather to it, to the presence of the LORD in Jerusalem, and they shall no longer stubbornly follow their own evil will. 18In those days the house of Judah shall join the house of Israel, and together they shall come from the land of the north to the land that I gave your ancestors for a heritage.

19 I thought
  how I would set you among
   my children,
 and give you a pleasant land,
  the most beautiful heritage of
   all the nations.
 And I thought you would call
  me, My Father,

 and would not turn from
  following me.
20 Instead, as a faithless wife
  leaves her husband,
 so you have been faithless to
  me, O house of Israel,
   says the LORD.

21 A voice on the bare heights[a]
  is heard,
 the plaintive weeping of
  Israel's children,
 because they have perverted
  their way,
 they have forgotten the LORD
  their God:
22 Return, O faithless children,
 I will heal your faithlessness.

"Here we come to you;
 for you are the LORD our
  God.
23 Truly the hills are[b] a delusion,
  the orgies on the mountains.
 Truly in the LORD our God
  is the salvation of Israel.
24 "But from our youth the shameful thing has devoured all for which our ancestors had labored, their flocks and their herds, their sons and their daughters. 25Let us lie down in our shame, and let our dishonor cover us; for we have sinned against the LORD our God, we and our ancestors, from our youth even to this day; and we have not obeyed the voice of the LORD our God."

4.1 IF you return, O Israel,
   says the LORD,
 if you return to me,
 if you remove your abominations
   from my presence,
  and do not waver,
2 and if you swear, "As the LORD
  lives!"
 in truth, in justice, and in
  uprightness,

aOr *the trails* bGk Syr Vg: Heb *Truly from the hills is*

then nations shall be blessed[a]
   by him,
  and by him they shall boast.
3  For thus says the Lord to the people of Judah and to the inhabitants of Jerusalem:
  Break up your fallow ground,
   and do not sow among
    thorns.
4  Circumcise yourselves to the
   Lord,
  remove the foreskin of your
   hearts,
   O people of Judah and
    inhabitants of Jerusalem,
  or else my wrath will go forth
   like fire,
  and burn with no one to
   quench it,
   because of the evil of your
    doings.

5  Declare in Judah, and proclaim in Jerusalem, and say:
  Blow the trumpet through the
   land;
   shout aloud[b] and say,
  "Gather together, and let us go
   into the fortified cities!"
6  Raise a standard toward Zion,
   flee for safety, do not delay,
  for I am bringing evil from the
   north,
   and a great destruction.
7  A lion has gone up from its
   thicket,
   a destroyer of nations has set
   out;
  he has gone out from his
   place
  to make your land a waste;
   your cities will be ruins
   without inhabitant.
8  Because of this put on
   sackcloth,
   lament and wail:
  "The fierce anger of the Lord

   has not turned away from
    us."

9On that day, says the Lord, courage shall fail the king and the officials; the priests shall be appalled and the prophets astounded. 10Then I said, "Ah, Lord God, how utterly you have deceived this people and Jerusalem, saying, 'It shall be well with you,' even while the sword is at the throat!"

11  At that time it will be said to this people and to Jerusalem: A hot wind comes from me out of the bare heights[c] in the desert toward my poor people, not to winnow or cleanse— 12a wind too strong for that. Now it is I who speak in judgment against them.
13  Look! He comes up like clouds,
   his chariots like the
    whirlwind;
  his horses are swifter than
   eagles—
   woe to us, for we are ruined!
14  O Jerusalem, wash your heart
   clean of wickedness
   so that you may be saved.
  How long shall your evil
   schemes
   lodge within you?
15  For a voice declares from Dan
   and proclaims disaster from
    Mount Ephraim.
16  Tell the nations, "Here they
   are!"
   Proclaim against Jerusalem,
  "Besiegers come from a distant
   land;
   they shout against the cities
    of Judah.
17  They have closed in around her
   like watchers of a field,
   because she has rebelled
    against me,
        says the Lord.
18  Your ways and your doings
   have brought this upon you.

---

a Or *shall bless themselves*  b Or *shout, take your weapons*: Heb *shout, fill* (your hand)  c Or *the trails*

This is your doom; how bitter it
    is!
It has reached your very
    heart."

## COLOSSIANS 1.1–20

**P**AUL, an apostle of Christ Jesus by the will of God, and Timothy our brother,

2 To the saints and faithful brothers and sisters[a] in Christ in Colossae:

Grace to you and peace from God our Father.

3 In our prayers for you we always thank God, the Father of our Lord Jesus Christ, [4]for we have heard of your faith in Christ Jesus and of the love that you have for all the saints, [5]because of the hope laid up for you in heaven. You have heard of this hope before in the word of the truth, the gospel [6]that has come to you. Just as it is bearing fruit and growing in the whole world, so it has been bearing fruit among yourselves from the day you heard it and truly comprehended the grace of God. [7]This you learned from Epaphras, our beloved fellow servant.[b] He is a faithful minister of Christ on your[c] behalf, [8]and he has made known to us your love in the Spirit.

9 For this reason, since the day we heard it, we have not ceased praying for you and asking that you may be filled with the knowledge of God's[d] will in all spiritual wisdom and understanding, [10]so that you may lead lives worthy of the Lord, fully pleasing to him, as you bear fruit in every good work and as you grow in the knowledge of God. [11]May you be made strong with all the strength that comes from his glorious power, and may you be prepared to endure everything with patience, while

joyfully [12]giving thanks to the Father, who has enabled[e] you[f] to share in the inheritance of the saints in the light. [13]He has rescued us from the power of darkness and transferred us into the kingdom of his beloved Son, [14]in whom we have redemption, the forgiveness of sins. [g]

15 He is the image of the invisible God, the firstborn of all creation; [16]for in[h] him all things in heaven and on earth were created, things visible and invisible, whether thrones or dominions or rulers or powers—all things have been created through him and for him. [17]He himself is before all things, and in[h] him all things hold together. [18]He is the head of the body, the church; he is the beginning, the firstborn from the dead, so that he might come to have first place in everything. [19]For in him all the fullness of God was pleased to dwell, [20]and through him God was pleased to reconcile to himself all things, whether on earth or in heaven, by making peace through the blood of his cross.

## PSALM 76. 1–12

*To the leader: with stringed instruments. A Psalm of Asaph. A Song.*

**I**N Judah God is known,
    his name is great in Israel.
2  His abode has been
      established in Salem,
    his dwelling place in Zion.
3  There he broke the flashing
      arrows,
    the shield, the sword, and the
      weapons of war.    *Selah*

4  Glorious are you, more majestic
    than the everlasting
      mountains. [i]
5  The stouthearted were stripped
    of their spoil;

a Gk *brothers*  b Gk *slave*  c Other ancient authorities read *our*  d Gk *his*  e Other ancient authorities read *called*  f Other ancient authorities read *us*  g Other ancient authorities add *through his blood*  h Or *by*  i Gk: Heb *the mountains of prey*

they sank into sleep;
   none of the troops
     was able to lift a hand.
6 At your rebuke, O God of
     Jacob,
   both rider and horse lay
     stunned.

7 But you indeed are awesome!
   Who can stand before you
   when once your anger is
     roused?
8 From the heavens you uttered
     judgment;
   the earth feared and was still
9 when God rose up to establish
     judgment,
   to save all the oppressed of
     the earth.    *Selah*

10 Human wrath serves only to
   praise you,

when you bind the last bit of
   your[a] wrath around you.
11 Make vows to the LORD your
     God, and perform them;
   let all who are around him
     bring gifts
   to the one who is awesome,
12 who cuts off the spirit of
     princes,
   who inspires fear in the kings
     of the earth.

## PROVERBS 24.21–22

**M**Y child, fear the LORD and
     the king,
   and do not disobey either
     of them;[b]
22 for disaster comes from them
     suddenly,
   and who knows the ruin that
     both can bring?

# OCTOBER 5

## JEREMIAH 4.19—6.15

**M**Y anguish, my anguish! I
     writhe in pain!
   Oh, the walls of my heart!
My heart is beating wildly;
   I cannot keep silent;
for I[c] hear the sound of the
     trumpet,
   the alarm of war.
20 Disaster overtakes disaster,
   the whole land is laid waste.
Suddenly my tents are
     destroyed,
   my curtains in a moment.
21 How long must I see the
     standard,

   and hear the sound of the
     trumpet?
22 "For my people are foolish,
   they do not know me;
they are stupid children,
   they have no understanding.
They are skilled in doing evil,
   but do not know how to do
     good."

23 I looked on the earth, and lo, it
     was waste and void;
   and to the heavens, and they
     had no light.
24 I looked on the mountains, and
     lo, they were quaking,

---

a Heb lacks *your*  b Gk: Heb *do not associate with those who change*  c Another reading is *for you,
O my soul,*

and all the hills moved to
    and fro.
25 I looked, and lo, there was no
    one at all,
  and all the birds of the air
    had fled.
26 I looked, and lo, the fruitful land
    was a desert,
  and all its cities were laid in
    ruins
  before the Lord, before his
    fierce anger.

27 For thus says the Lord: The whole land shall be a desolation; yet I will not make a full end.
28 Because of this the earth shall
    mourn,
  and the heavens above grow
    black;
  for I have spoken, I have
    purposed;
  I have not relented nor will I
    turn back.

29 At the noise of horseman and
    archer
  every town takes to flight;
  they enter thickets; they climb
    among rocks;
  all the towns are forsaken,
  and no one lives in them.
30 And you, O desolate one,
  what do you mean that you
    dress in crimson,
  that you deck yourself with
    ornaments of gold,
  that you enlarge your eyes
    with paint?
  In vain you beautify yourself.
  Your lovers despise you;
  they seek your life.
31 For I heard a cry as of a woman
    in labor,
  anguish as of one bringing
    forth her first child,
  the cry of daughter Zion gasping
    for breath,
  stretching out her hands,

  "Woe is me! I am fainting
    before killers!"

5.1 Run to and fro through the
    streets of Jerusalem,
  look around and take note!
  Search its squares and see
    if you can find one person
  who acts justly
    and seeks truth—
  so that I may pardon
    Jerusalem. [a]
2 Although they say, "As the
    Lord lives,"
  yet they swear falsely.
3 O Lord, do your eyes not look
    for truth?
  You have struck them,
    but they felt no anguish;
  you have consumed them,
    but they refused to take
    correction.
  They have made their faces
    harder than rock;
    they have refused to turn
    back.

4 Then I said, "These are only
    the poor,
    they have no sense;
  for they do not know the way of
    the Lord,
    the law of their God.
5 Let me go to the rich [b]
    and speak to them;
  surely they know the way of
    the Lord,
    the law of their God."
  But they all alike had broken
    the yoke,
    they had burst the bonds.

6 Therefore a lion from the forest
    shall kill them,
  a wolf from the desert shall
    destroy them.
  A leopard is watching against
    their cities;

a Heb *it*  b Or *the great*

everyone who goes out of
   them shall be torn in
   pieces—
because their transgressions
   are many,
   their apostasies are great.

7 How can I pardon you?
   Your children have forsaken
      me,
   and have sworn by those who
      are no gods.
When I fed them to the full,
   they committed adultery
   and trooped to the houses of
      prostitutes.
8 They were well-fed lusty
      stallions,
   each neighing for his
      neighbor's wife.
9 Shall I not punish them for
      these things?
         says the Lord;
   and shall I not bring
      retribution
   on a nation such as this?

10 Go up through her vine-rows
      and destroy,
   but do not make a full end;
strip away her branches,
   for they are not the Lord's.
11 For the house of Israel and the
      house of Judah
   have been utterly faithless to
      me,
         says the Lord.
12 They have spoken falsely of
      the Lord,
   and have said, "He will do
      nothing.
No evil will come upon us,
   and we shall not see sword or
      famine."
13 The prophets are nothing but
      wind,
   for the word is not in them.
Thus shall it be done to them!

14 Therefore thus says the Lord,
      the God of hosts:
Because they**a** have spoken
      this word,
I am now making my words in
      your mouth a fire,
   and this people wood, and the
      fire shall devour them.
15 I am going to bring upon you
   a nation from far away,
      O house of Israel,
         says the Lord.
It is an enduring nation,
   it is an ancient nation,
a nation whose language you do
      not know,
   nor can you understand what
      they say.
16 Their quiver is like an open
      tomb;
   all of them are mighty
      warriors.
17 They shall eat up your harvest
      and your food;
   they shall eat up your sons
      and your daughters;
they shall eat up your flocks and
      your herds;
   they shall eat up your vines
      and your fig trees;
they shall destroy with the
      sword
   your fortified cities in which
      you trust.

18 But even in those days, says the
Lord, I will not make a full end of you.
19 And when your people say, "Why has
the Lord our God done all these things
to us?" you shall say to them, "As you
have forsaken me and served foreign
gods in your land, so you shall serve
strangers in a land that is not yours."

20 Declare this in the house of
      Jacob,
   proclaim it in Judah:

a Heb *you*

21 Hear this, O foolish and
     senseless people,
  who have eyes, but do not
     see,
  who have ears, but do not
     hear.
22 Do you not fear me? says the
     LORD;
  Do you not tremble before
     me?
  I placed the sand as a boundary
     for the sea,
  a perpetual barrier that it
     cannot pass;
  though the waves toss, they
     cannot prevail,
  though they roar, they cannot
     pass over it.
23 But this people has a stubborn
     and rebellious heart;
  they have turned aside and
     gone away.
24 They do not say in their hearts,
  "Let us fear the LORD our
     God,
  who gives the rain in its season,
     the autumn rain and the
     spring rain,
  and keeps for us
     the weeks appointed for the
     harvest."
25 Your iniquities have turned
     these away,
  and your sins have deprived
     you of good.
26 For scoundrels are found among
     my people;
  they take over the goods of
     others.
  Like fowlers they set a trap; a
  they catch human beings.
27 Like a cage full of birds,
  their houses are full of
     treachery;
  therefore they have become
     great and rich,
28   they have grown fat and
     sleek.

They know no limits in deeds of
     wickedness;
  they do not judge with justice
  the cause of the orphan, to
     make it prosper,
  and they do not defend the
     rights of the needy.
29 Shall I not punish them for
     these things?
          says the LORD,
  and shall I not bring
     retribution
  on a nation such as this?

30 An appalling and horrible thing
     has happened in the land:
31 the prophets prophesy falsely,
     and the priests rule as the
     prophets direct; b
  my people love to have it so,
     but what will you do when the
     end comes?

6.1 FLEE for safety, O children of
     Benjamin,
  from the midst of Jerusalem!
  Blow the trumpet in Tekoa,
     and raise a signal on
     Beth-haccherem;
  for evil looms out of the north,
     and great destruction.
2 I have likened daughter Zion
     to the loveliest pasture. c
3 Shepherds with their flocks shall
     come against her.
  They shall pitch their tents
     around her;
     they shall pasture, all in
     their places.
4 "Prepare war against her;
  up, and let us attack at
     noon!"
  "Woe to us, for the day
     declines,
  the shadows of evening
     lengthen!"
5 "Up, and let us attack by night,
     and destroy her palaces!"

aMeaning of Heb uncertain   bOr *rule by their own authority*   cOr *I will destroy daughter Zion, the
loveliest pasture*

6 For thus says the LORD of
    hosts:
  Cut down her trees;
    cast up a siege ramp against
      Jerusalem.
  This is the city that must be
    punished; a
    there is nothing but
      oppression within her.
7 As a well keeps its water fresh,
    so she keeps fresh her
      wickedness;
  violence and destruction are
    heard within her;
    sickness and wounds are ever
      before me.
8 Take warning, O Jerusalem,
    or I shall turn from you in
      disgust,
  and make you a desolation,
    an uninhabited land.

9 Thus says the LORD of hosts:
  Glean b thoroughly as a vine
    the remnant of Israel;
  like a grape-gatherer, pass your
      hand again
    over its branches.

10 To whom shall I speak and give
      warning,
    that they may hear?
  See, their ears are closed, c
    they cannot listen.
  The word of the LORD is to
      them an object of scorn;
    they take no pleasure in it.
11 But I am full of the wrath of
      the LORD;
    I am weary of holding it in.

  Pour it out on the children in
      the street,
    and on the gatherings of
      young men as well;
  both husband and wife shall
      be taken,

the old folk and the very
    aged.
12 Their houses shall be turned
      over to others,
    their fields and wives
      together;
  for I will stretch out my hand
    against the inhabitants of
      the land,
                    says the LORD.

13 For from the least to the
      greatest of them,
    everyone is greedy for unjust
      gain;
  and from prophet to priest,
    everyone deals falsely.
14 They have treated the wound of
      my people carelessly,
    saying, "Peace, peace,"
    when there is no peace.
15 They acted shamefully, they
      committed abomination;
    yet they were not ashamed,
    they did not know how to
      blush.
  Therefore they shall fall among
      those who fall;
    at the time that I punish
      them, they shall be
      overthrown,
                    says the LORD.

# COLOSSIANS 1.21—2.7

AND you who were once es-
tranged and hostile in mind, doing evil deeds, 22he has now
reconciled d in his fleshly body e
through death, so as to present you
holy and blameless and irreproachable
before him— 23provided that you continue securely established and steadfast in the faith, without shifting from
the hope promised by the gospel that
you heard, which has been proclaimed
to every creature under heaven. I,
Paul, became a servant of this gospel.

a Or *the city of license*  b Cn: Heb *They shall glean*  c Heb *are uncircumcised*  d Other ancient
authorities read *you have now been reconciled*  e Gk *in the body of his flesh*

24 I am now rejoicing in my sufferings for your sake, and in my flesh I am completing what is lacking in Christ's afflictions for the sake of his body, that is, the church. 25I became its servant according to God's commission that was given to me for you, to make the word of God fully known, 26the mystery that has been hidden throughout the ages and generations but has now been revealed to his saints. 27To them God chose to make known how great among the Gentiles are the riches of the glory of this mystery, which is Christ in you, the hope of glory. 28It is he whom we proclaim, warning everyone and teaching everyone in all wisdom, so that we may present everyone mature in Christ. 29For this I toil and struggle with all the energy that he powerfully inspires within me.

2.1 FOR I want you to know how much I am struggling for you, and for those in Laodicea, and for all who have not seen me face to face. 2I want their hearts to be encouraged and united in love, so that they may have all the riches of assured understanding and have the knowledge of God's mystery, that is, Christ himself, a 3in whom are hidden all the treasures of wisdom and knowledge. 4I am saying this so that no one may deceive you with plausible arguments. 5For though I am absent in body, yet I am with you in spirit, and I rejoice to see your morale and the firmness of your faith in Christ.

6 As you therefore have received Christ Jesus the Lord, continue to live your lives b in him, 7rooted and built up in him and established in the faith, just as you were taught, abounding in thanksgiving.

## PSALM 77.1–20

*To the leader: according to Jeduthun. Of Asaph. A Psalm.*

I CRY aloud to God,
    aloud to God, that he may
      hear me.
2 In the day of my trouble I seek
    the Lord;
  in the night my hand is
    stretched out without
    wearying;
  my soul refuses to be
    comforted.
3 I think of God, and I moan;
  I meditate, and my spirit
    faints.     *Selah*

4 You keep my eyelids from
    closing;
  I am so troubled that I cannot
    speak.
5 I consider the days of old,
  and remember the years of
    long ago.
6 I commune c with my heart in
    the night;
  I meditate and search my
    spirit: d
7 "Will the Lord spurn forever,
  and never again be favorable?
8 Has his steadfast love ceased
    forever?
  Are his promises at an end
    for all time?
9 Has God forgotten to be
    gracious?
  Has he in anger shut up his
    compassion?"     *Selah*
10 And I say, "It is my grief
  that the right hand of the
    Most High has changed."

11 I will call to mind the deeds of
    the LORD;
  I will remember your
    wonders of old.

---

aOther ancient authorities read *of the mystery of God, both of the Father and of Christ*   bGk *to walk* cGk Syr: Heb *My music*   dSyr Jerome: Heb *my spirit searches*

12 I will meditate on all your work,
  and muse on your mighty
    deeds.
13 Your way, O God, is holy.
  What god is so great as our
    God?
14 You are the God who works
      wonders;
  you have displayed your
    might among the
      peoples.
15 With your strong arm you
      redeemed your people,
  the descendants of Jacob and
    Joseph.            *Selah*

16 When the waters saw you,
    O God,
  when the waters saw you,
    they were afraid;
  the very deep trembled.
17 The clouds poured out water;
  the skies thundered;
  your arrows flashed on every
    side.
18 The crash of your thunder was
    in the whirlwind;
  your lightnings lit up the
    world;
  the earth trembled and shook.
19 Your way was through the sea,
  your path, through the mighty
    waters;
  yet your footprints were
    unseen.
20 You led your people like a flock
  by the hand of Moses and
    Aaron.

## PROVERBS 24.23–25

THESE also are sayings of
the wise:

Partiality in judging is not good.
24 Whoever says to the wicked,
  "You are innocent,"
  will be cursed by peoples,
    abhorred by nations;
25 but those who rebuke the
      wicked will have delight,
  and a good blessing will come
    upon them.

# OCTOBER 6

## JEREMIAH 6.16—8.7

THUS says the LORD:
  Stand at the crossroads, and
    look,
  and ask for the ancient paths,
  where the good way lies; and
    walk in it,
  and find rest for your souls.
  But they said, "We will not walk
    in it."
17 Also I raised up sentinels for
    you:
  "Give heed to the sound of
    the trumpet!"
  But they said, "We will not give
    heed."
18 Therefore hear, O nations,
  and know, O congregation,
    what will happen to
    them.
19 Hear, O earth; I am going to
    bring disaster on this
    people,
  the fruit of their schemes,

because they have not given
    heed to my words;
and as for my teaching, they
    have rejected it.
20 Of what use to me is
    frankincense that comes
    from Sheba,
    or sweet cane from a distant
    land?
Your burnt offerings are not
    acceptable,
    nor are your sacrifices
    pleasing to me.
21 Therefore thus says the Lord:
See, I am laying before this
    people
    stumbling blocks against
    which they shall stumble;
parents and children together,
    neighbor and friend shall
    perish.

22 Thus says the Lord:
See, a people is coming from
    the land of the north,
    a great nation is stirring from
    the farthest parts of the
    earth.
23 They grasp the bow and the
    javelin,
    they are cruel and have no
    mercy,
    their sound is like the roaring
    sea;
they ride on horses,
    equipped like a warrior for
    battle,
    against you, O daughter Zion!

24 "We have heard news of them,
    our hands fall helpless;
anguish has taken hold of us,
    pain as of a woman in labor.
25 Do not go out into the field,
    or walk on the road;
for the enemy has a sword,
    terror is on every side."

26 O my poor people, put on
    sackcloth,
    and roll in ashes;
make mourning as for an
    only child,
    most bitter lamentation:
for suddenly the destroyer
    will come upon us.

27 I have made you a tester and a
    refiner[a] among my
    people
    so that you may know and
    test their ways.
28 They are all stubbornly
    rebellious,
    going about with slanders;
they are bronze and iron,
    all of them act corruptly.
29 The bellows blow fiercely,
    the lead is consumed by the
    fire;
in vain the refining goes on,
    for the wicked are not
    removed.
30 They are called "rejected
    silver,"
    for the Lord has rejected
    them.

7.1 The word that came to Jeremiah from the Lord: 2Stand in the gate of the Lord's house, and proclaim there this word, and say, Hear the word of the Lord, all you people of Judah, you that enter these gates to worship the Lord. 3Thus says the Lord of hosts, the God of Israel: Amend your ways and your doings, and let me dwell with you[b] in this place. 4Do not trust in these deceptive words: "This is[c] the temple of the Lord, the temple of the Lord, the temple of the Lord."

5 For if you truly amend your ways and your doings, if you truly act justly one with another, 6if you do not oppress the alien, the orphan, and the

widow, or shed innocent blood in this place, and if you do not go after other gods to your own hurt, [7]then I will dwell with you in this place, in the land that I gave of old to your ancestors forever and ever.

8  Here you are, trusting in deceptive words to no avail. [9]Will you steal, murder, commit adultery, swear falsely, make offerings to Baal, and go after other gods that you have not known, [10]and then come and stand before me in this house, which is called by my name, and say, "We are safe!"— only to go on doing all these abominations? [11]Has this house, which is called by my name, become a den of robbers in your sight? You know, I too am watching, says the LORD. [12]Go now to my place that was in Shiloh, where I made my name dwell at first, and see what I did to it for the wickedness of my people Israel. [13]And now, because you have done all these things, says the LORD, and when I spoke to you persistently, you did not listen, and when I called you, you did not answer, [14]therefore I will do to the house that is called by my name, in which you trust, and to the place that I gave to you and to your ancestors, just what I did to Shiloh. [15]And I will cast you out of my sight, just as I cast out all your kinsfolk, all the offspring of Ephraim.

16  As for you, do not pray for this people, do not raise a cry or prayer on their behalf, and do not intercede with me, for I will not hear you. [17]Do you not see what they are doing in the towns of Judah and in the streets of Jerusalem? [18]The children gather wood, the fathers kindle fire, and the women knead dough, to make cakes for the queen of heaven; and they pour out drink offerings to other gods, to provoke me to anger. [19]Is it I whom they provoke? says the LORD. Is it not themselves, to their own hurt? [20]Therefore thus says the Lord GOD: My anger and my wrath shall be poured out on this place, on human beings and animals, on the trees of the field and the fruit of the ground; it will burn and not be quenched.

21  Thus says the LORD of hosts, the God of Israel: Add your burnt offerings to your sacrifices, and eat the flesh. [22]For in the day that I brought your ancestors out of the land of Egypt, I did not speak to them or command them concerning burnt offerings and sacrifices. [23]But this command I gave them, "Obey my voice, and I will be your God, and you shall be my people; and walk only in the way that I command you, so that it may be well with you." [24]Yet they did not obey or incline their ear, but, in the stubbornness of their evil will, they walked in their own counsels, and looked backward rather than forward. [25]From the day that your ancestors came out of the land of Egypt until this day, I have persistently sent all my servants the prophets to them, day after day; [26]yet they did not listen to me, or pay attention, but they stiffened their necks. They did worse than their ancestors did.

27  So you shall speak all these words to them, but they will not listen to you. You shall call to them, but they will not answer you. [28]You shall say to them: This is the nation that did not obey the voice of the LORD their God, and did not accept discipline; truth has perished; it is cut off from their lips.

29  Cut off your hair and throw
      it away;
    raise a lamentation on the
        bare heights, [a]
  for the LORD has rejected and
      forsaken
    the generation that provoked
        his wrath.

30  For the people of Judah have done evil in my sight, says the LORD; they have set their abominations in the

a Or *the trails*

house that is called by my name, defiling it. ³¹And they go on building the high place ᵃ of Topheth, which is in the valley of the son of Hinnom, to burn their sons and their daughters in the fire—which I did not command, nor did it come into my mind. ³²Therefore, the days are surely coming, says the LORD, when it will no more be called Topheth, or the valley of the son of Hinnom, but the valley of Slaughter: for they will bury in Topheth until there is no more room. ³³The corpses of this people will be food for the birds of the air, and for the animals of the earth; and no one will frighten them away. ³⁴And I will bring to an end the sound of mirth and gladness, the voice of the bride and bridegroom in the cities of Judah and in the streets of Jerusalem; for the land shall become a waste.

8.1 AT that time, says the LORD, the bones of the kings of Judah, the bones of its officials, the bones of the priests, the bones of the prophets, and the bones of the inhabitants of Jerusalem shall be brought out of their tombs; ²and they shall be spread before the sun and the moon and all the host of heaven, which they have loved and served, which they have followed, and which they have inquired of and worshiped; and they shall not be gathered or buried; they shall be like dung on the surface of the ground. ³Death shall be preferred to life by all the remnant that remains of this evil family in all the places where I have driven them, says the LORD of hosts.

4  You shall say to them, Thus
        says the LORD:
    When people fall, do they not
        get up again?
    If they go astray, do they not
        turn back?

5  Why then has this people ᵇ
        turned away
    in perpetual backsliding?
    They have held fast to deceit,
        they have refused to return.
6  I have given heed and listened,
        but they do not speak
            honestly;
    no one repents of wickedness,
        saying, "What have I done!"
    All of them turn to their own
            course,
        like a horse plunging headlong
            into battle.
7  Even the stork in the heavens
        knows its times;
    and the turtledove, swallow, and
            crane ᶜ
        observe the time of their
            coming;
    but my people do not know
        the ordinance of the LORD.

## COLOSSIANS 2.8–23

SEE to it that no one takes you captive through philosophy and empty deceit, according to human tradition, according to the elemental spirits of the universe, ᵈ and not according to Christ. ⁹For in him the whole fullness of deity dwells bodily, ¹⁰and you have come to fullness in him, who is the head of every ruler and authority. ¹¹In him also you were circumcised with a spiritual circumcision, ᵉ by putting off the body of the flesh in the circumcision of Christ; ¹²when you were buried with him in baptism, you were also raised with him through faith in the power of God, who raised him from the dead. ¹³And when you were dead in trespasses and the uncircumcision of your flesh, God ᶠ made you ᵍ alive together with him, when he forgave us all our trespasses, ¹⁴erasing the record that stood against us with its

ᵃGk Tg: Heb *high places*   ᵇOne Ms Gk: MT *this people, Jerusalem,*   ᶜMeaning of Heb uncertain
ᵈOr *the rudiments of the world*   ᵉGk *a circumcision made without hands*   ᶠGk *he*   ᵍOther ancient
authorities read *made us*; others, *made*

legal demands. He set this aside, nailing it to the cross. [15]He disarmed[a] the rulers and authorities and made a public example of them, triumphing over them in it.

16 Therefore do not let anyone condemn you in matters of food and drink or of observing festivals, new moons, or sabbaths. [17]These are only a shadow of what is to come, but the substance belongs to Christ. [18]Do not let anyone disqualify you, insisting on self-abasement and worship of angels, dwelling[b] on visions,[c] puffed up without cause by a human way of thinking,[d] [19]and not holding fast to the head, from whom the whole body, nourished and held together by its ligaments and sinews, grows with a growth that is from God.

20 If with Christ you died to the elemental spirits of the universe,[e] why do you live as if you still belonged to the world? Why do you submit to regulations, [21]"Do not handle, Do not taste, Do not touch"? [22]All these regulations refer to things that perish with use; they are simply human commands and teachings. [23]These have indeed an appearance of wisdom in promoting self-imposed piety, humility, and severe treatment of the body, but they are of no value in checking self-indulgence.[f]

# PSALM 78.1–31

*A Maskil of Asaph.*

GIVE ear, O my people, to my
    teaching;
  incline your ears to the
    words of my mouth.
2 I will open my mouth in a
    parable;
  I will utter dark sayings from
    of old,
3 things that we have heard and
    known,

that our ancestors have told
  us.
4 We will not hide them from
    their children;
  we will tell to the coming
    generation
the glorious deeds of the LORD,
    and his might,
  and the wonders that he has
    done.

5 He established a decree in
    Jacob,
  and appointed a law in Israel,
which he commanded our
    ancestors
  to teach to their children;
6 that the next generation might
    know them,
  the children yet unborn,
and rise up and tell them to
    their children,
7   so that they should set their
    hope in God,
  and not forget the works of
    God,
  but keep his commandments;
8 and that they should not be like
    their ancestors,
  a stubborn and rebellious
    generation,
a generation whose heart was
    not steadfast,
  whose spirit was not faithful
    to God.

9 The Ephraimites, armed with[g]
    the bow,
  turned back on the day of
    battle.
10 They did not keep God's
    covenant,
  but refused to walk according
    to his law.
11 They forgot what he had done,
  and the miracles that he had
    shown them.

12 In the sight of their ancestors
      he worked marvels
   in the land of Egypt, in the
      fields of Zoan.
13 He divided the sea and let them
      pass through it,
   and made the waters stand
      like a heap.
14 In the daytime he led them with
      a cloud,
   and all night long with a fiery
      light.
15 He split rocks open in the
      wilderness,
   and gave them drink
      abundantly as from the
      deep.
16 He made streams come out of
      the rock,
   and caused waters to flow
      down like rivers.

17 Yet they sinned still more
      against him,
   rebelling against the Most
      High in the desert.
18 They tested God in their heart
   by demanding the food they
      craved.
19 They spoke against God,
      saying,
   "Can God spread a table in
      the wilderness?
20 Even though he struck the rock
      so that water gushed out
   and torrents overflowed,
   can he also give bread,
      or provide meat for his
      people?"

21 Therefore, when the Lord
      heard, he was full of
      rage;
   a fire was kindled against
      Jacob,
   his anger mounted against
      Israel,

22 because they had no faith in
      God,
   and did not trust his saving
      power.
23 Yet he commanded the skies
      above,
   and opened the doors of
      heaven;
24 he rained down on them manna
      to eat,
   and gave them the grain of
      heaven.
25 Mortals ate of the bread of
      angels;
   he sent them food in
      abundance.
26 He caused the east wind to
      blow in the heavens,
   and by his power he led out
      the south wind;
27 he rained flesh upon them like
      dust,
   winged birds like the sand of
      the seas;
28 he let them fall within their
      camp,
   all around their dwellings.
29 And they ate and were well
      filled,
   for he gave them what they
      craved.
30 But before they had satisfied
      their craving,
   while the food was still in
      their mouths,
31 the anger of God rose against
      them
   and he killed the strongest of
      them,
   and laid low the flower of
      Israel.


# PROVERBS 24.26

One who gives an honest
      answer
gives a kiss on the lips.

# OCTOBER 7

JEREMIAH 8.8—9.26

**H**ow can you say, "We are
            wise,
and the law of the Lord is
            with us,"
    when, in fact, the false pen of
            the scribes
        has made it into a lie?
9   The wise shall be put to shame,
        they shall be dismayed and
            taken;
    since they have rejected the
            word of the Lord,
        what wisdom is in them?
10  Therefore I will give their wives
            to others
        and their fields to conquerors,
    because from the least to the
            greatest
        everyone is greedy for unjust
            gain;
    from prophet to priest
        everyone deals falsely.
11  They have treated the wound of
            my people carelessly,
        saying, "Peace, peace,"
    when there is no peace.
12  They acted shamefully, they
            committed abomination;
        yet they were not at all
            ashamed,
        they did not know how to
            blush.
    Therefore they shall fall among
            those who fall;
        at the time when I punish
            them, they shall be
            overthrown,
                        says the Lord.
13  When I wanted to gather them,
            says the Lord,
        there are<sup>a</sup> no grapes on the
            vine,

nor figs on the fig tree;
    even the leaves are withered,
        and what I gave them has
            passed away from
            them. <sup>b</sup>

14  Why do we sit still?
    Gather together, let us go into
            the fortified cities
        and perish there;
    for the Lord our God has
            doomed us to perish,
        and has given us poisoned
            water to drink,
    because we have sinned
            against the Lord.
15  We look for peace, but find no
            good,
        for a time of healing, but
            there is terror instead.

16  The snorting of their horses is
            heard from Dan;
        at the sound of the neighing
            of their stallions
        the whole land quakes.
    They come and devour the land
            and all that fills it,
        the city and those who live in
            it.
17  See, I am letting snakes loose
            among you,
        adders that cannot be
            charmed,
        and they shall bite you,
                        says the Lord.

18  My joy is gone, grief is upon
            me,
        my heart is sick.
19  Hark, the cry of my poor people
        from far and wide in the land:
    "Is the Lord not in Zion?

---

<sup>a</sup>Or *I will make an end of them, says the Lord. There are*   <sup>b</sup>Meaning of Heb uncertain

Is her King not in her?"
("Why have they provoked me
to anger with their
images,
with their foreign idols?")
20 "The harvest is past, the
summer is ended,
and we are not saved."
21 For the hurt of my poor people
I am hurt,
I mourn, and dismay has
taken hold of me.

22 Is there no balm in Gilead?
Is there no physician there?
Why then has the health of my
poor people
not been restored?


9a.1 O THAT my head were a
spring of water,
and my eyes a fountain of
tears,
so that I might weep day and
night
for the slain of my poor
people!
2b O that I had in the desert
a traveler's lodging place,
that I might leave my people
and go away from them!
For they are all adulterers,
a band of traitors.
3 They bend their tongues like
bows;
they have grown strong in the
land for falsehood, and
not for truth;
for they proceed from evil to
evil,
and they do not know me,
says the LORD.

4 Beware of your neighbors,
and put no trust in any of
your kin; c

for all your kin d are
supplanters,
and every neighbor goes
around like a slanderer.
5 They all deceive their
neighbors,
and no one speaks the truth;
they have taught their tongues
to speak lies;
they commit iniquity and are
too weary to repent. e
6 Oppression upon oppression,
deceit f upon deceit!
They refuse to know me,
says the LORD.

7 Therefore thus says the LORD of
hosts:
I will now refine and test them,
for what else can I do with
my sinful people? g
8 Their tongue is a deadly arrow;
it speaks deceit through the
mouth.
They all speak friendly words to
their neighbors,
but inwardly are planning to
lay an ambush.
9 Shall I not punish them for
these things? says the
LORD;
and shall I not bring
retribution
on a nation such as this?

10 Take up h weeping and wailing
for the mountains,
and a lamentation for the
pastures of the
wilderness,
because they are laid waste so
that no one passes
through,
and the lowing of cattle is not
heard;
both the birds of the air and the
animals

a Ch 8.23 in Heb   b Ch 9.1 in Heb   c Heb *in a brother*   d Heb *for every brother*   e Cn Compare Gk:
Heb *they weary themselves with iniquity. 6 Your dwelling*   f Cn: Heb *Your dwelling in the midst of
deceit*   g Or *my poor people*   h Gk Syr: Heb *I will take up*

have fled and are gone.
11  I will make Jerusalem a heap
        of ruins,
    a lair of jackals;
    and I will make the towns of
        Judah a desolation,
      without inhabitant.

12  Who is wise enough to understand this? To whom has the mouth of the LORD spoken, so that they may declare it? Why is the land ruined and laid waste like a wilderness, so that no one passes through? 13And the LORD says: Because they have forsaken my law that I set before them, and have not obeyed my voice, or walked in accordance with it, 14but have stubbornly followed their own hearts and have gone after the Baals, as their ancestors taught them. 15Therefore thus says the LORD of hosts, the God of Israel: I am feeding this people with wormwood, and giving them poisonous water to drink. 16I will scatter them among nations that neither they nor their ancestors have known; and I will send the sword after them, until I have consumed them.

17  Thus says the LORD of hosts:
    Consider, and call for the
        mourning women to
        come;
      send for the skilled women
        to come;
18  let them quickly raise a dirge
        over us,
    so that our eyes may run
        down with tears,
    and our eyelids flow with
        water.
19  For a sound of wailing is heard
        from Zion:
    "How we are ruined!
    We are utterly shamed,
    because we have left the land,
      because they have cast down
        our dwellings."

20  Hear, O women, the word of
        the LORD,
    and let your ears receive the
        word of his mouth;
    teach to your daughters a dirge,
      and each to her neighbor
        a lament.
21  "Death has come up into our
        windows,
      it has entered our palaces,
    to cut off the children from
        the streets
      and the young men from
        the squares."
22  Speak! Thus says the LORD:
    "Human corpses shall fall
      like dung upon the open field,
    like sheaves behind the reaper,
      and no one shall gather
        them."

23  Thus says the LORD: Do not let the wise boast in their wisdom, do not let the mighty boast in their might, do not let the wealthy boast in their wealth; 24but let those who boast boast in this, that they understand and know me, that I am the LORD; I act with steadfast love, justice, and righteousness in the earth, for in these things I delight, says the LORD.
25  The days are surely coming, says the LORD, when I will attend to all those who are circumcised only in the foreskin: 26Egypt, Judah, Edom, the Ammonites, Moab, and all those with shaven temples who live in the desert. For all these nations are uncircumcised, and all the house of Israel is uncircumcised in heart.

# COLOSSIANS 3.1–17

So if you have been raised with Christ, seek the things that are above, where Christ is, seated at the right hand of God. 2Set your minds on things that are above, not on things that are on earth, 3for you have died, and your life is hidden with Christ in God. [4]When Christ who is your[a] life is revealed, then you also will be revealed with him in glory.

5 Put to death, therefore, whatever in you is earthly: fornication, impurity, passion, evil desire, and greed (which is idolatry). [6]On account of these the wrath of God is coming on those who are disobedient.[b] [7]These are the ways you also once followed, when you were living that life.[c] [8]But now you must get rid of all such things—anger, wrath, malice, slander, and abusive[d] language from your mouth. [9]Do not lie to one another, seeing that you have stripped off the old self with its practices [10]and have clothed yourselves with the new self, which is being renewed in knowledge according to the image of its creator. [11]In that renewal[e] there is no longer Greek and Jew, circumcised and uncircumcised, barbarian, Scythian, slave and free; but Christ is all and in all!

12 As God's chosen ones, holy and beloved, clothe yourselves with compassion, kindness, humility, meekness, and patience. [13]Bear with one another and, if anyone has a complaint against another, forgive each other; just as the Lord[f] has forgiven you, so you also must forgive. [14]Above all, clothe yourselves with love, which binds everything together in perfect harmony. [15]And let the peace of Christ rule in your hearts, to which indeed you were called in the one body. And be thankful. [16]Let the word of Christ[g] dwell in you richly; teach and admonish one another in all wisdom; and with gratitude in your hearts sing psalms, hymns, and spiritual songs to God.[h] [17]And whatever you do, in word or deed, do everything in the name of the Lord Jesus, giving thanks to God the Father through him.

## PSALM 78.32–55

IN spite of all this they still
    sinned;
  they did not believe in his
    wonders.
33 So he made their days vanish
    like a breath,
  and their years in terror.
34 When he killed them, they
    sought for him;
  they repented and sought
    God earnestly.
35 They remembered that God was
    their rock,
  the Most High God their
    redeemer.
36 But they flattered him with their
    mouths;
  they lied to him with their
    tongues.
37 Their heart was not steadfast
    toward him;
  they were not true to his
    covenant.
38 Yet he, being compassionate,
    forgave their iniquity,
  and did not destroy them;
often he restrained his anger,
    and did not stir up all his
    wrath.
39 He remembered that they were
    but flesh,
  a wind that passes and does
    not come again.
40 How often they rebelled against
    him in the wilderness
  and grieved him in the desert!
41 They tested God again and
    again,
  and provoked the Holy One of
    Israel.
42 They did not keep in mind his
    power,
  or the day when he redeemed
    them from the foe;

a Other authorities read *our*   b Other ancient authorities lack *on those who are disobedient* (Gk *the children of disobedience*)   c Or *living among such people*   d Or *filthy*   e Gk *its creator, 11 where*   f Other ancient authorities read *just as Christ*   g Other ancient authorities read *of God,* or *of the Lord*   h Other ancient authorities read *to the Lord*

43 when he displayed his signs in
     Egypt,
   and his miracles in the fields
     of Zoan.
44 He turned their rivers to blood,
     so that they could not drink of
     their streams.
45 He sent among them swarms of
     flies, which devoured
     them,
   and frogs, which destroyed
     them.
46 He gave their crops to the
     caterpillar,
   and the fruit of their labor to
     the locust.
47 He destroyed their vines with
     hail,
   and their sycamores with
     frost.
48 He gave over their cattle to the
     hail,
   and their flocks to
     thunderbolts.
49 He let loose on them his fierce
     anger,
   wrath, indignation, and
     distress,
   a company of destroying
     angels.
50 He made a path for his anger;
   he did not spare them from
     death,

but gave their lives over to
   the plague.
51 He struck all the firstborn in
     Egypt,
   the first issue of their
     strength in the tents of
     Ham.
52 Then he led out his people like
     sheep,
   and guided them in the
     wilderness like a flock.
53 He led them in safety, so that
     they were not afraid;
   but the sea overwhelmed
     their enemies.
54 And he brought them to his holy
     hill,
   to the mountain that his right
     hand had won.
55 He drove out nations before
     them;
   he apportioned them for a
     possession
   and settled the tribes of Israel
     in their tents.

## PROVERBS 24.27

PREPARE your work outside,
   get everything ready for you
     in the field;
   and after that build your
     house.

# OCTOBER 8



Hᴇᴀʀ the word that the Lᴏʀᴅ speaks to you, O house of Is- rael. ²Thus says the Lᴏʀᴅ:
Do not learn the way of the
nations,
or be dismayed at the signs of
the heavens;
for the nations are dismayed
at them.
3 For the customs of the peoples
are false:
a tree from the forest is cut
down,
and worked with an ax by the
hands of an artisan;
4 people deck it with silver and
gold;
they fasten it with hammer
and nails
so that it cannot move.
5 Their idolsᵃ are like scarecrows
in a cucumber field,
and they cannot speak;
they have to be carried,
for they cannot walk.
Do not be afraid of them,
for they cannot do evil,
nor is it in them to do good.

6 There is none like you, O Lᴏʀᴅ;
you are great, and your name
is great in might.
7 Who would not fear you, O King
of the nations?
For that is your due;
among all the wise ones of the
nations
and in all their kingdoms
there is no one like you.
8 They are both stupid and
foolish;
the instruction given by idols
is no better than wood!ᵇ
9 Beaten silver is brought from
Tarshish,
and gold from Uphaz.
They are the work of the
artisan and of the hands
of the goldsmith;
their clothing is blue and
purple;
they are all the product of
skilled workers.
10 But the Lᴏʀᴅ is the true God;
he is the living God and the
everlasting King.
At his wrath the earth quakes,
and the nations cannot endure
his indignation.

11 Thus shall you say to them: The gods who did not make the heavens and the earth shall perish from the earth and from under the heavens. ᶜ

12 It is he who made the earth by
his power,
who established the world by
his wisdom,
and by his understanding
stretched out the
heavens.
13 When he utters his voice, there
is a tumult of waters in
the heavens,
and he makes the mist rise
from the ends of the
earth.
He makes lightnings for the
rain,
and he brings out the wind
from his storehouses.
14 Everyone is stupid and without
knowledge;

ᵃHeb *They*   ᵇMeaning of Heb uncertain   ᶜThis verse is in Aramaic

goldsmiths are all put to
    shame by their idols;
for their images are false,
    and there is no breath in
    them.
15 They are worthless, a work of
    delusion;
at the time of their
    punishment they shall
    perish.
16 Not like these is the LORD, a the
    portion of Jacob,
for he is the one who formed
    all things,
and Israel is the tribe of his
    inheritance;
the LORD of hosts is his name.

17 Gather up your bundle from the
    ground,
    O you who live under siege!
18 For thus says the LORD:
I am going to sling out the
    inhabitants of the land
    at this time,
and I will bring distress on
    them,
    so that they shall feel it.

19 Woe is me because of my hurt!
    My wound is severe.
But I said, "Truly this is my
    punishment,
    and I must bear it."
20 My tent is destroyed,
    and all my cords are broken;
my children have gone from me,
    and they are no more;
there is no one to spread my
    tent again,
    and to set up my curtains.
21 For the shepherds are stupid,
    and do not inquire of the
    LORD;
therefore they have not
    prospered,
    and all their flock is scattered.

22 Hear, a noise! Listen, it is
    coming—
a great commotion from the
    land of the north
to make the cities of Judah a
    desolation,
    a lair of jackals.

23 I know, O LORD, that the way of
    human beings is not in
    their control,
that mortals as they walk
    cannot direct their steps.
24 Correct me, O LORD, but in
    just measure;
not in your anger, or you will
    bring me to nothing.

25 Pour out your wrath on the
    nations that do not know
    you,
and on the peoples that do
    not call on your name;
for they have devoured Jacob;
    they have devoured him and
    consumed him,
and have laid waste his
    habitation.

11.1 THE word that came to Jeremiah from the LORD: 2Hear the words of this covenant, and speak to the people of Judah and the inhabitants of Jerusalem. 3You shall say to them, Thus says the LORD, the God of Israel: Cursed be anyone who does not heed the words of this covenant, 4which I commanded your ancestors when I brought them out of the land of Egypt, from the iron-smelter, saying, Listen to my voice, and do all that I command you. So shall you be my people, and I will be your God, 5that I may perform the oath that I swore to your ancestors, to give them a land flowing with milk and honey, as at this day. Then I answered, "So be it, LORD."

a Heb lacks *the LORD*

6 And the Lord said to me: Proclaim all these words in the cities of Judah, and in the streets of Jerusalem: Hear the words of this covenant and do them. [7]For I solemnly warned your ancestors when I brought them up out of the land of Egypt, warning them persistently, even to this day, saying, Obey my voice. [8]Yet they did not obey or incline their ear, but everyone walked in the stubbornness of an evil will. So I brought upon them all the words of this covenant, which I commanded them to do, but they did not.

9 And the Lord said to me: Conspiracy exists among the people of Judah and the inhabitants of Jerusalem. [10]They have turned back to the iniquities of their ancestors of old, who refused to heed my words; they have gone after other gods to serve them; the house of Israel and the house of Judah have broken the covenant that I made with their ancestors. [11]Therefore, thus says the Lord, assuredly I am going to bring disaster upon them that they cannot escape; though they cry out to me, I will not listen to them. [12]Then the cities of Judah and the inhabitants of Jerusalem will go and cry out to the gods to whom they make offerings, but they will never save them in the time of their trouble. [13]For your gods have become as many as your towns, O Judah; and as many as the streets of Jerusalem are the altars you have set up to shame, altars to make offerings to Baal.

14 As for you, do not pray for this people, or lift up a cry or prayer on their behalf, for I will not listen when they call to me in the time of their trouble. [15]What right has my beloved in my house, when she has done vile deeds? Can vows[a] and sacrificial flesh avert your doom? Can you then exult? [16]The Lord once called you, "A green olive tree, fair with goodly fruit"; but with the roar of a great tempest he will set fire to it, and its branches will be consumed. [17]The Lord of hosts, who planted you, has pronounced evil against you, because of the evil that the house of Israel and the house of Judah have done, provoking me to anger by making offerings to Baal.

18 It was the Lord who made it
        known to me, and I
        knew;
    then you showed me their
        evil deeds.
19 But I was like a gentle lamb
        led to the slaughter.
    And I did not know it was
        against me
    that they devised schemes,
        saying,
    "Let us destroy the tree with
        its fruit,
    let us cut him off from the
        land of the living,
    so that his name will no
        longer be remembered!"
20 But you, O Lord of hosts, who
        judge righteously,
    who try the heart and the
        mind,
    let me see your retribution upon
        them,
    for to you I have committed
        my cause.

21 Therefore thus says the Lord concerning the people of Anathoth, who seek your life, and say, "You shall not prophesy in the name of the Lord, or you will die by our hand"— [22]therefore thus says the Lord of hosts: I am going to punish them; the young men shall die by the sword; their sons and their daughters shall die by famine; [23]and not even a remnant shall be left of them. For I will bring disaster upon the people of Anathoth, the year of their punishment.

aGk: Heb *Can many*

## COLOSSIANS 3.18—4.18

**W**IVES, be subject to your husbands, as is fitting in the Lord. ¹⁹Husbands, love your wives and never treat them harshly.

20 Children, obey your parents in everything, for this is your acceptable duty in the Lord. ²¹Fathers, do not provoke your children, or they may lose heart. ²²Slaves, obey your earthly masters[a] in everything, not only while being watched and in order to please them, but wholeheartedly, fearing the Lord.[a] ²³Whatever your task, put yourselves into it, as done for the Lord and not for your masters,[b] ²⁴since you know that from the Lord you will receive the inheritance as your reward; you serve[c] the Lord Christ. ²⁵For the wrongdoer will be paid back for whatever wrong has been done, and there is no partiality. 4.1Masters, treat your slaves justly and fairly, for you know that you also have a Master in heaven.

2 Devote yourselves to prayer, keeping alert in it with thanksgiving. ³At the same time pray for us as well that God will open to us a door for the word, that we may declare the mystery of Christ, for which I am in prison, ⁴so that I may reveal it clearly, as I should.

5 Conduct yourselves wisely toward outsiders, making the most of the time.[d] ⁶Let your speech always be gracious, seasoned with salt, so that you may know how you ought to answer everyone.

7 Tychicus will tell you all the news about me; he is a beloved brother, a faithful minister, and a fellow servant[e] in the Lord. ⁸I have sent him to you for this very purpose, so that you may know how we are[f] and that he may encourage your hearts; ⁹he is coming with Onesimus, the faithful and beloved brother, who is one of you. They will tell you about everything here.

10 Aristarchus my fellow prisoner greets you, as does Mark the cousin of Barnabas, concerning whom you have received instructions—if he comes to you, welcome him. ¹¹And Jesus who is called Justus greets you. These are the only ones of the circumcision among my co-workers for the kingdom of God, and they have been a comfort to me. ¹²Epaphras, who is one of you, a servant[e] of Christ Jesus, greets you. He is always wrestling in his prayers on your behalf, so that you may stand mature and fully assured in everything that God wills. ¹³For I testify for him that he has worked hard for you and for those in Laodicea and in Hierapolis. ¹⁴Luke, the beloved physician, and Demas greet you. ¹⁵Give my greetings to the brothers and sisters[g] in Laodicea, and to Nympha and the church in her house. ¹⁶And when this letter has been read among you, have it read also in the church of the Laodiceans; and see that you read also the letter from Laodicea. ¹⁷And say to Archippus, "See that you complete the task that you have received in the Lord."

18 I, Paul, write this greeting with my own hand. Remember my chains. Grace be with you.[h]

## PSALM 78.56—72

**Y**ET they tested the Most High God,
    and rebelled against him.
They did not observe his
    decrees,
57 but turned away and were
    faithless like their
    ancestors;

---

aIn Greek the same word is used for *master* and *Lord*  bGk *not for men*  cOr *you are slaves of,* or *be slaves of*  dOr *opportunity*  eGk *slave*  fOther authorities read *that I may know how you are*  gGk *brothers*  hOther ancient authorities add *Amen*

they twisted like a
  treacherous bow.
58 For they provoked him to anger
    with their high places;
  they moved him to jealousy
    with their idols.
59 When God heard, he was full of
    wrath,
  and he utterly rejected Israel.
60 He abandoned his dwelling at
    Shiloh,
  the tent where he dwelt
    among mortals,
61 and delivered his power to
    captivity,
  his glory to the hand of the
    foe.
62 He gave his people to the
    sword,
  and vented his wrath on his
    heritage.
63 Fire devoured their young men,
  and their girls had no
    marriage song.
64 Their priests fell by the sword,
  and their widows made no
    lamentation.
65 Then the Lord awoke as from
    sleep,
  like a warrior shouting
    because of wine.
66 He put his adversaries to rout;
  he put them to everlasting
    disgrace.

67 He rejected the tent of Joseph,
  he did not choose the tribe of
    Ephraim;
68 but he chose the tribe of Judah,
  Mount Zion, which he loves.
69 He built his sanctuary like the
    high heavens,
  like the earth, which he has
    founded forever.
70 He chose his servant David,
  and took him from the
    sheepfolds;
71 from tending the nursing ewes
    he brought him
  to be the shepherd of his
    people Jacob,
  of Israel, his inheritance.
72 With upright heart he tended
    them,
  and guided them with skillful
    hand.

# PROVERBS 24.28–29

Do not be a witness against
    your neighbor without
    cause,
  and do not deceive with your
    lips.
29 Do not say, "I will do to others
    as they have done to me;
  I will pay them back for what
    they have done."

# OCTOBER 9

JEREMIAH 12.1—14.10

YOU will be in the right,
    O LORD,
    when I lay charges against
      you;
  but let me put my case to
    you.
Why does the way of the guilty
    prosper?
Why do all who are
    treacherous thrive?
2 You plant them, and they take
    root;
  they grow and bring forth
    fruit;
you are near in their mouths
  yet far from their hearts.
3 But you, O LORD, know me;
  You see me and test me—my
    heart is with you.
Pull them out like sheep for the
    slaughter,
  and set them apart for the
    day of slaughter.
4 How long will the land mourn,
  and the grass of every field
    wither?
For the wickedness of those
    who live in it
  the animals and the birds are
    swept away,
  and because people said, "He
    is blind to our ways."<sup>a</sup>

5 If you have raced with
    foot-runners and they
    have wearied you,
  how will you compete with
    horses?
And if in a safe land you fall
    down,
  how will you fare in the
    thickets of the Jordan?

6 For even your kinsfolk and your
    own family,
  even they have dealt
    treacherously with you;
  they are in full cry after you;
do not believe them,
  though they speak friendly
    words to you.
7 I have forsaken my house,
  I have abandoned my
    heritage;
I have given the beloved of
    my heart
  into the hands of her
    enemies.
8 My heritage has become to me
  like a lion in the forest;
she has lifted up her voice
    against me—
  therefore I hate her.
9 Is the hyena greedy<sup>b</sup> for my
    heritage at my command?
  Are the birds of prey all
    around her?
Go, assemble all the wild
    animals;
  bring them to devour her.
10 Many shepherds have destroyed
    my vineyard,
  they have trampled down
    my portion,
they have made my pleasant
    portion
  a desolate wilderness.
11 They have made it a desolation;
  desolate, it mourns to me.
The whole land is made
    desolate,
  but no one lays it to heart.
12 Upon all the bare heights<sup>c</sup> in
    the desert
  spoilers have come;

---

a Gk: Heb *to our future*  b Cn: Heb *Is the hyena, the bird of prey*  c Or *the trails*

for the sword of the LORD
    devours
from one end of the land to
    the other;
no one shall be safe.
13  They have sown wheat and
    have reaped thorns,
they have tired themselves
    out but profit nothing.
They shall be ashamed of their[a]
    harvests
because of the fierce anger of
    the LORD.

14  Thus says the LORD concerning all my evil neighbors who touch the heritage that I have given my people Israel to inherit: I am about to pluck them up from their land, and I will pluck up the house of Judah from among them. 15And after I have plucked them up, I will again have compassion on them, and I will bring them again to their heritage and to their land, everyone of them. 16And then, if they will diligently learn the ways of my people, to swear by my name, "As the LORD lives," as they taught my people to swear by Baal, then they shall be built up in the midst of my people. 17But if any nation will not listen, then I will completely uproot it and destroy it, says the LORD.

13.1 THUS said the LORD to me, "Go and buy yourself a linen loincloth, and put it on your loins, but do not dip it in water." 2So I bought a loincloth according to the word of the LORD, and put it on my loins. 3And the word of the LORD came to me a second time, saying, 4"Take the loincloth that you bought and are wearing, and go now to the Euphrates,[b] and hide it there in a cleft of the rock." 5So I went, and hid it by the Euphrates,[c] as the LORD commanded me. 6And after many days the LORD said to me, "Go now to the Euphrates,[b] and take from there the loincloth that I commanded you to hide there." 7Then I went to the Euphrates,[b] and dug, and I took the loincloth from the place where I had hidden it. But now the loincloth was ruined; it was good for nothing.

8  Then the word of the LORD came to me: 9Thus says the LORD: Just so I will ruin the pride of Judah and the great pride of Jerusalem. 10This evil people, who refuse to hear my words, who stubbornly follow their own will and have gone after other gods to serve them and worship them, shall be like this loincloth, which is good for nothing. 11For as the loincloth clings to one's loins, so I made the whole house of Israel and the whole house of Judah cling to me, says the LORD, in order that they might be for me a people, a name, a praise, and a glory. But they would not listen.

12  You shall speak to them this word: Thus says the LORD, the God of Israel: Every wine-jar should be filled with wine. And they will say to you, "Do you think we do not know that every wine-jar should be filled with wine?" 13Then you shall say to them: Thus says the LORD: I am about to fill all the inhabitants of this land—the kings who sit on David's throne, the priests, the prophets, and all the inhabitants of Jerusalem—with drunkenness. 14And I will dash them one against another, parents and children together, says the LORD. I will not pity or spare or have compassion when I destroy them.

15  Hear and give ear; do not be
    haughty,
for the LORD has spoken.
16  Give glory to the LORD your
    God
before he brings darkness,

aHeb *your*  bOr *to Parah*; Heb *perath*  cOr *by Parah*; Heb *perath*

and before your feet stumble
  on the mountains at twilight;
while you look for light,
  he turns it into gloom
  and makes it deep darkness.
17 But if you will not listen,
  my soul will weep in secret
    for your pride;
  my eyes will weep bitterly and
    run down with tears,
  because the Lord's flock has
    been taken captive.

18 Say to the king and the queen
    mother;
  "Take a lowly seat,
for your beautiful crown
  has come down from your
    head."a
19 The towns of the Negeb are
    shut up
  with no one to open them;
all Judah is taken into exile,
  wholly taken into exile.

20 Lift up your eyes and see
  those who come from the
    north.
Where is the flock that was
    given you,
  your beautiful flock?
21 What will you say when they set
    as head over you
  those whom you have trained
to be your allies?
Will not pangs take hold of you,
  like those of a woman in
    labor?
22 And if you say in your heart,
  "Why have these things come
    upon me?"
  it is for the greatness of your
    iniquity
  that your skirts are lifted up,
  and you are violated.
23 Can Ethiopiansb change their
    skin
  or leopards their spots?

Then also you can do good
  who are accustomed to do
    evil.
24 I will scatter youc like chaff
  driven by the wind from
    the desert.
25 This is your lot,
  the portion I have measured
    out to you, says the
      Lord,
because you have forgotten me
  and trusted in lies.
26 I myself will lift up your skirts
    over your face,
  and your shame will be seen.
27 I have seen your abominations,
  your adulteries and neighings,
    your shameless
    prostitutions
on the hills of the
    countryside.
Woe to you, O Jerusalem!
  How long will it be
  before you are made clean?


14.1 The word of the Lord that came to
Jeremiah concerning the drought:
2 Judah mourns
  and her gates languish;
  they lie in gloom on the ground,
  and the cry of Jerusalem goes
    up.
3 Her nobles send their servants
    for water;
  they come to the cisterns,
they find no water,
  they return with their
    vessels empty.
They are ashamed and dismayed
  and cover their heads,
4 because the ground is cracked.
  Because there has been no
    rain on the land
the farmers are dismayed;
  they cover their heads.
5 Even the doe in the field
    forsakes her newborn
    fawn

aGk Syr Vg: Meaning of Heb uncertain   bOr *Nubians*; Heb *Cushites*   cHeb *them*

because there is no grass.
6 The wild asses stand on the
      bare heights, a
  they pant for air like jackals;
their eyes fail
  because there is no herbage.

7 Although our iniquities testify
      against us,
  act, O Lord, for your name's
      sake;
our apostasies indeed are many,
  and we have sinned against
      you.
8 O hope of Israel,
  its savior in time of trouble,
why should you be like a
      stranger in the land,
  like a traveler turning aside
      for the night?
9 Why should you be like
      someone confused,
  like a mighty warrior who
      cannot give help?
Yet you, O Lord, are in the
      midst of us,
  and we are called by your
      name;
  do not forsake us!

10 Thus says the Lord concerning
      this people:
Truly they have loved to
      wander,
  they have not restrained
      their feet;
therefore the Lord does not
      accept them,
  now he will remember their
      iniquity
  and punish their sins.

# 1 THESSALONIANS
## 1.1—2.8

PAUL, Silvanus, and Timothy,
To the church of the Thessalonians in God the Father and the
Lord Jesus Christ:

Grace to you and peace.

2 We always give thanks to God for all of you and mention you in our prayers, constantly 3remembering before our God and Father your work of faith and labor of love and steadfastness of hope in our Lord Jesus Christ. 4For we know, brothers and sistersb beloved by God, that he has chosen you, 5because our message of the gospel came to you not in word only, but also in power and in the Holy Spirit and with full conviction; just as you know what kind of persons we proved to be among you for your sake. 6And you became imitators of us and of the Lord, for in spite of persecution you received the word with joy inspired by the Holy Spirit, 7so that you became an example to all the believers in Macedonia and in Achaia. 8For the word of the Lord has sounded forth from you not only in Macedonia and Achaia, but in every place your faith in God has become known, so that we have no need to speak about it. 9For the people of those regionsc report about us what kind of welcome we had among you, and how you turned to God from idols, to serve a living and true God, 10and to wait for his Son from heaven, whom he raised from the dead—Jesus, who rescues us from the wrath that is coming.

2.1 You yourselves know, brothers and sisters, b that our coming to you was not in vain, 2but though we had already suffered and been shamefully mistreated at Philippi, as you know, we had courage in our God to declare to you the gospel of God in spite of great opposition. 3For our appeal does not spring from deceit or impure motives or trickery, 4but just as we have been approved by God to be entrusted with the message of the gospel, even so we speak, not to please mortals, but to

a Or *the trails*  b Gk *brothers*  c Gk *For they*

please God who tests our hearts. [5]As you know and as God is our witness, we never came with words of flattery or with a pretext for greed; [6]nor did we seek praise from mortals, whether from you or from others, [7]though we might have made demands as apostles of Christ. But we were gentle[a] among you, like a nurse tenderly caring for her own children. [8]So deeply do we care for you that we are determined to share with you not only the gospel of God but also our own selves, because you have become very dear to us.

## PSALM 79.1–13

*A Psalm of Asaph.*

O GOD, the nations have come
into your inheritance;
they have defiled your holy
temple;
they have laid Jerusalem in
ruins.
2   They have given the bodies of
your servants
to the birds of the air for
food,
the flesh of your faithful to
the wild animals of the
earth.
3   They have poured out their
blood like water
all around Jerusalem,
and there was no one to bury
them.
4   We have become a taunt to our
neighbors,
mocked and derided by those
around us.

5   How long, O LORD? Will you be
angry forever?
Will your jealous wrath burn
like fire?
6   Pour out your anger on the
nations
that do not know you,
and on the kingdoms
that do not call on your name.
7   For they have devoured Jacob
and laid waste his habitation.

8   Do not remember against us the
iniquities of our
ancestors;
let your compassion come
speedily to meet us,
for we are brought very low.
9   Help us, O God of our salvation,
for the glory of your name;
deliver us, and forgive our sins,
for your name's sake.
10   Why should the nations say,
"Where is their God?"
Let the avenging of the
outpoured blood of your
servants
be known among the nations
before our eyes.

11   Let the groans of the prisoners
come before you;
according to your great power
preserve those doomed
to die.
12   Return sevenfold into the bosom
of our neighbors
the taunts with which they
taunted you, O Lord!
13   Then we your people, the flock
of your pasture,
will give thanks to you
forever;
from generation to generation
we will recount your
praise.

## PROVERBS 24.30–34

I PASSED by the field of one who
was lazy,
by the vineyard of a stupid
person;
31   and see, it was all overgrown
with thorns;
the ground was covered with
nettles,

[a]Other ancient authorities read *infants*

and its stone wall was broken
    down.
32  Then I saw and considered it;
    I looked and received
      instruction.
33  A little sleep, a little slumber,

a little folding of the hands
    to rest,
34  and poverty will come upon you
    like a robber,
  and want, like an armed
    warrior.

# OCTOBER 10

## JEREMIAH 14.11—16.15

THE LORD said to me: Do not pray for the welfare of this people. [12]Although they fast, I do not hear their cry, and although they offer burnt offering and grain offering, I do not accept them; but by the sword, by famine, and by pestilence I consume them.

13 Then I said: "Ah, Lord GOD! Here are the prophets saying to them, 'You shall not see the sword, nor shall you have famine, but I will give you true peace in this place.' " [14]And the LORD said to me: The prophets are prophesying lies in my name; I did not send them, nor did I command them or speak to them. They are prophesying to you a lying vision, worthless divination, and the deceit of their own minds. [15]Therefore thus says the LORD concerning the prophets who prophesy in my name though I did not send them, and who say, "Sword and famine shall not come on this land": By sword and famine those prophets shall be consumed. [16]And the people to whom they prophesy shall be thrown out into the streets of Jerusalem, victims of famine and sword. There shall be no one to bury them—themselves, their wives, their sons, and their daughters. For I will pour out their wickedness upon them.

17  You shall say to them this word:
Let my eyes run down with
    tears night and day,
  and let them not cease,
for the virgin daughter—my
    people—is struck down
    with a crushing blow,
  with a very grievous wound.
18  If I go out into the field,
  look—those killed by the
    sword!
And if I enter the city,
  look—those sick with[a]
    famine!
For both prophet and priest ply
    their trade throughout
    the land,
  and have no knowledge.

19  Have you completely rejected
    Judah?
  Does your heart loathe Zion?
Why have you struck us down
  so that there is no healing for
    us?
We look for peace, but find no
    good;
  for a time of healing, but
    there is terror instead.

[a]Heb *look—the sicknesses of*

20 We acknowledge our
    wickedness, O Lord,
  the iniquity of our ancestors,
  for we have sinned against
    you.
21 Do not spurn us, for your
    name's sake;
  do not dishonor your glorious
    throne;
  remember and do not break
    your covenant with us.
22 Can any idols of the nations
    bring rain?
  Or can the heavens give
    showers?
Is it not you, O Lord our God?
  We set our hope on you,
  for it is you who do all this.

15.1 Then the Lord said to me: Though Moses and Samuel stood before me, yet my heart would not turn toward this people. Send them out of my sight, and let them go! 2And when they say to you, "Where shall we go?" you shall say to them: Thus says the Lord:
Those destined for pestilence,
    to pestilence,
  and those destined for the
    sword, to the sword;
those destined for famine, to
    famine,
  and those destined for
    captivity, to captivity.
3And I will appoint over them four kinds of destroyers, says the Lord: the sword to kill, the dogs to drag away, and the birds of the air and the wild animals of the earth to devour and destroy. 4I will make them a horror to all the kingdoms of the earth because of what King Manasseh son of Hezekiah of Judah did in Jerusalem.

5 Who will have pity on you,
    O Jerusalem,
  or who will bemoan you?
Who will turn aside
  to ask about your welfare?
6 You have rejected me, says
    the Lord,
  you are going backward;
so I have stretched out my hand
    against you and
    destroyed you—
  I am weary of relenting.
7 I have winnowed them with a
    winnowing fork
  in the gates of the land;
I have bereaved them, I have
    destroyed my people;
  they did not turn from
    their ways.
8 Their widows became more
    numerous
  than the sand of the seas;
I have brought against the
    mothers of youths
  a destroyer at noonday;
I have made anguish and terror
  fall upon her suddenly.
9 She who bore seven has
    languished;
  she has swooned away;
her sun went down while it was
    yet day;
  she has been shamed and
    disgraced.
And the rest of them I will give
    to the sword
  before their enemies,
        says the Lord.

10 Woe is me, my mother, that you ever bore me, a man of strife and contention to the whole land! I have not lent, nor have I borrowed, yet all of them curse me. 11The Lord said: Surely I have intervened in your life[a] for good, surely I have imposed enemies on you in a time of trouble and in a time of distress.[b] 12Can iron and bronze break iron from the north?

13 Your wealth and your treasures I will give as plunder, without price, for all your sins, throughout all your terri-

tory. [14]I will make you serve your enemies in a land that you do not know, for in my anger a fire is kindled that shall burn forever.

15 O Lord, you know;
 remember me and visit me,
 and bring down retribution for
 me on my persecutors.
In your forbearance do not take
 me away;
 know that on your account I
 suffer insult.
16 Your words were found, and I
 ate them,
 and your words became to
 me a joy
 and the delight of my heart;
for I am called by your name,
 O Lord, God of hosts.
17 I did not sit in the company of
 merrymakers,
 nor did I rejoice;
under the weight of your hand I
 sat alone,
 for you had filled me with
 indignation.
18 Why is my pain unceasing,
 my wound incurable,
 refusing to be healed?
Truly, you are to me like a
 deceitful brook,
 like waters that fail.

19 Therefore thus says the Lord:
If you turn back, I will take
 you back,
 and you shall stand before
 me.
If you utter what is precious,
 and not what is
 worthless,
 you shall serve as my mouth.
It is they who will turn to you,
 not you who will turn to
 them.
20 And I will make you to this
 people
 a fortified wall of bronze;

they will fight against you,
 but they shall not prevail
 over you,
for I am with you
 to save you and deliver you,
 says the Lord.
21 I will deliver you out of the
 hand of the wicked,
 and redeem you from the
 grasp of the ruthless.

16.1 The word of the Lord came to me: [2]You shall not take a wife, nor shall you have sons or daughters in this place. [3]For thus says the Lord concerning the sons and daughters who are born in this place, and concerning the mothers who bear them and the fathers who beget them in this land: [4]They shall die of deadly diseases. They shall not be lamented, nor shall they be buried; they shall become like dung on the surface of the ground. They shall perish by the sword and by famine, and their dead bodies shall become food for the birds of the air and for the wild animals of the earth.

5 For thus says the Lord: Do not enter the house of mourning, or go to lament, or bemoan them; for I have taken away my peace from this people, says the Lord, my steadfast love and mercy. [6]Both great and small shall die in this land; they shall not be buried, and no one shall lament for them; there shall be no gashing, no shaving of the head for them. [7]No one shall break bread[a] for the mourner, to offer comfort for the dead; nor shall anyone give them the cup of consolation to drink for their fathers or their mothers. [8]You shall not go into the house of feasting to sit with them, to eat and drink. [9]For thus says the Lord of hosts, the God of Israel: I am going to banish from this place, in your days and before your eyes, the voice of mirth and the voice

a Two Mss Gk: MT *break for them*

of gladness, the voice of the bridegroom and the voice of the bride.

10  And when you tell this people all these words, and they say to you, "Why has the Lord pronounced all this great evil against us? What is our iniquity? What is the sin that we have committed against the Lord our God?" [11]then you shall say to them: It is because your ancestors have forsaken me, says the Lord, and have gone after other gods and have served and worshiped them, and have forsaken me and have not kept my law; [12]and because you have behaved worse than your ancestors, for here you are, every one of you, following your stubborn evil will, refusing to listen to me. [13]Therefore I will hurl you out of this land into a land that neither you nor your ancestors have known, and there you shall serve other gods day and night, for I will show you no favor.

14  Therefore, the days are surely coming, says the Lord, when it shall no longer be said, "As the Lord lives who brought the people of Israel up out of the land of Egypt," [15]but "As the Lord lives who brought the people of Israel up out of the land of the north and out of all the lands where he had driven them." For I will bring them back to their own land that I gave to their ancestors.

# 1 THESSALONIANS
## 2.9—3.13

You remember our labor and toil, brothers and sisters; [a] we worked night and day, so that we might not burden any of you while we proclaimed to you the gospel of God. [10]You are witnesses, and God also, how pure, upright, and blameless our conduct was toward you believers. [11]As you know, we dealt with each one of you like a father with his children,

[12]urging and encouraging you and pleading that you lead a life worthy of God, who calls you into his own kingdom and glory.

13  We also constantly give thanks to God for this, that when you received the word of God that you heard from us, you accepted it not as a human word but as what it really is, God's word, which is also at work in you believers. [14]For you, brothers and sisters, [a] became imitators of the churches of God in Christ Jesus that are in Judea, for you suffered the same things from your own compatriots as they did from the Jews, [15]who killed both the Lord Jesus and the prophets, [b] and drove us out; they displease God and oppose everyone [16]by hindering us from speaking to the Gentiles so that they may be saved. Thus they have constantly been filling up the measure of their sins; but God's wrath has overtaken them at last. [c]

17  As for us, brothers and sisters, [a] when, for a short time, we were made orphans by being separated from you—in person, not in heart—we longed with great eagerness to see you face to face. [18]For we wanted to come to you—certainly I, Paul, wanted to again and again—but Satan blocked our way. [19]For what is our hope or joy or crown of boasting before our Lord Jesus at his coming? Is it not you? [20]Yes, you are our glory and joy!

[3.1] Therefore when we could bear it no longer, we decided to be left alone in Athens; [2]and we sent Timothy, our brother and co-worker for God in proclaiming[d] the gospel of Christ, to strengthen and encourage you for the sake of your faith, [3]so that no one would be shaken by these persecutions. Indeed, you yourselves know that this is what we are destined for. [4]In fact, when we were with you, we told you beforehand that we were to

[a] Gk *brothers*  [b] Other ancient authorities read *their own prophets*  [c] Or *completely* or *forever*
[d] Gk lacks *proclaiming*

suffer persecution; so it turned out, as you know. ⁵For this reason, when I could bear it no longer, I sent to find out about your faith; I was afraid that somehow the tempter had tempted you and that our labor had been in vain.

6 But Timothy has just now come to us from you, and has brought us the good news of your faith and love. He has told us also that you always remember us kindly and long to see us—just as we long to see you. ⁷For this reason, brothers and sisters,ᵃ during all our distress and persecution we have been encouraged about you through your faith. ⁸For we now live, if you continue to stand firm in the Lord. ⁹How can we thank God enough for you in return for all the joy that we feel before our God because of you? ¹⁰Night and day we pray most earnestly that we may see you face to face and restore whatever is lacking in your faith.

11 Now may our God and Father himself and our Lord Jesus direct our way to you. ¹²And may the Lord make you increase and abound in love for one another and for all, just as we abound in love for you. ¹³And may he so strengthen your hearts in holiness that you may be blameless before our God and Father at the coming of our Lord Jesus with all his saints.

## PSALM 80.1–19

*To the leader: on Lilies, a Covenant. Of Asaph. A Psalm.*

GIVE ear, O Shepherd of Israel,
  you who lead Joseph like a
    flock!
  You who are enthroned upon
      the cherubim, shine forth
2    before Ephraim and Benjamin
        and Manasseh.
    Stir up your might,
      and come to save us!

3  Restore us, O God;

ᵃGk *brothers*   ᵇSyr: Heb *strife*

let your face shine, that we
    may be saved.

4  O Lᴏʀᴅ God of hosts,
    how long will you be angry
      with your people's
        prayers?
5  You have fed them with the
        bread of tears,
    and given them tears to drink
      in full measure.
6  You make us the scornᵇ of our
        neighbors;
    our enemies laugh among
        themselves.

7  Restore us, O God of hosts;
    let your face shine, that we
        may be saved.

8  You brought a vine out of
        Egypt;
    you drove out the nations and
        planted it.
9  You cleared the ground for it;
    it took deep root and filled
        the land.
10  The mountains were covered
        with its shade,
    the mighty cedars with its
        branches;
11  it sent out its branches to the
        sea,
    and its shoots to the River.
12  Why then have you broken
        down its walls,
    so that all who pass along the
        way pluck its fruit?
13  The boar from the forest
        ravages it,
    and all that move in the field
        feed on it.

14  Turn again, O God of hosts;
    look down from heaven, and
        see;
    have regard for this vine,

15    the stock that your right hand
          planted. a
16    They have burned it with fire,
          they have cut it down; b
      may they perish at the rebuke
          of your countenance.
17    But let your hand be upon the
          one at your right hand,
      the one whom you made
          strong for yourself.
18    Then we will never turn back
          from you;
      give us life, and we will call
          on your name.

19    Restore us, O Lord God of
          hosts;
      let your face shine, that we
          may be saved.

## PROVERBS 25.1–5

These are other proverbs of Solomon that the officials of King Hezekiah of Judah copied.

2    It is the glory of God to conceal
          things,
      but the glory of kings is to
          search things out.
3    Like the heavens for height, like
          the earth for depth,
      so the mind of kings is
          unsearchable.
4    Take away the dross from the
          silver,
      and the smith has material for
          a vessel;
5    take away the wicked from the
          presence of the king,
      and his throne will be
          established in
          righteousness.

# OCTOBER 11

## JEREMIAH 16.16—18.23

I am now sending for many fishermen, says the Lord, and they shall catch them; and afterward I will send for many hunters, and they shall hunt them from every mountain and every hill, and out of the clefts of the rocks. 17For my eyes are on all their ways; they are not hidden from my presence, nor is their iniquity concealed from my sight. 18Andc I will doubly repay their iniquity and their sin, because they have polluted my land with the carcasses of their detestable idols, and have filled my inheritance with their abominations.

19    O Lord, my strength and my
          stronghold,
      my refuge in the day of
          trouble,
      to you shall the nations come
          from the ends of the earth
          and say:
      Our ancestors have inherited
          nothing but lies,
      worthless things in which
          there is no profit.

a Heb adds from verse 17 *and upon the one whom you made strong for yourself*   b Cn: Heb *it is cut down*   c Gk: Heb *And first*

20 Can mortals make for
themselves gods?
Such are no gods!

21 "Therefore I am surely going to teach them, this time I am going to teach them my power and my might, and they shall know that my name is the LORD."

17.1 THE sin of Judah is written with an iron pen; with a diamond point it is engraved on the tablet of their hearts, and on the horns of their altars, ²while their children remember their altars and their sacred poles,ᵃ beside every green tree, and on the high hills, ³on the mountains in the open country. Your wealth and all your treasures I will give for spoil as the price of your sinᵇ throughout all your territory. ⁴By your own act you shall lose the heritage that I gave you, and I will make you serve your enemies in a land that you do not know, for in my anger a fire is kindledᶜ that shall burn forever.

5 Thus says the LORD:
Cursed are those who trust in
mere mortals
and make mere flesh their
strength,
whose hearts turn away from
the LORD.
6 They shall be like a shrub in
the desert,
and shall not see when relief
comes.
They shall live in the parched
places of the wilderness,
in an uninhabited salt land.

7 Blessed are those who trust in
the LORD,
whose trust is the LORD.
8 They shall be like a tree planted
by water,
sending out its roots by
the stream.
It shall not fear when heat
comes,
and its leaves shall stay
green;
in the year of drought it is
not anxious,
and it does not cease to bear
fruit.

9 The heart is devious above all
else;
it is perverse—
who can understand it?
10 I the LORD test the mind
and search the heart,
to give to all according to
their ways,
according to the fruit of
their doings.

11 Like the partridge hatching what
it did not lay,
so are all who amass wealth
unjustly;
in mid-life it will leave them,
and at their end they will
prove to be fools.

12 O glorious throne, exalted from
the beginning,
shrine of our sanctuary!
13 O hope of Israel! O LORD!
All who forsake you shall be
put to shame;
those who turn away from youᵈ
shall be recorded in the
underworld,ᵉ
for they have forsaken the
fountain of living water,
the LORD.

14 Heal me, O LORD, and I shall
be healed;
save me, and I shall be
saved;
for you are my praise.

ᵃHeb *Asherim*  ᵇCn: Heb *spoil your high places for sin*  ᶜTwo Mss Theodotion: *you kindled*
ᵈHeb *me*  ᵉOr *in the earth*

15 See how they say to me,
  "Where is the word of the
    Lord?
  Let it come!"
16 But I have not run away from
    being a shepherd[a] in
    your service,
  nor have I desired the fatal
    day.
  You know what came from my
    lips;
  it was before your face.
17 Do not become a terror to me;
  you are my refuge in the day
    of disaster;
18 Let my persecutors be shamed,
    but do not let me be shamed;
  let them be dismayed,
    but do not let me be
      dismayed;
  bring on them the day of
    disaster;
    destroy them with double
      destruction!

19 Thus said the Lord to me: Go and stand in the People's Gate, by which the kings of Judah enter and by which they go out, and in all the gates of Jerusalem, 20 and say to them: Hear the word of the Lord, you kings of Judah, and all Judah, and all the inhabitants of Jerusalem, who enter by these gates. 21 Thus says the Lord: For the sake of your lives, take care that you do not bear a burden on the sabbath day or bring it in by the gates of Jerusalem. 22 And do not carry a burden out of your houses on the sabbath or do any work, but keep the sabbath day holy, as I commanded your ancestors. 23 Yet they did not listen or incline their ear; they stiffened their necks and would not hear or receive instruction.

24 But if you listen to me, says the Lord, and bring in no burden by the gates of this city on the sabbath day, but keep the sabbath day holy and do no work on it, 25 then there shall enter by the gates of this city kings[b] who sit on the throne of David, riding in chariots and on horses, they and their officials, the people of Judah and the inhabitants of Jerusalem; and this city shall be inhabited forever. 26 And people shall come from the towns of Judah and the places around Jerusalem, from the land of Benjamin, from the Shephelah, from the hill country, and from the Negeb, bringing burnt offerings and sacrifices, grain offerings and frankincense, and bringing thank offerings to the house of the Lord. 27 But if you do not listen to me, to keep the sabbath day holy, and to carry in no burden through the gates of Jerusalem on the sabbath day, then I will kindle a fire in its gates; it shall devour the palaces of Jerusalem and shall not be quenched.

18.1 The word that came to Jeremiah from the Lord: 2 "Come, go down to the potter's house, and there I will let you hear my words." 3 So I went down to the potter's house, and there he was working at his wheel. 4 The vessel he was making of clay was spoiled in the potter's hand, and he reworked it into another vessel, as seemed good to him.

5 Then the word of the Lord came to me: 6 Can I not do with you, O house of Israel, just as this potter has done? says the Lord. Just like the clay in the potter's hand, so are you in my hand, O house of Israel. 7 At one moment I may declare concerning a nation or a kingdom, that I will pluck up and break down and destroy it, 8 but if that nation, concerning which I have spoken, turns from its evil, I will change my mind about the disaster that I intended to bring on it. 9 And at another moment I may declare concerning a nation or a kingdom that I will build and plant it, 10 but if it does evil in my sight, not listening to my voice, then I will change

---

a Meaning of Heb uncertain   b Cn: Heb *kings and officials*

my mind about the good that I had intended to do to it. ¹¹Now, therefore, say to the people of Judah and the inhabitants of Jerusalem: Thus says the LORD: Look, I am a potter shaping evil against you and devising a plan against you. Turn now, all of you from your evil way, and amend your ways and your doings.

12  But they say, "It is no use! We will follow our own plans, and each of us will act according to the stubbornness of our evil will."

13 Therefore thus says the LORD:
Ask among the nations:
  Who has heard the like of
    this?
The virgin Israel has done
  a most horrible thing.
14 Does the snow of Lebanon
    leave
  the crags of Sirion? ᵃ
Do the mountainᵇ waters
    run dry, ᶜ
  the cold flowing streams?
15 But my people have forgotten
    me,
  they burn offerings to a
    delusion;
they have stumbledᵈ in their
    ways,
  in the ancient roads,
and have gone into bypaths,
  not the highway,
16 making their land a horror,
  a thing to be hissed at
    forever.
All who pass by it are horrified
  and shake their heads.
17 Like the wind from the east,
  I will scatter them before
    the enemy.
I will show them my back, not
    my face,
  in the day of their calamity.

18  Then they said, "Come, let us

make plots against Jeremiah—for instruction shall not perish from the priest, nor counsel from the wise, nor the word from the prophet. Come, let us bring charges against him, ᵉ and let us not heed any of his words."

19 Give heed to me, O LORD,
  and listen to what my
    adversaries say!
20 Is evil a recompense for good?
  Yet they have dug a pit for
    my life.
Remember how I stood before
    you
  to speak good for them,
  to turn away your wrath
    from them.
21 Therefore give their children
    over to famine;
  hurl them out to the power of
    the sword,
let their wives become childless
    and widowed.
May their men meet death by
    pestilence,
  their youths be slain by the
    sword in battle.
22 May a cry be heard from their
    houses,
  when you bring the marauder
    suddenly upon them!
For they have dug a pit to
    catch me,
  and laid snares for my feet.
23 Yet you, O LORD, know
  all their plotting to kill me.
Do not forgive their iniquity,
  do not blot out their sin from
    your sight.
Let them be tripped up before
    you;
  deal with them while you are
    angry.

ᵃCn: Heb *of the field*  ᵇCn: Heb *foreign*  ᶜCn: Heb *Are . . . plucked up?*  ᵈGk Syr Vg: Heb *they made them stumble*  ᵉHeb *strike him with the tongue*

## 1 THESSALONIANS 4.1—5.3

FINALLY, brothers and sisters,[a] we ask and urge you in the Lord Jesus that, as you learned from us how you ought to live and to please God (as, in fact, you are doing), you should do so more and more. [2]For you know what instructions we gave you through the Lord Jesus. [3]For this is the will of God, your sanctification: that you abstain from fornication; [4]that each one of you know how to control your own body[b] in holiness and honor, [5]not with lustful passion, like the Gentiles who do not know God; [6]that no one wrong or exploit a brother or sister[c] in this matter, because the Lord is an avenger in all these things, just as we have already told you beforehand and solemnly warned you. [7]For God did not call us to impurity but in holiness. [8]Therefore whoever rejects this rejects not human authority but God, who also gives his Holy Spirit to you.

9 Now concerning love of the brothers and sisters,[a] you do not need to have anyone write to you, for you yourselves have been taught by God to love one another; [10]and indeed you do love all the brothers and sisters[a] throughout Macedonia. But we urge you, beloved,[a] to do so more and more, [11]to aspire to live quietly, to mind your own affairs, and to work with your hands, as we directed you, [12]so that you may behave properly toward outsiders and be dependent on no one.

13 But we do not want you to be uninformed, brothers and sisters,[a] about those who have died,[d] so that you may not grieve as others do who have no hope. [14]For since we believe that Jesus died and rose again, even so, through Jesus, God will bring with him those who have died.[d] [15]For this we declare to you by the word of the Lord, that we who are alive, who are left until the coming of the Lord, will by no means precede those who have died.[d] [16]For the Lord himself, with a cry of command, with the archangel's call and with the sound of God's trumpet, will descend from heaven, and the dead in Christ will rise first. [17]Then we who are alive, who are left, will be caught up in the clouds together with them to meet the Lord in the air; and so we will be with the Lord forever. [18]Therefore encourage one another with these words.

[5.1] Now concerning the times and the seasons, brothers and sisters,[a] you do not need to have anything written to you. [2]For you yourselves know very well that the day of the Lord will come like a thief in the night. [3]When they say, "There is peace and security," then sudden destruction will come upon them, as labor pains come upon a pregnant woman, and there will be no escape!

## PSALM 81.1–16

*To the leader: according to The Gittith. Of Asaph.*

SING aloud to God our strength;
    shout for joy to the God of
        Jacob.
2  Raise a song, sound the
        tambourine,
    the sweet lyre with the harp.
3  Blow the trumpet at the new
        moon,
    at the full moon, on our
        festal day.
4  For it is a statute for Israel,
    an ordinance of the God of
        Jacob.
5  He made it a decree in Joseph,
    when he went out over[e] the
        land of Egypt.

    I hear a voice I had not known:

---

a Gk *brothers*  b Or *how to take a wife for himself*  c Gk *brother*  d Gk *fallen asleep*  e Or *against*

6 "I relieved your[a] shoulder of
    the burden;
  your[a] hands were freed from
    the basket.
7 In distress you called, and I
    rescued you;
  I answered you in the secret
    place of thunder;
  I tested you at the waters of
    Meribah.     *Selah*
8 Hear, O my people, while I
    admonish you;
  O Israel, if you would but
    listen to me!
9 There shall be no strange god
    among you;
  you shall not bow down to a
    foreign god.
10 I am the Lord your God,
  who brought you up out of
    the land of Egypt.
  Open your mouth wide and I
    will fill it.

11 "But my people did not listen to
    my voice;
  Israel would not submit to
    me.

12 So I gave them over to their
    stubborn hearts,
  to follow their own counsels.
13 O that my people would listen
    to me,
  that Israel would walk in my
    ways!
14 Then I would quickly subdue
    their enemies,
  and turn my hand against
    their foes.
15 Those who hate the Lord would
    cringe before him,
  and their doom would last
    forever.
16 I would feed you[b] with the
    finest of the wheat,
  and with honey from the rock
    I would satisfy you."

## PROVERBS 25.6–7a

Do not put yourself forward in
    the king's presence
  or stand in the place of the
    great;
7 for it is better to be told,
    "Come up here,"
  than to be put lower in the
    presence of a noble.

# OCTOBER 12

## JEREMIAH 19.1—21.14

Thus said the Lord: Go and buy a potter's earthenware jug. Take with you[c] some of the elders of the people and some of the senior priests, 2and go out to the valley of the son of Hinnom at the entry of the Potsherd Gate, and proclaim there the words that I tell you. 3You shall say: Hear the word of the Lord, O kings of Judah and inhabitants of Jerusalem. Thus says the Lord of hosts, the God of Israel: I am going to bring such disaster upon this place that the ears of everyone who hears of it will tingle. 4Because the people have forsaken me, and have profaned this place by making offerings in it to other gods whom nei-

[a] Heb *his*   [b] Cn Compare verse 16b: Heb *he would feed him*   [c] Syr Tg Compare Gk: Heb lacks *take with you*

ther they nor their ancestors nor the kings of Judah have known; and because they have filled this place with the blood of the innocent, [5]and gone on building the high places of Baal to burn their children in the fire as burnt offerings to Baal, which I did not command or decree, nor did it enter my mind. [6]Therefore the days are surely coming, says the LORD, when this place shall no more be called Topheth, or the valley of the son of Hinnom, but the valley of Slaughter. [7]And in this place I will make void the plans of Judah and Jerusalem, and will make them fall by the sword before their enemies, and by the hand of those who seek their life. I will give their dead bodies for food to the birds of the air and to the wild animals of the earth. [8]And I will make this city a horror, a thing to be hissed at; everyone who passes by it will be horrified and will hiss because of all its disasters. [9]And I will make them eat the flesh of their sons and the flesh of their daughters, and all shall eat the flesh of their neighbors in the siege, and in the distress with which their enemies and those who seek their life afflict them.

10  Then you shall break the jug in the sight of those who go with you, [11]and shall say to them: Thus says the LORD of hosts: So will I break this people and this city, as one breaks a potter's vessel, so that it can never be mended. In Topheth they shall bury until there is no more room to bury. [12]Thus will I do to this place, says the LORD, and to its inhabitants, making this city like Topheth. [13]And the houses of Jerusalem and the houses of the kings of Judah shall be defiled like the place of Topheth—all the houses upon whose roofs offerings have been made to the whole host of heaven, and libations have been poured out to other gods.

14  When Jeremiah came from Topheth, where the LORD had sent him to prophesy, he stood in the court of the LORD's house and said to all the people:

[15]Thus says the LORD of hosts, the God of Israel: I am now bringing upon this city and upon all its towns all the disaster that I have pronounced against it, because they have stiffened their necks, refusing to hear my words.

20.1 Now the priest Pashhur son of Immer, who was chief officer in the house of the LORD, heard Jeremiah prophesying these things. [2]Then Pashhur struck the prophet Jeremiah, and put him in the stocks that were in the upper Benjamin Gate of the house of the LORD. [3]The next morning when Pashhur released Jeremiah from the stocks, Jeremiah said to him, The LORD has named you not Pashhur but "Terror-all-around." [4]For thus says the LORD: I am making you a terror to yourself and to all your friends; and they shall fall by the sword of their enemies while you look on. And I will give all Judah into the hand of the king of Babylon; he shall carry them captive to Babylon, and shall kill them with the sword. [5]I will give all the wealth of this city, all its gains, all its prized belongings, and all the treasures of the kings of Judah into the hand of their enemies, who shall plunder them, and seize them, and carry them to Babylon. [6]And you, Pashhur, and all who live in your house, shall go into captivity, and to Babylon you shall go; there you shall die, and there you shall be buried, you and all your friends, to whom you have prophesied falsely.

7  O LORD, you have enticed me,
    and I was enticed;
  you have overpowered me,
    and you have prevailed.
  I have become a laughingstock
    all day long;
    everyone mocks me.
8  For whenever I speak, I must
      cry out,
    I must shout, "Violence and
      destruction!"

For the word of the LORD has
    become for me
  a reproach and derision all
    day long.
9  If I say, "I will not mention him,
    or speak any more in his
      name,"
  then within me there is
    something like a burning
    fire
  shut up in my bones;
  I am weary with holding it in,
    and I cannot.
10  For I hear many whispering:
    "Terror is all around!
  Denounce him! Let us denounce
    him!"
    All my close friends
    are watching for me to
      stumble.
  "Perhaps he can be enticed,
    and we can prevail against
      him,
    and take our revenge on
      him."
11  But the LORD is with me like a
    dread warrior;
    therefore my persecutors will
      stumble,
    and they will not prevail.
  They will be greatly shamed,
    for they will not succeed.
  Their eternal dishonor
    will never be forgotten.
12  O LORD of hosts, you test the
    righteous,
    you see the heart and the
      mind;
  let me see your retribution
    upon them,
    for to you I have committed
    my cause.

13  Sing to the LORD;
    praise the LORD!
  For he has delivered the life of
    the needy
    from the hands of evildoers.

14  Cursed be the day

  on which I was born!
  The day when my mother bore
    me,
    let it not be blessed!
15  Cursed be the man
    who brought the news to my
      father, saying,
  "A child is born to you, a son,"
    making him very glad.
16  Let that man be like the cities
    that the LORD overthrew
      without pity;
  let him hear a cry in the
    morning
    and an alarm at noon,
17  because he did not kill me in
    the womb;
    so my mother would have
      been my grave,
    and her womb forever great.
18  Why did I come forth from
    the womb
    to see toil and sorrow,
    and spend my days in shame?

21.1 THIS is the word that came to Jeremiah from the LORD, when King Zedekiah sent to him Pashhur son of Malchiah and the priest Zephaniah son of Maaseiah, saying, 2"Please inquire of the LORD on our behalf, for King Nebuchadrezzar of Babylon is making war against us; perhaps the LORD will perform a wonderful deed for us, as he has often done, and will make him withdraw from us."

3 Then Jeremiah said to them: 4Thus you shall say to Zedekiah: Thus says the LORD, the God of Israel: I am going to turn back the weapons of war that are in your hands and with which you are fighting against the king of Babylon and against the Chaldeans who are besieging you outside the walls; and I will bring them together into the center of this city. 5I myself will fight against you with outstretched hand and mighty arm, in anger, in fury, and in great wrath. 6And I will strike down the inhabitants of this city, both human be-

ings and animals; they shall die of a great pestilence. ⁷Afterward, says the LORD, I will give King Zedekiah of Judah, and his servants, and the people in this city—those who survive the pestilence, sword, and famine—into the hands of King Nebuchadrezzar of Babylon, into the hands of their enemies, into the hands of those who seek their lives. He shall strike them down with the edge of the sword; he shall not pity them, or spare them, or have compassion.

8 And to this people you shall say: Thus says the LORD: See, I am setting before you the way of life and the way of death. ⁹Those who stay in this city shall die by the sword, by famine, and by pestilence; but those who go out and surrender to the Chaldeans who are besieging you shall live and shall have their lives as a prize of war. ¹⁰For I have set my face against this city for evil and not for good, says the LORD: it shall be given into the hands of the king of Babylon, and he shall burn it with fire.

11 To the house of the king of Judah say: Hear the word of the LORD, ¹²O house of David! Thus says the LORD:

Execute justice in the morning,
   and deliver from the hand of
      the oppressor
   anyone who has been robbed,
 or else my wrath will go forth
      like fire,
   and burn, with no one to
      quench it,
   because of your evil doings.

13 See, I am against you,
      O inhabitant of the
      valley,
   O rock of the plain,
         says the LORD;
   you who say, "Who can come
      down against us,

or who can enter our places
      of refuge?"
14   I will punish you according to
      the fruit of your doings,
            says the LORD;
   I will kindle a fire in its
      forest,
   and it shall devour all that is
      around it.

# 1 THESSALONIANS 5.4–28

BUT you, beloved,ᵃ are not in darkness, for that day to surprise you like a thief; ⁵for you are all children of light and children of the day; we are not of the night or of darkness. ⁶So then let us not fall asleep as others do, but let us keep awake and be sober; ⁷for those who sleep sleep at night, and those who are drunk get drunk at night. ⁸But since we belong to the day, let us be sober, and put on the breastplate of faith and love, and for a helmet the hope of salvation. ⁹For God has destined us not for wrath but for obtaining salvation through our Lord Jesus Christ, ¹⁰who died for us, so that whether we are awake or asleep we may live with him. ¹¹Therefore encourage one another and build up each other, as indeed you are doing.

12 But we appeal to you, brothers and sisters,ᵃ to respect those who labor among you, and have charge of you in the Lord and admonish you; ¹³esteem them very highly in love because of their work. Be at peace among yourselves. ¹⁴And we urge you, beloved,ᵃ to admonish the idlers, encourage the faint hearted, help the weak, be patient with all of them. ¹⁵See that none of you repays evil for evil, but always seek to do good to one another and to all. ¹⁶Rejoice always, ¹⁷pray without ceasing, ¹⁸give thanks in all circumstances; for this is the will of God in Christ Jesus for you. ¹⁹Do not quench the Spirit. ²⁰Do

aGk *brothers*

not despise the words of prophets,[a] [21]but test everything; hold fast to what is good; [22]abstain from every form of evil.

23 May the God of peace himself sanctify you entirely; and may your spirit and soul and body be kept sound[b] and blameless at the coming of our Lord Jesus Christ. [24]The one who calls you is faithful, and he will do this.

25 Beloved,[c] pray for us.

26 Greet all the brothers and sisters[d] with a holy kiss. [27]I solemnly command you by the Lord that this letter be read to all of them.[e]

28 The grace of our Lord Jesus Christ be with you.[f]

## PSALM 82.1–8

*A Psalm of Asaph.*

**G**OD has taken his place in the
divine council;
in the midst of the gods he
holds judgment:
2 "How long will you judge
unjustly
and show partiality to the
wicked?              *Selah*
3 Give justice to the weak and the
orphan;
maintain the right of the lowly
and the destitute.
4 Rescue the weak and the
needy;
deliver them from the hand of
the wicked."

5 They have neither knowledge
nor understanding,
they walk around in darkness;
all the foundations of the
earth are shaken.

6 I say, "You are gods,
children of the Most High, all
of you;
7 nevertheless, you shall die like
mortals,
and fall like any prince."[g]

8 Rise up, O God, judge the
earth;
for all the nations belong to
you!

## PROVERBS 25.7b–10

**W**HAT your eyes have seen
8       do not hastily bring
into court;
for[h] what will you do in the
end,
when your neighbor puts you
to shame?
9 Argue your case with your
neighbor directly,
and do not disclose another's
secret;
10 or else someone who hears you
will bring shame upon
you,
and your ill repute will have
no end.

aGk *despise prophecies*   bOr *complete*   cGk *Brothers*   dGk *brothers*   eGk *to all the brothers*   fOther ancient authorities add *Amen*   gOr *fall as one man, O princes*   hCn: Heb *or else*

# OCTOBER 13

JEREMIAH 22.1—23.22

Hus says the Lord: Go down to the house of the king of Judah, and speak there this word, ²and say: Hear the word of the Lord, O King of Judah sitting on the throne of David—you, and your servants, and your people who enter these gates. ³Thus says the Lord: Act with justice and righteousness, and deliver from the hand of the oppressor anyone who has been robbed. And do no wrong or violence to the alien, the orphan, and the widow, or shed innocent blood in this place. ⁴For if you will indeed obey this word, then through the gates of this house shall enter kings who sit on the throne of David, riding in chariots and on horses, they, and their servants, and their people. ⁵But if you will not heed these words, I swear by myself, says the Lord, that this house shall become a desolation. ⁶For thus says the Lord concerning the house of the king of Judah:

You are like Gilead to me,
    like the summit of Lebanon;
but I swear that I will make you
        a desert,
    an uninhabited city. ᵃ
7  I will prepare destroyers
        against you,
    all with their weapons;
they shall cut down your
        choicest cedars
    and cast them into the fire.

8  And many nations will pass by this city, and all of them will say one to another, "Why has the Lord dealt in this way with that great city?" ⁹And they will answer, "Because they abandoned the covenant of the Lord their God, and worshiped other gods and served them."

10  Do not weep for him who is
        dead,
    nor bemoan him;
weep rather for him who
        goes away,
    for he shall return no more
    to see his native land.

11  For thus says the Lord concerning Shallum son of King Josiah of Judah, who succeeded his father Josiah, and who went away from this place: He shall return here no more, ¹²but in the place where they have carried him captive he shall die, and he shall never see this land again.

13  Woe to him who builds his
        house by
        unrighteousness,
    and his upper rooms by
        injustice;
who makes his neighbors work
        for nothing,
    and does not give them their
        wages;
14  who says, "I will build myself a
        spacious house
    with large upper rooms,"
and who cuts out windows for
        it,
    paneling it with cedar,
    and painting it with vermilion.
15  Are you a king
    because you compete in
        cedar?
Did not your father eat and
        drink
    and do justice and
        righteousness?
    Then it was well with him.

16  He judged the cause of the poor
       and needy;
     then it was well.
   Is not this to know me?
     says the LORD.
17  But your eyes and heart
     are only on your dishonest
       gain,
   for shedding innocent blood,
     and for practicing oppression
       and violence.
18  Therefore thus says the LORD concerning King Jehoiakim son of Josiah of Judah:
   They shall not lament for him,
       saying,
     "Alas, my brother!" or "Alas,
       sister!"
   They shall not lament for him,
       saying,
     "Alas, lord!" or "Alas, his
       majesty!"
19  With the burial of a donkey he
       shall be buried—
     dragged off and thrown out
       beyond the gates of
       Jerusalem.

20  Go up to Lebanon, and cry out,
     and lift up your voice in
       Bashan;
   cry out from Abarim,
     for all your lovers are
       crushed.
21  I spoke to you in your
       prosperity,
     but you said, "I will not
       listen."
   This has been your way from
       your youth,
     for you have not obeyed
       my voice.
22  The wind shall shepherd all your
       shepherds,
     and your lovers shall go into
       captivity;
   then you will be ashamed and
       dismayed

because of all your
       wickedness.
23  O inhabitant of Lebanon,
     nested among the cedars,
   how you will groan[a] when
       pangs come upon you,
     pain as of a woman in labor!

24  As I live, says the LORD, even if King Coniah son of Jehoiakim of Judah were the signet ring on my right hand, even from there I would tear you off [25]and give you into the hands of those who seek your life, into the hands of those of whom you are afraid, even into the hands of King Nebuchadrezzar of Babylon and into the hands of the Chaldeans. [26]I will hurl you and the mother who bore you into another country, where you were not born, and there you shall die. [27]But they shall not return to the land to which they long to return.
28  Is this man Coniah a despised
       broken pot,
     a vessel no one wants?
   Why are he and his offspring
       hurled out
     and cast away in a land that
       they do not know?
29  O land, land, land,
     hear the word of the LORD!
30  Thus says the LORD:
   Record this man as childless,
     a man who shall not succeed
       in his days;
   for none of his offspring shall
       succeed
     in sitting on the throne of
       David,
   and ruling again in Judah.

23.1  WOE to the shepherds who destroy and scatter the sheep of my pasture! says the LORD. [2]Therefore thus says the LORD, the God of Israel, concerning the shepherds who shepherd my peo-

a Gk Vg Syr: Heb *will be pitied*

ple: It is you who have scattered my flock, and have driven them away, and you have not attended to them. So I will attend to you for your evil doings, says the LORD. ³Then I myself will gather the remnant of my flock out of all the lands where I have driven them, and I will bring them back to their fold, and they shall be fruitful and multiply. ⁴I will raise up shepherds over them who will shepherd them, and they shall not fear any longer, or be dismayed, nor shall any be missing, says the LORD.

5  The days are surely coming, says the LORD, when I will raise up for David a righteous Branch, and he shall reign as king and deal wisely, and shall execute justice and righteousness in the land. ⁶In his days Judah will be saved and Israel will live in safety. And this is the name by which he will be called: "The LORD is our righteousness."

7  Therefore, the days are surely coming, says the LORD, when it shall no longer be said, "As the LORD lives who brought the people of Israel up out of the land of Egypt," ⁸but "As the LORD lives who brought out and led the offspring of the house of Israel out of the land of the north and out of all the lands where heᵃ had driven them." Then they shall live in their own land.

9  Concerning the prophets:
My heart is crushed within me,
    all my bones shake;
I have become like a drunkard,
    like one overcome by wine,
because of the LORD
    and because of his holy
        words.
10  For the land is full of adulterers;
    because of the curse the land
        mourns,
    and the pastures of the
        wilderness are dried up.
Their course has been evil,
    and their might is not right.

11  Both prophet and priest are
        ungodly;
    even in my house I have
        found their wickedness,
                says the LORD.
12  Therefore their way shall be
        to them
    like slippery paths in the
        darkness,
    into which they shall be
        driven and fall;
for I will bring disaster upon
        them
    in the year of their
        punishment,
                says the LORD.
13  In the prophets of Samaria
    I saw a disgusting thing:
they prophesied by Baal
    and led my people Israel
        astray.
14  But in the prophets of Jerusalem
    I have seen a more shocking
        thing:
they commit adultery and walk
        in lies;
    they strengthen the hands of
        evildoers,
    so that no one turns from
        wickedness;
all of them have become like
        Sodom to me,
    and its inhabitants like
        Gomorrah.
15  Therefore thus says the LORD of
        hosts concerning the
        prophets:
"I am going to make them eat
        wormwood,
    and give them poisoned water
        to drink;
for from the prophets of
        Jerusalem
    ungodliness has spread
        throughout the land."

16  Thus says the LORD of hosts: Do not listen to the words of the prophets

ᵃGk: Heb *I*

who prophesy to you; they are deluding you. They speak visions of their own minds, not from the mouth of the LORD. [17]They keep saying to those who despise the word of the LORD, "It shall be well with you"; and to all who stubbornly follow their own stubborn hearts, they say, "No calamity shall come upon you."

18  For who has stood in the council
       of the LORD
    so as to see and to hear his
       word?
    Who has given heed to his
       word so as to proclaim
       it?
19  Look, the storm of the LORD!
       Wrath has gone forth,
    a whirling tempest;
       it will burst upon the head of
       the wicked.
20  The anger of the LORD will not
       turn back
    until he has executed and
       accomplished
    the intents of his mind.
    In the latter days you will
       understand it clearly.

21  I did not send the prophets,
       yet they ran;
    I did not speak to them,
       yet they prophesied.
22  But if they had stood in my
       council,
    then they would have
       proclaimed my words to
       my people,
    and they would have turned
       them from their evil way,
    and from the evil of their
       doings.

# 2 THESSALONIANS 1.1–12

PAUL, Silvanus, and Timothy,
To the church of the Thessalonians in God our Father and the Lord Jesus Christ:

2  Grace to you and peace from God our[a] Father and the Lord Jesus Christ.

3  We must always give thanks to God for you, brothers and sisters,[b] as is right, because your faith is growing abundantly, and the love of everyone of you for one another is increasing. [4]Therefore we ourselves boast of you among the churches of God for your steadfastness and faith during all your persecutions and the afflictions that you are enduring.

5  This is evidence of the righteous judgment of God, and is intended to make you worthy of the kingdom of God, for which you are also suffering. [6]For it is indeed just of God to repay with affliction those who afflict you, [7]and to give relief to the afflicted as well as to us, when the Lord Jesus is revealed from heaven with his mighty angels [8]in flaming fire, inflicting vengeance on those who do not know God and on those who do not obey the gospel of our Lord Jesus. [9]These will suffer the punishment of eternal destruction, separated from the presence of the Lord and from the glory of his might, [10]when he comes to be glorified by his saints and to be marveled at on that day among all who have believed, because our testimony to you was believed. [11]To this end we always pray for you, asking that our God will make you worthy of his call and will fulfill by his power every good resolve and work of faith, [12]so that the name of our Lord Jesus may be glorified in you, and you in him, according to the grace of our God and the Lord Jesus Christ.

[a]Other ancient authorities read *the*   [b]Gk *brothers*

## PSALM 83.1–18

*A Song. A Psalm of Asaph.*

O GOD, do not keep silence;
do not hold your peace or
be still, O God!
2 Even now your enemies are in
tumult;
those who hate you have
raised their heads.
3 They lay crafty plans against
your people;
they consult together against
those you protect.
4 They say, "Come, let us wipe
them out as a nation;
let the name of Israel be
remembered no more."
5 They conspire with one accord;
against you they make a
covenant—
6 the tents of Edom and the
Ishmaelites,
Moab and the Hagrites,
7 Gebal and Ammon and Amalek,
Philistia with the inhabitants
of Tyre;
8 Assyria also has joined them;
they are the strong arm of
the children of Lot. *Selah*

9 Do to them as you did to
Midian,
as to Sisera and Jabin at the
Wadi Kishon,
10 who were destroyed at En-dor,
who became dung for the
ground.
11 Make their nobles like Oreb and
Zeeb,
all their princes like Zebah
and Zalmunna,
12 who said, "Let us take the
pastures of God
for our own possession."

13 O my God, make them like
whirling dust, a
like chaff before the wind.
14 As fire consumes the forest,
as the flame sets the
mountains ablaze,
15 so pursue them with your
tempest
and terrify them with your
hurricane.
16 Fill their faces with shame,
so that they may seek your
name, O LORD.
17 Let them be put to shame and
dismayed forever;
let them perish in disgrace.
18 Let them know that you alone,
whose name is the LORD,
are the Most High over all
the earth.

## PROVERBS 25.11–14

A WORD fitly spoken
is like apples of gold in a
setting of silver.
12 Like a gold ring or an ornament
of gold
is a wise rebuke to a listening
ear.
13 Like the cold of snow in the
time of harvest
are faithful messengers to
those who send them;
they refresh the spirit of their
masters.
14 Like clouds and wind without
rain
is one who boasts of a gift
never given.

a Or *a tumbleweed*

# OCTOBER 14

## JEREMIAH 23.23—25.38

**A**M I a God near by, says the LORD, and not a God far off? <sup>24</sup>Who can hide in secret places so that I cannot see them? says the LORD. Do I not fill heaven and earth? says the LORD. <sup>25</sup>I have heard what the prophets have said who prophesy lies in my name, saying, "I have dreamed, I have dreamed!" <sup>26</sup>How long? Will the hearts of the prophets ever turn back—those who prophesy lies, and who prophesy the deceit of their own heart? <sup>27</sup>They plan to make my people forget my name by their dreams that they tell one another, just as their ancestors forgot my name for Baal. <sup>28</sup>Let the prophet who has a dream tell the dream, but let the one who has my word speak my word faithfully. What has straw in common with wheat? says the LORD. <sup>29</sup>Is not my word like fire, says the LORD, and like a hammer that breaks a rock in pieces? <sup>30</sup>See, therefore, I am against the prophets, says the LORD, who steal my words from one another. <sup>31</sup>See, I am against the prophets, says the LORD, who use their own tongues and say, "Says the LORD." <sup>32</sup>See, I am against those who prophesy lying dreams, says the LORD, and who tell them, and who lead my people astray by their lies and their recklessness, when I did not send them or appoint them; so they do not profit this people at all, says the LORD.

33 When this people, or a prophet, or a priest asks you, "What is the burden of the LORD?" you shall say to them, "You are the burden,[a] and I will cast you off, says the LORD." <sup>34</sup>And as for the prophet, priest, or the people who say, "The burden of the LORD," I will punish them and their households. <sup>35</sup>Thus shall you say to one another, among yourselves, "What has the LORD answered?" or "What has the LORD spoken?" <sup>36</sup>But "the burden of the LORD" you shall mention no more, for the burden is everyone's own word, and so you pervert the words of the living God, the LORD of hosts, our God. <sup>37</sup>Thus you shall ask the prophet, "What has the LORD answered you?" or "What has the LORD spoken?" <sup>38</sup>But if you say, "the burden of the LORD," thus says the LORD: Because you have said these words, "the burden of the LORD," when I sent to you, saying, You shall not say, "the burden of the LORD," <sup>39</sup>therefore, I will surely lift you up[b] and cast you away from my presence, you and the city that I gave to you and your ancestors. <sup>40</sup>And I will bring upon you everlasting disgrace and perpetual shame, which shall not be forgotten.

24.1 THE LORD showed me two baskets of figs placed before the temple of the LORD. This was after King Nebuchadrezzar of Babylon had taken into exile from Jerusalem King Jeconiah son of Jehoiakim of Judah, together with the officials of Judah, the artisans, and the smiths, and had brought them to Babylon. <sup>2</sup>One basket had very good figs, like first-ripe figs, but the other basket had very bad figs, so bad that they could not be eaten. <sup>3</sup>And the LORD said to me, "What do you see, Jeremiah?" I said, "Figs, the good figs very good, and the bad figs very bad, so bad that they cannot be eaten."

4 Then the word of the LORD came to me: <sup>5</sup>Thus says the LORD, the God of Israel: Like these good figs, so I will

regard as good the exiles from Judah, whom I have sent away from this place to the land of the Chaldeans. <sup>6</sup>I will set my eyes upon them for good, and I will bring them back to this land. I will build them up, and not tear them down; I will plant them, and not pluck them up. <sup>7</sup>I will give them a heart to know that I am the LORD; and they shall be my people and I will be their God, for they shall return to me with their whole heart.

8  But thus says the LORD: Like the bad figs that are so bad they cannot be eaten, so will I treat King Zedekiah of Judah, his officials, the remnant of Jerusalem who remain in this land, and those who live in the land of Egypt. <sup>9</sup>I will make them a horror, an evil thing, to all the kingdoms of the earth—a disgrace, a byword, a taunt, and a curse in all the places where I shall drive them. <sup>10</sup>And I will send sword, famine, and pestilence upon them, until they are utterly destroyed from the land that I gave to them and their ancestors.

<sup>25.1</sup> THE word that came to Jeremiah concerning all the people of Judah, in the fourth year of King Jehoiakim son of Josiah of Judah (that was the first year of King Nebuchadrezzar of Babylon), <sup>2</sup>which the prophet Jeremiah spoke to all the people of Judah and all the inhabitants of Jerusalem: <sup>3</sup>For twenty-three years, from the thirteenth year of King Josiah son of Amon of Judah, to this day, the word of the LORD has come to me, and I have spoken persistently to you, but you have not listened. <sup>4</sup>And though the LORD persistently sent you all his servants the prophets, you have neither listened nor inclined your ears to hear <sup>5</sup>when they said, "Turn now, everyone of you, from your evil way and wicked doings, and you will remain upon the land that the LORD has given to you and your ancestors from of old and forever; <sup>6</sup>do not go after other gods to serve and worship them, and do not provoke me to anger with the work of your hands. Then I will do you no harm." <sup>7</sup>Yet you did not listen to me, says the LORD, and so you have provoked me to anger with the work of your hands to your own harm.

8  Therefore thus says the LORD of hosts: Because you have not obeyed my words, <sup>9</sup>I am going to send for all the tribes of the north, says the LORD, even for King Nebuchadrezzar of Babylon, my servant, and I will bring them against this land and its inhabitants, and against all these nations around; I will utterly destroy them, and make them an object of horror and of hissing, and an everlasting disgrace. <sup>a</sup> <sup>10</sup>And I will banish from them the sound of mirth and the sound of gladness, the voice of the bridegroom and the voice of the bride, the sound of the millstones and the light of the lamp. <sup>11</sup>This whole land shall become a ruin and a waste, and these nations shall serve the king of Babylon seventy years. <sup>12</sup>Then after seventy years are completed, I will punish the king of Babylon and that nation, the land of the Chaldeans, for their iniquity, says the LORD, making the land an everlasting waste. <sup>13</sup>I will bring upon that land all the words that I have uttered against it, everything written in this book, which Jeremiah prophesied against all the nations. <sup>14</sup>For many nations and great kings shall make slaves of them also; and I will repay them according to their deeds and the work of their hands.

15  For thus the LORD, the God of Israel, said to me: Take from my hand this cup of the wine of wrath, and make all the nations to whom I send you drink it. <sup>16</sup>They shall drink and stagger and go out of their minds because of the sword that I am sending among them.

17  So I took the cup from the LORD's hand, and made all the nations to

---

a Gk Compare Syr: Heb *and everlasting desolations*

whom the Lord sent me drink it: [18]Jerusalem and the towns of Judah, its kings and officials, to make them a desolation and a waste, an object of hissing and of cursing, as they are today; [19]Pharaoh king of Egypt, his servants, his officials, and all his people; [20]all the mixed people; [a] all the kings of the land of Uz; all the kings of the land of the Philistines—Ashkelon, Gaza, Ekron, and the remnant of Ashdod; [21]Edom, Moab, and the Ammonites; [22]all the kings of Tyre, all the kings of Sidon, and the kings of the coastland across the sea; [23]Dedan, Tema, Buz, and all who have shaven temples; [24]all the kings of Arabia and all the kings of the mixed peoples[a] that live in the desert; [25]all the kings of Zimri, all the kings of Elam, and all the kings of Media; [26]all the kings of the north, far and near, one after another, and all the kingdoms of the world that are on the face of the earth. And after them the king of Sheshach[b] shall drink.

27 Then you shall say to them, Thus says the Lord of hosts, the God of Israel: Drink, get drunk and vomit, fall and rise no more, because of the sword that I am sending among you.

28 And if they refuse to accept the cup from your hand to drink, then you shall say to them: Thus says the Lord of hosts: You must drink! [29]See, I am beginning to bring disaster on the city that is called by my name, and how can you possibly avoid punishment? You shall not go unpunished, for I am summoning a sword against all the inhabitants of the earth, says the Lord of hosts.

30 You, therefore, shall prophesy against them all these words, and say to them:

The Lord will roar from on
  high,
    and from his holy habitation
    utter his voice;
he will roar mightily against
  his fold,
    and shout, like those who
    tread grapes,
  against all the inhabitants of
  the earth.
31  The clamor will resound to the
    ends of the earth,
    for the Lord has an
    indictment against the
    nations;
  he is entering into judgment
    with all flesh,
    and the guilty he will put to
    the sword,
                says the Lord.

32  Thus says the Lord of hosts:
  See, disaster is spreading
    from nation to nation,
  and a great tempest is stirring
    from the farthest parts of
    the earth!

33  Those slain by the Lord on that day shall extend from one end of the earth to the other. They shall not be lamented, or gathered, or buried; they shall become dung on the surface of the ground.

34  Wail, you shepherds, and cry
    out;
    roll in ashes, you lords of
    the flock,
  for the days of your slaughter
    have come—and your
    dispersions, [a]
  and you shall fall like a
    choice vessel.
35  Flight shall fail the shepherds,
    and there shall be no escape
    for the lords of the flock.
36  Hark! the cry of the shepherds,
    and the wail of the lords of
    the flock!
  For the Lord is despoiling their
    pasture,
37    and the peaceful folds are
    devastated,

---

[a]Meaning of Heb uncertain  [b]*Sheshach* is a cryptogram for *Babel*, Babylon

because of the fierce anger of
the Lord.
38   Like a lion he has left his
covert;
for their land has become
a waste
because of the cruel sword,
and because of his fierce
anger.

## 2 THESSALONIANS 2.1–17

**A**s to the coming of our Lord
Jesus Christ and our being
gathered together to him, we
beg you, brothers and sisters, a [2]not to
be quickly shaken in mind or alarmed,
either by spirit or by word or by letter,
as though from us, to the effect that the
day of the Lord is already here. [3]Let no
one deceive you in any way; for that
day will not come unless the rebellion
comes first and the lawless one[b] is revealed, the one destined for destruction. [c] [4]He opposes and exalts himself
above every so-called god or object of
worship, so that he takes his seat in the
temple of God, declaring himself to be
God. [5]Do you not remember that I told
you these things when I was still with
you? [6]And you know what is now re-
straining him, so that he may be revealed when his time comes. [7]For the
mystery of lawlessness is already at
work, but only until the one who now
restrains it is removed. [8]And then the
lawless one will be revealed, whom the
Lord Jesus[d] will destroy[e] with the
breath of his mouth, annihilating him by
the manifestation of his coming. [9]The
coming of the lawless one is apparent in
the working of Satan, who uses all
power, signs, lying wonders, [10]and every kind of wicked deception for those
who are perishing, because they refused to love the truth and so be saved.
[11]For this reason God sends them a
powerful delusion, leading them to believe what is false, [12]so that all who
have not believed the truth but took
pleasure in unrighteousness will be
condemned.

13   But we must always give thanks
to God for you, brothers and sisters[a]
beloved by the Lord, because God
chose you as the first fruits[f] for salvation through sanctification by the Spirit
and through belief in the truth. [14]For
this purpose he called you through our
proclamation of the good news, [g] so
that you may obtain the glory of our
Lord Jesus Christ. [15]So then, brothers
and sisters, [a] stand firm and hold fast
to the traditions that you were taught
by us, either by word of mouth or by
our letter.

16   Now may our Lord Jesus Christ
himself and God our Father, who loved
us and through grace gave us eternal
comfort and good hope, [17]comfort your
hearts and strengthen them in every
good work and word.

## PSALM 84.1–12

*To the leader: according to The Gittith. Of the
Korahites. A Psalm.*

**H**ow lovely is your dwelling
place,
O Lord of hosts!
2   My soul longs, indeed it faints
for the courts of the Lord;
my heart and my flesh sing for
joy
to the living God.

3   Even the sparrow finds a home,
and the swallow a nest for
herself,
where she may lay her
young,
at your altars, O Lord of hosts,
my King and my God.

---

aGk *brothers*   bGk *the man of lawlessness*; other ancient authorities read *the man of sin*   cGk *the son
of destruction*   dOther ancient authorities lack *Jesus*   eOther ancient authorities read *consume*
fOther ancient authorities read *from the beginning*   gOr *through our gospel*

4  Happy are those who live in
     your house,
   ever singing your praise.
                              *Selah*

5  Happy are those whose strength
     is in you,
   in whose heart are the
     highways to Zion. **a**
6  As they go through the valley of
     Baca
   they make it a place of
     springs;
   the early rain also covers it
     with pools.
7  They go from strength to
     strength;
   the God of gods will be seen
     in Zion.

8  O Lord God of hosts, hear my
     prayer;
   give ear, O God of Jacob!
                              *Selah*
9  Behold our shield, O God;

   look on the face of your
     anointed.

10  For a day in your courts is
      better
    than a thousand elsewhere.
    I would rather be a doorkeeper
      in the house of my God
    than live in the tents of
      wickedness.
11  For the Lord God is a sun and
      shield;
    he bestows favor and honor.
    No good thing does the Lord
      withhold
    from those who walk
      uprightly.
12  O Lord of hosts,
    happy is everyone who trusts
      in you.

## PROVERBS 25.15

WITH patience a ruler may be
     persuaded,
   and a soft tongue can
     break bones.

# OCTOBER 15

## JEREMIAH 26.1—27.22

AT the beginning of the reign of King Jehoiakim son of Josiah of Judah, this word came from the Lord: 2Thus says the Lord: Stand in the court of the Lord's house, and speak to all the cities of Judah that come to worship in the house of the Lord; speak to them all the words that I command you; do not hold back a word. 3It may be that they will listen, all of them, and will turn from their evil way, that I may change my mind about the disaster that I intend to bring on them because of their evil doings. 4You shall say to them: Thus says the Lord: If you will not listen to me, to walk in my law that I have set before you, 5and to heed the words of my servants the prophets whom I send to you urgently—though you have not heeded— 6then I will make this house like Shiloh, and I will make this city a curse for all the nations of the earth.

**a**Heb lacks *to Zion*

7 The priests and the prophets and all the people heard Jeremiah speaking these words in the house of the Lord. 8And when Jeremiah had finished speaking all that the Lord had commanded him to speak to all the people, then the priests and the prophets and all the people laid hold of him, saying, "You shall die! 9Why have you prophesied in the name of the Lord, saying, 'This house shall be like Shiloh, and this city shall be desolate, without inhabitant'?" And all the people gathered around Jeremiah in the house of the Lord.

10 When the officials of Judah heard these things, they came up from the king's house to the house of the Lord and took their seat in the entry of the New Gate of the house of the Lord. 11Then the priests and the prophets said to the officials and to all the people, "This man deserves the sentence of death because he has prophesied against this city, as you have heard with your own ears."

12 Then Jeremiah spoke to all the officials and all the people, saying, "It is the Lord who sent me to prophesy against this house and this city all the words you have heard. 13Now therefore amend your ways and your doings, and obey the voice of the Lord your God, and the Lord will change his mind about the disaster that he has pronounced against you. 14But as for me, here I am in your hands. Do with me as seems good and right to you. 15Only know for certain that if you put me to death, you will be bringing innocent blood upon yourselves and upon this city and its inhabitants, for in truth the Lord sent me to you to speak all these words in your ears."

16 Then the officials and all the people said to the priests and the prophets, "This man does not deserve the sentence of death, for he has spoken to us in the name of the Lord our God." 17And some of the elders of the land arose and said to all the assembled people, 18"Micah of Moresheth, who prophesied during the days of King Hezekiah of Judah, said to all the people of Judah: 'Thus says the Lord of hosts,

Zion shall be plowed as a field;
Jerusalem shall become a
heap of ruins,
and the mountain of the house
a wooded height.'

19Did King Hezekiah of Judah and all Judah actually put him to death? Did he not fear the Lord and entreat the favor of the Lord, and did not the Lord change his mind about the disaster that he had pronounced against them? But we are about to bring great disaster on ourselves!"

20 There was another man prophesying in the name of the Lord, Uriah son of Shemaiah from Kiriath-jearim. He prophesied against this city and against this land in words exactly like those of Jeremiah. 21And when King Jehoiakim, with all his warriors and all the officials, heard his words, the king sought to put him to death; but when Uriah heard of it, he was afraid and fled and escaped to Egypt. 22Then King Jehoiakim senta Elnathan son of Achbor and men with him to Egypt, 23and they took Uriah from Egypt and brought him to King Jehoiakim, who struck him down with the sword and threw his dead body into the burial place of the common people.

24 But the hand of Ahikam son of Shaphan was with Jeremiah so that he was not given over into the hands of the people to be put to death.

27.1 In the beginning of the reign of King Zedekiahb son of Josiah of Judah, this word came to Jeremiah from the Lord. 2Thus the Lord said to me: Make yourself a yoke of straps and bars, and put

aHeb adds *men to Egypt*   bAnother reading is *Jehoiakim*

them on your neck. [3]Send word[a] to the king of Edom, the king of Moab, the king of the Ammonites, the king of Tyre, and the king of Sidon by the hand of the envoys who have come to Jerusalem to King Zedekiah of Judah. [4]Give them this charge for their masters: Thus says the Lord of hosts, the God of Israel: This is what you shall say to your masters: [5]It is I who by my great power and my outstretched arm have made the earth, with the people and animals that are on the earth, and I give it to whomever I please. [6]Now I have given all these lands into the hand of King Nebuchadnezzar of Babylon, my servant, and I have given him even the wild animals of the field to serve him. [7]All the nations shall serve him and his son and his grandson, until the time of his own land comes; then many nations and great kings shall make him their slave.

8  But if any nation or kingdom will not serve this king, Nebuchadnezzar of Babylon, and put its neck under the yoke of the king of Babylon, then I will punish that nation with the sword, with famine, and with pestilence, says the Lord, until I have completed its[b] destruction by his hand. [9]You, therefore, must not listen to your prophets, your diviners, your dreamers,[c] your soothsayers, or your sorcerers, who are saying to you, 'You shall not serve the king of Babylon.' [10]For they are prophesying a lie to you, with the result that you will be removed far from your land; I will drive you out, and you will perish. [11]But any nation that will bring its neck under the yoke of the king of Babylon and serve him, I will leave on its own land, says the Lord, to till it and live there.

12  I spoke to King Zedekiah of Judah in the same way: Bring your necks under the yoke of the king of Babylon, and serve him and his people, and live.

[13]Why should you and your people die by the sword, by famine, and by pestilence, as the Lord has spoken concerning any nation that will not serve the king of Babylon? [14]Do not listen to the words of the prophets who are telling you not to serve the king of Babylon, for they are prophesying a lie to you. [15]I have not sent them, says the Lord, but they are prophesying falsely in my name, with the result that I will drive you out and you will perish, you and the prophets who are prophesying to you.

16  Then I spoke to the priests and to all this people, saying, Thus says the Lord: Do not listen to the words of your prophets who are prophesying to you, saying, "The vessels of the Lord's house will soon be brought back from Babylon," for they are prophesying a lie to you. [17]Do not listen to them; serve the king of Babylon and live. Why should this city become a desolation? [18]If indeed they are prophets, and if the word of the Lord is with them, then let them intercede with the Lord of hosts, that the vessels left in the house of the Lord, in the house of the king of Judah, and in Jerusalem may not go to Babylon. [19]For thus says the Lord of hosts concerning the pillars, the sea, the stands, and the rest of the vessels that are left in this city, [20]which King Nebuchadnezzar of Babylon did not take away when he took into exile from Jerusalem to Babylon King Jeconiah son of Jehoiakim of Judah, and all the nobles of Judah and Jerusalem— [21]thus says the Lord of hosts, the God of Israel, concerning the vessels left in the house of the Lord, in the house of the king of Judah, and in Jerusalem: [22]They shall be carried to Babylon, and there they shall stay, until the day when I give attention to them, says the Lord. Then I will bring them up and restore them to this place.

[a]Cn: Heb *send them*   [b]Heb *their*   [c]Gk Syr Vg: Heb *dreams*

## 2 THESSALONIANS 3.1–18

Finally, brothers and sisters,[a] pray for us, so that the word of the Lord may spread rapidly and be glorified everywhere, just as it is among you, [2]and that we may be rescued from wicked and evil people; for not all have faith. [3]But the Lord is faithful; he will strengthen you and guard you from the evil one.[b] [4]And we have confidence in the Lord concerning you, that you are doing and will go on doing the things that we command. [5]May the Lord direct your hearts to the love of God and to the steadfastness of Christ.

6 Now we command you, beloved,[a] in the name of our Lord Jesus Christ, to keep away from believers who are[c] living in idleness and not according to the tradition that they[d] received from us. [7]For you yourselves know how you ought to imitate us; we were not idle when we were with you, [8]and we did not eat anyone's bread without paying for it; but with toil and labor we worked night and day, so that we might not burden any of you. [9]This was not because we do not have that right, but in order to give you an example to imitate. [10]For even when we were with you, we gave you this command: Anyone unwilling to work should not eat. [11]For we hear that some of you are living in idleness, mere busybodies, not doing any work. [12]Now such persons we command and exhort in the Lord Jesus Christ to do their work quietly and to earn their own living. [13]Brothers and sisters,[e] do not be weary in doing what is right.

14 Take note of those who do not obey what we say in this letter; have nothing to do with them, so that they may be ashamed. [15]Do not regard them as enemies, but warn them as believers.[f]

16 Now may the Lord of peace himself give you peace at all times in all ways. The Lord be with all of you.

17 I, Paul, write this greeting with my own hand. This is the mark in every letter of mine; it is the way I write. [18]The grace of our Lord Jesus Christ be with all of you.[g]

## PSALM 85.1–13

*To the leader. Of the Korahites. A Psalm.*

Lord, you were favorable to
    your land;
  you restored the fortunes of
    Jacob.
[2] You forgave the iniquity of your
    people;
  you pardoned all their sin.
                *Selah*
[3] You withdrew all your wrath;
  you turned from your hot
    anger.

[4] Restore us again, O God of our
    salvation,
  and put away your indignation
    toward us.
[5] Will you be angry with us
    forever?
  Will you prolong your anger
    to all generations?
[6] Will you not revive us again,
  so that your people may
    rejoice in you?
[7] Show us your steadfast love,
    O Lord,
  and grant us your salvation.

[8] Let me hear what God the Lord
    will speak,
  for he will speak peace to his
    people,
  to his faithful, to those who
    turn to him in their
    hearts.[h]

---

aGk *brothers*　bOr *from evil*　cGk *from every brother who is*　dOther ancient authorities read *you*　eGk *Brothers*　fGk *a brother*　gOther ancient authorities add *Amen*　hGk: Heb *but let them not turn back to folly*

9 Surely his salvation is at hand
    for those who fear him,
  that his glory may dwell in
    our land.

10 Steadfast love and faithfulness
    will meet;
  righteousness and peace will
    kiss each other.
11 Faithfulness will spring up from
    the ground,
  and righteousness will look
    down from the sky.

12 The LORD will give what is
    good,
  and our land will yield its
    increase.
13 Righteousness will go before
    him,
  and will make a path for his
    steps.

## PROVERBS 25.16

IF you have found honey, eat only
    enough for you,
  or else, having too much, you
    will vomit it.

# OCTOBER 16

## JEREMIAH 28.1—29.32

IN that same year, at the beginning of the reign of King Zedekiah of Judah, in the fifth month of the fourth year, the prophet Hananiah son of Azzur, from Gibeon, spoke to me in the house of the LORD, in the presence of the priests and all the people, saying, 2"Thus says the LORD of hosts, the God of Israel: I have broken the yoke of the king of Babylon. 3Within two years I will bring back to this place all the vessels of the LORD's house, which King Nebuchadnezzar of Babylon took away from this place and carried to Babylon. 4I will also bring back to this place King Jeconiah son of Jehoiakim of Judah, and all the exiles from Judah who went to Babylon, says the LORD, for I will break the yoke of the king of Babylon."

5 Then the prophet Jeremiah spoke to the prophet Hananiah in the presence of the priests and all the people who were standing in the house of the LORD; 6and the prophet Jeremiah said, "Amen! May the LORD do so; may the LORD fulfill the words that you have prophesied, and bring back to this place from Babylon the vessels of the house of the LORD, and all the exiles. 7But listen now to this word that I speak in your hearing and in the hearing of all the people. 8The prophets who preceded you and me from ancient times prophesied war, famine, and pestilence against many countries and great kingdoms. 9As for the prophet who prophesies peace, when the word of that prophet comes true, then it will be known that the LORD has truly sent the prophet."

10 Then the prophet Hananiah took the yoke from the neck of the prophet Jeremiah, and broke it. 11And Hananiah spoke in the presence of all the people, saying, "Thus says the LORD: This is how I will break the yoke of King Nebuchadnezzar of Babylon from the neck of all the nations within two years." At this, the prophet Jeremiah went his way.

12 Sometime after the prophet

Hananiah had broken the yoke from the neck of the prophet Jeremiah, the word of the LORD came to Jeremiah: 13Go, tell Hananiah, Thus says the LORD: You have broken wooden bars only to forge iron bars in place of them! 14For thus says the LORD of hosts, the God of Israel: I have put an iron yoke on the neck of all these nations so that they may serve King Nebuchadnezzar of Babylon, and they shall indeed serve him; I have even given him the wild animals. 15And the prophet Jeremiah said to the prophet Hananiah, "Listen, Hananiah, the LORD has not sent you, and you made this people trust in a lie. 16Therefore thus says the LORD: I am going to send you off the face of the earth. Within this year you will be dead, because you have spoken rebellion against the LORD."

17 In that same year, in the seventh month, the prophet Hananiah died.

29.1 THESE are the words of the letter that the prophet Jeremiah sent from Jerusalem to the remaining elders among the exiles, and to the priests, the prophets, and all the people, whom Nebuchadnezzar had taken into exile from Jerusalem to Babylon. 2This was after King Jeconiah, and the queen mother, the court officials, the leaders of Judah and Jerusalem, the artisans, and the smiths had departed from Jerusalem. 3The letter was sent by the hand of Elasah son of Shaphan and Gemariah son of Hilkiah, whom King Zedekiah of Judah sent to Babylon to King Nebuchadnezzar of Babylon. It said: 4Thus says the LORD of hosts, the God of Israel, to all the exiles whom I have sent into exile from Jerusalem to Babylon: 5Build houses and live in them; plant gardens and eat what they produce. 6Take wives and have sons and daughters; take wives for your sons, and give your daughters in marriage, that they may bear sons and daughters; multiply there, and do not decrease. 7But seek the welfare of the city where I have sent you into exile, and pray to the LORD on its behalf, for in its welfare you will find your welfare. 8For thus says the LORD of hosts, the God of Israel: Do not let the prophets and the diviners who are among you deceive you, and do not listen to the dreams that they dream, a 9for it is a lie that they are prophesying to you in my name; I did not send them, says the LORD.

10 For thus says the LORD: Only when Babylon's seventy years are completed will I visit you, and I will fulfill to you my promise and bring you back to this place. 11For surely I know the plans I have for you, says the LORD, plans for your welfare and not for harm, to give you a future with hope. 12Then when you call upon me and come and pray to me, I will hear you. 13When you search for me, you will find me; if you seek me with all your heart, 14I will let you find me, says the LORD, and I will restore your fortunes and gather you from all the nations and all the places where I have driven you, says the LORD, and I will bring you back to the place from which I sent you into exile.

15 Because you have said, "The LORD has raised up prophets for us in Babylon,"— 16Thus says the LORD concerning the king who sits on the throne of David, and concerning all the people who live in this city, your kinsfolk who did not go out with you into exile: 17Thus says the LORD of hosts, I am going to let loose on them sword, famine, and pestilence, and I will make them like rotten figs that are so bad they cannot be eaten. 18I will pursue them with the sword, with famine, and with pestilence, and will make them a horror to all the kingdoms of the earth, to be an

a Cn: Heb *your dreams that you cause to dream*

object of cursing, and horror, and hissing, and a derision among all the nations where I have driven them, ¹⁹because they did not heed my words, says the Lord, when I persistently sent to you my servants the prophets, but they[a] would not listen, says the Lord. ²⁰But now, all you exiles whom I sent away from Jerusalem to Babylon, hear the word of the Lord: ²¹Thus says the Lord of hosts, the God of Israel, concerning Ahab son of Kolaiah and Zedekiah son of Maaseiah, who are prophesying a lie to you in my name: I am going to deliver them into the hand of King Nebuchadrezzar of Babylon, and he shall kill them before your eyes. ²²And on account of them this curse shall be used by all the exiles from Judah in Babylon: "The Lord make you like Zedekiah and Ahab, whom the king of Babylon roasted in the fire," ²³because they have perpetrated outrage in Israel and have committed adultery with their neighbors' wives, and have spoken in my name lying words that I did not command them; I am the one who knows and bears witness, says the Lord.

24 To Shemaiah of Nehelam you shall say: ²⁵Thus says the Lord of hosts, the God of Israel: In your own name you sent a letter to all the people who are in Jerusalem, and to the priest Zephaniah son of Maaseiah, and to all the priests, saying, ²⁶The Lord himself has made you priest instead of the priest Jehoiada, so that there may be officers in the house of the Lord to control any madman who plays the prophet, to put him in the stocks and the collar. ²⁷So now why have you not rebuked Jeremiah of Anathoth who plays the prophet for you? ²⁸For he has actually sent to us in Babylon, saying, "It will be a long time; build houses and live in them, and plant gardens and eat what they produce."

29 The priest Zephaniah read this letter in the hearing of the prophet Jeremiah. ³⁰Then the word of the Lord came to Jeremiah: ³¹Send to all the exiles, saying, Thus says the Lord concerning Shemaiah of Nehelam: Because Shemaiah has prophesied to you, though I did not send him, and has led you to trust in a lie, ³²therefore thus says the Lord: I am going to punish Shemaiah of Nehelam and his descendants; he shall not have anyone living among this people to see[b] the good that I am going to do to my people, says the Lord, for he has spoken rebellion against the Lord.

# 1 TIMOTHY 1.1–20

**P**aul, an apostle of Christ Jesus by the command of God our Savior and of Christ Jesus our hope,

2 To Timothy, my loyal child in the faith:

Grace, mercy, and peace from God the Father and Christ Jesus our Lord.

3 I urge you, as I did when I was on my way to Macedonia, to remain in Ephesus so that you may instruct certain people not to teach any different doctrine, ⁴and not to occupy themselves with myths and endless genealogies that promote speculations rather than the divine training[c] that is known by faith. ⁵But the aim of such instruction is love that comes from a pure heart, a good conscience, and sincere faith. ⁶Some people have deviated from these and turned to meaningless talk, ⁷desiring to be teachers of the law, without understanding either what they are saying or the things about which they make assertions.

8 Now we know that the law is good, if one uses it legitimately. ⁹This means understanding that the law is laid down not for the innocent but for the

---

aSyr: Heb *you*   bGk: Heb *and he shall not see*   cOr *plan*

lawless and disobedient, for the godless and sinful, for the unholy and profane, for those who kill their father or mother, for murderers, [10]fornicators, sodomites, slave traders, liars, perjurers, and whatever else is contrary to the sound teaching [11]that conforms to the glorious gospel of the blessed God, which he entrusted to me.

12  I am grateful to Christ Jesus our Lord, who has strengthened me, because he judged me faithful and appointed me to his service, [13]even though I was formerly a blasphemer, a persecutor, and a man of violence. But I received mercy because I had acted ignorantly in unbelief, [14]and the grace of our Lord overflowed for me with the faith and love that are in Christ Jesus. [15]The saying is sure and worthy of full acceptance, that Christ Jesus came into the world to save sinners—of whom I am the foremost. [16]But for that very reason I received mercy, so that in me, as the foremost, Jesus Christ might display the utmost patience, making me an example to those who would come to believe in him for eternal life. [17]To the King of the ages, immortal, invisible, the only God, be honor and glory forever and ever. [a] Amen.

18  I am giving you these instructions, Timothy, my child, in accordance with the prophecies made earlier about you, so that by following them you may fight the good fight, [19]having faith and a good conscience. By rejecting conscience, certain persons have suffered shipwreck in the faith; [20]among them are Hymenaeus and Alexander, whom I have turned over to Satan, so that they may learn not to blaspheme.

## PSALM 86. 1–17

*A Prayer of David.*

INCLINE your ear, O LORD, and
    answer me,
  for I am poor and needy.
2  Preserve my life, for I am
    devoted to you;
  save your servant who trusts
    in you.
  You are my God; [3]be gracious
    to me, O Lord,
  for to you do I cry all day
    long.
4  Gladden the soul of your
    servant,
  for to you, O Lord, I lift up
    my soul.
5  For you, O Lord, are good and
    forgiving,
  abounding in steadfast love to
    all who call on you.
6  Give ear, O LORD, to my
    prayer;
  listen to my cry of
    supplication.
7  In the day of my trouble I call
    on you,
  for you will answer me.

8  There is none like you among
    the gods, O Lord,
  nor are there any works like
    yours.
9  All the nations you have made
    shall come
  and bow down before you,
    O Lord,
  and shall glorify your name.
10  For you are great and do
    wondrous things;
  you alone are God.
11  Teach me your way, O LORD,
    that I may walk in your truth;
  give me an undivided heart to
    revere your name.

[a] Gk *to the ages of the ages*

12   I give thanks to you, O Lord
         my God, with my whole
         heart,
     and I will glorify your name
         forever.
13   For great is your steadfast love
         toward me;
     you have delivered my soul
         from the depths of Sheol.

14   O God, the insolent rise up
         against me;
     a band of ruffians seeks my
         life,
     and they do not set you
         before them.
15   But you, O Lord, are a God
         merciful and gracious,
     slow to anger and abounding
         in steadfast love and
         faithfulness.

16   Turn to me and be gracious to
         me;
     give your strength to your
         servant;
     save the child of your serving
         girl.
17   Show me a sign of your favor,
     so that those who hate me
         may see it and be put to
         shame,
     because you, Lord, have
         helped me and comforted
         me.

## PROVERBS 25.17

L ET your foot be seldom in your
     neighbor's house,
  otherwise the neighbor will
     become weary of you
     and hate you.

# OCTOBER 17

## JEREMIAH 30.1—31.26

T HE word that came to Jeremiah from the Lord: ²Thus says the Lord, the God of Israel: Write in a book all the words that I have spoken to you. ³For the days are surely coming, says the Lord, when I will restore the fortunes of my people, Israel and Judah, says the Lord, and I will bring them back to the land that I gave to their ancestors and they shall take possession of it.

4   These are the words that the Lord spoke concerning Israel and Judah:

5   Thus says the Lord:
    We have heard a cry of panic,
        of terror, and no peace.
6   Ask now, and see,
        can a man bear a child?
    Why then do I see every man
        with his hands on his loins
            like a woman in labor?
    Why has every face turned
        pale?
7   Alas! that day is so great
        there is none like it;
    it is a time of distress for Jacob;
        yet he shall be rescued from
            it.

8   On that day, says the Lord of hosts, I will break the yoke from off hisᵃ neck, and I will burst hisᵃ bonds, and strangers shall no more make a

ᵃ Cn: Heb *your*

servant of him. ⁹But they shall serve the Lord their God and David their king, whom I will raise up for them.

10 But as for you, have no fear,
        my servant Jacob, says
        the Lord,
    and do not be dismayed,
        O Israel;
    for I am going to save you from
        far away,
    and your offspring from the
        land of their captivity.
    Jacob shall return and have quiet
        and ease,
    and no one shall make him
        afraid.
11 For I am with you, says the
        Lord, to save you;
    I will make an end of all the
        nations
        among which I scattered you,
    but of you I will not make
        an end.
    I will chastise you in just
        measure,
    and I will by no means leave
        you unpunished.

12 For thus says the Lord:
    Your hurt is incurable,
        your wound is grievous.
13 There is no one to uphold your
        cause,
        no medicine for your wound,
        no healing for you.
14 All your lovers have forgotten
        you;
        they care nothing for you;
    for I have dealt you the blow of
        an enemy,
        the punishment of a merciless
        foe,
    because your guilt is great,
        because your sins are so
        numerous.
15 Why do you cry out over your
        hurt?
        Your pain is incurable.
    Because your guilt is great,

    because your sins are so
        numerous,
    I have done these things to
        you.
16 Therefore all who devour you
        shall be devoured,
    and all your foes, everyone of
        them, shall go into
        captivity;
    those who plunder you shall be
        plundered,
    and all who prey on you I will
        make a prey.
17 For I will restore health to you,
    and your wounds I will heal,
                    says the Lord,
    because they have called you
        an outcast:
    "It is Zion; no one cares for
        her!"

18 Thus says the Lord:
    I am going to restore the
        fortunes of the tents of
        Jacob,
    and have compassion on his
        dwellings;
    the city shall be rebuilt upon its
        mound,
    and the citadel set on its
        rightful site.
19 Out of them shall come
        thanksgiving,
    and the sound of
        merrymakers.
    I will make them many, and
        they shall not be few;
    I will make them honored,
        and they shall not be
        disdained.
20 Their children shall be as of old,
        their congregation shall be
        established before me;
    and I will punish all who
        oppress them.
21 Their prince shall be one of
        their own,
    their ruler shall come from
        their midst;

I will bring him near, and he
    shall approach me,
for who would otherwise dare
    to approach me?
        says the LORD.
22 And you shall be my people,
    and I will be your God.

23 Look, the storm of the LORD!
    Wrath has gone forth,
a whirling[a] tempest;
    it will burst upon the head of
      the wicked.
24 The fierce anger of the LORD
    will not turn back
until he has executed and
    accomplished
the intents of his mind.
In the latter days you will
    understand this.

31.1 AT that time, says the LORD, I will
be the God of all the families of Israel,
and they shall be my people.
2 Thus says the LORD:
The people who survived the
    sword
    found grace in the wilderness;
when Israel sought for rest,
3     the LORD appeared to him[b]
      from far away. [c]
I have loved you with an
    everlasting love;
    therefore I have continued my
      faithfulness to you.
4 Again I will build you, and you
    shall be built,
    O virgin Israel!
Again you shall take[d] your
    tambourines,
and go forth in the dance of
    the merrymakers.
5 Again you shall plant vineyards
    on the mountains of Samaria;
the planters shall plant,
    and shall enjoy the fruit.
6 For there shall be a day when
    sentinels will call

in the hill country of Ephraim:
"Come, let us go up to Zion,
    to the LORD our God."
7 For thus says the LORD:
Sing aloud with gladness for
    Jacob,
    and raise shouts for the chief
      of the nations;
proclaim, give praise, and say,
    "Save, O LORD, your people,
    the remnant of Israel."
8 See, I am going to bring them
    from the land of the
    north,
    and gather them from the
      farthest parts of the
      earth,
among them the blind and
    the lame,
    those with child and those in
      labor, together;
a great company, they shall
    return here.
9 With weeping they shall come,
    and with consolations[e] I will
      lead them back,
I will let them walk by brooks of
    water,
    in a straight path in which
      they shall not stumble;
for I have become a father to
    Israel,
    and Ephraim is my firstborn.

10 Hear the word of the LORD,
    O nations,
    and declare it in the
      coastlands far away;
say, "He who scattered Israel
    will gather him,
    and will keep him as a
      shepherd a flock."
11 For the LORD has ransomed
    Jacob,
    and has redeemed him from
      hands too strong for him.

a One Ms: Meaning of MT uncertain  b Gk: Heb *me*  c Or *to him long ago*  d Or *adorn yourself with*
e Gk Compare Vg Tg: Heb *supplications*

12 They shall come and sing aloud
       on the height of Zion,
   and they shall be radiant over
       the goodness of the
       Lord,
   over the grain, the wine, and
       the oil,
   and over the young of the
       flock and the herd;
   their life shall become like a
       watered garden,
   and they shall never languish
       again.
13 Then shall the young women
       rejoice in the dance,
   and the young men and the
       old shall be merry.
   I will turn their mourning into
       joy,
   I will comfort them, and give
       them gladness for
       sorrow.
14 I will give the priests their fill of
       fatness,
   and my people shall be
       satisfied with my bounty,
                   says the Lord.

15 Thus says the Lord:
   A voice is heard in Ramah,
       lamentation and bitter
       weeping.
   Rachel is weeping for her
       children;
   she refuses to be comforted
       for her children,
   because they are no more.
16 Thus says the Lord:
   Keep your voice from weeping,
       and your eyes from tears;
   for there is a reward for your
       work,
                   says the Lord:
   they shall come back from the
       land of the enemy;
17 there is hope for your future,
                   says the Lord:

your children shall come back
    to their own country.

18 Indeed I heard Ephraim
       pleading:
   "You disciplined me, and I took
       the discipline;
   I was like a calf untrained.
   Bring me back, let me come
       back,
       for you are the Lord my God.
19 For after I had turned away I
       repented;
   and after I was discovered, I
       struck my thigh;
   I was ashamed, and I was
       dismayed
   because I bore the disgrace of
       my youth."
20 Is Ephraim my dear son?
   Is he the child I delight in?
   As often as I speak against him,
       I still remember him.
   Therefore I am deeply moved
       for him;
   I will surely have mercy on
       him,
                   says the Lord.

21 Set up road markers for
       yourself,
   make yourself guideposts;
   consider well the highway,
       the road by which you went.
   Return, O virgin Israel,
       return to these your cities.
22 How long will you waver,
       O faithless daughter?
   For the Lord has created a new
       thing on the earth:
   a woman encompasses[a] a
       man.

23 Thus says the Lord of hosts, the
God of Israel: Once more they shall use
these words in the land of Judah and in
its towns when I restore their fortunes:

[a] Meaning of Heb uncertain

"The Lord bless you, O abode
   of righteousness,
   O holy hill!"
²⁴And Judah and all its towns shall live
there together, and the farmers and
those who wander[a] with their flocks.
²⁵ I will satisfy the weary,
      and all who are faint I will
         replenish.

26  Thereupon I awoke and looked,
and my sleep was pleasant to me.

## 1 TIMOTHY 2.1–15

FIRST of all, then, I urge that supplications, prayers, interces-
sions, and thanksgivings be
made for everyone, ²for kings and all
who are in high positions, so that we
may lead a quiet and peaceable life in all
godliness and dignity. ³This is right and
is acceptable in the sight of God our
Savior, ⁴who desires everyone to be
saved and to come to the knowledge of
the truth. ⁵For
      there is one God;
         there is also one mediator
            between God and
            humankind,
      Christ Jesus, himself human,
⁶       who gave himself a ransom
            for all
—this was attested at the right time.
⁷For this I was appointed a herald and
an apostle (I am telling the truth,[b] I am
not lying), a teacher of the Gentiles in
faith and truth.

8  I desire, then, that in every place
the men should pray, lifting up holy
hands without anger or argument; ⁹also
that the women should dress themselves modestly and decently in suitable clothing, not with their hair
braided, or with gold, pearls, or expen-
sive clothes, ¹⁰but with good works, as
is proper for women who profess reverence for God. ¹¹Let a woman[c] learn
in silence with full submission.
¹²I permit no woman[c] to teach or to
have authority over a man;[d] she is to
keep silent. ¹³For Adam was formed
first, then Eve; ¹⁴and Adam was not deceived, but the woman was deceived
and became a transgressor. ¹⁵Yet she
will be saved through childbearing, provided they continue in faith and love and
holiness, with modesty.

## PSALM 87.1–7

*Of the Korahites. A Psalm. A Song.*

ON the holy mount stands the
      city he founded;
²       the Lord loves the
      gates of Zion
   more than all the dwellings of
      Jacob.
³  Glorious things are spoken of
         you,
      O city of God.            *Selah*

⁴  Among those who know me I
         mention Rahab and
         Babylon;
      Philistia too, and Tyre, with
         Ethiopia[e]—
      "This one was born there,"
         they say.

⁵  And of Zion it shall be said,
      "This one and that one were
         born in it";
      for the Most High himself will
         establish it.
⁶  The Lord records, as he
         registers the peoples,
      "This one was born there."
                        *Selah*

⁷  Singers and dancers alike say,
      "All my springs are in you."

---

[a]Cn Compare Syr Vg Tg: Heb *and they shall wander*   [b]Other ancient authorities add *in Christ*
[c]Or *wife*   [d]Or *her husband*   [e]Or *Nubia*; Heb *Cush*

## PROVERBS 25.18–19

Like a war club, a sword, or a
    sharp arrow
is one who bears false
    witness against a
    neighbor.

19 Like a bad tooth or a lame foot
    is trust in a faithless person in
    time of trouble.

# OCTOBER 18

## JEREMIAH 31.27—32.44

The days are surely coming, says the Lord, when I will sow the house of Israel and the house of Judah with the seed of humans and the seed of animals. 28 And just as I have watched over them to pluck up and break down, to overthrow, destroy, and bring evil, so I will watch over them to build and to plant, says the Lord. 29 In those days they shall no longer say:

"The parents have eaten sour
    grapes,
and the children's teeth are
    set on edge."

30 But all shall die for their own sins; the teeth of everyone who eats sour grapes shall be set on edge.

31 The days are surely coming, says the Lord, when I will make a new covenant with the house of Israel and the house of Judah. 32 It will not be like the covenant that I made with their ancestors when I took them by the hand to bring them out of the land of Egypt— a covenant that they broke, though I was their husband,[a] says the Lord. 33 But this is the covenant that I will make with the house of Israel after those days, says the Lord: I will put my law within them, and I will write it on their hearts; and I will be their God, and they shall be my people. 34 No longer shall they teach one another, or say to each other, "Know the Lord," for they shall all know me, from the least of them to the greatest, says the Lord; for I will forgive their iniquity, and remember their sin no more.

35 Thus says the Lord,
    who gives the sun for light by
        day
    and the fixed order of the
        moon and the stars for
        light by night,
    who stirs up the sea so that its
        waves roar—
    the Lord of hosts is his name:
36 If this fixed order were ever
        to cease
    from my presence, says the
        Lord,
    then also the offspring of Israel
        would cease
    to be a nation before me
        forever.

37 Thus says the Lord:
    If the heavens above can be
        measured,
    and the foundations of the
        earth below can be
        explored,
    then I will reject all the offspring
        of Israel

a Or *master*

because of all they have done,
says the Lord.

38 The days are surely coming, says the Lord, when the city shall be rebuilt for the Lord from the tower of Hananel to the Corner Gate. ³⁹And the measuring line shall go out farther, straight to the hill Gareb, and shall then turn to Goah. ⁴⁰The whole valley of the dead bodies and the ashes, and all the fields as far as the Wadi Kidron, to the corner of the Horse Gate toward the east, shall be sacred to the Lord. It shall never again be uprooted or overthrown.

32.1 The word that came to Jeremiah from the Lord in the tenth year of King Zedekiah of Judah, which was the eighteenth year of Nebuchadrezzar. ²At that time the army of the king of Babylon was besieging Jerusalem, and the prophet Jeremiah was confined in the court of the guard that was in the palace of the king of Judah, ³where King Zedekiah of Judah had confined him. Zedekiah had said, "Why do you prophesy and say: Thus says the Lord: I am going to give this city into the hand of the king of Babylon, and he shall take it; ⁴King Zedekiah of Judah shall not escape out of the hands of the Chaldeans, but shall surely be given into the hands of the king of Babylon, and shall speak with him face to face and see him eye to eye; ⁵and he shall take Zedekiah to Babylon, and there he shall remain until I attend to him, says the Lord; though you fight against the Chaldeans, you shall not succeed?"

6 Jeremiah said, The word of the Lord came to me: ⁷Hanamel son of your uncle Shallum is going to come to you and say, "Buy my field that is at Anathoth, for the right of redemption by purchase is yours." ⁸Then my cousin Hanamel came to me in the court of the guard, in accordance with the word of the Lord, and said to me, "Buy my field that is at Anathoth in the land of Benjamin, for the right of possession and redemption is yours; buy it for yourself." Then I knew that this was the word of the Lord.

9 And I bought the field at Anathoth from my cousin Hanamel, and weighed out the money to him, seventeen shekels of silver. ¹⁰I signed the deed, sealed it, got witnesses, and weighed the money on scales. ¹¹Then I took the sealed deed of purchase, containing the terms and conditions, and the open copy; ¹²and I gave the deed of purchase to Baruch son of Neriah son of Mahseiah, in the presence of my cousin Hanamel, in the presence of the witnesses who signed the deed of purchase, and in the presence of all the Judeans who were sitting in the court of the guard. ¹³In their presence I charged Baruch, saying, ¹⁴Thus says the Lord of hosts, the God of Israel: Take these deeds, both this sealed deed of purchase and this open deed, and put them in an earthenware jar, in order that they may last for a long time. ¹⁵For thus says the Lord of hosts, the God of Israel: Houses and fields and vineyards shall again be bought in this land.

16 After I had given the deed of purchase to Baruch son of Neriah, I prayed to the Lord, saying: ¹⁷Ah Lord God! It is you who made the heavens and the earth by your great power and by your outstretched arm! Nothing is too hard for you. ¹⁸You show steadfast love to the thousandth generation, ᵃ but repay the guilt of parents into the laps of their children after them, O great and mighty God whose name is the Lord of hosts, ¹⁹great in counsel and mighty in deed; whose eyes are open to all the ways of mortals, rewarding all according to their ways and according to the fruit of their doings.

a Or *to thousands*

20You showed signs and wonders in the land of Egypt, and to this day in Israel and among all humankind, and have made yourself a name that continues to this very day. 21You brought your people Israel out of the land of Egypt with signs and wonders, with a strong hand and outstretched arm, and with great terror; 22and you gave them this land, which you swore to their ancestors to give them, a land flowing with milk and honey; 23and they entered and took possession of it. But they did not obey your voice or follow your law; of all you commanded them to do, they did nothing. Therefore you have made all these disasters come upon them. 24See, the siege ramps have been cast up against the city to take it, and the city, faced with sword, famine, and pestilence, has been given into the hands of the Chaldeans who are fighting against it. What you spoke has happened, as you yourself can see. 25Yet you, O Lord GOD, have said to me, "Buy the field for money and get witnesses"—though the city has been given into the hands of the Chaldeans.

26 The word of the LORD came to Jeremiah: 27See, I am the LORD, the God of all flesh; is anything too hard for me? 28Therefore, thus says the LORD: I am going to give this city into the hands of the Chaldeans and into the hand of King Nebuchadrezzar of Babylon, and he shall take it. 29The Chaldeans who are fighting against this city shall come, set it on fire, and burn it, with the houses on whose roofs offerings have been made to Baal and libations have been poured out to other gods, to provoke me to anger. 30For the people of Israel and the people of Judah have done nothing but evil in my sight from their youth; the people of Israel have done nothing but provoke me to anger by the work of their hands, says the LORD. 31This city has aroused my anger and wrath, from the day it was built until this day, so that I will remove it from my sight 32because of all the evil of the people of Israel and the people of Judah that they did to provoke me to anger—they, their kings and their officials, their priests and their prophets, the citizens of Judah and the inhabitants of Jerusalem. 33They have turned their backs to me, not their faces; though I have taught them persistently, they would not listen and accept correction. 34They set up their abominations in the house that bears my name, and defiled it. 35They built the high places of Baal in the valley of the son of Hinnom, to offer up their sons and daughters to Molech, though I did not command them, nor did it enter my mind that they should do this abomination, causing Judah to sin.

36 Now therefore thus says the LORD, the God of Israel, concerning this city of which you say, "It is being given into the hand of the king of Babylon by the sword, by famine, and by pestilence": 37See, I am going to gather them from all the lands to which I drove them in my anger and my wrath and in great indignation; I will bring them back to this place, and I will settle them in safety. 38They shall be my people, and I will be their God. 39I will give them one heart and one way, that they may fear me for all time, for their own good and the good of their children after them. 40I will make an everlasting covenant with them, never to draw back from doing good to them; and I will put the fear of me in their hearts, so that they may not turn from me. 41I will rejoice in doing good to them, and I will plant them in this land in faithfulness, with all my heart and all my soul.

42 For thus says the LORD: Just as I have brought all this great disaster upon this people, so I will bring upon them all the good fortune that I now promise them. 43Fields shall be bought in this land of which you are saying, It is a desolation, without human beings or animals; it has been given into the

hands of the Chaldeans. ⁴⁴Fields shall be bought for money, and deeds shall be signed and sealed and witnessed, in the land of Benjamin, in the places around Jerusalem, and in the cities of Judah, of the hill country, of the Shephelah, and of the Negeb; for I will restore their fortunes, says the LORD.

## 1 TIMOTHY 3.1–16

THE saying is sure: [a] whoever aspires to the office of bishop[b] desires a noble task. ²Now a bishop[c] must be above reproach, married only once, [d] temperate, sensible, respectable, hospitable, an apt teacher, ³not a drunkard, not violent but gentle, not quarrelsome, and not a lover of money. ⁴He must manage his own household well, keeping his children submissive and respectful in every way— ⁵for if someone does not know how to manage his own household, how can he take care of God's church? ⁶He must not be a recent convert, or he may be puffed up with conceit and fall into the condemnation of the devil. ⁷Moreover, he must be well thought of by outsiders, so that he may not fall into disgrace and the snare of the devil.

8 Deacons likewise must be serious, not double-tongued, not indulging in much wine, not greedy for money; ⁹they must hold fast to the mystery of the faith with a clear conscience. ¹⁰And let them first be tested; then, if they prove themselves blameless, let them serve as deacons. ¹¹Women[e] likewise must be serious, not slanderers, but temperate, faithful in all things. ¹²Let deacons be married only once, [f] and let them manage their children and their households well; ¹³for those who serve well as deacons gain a good standing for

themselves and great boldness in the faith that is in Christ Jesus.

14 I hope to come to you soon, but I am writing these instructions to you so that, ¹⁵if I am delayed, you may know how one ought to behave in the household of God, which is the church of the living God, the pillar and bulwark of the truth. ¹⁶Without any doubt, the mystery of our religion is great:

He[g] was revealed in flesh,
  vindicated[h] in spirit, [i]
    seen by angels,
  proclaimed among Gentiles,
    believed in throughout the
      world,
      taken up in glory.

## PSALM 88.1–18

*A Song. A Psalm of the Korahites. To the leader: according to Mahalath Leannoth. A Maskil of Heman the Ezrahite.*

O LORD, God of my salvation,
    when, at night, I cry out in
      your presence,
2   let my prayer come before you;
      incline your ear to my cry.

3   For my soul is full of troubles,
      and my life draws near to
        Sheol.
4   I am counted among those who
        go down to the Pit;
      I am like those who have no
        help,
5   like those forsaken among the
        dead,
      like the slain that lie in the
        grave,
      like those whom you remember
        no more,
      for they are cut off from your
        hand.
6   You have put me in the depths
        of the Pit,
      in the regions dark and deep.

aSome interpreters place these words at the end of the previous paragraph. Other ancient authorities read *The saying is commonly accepted*  bOr *overseer*  cOr *an overseer*  dGk *the husband of one wife*  eOr *Their wives*, or *Women deacons*  fGk *be husbands of one wife*  gGk *Who*; other ancient authorities read *God*; others, *Which*  hOr *justified*  iOr *by the Spirit*

7 Your wrath lies heavy upon me,
  and you overwhelm me with
    all your waves. *Selah*

8 You have caused my
    companions to shun me;
  you have made me a thing of
    horror to them.
  I am shut in so that I cannot
    escape;
9   my eye grows dim through
    sorrow.
  Every day I call on you,
    O Lord;
  I spread out my hands to you.
10 Do you work wonders for the
    dead?
  Do the shades rise up to
    praise you? *Selah*
11 Is your steadfast love declared
    in the grave,
  or your faithfulness in
    Abaddon?
12 Are your wonders known in the
    darkness,
  or your saving help in the
    land of forgetfulness?

13 But I, O Lord, cry out to you;
  in the morning my prayer
    comes before you.
14 O Lord, why do you cast me
    off?

  Why do you hide your face
    from me?
15 Wretched and close to death
    from my youth up,
  I suffer your terrors; I am
    desperate. [a]
16 Your wrath has swept over me;
  your dread assaults destroy
    me.
17 They surround me like a flood
    all day long;
  from all sides they close in on
    me.
18 You have caused friend and
    neighbor to shun me;
  my companions are in
    darkness.

# PROVERBS 25.20–22

LIKE vinegar on a wound[b]
  is one who sings songs to a
    heavy heart.
  Like a moth in clothing or a
    worm in wood,
  sorrow gnaws at the human
    heart. [c]
21 If your enemies are hungry,
    give them bread to eat;
  and if they are thirsty, give
    them water to drink;
22 for you will heap coals of fire on
    their heads,
  and the Lord will reward you.

[a]Meaning of Heb uncertain  [b]Gk: Heb *Like one who takes off a garment on a cold day, like vinegar on lye*  [c]Gk Syr Tg: Heb lacks *Like a moth . . . human heart*

# OCTOBER 19

JEREMIAH 33.1—34.22

THE word of the LORD came to Jeremiah a second time, while he was still confined in the court of the guard: <sup>2</sup>Thus says the LORD who made the earth, [a] the LORD who formed it to establish it—the LORD is his name: <sup>3</sup>Call to me and I will answer you, and will tell you great and hidden things that you have not known. <sup>4</sup>For thus says the LORD, the God of Israel, concerning the houses of this city and the houses of the kings of Judah that were torn down to make a defense against the siege ramps and before the sword: [b] <sup>5</sup>The Chaldeans are coming in to fight [c] and to fill them with the dead bodies of those whom I shall strike down in my anger and my wrath, for I have hidden my face from this city because of all their wickedness. <sup>6</sup>I am going to bring it recovery and healing; I will heal them and reveal to them abundance [b] of prosperity and security. <sup>7</sup>I will restore the fortunes of Judah and the fortunes of Israel, and rebuild them as they were at first. <sup>8</sup>I will cleanse them from all the guilt of their sin against me, and I will forgive all the guilt of their sin and rebellion against me. <sup>9</sup>And this city [d] shall be to me a name of joy, a praise and a glory before all the nations of the earth who shall hear of all the good that I do for them; they shall fear and tremble because of all the good and all the prosperity I provide for it.

10 Thus says the LORD: In this place of which you say, "It is a waste without human beings or animals," in the towns of Judah and the streets of Jerusalem that are desolate, without inhabitants, human or animal, there shall once more be heard <sup>11</sup>the voice of mirth and the voice of gladness, the voice of the bridegroom and the voice of the bride, the voices of those who sing, as they bring thank offerings to the house of the LORD:

"Give thanks to the LORD of
hosts,
for the LORD is good,
for his steadfast love endures
forever!"

For I will restore the fortunes of the land as at first, says the LORD.

12 Thus says the LORD of hosts: In this place that is waste, without human beings or animals, and in all its towns there shall again be pasture for shepherds resting their flocks. <sup>13</sup>In the towns of the hill country, of the Shephelah, and of the Negeb, in the land of Benjamin, the places around Jerusalem, and in the towns of Judah, flocks shall again pass under the hands of the one who counts them, says the LORD.

14 The days are surely coming, says the LORD, when I will fulfill the promise I made to the house of Israel and the house of Judah. <sup>15</sup>In those days and at that time I will cause a righteous Branch to spring up for David; and he shall execute justice and righteousness in the land. <sup>16</sup>In those days Judah will be saved and Jerusalem will live in safety. And this is the name by which it will be called: "The LORD is our righteousness."

17 For thus says the LORD: David shall never lack a man to sit on the throne of the house of Israel, <sup>18</sup>and the levitical priests shall never lack a man in my presence to offer burnt offerings, to make grain offerings, and to make sacrifices for all time.

19 The word of the LORD came to

Jeremiah: [20]Thus says the LORD: If any of you could break my covenant with the day and my covenant with the night, so that day and night would not come at their appointed time, [21]only then could my covenant with my servant David be broken, so that he would not have a son to reign on his throne, and my covenant with my ministers the Levites. [22]Just as the host of heaven cannot be numbered and the sands of the sea cannot be measured, so I will increase the offspring of my servant David, and the Levites who minister to me.

23 The word of the LORD came to Jeremiah: [24]Have you not observed how these people say, "The two families that the LORD chose have been rejected by him," and how they hold my people in such contempt that they no longer regard them as a nation? [25]Thus says the LORD: Only if I had not established my covenant with day and night and the ordinances of heaven and earth, [26]would I reject the offspring of Jacob and of my servant David and not choose any of his descendants as rulers over the offspring of Abraham, Isaac, and Jacob. For I will restore their fortunes, and will have mercy upon them.

**34.**1 THE word that came to Jeremiah from the LORD, when King Nebuchadrezzar of Babylon and all his army and all the kingdoms of the earth and all the peoples under his dominion were fighting against Jerusalem and all its cities: [2]"Thus says the LORD, the God of Israel: Go and speak to King Zedekiah of Judah and say to him: Thus says the LORD: I am going to give this city into the hand of the king of Babylon, and he shall burn it with fire. [3]And you yourself shall not escape from his hand, but shall surely be captured and handed over to him; you shall see the king of Babylon eye to eye and speak with him face to face; and you shall go to Babylon. [4]Yet hear the word of the LORD, O King Zedekiah of Judah! Thus says the LORD concerning you: You shall not die by the sword; [5]you shall die in peace. And as spices were burned[a] for your ancestors, the earlier kings who preceded you, so they shall burn spices[b] for you and lament for you, saying, "Alas, lord!" For I have spoken the word, says the LORD.

6 Then the prophet Jeremiah spoke all these words to Zedekiah king of Judah, in Jerusalem, [7]when the army of the king of Babylon was fighting against Jerusalem and against all the cities of Judah that were left, Lachish and Azekah; for these were the only fortified cities of Judah that remained.

8 The word that came to Jeremiah from the LORD, after King Zedekiah had made a covenant with all the people in Jerusalem to make a proclamation of liberty to them, [9]that all should set free their Hebrew slaves, male and female, so that no one should hold another Judean in slavery. [10]And they obeyed, all the officials and all the people who had entered into the covenant that all would set free their slaves, male or female, so that they would not be enslaved again; they obeyed and set them free. [11]But afterward they turned around and took back the male and female slaves they had set free, and brought them again into subjection as slaves. [12]The word of the LORD came to Jeremiah from the LORD: [13]Thus says the LORD, the God of Israel: I myself made a covenant with your ancestors when I brought them out of the land of Egypt, out of the house of slavery, saying, [14]"Every seventh year each of you must set free any Hebrews who have been sold to you and have served you six years; you must set them free from your service." But your ancestors did not listen to me or incline their ears to me. [15]You your-

a Heb *as there was burning*   b Heb *shall burn*

selves recently repented and did what was right in my sight by proclaiming liberty to one another, and you made a covenant before me in the house that is called by my name; [16]but then you turned around and profaned my name when each of you took back your male and female slaves, whom you had set free according to their desire, and you brought them again into subjection to be your slaves. [17]Therefore, thus says the LORD: You have not obeyed me by granting a release to your neighbors and friends; I am going to grant a release to you, says the LORD—a release to the sword, to pestilence, and to famine. I will make you a horror to all the kingdoms of the earth. [18]And those who transgressed my covenant and did not keep the terms of the covenant that they made before me, I will make like[a] the calf when they cut it in two and passed between its parts: [19]the officials of Judah, the officials of Jerusalem, the eunuchs, the priests, and all the people of the land who passed between the parts of the calf [20]shall be handed over to their enemies and to those who seek their lives. Their corpses shall become food for the birds of the air and the wild animals of the earth. [21]And as for King Zedekiah of Judah and his officials, I will hand them over to their enemies and to those who seek their lives, to the army of the king of Babylon, which has withdrawn from you. [22]I am going to command, says the LORD, and will bring them back to this city; and they will fight against it, and take it, and burn it with fire. The towns of Judah I will make a desolation without inhabitant.

## 1 TIMOTHY 4.1–16

Now the Spirit expressly says that in later[b] times some will renounce the faith by paying attention to deceitful spirits and teachings of demons, [2]through the hypocrisy of liars whose consciences are seared with a hot iron. [3]They forbid marriage and demand abstinence from foods, which God created to be received with thanksgiving by those who believe and know the truth. [4]For everything created by God is good, and nothing is to be rejected, provided it is received with thanksgiving; [5]for it is sanctified by God's word and by prayer.

6 If you put these instructions before the brothers and sisters,[c] you will be a good servant[d] of Christ Jesus, nourished on the words of the faith and of the sound teaching that you have followed. [7]Have nothing to do with profane myths and old wives' tales. Train yourself in godliness, [8]for, while physical training is of some value, godliness is valuable in every way, holding promise for both the present life and the life to come. [9]The saying is sure and worthy of full acceptance. [10]For to this end we toil and struggle,[e] because we have our hope set on the living God, who is the Savior of all people, especially of those who believe.

11 These are the things you must insist on and teach. [12]Let no one despise your youth, but set the believers an example in speech and conduct, in love, in faith, in purity. [13]Until I arrive, give attention to the public reading of scripture,[f] to exhorting, to teaching. [14]Do not neglect the gift that is in you, which was given to you through prophecy with the laying on of hands by the council of elders.[g] [15]Put these things into practice, devote yourself to them, so that all may see your progress. [16]Pay close attention to yourself and to your teaching; continue in these things, for in doing this you will save both yourself and your hearers.

aCn: Heb lacks *like*  bOr *the last*  cGk *brothers*  dOr *deacon*  eOther ancient authorities read *suffer reproach*  fGk *to the reading*  gGk *by the presbytery*

## PSALM 89.1–13

*A Maskil of Ethan the Ezrahite.*

I WILL sing of your steadfast love,
O LORD, [a] forever;
with my mouth I will proclaim
your faithfulness to all
generations.
2 I declare that your steadfast
love is established
forever;
your faithfulness is as firm as
the heavens.

3 You said, "I have made a
covenant with my chosen
one,
I have sworn to my servant
David:
4 'I will establish your
descendants forever,
and build your throne for all
generations.' "          *Selah*

5 Let the heavens praise your
wonders, O LORD,
your faithfulness in the
assembly of the holy
ones.
6 For who in the skies can be
compared to the LORD?
Who among the heavenly
beings is like the LORD,
7 a God feared in the council of
the holy ones,
great and awesome[b] above
all that are around him?
8 O LORD God of hosts,
who is as mighty as you,
O LORD?
Your faithfulness surrounds
you.
9 You rule the raging of the sea;
when its waves rise, you still
them.
10 You crushed Rahab like a
carcass;
you scattered your enemies
with your mighty arm.
11 The heavens are yours, the
earth also is yours;
the world and all that is in
it—you have founded
them.
12 The north and the south[c]—you
created them;
Tabor and Hermon joyously
praise your name.
13 You have a mighty arm;
strong is your hand, high your
right hand.

## PROVERBS 25.23–24

THE north wind produces rain,
and a backbiting tongue,
angry looks.
24 It is better to live in a corner of
the housetop
than in a house shared with a
contentious wife.

[a]Gk: Heb *the steadfast love of the LORD*   [b]Gk Syr: Heb *greatly awesome*   [c]Or *Zaphon and Yamin*

# OCTOBER 20



THE word that came to Jeremiah from the LORD in the days of King Jehoiakim son of Josiah of Judah: ²Go to the house of the Rechabites, and speak with them, and bring them to the house of the LORD, into one of the chambers; then offer them wine to drink. ³So I took Jaazaniah son of Jeremiah son of Habazziniah, and his brothers, and all his sons, and the whole house of the Rechabites. ⁴I brought them to the house of the LORD into the chamber of the sons of Hanan son of Igdaliah, the man of God, which was near the chamber of the officials, above the chamber of Maaseiah son of Shallum, keeper of the threshold. ⁵Then I set before the Rechabites pitchers full of wine, and cups; and I said to them, "Have some wine." ⁶But they answered, "We will drink no wine, for our ancestor Jonadab son of Rechab commanded us, 'You shall never drink wine, neither you nor your children; ⁷nor shall you ever build a house, or sow seed; nor shall you plant a vineyard, or even own one; but you shall live in tents all your days, that you may live many days in the land where you reside.' ⁸We have obeyed the charge of our ancestor Jonadab son of Rechab in all that he commanded us, to drink no wine all our days, ourselves, our wives, our sons, or our daughters, ⁹and not to build houses to live in. We have no vineyard or field or seed; ¹⁰but we have lived in tents, and have obeyed and done all that our ancestor Jonadab commanded us. ¹¹But when King Nebuchadrezzar of Babylon came up against the land, we said, 'Come, and let us go to Jerusalem for fear of the army of the Chaldeans and the army of the Arameans.' That is why we are living in Jerusalem."

12 Then the word of the LORD came to Jeremiah: ¹³Thus says the LORD of hosts, the God of Israel: Go and say to the people of Judah and the inhabitants of Jerusalem, Can you not learn a lesson and obey my words? says the LORD. ¹⁴The command has been carried out that Jonadab son of Rechab gave to his descendants to drink no wine; and they drink none to this day, for they have obeyed their ancestor's command. But I myself have spoken to you persistently, and you have not obeyed me. ¹⁵I have sent to you all my servants the prophets, sending them persistently, saying, 'Turn now everyone of you from your evil way, and amend your doings, and do not go after other gods to serve them, and then you shall live in the land that I gave to you and your ancestors.' But you did not incline your ear or obey me. ¹⁶The descendants of Jonadab son of Rechab have carried out the command that their ancestor gave them, but this people has not obeyed me. ¹⁷Therefore, thus says the LORD, the God of hosts, the God of Israel: I am going to bring on Judah and on all the inhabitants of Jerusalem every disaster that I have pronounced against them; because I have spoken to them and they have not listened, I have called to them and they have not answered.

18 But to the house of the Rechabites Jeremiah said: Thus says the LORD of hosts, the God of Israel: Because you have obeyed the command of your ancestor Jonadab, and kept all his precepts, and done all that he commanded you, ¹⁹therefore thus says the LORD of hosts, the God of Israel: Jonadab son of

Rechab shall not lack a descendant to stand before me for all time.

36.1 In the fourth year of King Jehoiakim son of Josiah of Judah, this word came to Jeremiah from the Lord: ²Take a scroll and write on it all the words that I have spoken to you against Israel and Judah and all the nations, from the day I spoke to you, from the days of Josiah until today. ³It may be that when the house of Judah hears of all the disasters that I intend to do to them, all of them may turn from their evil ways, so that I may forgive their iniquity and their sin.

4  Then Jeremiah called Baruch son of Neriah, and Baruch wrote on a scroll at Jeremiah's dictation all the words of the Lord that he had spoken to him. ⁵And Jeremiah ordered Baruch, saying, "I am prevented from entering the house of the Lord; ⁶so you go yourself, and on a fast day in the hearing of the people in the Lord's house you shall read the words of the Lord from the scroll that you have written at my dictation. You shall read them also in the hearing of all the people of Judah who come up from their towns. ⁷It may be that their plea will come before the Lord, and that all of them will turn from their evil ways, for great is the anger and wrath that the Lord has pronounced against this people." ⁸And Baruch son of Neriah did all that the prophet Jeremiah ordered him about reading from the scroll the words of the Lord in the Lord's house.

9  In the fifth year of King Jehoiakim son of Josiah of Judah, in the ninth month, all the people in Jerusalem and all the people who came from the towns of Judah to Jerusalem proclaimed a fast before the Lord. ¹⁰Then, in the hearing of all the people, Baruch read the words of Jeremiah from the scroll, in the house of the Lord, in the chamber of Gemariah son of Shaphan the secretary, which was in the upper court, at the entry of the New Gate of the Lord's house.

11  When Micaiah son of Gemariah son of Shaphan heard all the words of the Lord from the scroll, ¹²he went down to the king's house, into the secretary's chamber; and all the officials were sitting there: Elishama the secretary, Delaiah son of Shemaiah, Elnathan son of Achbor, Gemariah son of Shaphan, Zedekiah son of Hananiah, and all the officials. ¹³And Micaiah told them all the words that he had heard, when Baruch read the scroll in the hearing of the people. ¹⁴Then all the officials sent Jehudi son of Nethaniah son of Shelemiah son of Cushi to say to Baruch, "Bring the scroll that you read in the hearing of the people, and come." So Baruch son of Neriah took the scroll in his hand and came to them. ¹⁵And they said to him, "Sit down and read it to us." So Baruch read it to them. ¹⁶When they heard all the words, they turned to one another in alarm, and said to Baruch, "We certainly must report all these words to the king." ¹⁷Then they questioned Baruch, "Tell us now, how did you write all these words? Was it at his dictation?" ¹⁸Baruch answered them, "He dictated all these words to me, and I wrote them with ink on the scroll." ¹⁹Then the officials said to Baruch, "Go and hide, you and Jeremiah, and let no one know where you are."

20  Leaving the scroll in the chamber of Elishama the secretary, they went to the court of the king; and they reported all the words to the king. ²¹Then the king sent Jehudi to get the scroll, and he took it from the chamber of Elishama the secretary; and Jehudi read it to the king and all the officials who stood beside the king. ²²Now the king was sitting in his winter apartment (it was the ninth month), and there was a fire burning in the brazier before him. ²³As Jehudi read three or four columns,

the king<sup>a</sup> would cut them off with a penknife and throw them into the fire in the brazier, until the entire scroll was consumed in the fire that was in the brazier. [24]Yet neither the king, nor any of his servants who heard all these words, was alarmed, nor did they tear their garments. [25]Even when Elnathan and Delaiah and Gemariah urged the king not to burn the scroll, he would not listen to them. [26]And the king commanded Jerahmeel the king's son and Seraiah son of Azriel and Shelemiah son of Abdeel to arrest the secretary Baruch and the prophet Jeremiah. But the LORD hid them.

27  Now, after the king had burned the scroll with the words that Baruch wrote at Jeremiah's dictation, the word of the LORD came to Jeremiah: [28]Take another scroll and write on it all the former words that were in the first scroll, which King Jehoiakim of Judah has burned. [29]And concerning King Jehoiakim of Judah you shall say: Thus says the LORD, You have dared to burn this scroll, saying, Why have you written in it that the king of Babylon will certainly come and destroy this land, and will cut off from it human beings and animals? [30]Therefore thus says the LORD concerning King Jehoiakim of Judah: He shall have no one to sit upon the throne of David, and his dead body shall be cast out to the heat by day and the frost by night. [31]And I will punish him and his offspring and his servants for their iniquity; I will bring on them, and on the inhabitants of Jerusalem, and on the people of Judah, all the disasters with which I have threatened them—but they would not listen.

32  Then Jeremiah took another scroll and gave it to the secretary Baruch son of Neriah, who wrote on it at Jeremiah's dictation all the words of the scroll that King Jehoiakim of Judah had burned in the fire; and many similar words were added to them.

## 1 TIMOTHY 5.1–25

**D**o not speak harshly to an older man,<sup>b</sup> but speak to him as to a father, to younger men as brothers, [2]to older women as mothers, to younger women as sisters—with absolute purity.

3  Honor widows who are really widows. [4]If a widow has children or grandchildren, they should first learn their religious duty to their own family and make some repayment to their parents; for this is pleasing in God's sight. [5]The real widow, left alone, has set her hope on God and continues in supplications and prayers night and day; [6]but the widow<sup>c</sup> who lives for pleasure is dead even while she lives. [7]Give these commands as well, so that they may be above reproach. [8]And whoever does not provide for relatives, and especially for family members, has denied the faith and is worse than an unbeliever.

9  Let a widow be put on the list if she is not less than sixty years old and has been married only once;<sup>d</sup> [10]she must be well attested for her good works, as one who has brought up children, shown hospitality, washed the saints' feet, helped the afflicted, and devoted herself to doing good in every way. [11]But refuse to put younger widows on the list; for when their sensual desires alienate them from Christ, they want to marry, [12]and so they incur condemnation for having violated their first pledge. [13]Besides that, they learn to be idle, gadding about from house to house; and they are not merely idle, but also gossips and busybodies, saying what they should not say. [14]So I would have younger widows marry, bear children, and manage their households, so as to give the adversary no occasion to revile us. [15]For some have already

<sup>a</sup>Heb *he*  <sup>b</sup>Or *an elder,* or *a presbyter*  <sup>c</sup>Gk *she*  <sup>d</sup>Gk *the wife of one husband*

turned away to follow Satan. ¹⁶If any believing woman[a] has relatives who are really widows, let her assist them; let the church not be burdened, so that it can assist those who are real widows.

17  Let the elders who rule well be considered worthy of double honor,[b] especially those who labor in preaching and teaching; ¹⁸for the scripture says, "You shall not muzzle an ox while it is treading out the grain," and, "The laborer deserves to be paid." ¹⁹Never accept any accusation against an elder except on the evidence of two or three witnesses. ²⁰As for those who persist in sin, rebuke them in the presence of all, so that the rest also may stand in fear. ²¹In the presence of God and of Christ Jesus and of the elect angels, I warn you to keep these instructions without prejudice, doing nothing on the basis of partiality. ²²Do not ordain[c] anyone hastily, and do not participate in the sins of others; keep yourself pure.

23  No longer drink only water, but take a little wine for the sake of your stomach and your frequent ailments.

24  The sins of some people are conspicuous and precede them to judgment, while the sins of others follow them there. ²⁵So also good works are conspicuous; and even when they are not, they cannot remain hidden.

## PSALM 89. 14–37

Righteousness and justice are
  the foundation of your
    throne;
steadfast love and faithfulness
  go before you.
15  Happy are the people who know
    the festal shout,
  who walk, O Lord, in the
    light of your
    countenance;
16  they exult in your name all day
    long,

and extol[d] your
    righteousness.
17  For you are the glory of their
    strength;
  by your favor our horn is
    exalted.
18  For our shield belongs to the
    Lord,
  our king to the Holy One of
    Israel.

19  Then you spoke in a vision to
    your faithful one, and
    said:
  "I have set the crown[e] on
    one who is mighty,
  I have exalted one chosen
    from the people.
20  I have found my servant David;
    with my holy oil I have
    anointed him;
21  my hand shall always remain
    with him;
  my arm also shall strengthen
    him.
22  The enemy shall not outwit him,
    the wicked shall not humble
    him.
23  I will crush his foes before him
    and strike down those who
    hate him.
24  My faithfulness and steadfast
    love shall be with him;
  and in my name his horn shall
    be exalted.
25  I will set his hand on the sea
    and his right hand on the
    rivers.
26  He shall cry to me, 'You are my
    Father,
  my God, and the Rock of my
    salvation!'
27  I will make him the firstborn,
    the highest of the kings of the
    earth.
28  Forever I will keep my steadfast
    love for him,

aOther ancient authorities read *believing man or woman*; others, *believing man*  bOr *compensation*
cGk *Do not lay hands on*  dCn: Heb *are exalted in*  eCn: Heb *help*

and my covenant with him will
    stand firm.
29 I will establish his line forever,
    and his throne as long as the
        heavens endure.
30 If his children forsake my law
    and do not walk according to
        my ordinances,
31 if they violate my statutes
    and do not keep my
        commandments,
32 then I will punish their
        transgression with the
        rod
    and their iniquity with
        scourges;
33 but I will not remove from him
      my steadfast love,
    or be false to my faithfulness.
34 I will not violate my covenant,
    or alter the word that went
        forth from my lips.
35 Once and for all I have sworn
      by my holiness;

    I will not lie to David.
36 His line shall continue forever,
    and his throne endure before
      me like the sun.
37 It shall be established forever
    like the moon,
    an enduring witness in the
      skies."       *Selah*

## PROVERBS 25.25–27

LIKE cold water to a thirsty
      soul,
  so is good news from a far
      country.
26 Like a muddied spring or a
      polluted fountain
    are the righteous who give
      way before the wicked.
27 It is not good to eat much
      honey,
    or to seek honor on top of
      honor.

# OCTOBER 21

## JEREMIAH 37.1—38.28

ZEDEKIAH son of Josiah, whom King Nebuchadrezzar of Babylon made king in the land of Judah, succeeded Coniah son of Jehoiakim. 2But neither he nor his servants nor the people of the land listened to the words of the LORD that he spoke through the prophet Jeremiah.

3 King Zedekiah sent Jehucal son of Shelemiah and the priest Zephaniah son of Maaseiah to the prophet Jeremiah saying, "Please pray for us to the LORD our God." 4Now Jeremiah was still going in and out among the people, for he had not yet been put in prison. 5Meanwhile, the army of Pharaoh had come out of Egypt; and when the Chaldeans who were besieging Jerusalem heard news of them, they withdrew from Jerusalem.

6 Then the word of the LORD came to the prophet Jeremiah: 7Thus says the LORD, God of Israel: This is what the two of you shall say to the king of Judah, who sent you to me to inquire of me, Pharaoh's army, which set out to help you, is going to return to its own land, to Egypt. 8And the Chaldeans shall return and fight against this city; they shall take it and burn it with fire. 9Thus says the LORD: Do not deceive

yourselves, saying, "The Chaldeans will surely go away from us," for they will not go away. [10] Even if you defeated the whole army of Chaldeans who are fighting against you, and there remained of them only wounded men in their tents, they would rise up and burn this city with fire.

11 Now when the Chaldean army had withdrawn from Jerusalem at the approach of Pharaoh's army, [12] Jeremiah set out from Jerusalem to go to the land of Benjamin to receive his share of property[a] among the people there. [13] When he reached the Benjamin Gate, a sentinel there named Irijah son of Shelemiah son of Hananiah arrested the prophet Jeremiah saying, "You are deserting to the Chaldeans." [14] And Jeremiah said, "That is a lie; I am not deserting to the Chaldeans." But Irijah would not listen to him, and arrested Jeremiah and brought him to the officials. [15] The officials were enraged at Jeremiah, and they beat him and imprisoned him in the house of the secretary Jonathan, for it had been made a prison. [16] Thus Jeremiah was put in the cistern house, in the cells, and remained there many days.

17 Then King Zedekiah sent for him, and received him. The king questioned him secretly in his house, and said, "Is there any word from the Lord?" Jeremiah said, "There is!" Then he said, "You shall be handed over to the king of Babylon." [18] Jeremiah also said to King Zedekiah, "What wrong have I done to you or your servants or this people, that you have put me in prison? [19] Where are your prophets who prophesied to you, saying, 'The king of Babylon will not come against you and against this land'? [20] Now please hear me, my lord king: be good enough to listen to my plea, and do not send me back to the house of the secretary Jonathan to die there." [21] So

King Zedekiah gave orders, and they committed Jeremiah to the court of the guard; and a loaf of bread was given him daily from the bakers' street, until all the bread of the city was gone. So Jeremiah remained in the court of the guard.

[38.1] Now Shephatiah son of Mattan, Gedaliah son of Pashhur, Jucal son of Shelemiah, and Pashhur son of Malchiah heard the words that Jeremiah was saying to all the people, [2] Thus says the Lord, Those who stay in this city shall die by the sword, by famine, and by pestilence; but those who go out to the Chaldeans shall live; they shall have their lives as a prize of war, and live. [3] Thus says the Lord, This city shall surely be handed over to the army of the king of Babylon and be taken. [4] Then the officials said to the king, "This man ought to be put to death, because he is discouraging the soldiers who are left in this city, and all the people, by speaking such words to them. For this man is not seeking the welfare of this people, but their harm." [5] King Zedekiah said, "Here he is; he is in your hands; for the king is powerless against you." [6] So they took Jeremiah and threw him into the cistern of Malchiah, the king's son, which was in the court of the guard, letting Jeremiah down by ropes. Now there was no water in the cistern, but only mud, and Jeremiah sank in the mud.

7 Ebed-melech the Ethiopian,[b] a eunuch in the king's house, heard that they had put Jeremiah into the cistern. The king happened to be sitting at the Benjamin Gate, [8] So Ebed-melech left the king's house and spoke to the king, [9] "My lord king, these men have acted wickedly in all they did to the prophet Jeremiah by throwing him into the cistern to die there of hunger, for there is

a Meaning of Heb uncertain   b Or *Nubian*; Heb *Cushite*

no bread left in the city." ¹⁰Then the king commanded Ebed-melech the Ethiopian, ᵃ "Take three men with you from here, and pull the prophet Jeremiah up from the cistern before he dies." ¹¹So Ebed-melech took the men with him and went to the house of the king, to a wardrobe ofᵇ the storehouse, and took from there old rags and worn-out clothes, which he let down to Jeremiah in the cistern by ropes. ¹²Then Ebed-melech the Ethiopianᵃ said to Jeremiah, "Just put the rags and clothes between your armpits and the ropes." Jeremiah did so. ¹³Then they drew Jeremiah up by the ropes and pulled him out of the cistern. And Jeremiah remained in the court of the guard.

14 King Zedekiah sent for the prophet Jeremiah and received him at the third entrance of the temple of the Lord. The king said to Jeremiah, "I have something to ask you; do not hide anything from me." ¹⁵Jeremiah said to Zedekiah, "If I tell you, you will put me to death, will you not? And if I give you advice, you will not listen to me." ¹⁶So King Zedekiah swore an oath in secret to Jeremiah, "As the Lord lives, who gave us our lives, I will not put you to death or hand you over to these men who seek your life."

17 Then Jeremiah said to Zedekiah, "Thus says the Lord, the God of hosts, the God of Israel, If you will only surrender to the officials of the king of Babylon, then your life shall be spared, and this city shall not be burned with fire, and you and your house shall live. ¹⁸But if you do not surrender to the officials of the king of Babylon, then this city shall be handed over to the Chaldeans, and they shall burn it with fire, and you yourself shall not escape from their hand." ¹⁹King Zedekiah said to Jeremiah, "I am afraid of the Judeans who have deserted to the Chaldeans, for I might be handed over to them and they would abuse me." ²⁰Jeremiah said, "That will not happen. Just obey the voice of the Lord in what I say to you, and it shall go well with you, and your life shall be spared. ²¹But if you are determined not to surrender, this is what the Lord has shown me— ²²a vision of all the women remaining in the house of the king of Judah being led out to the officials of the king of Babylon and saying,

'Your trusted friends have
    seduced you
  and have overcome you;
Now that your feet are stuck in
    the mud,
    they desert you.'

²³All your wives and your children shall be led out to the Chaldeans, and you yourself shall not escape from their hand, but shall be seized by the king of Babylon; and this city shall be burned with fire."

24 Then Zedekiah said to Jeremiah, "Do not let anyone else know of this conversation, or you will die. ²⁵If the officials should hear that I have spoken with you, and they should come and say to you, 'Just tell us what you said to the king; do not conceal it from us, or we will put you to death. What did the king say to you?' ²⁶then you shall say to them, 'I was presenting my plea to the king not to send me back to the house of Jonathan to die there.' " ²⁷All the officials did come to Jeremiah and questioned him; and he answered them in the very words the king had commanded. So they stopped questioning him, for the conversation had not been overheard. ²⁸And Jeremiah remained in the court of the guard until the day that Jerusalem was taken.

ᵃOr *Nubian*; Heb *Cushite*   ᵇCn: Heb *to under*

## 1 TIMOTHY 6.1–21

**L**ET all who are under the yoke of slavery regard their masters as worthy of all honor, so that the name of God and the teaching may not be blasphemed. [2]Those who have believing masters must not be disrespectful to them on the ground that they are members of the church; [a] rather they must serve them all the more, since those who benefit by their service are believers and beloved. [b]

Teach and urge these duties. [3]Whoever teaches otherwise and does not agree with the sound words of our Lord Jesus Christ and the teaching that is in accordance with godliness, [4]is conceited, understanding nothing, and has a morbid craving for controversy and for disputes about words. From these come envy, dissension, slander, base suspicions, [5]and wrangling among those who are depraved in mind and bereft of the truth, imagining that godliness is a means of gain. [c] [6]Of course, there is great gain in godliness combined with contentment; [7]for we brought nothing into the world, so that[d] we can take nothing out of it; [8]but if we have food and clothing, we will be content with these. [9]But those who want to be rich fall into temptation and are trapped by many senseless and harmful desires that plunge people into ruin and destruction. [10]For the love of money is a root of all kinds of evil, and in their eagerness to be rich some have wandered away from the faith and pierced themselves with many pains.

11 But as for you, man of God, shun all this; pursue righteousness, godliness, faith, love, endurance, gentleness. [12]Fight the good fight of the faith; take hold of the eternal life, to which you were called and for which you made[e] the good confession in the presence of many witnesses. [13]In the presence of God, who gives life to all things, and of Christ Jesus, who in his testimony before Pontius Pilate made the good confession, I charge you [14]to keep the commandment without spot or blame until the manifestation of our Lord Jesus Christ, [15]which he will bring about at the right time—he who is the blessed and only Sovereign, the King of kings and Lord of lords. [16]It is he alone who has immortality and dwells in unapproachable light, whom no one has ever seen or can see; to him be honor and eternal dominion. Amen.

17  As for those who in the present age are rich, command them not to be haughty, or to set their hopes on the uncertainty of riches, but rather on God who richly provides us with everything for our enjoyment. [18]They are to do good, to be rich in good works, generous, and ready to share, [19]thus storing up for themselves the treasure of a good foundation for the future, so that they may take hold of the life that really is life.

20  Timothy, guard what has been entrusted to you. Avoid the profane chatter and contradictions of what is falsely called knowledge; [21]by professing it some have missed the mark as regards the faith.

Grace be with you. [f]

## PSALM 89.38–52

**B**UT now you have spurned and rejected him;
    you are full of wrath against
      your anointed.
39  You have renounced the
      covenant with your
      servant;

---

aGk *are brothers*   bOr *since they are believers and beloved, who devote themselves to good deeds*   cOther ancient authorities add *Withdraw yourself from such people*   dOther ancient authorities read *world—it is certain that*   eGk *confessed*   fThe Greek word for *you* here is plural; in other ancient authorities it is singular. Other ancient authorities add *Amen*

you have defiled his crown in
   the dust.
40 You have broken through all
   his walls;
   you have laid his strongholds
   in ruins.
41 All who pass by plunder him;
   he has become the scorn of
   his neighbors.
42 You have exalted the right hand
   of his foes;
   you have made all his
   enemies rejoice.
43 Moreover, you have turned
   back the edge of his
   sword,
   and you have not supported
   him in battle.
44 You have removed the scepter
   from his hand, a
   and hurled his throne to the
   ground.
45 You have cut short the days of
   his youth;
   you have covered him with
   shame. *Selah*

46 How long, O Lord? Will you
   hide yourself forever?
   How long will your wrath
   burn like fire?

47 Remember how short my time
   is— b
   for what vanity you have
   created all mortals!
48 Who can live and never see
   death?
   Who can escape the power of
   Sheol? *Selah*

49 Lord, where is your steadfast
   love of old,
   which by your faithfulness you
   swore to David?
50 Remember, O Lord, how your
   servant is taunted;
   how I bear in my bosom the
   insults of the peoples, c
51 with which your enemies taunt,
   O Lord,
   with which they taunted the
   footsteps of your
   anointed.

52 Blessed be the Lord forever.
   Amen and Amen.

## PROVERBS 25.28

**L**IKE a city breached, without
   walls,
is one who lacks self-control.

# OCTOBER 22

## JEREMIAH 39.1—41.18

**I**N the ninth year of King Zedekiah of Judah, in the tenth month, King Nebuchadrezzar of Babylon and all his army came against Jerusalem and besieged it; 2in the eleventh year of Zedekiah, in the fourth month, on the ninth day of the month, a breach was made in the city. 3When Jerusalem was taken, d all the officials of the king of Babylon came and sat in the middle gate: Nergal-sharezer, Samgar-nebo, Sarsechim the Rabsaris, Nergal-sharezer the Rabmag, with all the rest

a Cn: Heb *removed his cleanness*  b Meaning of Heb uncertain  c Cn: Heb *bosom all of many peoples*
d This clause has been transposed from 38.28

of the officials of the king of Babylon. [4]When King Zedekiah of Judah and all the soldiers saw them, they fled, going out of the city at night by way of the king's garden through the gate between the two walls; and they went toward the Arabah. [5]But the army of the Chaldeans pursued them, and overtook Zedekiah in the plains of Jericho; and when they had taken him, they brought him up to King Nebuchadrezzar of Babylon, at Riblah, in the land of Hamath; and he passed sentence on him. [6]The king of Babylon slaughtered the sons of Zedekiah at Riblah before his eyes; also the king of Babylon slaughtered all the nobles of Judah. [7]He put out the eyes of Zedekiah, and bound him in fetters to take him to Babylon. [8]The Chaldeans burned the king's house and the houses of the people, and broke down the walls of Jerusalem. [9]Then Nebuzaradan the captain of the guard exiled to Babylon the rest of the people who were left in the city, those who had deserted to him, and the people who remained. [10]Nebuzaradan the captain of the guard left in the land of Judah some of the poor people who owned nothing, and gave them vineyards and fields at the same time.

11 King Nebuchadrezzar of Babylon gave command concerning Jeremiah through Nebuzaradan, the captain of the guard, saying, [12]"Take him, look after him well and do him no harm, but deal with him as he may ask you." [13]So Nebuzaradan the captain of the guard, Nebushazban the Rabsaris, Nergal-sharezer the Rabmag, and all the chief officers of the king of Babylon sent [14]and took Jeremiah from the court of the guard. They entrusted him to Gedaliah son of Ahikam son of Shaphan to be brought home. So he stayed with his own people.

15 The word of the LORD came to Jeremiah while he was confined in the court of the guard: [16]Go and say to Ebed-melech the Ethiopian:[a] Thus says the LORD of hosts, the God of Israel: I am going to fulfill my words against this city for evil and not for good, and they shall be accomplished in your presence on that day. [17]But I will save you on that day, says the LORD, and you shall not be handed over to those whom you dread. [18]For I will surely save you, and you shall not fall by the sword; but you shall have your life as a prize of war, because you have trusted in me, says the LORD.

[40.1] THE word that came to Jeremiah from the LORD after Nebuzaradan the captain of the guard had let him go from Ramah, when he took him bound in fetters along with all the captives of Jerusalem and Judah who were being exiled to Babylon. [2]The captain of the guard took Jeremiah and said to him, "The LORD your God threatened this place with this disaster; [3]and now the LORD has brought it about, and has done as he said, because all of you sinned against the LORD and did not obey his voice. Therefore this thing has come upon you. [4]Now look, I have just released you today from the fetters on your hands. If you wish to come with me to Babylon, come, and I will take good care of you; but if you do not wish to come with me to Babylon, you need not come. See, the whole land is before you; go wherever you think it good and right to go. [5]If you remain,[b] then return to Gedaliah son of Ahikam son of Shaphan, whom the king of Babylon appointed governor of the towns of Judah, and stay with him among the people; or go wherever you think it right to go." So the captain of the guard gave him an allowance of food and a present, and let him go. [6]Then Jeremiah went to Gedaliah son of Ahikam at Mizpah, and

---

a Or *Nubian*; Heb *Cushite*   b Syr: Meaning of Heb uncertain

stayed with him among the people who were left in the land.

7 When all the leaders of the forces in the open country and their troops heard that the king of Babylon had appointed Gedaliah son of Ahikam governor in the land, and had committed to him men, women, and children, those of the poorest of the land who had not been taken into exile to Babylon, ⁸they went to Gedaliah at Mizpah—Ishmael son of Nethaniah, Johanan son of Kareah, Seraiah son of Tanhumeth, the sons of Ephai the Netophathite, Jezaniah son of the Maacathite, they and their troops. ⁹Gedaliah son of Ahikam son of Shaphan swore to them and their troops, saying, "Do not be afraid to serve the Chaldeans. Stay in the land and serve the king of Babylon, and it shall go well with you. ¹⁰As for me, I am staying at Mizpah to represent you before the Chaldeans who come to us; but as for you, gather wine and summer fruits and oil, and store them in your vessels, and live in the towns that you have taken over." ¹¹Likewise, when all the Judeans who were in Moab and among the Ammonites and in Edom and in other lands heard that the king of Babylon had left a remnant in Judah and had appointed Gedaliah son of Ahikam son of Shaphan as governor over them, ¹²then all the Judeans returned from all the places to which they had been scattered and came to the land of Judah, to Gedaliah at Mizpah; and they gathered wine and summer fruits in great abundance.

13 Now Johanan son of Kareah and all the leaders of the forces in the open country came to Gedaliah at Mizpah ¹⁴and said to him, "Are you at all aware that Baalis king of the Ammonites has sent Ishmael son of Nethaniah to take your life?" But Gedaliah son of Ahikam would not believe them. ¹⁵Then Johanan son of Kareah spoke secretly to Gedaliah at Mizpah, "Please let me go and kill Ishmael son of Nethaniah, and no one else will know. Why should he take your life, so that all the Judeans who are gathered around you would be scattered, and the remnant of Judah would perish?" ¹⁶But Gedaliah son of Ahikam said to Johanan son of Kareah, "Do not do such a thing, for you are telling a lie about Ishmael."

⁴¹·¹ Iɴ the seventh month, Ishmael son of Nethaniah son of Elishama, of the royal family, one of the chief officers of the king, came with ten men to Gedaliah son of Ahikam, at Mizpah. As they ate bread together there at Mizpah, ²Ishmael son of Nethaniah and the ten men with him got up and struck down Gedaliah son of Ahikam son of Shaphan with the sword and killed him, because the king of Babylon had appointed him governor in the land. ³Ishmael also killed all the Judeans who were with Gedaliah at Mizpah, and the Chaldean soldiers who happened to be there.

4 On the day after the murder of Gedaliah, before anyone knew of it, ⁵eighty men arrived from Shechem and Shiloh and Samaria, with their beards shaved and their clothes torn, and their bodies gashed, bringing grain offerings and incense to present at the temple of the Lᴏʀᴅ. ⁶And Ishmael son of Nethaniah came out from Mizpah to meet them, weeping as he came. As he met them, he said to them, "Come to Gedaliah son of Ahikam." ⁷When they reached the middle of the city, Ishmael son of Nethaniah and the men with him slaughtered them, and threw themᵃ into a cistern. ⁸But there were ten men among them who said to Ishmael, "Do not kill us, for we have stores of wheat, barley, oil, and honey hidden in the fields." So he refrained, and did not kill them along with their companions.

9 Now the cistern into which Ish-

---

ᵃSyr: Heb lacks *and threw them*; compare verse 9

mael had thrown all the bodies of the men whom he had struck down was the large cistern[a] that King Asa had made for defense against King Baasha of Israel; Ishmael son of Nethaniah filled that cistern with those whom he had killed. [10]Then Ishmael took captive all the rest of the people who were in Mizpah, the king's daughters and all the people who were left at Mizpah, whom Nebuzaradan, the captain of the guard, had committed to Gedaliah son of Ahikam. Ishmael son of Nethaniah took them captive and set out to cross over to the Ammonites.

11  But when Johanan son of Kareah and all the leaders of the forces with him heard of all the crimes that Ishmael son of Nethaniah had done, [12]they took all their men and went to fight against Ishmael son of Nethaniah. They came upon him at the great pool that is in Gibeon. [13]And when all the people who were with Ishmael saw Johanan son of Kareah and all the leaders of the forces with him, they were glad. [14]So all the people whom Ishmael had carried away captive from Mizpah turned around and came back, and went to Johanan son of Kareah. [15]But Ishmael son of Nethaniah escaped from Johanan with eight men, and went to the Ammonites. [16]Then Johanan son of Kareah and all the leaders of the forces with him took all the rest of the people whom Ishmael son of Nethaniah had carried away captive[b] from Mizpah after he had slain Gedaliah son of Ahikam—soldiers, women, children, and eunuchs, whom Johanan brought back from Gibeon. [c] [17]And they set out, and stopped at Geruth Chimham near Bethlehem, intending to go to Egypt [18]because of the Chaldeans; for they were afraid of them, because Ishmael son of Nethaniah had killed Gedaliah son of Ahikam, whom the king of Babylon had made governor over the land.

# 2 TIMOTHY 1.1–18

P AUL, an apostle of Christ Jesus by the will of God, for the sake of the promise of life that is in Christ Jesus,

2  To Timothy, my beloved child:
Grace, mercy, and peace from God the Father and Christ Jesus our Lord.

3  I am grateful to God—whom I worship with a clear conscience, as my ancestors did—when I remember you constantly in my prayers night and day. [4]Recalling your tears, I long to see you so that I may be filled with joy. [5]I am reminded of your sincere faith, a faith that lived first in your grandmother Lois and your mother Eunice and now, I am sure, lives in you. [6]For this reason I remind you to rekindle the gift of God that is within you through the laying on of my hands; [7]for God did not give us a spirit of cowardice, but rather a spirit of power and of love and of self-discipline.

8  Do not be ashamed, then, of the testimony about our Lord or of me his prisoner, but join with me in suffering for the gospel, relying on the power of God, [9]who saved us and called us with a holy calling, not according to our works but according to his own purpose and grace. This grace was given to us in Christ Jesus before the ages began, [10]but it has now been revealed through the appearing of our Savior Christ Jesus, who abolished death and brought life and immortality to light through the gospel. [11]For this gospel I was appointed a herald and an apostle and a teacher, [d] [12]and for this reason I suffer as I do. But I am not ashamed, for I know the one in whom I have put my trust, and I am sure that he is able to guard until that day what I have en-

aGk: Heb whom he had killed by the hand of Gedaliah  bCn: Heb whom he recovered from Ishmael son of Nethaniah  cMeaning of Heb uncertain  dOther ancient authorities add of the Gentiles

trusted to him. [a] [13]Hold to the standard of sound teaching that you have heard from me, in the faith and love that are in Christ Jesus. [14]Guard the good treasure entrusted to you, with the help of the Holy Spirit living in us.

15 You are aware that all who are in Asia have turned away from me, including Phygelus and Hermogenes. [16]May the Lord grant mercy to the household of Onesiphorus, because he often refreshed me and was not ashamed of my chain; [17]when he arrived in Rome, he eagerly[b] searched for me and found me [18]—may the Lord grant that he will find mercy from the Lord on that day! And you know very well how much service he rendered in Ephesus.

# PSALM 90.1—91.16

*A Prayer of Moses, the man of God.*

Lord, you have been our
      dwelling place[c]
  in all generations.
2 Before the mountains were
      brought forth,
  or ever you had formed the
      earth and the world,
  from everlasting to
      everlasting you are God.

3 You turn us[d] back to dust,
  and say, "Turn back, you
      mortals."
4 For a thousand years in your
      sight
  are like yesterday when it is
      past,
  or like a watch in the night.

5 You sweep them away; they are
      like a dream,
  like grass that is renewed in
      the morning;
6 in the morning it flourishes and
      is renewed;

  in the evening it fades and
      withers.

7 For we are consumed by your
      anger;
  by your wrath we are
      overwhelmed.
8 You have set our iniquities
      before you,
  our secret sins in the light of
      your countenance.

9 For all our days pass away
      under your wrath;
  our years come to an end[e]
      like a sigh.
10 The days of our life are seventy
      years,
  or perhaps eighty, if we are
      strong;
  even then their span[f] is only
      toil and trouble;
  they are soon gone, and we
      fly away.

11 Who considers the power of
      your anger?
  Your wrath is as great as the
      fear that is due you.
12 So teach us to count our days
  that we may gain a wise
      heart.

13 Turn, O Lord! How long?
  Have compassion on your
      servants!
14 Satisfy us in the morning with
      your steadfast love,
  so that we may rejoice and be
      glad all our days.
15 Make us glad as many days as
      you have afflicted us,
  and as many years as we
      have seen evil.
16 Let your work be manifest to
      your servants,
  and your glorious power to
      their children.

[a]Or *what has been entrusted to me*  [b]Or *promptly*  [c]Another reading is *our refuge*  [d]Heb *humankind*  [e]Syr: Heb *we bring our years to an end*  [f]Cn Compare Gk Syr Jerome Tg: Heb *pride*

17 Let the favor of the Lord our
   God be upon us,
   and prosper for us the work
   of our hands—
   O prosper the work of our
   hands!

91.1 You who live in the shelter of
   the Most High,
   who abide in the shadow of
   the Almighty, a
2 will say to the LORD, "My
   refuge and my fortress;
   my God, in whom I trust."
3 For he will deliver you from the
   snare of the fowler
   and from the deadly
   pestilence;
4 he will cover you with his
   pinions,
   and under his wings you will
   find refuge;
   his faithfulness is a shield and
   buckler.
5 You will not fear the terror of
   the night,
   or the arrow that flies by day,
6 or the pestilence that stalks in
   darkness,
   or the destruction that wastes
   at noonday.

7 A thousand may fall at your
   side,
   ten thousand at your right
   hand,
   but it will not come near you.
8 You will only look with your
   eyes
   and see the punishment of the
   wicked.

9 Because you have made the
   LORD your refuge, b

the Most High your dwelling
   place,
10 no evil shall befall you,
   no scourge come near your
   tent.

11 For he will command his angels
   concerning you
   to guard you in all your ways.
12 On their hands they will bear
   you up,
   so that you will not dash your
   foot against a stone.
13 You will tread on the lion and
   the adder,
   the young lion and the
   serpent you will trample
   under foot.

14 Those who love me, I will
   deliver;
   I will protect those who know
   my name.
15 When they call to me, I will
   answer them;
   I will be with them in trouble,
   I will rescue them and honor
   them.
16 With long life I will satisfy them,
   and show them my salvation.

## PROVERBS 26.1–2

L IKE snow in summer or rain in
   harvest,
   so honor is not fitting for a
   fool.
2 Like a sparrow in its flitting, like
   a swallow in its flying,
   an undeserved curse goes
   nowhere.

a Traditional rendering of Heb *Shaddai*   b Cn: Heb *Because you, LORD, are my refuge; you have made*

# OCTOBER 23



THEN all the commanders of the forces, and Johanan son of Kareah and Azariah[a] son of Hoshaiah, and all the people from the least to the greatest, approached [2]the prophet Jeremiah and said, "Be good enough to listen to our plea, and pray to the LORD your God for us—for all this remnant. For there are only a few of us left out of many, as your eyes can see. [3]Let the LORD your God show us where we should go and what we should do." [4]The prophet Jeremiah said to them, "Very well: I am going to pray to the LORD your God as you request, and whatever the LORD answers you I will tell you; I will keep nothing back from you." [5]They in their turn said to Jeremiah, "May the LORD be a true and faithful witness against us if we do not act according to everything that the LORD your God sends us through you. [6]Whether it is good or bad, we will obey the voice of the LORD our God to whom we are sending you, in order that it may go well with us when we obey the voice of the LORD our God."

7 At the end of ten days the word of the LORD came to Jeremiah. [8]Then he summoned Johanan son of Kareah and all the commanders of the forces who were with him, and all the people from the least to the greatest, [9]and said to them, "Thus says the LORD, the God of Israel, to whom you sent me to present your plea before him: [10]If you will only remain in this land, then I will build you up and not pull you down; I will plant you, and not pluck you up; for I am sorry for the disaster that I have brought upon you. [11]Do not be afraid of the king of Babylon, as you have been; do not be afraid of him, says the LORD, for I am with you, to save you and to rescue you from his hand. [12]I will grant you mercy, and he will have mercy on you and restore you to your native soil. [13]But if you continue to say, 'We will not stay in this land,' thus disobeying the voice of the LORD your God [14]and saying, 'No, we will go to the land of Egypt, where we shall not see war, or hear the sound of the trumpet, or be hungry for bread, and there we will stay,' [15]then hear the word of the LORD, O remnant of Judah. Thus says the LORD of hosts, the God of Israel: If you are determined to enter Egypt and go to settle there, [16]then the sword that you fear shall overtake you there, in the land of Egypt; and the famine that you dread shall follow close after you into Egypt; and there you shall die. [17]All the people who have determined to go to Egypt to settle there shall die by the sword, by famine, and by pestilence; they shall have no remnant or survivor from the disaster that I am bringing upon them.

18 "For thus says the LORD of hosts, the God of Israel: Just as my anger and my wrath were poured out on the inhabitants of Jerusalem, so my wrath will be poured out on you when you go to Egypt. You shall become an object of execration and horror, of cursing and ridicule. You shall see this place no more. [19]The LORD has said to you, O remnant of Judah, Do not go to Egypt. Be well aware that I have warned you today [20]that you have made a fatal mistake. For you yourselves sent me to the LORD your God, saying, 'Pray for us to the LORD our God, and whatever the LORD our God says, tell

a Gk: Heb *Jezaniah*

us and we will do it.' <sup>21</sup>So I have told you today, but you have not obeyed the voice of the LORD your God in anything that he sent me to tell you. <sup>22</sup>Be well aware, then, that you shall die by the sword, by famine, and by pestilence in the place where you desire to go and settle."

<sup>43.1</sup> WHEN Jeremiah finished speaking to all the people all these words of the LORD their God, with which the LORD their God had sent him to them, <sup>2</sup>Azariah son of Hoshaiah and Johanan son of Kareah and all the other insolent men said to Jeremiah, "You are telling a lie. The LORD our God did not send you to say, 'Do not go to Egypt to settle there'; <sup>3</sup>but Baruch son of Neriah is inciting you against us, to hand us over to the Chaldeans, in order that they may kill us or take us into exile in Babylon." <sup>4</sup>So Johanan son of Kareah and all the commanders of the forces and all the people did not obey the voice of the LORD, to stay in the land of Judah. <sup>5</sup>But Johanan son of Kareah and all the commanders of the forces took all the remnant of Judah who had returned to settle in the land of Judah from all the nations to which they had been driven— <sup>6</sup>the men, the women, the children, the princesses, and everyone whom Nebuzaradan the captain of the guard had left with Gedaliah son of Ahikam son of Shaphan; also the prophet Jeremiah and Baruch son of Neriah. <sup>7</sup>And they came into the land of Egypt, for they did not obey the voice of the LORD. And they arrived at Tahpanhes.

8  Then the word of the LORD came to Jeremiah in Tahpanhes: <sup>9</sup>Take some large stones in your hands, and bury them in the clay pavement<sup>a</sup> that is at the entrance to Pharaoh's palace in Tahpanhes. Let the Judeans see you do it, <sup>10</sup>and say to them, Thus says the LORD of hosts, the God of Israel: I am going to send and take my servant King Nebuchadrezzar of Babylon, and he<sup>b</sup> will set his throne above these stones that I have buried, and he will spread his royal canopy over them. <sup>11</sup>He shall come and ravage the land of Egypt, giving

> those who are destined for
>> pestilence, to pestilence,
> and those who are destined
>> for captivity, to captivity,
> and those who are destined
>> for the sword, to the
>> sword.

<sup>12</sup>He<sup>c</sup> shall kindle a fire in the temples of the gods of Egypt; and he shall burn them and carry them away captive; and he shall pick clean the land of Egypt, as a shepherd picks his cloak clean of vermin; and he shall depart from there safely. <sup>13</sup>He shall break the obelisks of Heliopolis, which is in the land of Egypt; and the temples of the gods of Egypt he shall burn with fire.

<sup>44.1</sup> THE word that came to Jeremiah for all the Judeans living in the land of Egypt, at Migdol, at Tahpanhes, at Memphis, and in the land of Pathros, <sup>2</sup>Thus says the LORD of hosts, the God of Israel: You yourselves have seen all the disaster that I have brought on Jerusalem and on all the towns of Judah. Look at them; today they are a desolation, without an inhabitant in them, <sup>3</sup>because of the wickedness that they committed, provoking me to anger, in that they went to make offerings and serve other gods that they had not known, neither they, nor you, nor your ancestors. <sup>4</sup>Yet I persistently sent to you all my servants the prophets, saying, "I beg you not to do this abominable thing that I hate!" <sup>5</sup>But they did not listen or incline their ear, to turn from their wickedness and make no offerings to other gods. <sup>6</sup>So my wrath and my anger were poured out and kindled in

<sup>a</sup>Meaning of Heb uncertain   <sup>b</sup>Gk Syr: Heb *I*   <sup>c</sup>Gk Syr Vg: Heb *I*

the towns of Judah and in the streets of Jerusalem; and they became a waste and a desolation, as they still are today. ⁷And now thus says the Lᴏʀᴅ God of hosts, the God of Israel: Why are you doing such great harm to yourselves, to cut off man and woman, child and infant, from the midst of Judah, leaving yourselves without a remnant? ⁸Why do you provoke me to anger with the works of your hands, making offerings to other gods in the land of Egypt where you have come to settle? Will you be cut off and become an object of cursing and ridicule among all the nations of the earth? ⁹Have you forgotten the crimes of your ancestors, of the kings of Judah, of theirᵃ wives, your own crimes and those of your wives, which they committed in the land of Judah and in the streets of Jerusalem? ¹⁰They have shown no contrition or fear to this day, nor have they walked in my law and my statutes that I set before you and before your ancestors.

11 Therefore thus says the Lᴏʀᴅ of hosts, the God of Israel: I am determined to bring disaster on you, to bring all Judah to an end. ¹²I will take the remnant of Judah who are determined to come to the land of Egypt to settle, and they shall perish, everyone; in the land of Egypt they shall fall; by the sword and by famine they shall perish; from the least to the greatest, they shall die by the sword and by famine; and they shall become an object of execration and horror, of cursing and ridicule. ¹³I will punish those who live in the land of Egypt, as I have punished Jerusalem, with the sword, with famine, and with pestilence, ¹⁴so that none of the remnant of Judah who have come to settle in the land of Egypt shall escape or survive or return to the land of Judah. Although they long to go back to live there, they shall not go back, except some fugitives.

15 Then all the men who were aware that their wives had been making offerings to other gods, and all the women who stood by, a great assembly, all the people who lived in Pathros in the land of Egypt, answered Jeremiah: ¹⁶"As for the word that you have spoken to us in the name of the Lᴏʀᴅ, we are not going to listen to you. ¹⁷Instead, we will do everything that we have vowed, make offerings to the queen of heaven and pour out libations to her, just as we and our ancestors, our kings and our officials, used to do in the towns of Judah and in the streets of Jerusalem. We used to have plenty of food, and prospered, and saw no misfortune. ¹⁸But from the time we stopped making offerings to the queen of heaven and pouring out libations to her, we have lacked everything and have perished by the sword and by famine." ¹⁹And the women said, ᵇ "Indeed we will go on making offerings to the queen of heaven and pouring out libations to her; do you think that we made cakes for her, marked with her image, and poured out libations to her without our husbands' being involved?"

20 Then Jeremiah said to all the people, men and women, all the people who were giving him this answer: ²¹"As for the offerings that you made in the towns of Judah and in the streets of Jerusalem, you and your ancestors, your kings and your officials, and the people of the land, did not the Lᴏʀᴅ remember them? Did it not come into his mind? ²²The Lᴏʀᴅ could no longer bear the sight of your evil doings, the abominations that you committed; therefore your land became a desolation and a waste and a curse, without inhabitant, as it is to this day. ²³It is because you burned offerings, and because you sinned against the Lᴏʀᴅ and did not obey the voice of the Lᴏʀᴅ or walk in his law and in his statutes and in his de-

---

ᵃHeb *his*   ᵇCompare Syr: Heb lacks *And the women said*

crees, that this disaster has befallen you, as is still evident today."

## 2 TIMOTHY 2.1–21

YOU then, my child, be strong in the grace that is in Christ Jesus; ²and what you have heard from me through many witnesses entrust to faithful people who will be able to teach others as well. ³Share in suffering like a good soldier of Christ Jesus. ⁴No one serving in the army gets entangled in everyday affairs; the soldier's aim is to please the enlisting officer. ⁵And in the case of an athlete, no one is crowned without competing according to the rules. ⁶It is the farmer who does the work who ought to have the first share of the crops. ⁷Think over what I say, for the Lord will give you understanding in all things.

8 Remember Jesus Christ, raised from the dead, a descendant of David—that is my gospel, ⁹for which I suffer hardship, even to the point of being chained like a criminal. But the word of God is not chained. ¹⁰Therefore I endure everything for the sake of the elect, so that they may also obtain the salvation that is in Christ Jesus, with eternal glory. ¹¹The saying is sure:

> If we have died with him, we
>      will also live with him;
> 12  if we endure, we will also reign
>      with him;
>      if we deny him, he will also
>      deny us;
> 13  if we are faithless, he remains
>      faithful—
>      for he cannot deny himself.

14 Remind them of this, and warn them before God[a] that they are to avoid wrangling over words, which does no good but only ruins those who are listening. ¹⁵Do your best to present yourself to God as one approved by him, a worker who has no need to be ashamed, rightly explaining the word of truth. ¹⁶Avoid profane chatter, for it will lead people into more and more impiety, ¹⁷and their talk will spread like gangrene. Among them are Hymenaeus and Philetus, ¹⁸who have swerved from the truth by claiming that the resurrection has already taken place. They are upsetting the faith of some. ¹⁹But God's firm foundation stands, bearing this inscription: "The Lord knows those who are his," and, "Let everyone who calls on the name of the Lord turn away from wickedness."

20 In a large house there are utensils not only of gold and silver but also of wood and clay, some for special use, some for ordinary. ²¹All who cleanse themselves of the things I have mentioned[b] will become special utensils, dedicated and useful to the owner of the house, ready for every good work.

## PSALM 92.1—93.5

*A Psalm. A Song for the Sabbath Day.*

IT is good to give thanks to the
      LORD,
   to sing praises to your name,
      O Most High;
2  to declare your steadfast love in
      the morning,
   and your faithfulness by night,
3  to the music of the lute and the
      harp,
   to the melody of the lyre.
4  For you, O LORD, have made
      me glad by your work;
   at the works of your hands I
      sing for joy.

5  How great are your works,
      O LORD!
   Your thoughts are very deep!
6  The dullard cannot know,
   the stupid cannot understand
      this:
7  though the wicked sprout like
      grass

[a] Other ancient authorities read *the Lord*   [b] Gk *of these things*

and all evildoers flourish,
they are doomed to destruction
forever,
8    but you, O LORD, are on high
forever.
9  For your enemies, O LORD,
for your enemies shall perish;
all evildoers shall be
scattered.

10    But you have exalted my horn
like that of the wild ox;
you have poured over me[a]
fresh oil.
11  My eyes have seen the downfall
of my enemies;
my ears have heard the doom
of my evil assailants.

12    The righteous flourish like the
palm tree,
and grow like a cedar in
Lebanon.
13  They are planted in the house of
the LORD;
they flourish in the courts of
our God.
14  In old age they still produce
fruit;
they are always green and full
of sap,
15  showing that the LORD is
upright;
he is my rock, and there is
no unrighteousness in
him.

93.1  The LORD is king, he is robed in
majesty;
the LORD is robed, he is
girded with strength.
He has established the world; it
shall never be moved;
2    your throne is established
from of old;
you are from everlasting.

3  The floods have lifted up,
O LORD,
the floods have lifted up their
voice;
the floods lift up their roaring.
4  More majestic than the thunders
of mighty waters,
more majestic than the
waves[b] of the sea,
majestic on high is the LORD!

5  Your decrees are very sure;
holiness befits your house,
O LORD, forevermore.

# PROVERBS 26.3–5

A WHIP for the horse, a bridle
for the donkey,
and a rod for the back of
fools.
4  Do not answer fools according
to their folly,
or you will be a fool yourself.
5  Answer fools according to their
folly,
or they will be wise in their
own eyes.

---

[a]Syr: Meaning of Heb uncertain   [b]Cn: Heb *majestic are the waves*

## JEREMIAH 44.24—47.7

JEREMIAH said to all the people and all the women, "Hear the word of the LORD, all you Judeans who are in the land of Egypt, 25Thus says the LORD of hosts, the God of Israel: You and your wives have accomplished in deeds what you declared in words, saying, 'We are determined to perform the vows that we have made, to make offerings to the queen of heaven and to pour out libations to her.' By all means, keep your vows and make your libations! 26Therefore hear the word of the LORD, all you Judeans who live in the land of Egypt: Lo, I swear by my great name, says the LORD, that my name shall no longer be pronounced on the lips of any of the people of Judah in all the land of Egypt, saying, 'As the Lord GOD lives.' 27I am going to watch over them for harm and not for good; all the people of Judah who are in the land of Egypt shall perish by the sword and by famine, until not one is left. 28And those who escape the sword shall return from the land of Egypt to the land of Judah, few in number; and all the remnant of Judah, who have come to the land of Egypt to settle, shall know whose words will stand, mine or theirs! 29This shall be the sign to you, says the LORD, that I am going to punish you in this place, in order that you may know that my words against you will surely be carried out: 30Thus says the LORD, I am going to give Pharaoh Hophra, king of Egypt, into the hands of his enemies, those who seek his life, just as I gave King Zedekiah of Judah into the hand of King Nebuchadrezzar of Babylon, his enemy who sought his life."

45.1 THE word that the prophet Jeremiah spoke to Baruch son of Neriah, when he wrote these words in a scroll at the dictation of Jeremiah, in the fourth year of King Jehoiakim son of Josiah of Judah: 2Thus says the LORD, the God of Israel, to you, O Baruch: 3You said, "Woe is me! The LORD has added sorrow to my pain; I am weary with my groaning, and I find no rest." 4Thus you shall say to him, "Thus says the LORD: I am going to break down what I have built, and pluck up what I have planted—that is, the whole land. 5And you, do you seek great things for yourself? Do not seek them; for I am going to bring disaster upon all flesh, says the LORD; but I will give you your life as a prize of war in every place to which you may go."

46.1 THE word of the LORD that came to the prophet Jeremiah concerning the nations.

2 Concerning Egypt, about the army of Pharaoh Neco, king of Egypt, which was by the river Euphrates at Carchemish and which King Nebuchadrezzar of Babylon defeated in the fourth year of King Jehoiakim son of Josiah of Judah:

3 Prepare buckler and shield,
    and advance for battle!
4 Harness the horses;
    mount the steeds!
Take your stations with your
      helmets,
    whet your lances,
    put on your coats of mail!
5 Why do I see them terrified?
    They have fallen back;
their warriors are beaten down,
    and have fled in haste.
They do not look back—
    terror is all around!
            says the LORD.
6 The swift cannot flee away,

nor can the warrior escape;
in the north by the river
    Euphrates
they have stumbled and
    fallen.

7 Who is this, rising like the Nile,
    like rivers whose waters
        surge?
8 Egypt rises like the Nile,
    like rivers whose waters
        surge.
It said, Let me rise, let me
    cover the earth,
let me destroy cities and their
    inhabitants.
9 Advance, O horses,
    and dash madly, O chariots!
Let the warriors go forth:
    Ethiopia[a] and Put who carry
        the shield,
    the Ludim, who draw[b] the
        bow.
10 That day is the day of the Lord
    God of hosts,
a day of retribution,
to gain vindication from his
    foes.
The sword shall devour and
    be sated,
and drink its fill of their blood.
For the Lord God of hosts holds
    a sacrifice
in the land of the north by the
    river Euphrates.
11 Go up to Gilead, and take balm,
    O virgin daughter Egypt!
In vain you have used many
    medicines;
there is no healing for you.
12 The nations have heard of
    your shame,
and the earth is full of your
    cry;
for warrior has stumbled against
    warrior;
both have fallen together.

13 The word that the Lord spoke to the prophet Jeremiah about the coming of King Nebuchadrezzar of Babylon to attack the land of Egypt:
14 Declare in Egypt, and proclaim
    in Migdol;
proclaim in Memphis and
    Tahpanhes;
Say, "Take your stations and
    be ready,
for the sword shall devour
    those around you."
15 Why has Apis fled?[c]
Why did your bull not stand?
    —because the Lord thrust
    him down.
16 Your multitude stumbled[d] and
    fell,
and one said to another,[e]
"Come, let us go back to our
    own people
and to the land of our birth,
because of the destroying
    sword."
17 Give Pharaoh, king of Egypt,
    the name
"Braggart who missed his
    chance."

18 As I live, says the King,
    whose name is the Lord of
        hosts,
one is coming
    like Tabor among the
        mountains,
    and like Carmel by the sea.
19 Pack your bags for exile,
    sheltered daughter Egypt!
For Memphis shall become a
    waste,
a ruin, without inhabitant.

20 A beautiful heifer is Egypt—
    a gadfly from the north lights
    upon her.
21 Even her mercenaries in her
    midst

[a] Or Nubia; Heb Cush   [b] Cn: Heb who grasp, who draw   [c] Gk: Heb Why was it swept away
[d] Gk: Meaning of Heb uncertain   [e] Gk: Heb and fell one to another and they said

are like fatted calves;
they too have turned and fled
together,
they did not stand;
for the day of their calamity has
come upon them,
the time of their punishment.

22 She makes a sound like a snake
gliding away;
for her enemies march in
force,
and come against her with axes,
like those who fell trees.
23 They shall cut down her forest,
says the LORD,
though it is impenetrable,
because they are more
numerous
than locusts;
they are without number.
24 Daughter Egypt shall be put
to shame;
she shall be handed over to a
people from the north.

25 The LORD of hosts, the God of Israel, said: See, I am bringing punishment upon Amon of Thebes, and Pharaoh, and Egypt and her gods and her kings, upon Pharaoh and those who trust in him. 26I will hand them over to those who seek their life, to King Nebuchadrezzar of Babylon and his officers. Afterward Egypt shall be inhabited as in the days of old, says the LORD.

27 But as for you, have no fear,
my servant Jacob,
and do not be dismayed,
O Israel;
for I am going to save you from
far away,
and your offspring from the
land of their captivity.
Jacob shall return and have quiet
and ease,
and no one shall make him
afraid.

28 As for you, have no fear, my
servant Jacob,
says the LORD,
for I am with you.
I will make an end of all the
nations
among which I have banished
you,
but I will not make an end
of you!
I will chastise you in just
measure,
and I will by no means leave
you unpunished.

47.1 THE word of the LORD that came to the prophet Jeremiah concerning the Philistines, before Pharaoh attacked Gaza:
2 Thus says the LORD:
See, waters are rising out of
the north
and shall become an
overflowing torrent;
they shall overflow the land and
all that fills it,
the city and those who live in
it.
People shall cry out,
and all the inhabitants of the
land shall wail.
3 At the noise of the stamping of
the hoofs of his stallions,
at the clatter of his chariots,
at the rumbling of their
wheels,
parents do not turn back for
children,
so feeble are their hands,
4 because of the day that is
coming
to destroy all the Philistines,
to cut off from Tyre and Sidon
every helper that remains.
For the LORD is destroying the
Philistines,
the remnant of the coastland
of Caphtor.
5 Baldness has come upon Gaza,
Ashkelon is silenced.

O remnant of their power!<sup>a</sup>
   How long will you gash
     yourselves?
6  Ah, sword of the LORD!
   How long until you are quiet?
  Put yourself into your scabbard,
   rest and be still!
7  How can it[b] be quiet,
   when the LORD has given it
     an order?
  Against Ashkelon and against
     the seashore—
   there he has appointed it.

## 2 TIMOTHY 2.22—3.17

SHUN youthful passions and pursue righteousness, faith, love, and peace, along with those who call on the Lord from a pure heart. 23Have nothing to do with stupid and senseless controversies; you know that they breed quarrels. 24And the Lord's servant[c] must not be quarrelsome but kindly to everyone, an apt teacher, patient, 25correcting opponents with gentleness. God may perhaps grant that they will repent and come to know the truth, 26and that they may escape from the snare of the devil, having been held captive by him to do his will. [d]

3.1 You must understand this, that in the last days distressing times will come. 2For people will be lovers of themselves, lovers of money, boasters, arrogant, abusive, disobedient to their parents, ungrateful, unholy, 3inhuman, implacable, slanderers, profligates, brutes, haters of good, 4treacherous, reckless, swollen with conceit, lovers of pleasure rather than lovers of God, 5holding to the outward form of godliness but denying its power. Avoid them! 6For among them are those who make their way into households and captivate silly women, overwhelmed by their sins and swayed by all kinds of desires, 7who are always being instructed and can never arrive at a knowledge of the truth. 8As Jannes and Jambres opposed Moses, so these people, of corrupt mind and counterfeit faith, also oppose the truth. 9But they will not make much progress, because, as in the case of those two men, [e] their folly will become plain to everyone.

10 Now you have observed my teaching, my conduct, my aim in life, my faith, my patience, my love, my steadfastness, 11my persecutions and suffering the things that happened to me in Antioch, Iconium, and Lystra. What persecutions I endured! Yet the Lord rescued me from all of them. 12Indeed, all who want to live a godly life in Christ Jesus will be persecuted. 13But wicked people and impostors will go from bad to worse, deceiving others and being deceived. 14But as for you, continue in what you have learned and firmly believed, knowing from whom you learned it, 15and how from childhood you have known the sacred writings that are able to instruct you for salvation through faith in Christ Jesus. 16All scripture is inspired by God and is[f] useful for teaching, for reproof, for correction, and for training in righteousness, 17so that everyone who belongs to God may be proficient, equipped for every good work.

## PSALM 94.1–23

O LORD, you God of vengeance,
  you God of vengeance,
   shine forth!
2  Rise up, O judge of the earth;
   give to the proud what they
     deserve!
3  O LORD, how long shall the
     wicked,
   how long shall the wicked
     exult?

aGk: Heb *their valley*  bGk Vg: Heb *you*  cGk *slave*  dOr *by him, to do his* (that is, God's) *will*
eGk lacks *two men*  fOr *Every scripture inspired by God is also*

4  They pour out their arrogant
       words;
   all the evildoers boast.
5  They crush your people,
       O LORD,
   and afflict your heritage.
6  They kill the widow and the
       stranger,
   they murder the orphan,
7  and they say, "The LORD does
       not see;
   the God of Jacob does not
       perceive."

8  Understand, O dullest of the
       people;
   fools, when will you be wise?
9  He who planted the ear, does
       he not hear?
   He who formed the eye, does
       he not see?
10 He who disciplines the nations,
   he who teaches knowledge to
       humankind,
   does he not chastise?
11 The LORD knows our thoughts, a
       that they are but an empty
       breath.

12 Happy are those whom you
       discipline, O LORD,
   and whom you teach out of
       your law,
13 giving them respite from days of
       trouble,
   until a pit is dug for the
       wicked.
14 For the LORD will not forsake
       his people;
   he will not abandon his
       heritage;
15 for justice will return to the
       righteous,
   and all the upright in heart
       will follow it.

16 Who rises up for me against the
       wicked?

Who stands up for me against
       evildoers?
17 If the LORD had not been my
       help,
   my soul would soon have
       lived in the land of
       silence.
18 When I thought, "My foot is
       slipping,"
   your steadfast love, O LORD,
       held me up.
19 When the cares of my heart are
       many,
   your consolations cheer my
       soul.
20 Can wicked rulers be allied
       with you,
   those who contrive mischief
       by statute?
21 They band together against the
       life of the righteous,
   and condemn the innocent to
       death.
22 But the LORD has become my
       stronghold,
   and my God the rock of my
       refuge.
23 He will repay them for their
       iniquity
   and wipe them out for their
       wickedness;
   the LORD our God will wipe
       them out.

## PROVERBS 26.6–8

IT is like cutting off one's foot and
       drinking down
       violence,
   to send a message by a fool.
7  The legs of a disabled person
       hang limp;
   so does a proverb in the
       mouth of a fool.
8  It is like binding a stone in a
       sling
   to give honor to a fool.

a Heb *the thoughts of humankind*

# OCTOBER 25

JEREMIAH 48.1—49.22

Concerning Moab.

Thus says the Lord of hosts, the God of Israel:

Alas for Nebo, it is laid waste!
    Kiriathaim is put to shame, it
      is taken;
the fortress is put to shame and
      broken down;
2   the renown of Moab is no
      more.
In Heshbon they planned evil
      against her:
    "Come, let us cut her off
      from being a nation!"
You also, O Madmen, shall be
      brought to silence; [a]
the sword shall pursue you.

3   Hark! a cry from Horonaim,
    "Desolation and great
      destruction!"
4   "Moab is destroyed!"
    her little ones cry out.
5   For at the ascent of Luhith
    they go[b] up weeping bitterly;
for at the descent of Horonaim
    they have heard the
      distressing cry of
      anguish.
6   Flee! Save yourselves!
    Be like a wild ass[c] in the
      desert!

7   Surely, because you trusted in
      your strongholds[d] and
      your treasures,
    you also shall be taken;
Chemosh shall go out into exile,
    with his priests and his
      attendants.

8   The destroyer shall come upon
      every town,
    and no town shall escape;
the valley shall perish,
    and the plain shall be
      destroyed,
    as the Lord has spoken.

9   Set aside salt for Moab,
    for she will surely fall;
her towns shall become a
      desolation,
    with no inhabitant in them.

10   Accursed is the one who is slack in doing the work of the Lord; and accursed is the one who keeps back the sword from bloodshed.

11   Moab has been at ease from his
      youth,
    settled like wine[e] on its
      dregs;
he has not been emptied from
      vessel to vessel,
    nor has he gone into exile;
therefore his flavor has
      remained
    and his aroma is unspoiled.
12   Therefore, the time is surely coming, says the Lord, when I shall send to him decanters to decant him, and empty his vessels, and break his[f] jars in pieces. 13Then Moab shall be ashamed of Chemosh, as the house of Israel was ashamed of Bethel, their confidence.

14   How can you say, "We are
      heroes
    and mighty warriors"?
15   The destroyer of Moab and his
      towns has come up,

---

[a] The place-name *Madmen* sounds like the Hebrew verb *to be silent*  [b] Cn: Heb *he goes*  [c] Gk Aquila: Heb *like Aroer*  [d] Gk: Heb *works*  [e] Heb lacks *like wine*  [f] Gk Aquila: Heb *their*

and the choicest of his young
men have gone down to
slaughter,
says the King, whose name is
the Lord of hosts.
16 The calamity of Moab is near
at hand
and his doom approaches
swiftly.
17 Mourn over him, all you his
neighbors,
and all who know his name;
say, "How the mighty scepter is
broken,
the glorious staff!"

18 Come down from glory,
and sit on the parched
ground,
enthroned daughter Dibon!
For the destroyer of Moab has
come up against you;
he has destroyed your
strongholds.
19 Stand by the road and watch,
you inhabitant of Aroer!
Ask the man fleeing and the
woman escaping;
say, "What has happened?"
20 Moab is put to shame, for it is
broken down;
wail and cry!
Tell it by the Arnon,
that Moab is laid waste.

21 Judgment has come upon the tableland, upon Holon, and Jahzah, and
Mephaath, 22 and Dibon, and Nebo, and
Beth-diblathaim, 23 and Kiriathaim, and
Beth-gamul, and Beth-meon, 24 and Kerioth, and Bozrah, and all the towns of
the land of Moab, far and near. 25 The
horn of Moab is cut off, and his arm is
broken, says the Lord.

26 Make him drunk, because he
magnified himself against the Lord; let
Moab wallow in his vomit; he too shall
become a laughingstock. 27 Israel was a
laughingstock for you, though he was
not caught among thieves; but whenever you spoke of him you shook your
head!

28 Leave the towns, and live on
the rock,
O inhabitants of Moab!
Be like the dove that nests
on the sides of the mouth of
a gorge.
29 We have heard of the pride of
Moab—
he is very proud—
of his loftiness, his pride, and
his arrogance,
and the haughtiness of his
heart.
30 I myself know his insolence,
says the Lord;
his boasts are false,
his deeds are false.
31 Therefore I wail for Moab;
I cry out for all Moab;
for the people of Kir-heres I
mourn.
32 More than for Jazer I weep for
you,
O vine of Sibmah!
Your branches crossed over the
sea,
reached as far as Jazer; a
upon your summer fruits and
your vintage
the destroyer has fallen.
33 Gladness and joy have been
taken away
from the fruitful land of Moab;
I have stopped the wine from
the wine presses;
no one treads them with
shouts of joy;
the shouting is not the shout
of joy.

34 Heshbon and Elealeh cry out; b
as far as Jahaz they utter their voice,
from Zoar to Horonaim and Eglath-

a Two Mss and Isa 16.8: MT *the sea of Jazer*   b Cn: Heb *From the cry of Heshbon to Elealeh*

shelishiyah. For even the waters of Nimrim have become desolate. [35]And I will bring to an end in Moab, says the LORD, those who offer sacrifice at a high place and make offerings to their gods. [36]Therefore my heart moans for Moab like a flute, and my heart moans like a flute for the people of Kir-heres; for the riches they gained have perished.

37 For every head is shaved and every beard cut off; on all the hands there are gashes, and on the loins sackcloth. [38]On all the housetops of Moab and in the squares there is nothing but lamentation; for I have broken Moab like a vessel that no one wants, says the LORD. [39]How it is broken! How they wail! How Moab has turned his back in shame! So Moab has become a derision and a horror to all his neighbors.

40 For thus says the LORD:
Look, he shall swoop down like
    an eagle,
    and spread his wings against
    Moab;
41 the towns[a] shall be taken
    and the strongholds seized.
The hearts of the warriors of
    Moab, on that day,
    shall be like the heart of a
    woman in labor.
42 Moab shall be destroyed as
    a people,
    because he magnified himself
    against the LORD.
43 Terror, pit, and trap
    are before you, O inhabitants
    of Moab!
        says the LORD.
44 Everyone who flees from the
    terror
    shall fall into the pit,
and everyone who climbs out of
    the pit
    shall be caught in the trap.
For I will bring these things[b]
    upon Moab

    in the year of their
    punishment,
        says the LORD.

45 In the shadow of Heshbon
    fugitives stop exhausted;
for a fire has gone out from
    Heshbon,
    a flame from the house of
    Sihon;
it has destroyed the forehead
    of Moab,
    the scalp of the people of
    tumult.[c]
46 Woe to you, O Moab!
    The people of Chemosh have
    perished,
for your sons have been taken
    captive,
    and your daughters into
    captivity.
47 Yet I will restore the fortunes
    of Moab
    in the latter days, says the
    LORD.
Thus far is the judgment on
    Moab.

49.1 CONCERNING the Ammonites.

Thus says the LORD:
    Has Israel no sons?
        Has he no heir?
Why then has Milcom
        dispossessed Gad,
    and his people settled in its
    towns?
2 Therefore, the time is surely
    coming,
    says the LORD,
when I will sound the battle
    alarm
    against Rabbah of the
    Ammonites;
it shall become a desolate
    mound,
    and its villages shall be
    burned with fire;

aOr *Kerioth*  bGk Syr: Heb *bring upon it*  cOr *of Shaon*

then Israel shall dispossess
  those who dispossessed
  him,
  says the LORD.

3  Wail, O Heshbon, for Ai is laid
  waste!
  Cry out, O daughters[a] of
  Rabbah!
Put on sackcloth,
  lament, and slash yourselves
  with whips![b]
For Milcom shall go into exile,
  with his priests and his
  attendants.
4  Why do you boast in your
  strength?
  Your strength is ebbing,
O faithless daughter.
  You trusted in your
  treasures, saying,
  "Who will attack me?"
5  I am going to bring terror
  upon you,
  says the Lord GOD of hosts,
  from all your neighbors,
and you will be scattered, each
  headlong,
  with no one to gather the
  fugitives.

6  But afterward I will restore the
fortunes of the Ammonites, says the
LORD.

7  Concerning Edom.

Thus says the LORD of hosts:
  Is there no longer wisdom in
  Teman?
  Has counsel perished from
  the prudent?
  Has their wisdom vanished?
8  Flee, turn back, get down low,
  inhabitants of Dedan!
For I will bring the calamity of
  Esau upon him,
  the time when I punish him.
9  If grape-gatherers came to you,
  would they not leave
  gleanings?
If thieves came by night,
  even they would pillage only
  what they wanted.
10  But as for me, I have stripped
  Esau bare,
  I have uncovered his hiding
  places,
  and he is not able to conceal
  himself.
His offspring are destroyed,
  his kinsfolk
  and his neighbors; and he is
  no more.
11  Leave your orphans, I will keep
  them alive;
  and let your widows trust in
  me.

12  For thus says the LORD: If those
who do not deserve to drink the cup
still have to drink it, shall you be the
one to go unpunished? You shall not go
unpunished; you must drink it. [13]For by
myself I have sworn, says the LORD,
that Bozrah shall become an object of
horror and ridicule, a waste, and an object of cursing; and all her towns shall
be perpetual wastes.
14  I have heard tidings from the
  LORD,
  and a messenger has been
  sent among the nations:
"Gather yourselves together and
  come against her,
  and rise up for battle!"
15  For I will make you least among
  the nations,
  despised by humankind.
16  The terror you inspire
  and the pride of your heart
  have deceived you,
you who live in the clefts of
  the rock,[c]
  who hold the height of the
  hill.
Although you make your nest as
  high as the eagle's,

from there I will bring you
down,

    says the LORD.

17 Edom shall become an object of horror; everyone who passes by it will be horrified and will hiss because of all its disasters. [18]As when Sodom and Gomorrah and their neighbors were overthrown, says the LORD, no one shall live there, nor shall anyone settle in it. [19]Like a lion coming up from the thickets of the Jordan against a perennial pasture, I will suddenly chase Edom[a] away from it; and I will appoint over it whomever I choose. [b] For who is like me? Who can summon me? Who is the shepherd who can stand before me? [20]Therefore hear the plan that the LORD has made against Edom and the purposes that he has formed against the inhabitants of Teman: Surely the little ones of the flock shall be dragged away; surely their fold shall be appalled at their fate. [21]At the sound of their fall the earth shall tremble; the sound of their cry shall be heard at the Red Sea. [c] [22]Look, he shall mount up and swoop down like an eagle, and spread his wings against Bozrah, and the heart of the warriors of Edom in that day shall be like the heart of a woman in labor.

## 2 TIMOTHY 4.1–22

IN the presence of God and of Christ Jesus, who is to judge the living and the dead, and in view of his appearing and his kingdom, I solemnly urge you: [2]proclaim the message; be persistent whether the time is favorable or unfavorable; convince, rebuke, and encourage, with the utmost patience in teaching. [3]For the time is coming when people will not put up with sound doctrine, but having itching ears, they will accumulate for themselves teachers to suit their own desires, [4]and will turn away from listening to the truth and wander away to myths. [5]As for you, always be sober, endure suffering, do the work of an evangelist, carry out your ministry fully.

6 As for me, I am already being poured out as a libation, and the time of my departure has come. [7]I have fought the good fight, I have finished the race, I have kept the faith. [8]From now on there is reserved for me the crown of righteousness, which the Lord, the righteous judge, will give me on that day, and not only to me but also to all who have longed for his appearing.

9 Do your best to come to me soon, [10]for Demas, in love with this present world, has deserted me and gone to Thessalonica; Crescens has gone to Galatia, [d] Titus to Dalmatia. [11]Only Luke is with me. Get Mark and bring him with you, for he is useful in my ministry. [12]I have sent Tychicus to Ephesus. [13]When you come, bring the cloak that I left with Carpus at Troas, also the books, and above all the parchments. [14]Alexander the coppersmith did me great harm; the Lord will pay him back for his deeds. [15]You also must beware of him, for he strongly opposed our message.

16 At my first defense no one came to my support, but all deserted me. May it not be counted against them! [17]But the Lord stood by me and gave me strength, so that through me the message might be fully proclaimed and all the Gentiles might hear it. So I was rescued from the lion's mouth. [18]The Lord will rescue me from every evil attack and save me for his heavenly kingdom. To him be the glory forever and ever. Amen.

19 Greet Prisca and Aquila, and the household of Onesiphorus. [20]Erastus remained in Corinth; Trophimus I left ill

in Miletus. [21]Do your best to come before winter. Eubulus sends greetings to you, as do Pudens and Linus and Claudia and all the brothers and sisters. [a]

22 The Lord be with your spirit. Grace be with you. [b]

## PSALM 95.1—96.13

O COME, let us sing to the LORD;
  let us make a joyful noise to
    the rock of our salvation!
2 Let us come into his presence
    with thanksgiving;
  let us make a joyful noise to
    him with songs of praise!
3 For the LORD is a great God,
    and a great King above all
      gods.
4 In his hand are the depths of
      the earth;
  the heights of the mountains
    are his also.
5 The sea is his, for he made it,
    and the dry land, which his
      hands have formed.

6 O come, let us worship and bow
      down,
  let us kneel before the LORD,
    our Maker!
7 For he is our God,
    and we are the people of his
      pasture,
  and the sheep of his hand.

  O that today you would listen to
      his voice!
8   Do not harden your hearts, as
      at Meribah,
  as on the day at Massah in
      the wilderness,
9 when your ancestors tested me,
    and put me to the proof,
      though they had seen my
        work.
10 For forty years I loathed that
      generation

and said, "They are a people
    whose hearts go astray,
  and they do not regard my
      ways."
11 Therefore in my anger I swore,
    "They shall not enter my
      rest."

96.1 O sing to the LORD a new song;
    sing to the LORD, all the
      earth.
2 Sing to the LORD, bless his
      name;
  tell of his salvation from day
      to day.
3 Declare his glory among the
      nations,
  his marvelous works among
    all the peoples.
4 For great is the LORD, and
      greatly to be praised;
  he is to be revered above
    all gods.
5 For all the gods of the peoples
      are idols,
  but the LORD made the
      heavens.
6 Honor and majesty are before
      him;
  strength and beauty are in his
      sanctuary.

7 Ascribe to the LORD, O families
    of the peoples,
  ascribe to the LORD glory and
      strength.
8 Ascribe to the LORD the glory
    due his name;
  bring an offering, and come
    into his courts.
9 Worship the LORD in holy
      splendor;
  tremble before him, all the
      earth.

10 Say among the nations, "The
    LORD is king!

a Gk all the brothers   b The Greek word for you here is plural. Other ancient authorities add Amen

The world is firmly
established; it shall never
be moved.
He will judge the peoples with
equity."
11 Let the heavens be glad, and let
the earth rejoice;
let the sea roar, and all that
fills it;
12 let the field exult, and
everything in it.
Then shall all the trees of the
forest sing for joy
13 before the Lord; for he is
coming,
for he is coming to judge the
earth.
He will judge the world with
righteousness,
and the peoples with his
truth.

## PROVERBS 26.9–12

Like a thornbush brandished by
the hand of a drunkard
is a proverb in the mouth of
a fool.
10 Like an archer who wounds
everybody
is one who hires a passing
fool or drunkard. a
11 Like a dog that returns to its
vomit
is a fool who reverts to his
folly.
12 Do you see persons wise in
their own eyes?
There is more hope for fools
than for them.

# OCTOBER 26

## JEREMIAH 49.23—50.46

Concerning Damascus.

Hamath and Arpad are
confounded,
for they have heard bad
news;
they melt in fear, they are
troubled like the sea b
that cannot be quiet.
24 Damascus has become feeble,
she turned to flee,
and panic seized her;
anguish and sorrows have taken
hold of her,
as of a woman in labor.
25 How the famous city is
forsaken, c

the joyful town! d
26 Therefore her young men shall
fall in her squares,
and all her soldiers shall be
destroyed in that day,
says the Lord of hosts.
27 And I will kindle a fire at the
wall of Damascus,
and it shall devour the
strongholds of
Ben-hadad.

28 Concerning Kedar and the kingdoms of Hazor that King Nebuchadrezzar of Babylon defeated.

Thus says the Lord:
Rise up, advance against Kedar!

aMeaning of Heb uncertain   bCn: Heb *there is trouble in the sea*   cVg: Heb *is not forsaken*   dSyr Vg
Tg: Heb *the town of my joy*

Destroy the people of the
    east!
29  Take their tents and their
    flocks,
    their curtains and all their
      goods;
carry off their camels for
    yourselves,
and a cry shall go up: "Terror
    is all around!"
30  Flee, wander far away, hide in
    deep places,
    O inhabitants of Hazor!
          says the LORD.
For King Nebuchadrezzar of
    Babylon
has made a plan against you
and formed a purpose against
    you.

31  Rise up, advance against a
    nation at ease,
    that lives secure,
          says the LORD,
that has no gates or bars,
    that lives alone.
32  Their camels shall become
    booty,
    their herds of cattle a spoil.
I will scatter to every wind
    those who have shaven
      temples,
and I will bring calamity
    against them from every side,
          says the LORD.
33  Hazor shall become a lair of
    jackals,
    an everlasting waste;
no one shall live there,
    nor shall anyone settle in it.

34  The word of the LORD that came
to the prophet Jeremiah concerning
Elam, at the beginning of the reign of
King Zedekiah of Judah.

35  Thus says the LORD of hosts: I
am going to break the bow of Elam, the
mainstay of their might; 36and I will
bring upon Elam the four winds from
the four quarters of heaven; and I will
scatter them to all these winds, and
there shall be no nation to which the
exiles from Elam shall not come.
37I will terrify Elam before their enemies, and before those who seek their
life; I will bring disaster upon them, my
fierce anger, says the LORD. I will send
the sword after them, until I have consumed them; 38and I will set my throne
in Elam, and destroy their king and officials, says the LORD.

39  But in the latter days I will restore the fortunes of Elam, says the
LORD.

50.1 THE word that the LORD spoke concerning Babylon, concerning the land of
the Chaldeans, by the prophet Jeremiah:
2  Declare among the nations
    and proclaim,
    set up a banner and proclaim,
    do not conceal it, say:
Babylon is taken,
    Bel is put to shame,
    Merodach is dismayed.
Her images are put to shame,
    her idols are dismayed.
3  For out of the north a nation has
come up against her; it shall make her
land a desolation, and no one shall live
in it; both human beings and animals
shall flee away.

4  In those days and in that time,
says the LORD, the people of Israel shall
come, they and the people of Judah together; they shall come weeping as
they seek the LORD their God. 5They
shall ask the way to Zion, with faces
turned toward it, and they shall come
and joina themselves to the LORD by an
everlasting covenant that will never be
forgotten.

6  My people have been lost sheep;

aGk: Heb *toward it. Come! They shall join*

their shepherds have led them astray,
turning them away on the mountains;
from mountain to hill they have gone,
they have forgotten their fold. ⁷All who
found them have devoured them, and
their enemies have said, "We are not
guilty, because they have sinned
against the LORD, the true pasture, the
LORD, the hope of their ancestors."

8 Flee from Babylon, and go out of
the land of the Chaldeans, and be like
male goats leading the flock. ⁹For I am
going to stir up and bring against Babylon a company of great nations from
the land of the north; and they shall array themselves against her; from there
she shall be taken. Their arrows are
like the arrows of a skilled warrior who
does not return empty-handed. ¹⁰Chal-
dea shall be plundered; all who plunder
her shall be sated, says the LORD.

11  Though you rejoice, though
         you exult,
      O plunderers of my heritage,
   though you frisk about like a
         heifer on the grass,
      and neigh like stallions,
12   your mother shall be utterly
         shamed,
      and she who bore you shall
         be disgraced.
   Lo, she shall be the last of the
         nations,
      a wilderness, dry land, and
         a desert.
13   Because of the wrath of the
         LORD she shall not be
         inhabited,
      but shall be an utter
         desolation;
   everyone who passes by
         Babylon shall be appalled
      and hiss because of all her
         wounds.
14   Take up your positions around
         Babylon,
      all you that bend the bow;
   shoot at her, spare no arrows,
      for she has sinned against
         the LORD.
15   Raise a shout against her from
         all sides,
      "She has surrendered;
   her bulwarks have fallen,
      her walls are thrown down."
   For this is the vengeance of
         the LORD:
      take vengeance on her,
      do to her as she has done.
16   Cut off from Babylon the sower,
      and the wielder of the sickle
         in time of harvest;
   because of the destroying sword
      all of them shall return to
         their own people,
      and all of them shall flee to
         their own land.

17 Israel is a hunted sheep driven
away by lions. First the king of Assyria
devoured it, and now at the end King
Nebuchadrezzar of Babylon has
gnawed its bones. ¹⁸Therefore, thus
says the LORD of hosts, the God of Israel: I am going to punish the king of
Babylon and his land, as I punished the
king of Assyria. ¹⁹I will restore Israel
to its pasture, and it shall feed on Carmel and in Bashan, and on the hills of
Ephraim and in Gilead its hunger shall
be satisfied. ²⁰In those days and at that
time, says the LORD, the iniquity of Israel shall be sought, and there shall be
none; and the sins of Judah, and none
shall be found; for I will pardon the remnant that I have spared.

21   Go up to the land of
         Merathaim; a
      go up against her,
   and attack the inhabitants of
         Pekod b
      and utterly destroy the last
         of them, c

---

a Or *of Double Rebellion*   b Or *of Punishment*   c Tg: Heb *destroy after them* says the Lord;

do all that I have commanded
you.
22  The noise of battle is in the
land,
and great destruction!
23  How the hammer of the whole
earth
is cut down and broken!
How Babylon has become
a horror among the nations!
24  You set a snare for yourself and
you were caught,
O Babylon,
but you did not know it;
you were discovered and
seized,
because you challenged the
Lord.
25  The Lord has opened his
armory,
and brought out the weapons
of his wrath,
for the Lord God of hosts has a
task to do
in the land of the Chaldeans.
26  Come against her from every
quarter;
open her granaries;
pile her up like heaps of grain,
and destroy her utterly;
let nothing be left of her.
27  Kill all her bulls,
let them go down to the
slaughter.
Alas for them, their day has
come,
the time of their punishment!

28  Listen! Fugitives and refugees from the land of Babylon are coming to declare in Zion the vengeance of the Lord our God, vengeance for his temple.

29  Summon archers against Babylon, all who bend the bow. Encamp all around her; let no one escape. Repay her according to her deeds; just as she has done, do to her—for she has arrogantly defied the Lord, the Holy One of Israel.  30Therefore her young men shall fall in her squares, and all her soldiers shall be destroyed on that day, says the Lord.

31  I am against you, O arrogant
one,
says the Lord God of hosts;
for your day has come,
the time when I will punish
you.
32  The arrogant one shall stumble
and fall,
with no one to raise him up,
and I will kindle a fire in his
cities,
and it will devour everything
around him.

33  Thus says the Lord of hosts: The people of Israel are oppressed, and so too are the people of Judah; all their captors have held them fast and refuse to let them go.  34Their Redeemer is strong; the Lord of hosts is his name. He will surely plead their cause, that he may give rest to the earth, but unrest to the inhabitants of Babylon.

35  A sword against the Chaldeans,
says the Lord,
and against the inhabitants of
Babylon,
and against her officials and
her sages!
36  A sword against the diviners,
so that they may become
fools!
A sword against her warriors,
so that they may be
destroyed!
37  A sword against her[a] horses
and against her[a]
chariots,

aCn: Heb *his*

and against all the foreign
    troops in her midst,
so that they may become
    women!
A sword against all her
    treasures,
    that they may be plundered!
38  A drought[a] against her waters,
    that they may be dried up!
For it is a land of images,
    and they go mad over idols.

39  Therefore wild animals shall live with hyenas in Babylon,[b] and ostriches shall inhabit her; she shall never again be peopled, or inhabited for all generations. 40As when God overthrew Sodom and Gomorrah and their neighbors, says the LORD, so no one shall live there, nor shall anyone settle in her.

41  Look, a people is coming from
    the north;
a mighty nation and many
    kings
are stirring from the farthest
    parts of the earth.
42  They wield bow and spear,
    they are cruel and have
      no mercy.
The sound of them is like the
    roaring sea;
    they ride upon horses,
set in array as a warrior for
    battle,
    against you, O daughter
      Babylon!

43  The king of Babylon heard news
    of them,
    and his hands fell helpless;
anguish seized him,
    pain like that of a woman
      in labor.

44  Like a lion coming up from the thickets of the Jordan against a perennial pasture, I will suddenly chase them away from her; and I will appoint over her whomever I choose.[c] For who is like me? Who can summon me? Who is the shepherd who can stand before me? 45Therefore hear the plan that the LORD has made against Babylon, and the purposes that he has formed against the land of the Chaldeans: Surely the little ones of the flock shall be dragged away; surely their[d] fold shall be appalled at their fate. 46At the sound of the capture of Babylon the earth shall tremble, and her cry shall be heard among the nations.

## TITUS 1.1–16

PAUL, a servant[e] of God and an apostle of Jesus Christ, for the sake of the faith of God's elect and the knowledge of the truth that is in accordance with godliness, 2in the hope of eternal life that God, who never lies, promised before the ages began— 3in due time he revealed his word through the proclamation with which I have been entrusted by the command of God our Savior,

4  To Titus, my loyal child in the faith we share:

Grace[f] and peace from God the Father and Christ Jesus our Savior.

5  I left you behind in Crete for this reason, so that you should put in order what remained to be done, and should appoint elders in every town, as I directed you: 6someone who is blameless, married only once,[g] whose children are believers, not accused of debauchery and not rebellious. 7For a bishop,[h] as God's steward, must be blameless; he must not be arrogant or quick-tempered or addicted to wine or violent or greedy for gain; 8but he must be hospitable, a lover of goodness, pru-

aAnother reading is *A sword*  bHeb lacks *in Babylon*  cOr *and I will single out the choicest of her rams*: Meaning of Heb uncertain  dSyr Gk Tg Compare 49.20: Heb lacks *their*  eGk *slave*  fOther ancient authorities read *Grace, mercy,*  gGk *husband of one wife*  hOr *an overseer*

dent, upright, devout, and self-controlled. ⁹He must have a firm grasp of the word that is trustworthy in accordance with the teaching, so that he may be able both to preach with sound doctrine and to refute those who contradict it.

10 There are also many rebellious people, idle talkers and deceivers, especially those of the circumcision; ¹¹they must be silenced, since they are upsetting whole families by teaching for sordid gain what it is not right to teach. ¹²It was one of them, their very own prophet, who said,

"Cretans are always liars,
  vicious brutes, lazy
  gluttons."

¹³That testimony is true. For this reason rebuke them sharply, so that they may become sound in the faith, ¹⁴not paying attention to Jewish myths or to commandments of those who reject the truth. ¹⁵To the pure all things are pure, but to the corrupt and unbelieving nothing is pure. Their very minds and consciences are corrupted. ¹⁶They profess to know God, but they deny him by their actions. They are detestable, disobedient, unfit for any good work.

## PSALM 97.1—98.9

THE LORD is king! Let the earth
    rejoice;
  let the many coastlands be
    glad!
2  Clouds and thick darkness are
    all around him;
  righteousness and justice are
    the foundation of his
    throne.
3  Fire goes before him,
  and consumes his adversaries
    on every side.
4  His lightnings light up the world;
  the earth sees and trembles.
5  The mountains melt like wax
    before the LORD,

before the Lord of all the
    earth.

6  The heavens proclaim his
    righteousness;
  and all the peoples behold his
    glory.
7  All worshipers of images are put
    to shame,
  those who make their boast in
    worthless idols;
  all gods bow down before
    him.
8  Zion hears and is glad,
  and the towns ᵃ of Judah
    rejoice,
  because of your judgments,
    O God.
9  For you, O LORD, are most high
    over all the earth;
  you are exalted far above
    all gods.

10  The LORD loves those who
    hate ᵇ evil;
  he guards the lives of his
    faithful;
  he rescues them from the
    hand of the wicked.
11  Light dawns ᶜ for the righteous,
  and joy for the upright in
    heart.
12  Rejoice in the LORD, O you
    righteous,
  and give thanks to his holy
    name!

*A Psalm.*
98.1  O sing to the LORD a new song,
  for he has done marvelous
    things.
  His right hand and his holy arm
    have gotten him victory.
2  The LORD has made known his
    victory;
  he has revealed his
    vindication in the sight of
    the nations.

ᵃHeb *daughters*  ᵇCn: Heb *You who love the LORD hate*  ᶜGk Syr Jerome: Heb *is sown*

3  He has remembered his
       steadfast love and
       faithfulness
   to the house of Israel.
   All the ends of the earth have
       seen
       the victory of our God.

4  Make a joyful noise to the LORD,
       all the earth;
       break forth into joyous song
       and sing praises.
5  Sing praises to the LORD with
       the lyre,
       with the lyre and the sound of
       melody.
6  With trumpets and the sound of
       the horn
       make a joyful noise before the
       King, the LORD.

7  Let the sea roar, and all that
       fills it;
       the world and those who live
       in it.
8  Let the floods clap their hands;

   let the hills sing together for
       joy
9  at the presence of the LORD, for
       he is coming
       to judge the earth.
   He will judge the world with
       righteousness,
       and the peoples with equity.


## PROVERBS 26.13–16

THE lazy person says, "There is
   a lion in the road!
   There is a lion in the
       streets!"
14  As a door turns on its hinges,
       so does a lazy person in bed.
15  The lazy person buries a hand in
       the dish,
       and is too tired to bring it
       back to the mouth.
16  The lazy person is wiser in
       self-esteem
       than seven who can answer
       discreetly.


# OCTOBER 27

## JEREMIAH 51.1–53

THUS says the LORD:
   I am going to stir up a
       destructive wind[a]
   against Babylon
   and against the inhabitants of
       Leb-qamai;[b]
2  and I will send winnowers to
       Babylon,
       and they shall winnow her.
   They shall empty her land
       when they come against her
       from every side

   on the day of trouble.
3  Let not the archer bend his
       bow,
       and let him not array himself
       in his coat of mail.
   Do not spare her young men;
       utterly destroy her entire
       army.
4  They shall fall down slain in the
       land of the Chaldeans,
       and wounded in her streets.
5  Israel and Judah have not been
       forsaken

a Or *stir up the spirit of a destroyer*   b *Leb-qamai* is a cryptogram for *Kasdim*, Chaldea

by their God, the Lord of
hosts,
though their land is full of guilt
before the Holy One of Israel.

6 Flee from the midst of Babylon,
save your lives, each of you!
Do not perish because of her
guilt,
for this is the time of the
Lord's vengeance;
he is repaying her what is
due.
7 Babylon was a golden cup in the
Lord's hand,
making all the earth drunken;
the nations drank of her wine,
and so the nations went mad.
8 Suddenly Babylon has fallen and
is shattered;
wail for her!
Bring balm for her wound;
perhaps she may be healed.
9 We tried to heal Babylon,
but she could not be healed.
Forsake her, and let each of us
go
to our own country;
for her judgment has reached up
to heaven
and has been lifted up even to
the skies.
10 The Lord has brought forth our
vindication;
come, let us declare in Zion
the work of the Lord our
God.

11 Sharpen the arrows!
Fill the quivers!
The Lord has stirred up the spirit of the
kings of the Medes, because his purpose concerning Babylon is to destroy
it, for that is the vengeance of the Lord,
vengeance for his temple.
12 Raise a standard against the
walls of Babylon;
make the watch strong;

post sentinels;
prepare the ambushes;
for the Lord has both planned
and done
what he spoke concerning the
inhabitants of Babylon.
13 You who live by mighty waters,
rich in treasures,
your end has come,
the thread of your life is cut.
14 The Lord of hosts has sworn
by himself:
Surely I will fill you with troops
like a swarm of locusts,
and they shall raise a shout of
victory over you.

15 It is he who made the earth by
his power,
who established the world by
his wisdom,
and by his understanding
stretched out the
heavens.
16 When he utters his voice there
is a tumult of waters in
the heavens,
and he makes the mist rise
from the ends of the
earth.
He makes lightnings for the
rain,
and he brings out the wind
from his storehouses.
17 Everyone is stupid and without
knowledge;
goldsmiths are all put to
shame by their idols;
for their images are false,
and there is no breath in
them.
18 They are worthless, a work of
delusion;
at the time of their
punishment they shall
perish.
19 Not like these is the Lord, a the
portion of Jacob,

a Heb lacks the Lord

for he is the one who formed
    all things,
and Israel is the tribe of his
    inheritance;
    the Lord of hosts is his name.

20 You are my war club, my
    weapon of battle:
with you I smash nations;
    with you I destroy kingdoms;
21 with you I smash the horse and
    its rider;
    with you I smash the chariot
    and the charioteer;
22 with you I smash man and
    woman;
    with you I smash the old man
    and the boy;
    with you I smash the young man
    and the girl;
23     with you I smash shepherds
    and their flocks;
with you I smash farmers and
    their teams;
    with you I smash governors
    and deputies.

24 I will repay Babylon and all the inhabitants of Chaldea before your very eyes for all the wrong that they have done in Zion, says the Lord.

25 I am against you, O destroying
    mountain,
        says the Lord,
    that destroys the whole
    earth;
I will stretch out my hand
    against you,
    and roll you down from the
    crags,
    and make you a burned-out
    mountain.
26 No stone shall be taken from
    you for a corner
    and no stone for a foundation,
but you shall be a perpetual
    waste,
    says the Lord.

27 Raise a standard in the land,
    blow the trumpet among the
    nations;
prepare the nations for war
    against her,
    summon against her the
    kingdoms,
    Ararat, Minni, and Ashkenaz;
appoint a marshal against her,
    bring up horses like bristling
    locusts.
28 Prepare the nations for war
    against her,
    the kings of the Medes, with
    their governors and
    deputies,
    and every land under their
    dominion.
29 The land trembles and writhes,
    for the Lord's purposes
    against Babylon stand,
to make the land of Babylon a
    desolation,
    without inhabitant.
30 The warriors of Babylon have
    given up fighting,
they remain in their
    strongholds;
their strength has failed,
    they have become women;
her buildings are set on fire,
    her bars are broken.
31 One runner runs to meet
    another,
    and one messenger to meet
    another,
to tell the king of Babylon
    that his city is taken from end
    to end:
32 the fords have been seized,
    the marshes have been
    burned with fire,
    and the soldiers are in panic.
33 For thus says the Lord of
    hosts, the God of Israel:
Daughter Babylon is like a
    threshing floor
    at the time when it is
    trodden;

yet a little while
   and the time of her harvest
     will come.

34 "King Nebuchadrezzar of
     Babylon has devoured
     me,
   he has crushed me;
he has made me an empty
     vessel,
   he has swallowed me like
     a monster;
he has filled his belly with my
     delicacies,
   he has spewed me out.
35 May my torn flesh be avenged
     on Babylon,"
   the inhabitants of Zion shall
     say.
"May my blood be avenged on
     the inhabitants of
     Chaldea,"
   Jerusalem shall say.
36 Therefore thus says the LORD:
I am going to defend your cause
   and take vengeance for you.
I will dry up her sea
   and make her fountain dry;
37 and Babylon shall become a
     heap of ruins,
   a den of jackals,
an object of horror and of
     hissing,
   without inhabitant.

38 Like lions they shall roar
     together;
   they shall growl like lions'
     whelps.
39 When they are inflamed, I will
     set out their drink
   and make them drunk, until
     they become merry
and then sleep a perpetual sleep
   and never wake, says the
     LORD.
40 I will bring them down like

lambs to the slaughter,
   like rams and goats.

41 How Sheshach[a] is taken,
   the pride of the whole earth
     seized!
How Babylon has become
   an object of horror among the
     nations!
42 The sea has risen over Babylon;
   she has been covered by its
     tumultuous waves.
43 Her cities have become an
     object of horror,
   a land of drought and a
     desert,
a land in which no one lives,
   and through which no mortal
     passes.
44 I will punish Bel in Babylon,
   and make him disgorge what
     he has swallowed.
The nations shall no longer
     stream to him;
   the wall of Babylon has fallen.

45 Come out of her, my people!
   Save your lives, each of you,
   from the fierce anger of the
     LORD!
46 Do not be fainthearted or fearful
   at the rumors heard in
     the land—
one year one rumor comes,
   the next year another,
rumors of violence in the land
   and of ruler against ruler.

47 Assuredly, the days are coming
   when I will punish the images
     of Babylon;
her whole land shall be put to
     shame,
   and all her slain shall fall in
     her midst.
48 Then the heavens and the
     earth,
   and all that is in them,

---

a*Sheshach* is a cryptogram for *Babel*, Babylon

shall shout for joy over Babylon;
  for the destroyers shall come
    against them out of
    the north,
        says the Lord.
49 Babylon must fall for the slain of
    Israel,
  as the slain of all the earth
    have fallen because of
    Babylon.

50 You survivors of the sword,
    go, do not linger!
  Remember the Lord in a distant
    land,
  and let Jerusalem come into
    your mind:
51 We are put to shame, for we
    have heard insults;
  dishonor has covered our
    face,
  for aliens have come
    into the holy places of the
    Lord's house.

52 Therefore the time is surely
    coming, says the Lord,
  when I will punish her idols,
  and through all her land
    the wounded shall groan.
53 Though Babylon should mount
    up to heaven,
  and though she should fortify
    her strong height,
  from me destroyers would come
    upon her,
  says the Lord.

## TITUS 2.1–14

**B**UT as for you, teach what is consistent with sound doctrine. [2]Tell the older men to be temperate, serious, prudent, and sound in faith, in love, and in endurance.

3 Likewise, tell the older women to be reverent in behavior, not to be slanderers or slaves to drink; they are to teach what is good, [4]so that they may encourage the young women to love their husbands, to love their children, [5]to be self-controlled, chaste, good managers of the household, kind, being submissive to their husbands, so that the word of God may not be discredited.

6 Likewise, urge the younger men to be self-controlled. [7]Show yourself in all respects a model of good works, and in your teaching show integrity, gravity, [8]and sound speech that cannot be censured; then any opponent will be put to shame, having nothing evil to say of us.

9 Tell slaves to be submissive to their masters and to give satisfaction in every respect; they are not to talk back, [10]not to pilfer, but to show complete and perfect fidelity, so that in everything they may be an ornament to the doctrine of God our Savior.

11 For the grace of God has appeared, bringing salvation to all, [a] [12]training us to renounce impiety and worldly passions, and in the present age to live lives that are self-controlled, upright, and godly, [13]while we wait for the blessed hope and the manifestation of the glory of our great God and Savior, [b] Jesus Christ. [14]He it is who gave himself for us that he might redeem us from all iniquity and purify for himself a people of his own who are zealous for good deeds.

## PSALM 99.1–9

**T**HE Lord is king; let the
    peoples tremble!
  He sits enthroned upon the
    cherubim; let the earth
    quake!
2 The Lord is great in Zion;
  he is exalted over all the
    peoples.
3 Let them praise your great and
    awesome name.
  Holy is he!

[a] *Or* has appeared to all, bringing salvation    [b] *Or* of the great God and our Savior

4 Mighty King, a lover of justice,
   you have established equity;
you have executed justice
   and righteousness in Jacob.
5 Extol the LORD our God;
   worship at his footstool.
   Holy is he!

6 Moses and Aaron were among
      his priests,
   Samuel also was among those
      who called on his name.
   They cried to the LORD, and
      he answered them.
7 He spoke to them in the pillar
      of cloud;
   they kept his decrees,
   and the statutes that he gave
      them.

8 O LORD our God, you answered
      them;
   you were a forgiving God to
      them,
   but an avenger of their
      wrongdoings.
9 Extol the LORD our God,
   and worship at his holy
      mountain;
   for the LORD our God is holy.

## PROVERBS 26.17

Like somebody who takes a
      passing dog by the
      ears
is one who meddles in the
   quarrel of another.

# OCTOBER 28

## JEREMIAH 51.54—52.34

Listen!—a cry from Babylon!
   A great crashing from the
      land of the Chaldeans!
55 For the LORD is laying Babylon
      waste,
   and stilling her loud clamor.
   Their waves roar like mighty
      waters,
   the sound of their clamor
      resounds;
56 for a destroyer has come
      against her,
   against Babylon;
   her warriors are taken,
      their bows are broken;
   for the LORD is a God of
      recompense,
      he will repay in full.

57 I will make her officials and her
      sages drunk,
   also her governors, her
      deputies, and her
      warriors;
   they shall sleep a perpetual
      sleep and never wake,
   says the King, whose name is
      the LORD of hosts.

58 Thus says the LORD of hosts:
   The broad wall of Babylon
      shall be leveled to the
      ground,
   and her high gates
      shall be burned with fire.
   The peoples exhaust themselves
      for nothing,

a Cn: Heb *And a king's strength*

and the nations weary
themselves only for
fire. [a]

59 The word that the prophet Jeremiah commanded Seraiah son of Neriah son of Mahseiah, when he went with King Zedekiah of Judah to Babylon, in the fourth year of his reign. Seraiah was the quartermaster. [60]Jeremiah wrote in a[b] scroll all the disasters that would come on Babylon, all these words that are written concerning Babylon. [61]And Jeremiah said to Seraiah: "When you come to Babylon, see that you read all these words, [62]and say, 'O LORD, you yourself threatened to destroy this place so that neither human beings nor animals shall live in it, and it shall be desolate forever.' [63]When you finish reading this scroll, tie a stone to it, and throw it into the middle of the Euphrates, [64]and say, 'Thus shall Babylon sink, to rise no more, because of the disasters that I am bringing on her.' "[c]

Thus far are the words of Jeremiah.

52.1 ZEDEKIAH was twenty-one years old when he began to reign; he reigned eleven years in Jerusalem. His mother's name was Hamutal daughter of Jeremiah of Libnah. [2]He did what was evil in the sight of the LORD, just as Jehoiakim had done. [3]Indeed, Jerusalem and Judah so angered the LORD that he expelled them from his presence.

Zedekiah rebelled against the king of Babylon. [4]And in the ninth year of his reign, in the tenth month, on the tenth day of the month, King Nebuchadrezzar of Babylon came with all his army against Jerusalem, and they laid siege to it; they built siegeworks against it all around. [5]So the city was besieged until the eleventh year of King Zedekiah. [6]On the ninth day of the fourth month the famine became so severe in the city

that there was no food for the people of the land. [7]Then a breach was made in the city wall; [d] and all the soldiers fled and went out from the city by night by the way of the gate between the two walls, by the king's garden, though the Chaldeans were all around the city. They went in the direction of the Arabah. [8]But the army of the Chaldeans pursued the king, and overtook Zedekiah in the plains of Jericho; and all his army was scattered, deserting him. [9]Then they captured the king, and brought him up to the king of Babylon at Riblah in the land of Hamath, and he passed sentence on him. [10]The king of Babylon killed the sons of Zedekiah before his eyes, and also killed all the officers of Judah at Riblah. [11]He put out the eyes of Zedekiah, and bound him in fetters, and the king of Babylon took him to Babylon, and put him in prison until the day of his death.

12 In the fifth month, on the tenth day of the month—which was the nineteenth year of King Nebuchadrezzar, king of Babylon—Nebuzaradan the captain of the bodyguard who served the king of Babylon, entered Jerusalem. [13]He burned the house of the LORD, the king's house, and all the houses of Jerusalem; every great house he burned down. [14]All the army of the Chaldeans, who were with the captain of the guard, broke down all the walls around Jerusalem. [15]Nebuzaradan the captain of the guard carried into exile some of the poorest of the people and the rest of the people who were left in the city and the deserters who had defected to the king of Babylon, together with the rest of the artisans. [16]But Nebuzaradan the captain of the guard left some of the poorest people of the land to be vinedressers and tillers of the soil.

17 The pillars of bronze that were in the house of the LORD, and the stands

aGk Syr Compare Hab 2.13: Heb *and the nations for fire, and they are weary*   bOr *one*   cGk: Heb *on her. And they shall weary themselves*   dHeb lacks *wall*

and the bronze sea that were in the house of the LORD, the Chaldeans broke in pieces, and carried all the bronze to Babylon. 18They took away the pots, the shovels, the snuffers, the basins, the ladles, and all the vessels of bronze used in the temple service. 19The captain of the guard took away the small bowls also, the firepans, the basins, the pots, the lampstands, the ladles, and the bowls for libation, both those of gold and those of silver. 20As for the two pillars, the one sea, the twelve bronze bulls that were under the sea, and the stands, a which King Solomon had made for the house of the LORD, the bronze of all these vessels was beyond weighing. 21As for the pillars, the height of the one pillar was eighteen cubits, its circumference was twelve cubits; it was hollow and its thickness was four fingers. 22Upon it was a capital of bronze; the height of the one capital was five cubits; latticework and pomegranates, all of bronze, encircled the top of the capital. And the second pillar had the same, with pomegranates. 23There were ninety-six pomegranates on the sides; all the pomegranates encircling the latticework numbered one hundred.

24 The captain of the guard took the chief priest Seraiah, the second priest Zephaniah, and the three guardians of the threshold; 25and from the city he took an officer who had been in command of the soldiers, and seven men of the king's council who were found in the city; the secretary of the commander of the army who mustered the people of the land; and sixty men of the people of the land who were found inside the city. 26Then Nebuzaradan the captain of the guard took them, and brought them to the king of Babylon at Riblah. 27And the king of Babylon struck them down, and put them to death at Riblah in the land of Hamath.

So Judah went into exile out of its land.

28 This is the number of the people whom Nebuchadrezzar took into exile: in the seventh year, three thousand twenty-three Judeans; 29in the eighteenth year of Nebuchadrezzar he took into exile from Jerusalem eight hundred thirty-two persons; 30in the twenty-third year of Nebuchadrezzar, Nebuzaradan the captain of the guard took into exile of the Judeans seven hundred forty-five persons; all the persons were four thousand six hundred.

31 In the thirty-seventh year of the exile of King Jehoiachin of Judah, in the twelfth month, on the twenty-fifth day of the month, King Evil-merodach of Babylon, in the year he began to reign, showed favor to King Jehoiachin of Judah and brought him out of prison; 32he spoke kindly to him, and gave him a seat above the seats of the other kings who were with him in Babylon. 33So Jehoiachin put aside his prison clothes, and every day of his life he dined regularly at the king's table. 34For his allowance, a regular daily allowance was given him by the king of Babylon, as long as he lived, up to the day of his death.

# TITUS 2.15—3.15

**D**ECLARE these things; exhort and reprove with all authority. b Let no one look down on you.

3.1 REMIND them to be subject to rulers and authorities, to be obedient, to be ready for every good work, 2to speak evil of no one, to avoid quarreling, to be gentle, and to show every courtesy to everyone. 3For we ourselves were once foolish, disobedient, led astray, slaves to various passions and pleasures, passing our days in malice and envy, despicable, hating one another.

a Cn: Heb *that were under the stands*   b Gk *commandment*

4But when the goodness and loving kindness of God our Savior appeared, 5he saved us, not because of any works of righteousness that we had done, but according to his mercy, through the watera of rebirth and renewal by the Holy Spirit. 6This Spirit he poured out on us richly through Jesus Christ our Savior, 7so that, having been justified by his grace, we might become heirs according to the hope of eternal life. 8The saying is sure.

I desire that you insist on these things, so that those who have come to believe in God may be careful to devote themselves to good works; these things are excellent and profitable to everyone. 9But avoid stupid controversies, genealogies, dissensions, and quarrels about the law, for they are unprofitable and worthless. 10After a first and second admonition, have nothing more to do with anyone who causes divisions, 11since you know that such a person is perverted and sinful, being self-condemned.

12 When I send Artemas to you, or Tychicus, do your best to come to me at Nicopolis, for I have decided to spend the winter there. 13Make every effort to send Zenas the lawyer and Apollos on their way, and see that they lack nothing. 14And let people learn to devote themselves to good works in order to meet urgent needs, so that they may not be unproductive.

15 All who are with me send greetings to you. Greet those who love us in the faith.

Grace be with all of you. b

## PSALM 100.1–5

*A Psalm of thanksgiving.*

MAKE a joyful noise to the
LORD, all the earth.
2    Worship the LORD
with gladness;
come into his presence with
singing.

3    Know that the LORD is God.
It is he that made us, and we
are his; c
we are his people, and the
sheep of his pasture.

4    Enter his gates with
thanksgiving,
and his courts with praise.
Give thanks to him, bless his
name.

5    For the LORD is good;
his steadfast love endures
forever,
and his faithfulness to all
generations.

## PROVERBS 26.18–19

LIKE a maniac who shoots
deadly firebrands and
arrows,
19    so is one who deceives a
neighbor
and says, "I am only joking!"

---

aGk *washing*    bOther ancient authorities add *Amen*    cAnother reading is *and not we ourselves*

## LAMENTATIONS 1.1—2.19

**H**ow lonely sits the city
that once was full of
people!
How like a widow she has
become,
she that was great among the
nations!
She that was a princess among
the provinces
has become a vassal.

2 She weeps bitterly in the night,
with tears on her cheeks;
among all her lovers
she has no one to comfort
her;
all her friends have dealt
treacherously with her,
they have become her
enemies.

3 Judah has gone into exile with
suffering
and hard servitude;
she lives now among the
nations,
and finds no resting place;
her pursuers have all overtaken
her
in the midst of her distress.

4 The roads to Zion mourn,
for no one comes to the
festivals;
all her gates are desolate,
her priests groan;
her young girls grieve, a
and her lot is bitter.

5 Her foes have become the
masters,
her enemies prosper,
because the LORD has made
her suffer
for the multitude of her
transgressions;
her children have gone away,
captives before the foe.

6 From daughter Zion has
departed
all her majesty.
Her princes have become
like stags
that find no pasture;
they fled without strength
before the pursuer.

7 Jerusalem remembers,
in the days of her affliction
and wandering,
all the precious things
that were hers in days of old.
When her people fell into the
hand of the foe,
and there was no one to help
her,
the foe looked on mocking
over her downfall.

8 Jerusalem sinned grievously,
so she has become a
mockery;
all who honored her despise
her,
for they have seen her
nakedness;
she herself groans,
and turns her face away.

9 Her uncleanness was in her
skirts;
she took no thought of her
future;
her downfall was appalling,

a Meaning of Heb uncertain

with none to comfort her.
"O Lord, look at my affliction,
for the enemy has
triumphed!"

10 Enemies have stretched out
their hands
over all her precious things;
she has even seen the nations
invade her sanctuary,
those whom you forbade
to enter your congregation.

11 All her people groan
as they search for bread;
they trade their treasures for
food
to revive their strength.
Look, O Lord, and see
how worthless I have
become.

12 Is it nothing to you, a all you
who pass by?
Look and see
if there is any sorrow like my
sorrow,
which was brought upon me,
which the Lord inflicted
on the day of his fierce anger.

13 From on high he sent fire;
it went deep into my bones;
he spread a net for my feet;
he turned me back;
he has left me stunned,
faint all day long.

14 My transgressions were bounda
into a yoke;
by his hand they were
fastened together;
they weigh on my neck,
sapping my strength;
the Lord handed me over
to those whom I cannot
withstand.

15 The Lord has rejected
all my warriors in the midst
of me;
he proclaimed a time against me
to crush my young men;
the Lord has trodden as in a
wine press
the virgin daughter Judah.

16 For these things I weep;
my eyes flow with tears;
for a comforter is far from me,
one to revive my courage;
my children are desolate,
for the enemy has prevailed.

17 Zion stretches out her hands,
but there is no one to
comfort her;
the Lord has commanded
against Jacob
that his neighbors should
become his foes;
Jerusalem has become
a filthy thing among them.

18 The Lord is in the right,
for I have rebelled against
his word;
but hear, all you peoples,
and behold my suffering;
my young women and young
men
have gone into captivity.

19 I called to my lovers
but they deceived me;
my priests and elders
perished in the city
while seeking food
to revive their strength.

20 See, O Lord, how distressed I
am;
my stomach churns,
my heart is wrung within me,

a Meaning of Heb uncertain

because I have been very
    rebellious.
In the street the sword
    bereaves;
  in the house it is like death.

21  They heard how I was groaning,
    with no one to comfort me.
  All my enemies heard of my
    trouble;
    they are glad that you have
    done it.
  Bring on the day you have
    announced,
    and let them be as I am.

22  Let all their evil doing come
    before you;
    and deal with them
  as you have dealt with me
    because of all my
    transgressions;
  for my groans are many
    and my heart is faint.

2.1  How the Lord in his anger
    has humiliated[a] daughter
    Zion!
  He has thrown down from
    heaven to earth
    the splendor of Israel;
  he has not remembered his
    footstool
    in the day of his anger.

2  The Lord has destroyed without
    mercy
    all the dwellings of Jacob;
  in his wrath he has broken down
    the strongholds of daughter
    Judah;
  he has brought down to the
    ground in dishonor
    the kingdom and its rulers.

3  He has cut down in fierce anger
    all the might of Israel;

he has withdrawn his right hand
    from them
    in the face of the enemy;
he has burned like a flaming fire
    in Jacob,
    consuming all around.

4  He has bent his bow like an
    enemy,
    with his right hand set like a
    foe;
  he has killed all in whom we
    took pride
    in the tent of daughter Zion;
  he has poured out his fury like
    fire.

5  The Lord has become like an
    enemy;
    he has destroyed Israel;
  He has destroyed all its palaces,
    laid in ruins its strongholds,
  and multiplied in daughter Judah
    mourning and lamentation.

6  He has broken down his booth
    like a garden,
    he has destroyed his
    tabernacle;
  the Lord has abolished in Zion
    festival and sabbath,
  and in his fierce indignation has
    spurned
    king and priest.

7  The Lord has scorned his altar,
    disowned his sanctuary;
  he has delivered into the hand
    of the enemy
    the walls of her palaces;
  a clamor was raised in the
    house of the Lord
    as on a day of festival.

8  The Lord determined to lay
    in ruins
    the wall of daughter Zion;
  he stretched the line;

[a] Meaning of Heb uncertain

he did not withhold his hand
    from destroying;
he caused rampart and wall
    to lament;
they languish together.

9  Her gates have sunk into
        the ground;
    he has ruined and broken
        her bars;
    her king and princes are among
        the nations;
    guidance is no more,
    and her prophets obtain
        no vision from the Lord.

10  The elders of daughter Zion
        sit on the ground in silence;
    they have thrown dust on
        their heads
        and put on sackcloth;
    the young girls of Jerusalem
        have bowed their heads to
        the ground.

11  My eyes are spent with
        weeping;
        my stomach churns;
    my bile is poured out on the
        ground
        because of the destruction of
        my people,
    because infants and babes faint
        in the streets of the city.

12  They cry to their mothers,
        "Where is bread and wine?"
    as they faint like the wounded
        in the streets of the city,
    as their life is poured out
        on their mothers' bosom.

13  What can I say for you, to what
        compare you,
        O daughter Jerusalem?
    To what can I liken you, that I
        may comfort you,
        O virgin daughter Zion?

For vast as the sea is your ruin;
    who can heal you?

14  Your prophets have seen for
        you
        false and deceptive visions;
    they have not exposed your
        iniquity
        to restore your fortunes,
    but have seen oracles for you
        that are false and misleading.

15  All who pass along the way
        clap their hands at you;
    they hiss and wag their heads
        at daughter Jerusalem;
    "Is this the city that was called
        the perfection of beauty,
        the joy of all the earth?"

16  All your enemies
        open their mouths against
        you;
    they hiss, they gnash their
        teeth,
        they cry: "We have devoured
        her!
    Ah, this is the day we longed
        for;
        at last we have seen it!"

17  The Lord has done what he
        purposed,
        he has carried out his threat;
    as he ordained long ago,
        he has demolished without
        pity;
    he has made the enemy rejoice
        over you,
        and exalted the might of
        your foes.

18  Cry aloud[a] to the Lord!
        O wall of daughter Zion!
    Let tears stream down like a
        torrent
        day and night!
    Give yourself no rest,

[a] Cn: Heb *Their heart cried*

your eyes no respite!

19  Arise, cry out in the night,
       at the beginning of the
           watches!
    Pour out your heart like water
       before the presence of the
           Lord!
    Lift your hands to him
       for the lives of your children,
    who faint for hunger
       at the head of every street.

## PHILEMON 1.1–25

PAUL, a prisoner of Christ Jesus, and Timothy our brother, [a]

To Philemon our dear friend and co-worker, [2]to Apphia our sister, [b] to Archippus our fellow soldier, and to the church in your house:

3  Grace to you and peace from God our Father and the Lord Jesus Christ.

4  When I remember you[c] in my prayers, I always thank my God [5]because I hear of your love for all the saints and your faith toward the Lord Jesus. [6]I pray that the sharing of your faith may become effective when you perceive all the good that we[d] may do for Christ. [7]I have indeed received much joy and encouragement from your love, because the hearts of the saints have been refreshed through you, my brother.

8  For this reason, though I am bold enough in Christ to command you to do your duty, [9]yet I would rather appeal to you on the basis of love—and I, Paul, do this as an old man, and now also as a prisoner of Christ Jesus. [e] [10]I am appealing to you for my child, Onesimus, whose father I have become during my imprisonment. [11]Formerly he was useless to you, but now he is indeed useful[f] both to you and to me. [12]I am

sending him, that is, my own heart, back to you. [13]I wanted to keep him with me, so that he might be of service to me in your place during my imprisonment for the gospel; [14]but I preferred to do nothing without your consent, in order that your good deed might be voluntary and not something forced. [15]Perhaps this is the reason he was separated from you for a while, so that you might have him back forever, [16]no longer as a slave but more than a slave, a beloved brother—especially to me but how much more to you, both in the flesh and in the Lord.

17  So if you consider me your partner, welcome him as you would welcome me. [18]If he has wronged you in any way, or owes you anything, charge that to my account. [19]I, Paul, am writing this with my own hand: I will repay it. I say nothing about your owing me even your own self. [20]Yes, brother, let me have this benefit from you in the Lord! Refresh my heart in Christ. [21]Confident of your obedience, I am writing to you, knowing that you will do even more than I say.

22  One thing more—prepare a guest room for me, for I am hoping through your prayers to be restored to you.

23  Epaphras, my fellow prisoner in Christ Jesus, sends greetings to you, [g] [24]and so do Mark, Aristarchus, Demas, and Luke, my fellow workers.

25  The grace of the Lord Jesus Christ be with your spirit. [h]

## PSALM 101.1–8

*Of David. A Psalm.*

I WILL sing of loyalty and of justice;
    to you, O LORD, I will sing.
2    I will study the way that is
         blameless.

---

[a]Gk *the brother*  [b]Gk *the sister*  [c]From verse 4 through verse 21, *you* is singular  [d]Other ancient authorities read *you* (plural)  [e]Or *as an ambassador of Christ Jesus, and now also his prisoner* [f]The name Onesimus means *useful* or (compare verse 20) *beneficial*  [g]Here *you* is singular  [h]Other ancient authorities add *Amen*

When shall I attain it?

I will walk with integrity of
heart
within my house;
3  I will not set before my eyes
anything that is base.

I hate the work of those who
fall away;
it shall not cling to me.
4  Perverseness of heart shall be
far from me;
I will know nothing of evil.

5  One who secretly slanders a
neighbor
I will destroy.
A haughty look and an arrogant
heart
I will not tolerate.

6  I will look with favor on the
faithful in the land,

so that they may live with
me;
whoever walks in the way that
is blameless
shall minister to me.

7  No one who practices deceit
shall remain in my house;
no one who utters lies
shall continue in my presence.

8  Morning by morning I will
destroy
all the wicked in the land,
cutting off all evildoers
from the city of the Lord.

## PROVERBS 26.20

**F**OR lack of wood the fire goes
out,
and where there is no
whisperer, quarreling
ceases.

# OCTOBER 30

## LAMENTATIONS 2.20—3.66

**L**OOK, O LORD, and consider!
To whom have you done
this?
Should women eat their
offspring,
the children they have borne?
Should priest and prophet be
killed
in the sanctuary of the Lord?

21  The young and the old are lying
on the ground in the streets;
my young women and my
young men

have fallen by the sword;
in the day of your anger you
have killed them,
slaughtering without mercy.

22  You invited my enemies from
all around
as if for a day of festival;
and on the day of the anger of
the Lord
no one escaped or survived;
those whom I bore and reared
my enemy has destroyed.

3.1 I AM one who has seen affliction
        under the rod of God's [a]
        wrath;
2  he has driven and brought me
        into darkness without any
        light;
3  against me alone he turns
        his hand,
        again and again, all day long.

4  He has made my flesh and my
        skin waste away,
        and broken my bones;
5  he has besieged and enveloped
        me
        with bitterness and
        tribulation;
6  he has made me sit in darkness
        like the dead of long ago.

7  He has walled me about so that
        I cannot escape;
        he has put heavy chains on
        me;
8  though I call and cry for help,
        he shuts out my prayer;
9  he has blocked my ways with
        hewn stones,
        he has made my paths
        crooked.

10  He is a bear lying in wait for
        me,
        a lion in hiding;
11  he led me off my way and tore
        me to pieces;
        he has made me desolate;
12  he bent his bow and set me
        as a mark for his arrow.

13  He shot into my vitals
        the arrows of his quiver;
14  I have become the laughingstock
        of all my people,
        the object of their taunt-songs
        all day long.
15  He has filled me with bitterness,

he has sated me with
        wormwood.
16  He has made my teeth grind
        on gravel,
        and made me cower in ashes;
17  my soul is bereft of peace;
        I have forgotten what
        happiness is;
18  so I say, "Gone is my glory,
        and all that I had hoped for
        from the LORD."

19  The thought of my affliction and
        my homelessness
        is wormwood and gall!
20  My soul continually thinks of it
        and is bowed down within
        me.
21  But this I call to mind,
        and therefore I have hope:

22  The steadfast love of the LORD
        never ceases, [b]
        his mercies never come to an
        end;
23  they are new every morning;
        great is your faithfulness.
24  "The LORD is my portion," says
        my soul,
        "therefore I will hope in him."

25  The LORD is good to those who
        wait for him,
        to the soul that seeks him.
26  It is good that one should wait
        quietly
        for the salvation of the LORD.
27  It is good for one to bear
        the yoke in youth,
28  to sit alone in silence
        when the Lord has imposed
        it,
29  to put one's mouth to the dust
        (there may yet be hope),
30  to give one's cheek to the
        smiter,
        and be filled with insults.

aHeb *his*   bSyr Tg: Heb LORD, *we are not cut off*

31 For the Lord will not
   reject forever.
32 Although he causes grief, he will
       have compassion
   according to the abundance of
       his steadfast love;
33 for he does not willingly afflict
   or grieve anyone.

34 When all the prisoners of the
       land
   are crushed under foot,
35 when human rights are
       perverted
   in the presence of the Most
       High,
36 when one's case is subverted
   —does the Lord not see it?

37 Who can command and have
       it done,
   if the Lord has not ordained
       it?
38 Is it not from the mouth of the
       Most High
   that good and bad come?
39 Why should any who draw
       breath complain
   about the punishment of
       their sins?

40 Let us test and examine our
       ways,
   and return to the Lord.
41 Let us lift up our hearts as well
       as our hands
   to God in heaven.
42 We have transgressed and
       rebelled,
   and you have not forgiven.

43 You have wrapped yourself with
       anger and pursued us,
   killing without pity;
44 you have wrapped yourself with
       a cloud
   so that no prayer can pass
       through.
45 You have made us filth and
       rubbish
   among the peoples.

46 All our enemies
   have opened their mouths
       against us;
47 panic and pitfall have come
       upon us,
   devastation and destruction.
48 My eyes flow with rivers of
       tears
   because of the destruction of
       my people.

49 My eyes will flow without
       ceasing,
   without respite,
50 until the Lord from heaven
   looks down and sees.
51 My eyes cause me grief
   at the fate of all the young
       women in my city.

52 Those who were my enemies
       without cause
   have hunted me like a bird;
53 they flung me alive into a pit
   and hurled stones on me;
54 water closed over my head;
   I said, "I am lost."

55 I called on your name, O Lord,
   from the depths of the pit;
56 you heard my plea, "Do not
       close your ear
   to my cry for help, but give
       me relief!"
57 You came near when I called
       on you;
   you said, "Do not fear!"

58 You have taken up my cause,
       O Lord,
   you have redeemed my life.
59 You have seen the wrong done
       to me, O Lord;
   judge my cause.
60 You have seen all their malice,
   all their plots against me.

61  You have heard their taunts,
        O Lord,
    all their plots against me.
62  The whispers and murmurs of
        my assailants
    are against me all day long.
63  Whether they sit or rise—see,
    I am the object of their
        taunt-songs.

64  Pay them back for their deeds,
        O Lord,
    according to the work of their
        hands!
65  Give them anguish of heart;
    your curse be on them!
66  Pursue them in anger and
        destroy them
    from under the Lord's
        heavens.

## HEBREWS 1.1–14

Long ago God spoke to our ancestors in many and various ways by the prophets, 2but in these last days he has spoken to us by a Son,a whom he appointed heir of all things, through whom he also created the worlds. 3He is the reflection of God's glory and the exact imprint of God's very being, and he sustainsb all things by his powerful word. When he had made purification for sins, he sat down at the right hand of the Majesty on high, 4having become as much superior to angels as the name he has inherited is more excellent than theirs.

5  For to which of the angels did God ever say,
    "You are my Son;
        today I have begotten you"?
Or again,
    "I will be his Father,
        and he will be my Son"?
6And again, when he brings the firstborn into the world, he says,

    "Let all God's angels worship
        him."
7Of the angels he says,
    "He makes his angels winds,
        and his servants flames of
            fire."
8But of the Son he says,
    "Your throne, O God,c is
        forever and ever,
    and the righteous scepter is
        the scepter of yourd
            kingdom.
9   You have loved righteousness
        and hated wickedness;
    therefore God, your God, has
        anointed you
    with the oil of gladness
        beyond your
            companions."
10And,
    "In the beginning, Lord, you
        founded the earth,
    and the heavens are the work
        of your hands;
11  they will perish, but you remain;
    they will all wear out like
        clothing;
12  like a cloak you will roll them
        up,
    and like clothinge they will be
        changed.
    But you are the same,
        and your years will never
            end."
13But to which of the angels has he ever said,
    "Sit at my right hand
        until I make your enemies a
            footstool for your feet"?
14Are not all angelsf spirits in the divine service, sent to serve for the sake of those who are to inherit salvation?

aOr *the Son*  bOr *bears along*  cOr *God is your throne*  dOther ancient authorities read *his*  eOther ancient authorities lack *like clothing*  fGk *all of them*

## PSALM 102.1–28

*A prayer of one afflicted, when faint and pleading before the* Lord.

**H**ear my prayer, O Lord;
  let my cry come to you.
2  Do not hide your face
    from me
  in the day of my distress.
Incline your ear to me;
  answer me speedily in the
    day when I call.

3  For my days pass away like
    smoke,
  and my bones burn like a
    furnace.
4  My heart is stricken and
    withered like grass;
  I am too wasted to eat my
    bread.
5  Because of my loud groaning
  my bones cling to my skin.
6  I am like an owl of the
    wilderness,
  like a little owl of the waste
    places.
7  I lie awake;
  I am like a lonely bird on the
    housetop.
8  All day long my enemies taunt
    me;
  those who deride me use my
    name for a curse.
9  For I eat ashes like bread,
  and mingle tears with my
    drink,
10  because of your indignation and
    anger;
  for you have lifted me up and
    thrown me aside.
11  My days are like an evening
    shadow;
  I wither away like grass.

12  But you, O Lord, are enthroned
    forever;
  your name endures to all
    generations.
13  You will rise up and have
    compassion on Zion,

for it is time to favor it;
  the appointed time has come.
14  For your servants hold its
    stones dear,
  and have pity on its dust.
15  The nations will fear the name
    of the Lord,
  and all the kings of the earth
    your glory.
16  For the Lord will build up Zion;
  he will appear in his glory.
17  He will regard the prayer of the
    destitute,
  and will not despise their
    prayer.

18  Let this be recorded for a
    generation to come,
  so that a people yet unborn
    may praise the Lord:
19  that he looked down from his
    holy height,
  from heaven the Lord looked
    at the earth,
20  to hear the groans of the
    prisoners,
  to set free those who were
    doomed to die;
21  so that the name of the Lord
    may be declared in Zion,
  and his praise in Jerusalem,
22  when peoples gather together,
  and kingdoms, to worship the
    Lord.

23  He has broken my strength in
    midcourse;
  he has shortened my days.
24  "O my God," I say, "do not
    take me away
  at the mid-point of my life,
you whose years endure
  throughout all generations."

25  Long ago you laid the foundation
    of the earth,
  and the heavens are the work
    of your hands.
26  They will perish, but you
    endure;

they will all wear out like a
  garment.
You change them like clothing,
  and they pass away;
27  but you are the same, and
  your years have no end.
28 The children of your servants
  shall live secure;
their offspring shall be
  established in your
  presence.

## PROVERBS 26.21–22

As charcoal is to hot embers
  and wood to fire,
so is a quarrelsome person
  for kindling strife.
22 The words of a whisperer are
  like delicious morsels;
they go down into the inner
  parts of the body.

# OCTOBER 31

## LAMENTATIONS 4.1—5.22

How the gold has grown dim,
  how the pure gold is
  changed!
The sacred stones lie scattered
  at the head of every street.

2 The precious children of Zion,
  worth their weight in fine
  gold—
how they are reckoned as
  earthen pots,
the work of a potter's hands!

3 Even the jackals offer the breast
  and nurse their young,
but my people has become
  cruel,
like the ostriches in the
  wilderness.

4 The tongue of the infant sticks
  to the roof of its mouth for
  thirst;
the children beg for food,
  but no one gives them
  anything.

5 Those who feasted on delicacies
  perish in the streets;
those who were brought up
  in purple
cling to ash heaps.

6 For the chastisement[a] of my
  people has been greater
than the punishment[b] of
  Sodom,
which was overthrown in a
  moment,
though no hand was laid on
  it. [c]

7 Her princes were purer than
  snow,
  whiter than milk;
their bodies were more ruddy
  than coral,
their hair[c] like sapphire. [d]

a Or *iniquity*  b Or *sin*  c Meaning of Heb uncertain  d Or *lapis lazuli*

8 Now their visage is blacker
        than soot;
    they are not recognized in
        the streets.
    Their skin has shriveled on
        their bones;
    it has become as dry as
        wood.

9 Happier were those pierced by
        the sword
    than those pierced by hunger,
    whose life drains away, deprived
    of the produce of the field.

10 The hands of compassionate
        women
    have boiled their own
        children;
    they became their food
        in the destruction of my
        people.

11 The LORD gave full vent to
        his wrath;
    he poured out his hot anger,
    and kindled a fire in Zion
        that consumed its foundations.

12 The kings of the earth did
        not believe,
    nor did any of the inhabitants
        of the world,
    that foe or enemy could enter
        the gates of Jerusalem.

13 It was for the sins of her
        prophets
    and the iniquities of her
        priests,
    who shed the blood of the
        righteous
    in the midst of her.

14 Blindly they wandered through
        the streets,
    so defiled with blood
    that no one was able
        to touch their garments.

15 "Away! Unclean!" people
        shouted at them;
    "Away! Away! Do not touch!"
    So they became fugitives and
        wanderers;
    it was said among the nations,
    "They shall stay here no
        longer."

16 The LORD himself has scattered
        them,
    he will regard them no more;
    no honor was shown to the
        priests,
    no favor to the elders.

17 Our eyes failed, ever watching
        vainly for help;
    we were watching eagerly
        for a nation that could not
        save.

18 They dogged our steps
        so that we could not walk in
        our streets;
    our end drew near; our days
        were numbered;
    for our end had come.

19 Our pursuers were swifter
        than the eagles in the
        heavens;
    they chased us on the
        mountains,
        they lay in wait for us in the
        wilderness.

20 The LORD's anointed, the breath
        of our life,
    was taken in their pits—
    the one of whom we said,
        "Under his shadow
    we shall live among the
        nations."

21 Rejoice and be glad, O daughter
        Edom,
    you that live in the land of
        Uz;

but to you also the cup shall
    pass;
you shall become drunk and
    strip yourself bare.

22 The punishment of your iniquity,
    O daughter Zion, is
    accomplished,
he will keep you in exile
    no longer;
but your iniquity, O daughter
    Edom, he will punish,
he will uncover your sins.

5.1 REMEMBER, O LORD, what has
    befallen us;
look, and see our disgrace!
2 Our inheritance has been turned
    over to strangers,
our homes to aliens.
3 We have become orphans,
    fatherless;
our mothers are like widows.
4 We must pay for the water
    we drink;
the wood we get must be
    bought.
5 With a yoke[a] on our necks we
    are hard driven;
we are weary, we are given
    no rest.
6 We have made a pact with[b]
    Egypt and Assyria,
to get enough bread.
7 Our ancestors sinned; they are
    no more,
and we bear their iniquities.
8 Slaves rule over us;
there is no one to deliver us
    from their hand.
9 We get our bread at the peril of
    our lives,
because of the sword in the
    wilderness.
10 Our skin is black as an oven
from the scorching heat
    of famine.
11 Women are raped in Zion,

    virgins in the towns of Judah.
12 Princes are hung up by
    their hands;
no respect is shown to the
    elders.
13 Young men are compelled to
    grind,
and boys stagger under loads
    of wood.
14 The old men have left the city
    gate,
the young men their music.
15 The joy of our hearts has
    ceased;
our dancing has been turned
    to mourning.
16 The crown has fallen from
    our head;
woe to us, for we have
    sinned!
17 Because of this our hearts are
    sick,
because of these things our
    eyes have grown dim:
18 because of Mount Zion, which
    lies desolate;
jackals prowl over it.

19 But you, O LORD, reign forever;
your throne endures to all
    generations.
20 Why have you forgotten us
    completely?
Why have you forsaken us
    these many days?
21 Restore us to yourself, O LORD,
    that we may be restored;
renew our days as of old—
22 unless you have utterly rejected
    us,
and are angry with us beyond
    measure.

## HEBREWS 2.1–18

THEREFORE we must pay greater attention to what we have heard, so that we do not drift away from it. 2For if the message de-

---

[a] Symmachus: Heb lacks *With a yoke*  [b] Heb *have given the hand to*

clared through angels was valid, and every transgression or disobedience received a just penalty, [3]how can we escape if we neglect so great a salvation? It was declared at first through the Lord, and it was attested to us by those who heard him, [4]while God added his testimony by signs and wonders and various miracles, and by gifts of the Holy Spirit, distributed according to his will.

5 Now God[a] did not subject the coming world, about which we are speaking, to angels. [6]But someone has testified somewhere,

> "What are human beings that
> you are mindful of
> them, [b]
> or mortals, that you care for
> them?[c]

7 You have made them for a little
> while lower[d] than the
> angels;
> you have crowned them with
> glory and honor, [e]

8 subjecting all things under
> their feet."

Now in subjecting all things to them, God[a] left nothing outside their control. As it is, we do not yet see everything in subjection to them, [9]but we do see Jesus, who for a little while was made lower[f] than the angels, now crowned with glory and honor because of the suffering of death, so that by the grace of God[g] he might taste death for everyone.

10 It was fitting that God, [a] for whom and through whom all things exist, in bringing many children to glory, should make the pioneer of their salvation perfect through sufferings. [11]For the one who sanctifies and those who are sanctified all have one Father.[h] For this reason Jesus[a] is not ashamed to call them brothers and sisters,[i] [12]saying,

> "I will proclaim your name to
> my brothers and
> sisters, [i]
> in the midst of the
> congregation I will praise
> you."

[13]And again,
> "I will put my trust in him."
And again,
> "Here am I and the children
> whom God has given
> me."

14 Since, therefore, the children share flesh and blood, he himself likewise shared the same things, so that through death he might destroy the one who has the power of death, that is, the devil, [15]and free those who all their lives were held in slavery by the fear of death. [16]For it is clear that he did not come to help angels, but the descendants of Abraham. [17]Therefore he had to become like his brothers and sisters[i] in every respect, so that he might be a merciful and faithful high priest in the service of God, to make a sacrifice of atonement for the sins of the people. [18]Because he himself was tested by what he suffered, he is able to help those who are being tested.

## PSALM 103.1–22

*Of David.*

B LESS the LORD, O my soul,
> and all that is within me,
> bless his holy name.

2 Bless the LORD, O my soul,
> and do not forget all his
> benefits—

3 who forgives all your iniquity,
> who heals all your diseases,

[a]Gk *he*   [b]Gk *What is man that you are mindful of him?*   [c]Gk *or the son of man that you care for him?* In the Hebrew of Psalm 8.4-6 both *man* and *son of man* refer to all humankind   [d]Or *them only a little lower*   [e]Other ancient authorities add *and set them over the works of your hands*   [f]Or *who was made a little lower*   [g]Other ancient authorities read *apart from God*   [h]Gk *are all of one*   [i]Gk *brothers*

4 who redeems your life from the
    Pit,
  who crowns you with
    steadfast love and mercy,
5 who satisfies you with good as
    long as you live[a]
  so that your youth is renewed
    like the eagle's.

6 The LORD works vindication
    and justice for all who are
    oppressed.
7 He made known his ways to
    Moses,
  his acts to the people of
    Israel.
8 The LORD is merciful and
    gracious,
  slow to anger and abounding
    in steadfast love.
9 He will not always accuse,
  nor will he keep his anger
    forever.
10 He does not deal with us
    according to our sins,
  nor repay us according to our
    iniquities.
11 For as the heavens are high
    above the earth,
  so great is his steadfast love
    toward those who fear
    him;
12 as far as the east is from the
    west,
  so far he removes our
    transgressions from us.
13 As a father has compassion for
    his children,
  so the LORD has compassion
    for those who fear him.
14 For he knows how we were
    made;

he remembers that we are
    dust.
15 As for mortals, their days are
    like grass;
  they flourish like a flower of
    the field;
16 for the wind passes over it, and
    it is gone,
  and its place knows it no
    more.
17 But the steadfast love of the
    LORD is from everlasting
    to everlasting
  on those who fear him,
  and his righteousness to
    children's children,
18 to those who keep his covenant
  and remember to do his
    commandments.

19 The LORD has established his
    throne in the heavens,
  and his kingdom rules over
    all.
20 Bless the LORD, O you his
    angels,
  you mighty ones who do his
    bidding,
  obedient to his spoken word.
21 Bless the LORD, all his hosts,
  his ministers that do his will.
22 Bless the LORD, all his works,
  in all places of his dominion.
  Bless the LORD, O my soul.

## PROVERBS 26.23

LIKE the glaze[b] covering an
    earthen vessel
are smooth[c] lips with an
    evil heart.

[a] Meaning of Heb uncertain    [b] Cn: Heb *silver of dross*    [c] Gk: Heb *burning*

## EZEKIEL 1.1—3.15

IN the thirtieth year, in the fourth month, on the fifth day of the month, as I was among the exiles by the river Chebar, the heavens were opened, and I saw visions of God. ²On the fifth day of the month (it was the fifth year of the exile of King Jehoiachin), ³the word of the LORD came to the priest Ezekiel son of Buzi, in the land of the Chaldeans by the river Chebar; and the hand of the LORD was on him there.

4 As I looked, a stormy wind came out of the north: a great cloud with brightness around it and fire flashing forth continually, and in the middle of the fire, something like gleaming amber. ⁵In the middle of it was something like four living creatures. This was their appearance: they were of human form. ⁶Each had four faces, and each of them had four wings. ⁷Their legs were straight, and the soles of their feet were like the sole of a calf's foot; and they sparkled like burnished bronze. ⁸Under their wings on their four sides they had human hands. And the four had their faces and their wings thus: ⁹their wings touched one another; each of them moved straight ahead, without turning as they moved. ¹⁰As for the appearance of their faces: the four had the face of a human being, the face of a lion on the right side, the face of an ox on the left side, and the face of an eagle; ¹¹such were their faces. Their wings were spread out above; each creature had two wings, each of which touched the wing of another, while two covered their bodies. ¹²Each moved straight ahead; wherever the spirit would go, they went, without turning as they went. ¹³In the middle ofᵃ the living creatures there was something that looked like burning coals of fire, like torches moving to and fro among the living creatures; the fire was bright, and lightning issued from the fire. ¹⁴The living creatures darted to and fro, like a flash of lightning.

15 As I looked at the living creatures, I saw a wheel on the earth beside the living creatures, one for each of the four of them. ᵇ ¹⁶As for the appearance of the wheels and their construction: their appearance was like the gleaming of beryl; and the four had the same form, their construction being something like a wheel within a wheel. ¹⁷When they moved, they moved in any of the four directions without veering as they moved. ¹⁸Their rims were tall and awesome, for the rims of all four were full of eyes all around. ¹⁹When the living creatures moved, the wheels moved beside them; and when the living creatures rose from the earth, the wheels rose. ²⁰Wherever the spirit would go, they went, and the wheels rose along with them; for the spirit of the living creatures was in the wheels. ²¹When they moved, the others moved; when they stopped, the others stopped; and when they rose from the earth, the wheels rose along with them; for the spirit of the living creatures was in the wheels.

22 Over the heads of the living creatures there was something like a dome, shining like crystal, ᶜ spread out above their heads. ²³Under the dome their wings were stretched out straight, one toward another; and each of the creatures had two wings covering its body. ²⁴When they moved, I

ᵃGk OL: Heb *And the appearance of*  ᵇHeb *of their faces*  ᶜGk: Heb *like the awesome crystal* heard the sound of their wings like the sound of mighty waters, like the thunder of the Almighty,[a] a sound of tumult like the sound of an army; when they stopped, they let down their wings. [25]And there came a voice from above the dome over their heads; when they stopped, they let down their wings.

26 And above the dome over their heads there was something like a throne, in appearance like sapphire;[b] and seated above the likeness of a throne was something that seemed like a human form. [27]Upward from what appeared like the loins I saw something like gleaming amber, something that looked like fire enclosed all around; and downward from what looked like the loins I saw something that looked like fire, and there was a splendor all around. [28]Like the bow in a cloud on a rainy day, such was the appearance of the splendor all around. This was the appearance of the likeness of the glory of the LORD.

When I saw it, I fell on my face, and I heard the voice of someone speaking.

[2.1] He said to me: O mortal,[c] stand up on your feet, and I will speak with you. [2]And when he spoke to me, a spirit entered into me and set me on my feet; and I heard him speaking to me. [3]He said to me, Mortal, I am sending you to the people of Israel, to a nation[d] of rebels who have rebelled against me; they and their ancestors have transgressed against me to this very day. [4]The descendants are impudent and stubborn. I am sending you to them, and you shall say to them, "Thus says the Lord GOD." [5]Whether they hear or refuse to hear (for they are a rebellious house), they shall know that there has been a prophet among them. [6]And you, O mortal, do not be afraid of them, and do not be afraid of their words, though briers and thorns surround you and you live among scorpions; do not be afraid of their words, and do not be dismayed at their looks, for they are a rebellious house. [7]You shall speak my words to them, whether they hear or refuse to hear; for they are a rebellious house.

8 But you, mortal, hear what I say to you; do not be rebellious like that rebellious house; open your mouth and eat what I give you. [9]I looked, and a hand was stretched out to me, and a written scroll was in it. [10]He spread it before me; it had writing on the front and on the back, and written on it were words of lamentation and mourning and woe.

[3.1] HE said to me, O mortal, eat what is offered to you; eat this scroll, and go, speak to the house of Israel. [2]So I opened my mouth, and he gave me the scroll to eat. [3]He said to me, Mortal, eat this scroll that I give you and fill your stomach with it. Then I ate it; and in my mouth it was as sweet as honey.

4 He said to me: Mortal, go to the house of Israel and speak my very words to them. [5]For you are not sent to a people of obscure speech and difficult language, but to the house of Israel— [6]not to many peoples of obscure speech and difficult language, whose words you cannot understand. Surely, if I sent you to them, they would listen to you. [7]But the house of Israel will not listen to you, for they are not willing to listen to me; because all the house of Israel have a hard forehead and a stubborn heart. [8]See, I have made your face hard against their faces, and your forehead hard against their foreheads. [9]Like the hardest stone, harder than flint, I have made your forehead; do not fear them or be dismayed at their looks, for they are a rebellious house. [10]He said to me: Mortal, all my words that I shall speak to you receive in your heart and hear

with your ears; [11]then go to the exiles, to your people, and speak to them. Say to them, "Thus says the Lord God"; whether they hear or refuse to hear.

12 Then the spirit lifted me up, and as the glory of the Lord rose[a] from its place, I heard behind me the sound of loud rumbling; [13]it was the sound of the wings of the living creatures brushing against one another, and the sound of the wheels beside them, that sounded like a loud rumbling. [14]The spirit lifted me up and bore me away; I went in bitterness in the heat of my spirit, the hand of the Lord being strong upon me. [15]I came to the exiles at Tel-abib, who lived by the river Chebar.[b] And I sat there among them, stunned, for seven days.

## HEBREWS 3.1–19

THEREFORE, brothers and sisters,[c] holy partners in a heavenly calling, consider that Jesus, the apostle and high priest of our confession, [2]was faithful to the one who appointed him, just as Moses also "was faithful in all[d] God's[e] house." [3]Yet Jesus[f] is worthy of more glory than Moses, just as the builder of a house has more honor than the house itself. [4](For every house is built by someone, but the builder of all things is God.) [5]Now Moses was faithful in all God's[e] house as a servant, to testify to the things that would be spoken later. [6]Christ, however, was faithful over God's[e] house as a son, and we are his house if we hold firm[g] the confidence and the pride that belong to hope.

7 Therefore, as the Holy Spirit says,

"Today, if you hear his voice,
8   do not harden your hearts as in
    the rebellion,

    as on the day of testing in the
    wilderness,
9   where your ancestors put me to
    the test,
  though they had seen my
    works [10]for forty years.
Therefore I was angry with that
  generation,
and I said, 'They always go
  astray in their hearts,
and they have not known
  my ways.'
11   As in my anger I swore,
  'They will not enter my
    rest.'"

[12]Take care, brothers and sisters,[c] that none of you may have an evil, unbelieving heart that turns away from the living God. [13]But exhort one another every day, as long as it is called "today," so that none of you may be hardened by the deceitfulness of sin. [14]For we have become partners of Christ, if only we hold our first confidence firm to the end. [15]As it is said,

"Today, if you hear his voice,
  do not harden your hearts as in
    the rebellion."

[16]Now who were they who heard and yet were rebellious? Was it not all those who left Egypt under the leadership of Moses? [17]But with whom was he angry forty years? Was it not those who sinned, whose bodies fell in the wilderness? [18]And to whom did he swear that they would not enter his rest, if not to those who were disobedient? [19]So we see that they were unable to enter because of unbelief.

## PSALM 104.1–23

BLESS the Lord, O my soul.
  O Lord my God, you are
    very great.
You are clothed with honor and
  majesty,

aCn: Heb *and blessed be the glory of the* Lord   bTwo Mss Syr: Heb *Chebar, and to where they lived.* Another reading is *Chebar, and I sat where they sat*   cGk *brothers*   dOther ancient authorities lack *all*   eGk *his*   fGk *this one*   gOther ancient authorities add *to the end*

2     wrapped in light as with a
          garment.
    You stretch out the heavens like
          a tent,
3     you set the beams of your<sup>a</sup>
          chambers on the waters,
    you make the clouds your<sup>a</sup>
          chariot,
      you ride on the wings of the
          wind,
4   you make the winds your<sup>a</sup>
          messengers,
      fire and flame your<sup>a</sup>
          ministers.

5   You set the earth on its
          foundations,
      so that it shall never be
          shaken.
6   You cover it with the deep as
          with a garment;
      the waters stood above the
          mountains.
7   At your rebuke they flee;
      at the sound of your thunder
          they take to flight.
8   They rose up to the mountains,
          ran down to the valleys
      to the place that you
          appointed for them.
9   You set a boundary that they
          may not pass,
      so that they might not again
          cover the earth.

10  You make springs gush forth in
          the valleys;
      they flow between the hills,
11  giving drink to every wild
          animal;
      the wild asses quench their
          thirst.
12  By the streams<sup>b</sup> the birds of
          the air have their
          habitation;
      they sing among the
          branches.

13  From your lofty abode you
          water the mountains;
      the earth is satisfied with the
          fruit of your work.
14  You cause the grass to grow for
          the cattle,
      and plants for people to
          use,<sup>c</sup>
      to bring forth food from the
          earth,
15    and wine to gladden the
          human heart,
    oil to make the face shine,
      and bread to strengthen the
          human heart.
16  The trees of the LORD are
          watered abundantly,
      the cedars of Lebanon that he
          planted.
17  In them the birds build their
          nests;
      the stork has its home in the
          fir trees.
18  The high mountains are for the
          wild goats;
      the rocks are a refuge for the
          coneys.
19  You have made the moon to
          mark the seasons;
      the sun knows its time for
          setting.
20  You make darkness, and it is
          night,
      when all the animals of the
          forest come creeping
          out.
21  The young lions roar for their
          prey,
      seeking their food from God.
22  When the sun rises, they
          withdraw
      and lie down in their dens.
23  People go out to their work
      and to their labor until the
          evening.

<sup>a</sup>Heb *his*   <sup>b</sup>Heb *By them*   <sup>c</sup>Or *to cultivate*

## PROVERBS 26.24–26

An enemy dissembles in
speaking
while harboring deceit
within;
25 when an enemy speaks
graciously, do not
believe it,
for there are seven
abominations concealed
within;
26 though hatred is covered with
guile,
the enemy's wickedness will
be exposed in the
assembly.

# NOVEMBER 2

## EZEKIEL 3.16—6.14

At the end of seven days, the word of the Lord came to me: 17Mortal, I have made you a sentinel for the house of Israel; whenever you hear a word from my mouth, you shall give them warning from me. 18If I say to the wicked, "You shall surely die," and you give them no warning, or speak to warn the wicked from their wicked way, in order to save their life, those wicked persons shall die for their iniquity; but their blood I will require at your hand. 19But if you warn the wicked, and they do not turn from their wickedness, or from their wicked way, they shall die for their iniquity; but you will have saved your life. 20Again, if the righteous turn from their righteousness and commit iniquity, and I lay a stumbling block before them, they shall die; because you have not warned them, they shall die for their sin, and their righteous deeds that they have done shall not be remembered; but their blood I will require at your hand. 21If, however, you warn the righteous not to sin, and they do not sin, they shall surely live, because they took warning; and you will have saved your life.

22 Then the hand of the Lord was upon me there; and he said to me, Rise up, go out into the valley, and there I will speak with you. 23So I rose up and went out into the valley; and the glory of the Lord stood there, like the glory that I had seen by the river Chebar; and I fell on my face. 24The spirit entered into me, and set me on my feet; and he spoke with me and said to me: Go, shut yourself inside your house. 25As for you, mortal, cords shall be placed on you, and you shall be bound with them, so that you cannot go out among the people; 26and I will make your tongue cling to the roof of your mouth, so that you shall be speechless and unable to reprove them; for they are a rebellious house. 27But when I speak with you, I will open your mouth, and you shall say to them, "Thus says the Lord God"; let those who will hear, hear; and let those who refuse to hear, refuse; for they are a rebellious house.

4.1 And you, O mortal, take a brick and set it before you. On it portray a city, Jerusalem; 2and put siegeworks against it, and build a siege wall against it, and cast up a ramp against it; set camps also against it, and plant battering rams against it all around. ³Then take an iron plate and place it as an iron wall between you and the city; set your face toward it, and let it be in a state of siege, and press the siege against it. This is a sign for the house of Israel.

4 Then lie on your left side, and place the punishment of the house of Israel upon it; you shall bear their punishment for the number of the days that you lie there. ⁵For I assign to you a number of days, three hundred ninety days, equal to the number of the years of their punishment; and so you shall bear the punishment of the house of Israel. ⁶When you have completed these, you shall lie down a second time, but on your right side, and bear the punishment of the house of Judah; forty days I assign you, one day for each year. ⁷You shall set your face toward the siege of Jerusalem, and with your arm bared you shall prophesy against it. ⁸See, I am putting cords on you so that you cannot turn from one side to the other until you have completed the days of your siege.

9 And you, take wheat and barley, beans and lentils, millet and spelt; put them into one vessel, and make bread for yourself. During the number of days that you lie on your side, three hundred ninety days, you shall eat it. ¹⁰The food that you eat shall be twenty shekels a day by weight; at fixed times you shall eat it. ¹¹And you shall drink water by measure, one-sixth of a hin; at fixed times you shall drink. ¹²You shall eat it as a barley-cake, baking it in their sight on human dung. ¹³The Lᴏʀᴅ said, "Thus shall the people of Israel eat their bread, unclean, among the nations to which I will drive them." ¹⁴Then I said, "Ah Lord Gᴏᴅ! I have never defiled myself; from my youth up until now I have never eaten what died of itself or was torn by animals, nor has carrion flesh come into my mouth."

¹⁵Then he said to me, "See, I will let you have cow's dung instead of human dung, on which you may prepare your bread."

16 Then he said to me, Mortal, I am going to break the staff of bread in Jerusalem; they shall eat bread by weight and with fearfulness; and they shall drink water by measure and in dismay. ¹⁷Lacking bread and water, they will look at one another in dismay, and waste away under their punishment.

5.1 Aɴᴅ you, O mortal, take a sharp sword; use it as a barber's razor and run it over your head and your beard; then take balances for weighing, and divide the hair. ²One third of the hair you shall burn in the fire inside the city, when the days of the siege are completed; one third you shall take and strike with the sword all around the city; ᵃ and one third you shall scatter to the wind, and I will unsheathe the sword after them. ³Then you shall take from these a small number, and bind them in the skirts of your robe. ⁴From these, again, you shall take some, throw them into the fire and burn them up; from there a fire will come out against all the house of Israel.

5 Thus says the Lord Gᴏᴅ: This is Jerusalem; I have set her in the center of the nations, with countries all around her. ⁶But she has rebelled against my ordinances and my statutes, becoming more wicked than the nations and the countries all around her, rejecting my ordinances and not following my statutes. ⁷Therefore thus says the Lord Gᴏᴅ: Because you are more turbulent than the nations that are all around you, and have not followed my statutes or kept my ordinances, but have acted according to the ordinances of the nations that are all around you; ⁸therefore thus says the Lord Gᴏᴅ: I, I myself, am coming against you; I will execute judg-

ᵃHeb *it*

ments among you in the sight of the nations. ⁹And because of all your abominations, I will do to you what I have never yet done, and the like of which I will never do again. ¹⁰Surely, parents shall eat their children in your midst, and children shall eat their parents; I will execute judgments on you, and any of you who survive I will scatter to every wind. ¹¹Therefore, as I live, says the Lord God, surely, because you have defiled my sanctuary with all your detestable things and with all your abominations—therefore I will cut you down;ᵃ my eye will not spare, and I will have no pity. ¹²One third of you shall die of pestilence or be consumed by famine among you; one third shall fall by the sword around you; and one third I will scatter to every wind and will unsheathe the sword after them.

13 My anger shall spend itself, and I will vent my fury on them and satisfy myself; and they shall know that I, the Lord, have spoken in my jealousy, when I spend my fury on them. ¹⁴Moreover I will make you a desolation and an object of mocking among the nations around you, in the sight of all that pass by. ¹⁵You shall beᵇ a mockery and a taunt, a warning and a horror, to the nations around you, when I execute judgments on you in anger and fury, and with furious punishments—I, the Lord, have spoken— ¹⁶when I loose against youᶜ my deadly arrows of famine, arrows for destruction, which I will let loose to destroy you, and when I bring more and more famine upon you, and break your staff of bread. ¹⁷I will send famine and wild animals against you, and they will rob you of your children; pestilence and bloodshed shall pass through you; and I will bring the sword upon you. I, the Lord, have spoken.

⁶·¹ The word of the Lord came to me: ²O mortal, set your face toward the mountains of Israel, and prophesy against them, ³and say, You mountains of Israel, hear the word of the Lord God! Thus says the Lord God to the mountains and the hills, to the ravines and the valleys: I, I myself will bring a sword upon you, and I will destroy your high places. ⁴Your altars shall become desolate, and your incense stands shall be broken; and I will throw down your slain in front of your idols. ⁵I will lay the corpses of the people of Israel in front of their idols; and I will scatter your bones around your altars. ⁶Wherever you live, your towns shall be waste and your high places ruined, so that your altars will be waste and ruined,ᵈ your idols broken and destroyed, your incense stands cut down, and your works wiped out. ⁷The slain shall fall in your midst; then you shall know that I am the Lord.

8 But I will spare some. Some of you shall escape the sword among the nations and be scattered through the countries. ⁹Those of you who escape shall remember me among the nations where they are carried captive, how I was crushed by their wanton heart that turned away from me, and their wanton eyes that turned after their idols. Then they will be loathsome in their own sight for the evils that they have committed, for all their abominations. ¹⁰And they shall know that I am the Lord; I did not threaten in vain to bring this disaster upon them.

11 Thus says the Lord God: Clap your hands and stamp your foot, and say, Alas for all the vile abominations of the house of Israel! For they shall fall by the sword, by famine, and by pestilence. ¹²Those far off shall die of pestilence; those nearby shall fall by the sword; and any who are left and are

ᵃAnother reading is *I will withdraw*  ᵇGk Syr Vg Tg: Heb *It shall be*  ᶜHeb *them*  ᵈSyr Vg Tg: Heb *and be made guilty* spared shall die of famine. Thus I will spend my fury upon them. 13And you shall know that I am the LORD, when their slain lie among their idols around their altars, on every high hill, on all the mountain tops, under every green tree, and under every leafy oak, wherever they offered pleasing odor to all their idols. 14I will stretch out my hand against them, and make the land desolate and waste, throughout all their settlements, from the wilderness to Riblah. a Then they shall know that I am the LORD.

## HEBREWS 4.1–13

THEREFORE, while the promise of entering his rest is still open, let us take care that none of you should seem to have failed to reach it. 2For indeed the good news came to us just as to them; but the message they heard did not benefit them, because they were not united by faith with those who listened. b 3For we who have believed enter that rest, just as Godc has said,

"As in my anger I swore,
'They shall not enter my rest,' "
though his works were finished at the foundation of the world. 4For in one place it speaks about the seventh day as follows, "And God rested on the seventh day from all his works." 5And again in this place it says, "They shall not enter my rest." 6Since therefore it remains open for some to enter it, and those who formerly received the good news failed to enter because of disobedience, 7again he sets a certain day— "today"—saying through David much later, in the words already quoted,

"Today, if you hear his voice,
do not harden your hearts."
8For if Joshua had given them rest, Godc would not speak later about another day. 9So then, a sabbath rest still remains for the people of God; 10for those who enter God's rest also cease from their labors as God did from his. 11Let us therefore make every effort to enter that rest, so that no one may fall through such disobedience as theirs.

12  Indeed, the word of God is living and active, sharper than any two-edged sword, piercing until it divides soul from spirit, joints from marrow; it is able to judge the thoughts and intentions of the heart. 13And before him no creature is hidden, but all are naked and laid bare to the eyes of the one to whom we must render an account.

## PSALM 104.24–35

O LORD, how manifold are your
      works!
   In wisdom you have made
      them all;
   the earth is full of your
      creatures.
25   Yonder is the sea, great and
      wide,
   creeping things innumerable
      are there,
   living things both small and
      great.
26   There go the ships,
   and Leviathan that you
      formed to sport in it.

27   These all look to you
   to give them their food in due
      season;
28   when you give to them, they
      gather it up;
   when you open your hand,
      they are filled with good
      things.
29   When you hide your face, they
      are dismayed;
   when you take away their
      breath, they die
   and return to their dust.
30   When you send forth your

aAnother reading is *Diblah*   bOther ancient authorities read *it did not meet with faith in those who listened*   cGk *he*

spirit,[a] they are created;
and you renew the face of the
ground.

31 May the glory of the LORD
endure forever;
may the LORD rejoice in his
works—
32 who looks on the earth and it
trembles,
who touches the mountains
and they smoke.
33 I will sing to the LORD as long as
I live;
I will sing praise to my God
while I have being.

34 May my meditation be pleasing
to him,
for I rejoice in the LORD.
35 Let sinners be consumed from
the earth,
and let the wicked be no
more.
Bless the LORD, O my soul.
Praise the LORD!

## PROVERBS 26.27

WHOEVER digs a pit will fall
into it,
and a stone will come back
on the one who starts it
rolling.

# NOVEMBER 3

## EZEKIEL 7.1—9.11

THE word of the LORD came to me: [2]You, O mortal, thus says the Lord GOD to the land of Israel:
An end! The end has come
upon the four corners of the
land.
3 Now the end is upon you,
I will let loose my anger
upon you;
I will judge you according to
your ways,
I will punish you for all your
abominations.
4 My eye will not spare you, I
will have no pity.
I will punish you for your
ways,
while your abominations are
among you.
Then you shall know that I am the
LORD.

5 Thus says the Lord GOD:
Disaster after disaster! See,
it comes.
6 An end has come, the end
has come.
It has awakened against you;
see, it comes!
7 Your doom[b] has come to you,
O inhabitant of the land.
The time has come, the day
is near—
of tumult, not of reveling on
the mountains.
8 Soon now I will pour out my
wrath upon you;
I will spend my anger
against you.
I will judge you according to
your ways,
and punish you for all your
abominations.

a Or *your breath*   b Meaning of Heb uncertain

9 My eye will not spare; I will
        have no pity.
    I will punish you according to
        your ways,
    while your abominations are
        among you.
Then you shall know that it is I the LORD
who strike.
10  See, the day! See, it comes!
        Your doom[a] has gone out.
    The rod has blossomed, pride
        has budded.
11      Violence has grown into a rod
        of wickedness.
    None of them shall remain,
        not their abundance, not their
        wealth;
        no pre-eminence among
        them. [a]
12  The time has come, the day
        draws near;
    let not the buyer rejoice, nor
        the seller mourn,
    for wrath is upon all their
        multitude.
13For the sellers shall not return to
what has been sold as long as they remain alive. For the vision concerns all
their multitude; it shall not be revoked.
Because of their iniquity, they cannot
maintain their lives. [a]
14  They have blown the horn and
        made everything ready;
    but no one goes to battle,
    for my wrath is upon all their
        multitude.
15  The sword is outside, pestilence
        and famine are inside;
    those in the field die by
        the sword;
    those in the city—famine and
        pestilence devour them.
16  If any survivors escape,
        they shall be found on the
        mountains
        like doves of the valleys,
    all of them moaning over
        their iniquity.

17  All hands shall grow feeble,
        all knees turn to water.
18  They shall put on sackcloth,
        horror shall cover them.
    Shame shall be on all faces,
        baldness on all their heads.
19  They shall fling their silver into
        the streets,
        their gold shall be treated as
        unclean.
Their silver and gold cannot save them
on the day of the wrath of the LORD.
They shall not satisfy their hunger or fill
their stomachs with it. For it was the
stumbling block of their iniquity.
20From their[b] beautiful ornament, in
which they took pride, they made their
abominable images, their detestable
things; therefore I will make of it an unclean thing to them.
21  I will hand it over to strangers
        as booty,
    to the wicked of the earth
        as plunder;
        they shall profane it.
22  I will avert my face from them,
        so that they may profane my
        treasured[c] place;
    the violent shall enter it,
        they shall profane it.
23  Make a chain![a]
    For the land is full of bloody
        crimes;
        the city is full of violence.
24  I will bring the worst of the
        nations
        to take possession of their
        houses.
    I will put an end to the
        arrogance of the strong,
    and their holy places shall be
        profaned.
25  When anguish comes, they will
        seek peace,
        but there shall be none.
26  Disaster comes upon disaster,
        rumor follows rumor;

aMeaning of Heb uncertain   bSyr Symmachus: Heb *its*   cOr *secret*

they shall keep seeking a vision
    from the prophet;
instruction shall perish from
    the priest,
and counsel from the elders.
27 The king shall mourn,
    the prince shall be wrapped
      in despair,
and the hands of the people of
    the land shall tremble.
According to their way I will
    deal with them;
according to their own
    judgments I will judge
    them.
And they shall know that I am the Lord.

8.1 In the sixth year, in the sixth month, on the fifth day of the month, as I sat in my house, with the elders of Judah sitting before me, the hand of the Lord God fell upon me there. 2I looked, and there was a figure that looked like a human being;a below what appeared to be its loins it was fire, and above the loins it was like the appearance of brightness, like gleaming amber. 3It stretched out the form of a hand, and took me by a lock of my head; and the spirit lifted me up between earth and heaven, and brought me in visions of God to Jerusalem, to the entrance of the gateway of the inner court that faces north, to the seat of the image of jealousy, which provokes to jealousy. 4And the glory of the God of Israel was there, like the vision that I had seen in the valley.

5 Then Godb said to me, "O mortal, lift up your eyes now in the direction of the north." So I lifted up my eyes toward the north, and there, north of the altar gate, in the entrance, was this image of jealousy. 6He said to me, "Mortal, do you see what they are doing, the great abominations that the house of Israel are committing here, to drive me far from my sanctuary? Yet you will see still greater abominations."

7 And he brought me to the entrance of the court; I looked, and there was a hole in the wall. 8Then he said to me, "Mortal, dig through the wall"; and when I dug through the wall, there was an entrance. 9He said to me, "Go in, and see the vile abominations that they are committing here." 10So I went in and looked; there, portrayed on the wall all around, were all kinds of creeping things, and loathsome animals, and all the idols of the house of Israel. 11Before them stood seventy of the elders of the house of Israel, with Jaazaniah son of Shaphan standing among them. Each had his censer in his hand, and the fragrant cloud of incense was ascending. 12Then he said to me, "Mortal, have you seen what the elders of the house of Israel are doing in the dark, each in his room of images? For they say, 'The Lord does not see us, the Lord has forsaken the land.' " 13He said also to me, "You will see still greater abominations that they are committing."

14 Then he brought me to the entrance of the north gate of the house of the Lord; women were sitting there weeping for Tammuz. 15Then he said to me, "Have you seen this, O mortal? You will see still greater abominations than these."

16 And he brought me into the inner court of the house of the Lord; there, at the entrance of the temple of the Lord, between the porch and the altar, were about twenty-five men, with their backs to the temple of the Lord, and their faces toward the east, prostrating themselves to the sun toward the east. 17Then he said to me, "Have you seen this, O mortal? Is it not bad enough that the house of Judah commits the abominations done here? Must they fill the land with violence,

aGk: Heb *like fire*   bHeb *he*

and provoke my anger still further? See, they are putting the branch to their nose! [18]Therefore I will act in wrath; my eye will not spare, nor will I have pity; and though they cry in my hearing with a loud voice, I will not listen to them."

[9.1] THEN he cried in my hearing with a loud voice, saying, "Draw near, you executioners of the city, each with his destroying weapon in his hand." [2]And six men came from the direction of the upper gate, which faces north, each with his weapon for slaughter in his hand; among them was a man clothed in linen, with a writing case at his side. They went in and stood beside the bronze altar.

3 Now the glory of the God of Israel had gone up from the cherub on which it rested to the threshold of the house. The LORD called to the man clothed in linen, who had the writing case at his side; [4]and said to him, "Go through the city, through Jerusalem, and put a mark on the foreheads of those who sigh and groan over all the abominations that are committed in it." [5]To the others he said in my hearing, "Pass through the city after him, and kill; your eye shall not spare, and you shall show no pity. [6]Cut down old men, young men and young women, little children and women, but touch no one who has the mark. And begin at my sanctuary." So they began with the elders who were in front of the house. [7]Then he said to them, "Defile the house, and fill the courts with the slain. Go!" So they went out and killed in the city. [8]While they were killing, and I was left alone, I fell prostrate on my face and cried out, "Ah Lord GOD! will you destroy all who remain of Israel as you pour out your wrath upon Jerusalem?" [9]He said to me, "The guilt of the house of Israel and Judah is exceedingly great;

the land is full of bloodshed and the city full of perversity; for they say, 'The LORD has forsaken the land, and the LORD does not see.' [10]As for me, my eye will not spare, nor will I have pity, but I will bring down their deeds upon their heads."

11 Then the man clothed in linen, with the writing case at his side, brought back word, saying, "I have done as you commanded me."

# HEBREWS 4.14—5.14

SINCE, then, we have a great high priest who has passed through the heavens, Jesus, the Son of God, let us hold fast to our confession. [15]For we do not have a high priest who is unable to sympathize with our weaknesses, but we have one who in every respect has been tested[a] as we are, yet without sin. [16]Let us therefore approach the throne of grace with boldness, so that we may receive mercy and find grace to help in time of need.

[5.1] EVERY high priest chosen from among mortals is put in charge of things pertaining to God on their behalf, to offer gifts and sacrifices for sins. [2]He is able to deal gently with the ignorant and wayward, since he himself is subject to weakness; [3]and because of this he must offer sacrifice for his own sins as well as for those of the people. [4]And one does not presume to take this honor, but takes it only when called by God, just as Aaron was.

5 So also Christ did not glorify himself in becoming a high priest, but was appointed by the one who said to him,

"You are my Son,
today I have begotten you";
[6]as he says also in another place,
"You are a priest forever,
according to the order of
Melchizedek."

7 In the days of his flesh, Jesus[b]

aOr *tempted*  bGk *he*

offered up prayers and supplications, with loud cries and tears, to the one who was able to save him from death, and he was heard because of his reverent submission. ⁸Although he was a Son, he learned obedience through what he suffered; ⁹and having been made perfect, he became the source of eternal salvation for all who obey him, ¹⁰having been designated by God a high priest according to the order of Melchizedek.

11 About this[a] we have much to say that is hard to explain, since you have become dull in understanding. ¹²For though by this time you ought to be teachers, you need someone to teach you again the basic elements of the oracles of God. You need milk, not solid food; ¹³for everyone who lives on milk, being still an infant, is unskilled in the word of righteousness. ¹⁴But solid food is for the mature, for those whose faculties have been trained by practice to distinguish good from evil.

## PSALM 105.1–15

O GIVE thanks to the LORD, call
    on his name,
make known his deeds
    among the peoples.
2  Sing to him, sing praises to him;
    tell of all his wonderful works.
3  Glory in his holy name;
    let the hearts of those who
      seek the LORD rejoice.
4  Seek the LORD and his strength;
    seek his presence continually.
5  Remember the wonderful works
      he has done,
    his miracles, and the
      judgments he uttered,
6  O offspring of his servant
      Abraham,[b]

children of Jacob, his chosen
    ones.
7  He is the LORD our God;
    his judgments are in all the
      earth.
8  He is mindful of his covenant
      forever,
    of the word that he
      commanded, for a
      thousand generations,
9  the covenant that he made with
      Abraham,
    his sworn promise to Isaac,
10  which he confirmed to Jacob as
      a statute,
    to Israel as an everlasting
      covenant,
11  saying, "To you I will give the
      land of Canaan
    as your portion for an
      inheritance."

12  When they were few in number,
    of little account, and
      strangers in it,
13  wandering from nation to nation,
    from one kingdom to another
      people,
14  he allowed no one to oppress
      them;
    he rebuked kings on their
      account,
15  saying, "Do not touch my
      anointed ones;
    do my prophets no harm."

## PROVERBS 26.28

A LYING tongue hates its
    victims,
and a flattering mouth
    works ruin.

a Or *him*  b Another reading is *Israel* (compare 1 Chr 16.13)

## EZEKIEL 10.1—11.25

THEN I looked, and above the dome that was over the heads of the cherubim there appeared above them something like a sapphire,[a] in form resembling a throne. [2]He said to the man clothed in linen, "Go within the wheelwork underneath the cherubim; fill your hands with burning coals from among the cherubim, and scatter them over the city." He went in as I looked on. [3]Now the cherubim were standing on the south side of the house when the man went in; and a cloud filled the inner court. [4]Then the glory of the LORD rose up from the cherub to the threshold of the house; the house was filled with the cloud, and the court was full of the brightness of the glory of the LORD. [5]The sound of the wings of the cherubim was heard as far as the outer court, like the voice of God Almighty[b] when he speaks.

6 When he commanded the man clothed in linen, "Take fire from within the wheelwork, from among the cherubim," he went in and stood beside a wheel. [7]And a cherub stretched out his hand from among the cherubim to the fire that was among the cherubim, took some of it and put it into the hands of the man clothed in linen, who took it and went out. [8]The cherubim appeared to have the form of a human hand under their wings.

9 I looked, and there were four wheels beside the cherubim, one beside each cherub; and the appearance of the wheels was like gleaming beryl. [10]And as for their appearance, the four looked alike, something like a wheel within a wheel. [11]When they moved, they moved in any of the four directions without veering as they moved; but in whatever direction the front wheel faced, the others followed without veering as they moved. [12]Their entire body, their rims, their spokes, their wings, and the wheels—the wheels of the four of them—were full of eyes all around. [13]As for the wheels, they were called in my hearing "the wheelwork." [14]Each one had four faces: the first face was that of the cherub, the second face was that of a human being, the third that of a lion, and the fourth that of an eagle.

15 The cherubim rose up. These were the living creatures that I saw by the river Chebar. [16]When the cherubim moved, the wheels moved beside them; and when the cherubim lifted up their wings to rise up from the earth, the wheels at their side did not veer. [17]When they stopped, the others stopped, and when they rose up, the others rose up with them; for the spirit of the living creatures was in them.

18 Then the glory of the LORD went out from the threshold of the house and stopped above the cherubim. [19]The cherubim lifted up their wings and rose up from the earth in my sight as they went out with the wheels beside them. They stopped at the entrance of the east gate of the house of the LORD; and the glory of the God of Israel was above them.

20 These were the living creatures that I saw underneath the God of Israel by the river Chebar; and I knew that they were cherubim. [21]Each had four faces, each four wings, and underneath their wings something like human hands. [22]As for what their faces were like, they were the same faces whose

appearance I had seen by the river Chebar. Each one moved straight ahead.

11.1 THE spirit lifted me up and brought me to the east gate of the house of the LORD, which faces east. There, at the entrance of the gateway, were twenty-five men; among them I saw Jaazaniah son of Azzur, and Pelatiah son of Benaiah, officials of the people. [2]He said to me, "Mortal, these are the men who devise iniquity and who give wicked counsel in this city; [3]they say, 'The time is not near to build houses; this city is the pot, and we are the meat.' [4]Therefore prophesy against them; prophesy, O mortal."

5 Then the spirit of the LORD fell upon me, and he said to me, "Say, Thus says the LORD: This is what you think, O house of Israel; I know the things that come into your mind. [6]You have killed many in this city, and have filled its streets with the slain. [7]Therefore thus says the Lord GOD: The slain whom you have placed within it are the meat, and this city is the pot; but you shall be taken out of it. [8]You have feared the sword; and I will bring the sword upon you, says the Lord GOD. [9]I will take you out of it and give you over to the hands of foreigners, and execute judgments upon you. [10]You shall fall by the sword; I will judge you at the border of Israel. And you shall know that I am the LORD. [11]This city shall not be your pot, and you shall not be the meat inside it; I will judge you at the border of Israel. [12]Then you shall know that I am the LORD, whose statutes you have not followed, and whose ordinances you have not kept, but you have acted according to the ordinances of the nations that are around you."

13 Now, while I was prophesying, Pelatiah son of Benaiah died. Then I fell down on my face, cried with a loud voice, and said, "Ah Lord GOD! will you make a full end of the remnant of Israel?"

14 Then the word of the LORD came to me: [15]Mortal, your kinsfolk, your own kin, your fellow exiles, [a] the whole house of Israel, all of them, are those of whom the inhabitants of Jerusalem have said, "They have gone far from the LORD; to us this land is given for a possession." [16]Therefore say: Thus says the Lord GOD: Though I removed them far away among the nations, and though I scattered them among the countries, yet I have been a sanctuary to them for a little while[b] in the countries where they have gone. [17]Therefore say: Thus says the Lord GOD: I will gather you from the peoples, and assemble you out of the countries where you have been scattered, and I will give you the land of Israel. [18]When they come there, they will remove from it all its detestable things and all its abominations. [19]I will give them one[c] heart, and put a new spirit within them; I will remove the heart of stone from their flesh and give them a heart of flesh, [20]so that they may follow my statutes and keep my ordinances and obey them. Then they shall be my people, and I will be their God. [21]But as for those whose heart goes after their detestable things and their abominations, [d] I will bring their deeds upon their own heads, says the Lord GOD.

22 Then the cherubim lifted up their wings, with the wheels beside them; and the glory of the God of Israel was above them. [23]And the glory of the LORD ascended from the middle of the city, and stopped on the mountain east of the city. [24]The spirit lifted me up and brought me in a vision by the spirit of God into Chaldea, to the exiles. Then the vision that I had seen left me. [25]And I told the exiles all the things that the LORD had shown me.

aGk Syr: Heb *people of your kindred*   bOr *to some extent*   cAnother reading is *a new*   dCn: Heb *And to the heart of their detestable things and their abominations their heart goes*

## HEBREWS 6.1–20

**T**HEREFORE let us go on toward perfection,[a] leaving behind the basic teaching about Christ, and not laying again the foundation: repentance from dead works and faith toward God, [2]instruction about baptisms, laying on of hands, resurrection of the dead, and eternal judgment. [3]And we will do[b] this, if God permits. [4]For it is impossible to restore again to repentance those who have once been enlightened, and have tasted the heavenly gift, and have shared in the Holy Spirit, [5]and have tasted the goodness of the word of God and the powers of the age to come, [6]and then have fallen away, since on their own they are crucifying again the Son of God and are holding him up to contempt. [7]Ground that drinks up the rain falling on it repeatedly, and that produces a crop useful to those for whom it is cultivated, receives a blessing from God. [8]But if it produces thorns and thistles, it is worthless and on the verge of being cursed; its end is to be burned over.

9 Even though we speak in this way, beloved, we are confident of better things in your case, things that belong to salvation. [10]For God is not unjust; he will not overlook your work and the love that you showed for his sake[c] in serving the saints, as you still do. [11]And we want each one of you to show the same diligence so as to realize the full assurance of hope to the very end, [12]so that you may not become sluggish, but imitators of those who through faith and patience inherit the promises.

13 When God made a promise to Abraham, because he had no one greater by whom to swear, he swore by himself, [14]saying, "I will surely bless you and multiply you." [15]And thus Abraham,[d] having patiently endured, obtained the promise. [16]Human beings, of course, swear by someone greater than themselves, and an oath given as confirmation puts an end to all dispute. [17]In the same way, when God desired to show even more clearly to the heirs of the promise the unchangeable character of his purpose, he guaranteed it by an oath, [18]so that through two unchangeable things, in which it is impossible that God would prove false, we who have taken refuge might be strongly encouraged to seize the hope set before us. [19]We have this hope, a sure and steadfast anchor of the soul, a hope that enters the inner shrine behind the curtain, [20]where Jesus, a forerunner on our behalf, has entered, having become a high priest forever according to the order of Melchizedek.

## PSALM 105.16–36

**W**HEN he summoned famine against the land,
    and broke every staff of
      bread,
17  he had sent a man ahead of
      them,
    Joseph, who was sold as a
      slave.
18  His feet were hurt with fetters,
    his neck was put in a collar of
      iron;
19  until what he had said came to
      pass,
    the word of the LORD kept
      testing him.
20  The king sent and released him;
    the ruler of the peoples set
      him free.
21  He made him lord of his house,
    and ruler of all his
      possessions,
22  to instruct[e] his officials at his
      pleasure,
    and to teach his elders
      wisdom.

---

[a]Or *toward maturity*  [b]Other ancient authorities read *let us do*  [c]Gk *for his name*  [d]Gk *he*  [e]Gk Syr Jerome: Heb *to bind*

23 Then Israel came to Egypt;
    Jacob lived as an alien in the
      land of Ham.
24 And the LORD made his people
    very fruitful,
    and made them stronger than
      their foes,
25 whose hearts he then turned to
    hate his people,
    to deal craftily with his
      servants.

26 He sent his servant Moses,
    and Aaron whom he had
      chosen.
27 They performed his signs
    among them,
    and miracles in the land of
      Ham.
28 He sent darkness, and made the
    land dark;
    they rebelled[a] against his
      words.
29 He turned their waters into
    blood,
    and caused their fish to die.
30 Their land swarmed with frogs,
    even in the chambers of their
      kings.
31 He spoke, and there came
    swarms of flies,

    and gnats throughout their
      country.
32 He gave them hail for rain,
    and lightning that flashed
      through their land.
33 He struck their vines and fig
    trees,
    and shattered the trees of
      their country.
34 He spoke, and the locusts
    came,
    and young locusts without
      number;
35 they devoured all the vegetation
    in their land,
    and ate up the fruit of their
      ground.
36 He struck down all the firstborn
    in their land,
    the first issue of all their
      strength.

## PROVERBS 27.1–2

**D**o not boast about tomorrow,
    for you do not know what a
      day may bring.
2 Let another praise you, and not
    your own mouth—
    a stranger, and not your own
      lips.

# NOVEMBER 5

## EZEKIEL 12.1—14.11

**T**HE word of the LORD came to me: 2Mortal, you are living in the midst of a rebellious house, who have eyes to see but do not see, who have ears to hear but do not hear; 3for they are a rebellious house. Therefore, mortal, prepare for yourself an exile's baggage, and go into exile by day in their sight; you shall go like an exile from your place to another place in their sight. Perhaps they will understand, though they are a rebellious house. 4You shall bring out your bag-

a Cn Compare Gk Syr: Heb *they did not rebel*

gage by day in their sight, as baggage for exile; and you shall go out yourself at evening in their sight, as those do who go into exile. [5]Dig through the wall in their sight, and carry the baggage through it. [6]In their sight you shall lift the baggage on your shoulder, and carry it out in the dark; you shall cover your face, so that you may not see the land; for I have made you a sign for the house of Israel.

7 I did just as I was commanded. I brought out my baggage by day, as baggage for exile, and in the evening I dug through the wall with my own hands; I brought it out in the dark, carrying it on my shoulder in their sight.

8 In the morning the word of the Lord came to me: [9]Mortal, has not the house of Israel, the rebellious house, said to you, "What are you doing?" [10]Say to them, "Thus says the Lord God: This oracle concerns the prince in Jerusalem and all the house of Israel in it." [11]Say, "I am a sign for you: as I have done, so shall it be done to them; they shall go into exile, into captivity." [12]And the prince who is among them shall lift his baggage on his shoulder in the dark, and shall go out; he[a] shall dig through the wall and carry it through; he shall cover his face, so that he may not see the land with his eyes. [13]I will spread my net over him, and he shall be caught in my snare; and I will bring him to Babylon, the land of the Chaldeans, yet he shall not see it; and he shall die there. [14]I will scatter to every wind all who are around him, his helpers and all his troops; and I will unsheathe the sword behind them. [15]And they shall know that I am the Lord, when I disperse them among the nations and scatter them through the countries. [16]But I will let a few of them escape from the sword, from famine and pestilence, so that they may tell of all their abominations among the nations where they go;

then they shall know that I am the Lord.

17 The word of the Lord came to me: [18]Mortal, eat your bread with quaking, and drink your water with trembling and with fearfulness; [19]and say to the people of the land, Thus says the Lord God concerning the inhabitants of Jerusalem in the land of Israel: They shall eat their bread with fearfulness, and drink their water in dismay, because their land shall be stripped of all it contains, on account of the violence of all those who live in it. [20]The inhabited cities shall be laid waste, and the land shall become a desolation; and you shall know that I am the Lord.

21 The word of the Lord came to me: [22]Mortal, what is this proverb of yours about the land of Israel, which says, "The days are prolonged, and every vision comes to nothing"? [23]Tell them therefore, "Thus says the Lord God: I will put an end to this proverb, and they shall use it no more as a proverb in Israel." But say to them, The days are near, and the fulfillment of every vision. [24]For there shall no longer be any false vision or flattering divination within the house of Israel. [25]But I the Lord will speak the word that I speak, and it will be fulfilled. It will no longer be delayed; but in your days, O rebellious house, I will speak the word and fulfill it, says the Lord God.

26 The word of the Lord came to me: [27]Mortal, the house of Israel is saying, "The vision that he sees is for many years ahead; he prophesies for distant times." [28]Therefore say to them, Thus says the Lord God: None of my words will be delayed any longer, but the word that I speak will be fulfilled, says the Lord God.

13.1 The word of the Lord came to me: [2]Mortal, prophesy against the prophets of Israel who are prophesying; say to

a Gk Syr: Heb *they*

those who prophesy out of their own imagination: "Hear the word of the LORD!" [3]Thus says the Lord GOD, Alas for the senseless prophets who follow their own spirit, and have seen nothing! [4]Your prophets have been like jackals among ruins, O Israel. [5]You have not gone up into the breaches, or repaired a wall for the house of Israel, so that it might stand in battle on the day of the LORD. [6]They have envisioned falsehood and lying divination; they say, "Says the LORD," when the LORD has not sent them, and yet they wait for the fulfillment of their word! [7]Have you not seen a false vision or uttered a lying divination, when you have said, "Says the LORD," even though I did not speak?

[8] Therefore thus says the Lord GOD: Because you have uttered falsehood and envisioned lies, I am against you, says the Lord GOD. [9]My hand will be against the prophets who see false visions and utter lying divinations; they shall not be in the council of my people, nor be enrolled in the register of the house of Israel, nor shall they enter the land of Israel; and you shall know that I am the Lord GOD. [10]Because, in truth, because they have misled my people, saying, "Peace," when there is no peace; and because, when the people build a wall, these prophets[a] smear whitewash on it. [11]Say to those who smear whitewash on it that it shall fall. There will be a deluge of rain,[b] great hailstones will fall, and a stormy wind will break out. [12]When the wall falls, will it not be said to you, "Where is the whitewash you smeared on it?" [13]Therefore thus says the Lord GOD: In my wrath I will make a stormy wind break out, and in my anger there shall be a deluge of rain, and hailstones in wrath to destroy it. [14]I will break down the wall that you have smeared with whitewash, and bring it to the ground, so that its foundation will be laid bare; when it falls, you shall perish within it; and you shall know that I am the LORD. [15]Thus I will spend my wrath upon the wall, and upon those who have smeared it with whitewash; and I will say to you, The wall is no more, nor those who smeared it— [16]the prophets of Israel who prophesied concerning Jerusalem and saw visions of peace for it, when there was no peace, says the Lord GOD.

[17] As for you, mortal, set your face against the daughters of your people, who prophesy out of their own imagination; prophesy against them [18]and say, Thus says the Lord GOD: Woe to the women who sew bands on all wrists, and make veils for the heads of persons of every height, in the hunt for human lives! Will you hunt down lives among my people, and maintain your own lives? [19]You have profaned me among my people for handfuls of barley and for pieces of bread, putting to death persons who should not die and keeping alive persons who should not live, by your lies to my people, who listen to lies.

[20] Therefore thus says the Lord GOD: I am against your bands with which you hunt lives;[c] I will tear them from your arms, and let the lives go free, the lives that you hunt down like birds. [21]I will tear off your veils, and save my people from your hands; they shall no longer be prey in your hands; and you shall know that I am the LORD. [22]Because you have disheartened the righteous falsely, although I have not disheartened them, and you have encouraged the wicked not to turn from their wicked way and save their lives; [23]therefore you shall no longer see false visions or practice divination; I will save my people from your hand. Then you will know that I am the LORD.

aHeb *they*   bHeb *rain and you*   cGk Syr: Heb *lives for birds*

14.1 CERTAIN elders of Israel came to me and sat down before me. ²And the word of the LORD came to me: ³Mortal, these men have taken their idols into their hearts, and placed their iniquity as a stumbling block before them; shall I let myself be consulted by them? ⁴Therefore speak to them, and say to them, Thus says the Lord GOD: Any of those of the house of Israel who take their idols into their hearts and place their iniquity as a stumbling block before them, and yet come to the prophet—I the LORD will answer those who come with the multitude of their idols, ⁵in order that I may take hold of the hearts of the house of Israel, all of whom are estranged from me through their idols.

6 Therefore say to the house of Israel, Thus says the Lord GOD: Repent and turn away from your idols; and turn away your faces from all your abominations. ⁷For any of those of the house of Israel, or of the aliens who reside in Israel, who separate themselves from me, taking their idols into their hearts and placing their iniquity as a stumbling block before them, and yet come to a prophet to inquire of me by him, I the LORD will answer them myself. ⁸I will set my face against them; I will make them a sign and a byword and cut them off from the midst of my people; and you shall know that I am the LORD. 9 If a prophet is deceived and speaks a word, I, the LORD, have deceived that prophet, and I will stretch out my hand against him, and will destroy him from the midst of my people Israel. ¹⁰And they shall bear their punishment—the punishment of the inquirer and the punishment of the prophet shall be the same— ¹¹so that the house of Israel may no longer go astray from me, nor defile themselves any more with all their transgressions. Then they shall be my people, and I will be their God, says the Lord GOD.

## HEBREWS 7.1–17

THIS "King Melchizedek of Salem, priest of the Most High God, met Abraham as he was returning from defeating the kings and blessed him"; ²and to him Abraham apportioned "one-tenth of everything." His name, in the first place, means "king of righteousness"; next he is also king of Salem, that is, "king of peace." ³Without father, without mother, without genealogy, having neither beginning of days nor end of life, but resembling the Son of God, he remains a priest forever.

4 See how great he is! Even[a] Abraham the patriarch gave him a tenth of the spoils. ⁵And those descendants of Levi who receive the priestly office have a commandment in the law to collect tithes[b] from the people, that is, from their kindred, [c] though these also are descended from Abraham. ⁶But this man, who does not belong to their ancestry, collected tithes[b] from Abraham and blessed him who had received the promises. ⁷It is beyond dispute that the inferior is blessed by the superior. ⁸In the one case, tithes are received by those who are mortal; in the other, by one of whom it is testified that he lives. ⁹One might even say that Levi himself, who receives tithes, paid tithes through Abraham, ¹⁰for he was still in the loins of his ancestor when Melchizedek met him.

11 Now if perfection had been attainable through the levitical priesthood—for the people received the law under this priesthood—what further need would there have been to speak of another priest arising according to the order of Melchizedek, rather than one according to the order of Aaron? ¹²For when there is a change in the priesthood, there is necessarily a change in the law as well. ¹³Now the

a Other ancient authorities lack *Even*   b Or *a tenth*   c Gk *brothers*

one of whom these things are spoken belonged to another tribe, from which no one has ever served at the altar. [14]For it is evident that our Lord was descended from Judah, and in connection with that tribe Moses said nothing about priests.

15 It is even more obvious when another priest arises, resembling Melchizedek, [16]one who has become a priest, not through a legal requirement concerning physical descent, but through the power of an indestructible life. [17]For it is attested of him,

"You are a priest forever,
according to the order of
Melchizedek."

## PSALM 105.37–45

THEN he brought Israel[a] out
with silver and gold,
and there was no one among
their tribes who
stumbled.
[38] Egypt was glad when they
departed,
for dread of them had fallen
upon it.
[39] He spread a cloud for a
covering,
and fire to give light by night.
[40] They asked, and he brought
quails,
and gave them food from
heaven in abundance.
[41] He opened the rock, and water
gushed out;
it flowed through the desert
like a river.
[42] For he remembered his holy
promise,
and Abraham, his servant.

[43] So he brought his people out
with joy,
his chosen ones with singing.
[44] He gave them the lands of the
nations,
and they took possession of
the wealth of the
peoples,
[45] that they might keep his
statutes
and observe his laws.
Praise the LORD!

## PROVERBS 27.3

A STONE is heavy, and sand is
weighty,
but a fool's provocation is
heavier than both.

# NOVEMBER 6

## EZEKIEL 14.12—16.43a

THE word of the LORD came to me: [13]Mortal, when a land sins against me by acting faithlessly, and I stretch out my hand against it, and break its staff of bread and send famine upon it, and cut off from it human beings and animals, [14]even if Noah, Daniel,[b] and Job, these three, were in it, they would save only their own lives by their righteousness, says the Lord GOD. [15]If I send wild animals through the land to ravage it, so that it is made desolate, and no one may pass through

aHeb *them*   bOr, as otherwise read, *Danel*

because of the animals; <sup>16</sup>even if these three men were in it, as I live, says the Lord God, they would save neither sons nor daughters; they alone would be saved, but the land would be desolate. <sup>17</sup>Or if I bring a sword upon that land and say, 'Let a sword pass through the land,' and I cut off human beings and animals from it; <sup>18</sup>though these three men were in it, as I live, says the Lord God, they would save neither sons nor daughters, but they alone would be saved. <sup>19</sup>Or if I send a pestilence into that land, and pour out my wrath upon it with blood, to cut off humans and animals from it; <sup>20</sup>even if Noah, Daniel, a and Job were in it, as I live, says the Lord God, they would save neither son nor daughter; they would save only their own lives by their righteousness.

21 For thus says the Lord God: How much more when I send upon Jerusalem my four deadly acts of judgment, sword, famine, wild animals, and pestilence, to cut off humans and animals from it! <sup>22</sup>Yet, survivors shall be left in it, sons and daughters who will be brought out; they will come out to you. When you see their ways and their deeds, you will be consoled for the evil that I have brought upon Jerusalem, for all that I have brought upon it. <sup>23</sup>They shall console you, when you see their ways and their deeds; and you shall know that it was not without cause that I did all that I have done in it, says the Lord God.


<sup>15.1</sup> The word of the Lord came to me:

<sup>2</sup>  O mortal, how does the wood of
      the vine surpass all
      other wood—
   the vine branch that is among
      the trees of the forest?
<sup>3</sup>  Is wood taken from it to make
      anything?
   Does one take a peg from it

on which to hang any
      object?
<sup>4</sup>  It is put in the fire for fuel;
   when the fire has consumed
      both ends of it
   and the middle of it is
      charred,
   is it useful for anything?
<sup>5</sup>  When it was whole it was used
      for nothing;
   how much less—when the
      fire has consumed it,
   and it is charred—
   can it ever be used for
      anything!

6 Therefore thus says the Lord God: Like the wood of the vine among the trees of the forest, which I have given to the fire for fuel, so I will give up the inhabitants of Jerusalem. <sup>7</sup>I will set my face against them; although they escape from the fire, the fire shall still consume them; and you shall know that I am the Lord, when I set my face against them. <sup>8</sup>And I will make the land desolate, because they have acted faithlessly, says the Lord God.


<sup>16.1</sup> The word of the Lord came to me: <sup>2</sup>Mortal, make known to Jerusalem her abominations, <sup>3</sup>and say, Thus says the Lord God to Jerusalem: Your origin and your birth were in the land of the Canaanites; your father was an Amorite, and your mother a Hittite. <sup>4</sup>As for your birth, on the day you were born your navel cord was not cut, nor were you washed with water to cleanse you, nor rubbed with salt, nor wrapped in cloths. <sup>5</sup>No eye pitied you, to do any of these things for you out of compassion for you; but you were thrown out in the open field, for you were abhorred on the day you were born.

6 I passed by you, and saw you flailing about in your blood. As you lay in your blood, I said to you, "Live! <sup>7</sup>and

---

a Or, as otherwise read, *Danel*

grow up[a] like a plant of the field." You grew up and became tall and arrived at full womanhood;[b] your breasts were formed, and your hair had grown; yet you were naked and bare.

8  I passed by you again and looked on you; you were at the age for love. I spread the edge of my cloak over you, and covered your nakedness: I pledged myself to you and entered into a covenant with you, says the Lord God, and you became mine. [9]Then I bathed you with water and washed off the blood from you, and anointed you with oil. [10]I clothed you with embroidered cloth and with sandals of fine leather; I bound you in fine linen and covered you with rich fabric.[c] [11]I adorned you with ornaments: I put bracelets on your arms, a chain on your neck, [12]a ring on your nose, earrings in your ears, and a beautiful crown upon your head. [13]You were adorned with gold and silver, while your clothing was of fine linen, rich fabric,[c] and embroidered cloth. You had choice flour and honey and oil for food. You grew exceedingly beautiful, fit to be a queen. [14]Your fame spread among the nations on account of your beauty, for it was perfect because of my splendor that I had bestowed on you, says the Lord God.

15  But you trusted in your beauty, and played the whore because of your fame, and lavished your whorings on any passer-by.[d] [16]You took some of your garments, and made for yourself colorful shrines, and on them played the whore; nothing like this has ever been or ever shall be.[c] [17]You also took your beautiful jewels of my gold and my silver that I had given you, and made for yourself male images, and with them played the whore; [18]and you took your embroidered garments to cover them, and set my oil and my incense before them. [19]Also my bread that I gave you—I fed you with choice flour and oil and honey—you set it before them as a pleasing odor; and so it was, says the Lord God. [20]You took your sons and your daughters, whom you had borne to me, and these you sacrificed to them to be devoured. As if your whorings were not enough! [21]You slaughtered my children and delivered them up as an offering to them. [22]And in all your abominations and your whorings you did not remember the days of your youth, when you were naked and bare, flailing about in your blood.

23  After all your wickedness (woe, woe to you! says the Lord God), [24]you built yourself a platform and made yourself a lofty place in every square; [25]at the head of every street you built your lofty place and prostituted your beauty, offering yourself to every passer-by, and multiplying your whoring. [26]You played the whore with the Egyptians, your lustful neighbors, multiplying your whoring, to provoke me to anger. [27]Therefore I stretched out my hand against you, reduced your rations, and gave you up to the will of your enemies, the daughters of the Philistines, who were ashamed of your lewd behavior. [28]You played the whore with the Assyrians, because you were insatiable; you played the whore with them, and still you were not satisfied. [29]You multiplied your whoring with Chaldea, the land of merchants; and even with this you were not satisfied.

30  How sick is your heart, says the Lord God, that you did all these things, the deeds of a brazen whore; [31]building your platform at the head of every street, and making your lofty place in every square! Yet you were not like a whore, because you scorned payment. [32]Adulterous wife, who receives strangers instead of her husband! [33]Gifts are given to all whores; but you gave your gifts to all your lovers, bribing them to come to you from all around

[a]Gk Syr: Heb *Live! I made you a myriad*  [b]Cn: Heb *ornament of ornaments*  [c]Meaning of Heb uncertain  [d]Heb adds *let it be his*

for your whorings. ³⁴So you were different from other women in your whorings: no one solicited you to play the whore; and you gave payment, while no payment was given to you; you were different.

35 Therefore, O whore, hear the word of the LORD: ³⁶Thus says the Lord GOD, Because your lust was poured out and your nakedness uncovered in your whoring with your lovers, and because of all your abominable idols, and because of the blood of your children that you gave to them, ³⁷therefore, I will gather all your lovers, with whom you took pleasure, all those you loved and all those you hated; I will gather them against you from all around, and will uncover your nakedness to them, so that they may see all your nakedness. ³⁸I will judge you as women who commit adultery and shed blood are judged, and bring blood upon you in wrath and jealousy. ³⁹I will deliver you into their hands, and they shall throw down your platform and break down your lofty places; they shall strip you of your clothes and take your beautiful objects and leave you naked and bare. ⁴⁰They shall bring up a mob against you, and they shall stone you and cut you to pieces with their swords. ⁴¹They shall burn your houses and execute judgments on you in the sight of many women; I will stop you from playing the whore, and you shall also make no more payments. ⁴²So I will satisfy my fury on you, and my jealousy shall turn away from you; I will be calm, and will be angry no longer. ⁴³Because you have not remembered the days of your youth, but have enraged me with all these things; therefore, I have returned your deeds upon your head, says the Lord GOD.

## HEBREWS 7.18–28

THERE is, on the one hand, the abrogation of an earlier commandment because it was weak and ineffectual ¹⁹(for the law made nothing perfect); there is, on the other hand, the introduction of a better hope, through which we approach God.

20 This was confirmed with an oath; for others who became priests took their office without an oath, ²¹but this one became a priest with an oath, because of the one who said to him,

"The Lord has sworn
　and will not change his mind,
'You are a priest forever' "—
²²accordingly Jesus has also become the guarantee of a better covenant.

23 Furthermore, the former priests were many in number, because they were prevented by death from continuing in office; ²⁴but he holds his priesthood permanently, because he continues forever. ²⁵Consequently he is able for all time to save[a] those who approach God through him, since he always lives to make intercession for them.

26 For it was fitting that we should have such a high priest, holy, blameless, undefiled, separated from sinners, and exalted above the heavens. ²⁷Unlike the other[b] high priests, he has no need to offer sacrifices day after day, first for his own sins, and then for those of the people; this he did once for all when he offered himself. ²⁸For the law appoints as high priests those who are subject to weakness, but the word of the oath, which came later than the law, appoints a Son who has been made perfect forever.

[a] Or *able to save completely*　[b] Gk lacks *other*

## PSALM 106.1–12

**P**RAISE the LORD!
O give thanks to the LORD,
     for he is good;
  for his steadfast love endures
     forever.
2  Who can utter the mighty
     doings of the LORD,
  or declare all his praise?
3  Happy are those who observe
     justice,
  who do righteousness at all
     times.

4  Remember me, O LORD, when
     you show favor to your
     people;
  help me when you deliver
     them;
5  that I may see the prosperity of
     your chosen ones,
  that I may rejoice in the
     gladness of your nation,
  that I may glory in your
     heritage.

6  Both we and our ancestors have
     sinned;
  we have committed iniquity,
     have done wickedly.
7  Our ancestors, when they were
     in Egypt,
  did not consider your
     wonderful works;
  they did not remember the
     abundance of your
     steadfast love,
  but rebelled against the Most
     High[a] at the Red Sea.[b]
8  Yet he saved them for his
     name's sake,
  so that he might make known
     his mighty power.
9  He rebuked the Red Sea,[b] and
     it became dry;
  he led them through the deep
     as through a desert.
10  So he saved them from the hand
     of the foe,
  and delivered them from the
     hand of the enemy.
11  The waters covered their
     adversaries;
  not one of them was left.
12  Then they believed his words;
  they sang his praise.

## PROVERBS 27.4–6

**W**RATH is cruel, anger is
     overwhelming,
  but who is able to stand
     before jealousy?
5  Better is open rebuke
  than hidden love.
6  Well meant are the wounds a
     friend inflicts,
  but profuse are the kisses of
     an enemy.

**a** Cn Compare 78.17, 56: Heb *rebelled at the sea*   **b** Or *Sea of Reeds*

## EZEKIEL 16.43b—17.24

Have you not committed lewdness beyond all your abominations? [44]See, everyone who uses proverbs will use this proverb about you, "Like mother, like daughter." [45]You are the daughter of your mother, who loathed her husband and her children; and you are the sister of your sisters, who loathed their husbands and their children. Your mother was a Hittite and your father an Amorite. [46]Your elder sister is Samaria, who lived with her daughters to the north of you; and your younger sister, who lived to the south of you, is Sodom with her daughters. [47]You not only followed their ways, and acted according to their abominations; within a very little time you were more corrupt than they in all your ways. [48]As I live, says the Lord God, your sister Sodom and her daughters have not done as you and your daughters have done. [49]This was the guilt of your sister Sodom: she and her daughters had pride, excess of food, and prosperous ease, but did not aid the poor and needy. [50]They were haughty, and did abominable things before me; therefore I removed them when I saw it. [51]Samaria has not committed half your sins; you have committed more abominations than they, and have made your sisters appear righteous by all the abominations that you have committed. [52]Bear your disgrace, you also, for you have brought about for your sisters a more favorable judgment; because of your sins in which you acted more abominably than they, they are more in the right than you. So be ashamed, you also, and bear your disgrace, for you have made your sisters appear righteous.

53  I will restore their fortunes, the fortunes of Sodom and her daughters and the fortunes of Samaria and her daughters, and I will restore your own fortunes along with theirs, [54]in order that you may bear your disgrace and be ashamed of all that you have done, becoming a consolation to them. [55]As for your sisters, Sodom and her daughters shall return to their former state, Samaria and her daughters shall return to their former state, and you and your daughters shall return to your former state. [56]Was not your sister Sodom a byword in your mouth in the day of your pride, [57]before your wickedness was uncovered? Now you are a mockery to the daughters of Aram[a] and all her neighbors, and to the daughters of the Philistines, those all around who despise you. [58]You must bear the penalty of your lewdness and your abominations, says the Lord.

59  Yes, thus says the Lord God: I will deal with you as you have done, you who have despised the oath, breaking the covenant; [60]yet I will remember my covenant with you in the days of your youth, and I will establish with you an everlasting covenant. [61]Then you will remember your ways, and be ashamed when I[b] take your sisters, both your elder and your younger, and give them to you as daughters, but not on account of my[c] covenant with you. [62]I will establish my covenant with you, and you shall know that I am the Lord, [63]in order that you may remember and be confounded, and never open your mouth again because of your shame,

---

[a]Another reading is *Edom*  [b]Syr: Heb *you*  [c]Heb lacks *my*

when I forgive you all that you have done, says the Lord GOD.

**17.1** THE word of the LORD came to me: <sup>2</sup>O mortal, propound a riddle, and speak an allegory to the house of Israel. <sup>3</sup>Say: Thus says the Lord GOD:
A great eagle, with great wings
      and long pinions,
  rich in plumage of many
      colors,
  came to the Lebanon.
He took the top of the cedar,
<sup>4</sup>    broke off its topmost shoot;
He carried it to a land of trade,
  set it in a city of merchants.
<sup>5</sup> Then he took a seed from the
      land,
  placed it in fertile soil;
A plant[a] by abundant waters,
  he set it like a willow twig.
<sup>6</sup> It sprouted and became a vine
  spreading out, but low;
Its branches turned toward him,
  its roots remained where it
      stood.
So it became a vine;
  it brought forth branches,
  put forth foliage.

<sup>7</sup> There was another great eagle,
  with great wings and much
      plumage.
And see! This vine stretched
      out
  its roots toward him;
It shot out its branches toward
      him,
  so that he might water it.
From the bed where it was
      planted
<sup>8</sup>    it was transplanted
  to good soil by abundant waters,
    so that it might produce
      branches
    and bear fruit
    and become a noble vine.
<sup>9</sup>Say: Thus says the Lord GOD:

Will it prosper?
Will he not pull up its roots,
  cause its fruit to rot[a] and
      wither,
  its fresh sprouting leaves to
      fade?
No strong arm or mighty army
    will be needed
  to pull it from its roots.
<sup>10</sup>  When it is transplanted, will
    it thrive?
When the east wind strikes it,
  will it not utterly wither,
  wither on the bed where
    it grew?

11 Then the word of the LORD came to me: <sup>12</sup>Say now to the rebellious house: Do you not know what these things mean? Tell them: The king of Babylon came to Jerusalem, took its king and its officials, and brought them back with him to Babylon. <sup>13</sup>He took one of the royal offspring and made a covenant with him, putting him under oath (he had taken away the chief men of the land), <sup>14</sup>so that the kingdom might be humble and not lift itself up, and that by keeping his covenant it might stand. <sup>15</sup>But he rebelled against him by sending ambassadors to Egypt, in order that they might give him horses and a large army. Will he succeed? Can one escape who does such things? Can he break the covenant and yet escape? <sup>16</sup>As I live, says the Lord GOD, surely in the place where the king resides who made him king, whose oath he despised, and whose covenant with him he broke—in Babylon he shall die. <sup>17</sup>Pharaoh with his mighty army and great company will not help him in war, when ramps are cast up and siege walls built to cut off many lives. <sup>18</sup>Because he despised the oath and broke the covenant, because he gave his hand and yet did all these things, he shall not escape. <sup>19</sup>Therefore thus says the Lord GOD: As I live, I will surely return upon

[a] Meaning of Heb uncertain

his head my oath that he despised, and my covenant that he broke. [20]I will spread my net over him, and he shall be caught in my snare; I will bring him to Babylon and enter into judgment with him there for the treason he has committed against me. [21]All the pick[a] of his troops shall fall by the sword, and the survivors shall be scattered to every wind; and you shall know that I, the LORD, have spoken.

22  Thus says the Lord GOD:
   I myself will take a sprig
      from the lofty top of a cedar;
      I will set it out.
   I will break off a tender one
      from the topmost of its
         young twigs;
   I myself will plant it
      on a high and lofty mountain.
23  On the mountain height of Israel
      I will plant it,
   in order that it may produce
         boughs and bear fruit,
      and become a noble cedar.
   Under it every kind of bird
      will live;
      in the shade of its branches
         will nest
      winged creatures of every
         kind.
24  All the trees of the field shall
      know
      that I am the LORD.
   I bring low the high tree,
      I make high the low tree;
   I dry up the green tree
      and make the dry tree
         flourish.
   I the LORD have spoken;
      I will accomplish it.

# HEBREWS 8.1–13

Now the main point in what we are saying is this: we have such a high priest, one who is seated at the right hand of the throne of the Majesty in the heavens, [2]a minister in the sanctuary and the true tent[b] that the Lord, and not any mortal, has set up. [3]For every high priest is appointed to offer gifts and sacrifices; hence it is necessary for this priest also to have something to offer. [4]Now if he were on earth, he would not be a priest at all, since there are priests who offer gifts according to the law. [5]They offer worship in a sanctuary that is a sketch and shadow of the heavenly one; for Moses, when he was about to erect the tent,[b] was warned, "See that you make everything according to the pattern that was shown you on the mountain." [6]But Jesus[c] has now obtained a more excellent ministry, and to that degree he is the mediator of a better covenant, which has been enacted through better promises. [7]For if that first covenant had been faultless, there would have been no need to look for a second one.

8  God[d] finds fault with them when he says:
   "The days are surely coming,
      says the Lord,
   when I will establish a new
         covenant with the house
         of Israel
   and with the house of Judah;
9   not like the covenant that I
         made with their
         ancestors,
   on the day when I took them
         by the hand to lead them
         out of the land of Egypt;
   for they did not continue in
         my covenant,
   and so I had no concern for
         them, says the Lord.
10  This is the covenant that I will
         make with the house
         of Israel
   after those days, says the
         Lord:
   I will put my laws in their
         minds,

and write them on their
   hearts,
and I will be their God,
   and they shall be my people.
11 And they shall not teach
   one another
   or say to each other, 'Know
    the Lord,'
for they shall all know me,
   from the least of them to
   the greatest.
12 For I will be merciful toward
   their iniquities,
   and I will remember their sins
   no more."

13In speaking of "a new covenant," he has made the first one obsolete. And what is obsolete and growing old will soon disappear.

## PSALM 106.13–31

Bᴜᴛ they soon forgot his
   works;
   they did not wait for his
   counsel.
14 But they had a wanton craving
   in the wilderness,
   and put God to the test in the
   desert;
15 he gave them what they asked,
   but sent a wasting disease
   among them.

16 They were jealous of Moses in
   the camp,
   and of Aaron, the holy one of
   the Lᴏʀᴅ.
17 The earth opened and
   swallowed up Dathan,
   and covered the faction of
   Abiram.
18 Fire also broke out in their
   company;
   the flame burned up the
   wicked.

19 They made a calf at Horeb
   and worshiped a cast image.
20 They exchanged the glory of
   Godᵃ
   for the image of an ox that
   eats grass.
21 They forgot God, their Savior,
   who had done great things in
   Egypt,
22 wondrous works in the land of
   Ham,
   and awesome deeds by the
   Red Sea. ᵇ
23 Therefore he said he would
   destroy them—
   had not Moses, his chosen
   one,
stood in the breach before him,
   to turn away his wrath from
   destroying them.

24 Then they despised the pleasant
   land,
   having no faith in his promise.
25 They grumbled in their tents,
   and did not obey the voice of
   the Lᴏʀᴅ.
26 Therefore he raised his hand
   and swore to them
   that he would make them fall
   in the wilderness,
27 and would disperseᶜ their
   descendants among the
   nations,
   scattering them over the
   lands.

28 Then they attached themselves
   to the Baal of Peor,
   and ate sacrifices offered to
   the dead;
29 they provoked the Lᴏʀᴅ to
   anger with their deeds,
   and a plague broke out among
   them.
30 Then Phinehas stood up and
   interceded,
   and the plague was stopped.

ᵃCompare Gk Mss: Heb *exchanged their glory*  ᵇOr *Sea of Reeds*  ᶜSyr Compare Ezek 20.23: Heb *cause to fall*

<sup>31</sup> And that has been reckoned to
      him as righteousness
    from generation to generation
      forever.

## PROVERBS 27.7–9

THE sated appetite spurns
      honey,
but to a ravenous appetite
    even the bitter is sweet.

<sup>8</sup> Like a bird that strays from
      its nest
    is one who strays from home.
<sup>9</sup> Perfume and incense make the
      heart glad,
    but the soul is torn by
      trouble. [a]

# NOVEMBER 8

## EZEKIEL 18.1—19.14

THE word of the LORD came to me: <sup>2</sup>What do you mean by repeating this proverb concerning the land of Israel, "The parents have eaten sour grapes, and the children's teeth are set on edge"? <sup>3</sup>As I live, says the Lord GOD, this proverb shall no more be used by you in Israel. <sup>4</sup>Know that all lives are mine; the life of the parent as well as the life of the child is mine: it is only the person who sins that shall die.

5 If a man is righteous and does what is lawful and right— <sup>6</sup>if he does not eat upon the mountains or lift up his eyes to the idols of the house of Israel, does not defile his neighbor's wife or approach a woman during her menstrual period, <sup>7</sup>does not oppress anyone, but restores to the debtor his pledge, commits no robbery, gives his bread to the hungry and covers the naked with a garment, <sup>8</sup>does not take advance or accrued interest, withholds his hand from iniquity, executes true justice between contending parties, <sup>9</sup>follows my statutes, and is careful to observe my ordinances, acting faithfully—such a one is righteous; he shall surely live, says the Lord GOD.

10 If he has a son who is violent, a shedder of blood, <sup>11</sup>who does any of these things (though his father[b] does none of them), who eats upon the mountains, defiles his neighbor's wife, <sup>12</sup>oppresses the poor and needy, commits robbery, does not restore the pledge, lifts up his eyes to the idols, commits abomination, <sup>13</sup>takes advance or accrued interest; shall he then live? He shall not. He has done all these abominable things; he shall surely die; his blood shall be upon himself.

14 But if this man has a son who sees all the sins that his father has done, considers, and does not do likewise, <sup>15</sup>who does not eat upon the mountains or lift up his eyes to the idols of the house of Israel, does not defile his neighbor's wife, <sup>16</sup>does not wrong anyone, exacts no pledge, commits no robbery, but gives his bread to the hungry and covers the naked with a garment, <sup>17</sup>withholds his hand from iniquity,[c] takes no advance or accrued interest, observes my ordinances, and

follows my statutes; he shall not die for his father's iniquity; he shall surely live. [18]As for his father, because he practiced extortion, robbed his brother, and did what is not good among his people, he dies for his iniquity.

19 Yet you say, "Why should not the son suffer for the iniquity of the father?" When the son has done what is lawful and right, and has been careful to observe all my statutes, he shall surely live. [20]The person who sins shall die. A child shall not suffer for the iniquity of a parent, nor a parent suffer for the iniquity of a child; the righteousness of the righteous shall be his own, and the wickedness of the wicked shall be his own.

21 But if the wicked turn away from all their sins that they have committed and keep all my statutes and do what is lawful and right, they shall surely live; they shall not die. [22]None of the transgressions that they have committed shall be remembered against them; for the righteousness that they have done they shall live. [23]Have I any pleasure in the death of the wicked, says the Lord God, and not rather that they should turn from their ways and live? [24]But when the righteous turn away from their righteousness and commit iniquity and do the same abominable things that the wicked do, shall they live? None of the righteous deeds that they have done shall be remembered; for the treachery of which they are guilty and the sin they have committed, they shall die.

25 Yet you say, "The way of the Lord is unfair." Hear now, O house of Israel: Is my way unfair? Is it not your ways that are unfair? [26]When the righteous turn away from their righteousness and commit iniquity, they shall die for it; for the iniquity that they have committed they shall die. [27]Again, when the wicked turn away from the wickedness they have committed and do what is lawful and right, they shall save their life. [28]Because they considered and turned away from all the transgressions that they had committed, they shall surely live; they shall not die. [29]Yet the house of Israel says, "The way of the Lord is unfair." O house of Israel, are my ways unfair? Is it not your ways that are unfair?

30 Therefore I will judge you, O house of Israel, all of you according to your ways, says the Lord God. Repent and turn from all your transgressions; otherwise iniquity will be your ruin. [a] [31]Cast away from you all the transgressions that you have committed against me, and get yourselves a new heart and a new spirit! Why will you die, O house of Israel? [32]For I have no pleasure in the death of anyone, says the Lord God. Turn, then, and live.

[19.1] As for you, raise up a lamentation for the princes of Israel, [2]and say:
> What a lioness was your mother
>     among lions!
> She lay down among young
>     lions,
>     rearing her cubs.
> [3] She raised up one of her cubs;
>     he became a young lion,
> and he learned to catch prey;
>     he devoured humans.
> [4] The nations sounded an alarm
>     against him;
>     he was caught in their pit;
> and they brought him with
>     hooks
>     to the land of Egypt.
> [5] When she saw that she was
>     thwarted,
>     that her hope was lost,
> she took another of her cubs
>     and made him a young lion.
> [6] He prowled among the lions;

---

he became a young lion,
    and he learned to catch prey;
    he devoured people.
7 And he ravaged their
    strongholds, a
    and laid waste their towns;
    the land was appalled, and all in
      it,
    at the sound of his roaring.
8 The nations set upon him
    from the provinces all around;
    they spread their net over him;
    he was caught in their pit.
9 With hooks they put him in a
    cage,
    and brought him to the king
      of Babylon;
    they brought him into
      custody,
    so that his voice should be
      heard no more
    on the mountains of Israel.
10 Your mother was like a vine in
    a vineyard b
    transplanted by the water,
    fruitful and full of branches
    from abundant water.
11 Its strongest stem became
    a ruler's scepter; c
    it towered aloft
    among the thick boughs;
    it stood out in its height
    with its mass of branches.
12 But it was plucked up in fury,
    cast down to the ground;
    the east wind dried it up;
    its fruit was stripped off,
    its strong stem was withered;
    the fire consumed it.
13 Now it is transplanted into
    the wilderness,
    into a dry and thirsty land.
14 And fire has gone out from
    its stem,
    has consumed its branches
    and fruit,
    so that there remains in it no
    strong stem,

no scepter for ruling.
This is a lamentation, and it is used as a lamentation.

## HEBREWS 9.1–10

Now even the first covenant had regulations for worship and an earthly sanctuary. ²For a tent d was constructed, the first one, in which were the lampstand, the table, and the bread of the Presence; e this is called the Holy Place. ³Behind the second curtain was a tent d called the Holy of Holies. ⁴In it stood the golden altar of incense and the ark of the covenant overlaid on all sides with gold, in which there were a golden urn holding the manna, and Aaron's rod that budded, and the tablets of the covenant; ⁵above it were the cherubim of glory overshadowing the mercy seat. f Of these things we cannot speak now in detail.

6 Such preparations having been made, the priests go continually into the first tent d to carry out their ritual duties; ⁷but only the high priest goes into the second, and he but once a year, and not without taking the blood that he offers for himself and for the sins committed unintentionally by the people. ⁸By this the Holy Spirit indicates that the way into the sanctuary has not yet been disclosed as long as the first tent d is still standing. ⁹This is a symbol g of the present time, during which gifts and sacrifices are offered that cannot perfect the conscience of the worshiper, ¹⁰but deal only with food and drink and various baptisms, regulations for the body imposed until the time comes to set things right.

a Heb *his widows*  b Cn: Heb *in your blood*  c Heb *Its strongest stems became rulers' scepters*
d Or *tabernacle*  e Gk *the presentation of the loaves*  f Or *the place of atonement*  g Gk *parable*

## PSALM 106.32–48

**T**HEY angered the LORD [a] at the
    waters of Meribah,
  and it went ill with Moses on
    their account;
33 for they made his spirit bitter,
  and he spoke words that
    were rash.

34 They did not destroy the
    peoples,
  as the LORD commanded
    them,
35 but they mingled with the
    nations
  and learned to do as they did.
36 They served their idols,
  which became a snare to
    them.
37 They sacrificed their sons
  and their daughters to the
    demons;
38 they poured out innocent blood,
  the blood of their sons and
    daughters,
  whom they sacrificed to the
    idols of Canaan;
  and the land was polluted with
    blood.
39 Thus they became unclean by
    their acts,
  and prostituted themselves in
    their doings.

40 Then the anger of the LORD was
    kindled against his
    people,
  and he abhorred his heritage;
41 he gave them into the hand of
    the nations,
  so that those who hated them
    ruled over them.
42 Their enemies oppressed them,
  and they were brought into
    subjection under their
    power.

43 Many times he delivered them,
  but they were rebellious in
    their purposes,
  and were brought low through
    their iniquity.
44 Nevertheless he regarded their
    distress
  when he heard their cry.
45 For their sake he remembered
    his covenant,
  and showed compassion
    according to the
    abundance of his
    steadfast love.
46 He caused them to be pitied
  by all who held them captive.

47 Save us, O LORD our God,
  and gather us from among the
    nations,
  that we may give thanks to your
    holy name
  and glory in your praise.

48 Blessed be the LORD, the God
    of Israel,
  from everlasting to
    everlasting.
  And let all the people say,
    "Amen."
  Praise the LORD!

## PROVERBS 27.10

**D**o not forsake your friend or
    the friend of your
    parent;
  do not go to the house of
    your kindred in the day
    of your calamity.
  Better is a neighbor who is
    nearby
  than kindred who are far
    away.

a Heb *him*

## EZEKIEL 20.1–49

In the seventh year, in the fifth month, on the tenth day of the month, certain elders of Israel came to consult the LORD, and sat down before me. ²And the word of the LORD came to me: ³Mortal, speak to the elders of Israel, and say to them: Thus says the Lord GOD: Why are you coming? To consult me? As I live, says the Lord GOD, I will not be consulted by you. ⁴Will you judge them, mortal, will you judge them? Then let them know the abominations of their ancestors, ⁵and say to them: Thus says the Lord GOD: On the day when I chose Israel, I swore to the offspring of the house of Jacob—making myself known to them in the land of Egypt—I swore to them, saying, I am the LORD your God. ⁶On that day I swore to them that I would bring them out of the land of Egypt into a land that I had searched out for them, a land flowing with milk and honey, the most glorious of all lands. ⁷And I said to them, Cast away the detestable things your eyes feast on, every one of you, and do not defile yourselves with the idols of Egypt; I am the LORD your God. ⁸But they rebelled against me and would not listen to me; not one of them cast away the detestable things their eyes feasted on, nor did they forsake the idols of Egypt.

Then I thought I would pour out my wrath upon them and spend my anger against them in the midst of the land of Egypt. ⁹But I acted for the sake of my name, that it should not be profaned in the sight of the nations among whom they lived, in whose sight I made myself known to them in bringing them out of the land of Egypt. ¹⁰So I led them out of the land of Egypt and brought them into the wilderness. ¹¹I gave them my statutes and showed them my ordinances, by whose observance everyone shall live. ¹²Moreover I gave them my sabbaths, as a sign between me and them, so that they might know that I the LORD sanctify them. ¹³But the house of Israel rebelled against me in the wilderness; they did not observe my statutes but rejected my ordinances, by whose observance everyone shall live; and my sabbaths they greatly profaned.

Then I thought I would pour out my wrath upon them in the wilderness, to make an end of them. ¹⁴But I acted for the sake of my name, so that it should not be profaned in the sight of the nations, in whose sight I had brought them out. ¹⁵Moreover I swore to them in the wilderness that I would not bring them into the land that I had given them, a land flowing with milk and honey, the most glorious of all lands, ¹⁶because they rejected my ordinances and did not observe my statutes, and profaned my sabbaths; for their heart went after their idols. ¹⁷Nevertheless my eye spared them, and I did not destroy them or make an end of them in the wilderness.

18   I said to their children in the wilderness, Do not follow the statutes of your parents, nor observe their ordinances, nor defile yourselves with their idols. ¹⁹I the LORD am your God; follow my statutes, and be careful to observe my ordinances, ²⁰and hallow my sabbaths that they may be a sign between me and you, so that you may know that I the LORD am your God. ²¹But the children rebelled against me; they did not follow my statutes, and were not careful to observe my ordinances, by whose observance everyone shall live; they profaned my sabbaths.

Then I thought I would pour out my wrath upon them and spend my anger against them in the wilderness. 22But I withheld my hand, and acted for the sake of my name, so that it should not be profaned in the sight of the nations, in whose sight I had brought them out. 23Moreover I swore to them in the wilderness that I would scatter them among the nations and disperse them through the countries, 24because they had not executed my ordinances, but had rejected my statutes and profaned my sabbaths, and their eyes were set on their ancestors' idols. 25Moreover I gave them statutes that were not good and ordinances by which they could not live. 26I defiled them through their very gifts, in their offering up all their first-born, in order that I might horrify them, so that they might know that I am the LORD.

27 Therefore, mortal, speak to the house of Israel and say to them, Thus says the Lord GOD: In this again your ancestors blasphemed me, by dealing treacherously with me. 28For when I had brought them into the land that I swore to give them, then wherever they saw any high hill or any leafy tree, there they offered their sacrifices and presented the provocation of their offering; there they sent up their pleasing odors, and there they poured out their drink offerings. 29(I said to them, What is the high place to which you go? So it is called Bamah<sup>a</sup> to this day.) 30Therefore say to the house of Israel, Thus says the Lord GOD: Will you defile yourselves after the manner of your ancestors and go astray after their detestable things? 31When you offer your gifts and make your children pass through the fire, you defile yourselves with all your idols to this day. And shall I be consulted by you, O house of Israel? As I live, says the Lord GOD, I will not be consulted by you.

32 What is in your mind shall never happen—the thought, "Let us be like the nations, like the tribes of the countries, and worship wood and stone."

33 As I live, says the Lord GOD, surely with a mighty hand and an outstretched arm, and with wrath poured out, I will be king over you. 34I will bring you out from the peoples and gather you out of the countries where you are scattered, with a mighty hand and an outstretched arm, and with wrath poured out; 35and I will bring you into the wilderness of the peoples, and there I will enter into judgment with you face to face. 36As I entered into judgment with your ancestors in the wilderness of the land of Egypt, so I will enter into judgment with you, says the Lord GOD. 37I will make you pass under the staff, and will bring you within the bond of the covenant. 38I will purge out the rebels among you, and those who transgress against me; I will bring them out of the land where they reside as aliens, but they shall not enter the land of Israel. Then you shall know that I am the LORD.

39 As for you, O house of Israel, thus says the Lord GOD: Go serve your idols, everyone of you now and hereafter, if you will not listen to me; but my holy name you shall no more profane with your gifts and your idols.

40 For on my holy mountain, the mountain height of Israel, says the Lord GOD, there all the house of Israel, all of them, shall serve me in the land; there I will accept them, and there I will require your contributions and the choicest of your gifts, with all your sacred things. 41As a pleasing odor I will accept you, when I bring you out from the peoples, and gather you out of the countries where you have been scattered; and I will manifest my holiness among you in the sight of the nations. 42You shall know that I am the LORD,

---

<sup>a</sup> That is *High Place*

when I bring you into the land of Israel, the country that I swore to give to your ancestors. [43]There you shall remember your ways and all the deeds by which you have polluted yourselves; and you shall loathe yourselves for all the evils that you have committed. [44]And you shall know that I am the LORD, when I deal with you for my name's sake, not according to your evil ways, or corrupt deeds, O house of Israel, says the Lord GOD.

45[a] The word of the LORD came to me: [46]Mortal, set your face toward the south, preach against the south, and prophesy against the forest land in the Negeb; [47]say to the forest of the Negeb, Hear the word of the LORD: Thus says the Lord GOD, I will kindle a fire in you, and it shall devour every green tree in you and every dry tree; the blazing flame shall not be quenched, and all faces from south to north shall be scorched by it. [48]All flesh shall see that I the LORD have kindled it; it shall not be quenched. [49]Then I said, "Ah Lord GOD! they are saying of me, 'Is he not a maker of allegories?' "

## HEBREWS 9.11–28

**B**UT when Christ came as a high priest of the good things that have come, [b] then through the greater and perfect[c] tent[d] (not made with hands, that is, not of this creation), [12]he entered once for all into the Holy Place, not with the blood of goats and calves, but with his own blood, thus obtaining eternal redemption. [13]For if the blood of goats and bulls, with the sprinkling of the ashes of a heifer, sanctifies those who have been defiled so that their flesh is purified, [14]how much more will the blood of Christ, who through the eternal Spirit[e] offered himself without blemish to God, purify our[f] conscience from dead works to worship the living God!

15  For this reason he is the mediator of a new covenant, so that those who are called may receive the promised eternal inheritance, because a death has occurred that redeems them from the transgressions under the first covenant.[g]  [16]Where a will[g] is involved, the death of the one who made it must be established. [17]For a will[g] takes effect only at death, since it is not in force as long as the one who made it is alive. [18]Hence not even the first covenant was inaugurated without blood. [19]For when every commandment had been told to all the people by Moses in accordance with the law, he took the blood of calves and goats,[h] with water and scarlet wool and hyssop, and sprinkled both the scroll itself and all the people, [20]saying, "This is the blood of the covenant that God has ordained for you." [21]And in the same way he sprinkled with the blood both the tent[d] and all the vessels used in worship. [22]Indeed, under the law almost everything is purified with blood, and without the shedding of blood there is no forgiveness of sins.

23  Thus it was necessary for the sketches of the heavenly things to be purified with these rites, but the heavenly things themselves need better sacrifices than these. [24]For Christ did not enter a sanctuary made by human hands, a mere copy of the true one, but he entered into heaven itself, now to appear in the presence of God on our behalf. [25]Nor was it to offer himself again and again, as the high priest enters the Holy Place year after year with blood that is not his own; [26]for then he would have had to suffer again and again since the foundation of the world.

aCh 21.1 in Heb   bOther ancient authorities read *good things to come*   cGk *more perfect*
dOr *tabernacle*   eOther ancient authorities read *Holy Spirit*   fOther ancient authorities read *your*
gThe Greek word used here means both *covenant* and *will*   hOther ancient authorities lack *and goats*

But as it is, he has appeared once for all at the end of the age to remove sin by the sacrifice of himself. ²⁷And just as it is appointed for mortals to die once, and after that the judgment, ²⁸so Christ, having been offered once to bear the sins of many, will appear a second time, not to deal with sin, but to save those who are eagerly waiting for him.

## PSALM 107.1–43

O GIVE thanks to the LORD, for
    he is good;
for his steadfast love
    endures forever.
2  Let the redeemed of the LORD
        say so,
    those he redeemed from
        trouble
3  and gathered in from the lands,
    from the east and from the
        west,
    from the north and from the
        south. ᵃ

4  Some wandered in desert
        wastes,
    finding no way to an inhabited
        town;
5  hungry and thirsty,
    their soul fainted within them.
6  Then they cried to the LORD in
        their trouble,
    and he delivered them from
        their distress;
7  he led them by a straight way,
    until they reached an
        inhabited town.
8  Let them thank the LORD for his
        steadfast love,
    for his wonderful works to
        humankind.
9  For he satisfies the thirsty,
    and the hungry he fills with
        good things.

10  Some sat in darkness and in
        gloom,
    prisoners in misery and in
        irons,
11  for they had rebelled against the
        words of God,
    and spurned the counsel of
        the Most High.
12  Their hearts were bowed down
        with hard labor;
    they fell down, with no one
        to help.
13  Then they cried to the LORD in
        their trouble,
    and he saved them from their
        distress;
14  he brought them out of
        darkness and gloom,
    and broke their bonds
        asunder.
15  Let them thank the LORD for his
        steadfast love,
    for his wonderful works to
        humankind.
16  For he shatters the doors of
        bronze,
    and cuts in two the bars of
        iron.

17  Some were sickᵇ through their
        sinful ways,
    and because of their iniquities
        endured affliction;
18  they loathed any kind of food,
    and they drew near to the
        gates of death.
19  Then they cried to the LORD in
        their trouble,
    and he saved them from their
        distress;
20  he sent out his word and healed
        them,
    and delivered them from
        destruction.
21  Let them thank the LORD for his
        steadfast love,

ᵃCn: Heb *sea*   ᵇCn: Heb *fools*

for his wonderful works to
    humankind.
22 And let them offer thanksgiving
    sacrifices,
    and tell of his deeds with
    songs of joy.

23 Some went down to the sea
    in ships,
    doing business on the mighty
    waters;
24 they saw the deeds of the LORD,
    his wondrous works in the
    deep.
25 For he commanded and raised
    the stormy wind,
    which lifted up the waves of
    the sea.
26 They mounted up to heaven,
    they went down to the
    depths;
    their courage melted away in
    their calamity;
27 they reeled and staggered like
    drunkards,
    and were at their wits' end.
28 Then they cried to the LORD in
    their trouble,
    and he brought them out from
    their distress;
29 he made the storm be still,
    and the waves of the sea
    were hushed.
30 Then they were glad because
    they had quiet,
    and he brought them to their
    desired haven.
31 Let them thank the LORD for his
    steadfast love,
    for his wonderful works to
    humankind.
32 Let them extol him in the
    congregation of the
    people,
    and praise him in the
    assembly of the elders.

33 He turns rivers into a desert,
    springs of water into thirsty
    ground,
34 a fruitful land into a salty waste,
    because of the wickedness of
    its inhabitants.
35 He turns a desert into pools of
    water,
    a parched land into springs of
    water.
36 And there he lets the hungry
    live,
    and they establish a town to
    live in;
37 they sow fields, and plant
    vineyards,
    and get a fruitful yield.
38 By his blessing they multiply
    greatly,
    and he does not let their
    cattle decrease.

39 When they are diminished and
    brought low
    through oppression, trouble,
    and sorrow,
40 he pours contempt on princes
    and makes them wander in
    trackless wastes;
41 but he raises up the needy out
    of distress,
    and makes their families like
    flocks.
42 The upright see it and are glad;
    and all wickedness stops its
    mouth.
43 Let those who are wise give
    heed to these things,
    and consider the steadfast
    love of the LORD.

# PROVERBS 27.11

**B**E wise, my child, and make
    my heart glad,
    so that I may answer
    whoever reproaches me.

## EZEKIEL 21ᵃ.1—22.31

**T**HE word of the LORD came to me: ²Mortal, set your face toward Jerusalem and preach against the sanctuaries; prophesy against the land of Israel ³and say to the land of Israel, Thus says the LORD: I am coming against you, and will draw my sword out of its sheath, and will cut off from you both righteous and wicked. ⁴Because I will cut off from you both righteous and wicked, therefore my sword shall go out of its sheath against all flesh from south to north; ⁵and all flesh shall know that I the LORD have drawn my sword out of its sheath; it shall not be sheathed again. ⁶Moan therefore, mortal; moan with breaking heart and bitter grief before their eyes. ⁷And when they say to you, "Why do you moan?" you shall say, "Because of the news that has come. Every heart will melt and all hands will be feeble, every spirit will faint and all knees will turn to water. See, it comes and it will be fulfilled," says the Lord GOD.

8 And the word of the LORD came to me: ⁹Mortal, prophesy and say: Thus says the Lord; Say:

A sword, a sword is sharpened,
   it is also polished;
10 It is sharpened for slaughter,
   honed to flash like lightning!
How can we make merry?
   You have despised the rod,
   and all discipline. ᵇ
11 The swordᶜ is given to be
      polished,
   to be grasped in the hand;
It is sharpened, the sword is
      polished,
   to be placed in the slayer's
      hand.

12 Cry and wail, O mortal,
   for it is against my people;
it is against all Israel's princes;
   they are thrown to the
      sword,
   together with my people.
   Ah! Strike the thigh!
13 For consider: What! If you despise the rod, will it not happen?ᵇ says the Lord GOD.
14 And you, mortal, prophesy;
   Strike hand to hand.
Let the sword fall twice, thrice;
   it is a sword for killing.
A sword for great slaughter—
   it surrounds them;
15 therefore hearts melt
   and many stumble.
At all their gates I have set
   the pointᵇ of the sword.
Ah! It is made for flashing,
   it is polishedᵈ for slaughter.
16 Attack to the right!
   Engage to the left!
   Wherever your edge is
      directed.
17 I too will strike hand to hand,
   I will satisfy my fury;
   I the LORD have spoken.

18 The word of the LORD came to me: ¹⁹Mortal, mark out two roads for the sword of the king of Babylon to come; both of them shall issue from the same land. And make a signpost, make it for a fork in the road leading to a city; ²⁰mark out the road for the sword to come to Rabbah of the Ammonites or to Judah and toᵉ Jerusalem the fortified. ²¹For the king of Babylon stands at the parting of the way, at the fork in the two roads, to use divination; he shakes the arrows, he consults the teraphim,ᶠ he inspects the liver. ²²Into his right

aCh 21.6 in Heb   bMeaning of Heb uncertain   cHeb *It*   dTg: Heb *wrapped up*   eGk Syr: Heb *Judah*   f*Or the household gods* hand comes the lot for Jerusalem, to set battering rams, to call out for slaughter, for raising the battle cry, to set battering rams against the gates, to cast up ramps, to build siege towers. ²³But to them it will seem like a false divination; they have sworn solemn oaths; but he brings their guilt to remembrance, bringing about their capture.

24 Therefore thus says the Lord God: Because you have brought your guilt to remembrance, in that your transgressions are uncovered, so that in all your deeds your sins appear— because you have come to remembrance, you shall be taken in hand. ª

25 As for you, vile, wicked prince
        of Israel,
    you whose day has come,
    the time of final punishment,
26 thus says the Lord God:
    Remove the turban, take off
        the crown;
        things shall not remain as
            they are.
    Exalt that which is low,
        abase that which is high.
27 A ruin, a ruin, a ruin—
        I will make it!
        (Such has never occurred.)
    Until he comes whose right it
        is;
        to him I will give it.

28 As for you, mortal, prophesy, and say, Thus says the Lord God concerning the Ammonites, and concerning their reproach; say:

    A sword, a sword! Drawn for
        slaughter
    Polished to consume, ᵇ to
        flash like lightning.
29 Offering false visions for you,
        divining lies for you,
    they place you over the necks
        of the vile, wicked ones—
    those whose day has come,
        the time of final punishment.

30 Return it to its sheath!
    In the place where you were
        created,
        in the land of your origin,
        I will judge you.
31 I will pour out my indignation
        upon you,
    with the fire of my wrath
        I will blow upon you.
    I will deliver you into brutish
        hands,
        those skillful to destroy.
32 You shall be fuel for the fire,
        your blood shall enter the
            earth;
    You shall be remembered no
        more,
        for I the Lord have spoken.


22.1 The word of the Lord came to me: ²You, mortal, will you judge, will you judge the bloody city? Then declare to it all its abominable deeds. ³You shall say, Thus says the Lord God: A city! Shedding blood within itself; its time has come; making its idols, defiling itself. ⁴You have become guilty by the blood that you have shed, and defiled by the idols that you have made; you have brought your day near, the appointed time of your years has come. Therefore I have made you a disgrace before the nations, and a mockery to all the countries. ⁵Those who are near and those who are far from you will mock you, you infamous one, full of tumult.

6 The princes of Israel in you, everyone according to his power, have been bent on shedding blood. ⁷Father and mother are treated with contempt in you; the alien residing within you suffers extortion; the orphan and the widow are wronged in you. ⁸You have despised my holy things, and profaned my sabbaths. ⁹In you are those who slander to shed blood, those in you who eat upon the mountains, who commit lewdness in your midst. ¹⁰In you they

ª Or *be taken captive*   ᵇ Cn: Heb *to contain*

uncover their fathers' nakedness; in you they violate women in their menstrual periods. [11]One commits abomination with his neighbor's wife; another lewdly defiles his daughter-in-law; another in you defiles his sister, his father's daughter. [12]In you, they take bribes to shed blood; you take both advance interest and accrued interest, and make gain of your neighbors by extortion; and you have forgotten me, says the Lord God.

13 See, I strike my hands together at the dishonest gain you have made, and at the blood that has been shed within you. [14]Can your courage endure, or can your hands remain strong in the days when I shall deal with you? I the Lord have spoken, and I will do it. [15]I will scatter you among the nations and disperse you through the countries, and I will purge your filthiness out of you. [16]And I[a] shall be profaned through you in the sight of the nations; and you shall know that I am the Lord.

17 The word of the Lord came to me: [18]Mortal, the house of Israel has become dross to me; all of them, silver,[b] bronze, tin, iron, and lead. In the smelter they have become dross. [19]Therefore thus says the Lord God: Because you have all become dross, I will gather you into the midst of Jerusalem. [20]As one gathers silver, bronze, iron, lead, and tin into a smelter, to blow the fire upon them in order to melt them; so I will gather you in my anger and in my wrath, and I will put you in and melt you. [21]I will gather you and blow upon you with the fire of my wrath, and you shall be melted within it. [22]As silver is melted in a smelter, so you shall be melted in it; and you shall know that I the Lord have poured out my wrath upon you.

23 The word of the Lord came to me: [24]Mortal, say to it: You are a land that is not cleansed, not rained upon in the day of indignation. [25]Its princes[c] within it are like a roaring lion tearing the prey; they have devoured human lives; they have taken treasure and precious things; they have made many widows within it. [26]Its priests have done violence to my teaching and have profaned my holy things; they have made no distinction between the holy and the common, neither have they taught the difference between the unclean and the clean, and they have disregarded my sabbaths, so that I am profaned among them. [27]Its officials within it are like wolves tearing the prey, shedding blood, destroying lives to get dishonest gain. [28]Its prophets have smeared whitewash on their behalf, seeing false visions and divining lies for them, saying, "Thus says the Lord God," when the Lord has not spoken. [29]The people of the land have practiced extortion and committed robbery; they have oppressed the poor and needy, and have extorted from the alien without redress. [30]And I sought for anyone among them who would repair the wall and stand in the breach before me on behalf of the land, so that I would not destroy it; but I found no one. [31]Therefore I have poured out my indignation upon them; I have consumed them with the fire of my wrath; I have returned their conduct upon their heads, says the Lord God.

## HEBREWS 10.1–18

SINCE the law has only a shadow of the good things to come and not the true form of these realities, it[d] can never, by the same sacrifices that are continually offered year after year, make perfect those who approach. [2]Otherwise, would they not have ceased being offered, since the worshipers, cleansed once for all, would no longer have any conscious-

---

aGk Syr Vg: Heb *you*   bTransposed from the end of the verse; compare verse 20   cGk: Heb *indignation.* 25A *conspiracy of its prophets*   dOther ancient authorities read *they*

ness of sin? [3]But in these sacrifices there is a reminder of sin year after year. [4]For it is impossible for the blood of bulls and goats to take away sins. [5]Consequently, when Christ[a] came into the world, he said,

"Sacrifices and offerings you
        have not desired,
    but a body you have prepared
        for me;
[6]  in burnt offerings and sin
        offerings
    you have taken no pleasure.
[7]  Then I said, 'See, God, I have
        come to do your will, O
        God'
    (in the scroll of the book[b] it
        is written of me)."

[8]When he said above, "You have neither desired nor taken pleasure in sacrifices and offerings and burnt offerings and sin offerings" (these are offered according to the law), [9]then he added, "See, I have come to do your will." He abolishes the first in order to establish the second. [10]And it is by God's will[c] that we have been sanctified through the offering of the body of Jesus Christ once for all.

11  And every priest stands day after day at his service, offering again and again the same sacrifices that can never take away sins. [12]But when Christ[d] had offered for all time a single sacrifice for sins, "he sat down at the right hand of God," [13]and since then has been waiting "until his enemies would be made a footstool for his feet." [14]For by a single offering he has perfected for all time those who are sanctified. [15]And the Holy Spirit also testifies to us, for after saying,

[16]  "This is the covenant that I will
        make with them
    after those days, says the
        Lord:
    I will put my laws in their
        hearts,
    and I will write them on
        their minds,"
[17]he also adds,
    "I will remember[e] their sins
        and their lawless deeds
        no more."
[18]Where there is forgiveness of these, there is no longer any offering for sin.

## PSALM 108.1–13

*A Song. A Psalm of David.*

**M**y heart is steadfast, O God,
        my heart is
        steadfast;[f]
    I will sing and make melody.
    Awake, my soul![g]
[2]  Awake, O harp and lyre!
    I will awake the dawn.
[3]  I will give thanks to you,
        O LORD, among the
        peoples,
    and I will sing praises to you
        among the nations.
[4]  For your steadfast love is higher
        than the heavens,
    and your faithfulness reaches
        to the clouds.

[5]  Be exalted, O God, above the
        heavens,
    and let your glory be over all
        the earth.
[6]  Give victory with your right
        hand, and answer me,
    so that those whom you love
        may be rescued.

[7]  God has promised in his
        sanctuary:[h]
    "With exultation I will divide
        up Shechem,
    and portion out the Vale of
        Succoth.

---

[a]Gk *he*   [b]Meaning of Gk uncertain   [c]Gk *by that will*   [d]Gk *this one*   [e]Gk *on their minds and I will remember*   [f]Heb Mss Gk Syr: MT lacks *my heart is steadfast*   [g]Compare 57.8: Heb *also my soul*
[h]Or *by his holiness*

8  Gilead is mine; Manasseh is
      mine;
   Ephraim is my helmet;
   Judah is my scepter.
9  Moab is my washbasin;
      on Edom I hurl my shoe;
      over Philistia I shout in
      triumph."

10  Who will bring me to the
      fortified city?
    Who will lead me to Edom?
11  Have you not rejected us,
      O God?

   You do not go out, O God,
      with our armies.
12  O grant us help against the foe,
      for human help is worthless.
13  With God we shall do valiantly;
      it is he who will tread down
      our foes.

## PROVERBS 27.12

THE clever see danger and hide;
but the simple go on, and
suffer for it.

# NOVEMBER 11

## EZEKIEL 23.1–49

THE word of the LORD came to me: [2]Mortal, there were two women, the daughters of one mother; [3]they played the whore in Egypt; they played the whore in their youth; their breasts were caressed there, and their virgin bosoms were fondled. [4]Oholah was the name of the elder and Oholibah the name of her sister. They became mine, and they bore sons and daughters. As for their names, Oholah is Samaria, and Oholibah is Jerusalem.

5  Oholah played the whore while she was mine; she lusted after her lovers the Assyrians, warriors[a] [6]clothed in blue, governors and commanders, all of them handsome young men, mounted horsemen. [7]She bestowed her favors upon them, the choicest men of Assyria all of them; and she defiled herself with all the idols of everyone for whom she lusted. [8]She did not give up her whorings that she had practiced since Egypt; for in her youth men had lain with her and fondled her virgin bosom and poured out their lust upon her. [9]Therefore I delivered her into the hands of her lovers, into the hands of the Assyrians, for whom she lusted. [10]These uncovered her nakedness; they seized her sons and her daughters; and they killed her with the sword. Judgment was executed upon her, and she became a byword among women.

11  Her sister Oholibah saw this, yet she was more corrupt than she in her lusting and in her whorings, which were worse than those of her sister. [12]She lusted after the Assyrians, governors and commanders, warriors[a] clothed in full armor, mounted horsemen, all of them handsome young men. [13]And I saw that she was defiled; they both took the same way. [14]But she carried her whorings further; she saw male figures carved on the wall, images of the Chaldeans portrayed in vermil-

a Meaning of Heb uncertain

ion, [15]with belts around their waists, with flowing turbans on their heads, all of them looking like officers—a picture of Babylonians whose native land was Chaldea. [16]When she saw them she lusted after them, and sent messengers to them in Chaldea. [17]And the Babylonians came to her into the bed of love, and they defiled her with their lust; and after she defiled herself with them, she turned from them in disgust. [18]When she carried on her whorings so openly and flaunted her nakedness, I turned in disgust from her, as I had turned from her sister. [19]Yet she increased her whorings, remembering the days of her youth, when she played the whore in the land of Egypt [20]and lusted after her paramours there, whose members were like those of donkeys, and whose emission was like that of stallions. [21]Thus you longed for the lewdness of your youth, when the Egyptians[a] fondled your bosom and caressed[b] your young breasts.

22 Therefore, O Oholibah, thus says the Lord GOD: I will rouse against you your lovers from whom you turned in disgust, and I will bring them against you from every side: [23]the Babylonians and all the Chaldeans, Pekod and Shoa and Koa, and all the Assyrians with them, handsome young men, governors and commanders all of them, officers and warriors,[c] all of them riding on horses. [24]They shall come against you from the north[d] with chariots and wagons and a host of peoples; they shall set themselves against you on every side with buckler, shield, and helmet, and I will commit the judgment to them, and they shall judge you according to their ordinances. [25]I will direct my indignation against you, in order that they may deal with you in fury. They shall cut off your nose and your ears, and your survivors shall fall by the sword. They shall seize your sons and your daughters, and your survivors shall be devoured by fire. [26]They shall also strip you of your clothes and take away your fine jewels. [27]So I will put an end to your lewdness and your whoring brought from the land of Egypt; you shall not long for them, or remember Egypt any more. [28]For thus says the Lord GOD: I will deliver you into the hands of those whom you hate, into the hands of those from whom you turned in disgust; [29]and they shall deal with you in hatred, and take away all the fruit of your labor, and leave you naked and bare, and the nakedness of your whorings shall be exposed. Your lewdness and your whorings [30]have brought this upon you, because you played the whore with the nations, and polluted yourself with their idols. [31]You have gone the way of your sister; therefore I will give her cup into your hand.
[32]Thus says the Lord GOD:

You shall drink your sister's
   cup,
  deep and wide;
you shall be scorned and
   derided,
  it holds so much.
33  You shall be filled with
   drunkenness and sorrow.
A cup of horror and desolation
  is the cup of your sister
   Samaria;
34  you shall drink it and drain it
   out,
  and gnaw its sherds,
  and tear out your breasts;

for I have spoken, says the Lord GOD. [35]Therefore thus says the Lord GOD: Because you have forgotten me and cast me behind your back, therefore bear the consequences of your lewdness and whorings.

36 The LORD said to me: Mortal, will you judge Oholah and Oholibah? Then declare to them their abominable deeds. [37]For they have committed

---

[a]Two Mss: MT *from Egypt*   [b]Cn: Heb *for the sake of*   [c]Compare verses 6 and 12: Heb *officers and called ones*   [d]Gk: Meaning of Heb uncertain

adultery, and blood is on their hands; with their idols they have committed adultery; and they have even offered up to them for food the children whom they had borne to me. ³⁸Moreover this they have done to me: they have defiled my sanctuary on the same day and profaned my sabbaths. ³⁹For when they had slaughtered their children for their idols, on the same day they came into my sanctuary to profane it. This is what they did in my house.

40 They even sent for men to come from far away, to whom a messenger was sent, and they came. For them you bathed yourself, painted your eyes, and decked yourself with ornaments; ⁴¹you sat on a stately couch, with a table spread before it on which you had placed my incense and my oil. ⁴²The sound of a raucous multitude was around her, with many of the rabble brought in drunken from the wilderness; and they put bracelets on the arms ͣ of the women, and beautiful crowns upon their heads.

43 Then I said, Ah, she is worn out with adulteries, but they carry on their sexual acts with her. ⁴⁴For they have gone in to her, as one goes in to a whore. Thus they went in to Oholah and to Oholibah, wanton women. ⁴⁵But righteous judges shall declare them guilty of adultery and of bloodshed; because they are adulteresses and blood is on their hands.

46 For thus says the Lord GOD: Bring up an assembly against them, and make them an object of terror and of plunder. ⁴⁷The assembly shall stone them and with their swords they shall cut them down; they shall kill their sons and their daughters, and burn up their houses. ⁴⁸Thus will I put an end to lewdness in the land, so that all women may take warning and not commit lewdness as you have done. ⁴⁹They shall repay you for your lewdness, and you shall bear the penalty for your sinful idolatry; and you shall know that I am the Lord GOD.

## HEBREWS 10. 19–39

THEREFORE, my friends, ᵇ since we have confidence to enter the sanctuary by the blood of Jesus, ²⁰by the new and living way that he opened for us through the curtain (that is, through his flesh), ²¹and since we have a great priest over the house of God, ²²let us approach with a true heart in full assurance of faith, with our hearts sprinkled clean from an evil conscience and our bodies washed with pure water. ²³Let us hold fast to the confession of our hope without wavering, for he who has promised is faithful. ²⁴And let us consider how to provoke one another to love and good deeds, ²⁵not neglecting to meet together, as is the habit of some, but encouraging one another, and all the more as you see the Day approaching.

26 For if we willfully persist in sin after having received the knowledge of the truth, there no longer remains a sacrifice for sins, ²⁷but a fearful prospect of judgment, and a fury of fire that will consume the adversaries. ²⁸Anyone who has violated the law of Moses dies without mercy "on the testimony of two or three witnesses." ²⁹How much worse punishment do you think will be deserved by those who have spurned the Son of God, profaned the blood of the covenant by which they were sanctified, and outraged the Spirit of grace? ³⁰For we know the one who said, "Vengeance is mine, I will repay." And again, "The Lord will judge his people." ³¹It is a fearful thing to fall into the hands of the living God.

32 But recall those earlier days when, after you had been enlightened, you endured a hard struggle with sufferings, ³³sometimes being publicly ex-

ͣHeb *hands*  ᵇGk *Therefore, brothers*

posed to abuse and persecution, and sometimes being partners with those so treated. 34For you had compassion for those who were in prison, and you cheerfully accepted the plundering of your possessions, knowing that you yourselves possessed something better and more lasting. 35Do not, therefore, abandon that confidence of yours; it brings a great reward. 36For you need endurance, so that when you have done the will of God, you may receive what was promised.

37 For yet "in a very little while,
    the one who is coming will
      come and will not delay;
38 but my righteous one will live
    by faith.
    My soul takes no pleasure in
      anyone who shrinks
      back."

39But we are not among those who shrink back and so are lost, but among those who have faith and so are saved.

## PSALM 109.1–31

*To the leader. Of David. A Psalm.*

**D**o not be silent, O God of my
    praise.
2  For wicked and deceitful
    mouths are opened
    against me,
    speaking against me with
      lying tongues.
3  They beset me with words of
    hate,
    and attack me without cause.
4  In return for my love they
    accuse me,
    even while I make prayer for
      them. a
5  So they reward me evil for
    good,
    and hatred for my love.

6  They say, b "Appoint a wicked
    man against him;

    let an accuser stand on his
      right.
7  When he is tried, let him be
    found guilty;
    let his prayer be counted as
      sin.
8  May his days be few;
    may another seize his
      position.
9  May his children be orphans,
    and his wife a widow.
10  May his children wander about
    and beg;
    may they be driven out ofc
      the ruins they inhabit.
11  May the creditor seize all that
    he has;
    may strangers plunder the
      fruits of his toil.
12  May there be no one to do him
    a kindness,
    nor anyone to pity his
      orphaned children.
13  May his posterity be cut off;
    may his name be blotted out
      in the second generation.
14  May the iniquity of his fatherd
    be remembered before
      the LORD,
    and do not let the sin of his
      mother be blotted out.
15  Let them be before the LORD
    continually,
    and may hise memory be cut
      off from the earth.
16  For he did not remember to
    show kindness,
    but pursued the poor and
      needy
    and the brokenhearted to
      their death.
17  He loved to curse; let curses
    come on him.
    He did not like blessing; may
      it be far from him.
18  He clothed himself with cursing
    as his coat,

may it soak into his body like
    water,
like oil into his bones.
19 May it be like a garment that he
    wraps around himself,
like a belt that he wears
    every day."

20 May that be the reward of my
    accusers from the Lord,
of those who speak evil
    against my life.
21 But you, O Lord my Lord,
    act on my behalf for your
    name's sake;
because your steadfast love is
    good, deliver me.
22 For I am poor and needy,
    and my heart is pierced
    within me.
23 I am gone like a shadow at
    evening;
I am shaken off like a locust.
24 My knees are weak through
    fasting;
my body has become gaunt.
25 I am an object of scorn to my
    accusers;
when they see me, they
    shake their heads.

26 Help me, O Lord my God!

Save me according to your
    steadfast love.
27 Let them know that this is your
    hand;
you, O Lord, have done it.
28 Let them curse, but you will
    bless.
Let my assailants be put to
    shame; [a] may your
    servant be glad.
29 May my accusers be clothed
    with dishonor;
may they be wrapped in their
    own shame as in a
    mantle.
30 With my mouth I will give great
    thanks to the Lord;
I will praise him in the midst
    of the throng.
31 For he stands at the right hand
    of the needy,
to save them from those who
    would condemn them to
    death.

## PROVERBS 27.13

TAKE the garment of one who
    has given surety for a
    stranger;
seize the pledge given as
    surety for foreigners. [b]

# NOVEMBER 12

## EZEKIEL 24.1—26.21

IN the ninth year, in the tenth month, on the tenth day of the month, the word of the Lord came to me: 2Mortal, write down the name of this day, this very day. The king of Babylon has laid siege to Jerusalem this very day. 3And utter an allegory to the rebellious house and say to them, Thus says the Lord God:

Set on the pot, set it on,
    pour in water also;

a Gk: Heb *They have risen up and have been put to shame*  b Vg and 20.16: Heb *for a foreign woman*

4 put in it the pieces,
   all the good pieces, the thigh
    and the shoulder;
  fill it with choice bones.
5 Take the choicest one of the
   flock,
   pile the logs[a] under it;
  boil its pieces,[b]
   seethe[c] also its bones in it.

6 Therefore thus says the Lord God:
  Woe to the bloody city,
   the pot whose rust is in it,
   whose rust has not gone out
    of it!
  Empty it piece by piece,
   making no choice at all.[d]
7 For the blood she shed is inside
   it;
   she placed it on a bare rock;
  she did not pour it out on the
    ground,
   to cover it with earth.
8 To rouse my wrath, to take
   vengeance,
   I have placed the blood she
    shed
  on a bare rock,
   so that it may not be
    covered.
9 Therefore thus says the Lord God:
  Woe to the bloody city!
   I will even make the pile
    great.
10 Heap up the logs, kindle
   the fire;
   boil the meat well, mix in
    the spices,
  let the bones be burned.
11 Stand it empty upon the coals,
   so that it may become hot, its
    copper glow,
   its filth melt in it, its rust
    be consumed.
12 In vain I have wearied myself;[e]
   its thick rust does not depart.

  To the fire with its rust![f]
13 Yet, when I cleansed you in
   your filthy lewdness,
  you did not become clean
   from your filth;
  you shall not again be cleansed
   until I have satisfied my fury
    upon you.

14 I the Lord have spoken; the time is coming, I will act. I will not refrain, I will not spare, I will not relent. According to your ways and your doings I will judge you, says the Lord God.

15 The word of the Lord came to me: 16 Mortal, with one blow I am about to take away from you the delight of your eyes; yet you shall not mourn or weep, nor shall your tears run down. 17 Sigh, but not aloud; make no mourning for the dead. Bind on your turban, and put your sandals on your feet; do not cover your upper lip or eat the bread of mourners.[g] 18 So I spoke to the people in the morning, and at evening my wife died. And on the next morning I did as I was commanded.

19 Then the people said to me, "Will you not tell us what these things mean for us, that you are acting this way?" 20 Then I said to them: The word of the Lord came to me: 21 Say to the house of Israel, Thus says the Lord God: I will profane my sanctuary, the pride of your power, the delight of your eyes, and your heart's desire; and your sons and your daughters whom you left behind shall fall by the sword. 22 And you shall do as I have done; you shall not cover your upper lip or eat the bread of mourners.[g] 23 Your turbans shall be on your heads and your sandals on your feet; you shall not mourn or weep, but you shall pine away in your iniquities and groan to one another. 24 Thus Ezekiel shall be a sign to you; you shall do just as he has done. When

---

[a] Compare verse 10: Heb *the bones*   [b] Two Mss: Heb *its boilings*   [c] Cn: Heb *its bones seethe*
[d] Heb *piece, no lot has fallen on it*   [e] Cn: Meaning of Heb uncertain   [f] Meaning of Heb uncertain
[g] Vg Tg: Heb *of men*

this comes, then you shall know that I am the Lord God.

25 And you, mortal, on the day when I take from them their stronghold, their joy and glory, the delight of their eyes and their heart's affection, and also[a] their sons and their daughters, [26]on that day, one who has escaped will come to you to report to you the news. [27]On that day your mouth shall be opened to the one who has escaped, and you shall speak and no longer be silent. So you shall be a sign to them; and they shall know that I am the Lord.

25.[1] The word of the Lord came to me: [2]Mortal, set your face toward the Ammonites and prophesy against them. [3]Say to the Ammonites, Hear the word of the Lord God: Thus says the Lord God, Because you said, "Aha!" over my sanctuary when it was profaned, and over the land of Israel when it was made desolate, and over the house of Judah when it went into exile; [4]therefore I am handing you over to the people of the east for a possession. They shall set their encampments among you and pitch their tents in your midst; they shall eat your fruit, and they shall drink your milk. [5]I will make Rabbah a pasture for camels and Ammon a fold for flocks. Then you shall know that I am the Lord. [6]For thus says the Lord God: Because you have clapped your hands and stamped your feet and rejoiced with all the malice within you against the land of Israel, [7]therefore I have stretched out my hand against you, and will hand you over as plunder to the nations. I will cut you off from the peoples and will make you perish out of the countries; I will destroy you. Then you shall know that I am the Lord.

8 Thus says the Lord God: Because Moab[b] said, The house of Judah is like all the other nations, [9]therefore I will lay open the flank of Moab from the towns[c] on its frontier, the glory of the country, Beth-jeshimoth, Baal-meon, and Kiriathaim. [10]I will give it along with Ammon to the people of the east as a possession. Thus Ammon shall be remembered no more among the nations, [11]and I will execute judgments upon Moab. Then they shall know that I am the Lord.

12 Thus says the Lord God: Because Edom acted revengefully against the house of Judah and has grievously offended in taking vengeance upon them, [13]therefore thus says the Lord God, I will stretch out my hand against Edom, and cut off from it humans and animals, and I will make it desolate; from Teman even to Dedan they shall fall by the sword. [14]I will lay my vengeance upon Edom by the hand of my people Israel; and they shall act in Edom according to my anger and according to my wrath; and they shall know my vengeance, says the Lord God.

15 Thus says the Lord God: Because with unending hostilities the Philistines acted in vengeance, and with malice of heart took revenge in destruction; [16]therefore thus says the Lord God, I will stretch out my hand against the Philistines, cut off the Cherethites, and destroy the rest of the seacoast. [17]I will execute great vengeance on them with wrathful punishments. Then they shall know that I am the Lord, when I lay my vengeance on them.

26.[1] In the eleventh year, on the first day of the month, the word of the Lord came to me: [2]Mortal, because Tyre said concerning Jerusalem,

"Aha, broken is the gateway of
the peoples;
it has swung open to me;
I shall be replenished,

now that it is wasted."
³Therefore, thus says the Lord God:
  See, I am against you, O Tyre!
    I will hurl many nations
      against you,
    as the sea hurls its waves.
  4 They shall destroy the walls
      of Tyre
    and break down its towers.
    I will scrape its soil from it
    and make it a bare rock.
  5 It shall become, in the midst of
      the sea,
    a place for spreading nets.
  I have spoken, says the Lord God.
    It shall become plunder for
      the nations,
  6     and its daughter-towns in
      the country
    shall be killed by the sword.
Then they shall know that I am the
Lord.

7 For thus says the Lord God: I will
bring against Tyre from the north King
Nebuchadrezzar of Babylon, king of
kings, together with horses, chariots,
cavalry, and a great and powerful army.
  8 Your daughter-towns in the
      country
    he shall put to the sword.
    He shall set up a siege wall
      against you,
    cast up a ramp against you,
    and raise a roof of shields
      against you.
  9 He shall direct the shock of his
      battering rams against
      your walls
    and break down your towers
      with his axes.
  10 His horses shall be so many
    that their dust shall cover
      you.
    At the noise of cavalry, wheels,
      and chariots
    your very walls shall shake,
    when he enters your gates

like those entering a
  breached city.
  11 With the hoofs of his horses
    he shall trample all your
      streets.
    He shall put your people to
      the sword,
    and your strong pillars shall
      fall to the ground.
  12 They will plunder your riches
    and loot your merchandise;
    they shall break down your
      walls
    and destroy your fine houses.
    Your stones and timber and soil
    they shall cast into the water.
  13 I will silence the music of
      your songs;
    the sound of your lyres shall
      be heard no more.
  14 I will make you a bare rock;
    you shall be a place for
      spreading nets.
    You shall never again be rebuilt,
    for I the Lord have spoken,
    says the Lord God.

15 Thus says the Lord God to
Tyre: Shall not the coastlands shake at
the sound of your fall, when the
wounded groan, when slaughter goes
on within you? ¹⁶Then all the princes of
the sea shall step down from their
thrones; they shall remove their robes
and strip off their embroidered garments. They shall clothe themselves
with trembling, and shall sit on the
ground; they shall tremble every moment, and be appalled at you. ¹⁷And
they shall raise a lamentation over you,
and say to you:
  How you have vanished[a] from
      the seas,
    O city renowned,
  once mighty on the sea,
    you and your inhabitants, [b]
  who imposed your[c] terror
    on all the mainland![d]
  18 Now the coastlands tremble

[a]Gk OL Aquila: Heb *have vanished, O inhabited one,*   [b]Heb *it and its inhabitants*   [c]Heb *their*
[d]Cn: Heb *its inhabitants*

on the day of your fall;
the coastlands by the sea
are dismayed at your passing.

19 For thus says the Lord GOD: When I make you a city laid waste, like cities that are not inhabited, when I bring up the deep over you, and the great waters cover you, [20]then I will thrust you down with those who descend into the Pit, to the people of long ago, and I will make you live in the world below, among primeval ruins, with those who go down to the Pit, so that you will not be inhabited or have a place[a] in the land of the living. [21]I will bring you to a dreadful end, and you shall be no more; though sought for, you will never be found again, says the Lord GOD.

## HEBREWS 11.1–16

Now faith is the assurance of things hoped for, the conviction of things not seen. [2]Indeed, by faith[b] our ancestors received approval. [3]By faith we understand that the worlds were prepared by the word of God, so that what is seen was made from things that are not visible.[c]

4 By faith Abel offered to God a more acceptable[d] sacrifice than Cain's. Through this he received approval as righteous, God himself giving approval to his gifts; he died, but through his faith[e] he still speaks. [5]By faith Enoch was taken so that he did not experience death; and "he was not found, because God had taken him." For it was attested before he was taken away that "he had pleased God." [6]And without faith it is impossible to please God, for whoever would approach him must believe that he exists and that he rewards those who seek him. [7]By faith Noah, warned by God about events as yet unseen, respected the warning and built an ark to save his household; by this he condemned the world and became an heir to the righteousness that is in accordance with faith.

8 By faith Abraham obeyed when he was called to set out for a place that he was to receive as an inheritance; and he set out, not knowing where he was going. [9]By faith he stayed for a time in the land he had been promised, as in a foreign land, living in tents, as did Isaac and Jacob, who were heirs with him of the same promise. [10]For he looked forward to the city that has foundations, whose architect and builder is God. [11]By faith he received power of procreation, even though he was too old—and Sarah herself was barren—because he considered him faithful who had promised.[f] [12]Therefore from one person, and this one as good as dead, descendants were born, "as many as the stars of heaven and as the innumerable grains of sand by the seashore."

13 All of these died in faith without having received the promises, but from a distance they saw and greeted them. They confessed that they were strangers and foreigners on the earth, [14]for people who speak in this way make it clear that they are seeking a homeland. [15]If they had been thinking of the land that they had left behind, they would have had opportunity to return. [16]But as it is, they desire a better country, that is, a heavenly one. Therefore God is not ashamed to be called their God; indeed, he has prepared a city for them.

## PSALM 110.1–7

*Of David. A Psalm.*

THE LORD says to my lord,
"Sit at my right hand
until I make your enemies
your footstool."

2   The Lord sends out from Zion
     your mighty scepter.
     Rule in the midst of your
       foes.
3  Your people will offer
      themselves willingly
  on the day you lead your
     forces
  on the holy mountains. a
  From the womb of the morning,
  like dew, your youth b will
      come to you.
4   The Lord has sworn and will
     not change his mind,
  "You are a priest forever
     according to the order of
     Melchizedek." c

5   The Lord is at your right hand;
    he will shatter kings on the
     day of his wrath.

6   He will execute judgment among
     the nations,
    filling them with corpses;
  he will shatter heads
    over the wide earth.
7   He will drink from the stream
     by the path;
  therefore he will lift up his
    head.

## PROVERBS 27.14

WHOEVER blesses a neighbor
    with a loud voice,
rising early in the
    morning,
will be counted as cursing.

# NOVEMBER 13

## EZEKIEL 27.1—28.26

THE word of the Lord came to me: ²Now you, mortal, raise a lamentation over Tyre, ³and say to Tyre, which sits at the entrance to the sea, merchant of the peoples on many coastlands, Thus says the Lord God:
  O Tyre, you have said,
    "I am perfect in beauty."
4   Your borders are in the heart of
     the seas;
  your builders made perfect
    your beauty.
5   They made all your planks
    of fir trees from Senir;
  they took a cedar from Lebanon
    to make a mast for you.
6   From oaks of Bashan
    they made your oars;

    they made your deck of pines d
    from the coasts of Cyprus,
    inlaid with ivory.
7   Of fine embroidered linen
     from Egypt
  was your sail,
    serving as your ensign;
  blue and purple from the coasts
    of Elishah
  was your awning.
8   The inhabitants of Sidon and
    Arvad
  were your rowers;
  skilled men of Zemer e were
    within you,
  they were your pilots.
9   The elders of Gebal and its
    artisans were within you,
  caulking your seams;

a Another reading is *in holy splendor*  b Cn: Heb *the dew of your youth*  c Or *forever, a rightful king by my edict*  d Or *boxwood*  e Cn Compare Gen 10.18: Heb *your skilled men, O Tyre*

all the ships of the sea with
  their mariners were
  within you,
to barter for your wares.
10  Paras[a] and Lud and Put
  were in your army,
  your mighty warriors;
  they hung shield and helmet
    in you;
  they gave you splendor.
11  Men of Arvad and Helech[b]
  were on your walls all around;
  men of Gamad were at
    your towers.
  They hung their quivers all
    around your walls;
  they made perfect your
    beauty.

12  Tarshish did business with you out of the abundance of your great wealth; silver, iron, tin, and lead they exchanged for your wares. [13]Javan, Tubal, and Meshech traded with you; they exchanged human beings and vessels of bronze for your merchandise. [14]Beth-togarmah exchanged for your wares horses, war horses, and mules. [15]The Rhodians[c] traded with you; many coastlands were your own special markets; they brought you in payment ivory tusks and ebony. [16]Edom[d] did business with you because of your abundant goods; they exchanged for your wares turquoise, purple, embroidered work, fine linen, coral, and rubies. [17]Judah and the land of Israel traded with you; they exchanged for your merchandise wheat from Minnith, millet, [e] honey, oil, and balm. [18]Damascus traded with you for your abundant goods—because of your great wealth of every kind—wine of Helbon, and white wool. [19]Vedan and Javan from Uzal[e] entered into trade for your wares; wrought iron, cassia, and sweet cane were bartered for your merchandise. [20]Dedan traded with you in saddlecloths for riding. [21]Arabia and all the princes of Kedar were your favored dealers in lambs, rams, and goats; in these they did business with you. [22]The merchants of Sheba and Raamah traded with you; they exchanged for your wares the best of all kinds of spices, and all precious stones, and gold. [23]Haran, Canneh, Eden, the merchants of Sheba, Asshur, and Chilmad traded with you. [24]These traded with you in choice garments, in clothes of blue and embroidered work, and in carpets of colored material, bound with cords and made secure; in these they traded with you. [f] [25]The ships of Tarshish traveled for you in your trade.

  So you were filled and heavily
    laden
    in the heart of the seas.
26  Your rowers have brought you
    into the high seas.
  The east wind has wrecked you
    in the heart of the seas.
27  Your riches, your wares, your
    merchandise,
  your mariners and your pilots,
  your caulkers, your dealers in
    merchandise,
  and all your warriors within
    you,
  with all the company
    that is with you,
  sink into the heart of the seas
    on the day of your ruin.
28  At the sound of the cry of
    your pilots
    the countryside shakes,
29  and down from their ships
    come all that handle the oar.
  The mariners and all the pilots
    of the sea
    stand on the shore
30  and wail aloud over you,
    and cry bitterly.
  They throw dust on their heads
    and wallow in ashes;
31  they make themselves bald for
    you,

---

aOr *Persia*  bOr *and your army*  cGk: Heb *The Dedanites*  dAnother reading is *Aram*  eMeaning of Heb uncertain  fCn: Heb *in your market*

and put on sackcloth,
and they weep over you in
bitterness of soul,
with bitter mourning.
32 In their wailing they raise a
lamentation for you,
and lament over you:
"Who was ever destroyed a
like Tyre
in the midst of the sea?
33 When your wares came from
the seas,
you satisfied many peoples;
with your abundant wealth and
merchandise
you enriched the kings of
the earth.
34 Now you are wrecked by the
seas,
in the depths of the waters;
your merchandise and all your
crew
have sunk with you.
35 All the inhabitants of the
coastlands
are appalled at you;
and their kings are horribly
afraid,
their faces are convulsed.
36 The merchants among the
peoples hiss at you;
you have come to a dreadful
end
and shall be no more
forever."

28.1 THE word of the LORD came to me:
2Mortal, say to the prince of Tyre,
Thus says the Lord GOD:
Because your heart is proud
and you have said, "I am a
god;
I sit in the seat of the gods,
in the heart of the seas,"
yet you are but a mortal, and
no god,
though you compare your
mind

with the mind of a god.
3 You are indeed wiser than
Daniel; b
no secret is hidden from you;
4 by your wisdom and your
understanding
you have amassed wealth
for yourself,
and have gathered gold and
silver
into your treasuries.
5 By your great wisdom in trade
you have increased your
wealth,
and your heart has become
proud in your wealth.
6 Therefore thus says the Lord
GOD:
Because you compare your mind
with the mind of a god,
7 therefore, I will bring strangers
against you,
the most terrible of the
nations;
they shall draw their swords
against the beauty of
your wisdom
and defile your splendor.
8 They shall thrust you down to
the Pit,
and you shall die a violent
death
in the heart of the seas.
9 Will you still say, "I am a god,"
in the presence of those who
kill you,
though you are but a mortal,
and no god,
in the hands of those who
wound you?
10 You shall die the death of the
uncircumcised
by the hand of foreigners;
for I have spoken, says the
Lord GOD.
11 Moreover the word of the LORD
came to me: 12Mortal, raise a lamentation over the king of Tyre, and say to

aTg Vg: Heb *like silence*   bOr, as otherwise read, *Danel*

him, Thus says the Lord GOD:
   You were the signet of
      perfection, **a**
    full of wisdom and perfect in
      beauty.
13 You were in Eden, the garden
      of God;
    every precious stone was
      your covering,
  carnelian, chrysolite, and
      moonstone,
    beryl, onyx, and jasper,
  sapphire, **b** turquoise, and
      emerald;
    and worked in gold were your
      settings
    and your engravings. **a**
  On the day that you were
      created
    they were prepared.
14 With an anointed cherub as
      guardian I placed you; **a**
    you were on the holy
      mountain of God;
    you walked among the stones
      of fire.
15 You were blameless in your
      ways
    from the day that you were
      created,
    until iniquity was found in
      you.
16 In the abundance of your trade
    you were filled with violence,
      and you sinned;
    so I cast you as a profane thing
      from the mountain of
      God,
    and the guardian cherub
      drove you out
    from among the stones of
      fire.
17 Your heart was proud because
      of your beauty;
    you corrupted your wisdom
      for the sake of your
      splendor.
  I cast you to the ground;

    I exposed you before kings,
      to feast their eyes on you.
18 By the multitude of your
      iniquities,
    in the unrighteousness of
      your trade,
    you profaned your
      sanctuaries.
  So I brought out fire from
      within you;
    it consumed you,
  and I turned you to ashes on
      the earth
    in the sight of all who saw
      you.
19 All who know you among the
      peoples
    are appalled at you;
  you have come to a dreadful end
    and shall be no more forever.
20 The word of the LORD came to
me: 21Mortal, set your face toward Sidon, and prophesy against it, 22and say,
Thus says the Lord GOD:
  I am against you, O Sidon,
    and I will gain glory in your
      midst.
  They shall know that I am
      the LORD
    when I execute judgments in
      it,
    and manifest my holiness in
      it;
23 for I will send pestilence into it,
    and bloodshed into its streets;
  and the dead shall fall in its
      midst,
    by the sword that is against it
      on every side.
  And they shall know that I am
      the LORD.
24 The house of Israel shall no longer find a pricking brier or a piercing
thorn among all their neighbors who
have treated them with contempt. And
they shall know that I am the Lord GOD.
25 Thus says the Lord GOD: When
I gather the house of Israel from the

---

**a** Meaning of Heb uncertain  **b** Or *lapis lazuli*

peoples among whom they are scattered, and manifest my holiness in them in the sight of the nations, then they shall settle on their own soil that I gave to my servant Jacob. ²⁶They shall live in safety in it, and shall build houses and plant vineyards. They shall live in safety, when I execute judgments upon all their neighbors who have treated them with contempt. And they shall know that I am the LORD their God.

## HEBREWS 11.17–31

**B**Y faith Abraham, when put to the test, offered up Isaac. He who had received the promises was ready to offer up his only son, ¹⁸of whom he had been told, "It is through Isaac that descendants shall be named for you." ¹⁹He considered the fact that God is able even to raise someone from the dead—and figuratively speaking, he did receive him back. ²⁰By faith Isaac invoked blessings for the future on Jacob and Esau. ²¹By faith Jacob, when dying, blessed each of the sons of Joseph, "bowing in worship over the top of his staff." ²²By faith Joseph, at the end of his life, made mention of the exodus of the Israelites and gave instructions about his burial. ᵃ

23 By faith Moses was hidden by his parents for three months after his birth, because they saw that the child was beautiful; and they were not afraid of the king's edict. ᵇ ²⁴By faith Moses, when he was grown up, refused to be called a son of Pharaoh's daughter, ²⁵choosing rather to share ill-treatment with the people of God than to enjoy the fleeting pleasures of sin. ²⁶He considered abuse suffered for the Christᶜ to be greater wealth than the treasures of Egypt, for he was looking ahead to the reward. ²⁷By faith he left Egypt, unafraid of the king's anger; for he persevered as thoughᵈ he saw him who is invisible. ²⁸By faith he kept the Passover and the sprinkling of blood, so that the destroyer of the firstborn would not touch the firstborn of Israel. ᵉ

29 By faith the people passed through the Red Sea as if it were dry land, but when the Egyptians attempted to do so they were drowned. ³⁰By faith the walls of Jericho fell after they had been encircled for seven days. ³¹By faith Rahab the prostitute did not perish with those who were disobedient,ᶠ because she had received the spies in peace.

## PSALM 111.1–10

**P**RAISE the LORD!
    I will give thanks to the
      LORD with my whole
      heart,
    in the company of the upright,
      in the congregation.
2  Great are the works of the
      LORD,
    studied by all who delight
      in them.
3  Full of honor and majesty is
      his work,
    and his righteousness endures
      forever.
4  He has gained renown by his
      wonderful deeds;
    the LORD is gracious and
      merciful.
5  He provides food for those who
      fear him;
    he is ever mindful of his
      covenant.
6  He has shown his people the
      power of his works,
    in giving them the heritage of
      the nations.

ᵃGk *his bones*  ᵇOther ancient authorities add *By faith Moses, when he was grown up, killed the Egyptian, because he observed the humiliation of his people* (Gk *brothers*)  ᶜOr *the Messiah*
ᵈOr *because*  ᵉGk *would not touch them*  ᶠOr *unbelieving*

7 The works of his hands are
    faithful and just;
  all his precepts are
    trustworthy.
8 They are established forever
    and ever,
  to be performed with
    faithfulness and
    uprightness.
9 He sent redemption to his
    people;
  he has commanded his
    covenant forever.
  Holy and awesome is his
    name.

10 The fear of the LORD is the
    beginning of wisdom;
  all those who practice it[a]
    have a good
    understanding.
  His praise endures forever.

## PROVERBS 27.15–16

A CONTINUAL dripping on a
    rainy day
and a contentious wife are
    alike;
16 to restrain her is to restrain
    the wind
  or to grasp oil in the right
    hand. [b]

# NOVEMBER 14

## EZEKIEL 29.1—30.26

IN the tenth year, in the tenth month, on the twelfth day of the month, the word of the LORD came to me: 2Mortal, set your face against Pharaoh king of Egypt, and prophesy against him and against all Egypt; 3speak, and say, Thus says the Lord GOD:

I am against you,
  Pharaoh king of Egypt,
the great dragon sprawling
  in the midst of its channels,
saying, "My Nile is my own;
  I made it for myself."
4 I will put hooks in your jaws,
  and make the fish of your
    channels stick to your
    scales.
I will draw you up from your
    channels,
with all the fish of your
    channels
sticking to your scales.
5 I will fling you into the
    wilderness,
  you and all the fish of your
    channels;
you shall fall in the open field,
  and not be gathered and
    buried.
To the animals of the earth and
    to the birds of the air
I have given you as food.
6 Then all the inhabitants of Egypt
    shall know
  that I am the LORD
because you[c] were a staff
    of reed
to the house of Israel;
7 when they grasped you with the
    hand, you broke,
  and tore all their shoulders;

aGk Syr: Heb *them*  bMeaning of Heb uncertain  cGk Syr Vg: Heb *they*

and when they leaned on you,
you broke,
and made all their legs
unsteady. [a]
8 Therefore, thus says the Lord God: I will bring a sword upon you, and will cut off from you human being and animal; [9]and the land of Egypt shall be a desolation and a waste. Then they shall know that I am the LORD.

Because you[b] said, "The Nile is mine, and I made it," [10]therefore, I am against you, and against your channels, and I will make the land of Egypt an utter waste and desolation, from Migdol to Syene, as far as the border of Ethiopia. [c] [11]No human foot shall pass through it, and no animal foot shall pass through it; it shall be uninhabited forty years. [12]I will make the land of Egypt a desolation among desolated countries; and her cities shall be a desolation forty years among cities that are laid waste. I will scatter the Egyptians among the nations, and disperse them among the countries.

13 Further, thus says the Lord God: At the end of forty years I will gather the Egyptians from the peoples among whom they were scattered; [14]and I will restore the fortunes of Egypt, and bring them back to the land of Pathros, the land of their origin; and there they shall be a lowly kingdom. [15]It shall be the most lowly of the kingdoms, and never again exalt itself above the nations; and I will make them so small that they will never again rule over the nations. [16]The Egyptians[d] shall never again be the reliance of the house of Israel; they will recall their iniquity, when they turned to them for aid. Then they shall know that I am the Lord God.

17 In the twenty-seventh year, in the first month, on the first day of the month, the word of the LORD came to me: [18]Mortal, King Nebuchadrezzar of Babylon made his army labor hard against Tyre; every head was made bald and every shoulder was rubbed bare; yet neither he nor his army got anything from Tyre to pay for the labor that he had expended against it. [19]Therefore thus says the Lord God: I will give the land of Egypt to King Nebuchadrezzar of Babylon; and he shall carry off its wealth and despoil it and plunder it; and it shall be the wages for his army. [20]I have given him the land of Egypt as his payment for which he labored, because they worked for me, says the Lord God.

21 On that day I will cause a horn to sprout up for the house of Israel, and I will open your lips among them. Then they shall know that I am the LORD.

30.1 THE word of the LORD came to me: [2]Mortal, prophesy, and say, Thus says the Lord God:
    Wail, "Alas for the day!"
3       For a day is near,
        the day of the LORD is near;
    it will be a day of clouds,
        a time of doom[e] for the
            nations.
4   A sword shall come upon Egypt,
        and anguish shall be in
            Ethiopia, [c]
    when the slain fall in Egypt,
        and its wealth is carried
            away,
        and its foundations are
            torn down.
[5]Ethiopia, [c] and Put, and Lud, and all Arabia, and Libya, [f] and the people of the allied land[g] shall fall with them by the sword.

6   Thus says the LORD:
    Those who support Egypt shall
        fall,
        and its proud might shall
            come down;
    from Migdol to Syene

a Syr: Heb *stand*   b Gk Syr Vg: Heb *he*   c Or *Nubia*; Heb *Cush*   d Heb *It*   e Heb lacks *of doom*
f Compare Gk Syr Vg: Heb *Cub*   g Meaning of Heb uncertain

they shall fall within it by
the sword,
says the Lord God.
7 They shall be desolated among
other desolated
countries,
and their cities shall lie among
cities laid waste.
8 Then they shall know that I am
the Lord,
when I have set fire to
Egypt,
and all who help it are
broken.

9 On that day, messengers shall go out from me in ships to terrify the unsuspecting Ethiopians;[a] and anguish shall come upon them on the day of Egypt's doom;[b] for it is coming!

10 Thus says the Lord God:
I will put an end to the hordes
of Egypt,
by the hand of King
Nebuchadrezzar of
Babylon.
11 He and his people with him, the
most terrible of the
nations,
shall be brought in to destroy
the land;
and they shall draw their swords
against Egypt,
and fill the land with the slain.
12 I will dry up the channels,
and will sell the land into the
hand of evildoers;
I will bring desolation upon the
land and everything in it
by the hand of foreigners;
I the Lord have spoken.

13 Thus says the Lord God:
I will destroy the idols
and put an end to the images
in Memphis;
there shall no longer be a prince
in the land of Egypt;

so I will put fear in the land
of Egypt.
14 I will make Pathros a desolation,
and will set fire to Zoan,
and will execute acts of
judgment on Thebes.
15 I will pour my wrath upon
Pelusium,
the stronghold of Egypt,
and cut off the hordes of
Thebes.
16 I will set fire to Egypt;
Pelusium shall be in great
agony;
Thebes shall be breached,
and Memphis face adversaries
by day.
17 The young men of On and of
Pi-beseth shall fall by
the sword;
and the cities themselves[c]
shall go into captivity.
18 At Tehaphnehes the day shall
be dark,
when I break there the
dominion of Egypt,
and its proud might shall come
to an end;
the city[d] shall be covered by
a cloud,
and its daughter-towns shall
go into captivity.
19 Thus I will execute acts of
judgment on Egypt.
Then they shall know that I
am the Lord.

20 In the eleventh year, in the first month, on the seventh day of the month, the word of the Lord came to me: 21Mortal, I have broken the arm of Pharaoh king of Egypt; it has not been bound up for healing or wrapped with a bandage, so that it may become strong to wield the sword. 22Therefore thus says the Lord God: I am against Pharaoh king of Egypt, and will break his arms, both the strong arm and the one that was broken; and I will make the

sword fall from his hand. ²³I will scatter the Egyptians among the nations, and disperse them throughout the lands. ²⁴I will strengthen the arms of the king of Babylon, and put my sword in his hand; but I will break the arms of Pharaoh, and he will groan before him with the groans of one mortally wounded. ²⁵I will strengthen the arms of the king of Babylon, but the arms of Pharaoh shall fall. And they shall know that I am the LORD, when I put my sword into the hand of the king of Babylon. He shall stretch it out against the land of Egypt, ²⁶and I will scatter the Egyptians among the nations and disperse them throughout the countries. Then they shall know that I am the LORD.

## HEBREWS 11.32—12.13

AND what more should I say? For time would fail me to tell of Gideon, Barak, Samson, Jephthah, of David and Samuel and the prophets— ³³who through faith conquered kingdoms, administered justice, obtained promises, shut the mouths of lions, ³⁴quenched raging fire, escaped the edge of the sword, won strength out of weakness, became mighty in war, put foreign armies to flight. ³⁵Women received their dead by resurrection. Others were tortured, refusing to accept release, in order to obtain a better resurrection. ³⁶Others suffered mocking and flogging, and even chains and imprisonment. ³⁷They were stoned to death, they were sawn in two, ᵃ they were killed by the sword; they went about in skins of sheep and goats, destitute, persecuted, tormented— ³⁸of whom the world was not worthy. They wandered in deserts and mountains, and in caves and holes in the ground.

39 Yet all these, though they were commended for their faith, did not receive what was promised, ⁴⁰since God had provided something better so that they would not, apart from us, be made perfect.

12.1 THEREFORE, since we are surrounded by so great a cloud of witnesses, let us also lay aside every weight and the sin that clings so closely, ᵇ and let us run with perseverance the race that is set before us, ²looking to Jesus the pioneer and perfecter of our faith, who for the sake ofᶜ the joy that was set before him endured the cross, disregarding its shame, and has taken his seat at the right hand of the throne of God.

3 Consider him who endured such hostility against himself from sinners, ᵈ so that you may not grow weary or lose heart. ⁴In your struggle against sin you have not yet resisted to the point of shedding your blood. ⁵And you have forgotten the exhortation that addresses you as children—

> "My child, do not regard lightly
>> the discipline of the
>> Lord,
>> or lose heart when you are
>> punished by him;
> 6 for the Lord disciplines those
>> whom he loves,
>> and chastises every child
>> whom he accepts."

⁷Endure trials for the sake of discipline. God is treating you as children; for what child is there whom a parent does not discipline? ⁸If you do not have that discipline in which all children share, then you are illegitimate and not his children. ⁹Moreover, we had human parents to discipline us, and we respected them. Should we not be even more willing to be subject to the Father of spirits and live? ¹⁰For they disciplined us for a short time as seemed

---

ᵃOther ancient authorities add *they were tempted*  ᵇOther ancient authorities read *sin that easily distracts*  ᶜOr *who instead of*  ᵈOther ancient authorities read *such hostility from sinners against themselves*

best to them, but he disciplines us for our good, in order that we may share his holiness. [11]Now, discipline always seems painful rather than pleasant at the time, but later it yields the peaceful fruit of righteousness to those who have been trained by it.

12 Therefore lift your drooping hands and strengthen your weak knees, [13]and make straight paths for your feet, so that what is lame may not be put out of joint, but rather be healed.

## PSALM 112.1–10

PRAISE the LORD!
Happy are those who fear
    the LORD,
who greatly delight in his
    commandments.
2  Their descendants will be
    mighty in the land;
the generation of the upright
    will be blessed.
3  Wealth and riches are in their
    houses,
and their righteousness
    endures forever.
4  They rise in the darkness as a
    light for the upright;
they are gracious, merciful,
    and righteous.
5  It is well with those who deal
    generously and lend,

who conduct their affairs with
    justice.
6  For the righteous will never
    be moved;
they will be remembered
    forever.
7  They are not afraid of evil
    tidings;
their hearts are firm, secure
    in the LORD.
8  Their hearts are steady, they
    will not be afraid;
in the end they will look in
    triumph on their foes.
9  They have distributed freely,
    they have given to the
    poor;
their righteousness endures
    forever;
their horn is exalted in honor.
10  The wicked see it and are
    angry;
they gnash their teeth and
    melt away;
the desire of the wicked
    comes to nothing.

## PROVERBS 27.17

IRON sharpens iron,
and one person sharpens the
    wits[a] of another.

a Heb *face*

# NOVEMBER 15

EZEKIEL 31.1—32.32

IN the eleventh year, in the third month, on the first day of the month, the word of the LORD came to me: [2]Mortal, say to Pharaoh king of Egypt and to his hordes:

Whom are you like in your
  greatness?
3    Consider Assyria, a cedar
      of Lebanon,
with fair branches and forest
    shade,
  and of great height,
  its top among the clouds. [a]
4  The waters nourished it,
    the deep made it grow tall,
making its rivers flow [b]
    around the place it was
    planted,
sending forth its streams
    to all the trees of the field.
5  So it towered high
    above all the trees of the
    field;
  its boughs grew large
    and its branches long,
    from abundant water in
    its shoots.
6  All the birds of the air
    made their nests in its
    boughs;
  under its branches all the
    animals of the field
    gave birth to their young;
  and in its shade
    all great nations lived.
7  It was beautiful in its greatness,
    in the length of its branches;
  for its roots went down
    to abundant water.
8  The cedars in the garden of God
    could not rival it,

nor the fir trees equal its
    boughs;
the plane trees were as nothing
    compared with its branches;
no tree in the garden of God
    was like it in beauty.
9  I made it beautiful
    with its mass of branches,
  the envy of all the trees of
    Eden
    that were in the garden of
    God.
10  Therefore thus says the Lord GOD: Because it [c] towered high and set its top among the clouds, [a] and its heart was proud of its height, [11]I gave it into the hand of the prince of the nations; he has dealt with it as its wickedness deserves. I have cast it out. [12]Foreigners from the most terrible of the nations have cut it down and left it. On the mountains and in all the valleys its branches have fallen, and its boughs lie broken in all the watercourses of the land; and all the peoples of the earth went away from its shade and left it.
13  On its fallen trunk settle
    all the birds of the air,
  and among its boughs lodge
    all the wild animals.
[14]All this is in order that no trees by the waters may grow to lofty height or set their tops among the clouds, [a] and that no trees that drink water may reach up to them in height.

For all of them are handed over
    to death,
  to the world below;
along with all mortals,
    with those who go down to
    the Pit.
15  Thus says the Lord GOD: On the day it went down to Sheol I closed the

deep over it and covered it; I restrained its rivers, and its mighty waters were checked. I clothed Lebanon in gloom for it, and all the trees of the field fainted because of it. ¹⁶I made the nations quake at the sound of its fall, when I cast it down to Sheol with those who go down to the Pit; and all the trees of Eden, the choice and best of Lebanon, all that were well watered, were consoled in the world below. ¹⁷They also went down to Sheol with it, to those killed by the sword, along with its allies,ᵃ those who lived in its shade among the nations.

18 Which among the trees of Eden was like you in glory and in greatness? Now you shall be brought down with the trees of Eden to the world below; you shall lie among the uncircumcised, with those who are killed by the sword. This is Pharaoh and all his horde, says the Lord God.

³²·¹ In the twelfth year, in the twelfth month, on the first day of the month, the word of the Lord came to me: ²Mortal, raise a lamentation over Pharaoh king of Egypt, and say to him:
You consider yourself a lion
among the nations,
but you are like a dragon in
the seas;
you thrash about in your
streams,
trouble the water with your
feet,
and foul yourᵇ streams.
3 Thus says the Lord God:
In an assembly of many
peoples
I will throw my net over you;
and Iᶜ will haul you up in
my dragnet.
4 I will throw you on the ground,
on the open field I will fling
you,
and will cause all the birds of
the air to settle on you,
and I will let the wild animals
of the whole earth gorge
themselves with you.
5 I will strew your flesh on the
mountains,
and fill the valleys with your
carcass.ᵈ
6 I will drench the land with your
flowing blood
up to the mountains,
and the watercourses will be
filled with you.
7 When I blot you out, I will
cover the heavens,
and make their stars dark;
I will cover the sun with a
cloud,
and the moon shall not give
its light.
8 All the shining lights of the
heavens
I will darken above you,
and put darkness on your
land,
says the Lord God.
9 I will trouble the hearts of many
peoples,
as I carry you captiveᵉ
among the nations,
into countries you have not
known.
10 I will make many peoples
appalled at you;
their kings shall shudder
because of you.
When I brandish my sword
before them,
they shall tremble every
moment
for their lives, each one of
them,
on the day of your downfall.
11 For thus says the Lord God:
The sword of the king of
Babylon shall come
against you.

ᵃHeb *its arms*  ᵇHeb *their*  ᶜGk Vg: Heb *they*  ᵈSymmachus Syr Vg: Heb *your height*  ᵉGk: Heb *bring your destruction*

12 I will cause your hordes to fall
    by the swords of mighty
        ones,
    all of them most terrible
        among the nations.
    They shall bring to ruin the
        pride of Egypt,
    and all its hordes shall perish.
13 I will destroy all its livestock
    from beside abundant waters;
    and no human foot shall trouble
        them any more,
    nor shall the hoofs of cattle
        trouble them.
14 Then I will make their waters
        clear,
    and cause their streams to
        run like oil, says the
        Lord GOD.
15 When I make the land of Egypt
        desolate
    and when the land is stripped
        of all that fills it,
    when I strike down all who live
        in it,
    then they shall know that I
        am the LORD.
16 This is a lamentation; it shall
        be chanted.
    The women of the nations
        shall chant it.
    Over Egypt and all its hordes
        they shall chant it,
    says the Lord GOD.

17 In the twelfth year, in the first month, a on the fifteenth day of the month, the word of the LORD came to me:

18 Mortal, wail over the hordes
        of Egypt,
    and send them down,
    with Egypt b and the daughters
        of majestic nations,
    to the world below,
    with those who go down to
        the Pit.
19 "Whom do you surpass in
        beauty?

    Go down! Be laid to rest with
        the uncircumcised!"

20 They shall fall among those who are killed by the sword. Egypt c has been handed over to the sword; carry away both it and its hordes. 21 The mighty chiefs shall speak of them, with their helpers, out of the midst of Sheol: "They have come down, they lie still, the uncircumcised, killed by the sword."

22 Assyria is there, and all its company, their graves all around it, all of them killed, fallen by the sword. 23 Their graves are set in the uttermost parts of the Pit. Its company is all around its grave, all of them killed, fallen by the sword, who spread terror in the land of the living.

24 Elam is there, and all its hordes around its grave; all of them killed, fallen by the sword, who went down uncircumcised into the world below, who spread terror in the land of the living. They bear their shame with those who go down to the Pit. 25 They have made Elam b a bed among the slain with all its hordes, their graves all around it, all of them uncircumcised, killed by the sword; for terror of them was spread in the land of the living, and they bear their shame with those who go down to the Pit; they are placed among the slain.

26 Meshech and Tubal are there, and all their multitude, their graves all around them, all of them uncircumcised, killed by the sword; for they spread terror in the land of the living. 27 And they do not lie with the fallen warriors of long ago d who went down to Sheol with their weapons of war, whose swords were laid under their heads, and whose shields e are upon their bones; for the terror of the warriors was in the land of the living. 28 So you shall be broken and lie among the

a Gk: Heb lacks *in the first month*   b Heb *it*   c Heb *It*   d Gk Old Latin: Heb *of the uncircumcised*
e Cn: Heb *iniquities*

uncircumcised, with those who are killed by the sword.

29 Edom is there, its kings and all its princes, who for all their might are laid with those who are killed by the sword; they lie with the uncircumcised, with those who go down to the Pit.

30 The princes of the north are there, all of them, and all the Sidonians, who have gone down in shame with the slain, for all the terror that they caused by their might; they lie uncircumcised with those who are killed by the sword, and bear their shame with those who go down to the Pit.

31 When Pharaoh sees them, he will be consoled for all his hordes— Pharaoh and all his army, killed by the sword, says the Lord God. [32] For he[a] spread terror in the land of the living; therefore he shall be laid to rest among the uncircumcised, with those who are slain by the sword—Pharaoh and all his multitude, says the Lord God.

## HEBREWS 12.14–29

PURSUE peace with everyone, and the holiness without which no one will see the Lord. [15] See to it that no one fails to obtain the grace of God; that no root of bitterness springs up and causes trouble, and through it many become defiled. [16] See to it that no one becomes like Esau, an immoral and godless person, who sold his birthright for a single meal. [17] You know that later, when he wanted to inherit the blessing, he was rejected, for he found no chance to repent,[b] even though he sought the blessing[c] with tears.

18 You have not come to something[d] that can be touched, a blazing fire, and darkness, and gloom, and a tempest, [19] and the sound of a trumpet, and a voice whose words made the hearers beg that not another word be spoken to them. [20] (For they could not endure the order that was given, "If even an animal touches the mountain, it shall be stoned to death." [21] Indeed, so terrifying was the sight that Moses said, "I tremble with fear.") [22] But you have come to Mount Zion and to the city of the living God, the heavenly Jerusalem, and to innumerable angels in festal gathering, [23] and to the assembly[e] of the firstborn who are enrolled in heaven, and to God the judge of all, and to the spirits of the righteous made perfect, [24] and to Jesus, the mediator of a new covenant, and to the sprinkled blood that speaks a better word than the blood of Abel.

25 See that you do not refuse the one who is speaking; for if they did not escape when they refused the one who warned them on earth, how much less will we escape if we reject the one who warns from heaven! [26] At that time his voice shook the earth; but now he has promised, "Yet once more I will shake not only the earth but also the heaven." [27] This phrase, "Yet once more," indicates the removal of what is shaken— that is, created things—so that what cannot be shaken may remain. [28] Therefore, since we are receiving a kingdom that cannot be shaken, let us give thanks, by which we offer to God an acceptable worship with reverence and awe; [29] for indeed our God is a consuming fire.

## PSALM 113.1—114.8

PRAISE the Lord!
Praise, O servants of the
   Lord;
praise the name of the Lord.

2 Blessed be the name of the
   Lord
from this time on and
   forevermore.

---

aCn: Heb *I*   bOr *no chance to change his father's mind*   cGk *it*   dOther ancient authorities read *a mountain*   eOr *angels, and to the festal gathering* 23*and assembly*

3 From the rising of the sun to its
     setting
    the name of the Lord is to be
     praised.
4 The Lord is high above all
     nations,
    and his glory above the
     heavens.

5 Who is like the Lord our God,
    who is seated on high,
6 who looks far down
    on the heavens and the earth?
7 He raises the poor from the
     dust,
    and lifts the needy from the
     ash heap,
8 to make them sit with princes,
    with the princes of his people.
9 He gives the barren woman a
     home,
    making her the joyous mother
     of children.
Praise the Lord!

114.1 When Israel went out from
     Egypt,
    the house of Jacob from a
     people of strange
     language,
2 Judah became God's[a]
     sanctuary,
    Israel his dominion.

3 The sea looked and fled;
    Jordan turned back.
4 The mountains skipped like
     rams,
    the hills like lambs.

5 Why is it, O sea, that you flee?
    O Jordan, that you turn back?
6 O mountains, that you skip like
     rams?
    O hills, like lambs?

7 Tremble, O earth, at the
     presence of the Lord,
    at the presence of the God of
     Jacob,
8 who turns the rock into a pool
     of water,
    the flint into a spring of
     water.

# PROVERBS 27.18–20

ANYONE who tends a fig tree
    will eat its fruit,
and anyone who takes care
    of a master will be
    honored.
19 Just as water reflects the face,
    so one human heart reflects
     another.
20 Sheol and Abaddon are never
     satisfied,
    and human eyes are never
     satisfied.

a Heb *his*

# NOVEMBER 16

## EZEKIEL 33.1—34.31

THE word of the LORD came to me: <sup>2</sup>O Mortal, speak to your people and say to them, If I bring the sword upon a land, and the people of the land take one of their number as their sentinel; <sup>3</sup>and if the sentinel sees the sword coming upon the land and blows the trumpet and warns the people; <sup>4</sup>then if any who hear the sound of the trumpet do not take warning, and the sword comes and takes them away, their blood shall be upon their own heads. <sup>5</sup>They heard the sound of the trumpet and did not take warning; their blood shall be upon themselves. But if they had taken warning, they would have saved their lives. <sup>6</sup>But if the sentinel sees the sword coming and does not blow the trumpet, so that the people are not warned, and the sword comes and takes any of them, they are taken away in their iniquity, but their blood I will require at the sentinel's hand.

7 So you, mortal, I have made a sentinel for the house of Israel; whenever you hear a word from my mouth, you shall give them warning from me. <sup>8</sup>If I say to the wicked, "O wicked ones, you shall surely die," and you do not speak to warn the wicked to turn from their ways, the wicked shall die in their iniquity, but their blood I will require at your hand. <sup>9</sup>But if you warn the wicked to turn from their ways, and they do not turn from their ways, the wicked shall die in their iniquity, but you will have saved your life.

10 Now you, mortal, say to the house of Israel, Thus you have said: "Our transgressions and our sins weigh upon us, and we waste away because of them; how then can we live?" <sup>11</sup>Say to them, As I live, says the Lord GOD, I have no pleasure in the death of the wicked, but that the wicked turn from their ways and live; turn back, turn back from your evil ways; for why will you die, O house of Israel? <sup>12</sup>And you, mortal, say to your people, The righteousness of the righteous shall not save them when they transgress; and as for the wickedness of the wicked, it shall not make them stumble when they turn from their wickedness; and the righteous shall not be able to live by their righteousness[a] when they sin. <sup>13</sup>Though I say to the righteous that they shall surely live, yet if they trust in their righteousness and commit iniquity, none of their righteous deeds shall be remembered; but in the iniquity that they have committed they shall die. <sup>14</sup>Again, though I say to the wicked, "You shall surely die," yet if they turn from their sin and do what is lawful and right— <sup>15</sup>if the wicked restore the pledge, give back what they have taken by robbery, and walk in the statutes of life, committing no iniquity—they shall surely live, they shall not die. <sup>16</sup>None of the sins that they have committed shall be remembered against them; they have done what is lawful and right, they shall surely live.

17 Yet your people say, "The way of the Lord is not just," when it is their own way that is not just. <sup>18</sup>When the righteous turn from their righteousness, and commit iniquity, they shall die for it.[b] <sup>19</sup>And when the wicked turn from their wickedness, and do what is lawful and right, they shall live by it.[b] <sup>20</sup>Yet you say, "The way of the Lord is not just." O house of Israel, I will judge all of you according to your ways!

<sub>a</sub>Heb *by it*   <sub>b</sub>Heb *them*

21 In the twelfth year of our exile, in the tenth month, on the fifth day of the month, someone who had escaped from Jerusalem came to me and said, "The city has fallen." [22]Now the hand of the LORD had been upon me the evening before the fugitive came; but he had opened my mouth by the time the fugitive came to me in the morning; so my mouth was opened, and I was no longer unable to speak.

23 The word of the LORD came to me: [24]Mortal, the inhabitants of these waste places in the land of Israel keep saying, "Abraham was only one man, yet he got possession of the land; but we are many; the land is surely given us to possess." [25]Therefore say to them, Thus says the Lord GOD: You eat flesh with the blood, and lift up your eyes to your idols, and shed blood; shall you then possess the land? [26]You depend on your swords, you commit abominations, and each of you defiles his neighbor's wife; shall you then possess the land? [27]Say this to them, Thus says the Lord GOD: As I live, surely those who are in the waste places shall fall by the sword; and those who are in the open field I will give to the wild animals to be devoured; and those who are in strongholds and in caves shall die by pestilence. [28]I will make the land a desolation and a waste, and its proud might shall come to an end; and the mountains of Israel shall be so desolate that no one will pass through. [29]Then they shall know that I am the LORD, when I have made the land a desolation and a waste because of all their abominations that they have committed.

30 As for you, mortal, your people who talk together about you by the walls, and at the doors of the houses, say to one another, each to a neighbor, "Come and hear what the word is that comes from the LORD." [31]They come to you as people come, and they sit before you as my people, and they hear your words, but they will not obey them. For flattery is on their lips, but their heart is set on their gain. [32]To them you are like a singer of love songs, [a] one who has a beautiful voice and plays well on an instrument; they hear what you say, but they will not do it. [33]When this comes—and come it will!—then they shall know that a prophet has been among them.

34.1 THE word of the LORD came to me: [2]Mortal, prophesy against the shepherds of Israel: prophesy, and say to them—to the shepherds: Thus says the Lord GOD: Ah, you shepherds of Israel who have been feeding yourselves! Should not shepherds feed the sheep? [3]You eat the fat, you clothe yourselves with the wool, you slaughter the fatlings; but you do not feed the sheep. [4]You have not strengthened the weak, you have not healed the sick, you have not bound up the injured, you have not brought back the strayed, you have not sought the lost, but with force and harshness you have ruled them. [5]So they were scattered, because there was no shepherd; and scattered, they became food for all the wild animals. [6]My sheep were scattered, they wandered over all the mountains and on every high hill; my sheep were scattered over all the face of the earth, with no one to search or seek for them.

7 Therefore, you shepherds, hear the word of the LORD: [8]As I live, says the Lord GOD, because my sheep have become a prey, and my sheep have become food for all the wild animals, since there was no shepherd; and because my shepherds have not searched for my sheep, but the shepherds have fed themselves, and have not fed my sheep; [9]therefore, you shepherds, hear the word of the LORD: [10]Thus says the Lord GOD, I am against the shep-

a Cn: Heb *like a love song*

herds; and I will demand my sheep at their hand, and put a stop to their feeding the sheep; no longer shall the shepherds feed themselves. I will rescue my sheep from their mouths, so that they may not be food for them.

11  For thus says the Lord GOD: I myself will search for my sheep, and will seek them out. 12As shepherds seek out their flocks when they are among their scattered sheep, so I will seek out my sheep. I will rescue them from all the places to which they have been scattered on a day of clouds and thick darkness. 13I will bring them out from the peoples and gather them from the countries, and will bring them into their own land; and I will feed them on the mountains of Israel, by the watercourses, and in all the inhabited parts of the land. 14I will feed them with good pasture, and the mountain heights of Israel shall be their pasture; there they shall lie down in good grazing land, and they shall feed on rich pasture on the mountains of Israel. 15I myself will be the shepherd of my sheep, and I will make them lie down, says the Lord GOD. 16I will seek the lost, and I will bring back the strayed, and I will bind up the injured, and I will strengthen the weak, but the fat and the strong I will destroy. I will feed them with justice.

17  As for you, my flock, thus says the Lord GOD: I shall judge between sheep and sheep, between rams and goats: 18Is it not enough for you to feed on the good pasture, but you must tread down with your feet the rest of your pasture? When you drink of clear water, must you foul the rest with your feet? 19And must my sheep eat what you have trodden with your feet, and drink what you have fouled with your feet?

20  Therefore, thus says the Lord GOD to them: I myself will judge between the fat sheep and the lean sheep.

21Because you pushed with flank and shoulder, and butted at all the weak animals with your horns until you scattered them far and wide, 22I will save my flock, and they shall no longer be ravaged; and I will judge between sheep and sheep.

23  I will set up over them one shepherd, my servant David, and he shall feed them: he shall feed them and be their shepherd. 24And I, the LORD, will be their God, and my servant David shall be prince among them; I, the LORD, have spoken.

25  I will make with them a covenant of peace and banish wild animals from the land, so that they may live in the wild and sleep in the woods securely. 26I will make them and the region around my hill a blessing; and I will send down the showers in their season; they shall be showers of blessing. 27The trees of the field shall yield their fruit, and the earth shall yield its increase. They shall be secure on their soil; and they shall know that I am the LORD, when I break the bars of their yoke, and save them from the hands of those who enslaved them. 28They shall no more be plunder for the nations, nor shall the animals of the land devour them; they shall live in safety, and no one shall make them afraid. 29I will provide for them a splendid vegetation so that they shall no more be consumed with hunger in the land, and no longer suffer the insults of the nations. 30They shall know that I, the LORD their God, am with them, and that they, the house of Israel, are my people, says the Lord GOD. 31You are my sheep, the sheep of my pasturea and I am your God, says the Lord GOD.

aGk OL: Heb *pasture, you are people*

## HEBREWS 13.1–25

Let mutual love continue. [2]Do not neglect to show hospitality to strangers, for by doing that some have entertained angels without knowing it. [3]Remember those who are in prison, as though you were in prison with them; those who are being tortured, as though you yourselves were being tortured. [a] [4]Let marriage be held in honor by all, and let the marriage bed be kept undefiled; for God will judge fornicators and adulterers. [5]Keep your lives free from the love of money, and be content with what you have; for he has said, "I will never leave you or forsake you." [6]So we can say with confidence,

"The Lord is my helper;
　I will not be afraid.
　What can anyone do to me?"

7 Remember your leaders, those who spoke the word of God to you; consider the outcome of their way of life, and imitate their faith. [8]Jesus Christ is the same yesterday and today and forever. [9]Do not be carried away by all kinds of strange teachings; for it is well for the heart to be strengthened by grace, not by regulations about food, [b] which have not benefited those who observe them. [10]We have an altar from which those who officiate in the tent[c] have no right to eat. [11]For the bodies of those animals whose blood is brought into the sanctuary by the high priest as a sacrifice for sin are burned outside the camp. [12]Therefore Jesus also suffered outside the city gate in order to sanctify the people by his own blood. [13]Let us then go to him outside the camp and bear the abuse he endured. [14]For here we have no lasting city, but we are looking for the city that is to come. [15]Through him, then, let us continually offer a sacrifice of praise to God, that is, the fruit of lips that confess his name. [16]Do not neglect to do good and to share what you have, for such sacrifices are pleasing to God.

17 Obey your leaders and submit to them, for they are keeping watch over your souls and will give an account. Let them do this with joy and not with sighing—for that would be harmful to you.

18 Pray for us; we are sure that we have a clear conscience, desiring to act honorably in all things. [19]I urge you all the more to do this, so that I may be restored to you very soon.

20 Now may the God of peace, who brought back from the dead our Lord Jesus, the great shepherd of the sheep, by the blood of the eternal covenant, [21]make you complete in everything good so that you may do his will, working among us[d] that which is pleasing in his sight, through Jesus Christ, to whom be the glory forever and ever. Amen.

22 I appeal to you, brothers and sisters, [e] bear with my word of exhortation, for I have written to you briefly. [23]I want you to know that our brother Timothy has been set free; and if he comes in time, he will be with me when I see you. [24]Greet all your leaders and all the saints. Those from Italy send you greetings. [25]Grace be with all of you. [f]

## PSALM 115.1–18

Not to us, O Lord, not to us,
　　but to your name give
　　glory,
　for the sake of your steadfast
　　love and your
　　faithfulness.
2　Why should the nations say,
　　"Where is their God?"

---

a Gk *were in the body*　b Gk *not by foods*　c Or *tabernacle*　d Other ancient authorities read *you*
e Gk *brothers*　f Other ancient authorities add *Amen*

3  Our God is in the heavens;
      he does whatever he pleases.
4  Their idols are silver and gold,
      the work of human hands.
5  They have mouths, but do not
         speak;
      eyes, but do not see.
6  They have ears, but do not
         hear;
      noses, but do not smell.
7  They have hands, but do not
         feel;
      feet, but do not walk;
      they make no sound in their
         throats.
8  Those who make them are like
         them;
      so are all who trust in them.

9  O Israel, trust in the LORD!
      He is their help and their
         shield.
10  O house of Aaron, trust in the
         LORD!
      He is their help and their
         shield.
11  You who fear the LORD, trust in
         the LORD!
      He is their help and their
         shield.

12  The LORD has been mindful of
         us; he will bless us;
      he will bless the house of
         Israel;
      he will bless the house of
         Aaron;

13  he will bless those who fear the
         LORD,
      both small and great.

14  May the LORD give you
         increase,
      both you and your children.
15  May you be blessed by the
         LORD,
      who made heaven and earth.

16  The heavens are the LORD's
         heavens,
      but the earth he has given to
         human beings.
17  The dead do not praise the
         LORD,
      nor do any that go down into
         silence.
18  But we will bless the LORD
      from this time on and
         forevermore.
   Praise the LORD!


## PROVERBS 27.21–22

THE crucible is for silver, and
      the furnace is for gold,
   so a person is tested<sup>a</sup> by
      being praised.
22  Crush a fool in a mortar with a
         pestle
      along with crushed grain,
      but the folly will not be
         driven out.

a Heb lacks *is tested*

# NOVEMBER 17

## EZEKIEL 35.1—36.38

THE word of the LORD came to me: [2]Mortal, set your face against Mount Seir, and prophesy against it, [3]and say to it, Thus says the Lord GOD:

I am against you, Mount Seir;
    I stretch out my hand
        against you
    to make you a desolation and
        a waste.
[4]  I lay your towns in ruins;
    you shall become a
        desolation,
    and you shall know that I am
        the LORD.

[5]Because you cherished an ancient enmity, and gave over the people of Israel to the power of the sword at the time of their calamity, at the time of their final punishment; [6]therefore, as I live, says the Lord GOD, I will prepare you for blood, and blood shall pursue you; since you did not hate bloodshed, bloodshed shall pursue you. [7]I will make Mount Seir a waste and a desolation; and I will cut off from it all who come and go. [8]I will fill its mountains with the slain; on your hills and in your valleys and in all your watercourses those killed with the sword shall fall. [9]I will make you a perpetual desolation, and your cities shall never be inhabited. Then you shall know that I am the LORD.

10 Because you said, "These two nations and these two countries shall be mine, and we will take possession of them,"—although the LORD was there— [11]therefore, as I live, says the Lord GOD, I will deal with you according to the anger and envy that you showed because of your hatred against them;

and I will make myself known among you,[a] when I judge you. [12]You shall know that I, the LORD, have heard all the abusive speech that you uttered against the mountains of Israel, saying, "They are laid desolate, they are given us to devour." [13]And you magnified yourselves against me with your mouth, and multiplied your words against me; I heard it. [14]Thus says the Lord GOD: As the whole earth rejoices, I will make you desolate. [15]As you rejoiced over the inheritance of the house of Israel, because it was desolate, so I will deal with you; you shall be desolate, Mount Seir, and all Edom, all of it. Then they shall know that I am the LORD.

[36.1] AND you, mortal, prophesy to the mountains of Israel, and say: O mountains of Israel, hear the word of the LORD. [2]Thus says the Lord GOD: Because the enemy said of you, "Aha!" and, "The ancient heights have become our possession," [3]therefore prophesy, and say: Thus says the Lord GOD: Because they made you desolate indeed, and crushed you from all sides, so that you became the possession of the rest of the nations, and you became an object of gossip and slander among the people; [4]therefore, O mountains of Israel, hear the word of the Lord GOD: Thus says the Lord GOD to the mountains and the hills, the watercourses and the valleys, the desolate wastes and the deserted towns, which have become a source of plunder and an object of derision to the rest of the nations all around; [5]therefore thus says the Lord GOD: I am speaking in my hot jealousy against the rest of the nations, and

a Gk: Heb *them*

against all Edom, who, with whole-hearted joy and utter contempt, took my land as their possession, because of its pasture, to plunder it. 6Therefore prophesy concerning the land of Israel, and say to the mountains and hills, to the watercourses and valleys, Thus says the Lord God: I am speaking in my jealous wrath, because you have suffered the insults of the nations; 7therefore thus says the Lord God: I swear that the nations that are all around you shall themselves suffer insults.

8 But you, O mountains of Israel, shall shoot out your branches, and yield your fruit to my people Israel; for they shall soon come home. 9See now, I am for you; I will turn to you, and you shall be tilled and sown; 10and I will multiply your population, the whole house of Israel, all of it; the towns shall be inhabited and the waste places rebuilt; 11and I will multiply human beings and animals upon you. They shall increase and be fruitful; and I will cause you to be inhabited as in your former times, and will do more good to you than ever before. Then you shall know that I am the Lord. 12I will lead people upon you—my people Israel—and they shall possess you, and you shall be their inheritance. No longer shall you bereave them of children.

13 Thus says the Lord God: Because they say to you, "You devour people, and you bereave your nation of children," 14therefore you shall no longer devour people and no longer bereave your nation of children, says the Lord God; 15and no longer will I let you hear the insults of the nations, no longer shall you bear the disgrace of the peoples; and no longer shall you cause your nation to stumble, says the Lord God.

16 The word of the Lord came to me: 17Mortal, when the house of Israel lived on their own soil, they defiled it with their ways and their deeds; their conduct in my sight was like the uncleanness of a woman in her menstrual period. 18So I poured out my wrath upon them for the blood that they had shed upon the land, and for the idols with which they had defiled it. 19I scattered them among the nations, and they were dispersed through the countries; in accordance with their conduct and their deeds I judged them. 20But when they came to the nations, wherever they came, they profaned my holy name, in that it was said of them, "These are the people of the Lord, and yet they had to go out of his land." 21But I had concern for my holy name, which the house of Israel had profaned among the nations to which they came.

22 Therefore say to the house of Israel, Thus says the Lord God: It is not for your sake, O house of Israel, that I am about to act, but for the sake of my holy name, which you have profaned among the nations to which you came. 23I will sanctify my great name, which has been profaned among the nations, and which you have profaned among them; and the nations shall know that I am the Lord, says the Lord God, when through you I display my holiness before their eyes. 24I will take you from the nations, and gather you from all the countries, and bring you into your own land. 25I will sprinkle clean water upon you, and you shall be clean from all your uncleannesses, and from all your idols I will cleanse you. 26A new heart I will give you, and a new spirit I will put within you; and I will remove from your body the heart of stone and give you a heart of flesh. 27I will put my spirit within you, and make you follow my statutes and be careful to observe my ordinances. 28Then you shall live in the land that I gave to your ancestors; and you shall be my people, and I will be your God. 29I will save you from all your uncleannesses, and I will summon the grain and make it abundant and lay no famine upon you. 30I will make the fruit of the

tree and the produce of the field abundant, so that you may never again suffer the disgrace of famine among the nations. [31]Then you shall remember your evil ways, and your dealings that were not good; and you shall loathe yourselves for your iniquities and your abominable deeds. [32]It is not for your sake that I will act, says the Lord GOD; let that be known to you. Be ashamed and dismayed for your ways, O house of Israel.

33  Thus says the Lord GOD: On the day that I cleanse you from all your iniquities, I will cause the towns to be inhabited, and the waste places shall be rebuilt. [34]The land that was desolate shall be tilled, instead of being the desolation that it was in the sight of all who passed by. [35]And they will say, "This land that was desolate has become like the garden of Eden; and the waste and desolate and ruined towns are now inhabited and fortified." [36]Then the nations that are left all around you shall know that I, the LORD, have rebuilt the ruined places, and replanted that which was desolate; I, the LORD, have spoken, and I will do it.

37  Thus says the Lord GOD: I will also let the house of Israel ask me to do this for them: to increase their population like a flock. [38]Like the flock for sacrifices, [a] like the flock at Jerusalem during her appointed festivals, so shall the ruined towns be filled with flocks of people. Then they shall know that I am the LORD.

# JAMES 1.1–18

JAMES, a servant[b] of God and of the Lord Jesus Christ,

To the twelve tribes in the Dispersion:

Greetings.

2  My brothers and sisters, [c] whenever you face trials of any kind, consider it nothing but joy, [3]because you know that the testing of your faith produces endurance; [4]and let endurance have its full effect, so that you may be mature and complete, lacking in nothing.

5  If any of you is lacking in wisdom, ask God, who gives to all generously and ungrudgingly, and it will be given you. [6]But ask in faith, never doubting, for the one who doubts is like a wave of the sea, driven and tossed by the wind; [7, 8]for the doubter, being double-minded and unstable in every way, must not expect to receive anything from the Lord.

9  Let the believer[d] who is lowly boast in being raised up, [10]and the rich in being brought low, because the rich will disappear like a flower in the field. [11]For the sun rises with its scorching heat and withers the field; its flower falls, and its beauty perishes. It is the same way with the rich; in the midst of a busy life, they will wither away.

12  Blessed is anyone who endures temptation. Such a one has stood the test and will receive the crown of life that the Lord[e] has promised to those who love him. [13]No one, when tempted, should say, "I am being tempted by God"; for God cannot be tempted by evil and he himself tempts no one. [14]But one is tempted by one's own desire, being lured and enticed by it; [15]then, when that desire has conceived, it gives birth to sin, and that sin, when it is fully grown, gives birth to death. [16]Do not be deceived, my beloved. [f]

17  Every generous act of giving, with every perfect gift, is from above, coming down from the Father of lights, with whom there is no variation or

a Heb *flock of holy things*   b Gk *slave*   c Gk *brothers*   d Gk *brother*   e Gk *he*; other ancient authorities read *God*   f Gk *my beloved brothers*

shadow due to change. [a] [18]In fulfillment of his own purpose he gave us birth by the word of truth, so that we would become a kind of first fruits of his creatures.

## PSALM 116.1–19

I LOVE the LORD, because he has heard
   my voice and my
     supplications.
2 Because he inclined his ear to
   me,
   therefore I will call on him as
     long as I live.
3 The snares of death
     encompassed me;
   the pangs of Sheol laid hold
     on me;
   I suffered distress and
     anguish.
4 Then I called on the name of
     the LORD:
   "O LORD, I pray, save my
     life!"

5 Gracious is the LORD, and
     righteous;
   our God is merciful.
6 The LORD protects the simple;
   when I was brought low, he
     saved me.
7 Return, O my soul, to your
     rest,
   for the LORD has dealt
     bountifully with you.

8 For you have delivered my soul
     from death,
   my eyes from tears,
   my feet from stumbling.
9 I walk before the LORD
   in the land of the living.
10 I kept my faith, even when I
     said,
   "I am greatly afflicted";
11 I said in my consternation,
   "Everyone is a liar."

12 What shall I return to the LORD
   for all his bounty to me?
13 I will lift up the cup of salvation
   and call on the name of the
     LORD,
14 I will pay my vows to the LORD
   in the presence of all his
     people.
15 Precious in the sight of the
     LORD
   is the death of his faithful
     ones.
16 O LORD, I am your servant;
   I am your servant, the child
     of your serving girl.
   You have loosed my bonds.
17 I will offer to you a thanksgiving
     sacrifice
   and call on the name of the
     LORD.
18 I will pay my vows to the LORD
   in the presence of all his
     people,
19 in the courts of the house of
     the LORD,
   in your midst, O Jerusalem.
Praise the LORD!

## PROVERBS 27.23–27

K NOW well the condition of
     your flocks,
   and give attention to your
     herds;
24 for riches do not last forever,
   nor a crown for all
     generations.
25 When the grass is gone, and
     new growth appears,
   and the herbage of the
     mountains is gathered,
26 the lambs will provide your
     clothing,
   and the goats the price of a
     field;

---

a Other ancient authorities read *variation due to a shadow of turning*

27  there will be enough goats' milk
        for your food,
      for the food of your household

      and nourishment for your
          servant-girls.

# NOVEMBER 18

## EZEKIEL 37.1—38.23

THE hand of the LORD came upon me, and he brought me out by the spirit of the LORD and set me down in the middle of a valley; it was full of bones. [2]He led me all around them; there were very many lying in the valley, and they were very dry. [3]He said to me, "Mortal, can these bones live?" I answered, "O Lord GOD, you know." [4]Then he said to me, "Prophesy to these bones, and say to them: O dry bones, hear the word of the LORD. [5]Thus says the Lord GOD to these bones: I will cause breath[a] to enter you, and you shall live. [6]I will lay sinews on you, and will cause flesh to come upon you, and cover you with skin, and put breath[a] in you, and you shall live; and you shall know that I am the LORD."

7  So I prophesied as I had been commanded; and as I prophesied, suddenly there was a noise, a rattling, and the bones came together, bone to its bone. [8]I looked, and there were sinews on them, and flesh had come upon them, and skin had covered them; but there was no breath in them. [9]Then he said to me, "Prophesy to the breath, prophesy, mortal, and say to the breath:[b] Thus says the Lord GOD: Come from the four winds, O breath,[b] and breathe upon these slain, that they may live." [10]I prophesied as he commanded me, and the breath came into them, and they lived, and stood on their feet, a vast multitude.

11  Then he said to me, "Mortal, these bones are the whole house of Israel. They say, 'Our bones are dried up, and our hope is lost; we are cut off completely.' [12]Therefore prophesy, and say to them, Thus says the Lord GOD: I am going to open your graves, and bring you up from your graves, O my people; and I will bring you back to the land of Israel. [13]And you shall know that I am the LORD, when I open your graves, and bring you up from your graves, O my people. [14]I will put my spirit within you, and you shall live, and I will place you on your own soil; then you shall know that I, the LORD, have spoken and will act," says the LORD.

15  The word of the LORD came to me: [16]Mortal, take a stick and write on it, "For Judah, and the Israelites associated with it"; then take another stick and write on it, "For Joseph (the stick of Ephraim) and all the house of Israel associated with it"; [17]and join them together into one stick, so that they may become one in your hand. [18]And when your people say to you, "Will you not show us what you mean by these?" [19]say to them, Thus says the Lord GOD: I am about to take the stick of Joseph (which is in the hand of Ephraim) and the tribes of Israel associated with it; and I will put the stick of Judah upon it,[c] and make them one stick, in order that they may be one in my hand.

a Or *spirit*   b Or *wind* or *spirit*   c Heb *I will put them upon it*

<sup>20</sup>When the sticks on which you write are in your hand before their eyes, <sup>21</sup>then say to them, Thus says the Lord God: I will take the people of Israel from the nations among which they have gone, and will gather them from every quarter, and bring them to their own land. <sup>22</sup>I will make them one nation in the land, on the mountains of Israel; and one king shall be king over them all. Never again shall they be two nations, and never again shall they be divided into two kingdoms. <sup>23</sup>They shall never again defile themselves with their idols and their detestable things, or with any of their transgressions. I will save them from all the apostasies into which they have fallen, <sup>a</sup> and will cleanse them. Then they shall be my people, and I will be their God.

24  My servant David shall be king over them; and they shall all have one shepherd. They shall follow my ordinances and be careful to observe my statutes. <sup>25</sup>They shall live in the land that I gave to my servant Jacob, in which your ancestors lived; they and their children and their children's children shall live there forever; and my servant David shall be their prince forever. <sup>26</sup>I will make a covenant of peace with them; it shall be an everlasting covenant with them; and I will bless<sup>b</sup> them and multiply them, and will set my sanctuary among them forevermore. <sup>27</sup>My dwelling place shall be with them; and I will be their God, and they shall be my people. <sup>28</sup>Then the nations shall know that I the Lord sanctify Israel, when my sanctuary is among them forevermore.

**38.**<sup>1</sup> The word of the Lord came to me: <sup>2</sup>Mortal, set your face toward Gog, of the land of Magog, the chief prince of Meshech and Tubal. Prophesy against him <sup>3</sup>and say: Thus says the Lord God: I am against you, O Gog, chief prince of Meshech and Tubal; <sup>4</sup>I will turn you around and put hooks into your jaws, and I will lead you out with all your army, horses and horsemen, all of them clothed in full armor, a great company, all of them with shield and buckler, wielding swords. <sup>5</sup>Persia, Ethiopia, <sup>c</sup> and Put are with them, all of them with buckler and helmet; <sup>6</sup>Gomer and all its troops; Beth-togarmah from the remotest parts of the north with all its troops—many peoples are with you.

7  Be ready and keep ready, you and all the companies that are assembled around you, and hold yourselves in reserve for them. <sup>8</sup>After many days you shall be mustered; in the latter years you shall go against a land restored from war, a land where people were gathered from many nations on the mountains of Israel, which had long lain waste; its people were brought out from the nations and now are living in safety, all of them. <sup>9</sup>You shall advance, coming on like a storm; you shall be like a cloud covering the land, you and all your troops, and many peoples with you.

10  Thus says the Lord God: On that day thoughts will come into your mind, and you will devise an evil scheme. <sup>11</sup>You will say, "I will go up against the land of unwalled villages; I will fall upon the quiet people who live in safety, all of them living without walls, and having no bars or gates"; <sup>12</sup>to seize spoil and carry off plunder; to assail the waste places that are now inhabited, and the people who were gathered from the nations, who are acquiring cattle and goods, who live at the center<sup>d</sup> of the earth. <sup>13</sup>Sheba and Dedan and the merchants of Tarshish and all its young warriors<sup>e</sup> will say to you, "Have you come to seize spoil? Have you assembled your horde to carry off plunder, to carry away silver and gold, to take away cattle and

<sup>a</sup>Another reading is *from all the settlements in which they have sinned*   <sup>b</sup>Tg: Heb *give*   <sup>c</sup>Or *Nubia;* Heb *Cush*   <sup>d</sup>Heb *navel*   <sup>e</sup>Heb *young lions*

goods, to seize a great amount of booty?"

14 Therefore, mortal, prophesy, and say to Gog: Thus says the Lord God: On that day when my people Israel are living securely, you will rouse yourself[a] [15]and come from your place out of the remotest parts of the north, you and many peoples with you, all of them riding on horses, a great horde, a mighty army; [16]you will come up against my people Israel, like a cloud covering the earth. In the latter days I will bring you against my land, so that the nations may know me, when through you, O Gog, I display my holiness before their eyes.

17 Thus says the Lord God: Are you he of whom I spoke in former days by my servants the prophets of Israel, who in those days prophesied for years that I would bring you against them? [18]On that day, when Gog comes against the land of Israel, says the Lord God, my wrath shall be aroused. [19]For in my jealousy and in my blazing wrath I declare: On that day there shall be a great shaking in the land of Israel; [20]the fish of the sea, and the birds of the air, and the animals of the field, and all creeping things that creep on the ground, and all human beings that are on the face of the earth, shall quake at my presence, and the mountains shall be thrown down, and the cliffs shall fall, and every wall shall tumble to the ground. [21]I will summon the sword against Gog[b] in[c] all my mountains, says the Lord God; the swords of all will be against their comrades. [22]With pestilence and bloodshed I will enter into judgment with him; and I will pour down torrential rains and hailstones, fire and sulfur, upon him and his troops and the many peoples that are with him. [23]So I will display my greatness and my holiness and make myself known in the eyes of many na-

tions. Then they shall know that I am the Lord.

## JAMES 1.19—2.17

You must understand this, my beloved:[d] let everyone be quick to listen, slow to speak, slow to anger; [20]for your anger does not produce God's righteousness. [21]Therefore rid yourselves of all sordidness and rank growth of wickedness, and welcome with meekness the implanted word that has the power to save your souls.

22 But be doers of the word, and not merely hearers who deceive themselves. [23]For if any are hearers of the word and not doers, they are like those who look at themselves[e] in a mirror; [24]for they look at themselves and, on going away, immediately forget what they were like. [25]But those who look into the perfect law, the law of liberty, and persevere, being not hearers who forget but doers who act—they will be blessed in their doing.

26 If any think they are religious, and do not bridle their tongues but deceive their hearts, their religion is worthless. [27]Religion that is pure and undefiled before God, the Father, is this: to care for orphans and widows in their distress, and to keep oneself unstained by the world.

2.1 My brothers and sisters,[f] do you with your acts of favoritism really believe in our glorious Lord Jesus Christ?[g] [2]For if a person with gold rings and in fine clothes comes into your assembly, and if a poor person in dirty clothes also comes in, [3]and if you take notice of the one wearing the fine clothes and say, "Have a seat here, please," while to the one who is poor you say, "Stand there," or, "Sit at my

---

[a]Gk: Heb *will you not know?*  [b]Heb *him*  [c]Heb *to* or *for*  [d]Gk *my beloved brothers*  [e]Gk *at the face of his birth*  [f]Gk *My brothers*  [g]Or *hold the faith of our glorious Lord Jesus Christ without acts of favoritism*

feet,"[a] [4]have you not made distinctions among yourselves, and become judges with evil thoughts? [5]Listen, my beloved brothers and sisters.[b] Has not God chosen the poor in the world to be rich in faith and to be heirs of the kingdom that he has promised to those who love him? [6]But you have dishonored the poor. Is it not the rich who oppress you? Is it not they who drag you into court? [7]Is it not they who blaspheme the excellent name that was invoked over you?

8  You do well if you really fulfill the royal law according to the scripture, "You shall love your neighbor as yourself." [9]But if you show partiality, you commit sin and are convicted by the law as transgressors. [10]For whoever keeps the whole law but fails in one point has become accountable for all of it. [11]For the one who said, "You shall not commit adultery," also said, "You shall not murder." Now if you do not commit adultery but if you murder, you have become a transgressor of the law. [12]So speak and so act as those who are to be judged by the law of liberty. [13]For judgment will be without mercy to anyone who has shown no mercy; mercy triumphs over judgment.

14  What good is it, my brothers and sisters,[b] if you say you have faith but do not have works? Can faith save you? [15]If a brother or sister is naked and lacks daily food, [16]and one of you says to them, "Go in peace; keep warm and eat your fill," and yet you do not supply their bodily needs, what is the good of that? [17]So faith by itself, if it has no works, is dead.

## PSALM 117.1–2

Praise the Lord, all you
    nations!
    Extol him, all you peoples!
2  For great is his steadfast love
    toward us,
    and the faithfulness of the
        Lord endures forever.
Praise the Lord!

## PROVERBS 28.1

The wicked flee when no one
    pursues,
    but the righteous are as bold
    as a lion.

# NOVEMBER 19

## EZEKIEL 39.1—40.27

And you, mortal, prophesy against Gog, and say: Thus says the Lord God: I am against you, O Gog, chief prince of Meshech and Tubal! [2]I will turn you around and drive you forward, and bring you up from the remotest parts of the north, and lead you against the mountains of Israel. [3]I will strike your bow from your left hand, and will make your arrows drop out of your right hand. [4]You shall fall upon the mountains of Israel, you and all your troops and the peoples that are with you; I will give you to birds of prey of every kind and to the wild animals to be devoured. [5]You shall fall in the open field; for I have spoken, says

[a]Gk *Sit under my footstool*   [b]Gk *brothers*

the Lord GOD. [6]I will send fire on Magog and on those who live securely in the coastlands; and they shall know that I am the LORD.

7 My holy name I will make known among my people Israel; and I will not let my holy name be profaned any more; and the nations shall know that I am the LORD, the Holy One in Israel. [8]It has come! It has happened, says the Lord GOD. This is the day of which I have spoken.

9 Then those who live in the towns of Israel will go out and make fires of the weapons and burn them—bucklers and shields, bows and arrows, handpikes and spears—and they will make fires of them for seven years. [10]They will not need to take wood out of the field or cut down any trees in the forests, for they will make their fires of the weapons; they will despoil those who despoiled them, and plunder those who plundered them, says the Lord GOD.

11 On that day I will give to Gog a place for burial in Israel, the Valley of the Travelers[a] east of the sea; it shall block the path of the travelers, for there Gog and all his horde will be buried; it shall be called the Valley of Hamon-gog. [b] [12]Seven months the house of Israel shall spend burying them, in order to cleanse the land. [13]All the people of the land shall bury them; and it will bring them honor on the day that I show my glory, says the Lord GOD. [14]They will set apart men to pass through the land regularly and bury any invaders[c] who remain on the face of the land, so as to cleanse it; for seven months they shall make their search. [15]As the searchers[c] pass through the land, anyone who sees a human bone shall set up a sign by it, until the buriers have buried it in the Valley of Hamon-gog. [b] [16](A city Hamonah[d] is there also.) Thus they shall cleanse the land.

17 As for you, mortal, thus says the Lord GOD: Speak to the birds of every kind and to all the wild animals: Assemble and come, gather from all around to the sacrificial feast that I am preparing for you, a great sacrificial feast on the mountains of Israel, and you shall eat flesh and drink blood. [18]You shall eat the flesh of the mighty, and drink the blood of the princes of the earth—of rams, of lambs, and of goats, of bulls, all of them fatlings of Bashan. [19]You shall eat fat until you are filled, and drink blood until you are drunk, at the sacrificial feast that I am preparing for you. [20]And you shall be filled at my table with horses and charioteers,[e] with warriors and all kinds of soldiers, says the Lord GOD.

21 I will display my glory among the nations; and all the nations shall see my judgment that I have executed, and my hand that I have laid on them. [22]The house of Israel shall know that I am the LORD their God, from that day forward. [23]And the nations shall know that the house of Israel went into captivity for their iniquity, because they dealt treacherously with me. So I hid my face from them and gave them into the hand of their adversaries, and they all fell by the sword. [24]I dealt with them according to their uncleanness and their transgressions, and hid my face from them.

25 Therefore thus says the Lord GOD: Now I will restore the fortunes of Jacob, and have mercy on the whole house of Israel; and I will be jealous for my holy name. [26]They shall forget[f] their shame, and all the treachery they have practiced against me, when they live securely in their land with no one to make them afraid, [27]when I have brought them back from the peoples and gathered them from their enemies' lands, and through them have displayed my holiness in the sight of many nations. [28]Then they shall know that I am

a Or *of the Abarim*   b That is, *the Horde of Gog*   c Heb *travelers*   d That is *The Horde*   e Heb *chariots*
f Another reading is *They shall bear*

the LORD their God because I sent them into exile among the nations, and then gathered them into their own land. I will leave none of them behind; <sup>29</sup>and I will never again hide my face from them, when I pour out my spirit upon the house of Israel, says the Lord GOD.

<sup>40.1</sup> IN the twenty-fifth year of our exile, at the beginning of the year, on the tenth day of the month, in the fourteenth year after the city was struck down, on that very day, the hand of the LORD was upon me, and he brought me there. <sup>2</sup>He brought me, in visions of God, to the land of Israel, and set me down upon a very high mountain, on which was a structure like a city to the south. <sup>3</sup>When he brought me there, a man was there, whose appearance shone like bronze, with a linen cord and a measuring reed in his hand; and he was standing in the gateway. <sup>4</sup>The man said to me, "Mortal, look closely and listen attentively, and set your mind upon all that I shall show you, for you were brought here in order that I might show it to you; declare all that you see to the house of Israel."

5 Now there was a wall all around the outside of the temple area. The length of the measuring reed in the man's hand was six long cubits, each being a cubit and a handbreadth in length; so he measured the thickness of the wall, one reed; and the height, one reed. <sup>6</sup>Then he went into the gateway facing east, going up its steps, and measured the threshold of the gate, one reed deep.<sup>a</sup> There were <sup>7</sup>recesses, and each recess was one reed wide and one reed deep; and the space between the recesses, five cubits; and the threshold of the gate by the vestibule of the gate at the inner end was one reed deep. <sup>8</sup>Then he measured the inner vestibule of the gateway, one cu-

bit. <sup>9</sup>Then he measured the vestibule of the gateway, eight cubits; and its pilasters, two cubits; and the vestibule of the gate was at the inner end. <sup>10</sup>There were three recesses on either side of the east gate; the three were of the same size; and the pilasters on either side were of the same size. <sup>11</sup>Then he measured the width of the opening of the gateway, ten cubits; and the width of the gateway, thirteen cubits. <sup>12</sup>There was a barrier before the recesses, one cubit on either side; and the recesses were six cubits on either side. <sup>13</sup>Then he measured the gate from the back<sup>b</sup> of the one recess to the back<sup>b</sup> of the other, a width of twenty-five cubits, from wall to wall.<sup>c</sup> <sup>14</sup>He measured<sup>d</sup> also the vestibule, twenty cubits; and the gate next to the pilaster on every side of the court.<sup>e</sup> <sup>15</sup>From the front of the gate at the entrance to the end of the inner vestibule of the gate was fifty cubits. <sup>16</sup>The recesses and their pilasters had windows, with shutters<sup>e</sup> on the inside of the gateway all around, and the vestibules also had windows on the inside all around; and on the pilasters were palm trees.

17 Then he brought me into the outer court; there were chambers there, and a pavement, all around the court; thirty chambers fronted on the pavement. <sup>18</sup>The pavement ran along the side of the gates, corresponding to the length of the gates; this was the lower pavement. <sup>19</sup>Then he measured the distance from the inner front of<sup>f</sup> the lower gate to the outer front of the inner court, one hundred cubits.<sup>g</sup>

20 Then he measured the gate of the outer court that faced north—its depth and width. <sup>21</sup>Its recesses, three on either side, and its pilasters and its vestibule were of the same size as those of the first gate; its depth was fifty cubits, and its width twenty-five

<sup>a</sup>Heb *deep, and one threshold, one reed deep*   <sup>b</sup>Gk: Heb *roof*   <sup>c</sup>Heb *opening facing opening*
<sup>d</sup>Heb *made*   <sup>e</sup>Meaning of Heb uncertain   <sup>f</sup>Compare Gk: Heb *from before*   <sup>g</sup>Heb adds *the east and the north*

cubits. <sup>22</sup>Its windows, its vestibule, and its palm trees were of the same size as those of the gate that faced toward the east. Seven steps led up to it; and its vestibule was on the inside.<sup>a</sup> <sup>23</sup>Opposite the gate on the north, as on the east, was a gate to the inner court; he measured from gate to gate, one hundred cubits.

24 Then he led me toward the south, and there was a gate on the south; and he measured its pilasters and its vestibule; they had the same dimensions as the others. <sup>25</sup>There were windows all around in it and in its vestibule, like the windows of the others; its depth was fifty cubits, and its width twenty-five cubits. <sup>26</sup>There were seven steps leading up to it; its vestibule was on the inside.<sup>a</sup> It had palm trees on its pilasters, one on either side. <sup>27</sup>There was a gate on the south of the inner court; and he measured from gate to gate toward the south, one hundred cubits.

## JAMES 2.18—3.18

**B**UT someone will say, "You have faith and I have works." Show me your faith apart from your works, and I by my works will show you my faith. <sup>19</sup>You believe that God is one; you do well. Even the demons believe—and shudder. <sup>20</sup>Do you want to be shown, you senseless person, that faith apart from works is barren? <sup>21</sup>Was not our ancestor Abraham justified by works when he offered his son Isaac on the altar? <sup>22</sup>You see that faith was active along with his works, and faith was brought to completion by the works. <sup>23</sup>Thus the scripture was fulfilled that says, "Abraham believed God, and it was reckoned to him as righteousness," and he was called the friend of God. <sup>24</sup>You see that a person is justified by works and not by faith alone. <sup>25</sup>Likewise, was not Rahab the prostitute also justified by works when she welcomed the messengers and sent them out by another road? <sup>26</sup>For just as the body without the spirit is dead, so faith without works is also dead.

<sup>3.1</sup> NOT many of you should become teachers, my brothers and sisters,<sup>b</sup> for you know that we who teach will be judged with greater strictness. <sup>2</sup>For all of us make many mistakes. Anyone who makes no mistakes in speaking is perfect, able to keep the whole body in check with a bridle. <sup>3</sup>If we put bits into the mouths of horses to make them obey us, we guide their whole bodies. <sup>4</sup>Or look at ships: though they are so large that it takes strong winds to drive them, yet they are guided by a very small rudder wherever the will of the pilot directs. <sup>5</sup>So also the tongue is a small member, yet it boasts of great exploits.

How great a forest is set ablaze by a small fire! <sup>6</sup>And the tongue is a fire. The tongue is placed among our members as a world of iniquity; it stains the whole body, sets on fire the cycle of nature,<sup>c</sup> and is itself set on fire by hell.<sup>d</sup> <sup>7</sup>For every species of beast and bird, of reptile and sea creature, can be tamed and has been tamed by the human species, <sup>8</sup>but no one can tame the tongue—a restless evil, full of deadly poison. <sup>9</sup>With it we bless the Lord and Father, and with it we curse those who are made in the likeness of God. <sup>10</sup>From the same mouth come blessing and cursing. My brothers and sisters,<sup>e</sup> this ought not to be so. <sup>11</sup>Does a spring pour forth from the same opening both fresh and brackish water? <sup>12</sup>Can a fig tree, my brothers and sisters,<sup>f</sup> yield olives, or a grapevine figs? No more can salt water yield fresh.

13 Who is wise and understanding

<sup>a</sup>Gk: Heb *before them*  <sup>b</sup>Gk *brothers*  <sup>c</sup>Or *wheel of birth*  <sup>d</sup>Gk *Gehenna*  <sup>e</sup>Gk *My brothers*  <sup>f</sup>Gk *my brothers*

among you? Show by your good life that your works are done with gentleness born of wisdom. 14But if you have bitter envy and selfish ambition in your hearts, do not be boastful and false to the truth. 15Such wisdom does not come down from above, but is earthly, unspiritual, devilish. 16For where there is envy and selfish ambition, there will also be disorder and wickedness of every kind. 17But the wisdom from above is first pure, then peaceable, gentle, willing to yield, full of mercy and good fruits, without a trace of partiality or hypocrisy. 18And a harvest of righteousness is sown in peace for[a] those who make peace.

## PSALM 118. 1–18

O GIVE thanks to the LORD, for he is good;
>his steadfast love endures forever!

2 Let Israel say,
>"His steadfast love endures forever."
3 Let the house of Aaron say,
>"His steadfast love endures forever."
4 Let those who fear the LORD say,
>"His steadfast love endures forever."

5 Out of my distress I called on the LORD;
>the LORD answered me and set me in a broad place.
6 With the LORD on my side I do not fear.
>What can mortals do to me?
7 The LORD is on my side to help me;
>I shall look in triumph on those who hate me.
8 It is better to take refuge in the LORD

than to put confidence in mortals.
9 It is better to take refuge in the LORD
>than to put confidence in princes.

10 All nations surrounded me;
>in the name of the LORD I cut them off!
11 They surrounded me,
>surrounded me on every side;
>in the name of the LORD I cut them off!
12 They surrounded me like bees;
>they blazed[b] like a fire of thorns;
>in the name of the LORD I cut them off!
13 I was pushed hard,[c] so that I was falling,
>but the LORD helped me.
14 The LORD is my strength and my might;
>he has become my salvation.

15 There are glad songs of victory in the tents of the righteous:
>"The right hand of the LORD does valiantly;
16 the right hand of the LORD is exalted;
>the right hand of the LORD does valiantly."
17 I shall not die, but I shall live, and recount the deeds of the LORD.
18 The LORD has punished me severely,
>but he did not give me over to death.

aOr *by*   bGk: Heb *were extinguished*   cGk Syr Jerome: Heb *You pushed me hard*

## PROVERBS 28.2

**W**HEN a land rebels
it has many rulers;
but with an intelligent
ruler
there is lasting order. [a]

# NOVEMBER 20

## EZEKIEL 40.28—41.26

**T**HEN he [God's messenger] brought me to the inner court by the south gate, and he measured the south gate; it was of the same dimensions as the others. [29]Its recesses, its pilasters, and its vestibule were of the same size as the others; and there were windows all around in it and in its vestibule; its depth was fifty cubits, and its width twenty-five cubits. [30]There were vestibules all around, twenty-five cubits deep and five cubits wide. [31]Its vestibule faced the outer court, and palm trees were on its pilasters, and its stairway had eight steps.

32 Then he brought me to the inner court on the east side, and he measured the gate; it was of the same size as the others. [33]Its recesses, its pilasters, and its vestibule were of the same dimensions as the others; and there were windows all around in it and in its vestibule; its depth was fifty cubits, and its width twenty-five cubits. [34]Its vestibule faced the outer court, and it had palm trees on its pilasters, on either side; and its stairway had eight steps.

35 Then he brought me to the north gate, and he measured it; it had the same dimensions as the others. [36]Its recesses, its pilasters, and its ves-tibule were of the same size as the others; [b] and it had windows all around. Its depth was fifty cubits, and its width twenty-five cubits. [37]Its vestibule [c] faced the outer court, and it had palm trees on its pilasters, on either side; and its stairway had eight steps.

38 There was a chamber with its door in the vestibule of the gate, [d] where the burnt offering was to be washed. [39]And in the vestibule of the gate were two tables on either side, on which the burnt offering and the sin offering and the guilt offering were to be slaughtered. [40]On the outside of the vestibule [e] at the entrance of the north gate were two tables; and on the other side of the vestibule of the gate were two tables. [41]Four tables were on the inside, and four tables on the outside of the side of the gate, eight tables, on which the sacrifices were to be slaughtered. [42]There were also four tables of hewn stone for the burnt offering, a cubit and a half long, and one cubit and a half wide, and one cubit high, on which the instruments were to be laid with which the burnt offerings and the sacrifices were slaughtered. [43]There were pegs, one handbreadth long, fastened all around the inside. And on the tables the flesh of the offering was to be laid.

[a]Meaning of Heb uncertain   [b]One Ms: Compare verses 29 and 33: MT lacks *were of the same size as the others*   [c]Gk Vg Compare verses 26, 31, 34: Heb *pilasters*   [d]Cn: Heb *at the pilasters of the gates*   [e]Cn: Heb *to him who goes up*

44 On the outside of the inner gateway there were chambers for the singers in the inner court, one[a] at the side of the north gate facing south, the other at the side of the east gate facing north. [45]He said to me, "This chamber that faces south is for the priests who have charge of the temple, [46]and the chamber that faces north is for the priests who have charge of the altar; these are the descendants of Zadok, who alone among the descendants of Levi may come near to the LORD to minister to him." [47]He measured the court, one hundred cubits deep, and one hundred cubits wide, a square; and the altar was in front of the temple.

48 Then he brought me to the vestibule of the temple and measured the pilasters of the vestibule, five cubits on either side; and the width of the gate was fourteen cubits; and the sidewalls of the gate were three cubits[b] on either side. [49]The depth of the vestibule was twenty cubits, and the width twelve[c] cubits; ten steps led up[d] to it; and there were pillars beside the pilasters on either side.

41.1 THEN he brought me to the nave, and measured the pilasters; on each side six cubits was the width of the pilasters. [e] [2]The width of the entrance was ten cubits; and the sidewalls of the entrance were five cubits on either side. He measured the length of the nave, forty cubits, and its width, twenty cubits. [3]Then he went into the inner room and measured the pilasters of the entrance, two cubits; and the width of the entrance, six cubits; and the sidewalls[f] of the entrance, seven cubits. [4]He measured the depth of the room, twenty cubits, and its width, twenty cubits, beyond the nave. And he said to me, This is the most holy place.

5 Then he measured the wall of the temple, six cubits thick; and the width of the side chambers, four cubits, all around the temple. [6]The side chambers were in three stories, one over another, thirty in each story. There were offsets[g] all around the wall of the temple to serve as supports for the side chambers, so that they should not be supported by the wall of the temple. [7]The passageway[h] of the side chambers widened from story to story; for the structure was supplied with a stairway all around the temple. For this reason the structure became wider from story to story. One ascended from the bottom story to the uppermost story by way of the middle one. [8]I saw also that the temple had a raised platform all around; the foundations of the side chambers measured a full reed of six long cubits. [9]The thickness of the outer wall of the side chambers was five cubits; and the free space between the side chambers of the temple [10]and the chambers of the court was a width of twenty cubits all around the temple on every side. [11]The side chambers opened onto the area left free, one door toward the north, and another door toward the south; and the width of the part that was left free was five cubits all around.

12 The building that was facing the temple yard on the west side was seventy cubits wide; and the wall of the building was five cubits thick all around, and its depth ninety cubits.

13 Then he measured the temple, one hundred cubits deep; and the yard and the building with its walls, one hundred cubits deep; [14]also the width of the east front of the temple and the yard, one hundred cubits.

15 Then he measured the depth of the building facing the yard at the west,

---

aHeb lacks *one*  bGk: Heb *and the width of the gate was three cubits*  cGk: Heb *eleven*  dGk: Heb *and by steps that went up*  eCompare Gk: Heb *tent*  fGk: Heb *width*  gGk Compare 1 Kings 6.6: Heb *they entered*  hCn: Heb *it was surrounded*

together with its galleries[a] on either side, one hundred cubits.

The nave of the temple and the inner room and the outer[b] vestibule [16]were paneled,[c] and, all around, all three had windows with recessed[d] frames. Facing the threshold the temple was paneled with wood all around, from the floor up to the windows (now the windows were covered), [17]to the space above the door, even to the inner room, and on the outside. And on all the walls all around in the inner room and the nave there was a pattern.[e] [18]It was formed of cherubim and palm trees, a palm tree between cherub and cherub. Each cherub had two faces: [19]a human face turned toward the palm tree on the one side, and the face of a young lion turned toward the palm tree on the other side. They were carved on the whole temple all around; [20]from the floor to the area above the door, cherubim and palm trees were carved on the wall.[f]

21 The doorposts of the nave were square. In front of the holy place was something resembling [22]an altar of wood, three cubits high, two cubits long, and two cubits wide;[g] its corners, its base,[h] and its walls were of wood. He said to me, "This is the table that stands before the LORD." [23]The nave and the holy place had each a double door. [24]The doors had two leaves apiece, two swinging leaves for each door. [25]On the doors of the nave were carved cherubim and palm trees, such as were carved on the walls; and there was a canopy of wood in front of the vestibule outside. [26]And there were recessed windows and palm trees on either side, on the sidewalls of the vestibule.[i]

## JAMES 4.1–17

THOSE conflicts and disputes among you, where do they come from? Do they not come from your cravings that are at war within you? [2]You want something and do not have it; so you commit murder. And you covet[j] something and cannot obtain it; so you engage in disputes and conflicts. You do not have, because you do not ask. [3]You ask and do not receive, because you ask wrongly, in order to spend what you get on your pleasures. [4]Adulterers! Do you not know that friendship with the world is enmity with God? Therefore whoever wishes to be a friend of the world becomes an enemy of God. [5]Or do you suppose that it is for nothing that the scripture says, "God[k] yearns jealously for the spirit that he has made to dwell in us"? [6]But he gives all the more grace; therefore it says,

"God opposes the proud,
    but gives grace to the
        humble."

[7]Submit yourselves therefore to God. Resist the devil, and he will flee from you. [8]Draw near to God, and he will draw near to you. Cleanse your hands, you sinners, and purify your hearts, you double-minded. [9]Lament and mourn and weep. Let your laughter be turned into mourning and your joy into dejection. [10]Humble yourselves before the Lord, and he will exalt you.

11 Do not speak evil against one another, brothers and sisters.[l] Whoever speaks evil against another or judges another, speaks evil against the law and judges the law; but if you judge the law, you are not a doer of the law but a judge. [12]There is one lawgiver and judge who is able to save and to

---

[a]Cn: Meaning of Heb uncertain   [b]Gk: Heb *of the court*   [c]Gk: Heb *the thresholds*   [d]Cn Compare Gk 1 Kings 6.4: Meaning of Heb uncertain   [e]Heb *measures*   [f]Cn Compare verse 25: Heb *and the wall* [g]Gk: Heb lacks *two cubits wide*   [h]Gk: Heb *length*   [i]Cn: Heb *vestibule. And the side chambers of the temple and the canopies*   [j]Or *you murder and you covet*   [k]Gk *He*   [l]Gk *brothers*

destroy. So who, then, are you to judge your neighbor?

13 Come now, you who say, "Today or tomorrow we will go to such and such a town and spend a year there, doing business and making money." $^{14}$Yet you do not even know what tomorrow will bring. What is your life? For you are a mist that appears for a little while and then vanishes. $^{15}$Instead you ought to say, "If the Lord wishes, we will live and do this or that." $^{16}$As it is, you boast in your arrogance; all such boasting is evil. $^{17}$Anyone, then, who knows the right thing to do and fails to do it, commits sin.

## PSALM 118.19–29

OPEN to me the gates of
   righteousness,
   that I may enter through
    them
  and give thanks to the Lord.

20 This is the gate of the Lord;
   the righteous shall enter
    through it.

21 I thank you that you have
    answered me
   and have become my
    salvation.
22 The stone that the builders
    rejected
   has become the chief
    cornerstone.
23 This is the Lord's doing;
   it is marvelous in our eyes.
24 This is the day that the Lord
   has made;

let us rejoice and be glad in
   it. a
25 Save us, we beseech you,
   O Lord!
  O Lord, we beseech you,
   give us success!

26 Blessed is the one who comes
   in the name of the
    Lord. b
  We bless you from the house
   of the Lord.
27 The Lord is God,
  and he has given us light.
  Bind the festal procession with
    branches,
  up to the horns of the altar. c

28 You are my God, and I will give
    thanks to you;
  you are my God, I will extol
   you.

29 O give thanks to the Lord, for
   he is good,
  for his steadfast love endures
   forever.

## PROVERBS 28.3–5

A RULER$^d$ who oppresses the
    poor
  is a beating rain that leaves
   no food.
4 Those who forsake the law
   praise the wicked,
  but those who keep the law
   struggle against them.
5 The evil do not understand
   justice,
  but those who seek the Lord
   understand it completely.

a Or *in him*  b Or *Blessed in the name of the Lord is the one who comes*  c Meaning of Heb uncertain
d cn: heb *A poor person*

## EZEKIEL 42.1—43.27

**T**HEN he [God's messenger] led me out into the outer court, toward the north, and he brought me to the chambers that were opposite the temple yard and opposite the building on the north. [2]The length of the building that was on the north side[a] was[b] one hundred cubits, and the width fifty cubits. [3]Across the twenty cubits that belonged to the inner court, and facing the pavement that belonged to the outer court, the chambers rose[c] gallery[d] by gallery[d] in three stories. [4]In front of the chambers was a passage on the inner side, ten cubits wide and one hundred cubits deep, [e] and its[f] entrances were on the north. [5]Now the upper chambers were narrower, for the galleries[d] took more away from them than from the lower and middle chambers in the building. [6]For they were in three stories, and they had no pillars like the pillars of the outer[g] court; for this reason the upper chambers were set back from the ground more than the lower and the middle ones. [7]There was a wall outside parallel to the chambers, toward the outer court, opposite the chambers, fifty cubits long. [8]For the chambers on the outer court were fifty cubits long, while those opposite the temple were one hundred cubits long. [9]At the foot of these chambers ran a passage that one entered from the east in order to enter them from the outer court. [10]The width of the passage[h] is fixed by the wall of the court.

On the south[i] also, opposite the vacant area and opposite the building, there were chambers [11]with a passage in front of them; they were similar to the chambers on the north, of the same length and width, with the same exits[j] and arrangements and doors. [12]So the entrances of the chambers to the south were entered through the entrance at the head of the corresponding passage, from the east, along the matching wall. [d]

13 Then he said to me, "The north chambers and the south chambers opposite the vacant area are the holy chambers, where the priests who approach the LORD shall eat the most holy offerings; there they shall deposit the most holy offerings—the grain offering, the sin offering, and the guilt offering, for the place is holy. [14]When the priests enter the holy place, they shall not go out of it into the outer court without laying there the vestments in which they minister, for these are holy; they shall put on other garments before they go near to the area open to the people."

15 When he had finished measuring the interior of the temple area, he led me out by the gate that faces east, and measured the temple area all around. [16]He measured the east side with the measuring reed, five hundred cubits by the measuring reed. [17]Then he turned and measured[k] the north side, five hundred cubits by the measuring reed. [18]Then he turned and measured[k] the south side, five hundred cubits by the measuring reed. [19]Then he turned to the west side and measured, five hundred cubits by the measuring reed. [20]He measured it on the four sides. It had a wall around it, five hundred cubits long and five hundred cubits wide, to

---

[a]Gk: Heb *door*   [b]Gk: Heb *before the length*   [c]Heb lacks *the chambers rose*   [d]Meaning of Heb uncertain   [e]Gk Syr: Heb *a way of one cubit*   [f]Heb *their*   [g]Gk: Heb lacks *outer*   [h]Heb lacks *of the passage*   [i]Gk: Heb *east*   [j]Heb *and all their exits*   [k]Gk: Heb *measuring reed all around. He measured*

make a separation between the holy and the common.

**43.1** THEN he brought me to the gate, the gate facing east. ²And there, the glory of the God of Israel was coming from the east; the sound was like the sound of mighty waters; and the earth shone with his glory. ³The[a] vision I saw was like the vision that I had seen when he came to destroy the city, and[b] like the vision that I had seen by the river Chebar; and I fell upon my face. ⁴As the glory of the LORD entered the temple by the gate facing east, ⁵the spirit lifted me up, and brought me into the inner court; and the glory of the LORD filled the temple.

6 While the man was standing beside me, I heard someone speaking to me out of the temple. ⁷He said to me: Mortal, this is the place of my throne and the place for the soles of my feet, where I will reside among the people of Israel forever. The house of Israel shall no more defile my holy name, neither they nor their kings, by their whoring, and by the corpses of their kings at their death.[c] ⁸When they placed their threshold by my threshold and their doorposts beside my doorposts, with only a wall between me and them, they were defiling my holy name by their abominations that they committed; therefore I have consumed them in my anger. ⁹Now let them put away their idolatry and the corpses of their kings far from me, and I will reside among them forever.

10 As for you, mortal, describe the temple to the house of Israel, and let them measure the pattern; and let them be ashamed of their iniquities. ¹¹When they are ashamed of all that they have done, make known to them the plan of the temple, its arrangement, its exits and its entrances, and its whole form—all its ordinances and its entire plan and all its laws; and write it down in their sight, so that they may observe and follow the entire plan and all its ordinances. ¹²This is the law of the temple: the whole territory on the top of the mountain all around shall be most holy. This is the law of the temple.

13 These are the dimensions of the altar by cubits (the cubit being one cubit and a handbreadth): its base shall be one cubit high,[d] and one cubit wide, with a rim of one span around its edge. This shall be the height of the altar: ¹⁴From the base on the ground to the lower ledge, two cubits, with a width of one cubit; and from the smaller ledge to the larger ledge, four cubits, with a width of one cubit; ¹⁵and the altar hearth, four cubits; and from the altar hearth projecting upward, four horns. ¹⁶The altar hearth shall be square, twelve cubits long by twelve wide. ¹⁷The ledge also shall be square, fourteen cubits long by fourteen wide, with a rim around it half a cubit wide, and its surrounding base, one cubit. Its steps shall face east.

18 Then he said to me: Mortal, thus says the Lord GOD: These are the ordinances for the altar: On the day when it is erected for offering burnt offerings upon it and for dashing blood against it, ¹⁹you shall give to the levitical priests of the family of Zadok, who draw near to me to minister to me, says the Lord GOD, a bull for a sin offering. ²⁰And you shall take some of its blood, and put it on the four horns of the altar, and on the four corners of the ledge, and upon the rim all around; thus you shall purify it and make atonement for it. ²¹You shall also take the bull of the sin offering, and it shall be burnt in the appointed place belonging to the temple, outside the sacred area.

22 On the second day you shall offer a male goat without blemish for a sin

<hr>

a Gk: Heb *Like the vision*   b Syr: Heb *and the visions*   c Or *on their high places*   d Gk: Heb lacks *high* offering; and the altar shall be purified, as it was purified with the bull. <sup>23</sup>When you have finished purifying it, you shall offer a bull without blemish and a ram from the flock without blemish. <sup>24</sup>You shall present them before the Lord, and the priests shall throw salt on them and offer them up as a burnt offering to the Lord. <sup>25</sup>For seven days you shall provide daily a goat for a sin offering; also a bull and a ram from the flock, without blemish, shall be provided. <sup>26</sup>Seven days shall they make atonement for the altar and cleanse it, and so consecrate it. <sup>27</sup>When these days are over, then from the eighth day onward the priests shall offer upon the altar your burnt offerings and your offerings of well-being; and I will accept you, says the Lord God.

## JAMES 5.1–20

Come now, you rich people, weep and wail for the miseries that are coming to you. <sup>2</sup>Your riches have rotted, and your clothes are moth-eaten. <sup>3</sup>Your gold and silver have rusted, and their rust will be evidence against you, and it will eat your flesh like fire. You have laid up treasure[a] for the last days. <sup>4</sup>Listen! The wages of the laborers who mowed your fields, which you kept back by fraud, cry out, and the cries of the harvesters have reached the ears of the Lord of hosts. <sup>5</sup>You have lived on the earth in luxury and in pleasure; you have fattened your hearts in a day of slaughter. <sup>6</sup>You have condemned and murdered the righteous one, who does not resist you.

7 Be patient, therefore, beloved,[b] until the coming of the Lord. The farmer waits for the precious crop from the earth, being patient with it until it receives the early and the late rains. <sup>8</sup>You also must be patient. Strengthen your hearts, for the coming of the Lord is near.[c] <sup>9</sup>Beloved,[d] do not grumble against one another, so that you may not be judged. See, the Judge is standing at the doors! <sup>10</sup>As an example of suffering and patience, beloved,[b] take the prophets who spoke in the name of the Lord. <sup>11</sup>Indeed we call blessed those who showed endurance. You have heard of the endurance of Job, and you have seen the purpose of the Lord, how the Lord is compassionate and merciful.

12 Above all, my beloved,[b] do not swear, either by heaven or by earth or by any other oath, but let your "Yes" be yes and your "No" be no, so that you may not fall under condemnation.

13 Are any among you suffering? They should pray. Are any cheerful? They should sing songs of praise. <sup>14</sup>Are any among you sick? They should call for the elders of the church and have them pray over them, anointing them with oil in the name of the Lord. <sup>15</sup>The prayer of faith will save the sick, and the Lord will raise them up; and anyone who has committed sins will be forgiven. <sup>16</sup>Therefore confess your sins to one another, and pray for one another, so that you may be healed. The prayer of the righteous is powerful and effective. <sup>17</sup>Elijah was a human being like us, and he prayed fervently that it might not rain, and for three years and six months it did not rain on the earth. <sup>18</sup>Then he prayed again, and the heaven gave rain and the earth yielded its harvest.

19 My brothers and sisters,[e] if anyone among you wanders from the truth and is brought back by another, <sup>20</sup>you should know that whoever brings back a sinner from wandering will save the sinner's[f] soul from death and will cover a multitude of sins.

[a]Or *will eat your flesh, since you have stored up fire*   [b]Gk *brothers*   [c]Or *is at hand*   [d]Gk *Brothers*   [e]Gk *My brothers*   [f]Gk *his*

## PSALM 119.1–16

Happy are those whose way is
blameless,
who walk in the law of the
Lord.
2 Happy are those who keep his
decrees,
who seek him with their
whole heart,
3 who also do no wrong,
but walk in his ways.
4 You have commanded your
precepts
to be kept diligently.
5 O that my ways may be
steadfast
in keeping your statutes!
6 Then I shall not be put to
shame,
having my eyes fixed on all
your commandments.
7 I will praise you with an upright
heart,
when I learn your righteous
ordinances.
8 I will observe your statutes;
do not utterly forsake me.

9 How can young people keep
their way pure?
By guarding it according to
your word.

10 With my whole heart I seek
you;
do not let me stray from your
commandments.
11 I treasure your word in my
heart,
so that I may not sin against
you.
12 Blessed are you, O Lord;
teach me your statutes.
13 With my lips I declare
all the ordinances of your
mouth.
14 I delight in the way of your
decrees
as much as in all riches.
15 I will meditate on your
precepts,
and fix my eyes on your
ways.
16 I will delight in your statutes;
I will not forget your word.

## PROVERBS 28.6–7

Better to be poor and walk in
integrity
than to be crooked in one's
ways even though rich.
7 Those who keep the law are
wise children,
but companions of gluttons
shame their parents.

# NOVEMBER 22

## EZEKIEL 44.1—45.12

Then he [God's messenger] brought me back to the outer gate of the sanctuary, which faces east; and it was shut. 2The Lord said to me: This gate shall remain shut; it shall not be opened, and no one shall enter by it; for the Lord, the God of Israel, has entered by it; therefore it shall remain shut. 3Only the prince, because he is a prince, may sit in it to eat food before the Lord; he shall enter by way of the vestibule of the gate, and shall go out by the same way.

4 Then he brought me by way of the north gate to the front of the temple; and I looked, and lo! the glory of the Lord filled the temple of the Lord; and I fell upon my face. ⁵The Lord said to me: Mortal, mark well, look closely, and listen attentively to all that I shall tell you concerning all the ordinances of the temple of the Lord and all its laws; and mark well those who may be admitted to[a] the temple and all those who are to be excluded from the sanctuary. ⁶Say to the rebellious house,[b] to the house of Israel, Thus says the Lord God: O house of Israel, let there be an end to all your abominations ⁷in admitting foreigners, uncircumcised in heart and flesh, to be in my sanctuary, profaning my temple when you offer to me my food, the fat and the blood. You[c] have broken my covenant with all your abominations. ⁸And you have not kept charge of my sacred offerings; but you have appointed foreigners[d] to act for you in keeping my charge in my sanctuary.

9 Thus says the Lord God: No foreigner, uncircumcised in heart and flesh, of all the foreigners who are among the people of Israel, shall enter my sanctuary. ¹⁰But the Levites who went far from me, going astray from me after their idols when Israel went astray, shall bear their punishment. ¹¹They shall be ministers in my sanctuary, having oversight at the gates of the temple, and serving in the temple; they shall slaughter the burnt offering and the sacrifice for the people, and they shall attend on them and serve them. ¹²Because they ministered to them before their idols and made the house of Israel stumble into iniquity, therefore I have sworn concerning them, says the Lord God, that they shall bear their punishment. ¹³They shall not come near to me, to serve me as priest, nor come near any of my sacred offerings, the things that are most sacred; but they shall bear their shame, and the consequences of the abominations that they have committed. ¹⁴Yet I will appoint them to keep charge of the temple, to do all its chores, all that is to be done in it.

15 But the levitical priests, the descendants of Zadok, who kept the charge of my sanctuary when the people of Israel went astray from me, shall come near to me to minister to me; and they shall attend me to offer me the fat and the blood, says the Lord God. ¹⁶It is they who shall enter my sanctuary, it is they who shall approach my table, to minister to me, and they shall keep my charge. ¹⁷When they enter the gates of the inner court, they shall wear linen vestments; they shall have nothing of wool on them, while they minister at the gates of the inner court, and within. ¹⁸They shall have linen turbans on their heads, and linen undergarments on their loins; they shall not bind themselves with anything that causes sweat. ¹⁹When they go out into the outer court to the people, they shall remove the vestments in which they have been ministering, and lay them in the holy chambers; and they shall put on other garments, so that they may not communicate holiness to the people with their vestments. ²⁰They shall not shave their heads or let their locks grow long; they shall only trim the hair of their heads. ²¹No priest shall drink wine when he enters the inner court. ²²They shall not marry a widow, or a divorced woman, but only a virgin of the stock of the house of Israel, or a widow who is the widow of a priest. ²³They shall teach my people the difference between the holy and the common, and show them how to distinguish between the unclean and the clean. ²⁴In a controversy they shall act as judges, and they shall decide it according to my judg-

a Cn: Heb *the entrance of*  b Gk: Heb lacks *house*  c Gk Syr Vg: Heb *They*  d Heb lacks *foreigners* ments. They shall keep my laws and my statutes regarding all my appointed festivals, and they shall keep my sabbaths holy. 25They shall not defile themselves by going near to a dead person; for father or mother, however, and for son or daughter, and for brother or unmarried sister they may defile themselves. 26After he has become clean, they shall count seven days for him. 27On the day that he goes into the holy place, into the inner court, to minister in the holy place, he shall offer his sin offering, says the Lord GOD.

28 This shall be their inheritance: I am their inheritance; and you shall give them no holding in Israel; I am their holding. 29They shall eat the grain offering, the sin offering, and the guilt offering; and every devoted thing in Israel shall be theirs. 30The first of all the first fruits of all kinds, and every offering of all kinds from all your offerings, shall belong to the priests; you shall also give to the priests the first of your dough, in order that a blessing may rest on your house. 31The priests shall not eat of anything, whether bird or animal, that died of itself or was torn by animals.

45.1 WHEN you allot the land as an inheritance, you shall set aside for the LORD a portion of the land as a holy district, twenty-five thousand cubits long and twenty[a] thousand cubits wide; it shall be holy throughout its entire extent. 2Of this, a square plot of five hundred by five hundred cubits shall be for the sanctuary, with fifty cubits for an open space around it. 3In the holy district you shall measure off a section twenty-five thousand cubits long and ten thousand wide, in which shall be the sanctuary, the most holy place. 4It shall be a holy portion of the land; it shall be for the priests, who minister in the sanctuary and approach the LORD to minister to him; and it shall be both a place for their houses and a holy place for the sanctuary. 5Another section, twenty-five thousand cubits long and ten thousand cubits wide, shall be for the Levites who minister at the temple, as their holding for cities to live in. [b]

6 Alongside the portion set apart as the holy district you shall assign as a holding for the city an area five thousand cubits wide, and twenty-five thousand cubits long; it shall belong to the whole house of Israel.

7 And to the prince shall belong the land on both sides of the holy district and the holding of the city, alongside the holy district and the holding of the city, on the west and on the east, corresponding in length to one of the tribal portions, and extending from the western to the eastern boundary 8of the land. It is to be his property in Israel. And my princes shall no longer oppress my people; but they shall let the house of Israel have the land according to their tribes.

9 Thus says the Lord GOD: Enough, O princes of Israel! Put away violence and oppression, and do what is just and right. Cease your evictions of my people, says the Lord GOD.

10 You shall have honest balances, an honest ephah, and an honest bath. [c] 11The ephah and the bath shall be of the same measure, the bath containing one-tenth of a homer, and the ephah one-tenth of a homer; the homer shall be the standard measure. 12The shekel shall be twenty gerahs. Twenty shekels, twenty-five shekels, and fifteen shekels shall make a mina for you.

# 1 PETER 1.1–12

PETER, an apostle of Jesus Christ, To the exiles of the Dispersion in Pontus, Galatia, Cappadocia, Asia, and Bithynia, 2who have been chosen and destined by God the Father

aGk: Heb *ten*   bGk: Heb *as their holding, twenty chambers*   cA Heb measure of volume

and sanctified by the Spirit to be obedient to Jesus Christ and to be sprinkled with his blood:

May grace and peace be yours in abundance.

3 Blessed be the God and Father of our Lord Jesus Christ! By his great mercy he has given us a new birth into a living hope through the resurrection of Jesus Christ from the dead, [4]and into an inheritance that is imperishable, undefiled, and unfading, kept in heaven for you, [5]who are being protected by the power of God through faith for a salvation ready to be revealed in the last time. [6]In this you rejoice, [a] even if now for a little while you have had to suffer various trials, [7]so that the genuineness of your faith—being more precious than gold that, though perishable, is tested by fire—may be found to result in praise and glory and honor when Jesus Christ is revealed. [8]Although you have not seen[b] him, you love him; and even though you do not see him now, you believe in him and rejoice with an indescribable and glorious joy, [9]for you are receiving the outcome of your faith, the salvation of your souls.

10 Concerning this salvation, the prophets who prophesied of the grace that was to be yours made careful search and inquiry, [11]inquiring about the person or time that the Spirit of Christ within them indicated when it testified in advance to the sufferings destined for Christ and the subsequent glory. [12]It was revealed to them that they were serving not themselves but you, in regard to the things that have now been announced to you through those who brought you good news by the Holy Spirit sent from heaven—things into which angels long to look!

## PSALM 119.17–32

**D**EAL bountifully with your
   servant,
  so that I may live and
   observe your word.
18 Open my eyes, so that I may
   behold
  wondrous things out of your
   law.
19 I live as an alien in the land;
  do not hide your
   commandments from me.
20 My soul is consumed with
   longing
  for your ordinances at all
   times.
21 You rebuke the insolent,
   accursed ones,
  who wander from your
   commandments;
22 take away from me their scorn
   and contempt,
  for I have kept your decrees.
23 Even though princes sit plotting
   against me,
  your servant will meditate on
   your statutes.
24 Your decrees are my delight,
  they are my counselors.

25 My soul clings to the dust;
  revive me according to your
   word.
26 When I told of my ways, you
   answered me;
  teach me your statutes.
27 Make me understand the way of
   your precepts,
  and I will meditate on your
   wondrous works.
28 My soul melts away for sorrow;
  strengthen me according to
   your word.
29 Put false ways far from me;
  and graciously teach me
   your law.

---

a Or *Rejoice in this*  b Other ancient authorities read *known*

30  I have chosen the way of
    faithfulness;
      I set your ordinances before
      me.
31  I cling to your decrees, O LORD;
      let me not be put to shame.
32  I run the way of your
    commandments,
      for you enlarge my
      understanding.

9  When one will not listen to
    the law,
      even one's prayers are an
      abomination.
10  Those who mislead the upright
    into evil ways
      will fall into pits of their own
      making,
      but the blameless will have a
      goodly inheritance.

## PROVERBS 28.8–10

ONE who augments wealth by exorbitant interest gathers it for another who is kind to the poor.

# NOVEMBER 23

## EZEKIEL 45.13—46.24

THIS is the offering that you shall make: one-sixth of an ephah from each homer of wheat, and one-sixth of an ephah from each homer of barley, 14and as the fixed portion of oil, a one-tenth of a bath from each cor (the cor, b like the homer, contains ten baths); 15and one sheep from every flock of two hundred, from the pastures of Israel. This is the offering for grain offerings, burnt offerings, and offerings of well-being, to make atonement for them, says the Lord GOD. 16All the people of the land shall join with the prince in Israel in making this offering. 17But this shall be the obligation of the prince regarding the burnt offerings, grain offerings, and drink offerings, at the festivals, the new moons, and the sabbaths, all the appointed festivals of the house of Israel: he shall provide the sin offerings, grain offerings, the burnt offerings, and the offerings of well-being, to make atonement for the house of Israel.

18  Thus says the Lord GOD: In the first month, on the first day of the month, you shall take a young bull without blemish, and purify the sanctuary. 19The priest shall take some of the blood of the sin offering and put it on the doorposts of the temple, the four corners of the ledge of the altar, and the posts of the gate of the inner court. 20You shall do the same on the seventh day of the month for anyone who has sinned through error or ignorance; so you shall make atonement for the temple.

21  In the first month, on the fourteenth day of the month, you shall celebrate the festival of the passover, and for seven days unleavened bread shall

aCn: Heb *oil, the bath the oil*   bVg: Heb *homer*

be eaten. [22]On that day the prince shall provide for himself and all the people of the land a young bull for a sin offering. [23]And during the seven days of the festival he shall provide as a burnt offering to the LORD seven young bulls and seven rams without blemish, on each of the seven days; and a male goat daily for a sin offering. [24]He shall provide as a grain offering an ephah for each bull, an ephah for each ram, and a hin of oil to each ephah. [25]In the seventh month, on the fifteenth day of the month and for the seven days of the festival, he shall make the same provision for sin offerings, burnt offerings, and grain offerings, and for the oil.

**46.**[1]THUS says the Lord GOD: The gate of the inner court that faces east shall remain closed on the six working days; but on the sabbath day it shall be opened and on the day of the new moon it shall be opened. [2]The prince shall enter by the vestibule of the gate from outside, and shall take his stand by the post of the gate. The priests shall offer his burnt offering and his offerings of well-being, and he shall bow down at the threshold of the gate. Then he shall go out, but the gate shall not be closed until evening. [3]The people of the land shall bow down at the entrance of that gate before the LORD on the sabbaths and on the new moons. [4]The burnt offering that the prince offers to the LORD on the sabbath day shall be six lambs without blemish and a ram without blemish; [5]and the grain offering with the ram shall be an ephah, and the grain offering with the lambs shall be as much as he wishes to give, together with a hin of oil to each ephah. [6]On the day of the new moon he shall offer a young bull without blemish, and six lambs and a ram, which shall be without blemish; [7]as a grain offering he shall provide an ephah with the bull and an ephah with

the ram, and with the lambs as much as he wishes, together with a hin of oil to each ephah. [8]When the prince enters, he shall come in by the vestibule of the gate, and he shall go out by the same way.

9  When the people of the land come before the LORD at the appointed festivals, whoever enters by the north gate to worship shall go out by the south gate; and whoever enters by the south gate shall go out by the north gate: they shall not return by way of the gate by which they entered, but shall go out straight ahead. [10]When they come in, the prince shall come in with them; and when they go out, he shall go out.

11  At the festivals and the appointed seasons the grain offering with a young bull shall be an ephah, and with a ram an ephah, and with the lambs as much as one wishes to give, together with a hin of oil to an ephah. [12]When the prince provides a freewill offering, either a burnt offering or offerings of well-being as a freewill offering to the LORD, the gate facing east shall be opened for him; and he shall offer his burnt offering or his offerings of well-being as he does on the sabbath day. Then he shall go out, and after he has gone out the gate shall be closed.

13  He shall provide a lamb, a yearling, without blemish, for a burnt offering to the LORD daily; morning by morning he shall provide it. [14]And he shall provide a grain offering with it morning by morning regularly, one-sixth of an ephah, and one-third of a hin of oil to moisten the choice flour, as a grain offering to the LORD; this is the ordinance for all time. [15]Thus the lamb and the grain offering and the oil shall be provided, morning by morning, as a regular burnt offering.

16  Thus says the Lord GOD: If the prince makes a gift to any of his sons out of his inheritance,[a] it shall belong

---

aGk: Heb *it is his inheritance*

to his sons, it is their holding by inheritance. [17]But if he makes a gift out of his inheritance to one of his servants, it shall be his to the year of liberty; then it shall revert to the prince; only his sons may keep a gift from his inheritance. [18]The prince shall not take any of the inheritance of the people, thrusting them out of their holding; he shall give his sons their inheritance out of his own holding, so that none of my people shall be dispossessed of their holding.

19 Then he brought me through the entrance, which was at the side of the gate, to the north row of the holy chambers for the priests; and there I saw a place at the extreme western end of them. [20]He said to me, "This is the place where the priests shall boil the guilt offering and the sin offering, and where they shall bake the grain offering, in order not to bring them out into the outer court and so communicate holiness to the people."

21 Then he brought me out to the outer court, and led me past the four corners of the court; and in each corner of the court there was a court— [22]in the four corners of the court were small[a] courts, forty cubits long and thirty wide; the four were of the same size. [23]On the inside, around each of the four courts[b] was a row of masonry, with hearths made at the bottom of the rows all around. [24]Then he said to me, "These are the kitchens where those who serve at the temple shall boil the sacrifices of the people."

you formerly had in ignorance. [15]Instead, as he who called you is holy, be holy yourselves in all your conduct; [16]for it is written, "You shall be holy, for I am holy."

17 If you invoke as Father the one who judges all people impartially according to their deeds, live in reverent fear during the time of your exile. [18]You know that you were ransomed from the futile ways inherited from your ancestors, not with perishable things like silver or gold, [19]but with the precious blood of Christ, like that of a lamb without defect or blemish. [20]He was destined before the foundation of the world, but was revealed at the end of the ages for your sake. [21]Through him you have come to trust in God, who raised him from the dead and gave him glory, so that your faith and hope are set on God.

22 Now that you have purified your souls by your obedience to the truth[d] so that you have genuine mutual love, love one another deeply[e] from the heart.[f] [23]You have been born anew, not of perishable but of imperishable seed, through the living and enduring word of God.[g] [24]For

"All flesh is like grass
    and all its glory like the
        flower of grass.
The grass withers,
    and the flower falls,
25  but the word of the Lord
        endures forever."
That word is the good news that was announced to you.

# 1 PETER 1.13—2.10

THEREFORE prepare your minds for action;[c] discipline yourselves; set all your hope on the grace that Jesus Christ will bring you when he is revealed. [14]Like obedient children, do not be conformed to the desires that

2.1 RID yourselves, therefore, of all malice, and all guile, insincerity, envy, and all slander. [2]Like newborn infants, long for the pure, spiritual milk, so that by it you may grow into salvation— [3]if indeed you have tasted that the Lord is good.

[a]Gk Syr Vg: Meaning of Heb uncertain  [b]Heb *the four of them*  [c]Gk *gird up the loins of your mind*  [d]Other ancient authorities add *through the Spirit*  [e]Or *constantly*  [f]Other ancient authorities read *a pure heart*  [g]Or *through the word of the living and enduring God*

4 Come to him, a living stone, though rejected by mortals yet chosen and precious in God's sight, and [5]like living stones, let yourselves be built[a] into a spiritual house, to be a holy priesthood, to offer spiritual sacrifices acceptable to God through Jesus Christ. [6]For it stands in scripture:

"See, I am laying in Zion a
    stone,
  a cornerstone chosen and
    precious;
and whoever believes in him[b]
    will not be put to
    shame."

[7]To you then who believe, he is precious; but for those who do not believe,

"The stone that the builders
    rejected
  has become the very head of
    the corner,"

[8]and

"A stone that makes them
    stumble,
  and a rock that makes them
    fall."

They stumble because they disobey the word, as they were destined to do.

9 But you are a chosen race, a royal priesthood, a holy nation, God's own people,[c] in order that you may proclaim the mighty acts of him who called you out of darkness into his marvelous light.

[10] Once you were not a people,
  but now you are God's
    people;
once you had not received
    mercy,
but now you have received
    mercy.

## PSALM 119.33–48

Teach me, O Lord, the way of
    your statutes,
  and I will observe it to the
    end.

34 Give me understanding, that I
    may keep your law
  and observe it with my whole
    heart.
35 Lead me in the path of your
    commandments,
  for I delight in it.
36 Turn my heart to your decrees,
  and not to selfish gain.
37 Turn my eyes from looking at
    vanities;
  give me life in your ways.
38 Confirm to your servant your
    promise,
  which is for those who fear
    you.
39 Turn away the disgrace that I
    dread,
  for your ordinances are good.
40 See, I have longed for your
    precepts;
  in your righteousness give
    me life.

41 Let your steadfast love come to
    me, O Lord,
  your salvation according to
    your promise.
42 Then I shall have an answer for
    those who taunt me,
  for I trust in your word.
43 Do not take the word of truth
    utterly out of my mouth,
  for my hope is in your
    ordinances.
44 I will keep your law continually,
  forever and ever.
45 I shall walk at liberty,
  for I have sought your
    precepts.
46 I will also speak of your decrees
    before kings,
  and shall not be put to shame;
47 I find my delight in your
    commandments,
  because I love them.

[a]Or *you yourselves are being built*  [b]Or *it*  [c]Gk *a people for his possession*

<sup>48</sup> I revere your commandments,
    which I love,
    and I will meditate on your
      statutes.

## PROVERBS 28.11

THE rich is wise in self-esteem, but an intelligent poor person sees through the pose.

# NOVEMBER 24

## EZEKIEL 47.1—48.35

THEN he [God's messenger] brought me back to the entrance of the temple; there, water was flowing from below the threshold of the temple toward the east (for the temple faced east); and the water was flowing down from below the south end of the threshold of the temple, south of the altar. <sup>2</sup>Then he brought me out by way of the north gate, and led me around on the outside to the outer gate that faces toward the east;[a] and the water was coming out on the south side.

3 Going on eastward with a cord in his hand, the man measured one thousand cubits, and then led me through the water; and it was ankle-deep. <sup>4</sup>Again he measured one thousand, and led me through the water; and it was knee-deep. Again he measured one thousand, and led me through the water; and it was up to the waist. <sup>5</sup>Again he measured one thousand, and it was a river that I could not cross, for the water had risen; it was deep enough to swim in, a river that could not be crossed. <sup>6</sup>He said to me, "Mortal, have you seen this?"

Then he led me back along the bank of the river. <sup>7</sup>As I came back, I saw on the bank of the river a great many trees on the one side and on the other. <sup>8</sup>He said to me, "This water flows toward the eastern region and goes down into the Arabah; and when it enters the sea, the sea of stagnant waters, the water will become fresh. <sup>9</sup>Wherever the river goes,[b] every living creature that swarms will live, and there will be very many fish, once these waters reach there. It will become fresh; and everything will live where the river goes. <sup>10</sup>People will stand fishing beside the sea[c] from En-gedi to En-eglaim; it will be a place for the spreading of nets; its fish will be of a great many kinds, like the fish of the Great Sea. <sup>11</sup>But its swamps and marshes will not become fresh; they are to be left for salt. <sup>12</sup>On the banks, on both sides of the river, there will grow all kinds of trees for food. Their leaves will not wither nor their fruit fail, but they will bear fresh fruit every month, because the water for them flows from the sanctuary. Their fruit will be for food, and their leaves for healing."

13 Thus says the Lord GOD: These are the boundaries by which you shall divide the land for inheritance among the twelve tribes of Israel. Joseph shall have two portions. <sup>14</sup>You shall divide it equally; I swore to give it to your ancestors, and this land shall fall to you as your inheritance.

---

aMeaning of Heb uncertain   bGk Syr Vg Tg: Heb *the two rivers go*   cHeb *it*

15 This shall be the boundary of the land: On the north side, from the Great Sea by way of Hethlon to Lebo-hamath, and on to Zedad, [a] 16Berothah, Sibraim (which lies between the border of Damascus and the border of Hamath), as far as Hazer-hatticon, which is on the border of Hauran. 17So the boundary shall run from the sea to Hazar-enon, which is north of the border of Damascus, with the border of Hamath to the north. [b] This shall be the north side.

18 On the east side, between Hauran and Damascus; along the Jordan between Gilead and the land of Israel; to the eastern sea and as far as Tamar. [c] This shall be the east side.

19 On the south side, it shall run from Tamar as far as the waters of Meribath-kadesh, from there along the Wadi of Egypt[d] to the Great Sea. This shall be the south side.

20 On the west side, the Great Sea shall be the boundary to a point opposite Lebo-hamath. This shall be the west side.

21 So you shall divide this land among you according to the tribes of Israel. 22You shall allot it as an inheritance for yourselves and for the aliens who reside among you and have begotten children among you. They shall be to you as citizens of Israel; with you they shall be allotted an inheritance among the tribes of Israel. 23In whatever tribe aliens reside, there you shall assign them their inheritance, says the Lord GOD.

48.1 THESE are the names of the tribes: Beginning at the northern border, on the Hethlon road,[e] from Lebo-hamath, as far as Hazar-enon (which is on the border of Damascus, with Hamath to the north), and[f] extending from the east side to the west,[g] Dan, one portion. 2Adjoining the territory of Dan, from the east side to the west, Asher, one portion. 3Adjoining the territory of Asher, from the east side to the west, Naphtali, one portion. 4Adjoining the territory of Naphtali, from the east side to the west, Manasseh, one portion. 5Adjoining the territory of Manasseh, from the east side to the west, Ephraim, one portion. 6Adjoining the territory of Ephraim, from the east side to the west, Reuben, one portion. 7Adjoining the territory of Reuben, from the east side to the west, Judah, one portion.

8 Adjoining the territory of Judah, from the east side to the west, shall be the portion that you shall set apart, twenty-five thousand cubits in width, and in length equal to one of the tribal portions, from the east side to the west, with the sanctuary in the middle of it. 9The portion that you shall set apart for the LORD shall be twenty-five thousand cubits in length, and twenty[h] thousand in width. 10These shall be the allotments of the holy portion: the priests shall have an allotment measuring twenty-five thousand cubits on the northern side, ten thousand cubits in width on the western side, ten thousand in width on the eastern side, and twenty-five thousand in length on the southern side, with the sanctuary of the LORD in the middle of it. 11This shall be for the consecrated priests, the descendants[i] of Zadok, who kept my charge, who did not go astray when the people of Israel went astray, as the Levites did. 12It shall belong to them as a special portion from the holy portion of the land, a most holy place, adjoining the territory of the Levites. 13Alongside the territory of the priests, the Levites shall have an allotment twenty-five thousand cubits in length

aGk: Heb *Lebo-zedad, 16Hamath*   bMeaning of Heb uncertain   cCompare Syr: Heb *you shall measure*   dHeb lacks *of Egypt*   eCompare 47.15: Heb *by the side of the way*   fCn: Heb *and they shall be his*   gGk Compare verses 2-8: Heb *the east side the west*   hCompare 45.1: Heb *ten*   iOne Ms Gk: Heb *of the descendants*

and ten thousand in width. The whole length shall be twenty-five thousand cubits and the width twenty[a] thousand. [14]They shall not sell or exchange any of it; they shall not transfer this choice portion of the land, for it is holy to the LORD.

15 The remainder, five thousand cubits in width and twenty-five thousand in length, shall be for ordinary use for the city, for dwellings and for open country. In the middle of it shall be the city; [16]and these shall be its dimensions: the north side four thousand five hundred cubits, the south side four thousand five hundred, the east side four thousand five hundred, and the west side four thousand and five hundred. [17]The city shall have open land: on the north two hundred fifty cubits, on the south two hundred fifty, on the east two hundred fifty, on the west two hundred fifty. [18]The remainder of the length alongside the holy portion shall be ten thousand cubits to the east, and ten thousand to the west, and it shall be alongside the holy portion. Its produce shall be food for the workers of the city. [19]The workers of the city, from all the tribes of Israel, shall cultivate it. [20]The whole portion that you shall set apart shall be twenty-five thousand cubits square, that is, the holy portion together with the property of the city.

21 What remains on both sides of the holy portion and of the property of the city shall belong to the prince. Extending from the twenty-five thousand cubits of the holy portion to the east border, and westward from the twenty-five thousand cubits to the west border, parallel to the tribal portions, it shall belong to the prince. The holy portion with the sanctuary of the temple in the middle of it, [22]and the property of the Levites and of the city, shall be in the middle of that which belongs to the prince. The portion of the prince shall lie between the territory of Judah and the territory of Benjamin.

23 As for the rest of the tribes: from the east side to the west, Benjamin, one portion. [24]Adjoining the territory of Benjamin, from the east side to the west, Simeon, one portion. [25]Adjoining the territory of Simeon, from the east side to the west, Issachar, one portion. [26]Adjoining the territory of Issachar, from the east side to the west, Zebulun, one portion. [27]Adjoining the territory of Zebulun, from the east side to the west, Gad, one portion. [28]And adjoining the territory of Gad to the south, the boundary shall run from Tamar to the waters of Meribath-kadesh, from there along the Wadi of Egypt[b] to the Great Sea. [29]This is the land that you shall allot as an inheritance among the tribes of Israel, and these are their portions, says the Lord GOD.

30 These shall be the exits of the city: On the north side, which is to be four thousand five hundred cubits by measure, [31]three gates, the gate of Reuben, the gate of Judah, and the gate of Levi, the gates of the city being named after the tribes of Israel. [32]On the east side, which is to be four thousand five hundred cubits, three gates, the gate of Joseph, the gate of Benjamin, and the gate of Dan. [33]On the south side, which is to be four thousand five hundred cubits by measure, three gates, the gate of Simeon, the gate of Issachar, and the gate of Zebulun. [34]On the west side, which is to be four thousand five hundred cubits, three gates,[c] the gate of Gad, the gate of Asher, and the gate of Naphtali. [35]The circumference of the city shall be eighteen thousand cubits. And the name of the city from that time on shall be, The LORD is There.

[a]Gk: Heb *ten*   [b]Heb lacks *of Egypt*   [c]One Ms Gk Syr: MT *their gates three*

## 1 PETER 2.11—3.7

**B**ELOVED, I urge you as aliens and exiles to abstain from the desires of the flesh that wage war against the soul. [12]Conduct yourselves honorably among the Gentiles, so that, though they malign you as evildoers, they may see your honorable deeds and glorify God when he comes to judge. [a]

13 For the Lord's sake accept the authority of every human institution, [b] whether of the emperor as supreme, [14]or of governors, as sent by him to punish those who do wrong and to praise those who do right. [15]For it is God's will that by doing right you should silence the ignorance of the foolish. [16]As servants[c] of God, live as free people, yet do not use your freedom as a pretext for evil. [17]Honor everyone. Love the family of believers. [d] Fear God. Honor the emperor.

18 Slaves, accept the authority of your masters with all deference, not only those who are kind and gentle but also those who are harsh. [19]For it is a credit to you if, being aware of God, you endure pain while suffering unjustly. [20]If you endure when you are beaten for doing wrong, what credit is that? But if you endure when you do right and suffer for it, you have God's approval. [21]For to this you have been called, because Christ also suffered for you, leaving you an example, so that you should follow in his steps.
22 "He committed no sin,
and no deceit was found in
his mouth."
[23]When he was abused, he did not return abuse; when he suffered, he did not threaten; but he entrusted himself to the one who judges justly. [24]He himself bore our sins in his body on the cross, [e] so that, free from sins, we might live for righteousness; by his wounds[f] you have been healed. [25]For you were going astray like sheep, but now you have returned to the shepherd and guardian of your souls.

[3.1] WIVES, in the same way, accept the authority of your husbands, so that, even if some of them do not obey the word, they may be won over without a word by their wives' conduct, [2]when they see the purity and reverence of your lives. [3]Do not adorn yourselves outwardly by braiding your hair, and by wearing gold ornaments or fine clothing; [4]rather, let your adornment be the inner self with the lasting beauty of a gentle and quiet spirit, which is very precious in God's sight. [5]It was in this way long ago that the holy women who hoped in God used to adorn themselves by accepting the authority of their husbands. [6]Thus Sarah obeyed Abraham and called him lord. You have become her daughters as long as you do what is good and never let fears alarm you.

7 Husbands, in the same way, show consideration for your wives in your life together, paying honor to the woman as the weaker sex, [g] since they too are also heirs of the gracious gift of life—so that nothing may hinder your prayers.

## PSALM 119.49–64

**R**EMEMBER your word to your
servant,
in which you have made
me hope.
50 This is my comfort in my
distress,
that your promise gives me
life.
51 The arrogant utterly deride me,
but I do not turn away from
your law.
52 When I think of your ordinances
from of old,

I take comfort, O LORD.
53 Hot indignation seizes me
        because of the wicked,
    those who forsake your law.
54 Your statutes have been my
        songs
    wherever I make my home.
55 I remember your name in the
        night, O LORD,
    and keep your law.
56 This blessing has fallen to me,
    for I have kept your precepts.

57 The LORD is my portion;
    I promise to keep your
        words.
58 I implore your favor with all my
        heart;
    be gracious to me according
        to your promise.
59 When I think of your ways,
    I turn my feet to your
        decrees;
60 I hurry and do not delay
    to keep your commandments.
61 Though the cords of the wicked
        ensnare me,

I do not forget your law.
62 At midnight I rise to praise you,
    because of your righteous
        ordinances.
63 I am a companion of all who fear
        you,
    of those who keep your
        precepts.
64 The earth, O LORD, is full of
        your steadfast love;
    teach me your statutes.

## PROVERBS 28.12–13

WHEN the righteous triumph,
        there is great glory,
    but when the wicked
        prevail, people go into
        hiding.
13 No one who conceals
        transgressions will
        prosper,
    but one who confesses and
        forsakes them will obtain
        mercy.

# NOVEMBER 25

## DANIEL 1.1—2.23

IN the third year of the reign of King Jehoiakim of Judah, King Nebuchadnezzar of Babylon came to Jerusalem and besieged it. 2The Lord let King Jehoiakim of Judah fall into his power, as well as some of the vessels of the house of God. These he brought to the land of Shinar,a and placed the vessels in the treasury of his gods.

3 Then the king commanded his palace master Ashpenaz to bring some of the Israelites of the royal family and of the nobility, 4young men without physical defect and handsome, versed in every branch of wisdom, endowed with knowledge and insight, and competent to serve in the king's palace; they were to be taught the literature and language of the Chaldeans. 5The king assigned them a daily portion of the royal rations of food and wine. They were to be educated for three years, so that at the end of that time they could be stationed in the king's court. 6Among them were Daniel, Hananiah,

a Gk Theodotion: Heb adds *to the house of his own gods*

Mishael, and Azariah, from the tribe of Judah. [7]The palace master gave them other names: Daniel he called Belteshazzar, Hananiah he called Shadrach, Mishael he called Meshach, and Azariah he called Abednego.

8 But Daniel resolved that he would not defile himself with the royal rations of food and wine; so he asked the palace master to allow him not to defile himself. [9]Now God allowed Daniel to receive favor and compassion from the palace master. [10]The palace master said to Daniel, "I am afraid of my lord the king; he has appointed your food and your drink. If he should see you in poorer condition than the other young men of your own age, you would endanger my head with the king." [11]Then Daniel asked the guard whom the palace master had appointed over Daniel, Hananiah, Mishael, and Azariah: [12]"Please test your servants for ten days. Let us be given vegetables to eat and water to drink. [13]You can then compare our appearance with the appearance of the young men who eat the royal rations, and deal with your servants according to what you observe." [14]So he agreed to this proposal and tested them for ten days. [15]At the end of ten days it was observed that they appeared better and fatter than all the young men who had been eating the royal rations. [16]So the guard continued to withdraw their royal rations and the wine they were to drink, and gave them vegetables. [17]To these four young men God gave knowledge and skill in every aspect of literature and wisdom; Daniel also had insight into all visions and dreams.

18 At the end of the time that the king had set for them to be brought in, the palace master brought them into the presence of Nebuchadnezzar, [19]and the king spoke with them. And among them all, no one was found to compare with Daniel, Hananiah, Mishael, and Azariah; therefore they were stationed in the king's court. [20]In every matter of wisdom and understanding concerning which the king inquired of them, he found them ten times better than all the magicians and enchanters in his whole kingdom. [21]And Daniel continued there until the first year of King Cyrus.

2.1 In the second year of Nebuchadnezzar's reign, Nebuchadnezzar dreamed such dreams that his spirit was troubled and his sleep left him. [2]So the king commanded that the magicians, the enchanters, the sorcerers, and the Chaldeans be summoned to tell the king his dreams. When they came in and stood before the king, [3]he said to them, "I have had such a dream that my spirit is troubled by the desire to understand it." [4]The Chaldeans said to the king (in Aramaic),[a] "O king, live forever! Tell your servants the dream, and we will reveal the interpretation." [5]The king answered the Chaldeans, "This is a public decree: if you do not tell me both the dream and its interpretation, you shall be torn limb from limb, and your houses shall be laid in ruins. [6]But if you do tell me the dream and its interpretation, you shall receive from me gifts and rewards and great honor. Therefore tell me the dream and its interpretation." [7]They answered a second time, "Let the king first tell his servants the dream, then we can give its interpretation." [8]The king answered, "I know with certainty that you are trying to gain time, because you see I have firmly decreed: [9]if you do not tell me the dream, there is but one verdict for you. You have agreed to speak lying and misleading words to me until things take a turn. Therefore, tell me the dream, and I shall know that you can give me its interpretation." [10]The Chaldeans answered the king, "There is no

---

a The text from this point to the end of chapter 7 is in Aramaic

one on earth who can reveal what the king demands! In fact no king, however great and powerful, has ever asked such a thing of any magician or enchanter or Chaldean. [11]The thing that the king is asking is too difficult, and no one can reveal it to the king except the gods, whose dwelling is not with mortals."

12 Because of this the king flew into a violent rage and commanded that all the wise men of Babylon be destroyed. [13]The decree was issued, and the wise men were about to be executed; and they looked for Daniel and his companions, to execute them. [14]Then Daniel responded with prudence and discretion to Arioch, the king's chief executioner, who had gone out to execute the wise men of Babylon; [15]he asked Arioch, the royal official, "Why is the decree of the king so urgent?" Arioch then explained the matter to Daniel. [16]So Daniel went in and requested that the king give him time and he would tell the king the interpretation.

17 Then Daniel went to his home and informed his companions, Hananiah, Mishael, and Azariah, [18]and told them to seek mercy from the God of heaven concerning this mystery, so that Daniel and his companions with the rest of the wise men of Babylon might not perish. [19]Then the mystery was revealed to Daniel in a vision of the night, and Daniel blessed the God of heaven.

20 Daniel said:
"Blessed be the name of God
    from age to age,
  for wisdom and power are
    his.
21 He changes times and seasons,
    deposes kings and sets up
      kings;
  he gives wisdom to the wise
    and knowledge to those who
      have understanding.

22 He reveals deep and hidden
      things;
  he knows what is in the
      darkness,
  and light dwells with him.
23 To you, O God of my
      ancestors,
  I give thanks and praise,
  for you have given me wisdom
      and power,
  and have now revealed to me
      what we asked of you,
  for you have revealed to us
      what the king ordered."

# 1 PETER 3.8—4.6

FINALLY, all of you, have unity of spirit, sympathy, love for one another, a tender heart, and a humble mind. [9]Do not repay evil for evil or abuse for abuse; but, on the contrary, repay with a blessing. It is for this that you were called—that you might inherit a blessing. [10]For
"Those who desire life
    and desire to see good days,
  let them keep their tongues
      from evil
    and their lips from speaking
      deceit;
11 let them turn away from evil
      and do good;
  let them seek peace and
      pursue it.
12 For the eyes of the Lord are on
      the righteous,
    and his ears are open to
      their prayer.
  But the face of the Lord is
      against those who do
      evil."

13 Now who will harm you if you are eager to do what is good? [14]But even if you do suffer for doing what is right, you are blessed. Do not fear what they fear, [a] and do not be intimidated, [15]but in your hearts sanctify Christ as Lord. Always be ready to

a Gk *their fear*

make your defense to anyone who demands from you an accounting for the hope that is in you; [16]yet do it with gentleness and reverence.[a] Keep your conscience clear, so that, when you are maligned, those who abuse you for your good conduct in Christ may be put to shame. [17]For it is better to suffer for doing good, if suffering should be God's will, than to suffer for doing evil. [18]For Christ also suffered[b] for sins once for all, the righteous for the unrighteous, in order to bring you[c] to God. He was put to death in the flesh, but made alive in the spirit, [19]in which also he went and made a proclamation to the spirits in prison, [20]who in former times did not obey, when God waited patiently in the days of Noah, during the building of the ark, in which a few, that is, eight persons, were saved through water. [21]And baptism, which this prefigured, now saves you—not as a removal of dirt from the body, but as an appeal to God for[d] a good conscience, through the resurrection of Jesus Christ, [22]who has gone into heaven and is at the right hand of God, with angels, authorities, and powers made subject to him.

[4.1] SINCE therefore Christ suffered in the flesh,[e] arm yourselves also with the same intention (for whoever has suffered in the flesh has finished with sin), [2]so as to live for the rest of your earthly life[f] no longer by human desires but by the will of God. [3]You have already spent enough time in doing what the Gentiles like to do, living in licentiousness, passions, drunkenness, revels, carousing, and lawless idolatry. [4]They are surprised that you no longer join them in the same excesses of dissipation, and so they blaspheme.[g] [5]But they will have to give an accounting to him who stands ready to judge the living and the dead. [6]For this is the reason

the gospel was proclaimed even to the dead, so that, though they had been judged in the flesh as everyone is judged, they might live in the spirit as God does.

## PSALM 119.65–80

Y OU have dealt well with your servant,
   O LORD, according to your word.
66 Teach me good judgment and knowledge,
   for I believe in your commandments.
67 Before I was humbled I went astray,
   but now I keep your word.
68 You are good and do good;
   teach me your statutes.
69 The arrogant smear me with lies,
   but with my whole heart I keep your precepts.
70 Their hearts are fat and gross,
   but I delight in your law.
71 It is good for me that I was humbled,
   so that I might learn your statutes.
72 The law of your mouth is better to me
   than thousands of gold and silver pieces.

73 Your hands have made and fashioned me;
   give me understanding that I may learn your commandments.
74 Those who fear you shall see me and rejoice,
   because I have hoped in your word.
75 I know, O LORD, that your judgments are right,

---

a Or *respect*  b Other ancient authorities read *died*  c Other ancient authorities read *us*  d Or *a pledge to God from*  e Other ancient authorities add *for us*; others, *for you*  f Gk *rest of the time in the flesh*  g Or *they malign you*

and that in faithfulness you
   have humbled me.
76 Let your steadfast love become
   my comfort
   according to your promise to
   your servant.
77 Let your mercy come to me,
   that I may live;
   for your law is my delight.
78 Let the arrogant be put to
   shame,
   because they have subverted
   me with guile;
   as for me, I will meditate on
   your precepts.

79 Let those who fear you turn to
   me,
   so that they may know your
   decrees.
80 May my heart be blameless in
   your statutes,
   so that I may not be put to
   shame.

## PROVERBS 28.14

HAPPY is the one who is never
   without fear,
but one who is
   hard-hearted will fall into
   calamity.

# NOVEMBER 26

## DANIEL 2.24—3.30

THEREFORE Daniel went to Arioch, whom the king had appointed to destroy the wise men of Babylon, and said to him, "Do not destroy the wise men of Babylon; bring me in before the king, and I will give the king the interpretation."

25 Then Arioch quickly brought Daniel before the king and said to him: "I have found among the exiles from Judah a man who can tell the king the interpretation." 26The king said to Daniel, whose name was Belteshazzar, "Are you able to tell me the dream that I have seen and its interpretation?" 27Daniel answered the king, "No wise men, enchanters, magicians, or diviners can show to the king the mystery that the king is asking, 28but there is a God in heaven who reveals mysteries, and he has disclosed to King Nebuchadnezzar what will happen at the end of days. Your dream and the visions of your head as you lay in bed were these: 29To you, O king, as you lay in bed, came thoughts of what would be hereafter, and the revealer of mysteries disclosed to you what is to be. 30But as for me, this mystery has not been revealed to me because of any wisdom that I have more than any other living being, but in order that the interpretation may be known to the king and that you may understand the thoughts of your mind.

31 "You were looking, O king, and lo! there was a great statue. This statue was huge, its brilliance extraordinary; it was standing before you, and its appearance was frightening. 32The head of that statue was of fine gold, its chest and arms of silver, its middle and thighs of bronze, 33its legs of iron, its feet partly of iron and partly of clay. 34As you looked on, a stone was cut out, not by human hands, and it struck the statue on its feet of iron and clay

and broke them in pieces. [35]Then the iron, the clay, the bronze, the silver, and the gold, were all broken in pieces and became like the chaff of the summer threshing floors; and the wind carried them away, so that not a trace of them could be found. But the stone that struck the statue became a great mountain and filled the whole earth.

36 "This was the dream; now we will tell the king its interpretation. [37]You, O king, the king of kings—to whom the God of heaven has given the kingdom, the power, the might, and the glory, [38]into whose hand he has given human beings, wherever they live, the wild animals of the field, and the birds of the air, and whom he has established as ruler over them all—you are the head of gold. [39]After you shall arise another kingdom inferior to yours, and yet a third kingdom of bronze, which shall rule over the whole earth. [40]And there shall be a fourth kingdom, strong as iron; just as iron crushes and smashes everything,[a] it shall crush and shatter all these. [41]As you saw the feet and toes partly of potter's clay and partly of iron, it shall be a divided kingdom; but some of the strength of iron shall be in it, as you saw the iron mixed with the clay. [42]As the toes of the feet were part iron and part clay, so the kingdom shall be partly strong and partly brittle. [43]As you saw the iron mixed with clay, so will they mix with one another in marriage,[b] but they will not hold together, just as iron does not mix with clay. [44]And in the days of those kings the God of heaven will set up a kingdom that shall never be destroyed, nor shall this kingdom be left to another people. It shall crush all these kingdoms and bring them to an end, and it shall stand forever; [45]just as you saw that a stone was cut from the mountain not by hands, and that it crushed the iron, the bronze, the clay,

the silver, and the gold. The great God has informed the king what shall be hereafter. The dream is certain, and its interpretation trustworthy."

46 Then King Nebuchadnezzar fell on his face, worshiped Daniel, and commanded that a grain offering and incense be offered to him. [47]The king said to Daniel, "Truly, your God is God of gods and Lord of kings and a revealer of mysteries, for you have been able to reveal this mystery!" [48]Then the king promoted Daniel, gave him many great gifts, and made him ruler over the whole province of Babylon and chief prefect over all the wise men of Babylon. [49]Daniel made a request of the king, and he appointed Shadrach, Meshach, and Abednego over the affairs of the province of Babylon. But Daniel remained at the king's court.

3.1 KING Nebuchadnezzar made a golden statue whose height was sixty cubits and whose width was six cubits; he set it up on the plain of Dura in the province of Babylon. [2]Then King Nebuchadnezzar sent for the satraps, the prefects, and the governors, the counselors, the treasurers, the justices, the magistrates, and all the officials of the provinces to assemble and come to the dedication of the statue that King Nebuchadnezzar had set up. [3]So the satraps, the prefects, and the governors, the counselors, the treasurers, the justices, the magistrates, and all the officials of the provinces, assembled for the dedication of the statue that King Nebuchadnezzar had set up. When they were standing before the statue that Nebuchadnezzar had set up, [4]the herald proclaimed aloud, "You are commanded, O peoples, nations, and languages, [5]that when you hear the sound of the horn, pipe, lyre, trigon, harp, drum, and entire musical ensemble, you are to fall down and worship the

---

a Gk Theodotion Syr Vg: Aram adds *and like iron that crushes*   b Aram *by human seed*

golden statue that King Nebuchadnezzar has set up. [6]Whoever does not fall down and worship shall immediately be thrown into a furnace of blazing fire." [7]Therefore, as soon as all the peoples heard the sound of the horn, pipe, lyre, trigon, harp, drum, and entire musical ensemble, all the peoples, nations, and languages fell down and worshiped the golden statue that King Nebuchadnezzar had set up.

8 Accordingly, at this time certain Chaldeans came forward and denounced the Jews. [9]They said to King Nebuchadnezzar, "O king, live forever! [10]You, O king, have made a decree, that everyone who hears the sound of the horn, pipe, lyre, trigon, harp, drum, and entire musical ensemble, shall fall down and worship the golden statue, [11]and whoever does not fall down and worship shall be thrown into a furnace of blazing fire. [12]There are certain Jews whom you have appointed over the affairs of the province of Babylon: Shadrach, Meshach, and Abednego. These pay no heed to you, O King. They do not serve your gods and they do not worship the golden statue that you have set up."

13 Then Nebuchadnezzar in furious rage commanded that Shadrach, Meshach, and Abednego be brought in; so they brought those men before the king. [14]Nebuchadnezzar said to them, "Is it true, O Shadrach, Meshach, and Abednego, that you do not serve my gods and you do not worship the golden statue that I have set up? [15]Now if you are ready when you hear the sound of the horn, pipe, lyre, trigon, harp, drum, and entire musical ensemble to fall down and worship the statue that I have made, well and good.[a] But if you do not worship, you shall immediately be thrown into a furnace of blazing fire,

and who is the god that will deliver you out of my hands?"

16 Shadrach, Meshach, and Abednego answered the king, "O Nebuchadnezzar, we have no need to present a defense to you in this matter. [17]If our God whom we serve is able to deliver us from the furnace of blazing fire and out of your hand, O king, let him deliver us.[b] [18]But if not, be it known to you, O king, that we will not serve your gods and we will not worship the golden statue that you have set up."

19 Then Nebuchadnezzar was so filled with rage against Shadrach, Meshach, and Abednego that his face was distorted. He ordered the furnace heated up seven times more than was customary, [20]and ordered some of the strongest guards in his army to bind Shadrach, Meshach, and Abednego and to throw them into the furnace of blazing fire. [21]So the men were bound, still wearing their tunics,[c] their trousers,[c] their hats, and their other garments, and they were thrown into the furnace of blazing fire. [22]Because the king's command was urgent and the furnace was so overheated, the raging flames killed the men who lifted Shadrach, Meshach, and Abednego. [23]But the three men, Shadrach, Meshach, and Abednego, fell down, bound, into the furnace of blazing fire.

24 Then King Nebuchadnezzar was astonished and rose up quickly. He said to his counselors, "Was it not three men that we threw bound into the fire?" They answered the king, "True, O king." [25]He replied, "But I see four men unbound, walking in the middle of the fire, and they are not hurt; and the fourth has the appearance of a god."[d] [26]Nebuchadnezzar then approached the door of the furnace of blazing fire and said, "Shadrach, Meshach, and Abed-

[a]Aram lacks *well and good*   [b]Or *If our God whom we serve is able to deliver us, he will deliver us from the furnace of blazing fire and out of your hand, O king.*   [c]Meaning of Aram word uncertain
[d]Aram *a son of the gods*

nego, servants of the Most High God, come out! Come here!" So Shadrach, Meshach, and Abednego came out from the fire. [27]And the satraps, the prefects, the governors, and the king's counselors gathered together and saw that the fire had not had any power over the bodies of those men; the hair of their heads was not singed, their tunics[a] were not harmed, and not even the smell of fire came from them. [28]Nebuchadnezzar said, "Blessed be the God of Shadrach, Meshach, and Abednego, who has sent his angel and delivered his servants who trusted in him. They disobeyed the king's command and yielded up their bodies rather than serve and worship any god except their own God. [29]Therefore I make a decree: Any people, nation, or language that utters blasphemy against the God of Shadrach, Meshach, and Abednego shall be torn limb from limb, and their houses laid in ruins; for there is no other god who is able to deliver in this way." [30]Then the king promoted Shadrach, Meshach, and Abednego in the province of Babylon.

# 1 PETER 4.7—5.14

THE end of all things is near;[b] therefore be serious and discipline yourselves for the sake of your prayers. [8]Above all, maintain constant love for one another, for love covers a multitude of sins. [9]Be hospitable to one another without complaining. [10]Like good stewards of the manifold grace of God, serve one another with whatever gift each of you has received. [11]Whoever speaks must do so as one speaking the very words of God; whoever serves must do so with the strength that God supplies, so that God may be glorified in all things through Jesus Christ. To him belong the glory and the power forever and ever. Amen.

12 Beloved, do not be surprised at the fiery ordeal that is taking place among you to test you, as though something strange were happening to you. [13]But rejoice insofar as you are sharing Christ's sufferings, so that you may also be glad and shout for joy when his glory is revealed. [14]If you are reviled for the name of Christ, you are blessed, because the spirit of glory,[c] which is the Spirit of God, is resting on you.[d] [15]But let none of you suffer as a murderer, a thief, a criminal, or even as a mischief maker. [16]Yet if any of you suffers as a Christian, do not consider it a disgrace, but glorify God because you bear this name. [17]For the time has come for judgment to begin with the household of God; if it begins with us, what will be the end for those who do not obey the gospel of God? [18]And

"If it is hard for the righteous
        to be saved,
   what will become of the
        ungodly and the
        sinners?"

[19]Therefore, let those suffering in accordance with God's will entrust themselves to a faithful Creator, while continuing to do good.

[5.1]Now as an elder myself and a witness of the sufferings of Christ, as well as one who shares in the glory to be revealed, I exhort the elders among you [2]to tend the flock of God that is in your charge, exercising the oversight,[e] not under compulsion but willingly, as God would have you do it[f]—not for sordid gain but eagerly. [3]Do not lord it over those in your charge, but be examples to the flock. [4]And when the chief shepherd appears, you will win the crown of glory that never fades away. ⁵In the same way, you who are younger must accept the authority of the elders.ᵃ And all of you must clothe yourselves with humility in your dealings with one another, for

"God opposes the proud,
but gives grace to the
humble."

6 Humble yourselves therefore under the mighty hand of God, so that he may exalt you in due time. ⁷Cast all your anxiety on him, because he cares for you. ⁸Discipline yourselves, keep alert.ᵇ Like a roaring lion your adversary the devil prowls around, looking for someone to devour. ⁹Resist him, steadfast in your faith, for you know that your brothers and sistersᶜ in all the world are undergoing the same kinds of suffering. ¹⁰And after you have suffered for a little while, the God of all grace, who has called you to his eternal glory in Christ, will himself restore, support, strengthen, and establish you. ¹¹To him be the power forever and ever. Amen.

12 Through Silvanus, whom I consider a faithful brother, I have written this short letter to encourage you and to testify that this is the true grace of God. Stand fast in it. ¹³Your sister churchᵈ in Babylon, chosen together with you, sends you greetings; and so does my son Mark. ¹⁴Greet one another with a kiss of love.

Peace to all of you who are in Christ.ᵉ

## PSALM 119.81–96

**M**Y soul languishes for your
salvation;
I hope in your word.
82 My eyes fail with watching for
your promise;
I ask, "When will you comfort
me?"

83 For I have become like a
wineskin in the smoke,
yet I have not forgotten your
statutes.
84 How long must your servant
endure?
When will you judge those
who persecute me?
85 The arrogant have dug pitfalls
for me;
they flout your law.
86 All your commandments are
enduring;
I am persecuted without
cause; help me!
87 They have almost made an end
of me on earth;
but I have not forsaken your
precepts.
88 In your steadfast love spare my
life,
so that I may keep the
decrees of your mouth.

89 The LORD exists forever;
your word is firmly fixed in
heaven.
90 Your faithfulness endures to all
generations;
you have established the
earth, and it stands fast.
91 By your appointment they stand
today,
for all things are your
servants.
92 If your law had not been my
delight,
I would have perished in my
misery.
93 I will never forget your
precepts,
for by them you have given
me life.
94 I am yours; save me,
for I have sought your
precepts.
95 The wicked lie in wait to
destroy me,

ᵃOr *of those who are older*   ᵇOr *be vigilant*   ᶜGk *your brotherhood*   ᵈGk *She who is*   ᵉOther ancient authorities add *Amen*

but I consider your decrees.
96 I have seen a limit to all
    perfection,
  but your commandment is
    exceedingly broad.

## PROVERBS 28.15–16

LIKE a roaring lion or a charging
    bear
  is a wicked ruler over a poor
    people.
16 A ruler who lacks understanding
    is a cruel oppressor;
  but one who hates unjust gain
    will enjoy a long life.

# NOVEMBER 27

## DANIEL 4a.1–37

KING Nebuchadnezzar to all peoples, nations, and languages that live throughout the earth: May you have abundant prosperity! [2]The signs and wonders that the Most High God has worked for me I am pleased to recount.

3 How great are his signs,
    how mighty his wonders!
  His kingdom is an everlasting
    kingdom,
  and his sovereignty is from
    generation to generation.

4b I, Nebuchadnezzar, was living at ease in my home and prospering in my palace. [5]I saw a dream that frightened me; my fantasies in bed and the visions of my head terrified me. [6]So I made a decree that all the wise men of Babylon should be brought before me, in order that they might tell me the interpretation of the dream. [7]Then the magicians, the enchanters, the Chaldeans, and the diviners came in, and I told them the dream, but they could not tell me its interpretation. [8]At last Daniel came in before me—he who was named Belteshazzar after the name of my god, and who is endowed with a spirit of the holy godsc—and I told him the dream: [9]"O Belteshazzar, chief of the magicians, I know that you are endowed with a spirit of the holy godsc and that no mystery is too difficult for you. Heard the dream that I saw; tell me its interpretation.

10e Upon my bed this is what I
    saw;
  there was a tree at the center
    of the earth,
  and its height was great.
11 The tree grew great and strong,
    its top reached to heaven,
  and it was visible to the ends
    of the whole earth.
12 Its foliage was beautiful,
    its fruit abundant,
  and it provided food for all.
  The animals of the field found
    shade under it,
  the birds of the air nested in
    its branches,
  and from it all living beings
    were fed.

aCh 3.31 in Aram   bCh 4.1 in Aram   cOr *a holy, divine spirit*   dTheodotion: Aram *The visions of*
eTheodotion Syr Compare Gk: Aram adds *The visions of my head*

[13]I continued looking, in the visions of my head as I lay in bed, and there was a holy watcher, coming down from heaven. [14]He cried aloud and said:

'Cut down the tree and chop off
its branches,
strip off its foliage and scatter
its fruit.
Let the animals flee from
beneath it
and the birds from its
branches.
[15] But leave its stump and roots in
the ground,
with a band of iron and
bronze,
in the tender grass of the
field.
Let him be bathed with the dew
of heaven.
and let his lot be with the
animals of the field
in the grass of the earth.
[16] Let his mind be changed from
that of a human,
and let the mind of an animal
be given to him.
And let seven times pass
over him.
[17] The sentence is rendered by
decree of the watchers,
the decision is given by order
of the holy ones,
in order that all who live
may know
that the Most High is
sovereign over the
kingdom of mortals;
he gives it to whom he will
and sets over it the lowliest
of human beings.'

[18]This is the dream that I, King Nebuchadnezzar, saw. Now you, Belteshazzar, declare the interpretation, since all the wise men of my kingdom are unable to tell me the interpretation. You are able, however, for you are endowed with a spirit of the holy gods."[a]

19 Then Daniel, who was called Belteshazzar, was severely distressed for a while. His thoughts terrified him. The king said, "Belteshazzar, do not let the dream or the interpretation terrify you." Belteshazzar answered, "My lord, may the dream be for those who hate you, and its interpretation for your enemies! [20]The tree that you saw, which grew great and strong, so that its top reached to heaven and was visible to the end of the whole earth, [21]whose foliage was beautiful and its fruit abundant, and which provided food for all, under which animals of the field lived, and in whose branches the birds of the air had nests— [22]it is you, O king! You have grown great and strong. Your greatness has increased and reaches to heaven, and your sovereignty to the ends of the earth. [23]And whereas the king saw a holy watcher coming down from heaven and saying, 'Cut down the tree and destroy it, but leave its stump and roots in the ground, with a band of iron and bronze, in the grass of the field; and let him be bathed with the dew of heaven, and let his lot be with the animals of the field, until seven times pass over him'— [24]this is the interpretation, O king, and it is a decree of the Most High that has come upon my lord the king: [25]You shall be driven away from human society, and your dwelling shall be with the wild animals. You shall be made to eat grass like oxen, you shall be bathed with the dew of heaven, and seven times shall pass over you, until you have learned that the Most High has sovereignty over the kingdom of mortals, and gives it to whom he will. [26]As it was commanded to leave the stump and roots of the tree, your kingdom shall be reestablished for you from the time that you learn that Heaven is sovereign.

a Or *a holy, divine spirit*

27Therefore, O king, may my counsel be acceptable to you: atone for[a] your sins with righteousness, and your iniquities with mercy to the oppressed, so that your prosperity may be prolonged."

28 All this came upon King Nebuchadnezzar. 29At the end of twelve months he was walking on the roof of the royal palace of Babylon, 30and the king said, "Is this not magnificent Babylon, which I have built as a royal capital by my mighty power and for my glorious majesty?" 31While the words were still in the king's mouth, a voice came from heaven: "O King Nebuchadnezzar, to you it is declared: The kingdom has departed from you! 32You shall be driven away from human society, and your dwelling shall be with the animals of the field. You shall be made to eat grass like oxen, and seven times shall pass over you, until you have learned that the Most High has sovereignty over the kingdom of mortals and gives it to whom he will." 33Immediately the sentence was fulfilled against Nebuchadnezzar. He was driven away from human society, ate grass like oxen, and his body was bathed with the dew of heaven, until his hair grew as long as eagles' feathers and his nails became like birds' claws.

34 When that period was over, I, Nebuchadnezzar, lifted my eyes to heaven, and my reason returned to me.
I blessed the Most High,
    and praised and honored the
        one who lives forever.
For his sovereignty is an
        everlasting sovereignty,
    and his kingdom endures from
        generation to generation.
35 All the inhabitants of the earth
        are accounted as nothing,
    and he does what he wills
        with the host of heaven
    and the inhabitants of the
        earth.
    There is no one who can stay
        his hand
    or say to him, "What are you
        doing?"

36At that time my reason returned to me; and my majesty and splendor were restored to me for the glory of my kingdom. My counselors and my lords sought me out, I was re-established over my kingdom, and still more greatness was added to me. 37Now I, Nebuchadnezzar, praise and extol and honor the King of heaven,
    for all his works are truth,
        and his ways are justice;
    and he is able to bring low
        those who walk in pride.

## 2 PETER 1.1–21

SIMEON[b] Peter, a servant[c] and apostle of Jesus Christ,

To those who have received a faith as precious as ours through the righteousness of our God and Savior Jesus Christ:[d]

2 May grace and peace be yours in abundance in the knowledge of God and of Jesus our Lord.

3 His divine power has given us everything needed for life and godliness, through the knowledge of him who called us by[e] his own glory and goodness. 4Thus he has given us, through these things, his precious and very great promises, so that through them you may escape from the corruption that is in the world because of lust, and may become participants of the divine nature. 5For this very reason, you must make every effort to support your faith with goodness, and goodness with knowledge, 6and knowledge with self-control, and self-control with endurance, and endurance with godliness, 7and godliness with mutual[f] affection,

[a]Aram *break off*  [b]other ancient authorities read *Simon*  [c]Gk *slave*  [d]Or *of our God and the Savior Jesus Christ*  [e]Other ancient authorities read *through*  [f]Gk *brotherly*

and mutual<sup>a</sup> affection with love. ⁸For if these things are yours and are increasing among you, they keep you from being ineffective and unfruitful in the knowledge of our Lord Jesus Christ. ⁹For anyone who lacks these things is nearsighted and blind, and is forgetful of the cleansing of past sins. ¹⁰Therefore, brothers and sisters,<sup>b</sup> be all the more eager to confirm your call and election, for if you do this, you will never stumble. ¹¹For in this way, entry into the eternal kingdom of our Lord and Savior Jesus Christ will be richly provided for you.

12 Therefore I intend to keep on reminding you of these things, though you know them already and are established in the truth that has come to you. ¹³I think it right, as long as I am in this body,<sup>c</sup> to refresh your memory, ¹⁴since I know that my death<sup>d</sup> will come soon, as indeed our Lord Jesus Christ has made clear to me. ¹⁵And I will make every effort so that after my departure you may be able at any time to recall these things.

16 For we did not follow cleverly devised myths when we made known to you the power and coming of our Lord Jesus Christ, but we had been eyewitnesses of his majesty. ¹⁷For he received honor and glory from God the Father when that voice was conveyed to him by the Majestic Glory, saying, "This is my Son, my Beloved,<sup>e</sup> with whom I am well pleased." ¹⁸We ourselves heard this voice come from heaven, while we were with him on the holy mountain.

19 So we have the prophetic message

more fully confirmed. You will do well to be attentive to this as to a lamp shining in a dark place, until the day dawns and the morning star rises in your hearts. ²⁰First of all you must understand this, that no prophecy of scripture is a matter of one's own interpretation, ²¹because no prophecy ever came by human will, but men and women moved by the Holy Spirit spoke from God.<sup>f</sup>

## PSALM 119.97–112

O<sup>H</sup>, how I love your law!
    It is my meditation all day
      long.
98  Your commandment makes me
      wiser than my enemies,
  for it is always with me.
99  I have more understanding than
      all my teachers,
  for your decrees are my
      meditation.
100  I understand more than the
      aged,
  for I keep your precepts.
101  I hold back my feet from every
      evil way,
  in order to keep your word.
102  I do not turn away from your
      ordinances,
  for you have taught me.
103  How sweet are your words to
      my taste,
  sweeter than honey to my
      mouth!
104  Through your precepts I get
      understanding;
  therefore I hate every false
      way.

105  Your word is a lamp to my feet
  and a light to my path.
106  I have sworn an oath and
      confirmed it,
  to observe your righteous
      ordinances.
107  I am severely afflicted;
  give me life, O Lord,
      according to your word.
108  Accept my offerings of praise,
      O Lord,
  and teach me your
      ordinances.

<sup>a</sup>Gk *brotherly*  <sup>b</sup>Gk *brothers*  <sup>c</sup>Gk *tent*  <sup>d</sup>Gk *the putting off of my tent*  <sup>e</sup>Other ancient authorities read *my beloved Son*  <sup>f</sup>Other ancient authorities read *but moved by the Holy Spirit saints of God spoke*

109   I hold my life in my hand
      continually,
  but I do not forget your law.
110   The wicked have laid a snare
      for me,
  but I do not stray from your
      precepts.
111   Your decrees are my heritage
      forever;
  they are the joy of my heart.
112   I incline my heart to perform
      your statutes
  forever, to the end.

## PROVERBS 28.17–18

IF someone is burdened with the
      blood of another,
  let that killer be a fugitive
      until death;
  let no one offer assistance.
18   One who walks in integrity will
      be safe,
  but whoever follows crooked
      ways will fall into the
      Pit. [a]

# NOVEMBER 28

## DANIEL 5.1–31

KING Belshazzar made a great festival for a thousand of his lords, and he was drinking wine in the presence of the thousand.

2 Under the influence of the wine, Belshazzar commanded that they bring in the vessels of gold and silver that his father Nebuchadnezzar had taken out of the temple in Jerusalem, so that the king and his lords, his wives, and his concubines might drink from them. [3]So they brought in the vessels of gold and silver[b] that had been taken out of the temple, the house of God in Jerusalem, and the king and his lords, his wives, and his concubines drank from them. [4]They drank the wine and praised the gods of gold and silver, bronze, iron, wood, and stone.

5 Immediately the fingers of a human hand appeared and began writing on the plaster of the wall of the royal palace, next to the lampstand. The king was watching the hand as it wrote. [6]Then the king's face turned pale, and his thoughts terrified him. His limbs gave way, and his knees knocked together. [7]The king cried aloud to bring in the enchanters, the Chaldeans, and the diviners; and the king said to the wise men of Babylon, "Whoever can read this writing and tell me its interpretation shall be clothed in purple, have a chain of gold around his neck, and rank third in the kingdom." [8]Then all the king's wise men came in, but they could not read the writing or tell the king the interpretation. [9]Then King Belshazzar became greatly terrified and his face turned pale, and his lords were perplexed.

10 The queen, when she heard the discussion of the king and his lords, came into the banqueting hall. The queen said, "O king, live forever! Do not let your thoughts terrify you or your face grow pale. [11]There is a man in your kingdom who is endowed with a spirit of the holy gods.[c] In the days

a Syr: Heb *fall all at once*    b Theodotion Vg: Aram lacks *and silver*    c Or *a holy, divine spirit*

of your father he was found to have enlightenment, understanding, and wisdom like the wisdom of the gods. Your father, King Nebuchadnezzar, made him chief of the magicians, enchanters, Chaldeans, and diviners, [a] 12because an excellent spirit, knowledge, and understanding to interpret dreams, explain riddles, and solve problems were found in this Daniel, whom the king named Belteshazzar. Now let Daniel be called, and he will give the interpretation."

13 Then Daniel was brought in before the king. The king said to Daniel, "So you are Daniel, one of the exiles of Judah, whom my father the king brought from Judah? 14I have heard of you that a spirit of the gods[b] is in you, and that enlightenment, understanding, and excellent wisdom are found in you. 15Now the wise men, the enchanters, have been brought in before me to read this writing and tell me its interpretation, but they were not able to give the interpretation of the matter. 16But I have heard that you can give interpretations and solve problems. Now if you are able to read the writing and tell me its interpretation, you shall be clothed in purple, have a chain of gold around your neck, and rank third in the kingdom."

17 Then Daniel answered in the presence of the king, "Let your gifts be for yourself, or give your rewards to someone else! Nevertheless I will read the writing to the king and let him know the interpretation. 18O king, the Most High God gave your father Nebuchadnezzar kingship, greatness, glory, and majesty. 19And because of the greatness that he gave him, all peoples, nations, and languages trembled and feared before him. He killed those he wanted to kill, kept alive those he wanted to keep alive, honored those he wanted to honor, and degraded those he wanted to degrade. 20But when his heart was lifted up and his spirit was hardened so that he acted proudly, he was deposed from his kingly throne, and his glory was stripped from him. 21He was driven from human society, and his mind was made like that of an animal. His dwelling was with the wild asses, he was fed grass like oxen, and his body was bathed with the dew of heaven, until he learned that the Most High God has sovereignty over the kingdom of mortals, and sets over it whomever he will. 22And you, Belshazzar his son, have not humbled your heart, even though you knew all this! 23You have exalted yourself against the Lord of heaven! The vessels of his temple have been brought in before you, and you and your lords, your wives and your concubines have been drinking wine from them. You have praised the gods of silver and gold, of bronze, iron, wood, and stone, which do not see or hear or know; but the God in whose power is your very breath, and to whom belong all your ways, you have not honored.

24 "So from his presence the hand was sent and this writing was inscribed. 25And this is the writing that was inscribed: MENE, MENE, TEKEL, and PARSIN. 26This is the interpretation of the matter: MENE, God has numbered the days of[c] your kingdom and brought it to an end; 27TEKEL, you have been weighed on the scales and found wanting; 28PERES, [d] your kingdom is divided and given to the Medes and Persians."

29 Then Belshazzar gave the command, and Daniel was clothed in purple, a chain of gold was put around his neck, and a proclamation was made concerning him that he should rank third in the kingdom.

30 That very night Belshazzar, the Chaldean king, was killed. 31[e]And Da-

---

[a] Aram adds *the king your father*  [b] Or *a divine spirit*  [c] Aram lacks *the days of*  [d] The singular of *Parsin*  [e] Ch 6.1 in Aram

rius the Mede received the kingdom, being about sixty-two years old.

## 2 PETER 2.1–22

But false prophets also arose among the people, just as there will be false teachers among you, who will secretly bring in destructive opinions. They will even deny the Master who bought them—bringing swift destruction on themselves. [2]Even so, many will follow their licentious ways, and because of these teachers[a] the way of truth will be maligned. [3]And in their greed they will exploit you with deceptive words. Their condemnation, pronounced against them long ago, has not been idle, and their destruction is not asleep.

4 For if God did not spare the angels when they sinned, but cast them into hell[b] and committed them to chains[c] of deepest darkness to be kept until the judgment; [5]and if he did not spare the ancient world, even though he saved Noah, a herald of righteousness, with seven others, when he brought a flood on a world of the ungodly; [6]and if by turning the cities of Sodom and Gomorrah to ashes he condemned them to extinction[d] and made them an example of what is coming to the ungodly;[e] [7]and if he rescued Lot, a righteous man greatly distressed by the licentiousness of the lawless [8](for that righteous man, living among them day after day, was tormented in his righteous soul by their lawless deeds that he saw and heard), [9]then the Lord knows how to rescue the godly from trial, and to keep the unrighteous under punishment until the day of judgment [10]—especially those who indulge their flesh in depraved lust, and who despise authority.

Bold and willful, they are not afraid to slander the glorious ones,[f] [11]whereas angels, though greater in might and power, do not bring against them a slanderous judgment from the Lord.[g] [12]These people, however, are like irrational animals, mere creatures of instinct, born to be caught and killed. They slander what they do not understand, and when those creatures are destroyed,[h] they also will be destroyed, [13]suffering[i] the penalty for doing wrong. They count it a pleasure to revel in the daytime. They are blots and blemishes, reveling in their dissipation[j] while they feast with you. [14]They have eyes full of adultery, insatiable for sin. They entice unsteady souls. They have hearts trained in greed. Accursed children! [15]They have left the straight road and have gone astray, following the road of Balaam son of Bosor,[k] who loved the wages of doing wrong, [16]but was rebuked for his own transgression; a speechless donkey spoke with a human voice and restrained the prophet's madness.

17 These are waterless springs and mists driven by a storm; for them the deepest darkness has been reserved. [18]For they speak bombastic nonsense, and with licentious desires of the flesh they entice people who have just[l] escaped from those who live in error. [19]They promise them freedom, but they themselves are slaves of corruption; for people are slaves to whatever masters them. [20]For if, after they have escaped the defilements of the world through the knowledge of our Lord and Savior Jesus Christ, they are again entangled in them and overpowered, the last state

---

[a]Gk *because of them*   [b]Gk *Tartaros*   [c]Other ancient authorities read *pits*   [d]Other ancient authorities lack *to extinction*   [e]Other ancient authorities read *an example to those who were to be ungodly*   [f]Or *angels*; Gk *glories*   [g]Other ancient authorities read *before the Lord*; others lack the phrase   [h]Gk *in their destruction*   [i]Other ancient authorities read *receiving*   [j]Other ancient authorities read *love feasts*   [k]Other ancient authorities read *Beor*   [l]Other ancient authorities read *actually*

has become worse for them than the first. <sup>21</sup>For it would have been better for them never to have known the way of righteousness than, after knowing it, to turn back from the holy commandment that was passed on to them. <sup>22</sup>It has happened to them according to the true proverb,

"The dog turns back to its
own vomit,"

and,

"The sow is washed only to
wallow in the mud."

## PSALM 119.113–128

I HATE the double-minded,
but I love your law.
<sup>114</sup> You are my hiding place
and my shield;
I hope in your word.
<sup>115</sup> Go away from me, you
evildoers,
that I may keep the
commandments of my
God.
<sup>116</sup> Uphold me according to your
promise, that I may live,
and let me not be put to
shame in my hope.
<sup>117</sup> Hold me up, that I may be safe
and have regard for your
statutes continually.
<sup>118</sup> You spurn all who go astray
from your statutes;
for their cunning is in vain.
<sup>119</sup> All the wicked of the earth you
count as dross;
therefore I love your decrees.
<sup>120</sup> My flesh trembles for fear of
you,
and I am afraid of your
judgments.

<sup>121</sup> I have done what is just and
right;
do not leave me to my
oppressors.
<sup>122</sup> Guarantee your servant's
well-being;
do not let the godless oppress
me.
<sup>123</sup> My eyes fail from watching for
your salvation,
and for the fulfillment of your
righteous promise.
<sup>124</sup> Deal with your servant
according to your
steadfast love,
and teach me your statutes.
<sup>125</sup> I am your servant; give me
understanding,
so that I may know your
decrees.
<sup>126</sup> It is time for the LORD to act,
for your law has been broken.
<sup>127</sup> Truly I love your
commandments
more than gold, more than
fine gold.
<sup>128</sup> Truly I direct my steps by all
your precepts; <sup>a</sup>
I hate every false way.

## PROVERBS 28.19–20

A NYONE who tills the land will
have plenty of bread,
but one who follows
worthless pursuits will
have plenty of poverty.
<sup>20</sup> The faithful will abound with
blessings,
but one who is in a hurry to
be rich will not go
unpunished.

<sup>a</sup>Gk Jerome: Meaning of Heb uncertain

## DANIEL 6.1–28

IT pleased Darius to set over the kingdom one hundred twenty satraps, stationed throughout the whole kingdom, ²and over them three presidents, including Daniel; to these the satraps gave account, so that the king might suffer no loss. ³Soon Daniel distinguished himself above all the other presidents and satraps because an excellent spirit was in him, and the king planned to appoint him over the whole kingdom. ⁴So the presidents and the satraps tried to find grounds for complaint against Daniel in connection with the kingdom. But they could find no grounds for complaint or any corruption, because he was faithful, and no negligence or corruption could be found in him. ⁵The men said, "We shall not find any ground for complaint against this Daniel unless we find it in connection with the law of his God."

6 So the presidents and satraps conspired and came to the king and said to him, "O King Darius, live forever! ⁷All the presidents of the kingdom, the prefects and the satraps, the counselors and the governors are agreed that the king should establish an ordinance and enforce an interdict, that whoever prays to anyone, divine or human, for thirty days, except to you, O king, shall be thrown into a den of lions. ⁸Now, O king, establish the interdict and sign the document, so that it cannot be changed, according to the law of the Medes and the Persians, which cannot be revoked." ⁹Therefore King Darius signed the document and interdict.

10 Although Daniel knew that the document had been signed, he continued to go to his house, which had windows in its upper room open toward Jerusalem, and to get down on his knees three times a day to pray to his God and praise him, just as he had done previously. ¹¹The conspirators came and found Daniel praying and seeking mercy before his God. ¹²Then they approached the king and said concerning the interdict, "O king! Did you not sign an interdict, that anyone who prays to anyone, divine or human, within thirty days except to you, O king, shall be thrown into a den of lions?" The king answered, "The thing stands fast, according to the law of the Medes and Persians, which cannot be revoked." ¹³Then they responded to the king, "Daniel, one of the exiles from Judah, pays no attention to you, O king, or to the interdict you have signed, but he is saying his prayers three times a day."

14 When the king heard the charge, he was very much distressed. He was determined to save Daniel, and until the sun went down he made every effort to rescue him. ¹⁵Then the conspirators came to the king and said to him, "Know, O king, that it is a law of the Medes and Persians that no interdict or ordinance that the king establishes can be changed."

16 Then the king gave the command, and Daniel was brought and thrown into the den of lions. The king said to Daniel, "May your God, whom you faithfully serve, deliver you!" ¹⁷A stone was brought and laid on the mouth of the den, and the king sealed it with his own signet and with the signet of his lords, so that nothing might be changed concerning Daniel. ¹⁸Then the king went to his palace and spent the night fasting; no food was brought to him, and sleep fled from him.

19 Then, at break of day, the king got up and hurried to the den of lions. ²⁰When he came near the den where

Daniel was, he cried out anxiously to Daniel, "O Daniel, servant of the living God, has your God whom you faithfully serve been able to deliver you from the lions?" 21Daniel then said to the king, "O king, live forever! 22My God sent his angel and shut the lions' mouths so that they would not hurt me, because I was found blameless before him; and also before you, O king, I have done no wrong." 23Then the king was exceedingly glad and commanded that Daniel be taken up out of the den. So Daniel was taken up out of the den, and no kind of harm was found on him, because he had trusted in his God. 24The king gave a command, and those who had accused Daniel were brought and thrown into the den of lions—they, their children, and their wives. Before they reached the bottom of the den the lions overpowered them and broke all their bones in pieces.

25 Then King Darius wrote to all peoples and nations of every language throughout the whole world: "May you have abundant prosperity! 26I make a decree, that in all my royal dominion people should tremble and fear before the God of Daniel:

For he is the living God,
    enduring forever.
His kingdom shall never be
        destroyed,
    and his dominion has no end.
27  He delivers and rescues,
    he works signs and wonders
        in heaven and on earth;
    for he has saved Daniel
        from the power of the lions."
28So this Daniel prospered during the reign of Darius and the reign of Cyrus the Persian.

## 2 PETER 3.1–18

THIS is now, beloved, the second letter I am writing to you; in them I am trying to arouse your sincere intention by reminding you 2that you should remember the words spoken in the past by the holy prophets, and the commandment of the Lord and Savior spoken through your apostles. 3First of all you must understand this, that in the last days scoffers will come, scoffing and indulging their own lusts 4and saying, "Where is the promise of his coming? For ever since our ancestors died,a all things continue as they were from the beginning of creation!" 5They deliberately ignore this fact, that by the word of God heavens existed long ago and an earth was formed out of water and by means of water, 6through which the world of that time was deluged with water and perished. 7But by the same word the present heavens and earth have been reserved for fire, being kept until the day of judgment and destruction of the godless.

8 But do not ignore this one fact, beloved, that with the Lord one day is like a thousand years, and a thousand years are like one day. 9The Lord is not slow about his promise, as some think of slowness, but is patient with you,b not wanting any to perish, but all to come to repentance. 10But the day of the Lord will come like a thief, and then the heavens will pass away with a loud noise, and the elements will be dissolved with fire, and the earth and everything that is done on it will be disclosed.c

11 Since all these things are to be dissolved in this way, what sort of persons ought you to be in leading lives of holiness and godliness, 12waiting for and hasteningd the coming of the day

---

aGk *our fathers fell asleep*   bOther ancient authorities read *on your account*   cOther ancient authorities read *will be burned up*   dOr *earnestly desiring*

of God, because of which the heavens will be set ablaze and dissolved, and the elements will melt with fire? [13]But, in accordance with his promise, we wait for new heavens and a new earth, where righteousness is at home.

14 Therefore, beloved, while you are waiting for these things, strive to be found by him at peace, without spot or blemish; [15]and regard the patience of our Lord as salvation. So also our beloved brother Paul wrote to you according to the wisdom given him, [16]speaking of this as he does in all his letters. There are some things in them hard to understand, which the ignorant and unstable twist to their own destruction, as they do the other scriptures. [17]You therefore, beloved, since you are forewarned, beware that you are not carried away with the error of the lawless and lose your own stability. [18]But grow in the grace and knowledge of our Lord and Savior Jesus Christ. To him be the glory both now and to the day of eternity. Amen. [a]

## PSALM 119. 129–152

Your decrees are wonderful;
     therefore my soul keeps
          them.
130  The unfolding of your words
          gives light;
     it imparts understanding to
          the simple.
131  With open mouth I pant,
     because I long for your
          commandments.
132  Turn to me and be gracious to
          me,
     as is your custom toward
          those who love your
          name.
133  Keep my steps steady
          according to your
          promise,
     and never let iniquity have
          dominion over me.

134  Redeem me from human
          oppression,
     that I may keep your
          precepts.
135  Make your face shine upon
          your servant,
     and teach me your statutes.
136  My eyes shed streams of tears
     because your law is not kept.

137  You are righteous, O LORD,
     and your judgments are right.
138  You have appointed your
          decrees in righteousness
     and in all faithfulness.
139  My zeal consumes me
     because my foes forget your
          words.
140  Your promise is well tried,
     and your servant loves it.
141  I am small and despised,
     yet I do not forget your
          precepts.
142  Your righteousness is an
          everlasting
          righteousness,
     and your law is the truth.
143  Trouble and anguish have come
          upon me,
     but your commandments are
          my delight.
144  Your decrees are righteous
          forever;
     give me understanding that I
          may live.

145  With my whole heart I cry;
          answer me, O LORD.
     I will keep your statutes.
146  I cry to you; save me,
     that I may observe your
          decrees.
147  I rise before dawn and cry
          for help;
     I put my hope in your words.
148  My eyes are awake before
          each watch of the night,

a Other ancient authorities lack *Amen*

that I may meditate on your
      promise.
149  In your steadfast love hear my
      voice;
      O Lord, in your justice
      preserve my life.
150  Those who persecute me with
      evil purpose draw near;
      they are far from your law.
151  Yet you are near, O Lord,
      and all your commandments
      are true.
152  Long ago I learned from your
      decrees

that you have established
      them forever.

## PROVERBS 28.21–22

To show partiality is not
      good—
      yet for a piece of bread a
      person may do wrong.
22  The miser is in a hurry to get
      rich
      and does not know that loss
      is sure to come.

# NOVEMBER 30

## DANIEL 7.1–28

In the first year of King Belshazzar of Babylon, Daniel had a dream and visions of his head as he lay in bed. Then he wrote down the dream:[a] 2I,[b] Daniel, saw in my vision by night the four winds of heaven stirring up the great sea, 3and four great beasts came up out of the sea, different from one another. 4The first was like a lion and had eagles' wings. Then, as I watched, its wings were plucked off, and it was lifted up from the ground and made to stand on two feet like a human being; and a human mind was given to it. 5Another beast appeared, a second one, that looked like a bear. It was raised up on one side, had three tusks[c] in its mouth among its teeth and was told, "Arise, devour many bodies!" 6After this, as I watched, another appeared, like a leopard. The beast had four wings of a bird on its back and four heads; and dominion was given to it. 7After this I saw in the visions by night a fourth beast, terrifying and dreadful and exceedingly strong. It had great iron teeth and was devouring, breaking in pieces, and stamping what was left with its feet. It was different from all the beasts that preceded it, and it had ten horns. 8I was considering the horns, when another horn appeared, a little one coming up among them; to make room for it, three of the earlier horns were plucked up by the roots. There were eyes like human eyes in this horn, and a mouth speaking arrogantly.

9  As I watched,
      thrones were set in place,
      and an Ancient One[d] took
      his throne,
      his clothing was white as snow,
      and the hair of his head like
      pure wool;
      his throne was fiery flames,
      and its wheels were burning
      fire.

aQ Ms Theodotion: MT adds *the beginning of the words; he said*   bTheodotion: Aram *Daniel answered and said, "I*   cOr *ribs*   dAram *an Ancient of Days*

10   A stream of fire issued
        and flowed out from his
        presence.
     A thousand thousands served
        him,
        and ten thousand times ten
        thousand stood
        attending him.
     The court sat in judgment,
        and the books were opened.

¹¹I watched then because of the noise of the arrogant words that the horn was speaking. And as I watched, the beast was put to death, and its body destroyed and given over to be burned with fire. ¹²As for the rest of the beasts, their dominion was taken away, but their lives were prolonged for a season and a time. ¹³As I watched in the night visions,

     I saw one like a human beingᵃ
        coming with the clouds
        of heaven.
     And he came to the Ancient
        Oneᵇ
        and was presented before
        him.

14   To him was given dominion
        and glory and kingship,
     that all peoples, nations, and
        languages
        should serve him.
     His dominion is an everlasting
        dominion
        that shall not pass away,
     and his kingship is one
        that shall never be destroyed.

15   As for me, Daniel, my spirit was troubled within me, ᶜ and the visions of my head terrified me. ¹⁶I approached one of the attendants to ask him the truth concerning all this. So he said that he would disclose to me the interpretation of the matter: ¹⁷"As for these four great beasts, four kings shall arise out of the earth. ¹⁸But the holy ones of the Most High shall receive the kingdom and possess the kingdom forever— forever and ever."

19   Then I desired to know the truth concerning the fourth beast, which was different from all the rest, exceedingly terrifying, with its teeth of iron and claws of bronze, and which devoured and broke in pieces, and stamped what was left with its feet; ²⁰and concerning the ten horns that were on its head, and concerning the other horn, which came up and to make room for which three of them fell out—the horn that had eyes and a mouth that spoke arrogantly, and that seemed greater than the others. ²¹As I looked, this horn made war with the holy ones and was prevailing over them, ²²until the Ancient Oneᵇ came; then judgment was given for the holy ones of the Most High, and the time arrived when the holy ones gained possession of the kingdom.

23   This is what he said: "As for the fourth beast,

        there shall be a fourth kingdom
           on earth
        that shall be different from all
           the other kingdoms;
        it shall devour the whole earth,
           and trample it down, and
           break it to pieces.

24   As for the ten horns,
        out of this kingdom ten kings
           shall arise,
        and another shall arise after
           them.
     This one shall be different from
        the former ones,
        and shall put down three
        kings.

25   He shall speak words against
        the Most High,
        shall wear out the holy ones
        of the Most High,
        and shall attempt to change
        the sacred seasons and
        the law;

---

ᵃ Aram *one like a son of man*   ᵇ Aram *the Ancient of Days*   ᶜ Aram *troubled in its sheath*

and they shall be given into
    his power
      for a time, two times, <sup>a</sup> and
      half a time.
26  Then the court shall sit in
    judgment,
    and his dominion shall be
      taken away,
    to be consumed and totally
      destroyed.
27  The kingship and dominion
    and the greatness of the
      kingdoms under the
      whole heaven
    shall be given to the people of
      the holy ones of the
      Most High;
    their kingdom shall be an
      everlasting kingdom,
    and all dominions shall serve
      and obey them."

28  Here the account ends. As for me, Daniel, my thoughts greatly terrified me, and my face turned pale; but I kept the matter in my mind.

# 1 JOHN 1.1–10

WE declare to you what was from the beginning, what we have heard, what we have seen with our eyes, what we have looked at and touched with our hands, concerning the word of life— <sup>2</sup>this life was revealed, and we have seen it and testify to it, and declare to you the eternal life that was with the Father and was revealed to us— <sup>3</sup>we declare to you what we have seen and heard so that you also may have fellowship with us; and truly our fellowship is with the Father and with his Son Jesus Christ. <sup>4</sup>We are writing these things so that our<sup>b</sup> joy may be complete.

5 This is the message we have heard from him and proclaim to you, that God is light and in him there is no darkness at all. <sup>6</sup>If we say that we have fellowship with him while we are walk-

ing in darkness, we lie and do not do what is true; <sup>7</sup>but if we walk in the light as he himself is in the light, we have fellowship with one another, and the blood of Jesus his Son cleanses us from all sin. <sup>8</sup>If we say that we have no sin, we deceive ourselves, and the truth is not in us. <sup>9</sup>If we confess our sins, he who is faithful and just will forgive us our sins and cleanse us from all unrighteousness. <sup>10</sup>If we say that we have not sinned, we make him a liar, and his word is not in us.

# PSALM 119.153–176

LOOK on my misery and rescue
    me,
  for I do not forget your law.
154  Plead my cause and redeem
    me;
    give me life according to your
      promise.
155  Salvation is far from the
    wicked,
    for they do not seek your
      statutes.
156  Great is your mercy, O Lord;
    give me life according to your
      justice.
157  Many are my persecutors and
    my adversaries,
    yet I do not swerve from
      your decrees.
158  I look at the faithless with
    disgust,
    because they do not keep
      your commands.
159  Consider how I love your
    precepts;
    preserve my life according to
      your steadfast love.
160  The sum of your word is truth;
    and every one of your
      righteous ordinances
      endures forever.

161  Princes persecute me without
    cause,

<sup>a</sup>Aram *a time, times*   <sup>b</sup>Other ancient authorities read *your*

but my heart stands in awe of
    your words.
162  I rejoice at your word
    like one who finds great spoil.
163  I hate and abhor falsehood,
    but I love your law.
164  Seven times a day I praise you
    for your righteous ordinances.
165  Great peace have those who
    love your law;
    nothing can make them
    stumble.
166  I hope for your salvation,
    O Lord,
    and I fulfill your
    commandments.
167  My soul keeps your decrees;
    I love them exceedingly.
168  I keep your precepts and
    decrees,
    for all my ways are before
    you.

169  Let my cry come before you,
    O Lord;
    give me understanding
    according to your word.
170  Let my supplication come
    before you;
    deliver me according to your
    promise.
171  My lips will pour forth praise,

because you teach me your
    statutes.
172  My tongue will sing of your
    promise,
    for all your commandments
    are right.
173  Let your hand be ready to help
    me,
    for I have chosen your
    precepts.
174  I long for your salvation,
    O Lord,
    and your law is my delight.
175  Let me live that I may praise
    you,
    and let your ordinances help
    me.
176  I have gone astray like a lost
    sheep; seek out your
    servant,
    for I do not forget your
    commandments.

## PROVERBS 28.23–24

Whoever rebukes a person
    will afterward find
    more favor
than one who flatters with
    the tongue.
24  Anyone who robs father or
    mother
    and says, "That is no crime,"
    is partner to a thug.

# DECEMBER 1

## DANIEL 8.1–27

In the third year of the reign of King Belshazzar a vision appeared to me, Daniel, after the one that had appeared to me at first. 2In the vision I was looking and saw myself in Susa the capital, in the province of Elam, a and I was by the river Ulai. b 3I looked up and saw a ram standing beside the river. c It had two horns. Both horns

a Gk Theodotion: MT Q Ms repeat *in the vision I was looking*  b Or *the Ulai Gate*  c Or *gate*

were long, but one was longer than the other, and the longer one came up second. ⁴I saw the ram charging westward and northward and southward. All beasts were powerless to withstand it, and no one could rescue from its power; it did as it pleased and became strong.

5 As I was watching, a male goat appeared from the west, coming across the face of the whole earth without touching the ground. The goat had a horn[a] between its eyes. ⁶It came toward the ram with the two horns that I had seen standing beside the river,[b] and it ran at it with savage force. ⁷I saw it approaching the ram. It was enraged against it and struck the ram, breaking its two horns. The ram did not have power to withstand it; it threw the ram down to the ground and trampled upon it, and there was no one who could rescue the ram from its power. ⁸Then the male goat grew exceedingly great; but at the height of its power, the great horn was broken, and in its place there came up four prominent horns toward the four winds of heaven.

9 Out of one of them came another[c] horn, a little one, which grew exceedingly great toward the south, toward the east, and toward the beautiful land. ¹⁰It grew as high as the host of heaven. It threw down to the earth some of the host and some of the stars, and trampled on them. ¹¹Even against the prince of the host it acted arrogantly; it took the regular burnt offering away from him and overthrew the place of his sanctuary. ¹²Because of wickedness, the host was given over to it together with the regular burnt offering;[d] it cast truth to the ground, and kept prospering in what it did. ¹³Then I heard a holy one speaking, and another holy one said to the one that spoke, "For how long is this vision concerning the regular burnt offering, the transgression that makes desolate, and the giving over of the sanctuary and host to be trampled?"[d] ¹⁴And he answered him,[e] "For two thousand three hundred evenings and mornings; then the sanctuary shall be restored to its rightful state."

15 When I, Daniel, had seen the vision, I tried to understand it. Then someone appeared standing before me, having the appearance of a man, ¹⁶and I heard a human voice by the Ulai, calling, "Gabriel, help this man understand the vision." ¹⁷So he came near where I stood; and when he came, I became frightened and fell prostrate. But he said to me, "Understand, O mortal,[f] that the vision is for the time of the end."

18 As he was speaking to me, I fell into a trance, face to the ground; then he touched me and set me on my feet. ¹⁹He said, "Listen, and I will tell you what will take place later in the period of wrath; for it refers to the appointed time of the end. ²⁰As for the ram that you saw with the two horns, these are the kings of Media and Persia. ²¹The male goat[g] is the king of Greece, and the great horn between its eyes is the first king. ²²As for the horn that was broken, in place of which four others arose, four kingdoms shall arise from his[h] nation, but not with his power.

23 At the end of their rule,
   when the transgressions have
      reached their full
        measure,
  a king of bold countenance
      shall arise,
     skilled in intrigue.
24 He shall grow strong in
      power,[i]
   shall cause fearful destruction,

---

a Theodotion: Gk *one horn*; Heb *a horn of vision*  b Or *gate*  c Cn Compare 7.8: Heb *one*  d Meaning of Heb uncertain  e Gk Theodotion Syr Vg: Heb *me*  f Heb *son of man*  g Or *shaggy male goat* h Gk Theodotion Vg: Heb *the*  i Theodotion and one Gk Ms: Heb repeats (from 8.22) *but not with his power*

and shall succeed in what
    he does.
He shall destroy the powerful
    and the people of the holy
        ones.
25 By his cunning
    he shall make deceit prosper
        under his hand,
    and in his own mind he shall
        be great.
Without warning he shall
        destroy many
    and shall even rise up against
        the Prince of princes.
But he shall be broken, and not
        by human hands.
26The vision of the evenings and the mornings that has been told is true. As for you, seal up the vision, for it refers to many days from now."

27 So I, Daniel, was overcome and lay sick for some days; then I arose and went about the king's business. But I was dismayed by the vision and did not understand it.

# 1 JOHN 2.1–17

My little children, I am writing these things to you so that you may not sin. But if anyone does sin, we have an advocate with the Father, Jesus Christ the righteous; 2and he is the atoning sacrifice for our sins, and not for ours only but also for the sins of the whole world.

3 Now by this we may be sure that we know him, if we obey his commandments. 4Whoever says, "I have come to know him," but does not obey his commandments, is a liar, and in such a person the truth does not exist; 5but whoever obeys his word, truly in this person the love of God has reached perfection. By this we may be sure that we are in him: 6whoever says, "I abide in him," ought to walk just as he walked.

7 Beloved, I am writing you no new commandment, but an old commandment that you have had from the beginning; the old commandment is the word that you have heard. 8Yet I am writing you a new commandment that is true in him and in you, becausea the darkness is passing away and the true light is already shining. 9Whoever says, "I am in the light," while hating a brother or sister,b is still in the darkness. 10Whoever loves a brother or sisterc lives in the light, and in such a persond there is no cause for stumbling. 11But whoever hates another believere is in the darkness, walks in the darkness, and does not know the way to go, because the darkness has brought on blindness.

12 I am writing to you, little
      children,
    because your sins are
      forgiven on account of
      his name.
13 I am writing to you, fathers,
    because you know him who is
      from the beginning.
I am writing to you, young
      people,
    because you have conquered
      the evil one.
14 I write to you, children,
    because you know the
      Father.
I write to you, fathers,
    because you know him who is
      from the beginning.
I write to you, young people,
    because you are strong
    and the word of God abides
      in you,
    and you have overcome the
      evil one.

15 Do not love the world or the things in the world. The love of the Father is not in those who love the world; 16for all that is in the world—the desire of the flesh, the desire of the eyes, the pride in riches—comes not from the Father but from the world. 17And the

aOr that  bGk hating a brother  cGk loves a brother  dOr in it  eGk hates a brother

world and its desire[a] are passing away, but those who do the will of God live forever.

## PSALM 120.1–7

*A Song of Ascents.*

IN my distress I cry to the LORD,
 that he may answer me:
 [2] "Deliver me, O LORD,
 from lying lips,
 from a deceitful tongue."

3 What shall be given to you?
 And what more shall be done
 to you,
 you deceitful tongue?
4 A warrior's sharp arrows,
 with glowing coals of the
 broom tree!

5 Woe is me, that I am an alien in
 Meshech,
 that I must live among the
 tents of Kedar.
6 Too long have I had my dwelling
 among those who hate peace.
7 I am for peace;
 but when I speak,
 they are for war.

## PROVERBS 28.25–26

THE greedy person stirs up
 strife,
 but whoever trusts in the
 LORD will be enriched.
26 Those who trust in their own
 wits are fools;
 but those who walk in wisdom
 come through safely.

# DECEMBER 2

## DANIEL 9.1—11.1

IN the first year of Darius son of Ahasuerus, by birth a Mede, who became king over the realm of the Chaldeans— [2]in the first year of his reign, I, Daniel, perceived in the books the number of years that, according to the word of the LORD to the prophet Jeremiah, must be fulfilled for the devastation of Jerusalem, namely, seventy years.

3 Then I turned to the Lord God, to seek an answer by prayer and supplication with fasting and sackcloth and ashes. [4]I prayed to the LORD my God and made confession, saying,

"Ah, Lord, great and awesome God, keeping covenant and steadfast love with those who love you and keep your commandments, [5]we have sinned and done wrong, acted wickedly and rebelled, turning aside from your commandments and ordinances. [6]We have not listened to your servants the prophets, who spoke in your name to our kings, our princes, and our ancestors, and to all the people of the land.

7 "Righteousness is on your side, O Lord, but open shame, as at this day, falls on us, the people of Judah, the inhabitants of Jerusalem, and all Israel, those who are near and those who are far away, in all the lands to which you have driven them, because of the treachery that they have committed against you. [8]Open shame, O LORD,

a Or *the desire for it*

falls on us, our kings, our officials, and our ancestors, because we have sinned against you. [9]To the Lord our God belong mercy and forgiveness, for we have rebelled against him, [10]and have not obeyed the voice of the Lord our God by following his laws, which he set before us by his servants the prophets.

11 "All Israel has transgressed your law and turned aside, refusing to obey your voice. So the curse and the oath written in the law of Moses, the servant of God, have been poured out upon us, because we have sinned against you. [12]He has confirmed his words, which he spoke against us and against our rulers, by bringing upon us a calamity so great that what has been done against Jerusalem has never before been done under the whole heaven. [13]Just as it is written in the law of Moses, all this calamity has come upon us. We did not entreat the favor of the Lord our God, turning from our iniquities and reflecting on his[a] fidelity. [14]So the Lord kept watch over this calamity until he brought it upon us. Indeed, the Lord our God is right in all that he has done; for we have disobeyed his voice.

15 "And now, O Lord our God, who brought your people out of the land of Egypt with a mighty hand and made your name renowned even to this day—we have sinned, we have done wickedly. [16]O Lord, in view of all your righteous acts, let your anger and wrath, we pray, turn away from your city Jerusalem, your holy mountain; because of our sins and the iniquities of our ancestors, Jerusalem and your people have become a disgrace among all our neighbors. [17]Now therefore, O our God, listen to the prayer of your servant and to his supplication, and for your own sake, Lord,[b] let your face shine upon your desolated sanctuary. [18]Incline your ear, O my God, and

hear. Open your eyes and look at our desolation and the city that bears your name. We do not present our supplication before you on the ground of our righteousness, but on the ground of your great mercies. [19]O Lord, hear; O Lord, forgive; O Lord, listen and act and do not delay! For your own sake, O my God, because your city and your people bear your name!"

20 While I was speaking, and was praying and confessing my sin and the sin of my people Israel, and presenting my supplication before the Lord my God on behalf of the holy mountain of my God— [21]while I was speaking in prayer, the man Gabriel, whom I had seen before in a vision, came to me in swift flight at the time of the evening sacrifice. [22]He came[c] and said to me, "Daniel, I have now come out to give you wisdom and understanding. [23]At the beginning of your supplications a word went out, and I have come to declare it, for you are greatly beloved. So consider the word and understand the vision:

24 "Seventy weeks are decreed for your people and your holy city: to finish the transgression, to put an end to sin, and to atone for iniquity, to bring in everlasting righteousness, to seal both vision and prophet, and to anoint a most holy place. [d] [25]Know therefore and understand: from the time that the word went out to restore and rebuild Jerusalem until the time of an anointed prince, there shall be seven weeks; and for sixty-two weeks it shall be built again with streets and moat, but in a troubled time. [26]After the sixty-two weeks, an anointed one shall be cut off and shall have nothing, and the troops of the prince who is to come shall destroy the city and the sanctuary. Its[e] end shall come with a flood, and to the end there shall be war. Desolations are decreed. [27]He shall make a strong covenant with

aHeb *your*   bTheodotion Vg Compare Syr: Heb *for the Lord's sake*   cGk Syr: Heb *He made to understand*   dOr *thing* or *one*   eOr *His*

many for one week, and for half of the week he shall make sacrifice and offering cease; and in their place[a] shall be an abomination that desolates, until the decreed end is poured out upon the desolator."

10.1 In the third year of King Cyrus of Persia a word was revealed to Daniel, who was named Belteshazzar. The word was true, and it concerned a great conflict. He understood the word, having received understanding in the vision.

2 At that time I, Daniel, had been mourning for three weeks. [3]I had eaten no rich food, no meat or wine had entered my mouth, and I had not anointed myself at all, for the full three weeks. [4]On the twenty-fourth day of the first month, as I was standing on the bank of the great river (that is, the Tigris), [5]I looked up and saw a man clothed in linen, with a belt of gold from Uphaz around his waist. [6]His body was like beryl, his face like lightning, his eyes like flaming torches, his arms and legs like the gleam of burnished bronze, and the sound of his words like the roar of a multitude. [7]I, Daniel, alone saw the vision; the people who were with me did not see the vision, though a great trembling fell upon them, and they fled and hid themselves. [8]So I was left alone to see this great vision. My strength left me, and my complexion grew deathly pale, and I retained no strength. [9]Then I heard the sound of his words; and when I heard the sound of his words, I fell into a trance, face to the ground.

10 But then a hand touched me and roused me to my hands and knees. [11]He said to me, "Daniel, greatly beloved, pay attention to the words that I am going to speak to you. Stand on your feet, for I have now been sent to you." So while he was speaking this word to me, I stood up trembling. [12]He said to me, "Do not fear, Daniel, for from the first day that you set your mind to gain understanding and to humble yourself before your God, your words have been heard, and I have come because of your words. [13]But the prince of the kingdom of Persia opposed me twenty-one days. So Michael, one of the chief princes, came to help me, and I left him there with the prince of the kingdom of Persia, [b] [14]and have come to help you understand what is to happen to your people at the end of days. For there is a further vision for those days."

15 While he was speaking these words to me, I turned my face toward the ground and was speechless. [16]Then one in human form touched my lips, and I opened my mouth to speak, and said to the one who stood before me, "My lord, because of the vision such pains have come upon me that I retain no strength. [17]How can my lord's servant talk with my lord? For I am shaking, [c] no strength remains in me, and no breath is left in me."

18 Again one in human form touched me and strengthened me. [19]He said, "Do not fear, greatly beloved, you are safe. Be strong and courageous!" When he spoke to me, I was strengthened and said, "Let my lord speak, for you have strengthened me." [20]Then he said, "Do you know why I have come to you? Now I must return to fight against the prince of Persia, and when I am through with him, the prince of Greece will come. [21]But I am to tell you what is inscribed in the book of truth. There is no one with me who contends against these princes except Michael, your prince. 11.1 As for me, in the first year of Darius the Mede, I stood up to support and strengthen him.

[a]Cn: Meaning of Heb uncertain  [b]Gk Theodotion: Heb *I was left there with the kings of Persia*  [c]Gk: Heb *from now*

## 1 JOHN 2.18—3.3

**C**HILDREN, it is the last hour! As you have heard that antichrist is coming, so now many antichrists have come. From this we know that it is the last hour. [19]They went out from us, but they did not belong to us; for if they had belonged to us, they would have remained with us. But by going out they made it plain that none of them belongs to us. [20]But you have been anointed by the Holy One, and all of you have knowledge.[a] [21]I write to you, not because you do not know the truth, but because you know it, and you know that no lie comes from the truth. [22]Who is the liar but the one who denies that Jesus is the Christ?[b] This is the antichrist, the one who denies the Father and the Son. [23]No one who denies the Son has the Father; everyone who confesses the Son has the Father also. [24]Let what you heard from the beginning abide in you. If what you heard from the beginning abides in you, then you will abide in the Son and in the Father. [25]And this is what he has promised us,[c] eternal life.

26  I write these things to you concerning those who would deceive you. [27]As for you, the anointing that you received from him abides in you, and so you do not need anyone to teach you. But as his anointing teaches you about all things, and is true and is not a lie, and just as it has taught you, abide in him.[d]

28  And now, little children, abide in him, so that when he is revealed we may have confidence and not be put to shame before him at his coming.

29  If you know that he is righteous, you may be sure that everyone who does right has been born of him. [3.1]See what love the Father has given us, that we should be called children of God; and that is what we are. The reason the world does not know us is that it did not know him. [2]Beloved, we are God's children now; what we will be has not yet been revealed. What we do know is this: when he[d] is revealed, we will be like him, for we will see him as he is. [3]And all who have this hope in him purify themselves, just as he is pure.

## PSALM 121.1–8

*A Song of Ascents.*

**I** LIFT up my eyes to the hills—
from where will my help
come?
2  My help comes from the LORD,
who made heaven and earth.

3  He will not let your foot be
moved;
he who keeps you will not
slumber.
4  He who keeps Israel
will neither slumber nor
sleep.

5  The LORD is your keeper;
the LORD is your shade at
your right hand.
6  The sun shall not strike you
by day,
nor the moon by night.

7  The LORD will keep you from
all evil;
he will keep your life.
8  The LORD will keep
your going out and your
coming in
from this time on and
forevermore.

---

[a]Other ancient authorities read *you know all things*  [b]Or *the Messiah*  [c]Other ancient authorities read *you*  [d]Or *it*

PROVERBS 28.27–28

WHOEVER gives to the poor will lack nothing, but one who turns a blind eye will get many a curse.

28 When the wicked prevail, people
go into hiding;
but when they perish, the
righteous increase.

# DECEMBER 3

## DANIEL 11.2–35

"Now I [God's messenger] will announce the truth to you. Three more kings shall arise in Persia. The fourth shall be far richer than all of them, and when he has become strong through his riches, he shall stir up all against the kingdom of Greece. 3Then a warrior king shall arise, who shall rule with great dominion and take action as he pleases. 4And while still rising in power, his kingdom shall be broken and divided toward the four winds of heaven, but not to his posterity, nor according to the dominion with which he ruled; for his kingdom shall be uprooted and go to others besides these.

5 "Then the king of the south shall grow strong, but one of his officers shall grow stronger than he and shall rule a realm greater than his own realm. 6After some years they shall make an alliance, and the daughter of the king of the south shall come to the king of the north to ratify the agreement. But she shall not retain her power, and his offspring shall not endure. She shall be given up, she and her attendants and her child and the one who supported her.

"In those times 7a branch from her roots shall rise up in his place. He shall come against the army and enter the fortress of the king of the north, and he shall take action against them and prevail. 8Even their gods, with their idols and with their precious vessels of silver and gold, he shall carry off to Egypt as spoils of war. For some years he shall refrain from attacking the king of the north; 9then the latter shall invade the realm of the king of the south, but will return to his own land.

10 "His sons shall wage war and assemble a multitude of great forces, which shall advance like a flood and pass through, and again shall carry the war as far as his fortress. 11Moved with rage, the king of the south shall go out and do battle against the king of the north, who shall muster a great multitude, which shall, however, be defeated by his enemy. 12When the multitude has been carried off, his heart shall be exalted, and he shall overthrow tens of thousands, but he shall not prevail. 13For the king of the north shall again raise a multitude, larger than the former, and after some yearsa he shall advance with a great army and abundant supplies.

14 "In those times many shall rise against the king of the south. The law-

aHeb *and at the end of the times years*

less among your own people shall lift themselves up in order to fulfill the vision, but they shall fail. [15]Then the king of the north shall come and throw up siegeworks, and take a well-fortified city. And the forces of the south shall not stand, not even his picked troops, for there shall be no strength to resist. [16]But he who comes against him shall take the actions he pleases, and no one shall withstand him. He shall take a position in the beautiful land, and all of it shall be in his power. [17]He shall set his mind to come with the strength of his whole kingdom, and he shall bring terms of peace[a] and perform them. In order to destroy the kingdom,[b] he shall give him a woman in marriage; but it shall not succeed or be to his advantage. [18]Afterward he shall turn to the coastlands, and shall capture many. But a commander shall put an end to his insolence; indeed,[c] he shall turn his insolence back upon him. [19]Then he shall turn back toward the fortresses of his own land, but he shall stumble and fall, and shall not be found.

20 "Then shall arise in his place one who shall send an official for the glory of the kingdom; but within a few days he shall be broken, though not in anger or in battle. [21]In his place shall arise a contemptible person on whom royal majesty had not been conferred; he shall come in without warning and obtain the kingdom through intrigue. [22]Armies shall be utterly swept away and broken before him, and the prince of the covenant as well. [23]And after an alliance is made with him, he shall act deceitfully and become strong with a small party. [24]Without warning he shall come into the richest parts[d] of the province and do what none of his predecessors had ever done, lavishing plunder, spoil, and wealth on them. He shall devise plans against strongholds, but only for a time. [25]He shall stir up his power and determination against the king of the south with a great army, and the king of the south shall wage war with a much greater and stronger army. But he shall not succeed, for plots shall be devised against him [26]by those who eat of the royal rations. They shall break him, his army shall be swept away, and many shall fall slain. [27]The two kings, their minds bent on evil, shall sit at one table and exchange lies. But it shall not succeed, for there remains an end at the time appointed. [28]He shall return to his land with great wealth, but his heart shall be set against the holy covenant. He shall work his will, and return to his own land.

29 "At the time appointed he shall return and come into the south, but this time it shall not be as it was before. [30]For ships of Kittim shall come against him, and he shall lose heart and withdraw. He shall be enraged and take action against the holy covenant. He shall turn back and pay heed to those who forsake the holy covenant. [31]Forces sent by him shall occupy and profane the temple and fortress. They shall abolish the regular burnt offering and set up the abomination that makes desolate. [32]He shall seduce with intrigue those who violate the covenant; but the people who are loyal to their God shall stand firm and take action. [33]The wise among the people shall give understanding to many; for some days, however, they shall fall by sword and flame, and suffer captivity and plunder. [34]When they fall victim, they shall receive a little help, and many shall join them insincerely. [35]Some of the wise shall fall, so that they may be refined, purified, and cleansed,[e] until the time of the end, for there is still an interval until the time appointed.

[a]Gk: Heb *kingdom, and upright ones with him*   [b]Heb *it*   [c]Meaning of Heb uncertain   [d]Or *among the richest men*   [e]Heb *made them white*

## 1 JOHN 3.4–24

EVERYONE who commits sin is guilty of lawlessness; sin is lawlessness. <sup>5</sup>You know that he was revealed to take away sins, and in him there is no sin. <sup>6</sup>No one who abides in him sins; no one who sins has either seen him or known him. <sup>7</sup>Little children, let no one deceive you. Everyone who does what is right is righteous, just as he is righteous. <sup>8</sup>Everyone who commits sin is a child of the devil; for the devil has been sinning from the beginning. The Son of God was revealed for this purpose, to destroy the works of the devil. <sup>9</sup>Those who have been born of God do not sin, because God's seed abides in them;<sup>a</sup> they cannot sin, because they have been born of God. <sup>10</sup>The children of God and the children of the devil are revealed in this way: all who do not do what is right are not from God, nor are those who do not love their brothers and sisters.<sup>b</sup>

11 For this is the message you have heard from the beginning, that we should love one another. <sup>12</sup>We must not be like Cain who was from the evil one and murdered his brother. And why did he murder him? Because his own deeds were evil and his brother's righteous. <sup>13</sup>Do not be astonished, brothers and sisters,<sup>c</sup> that the world hates you. <sup>14</sup>We know that we have passed from death to life because we love one another. Whoever does not love abides in death. <sup>15</sup>All who hate a brother or sister<sup>b</sup> are murderers, and you know that murderers do not have eternal life abiding in them. <sup>16</sup>We know love by this, that he laid down his life for us—and we ought to lay down our lives for one another. <sup>17</sup>How does God's love abide in anyone who has the world's goods and sees a brother or sister<sup>d</sup> in need and yet refuses help? 18 Little children, let us love, not in word or speech, but in truth and action.

<sup>19</sup>And by this we will know that we are from the truth and will reassure our hearts before him <sup>20</sup>whenever our hearts condemn us; for God is greater than our hearts, and he knows everything. <sup>21</sup>Beloved, if our hearts do not condemn us, we have boldness before God; <sup>22</sup>and we receive from him whatever we ask, because we obey his commandments and do what pleases him.

23 And this is his commandment, that we should believe in the name of his Son Jesus Christ and love one another, just as he has commanded us. <sup>24</sup>All who obey his commandments abide in him, and he abides in them. And by this we know that he abides in us, by the Spirit that he has given us.

## PSALM 122.1–9

*A Song of Ascents. Of David.*

I WAS glad when they said to me,
  "Let us go to the house of
    the LORD!"
2 Our feet are standing
  within your gates,
    O Jerusalem.

3 Jerusalem—built as a city
  that is bound firmly together.
4 To it the tribes go up,
  the tribes of the LORD,
as was decreed for Israel,
  to give thanks to the name of
    the LORD.
5 For there the thrones for
    judgment were set up,
  the thrones of the house of
    David.

6 Pray for the peace of Jerusalem:
  "May they prosper who love
    you.
7 Peace be within your walls,
  and security within your
    towers."
8 For the sake of my relatives and
    friends

<sup>a</sup>Or *because the children of God abide in him*  <sup>b</sup>Gk *his brother*  <sup>c</sup>Gk *brothers*  <sup>d</sup>Gk *brother*

> I will say, "Peace be within
> you."
> 9  For the sake of the house of the
> LORD our God,
> I will seek your good.

**PROVERBS 29.1**

ONE who is often reproved, yet remains stubborn, will suddenly be broken beyond healing.

# DECEMBER 4

## DANIEL 11.36—12.13

"THE king shall act as he pleases. He shall exalt himself and consider himself greater than any god, and shall speak horrendous things against the God of gods. He shall prosper until the period of wrath is completed, for what is determined shall be done. <sup>37</sup>He shall pay no respect to the gods of his ancestors, or to the one beloved by women; he shall pay no respect to any other god, for he shall consider himself greater than all. <sup>38</sup>He shall honor the god of fortresses instead of these; a god whom his ancestors did not know he shall honor with gold and silver, with precious stones and costly gifts. <sup>39</sup>He shall deal with the strongest fortresses by the help of a foreign god. Those who acknowledge him he shall make more wealthy, and shall appoint them as rulers over many, and shall distribute the land for a price.

40  "At the time of the end the king of the south shall attack him. But the king of the north shall rush upon him like a whirlwind, with chariots and horsemen, and with many ships. He shall advance against countries and pass through like a flood. <sup>41</sup>He shall come into the beautiful land, and tens of thousands shall fall victim, but Edom and Moab and the main part of the Ammonites shall escape from his power. <sup>42</sup>He shall stretch out his hand against the countries, and the land of Egypt shall not escape. <sup>43</sup>He shall become ruler of the treasures of gold and of silver, and all the riches of Egypt; and the Libyans and the Ethiopians[a] shall follow in his train. <sup>44</sup>But reports from the east and the north shall alarm him, and he shall go out with great fury to bring ruin and complete destruction to many. <sup>45</sup>He shall pitch his palatial tents between the sea and the beautiful holy mountain. Yet he shall come to his end, with no one to help him.

<sup>12.1</sup> "AT that time Michael, the great prince, the protector of your people, shall arise. There shall be a time of anguish, such as has never occurred since nations first came into existence. But at that time your people shall be delivered, everyone who is found written in the book. <sup>2</sup>Many of those who sleep in the dust of the earth[b] shall awake, some to everlasting life, and some to shame and everlasting contempt. <sup>3</sup>Those who are wise shall shine like the brightness of the sky,[c] and those who lead many to righteousness, like the stars forever and ever. <sup>4</sup>But you,

a Or *Nubians*; Heb *Cushites*  b Or *the land of dust*  c Or *dome*

Daniel, keep the words secret and the book sealed until the time of the end. Many shall be running back and forth, and evil[a] shall increase."

5 Then I, Daniel, looked, and two others appeared, one standing on this bank of the stream and one on the other. ⁶One of them said to the man clothed in linen, who was upstream, "How long shall it be until the end of these wonders?" ⁷The man clothed in linen, who was upstream, raised his right hand and his left hand toward heaven. And I heard him swear by the one who lives forever that it would be for a time, two times, and half a time,[b] and that when the shattering of the power of the holy people comes to an end, all these things would be accomplished. ⁸I heard but could not understand; so I said, "My lord, what shall be the outcome of these things?" ⁹He said, "Go your way, Daniel, for the words are to remain secret and sealed until the time of the end. ¹⁰Many shall be purified, cleansed, and refined, but the wicked shall continue to act wickedly. None of the wicked shall understand, but those who are wise shall understand. ¹¹From the time that the regular burnt offering is taken away and the abomination that desolates is set up, there shall be one thousand two hundred ninety days. ¹²Happy are those who persevere and attain the thousand three hundred thirty-five days. ¹³But you, go your way,[c] and rest; you shall rise for your reward at the end of the days."

# 1 JOHN 4.1–21

**B**ELOVED, do not believe every spirit, but test the spirits to see whether they are from God; for many false prophets have gone out into the world. ²By this you know the Spirit of God: every spirit that confesses that Jesus Christ has come in the flesh is from God, ³and every spirit that does not confess Jesus[d] is not from God. And this is the spirit of the antichrist, of which you have heard that it is coming; and now it is already in the world. ⁴Little children, you are from God, and have conquered them; for the one who is in you is greater than the one who is in the world. ⁵They are from the world; therefore what they say is from the world, and the world listens to them. ⁶We are from God. Whoever knows God listens to us, and whoever is not from God does not listen to us. From this we know the spirit of truth and the spirit of error.

7 Beloved, let us love one another, because love is from God; everyone who loves is born of God and knows God. ⁸Whoever does not love does not know God, for God is love. ⁹God's love was revealed among us in this way: God sent his only Son into the world so that we might live through him. ¹⁰In this is love, not that we loved God but that he loved us and sent his Son to be the atoning sacrifice for our sins. ¹¹Beloved, since God loved us so much, we also ought to love one another. ¹²No one has ever seen God; if we love one another, God lives in us, and his love is perfected in us.

13 By this we know that we abide in him and he in us, because he has given us of his Spirit. ¹⁴And we have seen and do testify that the Father has sent his Son as the Savior of the world. ¹⁵God abides in those who confess that Jesus is the Son of God, and they abide in God. ¹⁶So we have known and believe the love that God has for us.

God is love, and those who abide in love abide in God, and God abides in them. ¹⁷Love has been perfected among us in this: that we may have boldness on the day of judgment, because as he is, so are we in this world.

a Cn Compare Gk: Heb *knowledge*   b Heb *a time, times, and a half*   c Gk Theodotion: Heb adds *to the end*   d Other ancient authorities read *does away with Jesus* (Gk *dissolves Jesus*)

[18]There is no fear in love, but perfect love casts out fear; for fear has to do with punishment, and whoever fears has not reached perfection in love. [19]We love[a] because he first loved us. [20]Those who say, "I love God," and hate their brothers or sisters,[b] are liars; for those who do not love a brother or sister[c] whom they have seen, cannot love God whom they have not seen. [21]The commandment we have from him is this: those who love God must love their brothers and sisters[b] also.

## PSALM 123.1–4

*A Song of Ascents.*

To you I lift up my eyes,
  O you who are enthroned in
    the heavens!
2  As the eyes of servants
    look to the hand of their
      master,
  as the eyes of a maid
    to the hand of her mistress,
  so our eyes look to the Lord
    our God,
    until he has mercy upon us.

3  Have mercy upon us, O Lord,
    have mercy upon us,
  for we have had more than
    enough of contempt.
4  Our soul has had more than its
    fill
  of the scorn of those who are
    at ease,
  of the contempt of the proud.

## PROVERBS 29.2–4

When the righteous are in authority, the people rejoice;
  but when the wicked rule, the
    people groan.
3  A child who loves wisdom
    makes a parent glad,
  but to keep company with
    prostitutes is to squander
    one's substance.
4  By justice a king gives stability
    to the land,
  but one who makes heavy
    exactions ruins it.

# DECEMBER 5

## HOSEA 1.1—3.5

The word of the Lord that came to Hosea son of Beeri, in the days of Kings Uzziah, Jotham, Ahaz, and Hezekiah of Judah, and in the days of King Jeroboam son of Joash of Israel.

2 When the Lord first spoke through Hosea, the Lord said to Hosea, "Go, take for yourself a wife of whoredom and have children of whoredom, for the land commits great whoredom by forsaking the Lord." [3]So he went and took Gomer daughter of Diblaim, and she conceived and bore him a son.

4 And the Lord said to him, "Name him Jezreel;[d] for in a little while I will punish the house of Jehu for the blood of Jezreel, and I will put an end to the kingdom of the house of Israel. [5]On that day I will break the bow of Israel in the valley of Jezreel."

[a]Other ancient authorities add *him;* others add *God*  [b]Gk *brothers*  [c]Gk *brother*  [d]That is *God sows*

6 She conceived again and bore a daughter. Then the LORD said to him, "Name her Lo-ruhamah,ᵃ for I will no longer have pity on the house of Israel or forgive them. ⁷But I will have pity on the house of Judah, and I will save them by the LORD their God; I will not save them by bow, or by sword, or by war, or by horses, or by horsemen."

8 When she had weaned Lo-ruhamah, she conceived and bore a son. ⁹Then the LORD said, "Name him Lo-ammi,ᵇ for you are not my people and I am not your God."ᶜ

10ᵈ Yet the number of the people of Israel shall be like the sand of the sea, which can be neither measured nor numbered; and in the place where it was said to them, "You are not my people," it shall be said to them, "Children of the living God." ¹¹The people of Judah and the people of Israel shall be gathered together, and they shall appoint for themselves one head; and they shall take possession ofᵉ the land, for great shall be the day of Jezreel.

2f.1 SAY to your brother,ᵍ Ammi,ʰ
and to your sister,ⁱ Ruhamah.ʲ
2  Plead with your mother,
        plead—
    for she is not my wife,
    and I am not her husband—
  that she put away her whoring
        from her face,
    and her adultery from
        between her breasts,
3  or I will strip her naked
    and expose her as in the day
        she was born,
  and make her like a wilderness,
    and turn her into a parched
        land,
    and kill her with thirst.
4  Upon her children also I will
        have no pity,

because they are children of whoredom.
5  For their mother has played
        the whore;
    she who conceived them has
        acted shamefully.
  For she said, "I will go after
        my lovers;
    they give me my bread and
        my water,
    my wool and my flax, my oil
        and my drink."
6  Therefore I will hedge up herᵏ
        way with thorns;
    and I will build a wall
        against her,
    so that she cannot find her
        paths.
7  She shall pursue her lovers,
        but not overtake them;
  and she shall seek them,
        but shall not find them.
  Then she shall say, "I will go
        and return to my first
        husband,
    for it was better with me then
        than now."
8  She did not know
    that it was I who gave her
        the grain, the wine, and the
        oil,
  and who lavished upon her
        silver
    and gold that they used for
        Baal.
9  Therefore I will take back
        my grain in its time,
    and my wine in its season;
  and I will take away my wool
        and my flax,
    which were to cover her
        nakedness.
10  Now I will uncover her shame
    in the sight of her lovers,
        and no one shall rescue her
        out of my hand.

ᵃThat is *Not pitied*  ᵇThat is *Not my people*  ᶜHeb *I am not yours*  ᵈCh 2.1 in Heb  ᵉHeb *rise up from*  ᶠCh 2.3 in Heb  ᵍGk: Heb *brothers*  ʰThat is *My People*  ⁱGk Vg: Heb *sisters*  ʲThat is *Pitied*  ᵏGk Syr: Heb *your*

11  I will put an end to all her
        mirth,
    her festivals, her new moons,
        her sabbaths,
    and all her appointed festivals.
12  I will lay waste her vines and
        her fig trees,
    of which she said,
    "These are my pay,
        which my lovers have given
        me."
    I will make them a forest,
        and the wild animals shall
        devour them.
13  I will punish her for the festival
        days of the Baals,
    when she offered incense to
        them
    and decked herself with her ring
        and jewelry,
        and went after her lovers,
        and forgot me, says the LORD.


14  Therefore, I will now allure her,
        and bring her into the
        wilderness,
    and speak tenderly to her.
15  From there I will give her her
        vineyards,
    and make the Valley of Achor
        a door of hope.
    There she shall respond as in
        the days of her youth,
    as at the time when she came
        out of the land of Egypt.
16On that day, says the LORD, you will
call me, "My husband," and no longer
will you call me, "My Baal."a 17For I
will remove the names of the Baals
from her mouth, and they shall be mentioned by name no more. 18I will make
for youb a covenant on that day with
the wild animals, the birds of the air,
and the creeping things of the ground;
and I will abolishc the bow, the sword,
and war from the land; and I will make
you lie down in safety. 19And I will take
you for my wife forever; I will take you

for my wife in righteousness and in justice, in steadfast love, and in mercy.
20I will take you for my wife in faithfulness; and you shall know the LORD.
21  On that day I will answer, says
        the LORD,
    I will answer the heavens
    and they shall answer the
        earth;
22  and the earth shall answer the
        grain, the wine, and the
        oil,
    and they shall answer
        Jezreel;d
23      and I will sow hime for
        myself in the land.
    And I will have pity on
        Lo-ruhamah,f
    and I will say to Lo-ammi,g
        "You are my people";
    and he shall say, "You are my
        God."

3.1 THE LORD said to me again, "Go, love
a woman who has a lover and is an adulteress, just as the LORD loves the people of Israel, though they turn to other
gods and love raisin cakes." 2So I
bought her for fifteen shekels of silver
and a homer of barley and a measure of
wine.h 3And I said to her, "You must
remain as mine for many days; you shall
not play the whore, you shall not have
intercourse with a man, nor I with
you." 4For the Israelites shall remain
many days without king or prince, without sacrifice or pillar, without ephod or
teraphim. 5Afterward the Israelites
shall return and seek the LORD their
God, and David their king; they shall
come in awe to the LORD and to his
goodness in the latter days.

aThat is, *"My master"*  bHeb *them*  cHeb *break*  dThat is *God sows*  eCn: Heb *her*  fThat is *Not
pitied*  gThat is *Not my people*  hGk: Heb *a homer of barley and a lethech of barley*

## 1 JOHN 5.1–21

**E**VERYONE who believes that Jesus is the Christ[a] has been born of God, and everyone who loves the parent loves the child. [2]By this we know that we love the children of God, when we love God and obey his commandments. [3]For the love of God is this, that we obey his commandments. And his commandments are not burdensome, [4]for whatever is born of God conquers the world. And this is the victory that conquers the world, our faith. [5]Who is it that conquers the world but the one who believes that Jesus is the Son of God?

6 This is the one who came by water and blood, Jesus Christ, not with the water only but with the water and the blood. And the Spirit is the one that testifies, for the Spirit is the truth. [7]There are three that testify:[b] [8]the Spirit and the water and the blood, and these three agree. [9]If we receive human testimony, the testimony of God is greater; for this is the testimony of God that he has testified to his Son. [10]Those who believe in the Son of God have the testimony in their hearts. Those who do not believe in God[c] have made him a liar by not believing in the testimony that God has given concerning his Son. [11]And this is the testimony: God gave us eternal life, and this life is in his Son. [12]Whoever has the Son has life; whoever does not have the Son of God does not have life.

13 I write these things to you who believe in the name of the Son of God, so that you may know that you have eternal life.

14 And this is the boldness we have in him, that if we ask anything according to his will, he hears us. [15]And if we know that he hears us in whatever we ask, we know that we have obtained the requests made of him. [16]If you see your brother or sister[d] committing what is not a mortal sin, you will ask, and God[e] will give life to such a one—to those whose sin is not mortal. There is sin that is mortal; I do not say that you should pray about that. [17]All wrongdoing is sin, but there is sin that is not mortal.

18 We know that those who are born of God do not sin, but the one who was born of God protects them, and the evil one does not touch them. [19]We know that we are God's children, and that the whole world lies under the power of the evil one. [20]And we know that the Son of God has come and has given us understanding so that we may know him who is true;[f] and we are in him who is true, in his Son Jesus Christ. He is the true God and eternal life.

21 Little children, keep yourselves from idols.[g]

## PSALM 124.1–8

*A Song of Ascents. Of David.*

**I**F it had not been the LORD who
      was on our side
    —let Israel now say—
2  if it had not been the LORD who
      was on our side,
    when our enemies attacked
      us,
3  then they would have swallowed
      us up alive,
    when their anger was kindled
      against us;
4  then the flood would have swept
      us away,
    the torrent would have gone
      over us;
5  then over us would have gone
      the raging waters.

6 Blessed be the LORD,

---

aOr *the Messiah*  bA few other authorities read (with variations) *7There are three that testify in heaven, the Father, the Word, and the Holy Spirit, and these three are one. 8And there are three that testify on earth:*  cOther ancient authorities read *in the Son*  dGk *your brother*  eGk *he*  fOther ancient authorities read *know the true God*  gOther ancient authorities add *Amen*

who has not given us
as prey to their teeth.
7 We have escaped like a bird
from the snare of the fowlers;
the snare is broken,
and we have escaped.

8 Our help is in the name of
the LORD,
who made heaven and earth.

## PROVERBS 29.5–8

WHOEVER flatters a neighbor
is spreading a net for the
neighbor's feet.
6 In the transgression of the evil
there is a snare,
but the righteous sing and
rejoice.
7 The righteous know the rights
of the poor;
the wicked have no such
understanding.
8 Scoffers set a city aflame,
but the wise turn away wrath.

# DECEMBER 6

## HOSEA 4.1—5.15

HEAR the word of the LORD,
O people of Israel;
for the LORD has an
indictment against the
inhabitants of the land.
There is no faithfulness or
loyalty,
and no knowledge of God in
the land.
2 Swearing, lying, and murder,
and stealing and adultery
break out;
bloodshed follows bloodshed.
3 Therefore the land mourns,
and all who live in it languish;
together with the wild animals
and the birds of the air,
even the fish of the sea are
perishing.

4 Yet let no one contend,
and let none accuse,

for with you is my contention,
O priest. a
5 You shall stumble by day;
the prophet also shall stumble
with you by night,
and I will destroy your
mother.
6 My people are destroyed for
lack of knowledge;
because you have rejected
knowledge,
I reject you from being a
priest to me.
And since you have forgotten
the law of your God,
I also will forget your
children.

7 The more they increased,
the more they sinned against
me;
they changed b their glory
into shame.

aCn: Meaning of Heb uncertain   bAncient Heb tradition: MT *I will change*

8 They feed on the sin of my
        people;
    they are greedy for their
        iniquity.
9 And it shall be like people,
        like priest;
    I will punish them for their
        ways,
    and repay them for their
        deeds.
10 They shall eat, but not be
        satisfied;
    they shall play the whore, but
        not multiply;
    because they have forsaken
        the LORD
    to devote themselves to
        11 whoredom.

    Wine and new wine
        take away the understanding.
12 My people consult a piece of
        wood,
    and their divining rod gives
        them oracles.
    For a spirit of whoredom has
        led them astray,
    and they have played the
        whore, forsaking their
        God.
13 They sacrifice on the tops of the
        mountains,
    and make offerings upon
        the hills,
    under oak, poplar, and
        terebinth,
    because their shade is good.

    Therefore your daughters play
        the whore,
    and your daughters-in-law
        commit adultery.
14 I will not punish your daughters
        when they play the
        whore,
    nor your daughters-in-law
        when they commit
        adultery;

for the men themselves go aside
        with whores,
    and sacrifice with temple
        prostitutes;
    thus a people without
        understanding comes to
        ruin.

15 Though you play the whore,
        O Israel,
    do not let Judah become
        guilty.
    Do not enter into Gilgal,
        or go up to Beth-aven,
    and do not swear, "As the
        LORD lives."
16 Like a stubborn heifer,
        Israel is stubborn;
    can the LORD now feed them
        like a lamb in a broad
        pasture?

17 Ephraim is joined to idols—
        let him alone.
18 When their drinking is ended,
        they indulge in sexual
        orgies;
    they love lewdness more than
        their glory. a
19 A wind has wrapped them b in
        its wings,
    and they shall be ashamed
        because of their altars. c

5.1 HEAR this, O priests!
        Give heed, O house of Israel!
    Listen, O house of the king!
        For the judgment pertains to
        you;
    for you have been a snare at
        Mizpah,
    and a net spread upon Tabor,
2    and a pit dug deep in Shittim; d
        but I will punish all of them.

3 I know Ephraim,
        and Israel is not hidden from
        me;

aCn Compare Gk: Meaning of Heb uncertain   bHeb *her*   cGk Syr: Heb *sacrifices*   dCn: Meaning of
Heb uncertain

for now, O Ephraim, you have
  played the whore;
Israel is defiled.
4   Their deeds do not permit them
      to return to their God.
  For the spirit of whoredom is
      within them,
    and they do not know the
      LORD.

5   Israel's pride testifies against
      him;
    Ephraim[a] stumbles in his
      guilt;
    Judah also stumbles with
      them.
6   With their flocks and herds they
      shall go
    to seek the LORD,
  but they will not find him;
    he has withdrawn from them.
7   They have dealt faithlessly with
      the LORD;
    for they have borne
      illegitimate children.
  Now the new moon shall
      devour them along with
      their fields.

8   Blow the horn in Gibeah,
    the trumpet in Ramah.
  Sound the alarm at Beth-aven;
    look behind you, Benjamin!
9   Ephraim shall become a
      desolation
    in the day of punishment;
  among the tribes of Israel
    I declare what is sure.
10  The princes of Judah have
      become
    like those who remove the
      landmark;
  on them I will pour out
    my wrath like water.
11  Ephraim is oppressed, crushed
      in judgment,
    because he was determined
      to go after vanity. [b]

12  Therefore I am like maggots to
      Ephraim,
    and like rottenness to the
      house of Judah.
13  When Ephraim saw his
      sickness,
    and Judah his wound,
  then Ephraim went to Assyria,
    and sent to the great king. [c]
  But he is not able to cure you
    or heal your wound.
14  For I will be like a lion to
      Ephraim,
    and like a young lion to the
      house of Judah.
  I myself will tear and go away;
    I will carry off, and no one
      shall rescue.
15  I will return again to my place
    until they acknowledge their
      guilt and seek my face.
  In their distress they will beg
    my favor:

# 2 JOHN 1.1–13

THE elder to the elect lady and her children, whom I love in the truth, and not only I but also all who know the truth, [2]because of the truth that abides in us and will be with us forever:

3  Grace, mercy, and peace will be with us from God the Father and from[d] Jesus Christ, the Father's Son, in truth and love.

4  I was overjoyed to find some of your children walking in the truth, just as we have been commanded by the Father. [5]But now, dear lady, I ask you, not as though I were writing you a new commandment, but one we have had from the beginning, let us love one another. [6]And this is love, that we walk according to his commandments; this is the commandment just as you have heard it from the beginning—you must walk in it.

aHeb *Israel and Ephraim*   bGk: Meaning of Heb uncertain   cCn: Heb *to a king who will contend*
dOther ancient authorities add *the Lord*

7 Many deceivers have gone out into the world, those who do not confess that Jesus Christ has come in the flesh; any such person is the deceiver and the antichrist! ⁸Be on your guard, so that you do not lose what we[a] have worked for, but may receive a full reward. ⁹Everyone who does not abide in the teaching of Christ, but goes beyond it, does not have God; whoever abides in the teaching has both the Father and the Son. ¹⁰Do not receive into the house or welcome anyone who comes to you and does not bring this teaching; ¹¹for to welcome is to participate in the evil deeds of such a person.

12 Although I have much to write to you, I would rather not use paper and ink; instead I hope to come to you and talk with you face to face, so that our joy may be complete.

13 The children of your elect sister send you their greetings. [b]

## PSALM 125.1–5

*A Song of Ascents.*

THOSE who trust in the LORD are
    like Mount Zion,
which cannot be moved, but
    abides forever.
2  As the mountains surround
    Jerusalem,

so the LORD surrounds his
    people,
from this time on and
    forevermore.
3  For the scepter of wickedness
    shall not rest
on the land allotted to the
    righteous,
so that the righteous might not
    stretch out
their hands to do wrong.
4  Do good, O LORD, to those who
    are good,
and to those who are upright
    in their hearts.
5  But those who turn aside to
    their own crooked ways
the LORD will lead away with
    evildoers.
Peace be upon Israel!

## PROVERBS 29.9–11

IF the wise go to law with fools,
    there is ranting and ridicule
    without relief.
10  The bloodthirsty hate the
    blameless,
and they seek the life of the
    upright.
11  A fool gives full vent to anger,
    but the wise quietly holds
    it back.

# DECEMBER 7

## HOSEA 6.1—9.17

"COME, let us return to the
    LORD;
for it is he who has torn,
    and he will heal us;
he has struck down, and he
    will bind us up.

2  After two days he will revive
    us;
on the third day he will raise
    us up,
that we may live before him.
3  Let us know, let us press on to
    know the LORD;

a Other ancient authorities read *you*  b Other ancient authorities add *Amen*

his appearing is as sure as
  the dawn;
he will come to us like the
  showers,
like the spring rains that
  water the earth."
4 What shall I do with you,
    O Ephraim?
  What shall I do with you,
    O Judah?
  Your love is like a morning
    cloud,
  like the dew that goes
    away early.
5 Therefore I have hewn them by
    the prophets,
  I have killed them by the
    words of my mouth,
  and my[a] judgment goes forth
    as the light.
6 For I desire steadfast love and
    not sacrifice,
  the knowledge of God rather
    than burnt offerings.

7 But at[b] Adam they
    transgressed the
    covenant;
  there they dealt faithlessly
    with me.
8 Gilead is a city of evildoers,
    tracked with blood.
9 As robbers lie in wait[c] for
    someone,
  so the priests are banded
    together;[d]
  they murder on the road to
    Shechem,
  they commit a monstrous
    crime.
10 In the house of Israel I have
    seen a horrible thing;
  Ephraim's whoredom is there,
    Israel is defiled.

11 For you also, O Judah, a
    harvest is appointed.

When I would restore the
  fortunes of my people,

7.1 WHEN I would heal Israel,
    the corruption of Ephraim is
      revealed,
    and the wicked deeds of
      Samaria;
  for they deal falsely,
    the thief breaks in,
    and the bandits raid outside.
2 But they do not consider
    that I remember all their
      wickedness.
  Now their deeds surround
    them,
    they are before my face.
3 By their wickedness they make
    the king glad,
    and the officials by their
      treachery.
4 They are all adulterers;
    they are like a heated oven,
  whose baker does not need to
    stir the fire,
    from the kneading of the
      dough until it is
      leavened.
5 On the day of our king the
    officials
    became sick with the heat
      of wine;
    he stretched out his hand
      with mockers.
6 For they are kindled[e] like an
    oven, their heart burns
      within them;
    all night their anger smolders;
    in the morning it blazes like a
      flaming fire.
7 All of them are hot as an oven,
    and they devour their rulers.
  All their kings have fallen;
    none of them calls upon me.
8 Ephraim mixes himself with
    the peoples;

Ephraim is a cake not turned.
9 Foreigners devour his strength,
    but he does not know it;
  gray hairs are sprinkled upon
      him,
    but he does not know it.
10 Israel's pride testifies against a
      him;
    yet they do not return to the
      Lord their God,
    or seek him, for all this.

11 Ephraim has become like a
      dove,
    silly and without sense;
    they call upon Egypt, they go
      to Assyria.
12 As they go, I will cast my net
      over them;
    I will bring them down like
      birds of the air;
    I will discipline them
      according to the report
      made to their
      assembly. b
13 Woe to them, for they have
      strayed from me!
    Destruction to them, for they
      have rebelled against me!
    I would redeem them,
    but they speak lies against
      me.

14 They do not cry to me from
      the heart,
    but they wail upon their beds;
    they gash themselves for grain
      and wine;
    they rebel against me.
15 It was I who trained and
      strengthened their arms,
    yet they plot evil against me.
16 They turn to that which does
      not profit; c
    they have become like a
      defective bow;
    their officials shall fall by
      the sword

because of the rage of their
    tongue.
  So much for their babbling in
      the land of Egypt.

8.1 Set the trumpet to your lips!
    One like a vulture b is over
        the house of the Lord,
  because they have broken my
      covenant,
    and transgressed my law.
2 Israel cries to me,
    "My God, we—Israel—know
      you!"
3 Israel has spurned the good;
    the enemy shall pursue him.

4 They made kings, but not
      through me;
    they set up princes, but
      without my knowledge.
  With their silver and gold they
      made idols
    for their own destruction.
5 Your calf is rejected, O Samaria.
    My anger burns against them.
  How long will they be incapable
      of innocence?
6   For it is from Israel,
  an artisan made it;
    it is not God.
  The calf of Samaria
    shall be broken to pieces. d

7 For they sow the wind,
    and they shall reap the
      whirlwind.
  The standing grain has no
      heads,
    it shall yield no meal;
  if it were to yield,
    foreigners would devour it.
8 Israel is swallowed up;
    now they are among the
      nations
    as a useless vessel.

a Or *humbles*  b Meaning of Heb uncertain  c Cn: Meaning of Heb uncertain  d Or *shall go up in flames*

9 For they have gone up to
    Assyria,
  a wild ass wandering alone;
  Ephraim has bargained
    for lovers.
10 Though they bargain with
    the nations,
  I will now gather them up.
  They shall soon writhe
    under the burden of kings
    and princes.

11 When Ephraim multiplied altars
    to expiate sin,
  they became to him altars for
    sinning.
12 Though I write for him the
    multitude of my
    instructions,
  they are regarded as a
    strange thing.
13 Though they offer choice
    sacrifices, [a]
  though they eat flesh,
  the LORD does not accept
    them.
  Now he will remember their
    iniquity,
  and punish their sins;
  they shall return to Egypt.
14 Israel has forgotten his Maker,
  and built palaces;
  and Judah has multiplied fortified
    cities;
  but I will send a fire upon
    his cities,
  and it shall devour his
    strongholds.

9.1 Do not rejoice, O Israel!
  Do not exult [b] as other
    nations do;
  for you have played the whore,
    departing from your God.
  You have loved a prostitute's
    pay
  on all threshing floors.

2 Threshing floor and wine vat
    shall not feed them,
  and the new wine shall fail
    them.
3 They shall not remain in the
    land of the LORD;
  but Ephraim shall return to
    Egypt,
  and in Assyria they shall eat
    unclean food.

4 They shall not pour drink
    offerings of wine to the
    LORD,
  and their sacrifices shall not
    please him.
  Such sacrifices shall be like
    mourners' bread;
  all who eat of it shall be
    defiled;
  for their bread shall be for their
    hunger only;
  it shall not come to the house
    of the LORD.

5 What will you do on the day of
    appointed festival,
  and on the day of the festival
    of the LORD?
6 For even if they escape
    destruction,
  Egypt shall gather them,
  Memphis shall bury them.
  Nettles shall possess their
    precious things of
    silver; [c]
  thorns shall be in their tents.

7 The days of punishment have
    come,
  the days of recompense
    have come;
  Israel cries, [d]
  "The prophet is a fool,
  the man of the spirit is mad!"
  Because of your great iniquity,
    your hostility is great.

aCn: Meaning of Heb uncertain  bGk: Heb *To exultation*  cMeaning of Heb uncertain
dCn Compare Gk: Heb *shall know*

8 The prophet is a sentinel for my
        God over Ephraim,
    yet a fowler's snare is on all
        his ways,
    and hostility in the house of
        his God.
9 They have deeply corrupted
        themselves
    as in the days of Gibeah;
    he will remember their iniquity,
        he will punish their sins.

10 Like grapes in the wilderness,
        I found Israel.
    Like the first fruit on the fig
        tree,
    in its first season,
    I saw your ancestors.
    But they came to Baal-peor,
        and consecrated themselves
            to a thing of shame,
        and became detestable like
            the thing they loved.
11 Ephraim's glory shall fly away
        like a bird—
    no birth, no pregnancy, no
        conception!
12 Even if they bring up children,
    I will bereave them until no
        one is left.
    Woe to them indeed
        when I depart from them!
13 Once I saw Ephraim as a young
        palm planted in a lovely
            meadow, a
    but now Ephraim must lead
        out his children for
            slaughter.
14 Give them, O LORD—
        what will you give?
    Give them a miscarrying womb
        and dry breasts.

15 Every evil of theirs began at
        Gilgal;
    there I came to hate them.
    Because of the wickedness of
        their deeds

I will drive them out of
        my house.
    I will love them no more;
        all their officials are rebels. b

16 Ephraim is stricken,
        their root is dried up,
        they shall bear no fruit.
    Even though they give birth,
        I will kill the cherished
            offspring of their womb.
17 Because they have not listened
        to him,
    my God will reject them;
        they shall become wanderers
            among the nations.

# 3 JOHN 1.1–15

THE elder to the beloved Gaius, whom I love in truth.

2 Beloved, I pray that all may go well with you and that you may be in good health, just as it is well with your soul. 3I was overjoyed when some of the friends b arrived and testified to your faithfulness to the truth, namely how you walk in the truth. 4I have no greater joy than this, to hear that my children are walking in the truth.

5 Beloved, you do faithfully whatever you do for the friends, b even though they are strangers to you; 6they have testified to your love before the church. You will do well to send them on in a manner worthy of God; 7for they began their journey for the sake of Christ, c accepting no support from non-believers. d 8Therefore we ought to support such people, so that we may become co-workers with the truth.

9 I have written something to the church; but Diotrephes, who likes to put himself first, does not acknowledge our authority. 10So if I come, I will call attention to what he is doing in spreading false charges against us. And not content with those charges, he refuses to welcome the friends, b and even

aMeaning of Heb uncertain   bGk *brothers*   cGk *for the sake of the name*   dGk *the Gentiles* prevents those who want to do so and expels them from the church.

11  Beloved, do not imitate what is evil but imitate what is good. Whoever does good is from God; whoever does evil has not seen God. [12]Everyone has testified favorably about Demetrius, and so has the truth itself. We also testify for him, [a] and you know that our testimony is true.

13  I have much to write to you, but I would rather not write with pen and ink; [14]instead I hope to see you soon, and we will talk together face to face.

15  Peace to you. The friends send you their greetings. Greet the friends there, each by name.

## PSALM 126.1–6

*A Song of Ascents.*

WHEN the Lord restored the
fortunes of Zion, [b]
we were like those who
dream.
[2]  Then our mouth was filled with
laughter,
and our tongue with shouts
of joy;
then it was said among the
nations,
"The Lord has done great
things for them."
[3]  The Lord has done great things
for us,
and we rejoiced.

[4]  Restore our fortunes, O Lord,
like the watercourses in the
Negeb.
[5]  May those who sow in tears
reap with shouts of joy.
[6]  Those who go out weeping,
bearing the seed for sowing,
shall come home with shouts of
joy,
carrying their sheaves.

## PROVERBS 29.12–14

IF a ruler listens to falsehood,
all his officials will be wicked.
[13]  The poor and the oppressor
have this in common:
the Lord gives light to the
eyes of both.
[14]  If a king judges the poor with
equity,
his throne will be established
forever.

# DECEMBER 8

## HOSEA 10.1—14.9

ISRAEL is a luxuriant vine
that yields its fruit.
The more his fruit increased
the more altars he built;
as his country improved,
he improved his pillars.
[2]  Their heart is false;
now they must bear their
guilt.
The Lord [c] will break down
their altars,
and destroy their pillars.

[3]  For now they will say:
"We have no king,
for we do not fear the Lord,

[a]Gk lacks *for him*   [b]Or *brought back those who returned to Zion*   [c]Heb *he*

and a king—what could he do
    for us?"
4 They utter mere words;
    with empty oaths they make
        covenants;
    so litigation springs up like
        poisonous weeds
    in the furrows of the field.
5 The inhabitants of Samaria
        tremble
    for the calf[a] of Beth-aven.
    Its people shall mourn for it,
    and its idolatrous priests shall
        wail[b] over it,
    over its glory that has
        departed from it.
6 The thing itself shall be carried
        to Assyria
    as tribute to the great king. [c]
    Ephraim shall be put to shame,
    and Israel shall be ashamed of
        his idol. [d]

7 Samaria's king shall perish
    like a chip on the face of
        the waters.
8 The high places of Aven, the sin
        of Israel,
    shall be destroyed.
    Thorn and thistle shall grow up
        on their altars.
    They shall say to the mountains,
        Cover us,
    and to the hills, Fall on us.

9 Since the days of Gibeah you
        have sinned, O Israel;
    there they have continued.
    Shall not war overtake them
        in Gibeah?
10 I will come[e] against the
        wayward people to
        punish them;
    and nations shall be gathered
        against them
    when they are punished[f] for
        their double iniquity.

11 Ephraim was a trained heifer
        that loved to thresh,
    and I spared her fair neck;
    but I will make Ephraim break
        the ground;
    Judah must plow;
    Jacob must harrow for
        himself.
12 Sow for yourselves
        righteousness;
    reap steadfast love;
    break up your fallow ground;
    for it is time to seek the LORD,
    that he may come and rain
        righteousness upon you.

13 You have plowed wickedness,
    you have reaped injustice,
    you have eaten the fruit of
        lies.
    Because you have trusted in
        your power
    and in the multitude of your
        warriors,
14 therefore the tumult of war shall
        rise against your people,
    and all your fortresses shall
        be destroyed,
    as Shalman destroyed
        Beth-arbel on the day of
        battle
    when mothers were dashed in
        pieces with their
        children.
15 Thus it shall be done to you,
        O Bethel,
    because of your great
        wickedness.
    At dawn the king of Israel
        shall be utterly cut off.

11.1 WHEN Israel was a child, I
        loved him,
    and out of Egypt I called my
        son.
2 The more I[g] called them,

---

a Gk Syr: Heb *calves*   b Cn: Heb *exult*   c Cn: Heb *to a king who will contend*   d Cn: Heb *counsel*
e Cn Compare Gk: Heb *In my desire*   f Gk: Heb *bound*   g Gk: Heb *they*

the more they went from
    me; **a**
they kept sacrificing to the
    Baals,
    and offering incense to idols.

3 Yet it was I who taught Ephraim
    to walk,
    I took them up in my **b** arms;
    but they did not know that I
    healed them.
4 I led them with cords of human
    kindness,
    with bands of love.
I was to them like those
    who lift infants to their
    cheeks. **c**
I bent down to them and
    fed them.

5 They shall return to the land of
    Egypt,
    and Assyria shall be their
    king,
because they have refused to
    return to me.
6 The sword rages in their cities,
    it consumes their
    oracle-priests,
and devours because of their
    schemes.
7 My people are bent on turning
    away from me.
To the Most High they call,
    but he does not raise them up
    at all. **d**

8 How can I give you up,
    Ephraim?
How can I hand you over,
    O Israel?
How can I make you like
    Admah?
How can I treat you like
    Zeboiim?
My heart recoils within me;
    my compassion grows warm
    and tender.

9 I will not execute my fierce
    anger;
    I will not again destroy
    Ephraim;
for I am God and no mortal,
    the Holy One in your midst,
    and I will not come in
    wrath. **d**

10 They shall go after the Lord,
    who roars like a lion;
when he roars,
    his children shall come
    trembling from the west.
11 They shall come trembling like
    birds from Egypt,
    and like doves from the land
    of Assyria;
    and I will return them to their
    homes, says the Lord.

12e Ephraim has surrounded me
    with lies,
    and the house of Israel with
    deceit;
but Judah still walks **f** with God,
    and is faithful to the Holy
    One.

12.1 Ephraim herds the wind,
    and pursues the east wind all
    day long;
they multiply falsehood and
    violence;
they make a treaty with
    Assyria,
and oil is carried to Egypt.

2 The Lord has an indictment
    against Judah,
and will punish Jacob
    according to his ways,
and repay him according to
    his deeds.
3 In the womb he tried to
    supplant his brother,
and in his manhood he strove
    with God.

aGk: Heb *them*  bGk Syr Vg: Heb *his*  cOr *who ease the yoke on their jaws*  dMeaning of Heb uncertain  eCh 12.1 in Heb  fHeb *roams* or *rules*

4 He strove with the angel and
    prevailed,
      he wept and sought his favor;
    he met him at Bethel,
      and there he spoke with
        him. a
5 The Lord the God of hosts,
      the Lord is his name!
6 But as for you, return to your
    God,
      hold fast to love and justice,
      and wait continually for
        your God.

7 A trader, in whose hands are
      false balances,
      he loves to oppress.
8 Ephraim has said, "Ah, I am
    rich,
      I have gained wealth for
        myself;
    in all of my gain
      no offense has been found in
        me
      that would be sin."b
9 I am the Lord your God
      from the land of Egypt;
    I will make you live in tents
      again,
      as in the days of the
        appointed festival.

10 I spoke to the prophets;
      it was I who multiplied
        visions,
      and through the prophets I
        will bring destruction.
11 In Gileadc there is iniquity,
      they shall surely come to
        nothing.
    In Gilgal they sacrifice bulls,
      so their altars shall be like
        stone heaps
      on the furrows of the field.
12 Jacob fled to the land of Aram,
      there Israel served for a wife,

    and for a wife he guarded
      sheep. d
13 By a prophet the Lord brought
      Israel up from Egypt,
    and by a prophet he was
      guarded.
14 Ephraim has given bitter
    offense,
      so his Lord will bring his
        crimes down on him
    and pay him back for his
      insults.

13.1 When Ephraim spoke, there
      was trembling;
      he was exalted in Israel;
    but he incurred guilt through
      Baal and died.
2 And now they keep on sinning
      and make a cast image for
        themselves,
    idols of silver made according to
      their understanding,
    all of them the work of
      artisans.
    "Sacrifice to these," they say. e
    People are kissing calves!
3 Therefore they shall be like the
      morning mist
      or like the dew that goes
        away early,
    like chaff that swirls from the
      threshing floor
      or like smoke from a window.

4 Yet I have been the Lord your
    God
      ever since the land of Egypt;
    you know no God but me,
      and besides me there is no
        savior.
5 It was I who fedf you in the
      wilderness,
      in the land of drought.
6 When I fedg them, they were
      satisfied;

aGk Syr: Heb *us*   bMeaning of Heb uncertain   cCompare Syr: Heb *Gilead*   dHeb lacks *sheep*
eCn Compare Gk: Heb *To these they say sacrifices of people*   fGk Syr: Heb *knew*   gCn: Heb
*according to their pasture*

they were satisfied, and their
        heart was proud;
    therefore they forgot me.
7   So I will become like a lion
        to them,
    like a leopard I will lurk
        beside the way.
8   I will fall upon them like a bear
        robbed of her cubs,
    and will tear open the
        covering of their heart;
    there I will devour them like
        a lion,
    as a wild animal would
        mangle them.

9   I will destroy you, O Israel;
        who can help you?[a]
10  Where now is[b] your king, that
        he may save you?
    Where in all your cities are
        your rulers,
    of whom you said,
        "Give me a king and rulers"?
11  I gave you a king in my anger,
        and I took him away in
        my wrath.

12  Ephraim's iniquity is bound up;
        his sin is kept in store.
13  The pangs of childbirth come
        for him,
    but he is an unwise son;
    for at the proper time he does
        not present himself
    at the mouth of the womb.

14  Shall I ransom them from the
        power of Sheol?
    Shall I redeem them from
        Death?
    O Death, where are[c] your
        plagues?
    O Sheol, where is[c] your
        destruction?
    Compassion is hidden from
        my eyes.

15  Although he may flourish among
        rushes, [d]
    the east wind shall come, a
        blast from the LORD,
    rising from the wilderness;
    and his fountain shall dry up,
        his spring shall be parched.
    It shall strip his treasury
        of every precious thing.
16e Samaria shall bear her guilt,
        because she has rebelled
        against her God;
    they shall fall by the sword,
        their little ones shall be
        dashed in pieces,
    and their pregnant women
        ripped open.

14.1 RETURN, O Israel, to the LORD
        your God,
    for you have stumbled
        because of your iniquity.
2   Take words with you
        and return to the LORD;
    say to him,
        "Take away all guilt;
    accept that which is good,
        and we will offer
        the fruit[f] of our lips.
3   Assyria shall not save us;
        we will not ride upon horses;
    we will say no more, 'Our God,'
        to the work of our hands.
    In you the orphan finds mercy."

4   I will heal their disloyalty;
        I will love them freely,
        for my anger has turned
        from them.
5   I will be like the dew to Israel;
        he shall blossom like the lily,
        he shall strike root like the
        forests of Lebanon. [g]
6   His shoots shall spread out;
        his beauty shall be like the
        olive tree,

aGk Syr: Heb *for in me is your help*   bGk Syr Vg: Heb *I will be*   cGk Syr: Heb *I will be*
dOr *among brothers*   eCh 14.1 in Heb   fGk Syr: Heb *bulls*   gCn: Heb *like Lebanon*

and his fragrance like that of
   Lebanon.
7 They shall again live beneath
   my[a] shadow,
  they shall flourish as a
   garden;[b]
 they shall blossom like the vine,
  their fragrance shall be like
   the wine of Lebanon.

8 O Ephraim, what have I[c] to do
   with idols?
  It is I who answer and look
   after you. [d]
 I am like an evergreen cypress;
  your faithfulness[e] comes
   from me.
9 Those who are wise understand
   these things;
  those who are discerning
   know them.
 For the ways of the LORD are
   right,
  and the upright walk in them,
  but transgressors stumble
   in them.

# JUDE 1.1–25

JUDE,[f] a servant[g] of Jesus Christ and brother of James,

To those who are called, who are beloved[h] in[i] God the Father and kept safe for[i] Jesus Christ:

2 May mercy, peace, and love be yours in abundance.

3 Beloved, while eagerly preparing to write to you about the salvation we share, I find it necessary to write and appeal to you to contend for the faith that was once for all entrusted to the saints. [4]For certain intruders have stolen in among you, people who long ago were designated for this condemnation as ungodly, who pervert the grace of our God into licentiousness and deny our only Master and Lord, Jesus Christ.[j]

5 Now I desire to remind you, though you are fully informed, that the Lord, who once for all saved[k] a people out of the land of Egypt, afterward destroyed those who did not believe. [6]And the angels who did not keep their own position, but left their proper dwelling, he has kept in eternal chains in deepest darkness for the judgment of the great Day. [7]Likewise, Sodom and Gomorrah and the surrounding cities, which, in the same manner as they, indulged in sexual immorality and pursued unnatural lust,[l] serve as an example by undergoing a punishment of eternal fire.

8 Yet in the same way these dreamers also defile the flesh, reject authority, and slander the glorious ones. [m] [9]But when the archangel Michael contended with the devil and disputed about the body of Moses, he did not dare to bring a condemnation of slander[n] against him, but said, "The Lord rebuke you!" [10]But these people slander whatever they do not understand, and they are destroyed by those things that, like irrational animals, they know by instinct. [11]Woe to them! For they go the way of Cain, and abandon themselves to Balaam's error for the sake of gain, and perish in Korah's rebellion. [12]These are blemishes[o] on your love-feasts, while they feast with you without fear, feeding themselves. [p] They are waterless clouds carried along by the winds; autumn trees without fruit, twice dead, uprooted; [13]wild waves of the sea, casting up the foam of their own shame; wan-

---

aHeb *his*  bCn: Heb *they shall grow grain*  cOr *What more has Ephraim*  dHeb *him*  eHeb *your fruit*
fGk *judas*  gGk *slave*  hOther ancient authorities read *sanctified*  iOr *by*  jOr *the only Master and*
*our Lord Jesus Christ*  kOther ancient authorities read *though you were once for all fully informed,*
*that Jesus* (or *Joshua*) *who saved*  lGk *went after other flesh*  mOr *angels; Gk glories*
nOr *condemnation for blasphemy*  oOr *reefs*  pOr *without fear. They are shepherds who care only for*
*themselves*

dering stars, for whom the deepest darkness has been reserved forever.

14 It was also about these that Enoch, in the seventh generation from Adam, prophesied, saying, "See, the Lord is coming[a] with ten thousands of his holy ones, [15]to execute judgment on all, and to convict everyone of all the deeds of ungodliness that they have committed in such an ungodly way, and of all the harsh things that ungodly sinners have spoken against him." [16]These are grumblers and malcontents; they indulge their own lusts; they are bombastic in speech, flattering people to their own advantage.

17 But you, beloved, must remember the predictions of the apostles of our Lord Jesus Christ; [18]for they said to you, "In the last time there will be scoffers, indulging their own ungodly lusts." [19]It is these worldly people, devoid of the Spirit, who are causing divisions. [20]But you, beloved, build yourselves up on your most holy faith; pray in the Holy Spirit; [21]keep yourselves in the love of God; look forward to the mercy of our Lord Jesus Christ that leads to[b] eternal life. [22]And have mercy on some who are wavering; [23]save others by snatching them out of the fire; and have mercy on still others with fear, hating even the tunic defiled by their bodies. [c]

24 Now to him who is able to keep you from falling, and to make you stand without blemish in the presence of his glory with rejoicing, [25]to the only God our Savior, through Jesus Christ our Lord, be glory, majesty, power, and authority, before all time and now and forever. Amen.

## PSALM 127.1–5

*A Song of Ascents. Of Solomon.*

UNLESS the LORD builds the
house,
those who build it labor in
vain.
Unless the LORD guards the city,
the guard keeps watch in
vain.
2 It is in vain that you rise up
early
and go late to rest,
eating the bread of anxious toil;
for he gives sleep to his
beloved. [d]

3 Sons are indeed a heritage from
the LORD,
the fruit of the womb a
reward.
4 Like arrows in the hand of a
warrior
are the sons of one's youth.
5 Happy is the man who has
his quiver full of them.
He shall not be put to shame
when he speaks with his
enemies in the gate.

## PROVERBS 29.15–17

THE rod and reproof give
wisdom,
but a mother is disgraced by
a neglected child.
16 When the wicked are in
authority, transgression
increases,
but the righteous will look
upon their downfall.
17 Discipline your children, and
they will give you rest;
they will give delight to your
heart.

---

[a]Gk *came*  [b]Gk *Christ to*  [c]Gk *by the flesh.* The Greek text of verses 22-23 is uncertain at several points  [d]Or *for he provides for his beloved during sleep*

# DECEMBER 9

JOEL 1.1—3.21

**T**HE word of the Lord that came to Joel son of Pethuel:

2 Hear this, O elders,
   give ear, all inhabitants of
      the land!
Has such a thing happened in
      your days,
   or in the days of your
      ancestors?
3 Tell your children of it,
   and let your children tell their
      children,
   and their children another
      generation.

4 What the cutting locust left,
   the swarming locust has
      eaten.
What the swarming locust left,
   the hopping locust has eaten,
and what the hopping locust left,
   the destroying locust has
      eaten.

5 Wake up, you drunkards, and
      weep;
   and wail, all you
      wine-drinkers,
over the sweet wine,
   for it is cut off from your
      mouth.
6 For a nation has invaded my
      land,
   powerful and innumerable;
its teeth are lions' teeth,
   and it has the fangs of a
      lioness.
7 It has laid waste my vines,
   and splintered my fig trees;
it has stripped off their bark and
      thrown it down;
   their branches have turned
      white.

8 Lament like a virgin dressed in
      sackcloth
   for the husband of her youth.
9 The grain offering and the drink
      offering are cut off
   from the house of the Lord.
The priests mourn,
   the ministers of the Lord.
10 The fields are devastated,
   the ground mourns;
for the grain is destroyed,
   the wine dries up,
   the oil fails.

11 Be dismayed, you farmers,
   wail, you vinedressers,
over the wheat and the barley;
   for the crops of the field
      are ruined.
12 The vine withers,
   the fig tree droops.
Pomegranate, palm, and apple—
   all the trees of the field are
      dried up;
surely, joy withers away
   among the people.

13 Put on sackcloth and lament,
      you priests;
   wail, you ministers of the
      altar.
Come, pass the night in
      sackcloth,
   you ministers of my God!
Grain offering and drink offering
   are withheld from the house
      of your God.

14 Sanctify a fast,
   call a solemn assembly.
Gather the elders
   and all the inhabitants of
      the land

to the house of the LORD your
    God,
  and cry out to the LORD.

15 Alas for the day!
  For the day of the LORD is near,
    and as destruction from the
      Almighty[a] it comes.
16 Is not the food cut off
    before our eyes,
  joy and gladness
    from the house of our God?

17 The seed shrivels under the
    clods, [b]
    the storehouses are desolate;
  the granaries are ruined
    because the grain has failed.
18 How the animals groan!
  The herds of cattle wander
    about
  because there is no pasture for
    them;
    even the flocks of sheep are
    dazed. [c]

19 To you, O LORD, I cry.
  For fire has devoured
    the pastures of the
    wilderness,
  and flames have burned
    all the trees of the field.
20 Even the wild animals cry to
    you
    because the watercourses are
    dried up,
  and fire has devoured
    the pastures of the
    wilderness.

2.1 BLOW the trumpet in Zion;
    sound the alarm on my holy
    mountain!
  Let all the inhabitants of the
    land tremble,
    for the day of the LORD is
    coming, it is near—
2 a day of darkness and gloom,

    a day of clouds and thick
    darkness!
  Like blackness spread upon the
    mountains
    a great and powerful army
    comes;
  their like has never been from
    of old,
    nor will be again after them
    in ages to come.

3 Fire devours in front of them,
    and behind them a flame
    burns.
  Before them the land is like the
    garden of Eden,
    but after them a desolate
    wilderness,
  and nothing escapes them.

4 They have the appearance of
    horses,
    and like war-horses they
    charge.
5 As with the rumbling of
    chariots,
    they leap on the tops of the
    mountains,
  like the crackling of a flame of
    fire
    devouring the stubble,
  like a powerful army
    drawn up for battle.

6 Before them peoples are in
    anguish,
    all faces grow pale. [b]
7 Like warriors they charge,
    like soldiers they scale the
    wall.
  Each keeps to its own course,
    they do not swerve from[d]
    their paths.
8 They do not jostle one another,
    each keeps to its own track;
  they burst through the weapons
    and are not halted.
9 They leap upon the city,

a Traditional rendering of Heb *Shaddai*  b Meaning of Heb uncertain  c Compare Gk Syr Vg: Meaning
of Heb uncertain  d Gk Syr Vg: Heb *they do not take a pledge along*

they run upon the walls;
they climb up into the houses,
  they enter through the
    windows like a thief.

10 The earth quakes before them,
    the heavens tremble.
The sun and the moon are
    darkened,
  and the stars withdraw their
    shining.
11 The Lord utters his voice
    at the head of his army;
how vast is his host!
  Numberless are those who
    obey his command.
Truly the day of the Lord is
    great;
  terrible indeed—who can
    endure it?

12 Yet even now, says the Lord,
    return to me with all your
      heart,
  with fasting, with weeping, and
    with mourning;
13   rend your hearts and not
      your clothing.
Return to the Lord, your God,
  for he is gracious and
    merciful,
slow to anger, and abounding in
    steadfast love,
  and relents from punishing.
14 Who knows whether he will not
      turn and relent,
  and leave a blessing behind
      him,
a grain offering and a drink
    offering
  for the Lord, your God?

15 Blow the trumpet in Zion;
    sanctify a fast;
call a solemn assembly;
16   gather the people.
Sanctify the congregation;
    assemble the aged;
gather the children,
    even infants at the breast.

Let the bridegroom leave his
    room,
  and the bride her canopy.

17 Between the vestibule and the
      altar
  let the priests, the ministers
    of the Lord, weep.
Let them say, "Spare your
    people, O Lord,
  and do not make your
      heritage a mockery,
  a byword among the nations.
Why should it be said among the
    peoples,
  'Where is their God?' "

18 Then the Lord became jealous
      for his land,
  and had pity on his people.
19 In response to his people the
      Lord said:
I am sending you
    grain, wine, and oil,
  and you will be satisfied;
and I will no more make you
  a mockery among the nations.

20 I will remove the northern army
      far from you,
  and drive it into a parched
      and desolate land,
its front into the eastern sea,
  and its rear into the western
      sea;
its stench and foul smell will
    rise up.
  Surely he has done great
    things!

21 Do not fear, O soil;
    be glad and rejoice,
  for the Lord has done great
    things!
22 Do not fear, you animals of
    the field,
  for the pastures of the
      wilderness are green;
the tree bears its fruit,

the fig tree and vine give
their full yield.

23  O children of Zion, be glad
and rejoice in the LORD your
God;
for he has given the early rain[a]
for your vindication,
he has poured down for you
abundant rain,
the early and the later rain,
as before.
24  The threshing floors shall be full
of grain,
the vats shall overflow with
wine and oil.

25  I will repay you for the years
that the swarming locust has
eaten,
the hopper, the destroyer, and
the cutter,
my great army, which I sent
against you.

26  You shall eat in plenty and be
satisfied,
and praise the name of the
LORD your God,
who has dealt wondrously
with you.
And my people shall never again
be put to shame.
27  You shall know that I am in the
midst of Israel,
and that I, the LORD, am your
God and there is no
other.
And my people shall never again
be put to shame.

28[b] Then afterward
I will pour out my spirit on
all flesh;
your sons and your daughters
shall prophesy,
your old men shall dream
reams,

and your young men shall
see visions.
29  Even on the male and female
slaves,
in those days, I will pour out
my spirit.

30  I will show portents in the heavens and on the earth, blood and fire and columns of smoke. [31]The sun shall be turned to darkness, and the moon to blood, before the great and terrible day of the LORD comes. [32]Then everyone who calls on the name of the LORD shall be saved; for in Mount Zion and in Jerusalem there shall be those who escape, as the LORD has said, and among the survivors shall be those whom the LORD calls.

[3c.1] FOR then, in those days and at that time, when I restore the fortunes of Judah and Jerusalem, [2]I will gather all the nations and bring them down to the valley of Jehoshaphat, and I will enter into judgment with them there, on account of my people and my heritage Israel, because they have scattered them among the nations. They have divided my land, [3]and cast lots for my people, and traded boys for prostitutes, and sold girls for wine, and drunk it down.

4  What are you to me, O Tyre and Sidon, and all the regions of Philistia? Are you paying me back for something? If you are paying me back, I will turn your deeds back upon your own heads swiftly and speedily. [5]For you have taken my silver and my gold, and have carried my rich treasures into your temples. [d] [6]You have sold the people of Judah and Jerusalem to the Greeks, removing them far from their own border. [7]But now I will rouse them to leave the places to which you have sold them, and I will turn your deeds back upon your own heads. [8]I will sell your sons and your daughters into the hand of the

[a]Meaning of Heb uncertain   [b]Ch 3.1 in Heb   [c]Ch 4.1 in Heb   [d]Or *palaces*

people of Judah, and they will sell them to the Sabeans, to a nation far away; for the LORD has spoken.

9 Proclaim this among the nations:
Prepare war, a
    stir up the warriors.
Let all the soldiers draw near,
    let them come up.
10 Beat your plowshares into
        swords,
    and your pruning hooks into
        spears;
    let the weakling say, "I am a
        warrior."

11 Come quickly, b
    all you nations all around,
    gather yourselves there.
Bring down your warriors,
        O LORD.
12 Let the nations rouse
        themselves,
    and come up to the valley of
        Jehoshaphat;
for there I will sit to judge
    all the neighboring nations.

13 Put in the sickle,
    for the harvest is ripe.
Go in, tread,
    for the wine press is full.
The vats overflow,
    for their wickedness is great.

14 Multitudes, multitudes,
    in the valley of decision!
For the day of the LORD is near
    in the valley of decision.
15 The sun and the moon are
        darkened,
    and the stars withdraw their
        shining.

16 The LORD roars from Zion,
    and utters his voice from
        Jerusalem,

and the heavens and the earth
        shake.
But the LORD is a refuge for his
        people,
    a stronghold for the people of
        Israel.

17 So you shall know that I, the
        LORD your God,
    dwell in Zion, my holy
        mountain.
And Jerusalem shall be holy,
    and strangers shall never
        again pass through it.

18 In that day
the mountains shall drip sweet
        wine,
    the hills shall flow with milk,
and all the stream beds of Judah
    shall flow with water;
a fountain shall come forth from
        the house of the LORD
and water the Wadi Shittim.

19 Egypt shall become a desolation
    and Edom a desolate
        wilderness,
because of the violence done to
        the people of Judah,
    in whose land they have shed
        innocent blood.
20 But Judah shall be inhabited
        forever,
    and Jerusalem to all
        generations.
21 I will avenge their blood, and I
        will not clear the guilty, c
for the LORD dwells in Zion.

# REVELATION 1.1–20

THE revelation of Jesus Christ, which God gave him to show his servants d what must soon take place; he made e it known by sending his angel to his servant f John, 2 who testified to the word of God and to the

aHeb *sanctify war*   bMeaning of Heb uncertain   cGk Syr: Heb *I will hold innocent their blood that I have not held innocent*   dGk *slaves*   eGk *and he made*   fGk *slave*

testimony of Jesus Christ, even to all that he saw.

3 Blessed is the one who reads aloud the words of the prophecy, and blessed are those who hear and who keep what is written in it; for the time is near.

4 John to the seven churches that are in Asia:

Grace to you and peace from him who is and who was and who is to come, and from the seven spirits who are before his throne, [5]and from Jesus Christ, the faithful witness, the first-born of the dead, and the ruler of the kings of the earth.

To him who loves us and freed[a] us from our sins by his blood, [6]and made[b] us to be a kingdom, priests serving[c] his God and Father, to him be glory and dominion forever and ever. Amen.

[7] Look! He is coming with the clouds;
   every eye will see him,
even those who pierced him;
and on his account all the
   tribes of the earth will
   wail.
So it is to be. Amen.

8 "I am the Alpha and the Omega," says the Lord God, who is and who was and who is to come, the Almighty.

9 I, John, your brother who share with you in Jesus the persecution and the kingdom and the patient endurance, was on the island called Patmos because of the word of God and the testimony of Jesus.[d] [10]I was in the spirit[e] on the Lord's day, and I heard behind me a loud voice like a trumpet [11]saying, "Write in a book what you see and send it to the seven churches, to Ephesus, to Smyrna, to Pergamum, to Thyatira, to Sardis, to Philadelphia, and to Laodicea."

12 Then I turned to see whose voice it was that spoke to me, and on turning I saw seven golden lampstands, [13]and in the midst of the lampstands I saw one like the Son of Man, clothed with a long robe and with a golden sash across his chest. [14]His head and his hair were white as white wool, white as snow; his eyes were like a flame of fire, [15]his feet were like burnished bronze, refined as in a furnace, and his voice was like the sound of many waters. [16]In his right hand he held seven stars, and from his mouth came a sharp, two-edged sword, and his face was like the sun shining with full force.

17 When I saw him, I fell at his feet as though dead. But he placed his right hand on me, saying, "Do not be afraid; I am the first and the last, [18]and the living one. I was dead, and see, I am alive forever and ever; and I have the keys of Death and of Hades. [19]Now write what you have seen, what is, and what is to take place after this. [20]As for the mystery of the seven stars that you saw in my right hand, and the seven golden lampstands: the seven stars are the angels of the seven churches, and the seven lampstands are the seven churches.

## PSALM 128.1–6

*A Song of Ascents.*

**H**APPY is everyone who fears
   the LORD,
   who walks in his ways.
[2] You shall eat the fruit of the
   labor of your hands;
   you shall be happy, and it
     shall go well with you.

[3] Your wife will be like a fruitful
   vine
   within your house;
   your children will be like olive
     shoots
   around your table.

[a]Other ancient authorities read *washed*   [b]Gk *and he made*   [c]Gk *priests to*   [d]Or *testimony to Jesus*   [e]Or *in the Spirit*

4   Thus shall the man be blessed
      who fears the Lord.

5   The Lord bless you from Zion.
      May you see the prosperity
         of Jerusalem
      all the days of your life.
6   May you see your children's
         children.
      Peace be upon Israel!

## PROVERBS 29.18

Where there is no prophecy,
      the people cast off
         restraint,
   but happy are those who keep
      the law.

# DECEMBER 10

## AMOS 1.1—3.15

The words of Amos, who was among the shepherds of Tekoa, which he saw concerning Israel in the days of King Uzziah of Judah and in the days of King Jeroboam son of Joash of Israel, two years[a] before the earthquake.
2 And he said:
   The Lord roars from Zion,
      and utters his voice from
         Jerusalem;
   the pastures of the shepherds
         wither,
      and the top of Carmel dries
         up.

3   Thus says the Lord:
   For three transgressions of
         Damascus,
      and for four, I will not revoke
         the punishment;[b]
   because they have threshed
         Gilead
      with threshing sledges of
         iron.
4   So I will send a fire on the
         house of Hazael,
   and it shall devour the
         strongholds of
         Ben-hadad.
5   I will break the gate bars of
         Damascus,
      and cut off the inhabitants
         from the Valley of Aven,
   and the one who holds the
         scepter from Beth-eden;
      and the people of Aram shall
         go into exile to Kir,
                  says the Lord.

6   Thus says the Lord:
   For three transgressions of
         Gaza,
      and for four, I will not revoke
         the punishment;[b]
   because they carried into exile
         entire communities,
      to hand them over to Edom.
7   So I will send a fire on the wall
         of Gaza,
      fire that shall devour its
         strongholds.
8   I will cut off the inhabitants from
         Ashdod,
      and the one who holds the
         scepter from Ashkelon;

a Or *during two years*   b Heb *cause it to return*

I will turn my hand against
Ekron,
and the remnant of the
Philistines shall perish,
says the Lord God.

9   Thus says the Lord:
For three transgressions of
Tyre,
and for four, I will not revoke
the punishment; a
because they delivered entire
communities over to
Edom,
and did not remember the
covenant of kinship.
10   So I will send a fire on the wall
of Tyre,
fire that shall devour its
strongholds.

11   Thus says the Lord:
For three transgressions of
Edom,
and for four, I will not revoke
the punishment; a
because he pursued his brother
with the sword
and cast off all pity;
he maintained his anger
perpetually, b
and kept his wrath c forever.
12   So I will send a fire on Teman,
and it shall devour the
strongholds of Bozrah.

13   Thus says the Lord:
For three transgressions of the
Ammonites,
and for four, I will not revoke
the punishment; a
because they have ripped open
pregnant women in
Gilead
in order to enlarge their
territory.
14   So I will kindle a fire against the
wall of Rabbah,

fire that shall devour its
strongholds,
with shouting on the day of
battle,
with a storm on the day of
the whirlwind;
15   then their king shall go into
exile,
he and his officials together,
says the Lord.

2.1   Thus says the Lord:
For three transgressions of
Moab,
and for four, I will not revoke
the punishment; a
because he burned to lime
the bones of the king of
Edom.
2   So I will send a fire on Moab,
and it shall devour the
strongholds of Kerioth,
and Moab shall die amid uproar,
amid shouting and the sound
of the trumpet;
3   I will cut off the ruler from its
midst,
and will kill all its officials
with him,
says the Lord.

4   Thus says the Lord:
For three transgressions of
Judah,
and for four, I will not revoke
the punishment; a
because they have rejected the
law of the Lord,
and have not kept his
statutes,
but they have been led astray
by the same lies
after which their ancestors
walked.
5   So I will send a fire on Judah,
and it shall devour the
strongholds of Jerusalem.

a Heb *cause it to return*   b Syr Vg: Heb *and his anger tore perpetually*   c Gk Syr Vg: Heb *and his
wrath kept*

6  Thus says the Lord:
    For three transgressions of
        Israel,
      and for four, I will not revoke
        the punishment; **a**
    because they sell the righteous
        for silver,
      and the needy for a pair of
        sandals—
7  they who trample the head of
        the poor into the dust of
        the earth,
      and push the afflicted out of
        the way;
    father and son go in to the
        same girl,
      so that my holy name is
        profaned;
8  they lay themselves down
        beside every altar
      on garments taken in pledge;
    and in the house of their God
        they drink
      wine bought with fines they
        imposed.

9  Yet I destroyed the Amorite
        before them,
      whose height was like the
        height of cedars,
      and who was as strong as
        oaks;
    I destroyed his fruit above,
      and his roots beneath.
10  Also I brought you up out of the
        land of Egypt,
      and led you forty years in
        the wilderness,
    to possess the land of the
        Amorite.
11  And I raised up some of your
        children to be prophets
      and some of your youths to
        be nazirites. **b**
    Is it not indeed so, O people
        of Israel?
                    says the Lord.

12  But you made the nazirites **b**
        drink wine,
      and commanded the prophets,
        saying, "You shall not
        prophesy."

13  So, I will press you down in
        your place,
      just as a cart presses down
        when it is full of sheaves. **c**
14  Flight shall perish from the
        swift,
      and the strong shall not retain
        their strength,
      nor shall the mighty save
        their lives;
15  those who handle the bow shall
        not stand,
      and those who are swift of
        foot shall not save
        themselves,
      nor shall those who ride
        horses save their lives;
16  and those who are stout of
        heart among the mighty
      shall flee away naked in
        that day,
                    says the Lord.

3.1  Hear this word that the Lord has
spoken against you, O people of Israel,
against the whole family that I brought
up out of the land of Egypt:
2  You only have I known
        of all the families of the earth;
    therefore I will punish you
        for all your iniquities.

3  Do two walk together
      unless they have made an
        appointment?
4  Does a lion roar in the forest,
      when it has no prey?
    Does a young lion cry out from
        its den,
      if it has caught nothing?

---

**a**Heb *cause it to return*   **b**That is, *those separated* or *those consecrated*   **c**Meaning of Heb uncertain

5 Does a bird fall into a snare on
        the earth,
    when there is no trap for it?
Does a snare spring up from
        the ground,
    when it has taken nothing?
6 Is a trumpet blown in a city,
    and the people are not afraid?
Does disaster befall a city,
    unless the Lord has done it?
7 Surely the Lord God does
        nothing,
    without revealing his secret
    to his servants the prophets.
8 The lion has roared;
    who will not fear?
The Lord God has spoken;
    who can but prophesy?

9 Proclaim to the strongholds
        in Ashdod,
    and to the strongholds in the
        land of Egypt,
and say, "Assemble yourselves
        on Mount[a] Samaria,
    and see what great tumults
        are within it,
    and what oppressions are in
        its midst."
10 They do not know how to do
        right, says the Lord,
    those who store up violence
        and robbery in their
        strongholds.
11 Therefore thus says the Lord
        God:
An adversary shall surround
        the land,
    and strip you of your defense;
    and your strongholds shall be
        plundered.

12 Thus says the Lord: As the
shepherd rescues from the mouth of
the lion two legs, or a piece of an ear,
so shall the people of Israel who live in
Samaria be rescued, with the corner of
a couch and part[b] of a bed.

13 Hear, and testify against the
        house of Jacob,
    says the Lord God, the God
        of hosts:
14 On the day I punish Israel for
        its transgressions,
    I will punish the altars of
        Bethel,
and the horns of the altar shall
        be cut off
    and fall to the ground.
15 I will tear down the winter
        house as well as the
        summer house;
    and the houses of ivory shall
        perish,
and the great houses[c] shall
        come to an end,
                    says the Lord.

## REVELATION 2.1–17

To the angel of the church in Ephesus write: These are the words of him who holds the seven stars in his right hand, who walks among the seven golden lampstands: 2 "I know your works, your toil and your patient endurance. I know that you cannot tolerate evildoers; you have tested those who claim to be apostles but are not, and have found them to be false. [3]I also know that you are enduring patiently and bearing up for the sake of my name, and that you have not grown weary. [4]But I have this against you, that you have abandoned the love you had at first. [5]Remember then from what you have fallen; repent, and do the works you did at first. If not, I will come to you and remove your lampstand from its place, unless you repent. [6]Yet this is to your credit: you hate the works of the Nicolaitans, which I also hate. [7]Let anyone who has an ear listen to what the Spirit is saying to the churches. To everyone who conquers,

aGk Syr: Heb *the mountains of*  bMeaning of Heb uncertain  cOr *many houses*

I will give permission to eat from the tree of life that is in the paradise of God.

8 "And to the angel of the church in Smyrna write: These are the words of the first and the last, who was dead and came to life:

9 "I know your affliction and your poverty, even though you are rich. I know the slander on the part of those who say that they are Jews and are not, but are a synagogue of Satan. [10]Do not fear what you are about to suffer. Beware, the devil is about to throw some of you into prison so that you may be tested, and for ten days you will have affliction. Be faithful until death, and I will give you the crown of life. [11]Let anyone who has an ear listen to what the Spirit is saying to the churches. Whoever conquers will not be harmed by the second death.

12 "And to the angel of the church in Pergamum write: These are the words of him who has the sharp two-edged sword:

13 "I know where you are living, where Satan's throne is. Yet you are holding fast to my name, and you did not deny your faith in me[a] even in the days of Antipas my witness, my faithful one, who was killed among you, where Satan lives. [14]But I have a few things against you: you have some there who hold to the teaching of Balaam, who taught Balak to put a stumbling block before the people of Israel, so that they would eat food sacrificed to idols and practice fornication. [15]So you also have some who hold to the teaching of the Nicolaitans. [16]Repent then. If not, I will come to you soon and make war against them with the sword of my mouth. [17]Let anyone who has an ear listen to what the Spirit is saying to the churches. To everyone who conquers I will give some of the hidden manna, and I will give a white stone, and on the

[a]Or *deny my faith*

white stone is written a new name that no one knows except the one who receives it.

## PSALM 129.1–8

*A Song of Ascents.*

"Often have they attacked me
        from my youth"
    —let Israel now say—
2   "often have they attacked me
        from my youth,
      yet they have not prevailed
        against me.
3   The plowers plowed on my
        back;
      they made their furrows
        long."
4   The Lord is righteous;
      he has cut the cords of the
        wicked.
5   May all who hate Zion
      be put to shame and turned
        backward.
6   Let them be like the grass on
        the housetops
      that withers before it grows
        up,
7   with which reapers do not fill
        their hands
      or binders of sheaves their
        arms,
8   while those who pass by do not
        say,
      "The blessing of the Lord be
        upon you!
      We bless you in the name of
        the Lord!"

## PROVERBS 29.19–20

By mere words servants are
        not disciplined,
    for though they understand,
        they will not give heed.
20   Do you see someone who is
        hasty in speech?
      There is more hope for a fool
        than for anyone like that.

# DECEMBER 11



Hear this word, you cows
of Bashan
who are on Mount Samaria,
who oppress the poor, who
crush the needy,
who say to their husbands,
"Bring something to
drink!"
2 The Lord God has sworn by
his holiness:
The time is surely coming
upon you,
when they shall take you away
with hooks,
even the last of you with
fishhooks.
3 Through breaches in the wall
you shall leave,
each one straight ahead;
and you shall be flung out into
Harmon, a
says the Lord.
4 Come to Bethel—and
transgress;
to Gilgal—and multiply
transgression;
bring your sacrifices every
morning,
your tithes every three days;
5 bring a thank offering of
leavened bread,
and proclaim freewill
offerings, publish them;
for so you love to do,
O people of Israel!
says the Lord God.

6 I gave you cleanness of teeth in
all your cities,
and lack of bread in all your
places,
yet you did not return to me,
says the Lord.
7 And I also withheld the rain
from you
when there were still three
months to the harvest;
I would send rain on one city,
and send no rain on another
city;
one field would be rained upon,
and the field on which it did
not rain withered;
8 so two or three towns
wandered to one town
to drink water, and were not
satisfied;
yet you did not return to me,
says the Lord.

9 I struck you with blight and
mildew;
I laid waste b your gardens
and your vineyards;
the locust devoured your fig
trees and your olive
trees;
yet you did not return to me,
says the Lord.

10 I sent among you a pestilence
after the manner of
Egypt;
I killed your young men with
the sword;
I carried away your horses; c
and I made the stench of your
camp go up into your
nostrils;
yet you did not return to me,
says the Lord.

aMeaning of Heb uncertain   bCn: Heb *the multitude of*   cHeb *with the captivity of your horses*

11 I overthrew some of you,
  as when God overthrew
    Sodom and Gomorrah,
  and you were like a brand
    snatched from the fire;
  yet you did not return to me,
      says the LORD.

12 Therefore thus I will do to you,
    O Israel;
  because I will do this to you,
  prepare to meet your God,
    O Israel!

13 For lo, the one who forms the
    mountains, creates the
    wind,
  reveals his thoughts to
    mortals,
  makes the morning darkness,
  and treads on the heights of
    the earth—
  the LORD, the God of hosts, is
    his name!

5.1 HEAR this word that I take up over
you in lamentation, O house of Israel:
2 Fallen, no more to rise,
  is maiden Israel;
  forsaken on her land,
    with no one to raise her up.

3 For thus says the Lord GOD:
The city that marched out
  a thousand
  shall have a hundred left,
and that which marched out
  a hundred
  shall have ten left. a

4 For thus says the LORD to the
  house of Israel:
Seek me and live;
5   but do not seek Bethel,
and do not enter into Gilgal
  or cross over to Beer-sheba;
for Gilgal shall surely go into
  exile,

and Bethel shall come to
  nothing.
6 Seek the LORD and live,
  or he will break out against
    the house of Joseph like
    fire,
  and it will devour Bethel, with
    no one to quench it.
7 Ah, you that turn justice to
    wormwood,
  and bring righteousness to
    the ground!

8 The one who made the Pleiades
    and Orion,
  and turns deep darkness into
    the morning,
  and darkens the day into
    night,
  who calls for the waters of the
    sea,
  and pours them out on the
    surface of the earth,
  the LORD is his name,
9 who makes destruction flash out
    against the strong,
  so that destruction comes
    upon the fortress.

10 They hate the one who
    reproves in the gate,
  and they abhor the one who
    speaks the truth.
11 Therefore because you trample
    on the poor
  and take from them levies
    of grain,
  you have built houses of
    hewn stone,
  but you shall not live in them;
  you have planted pleasant
    vineyards,
  but you shall not drink
    their wine.
12 For I know how many are your
    transgressions,

a Heb adds *to the house of Israel*

and how great are your
    sins—
you who afflict the righteous,
    who take a bribe,
and push aside the needy in
    the gate.
13   Therefore the prudent will keep
        silent in such a time;
    for it is an evil time.

14   Seek good and not evil,
        that you may live;
    and so the LORD, the God of
        hosts, will be with you,
    just as you have said.
15   Hate evil and love good,
        and establish justice in the
            gate;
    it may be that the LORD, the
        God of hosts,
    will be gracious to the
        remnant of Joseph.

16   Therefore thus says the LORD,
        the God of hosts, the
        Lord:
    In all the squares there shall be
        wailing;
        and in all the streets they
            shall say, "Alas! alas!"
    They shall call the farmers to
        mourning,
        and those skilled in
            lamentation, to wailing;
17   in all the vineyards there shall
        be wailing,
    for I will pass through the
        midst of you,
                says the LORD.

18   Alas for you who desire the day
        of the LORD!
    Why do you want the day of
        the LORD?
    It is darkness, not light;
19       as if someone fled from a lion,
        and was met by a bear;

or went into the house and
    rested a hand against the
    wall,
and was bitten by a snake.
20   Is not the day of the LORD
        darkness, not light,
    and gloom with no brightness
        in it?

21   I hate, I despise your festivals,
        and I take no delight in your
            solemn assemblies.
22   Even though you offer me your
        burnt offerings and grain
            offerings,
    I will not accept them;
    and the offerings of well-being
        of your fatted animals
    I will not look upon.
23   Take away from me the noise of
        your songs;
    I will not listen to the melody
        of your harps.
24   But let justice roll down like
        waters,
    and righteousness like an
        ever-flowing stream.

25   Did you bring to me sacrifices
and offerings the forty years in the wilderness, O house of Israel? 26 You shall
take up Sakkuth your king, and Kaiwan
your star-god, your images, a which
you made for yourselves; 27 therefore I
will take you into exile beyond Damascus, says the LORD, whose name is the
God of hosts.

6.1   ALAS for those who are at
        ease in Zion,
    and for those who feel secure
        on Mount Samaria,
    the notables of the first of the
        nations,
    to whom the house of Israel
        resorts!
2   Cross over to Calneh, and see;

a Heb *your images, your star-god*

from there go to Hamath
    the great;
then go down to Gath of the
    Philistines.
Are you better[a] than these
    kingdoms?
  Or is your[b] territory greater
    than their[c] territory,
3 O you that put far away the
    evil day,
  and bring near a reign of
    violence?

4 Alas for those who lie on beds
    of ivory,
  and lounge on their couches,
and eat lambs from the flock,
  and calves from the stall;
5 who sing idle songs to the
    sound of the harp,
  and like David improvise on
    instruments of music;
6 who drink wine from bowls,
  and anoint themselves with
    the finest oils,
  but are not grieved over the
    ruin of Joseph!
7 Therefore they shall now be the
    first to go into exile,
  and the revelry of the
    loungers shall pass away.

8 The Lord GOD has sworn by
    himself
(says the LORD, the God of
    hosts):
I abhor the pride of Jacob
  and hate his strongholds;
  and I will deliver up the city
    and all that is in it.

9 If ten people remain in one house, they shall die. [10]And if a relative, one who burns the dead,[d] shall take up the body to bring it out of the house, and shall say to someone in the innermost parts of the house, "Is anyone else with you?" the answer will come, "No."

Then the relative[e] shall say, "Hush! We must not mention the name of the LORD."

11 See, the LORD commands,
  and the great house shall be
    shattered to bits,
  and the little house to pieces.
12 Do horses run on rocks?
  Does one plow the sea with
    oxen?[f]
But you have turned justice
    into poison
  and the fruit of righteousness
    into wormwood—
13 you who rejoice in Lo-debar,[g]
  who say, "Have we not by
    our own strength
  taken Karnaim[h] for
    ourselves?"
14 Indeed, I am raising up against
    you a nation,
  O house of Israel, says the
    LORD, the God of hosts,
and they shall oppress you from
    Lebo-hamath
  to the Wadi Arabah.

## REVELATION 2.18—3.6

"AND to the angel of the church in Thyatira write: These are the words of the Son of God, who has eyes like a flame of fire, and whose feet are like burnished bronze:

19 "I know your works—your love, faith, service, and patient endurance. I know that your last works are greater than the first. [20]But I have this against you: you tolerate that woman Jezebel, who calls herself a prophet and is teaching and beguiling my servants[i] to practice fornication and to eat food sacrificed to idols. [21]I gave her time to repent, but she refuses to repent of her fornication. [22]Beware, I am throwing her on a bed, and those who commit adultery with her I am throwing into

aOr *Are they better*  bHeb *their*  cHeb *your*  dOr *who makes a burning for him*  eHeb *he*  fOr *Does one plow them with oxen*  gOr *in a thing of nothingness*  hOr *horns*  iGk *slaves*

great distress, unless they repent of her doings; <sup>23</sup>and I will strike her children dead. And all the churches will know that I am the one who searches minds and hearts, and I will give to each of you as your works deserve. <sup>24</sup>But to the rest of you in Thyatira, who do not hold this teaching, who have not learned what some call 'the deep things of Satan,' to you I say, I do not lay on you any other burden; <sup>25</sup>only hold fast to what you have until I come. <sup>26</sup>To everyone who conquers and continues to do my works to the end,

I will give authority over
    the nations;
<sup>27</sup> to rule[a] them with an iron rod,
    as when clay pots are
        shattered—

<sup>28</sup>even as I also received authority from my Father. To the one who conquers I will also give the morning star. <sup>29</sup>Let anyone who has an ear listen to what the Spirit is saying to the churches.

<sup>3.1</sup> "AND to the angel of the church in Sardis write: These are the words of him who has the seven spirits of God and the seven stars:

"I know your works; you have a name of being alive, but you are dead. <sup>2</sup>Wake up, and strengthen what remains and is on the point of death, for I have not found your works perfect in the sight of my God. <sup>3</sup>Remember then what you received and heard; obey it, and repent. If you do not wake up, I will come like a thief, and you will not know at what hour I will come to you. <sup>4</sup>Yet you have still a few persons in Sardis who have not soiled their clothes; they will walk with me, dressed in white, for they are worthy. <sup>5</sup>If you conquer, you will be clothed like them in white robes, and I will not blot your name out of the book of life; I will confess your name before my Father and before his an-

gels. <sup>6</sup>Let anyone who has an ear listen to what the Spirit is saying to the churches.

## PSALM 130.1–8

*A Song of Ascents.*

OUT of the depths I cry to you,
        O LORD.
<sup>2</sup>        Lord, hear my voice!
Let your ears be attentive
    to the voice of my
        supplications!

<sup>3</sup> If you, O LORD, should mark
        iniquities,
    Lord, who could stand?
<sup>4</sup> But there is forgiveness with
        you,
    so that you may be revered.

<sup>5</sup> I wait for the LORD, my soul
        waits,
    and in his word I hope;
<sup>6</sup> my soul waits for the Lord
    more than those who watch
        for the morning,
    more than those who watch
        for the morning.

<sup>7</sup> O Israel, hope in the LORD!
    For with the LORD there is
        steadfast love,
    and with him is great power
        to redeem.
<sup>8</sup> It is he who will redeem Israel
    from all its iniquities.

## PROVERBS 29.21–22

A SLAVE pampered from
        childhood
    will come to a bad end. [b]
<sup>22</sup> One given to anger stirs up
        strife,
    and the hothead causes much
        transgression.

---

a Or *to shepherd*   b Vg: Meaning of Heb uncertain

# DECEMBER 12

## AMOS 7.1—9.15

THIS is what the Lord GOD showed me: he was forming locusts at the time the latter growth began to sprout (it was the latter growth after the king's mowings). 2When they had finished eating the grass of the land, I said,

"O Lord GOD, forgive, I beg
        you!
    How can Jacob stand?
    He is so small!"
3    The LORD relented concerning
        this;
    "It shall not be," said the
        LORD.

4 This is what the Lord GOD showed me: the Lord GOD was calling for a shower of fire,a and it devoured the great deep and was eating up the land. 5Then I said,

"O Lord GOD, cease, I beg you!
    How can Jacob stand?
    He is so small!"
6    The LORD relented concerning
        this;
    "This also shall not be," said
        the Lord GOD.

7 This is what he showed me: the Lord was standing beside a wall built with a plumb line, with a plumb line in his hand. 8And the LORD said to me, "Amos, what do you see?" And I said, "A plumb line." Then the Lord said,

    "See, I am setting a plumb line
        in the midst of my people
        Israel;
    I will never again pass them
        by;
9    the high places of Isaac shall be
        made desolate,

    and the sanctuaries of Israel
        shall be laid waste,
    and I will rise against the
        house of Jeroboam with
        the sword."

10 Then Amaziah, the priest of Bethel, sent to King Jeroboam of Israel, saying, "Amos has conspired against you in the very center of the house of Israel; the land is not able to bear all his words. 11For thus Amos has said,

    'Jeroboam shall die by the
        sword,
    and Israel must go into exile
        away from his land.' "
12And Amaziah said to Amos, "O seer, go, flee away to the land of Judah, earn your bread there, and prophesy there; 13but never again prophesy at Bethel, for it is the king's sanctuary, and it is a temple of the kingdom."

14 Then Amos answered Amaziah, "I amb no prophet, nor a prophet's son; but I amb a herdsman, and a dresser of sycamore trees, 15and the LORD took me from following the flock, and the LORD said to me, 'Go, prophesy to my people Israel.'
16    "Now therefore hear the word
        of the LORD.
    You say, 'Do not prophesy
        against Israel,
    and do not preach against the
        house of Isaac.'
17    Therefore thus says the LORD:
    'Your wife shall become a
        prostitute in the city,
    and your sons and your
        daughters shall fall by
        the sword,

---

aOr *for a judgment by fire*  bOr *was*

and your land shall be
    parceled out by line;
you yourself shall die in an
    unclean land,
and Israel shall surely go into
    exile away from its
    land.' "

**8.**1 This is what the Lord God showed me—a basket of summer fruit.[a] 2He said, "Amos, what do you see?" And I said, "A basket of summer fruit."[a] Then the Lord said to me,

"The end[b] has come upon my
    people Israel;
I will never again pass them
    by.
3 The songs of the temple[c] shall
    become wailings in
    that day,"
         says the Lord God;
"the dead bodies shall be many,
    cast out in every place. Be
    silent!"

4 Hear this, you that trample on
    the needy,
    and bring to ruin the poor of
    the land,
5 saying, "When will the new
    moon be over
    so that we may sell grain;
and the sabbath,
    so that we may offer wheat
    for sale?
We will make the ephah small
    and the shekel great,
    and practice deceit with false
    balances,
6 buying the poor for silver
    and the needy for a pair of
    sandals,
    and selling the sweepings of
    the wheat."

7 The Lord has sworn by the
    pride of Jacob:

Surely I will never forget any of
    their deeds.
8 Shall not the land tremble on
    this account,
    and everyone mourn who
    lives in it,
and all of it rise like the Nile,
    and be tossed about and sink
    again, like the Nile of
    Egypt?

9 On that day, says the Lord
    God,
    I will make the sun go down
    at noon,
    and darken the earth in
    broad daylight.
10 I will turn your feasts into
    mourning,
    and all your songs into
    lamentation;
I will bring sackcloth on all loins,
    and baldness on every head;
I will make it like the mourning
    for an only son,
    and the end of it like a
    bitter day.

11 The time is surely coming, says
    the Lord God,
    when I will send a famine on
    the land;
not a famine of bread, or a
    thirst for water,
but of hearing the words of
    the Lord.
12 They shall wander from sea to
    sea,
    and from north to east;
they shall run to and fro,
    seeking the word of the
    Lord,
    but they shall not find it.

13 In that day the beautiful young
    women and the young
    men
    shall faint for thirst.

aHeb *qayits*  bHeb *qets*  cOr *palace*

14   Those who swear by Ashimah
           of Samaria,
       and say, "As your god lives,
           O Dan,"
       and, "As the way of Beer-sheba
           lives"—
       they shall fall, and never
           rise again.


9.1 I saw the Lord standing beside a the
altar, and he said:
       Strike the capitals until the
           thresholds shake,
       and shatter them on the
           heads of all the people; b
       and those who are left I will kill
           with the sword;
       not one of them shall flee
           away,
       not one of them shall escape.


2   Though they dig into Sheol,
       from there shall my hand
           take them;
       though they climb up to heaven,
           from there I will bring
           them down.
3   Though they hide themselves on
           the top of Carmel,
       from there I will search out
           and take them;
       and though they hide from my
           sight at the bottom of
           the sea,
       there I will command the
           sea-serpent, and it
           shall bite them.
4   And though they go into
           captivity in front of their
           enemies,
       there I will command the
           sword, and it shall kill
           them;
       and I will fix my eyes on them
           for harm and not for good.


5   The Lord, God of hosts,

he who touches the earth and
           it melts,
       and all who live in it mourn,
   and all of it rises like the Nile,
       and sinks again, like the Nile
           of Egypt;
6   who builds his upper chambers
           in the heavens,
       and founds his vault upon
           the earth;
   who calls for the waters of the
           sea,
       and pours them out upon the
           surface of the earth—
   the Lord is his name.

7   Are you not like the
           Ethiopians c to me,
       O people of Israel? says the
           Lord.
   Did I not bring Israel up from
           the land of Egypt,
       and the Philistines from
           Caphtor and the
           Arameans from Kir?
8   The eyes of the Lord God are
           upon the sinful kingdom,
       and I will destroy it from the
           face of the earth
       —except that I will not
           utterly destroy the house
           of Jacob,
                   says the Lord.

9   For lo, I will command,
       and shake the house of Israel
           among all the nations
   as one shakes with a sieve,
       but no pebble shall fall to
           the ground.
10   All the sinners of my people
           shall die by the sword,
       who say, "Evil shall not
           overtake or meet us."

11   On that day I will raise up
       the booth of David that is
           fallen,

a Or on   b Heb all of them   c Or Nubians; Heb Cushites

and repair its<sup>a</sup> breaches,
   and raise up its<sup>b</sup> ruins,
   and rebuild it as in the days
     of old;
12  in order that they may possess
     the remnant of Edom
   and all the nations who are
     called by my name,
   says the LORD who does this.

13  The time is surely coming, says
     the LORD,
   when the one who plows shall
     overtake the one who
     reaps,
   and the treader of grapes the
     one who sows the seed;
the mountains shall drip
     sweet wine,
   and all the hills shall flow with
     it.
14  I will restore the fortunes of my
     people Israel,
   and they shall rebuild the
     ruined cities and inhabit
     them;
they shall plant vineyards and
     drink their wine,
   and they shall make gardens
     and eat their fruit.
15  I will plant them upon their land,
   and they shall never again be
     plucked up
out of the land that I have
     given them,
     says the LORD your God.

# REVELATION 3.7–22

"**A**ND to the angel of the church in Philadelphia write:
These are the words of the
   holy one, the true one,
who has the key of David,
who opens and no one will
   shut,
who shuts and no one
   opens:
8  "I know your works. Look, I have set before you an open door, which no one is able to shut. I know that you have but little power, and yet you have kept my word and have not denied my name. ⁹I will make those of the synagogue of Satan who say that they are Jews and are not, but are lying—I will make them come and bow down before your feet, and they will learn that I have loved you. ¹⁰Because you have kept my word of patient endurance, I will keep you from the hour of trial that is coming on the whole world to test the inhabitants of the earth. ¹¹I am coming soon; hold fast to what you have, so that no one may seize your crown. ¹²If you conquer, I will make you a pillar in the temple of my God; you will never go out of it. I will write on you the name of my God, and the name of the city of my God, the new Jerusalem that comes down from my God out of heaven, and my own new name. ¹³Let anyone who has an ear listen to what the Spirit is saying to the churches.

14  "And to the angel of the church in Laodicea write: The words of the Amen, the faithful and true witness, the origin<sup>c</sup> of God's creation:

15  "I know your works; you are neither cold nor hot. I wish that you were either cold or hot. ¹⁶So, because you are lukewarm, and neither cold nor hot, I am about to spit you out of my mouth. ¹⁷For you say, 'I am rich, I have prospered, and I need nothing.' You do not realize that you are wretched, pitiable, poor, blind, and naked. ¹⁸Therefore I counsel you to buy from me gold refined by fire so that you may be rich; and white robes to clothe you and to keep the shame of your nakedness from being seen; and salve to anoint your eyes so that you may see. ¹⁹I reprove and discipline those whom I love. Be earnest, therefore, and repent. ²⁰Listen! I am standing at the door,

aGk: Heb *their*  bGk: Heb *his*  cOr *beginning*

knocking; if you hear my voice and open the door, I will come in to you and eat with you, and you with me. ²¹To the one who conquers I will give a place with me on my throne, just as I myself conquered and sat down with my Father on his throne. ²²Let anyone who has an ear listen to what the Spirit is saying to the churches."

## PSALM 131.1–3

*A Song of Ascents. Of David.*

O LORD, my heart is not lifted up,
  my eyes are not raised too high;
I do not occupy myself with things
  too great and too marvelous for me.
² But I have calmed and quieted my soul,
  like a weaned child with its mother;
  my soul is like the weaned child that is with me. ᵃ

³ O Israel, hope in the LORD
  from this time on and forevermore.

## PROVERBS 29.23

A PERSON'S pride will bring humiliation,
  but one who is lowly in spirit will obtain honor.

# DECEMBER 13

## OBADIAH 1.1–21

THE vision of Obadiah.

Thus says the Lord GOD concerning Edom:
We have heard a report from the LORD,
  and a messenger has been sent among the nations:
"Rise up! Let us rise against it for battle!"
² I will surely make you least among the nations;
  you shall be utterly despised.
³ Your proud heart has deceived you,
  you that live in the clefts of the rock, ᵇ
  whose dwelling is in the heights.
You say in your heart,
  "Who will bring me down to the ground?"
⁴ Though you soar aloft like the eagle,
  though your nest is set among the stars,
  from there I will bring you down,
      says the LORD.

⁵ If thieves came to you,
  if plunderers by night
  —how you have been destroyed!—
  would they not steal only what they wanted?
If grape-gatherers came to you,
  would they not leave gleanings?
⁶ How Esau has been pillaged,
  his treasures searched out!

ᵃOr *my soul within me is like a weaned child*   ᵇOr *clefts of Sela*

7 All your allies have deceived
you,
they have driven you to
the border;
your confederates have
prevailed against you;
those who ate<sup>a</sup> your bread
have set a trap for you—
there is no understanding of
it.
8 On that day, says the LORD,
I will destroy the wise out
of Edom,
and understanding out of
Mount Esau.
9 Your warriors shall be
shattered, O Teman,
so that everyone from Mount
Esau will be cut off.
10 For the slaughter and violence
done to your brother
Jacob,
shame shall cover you,
and you shall be cut off
forever.
11 On the day that you stood
aside,
on the day that strangers
carried off his wealth,
and foreigners entered his gates
and cast lots for Jerusalem,
you too were like one of
them.
12 But you should not have
gloated<sup>b</sup> over<sup>c</sup> your
brother
on the day of his misfortune;
you should not have rejoiced
over the people of Judah
on the day of their ruin;
you should not have boasted
on the day of distress.
13 You should not have entered the
gate of my people
on the day of their calamity;
you should not have joined in
the gloating over
Judah's<sup>d</sup> disaster

on the day of his calamity;
you should not have looted
his goods
on the day of his calamity.
14 You should not have stood at
the crossings
to cut off his fugitives;
you should not have handed
over his survivors
on the day of distress.
15 For the day of the LORD is near
against all the nations.
As you have done, it shall be
done to you;
your deeds shall return on
your own head.
16 For as you have drunk on my
holy mountain,
all the nations around you
shall drink;
they shall drink and gulp
down, <sup>e</sup>
and shall be as though they
had never been.
17 But on Mount Zion there shall
be those that escape,
and it shall be holy;
and the house of Jacob shall
take possession of those
who dispossessed them.
18 The house of Jacob shall be a
fire,
the house of Joseph a flame,
and the house of Esau
stubble;
they shall burn them and
consume them,
and there shall be no survivor
of the house of Esau;
for the LORD has spoken.
19 Those of the Negeb shall
possess Mount Esau,
and those of the Shephelah
the land of the
Philistines;
they shall possess the land of

<sup>a</sup>Cn: Heb lacks *those who ate*  <sup>b</sup>Heb *But do not gloat* (and similarly through verse 14)  <sup>c</sup>Heb *on the day of*  <sup>d</sup>Heb *his*  <sup>e</sup>Meaning of Heb uncertain

Ephraim and the land
of Samaria,
and Benjamin shall possess
Gilead.
20 The exiles of the Israelites who
are in Halah[a]
shall possess[b] Phoenicia as
far as Zarephath;
and the exiles of Jerusalem who
are in Sepharad
shall possess the towns of
the Negeb.
21 Those who have been saved[c]
shall go up to Mount
Zion
to rule Mount Esau;
and the kingdom shall be
the LORD's.

# REVELATION 4.1–11

**A**FTER this I looked, and there in heaven a door stood open! And the first voice, which I had heard speaking to me like a trumpet, said, "Come up here, and I will show you what must take place after this." $^2$At once I was in the spirit,[d] and there in heaven stood a throne, with one seated on the throne! $^3$And the one seated there looks like jasper and carnelian, and around the throne is a rainbow that looks like an emerald. $^4$Around the throne are twenty-four thrones, and seated on the thrones are twenty-four elders, dressed in white robes, with golden crowns on their heads. $^5$Coming from the throne are flashes of lightning, and rumblings and peals of thunder, and in front of the throne burn seven flaming torches, which are the seven spirits of God; $^6$and in front of the throne there is something like a sea of glass, like crystal.

Around the throne, and on each side of the throne, are four living creatures, full of eyes in front and behind: $^7$the first living creature like a lion, the second living creature like an ox, the third living creature with a face like a human face, and the fourth living creature like a flying eagle. $^8$And the four living creatures, each of them with six wings, are full of eyes all around and inside. Day and night without ceasing they sing,

"Holy, holy, holy,
the Lord God the Almighty,
who was and is and is to
come."

$^9$And whenever the living creatures give glory and honor and thanks to the one who is seated on the throne, who lives forever and ever, $^{10}$the twenty-four elders fall before the one who is seated on the throne and worship the one who lives forever and ever; they cast their crowns before the throne, singing,

11 "You are worthy, our Lord
and God,
to receive glory and honor
and power,
for you created all things,
and by your will they existed
and were created."

# PSALM 132.1–18

*A Song of Ascents.*

**O** LORD, remember in David's
favor
all the hardships he
endured;
2 how he swore to the LORD
and vowed to the Mighty One
of Jacob,
3 "I will not enter my house
or get into my bed;
4 I will not give sleep to my eyes
or slumber to my eyelids,
5 until I find a place for the LORD,
a dwelling place for the
Mighty One of Jacob."

6 We heard of it in Ephrathah;

we found it in the fields of
   Jaar.
7  "Let us go to his dwelling place;
   let us worship at his
      footstool."

8  Rise up, O Lord, and go to your
      resting place,
   you and the ark of your
      might.
9  Let your priests be clothed with
      righteousness,
   and let your faithful shout
      for joy.
10 For your servant David's sake
   do not turn away the face of
      your anointed one.

11 The Lord swore to David a sure
      oath
   from which he will not turn
      back:
   "One of the sons of your body
   I will set on your throne.
12 If your sons keep my covenant
   and my decrees that I shall
      teach them,
   their sons also, forevermore,
   shall sit on your throne."

13 For the Lord has chosen Zion;

he has desired it for his
      habitation:
14 "This is my resting place
      forever;
   here I will reside, for I have
      desired it.
15 I will abundantly bless its
      provisions;
   I will satisfy its poor with
      bread.
16 Its priests I will clothe with
      salvation,
   and its faithful will shout for
      joy.
17 There I will cause a horn to
      sprout up for David;
   I have prepared a lamp for
      my anointed one.
18 His enemies I will clothe with
      disgrace,
   but on him, his crown will
      gleam."

## PROVERBS 29.24–25

To be a partner of a thief is to
      hate one's own life;
   one hears the victim's curse,
      but discloses nothing. a
25 The fear of others b lays a
      snare,
   but one who trusts in the
      Lord is secure.

# DECEMBER 14

## JONAH 1.1—4.11

Now the word of the Lord came
to Jonah son of Amittai, saying,
2"Go at once to Nineveh, that
great city, and cry out against it; for
their wickedness has come up before
me." 3But Jonah set out to flee to Tarshish from the presence of the Lord.
He went down to Joppa and found a ship
going to Tarshish; so he paid his fare
and went on board, to go with them to

a Meaning of Heb uncertain   b Or *human fear*

Tarshish, away from the presence of the Lord.

4 But the Lord hurled a great wind upon the sea, and such a mighty storm came upon the sea that the ship threatened to break up. [5]Then the mariners were afraid, and each cried to his god. They threw the cargo that was in the ship into the sea, to lighten it for them. Jonah, meanwhile, had gone down into the hold of the ship and had lain down, and was fast asleep. [6]The captain came and said to him, "What are you doing sound asleep? Get up, call on your god! Perhaps the god will spare us a thought so that we do not perish."

7 The sailors[a] said to one another, "Come, let us cast lots, so that we may know on whose account this calamity has come upon us." So they cast lots, and the lot fell on Jonah. [8]Then they said to him, "Tell us why this calamity has come upon us. What is your occupation? Where do you come from? What is your country? And of what people are you?" [9]"I am a Hebrew," he replied. "I worship the Lord, the God of heaven, who made the sea and the dry land." [10]Then the men were even more afraid, and said to him, "What is this that you have done!" For the men knew that he was fleeing from the presence of the Lord, because he had told them so.

11 Then they said to him, "What shall we do to you, that the sea may quiet down for us?" For the sea was growing more and more tempestuous. [12]He said to them, "Pick me up and throw me into the sea; then the sea will quiet down for you; for I know it is because of me that this great storm has come upon you." [13]Nevertheless the men rowed hard to bring the ship back to land, but they could not, for the sea grew more and more stormy against them. [14]Then they cried out to the Lord, "Please, O Lord, we pray, do not let us perish on account of this man's life. Do not make us guilty of innocent blood; for you, O Lord, have done as it pleased you." [15]So they picked Jonah up and threw him into the sea; and the sea ceased from its raging. [16]Then the men feared the Lord even more, and they offered a sacrifice to the Lord and made vows.

17[b] But the Lord provided a large fish to swallow up Jonah; and Jonah was in the belly of the fish three days and three nights.

2.1 Then Jonah prayed to the Lord his God from the belly of the fish, [2]saying,

"I called to the Lord out of my
    distress,
  and he answered me;
out of the belly of Sheol I cried,
  and you heard my voice.
3 You cast me into the deep,
  into the heart of the seas,
  and the flood surrounded me;
all your waves and your billows
  passed over me.
4 Then I said, 'I am driven away
  from your sight;
how[c] shall I look again
  upon your holy temple?'
5 The waters closed in over me;
  the deep surrounded me;
weeds were wrapped around
    my head
6   at the roots of the mountains.
I went down to the land
  whose bars closed upon me
    forever;
yet you brought up my life from
    the Pit,
  O Lord my God.
7 As my life was ebbing away,
  I remembered the Lord;
and my prayer came to you,
  into your holy temple.
8 Those who worship vain idols
  forsake their true loyalty.

---

aHeb *They*  bCh 2.1 in Heb  cTheodotion: Heb *surely*

<sup>9</sup> But I with the voice of
   thanksgiving
   will sacrifice to you;
   what I have vowed I will pay.
      Deliverance belongs to the
         LORD!"
<sup>10</sup>Then the LORD spoke to the fish, and it spewed Jonah out upon the dry land.

<sup>3.1</sup> THE word of the LORD came to Jonah a second time, saying, <sup>2</sup>"Get up, go to Nineveh, that great city, and proclaim to it the message that I tell you." <sup>3</sup>So Jonah set out and went to Nineveh, according to the word of the LORD. Now Nineveh was an exceedingly large city, a three days' walk across. <sup>4</sup>Jonah began to go into the city, going a day's walk. And he cried out, "Forty days more, and Nineveh shall be overthrown!" <sup>5</sup>And the people of Nineveh believed God; they proclaimed a fast, and everyone, great and small, put on sackcloth.

<sup>6</sup> When the news reached the king of Nineveh, he rose from his throne, removed his robe, covered himself with sackcloth, and sat in ashes. <sup>7</sup>Then he had a proclamation made in Nineveh: "By the decree of the king and his nobles: No human being or animal, no herd or flock, shall taste anything. They shall not feed, nor shall they drink water. <sup>8</sup>Human beings and animals shall be covered with sackcloth, and they shall cry mightily to God. All shall turn from their evil ways and from the violence that is in their hands. <sup>9</sup>Who knows? God may relent and change his mind; he may turn from his fierce anger, so that we do not perish."

<sup>10</sup> When God saw what they did, how they turned from their evil ways, God changed his mind about the calamity that he had said he would bring upon them; and he did not do it.

<sup>4.1</sup> BUT this was very displeasing to Jonah, and he became angry. <sup>2</sup>He prayed to the LORD and said, "O LORD! Is not this what I said while I was still in my own country? That is why I fled to Tarshish at the beginning; for I knew that you are a gracious God and merciful, slow to anger, and abounding in steadfast love, and ready to relent from punishing. <sup>3</sup>And now, O LORD, please take my life from me, for it is better for me to die than to live." <sup>4</sup>And the LORD said, "Is it right for you to be angry?" <sup>5</sup>Then Jonah went out of the city and sat down east of the city, and made a booth for himself there. He sat under it in the shade, waiting to see what would become of the city.

<sup>6</sup> The LORD God appointed a bush, <sup>a</sup> and made it come up over Jonah, to give shade over his head, to save him from his discomfort; so Jonah was very happy about the bush. <sup>7</sup>But when dawn came up the next day, God appointed a worm that attacked the bush, so that it withered. <sup>8</sup>When the sun rose, God prepared a sultry east wind, and the sun beat down on the head of Jonah so that he was faint and asked that he might die. He said, "It is better for me to die than to live."

<sup>9</sup> But God said to Jonah, "Is it right for you to be angry about the bush?" And he said, "Yes, angry enough to die." <sup>10</sup>Then the LORD said, "You are concerned about the bush, for which you did not labor and which you did not grow; it came into being in a night and perished in a night. <sup>11</sup>And should I not be concerned about Nineveh, that great city, in which there are more than a hundred and twenty thousand persons who do not know their right hand from their left, and also many animals?"

## REVELATION 5.1–14

THEN I saw in the right hand of the one seated on the throne a scroll written on the inside and on the back, sealed<sup>b</sup> with seven seals; <sup>2</sup>and I

---

<sup>a</sup>Heb *qiqayon*, possibly *the castor bean plant*   <sup>b</sup>Or *written on the inside, and sealed on the back*

saw a mighty angel proclaiming with a loud voice, "Who is worthy to open the scroll and break its seals?" ³And no one in heaven or on earth or under the earth was able to open the scroll or to look into it. ⁴And I began to weep bitterly because no one was found worthy to open the scroll or to look into it. ⁵Then one of the elders said to me, "Do not weep. See, the Lion of the tribe of Judah, the Root of David, has conquered, so that he can open the scroll and its seven seals."

6 Then I saw between the throne and the four living creatures and among the elders a Lamb standing as if it had been slaughtered, having seven horns and seven eyes, which are the seven spirits of God sent out into all the earth. ⁷He went and took the scroll from the right hand of the one who was seated on the throne. ⁸When he had taken the scroll, the four living creatures and the twenty-four elders fell before the Lamb, each holding a harp and golden bowls full of incense, which are the prayers of the saints. ⁹They sing a new song:

"You are worthy to take the
scroll
and to open its seals,
for you were slaughtered and by
your blood you ransomed
for God
saints from ᵃ every tribe and
language and people
and nation;
10 you have made them to be a
kingdom and priests
serving ᵇ our God,
and they will reign on earth."

11 Then I looked, and I heard the voice of many angels surrounding the throne and the living creatures and the elders; they numbered myriads of myriads and thousands of thousands, ¹²singing with full voice,

"Worthy is the Lamb that was
slaughtered
to receive power and wealth and
wisdom and might
and honor and glory and
blessing!"
¹³Then I heard every creature in heaven and on earth and under the earth and in the sea, and all that is in them, singing,

"To the one seated on the
throne and to the Lamb
be blessing and honor and glory
and might
forever and ever!"
¹⁴And the four living creatures said, "Amen!" And the elders fell down and worshiped.

## PSALM 133.1–3

*A Song of Ascents.*

**H**ow very good and pleasant it is
when kindred live together
in unity!
2 It is like the precious oil on the
head,
running down upon the beard,
on the beard of Aaron,
running down over the collar
of his robes.
3 It is like the dew of Hermon,
which falls on the mountains
of Zion.
For there the LORD ordained his
blessing,
life forevermore.

---

ᵃGk *ransomed for God from*    ᵇGk *priests to*

## PROVERBS 29.26–27

**M**ANY seek the favor of a
    ruler,
  but it is from the LORD
    that one gets justice.

27 The unjust are an abomination
    to the righteous,
  but the upright are an
    abomination to the
    wicked.

# DECEMBER 15

## MICAH 1.1—4.13

**T**HE word of the LORD that came to
Micah of Moresheth in the days
of Kings Jotham, Ahaz, and
Hezekiah of Judah, which he saw concerning Samaria and Jerusalem.

2 Hear, you peoples, all of you;
    listen, O earth, and all that is
      in it;
  and let the Lord GOD be a
      witness against you,
    the Lord from his holy
      temple.
3 For lo, the LORD is coming out
      of his place,
    and will come down and tread
      upon the high places of
      the earth.
4 Then the mountains will melt
      under him
    and the valleys will burst
      open,
  like wax near the fire,
    like waters poured down a
      steep place.
5 All this is for the transgression
      of Jacob
    and for the sins of the house
      of Israel.
  What is the transgression of
      Jacob?
    Is it not Samaria?
  And what is the high place[a]
      of Judah?
    Is it not Jerusalem?

6 Therefore I will make Samaria a
      heap in the open
      country,
    a place for planting vineyards.
  I will pour down her stones into
      the valley,
    and uncover her foundations.
7 All her images shall be beaten
      to pieces,
    all her wages shall be burned
      with fire,
    and all her idols I will lay
      waste;
  for as the wages of a prostitute
      she gathered them,
    and as the wages of a
      prostitute they shall again
      be used.

8 For this I will lament and wail;
    I will go barefoot and naked;
  I will make lamentation like
      the jackals,
    and mourning like the
      ostriches.
9 For her wound[b] is incurable.
    It has come to Judah;
  it has reached to the gate of
      my people,
    to Jerusalem.

10 Tell it not in Gath,
    weep not at all;
  in Beth-leaphrah
    roll yourselves in the dust.
11 Pass on your way,

---

[a]Heb *what are the high places*   [b]Gk Syr Vg: Heb *wounds*

inhabitants of Shaphir,
   in nakedness and shame;
the inhabitants of Zaanan
   do not come forth;
Beth-ezel is wailing
   and shall remove its support
      from you.
12 For the inhabitants of Maroth
   wait anxiously for good,
yet disaster has come down
      from the LORD
   to the gate of Jerusalem.
13 Harness the steeds to the
      chariots,
   inhabitants of Lachish;
it was the beginning of sin
   to daughter Zion,
for in you were found
   the transgressions of Israel.
14 Therefore you shall give
      parting gifts
   to Moresheth-gath;
the houses of Achzib shall be
      a deception
   to the kings of Israel.
15 I will again bring a conqueror
      upon you,
   inhabitants of Mareshah;
the glory of Israel
   shall come to Adullam.
16 Make yourselves bald and cut
      off your hair
   for your pampered children;
make yourselves as bald as
      the eagle,
   for they have gone from you
      into exile.

2.1 ALAS for those who devise
      wickedness
and evil deeds[a] on their
      beds!
When the morning dawns, they
      perform it,
   because it is in their power.
2 They covet fields, and seize
      them;
   houses, and take them away;

they oppress householder
      and house,
   people and their inheritance.
3 Therefore thus says the LORD:
Now, I am devising against this
      family an evil
   from which you cannot
      remove your necks;
and you shall not walk haughtily,
   for it will be an evil time.
4 On that day they shall take up a
      taunt song against you,
   and wail with bitter
      lamentation,
and say, "We are utterly ruined;
   the LORD [b] alters the
      inheritance of my people;
how he removes it from me!
   Among our captors[c] he
      parcels out our fields."
5 Therefore you will have no one
      to cast the line by lot
   in the assembly of the LORD.

6 "Do not preach"—thus they
      preach—
   "one should not preach of
      such things;
   disgrace will not overtake
      us."
7 Should this be said, O house
      of Jacob?
   Is the LORD's patience
      exhausted?
   Are these his doings?
Do not my words do good
   to one who walks uprightly?
8 But you rise up against my
      people[d] as an enemy;
   you strip the robe from the
      peaceful, [e]
from those who pass by
      trustingly
   with no thought of war.
9 The women of my people you
      drive out
   from their pleasant houses;

aCn: Heb *work evil*  bHeb *he*  cCn: Heb *the rebellious*  dCn: Heb *But yesterday my people rose*
eCn: Heb *from before a garment*

from their young children you
take away
my glory forever.
10 Arise and go;
for this is no place to rest,
because of uncleanness that
destroys
with a grievous destruction. a
11 If someone were to go about
uttering empty
falsehoods,
saying, "I will preach to you
of wine and strong
drink,"
such a one would be the
preacher for this people!

12 I will surely gather all of you,
O Jacob,
I will gather the survivors
of Israel;
I will set them together
like sheep in a fold,
like a flock in its pasture;
it will resound with people.
13 The one who breaks out will go
up before them;
they will break through and
pass the gate,
going out by it.
Their king will pass on before
them,
the LORD at their head.

3.1 AND I said:
Listen, you heads of Jacob
and rulers of the house of
Israel!
Should you not know justice?—
2 you who hate the good and
love the evil,
who tear the skin off my
people, b
and the flesh off their bones;
3 who eat the flesh of my people,
flay their skin off them,
break their bones in pieces,

and chop them up like meat c
in a kettle,
like flesh in a caldron.

4 Then they will cry to the LORD,
but he will not answer them;
he will hide his face from them
at that time,
because they have acted
wickedly.

5 Thus says the LORD concerning
the prophets
who lead my people astray,
who cry "Peace"
when they have something to
eat,
but declare war against those
who put nothing into their
mouths.
6 Therefore it shall be night to
you, without vision,
and darkness to you, without
revelation.
The sun shall go down upon
the prophets,
and the day shall be black
over them;
7 the seers shall be disgraced,
and the diviners put to
shame;
they shall all cover their lips,
for there is no answer from
God.
8 But as for me, I am filled
with power,
with the spirit of the LORD,
and with justice and might,
to declare to Jacob his
transgression
and to Israel his sin.

9 Hear this, you rulers of the
house of Jacob
and chiefs of the house of
Israel,
who abhor justice
and pervert all equity,

aMeaning of Heb uncertain   bHeb *from them*   cGk: Heb *as*

10 who build Zion with blood
    and Jerusalem with wrong!
11 Its rulers give judgment for a
    bribe,
    its priests teach for a price,
    its prophets give oracles
    for money;
    yet they lean upon the LORD
    and say,
    "Surely the LORD is with us!
    No harm shall come upon us."
12 Therefore because of you
    Zion shall be plowed as a
    field;
    Jerusalem shall become a heap
    of ruins,
    and the mountain of the house
    a wooded height.

4.1 IN days to come
    the mountain of the LORD's
    house
    shall be established as the
    highest of the mountains,
    and shall be raised up above
    the hills.
    Peoples shall stream to it,
2   and many nations shall come
    and say:
    "Come, let us go up to the
    mountain of the LORD,
    to the house of the God of
    Jacob;
    that he may teach us his ways
    and that we may walk in
    his paths."
    For out of Zion shall go forth
    instruction,
    and the word of the LORD
    from Jerusalem.
3 He shall judge between many
    peoples,
    and shall arbitrate between
    strong nations far away;
    they shall beat their swords into
    plowshares,
    and their spears into pruning
    hooks;

    nation shall not lift up sword
    against nation,
    neither shall they learn war
    any more;
4 but they shall all sit under their
    own vines and under
    their own fig trees,
    and no one shall make
    them afraid;
    for the mouth of the LORD of
    hosts has spoken.

5 For all the peoples walk,
    each in the name of its god,
    but we will walk in the name of
    the LORD our God
    forever and ever.

6 In that day, says the LORD,
    I will assemble the lame
    and gather those who have been
    driven away,
    and those whom I have
    afflicted.
7 The lame I will make the
    remnant,
    and those who were cast off,
    a strong nation;
    and the LORD will reign over
    them in Mount Zion
    now and forevermore.

8 And you, O tower of the flock,
    hill of daughter Zion,
    to you it shall come,
    the former dominion shall
    come,
    the sovereignty of daughter
    Jerusalem.

9 Now why do you cry aloud?
    Is there no king in you?
    Has your counselor perished,
    that pangs have seized you
    like a woman in labor?
10 Writhe and groan, a O daughter
    Zion,
    like a woman in labor;

a Meaning of Heb uncertain

for now you shall go forth from
   the city
  and camp in the open
   country;
  you shall go to Babylon.
There you shall be rescued,
  there the Lᴏʀᴅ will redeem
   you
  from the hands of your
   enemies.

11 Now many nations
  are assembled against you,
  saying, "Let her be profaned,
   and let our eyes gaze upon
   Zion."
12 But they do not know
  the thoughts of the Lᴏʀᴅ;
  they do not understand his plan,
   that he has gathered them as
   sheaves to the threshing
   floor.
13 Arise and thresh,
  O daughter Zion,
  for I will make your horn iron
  and your hoofs bronze;
  you shall beat in pieces many
   peoples,
  and shall[a] devote their gain
   to the Lᴏʀᴅ,
  their wealth to the Lord of
   the whole earth.

# REVELATION 6.1–17

Tʜᴇɴ I saw the Lamb open one of the seven seals, and I heard one of the four living creatures call out, as with a voice of thunder, "Come!"[b] [2]I looked, and there was a white horse! Its rider had a bow; a crown was given to him, and he came out conquering and to conquer.

3 When he opened the second seal, I heard the second living creature call out, "Come!"[b] [4]And out came[c] another horse, bright red; its rider was permitted to take peace from the earth, so that people would slaughter one another; and he was given a great sword.

5 When he opened the third seal, I heard the third living creature call out, "Come!"[b] I looked, and there was a black horse! Its rider held a pair of scales in his hand, [6]and I heard what seemed to be a voice in the midst of the four living creatures saying, "A quart of wheat for a day's pay,[d] and three quarts of barley for a day's pay,[d] but do not damage the olive oil and the wine!"

7 When he opened the fourth seal, I heard the voice of the fourth living creature call out, "Come!"[b] [8]I looked and there was a pale green horse! Its rider's name was Death, and Hades followed with him; they were given authority over a fourth of the earth, to kill with sword, famine, and pestilence, and by the wild animals of the earth.

9 When he opened the fifth seal, I saw under the altar the souls of those who had been slaughtered for the word of God and for the testimony they had given; [10]they cried out with a loud voice, "Sovereign Lord, holy and true, how long will it be before you judge and avenge our blood on the inhabitants of the earth?" [11]They were each given a white robe and told to rest a little longer, until the number would be complete both of their fellow servants[e] and of their brothers and sisters,[f] who were soon to be killed as they themselves had been killed.

12 When he opened the sixth seal, I looked, and there came a great earthquake; the sun became black as sackcloth, the full moon became like blood, [13]and the stars of the sky fell to the earth as the fig tree drops its winter fruit when shaken by a gale. [14]The sky vanished like a scroll rolling itself up, and every mountain and island was removed from its place. [15]Then the kings of the earth and the magnates and the

a Gk Syr Tg: Heb *and I will*  b Or *"Go!"*  c Or *went*  d Gk *a denarius*  e Gk *slaves*  f Gk *brothers*

generals and the rich and the powerful, and everyone, slave and free, hid in the caves and among the rocks of the mountains, [16]calling to the mountains and rocks, "Fall on us and hide us from the face of the one seated on the throne and from the wrath of the Lamb; [17]for the great day of their wrath has come, and who is able to stand?"

## PSALM 134.1–3

*A Song of Ascents.*

COME, bless the LORD, all you
    servants of the LORD,
who stand by night in the
    house of the LORD!
2  Lift up your hands to the holy
    place,
  and bless the LORD.

3  May the LORD, maker of heaven
    and earth,
  bless you from Zion.

## PROVERBS 30.1–4

THE words of Agur son of Jakeh. An oracle.

Thus says the man: I am weary,
  O God,
  I am weary, O God. How can
    I prevail? [a]
2  Surely I am too stupid to be
    human;
  I do not have human
    understanding.
3  I have not learned wisdom,
    nor have I knowledge of the
    holy ones. [b]
4  Who has ascended to heaven
    and come down?
  Who has gathered the wind in
    the hollow of the hand?
  Who has wrapped up the waters
    in a garment?
  Who has established all the
    ends of the earth?
  What is the person's name?
  And what is the name of the
    person's child?
  Surely you know!

# DECEMBER 16

## MICAH 5c.1—7.20

Now you are walled around
    with a wall; [d]
  siege is laid against us;
with a rod they strike the ruler
    of Israel
  upon the cheek.

2[e] But you, O Bethlehem of
    Ephrathah,
  who are one of the little clans
    of Judah,
from you shall come forth for
    me
  one who is to rule in Israel,
  whose origin is from of old,

from ancient days.
3 Therefore he shall give them up
        until the time
    when she who is in labor has
        brought forth;
    then the rest of his kindred shall
        return
    to the people of Israel.
4 And he shall stand and feed his
        flock in the strength of
        the Lord,
    in the majesty of the name of
        the Lord his God.
    And they shall live secure, for
        now he shall be great
    to the ends of the earth;
5 and he shall be the one of
        peace.

    If the Assyrians come into
        our land
    and tread upon our soil, a
    we will raise against them seven
        shepherds
    and eight installed as rulers.
6 They shall rule the land of
        Assyria with the sword,
    and the land of Nimrod with
        the drawn sword; b
    theyc shall rescue us from the
        Assyrians
    if they come into our land
    or tread within our border.

7 Then the remnant of Jacob,
        surrounded by many peoples,
    shall be like dew from the Lord,
        like showers on the grass,
    which do not depend upon
        people
    or wait for any mortal.
8 And among the nations the
        remnant of Jacob,
        surrounded by many peoples,
    shall be like a lion among the
        animals of the forest,
    like a young lion among the
        flocks of sheep,

which, when it goes through,
        treads down
    and tears in pieces, with no
        one to deliver.
9 Your hand shall be lifted up over
        your adversaries,
    and all your enemies shall be
        cut off.

10 In that day, says the Lord,
        I will cut off your horses from
        among you
    and will destroy your
        chariots;
11 and I will cut off the cities of
        your land
    and throw down all your
        strongholds;
12 and I will cut off sorceries from
        your hand,
    and you shall have no more
        soothsayers;
13 and I will cut off your images
        and your pillars from among
        you,
    and you shall bow down no
        more
    to the work of your hands;
14 and I will uproot your sacred
        polesd from among you
    and destroy your towns.
15 And in anger and wrath I will
        execute vengeance
    on the nations that did not
        obey.


6.1 Hear what the Lord says:
        Rise, plead your case before
        the mountains,
    and let the hills hear your
        voice.
2 Hear, you mountains, the
        controversy of the Lord,
    and you enduring foundations
        of the earth;
    for the Lord has a controversy
        with his people,

aGk: Heb *in our palaces*   bCn: Heb *in its entrances*   cHeb *he*   dHeb *Asherim*

and he will contend with
   Israel.

3 "O my people, what have I done
     to you?
  In what have I wearied you?
     Answer me!
4 For I brought you up from the
     land of Egypt,
  and redeemed you from the
     house of slavery;
  and I sent before you Moses,
     Aaron, and Miriam.
5 O my people, remember now
     what King Balak of Moab
     devised,
  what Balaam son of Beor
     answered him,
  and what happened from Shittim
     to Gilgal,
  that you may know the saving
     acts of the Lord."

6 "With what shall I come before
     the Lord,
  and bow myself before God
     on high?
  Shall I come before him with
     burnt offerings,
  with calves a year old?
7 Will the Lord be pleased with
     thousands of rams,
     with ten thousands of rivers
     of oil?
  Shall I give my firstborn for my
     transgression,
     the fruit of my body for the
     sin of my soul?"
8 He has told you, O mortal, what
     is good;
  and what does the Lord
     require of you
  but to do justice, and to love
     kindness,
  and to walk humbly with
     your God?

9 The voice of the Lord cries to
     the city
  (it is sound wisdom to fear
     your name):
  Hear, O tribe and assembly of
     the city!a
10   Can I forgetb the treasures
     of wickedness in the
     house of the wicked,
  and the scant measure that is
     accursed?
11 Can I tolerate wicked scales
  and a bag of dishonest
     weights?
12 Yourc wealthy are full of
     violence;
  yourd inhabitants speak lies,
  with tongues of deceit in
     their mouths.
13 Therefore I have begune to
     strike you down,
  making you desolate because
     of your sins.
14 You shall eat, but not be
     satisfied,
  and there shall be a gnawing
     hunger within you;
  you shall put away, but not
     save,
  and what you save, I will
     hand over to the sword.
15 You shall sow, but not reap;
  you shall tread olives, but not
     anoint yourselves with
     oil;
  you shall tread grapes, but
     not drink wine.
16 For you have kept the statutes
     of Omrif
  and all the works of the house
     of Ahab,
  and you have followed their
     counsels.

---

aCn Compare Gk: Heb *tribe, and who has appointed it yet?*  bCn: Meaning of Heb uncertain
cHeb *Whose*  dHeb *whose*  eGk Syr Vg: Heb *have made sick*  fGk Syr Vg Tg: Heb *the statutes of Omri are kept*

Therefore I will make you a
    desolation, and your[a]
    inhabitants an object
    of hissing;
  so you shall bear the scorn of
    my people.

7.1 WOE is me! For I have become
    like one who,
  after the summer fruit has
    been gathered,
  after the vintage has been
    gleaned,
  finds no cluster to eat;
  there is no first-ripe fig for
    which I hunger.
2 The faithful have disappeared
    from the land,
  and there is no one left who
    is upright;
  they all lie in wait for blood,
  and they hunt each other
    with nets.
3 Their hands are skilled to do
    evil;
  the official and the judge ask
    for a bribe,
  and the powerful dictate what
    they desire;
  thus they pervert justice. [b]
4 The best of them is like a brier,
  the most upright of them a
    thorn hedge.
  The day of their[c] sentinels, of
    their[c] punishment,
    has come;
  now their confusion is at
    hand.
5 Put no trust in a friend,
  have no confidence in a
    loved one;
  guard the doors of your mouth
  from her who lies in your
    embrace;
6 for the son treats the father
    with contempt,
  the daughter rises up against
    her mother,

the daughter-in-law against her
    mother-in-law;
  your enemies are members of
    your own household.
7 But as for me, I will look to
    the LORD,
  I will wait for the God of my
    salvation;
  my God will hear me.

8 Do not rejoice over me, O my
    enemy;
  when I fall, I shall rise;
  when I sit in darkness,
  the LORD will be a light to me.
9 I must bear the indignation of
    the LORD,
  because I have sinned
    against him,
  until he takes my side
  and executes judgment for
    me.
  He will bring me out to the
    light;
  I shall see his vindication.
10 Then my enemy will see,
  and shame will cover her who
    said to me,
  "Where is the LORD your
    God?"
  My eyes will see her downfall;[d]
  now she will be trodden down
  like the mire of the streets.

11 A day for the building of your
    walls!
  In that day the boundary shall
    be far extended.
12 In that day they will come to
    you
  from Assyria to[e] Egypt,
  and from Egypt to the River,
  from sea to sea and from
    mountain to mountain.
13 But the earth will be desolate
  because of its inhabitants,
  for the fruit of their doings.

[a] Heb *its*    [b] Cn: Heb *they weave it*    [c] Heb *your*    [d] Heb lacks *downfall*    [e] One Ms: MT *Assyria and cities of*

14 Shepherd your people with
       your staff,
    the flock that belongs to you,
    which lives alone in a forest
       in the midst of a garden land;
    let them feed in Bashan and
       Gilead
       as in the days of old.
15 As in the days when you came
       out of the land of Egypt,
    show us<sup>a</sup> marvelous things.
16 The nations shall see and be
       ashamed
    of all their might;
    they shall lay their hands on
       their mouths;
    their ears shall be deaf;
17 they shall lick dust like a snake,
    like the crawling things of
       the earth;
    they shall come trembling out of
       their fortresses;
    they shall turn in dread to the
       LORD our God,
    and they shall stand in fear
       of you.

18 Who is a God like you,
       pardoning iniquity
    and passing over the
       transgression
    of the remnant of your<sup>b</sup>
       possession?
    He does not retain his anger
       forever,
    because he delights in
       showing clemency.
19 He will again have compassion
       upon us;
    he will tread our iniquities
       under foot.
    You will cast all our<sup>c</sup> sins
       into the depths of the sea.
20 You will show faithfulness to
       Jacob
    and unswerving loyalty to
       Abraham,

as you have sworn to our
    ancestors
from the days of old.

## REVELATION 7.1–17

AFTER this I saw four angels standing at the four corners of the earth, holding back the four winds of the earth so that no wind could blow on earth or sea or against any tree. ²I saw another angel ascending from the rising of the sun, having the seal of the living God, and he called with a loud voice to the four angels who had been given power to damage earth and sea, ³saying, "Do not damage the earth or the sea or the trees, until we have marked the servants<sup>d</sup> of our God with a seal on their foreheads."

4 And I heard the number of those who were sealed, one hundred forty-four thousand, sealed out of every tribe of the people of Israel:
5 From the tribe of Judah twelve
       thousand sealed,
    from the tribe of Reuben twelve
       thousand,
    from the tribe of Gad twelve
       thousand,
6 from the tribe of Asher twelve
       thousand,
    from the tribe of Naphtali twelve
       thousand,
    from the tribe of Manasseh
       twelve thousand,
7 from the tribe of Simeon twelve
       thousand,
    from the tribe of Levi twelve
       thousand,
    from the tribe of Issachar twelve
       thousand,
8 from the tribe of Zebulun twelve
       thousand,
    from the tribe of Joseph twelve
       thousand,
    from the tribe of Benjamin twelve
       thousand sealed.
9 After this I looked, and there was

aCn: Heb *I will show him*   bHeb *his*   cGk Syr Vg Tg: Heb *their*   dGk *slaves* a great multitude that no one could count, from every nation, from all tribes and peoples and languages, standing before the throne and before the Lamb, robed in white, with palm branches in their hands. ¹⁰They cried out in a loud voice, saying,

> "Salvation belongs to our God
> who is seated on the
> throne, and to the
> Lamb!"

¹¹And all the angels stood around the throne and around the elders and the four living creatures, and they fell on their faces before the throne and worshiped God, ¹²singing,

> "Amen! Blessing and glory
> and wisdom
> and thanksgiving and honor
> and power and might
> be to our God forever and ever!
> Amen."

13 Then one of the elders addressed me, saying, "Who are these, robed in white, and where have they come from?" ¹⁴I said to him, "Sir, you are the one that knows." Then he said to me, "These are they who have come out of the great ordeal; they have washed their robes and made them white in the blood of the Lamb.

¹⁵  For this reason they are before
> the throne of God,
> and worship him day and
> night within his temple,
> and the one who is seated on
> the throne will shelter
> them.

¹⁶  They will hunger no more, and
> thirst no more;
> the sun will not strike them,
> nor any scorching heat;

¹⁷  for the Lamb at the center of
> the throne will be their
> shepherd,
> and he will guide them to
> springs of the water of
> life,
> and God will wipe away every
> tear from their eyes."

## PSALM 135.1–21

**P**RAISE the LORD!
> Praise the name of the
> LORD;
> give praise, O servants of
> the LORD,

2  you that stand in the house of
> the LORD,
> in the courts of the house of
> our God.

3  Praise the LORD, for the LORD
> is good;
> sing to his name, for he is
> gracious.

4  For the LORD has chosen Jacob
> for himself,
> Israel as his own possession.

5  For I know that the LORD is
> great;
> our Lord is above all gods.

6  Whatever the LORD pleases he
> does,
> in heaven and on earth,
> in the seas and all deeps.

7  He it is who makes the clouds
> rise at the end of the
> earth;
> he makes lightnings for the
> rain
> and brings out the wind from
> his storehouses.

8  He it was who struck down the
> firstborn of Egypt,
> both human beings and
> animals;

9  he sent signs and wonders
> into your midst, O Egypt,
> against Pharaoh and all his
> servants.

10  He struck down many nations
> and killed mighty kings—

11  Sihon, king of the Amorites,
> and Og, king of Bashan,
> and all the kingdoms of
> Canaan—

12  and gave their land as a
> heritage,

a heritage to his people
Israel.

13 Your name, O Lord, endures
forever,
your renown, O Lord,
throughout all ages.
14 For the Lord will vindicate his
people,
and have compassion on his
servants.

15 The idols of the nations are
silver and gold,
the work of human hands.
16 They have mouths, but they do
not speak;
they have eyes, but they do
not see;
17 they have ears, but they do not
hear,
and there is no breath in their
mouths.
18 Those who make them
and all who trust them
shall become like them.

19 O house of Israel, bless the
Lord!
O house of Aaron, bless the
Lord!
20 O house of Levi, bless the
Lord!
You that fear the Lord, bless
the Lord!
21 Blessed be the Lord from Zion,
he who resides in Jerusalem.
Praise the Lord!

## PROVERBS 30.5–6

Every word of God proves
true;
he is a shield to those who
take refuge in him.
6 Do not add to his words,
or else he will rebuke you,
and you will be found a
liar.

# DECEMBER 17

## NAHUM 1.1—3.19

An oracle concerning Nineveh.
The book of the vision of Nahum of Elkosh.

2 A jealous and avenging God is
the Lord,
the Lord is avenging and
wrathful;
the Lord takes vengeance on his
adversaries
and rages against his
enemies.

3 The Lord is slow to anger but
great in power,
and the Lord will by no
means clear the guilty.

His way is in whirlwind and
storm,
and the clouds are the dust of
his feet.
4 He rebukes the sea and makes
it dry,
and he dries up all the rivers;
Bashan and Carmel wither,

and the bloom of Lebanon
    fades.
5  The mountains quake before
    him,
  and the hills melt;
the earth heaves before him,
    the world and all who live in
    it.

6  Who can stand before his
    indignation?
  Who can endure the heat of
    his anger?
His wrath is poured out like
    fire,
  and by him the rocks are
    broken in pieces.
7  The LORD is good,
  a stronghold in a day of
    trouble;
he protects those who take
    refuge in him,
8    even in a rushing flood.
He will make a full end of his
    adversaries, a
  and will pursue his enemies
    into darkness.
9  Why do you plot against the
    LORD?
  He will make an end;
  no adversary will rise up
    twice.
10  Like thorns they are entangled,
    like drunkards they are
    drunk;
  they are consumed like dry
    straw.
11  From you one has gone out
    who plots evil against the
    LORD,
    who counsels wickedness.

12  Thus says the LORD,
  "Though they are at full
    strength and many, b
  they will be cut off and
    pass away.
Though I have afflicted you,
  I will afflict you no more.
13  And now I will break off his
    yoke from you
  and snap the bonds that
    bind you."

14  The LORD has commanded
    concerning you:
  "Your name shall be
    perpetuated no longer;
from the house of your gods I
    will cut off
  the carved image and the
    cast image.
I will make your grave, for you
    are worthless."

15c  Look! On the mountains the
    feet of one
  who brings good tidings,
  who proclaims peace!
Celebrate your festivals,
    O Judah,
  fulfill your vows,
for never again shall the wicked
    invade you;
  they are utterly cut off.

2.1  A SHATTERER d has come up
    against you.
  Guard the ramparts;
  watch the road;
gird your loins;
  collect all your strength.

2  (For the LORD is restoring the
    majesty of Jacob,
  as well as the majesty of
    Israel,
though ravagers have ravaged
    them
  and ruined their branches.)

3  The shields of his warriors are
    red;
  his soldiers are clothed in
    crimson.

a Gk: Heb *of her place*  b Meaning of Heb uncertain  c Ch 2.1 in Heb  d Cn: Heb *scatterer*

The metal on the chariots
  flashes
on the day when he musters
  them;
the chargers[a] prance.
4  The chariots race madly through
  the streets,
they rush to and fro through
  the squares;
their appearance is like torches,
  they dart like lightning.
5  He calls his officers;
  they stumble as they come
  forward;
they hasten to the wall,
  and the mantelet[b] is set up.
6  The river gates are opened,
  the palace trembles.
7  It is decreed[b] that the city[c]
  be exiled,
  its slave women led away,
moaning like doves
  and beating their breasts.
8  Nineveh is like a pool
  whose waters[d] run away.
"Halt! Halt!"—
  but no one turns back.
9  "Plunder the silver,
  plunder the gold!
There is no end of treasure!
  An abundance of every
  precious thing!"

10  Devastation, desolation, and
  destruction!
  Hearts faint and knees
  tremble,
all loins quake,
  all faces grow pale!
11  What became of the lions' den,
  the cave[e] of the young lions,
where the lion goes,
  and the lion's cubs, with no
  one to disturb them?
12  The lion has torn enough for
  his whelps
and strangled prey for his
  lionesses;

he has filled his caves with prey
  and his dens with torn flesh.

13  See, I am against you, says the
LORD of hosts, and I will burn your[f]
chariots in smoke, and the sword shall
devour your young lions; I will cut off
your prey from the earth, and the voice
of your messengers shall be heard no
more.

3.1  AH! City of bloodshed,
  utterly deceitful, full of
  booty—
  no end to the plunder!
2  The crack of whip and rumble
  of wheel,
  galloping horse and bounding
  chariot!
3  Horsemen charging,
  flashing sword and glittering
  spear,
piles of dead,
  heaps of corpses,
dead bodies without end—
  they stumble over the bodies!
4  Because of the countless
  debaucheries of
  the prostitute,
  gracefully alluring, mistress
  of sorcery,
who enslaves[g] nations through
  her debaucheries,
  and peoples through her
  sorcery,
5  I am against you,
  says the LORD of hosts,
  and will lift up your skirts
  over your face;
and I will let nations look on
  your nakedness
  and kingdoms on your shame.
6  I will throw filth at you
  and treat you with contempt,
  and make you a spectacle.
7  Then all who see you will shrink
  from you and say,

aCn Compare Gk Syr: Heb *cypresses*  bMeaning of Heb uncertain  cHeb *it*  dCn Compare Gk: Heb
*a pool, from the days that she has become, and they*  eCn: Heb *pasture*  fHeb *her*  gHeb *sells*

"Nineveh is devastated; who
  will bemoan her?"
Where shall I seek comforters
  for you?

8  Are you better than Thebesᵃ
  that sat by the Nile,
with water around her,
  her rampart a sea,
  water her wall?
9  Ethiopiaᵇ was her strength,
  Egypt too, and that without
    limit;
  Put and the Libyans were
    herᶜ helpers.

10  Yet she became an exile,
  she went into captivity;
even her infants were dashed
    in pieces
  at the head of every street;
lots were cast for her nobles,
  all her dignitaries were bound
    in fetters.
11  You also will be drunken,
  you will go into hiding; ᵈ
you will seek
  a refuge from the enemy.
12  All your fortresses are like fig
    trees
  with first-ripe figs—
if shaken they fall
  into the mouth of the eater.
13  Look at your troops:
  they are women in your
    midst.
The gates of your land
  are wide open to your foes;
fire has devoured the bars of
    your gates.

14  Draw water for the siege,
  strengthen your forts;
trample the clay,
  tread the mortar,
  take hold of the brick mold!
15  There the fire will devour you,
  the sword will cut you off.

It will devour you like the
    locust.

Multiply yourselves like the
    locust,
  multiply like the grasshopper!
16  You increased your merchants
  more than the stars of the
    heavens.
  The locust sheds its skin and
    flies away.
17  Your guards are like
    grasshoppers,
  your scribes like swarmsᵈ
    of locusts
settling on the fences
  on a cold day—
when the sun rises, they fly
    away;
  no one knows where they
    have gone.

18  Your shepherds are asleep,
  O king of Assyria;
  your nobles slumber.
Your people are scattered on
    the mountains
  with no one to gather them.
19  There is no assuaging your
    hurt,
  your wound is mortal.
All who hear the news about
    you
  clap their hands over you.
For who has ever escaped
  your endless cruelty?

# REVELATION 8.1–13

WHEN the Lamb opened the
seventh seal, there was silence in heaven for about half
an hour. ²And I saw the seven angels
who stand before God, and seven trumpets were given to them.

3  Another angel with a golden censer came and stood at the altar; he was
given a great quantity of incense to of-

---

ᵃHeb *No-amon*   ᵇOr *Nubia*; Heb *Cush*   ᶜGk: Heb *your*   ᵈMeaning of Heb uncertain

fer with the prayers of all the saints on the golden altar that is before the throne. ⁴And the smoke of the incense, with the prayers of the saints, rose before God from the hand of the angel. ⁵Then the angel took the censer and filled it with fire from the altar and threw it on the earth; and there were peals of thunder, rumblings, flashes of lightning, and an earthquake.

6 Now the seven angels who had the seven trumpets made ready to blow them.

7 The first angel blew his trumpet, and there came hail and fire, mixed with blood, and they were hurled to the earth; and a third of the earth was burned up, and a third of the trees were burned up, and all green grass was burned up.

8 The second angel blew his trumpet, and something like a great mountain, burning with fire, was thrown into the sea. ⁹A third of the sea became blood, a third of the living creatures in the sea died, and a third of the ships were destroyed.

10 The third angel blew his trumpet, and a great star fell from heaven, blazing like a torch, and it fell on a third of the rivers and on the springs of water. ¹¹The name of the star is Wormwood. A third of the waters became wormwood, and many died from the water, because it was made bitter.

12 The fourth angel blew his trumpet, and a third of the sun was struck, and a third of the moon, and a third of the stars, so that a third of their light was darkened; a third of the day was kept from shining, and likewise the night.

13 Then I looked, and I heard an eagle crying with a loud voice as it flew in midheaven, "Woe, woe, woe to the inhabitants of the earth, at the blasts of the other trumpets that the three angels are about to blow!"

## PSALM 136.1–26

O GIVE thanks to the LORD, for
    he is good,
  for his steadfast love
    endures forever.
2 O give thanks to the God of
    gods,
  for his steadfast love endures
    forever.
3 O give thanks to the Lord of
    lords,
  for his steadfast love endures
    forever;

4 who alone does great wonders,
  for his steadfast love endures
    forever;
5 who by understanding made the
    heavens,
  for his steadfast love endures
    forever;
6 who spread out the earth on the
    waters,
  for his steadfast love endures
    forever;
7 who made the great lights,
  for his steadfast love endures
    forever;
8 the sun to rule over the day,
  for his steadfast love endures
    forever;
9 the moon and stars to rule over
    the night,
  for his steadfast love endures
    forever;

10 who struck Egypt through their
    firstborn,
  for his steadfast love endures
    forever;
11 and brought Israel out from
    among them,
  for his steadfast love endures
    forever;
12 with a strong hand and an
    outstretched arm,
  for his steadfast love endures
    forever;

13 who divided the Red Sea[a] in
    two,
        for his steadfast love endures
        forever;
14 and made Israel pass through
    the midst of it,
        for his steadfast love endures
        forever;
15 but overthrew Pharaoh and his
    army in the Red Sea,[a]
        for his steadfast love endures
        forever;
16 who led his people through the
    wilderness,
        for his steadfast love endures
        forever;
17 who struck down great kings,
        for his steadfast love endures
        forever;
18 and killed famous kings,
        for his steadfast love endures
        forever;
19 Sihon, king of the Amorites,
        for his steadfast love endures
        forever;
20 and Og, king of Bashan,
        for his steadfast love endures
        forever;
21 and gave their land as a
    heritage,
        for his steadfast love endures
        forever;
22 a heritage to his servant Israel,
        for his steadfast love endures
        forever.

23 It is he who remembered us in
    our low estate,
        for his steadfast love endures
        forever;
24 and rescued us from our foes,
        for his steadfast love endures
        forever;
25 who gives food to all flesh,
        for his steadfast love endures
        forever.

26 O give thanks to the God of
    heaven,
        for his steadfast love endures
        forever.

## PROVERBS 30.7–9

Two things I ask of you;
    do not deny them to me
        before I die:
8 Remove far from me falsehood
    and lying;
        give me neither poverty nor
        riches;
        feed me with the food that
        I need,
9 or I shall be full, and deny you,
    and say, "Who is the LORD?"
    or I shall be poor, and steal,
    and profane the name of my
        God.

[a] Or *Sea of Reeds*

# DECEMBER 18

HABAKKUK 1.1—3.19

THE oracle that the prophet Habakkuk saw.

2  O LORD, how long shall I cry
        for help,
    and you will not listen?
    Or cry to you "Violence!"
    and you will not save?
3  Why do you make me see
        wrongdoing
    and look at trouble?
    Destruction and violence are
        before me;
    strife and contention arise.
4  So the law becomes slack
    and justice never prevails.
    The wicked surround the
        righteous—
    therefore judgment comes
        forth perverted.

5  Look at the nations, and see!
    Be astonished! Be astounded!
    For a work is being done in
        your days
    that you would not believe if
        you were told.
6  For I am rousing the Chaldeans,
    that fierce and impetuous
        nation,
    who march through the breadth
        of the earth
    to seize dwellings not their
        own.
7  Dread and fearsome are they;
    their justice and dignity
        proceed from
        themselves.
8  Their horses are swifter than
        leopards,
    more menacing than wolves
        at dusk;

their horses charge.
Their horsemen come from
        far away;
    they fly like an eagle swift
        to devour.
9  They all come for violence,
    with faces pressing[a] forward;
    they gather captives like
        sand.
10  At kings they scoff,
    and of rulers they make
        sport.
    They laugh at every fortress,
    and heap up earth to take it.
11  Then they sweep by like the
        wind;
    they transgress and become
        guilty;
    their own might is their god!

12  Are you not from of old,
    O LORD my God, my Holy
        One?
    You[b] shall not die.
    O LORD, you have marked them
        for judgment;
    and you, O Rock, have
        established them for
        punishment.
13  Your eyes are too pure to
        behold evil,
    and you cannot look on
        wrongdoing;
    why do you look on the
        treacherous,
    and are silent when the
        wicked swallow
    those more righteous than
        they?
14  You have made people like the
        fish of the sea,
    like crawling things that have
        no ruler.

a Meaning of Heb uncertain   b Ancient Heb tradition: MT *We*

15 The enemya brings all of them
    up with a hook;
  he drags them out with his
    net,
  he gathers them in his seine;
    so he rejoices and exults.
16 Therefore he sacrifices to his
    net
  and makes offerings to his
    seine;
  for by them his portion is lavish,
    and his food is rich.
17 Is he then to keep on emptying
    his net,
  and destroying nations
    without mercy?

2.1 I WILL stand at my watchpost,
    and station myself on the
    rampart;
  I will keep watch to see what
    he will say to me,
  and what heb will answer
    concerning my complaint.
2 Then the LORD answered me
    and said:
  Write the vision;
    make it plain on tablets,
    so that a runner may read it.
3 For there is still a vision for the
    appointed time;
  it speaks of the end, and does
    not lie.
  If it seems to tarry, wait for it;
    it will surely come, it will
    not delay.
4 Look at the proud!
  Their spirit is not right in
    them,
  but the righteous live by
    their faith. c
5 Moreover, wealthd is
    treacherous;
  the arrogant do not endure.
  They open their throats wide
    as Sheol;
  like Death they never have
    enough.

  They gather all nations for
    themselves,
  and collect all peoples as
    their own.

6 Shall not everyone taunt such
people and, with mocking riddles, say
about them,
  "Alas for you who heap up what
    is not your own!"
  How long will you load
    yourselves with goods
    taken in pledge?
7 Will not your own creditors
    suddenly rise,
  and those who make you
    tremble wake up?
  Then you will be booty for
    them.
8 Because you have plundered
    many nations,
  all that survive of the peoples
    shall plunder you—
  because of human bloodshed,
    and violence to the
    earth,
  to cities and all who live in
    them.

9 "Alas for you who get evil gain
    for your houses,
  setting your nest on high
  to be safe from the reach of
    harm!"
10 You have devised shame for
    your house
  by cutting off many peoples;
  you have forfeited your life.
11 The very stones will cry out
    from the wall,
  and the plastere will respond
    from the woodwork.

12 "Alas for you who build a town
    by bloodshed,
  and found a city on iniquity!"
13 Is it not from the LORD of hosts
    that peoples labor only to
    feed the flames,

aHeb *He*   bSyr: Heb *I*   cOr *faithfulness*   dOther Heb Mss read *wine*   eOr *beam*

and nations weary themselves
for nothing?
14 But the earth will be filled
with the knowledge of the
glory of the LORD,
as the waters cover the sea.

15 "Alas for you who make your
neighbors drink,
pouring out your wrath[a] until
they are drunk,
in order to gaze on their
nakedness!"
16 You will be sated with contempt
instead of glory.
Drink, you yourself, and
stagger![b]
The cup in the LORD's right hand
will come around to you,
and shame will come upon
your glory!
17 For the violence done to
Lebanon will overwhelm
you;
the destruction of the animals
will terrify you—[c]
because of human bloodshed and
violence to the earth,
to cities and all who live in
them.

18 What use is an idol
once its maker has shaped
it—
a cast image, a teacher of
lies?
For its maker trusts in what has
been made,
though the product is only an
idol that cannot speak!
19 Alas for you who say to the
wood, "Wake up!"
to silent stone, "Rouse
yourself!"
Can it teach?
See, it is gold and silver plated,
and there is no breath in it
at all.

20 But the LORD is in his holy
temple;
let all the earth keep silence
before him!

3.1 A PRAYER of the prophet Habakkuk
according to Shigionoth.

2 O LORD, I have heard of your
renown,
and I stand in awe, O LORD,
of your work.
In our own time revive it;
in our own time make it
known;
in wrath may you remember
mercy.
3 God came from Teman,
the Holy One from Mount
Paran. _Selah_
His glory covered the heavens,
and the earth was full of
his praise.
4 The brightness was like the
sun;
rays came forth from his
hand,
where his power lay hidden.
5 Before him went pestilence,
and plague followed close
behind.
6 He stopped and shook the
earth;
he looked and made the
nations tremble.
The eternal mountains were
shattered;
along his ancient pathways
the everlasting hills sank low.
7 I saw the tents of Cushan under
affliction;
the tent-curtains of the land
of Midian trembled.
8 Was your wrath against the
rivers, [d] O LORD?

[a]Or _poison_   [b]Q Ms Gk: MT _be uncircumcised_   [c]Gk Syr: Meaning of Heb uncertain   [d]Or _against
River_

Or your anger against the
    rivers, [a]
or your rage against the
    sea, [b]
when you drove your horses,
    your chariots to victory?
9 You brandished your naked
    bow,
    sated[c] were the arrows at
        your command. [d]   *Selah*
    You split the earth with
        rivers.
10 The mountains saw you,
    and writhed;
    a torrent of water swept by;
    the deep gave forth its voice.
    The sun[e] raised high its
        hands;
11 the moon[f] stood still in its
    exalted place,
    at the light of your arrows
        speeding by,
    at the gleam of your flashing
        spear.
12 In fury you trod the earth,
    in anger you trampled
        nations.
13 You came forth to save your
    people,
    to save your anointed.
    You crushed the head of the
        wicked house,
    laying it bare from foundation
        to roof. [d]   *Selah*
14 You pierced with his own
    arrows the head[g] of his
    warriors, [h]
    who came like a whirlwind to
        scatter us, [i]
    gloating as if ready to devour
        the poor who were in
        hiding.
15 You trampled the sea with
    your horses,
    churning the mighty waters.

16 I hear, and I tremble within;

my lips quiver at the sound.
Rottenness enters into my
    bones,
    and my steps tremble[j]
    beneath me.
I wait quietly for the day of
    calamity
    to come upon the people who
    attack us.

17 Though the fig tree does not
    blossom,
    and no fruit is on the vines;
    though the produce of the
        olive fails
    and the fields yield no food;
    though the flock is cut off from
        the fold
    and there is no herd in the
        stalls,
18 yet I will rejoice in the LORD;
    I will exult in the God of my
        salvation.
19 GOD, the Lord, is my strength;
    he makes my feet like the
        feet of a deer,
    and makes me tread upon the
        heights. [k]

To the leader: with stringed[l]
    instruments.

# REVELATION 9.1–21

AND the fifth angel blew his trumpet, and I saw a star that had fallen from heaven to earth, and he was given the key to the shaft of the bottomless pit; ²he opened the shaft of the bottomless pit, and from the shaft rose smoke like the smoke of a great furnace, and the sun and the air were darkened with the smoke from the shaft. ³Then from the smoke came locusts on the earth, and they were given authority like the authority of scorpions of the earth. ⁴They were told

---

aOr *against River*  bOr *against Sea*  cCn: Heb *oaths*  dMeaning of Heb uncertain  eHeb *It*
fHeb *sun, moon*  gOr *leader*  hVg Compare Gk Syr: Meaning of Heb uncertain  iHeb *me*
jCn Compare Gk: Meaning of Heb uncertain  kHeb *my heights*  lHeb *my stringed*

not to damage the grass of the earth or any green growth or any tree, but only those people who do not have the seal of God on their foreheads. [5]They were allowed to torture them for five months, but not to kill them, and their torture was like the torture of a scorpion when it stings someone. [6]And in those days people will seek death but will not find it; they will long to die, but death will flee from them.

7  In appearance the locusts were like horses equipped for battle. On their heads were what looked like crowns of gold; their faces were like human faces, [8]their hair like women's hair, and their teeth like lions' teeth; [9]they had scales like iron breastplates, and the noise of their wings was like the noise of many chariots with horses rushing into battle. [10]They have tails like scorpions, with stingers, and in their tails is their power to harm people for five months. [11]They have as king over them the angel of the bottomless pit; his name in Hebrew is Abaddon, [a] and in Greek he is called Apollyon. [b]

12  The first woe has passed. There are still two woes to come.

13  Then the sixth angel blew his trumpet, and I heard a voice from the four[c] horns of the golden altar before God, [14]saying to the sixth angel who had the trumpet, "Release the four angels who are bound at the great river Euphrates." [15]So the four angels were released, who had been held ready for the hour, the day, the month, and the year, to kill a third of humankind. [16]The number of the troops of cavalry was two hundred million; I heard their number. [17]And this was how I saw the horses in my vision: the riders wore breastplates the color of fire and of sapphire[d] and of sulfur; the heads of the horses were like lions' heads, and fire and smoke and sulfur came out of their mouths. [18]By these three plagues a third of humankind was killed, by the fire and smoke and sulfur coming out of their mouths. [19]For the power of the horses is in their mouths and in their tails; their tails are like serpents, having heads; and with them they inflict harm.

20  The rest of humankind, who were not killed by these plagues, did not repent of the works of their hands or give up worshiping demons and idols of gold and silver and bronze and stone and wood, which cannot see or hear or walk. [21]And they did not repent of their murders or their sorceries or their fornication or their thefts.

## PSALM 137.1–9

By the rivers of Babylon—
  there we sat down and there
    we wept
  when we remembered Zion.
2  On the willows[e] there
    we hung up our harps.
3  For there our captors
    asked us for songs,
and our tormentors asked for
      mirth, saying,
  "Sing us one of the songs of
    Zion!"

4  How could we sing the LORD's
      song
  in a foreign land?
5  If I forget you, O Jerusalem,
    let my right hand wither!
6  Let my tongue cling to the roof
      of my mouth,
    if I do not remember you,
  if I do not set Jerusalem
    above my highest joy.

7  Remember, O LORD, against the
      Edomites
  the day of Jerusalem's fall,
  how they said, "Tear it down!
      Tear it down!

aThat is, *Destruction*  bThat is, *Destroyer*  cOther ancient authorities lack *four*  dGk *hyacinth*  eOr *poplars*

Down to its foundations!"
8 O daughter Babylon, you
    devastator!a
  Happy shall they be who pay
    you back
  what you have done to us!
9  Happy shall they be who take
    your little ones
  and dash them against the
    rock!

## PROVERBS 30.10

Do not slander a servant to a
    master,
  or the servant will curse
    you, and you will be held
    guilty.

# DECEMBER 19

## ZEPHANIAH 1.1—3.20

THE word of the LORD that came to Zephaniah son of Cushi son of Gedaliah son of Amariah son of Hezekiah, in the days of King Josiah son of Amon of Judah.

2  I will utterly sweep away
    everything
  from the face of the earth,
    says the LORD.
3  I will sweep away humans and
    animals;
  I will sweep away the birds of
    the air
  and the fish of the sea.
  I will make the wicked
    stumble. b
  I will cut off humanity
  from the face of the earth,
    says the LORD.
4  I will stretch out my hand
    against Judah,
  and against all the inhabitants
    of Jerusalem;
  and I will cut off from this place
    every remnant of Baal
  and the name of the
    idolatrous priests; c

5  those who bow down on the
    roofs
  to the host of the heavens;
  those who bow down and swear
    to the LORD,
  but also swear by Milcom; d
6  those who have turned back
    from following the LORD,
  who have not sought the LORD
    or inquired of him.

7  Be silent before the Lord GOD!
  For the day of the LORD is
    at hand;
  the LORD has prepared a
    sacrifice,
  he has consecrated his
    guests.
8  And on the day of the LORD's
    sacrifice
  I will punish the officials and the
    king's sons
  and all who dress themselves
    in foreign attire.
9  On that day I will punish
  all who leap over the
    threshold,
  who fill their master's house
  with violence and fraud.

aOr *you who are devastated*  bCn: Heb *sea, and those who cause the wicked to stumble*  cCompare
Gk: Heb *the idolatrous priests with the priests*  dGk Mss Syr Vg: Heb *Malcam* (or, *their king*)

10 On that day, says the LORD,
   a cry will be heard from the
      Fish Gate,
  a wail from the Second Quarter,
  a loud crash from the hills.
11 The inhabitants of the Mortar
     wail,
   for all the traders have
      perished;
   all who weigh out silver are
      cut off.
12 At that time I will search
     Jerusalem with lamps,
  and I will punish the people
  who rest complacently**a** on
     their dregs,
   those who say in their hearts,
  "The LORD will not do good,
   nor will he do harm."
13 Their wealth shall be plundered,
   and their houses laid waste.
  Though they build houses,
   they shall not inhabit them;
  though they plant vineyards,
   they shall not drink wine
     from them.

14 The great day of the LORD is
     near,
   near and hastening fast;
  the sound of the day of the
     LORD is bitter,
   the warrior cries aloud there.
15 That day will be a day of wrath,
   a day of distress and anguish,
  a day of ruin and devastation,
   a day of darkness and gloom,
  a day of clouds and thick
     darkness,
16   a day of trumpet blast and
     battle cry
  against the fortified cities
   and against the lofty
     battlements.

17 I will bring such distress upon
     people

  that they shall walk like
     the blind;
  because they have sinned
     against the LORD,
  their blood shall be poured out
     like dust,
  and their flesh like dung.
18 Neither their silver nor their
     gold
   will be able to save them
   on the day of the LORD's
     wrath;
  in the fire of his passion
   the whole earth shall be
     consumed;
  for a full, a terrible end
   he will make of all the
     inhabitants of the earth.

2.1 GATHER together, gather,
   O shameless nation,
2 before you are driven away
   like the drifting chaff, **b**
  before there comes upon you
   the fierce anger of the LORD,
  before there comes upon you
   the day of the LORD's wrath.
3 Seek the LORD, all you humble
   of the land,
  who do his commands;
  seek righteousness, seek
     humility;
   perhaps you may be hidden
   on the day of the LORD's
     wrath.
4 For Gaza shall be deserted,
   and Ashkelon shall become a
     desolation;
  Ashdod's people shall be driven
     out at noon,
   and Ekron shall be uprooted.

5 Ah, inhabitants of the seacoast,
   you nation of the Cherethites!
  The word of the LORD is
     against you,
   O Canaan, land of the
     Philistines;

**a**Heb *who thicken*   **b**Cn Compare Gk Syr: Heb *before a decree is born; like chaff a day has passed away*

and I will destroy you until no
  inhabitant is left.
6 And you, O seacoast, shall be
    pastures,
  meadows for shepherds
  and folds for flocks.
7 The seacoast shall become the
    possession
  of the remnant of the house
    of Judah,
  on which they shall pasture,
and in the houses of Ashkelon
  they shall lie down at
    evening.
For the Lord their God will be
  mindful of them
  and restore their fortunes.

8 I have heard the taunts of Moab
  and the revilings of the
    Ammonites,
how they have taunted my
  people
  and made boasts against
    their territory.
9 Therefore, as I live, says the
    Lord of hosts,
  the God of Israel,
Moab shall become like Sodom
  and the Ammonites like
    Gomorrah,
a land possessed by nettles and
  salt pits,
  and a waste forever.
The remnant of my people shall
  plunder them,
  and the survivors of my
    nation shall possess
    them.
10 This shall be their lot in return
    for their pride,
  because they scoffed and
    boasted
  against the people of the Lord
    of hosts.
11 The Lord will be terrible
    against them;

he will shrivel all the gods of
  the earth,
and to him shall bow down,
  each in its place,
  all the coasts and islands of
    the nations.

12 You also, O Ethiopians, a
  shall be killed by my sword.

13 And he will stretch out his hand
    against the north,
  and destroy Assyria;
and he will make Nineveh a
  desolation,
  a dry waste like the desert.
14 Herds shall lie down in it,
  every wild animal; b
the desert owlc and the
    screech owlc
  shall lodge on its capitals;
the owld shall hoot at the
    window,
  the ravene croak on the
    threshold;
  for its cedar work will be
    laid bare.
15 Is this the exultant city
    that lived secure,
  that said to itself,
    "I am, and there is no one
      else"?
What a desolation it has
    become,
  a lair for wild animals!
Everyone who passes by it
  hisses and shakes the fist.

3.1 Ah, soiled, defiled,
    oppressing city!
2 It has listened to no voice;
  it has accepted no correction.
It has not trusted in the Lord;
  it has not drawn near to its
    God.

3 The officials within it
  are roaring lions;

aOr *Nubians*; Heb *Cushites*   bTg Compare Gk: Heb *nation*   cMeaning of Heb uncertain   dCn: Heb
*a voice*   eGk Vg: Heb *desolation*

its judges are evening wolves
    that leave nothing until
      the morning.
4 Its prophets are reckless,
    faithless persons;
  its priests have profaned what
      is sacred,
    they have done violence to
      the law.
5 The Lord within it is righteous;
    he does no wrong.
  Every morning he renders his
      judgment,
    each dawn without fail;
    but the unjust knows no
      shame.

6 I have cut off nations;
    their battlements are in ruins;
  I have laid waste their streets
    so that no one walks in them;
  their cities have been made
      desolate,
    without people, without
      inhabitants.
7 I said, "Surely the city[a] will
      fear me,
    it will accept correction;
  it will not lose sight[b]
    of all that I have brought
      upon it."
  But they were the more eager
    to make all their deeds
      corrupt.

8 Therefore wait for me, says
      the Lord,
    for the day when I arise as
    a witness.
  For my decision is to gather
      nations,
    to assemble kingdoms,
  to pour out upon them my
      indignation,
    all the heat of my anger;
  for in the fire of my passion
    all the earth shall be
      consumed.

9 At that time I will change the
      speech of the peoples
    to a pure speech,
  that all of them may call on the
      name of the Lord
    and serve him with one
      accord.
10 From beyond the rivers of
      Ethiopia[c]
    my suppliants, my scattered
      ones,
    shall bring my offering.

11 On that day you shall not be put
      to shame
    because of all the deeds by
      which you have rebelled
      against me;
  for then I will remove from
      your midst
    your proudly exultant ones,
  and you shall no longer be
      haughty
    in my holy mountain.
12 For I will leave in the midst of
      you
    a people humble and lowly.
  They shall seek refuge in the
      name of the Lord—
13     the remnant of Israel;
  they shall do no wrong
    and utter no lies,
  nor shall a deceitful tongue
    be found in their mouths.
  Then they will pasture and
    lie down,
    and no one shall make them
      afraid.

14 Sing aloud, O daughter Zion;
    shout, O Israel!
  Rejoice and exult with all
      your heart,
    O daughter Jerusalem!
15 The Lord has taken away the
      judgments against you,

a Heb *it*  b Gk Syr: Heb *its dwelling will not be cut off*  c Or *Nubia*; Heb *Cush*

he has turned away your
   enemies.
The king of Israel, the LORD, is
   in your midst;
   you shall fear disaster no
      more.
16 On that day it shall be said to
   Jerusalem:
Do not fear, O Zion;
   do not let your hands grow
      weak.
17 The LORD, your God, is in
   your midst,
   a warrior who gives victory;
he will rejoice over you with
   gladness,
   he will renew you[a] in his
      love;
he will exult over you with
   loud singing
18    as on a day of festival.[b]
I will remove disaster from
   you,[c]
   so that you will not bear
      reproach for it.
19 I will deal with all your
      oppressors
   at that time.
And I will save the lame
   and gather the outcast,
and I will change their shame
   into praise
and renown in all the earth.
20 At that time I will bring you
      home,
   at the time when I gather
      you;
for I will make you renowned
   and praised
among all the peoples of
   the earth,
when I restore your fortunes
   before your eyes, says the
   LORD.

## REVELATION 10.1–11

AND I saw another mighty angel coming down from heaven, wrapped in a cloud, with a rainbow over his head; his face was like the sun, and his legs like pillars of fire. ²He held a little scroll open in his hand. Setting his right foot on the sea and his left foot on the land, ³he gave a great shout, like a lion roaring. And when he shouted, the seven thunders sounded. ⁴And when the seven thunders had sounded, I was about to write, but I heard a voice from heaven saying, "Seal up what the seven thunders have said, and do not write it down." ⁵Then the angel whom I saw standing on the sea and the land

   raised his right hand to heaven
6    and swore by him who lives
      forever and ever,

who created heaven and what is in it, the earth and what is in it, and the sea and what is in it: "There will be no more delay, ⁷but in the days when the seventh angel is to blow his trumpet, the mystery of God will be fulfilled, as he announced to his servants[d] the prophets."

8 Then the voice that I had heard from heaven spoke to me again, saying, "Go, take the scroll that is open in the hand of the angel who is standing on the sea and on the land." ⁹So I went to the angel and told him to give me the little scroll; and he said to me, "Take it, and eat; it will be bitter to your stomach, but sweet as honey in your mouth." ¹⁰So I took the little scroll from the hand of the angel and ate it; it was sweet as honey in my mouth, but when I had eaten it, my stomach was made bitter.

11 Then they said to me, "You must prophesy again about many peoples and nations and languages and kings."

---

aGk Syr: Heb *he will be silent*  bGk Syr: Meaning of Heb uncertain  cCn: Heb *I will remove from you; they were*  dGk *slaves*

## PSALM 138.1–8

*Of David.*

**I** GIVE you thanks, O LORD, with
    my whole heart;
  before the gods I sing your
    praise;
2 I bow down toward your holy
    temple
  and give thanks to your name
    for your steadfast love
    and your faithfulness;
  for you have exalted your
    name and your word
    above everything. **a**
3 On the day I called, you
    answered me,
  you increased my strength of
    soul. **b**

4 All the kings of the earth shall
    praise you, O LORD,
  for they have heard the
    words of your mouth.
5 They shall sing of the ways of
    the LORD,
  for great is the glory of the
    LORD.
6 For though the LORD is high, he
    regards the lowly;
  but the haughty he perceives
    from far away.
7 Though I walk in the midst of
    trouble,
  you preserve me against the
    wrath of my enemies;
  you stretch out your hand,
    and your right hand delivers
    me.
8 The LORD will fulfill his purpose
    for me;
  your steadfast love, O LORD,
    endures forever.
  Do not forsake the work of
    your hands.

## PROVERBS 30.11–14

**T** HERE are those who curse
    their fathers
  and do not bless their
    mothers.
12 There are those who are pure
    in their own eyes
  yet are not cleansed of their
    filthiness.
13 There are those—how lofty are
    their eyes,
  how high their eyelids lift!
14 There are those whose teeth
    are swords,
  whose teeth are knives,
  to devour the poor from off the
    earth,
  the needy from among
    mortals.

**a** Cn: Heb *you have exalted your word above all your name*   **b** Syr Compare Gk Tg: Heb *you made me arrogant in my soul with strength*

# DECEMBER 20

## HAGGAI 1.1—2.23

In the second year of King Darius, in the sixth month, on the first day of the month, the word of the Lord came by the prophet Haggai to Zerubbabel son of Shealtiel, governor of Judah, and to Joshua son of Jehozadak, the high priest: ²Thus says the Lord of hosts: These people say the time has not yet come to rebuild the Lord's house. ³Then the word of the Lord came by the prophet Haggai, saying: ⁴Is it a time for you yourselves to live in your paneled houses, while this house lies in ruins? ⁵Now therefore thus says the Lord of hosts: Consider how you have fared. ⁶You have sown much, and harvested little; you eat, but you never have enough; you drink, but you never have your fill; you clothe yourselves, but no one is warm; and you that earn wages earn wages to put them into a bag with holes.

7 Thus says the Lord of hosts: Consider how you have fared. ⁸Go up to the hills and bring wood and build the house, so that I may take pleasure in it and be honored, says the Lord. ⁹You have looked for much, and, lo, it came to little; and when you brought it home, I blew it away. Why? says the Lord of hosts. Because my house lies in ruins, while all of you hurry off to your own houses. ¹⁰Therefore the heavens above you have withheld the dew, and the earth has withheld its produce. ¹¹And I have called for a drought on the land and the hills, on the grain, the new wine, the oil, on what the soil produces, on human beings and animals, and on all their labors.

12 Then Zerubbabel son of Shealtiel, and Joshua son of Jehozadak, the high priest, with all the remnant of the people, obeyed the voice of the Lord their God, and the words of the prophet Haggai, as the Lord their God had sent him; and the people feared the Lord. ¹³Then Haggai, the messenger of the Lord, spoke to the people with the Lord's message, saying, I am with you, says the Lord. ¹⁴And the Lord stirred up the spirit of Zerubbabel son of Shealtiel, governor of Judah, and the spirit of Joshua son of Jehozadak, the high priest, and the spirit of all the remnant of the people; and they came and worked on the house of the Lord of hosts, their God, ¹⁵on the twenty-fourth day of the month, in the sixth month.

2.1 In the second year of King Darius, ¹in the seventh month, on the twenty-first day of the month, the word of the Lord came by the prophet Haggai, saying: ²Speak now to Zerubbabel son of Shealtiel, governor of Judah, and to Joshua son of Jehozadak, the high priest, and to the remnant of the people, and say, ³Who is left among you that saw this house in its former glory? How does it look to you now? Is it not in your sight as nothing? ⁴Yet now take courage, O Zerubbabel, says the Lord; take courage, O Joshua, son of Jehozadak, the high priest; take courage, all you people of the land, says the Lord; work, for I am with you, says the Lord of hosts, ⁵according to the promise that I made you when you came out of Egypt. My spirit abides among you; do not fear. ⁶For thus says the Lord of hosts: Once again, in a little while, I will shake the heavens and the earth and the sea and the dry land; ⁷and I will shake all the nations, so that the treasure of all nations shall come, and I will fill this house with splendor, says the Lord of hosts. ⁸The silver is mine, and the gold is mine, says the Lord of hosts. ⁹The latter splendor of this house shall be greater than the former, says the Lord of hosts; and in this place I will give prosperity, says the Lord of hosts.

10 On the twenty-fourth day of the ninth month, in the second year of Darius, the word of the Lord came by the prophet Haggai, saying: ¹¹Thus says the Lord of hosts: Ask the priests for a ruling: ¹²If one carries consecrated meat in the fold of one's garment, and with the fold touches bread, or stew, or wine, or oil, or any kind of food, does it become holy? The priests answered, "No." ¹³Then Haggai said, "If one who is unclean by contact with a dead body touches any of these, does it become unclean?" The priests answered, "Yes, it becomes unclean." ¹⁴Haggai then said, So is it with this people, and with this nation before me, says the Lord; and so with every work of their hands; and what they offer there is unclean. ¹⁵But now, consider what will come to pass from this day on. Before a stone was placed upon a stone in the Lord's temple, ¹⁶how did you fare?ᵃ When one came to a heap of twenty measures, there were but ten; when one came to the winevat to draw fifty measures, there were but twenty. ¹⁷I struck you and all the products of your toil with blight and mildew and hail; yet you did not return to me, says the Lord. ¹⁸Consider from this day on, from the twenty-fourth day of the ninth month. Since the day that the foundation of the Lord's temple was laid, consider: ¹⁹Is there any seed left in the barn? Do the vine, the fig tree, the pomegranate, and the olive tree still yield nothing? From this day on I will bless you.

20 The word of the Lord came a second time to Haggai on the twenty-fourth day of the month: ²¹Speak to Zerubbabel, governor of Judah, saying, I am about to shake the heavens and the earth, ²²and to overthrow the throne of kingdoms; I am about to destroy the strength of the kingdoms of the nations, and overthrow the chariots and their riders; and the horses and their riders shall fall, every one by the sword of a comrade. ²³On that day, says the Lord of hosts, I will take you, O Zerubbabel my servant, son of Shealtiel, says the Lord, and make you like a signet ring; for I have chosen you, says the Lord of hosts.

## REVELATION 11.1–19

THEN I was given a measuring rod like a staff, and I was told, "Come and measure the temple of God and the altar and those who worship there, ²but do not measure the court outside the temple; leave that out, for it is given over to the nations, and they will trample over the holy city for forty-two months. ³And I will grant my two witnesses authority to prophesy for one thousand two hundred sixty days, wearing sackcloth."

4 These are the two olive trees and the two lampstands that stand before the Lord of the earth. ⁵And if anyone wants to harm them, fire pours from their mouth and consumes their foes; anyone who wants to harm them must be killed in this manner. ⁶They have authority to shut the sky, so that no rain may fall during the days of their prophesying, and they have authority over the waters to turn them into blood, and to strike the earth with every kind of plague, as often as they desire.

7 When they have finished their testimony, the beast that comes up from the bottomless pit will make war on them and conquer them and kill them, ⁸and their dead bodies will lie in the street of the great city that is propheticallyᵇ called Sodom and Egypt,

---

ᵃGk: Heb *since they were*  ᵇOr *allegorically*; Gk *spiritually*

where also their Lord was crucified. [9]For three and a half days members of the peoples and tribes and languages and nations will gaze at their dead bodies and refuse to let them be placed in a tomb; [10]and the inhabitants of the earth will gloat over them and celebrate and exchange presents, because these two prophets had been a torment to the inhabitants of the earth.

11  But after the three and a half days, the breath[a] of life from God entered them, and they stood on their feet, and those who saw them were terrified. [12]Then they[b] heard a loud voice from heaven saying to them, "Come up here!" And they went up to heaven in a cloud while their enemies watched them. [13]At that moment there was a great earthquake, and a tenth of the city fell; seven thousand people were killed in the earthquake, and the rest were terrified and gave glory to the God of heaven.

14  The second woe has passed. The third woe is coming very soon.

15  Then the seventh angel blew his trumpet, and there were loud voices in heaven, saying,

> "The kingdom of the world has
>     become the kingdom of
>     our Lord
>     and of his Messiah, [c]
> and he will reign forever and
>     ever."

16  Then the twenty-four elders who sit on their thrones before God fell on their faces and worshiped God, [17]singing,

> "We give you thanks, Lord
>     God Almighty,
>   who are and who were,
>   for you have taken your
>     great power
>   and begun to reign.
> [18]  The nations raged,
>   but your wrath has come,

>   and the time for judging
>     the dead,
> for rewarding your servants, [d]
>     the prophets
>   and saints and all who fear
>     your name,
>   both small and great,
> and for destroying those who
>     destroy the earth."

19  Then God's temple in heaven was opened, and the ark of his covenant was seen within his temple; and there were flashes of lightning, rumblings, peals of thunder, an earthquake, and heavy hail.

## PSALM 139.1–24

*To the leader. Of David. A Psalm.*

O LORD, you have searched me
    and known me.
[2]  You know when I sit
    down and when I rise up;
you discern my thoughts from
    far away.
[3]  You search out my path and my
    lying down,
  and are acquainted with all
    my ways.
[4]  Even before a word is on my
    tongue,
  O LORD, you know it
    completely.
[5]  You hem me in, behind and
    before,
  and lay your hand upon me.
[6]  Such knowledge is too
    wonderful for me;
  it is so high that I cannot
    attain it.

[7]  Where can I go from your
    spirit?
  Or where can I flee from your
    presence?
[8]  If I ascend to heaven, you are
    there;
  if I make my bed in Sheol,
    you are there.

---

9 If I take the wings of the
      morning
   and settle at the farthest
      limits of the sea,
10 even there your hand shall
      lead me,
   and your right hand shall hold
      me fast.
11 If I say, "Surely the darkness
      shall cover me,
   and the light around me
      become night,"
12 even the darkness is not dark
      to you;
   the night is as bright as the
      day,
   for darkness is as light to
      you.

13 For it was you who formed my
      inward parts;
   you knit me together in my
      mother's womb.
14 I praise you, for I am fearfully
      and wonderfully made.
   Wonderful are your works;
   that I know very well.
15    My frame was not hidden
      from you,
   when I was being made in
      secret,
      intricately woven in the
      depths of the earth.
16 Your eyes beheld my unformed
      substance.
   In your book were written
      all the days that were formed
      for me,
      when none of them as yet
      existed.
17 How weighty to me are your
      thoughts, O God!
   How vast is the sum of them!
18 I try to count them—they are
      more than the sand;
   I come to the end[a]—I am
      still with you.

19 O that you would kill the
      wicked, O God,
   and that the bloodthirsty
      would depart from me—
20 those who speak of you
      maliciously,
   and lift themselves up against
      you for evil![b]
21 Do I not hate those who hate
      you, O Lord?
   And do I not loathe those
      who rise up against you?
22 I hate them with perfect hatred;
   I count them my enemies.
23 Search me, O God, and know
      my heart;
   test me and know my
      thoughts.
24 See if there is any wicked[c] way
      in me,
   and lead me in the way
      everlasting. [d]

# PROVERBS 30.15–16

THE leech[e] has two daughters;
   "Give, give," they cry.
   Three things are never
      satisfied;
   four never say, "Enough":
16 Sheol, the barren womb,
   the earth ever thirsty for
      water,
   and the fire that never says,
      "Enough."[e]

# DECEMBER 21

## ZECHARIAH 1.1–21

In the eighth month, in the second year of Darius, the word of the Lord came to the prophet Zechariah son of Berechiah son of Iddo, saying: ²The Lord was very angry with your ancestors. ³Therefore say to them, Thus says the Lord of hosts: Return to me, says the Lord of hosts, and I will return to you, says the Lord of hosts. ⁴Do not be like your ancestors, to whom the former prophets proclaimed, "Thus says the Lord of hosts, Return from your evil ways and from your evil deeds." But they did not hear or heed me, says the Lord. ⁵Your ancestors, where are they? And the prophets, do they live forever? ⁶But my words and my statutes, which I commanded my servants the prophets, did they not overtake your ancestors? So they repented and said, "The Lord of hosts has dealt with us according to our ways and deeds, just as he planned to do."

7 On the twenty-fourth day of the eleventh month, the month of Shebat, in the second year of Darius, the word of the Lord came to the prophet Zechariah son of Berechiah son of Iddo; and Zechariah[a] said, ⁸In the night I saw a man riding on a red horse! He was standing among the myrtle trees in the glen; and behind him were red, sorrel, and white horses. ⁹Then I said, "What are these, my lord?" The angel who talked with me said to me, "I will show you what they are." ¹⁰So the man who was standing among the myrtle trees answered, "They are those whom the Lord has sent to patrol the earth." ¹¹Then they spoke to the angel of the Lord who was standing among the myrtle trees, "We have patrolled the earth, and lo, the whole earth remains at peace." ¹²Then the angel of the Lord said, "O Lord of hosts, how long will you withhold mercy from Jerusalem and the cities of Judah, with which you have been angry these seventy years?" ¹³Then the Lord replied with gracious and comforting words to the angel who talked with me. ¹⁴So the angel who talked with me said to me, Proclaim this message: Thus says the Lord of hosts; I am very jealous for Jerusalem and for Zion. ¹⁵And I am extremely angry with the nations that are at ease; for while I was only a little angry, they made the disaster worse. ¹⁶Therefore, thus says the Lord, I have returned to Jerusalem with compassion; my house shall be built in it, says the Lord of hosts, and the measuring line shall be stretched out over Jerusalem. ¹⁷Proclaim further: Thus says the Lord of hosts: My cities shall again overflow with prosperity; the Lord will again comfort Zion and again choose Jerusalem.

18[b] And I looked up and saw four horns. ¹⁹I asked the angel who talked with me, "What are these?" And he answered me, "These are the horns that have scattered Judah, Israel, and Jerusalem." ²⁰Then the Lord showed me four blacksmiths. ²¹And I asked, "What are they coming to do?" He answered, "These are the horns that scattered Judah, so that no head could be raised; but these have come to terrify them, to strike down the horns of the nations that lifted up their horns against the land of Judah to scatter its people."[c]

a Heb *and he*   b Ch 2.1 in Heb   c Heb *it*

## REVELATION 12.1–17

A GREAT portent appeared in heaven: a woman clothed with the sun, with the moon under her feet, and on her head a crown of twelve stars. ²She was pregnant and was crying out in birth pangs, in the agony of giving birth. ³Then another portent appeared in heaven: a great red dragon, with seven heads and ten horns, and seven diadems on his heads. ⁴His tail swept down a third of the stars of heaven and threw them to the earth. Then the dragon stood before the woman who was about to bear a child, so that he might devour her child as soon as it was born. ⁵And she gave birth to a son, a male child, who is to rule[a] all the nations with a rod of iron. But her child was snatched away and taken to God and to his throne; ⁶and the woman fled into the wilderness, where she has a place prepared by God, so that there she can be nourished for one thousand two hundred sixty days.

7 And war broke out in heaven; Michael and his angels fought against the dragon. The dragon and his angels fought back, ⁸but they were defeated, and there was no longer any place for them in heaven. ⁹The great dragon was thrown down, that ancient serpent, who is called the Devil and Satan, the deceiver of the whole world—he was thrown down to the earth, and his angels were thrown down with him.

10 Then I heard a loud voice in heaven, proclaiming,

"Now have come the salvation
    and the power
and the kingdom of our God
and the authority of his
    Messiah, [b]
for the accuser of our
    comrades[c] has been
    thrown down,
who accuses them day and
    night before our God.

¹¹ But they have conquered him by
    the blood of the Lamb
and by the word of their
    testimony,
for they did not cling to life
    even in the face of death.
¹² Rejoice then, you heavens
    and those who dwell in them!
But woe to the earth and the
    sea,
for the devil has come down
    to you
with great wrath,
    because he knows that his
    time is short!"

13 So when the dragon saw that he had been thrown down to the earth, he pursued[d] the woman who had given birth to the male child. ¹⁴But the woman was given the two wings of the great eagle, so that she could fly from the serpent into the wilderness, to her place where she is nourished for a time, and times, and half a time. ¹⁵Then from his mouth the serpent poured water like a river after the woman, to sweep her away with the flood. ¹⁶But the earth came to the help of the woman; it opened its mouth and swallowed the river that the dragon had poured from his mouth. ¹⁷Then the dragon was angry with the woman, and went off to make war on the rest of her children, those who keep the commandments of God and hold the testimony of Jesus.

## PSALM 140.1–13

*To the leader. A Psalm of David.*

D ELIVER me, O LORD, from
    evildoers;
    protect me from those who
    are violent,
² who plan evil things in their
    minds
and stir up wars continually.
³ They make their tongue sharp
    as a snake's,

---

a Or *to shepherd*  b Gk *Christ*  c Gk *brothers*  d Or *persecuted*

and under their lips is the
  venom of vipers.    *Selah*

4  Guard me, O LORD, from the
      hands of the wicked;
   protect me from the violent
   who have planned my
      downfall.
5  The arrogant have hidden a trap
      for me,
   and with cords they have
      spread a net, [a]
   along the road they have set
      snares for me.    *Selah*

6  I say to the LORD, "You are
      my God;
   give ear, O LORD, to the
      voice of my
      supplications."
7  O LORD, my Lord, my strong
      deliverer,
   you have covered my head in
      the day of battle.
8  Do not grant, O LORD, the
      desires of the wicked;
   do not further their evil
      plot. [b]    *Selah*

9  Those who surround me lift up
      their heads; [c]
   let the mischief of their lips
      overwhelm them!
10  Let burning coals fall on them!
    Let them be flung into pits,
      no more to rise!
11  Do not let the slanderer be
      established in the land;
    let evil speedily hunt down
      the violent!

12  I know that the LORD maintains
      the cause of the needy,
    and executes justice for the
      poor.
13  Surely the righteous shall give
      thanks to your name;
    the upright shall live in your
      presence.

## PROVERBS 30.17

THE eye that mocks a father
and scorns to obey a mother
will be pecked out by the
   ravens of the valley
and eaten by the vultures.

# DECEMBER 22

## ZECHARIAH 2[d].1—3.10

I LOOKED up and saw a man with a measuring line in his hand. [2]Then I asked, "Where are you going?" He answered me, "To measure Jerusalem, to see what is its width and what is its length." [3]Then the angel who talked with me came forward, and another angel came forward to meet him, [4]and said to him, "Run, say to that young man: Jerusalem shall be inhabited like villages without walls, because of the multitude of people and animals in it. [5]For I will be a wall of fire all around it, says the LORD, and I will be the glory within it."

6 Up, up! Flee from the land of the north, says the LORD; for I have spread you abroad like the four winds of heaven, says the LORD. [7]Up! Escape to

[a] Or *they have spread cords as a net*   [b] Heb adds *they are exalted*   [c] Cn Compare Gk: Heb *those who surround me are uplifted in head*; Heb divides verses 8 and 9 differently   [d] Ch 2.5 in Heb

Zion, you that live with daughter Babylon. [8]For thus said the Lord of hosts (after his glory[a] sent me) regarding the nations that plundered you: Truly, one who touches you touches the apple of my eye.[b] [9]See now, I am going to raise[c] my hand against them, and they shall become plunder for their own slaves. Then you will know that the Lord of hosts has sent me. [10]Sing and rejoice, O daughter Zion! For lo, I will come and dwell in your midst, says the Lord. [11]Many nations shall join themselves to the Lord on that day, and shall be my people; and I will dwell in your midst. And you shall know that the Lord of hosts has sent me to you. [12]The Lord will inherit Judah as his portion in the holy land, and will again choose Jerusalem.

13 Be silent, all people, before the Lord; for he has roused himself from his holy dwelling.

[3.1] Then he showed me the high priest Joshua standing before the angel of the Lord, and Satan[d] standing at his right hand to accuse him. [2]And the Lord said to Satan,[d] "The Lord rebuke you, O Satan![d] The Lord who has chosen Jerusalem rebuke you! Is not this man a brand plucked from the fire?" [3]Now Joshua was dressed with filthy clothes as he stood before the angel. [4]The angel said to those who were standing before him, "Take off his filthy clothes." And to him he said, "See, I have taken your guilt away from you, and I will clothe you with festal apparel." [5]And I said, "Let them put a clean turban on his head." So they put a clean turban on his head and clothed him with the apparel; and the angel of the Lord was standing by.

6 Then the angel of the Lord assured Joshua, saying [7]"Thus says the Lord of hosts: If you will walk in my ways and keep my requirements, then you shall rule my house and have charge of my courts, and I will give you the right of access among those who are standing here. [8]Now listen, Joshua, high priest, you and your colleagues who sit before you! For they are an omen of things to come: I am going to bring my servant the Branch. [9]For on the stone that I have set before Joshua, on a single stone with seven facets, I will engrave its inscription, says the Lord of hosts, and I will remove the guilt of this land in a single day. [10]On that day, says the Lord of hosts, you shall invite each other to come under your vine and fig tree."

## REVELATION 12.18—13.18

THEN the dragon[e] took his stand on the sand of the seashore. [13.1]And I saw a beast rising out of the sea, having ten horns and seven heads; and on its horns were ten diadems, and on its heads were blasphemous names. [2]And the beast that I saw was like a leopard, its feet were like a bear's, and its mouth was like a lion's mouth. And the dragon gave it his power and his throne and great authority. [3]One of its heads seemed to have received a death-blow, but its mortal wound[f] had been healed. In amazement the whole earth followed the beast. [4]They worshiped the dragon, for he had given his authority to the beast, and they worshiped the beast, saying, "Who is like the beast, and who can fight against it?"

5 The beast was given a mouth uttering haughty and blasphemous words, and it was allowed to exercise authority for forty-two months. [6]It opened its mouth to utter blasphemies against God, blaspheming his name and his dwelling, that is, those who dwell in heaven. [7]Also it was allowed to make war on the saints and to conquer

aCn: Heb *after glory he*   bHeb *his eye*   cOr *wave*   dOr *the Accuser;* Heb *the Adversary*   eGk *Then he;* other ancient authorities read *Then I stood*   fGk *the plague of its death*

them. [a] It was given authority over every tribe and people and language and nation, [8]and all the inhabitants of the earth will worship it, everyone whose name has not been written from the foundation of the world in the book of life of the Lamb that was slaughtered. [b]

9  Let anyone who has an ear listen:
[10]  If you are to be taken captive,
        into captivity you go;
    if you kill with the sword,
        with the sword you must be
            killed.
Here is a call for the endurance and faith of the saints.

11  Then I saw another beast that rose out of the earth; it had two horns like a lamb and it spoke like a dragon. [12]It exercises all the authority of the first beast on its behalf, and it makes the earth and its inhabitants worship the first beast, whose mortal wound[c] had been healed. [13]It performs great signs, even making fire come down from heaven to earth in the sight of all; [14]and by the signs that it is allowed to perform on behalf of the beast, it deceives the inhabitants of earth, telling them to make an image for the beast that had been wounded by the sword[d] and yet lived; [15]and it was allowed to give breath[e] to the image of the beast so that the image of the beast could even speak and cause those who would not worship the image of the beast to be killed. [16]Also it causes all, both small and great, both rich and poor, both free and slave, to be marked on the right hand or the forehead, [17]so that no one can buy or sell who does not have the mark, that is, the name of the beast or the number of its name. [18]This calls for wisdom: let anyone with understanding calculate the number of the beast, for it is the number of a person. Its number is six hundred sixty-six. [f]

## PSALM 141. 1–10

*A Psalm of David.*

I CALL upon you, O LORD; come
        quickly to me;
    give ear to my voice when I
        call to you.
2  Let my prayer be counted as
        incense before you,
    and the lifting up of my hands
        as an evening sacrifice.

3  Set a guard over my mouth,
        O LORD;
    keep watch over the door of
        my lips.
4  Do not turn my heart to any
        evil,
    to busy myself with wicked
        deeds
in company with those who
        work iniquity;
    do not let me eat of their
        delicacies.

5  Let the righteous strike me;
    let the faithful correct me.
Never let the oil of the wicked
        anoint my head, [g]
    for my prayer is continually[h]
        against their wicked
        deeds.
6  When they are given over to
        those who shall condemn
        them,
    then they shall learn that my
        words were pleasant.
7  Like a rock that one breaks
        apart and shatters on the
        land,
    so shall their bones be strewn
        at the mouth of Sheol. [i]

8  But my eyes are turned toward
        you, O GOD, my Lord;
    in you I seek refuge; do not
        leave me defenseless.

[a]Other ancient authorities lack this sentence  [b]Or *written in the book of life of the Lamb that was slaughtered from the foundation of the world*  [c]Gk *whose plague of its death*  [d]Or *that had received the plague of the sword*  [e]Or *spirit*  [f]Other ancient authorities read *six hundred sixteen*  [g]Gk: Meaning of Heb uncertain  [h]Cn: Heb *for continually and my prayer*  [i]Meaning of Heb of verses 5-7 is uncertain

9 Keep me from the trap that
    they have laid for me,
  and from the snares of
    evildoers.
10 Let the wicked fall into their
    own nets,
  while I alone escape.

## PROVERBS 30.18–20

THREE things are too wonderful
    for me;
  four I do not understand:
19 the way of an eagle in the sky,

  the way of a snake on a rock,
  the way of a ship on the high
    seas,
  and the way of a man with a
    girl.

20 This is the way of an
    adulteress:
  she eats, and wipes her
    mouth,
  and says, "I have done no
    wrong."

# DECEMBER 23

## ZECHARIAH 4.1—5.11

THE angel who talked with me came again, and wakened me, as one is wakened from sleep. 2He said to me, "What do you see?" And I said, "I see a lampstand all of gold, with a bowl on the top of it; there are seven lamps on it, with seven lips on each of the lamps that are on the top of it. 3And by it there are two olive trees, one on the right of the bowl and the other on its left." 4I said to the angel who talked with me, "What are these, my lord?" 5Then the angel who talked with me answered me, "Do you not know what these are?" I said, "No, my lord." 6He said to me, "This is the word of the LORD to Zerubbabel: Not by might, nor by power, but by my spirit, says the LORD of hosts. 7What are you, O great mountain? Before Zerubbabel you shall become a plain; and he shall bring out the top stone amid shouts of 'Grace, grace to it!' "

8 Moreover the word of the LORD came to me, saying, 9"The hands of Zerubbabel have laid the foundation of this house; his hands shall also complete it. Then you will know that the LORD of hosts has sent me to you. 10For whoever has despised the day of small things shall rejoice, and shall see the plummet in the hand of Zerubbabel.

"These seven are the eyes of the LORD, which range through the whole earth." 11Then I said to him, "What are these two olive trees on the right and the left of the lampstand?" 12And a second time I said to him, "What are these two branches of the olive trees, which pour out the oila through the two golden pipes?" 13He said to me, "Do you not know what these are?" I said, "No, my lord." 14Then he said, "These are the two anointed ones who stand by the Lord of the whole earth."

5.1 AGAIN I looked up and saw a flying scroll. 2And he said to me, "What do you see?" I answered, "I see a flying

aCn: Heb *gold*

scroll; its length is twenty cubits, and its width ten cubits." [3]Then he said to me, "This is the curse that goes out over the face of the whole land; for everyone who steals shall be cut off according to the writing on one side, and everyone who swears falsely[a] shall be cut off according to the writing on the other side. [4]I have sent it out, says the LORD of hosts, and it shall enter the house of the thief, and the house of anyone who swears falsely by my name; and it shall abide in that house and consume it, both timber and stones."

5 Then the angel who talked with me came forward and said to me, "Look up and see what this is that is coming out." [6]I said, "What is it?" He said, "This is a basket[b] coming out." And he said, "This is their iniquity[c] in all the land." [7]Then a leaden cover was lifted, and there was a woman sitting in the basket! [b] [8]And he said, "This is Wickedness." So he thrust her back into the basket, [b] and pressed the leaden weight down on its mouth. [9]Then I looked up and saw two women coming forward. The wind was in their wings; they had wings like the wings of a stork, and they lifted up the basket[b] between earth and sky. [10]Then I said to the angel who talked with me, "Where are they taking the basket?"[b] [11]He said to me, "To the land of Shinar, to build a house for it; and when this is prepared, they will set the basket[b] down there on its base."

# REVELATION 14.1–20

THEN I looked, and there was the Lamb, standing on Mount Zion! And with him were one hundred forty-four thousand who had his name and his Father's name written on their foreheads. [2]And I heard a voice from heaven like the sound of many waters and like the sound of loud thunder; the voice I heard was like the sound of harpists playing on their harps, [3]and they sing a new song before the throne and before the four living creatures and before the elders. No one could learn that song except the one hundred forty-four thousand who have been redeemed from the earth. [4]It is these who have not defiled themselves with women, for they are virgins; these follow the Lamb wherever he goes. They have been redeemed from humankind as first fruits for God and the Lamb, [5]and in their mouth no lie was found; they are blameless.

6 Then I saw another angel flying in midheaven, with an eternal gospel to proclaim to those who lived[d] on the earth—to every nation and tribe and language and people. [7]He said in a loud voice, "Fear God and give him glory, for the hour of his judgment has come; and worship him who made heaven and earth, the sea and the springs of water."

8 Then another angel, a second, followed, saying, "Fallen, fallen is Babylon the great! She has made all nations drink of the wine of the wrath of her fornication."

9 Then another angel, a third, followed them, crying with a loud voice, "Those who worship the beast and its image, and receive a mark on their foreheads or on their hands, [10]they will also drink the wine of God's wrath, poured unmixed into the cup of his anger, and they will be tormented with fire and sulfur in the presence of the holy angels and in the presence of the Lamb. [11]And the smoke of their torment goes up forever and ever. There is no rest day or night for those who worship the beast and its image and for anyone who receives the mark of its name."

12 Here is a call for the endurance of the saints, those who keep the com-

---

[a] The word *falsely* added from verse 4   [b] Heb *ephah*   [c] Gk Compare Syr: Heb *their eye*   [d] Gk *sit*

mandments of God and hold fast to the faith of[a] Jesus.

13  And I heard a voice from heaven saying, "Write this: Blessed are the dead who from now on die in the Lord." "Yes," says the Spirit, "they will rest from their labors, for their deeds follow them."

14  Then I looked, and there was a white cloud, and seated on the cloud was one like the Son of Man, with a golden crown on his head, and a sharp sickle in his hand! [15]Another angel came out of the temple, calling with a loud voice to the one who sat on the cloud, "Use your sickle and reap, for the hour to reap has come, because the harvest of the earth is fully ripe." [16]So the one who sat on the cloud swung his sickle over the earth, and the earth was reaped.

17  Then another angel came out of the temple in heaven, and he too had a sharp sickle. [18]Then another angel came out from the altar, the angel who has authority over fire, and he called with a loud voice to him who had the sharp sickle, "Use your sharp sickle and gather the clusters of the vine of the earth, for its grapes are ripe." [19]So the angel swung his sickle over the earth and gathered the vintage of the earth, and he threw it into the great wine press of the wrath of God. [20]And the wine press was trodden outside the city, and blood flowed from the wine press, as high as a horse's bridle, for a distance of about two hundred miles.[b]

## PSALM 142.1–7

*A Maskil of David. When he was in the cave. A Prayer.*

WITH my voice I cry to the Lord;
  with my voice I make
    supplication to the Lord.

2  I pour out my complaint before
      him;
    I tell my trouble before him.
3  When my spirit is faint,
    you know my way.

  In the path where I walk
    they have hidden a trap for
      me.
4  Look on my right hand and
      see—
    there is no one who takes
      notice of me;
  no refuge remains to me;
    no one cares for me.

5  I cry to you, O Lord;
    I say, "You are my refuge,
    my portion in the land of the
      living."
6  Give heed to my cry,
    for I am brought very low.

  Save me from my persecutors,
    for they are too strong for
      me.
7  Bring me out of prison,
    so that I may give thanks to
      your name.
  The righteous will surround me,
    for you will deal bountifully
      with me.

## PROVERBS 30.21–23

UNDER three things the earth
      trembles;
    under four it cannot bear
      up:
22  a slave when he becomes king,
    and a fool when glutted
      with food;
23  an unloved woman when she
      gets a husband,
    and a maid when she
      succeeds her mistress.

aOr *to their faith in*  bGk *one thousand six hundred stadia*

# DECEMBER 24

## ZECHARIAH 6.1—7.14

**A**ND again I looked up and saw four chariots coming out from between two mountains— mountains of bronze. ²The first chariot had red horses, the second chariot black horses, ³the third chariot white horses, and the fourth chariot dappled graya horses. ⁴Then I said to the angel who talked with me, "What are these, my lord?" ⁵The angel answered me, "These are the four windsb of heaven going out, after presenting themselves before the LORD of all the earth. ⁶The chariot with the black horses goes toward the north country, the white ones go toward the west country,c and the dappled ones go toward the south country." ⁷When the steeds came out, they were impatient to get off and patrol the earth. And he said, "Go, patrol the earth." So they patrolled the earth. ⁸Then he cried out to me, "Lo, those who go toward the north country have set my spirit at rest in the north country."

9 The word of the LORD came to me: ¹⁰Collect silver and goldd from the exiles—from Heldai, Tobijah, and Jedaiah—who have arrived from Babylon; and go the same day to the house of Josiah son of Zephaniah. ¹¹Take the silver and gold and make a crown,e and set it on the head of the high priest Joshua son of Jehozadak; ¹²say to him: Thus says the LORD of hosts: Here is a man whose name is Branch: for he shall branch out in his place, and he shall build the temple of the LORD. ¹³It is he that shall build the temple of the LORD; he shall bear royal honor, and shall sit and rule on his throne. There shall be a priest by his throne, with peaceful understanding between the two of them. ¹⁴And the crownf shall be in the care of Heldai,g Tobijah, Jedaiah, and Josiahh son of Zephaniah, as a memorial in the temple of the LORD.

15 Those who are far off shall come and help to build the temple of the LORD; and you shall know that the LORD of hosts has sent me to you. This will happen if you diligently obey the voice of the LORD your God.

7.1 IN the fourth year of King Darius, the word of the LORD came to Zechariah on the fourth day of the ninth month, which is Chislev. ²Now the people of Bethel had sent Sharezer and Regemmelech and their men, to entreat the favor of the LORD, ³and to ask the priests of the house of the LORD of hosts and the prophets, "Should I mourn and practice abstinence in the fifth month, as I have done for so many years?" ⁴Then the word of the LORD of hosts came to me: ⁵Say to all the people of the land and the priests: When you fasted and lamented in the fifth month and in the seventh, for these seventy years, was it for me that you fasted? ⁶And when you eat and when you drink, do you not eat and drink only for yourselves? ⁷Were not these the words that the LORD proclaimed by the former prophets, when Jerusalem was inhabited and in prosperity, along with the towns around it, and when the Negeb and the Shephelah were inhabited?

8 The word of the LORD came to Zechariah, saying: ⁹Thus says the LORD of hosts: Render true judgments, show kindness and mercy to one another;

aCompare Gk: Meaning of Heb uncertain   bOr *spirits*   cCn: Heb *go after them*   dCn Compare verse 11: Heb lacks *silver and gold*   eGk Mss Syr Tg: Heb *crowns*   fGk Syr: Heb *crowns*   gSyr Compare verse 10: Heb *Helem*   hSyr Compare verse 10: Heb *Hen*

¹⁰do not oppress the widow, the orphan, the alien, or the poor; and do not devise evil in your hearts against one another. ¹¹But they refused to listen, and turned a stubborn shoulder, and stopped their ears in order not to hear. ¹²They made their hearts adamant in order not to hear the law and the words that the LORD of hosts had sent by his spirit through the former prophets. Therefore great wrath came from the LORD of hosts. ¹³Just as, when I[a] called, they would not hear, so, when they called, I would not hear, says the LORD of hosts, ¹⁴and I scattered them with a whirlwind among all the nations that they had not known. Thus the land they left was desolate, so that no one went to and fro, and a pleasant land was made desolate.

## REVELATION 15.1–8

THEN I saw another portent in heaven, great and amazing: seven angels with seven plagues, which are the last, for with them the wrath of God is ended.

2 And I saw what appeared to be a sea of glass mixed with fire, and those who had conquered the beast and its image and the number of its name, standing beside the sea of glass with harps of God in their hands. ³And they sing the song of Moses, the servant[b] of God, and the song of the Lamb:
"Great and amazing are your
      deeds,
   Lord God the Almighty!
Just and true are your ways,
   King of the nations![c]
4 Lord, who will not fear
      and glorify your name?
   For you alone are holy.
   All nations will come
      and worship before you,
   for your judgments have been
      revealed."

5 After this I looked, and the temple of the tent[d] of witness in heaven was opened, ⁶and out of the temple came the seven angels with the seven plagues, robed in pure bright linen,[e] with golden sashes across their chests. ⁷Then one of the four living creatures gave the seven angels seven golden bowls full of the wrath of God, who lives forever and ever; ⁸and the temple was filled with smoke from the glory of God and from his power, and no one could enter the temple until the seven plagues of the seven angels were ended.

## PSALM 143.1–12

*A Psalm of David.*

HEAR my prayer, O LORD;
      give ear to my supplications
         in your faithfulness;
   answer me in your
         righteousness.
2 Do not enter into judgment with
         your servant,
   for no one living is righteous
         before you.

3 For the enemy has pursued me,
      crushing my life to the
         ground,
   making me sit in darkness like
         those long dead.
4 Therefore my spirit faints
         within me;
   my heart within me is
         appalled.

5 I remember the days of old,
      I think about all your deeds,
      I meditate on the works of
         your hands.
6 I stretch out my hands to you;
      my soul thirsts for you like a
         parched land.          *Selah*

7 Answer me quickly, O LORD;

    my spirit fails.
Do not hide your face from me,
    or I shall be like those who
    go down to the Pit.
8 Let me hear of your steadfast
    love in the morning,
    for in you I put my trust.
Teach me the way I should go,
    for to you I lift up my soul.

9 Save me, O LORD, from my
    enemies;
    I have fled to you for
    refuge. a
10 Teach me to do your will,
    for you are my God.
Let your good spirit lead me
    on a level path.

11 For your name's sake, O LORD,
    preserve my life.
In your righteousness bring
    me out of trouble.

12 In your steadfast love cut off my
    enemies,
    and destroy all my
    adversaries,
    for I am your servant.

## PROVERBS 30.24–28

Four things on earth are small,
    yet they are exceedingly
    wise:
25 the ants are a people without
    strength,
    yet they provide their food in
    the summer;
26 the badgers are a people
    without power,
    yet they make their homes in
    the rocks;
27 the locusts have no king,
    yet all of them march in rank;
28 the lizard b can be grasped in
    the hand,
    yet it is found in kings'
    palaces.

# DECEMBER 25

## ZECHARIAH 8.1–23

THE word of the LORD of hosts came to me, saying: 2Thus says the LORD of hosts: I am jealous for Zion with great jealousy, and I am jealous for her with great wrath. 3Thus says the LORD: I will return to Zion, and will dwell in the midst of Jerusalem; Jerusalem shall be called the faithful city, and the mountain of the LORD of hosts shall be called the holy mountain. 4Thus says the LORD of hosts: Old men and old women shall again sit in the streets of Jerusalem, each with staff in hand because of their great age. 5And the streets of the city shall be full of boys and girls playing in its streets. 6Thus says the LORD of hosts: Even though it seems impossible to the remnant of this people in these days, should it also seem impossible to me, says the LORD of hosts? 7Thus says the LORD of hosts: I will save my people from the east country and from the west country; 8and I will bring them to live in Jerusalem. They shall be my people and I will be their God, in faithfulness and in righteousness.

aOne Heb Ms Gk: MT *to you I have hidden*   bOr *spider*

9  Thus says the Lord of hosts: Let your hands be strong—you that have recently been hearing these words from the mouths of the prophets who were present when the foundation was laid for the rebuilding of the temple, the house of the Lord of hosts. 10For before those days there were no wages for people or for animals, nor was there any safety from the foe for those who went out or came in, and I set them all against one other. 11But now I will not deal with the remnant of this people as in the former days, says the Lord of hosts. 12For there shall be a sowing of peace; the vine shall yield its fruit, the ground shall give its produce, and the skies shall give their dew; and I will cause the remnant of this people to possess all these things. 13Just as you have been a cursing among the nations, O house of Judah and house of Israel, so I will save you and you shall be a blessing. Do not be afraid, but let your hands be strong.

14  For thus says the Lord of hosts: Just as I purposed to bring disaster upon you, when your ancestors provoked me to wrath, and I did not relent, says the Lord of hosts, 15so again I have purposed in these days to do good to Jerusalem and to the house of Judah; do not be afraid. 16These are the things that you shall do: Speak the truth to one another, render in your gates judgments that are true and make for peace, 17do not devise evil in your hearts against one another, and love no false oath; for all these are things that I hate, says the Lord.

18  The word of the Lord of hosts came to me, saying: 19Thus says the Lord of hosts: The fast of the fourth month, and the fast of the fifth, and the fast of the seventh, and the fast of the tenth, shall be seasons of joy and gladness, and cheerful festivals for the house of Judah: therefore love truth and peace.

20  Thus says the Lord of hosts: Peoples shall yet come, the inhabitants of many cities; 21the inhabitants of one city shall go to another, saying, "Come, let us go to entreat the favor of the Lord, and to seek the Lord of hosts; I myself am going." 22Many peoples and strong nations shall come to seek the Lord of hosts in Jerusalem, and to entreat the favor of the Lord. 23Thus says the Lord of hosts: In those days ten men from nations of every language shall take hold of a Jew, grasping his garment and saying, "Let us go with you, for we have heard that God is with you."

# REVELATION 16.1–21

THEN I heard a loud voice from the temple telling the seven angels, "Go and pour out on the earth the seven bowls of the wrath of God."

2  So the first angel went and poured his bowl on the earth, and a foul and painful sore came on those who had the mark of the beast and who worshiped its image.

3  The second angel poured his bowl into the sea, and it became like the blood of a corpse, and every living thing in the sea died.

4  The third angel poured his bowl into the rivers and the springs of water, and they became blood. 5And I heard the angel of the waters say,

"You are just, O Holy One, who
        are and were,
    for you have judged these
        things;
6  because they shed the blood of
        saints and prophets,
    you have given them blood to
        drink.
    It is what they deserve!"
7And I heard the altar respond,
    "Yes, O Lord God, the
        Almighty,
    your judgments are true and
        just!"

8  The fourth angel poured his bowl

on the sun, and it was allowed to scorch them with fire; [9]they were scorched by the fierce heat, but they cursed the name of God, who had authority over these plagues, and they did not repent and give him glory.

10 The fifth angel poured his bowl on the throne of the beast, and its kingdom was plunged into darkness; people gnawed their tongues in agony, [11]and cursed the God of heaven because of their pains and sores, and they did not repent of their deeds.

12 The sixth angel poured his bowl on the great river Euphrates, and its water was dried up in order to prepare the way for the kings from the east. [13]And I saw three foul spirits like frogs coming from the mouth of the dragon, from the mouth of the beast, and from the mouth of the false prophet. [14]These are demonic spirits, performing signs, who go abroad to the kings of the whole world, to assemble them for battle on the great day of God the Almighty. [15]("See, I am coming like a thief! Blessed is the one who stays awake and is clothed, [a] not going about naked and exposed to shame.") [16]And they assembled them at the place that in Hebrew is called Harmagedon.

17 The seventh angel poured his bowl into the air, and a loud voice came out of the temple, from the throne, saying, "It is done!" [18]And there came flashes of lightning, rumblings, peals of thunder, and a violent earthquake, such as had not occurred since people were upon the earth, so violent was that earthquake. [19]The great city was split into three parts, and the cities of the nations fell. God remembered great Babylon and gave her the wine-cup of the fury of his wrath. [20]And every island fled away, and no mountains were to be found; [21]and huge hailstones, each weighing about a hundred pounds, [b] dropped from heaven on people, until they cursed God for the plague of the hail, so fearful was that plague.

## PSALM 144. 1–15

*Of David.*

**B**LESSED be the LORD, my rock,
  who trains my hands for
    war, and my fingers for
    battle;
2  my rock[c] and my fortress,
    my stronghold and my
      deliverer,
  my shield, in whom I take
    refuge,
    who subdues the peoples[d]
      under me.

3  O LORD, what are human beings
    that you regard them,
  or mortals that you think of
    them?
4  They are like a breath;
    their days are like a passing
      shadow.

5  Bow your heavens, O LORD, and
    come down;
  touch the mountains so that
    they smoke.
6  Make the lightning flash and
    scatter them;
  send out your arrows and
    rout them.
7  Stretch out your hand from on
    high;
  set me free and rescue me
    from the mighty waters,
  from the hand of aliens,
8  whose mouths speak lies,
    and whose right hands are
      false.

9  I will sing a new song to you,
    O God;
  upon a ten-stringed harp I will
    play to you,

aGk *and keeps his robes*  bGk *weighing about a talent*  cWith 18.2 and 2 Sam 22.2: Heb *my steadfast love*  dHeb Mss Syr Aquila Jerome: MT *my people*

10  the one who gives victory to
        kings,
    who rescues his servant
        David.
11  Rescue me from the cruel
        sword,
    and deliver me from the hand
        of aliens,
    whose mouths speak lies,
        and whose right hands are
        false.

12  May our sons in their youth
        be like plants full grown,
    our daughters like corner pillars,
        cut for the building of a
        palace.
13  May our barns be filled,
        with produce of every kind;
    may our sheep increase by
        thousands,
        by tens of thousands in our
        fields,

14  and may our cattle be heavy
        with young.
    May there be no breach in the
        walls, a no exile,
        and no cry of distress in our
        streets.

15  Happy are the people to whom
        such blessings fall;
    happy are the people whose
        God is the Lord.

## PROVERBS 30.29–31

THREE things are stately in their
        stride;
    four are stately in their gait:
30  the lion, which is mightiest
        among wild animals
    and does not turn back
        before any;
31  the strutting rooster, b the
        he-goat,
    and a king striding before c
        his people.

# DECEMBER 26

## ZECHARIAH 9.1–17

An Oracle.

THE word of the Lord is against
        the land of Hadrach
    and will rest upon Damascus.
    For to the Lord belongs the
        capital d of Aram, e
    as do all the tribes of Israel;
2  Hamath also, which borders on
        it,
    Tyre and Sidon, though they
        are very wise.
3  Tyre has built itself a rampart,

    and heaped up silver like
        dust,
    and gold like the dirt of the
        streets.
4  But now, the Lord will strip it
        of its possessions
    and hurl its wealth into the
        sea,
    and it shall be devoured by
        fire.

5  Ashkelon shall see it and be
        afraid;

a Heb lacks *in the walls*   b Gk Syr Tg Compare Vg: Meaning of Heb uncertain   c Meaning of Heb uncertain   d Heb *eye*   e Cn: Heb *of Adam* (or *of humankind*)

Gaza too, and shall writhe in
anguish;
Ekron also, because its hopes
are withered.
The king shall perish from Gaza;
Ashkelon shall be uninhabited;
6 a mongrel people shall settle
in Ashdod,
and I will make an end of the
pride of Philistia.
7 I will take away its blood from
its mouth,
and its abominations from
between its teeth;
it too shall be a remnant for
our God;
it shall be like a clan in Judah,
and Ekron shall be like the
Jebusites.
8 Then I will encamp at my house
as a guard,
so that no one shall march to
and fro;
no oppressor shall again overrun
them,
for now I have seen with my
own eyes.

9 Rejoice greatly, O daughter
Zion!
Shout aloud, O daughter
Jerusalem!
Lo, your king comes to you;
triumphant and victorious is
he,
humble and riding on a donkey,
on a colt, the foal of a
donkey.
10 He a will cut off the chariot
from Ephraim
and the war horse from
Jerusalem;
and the battle bow shall be cut
off,
and he shall command peace
to the nations;
his dominion shall be from sea
to sea,

and from the River to the
ends of the earth.
11 As for you also, because of the
blood of my covenant
with you,
I will set your prisoners free
from the waterless pit.
12 Return to your stronghold,
O prisoners of hope;
today I declare that I will
restore to you double.
13 For I have bent Judah as my
bow;
I have made Ephraim its
arrow.
I will arouse your sons, O Zion,
against your sons, O Greece,
and wield you like a
warrior's sword.

14 Then the LORD will appear
over them,
and his arrow go forth like
lightning;
the Lord GOD will sound the
trumpet
and march forth in the
whirlwinds of the south.
15 The LORD of hosts will protect
them,
and they shall devour and
tread down the
slingers; b
they shall drink their blood c
like wine,
and be full like a bowl,
drenched like the corners of
the altar.

16 On that day the LORD their God
will save them
for they are the flock of
his people;
for like the jewels of a crown
they shall shine on his land.
17 For what goodness and beauty
are his!

a Gk: Heb *I*   b Cn: Heb *the slingstones*   c Gk: Heb *shall drink*

Grain shall make the young
>    men flourish,
and new wine the young
>    women.

## REVELATION 17.1–18

**T**HEN one of the seven angels who had the seven bowls came and said to me, "Come, I will show you the judgment of the great whore who is seated on many waters, [2]with whom the kings of the earth have committed fornication, and with the wine of whose fornication the inhabitants of the earth have become drunk." [3]So he carried me away in the spirit[a] into a wilderness, and I saw a woman sitting on a scarlet beast that was full of blasphemous names, and it had seven heads and ten horns. [4]The woman was clothed in purple and scarlet, and adorned with gold and jewels and pearls, holding in her hand a golden cup full of abominations and the impurities of her fornication; [5]and on her forehead was written a name, a mystery: "Babylon the great, mother of whores and of earth's abominations." [6]And I saw that the woman was drunk with the blood of the saints and the blood of the witnesses to Jesus.

When I saw her, I was greatly amazed. [7]But the angel said to me, "Why are you so amazed? I will tell you the mystery of the woman, and of the beast with seven heads and ten horns that carries her. [8]The beast that you saw was, and is not, and is about to ascend from the bottomless pit and go to destruction. And the inhabitants of the earth, whose names have not been written in the book of life from the foundation of the world, will be amazed when they see the beast, because it was and is not and is to come.

9 "This calls for a mind that has wisdom: the seven heads are seven mountains on which the woman is seated; also, they are seven kings, [10]of whom five have fallen, one is living, and the other has not yet come; and when he comes, he must remain only a little while. [11]As for the beast that was and is not, it is an eighth but it belongs to the seven, and it goes to destruction. [12]And the ten horns that you saw are ten kings who have not yet received a kingdom, but they are to receive authority as kings for one hour, together with the beast. [13]These are united in yielding their power and authority to the beast; [14]they will make war on the Lamb, and the Lamb will conquer them, for he is Lord of lords and King of kings, and those with him are called and chosen and faithful."

15 And he said to me, "The waters that you saw, where the whore is seated, are peoples and multitudes and nations and languages. [16]And the ten horns that you saw, they and the beast will hate the whore; they will make her desolate and naked; they will devour her flesh and burn her up with fire. [17]For God has put it into their hearts to carry out his purpose by agreeing to give their kingdom to the beast, until the words of God will be fulfilled. [18]The woman you saw is the great city that rules over the kings of the earth."

## PSALM 145.1–21

*Praise. Of David.*

**I** WILL extol you, my God and
>    King,
and bless your name forever
>    and ever.
2   Every day I will bless you,
>    and praise your name forever
>    and ever.
3   Great is the LORD, and greatly
>    to be praised;
his greatness is unsearchable.

4   One generation shall laud your
>    works to another,

and shall declare your mighty
    acts.
5 On the glorious splendor of your
    majesty,
    and on your wondrous works,
       I will meditate.
6 The might of your awesome
    deeds shall be
    proclaimed,
    and I will declare your
       greatness.
7 They shall celebrate the fame of
    your abundant goodness,
    and shall sing aloud of your
       righteousness.

8 The LORD is gracious and
    merciful,
    slow to anger and abounding
       in steadfast love.
9 The LORD is good to all,
    and his compassion is over all
       that he has made.

10 All your works shall give thanks
    to you, O LORD,
    and all your faithful shall
       bless you.
11 They shall speak of the glory of
    your kingdom,
    and tell of your power,
12 to make known to all people
    your[a] mighty deeds,
    and the glorious splendor of
       your[b] kingdom.
13 Your kingdom is an everlasting
    kingdom,
    and your dominion endures
       throughout all
       generations.

The LORD is faithful in all his
    words,
    and gracious in all his
       deeds. [c]
14 The LORD upholds all who are
    falling,
    and raises up all who are
       bowed down.
15 The eyes of all look to you,
    and you give them their food
       in due season.
16 You open your hand,
    satisfying the desire of every
       living thing.
17 The LORD is just in all his ways,
    and kind in all his doings.
18 The LORD is near to all who call
    on him,
    to all who call on him in truth.
19 He fulfills the desire of all who
    fear him;
    he also hears their cry, and
       saves them.
20 The LORD watches over all who
    love him,
    but all the wicked he will
       destroy.

21 My mouth will speak the praise
    of the LORD,
    and all flesh will bless his holy
       name forever and ever.

## PROVERBS 30.32

IF you have been foolish, exalting
    yourself,
    or if you have been devising
       evil,
    put your hand on your mouth.

a Gk Jerome Syr: Heb *his*  b Heb *his*  c These two lines supplied by Q Ms Gk Syr

# DECEMBER 27



**A**sk rain from the Lord
in the season of the
spring rain,
from the Lord who makes the
storm clouds,
who gives showers of rain
to you, <sup>a</sup>
the vegetation in the field
to everyone.
2 For the teraphim<sup>b</sup> utter
nonsense,
and the diviners see lies;
the dreamers tell false dreams,
and give empty consolation.
Therefore the people wander
like sheep;
they suffer for lack of a
shepherd.

3 My anger is hot against the
shepherds,
and I will punish the
leaders;<sup>c</sup>
for the Lord of hosts cares for
his flock, the house of
Judah,
and will make them like his
proud war horse.
4 Out of them shall come the
cornerstone,
out of them the tent peg,
out of them the battle bow,
out of them every
commander.
5 Together they shall be like
warriors in battle,
trampling the foe in the mud
of the streets;
they shall fight, for the Lord is
with them,
and they shall put to shame
the riders on horses.

6 I will strengthen the house
of Judah,
and I will save the house
of Joseph.
I will bring them back because I
have compassion on
them,
and they shall be as though I
had not rejected them;
for I am the Lord their God
and I will answer them.
7 Then the people of Ephraim
shall become like
warriors,
and their hearts shall be glad
as with wine.
Their children shall see it and
rejoice,
their hearts shall exult in
the Lord.

8 I will signal for them and gather
them in,
for I have redeemed them,
and they shall be as numerous
as they were before.
9 Though I scattered them among
the nations,
yet in far countries they shall
remember me,
and they shall rear their
children and return.
10 I will bring them home from the
land of Egypt,
and gather them from
Assyria;
I will bring them to the land of
Gilead and to Lebanon,
until there is no room for
them.
11 They<sup>d</sup> shall pass through the
sea of distress,

---

aHeb *them*   bOr *household gods*   cOr *male goats*   dGk: Heb *He*

and the waves of the sea shall
   be struck down,
and all the depths of the Nile
   dried up.
The pride of Assyria shall be
   laid low,
and the scepter of Egypt
   shall depart.
12  I will make them strong in
   the Lord,
and they shall walk in his
   name,
           says the Lord.

11.1 Open your doors, O Lebanon,
   so that fire may devour
      your cedars!
2  Wail, O cypress, for the cedar
   has fallen,
   for the glorious trees are
      ruined!
Wail, oaks of Bashan,
   for the thick forest has
      been felled!
3  Listen, the wail of the
   shepherds,
   for their glory is despoiled!
Listen, the roar of the lions,
   for the thickets of the Jordan
      are destroyed!

4  Thus said the Lord my God: Be a shepherd of the flock doomed to slaughter. [5]Those who buy them kill them and go unpunished; and those who sell them say, "Blessed be the Lord, for I have become rich"; and their own shepherds have no pity on them. [6]For I will no longer have pity on the inhabitants of the earth, says the Lord. I will cause them, every one, to fall each into the hand of a neighbor, and each into the hand of the king; and they shall devastate the earth, and I will deliver no one from their hand.

7  So, on behalf of the sheep merchants, I became the shepherd of the flock doomed to slaughter. I took two staffs; one I named Favor, the other I named Unity, and I tended the sheep. [8]In one month I disposed of the three shepherds, for I had become impatient with them, and they also detested me. [9]So I said, "I will not be your shepherd. What is to die, let it die; what is to be destroyed, let it be destroyed; and let those that are left devour the flesh of one another!" [10]I took my staff Favor and broke it, annulling the covenant that I had made with all the peoples. [11]So it was annulled on that day, and the sheep merchants, who were watching me, knew that it was the word of the Lord. [12]I then said to them, "If it seems right to you, give me my wages; but if not, keep them." So they weighed out as my wages thirty shekels of silver. [13]Then the Lord said to me, "Throw it into the treasury"[a]—this lordly price at which I was valued by them. So I took the thirty shekels of silver and threw them into the treasury[a] in the house of the Lord. [14]Then I broke my second staff Unity, annulling the family ties between Judah and Israel.

15  Then the Lord said to me: Take once more the implements of a worthless shepherd. [16]For I am now raising up in the land a shepherd who does not care for the perishing, or seek the wandering,[b] or heal the maimed, or nourish the healthy,[c] but devours the flesh of the fat ones, tearing off even their hoofs.
17  Oh, my worthless shepherd,
   who deserts the flock!
May the sword strike his arm
   and his right eye!
Let his arm be completely
      withered,
   his right eye utterly blinded!

aSyr: Heb *it to the potter*  bSyr Compare Gk Vg: Heb *the youth*  cMeaning of Heb uncertain

# REVELATION 18.1–24

AFTER this I saw another angel coming down from heaven, having great authority; and the earth was made bright with his splendor. <sup>2</sup>He called out with a mighty voice,

"Fallen, fallen is Babylon the
great!
It has become a dwelling
place of demons,
a haunt of every foul spirit,
a haunt of every foul bird,
a haunt of every foul and
hateful beast. [a]
3 For all the nations have drunk [b]
of the wine of the wrath of
her fornication,
and the kings of the earth have
committed fornication
with her,
and the merchants of the
earth have grown rich
from the power [c] of her
luxury."
4 Then I heard another voice from heaven saying,
"Come out of her, my people,
so that you do not take part
in her sins,
and so that you do not share
in her plagues;
5 for her sins are heaped high
as heaven,
and God has remembered
her iniquities.
6 Render to her as she herself
has rendered,
and repay her double for
her deeds;
mix a double draught for her
in the cup she mixed.
7 As she glorified herself and lived
luxuriously,
so give her a like measure of
torment and grief.
Since in her heart she says,

'I rule as a queen;
I am no widow,
and I will never see grief,'
8 therefore her plagues will come
in a single day—
pestilence and mourning
and famine—
and she will be burned with fire;
for mighty is the Lord God
who judges her."

9 And the kings of the earth, who committed fornication and lived in luxury with her, will weep and wail over her when they see the smoke of her burning; <sup>10</sup>they will stand far off, in fear of her torment, and say,

"Alas, alas, the great city,
Babylon, the mighty city!
For in one hour your judgment
has come."

11 And the merchants of the earth weep and mourn for her, since no one buys their cargo anymore, <sup>12</sup>cargo of gold, silver, jewels and pearls, fine linen, purple, silk and scarlet, all kinds of scented wood, all articles of ivory, all articles of costly wood, bronze, iron, and marble, <sup>13</sup>cinnamon, spice, incense, myrrh, frankincense, wine, olive oil, choice flour and wheat, cattle and sheep, horses and chariots, slaves—and human lives. [d]
14 "The fruit for which your soul
longed
has gone from you,
and all your dainties and
your splendor
are lost to you,
never to be found again!"
<sup>15</sup>The merchants of these wares, who gained wealth from her, will stand far off, in fear of her torment, weeping and mourning aloud,
16 "Alas, alas, the great city,
clothed in fine linen,
in purple and scarlet,

[a] Other ancient authorities lack the words *a haunt of every foul beast* and attach the words *and hateful* to the previous line so as to read *a haunt of every foul and hateful bird*   [b] Other ancient authorities read *she has made all nations drink*   [c] Or *resources*   [d] Or *chariots, and human bodies and souls*

adorned with gold,
  with jewels, and with
    pearls!
17 For in one hour all this wealth
    has been laid waste!"

And all shipmasters and seafarers, sailors and all whose trade is on the sea, stood far off 18and cried out as they saw the smoke of her burning,
  "What city was like the great
    city?"
19And they threw dust on their heads, as they wept and mourned, crying out,
  "Alas, alas, the great city,
    where all who had ships at
      sea
    grew rich by her wealth!
  For in one hour she has been
    laid waste.
20 Rejoice over her, O heaven,
    you saints and apostles and
      prophets!
  For God has given judgment for
    you against her."

21 Then a mighty angel took up a stone like a great millstone and threw it into the sea, saying,
  "With such violence Babylon the
    great city
  will be thrown down,
    and will be found no more;
22 and the sound of harpists and
      minstrels and of flutists
      and trumpeters
    will be heard in you no more;
  and an artisan of any trade
    will be found in you no more;
  and the sound of the millstone
    will be heard in you no more;
23 and the light of a lamp
    will shine in you no more;
  and the voice of bridegroom
      and bride
    will be heard in you no more;
  for your merchants were the
      magnates of the earth,
    and all nations were deceived
      by your sorcery.

24 And in you[a] was found the
      blood of prophets and of
      saints,
    and of all who have been
      slaughtered on earth."

## PSALM 146.1–10

**P**RAISE the LORD!
  Praise the LORD, O my soul!
2  I will praise the LORD as
      long as I live;
  I will sing praises to my God
    all my life long.

3  Do not put your trust in
      princes,
    in mortals, in whom there is
      no help.
4  When their breath departs, they
      return to the earth;
    on that very day their plans
      perish.

5  Happy are those whose help is
      the God of Jacob,
    whose hope is in the LORD
      their God,
6  who made heaven and earth,
    the sea, and all that is in
      them;
  who keeps faith forever;
7    who executes justice for the
      oppressed;
    who gives food to the hungry.

  The LORD sets the prisoners
      free;
8    the LORD opens the eyes of
      the blind.
  The LORD lifts up those who are
      bowed down;
    the LORD loves the righteous.
9  The LORD watches over the
      strangers;
    he upholds the orphan and the
      widow,
    but the way of the wicked he
      brings to ruin.

a Gk *her*

10   The Lord will reign forever,
        your God, O Zion, for all
            generations.
      Praise the Lord!

## PROVERBS 30.33

For as pressing milk produces
        curds,
    and pressing the nose
        produces blood,
      so pressing anger produces
        strife.

# DECEMBER 28

## ZECHARIAH 12.1—13.9

### An Oracle.

THE word of the Lord concerning Israel: Thus says the Lord, who stretched out the heavens and founded the earth and formed the human spirit within: ²See, I am about to make Jerusalem a cup of reeling for all the surrounding peoples; it will be against Judah also in the siege against Jerusalem. ³On that day I will make Jerusalem a heavy stone for all the peoples; all who lift it shall grievously hurt themselves. And all the nations of the earth shall come together against it. ⁴On that day, says the Lord, I will strike every horse with panic, and its rider with madness. But on the house of Judah I will keep a watchful eye, when I strike every horse of the peoples with blindness. ⁵Then the clans of Judah shall say to themselves, "The inhabitants of Jerusalem have strength through the Lord of hosts, their God."

6  On that day I will make the clans of Judah like a blazing pot on a pile of wood, like a flaming torch among sheaves; and they shall devour to the right and to the left all the surrounding peoples, while Jerusalem shall again be inhabited in its place, in Jerusalem.

7  And the Lord will give victory to the tents of Judah first, that the glory of the house of David and the glory of the inhabitants of Jerusalem may not be exalted over that of Judah. ⁸On that day the Lord will shield the inhabitants of Jerusalem so that the feeblest among them on that day shall be like David, and the house of David shall be like God, like the angel of the Lord, at their head. ⁹And on that day I will seek to destroy all the nations that come against Jerusalem.

10  And I will pour out a spirit of compassion and supplication on the house of David and the inhabitants of Jerusalem, so that, when they look on the one[a] whom they have pierced, they shall mourn for him, as one mourns for an only child, and weep bitterly over him, as one weeps over a firstborn. ¹¹On that day the mourning in Jerusalem will be as great as the mourning for Hadad-rimmon in the plain of Megiddo. ¹²The land shall mourn, each family by itself; the family of the house of David by itself, and their wives by themselves; the family of the house of Nathan by itself, and their wives by themselves; ¹³the family of the house of Levi by itself, and their wives by themselves; the family of the

a Heb *on me*

Shimeites by itself, and their wives by themselves; [14]and all the families that are left, each by itself, and their wives by themselves.

13.1 On that day a fountain shall be opened for the house of David and the inhabitants of Jerusalem, to cleanse them from sin and impurity.

2 On that day, says the Lord of hosts, I will cut off the names of the idols from the land, so that they shall be remembered no more; and also I will remove from the land the prophets and the unclean spirit. [3]And if any prophets appear again, their fathers and mothers who bore them will say to them, "You shall not live, for you speak lies in the name of the Lord"; and their fathers and their mothers who bore them shall pierce them through when they prophesy. [4]On that day the prophets will be ashamed, every one, of their visions when they prophesy; they will not put on a hairy mantle in order to deceive, [5]but each of them will say, "I am no prophet, I am a tiller of the soil; for the land has been my possession[a] since my youth." [6]And if anyone asks them, "What are these wounds on your chest?"[b] the answer will be "The wounds I received in the house of my friends."

7   "Awake, O sword, against my
            shepherd,
      against the man who is my
            associate,"
                  says the Lord of hosts.
      Strike the shepherd, that the
            sheep may be scattered;
      I will turn my hand against
            the little ones.
8   In the whole land, says the
            Lord,
      two-thirds shall be cut off
            and perish,

      and one-third shall be left
            alive.
9   And I will put this third into
            the fire,
      refine them as one refines
            silver,
      and test them as gold is
            tested.
      They will call on my name,
            and I will answer them.
      I will say, "They are my
            people";
      and they will say, "The Lord
            is our God."

# REVELATION 19.1–21

After this I heard what seemed to be the loud voice of a great multitude in heaven, saying,
      "Hallelujah!
      Salvation and glory and power
            to our God,
2           for his judgments are true
                  and just;
      he has judged the great whore
            who corrupted the earth with
                  her fornication,
      and he has avenged on her the
            blood of his servants."[c]
[3]Once more they said,
      "Hallelujah!
      The smoke goes up from her
            forever and ever."
[4]And the twenty-four elders and the four living creatures fell down and worshiped God who is seated on the throne, saying,
      "Amen. Hallelujah!"
5   And from the throne came a voice saying,
      "Praise our God,
            all you his servants, [c]
      and all who fear him,
            small and great."
[6]Then I heard what seemed to be the voice of a great multitude, like the sound of many waters and like the

---

[a]Cn: Heb *for humankind has caused me to possess*   [b]Heb *wounds between your hands*   [c]Gk *slaves*

sound of mighty thunderpeals, crying out,

   "Hallelujah!
   For the Lord our God
    the Almighty reigns.
7 Let us rejoice and exult
   and give him the glory,
 for the marriage of the Lamb
   has come,
 and his bride has made
   herself ready;
8 to her it has been granted to
   be clothed
 with fine linen, bright and
   pure"—

for the fine linen is the righteous deeds of the saints.

9 And the angel said[a] to me, "Write this: Blessed are those who are invited to the marriage supper of the Lamb." And he said to me, "These are true words of God." [10]Then I fell down at his feet to worship him, but he said to me, "You must not do that! I am a fellow servant[b] with you and your comrades[c] who hold the testimony of Jesus.[d] Worship God! For the testimony of Jesus[d] is the spirit of prophecy."

11 Then I saw heaven opened, and there was a white horse! Its rider is called Faithful and True, and in righteousness he judges and makes war. [12]His eyes are like a flame of fire, and on his head are many diadems; and he has a name inscribed that no one knows but himself. [13]He is clothed in a robe dipped in[e] blood, and his name is called The Word of God. [14]And the armies of heaven, wearing fine linen, white and pure, were following him on white horses. [15]From his mouth comes a sharp sword with which to strike down the nations, and he will rule[f] them with a rod of iron; he will tread the wine press of the fury of the wrath of God the Almighty. [16]On his robe and on his thigh he has a name inscribed, "King of kings and Lord of lords."

17 Then I saw an angel standing in the sun, and with a loud voice he called to all the birds that fly in midheaven, "Come, gather for the great supper of God, [18]to eat the flesh of kings, the flesh of captains, the flesh of the mighty, the flesh of horses and their riders—flesh of all, both free and slave, both small and great." [19]Then I saw the beast and the kings of the earth with their armies gathered to make war against the rider on the horse and against his army. [20]And the beast was captured, and with it the false prophet who had performed in its presence the signs by which he deceived those who had received the mark of the beast and those who worshiped its image. These two were thrown alive into the lake of fire that burns with sulfur. [21]And the rest were killed by the sword of the rider on the horse, the sword that came from his mouth; and all the birds were gorged with their flesh.

## PSALM 147.1–20

**P**RAISE the LORD!
  How good it is to sing
   praises to our God;
 for he is gracious, and a song
  of praise is fitting.
2 The LORD builds up Jerusalem;
  he gathers the outcasts of
   Israel.
3 He heals the brokenhearted,
  and binds up their wounds.
4 He determines the number of
  the stars;
 he gives to all of them their
  names.
5 Great is our Lord, and abundant
  in power;
 his understanding is beyond
  measure.

a Gk *he said*  b Gk *slave*  c Gk *brothers*  d Or *to Jesus*  e Other ancient authorities read *sprinkled with*
f Or *will shepherd*

6  The LORD lifts up the
        downtrodden;
    he casts the wicked to the
        ground.

7  Sing to the LORD with
        thanksgiving;
    make melody to our God on
        the lyre.
8  He covers the heavens with
        clouds,
    prepares rain for the earth,
    makes grass grow on the
        hills.
9  He gives to the animals their
        food,
    and to the young ravens when
        they cry.
10  His delight is not in the strength
        of the horse,
    nor his pleasure in the speed
        of a runner;ᵃ
11  but the LORD takes pleasure in
        those who fear him,
    in those who hope in his
        steadfast love.

12  Praise the LORD, O Jerusalem!
    Praise your God, O Zion!
13  For he strengthens the bars of
        your gates;
    he blesses your children
        within you.
14  He grants peaceᵇ within your
        borders;
    he fills you with the finest of
        wheat.
15  He sends out his command to
        the earth;
    his word runs swiftly.
16  He gives snow like wool;
    he scatters frost like ashes.
17  He hurls down hail like
        crumbs—
    who can stand before his
        cold?

18  He sends out his word, and
        melts them;
    he makes his wind blow, and
        the waters flow.
19  He declares his word to Jacob,
    his statutes and ordinances to
        Israel.
20  He has not dealt thus with any
        other nation;
    they do not know his
        ordinances.
Praise the LORD!

## PROVERBS 31.1–7

**T**HE words of King Lemuel. An
oracle that his mother taught
him:

2  No, my son! No, son of my
        womb!
    No, son of my vows!
3  Do not give your strength to
        women,
    your ways to those who
        destroy kings.
4  It is not for kings, O Lemuel,
    it is not for kings to drink
        wine,
    or for rulers to desireᶜ
        strong drink;
5  or else they will drink and
        forget what has been
        decreed,
    and will pervert the rights of
        all the afflicted.
6  Give strong drink to one who is
        perishing,
    and wine to those in bitter
        distress;
7  let them drink and forget their
        poverty,
    and remember their misery
        no more.

ᵃHeb *legs of a person*  ᵇOr *prosperity*  ᶜCn: Heb *where*

# DECEMBER 29

## ZECHARIAH 14.1–21

SEE, a day is coming for the LORD, when the plunder taken from you will be divided in your midst. [2]For I will gather all the nations against Jerusalem to battle, and the city shall be taken and the houses looted and the women raped; half the city shall go into exile, but the rest of the people shall not be cut off from the city. [3]Then the LORD will go forth and fight against those nations as when he fights on a day of battle. [4]On that day his feet shall stand on the Mount of Olives, which lies before Jerusalem on the east; and the Mount of Olives shall be split in two from east to west by a very wide valley; so that one half of the Mount shall withdraw northward, and the other half southward. [5]And you shall flee by the valley of the LORD's mountain,[a] for the valley between the mountains shall reach to Azal;[b] and you shall flee as you fled from the earthquake in the days of King Uzziah of Judah. Then the LORD my God will come, and all the holy ones with him.

6 On that day there shall not be[c] either cold or frost.[d] [7]And there shall be continuous day (it is known to the LORD), not day and not night, for at evening time there shall be light.

8 On that day living waters shall flow out from Jerusalem, half of them to the eastern sea and half of them to the western sea; it shall continue in summer as in winter.

9 And the LORD will become king over all the earth; on that day the LORD will be one and his name one.

10 The whole land shall be turned into a plain from Geba to Rimmon south of Jerusalem. But Jerusalem shall remain aloft on its site from the Gate of Benjamin to the place of the former gate, to the Corner Gate, and from the Tower of Hananel to the king's wine presses. [11]And it shall be inhabited, for never again shall it be doomed to destruction; Jerusalem shall abide in security.

12 This shall be the plague with which the LORD will strike all the peoples that wage war against Jerusalem: their flesh shall rot while they are still on their feet; their eyes shall rot in their sockets, and their tongues shall rot in their mouths. [13]On that day a great panic from the LORD shall fall on them, so that each will seize the hand of a neighbor, and the hand of the one will be raised against the hand of the other; [14]even Judah will fight at Jerusalem. And the wealth of all the surrounding nations shall be collected—gold, silver, and garments in great abundance. [15]And a plague like this plague shall fall on the horses, the mules, the camels, the donkeys, and whatever animals may be in those camps.

16 Then all who survive of the nations that have come against Jerusalem shall go up year after year to worship the King, the LORD of hosts, and to keep the festival of booths.[e] [17]If any of the families of the earth do not go up to Jerusalem to worship the King, the LORD of hosts, there will be no rain upon them. [18]And if the family of Egypt do not go up and present themselves, then on them shall[f] come the plague that the LORD inflicts on the nations that do not go up to keep the festival of booths.[e] [19]Such shall be the punishment of Egypt and the punishment of all

---

aHeb *my mountains*  bMeaning of Heb uncertain  cCn: Heb *there shall not be light*  dCompare Gk
Syr Vg Tg: Meaning of Heb uncertain  eOr *tabernacles*; Heb *succoth*  fGk Syr: Heb *shall not*

the nations that do not go up to keep the festival of booths. <sup>a</sup>

20 On that day there shall be inscribed on the bells of the horses, "Holy to the LORD." And the cooking pots in the house of the LORD shall be as holy as<sup>b</sup> the bowls in front of the altar; [21]and every cooking pot in Jerusalem and Judah shall be sacred to the LORD of hosts, so that all who sacrifice may come and use them to boil the flesh of the sacrifice. And there shall no longer be traders[c] in the house of the LORD of hosts on that day.

## REVELATION 20.1–15

THEN I saw an angel coming down from heaven, holding in his hand the key to the bottomless pit and a great chain. [2]He seized the dragon, that ancient serpent, who is the Devil and Satan, and bound him for a thousand years, [3]and threw him into the pit, and locked and sealed it over him, so that he would deceive the nations no more, until the thousand years were ended. After that he must be let out for a little while.

4 Then I saw thrones, and those seated on them were given authority to judge. I also saw the souls of those who had been beheaded for their testimony to Jesus[d] and for the word of God. They had not worshiped the beast or its image and had not received its mark on their foreheads or their hands. They came to life and reigned with Christ a thousand years. [5](The rest of the dead did not come to life until the thousand years were ended.) This is the first resurrection. [6]Blessed and holy are those who share in the first resurrection. Over these the second death has no power, but they will be priests of God and of Christ, and they will reign with him a thousand years.

7 When the thousand years are ended, Satan will be released from his prison [8]and will come out to deceive the nations at the four corners of the earth, Gog and Magog, in order to gather them for battle; they are as numerous as the sands of the sea. [9]They marched up over the breadth of the earth and surrounded the camp of the saints and the beloved city. And fire came down from heaven[e] and consumed them. [10]And the devil who had deceived them was thrown into the lake of fire and sulfur, where the beast and the false prophet were, and they will be tormented day and night forever and ever.

11 Then I saw a great white throne and the one who sat on it; the earth and the heaven fled from his presence, and no place was found for them. [12]And I saw the dead, great and small, standing before the throne, and books were opened. Also another book was opened, the book of life. And the dead were judged according to their works, as recorded in the books. [13]And the sea gave up the dead that were in it, Death and Hades gave up the dead that were in them, and all were judged according to what they had done. [14]Then Death and Hades were thrown into the lake of fire. This is the second death, the lake of fire; [15]and anyone whose name was not found written in the book of life was thrown into the lake of fire.

## PSALM 148.1–14

PRAISE the LORD!
Praise the LORD from the
    heavens;
  praise him in the heights!
2  Praise him, all his angels;
  praise him, all his host!

3  Praise him, sun and moon;
  praise him, all you shining
    stars!

---

a Or *tabernacles*; Heb *succoth*  b Heb *shall be like*  c Or *Canaanites*  d Or *for the testimony of Jesus*
e Other ancient authorities read *from God, out of heaven,* or *out of heaven from God*

4 Praise him, you highest
    heavens,
    and you waters above the
       heavens!

5 Let them praise the name of
    the LORD,
    for he commanded and they
       were created.
6 He established them forever
    and ever;
    he fixed their bounds, which
       cannot be passed. a

7 Praise the LORD from the earth,
    you sea monsters and all
       deeps,
8 fire and hail, snow and frost,
    stormy wind fulfilling his
       command!

9 Mountains and all hills,
    fruit trees and all cedars!
10 Wild animals and all cattle,
    creeping things and flying
       birds!

11 Kings of the earth and all
    peoples,
    princes and all rulers of the
       earth!
12 Young men and women alike,
    old and young together!

13 Let them praise the name of
    the LORD,
    for his name alone is exalted;
    his glory is above earth and
       heaven.
14 He has raised up a horn for his
    people,
    praise for all his faithful,
    for the people of Israel who
       are close to him.
Praise the LORD!

## PROVERBS 31.8–9

SPEAK out for those who cannot
    speak,
for the rights of all the
    destitute. b
9 Speak out, judge righteously,
    defend the rights of the poor
    and needy.

# DECEMBER 30

## MALACHI 1.1—2.17

AN oracle. The word of the LORD to Israel by Malachi. c

2 I have loved you, says the LORD. But you say, "How have you loved us?" Is not Esau Jacob's brother? says the LORD. Yet I have loved Jacob 3but I have hated Esau; I have made his hill country a desolation and his heritage a desert for jackals. 4If Edom says, "We are shattered but we will rebuild the ruins," the LORD of hosts says: They may build, but I will tear down, until they are called the wicked country, the people with whom the LORD is angry forever. 5Your own eyes shall see this, and you shall say, "Great is the LORD beyond the borders of Israel!"

6 A son honors his father, and servants their master. If then I am a father, where is the honor due me? And

a Or *he set a law that cannot pass away*  b Heb *all children of passing away*  c Or *by my messenger*

if I am a master, where is the respect due me? says the Lord of hosts to you, O priests, who despise my name. You say, "How have we despised your name?" [7]By offering polluted food on my altar. And you say, "How have we polluted it?"[a] By thinking that the Lord's table may be despised. [8]When you offer blind animals in sacrifice, is that not wrong? And when you offer those that are lame or sick, is that not wrong? Try presenting that to your governor; will he be pleased with you or show you favor? says the Lord of hosts. [9]And now implore the favor of God, that he may be gracious to us. The fault is yours. Will he show favor to any of you? says the Lord of hosts. [10]Oh, that someone among you would shut the temple[b] doors, so that you would not kindle fire on my altar in vain! I have no pleasure in you, says the Lord of hosts, and I will not accept an offering from your hands. [11]For from the rising of the sun to its setting my name is great among the nations, and in every place incense is offered to my name, and a pure offering; for my name is great among the nations, says the Lord of hosts. [12]But you profane it when you say that the Lord's table is polluted, and the food for it[c] may be despised. [13]"What a weariness this is," you say, and you sniff at me,[d] says the Lord of hosts. You bring what has been taken by violence or is lame or sick, and this you bring as your offering! Shall I accept that from your hand? says the Lord. [14]Cursed be the cheat who has a male in the flock and vows to give it, and yet sacrifices to the Lord what is blemished; for I am a great King, says the Lord of hosts, and my name is revered among the nations.

[2.1] And now, O priests, this command is for you. [2]If you will not listen, if you will not lay it to heart to give glory to my name, says the Lord of hosts, then I will send the curse on you and I will curse your blessings; indeed I have already cursed them,[e] because you do not lay it to heart. [3]I will rebuke your offspring, and spread dung on your faces, the dung of your offerings, and I will put you out of my presence.[f]

4 Know, then, that I have sent this command to you, that my covenant with Levi may hold, says the Lord of hosts. [5]My covenant with him was a covenant of life and well-being, which I gave him; this called for reverence, and he revered me and stood in awe of my name. [6]True instruction was in his mouth, and no wrong was found on his lips. He walked with me in integrity and uprightness, and he turned many from iniquity. [7]For the lips of a priest should guard knowledge, and people should seek instruction from his mouth, for he is the messenger of the Lord of hosts. [8]But you have turned aside from the way; you have caused many to stumble by your instruction; you have corrupted the covenant of Levi, says the Lord of hosts, [9]and so I make you despised and abased before all the people, inasmuch as you have not kept my ways but have shown partiality in your instruction.

10 Have we not all one father? Has not one God created us? Why then are we faithless to one another, profaning the covenant of our ancestors? [11]Judah has been faithless, and abomination has been committed in Israel and in Jerusalem; for Judah has profaned the sanctuary of the Lord, which he loves, and has married the daughter of a foreign god. [12]May the Lord cut off from the tents of Jacob anyone who does this—any to witness[g] or answer, or to bring an offering to the Lord of hosts.

13 And this you do as well: You cover the Lord's altar with tears, with weeping and groaning because he no

aGk: Heb *you*  bHeb lacks *temple*  cCompare Syr Tg: Heb *its fruit, its food*  dAnother reading is *at it*  eHeb *it*  fCn Compare Gk Syr: Heb *and he shall bear you to it*  gCn Compare Gk: Heb *arouse*

longer regards the offering or accepts it with favor at your hand. [14]You ask, "Why does he not?" Because the LORD was a witness between you and the wife of your youth, to whom you have been faithless, though she is your companion and your wife by covenant. [15]Did not one God make her?[a] Both flesh and spirit are his.[b] And what does the one God[c] desire? Godly offspring. So look to yourselves, and do not let anyone be faithless to the wife of his youth. [16]For I hate[d] divorce, says the LORD, the God of Israel, and covering one's garment with violence, says the LORD of hosts. So take heed to yourselves and do not be faithless.

17  You have wearied the LORD with your words. Yet you say, "How have we wearied him?" By saying, "All who do evil are good in the sight of the LORD, and he delights in them." Or by asking, "Where is the God of justice?"

# REVELATION 21.1–27

THEN I saw a new heaven and a new earth; for the first heaven and the first earth had passed away, and the sea was no more. [2]And I saw the holy city, the new Jerusalem, coming down out of heaven from God, prepared as a bride adorned for her husband. [3]And I heard a loud voice from the throne saying,

"See, the home[e] of God is
among mortals.
He will dwell[e] with them as
their God;[f]
they will be his peoples,[g]
and God himself will be
with them;[h]
[4]  he will wipe every tear from
their eyes.
Death will be no more;
mourning and crying and pain
will be no more,

for the first things have
passed away."

5  And the one who was seated on the throne said, "See, I am making all things new." Also he said, "Write this, for these words are trustworthy and true." [6]Then he said to me, "It is done! I am the Alpha and the Omega, the beginning and the end. To the thirsty I will give water as a gift from the spring of the water of life. [7]Those who conquer will inherit these things, and I will be their God and they will be my children. [8]But as for the cowardly, the faithless,[i] the polluted, the murderers, the fornicators, the sorcerers, the idolaters, and all liars, their place will be in the lake that burns with fire and sulfur, which is the second death."

9  Then one of the seven angels who had the seven bowls full of the seven last plagues came and said to me, "Come, I will show you the bride, the wife of the Lamb." [10]And in the spirit[j] he carried me away to a great, high mountain and showed me the holy city Jerusalem coming down out of heaven from God. [11]It has the glory of God and a radiance like a very rare jewel, like jasper, clear as crystal. [12]It has a great, high wall with twelve gates, and at the gates twelve angels, and on the gates are inscribed the names of the twelve tribes of the Israelites; [13]on the east three gates, on the north three gates, on the south three gates, and on the west three gates. [14]And the wall of the city has twelve foundations, and on them are the twelve names of the twelve apostles of the Lamb.

15  The angel[k] who talked to me had a measuring rod of gold to measure the city and its gates and walls. [16]The city lies foursquare, its length the same as its width; and he measured the city

---

aOr *Has he not made one?*  bCn: Heb *and a remnant of spirit was his*  cHeb *he*  dCn: Heb *he hates*
eGk *tabernacle*  fOther ancient authorities lack *as their God*  gOther ancient authorities read *people*
hOther ancient authorities add *and be their God*  iOr *the unbelieving*  jOr *in the Spirit*  kGk *He*

with his rod, fifteen hundred miles; [a] its length and width and height are equal. [17] He also measured its wall, one hundred forty-four cubits [b] by human measurement, which the angel was using. [18] The wall is built of jasper, while the city is pure gold, clear as glass. [19] The foundations of the wall of the city are adorned with every jewel; the first was jasper, the second sapphire, the third agate, the fourth emerald, [20] the fifth onyx, the sixth carnelian, the seventh chrysolite, the eighth beryl, the ninth topaz, the tenth chrysoprase, the eleventh jacinth, the twelfth amethyst. [21] And the twelve gates are twelve pearls, each of the gates is a single pearl, and the street of the city is pure gold, transparent as glass.

22 I saw no temple in the city, for its temple is the Lord God the Almighty and the Lamb. [23] And the city has no need of sun or moon to shine on it, for the glory of God is its light, and its lamp is the Lamb. [24] The nations will walk by its light, and the kings of the earth will bring their glory into it. [25] Its gates will never be shut by day—and there will be no night there. [26] People will bring into it the glory and the honor of the nations. [27] But nothing unclean will enter it, nor anyone who practices abomination or falsehood, but only those who are written in the Lamb's book of life.

# PSALM 149.1–9

**P**RAISE the Lord!
Sing to the Lord a new
song,
  his praise in the assembly of
  the faithful.
2 Let Israel be glad in its Maker;
  let the children of Zion rejoice
  in their King.
3 Let them praise his name with
  dancing,
    making melody to him with
    tambourine and lyre.

4 For the Lord takes pleasure in
  his people;
  he adorns the humble with
  victory.
5 Let the faithful exult in glory;
  let them sing for joy on their
  couches.
6 Let the high praises of God be
  in their throats
  and two-edged swords in
  their hands,
7 to execute vengeance on the
  nations
  and punishment on the
  peoples,
8 to bind their kings with fetters
  and their nobles with chains
  of iron,
9 to execute on them the
  judgment decreed.
  This is glory for all his faithful
  ones.
Praise the Lord!

# PROVERBS 31.10–24

**A** CAPABLE wife who can find?
She is far more precious
than jewels.
11 The heart of her husband trusts
  in her,
  and he will have no lack of
  gain.
12 She does him good, and not
  harm,
  all the days of her life.
13 She seeks wool and flax,
  and works with willing hands.
14 She is like the ships of the
  merchant,
  she brings her food from
  far away.
15 She rises while it is still night
  and provides food for her
  household
  and tasks for her
  servant-girls.
16 She considers a field and buys
  it;

[a] Gk *twelve thousand stadia*  [b] That is, almost seventy-five yards

with the fruit of her hands
  she plants a vineyard.
17 She girds herself with strength,
  and makes her arms strong.
18 She perceives that her
    merchandise is profitable.
  Her lamp does not go out
    at night.
19 She puts her hands to the
    distaff,
  and her hands hold the
    spindle.
20 She opens her hand to the poor,
  and reaches out her hands to
    the needy.

21 She is not afraid for her
    household when it
    snows,
  for all her household are
    clothed in crimson.
22 She makes herself coverings;
  her clothing is fine linen and
    purple.
23 Her husband is known in the
    city gates,
  taking his seat among the
    elders of the land.
24 She makes linen garments and
    sells them;
  she supplies the merchant
    with sashes.

# DECEMBER 31

## MALACHI 3.1—4.6

SEE, I am sending my messenger to prepare the way before me, and the Lord whom you seek will suddenly come to his temple. The messenger of the covenant in whom you delight—indeed, he is coming, says the LORD of hosts. 2But who can endure the day of his coming, and who can stand when he appears?

For he is like a refiner's fire and like fullers' soap; 3he will sit as a refiner and purifier of silver, and he will purify the descendants of Levi and refine them like gold and silver, until they present offerings to the LORD in righteousness. a 4Then the offering of Judah and Jerusalem will be pleasing to the LORD as in the days of old and as in former years.

5 Then I will draw near to you for judgment; I will be swift to bear witness against the sorcerers, against the adulterers, against those who swear falsely, against those who oppress the hired workers in their wages, the widow and the orphan, against those who thrust aside the alien, and do not fear me, says the LORD of hosts.

6 For I the LORD do not change; therefore you, O children of Jacob, have not perished. 7Ever since the days of your ancestors you have turned aside from my statutes and have not kept them. Return to me, and I will return to you, says the LORD of hosts. But you say, "How shall we return?"

8 Will anyone rob God? Yet you are robbing me! But you say, "How are we robbing you?" In your tithes and offerings! 9You are cursed with a curse, for you are robbing me—the whole nation of you! 10Bring the full tithe into the storehouse, so that there may be food in my house, and thus put me to the test, says the LORD of hosts; see if I will

a Or *right offerings to the LORD*

not open the windows of heaven for you and pour down for you an overflowing blessing. <sup>11</sup>I will rebuke the locust<sup>a</sup> for you, so that it will not destroy the produce of your soil; and your vine in the field shall not be barren, says the Lord of hosts. <sup>12</sup>Then all nations will count you happy, for you will be a land of delight, says the Lord of hosts.

13 You have spoken harsh words against me, says the Lord. Yet you say, "How have we spoken against you?" <sup>14</sup>You have said, "It is vain to serve God. What do we profit by keeping his command or by going about as mourners before the Lord of hosts? <sup>15</sup>Now we count the arrogant happy; evildoers not only prosper, but when they put God to the test they escape."

16 Then those who revered the Lord spoke with one another. The Lord took note and listened, and a book of remembrance was written before him of those who revered the Lord and thought on his name. <sup>17</sup>They shall be mine, says the Lord of hosts, my special possession on the day when I act, and I will spare them as parents spare their children who serve them. <sup>18</sup>Then once more you shall see the difference between the righteous and the wicked, between one who serves God and one who does not serve him.

<sup>4b.1</sup> See, the day is coming, burning like an oven, when all the arrogant and all evildoers will be stubble; the day that comes shall burn them up, says the Lord of hosts, so that it will leave them neither root nor branch. <sup>2</sup>But for you who revere my name the sun of righteousness shall rise, with healing in its wings. You shall go out leaping like calves from the stall. <sup>3</sup>And you shall tread down the wicked, for they will be ashes under the soles of your feet, on the day when I act, says the Lord of hosts.

4 Remember the teaching of my servant Moses, the statutes and ordinances that I commanded him at Horeb for all Israel.

5 Lo, I will send you the prophet Elijah before the great and terrible day of the Lord comes. <sup>6</sup>He will turn the hearts of parents to their children and the hearts of children to their parents, so that I will not come and strike the land with a curse. <sup>c</sup>

# REVELATION 22.1–21

THEN the angel<sup>d</sup> showed me the river of the water of life, bright as crystal, flowing from the throne of God and of the Lamb <sup>2</sup>through the middle of the street of the city. On either side of the river is the tree of life<sup>e</sup> with its twelve kinds of fruit, producing its fruit each month; and the leaves of the tree are for the healing of the nations. <sup>3</sup>Nothing accursed will be found there any more. But the throne of God and of the Lamb will be in it, and his servants<sup>f</sup> will worship him; <sup>4</sup>they will see his face, and his name will be on their foreheads. <sup>5</sup>And there will be no more night; they need no light of lamp or sun, for the Lord God will be their light, and they will reign forever and ever.

6 And he said to me, "These words are trustworthy and true, for the Lord, the God of the spirits of the prophets, has sent his angel to show his servants<sup>f</sup> what must soon take place."

7 "See, I am coming soon! Blessed is the one who keeps the words of the prophecy of this book."

8 I, John, am the one who heard and saw these things. And when I heard and saw them, I fell down to wor-

---

<sup>a</sup>Heb *devourer*   <sup>b</sup>Ch 4.1-6 are Ch 3.19-24 in Heb   <sup>c</sup>Or *a ban of utter destruction*   <sup>d</sup>Gk *he*   <sup>e</sup>Or *the Lamb. 2In the middle of the street of the city, and on either side of the river, is the tree of life*   <sup>f</sup>Gk *slaves*

ship at the feet of the angel who showed them to me; [9]but he said to me, "You must not do that! I am a fellow servant[a] with you and your comrades[b] the prophets, and with those who keep the words of this book. Worship God!"

10  And he said to me, "Do not seal up the words of the prophecy of this book, for the time is near. [11]Let the evildoer still do evil, and the filthy still be filthy, and the righteous still do right, and the holy still be holy."

12  "See, I am coming soon; my reward is with me, to repay according to everyone's work. [13]I am the Alpha and the Omega, the first and the last, the beginning and the end."

14  Blessed are those who wash their robes,[c] so that they will have the right to the tree of life and may enter the city by the gates. [15]Outside are the dogs and sorcerers and fornicators and murderers and idolaters, and everyone who loves and practices falsehood.

16  "It is I, Jesus, who sent my angel to you with this testimony for the churches. I am the root and the descendant of David, the bright morning star."

17  The Spirit and the bride say,
    "Come."
And let everyone who hears
    say, "Come."
And let everyone who is thirsty
    come.
Let anyone who wishes take the
    water of life as a gift.

18  I warn everyone who hears the words of the prophecy of this book: if anyone adds to them, God will add to that person the plagues described in this book; [19]if anyone takes away from the words of the book of this prophecy, God will take away that person's share in the tree of life and in the holy city, which are described in this book.

20  The one who testifies to these things says, "Surely I am coming soon."

Amen. Come, Lord Jesus!

21  The grace of the Lord Jesus be with all the saints. Amen. [d]

## PSALM 150.1–6

Praise the LORD!
Praise God in his sanctuary;
    praise him in his mighty
        firmament![e]
2  Praise him for his mighty deeds;
    praise him according to his
        surpassing greatness!

3  Praise him with trumpet sound;
    praise him with lute and harp!
4  Praise him with tambourine and
        dance;
    praise him with strings and
        pipe!
5  Praise him with clanging
        cymbals;
    praise him with loud clashing
        cymbals!
6  Let everything that breathes
        praise the LORD!
Praise the LORD!

## PROVERBS 31.25–31

Strength and dignity are her [an
        excellent wife's]
        clothing,
    and she laughs at the time
        to come.
26  She opens her mouth with
        wisdom,
    and the teaching of kindness
        is on her tongue.
27  She looks well to the ways of
        her household,
    and does not eat the bread of
        idleness.
28  Her children rise up and call her
        happy;

her husband too, and he
    praises her:
29 "Many women have done
    excellently,
but you surpass them all."
30 Charm is deceitful, and beauty
    is vain,

but a woman who fears the
    Lord is to be praised.
31 Give her a share in the fruit of
    her hands,
and let her works praise her
    in the city gates.

Now that you have reached your goal of reading through the Bible in this version, you may want to use *The Living Bible,* the New International Version, or the New American Standard editions of *The One Year Bible* for your daily reading next year. See your local Christian bookstore.

# The Bible Talks about Life

Cast all your anxiety on him, because he cares for you. *1 Peter 5:7*

AGITATION

Peace I leave with you; my peace I give to you. I do not give to you as the world gives. Do not let your hearts be troubled, and do not let them be afraid. *John 14:27*

Do not worry about anything, but in everything by prayer and supplication with thanksgiving let your requests be made known to God. And the peace of God, which surpasses all understanding, will guard your hearts and your minds in Christ Jesus. *Philippians 4:6, 7*

ANGER

Be angry but do not sin; do not let the sun go down on your anger, and do not make room for the devil. *Ephesians 4:26, 27*

You must understand this, my beloved: let everyone be quick to listen, slow to speak, slow to anger; for your anger does not produce God's righteousness. *James 1:19, 20*

DEPRESSION

I waited patiently for the LORD;
    he inclined to me and heard my cry.
He drew me up from the desolate pit,
    out of the miry bog,
and set my feet upon a rock,
    making my steps secure.
He put a new song in my mouth,
    a song of praise to our God.
Many will see and fear,
    and put their trust in the LORD. *Psalm 40:1–3*

When the righteous cry for help, the LORD hears,
    and rescues them from all their troubles.

Many are the afflictions of the righteous,
    but the LORD rescues them from them all. *Psalm 34:17, 19*

DISCOURAGEMENT

"Do not let your hearts be troubled. Believe in God, believe also in me. In my Father's house there are many dwelling places. If it were not so, would I have told you that I go to prepare a place for you? And if I go and prepare a place for you, I will come again and will take you to myself, so that where I am, there you may be also. *John 14:1–3*

"Be strong and bold; have no fear or dread of them, because it is the LORD your God who goes with you; he will not fail you or forsake you."
*Deuteronomy 31:6*

## ETERNAL LIFE

Jesus said to her, "I am the resurrection and the life. Those who believe in me, even though they die, will live, and everyone who lives and believes in me will never die. Do you believe this?"
*John 11:25, 26*

For we know that if the earthly tent we live in is destroyed, we have a building from God, a house not made with hands, eternal in the heavens. For in this tent we groan, longing to be clothed with our heavenly dwelling—if indeed, when we have taken it off we will not be found naked. For while we are still in this tent, we groan under our burden, because we wish not to be unclothed but to be further clothed, so that what is mortal may be swallowed up by life. He who has prepared us for this very thing is God, who has given us the Spirit as a guarantee.
*2 Corinthians 5:1–5*

I consider that the sufferings of this present time are not worth comparing with the glory about to be revealed to us.
*Romans 8:18*

## FEAR

Do not fear, for I am with you,
do not be afraid, for I am your God;
I will strengthen you, I will help you,
I will uphold you with my victorious right hand.
*Isaiah 41:10*

They are not afraid of evil tidings;
their hearts are firm, secure in the LORD.
Their hearts are steady, they will not be afraid;
in the end they will look in triumph on their foes.
*Psalm 112:7, 8*

You are a hiding place for me;
you preserve me from trouble;
you surround me with glad cries of deliverance.
*Psalm 32:7*

## FRUSTRATION

For you need endurance, so that when you have done the will of God, you may receive what was promised.
*Hebrews 10:36*

Those of steadfast mind you keep in peace—
in peace because they trust in you.
Trust in the LORD forever,
for in the LORD GOD
you have an everlasting rock.
*Isaiah 26:3, 4*

## GUILT

If we confess our sins, he who is faithful and just will forgive us our sins and cleanse us from all unrighteousness.
*1 John 1:9*

Come now, let us argue it out,
says the LORD:
though your sins are like scarlet,
they shall be like snow;

though they are red like crimson,
    they shall become like wool. *Isaiah 1:18*

I have swept away your transgressions like a cloud,
    and your sins like mist;
return to me, for I have redeemed you. *Isaiah 44:22*

In him we have redemption through his blood, the forgiveness of our trespasses, according to the riches of his grace that he lavished on us. With all wisdom and insight. *Ephesians 1:7, 8*

"For I will be merciful toward their iniquities,
    and I will remember their sins no more." *Hebrews 8:12*

## IMPATIENCE

Be still before the LORD, and wait patiently for him;
    do not fret over those who prosper in their way,
    over those who carry out evil devices. *Psalm 37:7*

Be patient, therefore, beloved, until the coming of the Lord. The farmer waits for the precious crop from the earth, being patient with it until it receives the early and the late rains. You also must be patient. Strengthen your hearts, for the coming of the Lord is near. *James 5:7, 8*

## INSECURITY

What then are we to say about these things? If God is for us, who is against us? He who did not withhold his own Son, but gave him up for all of us, will he not with him also give us everything else? *Romans 8:31, 32*

For I, the LORD your God,
    hold your right hand;
it is I who say to you, "Do not fear,
    I will help you." *Isaiah 41:13*

So we can say with confidence.
    "The Lord is my helper;
    I will not be afraid.
What can anyone do to me?" *Hebrews 13:16*

## JEALOUSY

But if you have bitter envy and selfish ambition in your hearts, do not be boastful and false to the truth. Such wisdom does not come down from above, but is earthly, unspiritual, devilish. For where there is envy and selfish ambition, there will also be disorder and wickedness of every kind. *James 3:14–16*

Do not be afraid when some become rich,
    when the wealth of their houses increases.
For when they die they will carry nothing away;
    their wealth will not go down after them. *Psalm 49:16, 17*

## LONELINESS

"I will not leave you orphaned; I am coming to you." *John 14:18*

## LOW SELF-ESTEEM

> So God created humankind in his image,
>> in the image of God he created them;
>>> male and female he created them.
>>>> *Genesis 1:27*

"The second is this, 'You shall love your neighbor as yourself.' There is no other commandment greater than these."

*Mark 12:31*

For by the grace given to me I say to everyone among you not to think of yourself more highly than you ought to think, but to think with sober judgment, each according to the measure of faith that God has assigned. For as in one body we have many members, and not all the members have the same function, so we, who are many, are one body in Christ, and individually we are members one of another.

*Romans 12:3–5*

## PAIN

He said, "Abba, Father, for you all things are possible; remove this cup from me; yet, not what I want, but what you want."

*Mark 14:36*

For this slight momentary affliction is preparing us for an eternal weight of glory beyond all measure.

*2 Corinthians 4:17*

Even considering the exceptional character of the revelations. Therefore, to keep me from being too elated, a thorn was given me in the flesh, a messenger of Satan to torment me, to keep me from being too elated. Three times I appealed to the Lord about this, that it would leave me, but he said to me, "My grace is sufficient for you, for power is made perfect in weakness." So, I will boast all the more gladly of my weaknesses, so that the power of Christ may dwell in me. Therefore I am content with weaknesses, insults, hardships, persecutions, and calamities for the sake of Christ; for whenever I am weak, then I am strong.

*2 Corinthians 12:7–10*

## PERSECUTION

"Blessed are those who are persecuted for righteousness' sake, for theirs is the kingdom of heaven.

"Blessed are you when people revile you and persecute you and utter all kinds of evil against you falsely on my account. Rejoice and be glad, for your reward is great in heaven, for in the same way they persecuted the prophets who were before you.

*Matthew 5:10–12*

But I say to you, Love your enemies and pray for those who persecute you, so that you may be children of your Father in heaven; for he makes his sun rise on the evil and on the good, and sends rain on the righteous and on the unrighteous.

*Matthew 5:44, 45*

## SICKNESS

Are any among you sick? They should call for the elders of the church and have them pray over them, anointing them with oil in the name of the Lord. The prayer of faith will save the sick, and the Lord will raise them up; and anyone who has committed sins will be forgiven.

*James 5:14, 15*

> The LORD sustains them on their sickbed;
>> in their illness you heal all their infirmities.
>>> *Psalm 41:3*

SUFFERING AND DEATH

But we do not want you to be uninformed, brothers and sisters, about those who have died, so that you may not grieve as others do who have no hope. For since we believe that Jesus died and rose again, even so, through Jesus, God will bring with him those who have died. *1 Thessalonians 4:13, 14*

The LORD is near to the brokenhearted,
    and saves the crushed in spirit.
Many are the afflictions of the righteous,
    but the LORD rescues them from them all. *Psalm 34:18, 19*

Listen, I will tell you a mystery! We will not all die, but we will all be changed, in a moment, in the twinkling of an eye, at the last trumpet. For the trumpet will sound, and the dead will be raised imperishable, and we will be changed. For this perishable body must put on imperishability, and this mortal body must put on immortality. When this perishable body puts on imperishability, and this mortal body puts on immortality, then the saying that is written will be fulfilled: "Death has been swallowed up in victory."

"Where, O death, is your victory?
Where, O death, is your sting?" *1 Corinthians 15:51–55*

TEMPTATION

No testing has overtaken you that is not common to everyone. God is faithful, and he will not let you be tested beyond your strength, but with the testing he will also provide the way out so that you may be able to endure it.
*1 Corinthians 10:13*

Because he himself was tested by what he suffered, he is able to help those who are being tested. *Hebrews 2:18*

Blessed is anyone who endures temptation. Such a one has stood the test and will receive the crown of life that the Lord has promised to those who love him. No one, when tempted, should say, "I am being tempted by God"; for God cannot be tempted by evil and he himself tempts no one. But one is tempted by one's own desire, being lured and enticed by it. *James 1:12–14*

Submit yourselves therefore to God. Resist the devil, and he will flee from you. *James 4:7*

WEARINESS

But those who wait for the LORD shall renew their strength,
    they shall mount up with wings like eagles.
they shall run and not be weary,
    they shall walk and not faint. *Isaiah 40:31*

"Come to me, all you that are weary and are carrying heavy burdens, and I will give you rest. Take my yoke upon you, and learn from me; for I am gentle and humble in heart, and you will find rest for your souls. For my yoke is easy, and my burden is light." *Matthew 11:28–30*

WORRY

Those of steadfast mind you keep in peace—
    in peace because they trust in you.

Trust in the LORD forever,
   for in the LORD GOD
     you have an everlasting rock.
*Isaiah 26:3, 4*

Cast all your anxiety on him, because he cares for you.
*1 Peter 5:7*

He said to his disciples. "Therefore I tell you, do not worry about your life, what you will eat, or about your body, what you will wear. For life is more than food, and the body more than clothing. Consider the ravens: they neither sow nor reap, they have neither storehouse nor barn, and yet God feeds them. Of how much more value are you than the birds! And can any of you by worrying add a single hour to your span of life? If then you are not able to do so small a thing as that, why do you worry about the rest? Consider the lilies, how they grow: they neither toil nor spin; yet I tell you, even Solomon in all his glory was not clothed like one of these. But if God so clothes the grass in the field, which is alive today and tomorrow is thrown into the oven, how much more will he clothe you—you of little faith!
*Luke 12:22–28*

## The Bible Talks about Relationships

Some friends play at friendship
   but a true friend sticks closer than one's nearest kin.
*Proverbs 18:24*

FRIENDS
   Whoever walks with the wise becomes wise,
     but the companion of fools suffers harm.
*Proverbs 13:20*

Do nothing from selfish ambition or conceit, but in humility regard others as better than yourselves. Let each of you look not to your own interests, but to the interests of others.
*Philippians 2:3, 4*

INJUSTICE
   For it is better to suffer for doing good, if suffering should be God's will, than to suffer for doing evil.
*1 Peter 3:17*

And after you have suffered for a little while, the God of all grace, who has called you to his eternal glory in Christ, will himself restore, support, strengthen, and establish you.
*1 Peter 5:10*

LOVE
"This is my commandment, that you love one another as I have loved you. No one has greater love than this, to lay down one's life for one's friends. You are my friends if you do what I command you. I do not call you servants any longer, because the servant does not know what the master is doing; but I have called you friends, because I have made known to you everything that I have heard from my Father. You did not choose me but I chose you. And I appointed you to go and bear fruit, fruit that will last, so that the Father will give you whatever you ask him in my name. I am giving you these commands so that you may love one another.
*John 15:12–17*

"For God so loved the world that he gave his only Son, so that everyone who believes in him may not perish but may have eternal life."
*John 3:16*

Beloved, let us love one another, because love is from God; everyone who loves is born of God and knows God. Whoever does not love does not know God, for God is love. God's love was revealed among us in this way: God sent his only Son into the world so that we might live through him. In this is love, not that we loved God but that he loved us and sent his Son to be the atoning sacrifice for our sins. Beloved, since God loved us so much, we also ought to love one another. No one has ever seen God; if we love one another, God lives in us, and his love is perfected in us. *1 John 4:7–12*

Love is patient; love is kind; love is not envious or boastful or arrogant or rude. It does not insist on its own way; it is not irritable or resentful; it does not rejoice in wrongdoing, but rejoices in the truth. It bears all things, believes all things, hopes all things, endures all things. And now faith, hope, and love abide, these three; and the greatest of these is love. *1 Corinthians 13:4–7, 13*

MARRIAGE

Be subject to one another out of reverence for Christ.

Wives, be subject to your husbands as you are to the Lord. For the husband is the head of the wife just as Christ is the head of the church, the body of which he is the Savior. Just as the church is subject to Christ, so also wives ought to be, in everything, to their husbands.

Husbands, love your wives, just as Christ loved the church and gave himself up for her, in order to make her holy by cleansing her with the washing of water by the word, so as to present the church to himself in splendor, without a spot or wrinkle or anything of the kind—yes, so that she may be holy and without blemish. In the same way, husbands should love their wives as they do their own bodies. He who loves his wife loves himself. *Ephesians 5:21–28*

Wives, in the same way, accept the authority of your husbands, so that, even if some of them do not obey the word, they may be won over without a word by their wives' conduct, when they see the purity and reverence of your lives.

Husbands, in the same way, show consideration for your wives in your life together, paying honor to the woman as the weaker sex, since they too are also heirs of the gracious gift of life—so that nothing may hinder your prayers. *1 Peter 3:1, 2, 7*

"And said, 'For this reason a man shall leave his father and mother and be joined to his wife, and the two shall become one flesh'? So they are no longer two, but one flesh. Therefore what God has joined together, let no one separate." *Matthew 19:5, 6*

"And I say to you, whoever divorces his wife, except for unchastity, and marries another commits adultery." *Matthew 19:9*

He said to them, "Whoever divorces his wife and marries another commits adultery against her; and if she divorces her husband and marries another, she commits adultery." *Mark 10:11, 12*

PARENTS AND CHILDREN

Children, obey your parents in the Lord, for this is right. Honor your father and mother"—this is the first commandment with a promise: "so that it may be well with you and you may live long on the earth."

And, fathers, do not provoke your children to anger, but bring them up in the discipline and instruction of the Lord. *Ephesians 6:1–4*

# The Bible Talks about the Future

> Your word is a lamp to my feet
>> and a light to my path.

Psalm 119:105

ASTROLOGY, HOROSCOPES, AND THE OCCULT

Now if people say to you, "Consult the ghosts and the familiar spirits that chirp and mutter; should not a people consult their gods, the dead on behalf of the living?"

Isaiah 8:19

> Stand fast in your enchantments
>> and your many sorceries,
>> with which you have labored from your youth;
> perhaps you may be able to succeed,
>> perhaps you may inspire terror.
> You are wearied with your many consultations;
>> let those who study the heavens
> stand up and save you,
>> those who gaze at the stars,
> and at each new moon predict
>> what shall befall you.

> See, they are like stubble,
>> the fire consumes them;
> they cannot deliver themselves
>> from the power of the flame.
> No coal for warming oneself is this,
>> no fire to sit before!

Isaiah 47:12–14

DIRECTION FOR LIFE

But be doers of the word, and not merely hearers who deceive themselves. For if any are hearers of the word and not doers, they are like those who look at themselves in a mirror; for they look at themselves and, on going away, immediately forget what they were like. But those who look into the perfect law, the law of liberty, and persevere, being not hearers who forget but doers who act—they will be blessed in their doing.

James 1:22–25

MONEY MANAGEMENT

And my God will fully satisfy every need of yours according to his riches in glory in Christ Jesus.

Philippians 4:19

The lover of money will not be satisfied with money; nor the lover of wealth, with gain. This also is vanity.

Ecclesiastes 5:10

Of course, there is great gain in godliness combined with contentment; for we brought nothing into the world, so that we can take nothing out of it; but if we have food and clothing, we will be content with these. But those who want to be rich fall into temptation and are trapped by many senseless and harmful desires that plunge people into ruin and destruction. For the love of money is a root of all kinds of evil, and in their eagerness to be rich some have wandered away from the faith and pierced themselves with many pains.

1 Timothy 6:6–10

TRUST
Trust in the LORD with all your heart,
    and do not rely on your own insight.
In all your ways acknowledge him,
    and he will make straight your paths.                    *Proverbs 3:5, 6*


I know what it is to have little, and I know what it is to have plenty. In any and all circumstances I have learned the secret of being well-fed and of going hungry, of having plenty and of being in need. I can do all things through him who strengthens me.                    *Philippians 4:12, 13*


## The Bible Talks about Faith

So faith comes from what is heard, and what is heard comes through the word of Christ.                    *Romans 10:17*


BEING BORN AGAIN

Jesus answered him, "Very truly, I tell you, no one can see the kingdom of God without being born from above. Jesus answered, "Very truly, I tell you, no one can enter the kingdom of God without being born of water and Spirit. What is born of the flesh is flesh, and what is born of the Spirit is spirit. Do not be astonished that I said to you, 'You must be born from above.'        *John 3:3, 5–7*

Blessed be the God and Father of our Lord Jesus Christ! By his great mercy he has given us a new birth into a living hope through the resurrection of Jesus Christ from the dead.                    *1 Peter 1:3*

Those who have been born of God do not sin, because God's seed abides in them; they cannot sin, because they have been born of God.        *1 John 3:9*


FINDING GOD

So that they would search for God and perhaps grope for him and find him—though indeed he is not far from each one of us. For 'In him we live and move and have our being'; as even some of your own poets have said, 'For we too are his offspring.'                    *Acts 17:27, 28*

For surely I know the plans I have for you, says the LORD, plans for your welfare and not for harm, to give you a future with hope. Then when you call upon me and come and pray to me, I will hear you. When you search for me, you will find me; if you seek me with all your heart.        *Jeremiah 29:11–13*


KNOWING GOD
To whom then will you liken God,
    or what likeness compare with him?

It is he who sits above the circle of the earth,
    and its inhabitants are like grasshoppers;
who stretches out the heavens like a curtain,
    and spreads them like a tent to live in;
who brings princes to naught,
    and makes the rulers of the earth as nothing.

Scarcely are they planted, scarcely sown,
    scarcely has their stem taken root in the earth,
when he blows upon them, and they wither,
    and the tempest carries them off like stubble.

To whom then will you compare me,
    or who is my equal? says the Holy One.
Lift up your eyes on high and see:
    Who created these?
He who brings out their host and numbers them,
    calling them all by name;
because he is great in strength,
    might in power,
    not one is missing.                                    *Isaiah 40:18, 22-26*

Beloved, let us love one another, because love is from God; everyone who loves is born of God and knows God. Whoever does not love does not know God, for God is love.                                    *1 John 4:7, 8*


KNOWING JESUS CHRIST

In the beginning was the Word, and the Word was with God, and the Word was God. He was in the beginning with God. All things came into being through him, and without him not one thing came into being. What has come into being in him was life, and the life was the light of all people. The light shines in the darkness, and the darkness did not overcome it.

There was a man sent from God, whose name was John. He came as a witness to testify to the light, so that all might believe through him. He himself was not the light, but he came to testify to the light. The true light, which enlightens everyone, was coming into the world.

He was in the world, and the world came into being through him; yet the world did not know him. He came to what was his own, and his own people did not accept him. But to all who received him, who believed in his name, he gave power to become children of God, who were born, not of blood or of the will of the flesh or of the will of man, but of God.

And the Word became flesh and lived among us, and we have seen his glory, the glory as of a father's only son, full of grace and truth.          *John 1:1–14*

He is the image of the invisible God, the firstborn of all creation; for in him all things in heaven and on earth were created, things visible and invisible, whether thrones or dominions or rulers or powers—all things have been created through him and for him. He himself is before all things, and in him all things hold together. He is the head of the body, the church; he is the beginning, the firstborn from the dead, so that he might come to have first place in everything. For in him all the fullness of God was pleased to dwell. And when you were dead in trespasses and the uncircumcision of our flesh, God made you alive together with him, when he forgave us all our trespasses, erasing the record that stood against us with its legal demands. He set this aside, nailing it to the cross.                                    *Colossians 1:15–19; 2:13, 14*

He is the reflection of God's glory and the exact imprint of God's very being, and he sustains all things by his powerful word. When he had made purification for sins, he sat down at the right hand of the Majesty on high.

But of the Son he says,
> "Your throne, O God, is forever and ever,
> and the righteous scepter is the scepter of your kingdom.

*Hebrews 1:3, 8*


KNOWING THE HOLY SPIRIT

But it is God who establishes us with you in Christ and has anointed us, by putting his seal on us and giving us his Spirit in our hearts as a first installment.

*2 Corinthians 1:21b, 22*

And those who are in the flesh cannot please God.

But you are not in the flesh; you are in the Spirit, since the Spirit of God dwells in you. Anyone who does not have the Spirit of Christ does not belong to him. But if Christ is in you, though the body is dead because of sin, the Spirit is life because of righteousness. If the Spirit of him who raised Jesus from the dead dwells in you, he who raised Christ from the dead will give life to your mortal bodies also through his Spirit that dwells in you. *Romans 8:8–11*

"If you love me, you will keep my commandments. And I will ask the Father, and he will give you another Advocate, to be with you forever. This is the Spirit of truth, whom the world cannot receive, because it neither sees him nor knows him. You know him, because he abides with you, and he will be in you.

But the Advocate, the Holy Spirit, whom the Father will send in my name, will teach you everything, and remind you of all that I have said to you.

*John 14:15–17, 26*


PRAYER

Therefore confess your sins to one another, and pray for one another, so that you may be healed. The prayer of the righteous is powerful and effective.

*James 5:16*

If you abide in me, and my words abide in you, ask for whatever you wish, and it will be done for you. *John 15:7*

"Ask, and it will be given you; search, and you will find; knock, and the door will be opened for you. For everyone who asks receives, and everyone who searches finds, and for everyone who knocks, the door will be opened.

*Matthew 7:7, 8*

If we confess our sins, he who is faithful and just will forgive us our sins and cleanse us from all unrighteousness. *1 John 1:9*

Phillipians
4:6-8

fear God =
the reference
God

Prov 28:1

Lisa

↳ The wicked
flee when no one
pursues, but the
righteous are bold as a
lion

Mark 15:34 = Jesus/why
Psalm 22:1 = David/why

Acts 13:36
Ps 138:8

sovereign;
sovereign =
chief, highest;
supreme in power or
authority; having independent
authority; effectual, excellent.

Romans 1:

Romans 10:8 ... confess
lips ..... believe ....
you will be saved

Psalm 138:8 The Lord will fulfill His
purpose for me .......

II Chron
19:3
Set your heart to seek God.

II Chron 20:20
".... believe in the Lord your (my) God
→ you (I) will be established.

I Cor 6: 11 .... But

Acts 10:35
2 Cor 10:5........9
take every thought
captive to obey Chr.
If you are
Remind y
 self
you belong
Christ

"... my power (God's power)
made perfect in weakness
I Cor 12:9b